SKILLS For SUCCESS

with Microsoft® Office 2016

CHANEY ADKINS | HAIN | HAWKINS | MURRE WOLF

PEARSON

Boston Columbus Indianapolis New York San Francisco
Amsterdam Cape Town Dubai London Madrid Milan Munich Paris Montréal Toronto
Delhi Mexico City São Paulo Sydney Hong Kong Seoul Singapore Taipei Tokyo

Library of Congress Cataloging-in-Publication Data

On file with the Library of Congress.

Editorial Director: *Andrew Gilfillan*
Executive Editor: *Jenifer Niles*
Team Lead, Project Management: *Laura Burgess*
Project Manager: *Anne Garcia*
Program Manager: *Emily Biberger*
Development Editor: *Nancy Lamm*
Editorial Assistant: *Michael Campbell*
Director of Product Marketing: *Maggie Waples*
Director of Field Marketing: *Leigh Ann Sims*
Product Marketing Manager: *Kaylee Carlson*
Field Marketing Managers: *Joanna Sabella & Molly Schmidt*
Marketing Assistant: *Kelli Fisher*
Efficacy Improvement & Quality Manager:
Senior Operations Specialist: *Diane Peirano*
Senior Art Director: *Diane Ernsberger*
Manager, Permissions: *Karen Sanatar*
Interior and Cover Design: *Studio Montage*
Cover Photo: *Courtesy of Shutterstock® Images*
Associate Director of Design: *Blair Brown*
Product Strategy Manager: *Eric Hakanson*
Vice President, Product Strategy: *Jason Fournier*
Digital Product Manager: *Zachary Alexander*
Media Project Manager, Production: *John Cassar*
Full-Service Project Management: *Cenveo Publisher Services*
Composition: *Cenveo Publisher Services*

Credits and acknowledgments borrowed from other sources and reproduced, with permission, in this textbook appear on appropriate page within text.

10 9 8 7 6 5 4 3 2 1
ISBN-10: 0-13-432078-6
ISBN-13: 978-0-13-432078-6

Contents in Brief

Table of Contents

Part 3 | Microsoft Office

Microsoft Word

Microsoft Excel

Microsoft Access

Microsoft PowerPoint

Series Reviewers

We'd like to thank the following people for their reviewing of Skills for Success series:

Focus Group Participants

Rose Volynskiy	*Howard Community College*
Fernando Paniagua	*The Community College of Baltimore County*
Jeff Roth	*Heald College*
William Bodine	*Mesa Community College*
Lex Mulder	*College of Western Idaho*
Kristy McAuliffe	*San Jacinto College South*
Jan Hime	*University of Nebraska, Lincoln*
Deb Fells	*Mesa Community College*

Reviewers

Barbara Anderson	*Lake Washington Institute of Technology*
Janet Anderson	*Lake Washington Institute of Technology*
Ralph Argiento	*Guilford Technical Community College*
Tanisha Arnett	*Pima County Community College*
Greg Ballinger	*Miami Dade College*
Autumn Becker	*Allegany College of Maryland*
Bob Benavides	*Collin College*
Howard Blauser	*North GA Technical College*
William Bodine	*Mesa Community College*
Nancy Bogage	*The Community College of Baltimore County*
Maria Bright	*San Jacinto College*
Adell Brooks	*Hinds Community College*
Judy Brown	*Western Illinois University*
Maria Brownlow	*Chaminade*
Jennifer Buchholz	*UW Washington County*
Kathea Buck	*Gateway Technical College*
LeAnn Cady	*Minnesota State College—Southeast Technical*
John Cameron	*Rio Hondo College*
Tammy Campbell	*Eastern Arizona College*
Patricia Christian	*Southwest Georgia Technical College*
Tina Cipriano	*Gateway Technical College*
Paulette Comet	*The Community College of Baltimore County*
Jean Condon	*Mid-Plains Community College*
Joy DePover	*Minneapolis. Com. & Tech College*
Gina Donovan	*County College of Morris*
Alina Dragne	*Flagler College*
Russ Dulaney	*Rasmussen College*
Mimi Duncan	*University of Missouri St. Louis*
Paula Jo Elson	*Sierra College*
Bernice Eng	*Brookdale Community College*
Jill Fall	*Gateway Technical College*
Deb Fells	*Mesa Community College*
Tushnelda C Fernandez	*Miami Dade College*
Jean Finley	*Asheville-Buncombe Technical Community College*
Jim Flannery	*Central Carolina Community College*
Alyssa Foskey	*Wiregrass Georgia Technical College*
David Freer	*Miami Dade College*
Marvin Ganote	*University of Dayton*
David Grant	*Paradise Valley Community College*
Clara Groeper	*Illinois Central College*
Carol Heeter	*Ivy Tech Community College*
Jan Hime	*University of Nebraska*
Marilyn Holden	*Gateway Technical College*
Ralph Hunsberger	*Bucks County Community College*
Juan Iglesias	*University of Texas at Brownsville*
Carl Eric Johnson	*Great Bay Community College*
Joan Johnson	*Lake Sumter Community College*
Mech Johnson	*UW Washington County*
Deborah Jones	*Southwest Georgia Technical College*
Hazel Kates	*Miami-Dade College, Kendall Campus*
Jane Klotzle	*Lake Sumter Community College*
Kurt Kominek	*Northeast State Community College*
Vivian Krenzke	*Gateway Technical College*
Renuka Kumar	*Community College of Baltimore County*
Lisa LaCaria	*Central Piedmont Community College*
Sue Lannen	*Brazosport College*
Freda Leonard	*Delgado Community College*
Susan Mahon	*Collin College*
Nicki Maines	*Mesa Community College*
Pam Manning	*Gateway Technical College*
Juan Marquez	*Mesa Community College*

Alysia Martinez	*Gateway Technical College*
Kristy McAuliffe	*San Jacinto College*
Robert McCloud	*Sacred Heart University*
Susan Miner	*Lehigh Carbon Community College*
Namdar Mogharreban	*Southern Illinois University*
Daniel Moix	*College of the Ouachitas*
Lindsey Moore	*Wiregrass Georgia Technical College*
Lex Mulder	*College of Western Idaho*
Patricia Newman	*Cuyamaca College*
Melinda Norris	*Coker College*
Karen Nunan	*Northeast State Community College*
Fernando Paniagua	*The Community College of Baltimore County*
Christine Parrish	*Southwest Georgia Technical College*
Linda Pennachio	*Mount Saint Mary College*
Amy Pezzimenti	*Ocean County College*
Leah Ramalingam	*Riversity City College*
Mary Rasley	*Lehigh Carbon Community College*
Cheryl Reuss	*Estrella Mountain Community College*
Wendy Revolinski	*Gateway Technical College*
Kenneth Rogers	*Cecil College*
Jeff Roth	*Heald College*
Diane Ruscito	*Brazosport College*
June Scott	*County College of Morris*
Vicky Seehusen	*MSU Denver*
Emily Shepard	*Central Carolina Community College*
Pamela Silvers	*A-B Tech*
Martha Soderholm	*York College*
Yaacov Sragovich	*Queensborough Community College*
Jody Sterr	*Blackhawk Technical College*
Julia Sweitzer	*Lake-Sumter Community College*
Laree Thomas	*Okefenokee Technical College*
Joyce Thompson	*Lehigh Carbon Community College*
Barbara Tietsort	*University of Cincinnati, Blue Ash College*
Rose Volynskiy	*Howard Community College*
Sandra Weber	*Gateway Technical College*
Steven Weitz	*Lehigh Carbon Community College*
Berthenia Williams	*Savannah Technical College*
David Wilson	*Parkland College*
Allan Wood	*Great Bay Community College*
Roger Yaeger	*Estrella Mountain Community College*

A Microsoft Office textbook that recognizes how students learn today

Skills for Success Office 2016

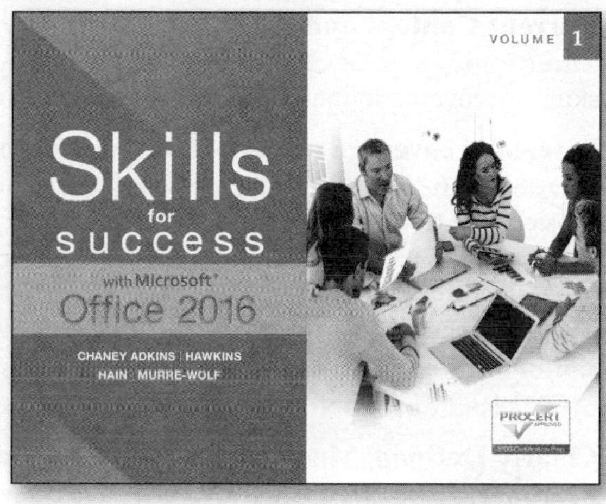

With Microsoft Office 2016, productivity is truly possible anywhere, anytime! Understanding this and being able to think and adapt to new environments is critical for today's learners. The *Skills for Success* series focuses on teaching essential productivity skills by providing a highly visual, step-by-step approach for learning Microsoft Office. This concise approach is very effective and provides the depth of skill coverage needed to succeed at work, school, and for MOS certification preparation. Using this approach, students learn the skills they need, and then put their knowledge to work through a progression of review, problem-solving, critical thinking projects, and proficiency demonstration with the NEW *Collaborating with Google* projects. For Office 2016, MOS exam objectives are also woven into the lessons, so students can review and prepare as they learn. Combine the visual approach and real-world projects of the text with the matching, live-in-the-application grader projects and high fidelity Office simulation training and assessments in MyITLab, and you have a truly effective learning approach!

Series Hallmarks

- **Highly Visual Two-Page Landscape Layout**—Gives students the visual illustrations right with the steps—no flipping pages
- **Clearly Outlined Skills**—Each skill is presented in a single two-page spread so that students can easily follow along
- **Numbered Steps and Bulleted Text**—Students don't read long paragraphs or text, but they will read information presented concisely
- **Wide Coverage of Skills**—Gives students the knowledge needed to learn the core skills for work success

Skills for Success with Microsoft Office 2016

Personalized, engaging, effective learning with MyITLab 2016

Using the *Grader* projects and MyITLab *simulations*, students receive immediate feedback on their work to ensure understanding and help students progress.

MyITLab® Grader **Live-in-the-application Grader Projects**—provide hands-on, autograded options for practice and assessment with immediate feedback and detailed performance comments. Grader projects cover all the skills taught in the chapter, including a new grader covering all four *More Skills.*

MyITLab® Simulation **MyITLab Simulation Trainings and Assessment** provide an interactive, highly-realistic simulated environment to practice the Microsoft skills and projects taught in the book. Students receive immediate assistance with the learning aids, *Read, Watch, Practice,* and *detailed click stream data* reports provide effective review of their work. In the simulation assessments, students demonstrate their understanding through a new scenario exam without learning aids.

Current Content and Essential Technology Coverage

Three Fundamental Chapters cover the latest technology concepts, key Windows 10 skills, and Internet Browsing with Edge and Chrome. Windows 10 skills are covered in the MyITLab Windows 10 simulations.

Extensive coverage of key skills students need for professional and personal success.

Chapters cover 10 Skills through real-world projects to meet the Learning Objectives and Outcomes. All 10 Skills are covered in the MyITLab grader projects and training and assessment simulations.

More Skills are now included in the text instead of online. These projects go beyond the main skills covered to provide additional training and to meet chapter learning objectives. NEW MyITLab grader project covers the skills from all four.

MOS Objective integration ensures students explore the MOS objectives as they are covered in the text for exam awareness and preparation.

Collaborating with Google projects—require students to apply their knowledge with another tool, replicating real-world work environments.

MOS appendix and icons in the text allow instructors to tailor preparation for Microsoft Office Specialist candidates by mapping MOS requirements to the text.

Clearly Defined, Measurable Learning Outcomes and Objectives

Learning *Outcomes* and *Objectives* have been clarified and expanded at the beginning of each chapter to define what students will learn, and are tied to the chapter assessments for clear measurement and efficacy.

Wide range of projects to ensure learning objectives and outcomes are achieved

Objective-based: Matching & Multiple choice, Discussion;

Review projects: Skills Review, Skills Assessments 1 & 2;

Problem-Solving: My Skills and Visual Skills Check;

Critical Thinking: Skills Challenges 1 & 2 and More Skills Assessment

Application Capstone Projects provided for each application help instructors ensure that students are ready to move on to the next application. Also delivered as grader projects in MyITLab.

Integrated Projects follow each application so that as students learn a new application, they also learn how to use it with other applications.

Office Online Projects provide hands-on experience with the web version of the Office applications to ensure students are familiar with the differences and become proficient with working between different versions of the tools.

Effective Learning Tools and Resources

Project Summary Chart—details the end of chapter projects from review, and problem-solving, to critical thinking, and demonstration of proficiency.

Skills Summary Chart lists all the Skills and Procedures and shortcut keys covered in the chapter making remembering what was covered easier!

Watch Skill Videos (formerly Student Training videos) are author-created training videos for each Skill in the chapter! Makes learning and remediation easier. Linked in ebook.

Biz Skills videos (e.g., Interviewing, Email Etiquette) one per chapter help teach students critical life and work skills! Linked in ebook.

Wide screen images with clear callouts provide better viewing and usability.

Application Introductions provide a brief overview of the application and put the chapters in context for students.

Stay Current

IT Innovation Station keeps you up to date with Office and Windows updates, news, and trends with help from your Pearson authors! Look for the IT "Innovation Station," articles on the MyITLab Community site. These monthly articles from Pearson authors on all things Microsoft Office, include tips for understanding automatic updates, adjusting to and utilizing new capabilities, and optimizing your Office course.

Skills for Success

with Microsoft® Office 2016 Volume 1

Application Introductions provide students with a concise overview of each application to put the chapters in context

Two Page Chapter Introduction—Briefs students on what is important and sets the stage for the project they will create

Learning Outcomes and Chapter Objectives clearly define what students will learn and achieve

Clock—Tells how much time students need to complete the chapter

File Summary—A quick summary of the files the students need to open and the names of the files they will turn in

Watch Skills Videos (formerly Student Training) for each Skill in the chapter provide a personal, instructor-led walk through

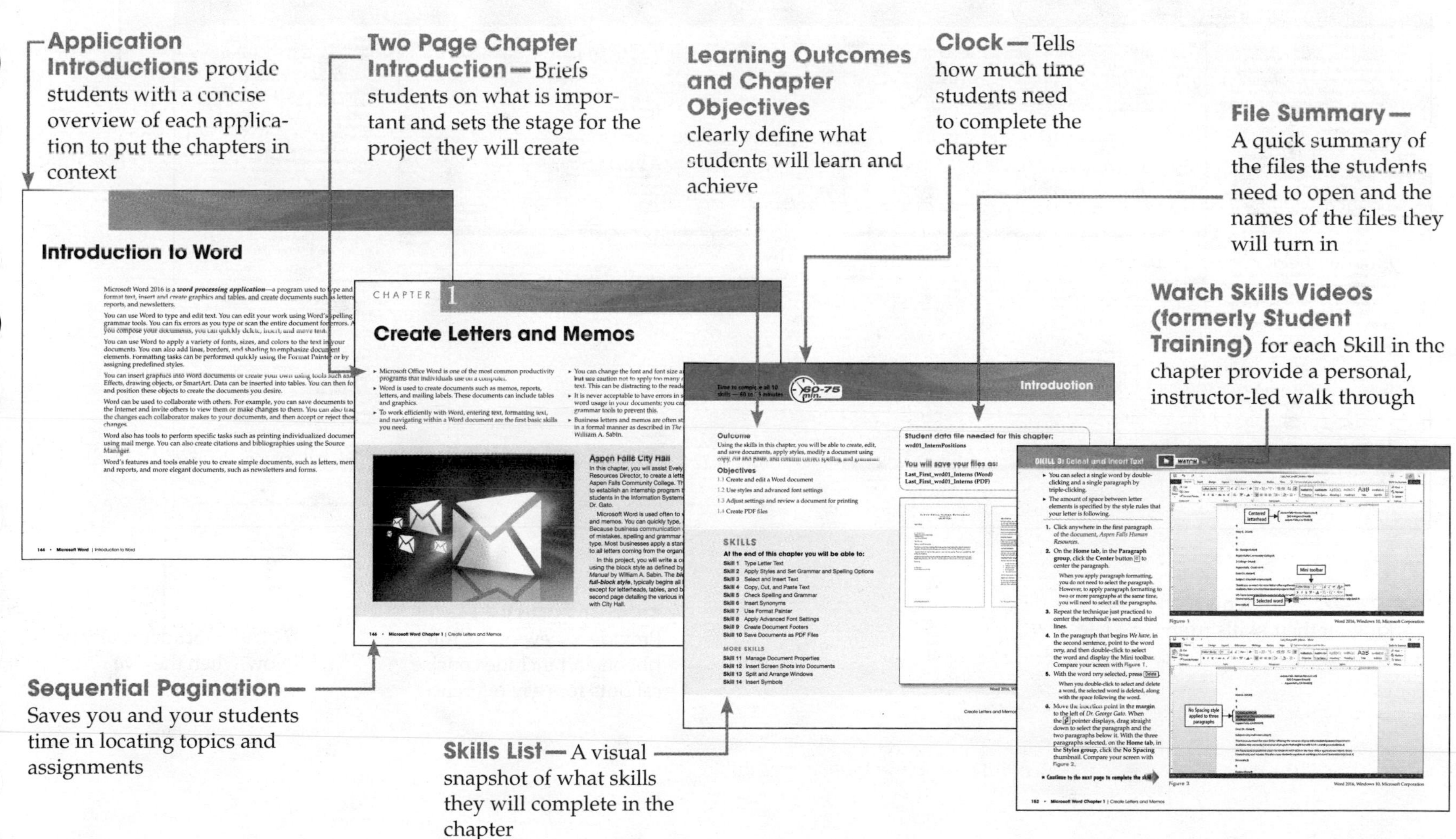

Sequential Pagination—Saves you and your students time in locating topics and assignments

Skills List—A visual snapshot of what skills they will complete in the chapter

Written for Today's Students—Skills are taught with numbered steps and bulleted text so students are less likely to skip valuable information

Two-Page Spreads—Each skill is presented in a concise, two-page spread to give students the visual illustration right with the steps—no flipping pages

Colored Text—Clearly shows what a student types

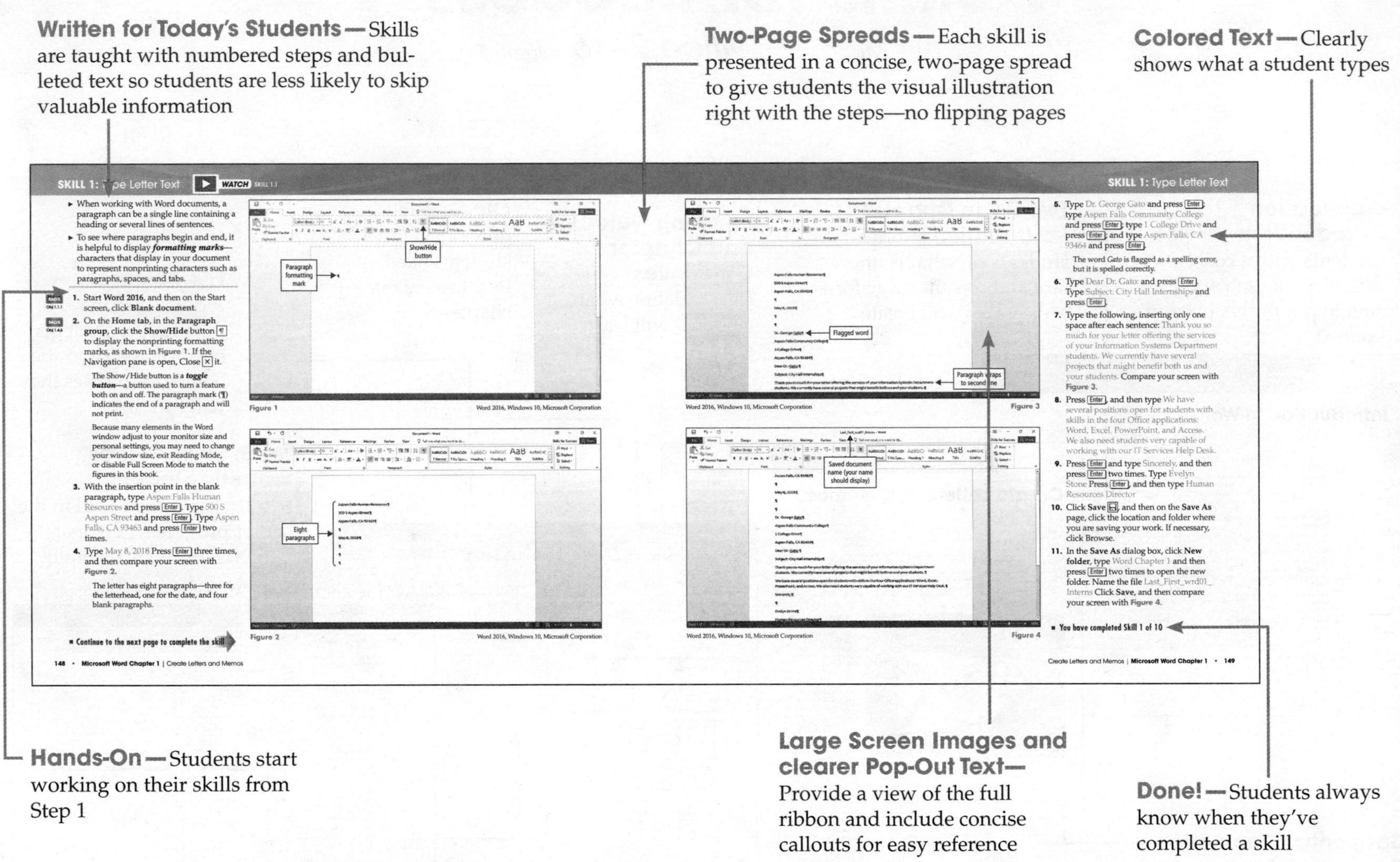
SKILL 1: Type Letter Text

WATCH SKILL 1.1

- When working with Word documents, a paragraph can be a single line containing a heading or several lines of sentences.
- To see where paragraphs begin and end, it is helpful to display ***formatting marks***—characters that display in your document to represent nonprinting characters such as paragraphs, spaces, and tabs.

MOS Obj 1.1.1

1. Start **Word 2016**, and then on the Start screen, click **Blank document**.

MOS Obj 1.4.6

2. On the **Home tab**, in the **Paragraph group**, click the **Show/Hide** button [¶] to display the nonprinting formatting marks, as shown in **Figure 1**. If the Navigation pane is open, Close [X] it.

   The Show/Hide button is a ***toggle button***—a button used to turn a feature both on and off. The paragraph mark (¶) indicates the end of a paragraph and will not print.

   Because many elements in the Word window adjust to your monitor size and personal settings, you may need to change your window size, exit Reading Mode, or disable Full Screen Mode to match the figures in this book.

3. With the insertion point in the blank paragraph, type Aspen Falls Human Resources and press [Enter]. Type 500 S Aspen Street and press [Enter]. Type Aspen Falls, CA 93463 and press [Enter] two times.
4. Type May 8, 2018 Press [Enter] three times, and then compare your screen with **Figure 2**.

   The letter has eight paragraphs—three for the letterhead, one for the date, and four blank paragraphs.

■ Continue to the next page to complete the skill

Figure 1 — Word 2016, Windows 10, Microsoft Corporation

Figure 2 — Word 2016, Windows 10, Microsoft Corporation

Figure 3 — Word 2016, Windows 10, Microsoft Corporation

Figure 4 — Word 2016, Windows 10, Microsoft Corporation

148 • Microsoft Word Chapter 1 | Create Letters and Memos

SKILL 1: Type Letter Text

5. Type Dr. George Gato and press [Enter]; type Aspen Falls Community College and press [Enter]; type 1 College Drive and press [Enter]; and type Aspen Falls, CA 93464 and press [Enter].

   The word *Gato* is flagged as a spelling error, but it is spelled correctly.

6. Type Dear Dr. Gato: and press [Enter]. Type Subject: City Hall Internships and press [Enter].
7. Type the following, inserting only one space after each sentence: Thank you so much for your letter offering the services of your Information Systems Department students. We currently have several projects that might benefit both us and your students. Compare your screen with **Figure 3**.
8. Press [Enter], and then type We have several positions open for students with skills in the four Office applications: Word, Excel, PowerPoint, and Access. We also need students very capable of working with our IT Services Help Desk.
9. Press [Enter] and type Sincerely, and then press [Enter] two times. Type Evelyn Stone Press [Enter], and then type Human Resources Director
10. Click **Save** [💾], and then on the **Save As** page, click the location and folder where you are saving your work. If necessary, click Browse.
11. In the **Save As** dialog box, click **New folder**, type Word Chapter 1 and then press [Enter] two times to open the new folder. Name the file Last_First_wrd01_Interns Click **Save**, and then compare your screen with **Figure 4**.

■ You have completed Skill 1 of 10

Create Letters and Memos | Microsoft Word Chapter 1 • 149

Hands-On—Students start working on their skills from Step 1

Large Screen Images and clearer Pop-Out Text—Provide a view of the full ribbon and include concise callouts for easy reference

Done!—Students always know when they've completed a skill

More Skills—Additional skills previously provided online are now included in the chapter to ensure students learn these important skills.

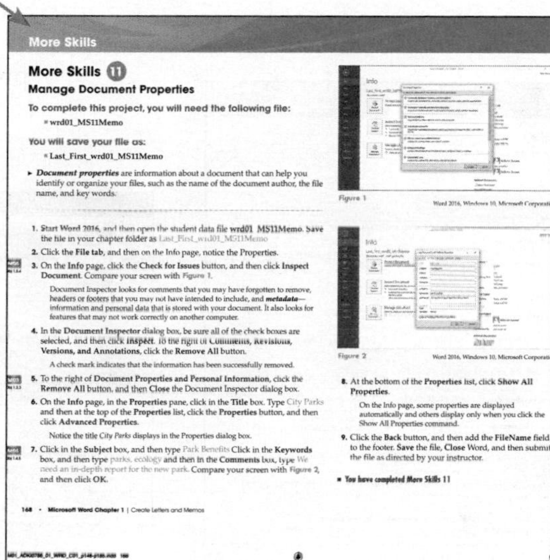

BizSkills Videos—Covering the important business skills students need to succeed: *Communication, Dress for Success, Interview Prep*, and more

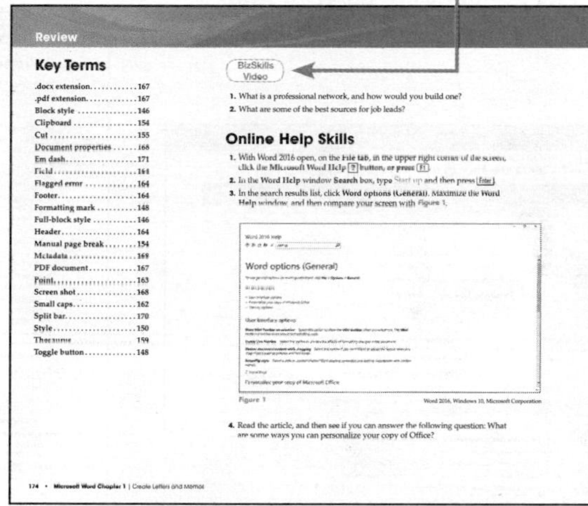

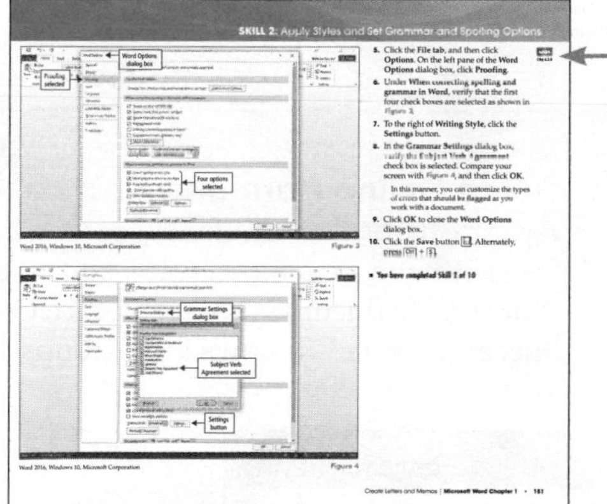

MOS Objectives—Integrated into the text for quick review and exam prep.

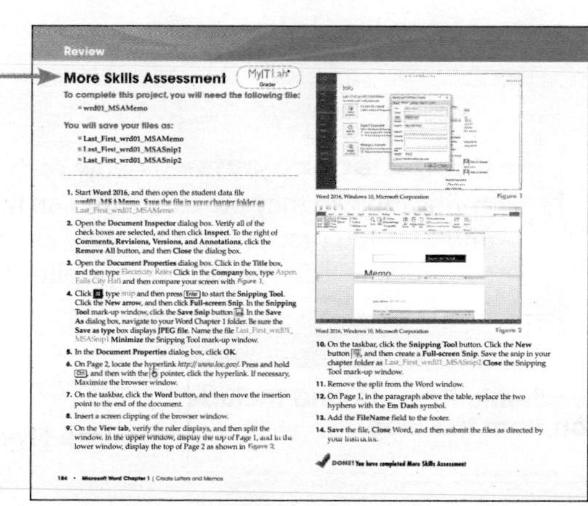

More Skills Assessment— MyITLab® Grader
Covers the core skills from the the four More Skills projects in a linear project that tells students what to do, but not necessarily how to do it.

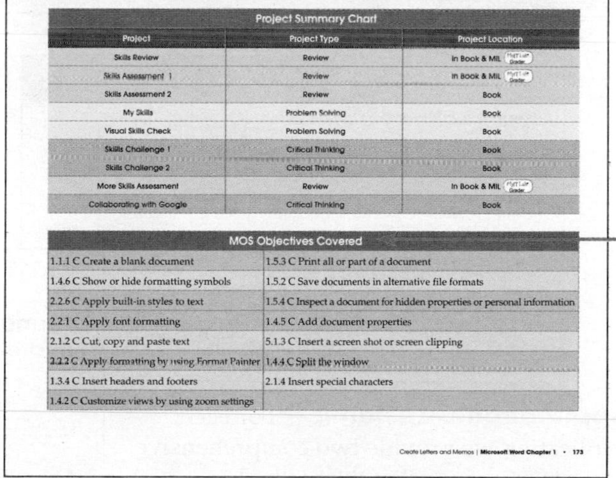

NEW MOS Summary table—Provides quick overview of objectives covered.

NEW Collaborating with Google— Hands-on projects that allow students to apply the skills they have learned in a Google project to demonstrate proficiency.

Skills and Procedures Summary Chart— Provides a quick review of the skills and tasks covered in each chapter

NEW Project Summary Chart— Provides an overview of project types and locations.

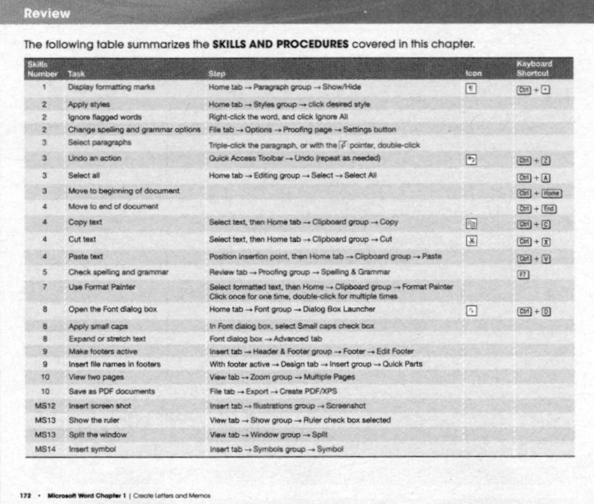

Review

The following table summarizes the **SKILLS AND PROCEDURES** covered in this chapter.

Skills Number	Task	Step	Icon	Keyboard Shortcut
1	Display formatting marks	Home tab → Paragraph group → Show/Hide		Ctrl + *
2	Apply styles	Home tab → Styles group → click desired style		
2	Ignore flagged words	Right-click the word, and click Ignore All		
2	Change spelling and grammar options	File tab → Options → Proofing page → Settings button		
3	Select paragraphs	Triple-click the paragraph, or with the pointer, double-click		
3	Undo an action	Quick Access Toolbar → Undo (repeat as needed)		Ctrl + Z
3	Select all	Home tab → Editing group → Select → Select All		Ctrl + A
3	Move to beginning of document			Ctrl + Home
4	Move to end of document			Ctrl + End
4	Copy text	Select text, then Home tab → Clipboard group → Copy		Ctrl + C
4	Cut text	Select text, then Home tab → Clipboard group → Cut		Ctrl + X
4	Paste text	Position insertion point, then Home tab → Clipboard group → Paste		Ctrl + V
5	Check spelling and grammar	Review tab → Proofing group → Spelling & Grammar		F7
7	Use Format Painter	Select formatted text, then Home → Clipboard group → Format Painter Click once for one time, double-click for multiple times		
8	Open the Font dialog box	Home tab → Font group → Dialog Box Launcher		Ctrl + D
8	Apply small caps	In Font dialog box, select Small caps check box		
8	Expand or stretch text	Font dialog box → Advanced tab		
9	Make footers active	Insert tab → Header & Footer group → Footer → Edit Footer		
9	Insert file names in footers	With footer active → Design tab → Insert group → Quick Parts		
10	View two pages	View tab → Zoom group → Multiple Pages		
10	Save as PDF documents	File tab → Export → Create PDF/XPS		
MS12	Insert screen shot	Insert tab → Illustrations group → Screenshot		
MS13	Show the ruler	View tab → Show group → Ruler check box selected		
MS13	Split the window	View tab → Window group → Split		
MS14	Insert symbol	Insert tab → Symbols group → Symbol		

172 • Microsoft Word Chapter 1 | Create Letters and Memos

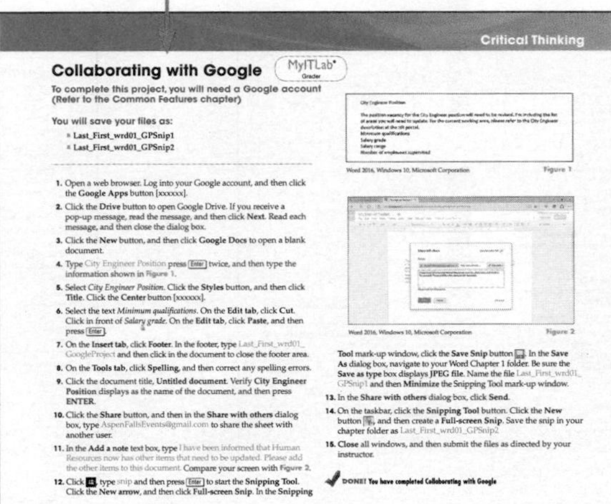

Critical Thinking

Collaborating with Google

To complete this project, you will need a Google account (Refer to the Common Features chapter)

You will save your files as:

- Last_First_wrd01_GPSnip1
- Last_First_wrd01_GPSnip2

DONE! You have completed Collaborating with Google

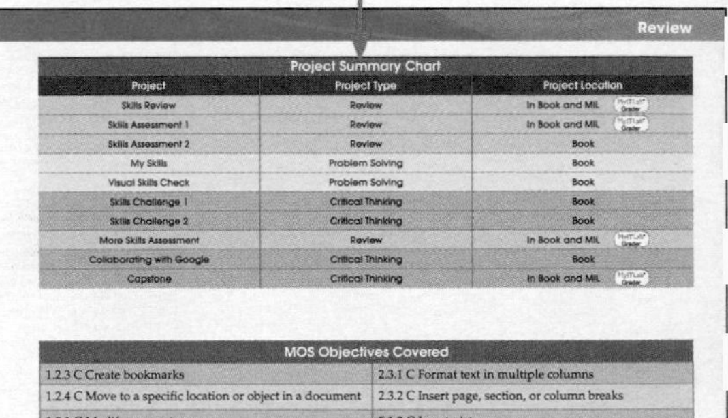

Review

Project	Project Type	Project Location
Skills Review	Review	In Book and MIL (MyITLab Grader)
Skills Assessment 1	Review	In Book and MIL (MyITLab Grader)
Skills Assessment 2	Review	Book
My Skills	Problem Solving	Book
Visual Skills Check	Problem Solving	Book
Skills Challenge 1	Critical Thinking	Book
Skills Challenge 2	Critical Thinking	Book
More Skills Assessment	Review	In Book and MIL (MyITLab Grader)
Collaborating with Google	Critical Thinking	Book
Capstone	Critical Thinking	In Book and MIL (MyITLab Grader)

MOS Objectives Covered

1.2.3 C Create bookmarks	2.3.1 C Format text in multiple columns
1.2.4 C Move to a specific location or object in a document	2.3.2 C Insert page, section, or column breaks
1.3.1 C Modify page setup	5.1.2 C Insert pictures
1.3.2 C Apply document themes	5.2.4 C Format objects
1.4.1 C Change document views	5.2.6 C Apply a picture style
1.4.2 C Customize views by using zoom settings	5.3.1 C Create a SmartArt graphic
1.4.6 C Show or hide formatting symbols	5.3.2 C Format a SmartArt graphic
1.5.2 C Save documents in alternative file formats	5.3.3 C Modify SmartArt graphic content
2.2.1 C Apply font formatting	

Create Newsletters and Mail Merge Documents | Microsoft Word Chapter 4 • 293

CAPSTONE PROJECT

To complete this project, you will need the following files:
wrd_CAPVisitUs
wrd_CAPFestival

You will save your file as:
Last_First_wrd_CAPVisitUs

Integrated Projects— Follow each application so they are easier to manage and provide practice immediately after students work with each new application.

Office Online (formerly Web App) Projects— Students use Cloud computing to save files; create, edit, and share Office documents using Office Online; and create Windows Live groups.

INTEGRATED PROJECT 1

Format Academic Reports and Include Information from the Web

Aspen Falls City Hall

OFFICE ONLINE PROJECT

Create Flyers Using Word Online

Aspen Falls City Hall

Application Capstones— For each application we provide two comprehensive projects covering all of the Skills. The capstones are available as a Homework and Assessment version, with the Assessment version earning a MIL Badge. Also available as a Grader project in MyITLab.

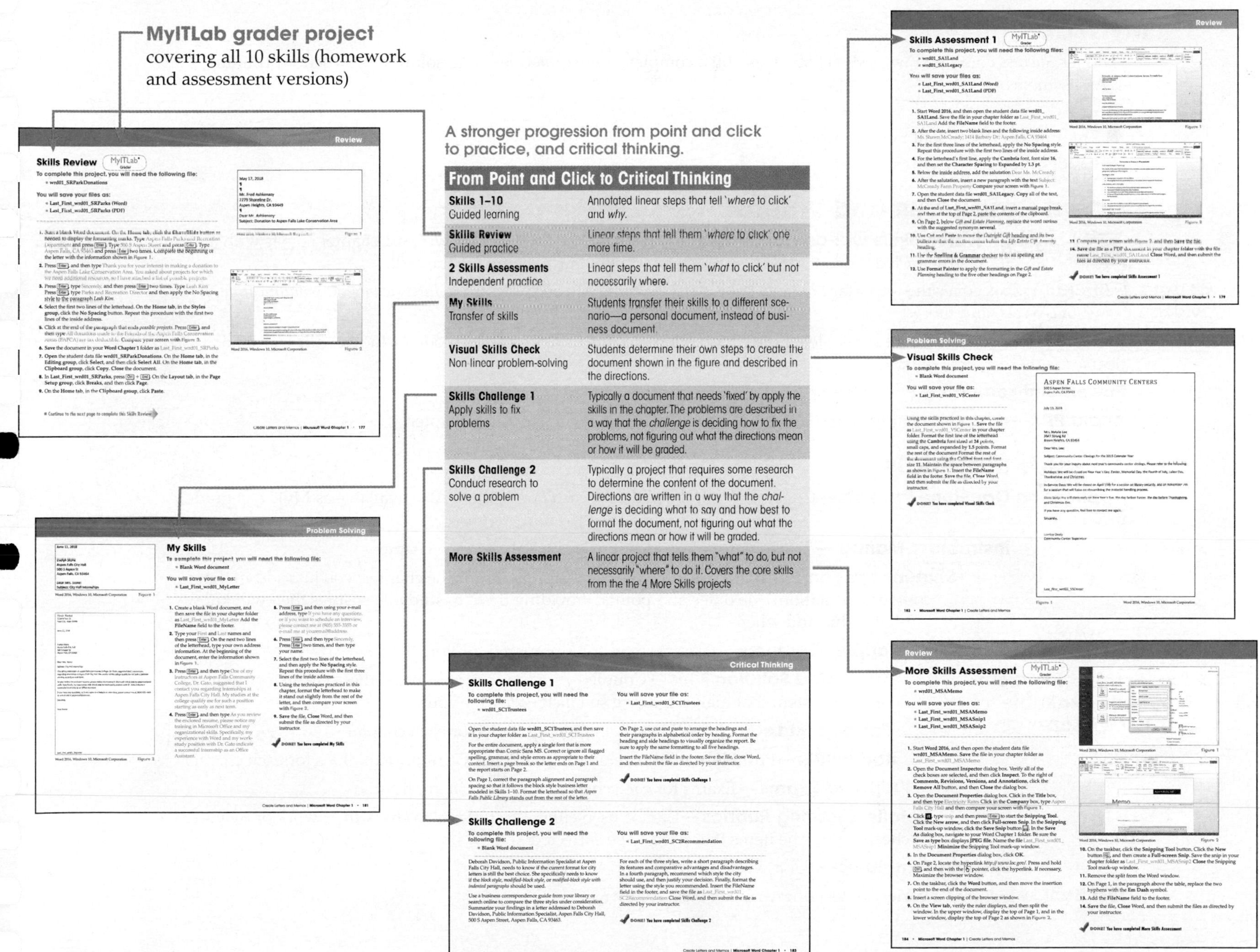

From Point and Click to Critical Thinking

Skills 1–10 Guided learning	Annotated linear steps that tell '*where* to click' and *why*.
Skills Review Guided practice	Linear steps that tell them '*where* to click' one more time.
2 Skills Assessments Independent practice	Linear steps that tell them '*what* to click' but not necessarily where.
My Skills Transfer of skills	Students transfer their skills to a different scenario—a personal document, instead of business document.
Visual Skills Check Non linear problem-solving	Students determine their own steps to create the document shown in the figure and described in the directions.
Skills Challenge 1 Apply skills to fix problems	Typically a document that needs 'fixed' by apply the skills in the chapter. The problems are described in a way that the *challenge* is deciding how to fix the problems, not figuring out what the directions mean or how it will be graded.
Skills Challenge 2 Conduct research to solve a problem	Typically a project that requires some research to determine the content of the document. Directions are written in a way that the *challenge* is deciding what to say and how best to format the document, not figuring out what the directions mean or how it will be graded.
More Skills Assessment	A linear project that tells them "what" to do, but not necessarily "where" to do it. Covers the core skills from the the 4 More Skills projects

MyITLab (MyITLab®)

Skills for Success combined with MyITLab gives you a completely integrated learning solution: Instruction, Training, & Assessment

- eText
- Training & Assessment Simulations
- Grader Projects

Student Resources and Videos!

WATCH **Watch Skills videos (formerly Student Training)**—Each skill within a chapter comes with an instructor-led video that walks students through how to complete the skill.

BizSkills Video — BizSKill Videos cover the important business skills students need to be successful—*Interviewing, Communication, Dressing for Success,* and more.

Student Data Files—are all available on the Companion Website using the access code included with your book. pearsonhighered.com/skills

PowerPoint Lectures—PowerPoint presentations for each chapter

Audio PPTs—Provide an audio version of the PowerPoint presentations for each chapter

Instructor Materials

Application Capstone Projects—Covering all of the Skills for each application. Also available as MyITLab grader projects

Instructor's Manual—Teaching tips and additional resources for each chapter

Student Assignment Tracker—Lists all the assignments for the chapter; you just add in the course information, due dates and points. Providing these to students ensures they will know what is due and when

Scripted Lectures—Classroom lectures prepared for you

Annotated Solution Files—Coupled with the scoring rubrics, these create a grading and scoring system that makes grading so much easier for you

PowerPoint Lectures—PowerPoint presentations for each chapter

Audio PPTs—Provide an audio version of the PowerPoint presentations for each chapter

Prepared Exams—Exams for each chapter and for each application

Detailed Scoring Rubrics—Can be used either by students to check their work or by you as a quick check-off for the items that need to be corrected

Syllabus Templates—For 8-week, 12-week, and 16-week courses

Test Bank—Includes a variety of test questions for each chapter

All Student and Instructor Materials available in MyITLab.

Margo Chaney Adkins is an Assistant Professor of Information Technology at Carroll Community College in Westminster, Maryland. She holds a bachelor's degree in Information Systems and master's degree in Post-Secondary Education from Salisbury University. She teaches computer application and office technology courses, both online and in the classroom. She enjoys athletic activities, gardening, and traveling with her husband.

Catherine Hain is an instructor at Central New Mexico Community College in Albuquerque, New Mexico. She teaches computer applications classes in the Business and Information Technology School, both in the classroom and through the distance learning office. Catherine holds a bachelor's degree in Management and Marketing and a master's degree in Business Administration.

Lisa Hawkins is a Professor of Computer and Information Sciences at Frederick Community College in Maryland. She earned a PhD in Information Technology from Capella University. Lisa has also worked as a database administrator, E-commerce manager, and systems administrator. She enjoys adventure sports, gardening, and making glass beads.

Stephanie Murre Wolf is a Technology and Computer Applications instructor at Moraine Park Technical College in Wisconsin. She is a graduate of Alverno College and enjoys teaching, writing curriculum, and authoring textbooks. In addition to classroom instruction, Stephanie actively performs corporate training in technology. She is married and has two sons; together, the family enjoys the outdoors.

A Special Thank You Pearson Prentice Hall gratefully acknowledges the contribution made by Shelley Gaskin to the first edition publication of this series—*Skills for Success with Office 2007*. The series has truly benefited from her dedication toward developing a textbook that aims to help students and instructors. We thank her for her continued support of this series.

CHAPTER 1

Getting Started with Computer Concepts

- The computer is a system with many parts that perform specific functions. Understanding how these functions work helps you to become more effective when using computers to accomplish tasks.
- There are many types of computers, but they all work in a similar manner.
- Understanding how a computer works requires an understanding of the main purpose of the hardware and software on that computer.
- Networks, the Internet, and the cloud have become integral parts of most computer systems.
- Understanding computers as systems also helps you to make informed decisions when solving problems, upgrading, or purchasing a computer.

violetkaipa/Fotolia

Introduction

Computers are an integral part of daily life. You interact with them when online banking, searching for information, shopping, registering for classes, interacting with others via social media, or video chatting.

Because you interact with computers on a daily basis, it is important to become knowledgeable about computers: how they work, how to troubleshoot problems, and how to make an informed decision when purchasing a computer system. Solid working knowledge about computers enhances your career possibilities and also makes your daily life easier.

This chapter will familiarize you with some of the fundamentals of a computer system, such as computer hardware and software, different types of computers, basics of computer networks, an overview of saving and storage, and an understanding of cloud computing as well as an introduction to Office 365. All of these concepts can help you understand how to work with computers and how to make informed decisions when purchasing computer systems.

Time to complete all 10 skills — 60–90 minutes

Outcome

Using the concepts in this chapter, you will be able to answer questions like these:

1 What is the difference between a reader, tablet, ultrabook, notebook, and desktop computer?
2 How do keyboards, mice, and touch screens work?
3 What is random access memory (RAM)?
4 What is the difference between a hard disk drive and a solid-state disk drive?
5 What is the difference between desktop applications and Windows 10 Store apps?
6 What is a web app?
7 How is each type of productivity software used?
8 What do I need to set up a home network and connect to the Internet?
9 What is the cloud, and how is it used?
10 How can I share my files, photographs, songs, and videos?
11 What is Office 365, and how is it different than the desktop version of Microsoft Office?
12 What is the first step in purchasing a computer system?
13 What specifications do I need to know when purchasing a computer?

Student data file needed for this chapter:

No documents are needed or created in this chapter.

CONCEPTS

At the end of this chapter, you will better understand the following concepts:

Concept 1 The Computer Is a System
Concept 2 Common Operating Systems
Concept 3 Input Devices
Concept 4 Storage Devices
Concept 5 Apps and Applications
Concept 6 Networks
Concept 7 Cloud Computing
Concept 8 Share Files with Others
Concept 9 Office 365
Concept 10 Buying a Computer

- A computer is a system comprised of smaller components working together to perform four basic functions: input, processing, output, and storage.
- Because you interact with computers on a daily basis, it is important to have an understanding of how they work.

1. ***What is a computer?*** Computers can be classified and defined in several ways. A ***computer*** is commonly defined as a programmable electronic device that can receive input, process, produce output, and store data. For example, to create a letter on a computer, you type on a keyboard (input) using software that converts the input into a document (processing) that displays on a screen (output). The characters you type and the formatting choices you make are stored in the computer's temporary or permanent memory. In this way, the four computer functions work as a system as shown in **Figure 1**.
2. ***How do the four basic computer functions work together?*** The four basic computer functions work together in a cycle called the ***information processing cycle***. The four functions are summarized in the table shown in **Figure 2**.
3. ***What is software? Software*** is a set of instructions stored on your computer. The central processing unit (CPU) processes data according to these instructions. ***Operating system software*** controls the way the computer works while it is running. You use ***application software*** to accomplish specific tasks such as word processing and surfing the Internet.

■ Continue to the next page to complete the concept

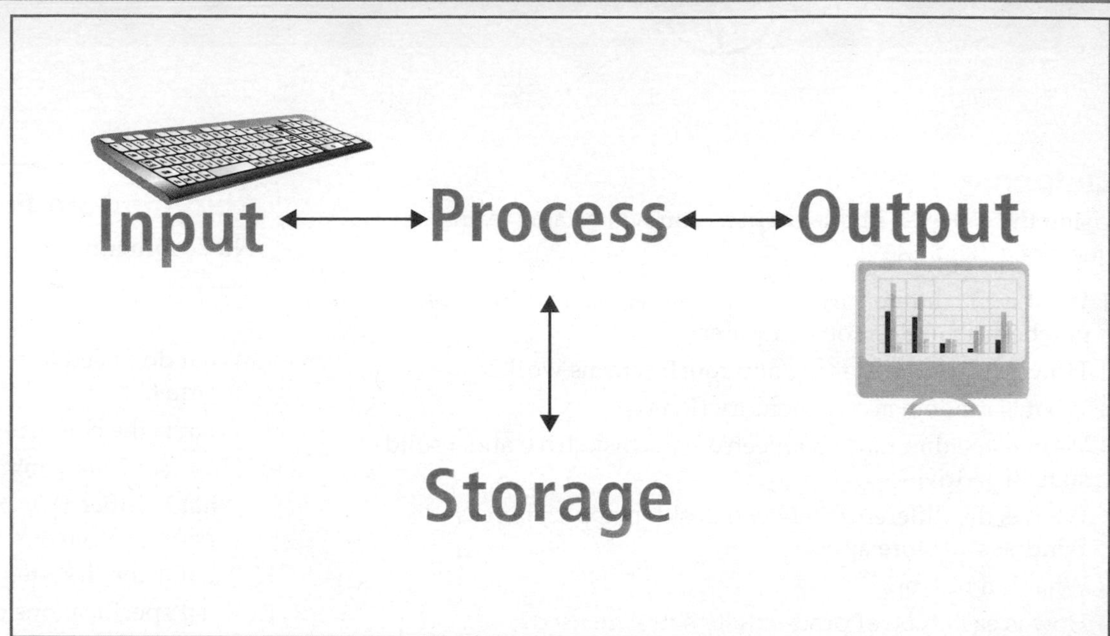

Figure 1 Claire Cordier/Dorling Kindersley Ltd.; Dorling Kindersley Ltd.

Information Processing Cycle	
Basic Function	**Description**
Input	The process of gathering information from the user or other sources through an ***input device***—hardware that provides information to the computer, such as keyboards, mice, touch displays, and microphones.
Processing	Transforming, managing, and making decisions about data and information. Most processing occurs in the ***central processing unit*** (***CPU***)—the hardware responsible for controlling the computer commands and operations.
Output	The display of information through an ***output device***—hardware that provides information to the user, such as monitors, speakers, and printers.
Storage	The location where data resides on a computer. ***Random Access Memory*** (***RAM***) is an electronic chip that provides temporary storage. Long-term data are written to a ***storage device***—hardware that stores information while the computer is in use or after it is powered off. Storage devices include magnetic hard drives, solid-state drives, optical drives, USB flash drives, and other types of permanent storage.

Figure 2

Luisa Leal/Fotolia

Figure 3

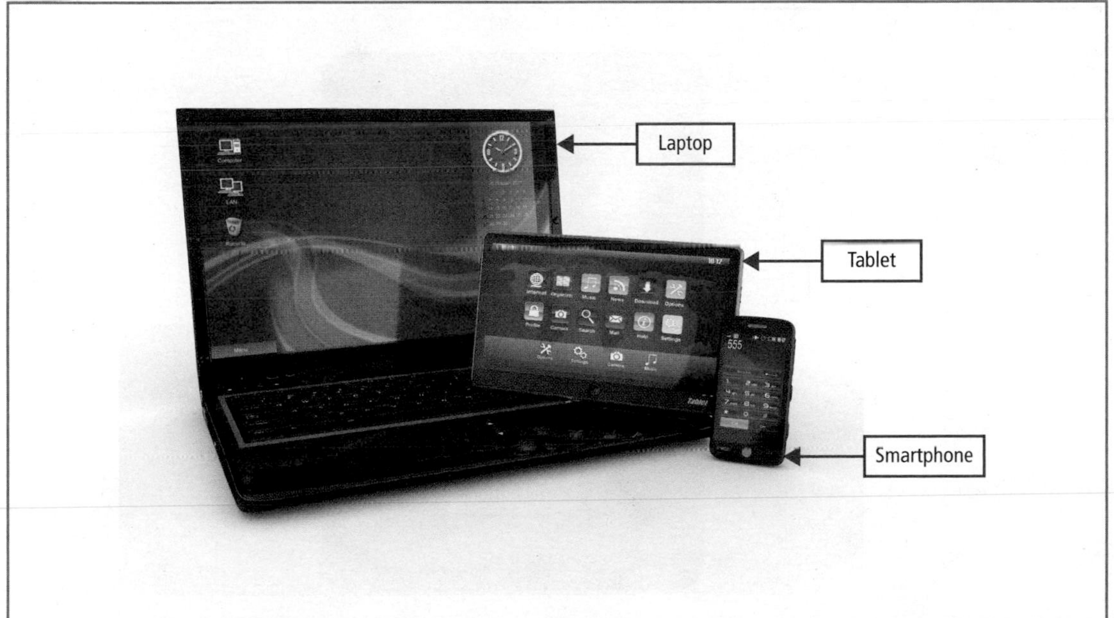

Maxx-Studio/Shutterstock

Figure 4

4. What types of computers are there?

   Desktop computer: A computer designed to be placed permanently on a desk or at a work station. Desktop computers typically have larger monitors and more computing power than other personal devices. A desktop computer is shown in **Figure 3**.

   Laptop: A portable computer with a built-in screen, keyboard, and touchpad. Laptops range from 13 to 20 inches in width and weigh 3 pounds or more. Ultrabooks weigh less than 3 pounds.

   Tablet: A portable computer built around a single touch screen. Tablets typically range from 7 to 13 inches in width and weigh between 1 and 2 pounds.

   Reader: A tablet-like computer designed around entertainment features, such as books and movies. The other types of tasks that can be performed on a reader are very limited.

   Smartphone: A cellular phone with an operating system. Smartphones have touch screens like a tablet and are small enough to be carried in a pocket.

5. ***What is a personal computing device?*** Portable computers like a smartphone or tablet are often referred to as ***devices***. The relative sizes of common devices are shown in **Figure 4**.

6. ***What other types of computers are there?*** There are many other types of computers such as the following:

   Server: A computer dedicated to providing services to other computers on a network.

   Embedded computer: A small, specialized computer built into a larger component, such as an automobile and an appliance.

■ **You have completed Concept 1 of 10**

- The operating system is the gateway between the computer hardware and the application software you have installed on the computer.
- Soon after you turn on a computer, control is given to the operating system. The operating system continues running until you turn the computer off.

1. ***What is a graphical user interface?*** Operating systems provide a ***graphical user interface*** (***GUI***)—a visual system used to interact with the computer. GUI elements include icons, buttons, tiles, windows, dialog boxes, menus, and ribbons. It is through these graphical elements that you instruct the computer to perform tasks.
2. ***What is a desktop?*** Many, but not all, operating systems provide a ***desktop***—a GUI element that simulates a real desktop in which files are placed. Both files and programs can be opened in windows—similar to opening a file drawer/cabinet in your office and selecting a file folder with items inside that you can arrange on top of your work area. The Windows 10 desktop is shown in **Figure 1**.
3. ***Do all operating systems have desktops?*** Several operating systems do not provide a desktop. Instead, you interact with icons or tiles on a screen. **Figure 2** shows a tablet operating system without a desktop.
4. ***What is a file system?*** Operating systems provide a ***file system***—an organized method to save and retrieve files. Desktop computer operating systems provide a way for you to manage your files directly, while many mobile device operating systems limit the files you can see.

■ **Continue to the next page to complete the concept**

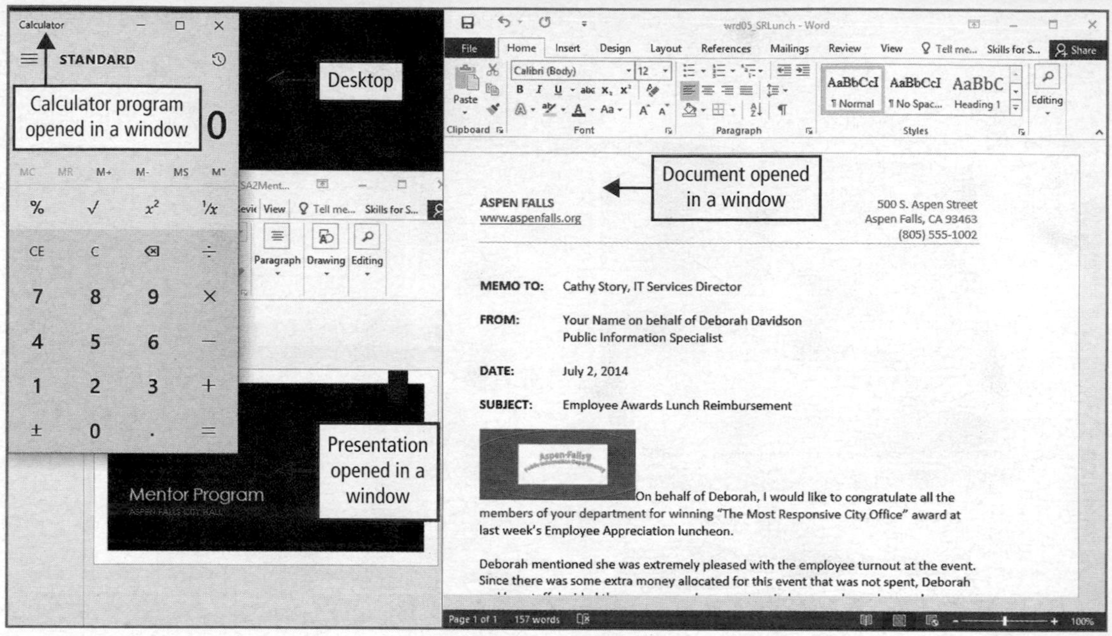

Figure 1 Office 2016, Windows 10, Microsoft Corporation

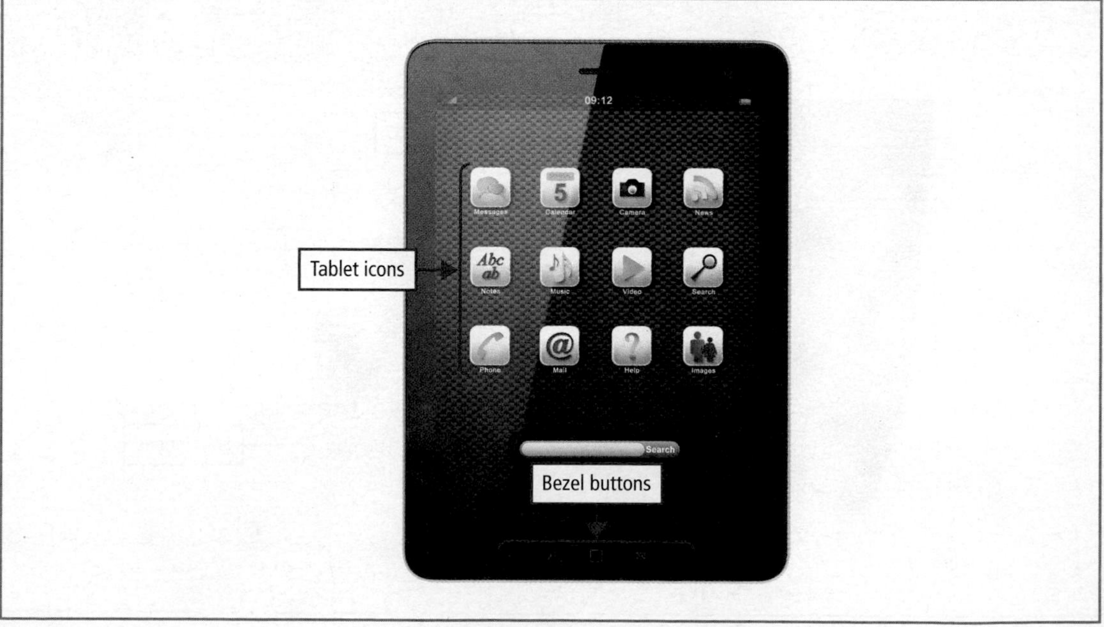

Figure 2 Maksim Kabakou/Fotolia

Office 2016, Windows 10, Microsoft Corporation

Figure 3

Common Operating Systems	
Name	**Description**
Apple iOS	A mobile operating system (OS) designed for iPads, iPhones, and other Apple devices.
Google Android	A Linux-based OS designed by Google for smartphones and tablets with many versions.
Google Chrome OS	A Linux-based OS designed by Google for Chromebooks for users to access the web and/or installed applications when offline.
Linux	A Unix-based OS built as ***open source software***—software that can be sold or given away as long as the source code is provided for free.
Mac OS X	A UNIX-based OS designed for Macintosh notebooks and computers.
Microsoft Windows 8.0/8.1	A Microsoft OS designed for computers, laptops, and tablets with Intel-based processors.
Microsoft Windows 10	A Microsoft OS designed and used between computers, ***embedded systems***—computer hardware and software used to control many devices—HoloLens, laptops, smartphones, Surface Hub, tablets, and Xbox One.

Figure 4

5. ***Does Windows 10 provide a desktop?*** Windows 10 provides a desktop. It is the screen you see after logging in to your computer, as shown in **Figure 3**. You may see the Recycle Bin icon and Edge shortcut.

   The Windows 10 Start menu displays tiles. When you click or tap a tile that is a running program, a larger view of the program fills the screen. For example, the Bing weather tile displays current weather information in its tile. In full-screen mode, it displays even more information. When you click or tap a tile that represents a file, web page, or program that is not currently running, that file, web page, or program opens.

   By providing a Start menu and a desktop, the Windows 10 operating system can perform similarly on a desktop computer, laptop, tablet, or smartphone.

6. ***What are the common operating systems?*** Several operating systems are available depending on the type of computer or device. However, not all computers will run with an operating system other than the one for which it was designed. The common operating systems are summarized in the table shown in **Figure 4**.

7. ***What are utility programs?*** Operating systems provide ***utility programs***—small programs designed to perform routine tasks or computer housekeeping tasks. Other utility programs can be purchased and installed by the computer user.

■ **You have completed Concept 2 of 10**

▶ The methods you use to work with a computer depend on the types of input devices that your computer, operating system, and application software support.

1. ***How do keyboards work? Keyboards*** are input devices used to type characters and perform common commands. In addition to typing, you can perform common tasks using ***keyboard shortcuts***—combinations of Ctrl, Alt, ⊞, and character keys that perform commands when pressed. Other keys perform commands, such as the function or "F" keys, PageUp, and PrintScreen. Keyboards vary by manufacturer, but common keyboard areas are shown in **Figure 1**.
2. ***How do mice work? Mice*** are input devices used to point to and click screen elements. The mouse controls the position of a pointer on the screen, and commands are performed when the left or right mouse button is clicked. Typically, ***click*** means to press the left mouse button, and ***right-click*** means to press the right mouse button. Most mice also have a scroll wheel, which can be used to move up or down within windows. A typical mouse is shown in **Figure 2**.
3. ***How do keyboards and mice connect to computers?*** External input devices may connect to your computer using a wire or wirelessly using ***Bluetooth***—a wireless technology that connects devices using radio waves over short distances. Some keyboards are ***onscreen keyboards***—virtual keyboards that display on a touch screen—and others connect to or are part of the computer itself.

■ **Continue to the next page to complete the concept**

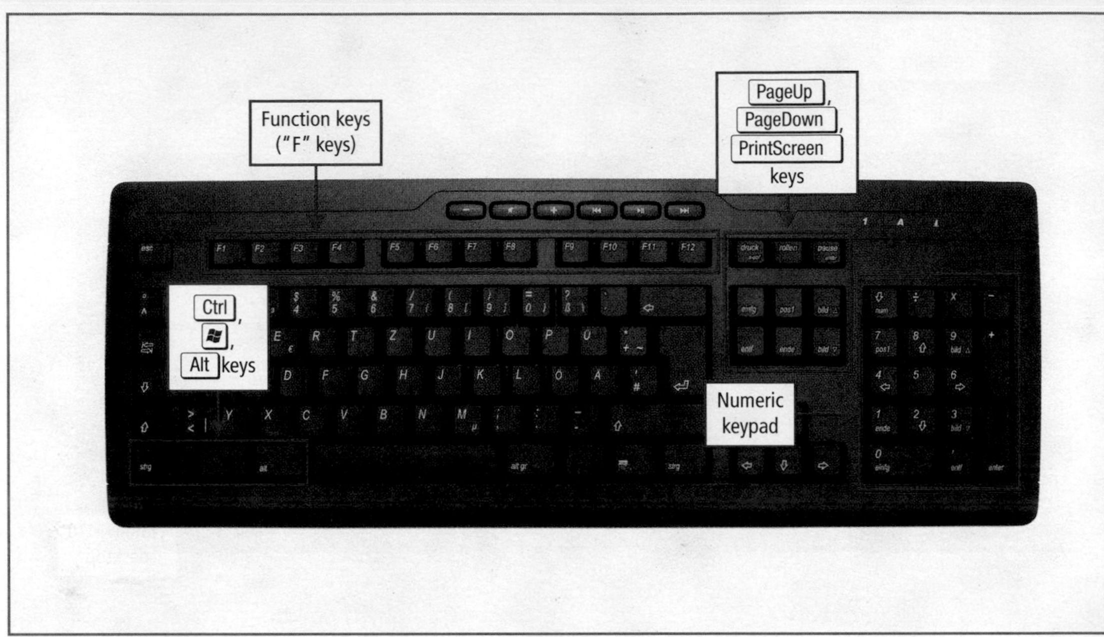

Figure 1 Baciu/Shutterstock

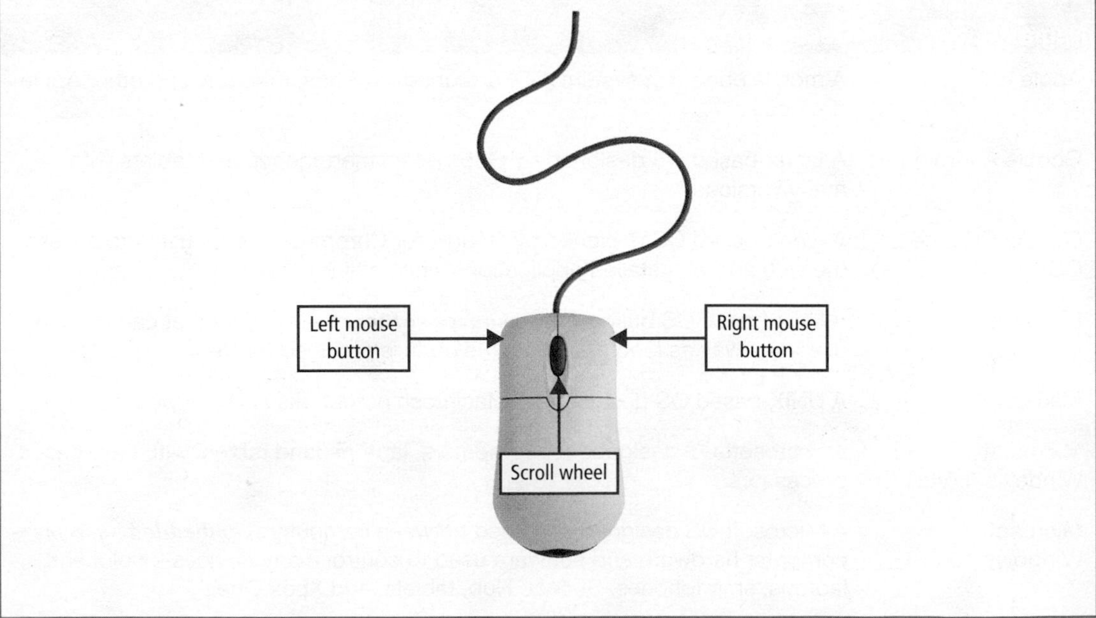

Figure 2 Dimedrol68/Fotolia

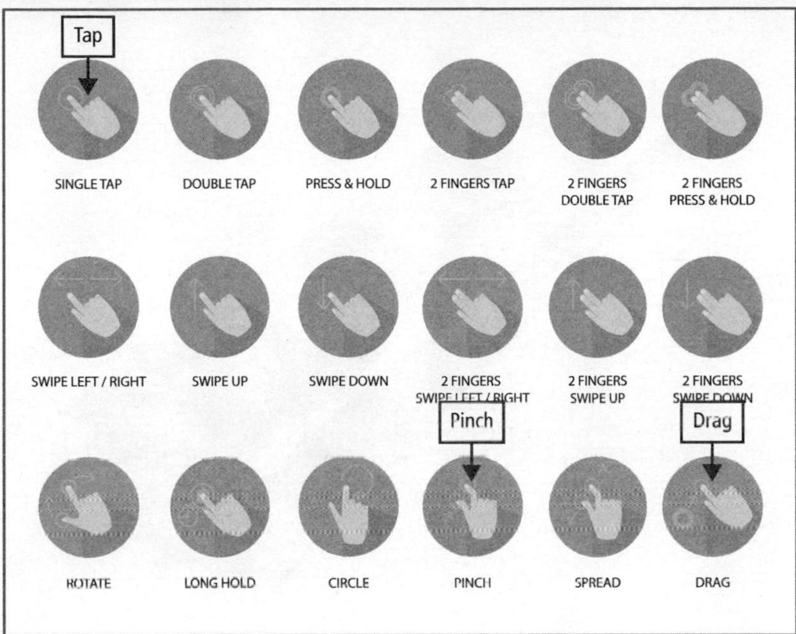

Redlinevector/Fotolia

Figure 3

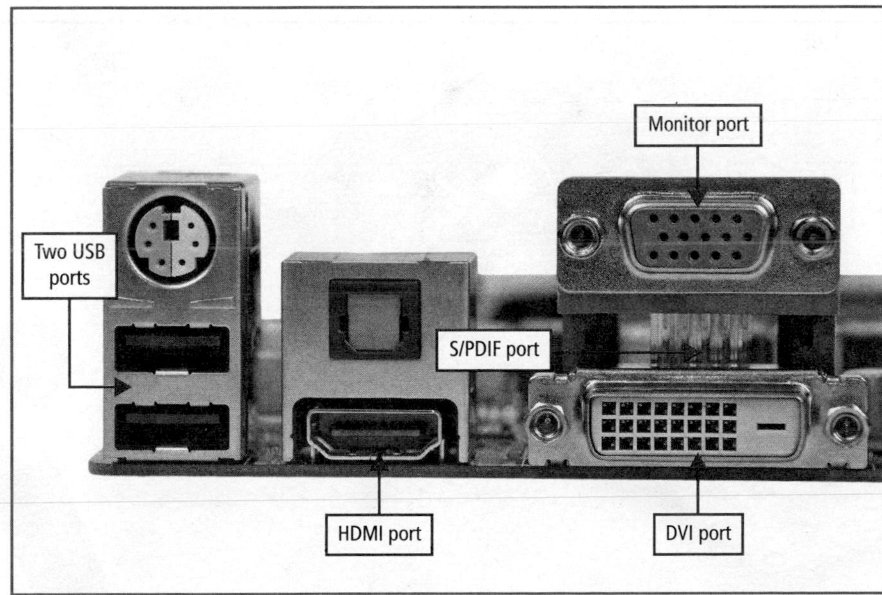

Hellen Sergeyeva/Shutterstock

Figure 4

4. ***How do touchpads work?*** Some computers have a built-in ***touchpad***—a flat area on which you can move the finger to position the pointer. Many touchpads can be pressed similar to pressing the left and right buttons on a mouse.
5. ***How do touch screens work?*** Touch screens can accept input when you touch them with your finger or a ***stylus***—a pen-like pointing device used with touch screens. Touch screens use ***gestures***—bodily motions that are interpreted as commands. Common gestures are described in **Figure 3**.
6. ***Are there other input devices?*** There are many ways a computer can accept input from users. ***Speech recognition*** performs commands or types text based on words spoken into a microphone. Most newer computers have a webcam already installed. If not, cameras can be attached to a computer for recording video or for transmitting video during video conferences or live chats. ***Scanners*** can convert paper images into a digital image, and ***fingerprint scanners*** read fingerprints to authorize computer users.
7. ***What are ports? Ports*** are the connectors on the outside of the computer to which you connect external devices. Ports are designed so that only the right type of connector can be used. For example, USB ports can accept connections from USB keyboards, mice, and flash drives. An external monitor has ports for each video standard it can accept. Common ports are shown in **Figure 4**.

■ **You have completed Concept 3 of 10**

- Data is stored in the short-term and long-term memory of a computer.
- Storage devices include random access memory (RAM), internal and external hard drives, USB flash drives, DVD-RW drives, and the cloud.

1. ***How does RAM work?*** RAM acts as the computer's short-term memory. RAM is stored in chips similar to those shown in **Figure 1**. These chips maintain data storage by the flow of electricity, and the data is erased when the power to the computer is turned off. You need to save files to a long-term storage location if you want to use them in the future.
2. ***What is a hard disk drive?*** A ***hard disk drive*** (***HDD***) is a common long term storage device in desktop computers. Traditional hard disk drives write and read data stored as magnetic tracks on platters inside a drive similar to those shown in **Figure 2**.
3. ***What is the difference between a solid-state drive and a magnetic disk drive?*** A ***solid-state drive*** (***SSD***) stores data using electricity and retains the data when the power is turned off. Although both the SSD and the magnetic disk drive can store the same amount of data, the SSD is more costly. Any storage drive connected to an eSATA port is known as an ***external drive***.
4. ***What is a USB flash drive?*** A ***USB flash drive*** is a small, portable, solid-state drive about the size of the human thumb. For this reason, they are sometimes referred to as ***thumb drives***.

■ Continue to the next page to complete the concept

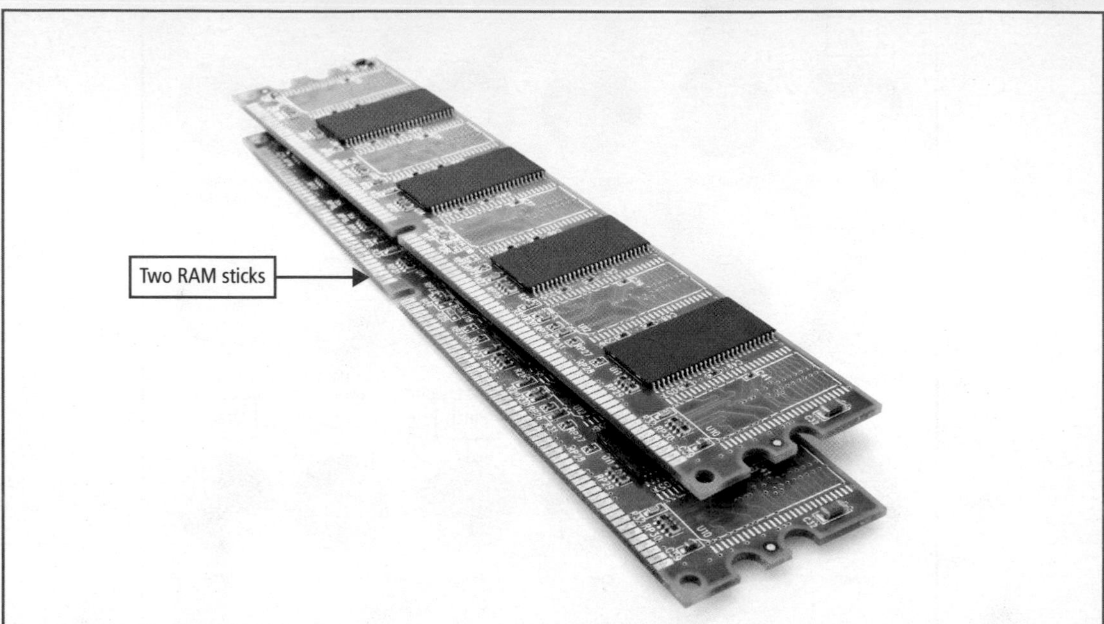

Figure 1 Vladimir Vydrin/Fotolia

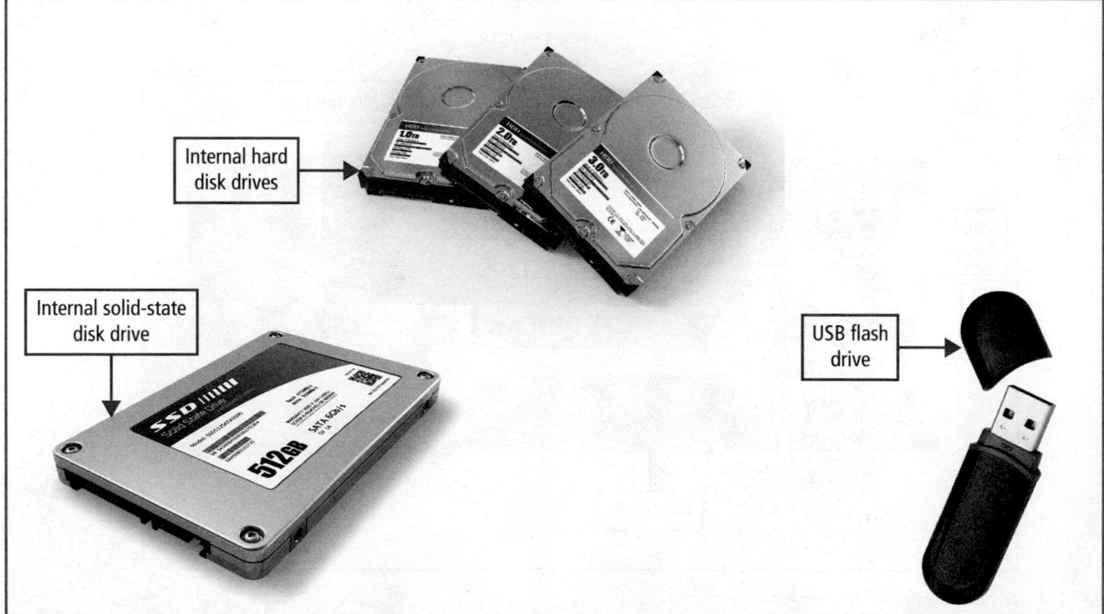

Figure 2 Maksym Yemelyanov/Fotolia; Oleksiy Mark/Fotolia

Common Storage Sizes	
Name	**Description**
Kilobyte (KB)	One thousand bytes (1 page of text)
Megabyte (MB)	One million bytes (100 pages of text)
Gigabyte (GB)	One billion bytes (100,000 pages of text)
Terabyte (TB)	One trillion bytes (1,000,000,000 pages of text)
Petabyte (PB)	One thousand terabytes or one million gigabytes
Exabyte (EB)	One million terabytes or one billion gigabytes
Zettabyte (ZB)	One sextillion
Yottabyte (YB)	One septillion
Computer Data Storage	
Typical Range	**Drive Types**
4 GB – 17 GB	DVD
500 GB – 8 TB	Internal hard drives External solid-state drives
500 GB – 6 TB	MAC external hard drives
64 GB – 200 GB	Flash memory cards
8 GB – 256 or more GB	USB flash drives
2 GB – Unlimited	Personal cloud storage

Figure 3

Office 2016, Windows 10, Microsoft Corporation

Figure 4

5. ***What are other common storage devices?*** A ***DVD drive*** uses optical laser technology to read and write data on a ***DVD***—a type of data storage, in this case optical. ***Flash-based memory cards*** are solid-state drives designed for devices such as digital cameras and video recorders. Many computers have ***card readers***—ports designed to accept flash-based memory cards.
6. ***How is storage capacity measured?*** Most common storage devices measure their capacity in either gigabytes or terabytes. Each ***gigabyte*** (***GB***) can store about 1,000,000,000 bytes, or 1,000 digital photos. A ***terabyte*** (***TB***) is one trillion bytes, or approximately 1,000 gigabytes. A 1 terabyte hard drive can store approximately 1,000,000 digital photos. These and other relative capacities are summarized in **Figure 3**.
7. ***What is a network drive?*** Large organizations often have ***network drives***—hard drives that are accessed through a network. Your school or organization may ask you to save your work to a network drive. In the Windows operating system, these drives often display in the File Explorer, on the Computer tab, on This PC.
8. ***How can I identify drives?*** In a Windows file system, each drive is assigned a unique volume letter. The internal drive that stores the operating system is commonly assigned the letter "C" and is often called the ***C drive*** as shown in **Figure 4**. Optical drives often are assigned the letter "D," and USB flash drives are assigned the next available letter. Network drives are often assigned the highest letters.

■ **You have completed Concept 4 of 10**

- Most businesses, schools, and home users purchase and install applications on their computers.
- Applications are also referred to as ***programs***.

1. ***Can I just use the software that comes with my operating system?*** Most operating systems do include software to complete common tasks. However, most computer users desire or need additional features beyond the capabilities of these types of programs. Some applications that come with Windows 10 are shown in **Figure 1**. Additional applications may be downloaded.
2. ***What is the difference between Microsoft Office and Microsoft Windows? Microsoft Office*** is a suite of productivity programs that is purchased separately from the operating system. The most common Office programs are Word, Excel, Access, PowerPoint, and Outlook. Many new Windows computers provide a trial version of Office, which you can then pay for after the trial period has expired. Others have Office preinstalled for an extra fee.
3. ***Are there free programs that I can use?*** Most of the features provided by commercial software can also be found in free software. Extra caution is needed when installing free software to ensure that the source can be trusted.
4. ***What is productivity software? Productivity software*** is used to accomplish tasks such as reading and composing e-mail, creating documents, and managing tasks. Common productivity application types are summarized in the table shown in **Figure 2**.

■ Continue to the next page to complete the concept

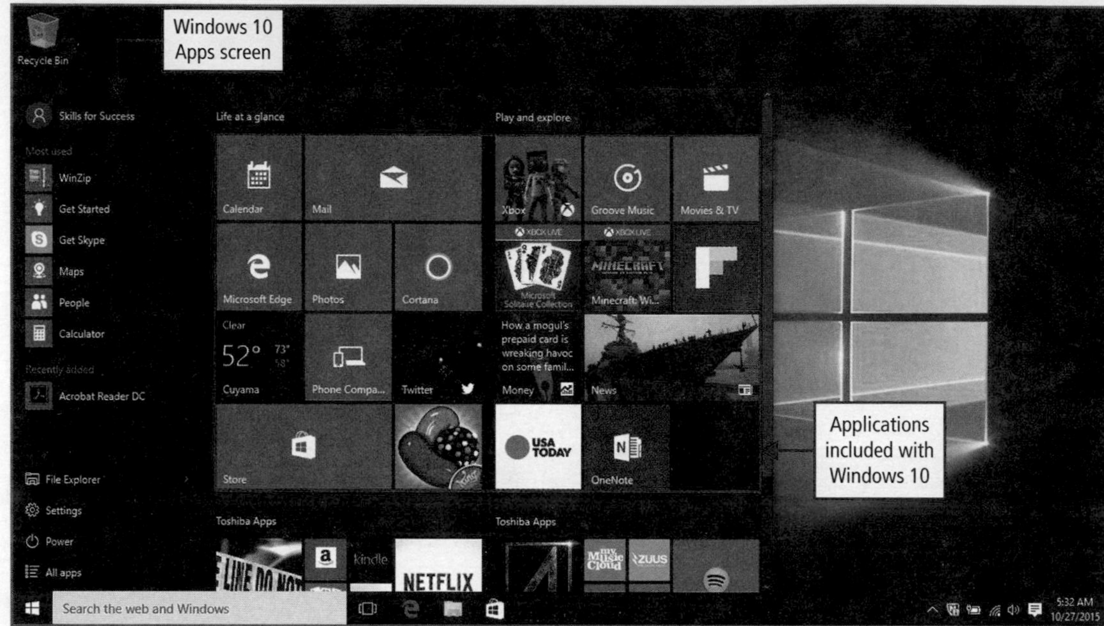

Figure 1

Office 2016, Windows 10, Microsoft Corporation

Common Productivity Application Types	
Application Type	**Purpose**
Word processing software	To create, edit, format, and print documents.
Spreadsheet software	To organize information in a tabular structure with numeric data, labels, formulas for calculations, and charts.
Presentation software	To arrange information in slides that can be projected on a large screen in front of an audience.
Database software	To store large amounts of data and retrieve that data in useful and meaningful ways.
E-mail software	To receive and send e-mail. Many e-mail programs also include tools for managing appointments, contacts, and tasks.
Browser software	To view web pages on the World Wide Web.

Figure 2

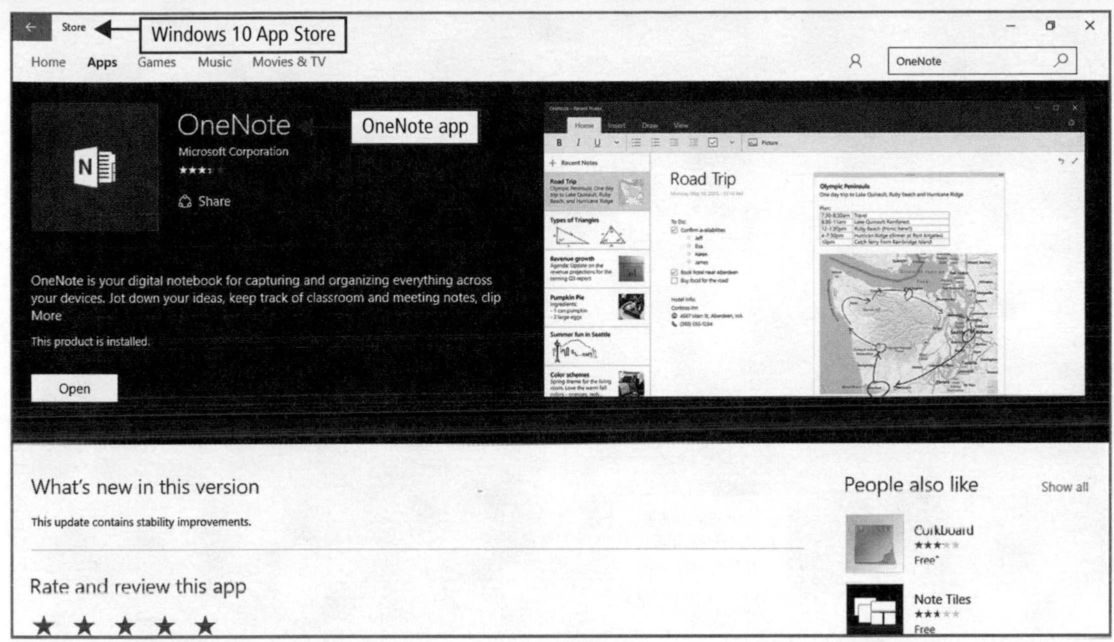

OneNote 2015, Microsoft Corporation

Figure 3

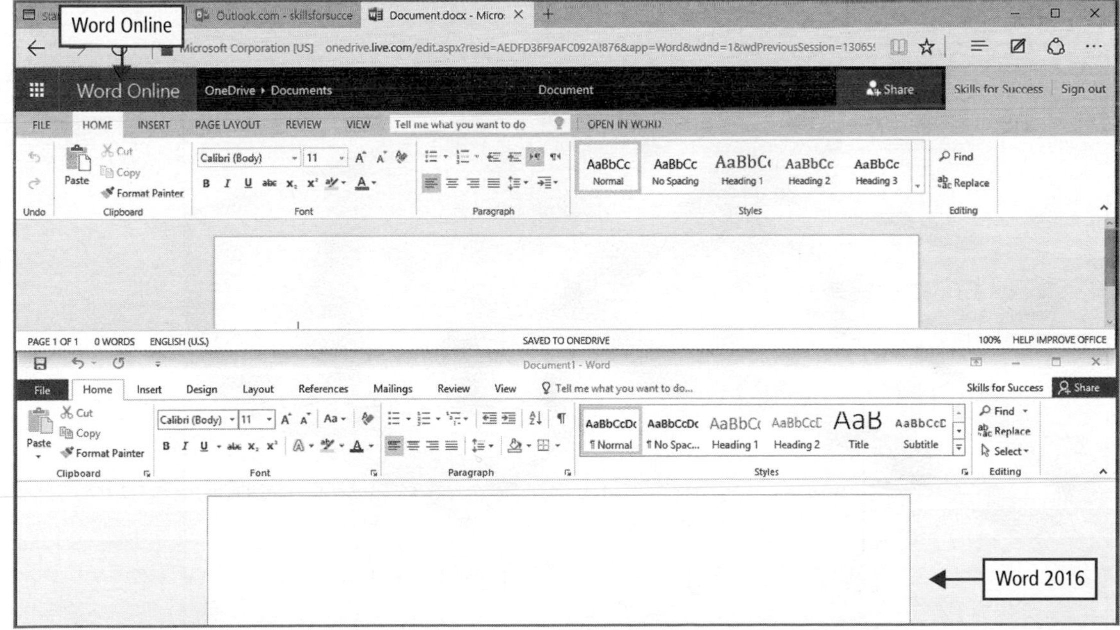

Word 2016, Windows 10, Microsoft Corporation

Figure 4

5. ***What is the difference between an app and an application?*** Increasingly, the term ***app*** refers to a program downloaded or purchased through the computer's or device's store. These programs tend to be smaller and less expensive than traditional applications. Some devices, such as smartphones and tablets, limit you to installing only apps from their store service.

   Windows 10 Store apps are downloaded and installed from the Windows 10 Store, and they run and display information in the Start menu. They usually have fewer features and a different interface than ***desktop applications***—programs that can display information on the desktop, but that are not actually "running" on the desktop. The Windows 10 Store is shown in **Figure 3**.

6. ***Why does some software seem to work on only one or two types of computers?*** The instructions stored in a program are designed to work with specific operating systems and hardware. Smartphone apps are typically written separately for iOS, Android, or Windows Phone 8.1. Desktop applications are often written for Windows, System X, or Linux.

   Microsoft Office has several versions. These versions include the subscription-based Office 365, Office 2016, and Office Online. **Figure 4** displays some of the differences between Word Online and Word 2016.

- **You have completed Concept 5 of 10**

▸ To share files, print, and connect to the Internet, homes and businesses with 20 or fewer computers can use a ***peer-to-peer network***—a small network that connects computers and devices without the need for a server.

1. ***What are the differences between a wired and a wireless network?*** Networks can be both wired or wireless. ***Wired networks*** transmit signals through wires, and ***wireless networks*** transmit signals via radio waves. Without the need to run wires to every computer, wireless networks can be less expensive to install. Wired networks can transmit data faster and more securely than wireless networks. Items that can be connected to a wireless home network are shown in **Figure 1**.
2. ***What do I need to connect my computers and devices to my network?*** Each device needs a ***network interface card*** (***NIC***). A wired NIC has a port for an RJ-11 or an RJ-45 connector. Wireless NICs have an antennae for sending and receiving radio signals. NICs can connect to a ***router***—a device for connecting networks—or to a ***switch***, which connects the devices on a network. Most home "routers" are a combination of a router and a switch. The network ports on a wired router are shown in **Figure 2**.
3. ***Is the Internet a network?*** The ***Internet*** is a collection of networks distributed throughout the world. Those networks may include services such as e-mail, on-demand video, and telephony.

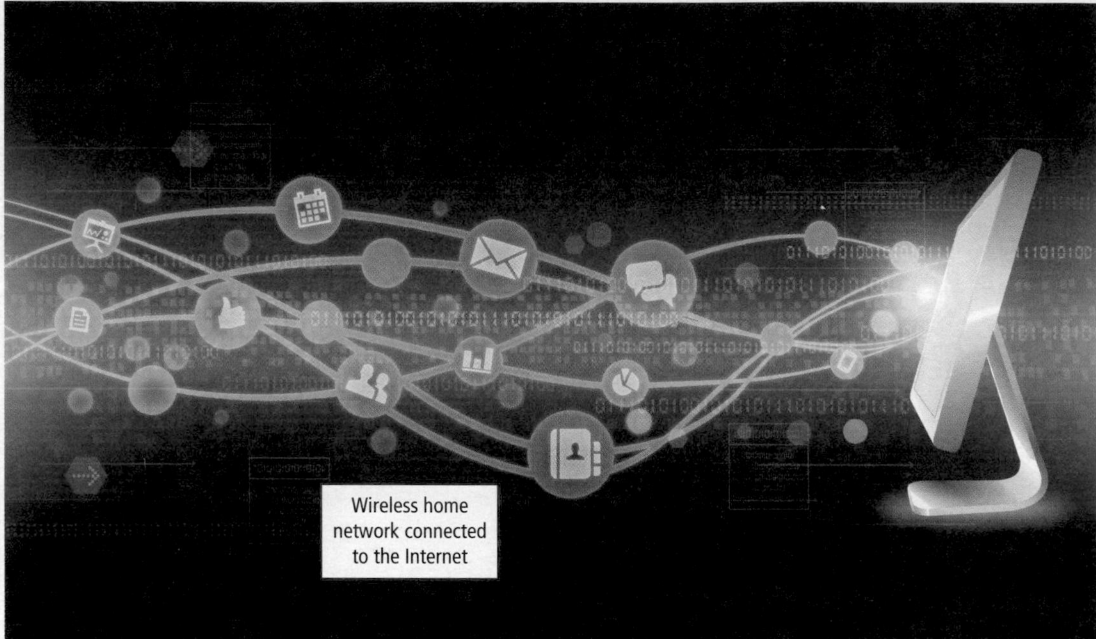

Figure 1 Apinan/Fotolia

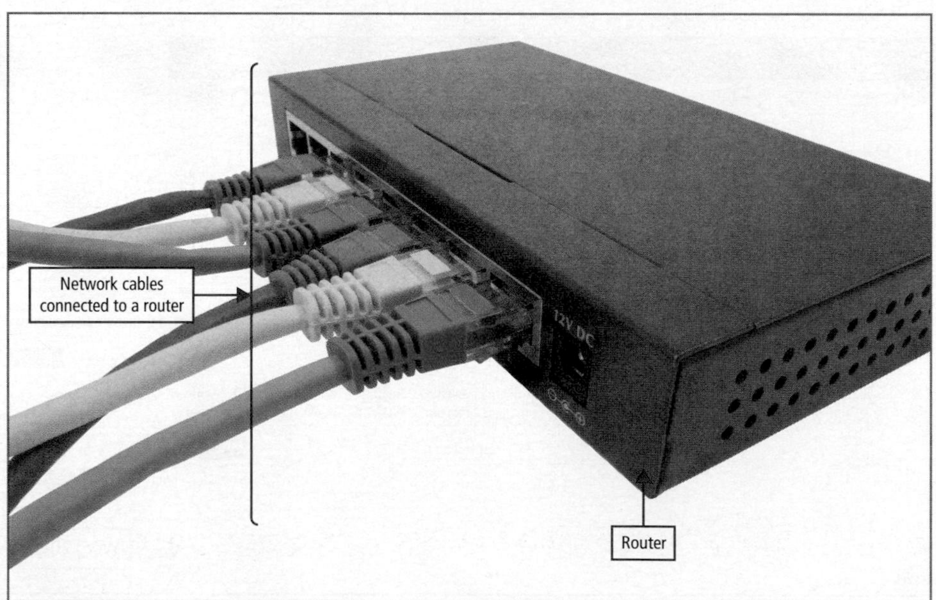

Figure 2 AVD/Fotolia

■ Continue to the next page to complete the concept

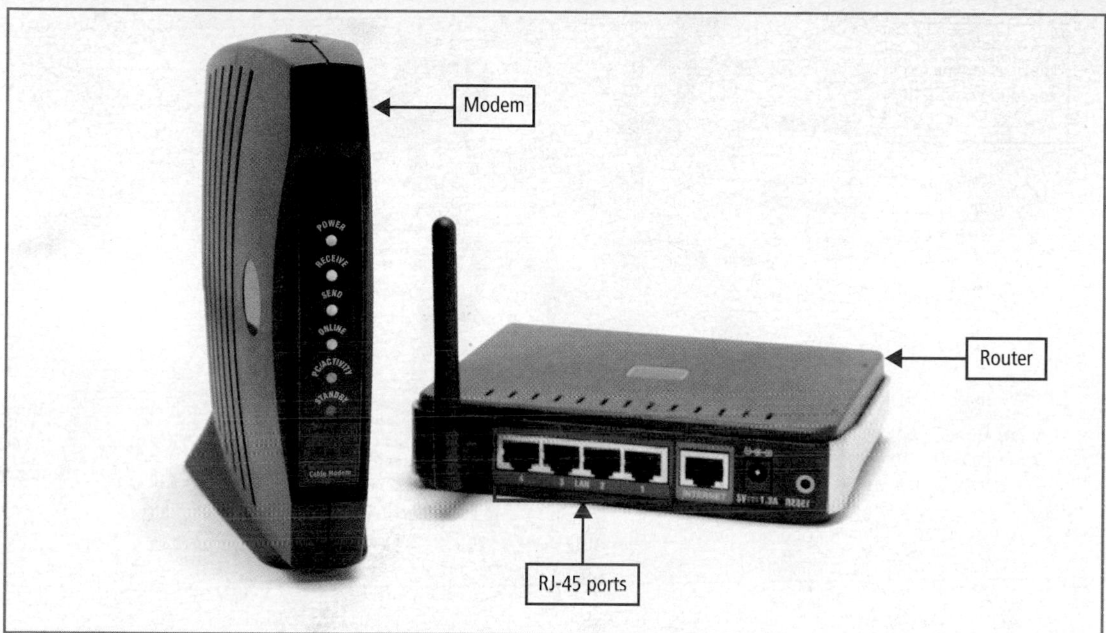

Norman Chan/Shutterstock

Figure 3

Advanced sharing settings
Control Panel > Network and Internet > Network and Sharing Center > Advanced sharing settings
Search Control Panel

Windows 10 Network and Sharing Center

Change sharing options for different network profiles

Windows creates a separate network profile for each network you use. You can choose specific options for each profile.

Private network settings

Private

Guest or Public (current profile)

Network discovery

When network discovery is on, this computer can see other network computers and devices and is visible to other network computers.

- Turn on network discovery
- Turn off network discovery

File and printer sharing

When file and printer sharing is on, files and printers that you have shared from this computer can be accessed by people on the network.

- Turn on file and printer sharing
- Turn off file and printer sharing

Public network setting

All Networks

Save changes Cancel

Windows 10, Microsoft Corporation

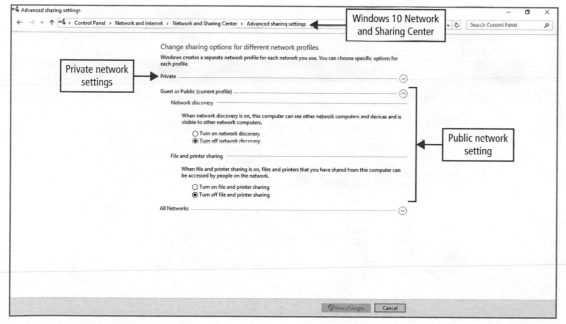

Figure 4

4. ***What do I need to connect my home network to the Internet?*** To connect to the Internet, you need to subscribe to an ***Internet service provider*** (***ISP***)—an organization that provides Internet connections, typically for a fee.

   Most routers are also a ***gateway***—a network device through which different networks communicate. The router needs to be connected to a ***modem***—a device that translates signals from analog to digital or digital to analog. A cable modem and a wireless router are shown in **Figure 3**.

5. ***What types of connections do ISP's provide?*** ISP connections vary depending on location. If you have cable TV, it is likely you can connect to an ISP via cable. DSL provides Internet connections via phone lines. ISP connections are also available using radio waves transmitted from satellites and line-of-sight radio towers.

6. ***What is an unsecured network?*** An ***unsecured network*** is a network that does not require a password to connect to it. Malicious persons sometimes connect to unsecured networks to obtain sensitive data, such as the user names and passwords of others using the network.

   Figure 4 shows the Network and Internet window in the Control Panel. In Windows, you can select the *HomeGroup and Sharing Options* link to limit the type of information you send over private or public networks. You should secure your own wireless network with a strong password and WPA2 encryption.

■ **You have completed Concept 6 of 10**

▸ ***Cloud computing*** is a service such as file storage or an application provided via the Internet. Collectively, these services are referred to as ***the cloud***.

1. ***How does the cloud work?*** The cloud works by storing your files, settings, and applications on servers connected to the Internet. Instead of opening files and applications stored on your own storage device, you open them by connecting to cloud servers. The data is then downloaded to your computer as you need it. When you save a document to the cloud, it is uploaded to a server.
2. ***What are the benefits of cloud computing?*** The main benefit of cloud computing is that you can access your files and programs from your computer, tablet, or smartphone in locations where you can connect via WiFi or have cell reception as diagrammed in **Figure 1**. For example, you can access your e-mail and work with documents from your desktop computer, tablet, or phone.

   Using the cloud provides additional backup. For example, if your computer or device fails or is lost, you can recover your data from the cloud after you fix or replace the device.
3. ***What are the disadvantages of cloud computing?*** Your device must be connected to the Internet, which is not always possible. Some services can provide limited functionality by storing copies of your files on your computer.
4. ***How does cloud storage work?*** You can save and open files stored on the cloud instead of your local drives. **Figure 2** shows Microsoft OneDrive.

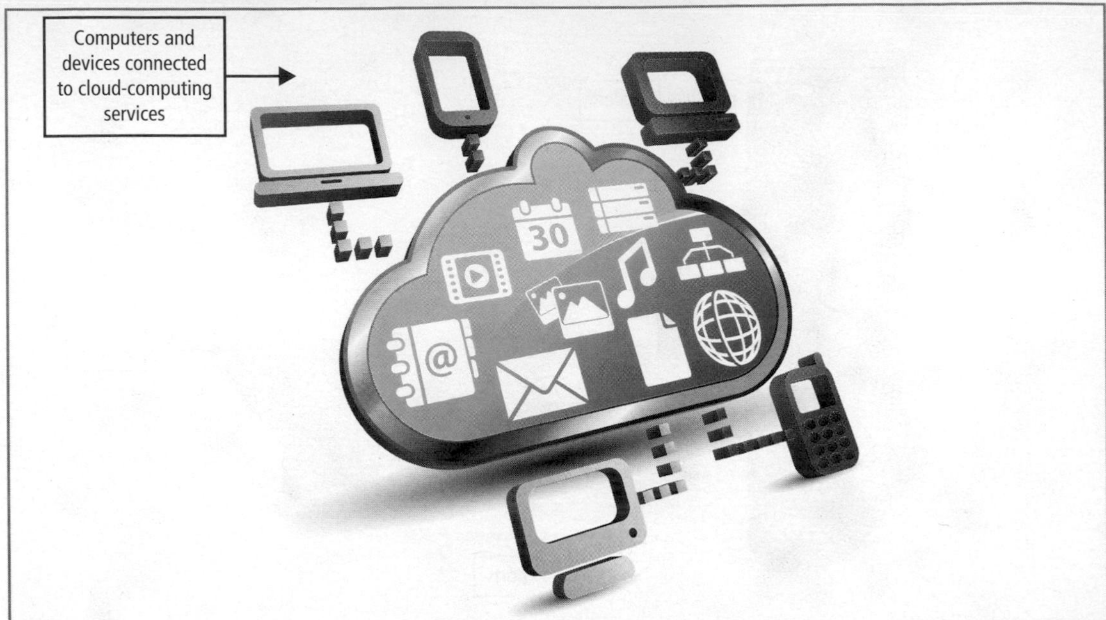

Figure 1 Spiral Media/Fotolia

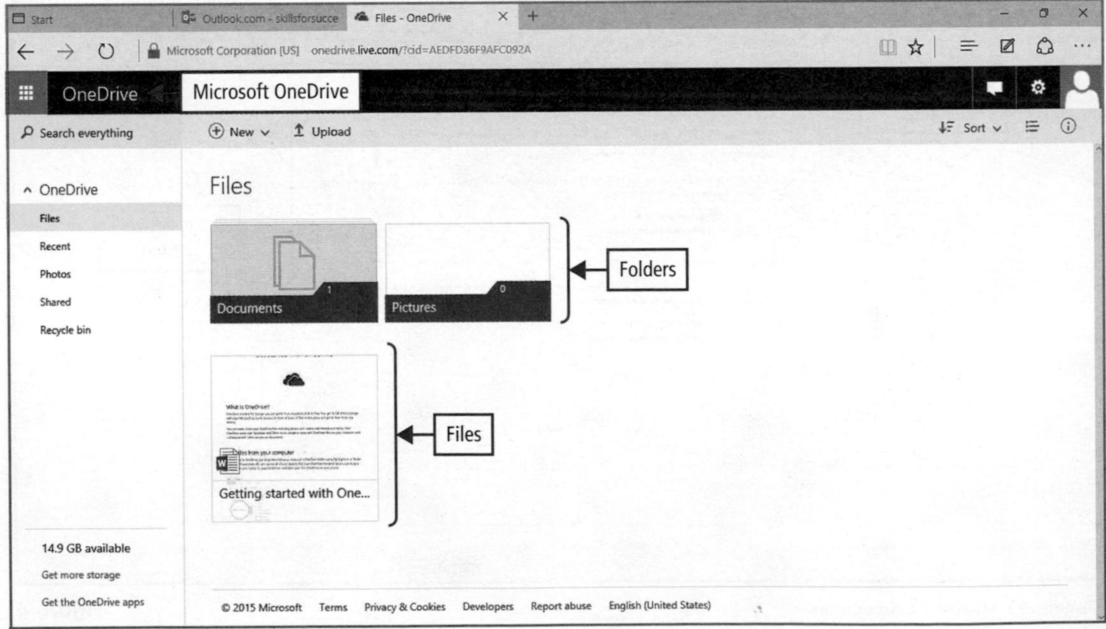

Figure 2 OneDrive 2015, Microsoft Corporation

■ **Continue to the next page to complete the concept**

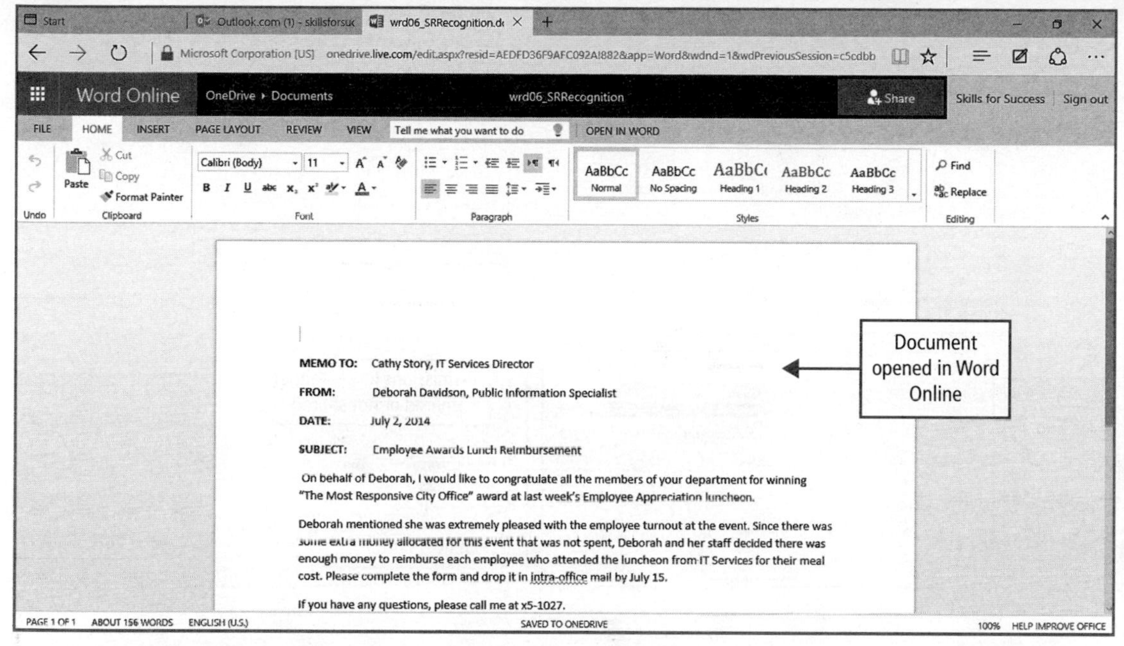

OneDrive 2015, Microsoft Corporation

Figure 3

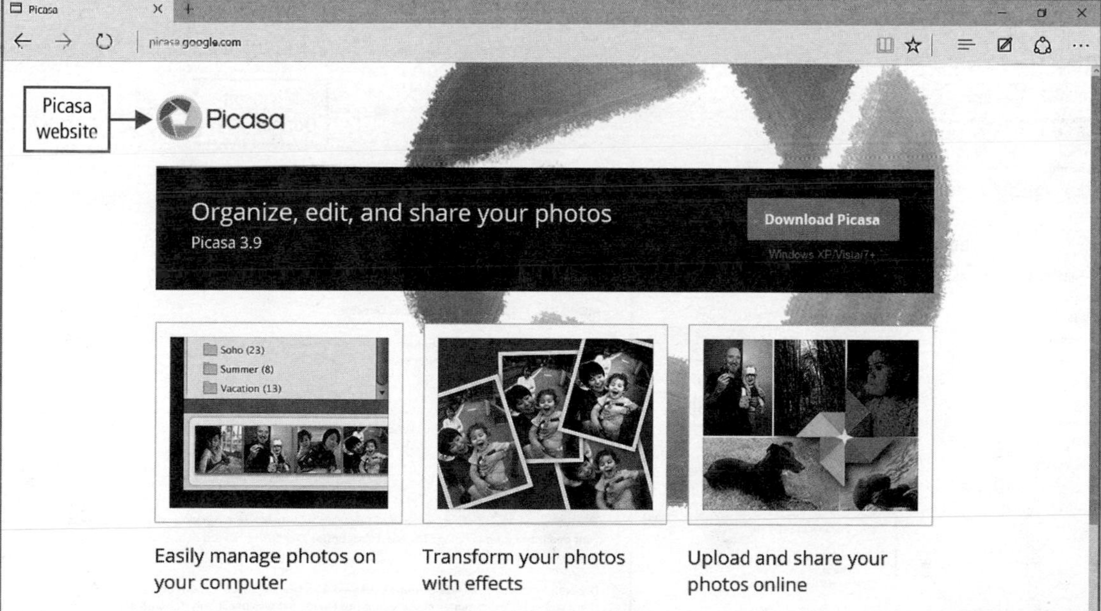

Picassa

Figure 4

5. ***How do online apps work? Online apps*** are programs that run in a web browser. Web apps are useful when you need to read, edit, and apply basic formatting from a computer that does not have the desktop application that made the document. For example, the Word Online app shown in **Figure 3** can be used to open and modify Word documents on computers that do not have Word installed.

   Common online apps include applications for word processing, spreadsheets, presentations, e-mail, and calendars.

6. ***What is streaming media? Streaming media*** is a cloud-based service that provides video and music as you watch or listen to it. The media are stored on the cloud so that you can play them from multiple devices. Many televisions and DVD players can also play streaming media.

7. ***What are cloud backups?*** A ***cloud backup*** is a service that copies your files to a server so that you can recover them, if needed. If you upgrade to a new device or computer, you can use these backups to move your data to the new device.

8. ***What is a web album? Web albums*** are cloud-based services that you use to store, organize, and share photos and video. You create albums by uploading them to a cloud-based service as shown in **Figure 4**. You can then make the album available to others. Some services provide applications to edit your photos.

■ **You have completed Concept 7 of 10**

▸ You can use your network, the Internet, and cloud computing to share with others.

1. ***What is sharing, and how is sharing used?*** One way to share is to provide access to files using a network. In the Control Panel, under the Network and Internet settings, the HomeGroup dialog box can be used to share your files with others on your network and is shown in **Figure 1**. ***HomeGroup*** is a Windows networking tool that makes it easy to share pictures, videos, music, documents, printers, and other devices. For example, you could use your laptop in your bedroom to print a file on the home network printer in your home office.

   When you share a file, you set a ***permission level***—the privilege to read, rename, delete, or change a file. Those with the ***read privilege*** can open the document, but they cannot save any changes they might make. Those without the read privilege will not be able to view the document at all.

   You can ***password protect*** shared files so that the correct password must be entered before the file can be opened. If no password is required, the shared file is considered to be ***public***.

2. ***How can I use e-mail to share with others?*** Electronic mail, or e-mail, can be used to share text, pictures, and files. You can attach files to e-mail messages or embed pictures into the messages. **Figure 2** shows an e-mail message with a file attached. In Outlook, the file can be previewed in the Reading pane or opened in the application that created it.

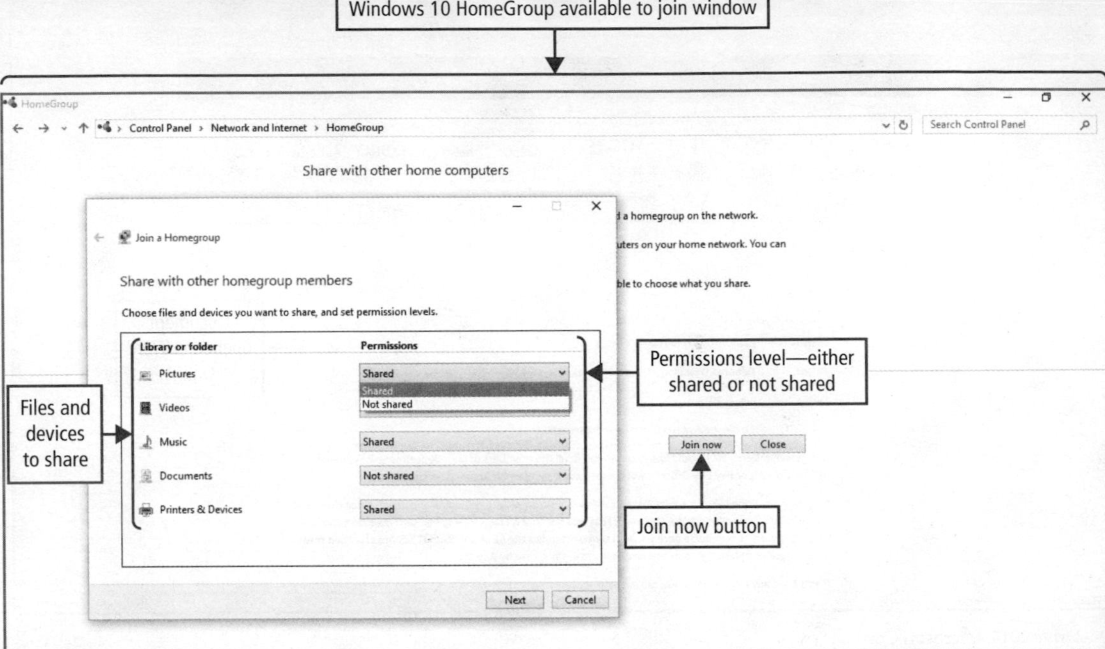

Figure 1 Office 2016, Windows 10, Microsoft Corporation

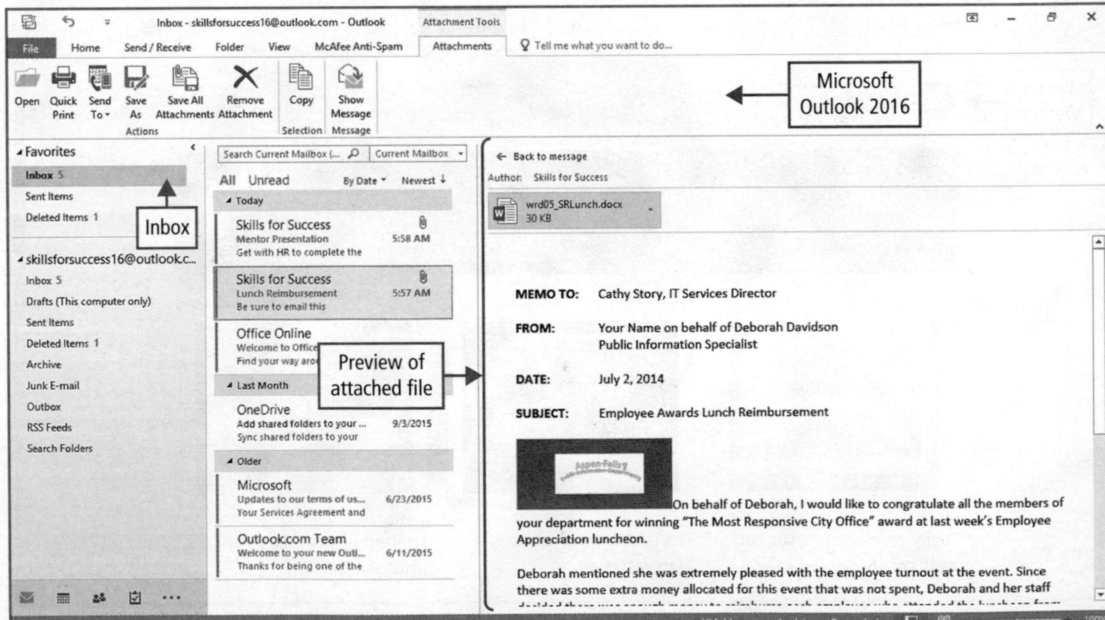

Figure 2 Office 2016, Windows 10, Microsoft Corporation

■ **Continue to the next page to complete the concept**

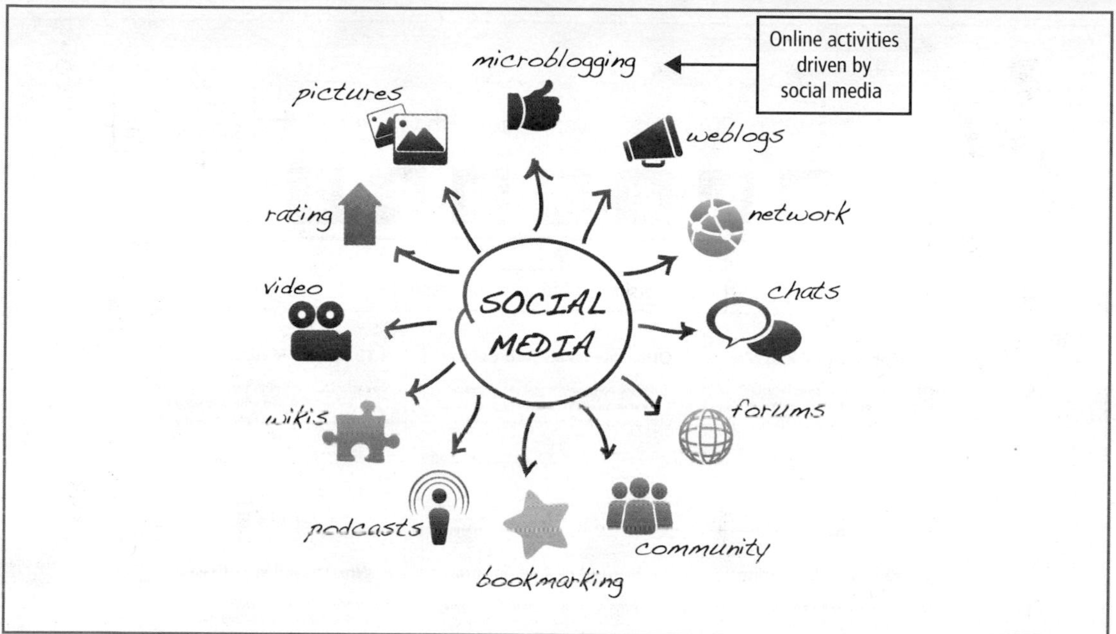

Arco/Fotolia

Figure 3

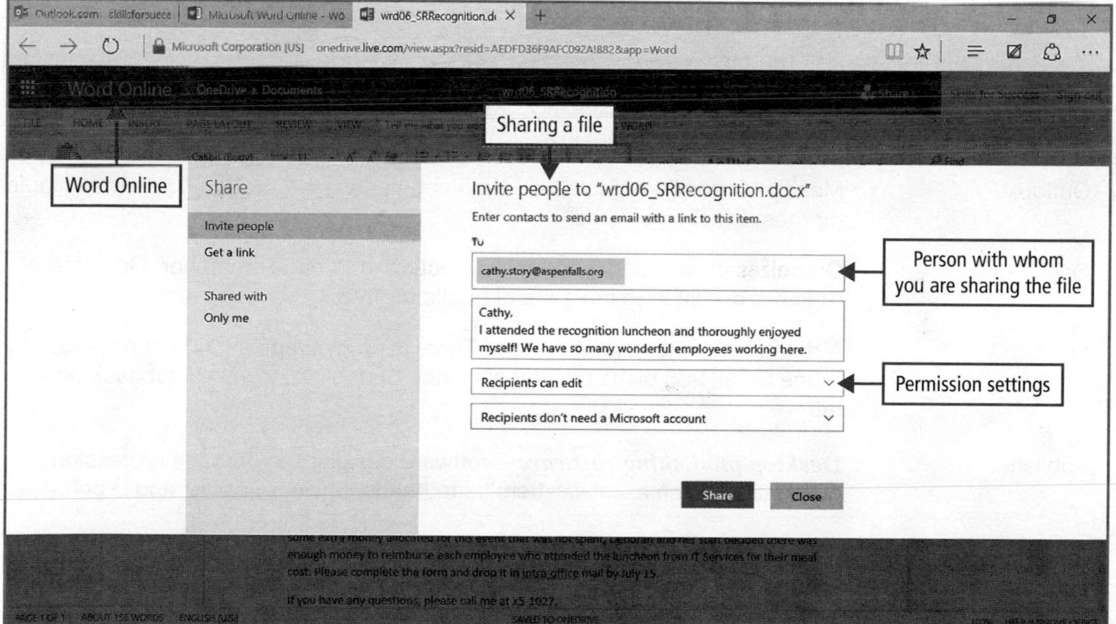

OneDrive 2015, Microsoft Corporation

Figure 4

3. ***How can I use social media to share files? Social media*** is a cloud service where content is shared through the interactions of people connected through social networks. The comments, photos, and videos that you share may only be seen by a few of your friends. However, because of the interconnectivity of social networking, interesting content may also be viewed by millions. The online content driven by social media is diagrammed in **Figure 3**.
4. ***How do you share files on the cloud?*** Saving files on the cloud makes it easy to share them. **Figure 4** shows a Word file stored at OneDrive and opened in Word Online. The dialog box is used to send an e-mail inviting others to share the document. They can then click a hyperlink provided in the e-mail message to open the file. If they make changes to the file, you will see those changes when you open the file the next time.

   You can also share OneDrive files by posting a link to your social media account such as Facebook and Twitter. Those who can see your posts can follow the link to open the document. The check boxes in the lower left corner are used to set the permission levels for the document that will be shared.

■ **You have completed Concept 8 of 10**

▸ ***Office 365*** is a cloud-based service built around the Office suite of programs. It combines traditional Office desktop applications with cloud services.

1. ***Is Office 365 an application?*** Office 365 is a collection of services, most of which can be purchased separately. When you purchase a subscription to Office 365, you can install the latest versions of Office programs on several computers from a web page, as shown in **Figure 1**. These programs are the same desktop programs that are purchased separately from an Office 365 subscription.
2. ***How do you buy Office 365?*** With Office 365, you pay a monthly fee to maintain a license to use the software and services. The cost of a subscription depends on the number of users and the types of Office 365 services required. Some subscription levels are designed for homes, and others are designed for businesses of various sizes and needs.
3. ***What Office applications are provided by Office 365?*** When you subscribe to Office 365, you receive additional Office applications that are not included in many home and small business editions of Office. These applications are described in the table shown in **Figure 2**.
4. ***What other cloud-based services come with Office 365?*** All plans include additional OneDrive storage. The amount of additional storage depends on the subscription level. Most plans also include Office for Mac.

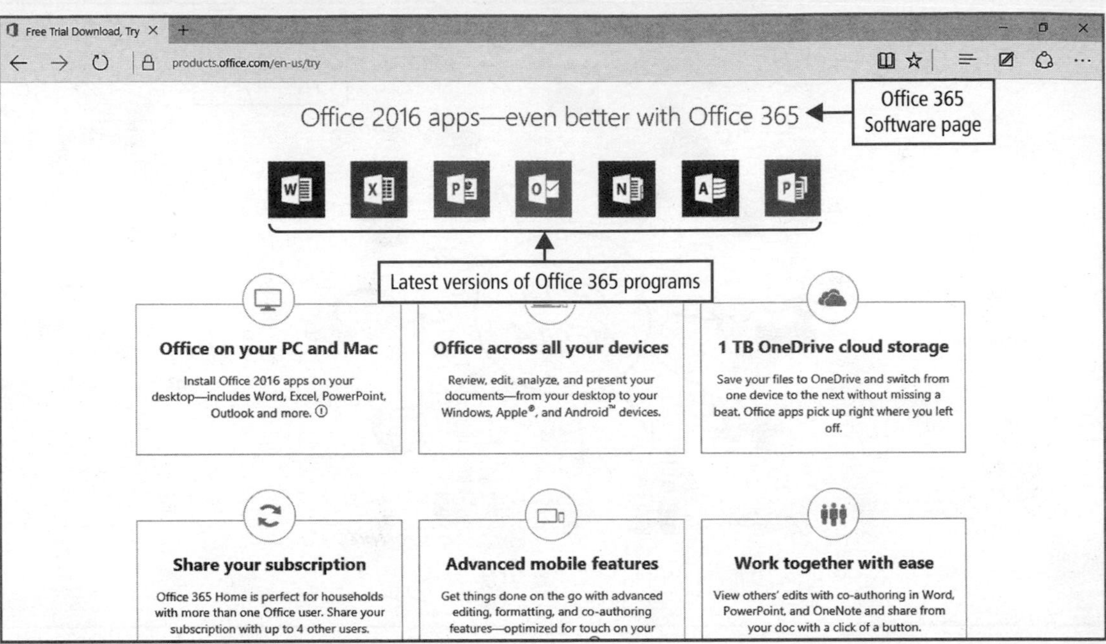

Figure 1 Microsoft Corporation

Office Applications

Application Type	Description
Word, Excel, PowerPoint	These three programs are included with most Office versions. The online version of each program is available to the general public for free.
Outlook	Manages e-mail, contacts, appointments, and tasks. Outlook.com is available for most Office 365 plans.
OneNote	Organizes ideas using a notebook, section, and page metaphor. OneNote Online is available to the general public for free.
Access	A database management system. There is no web app version of Access. Some Office 365 plans provide a service to publish Access databases on the web.
Publisher	***Desktop publishing software***—software designed to produce professional publications such as newsletters, letterheads, business cards, and brochures.

Figure 2

■ **Continue to the next page to complete the concept**

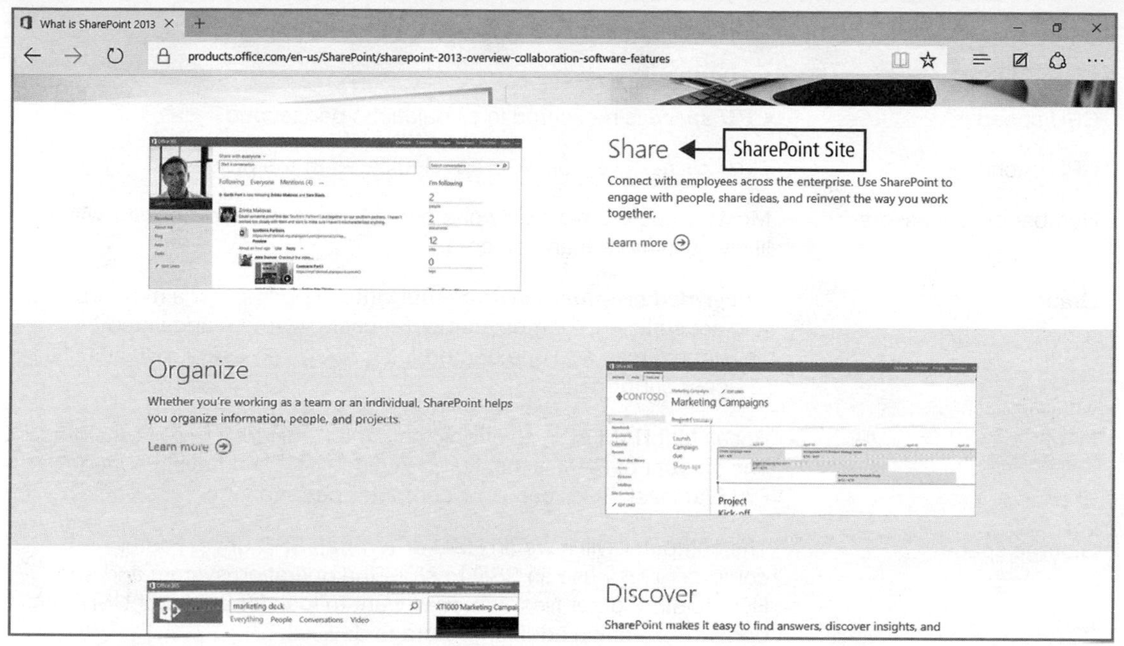

Microsoft Corporation

Figure 3

Choose Microsoft Office — products.office.com/en-us/buy/compare-microsoft-office-products

Comparison of Office 365 and Office 2016

	Office 365 Home	Office 365 Personal	Office Home & Student 2016	Office Home & Business 2016	Office Professional 2016
Fully installed Office applications ⓘ Word, Excel, PowerPoint, OneNote	✓ Also includes: Outlook (PC and Mac) Publisher, Access (PC only)	✓ Also includes: Outlook (PC and Mac) Publisher, Access (PC only)	✓	✓ Also Outlook	✓ Also Outlook, Publisher, Access
Installations available Compatible with Windows 7 or later, Office 2016 for Mac requires Mac OS X 10.10. Microsoft account required.	5 PCs or Macs	1 PC or Mac	1 PC	1 PC	1 PC
Tablets and phones ⓘ Get the optimized Office experience on your tablets and phones	✓ 5 tablets and 5 phones	✓ 1 tablet and 1 phone			
Offline storage Save documents to your PC or Mac	✓	✓	✓	✓	✓
OneDrive cloud storage Save documents online and access them from nearly anywhere	✓ 1 TB storage each for up to 5 users	✓ 1 TB storage for 1 user	✓ 15 GB	✓ 15 GB	✓ 15 GB
Skype ⓘ Calls to mobile phones and landlines	✓ 60 minutes/month for up to 5 users each	✓ 60 minutes/month for 1 user			

Microsoft Corporation

Figure 4

Office on Demand is a streaming version of Office that you can work with using a computer that does not have Office installed.

5. ***What business-oriented services come with Office 365?*** Office 365 provides access to several popular business services. These services can be managed from the Office 365 portal and eliminate the need for a business to purchase, install, and configure their own servers. Most business plans include ***hosted e-mail***— a service used to provide e-mail addresses and related resources.

   Other servers include ***SharePoint***—a web application server designed for organizations to develop an intranet. An ***intranet*** is a private network that is accessed only by individuals within the organization. A SharePoint site is shown in **Figure 3**. Office 365 also provides a server that can host a ***public website***—a website designed for public access.

6. ***What are the advantages of Office 365?*** Office 365 makes it easy to install and use Office on multiple devices with multiple users in multiple locations. An overview of Office 365 and Office 2016 products is shown in **Figure 4**.

   When you save your files to OneDrive, you will have access to your files and settings from any computer connected to the Internet. When you log on, you can use the desktop application, web apps, or Office on Demand to work with your documents.

■ **You have completed Concept 9 of 10**

► The more you understand how computer systems work, the better able you will be to make informed decisions when purchasing a computer.

1. ***What is the first step in deciding what computer to buy?*** The first step in purchasing a computer is to decide how you will use it. You need to determine what types of tasks you want to perform or apps you want to use. It is a good idea to make a list of the software you plan to buy and learn the operating system(s) needed to run your desired software.
2. ***Do I need a desktop or a mobile device?*** You need to decide if you want a computer that you can carry around with you. If you plan to work only when sitting at your desk, then a desktop computer may provide the most power for the least amount of money. Other factors to consider are summarized in the table shown in **Figure 1**.
3. ***Can I use a mobile device as my desktop computer?*** Many choose to use their laptop or tablet as their only computer. Although they may not be as powerful or easy to use as a desktop computer, they do perform most tasks very well. If you plan to use your computer for e-mail, browsing, word processing, or simple gaming, then this option may work.

   Because of their small screens, working with Office documents on smartphones can be challenging. A Word document displayed with a monitor size of 1280 x 720 is shown in **Figure 2**.

■ **Continue to the next page to complete the concept**

Common Computer Specifications

Component	Description
CPU speed	***CPU speed*** is measured in calculations per second.
CPU cache	***CPU caches*** are storage areas dedicated to the processor.
Number of processors	Most computers have only one processor, and that processor will likely have more than one core.
Graphics card	***Integrated graphics cards*** are built into the computer's motherboard and are sufficient for most computer users. Gamers and video developers may add one or more ***graphics processing units*** (***GPUs***) to boost performance.
RAM	Recall that RAM is an electronic chip that provides temporary storage. The amount of RAM is measured in gigabytes. Not having enough RAM (at least 4 GB) can slow computer performance.
Storage space	The computer will have an HDD drive or an SSD drive. Faster computers may use an SSD to store the operating system and an HDD to store other files. You may want to look for plenty of USB ports for attaching additional storage devices.

Figure 1

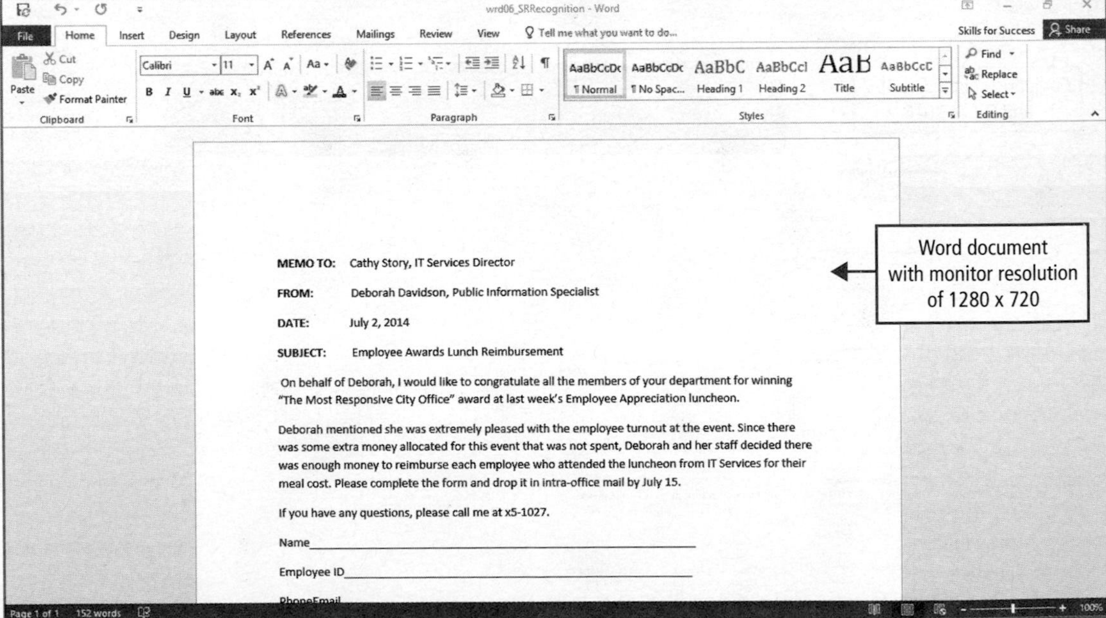

Figure 2

Word 2016, Windows 10, Microsoft Corporation

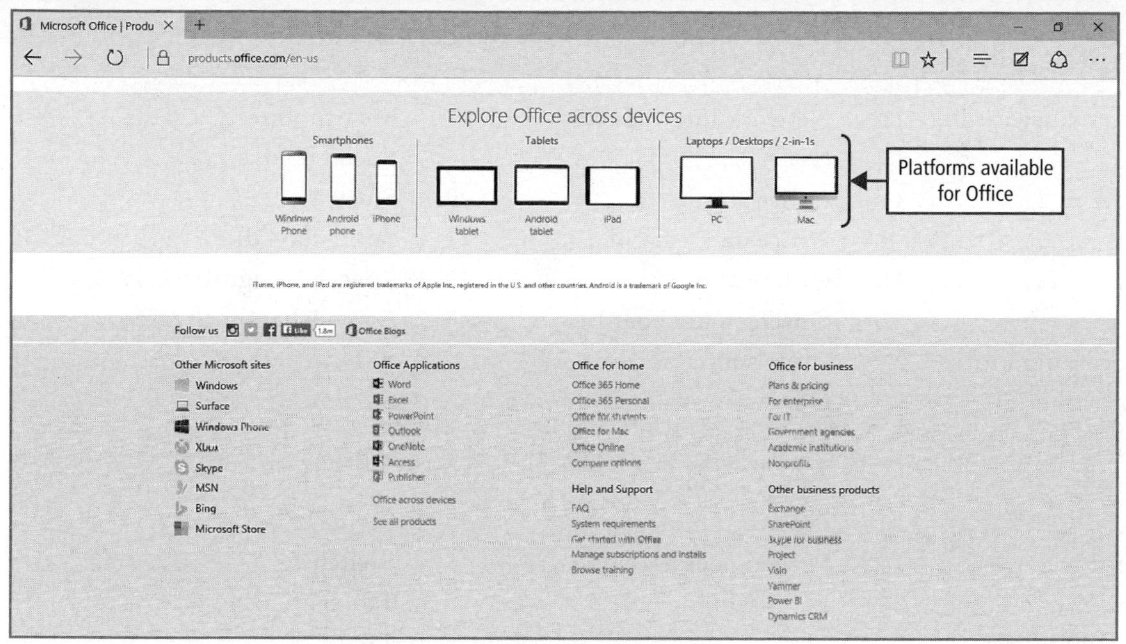

Microsoft Corporation

Figure 3

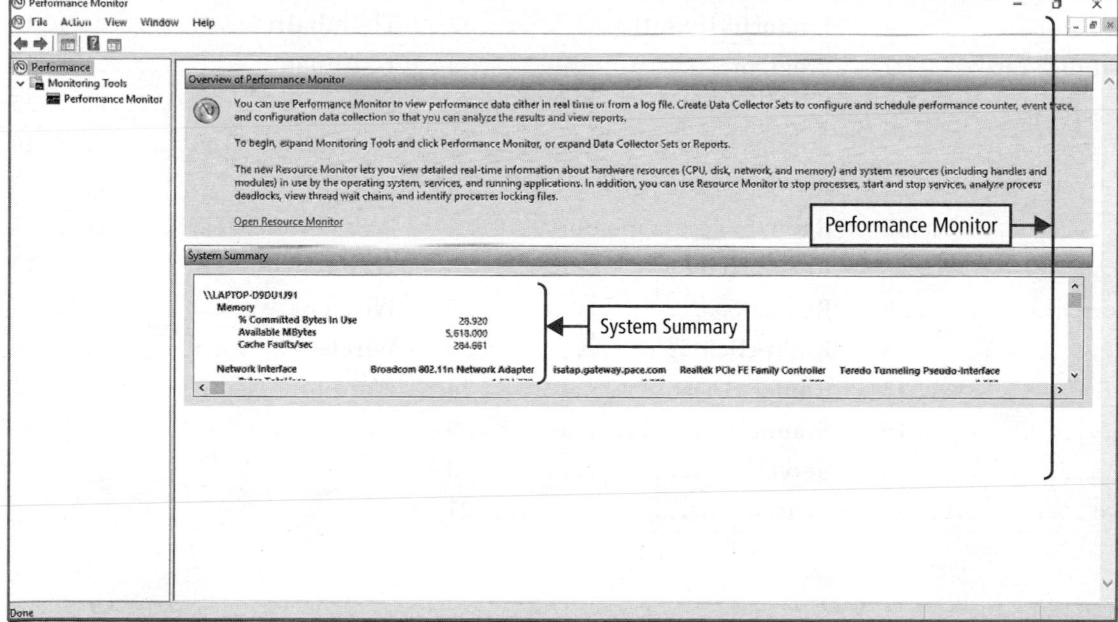

Windows 10, Microsoft Corporation

Figure 4

4. ***What operating system should I pick?*** Your list of planned software will determine your options for picking an operating system. For example, if you know that you will need Microsoft Word, your choices might be limited to an Android, Windows, or Macintosh computer or tablet.

   If you know that you will need Microsoft Office, an Office 365 subscription may be a good choice. You can use the subscription to install Office on multiple devices running Windows operating systems. Macintosh desktop and laptop computers are also supported.

   If you plan to use online apps instead of Office, iOS and Android tablets may be a good option. Microsoft Office runs on multiple platforms as shown in **Figure 3**.

5. ***How much storage will I need?*** If you mainly browse the Internet, check e-mail, and work with Office, you will need relatively little storage space. If you plan to store music, videos, and/or digital photos, then you will likely need a system with larger storage capacities.

6. ***How much computing power will I need?*** Generally, if you play high-end games, you will need far more computing power than others. If you do not plan to play games with three-dimensional (3D) graphics, you likely do not need a computer with faster CPUs or higher graphics capabilities. **Figure 4** shows the Performance Monitor settings of a non-gaming computer.

DONE! You have completed Concept 10 of 10, and your presentation is complete!

Key Terms

Online Help Skills

1. **Start** your web browser, for example, Microsoft Edge. In the **Address Bar**, type http://www.microsoft.com/en-us/windows and then press ENTER. If necessary, in the upper right corner of the window, click the Maximize ☐ button.
2. From the ribbon at the top, click **How to**. Scroll down and then under **Categories**, select **Security & privacy**.
3. Select **Protect your PC** and then and read through how you can protect your PC. Compare your screen with **Figure 1**.
4. Draft a short letter to a friend telling them how they can protect their PC using Windows 10.

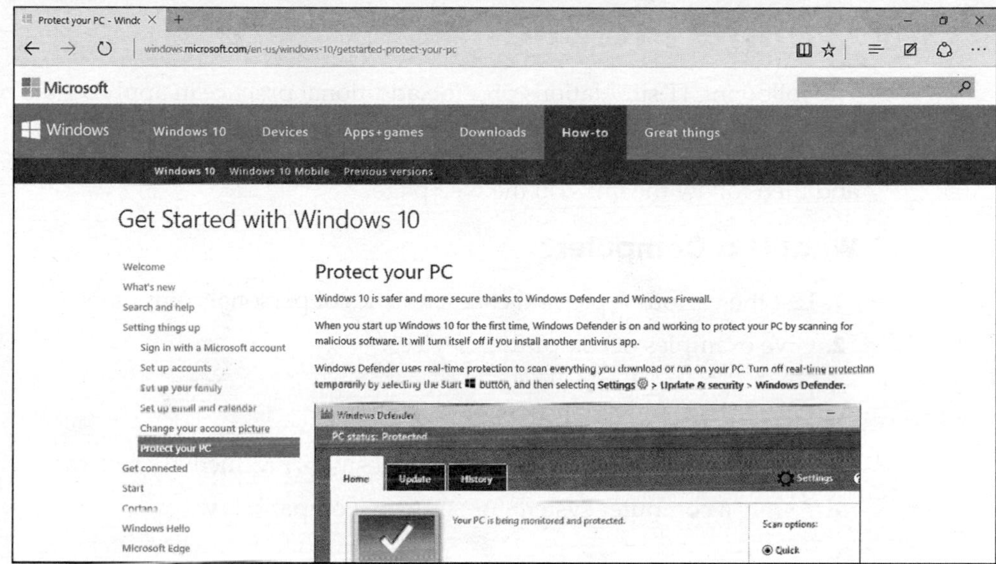

Microsoft Corporation

Figure 1

Online Practice

The following IT simulations provide additional practice in applying the concepts learned in this chapter. To begin, open your web browser, navigate to http://media.pearsoncmg.com/ph/bp/bp_mylabs/simulations/2012/IT/index.html and then follow the links on the web page.

What Is a Computer?

1. List the various types and characteristics of personal computers.
2. Give examples of computing devices.

Application Software

1. Identify the features and benefits of business productivity software.
2. Assess a computer system for software compatibility.

Hardware

1. Select hardware components appropriate to your needs.
2. Evaluate the advantages offered by devices desired in a computer system.

System Software

1. Identify basic features of the most common stand-alone operating systems.
2. Configure and modify basic features of the most common stand-alone operating systems.

Communicating and Sharing on the Web

1. Compose and respond to e-mail by following e-mail etiquette guidelines.
2. Create a letter to your instructor using Word Online.

Networks

1. Configure your computer's software to connect to a network.
2. Secure your network connection to minimize risks of online communication.

Security and Privacy

1. Demonstrate safe computing practices.
2. Differentiate between legitimate and potentially harmful e-mail.

Matching

Match each term in the second column with its correct definition in the first column by writing the letter of the term on the blank line in front of the correct definition.

___ **1.** The four basic computer functions that work together in a computer system: input, process, output, and storage.

___ **2.** The hardware responsible for controlling the computer commands and operations.

___ **3.** Computer hardware that stores information while the computer is in use or after it is powered off.

___ **4.** Software that controls the way the computer works while it is running.

___ **5.** Software used to accomplish specific tasks, such as word processing and surfing the Internet.

___ **6.** A collection of ports designed to accept flash-based memory cards.

___ **7.** Software that is downloaded and installed from the Windows 10 Store and run from the Start menu.

___ **8.** A card that connects a computer to a network.

___ **9.** A small network that connects computers and devices without the need for a server.

___ **10.** A collection of networks distributed throughout the world.

___ **11.** A device that translates signals from analog to digital or digital to analog

___ **12.** Services such as file storage or an application provided via the Internet.

___ **13.** A cloud-based service where content is shared through the interactions of people connected through social networks.

___ **14.** A cloud-based service built around the Office suite of programs.

___ **15.** A card attached to the computer's motherboard to improve the computer's graphic performance.

A Application
B Card reader
C Cloud computing
D Central processing unit (CPU)
E Graphics processing unit (GPU)
F Information processing cycle
G Internet
H Modem
I Network interface card (NIC)
J Office 365
K Operating system
L Peer-to-peer networking
M Social media
N Storage device
O Windows 10 Store app

Multiple Choice

MyITLab®

Choose the correct answer.

1. Computer hardware such as keyboards, mice, touch displays, and microphones.
   A. Input devices
   B. Output devices
   C. Storage devices
2. An electronic chip that provides temporary storage.
   A. CPU
   B. RAM
   C. Utility program
3. A bodily motion that is interpreted as a command.
   A. Gesture
   B. Speech recognition
   C. Thumb drive
4. A computer dedicated to providing services to other computers on a network.
   A. Desktop computer
   B. Reader
   C. Server
5. A drive that stores data using electricity and retains the data when the power is turned off.
   A. DVD
   B. Hard disk drive (HDD)
   C. Solid-state drive (SSD)
6. A unit of measure for devices that can store about 1,000 digital photos.
   A. Gigabyte
   B. Megabyte
   C. Terabyte
7. Software used to create, edit, format, and print documents containing primarily text and graphics.
   A. Presentation
   B. Spreadsheet
   C. Word processing
8. Software used to organize information in a tabular structure with numeric data, labels, formulas, and charts.
   A. Presentation
   B. Spreadsheet
   C. Word processing
9. A network that transmits signals via radio waves.
   A. Bluetooth network
   B. Wired network
   C. Wireless network
10. A device for connecting networks.
   A. Router
   B. Tablet
   C. USB flash drive
11. An organization that provides Internet connections, typically for a fee.
   A. ISP
   B. Hosted e-mail
   C. Social media
12. A Windows networking tool that makes it easy to share pictures, videos, music, documents, and devices such as printers.
   A. The cloud
   B. HomeGroup
   C. Web album
13. A permission level that allows you to open, but not change, a document.
   A. Password protected
   B. Read
   C. Share

14. A private network that is accessed only by individuals within the organization.
    A. Internet
    B. Intranet
    C. Public website

15. A storage area dedicated to the processor.
    A. Cache
    B. DVD
    C. USB external drive

Topics for Discussion

1. If you needed a computer for e-mail and word processing but could only buy a tablet or a desktop computer, which one would you buy? Why?

2. Given web apps, such as Word Online, and open source desktop applications, such as openoffice.org, do you think it is necessary to purchase Microsoft Office? Why, or why not?

Skills Challenge 1

To complete this project, you will need the following file:

- **Blank Word document**

You will save your file as:

- **Last_First_con01_SC1Compare**

Locate two different desktop or laptop computers available for purchase. You can research either an online seller or a local store. Gather the following information for both computers:

- Manufacturer
- Model name or number
- Desktop or laptop
- Operating system
- Processor brand and speed
- Hard drive capacity
- Number of HDMI outputs
- Number of USB ports
- System memory (RAM) and type of RAM
- Monitor or display size
- DVD drive (if included)
- Software
- Price
- Hyperlink to webpage if from an online seller, or scanned copy or advertisement if local store

Start Word and open a new, blank document. Type your first and last names, press Enter and then type Computer Comparison Report Press Enter twice. Using the list above as a guideline, type the information for the first computer you researched. Press Enter twice, and then type the same information for the second computer you researched. Press Enter twice and then type a paragraph that explains which computer you would recommend purchasing and why. Save the report as Last_First_con01_SC1Compare Close Word, and then submit the file as directed by your instructor.

DONE! You have completed Skills Challenge 1

Skills Challenge 2

To complete this project, you will need the following file:

- Blank Word document

You will save your file as:

- Last_First_con01_SC2Build

Start Word and open a new, blank document. Type your first and last names and then press Enter. Type Computer Custom Build and then press Enter twice. Write a short report describing an ideal setup for a computer used in your career field. In the report, answer the following questions, being sure to use proper sentence and paragraph structure. Which type of computer you would use (desktop, laptop, or tablet) and why? Which operating system would you use, and why? Would you select a touch screen or not, and why? How many USB ports would you include, and why? Would you add a DVD drive, and why? What types of software or apps would you add, and why? How much would you expect to spend? Save the report as Last_First_con01_SC2Build Close Word, and then submit the file as directed by your instructor.

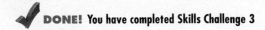

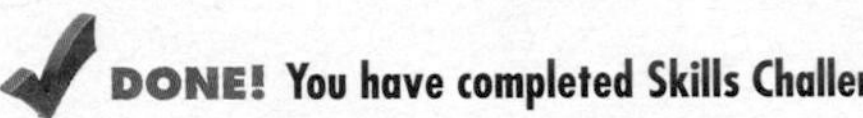
DONE! You have completed Skills Challenge 2

Skills Challenge 3

To complete this project, you will need the following file:

- con01_SC3MindMap

You will save your file as:

- Last_First_con01_SC3MindMap

Start Word. From your student files, open **con01_SC3MindMap**. Save as Last_First_con01_SC3MindMap In the **Input** shape, click in the blank line below **Description**. Type a short description or definition of input as it relates to basic computer functions. Click in the blank line below **Example of input device** and list one example of an input device. In the **Process** shape, click in the blank line below **Description**. Type a short description or definition of process as it relates to basic computer functions. Click in the blank line below **Where does most processing occur?** and answer the question. In the **Output** shape, click in the blank line below **Description**. Type a short description or definition of output as it relates to basic computer functions. Click in the blank line below **Example of output device** and list one example of an output device. In the **Storage** shape, click in the blank line below **Description**. Type a short description or definition of storage as it relates to basic computer functions. Click in the blank line below **Example of storage device** and list one example of storage device. Save the mind map. Close Word, and then submit the file as directed by your instructor.

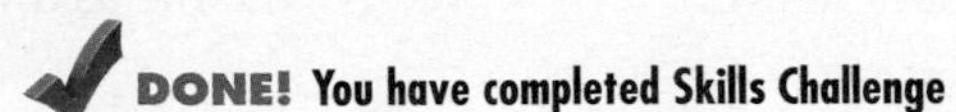
DONE! You have completed Skills Challenge 3

Skills Challenge 4

To complete this project, you will need the following file:

- **Blank Word document**

You will save your project as:

- **Last_First_con01_SC4Input**

Start Word and open a new, blank document. Type your first and last names and then press Enter. Type New Input Devices and then press Enter twice. Choose one of the following categories of input devices: keyboard, mouse, touch pad, speech recognition, scanner, or fingerprint scanner. Use a web browser to research new technology available for the category you selected. Write a short report describing the currently available device and then describe the new features or technology available for this device. Describe how the new device is used, or will be used, and the reason it is used. Describe the target market for the new device. List the computers with which this device is compatible and the estimated price. Provide at least two web addresses where this device could be researched or purchased. In your closing paragraph, explain whether you would or would not endorse this device and why. Save the report as Last_First_con01_SC4Input Close Word, and then submit the file as directed by your instructor.

DONE! You have completed Skills Challenge 4

Skills Challenge 5

To complete this project, you will need the following file:

- **Blank Word document**

You will save your project as:

- **Last_First_con01_SC5Cloud**

Start Word and open a new, blank document. Type your first and last names, and then press Enter. Type Cloud Computing and then press Enter twice. Write a short report describing how cloud computing is used in your career field, using an Internet browser to research as needed. Answer the following questions in proper sentence and paragraph format: What is cloud computing? In your career field, what type of information is stored in the cloud, and what type of apps are available? What are the benefits of cloud computing in your field? How has cloud computing changed your field? How will it continue to affect your field in the future? What are the disadvantages to cloud computing, and how are these disadvantages being addressed? How is information backed up, and why is this necessary? Save the report as Last_First_con01_SC5Cloud Close Word, and then submit the file as directed by your instructor.

DONE! You have completed Skills Challenge 5

CHAPTER 2

Getting Started with Windows 10

- You can sign in to your Windows 10 desktop with your username and password, a PIN, or a gesture. You can modify and customize multiple desktops, start programs and applications, search the Internet, and view updates.
- The Windows Start menu and Cortana allow you to perform tasks such as opening desktop applications and changing your computer settings.
- You can customize the Start menu and taskbar. Windows 10 adapts to whatever device you are using so that you can access the same information on your desktop computer, laptop, tablet, or smartphone.
- You can download, unzip, zip, and save student data files to your device or to OneDrive. You can organize your files and folders using File Explorer.
- Windows 10 allows you to search Help.

© Slickpics / Dreamtime.com

Aspen Falls City Hall

In this chapter, you will assist Cathy Story in IT Services to prepare a training program for city employees to learn and to use Windows 10. While most employees have been working with a previous version of Windows, you must learn about the new features and be ready to share about Cortana, the Action Center, and multiple desktops. Additionally, you need to see how backup and restore have changed.

Typically, you will begin working with Windows by signing in to the computer. When you sign in, your personalized changes to the desktop will display, and you will be able to access your files, programs, and apps. In this way, you use Windows to customize your computer experience.

In this project, you will sign in to Windows, and then work with several programs that are part of Windows 10. You will search for and copy files to new locations, as well as organize the files into folders. You will also customize the desktop and then return the computer to its original settings.

Time to complete all 10 skills — 60 to 90 minutes

Outcome

Using the skills in this chapter, you will be able to sign in to and search Windows 10, customize the Start menu and taskbar, manage Cortana settings, and access the Cortana notebook. You will also download, unzip, and zip data files, navigate and use File Explorer, obtain help, use the Action Center, modify the desktop, set a PIN, create a picture password, save to OneDrive, and backup and restore files.

Objectives

1 Customize Windows Options

2 Work with Apps

3 Use File Explorer

Student data files needed for this chapter:

win02_student_data_files (a folder containing files and folders)

You will save your files as:

Last_**First_win02_Snip** (PNG)
Last_First_win02_Zip (PNG)
Last_First_win02_Group (PNG)
Last_First_win02_Firewall (PNG)
Last_First_win02_History (PNG)

SKILLS

At the end of this chapter, you will be able to:

Skill 1 Sign In to Windows 10
Skill 2 Search Windows 10 and Customize the Start Menu and Taskbar
Skill 3 Manage Cortana Settings and Access the Cortana Notebook
Skill 4 Download, Unzip, and Zip Data Files
Skill 5 Navigate and Use File Explorer
Skill 6 Work with Files and Folders
Skill 7 Obtain Windows 10 Help and Use the Action Center
Skill 8 Modify the Desktop
Skill 9 Set a PIN or Create a Picture Password
Skill 10 Save to OneDrive and Back Up and Restore Files

MORE SKILLS

Skill 11 Use Windows Defender to Protect Your Computer from Malware
Skill 12 Install and Uninstall Programs
Skill 13 Modify Family Safety Settings
Skill 14 Perform a Disk Cleanup

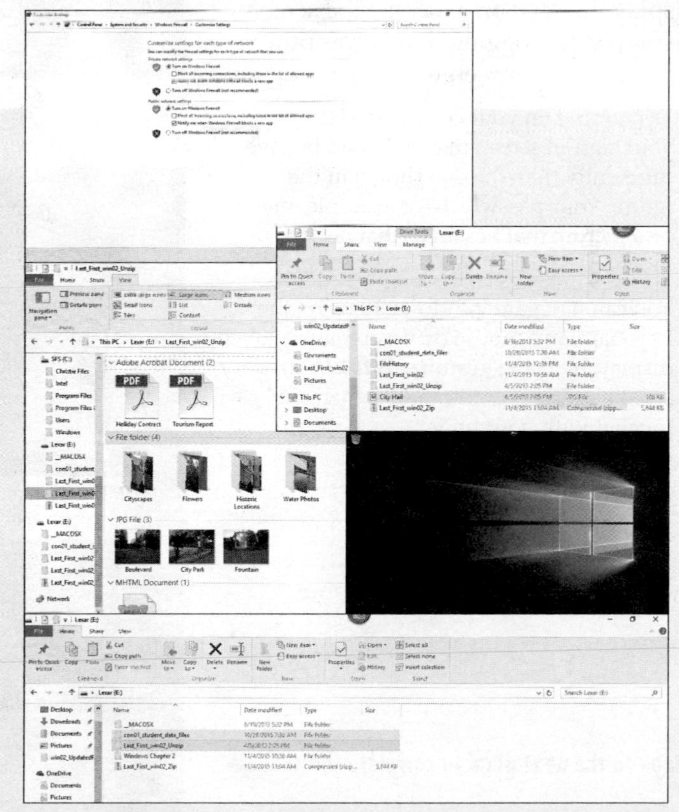

Office 2016, Windows 10, Microsoft Corporation

► To use Windows 10, you need to ***sign in***—the process of connecting to a device by keying a Microsoft account username and then entering a password or PIN or using a picture password.

1. If necessary, turn on your device, and then wait a few moments for the Windows 10 lock screen to display. Compare your screen with **Figure 1**.

   The ***lock screen*** is a screen that displays shortly after a computer or device is turned on that is running Windows 10. It may display after a period of inactivity or when not signed in to prevent unauthorized individuals from using your account.

2. Click the lock screen or press any key to display the ***sign-in screen***—the screen displayed for logging in to a computer. Compare your screen with **Figure 2**.

   Depending on your computer settings, your sign-in screen may look and behave differently than the one shown in the figure. Your password, for example, may be a picture that has areas that need to be touched or clicked in a certain order.

   You can navigate Windows 10 using the keyboard and mouse or, if you have a touch display, by using gestures. A ***touch display*** screen interprets commands when you touch it with your finger.

■ Continue to the next page to complete the skill

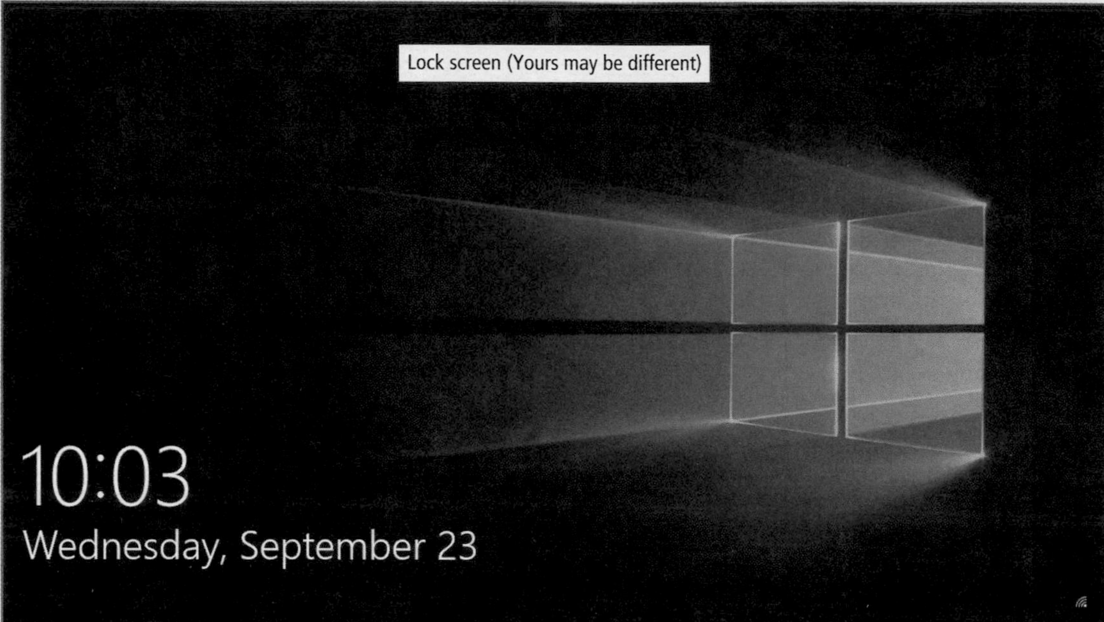

Figure 1 Windows 10, Microsoft Corporation

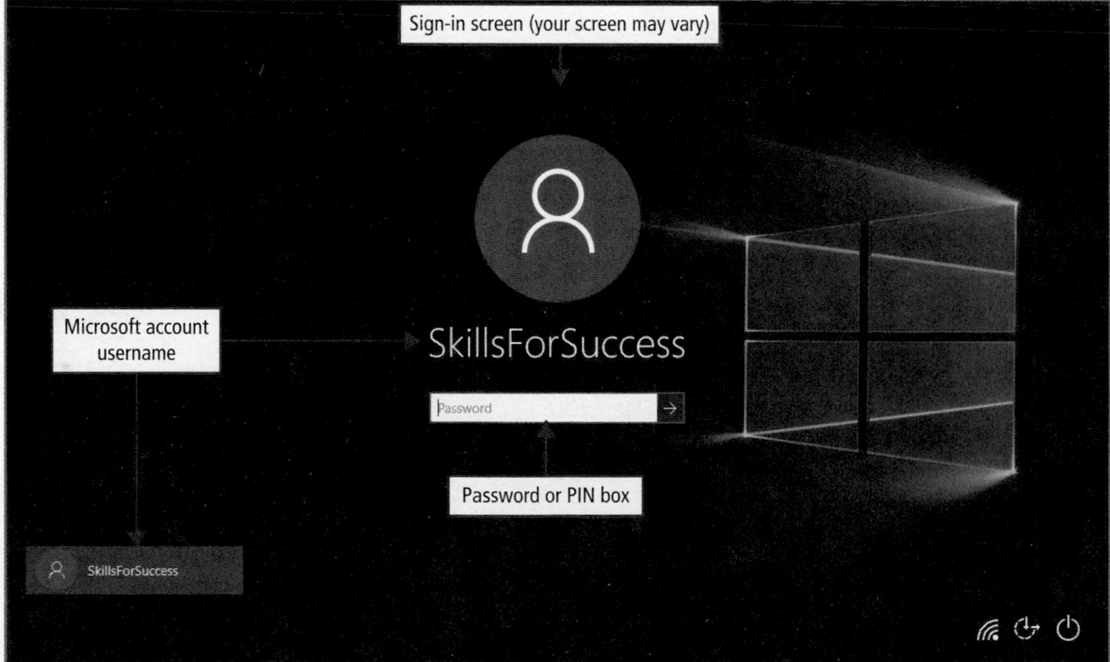

Figure 2 Windows 10, Microsoft Corporation

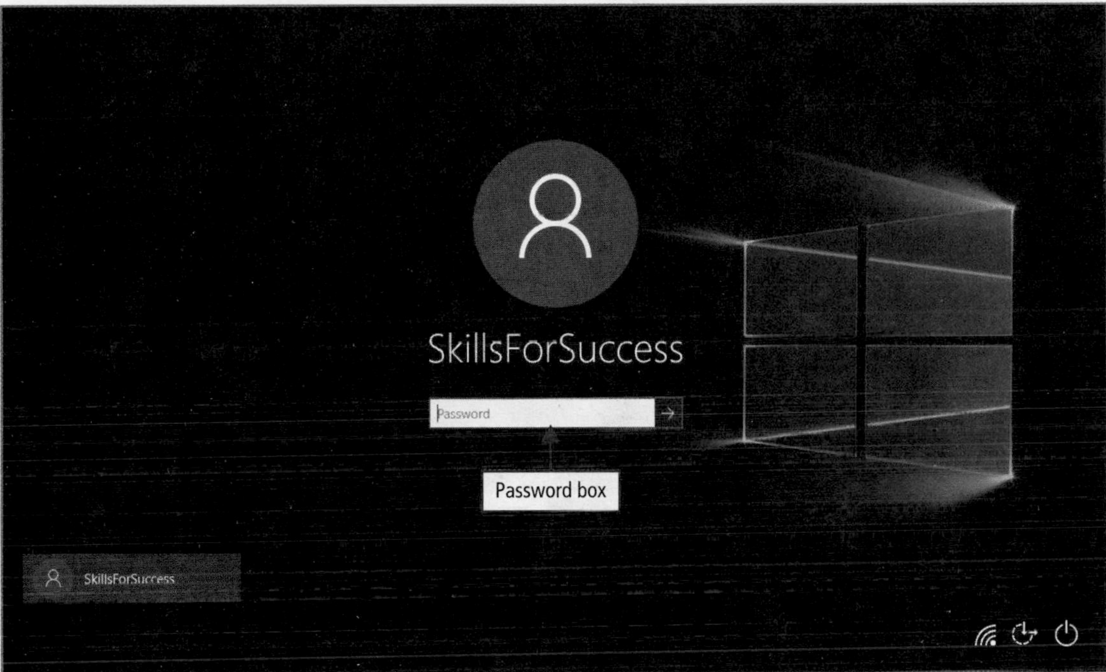

Windows 10, Microsoft Corporation

Figure 3

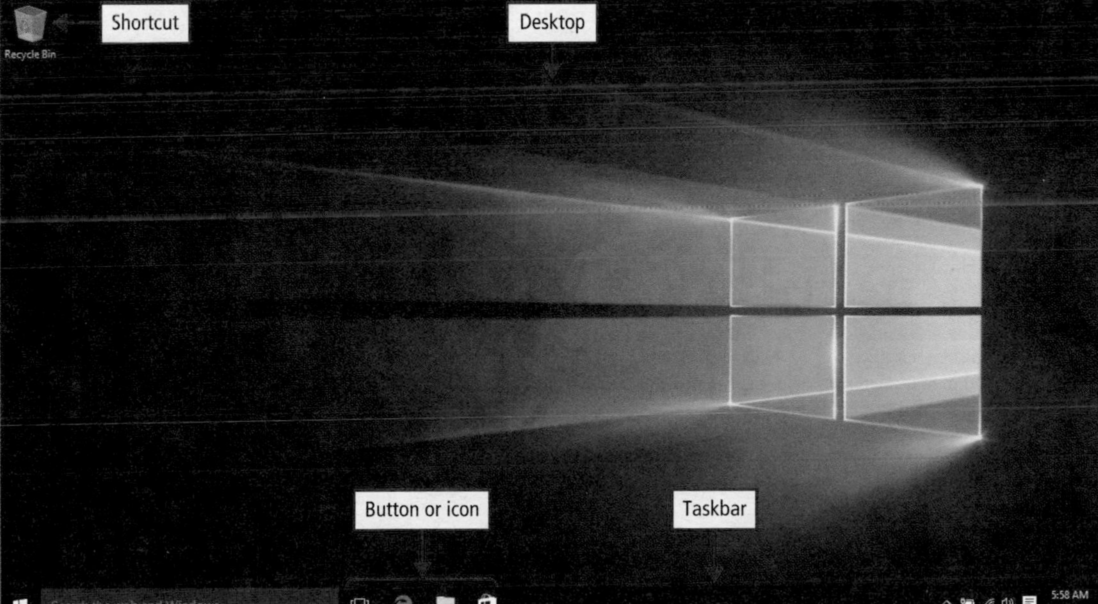

Windows 10, Microsoft Corporation

Figure 4

3. Select your username from the list of users. If a blank User Name box displays, type your Microsoft account username, and then compare your screen with **Figure 3**. In the **Password** box, type your password.

   To prevent unauthorized access to your data and computer settings, you should always keep your password confidential. For this reason, the password text characters are ***masked characters***—text that is hidden by displaying characters such as bullets.

4. If you do not recall your password and have already set up a ***PIN***, or ***personal identification number***—a four-digit code used for signing in to Windows 10—or simply wish to use your PIN, click **Sign-in options**, and then click the **PIN** button. Type your PIN to view the desktop.

5. Press Enter or ***tap***—touch the device display once with your finger—or click the arrow to complete the sign in. Compare your screen with **Figure 4**.

   The desktop displays ***icons***, or ***buttons***—picture representations for applications, files, folders, or commands on your device—and ***shortcuts***—links to specific applications, files, or folders. Since you will likely customize your desktop, your screen will be different.

   After signing in, the desktop displays, along with the ***taskbar***—a toolbar located at the bottom of the desktop used to view applications, files, or folders, search the Internet, and view updates.

■ **You have completed Skill 1 of 10**

- The ***Search box*** is located on the taskbar and used to find applications, files, computer settings, or results on the Internet.
- The Start menu and taskbar may display buttons used to open apps or programs.

1. Click the **Search** box. Type weather Right-click the **Weather** app. Select **Pin to taskbar**.

   Weather is an example of a ***Windows 10 Store app***—a program used to perform a similar set of tasks that run on the Start screen.

2. Repeat the technique from step 1 to pin the Snipping Tool to the taskbar, as shown in **Figure 1**. Click the **Desktop**.

   The ***Snipping Tool*** is an application that creates screen shots called ***snips***.

3. Click the **Start menu** button, click **All apps**, and then right-click the **Calculator** app. Click **Pin to Start**. Repeat this technique to pin *Maps* to the Start menu.

4. Click the **Start menu** button. Scroll down to view the *Calculator* and *Maps* tiles. Right-click the **Maps** app. Point to **Resize** as shown in **Figure 2**. Click **Wide**.

   To view the Maps tile, you may need to ***scroll***—placing the mouse in the ***Scroll bar***—an area at the far right or bottom of a window indicating there is more to be displayed—and moving the mouse up or down or side to side to view parts of the window that do not display at the same time.

■ Continue to the next page to complete the skill

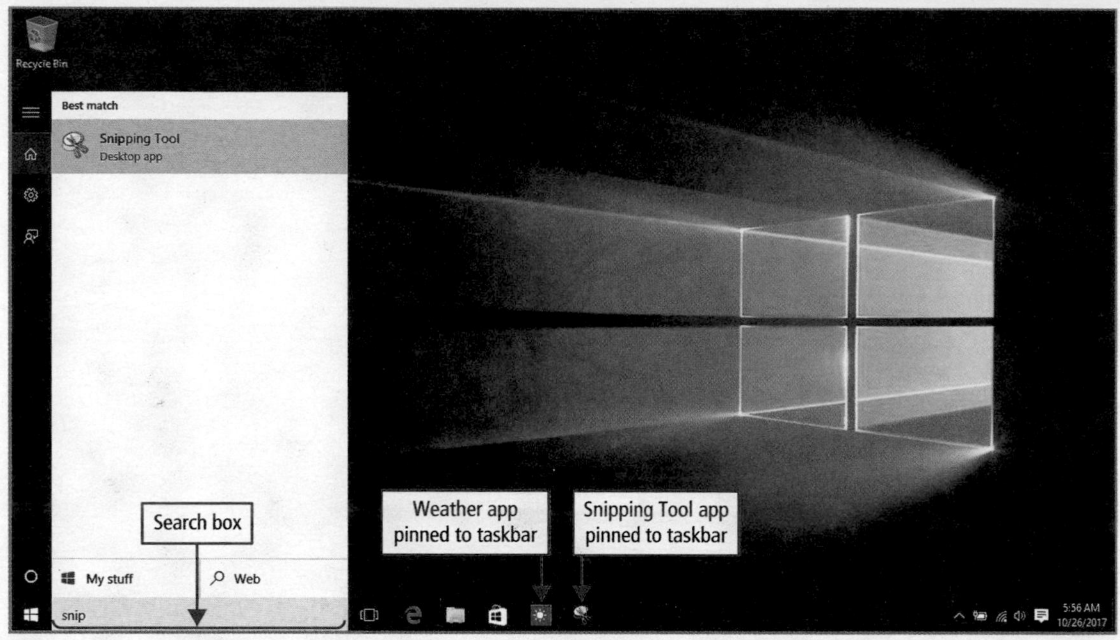

Figure 1

Windows 10, Microsoft Corporation

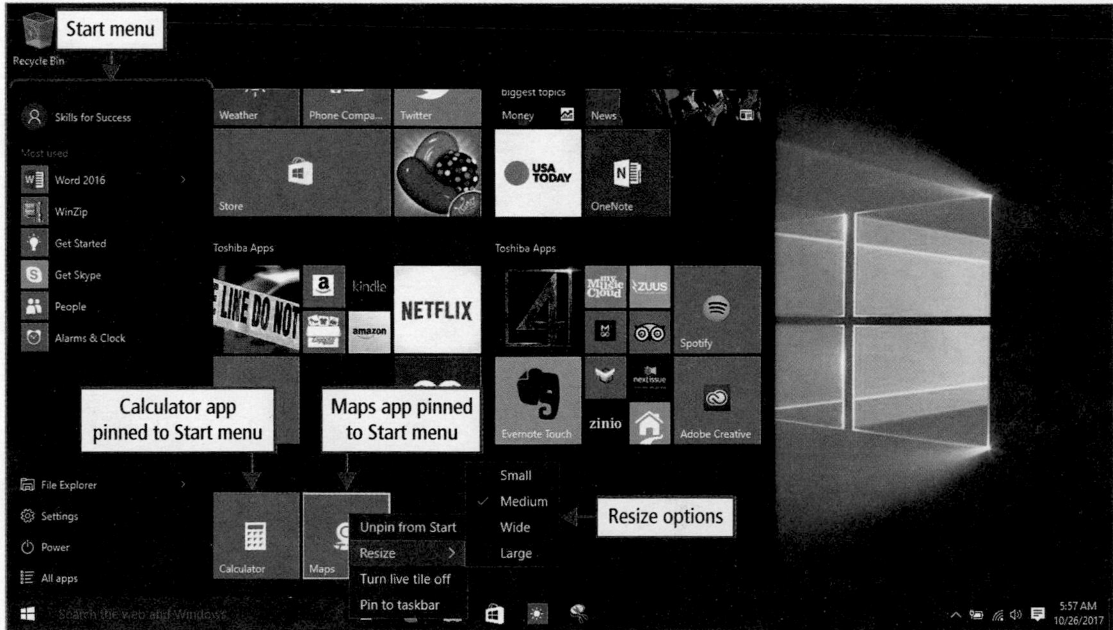

Figure 2

Windows 10, Microsoft Corporation

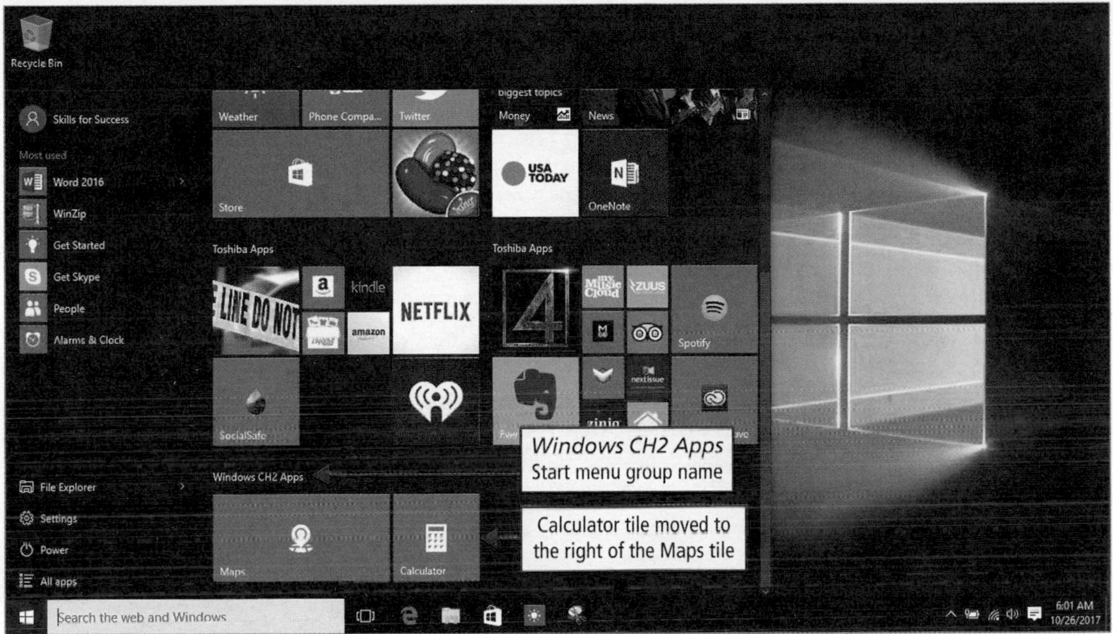

Windows 10, Microsoft Corporation

Figure 3

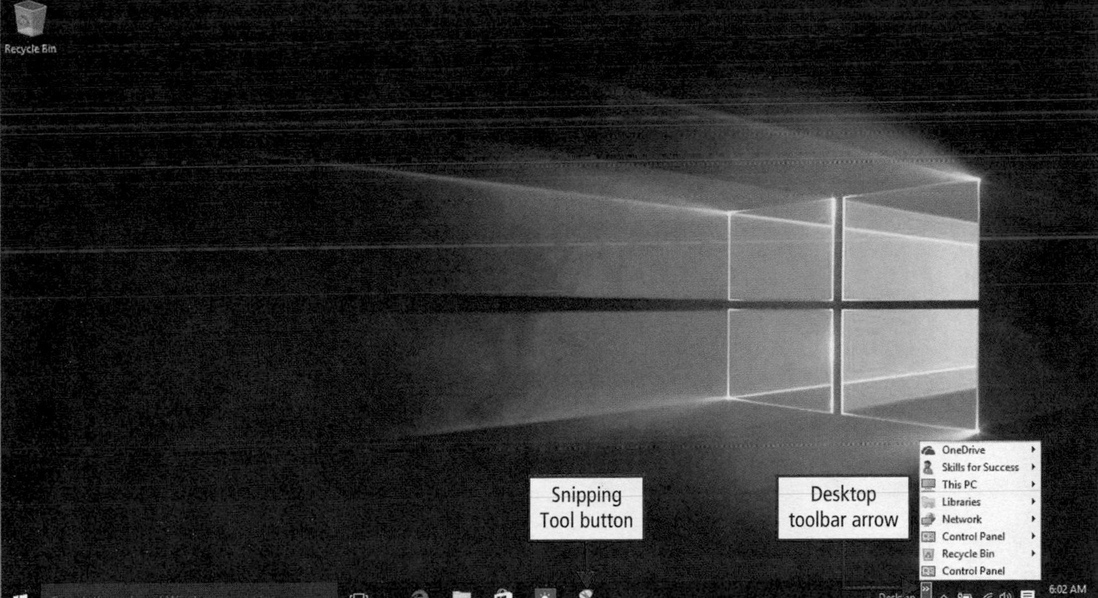

Windows 10, Microsoft Corporation

Figure 4

5. Drag the **Calculator** tile to the right of the **Maps** tile. Position the mouse pointer above the **Maps** tile, and then click the **Name Group** button. Type Windows CH2 Apps Press Enter. Compare your screen with **Figure 3**.
6. Right-click the taskbar. Point to **Toolbars**, and then click **Desktop**.

   The Desktop toolbar displays the default locations on the computer, as well as programs added to the Desktop.
7. On the taskbar, click the **Desktop toolbar arrow**, and then compare your screen with **Figure 4**.
8. On the taskbar, click the **Snipping Tool** button. In the **Snipping Tool** window, click the **New snip button arrow**, and then click **Full-screen Snip**. Click the **Save Snip** button. In the **Save as** dialog box, navigate to the location where you are saving your files, and then create a folder named Windows
9. **Save** the file in the folder as Last_First_win02_Snip Verify the *Save as type* is Portable Network Graphic (PNG). Click **Save**, and then click **Close** × two times.
10. Right-click the taskbar. Point to **Toolbars**, and then click **Desktop**.
11. In the taskbar, right-click the **Weather** button, and then click **Unpin this program from the taskbar**.
12. Click the **Start menu** button. Right-click the **Maps** tile, and then select **Unpin from Start**. Repeat this technique to unpin the *Calculator*. Click the **Desktop**.

■ **You have completed Skill 2 of 10**

- ***Cortana*** is a built-in feature of Windows 10 that opens apps, files, and settings, provides appointment reminders, and shares results of keyed or spoken questions or commands for items located on your devices and in Bing. For Cortana to recognize voice, you will need a microphone.
- Cortana is similar to having a personal assistant for your computer. Your personal preferences are stored in the ***Cortana Notebook***—a location on your device used to store results of previous searches. For example, the stored contact information for Maria Martinez.

1. In the **Search** box, type Cortana Select **Cortana & Search settings** and use the table in **Figure 1** to learn more. If necessary, type your First name.

   If you do not have a microphone, ask your instructor how to proceed.

2. Under *Cortana can give*, drag to **On**. Under *Hey Cortana*, drag to **On**. Under *Respond best:*, click **Learn my voice**, and then compare your screen with **Figure 2**. Click **Start**. Follow the six prompts for Cortana to learn your speaking patterns.
3. Speak Cortana, open File Explorer **Minimize** [−] the window.

   Alternately, in the taskbar, click File Explorer.

4. In the **Search** box, click the microphone. Speak Cortana, open Edge Type www.recreation.gov and then press [Enter].

■ **Continue to the next page to complete the skill**

Cortana Settings Setting	Purpose
Suggestions, ideas, reminders, alerts, and more	On – Cortana can offer suggestions, ideas, reminders, alerts, and search for files, programs, and applications. Off – Clear Cortana settings on the device, but not the Cortana Notebook.
Manage what Cortana knows about me in the cloud	Use this link to Bing.com where you will login with your Microsoft account and determine what favorites and interests you no longer want Cortana to access. Additionally, personal information from your device such as your calendar and contacts can be cleared so Cortana no longer has access to this information when making recommendations.
Hey Cortana	On – Cortana can respond to "Hey Cortana." This feature takes additional battery power. Off – To activate Cortana, you must click the Microphone button in the taskbar pane.
Find flights and more	On – Cortana searches tracking information such as flight schedules contained in messages on your device. Off – Cortana does not search tracking information.
Taskbar tidbits	On – Cortana shares Windows 10 hints, as well as various thoughts and greetings in the Search box via pop-up messages. Off – Cortana does not share hints, thoughts, and greetings in the Search box.
Bing Safe Search settings	Use this link to Bing.com to set restrictions on the adult content downloaded during searches. Choices include *Strict*, *Moderate*, and *Off*.
Other privacy settings	Use this link to view your computer privacy settings and update personal information settings.
Learn more about Cortana & Search	Use this link to windows.microsoft.com/en-us/windows-10/Cortana-privacy-faq to learn more about Cortana, Search, and privacy.

Figure 1

Windows 10, Microsoft Corporation

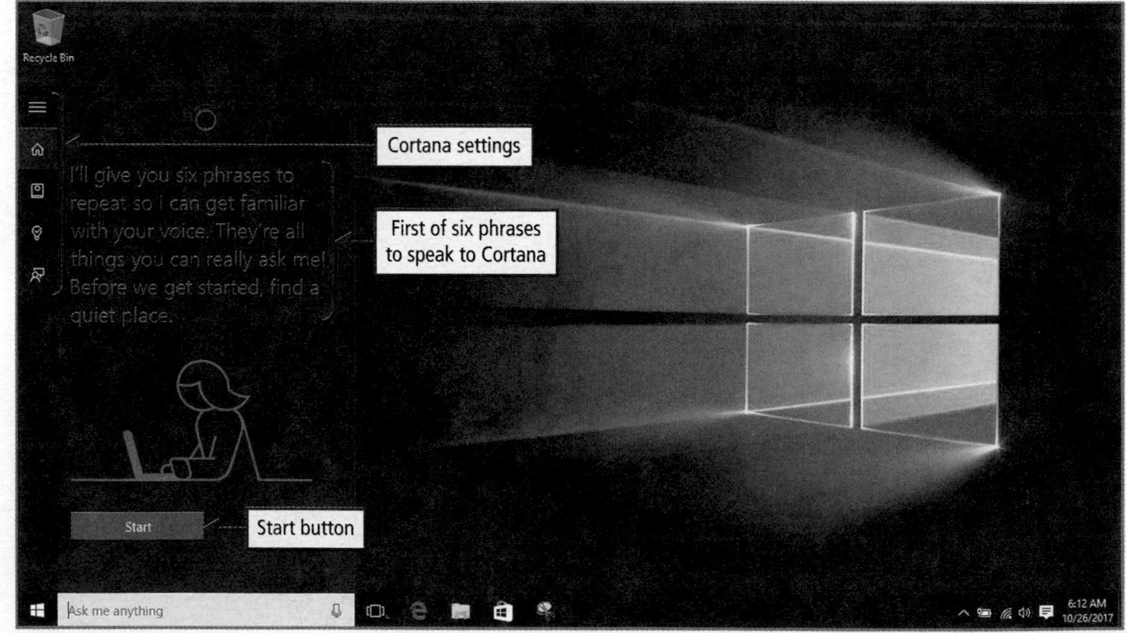

Figure 2

Windows 10, Microsoft Corporation

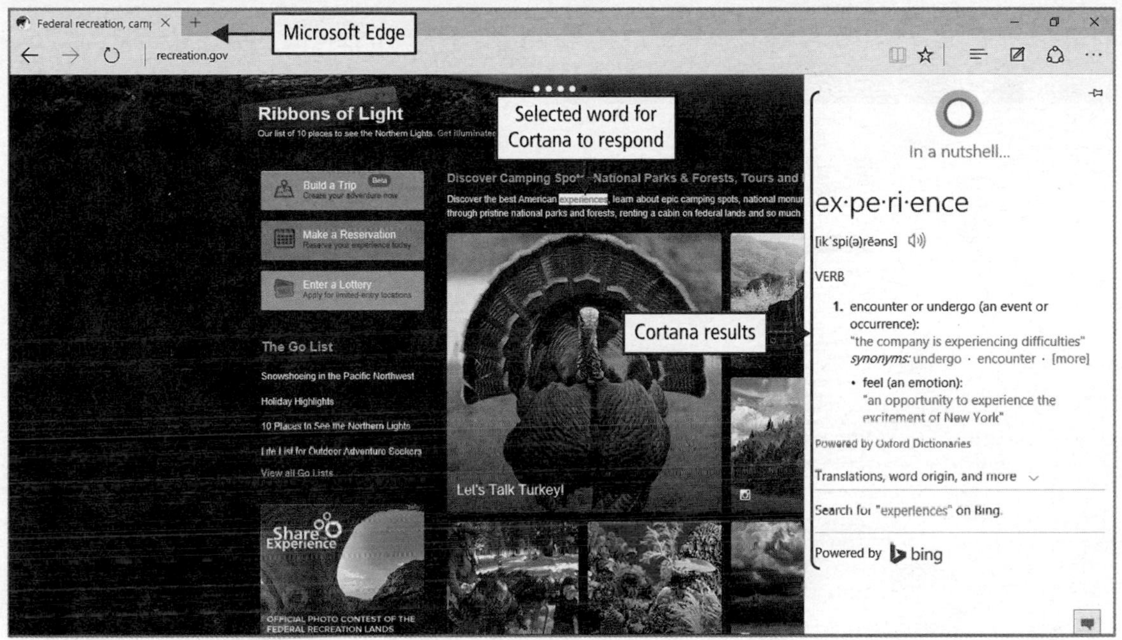

Windows 10, Microsoft Corporation

Figure 3

Windows 10, Microsoft Corporation

Figure 4

5. Select **experiences**, or another word, and then right-click **experiences**.
6. Select **Ask Cortana**. Compare your screen with **Figure 3**. **Close** [×] Edge.

   In this manner, Cortana can provide information about the selected word or phrase in a search.

7. Right-click the taskbar, click **Cortana**, and then click **Show Cortana icon**.
8. Click **Cortana** [icon], and then click **Notebook** [icon]. Select **About Me**. Click **Change my name**, and then type your First name. Click **Enter**. Click the **Hear how I'll say it** link, and then, if pronounced correctly, click **Sounds Good**. Click **Done**.
9. If your name is mispronounced, click the **That's wrong** button. Click the microphone, and then speak your name.
10. Click **Notebook** [icon], click **About Me**, and then click **Edit Favorites**. Click **Add** [+], and then type White House Select **White House**, and then drag the *Set as home* slider right to **On**. Click **Save** [icon], and then compare your screen with **Figure 4**.
11. Under *Favorites*, click **Home White House**. Under *Nearby*, click **See & Do**, and then click **Martin Luther King Jr. Memorial**. Click the **Favorites** button [★]. **Close** [×] the window.
12. Click **Cortana** [icon], and then click **Notebook** [icon]. Click **About Me**, and then click **Edit favorites**. Right-click **White House**, and then select **Delete**. Press [Esc]. Right-click the taskbar, click **Cortana** [icon], and then click **Show Search box**.

■ **You have completed Skill 3 of 10**

SKILL 4: Download, Unzip, and Zip Data Files

- Textbooks often provide files, known as ***student data files***, to complete projects.
- A ***compressed folder*** is a file or group of files reduced into a single file. They are also referred to as ***zipped folders***. ***Unzipping*** is the process of opening and extracting the files from the zipped folder.

1. If your instructor provided directions for accessing student data files, follow them, and then skip to Skill 5.
2. On the taskbar, click **Edge** . In the **Search** box, type pearsonhighered.com/skills Press Enter. Compare your screen with **Figure 1**.

   WinZip® and Stuffit Expander® are two programs that can unzip compressed files.
3. At the Pearson web page, locate and select the picture of your text. Under *Student Resources*, click the **Download Data Files** link. Locate and select **Technology Fundamentals Chapter 2: Getting Started with Windows 10** link.

   Browser settings determine what displays when you click a link to download files. In this case, you can open the file or view downloads.
4. In the **Edge** box, click **Open**. Compare your screen with **Figure 2**.
5. If necessary, insert your USB flash drive. Click the **win02_student_data_files** folder, and then on the **Extract tab**, click **Extract All**.

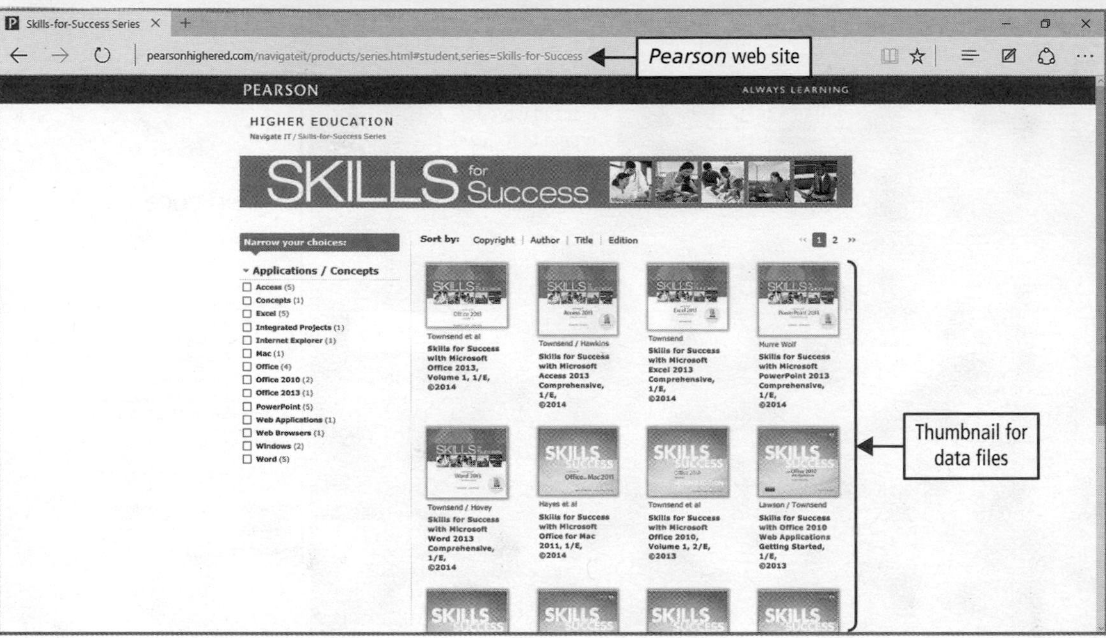

Figure 1

Windows 10, Microsoft Corporation

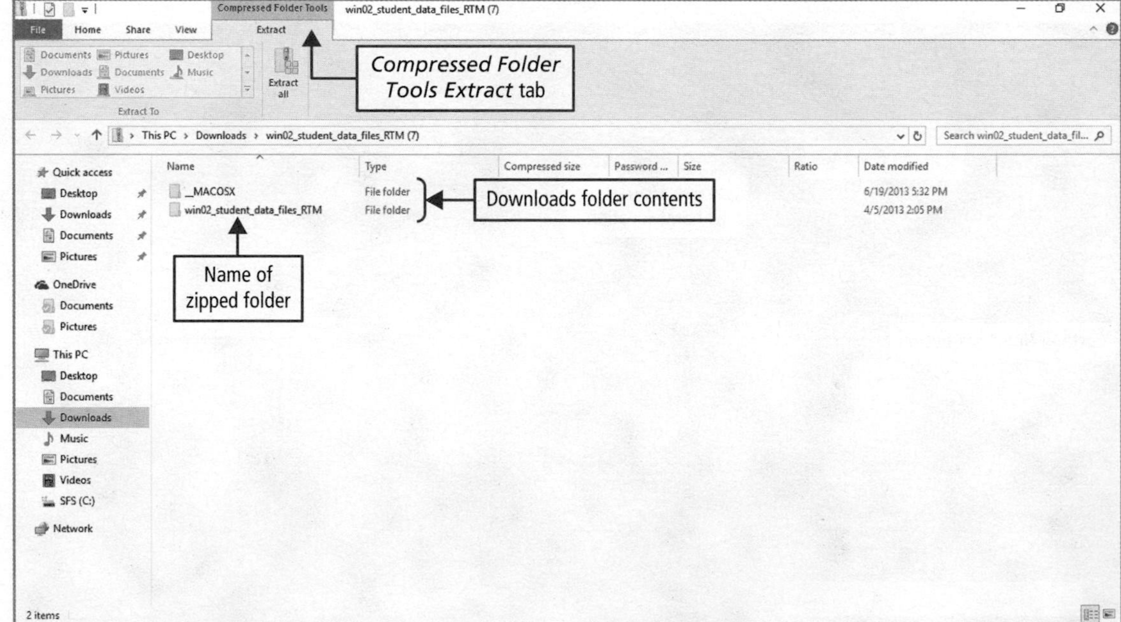

Figure 2

Office 2016, Windows 10, Microsoft Corporation

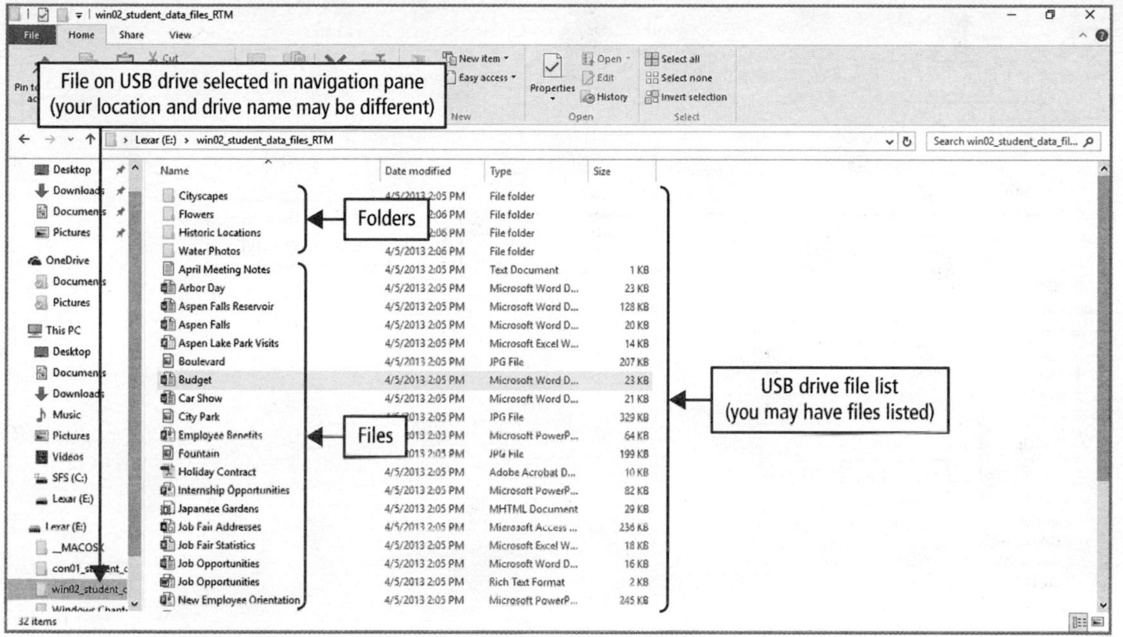

Office 2016, Windows 10, Microsoft Corporation

Figure 3

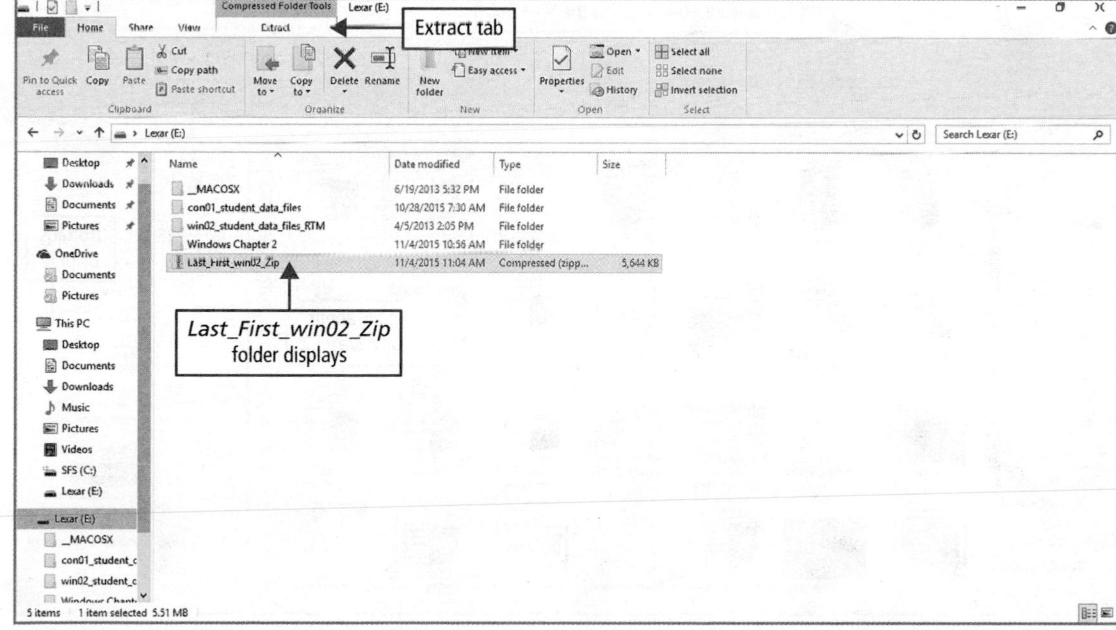

Office 2016, Windows 10, Microsoft Corporation

Figure 4

6. In the dialog box, click **Browse**. At the left of the dialog box, click **This PC**, and then click the link for your flash drive. Click **Select Folder**, and then click **Extract**.

   When files are unzipped, the files remain in the zipped folder and also display in the new, unzipped folder.

7. Double-click the **win02_student_data_files** folder, and then compare your screen with **Figure 3**.

   The student data files from the web page display as files that are unzipped.

8. On the **Home tab**, in the **Select group**, click **Select all**.
9. On the **Share tab**, in the **Send group**, click **Zip**. With the selected folder highlighted, type Last_First_win02_Zip and then press Enter. On the **Home tab**, in the **Clipboard group**, click **Cut**.

   A zipped folder is created.

10. Click the **Up arrow** ↑. In the **Clipboard group**, click **Paste**, and then compare your screen with **Figure 4**.
11. Click the **win02_student_data_files** folder. On the **Home tab**, in the **Organize group**, click **Rename**, and then type Last_First_win02_Unzip Press Enter
12. Repeat the technique from Skill 2 above to create a **Full-screen Snip**, and then save the file to your chapter folder as Last_First_win02_Zip
13. On the taskbar, right-click the **File Explorer** button, and then click **Close all windows**.
14. **Close** ✕ Edge. If a message displays, click the **Close all** button.

■ **You have completed Skill 4 of 10**

- ***File Explorer*** is a Windows application to view, find, and organize files and folders.
- File Explorer displays ***folder windows***—windows that show files and folders. Folder windows display a Navigation pane on the left and a file list on the right.
- ***Quick access*** displays a list of favorite and/or frequently-visited locations and files on your computer.

1. Open **File Explorer**. Select your flash drive, and then compare your screen with **Figure 1**. **Maximize** File Explorer.

   The ***This PC*** is used to access devices, drives, and folders on your computer.

2. Select the **Windows Chapter 2** folder. On the **Home tab**, in the **Organize group**, click the **Rename** button. Type Last_First_win02 and then press Enter twice.
3. Double-click the **Last_First_win02_Unzip** folder.

   Last_First_win02_Unzip is a ***parent folder***—the folder that contains student data files.

4. On the **View tab**, in the **Layout group**, point to—do not click—each of the commands to preview each setting, and then click **Large icons**.
5. Click the **Arbor Day** file. In the **Panes group**, click the **Details pane** button to display details about the document as shown in **Figure 2**.
6. On the **Home tab**, in the **Organize group**, click **Rename**. Type Last_First_win02_Arbor and then press Enter twice to save the name and open the file.

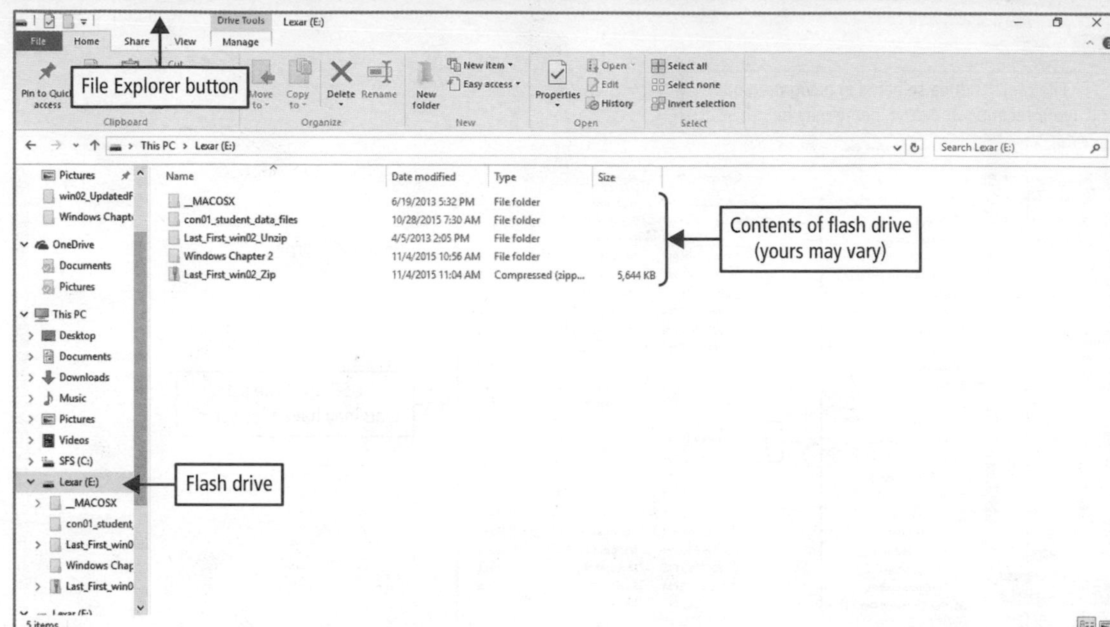

Figure 1

Office 2016, Windows 10, Microsoft Corporation

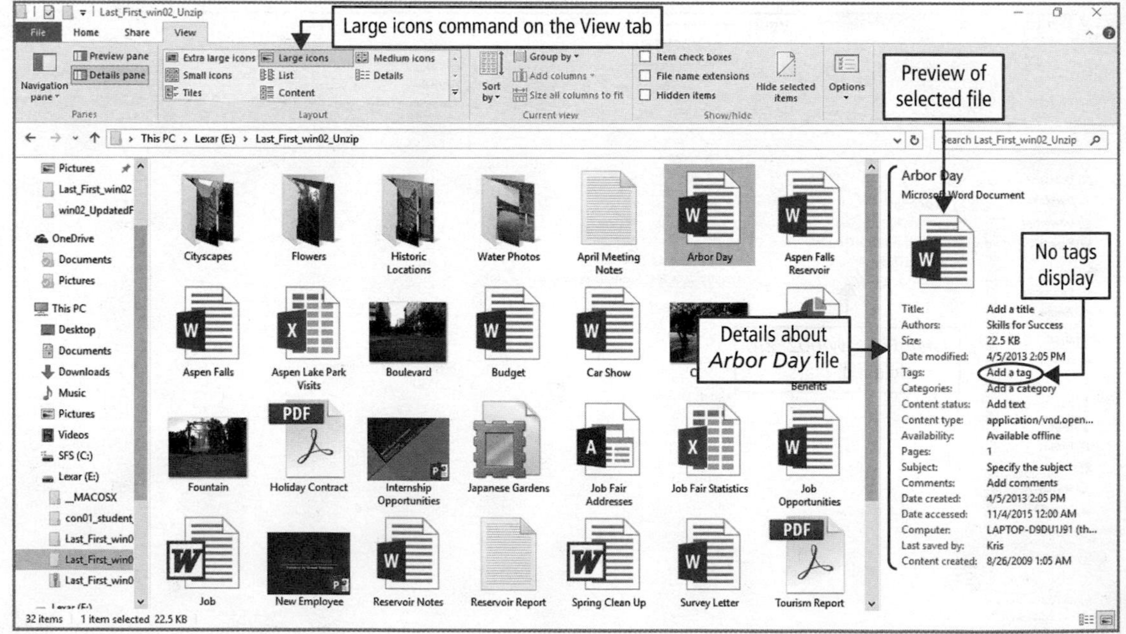

Figure 2

Office 2016, Windows 10, Microsoft Corporation

■ **Continue to the next page to complete the skill**

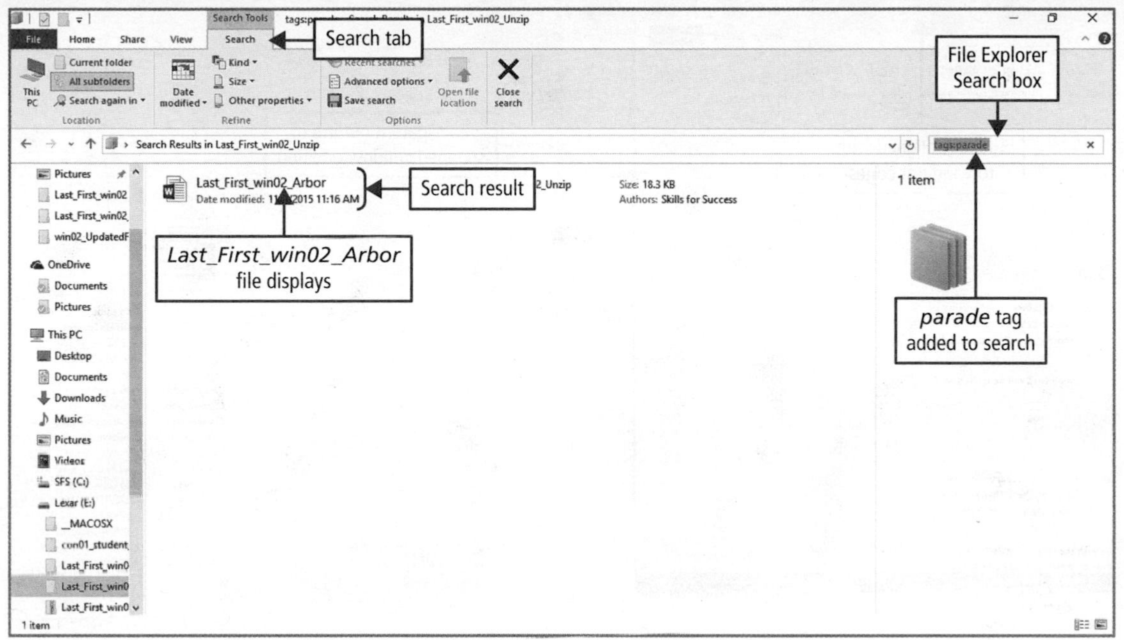

Office 2016, Windows 10, Microsoft Corporation

Figure 3

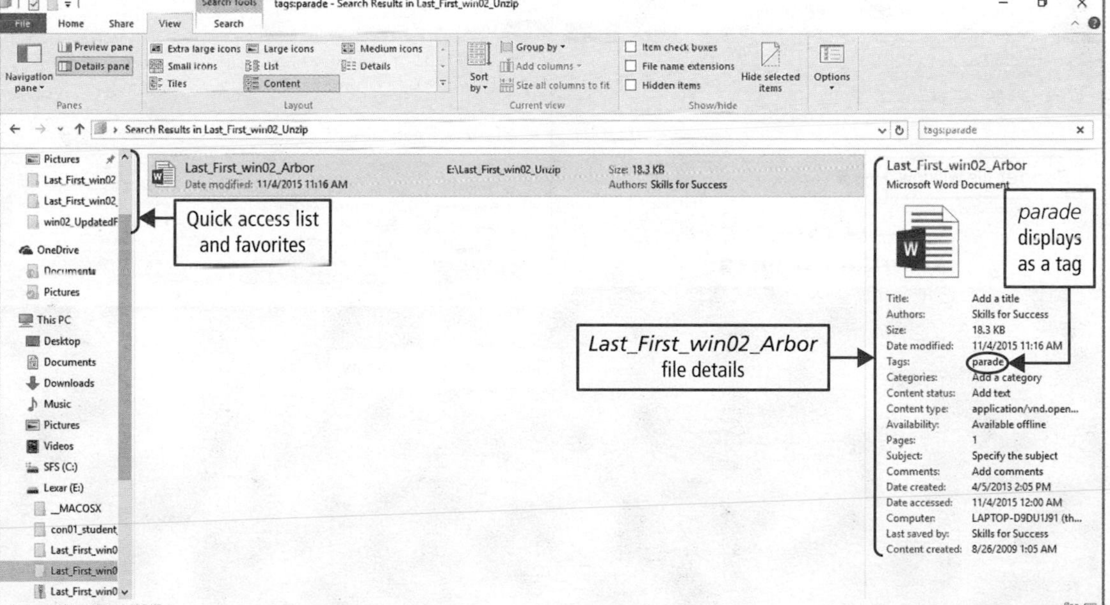

Office 2016, Windows 10, Microsoft Corporation

Figure 4

7. On the **File tab**, in the **Info group**, click **Properties**, and then click **Advanced Properties**.
8. In the dialog box, on the **Summary tab**, click the **Keywords** box. Type parade and then click **OK**. Click **Save**, and then **Close** [×] Word.

   Parade is a ***keyword*** or ***tag***—words or phrases to help identify the file when you do not know the file name during a File Explorer search.

9. Click the **File Explorer Search** box. On the **Search tab**, in the **Refine group**, click **Other properties**, and then click **Tags**. Type parade and then compare your screen with **Figure 3**.
10. Click the **Last_First_win02_Arbor** file, and then on the **View tab**, verify the **Details** pane displays. Compare your screen with **Figure 4**. On the **Search tab**, click **Close search**.
11. In the **Last_First_win02_Unzip** folder, click the **Cityscapes** folder, and then on the **Home tab**, in the **Clipboard group**, click **Pin to Quick access**.
12. In the navigation pane, under **Quick access**, click the **Cityscapes** folder. On the **View tab**, in the **Layout group**, click **Large icons**. In the **Quick access list**, right-click the **Cityscape** favorite, and then click **Unpin from Quick access**.
13. In the **Cityscapes** folder, click **Photo 4**, and then repeat the technique to rename the file to City Hall
14. Leave File Explorer open for the next skill.

■ **You have completed Skill 5 of 10**

- You can ***snap*** to quickly position a window to either half of the screen by dragging its title bar and the pointer to the screen's edge.
- When you delete a file, it is moved to the ***Recycle Bin***—an area on your drive that stores files you no longer need.

1. With **City Hall** selected, in the **Clipboard group**, click **Copy**.
2. Click the **Up arrow** [↑] twice. In the **Last_First_win02** folder, click below the folders to deselect the folders, and then click **Paste**.
3. Double-click the **Last_First_win02_ Unzip** folder. Click the **Budget** file, and then in the **Clipboard group**, click **Cut**. Click the **Up arrow** [↑], deselect all folders, and then click **Paste**.
4. **Open** the **Budget** file.
5. Point to the title bar of the *Budget* document, and then drag it to the left. When the [pointer] pointer is on the left edge of the screen and a transparent outline displays as shown in **Figure 1**, release the left mouse button to snap the window to the top left quarter of the screen. Repeat the technique to snap the **Last_First_ win02** folder window to the top right quarter of the screen.
6. In **File Explorer**, click the **Up arrow** [↑]. Click the **Last_First_win02** folder, and then click **Copy**. Click the blank space in **File Explorer**, and then click **Paste**. Compare your screen with **Figure 2**.

   When a copy of a folder is made in the same location as the previous folder, a new copy is created.

■ **Continue to the next page to complete the skill**

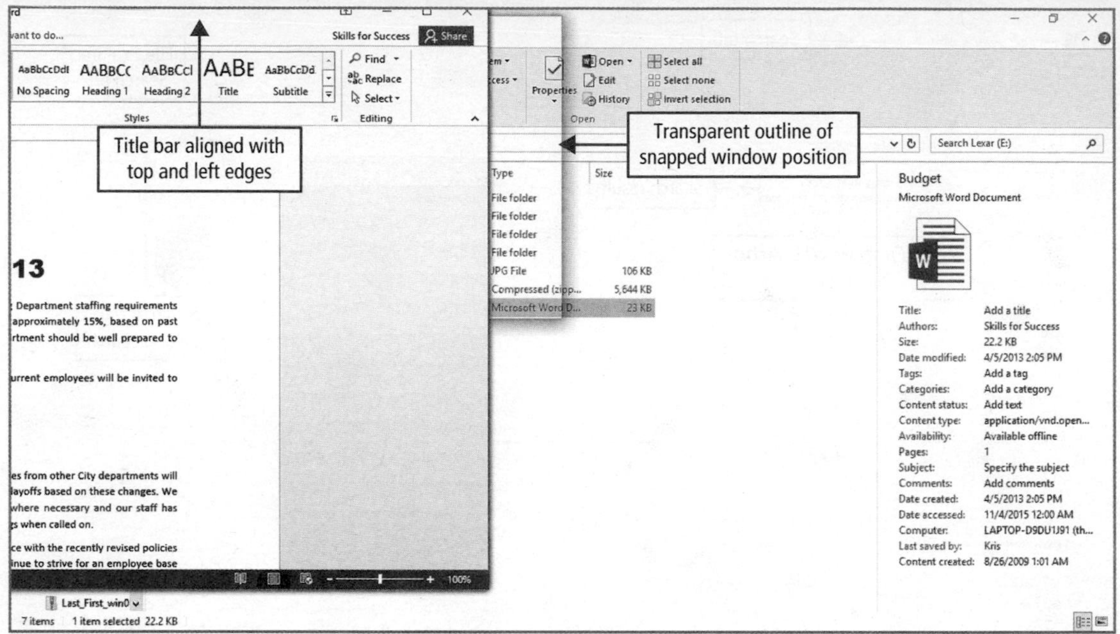

Figure 1 Office 2016, Windows 10, Microsoft Corporation

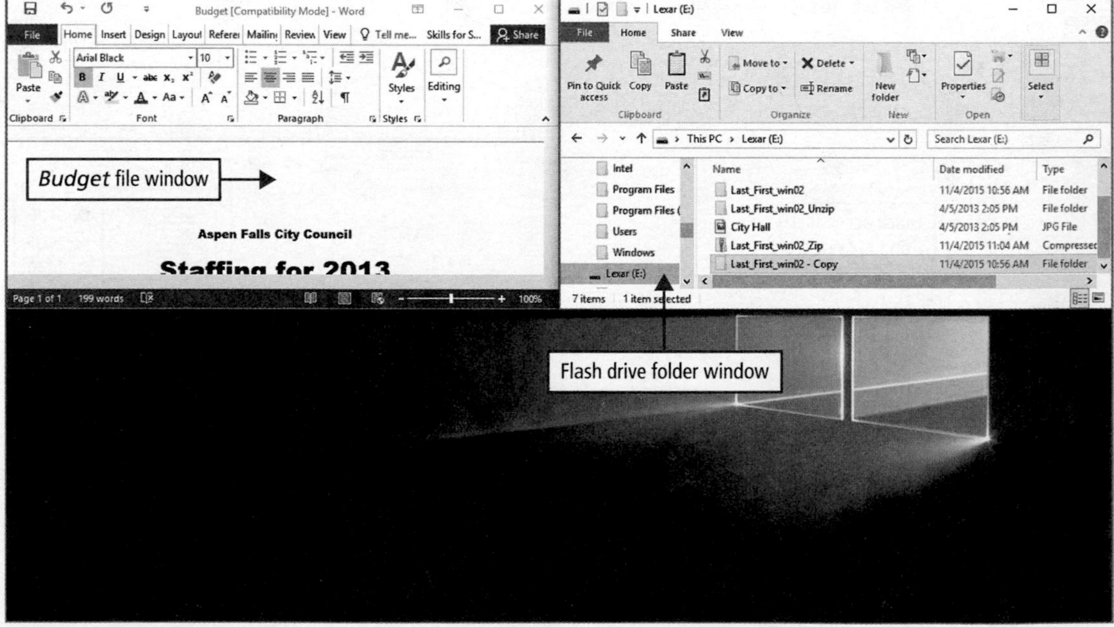

Figure 2 Office 2016, Windows 10, Microsoft Corporation

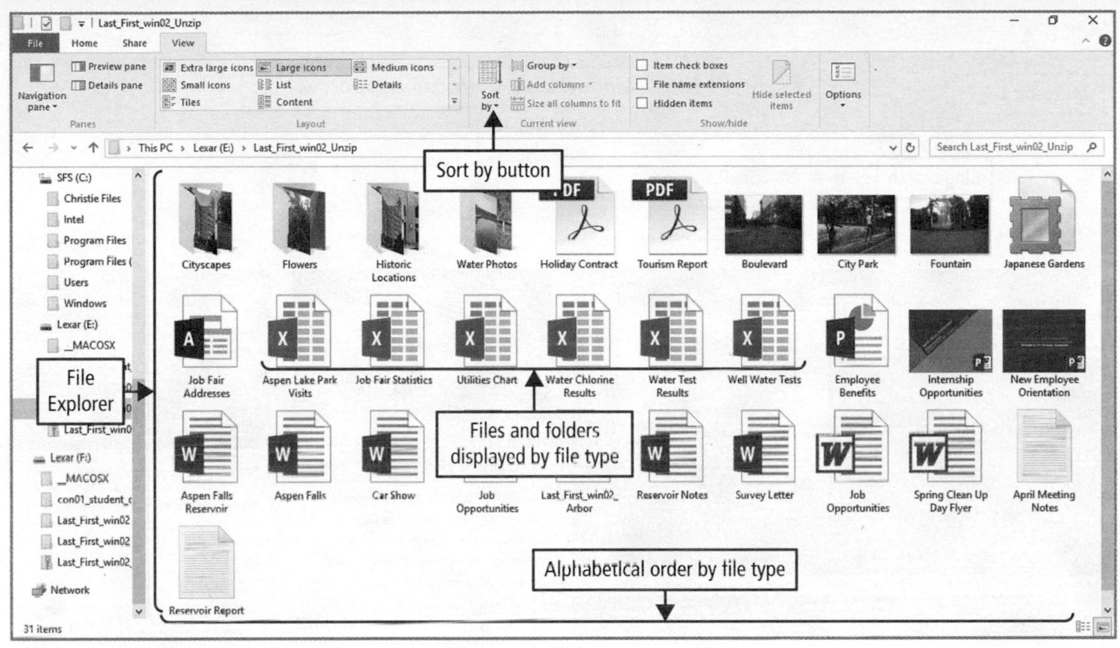

Office 2016, Windows 10, Microsoft Corporation

Figure 3

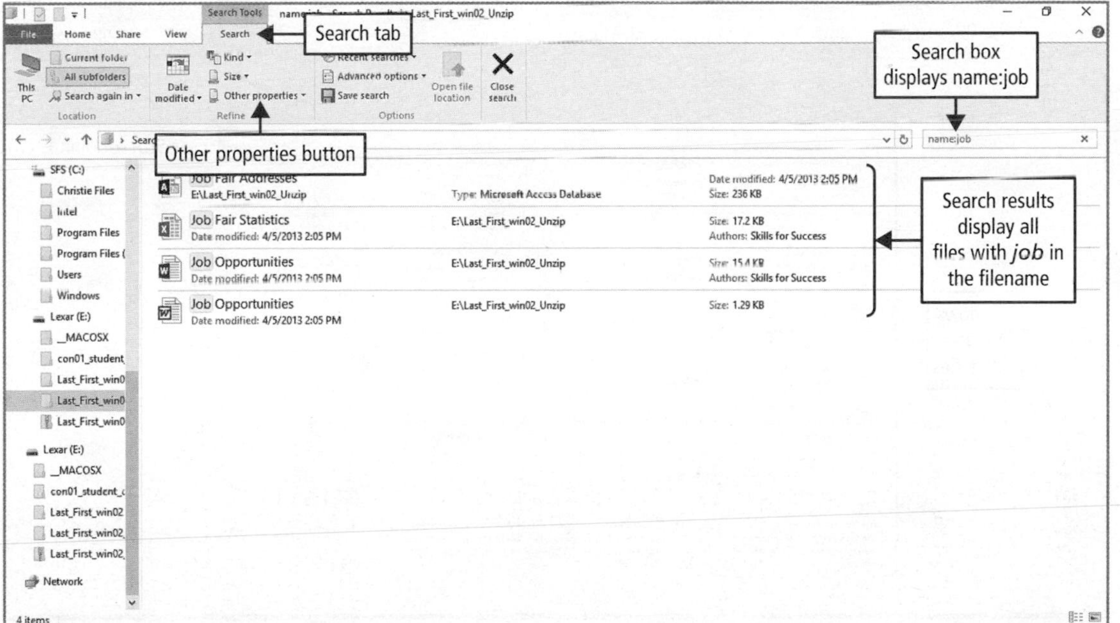

Office 2016, Windows 10, Microsoft Corporation

Figure 4

7. Open **Last_First_win02_Copy**. Click **Budget**, and then on the **Home tab**, in the **Organize group**, click the **Delete button arrow**. Click **Permanently Delete**. In the displayed message, click **Yes**. Click the **Up arrow** [↑], and then repeat the technique to delete the **Last_First_win02_Copy** folder.

   Files and folders on a flash drive are permanently deleted, while those located on the computer can go to the Recycle Bin to be restored later.

8. **Minimize** [–] Word. **Maximize** [□] File Explorer, and then double-click **Last_First_win02**. Open the **Last_First_win02 Unzip** folder.

9. On the **View tab**, in the **Panes group**, deselect **Details pane**. In the **Current view group**, click **Sort by**, and then click **Type**. Compare your screen with **Figure 3**.

10. In the **Current view group**, click **Group by**, and then select **Type**.

    The view changes to display files and folders in groups in alphabetical order by file type.

11. Repeat the technique from Skill 2 above to create a **Full-screen Snip**, and then save the file to your chapter folder as Last_First_win02_Group

12. Click **Group by**, and then click **(None)**.

13. Click the **Search** box. On the **Search tab**, in the **Refine group**, click the **Other properties** button, and then click **Name**. In the **Search** box, type job as shown in **Figure 4**.

14. On the **Search tab**, click the **Close Search** button. **Close** [×] File Explorer.

■ **You have completed Skill 6 of 10**

SKILL 2.7

- You can search the Microsoft Windows web site for help and support about Windows 10.
- You can visit the Action Center to view notifications, updates, and system information.

1. Open **Edge** [Edge icon], and then in the **Search** box, type windows.microsoft.com/support Click the first link in the list to the website as shown in **Figure 1**.

   windows.microsoft.com/en-US/windows/support or a similar site displays.

2. Scroll down, and then under *Categories*, select **Get Started** as shown in **Figure 2**.
3. At the left, click **Search and help**, and then click **Search for help**. Review how you can get Windows 10 help.
4. At the left, click **Apps and notifications**, and then click **Choose how updates are installed**. Review how you can customize the way updates are installed on your computer.
5. In the **Edge** bar, click [+] to open a new Edge tab. Type support.microsoft.com/en-us and then press Enter.
6. Click the **Search** box, type windows 10 firewall and then press Enter. Read about Windows Firewall.
7. In the **Windows Search** box, type firewall Select **Windows Firewall**. In the **Control Panel** window, click **Turn Windows Firewall on or off**.
8. Under **Private network settings**, select the **Turn on Windows Firewall** option button.

■ Continue to the next page to complete the skill

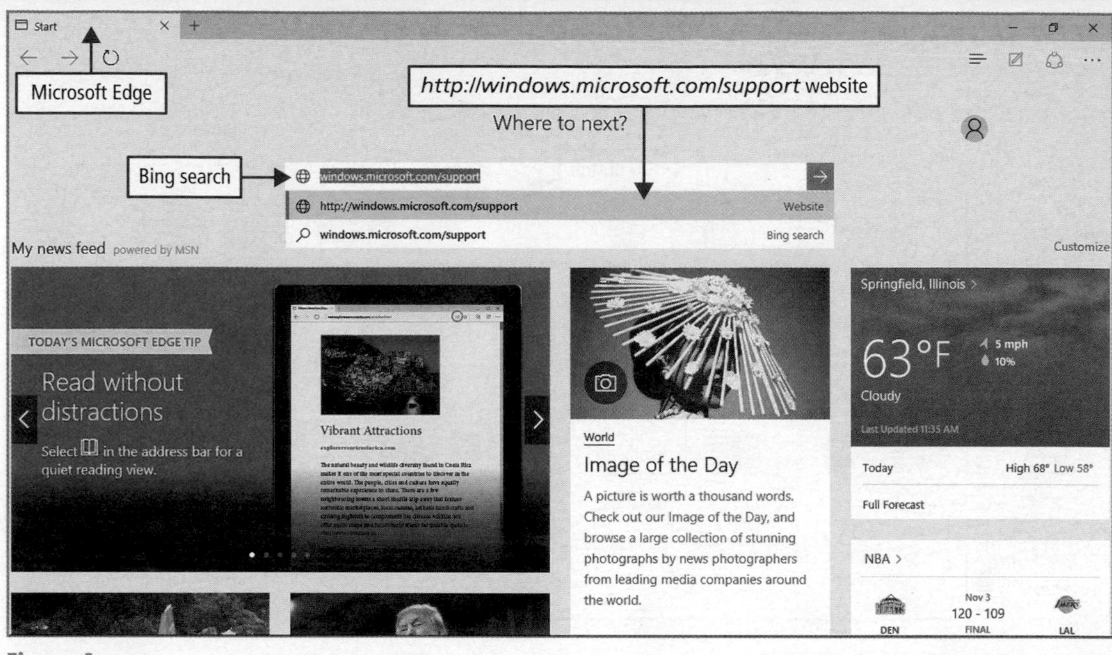

Figure 1 Windows 10, Microsoft Corporation

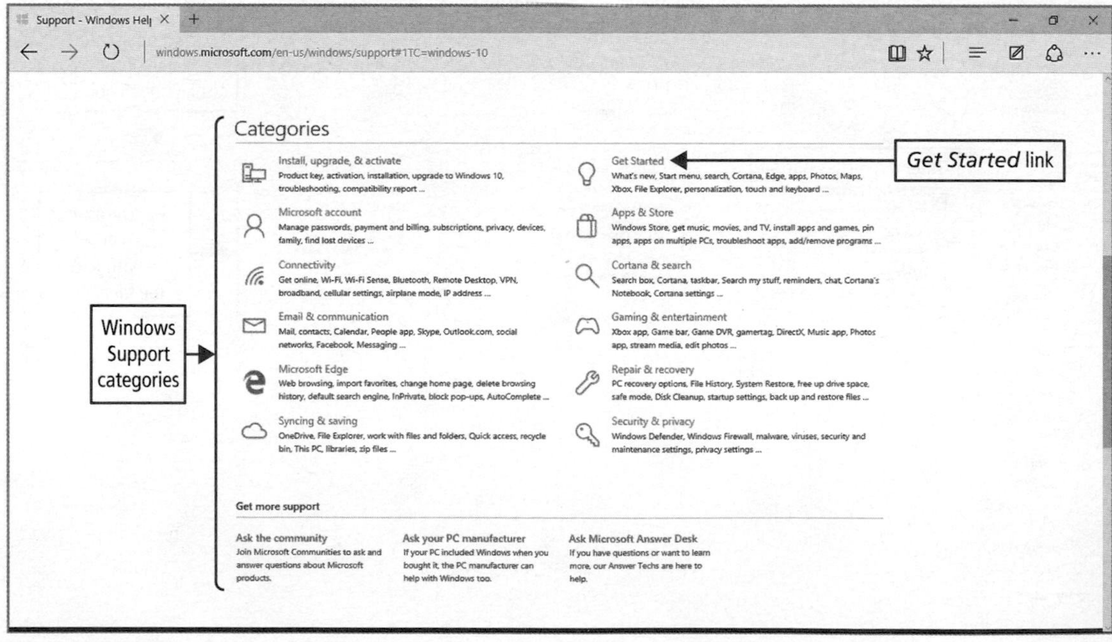

Figure 2 Windows 10, Microsoft Corporation

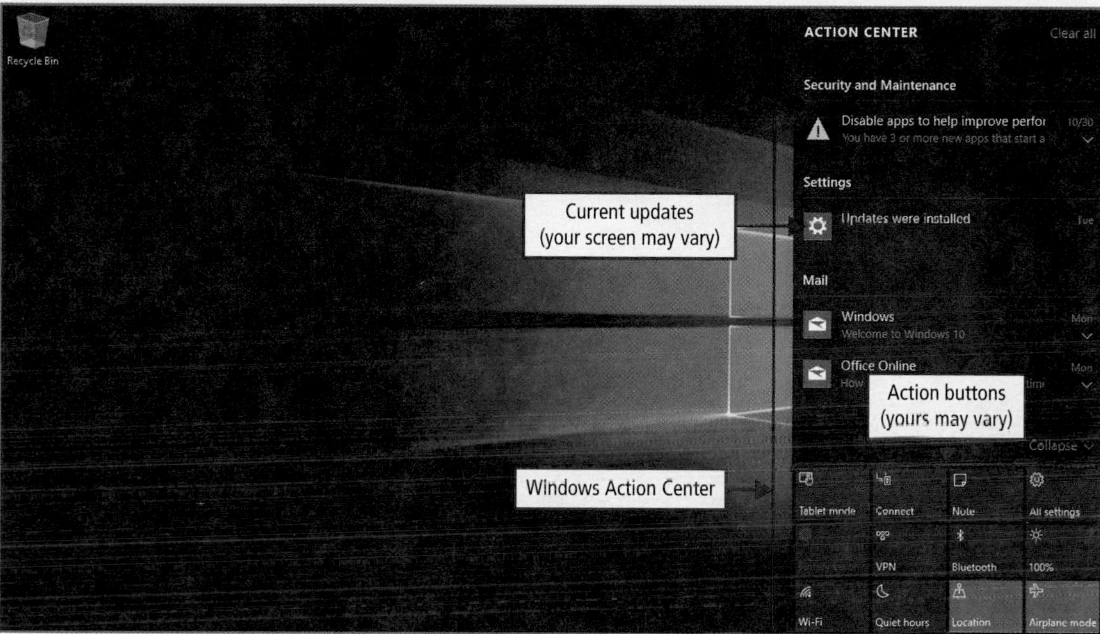

Windows 10, Microsoft Corporation

Figure 3

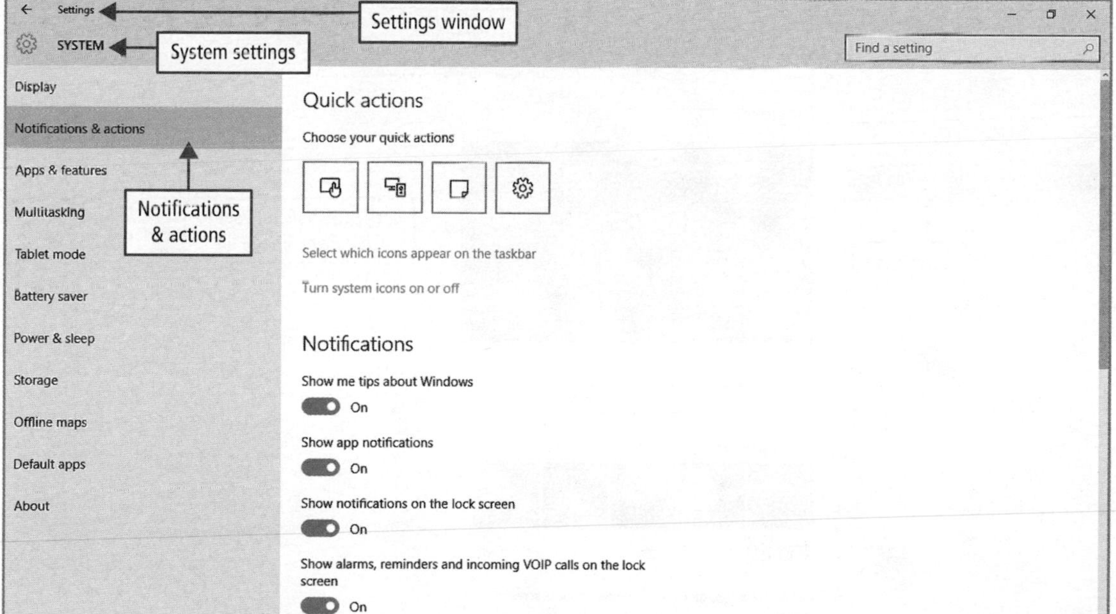

Windows 10, Microsoft Corporation

Figure 4

9. Repeat the technique from Skill 2 above to create a **Full-screen Snip**, and then save the file to your chapter folder as Last_First_win02_Firewall

10. **Close** [×] the Control Panel and Edge. In the message box, click **Close all**.

11. In the taskbar, click the **Notifications** button [icon] to display the Action Center as shown in **Figure 3**.

    The ***Action Center*** is used to let you know the status of various settings and apps as well as when you have updates for your device available to download. The Notifications button is white if you have notifications. You can customize the Action Center as desired.

12. In the **Action Center**, click **All settings**. In the **Settings** window, click **System**. Click **Notifications & actions**, and then view the current notification settings. Compare your screen with **Figure 4**.

    Notifications display for Windows 10 and the apps on your device.

    If you make any changes on your school device, be sure to return them to their original settings.

13. In the **Settings** window, click **Back** [←], and then click **Update & security**.

    Windows Update lets you know when your computer was last modified with newer settings. You can also check for any new updates and view what was recently downloaded or installed.

14. Under **Windows Update**, click the **Advanced options** link, and then click **View your update history**. **Close** [×] the Settings window.

■ **You have completed Skill 7 of 10**

- You can modify the desktop on your device by changing the background picture and lock screen image.
- You can use multiple desktops to organize apps, files, and folders.

1. Click the **Start menu** button, click **Settings**, and then click **Personalization**.
2. On the **Background tab**, record the current background. Click **Browse**.

   The ***Windows background*** is the image that displays on the desktop.
3. Open the **Last_First_win02_Unzip** folder. Double-click **Fountain**, click the **Choose a fit** box, and then click **Center**.
4. Click the **Colors tab**, and then compare your screen with **Figure 1**.

   The background color changes in the preview because the Choose a color option defaults to On. This means the tan color is automatically determined from the background image selected.
5. Click the **Lock Screen tab**, verify the **Background** is set to **Picture**, and then under **Choose your picture**, click **Browse**. In the **Unzip** folder, double-click **City Park**. Compare your screen with **Figure 2**.
6. **Close** the **Settings** window.
7. Click the **Start menu** button, click **Power**, and then click **Restart**. Wait until the power turns off and the lock screen displays to verify the new image displays.

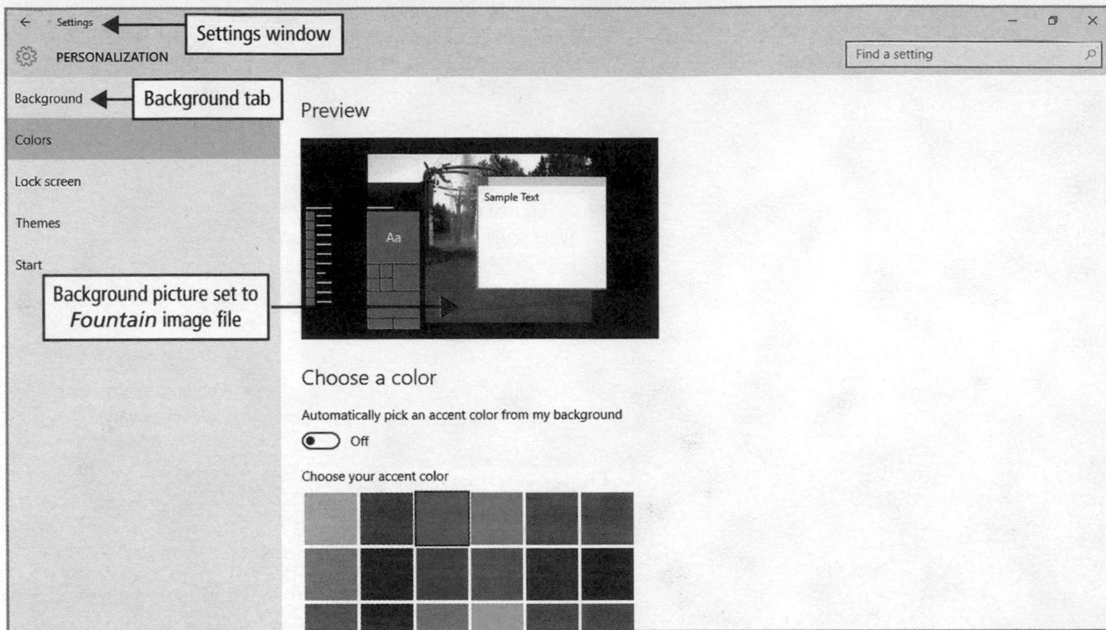

Figure 1

Windows 10, Microsoft Corporation

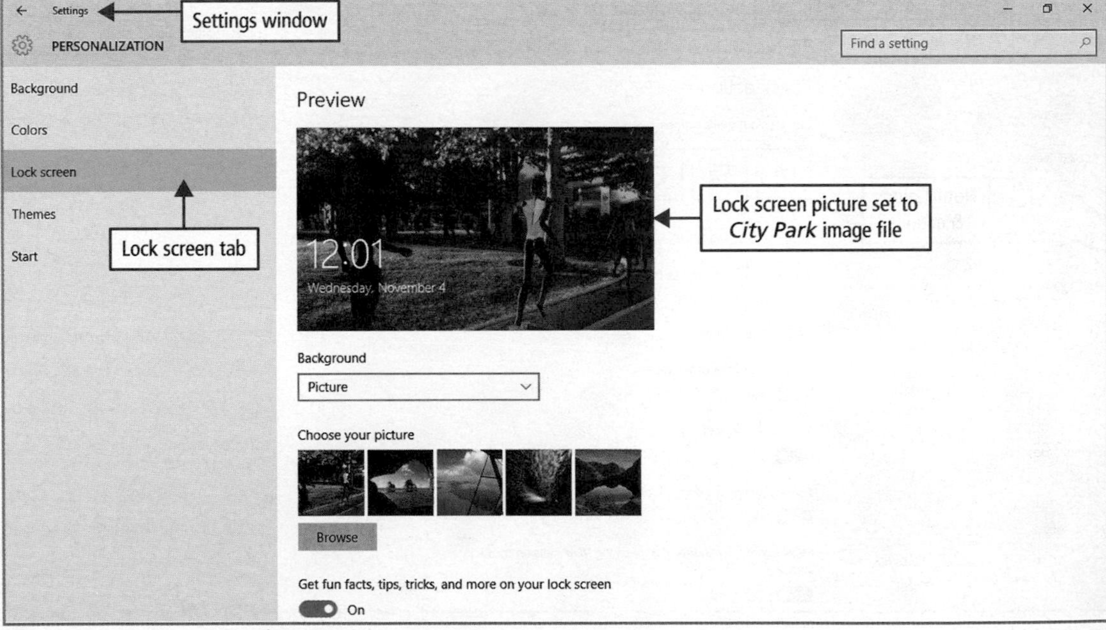

Figure 2

Windows 10, Microsoft Corporation

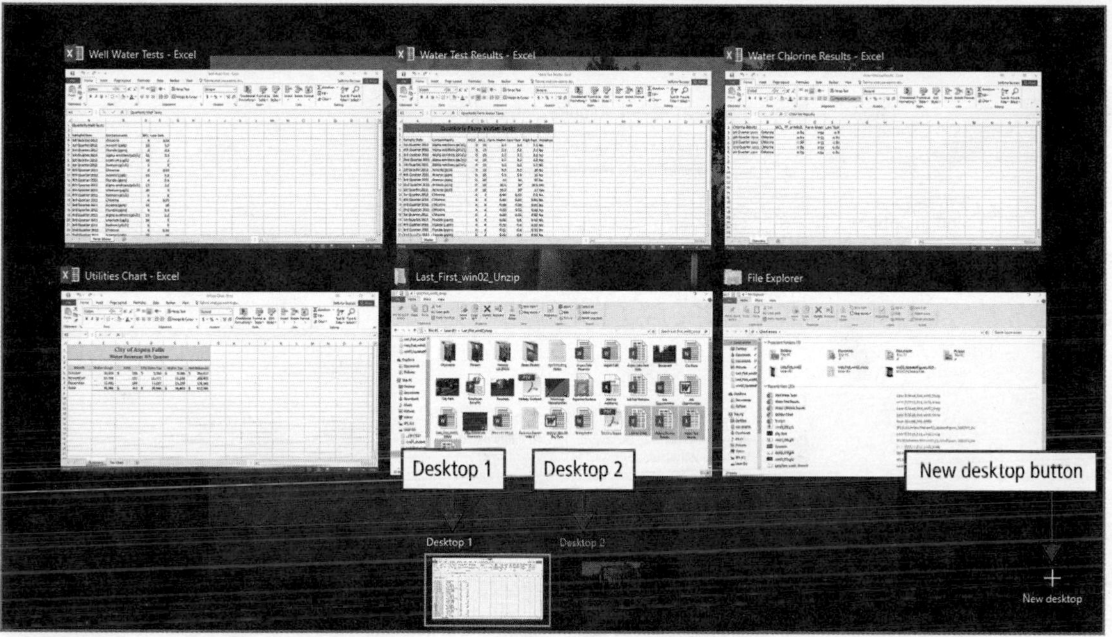

Windows 10, Microsoft Corporation

Figure 3

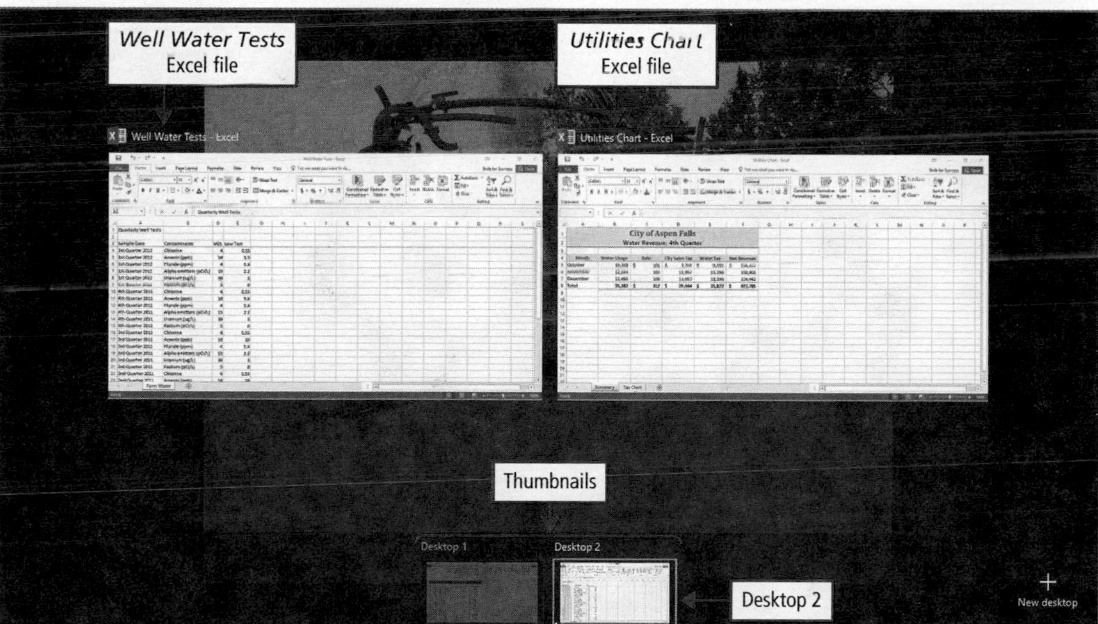

Windows 10, Microsoft Corporation

Figure 4

8. Open **File Explorer**, and then open the **Last_First_win02_Unzip** folder. Click **Utilities Chart**, press Shift, and then click **Well Water Tests**. On the **Home tab**, in the **Open group**, click **Open**.

9. On the taskbar, click **Task View**, and then click **New desktop**. Click the **Desktop 1** thumbnail as shown in **Figure 3**.

   Desktop 1 contains File Explorer, one Word document, and four Excel files. Desktop 2 contains your default settings. In this manner, you could organize Desktop 2 with apps required for a specific project.

10. Right-click the thumbnail for the **Utilities Chart**. Point to **Move to**, and then click **Desktop 2**. Repeat this technique to move *Well Water Tests* to **Desktop 2**. Select **Desktop 2** as shown in **Figure 4**.

    A ***thumbnail*** is a miniature window of the open app, file, or folder that when hovered over contains the Close button in the top-right corner.

11. Click **Desktop 1**. Click **Task View** to display the thumbnails, and then click **Desktop 2**.

12. Hover over **Desktop 2**, and then click **Close**. In the taskbar, right-click the **Word** button, and then click **Close window**. In the taskbar, right-click the **Excel** button, and then click **Close all windows**. **Close** File Explorer.

13. Reset the desktop and lock screen images to their original settings.

■ **You have completed Skill 8 of 10**

- You can modify your account settings so you sign in to Windows 10 with a PIN or, if you have a device with touch capabilities, a picture password.
- To login with a picture password, you use three ***gestures***—dragging with your finger over the touch screen to form circles, straight lines, and taps in a specific order.

1. Click the **Start menu** button, click **Settings**, and then click **Accounts**. Click **Sign-in options**, and then compare your screen with **Figure 1**.
2. Under **PIN**, click **Change**. Type your current PIN, and then press Tab twice. In the **New PIN** box, type 9513 Press Tab, and then type 9513 Click **OK**.
3. If you are not using a touch device, skip to step 13. Under **Picture password**, click **Add**.
4. In the **Create a picture password** box, type your Microsoft password, and then click **OK**.
5. Click **Choose new picture**, and then navigate to the student data files for this chapter. Open **Boulevard**, and then click **Use this picture** as shown in **Figure 2**.

   The boulevard image displays at the right.

■ Continue to the next page to complete the skill

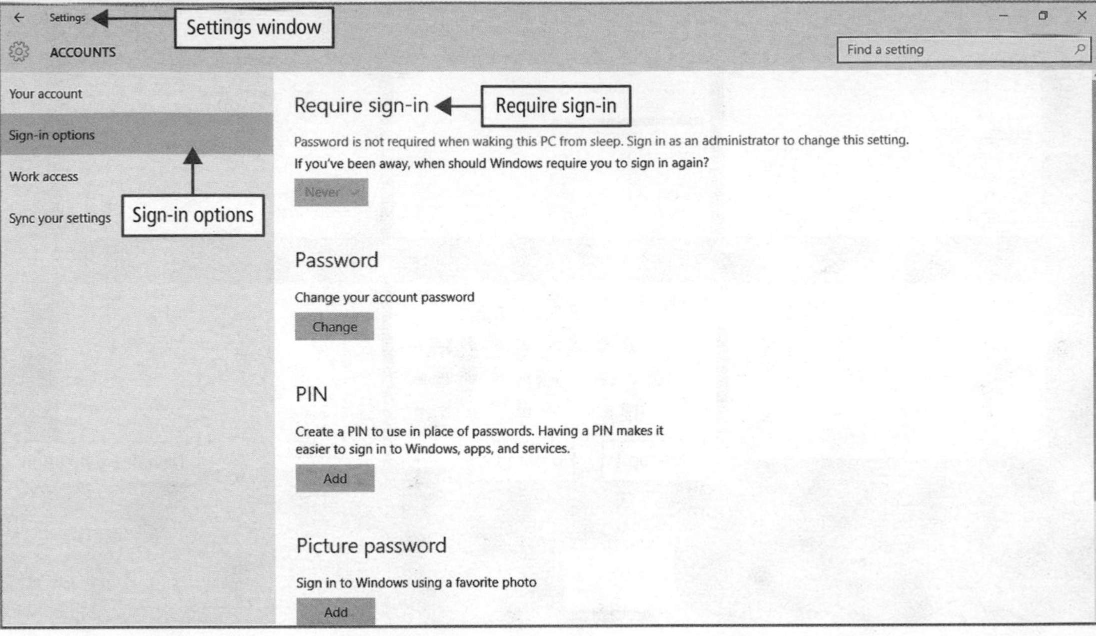

Figure 1

Windows 10, Microsoft Corporation

Figure 2

Windows 10, Microsoft Corporation

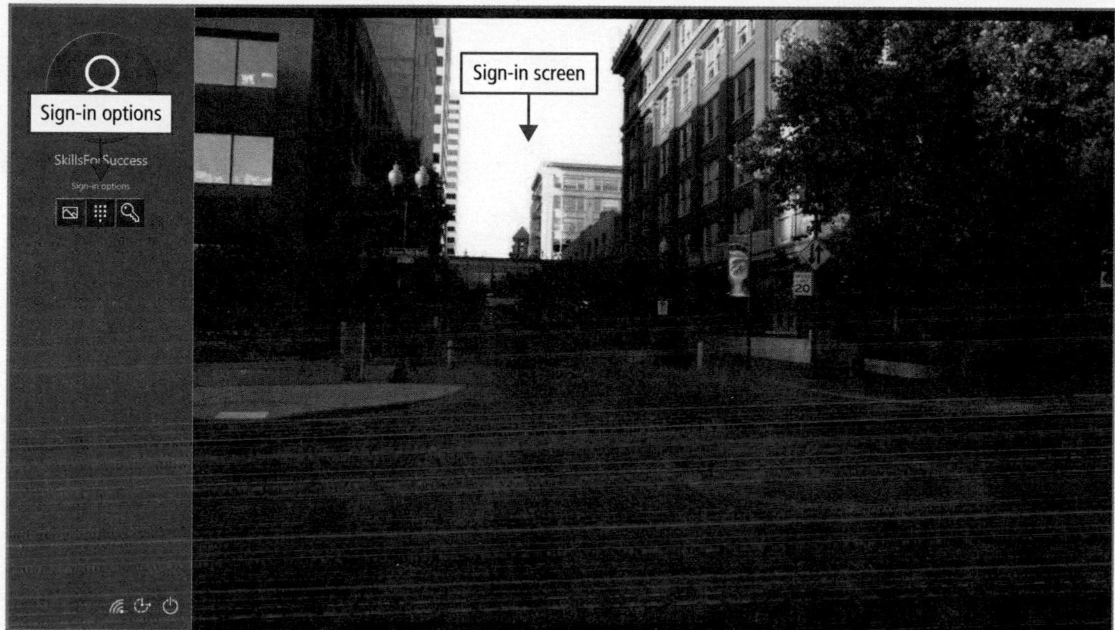

Windows 10, Microsoft Corporation

Figure 3

Windows 10, Microsoft Corporation

Figure 4

6. Use your finger on your screen to draw a straight line over the top of the walkway connecting the two buildings.

   Your first gesture is a line moving to the right. You are ready to create your second gesture.

7. Draw a circle around the outside edge of the manhole cover closest to the taskbar.
8. Tap the **Speed Limit 20** sign.
9. To confirm your gestures, repeat steps 6–8 until the *Congratulations* message displays, and then click **Finish**.
10. Click the **Start menu** button, click **Power**, and then click **Restart**.
11. Click the mouse, and then compare your screen with **Figure 3**. Repeat steps 6–8 to log in using the picture password.
12. Click the **Start menu** button, click **Power**, and then click **Restart**.
13. Click the mouse, and then to the left of the picture, click **Sign-in options**. Compare your screen with **Figure 4**.
14. Click the **PIN** button, and then type 9513
15. Click the **Start menu** button, click **Settings**, and then click **Accounts**. If desired, **Change** your PIN, and then under **Picture Password**, click **Remove**. **Close** the Settings window.

- **You have completed Skill 9 of 10**

SKILL 10: Save to OneDrive and Back Up and Restore Files

SKILL 2.10

- You should store files and folders to a separate location in case something happens to them. You can store to ***OneDrive***—a free storage space on the cloud that is automatically created when you create your Microsoft account.
- You can view a history of files so you can retrieve them if they are lost or damaged.

1. On the taskbar, click **File Explorer** , and then in the **Navigation** pane, click **OneDrive**. If necessary, in the **Microsoft OneDrive** dialog box, click **OK**. Compare your screen with **Figure 1**.

   Any files or folders you already saved to OneDrive now display in the OneDrive window.

2. In the taskbar, right-click **File Explorer** , and then click **File Explorer**. In the **File Explorer** window, click the **Restore** button .

   Here you can have two of the same window open.

   Restore is used to reduce the window size to what it was previously.

3. Under **Quick Access**, point to the **Last_First_win02** folder. Click and hold to drag the folder to the OneDrive window. Release the mouse button.

   In this manner, a copy of your folder has been placed in your OneDrive account and you have created a backup of your saved work to the cloud.

4. In the taskbar, right-click the **File Explorer** button . Click **Close all windows** as shown in **Figure 2**.

■ **Continue to the next page to complete the skill**

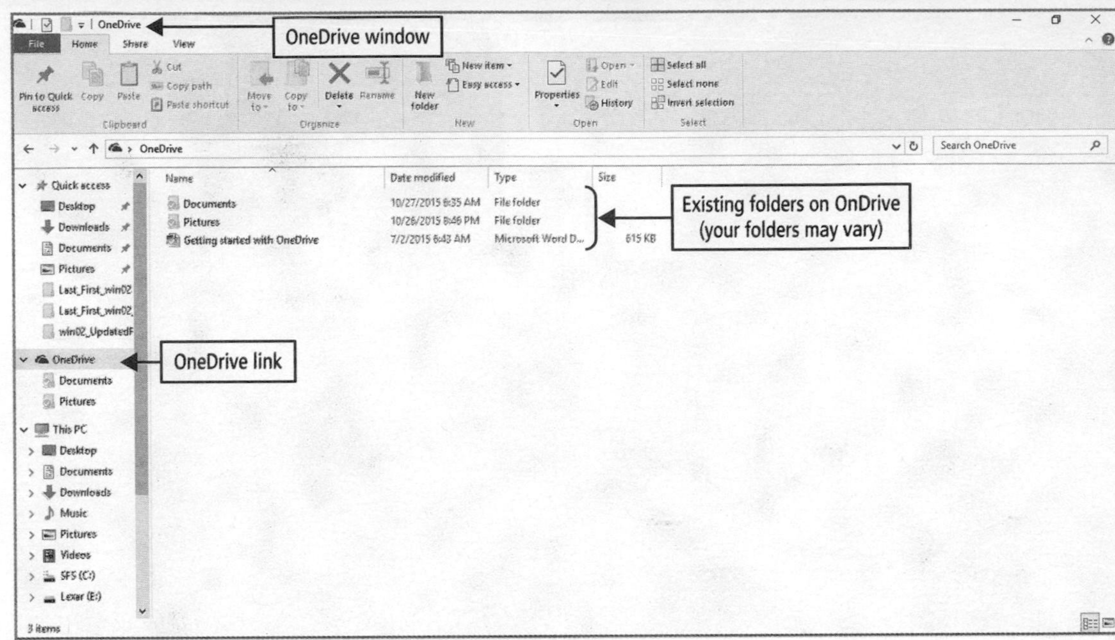

Figure 1

Windows 10, Microsoft Corporation

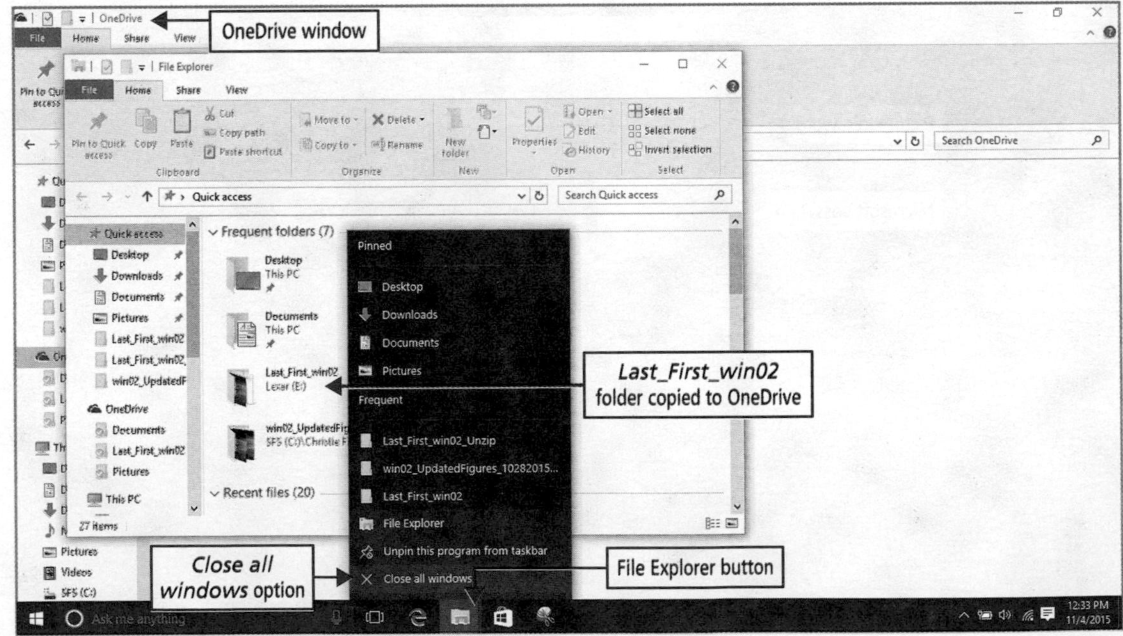

Figure 2

Windows 10, Microsoft Corporation

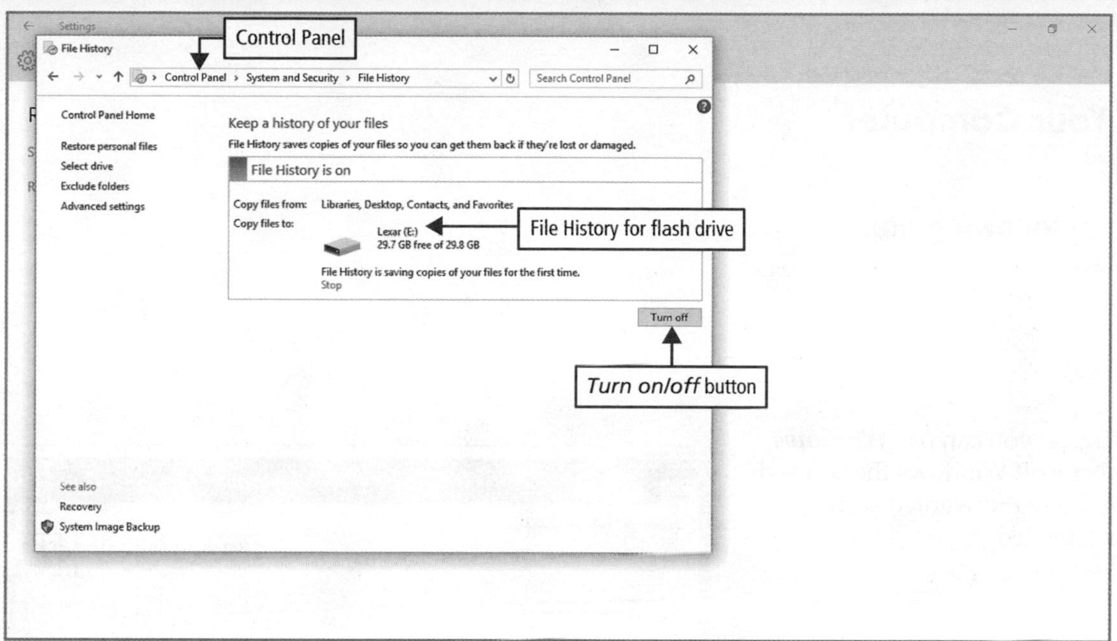

Windows 10, Microsoft Corporation

Figure 3

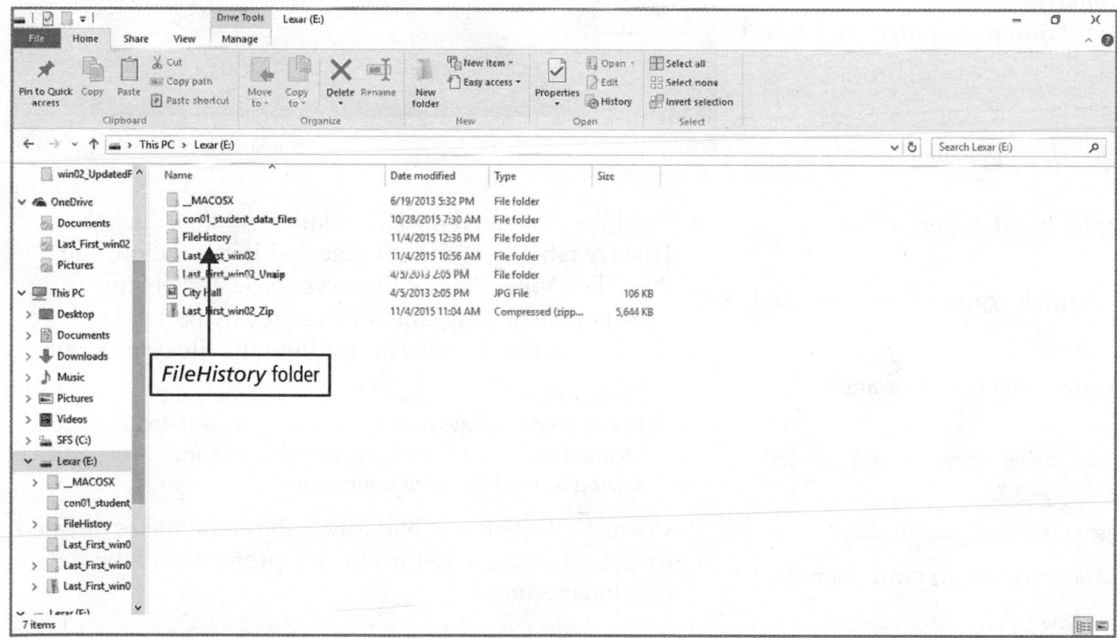

Windows 10, Microsoft Corporation

Figure 4

5. Click the **Start menu**, click **Settings**, and then click **Update & security**. Click **Backup**, and then select **More options**. If necessary, select a folder, and then click **Remove** to exclude the folder from being saved to your flash drive. Repeat this technique until only the folders you desire to back up display.
6. Select **Stop using drive**, and then click **See advanced settings**. In **File History**, click **Turn on**. Compare your screen with **Figure 3**. **Close** File History.

   The file history for your flash drive is turned on.
7. In the **Settings** window, click **Back up now**.

   This may take a while. When the backup is complete, the FileHistory file should display on your flash drive.
8. Open your flash drive, verify the FileHistory folder displays, and then compare your screen with **Figure 4**.
9. Repeat the technique from Skill 2 above to create a **Full-screen Snip**, and then save the file to your chapter folder as Last_First_win02_History
10. Delete the **FileHistory** folder. **Close** File Explorer, the Settings window, and any open windows. Reset any computer settings back to the default.
11. Click the **Start menu** button, click **Power**, and then click **Restart**.
12. Submit your files as directed by your instructor.

DONE! You have completed Skill 10 of 10, and your project is complete!

More Skills 11

Use Windows Defender to Protect Your Computer from Malware

To complete this project, you will need the following file:

- None

You will save your file as:

- Last_First_win02_MS11Defender

► When you download and open files you did not create, you can use ***Windows Defender***—software automatically included in Microsoft Windows that is used to check for and help prevent viruses, spyware, and other unwanted software from being installed on your device without your knowledge.

1. Speak Cortana, open Windows Defender **Maximize** [□] the window. Click the **Settings** link.
2. At the **Windows Defender** link, verify *Real-time protection*, *Cloud-based Protection*, and *Sample submission* are set to **On**. Scroll down, and then click **Use Windows Defender**.

   Real-time protection checks for malware all the time.

   Cloud-based protection sends Microsoft information about potential security problems found in Windows Defender.

   Sample submission sends Microsoft malware samples found on your PC so Microsoft can learn about potential security issues.
3. On the **Home tab**, under **Scan options**, verify the **Quick scan** option is selected as shown in **Figure 1**. Click **Scan now**.

   A ***quick scan*** checks only the areas on your PC that are most likely to be affected by viruses, spyware, and infected software.

   A ***full scan*** checks all files and running programs for viruses, spyware, and infected software. A full scan could take a while.

   A ***custom scan*** checks only the files, folders, and programs that you identify.
4. Read the scan details. Create a **Full-screen Snip**. Save the file to your chapter folder as Last_First_win02_MS11Defender
5. Click the **Update tab**, and then click the **Update button** to search for the most-recent virus and spyware definitions.

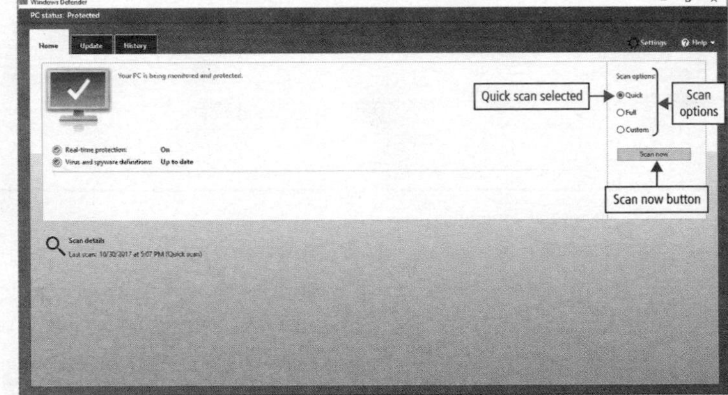

Figure 1 Windows 10, Microsoft Corporation

6. Read the displayed update details, and then click the **History tab**. Select the **All detected items** option, and then click **View details**. Observe the status of any detected file or program. If there are any issues, take action to either Remove or to Allow the file or program.

   Quarantined items are files and programs that were found to have a potential security issue that are isolated in a special location on your PC and prevented from running on your PC during a Windows Defender scan.
7. **Close** [×] the Settings window. Submit the file as directed by your instructor. Return the PC protection to the previous settings.

■ **You have completed More Skills 11**

More Skills 12

Install and Uninstall Programs

To complete this project, you will need the following file:

- None

You will save your file as:

- Last_First_win02_MS12Uninstall

- ▶ You can ***install***—add new programs to your computer. Before installing any new software, be sure you trust the manufacturer.
- ▶ You can also ***uninstall***—remove a program from your computer. When uninstall is selected, all related files that may be in other folder locations are removed.

1. Open **Edge**, type myitlab.com and then press Enter. Click the **STUDENTS** link as shown in **Figure 1**. On the Ribbon at the top, click the **Home Computer Set-up** link.
2. Click the **Microsoft Office 2016** link, scroll down, and then click **Run the Browser Tune-Up for PC** as shown in **Figure 2**.
3. Open, download, and then double-click the **Windows_ Office2016BrowserTuneUp** folder. Double-click **MyITLabForOffice2016** to run the Windows Installer Package. Click **Next** three times, and then wait for MyITLab's Launch Tool to install.
4. In the **User Account Control** dialog box, click **Yes**. **Close** [X] all open windows.

   The MyITLab browser tune up has been installed on your PC.

5. Click the **Start menu** button, and then click **Settings**.
6. Click **System**, and then at the left, select the **Apps & features** link. At the right, click the **Type an app name** box, and then type myitlab
7. At the bottom of the **Apps & features** pane, select **MyITLab Office 2016 Launch Tool**.
8. Create a **Full-screen Snip**, and then save the file to your chapter folder as Last_First_win02_MS12Uninstall
9. Click **Uninstall**. In the displayed message window, click **Uninstall**. In the **User Account Control** window, click **Yes**.

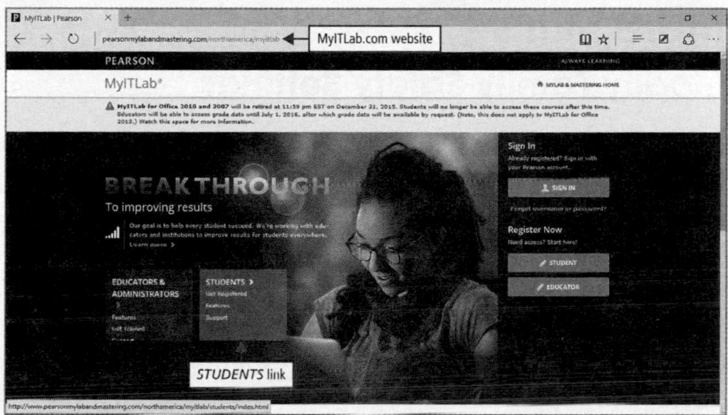

Pearson Education, Inc

Figure 1

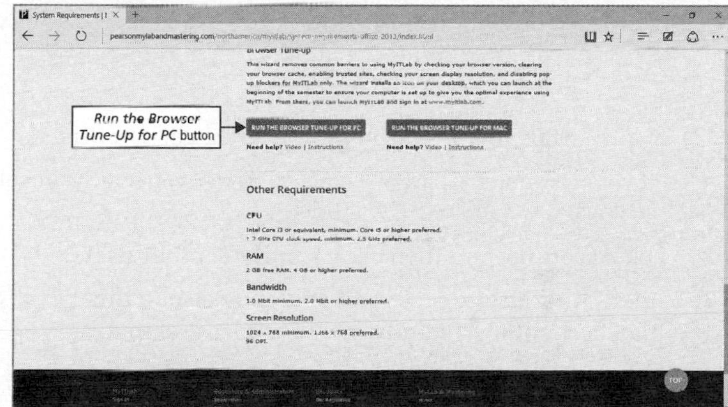

Pearson Education, Inc

Figure 2

The prompts to uninstall are created so only specified users with access to your PC can remove a program from your computer. Once the program is removed, you would need to install it again to run it on your PC.

10. **Close** [X] all open windows, and then submit the file as directed by your instructor.

■ **You have completed More Skills 12**

More Skills 13

Modify Family Safety Settings

To complete this project, you will need the following file:

- None

You will save your file as:

- Last_First_win02_MS13Family

- You can share your Windows 10 PC or other device with family members. You remain in control of your device when you provide them with access. You can also prevent them from accessing the device and/or specific settings.
- When a child is added to your device, you can adjust settings to help them safely navigate the Internet. You can view reports of their online connection, as well as set time limits for using the device.

---

1. Click the **Start menu** button, and then click **Settings**.

   If your computer is part of a home network, you may be unable to use family settings.

2. Click **Accounts**, and then click **Family & other users**.
3. Under **Other users**, click **Add someone else to this PC**. If you have an e-mail account for a family member, please skip to step 6.
4. Click the **The person I want to add doesn't have an email address** link.
5. In the **Let's create your account** box, use the table in **Figure 1** to create a new user account. Click **Next** two times, and then skip to step 8.
6. Under **Your family**, click **Add a family member**. Click the desired option button, and then type the e-mail address for the person.
7. Click **Next**. In the **Add this person** message box, click **Confirm**. Click **OK** if it is an existing e-mail address or **Close** if the e-mail address has to be verified. Review the e-mail account for the join invitation, and then sign in to Windows 10.

   If the person has not used Windows 10 on the device, follow the prompts to update.

8. Create a **Full-screen Snip**, and then save the file to your chapter folder as Last_First_win02_MS13Family

Create your account text	
First name	Brian
Last name	Carnival
E-mail address	bcarnival@aspenfalls.org
Password	BC395_afCA
Country	United States
Birth month	November
Birth day	13
Birth year	1976

Figure 1

9. If you are adding a family member, under **Your family**, click the **Manage family settings online** link. Turn on **Activity reporting** and **Email weekly reports to me**.

   Activity reporting is a family account feature that provides a report to the account owner with the length of time your child spent using the device and your child's online searches, including what apps and games have been installed and played.

   Web browsing is a family account feature used to restrict websites from your child's viewing.

   Apps, games & media is a family account feature used to determine what apps and games can be downloaded for a specific age.

   Screen time is a family account feature used to set the start time, end time, and total time the device can be used each day.

10. Click the family member to be blocked. Click **Block**.
11. **Close** the **Settings** window. Submit the file as directed by your instructor.

- **You have completed More Skills 13**

More Skills 14

Perform a Disk Cleanup

To complete this project, you will need the following file:

- **win02_Student_Data_Files**

You will save your file as:

- **Last_First_win02_MS14Optimize**

- The Start Menu in Windows 10 can be customized to display in full screen.
- ***Disk cleanup*** is a Windows feature that removes unnecessary files from the hard drive of the PC to allow for better storage and file retrieval.

---

1. Click the **Start** button, and then click **Settings**.
2. Click **Personalization**, click **Start**, and then drag the *Use Start full screen* slider right to **On**.
3. Click the **Search** box, and then type disk cleanup Press Enter, and then compare your screen with **Figure 1**.
4. In the list, click **Defragment and Optimize Drives** to open the desktop app.
5. In the **Optimize Drives** window, under **Drive**, select drive **C:**.

   Flash drives are not optimized because they may not always be connected to the device.

6. Click **Analyze**, and then wait for the drive to be analyzed.

   Depending on the number of files located on the hard drive, this could take a while.

7. Click **Optimize**, and then wait for the drive to be optimized. If it takes longer than 5 minutes, click **Stop**.

   Depending on the number of files located on the hard drive, this could take a while.

8. Create a **Full-screen Snip**, and then save to your chapter folder as Last_First_win02_MS14Optimize
9. **Close** the Optimize Drives window.
10. In the **Settings** window, at the **Start tab**, drag the *Use Start full screen* slider left to **Off**. **Close** the Settings window.
11. Submit the file as directed by your instructor.

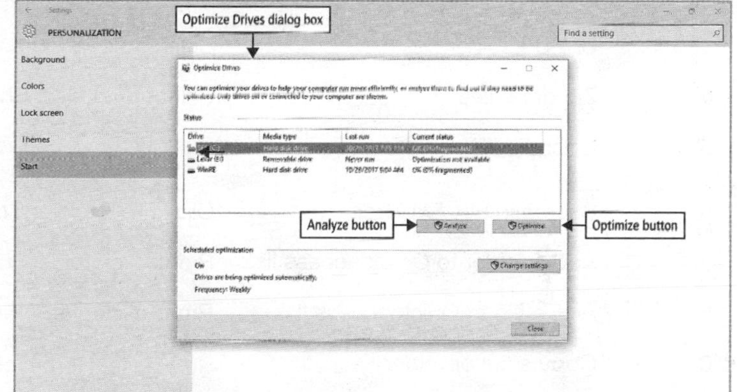

Windows 10, Microsoft Corporation

Figure 1

- **You have completed More Skills 14**

The following table summarizes the **SKILLS AND PROCEDURES** covered in this chapter.

Skills Number	Task	Steps	Icon	Keyboard Shortcut
1	Sign in	Click the lock screen. On the sign-in screen, select your username, type your password, and then click Submit		
2	Search in Windows 10	Click the Search box and type your request		
2	Customize the Start menu	Click the Start Menu. Right-click an app and pin to Start menu		
2	Customize the taskbar	Right-click an app and pin to taskbar		
3	Manage Cortana settings	Use the Search box to locate the Cortana & Search settings to turn on Cortana		
3	Access Cortana Notebook	In the Search box, click the Cortana circle, click Notebook		
4	Download a file	Navigate to the website, search for the website, and click the link to download the file(s)		
4	Unzip a folder	Select folder. Extract tab → Extract all		
4	Zip data files	Select data files. Share tab → Send group → Click Zip		
5	Open File Explorer	Click File Explorer icon		
5	Search in File Explorer	Click File Explorer Search box → Search tab → Refine group → Other properties → Tags		
5	Add a folder to Quick access list	Right-click folder→ Pin to Quick access		
5	Add a file to Quick access list	Right-click file → Pin to Quick access		
6	Copy a file or folder	Select file. Home tab → Clipboard group → Copy or press Ctrl and drag to move		Ctrl + C
6	Snap a window	Drag the window's title bar to the edge of the screen		
6	Cut a file or folder	Select file. Home tab → Clipboard group → Cut or drag to move to Recycle Bin		Ctrl + X
6	Paste a file or folder	Select location. Home tab → Clipboard group → Paste		Ctrl + V
7	Obtain Windows 10 Help	Navigate to the website, search for windows.microsoft.com/support		
7	Use the Action Center	In the taskbar, click the Notifications button		
8	Modify the desktop	Start menu → Settings → Personalization		
8	Use Desktop 2	On the Taskbar, click Task View		
9	Set a PIN	Start menu → Settings → Accounts		

Skills Number	Task	Steps	Icon	Keyboard Shortcut
9	Create a picture password	Start menu → Settings → Accounts		
10	Save to OneDrive	Open File Explorer → Click OneDrive in Navigation pane		
10	Back up a file	Start → Settings → Update & Security → Backup → More Options		
10	Restore a file	File Explorer→ Restore		
MS11	Use Windows Defender	Start → Settings → Windows Defender → Quick scan → Scan now		
MS12	Install a program	Navigate to the website, search for the program → Download the file → Open the file → Follow the prompts to install		
MS12	Uninstall a program	Start → Settings → System → Apps & features		
MS13	Modify family safety settings	Start → Settings → Accounts → Family & other users → Add a family member		
MS13	Manage family safety settings online	Start → Settings → Accounts → Family & other users→ Manage family settings online		
MS14	Perform a disk cleanup	Start → Settings → Personalization → Search for disk cleanup → click Defragment and Optimize Drives		

Project Summary Chart		
Project	**Project Type**	**Project Location**
Skills Review	Review	Book
Skills Assessment 1	Review	Book
Skills Assessment 2	Review	Book
Visual Skills Check	Problem Solving	Book
Skillls Challenge 1	Critical Thinking	Book
Skills Challenge 2	Critical Thinking	Book

Key Terms

Online Help Skills

1. Open **Microsoft Edge**, type https://support.microsoft.com and then press Enter. Type gesture and then select **Windows 10 touchpad gestures**.
2. In the displayed list, select **Touchpad gestures for Windows 10 - Windows Help**. Compare your screen with **Figure 1**.
3. Read through the list to answer the following questions: Other than tap and swipe, what other gestures can you use, and how might you use them?

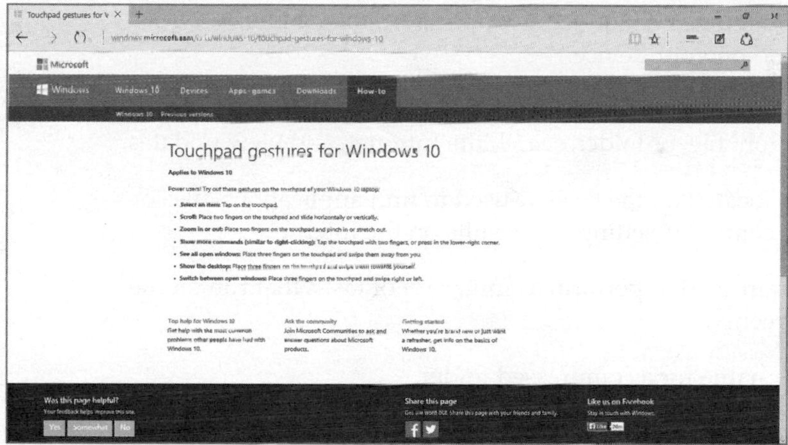

Microsoft Corporation

Figure 1

Matching 

Match each term in the second column with its correct definition in the first column by writing the letter of the term on the blank line in front of the correct definition.

___ **1.** The process of connecting to a device by keying a Microsoft account username and then entering a password or pin or using a picture password.

___ **2.** A screen that interprets commands when you touch it with your finger.

___ **3.** A picture representation for an application, file, folder, or command on your device.

___ **4.** A toolbar located at the bottom of the desktop used to view an application, file, or folder, search the Internet, and view updates.

___ **5.** An area located on the taskbar used to find applications, files or folders, computer settings, or results on the Internet.

___ **6.** A program used to perform a similar set of tasks that run on the Start screen.

___ **7.** Another name for a compressed folder.

___ **8.** The process of opening and extracting the files from the zipped folder.

___ **9.** A Windows application that is used to view, find, and organize files and folders.

___ **10.** A feature that is used to let you know the status of various settings and apps, as well as when you have updates for your device available to download.

A Action Center
B File Explorer
C Icon
D Search box
E Sign in
F Taskbar
G Touch display
H Unzip
I Windows 10 Store app
J Zipped

Multiple Choice

MyITLab®

Choose the correct answer.

1. A screen that displays shortly after a computer or device is turned on that is running Windows 10.
   - **A.** Lock
   - **B.** Password
   - **C.** Sign-in
2. Text that is hidden by displaying characters such as bullets.
   - **A.** Button
   - **B.** Masked character
   - **C.** Serif
3. A four-digit code used when signing in to Windows 10.
   - **A.** Keyword
   - **B.** PIN
   - **C.** Thumbnail
4. A built-in feature of Windows 10 that opens apps, files, and settings, provides appointment reminders, and shares results of keyed or spoken questions or commands for items located on your computer devices and in Bing.
   - **A.** Action Center
   - **B.** Calendar
   - **C.** Cortana
5. A list of favorite and/or frequently-visited locations and files on your computer displayed in File Explorer.
   - **A.** Action Center
   - **B.** Cortana Notebook
   - **C.** Quick Access
6. A word or phrase to help identify the file when you do not know the file name during a File Explorer search.
   - **A.** Gesture
   - **B.** Tag
   - **C.** Tap
7. To quickly position a window to either half of the screen by dragging the title bar and the pointer to the screen's edge.
   - **A.** Lock Screen
   - **B.** Snap
   - **C.** Snip
8. A miniature window of the open app, file, or folder that when hovered over contains the Close button in the top-right corner.
   - **A.** Keyword
   - **B.** PIN
   - **C.** Thumbnail
9. Dragging with your finger over the touch screen to form circles, straight lines, and taps in a specific order.
   - **A.** Gesture
   - **B.** Tag
   - **C.** Tap
10. A free storage space on the cloud that is automatically created when you create your Microsoft account.
    - **A.** Cortana Notebook
    - **B.** File Explorer
    - **C.** OneDrive

Topics for Discussion

1. Start the Store app, and view the apps that are available. Which apps would you like to add, and how do you think you might use them?
2. If your desktop computer had a touchscreen, do you think you would primarily use gestures like swipe and tap to navigate between apps and windows or use the mouse? Why?

Skills Review

To complete this project, you will need the following file:

- **win02_student_data_files (a folder containing several files)**

You will save your files as:

- **Last_First_win02_SRWater**
- **Last_First_win02_SRFile**

1. If necessary, turn on your computer and sign in.
2. On the **Start** menu, search for the **Alarms & Clock** app. Right-click the app, and then pin the app to the Start menu and to the taskbar. On the **Start** menu, resize the tile to **Large**.
3. Open the **Cortana Notebook**, click **About Me**. Click **Edit favorites**. Add and save Sacramento, California as a favorite. Set the location to **Home**.
4. Speak Cortana, Open Microsoft Edge and then search for pearsonhighered .com/skills Select the first thumbnail. Select **Organized by chapter**.
5. Download, open, and unzip the Windows 10 student data files. Extract the files to your flash drive. Rename the unzipped folder as Last_First_win02_SR as shown in **Figure 1**.
6. Open the renamed folder. Open the **Flowers** folder, and then change the view to **Large** icons. Click the **IMG_5294** file to select it, and then press Shift and, at the same time, click **IMG_5849** to select the nine images in the folder.
7. On the **Home tab**, click **Copy**. **Paste** the images in the parent directory **Last_First_win02_SR**.
8. Open the **Last_First_win02_SR** folder. On the **Home tab**, click **Select all**. On the **Share tab**, click **Zip**, and then save the folder as Last_First_win02_SRZip Compare your screen with **Figure 2**.
9. On the **View tab**, in the **Layout group**, click **Content**. Click the **Search** box, and then type name:water Press Enter. Click **Sort by**, and then select **Type**. Click **Group by**, and then click **Type**.
10. Create a **Full-screen Snip**, and then save the file to your chapter folder as Last_First_win02_SRWater On the **Search tab**, click **Close Search**.

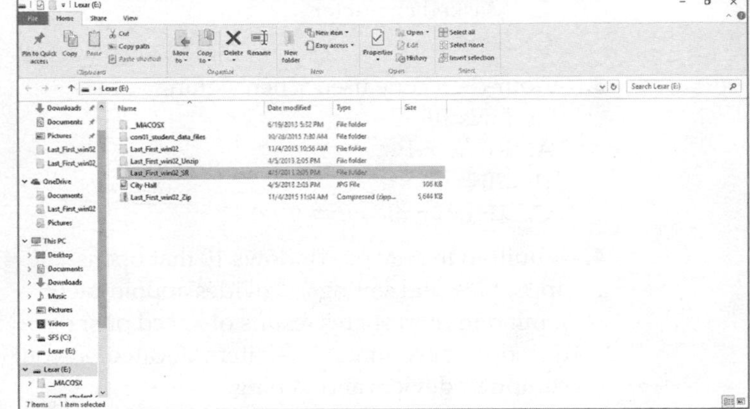

Figure 1 Windows 10, Microsoft Corporation

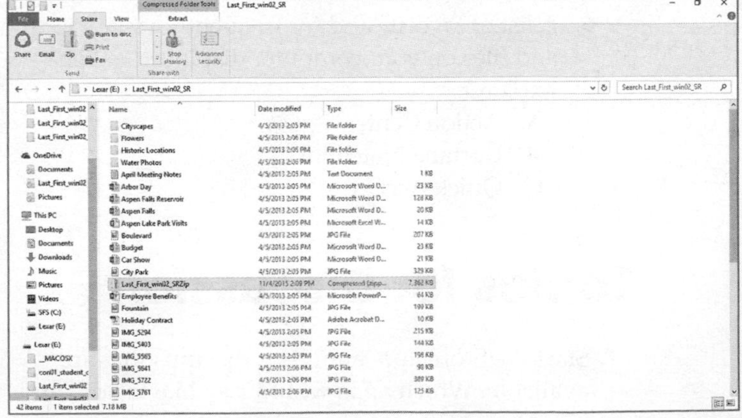

Figure 2 Windows 10, Microsoft Corporation

■ **Continue to the next page to complete this Skills Review**

11. Select the file **IMG_5761**, and then delete the image from the **Last_First_win02_SR** folder.
12. Move up one folder level. Select the **Last_First_win02_SR** folder, and then click **Copy**. Click the **OneDrive** folder and then click **Paste**.
13. Open **Edge**, and then search for and open windows.microsoft.com/support Select the **Get Started** link. Click the **Apps and notifications** link, and then select **Group apps into desktops**. Read **how to get the Alarm to Desktop 2**. **Close** [×] Edge.
14. In **Task** view, add a new Desktop2. Open Desktop2. From the taskbar, open the **Alarms & Clock** app, and then open the **Snipping Tool** app as shown in **Figure 3**. Delete Desktop 2.
15. On the **Start** menu, type Account and then click **Manage your account**. Click **Sign-in options**, and then under **PIN**, click **Add**. Type 3574 for the PIN.
16. Under **Picture password**, click **Add**. Verify your Microsoft password, and then click **Choose new picture**. From your student data files, choose **City Hall** (located in the Historic Locations folder on your flash drive) as the new picture, as shown in **Figure 4**. Use the City Hall image to create three gestures.
17. Click the **Start menu** button, click **Power**, and then click **Restart**. Login with your PIN. Repeat the technique to login with a picture password with a gesture.
18. Click the **Start menu** button, click **Settings**, and then click **Update & security**. On the **Backup tab**, click **More options**, and then click **See advanced settings**. Click **Advanced settings**, and then click the **Open File History** link. In **File History**, click **Turn on**. **Close** [×] the window.
19. Open **File Explorer**, and then open your flash drive. On the **View tab**, in the **Layout group**, click **Details**. Verify the **FileHistory** folder displays.
20. Create a **Full-screen Snip**, and then save the file to your chapter folder as Last_First_win02_SRFile
21. **Close** [×] any open windows. Reset any computer settings back to the default. Submit your files and folders as directed by your instructor.

DONE! You have completed this Skills Review

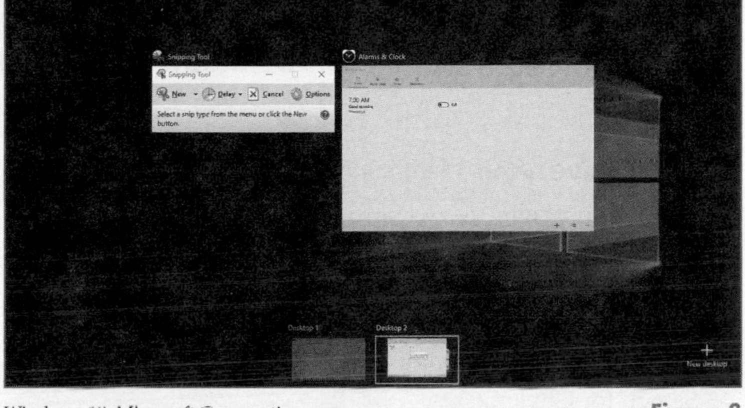

Windows 10, Microsoft Corporation **Figure 3**

Windows 10, Microsoft Corporation **Figure 4**

Skills Assessment 1

To complete this project, you will need the following file:

- None

You will save your files as:

- Last_First_win02_SA1Snip1
- Last_First_win02_SA1Snip2

---

1. Click the **Maps** tile to open the app, and then **Maximize** the window. Search for Cuyama, CA
2. Compare your screen to **Figure 1**.
3. Open the Snipping Tool. **Save** a Full Screen Snip as a JPEG file in your chapter folder as Last_First_win02_SA1Snip1
4. **Close** the Maps app window.
5. Display the **Personalization** window. In the second row of the gallery, click the second theme and then close the Settings dialog box. Compare your screen with **Figure 2**.
6. **Save** a Full Screen snip of the desktop in your chapter folder as Last_First_win02_SA1Snip2
7. **Close** all open windows, and then return the desktop to its original settings. Submit the files as directed by your instructor.

DONE! You have completed Skills Assessment 1

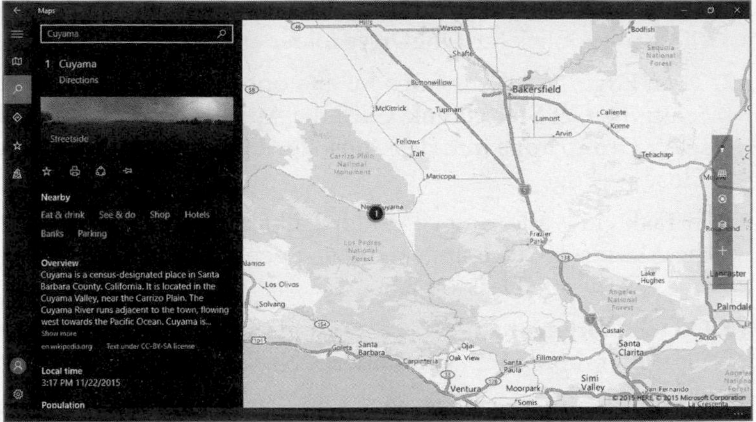

Figure 1 Windows 10, Microsoft Corporation

Figure 2 Windows 10, Microsoft Corporation

Skills Assessment 2

To complete this project, you will need the following file:

- **win02_student_data_files (a folder containing several files)**

You will save your files as:

- **Last_First_win02_SA2Snip1**
- **Last_First_win02_SA2Snip1**

---

1. Pin the **Snipping Tool** to the taskbar.
2. Start **WordPad**. Snap the **WordPad** window to the left edge of the desktop. In WordPad, type your First and Last name, and then press Enter.
3. **Open** the **File Explorer** folder window, and then snap the window between the right edge of the screen and the **WordPad** window.
4. In the **File Explorer** window, display your USB drive or storage device file list, and then create a new folder named Last_First_win02_SA2
5. Compare your screen with **Figure 1**.
6. Create a **Full-screen Snip**, and then **Save** the file in your chapter folder as Last_First_win02_SA2Snip1
7. **Maximize** the File Explorer window, and then display the **win02_student_data_files** folder. From the **Flowers** folder, Copy the nine *JPEG image* files to your **Last_First_win02_SA2** folder.
8. In your **Last_First_win02_SA2** folder, rename the file **IMG_5565** as RedBerries
9. Open your Last_First_win02_SA2 folder, and then sort by **Name** in ascending order. Create a **Full-screen Snip.** Save the snip in your **Last_First_win02_SA2** folder with the name Last_First_win02_SA2Snip2 Compare your screen to **Figure 2**.
10. **Close** all open windows, and then Unpin the **Snipping Tool** from the task bar. Return the desktop to its original settings. Submit the files as directed by your instructor.

DONE! **You have completed Skills Assessment 2**

Windows 10, Microsoft Corporation

Figure 1

Windows 10, Microsoft Corporation

Figure 2

Visual Skills Check

To complete this project, you will need the following file:

- None

You will save your files as:

- Last_First_win02_VSSnip1
- Last_First_win02_VSSnip2

On the **Start screen**, click the Weather tile. If asked to use your location, click **Block**. In the **City or ZIP code** box, type Cuyana California Take a Full screen snip. Save the file in your chapter folder as Last_First_win02_VSSnip1 Compare your screen with **Figure 1**.

Return to the Start screen, and then use the Maps app to search for California Take a Full screen snip. Save the file in your chapter folder as Last_First_win02_VSSnip2

Close all open windows, and then submit your files as directed by your instructor. Return the Start screen to its original settings.

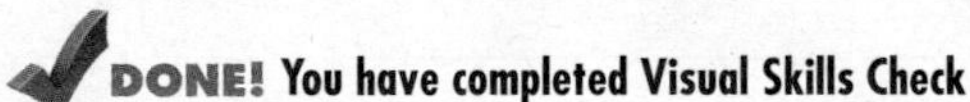

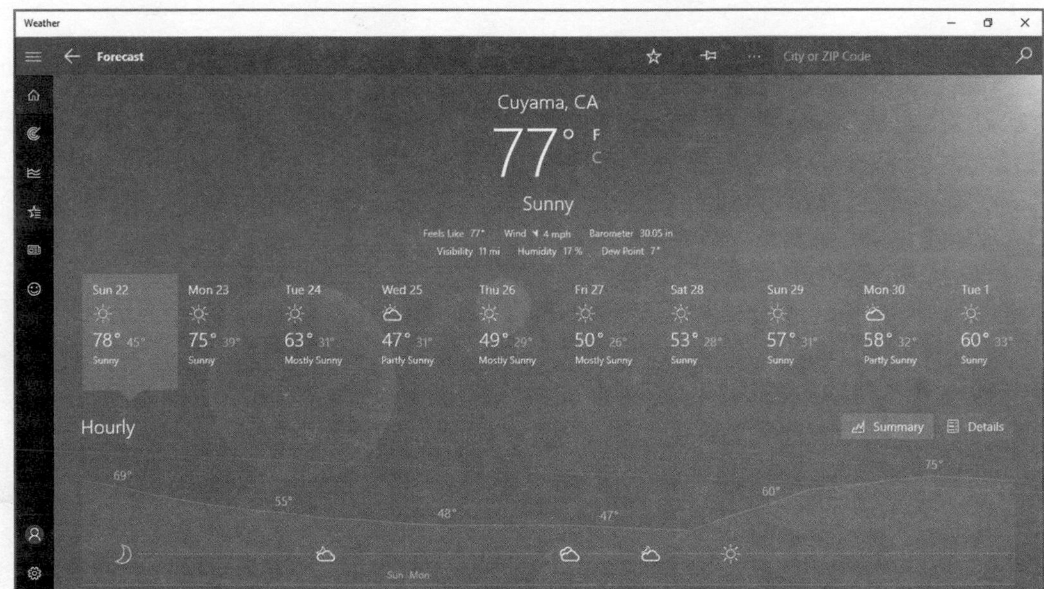

Figure 1

Windows 10, Microsoft Corporation

Skills Challenge 1

To complete this project, you will need the following folder:

- **win02_student_data_files**

You will save your file as:

- **Last_First_win02_SC1Folder**

The files in the folder *win02_student_data_files* contain work from several different projects. To organize these files, on your storage device, create a new folder named Skills Challenge 1 In the new folder, create three additional folders with the following names: Human Resources and Water Department and Events Search win02_student_data_files to find the three PowerPoint files **Employee Benefits, Internship Opportunities**, and **New Employee Orientation**. Copy these files into your Human Resources folder. Search again for files containing the word **Water** and copy these three Excel files into the Water Department folder. Copy the Arbor Day and Car Show files into the Events folder.

Select your **Skills Challenge 1** folder, and then create a zipped archive named Last_First_win02_SC1Folder Submit the compressed folder as directed by your instructor.

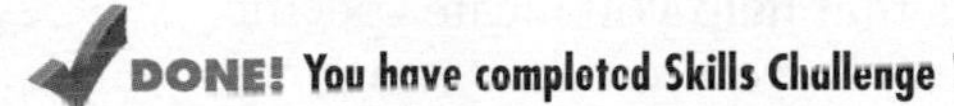

DONE! You have completed Skills Challenge 1

Skills Challenge 2

To complete this project, you will need the following file:

- **win02_student_data_files**

You will save your files as:

- **Last_First_win02_SC2Snip1**
- **Last_First_win02_SC2Snip2**

Open the win02_student_data_files folder. Sort the files by size, so that the largest files appear at the top of the window, and the smallest appear at the bottom. Take a Full screen snip, and then save the file in your chapter folder as Last_First_win02_SC2Snip1

Return to the win02_student_data_files folder and sort by type. Take a Full screen snip, and then save the file in your chapter folder as Last_First_win02_SC2Snip2 Close all open windows, and then submit the files as directed by your instructor.

DONE! You have completed Skills Challenge 2

CHAPTER 3

Browse the Internet

- ***Microsoft Edge*** is the default web browser in Windows 10 that replaces Internet Explorer. Other browsers include ***Google Chrome***, ***Mozilla Firefox***, and ***Apple Safari***.
- You can browse the Internet to locate and view web pages on the World Wide Web using devices such as desk computers, laptops, tablets, smart phones, and Xbox game consoles.
- Browsers provide navigation tools that help you locate specific information on a website. For example, you can save your favorite websites and return to them later. You can also revisit websites by navigating to them from a list of recently visited websites.
- When you need to print a web page, there is often a version of the page that is optimized for printing. You can also select part of the page and print just that selection.
- Internet browsers have several features that protect your online safety and privacy. These features can be adjusted to better meet your personal needs.

© HaywireMedia

Aspen Falls City Hall

In this chapter, you will use popular Internet browsers to conduct research for Aspen Falls City Hall, which provides essential services for the citizens and visitors of Aspen Falls, California. You will assist Todd Austin, Tourism Director, to locate information about National Parks that are a short drive from the city.

The Internet is a collection of networks distributed throughout the world. These networks may include services such as e-mail, on-demand video, and telephony. Microsoft Edge is one example of an Internet browser that can be used to search the ***World Wide Web***, also known as the ***WWW*** or the ***web***—a collection of linked pages designed to be viewed from devices, such as your laptop, tablet, or SmartPhone, connected to the Internet. Because so many websites and pages are available on the Internet, you may use web tools and search engines to locate, filter, and organize your information.

In this project, you will search and navigate through several websites, open multiple tabs, and organize a list of favorite websites. You will practice printing web pages and saving them as files on your local drive. You will also use Microsoft Edge to protect your online privacy and security while you browse the web.

Time to complete all 10 skills — 60 to 75 minutes

Introduction

Outcome

Using the skills in this chapter, you will be able to browse the Internet and protect your online privacy.

Objectives

1 Browse the Internet
2 Navigate and search websites
3 Add and organize favorites
4 Protect your online privacy

Student data files needed for this project:

None

You will save your files as:

Last_First_me03_Parks1.jpg
Last_First_me03_Parks2.jpg
Last_First_me03_Parks.MHT
Last_First_me03_Parks3.jpg
Last_First_me03_Parks4.jpg

SKILLS

At the end of this chapter, you will be able to:

Skill 1 Browse from the Desktop
Skill 2 Browse from the Start Menu and Add Favorites
Skill 3 Navigate and Search Websites
Skill 4 Use Accelerators and Search Providers
Skill 5 Manage Browser Tabs and Use Reading View
Skill 6 Organize Favorites
Skill 7 Print and Save Web Pages
Skill 8 View and Delete Browsing History
Skill 9 Protect Online Privacy
Skill 10 Create Web Notes

MORE SKILLS

Skill 11 Change Your Home Page
Skill 12 Add Navigation Tiles to the Start Menu
Skill 13 Use Internet Privacy Settings
Skill 14 Change Internet Security Settings

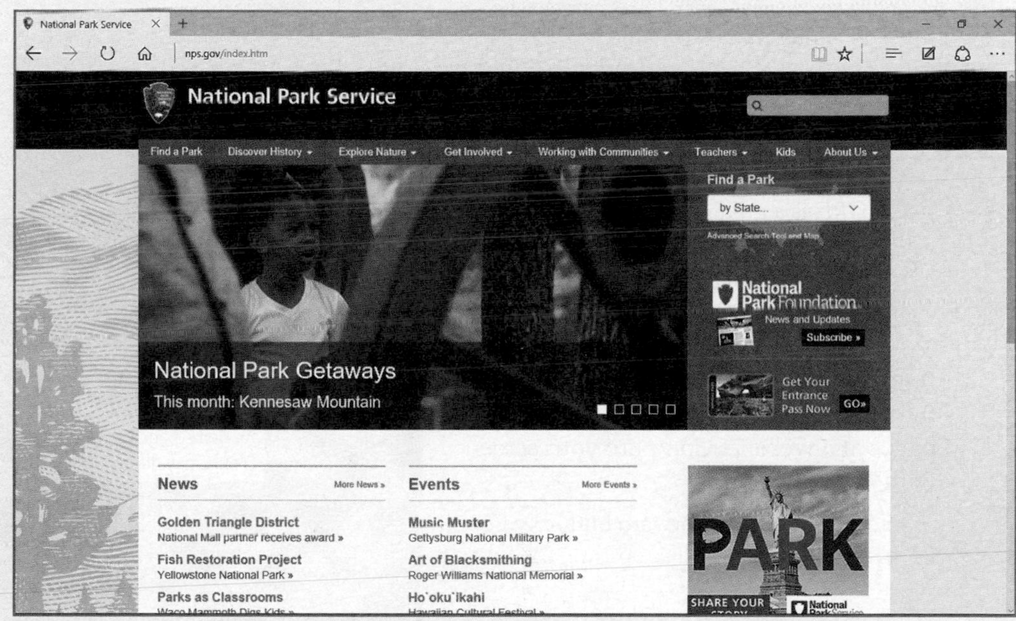

National Park Service website, 2015; Microsoft Edge 2016, Windows 10, Microsoft Corporation

- Programs used to navigate the World Wide Web are called ***web browsers***.
- To maximize the area devoted to the web page when viewed on mobile devices, Microsoft Edge displays buttons and commands only when you need them. For example, you can access multiple pages and other tools in the app commands area.

1. Display the Windows 10 desktop. Compare your screen with **Figure 1**.
2. On the taskbar, click the **Microsoft Edge** button. In the address bar, type nasa.gov

   If the Microsoft Edge button is not on your taskbar, you can open Microsoft Edge from the Start screen and navigate to the page.

   If you have a touch screen, you can tap the address bar instead of clicking.

   The *Where to next?* search bar can also be used to enter a website name.

   When you start the Microsoft Edge browser, the page that displays is called the ***default home page***.

   A ***Uniform Resource Locator***, also known as a *URL*, is a unique address of a page on the Internet.

   The text *nasa.gov* is a ***domain name***—a unique name assigned to a website on the World Wide Web.
3. Press Enter to display the ***home page***—the starting point for the remainder of the pages at a website. Compare your screen with **Figure 2**.

   Alternately, tap the Forward button →.

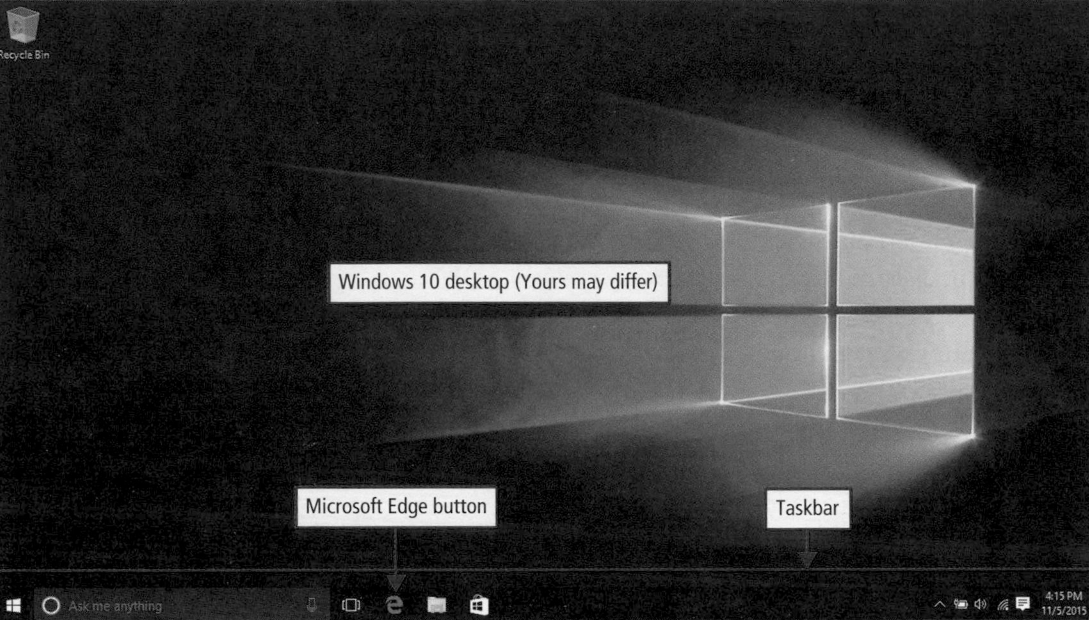

Figure 1 Microsoft Edge 2016, Windows 10, Microsoft Corporation

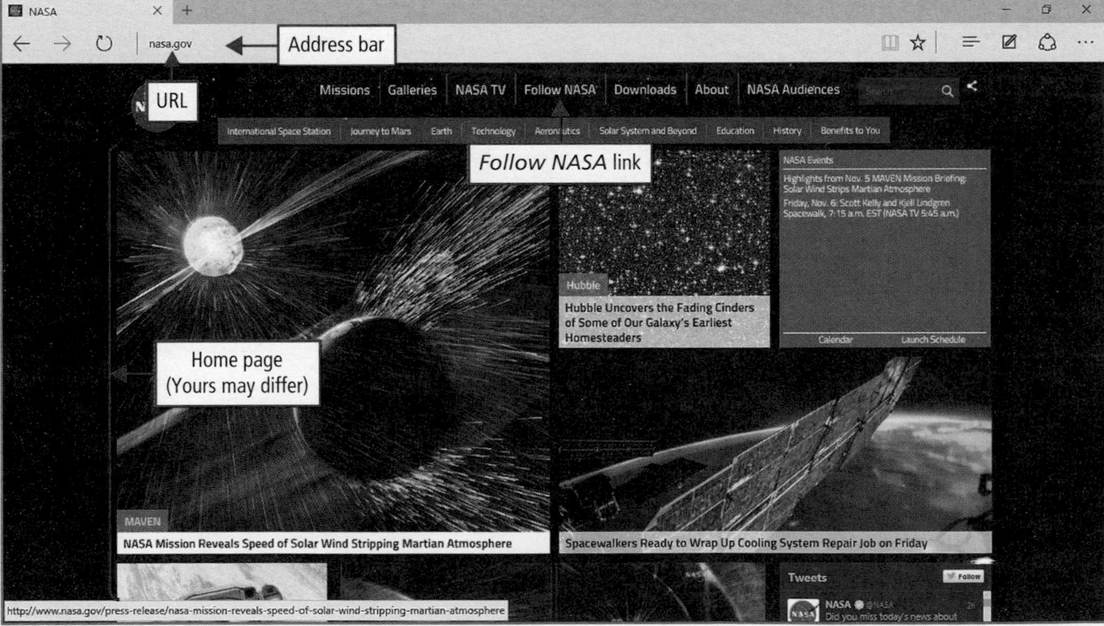

Figure 2 Microsoft Edge 2016, Windows 10, Microsoft Corporation

■ Continue to the next page to complete the skill

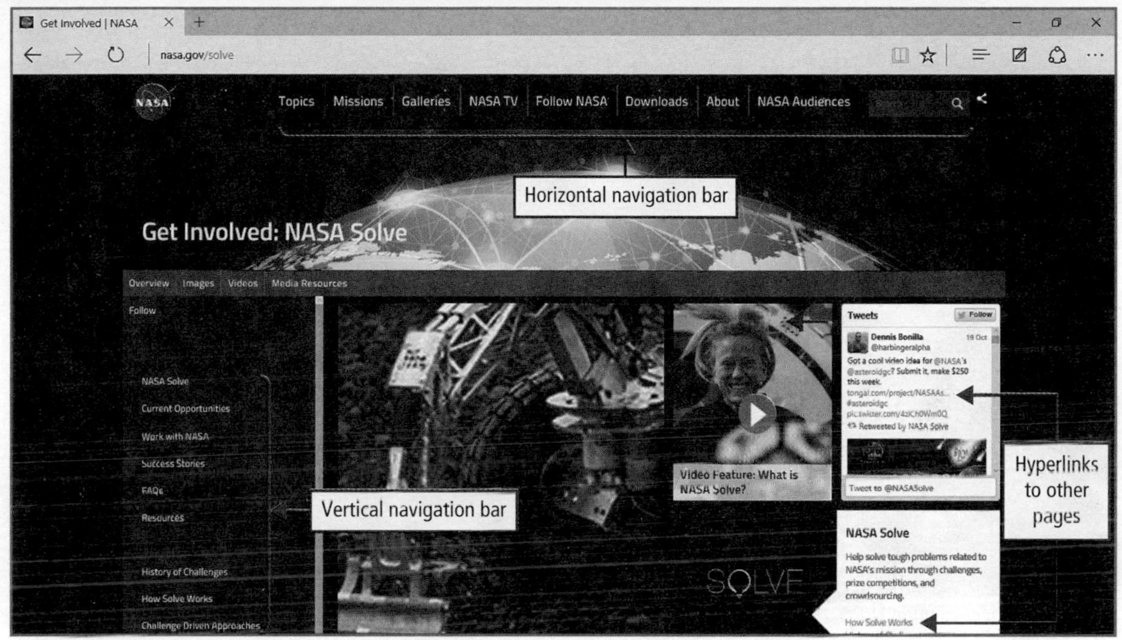

NASA website 2015; Microsoft Edge 2016, Windows 10, Microsoft Corporation

Figure 3

National Park Service website; Microsoft Edge 2016, Windows 10, Microsoft Corporation

Figure 4

4. ***Hover over***, or point to, the *Follow NASA* link to display additional information. Click the **Get Involved** link, and then compare your screen with **Figure 3**.

   Because the web is dynamic, the page on your computer may be different than the version shown in the figure. Here, the page displays ***hyperlinks***—any text or pictures that can be clicked to move to a new page or location.

   Most web pages have a ***navigation bar*** with hyperlinks to the main pages of the site. Here, the page has a horizontal navigation bar that spans across the page.

5. At the top of the browser, click the **New Tab** button [+]. Type nps.gov and then press [Enter] to navigate to the *National Park Service* home page. Compare your screen with **Figure 4**.

   The command bar includes *Back*, *Forward*, and *Refresh* buttons to move through your recently browsed pages and to ***refresh***—reload, or update, the current webpage with any changes that have been made since the browser session started.

6. At the top edge of the window, click the **Close** button [×]. Read the message in the dialog box, and then click **Close All**.

■ **You have completed Skill 1 of 10**

- You can open Microsoft Edge from an app on the Start menu.
- A *favorite* is a stored web address that can be clicked to quickly navigate to that page.

1. Click the **Start menu** button as shown in **Figure 1**. Click the **Microsoft Edge** tile.

   If the Microsoft Edge tile is not on your Start menu, you can open Microsoft Edge from the taskbar and navigate to the page.

2. Type np and then compare your screen with **Figure 2**. Press Enter to select the nps.gov website.

   When you type in the search or address bar, an Autocomplete list displays recently visited websites. You can navigate to these sites by clicking them. Here, the URL *http://nps.gov* has been typed previously. Your list may differ.

   Alternately, finish typing nps.gov and then press Enter.

   The National Park Service, NPS, provides a large ***website***—a collection of connected pages located at a single domain name. Large websites consist of hundreds or thousands of individual pages. The home page has search boxes and navigation bars to help you find information.

3. To the right of the address bar, in the command bar, click the **Favorites** button.

4. Verify the **Favorites** button is selected in the **Favorites Center**, and then in the **Name** box, replace the text with NPS Verify the *Create in* box displays *Favorites*.

■ Continue to the next page to complete the skill

Figure 1 Windows 10, Microsoft Corporation

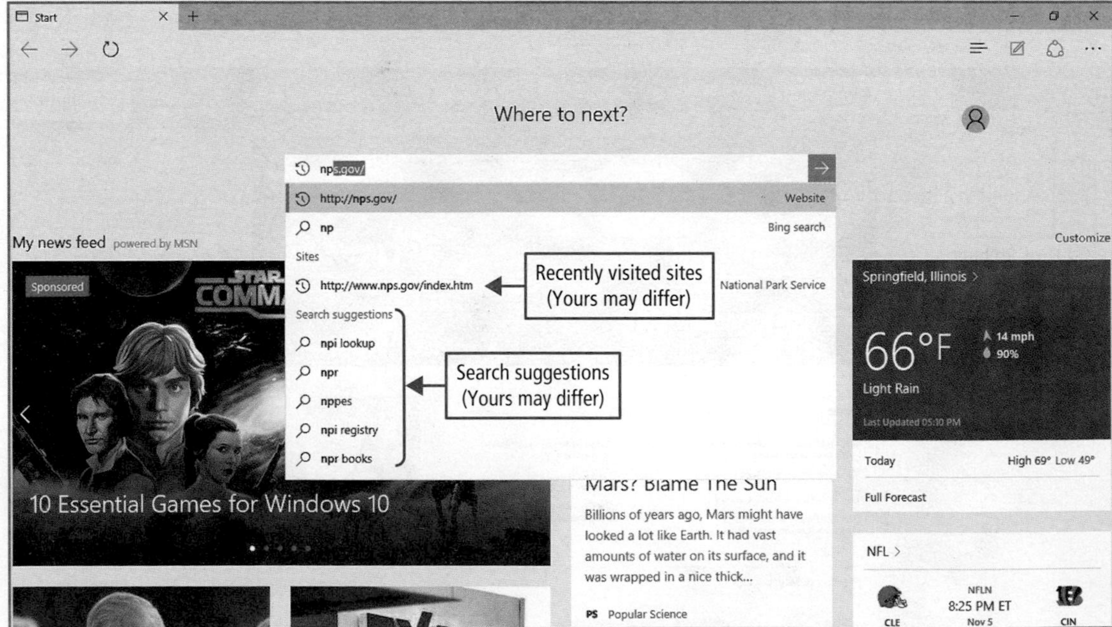

Figure 2 Windows 10, Microsoft Corporation

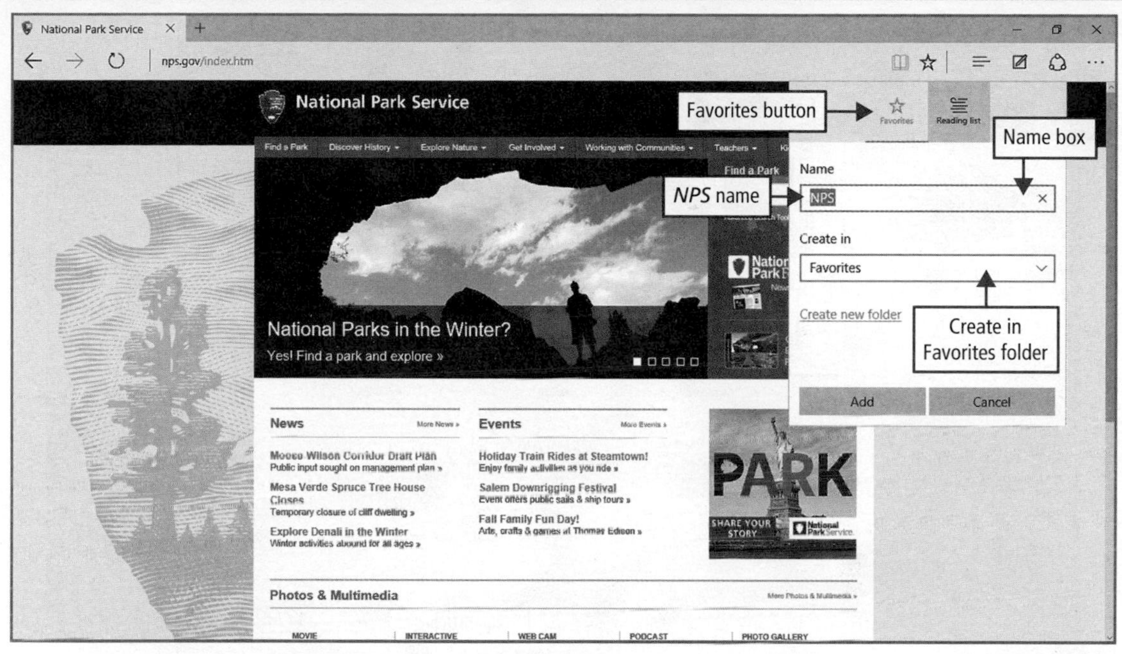

National Park Service website, 2015; Microsoft Edge 2016, Windows 10, Microsoft Corporation

Figure 3

National Park Service website, 2015; Microsoft Edge 2016, Windows 10, Microsoft Corporation

Figure 4

5. Click **Add**, and then compare your screen with **Figure 3**.
6. On the command bar, click the **Hub** button [≡]. If necessary, click the **Favorites** button [☆] to display the **Favorites Center**, and then compare your screen with **Figure 4**.
7. On the *NPS* home page, click any hyperlink. Click the **Hub** button [≡], and then click the **NPS** favorite.

   In this manner, you can return to your favorite pages quickly. In this case, *NPS*.
8. Click the **NPS Search** box, type point reyes and then press Enter.
9. Click the first **Point Reyes National Seashore** hyperlink. Add the link as a favorite with the name Point Reyes
10. Scroll down the *Point Reyes* page. Click the **Directions & Transportation** link. Add the link as a favorite with the name Travel
11. Click the **Back** button [←]. Scroll down the *Point Reyes* page. Click the **Operating Hours & Seasons** link. Add the link as a favorite with the name Hours
12. Click the **Hub** button [≡], and then click the **NPS** favorite.
13. Click the **NPS Search** box, type Sequoia & Kings and then press Enter.
14. In your list of search results, click the **Sequoia & Kings Canyon** hyperlink at *www.nps.gov/seki/index.htm*. Add this page to your Favorites with the default settings.
15. **Close** [×] Edge.

■ **You have completed Skill 2 of 10**

▸ Websites that contain many pages provide navigation bars, hyperlinks, and their own search boxes, all of which you can use to find the pages you need.

1. If necessary, on your Apple device, search for and download the **Apple Safari** browser for your operating system. Open **Safari**, and then type apple.com

2. Press Enter, and then scroll to the bottom of the page to view the page footer, as shown in **Figure 1**.

   Web page footers typically provide links to a site index, copyright information, and a link to contact the organization.

3. In the page footer, click the **Site Map** hyperlink. Compare your screen with **Figure 2**.

   A *site map*—sometimes called a *site index*—is a page of hyperlinks that outline a website.

4. On the **Site Map** page, click the **Apple Info** hyperlink. If that link is no longer available, click a different link.

   The pages displayed in this chapter may differ from your screen, because most websites update frequently. When appropriate, substitute similar links to perform each skill.

■ **Continue to the next page to complete the skill**

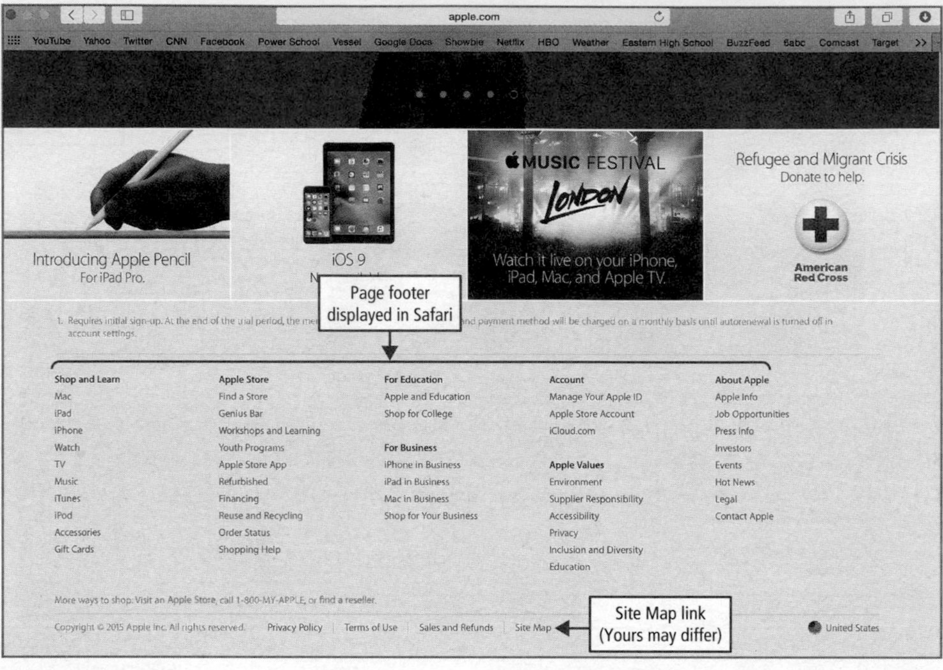

Figure 1 Screen shot reprinted with permission from Apple Inc

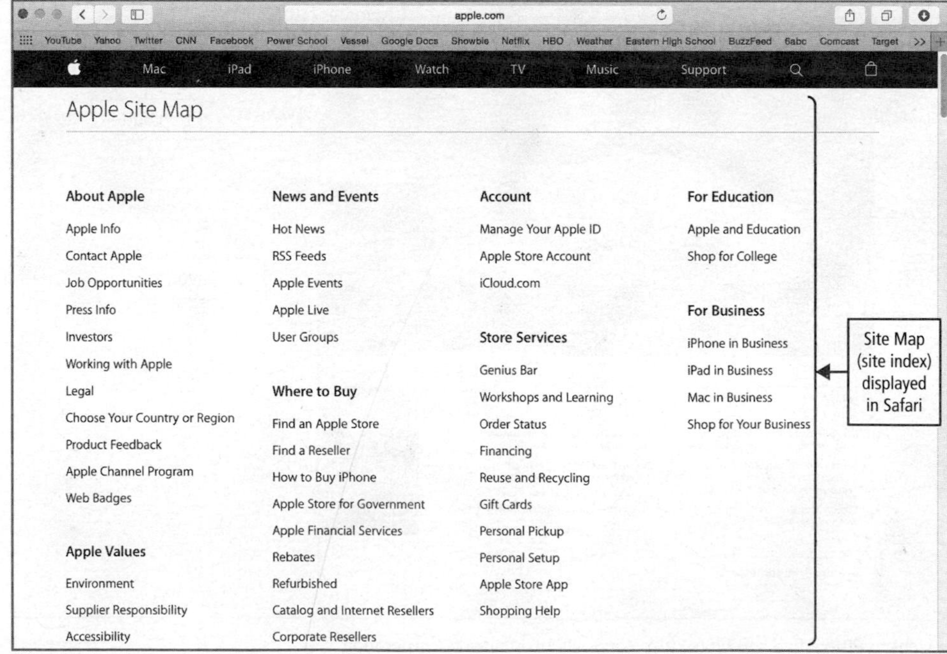

Figure 2 Screen shot reprinted with permission from Apple Inc

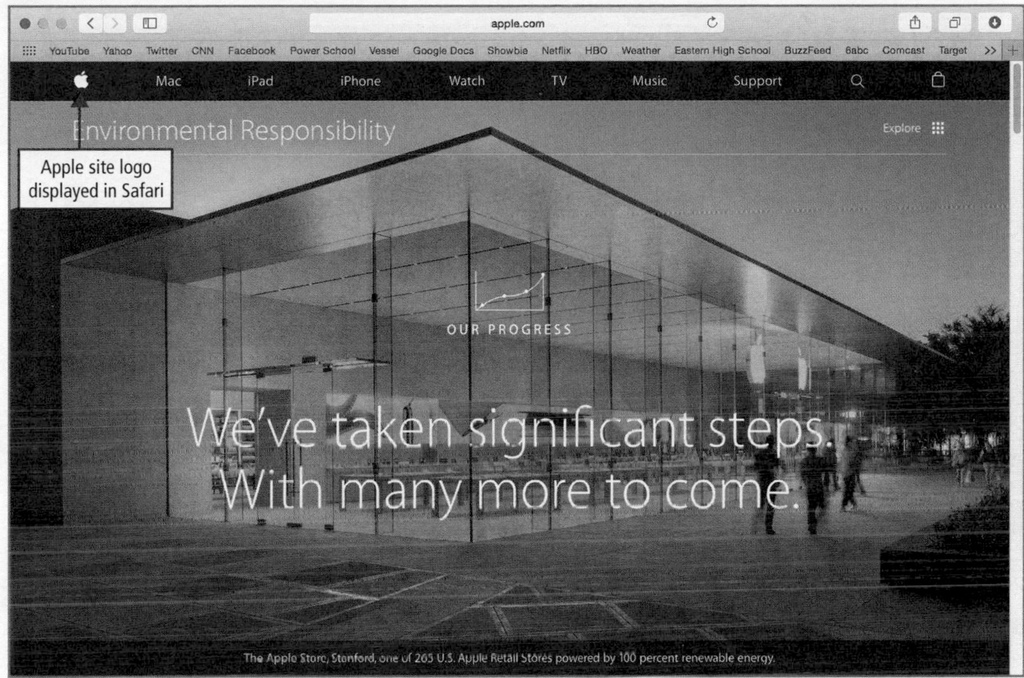

Screen shot reprinted with permission from Apple Inc

Figure 3

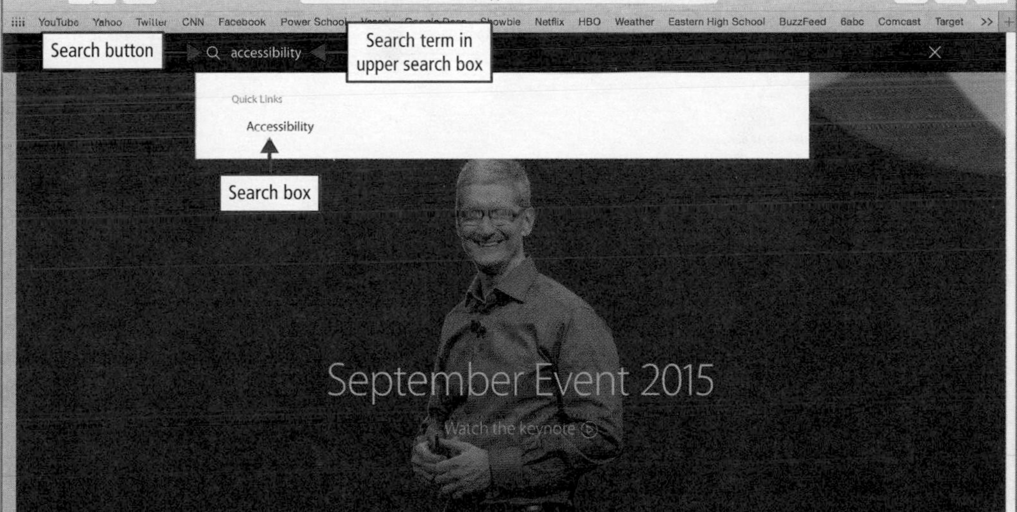

Microsoft Edge 2016, Windows 10, Microsoft Corporation

Figure 4

5. On the **Site Map**, click the **Environment** hyperlink. If that link is no longer available, click a different link.
6. In the top-right corner, click the **Explore** button, and then click the **Our Progress** thumbnail.

   In this manner, thumbnails display with the names of the page sections instead of the words.

   Alternately, in the address bar, type www.apple.com/environment/our-progress and then press Enter.
7. In the upper-left corner of the page header, click the **Apple** logo to return to the site's home page as shown in **Figure 3**.
8. On the home page, in the upper-right corner of the page header, click the search box, and then type accessibility as shown in **Figure 4**. Press Enter, and then select the *http://www.apple.com/accessibility* link.
9. **Close** ✕ Safari.

■ **You have completed Skill 3 of 10**

- An *accelerator* is a feature that searches the web for information related to text that you type/enter.
- A *search provider* is a website that provides a way for you to search for information on the World Wide Web.

1. If necessary, search for and download the Google Chrome browser for your operating system. Open **Chrome**. In the address bar, type www.nps.gov/pore and then press Enter.
2. If a message box displays, click **Close** ☒. Compare your screen with **Figure 1**.
3. On the *Points Reyes* website, select any occurrence of *Point Reyes*. Right-click on the selected text, and then click **Search Google for 'Point Reyes'**. Compare your screen with **Figure 2**.
4. In the **Google** menu, at the top left corner, click the word **Maps** to open the accelerator to display a map of Point Reyes in a new tab.

   If necessary, right-click Maps and then select Open link in new tab.

   When you click an accelerator, the page typically opens in a new tab. ***Tabbed browsing*** is a feature that you use to open multiple web pages in the same browser window. Each page can be viewed by clicking its tab.
5. Click the **Back** button ←. In the **Google** toolbar, click **More**, and then click **Apps**.

   The apps related to the search display, in this case, those for Point Reyes. Yours may differ.
6. **Close** ☒ Chrome.

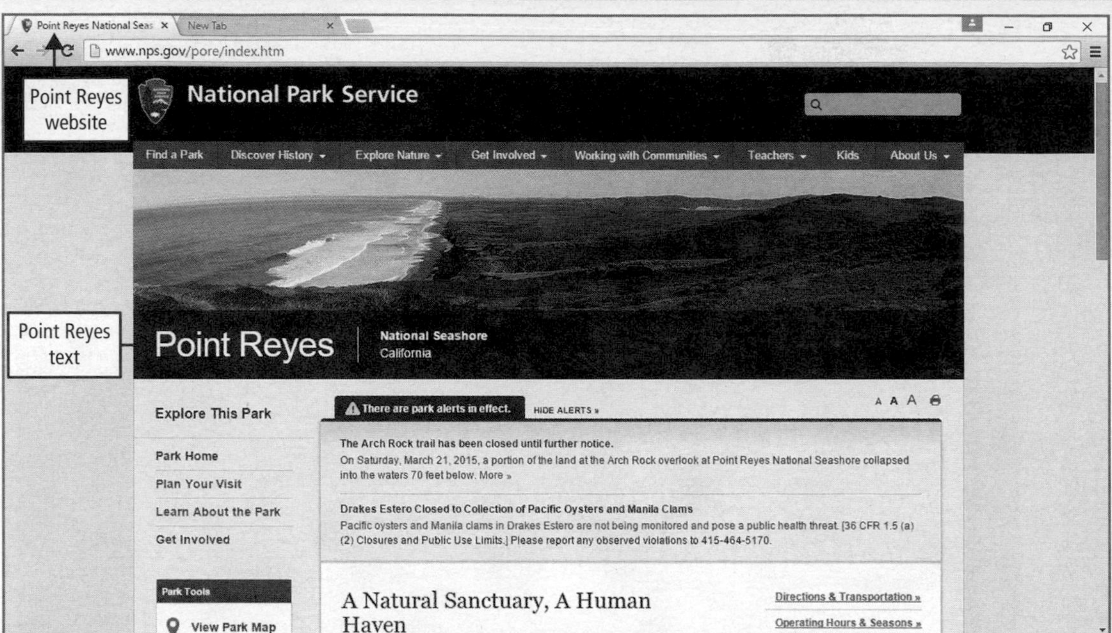

Figure 1 National Park Service website, 2015; Microsoft Edge 2016, Windows 10, Microsoft Corporation

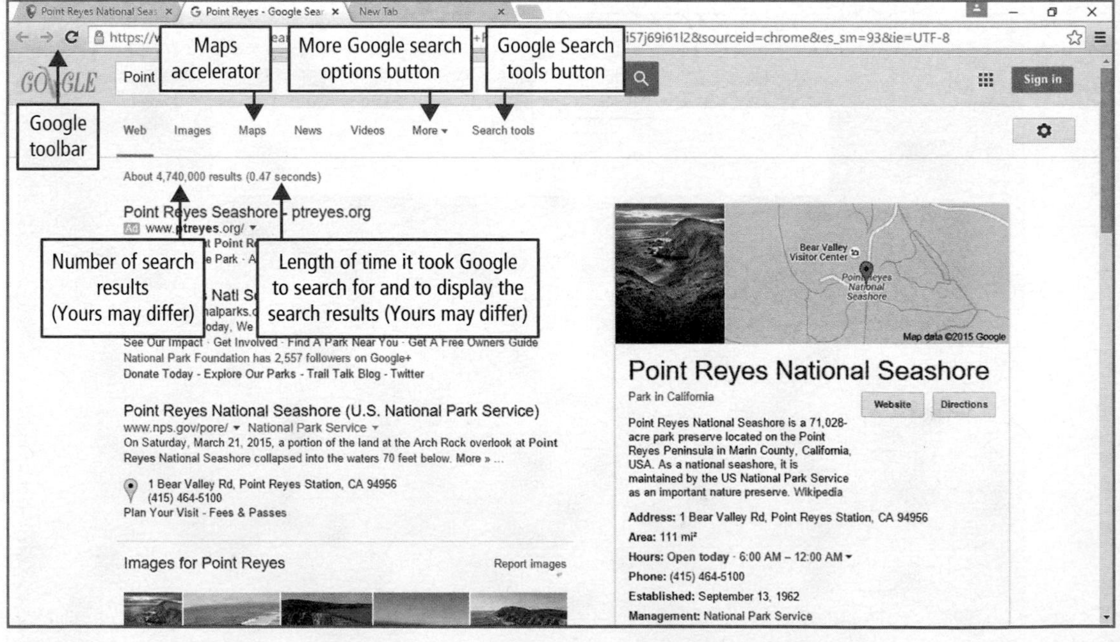

Figure 2 Microsoft Edge 2016, Windows 10, Microsoft Corporation

■ **Continue to the next page to complete the skill**

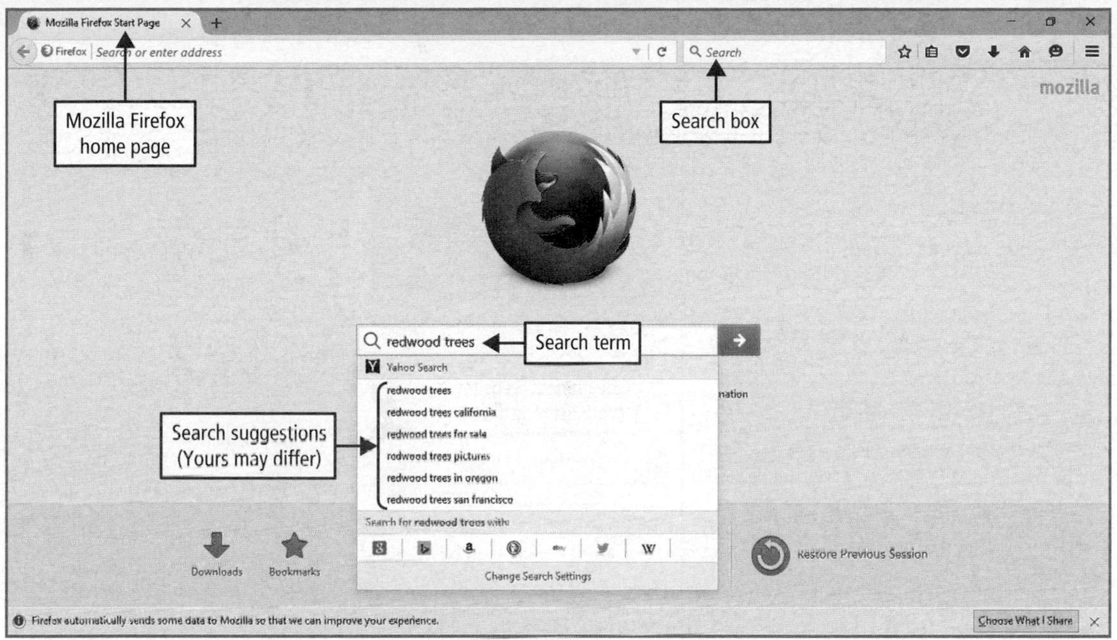

Mozilla firefox Inc.

Figure 3

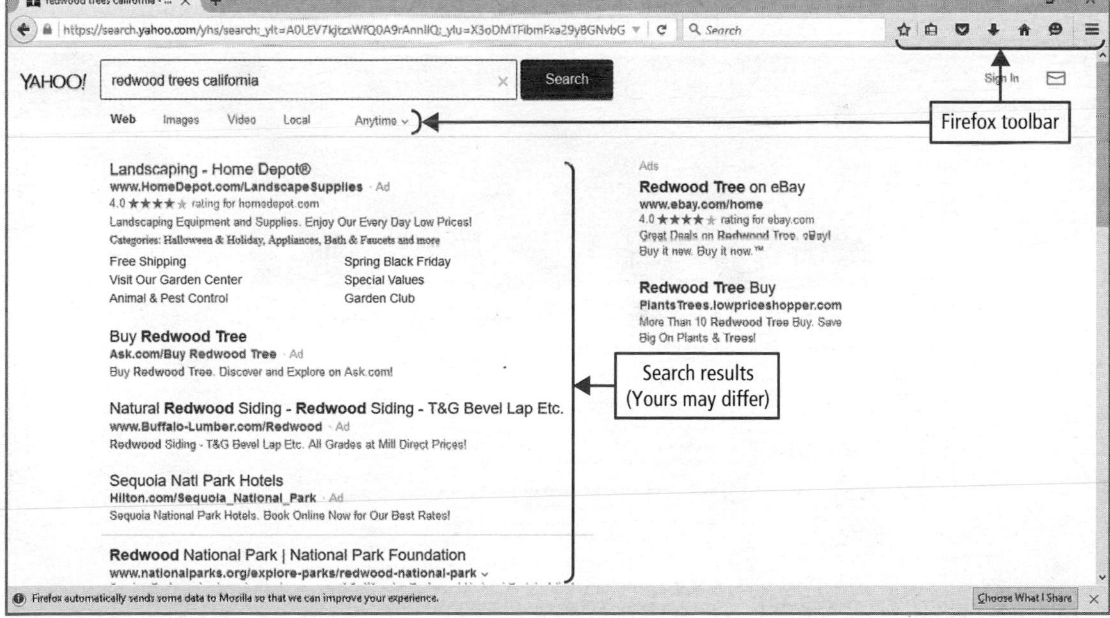

Mozilla firefox Inc.

Figure 4

7. If necessary, search for and download the Mozilla Firefox browser for your operating system. Open **Firefox**. If a message box displays, click **Not now**.
8. On the **Firefox** home page, in the search box, type redwood trees and then then compare your screen with **Figure 3**.

   Search suggestions are the words or phrases that display as you type in a search box.

9. In the list of search suggestions, click **redwood trees california**.
10. Scroll to the bottom of the search results, and then click the **Next** hyperlink to display a second page of results. Compare your screen with **Figure 4**.

    The top of the Firefox search page displays the Firefox toolbar that contains links that filter your search by media type. The default media type is web pages, but you can display results for other media such as video and images.

11. In the toolbar at the top of the page, click the **Images** link to display images related to the current search.
12. In the navigation bar at the top of the page, click the **Video** link to display videos related to the current search.

    In this manner, you can filter your search results to specific media such as web pages, images, or video.

13. In the navigation bar at the top of the page, click the **Web** link to return to the original search results.
14. **Close** [×] Mozilla Firefox.

■ **You have completed Skill 4 of 10**

- You can use a keyboard shortcut when clicking a hyperlink so that the page opens in a new tab.
- When you have multiple tabs open, you can rearrange the tabs in the tab row by dragging them. You can also view thumbnails of each open tab using the taskbar.

1. Open **Microsoft Edge**. At the end of the tabs row, to the right of the **Start tab**, click the **New Tab** button [+]. In the search box, type bing.com and then press [Enter].
2. In the **Bing** search box, type sequoia trees domain:gov

   The search will be limited to sites with the *gov* top-level domain. ***Top-level domains*** specify the organization type that sponsors a website and follow the period—often pronounced as *dot*—after a website's domain name. For example, federal and state government agencies use *.gov*, educational institutions use *.edu*, commercial entities use *.com*, and nonprofit organizations use *.org*. Most countries have their own top-level domain. A site from France, for example, may end with *.fr*.
3. Press [Enter] to complete the search, and then compare your screen with **Figure 1**.
4. Click the **www.nps.gov/seki/index.htm** link.
5. Drag the current tab—starting *Sequoia & Kings*—to the left of the first tab. The Start tab shifts to the right, as shown in **Figure 2**.

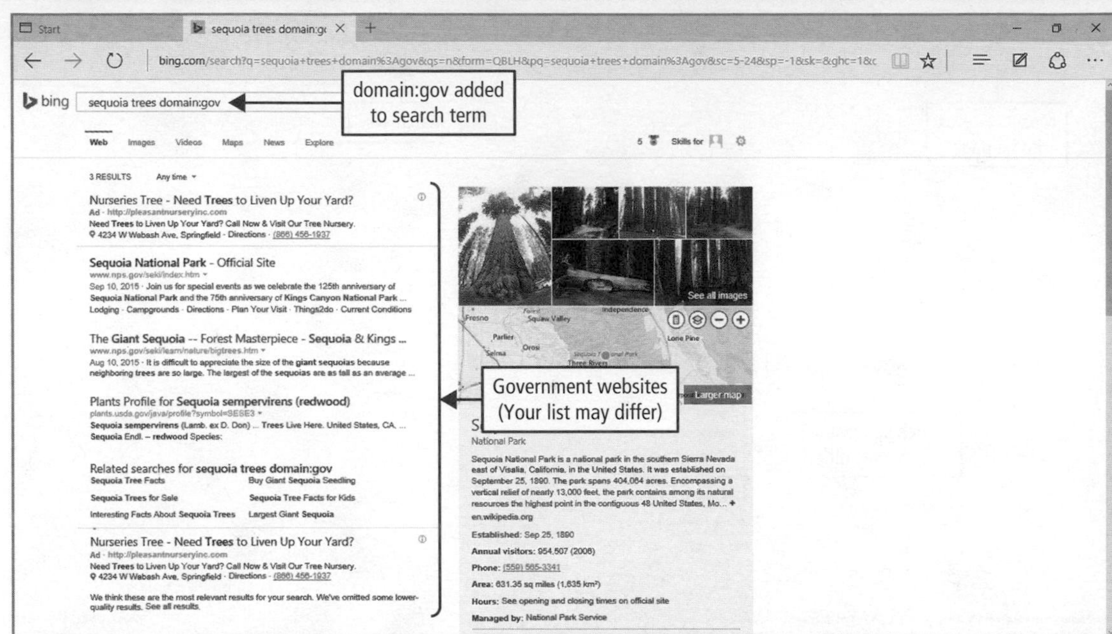

Figure 1 Microsoft Edge 2016, Windows 10, Microsoft Corporation

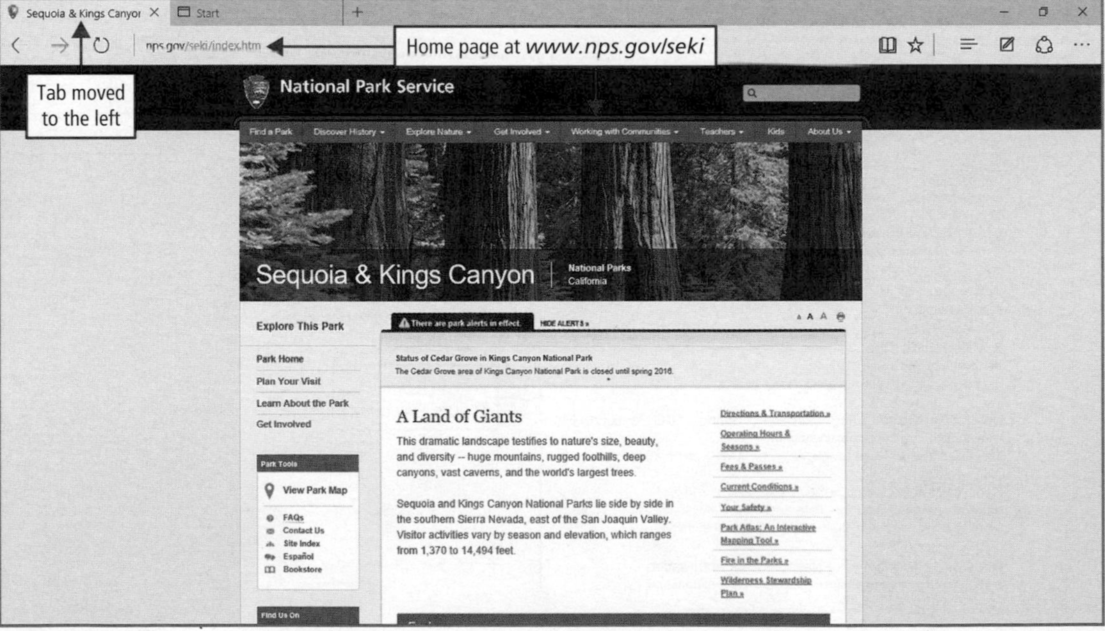

Figure 2 National Park Service website, 2015; Microsoft Edge 2016, Windows 10, Microsoft Corporation

■ Continue to the next page to complete the skill

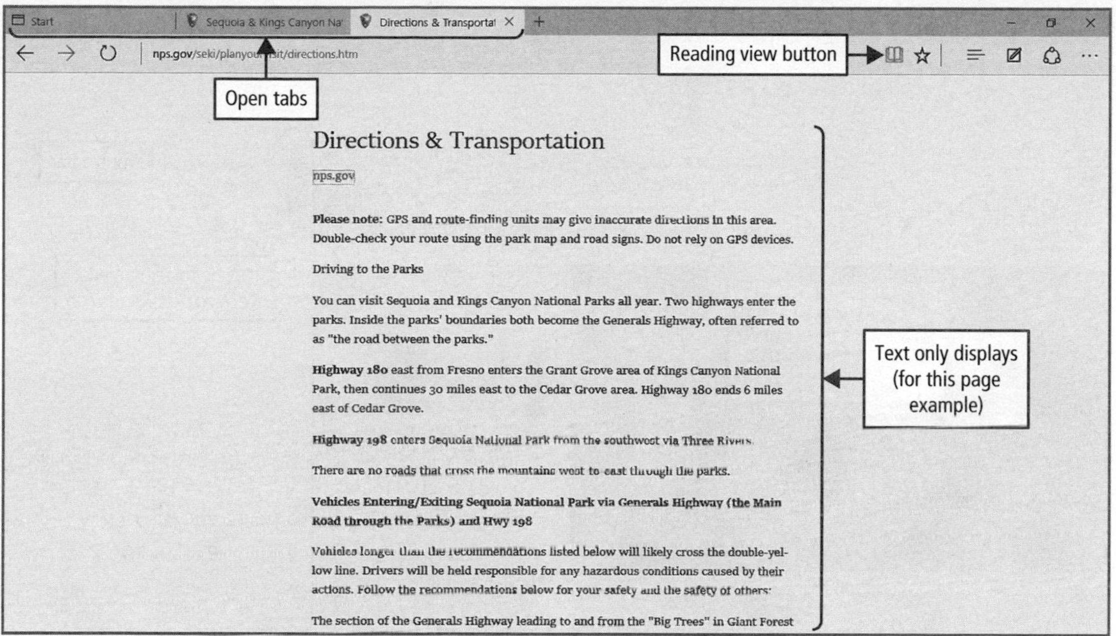

Start
Sequoia & Kings Canyon Na
Directions & Transportat
nps.gov/seki/planyourvisit/directions.htm
Reading view button
Open tabs
Directions & Transportation
nps.gov
Please note: GPS and route-finding units may give inaccurate directions in this area. Double-check your route using the park map and road signs. Do not rely on GPS devices.
Driving to the Parks
You can visit Sequoia and Kings Canyon National Parks all year. Two highways enter the parks. Inside the parks' boundaries both become the Generals Highway, often referred to as "the road between the parks."
Highway 180 east from Fresno enters the Grant Grove area of Kings Canyon National Park, then continues 30 miles east to the Cedar Grove area. Highway 180 ends 6 miles east of Cedar Grove.
Highway 198 enters Sequoia National Park from the southwest via Three Rivers.
There are no roads that cross the mountains west to east through the parks.
Vehicles Entering/Exiting Sequoia National Park via Generals Highway (the Main Road through the Parks) and Hwy 198
Vehicles longer than the recommendations listed below will likely cross the double-yellow line. Drivers will be held responsible for any hazardous conditions caused by their actions. Follow the recommendations below for your safety and the safety of others:
The section of the Generals Highway leading to and from the "Big Trees" in Giant Forest
Text only displays (for this page example)

National Park Service website, 2015; Microsoft Edge 2016, Windows 10, Microsoft Corporation

Figure 3

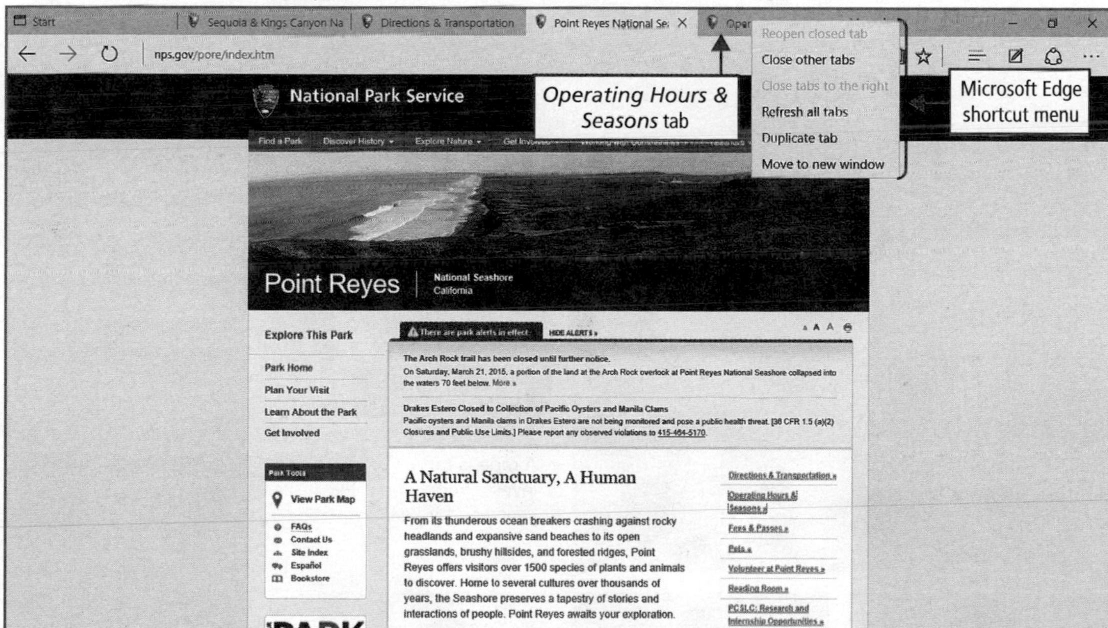

National Park Service website, 2015; Microsoft Edge 2016, Windows 10, Microsoft Corporation

Figure 4

6. On the page, locate the *Directions & Transportation* hyperlink. Press and hold down Shift and Ctrl, and then click **Directions & Transportation**.

   A new tab opens.

7. In the command bar, click the **Reading view** button. Compare your screen with **Figure 3**.

   The ***Reading view*** is a webpage view that provides the webpage text without the navigation bars and hyperlinks displayed.

8. On the tabs row, click the **New Tab** button. In the search box, type nps.gov/pore and then press Enter.

9. On the web page, right-click the **Operating Hours & Seasons** hyperlink. Click **Open in a new tab**, and then right-click the **Operating Hours & Seasons tab**, as shown in **Figure 4**.

10. Click the **Duplicate tab**, and then **Close** ✕ the second occurrence of the *Operating* tab and the *Start* tab.

11. Right-click the **Operating tab**, and then click **Reopen closed tab**.

    Tabs closed during the current browsing session can be reopened.

12. In the upper-right corner of the **Microsoft Edge** window, click the **Close** button ✕.

13. In the **Microsoft Edge** dialog box, read the message, and then click the **Close all** button to close all open tabs and exit Microsoft Edge.

    When closing the browser with multiple tabs open, a dialog box displays to ask if you want to close all of the open tabs.

■ **You have completed Skill 5 of 10**

SKILL 6: Organize Favorites

BROWSER 3.6

► Over time, your favorites list may become quite long and need to be organized.

1. Open **Microsoft Edge**, and then click the **Hub** button. If necessary, click the **Favorites** button.
2. Right-click the **Favorites Bar** folder, and then click **Create new folder**. Type Redwoods Research Press Enter, and then compare your screen with **Figure 1**.
3. Drag the *NPS* favorite link to the *Redwoods Research* folder. Repeat the process to add the links that begin *Point Reyes*, *Hours*, *Sequoia & Kings*, and *Travel* to the *Redwoods Research* folder.

   When the link is directly on top of the NPS folder, release the mouse.
4. Click the **Redwoods Research** folder to view the favorites. Compare your screen with **Figure 2**.
5. In the Windows search bar, type snip Right-click the **Snipping Tool**, click **Pin to taskbar**, and then click to open the Snipping Tool.
6. In the **Snipping Tool** window, click the **New arrow**, and then click **Full-screen Snip**. In the **Snipping Tool** markup window, click **Save Snip**.
7. In the **Save As** dialog box, navigate to the location where you will be saving your work for this project. On the **Save As** toolbar, click **New folder**, and then type Edge Chapter 3 Press Enter two times to accept the new folder name and open the folder.

■ Continue to the next page to complete the skill

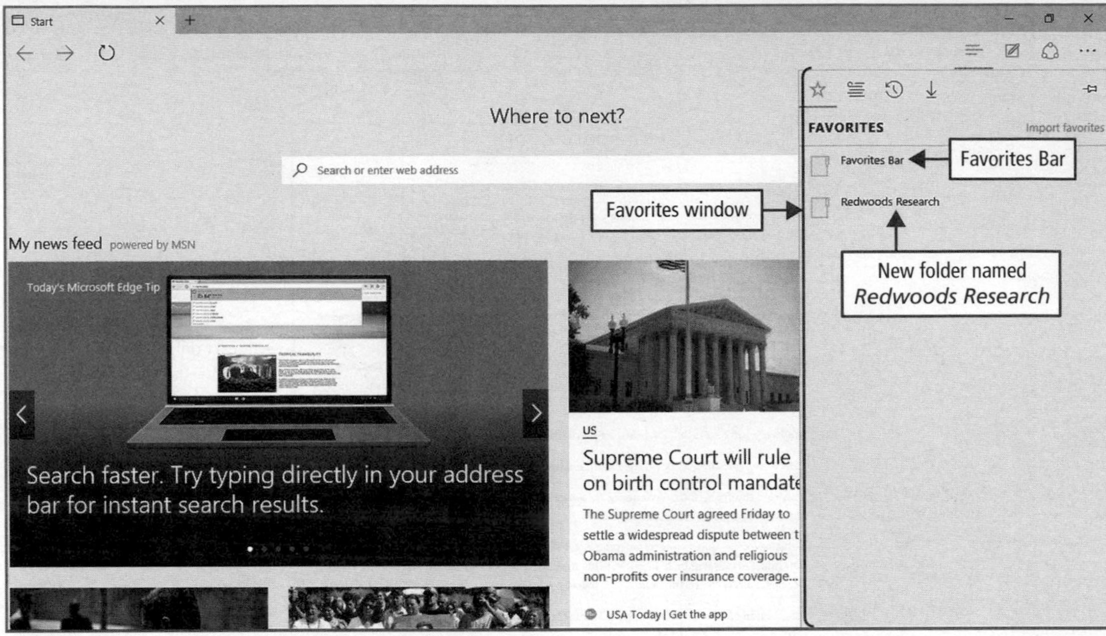

Figure 1 Windows 10, Microsoft Corporation

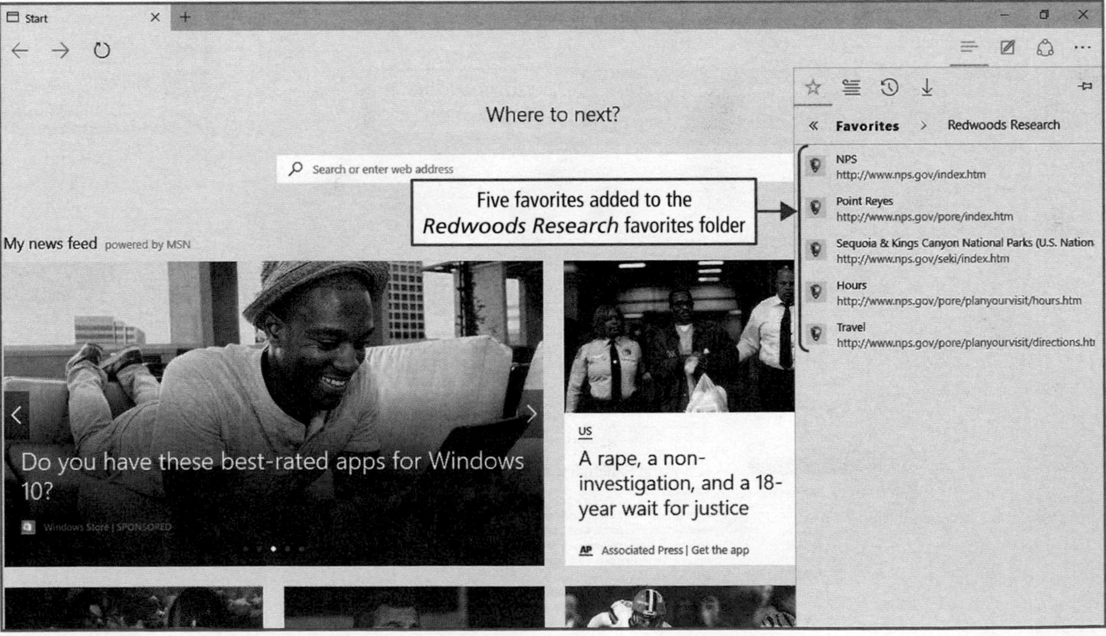

Figure 2 Windows 10, Microsoft Corporation

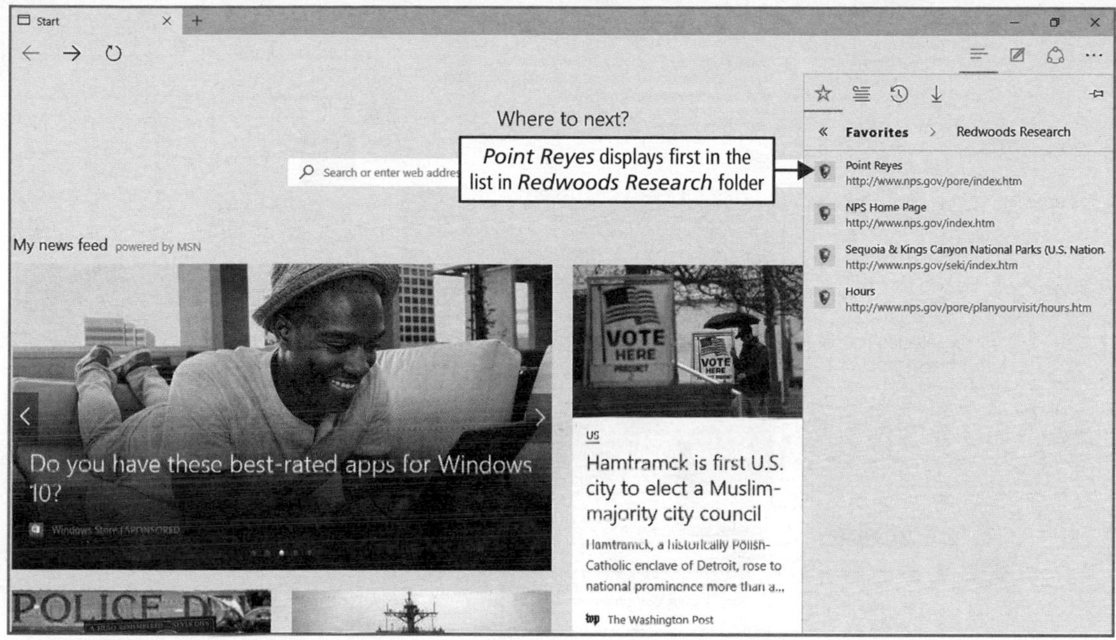

Windows 10, Microsoft Corporation

Figure 3

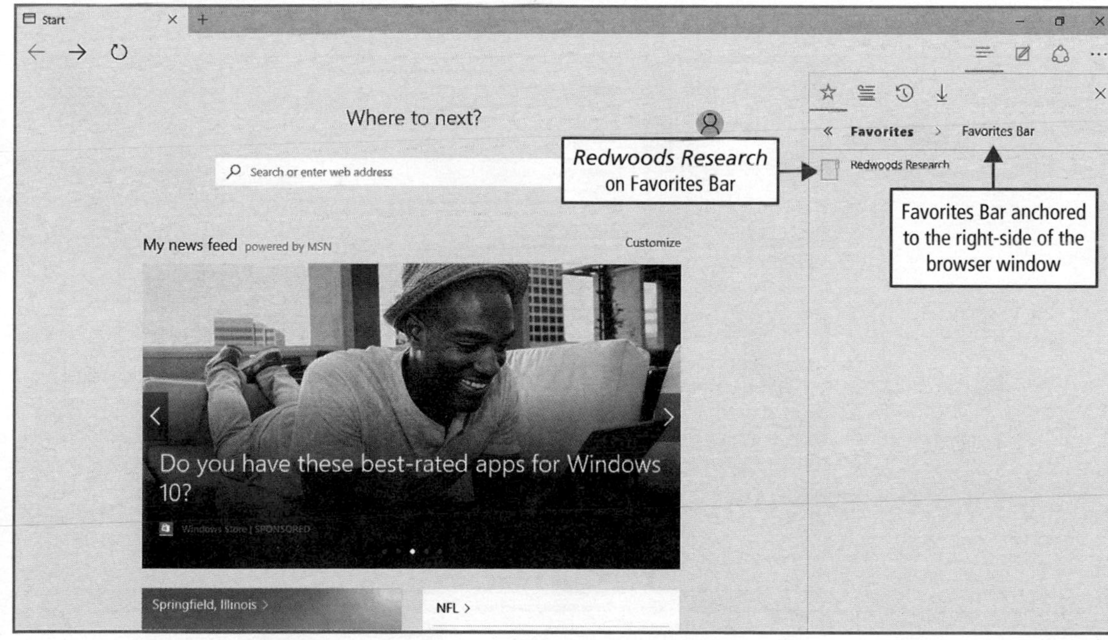

Windows 10, Microsoft Corporation

Figure 4

8. In the **Name** box, replace the text with Last_First_me03_Parks1 Be sure the **Save as type** button displays **JPEG file**, and then click **Save**. **Close** [X] the Snipping Tool window.
9. In Edge, right-click the **NPS** favorite link. Click **Rename**, type NPS Home Page and then press Enter to display the updated name.
10. Right-click the **Travel** favorite link, and then click **Remove**.
11. Drag the *Point Reyes* favorite so that it displays as the first favorite in the list as shown in **Figure 3**.
12. In the **Favorites Center**, click **Favorites**, and then drag the *Redwoods Research* folder to the **Favorites Bar** folder. In the **Favorites** navigation bar, click the push pin.

    The Favorites Bar is docked to the right-hand side of the browser window while the browser session is active.
13. Click **Favorites Bar**, and then compare your screen with **Figure 4**. **Close** [X] Microsoft Edge.

■ **You have completed Skill 6 of 10**

BROWSER 3.7

- When you need to store information on a web page, you can print the page, print a selection on the page, or save the page to your drive.

1. Open **Google Chrome**. In the search box, type nps.gov/pore and then press Enter.
2. On the webpage, scroll down, and then click the **Operating Hours & Seasons** link.
3. On the **Operating Hours & Seasons** webpage, under the *Bear Valley Visitor Center* heading, starting with *Operational Changes*, drag through all the paragraphs in the section. Compare your screen with **Figure 1**.
4. Right-click the selected text, and then from the shortcut menu, click **Print**. Compare your screen with **Figure 2**.
5. Start the **Snipping Tool**, and then create a **Full-screen Snip**. **Save** the snip in your chapter folder as a **.jpg** with the name Last_First_me03_Parks2
6. **Close** the Snipping Tool markup window. In the **Print** dialog box, click **Cancel**.
7. On the command bar, click the **Customize** button. Click **More Tools**, and then click **Save page as**.

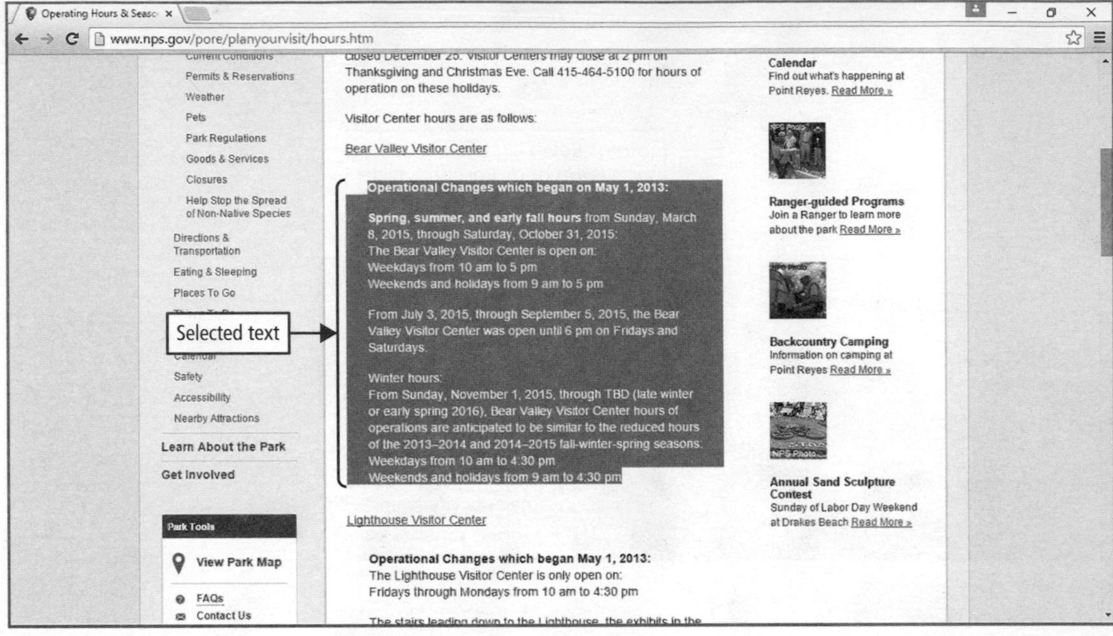

Figure 1 National Park Service website, 2015; Microsoft Edge 2016, Windows 10, Microsoft Corporation

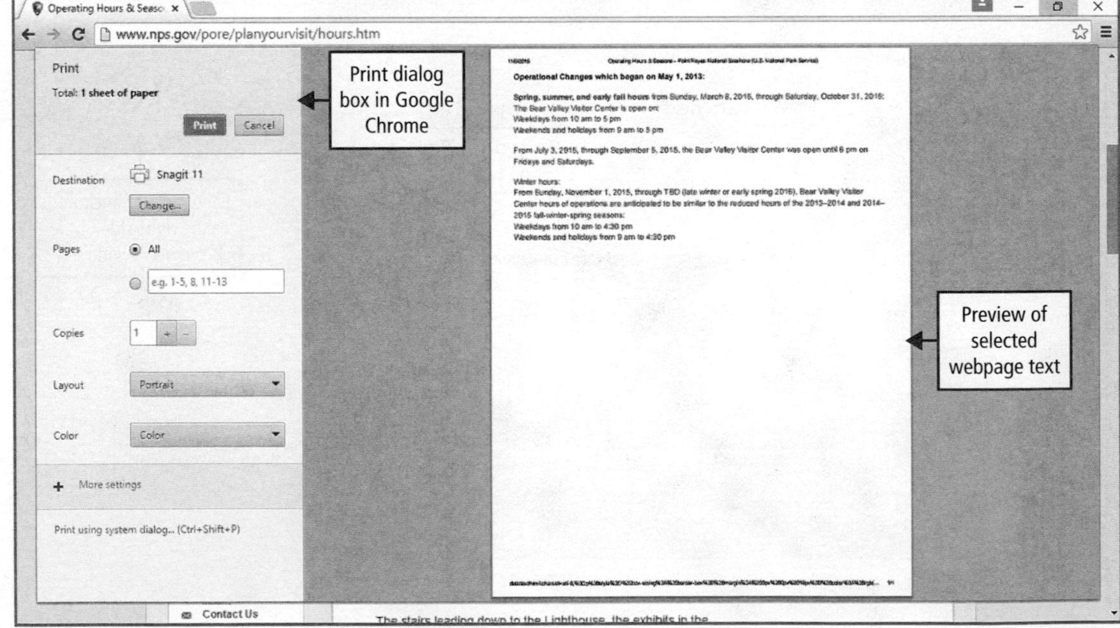

Figure 2 National Park Service website, 2015; Microsoft Edge 2016, Windows 10, Microsoft Corporation

■ Continue to the next page to complete the skill

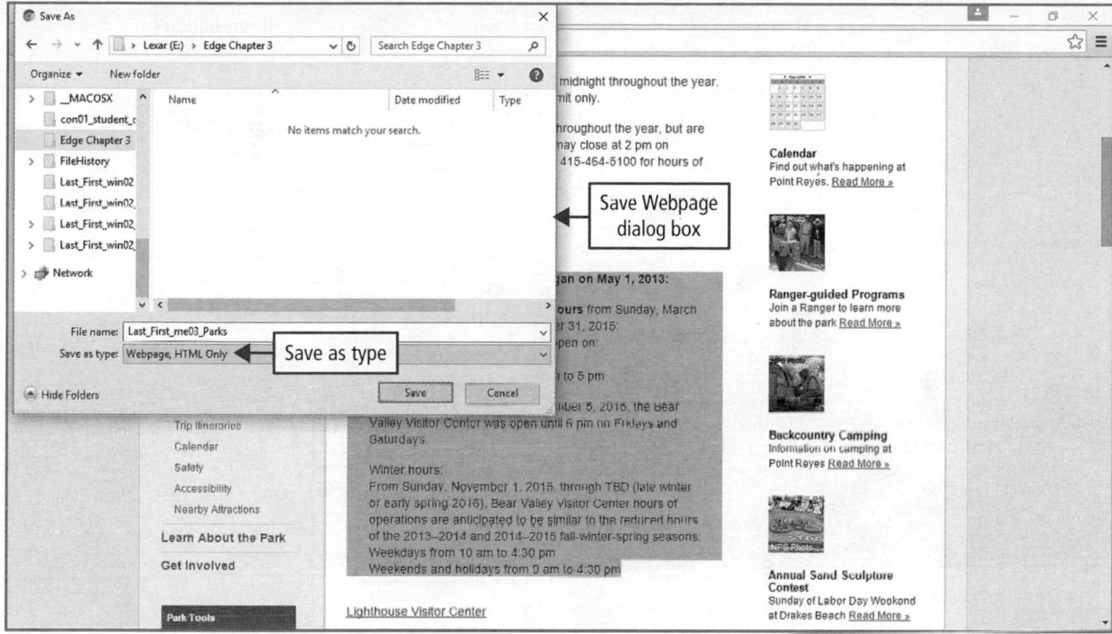

National Park Service website, 2015; Microsoft Edge 2016, Windows 10, Microsoft Corporation

Figure 3

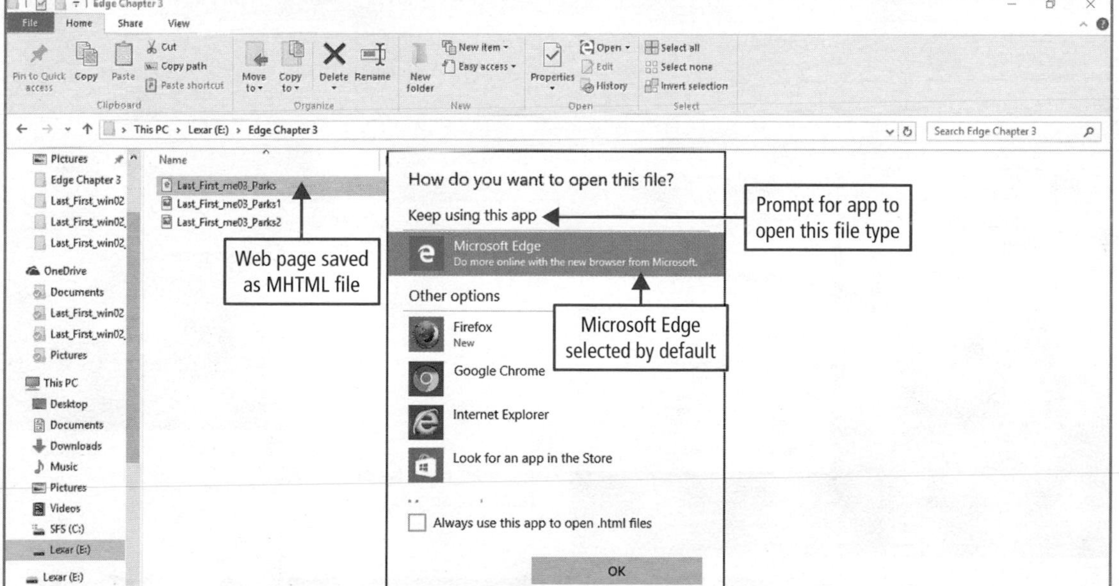

Windows 10, Microsoft Corporation

Figure 4

8. In the **Save As** dialog box, navigate to and then open your chapter folder. In the **File name** box, replace the text with Last_First_me03_Parks.MHT

9. If necessary, click the **Save as type** button, and then click **Webpage, HTML Only**. Compare your screen with **Figure 3**, and then click **Save**.

   A ***Web page archive*** is a file that saves the web page text and its pictures in a single file. These files are typically assigned the *.mht* file extension. Web archives are also known as ***MHTML files***.

10. On the taskbar, click the **File Explorer** button. In the **Navigation** pane, navigate to and then open your chapter folder. Double-click to open the MHT file, and then compare your screen with **Figure 4**. Verify *Microsoft Edge* is selected, and then click **OK**.

11. **Close** the File Explorer window, the MHT file, and Chrome.

12. Open **Microsoft Edge**. On the command bar, click the **Hub** button. If necessary, click the **Favorites** button, and then click the **Favorites Bar** folder. Right-click the **Redwoods Research** folder, and then click **Remove**. Keep Edge open.

■ **You have completed Skill 7 of 10**

SKILL 8: View and Delete Browsing History

► As you search the web, your browser stores information that helps you search more efficiently, also known as your ***browsing history***.

1. In Edge, in the **Favorites Center**, click the **History** button.
2. In the **History** list, click the **arrow** to the left of *Today* to expand the list. Compare your screen with **Figure 1**. In the **History** list, click **Bing (bing.com)**.

   From the History list, you can open a previously-viewed webpage by clicking its URL.

3. Repeat the steps to expand the *Today* history list, and then right-click the **nasa.gov** entry. In the shortcut menu, click **Delete all visits to nasa.gov**.

   In this manner, you can delete all occurrences of the website from your browser's history.

4. Right-click any **Bing (bing.com)** entry. In the shortcut menu, click **Delete**.

   In this manner, you can delete one occurrence of the Bing.com URL from your browser's history.

5. Click the address bar two times, type windows.microsoft.com and then press Enter.
6. **Close** Microsoft Edge. If a message box displays, click **Close All**. Open **Microsoft Edge** from the Start menu. Watch the search bar **Autocomplete** list as you type windows Compare your screen with **Figure 2**.

   As you type in the address bar, an Autocomplete list displays sites matching your history list. Your screen may differ.

■ Continue to the next page to complete the skill

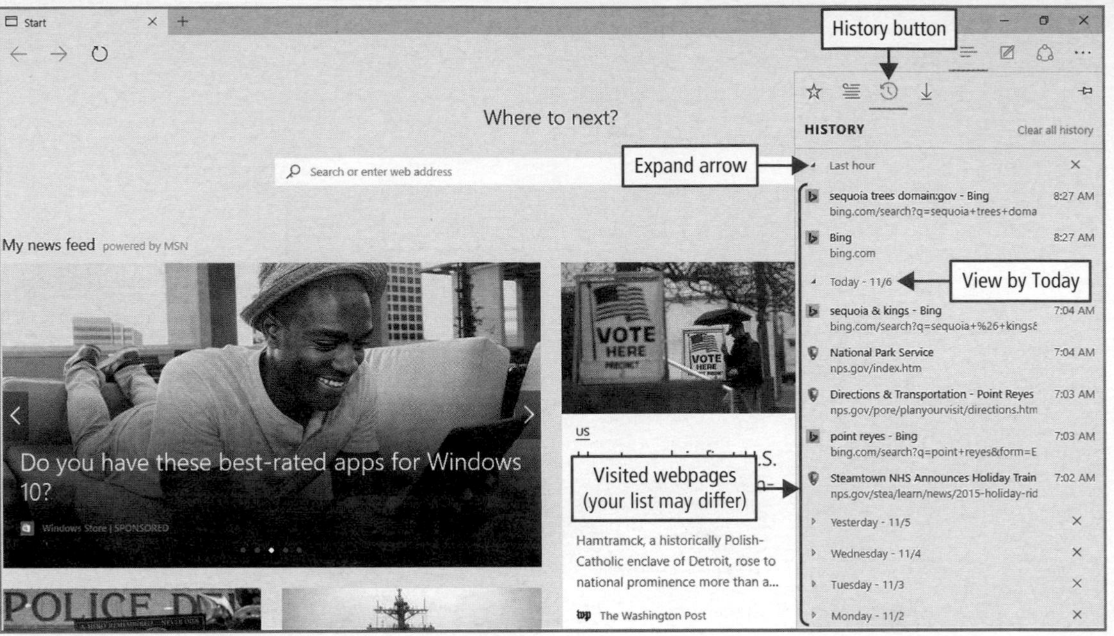

Figure 1

Windows 10, Microsoft Corporation

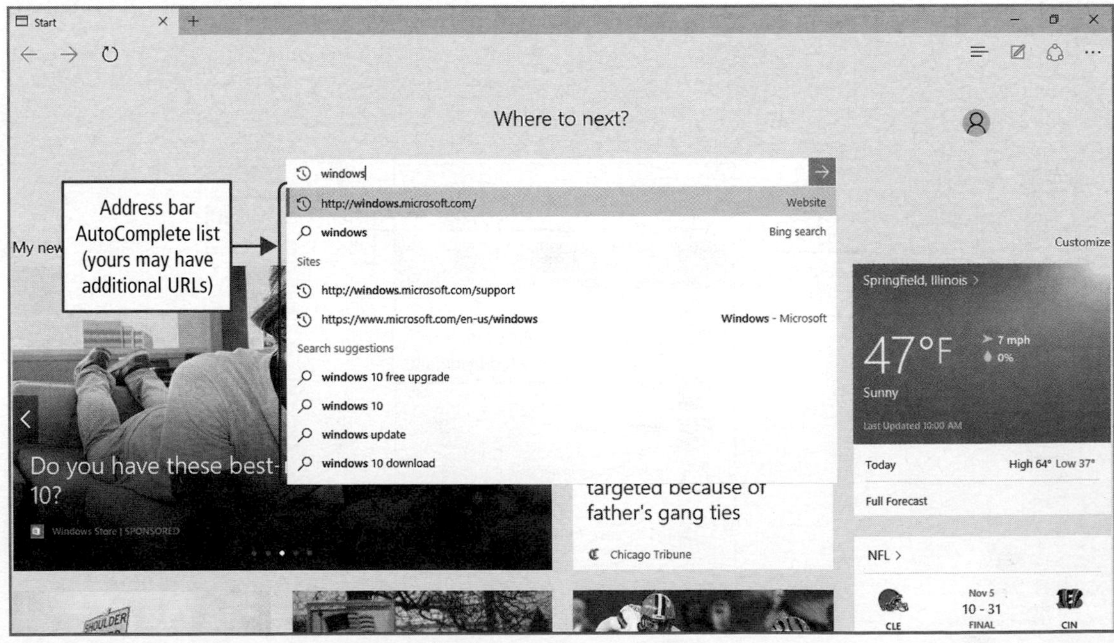

Figure 2

Windows 10, Microsoft Corporation

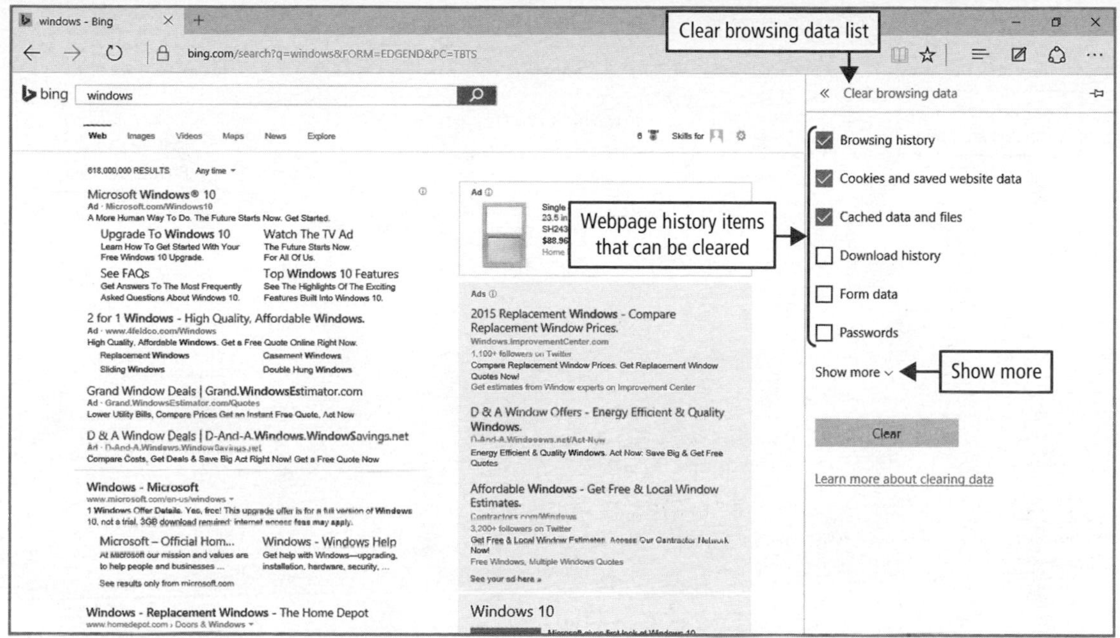

Windows 10, Microsoft Corporation

Figure 3

Browsing History Settings	
Category	**Purpose**
Browsing history	Websites you have previously visited.
Cookies and saved website data	Small text files written by some websites as you visit them. They are used to add functionality to pages or to analyze the way you use a website and to track what websites you visit next.
Cached data and files	Webpage data stored on your computer and used to decrease the time it takes for frequently-visited pages to display.
Download history	A list of all the files you have downloaded to your computer from the webpages you have visited.
Form data	Information that you have typed into forms, such as your logon name, e-mails address, and street address.
Passwords	A series of letters, numbers, symbols, and spaces that you type to gain access to a computer, file, or program to help ensure you are authorized.

Figure 4

7. In the address bar **Autocomplete** list, verify *http://windows.microsoft.com* displays. Press Enter.

   In this manner, your history list can help you navigate to websites quickly.

8. In the command bar, click the **More actions** button [...]. Click **Settings**. Under **Clear browsing data**, click the **Choose what to clear** button, and then compare your screen with **Figure 3**.

   In the Clear browsing data pane, you can choose which items from your browsing history to delete. The different options are summarized in **Figure 4**.

9. Create a **Full-screen Snip**. **Save** the snip as a **JPEG** file in your chapter folder with the name Last_First_me03_Parks3

10. **Close** [X] the Snipping Tool markup window.

11. Click the website to close the pane.

    To delete your browsing history, in the Clear browsing history pane, verify the Browsing history check box is selected. Deselect any other items that you do not want deleted, and then click the Clear button.

    When you are working on a ***public computer***—a computer that is available to others when you are not using it—it is a good idea to delete your browsing history, form data, and passwords before logging off the computer.

12. Click the address bar and leave Microsoft Edge open.

■ **You have completed Skill 8 of 10**

- You can protect your privacy with ***InPrivate Browsing***—a Microsoft Edge search window that limits the browsing history that is stored on your device. This feature may have a different name in another browser. For example, Google Chrome uses the name New incognito window.
- You can allow or prevent specific sites from writing cookies on your computer.

1. In the command bar, click the **More actions** button [...], and then click **New InPrivate window**. Compare your screen with **Figure 1**.

   When you start InPrivate Browsing, a new Microsoft Edge window opens. InPrivate Browsing is in effect only when that window is used.

2. On the **InPrivate browser tab**, take a few moments to read the information about InPrivate Browsing.
3. In the search bar, type nps.gov/muwo and then press [Enter]. **Close** [X] the message box.
4. In the command bar, click the **Hub** button [≡], and then click the **History** button [🕓]. Expand the *Last hour* list as shown in **Figure 2**.

   The history list does not display nps.gov/muwo.

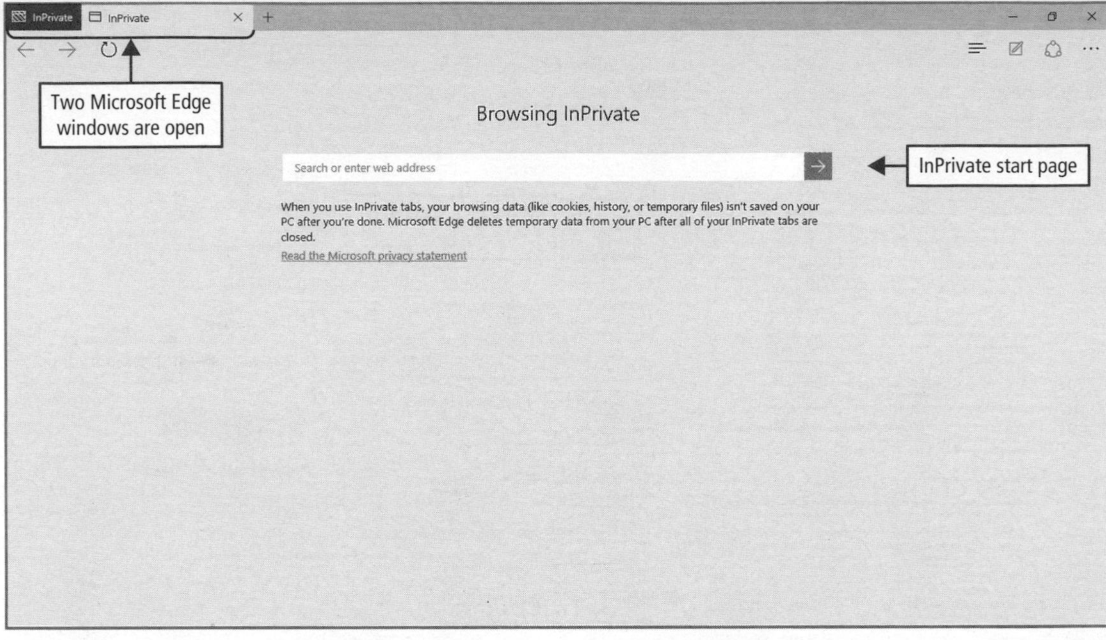

Figure 1 Microsoft Edge 2016, Windows 10, Microsoft Corporation

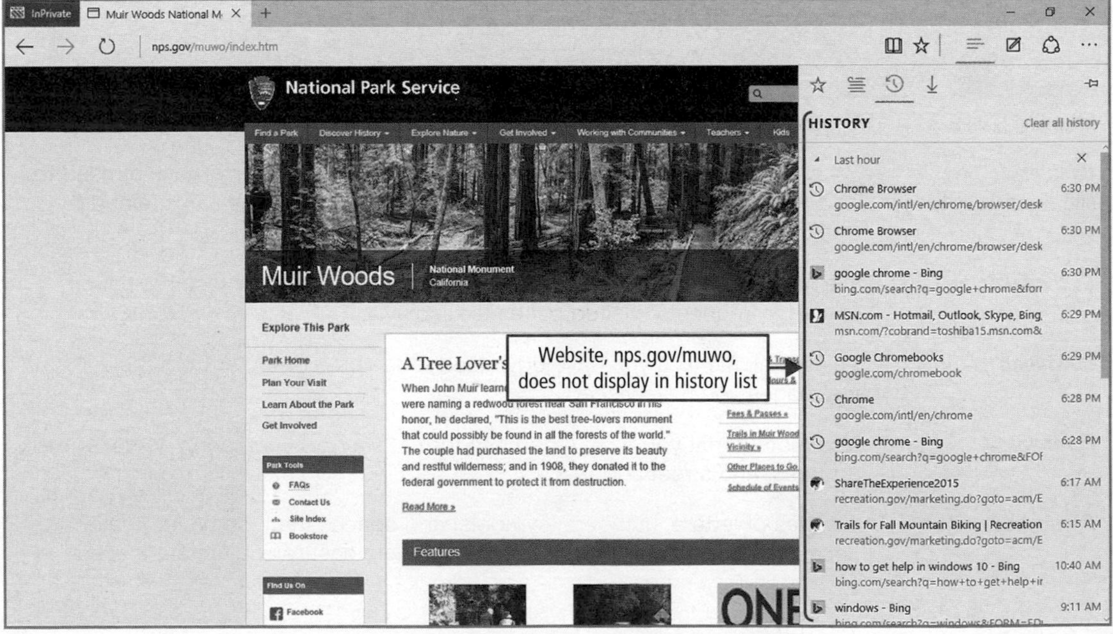

Figure 2 National Park Service website, 2015; Microsoft Edge 2016, Windows 10, Microsoft Corporation

■ **Continue to the next page to complete the skill**

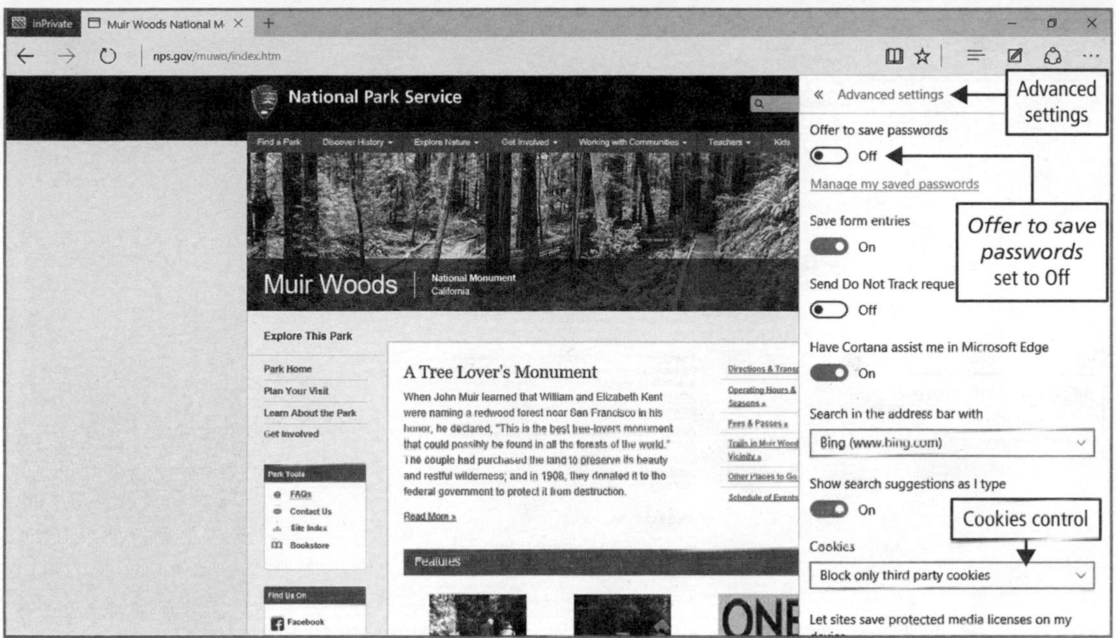

National Park Service website, 2015; Microsoft Edge 2016, Windows 10, Microsoft Corporation

Figure 3

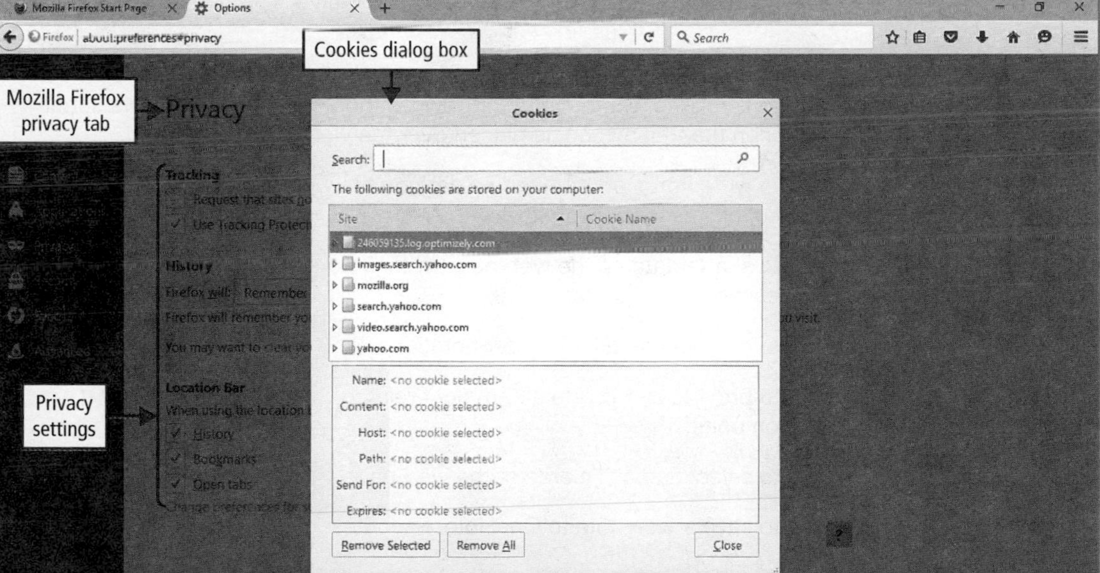

Mozilla firefox Inc.

Figure 4

5. In the command bar, click the **More actions** button [⋯] twice, and then click **Settings**. Scroll down, and then under **Advanced settings**, click **View advanced settings**.
6. Remember the original settings. View the settings, and then under **Offer to save passwords**, drag left to select **Off**.
7. Under **Cookies**, click and then select **Block only third party cookies**. Compare your screen with **Figure 3**. Return the *passwords* and *cookies* to their original settings.
8. **Minimize** [–] Edge. Open **Mozilla Firefox**. If a message displays, click **Not Now**. In the command bar, click the **Open menu** button [≡], and then click **Options**.
9. In the left navigation bar, click **Privacy**. Select the **remove individual cookies** hyperlink, and then compare your screen with **Figure 4**.
10. Under **Site**, scroll down and then select **google.com**. Click **Remove Selected**, and then click **Close**.
11. **Close** [×] Mozilla Firefox, and then in the dialog box, click **Close tabs**.
12. Right-click **Edge**, and then **Close** [×] the Microsoft Edge InPrivate window.
13. Open **Microsoft Edge**. Click the search bar, and then select the text. Type nps.gov/pore **Close** [×] the message box, and then click the **Operating Hours & Seasons** link.
14. Scroll to view the *Lighthouse Visitor Center* heading at the top of the window.

You have completed Skill 9 of 10

SKILL 10: Create Web Notes

WATCH BROWSER 3.10

► In Edge, as you search websites, you can create ***web notes***—items you can highlight, clip, or annotate to read about later. Web notes can be sent to OneNote or your Favorites or Reading list or shared through OneNote or e-mail.

1. On the command bar, click the **Make a Web Note** button. Compare your screen with **Figure 1**.
2. Point to the buttons to familiarize yourself with them and review the features in **Figure 2**.
3. Click the **Pan** button. Position the Pan symbol over the Lighthouse section. Drag the mouse to the bottom of the window.

   In this manner, you can view what comes before and after the text in the Web Note window.
4. Click the **Pen** button, and then click the **arrow**. Under **Color**, select the **magenta** color—the first color in the fourth row. Select the **smallest** size—the first button under **Size**.
5. Position the mouse at the top left corner of the paragraph that begins *The Lens Room*. Draw a box around the paragraph.
6. Click the **Highlighter** button, and then click the **arrow**. Select the **green** color—the first color in the second row. Select the **largest** size—the third button.
7. Position the mouse at the top left corner of the line that begins *The Lighthouse Visitor Center*.

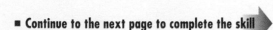

■ **Continue to the next page to complete the skill**

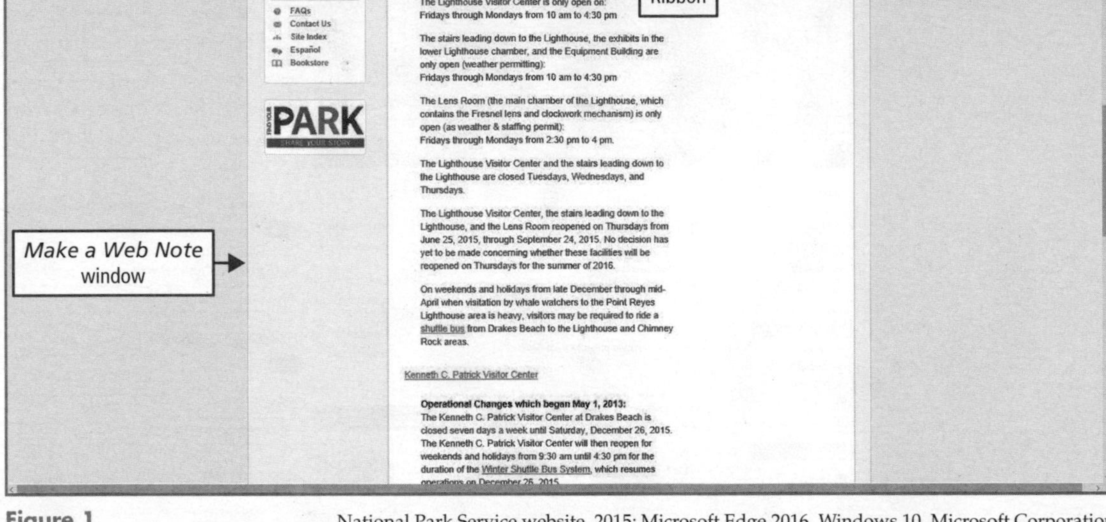

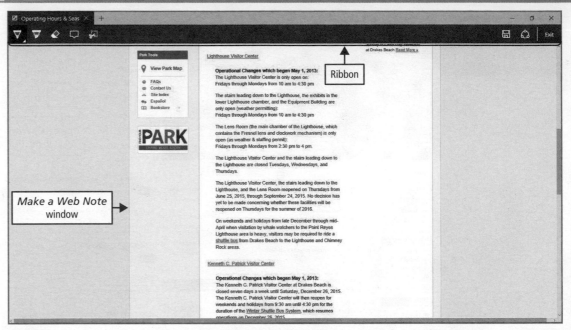

Figure 1 National Park Service website, 2015; Microsoft Edge 2016, Windows 10, Microsoft Corporation

Make a Web Note Buttons

Button Name	Purpose
Pan	Used to scroll the web page up or down without using the Windows scroll bars when the Pan symbol is placed over the web page.
Pen	Used to write notes or to underline data on the web page in 12 colors in three different thicknesses.
Highlighter	Used to shade data on the web page in six colors in three different thicknesses.
Eraser	Used to clear pen and highlighter notations.
Add a typed note	Used to provide and delete a comment related to the Web page at the insertion point.
Clip	Used to select a specific area of the web page.
Save Web Note	Used to save a web note to OneNote, Favorites, or Reading List
Share	Used to save a web note to OneNote or e-mail
Exit	Used to close the Web Note window

Figure 2

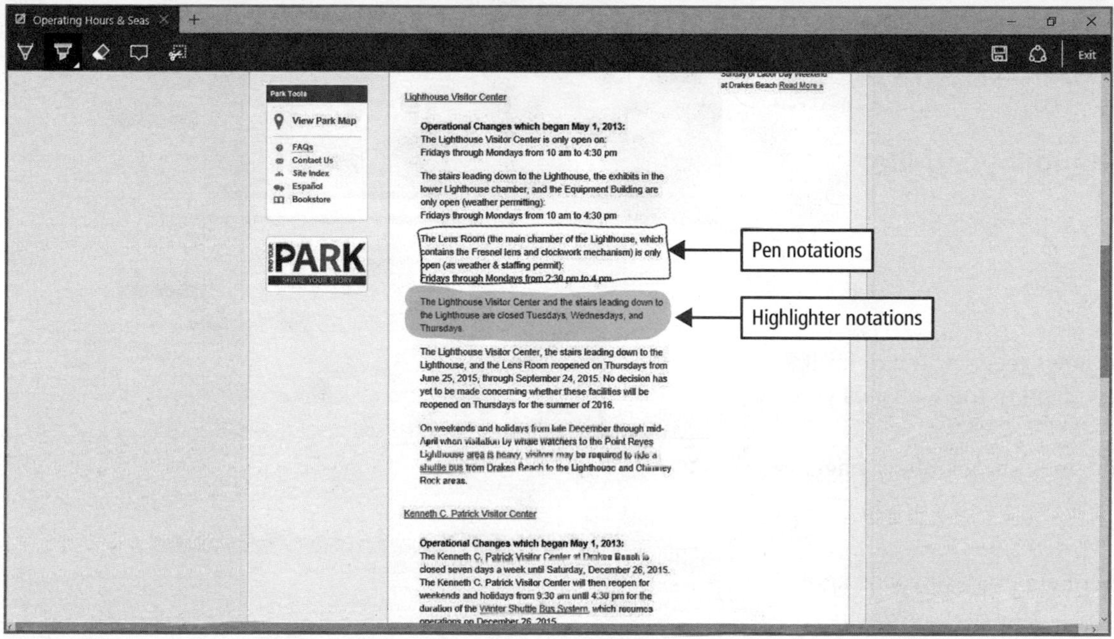

National Park Service website, 2015; Microsoft Edge 2016, Windows 10, Microsoft Corporation

Figure 3

National Park Service website, 2015; Microsoft Edge 2016, Windows 10, Microsoft Corporation

Figure 4

8. Drag to highlight the text as shown in **Figure 3**. Your highlighting may differ.

   Click the Eraser button to clear any unwanted pen and highlighter notations.

9. Click the **Save Web Note** button, and then click **Reading list**. In the **Name** box, select the text, type Hours and then click **Add**.
10. Click the **Add a typed note** button. Position the note to the right of *The Lens Room* and click. In the note, type Visit on weekends. as shown in **Figure 4**.
11. Click the **Save Web Note** button. In the **Name** box, select the text, type Weekend and then click **Add**. In the note, click the **Delete** button.
12. Click the **Clip** button. Select the lines that begin *Operational* through *Closed Tuesdays*. Click the **Save Web Note** button. In the **Name** box, select the text, type Changes and then click **Add**. Click **Exit**.
13. Click the **Hub** button, and then click **Reading List**.
14. Create a **Full-screen Snip**. **Save** the snip as a **JPEG** file in your chapter folder with the name Last_First_me03_Parks4 **Close** the Snipping Tool markup window.
15. Right-click the **Hours** Reading List entry, and then click **Remove**. Use the techniques practiced to clear any favorites, Favorites Bar, Reading List, and browsing history entries. **Close** all open windows.

DONE! You have completed Skill 10 of 10, and your project is complete!

More Skills 11

Change Your Home Page

To complete this project, you will need the following file:

- None

You will save your snip as:

- Last_First_me03_MS11Home

- When you open Microsoft Edge, your customized news feeds or the default MSN news feeds may display. Other browsers may display the websites you have previously visited.
- You can set your default home page to any website, including a blank page.

Figure 1 USA.gov, 2015

1. In the taskbar, click **Microsoft Edge** , and then navigate to www.usa.gov
2. In the address bar, click **More actions** [...], and then click **Settings**. Scroll to select the **View advanced settings** button. Compare your screen with **Figure 1**. Click the **View advanced settings** button.
3. Note the default setting for the **Show the home button** and the URL of your current default home page, so that you can restore them at the end of this project.
4. In the **Advanced settings** pane, under **Show the home slider**, move the slider right to **ON**.
   When a slider is turned on, the slider background is blue.
   When the slider is turned off, the slider background is white.
   The home button [Home] also displays in the address bar.
5. In the **Advanced settings** pane, in the box below the *Show the home button* slider, select the text, and then type http://www.aspenfalls.org Click **Save**.
6. In the address bar, click **Home** [Home] twice to display the default home page. Compare your screen with **Figure 2**.
7. Add a new tab.
8. To the right of the search bar, click the **Customize** link.
9. Under **Select language & content**, if necessary, select **United States (English)** as the default language.
10. Under **Choose your favorite topics**, click **Autos**. Press [Ctrl], and then click **Money**. Click **Save**.
    If necessary, click Refresh [Refresh], and then verify Autos and Money feeds display toward the top of the feeds.

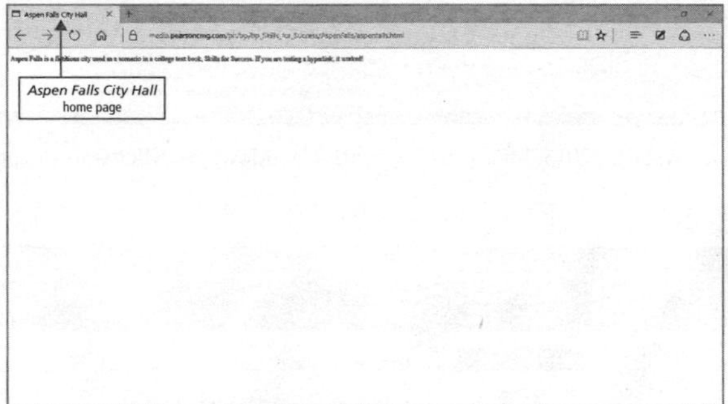

Figure 2 Pearson

11. Create a **Full-screen Snip**. **Save** [Save] the snip as a **JPEG** file in your **Internet Chapter 3** folder with the name Last_First_me03_MS11Home and then **Close** the Snipping Tool markup window.
12. Use the techniques practiced in this assignment to reset to your default home page. Remove any home page customizations by pressing [Ctrl] and clicking a news feed to remove it. When finished deselecting news feed categories, click **Save**.
13. **Close** [X] Microsoft Edge, and then submit the snip as directed by your instructor.

- **You have completed More Skills 11**

More Skills 12

Add Navigation Tiles to the Start Menu

To complete this project, you will need the following file:

- None

You will save your screen shot as:

- Last_First_me03_MS12Tiles

▶ You can add web pages to the Start menu as tiles.

---

1. In the taskbar, click **Microsoft Edge** . Type www.nps.gov to open the *National Park Service* home page.
2. In the **Edge** commands area, click the **More actions** button [···], and then click **Pin to Start**.
3. Open the **Start menu** . Use the scroll bar to verify the *National Park Service* tile displays.
4. Add a new tab [+].
5. Navigate to www.doi.gov to open the *U.S. Department of the Interior* home page.
6. On the command bar, click the **More actions** button [···], and then click **Pin to Start**.
7. **Close** [×] all open tabs in Microsoft Edge. Open the **Start menu**, and then scroll to verify the *U.S. Department of the Interior* tile has been added as shown in **Figure 1**.
8. On the **Start menu**, click the **National Park Service** tile to open the page in Microsoft Edge.
9. Return to the **Start menu**. Click the **U.S. Department of the Interior** tile to open the page.
10. **Close** [×] Microsoft Edge. If a message displays, click **Close all**.
11. On your keyboard, take a moment to locate the [PrintScreen] key, which is often located above the [Home] key.

    The [PrintScreen] key on the keyboard may display as [PrintScreen] or [Prt Scr] or something similar depending on your device.
12. On the **Start menu**, scroll to display the two tiles added in this project. Press [PrintScreen] to create a screen capture.
13. In the Windows search bar, type paint and then press [Enter].

Windows 10, Microsoft Corporation **Figure 1**

Paint is a drawing program that is installed with most versions of Windows.

14. On the **Home tab**, in the **Clipboard group**, click the **Paste** button to insert the screen capture.
15. On the **File tab**, point to **Save As**, and then click **JPEG Picture**. In the **Save As** dialog box, navigate to your **Internet Chapter 3** folder. Name the file Last_First_me03_MS12Tiles and then click **Save**.
16. On the **File tab**, click **Exit** to quit the Paint program.
17. On the **Start menu**, right-click the **National Park Service** tile, and then click **Unpin from Start**. Right-click the **U.S. Department of the Interior** tile, and then click **Unpin from Start**.
18. Submit the file as directed by your instructor.

■ **You have completed More Skills 12**

More Skills 13

Use Internet Privacy Settings

To complete this project, you will need the following file:

- None

You will save your snips as:

- Last_First_me03_MS13Track1
- Last_First_me03_MS13Track2

- ▶ ***Tracking cookies*** are cookies that gather information about your web browsing behaviors across multiple websites. They are used to provide ads and services based on your interests.
- ▶ If you do not wish to participate in tracking services, you can turn on Tracking Protection.
- ▶ ***Pop-ups*** are small windows that display in addition to the web page you are viewing.
- ▶ ***SmartScreen Filter*** is a feature that helps protect you from online threats.

---

1. In the taskbar, in the Windows search bar, type Internet Options Press Enter
2. In the **Internet Properties** dialog box, click the **Privacy tab**, and then click the **Settings** button.
3. In the **Pop-up Blocker Settings** dialog box, in the **Address of website to allow** box, type pearsonhighered.com Click the **Add** button.

   The site is now an *allowed site*.
4. Click the **Blocking level** drop-down list. Click **High: Block all pop-ups**.

   Pop-ups can add functionality, although some pop-ups display unwanted advertising. When the blocking level is set to high, only the sites you allow display pop-ups. Here, pages from pearsonhighered.com—such as MyITLab—can display pop-ups.
5. Create a **Full-screen Snip**. **Save** the snip as a **JPEG** file in your chapter folder as Last_First_me03_MS13Track1 **Close** the Snipping Tool markup window.
6. In the **Pop-up Blocker Settings** dialog box, under *Allowed sites*, click ***.pearsonhighered.com**. Click the **Remove** button.
7. Set the **Blocking level** to *Medium: Block most automatic pop-ups*. Close all open dialog boxes.
8. Open **Microsoft Edge**. In the address bar, type the IP address http://165.83.19.13

   Be wary of websites that display an IP address instead of a domain name. An ***IP address*** is a unique set of numbers assigned to each device on the Internet and are often used by ***Phishing websites***—dishonest sites posing as legitimate sites to gain personal information, such as your logon and bank account number.
9. Replace the IP address with nps.gov Press Enter. On the command bar, click the **More actions** button ···. Click **Open with Internet Explorer**.
10. In Internet Explorer, click the **Tools** button. Point to **Safety**, and then click **Check this website**. If necessary, click **OK** to check the site.
11. Create a **Full-screen Snip**. **Save** the snip in your chapter folder as Last_First_me03_MSTrack2
12. **Close** all open dialog boxes and windows. Submit the files as directed by your instructor.

- **You have completed More Skills 13**

More Skills 14

Change Internet Security Settings

To complete this project, you will need the following file:

- **None**

You will save your snip as:

- **Last_First_me03_MS14Security**

- Some sites use scripts and active content to download ***malware***—a type of program designed to harm your computer, control your computer, or discover private information.
- ***Scripts*** and ***active content*** are programs downloaded with a web page that provide additional functionality, such as dynamic content.

---

1. Open **Microsoft Edge**. Navigate to pearsonmylabandmastering.com
2. On the command bar, click the **More actions** button [...]. Click **Open with Internet Explorer**.
3. In Internet Explorer, click the **Tools** button, and then point to **Safety**. Click **ActiveX Filtering**.

   In Internet Explorer, you can use the Safety menu to filter ***ActiveX scripts***—a small program that allows Internet Explorer to load other software applications in the browser.
4. On the **Tools** menu, click **Internet options**. In the **Internet Options** dialog box, click the **Security tab**.

   Websites can be assigned to four zones. The ***Internet zone*** is the default security zone Internet Explorer applies to all websites. The ***Local intranet zone*** is designed for web content stored on internal networks that is accessed only by those within the organization. Sites that you trust to not harm your computer can be placed in the ***Trusted sites zone***. Sites that you explicitly do not trust can be placed in the ***Restricted sites zone***. ***Protected Mode*** is a feature that makes it more difficult for malware to be installed on your computer.
5. Review the security levels described in **Figure 1**.
6. On the **Security tab**, click **Trusted sites**. Click the **Sites** button. In the **Trusted sites** dialog box, clear the **Require server** check box. In the **Websites** box, verify *http://www.pearsonmylabandmastering.com* displays. Click **Add**.
7. Create a **Full-screen Snip**. **Save** the snip as a **JPEG** file in your chapter folder as Last_First_me03_MS14Security **Close** [X] the Snipping Tool window.

Internet Explorer Security Levels

Level	Description
High	No file downloads, scripts, or active content allowed.
Medium-high	Files can be downloaded, but a prompt must first display for approval. Some scripts and active content are classified as unsafe and are blocked.
Medium	Files can be downloaded, and a prompt displays before running any potentially unsafe scripts or active content.
Medium-low	This level is available only in the Local intranet and Trusted sites zones. A smaller range of scripts and active content are classified as unsafe.
Low	This level is available only in the Local intranet and Trusted sizes zones and should be applied only to a site you absolutely trust.

Figure 1

8. Click **http://www.pearsonmylabandmastering.com**. Click the **Remove** button. Click the **Close** button. In the **Internet Options** dialog box, click **Cancel**.
9. On the command bar, click the **Tools** button. Point to **Safety**. Click **ActiveX Filtering** to deselect it. **Close** [X] Internet Explorer.
10. **Close** [X] Microsoft Edge, and then submit the file as directed by your instructor.

- **You have completed More Skills 14**

Review

The following table summarizes the **SKILLS AND PROCEDURES** covered in this chapter.

Skills Number	Task	Step	Icon
1	Start Microsoft Edge from the desktop	On the taskbar, click the Microsoft Edge button	
1	Start Microsoft Edge from the Start menu	From the Start Menu, click the Microsoft Edge tile	
2	Create a favorite	In Microsoft Edge, click the Add to favorites or reading list button	
3	View a site map	In Apple Safari, scroll to the bottom, click the link for the Site Map or Site Index	
4	Search using an accelerator	In Google Chrome, type the word or words to search, click the desired accelerator button (i.e. Maps, Images, Videos, Web, etc.)	
5	Search from Bing	In Microsoft Edge, navigate to bing.com and type the search word(s) in the search box	
5	Limit results to a top-level domain	In Microsoft Edge, after the search term, type domain:gov or other top-level domain such as .org, .edu, or .com	
5	Open a new tab	In Microsoft Edge, on the Tabs row, click New Tab. Right-click a hyperlink, click Open in a new tab	+
6	Organize favorites	In Microsoft Edge, click the Hub button, right-click Favorites Bar, click Create new folder	
6	Create a snip	In Windows, from Start screen, type snip, locate the Snipping Tool application, press Enter. From New menu, click desired Snip type, click Save	
6	Rename a favorite	In Microsoft Edge, click the Favorites button, click the Favorites Bar, if necessary, click a folder, right-click a hyperlink, click Rename	
6	Move a favorite	In Microsoft Edge, click the Favorites button, click the Favorites Bar, if necessary, click a folder, click and drag a hyperlink to the desired location	
6	Dock the Favorites Bar	In Microsoft Edge, click the Favorites button, click the Favorites Bar, if necessary, click a folder, drag the desired folder to the Favorites Bar	
7	Print a web page selection	In Google Chrome, with the desired text highlighted, right-click, and from the shortcut menu, click Print	
7	Save a web page as an MHT file	In the Google Chrome command bar, click Customize, click Save page as. Click the Save as type button, click Webpage, HTML Only	
8	View browsing history	In Microsoft Edge, click the Hub button, click the History button	
8	Delete all occurrences of a URL from the browsing history	In Microsoft Edge, click the Hub button, click the History button, right-click the URL, click Delete all visits to (the URL)	
8	Delete single occurrence of a URL from the browsing history	In Microsoft Edge, click the Hub button, click the History button, right-click any URL, click Delete	

The following table summarizes the **SKILLS AND PROCEDURES** covered in this chapter.

Skills Number	Task	Step	Icon
8	Clear browsing history	In Microsoft Edge, in the command bar, click the More Actions button, click Settings, click the Choose what to clear button	...
8	Turn off save passwords	In Microsoft Edge, in the command bar, click the More Actions button, click Settings, click View advanced settings, drag Offer to save passwords to the left to select Off	...
8	Disable cookies	In Mozilla Firefox, in the command bar, click the Open menu button, click Options, click Privacy, select the remove individual cookies hyperlink	
9	Start an InPrivate session	In Microsoft Edge, in the command bar, click the More Actions button, click New InPrivate window, type your search	...
10	Open the Make a Web Note window	In Microsoft Edge, click the Make a Web Note button	
10	Pan a Web Note window	In Microsoft Edge, click the Make a Web Note button, click the Pan button	
10	Use pen for web notes	In Microsoft Edge, click the Make a Web Note button, click the Pen button, select color and size, move mouse to Web Note area	
10	Use highlighter for web notes	In Microsoft Edge, click the Make a Web Note button, click the Highlighter button, select color and size, move mouse to Web Note area	
10	Add a typed note to a web note	In Microsoft Edge, click the Make a Web Note button, click the Add a typed note button, type text	
10	Delete a typed note from a web note	In Microsoft Edge, in a Typed Note, click the Delete button	
10	Clip an area in web notes	In Microsoft Edge, click the Make a Web Note button, click the Clip button, select an area from the Web page	
10	Remove a web note entry from the Reading list	In Microsoft Edge, click the Hub button, right-click a Reading list entry	
MS 11	Change your home page	In Microsoft Edge, type a web page name. In the address bar, click More actions, click Settings, select View advanced settings, and move the *Show the home* slider button right to ON	...
MS 12	Add navigation tiles to the Start menu	In Microsoft Edge, type the web page name, click the More actions button, and then click Pin to Start	...
MS 13	Use Internet privacy settings	In the Windows search bar, type Internet Options and press Enter. In the Internet Properties dialog box, on the Privacy tab, click Settings	
MS 14	Change Internet security settings	In Microsoft Edge, type a web page name, click the More actions button, click Open with Internet Explorer. In Internet Explorer, click Tools, point to Safety, click Active X Filtering. On the Tools menu, click Internet options, click Security tab, click Trusted sites	...

Project Summary Chart		
Project	**Project Type**	**Project Location**
Skills Review	Review	Book
Skills Assessment 1	Review	Book
Skills Assessment 2	Review	Book
Visual Skills Check	Problem Solving	Book
Skillls Challenge 1	Critical Thinking	Book
Skills Challenge 2	Critical Thinking	Book

Key Terms

Accelerator 78
Active content 95
ActiveX scripts 95
Apple Safari 70
Browsing history 86
Cached data and files 87
Cookie 89
Default home page 72
Domain name 72
Download history 87
Favorite 74
Form data 87
Google Chrome 70
Home page 72
Hover over 73
Hyperlink 73
InPrivate Browsing 88
Internet zone 95
IP address 94
Local intranet zone 95
Malware 95
Microsoft Edge 70
Mozilla Firefox 70
MHTML file 85
Navigation bar 73
Paint 93
Password 87
Phishing websites 94
Pop-ups 94
Protected Mode 95
Public computer 87
Reading view 81
Refresh 73
Restricted sites zone 95
Scripts 95
Search provider 78
Search suggestion 79
Site index 76
Site map 76
SmartScreen Filter 94
Tabbed browsing 78
Top-level domain 80
Tracking cookies 94
Trusted sites zone 95
Uniform Resource Locator . . . 72
URL 72
Web 70
Web browser 72
Web note 90
Web page archive 85
Website 74
World Wide Web 70
WWW 70

Online Help Skills

1. Start **Microsoft Edge** . In the address bar, type windows.microsoft.com Click the Windows 10 drop-down, and then click **Microsoft Edge**. On the *Introducing Microsoft Edge* page, click the **Get started** button. Below the third picture, click **Cortana gives you instant search results and information**. Read about the dynamic duo—Cortana and Microsoft Edge. Compare your screen with **Figure 1**.

   Another option to get to the location is to open Edge, and then type windows.microsoft.com /en-US/windows-10/getstarted-dynamic-duo

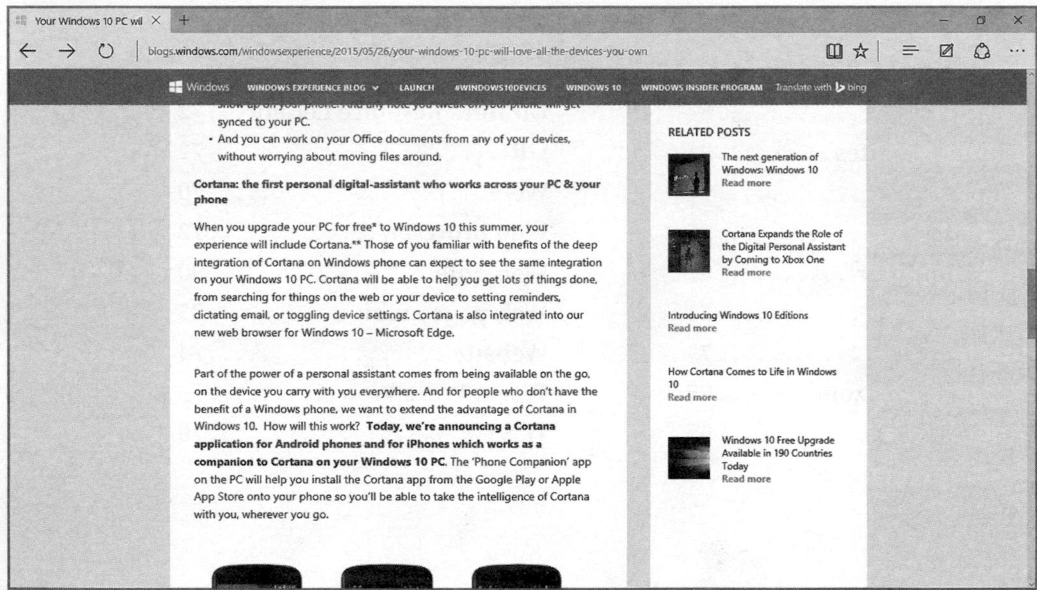

Figure 1 Microsoft Edge 2016, Windows 10, Microsoft Corporation

2. Read the page and expand each section to see if you can answer the following questions: What is Cortana? How can you access Cortana in Microsoft Edge? How can Cortana be used to learn more about a topic?

Matching 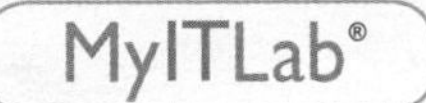

Match each term in the second column with its correct definition in the first column by writing the letter of the term on the blank line in front of the correct definition.

___ **1.** A unique name assigned to a website on the World Wide Web.

___ **2.** The starting point for the remainder of the pages at a website.

___ **3.** Any text or picture that can be clicked to move to a new page or location.

___ **4.** A stored web address that can be clicked to navigate to that page quickly.

___ **5.** A feature that searches the web for information related to text that you type/enter.

___ **6.** A feature that you use to open multiple web pages in the same browser window.

___ **7.** Letters, such as *.edu*, after a domain name that specify the type of organization sponsoring a website.

___ **8.** A file that saves web page text and pictures in a single file. These files are typically assigned the *.mht* file extension.

___ **9.** A Microsoft Edge window that limits the browsing history that is written.

___ **10.** A small text file written by a web site as you visit it.

A Accelerator
B Cookie
C Domain name
D Favorite
E Home page
F Hyperlink
G InPrivate Browsing
H Tabbed browsing
I Top-level domain
J Web archive

Multiple Choice

Choose the correct answer.

1. A stored web address that can be clicked to navigate to that page quickly.
   - **A.** Favorite
   - **B.** Quicklink
   - **C.** Top-level domain name
2. A vertical or horizontal bar with hyperlinks to the main pages of a website.
   - **A.** Accelerator
   - **B.** Navigation bar
   - **C.** Site index
3. A collection of linked pages designed to be viewed from any computer connected to the Internet.
   - **A.** Temporary Internet files
   - **B.** Web archive
   - **C.** World Wide Web
4. A website that provides a way for you to search for information on the web.
   - **A.** Accelerator
   - **B.** Search provider
   - **C.** Uniform Resource Locator
5. Letters after a domain name that specify the type of organization sponsoring a website—*.gov,* for example.
   - **A.** Cookie
   - **B.** Top-level domain
   - **C.** URL
6. The unique address of a page on the Internet.
   - **A.** Site index
   - **B.** Top-level domain
   - **C.** URL
7. The information that Microsoft Edge stores as you browse the web.
   - **A.** Browsing history
   - **B.** Site map
   - **C.** Wiki
8. A computer that is available to others when you are not using it.
   - **A.** Desktop computer
   - **B.** Mobile device
   - **C.** Public computer
9. A browsing session that writes cookies to RAM so that they are deleted when you close the window.
   - **A.** Accelerator
   - **B.** Active content
   - **C.** InPrivate Browsing
10. A unique set of numbers assigned to each computer on the Internet.
    - **A.** Location code
    - **B.** IP address
    - **C.** URL

Topics for Discussion

1. Consider the websites you might visit. Which sites should be added as favorites? Of those favorites, which ones would you add to the Favorites Bar?
2. In this chapter, you searched various websites. What is the importance of a site map or site index? When might you use one?

Skills Review

To complete this project, you will need the following file:

- None

You will save your files as:

- Last_First_me03_SRBLM1.MHT
- Last_First_me03_SRBLM2.jpg
- Last_First_me03_SRBLM3.jpg
- Last_First_me03_SRBLM4.jpb

1. Use the taskbar to open Microsoft Edge. Search for blm.gov Create a **Favorite** for this site with the default save options.
2. On the *Bureau of Land Management* home page vertical navigation bar, click **Visit Us**, and then click **Monuments**. Create a **Favorite** for this site with the default save options.
3. Display the **Site Map**, and then select the **California Site Map** hyperlink. Create a **Favorite** with the defaults shown in **Figure 1**.
4. Open a **New Tab**, and then use bing.com to search for carrizo plain domain:org Use the **Maps** accelerator, and then compare your screen with **Figure 2**. Save the page as a Favorite with the name Carrizo Plains
5. Open the *blm.gov* tab. In the site map, press Ctrl + Shift, and then click the **About BLM in California** hyperlink to open it.
6. Open **Reading view**, and then save the page as a Favorite with the default name.
7. From the Start menu, locate and select **Google Chrome**. Click the **Customize** button, and then select *New incognito window*.
8. Search for blm.gov In the left navigation bar, click the **What We Do** hyperlink, and then select *Energy*.

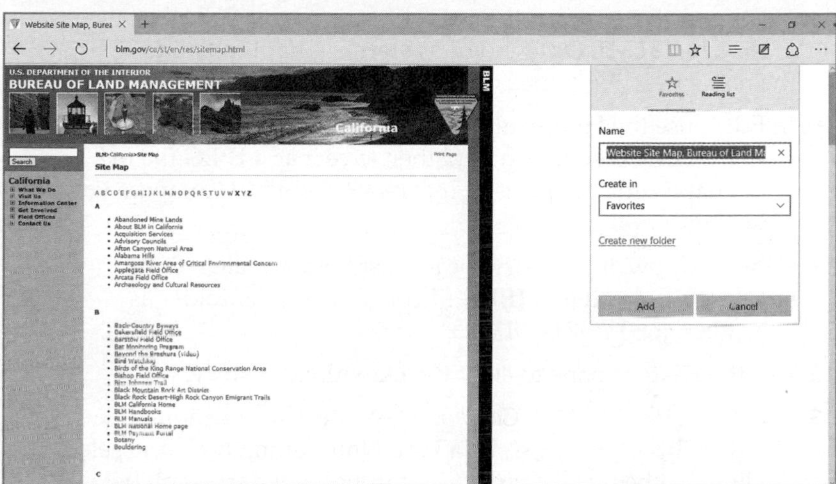

Bureau of Land Management website, 2015; Microsoft Edge 2016, Windows 10, Microsoft Corporation **Figure 1**

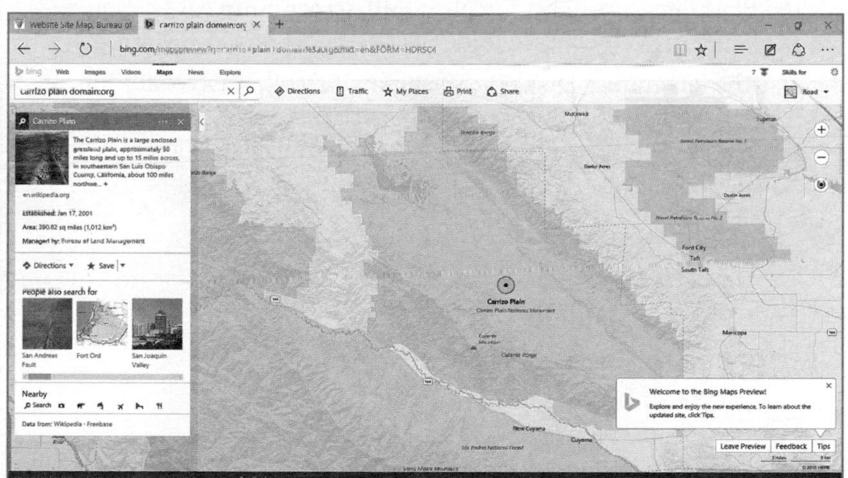

Microsoft Edge 2016, Windows 10, Microsoft Corporation **Figure 2**

■ Continue to the next page to complete this Skills Review

9. Select the paragraphs that begin *New Energy* through *Companies pay*, right-click, and then click **Print**. **Cancel** printing. Click the **Customize** button, and then click **Save page as**. Save the page as **Webpage, HTML Only** in your **Internet Chapter 3** folder with the name Last_First_me03_SRBLM1_MHT **Close** Chrome.
10. In Edge, use the **Hub** to alphabetize the favorites related to BLM. Create a **Full-screen Snip**, and then save it as a **JPEG** file in your chapter folder as Last_First_me03_SRBLM2 Compare your screen with **Figure 3**.
11. View the browsing history for the last hour. Create a **Full-screen Snip** saved as a **JPEG** file in your chapter folder as Last_First_me03_SRBLM3
12. Use the **History** pane to clear the **Download history**.
13. Open the *About BLM in California* favorite. **Close** Reading view. Use the **Clip** from the **Make a Web Note** command bar to select the line that begins *Department of* through the paragraph below the figure. Compare your screen with **Figure 4**. Save the clip as BLM Framework
14. Exit the **Make a Web Note** window. In the Reading List, display the *BLM Framework* clip. Create a **Full-screen Snip** saved as a **JPEG** file in your chapter folder as Last_First_me03_SRBLM4
15. Use the techniques learned to clear any favorites, Favorites Bar, Reading List, and browsing history entries. **Close** [×] all open windows. Submit your files as directed by your instructor.

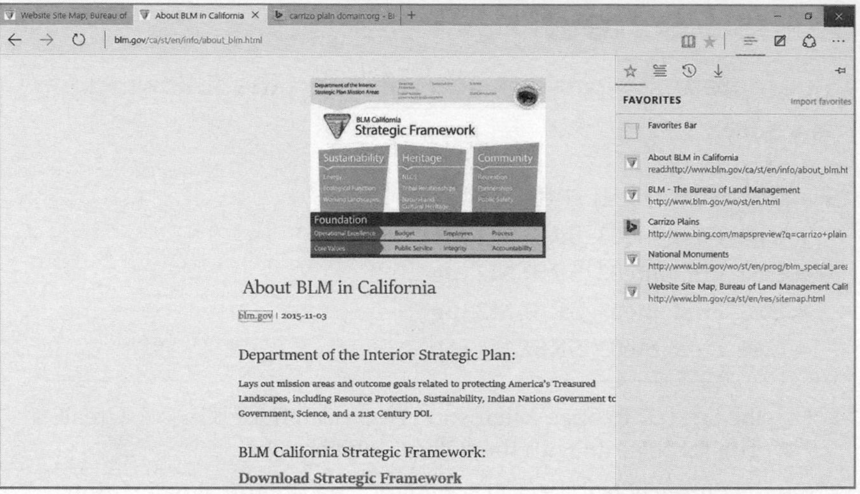

Figure 3 Bureau of Land Management website, 2015; Microsoft Edge 2016, Windows 10, Microsoft Corporation

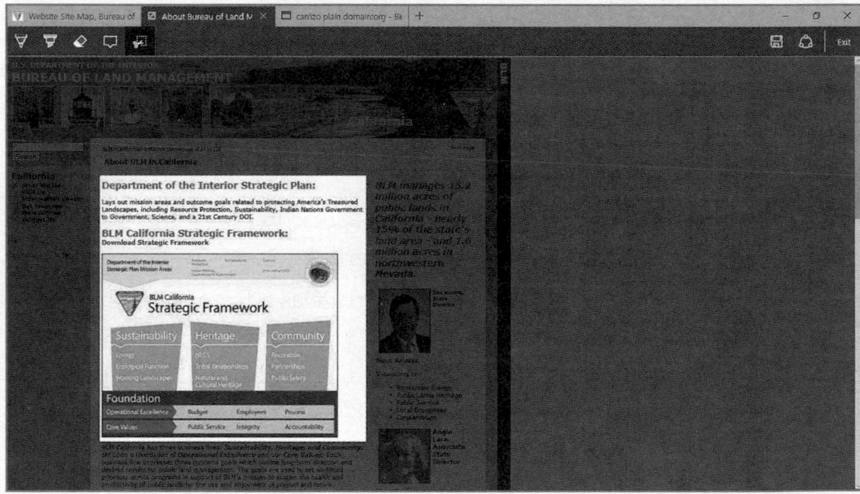

Figure 4 Bureau of Land Management website, 2015; Microsoft Edge 2016, Windows 10, Microsoft Corporation

Skills Assessment 1

To complete this project, you will need the following file:

- None

You will save your file as:

- Last_First_me03_SA1Snip

---

1. In **Microsoft Edge**, navigate to doi.gov to display the U.S. Department of Interior home page. In the site map, under **What We Do**, click **Native American Issues**.
2. Scroll down the page to display the **Other Issues of Concern** paragraph, and then click the paragraph's **Learn more** hyperlink. Add the page to your **Favorites** with the name BIE-Funded Schools.
3. Click the **Back** button, and then open the **Site Map** in a new tab. Compare your screen with **Figure 1**.
4. Create a **Full-Screen Snip**. **Save** the file in your chapter folder as Last_First_me03_SA1Snip.
5. **Close** all open windows, and then submit the file as directed by your instructor.

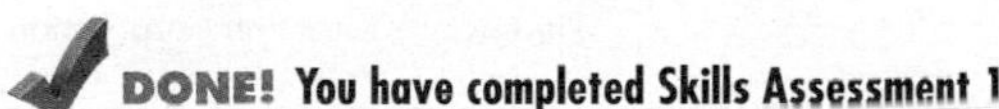

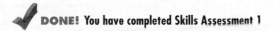

DONE! You have completed Skills Assessment 1

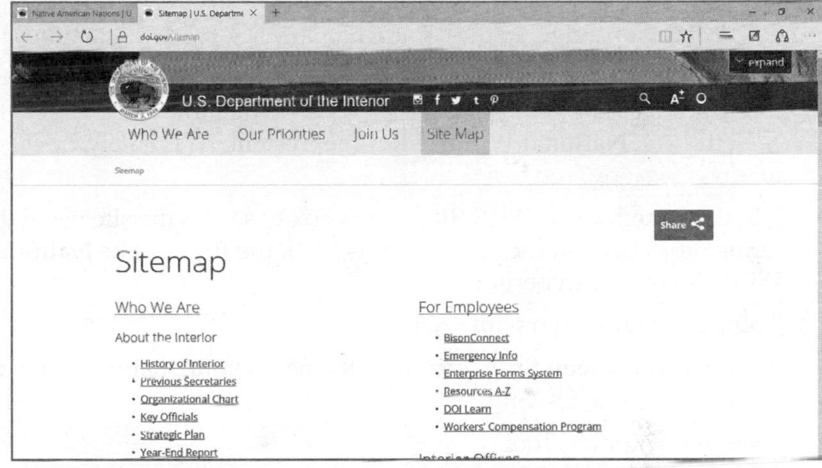

U.S. Department of Interior website, 2015; Microsoft Edge 2016, Windows 10, Microsoft Corporation

Figure 1

Skills Assessment 2

To complete this project, you will need the following file:

- None

You will save your files as:

- Last_First_me03_SA2Snip1
- Last_First_me03_SA2Snip2

---

1. Start **Microsoft Edge**. In the command bar, click the **More actions** button [···], and then click **New InPrivate window**.
2. In the address bar, type National Wildlife Refuge In the search results, click the link **National Wildlife Refuge System**. Alternately, navigate to www.fws.gov/refuges
3. Use the **Search the NWRS Site** search box to search the site using the terms Bitter Lake In the search results, click the **Bitter Lake National Wildlife Refuge** hyperlink.
4. Compare your screen with **Figure 1**.
5. Create a **Full-screen Snip**, and **Save** the file in your chapter folder as Last_First_me03_SA2Snip1
6. Close the Snipping Tool.
7. In the **InPrivate** window, click **Back** two times to return to *fws.gov/refuges*. Scroll to the bottom of the page, and then click **Privacy**. Compare your screen with **Figure 2**.
8. Create a **Full-screen Snip**, and save it as Last_First_me03_SA2Snip2
9. **Close** all open windows, and then submit the files as directed by your instructor.

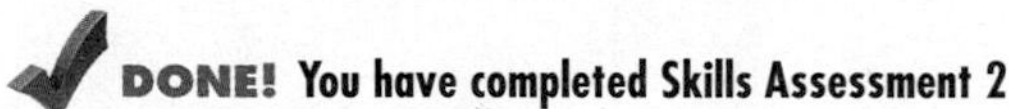

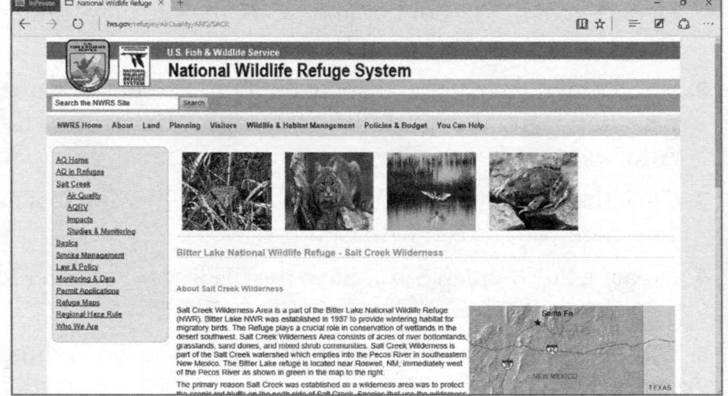

Figure 1 U.S. Fish and Wildlife Service website, 2015; Microsoft Edge 2016, Windows 10, Microsoft Corporation

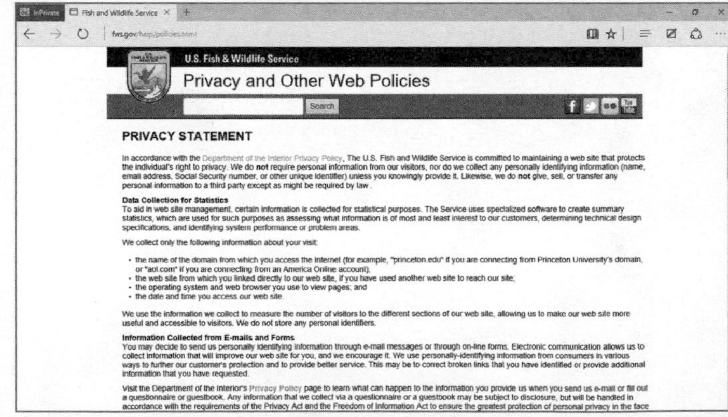

Figure 2 U.S. Fish and Wildlife Service website, 2015; Microsoft Edge 2016, Windows 10, Microsoft Corporation

Visual Skills Check

To complete this project, you will need the following file:

- None

You will save your file as:

- Last_First_me03_VSSnip

Use the skills you have practiced in this chapter to locate the home pages for the following government agencies: NOAA's National Ocean Service, U.S. Geological Survey, U.S. Forest Service, and the National Register of Historic Places. Open each home page in its own tab, as shown in **Figure 1**.

Add the tabs as a group to your Favorites in a folder named Agencies Open the **Organize Favorites** dialog box, and then display the **Agencies** folder, as shown in **Figure 1**. Create a **Full-screen Snip**. **Save** the snip in your chapter folder as Last_First_me03_VSSnip

In your **Favorites**, delete the **Agencies** folder. **Close** all open windows, and then submit the file as directed by your instructor.

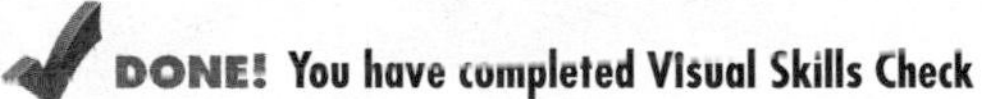

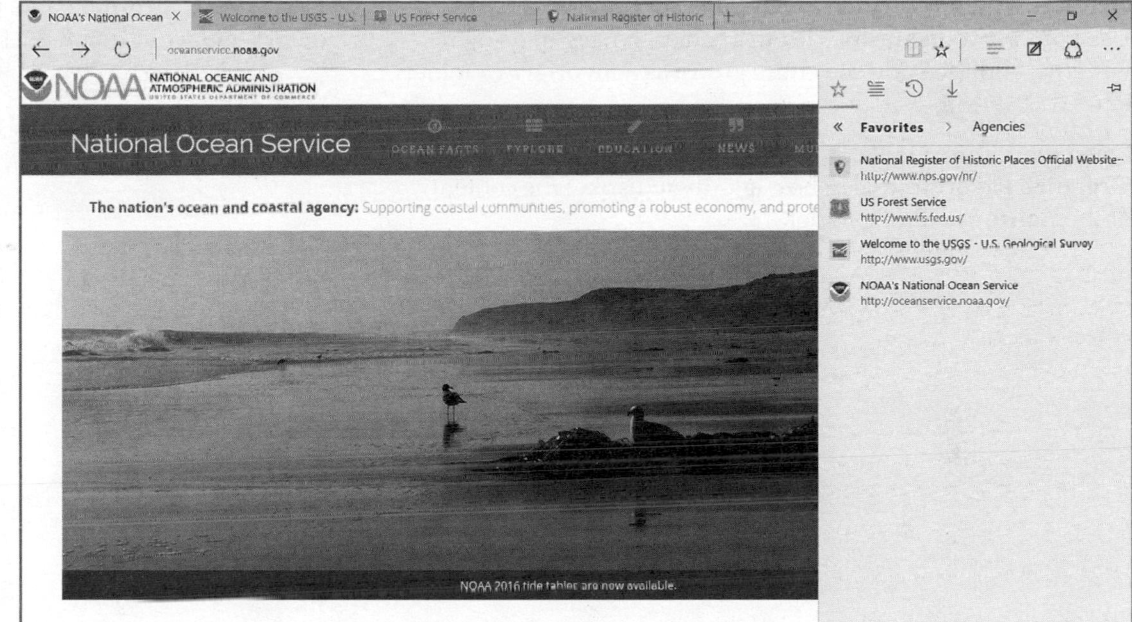

NOAA website, 2015; Microsoft Edge 2016, Windows 10, Microsoft Corporation

Figure 1

Skills Challenge 1

To complete this project, you will need the following file:

- **None**

You will save your file as:

- **Last_First_me03_SC1Snip**

Research national and state parks in California. Use the skills that you have practiced in this chapter to search at least eight websites with information about different California parks. Use your browsing history list to open each page in its own window, and then add the entire group as a favorite in a folder named California Parks

Open the **California Parks** favorite as a group, open the **Organize Favorites** dialog box, and then display the contents of the **California Parks** folder.

Create a **Full-screen Snip**, and then **Save** the snip in your chapter folder with the name Last_First_me03_SC1Snip Delete the **California Parks** favorites folder, and then **Close** all open windows. Submit the file as directed by your instructor.

DONE! You have completed Skills Challenge 1

Skills Challenge 2

To complete this project, you will need the following file:

- None

You will save your file as:

- Last_First_me03_SC2Snip

Use tools on the page at www.nws.noaa.gov to display the weekly weather forecast for your locality. When you are done, create a **Full-screen Snip**. **Save** the file in your chapter folder as Last_First_me03_SC2Snip **Close** all open windows, and then submit the file as directed by your instructor.

DONE! You have completed Skills Challenge 2

CHAPTER 1

Common Features of Office 2016

- Microsoft Office is a suite of several programs—Word, PowerPoint, Excel, Access, and others.
- Each Office program is used to create different types of personal and business documents.
- The programs in Office 2016 share common tools that you use in a consistent, easy-to-learn manner.
- Some common tasks include opening and saving files, entering and formatting text, inserting pictures, and printing your work.
- Because of the consistent design and layout of the Office applications, when you learn to use one Microsoft Office application, you can apply many of the same techniques when working in the other Microsoft Office applications.

lculig/Fotolia

Aspen Falls City Hall

In this project, you will create documents for the Aspen Falls City Hall, which provides essential services for the citizens and visitors of Aspen Falls, California. You will assist Janet Neal, Finance Director, to prepare a presentation for the City Council. The presentation will explain retail sales trends in the city. The information will help the council to predict revenue from local sales taxes.

Microsoft Office is a suite of tools designed for specific tasks. In this project, the data was originally stored in an Access database. You will use Word to write a memo to update your supervisor about the project's status. Next, you will use Excel to create a chart from that data, and then use PowerPoint to display the chart to an audience. In this way, each application performs a different function and creates a different type of document.

In this project, you will create a Word document, and open existing files in Excel and PowerPoint. You will write a memo, format an Excel worksheet, and update chart data, and then place a copy of the chart into a PowerPoint presentation. You will also format a database report in Access. In all four applications, you will apply the same formatting to provide a consistent look and feel.

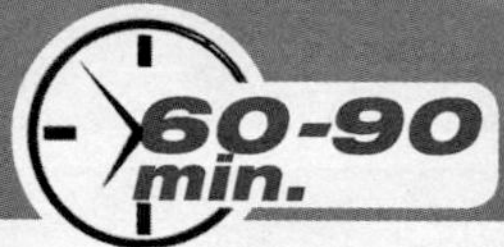

Outcome

Using the skills in this chapter, you will be able to open Office applications, save files, edit and format text and pictures, apply themes, use the Mini toolbar and Backstage view, format worksheets and reports, and paste objects into presentations.

Objectives

1 Explain the common features of Office 2016 applications

2 Modify documents

3 Prepare a presentation

4 Differentiate the uses of each Office 2016 application

5 Create Word, Excel, PowerPoint, and Access files for a presentation

Student data files needed for this chapter:

cf01_Memo (Word)
cf01_Parks (Word)
cf01_RetailChart (Excel)
cf01_RetailSlides (PowerPoint)
cf01_RetailData (Access)

You will save your files as:

Last_First_cf01_Parks (Word)
Last_First_cf01_Memo (Word)
Last_First_cf01_RetailMemo (Word)
Last_First_cf01_RetailChart (Excel)
Last_First_cf01_RetailSlides (PowerPoint)
Last_First_cf01_RetailData (Access)

SKILLS

At the end of this chapter, you will be able to:

Skill 1 Start Office Applications
Skill 2 Open and Save Student Data Files
Skill 3 Type and Edit Text
Skill 4 Format Text and Save Files
Skill 5 Apply Themes and Use the Mini Toolbar
Skill 6 Use Backstage View
Skill 7 Insert and Format Images
Skill 8 Format Worksheets
Skill 9 Copy and Paste Objects and Format Slides
Skill 10 Format Access Reports

MORE SKILLS

Skill 11 Store Files Online
Skill 12 Share Office Files
Skill 13 Install Office Add-ins
Skill 14 Customize the Ribbon and Options

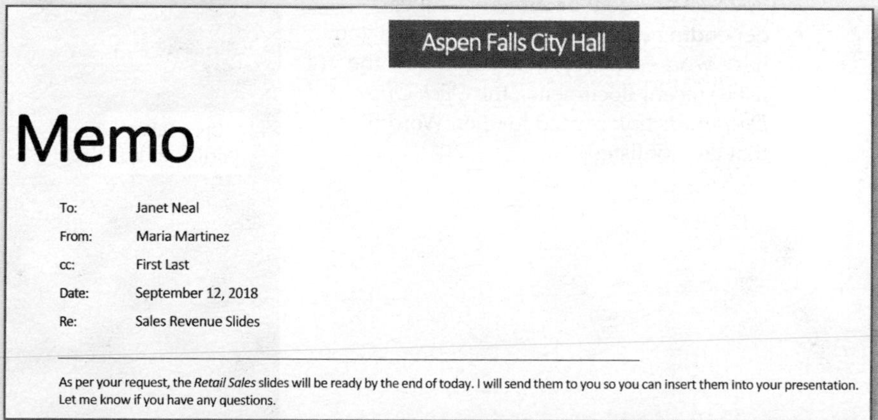

Office 2016, Windows 10, Microsoft Corporation

 WATCH SKILL 1.1

- The way that you start an Office application depends on what operating system you are using and how your computer is configured.
- Each application's start screen displays links to recently viewed documents and thumbnails of sample documents that you can open.

1. If necessary, turn on the computer, sign in, and navigate to the desktop. Take a few moments to familiarize yourself with the various methods for starting Office applications as summarized in **Figure 1**.

   One method that works in both Windows 8.1 and Windows 10 is to press ⊞ (the Windows key located between Ctrl and Alt) to display the Start menu or screen. With Start displayed, type the application name, verify that Word is selected, and then press Enter.

2. Use one of the methods described in the previous step to start **Word 2016**, and then take a few moments to familiarize yourself with the Word start screen as shown in **Figure 2**.

   Your list of recent documents will vary depending on what Word documents you have worked with previously. Below the list of recent documents, the *Open Other Documents* link is used to open Word files that are not listed.

Common Methods to Start Office 2016 Applications

Location	Description
Start screen tile	Click the application's tile
Desktop	Double-click the application's desktop icon
Taskbar	Click the application's taskbar button
Windows 10 Start menu	Click Start and look in pinned or most used apps. Or click All apps and locate the Office application or the Microsoft Office 2016 folder.
All locations	Press ⊞, type the application's name, select the correct application, and then press Enter.
Search the web and Windows	Type the application's name, and then press Enter

Figure 1

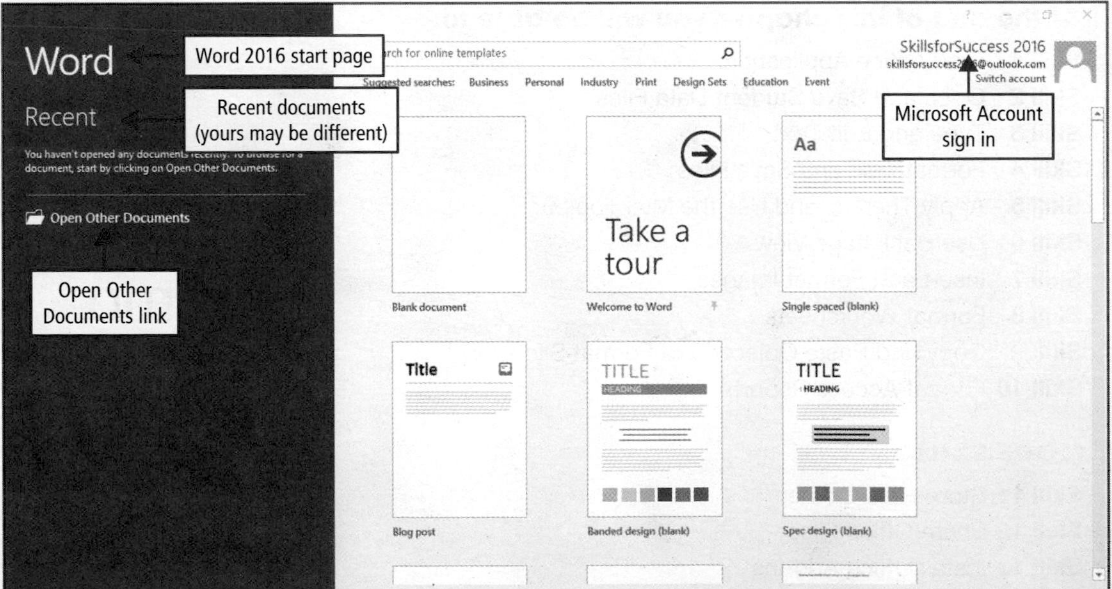

Figure 2

Word 2016, Windows 10, Microsoft Corporation

■ **Continue to the next page to complete the skill**

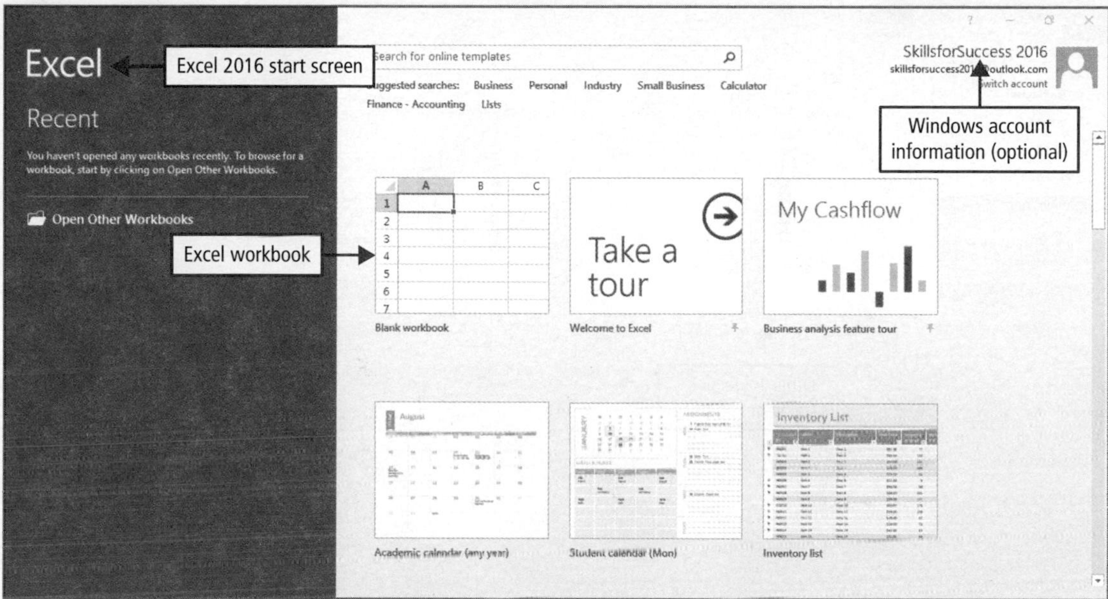

Excel 2016, Windows 10, Microsoft Corporation

Figure 3

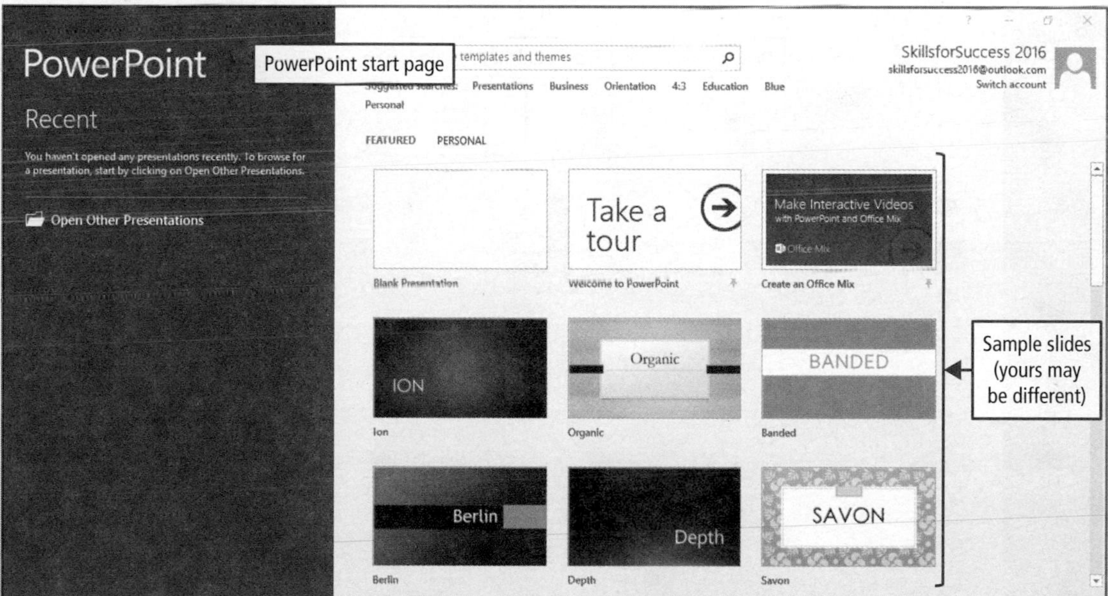

PowerPoint 2016, Windows 10, Microsoft Corporation

Figure 4

3. If desired, click **Sign in to get the most out of Office**, and then follow the onscreen directions to sign in using your Microsoft account.

   Logging in enables you to access Microsoft Cloud services such as opening and saving files stored on your OneDrive. Unless otherwise directed, signing in to your Microsoft account is optional in this book. To protect your privacy, you should sign in only if you are already signed in to Windows using a unique username, not a shared account. For example, many public computers share an account for guests. When you are logged in to your Microsoft account, your name and picture will display in the upper right corner of the window.

4. Using the technique just practiced, start **Excel 2016**, and then compare your screen with **Figure 3**.

   Worksheets are divided into ***cells***—boxes formed by the intersection of a row and column into which text, objects, and data can be inserted. In Excel, cells can contain text, formulas, and functions. Worksheets can also display charts based on the values in the cells.

5. Start **PowerPoint 2016**, and then compare your screen with **Figure 4**.

   PowerPoint presentations consist of ***slides***—individual pages in a presentation that can contain text, pictures, or other objects. PowerPoint slides are designed to be projected as you talk in front of a group of people. The PowerPoint start screen has thumbnails of several slides formatted in different ways.

■ **You have completed Skill 1 of 10**

► In this book, you will frequently open student data files.

1. Before beginning this skill, download the student data files for this chapter and unzip or copy them; use **Figure 1** as an example. Follow the instructions in the Getting Started with Windows 10 chapter or provided by your instructor.
2. On the taskbar, click the **Word** button. If necessary, start Word.
3. On the **Word** start page, click **Open Other Documents** to display the Open page. If you already had a blank document open, click the File tab instead.
4. On the **Open** page, click **This PC**, and then click the **Browse** button.
5. In the **Open** dialog box navigation pane, navigate to the student files for this chapter, and then compare your screen with **Figure 2**.
6. In the **Open** dialog box, select **cf01_Memo**, and then click the **Open** button.
7. If the **Protected View** message displays, click the **Enable Editing** button.

   Files downloaded from a website typically open in ***Protected View***—a view applied to files downloaded from the Internet that allows you to decide if the content is safe before working with the file.
8. On the **File tab**, click **Save As**. Click **Browse**. Navigate to the location where you will be saving your files. In the **Save As** dialog box, click the **New folder** button, and then type Common Features Chapter

   Save As is used to select the location where you want to save your work. You can choose to save to your OneDrive or other locations on your computer.

■ Continue to the next page to complete the skill

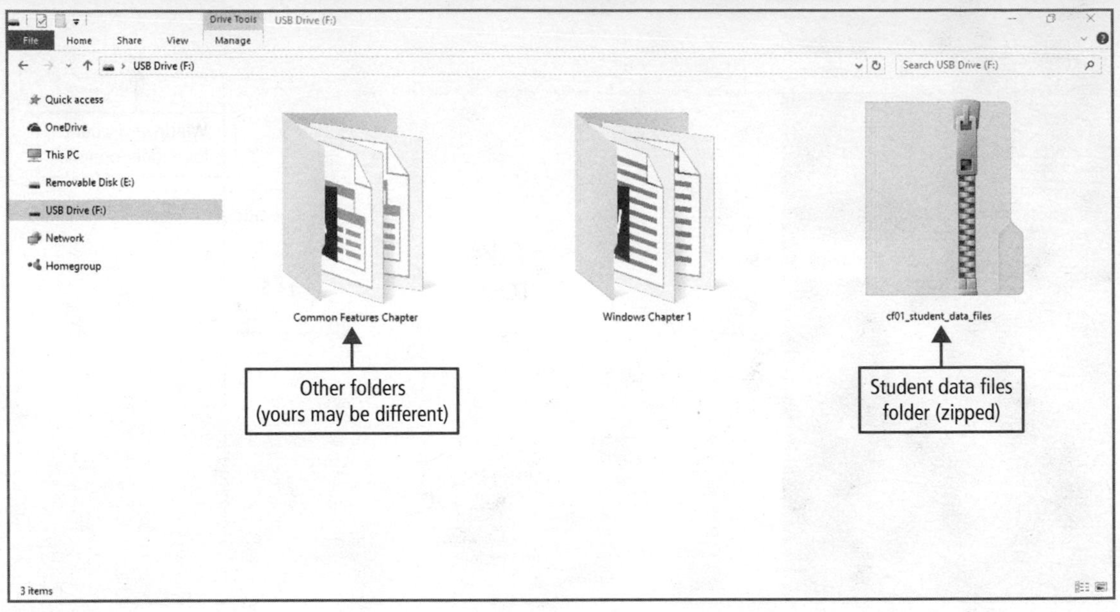

Figure 1 Word 2016, Windows 10, Microsoft Corporation

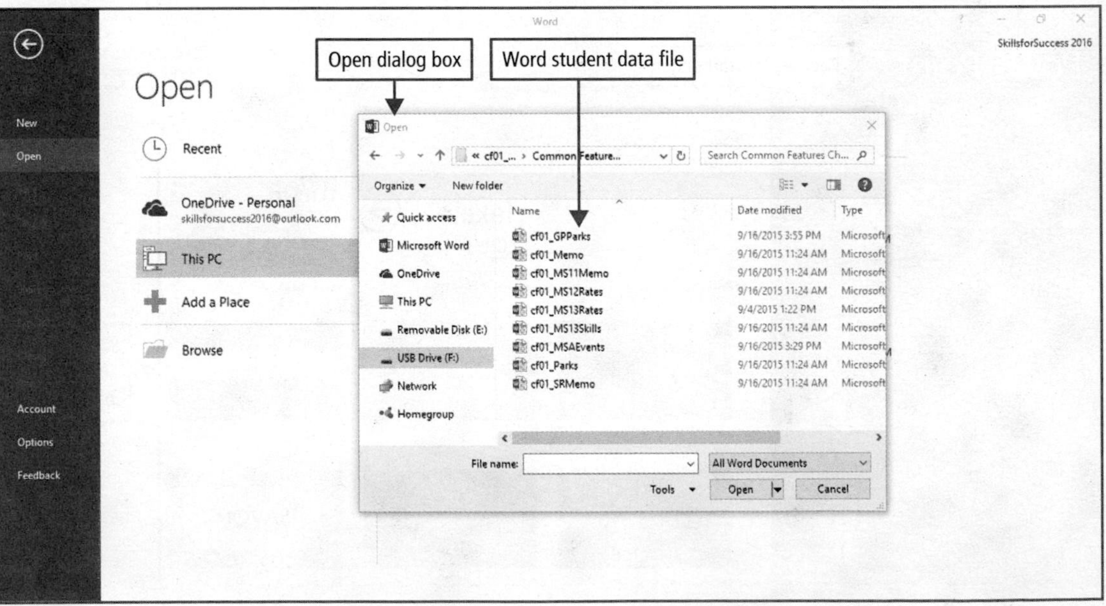

Figure 2 Word 2016, Windows 10, Microsoft Corporation

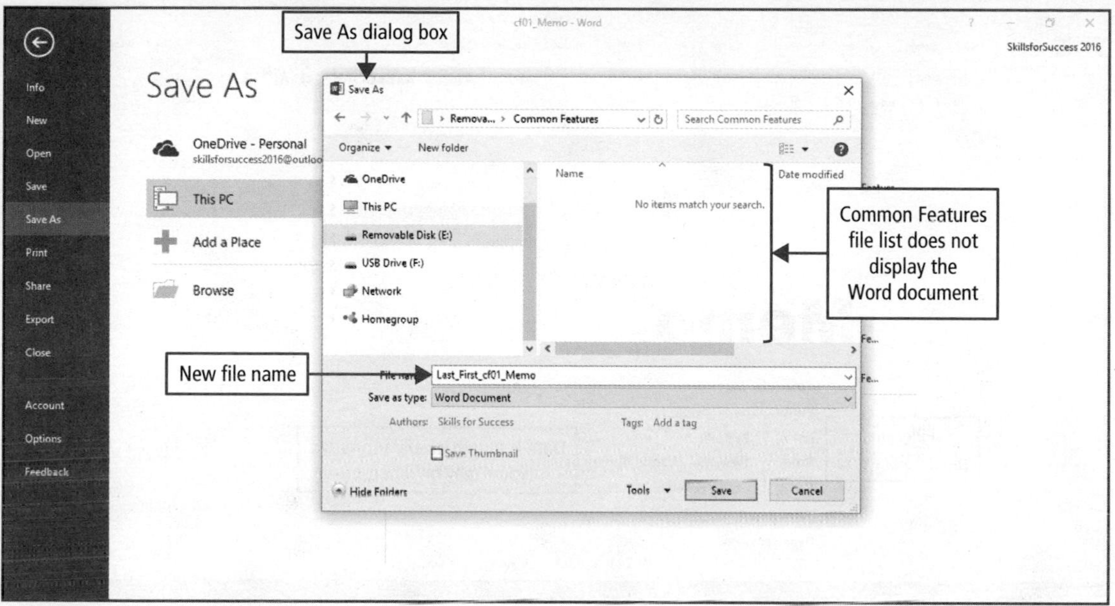

Word 2016, Windows 10, Microsoft Corporation

Figure 3

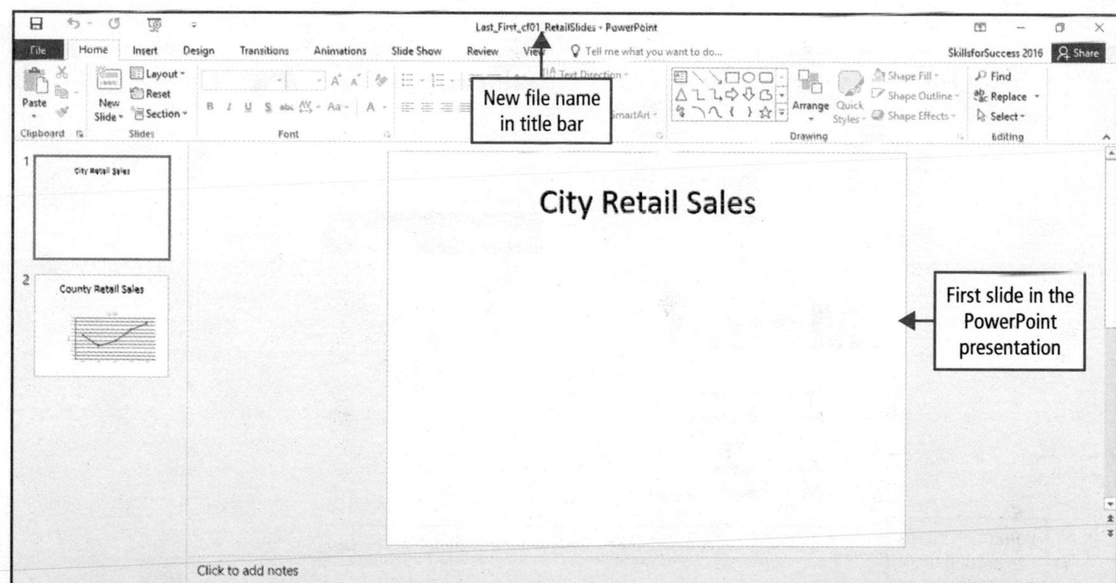

PowerPoint 2016, Windows 10, Microsoft Corporation

Figure 4

9. Press Enter twice. In the **File name** box, change the text to Last_First_cf01_Memo using your own name.

   In this book, you should substitute your first and last name whenever you see the text *Last_First* or *Your Name*.

10. Compare your screen with **Figure 3**, and then click the **Save** button.

    You can use Save As to create a copy of a file with a new name. The original student data file will remain unchanged.

    By default, the Save As dialog box displays only those files saved in the current application file format.

11. On the taskbar, click the **PowerPoint** button to return to the PowerPoint start screen. If necessary, start PowerPoint.

12. On the **PowerPoint 2016** start screen, click **Open Other Presentations** to display the Open page. If you already had a blank presentation open, click the File tab instead.

13. On the **Open** page, click **This PC**, and then click the **Browse** button. In the **Open** dialog box, navigate to the student files for this chapter, and then open **cf01_RetailSlides**. If necessary, enable the content.

14. On the **File tab**, click **Save As**, and then use the **Save As** page to navigate as needed to open your **Common Features Chapter** folder in the Save As dialog box.

    On most computers, your Word and Excel files will not display because the PowerPoint Save As dialog box is set to display only presentation files.

15. Type Last_First_cf01_RetailSlides and then click **Save**. Compare your screen with **Figure 4**.

- **You have completed Skill 2 of 10**

- New documents are stored in ***RAM***—the computer's temporary memory—until you save them to more permanent storage such as your hard drive, USB flash drive, or online storage.
- To ***edit*** is to insert, delete, or replace text in an Office document, workbook, or presentation.
- To edit text, position the ***insertion point***—a flashing vertical line that indicates where text will be inserted when you start typing—at the desired location or select the text you want to replace.

1. On the taskbar, click the **Word** button to return to the *Last_First_cf01_Memo* document.
2. Click the **Date** placeholder—*[Click to select date]*—and then click the **date arrow** to open the calendar. In the calendar, click the current date.

   Placeholders—are reserved, formatted spaces into which you enter your own text or objects. If no text is entered, the placeholder text will not print.
3. In the **Subject** placeholder, type Sales Tax Revenues Compare your screen with **Figure 1**.
4. Press Ctrl + End to place the insertion point in the **Type memo here** placeholder—*[Type memo here]*—and then type the following: As per your request, the Retail Sales slides will be ready by the end of today. I will send them to you so you can insert them into your presentation. Let me know if you have any questions. Compare your screen with **Figure 2**.

   Word determines whether the word will fit within the established margin. If it does not fit, Word moves the entire word to the beginning of the next line. This feature is called ***word wrap***.

■ Continue to the next page to complete the skill

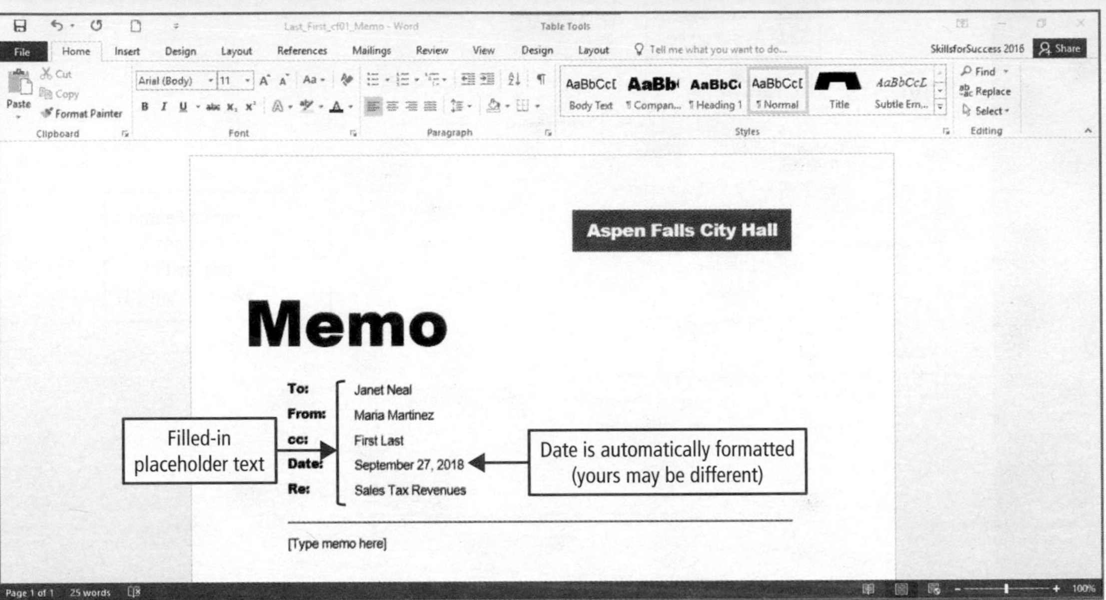

Figure 1

Word 2016, Windows 10, Microsoft Corporation

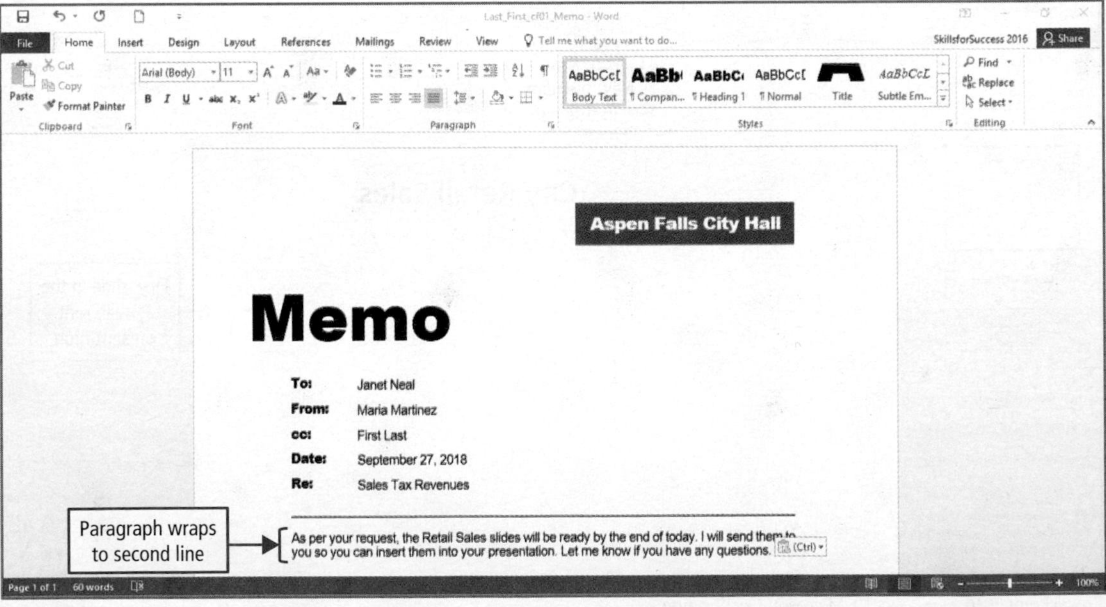

Figure 2

Word 2016, Windows 10, Microsoft Corporation

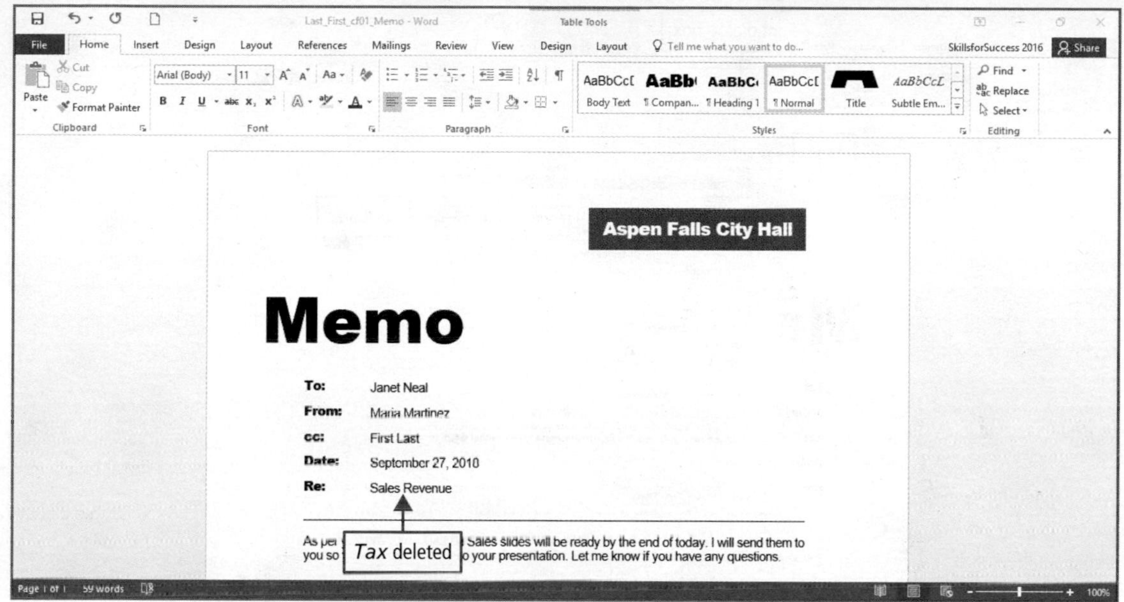

Word 2016, Windows 10, Microsoft Corporation

Figure 3

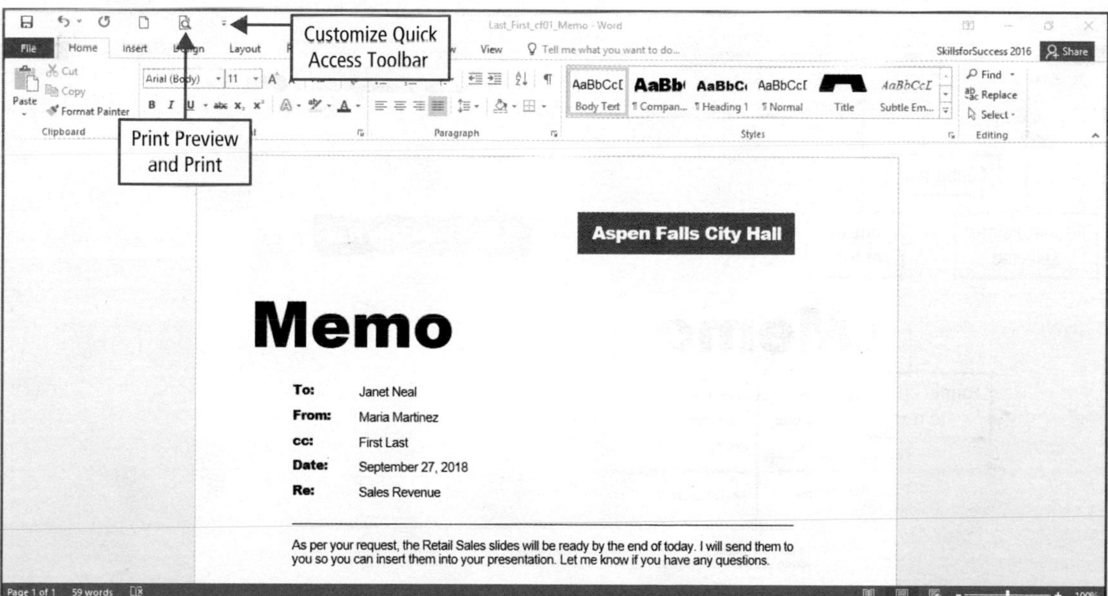

Word 2016, Windows 10, Microsoft Corporation

Figure 4

5. In the **Re:** line, click to the left of *Tax* to place the insertion point at the beginning of the word. Press Delete four times to delete the word *Tax* and the space following it.

   The Delete key deletes one letter at a time moving from left to right. The name on your keyboard may vary—for example, DEL, Del or Delete. Another option would be to ***double-click***— is to click the left mouse button two times quickly without moving the mouse—or to ***double-tap***—tap the screen in the same place two times quickly—the text to delete the word.

   After selecting text, the ***Mini toolbar***—a toolbar with common formatting commands—displays near the selection.

6. Click to the right of *Revenues*. Press Backspace one time to delete the letter *s*, and then compare your screen with **Figure 3**.

   The Backspace key deletes one letter at a time moving from right to left. The name on your keyboard may vary—for example, BACK, Backspace, or simply a left-facing arrow.

7. Press Ctrl + End. Type Thank you On the Quick Access Toolbar, and then click **Undo Typing**.

8. Click the **Customize Quick Access Toolbar** button, and then from the menu, click **Print Preview and Print** Compare your screen with **Figure 4**.

9. Click the **Print Preview and Print** button to view how the memo will look in printed form. Click the **Back** button to return to the document. Keep the file open for the next skill.

■ **You have completed Skill 3 of 10**

- To ***format*** is to change the appearance of the text—for example, changing the text color to red.
- The ***Format Painter*** copies formatting from selected text and applies that formatting to other text.

1. Select the text *Janet Neal*. On the **Home tab**, in the **Font group**, click the **Font Dialog Box Launcher** to open the Font dialog box. Compare your screen with **Figure 1**.
2. In the **Font dialog** box, under **Font**, scroll down until you can see the *Calibri* font. Click **Calibri**, and then under **Size**, click **12**. Click **OK**.
3. Verify that the text *Janet Neal* is selected. On the **Home tab**, in the **Clipboard group**, double-click the **Format Painter** button.
4. With the **Format Painter** selected, double-click the word **Maria** to apply the formatting from the text *Janet Neal*.
5. ***Drag***—press and hold the left mouse button while moving the mouse—to select the text **Martinez** to apply the formatting from the text *Janet Neal*. Use the techniques just practiced to apply the formatting to **First** and **Last** name, the **date**, and **Sales Revenue**. Compare your screen with **Figure 2**.

   The Calibri font and font size of 12 are copied from the text *Janet Neal* and applied to the other text.

■ **Continue to the next page to complete the skill**

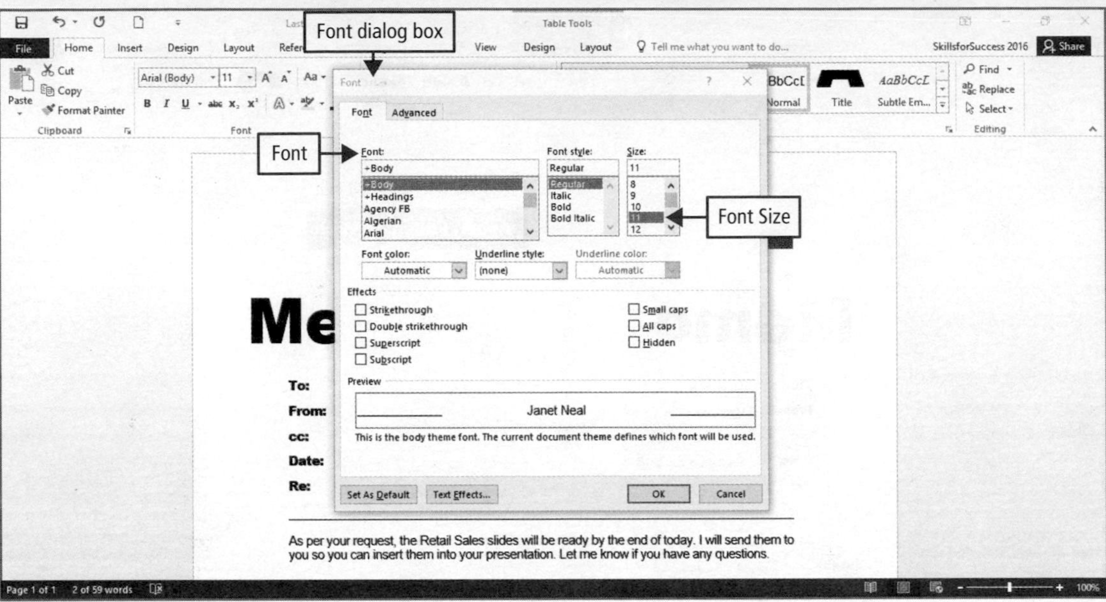

Figure 1 Word 2016, Windows 10, Microsoft Corporation

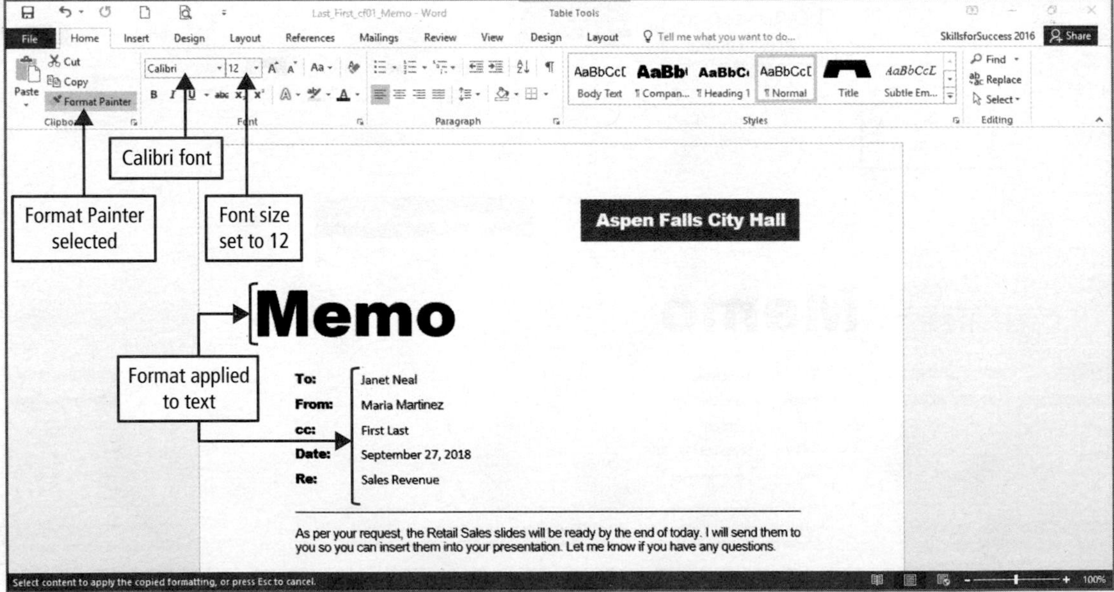

Figure 2 Word 2016, Windows 10, Microsoft Corporation

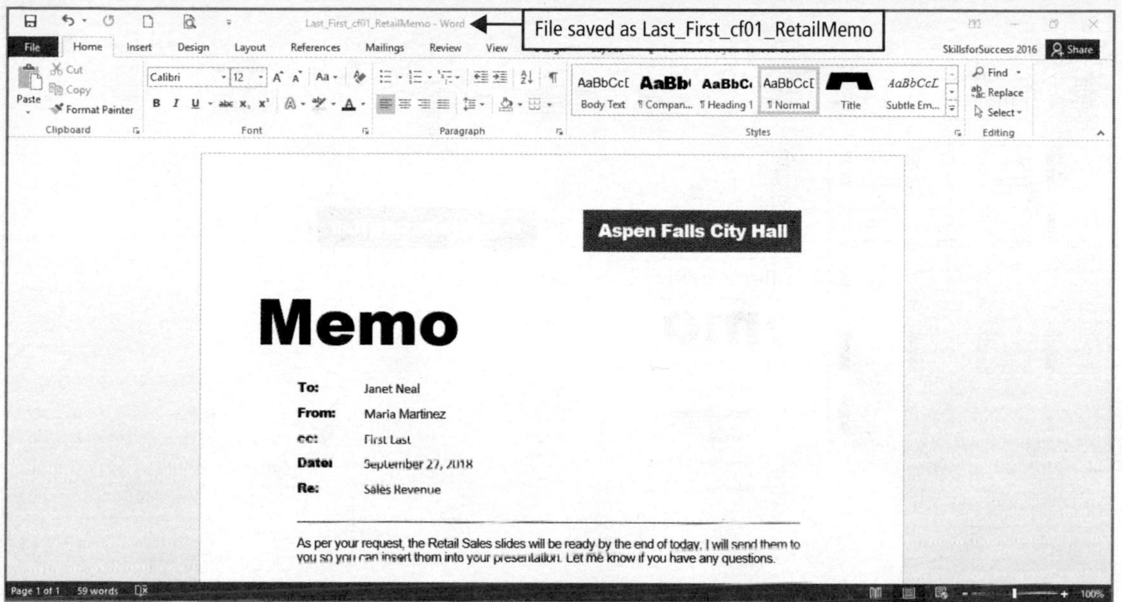

Word 2016, Windows 10, Microsoft Corporation

Figure 3

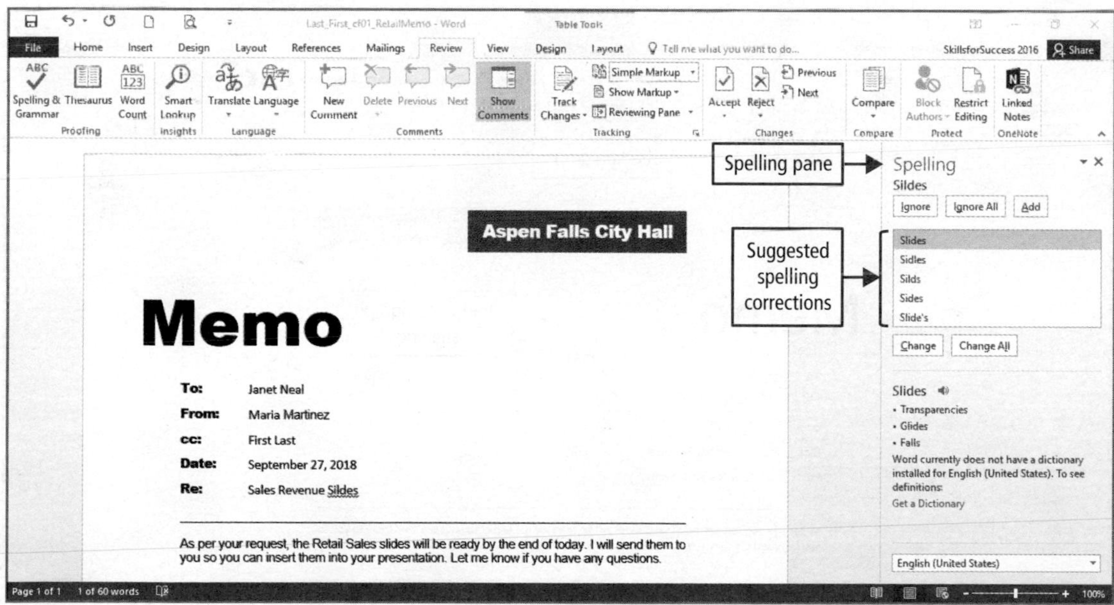

Word 2016, Windows 10, Microsoft Corporation

Figure 4

6. Click the **Format Painter** button to deselect it.

   When you single-click the format painter, you can apply the formatting to one other text selection. When you double-click the format painter, it will remain active until you click it again to deselect it.

7. In the **cc:** line, replace the text **First Last** with your first and last names. Click the **File tab**, and then click **Save As**.
8. Click **Browse** to navigate to your **Common Features Chapter** folder, and then in the **Save As** dialog box, change the **File name** to Last_First_cf01_RetailMemo
9. Click **Save**, and then compare your screen to **Figure 3**.
10. In the **Re:** line, click to the right of *Revenue* to place the insertion point at the end of the word. Type Sildes
11. Click the **Review tab**. In the **Proofing group**, click the **Spelling & Grammar** button. Compare your screen with **Figure 4**.

    The Spelling pane provides suggested spelling corrections.

12. In the **Spelling pane**, if necessary, click the first option **Slides**, and then click **Change** to correct the spelling of the word **Slides**. Read the dialog box message, and then click **OK**.

    After the document is saved, the name of the file displays on the title bar at the top of the window.

13. Leave the memo open for the next skill.

■ **You have completed Skill 4 of 10**

- When formatting an Office document, it is a good idea to pick a ***theme***—a prebuilt set of unified formatting choices including colors and fonts.

1. Click the **Design tab**. In the **Document Formatting group**, click the **Themes** button, and then compare your screen with **Figure 1**.

   Each theme displays as a thumbnail in a ***gallery***—a visual display of selections from which you can choose.

2. In the **Themes** gallery, point to—but do not click—each thumbnail to preview its formatting with ***Live Preview***—a feature that displays what the results of a formatting change will be if you select it.

3. In the **Themes** gallery, click the third theme in the second row—**Retrospect**.

   A ***font*** is a set of characters with the same design and shape. Each theme has two font categories—one for headings and one for body text.

4. Click anywhere in the text *Aspen Falls City Hall* to make it the active paragraph. With the insertion point in the paragraph, click the **Home tab**.

5. In the **Paragraph group**, click the **Shading arrow**. In the first row of the gallery under **Theme Colors**, click the sixth choice—**Orange, Accent 2**. Compare your screen with **Figure 2**.

   In all themes, the Accent 2 color is the sixth choice in the color gallery, but the color varies depending on the theme. Here, the Retrospect theme Accent 2 color is a shade of orange.

■ Continue to the next page to complete the skill

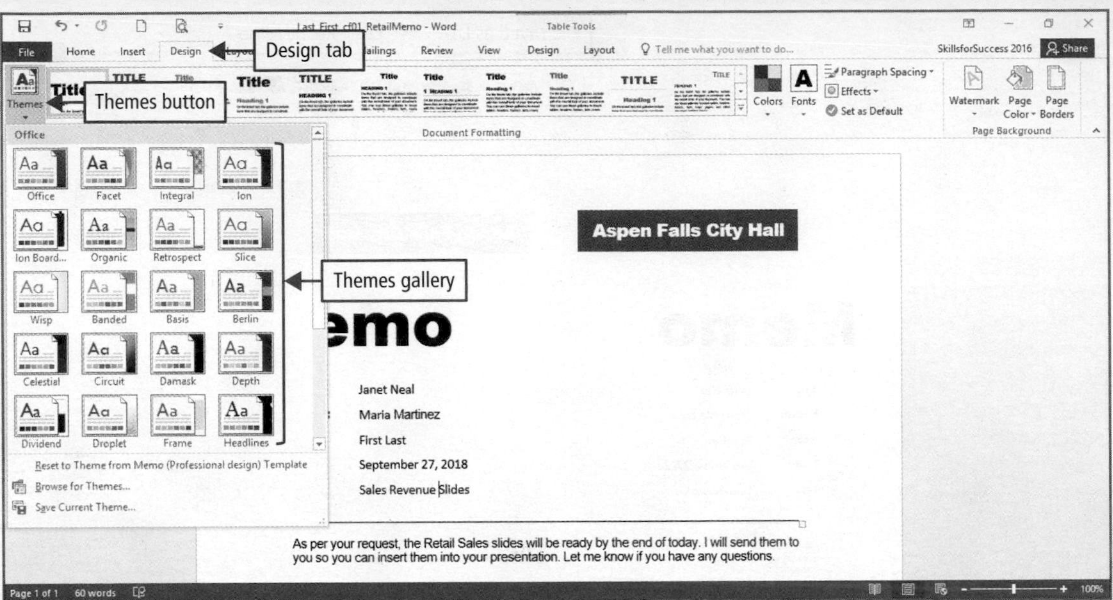

Figure 1

Word 2016, Windows 10, Microsoft Corporation

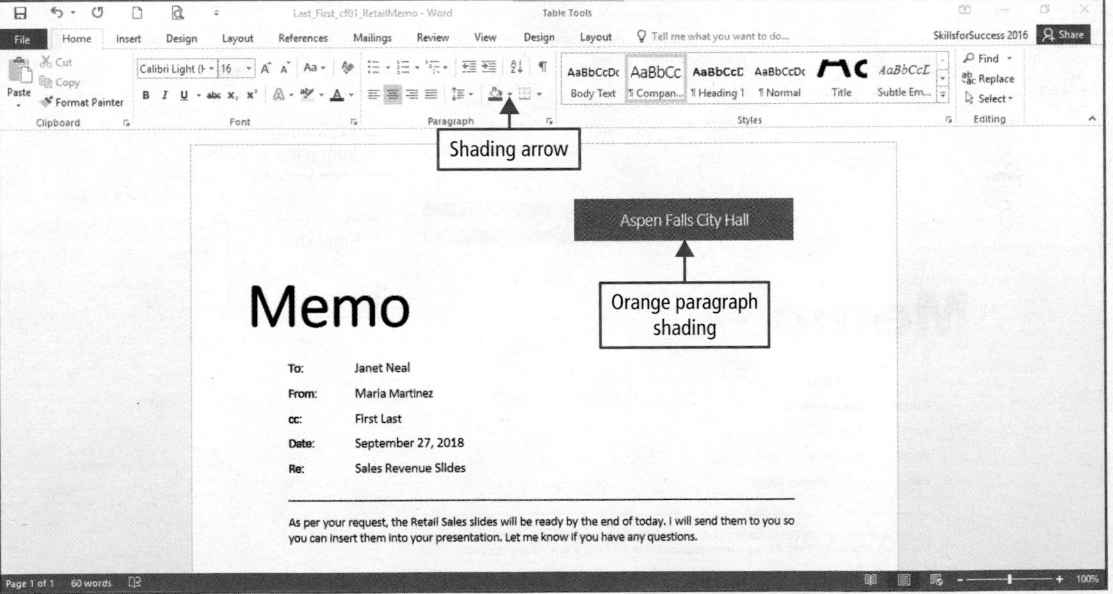

Figure 2

Word 2016, Windows 10, Microsoft Corporation

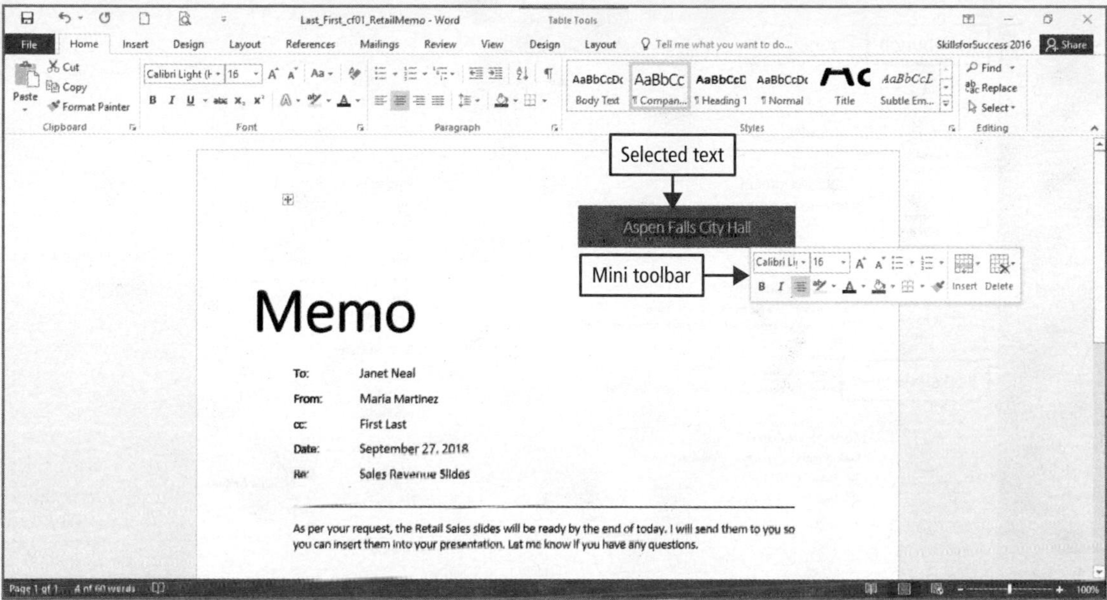

Word 2016, Windows 10, Microsoft Corporation

Figure 3

Word 2016, Windows 10, Microsoft Corporation

Figure 4

6. In the upper right corner, select the text *Aspen Falls City Hall*, and then compare your screen with **Figure 3**. To select by dragging with a touch display, tap in the text and then drag the selection handle.

   If the Mini toolbar does not display, you can right-click or tap the selected text.

7. On the Mini toolbar, click the **Font Size arrow** [11], and then from the list, click **20** to increase the size of the selected text. On the Mini toolbar, click the **Bold** button [B].

8. On the Mini toolbar, click the **Font Color arrow** [A], and then under **Theme colors**, click the first color in the first row—**White, Background 1**. Alternatively, on the Home tab, in the Font group, click the Font Color arrow.

9. In the paragraph that begins *As per your*, drag to select the text *Retail Sales*. From the Mini toolbar, click the **Italic** button [I].

   Alternatively, you can use a ***keyboard shortcut***—a combination of keys that performs a command. To apply italic, you could press [Ctrl] + [I].

10. Click a blank area of the document, and then compare your screen with **Figure 4**. Carefully check the memo for spelling errors. If spelling errors are found, use the techniques previously practiced to correct them.

11. **Save** [save icon] the file.

■ **You have completed Skill 5 of 10**

SKILL 6: Use Backstage View

- ***Backstage view*** is a collection of options on the File tab used to open, save, print, and perform other file management tasks. In Backstage view, you can return to the open document by clicking the Back button.

1. Click the **File tab**, and then compare your screen with **Figure 1**.
2. On the **File tab**, click **Print** to display the Print page. In the lower right corner of the **Print** page, click the **Zoom In** button until the zoom level displays **100%**, and then compare your screen with **Figure 2**.

   The Printer list displays available printers for your computer along with their status. For example, a printer may be offline because it is not turned on. The ***default printer*** is automatically selected when you do not choose a different printer—indicated by a check mark.

   In a school lab or office, it is a good idea to check the list of available printers and verify that the correct printer is selected. It is also important that you know where the printer is located so that you can retrieve your printout.

   The size of the print preview depends on the size of your monitor. When previewed on smaller monitors, some documents may not display accurately. If this happens, you can zoom in to see a more accurate view.
3. If you are printing your work for this project, note the location of the selected printer, click the **Print** button, and then retrieve your printouts from the printer.

■ **Continue to the next page to complete the skill**

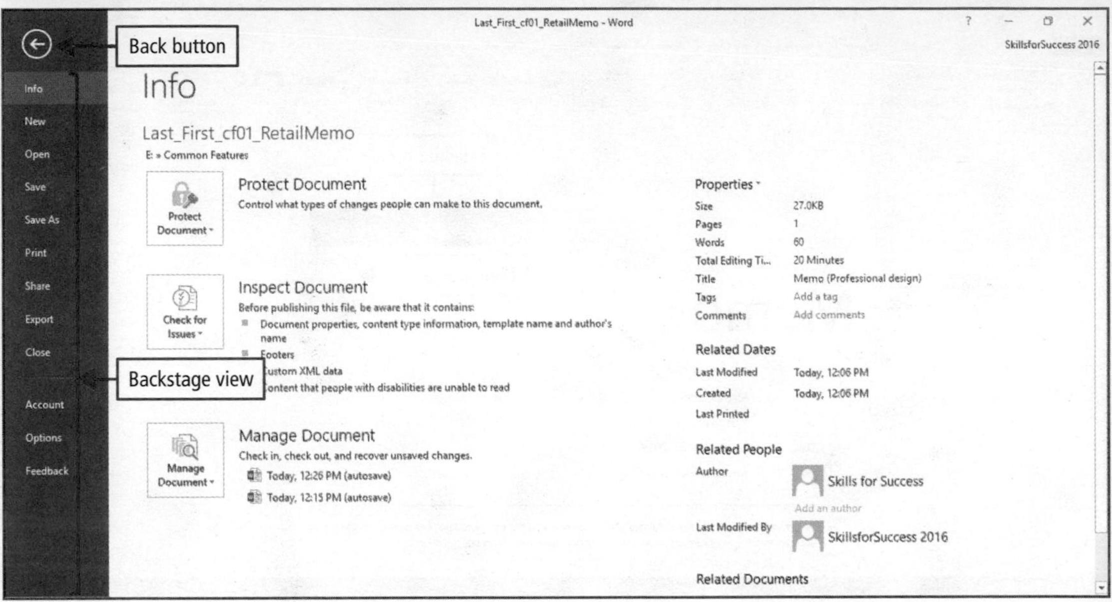

Figure 1 Word 2016, Windows 10, Microsoft Corporation

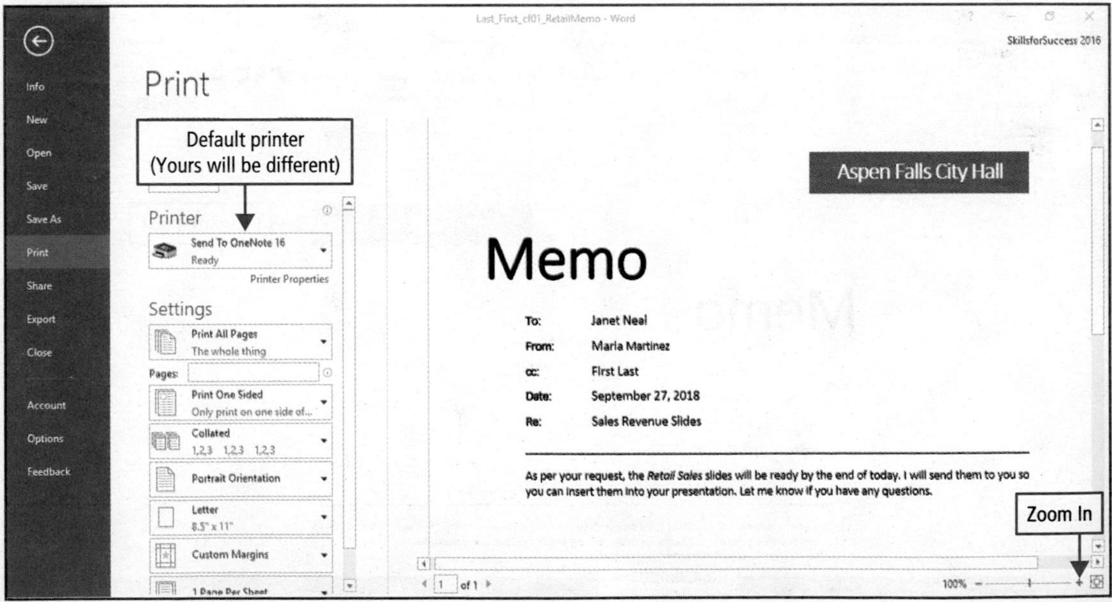

Figure 2 Word 2016, Windows 10, Microsoft Corporation

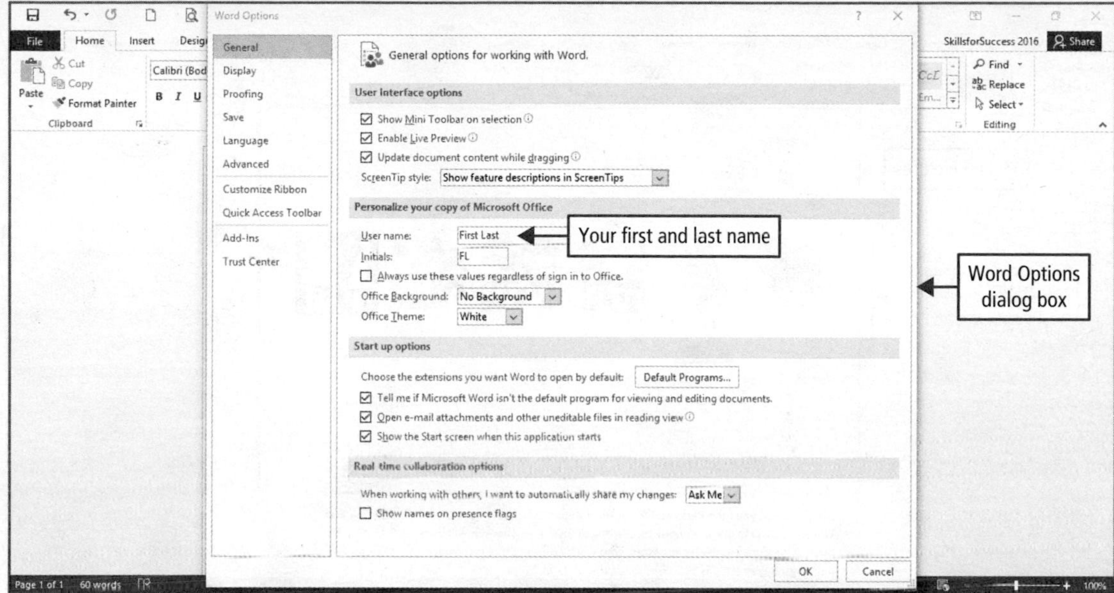

Word 2016, Windows 10, Microsoft Corporation

Figure 3

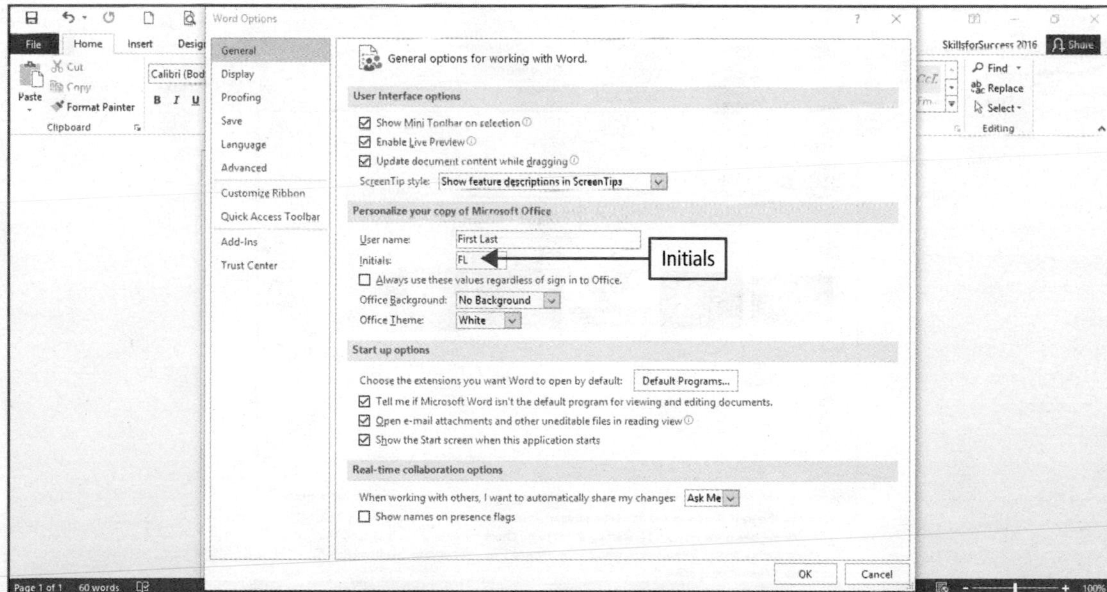

Word 2016, Windows 10, Microsoft Corporation

Figure 4

4. If necessary, click the **File tab**, and then click **Options**.
5. Under **Personalize your copy of Microsoft Office**, in the **User name** text box, replace the existing text with your First and Last name. Compare your screen with **Figure 3**.
6. Press Tab to select the text in the **Initials** text box, and then type your initials. Compare your screen to **Figure 4**, and then click **OK**.
7. Click the **Layout tab**. In the **Page Setup group**, click the **Margins** button.
8. Click the second option in the list—**Moderate**—to adjust the margins of the document.

   When changing the margins of the document, you should verify that the document will still print properly.

9. Click the **File tab**, and then click **Print**.
10. Under the **Settings** options, click the **Portrait Orientation** button, and then click **Landscape Orientation**.

    In Portrait Orientation, the page is taller than it is wide. In Landscape Orientation, the page is wider than it is tall.

11. Click the **Back** button, and then click **Save**. **Close** the file.

■ **You have completed Skill 6 of 10**

 WATCH SKILL 1.7

- You can insert images into documents from files or online resources.
- Images can be resized or rotated or the color of the picture can be changed. You can also add frames and artistic effects to images.

1. Start **Word 2016**, and then open the student data file **cf01_Parks**. On the **File tab**, click **Save As**. Click **Browse**, navigate to the folder for this chapter, and then save the file as Last_First_cf01_Parks
2. If the Security Warning message displays, enable the content.
3. If necessary, click the upper left portion of the document, to place the insertion point in the blank area above the *Park Events* title.
4. Click the **Insert tab**. In the **Illustrations group**, click the **Online Pictures** button.
5. In the **Insert Pictures** dialog box, in the **Bing Image Search** text box, type Forest and then press Enter. Compare your screen with **Figure 1**.
6. Scroll down to view the available images. Select an image of a forest. Compare your screen with **Figure 2**, and then click **Insert**. If you are unable to locate the image shown in the figure, choose a similar picture.
7. If necessary, scroll down so you can view the entire image. With the **Resize** pointer, drag the lower right corner of the image upward and to the left until the right edge of the image aligns with the space between the words *Park* and *Events* in the document title.

■ **Continue to the next page to complete the skill**

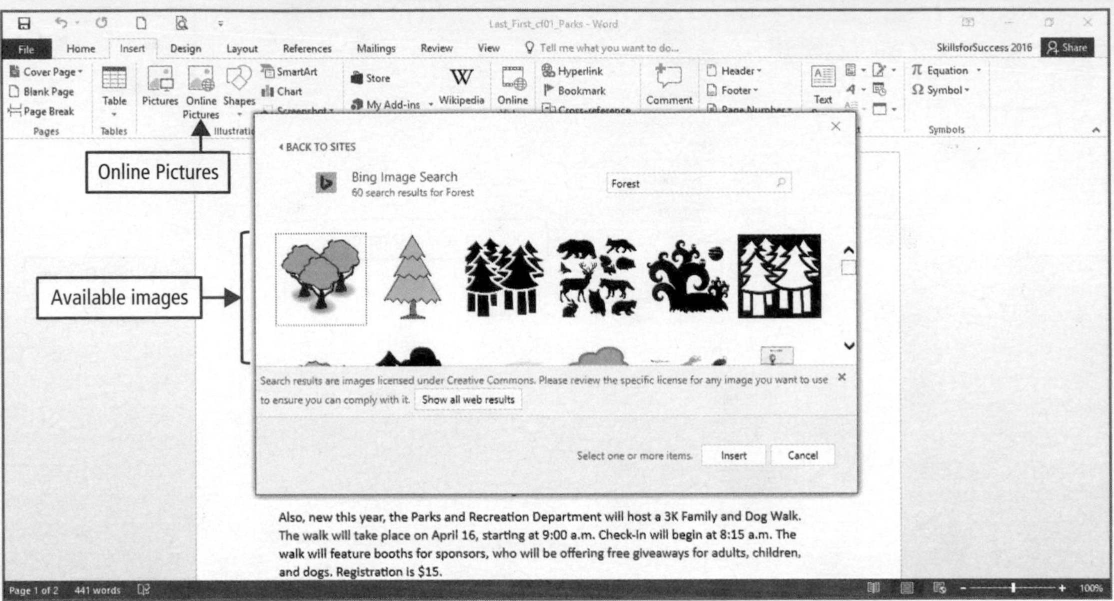

Figure 1 Word 2016, Windows 10, Microsoft Corporation

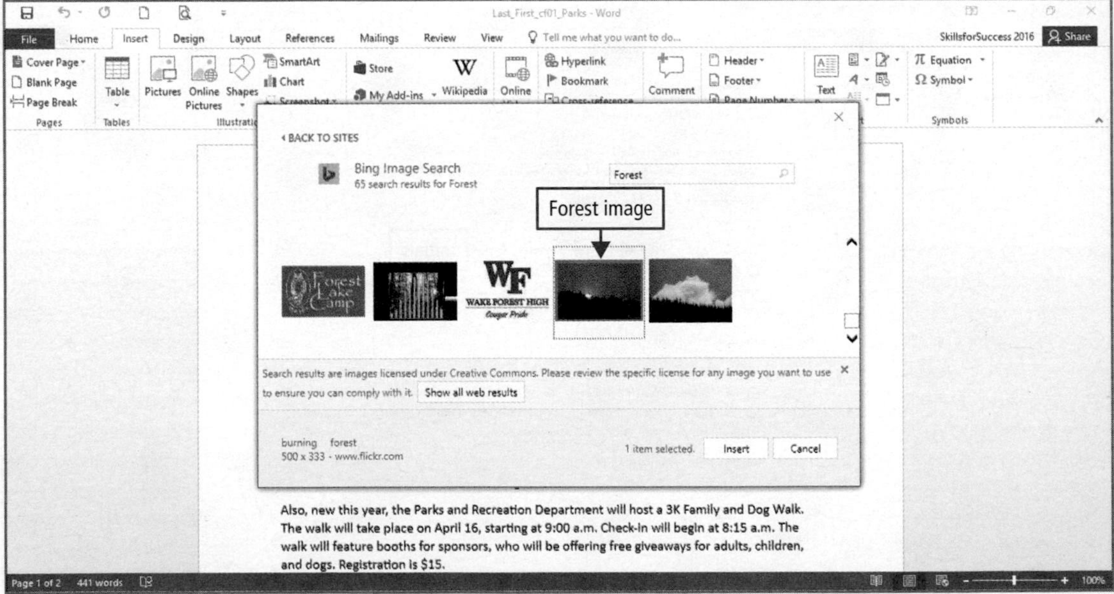

Figure 2 Word 2016, Windows 10, Microsoft Corporation

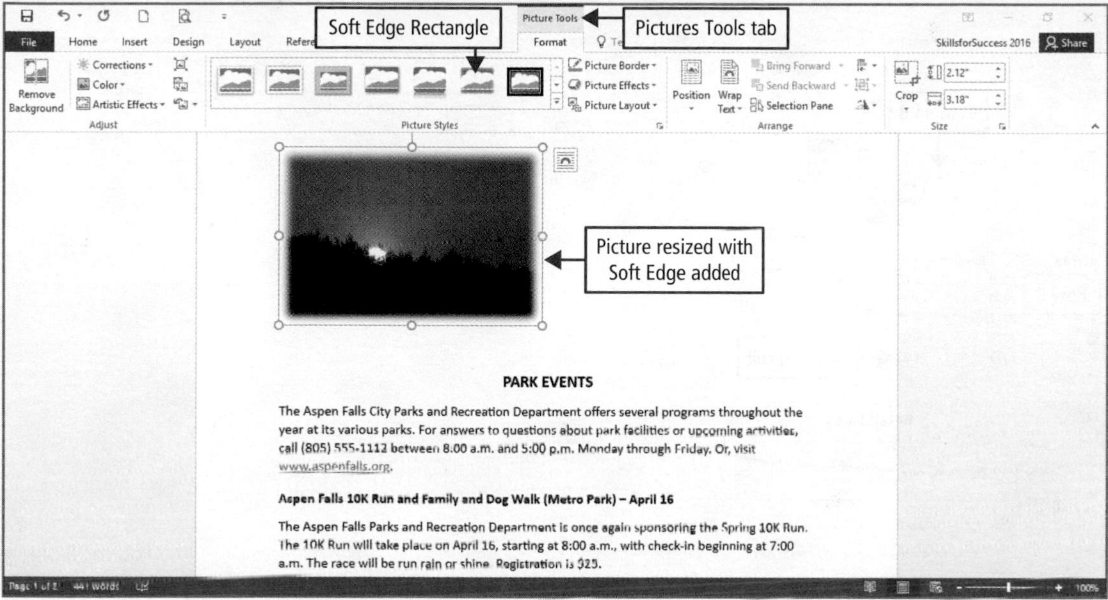

Lassedesignen/Fotolia; Word 2016, Windows 10, Microsoft Corporation

Figure 3

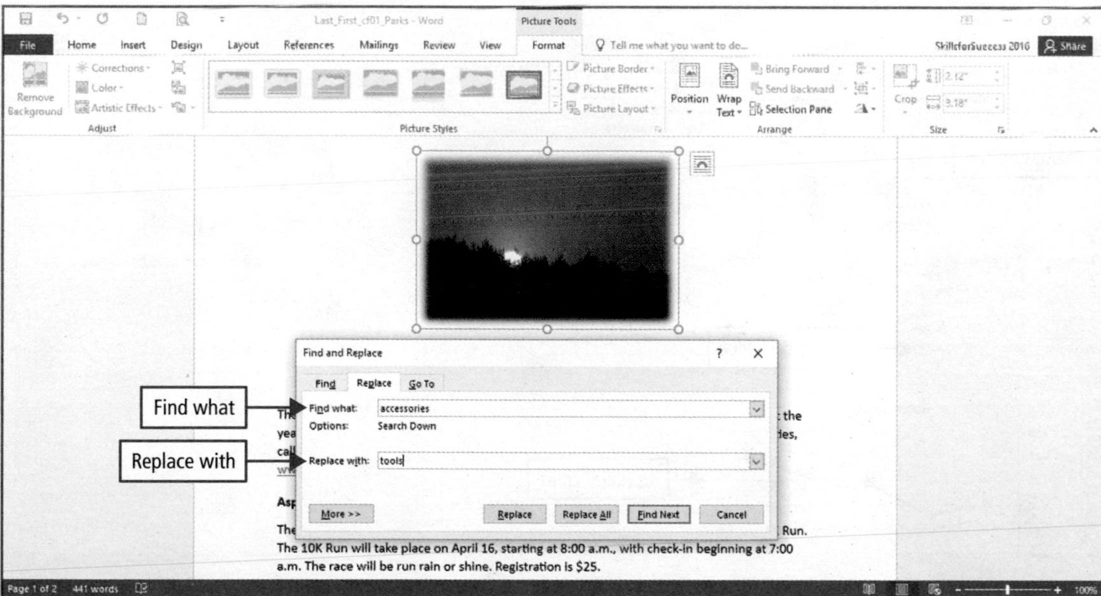

Lassedesignen/Fotolia; Word 2016, Windows 10, Microsoft Corporation

Figure 4

8. On the **Picture Tools Format tab**, in the **Picture Styles group**, click the sixth option—**Soft Edge Rectangle**. Compare your screen with **Figure 3**.

9. With the image still selected, press Ctrl + E to center the image on the page.

   Keyboard shortcuts can be used to edit text, change the position of images on a page, or navigate throughout the document.

10. Next to the **Format tab**, click **Tell me what you want to do...**, and then type Find and Replace Press Enter.

11. In the **Find and Replace dialog box**, in the **Find what** text box, type accessories In the **Replace with** text box, type tools and then compare your screen with **Figure 4**.

12. In the **Find and Replace dialog box**, click **Replace All**.

13. Read the message, and then click **Yes**. Read the next message, and then click **OK**.

14. In the **Find and Replace dialog box**, click **Close**.

15. Click **Save**, and then **Close** the file.

- **You have completed Skill 7 of 10**

- To keep formatting consistent across all Office files, the same themes are available in Word, Excel, PowerPoint, and Access.
- To format text in Excel, you select the cell that holds the text, and then click the desired formatting command.

1. On the taskbar, click the **Excel** button. On the **Start** screen, click **Open Other Workbooks**. Click **Browse** to navigate to the student data files, and then double-click **cf01_RetailChart**.
2. Click the **File tab**, and then click **Save As**. Navigate to the folder for this chapter, and then save the file as Last_First_cf01_RetailChart
3. Click cell **B9**—the intersection of column B and row 9—to select the cell. Compare your screen with **Figure 1**.

   A selected cell is indicated by a thick, dark-green border.
4. With cell **B9** selected, type 4.37 and then press Enter to update the chart.

   The chart is based on the data in columns A and B. When the data is changed, the chart changes to reflect the new values.
5. On the **Page Layout tab**, in the **Themes group**, click the **Themes** button, and then click the **Retrospect** thumbnail. Compare your screen with **Figure 2**.

   The Retrospect theme applies the same colors, fonts, and effects as the Retrospect theme of other Office applications. Here, the font was changed to Calibri.

■ **Continue to the next page to complete the skill**

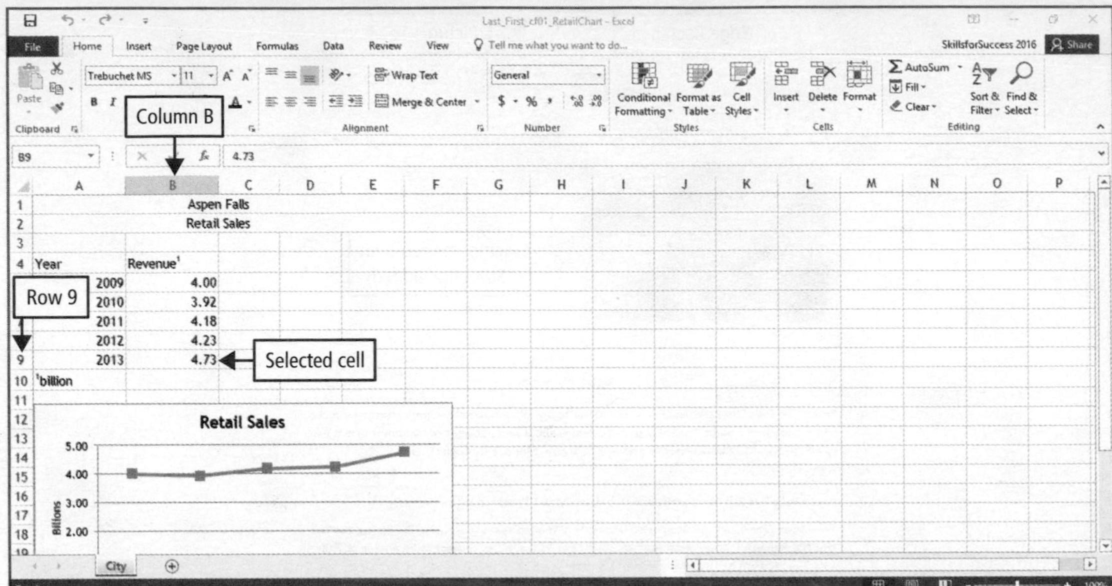

Figure 1 Excel 2016, Windows 10, Microsoft Corporation

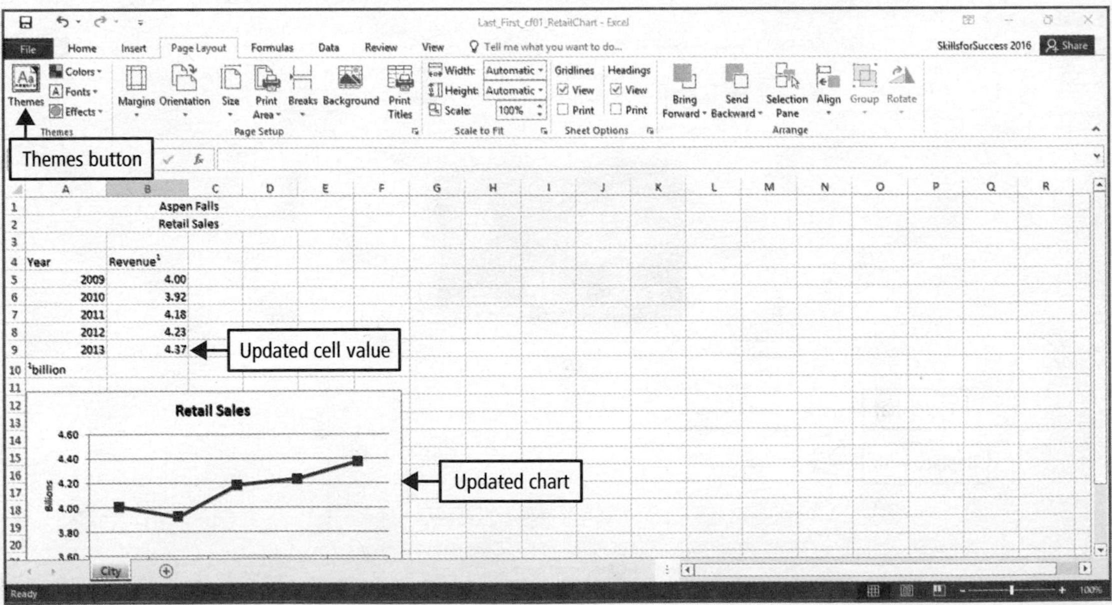

Figure 2 Excel 2016, Windows 10, Microsoft Corporation

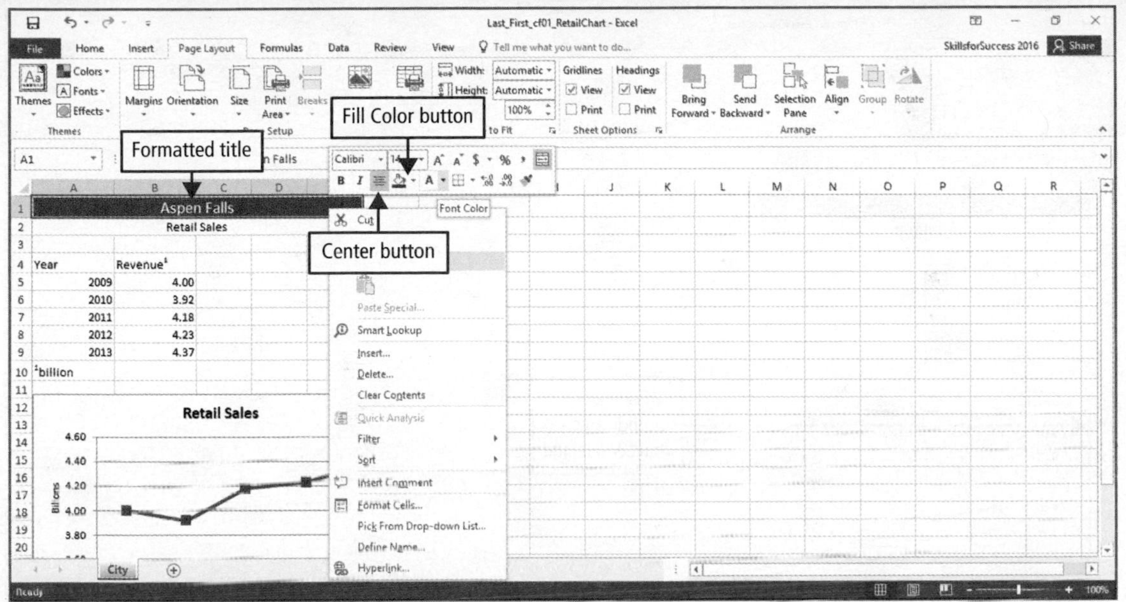

Excel 2016, Windows 10, Microsoft Corporation

Figure 3

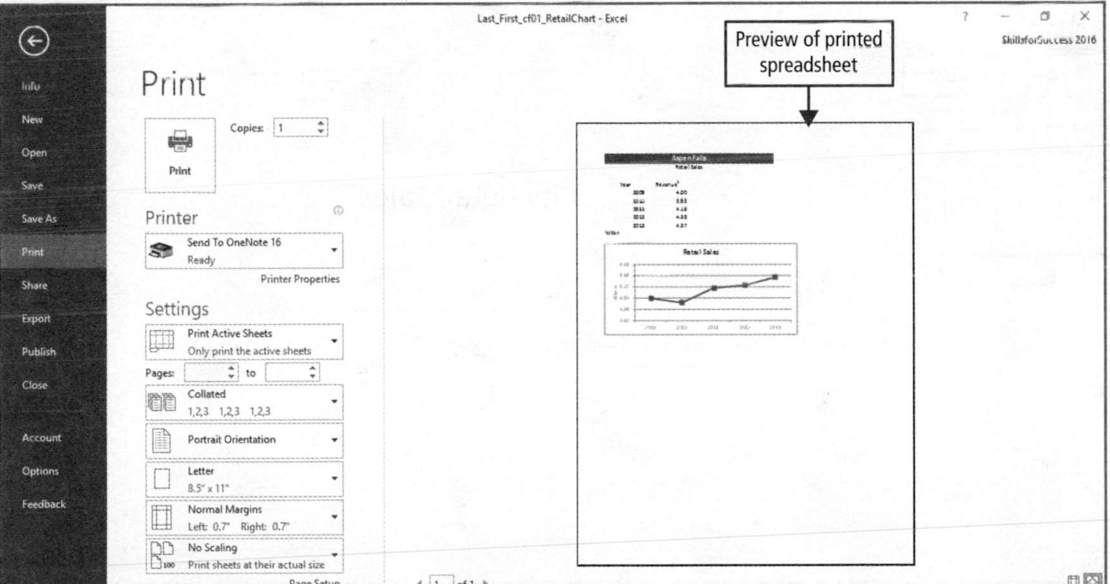

Excel 2016, Windows 10, Microsoft Corporation

Figure 4

6. Right-click cell **A1** containing the text *Aspen Falls* to display the Mini toolbar. Click the **Font Size arrow**, and then click **14** to increase the font size. Click the **Center** button to center the title.
7. With cell **A1** still selected, on the Mini toolbar, click the **Fill Color arrow**, and then under **Theme Colors**, click the sixth choice—**Orange, Accent 2**.
8. On the Mini toolbar, click the **Font Color arrow**, and then under **Theme Colors**, click the first choice—**White, Background 1**. Compare your screen with **Figure 3**.
9. Click cell **A4**. On the **Home tab**, in the **Alignment group**, click the **Center** button to center the text. In the **Clipboard group**, click the **Format Painter** button one time, click cell **B4** to apply the center format, and then turn off the Format Painter.
10. Click cell **A10**, and then in the **Font group**, change the **Font Size** to **9**.
11. On the **File tab**, click **Print**, and then compare your screen with **Figure 4**.

    The Excel Print page is used in the same manner as the Word Print page. Here, you can preview the document, select your printer, and verify that the worksheet will print on a single page. By default, the gridlines do not print.
12. If you are printing your work for this project, print the worksheet. Otherwise, click the **Back** button to return to Normal view.
13. Click **Save**.

■ **You have completed Skill 8 of 10**

SKILL 9: Copy and Paste Objects and Format Slides

- In Office, the ***copy*** command places a copy of the selected text or object in the ***Office Clipboard***—a temporary storage area that holds text or an object that has been cut or copied.
- The ***paste*** command inserts a copy of the text or object from the Office Clipboard.

1. In the Excel window, click the border of the chart to select the chart. Compare your screen with **Figure 1**.

   In Office, certain graphics such as charts and SmartArt display a thick border when they are selected.

2. Right-click a blank area of the chart, and then click the **Copy** button to place a copy of the chart into the Office Clipboard.
3. On the taskbar, click the **PowerPoint** button to return to the **Last_First_cf01_RetailSlides** presentation.
4. With **Slide 1** as the active slide, on the **Home tab**, in the **Clipboard group**, click the **Paste** button to insert the copied Excel chart. If you accidentally clicked the Paste arrow to display the Paste Options, click the Paste button that is above it. Click a blank area of the slide, and then compare your screen with **Figure 2**.
5. Click the **Design tab**, and then in the **Themes group**, click the **More** button. Point to the thumbnails to preview their formatting, and then under Office, click the seventh choice—**Retrospect**.

   In PowerPoint, themes are sets of colors, fonts, and effects optimized for viewing in a large room with the presentation projected onto a screen in front of the audience.

■ **Continue to the next page to complete the skill**

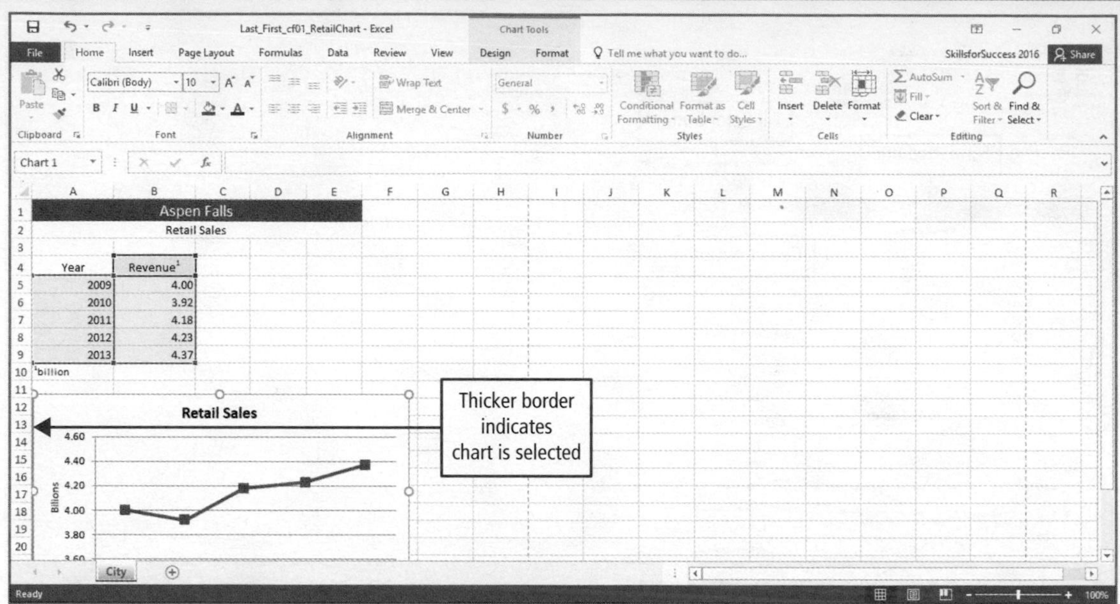

Figure 1

Excel 2016, Windows 10, Microsoft Corporation

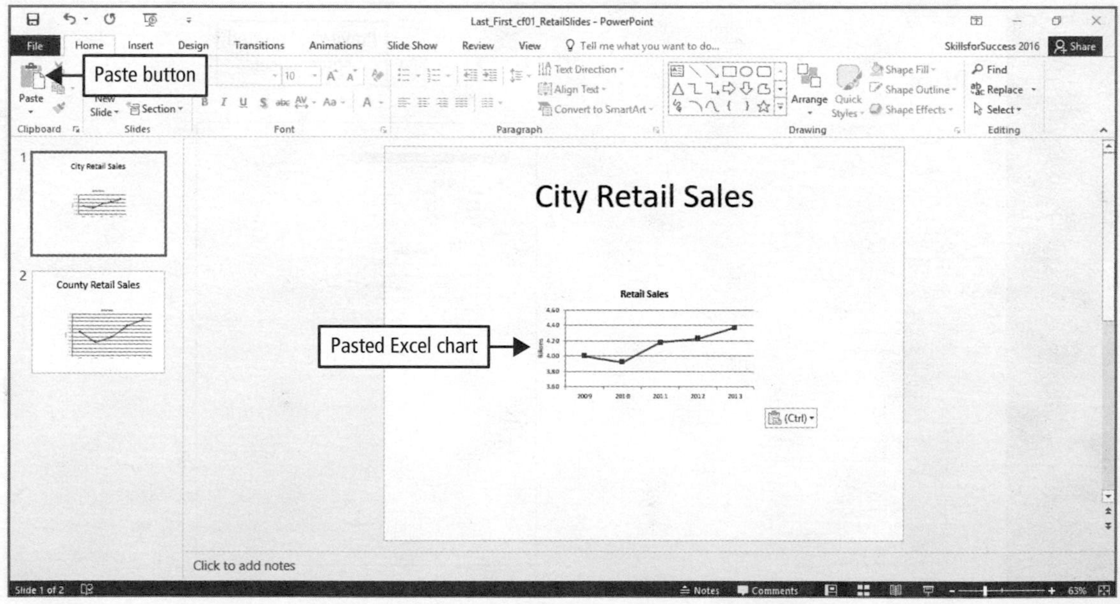

Figure 2

PowerPoint 2016, Windows 10, Microsoft Corporation

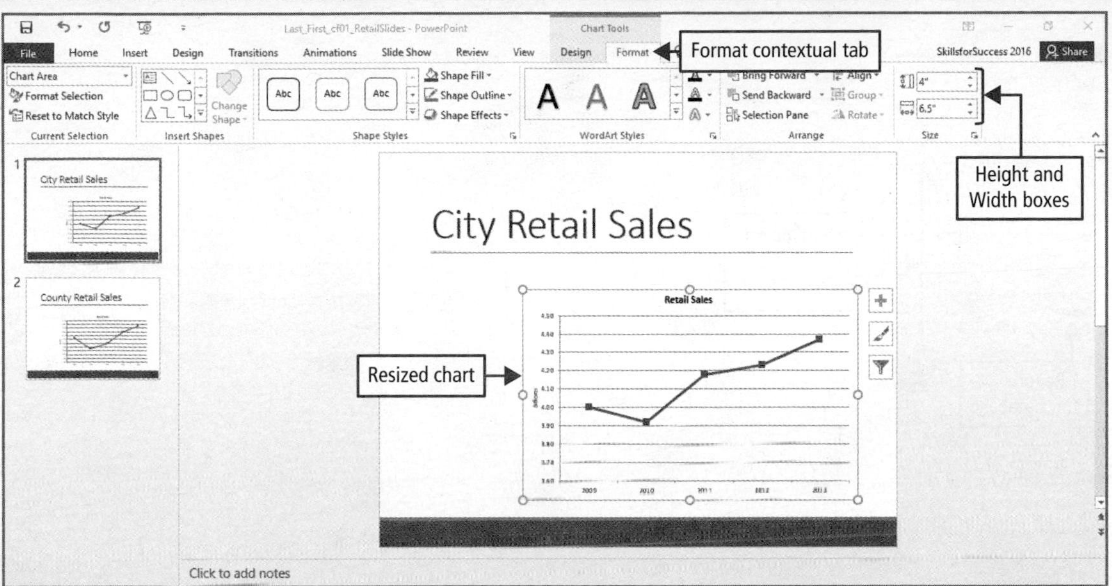

PowerPoint 2016, Windows 10, Microsoft Corporation

Figure 3

PowerPoint 2016, Windows 10, Microsoft Corporation

Figure 4

6. Drag to select the slide title text *City Retail Sales*. On the **Home tab**, in the **Font group**, click the **Font Size arrow**, and then click **60**. Alternatively, right-click the selected text, and then use the Mini toolbar to change the font size.
7. Click any area in the chart, and then click the border of the chart so that only the chart is selected.
8. Click the **Chart Tools Format tab**, and then in the **Size group**, click the **Shape Height arrow** until the value is **4"**. Repeat this technique to change the **Width** value to **6.5"**, and then compare your screen with **Figure 3**.

   The Format tab is a ***contextual tab***—a tab that displays on the ribbon only when a related object such as a graphic or chart is selected.

9. On the **File tab**, click **Print**. On the **Print** page, under **Settings**, click the **Full Page Slides** button. In the gallery, under **Handouts**, click **2 Slides**. Compare your screen with **Figure 4**.
10. If you are printing your work, click **Print** to print the handout. Otherwise, click **Save** to return to Normal view. **Close** PowerPoint.
11. On the taskbar, click the **Excel** button, and then **Close** Excel. If a message displays asking you to save changes, click Save.

■ **You have completed Skill 9 of 10**

- Access ***reports*** are database objects that present tables or query results in a way that is optimized for onscreen viewing or printing.

1. Start **Access 2016**, and then on the Start screen, click **Open Other Files**. On the **Open** page, click **Browse**.
2. In the **Open** dialog box, navigate to the student data files for this chapter. In the **Open** dialog box, select **cf01_RetailData**, and then click the **Open** button. If necessary, enable the content.
3. Take a few moments to familiarize yourself with the Access objects in the Navigation Pane as shown in **Figure 1**.

   Database files contain several different types of objects such as tables, queries, forms, and reports. Each object has a special purpose summarized in the table in **Figure 2**.

4. On the **File tab**, click **Save As**. With **Save Database As** selected, click the **Save As** button.
5. In the **Save As** dialog box, navigate to your **Common Features Chapter** folder. In the **File name** box, name the file Last_First_cf01_RetailData and then click **Save**. If a security message displays, click the Enable Content button.

   Malicious persons sometimes place objects in database files that could harm your computer. For this reason, the security message may display when you open a database that you did not create. You should click the Enable Content button only when you know the file is from a trusted source.

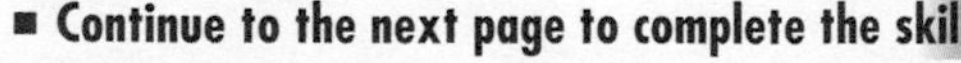
■ Continue to the next page to complete the skill

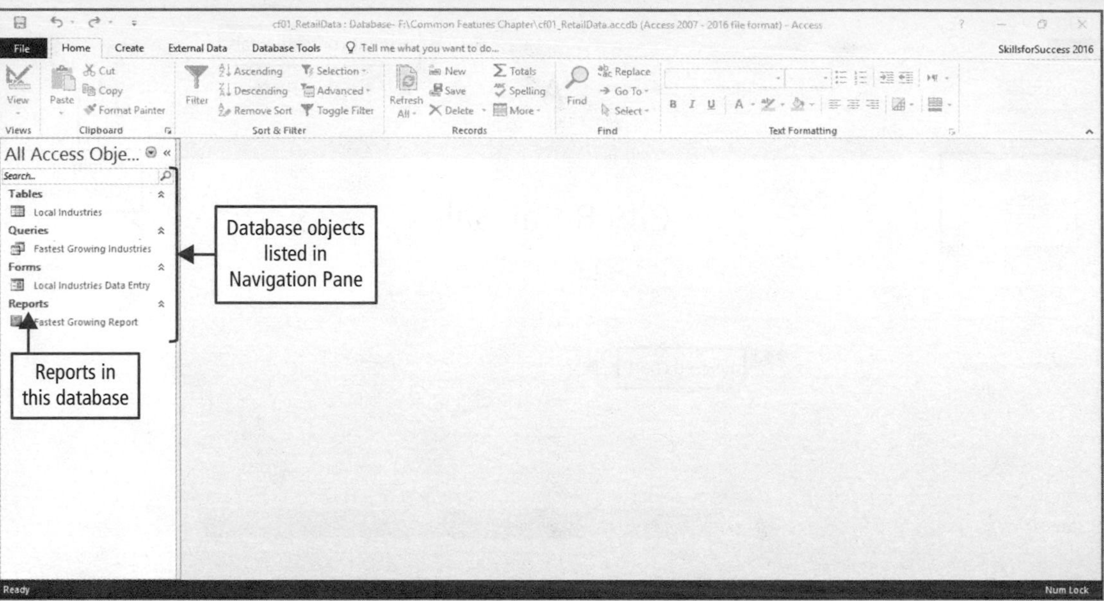

Figure 1

Access 2016, Windows 10, Microsoft Corporation

Common Database Objects

Object	Description
Table	Stores the database data so that records are in rows and fields are in columns.
Query	Displays a subset of data in response to a question.
Form	Used to find, update, and add table records.
Report	Presents tables or query results optimized for onscreen viewing or printing.

Figure 2

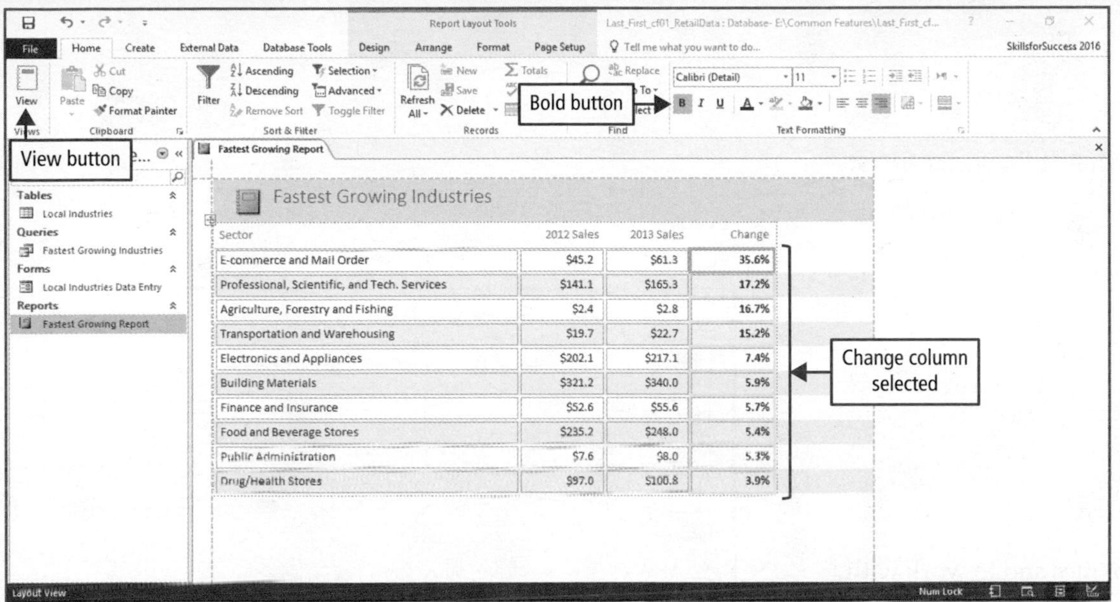

Access 2016, Windows 10, Microsoft Corporation

Figure 3

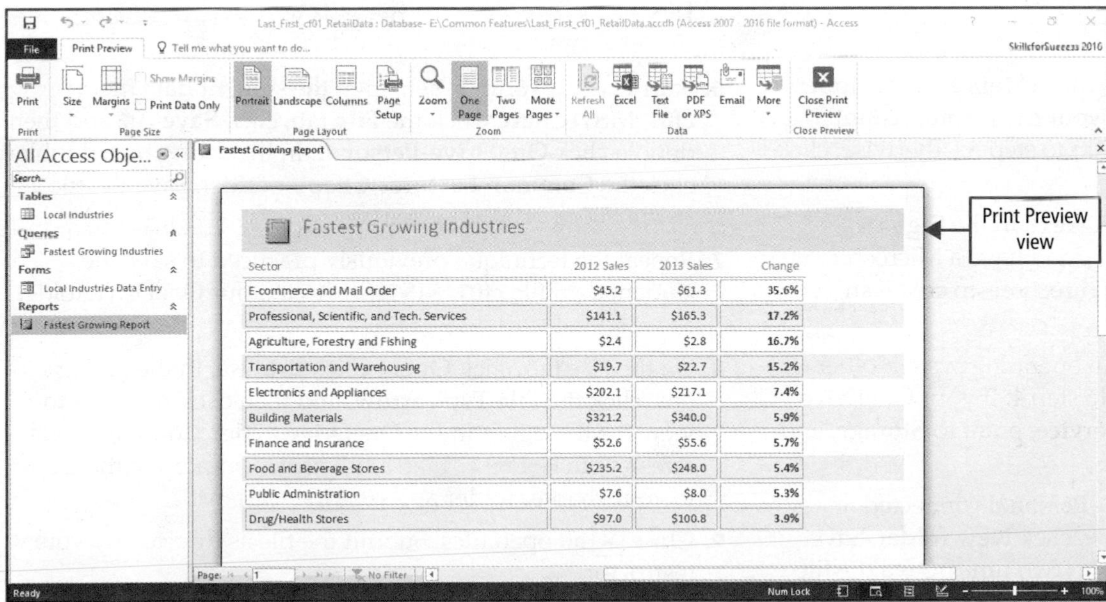

Access 2016, Windows 10, Microsoft Corporation

Figure 4

6. In the **Navigation Pane**, under **Reports**, double-click **Fastest Growing Report**.
7. On the **Home tab**, in the **Views group**, click the **View** button one time to switch to Layout view.
8. On the **Design tab**, in the **Themes group**, click **Themes**, and then click the seventh thumbnail—**Retrospect**.
9. Near the top of the **Change** column, click the first value—*35.6%*—to select all the values in the column.
10. Click the **Home tab**, and then in the **Text Formatting group**, click the **Bold** button. Compare your screen with **Figure 3**.
11. On the **Home tab**, click the **View arrow**, and then click **Print Preview**. Compare your screen with **Figure 4**. If necessary, in the Zoom group, click the One Page button to zoom to 100%.
12. If your instructor asked you to print your work, click the **Print** button, and then print the report.
13. **Save** the formatting changes, and then **Close** the report.

    Objects such as reports are opened and closed without closing the Access application itself.
14. **Close** Access, and then submit your printouts or files for this chapter as directed by your instructor.

DONE! You have completed Skill 10 of 10, and your file is complete!

More Skills 11

Store Files Online

To complete this project, you will need the following files:

- cf01_MS11Memo (Word)
- cf01_MS11Chart (Excel)
- cf01_MS11Slide (PowerPoint)

You will save your files as:

- Last_First_cf01_MS11Memo (Word)
- Last_First_cf01_MS11Chart (Excel)
- Last_First_cf01_MS11Slide (PowerPoint)
- Last_First_cf01_MS11Snip

- ▸ ***The Cloud***—an Internet technology used to store files and to work with programs that are stored in a central location.
- ▸ ***Microsoft account***—personal account that you use to access your files, settings, and online services from devices connected to the Internet.

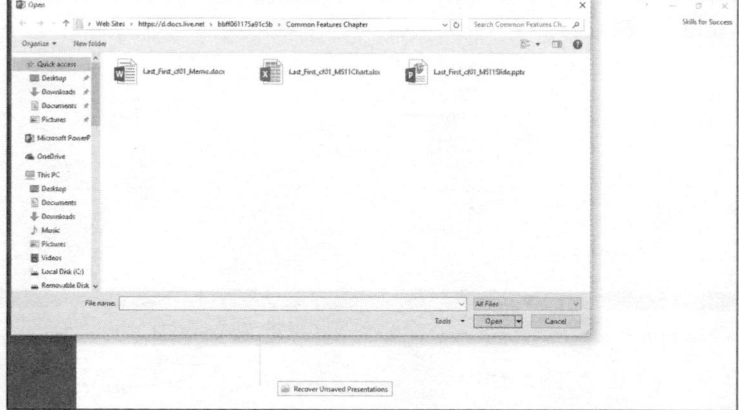

Figure 1 Office 2016, Windows 10, Microsoft Corporation

1. Start **Word 2016**. Open the student data file **cf01_MS11Memo**. In the upper right corner of the Word window, check to see if your Microsoft account name displays. If your account name displays, skip to step 3; otherwise, click **Sign In**.
2. In the dialog box, type your e-mail address. Click **Next**. In the **Sign in** screen, type your password. Click **Sign in**. If you don't have a Microsoft account, click **Sign up now**. Follow the onscreen directions to create an account.
3. On the **File tab**, click **Account**. If you are using an operating system other than Windows, this option is not available, skip to step 4. If your OneDrive is not listed as a connected service, click **Add a service**, point to **Storage**, and then click **OneDrive**.
4. Click **Save As**, and then double-click **OneDrive - Personal** connected to your Microsoft account. In the **Save As** dialog box, click **New folder**. Save the folder as Common Features Chapter Press Enter two times. Save the file as Last_First_cf01_MS11Memo
5. Replace the text *Your Name* with your First and Last names. **Save** the file. Notice the green arrow on the save button. This indicates the file is syncing to OneDrive.
6. Start **Excel 2016**, and then open the student data file **cf01_MS11Chart**. Click the **File tab**, click **Save As**, and then double-click **OneDrive-Personal**. In the dialog box, double-click the **Common Features Chapter** folder. Save the file as Last_First_cf01_MS11Chart
7. Repeat the technique previously practiced to save the student data file **cf01_MS11Slides** to your OneDrive folder as Last_First_cf01_MS11Slide
8. On the **File tab**, click **Open**. Click **Browse**. In the dialog box, click the **File Type arrow**, and then click **All Files** to view the three files in the OneDrive folder. Compare your screen with **Figure 1**. Take a full-screen snip. Save the snip to your chapter folder as Last_First_cf01_MS11Snip
9. **Close** all open files. Submit the file as directed by your instructor.

■ **You have completed More Skills 11**

More Skills 12

Share Office Files

To complete this project, you will need the following file:

- cf01_MS12Rates

You will save your files as:

- Last_First_cf01_MS12Rates
- Last_First_cf01_MS12Share

► If you are working on a team project, you can share files, and provide others with editing or viewing privileges.

► You can share files instead of sending them as an e-mail attachment.

1. Start **Word 2016**. Open the student data file **cf01_MS12Rates**. Replace the *From:* placeholder text in the memo with your First and Last names.
2. In the upper right corner of the window, click the **Share** button. In the **Share** pane, click the **Save to Cloud** button.
3. If you are signed in to your Microsoft account, skip to step 4. If your computer does not show your Microsoft account, then click **Add a Place**. In the **Add a Place** page, click **OneDrive**. In the dialog box, type your e-mail address. Click **Next**. In the **Sign in** screen, type your password. Click **Sign in**. If you don't have a Microsoft account, click **Sign up now**. Follow the onscreen directions to create an account.
4. Click **OneDrive - Personal** connected to your Microsoft account. If you completed the More Skills 11 project, then skip to step 5; otherwise, double-click **OneDrive - Personal** to open your online folders. Click **New folder**, and then rename the folder as Common Features Chapter
5. Double-click the **Common Features Chapter** folder to open it. Save the file as Last_First_cf01_MS12Rates
6. In the **Share** pane, type the e-mail address as directed by your instructor in the **Invite people** box. Verify that *Can edit* is displayed, and then type the message Please verify information is correct in the memo. Click the **arrow** to **Automatically share changes**, and then click **Always**. Compare your screen with **Figure 1**.

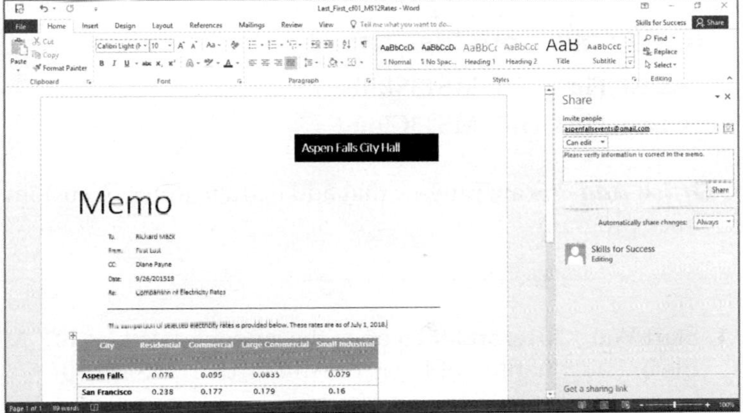

Word 2016, Windows 10, Microsoft Corporation

Figure 1

An e-mail is sent to the owner of the e-mail address with a link. Saving files to the cloud ensures a link is created to the file and revisions are updated in one location. Sharing options allow shared files to be edited or viewed. If changes are allowed, options for sharing changes can be set.

7. Click the **Share** button below the message to share the file. Once the share is processed, the account associated with the e-mail address you shared the file with displays at the bottom of the Share pane.
8. Press [Windows key], and type Snip Open the **Snipping Tool**, and then take a full-screen snip. Save the snip to your chapter folder as Last_First_cf01_MS12Share
9. **Save** [Save] the file, and then **Close** [X] Word. Submit the file as directed by your instructor.

■ **You have completed More Skills 12**

More Skills 13

Install Office Add-ins

To complete this project, you will need the following file:

- cf01_MS13Skills

You will save your files as:

- Last_First_cf01_MS13Skills
- Last_First_cf01_MS13Cloud

▶ ***Office Add-ins*** are plugins that add extra features or custom commands to Office programs.

---

1. Start **Word 2016**, and then open the student data file **cf01_MS13Skills**. Save the file in your chapter folder as Last_First_cf01_MS13Skills
2. Click the **File tab**, and then replace the *Author* with your First and Last names. Click the **Back arrow**, and then click the **Insert tab**. In the **Header & Footer group**, click the **Header arrow**, and then click **Edit Header**. On the **Header & Footer Tools Design tab**, in the **Insert group**, click the **Document Info** button. Click **Author** to insert the Author's name in the header.

   Word inserts the author's name found in the document properties. Since you revised this property in step 2, your name will display.

3. Click **Close Header and Footer**. Starting with the text *Desktop Applications*, drag to select both columns through the text *Clipboard*.
4. Click the **Insert tab**, and then in the **Add-ins group**, click the **Store** button. Compare your screen with **Figure 1**.

   The Office add-ins available for Word display in the window. When you open other Office applications, add-ins associated with those applications will display.

5. Use the scroll bar on the right side of the Office Add-ins window to review the Add-ins. Notice there are also categories on the left of the window that provide several additional choices. If you have clicked any of the categories, click the Back arrow until the *Finalize and Polish Your Documents* category displays.
6. Click **Pro Word Cloud**. In the **Office Add-ins** window, click **Trust It**.
7. In the **Pro Word Cloud** pane, click the **Font arrow**, scroll down, and then click **Silentina Movie**. Click the **Colors arrow**, and then click **Sun Set**. Click the **Layout arrow**, and then click **Half And Half**. Verify the **Remove common words** check box is selected, and then click the **Create Word Cloud** button.

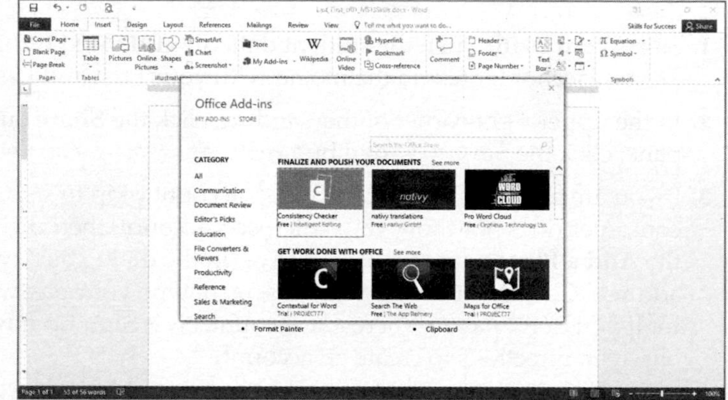

Figure 1 Word 2016, Windows 10, Microsoft Corporation

8. The word *cloud* will display in the top of the pane. Right-click the word **cloud**, and then click **Save Picture As**. Navigate to the folder for this chapter, and then save the file as Last_First_cf01_MS13Cloud
9. Close the **Pro Word Cloud** pane. **Save** [Save icon], and then **Close** [×] the file. Submit the files as directed by your instructor.

■ **You have completed More Skills 13**

More Skills 14

Customize the Ribbon and Options

To complete this project, you will need the following file:

- cf01_MS14Slide

You will save your file as:

- Last_First_cf01_MS14Ribbon

► The ***Ribbon*** contains commands placed in groups that are organized by tabs so that you can quickly find the tools you need.

---

1. Start **PowerPoint 2016**, and then open the student data file **cf01_MS14Slide**. Click the **Insert tab**. In the **Text group**, click the **Header & Footer** button. On the **Slide tab**, click the *Footer* check box. In the box, type your First and Last names, and then click **Apply**.
2. Click the **File tab**, and then click **Options**. Review the list, and then on the left, click **Save**. Under *Save presentations*, click the **arrow** to change **Save AutoRecover information every** to 5 minutes.
3. In the **PowerPoint Options** list, click **Customize Ribbon**. Compare your screen to **Figure 1**.

   Two panes display. In the left pane are the commands available to add to the ribbon. In the right pane are tabs and groups already added to the ribbon.

4. At the bottom of the right pane, click the **New Tab** button. Click **New Tab (Custom)**, and then click the **Rename** button. Type Common Features and then click **OK**. Click **New Group (Custom)**, click the **Rename** button, type Editing and then click **OK**.
5. In the left pane, click **Copy**, and then click the **Add** button. Notice the copy command appears in the *Editing (Custom)* group. Repeat this technique to add the commands **Cut**, **Font**, **Font Color**, **Font Size**, and **Format Painter**.
6. Click **Common Features (Custom),** and then click the **New Group** button. Click the **Rename** button, type Objects and click **OK**.
7. Repeat the technique previously practiced to add the commands **Add Table**, **Format Object**, **Insert Pictures**, and **Insert Text Box**. Click **OK** to close the Options window.
8. Review the tabs available, and then click the **Common Features tab** to view your new ribbon, groups, and commands.

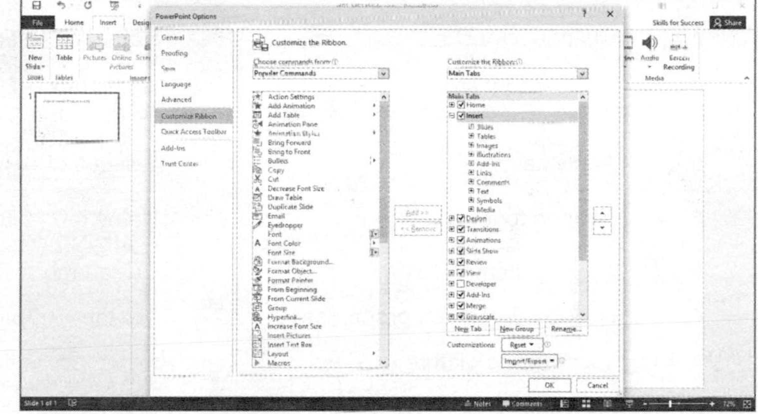

Access 2016, Windows 10, Microsoft Corporation

Figure 1

9. Press [Windows key], and then type Snip Open the **Snipping Tool**, and then take a full-screen snip. Save the snip to your chapter folder as Last_First_cf01_MS14Ribbon
10. Click the **File tab**, click **Options**, and then click **Customize Ribbon**. At the bottom of the right pane, click the **Reset arrow**, click **Reset all customizations**, and then click **Yes** to delete the customizations. Click **OK** to close the Options window. Notice the tab is removed from the ribbon.
11. **Close** [X] PowerPoint without saving the file. Submit the file as directed by your instructor.

- **You have completed More Skills 14**

Review

The following table summarizes the **SKILLS AND PROCEDURES** covered in this chapter.

Skills Number	Task	Step	Icon	Keyboard Shortcut
1	Start Office applications	Display Start menu or screen, and then type application name		
2	Create a new folder while saving	Save As dialog box toolbar → New folder		
2	Save	Quick Access Toolbar → Save		Ctrl + S
2	Open a file	File tab → Open		Ctrl + O
2	Save a file with new name and location	File tab → Save As		F12
3	Apply bold	Home tab → Text Formatting group → Bold	B	Ctrl + B
3	Preview the printed page	File tab → Print		Alt + Ctrl + I
4	Change a font	Home tab → Font group → Font arrow		Ctrl + Shift + F
4	Change font size	Home tab → Font group → Font Size arrow	11	Ctrl + < Ctrl + >
5	Apply italic	Select text → Mini toolbar → Italic	I	Ctrl + I
5	Change font color	Home tab → Font group → Font Color arrow	A	
5	Apply a theme	Design tab → Themes		
6	Change document properties	File tab → Options		
7	Insert online picture	Insert tab → Illustrations group → Online Pictures → Bing Image Search		
8	Fill Color	Mini toolbar → Fill Color arrow	abc	
8	Center align text	Select text → Mini toolbar → Center		Ctrl + E
9	Copy	Select text or object → Right-click → Copy		Ctrl + C
9	Paste	Home tab → Clipboard group → Paste		Ctrl + V
9	Save	File tab → Save		
10	Change report view	Home tab → View arrow		
MS11	Save files to OneDrive	File tab → OneDrive - Personal → Save		
MS11	View files in OneDrive	File tab → Open → Browse → All Files		
MS12	Share Office files	Share button → Sign in → Share		
MS13	Install Office Add-ins	Insert tab → Add-ins group → Store		
MS14	Customize Ribbon	File tab → Customize Ribbon		

Project Summary Chart		
Project	**Project Type**	**Project Location**
Skills Review	Review	In Book & MIL MyITLab® Grader
Skills Assessment 1	Review	In Book & MIL MyITLab® Grader
Skills Assessment 2	Review	Book
My Skills	Problem Solving	Book
Visual Skills Check	Problem Solving	Book
Skillls Challenge 1	Critical Thinking	Book
Skills Challenge 2	Critical Thinking	Book
More Skills Assessment	Review	In Book & MIL MyITLab® Grader
Collaborating with Google	Critical Thinking	Book

Key Terms

Matching 

Match each term in the second column with its correct definition in the first column by writing the letter of the term on the blank line in front of the correct definition.

___ **1.** An individual page in a presentation that can contain text, pictures, or other objects.

___ **2.** The tool used to copy formatting from selected text and apply it to other text in the document, worksheet, or slide.

___ **3.** A menu with options such as Copy or Paste, available after selected text is right-clicked.

___ **4.** To insert, delete, or replace text in an Office document, spreadsheet, or presentation.

___ **5.** A prebuilt set of unified formatting choices including colors, fonts, and effects.

___ **6.** To change the appearance of text.

___ **7.** A set of characters with the same design and shape.

___ **8.** A feature that displays the result of a formatting change if you select it.

___ **9.** A view applied to documents downloaded from the Internet that allows you to decide if the content is safe before working with the document.

___ **10.** A command that moves a copy of the selected text or object to the Office Clipboard.

A Format Painter
B Copy
C Edit
D Font
E Format
F Live Preview
G Protected
H Slide
I Shortcut Menu
J Theme

Multiple Choice 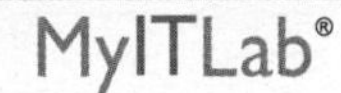

Choose the correct answer.

1. The flashing vertical line that indicates where text will be inserted when you start typing.
   - **A.** Cell reference
   - **B.** Insertion point
   - **C.** KeyTip
2. A reserved, formatted space into which you enter your own text or object.
   - **A.** Gallery
   - **B.** Placeholder
   - **C.** Title
3. Until you save a document, the document is stored here.
   - **A.** Office Clipboard
   - **B.** Live Preview
   - **C.** RAM
4. A collection of options on the File tab used to open, save, print, and perform other file management tasks.
   - **A.** Backstage view
   - **B.** Page Layout view
   - **C.** File gallery
5. A temporary storage area that holds text or an object that has been cut or copied.
   - **A.** Office Clipboard
   - **B.** Dialog box
   - **C.** Live Preview
6. A toolbar with common formatting buttons that displays after you select text.
   - **A.** Gallery toolbar
   - **B.** Mini toolbar
   - **C.** Taskbar toolbar
7. A command that inserts a copy of the text or object from the Office Clipboard.
   - **A.** Copy
   - **B.** Insert
   - **C.** Paste
8. A visual display of choices—typically thumbnails—from which you can choose.
   - **A.** Gallery
   - **B.** Options menu
   - **C.** Shortcut menu
9. A tab that displays on the ribbon only when a related object such as a graphic or chart is selected.
   - **A.** Contextual tab
   - **B.** File tab
   - **C.** Page Layout tab
10. A database object that presents tables or query results in a way that is optimized for onscreen viewing or printing.
    - **A.** Form
    - **B.** Report
    - **C.** Table

Topics for Discussion

1. You have briefly worked with four Microsoft Office programs: Word, Excel, PowerPoint, and Access. Based on your experience, describe the overall purpose of each program.
2. Many believe that computers enable offices to go paperless—that is, to share files electronically instead of printing and then distributing them. What are the advantages of sharing files electronically, and in what situations is it best to print documents?

Skills Review

To complete this project, you will need the following files:

- cf01_SRData (Access)
- cf01_SRChart (Excel)
- cf01_SRSlide (PowerPoint)
- cf01_SRMemo (Word)

You will save your files as:

- Last_First_cf01_SRData (Access)
- Last_First_cf01_SRChart (Excel)
- Last_First_cf01_SRSlide (PowerPoint)
- Last_First_cf01_SRMemo (Word)

---

1. Start **Access 2016**, and then click **Open Other Files**. Click **Browse**. In the **Open** dialog box, navigate to the student data files for this chapter and open **cf01_SRData**.
2. On the **File tab**, click **Save As**, and then click the **Save As** button. In the **Save As** dialog box, navigate to your chapter folder, and then save the file as Last_First_cf01_SRData Click **Save**. If necessary, enable the content.
3. In the **Navigation Pane**, double-click **Budget Report**, and then click the **View** button to switch to Layout view. On the **Design tab**, click **Themes**, and then click **Retrospect**.
4. Click the **View arrow**, click **Print Preview**, and then compare your screen with **Figure 1**. If you are printing this project, print the report.
5. Click **Save**, **Close** the report, and then **Close** Access.
6. Start **Excel 2016**, and then click **Open Other Workbooks**. Use the **Open** page to locate and open the student data file **cf01_SRChart**.
7. Navigate to your chapter folder, and then save the file as Last_First_cf01_SRChart
8. With **A1** selected, on the **Home tab**, in the **Font group**, click the **Font Size arrow**, and then click **24**.

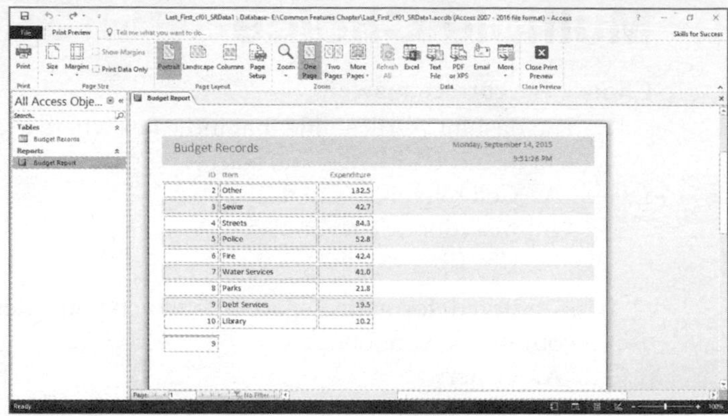

Figure 1 Access 2016, Windows 10, Microsoft Corporation

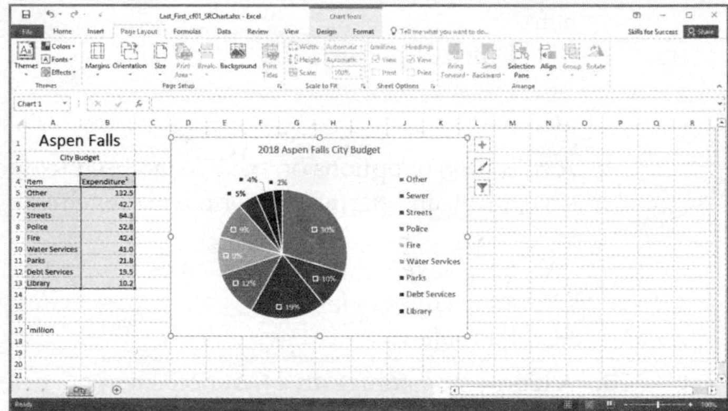

Figure 2 Excel 2016, Windows 10, Microsoft Corporation

9. On the **Page Layout tab**, click **Themes**, and then click **Retrospect**.
10. Click cell **B7**, and then type 84.3 Press Enter, and then click **Save**.
11. Click the border of the chart, and then compare your screen with **Figure 2**.

Continue to the next page to complete this Skills Review

12. On the **Home tab**, in the **Clipboard group**, click the **Copy** button.
13. Start **PowerPoint 2016**. Click **Open Other Presentations**, and then open the student data file **cf01_SRSlide**.
14. On the **File tab**, click **Save As**. Click **Browse**, and then save the file in your chapter folder as Last_First_cf01_SRSlide
15. On the **Home tab**, in the **Clipboard group**, click **Paste** to insert the chart.
16. On the **Design tab**, in the **Themes group**, click the **More** button, and then click the seventh choice—**Retrospect**. Compare your screen with **Figure 3**.
17. If you are printing this project, on the **File tab**, click **Print**, change the **Settings** to **Handouts, 1 Slide**, and then print the handout.
18. Click **Save**, and then **Close** PowerPoint.
19. Click cell **A4**. In the **Clipboard group**, click the **Format Painter**, and then click cell **B4**.
20. Click **Save**, and then **Close** Excel.
21. Start **Word 2016**, and then click **Open Other Documents**. Use the **Open** page to locate and open the student data file **cf01_SRMemo**.
22. On the **File tab**, click **Save As**. Click **Browse**, and then save the file in your chapter folder as Last_First_cf01_SRMemo
23. Click *[RECIPIENT NAME]*, and then type Janet Neal
24. Change *[YOUR NAME]* to your own name, and then change *[SUBJECT]* to City Budget
25. Change *[CLICK TO SELECT DATE]* to the current date, and then change *[NAME]* to Maria Martinez
26. Change *[Type your memo text here]* to the following: I am pleased to tell you that the city budget items that you requested are ready. I will send you the Access report and PowerPoint slide today.
27. Click to the left of *INTEROFFICE*, and then press Delete as needed to delete the word and the space following it.
28. On the **Design tab**, click the **Themes** button, and then click **Retrospect**.
29. Double-click the word *MEMORANDUM* to select it. On the Mini toolbar, click the **Font Color arrow**, and then click the fifth color—**Orange, Accent 1**.
30. With *MEMORANDUM* still selected, on the Mini toolbar, click the **Bold** button one time to remove the bold formatting from the selection, and then change the **Font Size** to **24**.
31. Click **Save**, and then compare your screen with **Figure 4**.

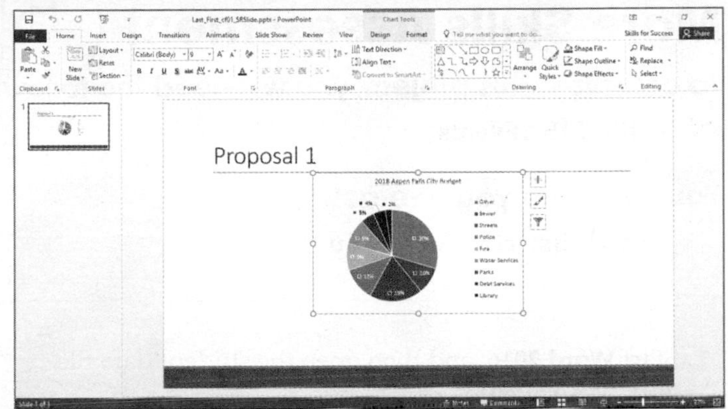

Access 2016, Windows 10, Microsoft Corporation **Figure 3**

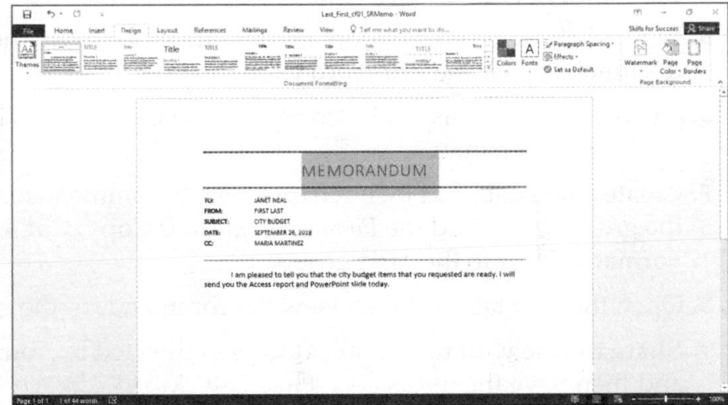

Word 2016, Windows 10, Microsoft Corporation **Figure 4**

32. Click the **File tab**, and then click **Options**. Replace the User name with your First and Last names. Close the dialog box to save the change.
33. If you are printing your work, print the memo. Click **Save**, and then **Close** Word. Submit your printouts or files as directed by your instructor.

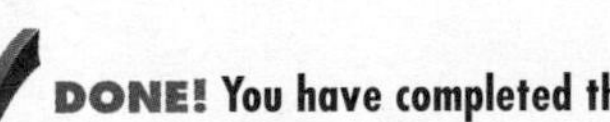

More Skills Assessment

To complete this project, you will need the following file:

- cf01_MSAEvents

You will save your file as:

- Last_First_cf01_MSASnip

---

1. Start **Word 2016**, and then open the student data file **cf01_MSAEvents**.
2. Starting with the text *Park Events*, drag to select the text through *October 2*.
3. Using **My Add-ins**, insert the **Pro Word Cloud** add-in.
4. Create a word cloud using the **Steelfish** font and **Bluebell Glade** colors. Click **Create Word Cloud**.
5. Right-click the word cloud image, and then paste it to the top of the document. Close the **Pro Word Cloud** pane.
6. Open **Word Options**, and then replace the User name with your First and Last names.
7. Create a new tab, and then rename the tab Common Features and the group Tasks Add the *Popular Commands* **Copy**, **Cut**, **Delete**, and **Format Painter** to the *Tasks* group.
8. Open the new tab, and then view the commands in the group.
9. **Share** the file with the e-mail address as directed by your instructor, and then **Save** the file as Last_First_cf01_MSAEvents to **OneDrive - Personal** linked to your account in the **Common Features Chapter** folder.
10. Set the share options to **Can edit**, and then type the message I've created the word cloud for the events flyer.
11. Edit the **Author** property, and then insert your First and Last names. Insert the **Document Info** property **Author** as the header, and then **Close** the header. Compare your screen with **Figure 1**.

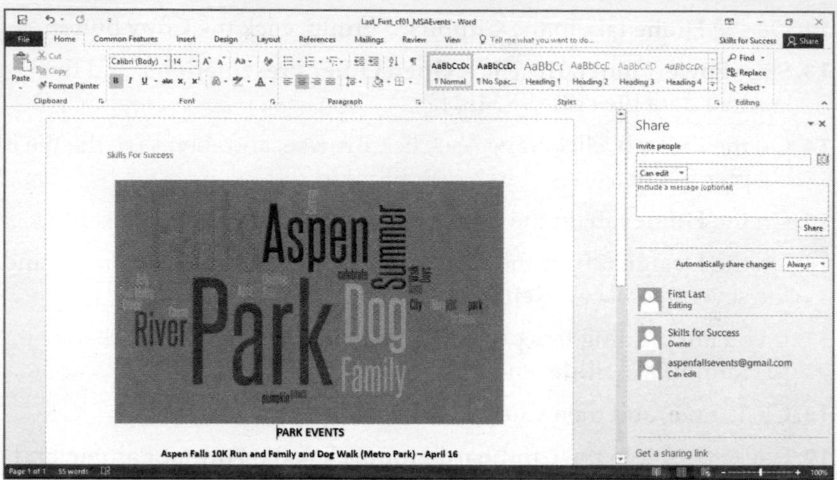

Figure 1 Word 2016, Windows 10, Microsoft Corporation

12. Click the **Common Features tab**, and then use the **Snipping Tool** to take a **Full-screen Snip** of your screen. **Save** the file as Last_First_cf01_MSASnip
13. **Close** the Snipping Tool window. **Save** the file, and then **Close** Word. Submit the file as directed by your instructor.

Collaborating with Google

To complete this project, you will need a Google account (refer to the Common Features chapter) and the following files:

- cf01_GPParks
- cf01_GPImage

You will save your file as:

- Last_First_cf01_GPParks

---

1. Open the **Google Chrome** web browser. If you already have a Google account, skip to step 2. In the upper right corner, click **Gmail**. In the next window, click **Create an account**. Follow the onscreen directions to create an account.
2. Log into your Google account, and then click the **Apps** button. Click **Drive** to open Google Drive.
3. Click **NEW**, and then click **File upload**. Navigate to the student data files, and then open **cf01_GPParks**.
4. Select the **cf01_GPParks** file in **Google Drive**. Click **More actions** [More], point to **Open with**, and then click **Google Docs**.
5. Position the insertion point after the title in the document. Click **Insert** on the menu, and then click **Image**. In the **Insert image** window, ensure **Upload** is selected. Click **Choose an Image to upload**, and then navigate to the student data files, click **cf01_GPImage**, and then click **Open**. Click the image, and then drag the lower middle sizing handle up until the image height is resized about 1 inch.
6. Drag to select the title text above image. On the toolbar, click the **Font arrow**, and then click **Georgia**. Click the **Font size arrow**, and then click **18**. Click **Text color**, and then click the third option in the second row—**orange**.
7. With the title text selected, click **Paint format**. Scroll down to the *Events* table. Drag to select the text *Parks and Recreation*, and then apply the **title format**.

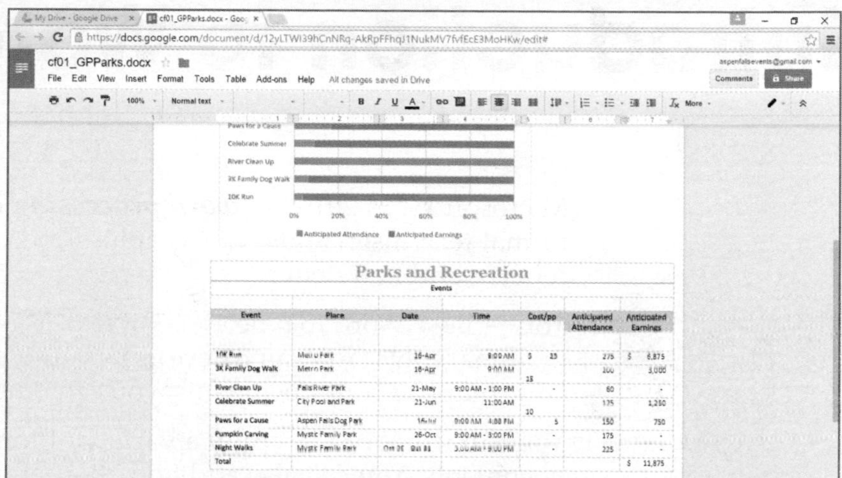

Google; Word 2016, Windows 10, Microsoft Corporation **Figure 1**

8. In the first column, drag to select the text *Event*. Click the **Font size arrow**, and then click **10**. Double-click **Paint format**, and then copy the format to the other column titles. Drag to select all of the column titles, and then click **Center**. Compare your screen with **Figure 1**.
9. Click the **File tab**, point to **Download as**, and then click **Microsoft Word (.docx)**. Open the downloaded file, click **Enable Editing**, and then save the file in the chapter folder as Last_First_cf01_GPParks
10. Close all windows, and then submit your file as directed by your instructor.

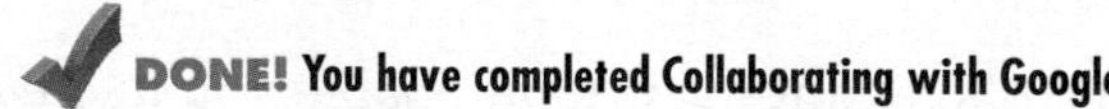

Introduction to Word

Microsoft Word 2016 is a ***word processing application***—a program used to type and format text, insert and create graphics and tables, and create documents such as letters, reports, and newsletters.

You can use Word to type and edit text. You can edit your work using Word's spelling and grammar tools. You can fix errors as you type or scan the entire document for errors. As you compose your documents, you can quickly delete, insert, and move text.

You can use Word to apply a variety of fonts, sizes, and colors to the text in your documents. You can also add lines, borders, and shading to emphasize document elements. Formatting tasks can be performed quickly using the Format Painter or by assigning predefined styles.

You can insert graphics into Word documents or create your own using tools such as Text Effects, drawing objects, or SmartArt. Data can be inserted into tables. You can then format and position these objects to create the documents you desire.

Word can be used to collaborate with others. For example, you can save documents to the Internet and invite others to view them or make changes to them. You can also track the changes each collaborator makes to your documents, and then accept or reject those changes.

Word also has tools to perform specific tasks such as printing individualized documents using mail merge. You can also create citations and bibliographies using the Source Manager.

Word's features and tools enable you to create simple documents, such as letters, memos, and reports, and more elegant documents, such as newsletters and forms.

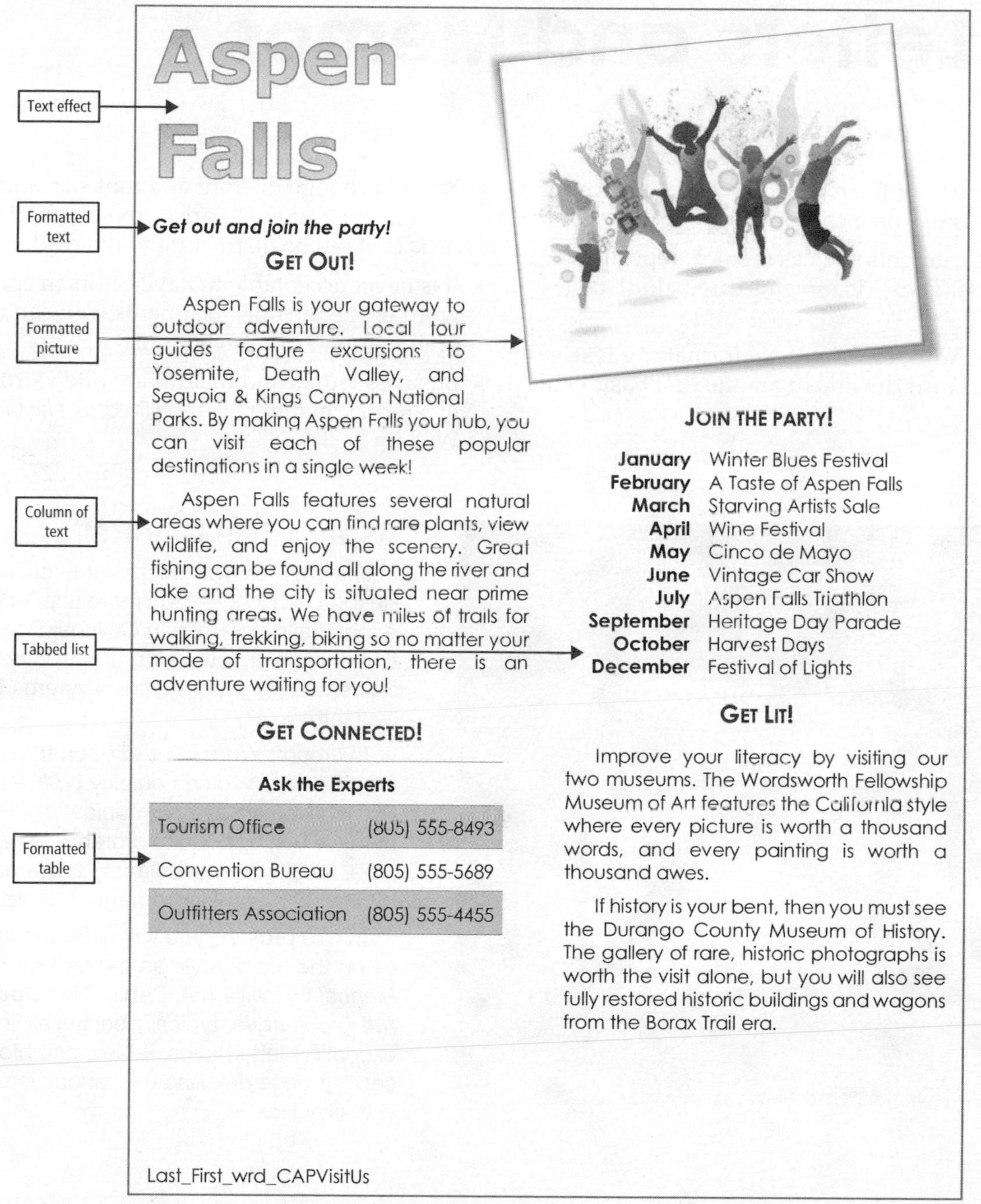
Text effect
Formatted text
Formatted picture
Column of text
Tabbed list
Formatted table
Aspen Falls
Get out and join the party!
GET OUT!
Aspen Falls is your gateway to outdoor adventure. Local tour guides feature excursions to Yosemite, Death Valley, and Sequoia & Kings Canyon National Parks. By making Aspen Falls your hub, you can visit each of these popular destinations in a single week!
Aspen Falls features several natural areas where you can find rare plants, view wildlife, and enjoy the scenery. Great fishing can be found all along the river and lake and the city is situated near prime hunting areas. We have miles of trails for walking, trekking, biking so no matter your mode of transportation, there is an adventure waiting for you!
GET CONNECTED!
Ask the Experts
Tourism Office (805) 555-8493
Convention Bureau (805) 555-5689
Outfitters Association (805) 555-4455
JOIN THE PARTY!
January Winter Blues Festival
February A Taste of Aspen Falls
March Starving Artists Sale
April Wine Festival
May Cinco de Mayo
June Vintage Car Show
July Aspen Falls Triathlon
September Heritage Day Parade
October Harvest Days
December Festival of Lights
GET LIT!
Improve your literacy by visiting our two museums. The Wordsworth Fellowship Museum of Art features the California style where every picture is worth a thousand words, and every painting is worth a thousand awes.
If history is your bent, then you must see the Durango County Museum of History. The gallery of rare, historic photographs is worth the visit alone, but you will also see fully restored historic buildings and wagons from the Borax Trail era.
Last_First_wrd_CAPVisitUs

CHAPTER 1

Create Letters and Memos

- Microsoft Office Word is one of the most common productivity programs that individuals use on a computer.
- Word is used to create documents such as memos, reports, letters, and mailing labels. These documents can include tables and graphics.
- To work efficiently with Word, entering text, formatting text, and navigating within a Word document are the first basic skills you need.
- You can change the font and font size and add emphasis to text, but use caution not to apply too many different formats to your text. This can be distracting to the reader.
- It is never acceptable to have errors in spelling, grammar, or word usage in your documents; you can use Word spelling and grammar tools to prevent this.
- Business letters and memos are often structured and formatted in a formal manner as described in *The Gregg Reference Manual* by William A. Sabin.

Julien Eichinger/Fotolia

Aspen Falls City Hall

In this chapter, you will assist Evelyn Stone, Human Resources Director, to create a letter to Dr. George Gato of Aspen Falls Community College. The purpose of the letter is to establish an internship program between City Hall and the students in the Information Systems Department chaired by Dr. Gato.

Microsoft Word is used often to write business letters and memos. You can quickly type, edit, and format text. Because business communication documents should be free of mistakes, spelling and grammar errors are flagged as you type. Most businesses apply a standard business letter format to all letters coming from the organization.

In this project, you will write a one-page business letter using the block style as defined by *The Gregg Reference Manual* by William A. Sabin. The ***block style***, also called the ***full-block style***, typically begins all lines at the left margin except for letterheads, tables, and block quotes. You will add a second page detailing the various internship positions available with City Hall.

Time to complete all 10 skills — 60 to 75 minutes

Outcome

Using the skills in this chapter, you will be able to create, edit, and save documents, apply styles, modify a document using copy, cut and paste, and confirm correct spelling and grammar.

Objectives

1.1 Create and edit a Word document

1.2 Use styles and advanced font settings

1.3 Adjust settings and review a document for printing

1.4 Create PDF files

Student data file needed for this chapter:

wrd01_InternPositions

You will save your files as:

Last_First_wrd01_Interns (Word)
Last_First_wrd01_Interns (PDF)

SKILLS

At the end of this chapter you will be able to:

Skill 1 Type Letter Text
Skill 2 Apply Styles and Set Grammar and Spelling Options
Skill 3 Select and Insert Text
Skill 4 Copy, Cut, and Paste Text
Skill 5 Check Spelling and Grammar
Skill 6 Insert Synonyms
Skill 7 Use Format Painter
Skill 8 Apply Advanced Font Settings
Skill 9 Create Document Footers
Skill 10 Save Documents as PDF Files

MORE SKILLS

Skill 11 Manage Document Properties
Skill 12 Insert Screen Shots into Documents
Skill 13 Split and Arrange Windows
Skill 14 Insert Symbols

ASPEN FALLS HUMAN RESOURCES
500 S Aspen Street
Aspen Falls, CA 93463

May 8, 2018

Dr. George Gato
Aspen Falls Community College
1 College Drive
Aspen Falls, CA 93464

Dear Dr. Gato:

Subject: City Hall Internships

Thank you so much for your letter offering the services of your Information Systems Department students. We currently have several projects that might benefit both City Hall and your students.

I have attached a description of the positions we are currently seeking. Please call me at (805) 555-1016 to discuss this further.

We have several positions open for students with skills in the four Office applications: Word, Excel, PowerPoint, and Access. We also need students capable of working with our IT Services Help Desk.

Sincerely,

Evelyn Stone
Human Resources Director

Last_First_wrd01_Interns

Word 2016, Windows 10, Microsoft Corporation

- When working with Word documents, a paragraph can be a single line containing a heading or several lines of sentences.
- To see where paragraphs begin and end, it is helpful to display ***formatting marks***—characters that display in your document to represent nonprinting characters such as paragraphs, spaces, and tabs.

1. Start **Word 2016**, and then on the Start screen, click **Blank document**.

2. On the **Home tab**, in the **Paragraph group**, click the **Show/Hide** button [¶] to display the nonprinting formatting marks, as shown in **Figure 1**. If the Navigation pane is open, Close [X] it.

   The Show/Hide button is a ***toggle button***—a button used to turn a feature both on and off. The paragraph mark (¶) indicates the end of a paragraph and will not print.

   Because many elements in the Word window adjust to your monitor size and personal settings, you may need to change your window size, exit Reading Mode, or disable Full Screen Mode to match the figures in this book.

3. With the insertion point in the blank paragraph, type Aspen Falls Human Resources and press [Enter]. Type 500 S Aspen Street and press [Enter]. Type Aspen Falls, CA 93463 and press [Enter] two times.

4. Type May 8, 2018 Press [Enter] three times, and then compare your screen with **Figure 2.**

   The letter has eight paragraphs—three for the letterhead, one for the date, and four blank paragraphs.

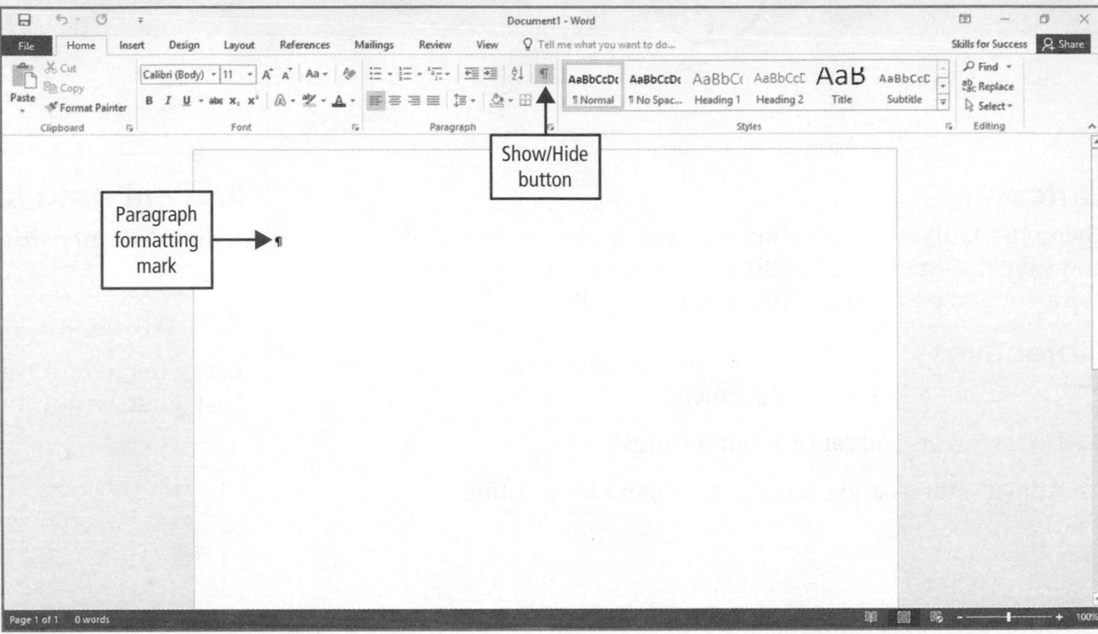

Figure 1

Word 2016, Windows 10, Microsoft Corporation

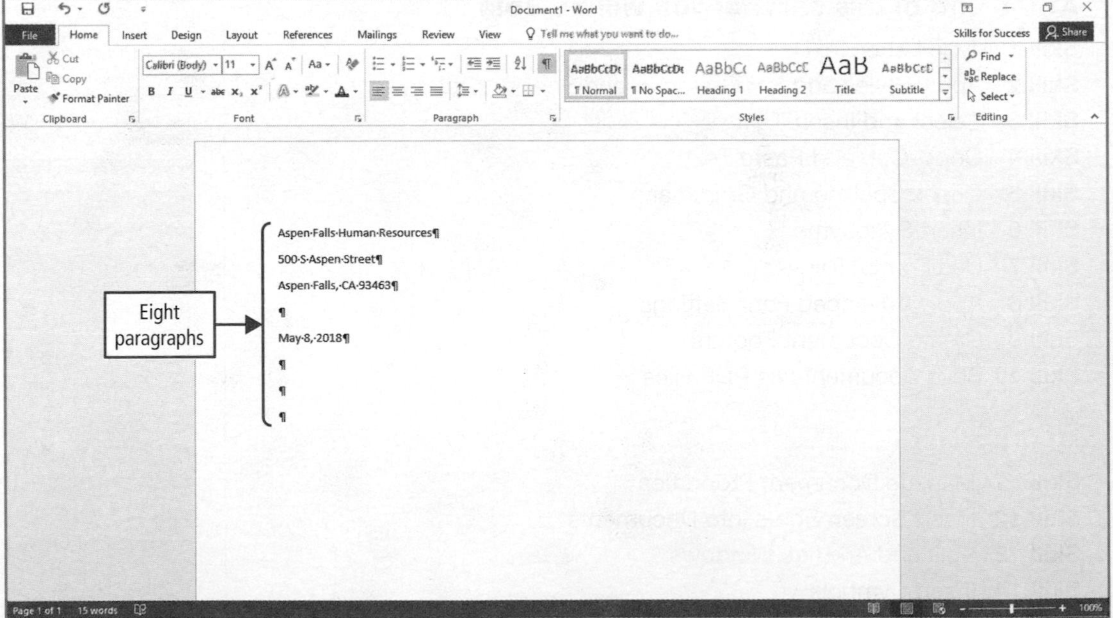

Figure 2

Word 2016, Windows 10, Microsoft Corporation

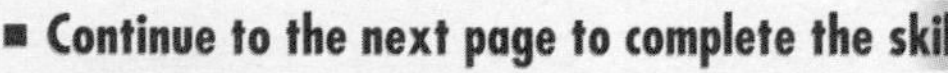
■ Continue to the next page to complete the skill

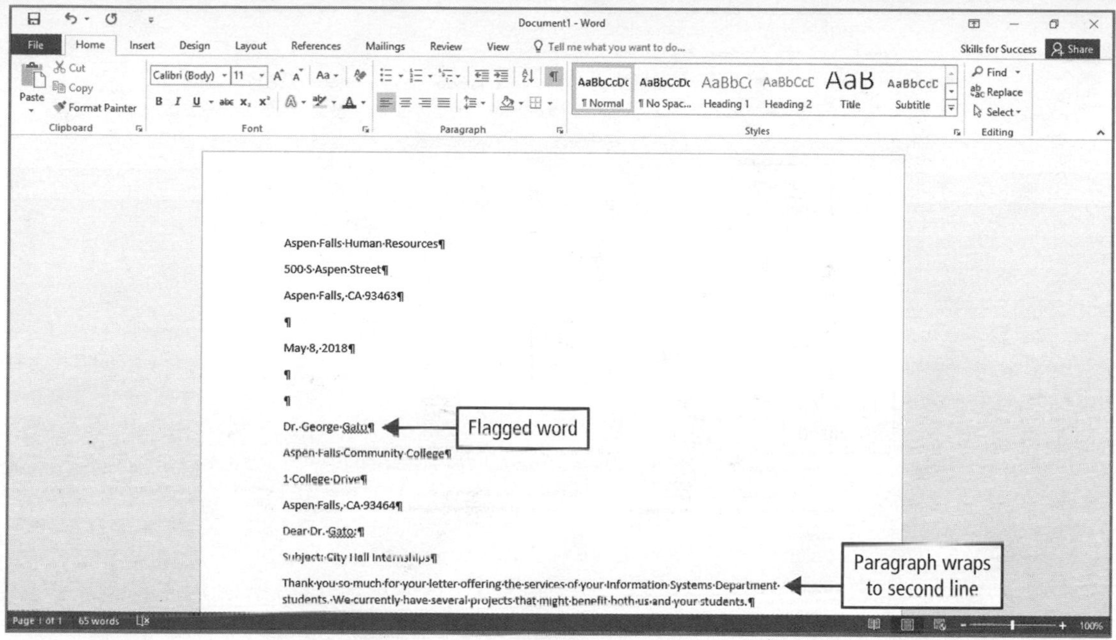

Word 2016, Windows 10, Microsoft Corporation

Figure 3

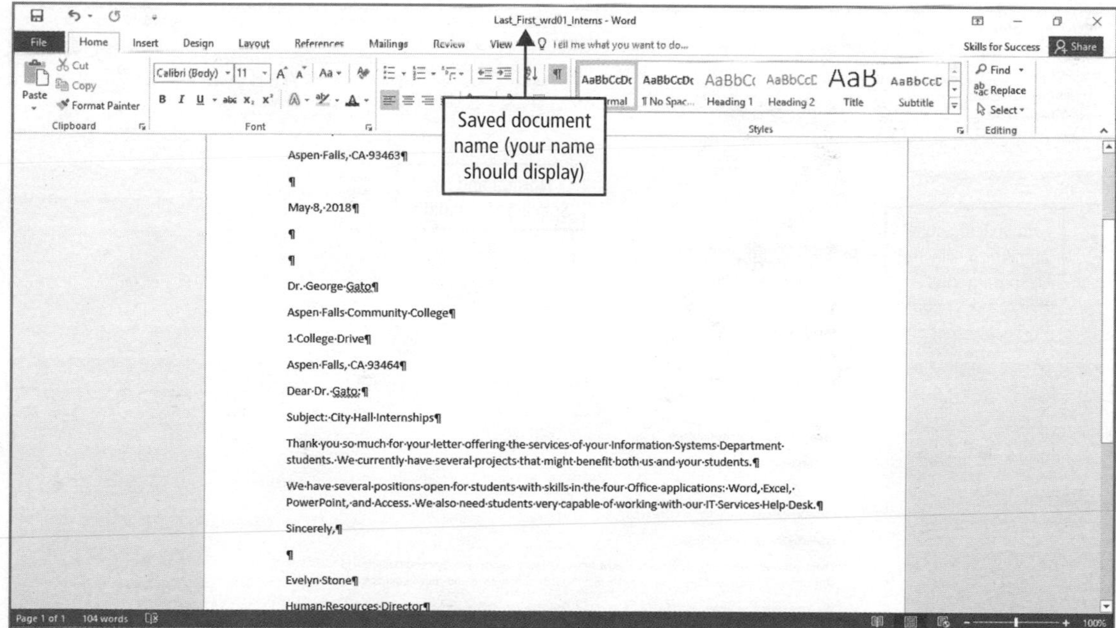

Word 2016, Windows 10, Microsoft Corporation

Figure 4

5. Type Dr. George Gato and press Enter; type Aspen Falls Community College and press Enter; type 1 College Drive and press Enter; and type Aspen Falls, CA 93464 and press Enter.

   The word *Gato* is flagged as a spelling error, but it is spelled correctly.

6. Type Dear Dr. Gato: and press Enter. Type Subject: City Hall Internships and press Enter.
7. Type the following, inserting only one space after each sentence: Thank you so much for your letter offering the services of your Information Systems Department students. We currently have several projects that might benefit both us and your students. Compare your screen with **Figure 3**.
8. Press Enter, and then type We have several positions open for students with skills in the four Office applications: Word, Excel, PowerPoint, and Access. We also need students very capable of working with our IT Services Help Desk.
9. Press Enter and type Sincerely, and then press Enter two times. Type Evelyn Stone Press Enter, and then type Human Resources Director
10. Click **Save** [icon], and then on the **Save As** page, click the location and folder where you are saving your work. If necessary, click Browse.
11. In the **Save As** dialog box, click **New folder**, type Word Chapter 1 and then press Enter two times to open the new folder. Name the file Last_First_wrd01_Interns Click **Save**, and then compare your screen with **Figure 4**.

■ **You have completed Skill 1 of 10**

SKILL 2: Apply Styles and Set Grammar and Spelling Options

SKILL 1.2

- You can format text quickly by applying ***styles***—pre-built collections of formatting settings that can be assigned to text.
- During the writing process, it is a good idea to look for ***flagged errors***—wavy lines indicating spelling or grammar errors. You can right-click these flagged errors to see a list of suggestions for fixing them.

1. In the inside address, right-click the word *Gato*, and then compare your screen with **Figure 1**.

   Red wavy lines indicate words that have been flagged as possible spelling errors, and the shortcut menu provides suggested spellings.

2. From the shortcut menu, click **Ignore All**, and verify that both instances of the word *Gato* are no longer flagged as spelling errors.
3. Hold down Ctrl, and then press Home, to move the insertion point to the beginning of the document.

MOS
Obj 2.2.6 C

4. Move the pointer to the left of the first line of the document to display the [pointer icon] pointer. Drag down to select the first two lines of the document. On the **Home tab**, in the **Styles group**, click the **No Spacing** thumbnail. Compare your screen with **Figure 2**.

   The Normal style has extra space after each paragraph. The No Spacing style does not apply this extra space after each paragraph, and the extra space between the lines of the letterhead have been removed.

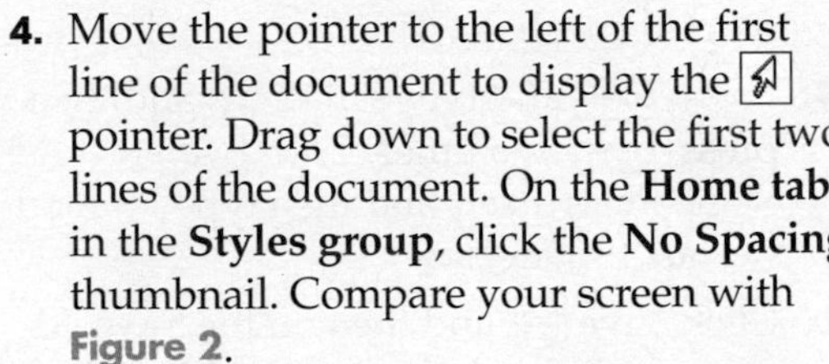

■ **Continue to the next page to complete the skill**

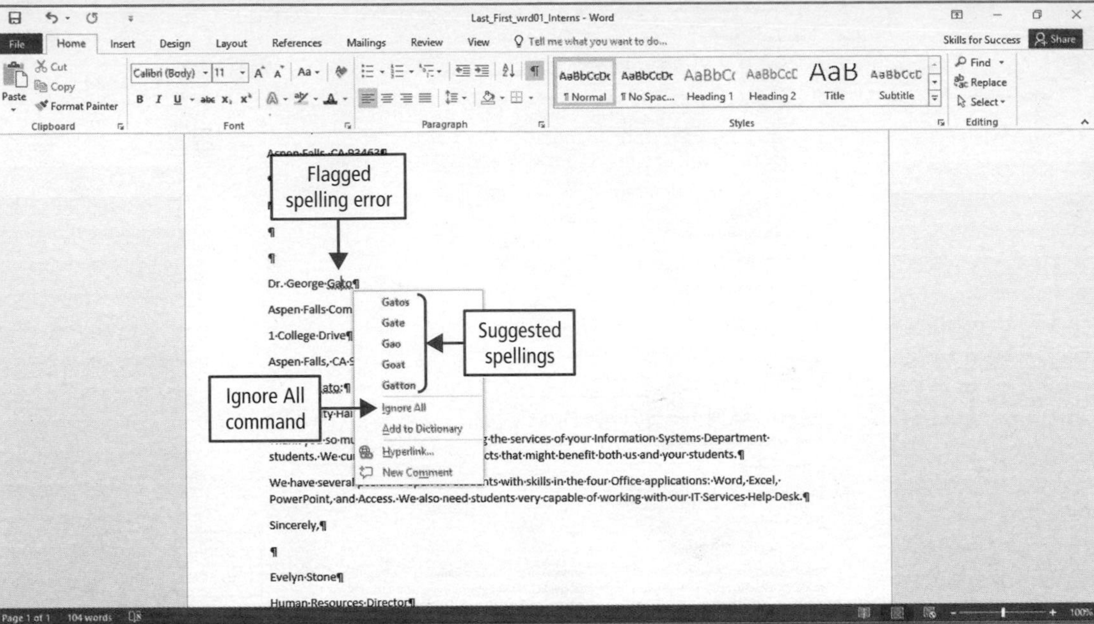

Figure 1

Word 2016, Windows 10, Microsoft Corporation

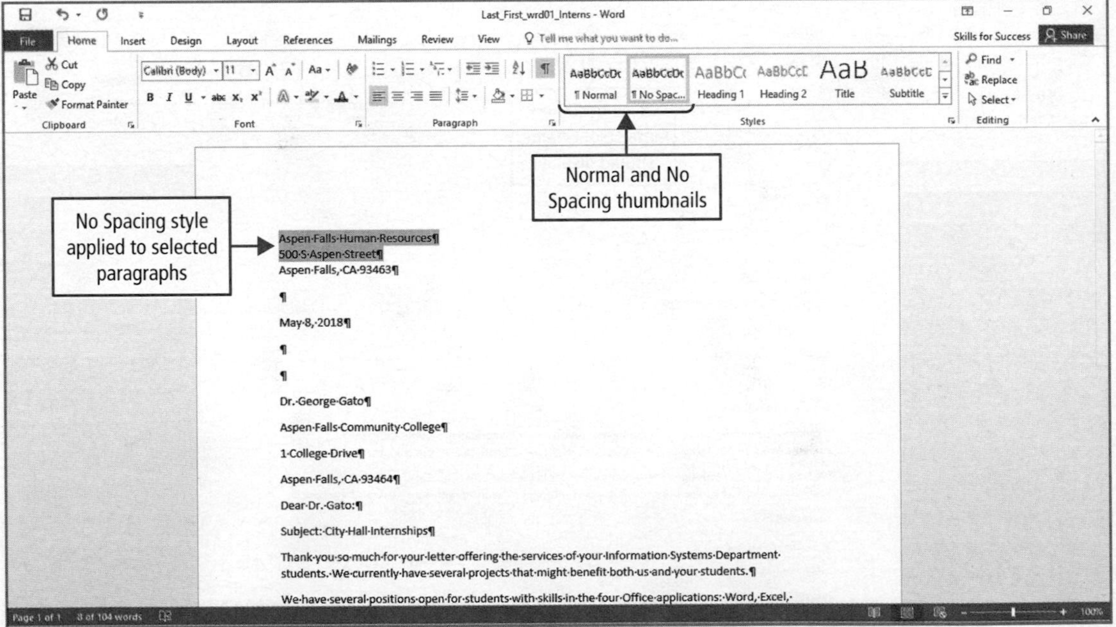

Figure 2

Word 2016, Windows 10, Microsoft Corporation

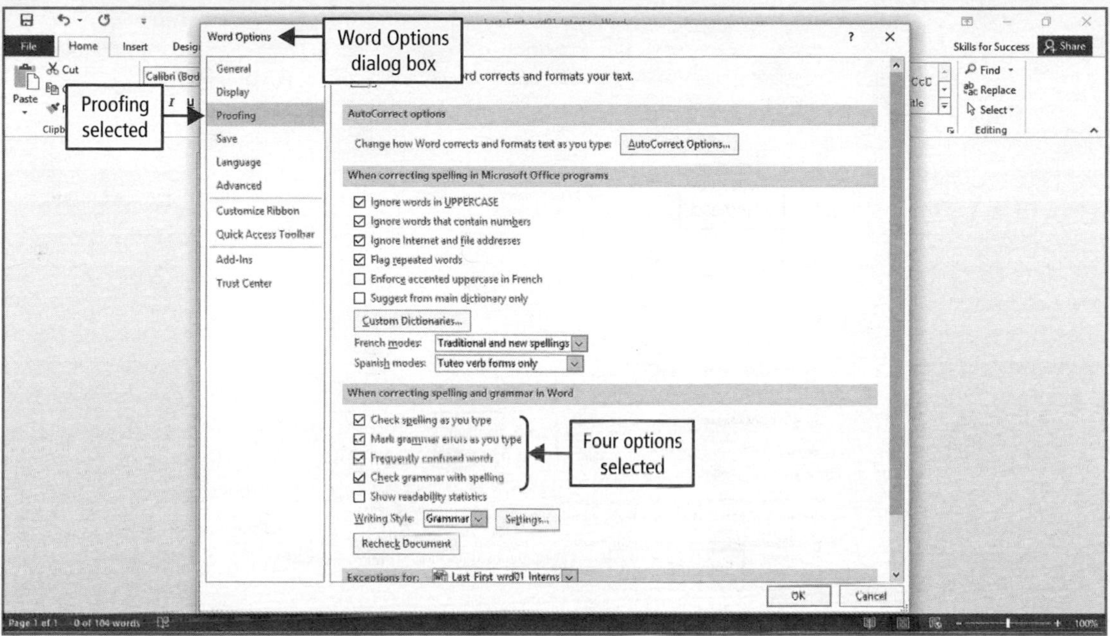

Word 2016, Windows 10, Microsoft Corporation

Figure 3

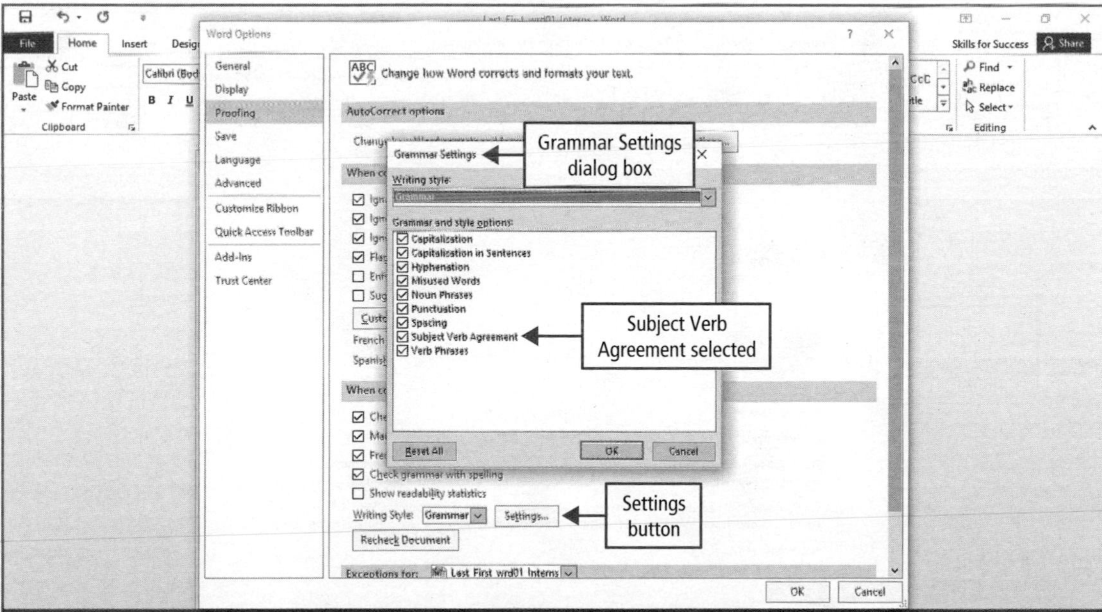

Word 2016, Windows 10, Microsoft Corporation

Figure 4

5. Click the **File tab**, and then click **Options**. On the left pane of the **Word Options** dialog box, click **Proofing**.
6. Under **When correcting spelling and grammar in Word**, verify that the first four check boxes are selected as shown in **Figure 3**.
7. To the right of **Writing Style**, click the **Settings** button.
8. In the **Grammar Settings** dialog box, verify the **Subject Verb Agreement** check box is selected. Compare your screen with **Figure 4**, and then click **OK**.

   In this manner, you can customize the types of errors that should be flagged as you work with a document.
9. Click **OK** to close the **Word Options** dialog box.
10. Click the **Save** button. Alternately, press Ctrl + S.

■ **You have completed Skill 2 of 10**

- You can select a single word by double-clicking and a single paragraph by triple-clicking.
- The amount of space between letter elements is specified by the style rules that your letter is following.

1. Click anywhere in the first paragraph of the document, *Aspen Falls Human Resources*.
2. On the **Home tab**, in the **Paragraph group**, click the **Center** button to center the paragraph.

   When you apply paragraph formatting, you do not need to select the paragraph. However, to apply paragraph formatting to two or more paragraphs at the same time, you will need to select all the paragraphs.

3. Repeat the technique just practiced to center the letterhead's second and third lines.
4. In the paragraph that begins *We have*, in the second sentence, point to the word *very*, and then double-click to select the word and display the Mini toolbar. Compare your screen with **Figure 1**.
5. With the word *very* selected, press Delete.

   When you double-click to select and delete a word, the selected word is deleted, along with the space following the word.

6. Move the insertion point in the margin to the left of *Dr. George Gato*. When the pointer displays, drag straight down to select the paragraph and the two paragraphs below it. With the three paragraphs selected, on the **Home tab**, in the **Styles group**, click the **No Spacing** thumbnail. Compare your screen with **Figure 2**.

■ **Continue to the next page to complete the skill**

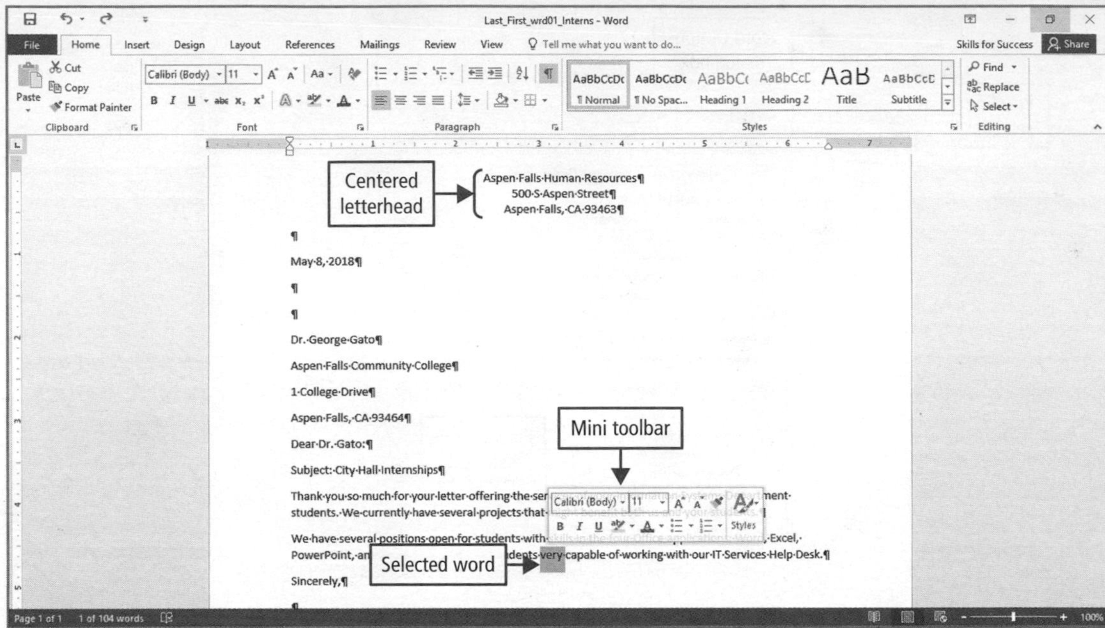

Figure 1 Word 2016, Windows 10, Microsoft Corporation

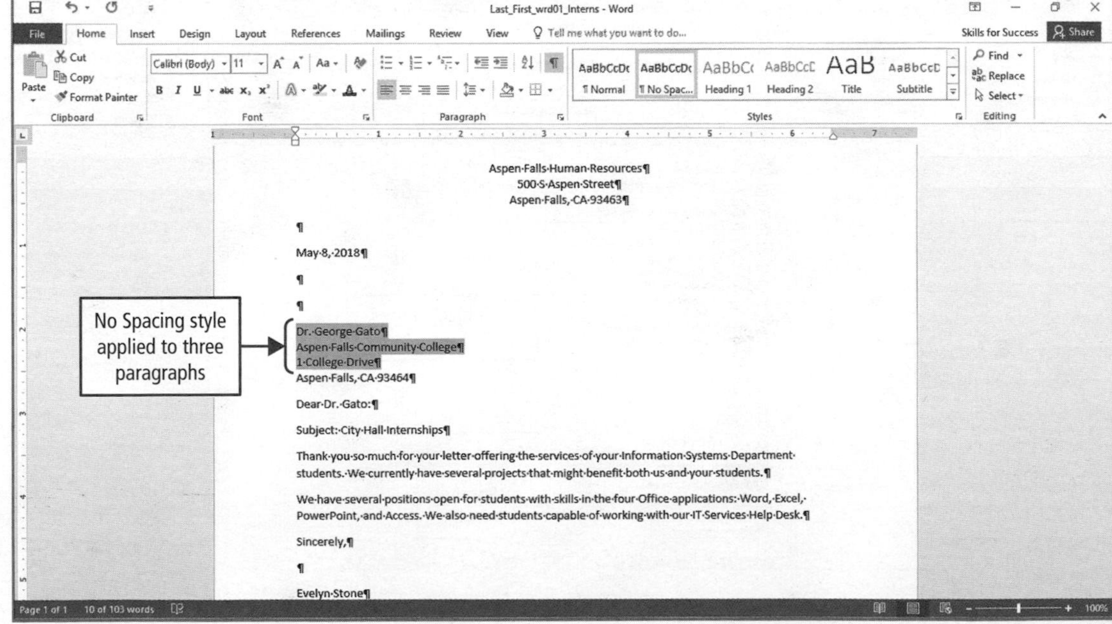

Figure 2 Word 2016, Windows 10, Microsoft Corporation

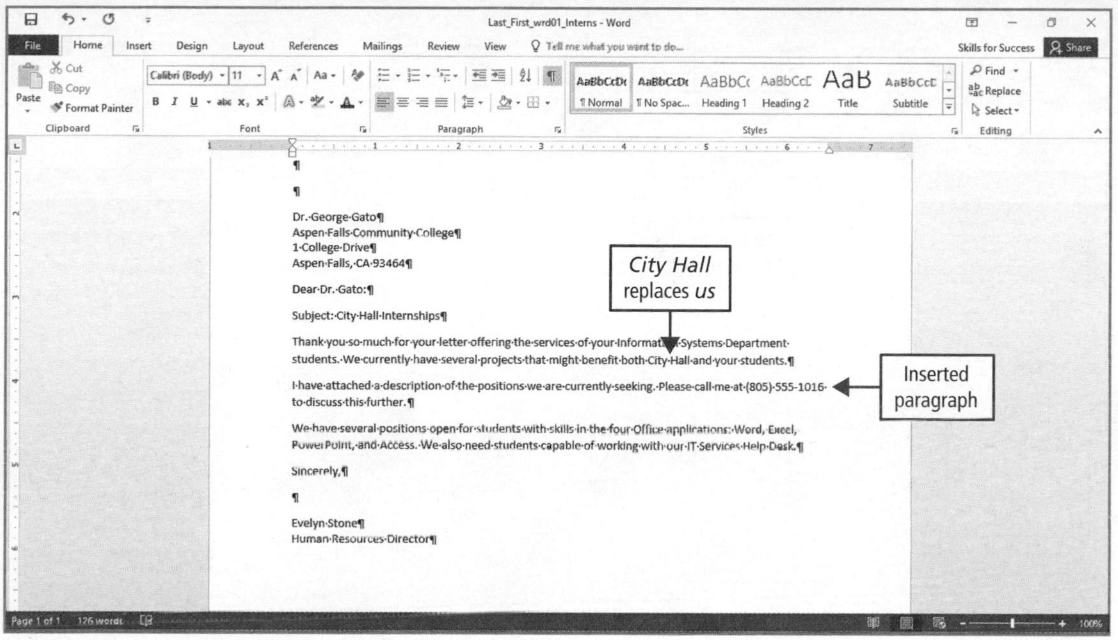

Word 2016, Windows 10, Microsoft Corporation

Figure 3

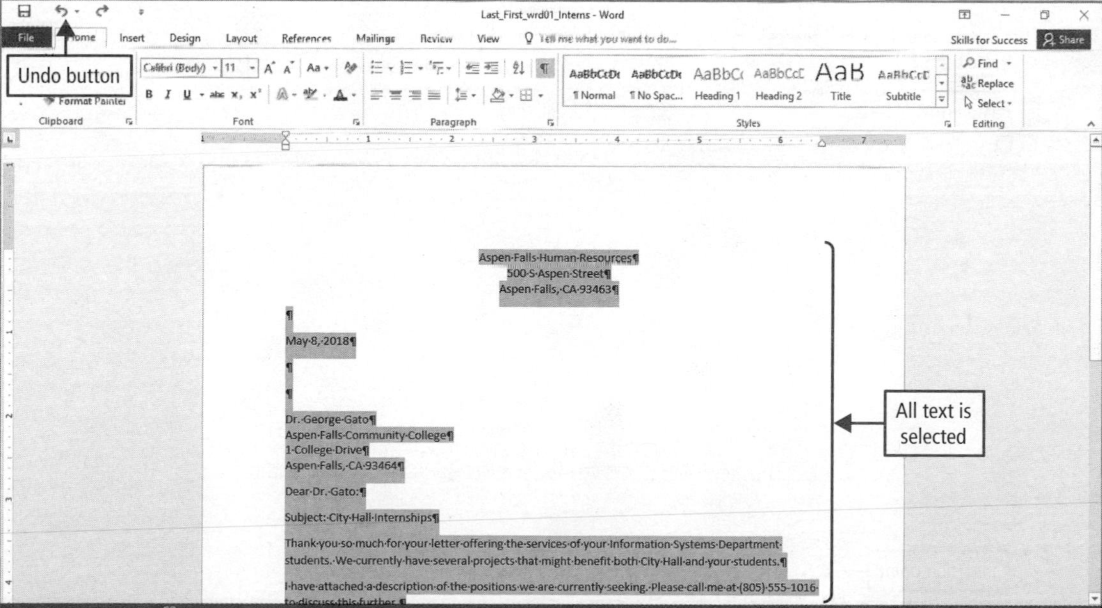

Word 2016, Windows 10, Microsoft Corporation

Figure 4

7. Triple-click the signature, *Evelyn Stone*, to select the paragraph, and then apply the **No Spacing** style.
8. In the paragraph that begins *Thank you*, double-click the word *us* to select it, and then type City Hall
9. In the paragraph that begins *Thank you*, click to position the insertion point at the end of the paragraph—following the period after *students*.
10. Press Enter one time, and then type I have attached a description of the positions we are currently seeking. Please call me at (805) 555-1016 to discuss this further. Compare your screen with **Figure 3**.
11. On the **Home tab**, in the **Editing group**, click **Select**, and then click **Select All** to select all of the text in the document. Alternately, press Ctrl + A.
12. On the **Home tab**, in the **Font group**, click the **Font arrow**. Scroll down the list of fonts, and then click **Cambria**.
13. Press Ctrl + Home, and then on the Quick Access Toolbar, click the **Undo** button one time to change the font back to Calibri. Compare your screen with **Figure 4**.

    As you work with a document, you need to be aware when text is selected. For example, if you start typing when the entire document is selected, all the text will be replaced with whatever new text you type. You can use the Undo button to fix this type of mistake.

14. Click anywhere in the document to deselect the text, and then **Save** the changes.

■ **You have completed Skill 3 of 10**

► The copy command places a copy of the selected text or object in the ***clipboard***—a temporary storage area that holds text or an object that has been cut or copied.

1. Press Ctrl + End to move the insertion point to the end of the document.
2. Click the **Layout tab**. In the **Page Setup group**, click **Breaks**, and then click **Page**. Alternately, press Ctrl + Enter. Compare your screen with **Figure 1**.

   A ***manual page break***—forcing a page to end at a location you specify—is added at the end of Page 1.
3. On the **File tab**, click **Open**. On the **Open** page, click the **Browse** button.
4. In the **Open** dialog box, navigate to the student files for this chapter. Click **wrd01_InternPositions**, and then click **Open**.
5. On the **Home tab**, in the **Editing group**, click **Select**, and then click **Select All**.

Obj 2.1.2 C

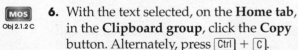

6. With the text selected, on the **Home tab**, in the **Clipboard group**, click the **Copy** button. Alternately, press Ctrl + C.
7. On the taskbar, point to the **Word** button. Click the **Last_First_wrd01_Interns** thumbnail to make it the active window.
8. With the insertion point still at the end of the document, click the **Home tab**. In the **Clipboard group**, click the **Paste arrow**, and then compare your screen with **Figure 2**.

   The Paste button has two parts—the Paste button and the Paste arrow that displays paste options.

■ **Continue to the next page to complete the skill**

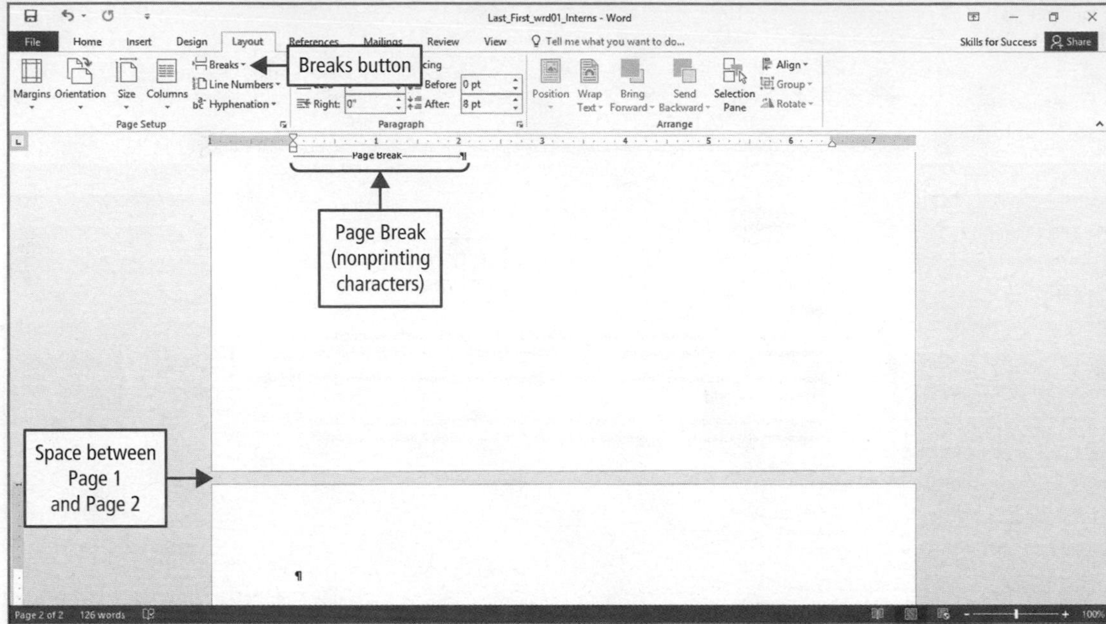

Figure 1

Word 2016, Windows 10, Microsoft Corporation

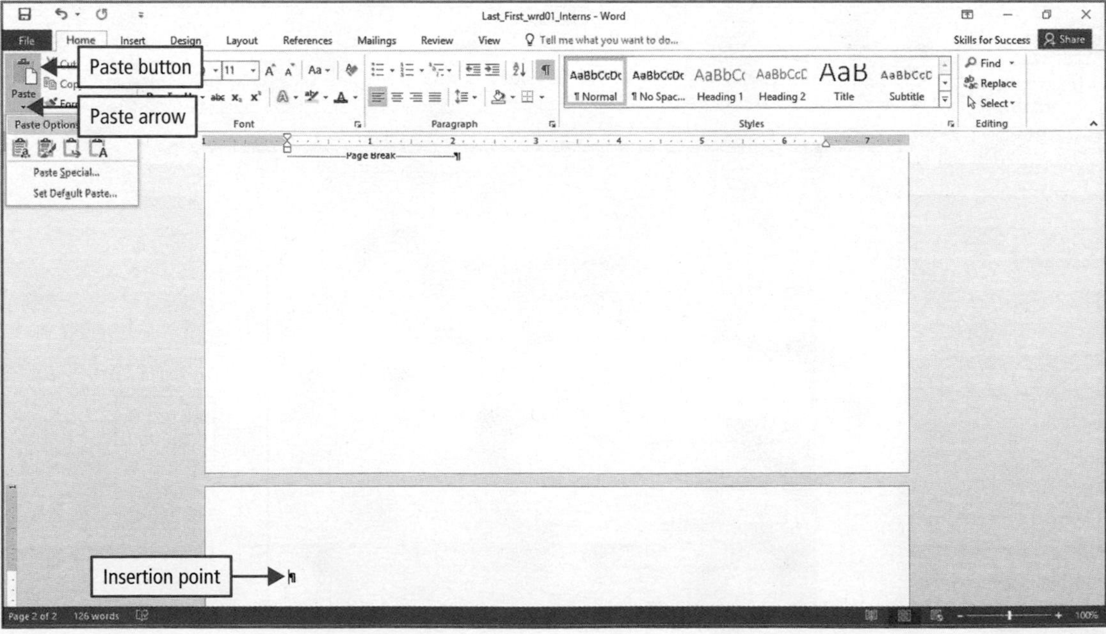

Figure 2

Word 2016, Windows 10, Microsoft Corporation

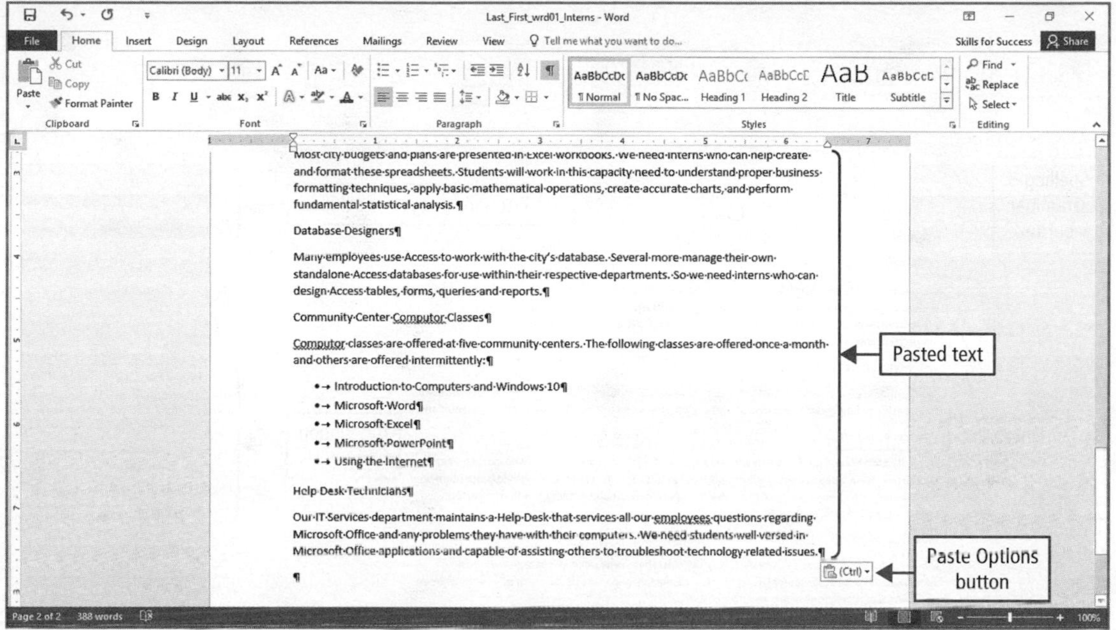

Word 2016, Windows 10, Microsoft Corporation

Figure 3

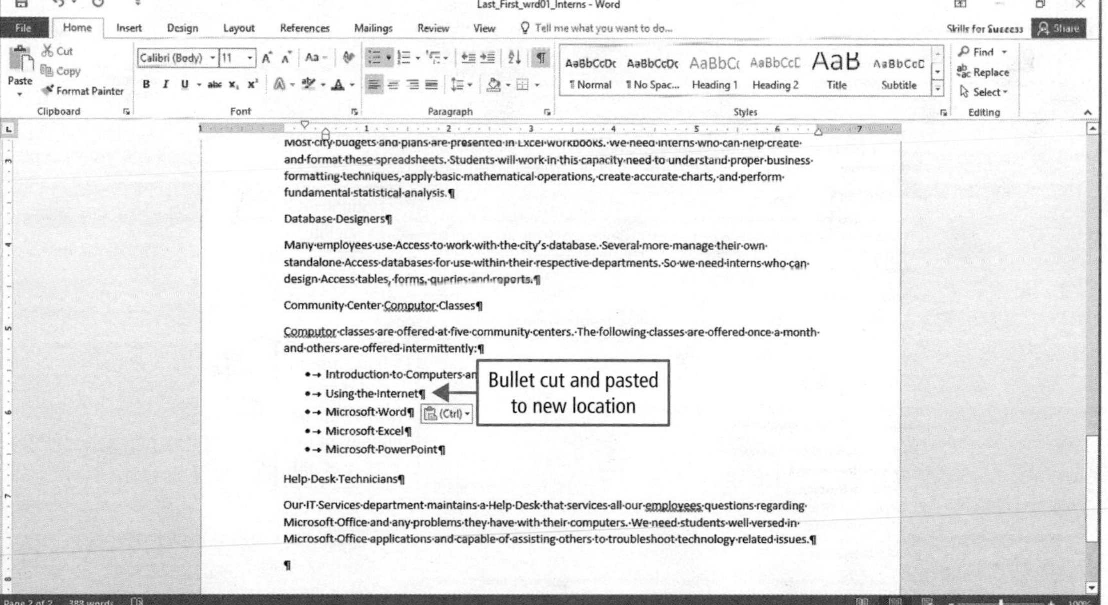

Word 2016, Windows 10, Microsoft Corporation

Figure 4

9. Click the **Paste** button, and then compare your screen with **Figure 3**.

   When you paste, you insert a copy of the text or object stored in the clipboard and the Paste Options button displays near the pasted text. The spelling and grammar errors in the pasted text will be corrected in the next skill.

10. Press Esc to hide the Paste Options button. In the bulleted text, select the paragraph *Using the Internet* including the paragraph mark.

11. On the **Home tab**, in the **Clipboard group**, click the **Cut** button. Alternately, press Ctrl + X.

    The ***cut*** command deletes the selected text or object and places a copy in the Office clipboard.

12. In the bulleted list, click to place the insertion point to the left of the text *Microsoft Word* and to the right of the bullet and tab formatting mark. In the **Clipboard group**, click **Paste**. Alternately, press Ctrl + V. Compare your screen with **Figure 4**.

    In this manner, you can move text by cutting it and then pasting it somewhere else.

13. On the taskbar, point to the **Word** button, point to the **wrd01_InternPositions** thumbnail, and then click the thumbnail's **Close** button ×.

14. Click in the letter document to make it the active window, and then **Save** the changes.

■ **You have completed Skill 4 of 10**

- When you are done typing the text of a document, it is a good idea to run the Spelling and Grammar checker to check for potential errors.

---

1. Press Ctrl + Home to place the insertion point at the beginning of the document.

2. Click the **Review tab**, and then in the **Proofing group**, click **Spelling & Grammar**. Alternately, press F7. Compare your screen with **Figure 1**.

   Spelling and grammar errors display in a task pane on the right side of the window. The first error is a grammar error indicating the verb *has* is not in the correct form. The checker suggests that the verb be changed to *have*.

3. In the **Grammar** pane, click the **Change** button to accept the suggested verb form change and move to the next error.

4. In the **Spelling** pane, click the **Delete** button to remove the repeated word *the*, and then compare your screen with **Figure 2**.

   When a misspelled word is encountered, you can replace it with one of the suggested spellings or add it to the custom dictionary. Words added to the custom dictionary will not be flagged as spelling errors. If you accidentally add a misspelled word to the dictionary, you can open the dictionary from the Options dialog box and delete the word.

   The Spelling task pane often displays definitions to help you decide if the suggested spelling is the correct choice. By signing in to your Microsoft account, you can access additional online dictionaries.

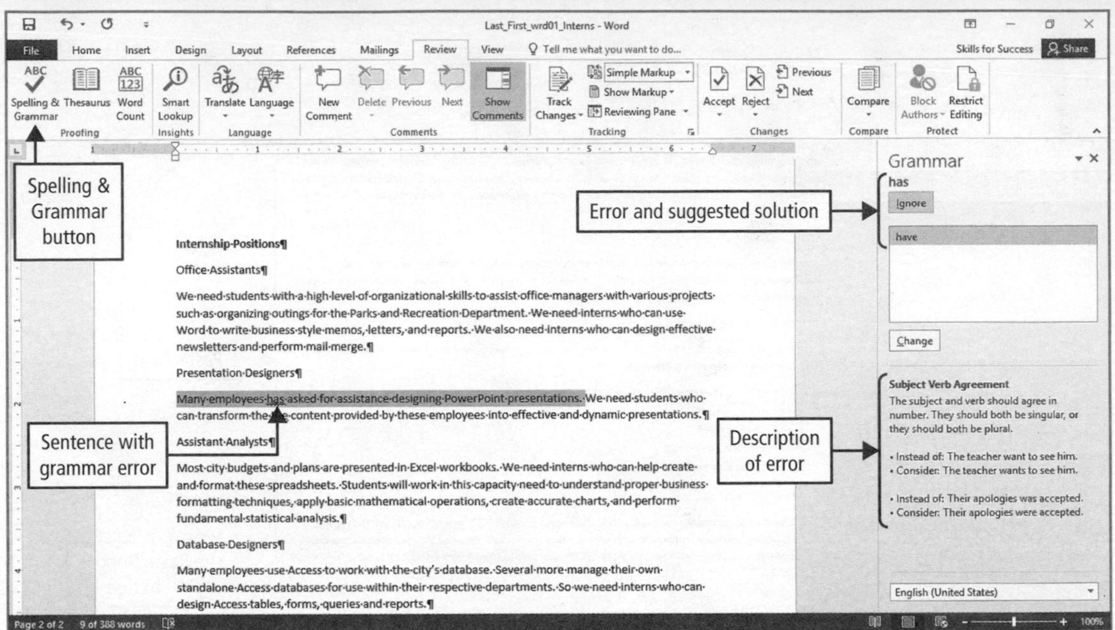

Figure 1 Word 2016, Windows 10, Microsoft Corporation

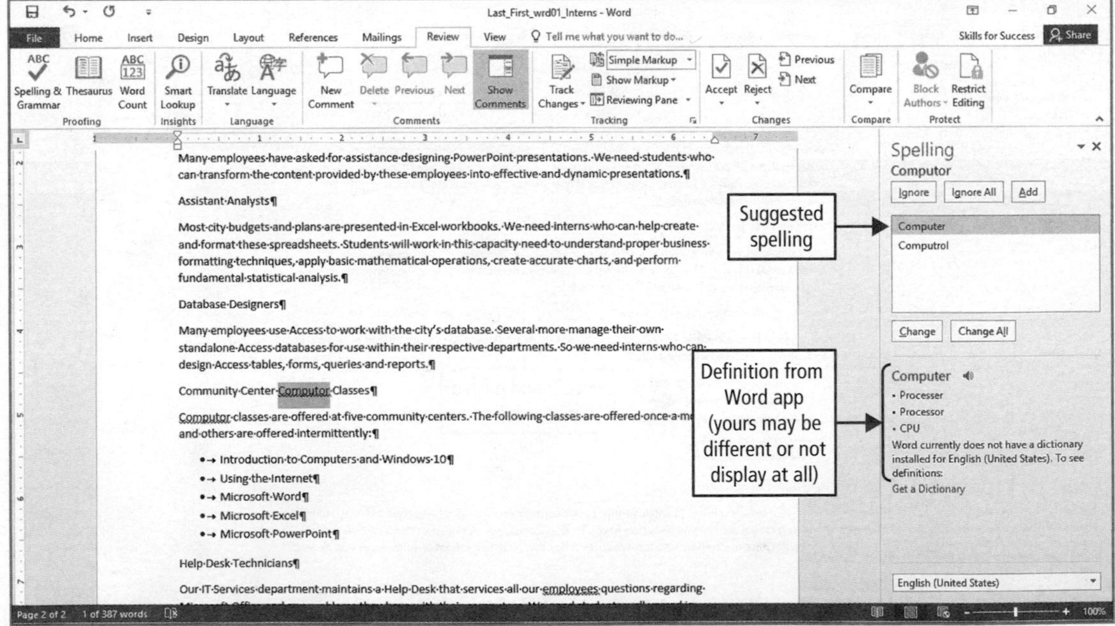

Figure 2 Word 2016, Windows 10, Microsoft Corporation

■ **Continue to the next page to complete the skill**

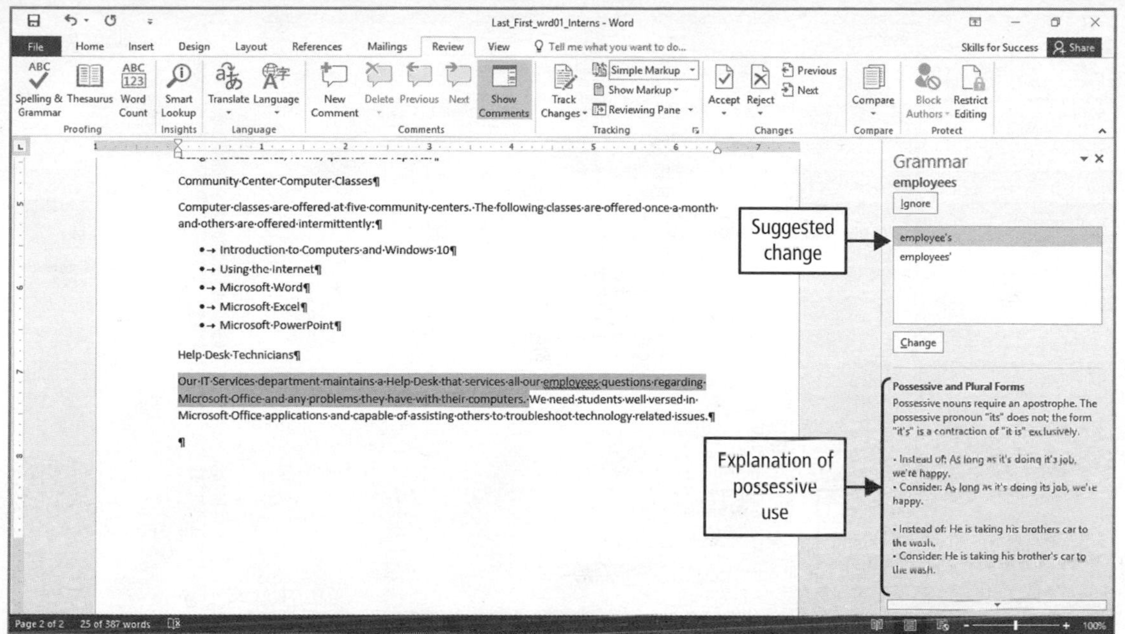

Word 2016, Windows 10, Microsoft Corporation

Figure 3

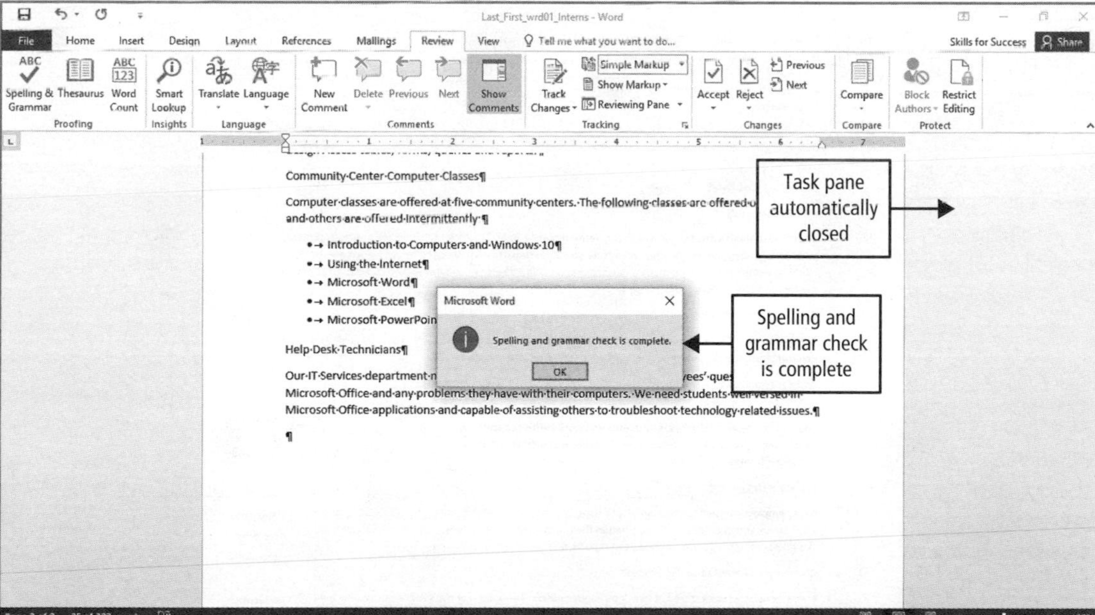

Word 2016, Windows 10, Microsoft Corporation

Figure 4

5. In the **Spelling** pane, click the **Change All** button to change both instances of the misspelled word, and then compare your screen with **Figure 3**.

   Many grammar errors are explained in the Grammar pane so that you can make an informed decision to ignore or accept the suggested change. Here, the word *employees* should have an apostrophe to indicate possessive use—*employees'*.

6. In the **Grammar** pane, click **employees'**, and then click the **Change** button to add the apostrophe. Compare your screen with **Figure 4**.

   When all flagged errors have been changed or ignored, a message displays indicating that the spelling and grammar check is complete. If you did not receive this message after completing this step, you may have typing errors, and you should fix them before continuing.

7. In the message indicating that the spelling and grammar check is complete, click **OK**, and then **Save** the file.

- **You have completed Skill 5 of 10**

- You can insert a synonym to replace a word with a different word.

1. On the **File tab**, click **Options**. In the **Word Options** dialog box, click **Proofing** to display the spelling and grammar options.
2. In the **Word Options** dialog box, click the **Recheck Document** button. Read the message that displays, and then click **Yes**. Compare your screen with **Figure 1**.
3. In the **Word Options** dialog box, click **OK**.
4. Press Ctrl + Home, and then notice that *Gato* is again flagged as a potential spelling error.

   By clicking the Recheck Document button, you can run the Spelling & Grammar checker again, and previously ignored errors will again be flagged.

5. Scroll as needed to display the heading *Database Designers* on Page 2.
6. Under the heading *Database Designers*, right-click the word *So*, point to **Synonyms**, and then compare your screen with **Figure 2**.
7. From the shortcut menu, click **Therefore**, and then notice that *Therefore* is flagged as a potential error. Right-click *Therefore*, and from the shortcut menu, click **Therefore**, to insert a comma.

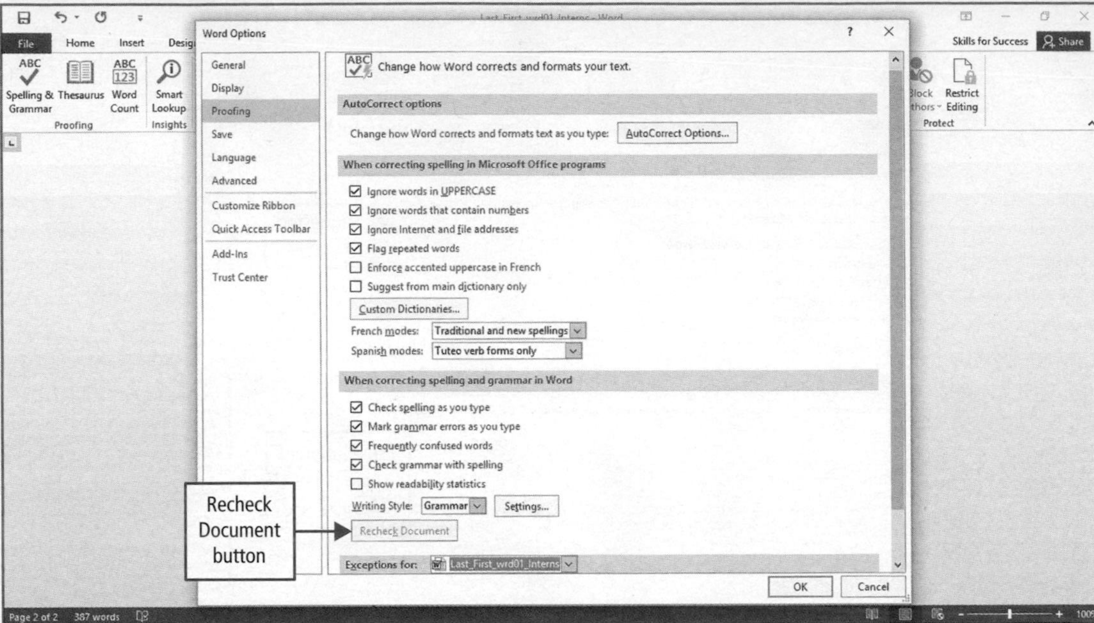

Figure 1

Word 2016, Windows 10, Microsoft Corporation

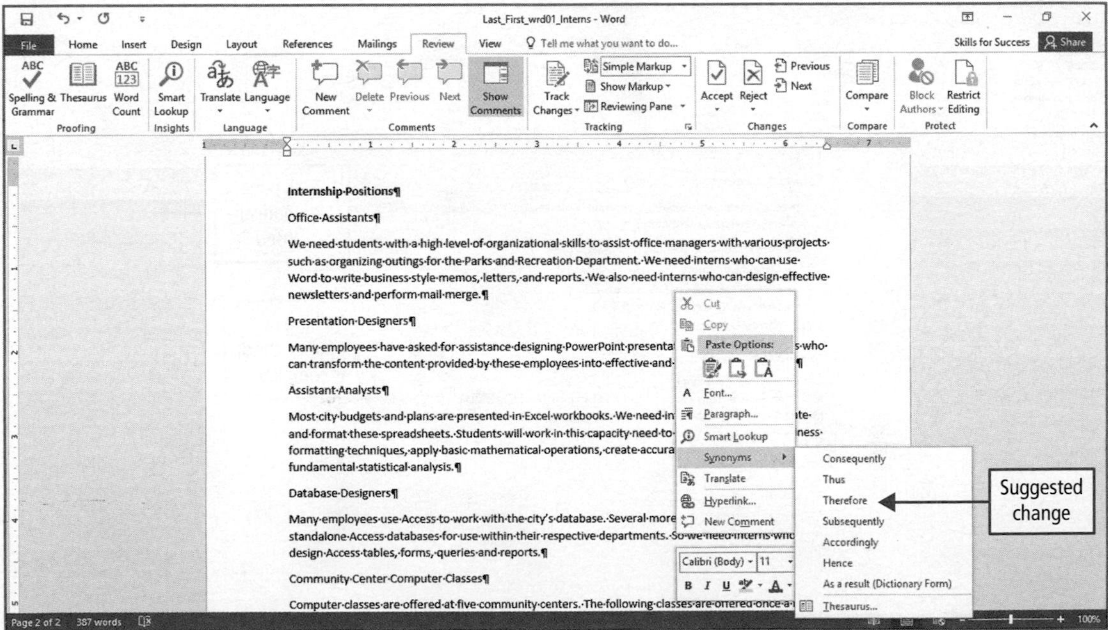

Figure 2

Word 2016, Windows 10, Microsoft Corporation

■ Continue to the next page to complete the skill

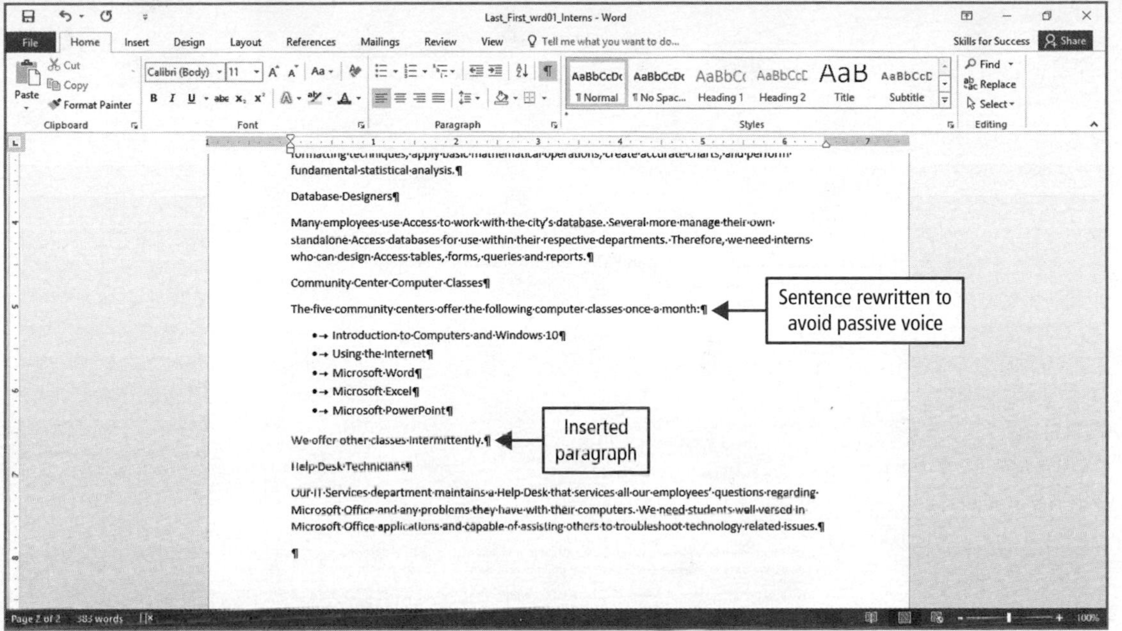

Word 2016, Windows 10, Microsoft Corporation

Figure 3

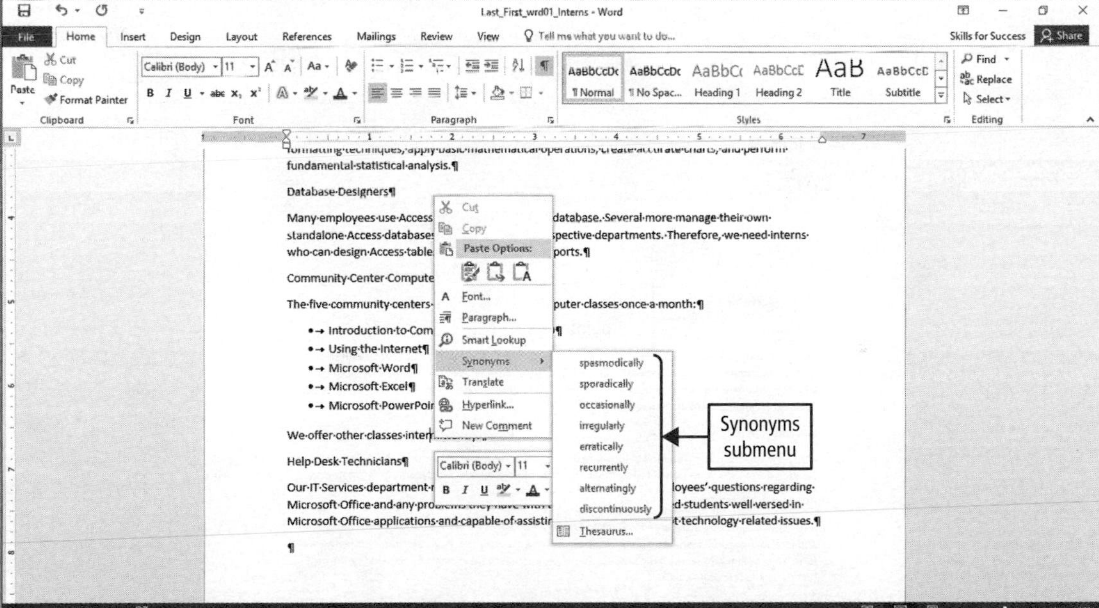

Word 2016, Windows 10, Microsoft Corporation

Figure 4

8. Point to the left of the paragraph starting *Computer classes are offered*, and then when the [pointer icon] pointer displays, double-click to select the entire paragraph.
9. With the entire paragraph selected, type the following: The five community centers offer the following computer classes once a month:
10. In the bulleted list, click to the right of *PowerPoint*, and then press Enter. On the **Home tab**, in the **Styles group**, click **Normal** to apply the default document formatting. Type We offer other classes intermittently. and then compare your screen with **Figure 3**.
11. Right-click the word *intermittently*, and then from the shortcut menu, point to **Synonyms**. Compare your screen with **Figure 4**.

    The Synonyms command displays a submenu with alternate word choices. In this manner, Word Thesaurus can be accessed quickly. A ***thesaurus*** lists words that have the same or similar meaning to the word you are looking up.
12. From the **Synonyms** submenu, click **occasionally** to replace the word *intermittently*.
13. **Save** [Save icon] the file.

■ **You have completed Skill 6 of 10**

- Formatting document text should help organize the document visually without detracting from its message.
- A set of formatting choices can be applied with Format Painter quickly and consistently.

Obj 2.2.1 C

1. Select the first paragraph of the letterhead, *Aspen Falls Human Resources*. On the **Home tab**, in the **Font group**, click the **Font Size arrow**, and then click **16**.
2. With the first paragraph still selected, click the **Font arrow**, click **Cambria**, and then apply **Bold** [B].
3. In the letterhead, drag to select the two paragraphs beginning with *500* and ending with *93463*. In the **Font group**, click the **Italic** button [I], and then compare your screen with **Figure 1**.

Obj 2.2.2 C

4. In the letterhead, click in the text *Aspen Falls Human Resources*. On the **Home tab**, in the **Clipboard group**, click the **Format Painter** button.
5. Press [PageDown] as needed to display the top of Page 2. With the icon, drag through the heading *Internship Positions*. Compare your screen with **Figure 2**, and then release the left mouse button.

   In this manner, you can copy a collection of formatting settings to other text in the document. When you release the left mouse button, Format Painter will no longer be active.

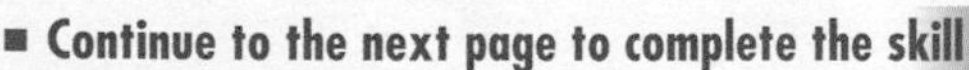

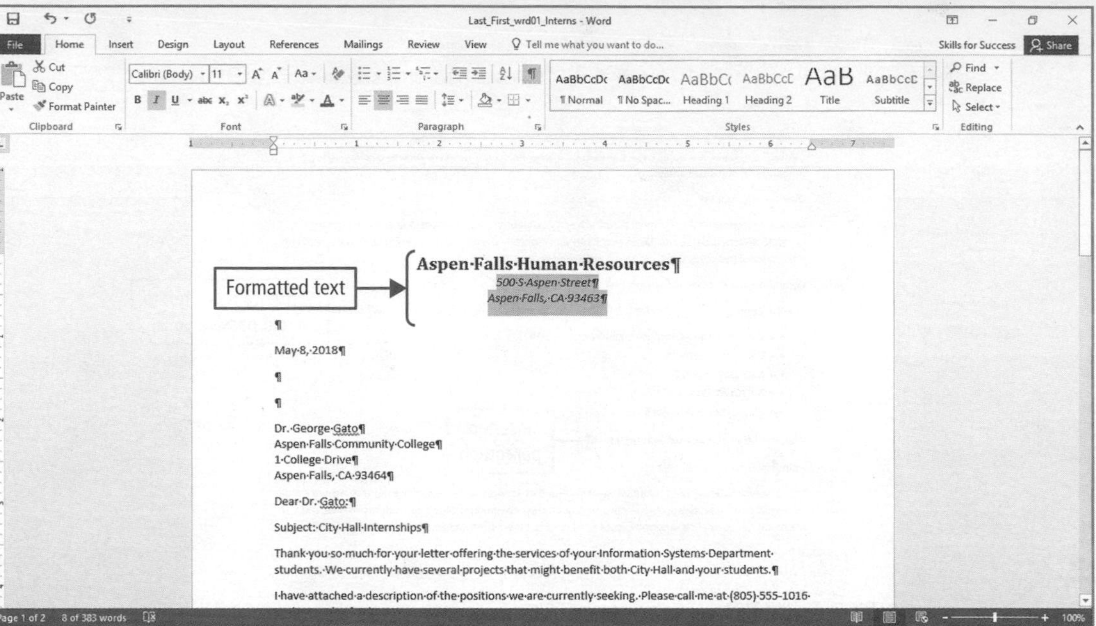

Figure 1

Word 2016, Windows 10, Microsoft Corporation

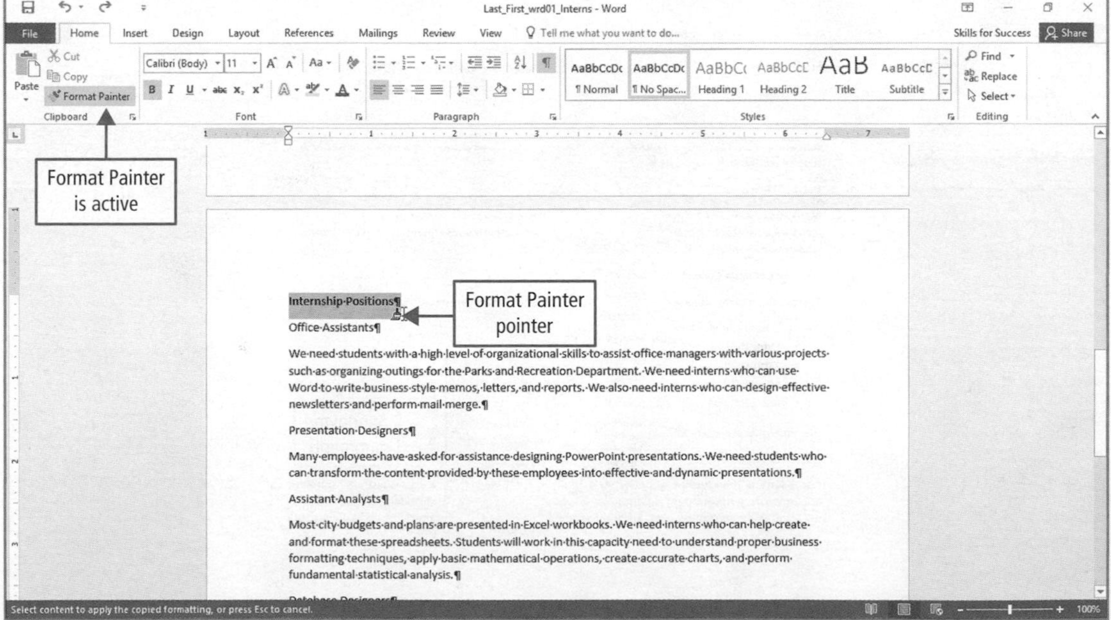

Figure 2

Word 2016, Windows 10, Microsoft Corporation

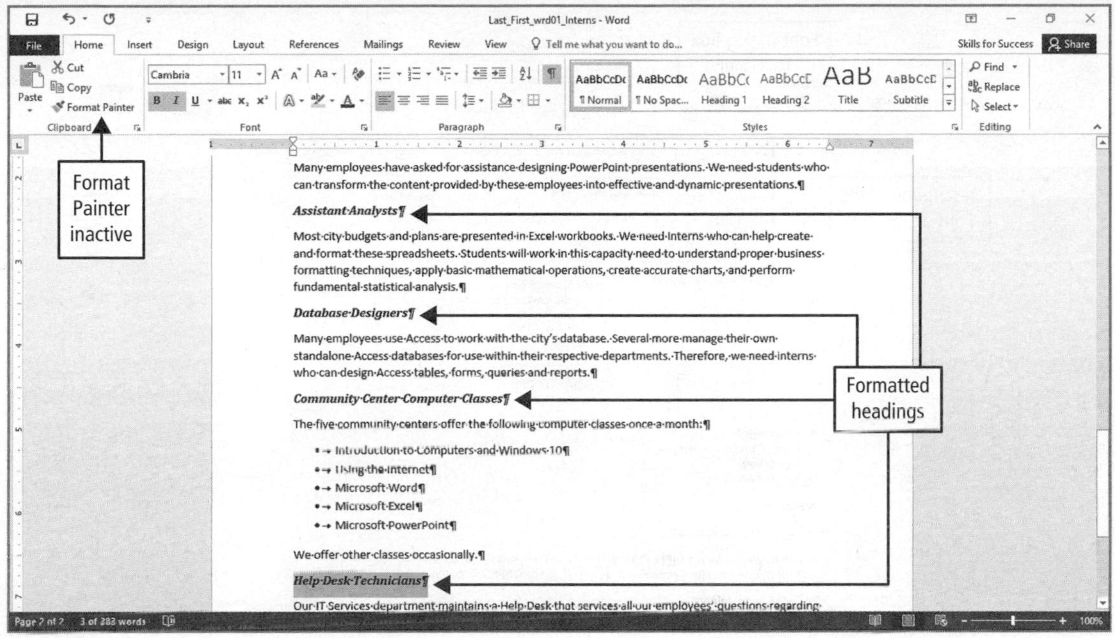

Word 2016, Windows 10, Microsoft Corporation

Figure 3

6. Near the top of Page 2, select the heading *Office Assistants*, and then apply the **Cambria** font, **Bold** [B], and **Italic** [I].
7. With the heading *Office Assistants* still selected, in the **Clipboard group**, double-click the **Format Painter** button. Drag through the *Presentation Designers* heading, and then notice that Format Painter remains active.
8. Drag through the *Assistant Analysts* heading to apply the formatting, and then repeat this technique to apply the formatting to the three remaining headings on Page 2.
9. In the **Clipboard group**, click the **Format Painter** button to release it, and then compare your screen with **Figure 3**.

   In this manner, you can use Format Painter multiple times to format headings and other document elements. You can also release Format Painter by pressing [Esc].
10. **Save** the file, and then take a moment to review the common formatting options as described in the table in **Figure 4**.

■ **You have completed Skill 7 of 10**

Common Formatting Options	
Format	**Description**
Font	A set of characters with a common design.
Font size	The size of the characters typically measured in points.
Bold	Extra thickness applied to characters to emphasize text.
Italic	A slant applied to characters to emphasize text.
Underline	A line under characters used to emphasize text.
Text efects	A set of decorative formatting applied to characters.
Highlight color	Shading applied to the background of characters.
Font color	The color applied to the characters.

Figure 4

SKILL 8: Apply Advanced Font Settings

SKILL 1.8

► Dialog boxes often contain commands that are not on the ribbon. Many of these dialog boxes can be launched from their Ribbon group. For example, the Font dialog box can be opened by clicking the Dialog Box Launcher in the Font group.

1. At the beginning of the letter, select the first paragraph, *Aspen Falls Human Resources*.
2. On the **Home tab**, in the **Font group**, point to—do not click—the **Font Dialog Box Launcher** [icon], and then compare your screen with **Figure 1**.

   When you point to a Dialog Box Launcher, the name of the dialog box and the name of the keyboard shortcut that opens it display. A thumbnail of the dialog box displays next to its description.
3. Click the **Font Dialog Box Launcher** [icon] to open the Font dialog box.
4. In the **Font** dialog box, under **Font style**, click **Regular** to remove the Bold font style.
5. Under **Effects**, select the **Small caps** check box, and then compare your screen with **Figure 2**.

   MOS Obj 2.2.1 C

   The ***small caps*** effect displays all characters in uppercase while making any character originally typed as an uppercase letter taller than the ones typed as lowercase characters. Small caps is an alternate to using bold or italic to emphasize text. A preview of the effect displays at the bottom of the Font dialog box.

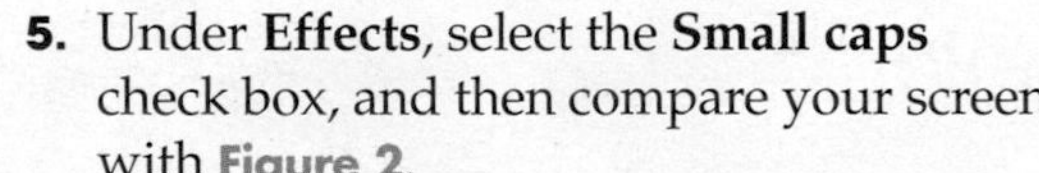

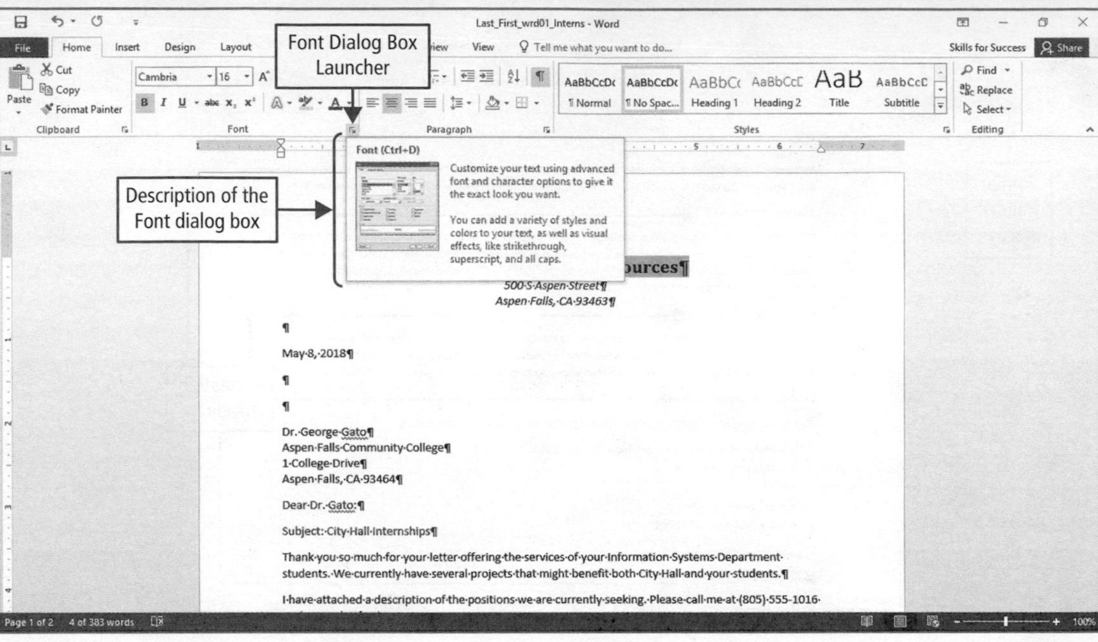

Figure 1

Word 2016, Windows 10, Microsoft Corporation

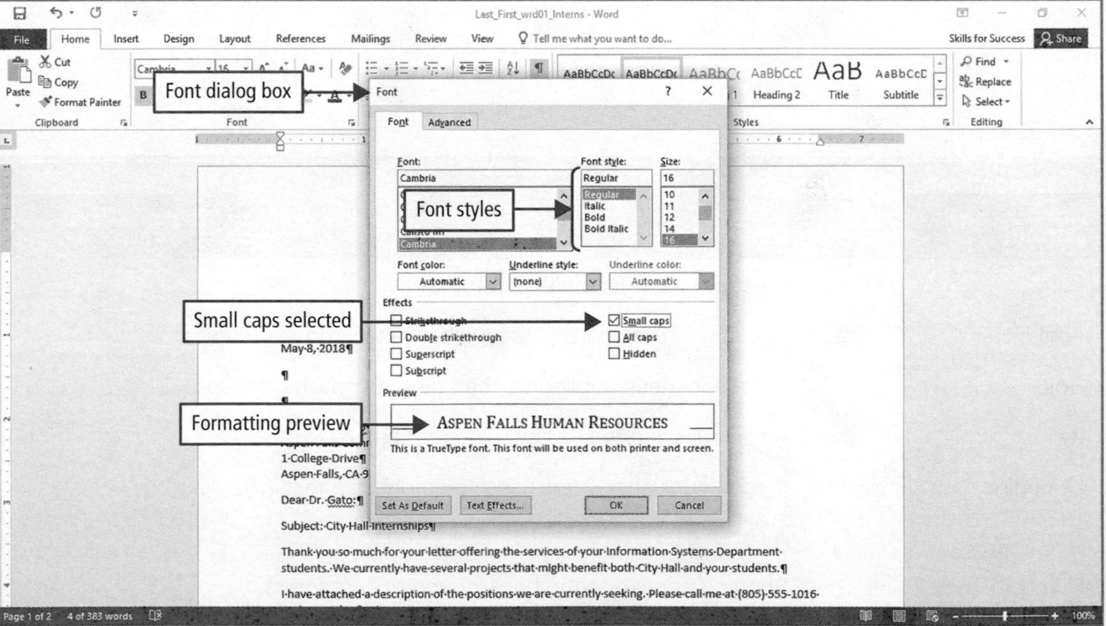

Figure 2

Word 2016, Windows 10, Microsoft Corporation

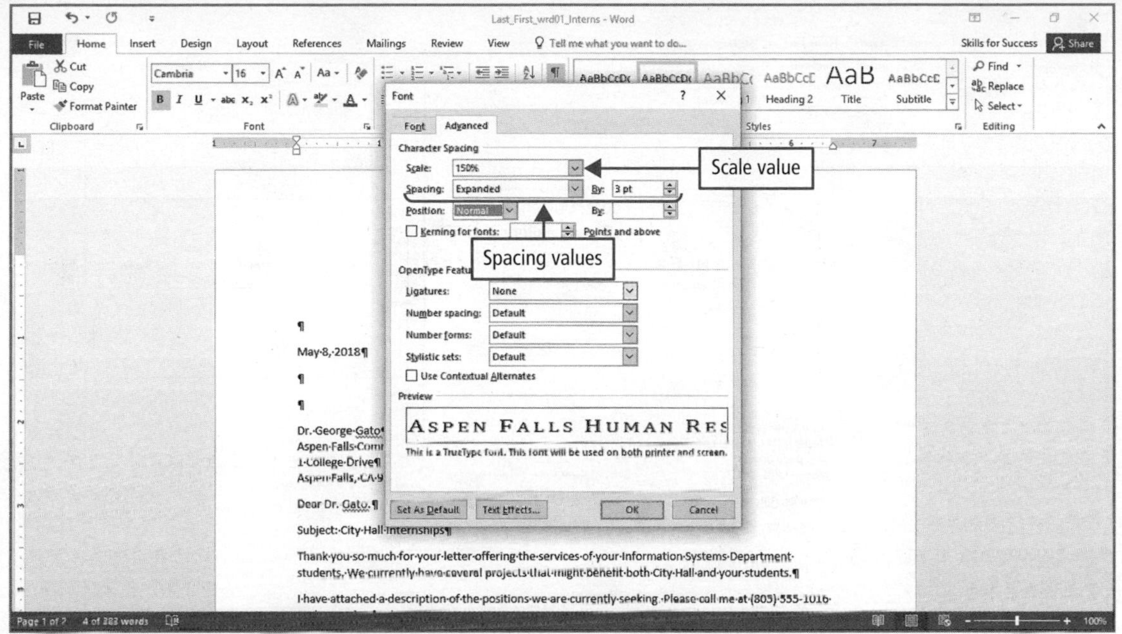

Word 2016, Windows 10, Microsoft Corporation

Figure 3

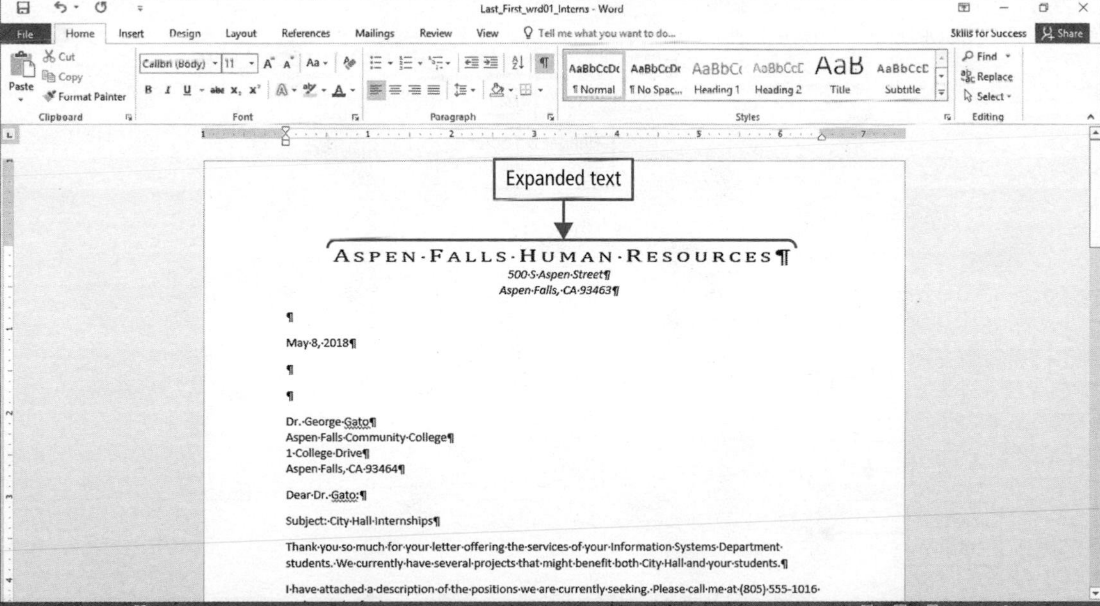

Word 2016, Windows 10, Microsoft Corporation

Figure 4

6. In the **Font** dialog box, click the **Advanced tab**.
7. On the **Advanced tab** of the **Font** dialog box, under **Character Spacing**, click the **Scale arrow**, and then click **150%**.
8. Under **Character Spacing**, click the **Spacing arrow**, and then click **Expanded**.
9. To the right of **Spacing**, in the **By** box, replace the value *1 pt* with 3 pt
10. Press Tab, and then compare your screen with **Figure 3**.

    Font sizes and the spacing between characters are measured in ***points***—a unit of measure with 72 points per inch. Here, the characters will have an additional 3 points of space between them.

11. Click **OK** to accept the changes and close the dialog box.
12. Click anywhere in the document to deselect the text, and then compare your screen with **Figure 4**.

    An organization's letterhead is typically formatted differently than the rest of the letter to make it stand out. Here, the text is centered and the department's name has been expanded and stretched.

13. **Save** the file.

■ **You have completed Skill 8 of 10**

- A ***header*** and ***footer*** are reserved areas for text, graphics, and fields that display at the top (header) or bottom (footer) of each page in a document.
- You can insert a built-in header or footer, or you can create your own custom header or footer.
- Throughout this book, you will insert the document file name in the footer of each document.

Obj 1.3.4 C

1. Press Ctrl + Home to move to the beginning of the document. On the **Insert tab**, in the **Header & Footer group**, click the **Footer** button.
2. Compare your screen with **Figure 1**, and then in the Footer gallery scroll down to view the built-in footers.

   You can quickly insert a footer by selecting a built-in footer from the Footer gallery.

3. Below the **Footer** gallery, click **Edit Footer**. Notice that at the bottom of Page 1, below **Footer**, the insertion point is blinking in the footer, and the **Header & Footer Tools Design tab** displays on the Ribbon, as shown in **Figure 2**.

   When you want to create or edit your own custom footer, you need to make the footer area active. You can do this using the Edit Footer command or by double-clicking in the footer area.

4. On the **Header & Footer Tools Design tab**, in the **Insert group**, click the **Quick Parts** button. From the displayed list, click **Field**.

   A ***field*** is a category of data—such as a file name, a page number, or the current date—that can be inserted into a document.

■ **Continue to the next page to complete the skill**

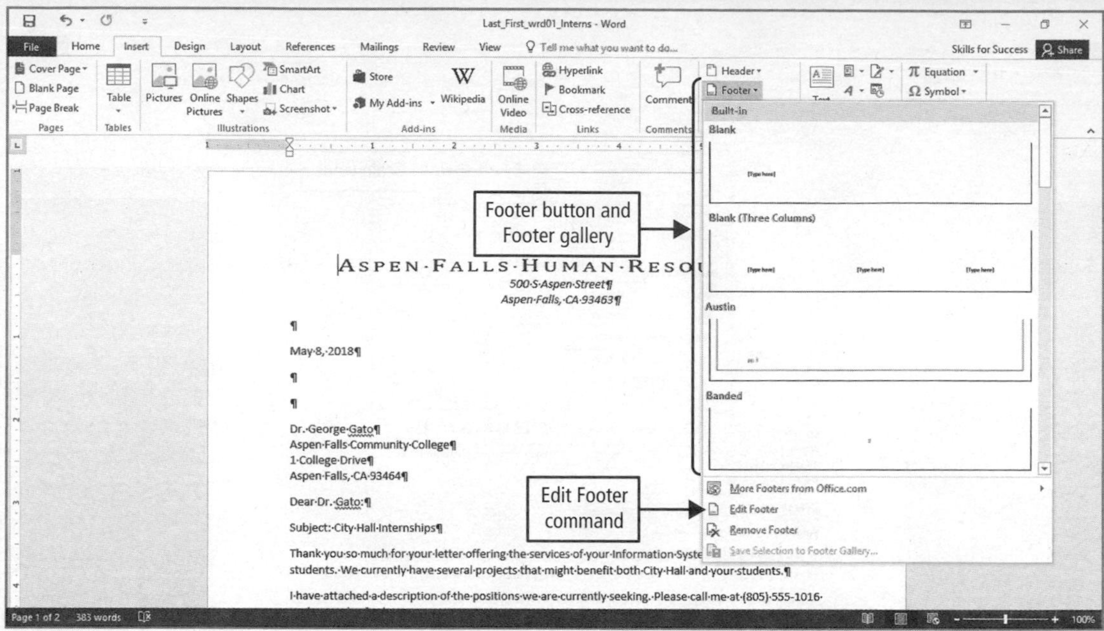

Figure 1

Word 2016, Windows 10, Microsoft Corporation

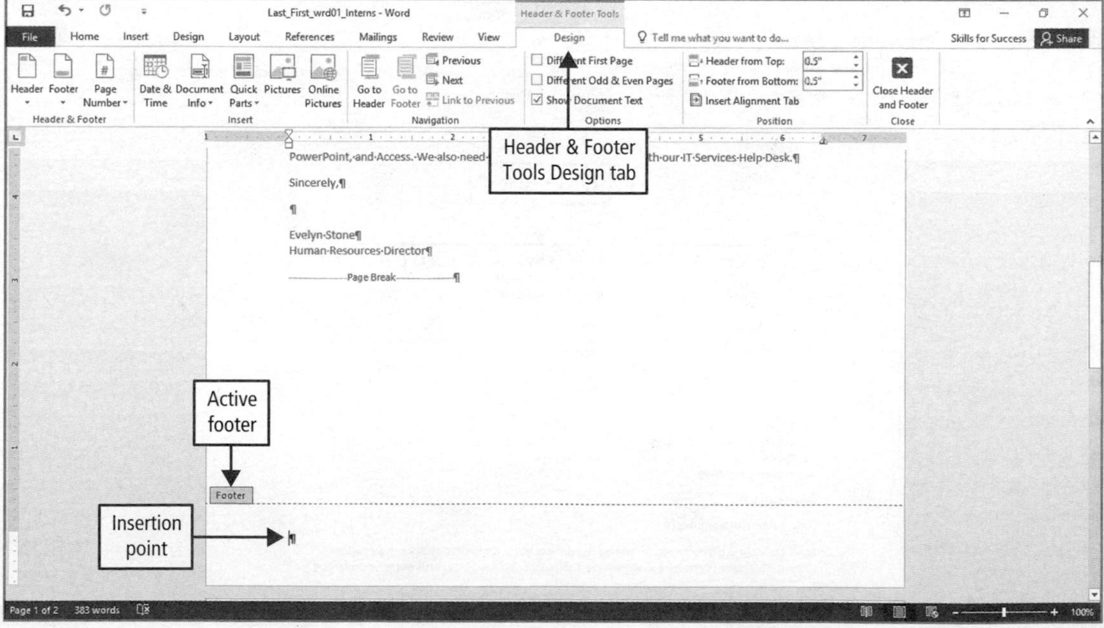

Figure 2

Word 2016, Windows 10, Microsoft Corporation

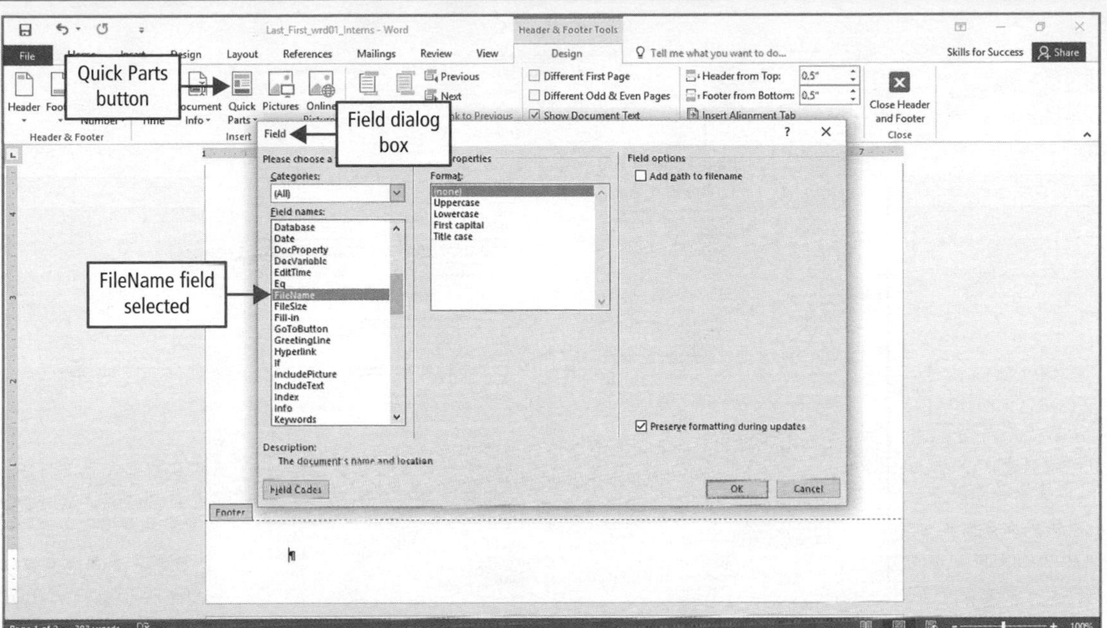

Word 2016, Windows 10, Microsoft Corporation

Figure 3

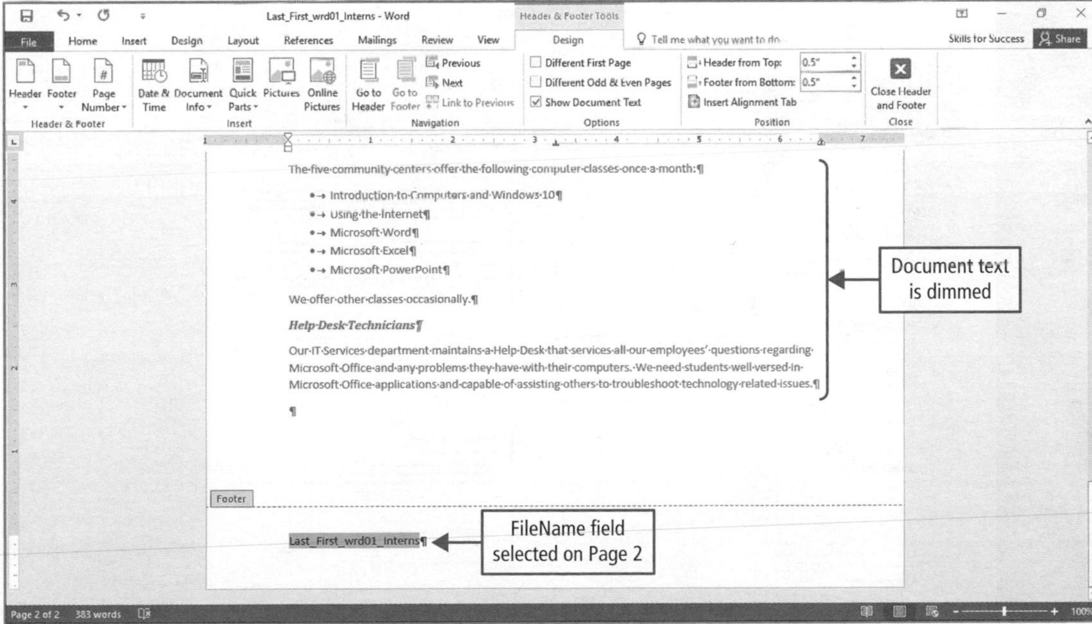

Word 2016, Windows 10, Microsoft Corporation

Figure 4

5. Under **Field names**, scroll down to see what types of fields are available, and then click the **FileName** field. Compare your screen with **Figure 3**.

   Spaces between multiple words in field names are removed to create a single word.

6. Under **Format**, be sure that **(none)** is selected, and then at the bottom of the **Field** dialog box, click **OK** to insert the file name in the footer.

7. Scroll to display the bottom of Page 2, click the **FileName** field one time to select it, and then compare your screen with **Figure 4**.

   By default, footers are inserted on each page of the document. When you select a field, it is shaded in gray.

8. On the **Header & Footer Tools Design tab**, click the **Close Header and Footer** button. Scroll to display the bottom of Page 1 and the top of Page 2, and then notice that the header and footer areas are inactive as indicated by the dimmed file name.

   While the document text is active, the footer text cannot be edited. When the footer area is active, the footer text is black, and the document text is dimmed and cannot be edited.

9. **Save** the file.

■ **You have completed Skill 9 of 10**

SKILL 10: Save Documents as PDF Files

- Before printing, it is a good idea to set the zoom level to view one or more pages without scrolling.
- You can save documents in different formats so that people who do not have Word can read them.

---

1. Press Ctrl + Home to move to the beginning of the document. On the **Home tab**, in the **Paragraph group**, click the **Show/Hide** button ¶ so that the formatting marks do not display.

   Because formatting marks do not print, hiding them gives you a better idea of how the printed page will look.

Obj 1.4.2 C

2. On the **View tab**, in the **Zoom group**, click **Multiple Pages**, and then compare your screen with **Figure 1**.

   When you zoom to display multiple pages, a best fit is calculated based on your monitor size. Here, two pages are displayed with a zoom level of 47 percent. If you have a different-sized monitor, your zoom percentage may be different.

3. In the **Zoom group**, click the **100%** button to return to your original zoom level.

Obj 1.5.3 C

4. On the **File tab**, click **Print**. On the **Print** page, click the **Next Page** button ▶ to preview Page 2, and then compare your screen with **Figure 2**.

5. If you are printing your work for this project, click the **Print** button to print the letter. Otherwise, click the **Back** button.

Obj 1.5.2 C

6. Click **Save**. Click the **File tab**, and then click **Export**. On the **Export** page, click the **Create PDF/XPS** button.

■ Continue to the next page to complete the skill

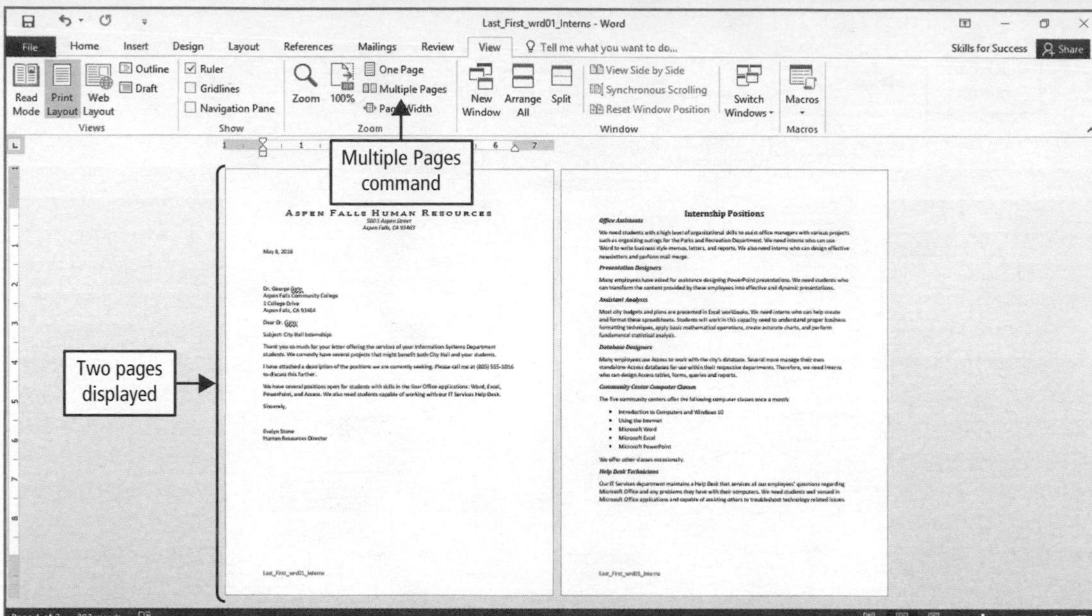

Figure 1 Word 2016, Windows 10, Microsoft Corporation

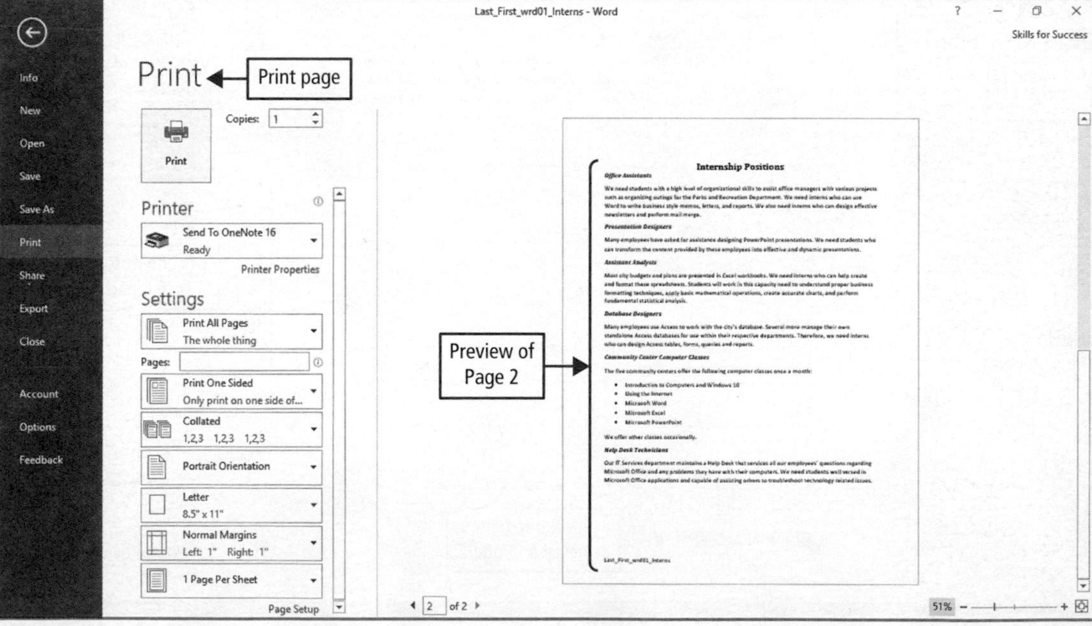

Figure 2 Word 2016, Windows 10, Microsoft Corporation

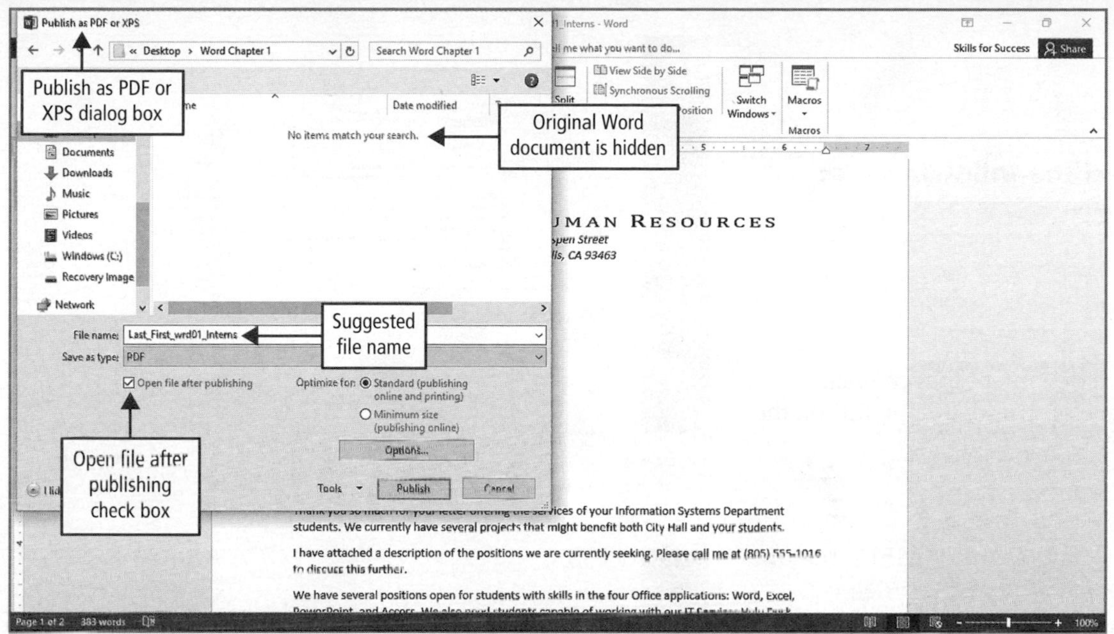

Word 2016, Windows 10, Microsoft Corporation

Figure 3

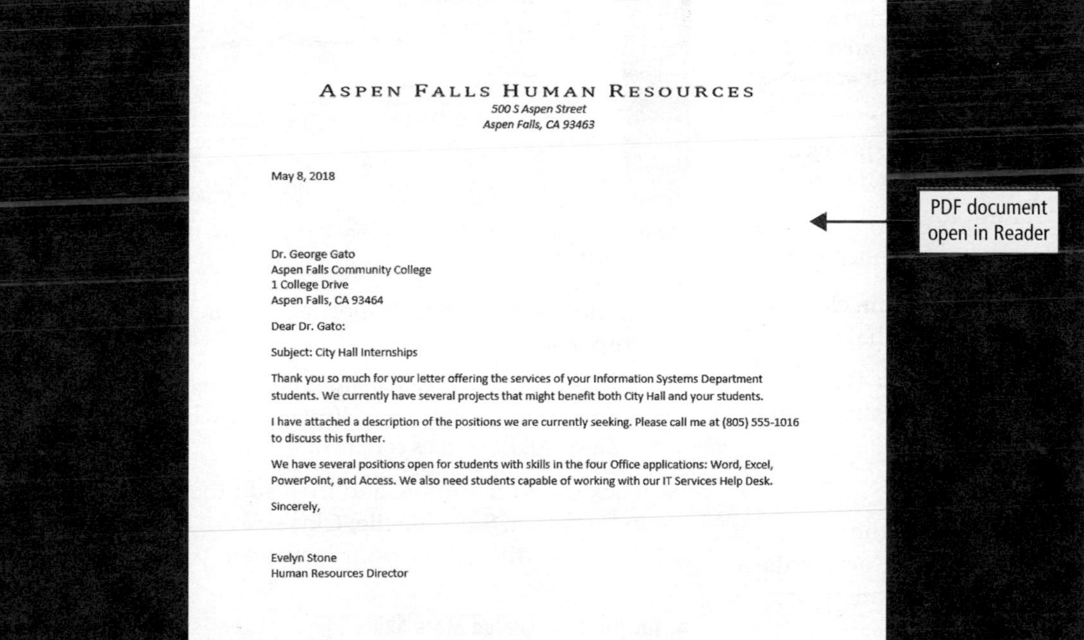

Word 2016, Windows 10, Microsoft Corporation

Figure 4

7. In the **Publish as PDF or XPS** dialog box, navigate to your **Word Chapter 1** folder. Notice that the Word document is not listed and the suggested file name is identical to the Word file name as shown in **Figure 3**.

   A ***PDF document*** is an image of a document that can be viewed using a PDF reader such as Adobe Acrobat Reader instead of the application that created the original document.

   Here, you can use the file name suggested in the dialog box because a PDF document file extension will be ***.pdf*** instead of ***.docx***—the file extension assigned to Word documents.

   The Word file is not listed in the dialog box because only files with the extensions .pdf and .xps will be listed. The original Word file is in the folder and will not be altered.

8. If necessary, select the **Open file after publishing** check box, and then click **Publish**.

9. Wait a few moments for the document to publish and display in your default PDF viewer. Compare your screen with **Figure 4**.

10. **Close** your PDF viewer application window.

11. **Close**  Word. If you are prompted to save changes, click Save. Submit your printout or files as directed by your instructor.

DONE! You have completed Skill 10 of 10, and your file is complete!

More Skills 11

Manage Document Properties

To complete this project, you will need the following file:

- wrd01_MS11Memo

You will save your file as:

- Last_First_wrd01_MS11Memo

▶ ***Document properties*** are information about a document that can help you identify or organize your files, such as the name of the document author, the file name, and key words.

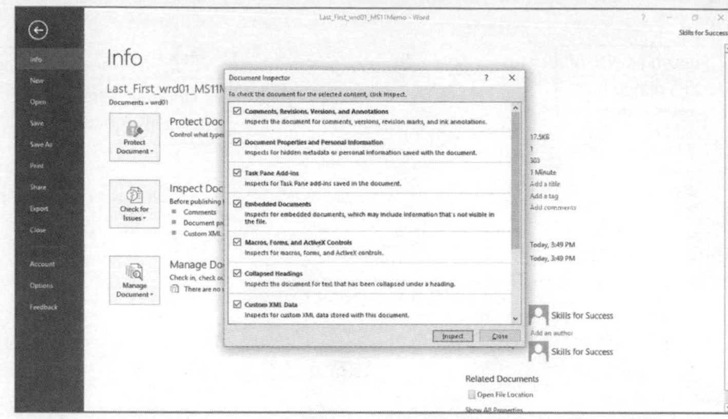

Figure 1 Word 2016, Windows 10, Microsoft Corporation

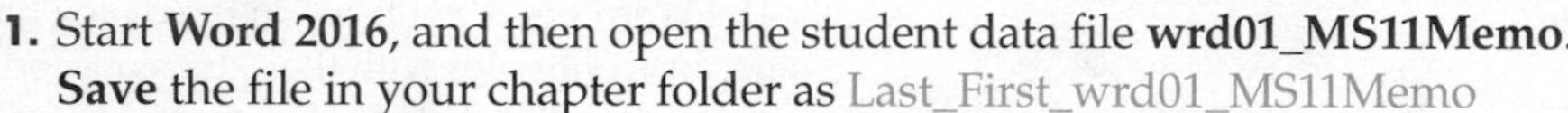

1. Start **Word 2016**, and then open the student data file **wrd01_MS11Memo**. **Save** the file in your chapter folder as Last_First_wrd01_MS11Memo
2. Click the **File tab**, and then on the Info page, notice the Properties.

MOS Obj 1.5.4 C

3. On the **Info** page, click the **Check for Issues** button, and then click **Inspect Document**. Compare your screen with **Figure 1**.

   Document Inspector looks for comments that you may have forgotten to remove, headers or footers that you may not have intended to include, and ***metadata***—information and personal data that is stored with your document. It also looks for features that may not work correctly on another computer.

4. In the **Document Inspector** dialog box, be sure all of the check boxes are selected, and then click **Inspect**. To the right of **Comments, Revisions, Versions, and Annotations**, click the **Remove All** button.

   A check mark indicates that the information has been successfully removed.

5. To the right of **Document Properties and Personal Information**, click the **Remove All** button, and then **Close** the Document Inspector dialog box.
6. On the **Info** page, in the **Properties** pane, click in the **Title** box. Type City Parks and then at the top of the **Properties** list, click the **Properties** button, and then click **Advanced Properties**.

   Notice the title *City Parks* displays in the Properties dialog box.

Obj 1.4.5 C

7. Click in the **Subject** box, and then type Park Benefits Click in the **Keywords** box, and then type parks, ecology and then in the **Comments** box, type We need an in-depth report for the new park. Compare your screen with **Figure 2**, and then click **OK**.

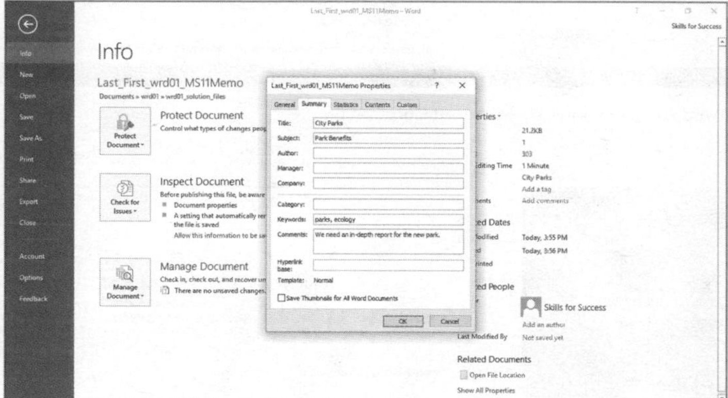

Figure 2 Word 2016, Windows 10, Microsoft Corporation

8. At the bottom of the **Properties** list, click **Show All Properties**.

   On the Info page, some properties are displayed automatically and others display only when you click the Show All Properties command.

9. Click the **Back** button, and then add the **FileName** field to the footer. **Save** the file, **Close** Word, and then submit the file as directed by your instructor.

■ **You have completed More Skills 11**

More Skills 12

Insert Screen Shots into Documents

To complete this project, you will need the following file:

- **wrd01_MS12Sites**

You will save your file as:

- **Last_First_wrd01_MS12Sites**

▶ A ***screen shot*** is a picture of your computer screen, a window, or a selected region saved as a file that can be printed or shared electronically.

---

1. Start **Word 2016**, and then open the student data file **wrd01_MS12Sites**. Save the file in your chapter folder as Last_First_wrd01_MS12Sites
2. On the **Insert tab**, in the **Header & Footer group**, click the **Footer** button, and then click **Edit Footer**. On the **Header & Footer Tools Design tab**, in the **Insert group**, click the **Document Info** button, and then click **File Name**. In the **Close group**, click the **Close Header and Footer** button. MOS Obj 1.3.4 C
3. In the memo, locate the hyperlink *www.aspenfalls.org*. Press and hold Ctrl, point to *www.aspenfalls.org*, and then with the pointer, click the hyperlink to open the page in a web browser. If necessary, Maximize the browser window.
4. On the taskbar, click the **Word** button to return to the Word document. Press Ctrl + End to move to the blank line at the end of the document.
5. Click the **Insert tab**, and then in the **Illustrations group**, click the **Screenshot** button. In the gallery, point to **Screen Clipping**, and then compare your screen with **Figure 1**. MOS Obj 5.1.3 C
6. Click **Screen Clipping**. Point at the top left corner of the window, and then drag from the top left corner to the bottom right corner to select and insert the clip.

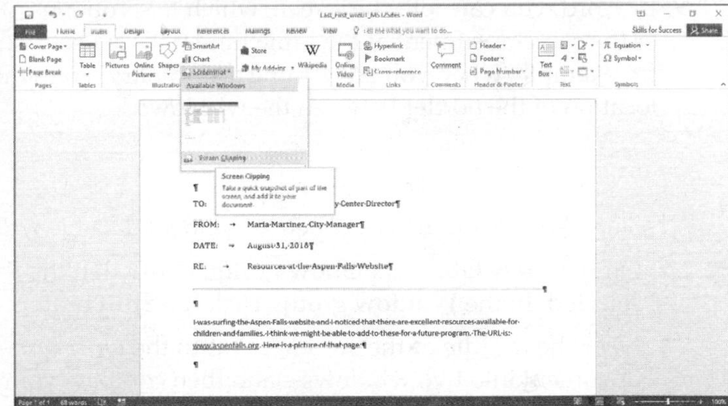

Word 2016, Windows 10, Microsoft Corporation **Figure 1**

7. **Save** the file, **Close** the open windows, and then submit the file as directed by your instructor.

■ **You have completed More Skills 12**

More Skills 13

Split and Arrange Windows

To complete this project, you will need the following files:

- wrd01_MS13Donations
- wrd01_MS13EstatePlanning

You will save your files as:

- Last_First_wrd01_MS13Snip1
- Last_First_wrd01_MS13Snip2

► In Word, you can split the screen, which lets you look at two different parts of the same document at the same time. This is useful in a long document, for example, when you are writing a summary. The split bar indicates the location of the border between the windows.

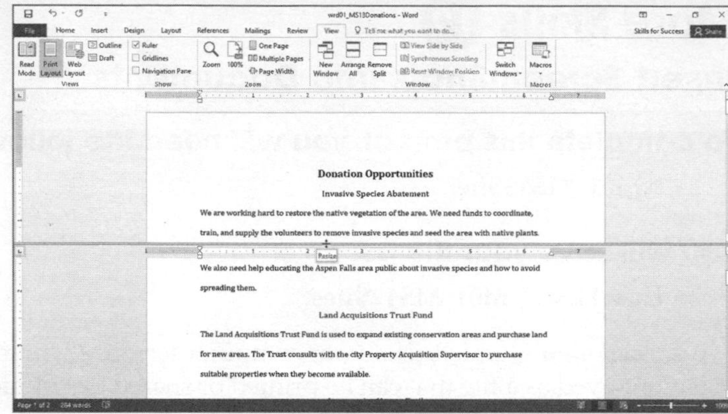

Figure 1 Word 2016, Windows 10, Microsoft Corporation

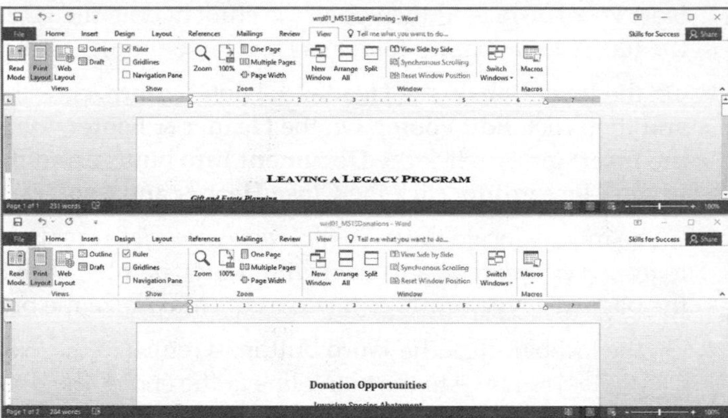

Figure 2 Word 2016, Windows 10, Microsoft Corporation

1. Start **Word 2016**, and then open the student data file **wrd01_MS13Donations**.

Obj 1.4.4 C

2. On the **View tab**, in the **Show group**, verify that the **Ruler** check box is selected. In the **Window group**, click the **Split** button.
3. Near the middle of the screen, point to the ***split bar***—a bar that splits a document into two windows—and then compare your screen with **Figure 1**.
4. With the [÷] pointer, drag down to move the split bar below the line that ends *how to avoid spreading them*.
5. In the lower window, scroll down to display the *Wildlife Viewing Blinds* subtitle.
6. Click [Start], type snip and then press [Enter]. In the **Snipping Tool** window, click the **New arrow**, and then click **Full-screen Snip**.
7. In the **Snipping Tool** mark-up window, click the **Save Snip** button. In the **Save As** dialog box, navigate to your chapter folder, and then **Save** the snip as Last_First_wrd01_MS13Snip1 **Minimize** the Snipping Tool mark-up window.
8. On the **View tab**, in the **Window group**, click the **Remove Split** button. Alternately, drag the split bar to the top or the bottom of the document window.
9. Open the student data file **wrd01_MS13EstatePlanning**.
10. On the **View tab**, in the **Window group**, click the **Arrange All** button. Notice that both documents display in their own window, and each window has a Ribbon as shown in **Figure 2**.

   You can view two different documents side by side to make comparisons between the two, use one as a source of information, or copy text from one document to another.

11. On the taskbar, click the **Snipping Tool** button. Click the **New** button, and then create a **Full-screen Snip**. **Save** the snip in your chapter folder with the name Last_First_wrd01_MS13Snip2 and then **Close** the Snipping Tool mark-up window.
12. **Close** Word, and then submit the files as directed by your instructor.

- **You have completed More Skills 13**

More Skills 14

Insert Symbols

To complete this document, you will need the following file:

- wrd01_MS14Training

You will save your file as:

- Last_First_wrd01_MS14Training

- When you insert a symbol, it is inserted at the position of the insertion point and the Symbol dialog box remains open.
- Symbols are inserted characters that are formatted in the same manner as letters you type.
- An ***em dash*** is the word processing name for a long dash in a sentence, which marks a break in thought, similar to a comma but stronger. An em dash is slightly wider than the width of the capital letter M in the existing font and font size.

---

1. Start **Word 2016**, and then open the student data file **wrd01_MS14Training**. Save the file in your chapter folder as Last_First_wrd01_MS14Training and then add the **FileName** field to the footer.
2. In the bulleted list, click to the right of *Microsoft Word*. On the **Insert tab**, in the **Symbols group**, click the **Symbol** button to display the Symbol gallery.

MOS Obj 2.1.4 C

3. Below the **Symbol** gallery, click **More Symbols** to open the Symbol dialog box, and then compare your screen with **Figure 1**.

   Each font has a separate set of associated symbols. You can view and search for additional symbols by changing the font. Your symbols may be different.

4. In the **Symbol** dialog box, click the **Special Characters tab** to display a list of common characters and symbol characters.
5. Click the **Registered** symbol ®, and then at the bottom of the dialog box, click **Insert**.
6. If necessary, move the **Symbol** dialog box so that you can see the bulleted list.
7. Click to the right of *Microsoft Excel*, and then insert a **Registered** symbol.
8. Move the **Symbol** dialog box so that you can see the two hyphens following the word *sessions*. Double-click the two hyphens to select them.
9. In the **Symbol** dialog box, click the **Em Dash**, and then click **Insert**.

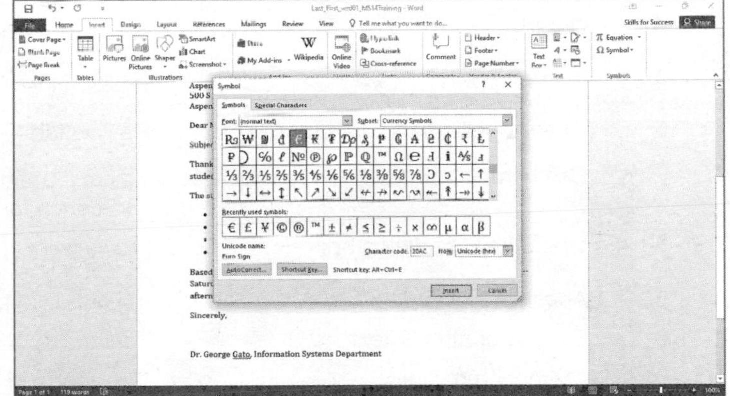

Word 2016, Windows 10, Microsoft Corporation

Figure 1

10. In the same paragraph, select the double hyphens to the right of *adults*, and then insert another em dash. **Close** the Symbol dialog box.
11. **Save** the file, **Close** Word, and then submit the file as directed by your instructor.

- **You have completed More Skills 14**

The following table summarizes the **SKILLS AND PROCEDURES** covered in this chapter.

Skills Number	Task	Step	Icon	Keyboard Shortcut
1	Display formatting marks	Home tab → Paragraph group → Show/Hide	¶	Ctrl + *
2	Apply styles	Home tab → Styles group → click desired style		
2	Ignore flagged words	Right-click the word, and click Ignore All		
2	Change spelling and grammar options	File tab → Options → Proofing page → Settings button		
3	Select paragraphs	Triple-click the paragraph, or with the [pointer] pointer, double-click		
3	Undo an action	Quick Access Toolbar → Undo (repeat as needed)		Ctrl + Z
3	Select all	Home tab → Editing group → Select → Select All		Ctrl + A
3	Move to beginning of document			Ctrl + Home
4	Move to end of document			Ctrl + End
4	Copy text	Select text, then Home tab → Clipboard group → Copy		Ctrl + C
4	Cut text	Select text, then Home tab → Clipboard group → Cut		Ctrl + X
4	Paste text	Position insertion point, then Home tab → Clipboard group → Paste		Ctrl + V
5	Check spelling and grammar	Review tab → Proofing group → Spelling & Grammar		F7
7	Use Format Painter	Select formatted text, then Home → Clipboard group → Format Painter Click once for one time, double-click for multiple times		
8	Open the Font dialog box	Home tab → Font group → Dialog Box Launcher		Ctrl + D
8	Apply small caps	In Font dialog box, select Small caps check box		
8	Expand or stretch text	Font dialog box → Advanced tab		
9	Make footers active	Insert tab → Header & Footer group → Footer → Edit Footer		
9	Insert file names in footers	With footer active → Header & Footer Tools Design tab → Insert group → Quick Parts		
10	View two pages	View tab → Zoom group → Multiple Pages		
10	Save as PDF documents	File tab → Export → Create PDF/XPS		
MS12	Insert screen shot	Insert tab → Illustrations group → Screenshot		
MS13	Show the ruler	View tab → Show group → Ruler check box selected		
MS13	Split the window	View tab → Window group → Split		
MS14	Insert symbol	Insert tab → Symbols group → Symbol		

Project Summary Chart		
Project	**Project Type**	**Project Location**
Skills Review	Review	In Book & MIL MyITLab® Grader
Skills Assessment 1	Review	In Book & MIL MyITLab® Grader
Skills Assessment 2	Review	Book
My Skills	Problem Solving	Book
Visual Skills Check	Problem Solving	Book
Skillls Challenge 1	Critical Thinking	Book
Skills Challenge 2	Critical Thinking	Book
More Skills Assessment	Review	In Book & MIL MyITLab® Grader
Collaborating with Google	Critical Thinking	Book

MOS Objectives Covered	
1.1.1 C Create a blank document	1.5.4 C Inspect a document for hidden properties or personal information
1.3.4 C Insert headers and footers	2.1.2 C Cut, copy and paste text
1.4.2 C Customize views by using zoom settings	2.1.4 C Insert special characters
1.4.4 C Split the window	2.2.1 C Apply font formatting
1.4.5 C Add document properties	2.2.2 C Apply formatting by using Format Painter
1.4.6 C Show or hide formatting symbols	2.2.6 C Apply built-in styles to text
1.5.2 C Save documents in alternative file formats	5.1.3 C Insert a screen shot or screen clipping
1.5.3 C Print all or part of a document	

Key Terms

1. What is a professional network, and how would you build one?
2. What are some of the best sources for job leads?

Online Help Skills

1. With Word 2016 open, on the **File tab**, in the upper right corner of the screen, click the **Microsoft Word Help** [?] button, or press [F1].
2. In the **Word Help** window **Search** box, type Start up and then press [Enter].
3. In the search results list, click **Word options (General)**. Maximize the **Word Help** window, and then compare your screen with **Figure 1**.

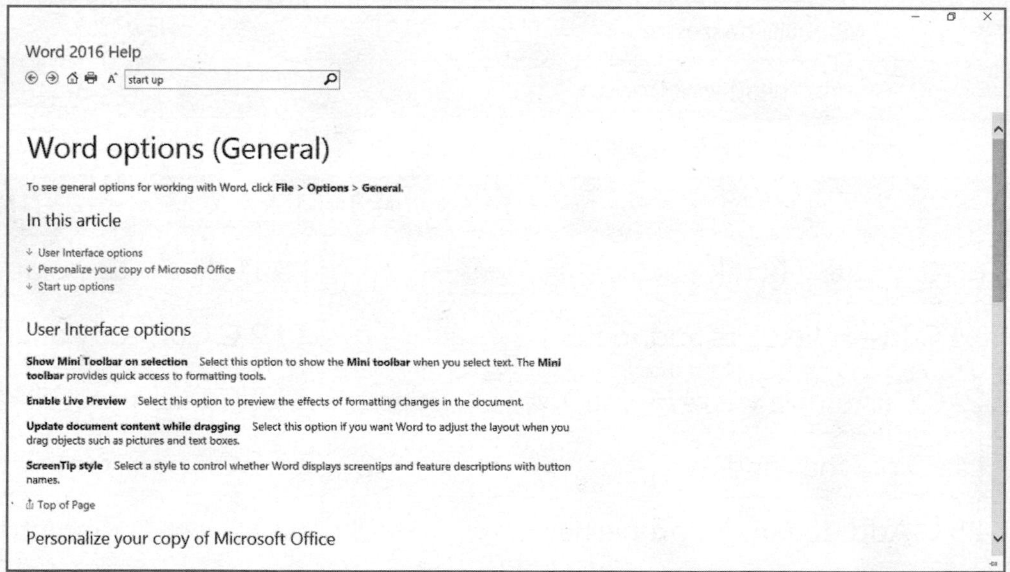

Figure 1 Word 2016, Windows 10, Microsoft Corporation

4. Read the article, and then see if you can answer the following question: What are some ways you can personalize your copy of Office?

Matching 

Match each term in the second column with its correct definition in the first column by writing the letter of the term on the blank line in front of the correct definition.

___ **1.** A character that indicates a paragraph, tab, or space on your screen, but that does not print when you print a Word document.

___ **2.** A pre-built collection of formatting settings that can be assigned to text.

___ **3.** A red wavy line indicates this type of error.

___ **4.** Forces a page to end, and places subsequent text at the top of the next page.

___ **5.** A command that deletes the selected text or object and places a copy in the Office Clipboard.

___ **6.** A reference that lists words that have the same or similar meaning to the word you are looking up.

___ **7.** A unit of measurement for font sizes.

___ **8.** A reserved area for text, graphics, and fields that displays at the top of each page in a document.

___ **9.** A category of data—such as a file name, the page number, or the current date—that can be inserted into a document.

___ **10.** An image of a document that can be viewed using a reader such as Adobe Acrobat Reader instead of the application that created the original document.

A Cut
B Field
C Formatting mark
D Header
E Manual page break
F PDF document
G Point
H Spelling
I Style
J Thesaurus

Multiple Choice

MyITLab®

Choose the correct answer.

1. A button used to turn a feature both on and off.
- **A.** Dialog Box Launcher
- **B.** Spin button
- **C.** Toggle button

2. To change Proofing settings, first display the:
- **A.** File tab
- **B.** Home tab
- **C.** Reference tab

3. In the Grammar Settings dialog box, which is a category that can be enabled or disabled?
- **A.** Check spelling as you type
- **B.** Small caps
- **C.** Subject Verb Agreement

4. A wavy line indicating a possible spelling, grammar, or style error.
- **A.** AutoComplete error
- **B.** Flagged error
- **C.** ScreenTip

5. This keyboard shortcut places the insertion point at the beginning of the document.
- **A.** Ctrl + A
- **B.** Ctrl + PageUp
- **C.** Ctrl + Home

6. The Spelling & Grammar button is located on this Ribbon tab.
- **A.** Home
- **B.** References
- **C.** Review

7. The Undo button is located here.
- **A.** Quick Access Toolbar
- **B.** Ribbon Home tab
- **C.** Ribbon Review tab

8. A font effect that displays all characters in uppercase while making any character originally typed as an uppercase letter taller than the ones typed as lowercase characters.
- **A.** CamelCase
- **B.** Small caps
- **C.** Uppercase

9. To view two pages at the same time, on the View tab, in the Zoom group, click this command.
- **A.** Fit Two
- **B.** Multiple Pages
- **C.** Two Pages

10. The typical file extension assigned to a Word document.
- **A.** .docx
- **B.** .pdf
- **C.** .xps

Topics for Discussion

1. Many organizations have professionally designed letterhead printed on sheets of paper. When writing a letter such as the one in this chapter, what would you need to do differently to accommodate stationery that already has your organization's name and address printed at the top? What might you need to do differently to print the letter?

2. When you check the spelling in a document, one of the options is to add unrecognized words to the dictionary. If you were working for a large company, what types of words do you think you would add to your dictionary?

Skills Review

To complete this project, you will need the following file:

- **wrd01_SRParkDonations**

You will save your files as:

- **Last_First_wrd01_SRParks (Word)**
- **Last_First_wrd01_SRParks (PDF)**

---

1. Start a blank Word document. On the **Home tab**, click the **Show/Hide** button as needed to display the formatting marks. Type Aspen Falls Parks and Recreation Department and press Enter. Type 500 S Aspen Street and press Enter. Type Aspen Falls, CA 93463 and press Enter two times. Complete the beginning of the letter with the information shown in **Figure 1**.

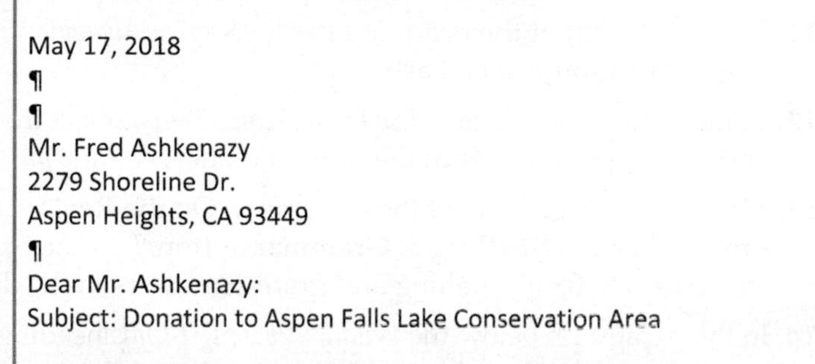

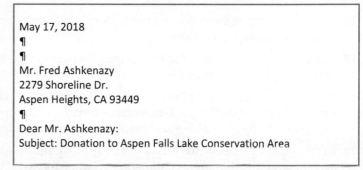

May 17, 2018
¶
¶
Mr. Fred Ashkenazy
2279 Shoreline Dr.
Aspen Heights, CA 93449
¶
Dear Mr. Ashkenazy:
Subject: Donation to Aspen Falls Lake Conservation Area

Word 2016, Windows 10, Microsoft Corporation **Figure 1**

2. Press Enter, and then type Thank you for your interest in making a donation to the Aspen Falls Lake Conservation Area. You asked about projects for which we need additional resources, so I have attached a list of possible projects.
3. Press Enter, type Sincerely, and then press Enter two times. Type Leah Kim Press Enter, type Parks and Recreation Director and then apply the No Spacing style to the paragraph *Leah Kim*.
4. Select the first two lines of the letterhead. On the **Home tab**, in the **Styles group**, click the **No Spacing** button. Repeat this procedure with the first two lines of the inside address.
5. Click at the end of the paragraph that ends *possible projects*. Press Enter, and then type All donations made to the Friends of the Aspen Falls Conservation Areas (FAFCA) are tax deductible. Compare your screen with **Figure 2**.

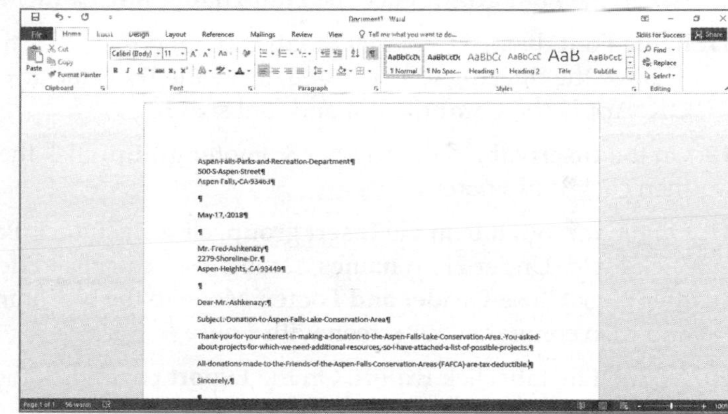

Word 2016, Windows 10, Microsoft Corporation **Figure 2**

6. **Save** the document in your **Word Chapter 1** folder as Last_First_wrd01_SRParks
7. **Open** the student data file **wrd01_SRParkDonations**. On the **Home tab**, in the **Editing group**, click **Select**, and then click **Select All**. On the **Home tab**, in the **Clipboard group**, click **Copy**. **Close** the document.
8. In **Last_First_wrd01_SRParks**, press Ctrl + End. On the **Layout tab**, in the **Page Setup group**, click **Breaks**, and then click **Page**.
9. On the **Home tab**, in the **Clipboard group**, click **Paste**.

■ **Continue to the next page to complete this Skills Review**

10. Select the heading *Land Acquisitions Trust Fund* and the paragraph that follows it. On the **Home tab**, in the **Clipboard group**, click **Cut** to remove the two paragraphs.
11. Click to the left of the heading *Invasive Species Abatement*, and then in the **Clipboard group**, click **Paste**.
12. In the paragraph starting *The Land Acquisitions*, select the text *is used to expand*, and then type expands In the same sentence, change *purchase* to purchases
13. Move to the beginning of the document. On the **Review tab**, in the **Proofing group**, click the **Spelling & Grammar** button. Use the **Spelling** and **Grammar** task panes to fix all spelling and grammar errors in the document.
14. In the paragraph below the *Wildlife Viewing Blinds* heading, right-click *inhabitants*, and then use the **Synonyms** submenu to change the word to **populations.**
15. Using the **Format Painter**, apply the formatting in the *Land Acquisitions Trust Fund* heading to the five other headings on the page. Compare your screen with **Figure 3**.
16. In the letterhead, select the paragraph starting *Aspen Falls Parks*. On the **Home tab**, in the **Font group**, click the **Font Dialog Box Launcher**.
17. In the **Font** dialog box, select **Small caps**, and then click the **Advanced tab**. Change the **Spacing** to **Expanded**, leave the **By** value at **1 pt**, and then click **OK**. Apply the **Cambria** font and font size **16**.
18. On the **Insert tab**, in the **Header & Footer group**, click the **Footer** button, and then click **Edit Footer**.
19. On the **Design tab**, in the **Insert group**, click the **Quick Parts** button, and then click **Field**. Under **Field names**, scroll down and click **FileName**. Click **OK**, and then click **Close Header and Footer**. Move to the beginning of the document, and then compare your screen with **Figure 4**.
20. On the **File tab**, click **Export**. On the **Export** page, click the **Create PDF/XPS** button.
21. In the **Publish as PDF or XPS** dialog box, navigate to your **Word Chapter 1** folder. Be sure the **Open file after publishing** check box is selected, and then click **Publish**.
22. View the document in a PDF viewer, and then **Close** the window.

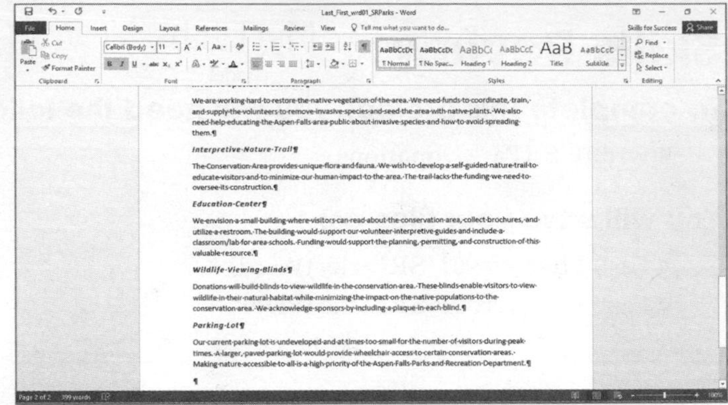

Figure 3 Word 2016, Windows 10, Microsoft Corporation

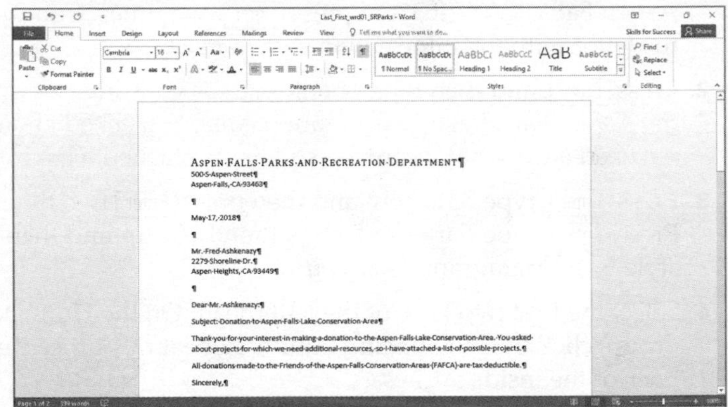

Figure 4 Word 2016, Windows 10, Microsoft Corporation

23. **Save** the file, **Close** Word, and then submit the files as directed by your instructor.

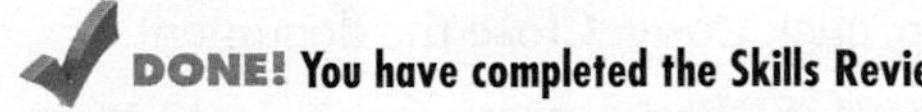
DONE! You have completed the Skills Review

Skills Assessment 1

To complete this project, you will need the following files:

- **wrd01_SA1Land**
- **wrd01_SA1Legacy**

You will save your files as:

- **Last_First_wrd01_SA1Land (Word)**
- **Last_First_wrd01_SA1Land (PDF)**

---

1. Start **Word 2016**, and then open the student data file **wrd01_SA1Land**. Save the file in your chapter folder as Last_First_wrd01_SA1Land Add the **FileName** field to the footer.
2. After the date, insert two blank lines and the following inside address: Ms. Shawn McCready; 1414 Barbary Dr.; Aspen Falls, CA 93464
3. For the first three lines of the letterhead, apply the **No Spacing** style. Repeat this procedure with the first two lines of the inside address.
4. For the letterhead's first line, apply the **Cambria** font, font size **16**, and then set the **Character Spacing** to **Expanded** by **1.3 pt**.
5. Below the inside address, add the salutation Dear Ms. McCready:
6. After the salutation, insert a new paragraph with the text Subject: McCready Farm Property Compare your screen with **Figure 1**.
7. Open the student data file **wrd01_SA1Legacy**. **Copy** all of the text, and then **Close** the document.
8. At the end of **Last_First_wrd01_SA1Land**, insert a manual page break, and then at the top of Page 2, paste the contents of the clipboard.
9. On Page 2, below *Gift and Estate Planning*, replace the word *various* with the suggested synonym **several**.
10. Use **Cut** and **Paste** to move the *Outright Gift* heading and its two bullets so that the section comes before the *Life Estate Gift Annuity* heading.
11. Use the **Spelling & Grammar** checker to fix all spelling and grammar errors in the document.
12. Use **Format Painter** to apply the formatting in the *Gift and Estate Planning* heading to the five other headings on Page 2.

Word 2016, Windows 10, Microsoft Corporation **Figure 1**

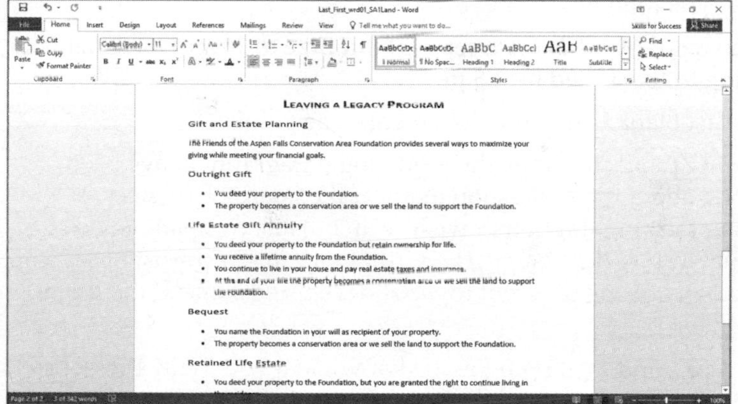

Word 2016, Windows 10, Microsoft Corporation **Figure 2**

13. Compare your screen with **Figure 2**, and then **Save** the file.
14. **Save** the file as a PDF document in your chapter folder with the file name Last_First_wrd01_SA1Land **Close** Word, and then submit the files as directed by your instructor.

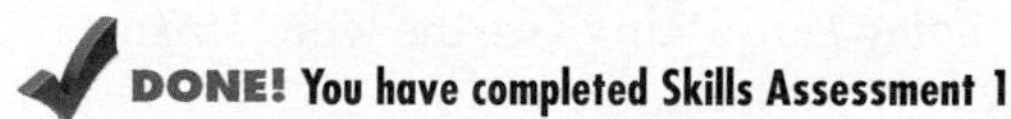

DONE! You have completed Skills Assessment 1

Skills Assessment 2

To complete this project, you will need the following files:

- wrd01_SA2Memo
- wrd01_SA2Topics

You will save your files as:

- Last_First_wrd01_SA2Memo (Word)
- Last_First_wrd01_SA2Memo (PDF)

---

1. Start **Word 2016**, and then open the student data file **wrd01_SA2Memo**. Save the file in your chapter folder as Last_First_wrd01_SA2Memo Add the **FileName** field to the footer.
2. With the insertion point in the blank paragraph at the top of the document, apply the **No Spacing** style, and then press Enter five times. Type Memorandum
3. For the word *Memorandum*, set the **Font Size** to **36** and the **Character Spacing** to **Expanded** by **2.5 pt**.
4. In the last blank line of the document, type Jamie:
5. Press Enter, and then type the following paragraph: I have been thinking about the suggestion made at the Board of Trustees meeting the other night that we hire an outside company to design a virtual tour of the library. The virtual tour might consist of several modules featuring different topics. I have listed some of the topics on the next page.
6. Press Enter, and then type Let me know what you think. Press Enter two times, type Doug and then compare your screen with **Figure 1**.
7. At the end of the document, insert a manual page break, and then on Page 2, copy and paste all of the text from the student data file **wrd01_SA2Topics**.
8. Cut the heading *Building Interior* and the paragraph that follows it, and then paste it before the *Building Exterior* heading.
9. Use the **Spelling & Grammar** checker to fix all spelling, grammar, and style errors in the document.
10. In the paragraph below *Building Exterior*, replace the word *striking* with the suggested synonym **prominent**.

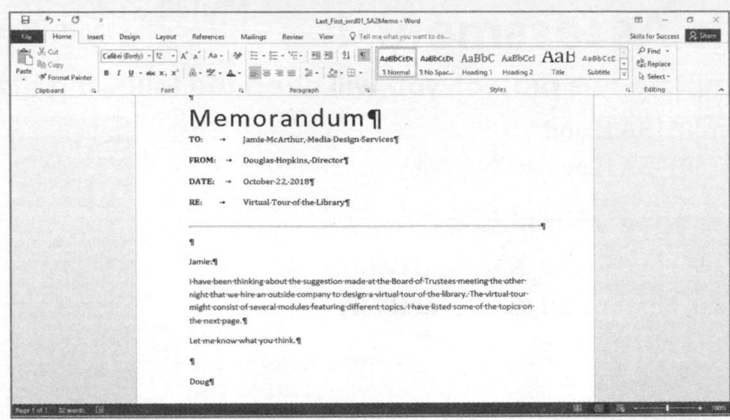

Word 2016, Windows 10, Microsoft Corporation **Figure 1**

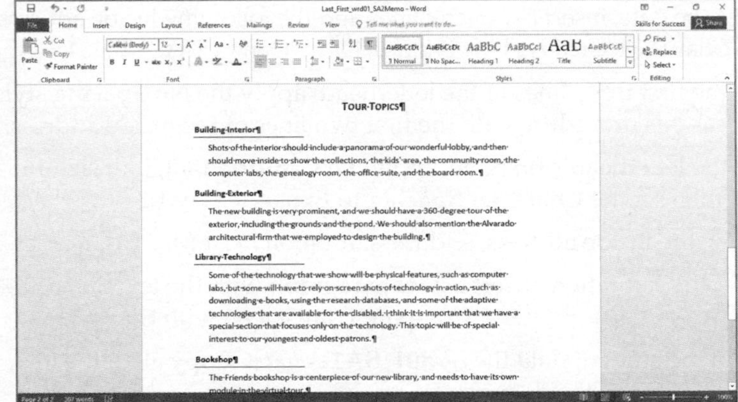

Word 2016, Windows 10, Microsoft Corporation **Figure 2**

11. Use **Format Painter** to apply the formatting in the *Building Interior* heading to the other four headings on Page 2.
12. Compare your screen with **Figure 2**, and then **Save** the file.
13. **Save** the file as a PDF document in your chapter folder with the name Last_First_wrd01_SA2Memo **Close** Word, and then submit the files as directed by your instructor.

June 11, 2018

Evelyn Stone
Aspen Falls City Hall
500 S Aspen St
Aspen Falls, CA 93464

Dear Mrs. Stone:
Subject: City Hall Internships

Word 2016, Windows 10, Microsoft Corporation **Figure 1**

Your Name
1234 N Your St
Your City, State 99999

June 11, 2018

Evelyn Stone
Aspen Falls City Hall
500 S Aspen St
Aspen Falls, CA 93464

Dear Mrs. Stone:

Subject: City Hall Internships

One of my instructors at Aspen Falls Community College, Dr. Gato, suggested that I contact you regarding internships at Aspen Falls City Hall. My studies at the college qualify me for such a position starting as early as next term.

As you review the enclosed resume, please notice my training in Microsoft Office and my organizational skills. Specifically, my experience with Word and my work-study position with Dr. Gato indicate a successful internship as an Office Assistant.

If you have any questions, or if you want to schedule an interview, please contact me at (805) 555-3355 or e-mail me at youremail@address.

Sincerely,

Your Name

Last_First_wrd01_MyLetter

Word 2016, Windows 10, Microsoft Corporation **Figure 2**

My Skills

To complete this project, you will need the following file:

- **Blank Word document**

You will save your file as:

- **Last_First_wrd01_MyLetter**

---

1. Create a blank Word document, and then save the file in your chapter folder as Last_First_wrd01_MyLetter Add the **FileName** field to the footer.
2. Type your First and Last names and then press Enter. On the next two lines of the letterhead, type your own address information. At the beginning of the document, enter the information shown in **Figure 1**.
3. Press Enter, and then type One of my instructors at Aspen Falls Community College, Dr. Gato, suggested that I contact you regarding internships at Aspen Falls City Hall. My studies at the college qualify me for such a position starting as early as next term.
4. Press Enter, and then type As you review the enclosed resume, please notice my training in Microsoft Office and my organizational skills. Specifically, my experience with Word and my work-study position with Dr. Gato indicate a successful internship as an Office Assistant.
5. Press Enter, and then using your e-mail address, type If you have any questions, or if you want to schedule an interview, please contact me at (805) 555-3355 or e-mail me at youremail@address.
6. Press Enter, and then type Sincerely, Press Enter two times, and then type your name.
7. Select the first two lines of the letterhead, and then apply the **No Spacing** style. Repeat this procedure with the first three lines of the inside address.
8. Using the techniques practiced in this chapter, format the letterhead to make it stand out slightly from the rest of the letter, and then compare your screen with **Figure 2**.
9. **Save** the file, **Close** Word, and then submit the file as directed by your instructor.

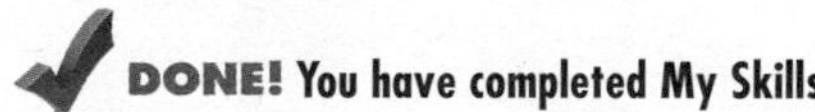
DONE! You have completed My Skills

Visual Skills Check

To complete this project, you will need the following file:

- **Blank Word document**

You will save your file as:

- **Last_First_wrd01_VSCenter**

Using the skills practiced in this chapter, create the document shown in **Figure 1**. **Save** the file as Last_First_wrd01_VSCenter in your chapter folder. Format the first line of the letterhead using the **Cambria** font sized at **24** points, small caps, and expanded by **1.5** points. Format the rest of the document using the **Calibri** font and font size **11**. Maintain the space between paragraphs as shown in **Figure 1**. Insert the **FileName** field in the footer. **Save** the file, **Close** Word, and then submit the file as directed by your instructor.

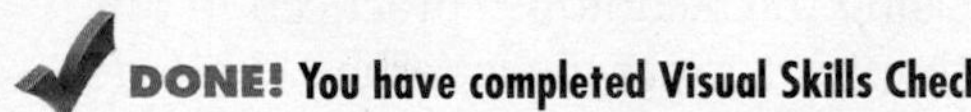
DONE! You have completed Visual Skills Check

ASPEN FALLS COMMUNITY CENTERS
500 S Aspen Street
Aspen Falls, CA 93463

July 13, 2018

Mrs. Natalie Lee
3947 Strong Rd
Aspen Heights, CA 93464

Dear Mrs. Lee:

Subject: Community Center Closings for the 2015 Calendar Year

Thank you for your inquiry about next year's community center closings. Please refer to the following:

Holidays: We will be closed on New Year's Day, Easter, Memorial Day, the Fourth of July, Labor Day, Thanksgiving, and Christmas.

In-Service Days: We will be closed on April 15th for a session on library security, and on November 7th for a session that will focus on streamlining the material handling process.

Close Early: We will close early on New Year's Eve, the day before Easter, the day before Thanksgiving, and Christmas Eve.

If you have any question, feel free to contact me again.

Sincerely,

Lorrine Deely
Community Center Supervisor

Last_First_wrd01_VSCenter

Figure 1

Word 2016, Windows 10, Microsoft Corporation

Skills Challenge 1

To complete this project, you will need the following file:

- wrd01_SC1Trustees

You will save your file as:

- Last_First_wrd01_SC1Trustees

Open the student data file **wrd01_SC1Trustees**, and then save it in your chapter folder as Last_First_wrd01_SC1Trustees

For the entire document, apply a single font that is more appropriate than Comic Sans MS. Correct or ignore all flagged spelling, grammar, and style errors as appropriate to their context. Insert a page break so the letter ends on Page 1 and the report starts on Page 2.

On Page 1, correct the paragraph alignment and paragraph spacing so that it follows the block style business letter modeled in Skills 1–10. Format the letterhead so that *Aspen Falls Public Library* stands out from the rest of the letter.

On Page 2, use cut and paste to arrange the headings and their paragraphs in alphabetical order by heading. Format the heading and side headings to visually organize the report. Be sure to apply the same formatting to all five headings.

Insert the FileName field in the footer. Save the file, close Word, and then submit the file as directed by your instructor.

DONE! You have completed Skills Challenge 1

Skills Challenge 2

To complete this project, you will need the following file:

- Blank Word document

You will save your file as:

- Last_First_wrd01_SC2Recommendation

Deborah Davidson, Public Information Specialist at Aspen Falls City Hall, needs to know if the current format for city letters is still the best choice. She specifically needs to know if the *block style*, *modified-block style*, or *modified-block style with indented paragraphs* should be used.

Use a business correspondence guide from your library or search online to compare the three styles under consideration. Summarize your findings in a letter addressed to Deborah Davidson, Public Information Specialist, Aspen Falls City Hall, 500 S Aspen Street, Aspen Falls, CA 93463.

For each of the three styles, write a short paragraph describing its features and comparative advantages and disadvantages. In a fourth paragraph, recommend which style the city should use, and then justify your decision. Finally, format the letter using the style you recommended. Insert the FileName field in the footer, and save the file as Last_First_wrd01_SC2Recommendation Close Word, and then submit the file as directed by your instructor.

DONE! You have completed Skills Challenge 2

More Skills Assessment

MyITLab®
Grader

To complete this project, you will need the following file:

- **wrd01_MSAMemo**

You will save your files as:

- **Last_First_wrd01_MSAMemo**
- **Last_First_wrd01_MSASnip1**
- **Last_First_wrd01_MSASnip2**

1. Start **Word 2016**, and then open the student data file **wrd01_MSAMemo. Save** the file in your chapter folder as Last_First_wrd01_MSAMemo
2. Open the **Document Inspector** dialog box. Verify all of the check boxes are selected, and then click **Inspect**. To the right of **Comments, Revisions, Versions, and Annotations**, click the **Remove All** button, and then **Close** the dialog box.
3. Open the **Document Properties** dialog box. Click in the **Title** box, and then type Electricity Rates Click in the **Company** box, type Aspen Falls City Hall and then compare your screen with **Figure 1**.
4. Click [Windows], type snip and then press Enter to start the **Snipping Tool**. Click the **New arrow**, and then click **Full-screen Snip**. In the **Snipping Tool** mark-up window, click the **Save Snip** button [Save]. In the **Save As** dialog box, navigate to your Word Chapter 1 folder. Be sure the **Save as type** box displays **JPEG file**. Name the file Last_First_wrd01_MSASnip1 **Minimize** the Snipping Tool mark-up window.
5. In the **Document Properties** dialog box, click **OK**.
6. On Page 2, locate the hyperlink *http:// www.loc.gov/*. Press and hold Ctrl, and then with the [pointer] pointer, click the hyperlink. If necessary, Maximize the browser window.
7. On the taskbar, click the **Word** button, and then move the insertion point to the end of the document.
8. Insert a screen clipping of the browser window.
9. On the **View tab**, verify the ruler displays, and then split the window. In the upper window, display the top of Page 1, and in the lower window, display the top of Page 2 as shown in **Figure 2**.

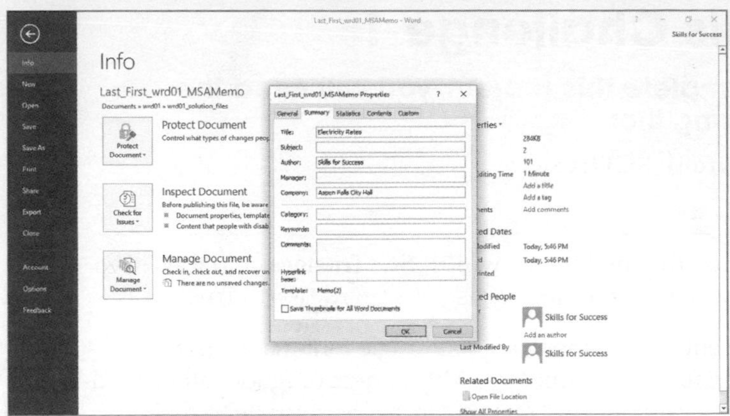

Word 2016, Windows 10, Microsoft Corporation **Figure 1**

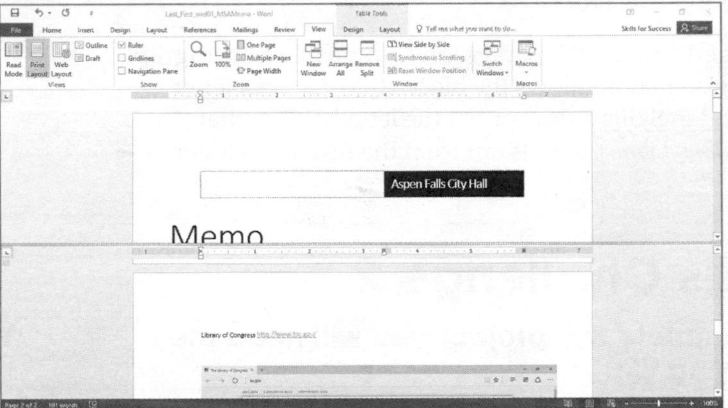

Word 2016, Windows 10, Microsoft Corporation **Figure 2**

10. On the taskbar, click the **Snipping Tool** button. Click the **New** button [New], and then create a **Full-screen Snip**. Save the snip in your chapter folder as Last_First_wrd01_MSASnip2 **Close** the Snipping Tool mark-up window.
11. Remove the split from the Word window.
12. On Page 1, in the paragraph above the table, replace the two hyphens with the **Em Dash** symbol.
13. Add the **FileName** field to the footer.
14. **Save** the file, **Close** Word, and then submit the files as directed by your instructor.

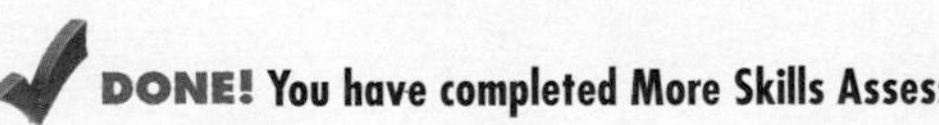
DONE! You have completed More Skills Assessment

Collaborating with Google

To complete this project, you will need a Google account (refer to the Common Features chapter)

You will save your files as:

- **Last_First_wrd01_GPSnip1**
- **Last_First_wrd01_GPSnip2**

---

1. Open a web browser. Log into your Google account, and then click the **Google Apps** button.
2. Click the **Drive** button to open Google Drive. If you receive a pop-up message, read the message, and then click **Next**. Read each message, and then close the dialog box.
3. Click the **New** button, and then click **Google Docs** to open a blank document.
4. Type City Engineer Position press Enter twice, and then type the information shown in **Figure 1**.
5. Select *City Engineer Position*. Click the **Styles** button, and then click **Title**. Click the **Center** button.
6. Select the text *Minimum qualifications*. On the **Edit tab**, click **Cut**. Click in front of *Salary grade*. On the **Edit tab**, click **Paste**, and then press Enter.
7. On the **Insert tab**, click **Footer**. In the footer, type Last_First_wrd01_GoogleProject and then click in the document to close the footer area.
8. On the **Tools tab**, click **Spelling**, and then correct any spelling errors.
9. Click the document title, **Untitled document**. Verify **City Engineer Position** displays as the name of the document, and then press Enter.
10. Click the **Share** button, and then in the **Share with others** dialog box, type AspenFallsEvents@gmail.com to share the sheet with another user.
11. In the **Add a note** text box, type I have been informed that Human Resources now has other items that need to be updated. Please add the other items to this document. Compare your screen with **Figure 2**.
12. Click the Start button, type snip and then press Enter to start the **Snipping Tool**. Click the **New arrow**, and then click **Full-screen Snip**. In the **Snipping Tool** mark-up window, click the **Save Snip** button. In the **Save As** dialog box, navigate to your Word Chapter 1 folder. Be sure the **Save as type** box displays **JPEG file**. Name the file Last_First_wrd01_GPSnip1 and then **Minimize** the Snipping Tool mark-up window.
13. In the **Share with others** dialog box, click **Send**.
14. On the taskbar, click the **Snipping Tool** button. Click the **New** button, and then create a **Full-screen Snip**. Save the snip in your chapter folder as Last_First_wrd01_GPSnip2
15. **Close** all windows, and then submit the files as directed by your instructor.

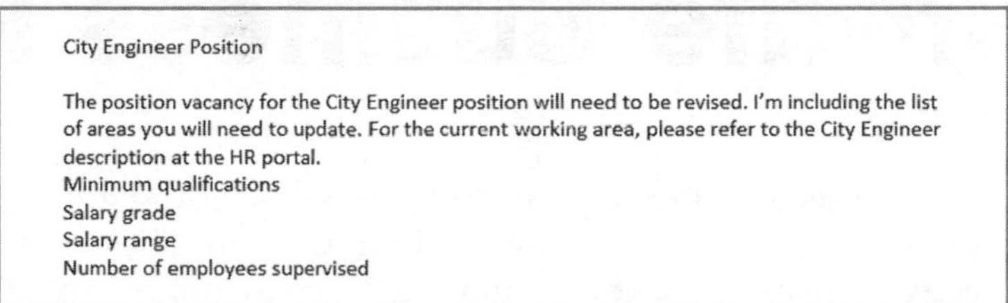

City Engineer Position

The position vacancy for the City Engineer position will need to be revised. I'm including the list of areas you will need to update. For the current working area, please refer to the City Engineer description at the HR portal.
Minimum qualifications
Salary grade
Salary range
Number of employees supervised

Figure 1

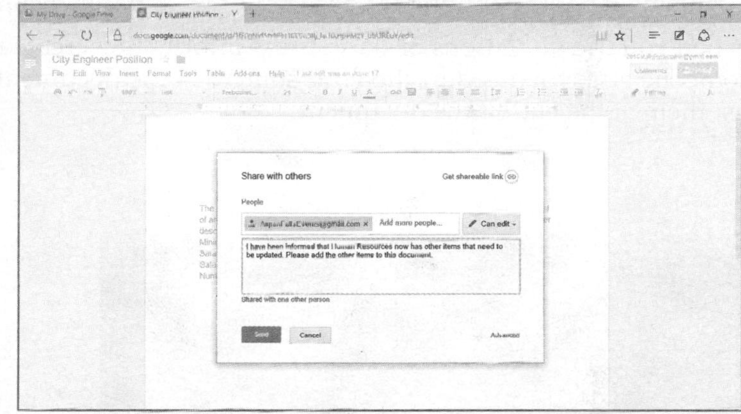

Figure 2

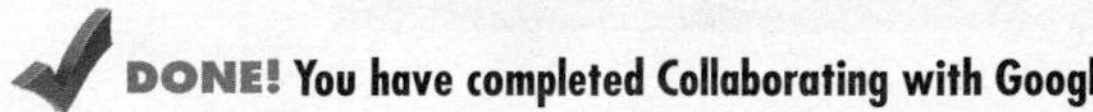

DONE! You have completed Collaborating with Google

CHAPTER 2

Create Business Reports

- Informal business reports are often formatted using guidelines in *The Gregg Reference Manual* by William A. Sabin. These guidelines specify the way the text is formatted, the way notes display, and the types of citations used.
- A footnote or endnote can be inserted when you have supplemental information that does not fit well in the document.
- When you use quotations or paraphrase information created by someone else, you need to cite your sources in the document and list them at the end of the document.
- Report style guidelines specify how headings and side headings should be formatted. Your guidelines should also specify how much space should be above and below paragraphs, how the first line should be indented, and how much space should be between each line.
- Document margins are the spaces that display on the outer edges of a printed page. All four page margins can be adjusted independently.
- Lists make information easier to understand. Use numbered lists when information is displayed in a sequence, and use bulleted lists when information can appear in any order.

Gam16/Fotolia

Aspen Falls City Hall

In this chapter, you will finish a report for Richard Mack, Aspen Falls Assistant City Manager. The report provides a cost-benefit analysis regarding LED lights and makes recommendations based on that analysis. The study was conducted at the request of the city in cooperation with the Durango County Museum of History located in Aspen Falls.

If someone has requested that you write a report for them, you should ask them for guidelines regarding length, style, and format. Academic reports typically follow a set of guidelines such as MLA or Chicago, whereas the guidelines for business reports vary. Reports are either formal or informal. Formal reports include front matter, such as a separate title page and a table of contents, and back matter, such as bibliographies and appendixes. Informal reports do not contain front matter, are short in length, and may have an optional bibliography.

In this project, you will edit and format an informal business report using the guidelines from *The Gregg Reference Manual* by William A. Sabin. You will edit text and then insert comments in footnotes. Following *The Chicago Manual of Style*, you will add sources to the document, cite those sources, and then insert a bibliography. Finally, you will format the document following standard guidelines for informal business reports.

Time to complete all 10 skills — 60 to 75 minutes

Outcome

Using the skills in this chapter, you will be able to create and modify a report; insert footnotes, citations, bibliographies, and bulleted and numbered lists; and modify paragraph formatting.

Objectives

2.1 Create an informal report

2.2 Organize a report using bulleted and numbered lists, and insert custom headers and footers

2.3 Insert and modify footnotes, citations, and bibliographies

2.4 Format a report using paragraph indents, line spacing, and page margins

SKILLS

At the end of this chapter you will be able to:

Skill 1 Find and Replace Text
Skill 2 Insert and Modify Footnotes
Skill 3 Add Sources
Skill 4 Insert Citations and Bibliographies
Skill 5 Format Bulleted and Numbered Lists
Skill 6 Set Paragraph Indents
Skill 7 Modify Line and Paragraph Spacing
Skill 8 Set Line and Page Break Options and Modify Styles
Skill 9 View Multiple Pages and Set Margins
Skill 10 Create Custom Headers and Footers

MORE SKILLS

Skill 11 Record AutoCorrect Entries
Skill 12 Use AutoFormat to Create Numbered Lists
Skill 13 Format and Customize Lists
Skill 14 Create Standard Outlines

Student data file needed for this chapter:

wrd02_LEDs

You will save your file as:

Last_First_wrd02_LEDs

LED LIGHTS

A Museum Exhibit Case Study

By Your Name

July 20, 2018

In April 2014, the Durango County Museum of History installed a small exhibit titled *Our heritage: Pictures from the past*. The collection consists of five daguerreotypes and several silver albumen prints. A study was made to measure the benefits and costs of using LED lights instead of traditional halogen lamps.

RISKS OF LIGHTING HISTORIC PHOTOGRAPHS

All lighting harms photographs. (Lavedrine 2003) It is the task of the conservator to minimize this harm so that the photographs can be viewed for a significant span of time, typically 50 to 100 years. For these reasons, historical photographs are displayed only periodically in rooms with significantly reduced lighting. These practices minimize the visitor experience and according to Hunt, reducing light levels diminishes color saturation and contrast. (Hunt 1952, 192)

In all lighting systems, ultraviolet light (UV) must be eliminated as that spectrum harms photographs the most. Halogen lights must have UV filters installed which adds to their cost and effectiveness. LED lamps do not emit UV light and do not need extra filters. According to a study by the Getty Conservation Institute, fading from LED lamps does not result in any more damage than conventional halogen lamps with ultraviolet filtering. They found that it is likely using LED lamps results in less fading of photographic materials. (Druzik and Miller 2015)

METHODOLOGY

In the new exhibit, 12 watt PAR38 20° lamps were utilized. The temperature rating for these lamps was 2700 Kelvin. Although the LED light output was significantly less than traditional halogen lamps, some screening was still needed. UV filters were not installed because LED lights do not emit any significant levels of ultra-violet light. This simplified the installation process.

- The Navigation pane can be used to find text quickly.
- When you need to find and then replace several instances of the same words or phrases, you can use the Find and Replace dialog box.

1. Start **Word 2016**, and then open the student data file **wrd02_LEDs**. If necessary, display the formatting marks.
2. On the **File tab**, click **Save As**, and then click **Browse**. In the **Save As** dialog box, navigate to the location where you are saving your files. Create a folder named Word Chapter 2 and then save the file as Last_First_wrd02_LEDs
3. On the **View tab**, in the **Show group**, select the **Navigation Pane** check box, and then compare your screen with **Figure 1**.
4. With the insertion point at the top of the document, press Enter five times. On the **Home tab**, in the **Styles group**, click the **Heading 1** thumbnail. Type LED LIGHTS and then press Enter. Type A Museum Exhibit Case Study and then press Enter.
5. Using your own name, type By Your Name and then press Enter. Type the current date, and then press Enter.
6. Click to place the insertion point to the left of the title. Press and hold Shift while clicking to the right of the date to select the four lines.
7. In the **Paragraph group**, click the **Center** button, and then compare your screen with **Figure 2**.

   In an informal report, there should be 2 inches of space above the title, and the title, subtitle, writer's name, and date should be centered.

■ **Continue to the next page to complete the skill**

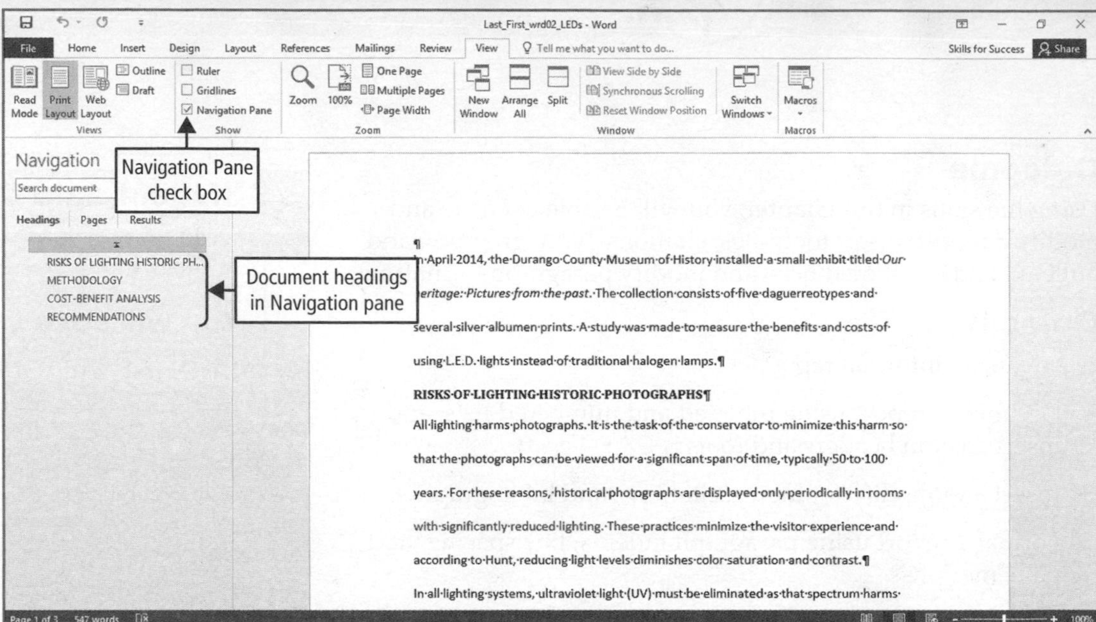

Figure 1

Word 2016, Windows 10, Microsoft Corporation

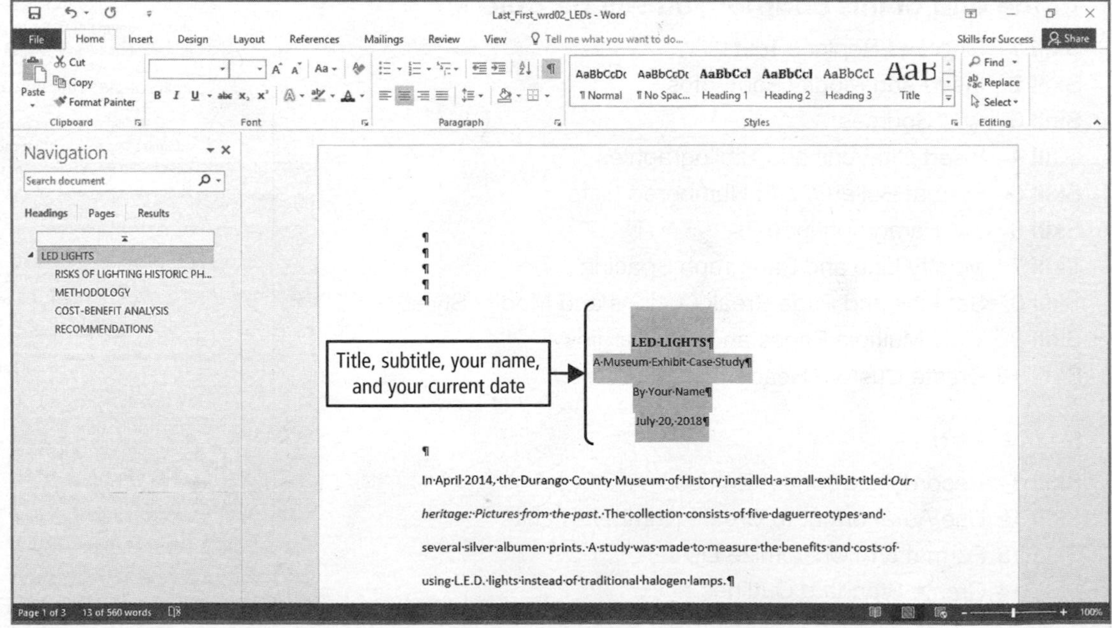

Figure 2

Word 2016, Windows 10, Microsoft Corporation

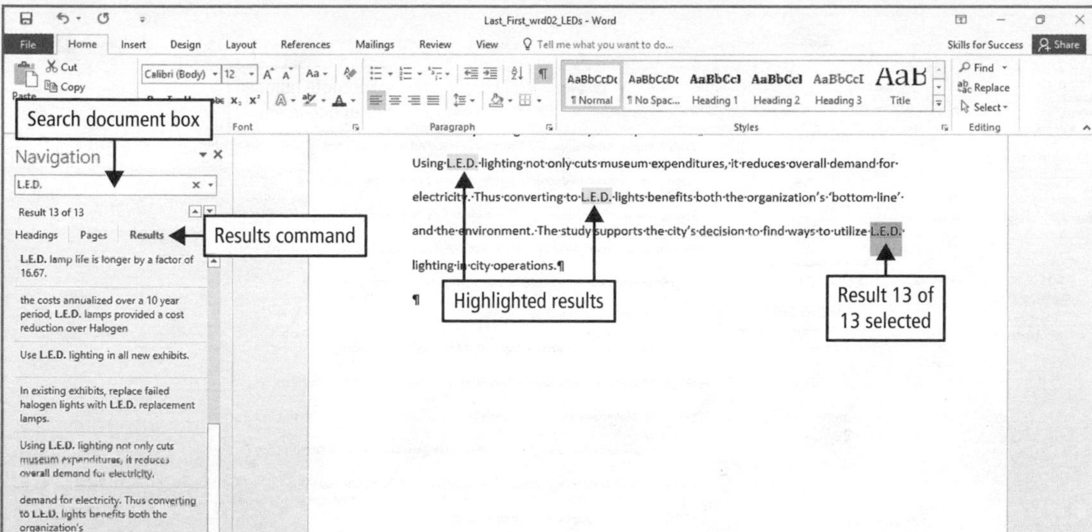

Word 2016, Windows 10, Microsoft Corporation

Figure 3

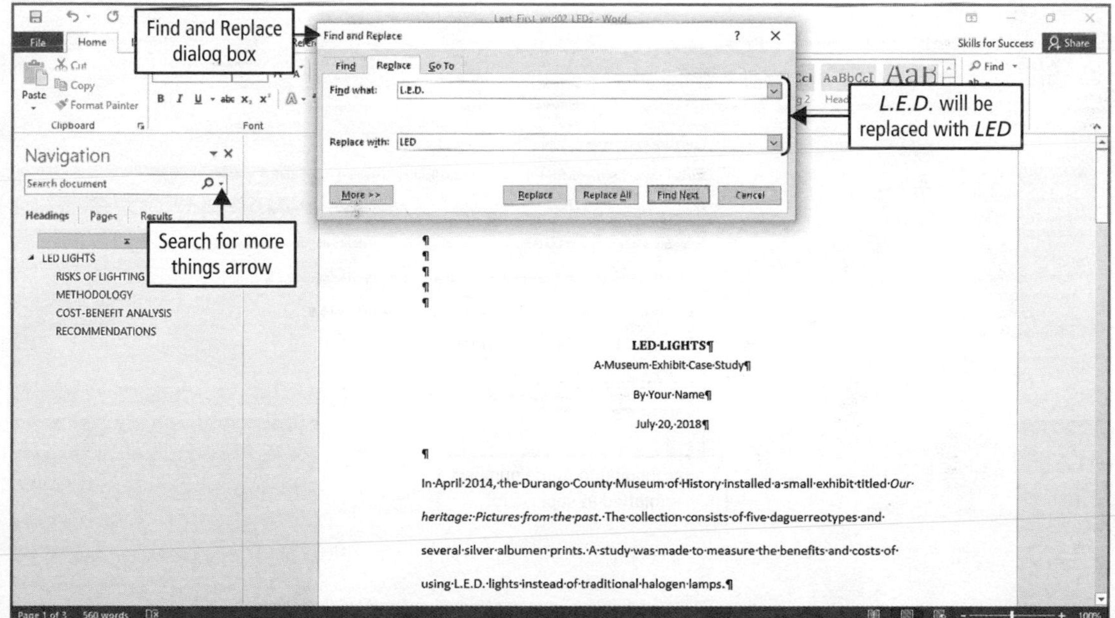

Word 2016, Windows 10, Microsoft Corporation

Figure 4

8. In the **Navigation** pane **Search document** box, type L.E.D. and then click **Results** to display the results. MOS Obj 1.2.1 C

9. Scroll to the bottom of the **Results** list, click the last search result, and then compare your screen with **Figure 3**.

   In this manner, you can quickly find and navigate to a word or phrase in a document. In the document, each instance of the searched text is highlighted.

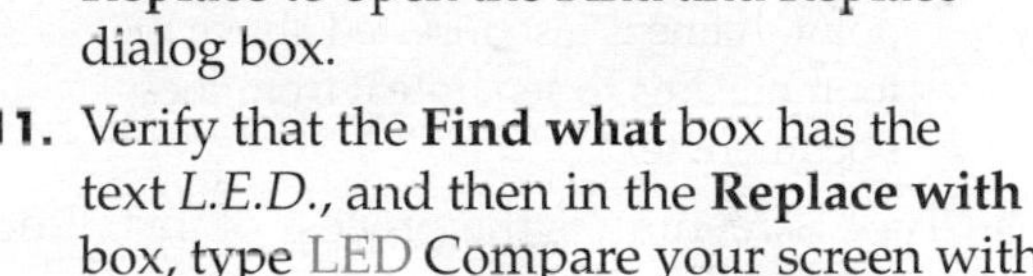

10. Click in the document, and then press Ctrl + Home to move the insertion point to the beginning of the document. In the **Navigation** pane, click the **Search for more things arrow**, and then click **Replace** to open the Find and Replace dialog box. MOS Obj 2.1.1 C

11. Verify that the **Find what** box has the text *L.E.D.*, and then in the **Replace with** box, type LED Compare your screen with **Figure 4**.

    When you open the Find and Replace dialog box from the Navigation pane, the word or phrase you want to find is automatically entered into the *Find what* box.

12. Click the **Find Next** button to select the next occurrence of *L.E.D.* Click the **Replace** button to replace the initials and move to the next occurrence. Click **Replace** to replace another occurrence of *L.E.D.* with *LED*.

    In this manner, you can replace each instance one at a time.

13. Click the **Replace All** button to replace the eleven remaining occurrences. Read the message that displays, click **OK**, and then **Close** the Find and Replace dialog box. **Save** the file.

- **You have completed Skill 1 of 10**

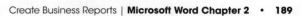

► A ***footnote*** is a note or comment placed at the bottom of the page. An ***endnote*** is a note or comment placed at the end of a section or a document.

1. In the **Navigation** pane, click the **Headings** command, and then click the **METHODOLOGY** heading to display that section of the report.

Obj 4.1.1 C

2. Click to the right of the period in the paragraph ending *output to the desired level.* Click the **References tab**, and then in the **Footnotes group**, click the **Insert Footnote** button.

   A footnote displays at the bottom of the page with a number *1* before the insertion point. A line is also inserted above the footnote area to separate it from the document text.

3. Type Screening is the process of installing layers of metal window screen. Compare your screen with **Figure 1**.

4. Navigate to the **COST-BENEFIT ANALYSIS** section, and then click to the right of the sentence ending *LED lamp life is longer by a factor of 16.67*.

5. Repeat the technique just practiced to insert a second footnote with the text Derived from industry standards. Compare your screen with **Figure 2**.

   Footnote numbers are inserted and formatted as ***superscript***—text that is positioned higher and smaller than the other text.

■ **Continue to the next page to complete the skill**

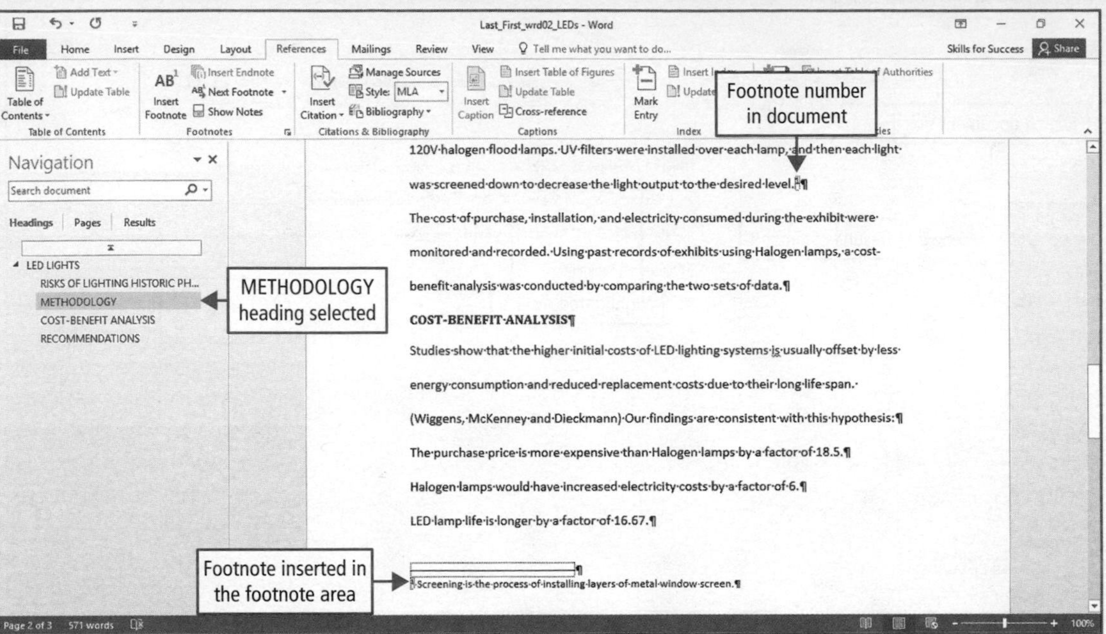

Figure 1 Word 2016, Windows 10, Microsoft Corporation

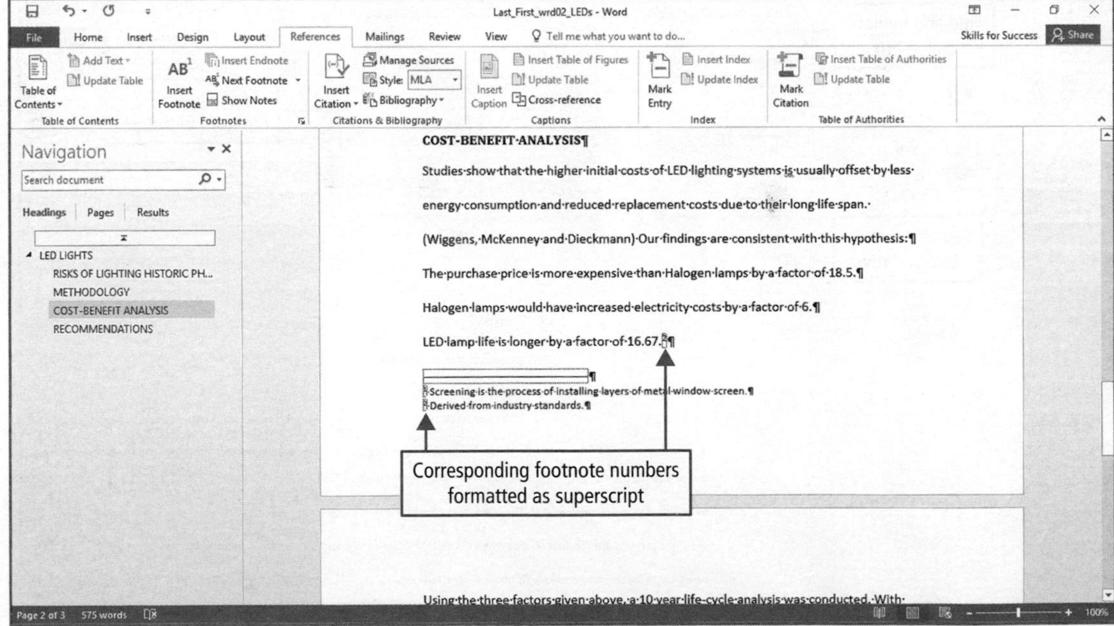

Figure 2 Word 2016, Windows 10, Microsoft Corporation

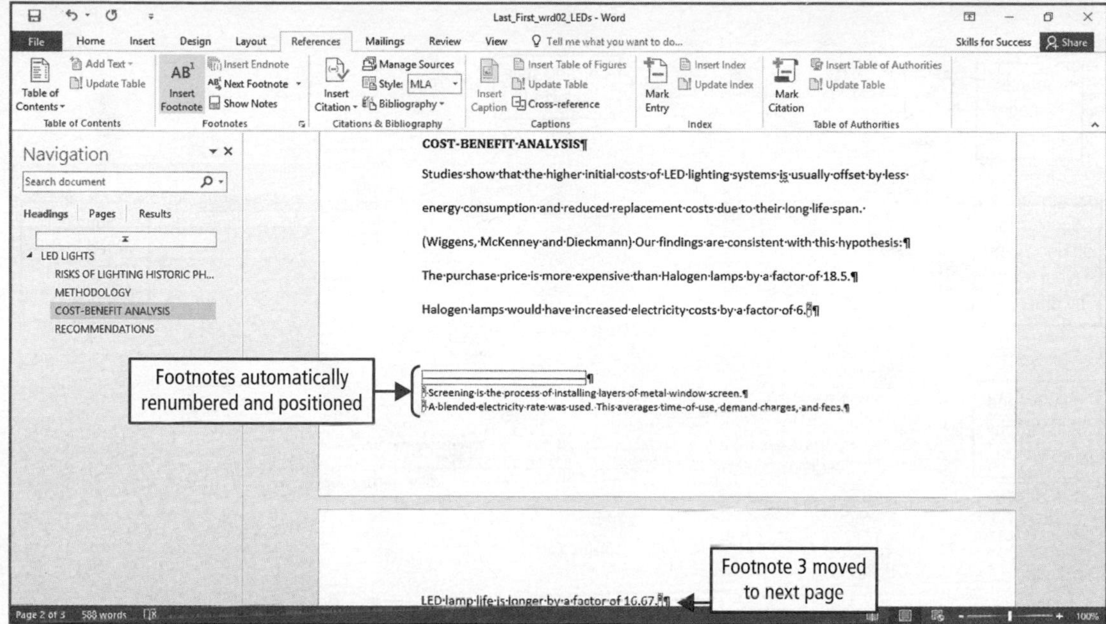

Word 2016, Windows 10, Microsoft Corporation

Figure 3

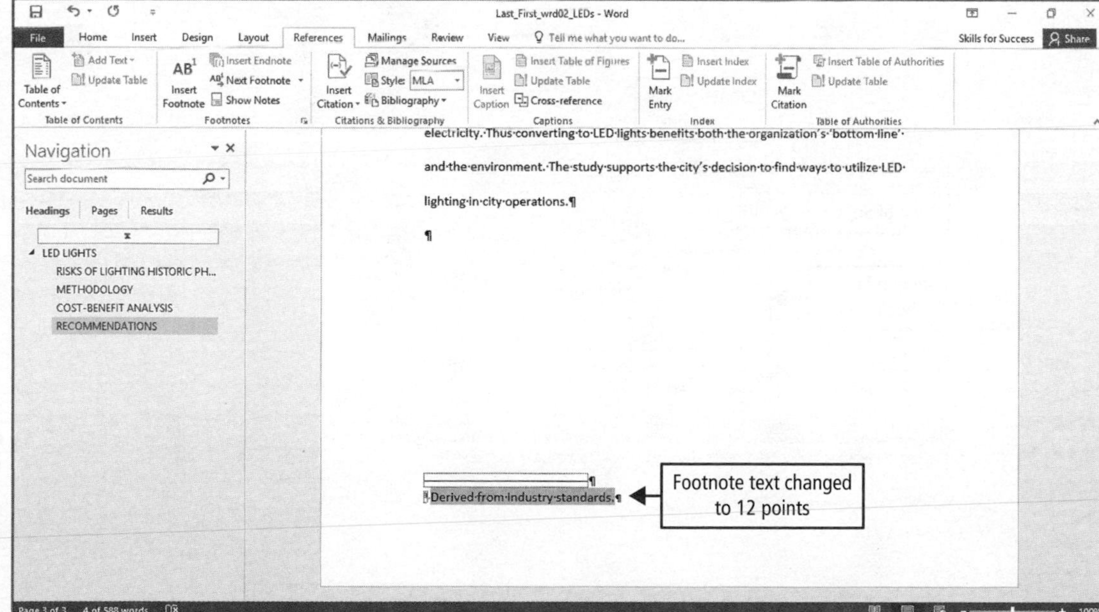

Word 2016, Windows 10, Microsoft Corporation

Figure 4

6. Above the footnotes, click to the right of the sentence ending *increased electricity costs by a factor of 6*. Insert another footnote with the text A blended electricity rate was used. This averages time-of-use, demand charges, and fees. Compare your screen with **Figure 3**.

   Footnotes automatically position themselves at the bottom of the correct page and adjust so that they are renumbered sequentially.

7. At the bottom of Page 2, select the text of the first footnote without selecting the footnote number. Change the font size to **12**.

   Most style manuals call for the footer text to be the same size as the document text. Footnote numbers are typically smaller than the report text.

8. Repeat the technique just practiced to change the text of the second footnote to **12** points. Take care to format just the text and not the footnote number.
9. Scroll to the bottom of Page 3 to display the third footnote, and then change the footnote text to **12** points.
10. Compare your screen with **Figure 4**, and then **Save** the file.

■ **You have completed Skill 2 of 10**

▶ A ***source*** is the reference used to find information or data.

1. On the **References tab**, in the **Citations & Bibliography group**, click the **Style arrow**, and then click **Chicago Sixteenth Edition**.
2. In the **Citations & Bibliography group**, click **Manage Sources**, and then under **Current List**, click the source starting *Wiggens*. Compare your screen with **Figure 1**.

   The Master List sources are available for all your documents, and the Current List sources are available only for a single document. The Preview pane displays citations and bibliography entries in the format for the selected style—here, Chicago Sixteenth Edition. The check mark indicates that the source has been cited in the document.

MOS Obj 4.1.3 C

3. Click the **New** button, and then verify the **Type of Source** is **Book**.
4. In the **Author** box, type Bertrand Lavedrine and then in the **Title** box, type A Guide to the Preventive Conservation of Photograph Collections
5. For the **Year**, type 2003 and for the **City**, type Los Angeles For the **Publisher**, type Getty Conservation Institute and then compare your screen with **Figure 2**.

   The Create Source dialog box displays the fields required by the Chicago style for the selected source type.

6. Click **OK**, and then in **Source Manager**, preview the new source's citation and bibliography entry.

   The author's last name followed by a comma was placed before the first name when you closed the dialog box.

7. Click the **New** button, and then change the **Type of Source** to **Journal Article**.

■ **Continue to the next page to complete the skill**

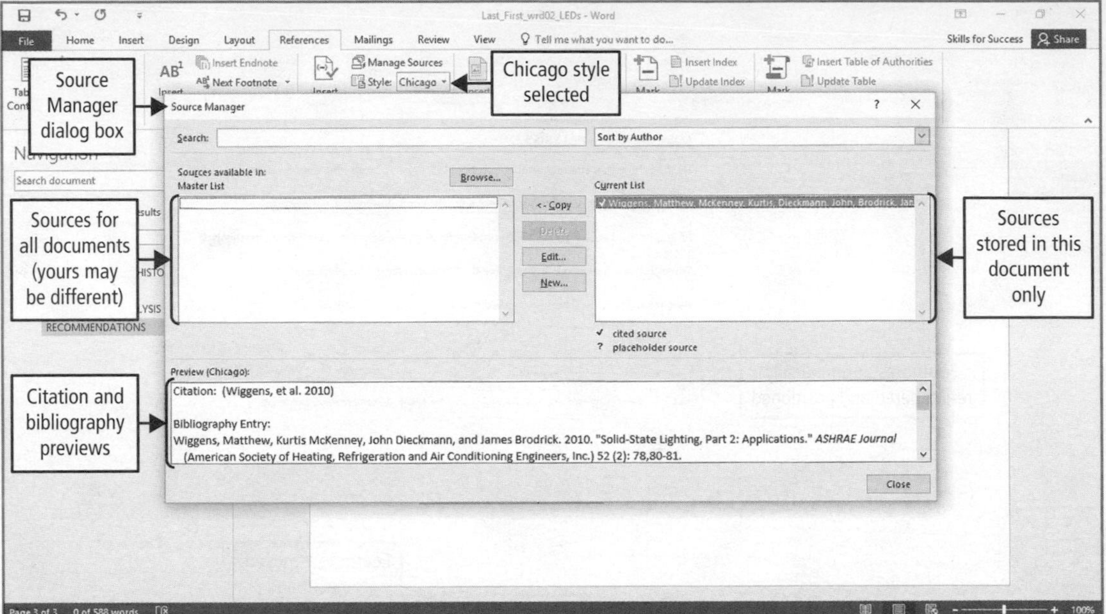

Figure 1

Word 2016, Windows 10, Microsoft Corporation

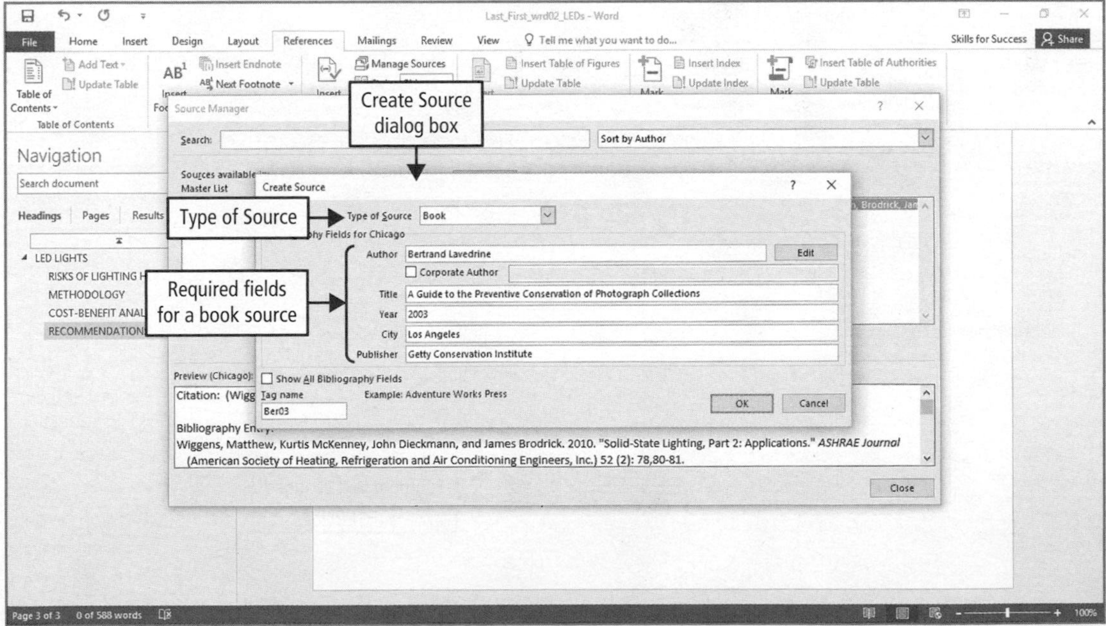

Figure 2

Word 2016, Windows 10, Microsoft Corporation

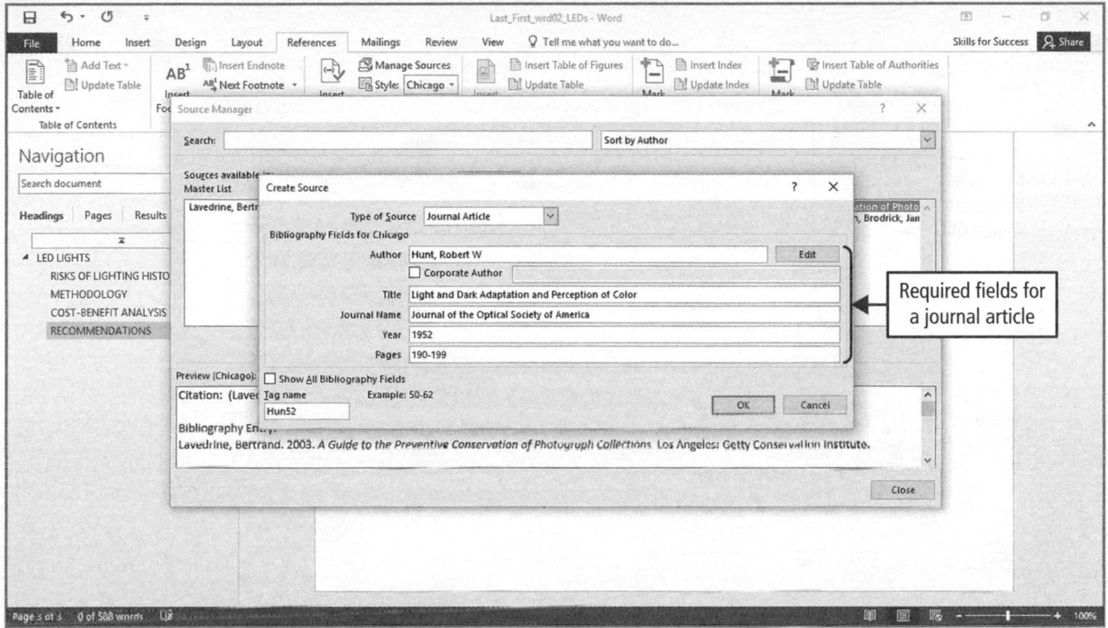

Word 2016, Windows 10, Microsoft Corporation

Figure 3

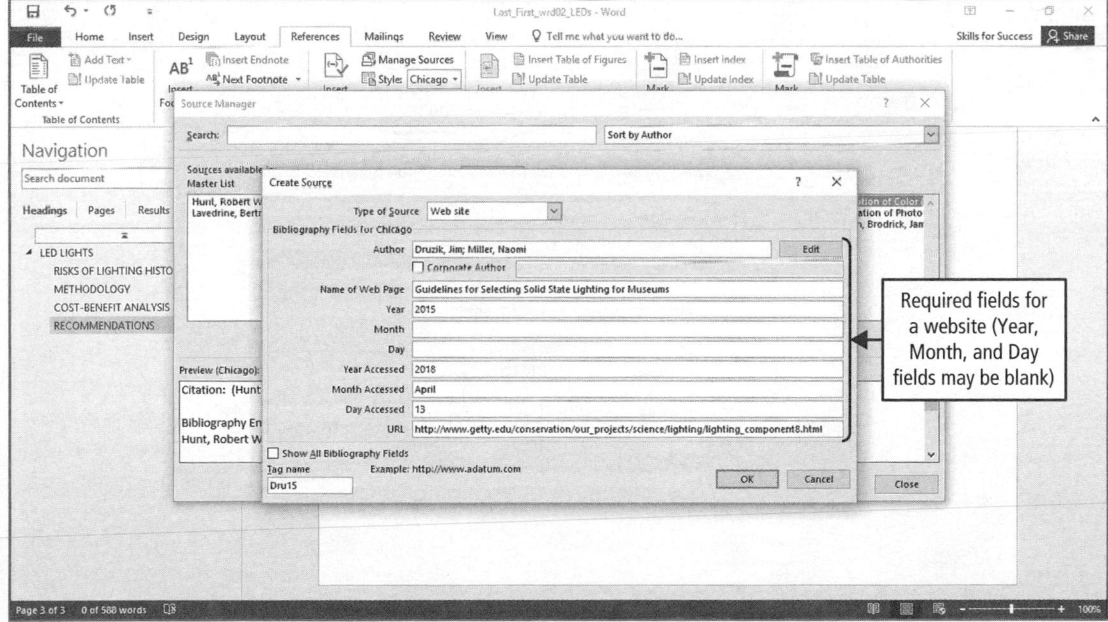

Word 2016, Windows 10, Microsoft Corporation

Figure 4

8. In the **Author** box, type Hunt, Robert W and then in the **Title** box, type Light and Dark Adaptation and Perception of Color
9. For the **Journal Name**, type Journal of the Optical Society of America and in the **Year** box, type 1952 In the **Pages** box, type 190-199 Compare your screen with **Figure 3**, and then click **OK**.
10. Click the **New** button, and then change the **Type of Source** to **Web site**.
11. In the **Author** box, type Druzik, Jim; Miller, Naomi and then in the **Name of Web Page** box, type Guidelines for Selecting Solid State Lighting for Museums
12. In the **Year** box, type 2015 In the **Year Accessed** box, type 2018 The **Month Accessed** is April and the **Day Accessed** is 13
13. In the **URL** box, type http://www.getty.edu/conservation/our_projects/science/lighting/lighting_component8.html Compare your screen with **Figure 4**, and then click **OK**.
14. In the **Source Manager** dialog box **Master List**, select the first source created in this skill. Verify you selected the title in the **Master List**—*not* the one in the Current List—and then click the **Delete** button. Repeat to delete the other two sources created in this skill from the **Master List**, and then click the **Close** button.

    When you add a new source, it is placed in both the Master and Current Lists. If you do not plan to use a source in other documents, it can be deleted from the Master List. However, take care to leave the sources in the Current List.

- **You have completed Skill 3 of 10**

SKILL 2.4

- When you quote or refer to information from another source, you need to credit that source.
- A ***bibliography*** is a compilation of sources referenced in a report and listed on a separate page.
- A ***citation*** is a note in the document that refers the reader to a source in the bibliography.

1. Navigate to the **RISKS OF LIGHTING HISTORIC PHOTOGRAPHS** section.

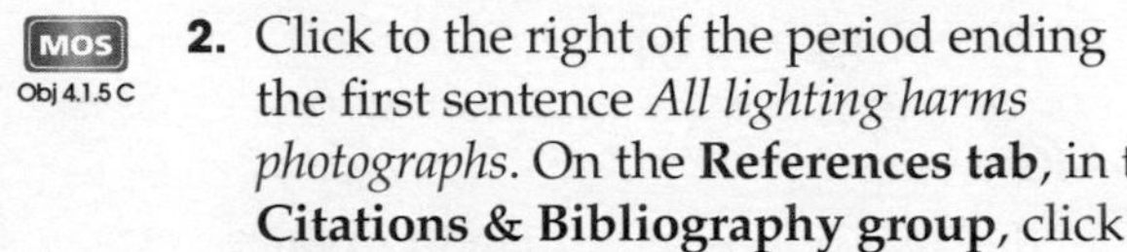

2. Click to the right of the period ending the first sentence *All lighting harms photographs*. On the **References tab**, in the **Citations & Bibliography group**, click **Insert Citation**, and then compare your screen with **Figure 1**.

   When you insert a citation field, the sources stored in Source Manager display in the gallery.

3. In the **Citation** gallery, click the **Lavedrine, Bertand** source to insert the citation.
4. In the same paragraph, click to the right of the period of the sentence ending *saturation and contrast*. Repeat the technique just practiced to insert the citation for **Hunt, Robert W**.
5. Click the citation just inserted, click the field's **Citation Options arrow**, and then click **Edit Citation**. In the **Pages** box, type 192 click **OK**, and then compare your screen with **Figure 2**.

   Many business reports use the ***author-date citation***, which contains the author's last name, the publication year, and the specific page number(s) if one is available.

■ **Continue to the next page to complete the skill**

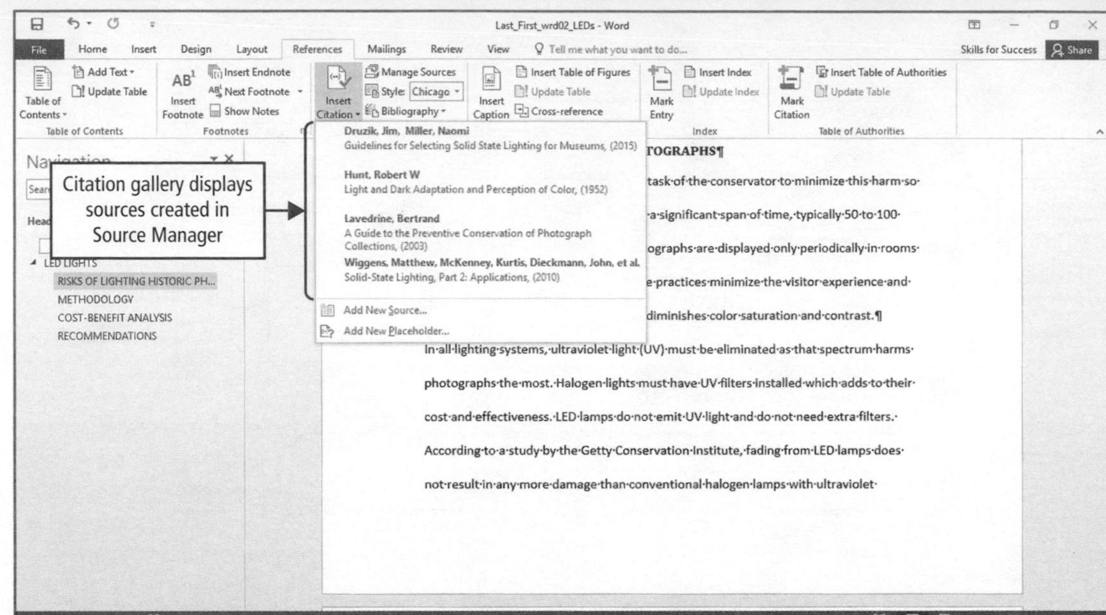

Figure 1

Word 2016, Windows 10, Microsoft Corporation

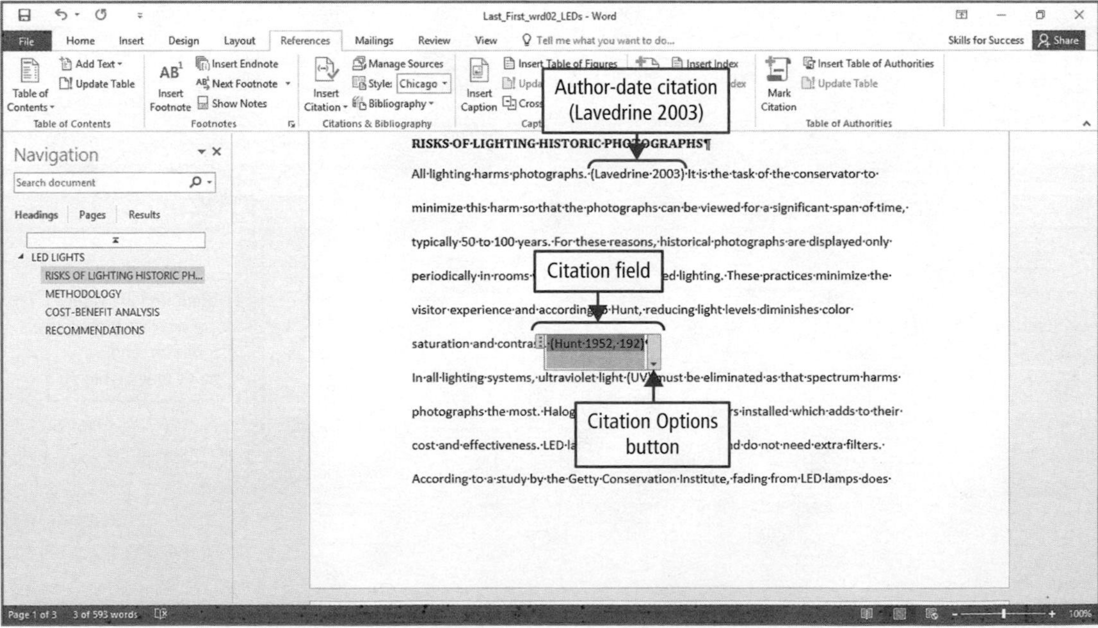

Figure 2

Word 2016, Windows 10, Microsoft Corporation

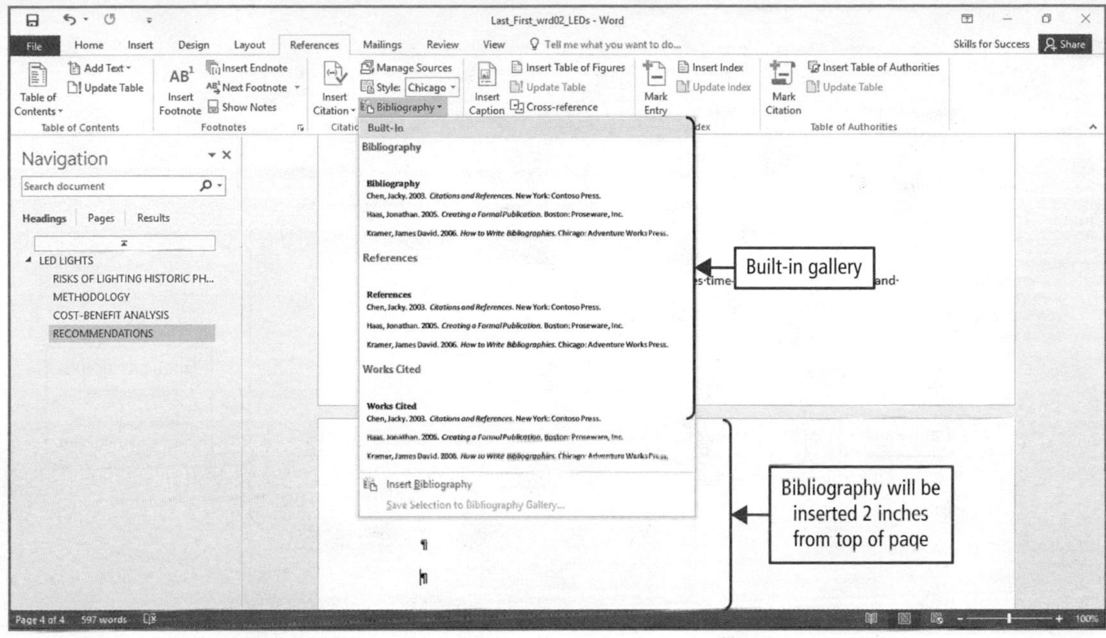

Word 2016, Windows 10, Microsoft Corporation

Figure 3

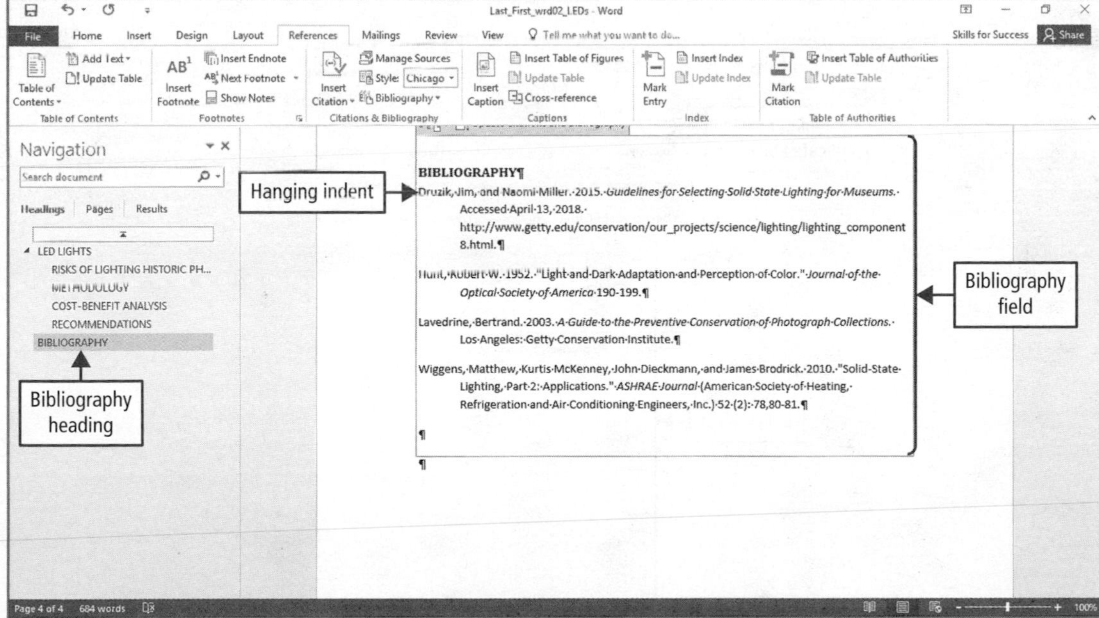

Word 2016, Windows 10, Microsoft Corporation

Figure 4

6. At the top of Page 2, click to the right of the period of the sentence ending *fading of photographic materials*, and then insert the citation for **Druzik, Jim, Miller, Naomi**.

7. Press Ctrl + End, and then press Ctrl + Enter to insert a manual page break and start a new page. Press Enter two times to create about 2 inches of space from the top of the page.

8. On the **References tab**, in the **Citations & Bibliography group**, click the **Bibliography** button, and then compare your screen with **Figure 3**.

9. From the gallery, click the **Bibliography** thumbnail to insert a bibliography field. If necessary, scroll up to display the inserted bibliography field.

   In the Chicago style, the Bibliography field displays each source using hanging indents. In a ***hanging indent***, the first line extends to the left of the rest of the paragraph.

10. Double-click the *Bibliography* title, and then type BIBLIOGRAPHY In the **Navigation** pane, verify that the *BIBLIOGRAPHY* title has been added as a level 1 heading. Compare your screen with **Figure 4**.

    In an informal report, the first-level headings should be uppercase and centered. You will center this title in a later skill.

11. **Save** the file.

    If you change the reference style or report sources, you can update the citation and bibliography fields by clicking the field and then selecting its update command.

■ **You have completed Skill 4 of 10**

► A ***bulleted list*** is a list of items with each item introduced by a symbol—such as a small circle or check mark—in which the list items can be presented in any order.

1. Navigate to the **COST-BENEFIT ANALYSIS** section.
2. If necessary, scroll down to display the bottom of Page 2 and the top of Page 3.
3. Point to the left of the paragraph that starts *The purchase price is more* to display the pointer, and then drag straight down to select the three paragraphs starting *The purchase price* and ending with *factor of 16.67* including the footnote number and paragraph marks. Compare your screen with **Figure 1**.

   When you select text with footnotes, the text in the footnotes area will not be selected.
4. If your ruler does not display, on the **View tab**, in the **Show group**, select the **Ruler** check box.
5. MOS Obj 3.3.1 C On the **Home tab**, in the **Paragraph group**, click the **Bullets arrow**, and then in the **Bullets** gallery, click the solid circle bullet.

   The Bullets gallery displays commonly used bullet characters, and the most recently used bullet displays at the top.
6. MOS Obj 3.3.4 C In the **Paragraph group**, click the **Increase Indent** button one time, and then compare your screen with **Figure 2**.

   In reports, lists are typically indented 0.5 inches on the left with a hanging indent set to 0.25 inches for the first line.

■ Continue to the next page to complete the skill

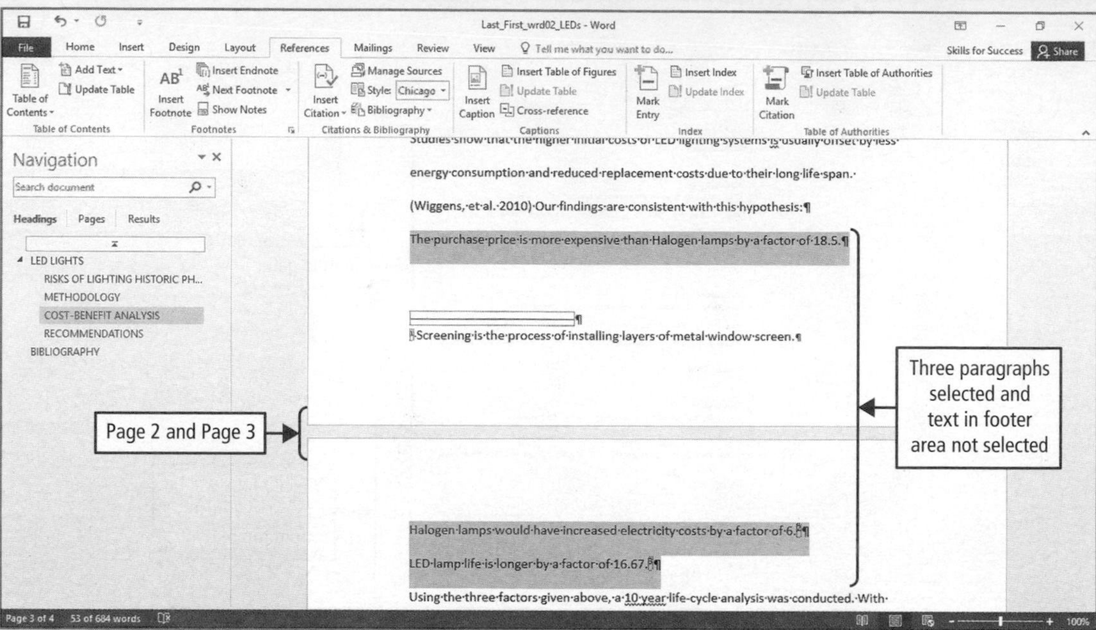

Figure 1 Word 2016, Windows 10, Microsoft Corporation

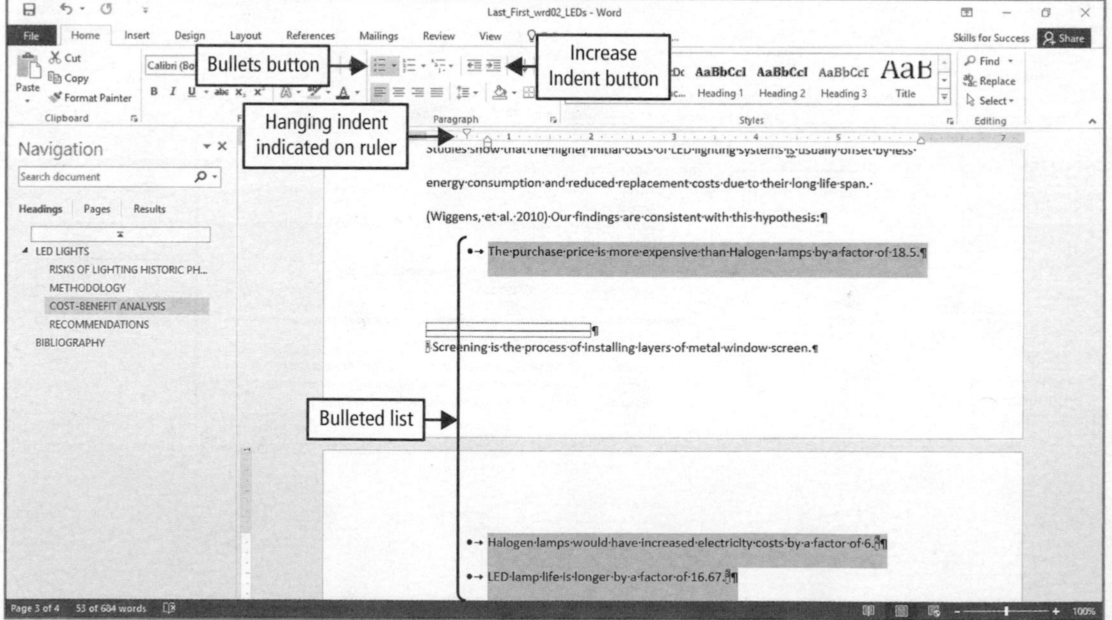

Figure 2 Word 2016, Windows 10, Microsoft Corporation

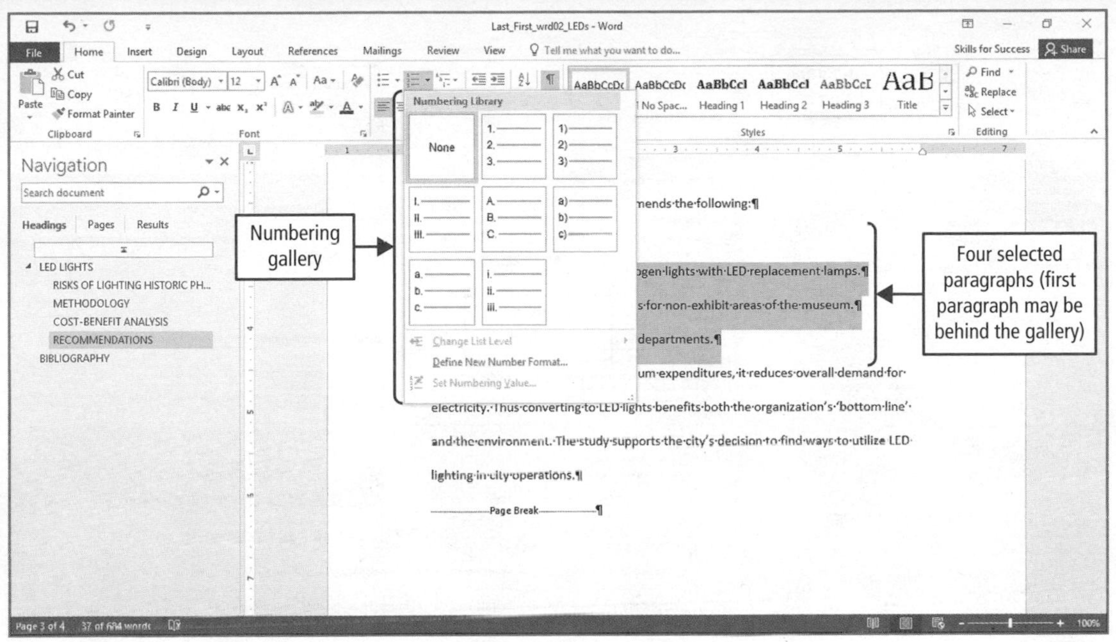

Word 2016, Windows 10, Microsoft Corporation

Figure 3

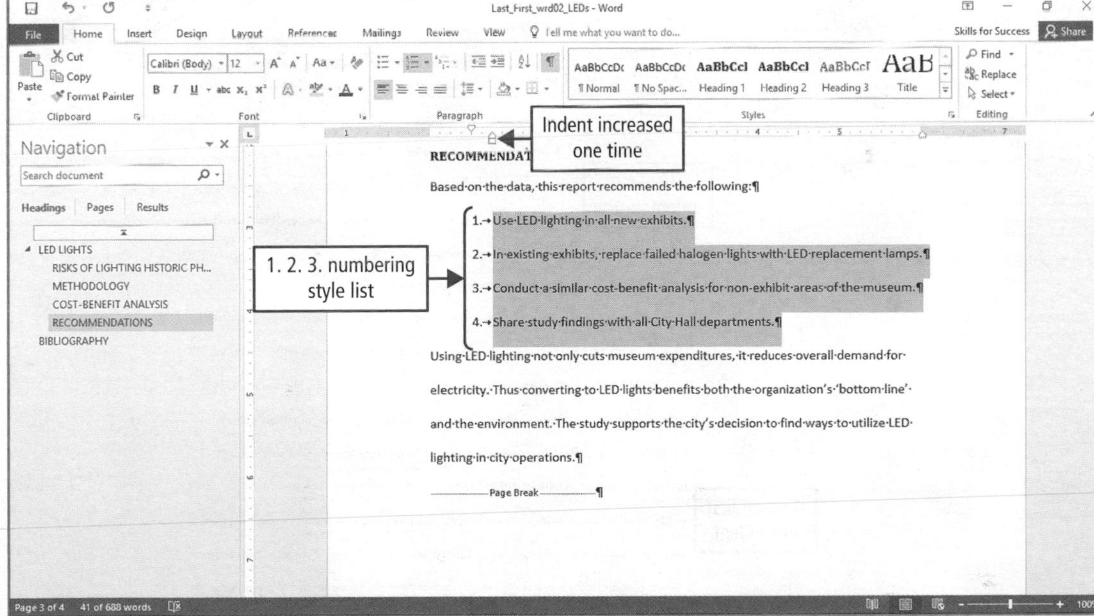

Word 2016, Windows 10, Microsoft Corporation

Figure 4

7. Navigate to the **RECOMMENDATIONS** section, and then select the four paragraphs beginning *Use LED lighting in all new* and ending with *City Hall departments*.
8. On the **Home tab**, in the **Paragraph group**, click the **Numbering arrow**, and then compare your screen with **Figure 3**.

   A ***numbered list*** is a list of items with each item introduced by a consecutive number or letter to indicate definite steps, a sequence of actions, or chronological order.

   The Numbering gallery displays common formats that can be used to enumerate lists. For all lists, you should refer to the style guidelines specified for your report. Certain bullet characters may be specified or a different numbering system may need to be applied.
9. In the **Numbering** gallery, click the thumbnail with the **1. 2. 3.** formatting.
10. In the **Paragraph group**, click the **Increase Indent** button one time, and then compare your screen with **Figure 4**.
11. **Save** the file.

- **You have completed Skill 5 of 10**

► An ***indent*** is the position of paragraph lines in relation to a page margin.

1. Navigate to the **LED LIGHTS** heading, and then click in the body paragraph that starts *In April 2014*.
2. On the **Home tab**, in the **Paragraph group**, click the **Paragraph Dialog Box Launcher** [launcher].

   The Paragraph dialog box has commands and settings that are not available in the Paragraph group.

MOS Obj 2.2.3 C

3. Under **Indentation**, click the **Special arrow**, and then click **First line**. Compare your screen with **Figure 1**.

   The ***first line indent*** is the location of the beginning of the first line of a paragraph in relation to the left edge of the remainder of the paragraph. In this case, the *By* box displays *0.5"*, which will indent the first line of the current paragraph one-half inch.
4. Click **OK** to indent the first line of the paragraph. On the ruler, verify that the **First Line Indent** marker is now at the **0.5 inch** mark.
5. Click in the paragraph starting *All lighting harms photographs*. Press F4 to repeat the previous task.

   The F4 keyboard shortcut repeats the last command. If you performed an additional task after setting the previous indent, you will need to set the indent using the Paragraph dialog box.
6. Click in the next paragraph starting *In all lighting systems*, press F4, and then compare your screen with **Figure 2**.

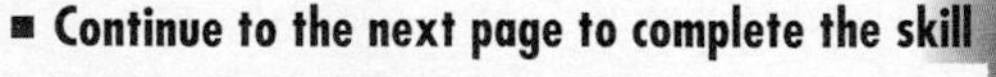

■ **Continue to the next page to complete the skill**

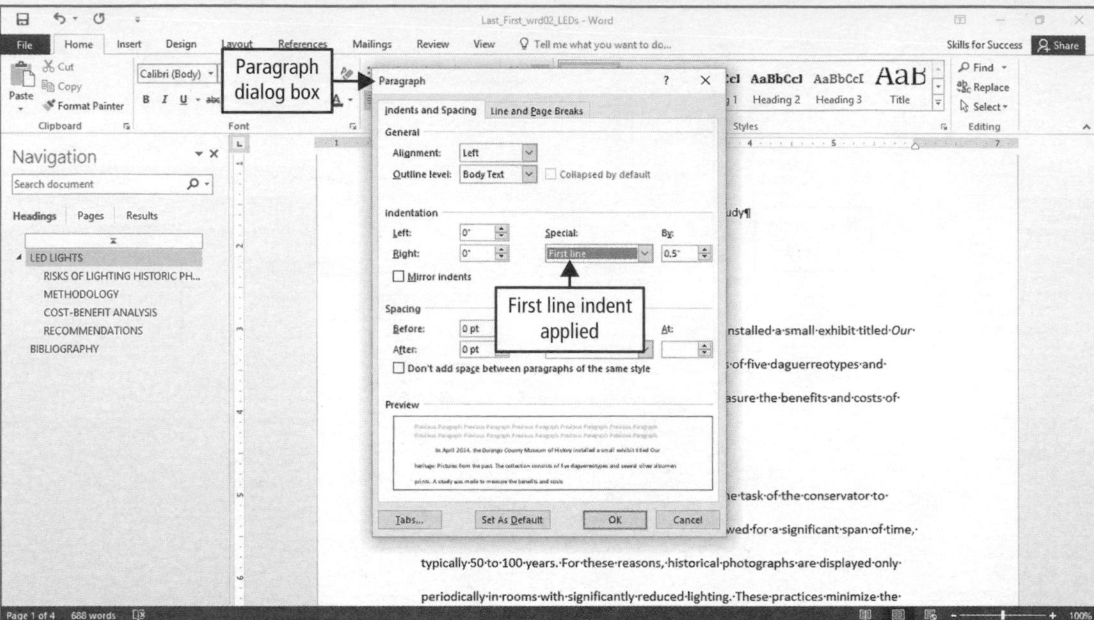

Figure 1 Word 2016, Windows 10, Microsoft Corporation

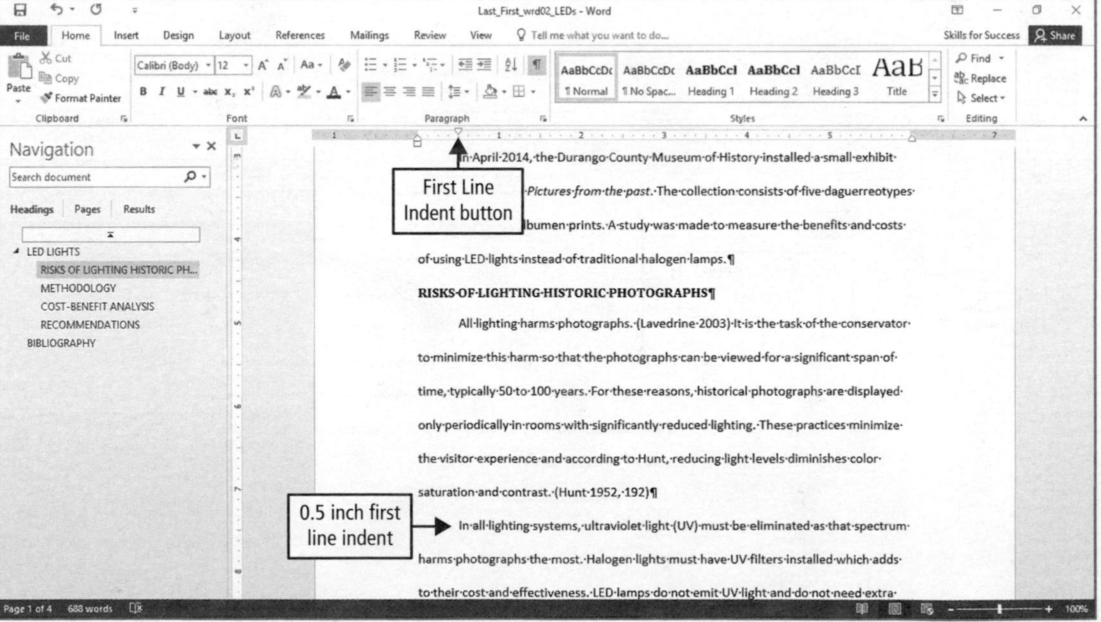

Figure 2 Word 2016, Windows 10, Microsoft Corporation

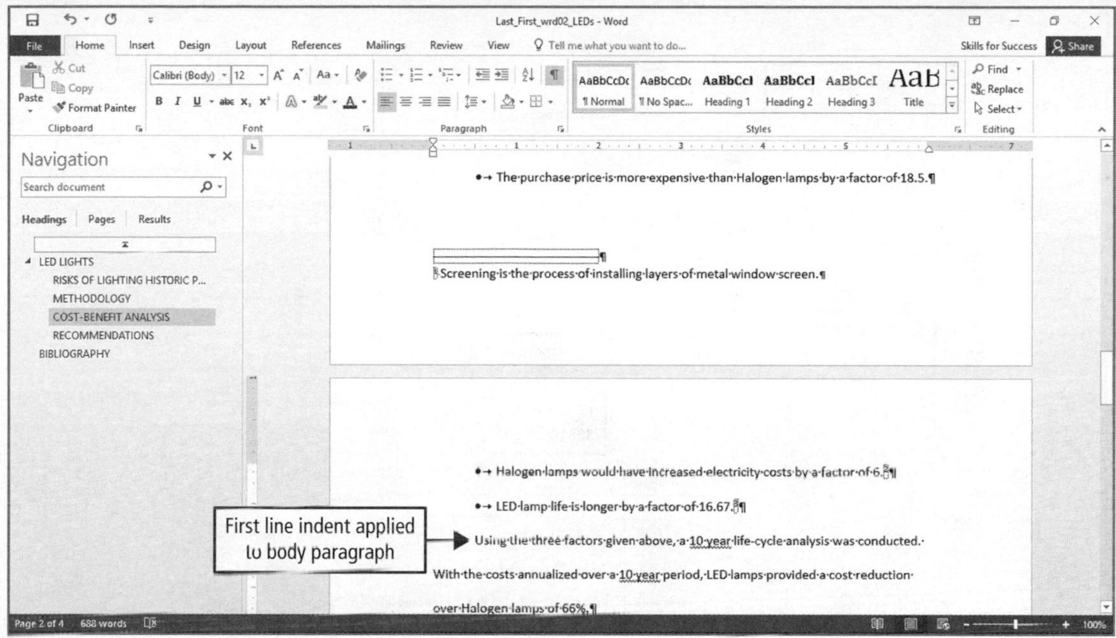

Word 2016, Windows 10, Microsoft Corporation

Figure 3

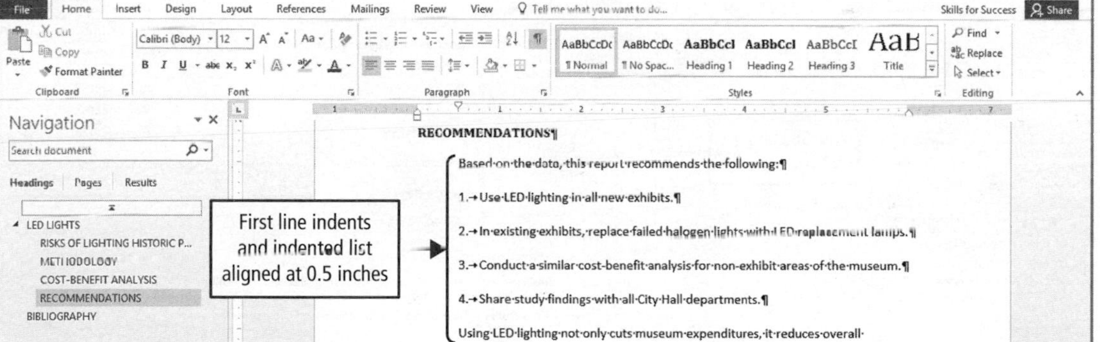

Word 2016, Windows 10, Microsoft Corporation

Figure 4

7. In the **METHODOLOGY** section, click in the first paragraph beginning *In the new exhibit*. On the ruler, drag the **First Line Indent** button to the **0.5 inch** mark on the ruler.

   In this manner, you can set the first line indent in the Paragraph dialog box or on the ruler.

8. Select the two paragraphs beginning *In the past* and *The cost of purchase*, and then repeat one of the techniques practiced in this skill to set a **0.5 inch** first line indent to both paragraphs.

9. Navigate to the **COST-BENEFIT ANALYSIS** section, and then apply a **0.5 inch** first line indent to the two paragraphs starting *Studies show that* and *Using the three factors*. Compare your screen with **Figure 3**.

   Recall that the bulleted list was indented to 0.5 inches in the previous skill and already has a hanging indent.

10. Navigate to the **RECOMMENDATIONS** section, and then apply a **0.5 inch** first line indent to the two paragraphs starting *Based on the data* and *Using LED lighting not only cuts*. Compare your screen with **Figure 4**.

    In a report, the paragraph first line indents and the bullets or numbers in a list should all align at the 0.5 inch mark.

11. **Save** the file.

■ **You have completed Skill 6 of 10**

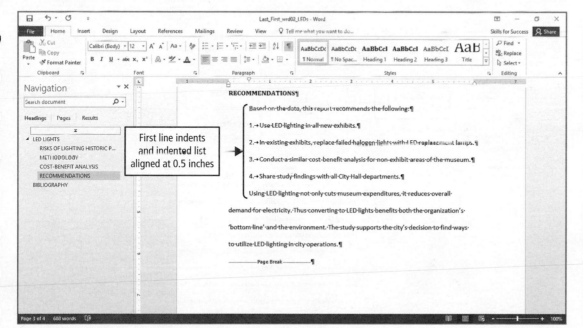

SKILL 7: Modify Line and Paragraph Spacing

► ***Line spacing*** is the vertical distance between lines of text in a paragraph, and ***paragraph spacing*** is the vertical distance above and below each paragraph. Both may need to be adjusted to match your report's style guide.

1. In the **Navigation** pane, click the **LED LIGHTS** heading. Select the title and the three paragraphs after it. On the **Home tab**, in the **Paragraph group**, click the **Paragraph Dialog Box Launcher** .

Obj 2.2.3 C

2. In the **Paragraph** dialog box, under **Spacing**, click the **Before up spin arrow** one time to change the value to **0 pt**, and then change the **After** value to **12 pt**.
3. Click the **Line spacing arrow**, and then click **Single**. Compare your screen with **Figure 1**, and then click **OK**.

   Reports should have a blank line between each element. The style guide you follow should specify if this should be done by inserting a blank paragraph or by adjusting the paragraph spacing.

4. Click in the body paragraph that begins *In April 2014*. In the **Paragraph group**, click the **Line and Paragraph Spacing** button , and then compare your screen with **Figure 2**.

   To increase readability in longer reports, the default line spacing should be 2.0, which is ***double-spacing***—the equivalent of a blank line of text displays between each line of text.

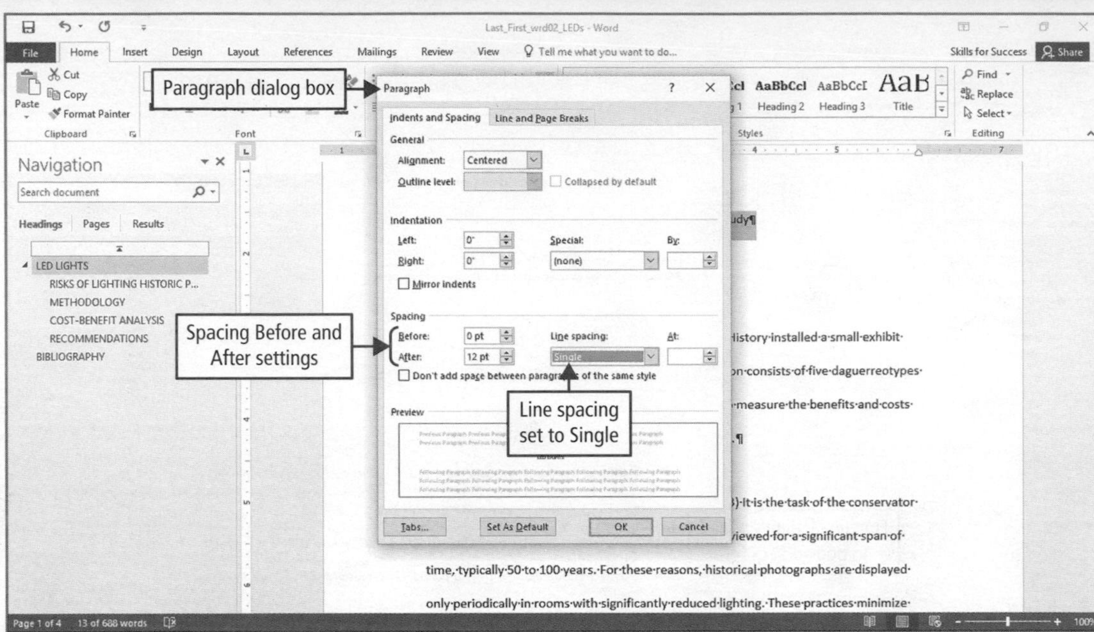

Figure 1 Word 2016, Windows 10, Microsoft Corporation

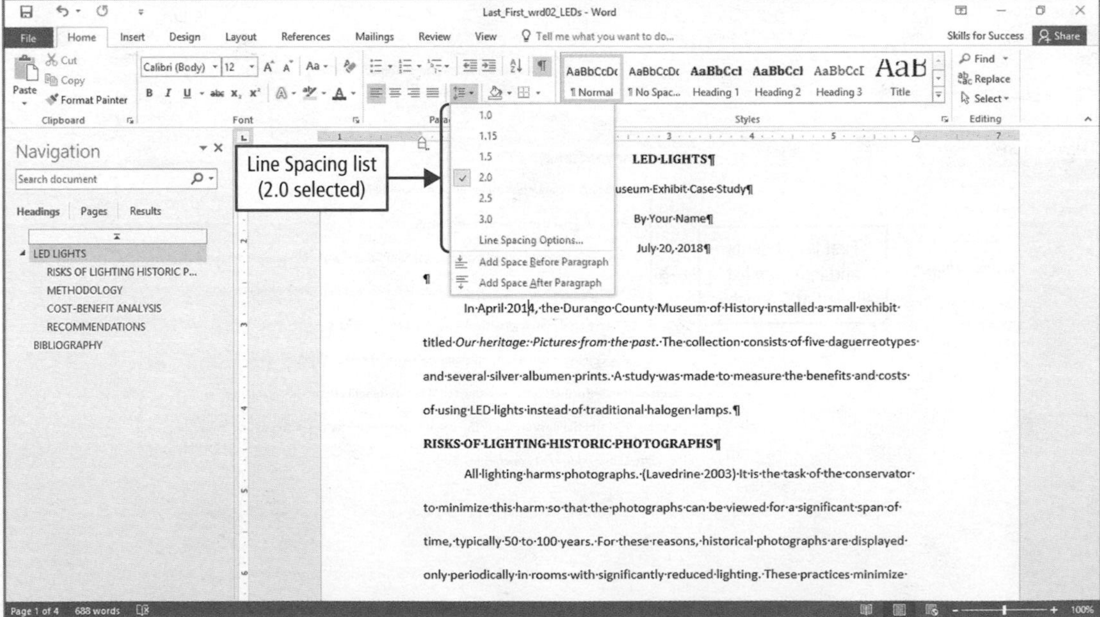

Figure 2 Word 2016, Windows 10, Microsoft Corporation

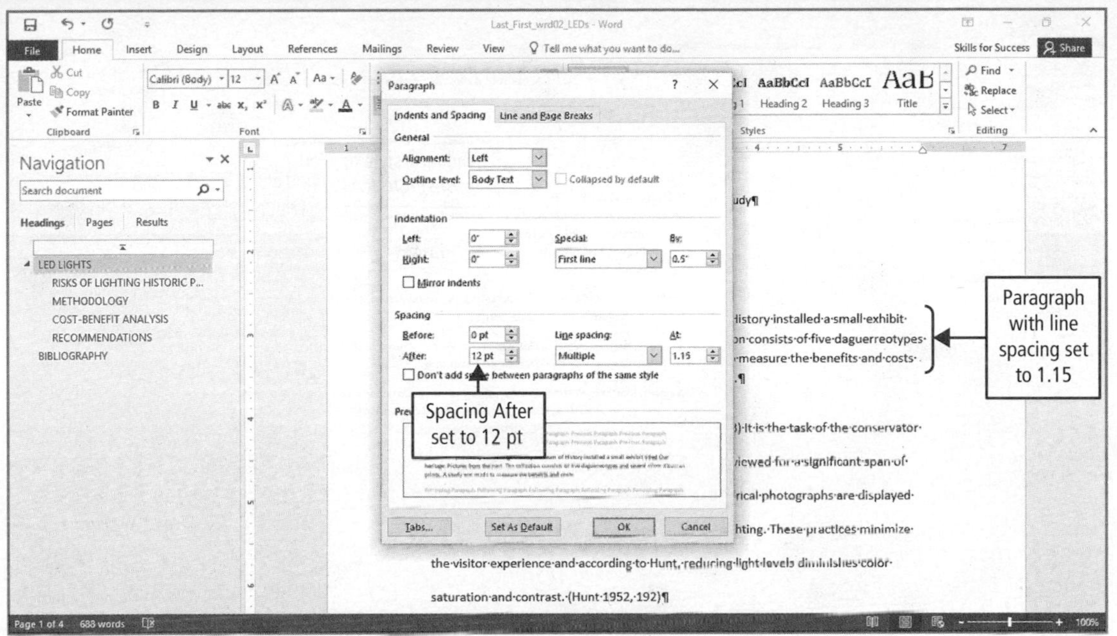

Word 2016, Windows 10, Microsoft Corporation

Figure 3

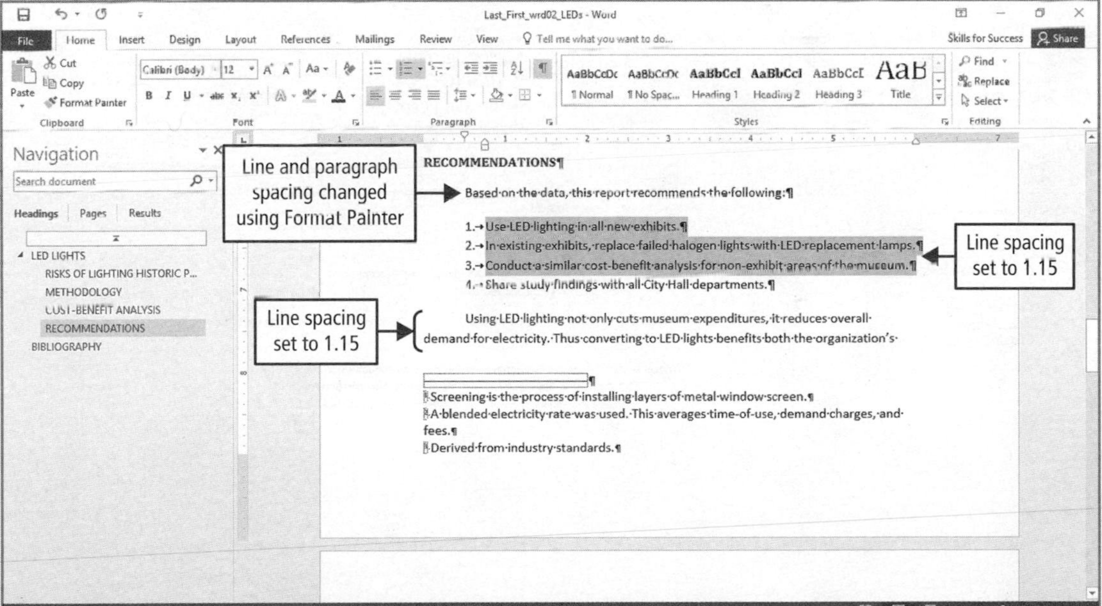

Word 2016, Windows 10, Microsoft Corporation

Figure 4

5. In the **Line and Paragraph Spacing** list, point to **1.15** to preview the setting, and then click **1.15**.

   In shorter, informal reports such as this report, you can reduce the amount of line spacing so that the report fits on fewer pages. Text with a line spacing of 1.15 has been found to be easier to read than single-spaced text.

6. Open the **Paragraph** dialog box, and then change the **After** setting to **12 pt**. Compare your screen with **Figure 3**, and then click **OK**.
7. With the insertion point still in the paragraph, double-click the **Format Painter** button. With the **Format Painter** pointer, click one time in the nine remaining body paragraphs—do not drag—to apply the line and paragraph spacing formatting. Do not apply the formatting to the headings, bulleted list items, numbered list items, or bibliography items. When you are done, click the **Format Painter** button so it is no longer active.
8. Navigate to the **COST-BENEFIT ANALYSIS** section, and then select the first two bulleted list items. In the **Paragraph group**, click the **Line and Paragraph Spacing** button, and then click **1.15**.
9. In the **RECOMMENDATIONS** section, select the first three numbered list items, and then set the **Line Spacing** to **1.15**. Compare your screen with **Figure 4**.
10. **Save** the file.

■ **You have completed Skill 7 of 10**

- You may need to adjust line and page break options to avoid problems when headings and paragraphs split across two pages.
- You can format elements quickly by modifying the styles assigned to them.

1. In the **Navigation** pane, click the **BIBLIOGRAPHY** header, and then compare your screen with **Figure 1**.

   The Bibliography header was assigned the Heading 1 style, but it does not have the same alignment and paragraph spacing as the document title.

2. Navigate to the document title, **LED LIGHTS**. With the insertion point in the title paragraph, on the **Home tab**, in the **Styles group**, right-click the **Heading 1** thumbnail. From the shortcut menu, click **Update Heading 1 to Match Selection**.

   Recall that for paragraph formatting, the paragraph does not actually need to be selected. Here, the Heading 1 style was updated based on the formatting of the paragraph the insertion point was in.

3. Navigate to the **BIBLIOGRAPHY** heading, and then compare your screen with **Figure 2**.

   The heading is now center aligned with 12 points of space below the paragraph. In this manner, you can format a document quickly by modifying its styles.

4. Navigate to the **METHODOLOGY** section. Click in the paragraph that begins *In the new exhibit*, and then open the **Paragraph** dialog box.

Continue to the next page to complete the skill

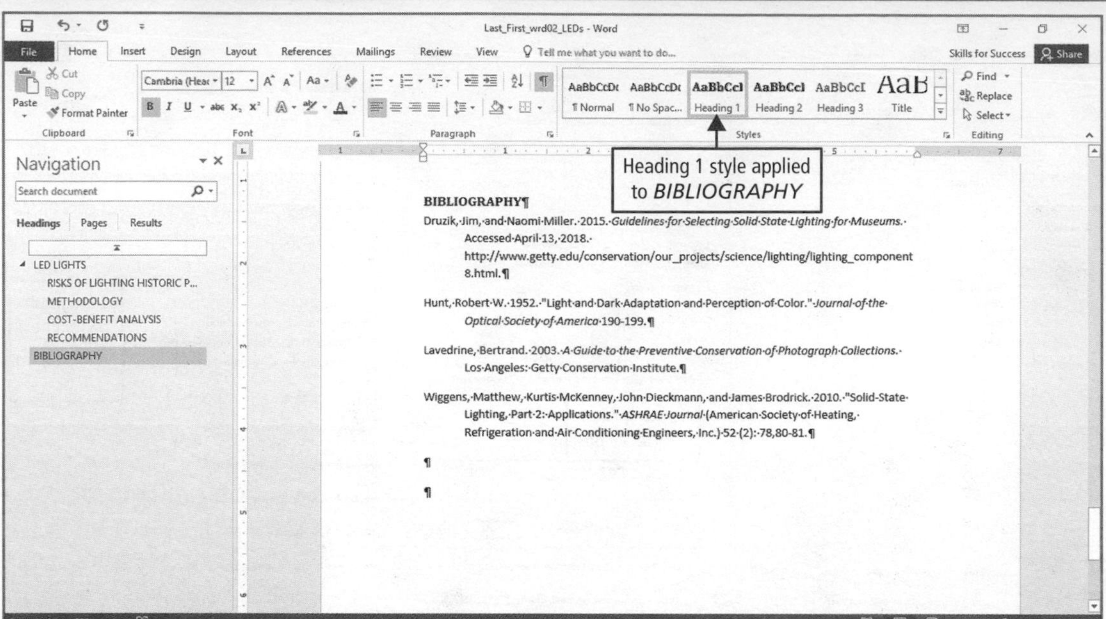

Figure 1 Word 2016, Windows 10, Microsoft Corporation

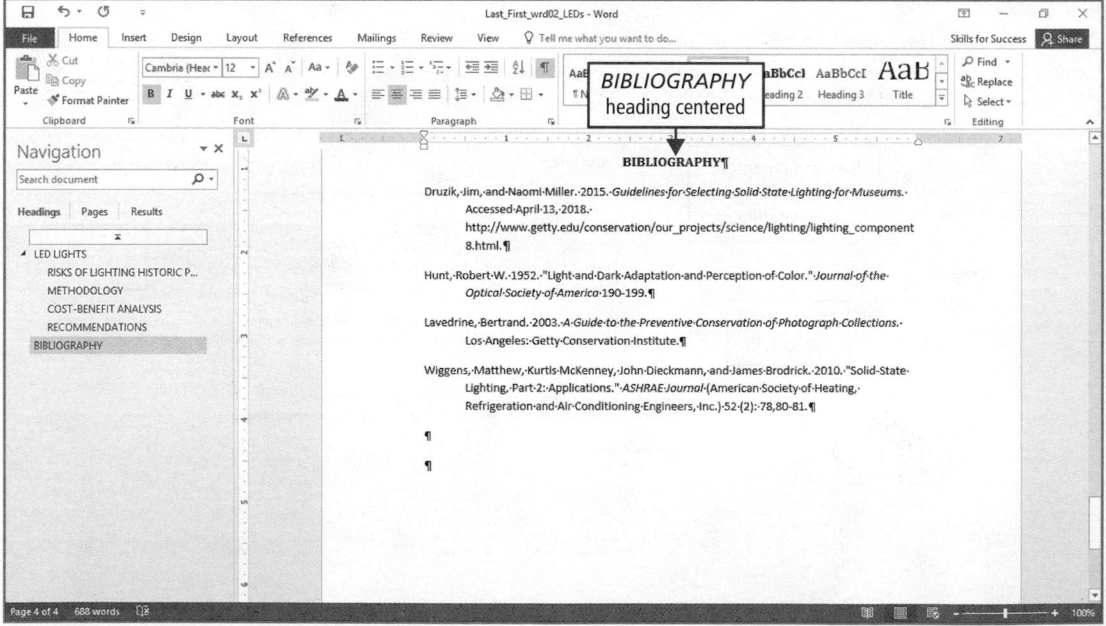

Figure 2 Word 2016, Windows 10, Microsoft Corporation

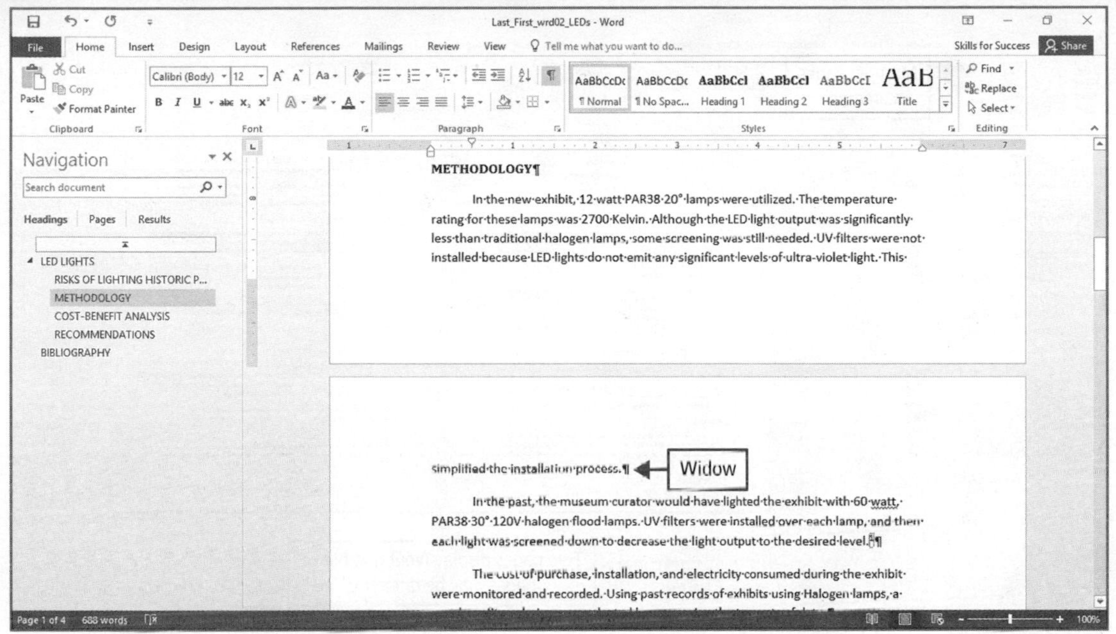

Word 2016, Windows 10, Microsoft Corporation

Figure 3

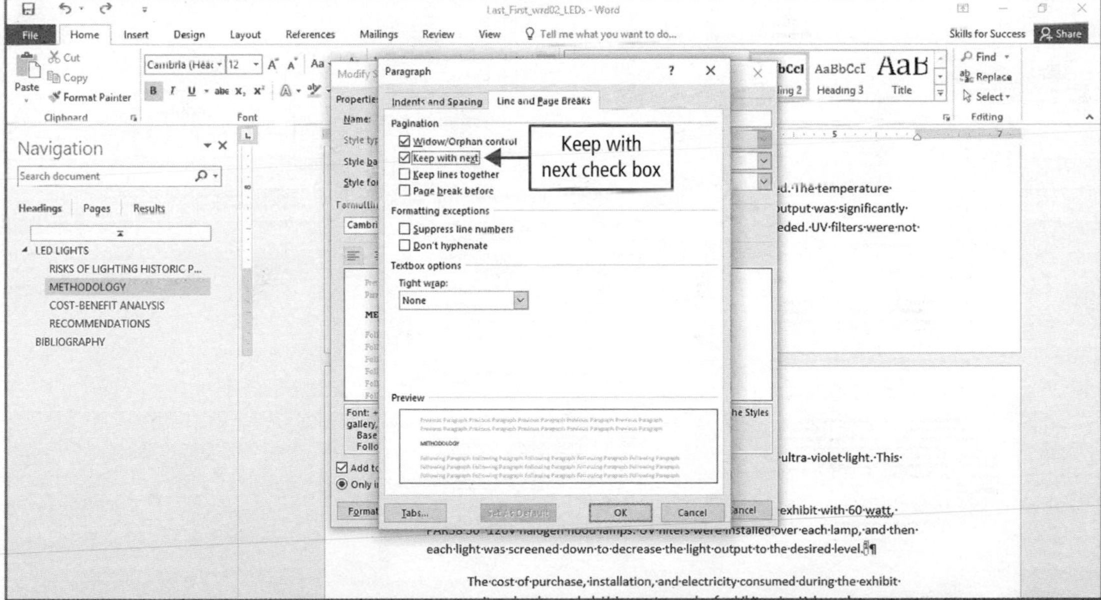

Word 2016, Windows 10, Microsoft Corporation

Figure 4

5. In the **Paragraph** dialog box, click the **Line and Page Breaks tab**, clear the **Widow/Orphan control** check box, and then click **OK**. Compare your screen with **Figure 3**.

   The top of Page 3 displays a ***widow***—the last line of a paragraph displays as the first line of a page. An ***orphan*** is the first line of a paragraph that displays as the last line of a page. Both widows and orphans should be avoided.

6. On the **Quick Access Toolbar**, click the **Undo** button to enable widow and orphan control. Alternately, press Ctrl + Z.

7. Click to place the insertion point in the *METHODOLOGY* header. In the **Styles group**, right-click the **Heading 2** thumbnail, and then from the shortcut menu, click **Modify**.

8. In the lower corner of the **Modify Style** dialog box, click the **Format** button, and then click **Paragraph**.

9. On the **Line and Page Breaks tab** of the **Paragraph** dialog box, select the **Keep with next** check box, and then compare your screen with **Figure 4**.

10. Click **OK** two times to close the dialog boxes and update the Heading 2 style.

    Headings should have the *Keep with next* option selected so that at least two lines of the paragraph that follows them always display on the same page as the heading. Here, the setting has been applied to all the document's side headings—Heading 2.

11. **Save** the file.

- **You have completed Skill 8 of 10**

- ***Margins*** are the spaces between the text and the top, bottom, left, and right edges of the paper.
- Viewing multiple pages on a single screen is useful when you need to evaluate the overall layout of a document.

Obj 1.4.1 C

1. Navigate to the **LED LIGHTS** heading. On the **View tab**, in the **Zoom group**, click **Multiple Pages**. Compare your screen with **Figure 1**.

   The number of pages that display when you view multiple pages depends on the dimensions of your monitor or window. On large monitors, your window may be large enough to display three pages and the text may be large enough to edit and format.

2. In the **Navigation** pane, click the **BIBLIOGRAPHY** heading. **Close** ☒ the Navigation pane, and then compare your screen with **Figure 2**.

   Depending on the audience, you may want to reduce the length of a report to as few pages as possible. Here, the end of the report body uses a small portion of Page 3. Reducing the size of the side margins may fit the report on three pages instead of four.

■ **Continue to the next page to complete the skill**

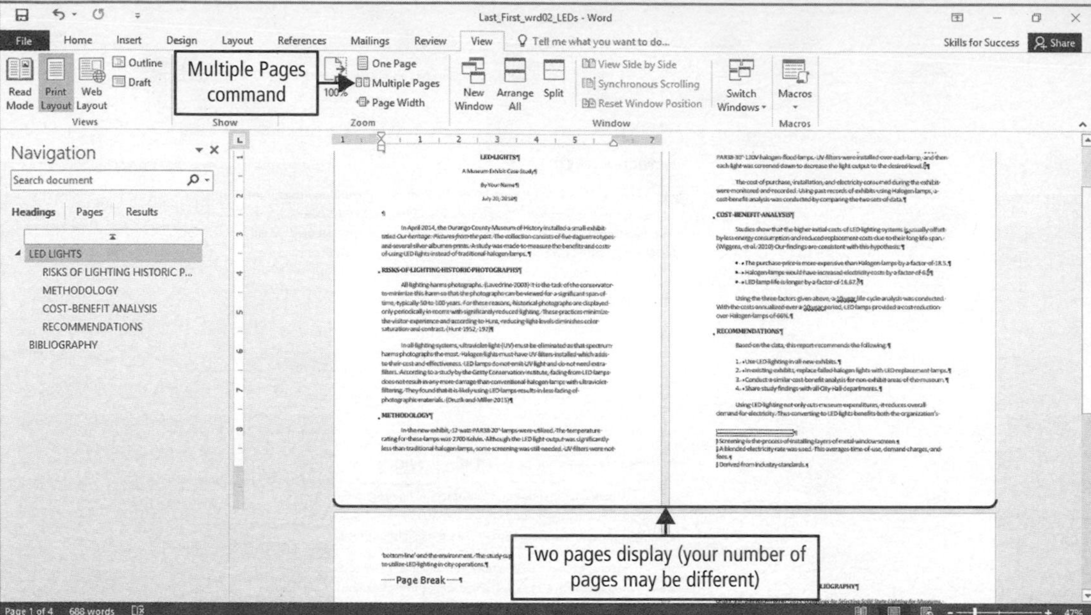

Figure 1

Word 2016, Windows 10, Microsoft Corporation

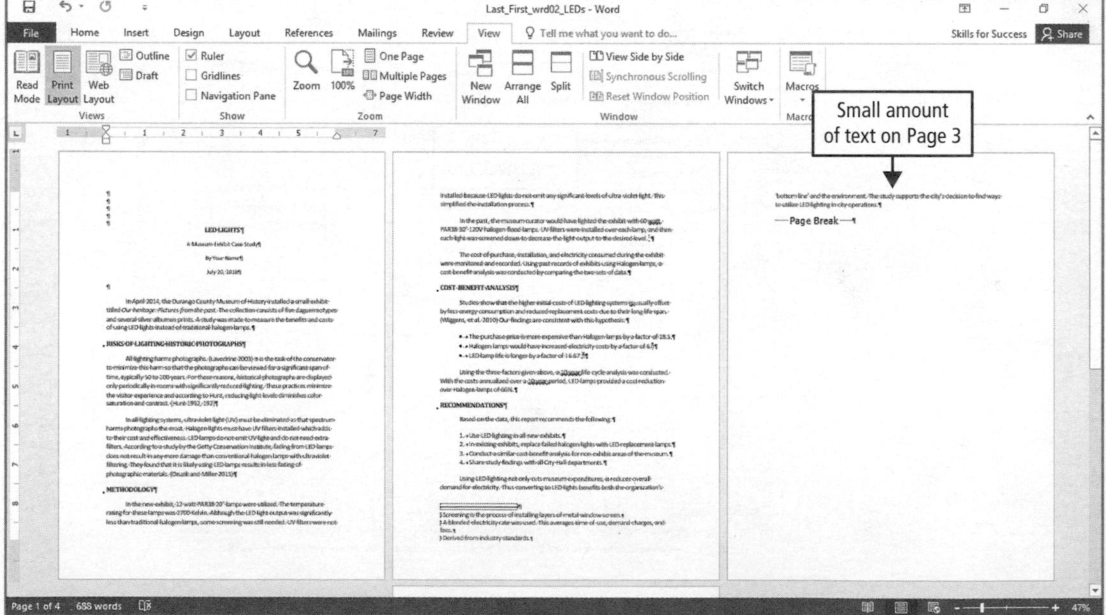

Figure 2

Word 2016, Windows 10, Microsoft Corporation

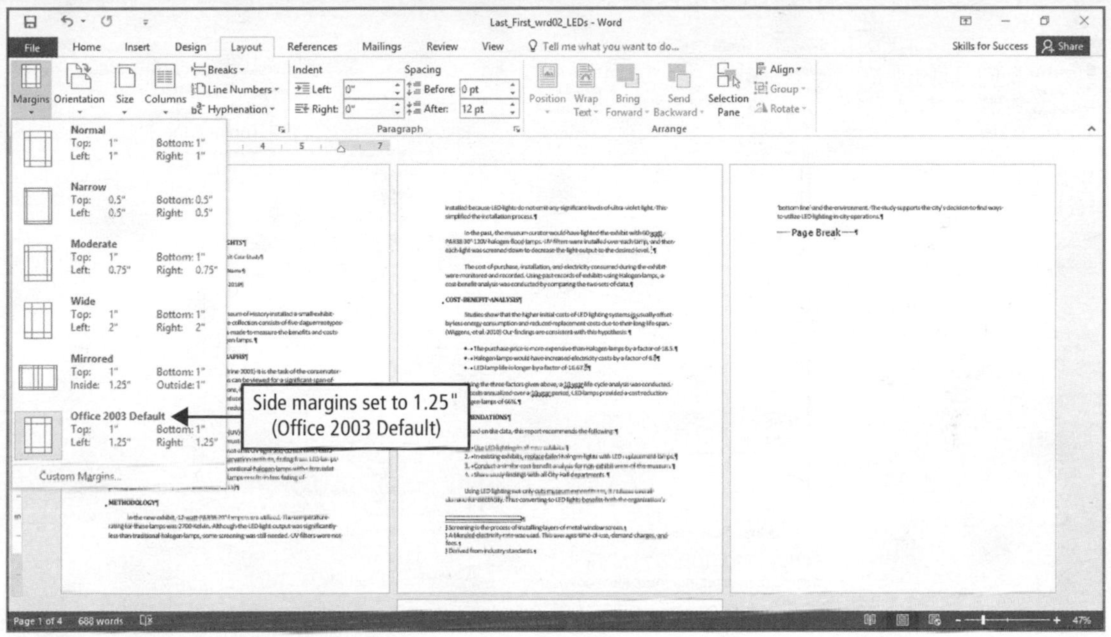

Word 2016, Windows 10, Microsoft Corporation

Figure 3

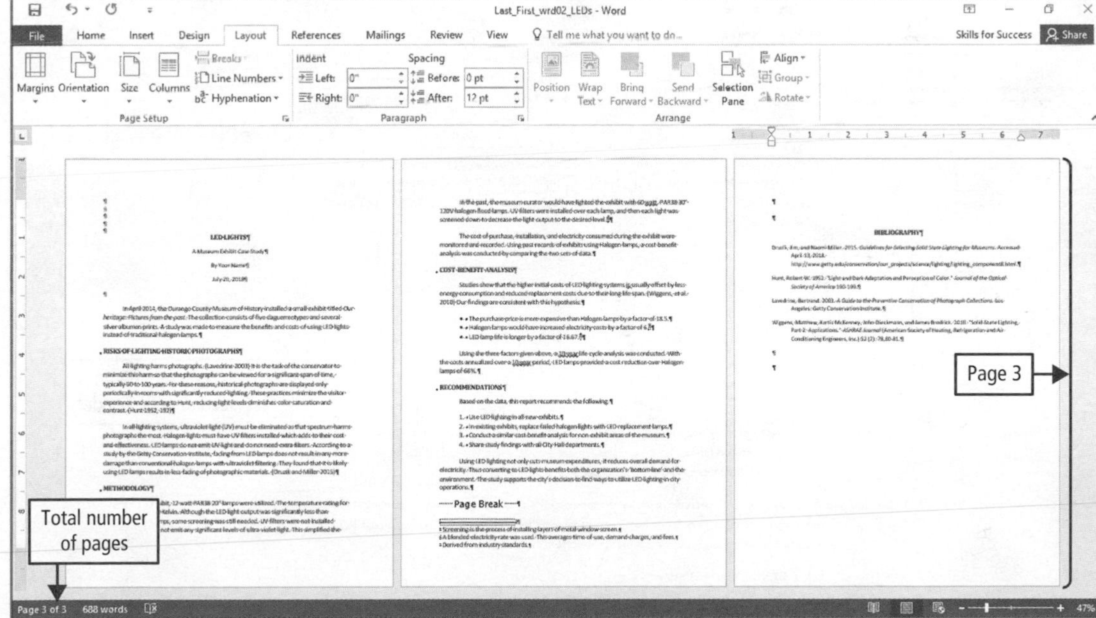

Word 2016, Windows 10, Microsoft Corporation

Figure 4

3. On the **Layout tab**, in the **Page Setup group**, click **Margins**, and then compare your screen with **Figure 3**.

   The Margins gallery displays thumbnails and descriptions of common margin settings. Here, the report is set to the default margin sizes used in an older version of Word—Office 2003 Default.

   In a report, the top and bottom margins are typically 1.0 inch each, and the side margins are 1.25 inches each. In a short informal report, you can change the side margins to 1 inch each if needed.

4. In the **Margins** gallery, click the **Normal** thumbnail to set the margins to 1 inch on all four sides. Compare your screen with **Figure 4**.

   With the smaller margins, the report title and body now fit on two pages, and the Bibliography is on the third page. Before setting the margins on a report, you should check the assigned style guidelines for the dimensions that you should use.

5. Scroll up to view Page 1 and Page 2, and then on the **View tab**, in the **Zoom group**, click **100%** to return to the default view.

   If you are working on a large monitor, you may still see two pages displayed with the 100% zoom level. If so, you can snap the window to either half of the screen to see only one page at a time.

6. **Save** the file.

■ **You have completed Skill 9 of 10**

SKILL 2.10

- Headers and footers can include text you type, fields, and graphics.
- On the first page of a document, you can set the headers and footers so that they do not display.

Obj 1.3.5 C

1. Press Ctrl + Home to move the insertion point to the beginning of the document. On the **Insert tab**, in the **Header & Footer group**, click **Page Number**. In the **Page Number** list, point to **Top of Page**, and then compare your screen with **Figure 1**.
2. In the **Page Number** gallery, use the vertical scroll bar to scroll through the page number options. When you are through, scroll to the top of the list. Under **Simple**, click **Plain Number 3** to insert the page number at the top and right margins.

   When you insert a pre-built page number in this manner, the header and footer areas are activated so that you can continue working with them.
3. Under **Header & Footer Tools**, on the **Design tab**, in the **Options group**, select the **Different First Page** check box, and notice the page number on Page 1 is removed.
4. Scroll to the top of Page 2, and verify that the page number displays, as shown in **Figure 2**.

   In reports where the body starts on the same page as the title, the page number is not included on the first page.

■ **Continue to the next page to complete the skill**

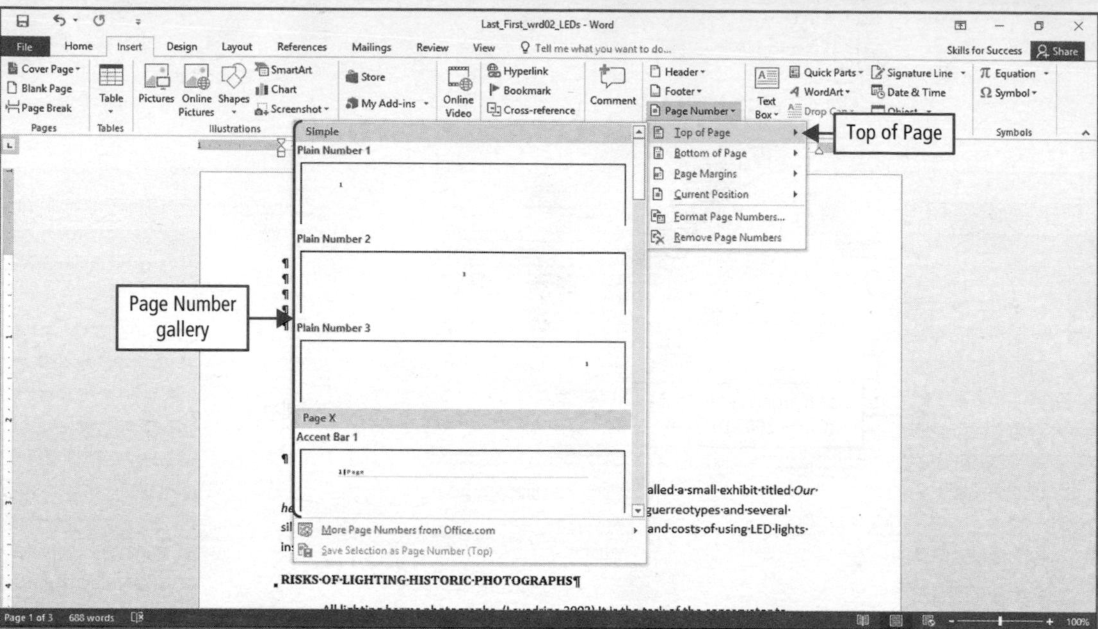

Figure 1 Word 2016, Windows 10, Microsoft Corporation

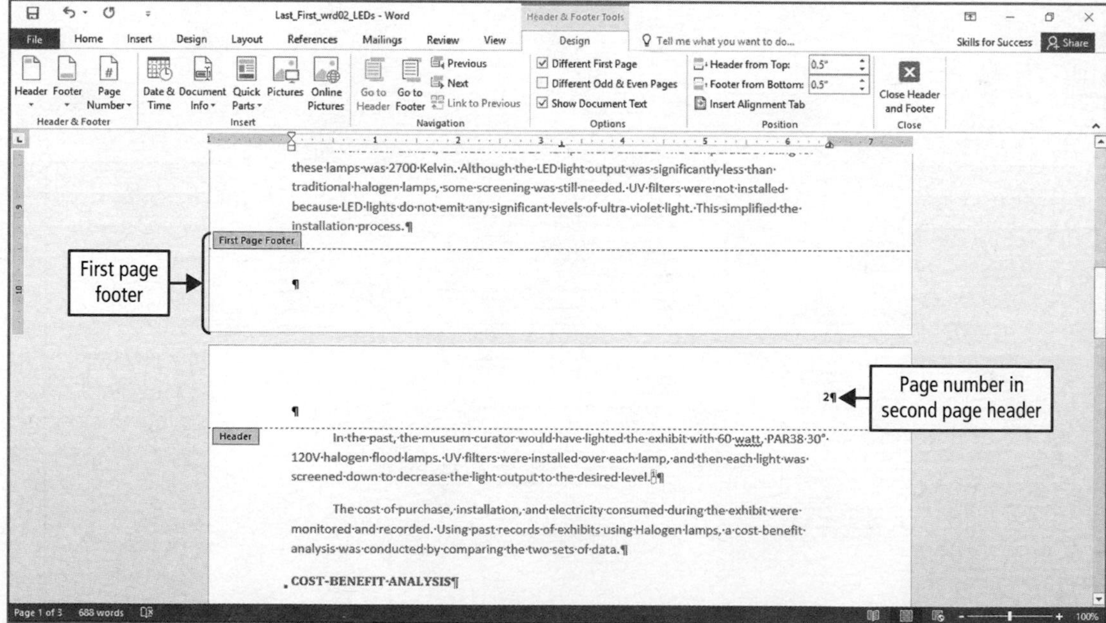

Figure 2 Word 2016, Windows 10, Microsoft Corporation

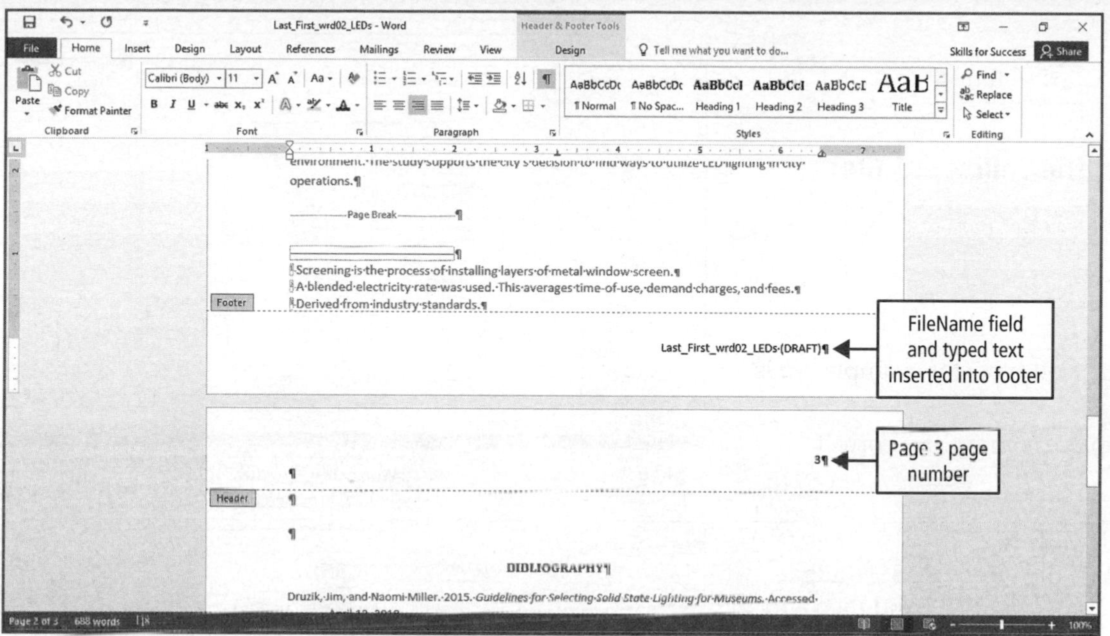

Word 2016, Windows 10, Microsoft Corporation

Figure 3

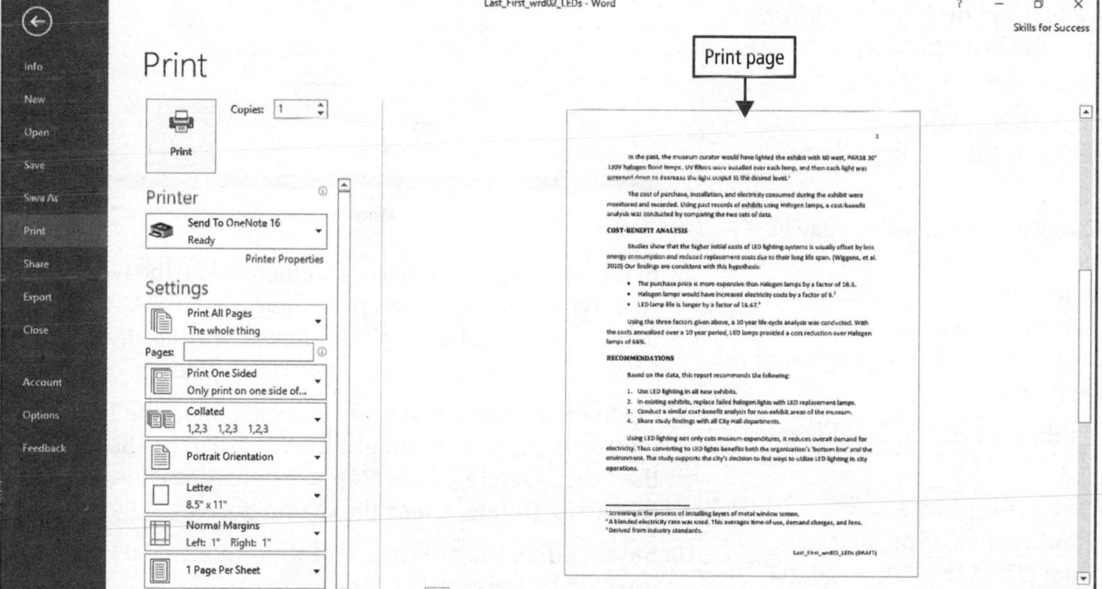

Word 2016, Windows 10, Microsoft Corporation

Figure 4

5. Scroll to the bottom of Page 2, and then click in the footer area. If you accidentally deactivated the header and footer areas, double-click the footer area.
6. In the **Insert group**, click the **Quick Parts** button, and then click **Field**. Under **Field names**, scroll down, click **FileName**, and then click **OK**.

   MOS Obj 1.3.4 C
7. Add a space, and then type (DRAFT) Be sure to include the parentheses.

   In this manner, headers and footers can contain both fields such as page numbers and file names and text that you type.
8. On the **Home tab**, in the **Paragraph group**, click the **Align Right** button, and then compare your screen with **Figure 3**.

   In a business setting, this footer would be removed before the report is published.
9. Double-click in the report body to deactivate the footer area. On the **File tab**, click **Print**, and then compare your screen with **Figure 4**.
10. If you are printing your work, print the report. Otherwise, click the **Back** button .
11. **Save** the file, **Close** Word, and then submit the file as directed by your instructor.

DONE! You have completed Skill 10 of 10 and your document is complete!

More Skills 11

Record AutoCorrect Entries

To complete this project, you will need the following file:

- wrd02_MS11Budget

You will save your file as:

- Last_First_wrd02_MS11Budget

- ***AutoCorrect*** corrects common spelling errors as you type; for example, *teh* is automatically corrected to *the*.
- AutoCorrect stores misspelled words in the Replace column and correct spellings in the With column.

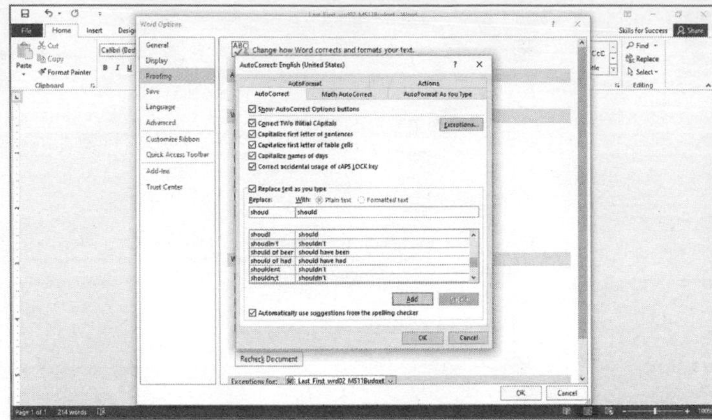

Figure 1 Word 2016, Windows 10, Microsoft Corporation

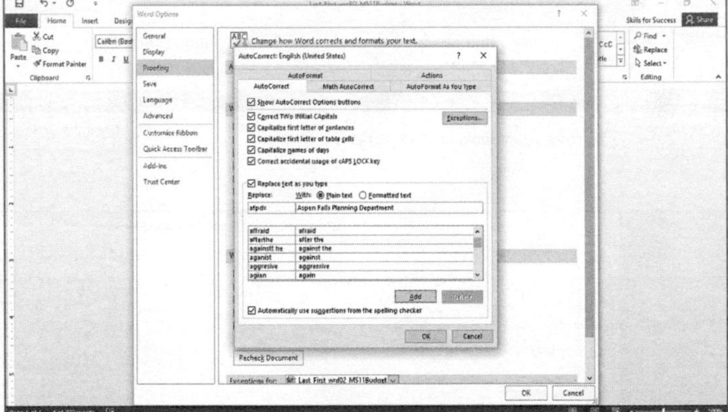

Figure 2 Word 2016, Windows 10, Microsoft Corporation

1. Start **Word 2016**, and then open the student data file **wrd02_MS11Budget**. Save the file in your folder as Last_First_wrd02_MS11Budget and then add the **FileName** field to the footer.
2. On the **File tab**, click **Options**. In the **Word Options** dialog box, click **Proofing**, and then click the **AutoCorrect Options** button.

Obj 2.1.3 C

3. On the **AutoCorrect tab**, verify that the **Replace text as you type** check box is selected. In the **Replace** box, type shoud and in the **With** box, type should Compare your screen with **Figure 1**.
4. Near the bottom of the **AutoCorrect** dialog box, click the **Add** button, and then click **OK**. If you see the Replace button, click it instead. Click **OK** to close the **Word Options** dialog box.

   If someone else has already added a correction, a Replace button will display in place of the Add button.
5. In the paragraph that begins *I just received*, click to position the insertion point between *Council* and the period. Type a comma, add a space, then type the following text exactly as written, and watch your screen when you misspell *shoud*: and I thought you shoud see the plans
6. In the paragraph that begins *In accordance*, select the text *Aspen Falls Planning Department*.
7. Open the **AutoCorrect** dialog box again. Notice that the phrase automatically displays in the *With* box. In the **Replace** box, type afpdx as shown in **Figure 2**. Click the **Add** button, and then click **OK**. If you see the Replace button, click it instead. Click **OK** to close the dialog box.

   When you create a shortcut, it is a good idea to use an acronym of the phrase, and then add another letter to create a word that will never be typed.
8. In the last paragraph, select and then delete the words *our own*. Type afpdx and then press Spacebar to use AutoCorrect to insert the text *Aspen Falls Planning Department*. If you have two spaces after the phrase, delete one.
9. Open the **AutoCorrect** dialog box again. In the **Replace** box, type afpdx to highlight the phrase in the list, and then click **Delete**. In the **Replace** box, type shoud and then click **Delete**. **Close** the dialog boxes.
10. **Save** the file, **Close** Word, and then submit the file as directed by your instructor.

- **You have completed More Skills 11**

More Skills 12

Use AutoFormat to Create Numbered Lists

To complete this project, you will need the following file:

- wrd02_MS12Permits

You will save your file as:

- Last_First_wrd02_MS12Permits

- You can create a numbered list using existing text or create the list as you type.
- The Word AutoCorrect option to create lists automatically can be turned on or off as desired.

---

1. Start **Word 2016**, and then open the student data file **wrd02_MS12Permits.** Save the file in your chapter folder as Last_First_wrd02_MS12Permits and then add the **FileName** field to the footer.
2. On the **File tab**, click **Options**. On the left side of the **Word Options** dialog box, click **Proofing**. Under **AutoCorrect options**, click the **AutoCorrect Options** button.
3. In the **AutoCorrect** dialog box, click the **AutoFormat As You Type tab**. Under **Apply as you type**, verify that the **Automatic numbered lists** check box is selected, as shown in **Figure 1**.

   The other check boxes that are selected on your computer may vary and do not need to be changed.
4. Click **OK** two times to close the dialog boxes, and then position the insertion point in the blank line between the memo's two body paragraphs.
5. Type 1. (include the period), and then press SpaceBar. Notice that the number is indented, a tab is added after the number, and the AutoCorrect Options button displays.
6. Click the **AutoCorrect Options** button to view the menu.

   In the AutoCorrect Options menu, you can turn off automatic numbering should you need that option.
7. Click the **AutoCorrect Options** button again to hide the menu.
8. Type the following list. Press Enter after each item except the last one.
   1. Notify the Planning Department at least 60 days prior to the event.
   2. Fill out and submit a permit request at least 30 days prior to the event.
   3. Meet with a Planning Department representative at least 14 days prior to the event.

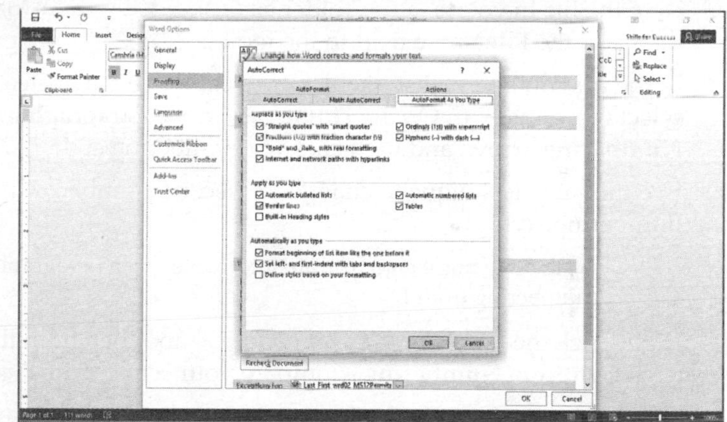

Word 2016, Windows 10, Microsoft Corporation **Figure 1**

   If you are typing a list and want the list to end, you can press Enter two times or click the Numbering button to turn off automatic numbering.

9. **Save** the file.
10. If you changed the Word Options settings in Step 3, repeat Steps 2–4 to clear the *Automatic numbered lists* check box. **Close** Word, and then submit the file as directed by your instructor.

- **You have completed More Skills 12**

More Skills 13

Format and Customize Lists

To complete this project, you will need the following file:

- wrd02_MS13Garden

You will save your file as:

- Last_First_wrd02_MS13Garden

▸ Numbered lists separated by other text can be formatted to display continuous numbering.

---

1. Start **Word 2016**, and then open the student data file **wrd02_MS13Garden**. Save the file in your chapter folder as Last_First_wrd02_MS13Garden and then add the **FileName** field to the footer.
2. In the first numbered list—which uses capital letters instead of numbers—select list items *A–C*. On the **Home tab**, in the **Paragraph group**, click the **Numbering arrow**, and then click the numbering style *1) 2) 3)*.
3. Use the same technique to change the second numbered list to the *1) 2) 3)* numbering style.

   Because the two numbered lists are interrupted by a paragraph, the second list starts numbering from 1.

Obj 3.3.5 C

4. Right-click the first item in the second list, and then from the shortcut menu, click **Continue Numbering**. Compare your screen with **Figure 1**.
5. Select the three items in the first numbered list. In the **Paragraph group**, click the **Increase Indent** button one time.

   When you change the numbering to *Continuous*, formatting edits made to one list affect the other lists. Here, the indents for both numbered lists increased.

6. With the first three items still selected, in the **Paragraph group**, click the **Decrease Indent** button one time to move both lists to the left margin.

   When you decrease the indent of a list, it moves to the left 0.5 inches. When you increase the indent, the list moves to the right 0.25 inches.

7. With the first three items still selected, in the **Paragraph group**, click the **Increase Indent** button one time to move both lists to their original position.
8. In the bulleted list, click at the end of the last item ending *garden beds*, and then press Enter. Type Trellises

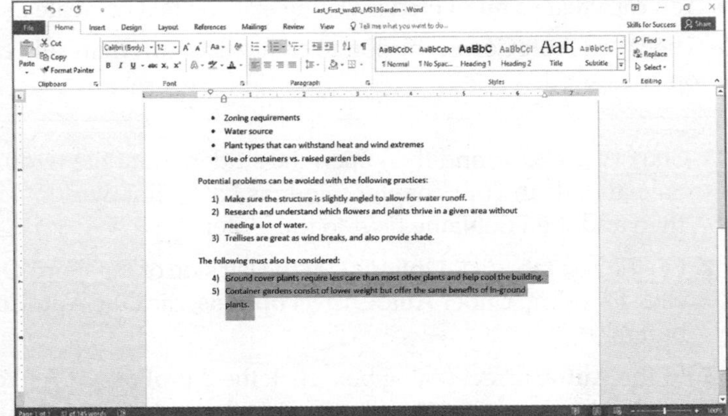

Figure 1 Word 2016, Windows 10, Microsoft Corporation

9. In the same list, click to the right of *Water source*, and then press Enter. Type Captured rainwater and then press Enter. Type Water tap on roof
10. Select the two list items *Captured rainwater* and *Water tap on roof*. In the **Paragraph group**, click the **Increase Indent** button to assign a different level than the rest of the list items.

    When you indent part of a list, the indent moves 0.5 inches and the symbol or number assigned to that level displays. Here, the circle symbol is assigned to second-level items.

11. **Save** the file, **Close** Word, and then submit the file as directed by your instructor.

- **You have completed More Skills 13**

More Skills 14

Create Standard Outlines

To complete this project, you will need the following file:

- wrd02_MS14Outline

You will save your file as:

- Last_First_wrd02_MS14Outline

▶ ***Outlines*** are used to plan and organize longer documents such as formal reports.

1. Start **Word 2016**, and then open the student data file **wrd02_MS14Outline**. Save the file in your chapter folder as Last_First_wrd02_MS14Outline and then add the **FileName** field to the footer.
2. In the third paragraph, replace the words *Your Name* with your First and Last name.
3. On the **File tab**, click **Options**. In the **Word Options** dialog box, click **Proofing**, and then click the **AutoCorrect Options** button.
4. In the **AutoCorrect** dialog box, click the **AutoFormat As You Type tab**, and then under **Apply as you type**, clear the **Automatic numbered lists** check box.
5. Under **Automatically as you type**, clear the **Set left- and first-indent with tabs and backspaces** check box. Compare your screen with **Figure 1**, and then click **OK** two times to close the dialog boxes.

   With these two AutoComplete features disabled, you can indent and number the outline following the standard outline format. You will enable these two settings at the end of the skill.
6. Click to the right of *Installation Procedures*.
7. Press Enter three times. Type IV. (include the period) press Tab, and then type COST BENEFIT ANALYSIS
8. Press Enter two times, and then press Tab. Type A. press Tab, and then type Initial Costs
9. Press Enter, and then press Tab. Type B. press Tab, and then type Long-Term Costs
10. Press Enter, and then press Tab two times. Type 1. press Tab, and then type Maintenance
11. Press Enter, and then press Tab two times. Type 2. press Tab, and then type Replacement

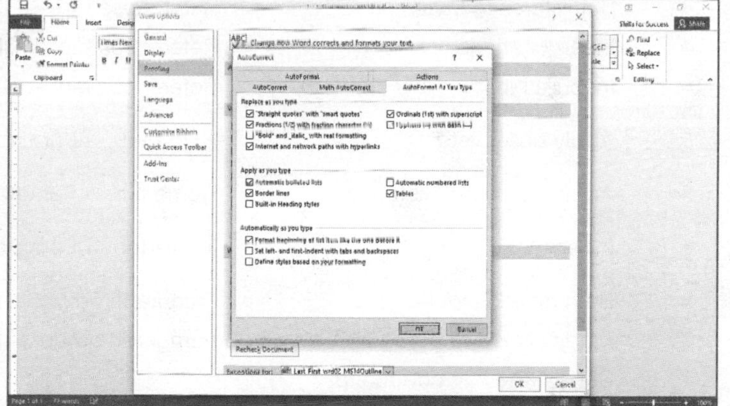

Word 2016, Windows 10, Microsoft Corporation **Figure 1**

12. Press Enter, and then press Tab. Type C. press Tab, and then type Overall Costs and Benefits
13. Press Enter three times. Type V. press Tab, and then type RECOMMENDATIONS Verify your outline fits on one page and your list levels align with the items above.
14. Reopen the **AutoCorrect** dialog box, click the **AutoFormat As You Type tab**, and then if they were selected previous to this skill, select the **Automatic numbered lists** and **Set left- and first-indent with tabs and backspaces** check boxes. Click **OK** to close the dialog boxes.
15. **Save** the file, **Close** Word, and then submit the file as directed by your instructor.

■ **You have completed More Skills 14**

Review

The following table summarizes the **SKILLS AND PROCEDURES** covered in this chapter.

Skills Number	Task	Step	Icon	Keyboard Shortcut
1	Find text	In the Navigation pane, use the search box and click Results		Ctrl + F
1	Find and replace text	In the Navigation pane, click the Search for more things arrow		Ctrl + H
1	Navigate by headings	In the Navigation pane, click Headings		
2	Insert footnotes	References tab → Footnotes group → Insert Footnote		Alt + Ctrl + F
3	Add or edit sources	References tab → Citations & Bibliography group → Manage Sources		
3	Set reference styles	References tab → Citations & Bibliography group → Style		
4	Insert citations	References tab → Citations & Bibliography group → Insert Citation		
4	Insert a bibliography	References tab → Citations & Bibliography group → Bibliography		
5	Apply bullet lists	Home tab → Paragraph group → Bullets arrow		
5	Apply numbered lists	Home tab → Paragraph group → Numbering arrow		
5	Indent lists	Home tab → Paragraph group → Increase Indent		
6	Set first line indents	Paragraph group → Paragraph Dialog Box Launcher → Special → First Line		
7	Modify line and paragraph spacing	Paragraph group → Paragraph Dialog Box Launcher		
7	Repeat the last command			F4
8	Enable widow and orphan control	Paragraph group → Paragraph Dialog Box Launcher → Line and Page Breaks tab		
8	Set keep with next control	Paragraph group → Paragraph Dialog Box Launcher → Line and Page Breaks tab		
8	Modify styles	Right-click style thumbnail in Styles group, and then click Modify. Click the Format button and open desired dialog box.		
8	Update styles	Click or select text with desired style formatting. Right-click the style's thumbnail in Styles group, and then click Update command.		
9	Change margins	Layout tab → Margins		
10	Add page numbers	Insert tab → Header & Footer group → Page Number		
10	Apply different first page headers and footers	Header & Footer Tools → Design tab → Different first page		
MS11	Insert AutoCorrect text	File tab → Options → Proofing → AutoCorrect Options		
MS12	Apply numbered lists using AutoFormat	File tab → Options → Proofing → AutoCorrect Options → AutoFormat As You Type tab → Automatic numbered lists check box selected		
MS13	Insert continuous numbering	Right-click first list item → Continue Numbering		
MS14	Apply standard outline	File tab → Options → Proofing → AutoCorrect Options → AutoFormat As You Type tab → Automatic numbered lists check box not selected		

Project Summary Chart

Project	Project Type	Project Location
Skills Review	Review	In Book & MIL MyITLab® Grader
Skills Assessment 1	Review	In Book & MIL MyITLab® Grader
Skills Assessment 2	Review	Book
My Skills	Problem Solving	Book
Visual Skills Check	Problem Solving	Book
Skillls Challenge 1	Critical Thinking	Book
Skills Challenge 2	Critical Thinking	Book
More Skills Assessment	Review	In Book & MIL MyITLab® Grader
Collaborating with Google	Critical Thinking	Book

MOS Objectives Covered

1.2.1 C Search for text	3.3.1 C Create a numbered or bulleted list
1.3.4 C Insert headers and footers	3.3.4 C Increase or decrease list levels
1.3.5 C Insert page numbers	3.3.5 C Restart or continue list numbering
1.4.1 C Change document views	4.1.1 C Insert footnotes and endnotes
2.1.1 C Find and replace text	4.1.3 C Create bibliography citations sources
2.1.3 C Replace text by using AutoCorrect	4.1.5 C Insert citations for bibliographies
2.2.3 C Set line and paragraph spacing and indentation	

Key Terms

1. What are some actions that you should take when attending a job fair?
2. What actions should be avoided when attending a job fair?

Online Help Skills

1. With Word 2016 open, on the **File tab**, in the upper right corner of the screen, click the **Microsoft Word Help** [?] button, or press [F1].
2. In the **Word Help** window **Search** box, type word count and then press [Enter].
3. In the search result list, click **Show the word count**. Maximize the **Word Help** window, and then compare your screen with **Figure 1**.

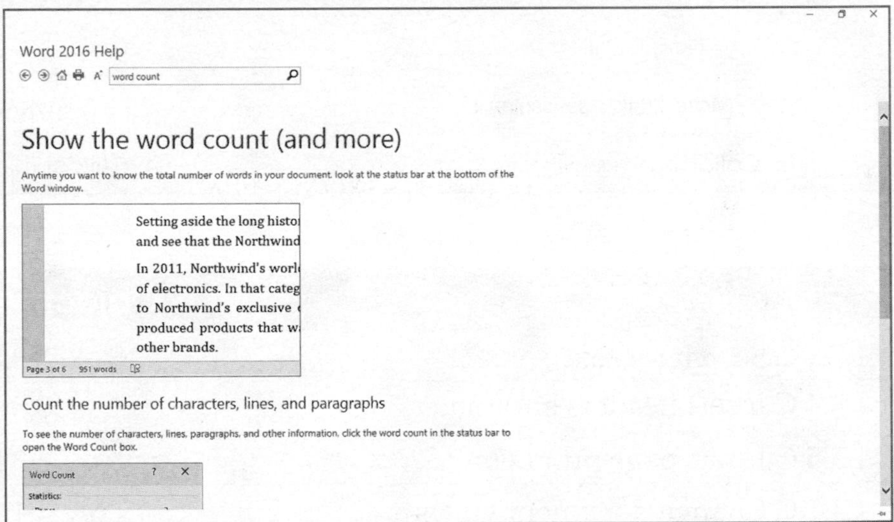

Figure 1 Word 2016, Windows 10, Microsoft Corporation

4. Read the article to see if you can find the answer to the following question: How can you find out how many words are in the document without counting the words in the footnotes?

Matching 

Match each term in the second column with its correct definition in the first column by writing the letter of the term on the blank line in front of the correct definition.

___ **1.** The pane used to find document text.

___ **2.** A comment or notation added to the end of a section or document.

___ **3.** The reference used to find information or data when writing a report.

___ **4.** The citation type used for the Chicago style.

___ **5.** A list of sources displayed on a separate page at the end of a report.

___ **6.** The type of list used for items that are in chronological or sequential order.

___ **7.** The equivalent of a blank line of text displayed between each line of text in a paragraph.

___ **8.** The vertical distance above and below each paragraph in a document.

___ **9.** The position of the first line of a paragraph relative to the text in the rest of the paragraph.

___ **10.** The space between the text and the top, bottom, left, and right edges of the paper when you print the document.

A Author-date
B Bibliography
C Double-spacing
D Endnote
E First line indent
F Margin
G Navigation
H Numbered
I Paragraph spacing
J Source

Multiple Choice

MyITLab®

Choose the correct answer.

1. To place a note on the same page as the comment or notation, which of the following should be used?
   A. Footnote
   B. Endnote
   C. Citation
2. This is placed in body paragraphs and points to an entry in the bibliography.
   A. Footnote
   B. Citation
   C. Endnote
3. The number of inches from the top edge of the paper to the beginning of the bibliography.
   A. 0.5 inches
   B. 1 inch
   C. 2 inches
4. In a Chicago style bibliography, this type of indent is used for each reference.
   A. Hanging indent
   B. First line indent
   C. Left alignment
5. Items that can be listed in any order are best presented using which of the following?
   A. Bulleted list
   B. Numbered list
   C. Outline list
6. The default line spacing in a long report.
   A. Custom
   B. Single
   C. Double
7. The vertical distance between lines in a paragraph.
   A. Spacing after
   B. Line spacing
   C. Text wrapping
8. The last line of a paragraph that displays as the first line of a page.
   A. Single
   B. Stray
   C. Widow
9. The pre-built setting that places all four margins at 1.0 inches.
   A. Narrow
   B. Normal
   C. Office 2003 Default
10. This type of alignment positions the text so that it is aligned with the right margin.
    A. Right
    B. Center
    C. Left

Topics for Discussion

1. You can build and save a list of master sources you have used in research papers and reports and display them using Manage Sources. What are the advantages of storing sources over time?
2. Paragraph text can be left aligned, centered, right aligned, or justified. Left alignment is most commonly used. In what situations would you use centered text? Justified text? Can you think of any situations where you might want to use right alignment?

Skills Review

To complete this project, you will need the following file:

- wrd02_SRWeb

You will save your file as:

- Last_First_wrd02_SRWeb

1. Start **Word 2016**, and then open the student data file **wrd02_SRWeb**. Save the file in your chapter folder as Last_First_wrd02_SRWeb If necessary, display the formatting marks and the Navigation pane.
2. Click to the right of *By*, add a space, and then type your name.
3. Click in the first body paragraph beginning *The city of Aspen Falls*. Click the **Paragraph Dialog Box Launcher**, and then in the **Paragraph** dialog box, under **Special**, select **First line**. Under **Spacing**, change the **After** value to **12 pt**, and then click **OK**. Click in the paragraph beginning *Color blindness varies*, and then press F4 to repeat the formatting.
4. Click in the side heading beginning *DESIGN FOR*. In the **Styles group**, right-click **Heading 2**, and then click **Modify**. In the **Modify Style** dialog box, click the **Format** button, and then click **Paragraph**. In the **Paragraph** dialog box, click the **Line and Page Breaks tab**, and then select the **Keep with next** check box. Click **OK** two times. Compare your screen with **Figure 1**.
5. On the **References tab**, in the **Citations & Bibliography group**, verify that **Chicago** is selected, and then click **Manage Sources**.
6. Select the source for **Bennett, Jean**, and then click the **Edit** button. Change the **Type of Source** to **Journal Article**. Add the **Journal Name** The New England Journal of Medicine and the **Pages** 2483-2484
7. Click **OK**, and then **Close** Source Manager. In the *DESIGN FOR COLOR BLINDNESS* section, click to the right of the sentence ending *degree of color blindness*. In the **Citations & Bibliography group**, click **Insert Citation**, and then click the **Bennett, Jean** source.
8. Right-click the citation just inserted, and then click **Edit Citation**. In the **Edit Citation** dialog box, type 2483 and then click **OK**. Deselect the citation, and then compare your screen with **Figure 2**.

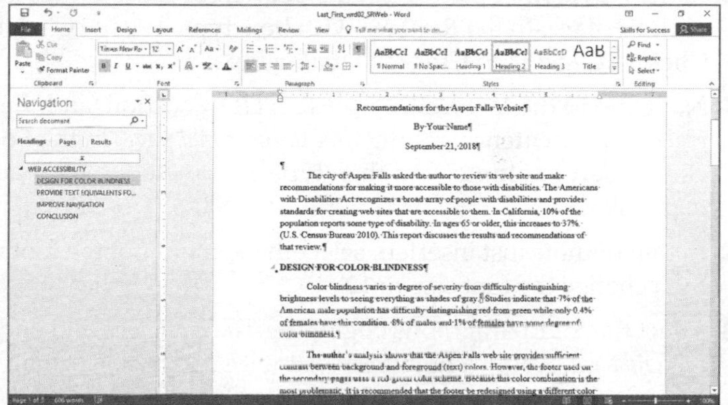

Figure 1 Word 2016, Windows 10, Microsoft Corporation

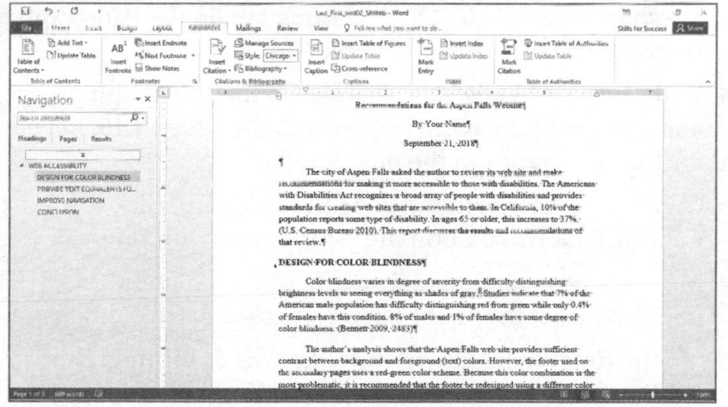

Figure 2 Word 2016, Windows 10, Microsoft Corporation

■ **Continue to the next page to complete this Skills Review**

9. In the **Navigation** pane search box, type web site and then click **Results**.
10. In the **Navigation** pane, click the **Search for more things arrow**, and then click **Replace**. In the **Replace with** box, type website Click **Replace All**. Click **OK**, and then **Close** the dialog box.
11. Navigate to the *IMPROVE NAVIGATION* section, and then click to the right of the sentence ending *link to the home page*. In the **Footnotes group**, click **Insert Footnote**, and then type This includes the logo on the home page itself.
12. In the footnote just inserted, select the text but not the footnote number, and then change the font size to **12**.
13. Select the four paragraphs beginning *The main logo* and ending with *using the keyboard*. Apply a numbered list with the **1. 2. 3.** format. In the **Paragraph group**, click the **Increase Indent** button one time.
14. In the *CONCLUSION* section, select the four paragraphs beginning *Anyone with a vision* and ending with *a portable device*. Apply a bulleted list with the solid round circle. On the **Home tab**, in the **Paragraph group**, click the **Increase Indent** button one time.
15. With the bulleted list still selected, in the **Paragraph group**, click the **Line and Paragraph Spacing** button, and then click **1.15**. Repeat this formatting for the paragraphs in the numbered list.
16. On the **Layout tab**, in the **Page Setup group**, click the **Margins** button, and then click **Normal**. Compare your screen with **Figure 3**.
17. Move to the end of the document, and then press Ctrl + Enter to insert a page break. At the top of Page 3, press Enter two times.
18. On the **References tab**, in the **Citations & Bibliography group**, click **Bibliography**, and then click the **Bibliography** thumbnail. Change the *Bibliography* heading to BIBLIOGRAPHY
19. On the **Insert tab**, in the **Header & Footer group**, click **Page Number**, point to **Top of Page**, and then click **Plain Number 3**. In the **Options group**, select the **Different First Page** check box.
20. Navigate to the Page 2 footer, and then click in the footer. Insert the **FileName** field, add a space, and then type (DRAFT) On the **Home tab**, in the **Paragraph group**, click the **Align Right** button, and then double-click in the document.
21. On the **View tab**, in the **Zoom group**, click **Multiple Pages**, and then compare your screen with **Figure 4**.

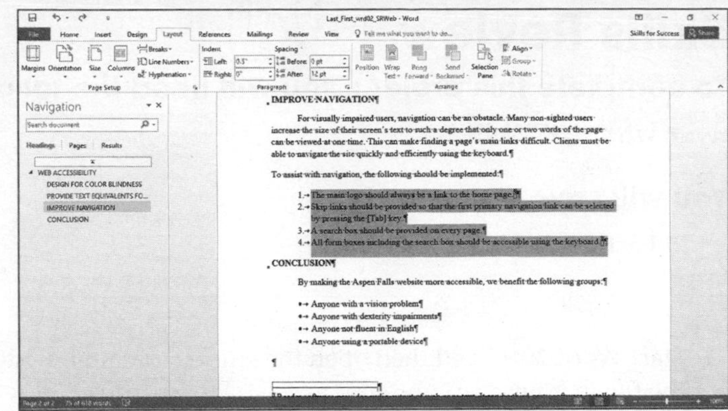

Word 2016, Windows 10, Microsoft Corporation **Figure 3**

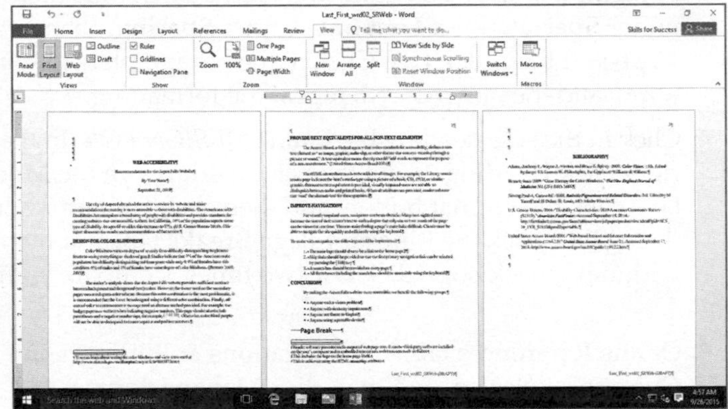

Word 2016, Windows 10, Microsoft Corporation **Figure 4**

22. In the **Zoom group** click **100%**, and then **Close** the Navigation pane.
23. **Save** the file, **Close** Word, and then submit the file as directed by your instructor.

DONE! You have completed this Skills Review

Skills Assessment 1

MyITLab®
Grader

To complete this project, you will need the following file:

- wrd02_SA1Tourism

You will save your file as:

- Last_First_wrd02_SA1Tourism

1. Start **Word 2016**, and then open the student data file **wrd02_SA1Tourism**. Save the file in your chapter folder as Last_First_wrd02_SA1Tourism
2. Click to the right of *By*, add a space, and then type your name.
3. Replace all occurrences of the phrase *City of Aspen Falls* with Aspen Falls
4. In the first body paragraph beginning *The Aspen Falls Tourism*, set a **0.5 inch** first line indent and the spacing after to **12 pt**. Repeat the same formatting to the paragraph beginning *The number of people visiting*.
5. Modify the **Heading 2** style so that **Keep with next** is enabled.
6. In the *DEMOGRAPHICS* section, apply a solid circle bullet to the four paragraphs beginning *Stay longer than* and ending with *drive to Aspen Falls*. Increase the list's indent to **0.5 inch** and set the line spacing to **1.15**.
7. Use **Source Manager** to edit the source for **Law, Christopher M.** Change the source type to **Journal Article**, and then add the **Journal Name** Urban Studies and the **Pages** 599-618
8. In the *DEVELOPMENT AREAS* section, after the sentence ending *is a recent practice*, insert a citation using **Law, Christopher M.** as the reference. Edit the citation field to include the pages 599-618
9. Apply a list with the **1. 2. 3.** format to the three paragraphs beginning *Agritourism* and ending with *Sports Tourism*. Increase the indent of the numbered list to **0.5 inch** and set the line spacing to **1.15**.
10. Insert a footnote after the list item *Agritourism* with the text Agritourism caters to those interested in visiting farms, ranches, and wineries. Change the font size of the footnote text to **12**.
11. In the blank paragraph below the *SUMMARY* section, insert a manual page break. Press Enter two times, and then insert the **Bibliography** built-in field. Change the bibliography's heading to BIBLIOGRAPHY

non-resident leisure visitors would have th... area.

DEVELOPMENT AREAS

Treating tourism as a growth indus... in recent years that the classifications of to... field. Currently, specialty tourism is seeing... seeing robust potential.

Given its location and economy, th... three specialty areas:

1. Agritourism[2]
2. Wildlife Tourism
3. Sports Tourism

According to the World Tourism O... of international tourism growth. (World T... leisure visitors from China is not mutually...

SUMMARY

The economic benefits from promo... would have a significant impact on the loc... local organizations enhance the visitor exp... conservation areas attract more visitors wh... improving venues for playing sports and o... resident and non-resident visitors.

[2] Agritourism caters to those interested in visiting farms, ranches, and wineries.

wrd02_COfig02 (DRAFT)

TRAVEL AND TOURISM

Trends for the Aspen Falls Metro Area

By Your Name

September 21, 2018

The Aspen Falls Tourism Department in cooperation with the Aspen Falls Chamber of Commerce surveyed random tourists[1] about their visit to Aspen Falls. Other key indicators were assembled from public records. These include airport arrivals and departures and room tax revenues. From this analysis trends, demographics, and recommendations are provided in this report.

TRENDS

The number of people visiting Aspen Falls grew about 10% last year, and for the first time topped the 1 million mark. Over the past 10 years, spending by convention and event attendees has risen consistently. However, this past year saw a decrease in business tourist spending of 4%. This decline was offset by an increase in spending from leisure visitors. Overall, spending by business and leisure tourists increased by over 9%.

DEMOGRAPHICS

The study shows that 60% of Aspen Falls tourists are from California—resident visitors. Further, non-resident tourists:

- Stay longer than resident visitors.
- Are slightly older than resident visitors.
- Have a higher average household income than resident visitors.
- Fly in instead of drive to Aspen Falls.

Other studies have shown that on average, leisure visitors travel with larger parties and stay longer than business visitors. (Tribe 2011) These demographics suggest that marketing to

[1] A tourist is any person staying for one or more nights in the Aspen Falls metro area outside of their regular residence. A tourist can be classified as either a business visitor or a leisure visitor.

Figure 1

12. In the header, insert the **Plain Number 3** page number so that it displays on all pages except for Page 1.
13. In the Page 2 footer, insert the **FileName** field, add a space, and then type (DRAFT) Align the footer paragraph with the right margin, and then close the footer.
14. Change the page margins to **Normal** (1 inch on all sides).
15. Compare your screen with **Figure 1**. **Save** the file, **Close** Word, and then submit the file as directed by your instructor.

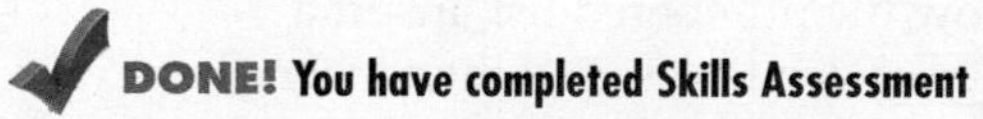
DONE! You have completed Skills Assessment 1

Skills Assessment 2

To complete this project, you will need the following file:

- **wrd02_SA2Wildlife**

You will save your file as:

- **Last_First_wrd02_SA2Wildlife**

---

1. Start **Word 2016**, and then open the student data file **wrd02_SA2Wildlife**. Save the file in your chapter folder as Last_First_wrd02_SA2Wildlife
2. Click to the right of *By*, add a space, and then type your name.
3. Replace all occurrences of the word *fisherman* with angler and then replace all occurrences of the word *fishermen* with anglers
4. In the first body paragraph beginning *This report summarizes*, set a **0.5 inch** first line indent and the spacing after to **12 pt**. Repeat the same formatting to the paragraph beginning *The 2017 survey was provided.*
5. Modify the **Heading 2** style so that **Widow/Orphan control** and **Keep with next** are enabled.
6. Use **Source Manager** to edit the source for **U.S. Fish & Wildlife Service**. Change the source type to **Document From Web site**, and then add the **URL** http://www.census.gov/prod/www/abs/fishing.html
7. In the *FINDINGS* section, after the sentence ending *with the state trend*, insert a citation using **U.S. Fish & Wildlife Service** as the reference.
8. In the same section, apply a solid circle bullet to the two paragraphs beginning *Each angler spent* and ending with *equipment and trip expenses*. Increase the list's indent to **0.5 inch** and set the line spacing to **1.15**.
9. At the end of the second bulleted list item, insert a footnote with the text Equipment includes binoculars, clothing, tents, and backpacking equipment. Change the footnote's text to **12** points.
10. In the *RECOMMENDATIONS* section, apply a list with the **1. 2. 3.** format to the six paragraphs beginning *Maintain existing natural areas* and ending with *wildlife recreation areas*. Increase the indent of the numbered list to **0.5 inch** and set the line spacing to **1.15**.
11. In the blank paragraph below the numbered list, insert a manual page break. Press Enter two times, and then insert the **Bibliography** built-in field. Change the bibliography's heading to BIBLIOGRAPHY
12. In the header, insert the **Plain Number 3** page number so that it displays on all pages except for Page 1.
13. In the Page 2 footer, insert the **FileName** field, add a space, and then type (DO NOT RELEASE YET) Align the footer paragraph with the right margin, and then close the footer.
14. Change the page margins to **Normal**.
15. Compare your screen with **Figure 1**. **Save** the file, **Close** Word, and then submit the file as directed by your instructor.

ASPEN FALLS WILDLIFE RECREATION

An Analysis of the 2017 Visitor and Citizen Surveys

By Your Name

October 5, 2018

This report summarizes the findings of the annual survey of Durango County residents about their wildlife recreation. In the Aspen Falls area, wildlife recreation opportunities are limited to fishing and wildlife observation. The two activities are not mutually exclusive. Wildlife observation includes watching, photographing, or painting wildlife. Based on the annual survey, recommendations have been provided to assist Aspen Falls Parks and Recreation managers formulate policies and procedures.

METHODOLOGY

The 2017 survey was provided online and via a scripted interview process. The citizenry were invited via several media including mailings, Parks and Recreation catalogs and flyers, and public service announcements on radio and TV. A random selection of citizens were called and invited to complete the survey over the phone. Non-residents were also surveyed in the field using the interview process.

FINDINGS

An overall increase in wildlife recreation indicates that it is a significant source of enjoyment for residents and non-residents alike. However, only 23% of anglers are from out of the area and 11% are from out of state. A far higher percentage of wildlife viewers were from out of the area—nearly 45%. This indicates that the Aspen Falls area wildlife viewing opportunities attract a significant number of visitors to the area.

Over the past 10 year period, angling has decreased by 36% while wildlife viewing has increased by nearly 83%. Currently, anglers still outnumber wildlife observers nearly 2 to 1. If current trends continue, it will be several years before the number of days spent wildlife viewing will be on par with angling. This trend is consistent with the state trend. (U.S. Fish & Wildlife Service 2015)

The study found the following e...

- Each angler spent an average...
- Each wildlife watcher spent ...

RECOMMENDATIONS

Based on the survey results, city... opportunities. Improving and expanding... greatest increase in wildlife recreation. S... habitat and healthy fish stocks. (Lau, La... also increase native plantings and natura... recreationists will be served.

To improve upland river habitat,...

1. Maintain existing natural are... areas. A natural area is defin... open fields for the primary p...
2. Maintain and introduce nativ... and cover plants for the prim...
3. Educate the populace on how... species, and protect natural a...
4. Provide wildlife photography... raising tool.
5. Sponsor volunteer based eve... invasive species, and plant n...
6. Improve field guides and ma...

[1] Trip expenses include food, fuel, and lodging. Angling equipment includes tents, clothing, and fishing gear.
[2] Equipment includes binoculars, clothing, tents, and backpacking equipment.

Last_First_wrd02_SA2Wildlife (DO NOT RELEASE YET)

Figure 1

DONE! You have completed Skills Assessment 2

PAYING FOR COLLEGE

Techniques for Saving Money

By Your Name

March 14, 2018

In the previous year, college tuition and fees at public colleges increased by over 8%. Students at private colleges saw increases of 3.2 to 4.5%. (Education & the Workforce Committee 2014). To counter this rise, students can employ several strategies to reduce the cost of attending college.

PURSUE SCHOLARSHIPS

Students should pursue all scholarship opportunities, not just those that are based on need. Scholarships based on academic achievement have been increasingly awarded in past years. (Silverstein 2015) Nearly all colleges provided merit-based scholarships to prospective students. Most states offer scholarships through their education offices. Finally, many schools offer grants and scholarships in special areas such as music, technology, math, and science.

Many companies and associations offer scholarships. For example, banks often provide scholarships or grants for students planning to work in the finance industry. Alumni organizations typically have scholarship programs. Parents should check with their employers to see if they provide assistance to children of employees.

Students should pursue all avenues for funding. For example, many schools have special scholarships for students who do not qualify for federal or state funding. Others may offer discounted tuition to older students. Typically, financial aid counselors can help students find scholarships, grants, and discounts.

STAY LOCAL

Students who attend local colleges can save considerable money on both housing and tuition. Students who live at home can save as much as $6000 per year (U.S. Government

2

Department of Education n.d.). Living at home also enables students to attend a community college for the first 1 or 2 years, which substantially lowers tuition costs. Tuition at local public colleges avoids the extra tuition typically charged to out-of-state residents.

WORK AND STUDY

Many students can leverage their income by working at a job coordinated through the college that they are attending. Some schools provide free room and board to students in exchange for the work they perform. Others provide discounts to student government leaders. Students should find their institution's placement office to find on and off campus jobs.

SERVE IN AN ARMED FORCE

Two programs pay for tuition and fees for those planning to be in a military service—Service Academy Scholarships and the Reserve Officers Training Corps (ROTC) Scholarship Program. Service Academy Scholarships are competitive scholarships that provide free tuition at a military academy. ROTC scholarships pay for tuition, textbooks, and a monthly living allowance. Both scholarships require a service commitment upon graduation.

TEST OUT

Receive college credit by testing through one of these test-out programs:

- Advanced Placement Program (APP)
- College-Level Examination Program (CLEP)
- Provenience Examination Program (PEP)

Some colleges give credit for life experiences.[1]

OTHER OPTIONS

Several other options include:

- Take transferable summer college courses at less expensive schools.
- Take advantage of accelerated 3-year programs when they are available
- Take the maximum number of allowed credits to reduce the number of quarters or semesters needed to graduate.

[1] Contact the Distance Education and Training Council at 1601 18th Street, NW, Washington, DC 20009, or call (202) 234-5100 for more information.

Figure 1

My Skills

To complete this project, you will need the following file:

- wrd02_MYCosts

You will save your file as:

- Last_First_wrd02_MYCosts

---

1. Start **Word 2016**, and then open the student data file **wrd02_MYCosts**. Save the file in your chapter folder as Last_First_wrd02_MYCosts
2. Click to the right of *By*, add a space, and then type your name.
3. Replace all occurrences of the word *you* with students
4. In the first body paragraph beginning *In the previous year*, set a **0.5 inch** first line indent and the spacing after to **12 pt**. Repeat the same formatting to the paragraph beginning *Students should pursue*.
5. Update the **Heading 1** style to match the formatting of the report title.
6. Use **Source Manager** to edit the source for **U.S. Government**. Change the source type to **Web site**, and then add the **URL** https://studentaid2.ed.gov/getmoney/pay_for_college/cost_35.html
7. In the *STAY LOCAL* section, after the sentence ending *$6000 per year*, insert a citation using **U.S. Government Department of Education** as the reference.
8. In the *TEST OUT* section, after the last sentence ending *credit for life experiences*, insert a footnote with the text Contact the Distance Education and Training Council at 1601 18th Street, NW, Washington, DC 20009, or call (202) 234-5100 for more information.
9. In the footnote just inserted, change the footnote text font size to **12**.
10. At the end of the document, apply a solid circle bullet to the three paragraphs beginning *Take transferable summer* and ending with *semesters needed to graduate*. Increase the indent of the list items to **0.5 inch** and set the line spacing to **1.15**.
11. In the blank paragraph below the last bulleted list, insert a manual page break. Press Enter two times, and then insert the **Bibliography** built-in field. Change the bibliography's heading to BIBLIOGRAPHY
12. In the header, insert the **Plain Number 3** page number so that it displays on all pages except for Page 1.
13. In the Page 2 footer, insert the **FileName** field, align the footer paragraph with the right margin, and then close the footer.
14. Change the page margins to **Normal** (1 inch on all sides).
15. Compare your screen with **Figure 1**. **Save** the file, **Close** Word, and then submit the file as directed by your instructor.

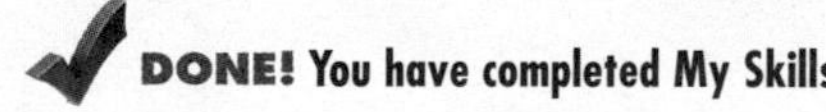
DONE! You have completed My Skills

Visual Skills Check

To complete this project, you will need the following file:

- **wrd02_VSSecurity**

You will save your file as:

- **Last_First_wrd02_VSSecurity**

Open the student data file **wrd02_VSSecurity**, and then save the file in your chapter folder as Last_First_wrd02_VSSecurity

To complete this document, set the margins to Office 2003 Default. Format the three lists as shown in **Figure 1**. The lists have been indented to 0.5 inch, line spacing is 1.15, and the spacing after is 12 pt.

The front matter is center aligned, the *By* line should display your own name, and the date should display your current date. The date paragraph's spacing after is set to 12 pt.

The body paragraph has a first line indent of 0.5 inches, spacing after of 12 pt, and line spacing of 1.15. At the end of the paragraph, a footnote has been inserted with the text Federal Trade Commission. Protecting Personal Information: A Guide for Business. Washington, November 2015. The footnote text is size 12, and the source title is italic.

Save the file, Close Word, and then submit the file as directed by your instructor.

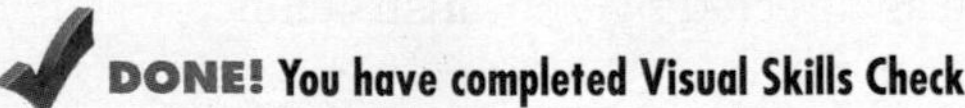

DONE! You have completed Visual Skills Check

SECURING DATA

A Summary for Aspen Falls City Government

By Your Name

October 12, 2018

Several laws require the city to keep sensitive data secure. Most notably are the Federal Trade Commission Act, Fair Credit Reporting Act, and the Gramm-Leach-Bliley Act. To comply with these laws and respect the rights of our citizens and those who do business with City Hall, the FTC recommends following these 5 key principles.[1]

1. Take stock. Know what personal information is stored on city systems.
2. Scale down. Keep only what we need to conduct city business.
3. Lock it. Prevent physical and virtual access to all information systems.
4. Pitch it. Dispose of all data that is no longer needed.
5. Plan ahead. Create an incident response plan.

PHYSICAL SECURITY

- Keep all paper documents, CDs, DVDs, and other storage medium in a locked room or locked file cabinet.
- Train employees to put away all files and log off their computer at the end of their shifts.
- Keep servers in locked rooms with access restricted only to authorized IT Department staff.
- Keep long term storage offsite and access should be limited only to those employees with a legitimate need for the data.
- Install alarms and institute a procedure for reporting unfamiliar persons on the premises.

VIRTUAL SECURITY

- Encrypt all sensitive information.
- Restrict employee privileges to install software.
- Keep anti-malware software up to date.
- Conduct periodic security audits including penetration testing.

[1] Federal Trade Commission. *Protecting Personal Information: A Guide for Business*. Washington, November 2015.

Figure 1

Skills Challenge 1

To complete this project, you will need the following file:

- **wrd02_SC1Aging**

You will save your file as:

- **Last_First_wrd02_SC1Aging**

Open the student data file **wrd02_SC1Aging**, and then save the file in your chapter folder as Last_First_wrd02_SC1Aging

Format the report following informal business report rules modeled in Skills 1–10. Take care to apply the appropriate paragraph spacing, paragraph line spacing, paragraph alignment, and indents for front matter, headings, body paragraphs, and lists. Adjust the font size of the footnotes to those used in an informal business report. Apply one of the pre-built margins accepted in an informal business report, making sure that the report fits within a total of three pages.

Insert your name in the By line and the FileName field in the footer. Adjust the page numbers to the correct format and placement. Save the file, Close Word, and then submit the file as directed by your instructor.

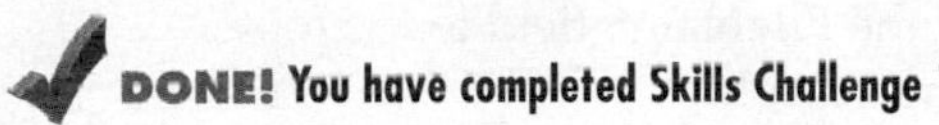
DONE! You have completed Skills Challenge 1

Skills Challenge 2

To complete this project, you will need the following file:

- **New blank Word document**

You will save your file as:

- **Last_First_wrd02_SC2Parks**

The Aspen Falls Planning Department is working with the Travel and Tourism Bureau to explore ways to use the city as the base of operation for tourists who want to visit important sites within a day's drive. Using the skills you practiced in this chapter, create a report on the nearby major nature attractions. These could include Yosemite National Park (250 miles), Death Valley National Park (200 miles), Sequoia National Forest (180 miles), and the Channel Islands National Park (40 miles). Research three of these sites, and write a report about the highlights of what a visitor might find at each. Include an introduction, a section for each of the three attractions, and a conclusion. Add your sources to Source Manager, and insert them in citations and a bibliography. Format the report as an informal business report.

Insert the FileName field in the footer, and check the entire document for grammar and spelling. Save the file in your chapter folder as Last_First_wrd02_SC2Parks Close Word, and then submit the file as directed by your instructor.

DONE! You have completed Skills Challenge 2

More Skills Assessment

To complete this project, you will need the following file:

- wrd02_MSATours

You will save your file as:

- Last_First_wrd02_MSATours

1. Start **Word 2016**, and then open the student data file **wrd02_MSATours**. Save the file in your folder as Last_First_wrd02_MSATours Add the **FileName** field to the footer, and then verify the formatting marks display.
2. Open the **AutoCorrect** dialog box. On the **AutoCorrect tab**, in the **Replace** box, type afx and in the **With** box, type Aspen Falls and then click the **Add** button. Compare your screen with **Figure 1**.
3. In the **AutoCorrect** dialog box, clear the **Automatic numbered lists** check box, and then clear the **Set left- and first-indent with tabs and backspaces** check box. Click **OK** two times to close the dialog boxes.
4. At the top of the document, in the paragraph beginning *The city wine region*, select and then delete the word *city*. Type afx and then press SpaceBar to replace *city* with *Aspen Falls*. At the end of the page, repeat this step in the paragraph beginning *For more information*.
5. Under the title *Wine Tours*, click in the blank line under the list item *Four hours*.
6. Type 2. (include the period) press Tab, and then type Group Size
7. Press Enter, and then press Tab. Type A. press Tab, and then type Four people
8. Press Enter, and then press Tab. Type B. press Tab, and then type Six people Verify your file fits on one page and your list levels align with the items above. Compare your screen with **Figure 2**.
9. Reopen the **AutoCorrect** dialog box. On the **AutoCorrect tab**, delete the phrase *afx*. If they were selected previous to this skill, select the **Automatic numbered lists** and **Set left- and first-indent with tabs and backspaces** check boxes. Click **OK** to close the dialog boxes.
10. Under the title *Activities*, select list items *A–C*. Change the numbering style to **1. 2. 3.**

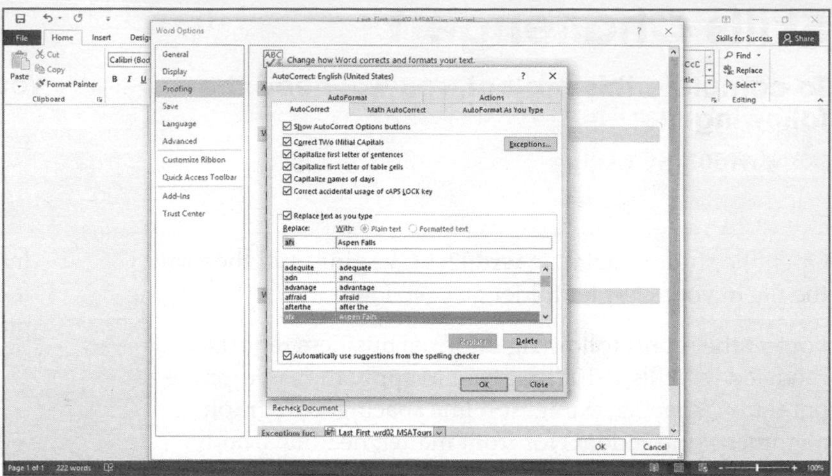

Figure 1 Word 2016, Windows 10, Microsoft Corporation

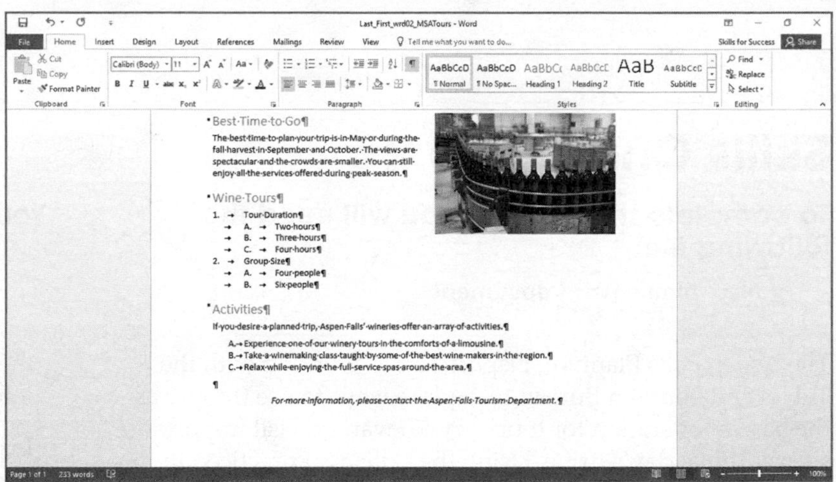

Figure 2 Word 2016, Windows 10, Microsoft Corporation

11. **Save** the file, **Close** Word, and then submit the file as directed by your instructor.

DONE! You have completed More Skills Assessment

Collaborating with Google

To complete this project, you will need a Google account (refer to the Common Features chapter) and the following file:

- wrd02_GPPlayground

You will save your file as:

- Last_First_wrd02_GPPlayground

1. Open a web browser. Log into your Google account, and then click the **Google Apps** button.
2. Click the **Drive** button to open Google Drive. If you receive a pop-up message, read the message, and then click **Next**. Read each message, and then close the dialog box.
3. Click the **New** button, click **Google Docs**, and then change the document title to Playground Proposal
4. In **Word 2016**, open the student data file **wrd02_GPPlayground**. Select and copy all the text and paste it in your Google Doc. At the top of the document, replace *Your Name* with your First and Last name.
5. Click the **Edit tab**, and then click **Find and replace**. In the **Find and replace** dialog box, **Find** all occurrences of play ground and **Replace with** playground
6. Click in the paragraph starting *The majority of*. On the **Format tab**, click **Line spacing**, and then click **Double**. Click to the right of the double quotes at the end of the paragraph. On the **Insert tab**, click **Footnote**, and then type StrongReach.com, Strong Reach, 2017, http://strongreach.org/ (accessed January 24, 2018). Compare your screen with **Figure 1**.
7. Under the title *ADA Compliance*, select the four requirements starting with *Wheelchair access*. On the **Format tab**, click **Lists**, and then click **Bulleted list**. In the gallery, click the first bullet style. Scroll down to the *Design Elements* title, and then repeat this technique to apply the bulleted list to the five ground covers. Compare your screen with **Figure 2**.
8. Under the document title *Playground Proposal*, click the **File tab**, click **Download as**, and then click **Microsoft Word (.docx)**. **Save** the file in your chapter folder as Last_First_wrd02_GPPlayground

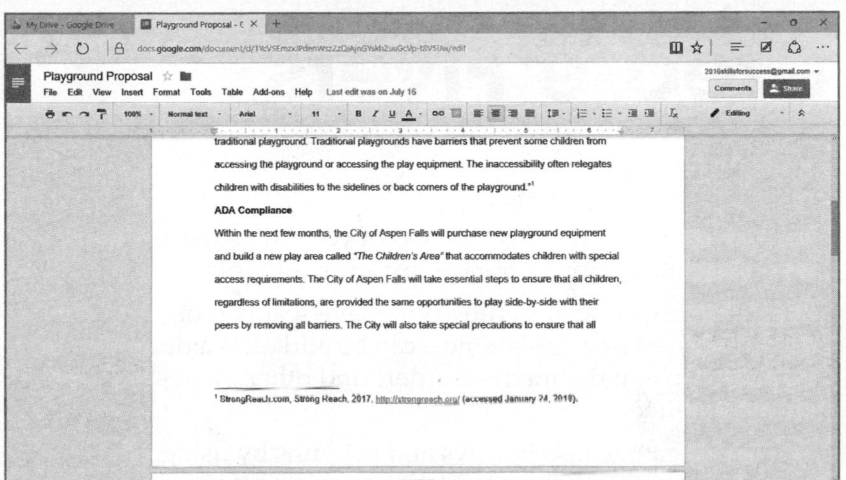

Figure 1

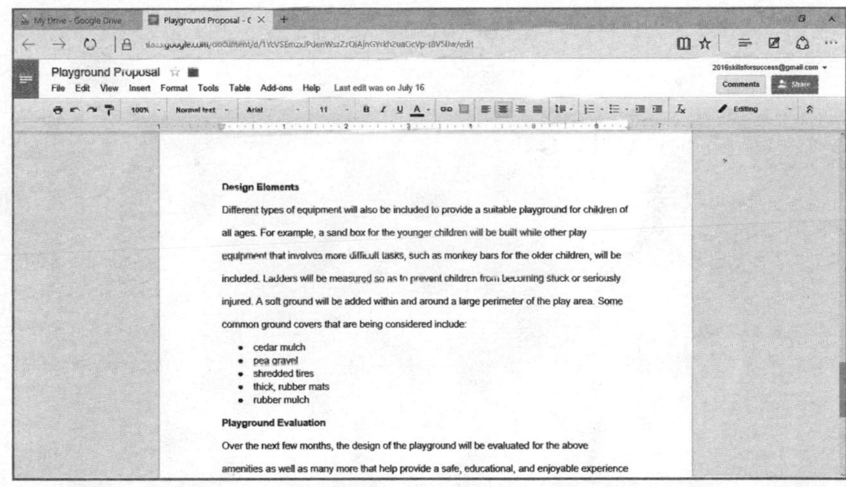

Figure 2

9. Start **Word 2016**, and then open the file **Last_First_wrd02_GPPlayground**. Insert the **FileName** field in the footer.
10. **Save** the file, **Close** the open windows, and then submit the file as directed by your instructor.

CHAPTER 3

Create Flyers

- You can enhance the effectiveness of your message and make your document more attractive by adding graphics.
- Digital images—such as those you have scanned or taken with a digital camera or a cell phone—can be added to a document and formatted using distinctive borders and other interesting and attractive effects.
- You can organize lists in rows and columns by using tabs.
- Word tables are used to organize lists and data in columns and rows without needing to create tab settings.
- You can use tables to summarize and emphasize information in an organized arrangement of rows and columns that make complex information easy to understand at a glance.
- You can format tables manually or apply a number of different formats quickly using built-in styles.

Alexey Klementiev/Fotolia

Aspen Falls City Hall

In this chapter, you will create a flyer for Carter Horikoshi, the Parks and Recreation Art Center Supervisor. The flyer will promote the art gallery and art classes provided at the Art Center. The flyer needs to describe the gallery hours, art classes, and the class fees.

An effective flyer organizes the content visually. For example, a prominent title and a graphic need to pull the reader's attention to the flyer. Subheadings should be smaller than the title, and the least prominent text should be used for the paragraphs, lists, or tables. The overall formatting and layout need to help the reader flow through the flyer's message, typically in a top to bottom direction. Wrapping text around graphics is an important technique to provide this flow.

Before formatting, you should select a theme, and then select choices from that theme's colors and fonts. In this manner, you can select formatting that works well together and does not detract from the flyer's desired look and feel. Placing content in tables or tabbed lists helps organize the flyer's message, and it is also a good idea to provide ample white space between flyer elements.

In this project, you will insert, resize, and move pictures, and apply picture styles and artistic effects. You will set tab stops and use tabs to enter data. You will also work with tables, add rows and columns, format the tables' contents, and modify their layout and design.

Time to complete all 10 skills — 45 to 60 minutes

Outcome

Using the skills in this chapter, you will be able to change the document layout, insert and modify pictures, insert tab stops and tabbed lists, and design tables.

Objectives

3.1 Insert and format pictures

3.2 Insert and modify tab stops

3.3 Create and format tables

Student data files needed for this chapter:

wrd03_Art
wrd03_ArtPhoto1
wrd03_ArtPhoto2
wrd03_ArtClasses

You will save your file as:

Last_First_wrd03_Art

SKILLS

At the end of this chapter, you will be able to:

Skill 1 Insert Text and Pictures from Files
Skill 2 Resize and Align Pictures
Skill 3 Apply Picture Styles and Artistic Effects
Skill 4 Set Tab Stops
Skill 5 Type Tabbed Lists
Skill 6 Apply Table Styles
Skill 7 Create Tables
Skill 8 Delete and Add Table Rows and Columns
Skill 9 Format Text in Table Cells
Skill 10 Format Tables

MORE SKILLS

Skill 11 Insert Text Boxes
Skill 12 Format with WordArt
Skill 13 Convert Text into Tables
Skill 14 Insert Drop Caps

Corbett Art Center

The Art Center gallery, located in the historic Corbett mansion, is open to the general. The gallery features local artists and the work of students taking classes at the center. The hours of operation are:

Day Hours
Monday – Wednesday ....noon to 5
Thursday – Friday ....noon to 8
Saturday ....11 to 5
Sunday ....Closed

The Art Center offers art classes throughout the year. Each class has a beginning, intermediate, and advanced section. Each section lasts two months. Art classes include the following:

Class	Starting Months	Description
Art History	January and July	Survey of medieval to modern art.
Drawing	February and August	Freehand drawing, light and shadow, composition, and perspective, and portrait
Watercolors	March and September	Washes, wet-in-wet, and dry brush
Painting	April and October	Acrylics, oils, and watercolors.
Sculpture	May and November	Medium, modeling, busts, and abstraction
Photography	June and December	Point and Shoot, DSLRs, Photoshop, Portraits, Landscapes, and Sports

Class fees are as follows:

Class Fees		
Group	Ages	Cost
Students	12 to 17	$ 64.00
Young Adults	18 to 24	78.00
Adults	25 to 59	125.00
Seniors	60+	38.00

Last_First_wrd03_Art

- You can insert text and pictures from other files into the document you are working on.
- By inserting pictures from files, you can include pictures taken with digital cameras, tablets, or cell phones. You can also include files created by scanners or downloaded from the web.

1. Start **Word 2016**, open the student file **wrd03_Art**, and if necessary, display the formatting marks. If your rulers do not display, on the View tab, in the Show group, select the Ruler check box.
2. On the **File tab**, click **Save As**, and then click **Browse**. In the **Save As** dialog box, navigate to the location where you are saving your files, create and open a folder named Word Chapter 3 and then **Save** the file as Last_First_wrd03_Art

MOS Obj 1.3.2 C

3. On the **Design tab**, in the **Document Formatting group**, click the **Themes** button, and then click the **Wisp** thumbnail.
4. Select the document title *Corbett Art Center*, change the **Font Size** to **26**, and then **Center** the title. Compare your screen with **Figure 1**.

MOS Obj 5.1.2 C

5. Position the insertion point to the left of *The Art Center gallery*. On the **Insert tab**, in the **Illustrations group**, click the **Pictures** button.
6. In the **Insert Picture** dialog box, navigate to your student files, select **wrd03_ArtPhoto1**, and then click **Insert**. Compare your screen with **Figure 2**.

   When you insert a picture, it is inserted as part of the paragraph the insertion point was in, and the Layout Options button displays to the right of the picture.

■ **Continue to the next page to complete the skill**

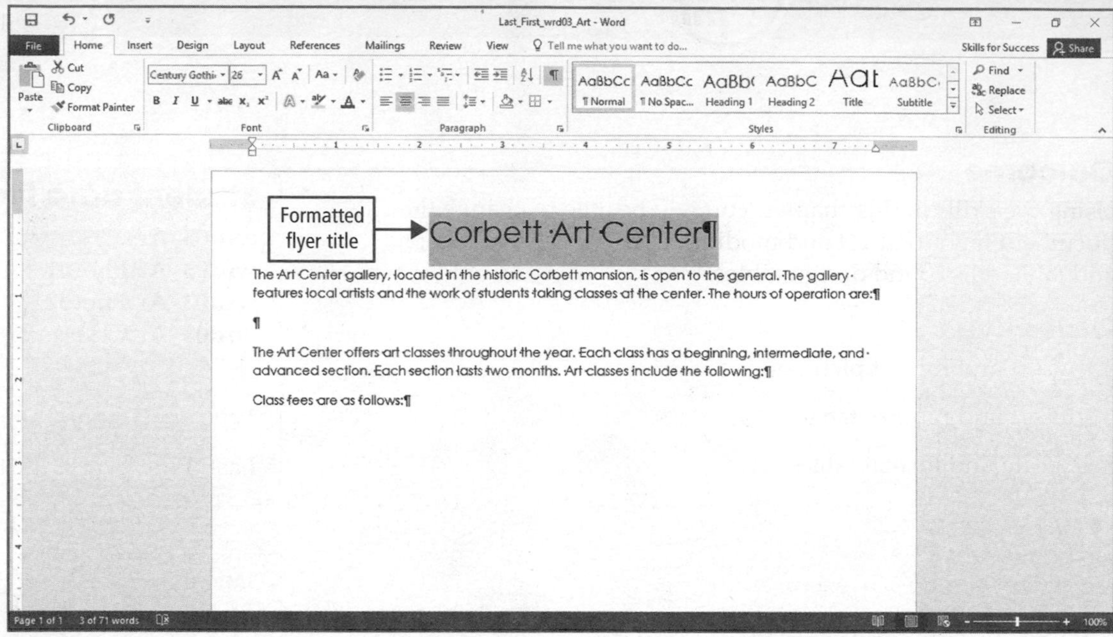

Figure 1 Word 2016, Windows 10, Microsoft Corporation

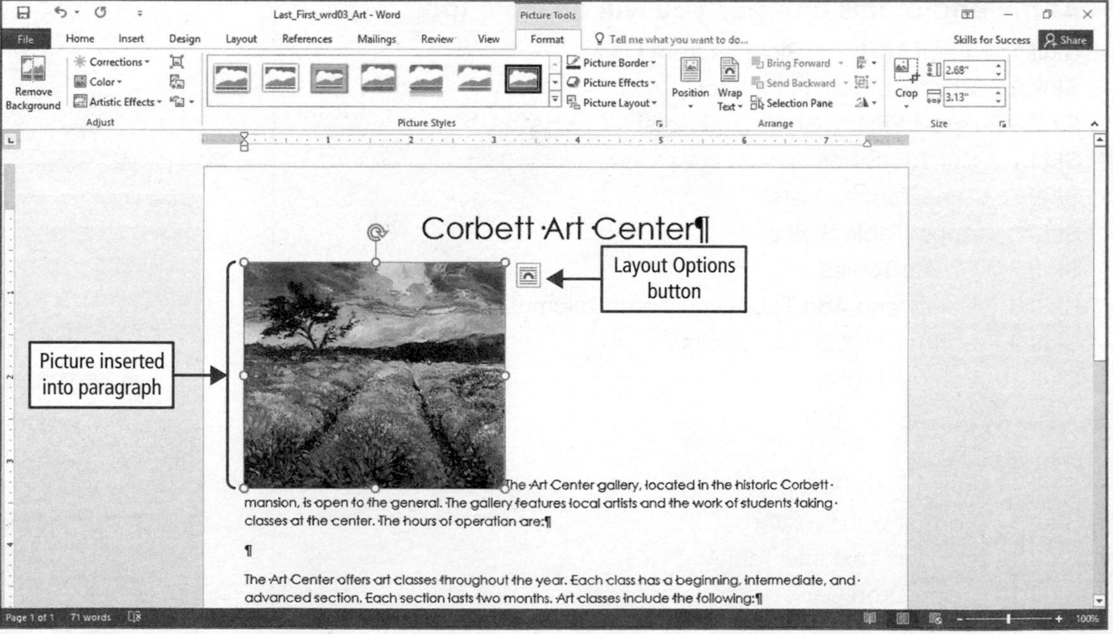

Figure 2 Word 2016, Windows 10, Microsoft Corporation

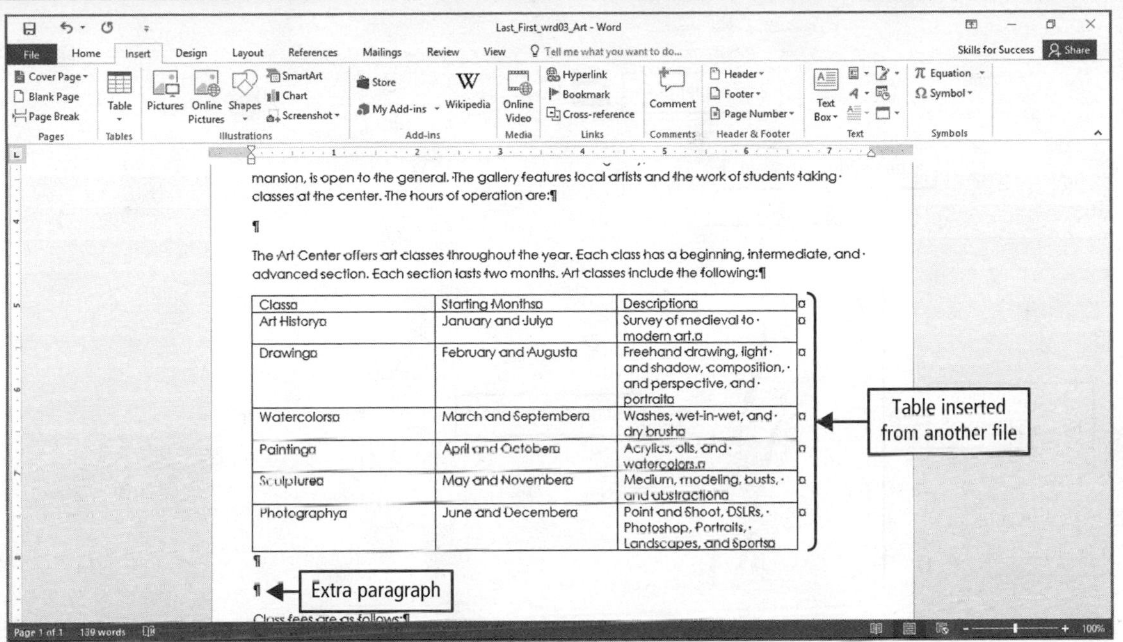

Word 2016, Windows 10, Microsoft Corporation

Figure 3

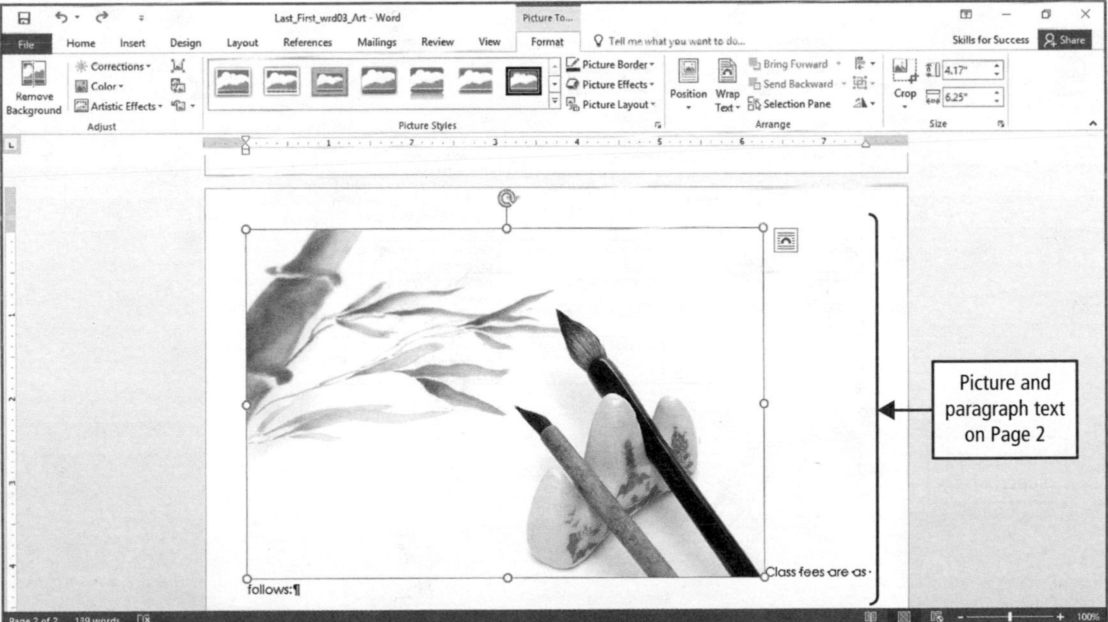

Julian Rovagnati/Fotolia; Word 2016, Windows 10, Microsoft Corporation

Figure 4

7. At the end of the paragraph that begins *The Art Center offers art classes*, click to position the insertion point to the right of the colon, and then press Enter.

8. On the **Insert tab**, in the **Text group**, click the **Object arrow**, and then click **Text from File**. MOS Obj 1.1.4 C

9. In the **Insert File** dialog box, navigate to your student files, select **wrd03_ArtClasses**, and then click **Insert** to insert the table. Compare your screen with **Figure 3**.

10. With the insertion point in the second blank paragraph below the inserted table, press Backspace to remove the extra blank paragraph that is created when you insert text from a file.

11. Position the insertion point to the left of *Class fees are as follows*, and then use the technique practiced previously to insert the **wrd03_ArtPhoto2** picture from the student data files for this chapter. Compare your screen with **Figure 4**.

    Because the picture is too large to fit in the available space at the bottom of the first page, a new page was added containing just the picture and the paragraph. You will move the picture in the next skill.

12. **Save** the file.

- **You have completed Skill 1 of 10**

- When you select a graphic, ***sizing handles***—small circles on an object's border—display and the Format contextual tab is added to the Ribbon.
- You can move graphics precisely using ***Alignment Guides***—lines that display when an object is aligned with document objects such as margins and headings.

1. On Page 2, be sure the **wrd03_ArtPhoto2** paint brushes picture is selected.
2. On the right border of the picture, locate the middle sizing handle. Point to the sizing handle to display the pointer, and then drag to the left to approximately **2 inches** on the horizontal ruler, as shown in **Figure 1**, and then release the left mouse button.

   When you size an image using the middle sizing handles, the picture does not resize proportionally.
3. On the **Format tab**, in the **Adjust group**, click the **Reset Picture arrow**, and then click **Reset Picture & Size**.
4. Point to the sizing handle in the lower right corner of the picture. When the pointer displays, drag up and to the left until the right border of the picture aligns at approximately **2 inches** on the horizontal ruler. Release the left mouse button, and then compare your screen with **Figure 2**.

   When you size an image using the corner sizing handles, the picture resizes proportionally.

■ Continue to the next page to complete the skill

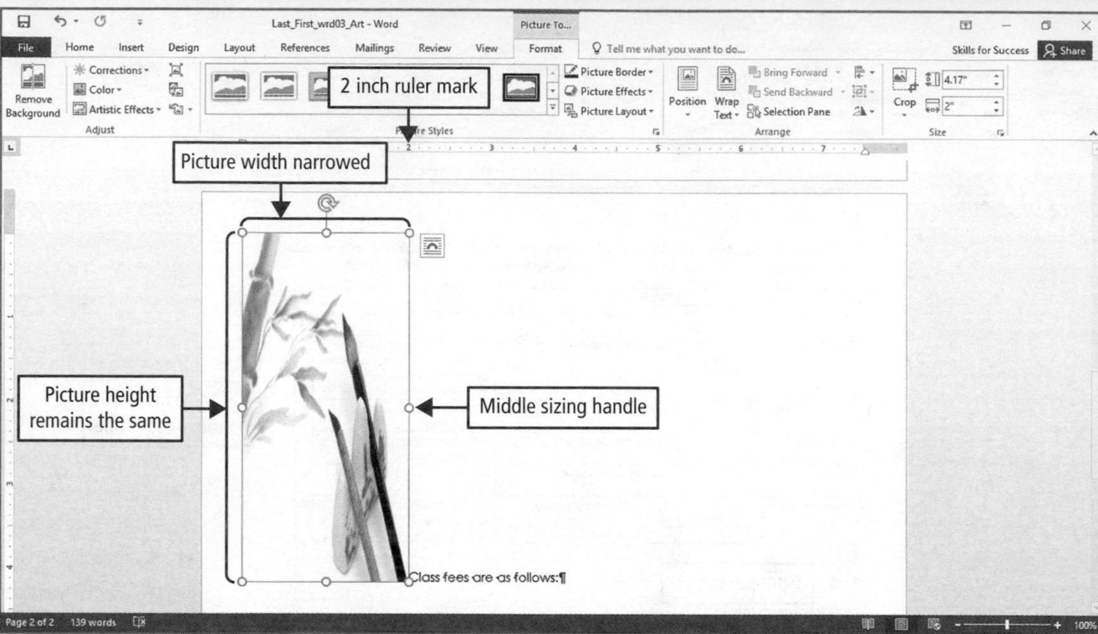

Figure 1

Julian Rovagnati/Fotolia; Word 2016, Windows 10, Microsoft Corporation

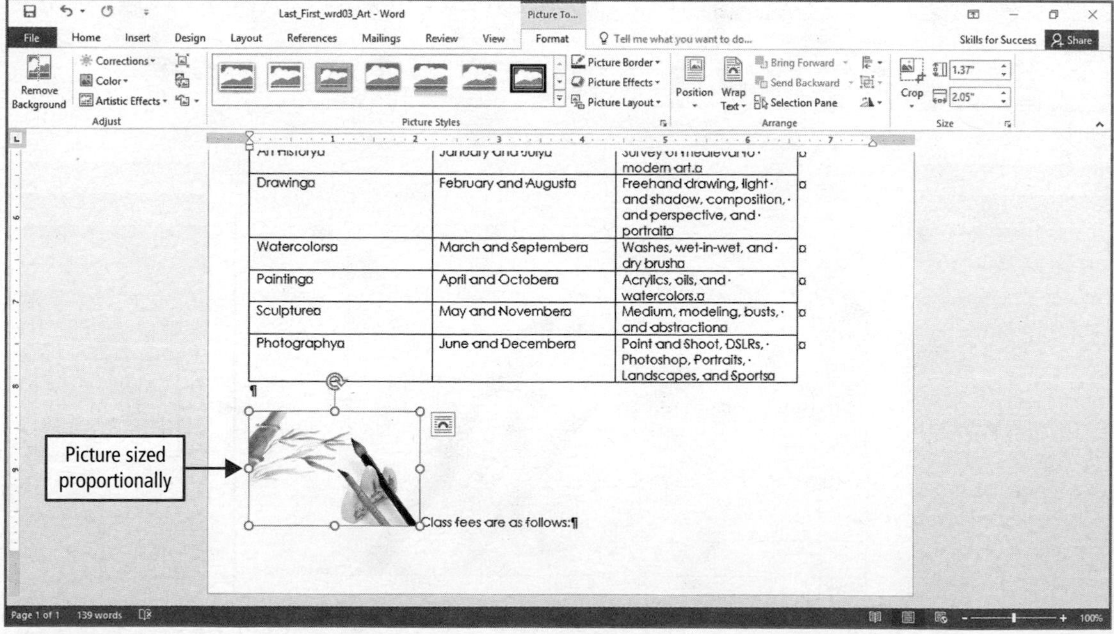

Figure 2

Julian Rovagnati/Fotolia; Word 2016, Windows 10, Microsoft Corporation

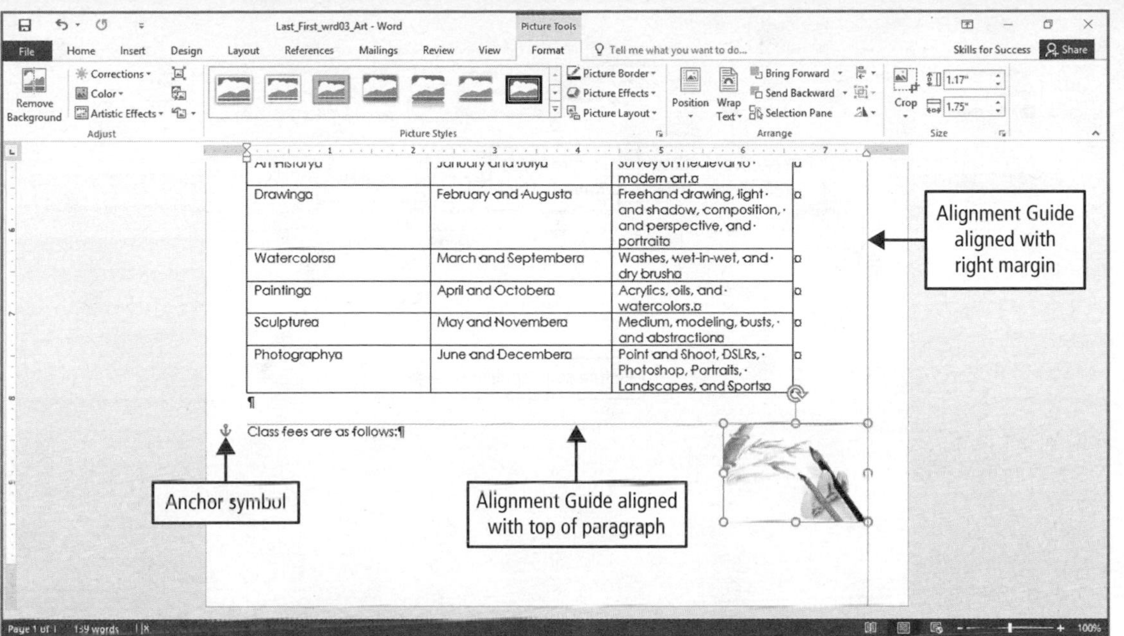

Julian Rovagnati/Fotolia; Word 2016, Windows 10, Microsoft Corporation

Figure 3

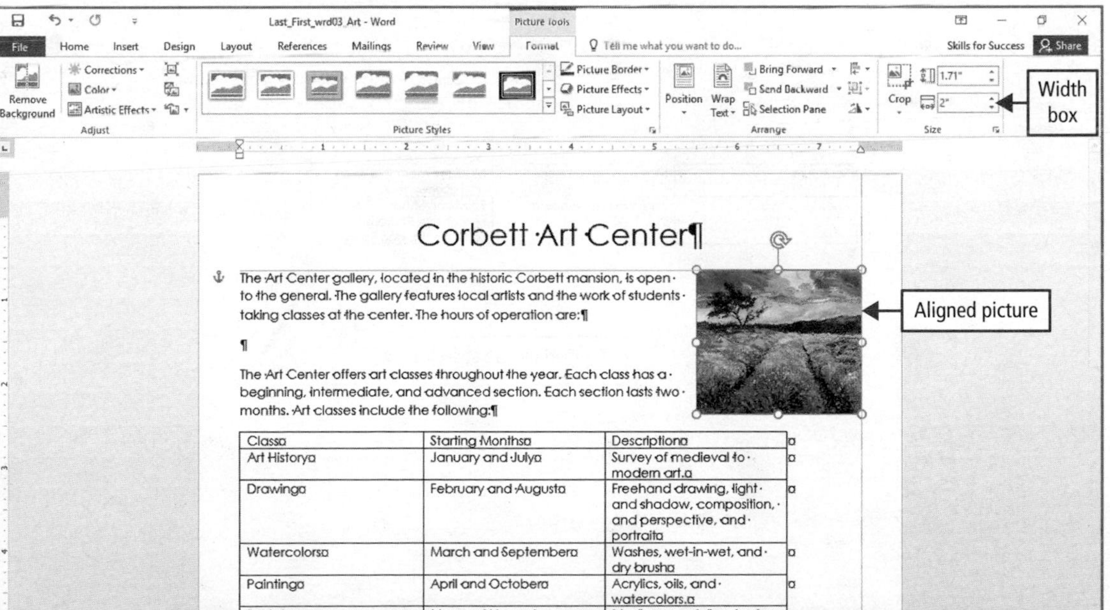

Word 2016, Windows 10, Microsoft Corporation

Figure 4

5. With the second picture still selected, on the **Format tab**, in the **Size group**, select the value in the **Width** box. Type 1.75 and then press Enter to change the size of the picture to 1.75 inches wide and approximately 1.17 inches in height.

MOS Obj 5.2.4 C

6. With the second picture still selected, click its **Layout Options** button, and then under **With Text Wrapping**, click the first thumbnail—**Square**.

MOS Obj 5.2.6 C

The Square text wrapping option changes the picture to a ***floating object***, which you can move independently of the surrounding text. An ***anchor*** symbol displays to the left of a paragraph to indicate which paragraph is associated with the picture.

7. Point to the picture to display the pointer. Drag the picture so that the Alignment Guides align with the right margin and the top of the paragraph that begins *Class fees*. Compare your screen with **Figure 3**, and then release the left mouse button.

MOS Obj 5.2.7 C

If your Alignment Guides do not display, on the Layout tab, in the Arrange group, click Align, and then click Use Alignment Guides.

8. Press Ctrl + Home, and then select the flower field picture. On the **Format tab**, in the **Size group**, change the **Width** to 2"

9. Repeat the technique practiced previously to change the picture's layout to **Square**.

10. Repeat the technique just practiced to position the picture as shown in **Figure 4**.

11. **Save** the file.

■ **You have completed Skill 2 of 10**

- You can add special effects to graphics to make them look like drawings or paintings.
- You can also apply built-in picture styles and then format that style's borders, effects, or layouts.

1. Press Ctrl + End, and then click the picture with the paint brushes.

Obj 5.2.5 C

2. On the **Format tab**, in the **Picture Styles group**, click the **More** button, and then point to several thumbnails to view them using Live Preview.
3. In the gallery, use ScreenTips text to locate and click the eighteenth thumbnail—**Perspective Shadow, White**—and then compare your screen with **Figure 1**.
4. In the **Picture Styles group**, click the **Picture Effects** button, point to **Bevel**, and then under **Bevel**, click the first effect in the second row—**Angle**.

   In this manner you can adjust the Picture Style settings applied in the Quick Style gallery. Here, the bevel setting assigned by the picture style was changed from Circle to Angle.

Obj 5.2.2 C

5. Click the **Picture Effects** button, point to **3-D Rotation**, and then under **Perspective**, click the first effect in the third row—**Perspective Contrasting Right**. Click in a paragraph to deselect the picture, and then compare your screen with **Figure 2**.

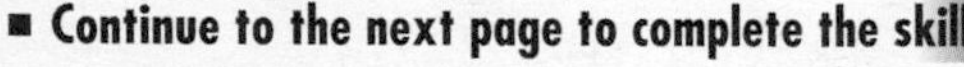
■ Continue to the next page to complete the skill

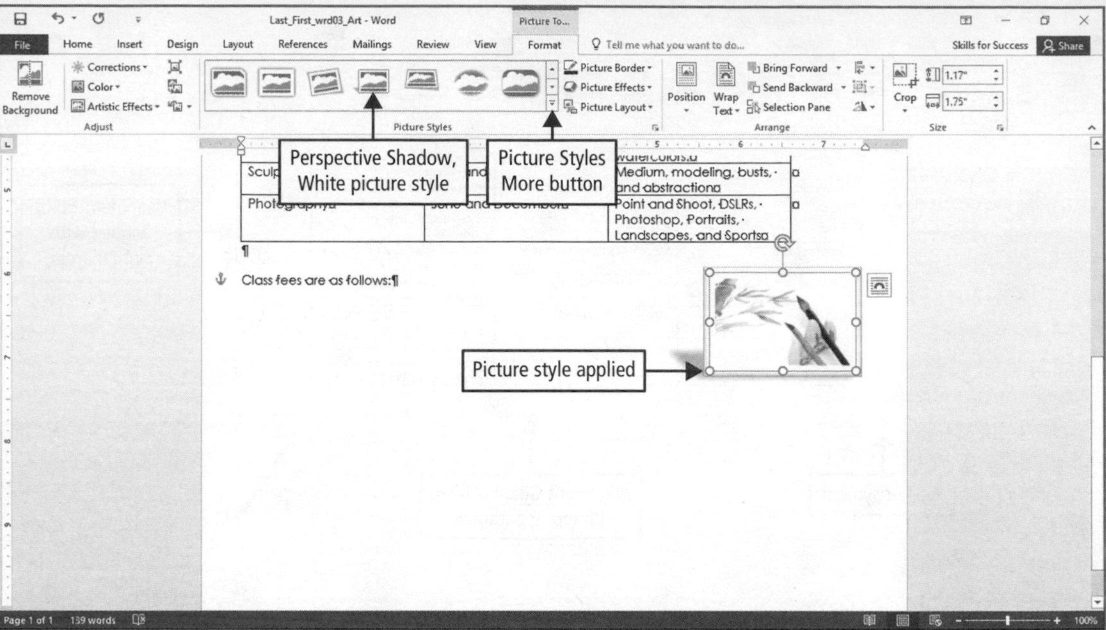

Figure 1

Julian Rovagnati/Fotolia; Word 2016, Windows 10, Microsoft Corporation

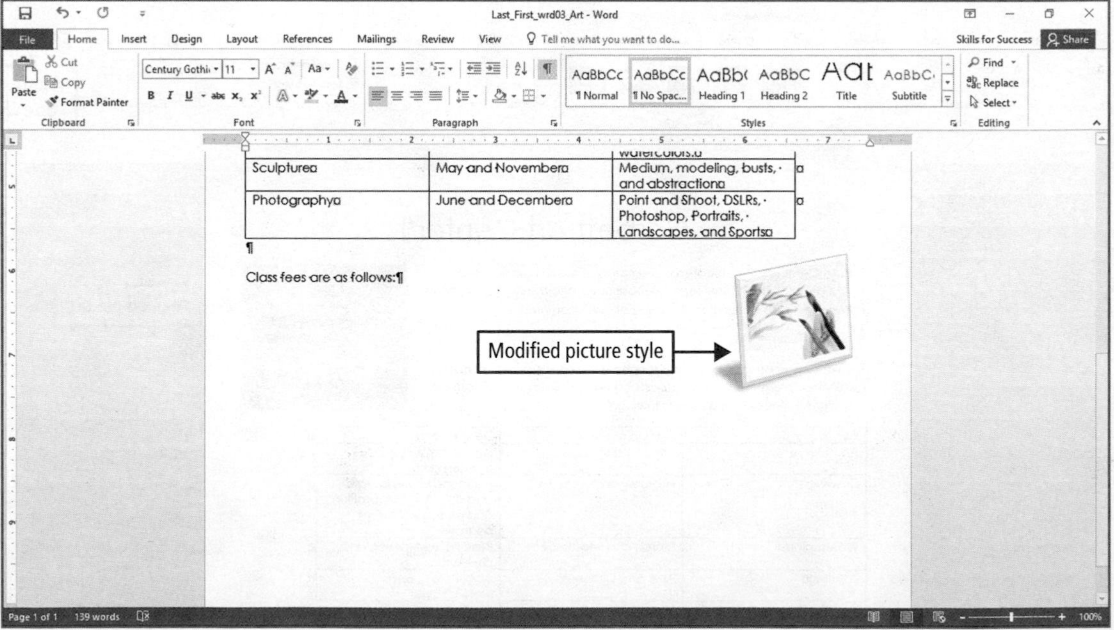

Figure 2

Julian Rovagnati/Fotolia; Word 2016, Windows 10, Microsoft Corporation

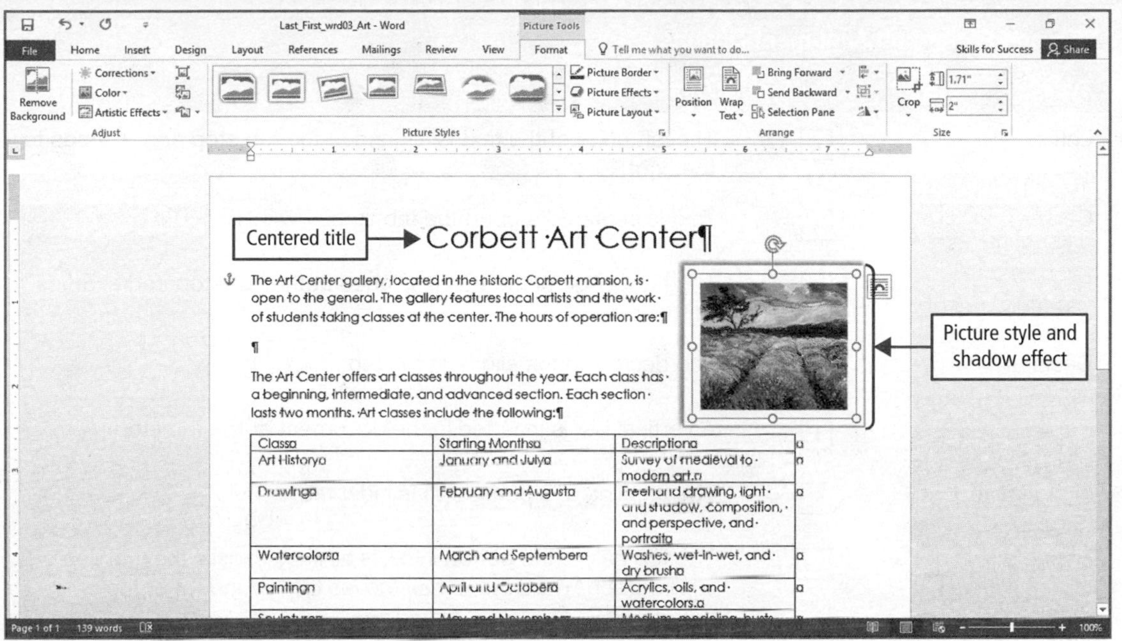

Word 2016, Windows 10, Microsoft Corporation

Figure 3

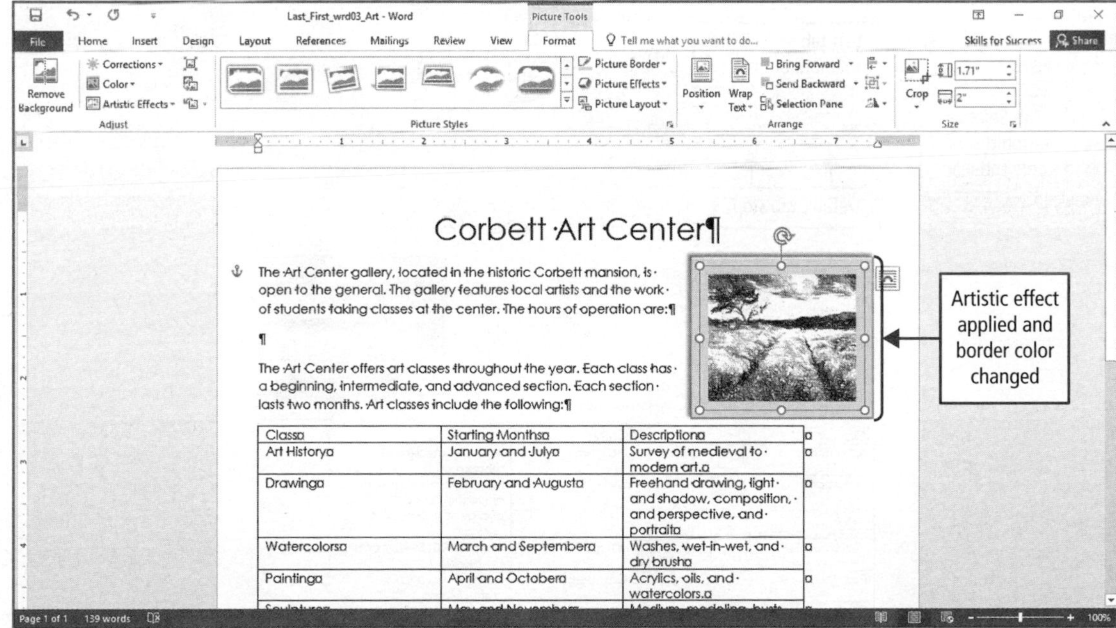

Word 2016, Windows 10, Microsoft Corporation

Figure 4

6. Press Ctrl + Home to move to the top of the document, select the flower field picture, and then apply the sixteenth picture style—**Moderate Frame, White**.

7. Click the **Picture Effects** button, point to **Shadow**, and then click the last thumbnail under **Outer—Offset Diagonal Top Left**.

   When applying shadow effects, all the shadows should be on the same side(s) of each graphic. Because the new style increased the size of the picture, the title has wrapped to the left and is no longer centered.

8. With the picture still selected, press ↓ approximately two times until the document title is centered. Compare your screen with **Figure 3**.

   To move objects in small precise increments, you can ***nudge*** them in this manner by selecting the object and then pressing one of the arrow keys.

9. In the **Adjust group**, click the **Artistic Effects** button. Point to several thumbnails in the gallery to preview available effects, and then click the fourth effect—**Pencil Sketch**.

   MOS Obj 5.2.1 C

10. With the picture still selected, in the **Picture Styles group**, click the **Picture Border** button. In the second row under **Theme Colors**, click the seventh color—**Brown, Accent 3, Lighter 80%**. Compare your screen with **Figure 4**.

11. **Save** the file.

■ **You have completed Skill 3 of 10**

- A ***tab stop*** is a specific location on a line of text and marked on the Word ruler to which you can move the insertion point by pressing Tab. Tabs are used to align and indent text.
- Tab stops can be set and modified using the ruler or in the Tabs dialog box.

---

1. Click in the blank paragraph below the paragraph starting *The Art Center gallery*.
2. At the left of the horizontal ruler, notice the **Tab Selector** button —the icon displayed in your button area may be different.
3. Click the button several times to view the various tab styles and paragraph alignment options available. Pause at each tab stop type, and then view the information in the table in **Figure 1** to see how each of the tab types is used.
4. With the insertion point still in the blank paragraph, click the **Tab Selector** button until the **Left Tab** icon displays.
5. On the horizontal ruler, point to the mark that indicates **0.25 inches**, and then click one time to insert a left tab stop. Compare your screen with **Figure 2**.

   The default tab stops are every half inch. When you add your own tab stop, it replaces the default tab stops up to that place on the ruler. To the right of that tab, the next half inch mark will be the next default tab stop.

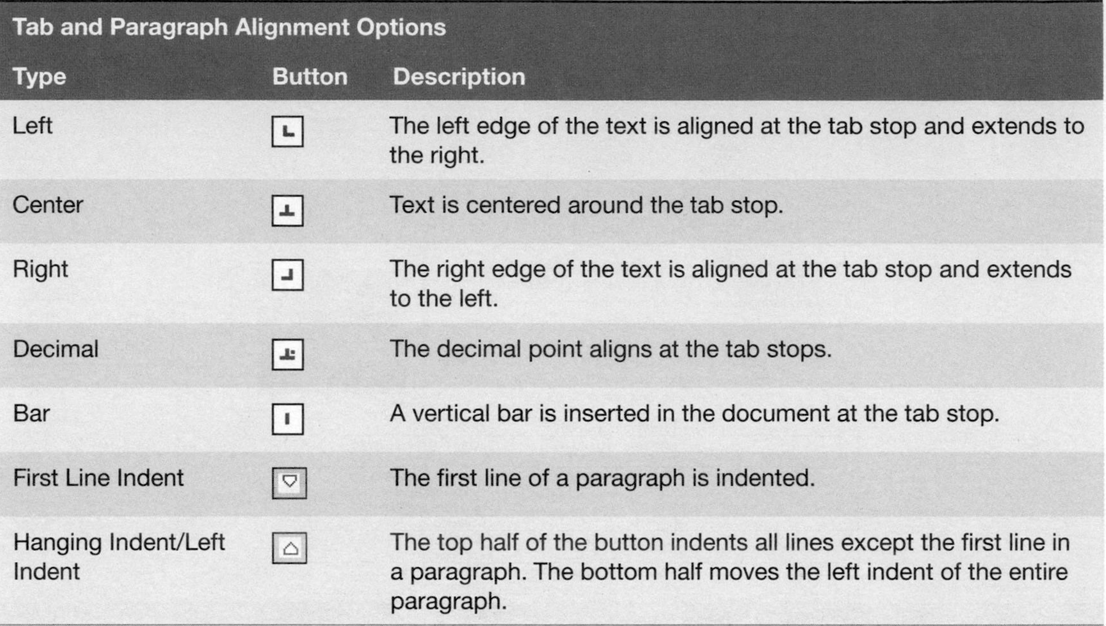

Tab and Paragraph Alignment Options

Type	Button	Description
Left		The left edge of the text is aligned at the tab stop and extends to the right.
Center		Text is centered around the tab stop.
Right		The right edge of the text is aligned at the tab stop and extends to the left.
Decimal		The decimal point aligns at the tab stops.
Bar		A vertical bar is inserted in the document at the tab stop.
First Line Indent		The first line of a paragraph is indented.
Hanging Indent/Left Indent		The top half of the button indents all lines except the first line in a paragraph. The bottom half moves the left indent of the entire paragraph.

Figure 1

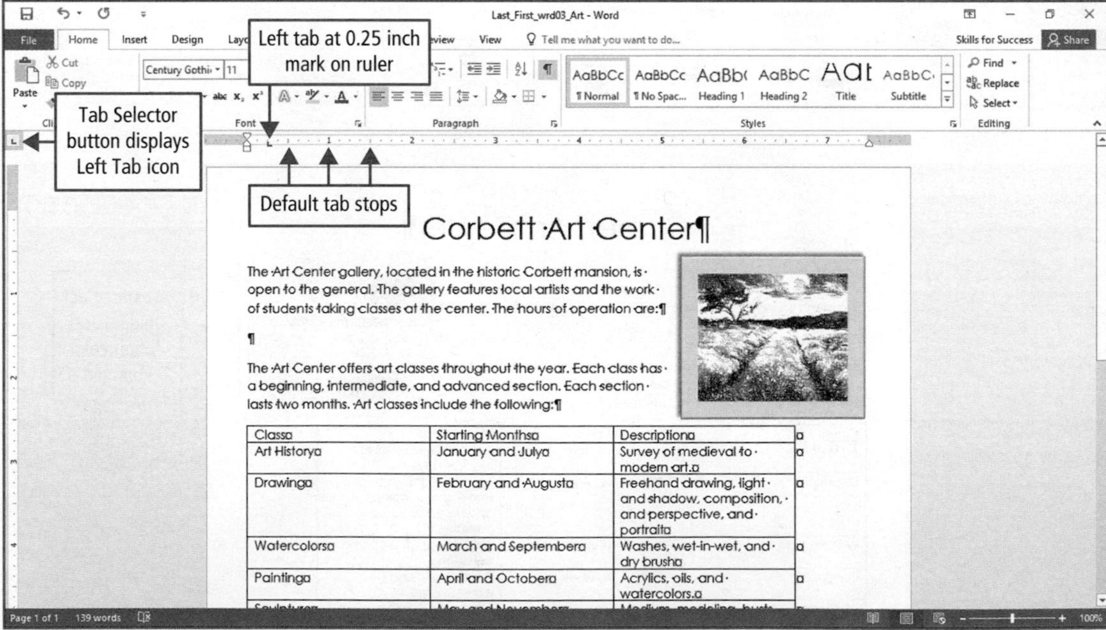

Figure 2

Word 2016, Windows 10, Microsoft Corporation

▪ **Continue to the next page to complete the skill**

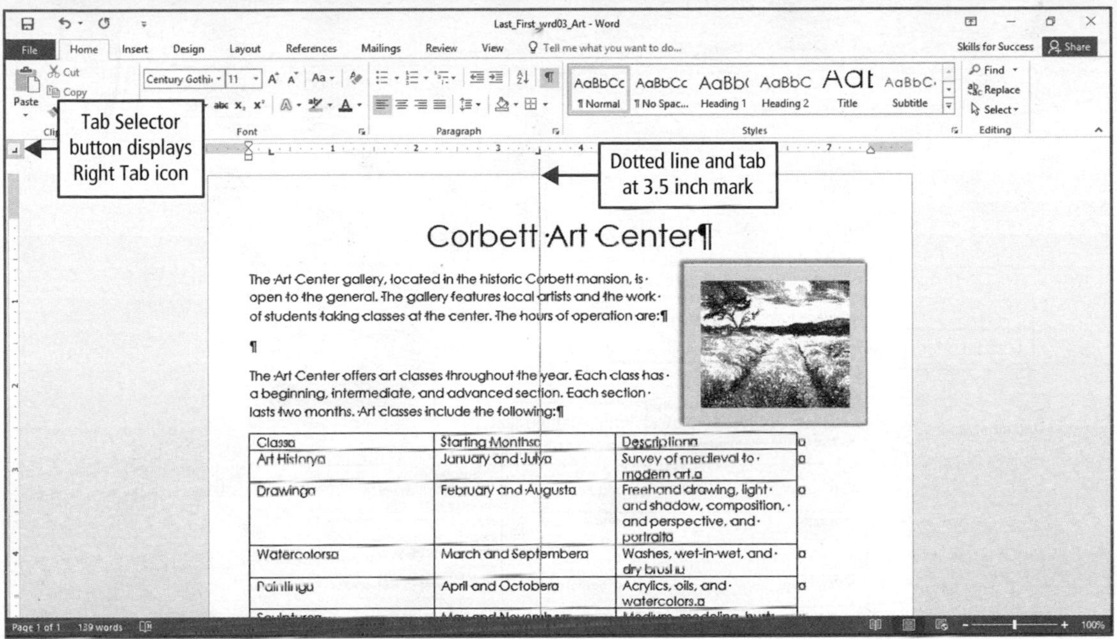

Word 2016, Windows 10, Microsoft Corporation

Figure 3

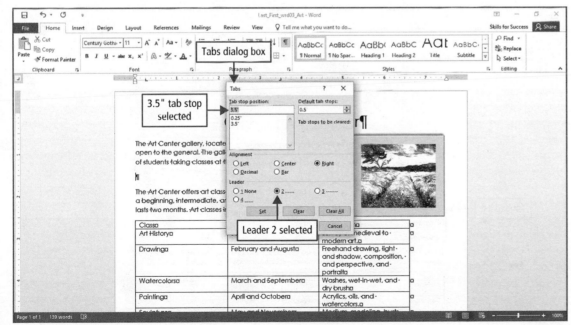

Word 2016, Windows 10, Microsoft Corporation

Figure 4

6. Click the **Tab Selector** button two times to display the **Right Tab** icon ⌟.
7. On the ruler, point to the mark that indicates **3.5 inches**. Click and hold down the mouse button. Notice that a dotted line indicates the tab location in the document, as shown in **Figure 3**. In this manner, you can determine whether the tab stop is exactly where you want it.
8. Release the mouse button to insert the right tab stop.
9. On the **Home tab**, in the **Paragraph group**, click the **Paragraph Dialog Box Launcher** ⧉. At the bottom of the **Paragraph** dialog box, click the **Tabs** button. Alternately, double-click a tab stop on the ruler.
10. In the **Tabs** dialog box, under **Tab stop position**, select the tab stop at **3.5"**. Under **Leader**, select the **2** option button to add a dot leader to the selected tab stop. Near the bottom of the dialog box, click the **Set** button, and then compare your screen with **Figure 4**.

    A ***leader*** is a series of characters that form a solid, dashed, or dotted line to fill the space preceding a tab stop; a ***leader character*** is the symbol used to fill the space. A ***dot leader*** is a series of evenly spaced dots that precede a tab stop.

11. In the **Tabs** dialog box, click **OK**, and then **Save** the file.

- **You have completed Skill 4 of 10**

SKILL 5: Type Tabbed Lists

SKILL 3.5

- The Tab key is used to move to the next tab stop in a line of text.
- When you want to relocate a tab stop, you can drag the tab stop marker to a new location on the ruler.

1. Be sure your insertion point is still in the blank paragraph and the tab stops you entered display on the horizontal ruler.
2. Press Tab to move the insertion point to the first tab stop you placed on the ruler. Type Day and then press Tab to move to the right tab with the dot leader that you created.
3. Type Hours and then press Enter. Compare your screen with **Figure 1**.

   When your insertion point is positioned at a right tab stop and you begin to type, the text moves to the left. When you press Enter, the new paragraph displays the same tab stop markers on the ruler as the previous paragraph.
4. Press Tab, type Monday - Wednesday and then press Tab. Type noon to 5 and then press Enter.
5. Press Tab, type Thursday - Friday and then press Tab. Type noon to 8 and then press Enter.
6. Press Tab, type Saturday and then press Tab. Type 11 to 5 and then press Enter.
7. Press Tab, type Sunday and then press Tab. Type Closed and then compare your screen with **Figure 2**.

■ Continue to the next page to complete the skill

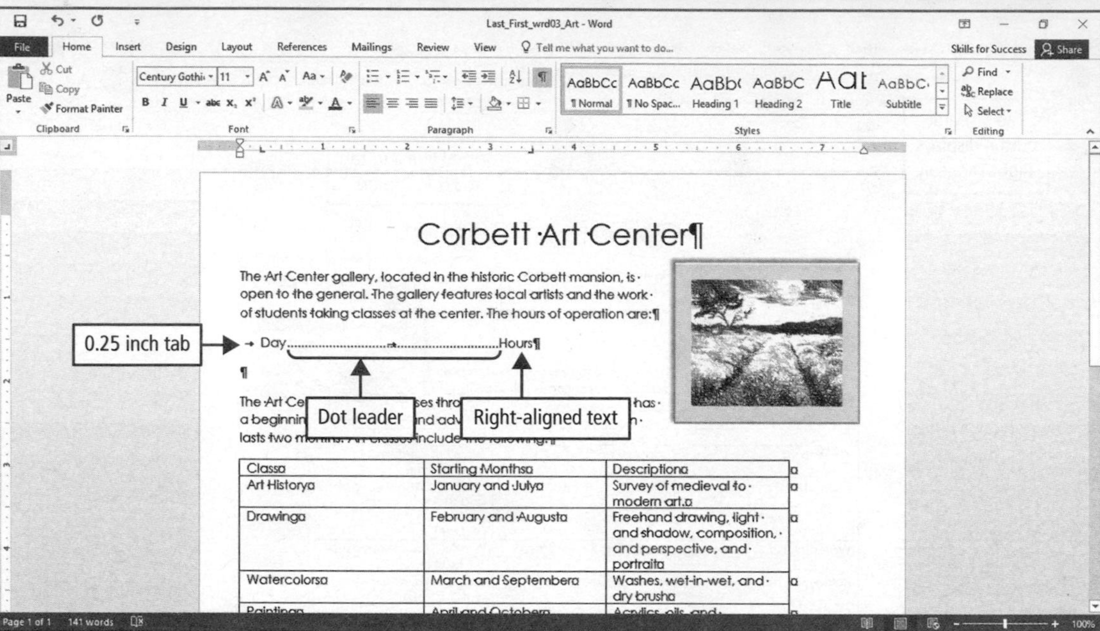

Figure 1

Word 2016, Windows 10, Microsoft Corporation

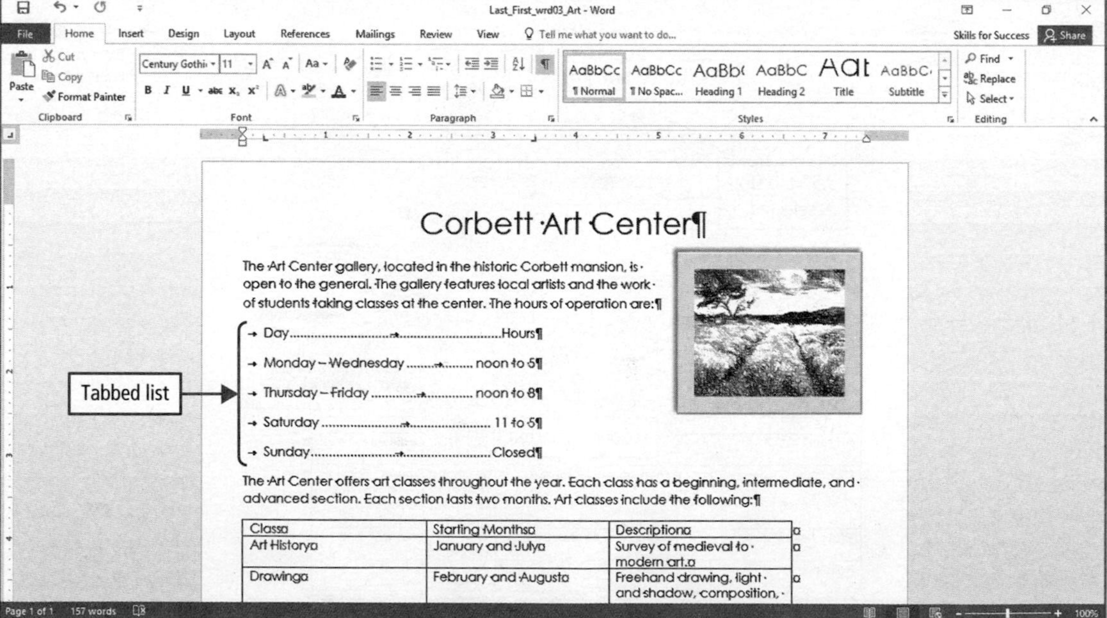

Figure 2

Word 2016, Windows 10, Microsoft Corporation

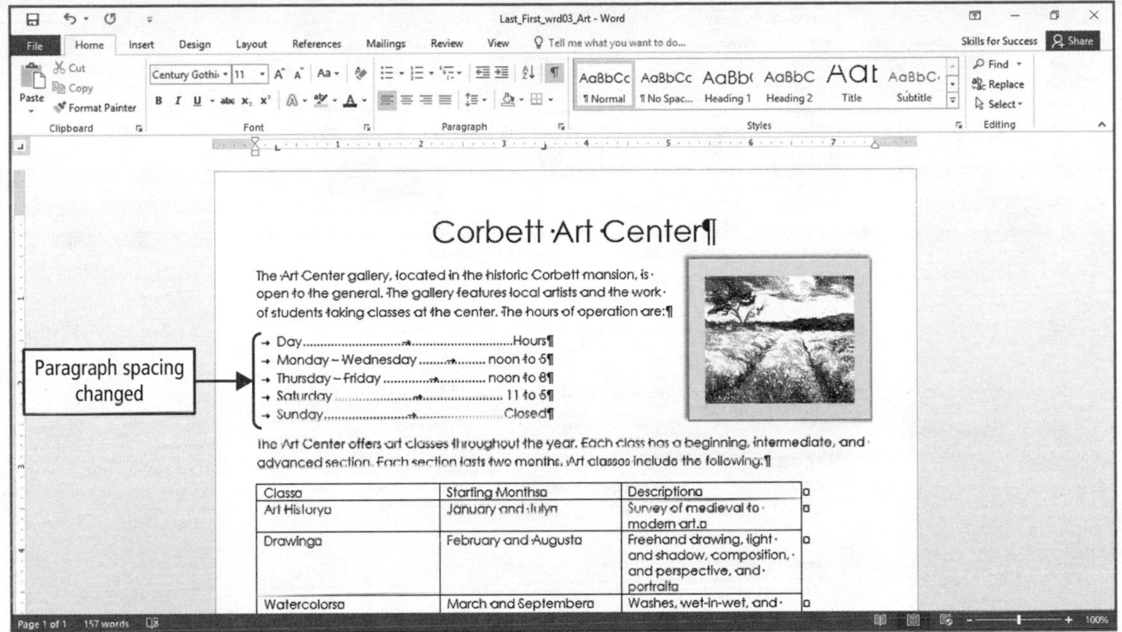

Word 2016, Windows 10, Microsoft Corporation

Figure 3

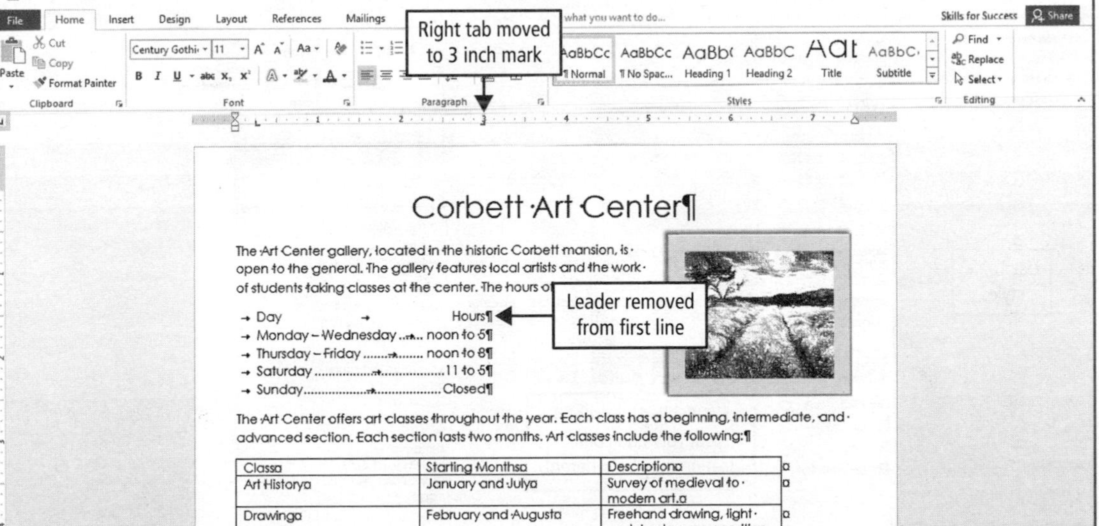

Word 2016, Windows 10, Microsoft Corporation

Figure 4

8. Select the first four paragraphs of the tabbed list starting with *Day* and ending with *11 to 5*. Do not select the paragraph that begins *Sunday*.
9. On the **Home tab**, in the **Paragraph group**, click the **Line Spacing** button, and then click **Remove Space After Paragraph**. Click anywhere in the document to deselect the text, and then compare your screen with **Figure 3**.
10. Select all five lines in the tabbed list. On the horizontal ruler, place the tip of the pointer over the right tab mark at **3.5 inches** on the horizontal ruler. When the ScreenTip *Right Tab* displays, drag left to move the tab mark to **3 inches**.
11. Click in the first line of the tabbed list. On the horizontal ruler, point to the right tab mark again. When the ScreenTip *Right Tab* displays, double-click to open the **Tabs** dialog box.
12. In the **Tabs** dialog box, select the **3"** tab stop, and then under **Leader**, click the **None** option button. Click **OK**, and then compare your screen with **Figure 4**.

    Tabs are added or changed only for the selected paragraphs. Here, the leader is removed only from the first line in the tabbed list.

13. **Save** the file.

■ **You have completed Skill 5 of 10**

SKILL 6: Apply Table Styles

SKILL 3.6

- Because tables can hold text, numbers, or graphics, they are often used to lay out and summarize data.
- You can format each table element individually, or you can apply table styles to the entire table.

1. Scroll as needed to display the entire table.

   A table consists of cells arranged in rows and columns. Here, the table contains seven rows and three columns.

Obj 3.1.4 C

2. Click in any cell in the table to display the Table Tools contextual tabs—Design and Layout. Below Table Tools, click the **Design tab**, and then in the **Table Styles group**, notice that a number of predesigned table styles are available.
3. Point to the fourth style—**Plain Table 3**—to preview the style, as shown in **Figure 1**.
4. In the **Table Styles group**, click the **More** button.
5. In the **Table Styles** gallery, use the vertical scroll bar to scroll to the bottom of the gallery. Under **List Tables**, locate the **List Table 4 - Accent 4** thumbnail, and then point to it, as shown in **Figure 2**.

   Because the width of the Table Styles gallery changes depending on the size of your window, the position of your thumbnails may be different than in the figure.
6. Click one time to apply the **List Table 4 - Accent 4** table style.

   You only need to click in a table to apply a table style. You do not need to select the table first.

■ **Continue to the next page to complete the skill**

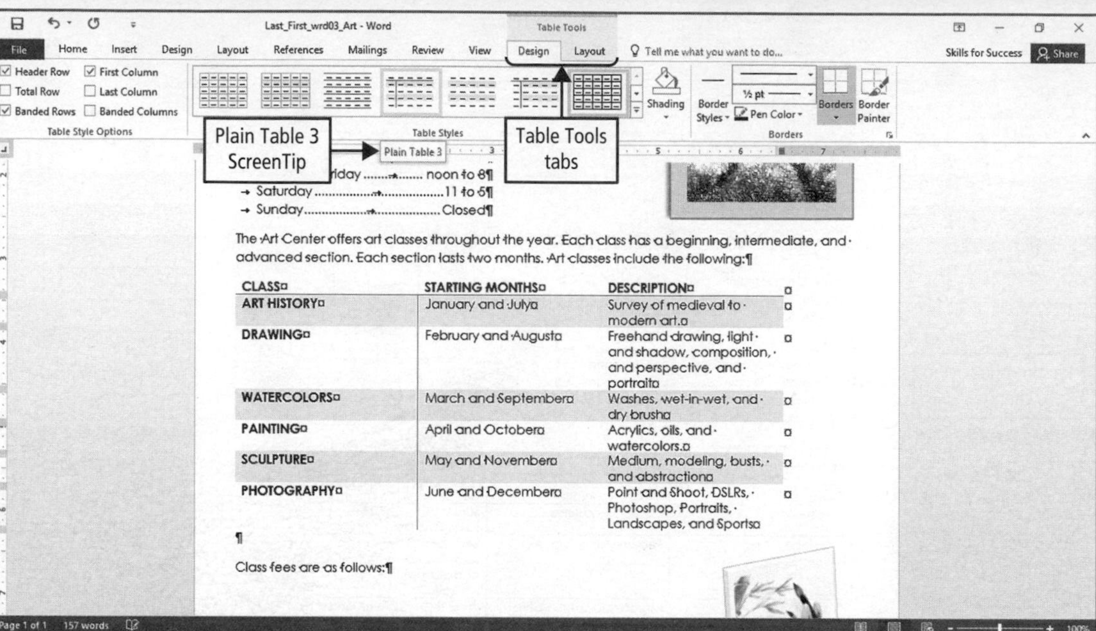

Figure 1

Word 2016, Windows 10, Microsoft Corporation

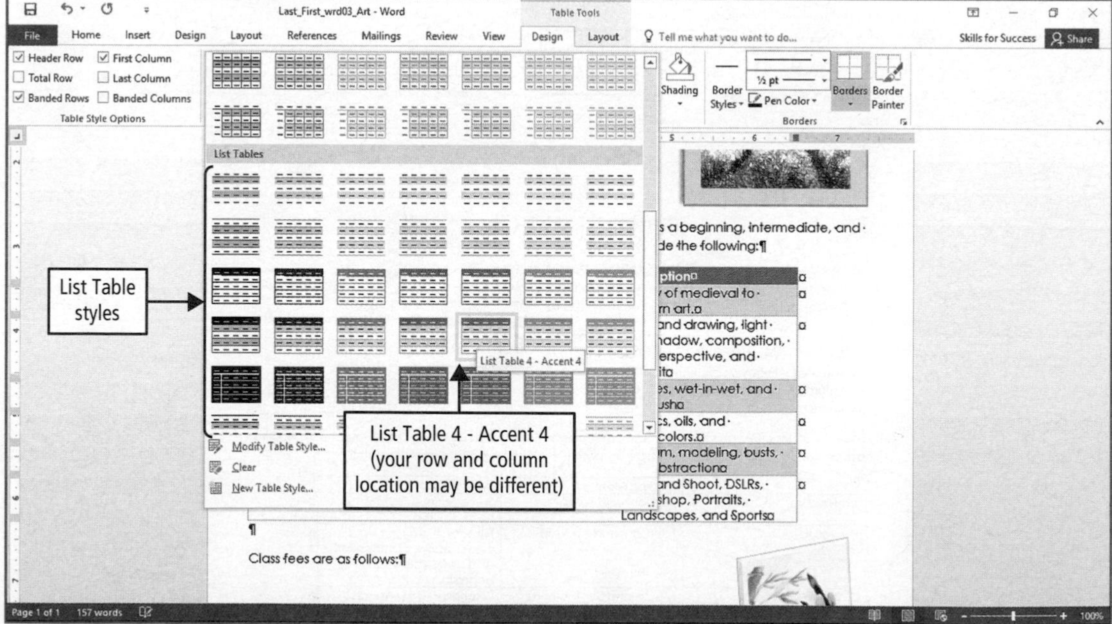

Figure 2

Word 2016, Windows 10, Microsoft Corporation

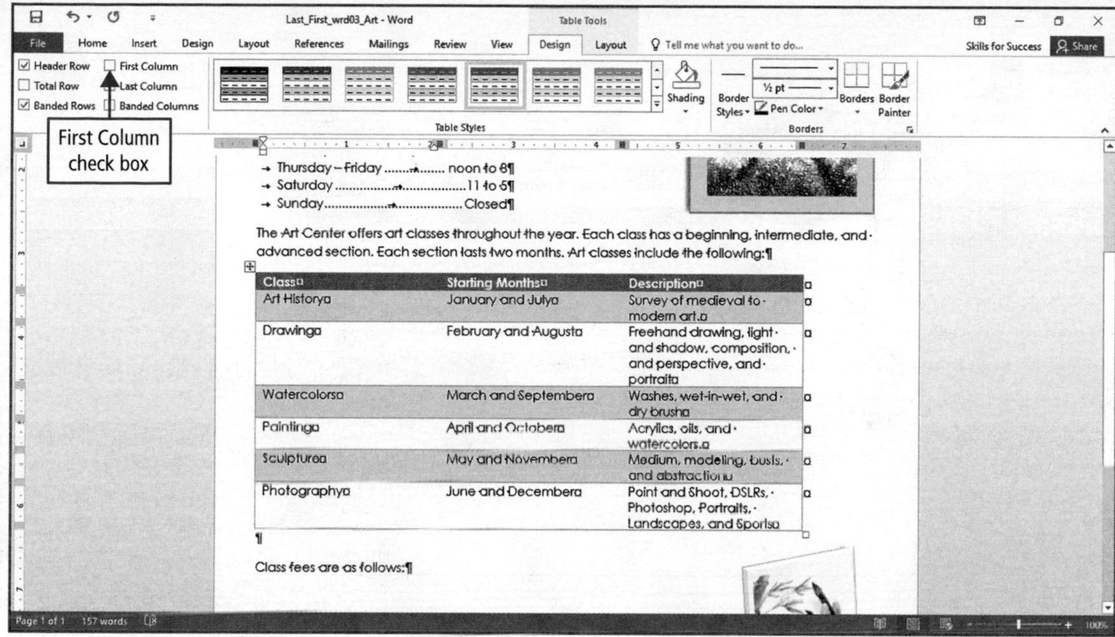

Word 2016, Windows 10, Microsoft Corporation

Figure 3

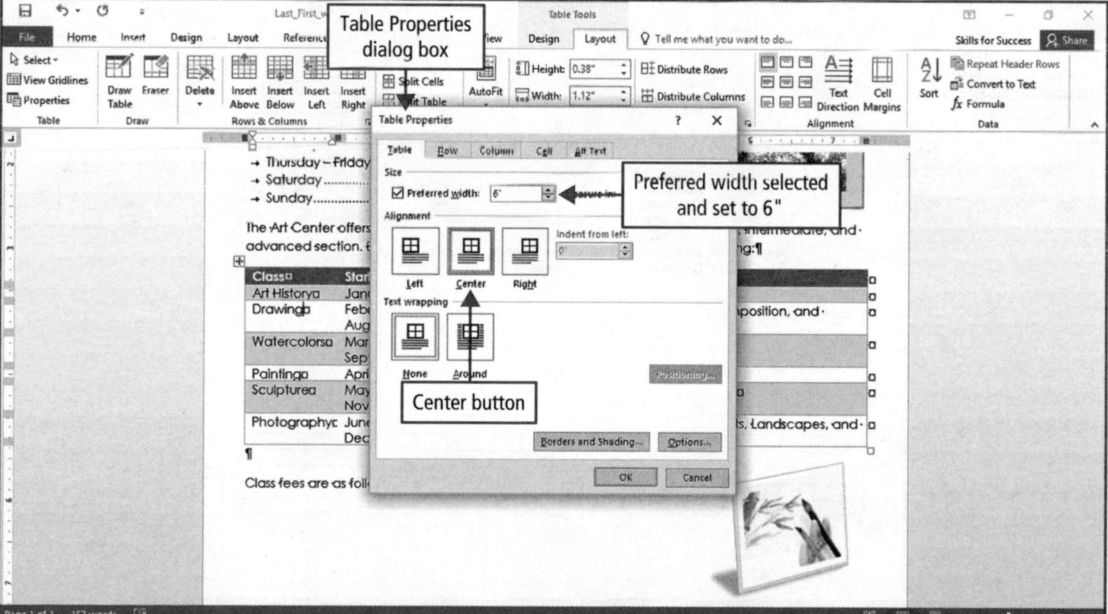

Word 2016, Windows 10, Microsoft Corporation

Figure 4

7. In the **Table Style Options group**, clear the **First Column** check box to remove the bold from the first column, as shown in **Figure 3**.

   In this manner, you can customize how a pre-built table style is applied to a table. Here, the formatting assigned to the first column was disabled.

8. Click the **Table Tools Layout tab**. In the **Cell Size group**, click the **AutoFit** button, and then click **AutoFit Contents**. MOS Obj 3.2.4 C

   The columns, which were all the same width, adjust to the best fit based on the content in the cells.

9. In the **Table group**, click the **Properties** button. In the **Table Properties** dialog box, be sure the **Table tab** is selected. Under **Size**, select the **Preferred width** check box. In the **Preferred width** box, change the existing value to **6"**.

10. In the **Table Properties** dialog box, under **Alignment**, click **Center**. Compare your screen with **Figure 4**, and then click **OK** to set the table width and to center the table between the left and right margins.

11. **Save** the file.

■ **You have completed Skill 6 of 10**

- To create a table using the Insert Table command, you need to specify the number of rows and columns you want to start with.
- A table created with the Insert Table command retains the formatting of the paragraph above the table and the columns are of equal width.

1. Press Ctrl + End, and then press Enter to create a new blank paragraph at the bottom of the document.

Obj 3.1.3 C

2. On the **Insert tab**, in the **Tables group**, click the **Table** button. In the fifth row, point to the second box, and then compare your screen with **Figure 1**.

   The top of the Table gallery displays the dimensions of the table, with the number of columns first, followed by the number of rows—in this instance, you are creating a 2x5 table.

3. Click one time to insert a **2x5 Table**. Scroll as needed to view the table just inserted, and then compare your screen with **Figure 2**.

   Like a graphic, a table is associated with a paragraph. Here, the table's paragraph formatting mark displays below the table.

   When no objects are in the way, an inserted table will extend from the left margin to the right margin. Here, the table wraps below the floating image that is attached to the paragraph above the table.

■ Continue to the next page to complete the skill

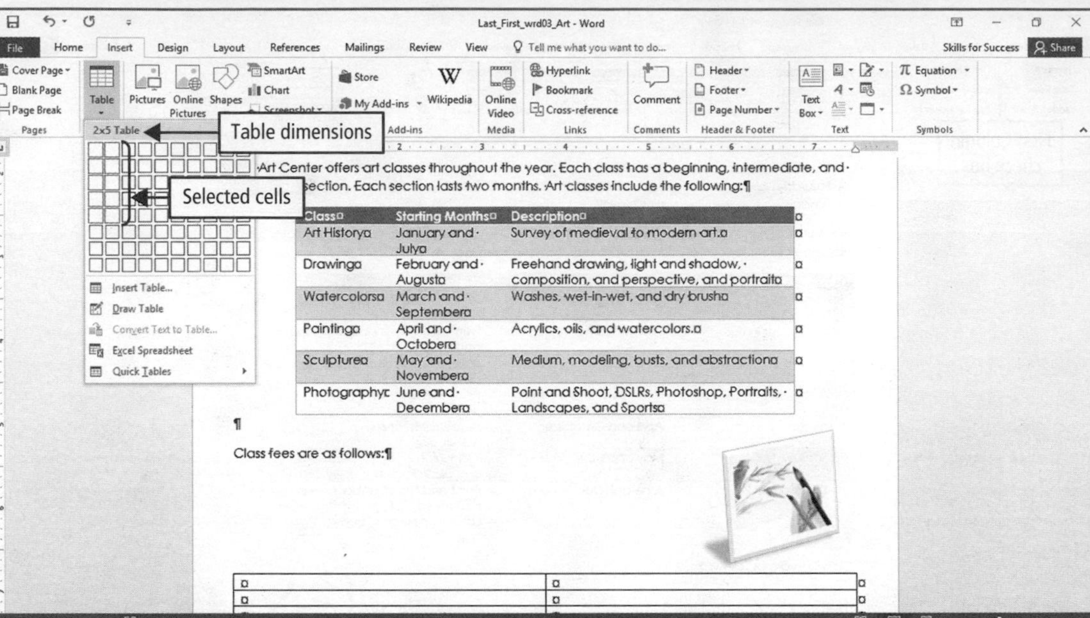

Figure 1

Julian Rovagnati/Fotolia; Word 2016, Windows 10, Microsoft Corporation

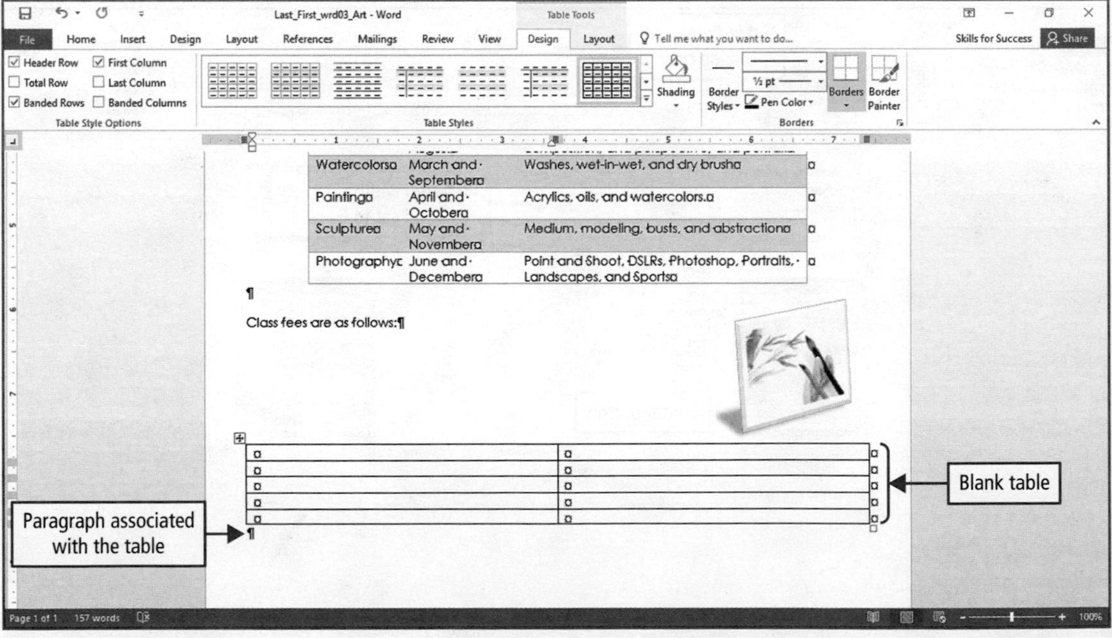

Figure 2

Julian Rovagnati/Fotolia; Word 2016, Windows 10, Microsoft Corporation

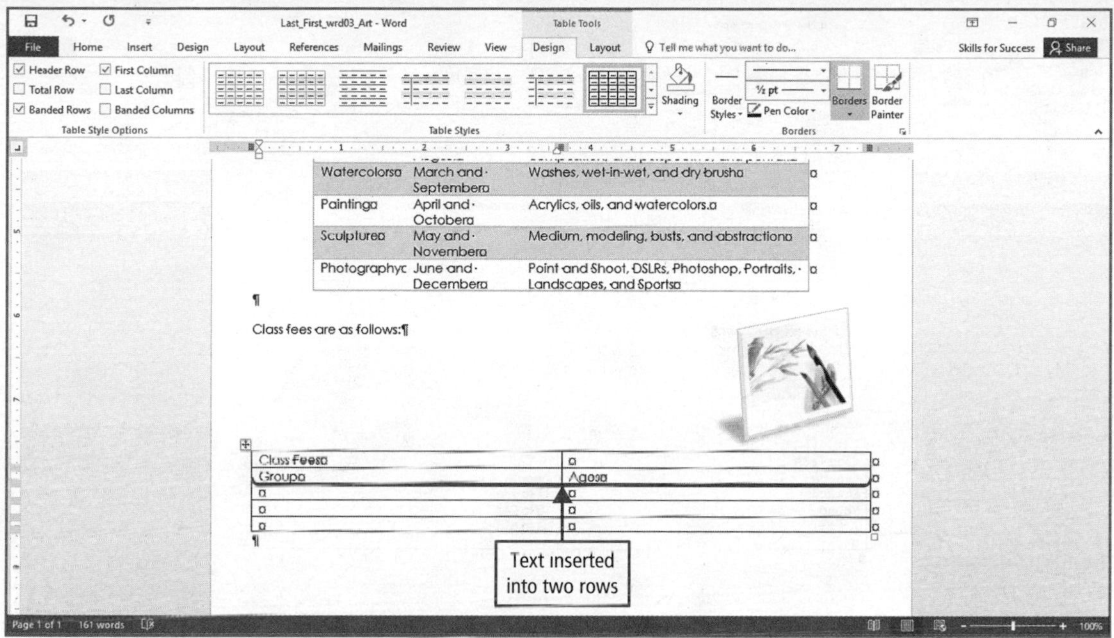

Julian Rovagnati/Fotolia; Word 2016, Windows 10, Microsoft Corporation

Figure 3

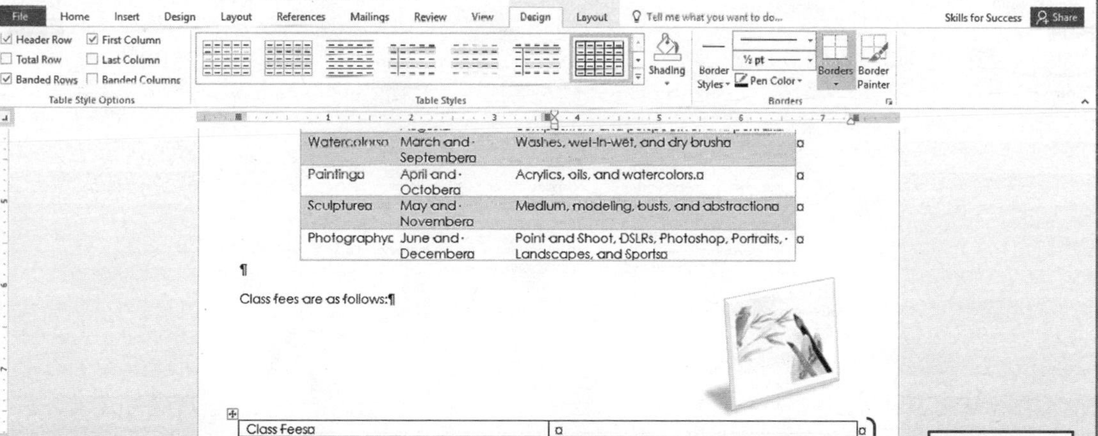

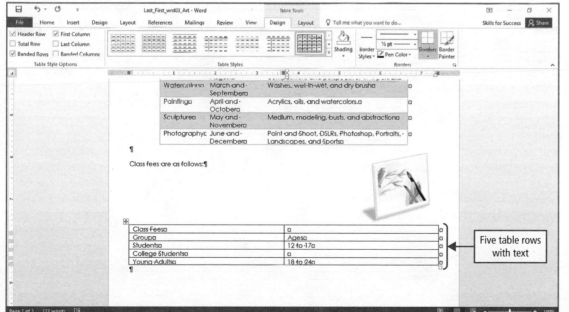

Julian Rovagnati/Fotolia; Word 2016, Windows 10, Microsoft Corporation

Figure 4

4. Be sure the insertion point is located in the upper left cell of the new table. Type Class Fees and then press Tab.

   You can use Tab or the arrow keys to move among cells in a table. When you press Enter, a second line in the same cell is created. If this happens, you can press Backspace to remove the inserted paragraph.

5. Press Tab again to move to the first cell in the second row. Type Group and then press Tab.
6. Type Ages and then press Tab. Compare your screen with **Figure 3**.
7. With the insertion point in the first cell of the third row, type Students and then press Tab. Type 12 to 17 and then press Tab.
8. In the first cell of the fourth row, type College Students and then press ↓.
9. In the first cell of the last row, type Young Adults and then press Tab. Type 18 to 24 and then compare your screen with **Figure 4**.
10. Save the file.

■ **You have completed Skill 7 of 10**

SKILL 8: Delete and Add Table Rows and Columns

- You can add rows to the beginning, middle, or end of a table, and you can delete one or more rows, if necessary.
- You can add columns to the left or right of the column that contains the insertion point.

1. In the fourth row of the table, click anywhere in the *College Students* cell.

   To delete a row, you need only position the insertion point anywhere in the row.

2. On the **Table Tools Layout tab**, in the **Rows & Columns group**, click the **Delete** button, and then click **Delete Rows**. If you accidentally click Delete Columns, on the Quick Access Toolbar, click the Undo button and try again.
3. Right-click the *Young Adults* cell. On the Mini toolbar, click the **Insert** button, and then click **Insert Below** to add a row.
4. Type Adults and then notice that although the entire row was selected when you started typing, the text was entered into the row's first cell. Press Tab, and then type 25 to 59 Press Tab to add a new row, and then compare your screen with **Figure 1**.

   When the insertion point is in the last cell, you can add another row by pressing Tab.

5. In the first cell of the new row, type Seniors and then press Tab. Type 60+ and then compare your screen with **Figure 2**.

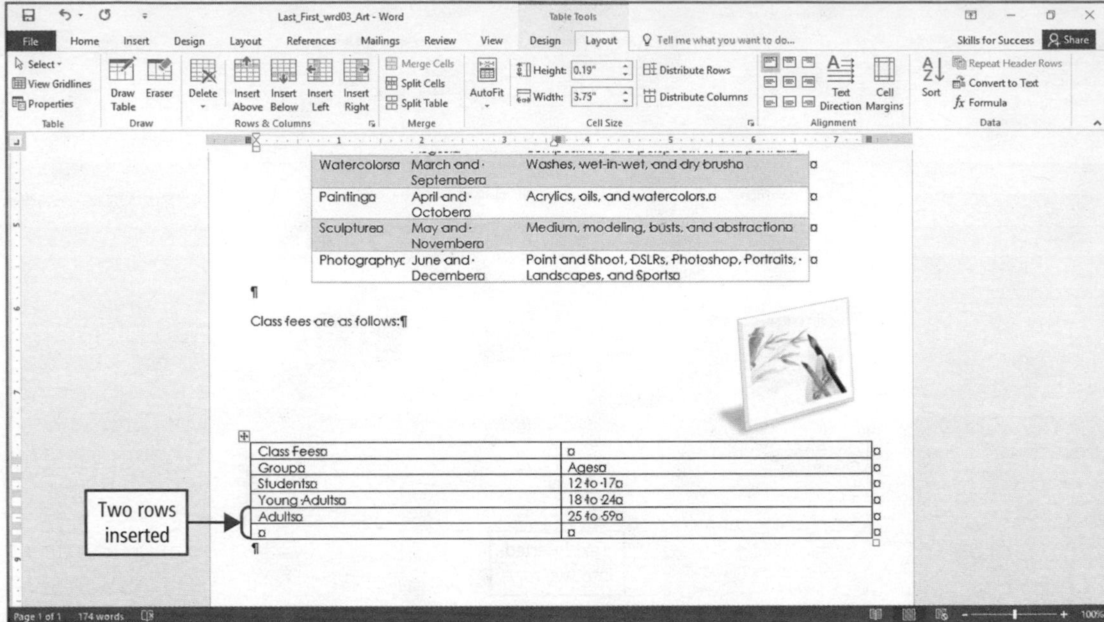

Figure 1 Julian Rovagnati/Fotolia; Word 2016, Windows 10, Microsoft Corporation

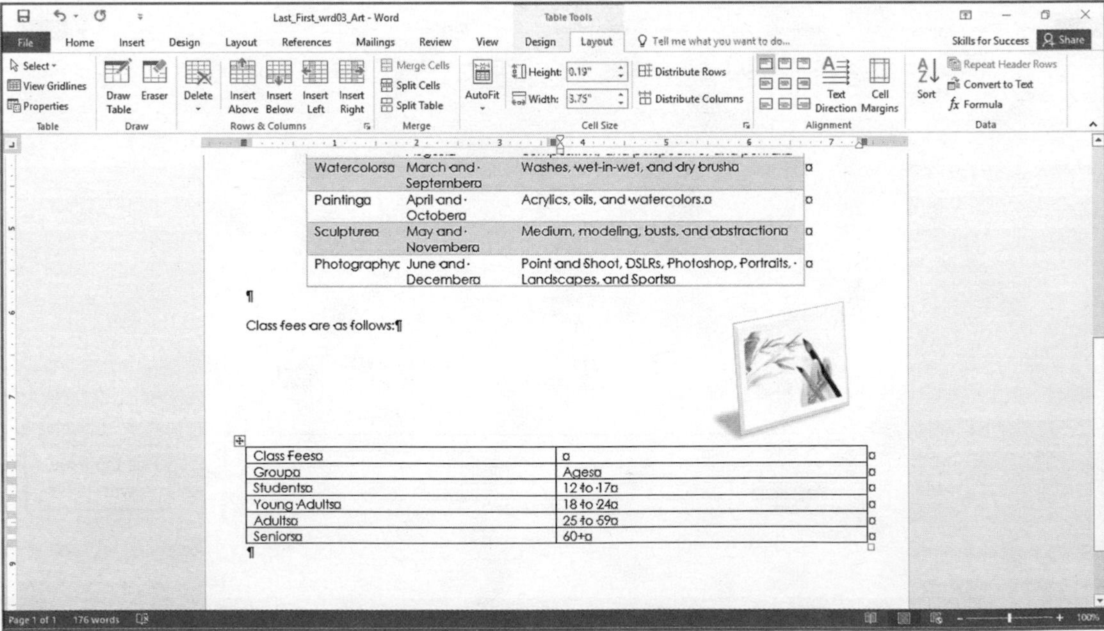

Figure 2 Julian Rovagnati/Fotolia; Word 2016, Windows 10, Microsoft Corporation

■ **Continue to the next page to complete the skill**

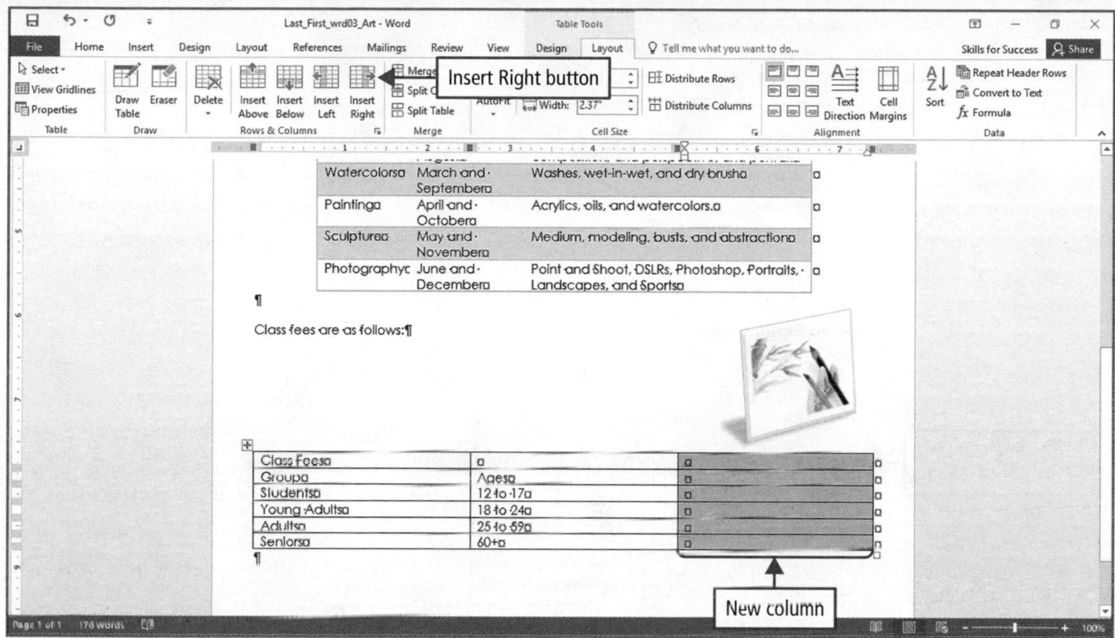

Julian Rovagnati/Fotolia; Word 2016, Windows 10, Microsoft Corporation

Figure 3

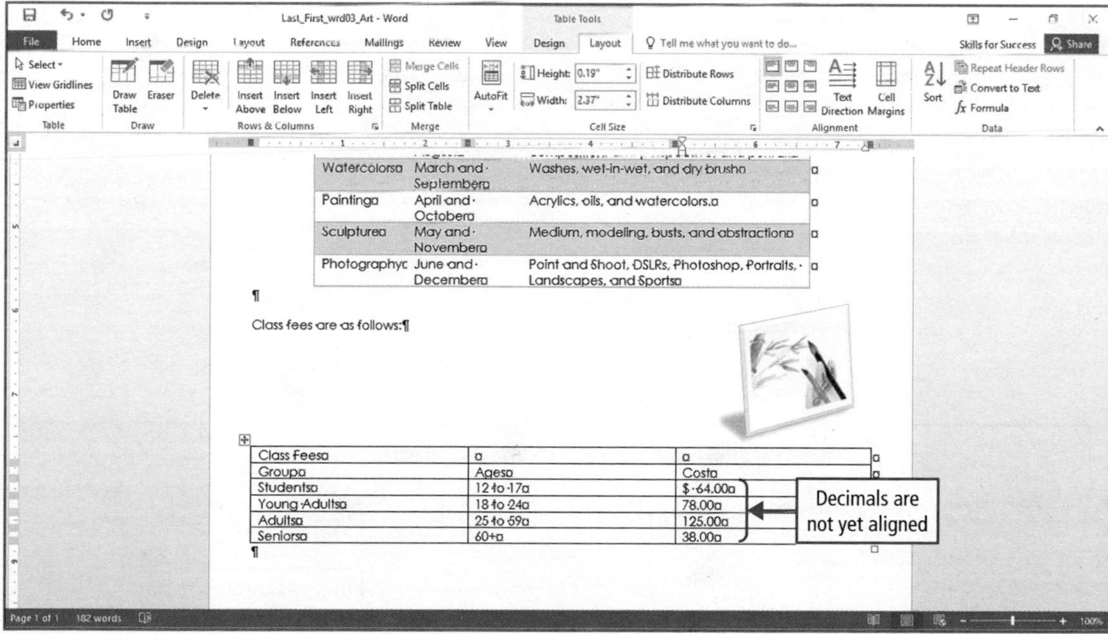

Julian Rovagnati/Fotolia; Word 2016, Windows 10, Microsoft Corporation

Figure 4

6. Be sure the insertion point is positioned in a cell in the second column of the table.
7. On the **Table Tools Layout tab**, in the **Rows & Columns group**, click the **Insert Right** button to insert a new column to the right of the column that contained the insertion point, as shown in **Figure 3**.

   An alternate method to insert rows and columns is to point to a table border and then click the Insert button that displays at the top of the column or beginning of the row. When you insert a new column, the existing columns are resized to fit within the width of the table.

8. In the new column, click in the second row, and then type Cost
9. Press [↓] to move to the next cell in the column, and then type 64.00
10. Press [↓], and then type 78.00 In the next cell down, type 125.00 and in the last cell of the table, type 38.00
11. In the third row, click to position the insertion point to the left of *64.00*. If the entire cell is selected, point closer to the *64.00* and click again. Type $ and then press [SpaceBar] two times. Compare your screen with **Figure 4**.

    A dollar sign is typically added only to the first row in a column of numbers and to the *Totals* row, if there is one. You will align the decimal points in this column in the next skill.

12. **Save** the file.

■ **You have completed Skill 8 of 10**

- Text in a table is formatted using the same techniques as text in paragraphs.
- When you apply paragraph formatting to text in a table, it is applied only to the cell the text is in.

1. Position the pointer in the left margin to the left of the first row of the lower table to display the pointer, and then click one time to select the row.
2. On the **Table Tools Design tab**, in the **Table Styles group**, click the **Shading arrow**, and then in the first row, click the seventh color—**Brown, Accent 3**.
3. With the entire row still selected, change the font size to **12**, and then change the font color to the first color in the first row—**White, Background 1**. Compare your screen with **Figure 1**.
4. Repeat the technique just practiced to select the second row of the table, and then apply the **Center** paragraph alignment.
5. With the second row still selected, change the font color to the eighth choice in the first row—**Olive Green, Accent 4**.
6. Click in the third cell in the third row—*$ 64.00*. Drag down to select the remaining cells in the column, and then apply the **Align Right** paragraph alignment. Compare your screen with **Figure 2**.

   Numbers are typically aligned to the right in table cells.

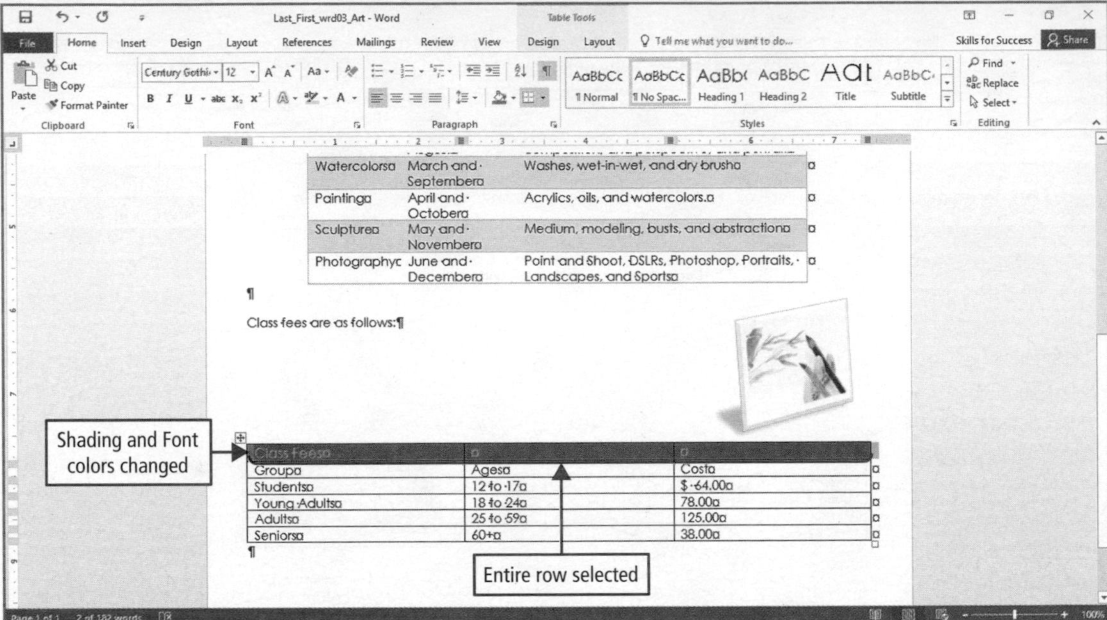

Figure 1 Julian Rovagnati/Fotolia; Word 2016, Windows 10, Microsoft Corporation

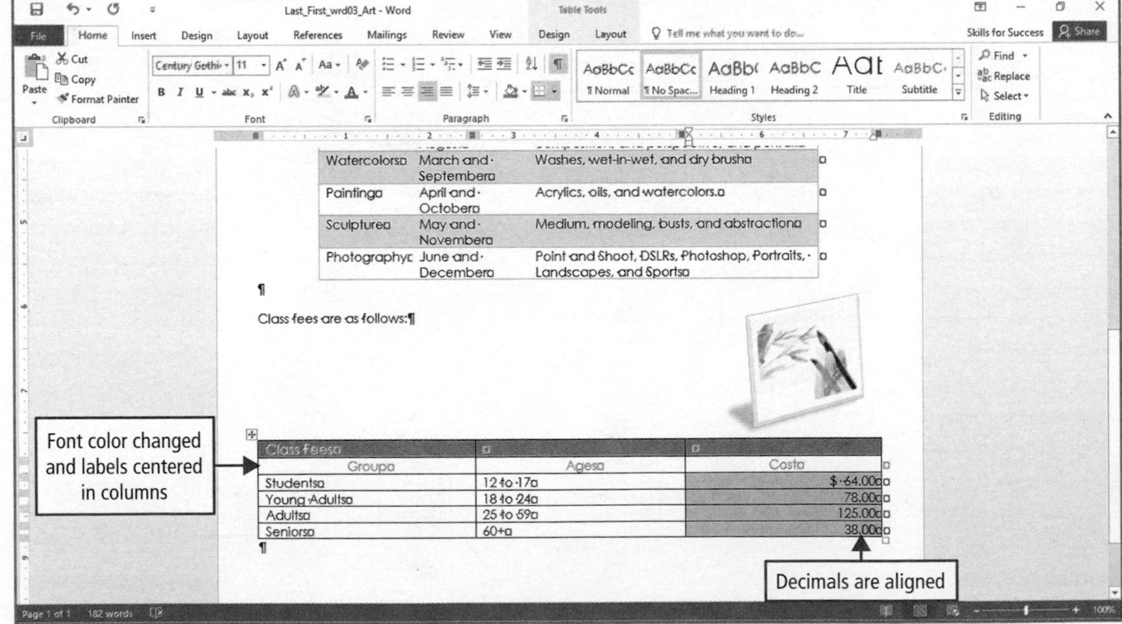

Figure 2 Julian Rovagnati/Fotolia; Word 2016, Windows 10, Microsoft Corporation

■ Continue to the next page to complete the skill

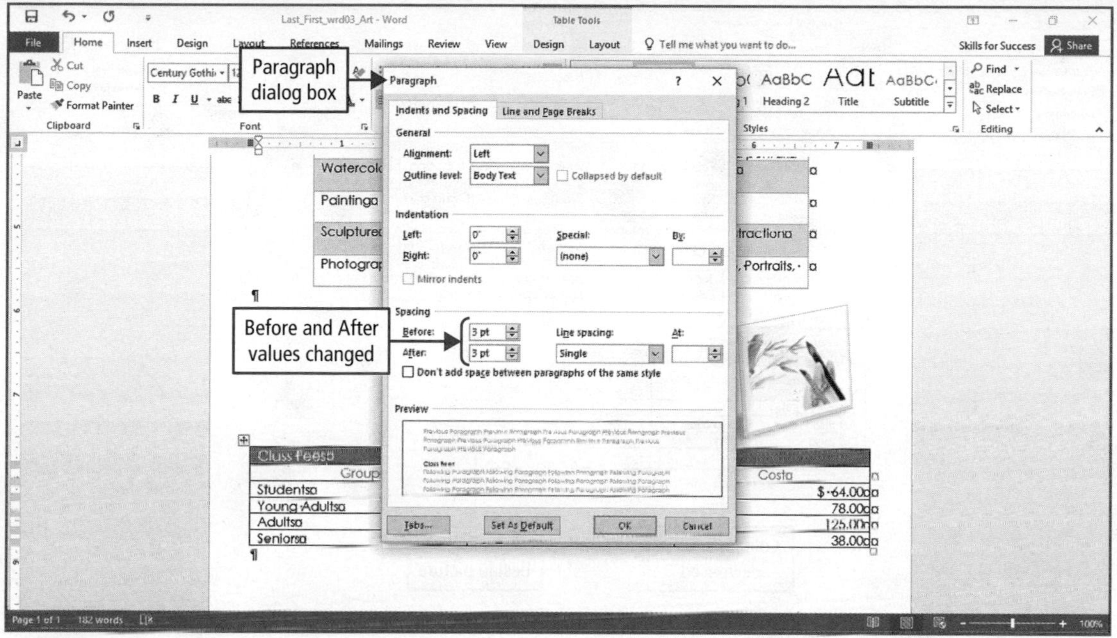

Word 2016, Windows 10, Microsoft Corporation

Figure 3

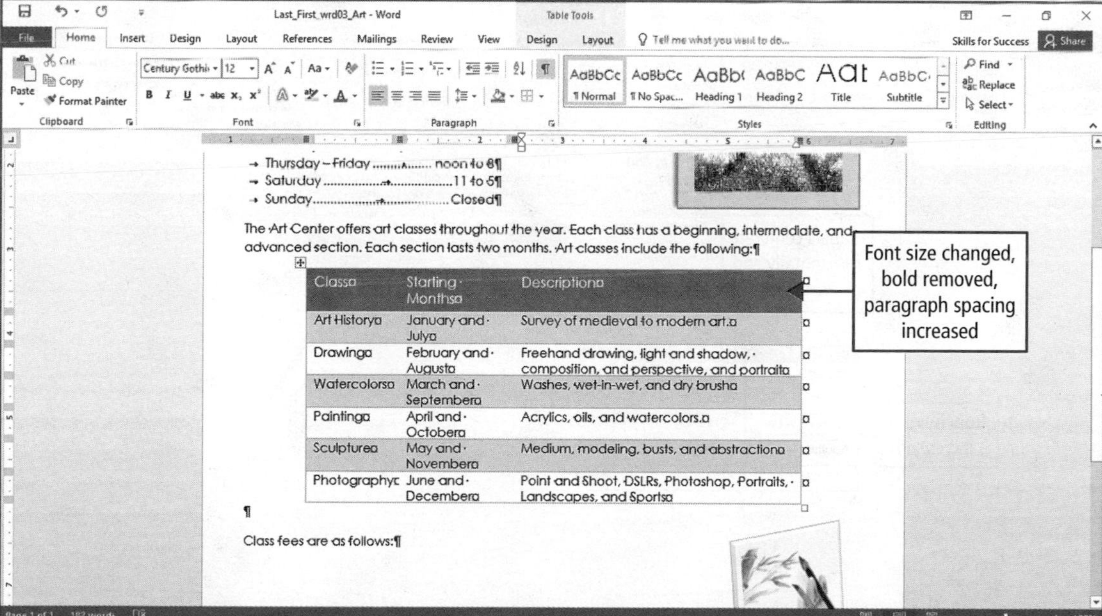

Word 2016, Windows 10, Microsoft Corporation

Figure 4

7. Click in the first cell—*Class Fees*. On the **Home tab**, in the **Paragraph group**, click the **Paragraph Dialog Box Launcher** . In the **Paragraph** dialog box, under **Spacing**, select the text in the **Before** box, and then type 3 pt Change the **After** value to 3 pt and then compare your screen with **Figure 3**.

   When you type numbers into the Before and After boxes without providing a unit of measure, the points unit will automatically be applied.

8. Click **OK** to accept the change and close the dialog box.
9. Scroll up to view the first table, select the first row, and then change the font size to **12**. Click the **Bold** button **B** to remove the bold, and then set the paragraph spacing **Before** and **After** to 3 pt
10. Click in another cell to deselect the row, and then compare your screen with **Figure 4**.
11. **Save** the file.

You have completed Skill 9 of 10

- To improve a table's readability, you can merge cells, change column widths, remove borders, and align text vertically.
- In a table, ***vertical alignment*** determines the space above and below a text or object in relation to the top and bottom of the cell.

1. In the upper table, click in any cell in the middle column. On the **Table Tools Layout tab**, in the **Cell Size group**, click the **Width up spin arrow** as needed to widen the middle column to **1.6"**.
2. In the lower table, repeat the technique just practiced to change the first column's width to **1.5"**, the second column's width to **1.2"**, and the third column's width to **0.8"**.

Obj 3.2.3 C

3. In the lower table, select the first row. On the **Layout tab**, in the **Merge group**, click the **Merge Cells** button.
4. On the **Layout tab**, in the **Alignment group**, click the **Align Top Center** button. Click to deselect the row, and then compare your screen with **Figure 1**.
5. In the lower table, point to the second row, and then with the pointer, drag down to select rows two through six. In the **Cell Size group**, change the **Height** value to **0.3"**.
6. Select the second row, and then in the **Alignment group**, click the **Align Center** button. Compare your screen with **Figure 2**.
7. In the first column of the lower table, select the four cells starting with *Students* and ending with *Seniors*. In the **Alignment group**, click the **Align Center Left** button.

■ **Continue to the next page to complete the skill**

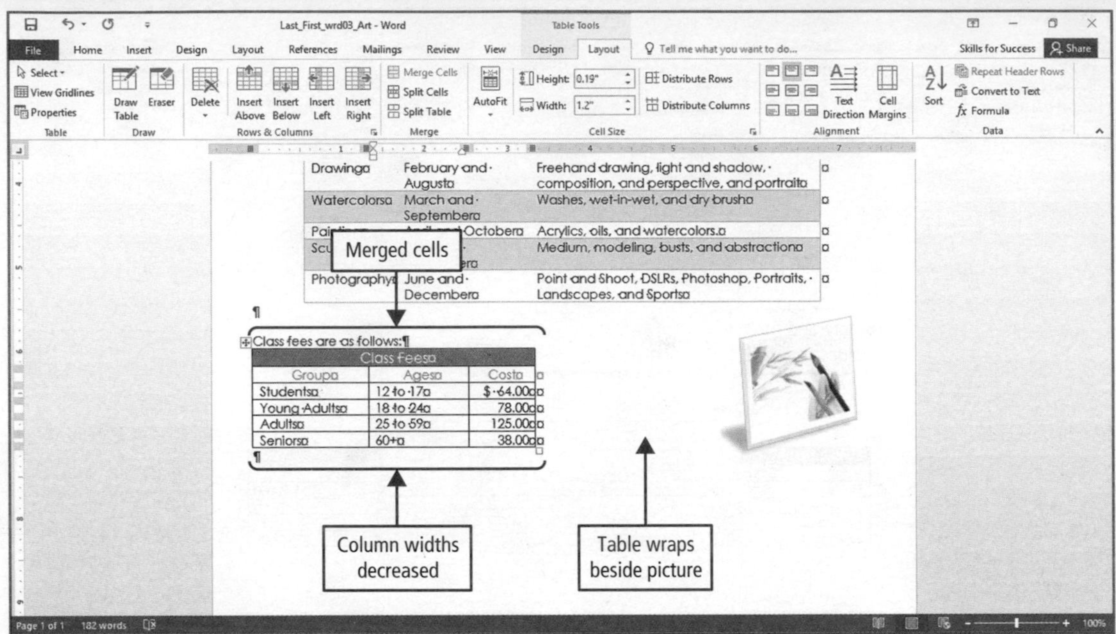

Figure 1 Julian Rovagnati/Fotolia; Word 2016, Windows 10, Microsoft Corporation

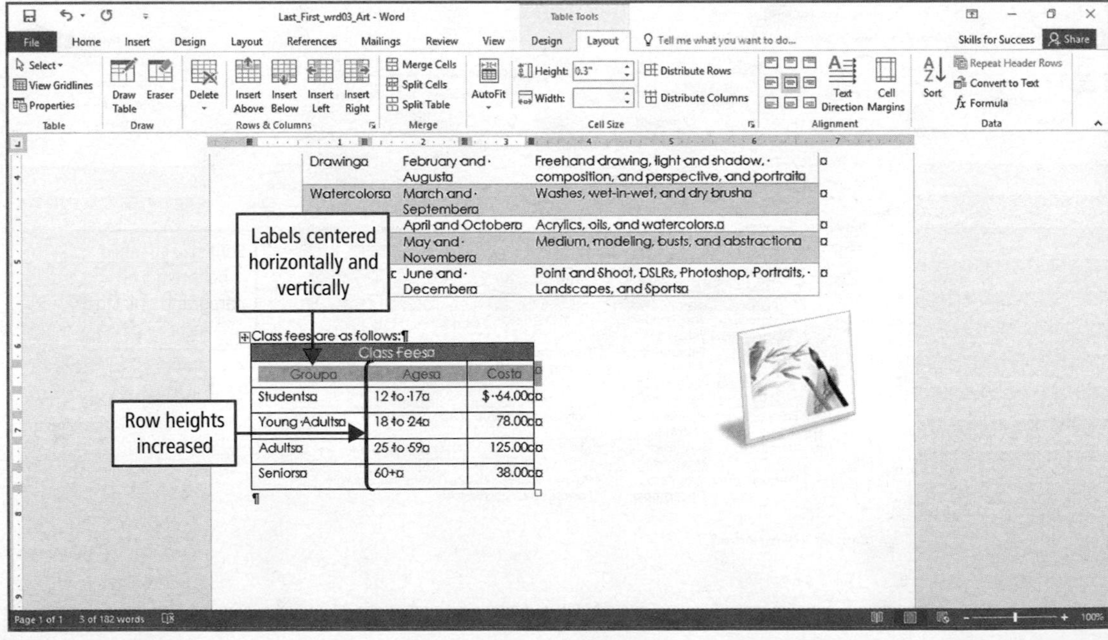

Figure 2 Julian Rovagnati/Fotolia; Word 2016, Windows 10, Microsoft Corporation

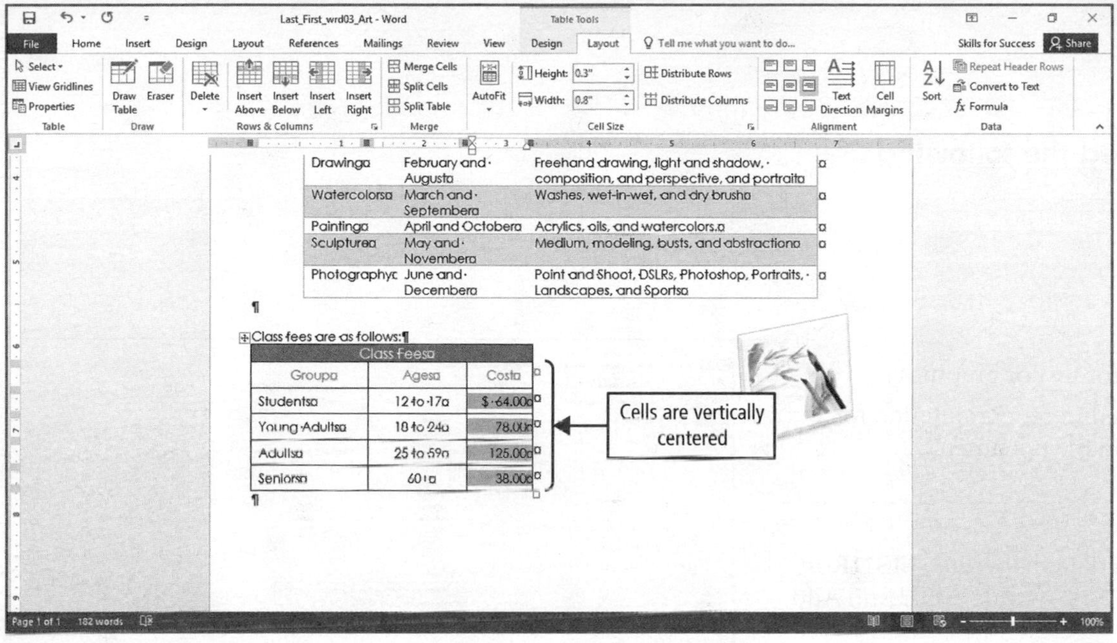

Julian Rovagnati/Fotolia; Word 2016, Windows 10, Microsoft Corporation

Figure 3

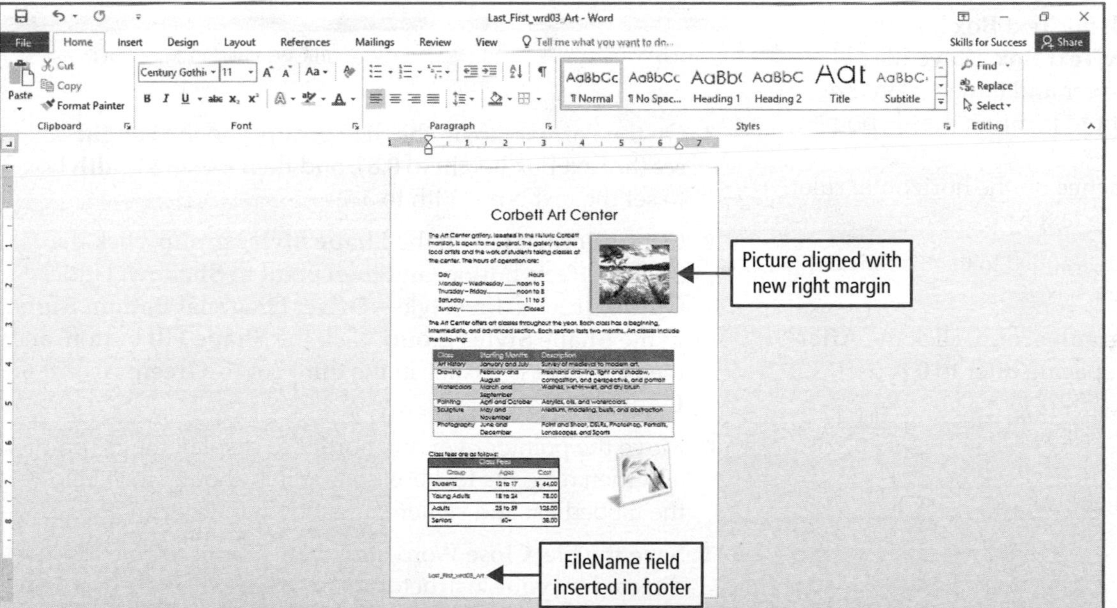

Word 2016, Windows 10, Microsoft Corporation

Figure 4

8. In the second column, select the cells starting with *12 to 17* and ending with *60+*. In the **Alignment group**, click the **Align Center** button.
9. In the third column, select the cells starting with *$ 64.00* and ending with *38.00*. In the **Alignment group**, click the **Align Center Right** button. Compare your screen with **Figure 3**.
10. Above and to the left of the lower table, click the **Table Selector** button to select the table.
11. On the **Table Tools Design tab**, in the **Borders group**, click the **Borders arrow**, and then notice that several types of borders are selected in the gallery.
12. In the **Border** gallery, click **Inside Vertical Border** to remove the border from the table. Click a cell to deselect the table, and then click the **Show/Hide** button to hide the formatting marks.
13. On the **View tab**, in the **Zoom group**, click **One Page**.
14. On the **Layout tab**, in the **Page Setup group**, click **Margins**, and then click **Normal** to increase the margin widths. Using the Alignment Guides, align the first picture with the right margin and the top of the first body paragraph.
15. Add the FileName field to the footer, deactivate the footer area, and then compare your screen with **Figure 4**.
16. **Save** the file, **Close** Word, and then submit the file as directed by your instructor.

DONE! You have completed Skill 10 of 10 and your document is complete!

More Skills 11

Insert Text Boxes

To complete this project, you will need the following file:

- wrd03_MS11Run

You will save your file as:

- Last_First_wrd03_MS11Run

- A ***text box*** is a movable, resizable container for text or graphics.
- Text boxes are useful because they can give a different orientation for document text and can be placed anywhere in the document.

---

1. Start **Word 2016**, and then open the student data file **wrd03_MS11Run**. **Save** the file in your chapter folder as Last_First_wrd03_MS11Run Add the **FileName** field to the footer.
2. Press Ctrl + End to move to the bottom of the document. If your rulers do not display, on the View tab, in the Show group, select the Ruler check box.

Obj 5.1.4 C

3. Click the **Insert tab**. In the **Text group**, click the **Text Box** button, and then below the **Text Box** gallery, click **Draw Text Box**. Move the [+] pointer to about **7.5 inches** on the vertical ruler and **0 inches** on the horizontal ruler. Drag down and to the right to position the [+] pointer at approximately **8.25 inches** on the vertical ruler and **3.25 inches** on the horizontal ruler, and then release the mouse button to insert a text box.

   A text box is inserted, a Format contextual tab is added to the Ribbon, and the insertion point displays inside the new text box.

4. Click the **Layout tab**, and then in the **Paragraph group**, click the **After down spin arrow** two times to change the spacing after to **0 pt**.
5. Type the following three paragraphs in the text box, pressing Enter following the first two paragraphs.

   Your registration must be received by April 25.
   The faster waves fill up very quickly.
   Register online at 10k.aspenfalls.org.

6. In the text box, select all three paragraphs of text, and then on the **Home tab**, in the **Paragraph group**, click the **Bullets** button. In the **Paragraph group**, click the **Decrease Indent** button.

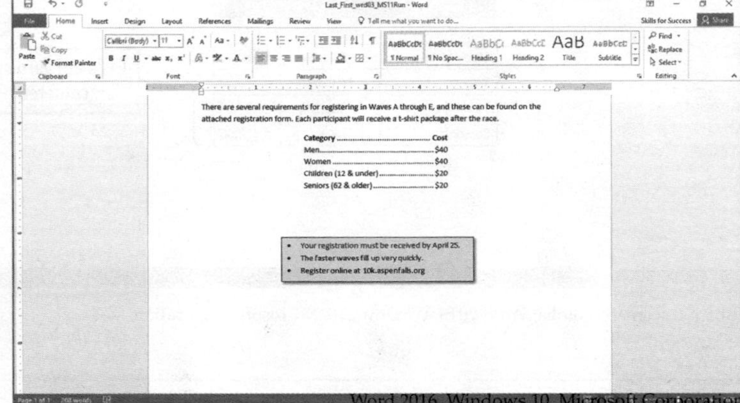

Figure 1 Word 2016, Windows 10, Microsoft Corporation

7. On the **Format tab**, in the **Size group**, use the **Height** box to set the text box height to **0.8"**, and then use the **Width** box to set the text box width to **3.5"**.
8. On the **Format tab**, in the **Shape Styles group**, click the **Shape Effects** button, and then point to **Shadow**. Under **Outer**, click the first style—**Offset Diagonal Bottom Right**. In the **Shape Styles group**, click the **Shape Fill** button, and then click the last color in the third row—**Green, Accent 6, Lighter 60%**.
9. Move the pointer over any border to display the [move] pointer, and then drag the text box so that it is about 1 inch below the tabbed list and centered as shown in **Figure 1**.
10. **Save** the file, **Close** Word, and then submit the file as directed by your instructor.

- **You have completed More Skills 11**

More Skills 12

Format with WordArt

To complete this project, you will need the following file:

- wrd03_MS12Spring

You will save your file as:

- Last_First_wrd03_MS12Spring

- ***WordArt*** is a set of graphic text styles that can be used to make text look like a graphic.
- WordArt is typically used only for titles or subheadings in informal documents such as flyers or posters.

---

1. Start **Word 2016**, and then open the student data file **wrd03_MS12Spring**. **Save** the file in your chapter folder as Last_First_wrd03_MS12Spring Add the **FileName** field to the footer, and then if necessary, display the formatting marks.
2. Select the title paragraph—*Aspen Falls Cleanup Day*—including the paragraph mark at the end of the paragraph.
3. Click the **Insert tab**. In the **Text group**, click the **WordArt** button, and then click the second style in the second row—**Gradient Fill - Blue, Accent 1, Reflection**. MOS Obj 2.2.7 C

   The effect is applied to the selected text. The text has sizing handles and is surrounded by a border in the same manner as a picture or other graphic object. Square text wrapping is also applied.
4. With the WordArt still selected, on the **Format tab**, in the **Size group**, click the **Width up spin arrow** to change the width to **6.2"**.
5. With the WordArt still selected, on the **Format tab**, in the **WordArt Styles group**, click the **Text Fill arrow** [A ▾], and then click the last color in the first row—**Green, Accent 6**. Deselect the WordArt, and then compare your screen with **Figure 1**.
6. **Save** the file, **Close** Word, and then submit the file as directed by your instructor.

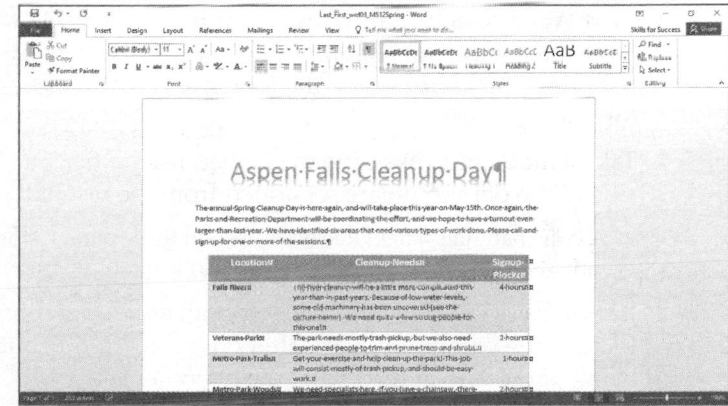

Word 2016, Windows 10, Microsoft Corporation **Figure 1**

■ **You have completed More Skills 12**

More Skills 13

Convert Text into Tables

To complete this project, you will need the following file:

- wrd03_MS13Tours

You will save your file as:

- Last_First_wrd03_MS13Tours

▸ Any text can be converted into a table. If the columns in each paragraph are separated by a ***separator character***—a character such a tab or comma designated as the character to separate columns of unformatted text—you can convert the text into a table with multiple columns.

---

1. Start **Word 2016**, and then open the student data file **wrd03_MS13Tours**. **Save** the file in your chapter folder as Last_First_wrd03_MS13Tours Add the **FileName** field to the footer, and then if necessary, display the formatting marks.
2. Take a moment to examine the tabbed list. Notice that the items on the left side of the paragraph are separated from the rest of the paragraph by tabs.

   A large hanging indent has been used in these paragraphs; however, hanging indents are not necessary to change text to a table.
3. Beginning with *Bird Watching*, select all six paragraphs in the tabbed list. Include the paragraph mark after *great for pictures!*, but do not include the blank paragraph at the end of the document.

Obj 3.1.1 C

4. Click the **Insert tab**. In the **Tables group**, click the **Table** button, and then click **Convert Text to Table**.
5. In the **Convert Text to Table** dialog box, be sure the **Number of columns** is set at **2**. Under **AutoFit behavior**, select the **AutoFit to contents** option button. Under **Separate text at**, verify the **Tabs** option button is selected.

   Because a tab separates the first and second columns in this list, it can be used as the separator character to designate in which table column each item should be placed.
6. At the bottom of the **Convert Text to Table** dialog box, click **OK** to convert the text into a table.
7. On the **Table Tools Layout tab**, in the **Table group**, click the **Properties** button. In the **Table Properties** dialog box, on the **Table tab**, select the **Preferred width** check box, and then in the **Preferred width** text box, type 6.5

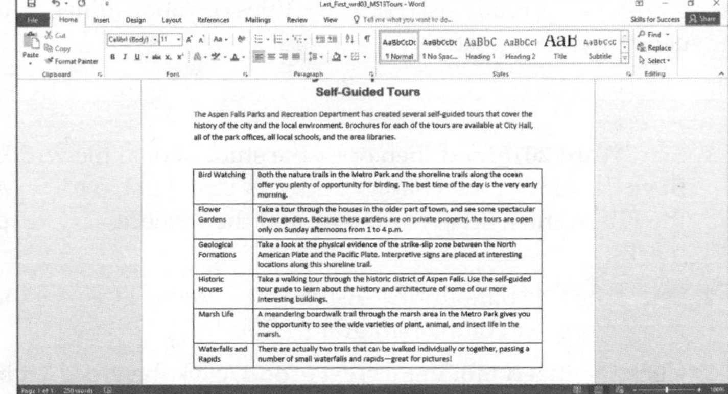

Figure 1 Word 2016, Windows 10, Microsoft Corporation

8. Under **Alignment**, in the **Indent from left** box, select the existing value, and then type 0 to remove the hanging indent formatting used by the tabbed list.
9. In the **Table Properties** dialog box, click **OK**. Click anywhere in the document to deselect the table, and then hide the formatting marks. Compare your screen with **Figure 1**.
10. **Save** the file, **Close** Word, and then submit the file as directed by your instructor.

- **You have completed More Skills 13**

More Skills 14

Insert Drop Caps

To complete this project, you will need the following file:

- wrd03_MS14Times

You will save your file as:

- Last_First_wrd03_MS14Times

- A ***drop cap*** is the first letter (or letters) of a paragraph, enlarged and either embedded in the text or placed in the left margin.
- A drop cap gives a document a professional look but should be used only one time in any document.

---

1. Start **Word 2016**, and then open the student data file **wrd03_MS14Times**. **Save** the file in your chapter folder as Last_First_wrd03_MS14Times Add the **FileName** field to the footer.
2. In the paragraph that begins *The Aspen Falls*, click to the left of *T*—the first letter of the paragraph.
3. Click the **Insert tab**. In the **Text group**, click the **Drop Cap** button, and then point to **In margin** to view the Live Preview of the letter enlarged and positioned in the margin.
4. In the **Drop Cap** gallery, click **Dropped** to position the drop cap in the text of the first paragraph.
5. With the drop cap still selected, in the **Text group**, click the **Drop Cap** button, and then click **Drop Cap Options**.
6. In the **Drop Cap** dialog box, under **Options**, click the **Font arrow**. Scroll down and click **Arial Rounded MT Bold**, and then click **OK**.
7. With the drop cap still selected, click the **Home tab**. In the **Font group**, click the **Text Effects** button. In the second row, click the second effect—**Gradient Fill - Tan, Accent 1, Reflection**.
8. Click anywhere in the document, and then if necessary, hide the formatting marks. Compare your screen with **Figure 1**.

   A drop cap can be formatted as text even though it is treated as a floating graphic.
9. **Save** the file, **Close** Word, and then submit the file as directed by your instructor.

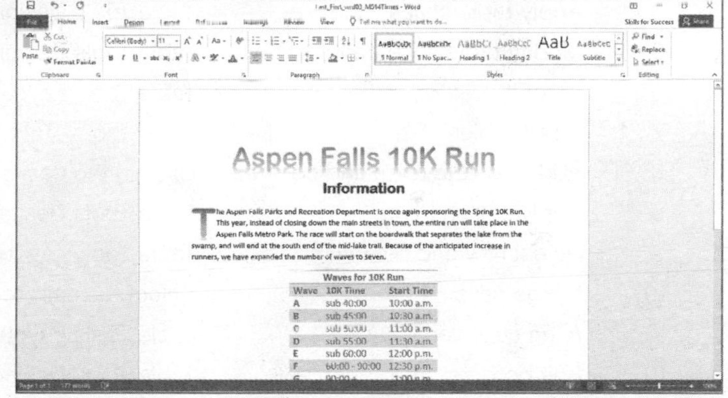

Word 2016, Windows 10, Microsoft Corporation

Figure 1

- **You have completed More Skills 14**

The following table summarizes the **SKILLS AND PROCEDURES** covered in this chapter.

Skills Number	Task	Step	Icon
1	Insert pictures	Insert tab → Illustrations group → Pictures	
1	Insert text from files	Insert tab → Text group → Object arrow, and click Text from File	
2	Resize pictures	Drag the corner resizing handles, or Format tab → Size group commands	
2	Reset pictures	Format tab → Adjust group → Reset Picture	
2	Float pictures	Select picture → Layout Options button → Square	
3	Set picture styles	Format tab → Picture Styles group commands	
3	Set artistic effects	Format tab → Adjust group → Artistic Effects	
4	Set tab stops	Click the Tab Selector to pick the desired tab, and then click the ruler at the desired location	
4	Add leaders to tabs	Home → Paragraph → Paragraph Dialog Box Launcher → Tabs button In the Tabs dialog box, select the desired tab, and then select the desired Leader option.	
6	Apply table styles	Table Tools Design tab → Table Styles group commands	
6	Modify table style options	Table Tools Design tab → select or clear Table Style Options group check boxes	
6	AutoFit cells	Table Tools Layout tab → Cell Size group → AutoFit	
7	Insert tables	Insert tab → Tables group → Table button → select the desired dimensions	
8	Add or delete rows and columns	Click in the desired cell → Mini toolbar Insert button	
9	Apply cell shading	Table Tools Design tab → Table Styles group → Shading	
9	Adjust row and column sizes	Table Tools Layout tab → Cell Size group commands	
10	Merge cells	Select the cells to be merged, and then Table Tools Layout tab → Merge group → Merge Cells	
10	Align cells vertically	Table Tools Layout tab → Alignment group commands	
10	Edit borders	Table Tools Design tab → Borders group → Borders	
MS11	Draw text box	Insert tab → Text group → Text Box button → Draw Text Box	
MS11	Apply shape effects to text box	Format tab → Shape Styles group → Shape Effects button → select the desired effect	
MS12	Insert WordArt	Insert tab → Text group → WordArt button → select the desired style	WordArt
MS12	Apply style to WordArt	Format tab → WordArt Styles group → select the desired style	
MS13	Convert text to table	Select the text to be converted, and then Insert tab → Tables group → Table button → Convert Text to Table	
MS13	Apply table properties	Table Tools Layout tab → Table group → Properties button	
MS14	Insert drop cap	Insert tab → Text group → Drop Cap button	
MS14	Apply drop cap format	Insert tab → Text group → Drop Cap button → Drop Cap Options	

Project Summary Chart		
Project	**Project Type**	**Project Location**
Skills Review	Review	In Book & MIL MyITLab® Grader
Skills Assessment 1	Review	In Book & MIL MyITLab® Grader
Skills Assessment 2	Review	Book
My Skills	Problem Solving	Book
Visual Skills Check	Problem Solving	Book
Skillls Challenge 1	Critical Thinking	Book
Skills Challenge 2	Critical Thinking	Book
More Skills Assessment	Review	In Book & MIL MyITLab® Grader
Collaborating with Google	Critical Thinking	Book

MOS Objectives Covered	
1.1.4 C Insert text from a file or external source	5.1.2 C Insert pictures
1.3.2 C Apply document themes	5.1.4 C Insert text boxes
2.2.7 C Change text to WordArt	5.2.1 C Apply artistic effects
3.1.1 C Convert text to tables	5.2.2 C Apply picture effects
3.1.3 C Create a table by specifying rows and columns	5.2.4 C Format objects
3.1.4 C Apply table styles	5.2.5 C Apply a picture style
3.2.3 C Merge and split cells	5.2.6 C Wrap text around objects
3.2.4 C Resize tables, rows, and columns	5.2.7 C Position objects

Key Terms

1. What types of questions should you have prepared for the interviewer?
2. What is the most important thing you can convey during an interview?

Online Help Skills

1. With Word 2016 open, on the **File tab**, in the upper right corner of the screen, click the **Microsoft Word Help** [?] button, or press [F1].
2. In the **Word Help** window **Search** box, type table borders and then press [Enter].
3. In the search result list, click **Remove borders from a table**. Maximize the Word Help window, and then compare your screen with **Figure 1**.

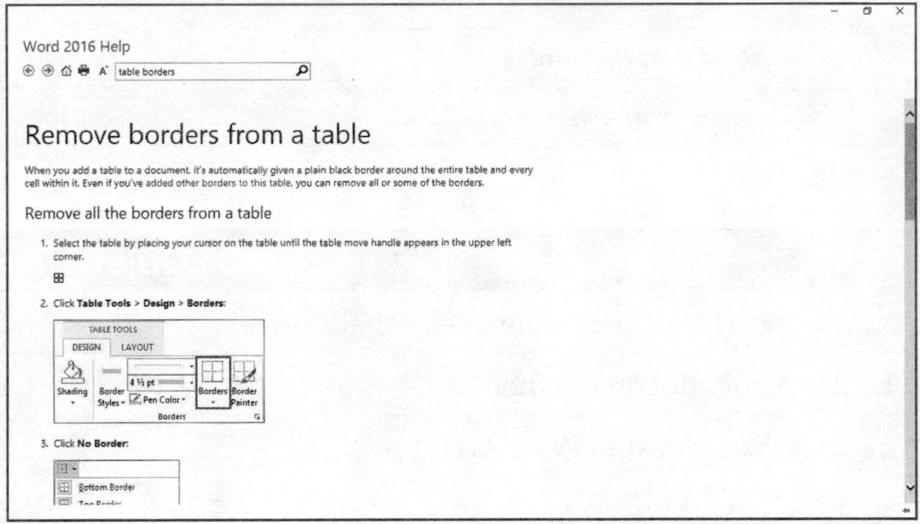

Figure 1 Word 2016, Windows 10, Microsoft Corporation

4. Read the article to answer the following questions: How can you remove all the table borders at the same time? How can you remove certain table borders?

Matching 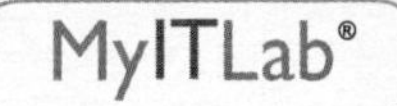

Match each term in the second column with its correct definition in the first column by writing the letter of the term on the blank line in front of the correct definition.

___ **1.** When you select a picture, this button displays next to the image so that you can change text wrapping settings quickly.

___ **2.** The layout option that sets a picture to "float" so that it can be moved independently of the paragraph.

___ **3.** The type of sizing handle used to resize a picture proportionally.

___ **4.** A line that displays when an object is aligned with a document object such as a margin or heading.

___ **5.** A prebuilt set of formatting options that can be applied to a graphic with a single click.

___ **6.** A specific location in the document, marked on the Word ruler, to which you can move using the Tab key.

___ **7.** A series of characters that form a solid, dashed, or dotted line that fills the space preceding a tab stop.

___ **8.** Information presented in rows and columns to summarize and present data effectively and efficiently.

___ **9.** A prebuilt set of formatting options that can be applied to a table with a single click.

___ **10.** The command used to make the size of the table columns reflect the data in the columns.

A Alignment Guide
B AutoFit Contents
C Corner
D Layout Options
E Leader
F Picture style
G Square
H Tab stop
I Table
J Table style

Multiple Choice

MyITLab®

Choose the correct answer.

1. When you select a picture, you can use these to change the picture's size.
   - A. Arrow keys
   - B. Sizing handles
   - C. Layout Options
2. The symbol that indicates which paragraph a picture is associated with.
   - A. Anchor
   - B. Paragraph mark
   - C. Em dash
3. To move a selected picture small distances using an arrow key.
   - A. Drag
   - B. Bump
   - C. Nudge
4. A series of evenly spaced dots that precede a tab.
   - A. Ellipsis
   - B. Tab stop position
   - C. Dot leader
5. When you make a change to a tab stop in the Tabs dialog box, click this button to apply the changes.
   - A. Set
   - B. Clear
   - C. Apply
6. The intersection of a row and column in a table.
   - A. Banded row
   - B. Cell
   - C. Banded column
7. This command can be used to make a picture look more like a drawing or a painting.
   - A. Artistic Effects
   - B. Change Picture
   - C. Compress Pictures
8. Use this key to move from one part of a table to another.
   - A. Alt
   - B. Tab
   - C. Ctrl
9. How many columns are in a 3x7 table?
   - A. 3
   - B. 7
   - C. 21
10. Numbers in a table are typically aligned this way.
    - A. Left
    - B. Center
    - C. Right

Topics for Discussion

1. Tables have largely taken the place of tabs in most documents. Can you think of any situations where you might want to use tabs instead of tables? What would you have to do to a table to make it look like a tabbed list?
2. Pictures add interest to your documents when used in moderation. What guidelines would you recommend for using pictures—or any other type of graphics—in a document?

Skills Review

To complete this project, you will need the following files:

- wrd03_SRAdventures
- wrd03_SRGeo
- wrd03_SRHikes

You will save your file as:

- Last_First_wrd03_SRAdventures

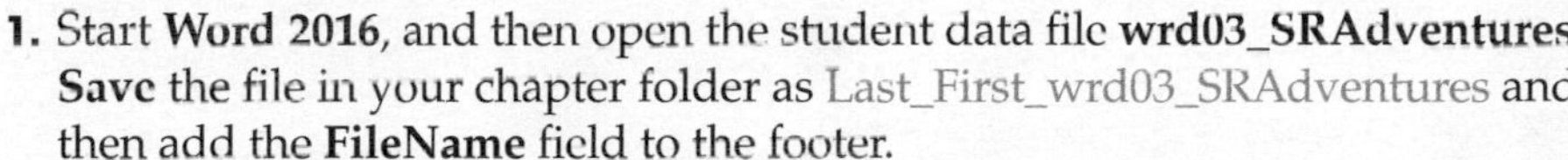

1. Start **Word 2016**, and then open the student data file **wrd03_SRAdventures**. **Save** the file in your chapter folder as Last_First_wrd03_SRAdventures and then add the **FileName** field to the footer.

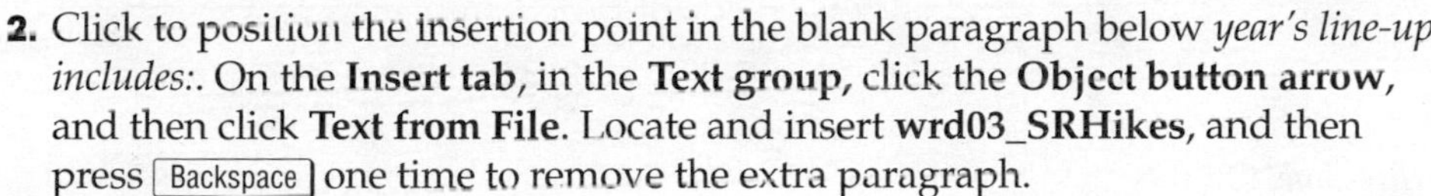

2. Click to position the insertion point in the blank paragraph below *year's line-up includes:*. On the **Insert tab**, in the **Text group,** click the **Object button arrow**, and then click **Text from File**. Locate and insert **wrd03_SRHikes**, and then press Backspace one time to remove the extra paragraph.
3. Right-click in the first row of the table. On the Mini toolbar, click the **Insert** button, and then click **Insert Above**. If necessary, on the **Table Tools Layout tab**, in the **Table group**, click the **View Gridlines** button to display the table gridlines.
4. In the first cell of the new row, type Hike and then press Tab. In the second cell, type Length and then press Tab. In the third cell, type Difficulty and then press Tab. In the last cell, type Description
5. With the insertion point in the table, click the **Table Tools Design tab**. In the **Table Styles group**, click the **More** button, and then under **Grid Tables**, click **Grid Table 7 Colorful - Accent 6**.
6. On the **Table Tools Layout tab**, in the **Cell Size group**, click the **AutoFit** button, and then click **AutoFit Contents**.
7. Click the **Table Selector** button to select the entire table. On the **Layout tab**, in the **Alignment group**, click the **Align Center Left** button.
8. Click in a cell in the second column, and then in the **Cell Size group**, click the **Width up spin arrow** to set the column width to **0.9"**. Compare your screen with **Figure 1**.

Word 2016, Windows 10, Microsoft Corporation **Figure 1**

Class	Date
Intro to Rock Climbing	March 22
Fitness through Climbing	March 29
Family Vertical Climbing	April 5

Figure 2

9. Click in the blank paragraph below the paragraph that ends *Climbing Center*. On the **Insert tab**, in the **Tables group**, click the **Table** button, and then insert a **2x4** table.
10. In the table just inserted, add the text as shown in **Figure 2**.

■ **Continue to the next page to complete this Skills Review**

11. On the **Table Tools Design tab**, apply the same table style you applied to the upper table—**Grid Table 7 Colorful - Accent 6**. On the **Table Tools Layout tab**, in the **Cell Size group**, click the **AutoFit** button, and then click **AutoFit Contents**.
12. Select the three cells that contain dates. On the **Home tab**, in the **Paragraph group**, click the **Align Right** button.
13. Press Ctrl + End to position the insertion point at the end of the document. On the left side of the horizontal ruler, click the **Tab Selector** button to display the Right Tab icon. Insert a right tab at **2.75 inches** on the horizontal ruler.
14. Double-click the tab mark. In the **Tabs** dialog box, under **Leader**, select **2**, click **Set**, and then click **OK**. Type the following tabbed list, pressing Tab before typing the text in the second column:

Friday	5:00 p.m. to 10:00 p.m.
Saturday	4:00 p.m. to 9:00 p.m.
Sunday	1:00 p.m. to 5:00 p.m.

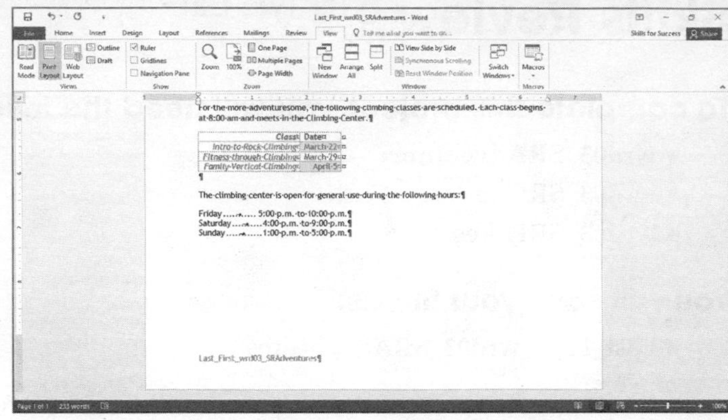

Figure 3 Word 2016, Windows 10, Microsoft Corporation

15. Compare your screen with **Figure 3**.
16. Click to the left of the paragraph that begins *For the more adventuresome*. On the **Insert tab**, in the **Illustrations group**, click the **Pictures** button, and then locate and insert **wrd03_SRGeo**.
17. On the **Format tab**, in the **Size group**, select the number in the **Width** box, type 2.5 and then press Enter.
18. Scroll up to display the bottom of Page 1. Click the picture's **Layout Options** button, and then under **With Text Wrapping**, click **Square**.
19. Drag the picture to the right and slightly up. When the Alignment Guides display and align with the top of the paragraph beginning *For the more adventuresome* and the right page margin, release the left mouse button.
20. On the **Format tab**, in the **Picture Styles group**, click the sixth thumbnail—**Soft Edge Rectangle**.
21. In the **Picture Styles group**, click the **Picture Effects** button, point to **3-D Rotation**, and then under **Perspective**, click the second to last choice—**Perspective Heroic Extreme Left**.
22. Click in the table. On the **Table Tools Layout tab**, in the **Table group**, click the **View Gridlines** button to deactivate the table gridlines. Hide the formatting marks, set the zoom level to **One Page**, and then compare your screen with **Figure 4**.
23. **Save** the file, **Close** Word, and then submit the file as directed by your instructor.

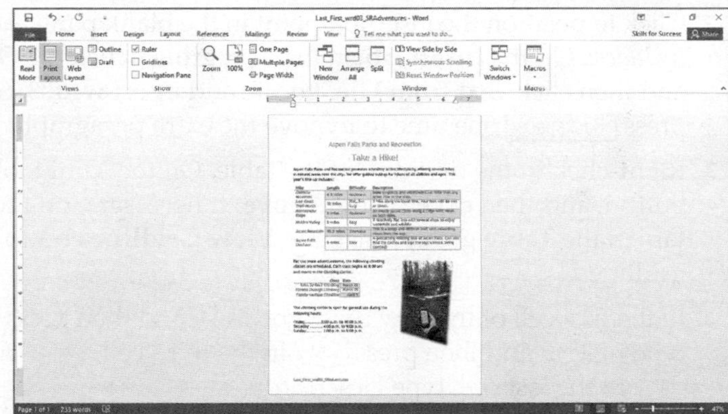

Figure 4 Henner Danke/Fotolia; Word 2016, Windows 10, Microsoft Corporation

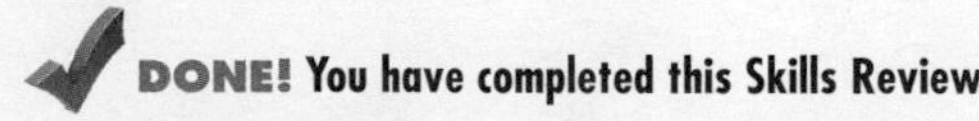

DONE! You have completed this Skills Review

Skills Assessment 1

MyITLab®
Grader

To complete this project, you will need the following files:

- wrd03_SA1Festival
- wrd03_SA1Photo
- wrd03_SA1Bands

You will save your file as:

- Last_First_wrd03_SA1Festival

---

1. Start **Word 2016**, and then open the student data file **wrd03_SA1Festival**. **Save** the file in your chapter folder as Last_First_wrd03_SA1Festival and then add the **FileName** field to the footer.
2. With the insertion point to the left of the flyer title, insert the picture from the student file **wrd03_SA1Photo**. Apply the **Square** layout, change the **Width** to **3.5"**, and then align the picture with the top of the title paragraph and the document's right margin. Apply the **Bevel Rectangle** picture style (the twenty-first choice), and then apply the **Preset** picture effect—**Preset** 5.
3. In the blank paragraph below *line-up includes the following:*, insert the text from the student file **wrd03_SA1Bands**, and then remove the second blank paragraph below the table. Add a fourth column, and then in cells two to seven, add the following times:

   4:00 p.m.
   7:00 p.m.
   12:00 p.m.
   4:00 p.m.
   7:00 p.m.
   2:00 p.m.

4. Add a new row below the table's last row, and then enter the following: Obia | Afro-Latin Groove | Sunday | 5:00 p.m.
5. Select the table, and then apply the **Grid Table 1 Light - Accent 2** table style. Change the font size to **14** and the row height to **0.3"**. Set the first row to **Align Center** and rows two to eight to **Align Center Left**.
6. In the first row, merge cells three and four, and then AutoFit the columns to their contents. Change the table's **Alignment** property to **Center** the table between the side margins.

A Taste of Aspen Falls

A Taste of Aspen Falls is an annual food and music event held in Aspen Falls City Park. This year features more than 50 food vendors and over 75 free concerts on 4 different stages. All concerts are free and no food item is over $7.95.

This year's artist line-up includes the following:

Band	Genre	Day and Time	
Noseeums	Eclectic Mix	Friday	4:00 p.m.
Fork in the Road	Electric Blues	Friday	7:00 p.m.
Hungary Creek	Folk-Americana	Saturday	12:00 p.m.
Green Sword	Mexi-Cali	Saturday	4:00 p.m.
Pete's Fork	Rock	Saturday	7:00 p.m.
Wendover	Acoustic Rock	Sunday	2:00 p.m.
Obia	Afro-Latin Groove	Sunday	5:00 p.m.

Plan your good times now!

Friday .... 4:00 to 10:00
Saturday......... 10:00 to 10:00
Sunday .... 10:00 to 8:00

Figure 1 Dawn Delaney/Getty Images

7. In the blank paragraph at the end of the document, set a left tab stop at **0.25 inches** and a right tab stop at **2.5 inches**. Add a dot leader to the right tab stop, and then enter the following text to create a tabbed list.

Friday	4:00 to 10:00
Saturday	10:00 to 10:00
Sunday	10:00 to 8:00

8. View your document as one page, and then compare your screen with **Figure 1**. **Save** the file, **Close** Word, and then submit the file as directed by your instructor.

DONE! You have completed Skills Assessment 1

Skills Assessment 2

To complete this project, you will need the following files:

- wrd03_SA2College
- wrd03_SA2Photo
- wrd03_SA2Prices

You will save your file as:

- Last_First_wrd03_SA2College

1. Start **Word 2016**, and then open the student data file **wrd03_SA2College**. **Save** the file in your chapter folder as Last_First_wrd03_SA2College Add the **FileName** field to the footer, and if necessary, display the formatting marks.
2. In the blank paragraph below *Several health care providers*, insert a 2x6 table, and then add the following text:

Provider	Plan(s)
Ultra Shield	PPO
Sunshine Health Cooperative	PPO, HMO
HealthWise Choice	PPO
United Southwest Health	HMO
Morgan Association Health Plan of CA	PPO

3. In the blank paragraph below *If you are considering*, insert the text from the student file **wrd03_SA2Prices**, and then remove the second blank paragraph below the table.
4. In the second table, add a new first row, and then enter the following column headings:

   Unit Type | Average Rate | Vacancy Rate

5. For both document tables, apply the **Grid Table 4 - Accent 5** table style, **AutoFit** the columns to their contents, and then change the **Alignment** property to **Center**.
6. In the second table, change the currency and percent values in the cells below *Average Rate* and *Vacancy Rate* to the **Align Right** paragraph alignment.
7. In the blank paragraph at the end of the document, click the **Tab Selector** to display the **Decimal Tab** icon, and then click the **1.25 inch** mark on the ruler. Enter the following text using the tab to align the decimal points in the second column.

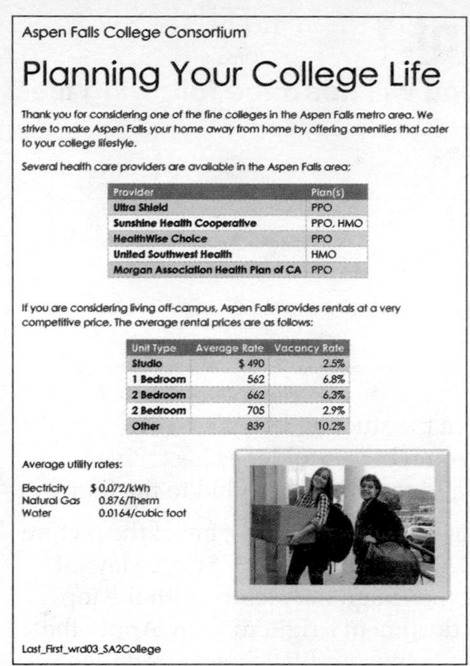

Aspen Falls College Consortium

Planning Your College Life

Thank you for considering one of the fine colleges in the Aspen Falls metro area. We strive to make Aspen Falls your home away from home by offering amenities that cater to your college lifestyle.

Several health care providers are available in the Aspen Falls area:

Provider	Plan(s)
Ultra Shield	PPO
Sunshine Health Cooperative	PPO, HMO
HealthWise Choice	PPO
United Southwest Health	HMO
Morgan Association Health Plan of CA	PPO

If you are considering living off-campus, Aspen Falls provides rentals at a very competitive price. The average rental prices are as follows:

Unit Type	Average Rate	Vacancy Rate
Studio	$ 490	2.5%
1 Bedroom	562	6.8%
2 Bedroom	662	6.3%
2 Bedroom	705	2.9%
Other	839	10.2%

Average utility rates:

Electricity $ 0.072/kWh
Natural Gas 0.876/Therm
Water 0.0164/cubic foot

Last_First_wrd03_SA2College

Mangostock/Fotolia

Figure 1

Electricity	$ 0.072/kWh
Natural Gas	0.876/Therm
Water	0.0164/cubic foot

8. With the insertion point to the left of the paragraph beginning *Average utility rates*, insert the picture from the student file **wrd03_SA2Photo**. Apply the **Square** layout, change the **Width** to **3"**, and then align the picture with the top of the *Average utility rates* paragraph and the document's right margin.
9. Apply the **Beveled Matte, White** picture style—the second choice, and then change the **Picture Border** color to the ninth choice in the second row—**Lavender, Accent 5, Lighter 80%**. View your document as one page, and then compare your screen with **Figure 1**.
10. **Save** the file, **Close** Word, and then submit the file as directed by your instructor.

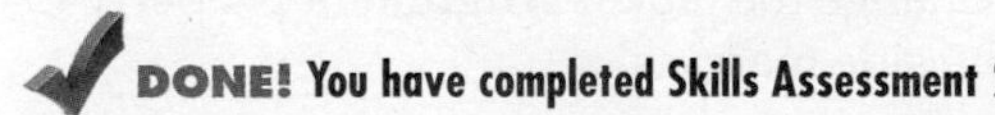

DONE! You have completed Skills Assessment 2

TUTORING

Math, English, and Computer Literacy

Reasonable Rates

Contact Your Name at (555) 555-5555

Flexible Hours

Your Name (555) 555-5555	Your Name (555) 555-5555	Your Name (555) 555-5555	Your Name (555) 555-5555	Your Name (555) 555-5555	Your Name (555) 555-5555	Your Name (555) 555-5555	Your Name (555) 555-5555	Your Name (555) 555-5555

Matthew Benoit/Fotolia

Figure 1

My Skills

To complete this project, you will need the following files:

- wrd03_MYFlyer
- wrd03_MYPhoto

You will save your file as:

- Last_First_wrd03_MYFlyer

1. Start **Word 2016**, and then open the student data file **wrd03_MYFlyer**. **Save** the file in your chapter folder as Last_First_wrd03_MYFlyer
2. Apply the **Organic** theme. Select all of the document text, and then change the font color to the ninth choice in the first row—**Orange, Accent 5**.
3. Select the flyer title, *Tutoring*. In the **Font Size** box, replace the existing value with 84 and then press Enter.
4. In the blank paragraph after the title, insert the picture from the student file **wrd03_MYPhoto**. Resize the picture proportionally by changing the width to **3.5"**.
5. For the picture, apply the nineteenth picture style—**Relaxed Perspective, White**.
6. In the first paragraph below the picture, change the font size to **26**. For the last three document paragraphs, change the font size to **18**.
7. Click the **Insert tab**. In the **Header & Footer group**, click the **Footer** button, and then click **Edit Footer**.
8. In the footer, insert a **9x1** table. In the first cell, type your First and Last name. Press Enter, and then type the phone number (555) 555-5555
9. Select the text taking care not to select the entire cell, and then on the **Home tab**, click the **Copy** button. Paste the text into the table's eight remaining cells. If you accidentally copied the cell, undo and select just the text before clicking Copy.
10. Select the entire table, and then click the **Table Tools Layout tab**. In the **Alignment group**, click the **Text Direction** button one time to rotate the text from top to bottom as indicated by the arrows in the Text Direction button.
11. Change the **Table Row Height** to **1.6"**, and then with the entire table selected, change the alignment to **Align Center** so that the text is centered both vertically and horizontally in the cells.
12. On the **Table Tools Layout tab**, in the **Table group**, click **Properties**. In the **Table Properties** dialog box, under **Alignment**, click **Center**. Under **Text wrapping**, click the **Around** button, and then click **OK**.
13. Double-click in the body to deactivate the footer area, and then click the **Layout tab**. In the **Page Setup group**, click the **Margins** button, and then click **Narrow**. View your document as one page, and then compare your screen with **Figure 1**.
14. **Save** the file, **Close** Word, and then submit the file as directed by your instructor.

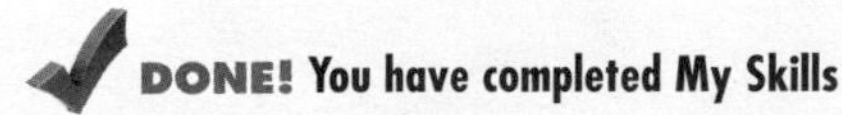
DONE! You have completed My Skills

Visual Skills Check

To complete this project, you will need the following files:

- **wrd03_VSConservation**
- **wrd03_VSPhoto**
- **wrd03_VSWildlife**

You will save your file as:

- **Last_First_wrd03_VSConservation**

Start **Word 2016**, and then open the student data file **wrd03_VSConservation. Save** the file in your chapter folder as Last_First_wrd03_VSConservation Add the **FileName** field in the footer.

Create the document shown in **Figure 1**. The picture is the student data file **wrd03_VSPhoto**, has the **Soft Edge Rectangle** picture style, and is **3 inches** wide. The table can be inserted from the student data file **wrd03_VSWildlife**, but you will need to add the last row and its text. The table is formatted with the **Grid Table 4 - Accent 5** table style, and the First Column table style option has been cleared. The cell sizes have been changed to AutoFit Contents, and the row headings are aligned Center Left in each cell. **Save** the file, **Close** Word, and then submit the file as directed by your instructor.

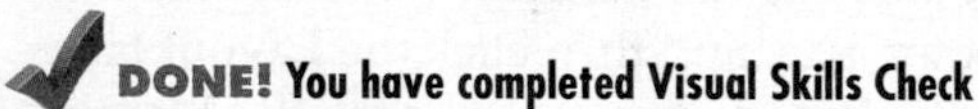

DONE! You have completed Visual Skills Check

Durango County
Conservation Futures Program

Aspen Falls Conservation Area

In 1994, the Durango County Commissioners created the Conservation Futures Program to preserve county natural areas in perpetuity. The program expands existing natural areas and creates new areas by acquiring properties nominated by county citizens. The Aspen Falls Conservation Area has returned the Aspen River to its natural meandering course benefiting wildlife, natural vegetation, and citizens alike.

The Aspen Falls Conservation Area features the following wildlife and plants:

Songbirds	Spring is an especially good time to observe songbirds during the breeding season. Over 100 species of birds have been spotted in the area.
Raptors	Attracted by the abundant forage fish found in the restored river, two nesting Bald eagle pairs live here year-round and several more nest each winter. Other raptors include osprey, red-tailed hawk, kestrel, and the long-eared owl.
Tule Elk	Approximately 25 elk visit the area to feed and can often be seen from the area's wildlife viewing blinds.
Beaver	Beaver are returning to the area. Their dams, diversions, and ponds attract birds, fish, and native plants which attract a wide array of wildlife to the area.
Sensitive Plants	Rare or endangered plants include Snow Mountain buckwheat, Drymaria-like western flax, Adobe lily, and Hall's madia.

Last_First_wrd03_VSConservation

Figure 1

V_Blinov/Fotolia

Skills Challenge 1

To complete this project, you will need the following file:

- wrd03_SC1Softball

You will save your file as:

- Last_First_wrd03_SC1Softball

The Aspen Falls Parks and Recreation Department has a Spring Softball flyer that needs updating. To update the flyer, open the student data file **wrd03_SC1Softball**, and then save the file in your chapter folder as Last_First_wrd03_SC1Softball Add the **FileName** field to the footer.

Improve the flyer by applying the skills practiced in this chapter. Assign a suitable theme, and then use the theme's fonts and colors to format the title in a manner demonstrated in this chapter's project. Create and format headings for each section. Use Online Pictures to insert a picture that complements the flyer's message. Size, position, and format the picture using picture styles or artistic effects so that the picture attracts the reader's eye to the flyer.

Organize the content using at least one table, a tabbed list, and a bulleted list. Format the table(s) in a manner that is consistent with the title formatting. In the tabbed list(s), assign a leader and alignment as appropriate to the content. Assign paragraph spacing to provide white space between flyer elements, and adjust the margins if needed so that the flyer displays on a single page. Save the file, close Word, and then submit the file as directed by your instructor.

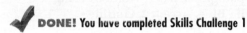

DONE! You have completed Skills Challenge 1

Skills Challenge 2

To complete this project, you will need the following file:

- New blank Word document

You will save your file as:

- Last_First_wrd03_SC2Resume

On the Word 2016 New page, search for and select the Basic Resume template provided by Microsoft Corporation. If that template is no longer available, select a different résumé template. Download the template, and then save the file in your chapter folder as Last_First_wrd03_SC2Resume Add the FileName field to the footer.

Create your own résumé by filling in the template. Using the skills you have practiced in this chapter, add or remove sections as appropriate and position the section featuring your strongest area (for example, experience, education, or skills) immediately below the objective. Reformat table cells and text as needed, and verify the résumé fits on a single page.

Check the entire document for grammar and spelling. Save the file, close Word, and then submit the file as directed by your instructor.

DONE! You have completed Skills Challenge 2

More Skills Assessment

To complete this project, you will need the following file:

- wrd03_MSAParks

You will save your file as:

- Last_First_wrd03_MSAParks

1. Start **Word 2016**, and then open the student data file **wrd03_MSAParks**. **Save** the file in your chapter folder as Last_First_wrd03_MSAParks Add the **FileName** field to the footer, and if necessary, display the formatting marks.
2. Select the title paragraph *City Parks and Recreation*, including the paragraph mark at the end of the paragraph. Insert WordArt using the third style in the first row—**Fill - Blue, Accent 2, Outline - Accent 2**.
3. Change the WordArt width to **6"**, and then change the fill color to the sixth choice in the second row—**Blue, Accent 2, Lighter 80%**.
4. In the paragraph that begins *Discover the outdoors*, click to the left of the letter *D*. Insert a **Drop Cap** with the **Dropped** position, and then change the drop cap font to **Arial Rounded MT Bold**. Click anywhere in the document, and then compare your screen with **Figure 1**.
5. Move to the end of the document, and then select all three paragraphs in the tabbed list. Include the paragraph mark after *October 25*. Convert the tabbed text to a table, and then **AutoFit** the table contents.
6. At the end of the document, draw a text box approximately **1"** in height and **2"** in width that aligns with the paragraph ending *Recreation Events* and the right margin. In the text box, type For questions about park facilities, call (805) 555-3666 between 8:00 a.m. and 5:00 p.m. Monday through Friday.
7. Set the text box height to **1"** and the width to **2.4"**, and then change the shape fill to the sixth choice in the second row—**Blue, Accent 2, Lighter 80%**. Click anywhere in the document, and then compare your screen with **Figure 2**.

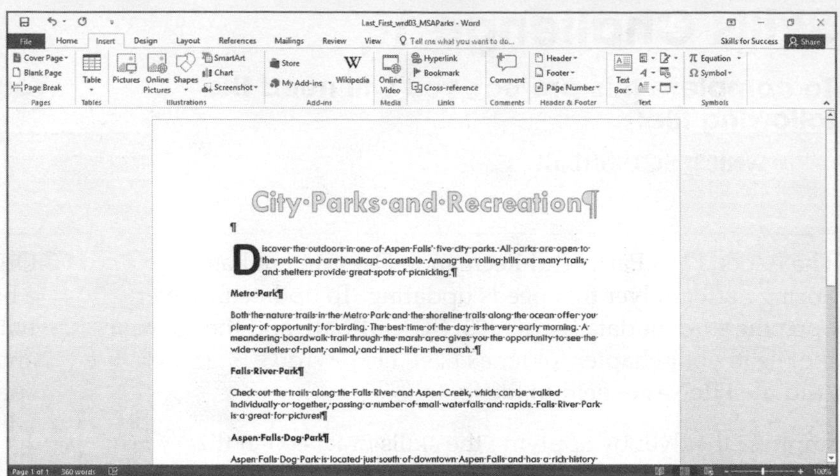

Figure 1 Word 2016, Windows 10, Microsoft Corporation

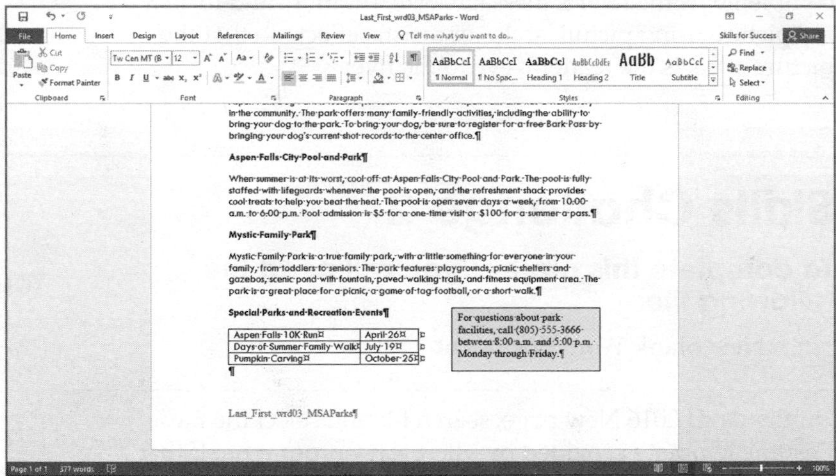

Figure 2 Word 2016, Windows 10, Microsoft Corporation

8. **Save** the file, **Close** Word, and then submit the file as directed by your instructor.

DONE! You have completed More Skills Assessment

Collaborating with Google

To complete this project, you will need a Google account (refer to the Common Features chapter) and the following file:

- wrd03_GPRecycle

You will save your file as:

- Last_First_wrd03_GPRecycle

1. Open a web browser. Log into your Google account, and then click the **Google Apps** button.
2. Click the **Drive** button to open Google Drive. Click the **New** button, and then click **Google Docs** to open a blank document.
3. In **Word 2016**, open the student data file **wrd03_GPRecycle**. Select and copy all the text from the file and paste it in your new Google document. In the Google document title box, type Recycling Bins
4. Place the insertion point in the blank line below the document title. Click the **Insert tab**, and then click **Image**. If necessary, click Search, and then type recycling bin Press Enter. Click on a recycling image, and then click the **Select** button. In your document, click the image to select it. Use the sizing handles to change the width to approximately **2.5"**, and then **Center** the image.
5. Move to the last blank line at the end of the document. Click the **Insert tab**, click **Table**, and then insert a **2x4** table. Type the following text in the table

Do Recycle	Do Not Place In Bin
Paper	Glass
Plastic	Food
Metal	Yard Waste

6. Select the word *Plastic*. Click the **Table tab**, and then click **Insert row below**. In the new row, type Small Appliances and Batteries
7. In the third row, select the words *Plastic* and *Food*. Click the **Table tab**, and then click **Table properties**. In the **Table properties** dialog box, select the **Column width** check box, and then in the **Column width** box, type 2 Under **Table alignment**, click the button, and then click **Center**. Click **OK**, and then click the blank line above the table. Compare your screen with **Figure 1**.

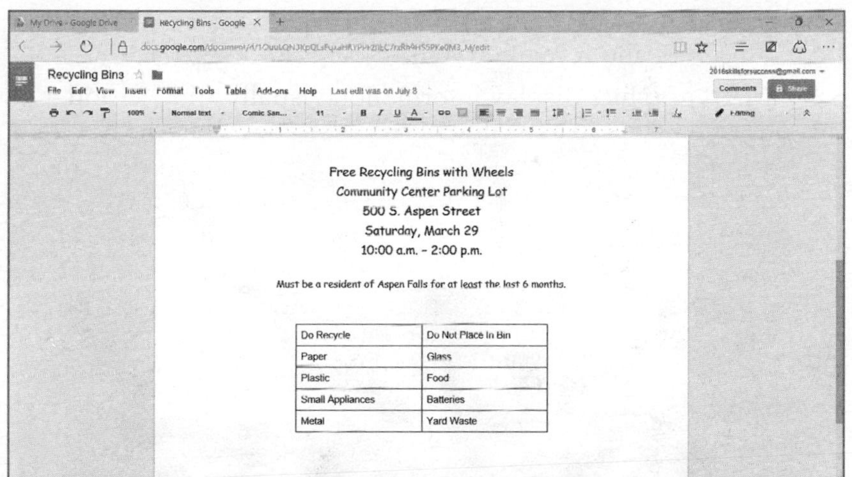

Figure 1

8. Under the document title *Recycling Bins*, click the **File tab**, point to **Download as**, and then click **Microsoft Word (.docx)**. **Save** the file in your chapter folder as Last_First_wrd03_GPRecycle
9. Start **Word 2016**, and then open the file **Last_First_wrd03_GPRecycle**. Insert the **FileName** field in the footer.
10. **Save** the file, **Close** all open windows, and then submit the file as directed by your instructor.

DONE! You have completed Collaborating with Google

CHAPTER 4

Create Newsletters and Mail Merge Documents

- Newsletters often display articles in two or three columns and have a title that spans across the columns. Text is typically easier to read when it is in columns.
- Online images can be downloaded from Bing Image Search and then inserted and formatted.
- SmartArt graphics display information visually and can add a professional look to a document.
- To draw attention to a small amount of text, you can add a border and shading to the paragraph.
- You can use the mail merge feature in Word to create mailing labels to distribute flyers or brochures.
- In a mail merge, you can take an existing list of names and addresses from other Office applications and insert them into a mailing labels document.

Kratuanoiy/Fotolia

Aspen Falls City Hall

In this chapter, you will assist Todd Austin, the Aspen Falls Tourism Director, to create a newsletter about the Aspen Falls Farmers' Market. The newsletter will be mailed to local farmers promoting their participation in the market. The newsletter will be mailed, so you will also create mailing labels with the addresses of local farms.

An effective newsletter uses large, attractive text and graphics to invite readers to read the articles. Subtitles, graphics, and other formatting can help those who only scan the newsletter to gain the information they desire. Word's library of SmartArt graphics can help you create graphics that communicate a message with very little text. You can save time by formatting as desired and then creating your own Quick Style based on that formatting. After the style is created, you apply that formatting with a single click.

In this project, you will create a one-page flyer with an artistic title and a two-column format. You will add text effects to the newsletter title, and add page and paragraph borders and shading. You will insert an online image and create a SmartArt graphic. Finally, you will create mailing labels by merging data from one file to a label template.

Time to complete all 10 skills — 60 to 90 minutes

Outcome

Using the skills in this chapter, you will be able to create a newsletter that includes columns, borders, shading, online pictures, and SmartArt. You will also be able to create merged labels.

Objectives

4.1 Modify a document using themes, columns, borders, and shading

4.2 Insert and modify images

4.3 Create and modify styles

4.4 Create and format mailing labels

Student data files needed for this chapter:

wrd04_Farmers
wrd04_FarmerAddressess (Excel)

You will save your files as:

Last_First_wrd04_Farmers
Last_First_wrd04_FarmerMain
Last_First_wrd04 FarmerMerge

SKILLS

At the end of this chapter, you will be able to:

Skill 1 Modify Themes and Create Columns
Skill 2 Modify Margins and Columns
Skill 3 Apply Text Effects
Skill 4 Create Styles
Skill 5 Add Borders and Shading to Paragraphs and Pages
Skill 6 Insert and Adjust Online Pictures
Skill 7 Insert SmartArt
Skill 8 Format SmartArt
Skill 9 Create Labels Using Mail Merge
Skill 10 Preview and Print Mail Merge Documents

MORE SKILLS

Skill 11 Optimize Documents for Read Mode
Skill 12 Work in Outline View
Skill 13 Create Bookmarks
Skill 14 Save Documents as Web Pages

Aspen Falls Farmers' Market

ASSOCIATION MEMBERSHIP

Currently, membership in the Farmers' Market association is required to become a vendor. All produce should be grown on a local area farm managed by the member seller. Exceptions include wild products such as huckleberries and mushrooms and baked goods at the discretion of the association board. Membership costs $20 annually and 5% of gross sales. Forms are available at the association website and through City Hall.

For further information, contact Arturo Schnabel at (805) 555-5454.

MARKET TIMES

The market will be open to the public 9:00 a.m. to 3:00 p.m. As a courtesy to our shoppers, vendors should off-load prior to 8:30 and should not break down their booths until after 3:00 p.m.

CANOPIES AND UMBRELLAS

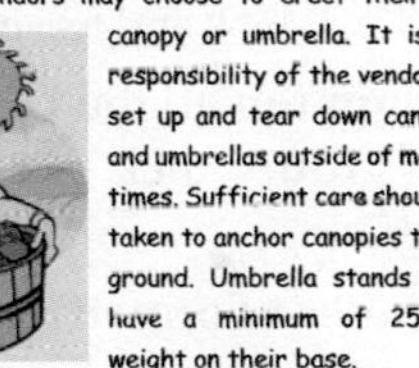

Vendors may choose to erect their own canopy or umbrella. It is the responsibility of the vendors to set up and tear down canopies and umbrellas outside of market times. Sufficient care should be taken to anchor canopies to the ground. Umbrella stands must have a minimum of 25 lbs. weight on their base.

OTHER RULES

Vendors will no longer be able to bring their pets to market. The market will not be a forum for political or religious activities. All booths will have signs that clearly identify the vendor by name and the prices of all products.

Last_First_wrd04_Farmers

- You can modify a theme by selecting a different set of colors, fonts, or effects.
- In a newsletter, multiple columns make text easier to read.

1. Start **Word 2016**, and then open the student data file **wrd04_Farmers**. Use **Save As** to create a folder named Word Chapter 4 and then **Save** the file as Last_First_wrd04_Farmers
2. If necessary, display the formatting marks, and then add the **FileName** field to the footer.
3. Click the **View tab**. In the **Show group**, verify the **Ruler** check box is selected. In the **Zoom group**, click **One Page**. Compare your screen with **Figure 1**.

   Because you are not editing text, it is typically best to view the entire page when working with the overall look and feel of a page.

4. On the **Design tab**, in the **Document Formatting group**, click **Themes**, and then click **Wisp**.
5. In the **Document Formatting group**, click the **Fonts** button. Scroll down the list of font sets, and then click **Century Gothic-Palatino Linotype**. Compare your screen with **Figure 2**.

   To improve readability in printed newsletters, body text is often given a ***serif font***—a font where the letters have extra details or hooks at the end of each stroke. Article titles and headings are often given a ***sans serif font***—a font where the letters do not have ***serifs***—the extra details or hooks at the end of each character stroke.

   Here, the colors and effects of the Wisp theme have been applied, but the default fonts have been changed to Century Gothic for headings and Palatino Linotype for body text.

■ **Continue to the next page to complete the skill**

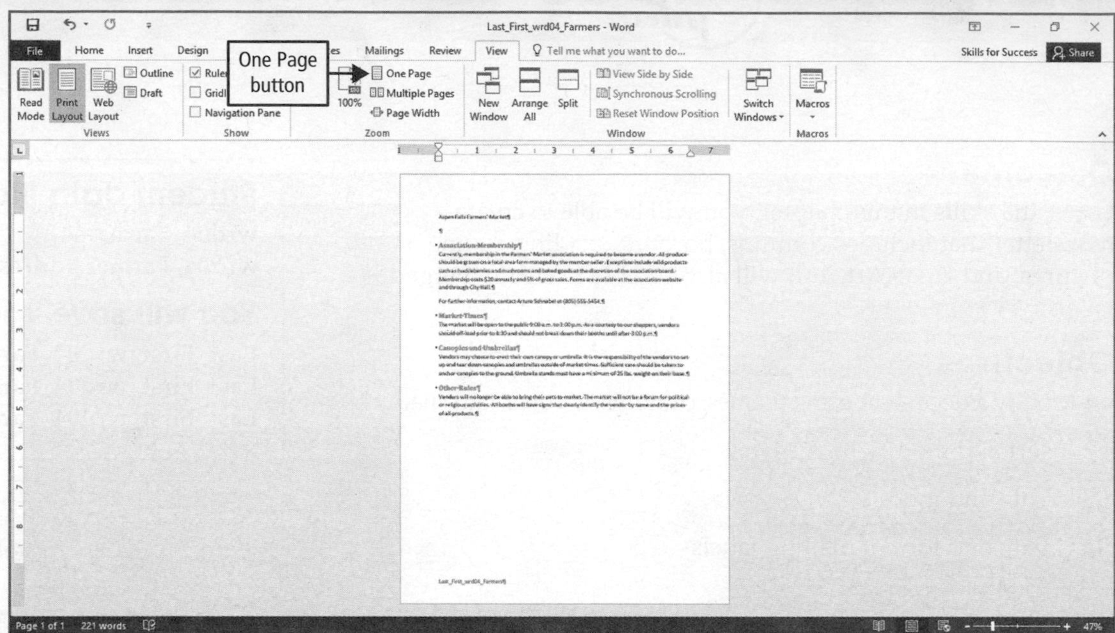

Figure 1 Word 2016, Windows 10, Microsoft Corporation

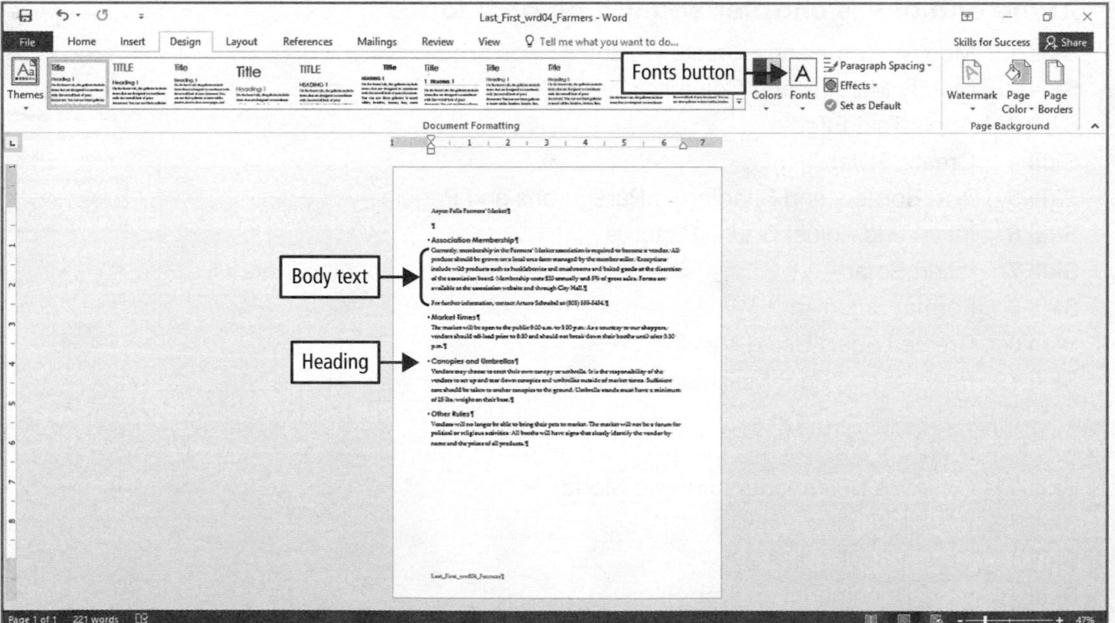

Figure 2 Word 2016, Windows 10, Microsoft Corporation

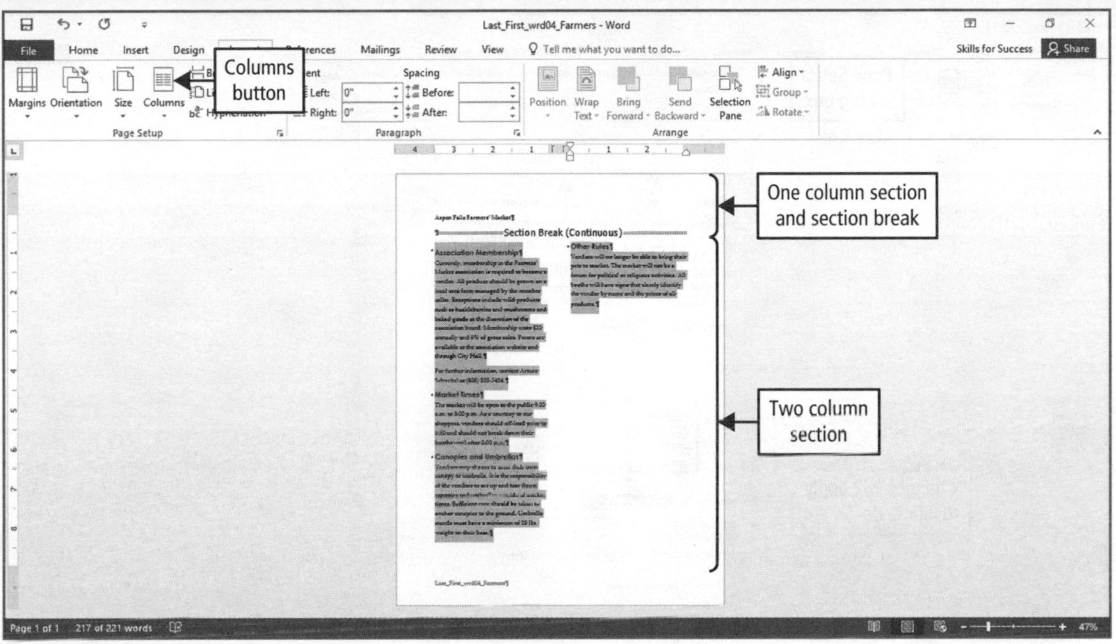

Word 2016, Windows 10, Microsoft Corporation

Figure 3

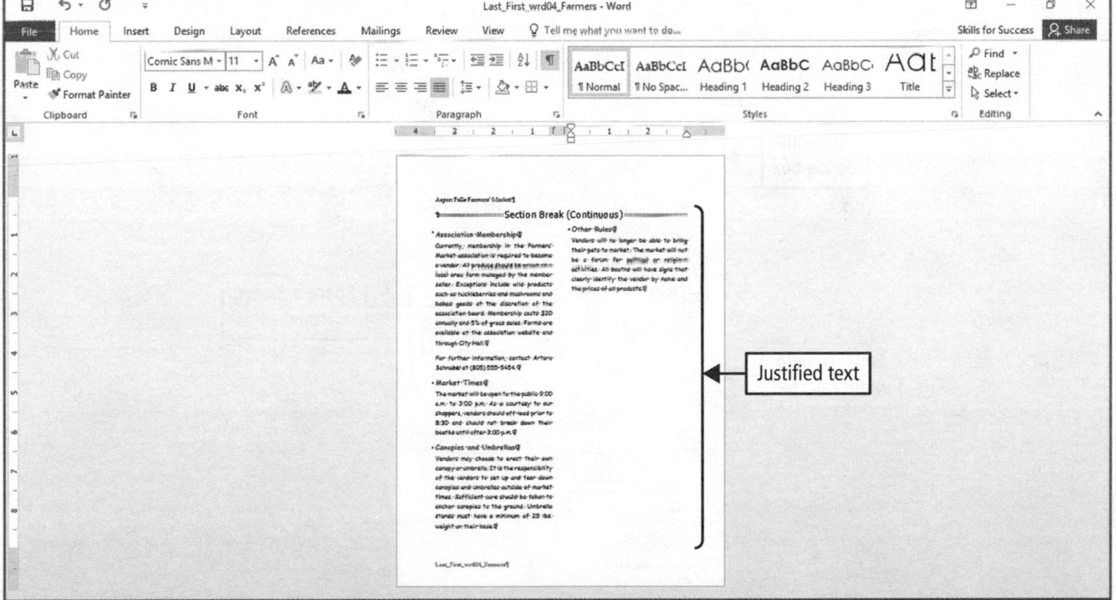

Word 2016, Windows 10, Microsoft Corporation

Figure 4

6. Locate the subtitle *Association Membership*, and then position the pointer to the left of the first word in the paragraph. Drag down to the end of the document—including the paragraph mark in the last paragraph.

7. Click the **Layout tab**. In the **Page Setup group**, click the **Columns** button, click **Two**, and then compare your screen with **Figure 3**.

Obj 2.3.1 C

   A section break displays above the two-column text. A ***section*** is a portion of a document that can be formatted differently from the rest of the document. A ***section break*** is a nonprinting character that marks the end of one section and the beginning of another section.

8. With the two columns of text still selected, on the **Home tab**, in the **Font group**, change the font to **Comic Sans MS**.

   Because this newsletter is only one page long, a serif font is not needed for the body text.

9. With the text still selected, in the **Paragraph group**, click the **Justify** button.

10. Click anywhere in the two-column text to deselect the text, and then compare your screen with **Figure 4**.

    Justified text aligns the text with both the left and right margins. Justified text is often used in documents with multiple columns, although some wide gaps can occur in the text.

11. **Save** the file.

■ **You have completed Skill 1 of 10**

- You can increase or decrease the space between the columns and apply custom margins to adjust the document layout.
- A ***column break*** is a nonprinting character that forces the text following the break to flow into the next column.

Obj 1.3.1 C

1. On the **Layout tab**, in the **Page Setup group**, click **Margins**, and then below the **Margins** gallery, click **Custom Margins** to open the Page Setup dialog box.
2. In the **Page Setup** dialog box, under **Margins**, use the **down spin arrows** to change the **Top** and **Bottom** margins to **0.8"**.
3. Under **Preview**, click the **Apply to arrow**, and then click **Whole document**. Compare your screen with **Figure 1**, and then click **OK** to accept the changes and to close the dialog box.

   Unless you specify otherwise, when documents have multiple sections, the Page Setup dialog box applies the changes only to the current section.

4. With the insertion point in the two columns of text, on the **Layout tab**, in the **Page Setup group**, click the **Columns** button. Below the **Columns** gallery, click **More Columns** to display the Columns dialog box. Compare your screen with **Figure 2**.

   When you set column options, you only need to place the insertion point in the section that the columns are applied to.

   The Columns dialog box can be used to set the number of columns and the distance between them. By default, the columns are of equal width with 0.5 inches of space between them.

■ **Continue to the next page to complete the skill**

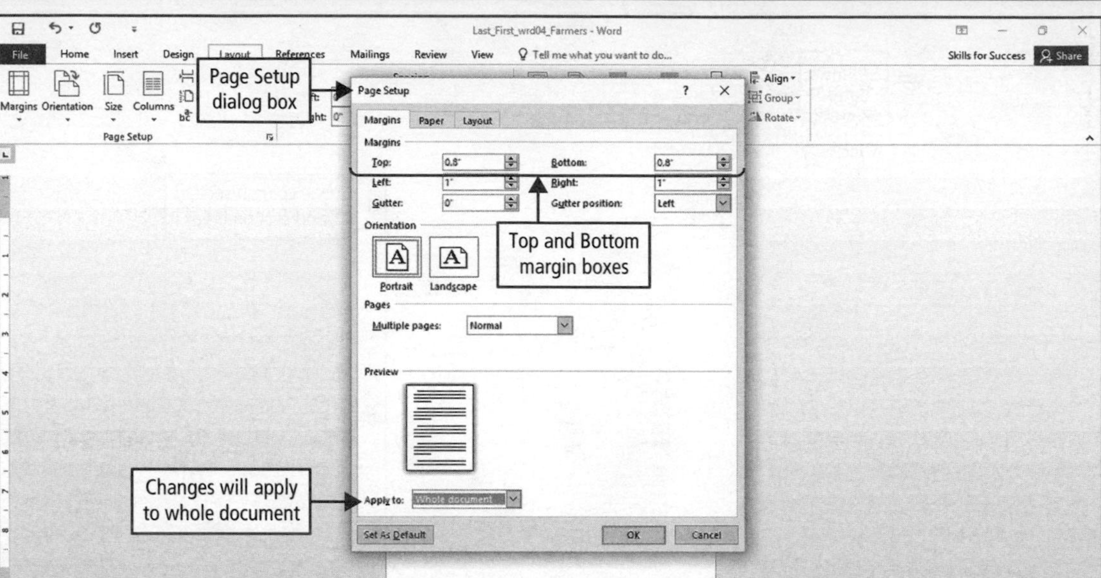

Figure 1 Word 2016, Windows 10, Microsoft Corporation

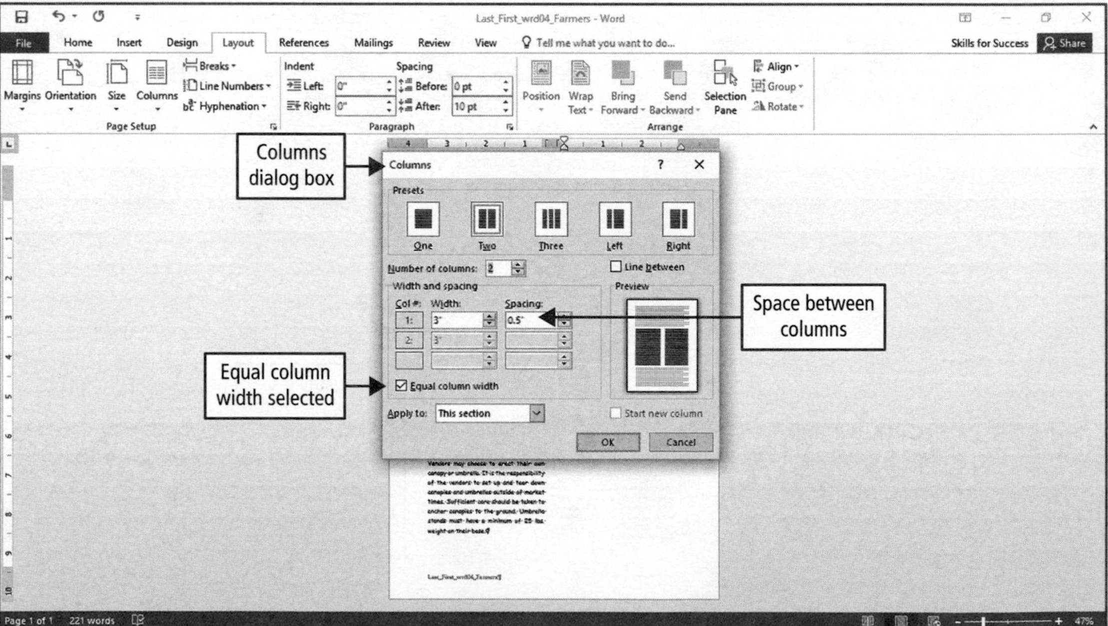

Figure 2 Word 2016, Windows 10, Microsoft Corporation

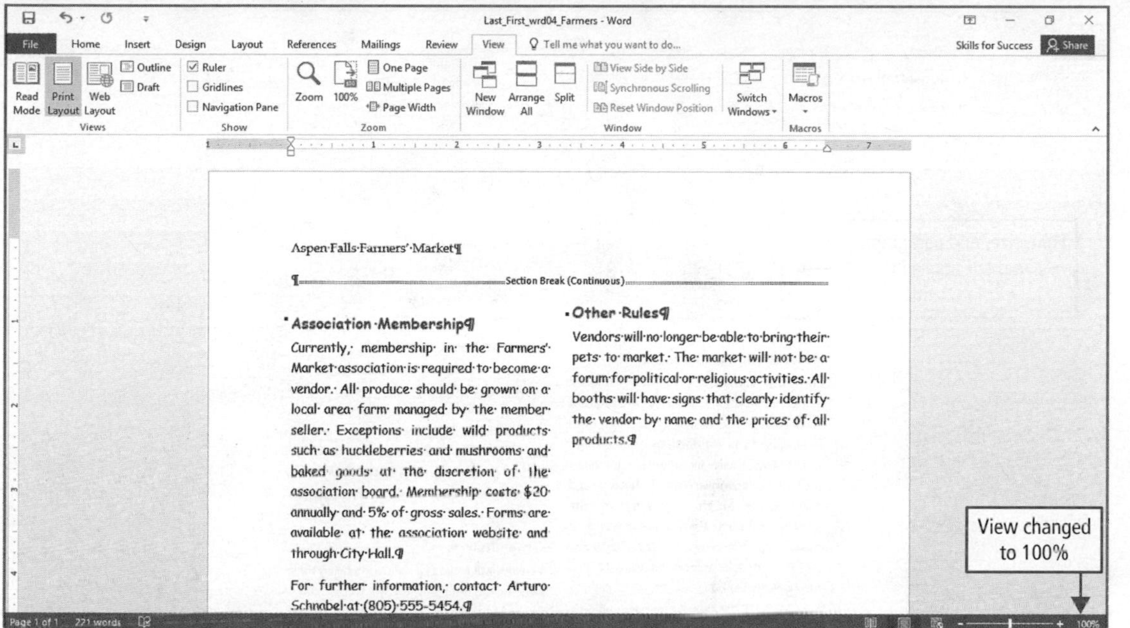

Word 2016, Windows 10, Microsoft Corporation

Figure 3

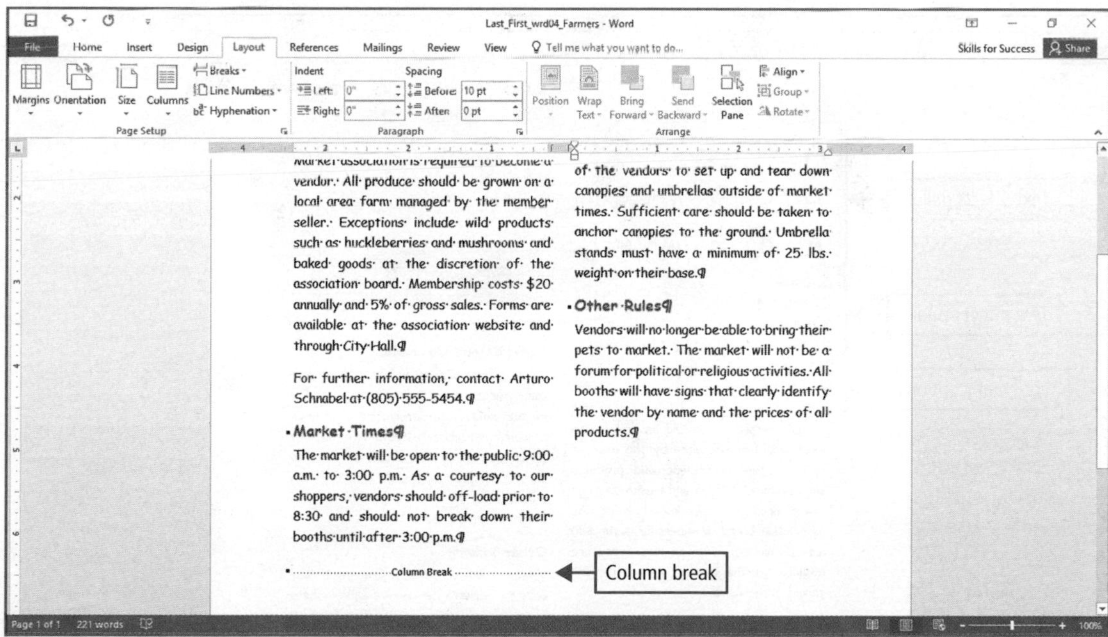

Word 2016, Windows 10, Microsoft Corporation

Figure 4

5. In the **Columns** dialog box, under **Width and spacing**, click the first **Spacing down spin arrow** two times to change the spacing between the columns to **0.3"**. Click **OK** to accept the changes and close the dialog box.

   Both columns will remain of equal width because the *Equal column width* check box is selected. When you decrease the spacing between columns, the width of each column is increased, in this case from 3.0 to 3.1 inches.

6. On the **View tab**, in the **Zoom group**, click **100%**. Press Ctrl + Home to move to the beginning of the document, and then compare your screen with **Figure 3**.

   Obj 1.4.2 C

   If you are working with a larger monitor, you may prefer to work with the document in One Page view instead of at 100%.

7. In the left column, click to position the insertion point to the left of the subtitle *Canopies and Umbrellas*.

8. On the **Layout tab**, in the **Page Setup group**, click the **Breaks** button. In the **Breaks** gallery, under **Page Breaks**, click **Column**.

   Obj 2.3.2 C

9. Scroll to display the column break at the bottom of column 1, and then compare your screen with **Figure 4**.

   Column breaks display as nonprinting characters, and after the break, the remaining text flows into the second column.

10. **Save** the file.

■ **You have completed Skill 2 of 10**

SKILL 3: Apply Text Effects

- ***Text effects*** are pre-built sets of decorative formats, such as outlines, shadows, text glow, and colors, that make text stand out in a document.
- You should use text effects sparingly, at most just for titles or subtitles.

1. At the top of the document, select the title *Aspen Falls Farmers' Market* including the paragraph mark.
2. With the title text selected, on the **Home tab**, in the **Font group**, click the **Font arrow** [Calibri (Body)], and then under **Theme Fonts**, click **Century Gothic**.

Obj 2.2.1 C

3. In the **Font group**, click in the **Font Size** box [11] to select the existing value. Type 30 and then press [Enter].

   By typing the desired size, you can assign a font size that is not included in the Font Size list.

4. On the **Home tab**, in the **Paragraph group**, click the **Center** button, and then compare your screen with **Figure 1**.

Obj 2.2.1 C

5. On the **Home tab**, in the **Font group**, click the **Text Effects** button. Compare your screen with **Figure 2**.

   The Text Effects gallery displays thumbnails of pre-built text effects and commands for applying individual text effects settings.

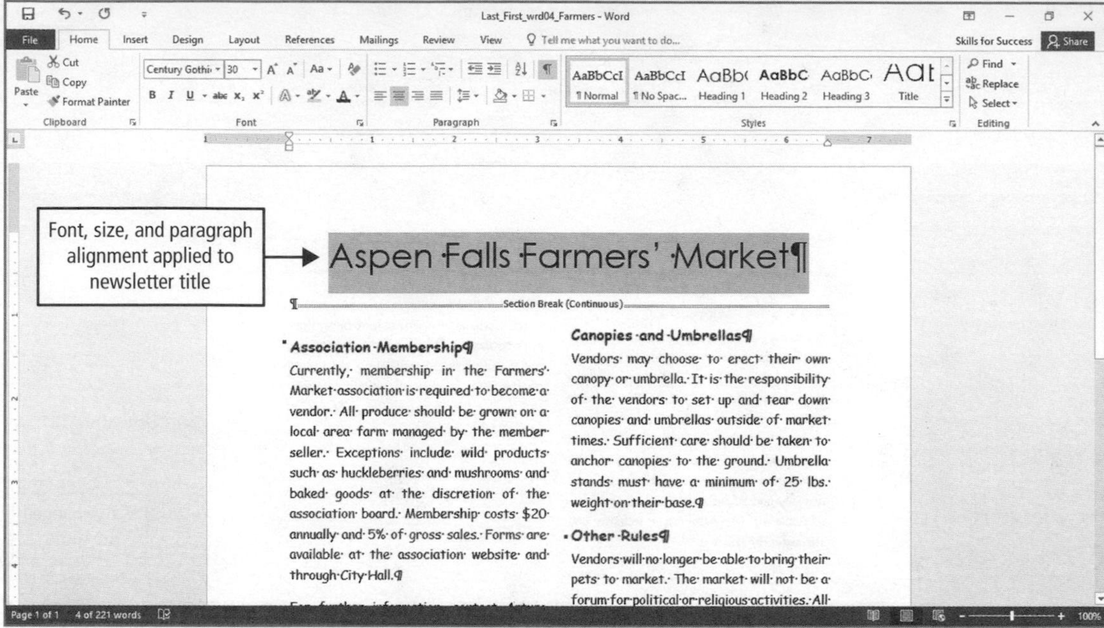

Figure 1

Word 2016, Windows 10, Microsoft Corporation

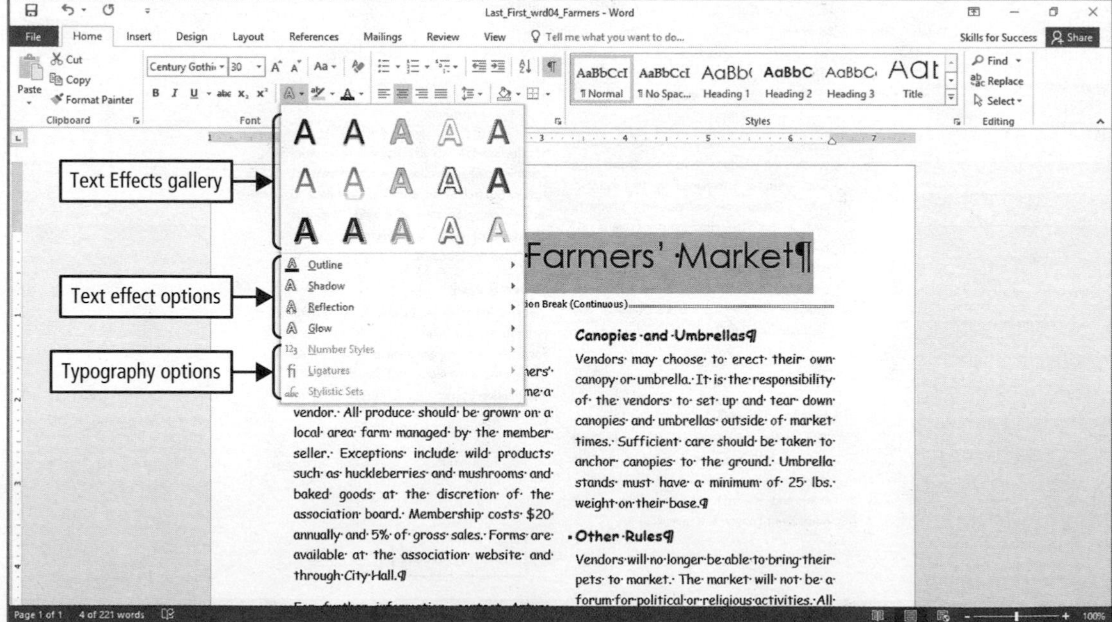

Figure 2

Word 2016, Windows 10, Microsoft Corporation

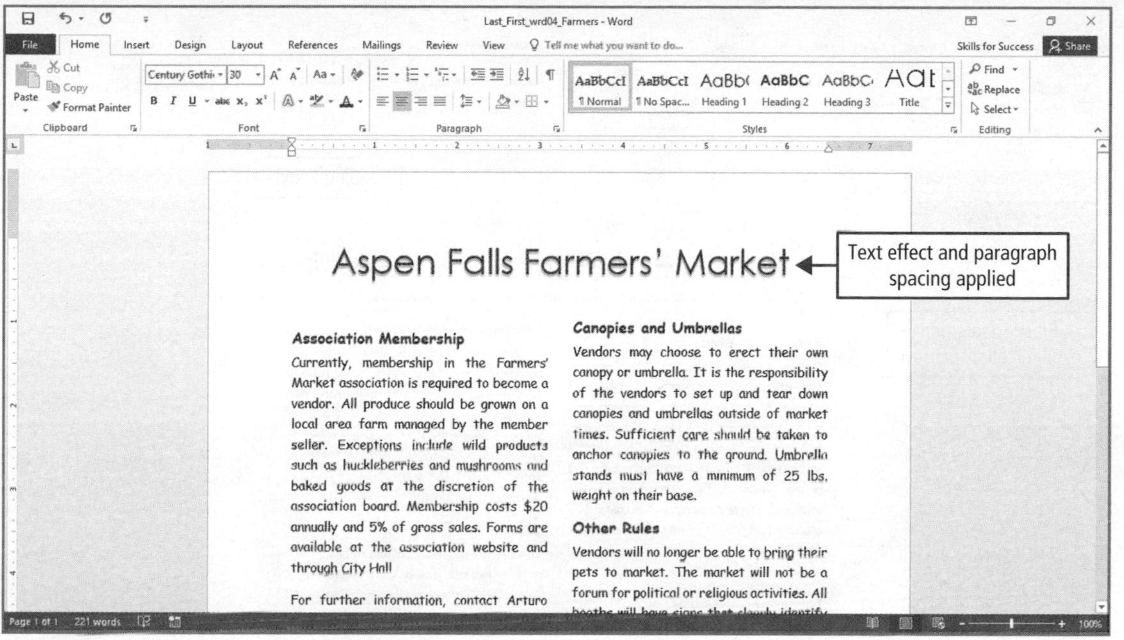

Word 2016, Windows 10, Microsoft Corporation

Figure 3

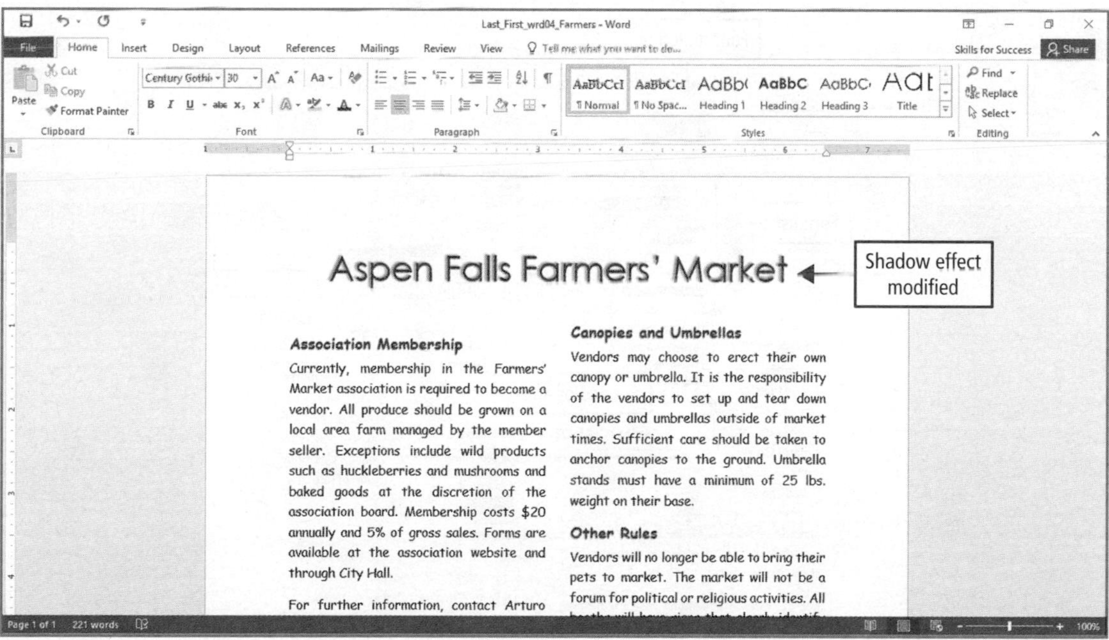

Word 2016, Windows 10, Microsoft Corporation

Figure 4

6. In the **Text Effects** gallery, in the first row, click the second thumbnail—**Fill - Dark Red, Accent 1, Shadow**.

7. On the **Home tab**, in the **Paragraph group**, click the **Show/Hide** button so that it is no longer selected.

   At times, it is helpful to format text with the nonprinting formatting marks hidden.

8. In the **Paragraph group**, click the **Paragraph Dialog Box Launcher**. In the **Paragraph** dialog box, change the **Spacing After** to **0 pt**, the **Line spacing** to **Single**, and then click **OK**. Click to deselect the text, and then compare your screen with **Figure 3**.

9. Select the newsletter title paragraph that begins *Aspen Falls*. In the **Fonts group**, click the **Text Effects** button. In the **Text Effects** gallery, point to **Outline**, and then point to several colors to preview the outline effects.

10. Repeat the technique just practiced to preview the shadow, reflection, and glow effects.

11. In the **Text Effects** gallery, point to **Shadow**, and then under **Outer**, click the last thumbnail—**Offset Diagonal Top Left**. Deselect the text, and then compare your screen with **Figure 4**.

    In this manner, you can modify the text effect settings. Here, the shadow's position and distance from the text were changed.

12. **Save** the file.

- **You have completed Skill 3 of 10**

- A ***Quick Style*** is a style that can be accessed from a Ribbon gallery of thumbnails.
- You can create and name your own styles, and then add them to the Style gallery so that you can apply them with a single click.

1. Display the formatting marks, and then at the top of the left column, click to place the insertion point in the subtitle *Association Membership*. Compare your screen with **Figure 1**.

   The subtitles in this newsletter have been assigned the Heading 2 style. The black square to the left of the subtitle indicates that it will always stay with the next paragraph. Recall that text assigned a Heading style can also be collapsed and expanded.

2. Select the subtitle *Association Membership* including the paragraph mark. On the **Home tab**, in the **Font group**, click the **Font Dialog Box Launcher** .
3. In the **Font** dialog box, change the font to **Century Gothic**, and the **Size** to **16**.
4. Click the **Font color arrow**, and then under **Theme Colors**, click the last color in the last row—**Green, Accent 6, Darker 50%**.

   MOS Obj 2.2.1 C

5. Under **Effects**, select the **Small caps** check box. Compare your screen with **Figure 2**, and then click **OK**.
6. With the text still selected, open the **Paragraph** dialog box. Under **General**, change the **Alignment** to **Centered**. Change the **Spacing Before** to **0 pt** and the **Spacing After** to **6 pt**. Change the **Line spacing** to **Single**, and then click **OK**.

■ **Continue to the next page to complete the skill**

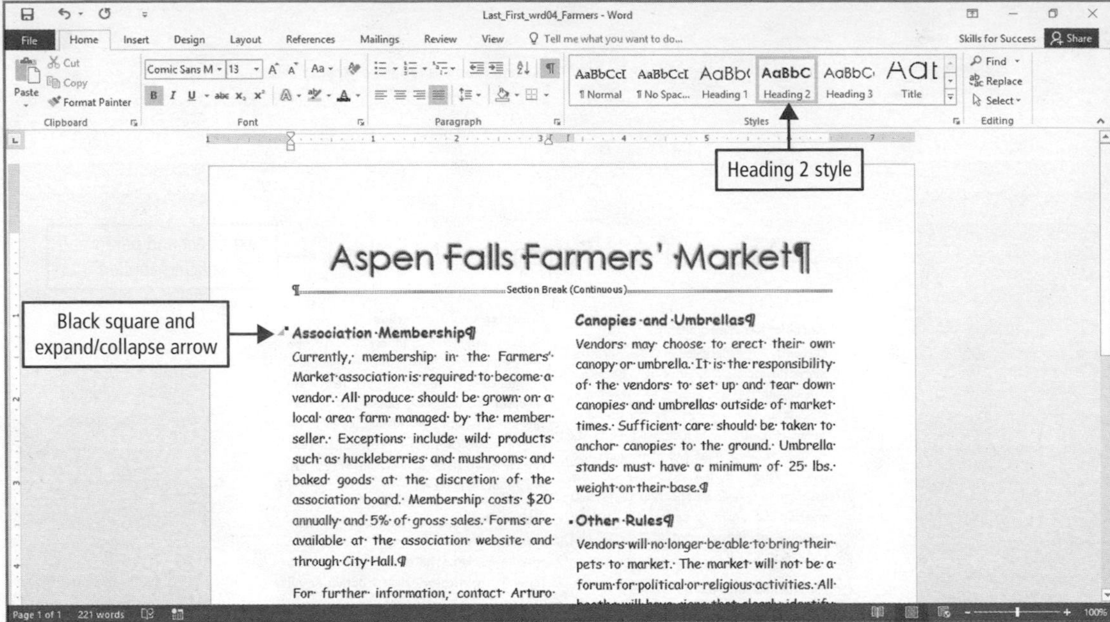

Figure 1

Word 2016, Windows 10, Microsoft Corporation

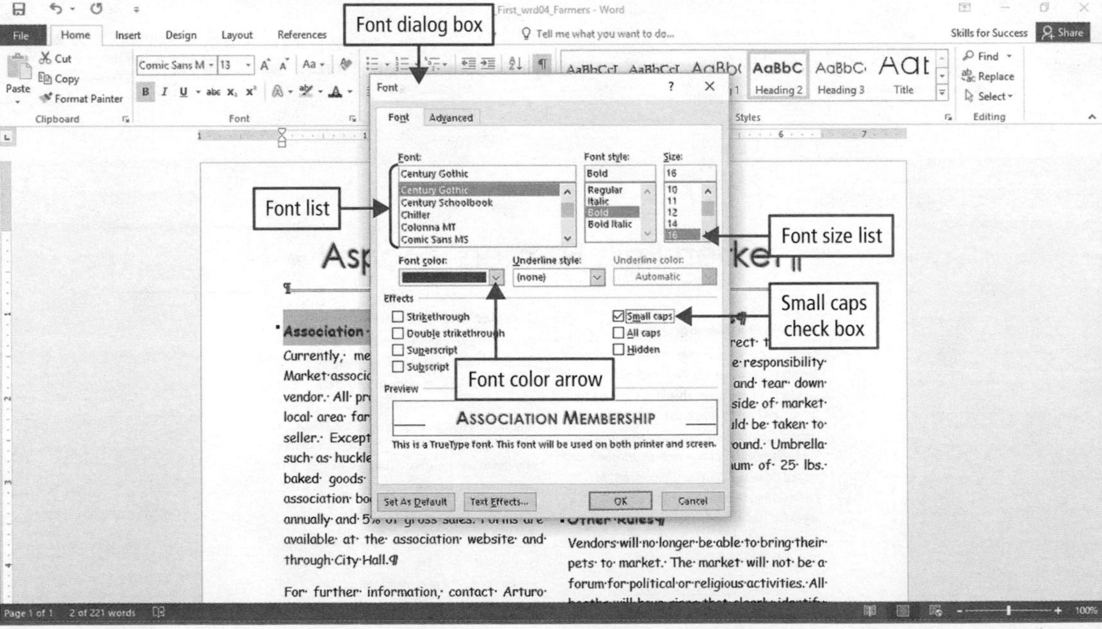

Figure 2

Word 2016, Windows 10, Microsoft Corporation

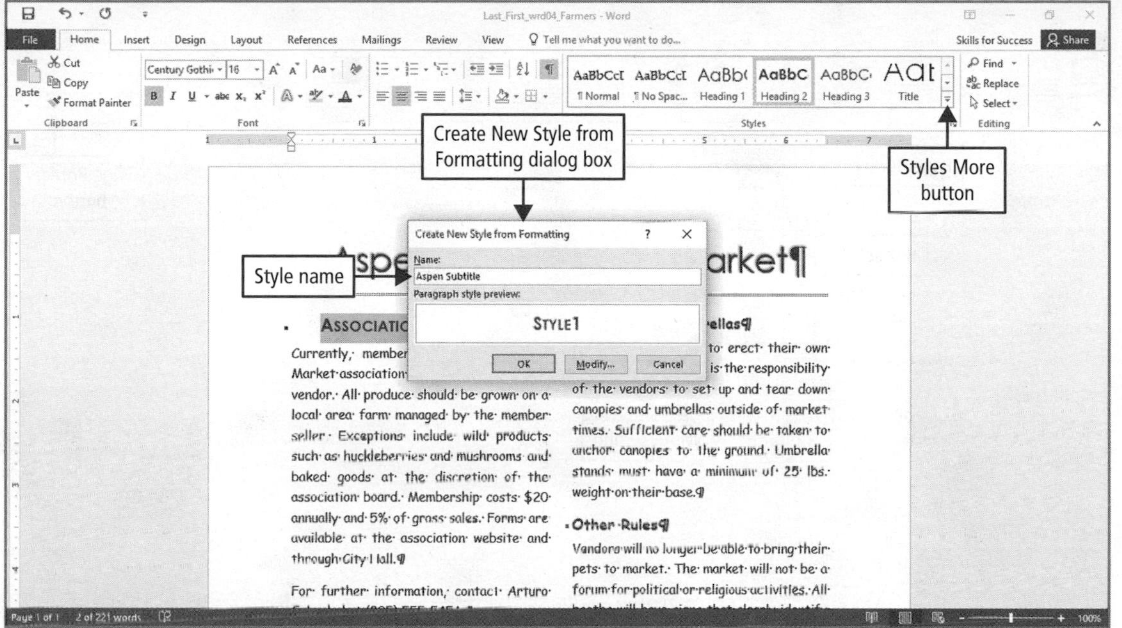

Word 2016, Windows 10, Microsoft Corporation

Figure 3

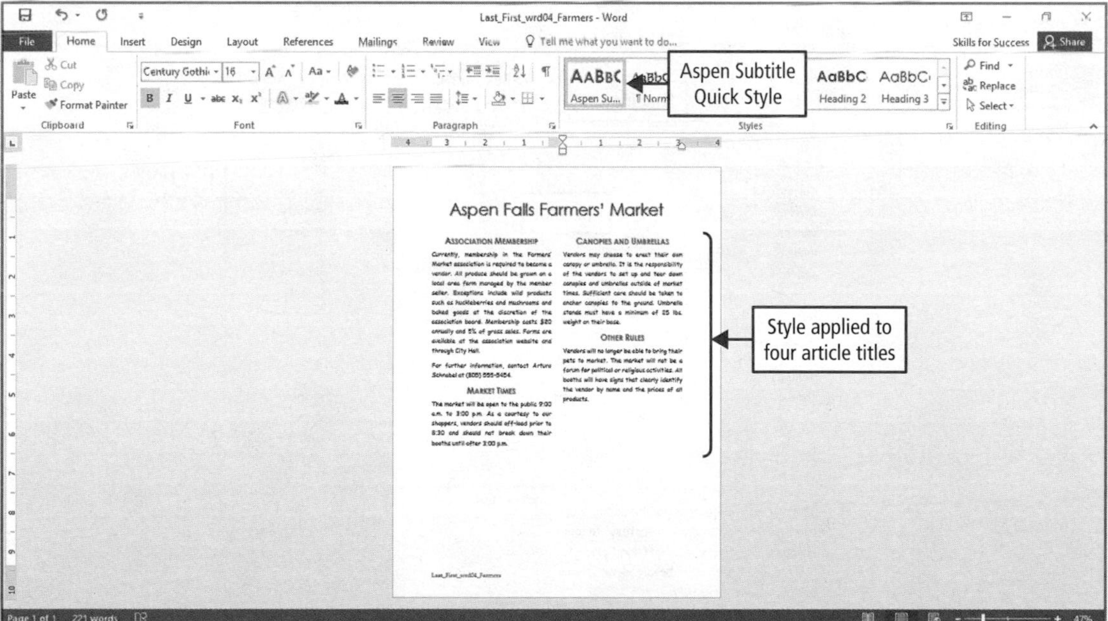

Word 2016, Windows 10, Microsoft Corporation

Figure 4

7. With the subtitle text still selected, on the **Home tab**, in the **Styles group**, click the **More arrow**, and then below the **Styles** gallery, click **Create a Style**.

8. In the **Create New Style from Formatting** dialog box, under **Name**, type Aspen Subtitle Compare your screen with **Figure 3**, and then click **OK** to add the style to the Styles gallery.

   When you create a style in this manner, the style is available only in the same document. In other documents, the style will not display in the Styles gallery.

9. Click to place the insertion point in the subtitle *Canopies and Umbrellas*. On the **Home tab**, in the **Styles group**, click the **Aspen Subtitle** thumbnail to apply the style.

10. Repeat the technique just practiced to apply the **Aspen Subtitle** style to the *Market Times* and *Other Rules* subtitles.

11. On the **View tab**, in the **Zoom group**, click **One Page**. Hide the formatting marks, and then compare your screen with **Figure 4**.

    The styles that you create can be modified and updated in the same manner that pre-built styles are updated.

12. **Save** the file.

■ **You have completed Skill 4 of 10**

- To make a paragraph stand out in a document, you can add a paragraph border or paragraph shading.
- You can use page borders to frame flyers or posters, giving the document a more professional look.

1. On the **Design tab**, in the **Page Background group**, click the **Page Borders** button.
2. In the **Borders and Shading** dialog box, on the **Page Border tab**, under **Setting**, click **Box**.
3. Click the **Color arrow**, and then in the first row under **Theme Colors**, click the last color—**Green, Accent 6**. Click the **Width arrow**, and then click **1½ pt**. Compare your screen with **Figure 1**, and then click **OK** to add the page border.
4. Change the **Zoom** to **100%**, and then display the formatting marks.
5. At the end of the first article, click in the paragraph starting *For further information*.
6. On the **Home tab**, in the **Paragraph group**, click the **Borders arrow**, and then at the bottom of the gallery, click **Borders and Shading**.
7. In the **Borders and Shading** dialog box, click the **Shading tab**. Click the **Fill arrow**, and then under **Theme Colors**, click the last color in the third row—**Green, Accent 6, Lighter 60%**. Compare your screen with **Figure 2**.

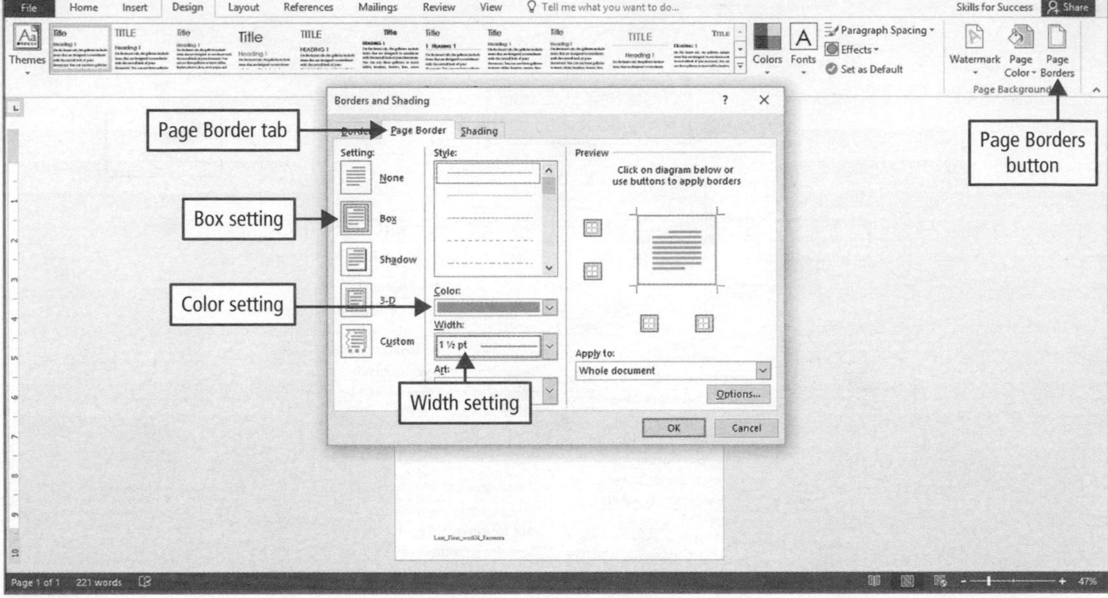

Figure 1

Word 2016, Windows 10, Microsoft Corporation

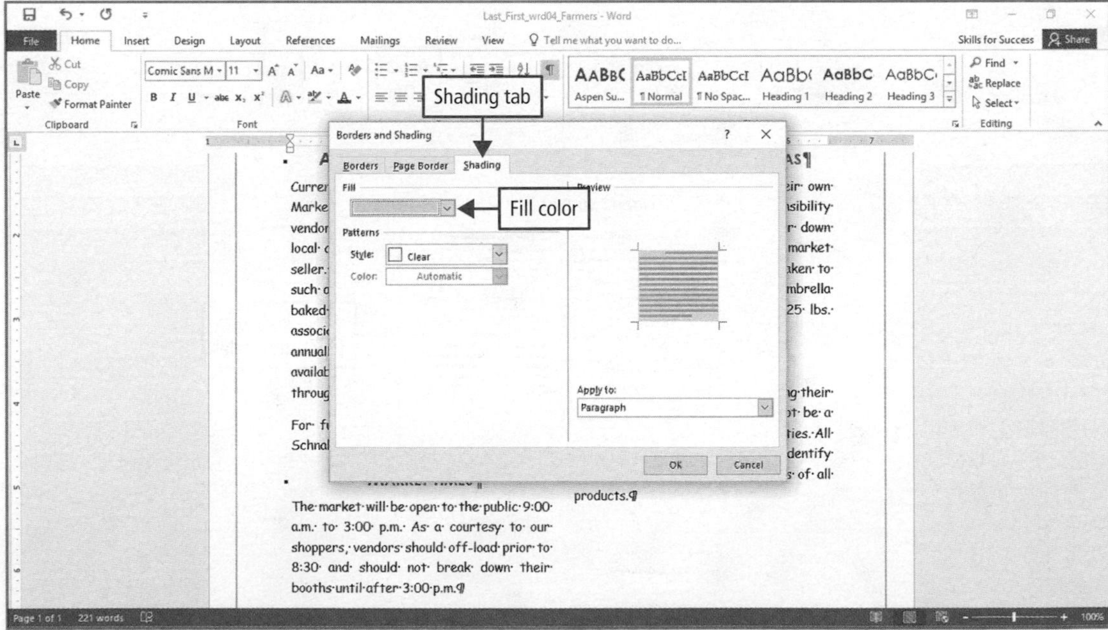

Figure 2

Word 2016, Windows 10, Microsoft Corporation

■ **Continue to the next page to complete the skill**

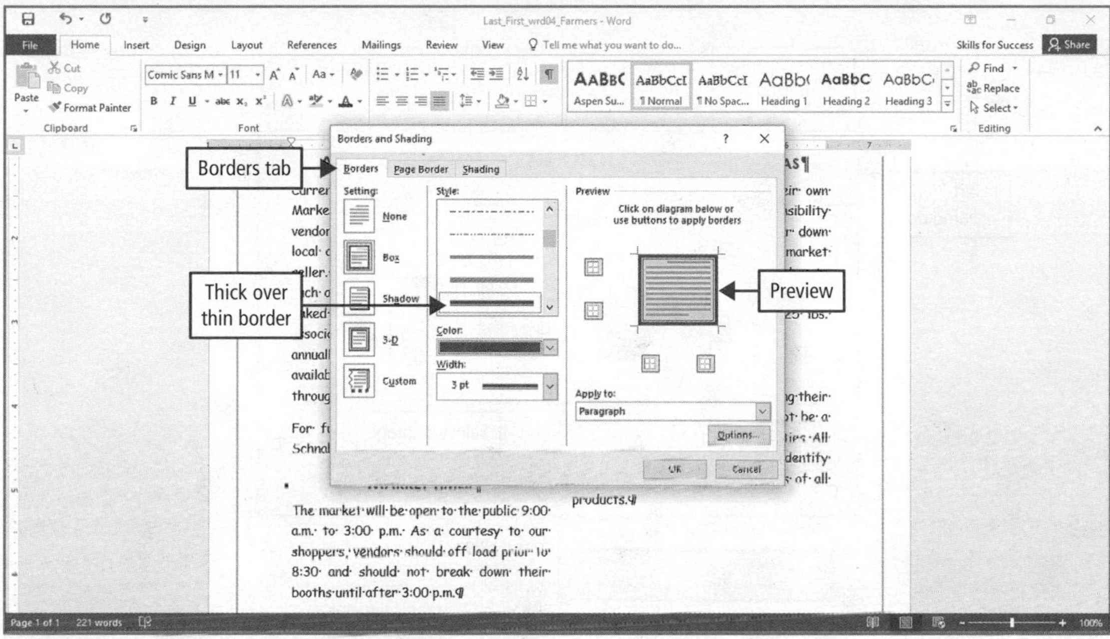

Word 2016, Windows 10, Microsoft Corporation

Figure 3

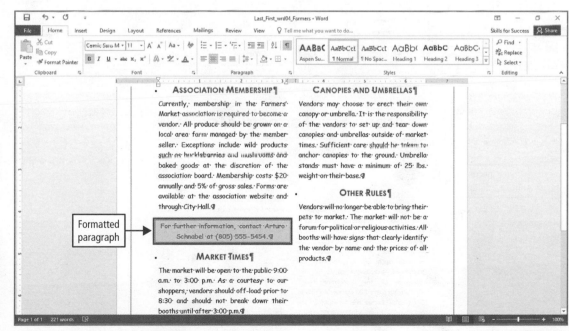

Word 2016, Windows 10, Microsoft Corporation

Figure 4

8. In the **Borders and Shading** dialog box, click the **Borders tab**.
9. On the **Borders tab**, under **Setting**, click **Box**. Under **Style**, scroll down and select the line style with a thick upper line and a thin bottom line.
10. Click the **Color arrow**, and then under **Theme Colors**, click the last color in the last row—**Green, Accent 6, Darker 50%**. Notice that a preview of the box border displays in the Preview area, as shown in **Figure 3**.
11. Click **OK** to apply the changes and close the dialog box.
12. **Center** the paragraph.
13. Select the text, and then in the **Font group**, click the **Bold** button **B**. Click the **Font Color arrow**, and then under **Theme Colors**, in the last row, click the first color—**White, Background 1, Darker 50%**. Deselect the text, and then compare your screen with **Figure 4**.
14. **Save** the file.

■ **You have completed Skill 5 of 10**

SKILL 6: Insert and Adjust Online Pictures

- An ***online image*** is a graphic, drawing, or photograph accessed from Bing Image Search or other online providers.
- You search for and select graphics in the Insert Pictures dialog box.

1. In the first article, click to position the insertion point to the left of *Currently, membership in*.

Obj 5.1.2 C

2. On the **Insert tab**, in the **Illustrations group**, click the **Online Pictures** button to display the Insert Pictures dialog box.

   The Insert Pictures dialog box is used to connect with online services such as Bing Image Search and your OneDrive. You may have additional providers listed, and if you are not signed in, your OneDrive may not display.

3. In the **Insert Pictures** dialog box, in the **Bing Image Search** box, type farmer and then click the **Search** button. If a message displays, close it. Browse the search results and click an image suitable for use in a newsletter about a farmer's market. Click the image, and then compare your screen with **Figure 1**.

   Because the online images available at Bing Image Search change frequently, your search results will likely be different than shown. If the image in Figure 1 is no longer available, choose a different image.

4. Click the **Insert** button to insert the image into the document. Compare your screen with **Figure 2**.

■ **Continue to the next page to complete the skill**

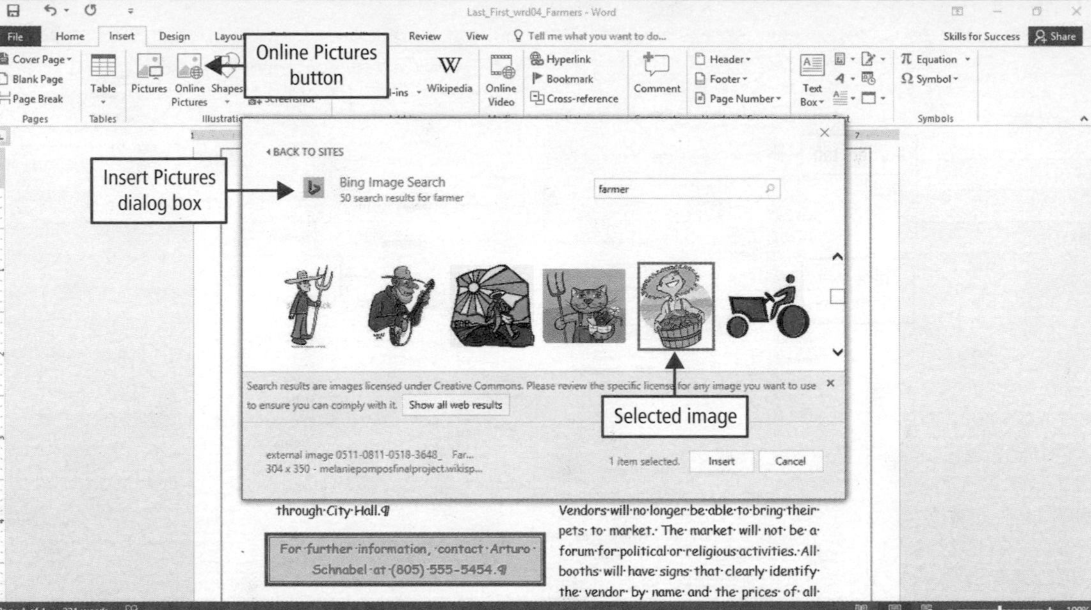

Figure 1

Word 2016, Windows 10, Microsoft Corporation

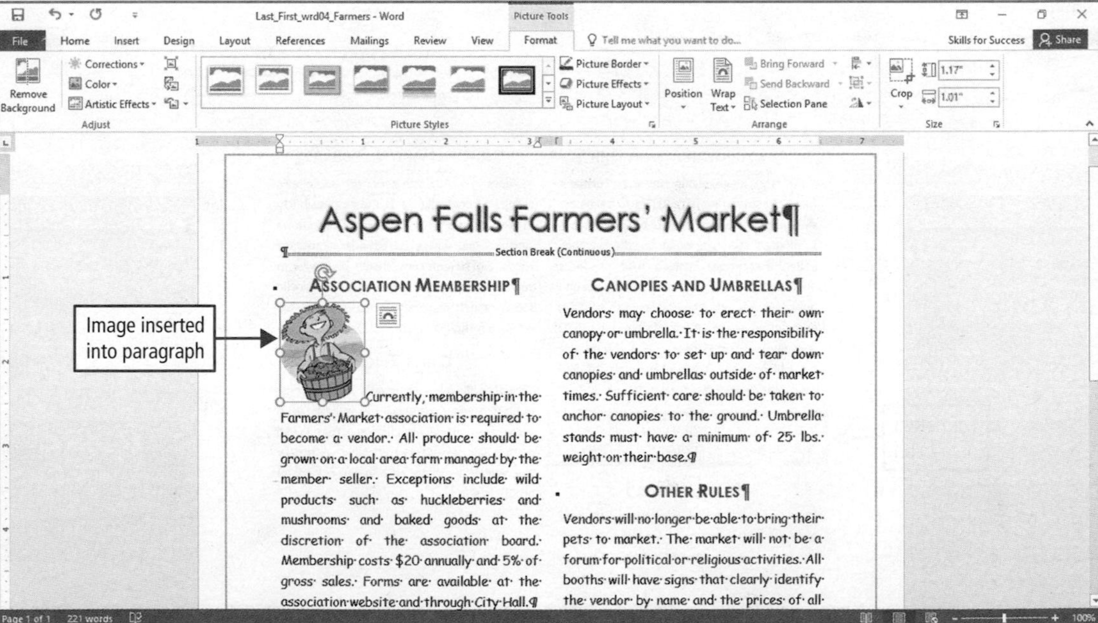

Figure 2

Word 2016, Windows 10, Microsoft Corporation

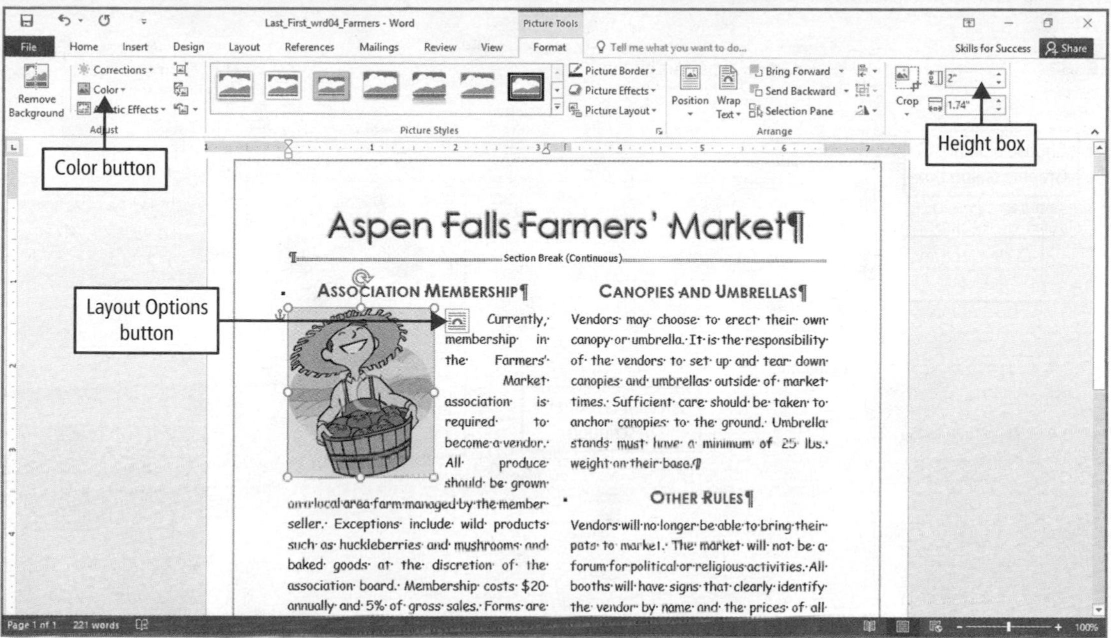

Word 2016, Windows 10, Microsoft Corporation

Figure 3

Word 2016, Windows 10, Microsoft Corporation

Figure 4

5. With the image selected, on the **Format tab**, in the **Adjust group**, click **Color**, and then point to several thumbnails to preview their effects.

MOS Obj 5.2.4 C

6. In the **Recolor** gallery, in the second row, click the last choice—**Green, Accent color 6 Dark**.

   You can change picture adjustments and styles to online images in the same manner you modify photographs. Here, the look and feel of the image has been changed using the same color tones as in the subtitles.

7. With the image selected, click the **Layout Options** button, and then under **With Text Wrapping**, click the first thumbnail—**Square**.

8. Click the **Layout Options** button again, and then click **See more**. In the **Layout** dialog box, on the **Size tab**, under **Scale**, clear the **Lock aspect ratio** check box, and then click **OK**. In the **Size group**, change the **Height** to **2"** and the **Width** to **1.74"**, and then click **OK**. Compare your screen with **Figure 3**.

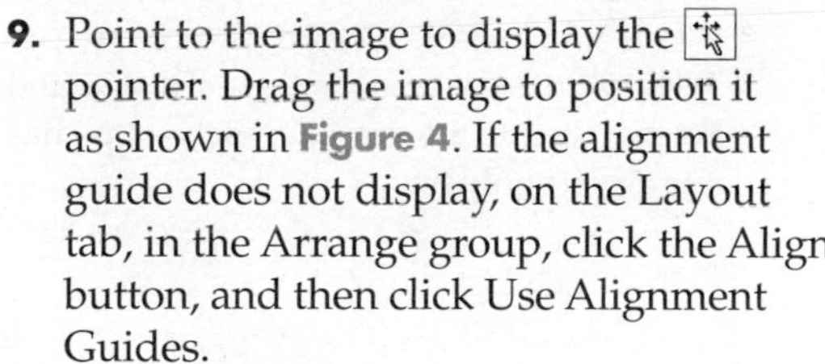

9. Point to the image to display the pointer. Drag the image to position it as shown in **Figure 4**. If the alignment guide does not display, on the Layout tab, in the Arrange group, click the Align button, and then click Use Alignment Guides.
10. **Save** the file.

■ **You have completed Skill 6 of 10**

- A ***SmartArt graphic*** is a pre-built visual representation of information.
- You can choose from many different SmartArt layouts to communicate your message or ideas.

1. Press Ctrl + End to move the insertion point to the end of the document. On the **Insert tab**, in the **Illustrations group**, click the **SmartArt** button.

MOS Obj 5.3.1 C

2. In the **Choose a SmartArt Graphic** dialog box, scroll down and look at the various types of layouts that are available.
3. On the left side of the dialog box, click **Cycle**. Click the first layout—**Basic Cycle**, and then compare your screen with **Figure 1**.
4. In the **Choose a SmartArt Graphic** dialog box, read the description of the selected layout, and then click **OK**. Compare your screen with **Figure 2**. If the Text pane displays to the left of the graphic, click the Text Pane button on the left border to close it.

   When SmartArt is selected, two SmartArt Tools contextual tabs display—Design and Format. Inside the graphic, each shape has a text placeholder.

■ **Continue to the next page to complete the skill**

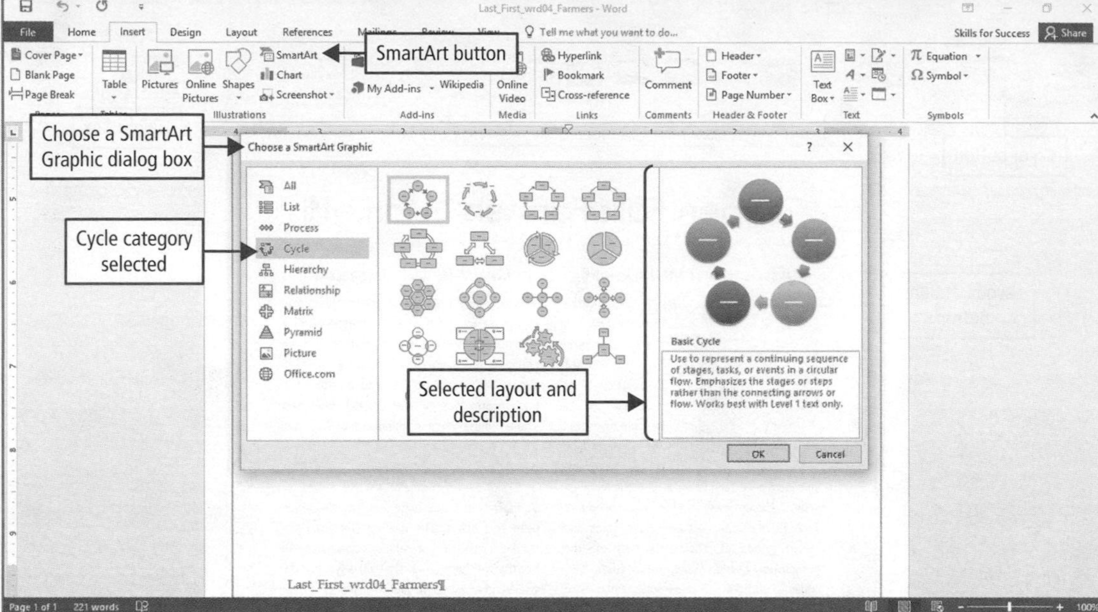

Figure 1 Word 2016, Windows 10, Microsoft Corporation

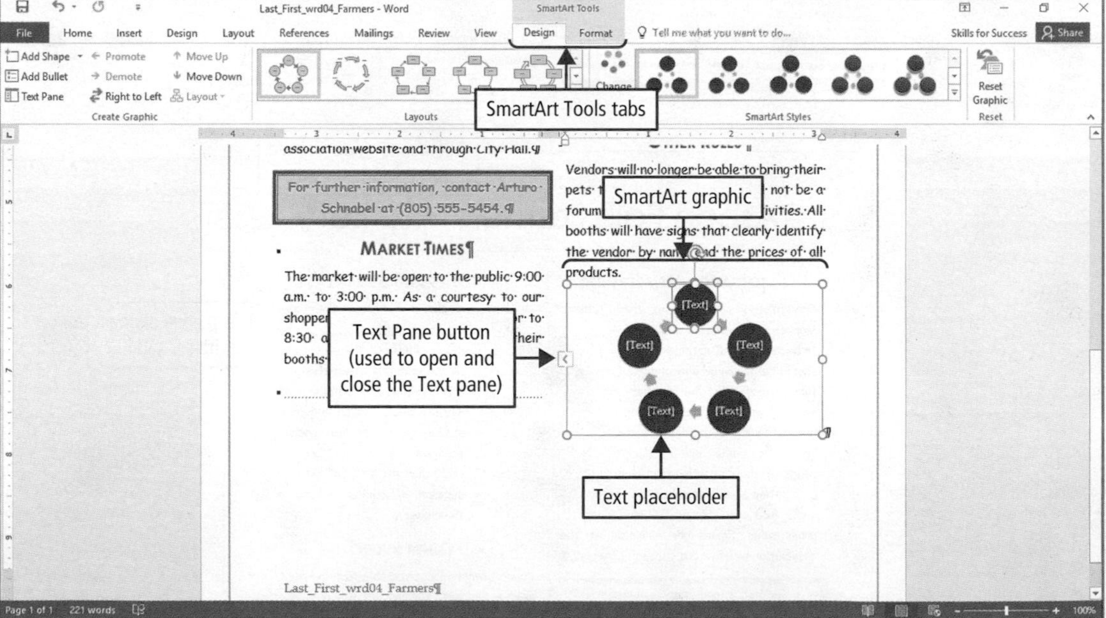

Figure 2 Word 2016, Windows 10, Microsoft Corporation

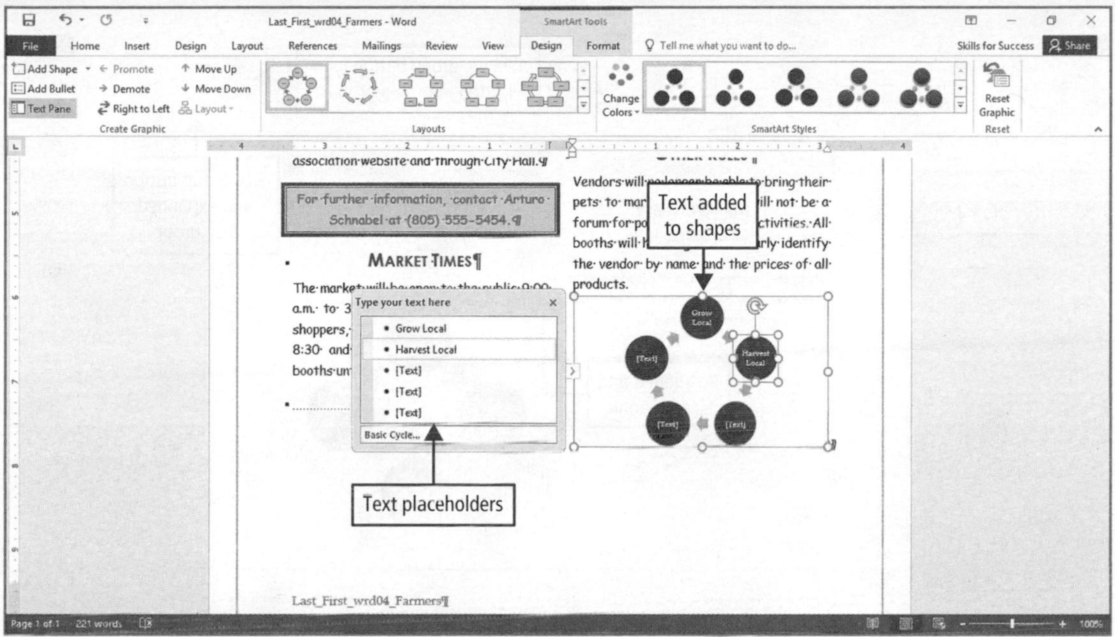

Word 2016, Windows 10, Microsoft Corporation

Figure 3

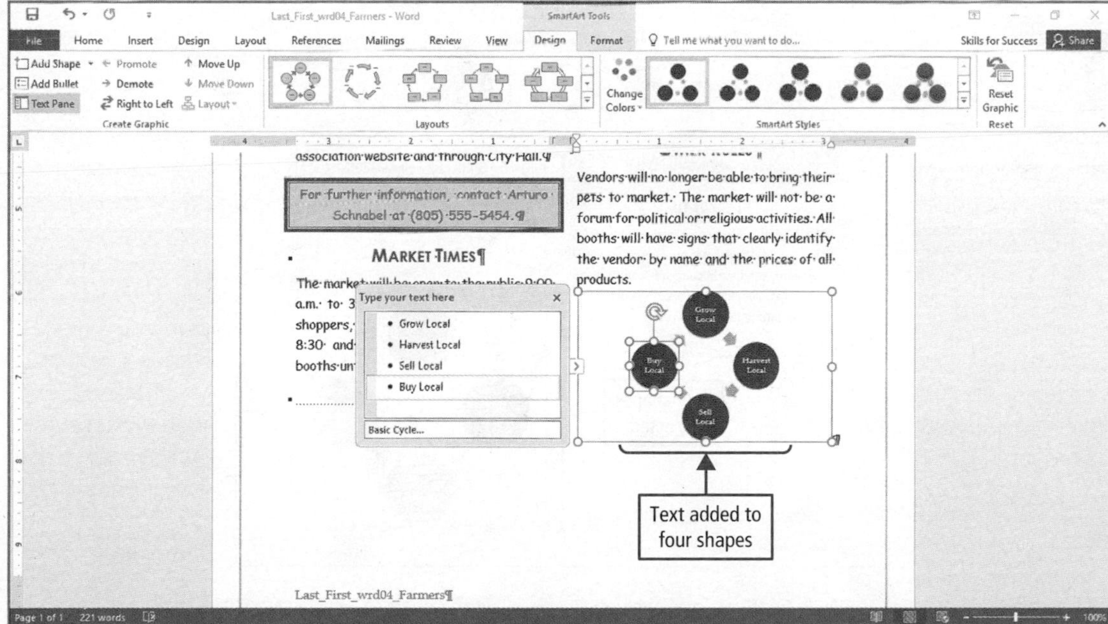

Word 2016, Windows 10, Microsoft Corporation

Figure 4

5. In the upper shape, click the **[Text]** placeholder, and then type Grow Local
6. In the middle-right shape, click the **[Text]** placeholder, and then type Harvest Local

   As you work with SmartArt, the shape and font sizes automatically adjust to the contents.

7. On the left border, click the **Text Pane** button, and then compare your screen with **Figure 3**.

   The Text pane displays text as bullets and provides an alternate method of entering text. In the pane, you can remove or add shapes by removing or adding bullets, and you can insert subordinate shapes by indenting bullets.

8. In the **Text** pane, click the first **[Text]** placeholder—the third bullet, and then type Sell Local Notice that while you type in the bulleted list, the text also displays in the third SmartArt shape.

   To move to the next [Text] shape in the Text pane, you can also press [↓] or [↑].

9. Press [↓] to move to the next bullet, and then type Buy Local
10. With the insertion point to the right of the text *Buy Local*, press [Delete] to remove the fifth shape, and then compare your screen with **Figure 4**.

MOS Obj 5.3.3 C

11. **Close** [X] the Text pane, and then **Save** [💾] the file.

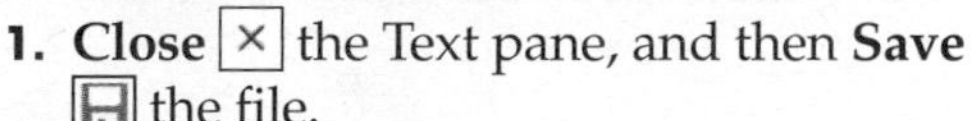

■ **You have completed Skill 7 of 10**

► You can resize an entire SmartArt graphic, or you can resize its individual shapes.

1. Click the border of the SmartArt graphic to select the graphic without selecting any of its shapes.
2. Click the **Format tab**, and then click the **Arrange group** button. Click **Position**, and then under **With Text Wrapping**, click the last thumbnail—**Position in Bottom Right with Square Text Wrapping**.

    On smaller monitors, some groups collapse and are accessed only by clicking a button. If you are working with a larger monitor, your Arrange and Size groups may not be collapsed.

Obj 5.3.2 C

3. If necessary, scroll down to display the SmartArt graphic. On the **Format tab**, click the **Size group** button. Change **Height** value to **2.7"**, and then compare your screen with **Figure 1**.

    When you change the height of a SmartArt graphic, the graphic width is not resized proportionally.

4. In the SmartArt graphic, click the first shape, and then click its border so that the border is a solid line. Press and hold Ctrl while clicking the other three shapes. Compare your screen with **Figure 2**.

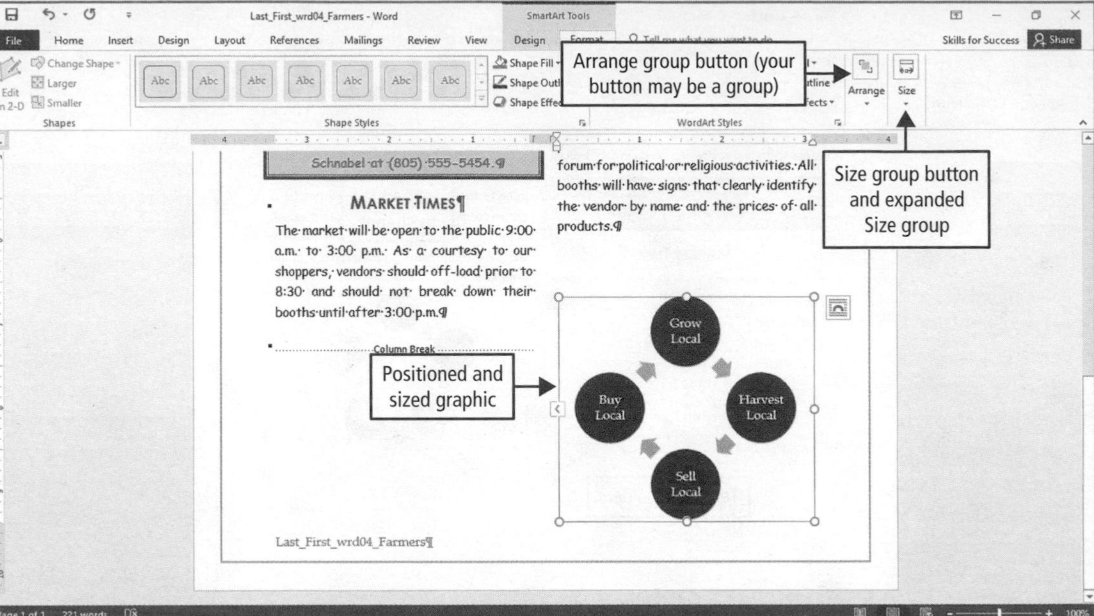

Figure 1

Word 2016, Windows 10, Microsoft Corporation

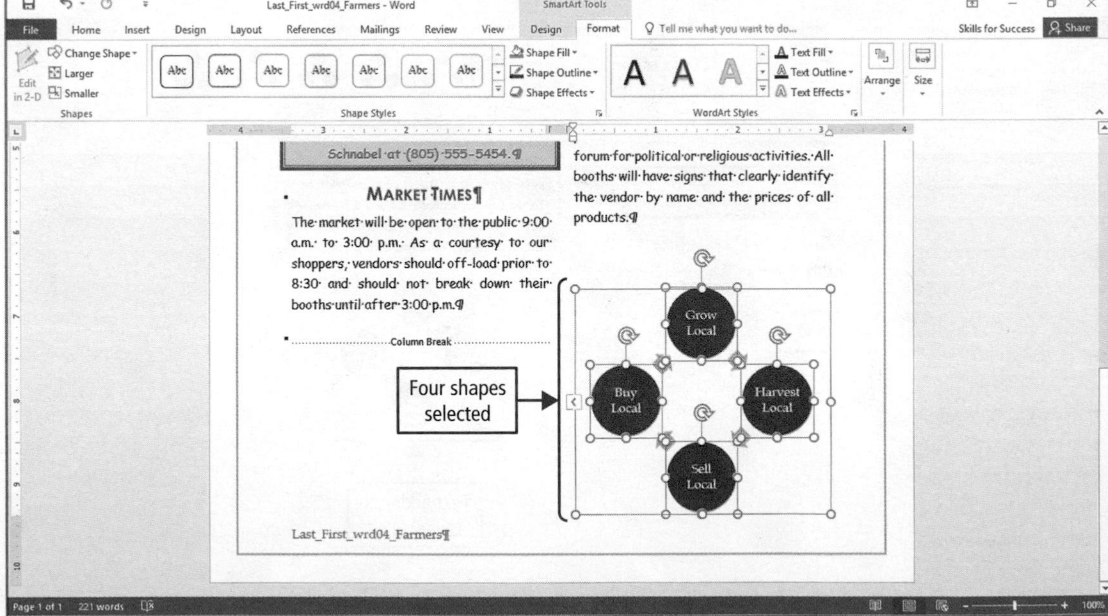

Figure 2

Word 2016, Windows 10, Microsoft Corporation

■ **Continue to the next page to complete the skill**

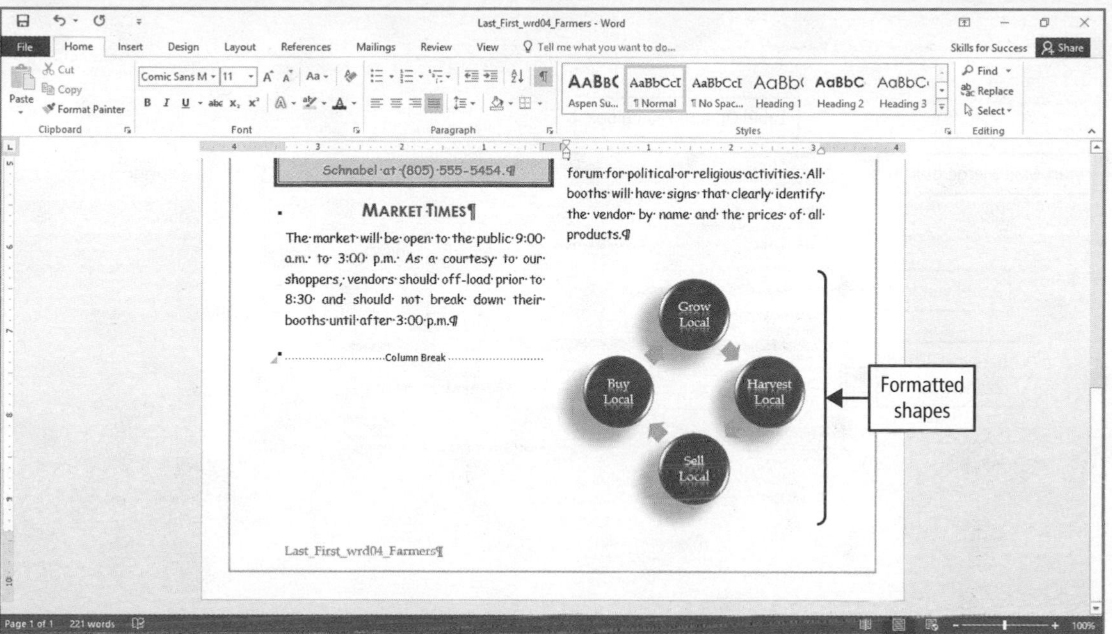

Word 2016, Windows 10, Microsoft Corporation

Figure 3

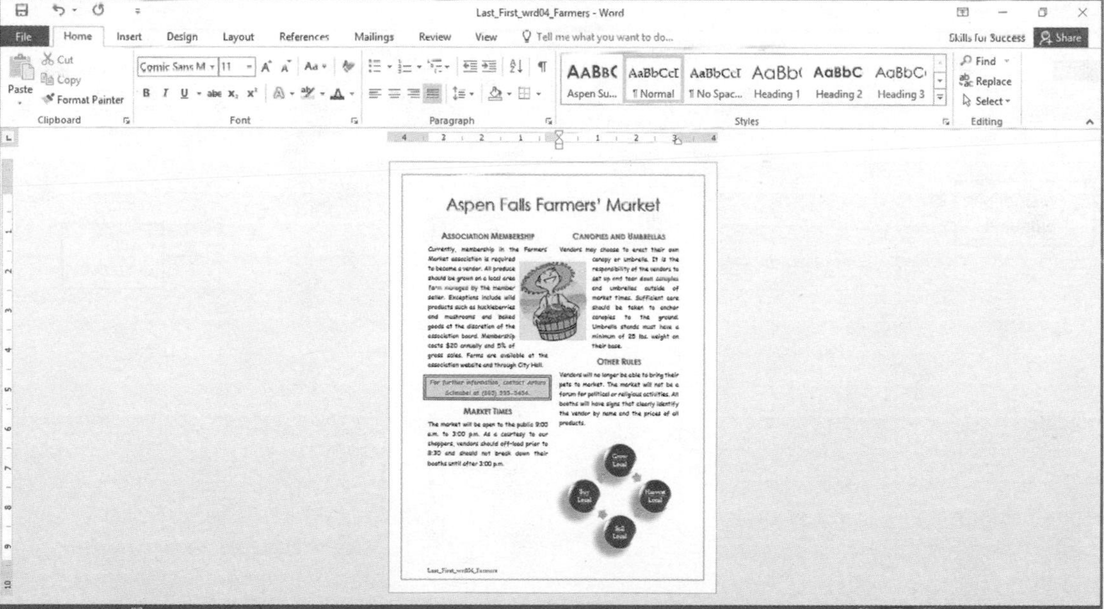

Word 2016, Windows 10, Microsoft Corporation

Figure 4

Obj 5.3.2 C

5. With all four shapes selected, on the **Format tab**, in the **Shape Styles group**, click the **Shape Fill** button. Under **Theme Colors**, click the last color in the last row—**Green, Accent 6, Darker 50%**.
6. In the **Shape Styles group**, click the **Shape Effects** button. Point to **Preset**, and then under **Presets**, click the first effect in the second row—**Preset 5**.
7. With all four shapes still selected, in the **WordArt Styles group**, click the **Text Effects** button. Point to **Reflection**, and then under **Reflection Variations**, click the first effect—**Tight Reflection, touching**.
8. Click in the document to deselect the SmartArt graphic, and then compare your screen with **Figure 3**.
9. On the **View tab**, in the **Zoom group**, click the **One Page** button. Hide the formatting marks, and then compare your screen with **Figure 4**.
10. In the **Zoom group**, click the **100%** button.
11. **Save** the file, and then **Close** the file.

- **You have completed Skill 8 of 10**

- The ***mail merge*** feature is used to customize letters or labels by combining a main document with a data source.
- The ***main document*** contains the text that remains constant; the ***data source*** contains the information—such as names and addresses—that changes with each letter or label in the main mail merge document.

1. Start **Word 2016**, and then on the start page, click **Blank document**. Save the file in your chapter folder as Last_First_wrd04_FarmerMain

   This file is the main document that will be linked to the data source.
2. Click the **Mailings tab**. In the **Start Mail Merge group**, click the **Start Mail Merge** button, and then click **Labels** to open the Label Options dialog box, as shown in **Figure 1**.
3. Under **Label information**, click the **Label vendors arrow**, scroll down, and then click **Avery US Letter**. Under **Product number**, click a label, and then press [5]. Scroll down and click **5160 Easy Peel Address Labels**, and then click **OK**.
4. Compare your screen with **Figure 2**. If necessary, display the formatting marks, and on the Table Tools Layout tab, in the Table group, select View Gridlines.

   The Avery 5160 address label has precut sheets with three columns of ten labels each.
5. On the **Mailings tab**, in the **Start Mail Merge group**, click the **Select Recipients** button, and then click **Use an Existing List**.

■ **Continue to the next page to complete the skill**

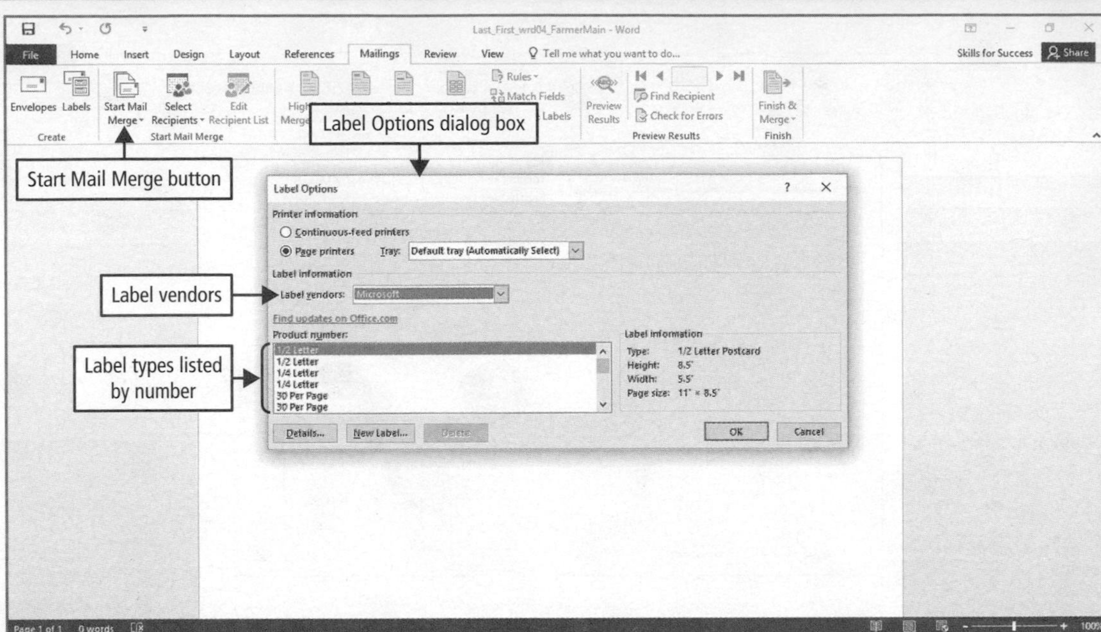

Figure 1 Word 2016, Windows 10, Microsoft Corporation

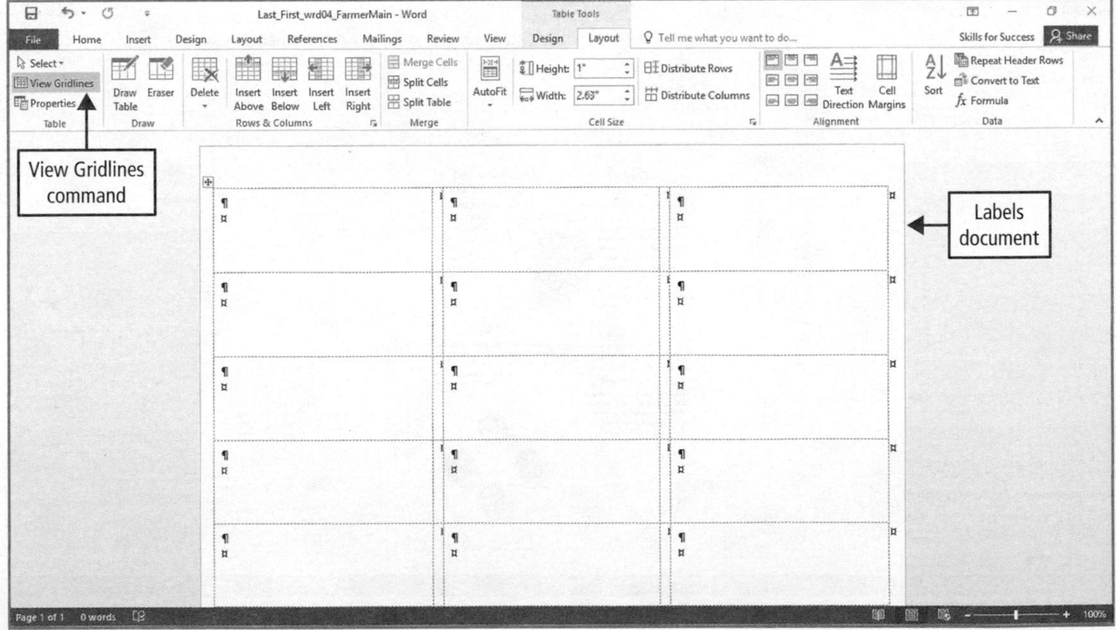

Figure 2 Word 2016, Windows 10, Microsoft Corporation

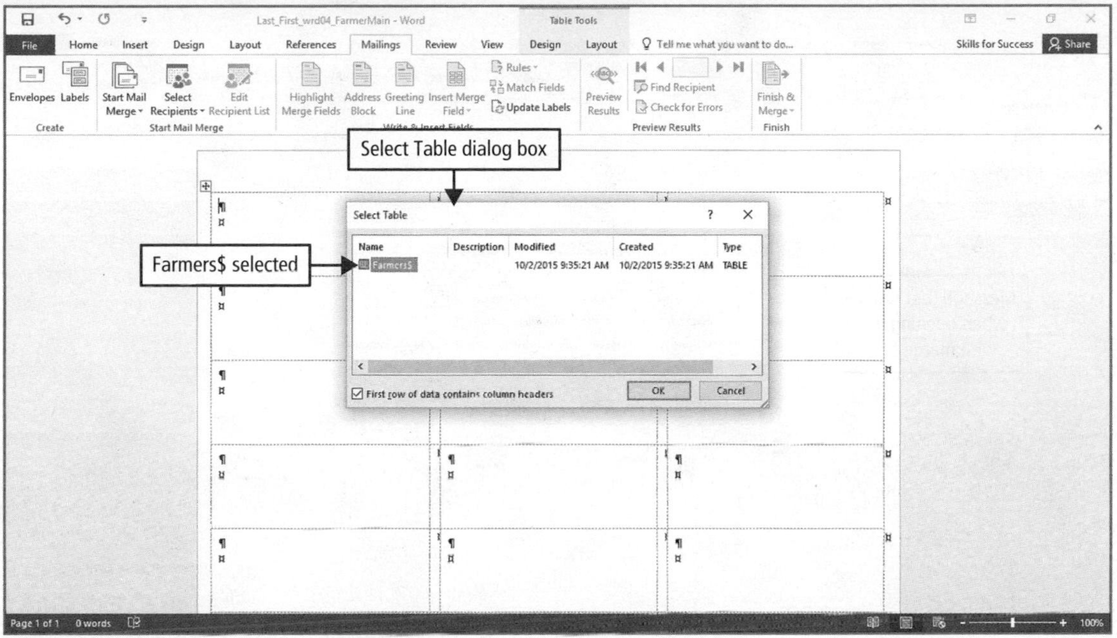

Word 2016, Windows 10, Microsoft Corporation

Figure 3

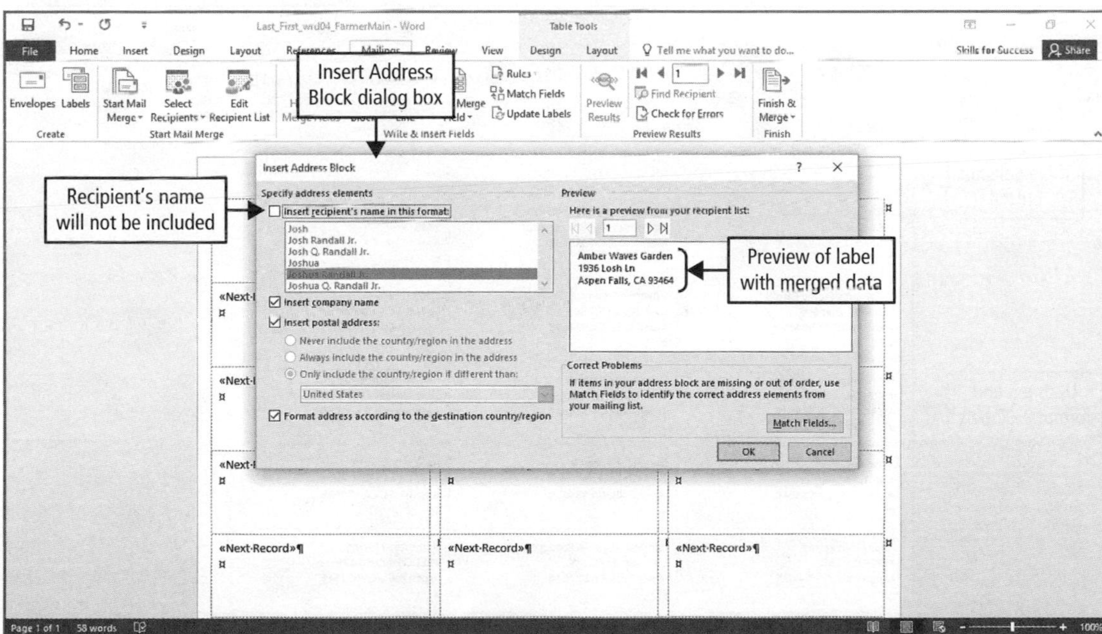

Word 2016, Windows 10, Microsoft Corporation

Figure 4

6. In the **Select Data Source** dialog box, navigate to the student data files, click **wrd04_FarmerAddresses**, and then click **Open**. Compare your screen with **Figure 3**.
7. In the **Select Table** dialog box, under **Name**, verify **Farmers$** is selected, and then click **OK**.
8. In the **Start Mail Merge group**, click the **Edit Recipient List** button. In the row of column headings, click the **Company** heading one time to sort the list by company names, and then click **OK**.
9. In the **Write & Insert Fields group**, click the **Address Block** button. In the **Insert Address Block** dialog box, under **Specify address elements**, clear the **Insert recipient's name in this format** check box. Compare your screen with **Figure 4**, and then click **OK**.

   Merge fields merge and display data from specific columns in the data source. They are surrounded by nonprinting characters—for example, «AddressBlock» and «Next Record».

10. **Save** [Save icon], and then **Close** [X] the file.

■ **You have completed Skill 9 of 10**

SKILL 10: Preview and Print Mail Merge Documents

► When you open a merge document, you need to confirm that you want to open the document. Confirmation runs an ***SQL select query***—a command that selects data from a data source based on the criteria you specify.

1. Start **Word 2016**, and then open **Last_First_wrd04_FarmerMain**. Compare your screen with **Figure 1**.

   The message informs you that data from the data source will be placed in the document. If you have moved to a different computer or are saving to a network drive, you may also be asked to locate the data source file—*Last_First_wrd04_FarmerAddresses*.

2. Read the message, and then click **Yes** to open the labels document.

   If you encounter a similar message when opening a document that you did not expect to contain merged data, you should click No to protect your privacy.

3. On the **Mailings tab**, in the **Preview Results group**, click the **Preview Results** button. In the **Write & Insert Fields group**, click **Update Labels**.

   The Update Labels command is used to fill in the data from the remaining rows in the data source.

4. Click the **Table Selector** button [⊞] to select all the labels. On the **Home tab**, open the **Paragraph** dialog box, change the **Spacing Before** to **0 pt**, and then click **OK**.

5. With the text still selected, click the **Table Tools Layout tab**, and then in the **Alignment group**, click the **Align Center Left** button [≡] to vertically center the label text. Deselect the table, and then compare your screen with **Figure 2**.

■ **Continue to the next page to complete the skill**

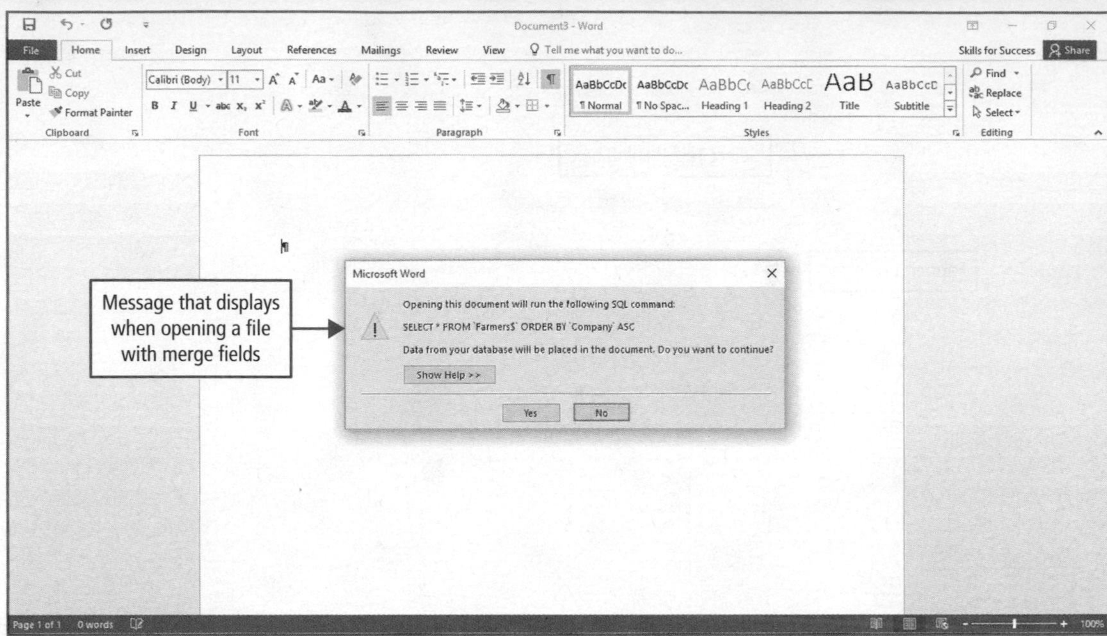

Figure 1 Word 2016, Windows 10, Microsoft Corporation

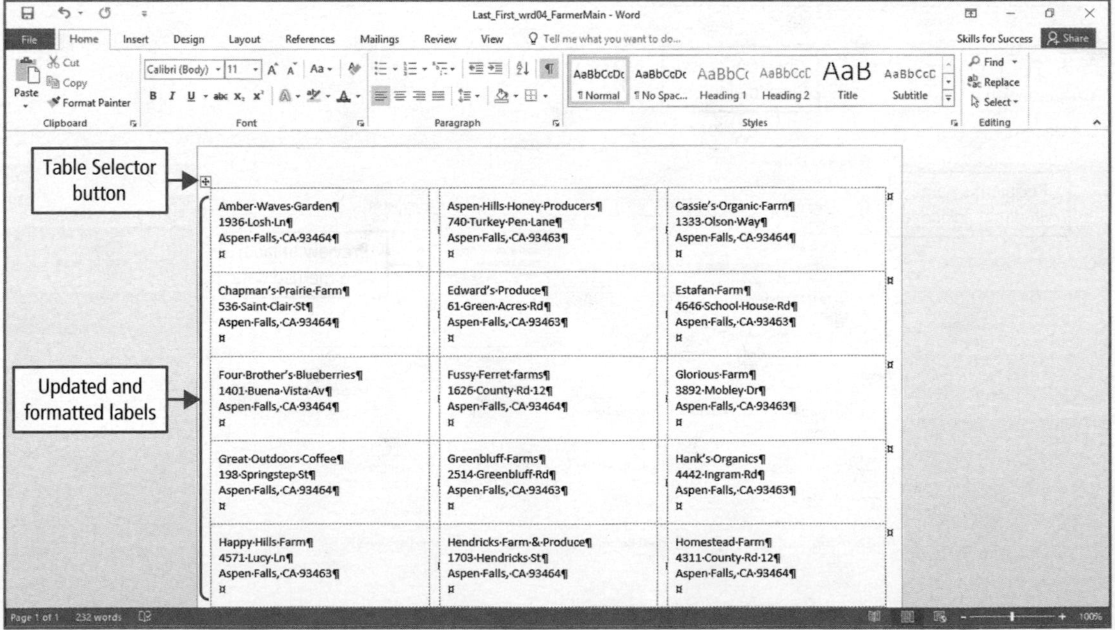

Figure 2 Word 2016, Windows 10, Microsoft Corporation

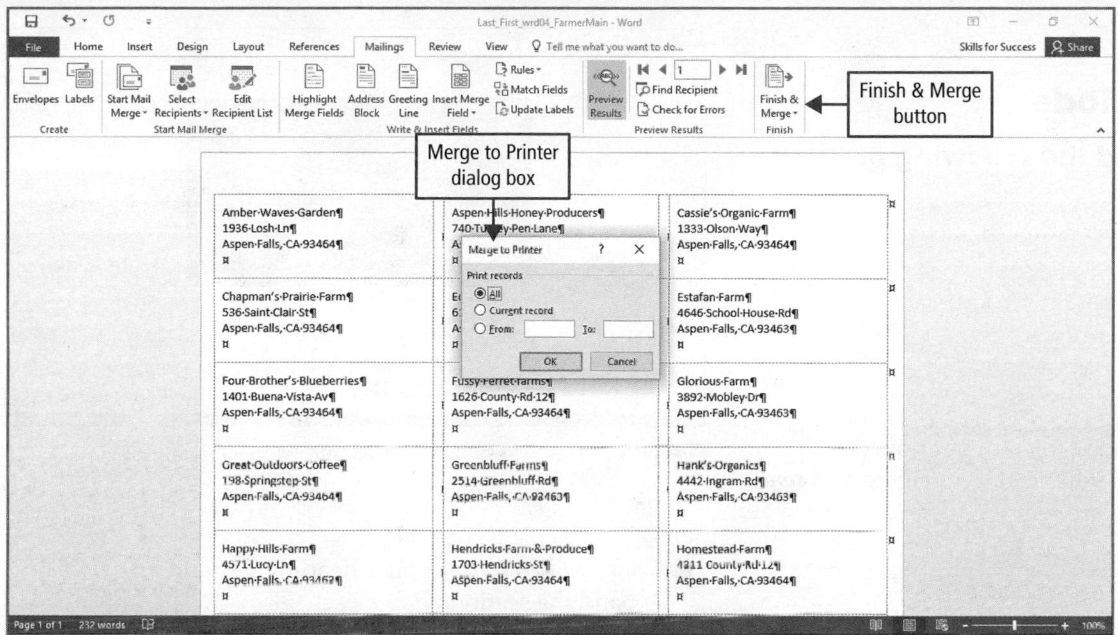

Word 2016, Windows 10, Microsoft Corporation

Figure 3

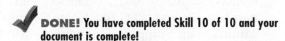

Word 2016, Windows 10, Microsoft Corporation

Figure 4

6. Click the **Mailings tab**. In the **Finish group**, click the **Finish & Merge** button, and then click **Print Documents**. Compare your screen with **Figure 3**.

   Typically a merge is completed by sending the document with its merged data to a printer with the label sheet(s) inserted into the appropriate printer tray.

7. In the **Merge to Printer** dialog box, click **Cancel**. In the **Finish group**, click the **Finish & Merge** button, and then click **Edit Individual Documents**. In the **Merge to New Document** dialog box, click **OK** to create a new document named *Labels1*.

   When you merge to a new document, the merge fields are replaced with the corresponding data from each row in the data source and the new document does not contain any merge fields.

8. **Save** the file in your chapter folder as Last_First_wrd04_FarmerMerge

9. Select the table, and then click the **Home tab**. In the **Font group**, click the **Change Case arrow** Aa, and then click **UPPERCASE**.

10. Click to deselect the table, and then hide the formatting marks. Press Ctrl + Home, and then compare your screen with **Figure 4**.

11. **Save** the file, **Close** Word, and then submit the files as directed by your instructor.

DONE! You have completed Skill 10 of 10 and your document is complete!

More Skills 11

Optimize Documents for Read Mode

To complete this project, you will need the following file:

- wrd04_MS11LEDs

You will save your files as:

- Last_First_wrd04_MS11LEDs
- Last_First_wrd04_MS11Snip1
- Last_First_wrd04_MS11Snip2

▸ ***Read Mode*** is a view that is used when you need to read, but not edit, electronic documents. In Read Mode, the tools you need to navigate and read a document are provided and the editing tools are removed.

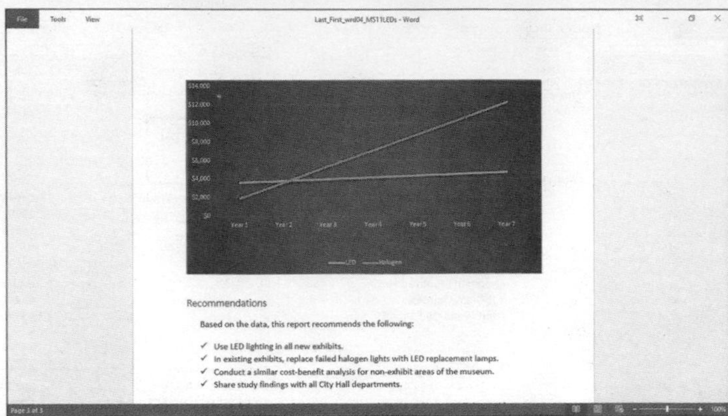

Figure 1 Word 2016, Windows 10, Microsoft Corporation

---

1. Start **Word 2016**, and then open the student data file **wrd04_MS11LEDs**. **Save** the file in your chapter folder as Last_First_wrd04_MS11LEDs Add the **FileName** field to the footer.
2. Move to the end of the document, and then click the subheading *Recommendations*. On the **Home tab**, in the **Styles group**, click **Heading 2**. Point to the subheading, and then click the **Collapse arrow** ◿ to collapse the section.

   When you assign Heading styles, those headings can be collapsed and expanded. Here, the hollow triangle indicates that the *Recommendations* heading is collapsed and the paragraphs associated with that section are hidden.

3. On the **View tab**, in the **Views group**, click **Read Mode**. MOS Obj 1.4.1 C
4. Click ⊞, type snip and then press Enter. In the **Snipping Tool** window, click the **New arrow**, and then click **Full-screen Snip**.
5. In the **Snipping Tool** mark-up window, click the **Save Snip** button 💾. In the **Save As** dialog box, navigate to your chapter folder. Be sure the **Save as type** box displays **JPEG file**. Name the snip Last_First_wrd04_MS11Snip1 **Minimize** the **Snipping Tool** mark-up window.
6. Double-click the chart, and then click the **Zoom** button 🔍.

   Objects such as charts and pictures can be represented by smaller thumbnails and then zoomed in this manner. This maximizes the amount of space for text, especially when viewed on a tablet.

7. Click anywhere outside the enlarged chart to return the document to Read Mode.
8. Click the *Recommendations* heading **Expand arrow** ▷ to expand the section.
9. Click the buttons on the sides of the pages.

   To move between pages, you can click the arrows on the sides of the pages, or press PageDown, PageUp, SpaceBar, and Backspace. If you are working with a touch display, you can swipe left or right to move between pages.

10. Click **View**, and then from the menu, point to **Layout**, and then click **Paper Layout**.

    When the Read Mode layout is set to paper, the page size is adjusted to a standard sheet of paper instead of to the size of the window.

11. Scroll to display the chart as shown in **Figure 1**, and then on the taskbar, click the **Snipping tool** icon. Click the **New** button, and then repeat the step to save a **Full-screen Snip** as Last_First_wrd04_MS11Snip2 **Close** the Snipping tool window.
12. Click **View**, and then click **Edit Document** to return to Print Layout view.  Obj 1.4.1 C
13. **Save** the file, **Close** Word, and then submit the files as directed by your instructor.

■ **You have completed More Skills 11**

More Skills 12

Work in Outline View

To complete this project, you will need the following file:

- wrd04_MS12Hotel

You will save your files as:

- Last_First_wrd04_MS12Hotel
- Last_First_wrd04_MS12Snip1
- Last_First_wrd04_MS12Snip2

▸ Use Outline view to display all of the headings and body text, collapse headings, or move headings and associated text.

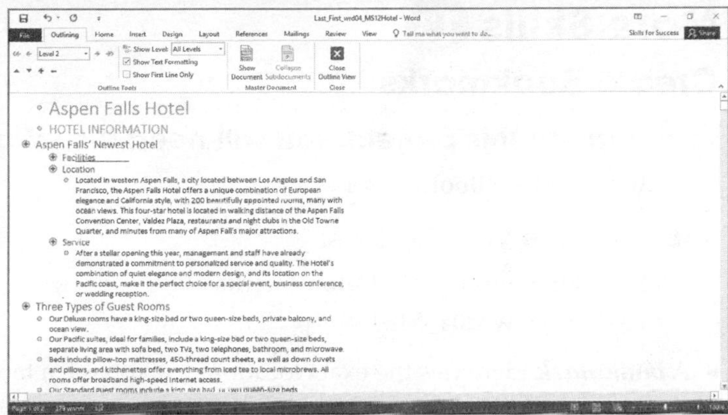

Word 2016, Windows 10, Microsoft Corporation **Figure 1**

---

1. Start **Word 2016**, and then open the student data file **wrd04_MS12Hotel**. **Save** the file in your chapter folder as Last_First_wrd04_MS12Hotel Add the **FileName** field to the footer, and then move to the beginning of the document.
2. On the **View tab**, in the **Views group**, click the **Outline** button. On the **Outlining tab**, in the **Outline Tools group**, verify that the **Show Text Formatting** check box is selected. MOS Obj 1.4.1 C
3. Click in the third paragraph *Aspen Falls' Newest Hotel*. On the **Outlining tab**, in the **Outline Tools group**, click the **Promote to Heading 1** button one time to assign the Level 1 outline level. Alternately, press Shift + Tab.

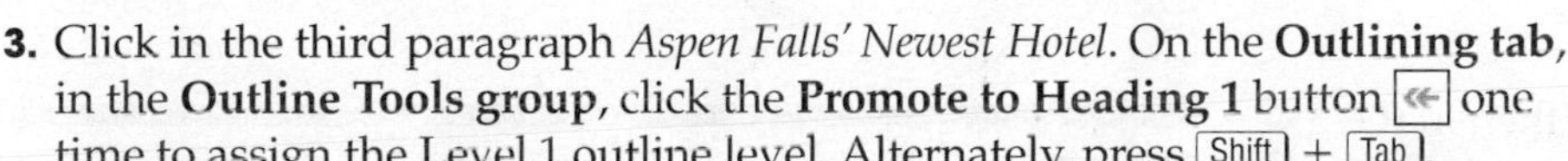

4. Repeat the technique to change the paragraphs *Three Types of Guest Rooms* and *Additional Hotel Facilities* to **Level 1** outline levels.
5. Just below the first Level 1 heading, click in the paragraph *Facilities*. In the **Outline Tools group**, click the **Outline Level arrow** Body Text, and then click **Level 2**.
6. Click in the paragraph *Location*. In the **Outline Tools group**, click the **Outline Level arrow** Body Text, and then click **Level 2**. Alternately, press the Promote arrow. Repeat this step to change *Service* to the **Level 2** outline level.
7. Click anywhere in the *Facilities* Level 2 heading. In the **Outline Tools group**, click the **Collapse** button. Alternately, double-click the plus sign to the left of the heading. Compare your screen with **Figure 1**.

   Expanding or collapsing levels can make long documents easier to organize. When you collapse an outline level, all the text associated with that level is hidden. The gray wavy line below the heading indicates that the text is hidden.

8. Open the **Snipping Tool** window, and then save a **Full-screen Snip** in your chapter folder as Last_First_wrd04_MS12Snip1 **Minimize** the **Snipping Tool** mark-up window.
9. In the **Outline Tools group**, click the **Show Level arrow**, and then click **Level 2**.

   When you specify which level to display, only the paragraphs that have been assigned outline levels equal to or higher than the selected level display.

10. Point to the plus sign to the left of *Location*. Click and drag up until a gray line displays above *Facilities*, and then release the mouse button. Double-click the plus sign to the left of *Location* to expand the section.

    The heading and all associated lower level headings and body text are moved and display.

11. On the taskbar, click the **Snipping tool** icon. Save a **Full-screen Snip** as Last_First_wrd04_MS12Snip2 **Close** the Snipping tool window.
12. In the **Outline Tools group**, click the **Show Level arrow**, and then click **All Levels**. In the **Close group**, click the **Close Outline View** button.
13. **Save** the file, **Close** Word, and then submit the files as directed by your instructor.

■ **You have completed More Skills 12**

More Skills 13

Create Bookmarks

To complete this project, you will need the following file:

- wrd04_MS13Bookmarks

You will save your files as:

- Last_First_wrd04_MS13Bookmarks
- Last_First_wrd04_MS13Snip

- ► A ***bookmark*** identifies the exact location of an object, a table, or text that you name for future reference.
- ► Bookmark names should briefly describe their destination and do not include spaces.

---

1. Start **Word 2016**, and then open the student data file **wrd04_MS13Bookmarks**. **Save** the file in your chapter folder as Last_First_wrd04_MS13Bookmarks Add the **FileName** field to the Page 2 footer.
2. On Page 2, select the *SITE INFORMATION* heading. On the **Insert tab**, in the **Links group**, click the **Bookmark** button. Type Site_Info Compare your screen with **Figure 1**, and then click **Add**. MOS Obj 1.2.3 C

   In a bookmark name, the underscore character is used between words instead of a space.

   Bookmark characters typically do not display in the document.
3. On Page 2, select the *ZONING INFORMATION* heading, and then in the **Links group**, click the **Bookmark** button. In the **Bookmark name** box, type Zoning_Info and then click **Add**.
4. Select the *Change in Classification* heading, and then repeat the technique just practiced to add a bookmark named Classification
5. On Page 3, add a bookmark to the *Commercial Zoning Requirement* heading named Commercial and then add a bookmark to the *FIRE STATION DESIGN ELEMENTS* heading named Design_Elements
6. On Page 3, select the fire station picture. In the **Links group**, click the **Bookmark** button, and then in the **Bookmark name** box, type Figure_1 In the displayed **Bookmark** dialog box, to the right of **Sort by**, select the **Location** option button, and then compare your screen with **Figure 2**.

   The bookmarks now display in the order in which they occur in the document.
7. Create a **Full-screen Snip**, and then **Save** it in your chapter folder as Last_First_wrd04_MS13Snip **Close** the Snipping Tool window.

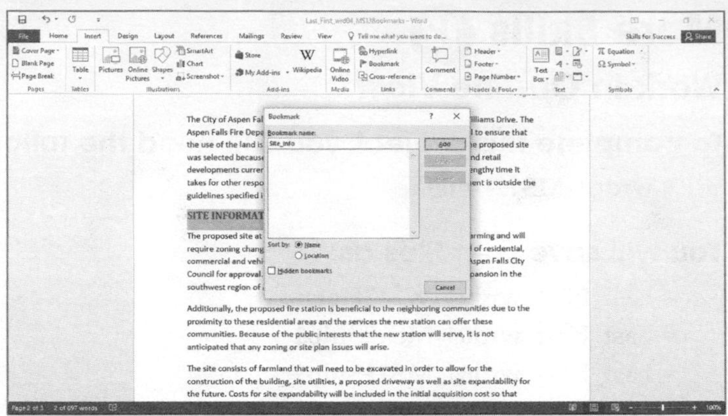

Figure 1 Word 2016, Windows 10, Microsoft Corporation

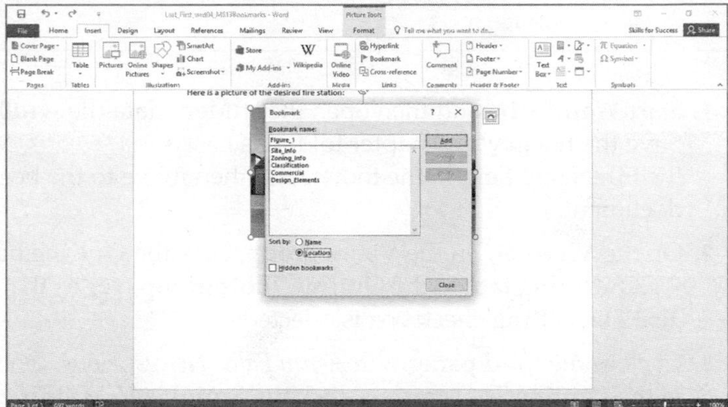

Figure 2 Word 2016, Windows 10, Microsoft Corporation

8. In the **Bookmark** dialog box, click **Add**.
9. In the **Links group**, click the **Bookmark** button. In the **Bookmark** dialog box, click the bookmark name *Zoning_Info*, and then click the **Go To** button. **Close** the dialog box. MOS Obj 1.2.4 C

   The Zoning Information section displays.
10. **Save** the file, **Close** Word, and then submit the files as directed by your instructor.

■ **You have completed More Skills 13**

More Skills 14

Save Documents as Web Pages

To complete this project, you will need the following file:

- wrd04_MS14Triathlon

You will save your file as:

- Last_First_wrd04_MS14Triathlon (MHT file)

▸ Word documents can be saved as web pages so that the document can be viewed in a web browser.

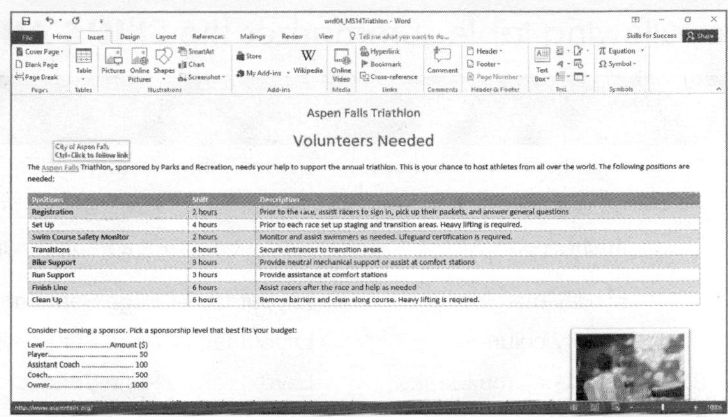

Word 2016, Windows 10, Microsoft Corporation **Figure 1**

1. Start **Word 2016**, and then open the student data file **wrd04_MS14Triathlon**.
2. Click the **View tab**, and then in the **Zoom group**, click the **One Page** button to view the entire page. In the **Views group**, click the **Web Layout** button. MOS Obj 1.4.1 C

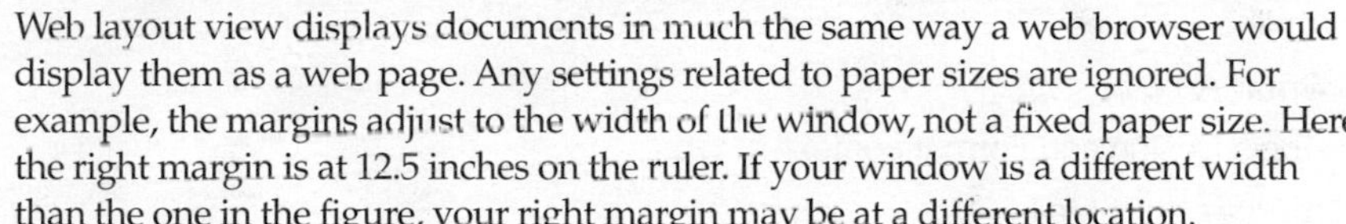

   Web layout view displays documents in much the same way a web browser would display them as a web page. Any settings related to paper sizes are ignored. For example, the margins adjust to the width of the window, not a fixed paper size. Here, the right margin is at 12.5 inches on the ruler. If your window is a different width than the one in the figure, your right margin may be at a different location.

3. In the paragraph that begins *The Aspen Falls Triathlon, sponsored by*, select the text *Aspen Falls*.
4. Click the **Insert tab**, and then in the **Links group**, click the **Hyperlink** button. In the **Insert Hyperlink** dialog box, in the **Address** box, type www.aspenfalls.org

   The text *http://* will automatically be inserted before any web address you type in the Address box.

5. In the upper right corner of the **Insert Hyperlink** dialog box, click the **ScreenTip** button. In the **Set Hyperlink ScreenTip** dialog box, type City of Aspen Falls and then click **OK** two times. Notice that the new hyperlink displays underlined and in blue text.
6. Point to the new hyperlink just inserted, and then compare your screen with **Figure 1**.

   A ScreenTip displays instructions for using the link, and the Internet address displays on the status bar.

7. Click the **File tab**, and then click **Export**. On the **Export** page, click **Change File Type**, and then under **Change File Type**, click **Single File Web Page** one time to select it.

MOS Obj 1.5.2 C

   When you save a document as a single file web page, it saves all the text and pictures in a single file called a ***web archive***. These files are typically assigned the *.mht* file extension. Web archives are also known as ***MHTML files***.

8. Click the **Save As** button. In the **Save As** dialog box, navigate to your chapter folder. In the **File name** box, name the file Last_First_wrd04_MS14Triathlon Near the bottom of the dialog box, click the **Change Title** button. In the **Enter Text** dialog box, under **Page title**, type City of Aspen Falls and then click **OK**. Click **Save** to create the web page.
9. Open **File Explorer**, navigate to your chapter folder, and then double-click **Last_First_wrd04_MS14Triathlon** to open the web page.

   The title you typed when you saved the file displays in the page's tab.

10. Move the pointer over the hyperlink to display the ScreenTip.
11. **Close** the open windows, and then submit the file as directed by your instructor.

- **You have completed More Skills 14**

The following table summarizes the **SKILLS AND PROCEDURES** covered in this chapter.

Skills Number	Task	Step	Icon	Keyboard Shortcut
1	Change the Fonts theme	Design tab → Document Formatting group → Fonts		
1	Create columns	Layout tab → Page Setup group → Columns		
1	Justify text	Home tab → Paragraph group → Justify		Ctrl + J
2	Modify margins	Layout tab → Page Setup group → Margins → Custom Margins		
2	Modify columns	Layout tab → Page Setup group → Columns → More Columns		
2	Insert column breaks	Layout tab → Page Setup group → Breaks → Column		Ctrl + Shift + Enter
3	Apply text effects	Home tab → Font group → Text Effects		
4	Create styles	Home tab → Styles group → More → Create a Style		
5	Add page borders	Design tab → Page Background group → Page Borders		
5	Apply paragraph borders and shading	Home tab → Paragraph group → Borders → Borders and Shading		
6	Insert Online Pictures	Insert tab → Illustrations group → Online Pictures		
7	Create SmartArt	Insert tab → Illustrations group → SmartArt		
8	Format SmartArt	Use the commands in the SmartArt Tools Design and Format contextual tabs		
9	Create mail merge labels	Mailings tab → Start Mail Merge group → Start Mail Merge → Labels		
9	Connect to a data source	Mailings tab → Start Mail Merge group → Select Recipients		
9	Insert merge fields	Mailings tab → Use the commands in the Write & Insert Fields group		
10	Preview mail merge	Mailings tab → Preview Results group → Preview Results		
10	Update labels	Mailings tab → Write & Insert Fields group → Update Labels		
10	Finish a mail merge	Mailings tab → Finish group → Finish & Merge → Print Documents or Edit Individual Documents		
MS11	Display Read Mode	View tab → Views group → Read Mode		
MS12	Display outline view	View tab → Views group → Outline		Alt + Ctrl + O
MS12	Promote a heading	Outlining tab → Outline Tools group → Promote	←	Alt + Shift + ←
MS12	Demote a heading	Outlining tab → Outline Tools group → Demote	→	Alt + Shift + →
MS13	Add bookmark	Insert tab → Links group → Bookmark		
MS13	Use Go To	Insert tab → Links group → Bookmark		F5 or Ctrl + G
MS14	Insert hyperlink	Insert tab → Links group → Hyperlink		Ctrl + K
MS14	Save as web page	File tab → Export → Change File Type → Single File Web Page		

Project Summary Chart		
Project	**Project Type**	**Project Location**
Skills Review	Review	In Book and MIL MyITLab® Grader
Skills Assessment 1	Review	In Book and MIL MyITLab® Grader
Skills Assessment 2	Review	Book
My Skills	Problem Solving	Book
Visual Skills Check	Problem Solving	Book
Skills Challenge 1	Critical Thinking	Book
Skills Challenge 2	Critical Thinking	Book
More Skills Assessment	Review	In Book and MIL MyITLab® Grader
Collaborating with Google	Critical Thinking	Book

MOS Objectives Covered	
1.2.3 C Create bookmarks	2.3.1 C Format text in multiple columns
1.2.4 C Move to a specific location or object in a document	2.3.2 C Insert page, section, or column breaks
1.3.1 C Modify page setup	5.1.2 C Insert pictures
1.3.2 C Apply document themes	5.2.4 C Format objects
1.4.1 C Change document views	5.2.6 C Apply a picture style
1.4.2 C Customize views by using zoom settings	5.3.1 C Create a SmartArt graphic
1.4.6 C Show or hide formatting symbols	5.3.2 C Format a SmartArt graphic
1.5.2 C Save documents in alternative file formats	5.3.3 C Modify SmartArt graphic content
2.2.1 C Apply font formatting	

Key Terms

BizSkills Video

1. What is the purpose of a cover letter, and what steps can you take to make one more effective?
2. Consider the various ways to organize resume information. Which layout do you think would be best for your particular education, skills, and experience?

Online Help Skills

1. With Word 2016 open, on the **File tab**, in the upper right corner of the screen, click the **Microsoft Word Help** [?] button, or press [F1].
2. In the **Word Help** window **Search** box, type mail merge list and then press [Enter].
3. In the search result list, click **Set up a mail merge list with Word or Outlook**. Maximize the Word Help window, and then compare your screen with **Figure 1**.

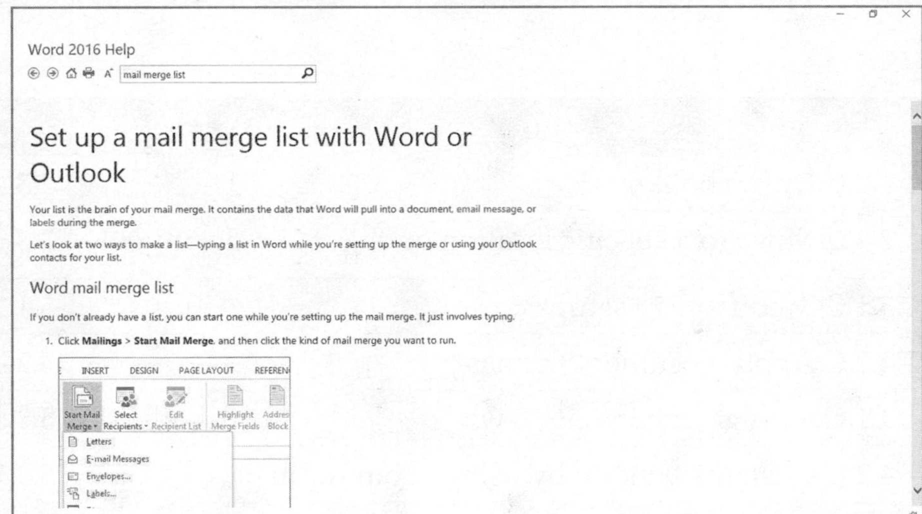

Figure 1 Word 2016, Windows 10, Microsoft Corporation

4. Explain the steps to change the order of columns. Why might you want to change the column order?

Matching

Match each term in the second column with its correct definition in the first column by writing the letter of the term on the blank line in front of the correct definition.

___ **1.** You can change the font set that a theme uses by clicking the Fonts button on this tab.

___ **2.** A portion of a document that can be formatted differently from the rest of the document.

___ **3.** In the Columns gallery, the command that displays the Columns dialog box.

___ **4.** Any style that displays in a Ribbon gallery.

___ **5.** A pre-built set of decorative formats that make text stand out in a document.

___ **6.** The command that forces text into the next column.

___ **7.** An extra detail or hook at the end of a character stroke.

___ **8.** A field that reserves space in a SmartArt shape but does not print until you insert your own text.

___ **9.** A feature that combines a main document and a data source to create customized letters or tables.

___ **10.** In mail merge, the command used to modify all labels based on changes made to the original label.

A Column break
B Design
C Mail merge
D More Columns
E Placeholder
F Quick Style
G Section
H Serif
I Text effects
J Update Labels

Multiple Choice

Choose the correct answer.

1. A font where the letters do not have serifs.
   A. Non serif
   B. Plain print
   C. Sans serif
2. The default width assigned to columns.
   A. Proportional
   B. Equal
   C. Unbalanced
3. A paragraph alignment that aligns the text with both the left and right margins.
   A. Center
   B. Justified
   C. Left/Right
4. This moves the text that follows it to the top of the next column.
   A. Page break
   B. Column break
   C. Continuous break
5. A type of break that is used to create a new section that can be formatted differently from the rest of the document.
   A. Page
   B. Column
   C. Continuous
6. To change the color of the background in a paragraph, add this to the text background.
   A. Shading
   B. A border
   C. Text emphasis
7. A pre-built visual representation of information in which you can enter your own text.
   A. Mail merge
   B. Online picture
   C. SmartArt
8. Used by a mail merge document, this file contains information such as names and addresses.
   A. Data source
   B. Main document
   C. Merge document
9. In a mail merge document, this document contains the text that remains constant.
   A. Data source
   B. Main document
   C. Merge document
10. When you open a mail merge document, a message displays informing that this will be run.
    A. Insert records query
    B. SQL select query
    C. Update fields query

Topics for Discussion

1. In this chapter, you practiced inserting an online image in a document. When do you think online images are most appropriate, and in what kind of documents might online images be inappropriate? If you had to create a set of rules for using online images in a document, what would the top three rules be?
2. In this chapter, you used the mail merge feature in Word to create mailing labels. With mail merge, you can also insert one field at a time—and the fields do not have to be just names and addresses. Can you think of any situations where you might want to insert fields in a letter or another document?

Skills Review

To complete this project, you will need the following files:

- wrd04_SRUtilities
- wrd04_SRaddresses (Excel)

You will save your files as:

- Last_First_wrd04_SRUtilities
- Last_First_wrd04_SRLabels

1. Start **Word 2016**, and then open the student data file **wrd04_SRUtilities**. **Save** the file in your chapter folder as Last_First_wrd04_SRUtilities Add the **FileName** field to the footer. If necessary, display the formatting marks.
2. Locate the subtitle *Take the Lead with LEDs*, and then select the document text from that point to the end of the document. On the **Layout tab**, in the **Page Setup group**, click the **Columns** button, and then click **Two**.
3. Position the insertion point at the beginning of the subtitle *Free Energy Audits*. On the **Layout tab**, in the **Page Setup group**, click the **Breaks** button, and then click **Column**. Compare your screen with **Figure 1**.
4. Select the title *Utility News*. On the **Home tab**, in the **Font group**, click the **Text Effects** button. Point to **Shadow**, and then click the first choice under **Outer—Offset Diagonal Bottom Right**.
5. Select the subtitle *Take the Lead with LEDs*, and then click the **Font Dialog Box Launcher**. Under **Effects**, select the **Small caps** check box, and then click **OK**. In the **Paragraph group**, click the **Center** button.
6. With the subtitle still selected, in the **Styles group**, click the **More** button, and then click **Create a Style**. In the **Create New Style from Formatting** dialog box, name the style Utility Subtitle and then press Enter.
7. Click in the second subtitle—*Free Energy Audits*. On the **Home tab**, in the **Styles group**, click the **Utility Subtitle** thumbnail. Compare your screen with **Figure 2**.
8. On the **Insert tab**, in the **Illustrations group**, click the **Online Pictures** button. In the **Insert Pictures** dialog box, in the **Bing Image Search** box, type architect and then press Enter.

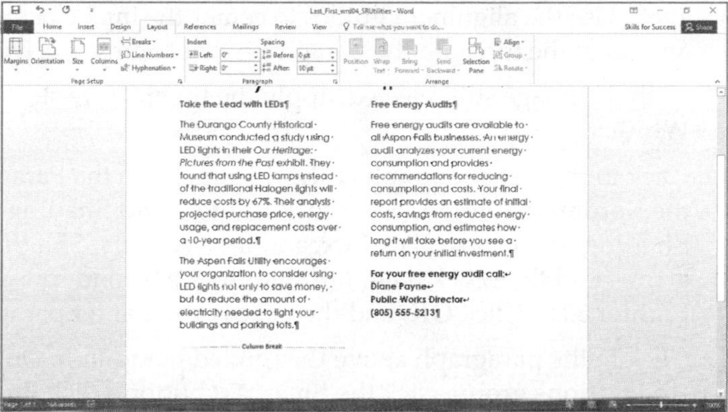

Word 2016, Windows 10, Microsoft Corporation

Figure 1

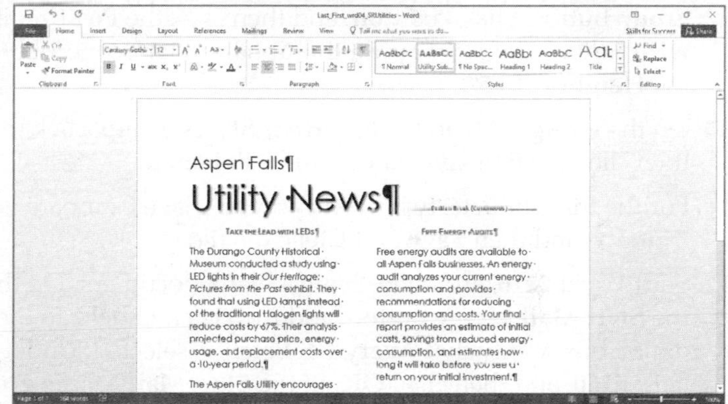

Word 2016, Windows 10, Microsoft Corporation

Figure 2

9. Click the image shown in **Figure 3** (or a similar image if this one is not available), and then click the **Insert** button.

■ **Continue to the next page to complete this Skills Review**

10. Click the image's **Layout Options** button, and then click **Square**. On the **Format tab**, in the **Size group**, change the **Width** to **1.5"** and the **Height** to **1.99"**. Use the alignment guides to center the image between the side margins and align the top with the paragraph that begins, *The Durango County*.
11. With the image still selected, apply the first picture style—**Simple Frame, White**.
12. Click in the last paragraph in the document. In the **Paragraph group**, click the **Borders arrow**, and then click **Borders and Shading**. In the **Borders and Shading** dialog box, click **Box**, and then click the **Shading tab**. Click the **Fill arrow**, and then click the ninth color in the second row—**Orange, Accent 5, Lighter 80%**. Click **OK**, and then apply the **Center** paragraph alignment.
13. Click in the paragraph above the shaded paragraph. On the **Insert tab**, in the **Illustrations group**, click the **SmartArt** button. Click **Process**, click the first layout—**Basic Process**, and then click **OK**.
14. Click the SmartArt's border, and then click the **Format tab**. Click the **Arrange group** button, click **Position**, and then click the **Position in Bottom Center with Square Text Wrapping** thumbnail. Change the **Width** to **6.2"** and verify the **Height** is **1.75"**.
15. On the **Design tab**, in the **SmartArt Styles group**, click the **More** button, and then click the first style under **3-D—Polished**.
16. For the three bullets, type Audit | Invest | Save Compare your document with **Figure 3**, and then **Save** and **Close** the file.
17. Start **Word 2016**, and then create a blank document. On the **Mailings tab**, click the **Start Mail Merge** button, and then click **Labels**. In the **Label Options** dialog box, verify that **Avery US Letter** is selected. Under **Product number**, click **5160**, and then click **OK**. In the **Start Mail Merge group**, click **Select Recipients**, click **Use an Existing List**, and then locate and open the student data file **wrd04_SRAddresses**.
18. In the **Write & Insert Fields group**, click the **Address Block** button, clear the **Insert recipients name in this format** check box, and then click **OK**. In the **Write & Insert Fields group**, click the **Update Labels** button.
19. In the **Finish group**, click the **Finish & Merge** button, click **Edit Individual Documents**, and then click **OK**. **Save** the file in your chapter folder as Last_First_wrd04_SRLabels Compare your document with **Figure 4**.
20. **Save** the file, and then **Close** all other Word documents without saving changes. Submit the files as directed by your instructor.

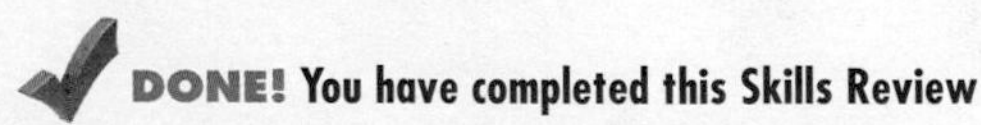
DONE! You have completed this Skills Review

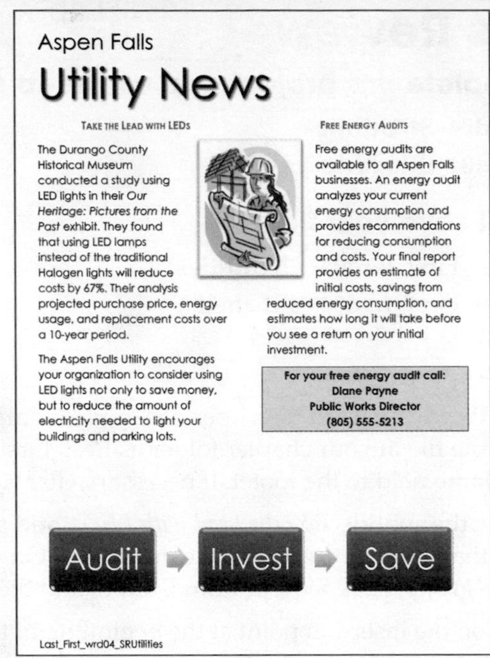
Aspen Falls

Utility News

TAKE THE LEAD WITH LEDs

The Durango County Historical Museum conducted a study using LED lights in their Our *Heritage: Pictures from the Past* exhibit. They found that using LED lamps instead of the traditional Halogen lights will reduce costs by 67%. Their analysis projected purchase price, energy usage, and replacement costs over a 10-year period.

The Aspen Falls Utility encourages your organization to consider using LED lights not only to save money, but to reduce the amount of electricity needed to light your buildings and parking lots.

FREE ENERGY AUDITS

Free energy audits are available to all Aspen Falls businesses. An energy audit analyzes your current energy consumption and provides recommendations for reducing consumption and costs. Your final report provides an estimate of initial costs, savings from reduced energy consumption, and estimates how long it will take before you see a return on your initial investment.

For your free energy audit call:
Diane Payne
Public Works Director
(805) 555-5213

Audit | Invest | Save

Last_First_wrd04_SRUtilities

Figure 3

Arcos Building Center 76952 N Cardinal Pl Aspen Falls, CA 93464	Aspen Falls Bank 2014 W Carmen Dr Aspen Falls, CA 93463	Aspen Falls Community College 76601 S Chaffee Av Aspen Falls, CA 93464
Aspen Falls Federal Credit Union 7395 E Belmont Av Aspen Falls, CA 93464	Boyd Center Shopping Club 19382 W Chaplin Av Aspen Falls, CA 93463	Brennan Travel Services 61993 W Adams St Aspen Falls, CA 93464
Bronze Star Studios 89132 N Alta Ter Aspen Falls, CA 93463	California Airlines 68044 E Allen St Aspen Falls, CA 93464	Cuddy Title 89459 N Cardinal Pl Aspen Falls, CA 93464
Dianne Financial Center 13578 S Brightview Av Aspen Falls, CA 93463	Dr. John Donachie 79655 E Ash St Aspen Falls, CA 93464	Durango County Historical Museum 43299 E Gore St Aspen Falls, CA 93464
Ellegood Development Corporation 28709 S Aiken Pl Aspen Falls, CA 93463	H3C Catering 29195 W Billings Ct Aspen Falls, CA 93463	Jeramy B. Slow Charitable Foundation 82165 S Alta Ter Aspen Falls, CA 93464
Lehman Instruments 26362 S Burnham Av Aspen Falls, CA 93464	McAboy Business Systems 48437 E Brookfield Dr Aspen Falls, CA 93463	Rhoton's 18790 W Cessna Pl Aspen Falls, CA 93464
Samway Investors LCC 81580 E Carmen Dr Aspen Falls, CA 93463	Scruton Business Products Centre 52520 W Center St Aspen Falls, CA 93463	Seaview Mall 88354 E Chaplin Av Aspen Falls, CA 93464
The Piliero Family 45096 S Cardinal Pl Aspen Falls, CA 93463	Toole Inn 99975 N Bellevue Av Aspen Falls, CA 93463	VC Botanical Services 80862 S Central Av Aspen Falls, CA 93464

Figure 4

Skills Assessment 1

To complete this project, you will need the following files:

- wrd04_SA1Racers
- wrd04_SA1Addresses (Excel)

You will save your files as:

- Last_First_wrd04_SA1Racers
- Last_First_wrd04_SA1Merged

1. Start **Word 2016**, and then open the student data file **wrd04_SA1Racers**. **Save** the file in your chapter folder as Last_First_wrd04_SA1Racers and then add the **FileName** field to the footer.
2. Apply the **Slice** theme, and then change the fonts theme to **Candara**. For the title *Aspen Falls Triathlon*, apply the last text effect—**Fill – Light Turquoise, Background 2, Inner Shadow**.
3. Search Online Pictures using the search phrase triathlon and then insert an appropriate image from the results. Compare your screen with **Figure 1**. If that image is not available, find a similar image. Set the graphic's height to **1.6"**, the width to **2.58"**, and its position to **Position in Top Left with Square Text Wrapping**. Recolor the picture to **Light Turquoise, Background color 2 Light** (first column, third row).
4. Starting with the subtitle *This Year's Race* and ending with the phone number, apply the two-column layout and change column spacing to **0.3"**. Insert a column break at the beginning of the *This Year's Sponsors* subtitle.
5. Create a new **Quick Style** named Racers Subtitle based on the *This Year's Race* subtitle, and then apply the style to the other subtitle—*This Year's Sponsors*.
6. For the paragraph starting *Consider becoming a sponsor*, apply a box border with a 1½ pt wide line and a border color of **Orange, Accent 5**—ninth column, first row. For the same paragraph, set the shading to **Orange, Accent 5, Lighter 80%**—ninth column, second row.
7. Insert a SmartArt graphic with the **Basic Timeline** layout—fourth column, fourth row under Process. Set the SmartArt's position to **Position in Bottom Center with Square Text Wrapping**. Change the height to **2"** and width to **5.6"**.

Aspen Falls Triathlon

THIS YEAR'S RACE

This year's triathlon will be better than ever! For the first time ever, we anticipate over 300 racers. Adding to the excitement, five professional males and 8 professional females will race. For these reasons, we expect significantly higher numbers of spectators and volunteers. Our sponsors will enjoy higher visibility than ever before!

If you are already a sponsor, please consider increasing your support either in money or donated services. If you are considering becoming a sponsor, it is not too late! With your help, we can make the annual running of the triathlon a truly memorable event for the Aspen Falls community.

THIS YEAR'S SPONSORS

A special thank you to this year's sponsors:

- A Touch of Amsterdam
- Allegro Runner's World
- Aspen Falls Bank
- Aspen Falls Community College
- Aspen Falls Federal Credit Union
- Brennan Travel Services
- California Airlines
- H3C Catering
- Koopman Construction
- Lehman Instruments
- Seaview Mall
- Ton Design Associates
- Toole Inn

Consider becoming a sponsor by calling Todd Austin, Tourism Director, (805) 555-1028.

Last_First_wrd04_SA1Racers

Figure 1

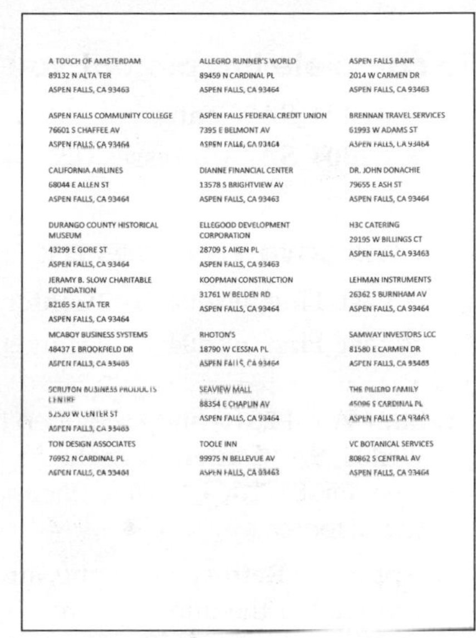
A TOUCH OF AMSTERDAM 89132 N ALTA TER ASPEN FALLS, CA 93463	ALLEGRO RUNNER'S WORLD 89459 N CARDINAL PL ASPEN FALLS, CA 93464	ASPEN FALLS BANK 2014 W CARMEN DR ASPEN FALLS, CA 93463
ASPEN FALLS COMMUNITY COLLEGE 76601 S CHAFFEE AV ASPEN FALLS, CA 93464	ASPEN FALLS FEDERAL CREDIT UNION 7395 E BELMONT AV ASPEN FALLS, CA 93464	BRENNAN TRAVEL SERVICES 61993 W ADAMS ST ASPEN FALLS, CA 93464
CALIFORNIA AIRLINES 68044 E ALLEN ST ASPEN FALLS, CA 93464	DIANNE FINANCIAL CENTER 13578 S BRIGHTVIEW AV ASPEN FALLS, CA 93463	DR. JOHN DONACHIE 79655 E ASH ST ASPEN FALLS, CA 93464
DURANGO COUNTY HISTORICAL MUSEUM 43299 E GORE ST ASPEN FALLS, CA 93464	ELLEGOOD DEVELOPMENT CORPORATION 28709 S AIKEN PL ASPEN FALLS, CA 93463	H3C CATERING 29195 W BILLINGS CT ASPEN FALLS, CA 93463
JERAMY B. SLOW CHARITABLE FOUNDATION 82165 S ALTA TER ASPEN FALLS, CA 93464	KOOPMAN CONSTRUCTION 31761 W BELDEN RD ASPEN FALLS, CA 93464	LEHMAN INSTRUMENTS 26362 S BURNHAM AV ASPEN FALLS, CA 93464
MCABOY BUSINESS SYSTEMS 48437 E BROOKFIELD DR ASPEN FALLS, CA 93463	RHOTON'S 18790 W CESSNA PL ASPEN FALLS, CA 93464	SAMWAY INVESTORS LCC 81580 E CARMEN DR ASPEN FALLS, CA 93463
SCRUTON BUSINESS PRODUCTS CENTRE 52520 W CENTER ST ASPEN FALLS, CA 93463	SEAVIEW MALL 88354 E CHAPLIN AV ASPEN FALLS, CA 93464	THE PILIERO FAMILY 45096 S CARDINAL PL ASPEN FALLS, CA 93463
TON DESIGN ASSOCIATES 76952 N CARDINAL PL ASPEN FALLS, CA 93464	TOOLE INN 99975 N BELLEVUE AV ASPEN FALLS, CA 93463	VC BOTANICAL SERVICES 80862 S CENTRAL AV ASPEN FALLS, CA 93464

Figure 2

8. Change the SmartArt text to Swim | Bike | Run as shown in **Figure 1**. **Save**, and then **Close** the file.
9. Create a blank document, and then start a **Labels** mail merge using **Avery US Letter** label **5160**. Use **wrd04_SA1Addresses** as the data source. Insert an **Address Block** clearing the option to include the recipient names, and then update the labels.
10. Merge the labels to a new document, and then edit that document by converting all the text to **UPPERCASE**. **Save** the file in your chapter folder as Last_First_wrd04_SA1Merged Compare your document with **Figure 2**, and then **Save** and **Close** the file. **Close** the original mail merge document without saving changes, and then submit the files as directed by your instructor.

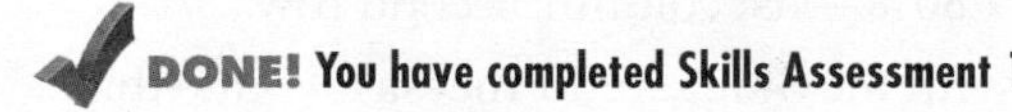

Skills Assessment 2

To complete this project, you will need the following files:

- wrd04_SA2Center
- wrd04_SA2Addresses (Excel)

You will save your files as:

- Last_First_wrd04_SA2Center
- Last_First_wrd04_SA2Merged

1. Start **Word 2016**, and then open the student data file **wrd04_SA2Center**. **Save** the file in your chapter folder as Last_First_wrd04_SA2Center and then add the **FileName** field to the footer.
2. Apply the **Retrospect** theme, and then change the fonts theme to **Corbel**. For the title *Community Center News*, apply the **Fill - White Outline - Accent 1, Shadow** text effect—fourth column, first row.
3. Search Online Pictures using the search phrase computer class and then insert an appropriate image from the results. Compare your screen with **Figure 1**. If that image is not available, find a similar image. Set the image's height to **1.2"**, the width to **2.07"**, and its position to **Position in Top Right with Square Text Wrapping**. Recolor the picture to **Green, Accent color 6 Light** (seventh column, third row).
4. Starting with the subtitle *Computer Labs* and ending with the last paragraph, apply the two-column layout and change column spacing to **0.7"**. Insert a column break at the beginning of the *Computer Classes* subtitle.
5. Create a new **Quick Style** named Center Subtitle based on the *Computer Labs* subtitle, and then apply the style to the other two subtitles—*Computer Classes* and *Room Rentals*.
6. For the paragraph starting *To enroll in a class*, apply a box border with a **1½ pt** wide line and a border color of **Brown, Accent 3**—seventh column, first row. For the same paragraph, set the shading to **Green, Accent 6, Lighter 80%**—last column, second row.
7. Insert a SmartArt graphic with the **Staggered Process** layout—third column, seventh row under Process. Change the SmartArt's position to **Position in Bottom Left with Square Text Wrapping**, and then change the shape's width and height to **3.0"**.

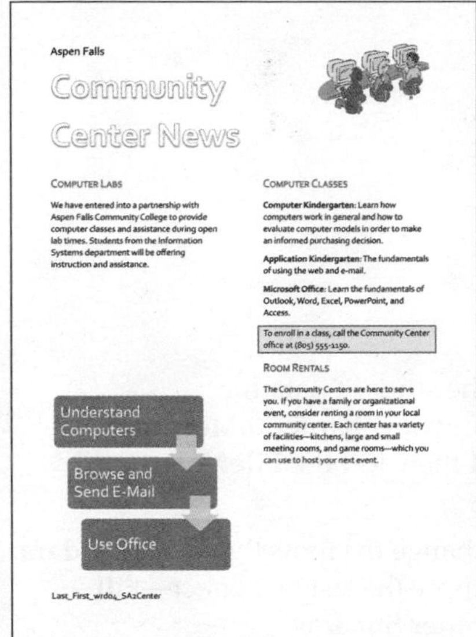

Aspen Falls

Community Center News

COMPUTER LABS

We have entered into a partnership with Aspen Falls Community College to provide computer classes and assistance during open lab times. Students from the Information Systems department will be offering instruction and assistance.

Understand Computers

Browse and Send E-Mail

Use Office

COMPUTER CLASSES

Computer Kindergarten: Learn how computers work in general and how to evaluate computer models in order to make an informed purchasing decision.

Application Kindergarten: The fundamentals of using the web and e-mail.

Microsoft Office: Learn the fundamentals of Outlook, Word, Excel, PowerPoint, and Access.

To enroll in a class, call the Community Center office at (805) 555-1150.

ROOM RENTALS

The Community Centers are here to serve you. If you have a family or organizational event, consider renting a room in your local community center. Each center has a variety of facilities—kitchens, large and small meeting rooms, and game rooms—which you can use to host your next event.

Last_First_wrd04_SA2Center

Figure 1

TAMMARA PEAGLER 79655 E ASH ST ASPEN FALLS, CA 93463	ANNIKA HOOBLER 89132 N ALTA TER ASPEN FALLS, CA 93463	LILLIANA CAYA 89459 N CARDINAL PL ASPEN FALLS, CA 93463
KLARA BURSIK 48437 E BROOKFIELD DR ASPEN FALLS, CA 93464	SHERA ACERRA 76952 N CARDINAL PL ASPEN FALLS, CA 93463	JAMEY HOUGHTLING 99119 N ALTA TER ASPEN FALLS, CA 93463
SIMONNE DESANTIS 74470 E BILLINGS CT ASPEN FALLS, CA 93464	MARSHA HEISER 46235 E CESSNA PL ASPEN FALLS, CA 93464	EMELDA LATTANZI 60374 E CESSNA PL ASPEN FALLS, CA 93463
RENATO PACHTER 3840 N BRIGHTVIEW AV ASPEN FALLS, CA 93463	DANILLE FLOOK 52377 N BAXTER ST ASPEN FALLS, CA 93463	MACK SPELL 2562 E BUTTERFLY AV ASPEN FALLS, CA 93463
BRENDON CATTELL 84206 E BELDEN RD ASPEN FALLS, CA 93464	ERWIN BREACH 88403 E ASH ST ASPEN FALLS, CA 93463	BASIL HASAS 7243 N BILLINGS AV ASPEN FALLS, CA 93464
TYRELL PEAVLER 27464 N CENTRAL AV ASPEN FALLS, CA 93464	DANE RHINEHARDT 71569 E BELDEN RD ASPEN FALLS, CA 93463	IRA FROSSARD 41328 N BURNHAM AV ASPEN FALLS, CA 93464
TYREE JENISON 77334 N BILLINGS AV ASPEN FALLS, CA 93464	JERE LEREW 84081 N BRIGHTVIEW AV ASPEN FALLS, CA 93464	BERTRAM CIUCCI 54337 E ADAMS ST ASPEN FALLS, CA 93464
TARA MIJANGOS 37080 E BROOKFIELD DR ASPEN FALLS, CA 93464	WILBER KASSAM 69664 N BAXTER ST ASPEN FALLS, CA 93464	SULEMA STIMPSON 83974 N CENTRAL AV ASPEN FALLS, CA 93464

Figure 2

8. In the SmartArt shapes, change the text to Understand Computers | Browse and Send E-Mail | Use Office as shown in **Figure 1**. **Save**, and then **Close** the file.
9. Create a blank document, and then start a **Labels** mail merge using **Avery US Letter** label **5160**. Use **wrd04_SA2Addresses** as the data source. Insert an **Address Block** accepting the default settings, and then update the labels.
10. Merge the labels to a new document, and then edit that document by converting all the text to uppercase. Save the file in your chapter folder as Last_First_wrd04_SA2Merged Compare your document with **Figure 2**, and then **Save** and **Close** the file. **Close** the original mail merge document without saving changes, and then submit the files as directed by your instructor.

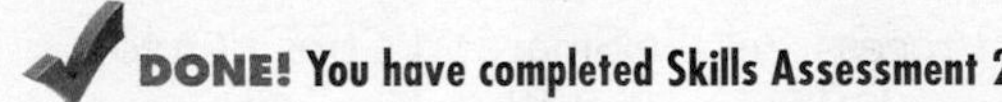

DONE! You have completed Skills Assessment 2

Martinez Family Reunion

PICNIC

This year's family reunion starts at Aspen Falls City Park with our traditional picnic. We have reserved Picnic Shelter B starting at 12:00 P.M. on July 21. You can arrive any time after that. As before, we ask each family to bring one main dish, one side dish, and a dessert. This year, we will provide all the plates, bowls, silverware, and glasses. We will also provide water, popular sodas, ice tea, and coffee. If you need a different beverage, please bring your own and keep in mind that alcohol is not allowed in the park.

Park facilities include electricity, plumbed restrooms, and most areas are handicap accessible. Plugins in our shelter are limited, so if you could bring your dish already hot or bring an alternate warming source, it would be very helpful.

Besides eating and socializing, we will be organizing our annual softball game. If you have a baseball glove, be sure to bring it. This year, the Riaz side of the family has boasted they can beat the Martinez side. Given the level of 'trash talk' already started, it sounds like this year's match up will be entertaining for all.

BANQUET

This year's dinner will be at the Central Community Center in Aspen Falls. It will be catered by Aspen Falls' very own H3C Catering. We have rented the game room, so kids of all ages will be able to find something fun to do. Each family is responsible for exhibiting their auction before and during the banquet.

AUCTION

To pay for expenses, each family needs to bring one item or package for the auction that follows the banquet. If last year is any indication, this year's items ought to bring out the bidding war mentality our family is known for!

If you have any question, contact Maria at (805) 555-8945.

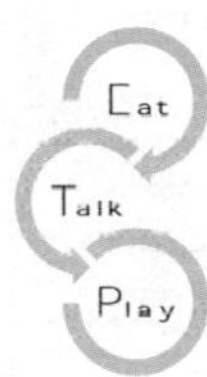

Last_First_wrd04_MYReunion

Figure 1

JULIO AULDRIDGE 7531 N NOTTY TIMBER WAY PASADENA, CA 91101	ARLETTA GLOGOWSKI 83514 N STARDUST ST CUDDEBACKVILLE, NY 12729	ALISSA JANCIK 770000 N LAGUNA SHORE LN STATE CENTER, IA 50247
DEANDRE MARTINEZ 7710 N CLEARWATER LN SAINT AUGUSTINE, FL 32086	MERIDITH MARTINEZ 50285 N ILLUMINATE AV GRANITE, CO 81228	ROCKY MARTINEZ 2738 N DEVON AV NEW BRAINTREE, MA 1531
JAE MARTINEZ 4886 N HOLLANDALE DR MURRAYSVILLE, WV 26153	YI MARTINEZ 4551 N OPUNTIA AV WILFORD HALL, TX 78236	SHIN MARTINEZ 37867 N STODDARD RD NESS CITY, KS 67560
HARLEY MIESZALA 3480 N DOBERMAN DR ROLLING PRAIRIE, IN 46371	KRYSTYNA MORATAYA 63110 N LABRADOR PL LIBERTY, NC 27298	JULIEANN PLESNARSKI 10466 N BANNER RIDGE ST WILBUR, WA 99185
IRVIN RIAZ 16589 N ROSEDALE PL GLEN BURNIE, MD 21061	SAUL RIAZ [illegible] N DAL MAR DR WATERFORD, MI 48328	TEODORO RIAZ 9150 N YONKERS AV ELTON, WI 54430
DARON RIAZ 1014 N DEERHORN AV KANAWHA FALLS, WV 25115	CHRISTOPHER RIAZ 1251 N BLUE DOWNS ST LAS VEGAS, NV 89118	DEREK RIIS 15467 N KLAMATH LN GREEN VILLAGE, NJ 7935
JOHNATHAN SWERDLOW 6484 N SEA BREEZE WAY HOLABIRD, SD 57540	LAVERNE VILLANVEVA 9908 N WELCH ST BEAUMONT, KS 67012	

Figure 2

My Skills

To complete this project, you will need the following files:

- wrd04_MYReunion
- wrd04_MYAddresses (Excel)

You will save your files as:

- Last_First_wrd04_MYReunion
- Last_First_wrd04_MYLabels

1. Start **Word 2016**, and then open the student data file **wrd04_MYReunion**. Save the file in your chapter folder as Last_First_wrd04_MYReunion and then add the **FileName** field to the footer.
2. Apply the **Facet** theme, and then change the fonts theme to **Arial**. For the title *Martinez Family Reunion*, apply the **Fill - White, Outline - Accent 1, Shadow** text effect—fourth column, first row, and then change the **Font size** to **32**.
3. Search Online Pictures using the search word picnic and then insert an appropriate image from the results. Compare your screen with **Figure 1**. If that image is not available, find a similar image. Set the image's height to **1"**, its width to **1.73"**, and its position to **Position in Top Left with Square Text Wrapping**. Recolor the picture to **Brown, Accent color 6 Dark**—seventh column, second row.
4. Starting with the subtitle *Picnic* and ending with the last paragraph, apply the two-column layout and change column spacing to **0.3"**. Insert a column break at the beginning of the *Banquet* subtitle.
5. Create a new **Quick Style** named Reunion Subtitle based on the *Picnic* subtitle, and then apply the style to the other two subtitles—*Banquet* and *Auction*.
6. For the paragraph starting *If you have any questions*, apply a box border with a **1½ pt** wide line and a border color of **Dark Green, Accent 2**—sixth column, first row. For the same paragraph, set the shading to **Dark Green, Accent 2, Lighter 80%**—sixth column, second row.
7. Insert a SmartArt graphic with the **Circle Arrow Process** layout—second column, eighth row. Set the SmartArt's position to **Position in Bottom Right with Square Text Wrapping**, and then change the graphic's height to **3.2"** and width to **3"**.
8. In the SmartArt shapes, change the text to Eat | Talk | Play as shown in **Figure 1**. **Save**, and then **Close** the file.
9. Create a blank document, and then start a **Labels** mail merge using **Avery US Letter** label **5160**. Use **wrd04_MYAddresses** as the data source. Insert an **Address Block** accepting the default settings, and then update the labels.
10. Merge the labels to a new document, and then edit that document by converting all the text to uppercase. Save the file in your chapter folder as Last_First_wrd04_MYLabels Compare your document with **Figure 2**, and then **Save** and **Close** the file. **Close** the original mail merge document without saving changes, and then submit the files as directed by your instructor.

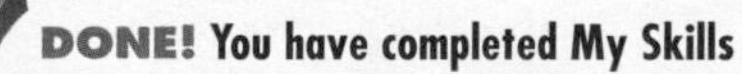

DONE! You have completed My Skills

Visual Skills Check

To complete this project, you will need the following file:

- **wrd04_VSRecycle**

You will save your file as:

- **Last_First_wrd04_VSRecycle**

Start **Word 2016**, and then open the student data file **wrd04_VSRecycle**. **Save** the file in your chapter folder as Last_First_wrd04_VSRecycle Add the **FileName** field in the footer.

To complete this project, format the file as shown in **Figure 1**. The theme is **Ion Boardroom** with the **Tw Cen MT** fonts theme. The title is **48** points, the text effect is **Gradient Fill - Lavender, Accent 1, Reflection**, and the font color has been changed to **Dark Purple, Text 2, Lighter 40%**. Search Online Pictures for an image related to recycling and then insert an appropriate image from the results. The image height has been set to **1"** and the width to **1.07"**, and **Square** text wrapping has been applied.

Apply the two-column layout with **0.7"** between columns, and then add a column break as shown in **Figure 1**. Use the formatting in the first subtitle to create a Quick Style named Recycle Subtitle and then apply that style to the second subtitle. The shaded paragraph uses the default **Shadow** border, and the fill color is **Lavender, Accent 5, Lighter 80%**.

Insert and format the SmartArt as shown in **Figure 1**. The layout is **Text Cycle**, the height is **4"**, and the width is **6.5"**. The SmartArt style has been changed to **Powder**. **Save** the file, **Close** Word, and then submit the file as directed by your instructor.

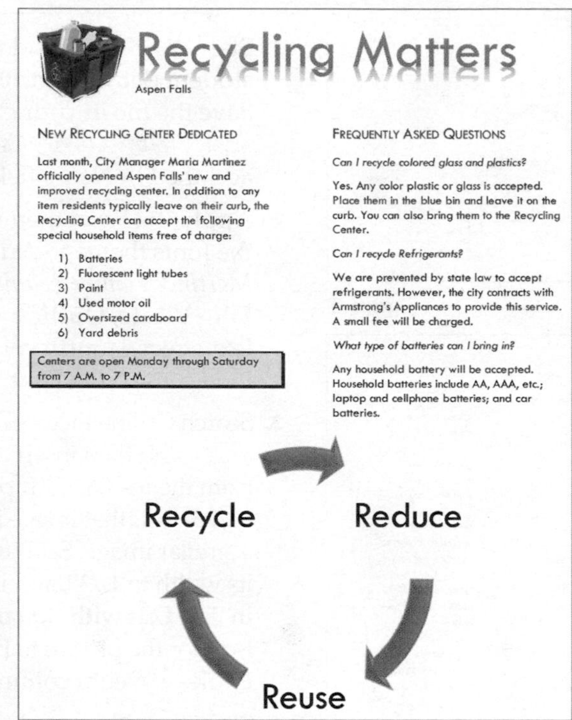

Recycling Matters

Aspen Falls

NEW RECYCLING CENTER DEDICATED

Last month, City Manager Maria Martinez officially opened Aspen Falls' new and improved recycling center. In addition to any item residents typically leave on their curb, the Recycling Center can accept the following special household items free of charge:

1) Batteries
2) Fluorescent light tubes
3) Paint
4) Used motor oil
5) Oversized cardboard
6) Yard debris

Centers are open Monday through Saturday from 7 A.M. to 7 P.M.

FREQUENTLY ASKED QUESTIONS

Can I recycle colored glass and plastics?

Yes. Any color plastic or glass is accepted. Place them in the blue bin and leave it on the curb. You can also bring them to the Recycling Center.

Can I recycle Refrigerants?

We are prevented by state law to accept refrigerants. However, the city contracts with Armstrong's Appliances to provide this service. A small fee will be charged.

What type of batteries can I bring in?

Any household battery will be accepted. Household batteries include AA, AAA, etc.; laptop and cellphone batteries; and car batteries.

Recycle

Reduce

Reuse

Figure 1

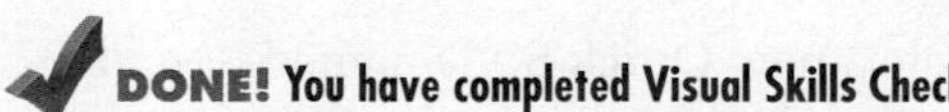

DONE! You have completed Visual Skills Check

Skills Challenge 1

To complete this project, you will need the following file:

- **wrd04_SC1Fire**

You will save your file as:

- **Last_First_wrd04_SC1Fire**

Open the student data file **wrd04_SC1Fire**, and then save the file in your chapter folder as Last_First_wrd04_SC1Fire Add the **FileName** field to the footer.

Using the techniques practiced in this chapter, format and lay out the document as a two-column newsletter. Apply text effects to the title so that it stands out from the rest of the text. Locate and insert an online image from Bing Image Search that works well with the newsletter theme of fire protection. Size, format, and position the image to pull the reader's eye from the title to the newsletter text. Format the subtitles so they stand out from the articles, and then create a style for that format. Apply the style to both subtitles. Replace the text *Air → Fuel → Heat* with a SmartArt graphic that illustrates this relationship as a triangle. Format, size, and position the graphic to fill the bottom of the newsletter.

Save the file, close Word, and then submit the file as directed by your instructor.

DONE! You have completed Skills Challenge 1

Skills Challenge 2

To complete this project, you will need the following file:

- **wrd04_SC2Addresses (Excel)**

You will save your file as:

- **Last_First_wrd04_SC2Merged**

Open a blank Word document, and then start the merge process to create Avery 5160 mailing labels. For the recipient's list, use the student data file **wrd04_SC2Addresses**. To complete the labels document, insert the Address Block, update all the labels, and then preview the labels. Merge the labels to a new document, and then save the merged document as Last_First_wrd04_SC2Merged Close the merged document, and then close the original document without saving it. Close Word, and then submit the file as directed by your instructor.

DONE! You have completed Skills Challenge 2

More Skills Assessment

To complete this project, you will need the following file:

- wrd04_MSAHousing

You will save your files as:

- Last_First_wrd04_MSAHousing
- Last_First_wrd04_MSASnip1
- Last_First_wrd04_MSASnip2
- Last_First_wrd04_MSAWebPage (MHT)

1. Start **Word 2016**, and then open the student data file **wrd04_MSAHousing**. **Save** the file in your chapter folder as Last_First_wrd04_MSAHousing Add the **FileName** field to the footer, and then at the top of Page 1, replace *Your Name* with your First and Last name.
2. On Page 1, collapse the *Introduction* section, and then display the document in **Read Mode**. On the **View tab**, click **Layout**, and then click **Column Layout**. Compare your screen with **Figure 1**.
3. Click [Windows icon], type snip and then press Enter. In the **Snipping Tool** window, click the **New arrow,** and then click **Full-screen Snip**.
4. In the **Snipping Tool** mark-up window, click the **Save Snip** button [icon]. In the **Save As** dialog box, navigate to your chapter folder. Be sure the **Save as type** box displays **JPEG file**. Name the snip Last_First_wrd04_MSASnip1 **Minimize** the **Snipping Tool** mark-up window.
5. Return to Print Layout view, and then display the document in **Outline** view.
6. Use the **Promote to Heading 1** button to promote the paragraphs beginning *The Crisis Is Also* and *Solutions Require*.
7. Show only **Level 1**, and then verify all five headings are displayed, as shown in **Figure 2**.
8. On the taskbar, click the **Snipping Tool** button. Click the **New** button [icon], and then repeat the previous step to create a **Full-screen Snip**. **Save** the file in your chapter folder as Last_First_wrd04_MSASnip2 and then **Close** the **Snipping Tool** mark-up window.
9. Return to Print Layout view, and then **Expand** the *Introduction* section.
10. Insert bookmarks for the five headings using the bookmark names Intro | Problem | Activities | Crisis | Solutions

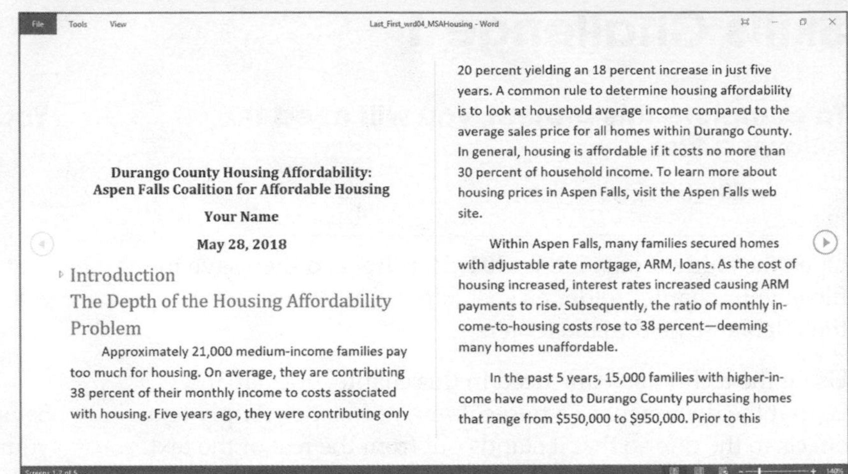

Figure 1 Word 2016, Windows 10, Microsoft Corporation

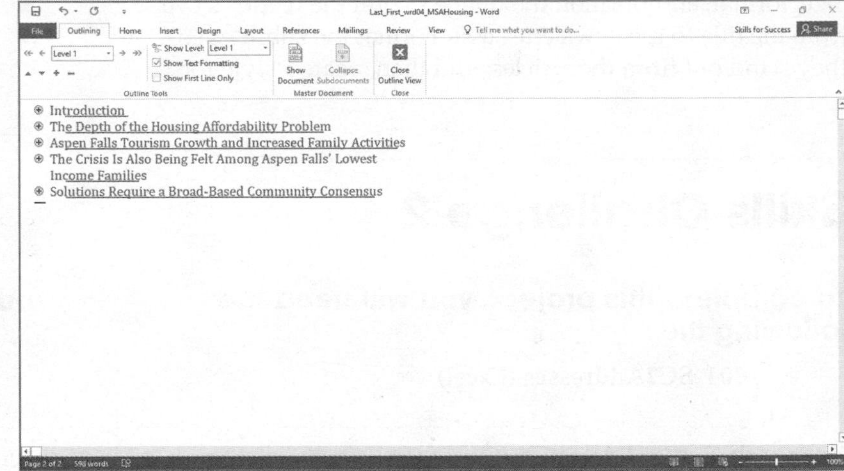

Figure 2 Word 2016, Windows 10, Microsoft Corporation

11. In the paragraph that begins *Approximately 21,000*, select the text at the end of the paragraph *Aspen Falls web site*. Insert a **Hyperlink** to the website *www.aspenfalls.org*, and then add the **ScreenTip** City of Aspen Falls
12. **Save** the file as a Word document, and then **Export** the file to save it as a **Single File Web Page** with the file name Last_First_wrd04_MSAWebPage **Close** Word, and then submit the files as directed by your instructor.

DONE! You have completed More Skills Assessment

Collaborating with Google

To complete this project, you will need a Google account (refer to the Common Features chapter) and the following file:

- **wrd04_GPExpenses**

You will save your file as:

- **Last_First_wrd04_GPExpenses**

---

1. Open a web browser. Log into your Google account, and then click the **Google Apps** button.
2. Click the **Drive** button. Click the **New** button, and then click **Google Docs**.
3. In **Word 2016**, open the student data file **wrd04_GPExpenses**. Select and copy all the text from the file and paste it in your new Google document. In the Google document **Untitled document** box, type Reimbursed Expenses and then press **Enter**.
4. Select the first paragraph beginning with *Aspen Falls*. Click the **Format tab**, click **Paragraph styles**, click **Heading 1**, and then click **Apply 'Heading 1'**.
5. Use the same technique to apply the **Heading 2** style to the paragraphs *Reimbursed Expenses* and *Reimbursement Guidelines*.
6. Select the table text beginning with *Item* and ending with *and be specific*. Click the **Table tab**, and then click **Table properties**. In the **Table properties** dialog box, click the **Cell background color arrow**, and then click the seventh color in the first row—**light gray 1**. Click **OK**.
7. Click the **File tab**, and then click **Page setup**. In the **Page setup** dialog box, change the **Top** margin to 1.5 and then click **OK**.
8. Press Ctrl + End to move to the end of the document. Click the **Insert tab**, and then click **Image**. If necessary, click Search. In the **Search** box, type conference and then press Enter. Click on an image, and then click **Select**. In your document, click the image to select it, and then below the image, click **Wrap text**. Use a corner sizing handle to change the width to approximately **2.5"**. Drag the image to the right side of the *Guidelines* list. If necessary, resize the image so the document is one page. Compare your screen with **Figure 1**.

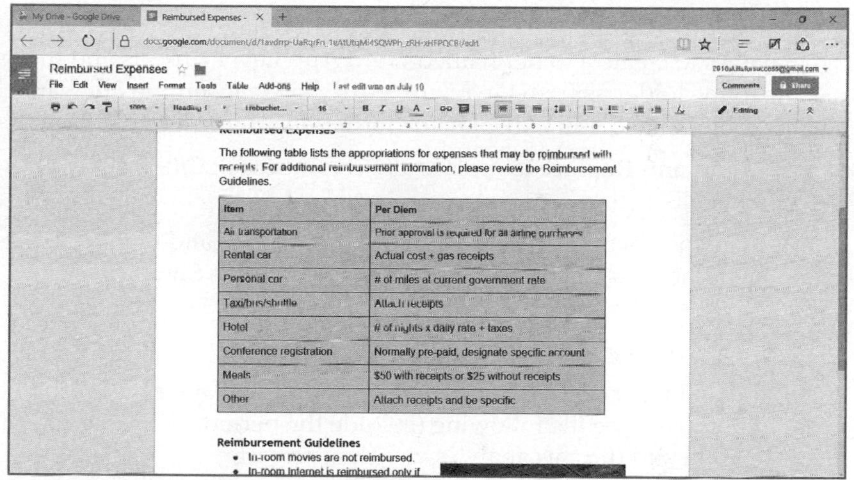

Figure 1

9. Under the document title *Reimbursed Expenses*, click the **File tab**, point to **Download as**, and then click **Microsoft Word (.docx)**. **Save** the file in your chapter folder as Last_First_wrd04_GPExpenses
10. Start **Word 2016**, and then open the file **Last_First_wrd04_GPExpenses**. Insert the **FileName** field in the footer.
11. **Save** the file, **Close** the open windows, and then submit the file as directed by your instructor.

DONE! You have completed Collaborating with Google

To complete this project, you will need the following files:

wrd_CAPVisitUs
wrd_CAPFestival

You will save your file as:

Last_First_wrd_CAPVisitUs

1. Start **Word 2016**, and then open the student data file **wrd_CAPVisitUs**. Use **Save As** to create a folder named Word App Level Projects and then save the file to the folder as Last_First_wrd_CAPVisitUs Insert the **FileName** field in the footer. If necessary, display the formatting marks.
2. Use **Find and Replace** to replace all occurrences of *City of Aspen Falls* with Aspen Falls
3. Change the document's theme to **Ion Boardroom**, and then in the first line of the letterhead, change the font size to **18**, apply the **Small caps** effect, and then set the character spacing to **Expanded** by **2 pt**.
4. In the letter greeting, change the word *Mrs.* to Ms.
5. In the first letter body paragraph, insert a footnote after the word *interns*. For the footnote, type the following (include the period): This intern is majoring in recreation and did this analysis as a class project.
6. Near the bottom of Page 1, after the text *City Hall*, insert a manual page break, and then compare your screen with **Figure 1**.
7. At the top of Page 2, delete the blank paragraph, and then select the text *Aspen Falls*. Change the **Font** to **Verdana** and the size to 42 and then apply the **Gradient Fill - Orange, Accent 4, Outline - Accent 4** text effect.
8. For the text *Get out and join the party!*, apply **Bold** and **Italic**.
9. For the newsletter articles, starting with *Get Out!* and ending with *Borax Trail era*, apply two columns of equal width with **0.3** spacing between them.
10. For the article title, *Get Out!*, apply the **Small caps** effect, and then change the font color to the fifth theme color—**Plum, Accent 1**. **Center** align the paragraph, change the **Spacing Before** to **12 pt**, and then compare your screen with **Figure 2**.

■ **Continue to the next page to complete the skill**

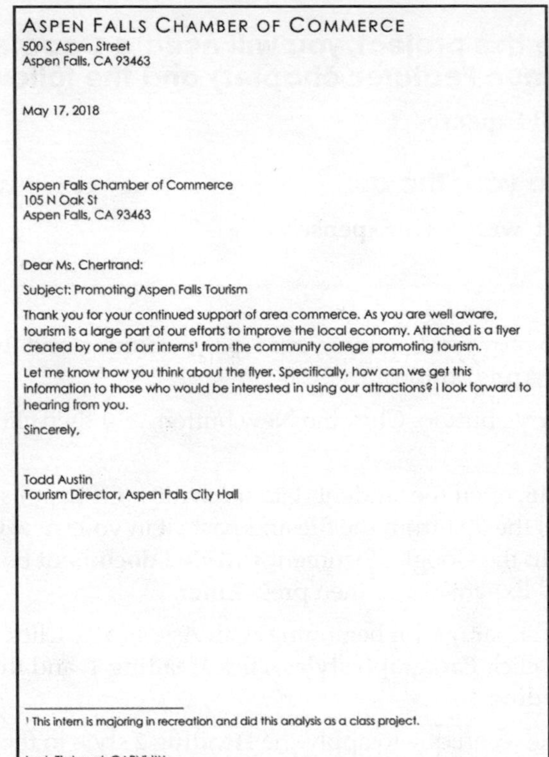

ASPEN FALLS CHAMBER OF COMMERCE
500 S Aspen Street
Aspen Falls, CA 93463

May 17, 2018

Aspen Falls Chamber of Commerce
105 N Oak St
Aspen Falls, CA 93463

Dear Ms. Chertrand:

Subject: Promoting Aspen Falls Tourism

Thank you for your continued support of area commerce. As you are well aware, tourism is a large part of our efforts to improve the local economy. Attached is a flyer created by one of our interns[1] from the community college promoting tourism.

Let me know how you think about the flyer. Specifically, how can we get this information to those who would be interested in using our attractions? I look forward to hearing from you.

Sincerely,

Todd Austin
Tourism Director, Aspen Falls City Hall

[1] This intern is majoring in recreation and did this analysis as a class project.

Last_First_wrd_CAPVisitUs

Figure 1

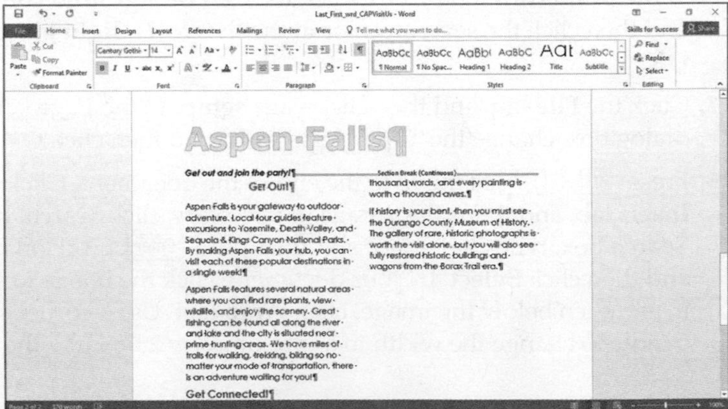

Figure 2

Word 2016, Windows 10, Microsoft Corporation

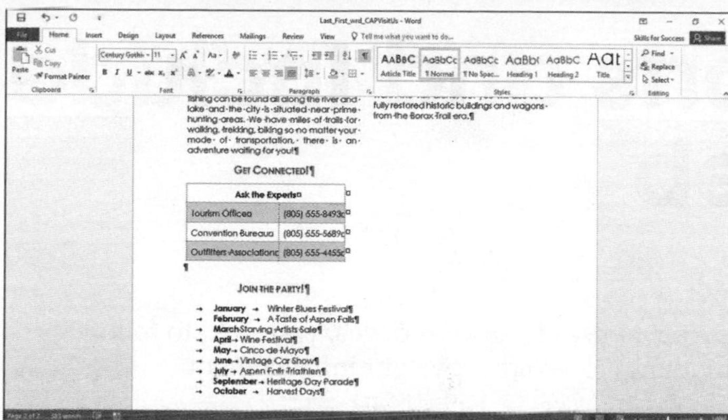

Word 2016, Windows 10, Microsoft Corporation **Figure 3**

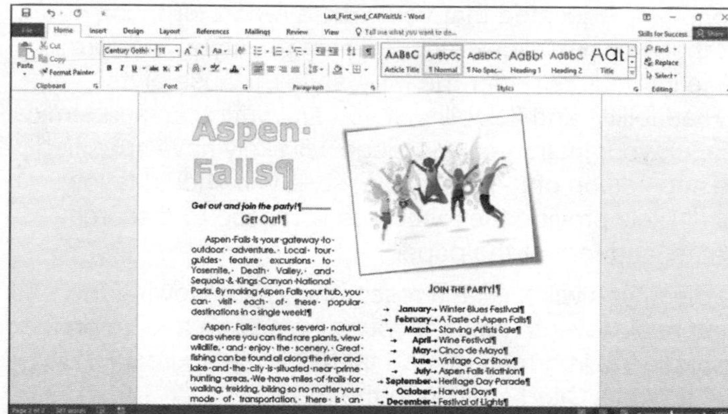

Word 2016, Windows 10, Microsoft Corporation **Figure 4**

11. Create a new style named Article Title based on the formatting applied to the *Get Out!* title in the previous step. Apply the **Article Title** style to the other three article titles.
12. In the first article, apply a first line indent of 0.25 inches to the paragraph beginning *Aspen Falls is your gateway*. In the same paragraph, set the line spacing to **Single** (1.0), and the **Spacing Before** and **Spacing After** the paragraph to **6 pt** each. Set the paragraph's alignment to **Justified**.
13. Use **Format Painter** to apply the formatting of the paragraph formatted in the previous step to the article paragraphs beginning *Aspen Falls features*, *Improve your literacy*, and *If history is your bent*.
14. In the **Get Connected!** article, delete the text *Phone numbers*, but not the paragraph mark, and then in the blank paragraph, insert a 2x3 table. In the table, add the following:

    Tourism Office | (805) 555-8493

    Convention Bureau | (805) 555-5689

    Outfitters Association | (805) 555-4455
15. Add a new row above the table, and then merge the new row's cells into one cell. In the new row, type Ask the Experts
16. For the table, apply the **List Table 2 - Accent 1** table style, and then clear the **First Column** table style option. Set the cell sizes to **AutoFit Contents**.
17. Select the table, and then set the **Height** to **0.3"**. Set the alignment of the first row to **Align Center** and the alignment of the cells in rows 2 to 4 to **Align Center Left**. Compare your screen with **Figure 3**.
18. On Page 2, insert the picture from the student data file **wrd_CAPFestival**. Set the picture's position to **Top Right with Square Text Wrapping**, and then set the **Width** to **3.0"**. Apply the **Rotated, White** picture style.
19. Insert a column break before the *Join the Party!* article title.
20. In the *Join the Party!* article, select the tabbed list, and then use the **Tabs** dialog box to add a **Right** tab at **1"** and a **Left** tab at **1.15"**.
21. After the last item in the tabbed list, add the following event:

    December | Festival of Lights
22. In the tabbed list, **Bold** the word *December*. Check the spelling and grammar, and then compare your screen with **Figure 4**.
23. Save the file, **Close** Word ×, and then submit the file as directed by your instructor.

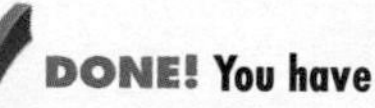

DONE! You have completed the Word Capstone Project

Format Academic Reports and Include Information from the Web

- When writing a research paper, you will often be required to use the style guidelines provided or designated by your school or instructor.
- Many colleges require that research papers follow guidelines based on those for academic books and journals. Commonly used style guidelines for research papers include the MLA (Modern Language Association) and the APA (American Psychological Association) style manuals.
- When copying content from web pages, you need to follow certain guidelines to avoid copyright infringement.
- When paraphrasing information written by someone else, you need to add a reference to show the source of the information.
- When citing the source of content copied from a web page, you can copy the website's address and paste it into your citation.

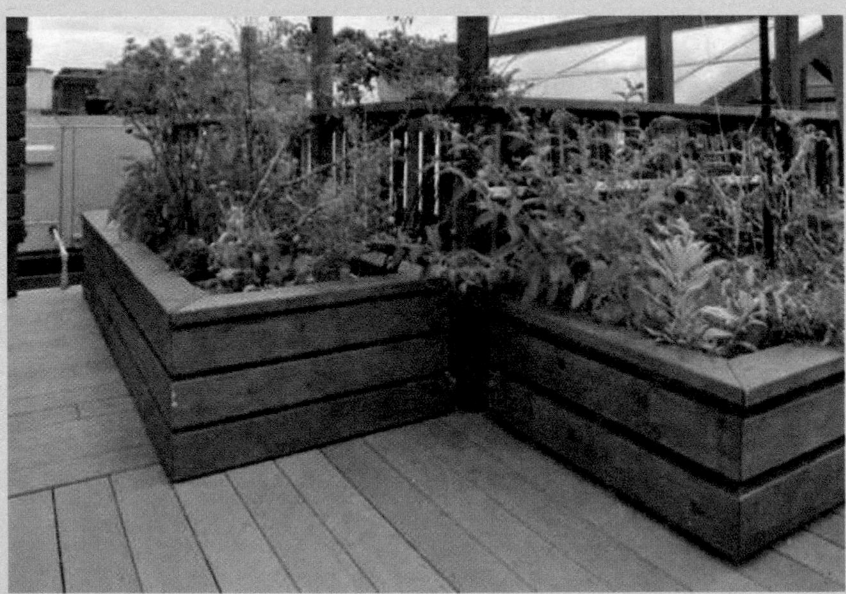

Alisonhancock/Fotolia

Aspen Falls City Hall

In this Integrated Project, you will write an academic report for Donald Norris, Aspen Falls City Engineer. The report provides a brief overview of the benefits and costs of rooftop gardens—gardens placed on top of buildings in the city.

If someone has requested that you write a report for them, you should ask them for guidelines regarding length, style, and format. Many college instructors prefer the MLA style because of its simplicity, readability, and flexibility. If you are writing an academic research paper, your instructor or college will likely have specified which style and edition of that particular style you should follow. They will also likely provide the resources you need to research, organize, write, and format the paper.

In this project, you will format a research paper following the MLA style manual, seventh edition. You will research a topic on the web, paraphrase the information, and then cite the source. Finally, you will add a Works Cited section to the report.

Time to complete this project — 30 to 60 minutes

Outcome

Using the skills in this project, you will be able to format a report.

Objectives

1.1 Create an academic report

1.2 Insert information from the web

1.3 Create a bibliography

To complete this project, you will need the following file:

wrd_IP01Rooftops

You will save your file as:

Last_First_wrd_IP01Rooftops

Lastname 1

Your Name

Donald Norris

Engineering

March 23, 2018

Rooftop Garden Benefits and Costs

Rooftop gardens are growing popular as people realize the benefits they offer. People living in urban areas, apartments, or residences with small gardening spaces now build gardens transforming the city scape into a beautiful and relaxing environment. In addition to these benefits, rooftop gardens can create savings that offset the cost of their initial investment and maintenance.

The main benefits and cost savings of rooftop gardens come from their insulating properties. Roof gardens are barriers between the outside and the building environment which reduces the energy need to cool and heat the building. Additionally, roof gardens reduce greenhouse gas emissions and reduce air pollution. (Environmental Protection Agency)

There are many options for the placement of a rooftop garden including wood-frame structures. However, the primary guiding principal is that roof gardens should be built on structures that are strong enough to support them. According to Osmundson, rooftop gardens work best with either steel-framed buildings or buildings built from reinforced concrete. (18)

Weaker structures or structures that require additional support be added can be transformed into a rooftop garden. However, these can cost significantly more to build depending on the initial weight-bearing capability of that structure.

The main consideration when designing a rooftop garden is to consider whether the structure can withstand not only the weight of the garden but also the water needed to maintain

SKILLS

At the end of this project, you will be able to:

- Format academic reports in the MLA style
- Search for information on the web
- Paraphrase information found on the web
- Avoid copyright infringement and plagiarism
- Copy URLs and add them to a list of references
- Insert and format bibliographies in the MLA style

1. Start **Word 2016**, and then open the student data file **wrd_IP01Rooftops**. **Save** the file in your **Word App Level Projects** folder as Last_First_wrd_IP01Rooftops If necessary, display the formatting marks.
2. With the insertion point at the beginning of the document and using your own name, type your First and Last name and then press Enter.
3. Type Donald Norris and then press Enter. Type Engineering and then press Enter. Type March 23, 2018 and then press Enter.
4. Type Rooftop Garden Benefits and Costs and then press Enter. Compare your screen with **Figure 1**.

   This paper follows the MLA guidelines. In an MLA research paper, the first four lines consist of your name, the person for whom the report was prepared, the name of the class or business, and the date. There is typically no cover page.

5. At the top of the document, double-click the header area. Type your Last name and then press SpaceBar. On the **Insert tab**, in the **Header & Footer group**, click the **Page Number** button, point to **Current Position**, and then click **Plain Number**.
6. On the **Home tab**, in the **Paragraph group**, click the **Align Right** button. Double-click below the header, and then compare your screen with **Figure 2**.
7. Press Ctrl + A, and then change the **Font Size** to **12** and the **Font** to **Times New Roman**.

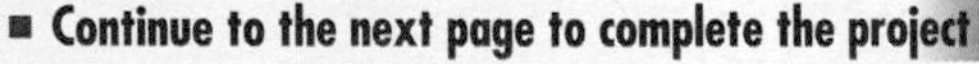

■ **Continue to the next page to complete the project**

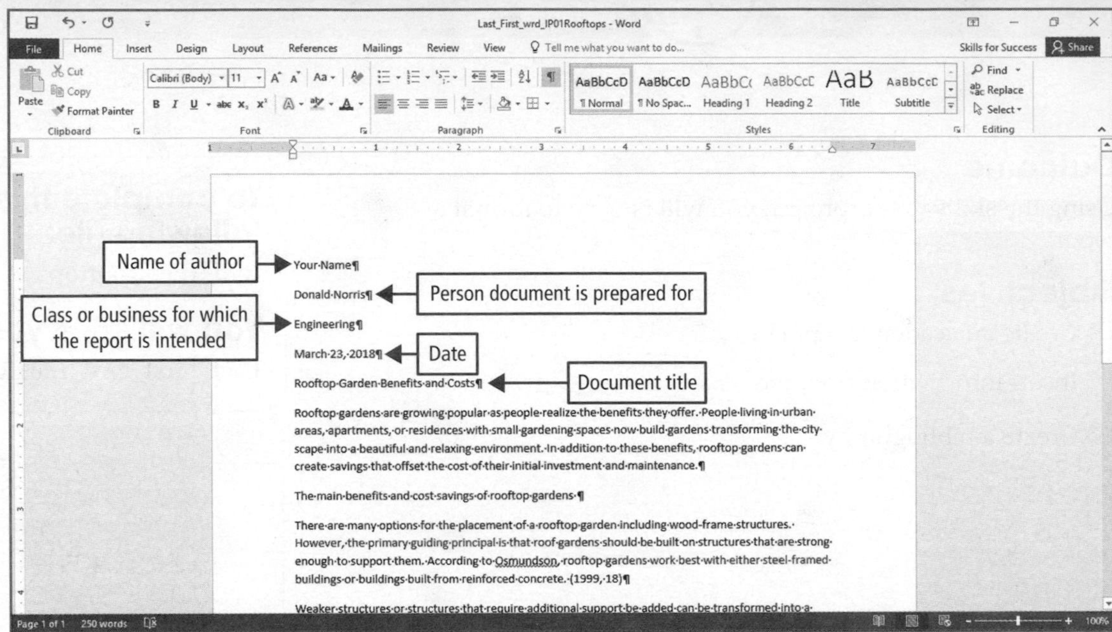

Figure 1 Word 2016, Windows 10, Microsoft Corporation

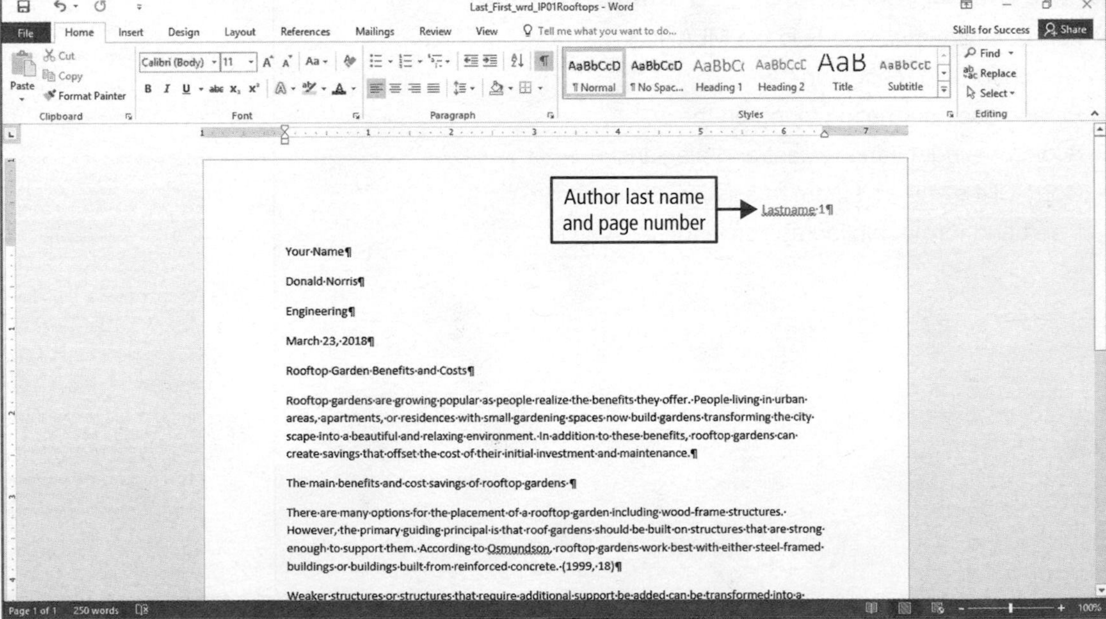

Figure 2 Word 2016, Windows 10, Microsoft Corporation

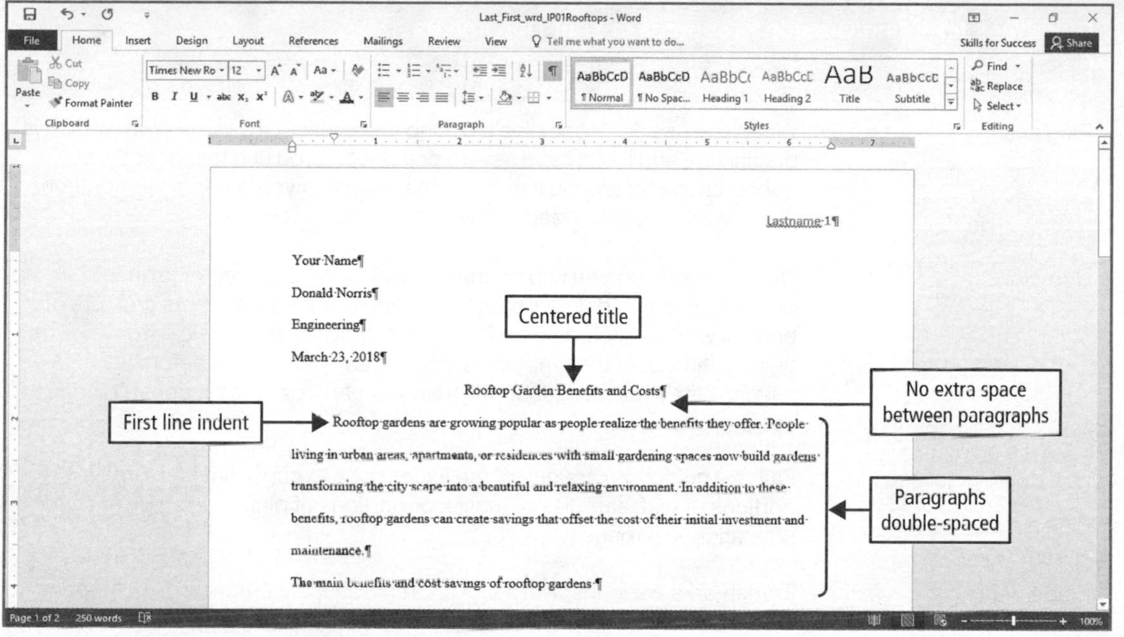

Word 2016, Windows 10, Microsoft Corporation

Figure 3

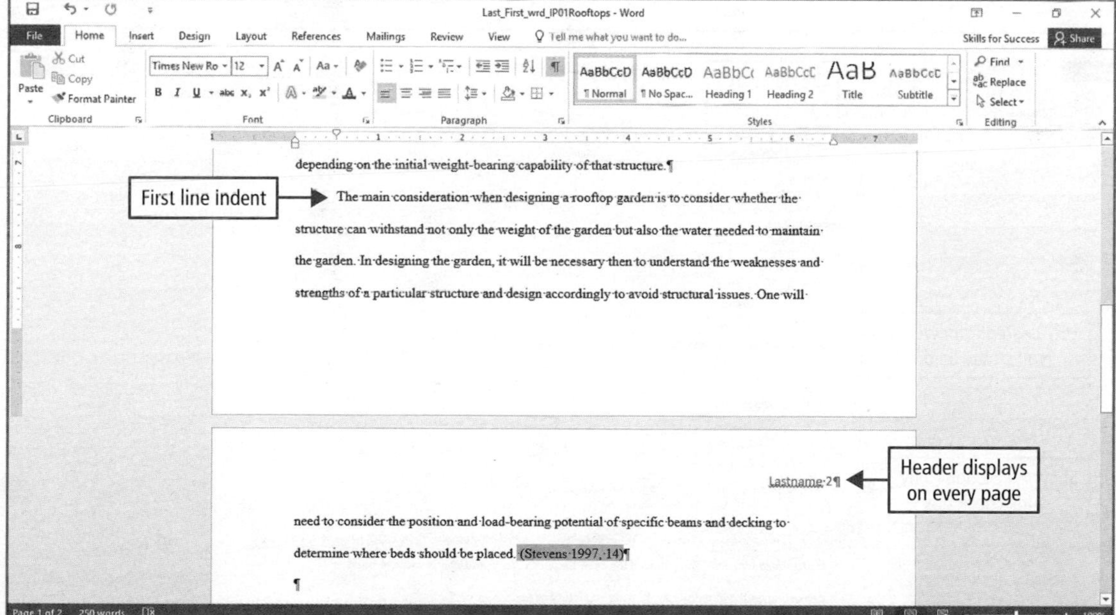

Word 2016, Windows 10, Microsoft Corporation

Figure 4

8. With the entire document still selected, click the **Line and Paragraph Spacing** button, and then click **2.0**. Click the **Line and Paragraph Spacing** button again, and then click **Remove Space After Paragraph**.

   In an MLA research paper, the margins are all set to 1 inch—the default for a new Word document. The rest of the text—including the title, any footnotes, and the references at the end of the document—is double-spaced, with no extra space between paragraphs.

9. Press Ctrl + Home. Click in the title that begins *Rooftop Garden Benefits*, and then click **Center**.

   The title and the Works Cited page headings are the only elements of the paper that are centered.

10. Click in the first paragraph below the title, and then click the **Paragraph Dialog Box Launcher**. In the **Paragraph** dialog box, under **Indentation**, click the **Special arrow**, click **First line**, and then click **OK**. Compare your screen with **Figure 3**.

    In MLA style, the first line of all body text paragraphs and notes are indented 0.5".

11. Click to the left of the paragraph that begins *The main benefits and cost savings*, scroll to the end of the document, hold down Shift, and then click to the right of the citation *(Stevens 1997, 14)*. Press F4 to repeat the First Line Indent command.

12. **Save** the document, deselect the text, scroll up to display the break between Pages 1 and 2, and then compare your screen with **Figure 4**.

■ **Continue to the next page to complete the project**

13. Open your web browser and navigate to www.epa.gov In the page's search box, type green roofs and then press Enter. Locate and read an article about the benefits of rooftop gardens.
14. Return to **Word**. Near the beginning of the document, locate the paragraph that begins *The main benefits and cost savings*. In your own words, complete the paragraph with two or three sentences that paraphrase the information you found on the main benefits and cost savings of rooftop gardens.
15. Take a moment to read the information in the table in **Figure 5**.
16. Return to the browser. In the **Address bar**, select and **Copy** the web address—the URL.
17. In the Word document, click the **References tab**. In the **Citations & Bibliography group**, click the **Style arrow**, and then click **MLA**.
18. Be sure the insertion point is at the end of the paragraph you wrote previously, and then add a space.
19. In the **Citations & Bibliography group**, click **Insert Citation**, and then click **Add New Source**.
20. Click the **Type of Source arrow**, and then click **Web site**. Select the **Corporate Author** check box, and then in the **Corporate Author** box, type Environmental Protection Agency
21. Select the **Show All Bibliography Fields** check box, scroll down the list, and then in the **URL** box, paste the URL that you copied. Compare your screen with **Figure 6**.

With MLA, the URL field is an optional field when citing sources for web pages.

■ **Continue to the next page to complete the project**

Guidelines for Using Outside Resources in Your Documents	
Issue	**Description**
Plagiarism	When you use someone else's writing and present it as your own work, it is plagiarism, and it can have severe penalties. If you use text directly, put quotation marks around it and cite the source. If you paraphrase someone else's work, you also need to cite the source.
Copyright	Nearly everything you find on the Internet or in books or magazines is probably protected under copyright laws. Copyright protects creators of original works—including text, art, photographs, and music—from unlicensed use of their materials. Always ask permission before you use anyone else's material. Just because you can download it doesn't mean you can use it.
Fair Use Guidelines	Fair use guidelines are one of the exceptions to copyright law. Small portions of text, samples of music, or portions of pictures can be used for educational purposes
Trademarks	Trademarks are icons, words, or short phrases that represent a company or product.

Figure 5

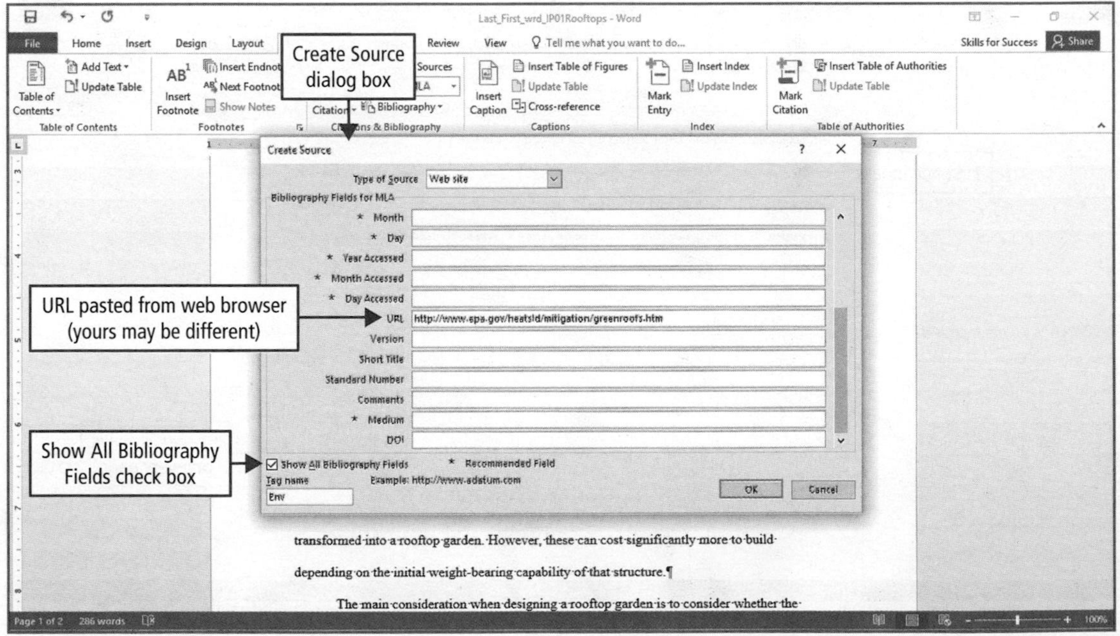

Figure 6

Word 2016, Windows 10, Microsoft Corporation

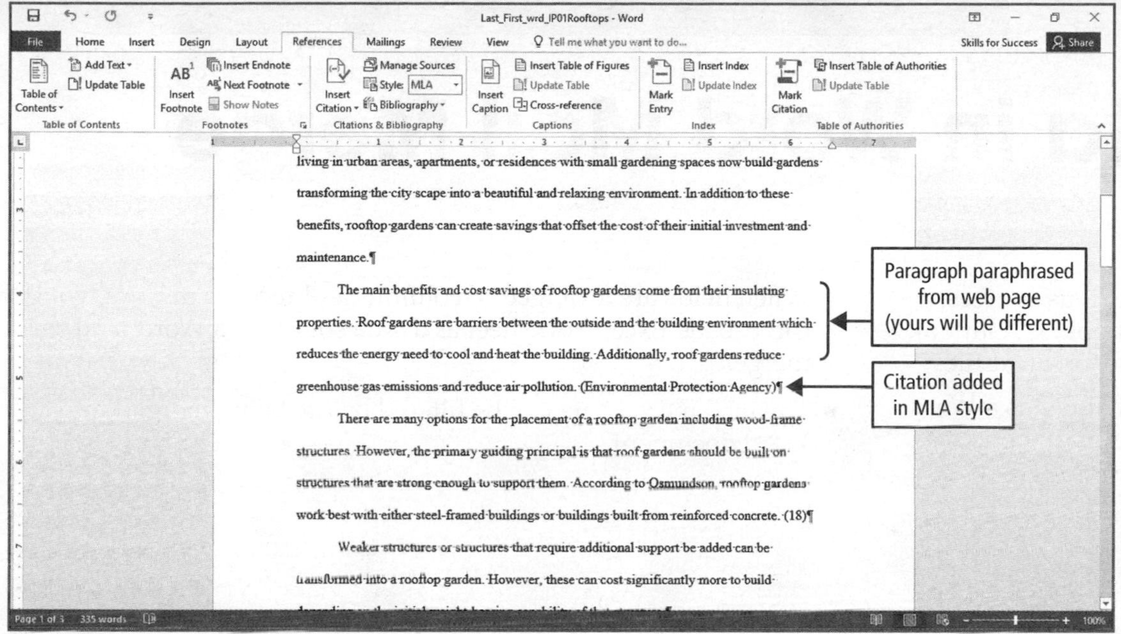

Word 2016, Windows 10, Microsoft Corporation

Figure 7

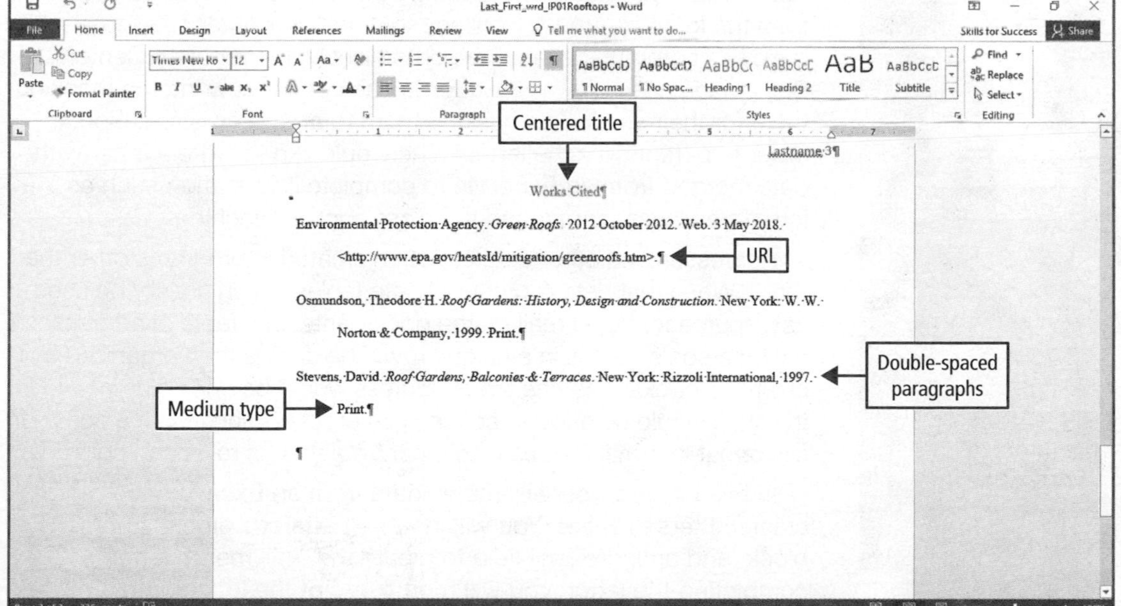

Word 2016, Windows 10, Microsoft Corporation

Figure 8

22. Clear the **Show All Bibliography Fields** check box, and then fill out the rest of the information if it is provided on the web page you selected. In the **Medium** box, type Web When you are done, click **OK**, and then compare your screen with **Figure 7**.

The MLA seventh edition citation style recommends that the medium be included. For example, a book may be in print, an eBook, or accessed from a website. Instructors often specify which mediums they will accept.

23. Press Ctrl + End, and then press Ctrl + Enter to create a new page.

24. On the **References tab**, in the **Citations & Bibliography group**, click the **Bibliography** button, and then click **Works Cited**. Press Backspace.

25. Select all of the text on the *Works Cited* page including the title. On the **Home tab**, change the **Font Size** to **12** and the **Font** to **Times New Roman**. Change the **Line and Paragraph Spacing** to **2.0**. Click the **Line and Paragraph Spacing** button again, and then click **Remove Space Before Paragraph**.

26. Select the *Works Cited* title, and then click **Center**. Check the spelling and grammar, and then compare your screen with **Figure 8**.

27. Save the file, **Close** Word, and then submit the file as directed by your instructor.

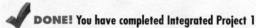

DONE! You have completed Integrated Project 1

INTEGRATED PROJECT 2

Use Excel Data in Word Mail Merge

- Mail merge enables you to select data from various sources. The data source could include an Excel workbook, an Outlook Contacts list, a Word table, an Access database, or a text file.
- Excel tables typically store data in the same manner as a Word table that has been set up as a data source in a mail merge.
- When fields are arranged in columns and records in rows, you can use the Excel worksheet as a data source in a Word mail merge.
- The mail merge data can be filtered before being merged into a Word document.

Alisonhancock/Fotolia

Aspen Falls City Hall

Aspen Falls City Hall has started a new program that uses interns from the local community college to teach computer classes at the city's community centers. Lorrine Deely, Community Center Supervisor, needs to mail a letter to each of the new interns thanking them for their service and asking them to attend an orientation. In order to personalize the letters, she would like to write a letter with data merged from an Excel file to complete information such as the intern's address, name, and the class each is teaching.

Addresses and other data are often created in programs other than Word. When that data is organized into tables, it can usually be used as a source for Word mail merge documents. In a table of addresses, each person's data is in a unique row. The data is then organized by column. For example, the street address would be one column, and the state would be another column. Excel spreadsheets are a common file format that makes it easy to organize data into rows and columns.

In this project, you will import data from an Excel workbook to create letters in Word. You will insert an address block, a name block, and an individual field to create the mail merge letter. After completing the letter, you will merge one of the letters into a new document to provide a document for your instructor to grade.

Time to complete this project — 30 to 60 minutes

Outcome

Using the skills in this project, you will be able to create personalized letters using the mail merge tool.

Objectives

2.1 Create and modify letters

2.2 Insert fields

2.3 Merge letters

To complete this project, you will need the following files:

wrd_IP02Instructors (Excel)
wrd_IP02Letter

You will save your files as:

Last_First_wrd_IP02Letter
Last_First_wrd_IP02LetterMerge

ASPEN FALLS HUMAN RESOURCES
500 S Street
Aspen Falls, CA 93463

June 18, 2018

76117 W Second St
Aspen Falls, CA 93463

Dear Mitchell Screen:

Thank you so much for agreeing to teach the Beginning Microsoft PowerPoint class at one of our community centers. Before you teach your first session, you need to attend an orientation.

The orientations will be at the Central Community Center, Room 110A next Thursday at 8:00 a.m. and 5:00 p.m. You may attend either session. If you cannot attend one of these sessions, please contact me to make other arrangements.

Thank you for your service to Aspen Falls, and I look forward to seeing you next week.

Sincerely,

Lorrine Deely
Community Center Supervisor

SKILLS

At the end of this project, you will be able to:

- Create letters using mail merge
- Use Excel spreadsheets as mail merge data sources
- Insert Address Block, Greeting Line, and individual merge fields
- Finish and merge letters into individual documents

1. Start **Word 2016**, and then open the student data file **wrd_IP02Letter**. Save the file in your **Word App Level Projects** folder as Last_First_wrd_IP02Letter If necessary, display the formatting marks.
2. Click the **Mailings tab**. In the **Start Mail Merge group**, click the **Start Mail Merge** button, and then click **Letters**.
3. In the **Start Mail Merge group**, click the **Select Recipients** button, and then click **Use an Existing List**.
4. In the **Select Data Source** dialog box, navigate to the student data files, click **wrd_IP02Instructors**, and then click **Open**. Compare your screen with **Figure 1**.

   Because Excel workbooks can contain multiple worksheets in a single workbook, the Select Table dialog box is used to select the desired worksheet. Here, the *Art_Instructors* worksheet contains the data that needs to be merged.

5. In the **Select Table** dialog box, be sure that **Art_Instructors** is selected, and then click **OK**.
6. In the letter, click to the left of the word *ADDRESS*. In the **Write & Insert Fields group**, click **Address Block**. In the **Insert Address Block** dialog box, clear the **Insert recipient's name in this format** check box, and then click **OK**. To the right of the merge field, delete the word *ADDRESS*.
7. In the **Preview Results group**, click the **Preview Results button**, and then compare your screen with **Figure 2**.

Continue to the next page to complete the project

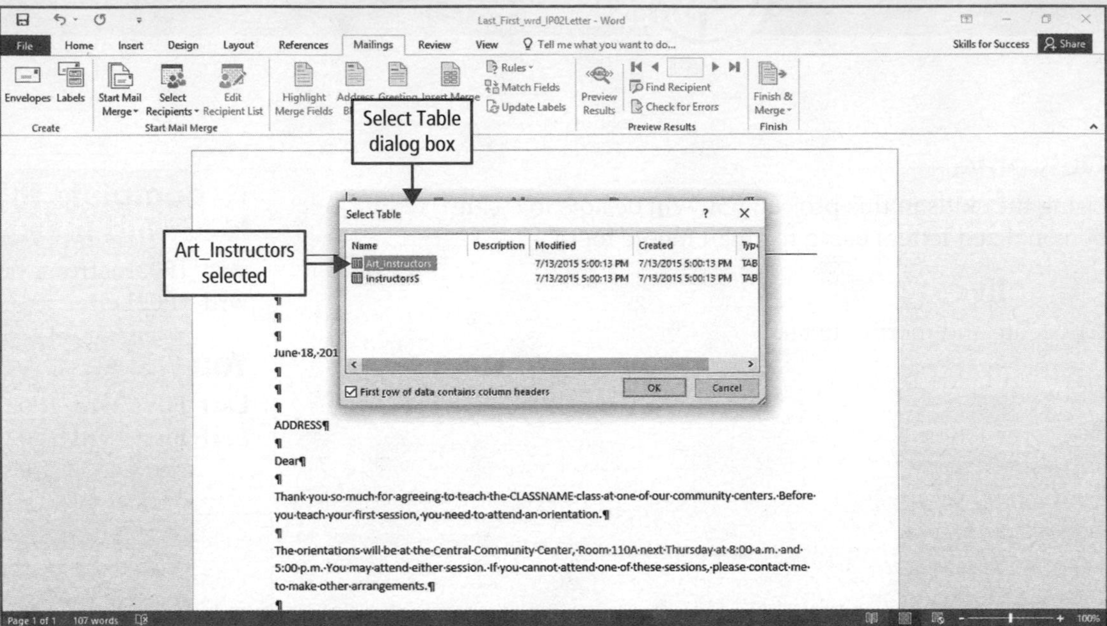

Figure 1

Word 2016, Windows 10, Microsoft Corporation

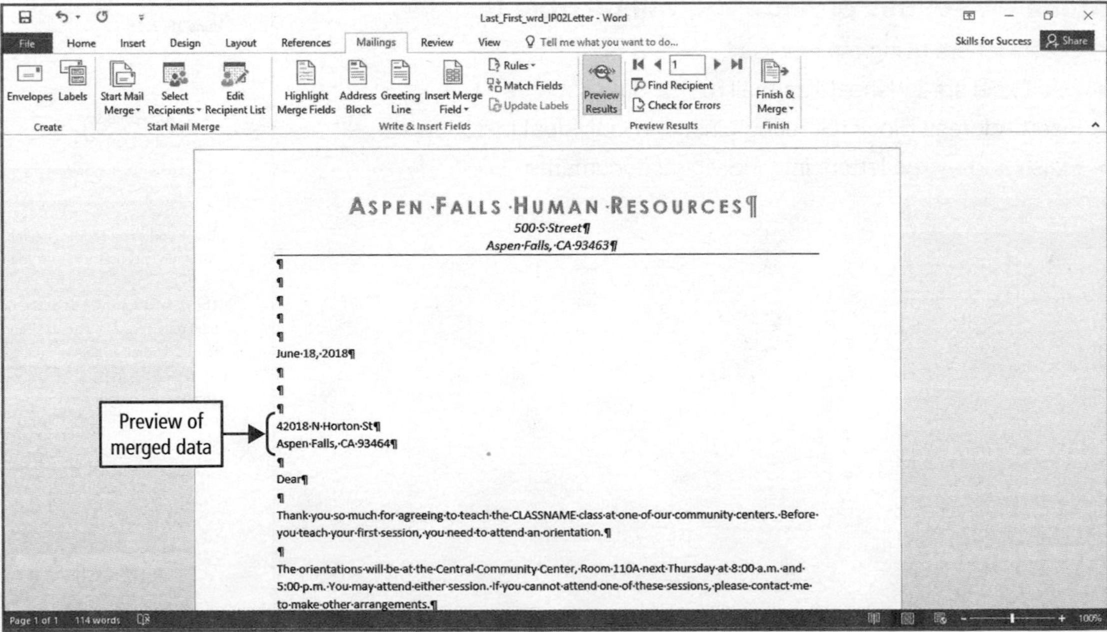

Figure 2

Word 2016, Windows 10, Microsoft Corporation

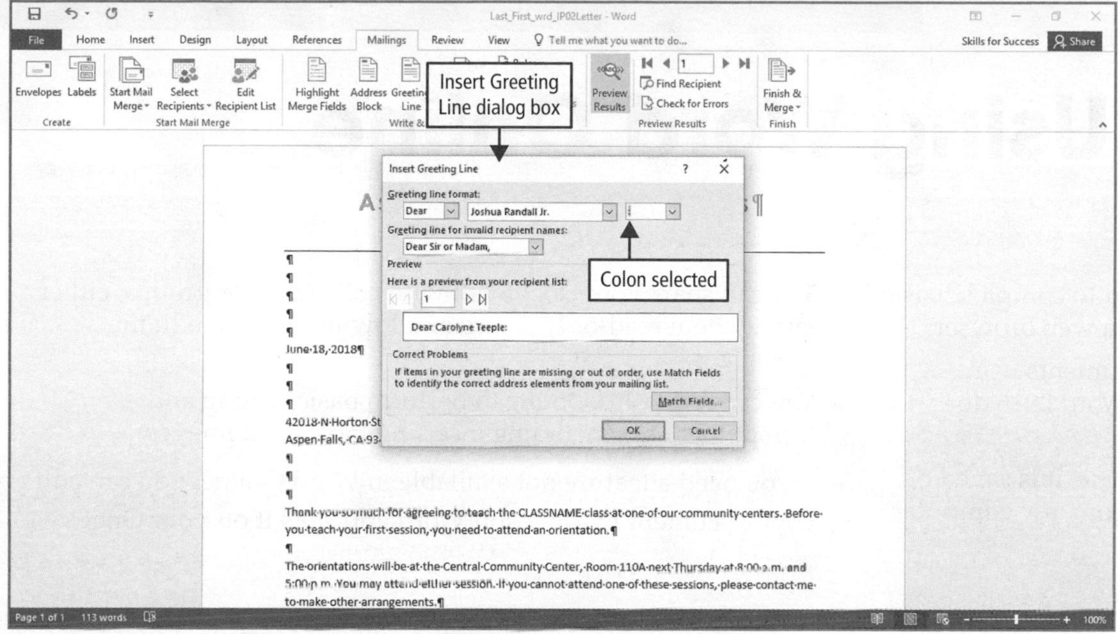

Word 2016, Windows 10, Microsoft Corporation

Figure 3

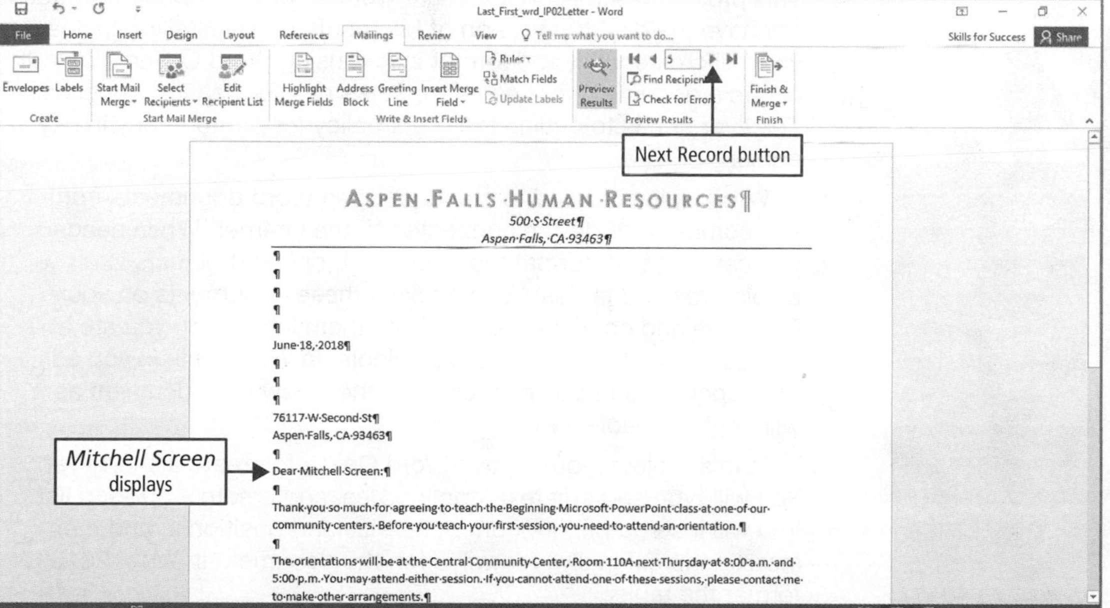

Word 2016, Windows 10, Microsoft Corporation

Figure 4

8. Click to the left of the word *Dear*, and then press Delete four times to delete the word. In the **Write & Insert Fields group**, click the **Greeting Line** button.
9. In the **Insert Greeting Line** dialog box, under **Greeting line format**, click the third arrow, and then click the colon (**:**). Compare your screen with **Figure 3**, and then click **OK**.
10. In the first body paragraph, double-click the word *CLASSNAME* to select it. In the **Write & Insert Fields group**, click the **Insert Merge Field button arrow**, and then click **Classes**. After the field just inserted, add a space.
11. In the **Preview Results group**, click the **Next Record** button ▶ four times to display the fifth letter—the letter for *Mitchell Screen*. Compare your screen with **Figure 4**.
12. In the **Finish group**, click the **Finish & Merge** button, and then click **Edit Individual Documents**. In the **Merge to New Document** dialog box, select the **Current record** option button, and then click **OK**.
13. **Save** the new merged document as Last_First_wrd_IP02LetterMerge and then **Close** the file.
14. Save the file *Last_First_wrd_IP02Letter*. **Close** ✕ Word, and then submit the files as directed by your instructor.

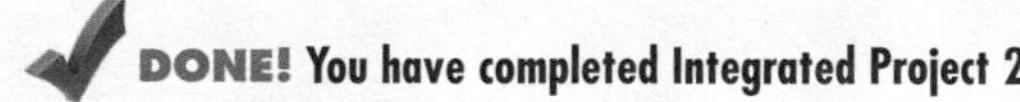

Create Flyers Using Word Online

- Word Online is a cloud-based application used to complete basic document editing and formatting tasks using a web browser.
- Word Online can be used to create or edit documents using a web browser instead of the Word program—Word 2016 does not need to be installed on your computer.
- When you create a document using Word Online, it is saved on your OneDrive so that you can work with it from any computer connected to the Internet.
- You can share your document with colleagues or groups, either giving them read-only access or allowing them to edit the document.
- You can use Word Online to perform basic editing and formatting tasks including inserting tables and images.
- If you need a feature not available in Word Online, you can edit your document in Microsoft Word and save it on your OneDrive.

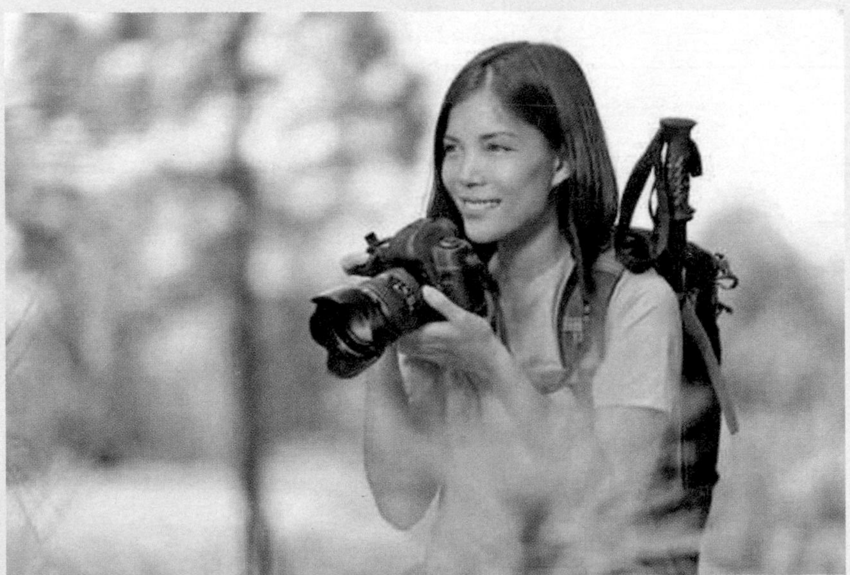

Maridav/Fotolia

Aspen Falls City Hall

This project assumes that you are working at a computer that does not have the desktop version of Microsoft Word installed. Instead, you will create, edit, and format a flyer using Word Online. You will create a document for Leah Kim, Parks and Recreation Supervisor. The flyer needs to outline the city's policy for photography in city parks.

Word Online is used to create or open Word documents from any computer or device connected to the Internet. When needed, you can edit text, format the document, or insert objects such as pictures and tables. You can save these documents on your OneDrive and continue working with them later when you are at a computer that has Word 2016 available. In Word Online, you edit your document in Editing View, and then view the document as it will print in Reading View.

In this project, you will use Word Online to create a short flyer. You will type and edit text, apply styles, and create a bulleted list. You will insert a picture from a file, size and position it, and then insert a table. Finally, you will open the document in Word 2016 to format the table.

Time to complete this project — 30 to 60 minutes

Outcome

Using the skills in this project, you will be able to create and edit a Word Online document.

Objectives

1 Create a Word Online document

2 Insert and format text

3 Insert and format pictures

4 Open and edit the Word Online document in Word 2016

SKILLS

At the end of this project, you will be able to:

- Create new Word documents from OneDrive
- Type text in Editing View
- Apply styles
- Add emphasis to text
- Change text alignment
- Insert pictures from files
- Create tables
- Switch to desktop Word to complete editing
- View documents in Reading View

To complete this project, you will need the following file:

wrd_WAPark

You will save your file as:

Last_First_wrd_WAPark

City of Aspen Falls Parks and Recreation

Photography Policy

We encourage photography in city parks and conservation area. If you are taking pictures as a recreational activity and will not earn more than $3,000 total revenue from the sale of the photographs, no fees or permits are needed. If you are not a hobby photographer, the following requirements must be met:

- Complete a photography permit application form.
- Provide proof of liability insurance.
- Pay a refundable damage deposit.
- Pay the permit fee as specified in the table below.
- Commercial photography in conservation areas is not allowed.

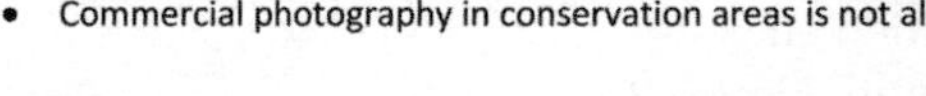

Photography fees:

Hobby Photography	No Fee
Commercial Photography	$200 per day
Motion Pictures or Feature Films	$625 per four hours

luchshen/Fotolia

1. Open a web browser, navigate to live.com and then log on to your Microsoft account. If you do not have an account, follow the links and directions on the page to create one.
2. After logging in, navigate as needed to display your **OneDrive** page, and then compare your screen with **Figure 1**.

   OneDrive and Office Online technologies are accessed through web pages that can change often, and the formatting and layout of some pages may often be different than the figures in this book. You may need to adapt the steps to complete the actions they describe.

3. On the toolbar, click **New**, and then click **Word document**. At the top of the screen, click the file name, and then name the file Last_First_wrd_WAPark Notice the *Saving* message on the status bar at the bottom of the screen.
4. On the **Home tab**, in the **Styles group**, click the **Heading 2** style, and then type City of Aspen Falls Parks and Recreation
5. Press Enter. In the **Styles group**, click the **Heading 1** style, and then type Photography Policy
6. Select the first two title lines, and then in the **Paragraph group**, click the **Center** button.
7. Select the text *Photography Policy*, and then in the **Font group**, click the **Font Size arrow** 11, and then click **24**. Compare your screen with **Figure 2**.

■ Continue to the next page to complete the project

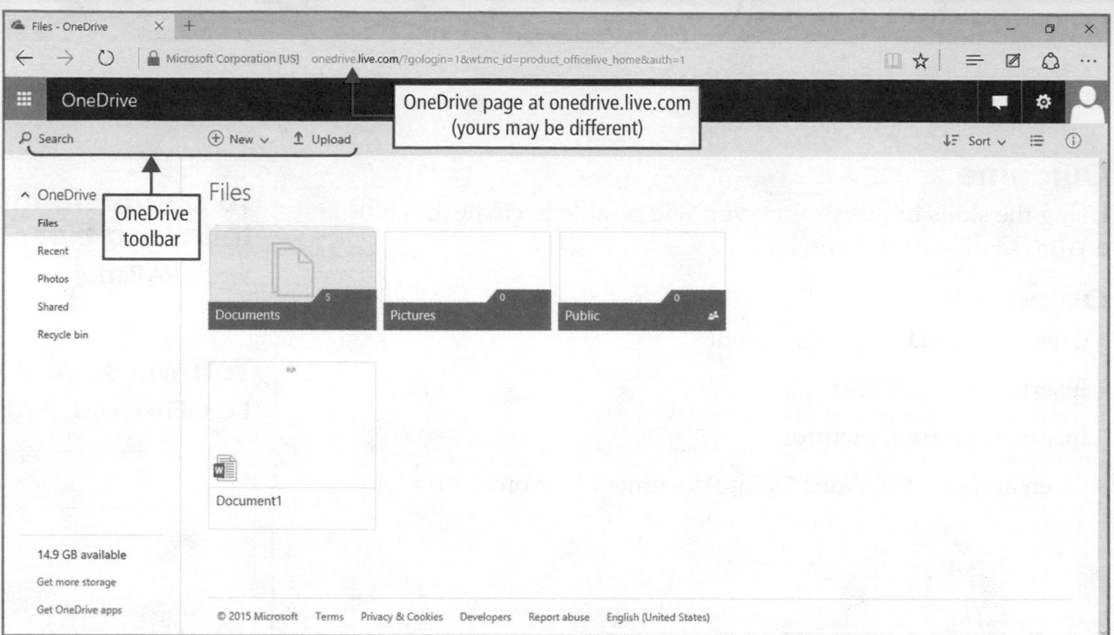

Figure 1

Word 2016, Windows 10, Microsoft Corporation

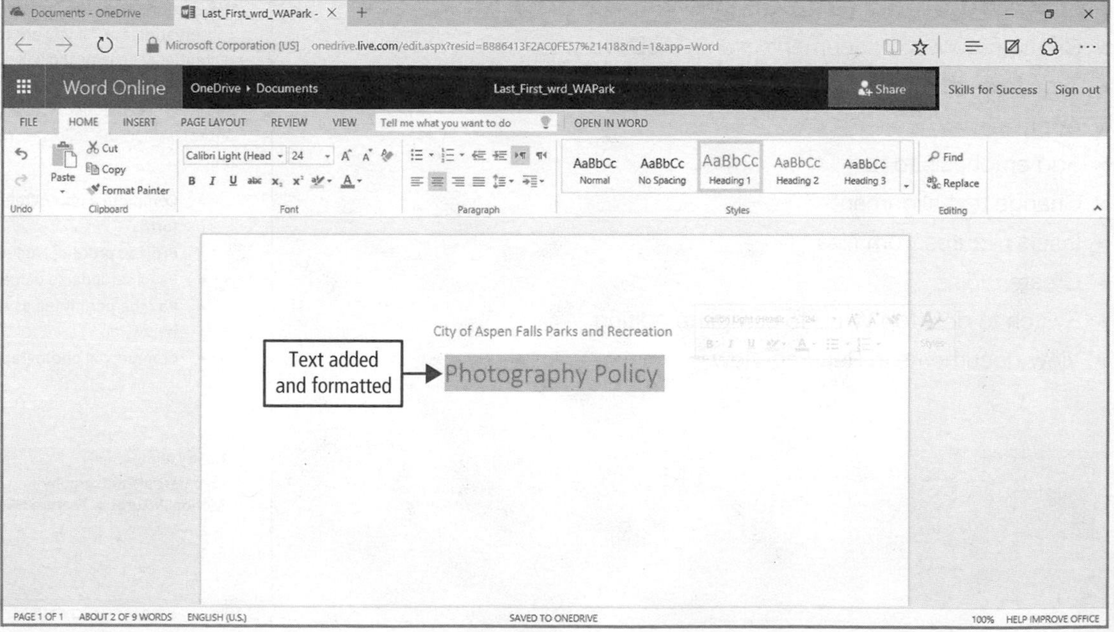

Figure 2

Word 2016, Windows 10, Microsoft Corporation

- Complete a photography permit application form.
- Provide proof of liability insurance.
- Pay a refundable damage deposit.
- Pay the permit fee as specified in the table below.
- Commercial photography in conservation areas is not allowed.

Figure 3

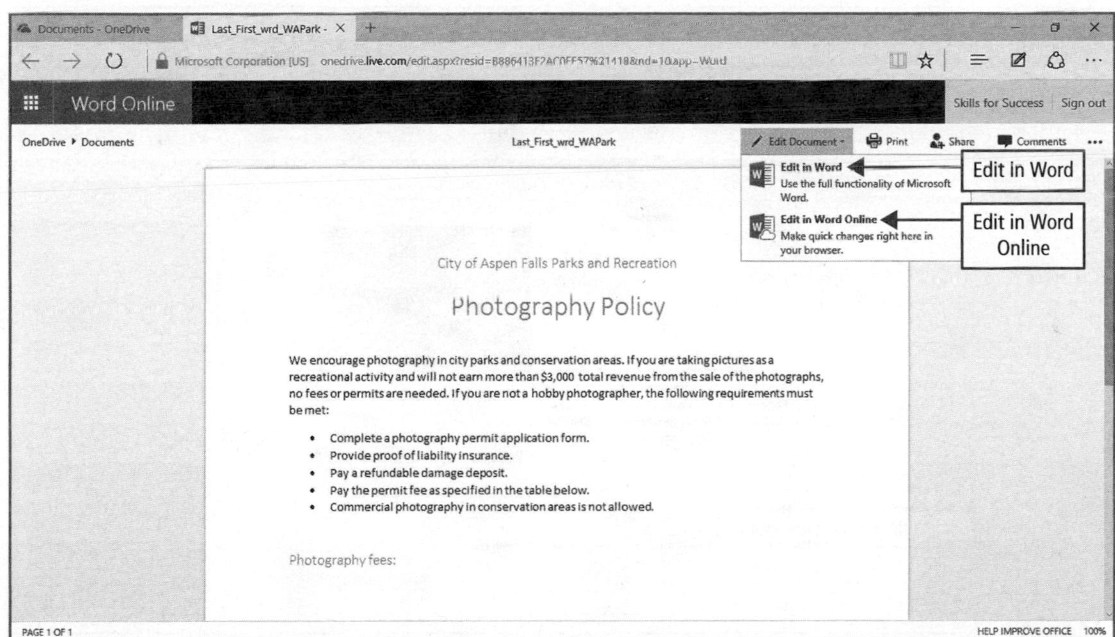

Word 2016, Windows 10, Microsoft Corporation

Figure 4

8. Position the insertion point to the right of *Policy*, and then press Enter two times.
9. In the **Styles group**, click **Normal**, and then type the following text: We encourage photography in city parks and conservation areas. If you are taking pictures as a recreational activity and will not earn more than $3,000 total revenue from the sale of the photographs, no fees or permits are needed. If you are not a hobby photographer, the following requirements must be met:
10. Press Enter, and then in the **Paragraph group**, click the **Bullets** button. Create a bulleted list using the text found in the table in **Figure 3**.
11. After typing the list, press Enter three times, and then type Photography fees:
12. With the insertion point in the *Photography fees* paragraph, apply the **Heading 2** style.
13. Click the **View tab**. In the **Documents Views group**, click the **Reading View** button.

    Reading View displays the document as it will print, but you cannot edit in this view.
14. Click **Edit Document**, compare your screen with **Figure 4**, and then click **Edit in Word Online**.
15. In the first bullet, position the insertion point to the right of the line that ends *permit application form*. Click the **Insert tab**, and then in the **Pictures group**, click the **Picture** button. In the **Choose File to Upload** dialog box, navigate to the student files for this project, and then open **wrd_WAPark**. Click the **Insert** button to close the dialog box.

■ **Continue to the next page to complete the project**

16. If necessary, click the picture to select it, and then click the **Format tab**. In the **Image Size group**, click in the **Scale** box. Type 75 and then press Enter to change the size of the picture to 75% of its original size. Compare your screen with **Figure 5**.

    When a picture is selected, the Format tab displays and the picture has a washed-out effect.

17. Click in the document, and then press Ctrl + End to move to the end of the document. Press Enter.
18. Click the **Insert tab**, and then in the **Tables group**, click the **Table** button. In the third row, click the second square to create a 2x3 table.
19. In the first table cell, type Hobby Photography and then press Tab. Type No Fee and then press Tab.
20. Type Commercial Photography and then press Tab. Type $200 per day and then press Tab.
21. Type Motion Pictures or Feature Films and then press Tab. Type $625 per four hours and then compare your screen with **Figure 6**.

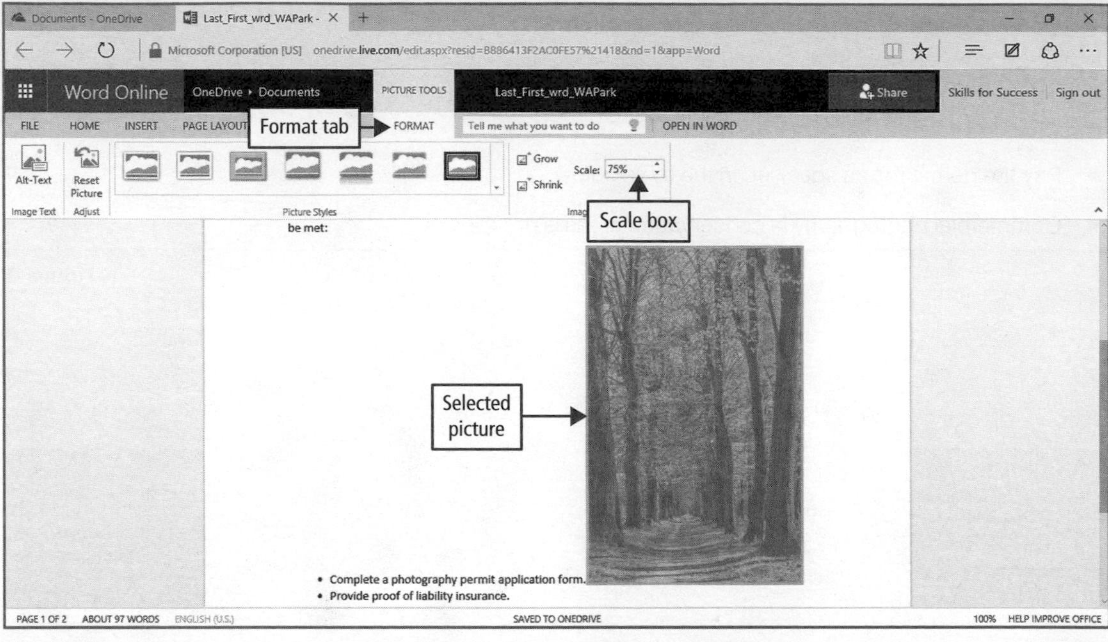

Figure 5

luchshen/Fotolia; Word 2016, Windows 10, Microsoft Corporation

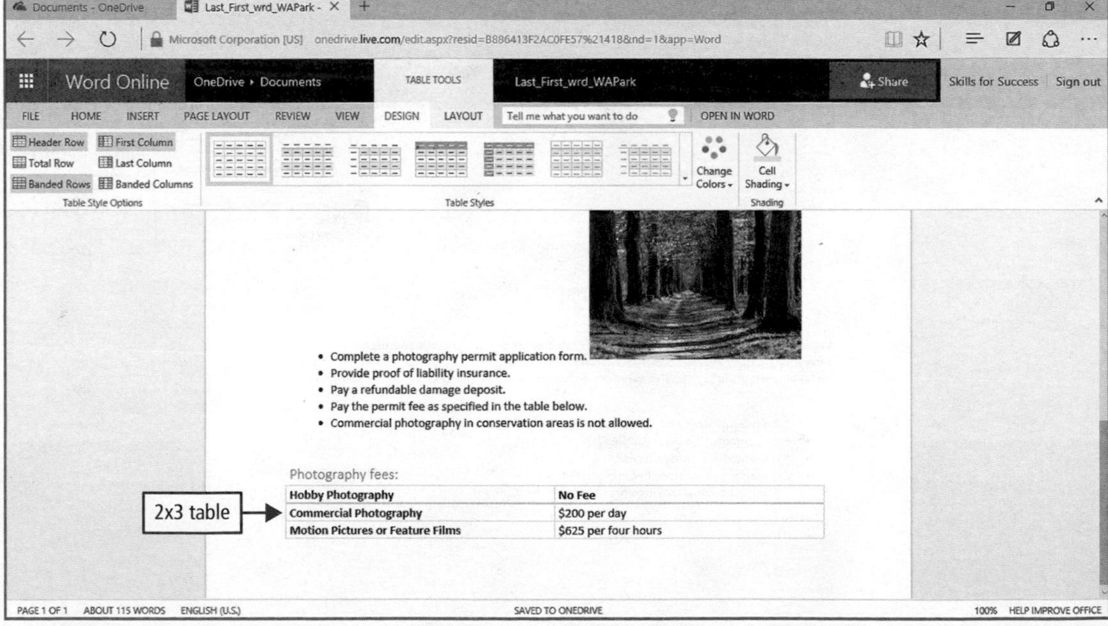

Figure 6

luchshen/Fotolia; Word 2016, Windows 10, Microsoft Corporation

■ **Continue to the next page to complete the project**

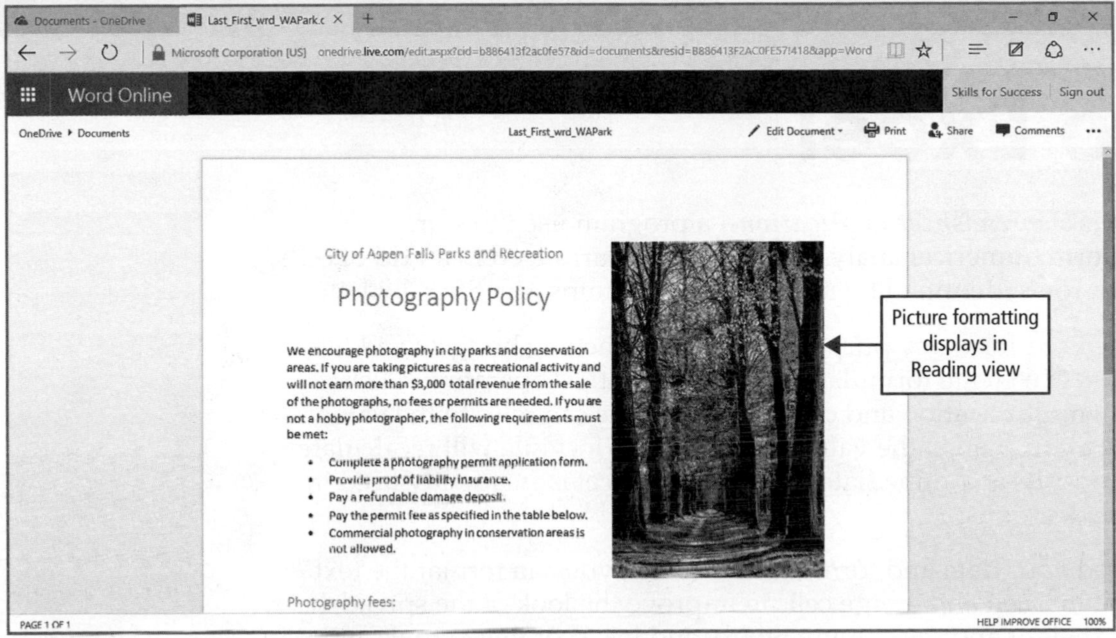

luchshen/Fotolia; Word 2016, Windows 10, Microsoft Corporation

Figure 7

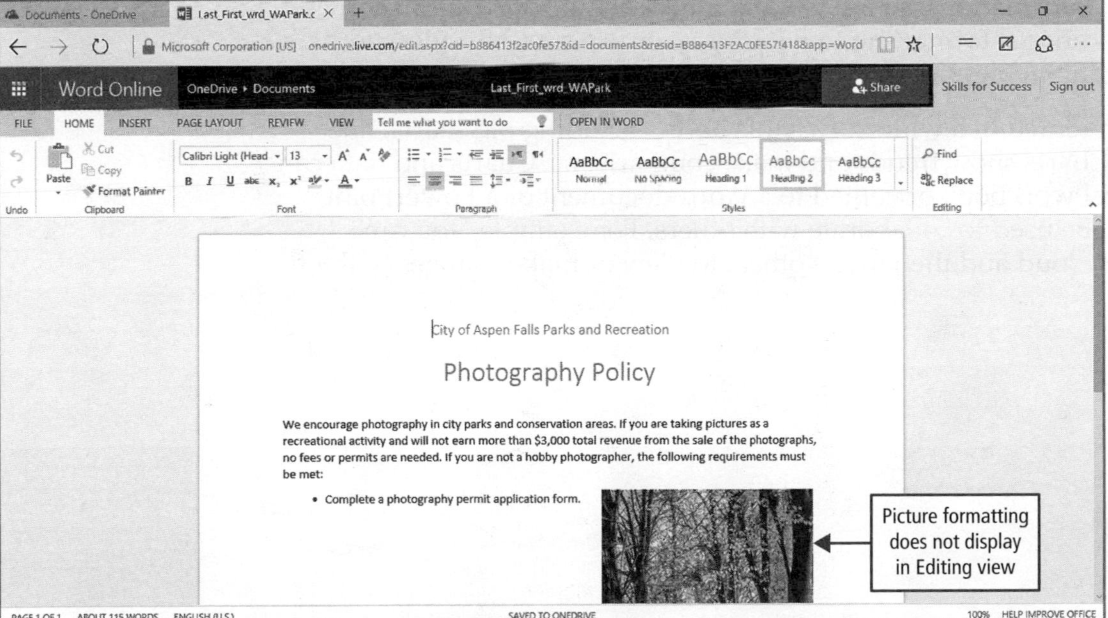

luchshen/Fotolia; Word 2016, Windows 10, Microsoft Corporation

Figure 8

22. To the right of the **Tell me what you want to do** box, click **OPEN IN WORD**. Read all messages that display, and then click **Allow** or **Yes** as needed to open the document in Word 2016.

23. If necessary, switch to Print Layout view. Click the picture to select it, and then click the **Format tab**. In the **Arrange group**, click the **Position** button, and then click the third thumbnail—**Position in Top Right with Square Text Wrapping**.

24. Click in the table, and then click the **Table Tools Design tab**. Click the **Table Styles More** button, and then under **Grid Tables**, click the fourth style in the second row—**Grid Table 2 - Accent 3**.

25. Save the file, and then **Close** Word 2016.

26. In the message that displays, click **Edit in Word Online**. On the **View tab**, click **Reading View**, and then compare your screen with **Figure 7**.

27. Click **Edit Document**, and then click **Edit in Word Online**. Compare your screen with **Figure 8**.

    Features not supported by Word Online will not be available in Edit view. Here, the picture layout does not display. These features however, do display in Reading view and when opened in Word 2016.

28. Submit the file as directed by your instructor.

29. In the top right corner of the browser window, click the **Sign out** link, and then **Close** the browser window.

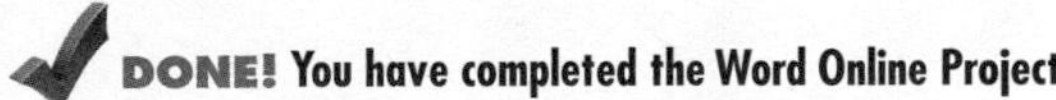

DONE! You have completed the Word Online Project

Introduction to Excel

Microsoft Excel 2016 is a ***spreadsheet application***—a program used to store information and to perform numerical analysis of data that is arranged in a grid of cells. This grid is organized in rows identified by numbers and columns identified by letters.

A spreadsheet can be used for many purposes including tracking budgets and summarizing results. You can create formulas using mathematical operations such as addition, subtraction, multiplication and division. Formulas can refer to the value stored in a cell and when you change the value of the cell, the formula will recalculate the results. Because the results are immediately displayed, Excel is frequently used in businesses to help make decisions.

Once you have entered your data and formulas into Excel, you can format the text and values, or wrap text in a cell and merge cells to improve the look of the spreadsheet. You can change the row height and the column width, and insert or delete rows and columns.

To help you find the information you are looking for more quickly, you can sort and filter data or apply conditional formatting to data. You can also use cell styles, borders, or font colors and shading to highlight important data.

Excel data can be presented in a wide variety of charts, including pie charts, line charts and bar charts. Charts show trends and make comparisons. Charts and data can be displayed in an Excel workbook or copied to a Word document or a PowerPoint presentation. Excel can be used to collaborate with others. For example, you can save workbooks to the Cloud and then invite others to view or make changes to the workbooks.

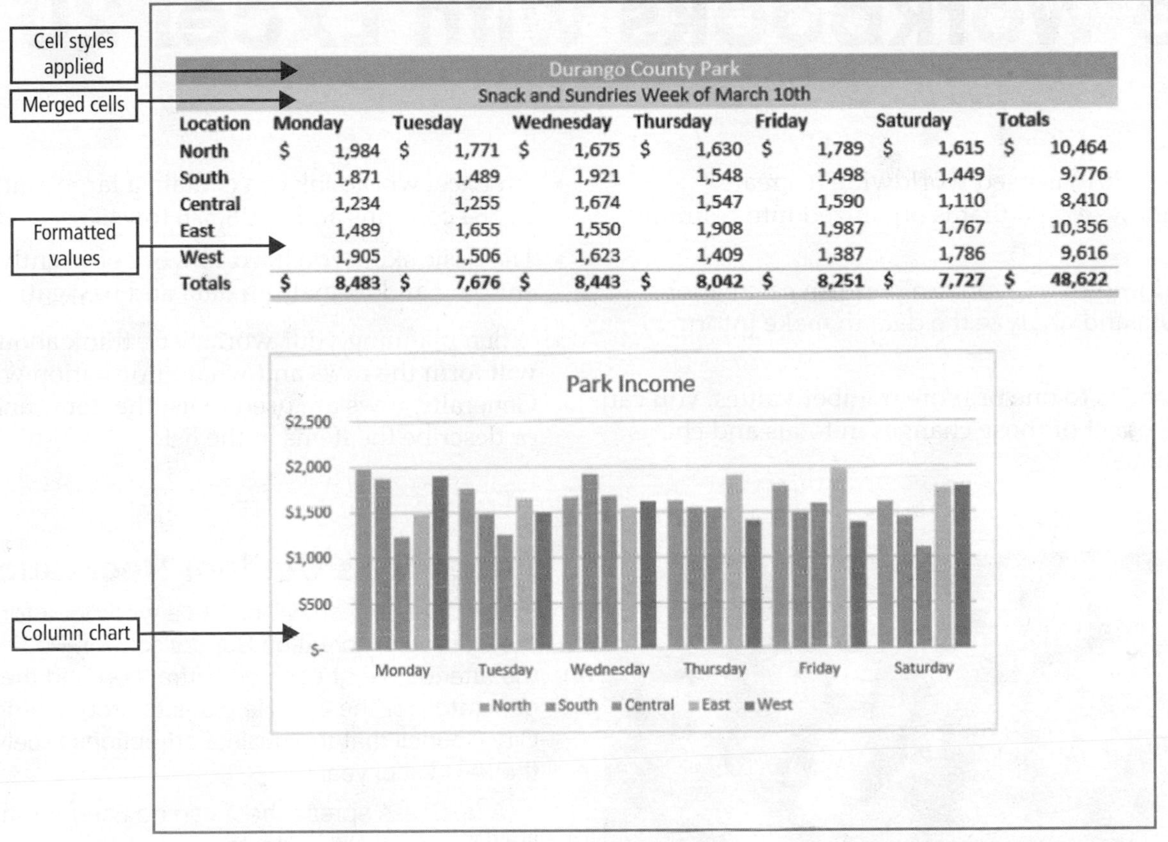

Durango County Park							
Snack and Sundries Week of March 10th							
Location	Monday	Tuesday	Wednesday	Thursday	Friday	Saturday	Totals
North	$ 1,984	$ 1,771	$ 1,675	$ 1,630	$ 1,789	$ 1,615	$ 10,464
South	1,871	1,489	1,921	1,548	1,498	1,449	9,776
Central	1,234	1,255	1,674	1,547	1,590	1,110	8,410
East	1,489	1,655	1,550	1,908	1,987	1,767	10,356
West	1,905	1,506	1,623	1,409	1,387	1,786	9,616
Totals	$ 8,483	$ 7,676	$ 8,443	$ 8,042	$ 8,251	$ 7,727	$ 48,622

CHAPTER 1

Create Workbooks with Excel 2016

- Microsoft Office Excel 2016 is used worldwide to create workbooks and to analyze data that is organized into columns and rows.
- After data is entered into Excel, you can perform calculations on the numerical data and analyze the data to make informed decisions.
- When you make changes to one or more number values, you can immediately see the effect of those changes in totals and charts that rely on those values.
- An Excel workbook can contain a large amount of data—up to 16,384 columns and 1,048,576 rows.
- The basic skills you need to work efficiently with Excel include entering and formatting data and navigating within Excel.
- When planning your worksheet, think about what information will form the rows and what information will form the columns. Generally, rows are used to list the items and columns to group or describe the items in the list.

Vlad_g/Fotolia

Aspen Falls Outdoor Recreation

In this chapter, you will create a workbook for Amado Pettinelli, the Outdoor Recreation Supervisor. Mr. Pettinelli wants to know the attendance at each city attraction and the revenue each venue generates for the city. He plans to recommend to the Aspen Falls City Council that the busiest attractions receive more city funding in the next fiscal year.

A business spreadsheet can be used for many purposes including tracking budgets, manufacture measurements, or employees. The spreadsheet data can be manipulated using arithmetic and mathematical formulas commonly used in the modern-day business world. If you are asked to create a spreadsheet, you need to know if the results of the data manipulation will be presented in numerical or graphical format.

In this project, you will create a new Excel workbook and enter data that displays the total number of visitors at the various city attractions in Aspen Falls. You will format the data, construct formulas, and insert functions. You will calculate the percentage of weekday visitors at each of the locations and insert a footer. Finally, you will check the spelling in the workbook.

Time to complete all 10 skills — 60 to 90 minutes

Outcome

Using the skills in this chapter, you will be able to create, edit, and save workbooks; create addition, subtraction, multiplication, and division formulas and functions; modify cell and worksheet formats; and apply print settings.

Objectives:

1.1 Create and enter data into worksheets

1.2 Construct basic functions and formulas

1.3 Apply cell formatting

1.4 Adjust settings and review worksheets for printing

Student data file needed for this chapter:

Blank Excel workbook

You will save your file as:

Last_First_exl01_Visitors

SKILLS

At the end of this chapter you will be able to:

Skill 1 Create and Save Workbooks

Skill 2 Enter Data and Merge and Center Titles

Skill 3 Construct Addition and Subtraction Formulas

Skill 4 Construct Multiplication and Division Formulas

Skill 5 Adjust Column Widths and Apply Cell Styles

Skill 6 Insert the SUM Function

Skill 7 AutoFill Formulas and Data

Skill 8 Format, Edit, and Check Spelling

Skill 9 Insert Footers and Adjust Page Settings

Skill 10 Display Formulas and Print Worksheets

MORE SKILLS

Skill 11 Set Print Areas

Skill 12 Fill Data with Flash Fill

Skill 13 Create Templates and Workbooks from Templates

Skill 14 Manage Document Properties

Aspen Falls Outdoor Recreation

Visitors to City Attractions

Location	Weekends	Weekdays	All Visitors	Difference	Entrance Fee	Total Fees
Zoo	3,169	1,739	4,908	1,430	$ 10	$ 49,080
Pool	5,338	3,352	8,690	1,986	10	86,900
Aquarium	9,027	3,868	12,895	5,159	12	154,740
Garden	4,738	2,788	7,526	1,950	4	30,104
Museum	3,876	913	4,789	2,963	11	52,679
Total	26,148	12,660	38,808			$ 373,503

Percent of Weekday Visitors	
Zoo	35.4%
Pool	38.6%
Aquarium	30.0%
Garden	37.0%
Museum	19.1%

Excel 2016, Windows 10, Microsoft Corporation

- An Excel ***workbook*** is a file that you can use to organize various kinds of related information. A workbook contains ***worksheets***, also called ***spreadsheets***—the primary documents that you use in Excel to store and work with data.
- The worksheet forms a grid of vertical columns and horizontal rows. The small box where one column and one row meet is a cell.

1. Start **Excel 2016**, and then click **Blank workbook**. In the lower right, notice the zoom level.

   Your zoom level should be 100%, but most figures in this chapter are zoomed to 120%.

2. Verify the cell in the upper left corner is the *active cell*—as shown in **Figure 1**.

   active cell—the cell outlined in green in which data is entered when you begin typing. In a worksheet, columns have alphabetical headings across the top, and rows have numerical headings down the left side. When a cell is active, the headings for the column and row in which the cell is located are shaded. The column letter and row number that identify a cell compose the ***cell address***, also called the ***cell reference***.

3. In cell **A1**, type Aspen Falls Outdoor Recreation and then press Enter to accept the entry.
4. In cell **A2**, type Visitors and then press Enter two times. Compare your screen with **Figure 2**.
5. In cell **A4**, type Location and press Tab to make the cell to the right—**B4**—active.

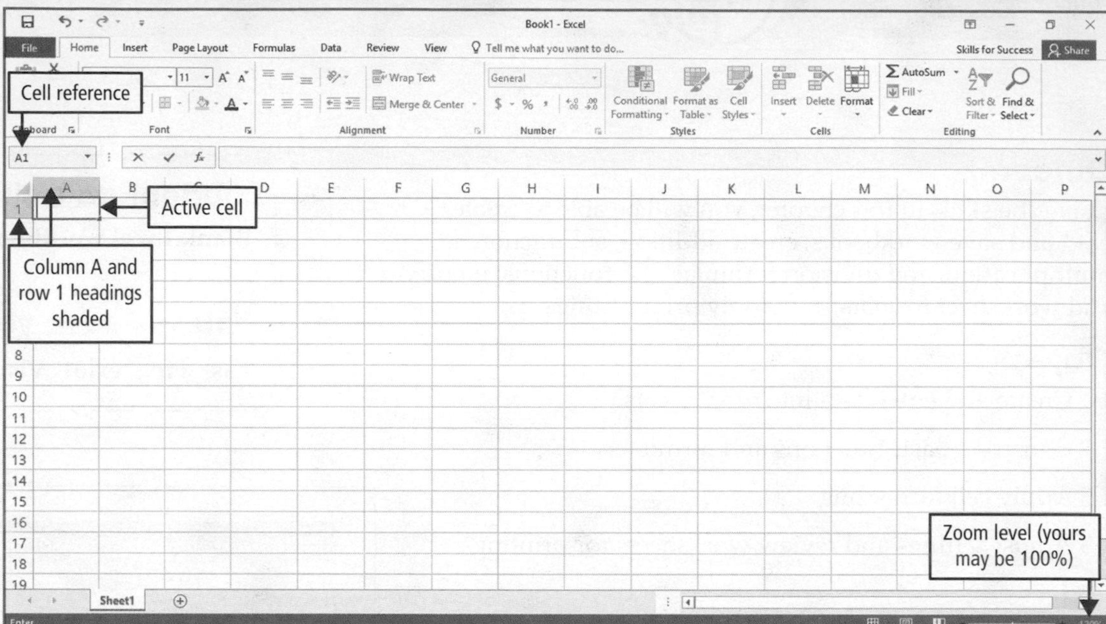

Figure 1

Excel 2016, Windows 10, Microsoft Corporation

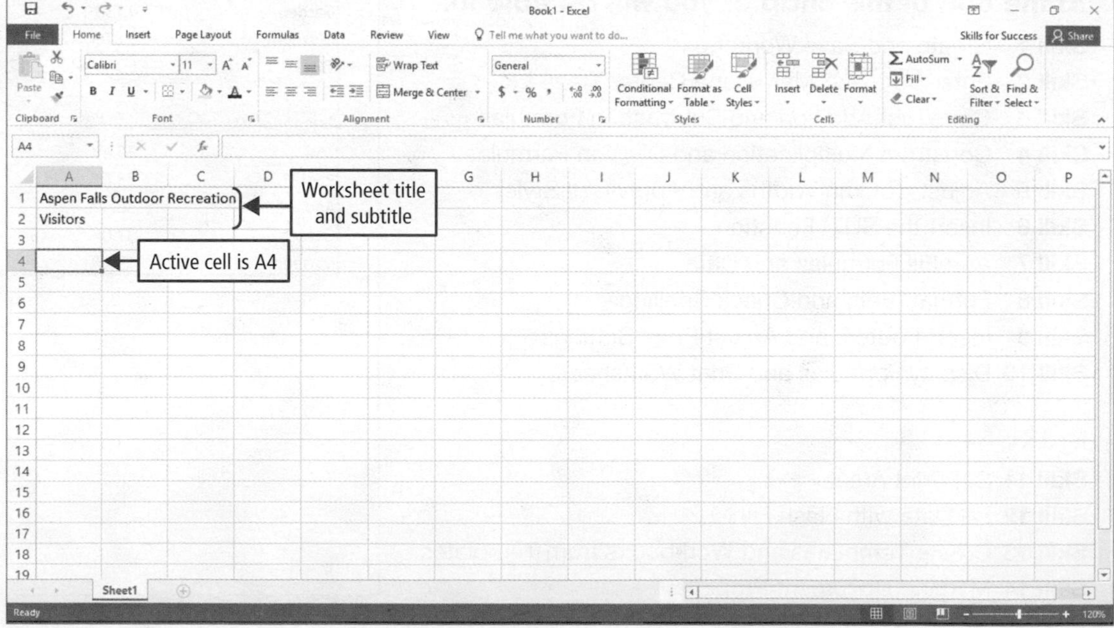

Figure 2

Excel 2016, Windows 10, Microsoft Corporation

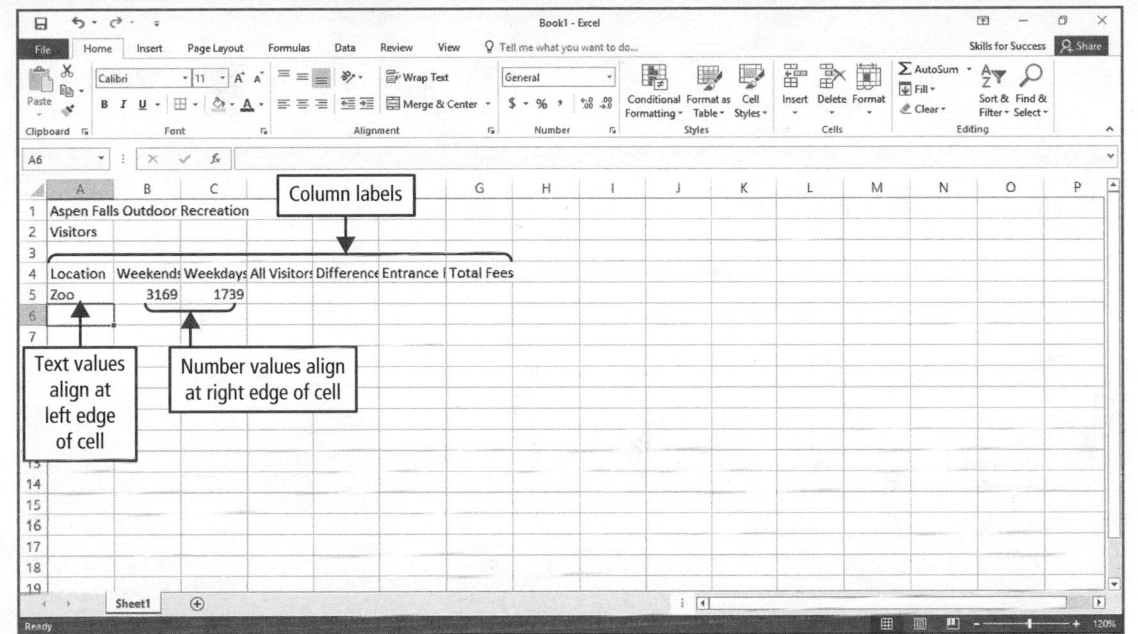

Excel 2016, Windows 10, Microsoft Corporation

Figure 3

Common Ways to Move or Scroll Through a Worksheet	
Key	**Description**
Enter	Move down one row.
Tab	Move one column to the right.
Shift + Tab	Move one column to the left.
↓ ↑ → ←	Move one cell in the direction of the arrow.
Ctrl + Home	Move to cell A1.
Ctrl + End	Move to the last row and last column farthest to the bottom right that contains data.

Figure 4

6. With cell **B4** the active cell, type the following labels, pressing Tab between each label:

   Weekends
   Weekdays
   All Visitors
   Difference
   Entrance Fee
   Total Fees

   Labels at the beginning of columns or rows help readers understand the data.

   To correct typing errors, click a cell and retype the data. The new typing will replace the existing data.

7. Click cell **A5**, type Zoo and then press Tab. Type 3169 and then press Tab. Type 1739 and then press Enter. Compare your screen with **Figure 3**.

   Data in a cell is called a ***value***. You can have a ***text value***—character data in a cell that usually labels number values, or a ***number value***—numeric data in a cell. A text value is often used as a ***label***. Text values align at the left cell edge, and number values align at the right cell edge.

8. Click **Save**, and then on the **Save As** page, click the **Browse** button. In the **Save As** dialog box, navigate to the location where you are saving your files. Click **New folder**, type Excel Chapter 1 and then press Enter two times. In the **File name** box, name the file Last_First_exl01_Visitors and then press Enter.

9. Take a few moments to familiarize yourself with common methods to move between cells as summarized in the table in **Figure 4**.

■ **You have completed Skill 1 of 10**

▸ To create an effective worksheet, you enter titles and subtitles and add labels for each row and column of data. It is a good idea to have the worksheet title and subtitle span across all the columns containing data.

1. In cell **A6**, type Aquarium and then press Tab.
2. In cell **B6**, type 9027 and then press Tab. In cell **C6**, type 3868 and then press Enter.
3. In row 7 and row 8, type the following data:

   Garden | 5738 | 2877

   Museum | 3876 | 913
4. In cell **A9**, type Total and then press Enter. Compare your screen with **Figure 1**.
5. Click cell **B1**, type Worksheet and then press Enter. Click cell **A1**, and then compare your screen with **Figure 2**.

   When text is too long to fit in a cell and the cell to the right of it contains data, the text will be ***truncated***—cut off. Here, the text in cell A1 is truncated.

   The ***formula bar*** is a bar below the ribbon that displays the value contained in the active cell and is used to enter or edit values or formulas.

   Data displayed in a cell is the ***displayed value***. Data displayed in the formula bar is the ***underlying value***. Displayed values often do not match their underlying values.
6. On the Quick Access Toolbar, click the **Undo** button to remove the text in cell B1.

   Long text in cells overlaps into other columns only when those cells are empty. Here, A1 text now overlaps B1 because that cell is empty.

■ Continue to the next page to complete the skill

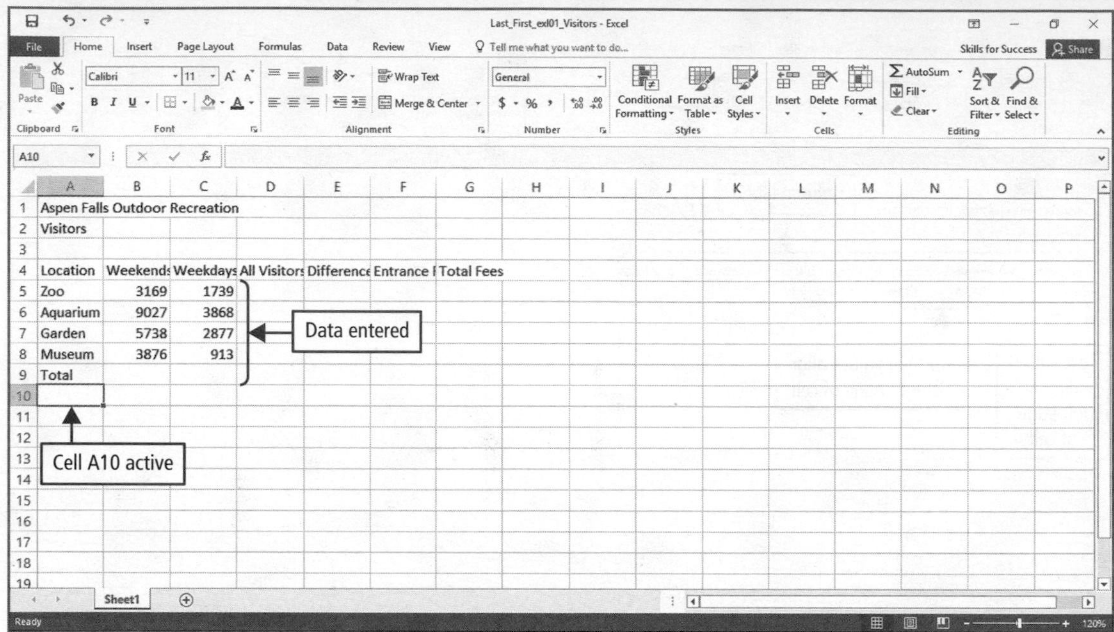

Figure 1

Excel 2016, Windows 10, Microsoft Corporation

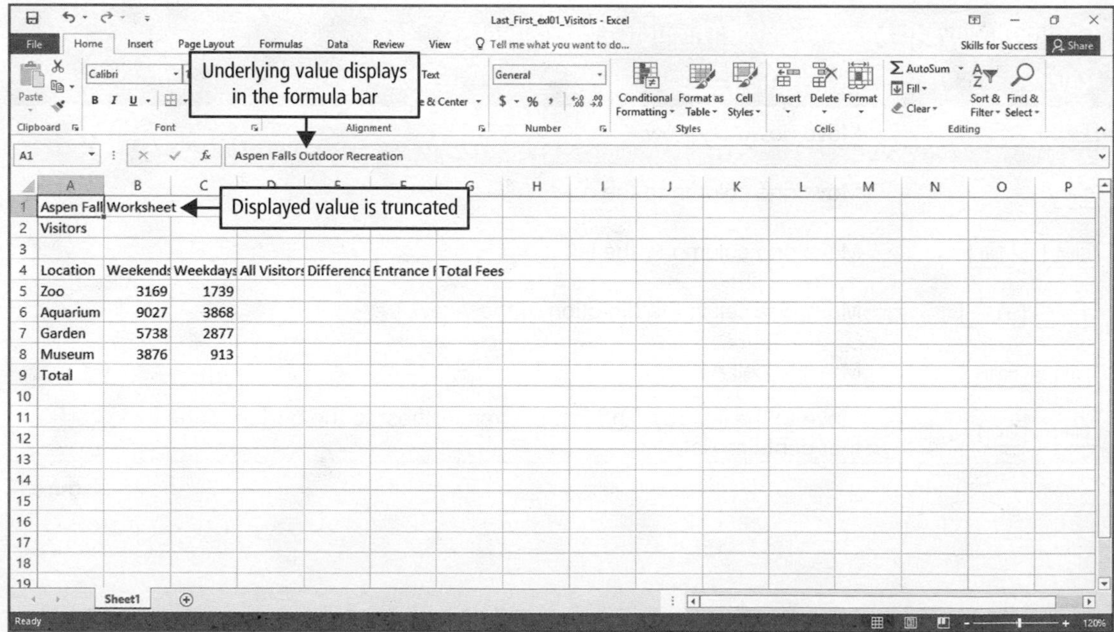

Figure 2

Excel 2016, Windows 10, Microsoft Corporation

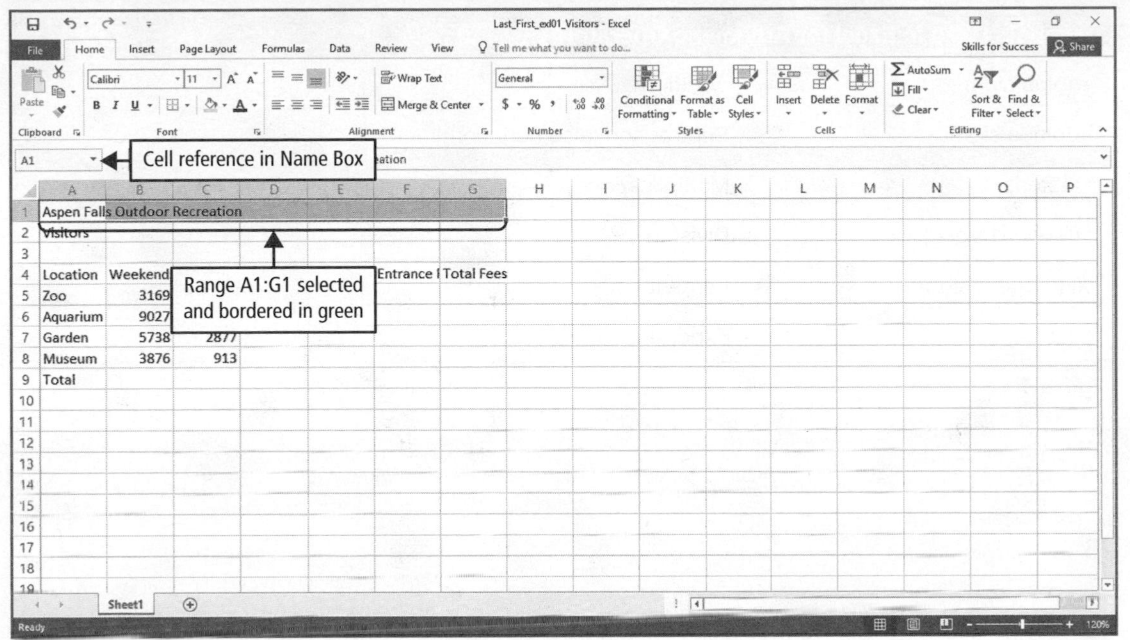

Excel 2016, Windows 10, Microsoft Corporation

Figure 3

Merge & Center button

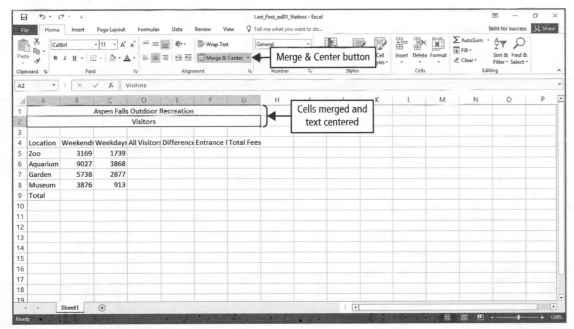

Cells merged and text centered

Excel 2016, Windows 10, Microsoft Corporation

Figure 4

7. Point to the middle of cell **A1** to display the [pointer icon] pointer. Hold down the left mouse button, and then drag to the right to select cells **A1** through **G1**. Compare your screen with **Figure 3**. To select a range on a touch screen, tap the cell, and then drag the selection handle. MOS Obj 1.2.2 C

   The selected range is referred to as *A1:G1* (A1 through G1). A ***range*** is two or more cells in a worksheet that are adjacent (next to each other). A colon (:) between two cell references indicates that the range includes the two cell references and all the cells between them. When you select a range, a thick green line surrounds the range, and all but the first cell in the range are shaded. The first cell reference will be displayed in the ***Name Box***—an area by the formula bar that displays the active cell reference.

8. On the **Home tab**, in the **Alignment group**, click the **Merge & Center** button [button icon]. MOS Obj 2.2.1 C

   The selected range, A1:G1, merges into one larger cell, and the data is centered in the new cell. The cells in B1 through G1 can no longer be selected individually because they are merged into cell A1.

9. Using the technique just practiced, merge and center the range **A2:G2**.

10. **Save** [save icon] the file, and then compare your screen with **Figure 4**.

■ **You have completed Skill 2 of 10**

SKILL 3: Construct Addition and Subtraction Formulas

- A cell's underlying value can be a text value, a number value, or a ***formula***—an equation that performs mathematical calculations on number values in the worksheet.
- Formulas begin with an equal sign and often include an ***arithmetic operator***—a symbol that specifies a mathematical operation such as addition or subtraction.

1. Study the symbols that Excel uses to perform mathematical operations, as summarized in the table in **Figure 1**.
2. In cell **D5**, type =B5+C5 and then press [Enter].

   When you include cell references in formulas, the values in those cells are inserted. Here, the total number of visitors for the zoo location equals the sum of the values in cells B5 and C5 (3169 + 1739 = 4908).

   When you type a formula, you might see a brief display of function names that match the first letter you type. This Excel feature, called ***Formula AutoComplete***, suggests values as you type a function.
3. In cell **D6**, type the formula to add cells B6 and C6, =B6+C6 and then press [Enter].
4. In cell **D7**, type = and then click cell **B7** to automatically insert *B7* into the formula. Compare your screen with **Figure 2**.

   Cell B7 is surrounded by a moving border indicating that it is part of an active formula.
5. Type + Click cell **C7**, and then press [Enter] to display the result *8615*.

   You can either type formulas or construct them by pointing and clicking in this manner.

■ **Continue to the next page to complete the skill**

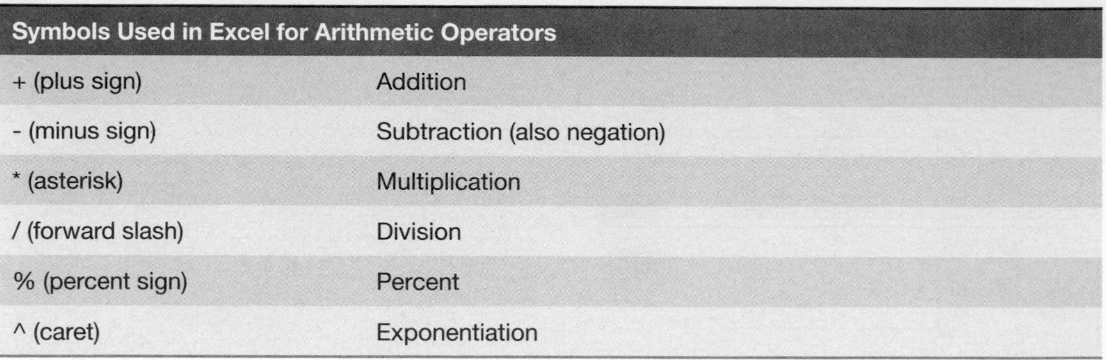

Symbols Used in Excel for Arithmetic Operators	
+ (plus sign)	Addition
- (minus sign)	Subtraction (also negation)
* (asterisk)	Multiplication
/ (forward slash)	Division
% (percent sign)	Percent
^ (caret)	Exponentiation

Figure 1

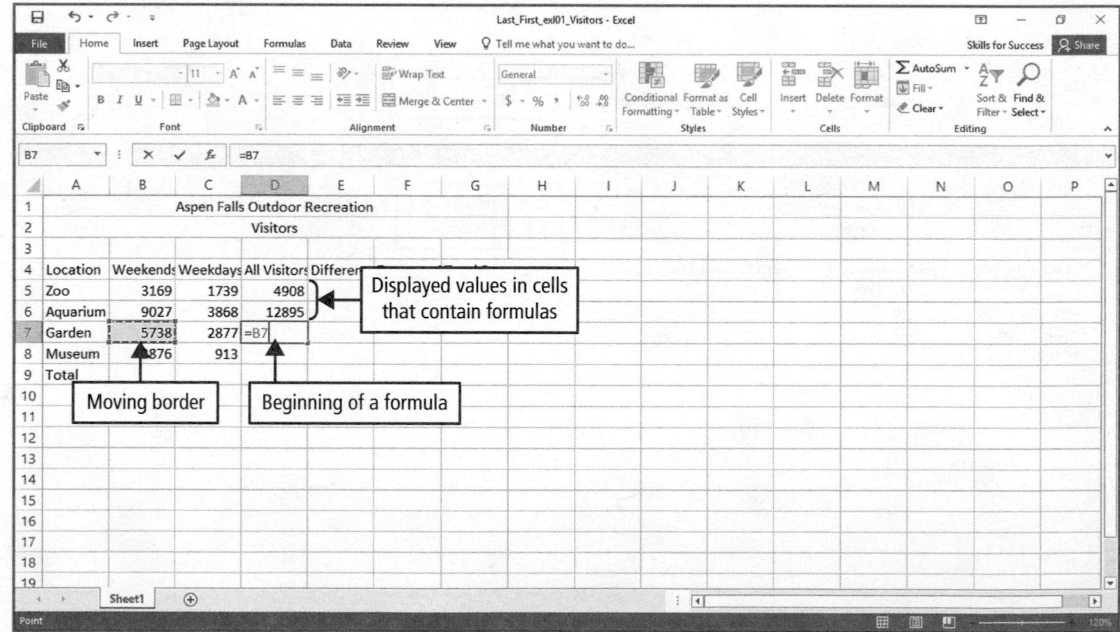

Figure 2

Excel 2016, Windows 10, Microsoft Corporation

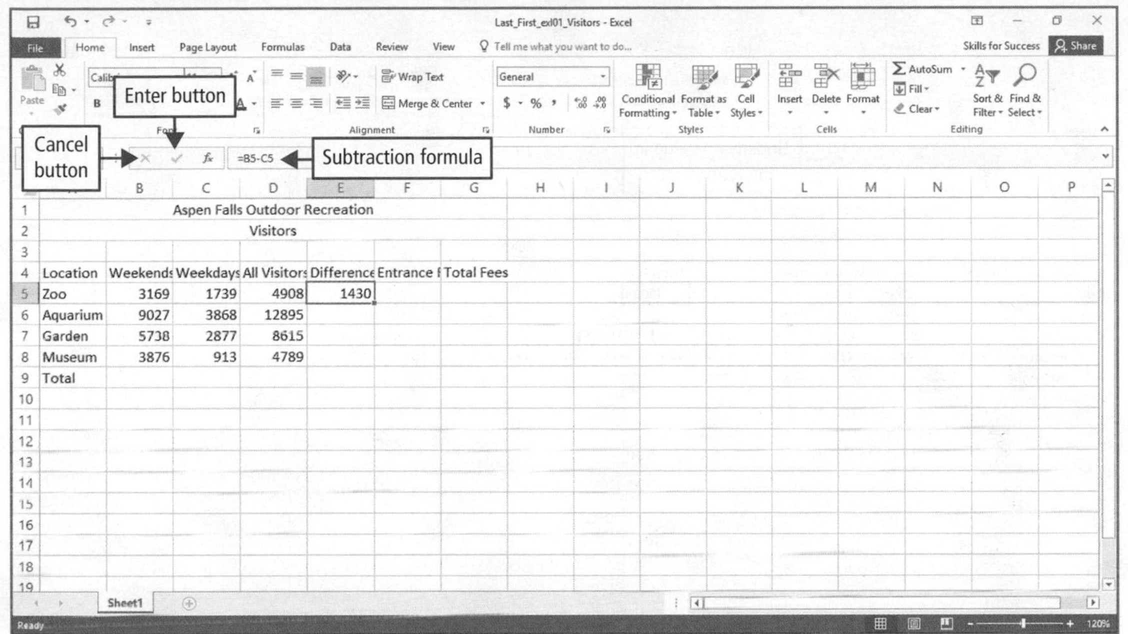

Excel 2016, Windows 10, Microsoft Corporation

Figure 3

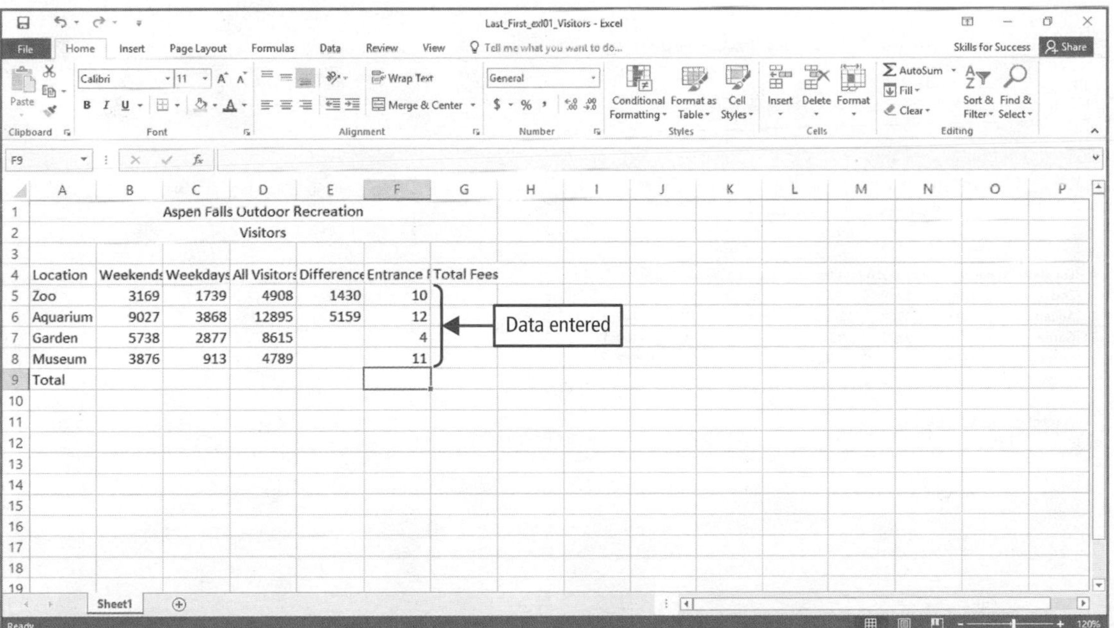

Excel 2016, Windows 10, Microsoft Corporation

Figure 4

6. In cell **D8**, use point and click to construct a formula that adds cells **B8** and **C8**. Press Enter when done.
7. In cell **E5**, type =B5-C5 On the formula bar, click the **Enter** button ✓ to confirm the entry while keeping cell **E5** the active cell, and then compare your screen with **Figure 3**.

   Here, the underlying value for cell E5 displays as a formula in the formula bar and displays as a value, *1430*, in the cell as a result of the formula.

   If you make an error entering a formula, you can click the Cancel button ✗ and then start over. Alternately, you can press the Esc key.
8. In cell **E6**, use point and click to enter the formula =B6-C6 to display the difference for the aquarium weekend and weekday visitors. (You will complete the column E formulas in Skill 7.)
9. In column **F**, type the following data as listed in the table below, and then compare your screen with **Figure 4**.

Cell	Value
F5	10
F6	12
F7	4
F8	11

10. Save the file.

- **You have completed Skill 3 of 10**

- The four most common operators for addition (+), subtraction (−), multiplication (*), and division (/) can be found on the number keypad at the right side of a standard keyboard or on the number keys at the top of a keyboard.

1. In cell **G5**, type =D5*F5 This formula multiplies the total zoo visitors by its entrance fee. On the formula bar, click the **Enter** button ✓, and then compare your screen with **Figure 1**.

   The ***underlying formula***—the formula as displayed in the formula bar—multiplies the value in cell D5 (*4908*) by the value in cell F5 (*10*) and displays the result in cell G5 (*49080*).

2. In the range **G6:G8**, enter the following formulas:

Cell	Formula
G6	=D6*F6
G7	=D7*F7
G8	=D8*F8

3. In cell **A11**, type Percent of Weekday Visitors and then press Enter. Compare your screen with **Figure 2**.

■ Continue to the next page to complete the skill

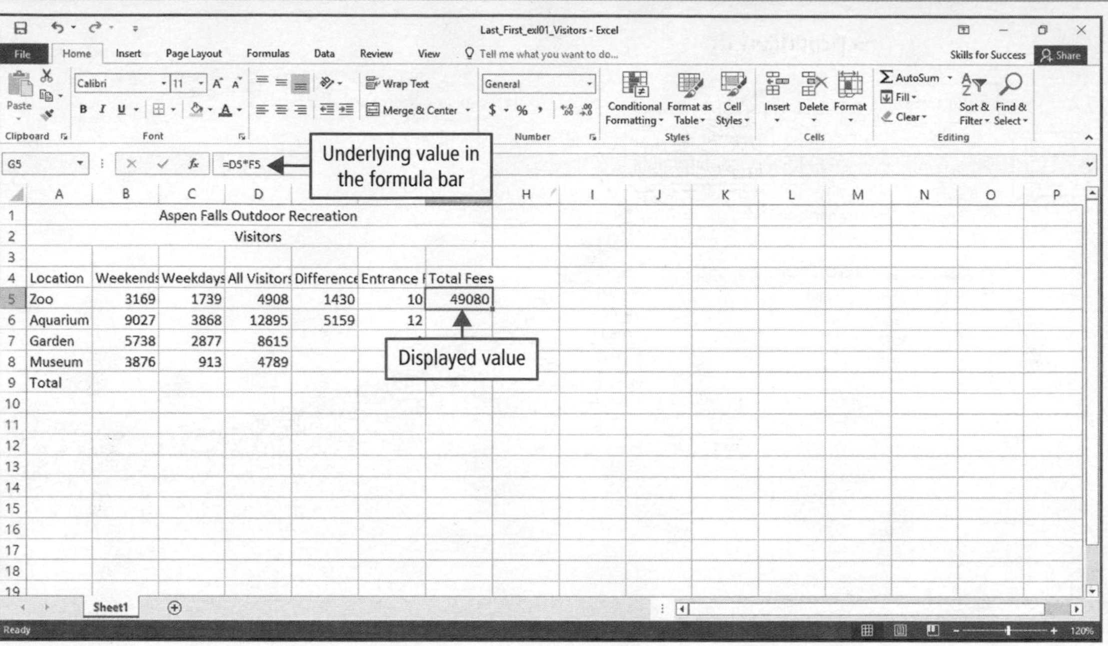

Figure 1

Excel 2016, Windows 10, Microsoft Corporation

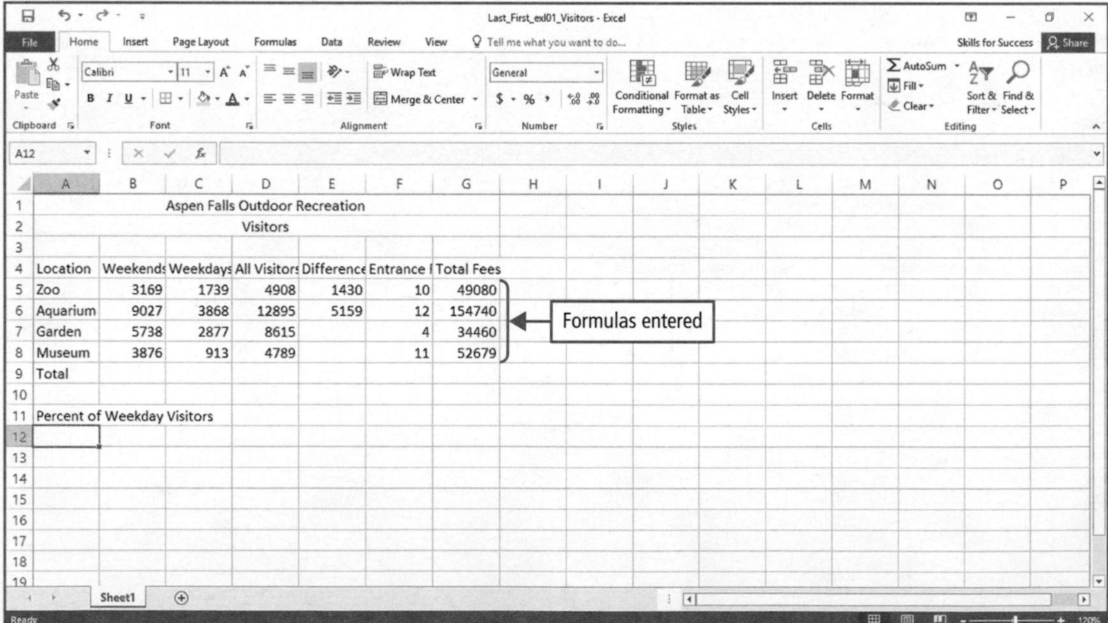

Figure 2

Excel 2016, Windows 10, Microsoft Corporation

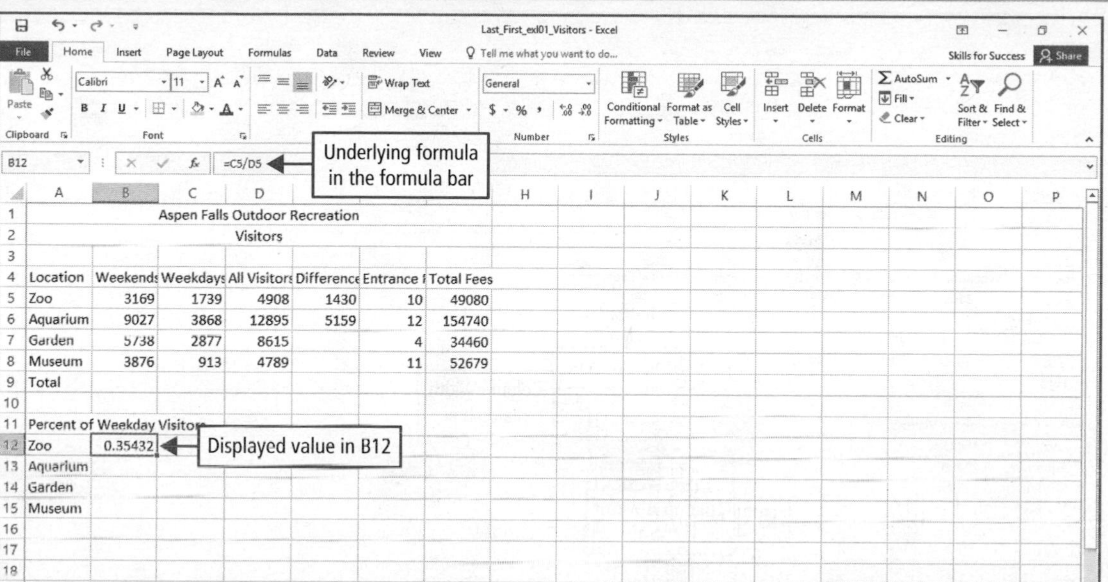

Excel 2016, Windows 10, Microsoft Corporation

Figure 3

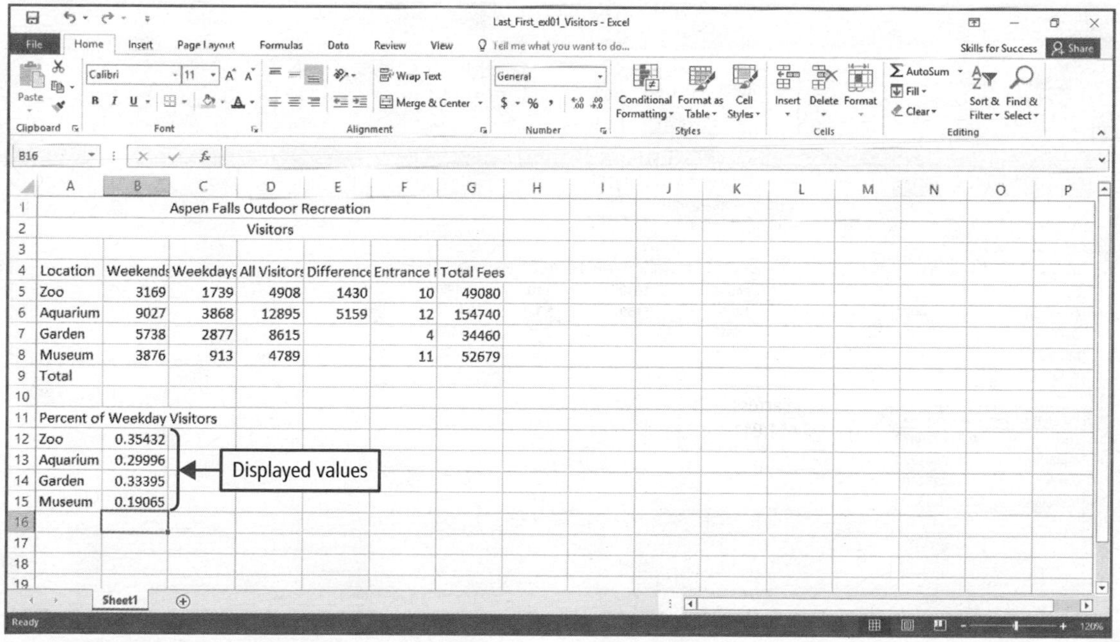

Excel 2016, Windows 10, Microsoft Corporation

Figure 4

Obj 2.1.2 C

4. Select the range **A5:A8**, and then on the **Home tab**, in the **Clipboard group**, click the **Copy** button. Click cell **A12**, and then in the **Clipboard group**, click the **Paste** button.

   The four location labels are copied to the range A12:A15.

5. Press Esc to remove the moving border around the copied cells.

6. In cell **B12**, construct the formula to divide the number of weekday zoo visitors by the total zoo visitors, =C5/D5 and then click the **Enter** button. Compare your screen with **Figure 3**.

   Percentages are calculated by taking the amount divided by the total and will be displayed in decimal format. Here, the underlying formula in B12 (*=C5/D5*) divides the weekday zoo visitors (*1739*) by the total zoo visitors (*4908*).

7. Construct the following formulas to calculate the percentage of weekday visitors for each location, and then compare your screen with **Figure 4**.

Cell	Formula
B13	=C6/D6
B14	=C7/D7
B15	=C8/D8

8. **Save** the file.

■ **You have completed Skill 4 of 10**

- The ***column heading*** is the letter that displays at the top of a column. The number that displays at the left of a row is the ***row heading***.
- ***Formatting*** is the process of specifying the appearance of cells or the overall layout of a worksheet.

Obj 1.3.7 C

1. Click cell **A4**. On the **Home tab**, in the **Cells group**, click the **Format** button, and then click **Column Width**. In the **Column Width** dialog box, type 13
2. Compare your screen with **Figure 1**, and then click **OK**.

   The default column width will display as 8.43 characters when formatted in the standard font. Here, the width is increased to display more characters.
3. Select the range **B4:G4**. In the **Cells group**, click the **Format** button, and then click **Column Width**. In the **Column Width** dialog box, type 12 and then click **OK**.

   As an alternate method, you can select the column range to format the column widths.
4. Select cells **A11:B11**. On the **Home tab**, in the **Alignment group**, click the **Merge & Center arrow**, and then on the displayed list, click **Merge Across**. Compare your screen with **Figure 2**.

   Merge Across merges the selected cells without centering them.

Obj 1.3.7 C

5. Click cell **A1** to select the merged and centered range A1:G1. In the **Cells group**, click the **Format** button, and then click **Row Height**. In the **Row Height** dialog box, type 22.5 and then click **OK**.

■ **Continue to the next page to complete the skill**

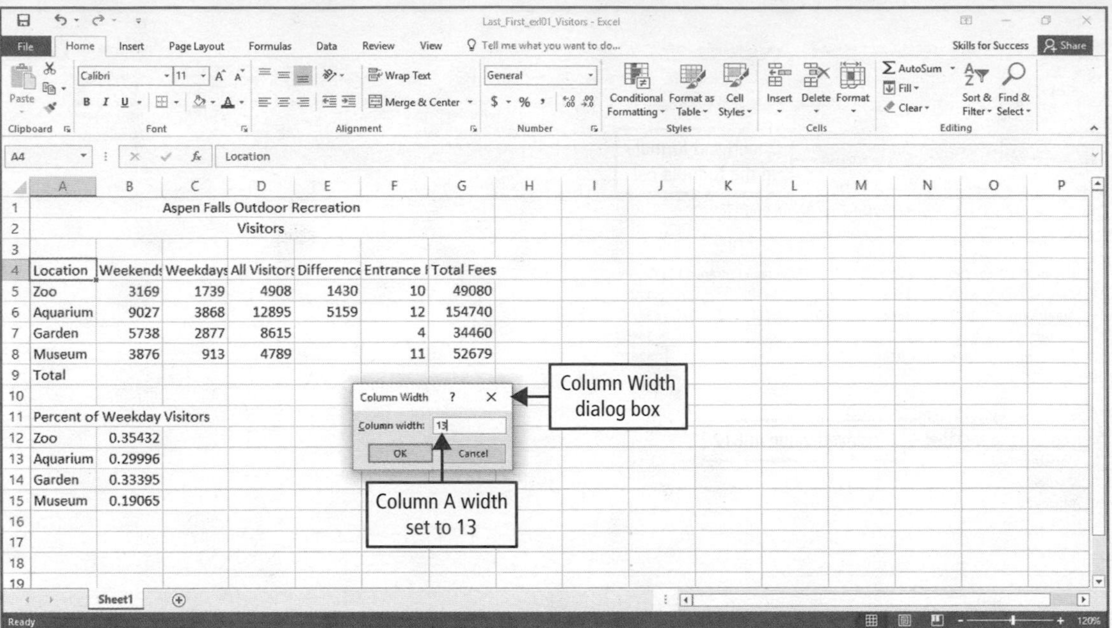

Figure 1

Excel 2016, Windows 10, Microsoft Corporation

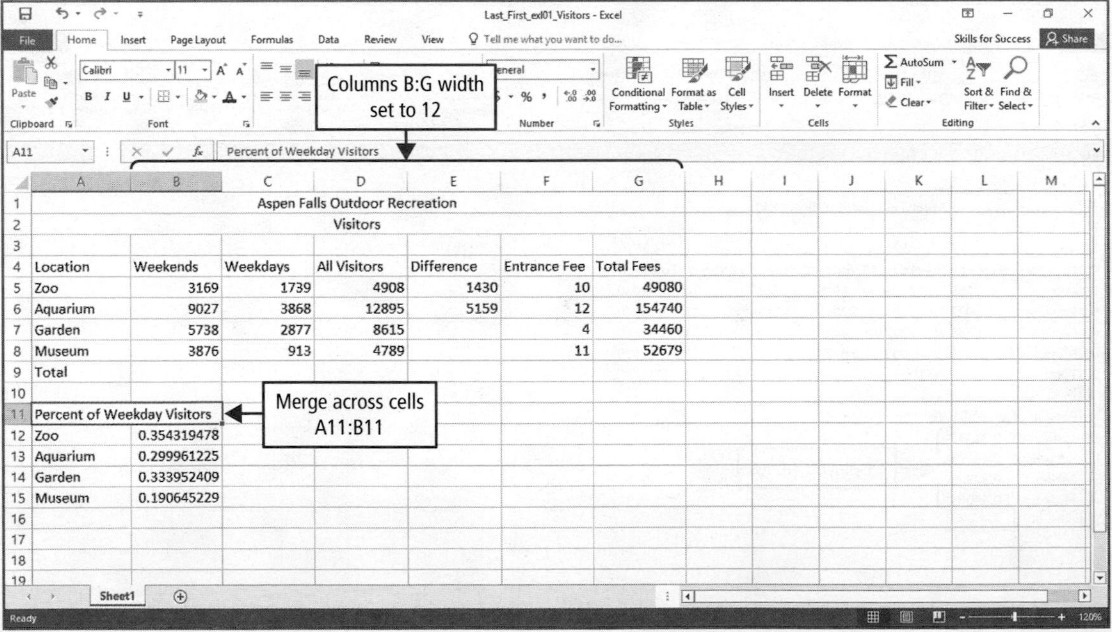

Figure 2

Excel 2016, Windows 10, Microsoft Corporation

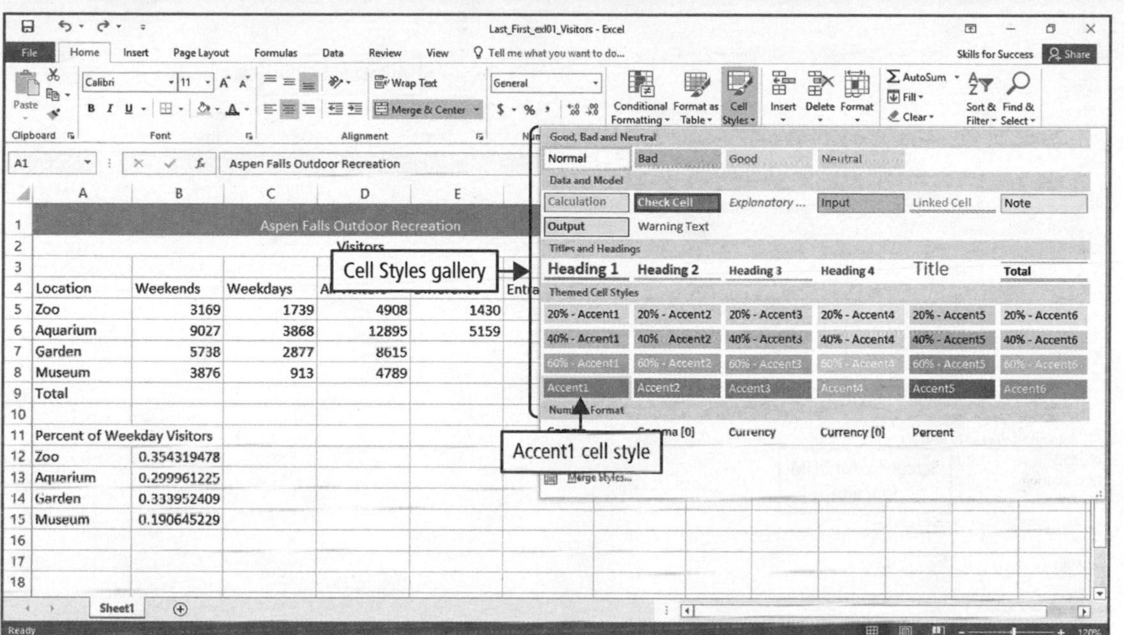

Excel 2016, Windows 10, Microsoft Corporation

Figure 3

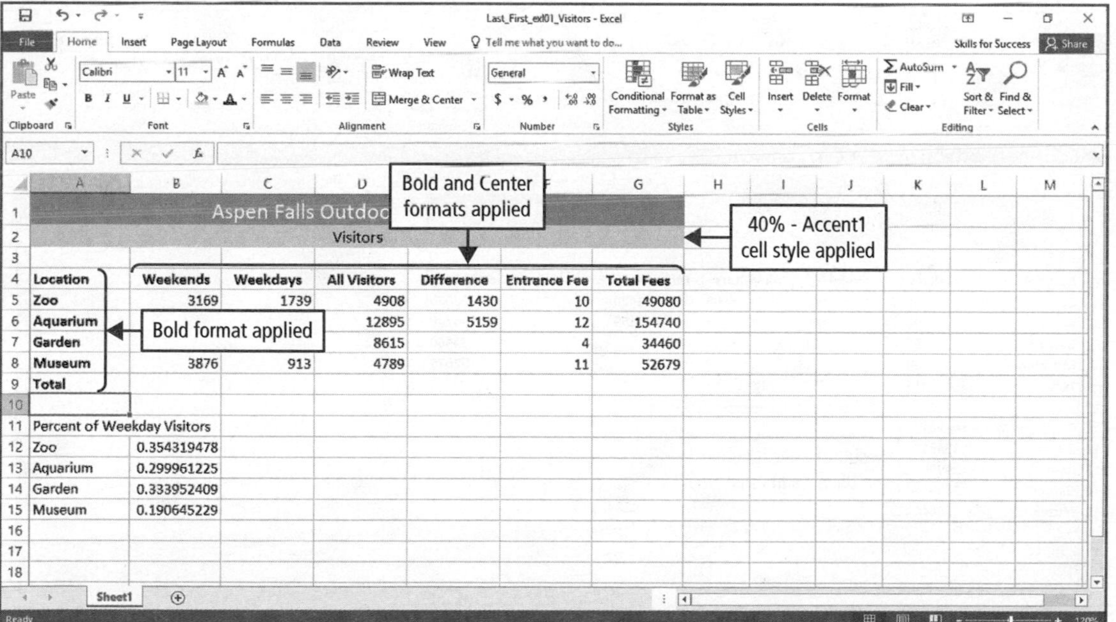

Excel 2016, Windows 10, Microsoft Corporation

Figure 4

MOS Obj 2.2.7 C

6. With **A1:G1** still selected, in the **Styles group**, click the **Cell Styles** button. In the **Cell Styles** gallery, under **Titles and Headings**, use Live Preview to view the title as you point to **Heading 1** and then **Heading 2**.

   A ***cell style*** is a prebuilt set of formatting characteristics, such as font, font size, font color, cell borders, and cell shading.

7. Under **Themed Cell Styles**, point to the **Accent1** style. Compare your screen with **Figure 3**, and then click **Accent1**.

MOS Obj 2.2.6 C

8. In the **Font group**, click the **Font Size arrow** [11], and then click **16**.
9. Click cell **A2**, and then using the technique you just practiced, apply the **40% - Accent1** cell style. In the **Font group**, click the **Increase Font Size** button [A^] one time to change the font size to **12**.
10. Select the range **B4:G4**. Right-click the selected range to display a shortcut menu and the Mini toolbar. On the Mini toolbar, click the **Bold** button [B] and then click the **Center** button [≡] to apply bold and to center the text within each of the selected cells.
11. Select the range **A4:A9**. Display the Mini toolbar, and then apply **Bold** to the selected range. Click cell **A10**, and then compare your screen with **Figure 4**.
12. **Save** [🖫] the file.

■ **You have completed Skill 5 of 10**

- You can create your own formulas, or you can use a ***function***—a prewritten Excel formula that takes a value or values, performs an operation, and returns a value or values.
- The AutoSum button is used to insert common summary functions into a worksheet.
- When cell references are used in a formula or function, the results are automatically recalculated whenever those cells are edited.

MOS Obj 4.1.2 C

1. Click cell **B9**. On the **Home tab**, in the **Editing group**, click the **AutoSum** button [Σ AutoSum], and then compare your screen with **Figure 1**.

   SUM is an Excel function that adds all the numbers in a range of cells. The range in parentheses, *(B5:B8)*, indicates the range of cells on which the SUM function will be performed.

   When the AutoSum button is used, Excel first looks *above* the selected cell for a range of cells to sum. If there is no data detected in the range above the selected cell, Excel then looks to the *left* and proposes a range of cells to sum. Here, the range B5:B8 is surrounded by a moving border, and *=SUM(B5:B8)* displays in cell B9.

2. Press [Enter] to display the function result—*21810*.
3. Select the range **C9:D9**. In the **Editing group**, click the **AutoSum** button [Σ AutoSum], and then compare your screen with **Figure 2**.

■ Continue to the next page to complete the skill

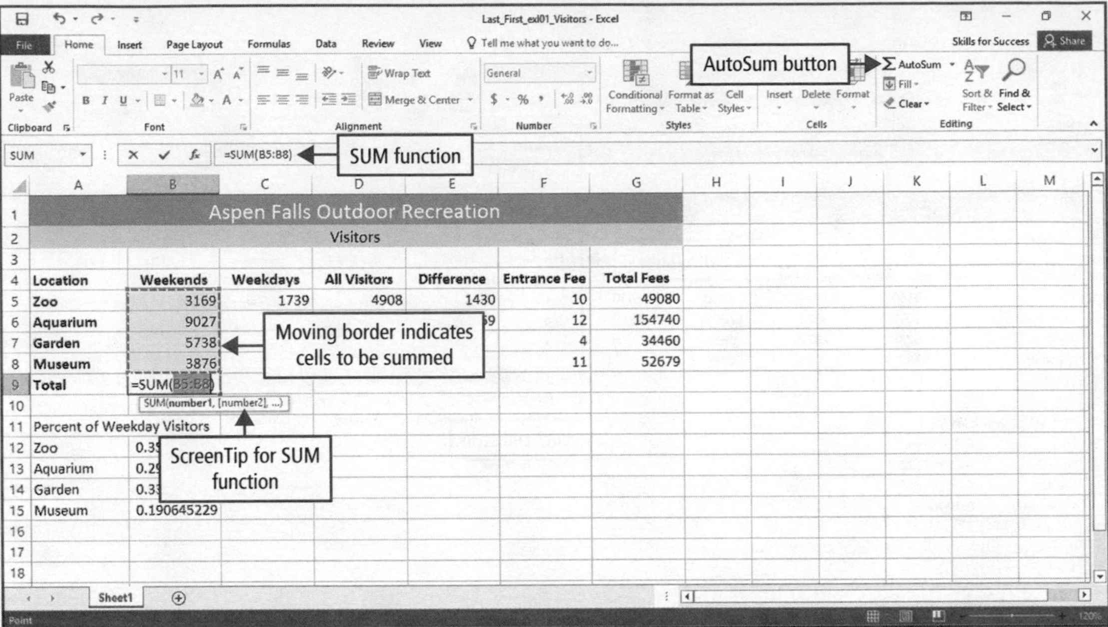

Figure 1 Excel 2016, Windows 10, Microsoft Corporation

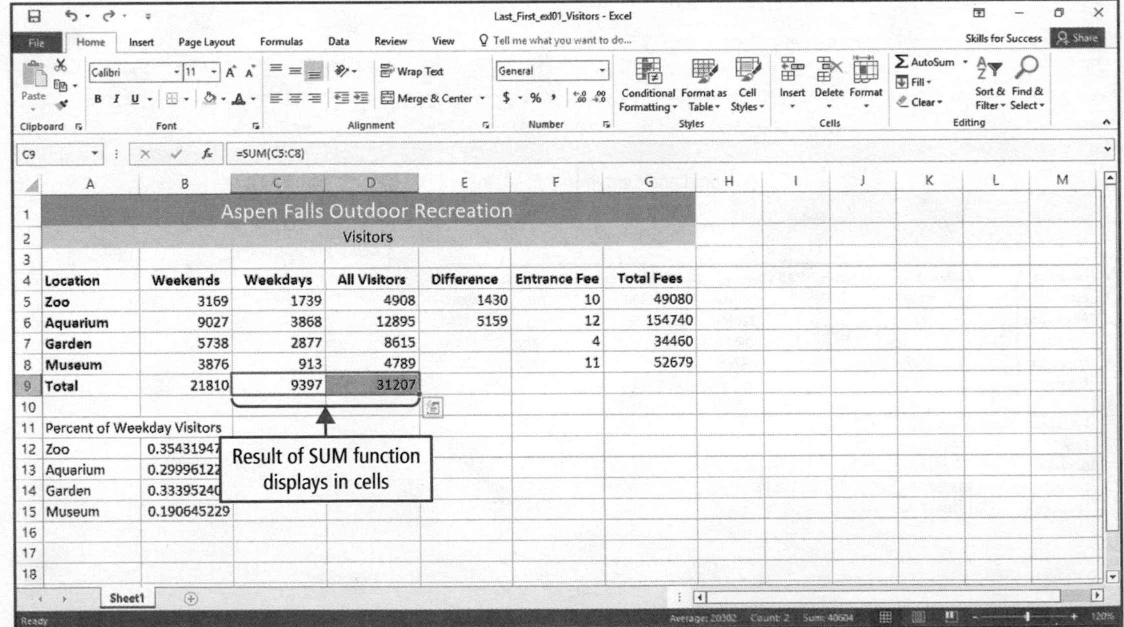

Figure 2 Excel 2016, Windows 10, Microsoft Corporation

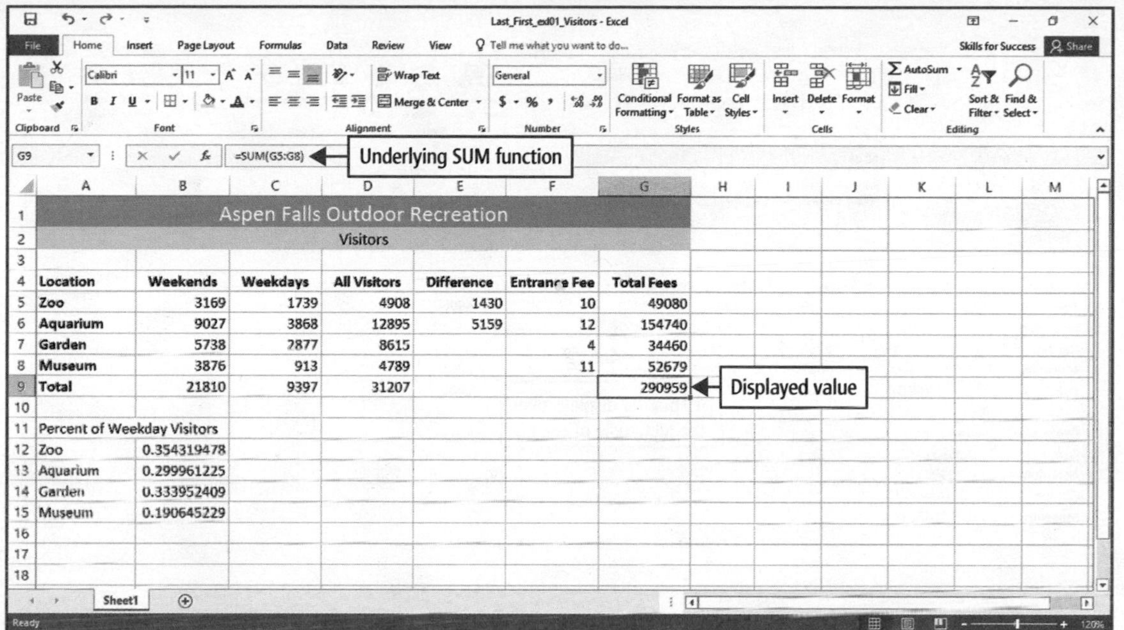

Excel 2016, Windows 10, Microsoft Corporation

Figure 3

B7 and C7 numeric values changed

Total Fees recalculated

Total values recalculated

Percent recalculated

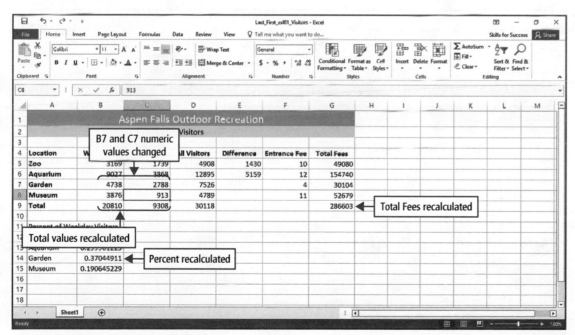

Excel 2016, Windows 10, Microsoft Corporation

Figure 4

4. Click cell **C9**, and then in the formula bar, verify that the SUM function adds the values in the range *C5:C8*.
5. Click cell **D9**, and then verify that the SUM function adds the values in the range *D5:D8*.
6. Using the technique just practiced, in cell **G9**, insert the SUM function to add the values in the range **G5:G8**. Select cell **G9**, and then compare your screen with **Figure 3**.
7. In cell **B7**, type 4738 Watch the total in cell **B9** update as you press Tab.

   In cell B9, the displayed value changed to 20810, but the underlying formula remained the same.
8. In cell C7, type 2788 and then press Enter to update the totals in cells C9, G7, and G9. Compare your screen with **Figure 4**.

   The amounts were recalculated when the data was changed because cell references were used in the functions.
9. **Save** the file.

- **You have completed Skill 6 of 10**

SKILL 1.7

▸ Text, numbers, formulas, and functions can be copied down rows and across columns to insert formulas and functions quickly.

▸ When a formula is copied to another cell, Excel adjusts the cell references relative to the new location of the formula.

Obj 2.1.4 C

1. Click cell **E6**. With cell **E6** selected, point to the ***fill handle***—the small green square in the lower right corner of the selection—until the [+] pointer displays, as shown in **Figure 1**.

   To use the fill handle, first select the cell that contains the content you want to copy—here the formula *=B6-C6*.

2. Drag the [+] pointer down to cell **E8**, and then release the mouse button.

Obj 4.1.1 C

3. Click cell **E7**, and verify on the formula bar that the formula copied from E6 changed to *=B7-C7*. Click cell **E8**, and then compare your screen with **Figure 2**.

   In each row, the cell references in the formula adjusted *relative to* the row number—B6 changed to B7 and then to B8. This adjustment is called a ***relative cell reference*** because it refers to cells based on their position *in relation to* (relative to) the cell that contains the formula.

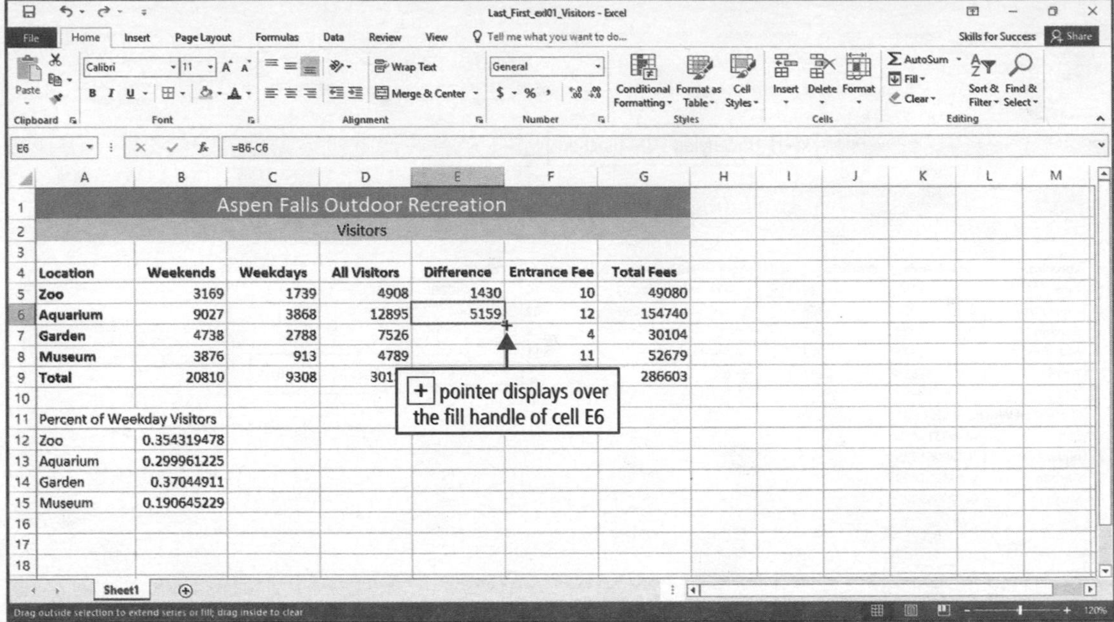

Figure 1

Excel 2016, Windows 10, Microsoft Corporation

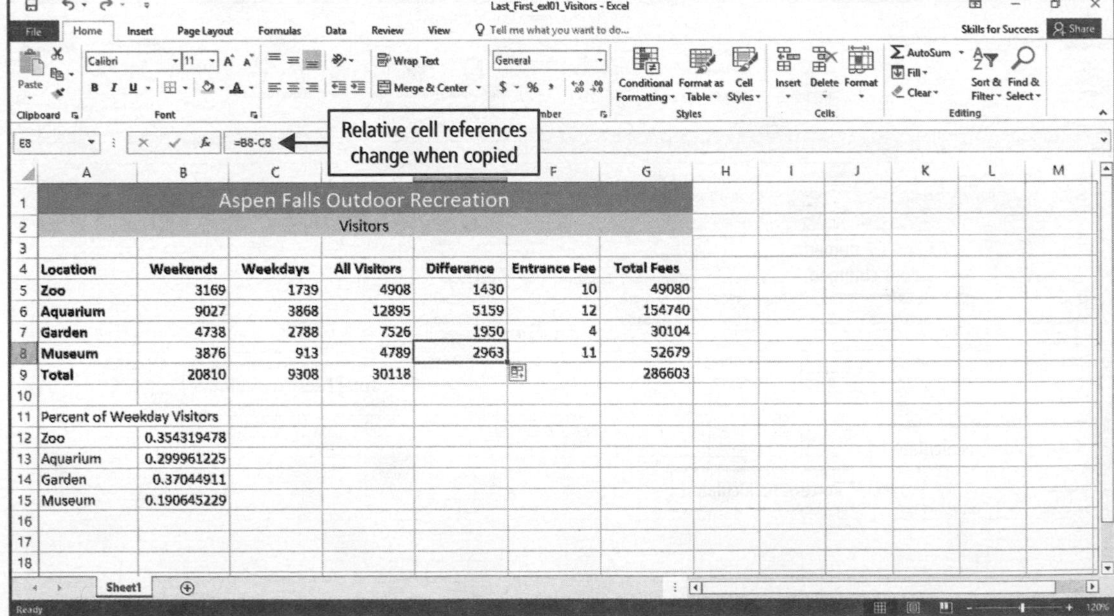

Figure 2

Excel 2016, Windows 10, Microsoft Corporation

■ **Continue to the next page to complete the skill**

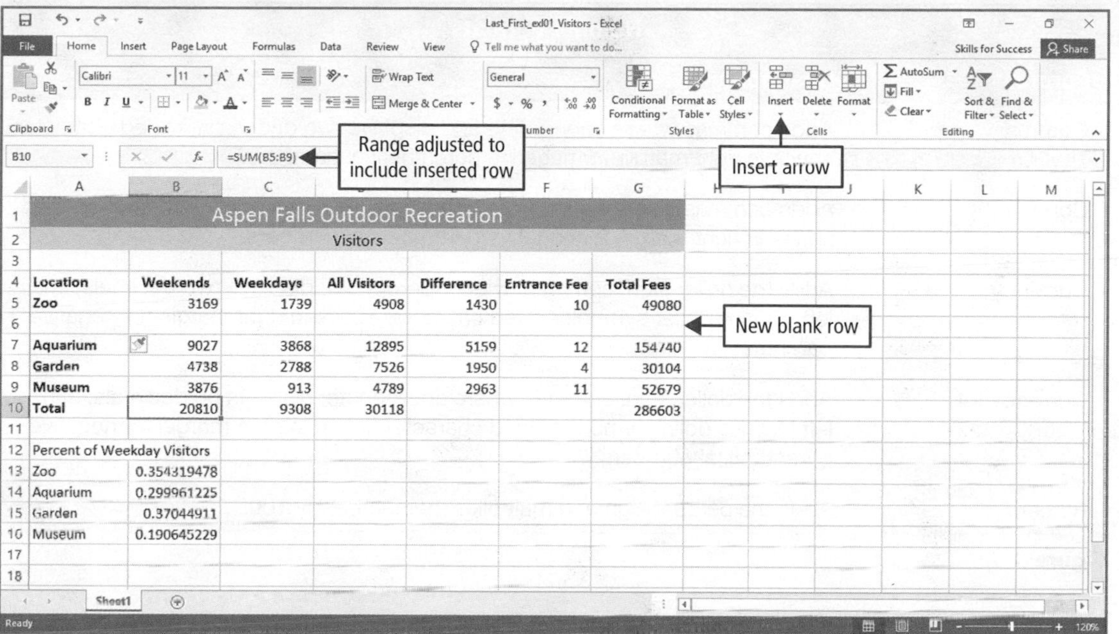

Excel 2016, Windows 10, Microsoft Corporation

Figure 3

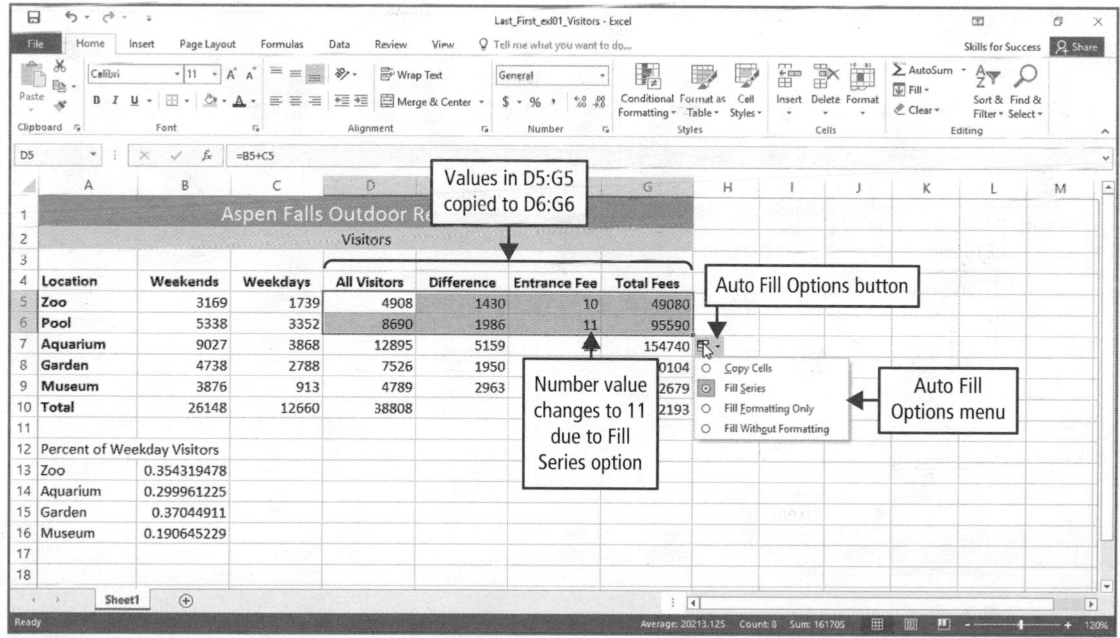

Excel 2016, Windows 10, Microsoft Corporation

Figure 4

4. Click cell **A6**. In the **Cells group**, click the **Insert arrow**, and then click **Insert Sheet Rows**. Click cell **B10**, and then compare your screen with **Figure 3**.

   When you insert a new row or column, the cell references and the ranges in formulas or in functions adjust to include the new row or column. Here, in cell B10, the range in the function automatically updated to include the new row in the range.

5. In cell **A6**, type Pool and then press Tab.

   By default, formatting (bold) from the row above is applied to an inserted row.

6. In cell **B6**, type 5338 and then press Tab to enter the value and update the column total in cell B10 to *26148*.

7. In cell **C6**, type 3352 and then press Tab.

8. Select cells **D5:G5**. Point to the fill handle until the + pointer displays, and then drag the + pointer down one row. Release the mouse button, and then click the **Auto Fill Options** button. Compare your screen with **Figure 4**.

   Three formulas and a number are copied. When you copy number values using the fill handle, the numbers automatically increment for each row or column. Here, the number value in cell F5 increased by one when it was copied to cell F6.

9. In the **Auto Fill Options** menu, click **Copy Cells**.

   With the Copy Cells option, number values are copied exactly and do not increment. Here, the number value in cell F6 changes to 10.

10. **Save** the file.

- **You have completed Skill 7 of 10**

► Always check spelling after you have completed formatting and editing worksheet data.

1. Click cell **A14**, and then repeat the technique used previously to insert a new row. In cell **A14**, type Pool and then press Enter.
2. Click cell **B13**, and then use the fill handle to copy the formula down to cell **B14**.
3. Double-click cell **A2** to edit the cell contents. Use the arrow keys to move to the right of the word *Visitors*. Add a space, type to City Attractions and then press Enter.

Obj 2.2.7 C

4. Select the range **F5:G5**. In the **Styles group**, click the **Cell Styles** button, and then under **Number Format**, click **Currency [0]**. Repeat this technique to apply the **Currency [0]** format to cell **G10**. Review Cell Style Number Formats as summarized in the table in **Figure 1**.

   When applying number formats, general practice is to apply the currency symbol to the top and bottom amounts.

5. Select the range **B5:E10**. Click the **Cell Styles** button, and then under **Number Format**, click **Comma [0]**. Repeat the technique to apply the **Comma [0]** format to the range **F6:G9**.

Obj 2.2.5 C

6. Select the range **B13:B17**. In the **Number group**, click the **Percent Style** button %, and then click the **Increase Decimal** button one time. Compare your screen with **Figure 2**.

   The Increase Decimal and Decrease Decimal buttons do not add or remove decimals; they change how the decimal values *display* in the cells.

■ **Continue to the next page to complete the skill**

Number Formats	
Format	**Description**
Comma	Adds commas where appropriate and displays two decimals. Added character space in right margin for negative parenthetical numbers.
Comma [0]	Adds commas where appropriate and displays no decimals. Added character space in right margin for negative parenthetical numbers.
Currency	Adds the dollar sign, commas where appropriate, displays two decimals, and left justifies dollar symbol. Added character space in right margin for negative parenthetical numbers.
Currency [0]	Adds the dollar sign, commas where appropriate, displays no decimals, and left justifies dollar symbol. Added character space in right margin for negative parenthetical numbers.
Percent	Adds the percent sign and multiplies the number by 100.

Figure 1

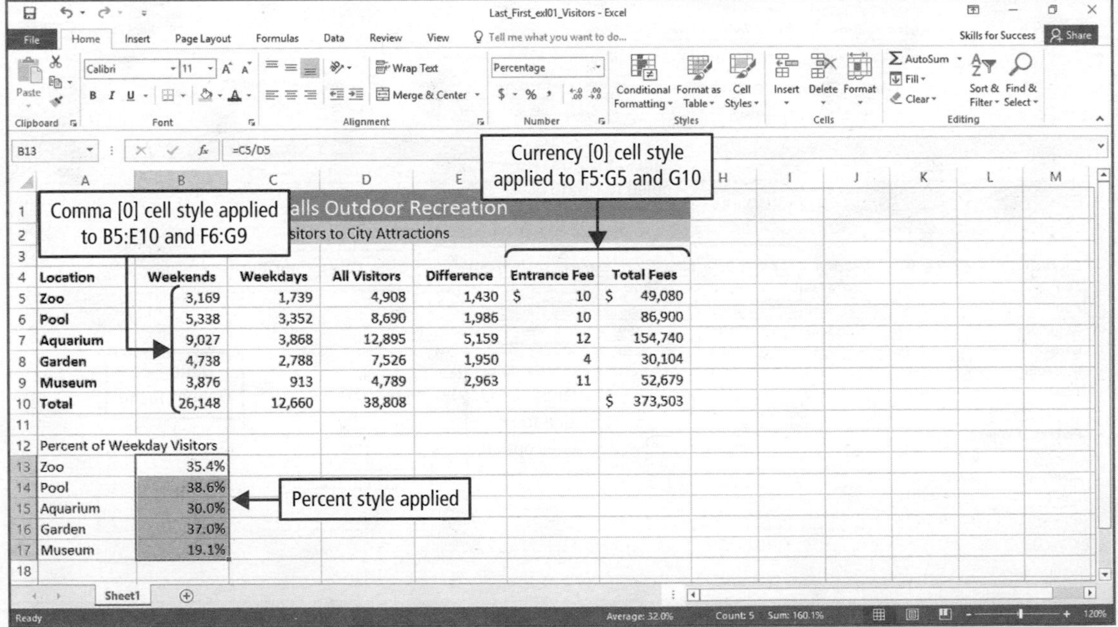

Figure 2

Excel 2016, Windows 10, Microsoft Corporation

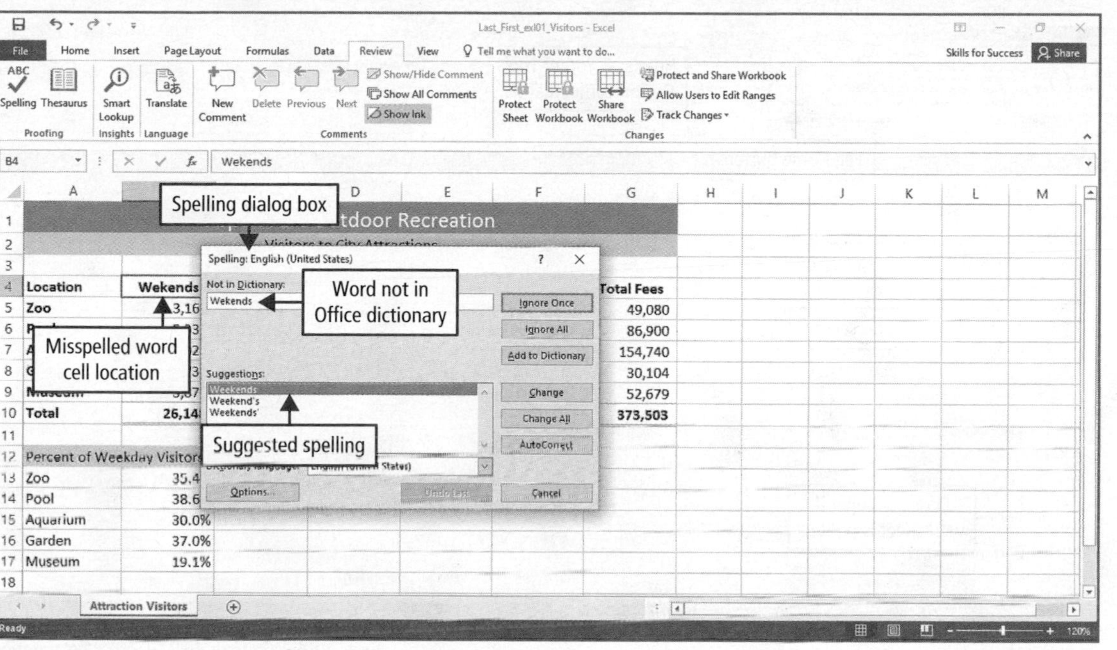

Excel 2016, Windows 10, Microsoft Corporation

Figure 3

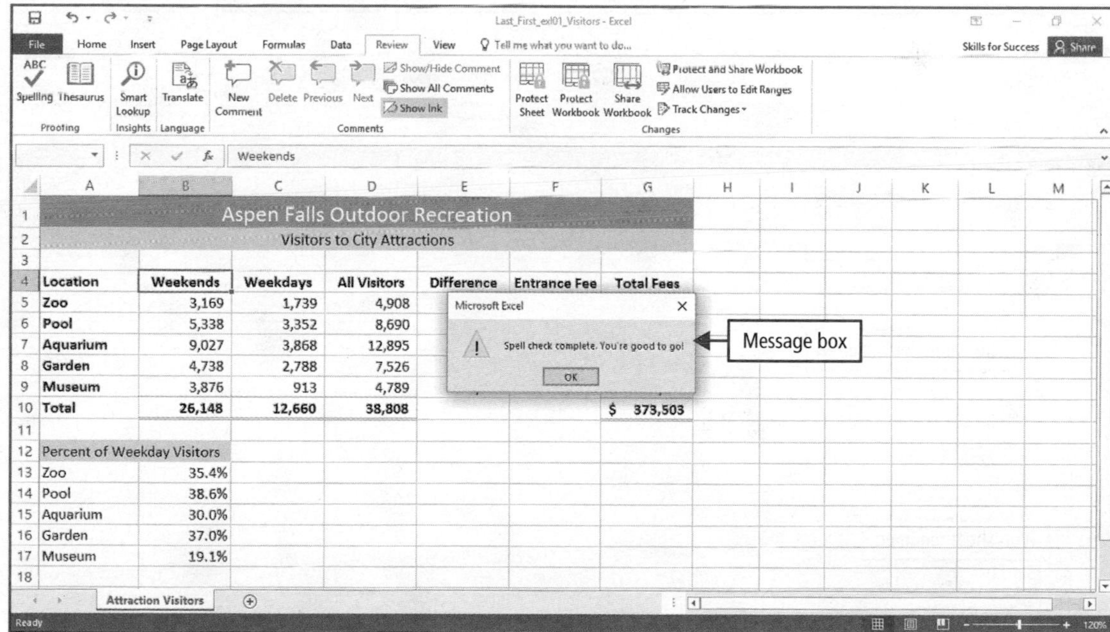

Excel 2016, Windows 10, Microsoft Corporation

Figure 4

Obj 2.2.7 C

7. Select the range **B10:D10**. Hold down Ctrl, and then click cell **G10**. Click the **Cell Styles** button. Under **Titles and Headings**, click the **Total** style.
8. Select cell **A12**, and then click the **Cell Styles** button. Under **Themed Cell Styles**, click **40% - Accent1**.
9. Press Ctrl + Home to make cell **A1** active. On the **Review tab**, in the **Proofing group**, click the **Spelling** button.

   The Spelling checker starts with the active cell and moves to the right and down. Making cell A1 the active cell verifies the spreadsheet is checked from the beginning.

   If the Spelling dialog box opens to reveal unrecognized words not in the Office dictionary, as shown in **Figure 3** (your screen may be different), the words not in the dictionary are not necessarily misspelled. Many proper nouns or less commonly used words are not in the Office dictionary.

   To correct a misspelled word and to move to the next word not in the Office dictionary, under Suggestions, verify that the correct spelling is selected, and then click the Change button.
10. Use the Spelling checker to correct any errors you may have made. When the **Spell check complete. You're good to go!** message box displays, as shown in **Figure 4**, click **OK**.

    When words you use often are not in the Office dictionary, you can click *Add to Dictionary* to add them.
11. **Save** the file.

- **You have completed Skill 8 of 10**

- In Excel, ***Page Layout view*** is used to adjust how a worksheet will look when it is printed.

Obj 1.4.6 C

1. Click the **Insert tab**, in the **Text group**, click the **Header & Footer** button to switch to **Page Layout view** and to display the **Header & Footer Tools Design** contextual tab.

Obj 1.3.8 C

2. On the **Design tab**, in the **Navigation group**, click the **Go to Footer** button to move to the Footer area. Click just above the word **Footer** to place the insertion point in the left section of the Footer area. Compare your screen with **Figure 1**.

3. In the **Header & Footer Elements group**, click the **File Name** button, and then click any cell in the workbook to view the file name, if necessary.

   Predefined headers and footers insert placeholders with instructions for printing. Here, the *&[File]* placeholder instructs Excel to insert the file name when the worksheet is printed.

Obj 1.3.2 C

4. At the bottom of your worksheet, right-click the **Sheet1** worksheet tab, and then from the shortcut menu, click **Rename**. Type Attraction Visitors and then press Enter to change the worksheet tab name. Compare your screen with **Figure 2**.

5. Click in the middle section of the Footer area, click the **Header & Footer Tools tab**, and then click the **Current Date** button. Click the right section of the Footer area, and then click the **Sheet Name** button. Click in a cell just above the footer to exit the Footer area, and then press Ctrl + Home.

Continue to the next page to complete the skill

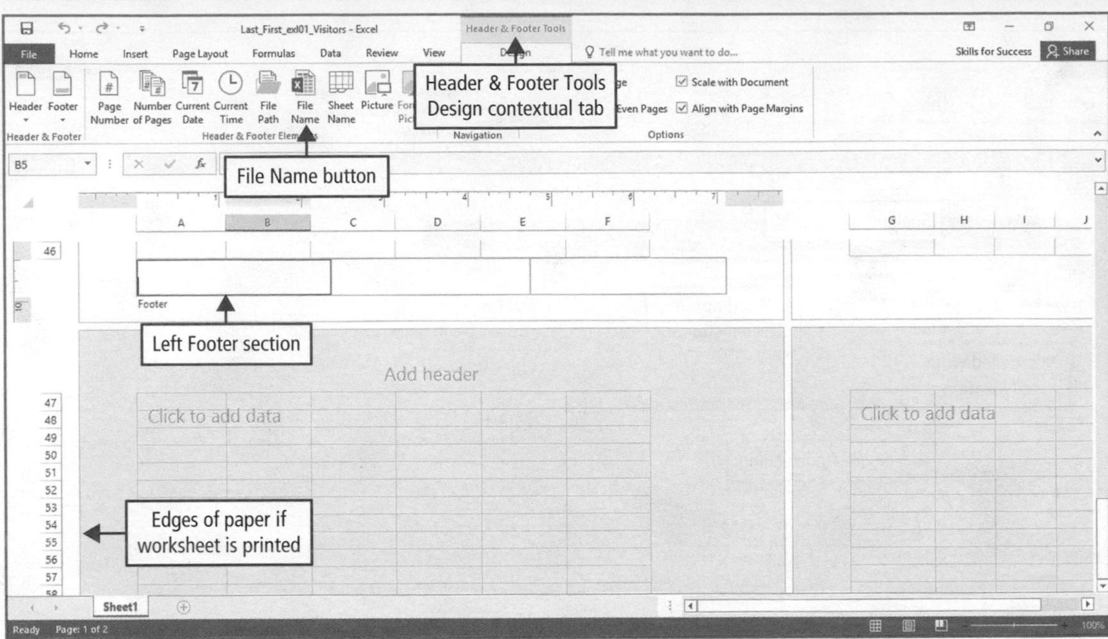

Figure 1

Excel 2016, Windows 10, Microsoft Corporation

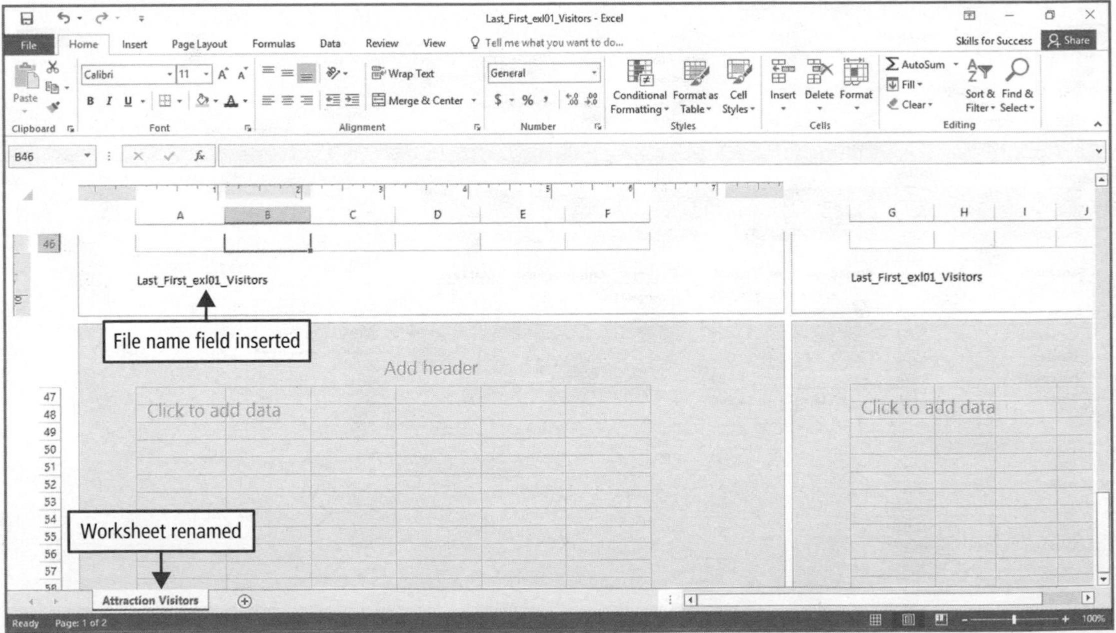

Figure 2

Excel 2016, Windows 10, Microsoft Corporation

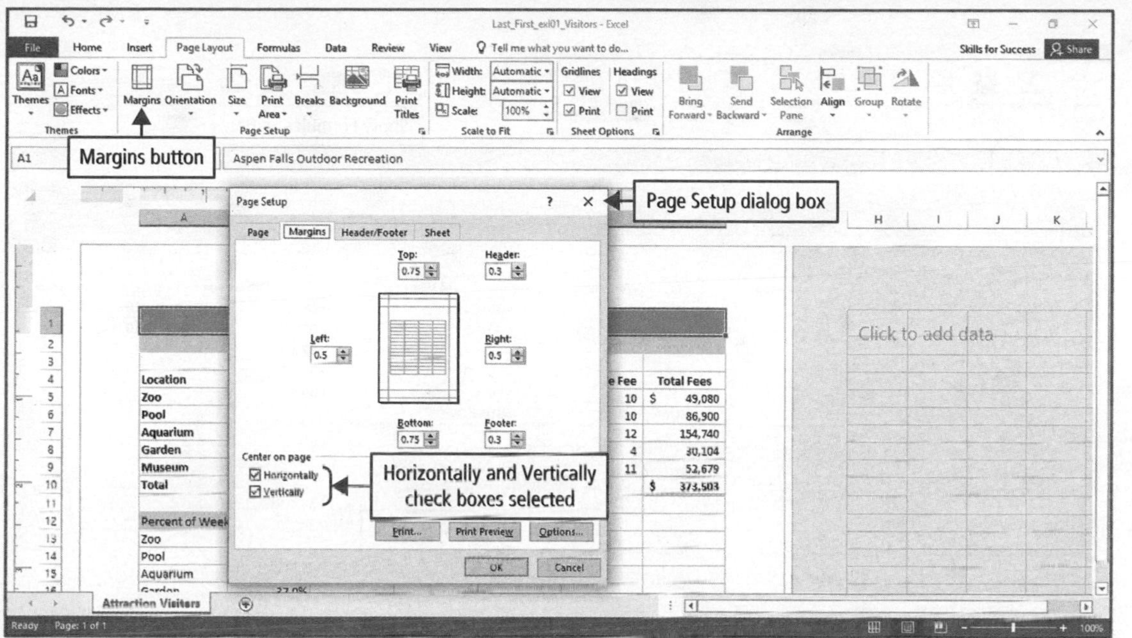

Excel 2016, Windows 10, Microsoft Corporation

Figure 3

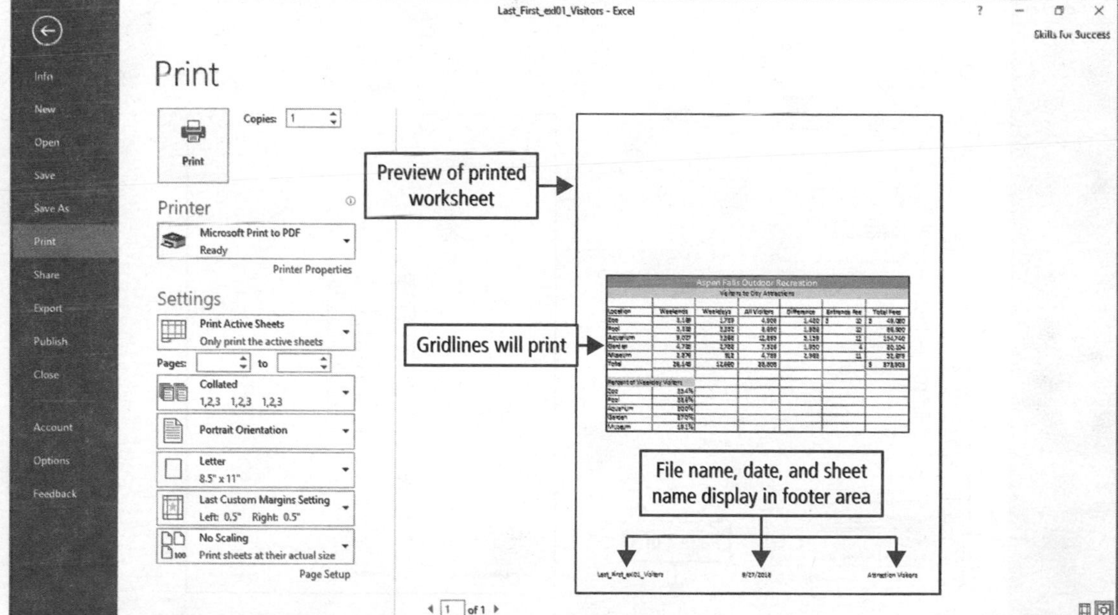

Excel 2016, Windows 10, Microsoft Corporation

Figure 4

6. Click the **Page Layout tab**. In the **Sheet Options group**, under **Gridlines**, select the **Print** check box. MOS Obj 1.3.4 C
7. In the **Page Setup group**, click the **Margins** button. Below the **Margins** gallery, click **Custom Margin**, and then type 0.5 in the **Left** and **Right** margins.
8. In the **Page Setup** dialog box, under **Center on page**, click to select the **Horizontally** and **Vertically** check boxes, and then compare your screen with **Figure 3**.
9. In the **Page Setup** dialog box, click **Print Preview**, and then compare your screen with **Figure 4**.
10. Click the **Back** button. On the lower right side of the status bar, click the **Normal** button to return to Normal view.  MOS Obj 1.4.4 C

    Normal view maximizes the number of cells visible on the screen. The page break—the dotted line between columns G and H—indicates where one page ends and a new page begins.

11. **Save** the file.

■ **You have completed Skill 9 of 10**

- Underlying formulas and functions can be displayed and printed.
- When formulas are displayed in cells, the orientation and worksheet scale may need to be changed so that the worksheet prints on a single page.

Obj 1.4.8 C

1. Click the **Formulas tab**. In the **Formula Auditing group**, click the **Show Formulas** button to display the underlying formulas in the cells. Compare your screen with **Figure 1**.

   Columns often become wider when formulas are displayed. Here, the printed worksheet extends to a third page.

2. Click the **File tab**, and then click **Print**.

   Below the preview of the printed page, *1 of 3* indicates that the worksheet will print on three pages.

3. In **Backstage** view, on the bottom of the **Print** page, click the **Next Page** button two times to view the second and third pages, and then compare your screen with **Figure 2**.

Obj 1.3.4 C

4. Click the **Back** button. On the **Page Layout tab**, in the **Page Setup group**, click the **Orientation** button, and then click **Landscape** so that the page orientation will be wider than it is tall.

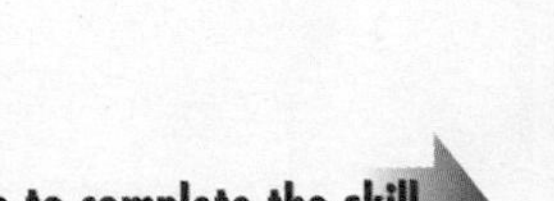

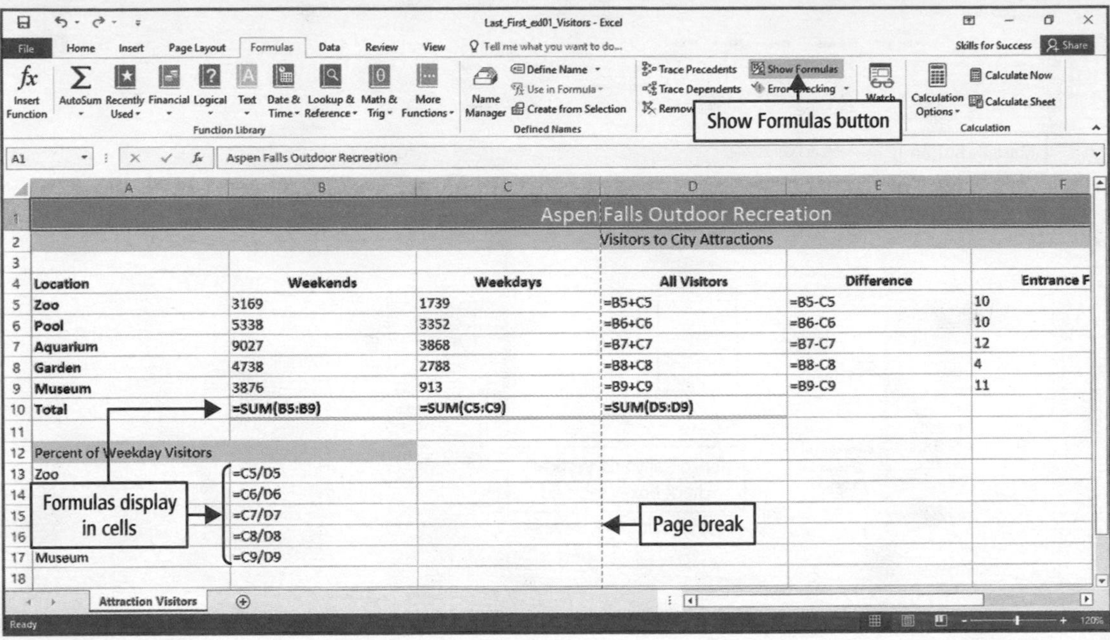

Figure 1

Excel 2016, Windows 10, Microsoft Corporation

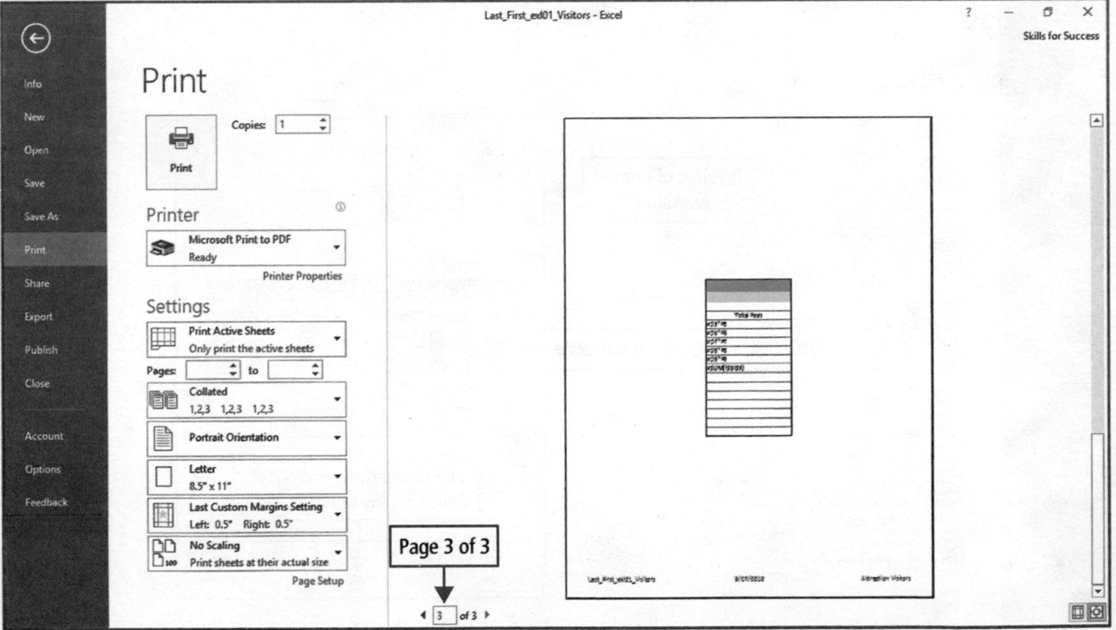

Figure 2

Excel 2016, Windows 10, Microsoft Corporation

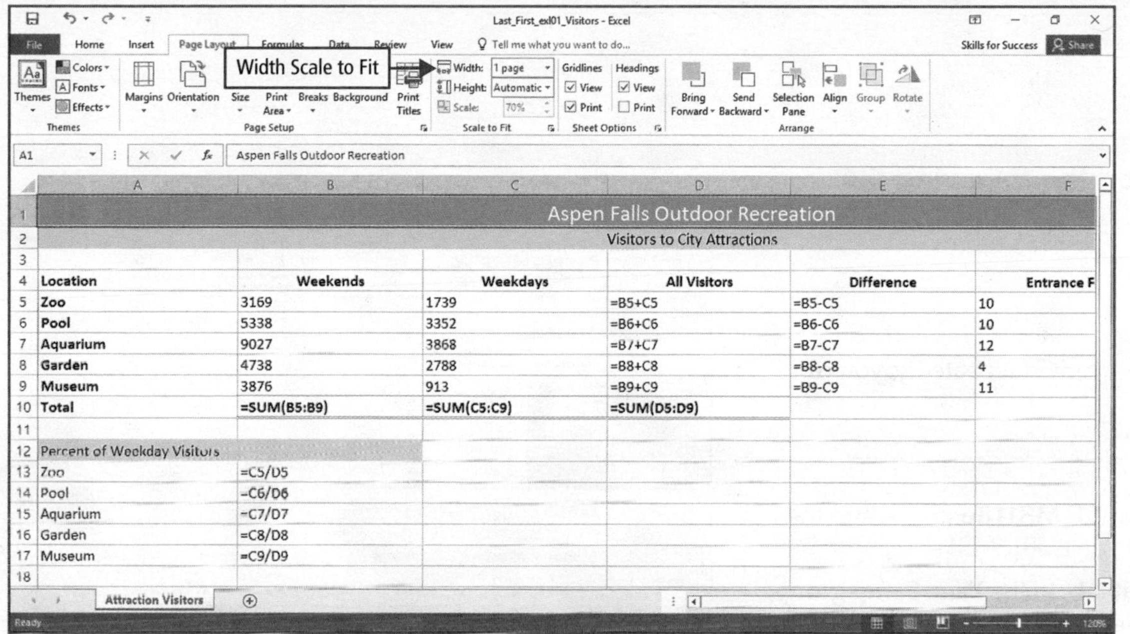

Excel 2016, Windows 10, Microsoft Corporation

Figure 3

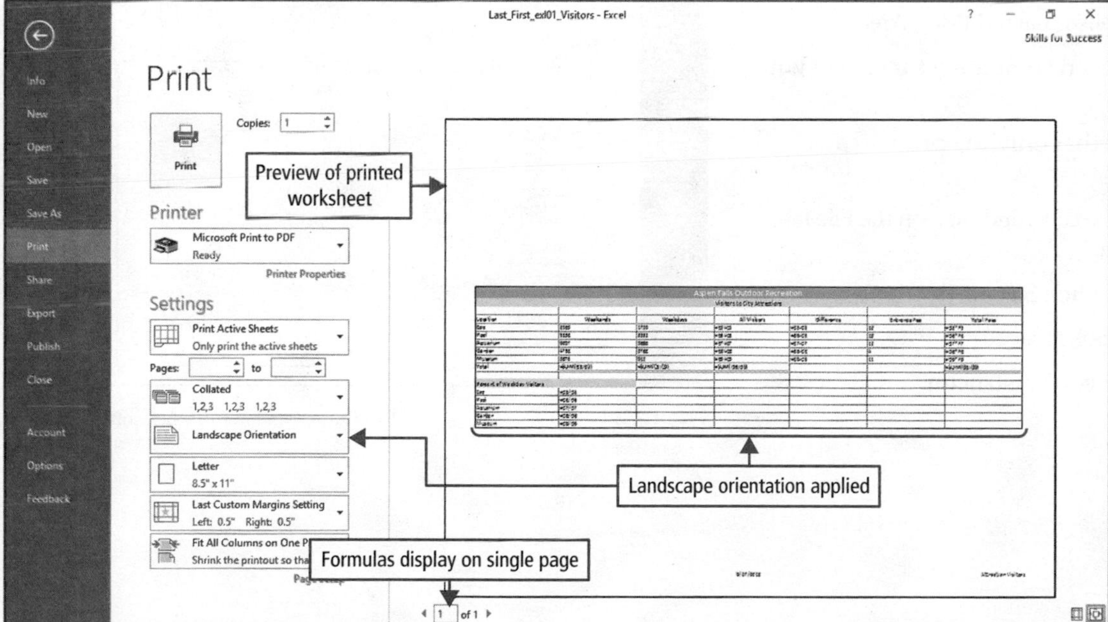

Excel 2016, Windows 10, Microsoft Corporation

Figure 4

5. In the **Scale to Fit group**, click the **Width arrow**, and then click **1 page**. Compare your screen with **Figure 3**. MOS Obj 1.5.4 C

   Scaling adjusts the size of the printed worksheet to fit on the number of pages that you specify.

6. Click the **File tab**, and then click **Print**. Compare your screen with **Figure 4**.

   1 of 1 displays at the bottom of the Print page to notify you that the worksheet will now print on one page.

7. If you are directed by your instructor to submit a printout with your formulas displayed, click the Print button.

8. Click the **Back** button. On the **Formulas tab**, in the **Formula Auditing group**, click the **Show Formulas** button to hide the formulas.

9. If you are printing your work, print the worksheet with the values displayed and formulas hidden. MOS Obj 1.4.4 C

10. **Save** the file, and then **Close** Excel. Submit the file as directed by your instructor.

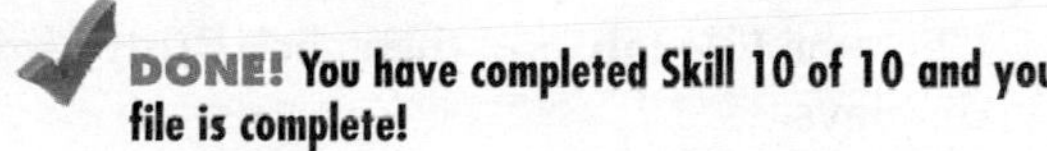

DONE! You have completed Skill 10 of 10 and your file is complete!

More Skills 11

Set Print Areas

To complete this project, you will need the following file:

- exl01_MS11Business

You will save your file as:

- Last_First_exl01_MS11Business

▸ If the same portion of a worksheet needs to be printed repeatedly, you can save time by setting a print area.

---

1. Start **Excel 2016**, open the student data file **exl01_MS11Business**, and then save the file in your chapter folder as Last_First_exl01_MS11Business

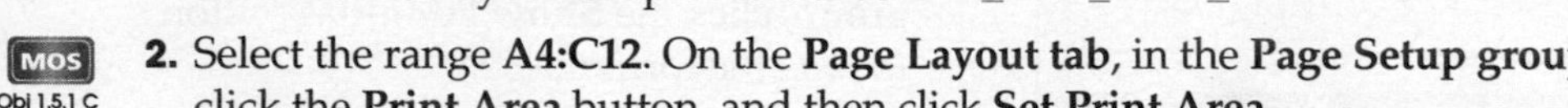

MOS Obj 1.5.1 C

2. Select the range **A4:C12**. On the **Page Layout tab**, in the **Page Setup group**, click the **Print Area** button, and then click **Set Print Area**.

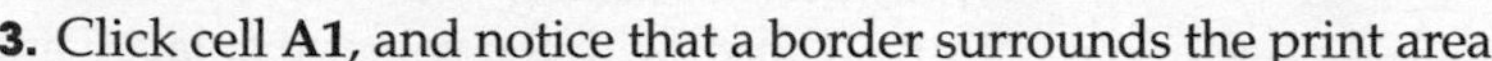

3. Click cell **A1**, and notice that a border surrounds the print area.

MOS Obj 1.2.2 C

4. Click the **Name Box arrow** above column A, and then click **Print_Area.**

   When a print area is set, the range of selected cells is named Print_Area.

5. Verify that the range **A4:C12** is selected, and then compare your screen with **Figure 1**.

6. Click the **File tab**, and then click **Print**. Verify that only the print area displays.

   To print a worksheet portion only once, select the cells, and then on the File tab, click Print. Under Settings, select Print Selection.

7. Compare your screen with **Figure 2**, and then click **Save** [Save].

   The print area setting is saved when the workbook is saved.

8. **Close** [X] Excel. Submit the file as directed by your instructor.

■ **You have completed More Skills 11**

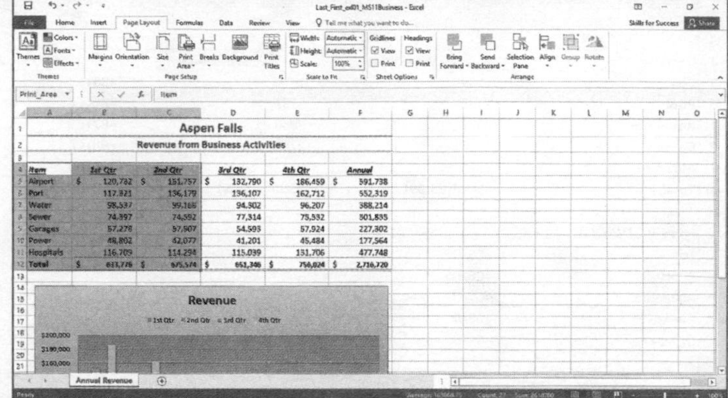

Figure 1 Excel 2016, Windows 10, Microsoft Corporation

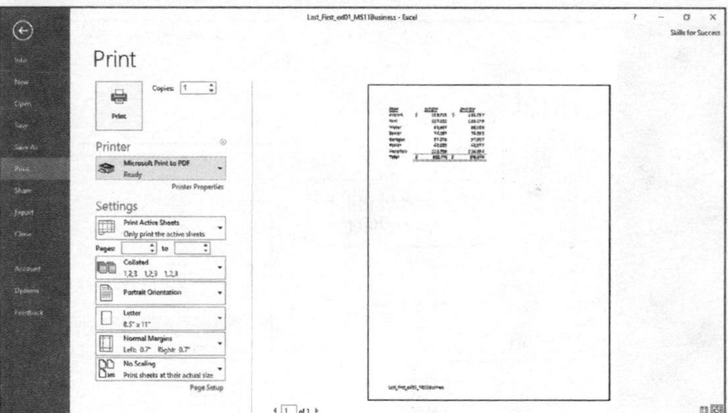

Figure 2 Excel 2016, Windows 10, Microsoft Corporation

More Skills 12

Fill Data with Flash Fill

To complete this project, you will need the following file:

- exl01_MS12Employees

You will save your file as:

- Last_First_exl01_MS12Employees

▶ ***Flash Fill*** recognizes a pattern in data and automatically enters the rest of the data.

---

1. Start **Excel 2016**, open the student data file **exl01_MS12Employees**, and then save the file in your chapter folder as Last_First_exl01_MS12Employees
2. Add the file name in the worksheet's left footer, and then return to **Normal** view. Press Ctrl + Home.

   Often, data imported from a database will place spaces between data instead of placing each field in a separate column.

3. Click cell **B4**, type Ron and then press Enter. In cell **B5**, type Re and then pause to preview all the employee first names in column B.

   Flash Fill recognizes the first name pattern in your data.

4. Press Enter to automatically fill all employee first names.
5. Using the technique just practiced, use Flash Fill to enter the last names into column **C** and the e-mail addresses into column **D**. Compare your screen with **Figure 1**.
6. **Save** the file, and then **Close** Excel. Submit the file as directed by your instructor.

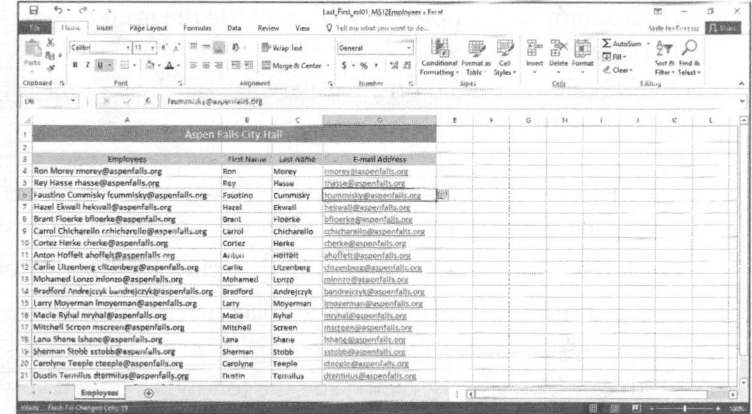

Excel 2016, Windows 10, Microsoft Corporation

Figure 1

■ **You have completed More Skills 12**

More Skills 13

Create Templates and Workbooks from Templates

To complete this project, you will need the following file:

- Blank Excel workbook

You will save your files as:

- Last_First_exl01_MS13Timecard
- Last_First_exl01_MS13Template

- A ***template***—a prebuilt workbook used as a pattern for creating new workbooks—is used to build workbooks without having to start from a blank workbook.
- When a template is opened, a copy of the file is created to keep the original template.
- A workbook submitted on a regular basis, such as a time card or an expense report, can be saved as a template.

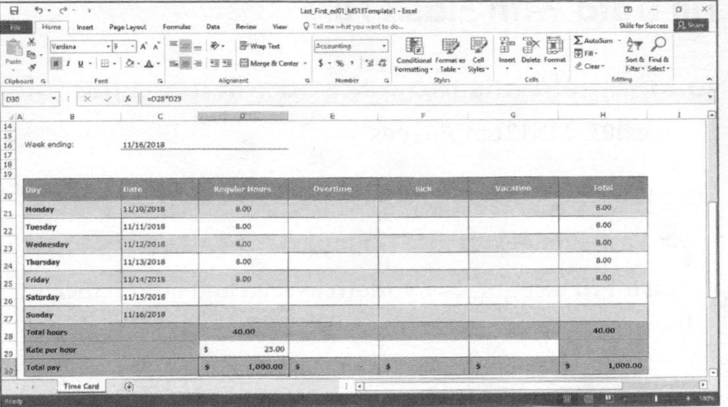

Figure 1 Excel 2016, Windows 10, Microsoft Corporation

1. Start **Excel 2016**. At the top of the window, in the search box, type time card and then press Enter. If necessary, scroll to find the **Time card** template.
2. Click the **Time card** template, and then click the **Create** button.

   If you are not able to locate this template, navigate to your student data files and open exl01_MS13Timecard.

3. With cell **C7** the active cell, type the following data using your name where indicated.

Title	Cell	Data
Employee	C7	Your First Last Name
[Street Address]	C9	500 S Aspen Street
[City, ST ZIP Code]	C13	Aspen Falls, CA 93463
Manager	G7	Maria Martinez
Employee phone	G9	(805) 555-9080

4. On the **File tab**, click **Save As**, and then in **Backstage** view, click the **Browse** button. In the **Save As** dialog box, click the **Save as type arrow**, and then click **Excel Template**. Save the file in your chapter folder as Last_First_exl01_MS13Template

   MOS Obj 1.5.2 C

   By default, Excel saves templates in the Templates folder.

5. Click **Save**, and then **Close** Excel.
6. Navigate to your chapter folder, and then open the file **Last_First_exl01_MS13Template** to create a new workbook.
7. In cell **C16**, type 11/16/2018 and then press Enter. Scroll down to display row **30**.

   When a date is entered in cell C16, functions in C21:C27 automatically display the corresponding dates.

Obj 2.1.4 C

8. In cell **D21**, type 8 and then, on the formula bar, click the **Enter** button. Fill the number 8 down through the cells **D22:D25**. Click the **Auto Fill Options** button, and then click **Fill Without Formatting**. In cell **D29**, type 25 and then press Enter. Compare your screen with **Figure 1**.

   When the regular hours are entered in cells D21:D25, the total hours in cell D28 are automatically calculated.

   Formatting symbols, such as the dollar sign in cell D29, are already formatted in a template.

9. Save the file as Last_First_exl01_MS13Timecard and then **Close** Excel. Submit the files as directed by your instructor.

- **You have completed More Skills 13**

More Skills 14

Manage Document Properties

To complete this project, you will need the following file:

- **exl01_MS14Revenue**

You will save your files as:

- **Last_First_exl01_MS14Revenue**
- **Last_First_exl01_MS14Snip**

- ***Document properties*** are details about a file that describe or identify the file, such as title, author, and keywords.
- The document properties are stored as part of the Excel file.

---

1. Start **Excel 2016**, open the student data file **exl01_MS14Revenue**, and then save the file in your chapter folder as Last_First_exl01_MS14Revenue
2. Click the **File tab**. In **Backstage** view, on the right side of the **Info** page, click the **Title** box, and then type Park Revenue
3. In the **Tags** box, type first half, park, revenue, chart
4. In the **Author** box, replace the existing text with your First and Last names.
5. Select the **Show All Properties** link.
6. In the **Status** box, type Draft
7. At the top of the right panel, click **Properties**, click **Advanced Properties**, and then ensure the **Summary tab** is selected.

Obj 1.4.6 C

8. In the **Company** box, type Aspen Falls In the **Comments** box, type Need to increase marketing effort
9. In the **Properties** dialog box, click **OK**.
10. Start the **Snipping Tool**, click the **New arrow**, and then click **Full-screen Snip**.
11. Click the **Save Snip** button. In the **Save As** dialog box, navigate to your chapter folder. **Save** the file as Last_First_exl01_MS14Snip and then **Close** the Snipping Tool window. Compare your screen with **Figure 1**.

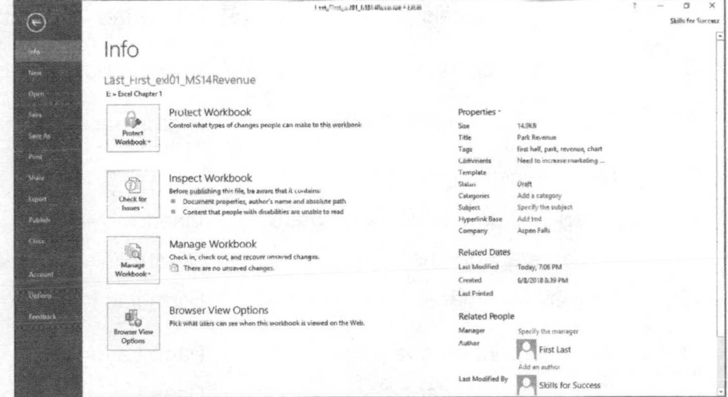

Excel 2016, Windows 10, Microsoft Corporation

Figure 1

12. **Close** the Document Information Panel. **Save** the file, and then **Close** Excel. Submit the files as directed by your instructor.

- **You have completed More Skills 14**

Review

The following table summarizes the **SKILLS AND PROCEDURES** covered in this chapter.

Skills Number	Task	Step	Icon	Keyboard Shortcut
2	Merge cells	Home tab → Alignment group → Merge & Center		
3	Accept a cell entry	Formula bar → Enter		Enter
5	Adjust column width	Home tab → Cells group → Format → Column Width		
5	Adjust row height	Home tab → Cells group → Format → Row Height		
5	Apply Cell Styles	Home tab → Styles group → Cell Styles		
6	Insert SUM function	Home tab → Editing group → AutoSum	Σ AutoSum	Alt + =
7	Insert a row	Home tab → Cells group → Insert → Insert Sheet Rows		
8	Check spelling	Review tab → Proofing group → Spelling		F7
8	Edit inside cells	Double-click		F2
8	Increase decimals	Home tab → Number group → Increase Decimal		
8	Decrease decimals	Home tab → Number group → Decrease Decimal		
9	Display workbook in Normal View	Status bar → Normal		
9	Move to cell A1			Ctrl + Home
9	Insert text and fields into footers	Insert tab → Text group → Header & Footer		
9	Rename a worksheet tab	Right-click worksheet tab → Rename		
10	Display formulas	Formulas tab → Formula Auditing group → Show Formulas		Ctrl + [']
10	Scale to print on one page	Page Layout tab → Scale to Fit group → Width / Height		
10	Change page orientation	Page Layout tab → Page Setup group → Orientation		
MS 11	Set print area	Page Layout tab → Page Setup group → Print Area		
MS 12	Flash Fill	Type Text → Home tab → Editing group → Fill		
MS 13	Create template	Excel Start Screen → Search box → Create		
MS 14	Document properties	File tab → Backstage view → Info		

Project Summary Chart

Project	Project Type	Project Location
Skills Review	Review	In Book & MIL MyITLab® Grader
Skills Assessment 1	Review	In Book & MIL MyITLab® Grader
Skills Assessment 2	Review	Book
My Skills	Problem Solving	Book
Visual Skills Check	Problem Solving	Book
Skillls Challenge 1	Critical Thinking	Book
Skills Challenge 2	Critical Thinking	Book
More Skills Assessment	Review	In Book & MIL MyITLab® Grader
Collaborating with Google	Critical Thinking	Book

MOS Objectives Covered

1.1.1 C Create a workbook	1.5.1 C Set a print area
1.2.2 C Navigate to a named cell, range, or workbook element	1.5.2 C Save workbooks in alternative file formats
1.3.2 C Rename a worksheet	1.5.4 C Set print scaling
1.3.4 C Modify page setup	2.1.2 C Copy and paste data
1.3.7 C Adjust column width	2.1.4 C Fill cells by using AutoFill
1.3.7 C Adjust row height	2.2.1 C Merge cells
1.3.8 C Insert headers and footers	2.2.5 C Apply number formats
1.4.4 C Change workbook views	2.2.7 C Apply cell styles
1.4.6 C Modify document properties	4.1.1 C Insert references
1.4.8 C Display formulas	4.1.2 C Perform calculations by using the SUM function

Key Terms

1. What are the best ways to network online?
2. What are some of the biggest pitfalls in using social media to communicate a personal brand?

Online Help Skills

1. Start **Excel 2016**, and then in the upper right corner of the start page, click the **Help** button [?].
2. In the **Excel Help** window **Search help** box, type broken formula and then press [Enter].
3. In the search result list, click **How to avoid broken formulas**, **Maximize** the Help window, and then compare your screen with **Figure 1**.

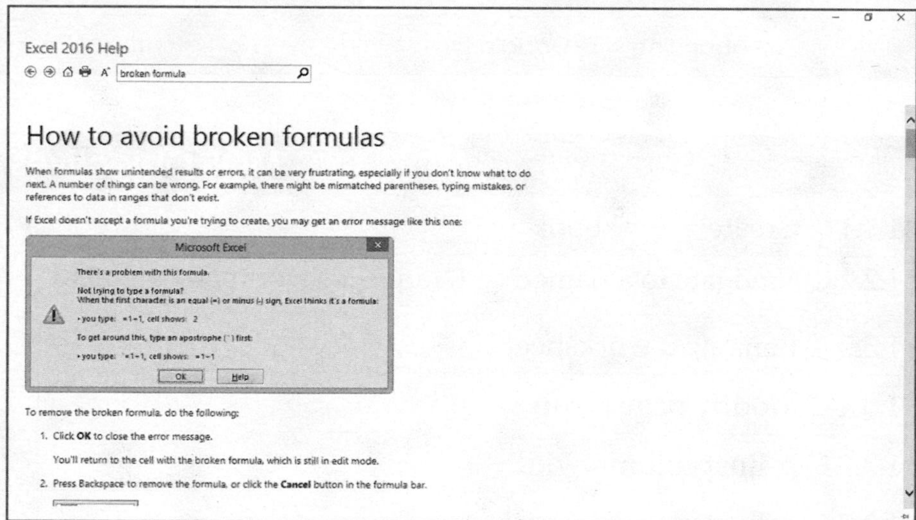

Figure 1 Excel 2016, Windows 10, Microsoft Corporation

4. Read the article to answer the following questions: How do you remove a broken formula? What sign does every function start with?

Matching 

Match each term in the second column with its correct definition in the first column by writing the letter of the term on the blank line in front of the correct definition.

___ **1.** An Excel file that contains one or more worksheets.

___ **2.** The primary document that you use in Excel to store and work with data.

___ **3.** The cell, surrounded by a green border, ready to receive data or be affected by the next Excel command.

___ **4.** The identification of a specific cell by its intersecting column letter and row number.

___ **5.** Data in a cell—text or numbers.

___ **6.** Data in a cell made up of text only.

___ **7.** Data in a cell made up of numbers only.

___ **8.** Two or more cells on a worksheet.

___ **9.** The Excel window area that displays the address of a selected cell.

___ **10.** An Excel feature that suggests values as you type a function.

A Active cell
B Cell reference
C Formula AutoComplete
D Name Box
E Number value
F Range
G Text value
H Value
I Workbook
J Worksheet

Multiple Choice 

Choose the correct answer.

1. An Excel window area that displays the value contained in the active cell.
   A. Formula bar
   B. Workbook
   C. Name Box
2. The column letter and row number that identify a cell.
   A. Cell window
   B. Cell address
   C. Cell file name
3. The data displayed in a cell.
   A. Viewed value
   B. Inspected value
   C. Displayed value
4. An equation that performs mathematical calculations on number values.
   A. Method
   B. Formula
   C. System
5. Page headers and footers can be changed in this view.
   A. Print preview
   B. Page Layout view
   C. Normal view
6. Symbols that specify mathematical operations such as addition or subtraction.
   A. Hyperlinks
   B. Bookmarks
   C. Arithmetic operators
7. The number that displays at the left of a row.
   A. Row heading
   B. Row name
   C. Row border
8. A prewritten Excel formula.
   A. Method
   B. Function
   C. Exponent
9. The small green square in the lower right corner of the active cell.
   A. Border
   B. Fill handle
   C. Edge
10. A view that maximizes the number of cells visible on the screen.
    A. Page Layout view
    B. Standard view
    C. Normal view

Topics for Discussion

1. What is the advantage of using cell references instead of actual number values in formulas and functions?
2. What are some things you can do to make your worksheet easier for others to read and understand?
3. According to the introduction to this chapter, how do you decide which information to put in columns and which to put in rows?

Skills Review

To complete this project, you will need the following file:

- Blank Excel document

You will save your file as:

- Last_First_exl01_SRFitness

1. Start **Excel 2016**. In cell **A1**, type Aspen Falls Fitness Events and then in cell **A2**, type Number of Participants In cell **A4**, type Department and then pressing Tab after each label, type Spring | Fall | Total Participants | Difference
2. In rows **5** through **9**, enter the following data starting in cell **A5**:

City Hall	185	140
Finance	147	136
IT Services	130	117
Engineering	169	147
City Council	195	152

3. In cell **D5**, type =B5+C5 and then in cell **E5**, type =B5-C5 Select the range **D5:E5**. Point to the fill handle, and then drag down through row **9**. Compare your screen with **Figure 1**.
4. **Save** the file in your chapter folder with the name Last_First_exl01_SRFitness
5. On the **Insert tab**, in the **Text group**, click the **Header & Footer** button. In the **Navigation group**, click the **Go to Footer** button, and then click in the left footer. In the **Header & Footer Elements group**, click the **File Name** button. Click in a cell just above the footer. On the lower right side of the status bar, click the **Normal** button, and then press Ctrl + Home.
6. In cell **A10**, type Total and then select the range **B10:D10**. On the **Home tab**, in the **Editing group**, click the **AutoSum** button.
7. Click cell **A7**. In the **Cells group**, click the **Insert arrow**, and then click **Insert Sheet Rows**. In the new row **7**, type the following data in columns **A:C**: Public Works | 95 | 87
8. Select the range **D6:E6**, and then use the fill handle to copy the formulas down one row.
9. In cell **A13**, type Fall Participants as Percent of Total
10. Select the range **A5:A10**, and then on the **Home tab**, in the **Clipboard group**, click the **Copy** button. Click cell **A14**, and then in the **Clipboard group**, click the **Paste** button. Press Esc, and then compare your screen with **Figure 2**.

■ Continue to the next page to complete this Skills Review

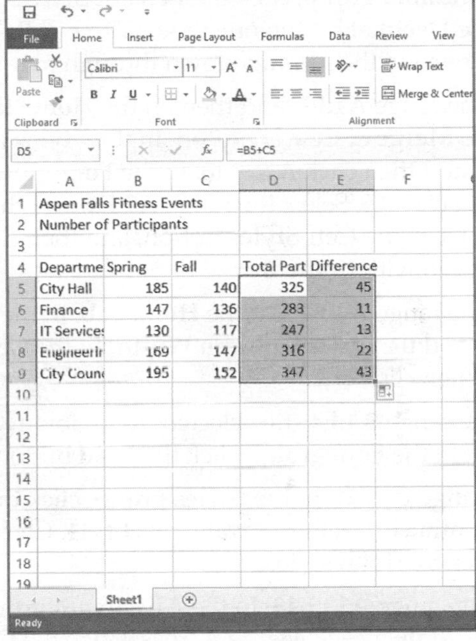

Excel 2016, Windows 10, Microsoft Corporation

Figure 1

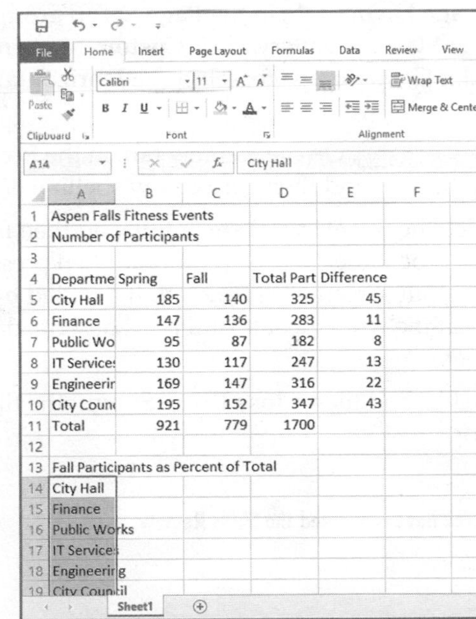

Excel 2016, Windows 10, Microsoft Corporation

Figure 2

11. In cell **B14**, type =C5/D5 and then on the formula bar, click the **Enter** button. In the **Number group**, click the **Percent Style** button, and then click the **Increase Decimal** button one time. With cell **B14** still the active cell, use the fill handle to copy the formula down through row **19**.
12. Select the range **A1:E1**, and then on the **Home tab**, in the **Alignment group**, click the **Merge & Center** button. In the **Styles group**, click the **Cell Styles** button, and then click **Accent6**. In the **Font group**, click the **Font Size arrow**, and then click **16**. Select the range **A2:E2**, and then click the **Merge & Center** button. Click the **Cell Styles** button, and then click **60% - Accent6**. Compare your screen with **Figure 3**.
13. Select the range **A4:E4**. On the **Home tab**, in the **Cells group**, click the **Format** button, and then click **Column Width**. In the **Column Width** dialog box, type 16 and then click **OK**.
14. With the range **A4:E4** still selected, hold down Ctrl, and then select the range **A5:A11**. In the **Font group**, click the **Bold** button.
15. Select range **B5:E11**. In the **Styles group**, click the **Cell Styles** button, and then click **Comma [0]**. Select the range **B11:D11**. Click the **Cell Styles** button, and then click the **Total** style.
16. Select the range **A13:B13**. In the **Alignment group**, click the **Merge & Center arrow**, and then click **Merge Across**. Click the **Cell Styles** button, and then click **40% - Accent6**.
17. On the **Page Layout tab**, in the **Page Setup group**, click the **Margins** button. Below the **Margins** gallery, click **Custom Margins**. In the **Page Setup** dialog box, under **Center on page**, select the **Horizontally** check box, and then click **OK**.
18. Press Ctrl + Home. On the **Review tab**, in the **Proofing group**, click the **Spelling** button, and then correct any spelling errors.
19. Right-click the **Sheet1 worksheet tab**, and then from the shortcut menu, click **Rename**. Type Fitness Participants and then press Enter. Press Ctrl + Home. Compare your screen with **Figure 4**. If directed by your instructor, display and format the worksheet formulas as described in Skill 10, and then print the worksheet.
20. **Save** the file, and then **Close** Excel. Submit the file as directed by your instructor.

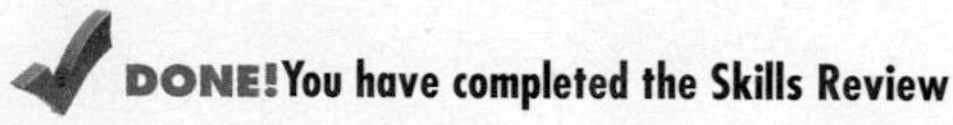

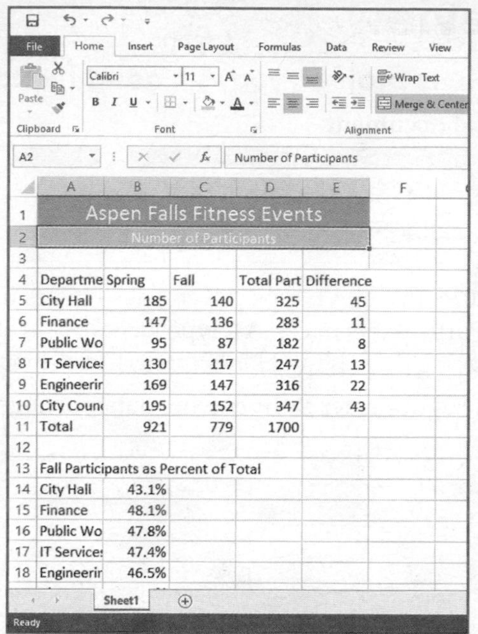

Figure 3 Excel 2016, Windows 10, Microsoft Corporation

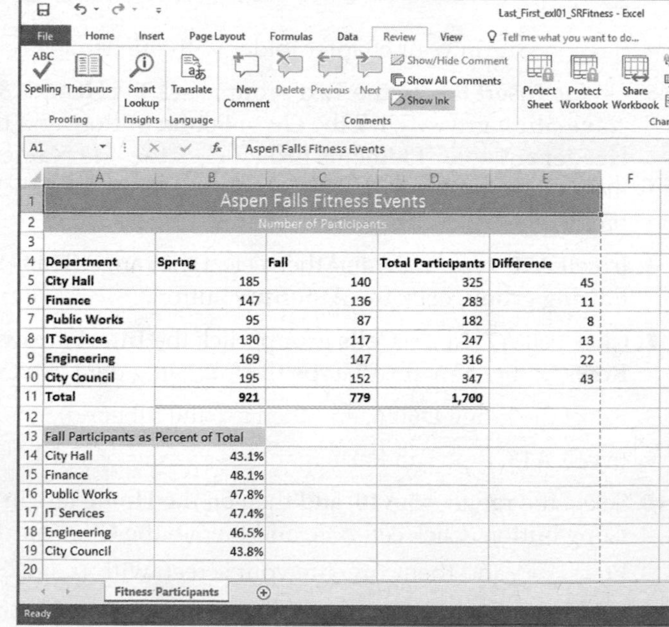

Figure 4 Excel 2016, Windows 10, Microsoft Corporation

Skills Assessment 1

MyITLab®
Grader

To complete this project, you will need the following file:

- exl01_SA1Path

You will save your file as:

- Last_First_exl01_SA1Path

1. Start **Excel 2016**. From your student data files, open **exl01_SA1Path**. Save the file in your chapter folder as Last_First_exl01_SA1Path Rename the **Sheet1** worksheet tab as Path Costs
2. Add the file name to the worksheet's left footer, add the current date to the center footer, and then in the right footer, insert the sheet name. Return to **Normal** view.
3. For the range **A1:E1**, merge and center and apply the **Accent5** cell style. Increase the font size to **18** points. For the range **A2:E2**, merge and center and apply the **40% - Accent5** cell style. Increase the width of column **A** to **20**. For all column and row labels **A4:E4**, **A5:A14**, and **A17:C17**, apply **Bold**.
4. For the range **E5:E13**, insert the **SUM** function to add the three costs for each row. In the range **B14:E14**, insert the **SUM** function to provide totals for each column.
5. Select the nonadjacent ranges **B5:E5** and **B14:E14**. Apply the **Currency [0]** cell style.
6. Select the range **B6:E13**, and then apply the **Comma [0]** cell style. Select the range **B14:E14**, and then apply the **Total** cell style.
7. Insert a new row above row **7**. In cell **A7**, type Aspen Lakes and as the costs for the new location, type 4763 | 18846 | 1498 Use the fill handle to copy the formula in cell **E6** to cell **E7**.
8. **Copy** the location names from the range **A5:A14** to the range **A19:A28**. In cell **A29**, type Total
9. In cells **B19** and **B20**, type .03 In cells **B21** and **B22**, type .05 In cell **B23**, type .06 Use the fill handle to copy the value in cell **B23** down through cell **B28**. Select the range **B19:B28**, and then apply the **Percent Style** cell style.
10. In cell **C19**, enter a formula that calculates the cost increase by multiplying cell **E5** by cell **B19**. Fill the formula in cell **C19** down through cell **C28**.

Aspen Falls								
Bike Path Construction Costs								
Location	**Brush Clearing**		**Paving**		**Landscaping**		**Total Cost**	
Cornish Forest	$	5,883	$	15,580	$	3,271	$	24,734
Haack Center		6,234		18,916		1,697		26,847
Aspen Lakes		4,763		18,846		1,498		25,107
Hamilton Hills Park		4,981		17,169		1,805		23,955
Hansen Hills		4,209		14,062		2,437		20,708
Plasek Park		3,247		12,691		3,971		19,909
Price Lakes		3,648		19,387		2,927		25,962
Rodman Creek		4,515		13,120		1,934		19,569
Schroder Brook		3,862		19,166		2,036		25,064
Terry Park		2,569		17,506		1,756		21,831
Total	**$**	**43,911**	**$**	**166,443**	**$**	**23,332**	**$**	**233,686**
Location	**Increase**		**Cost Increase**					
Cornish Forest		3%	$	742.02				
Haack Center		3%		805.41				
Aspen Lakes		5%		1,255.35				
Hamilton Hills Park		5%		1,197.75				
Hansen Hills		6%		1,242.48				
Plasek Park		6%		1,194.54				
Price Lakes		6%		1,557.72				
Rodman Creek		6%		1,174.14				
Schroder Brook		6%		1,503.84				
Terry Park		6%		1,309.86				
Total			**$**	**11,983.11**				

Figure 1

11. In cell **C29**, insert the **SUM** function to add the total cost increase, and then apply the **Total** cell style.
12. Select the range **C20:C28**, apply the **Comma [0]** cell style, and then increase the decimal two times.
13. Use **Page Setup** to center the worksheet **Horizontally**. Set the **Gridlines** to print.
14. Review and correct any spelling errors, ignoring proper names. Press Ctrl + Home.
15. **Save** the file, and then compare your screen with **Figure 1**.
16. **Close** the file, and then submit the file as directed by your instructor.

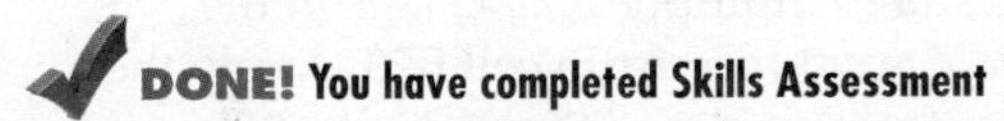
DONE! You have completed Skills Assessment 1

Skills Assessment 2

To complete this project, you will need the following file:

- exl01_SA2Guests

You will save your file as:

- Last_First_exl01_SA2Guests

1. Start **Excel 2016**. From the student data files, open **exl01_SA2Guests**. Save the file in your chapter folder as Last_First_exl01_SA2Guests
2. Rename the worksheet tab Aspen Lake Guests Add the file name to the worksheet's left footer, and then add the current date to the right footer. Return to **Normal** view.
3. In cell **D5**, construct a formula to add the *1st Qtr.* and *2nd Qtr.* guests who are *Over 70*. In cell **E5**, construct a formula to calculate the increase of guests from the *1st Qtr.* to the *2nd Qtr.* who are *Over 70*.
4. In cell **F5** for the *Over 70* row, construct a formula to divide *2nd Qtr.* guests by the *1st Half Total Guests*. Fill the formulas in **D5:F5** down through row **17**.
5. In cell **A18**, type Total and then in row **18**, insert the function to total columns **B:D**.
6. Insert a new row above row **15**, and then using the other rows as an example, enter the following data: 20 to 25 | 17196 | 19133
7. For the range **B5:E19**, apply the **Comma [0]** cell style, and then for the range **F5:F18**, apply the **Percent** cell style and display one decimal.
8. Merge and center the range **A1:F1**, and then apply the **Accent6** cell style. Increase the font size to **18**. Merge and center the range **A2:F2**, and then apply the **40% - Accent6** cell style. Increase the font size to **14**.
9. Increase the column widths of **A:C** to **11.00**, and then increase the column widths of **D:F** to **14.00**.
10. For the column and row labels, apply **Bold**. In the range **B19:D19**, apply the **Total** cell style.
11. For the range **A21:C21**, apply the **Merge Across** alignment and the **40% - Accent6** cell style.
12. In cell **C23**, construct a formula to multiply *Total Guests* in the *Over 70* row by the *Projected Percent Increase* in cell **B23**. Apply the **Comma [0]** cell style. Fill the formula down through row **36**.

Aspen Lake Recreation Area

Number of Guests

Ages	1st Quarter	2nd Quarter	Total Guests	2nd Quarter Increase	2nd Quarter as Percent of Total
Over 70	14,102	15,216	29,318	1,114	51.9%
65 to 70	15,125	17,854	32,979	2,729	54.1%
60 to 65	11,175	18,273	29,448	7,098	62.1%
55 to 60	15,110	16,572	31,682	1,462	52.3%
50 to 55	19,114	19,841	38,955	727	50.9%
45 to 50	18,475	21,418	39,893	2,943	53.7%
40 to 45	12,064	13,242	25,306	1,178	52.3%
35 to 40	14,628	16,232	30,860	1,604	52.6%
30 to 35	14,543	19,975	34,518	5,432	57.9%
25 to 30	17,933	19,724	37,657	1,791	52.4%
20 to 25	17,196	19,133	36,329	1,937	52.7%
15 to 20	30,516	32,597	63,113	2,081	51.6%
10 to 15	13,469	17,439	30,908	3,970	56.4%
Under 10	17,876	19,599	37,475	1,723	52.3%
Total	231,326	267,115	498,441		

Projected 2nd Half Guests

Ages	Projected Percentage Increase	Projected Increase in Guests
Over 70	2%	586
65 to 70	8%	2,638
60 to 65	4%	1,178
55 to 60	1%	317
50 to 55	5%	1,948
45 to 50	6%	2,394
40 to 45	9%	2,278
35 to 40	3%	926
30 to 35	6%	2,071
25 to 30	15%	5,649
20 to 25	14%	5,086
15 to 20	18%	11,360
10 to 15	21%	6,491
Under 10	23%	8,619

Figure 1

13. Review and correct any spelling errors.
14. Use **Page Setup** to center the page **Horizontally**, and then set the **Gridlines** to print.
15. If you are instructed to do so, display the worksheet formulas, scale the worksheet to print on one page, and then print with the formulas displayed.
16. Compare your screen with **Figure 1**. Save the file, and then **Close** Excel. Submit the file as directed by your instructor.

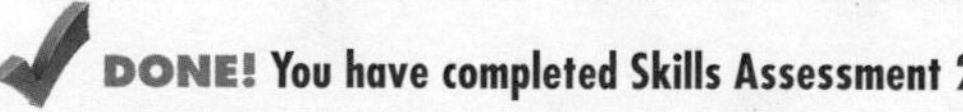

DONE! You have completed Skills Assessment 2

My College Enrollment				
Course Name	**Fall**	**Spring**	**Summer**	**Course Total**
Algebra	1,173	938	415	2,526
Intro to Computers	1,043	857	497	2,397
Biology	578	311	253	1,142
World History	688	549	372	1,609
American History	824	598	397	1,819
Management	367	228	103	698
English	1,292	1,125	573	2,990
Semester Total	**5,965**	**4,606**	**2,610**	**13,181**
Summer as a Percent of Total				
Algebra	16.4%			
Intro to Computers	20.7%			
Biology	22.2%			
World History	23.1%			
American History	21.8%			
Management	14.8%			
English	19.2%			

Figure 1

My Skills

To complete this project, you will need the following file:

- **exl01_MYCollege**

You will save your file as:

- **Last_First_exl01_MYCollege**

---

1. Start **Excel 2016**. From the student data files, open **exl01_MYCollege**. Save the file in your chapter folder as Last_First_exl01_MYCollege Rename the **Sheet1** worksheet tab as Enrollment
2. Add the file name to the worksheet's left footer, insert the sheet name in the right footer, and then return to **Normal** view.
3. For the range **A1:E1**, merge and center and apply the **Accent3** cell style, and then change the font size to 16
4. Increase the width of column **A** to 20 and then increase the width of columns **B:E** to 12
5. For the range **B3:E3**, center the labels. For all column and row labels, apply **Bold**.
6. For cell **E4**, insert the **SUM** function to provide the total for the row. Fill the formula in cell **E4** down through cell **E9**.
7. Insert the **SUM** function for the range **B10:E10** to provide totals for each column. With the range **B10:E10** still selected, apply the **Total** cell style.
8. For the range **B4:E10**, apply the **Comma [0]** cell style.
9. Insert a new row above row **7**. In cell **A7**, type World History and then as the enrollment for the new course, type 688 | 549 | 372 Fill the formula in cell **E6** to cell **E7**.
10. **Copy** the course names from the range **A4:A10** to the range **A15:A21**.
11. In cell **B15**, create a formula that calculates the summer semester as a percentage of the total course enrollment by dividing cell **D4** by cell **E4**. Apply the **Percent Style** cell style, and then display one decimal. Fill the formula in cell **B15** down through cell **B21**.
12. For the range **A14:B14**, merge across and apply the **40% - Accent3** cell style.
13. Use **Page Setup** to center the worksheet **Horizontally**.
14. Check and correct any spelling errors.
15. Compare your screen with **Figure 1**. If you are instructed to do so, display the worksheet formulas, and scale the worksheet to print on one page.
16. **Save** the file, and **then Close** Excel. Submit the file as directed by your instructor.

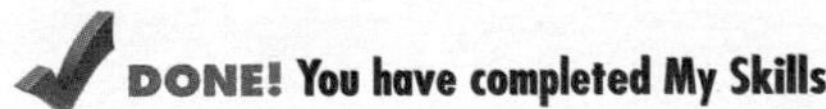
DONE! You have completed My Skills

Visual Skills Check

To complete this project, you will need the following file:

- **Blank Excel workbook**

You will save your file as:

- **Last_First_exl01_VSWorkers**

Start **Excel 2016.** Open a blank workbook, and then **Save** the file in your chapter folder as Last_First_exl01_VSWorkers Create the worksheet shown in **Figure 1**. The width of column **A** is **20** and the width of columns **B:F** is **13**. Construct formulas that display the results shown in columns **D** and **F**, row **13**, and the range **B16:B23**. The title uses the **Accent4** cell style, and the font size is **20**. The subtitle uses the **40% - Accent4** cell style, and the font size is **16**. The title and subtitle should be merged and centered. Using **Figure 1** as your guide, apply the **Currency [0]** cell style, the **Comma [0]** cell style, the **Total** cell style, the **Percent** cell style with one decimal place, and the **Bold** format. On the range **A15:C15**, use **Merge Across** and apply the **20% - Accent4** cell style. Rename the Sheet1 worksheet tab as Park Workers Check and correct any spelling errors. Add the file name to the left footer. **Save** the file, **Close** Excel, and then submit the file as directed by your instructor.

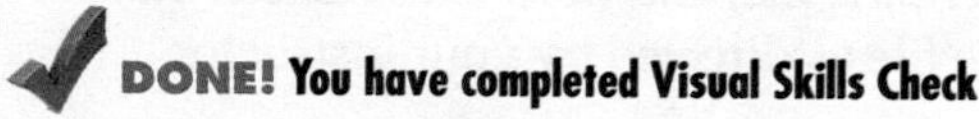
DONE! You have completed Visual Skills Check

Aspen Falls

Park Workers

	Price Park	Silkwood Park	Total Workers	Wage	Total Wages
Ticket Sellers	75	52	127	$ 15	$ 1,905
Security	92	79	171	25	4,275
Landscapers	19	11	30	20	600
Life Guards	23	23	46	15	690
Cashiers	73	58	131	15	1,965
Parking Attendants	15	11	26	15	390
Maintenance	21	28	49	20	980
Cleaning	29	17	46	18	828
Total	**347**	**279**	**626**		**$ 11,633**

Price Park as Percent of Total Workers	
Ticket Sellers	59.1%
Security	53.8%
Landscapers	63.3%
Life Guards	50.0%
Cashiers	55.7%
Parking Attendants	57.7%
Maintenance	42.9%
Cleaning	63.0%

Figure 1

Skills Challenge 1

To complete this project, you will need the following file:

- exl01_SC1Employees

You will save your file as:

- Last_First_exl01_SC1Employees

Start **Excel 2016**, and then from the student data files, open **exl01_SC1Employees**. Save the file in your chapter folder as Last_First_exl01_SC1Employees Duncan Chueng, the Park Operations Manager for Aspen Falls, wants to total and compare the number of employees at the city recreation areas. Using the skills you practiced in this chapter, correct the SUM function for each row and column. Format the worksheet using cell styles as practiced in this chapter. Merge and center the title across the correct columns. Correct the number formats. No decimals should display in rows 5:11. Adjust column widths as necessary to display all data. Set the gridlines to print, and center the data horizontally on the page. Add the file name in the worksheet's left footer, and check for spelling errors. Save the file, and then close Excel. Submit the file as directed by your instructor.

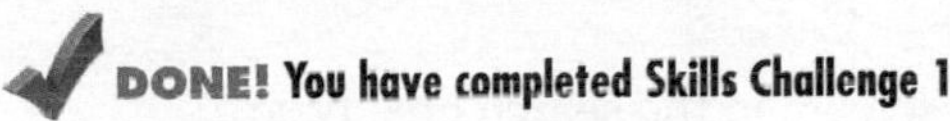

Skills Challenge 2

To complete this project, you will need the following file:

- exl01_SC2Painting

You will save your file as:

- Last_First_exl01_SC2Painting

Start **Excel 2016**, and then from the student data files, open **exl01_SC2Painting**. Save the file in your chapter folder as Last_First_exl01_SC2Painting The Art Center wants to total and compare the number of students enrolled in the painting classes in the different neighborhoods. Using the skills you practiced in this chapter, insert appropriate formulas and functions. Adjust column widths and row heights as necessary to display all data. Format the worksheet as appropriate. Add the file name in the worksheet's left footer, and check for spelling errors. Save the file, and then close Excel. Submit the file as directed by your instructor.

More Skills Assessment

To complete this project, you will need the following files:

- Blank Excel workbook
- exl01_MSAAnalysis

You will save your files as:

- Last_First_exl01_MSATemplate
- Last_First_exl01_MSACalendar
- Last_First_exl01_MSAAnalysis

---

1. Start **Excel 2016**. At the top of the screen, in the search box, type Academic calendar
2. Select the template, and then Create the template file. If necessary, scroll through and find the Academic calendar template. If you do not have an Internet connection, navigate to your student data files and open exl01_MSAAssessment.
3. Save your workbook as an Excel template in your chapter folder as Last_First_exl01_MSATemplate Create a new workbook using the template, and then save your workbook in your chapter folder as Last_First_exl01_MSACalendar
4. In cell **B1**, click the **spinner arrow** to change the start year to **2018**.
5. Click the merged cell **C1**, and then click the **arrow** in the lower right corner to display the months.
6. From the displayed list, click **September**. In the worksheet, scroll down to view the months that follow.
7. Select the four sample calendar entries in the nonadjacent range **E7:F7** and cells **B9** and **F13**. Delete the four entries.
8. Click cell **G5**, the cell for September 1. Enter your name, Last First
9. Enter or replace the following data in the cells.

Date	Cell	Data
September 4	C7	New Student Orientation
September 7	F7	Review Biology Lab Procedures
September 12	D9	Access data analysis due
September 14	F9	Draft of English paper due

2018 September

MONDAY	TUESDAY	WEDNESDAY	THURSDAY	FRIDAY	SATURDAY	SUNDAY
27	28	29	30	31	01 Last First	02
03	04 New Student Orientation	05	06	07 Review Biology Lab Procedures	08	09
10	11	12 Access data analysis due	13	14 Draft of English paper due	15	16
17	18	19	20	21	22	23
24	25	26	27	28	29	30
01	02	NOTES				

Figure 1

10. Set the print area for the range **A1:H15**, and then **Save** the workbook. Preview the document, and then compare your screen with **Figure 1**.
11. On the right side of the **Info** page, revise the **Title** to Calendar 2018
12. Enter calendar, academic, 2018 as **Tags**.
13. In the **Author** box, replace the existing text with your First and Last names, and then **Save** the workbook.
14. Open the student data file **exl01_MSAAnalysis**, and then save the file in your chapter folder as Last_First_exl01_MSAAnalysis
15. In cell **B4**, enter Anten In cell **B5**, enter Boy and then flash fill the list of first names in column B.
16. Repeat this technique to enter the last names into column **C** and the e-mail addresses into column **D**.
17. **Save** the file. Close all open windows, and then submit the files as directed by your instructor.

DONE! You have completed the More Skills Assessment

Collaborating with Google

To complete this project, you will need a Google account (refer to the Common Features chapter) and the following file:

- **exl01_GPCityFees**

You will save your file as:

- **Last_First_exl01_GPSnip**

---

1. Open the Google Chrome web browser. Log into your Google account, and then click **Google Apps** [icon].
2. Click **Drive** [icon] to open Google Drive. If you receive a pop-up message, read the message, and then click **Next**. Read each message, and then close the dialog box.
3. Click **New**, and then click **Google Sheets** to open a blank spreadsheet.
4. Open the workbook from the student data file **exl01_GPCityFees**. Copy the range **A1:F17** from the *City Fees* worksheet, and then paste it in cell **A1** of the blank Google worksheet.
5. Click the spreadsheet title, **Untitled spreadsheet**. Type Annual City Fees as the name of the spreadsheet, and then click **OK**. Rename the *Sheet1* worksheet tab as City Fees
6. Select the range **A1:F1**, click **Merge** [icon], and then click **Center** [icon]. Repeat this process to apply the same formatting to the range **A2:F2**.
7. Select the range **B10:D10**, and then insert the **SUM** function [icon] to calculate total fees. Repeat this technique to apply the **SUM** function to the range **E5:E9** to calculate the total for each location.
8. In the range **F5:F9**, enter a formula to calculate the difference, subtracting Overnight Fees from Total Fees.
9. Select the range **B5:F10**. Click **Format**. Point to **Number**, click the **Financial** number format, and then select **Decrease decimal places** [icon] two times.
10. Apply **Bold** [icon] format to all worksheet headings and row and column headings.

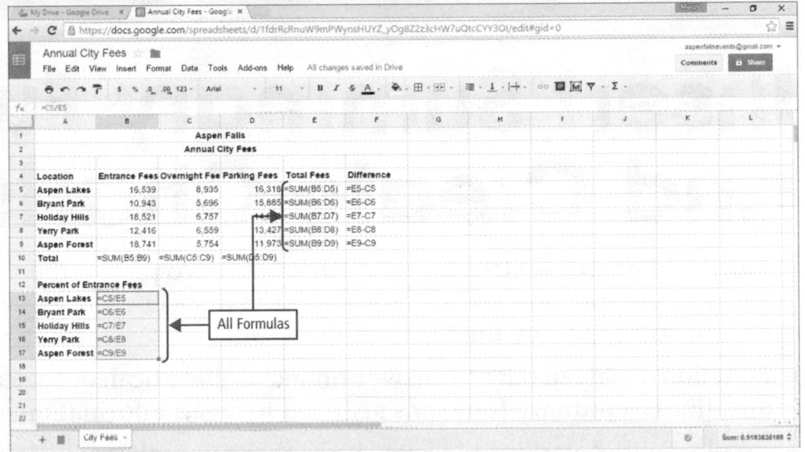

Figure 1

11. In the range **B13:B17**, enter a formula to calculate Overnight Fees divided by Total Fees for each location. With the range **B13:B17** still selected, point to **Format**, point to **Number**, and then click **Percent**.
12. Click **View**, select **All Formulas**, and then compare your screen with **Figure 1**.
13. Click **Share** [icon], and then in the **Share with others** dialog box, type AspenFallsEvents@gmail.com
14. In the **Add a note** text box, type Please review and contact me with any questions.
15. Click **Send**. Press [Windows key], type snip and then press [Enter] to start the **Snipping Tool**. Click the **New arrow**, and then click **Window Snip**. Point to the Windows Explorer window, and then when a red border displays around the window, click one time.
16. In the **Snipping Tool** mark-up window, click the **Save Snip** button [icon]. In the **Save As** dialog box, navigate to your Excel Chapter 1 folder. Be sure the **Save as type** box displays **JPEG file**. Name the file Last_First_exl01_GPSnip and then press [Enter].
17. Close all windows, and then submit the file as directed by your instructor.

DONE! You have completed Collaborating with Google

CHAPTER 2

Insert Summary Functions and Create Charts

- Functions are prewritten formulas that have two parts—the name of the function and the arguments that specify the values or cells to be used by the function.
- Functions analyze data to answer financial, statistical, or logical questions. Summary functions are used to recap information.
- Excel provides various types of charts that can make your data easier to understand.
- Column charts show data changes over a period of time or illustrate comparisons among items.
- Pie charts illustrate how each part relates to the whole. Pie charts display the relative sizes of items in a single data series.
- Charts can be enhanced with effects such as 3-D and soft shadows to create compelling graphical summaries.

Djile/Fotolia

Aspen Falls City Hall

In this chapter, you will finish a workbook for Thelma Perkins, a Risk Management Specialist in the Finance Department. The workbook displays the department expenditures for Aspen Falls. The City Council requires that the Finance Department present the departmental information annually for review and approval.

Companies use formulas and statistical functions to manipulate and summarize data to make better decisions. Summary results can include the data totals or averages. Results can be displayed graphically as charts, providing a visual representation of data. Commonly used chart types include line charts to illustrate trends over time or bar charts to illustrate comparisons among individual items. Based on the type of data selected, the Quick Analysis tools provide chart type options.

In this project, you will open an existing workbook, construct formulas containing absolute cell references, and AutoFill the formulas to other cells. You will insert the statistical functions AVERAGE, MAX, and MIN. You will create and format column charts and pie charts and insert WordArt. Finally, you will prepare the chart sheet and the worksheet to meet printing requirements.

Time to complete all 10 skills — 60 to 90 minutes

Introduction

Outcome

Using the skills in this chapter, you will be able to modify cell and number formats; create formulas using absolute cell references and average, minimum, and maximum functions; create, edit, and format pie and column charts; and update print settings for multiple worksheets.

Objectives

2.1 Construct statistical functions

2.2 Generate formulas using absolute cell references

2.3 Apply cell and number formatting

2.4 Create, edit, and format basic charts

2.5 Modify workbook print settings

Student data file needed for this chapter:

exl02_Expenditures

You will save your file as:

Last_First_exl02_Expenditures

SKILLS

At the end of this chapter you will be able to:

Skill 1 Align and Wrap Text
Skill 2 Apply Absolute Cell References
Skill 3 Format Numbers
Skill 4 Insert the AVERAGE Function
Skill 5 Insert the MIN and MAX Functions
Skill 6 Create Column Charts
Skill 7 Format Column Charts
Skill 8 Create and Format Pie Charts
Skill 9 Update Charts and Insert WordArt
Skill 10 Preview and Print Multiple Worksheets

MORE SKILLS

Skill 11 Validate Workbooks for Accessibility
Skill 12 Change Chart Types
Skill 13 Copy Excel Data to Word Documents
Skill 14 Create Line Charts

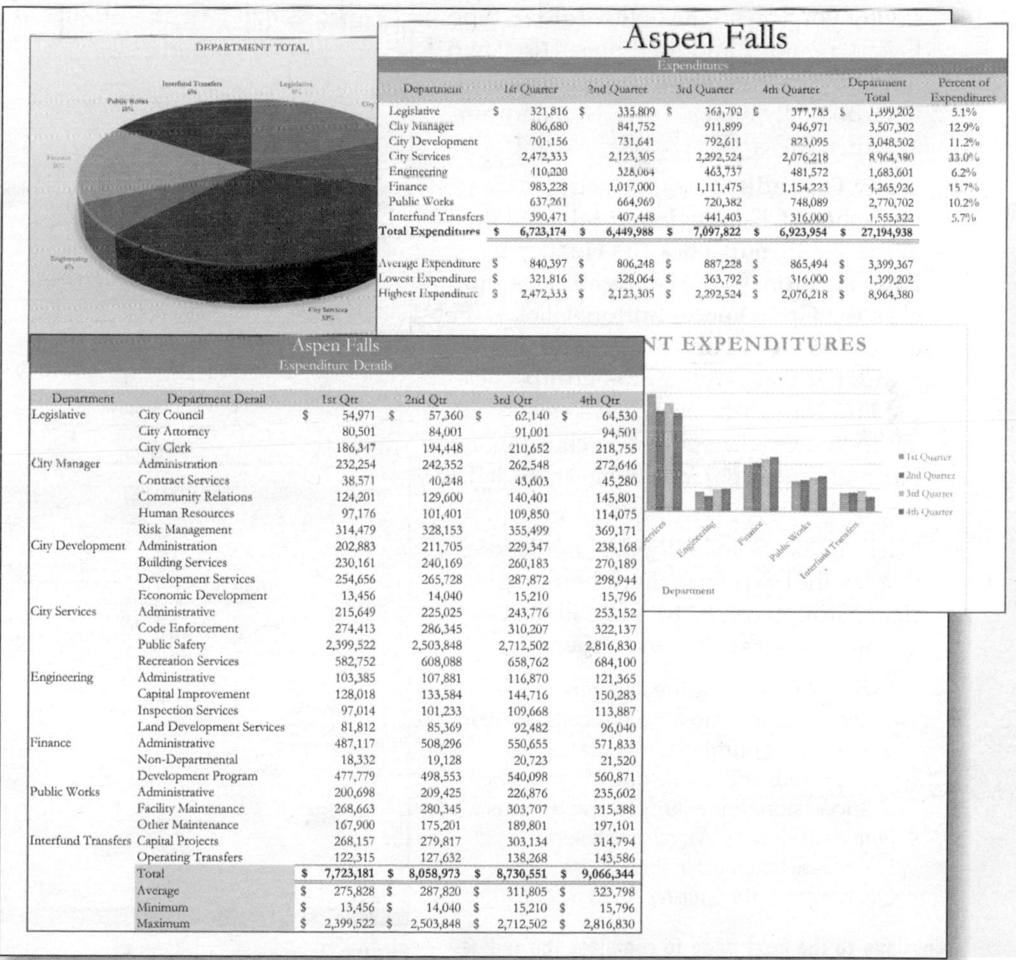

Aspen Falls

Expenditures

Department	1st Quarter	2nd Quarter	3rd Quarter	4th Quarter	Department Total	Percent of Expenditures
Legislative	$ 321,816	$ 335,809	$ 363,792	$ 377,785	$ 1,399,202	5.1%
City Manager	806,680	841,752	911,899	946,971	3,507,302	12.9%
City Development	701,156	731,641	792,611	823,095	3,048,502	11.2%
City Services	2,472,333	2,123,305	2,292,524	2,076,218	8,964,380	33.0%
Engineering	410,220	328,064	463,737	481,572	1,683,601	6.2%
Finance	983,228	1,017,000	1,111,475	1,154,223	4,265,926	15.7%
Public Works	637,261	664,969	720,382	748,089	2,770,702	10.2%
Interfund Transfers	390,471	407,448	441,403	316,000	1,555,322	5.7%
Total Expenditures	**$ 6,723,174**	**$ 6,449,988**	**$ 7,097,822**	**$ 6,923,954**	**$ 27,194,938**	
Average Expenditure	$ 840,397	$ 806,248	$ 887,228	$ 865,494	$ 3,399,367	
Lowest Expenditure	$ 321,816	$ 328,064	$ 363,792	$ 316,000	$ 1,399,202	
Highest Expenditure	$ 2,472,333	$ 2,123,305	$ 2,292,524	$ 2,076,218	$ 8,964,380	

Aspen Falls

Expenditure Details

Department	Department Detail	1st Qtr	2nd Qtr	3rd Qtr	4th Qtr
Legislative	City Council	$ 54,971	$ 57,360	$ 62,140	$ 64,530
	City Attorney	80,501	84,001	91,001	94,501
	City Clerk	186,347	194,448	210,652	218,755
City Manager	Administration	232,254	242,352	262,548	272,646
	Contract Services	38,571	40,248	43,603	45,280
	Community Relations	124,201	129,600	140,401	145,801
	Human Resources	97,176	101,401	109,850	114,075
	Risk Management	314,479	328,153	355,499	369,171
City Development	Administration	202,883	211,705	229,347	238,168
	Building Services	230,161	240,169	260,183	270,189
	Development Services	254,656	265,728	287,872	298,944
	Economic Development	13,456	14,040	15,210	15,796
City Services	Administrative	215,649	225,025	243,776	253,152
	Code Enforcement	274,413	286,345	310,207	322,137
	Public Safety	2,399,522	2,503,848	2,712,502	2,816,830
	Recreation Services	582,752	608,088	658,762	684,100
Engineering	Administrative	103,385	107,881	116,870	121,365
	Capital Improvement	128,018	133,584	144,716	150,283
	Inspection Services	97,014	101,233	109,668	113,887
	Land Development Services	81,812	85,369	92,482	96,040
Finance	Administrative	487,117	508,296	550,655	571,833
	Non-Departmental	18,332	19,128	20,723	21,520
	Development Program	477,779	498,553	540,098	560,871
Public Works	Administrative	200,698	209,425	226,876	235,602
	Facility Maintenance	268,663	280,345	303,707	315,388
	Other Maintenance	167,900	175,201	189,801	197,101
Interfund Transfers	Capital Projects	268,157	279,817	303,134	314,794
	Operating Transfers	122,315	127,632	138,268	143,586
	Total	**$ 7,723,181**	**$ 8,058,973**	**$ 8,730,551**	**$ 9,066,344**
	Average	$ 275,828	$ 287,820	$ 311,805	$ 323,798
	Minimum	$ 13,456	$ 14,040	$ 15,210	$ 15,796
	Maximum	$ 2,399,522	$ 2,503,848	$ 2,712,502	$ 2,816,830

▶ The ***Text wrap*** format displays text on multiple lines within a cell.

1. Start **Excel 2016**, open the student data file **exl02_Expenditures**, and then compare your screen with **Figure 1**.

   When columns in a worksheet are not wide enough, the labels in the cells will be truncated and values will display as # characters.

2. On the **File tab**, click **Save As**. On the **Save As** page, click the **Browse** button. Navigate to the location where you are saving your files. Click **New folder**, type Excel Chapter 2 and then press Enter two times. In the **File name** box, name the workbook Last_First_exl02_Expenditures and then press Enter.

3. Verify **Expenditures** is the active worksheet. Click the **Insert tab**, and then in the **Text group**, click the **Header & Footer** button. In the **Navigation group**, click the **Go to Footer** button. Click just above the word **Footer**, and then in the **Header & Footer Elements group**, click the **File Name** button. Click a cell above the footer. On the status bar, click the **Normal** button, and then press Ctrl + Home.

4. Click cell **B2**. Point at the fill handle to display the + pointer, and then drag right through cell **E2** to AutoFill the labels. Compare your screen with **Figure 2**.

   Excel's AutoFill feature can generate a series of values into adjacent cells. A ***series*** is a group of numbers, text, dates, or time periods that come one after another in succession. For example, the months *January, February, March* are a series. Likewise, *1st Quarter, 2nd Quarter, 3rd Quarter,* and *4th Quarter* form a series.

■ **Continue to the next page to complete the skill**

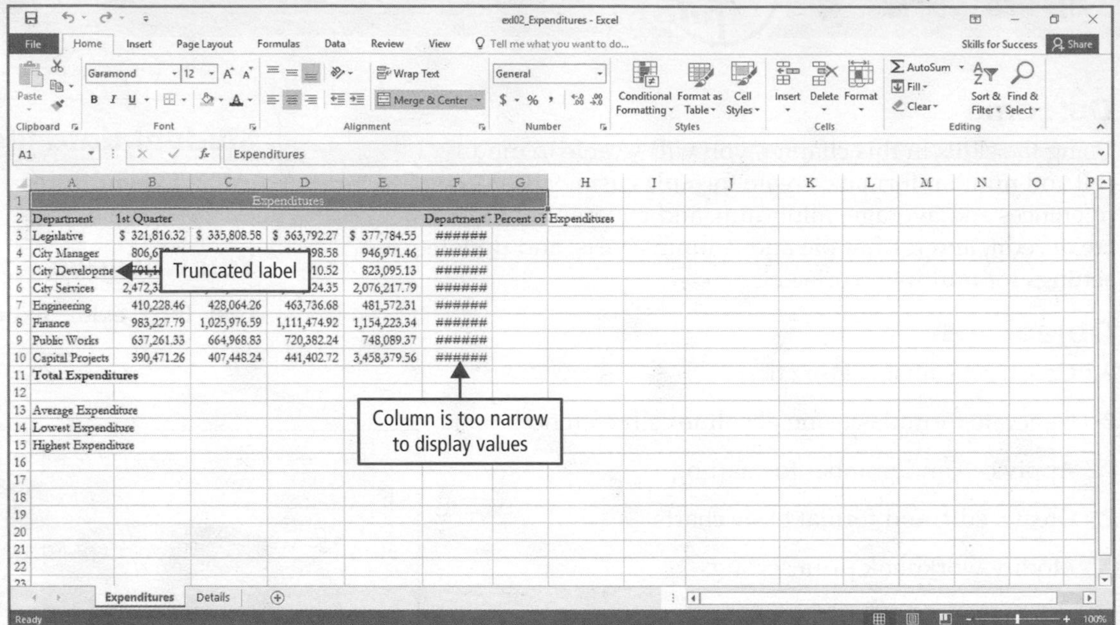

Figure 1 Excel 2016, Windows 10, Microsoft Corporation

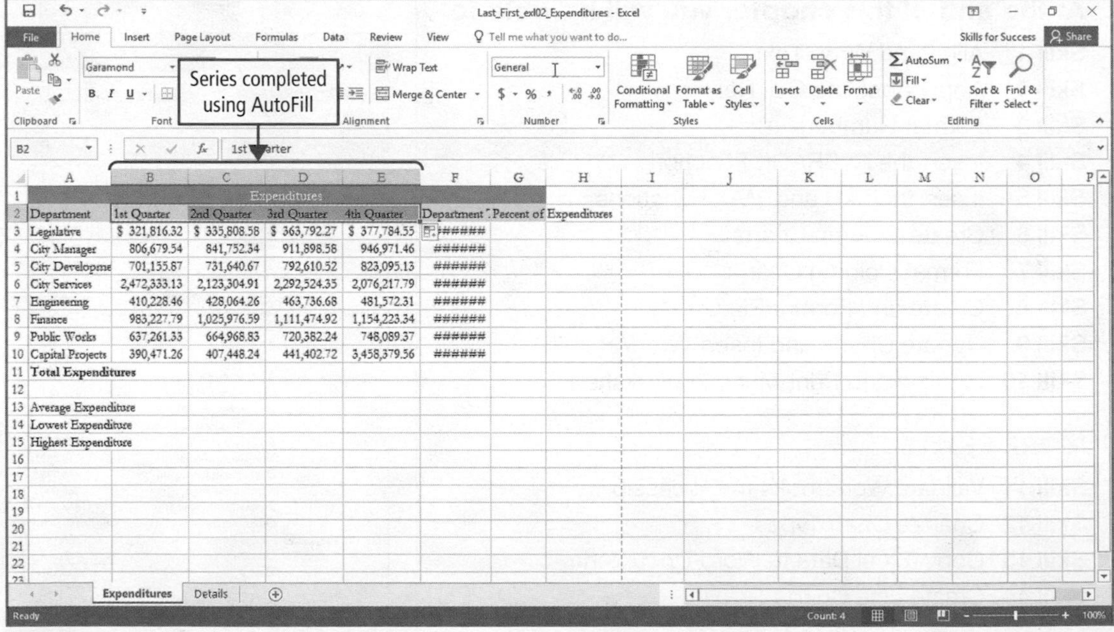

Figure 2 Excel 2016, Windows 10, Microsoft Corporation

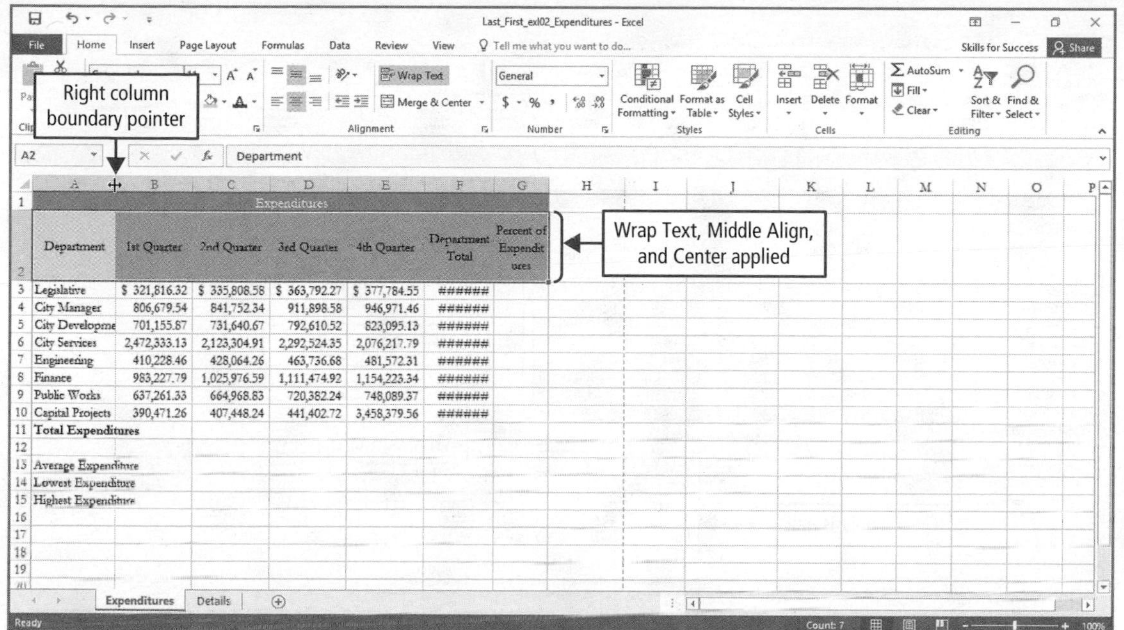

Excel 2016, Windows 10, Microsoft Corporation

Figure 3

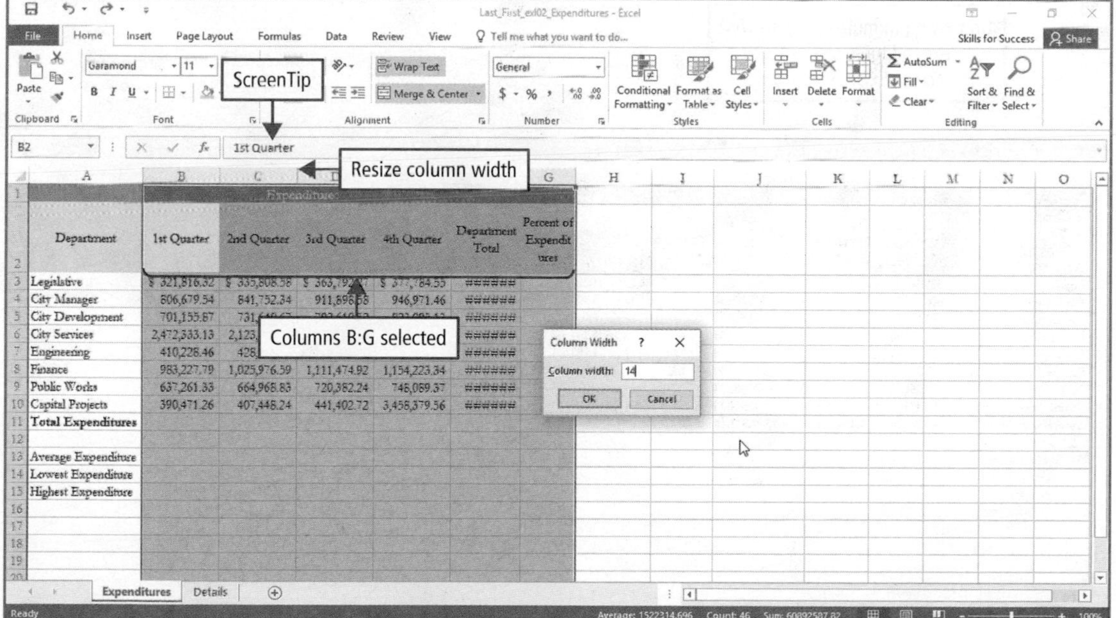

Excel 2016, Windows 10, Microsoft Corporation

Figure 4

5. Select the range **A2:G2**. On the **Home tab**, in the **Alignment group**, click the **Wrap Text** button, the **Middle Align** button, and the **Center** button.

Obj 2.2.4 C

MOS
Obj 2.2.2 C

6. In the column heading area, point to the right boundary of column **A** to display the pointer, as shown in **Figure 3**.
7. With the pointer displayed, double-click to **AutoFit** the column.

   AutoFit —automatically change the column width to accommodate the longest entry.

8. In the column heading area, click the column **B** heading, and then drag right through column **G** to select columns **B:G**. Right-click the boundary of column G to display the Column Width box, type 14 in the box, and then compare your screen with **Figure 4**. Click OK to change the width.
9. Select the range **A3:A10**, and then in the **Alignment group**, click the **Increase Indent** button.
10. **Save** the file.

- **You have completed Skill 1 of 10**

- The Quick Analysis button is used to apply conditional formatting or to insert charts and totals.
- Excel uses rules to check for formula errors. When a formula breaks a rule, the cell displays an ***error indicator***—a green triangle that indicates a possible error in a formula.
- An ***absolute cell reference*** is a cell reference address that remains the same when it is copied or filled to other cells. To make a cell reference absolute, insert a dollar sign ($) before the row and column references.

Obj 5.1.4 C

1. Select **B3:F10**, click the **Quick Analysis** button, and then compare your screen with **Figure 1**.
2. In the **Quick Analysis** gallery, click **Totals**, and then click the first option—**SUM**—to insert column totals.
3. Click cell **G3**, and then type =F3/F11 On the formula bar, click the **Enter** button. Double-click cell **G3** to display the range finder, and then compare your screen with **Figure 2**.

   The ***range finder*** outlines all of the cells referenced in a formula. It is useful for verifying which cells are used in a formula and for editing formulas.
4. Press Esc to close the range finder. Point to the **G3** fill handle, and then AutoFill the formula down through **G10** to display error values.

   Error values—messages that display whenever a formula or function cannot perform its calculations. The #DIV/0! error value displays in a cell whenever the underlying formula attempts to divide by zero.

■ **Continue to the next page to complete the skill**

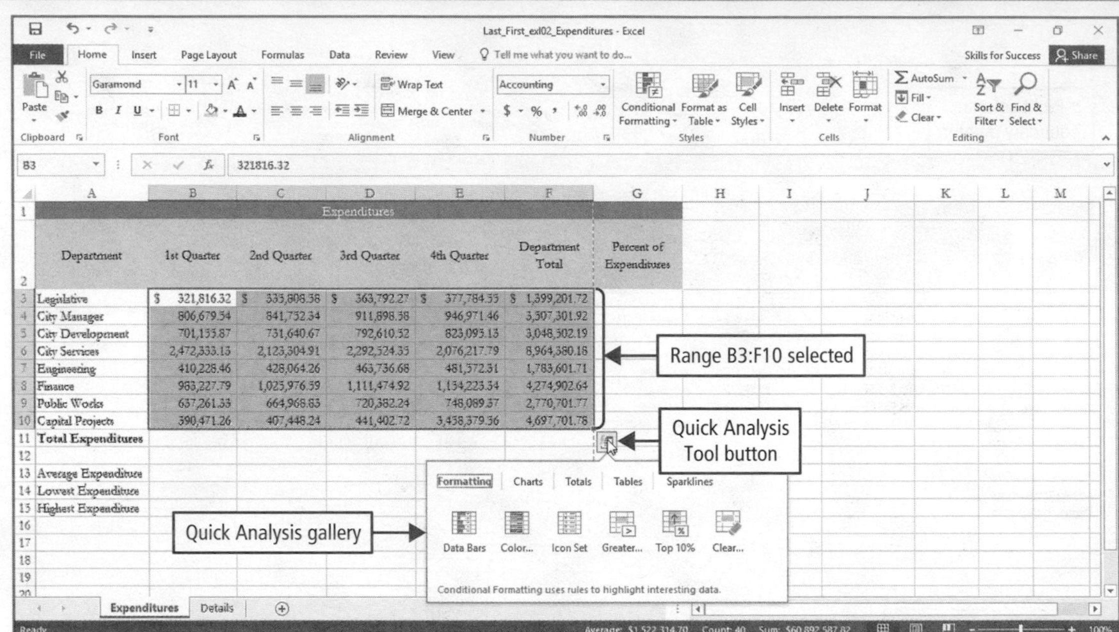

Figure 1

Excel 2016, Windows 10, Microsoft Corporation

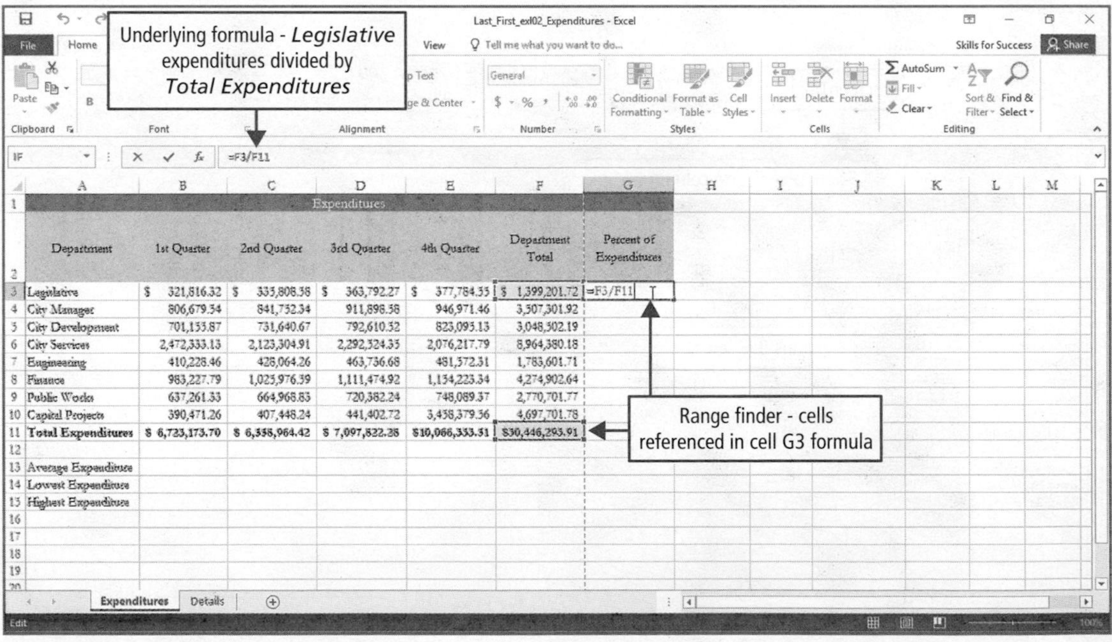

Figure 2

Excel 2016, Windows 10, Microsoft Corporation

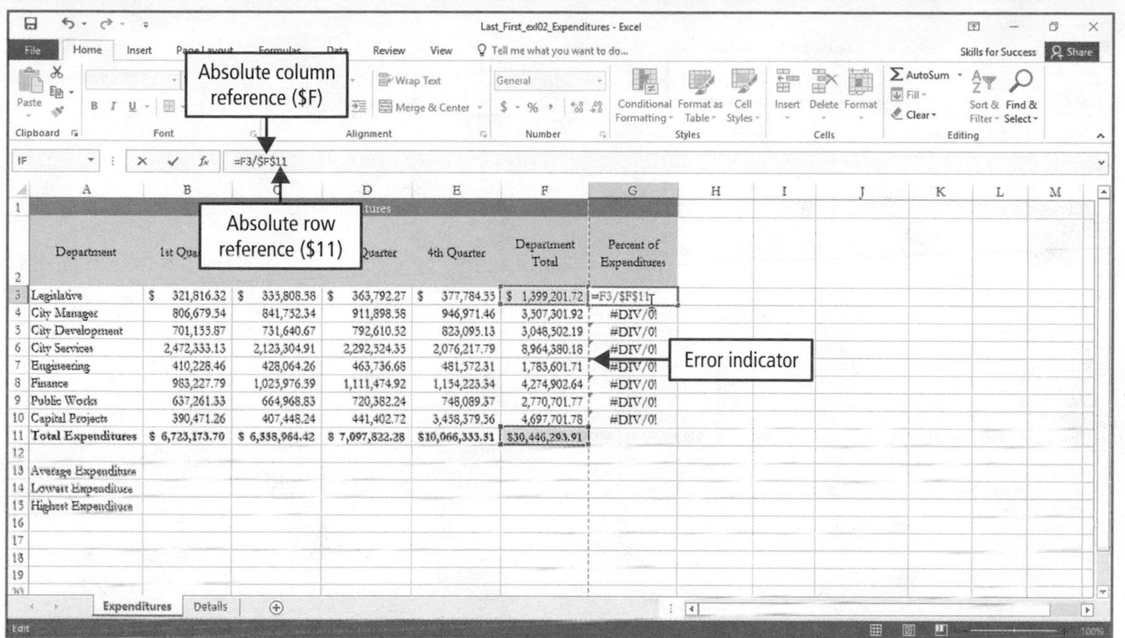

Excel 2016, Windows 10, Microsoft Corporation

Figure 3

Excel 2016, Windows 10, Microsoft Corporation

Figure 4

5. Click cell **G4**. To the left of the cell, point to the **Error Message** button [!] to display the ScreenTip—*The formula or function used is dividing by zero or empty cells.*

6. Double-click cell **G4** to display the range finder.

   The formula was copied with a relative cell reference. In the copied formula, the cell reference to cell F4 is correct, but the formula is dividing by the value in cell F12, an empty cell. In this calculation, the divisor must be cell F11.

7. Press Esc, and then double-click cell **G3**. In the formula, click after the reference to cell F11, and then press F4 to insert a dollar sign ($) before the column reference *F* and the row reference *11*, as shown in **Figure 3**.

Obj 4.1.1 C

   The dollar signs are used to indicate an absolute cell reference.

8. On the formula bar, click the **Enter** button [✓], and then AutoFill the formula in cell **G3** down through cell **G10**.

9. Click cell **G4**, and verify that the divisor refers to cell *$F$11*, as shown in **Figure 4**.

   The cell reference for the row *City Manager Department Total* changed relative to its row; however, the value used as the divisor—*Total Expenditures* in cell F11—remains absolute.

10. Press the [↓] two times and verify the contents of each cell. Notice that the divisor remains constant—$F$11—while the dividend changes relative to the row.

11. **Save** [💾] the file.

■ **You have completed Skill 2 of 10**

- A ***number format*** is a specific way that Excel displays numbers; for example, the number of decimals or whether commas and special symbols, such as dollar signs, display.
- By default, Excel displays the ***General format***—a number format that does not display commas or trailing zeros to the right of a decimal point.

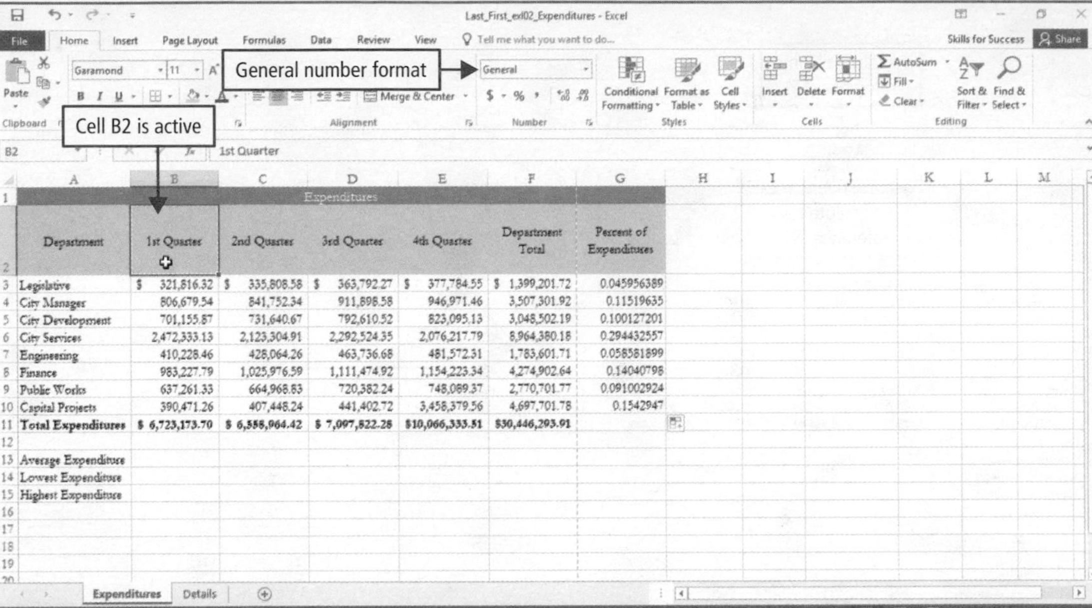

Figure 1 Excel 2016, Windows 10, Microsoft Corporation

1. Click cell **B2**, and then on the **Home tab**, in the **Number group**, notice that *General* displays. Compare your screen with **Figure 1**.
2. Select the range **B3:F3**, press Ctrl, and then select the range **B11:F11**. In the **Number group**, click the **Decrease Decimal** button two times to round the number and hide the decimals. Select the range **B4:F10**. In the **Number group**, click the **Decrease Decimal** button two times. Click cell **B6**, and then compare your screen with **Figure 2**.

   The Decrease Decimal button hides the displayed value decimals. The underlying value shows the decimals.

MOS Obj 2.2.5 C

3. Select the range **G3:G10**. In the **Number group**, click the **Percent Style** button %, and then click the **Increase Decimal** button one time to add one decimal to the applied Percent Style. In the **Alignment group**, click the **Center** button.

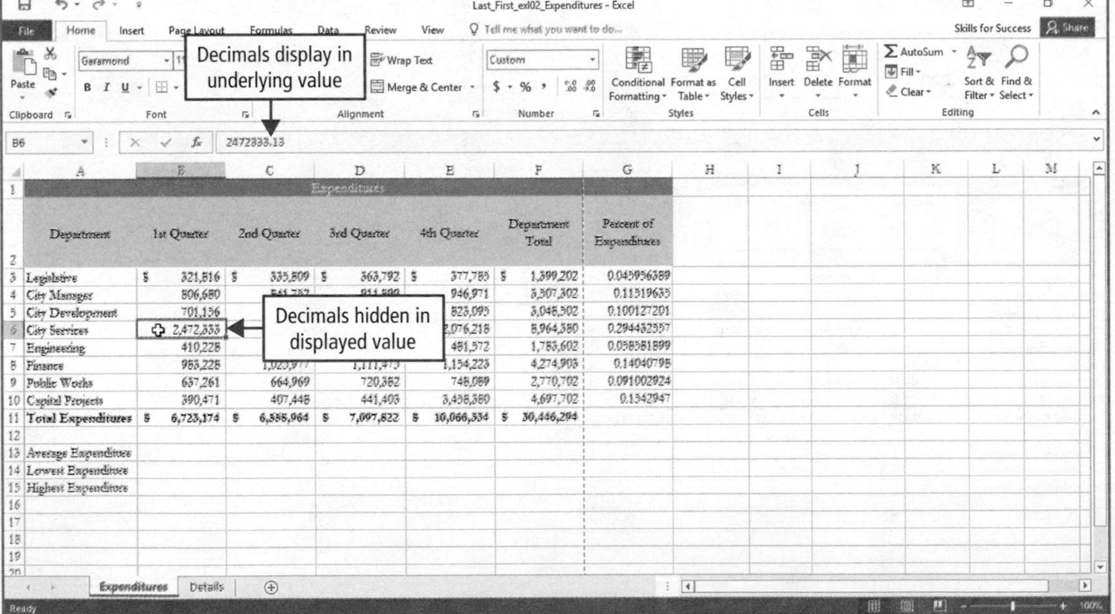

Figure 2 Excel 2016, Windows 10, Microsoft Corporation

■ Continue to the next page to complete the skill

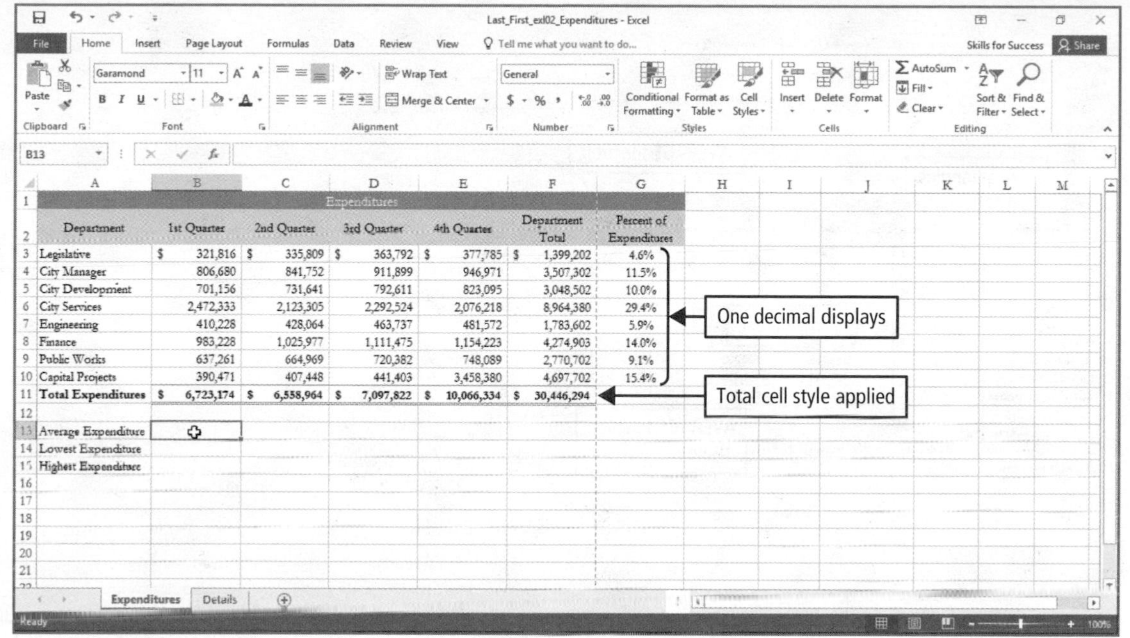

Excel 2016, Windows 10, Microsoft Corporation

Figure 3

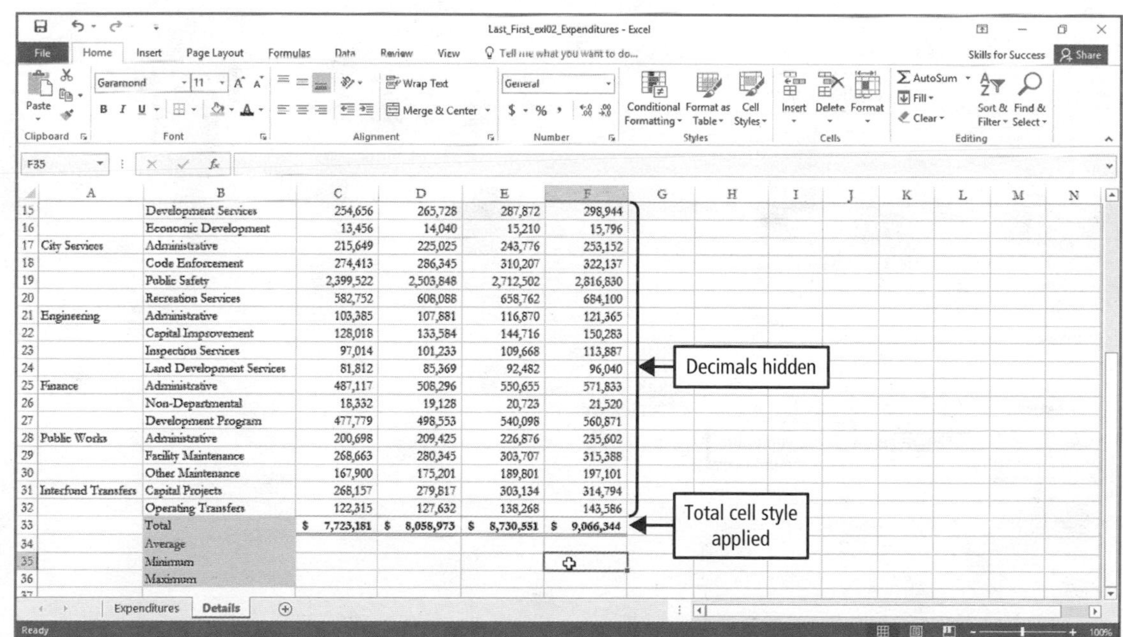

Excel 2016, Windows 10, Microsoft Corporation

Figure 4

4. Select the range **B11:F11**. In the **Styles group**, click the **Cell Styles** button, and then under **Titles and Headings**, click **Total**. Click cell **B13**, and then compare your screen with **Figure 3**.
5. Along the bottom of the Excel window, notice the worksheet tabs. Click the **Details** worksheet tab to make it the active worksheet.

   Worksheet tabs, the labels along the lower border of the workbook window that identify each worksheet.
6. Click cell **C5**. Hold down the Ctrl + Shift keys. With both keys held down, press the ↓ one time and the → one time to select the range C5:F32.
7. With the range **C5:F32** selected, click the **Quick Analysis** button. In the **Quick Analysis** gallery, click **Totals**, and then click the first option—**SUM**.
8. Select the range **C5:F5**, press Ctrl, and then select the range **C33:F33**. In the **Number group**, click the **Decrease Decimal** button two times. Select the range **C6:F32**. In the **Number group**, click the **Decrease Decimal** button two times.
9. Select the range **C33:F33**, and then apply the **Total** cell style. Click cell **F35**, and then compare your screen with **Figure 4**.

Obj 2.2.7 C

10. **Save** the file.

■ **You have completed Skill 3 of 10**

SKILL 4: Insert the AVERAGE Function

- ▶ ***Statistical functions*** are predefined formulas that describe a collection of data—for example, averages, maximums, and minimums.
- ▶ The ***AVERAGE function*** adds a group of values and then divides the result by the number of values in the group.

Obj 4.1.5 C

1. Click the **Expenditures** worksheet tab, and then click cell **B13**. On the **Home tab**, in the **Editing group**, click the **AutoSum arrow**, and then in the list of functions, click **Average**. Look in the formula bar and in cell B13 to verify that the range *B3:B12* is the suggested range of cells that will be averaged, as shown in **Figure 1**.

   The range in parentheses is the function ***argument***—the values that a function uses to perform operations or calculations. The arguments each function uses are specific to that function. Common arguments include numbers, text, cell references, and range names.

   When data is above or to the left of a selected cell, the function argument will automatically be entered. Often, you will need to edit the argument range.

2. With the function argument still active in cell B13, click cell **B3**. On the range finder, click a bottom corner sizing handle, and then drag down to select the argument range **B3:B10**, to exclude the *Total Expenditures* value in cell B11. On the formula bar, click the **Enter** button ✓ to display the result *$840,397*. Compare your screen with **Figure 2**.

■ **Continue to the next page to complete the skill**

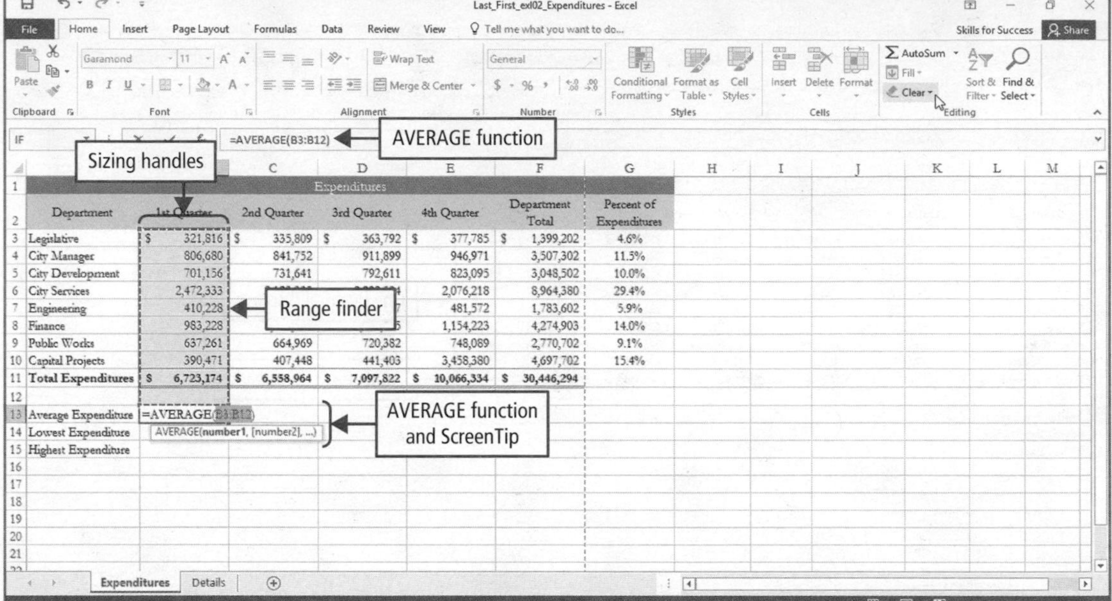

Figure 1

Excel 2016, Windows 10, Microsoft Corporation

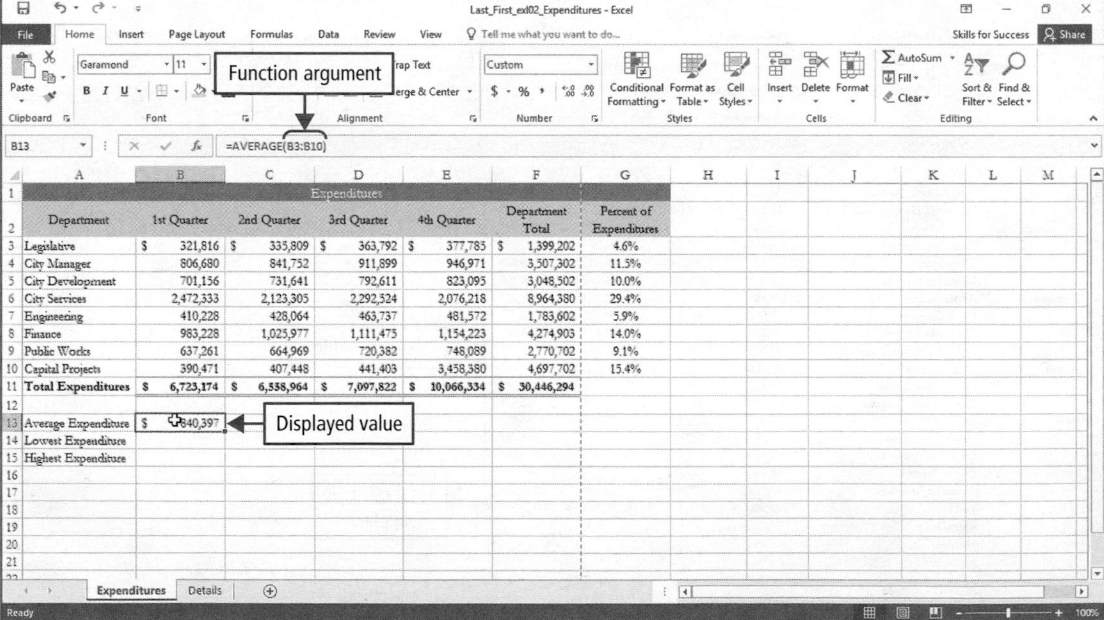

Figure 2

Excel 2016, Windows 10, Microsoft Corporation

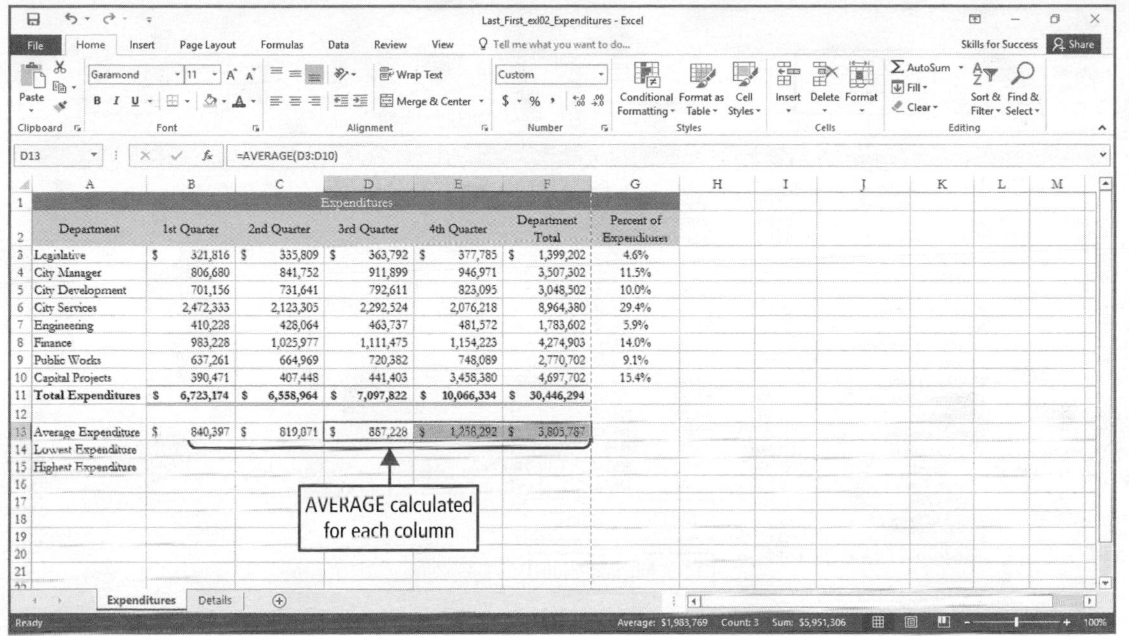

Excel 2016, Windows 10, Microsoft Corporation

Figure 3

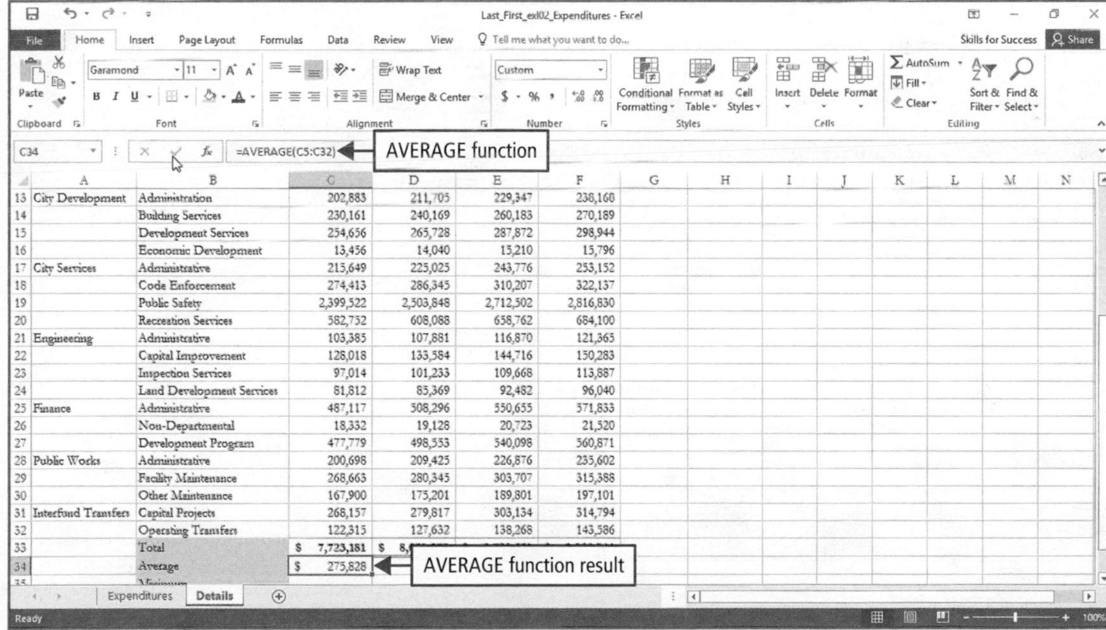

Excel 2016, Windows 10, Microsoft Corporation

Figure 4

3. Click cell **C13**. In the **Editing group**, click the **AutoSum arrow**, and then in the list of functions, click **Average**. In the formula bar and in the cell, notice that Excel proposes to average the value in cell *B13*, not the values in column C.
4. With cell reference **B13** highlighted in the function argument, click cell **C3**, and then use the range finder sizing handle to select the range **C3:C10**. On the formula bar, click the **Enter** button ✓ to display the result *$819,871*.
5. Click cell **D13**. Using the techniques just practiced, enter the **AVERAGE** function using the argument range **D3:D10**, and then on the formula bar, click the **Enter** button ✓.
6. Verify that cell *D13* is the active cell, and then AutoFill the function to the right through cell **F13**. Compare your sheet to **Figure 3**.
7. Click the **Details** worksheet tab, and then click cell **C34**. Enter the **AVERAGE** function using the argument range **C5:C32**. Do not include the *Total* value in cell *C33* in the function argument. Compare your sheet to **Figure 4**.
8. Display the worksheet footers, click in the left footer, and then click the **File Name** button. Click in the right footer, and then click the **Sheet Name** button. Click in a cell above the footer, and then press Ctrl + Home. Return to **Normal** view.
9. **Save** the file.

■ **You have completed Skill 4 of 10**

SKILL 5: Insert the MIN and MAX Functions

SKILL 2.5

- The ***MIN function*** returns the smallest value in a range of cells.
- The ***MAX function*** returns the largest value in a range of cells.

Obj 4.1.3 C

1. On the **Details** worksheet, click cell **C35**. Type =Mi and then in the **Formula AutoComplete** list, double-click **MIN**. With the insertion point blinking in the function argument, click cell **C32**, and then use the range finder top corner sizing handles to drag up and select the range **C5:C32**. Press Enter to display the result *$13,456*.

   The MIN function evaluates the range provided in the function argument—C5:C32—and then returns the lowest value—*$13,456*. Here, the *Total* and *Average* values in cells *C33* and *C34* should not be included in the argument range.

Obj 4.1.3 C

2. Verify that **C36** is the active cell. Type =Ma and then in the **Formula AutoComplete** list, double-click **MAX**. Using the technique just practiced, select the range **C5:C32**, and then on the formula bar, click the **Enter** button ✓ to display the result *$2,399,522*. Compare your screen with **Figure 1**.

   The MAX function evaluates all of the values in the range C5:C32 and then returns the highest value found in the range.

3. Select the range **C34:C36**. AutoFill the formulas to the right through column **F**, and then compare your screen with **Figure 2**.

   In this manner, you can AutoFill several different functions or formulas at the same time. Here, the different functions at the beginning of each row are filled across the columns.

■ **Continue to the next page to complete the skill**

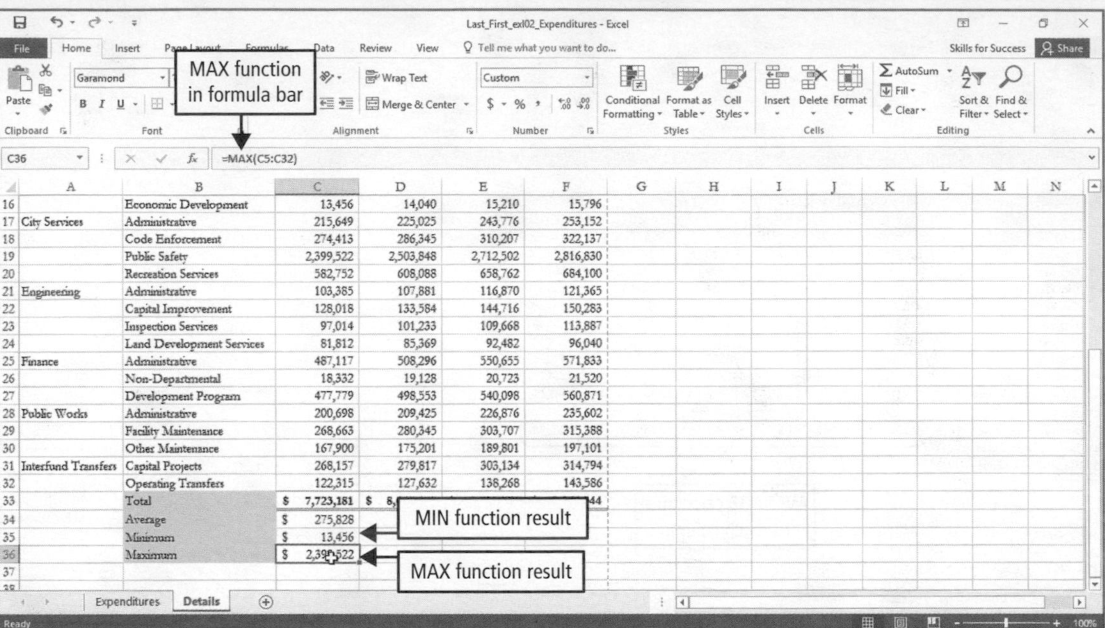

Figure 1

Excel 2016, Windows 10, Microsoft Corporation

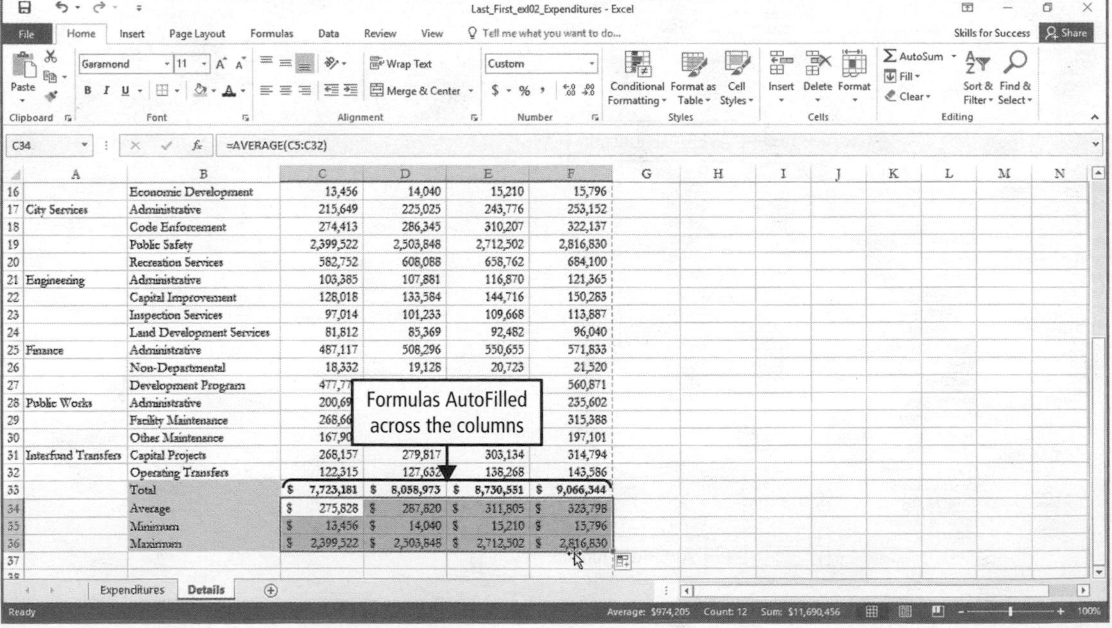

Figure 2

Excel 2016, Windows 10, Microsoft Corporation

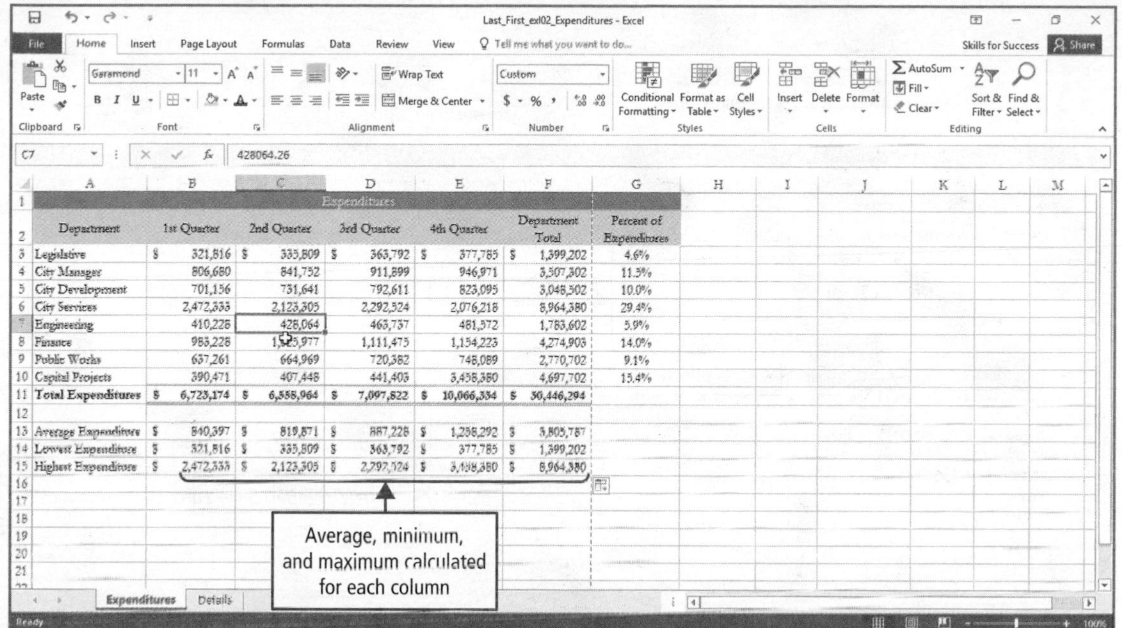

Excel 2016, Windows 10, Microsoft Corporation

Figure 3

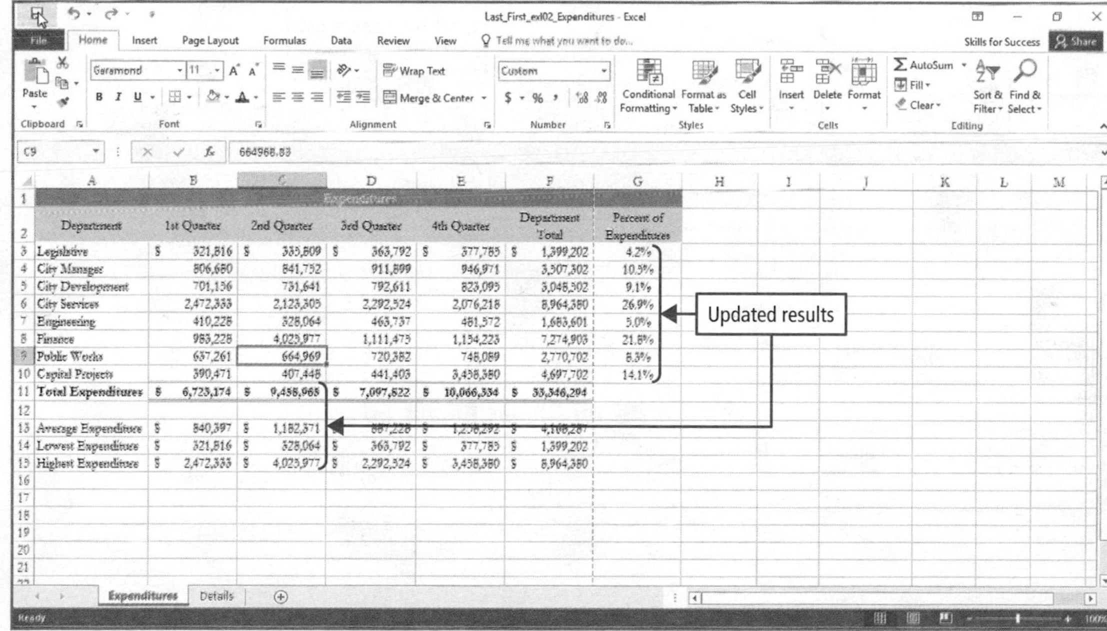

Excel 2016, Windows 10, Microsoft Corporation

Figure 4

4. Click the **Expenditures** worksheet tab. In cell **B14**, repeat the technique just practiced to insert the **MIN** function using the range **B3:B10** as the function argument in the parentheses. Verify that the result is *$321,816*.
5. In cell **B15**, insert the **MAX** function using the range **B3:B10** as the function argument. Verify that the result is *$2,472,333*. Take care that the argument range does not include the cells with the total expenditures or average expenditures.
6. AutoFill the formulas in **B14:B15** to the right through column **F**. Review the functions, and verify that the lowest and highest values in each column were selected from each of the ranges for the MIN and MAX functions. Click cell **C7**, and then compare your screen with **Figure 3**.
7. With cell **C7** as the active cell, type 328064 and then press Enter. In cell **C8**, type 4025977 and then press Enter. Verify that the MIN and MAX values in cells **C14** and **C15** and the SUM and AVERAGE functions were automatically updated. Compare your screen with **Figure 4**.
8. **Save** the file.

■ **You have completed Skill 5 of 10**

SKILL 6: Create Column Charts

SKILL 2.6

- A ***chart*** is a graphical representation of data used to show comparisons, patterns, and trends.
- A ***column chart*** is useful for illustrating comparisons among related numbers.

Obj 5.1.4 C

1. On the **Expenditures** worksheet, select the range **A2:E10**—do *not* include the *Department Total* column or the *Total Expenditures* row in your selection. Click the **Quick Analysis** button, and then in the **Quick Analysis** gallery, click **Charts**. Compare your screen with **Figure 1**.

Obj 5.1.1 C

2. In the **Quick Analysis** gallery, click the third chart—**Clustered Column**—to insert the chart and display the *Chart Tools* contextual tabs. Compare your screen with **Figure 2**.

When you insert a chart in this manner, an ***embedded chart***—a chart that is placed on the worksheet containing the data—is created. Embedded charts are beneficial when you want to view or print a chart with its source data.

An ***axis*** is a line bordering the chart plot area that is used as a frame of reference for measurement. The ***category axis*** is the axis that displays the category labels. A ***category label*** is nonnumeric text that identifies the categories of data. Here, the worksheet's row labels—the department names in A3:A10—are used for the category labels.

The ***value axis*** is the axis that displays the worksheet's numeric data.

The ***y-axis*** is the vertical axis of a chart, and the ***x-axis*** is the horizontal axis of a chart.

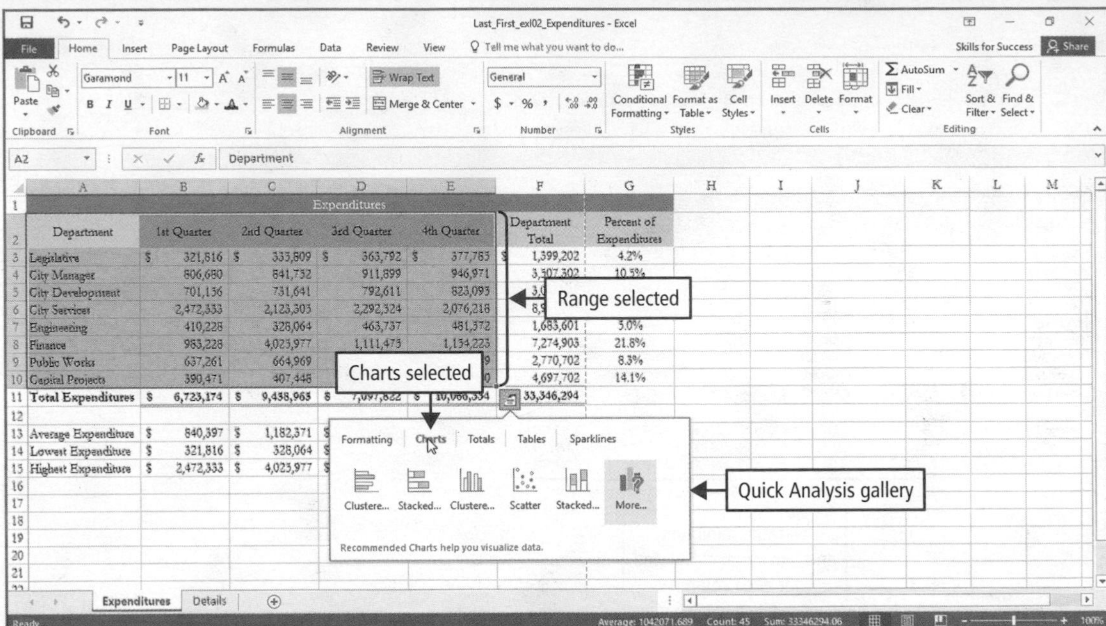

Figure 1

Excel 2016, Windows 10, Microsoft Corporation

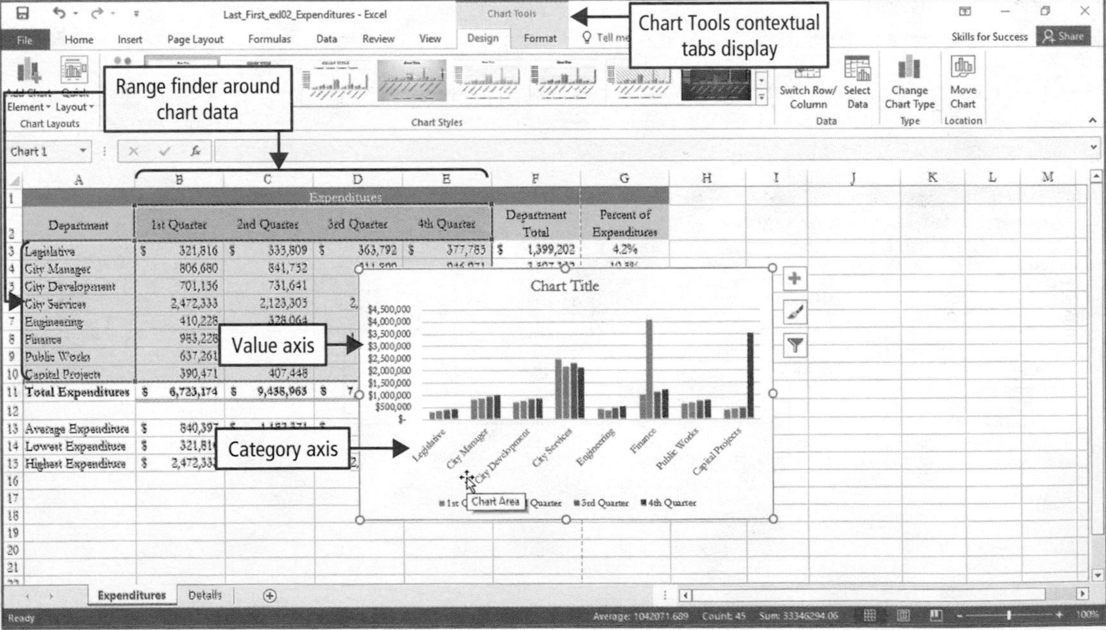

Figure 2

Excel 2016, Windows 10, Microsoft Corporation

■ Continue to the next page to complete the skill

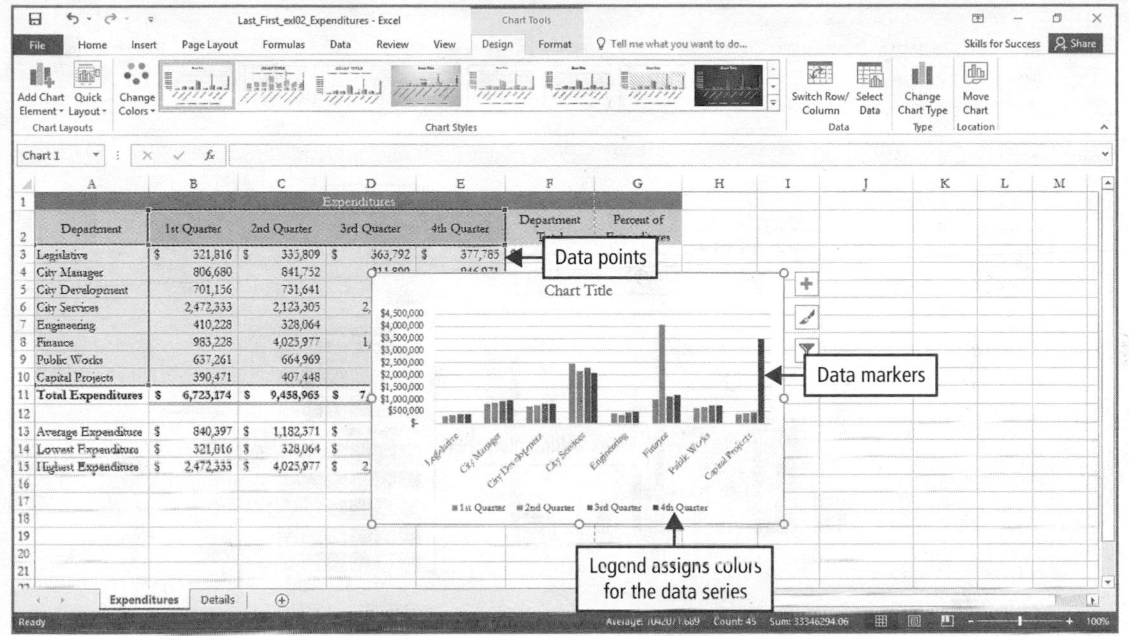

Excel 2016, Windows 10, Microsoft Corporation

Figure 3

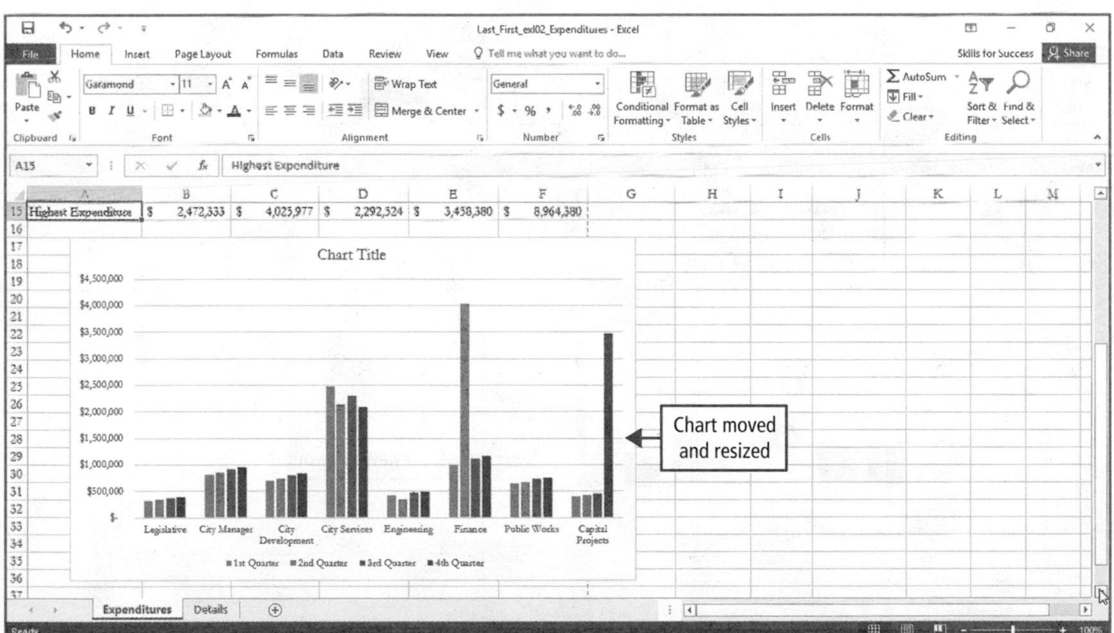

Excel 2016, Windows 10, Microsoft Corporation

Figure 4

3. On the left side of the chart, locate the numerical scale, and then on the bottom, locate the quarters displayed in the legend. Compare your screen with **Figure 3**.

   In the worksheet, each cell in the blue range finder is referred to as a ***data point***—a chart value that originates in a worksheet cell. Each data point is represented in a chart by a ***data marker***—a column, a bar, an area, a dot, a pie slice, or another symbol that represents a single data point.

   Data points that are related to one another form a ***data series***, and each data series has a unique color or pattern represented in the chart ***legend***—a box that identifies the patterns or colors that are assigned to the data series or categories in the chart. Here, each quarter is a different data series, and the legend shows the color assigned to each quarter.

4. With the chart selected, point to the upper border of the chart to display the pointer, and then move the chart to position its upper left corner in the middle of cell **A17**. If you are working with a touch screen, you can touch the chart and slide it to the correct position.

5. Scroll down to display row **36**. Point to the lower right corner of the chart to display the pointer, and then drag to resize the chart until the lower right chart corner is in the middle of cell **G36**. Click cell **G15**, and then compare your screen with **Figure 4**.

Obj 5.2.1 C

6. **Save** the file.

■ **You have completed Skill 6 of 10**

- You can modify the overall look of a chart by applying a ***chart layout***—a prebuilt set of chart elements that can include a title, a legend, or labels.
- You can modify the overall look of a chart by applying a ***chart style***—a prebuilt chart format that applies an overall visual look to a chart by modifying its graphic effects, colors, and backgrounds.

1. Click the border of the chart to select the chart and display the chart buttons.

Obj 5.2.3 C

2. To the right of the chart, click the **Chart Styles** button, and then click **Style 3**. At the top of the **Chart Styles** gallery, click the **Color tab**, and then under **Colorful**, click **Color 3**. Compare your screen with **Figure 1**.
3. Click the **Chart Styles** button to close the gallery.
4. On the **Design tab**, in the **Chart Layouts group**, click the **Quick Layout** button. Point at the different layouts to preview the layouts on the chart. Point at **Layout 9**, and then compare your screen with **Figure 2**.

Obj 5.2.2 C

5. In the **Quick Layout** gallery, click **Layout 9** to add the axes titles and to move the legend to the right side of the chart.

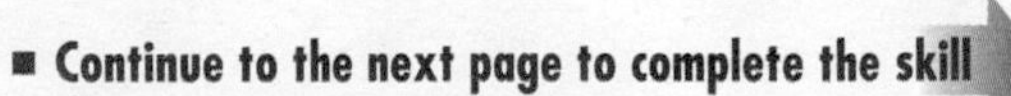
■ Continue to the next page to complete the skill

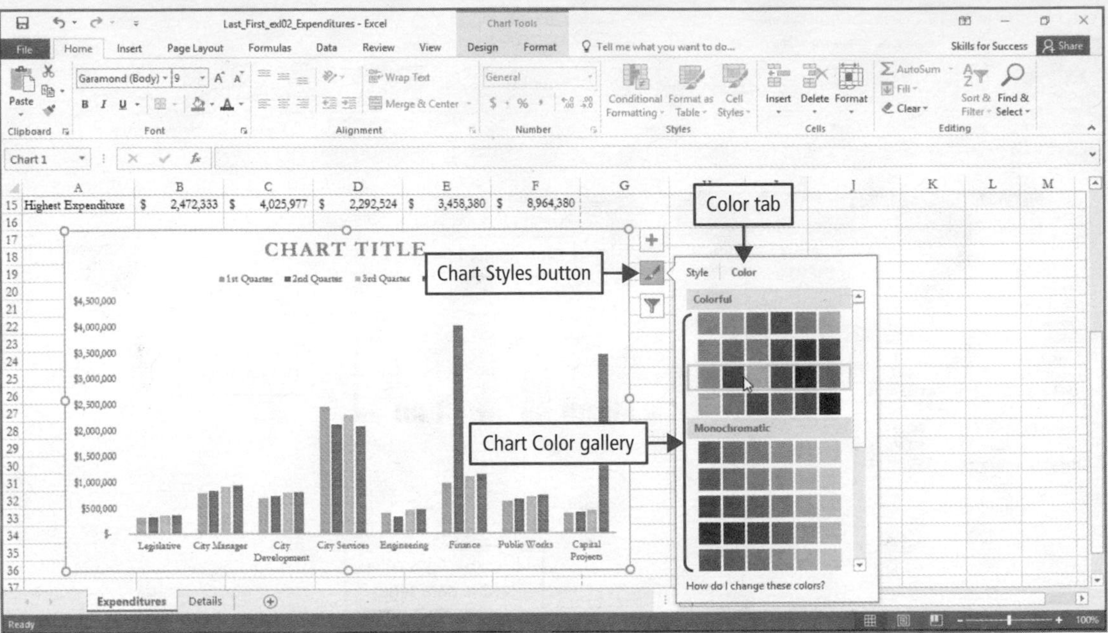

Figure 1

Excel 2016, Windows 10, Microsoft Corporation

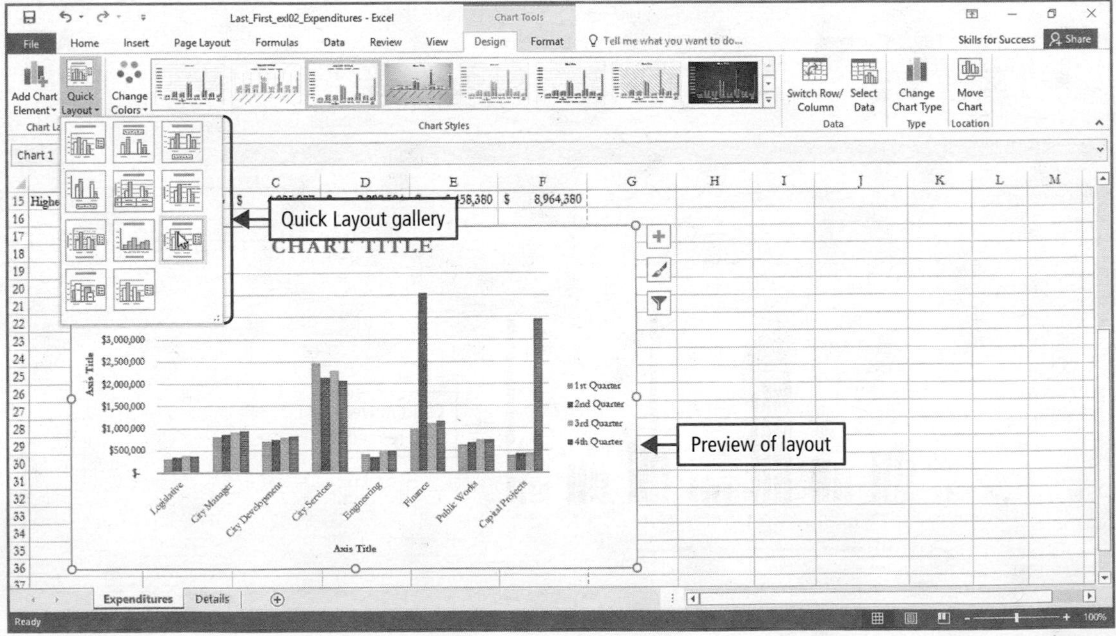

Figure 2

Excel 2016, Windows 10, Microsoft Corporation

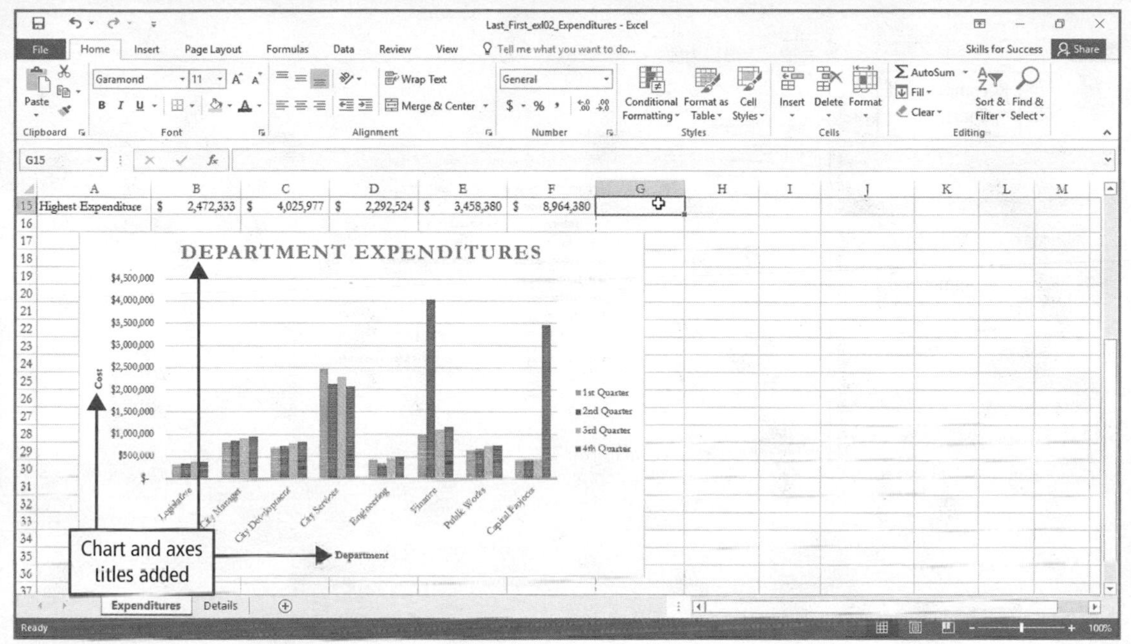

Excel 2016, Windows 10, Microsoft Corporation

Figure 3

6. At the top of the chart, click the text *Chart Title*, and then type Department Expenditures to insert the text into the formula bar. Press Enter to accept the text. Verify that your text replaced any text in the chart title.
7. Below the horizontal axis, click the text *Axis Title*, type Department and then press Enter.
8. To the left of the vertical axis, click the text *Axis Title*, type Cost and then press Enter.
9. Click cell **G15** to deselect the chart. **Save** the file, and then compare your screen with **Figure 3**.
10. Take a moment to examine the various types of charts available in Excel, as summarized in **Figure 4**.

- **You have completed Skill 7 of 10**

Chart Types Commonly Used in Excel	
Chart type	**Used to**
Column	Illustrate data changes over a period of time or illustrate comparisons among items.
Line	Illustrate trends over time, with time displayed along the horizontal axis and the data point values connected by a line.
Pie	Illustrate the relationship of parts to a whole.
Bar	Illustrate comparisons among individual items.
Area	Emphasize the magnitude of change over time.

Figure 4

 WATCH SKILL 2.8

- A ***pie chart*** displays the relationship of parts to a whole.
- A ***chart sheet*** is a workbook sheet that contains only a chart and is useful when you want to view a chart separately from the worksheet data.

1. Verify that *Expenditures* is the active sheet. Select the range **A2:A10**. Hold down Ctrl, and then select the nonadjacent range **F2:F10**.
2. On the **Insert tab**, in the **Charts group**, click the **Recommended Charts** button, and then compare your screen with **Figure 1**.

MOS Obj 5.1.1 C

3. In the **Insert Chart** dialog box, click the **Pie** thumbnail, and then click **OK**.

   Here, the row labels identify the slices of the pie chart, and the department totals are the data series that determine the size of each pie slice.

MOS Obj 5.2.4 C

4. On the **Design tab**, in the **Location group**, click the **Move Chart** button. In the **Move Chart** dialog box, select the **New sheet** option button. In the **New sheet** box, replace the highlighted text *Chart1* with Expenditure Chart as shown in **Figure 2**.
5. In the **Move Chart** dialog box, click **OK** to move the pie chart to a chart sheet.
6. On the **Design tab**, in the **Type group**, click the **Change Chart Type** button. In the **Change Chart Type** dialog box, click the **3-D Pie** thumbnail, and then click **OK**.

   The chart is changed from a two-dimensional chart to a three-dimensional chart. ***3-D***, which is short for ***three-dimensional***, refers to an image that appears to have all three spatial dimensions—length, width, and depth.

■ Continue to the next page to complete the skill

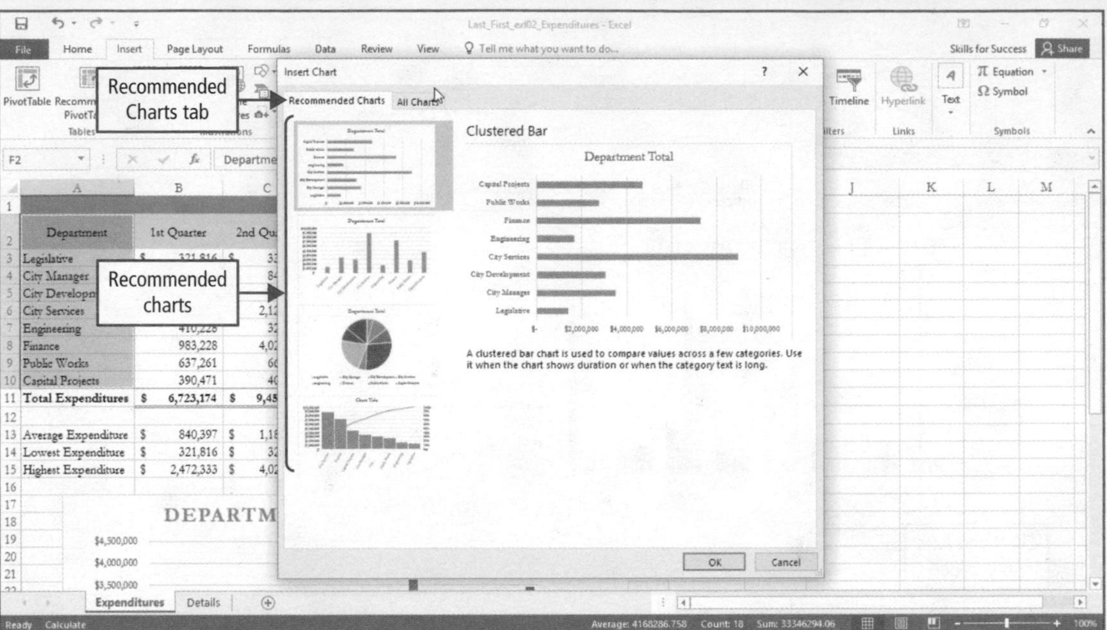

Figure 1

Excel 2016, Windows 10, Microsoft Corporation

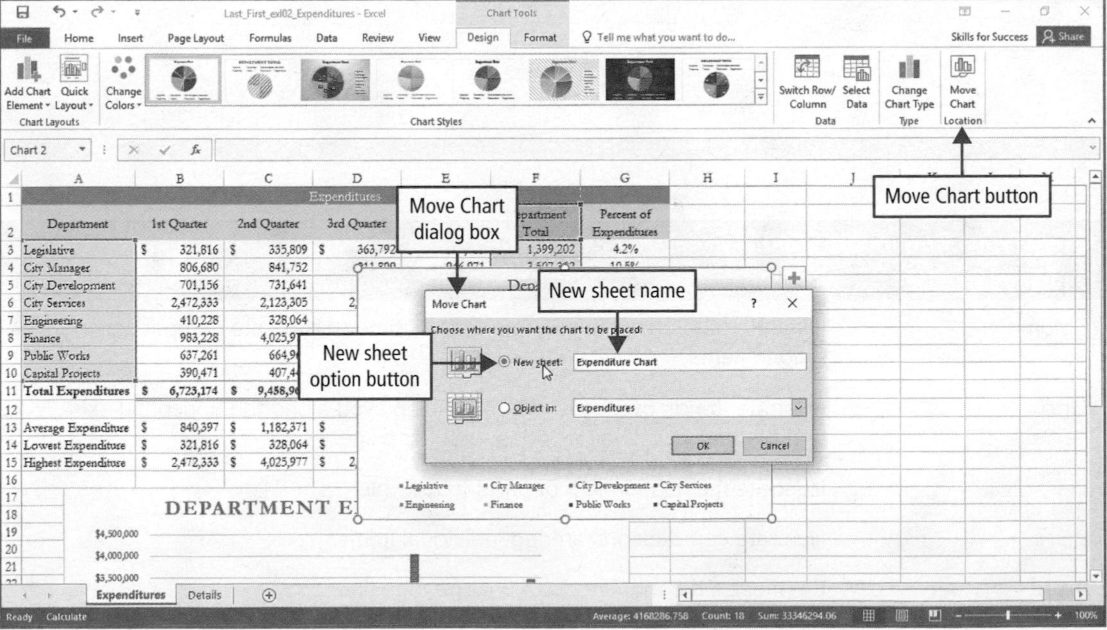

Figure 2

Excel 2016, Windows 10, Microsoft Corporation

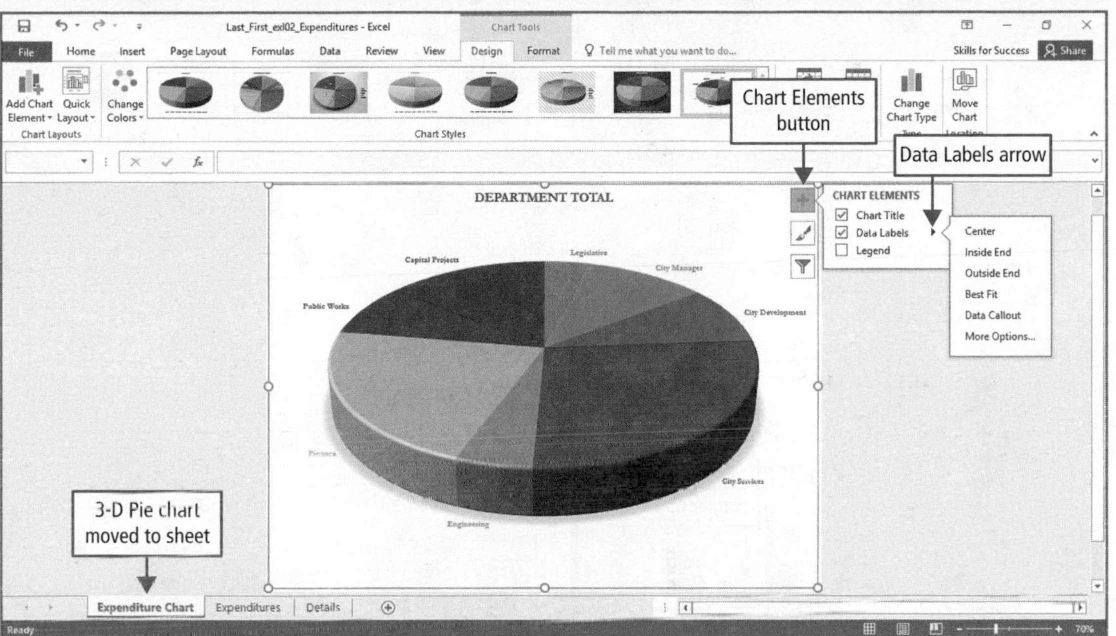

Excel 2016, Windows 10, Microsoft Corporation

Figure 3

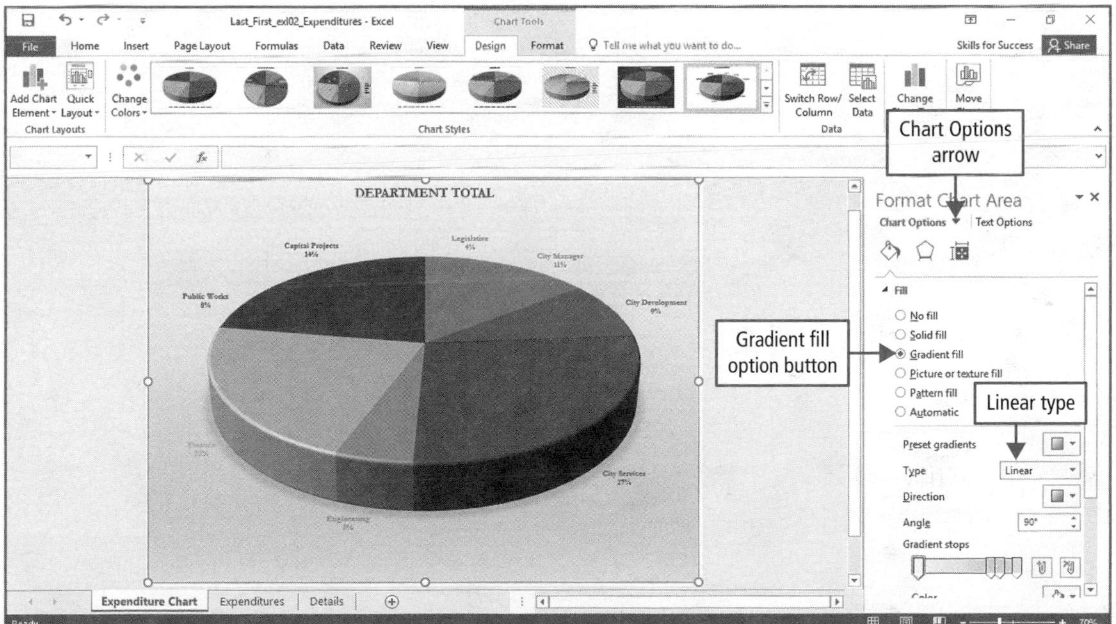

Excel 2016, Windows 10, Microsoft Corporation

Figure 4

7. To the right of the chart, click the **Chart Styles** button. In the **Chart Styles** gallery, scroll down, and then click **Style** 8. MOS Obj 5.2.3 C

8. To the right of the chart, click the **Chart Elements** button. Under **Chart Elements**, point at **Data Labels**, and then click the **Data Labels arrow**. Compare your screen with **Figure 3**. MOS Obj 5.2.2 C

9. In the **Data Labels** list, click **More Options** to open the Format Data Labels pane.

10. In the **Format Data Labels** pane, under **Label Contains**, select the **Percentage** check box. Verify that the **Category Name** check box is selected, and then clear any other check boxes.

11. At the top of the pane, click the **Label Options arrow**, and then click **Chart Area** to open the Format Chart Area pane. In the **Format Chart Area** pane, click the **Fill & Line** button, and then click **Fill**. Click the **Gradient fill** option button, and verify that the Type is Linear. Compare your screen with **Figure 4**.

12. **Close** the **Format Chart Area** pane.

13. On the **Insert tab**, in the **Text group**, click the **Header & Footer** button. In the **Page Setup** dialog box, click the **Custom Footer** button. Verify that the insertion point is in the **Left section** box, and then click the **Insert File Name** button. Click in the **Right section** box, and then click the **Insert Sheet Name** button. Click **OK** two times.

14. **Save** the file.

■ **You have completed Skill 8 of 10**

▶ A chart's data series and labels are linked to the source data in the worksheet. When worksheet values are changed, the chart is automatically updated.

1. Click the **Expenditures** worksheet tab to display the worksheet. Scroll as necessary to display row **8** at the top of the window and the chart at the bottom of the window. In the column chart, note the height of the *Finance* data marker for the 2nd Quarter and the *Capital Projects* data marker for the 4th Quarter.
2. Click cell **C8**. Type 1017000 and then press Enter to accept the new value. Notice the animation in the chart when changes are made to its source data. Compare your screen with **Figure 1**.
3. Click cell **E10**, type 316000 and then press Enter. In cell G10, the *Capital Projects* expenditure now represents 5.7% of the projected total.
4. Click the **Expenditure Chart** worksheet tab to display the pie chart. Verify that in the pie chart, the slice for *Capital Projects* displays 6%.

   When underlying data is changed, the pie chart percentages and pie slices are automatically recalculated and resized. On the chart, 5.7% is rounded up to 6%.
5. Right-click the *Capital Projects* data label to select all of the data labels, and then in the shortcut menu, click **Font**. In the **Size** box, type 11 Compare your screen with **Figure 2**, and then click **OK**.

■ Continue to the next page to complete the skill

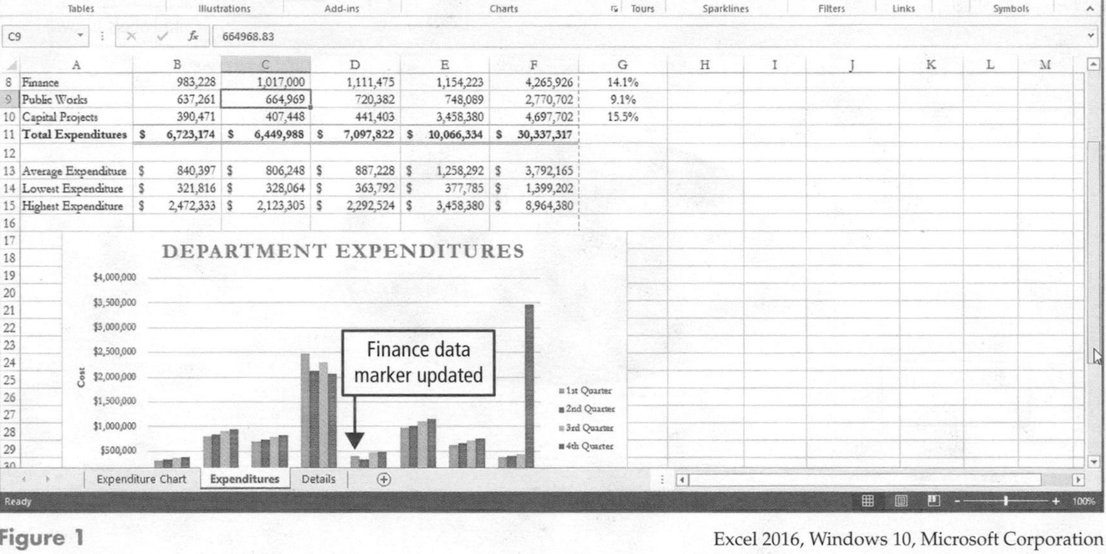

Figure 1 Excel 2016, Windows 10, Microsoft Corporation

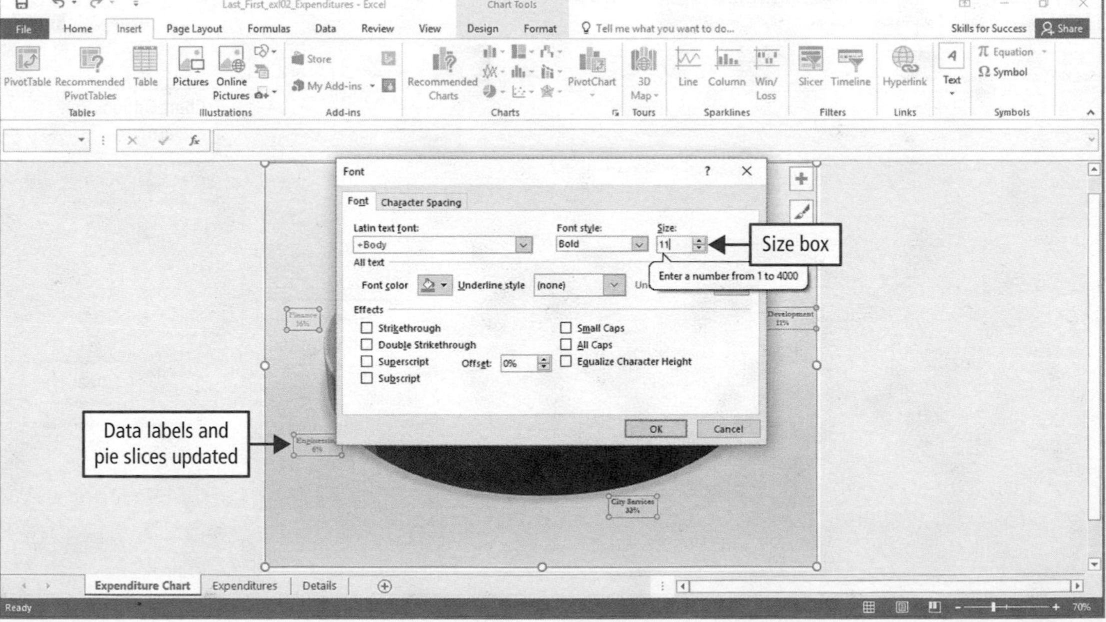

Figure 2 Excel 2016, Windows 10, Microsoft Corporation

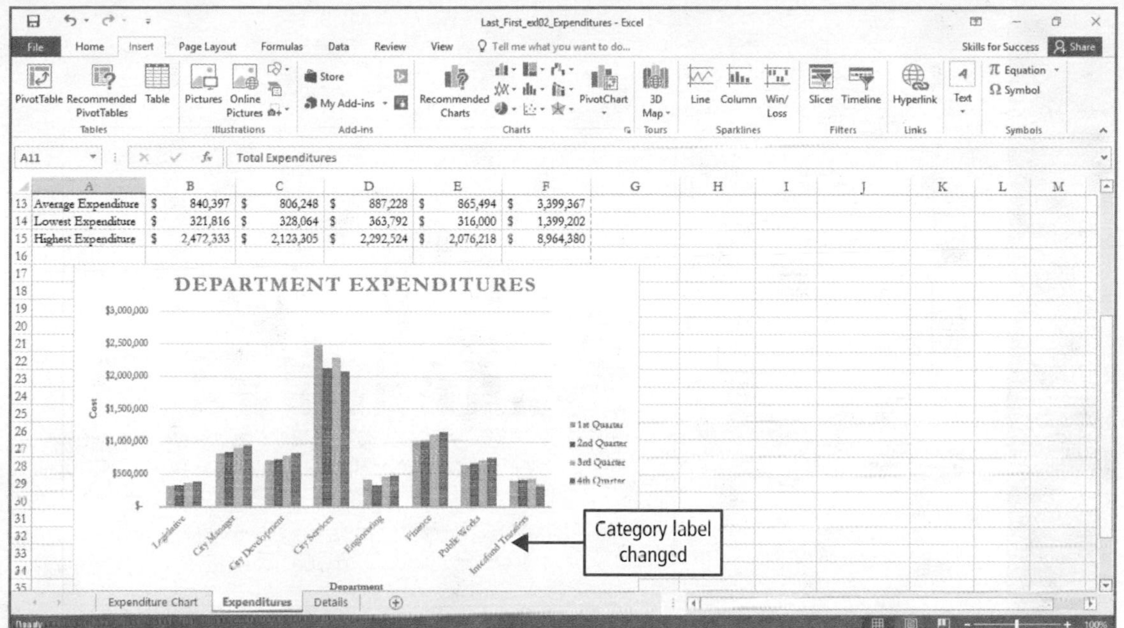

Excel 2016, Windows 10, Microsoft Corporation

Figure 3

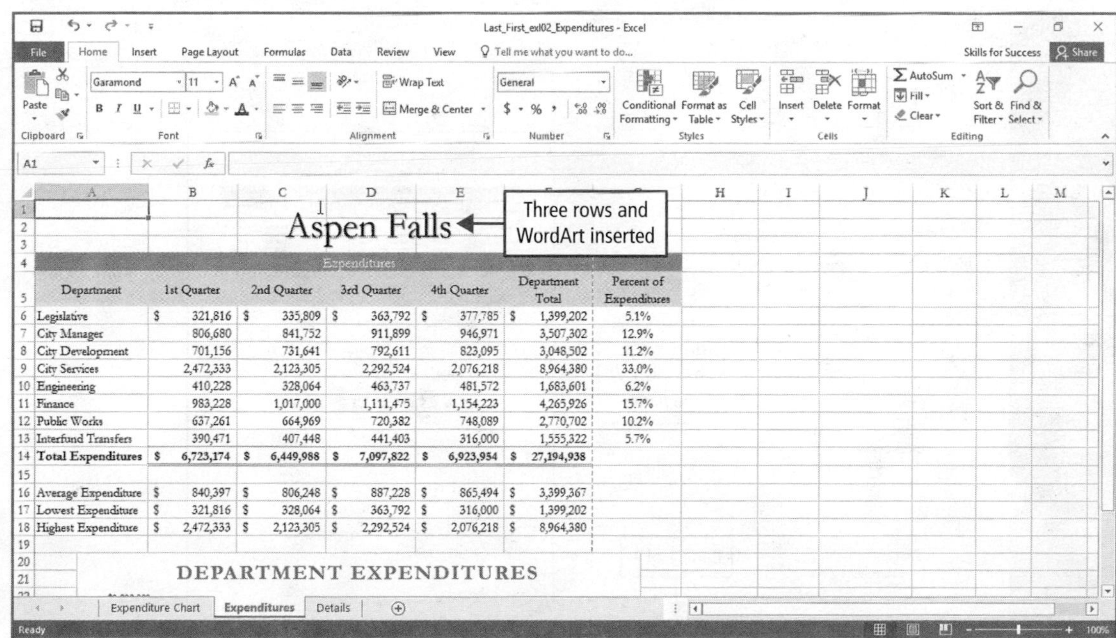

Excel 2016, Windows 10, Microsoft Corporation

Figure 4

6. Click the **Expenditures** worksheet tab, and then in cell **A10**, change *Capital Projects* to Interfund Transfers Press Enter, and then scroll down to verify that the column chart category label changed. Compare your screen with **Figure 3**.
7. Click the **Expenditure Chart** worksheet tab, and verify that the data label on the pie chart displays as *Interfund Transfers*.
8. Click the **Expenditures** worksheet tab. Scroll up, and then select the range **A1:G3**. On the **Home tab**, in the **Cells group**, click the **Insert arrow**, and then click **Insert Sheet Rows** to insert three blank rows.

MOS Obj 1.3.4 C

9. On the **Insert tab**, in the **Text group**, click the **Insert WordArt** button. In the **WordArt** gallery, click the first style in the first row—**Fill - Black, Text 1, Shadow**. Immediately type Aspen Falls
10. Select the WordArt text. On the Mini toolbar, click the **Font Size** button 11, and then click **32**.
11. Point to the bottom border of the WordArt box, and then with the pointer, drag to position the WordArt object to approximately the range **C1:E3**. Click cell **A1** to deselect the WordArt, and then compare your screen with **Figure 4**.
12. **Save** the file.

■ **You have completed Skill 9 of 10**

► Before you print an Excel worksheet, you can use Page Layout view to preview and adjust the printed document.

1. Verify that *Expenditures* is the active worksheet. Scroll down, and then click the column chart to select the chart. Click the **File tab**, and then click **Print**. Compare your screen with **Figure 1**.

   When an embedded chart is selected, only the chart will print.

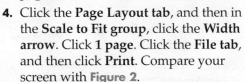

2. Click the **Back** button. Click cell **A19** to deselect the chart.
3. Click the **View tab**, and then in the **Workbook Views group**, click the **Page Layout** button. On the left side of the status bar, notice that *Page: 1 of 2* displays, informing you that the data and the column chart would print on two pages.
4. Click the **Page Layout tab**, and then in the **Scale to Fit group**, click the **Width arrow**. Click **1 page**. Click the **File tab**, and then click **Print**. Compare your screen with **Figure 2**.

   MOS Obj 1.5.4 C

   1 of 1 displays at the bottom of the screen, indicating that the WordArt, the data, and the column chart will all print on one page.

5. Click the **Back** button. On the status bar, click the **Normal** button, and then press Ctrl + Home to make cell **A1** the active cell.

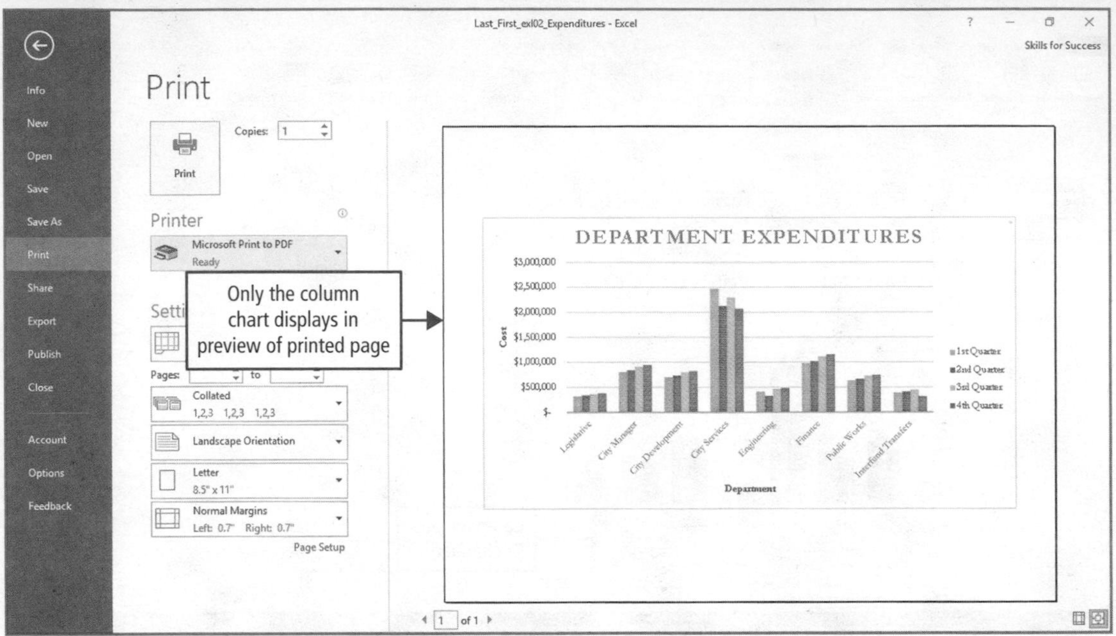

Figure 1 Excel 2016, Windows 10, Microsoft Corporation

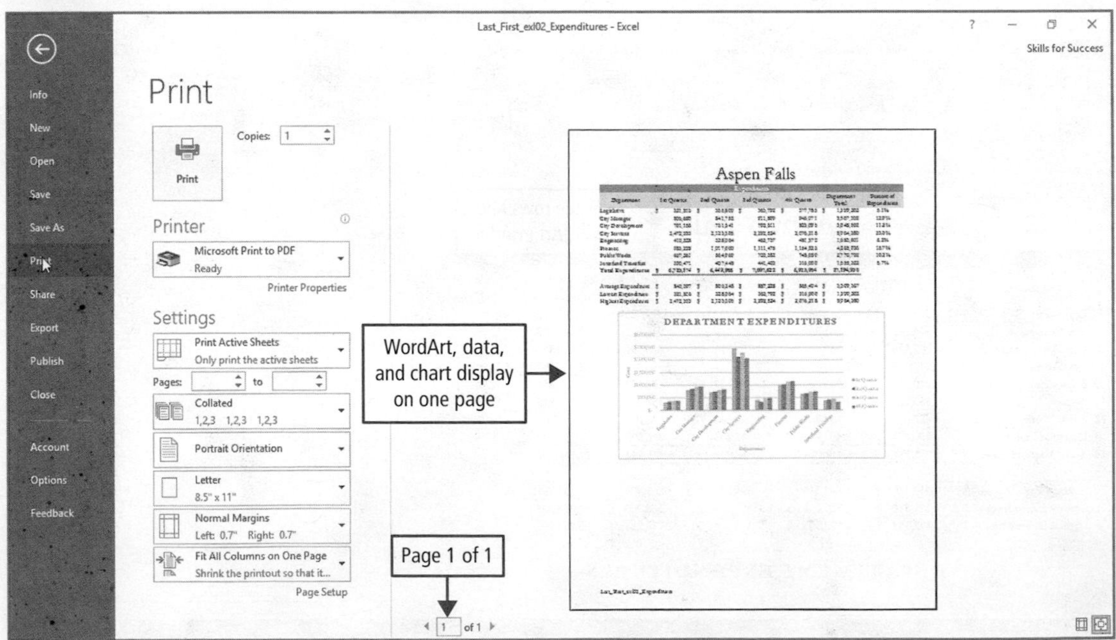

Figure 2 Excel 2016, Windows 10, Microsoft Corporation

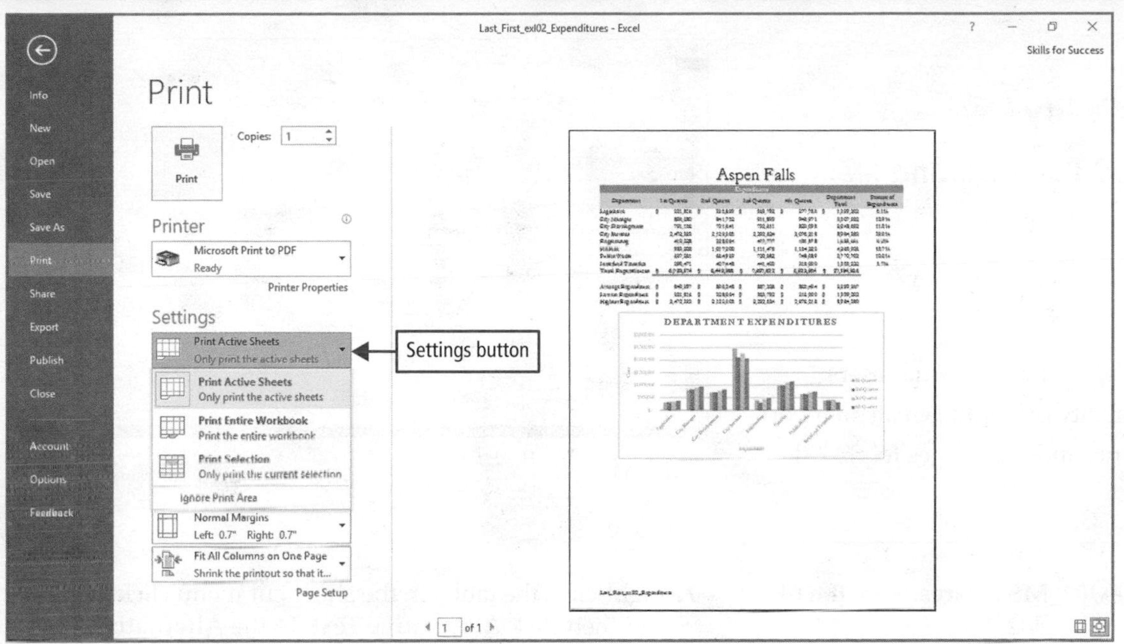

Excel 2016, Windows 10, Microsoft Corporation

Figure 3

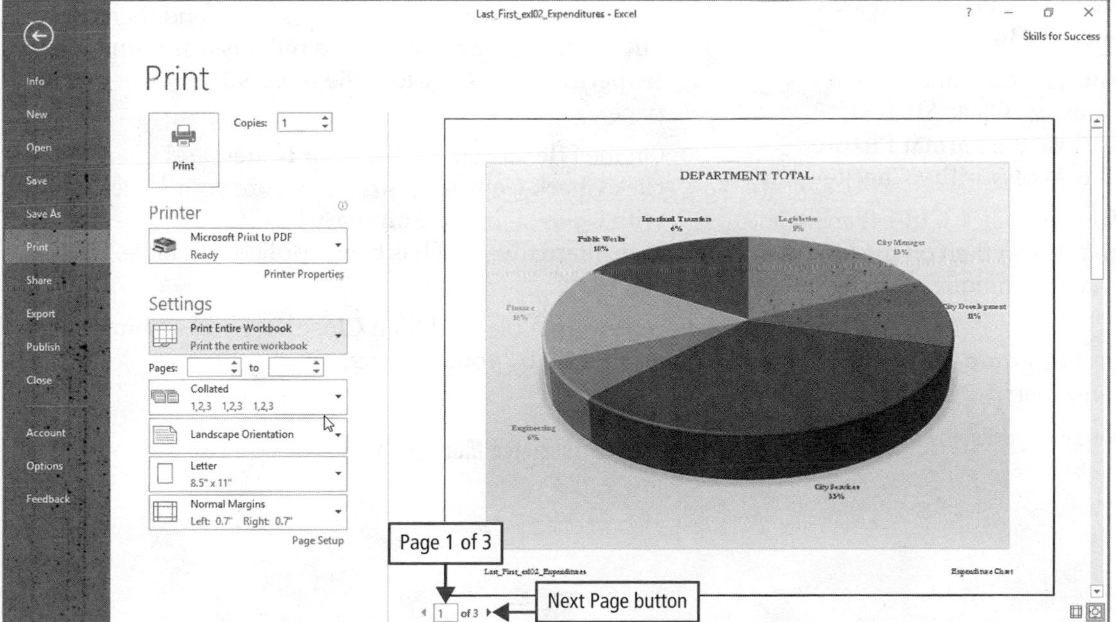

Excel 2016, Windows 10, Microsoft Corporation

Figure 4

6. Click the **Review tab**, and then in the **Proofing group**, click the **Spelling** button. Check the spelling of the worksheet. Click **Ignore All** for Interfund suggestion. When the message *Spell check complete. You're good to go!* displays, click **OK**.
7. **Save** the file.
8. Click the **File tab**, and then click **Print**. Under **Settings**, click the first button. Compare your screen with **Figure 3**.
9. On the displayed list, click **Print Entire Workbook**. Notice at the bottom of the screen that *1 of 3* displays and the chart sheet with the pie chart is the first page. Compare your screen with **Figure 4**.

Obj 1.5.3 C

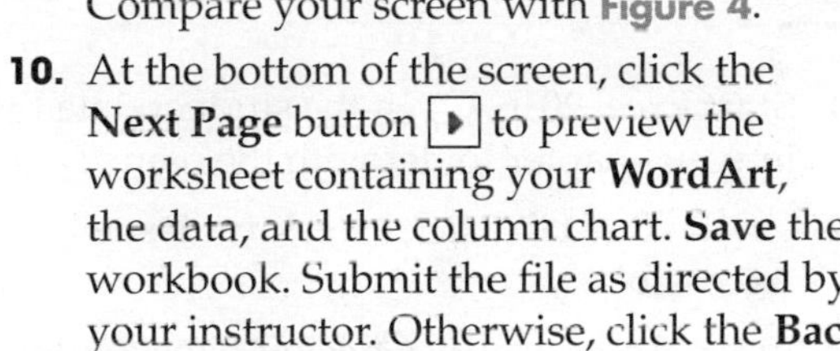

10. At the bottom of the screen, click the **Next Page** button to preview the worksheet containing your **WordArt**, the data, and the column chart. **Save** the workbook. Submit the file as directed by your instructor. Otherwise, click the **Back** button.
11. If instructed, print the formulas. Display the worksheet formulas, AutoFit the column widths, and then print the formulas.
12. **Close** Excel. Submit the file as directed by your instructor.

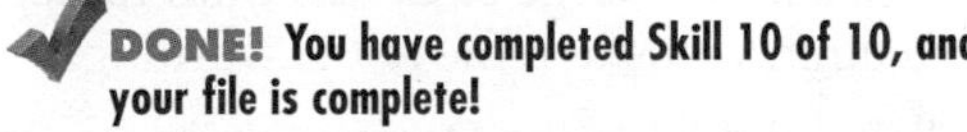

DONE! You have completed Skill 10 of 10, and your file is complete!

More Skills 11

Validate Workbooks for Accessibility

To complete this project, you will need the following file:

- exl02_MS11Fares

You will save your file as:

- Last_First_exl02_MS11Fares

- ***Accessibility***—technologies that adapt the display for nonvisual users.
- ***Accessibility Checker***—finds potential accessibility issues and creates a report.
- ***Alternative (Alt) text***—text used in documents and web pages to provide a text description of an object.

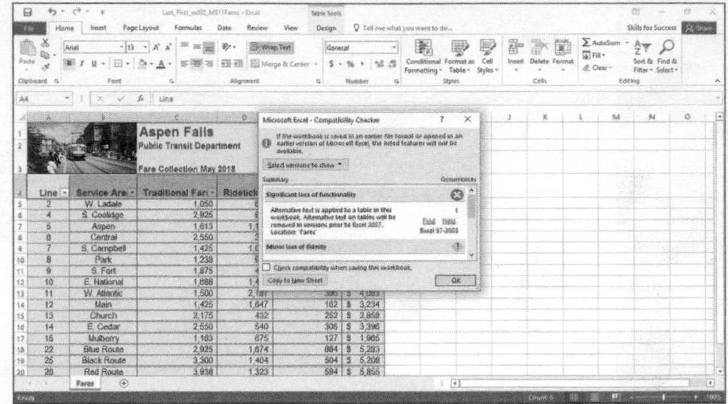

Figure 1 Excel 2016, Windows 10, Microsoft Corporation

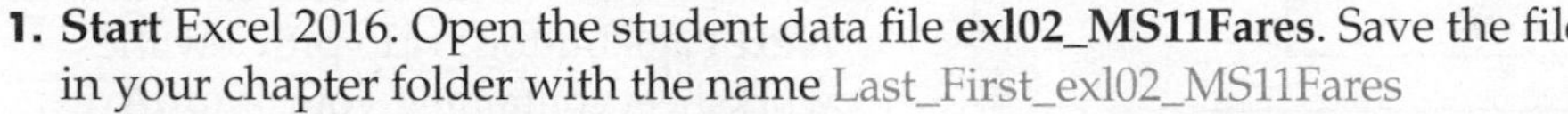

1. **Start** Excel 2016. Open the student data file **exl02_MS11Fares**. Save the file in your chapter folder with the name Last_First_exl02_MS11Fares

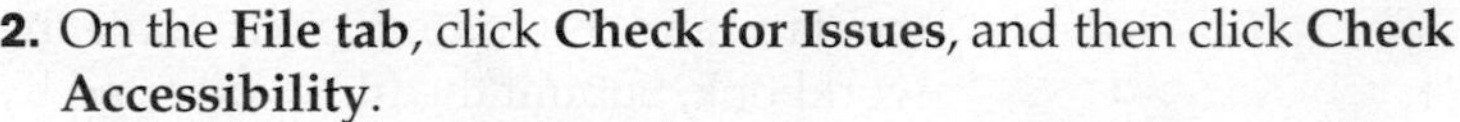

2. On the **File tab**, click **Check for Issues**, and then click **Check Accessibility**. MOS Obj 1.5.7 C
3. In the **Accessibility Checker** pane, under **Errors** click **Picture 1 (Fares)**. Under **Additional Information**, read **Why Fix** and **How To Fix**.
4. Right-click the image in cell **A1:B3**. Click **Format Picture**, and then in the **Format Picture** pane, click **Size & Properties** [icon]. Click **Alt Text**, and then in the **Title** box type Transit Picture Close the **Format Picture** pane. Notice the error no longer displays in the **Accessibility Checker** pane. MOS Obj 5.3.4 C

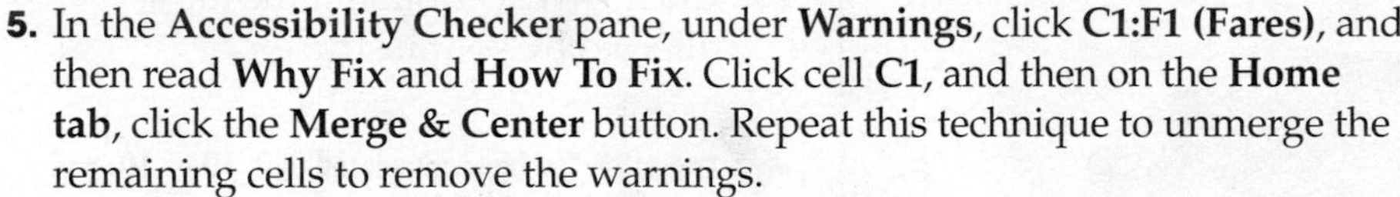

5. In the **Accessibility Checker** pane, under **Warnings**, click **C1:F1 (Fares)**, and then read **Why Fix** and **How To Fix**. Click cell **C1**, and then on the **Home tab**, click the **Merge & Center** button. Repeat this technique to unmerge the remaining cells to remove the warnings.
6. Click cell **A4**. On the **Design tab**, in the **Properties group**, click in the **Table Name** box. Replace the text with TableFares and then press Enter.

   Defining table names can assist in the navigation of a worksheet for people with disabilities.

7. Right-click the table. In the short-cut menu click **Table**, and then click **Alternative Text**. In the **Alternative Text** dialog box, with the insertion point in the **Title** box, type Fares Table In the **Description** box type The table provides fare collection information for line, service area, traditional fares, and ticket prices. and then click **OK**. Notice there are no accessibility issues found in the **Inspection Results**. Close the **Accessibility Checker** pane.
8. On the **File tab**, click **Check for Issues**, and then click **Check Compatibility**. Compare your screen with **Figure 1**. In the **Summary** box it is explained that Alternative text has been applied to a table. Click **OK**. MOS Obj 1.5.8 C

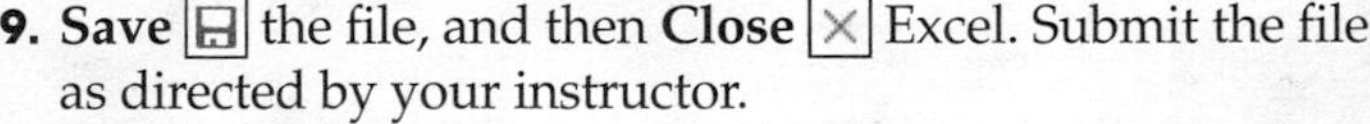

9. **Save** [icon] the file, and then **Close** [icon] Excel. Submit the file as directed by your instructor.

- **You have completed More Skills 11**

More Skills 12

Change Chart Types

To complete this project, you will need the following file:

- exl02_MS12Specials

You will save your files as:

- Last_First_exl02_MS12Specials

- ***Chart type*** is a specific design of how data is displayed or compared in a chart.
- In a ***bar chart***, the categories are displayed on the vertical axis, and the values are displayed on the horizontal axis. A bar chart illustrates comparisons among individual items.
- In a column chart, the values are displayed on the vertical axis, and the categories are displayed on the horizontal axis.

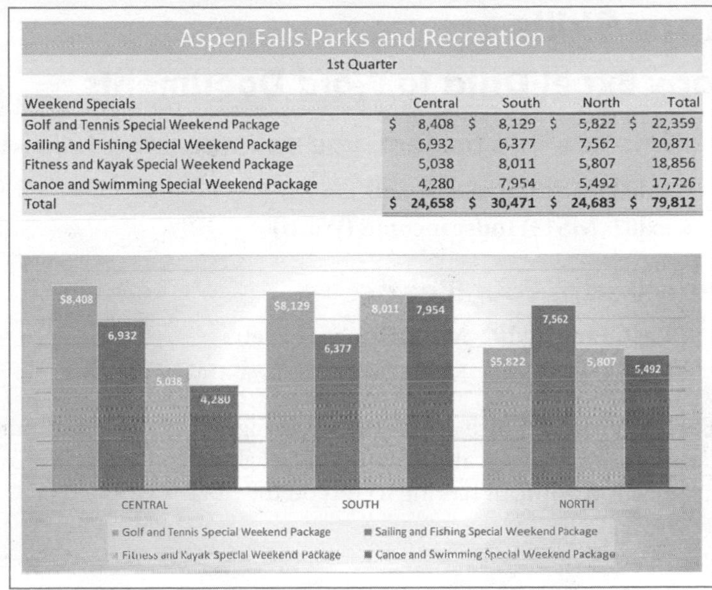

Aspen Falls Parks and Recreation

1st Quarter

Weekend Specials	Central	South	North	Total
Golf and Tennis Special Weekend Package	$ 8,408	$ 8,129	$ 5,822	$ 22,359
Sailing and Fishing Special Weekend Package	6,932	6,377	7,562	20,871
Fitness and Kayak Special Weekend Package	5,038	8,011	5,807	18,856
Canoe and Swimming Special Weekend Package	4,280	7,954	5,492	17,726
Total	$ 24,658	$ 30,471	$ 24,683	$ 79,812

Excel 2016, Windows 10, Microsoft Corporation

Figure 1

1. Start **Excel 2016**. Open the student data file **exl02_MS12Specials**, and then save the file in your chapter folder as Last_First_exl02_MS12Specials
2. Add the file name in the worksheet's left footer, and then return to Normal view.
3. Select the range **A4:D8**. Click the **Insert tab**, and then in the **Charts group**, click the **Recommended Charts** button. In the **Insert Chart** dialog box, verify that the **Clustered Bar** thumbnail is selected, and then click **OK**. MOS Obj 5.1.1 C

   Recall that each of the cells bordered in blue is referred to as a data point—a value that originates in a worksheet cell.

   Related data points form a data series; for example, there is a data series for *Central*, a data series for *South*, and a data series for *North*.
4. On the **Design tab**, in the **Type group**, click the **Change Chart Type** button. In the **Change Chart Type** dialog box, on the **All Charts tab**, click **Line** to preview the data in a line chart.
5. In the left pane of the **Change Chart Type** dialog box, click **Column**, and then under **Clustered Column**, click the second thumbnail, and then click **OK** to change the chart type.
6. Move the chart so that the upper left corner is inside the upper left corner of cell **A12**. Use the lower right sizing handle to resize the chart so that the chart covers the range **A12:E27**. MOS Obj 5.2.1 C
7. At the top right corner of the chart, click the **Chart Elements** button, and then clear the **Chart Title** check box.
8. At the top right corner of the chart, click the **Chart Styles** button. Scroll down, and then click the fourth thumbnail—**Style 4**. At the top of the **Chart Styles** gallery, click **Color**, and then click the fourth color in the **Colorful** section—**Color 4**. MOS Obj 5.2.3 C
9. Click cell **A10** to deselect the chart. Click the **File tab**, and then click **Print** to preview the printed page as shown in **Figure 1**.
10. **Save** the file, and then **Close** Excel. Submit the file as directed by your instructor.

- **You have completed More Skills 12**

More Skills 13

Copy Excel Data to Word Documents

To complete this project, you will need the following files:

- **exl02_MS13House (Excel)**
- **exl02_MS13HouseIncome (Word)**

You will save your files as:

- **Last_First_exl02_MS13House (Excel)**
- **Last_First_exl02_MS13HouseIncome (Word)**

▶ Each Microsoft Office application is designed for different purposes. Copying data from one application to another enables you to use the strengths of each application without having to retype the data.

---

1. Start **Excel 2016**. Open the student data file **exl02_MS13House**, and then save the file in your chapter folder as Last_First_exl02_MS13House
2. Start **Word 2016**. Open the student data file **exl02_MS13HouseIncome**, and then save the file in your chapter folder as Last_First_exl02_MS13HouseIncome
3. In the Word document, click the **Insert tab**. In the **Header & Footer group**, click the **Footer** button, and then click **Edit Footer**. On the **Header & Footer Tools Design tab**, in the **Insert group**, click the **Quick Parts** button, and then click **Field**. In the **Field** dialog box, under **Field names**, scroll down and then click **File Name**. Click the **OK** button. In the **Close group**, click the **Close Header and Footer** button.
4. At the bottom of the screen, on the taskbar, click the **Microsoft Excel** icon to display the Excel window. Select the range **A3:C6**, and then on the **Home tab**, in the **Clipboard group**, click the **Copy** button.
5. On the taskbar, click the **Microsoft Word** window. Press Ctrl + End to move to the end of the document. On the **Home tab**, in the **Clipboard group**, click the **Paste** button.
6. At the bottom of the screen, on the taskbar, click the **Microsoft Excel** icon to open the Excel window, and then press Esc to cancel the copy command.
7. Click the border of the chart to select the entire chart, and then on the **Home tab**, in the **Clipboard group**, click the **Copy** button.

MEMORANDUM

TO: Richard Mack, Assistant City Manager

FROM: Cyril Shore, Planning Council Director

DATE: November 25, 2018

RE: Aspen Falls Annual Household Income

Aspen Falls' mid-point (or median) household income was $56,332, about 17 percent higher than the United States and 11 percent higher than California as a whole. The average (or mean) household income for Aspen Falls was $63,965 or 21 percent higher than the nation and 15 percent higher than California as a whole. It is expected that Aspen Falls' income figures would be higher, reflecting a higher concentration of well-educated individuals. Following is the data and chart that reflect these numbers.

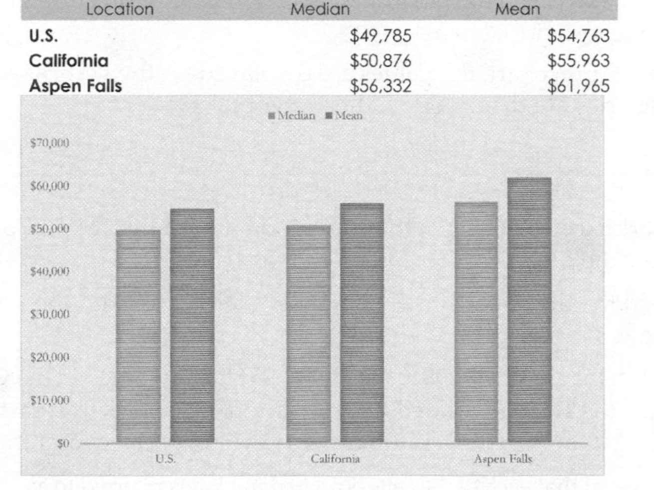

Location	Median	Mean
U.S.	$49,785	$54,763
California	$50,876	$55,963
Aspen Falls	$56,332	$61,965

Figure 1 Excel 2016, Windows 10, Microsoft Corporation

8. Display the **Microsoft Word** window. Verify the insertion point is at the end of the document. On the **Home tab**, in the **Clipboard group**, click the **Paste** button.
9. Click the **File tab**, and then click **Print**. Compare your screen with **Figure 1**.
10. **Save** the file, and then **Close** Word and Excel. Submit the files as directed by your instructor.

■ **You have completed More Skills 13**

More Skills 14

Create Line Charts

To complete this project, you will need the following file:

- exl02_MS14Growth

You will save your file as:

- Last_First_exl02_MS14Growth

► A *line chart*, allows you to compare more than one set of values, each group of values is connected by a different line.

1. Start **Excel 2016**. Open the student data file **exl02_MS14Growth**, and then save the file in your chapter folder as Last_First_exl02_MS14Growth
2. Select the range **A4:F7**. Click the **Insert tab**, and then in the **Charts group**, click the **Recommended Charts** button. In the **Insert Chart** dialog box, click the **All Charts tab**. Click **Line**, and then click the fourth chart—**Line with Markers**. Click **OK**. MOS Obj 5.1.1 C
3. On the **Design tab**, in the **Location group**, click the **Move Chart** button. In the displayed **Move Chart** dialog box, select the **New sheet** option button, replace the text with Growth Chart and then click **OK**.  Obj 5.2.4 C
4. On the **Design tab**, in the **Chart Layouts group**, click the **Quick Layout** button, and then click **Layout 6**. At the top right corner of the chart, click the **Chart Styles** button, and then click **Style 8**. Click the **Chart Styles** button to close the gallery. MOS Obj 5.2.3 C

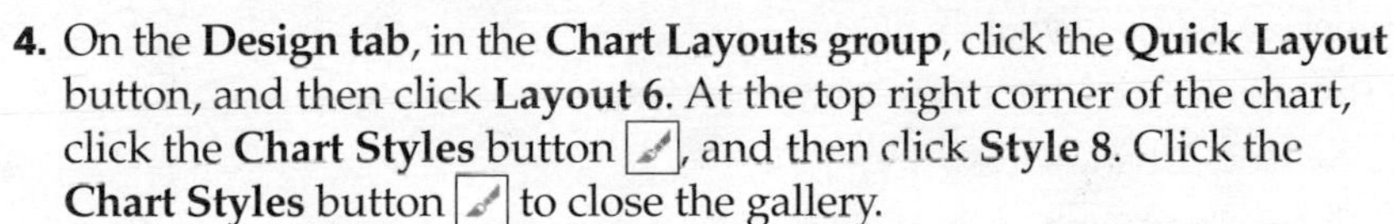

   The years display at the bottom of the chart, and the population growth is represented by the lines in the chart.
5. Click the **Format tab**. In the **Current Selection group**, click the **Chart Elements arrow**, and then click **Vertical (Value) Axis**. In the **Current Selection group**, click the **Format Selection** button to open the Format Axis pane.
6. In the **Format Axis** pane, under **Axis Options**, in the **Minimum** box, replace the number with 250000 Press Enter, and then watch the chart as the vertical axis minimum changes from 0 to 250,000. MOS Obj 5.2.2 C
7. In the **Format Axis** pane, scroll down and click **Tick Marks**. Scroll down and click the **Major type arrow**.
8. In the **Tick Marks** list, click **Cross** to display marks on the vertical axis.

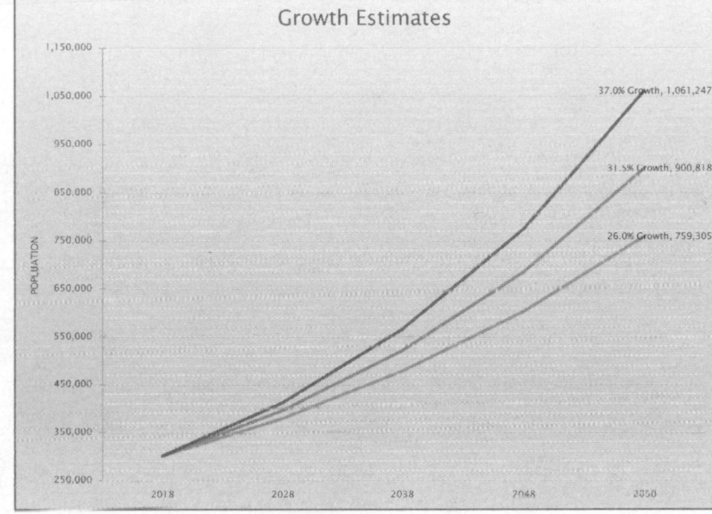

Excel 2016, Windows 10, Microsoft Corporation

Figure 1

9. In the **Format Axis** pane, click the **Axis Options arrow**, and then click **Chart Area** to display the Format Chart Area pane. Click the **Fill & Line** button, and then click **Fill**. Select the **Gradient fill** option button. **Close** the Format Chart Area pane.
10. At the top of the chart, click the **Chart Title**, type Growth Estimates and then press Enter.
11. At the left side of the chart, click the vertical **Axis Title**, type Population and then press Enter. Compare your screen with **Figure 1**. MOS Obj 5.2.2 C
12. **Save** the file, and then **Close** Excel. Submit the file as directed by your instructor.

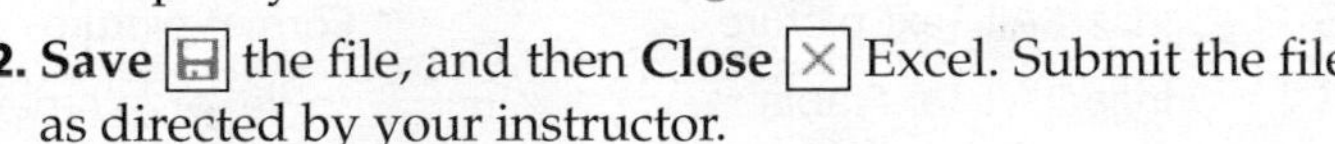

■ **You have completed More Skills 14**

Review

The following table summarizes the **SKILLS AND PROCEDURES** covered in this chapter.

Skills Number	Task	Step	Icon	Keyboard Shortcut
1	Wrap text	Home tab → Alignment group → Wrap Text		
1	Middle align text	Home tab → Alignment group → Middle Align		
1	Center text	Home tab → Alignment group → Center		
1	Increase indent	Home tab → Alignment group → Increase Indent		
2	Insert the SUM function	Quick Analysis button → Totals → SUM		
2	Create an absolute cell reference	Select cell reference → Type $		F4
3	Apply the Percent style	Home tab → Number group → Percent Style	%	
3	Increase the number of display decimals	Home tab → Number group → Increase Decimal		
4	Calculate an average	Home tab → Editing group → AutoSum arrow → Average		
5	Calculate a minimum	Home tab → Editing group → AutoSum arrow → Min		
5	Calculate a maximum	Home tab → Editing group → AutoSum arrow → Max		
6	Insert a chart using Quick Analysis	Quick Analysis button → Charts → select chart		
7	Apply a chart style	Chart Style → Style		
7	Apply a chart layout	Design tab → Chart Layouts group → Quick Layout → Layout		
8	Insert a recommended chart	Insert tab → Charts group → Recommended Charts→ select desired chart		
8	Move a chart to its own worksheet	Design tab → Locations group → Move Chart → New sheet		
8	Change the chart type	Design tab → Type group → Change Chart Type → Type		
8	Change chart data labels	Design tab → Locations group → Move Chart → New sheet		
9	Insert WordArt	Insert tab → Text group → WordArt		
10	Adjust scale page width	Page Layout tab → Scale to Fit group → Width arrow → Page		
10	Print an entire workbook	File tab → Print → Settings → Print Entire Workbook		
MS 11	Check accessibility	File tab → Check for Issues → Check Accessibility		
MS 11	Insert Alt Text picture	Format picture → Size & Properties → Alt Text		
MS 11	Insert Alt Text table	Table → Alternative Text		
MS 11	Check compatibility	File tab → Check for Issues → Check Compatibility		
MS 13	Copy Excel data to documents	Home tab → Clipboard Group → Copy		
MS 14	Create line charts	Insert tab → Chart Group → Line Chart		

Project Summary Chart

Project	Project Type	Project Location
Skills Review	Review	In Book & MIL MyITLab® Grader
Skills Assessment 1	Review	In Book & MIL MyITLab® Grader
Skills Assessment 2	Review	Book
My Skills	Problem Solving	Book
Visual Skills Check	Problem Solving	Book
Skillls Challenge 1	Critical Thinking	Book
Skills Challenge 2	Critical Thinking	Book
More Skills Assessment	Review	In Book & MIL MyITLab® Grader
Collaborating with Google	Critical Thinking	Book

MOS Objectives Covered

1.3.4 C Insert and deleting columns and rows	4.1.3 C Perform calculations by using the MIN and MAX functions
1.5.3 C Print individual worksheets	4.1.5 C Perform calculations by using the AVERAGE function
1.5.4 C Set print scaling	5.1.1 C Create a new chart
1.5.7 C Check accessibility	5.1.4 C Use Quick Analysis
1.5.8 C Inspect a workbook for compatibility issues	5.2.1 C Resize charts
2.2.2 C Modify cell alignment and indentation	5.2.2 C Add and modify chart elements
2.2.4 C Wrap text within cells	5.2.3 C Apply chart layouts and styles
2.2.5 C Apply number formats	5.2.4 C Move charts to a chart sheet
2.2.7 C Apply cell styles	5.3.4 C Add alternative text to objects for accessibility
4.1.1 C Insert references (relative, mixed, absolute, across worksheets)	

Key Terms

BizSkills Video

1. What are the best ways to network online?
2. What are some of the biggest pitfalls in using social media to communicate a personal brand?

Online Help Skills

1. Start **Excel 2016**, and then in the upper right corner of the start page, click the **Help** button [?].
2. In the **Excel Help** window **Search help** box, type Keyboard shortcuts and then press [Enter].
3. In the search result list, click **Keyboard shortcuts in Excel**. **Maximize** the Help window, and then compare your screen with **Figure 1**.

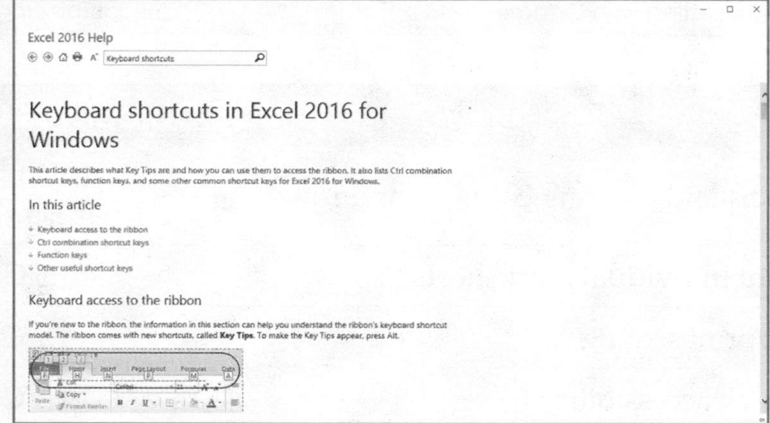

Figure 1 Excel 2016, Windows 10, Microsoft Corporation

4. Read the article to answer the following question: How can you use Key Tips to access the Ribbon?

Matching 

Match each term in the second column with its correct definition in the first column by writing the letter of the term on the blank line in front of the correct definition.

___ **1.** A command with which you can display text on multiple lines within a cell.

___ **2.** A cell reference that refers to a cell by its fixed position in a worksheet and does not change when the formula is copied.

___ **3.** Rules that specify the way numbers should display.

___ **4.** The default format applied to numbers.

___ **5.** The value(s) that determine(s) how a function should be used.

___ **6.** A graphical representation of data in a worksheet that shows comparisons, patterns, and trends.

___ **7.** A chart line that contains words as labels.

___ **8.** A chart line that contains numeric data.

___ **9.** The function that adds a group of values and then divides the result by the number of values in the group.

___ **10.** The Excel feature that outlines all of the cells referenced in a formula.

A Absolute cell reference
B Argument
C AVERAGE function
D Category axis
E Chart
F General format
G Number format
H Range finder
I Text wrap
J Value axis

Multiple Choice 

Choose the correct answer.

1. Automatically changing the column width to accommodate the longest column entry.
   A. Drag and drop
   B. AutoFit
   C. Auto adjust
2. A green triangle that indicates a possible error in a formula.
   A. Error indicator
   B. Message
   C. Dialog Box Launcher
3. A chart type useful for illustrating comparisons among related numbers.
   A. Pie chart
   B. Area chart
   C. Column chart
4. A chart placed on a worksheet with the source data.
   A. Chart sheet
   B. Column chart
   C. Embedded chart
5. The related data points in a chart.
   A. Column
   B. Data series
   C. Chart point
6. The box that identifies the patterns or colors assigned to the data series.
   A. Legend
   B. Dialog box
   C. Message box
7. A predesigned combination of chart elements.
   A. 3-D chart
   B. Chart layout
   C. Chart
8. A prebuilt chart format that applies an overall visual look to a chart.
   A. Data marker
   B. Chart finder
   C. Chart style
9. The chart type that best displays the relationship of parts to a whole.
   A. Pie chart
   B. Area chart
   C. Column chart
10. A worksheet that contains only a chart.
   A. Worksheet
   B. Chart area
   C. Chart sheet

Topics for Discussion

1. Search current newspapers and magazines for examples of charts. Which charts catch your eye, and why? Do the charts appeal to you because of their color or format? Is something intriguing revealed to you in the chart that you have never considered before? What are some formatting changes that you think make a chart interesting and valuable to a reader?
2. Do you think 3-D pie charts distort the data in a way that is misleading? Why or why not?

Skills Review

To complete this project, you will need the following file:

- **exl02_SRRevenue**

You will save your file as:

- **Last_First_exl02_SRRevenue**

---

1. Start **Excel 2016**, and open the file **exl02_SRRevenue**. **Save** the file in your chapter folder as Last_First_exl02_SRRevenue Add the file name in the worksheet's left footer and the sheet name in the right footer. Return to **Normal** view.
2. In the column heading area, point to the right boundary of column **A**, and then double-click to AutoFit the column width. Click the column **B** heading, and then drag right to select columns **B:F**. Click the right boundary of column B, and then drag to the right until the ScreenTip indicates *Width:13:00 (96 pixels)*.
3. Select the range **A1:F1**. On the **Home tab**, in the **Alignment group**, click the **Wrap Text**, **Middle Align**, and **Center** buttons.
4. Select the range **B2:E13**. Click the **Quick Analysis** button, click **Totals**, and then click the first option—**SUM**.
5. Select the nonadjacent ranges **B2:E2** and **B14:E14**. In the **Number group**, click the **Decrease Decimal** button two times. Select the range **B3:E13**. In the **Number group**, click the **Decrease Decimal** button two times. Select the range **B14:E14**. In the **Styles group**, click the **Cell Styles** button, and then click **Total**.
6. In cell **F2**, type=E2/$E$14 and then on the formula bar, click the **Enter** button. With cell F2 as the active cell, in the **Number group**, click the **Percent Style** button, and then click the **Increase Decimal** button once. In the **Alignment group**, click the **Center** button. AutoFill the formula in cell **F2** down through cell **F13**. Click cell **A15**, and then compare your screen with **Figure 1**.
7. Click cell **B16**. Type =Av and then in the **Formula AutoComplete** list, double-click **AVERAGE**. For the function argument, select the range **B2:B13**, and then press Enter. Using the same function argument range, in cell **B17**, enter the **MAX** function. Select the range **B16:B17**, and then AutoFill the formulas to the right through column **D**. Compare your screen with **Figure 2**.

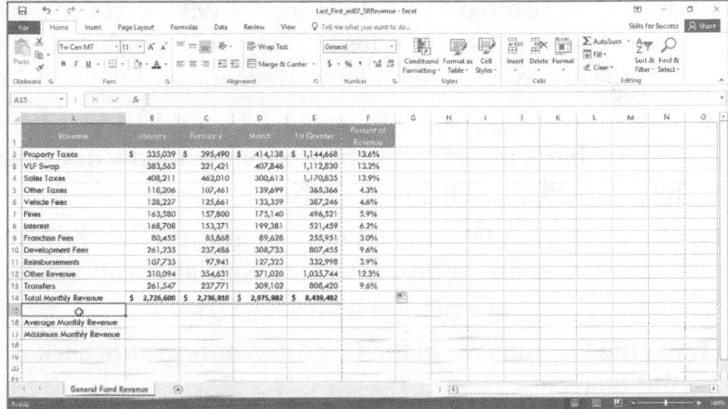

Figure 1 Excel 2016, Windows 10, Microsoft Corporation

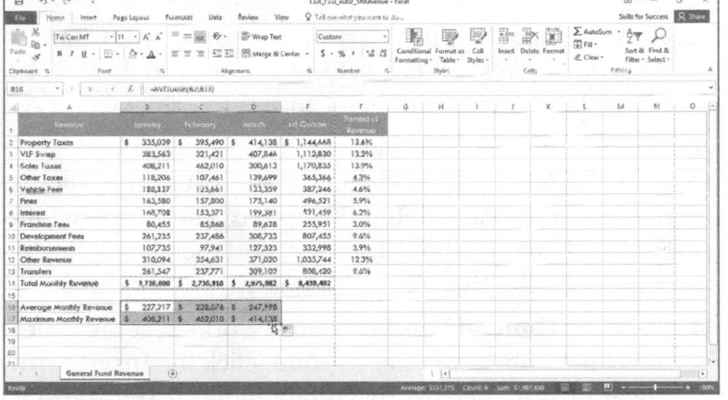

Figure 2 Excel 2016, Windows 10, Microsoft Corporation

■ **Continue to the next page to complete this Skills Review**

8. Select the range **A1:D13**. Click the **Quick Analysis** button, click **Charts**, and then click the **Clustered Column** thumbnail. Move and resize the chart to display in approximately the range **A19:F35**. At the top right corner of the chart, click the **Chart Styles** button, and then click the **Style 9** thumbnail. Select **Chart Title**, type General Fund Revenue and then press Enter.
9. Select the nonadjacent ranges **A1:A13** and **E1:E13**. Click the **Insert tab**, and then in the **Charts group**, click the **Recommended Charts** button. On the **All Charts tab**, click **Pie**, and then click **OK**.
10. On the **Design tab**, in the **Location group**, click the **Move Chart** button. In the **Move Chart** dialog box, select the **New sheet** option button, type the sheet name Revenue Chart and then click **OK**.
11. On the **Design tab**, in the **Chart Layouts group**, click the **Quick Layout** button, and then click **Layout 1**.
12. Click the **Chart Elements** button, click the **Data Labels arrow**, and then click **More Options**. In the **Format Data Labels** pane, under **Label Position**, click **Outside End**.
13. Click the **Label Options arrow**, and then click **Chart Area**. In the **Format Chart Area** pane, click the **Fill & Line** button, and then click **Fill**. Select the **Gradient fill** option button, and then **Close** the Format Chart Area pane. Compare your screen with **Figure 3**.
14. Click the **Insert tab**, and then in the **Text group**, click the **Header & Footer** button. In the **Page Setup** dialog box, click the **Custom Footer** button. Insert the **File Name** in the left section, and then insert the **Sheet Name** in the right section. Click **OK** twice.
15. Click the **General Fund Revenue worksheet tab**. Select the range **A1:A3**. On the **Home tab**, in the **Cells group**, click the **Insert arrow**, and then click **Insert Sheet Rows**. Click the **Insert tab**. In the **Text group**, click the **Insert WordArt** button, and then in the first row, click the second thumbnail—**Fill - Blue, Accent 1, Shadow**. Immediately type Aspen Falls Revenue Select the text in the WordArt. On the Mini toolbar, change the **Font Size** to **36**. Point to the bottom border of the WordArt, and then move the WordArt to center approximately within the range **A1:E3**.
16. Click cell **A1**. Click the **Page Layout tab**. In the **Scale to Fit group**, click the **Width arrow**, and then click the **1 page** button.
17. Click the **File tab**, and then click **Print**. Compare your screen with **Figure 4**.

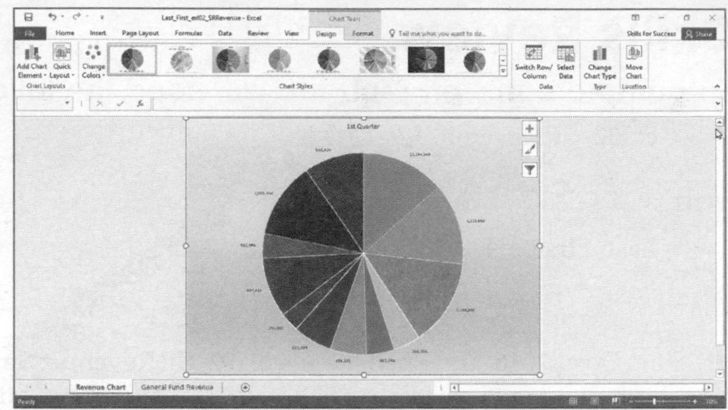

Excel 2016, Windows 10, Microsoft Corporation **Figure 3**

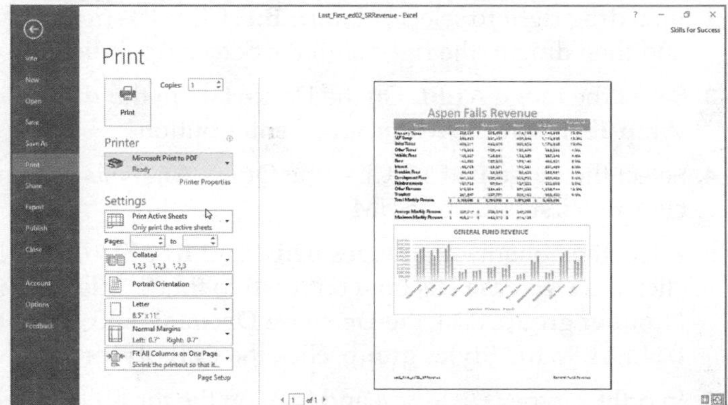

Excel 2016, Windows 10, Microsoft Corporation **Figure 4**

18. **Save** the file, and then **Close** Excel. Submit the file as directed by your instructor.

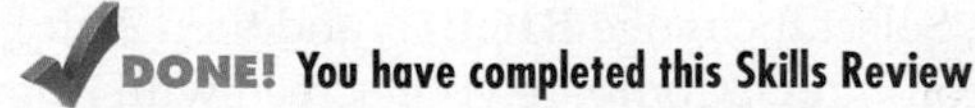

DONE! You have completed this Skills Review

Skills Assessment 1

To complete this project, you will need the following file:

- exl02_SA1Debt

You will save your file as:

- Last_First_exl02_SA1Debt

1. Start **Excel 2016**, and open the file **exl02_SA1Debt**. **Save** the workbook in your chapter folder as Last_First_exl02_SA1Debt Add the file name in the worksheet's left footer and the sheet name in the right footer. Return to **Normal** view.
2. Select the range **A2:I2**, and then apply the alignment **Wrap Text** and **Middle Align**.
3. Select the column headings **B:I**, and then AutoFit the column widths.
4. In the range **B8:I18**, insert the column totals, and then apply the **Total** cell style.
5. Select the nonadjacent ranges **B3:H3** and **B8:I18**, and then display no decimals. Select the range **B4:H7**, and then display no decimals.
6. In cell **I3**, calculate the *Percent of Total Debt*. In the formula, use an absolute cell reference when referring to cell **H8**. AutoFill the formula down through cell **I7**, and then format the results as percentages with one decimal place.
7. In the range **B10:G10**, insert a function to calculate the highest monthly debt. In the range **B11:G11**, insert a function to calculate the lowest monthly debt. In the range **B12:G12**, insert a function to calculate the average monthly debt.
8. Insert a **Pie** chart based on the nonadjacent ranges **A2:A7** and **H2:H7**. Move the pie chart to a chart sheet with the sheet name Debt Chart
9. For the pie chart, apply **Layout 6**, and then apply the **Chart Style 3**. Change the data label **Font Size** to **12**, and then position to **Center**. Add the file name in the chart sheet's left footer and the sheet name in the right footer.
10. On the **Debt** worksheet, insert a **Clustered Column** chart based on the range **A2:G7**. Move the chart below the data, and then resize the chart to approximately the range **A14:I28**. Apply the chart **Style 5**. Change the chart title to City Debt

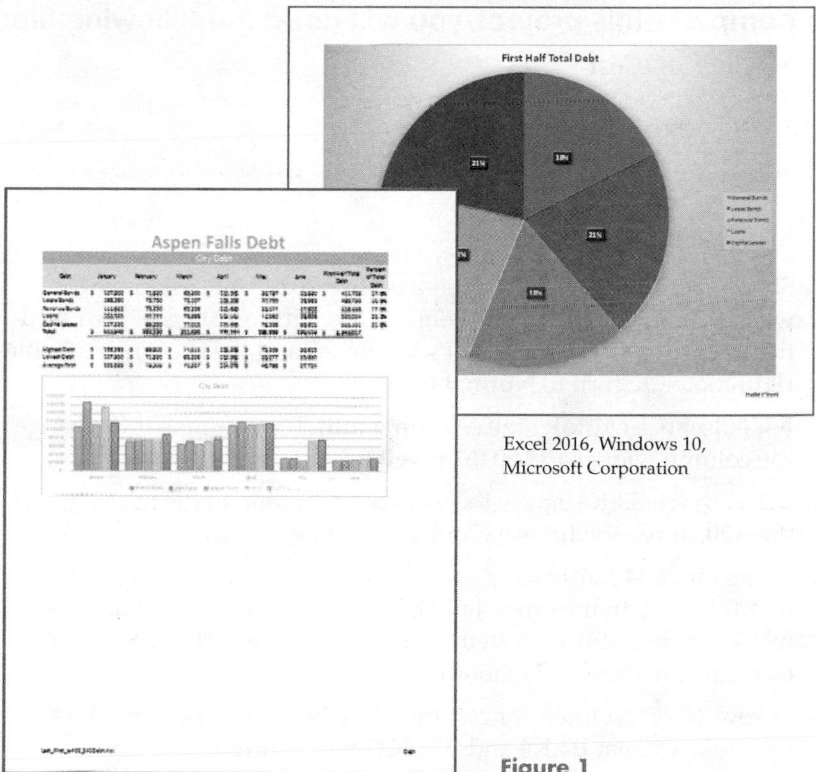

Excel 2016, Windows 10, Microsoft Corporation

Figure 1

11. Insert three sheet rows at the top of the worksheet. Insert **WordArt**, using the style **Fill - Gold, Accent 4, Soft Bevel**. Change the WordArt text to Aspen Falls Debt and then change the **Font Size** to **36**. Move the WordArt to the top of the worksheet, centering it above the data.
12. Adjust the **Scale to Fit** to fit the WordArt, data, and column chart on one page.
13. Revise the Print Settings to **Print Entire Workbook**, and then compare your screen with **Figure 1**.
14. **Save** the file, and then **Close** Excel. Submit the file as directed by your instructor.

DONE! You have completed Skills Assessment 1

Skills Assessment 2

To complete this project, you will need the following file:

- exl02_SA2Cost

You will save your file as:

- Last_First_exl02_SA2Cost

1. Start **Excel 2016**, and then open the file **exl02_SA2Cost**. **Save** the workbook in your chapter folder as Last_First_exl02_SA2Cost Add the file name in the worksheet's left footer and the sheet name in the right footer. Return to **Normal** view.
2. For column **A**, AutoFit the column width. For columns **B:K**, change the column width to **11.00 (82 pixels)**.
3. In the range **B3:K3**, apply the **Center** alignment. In the range **A4:A20**, apply the **Increase Indent** alignment.
4. In the range **I4:I20**, insert a function to calculate the average monthly cost. In the range **J4:J20**, insert a function to calculate the minimum monthly cost. In the range **K4:K20**, insert a function to calculate the maximum monthly cost.
5. In row **21**, insert totals for columns **B:K**, and then apply the **Total** cell style. Format **B4:K4** and **B21:K21** with Currency, no decimals. Format **B5:K20** with Comma, no decimals.
6. In cell **B22**, calculate the *Percent of First Half Costs*. In the formula, use an absolute cell reference when referring to cell **H21**. Format the result as a percentage and display two decimals. AutoFill the formula to the right through column **G**.
7. Insert a **Stacked Bar** chart based on the range **A3:G20**. Move the stacked bar chart to a chart sheet named Projected Costs Apply the chart **Style 11**. Change the chart title to Projected Monthly Costs Add the file name in the chart sheet's left footer and the sheet name in the right footer.
8. Click the **Cost worksheet tab**. Insert a **Pie** chart based on the nonadjacent ranges **A3:G3** and **A21:G21**. Move the pie chart to a chart sheet named Total Monthly Costs Apply the chart **Layout 1**. Change the data label position to **Data Callout**, and then change the data label **Font Size** to **12**.

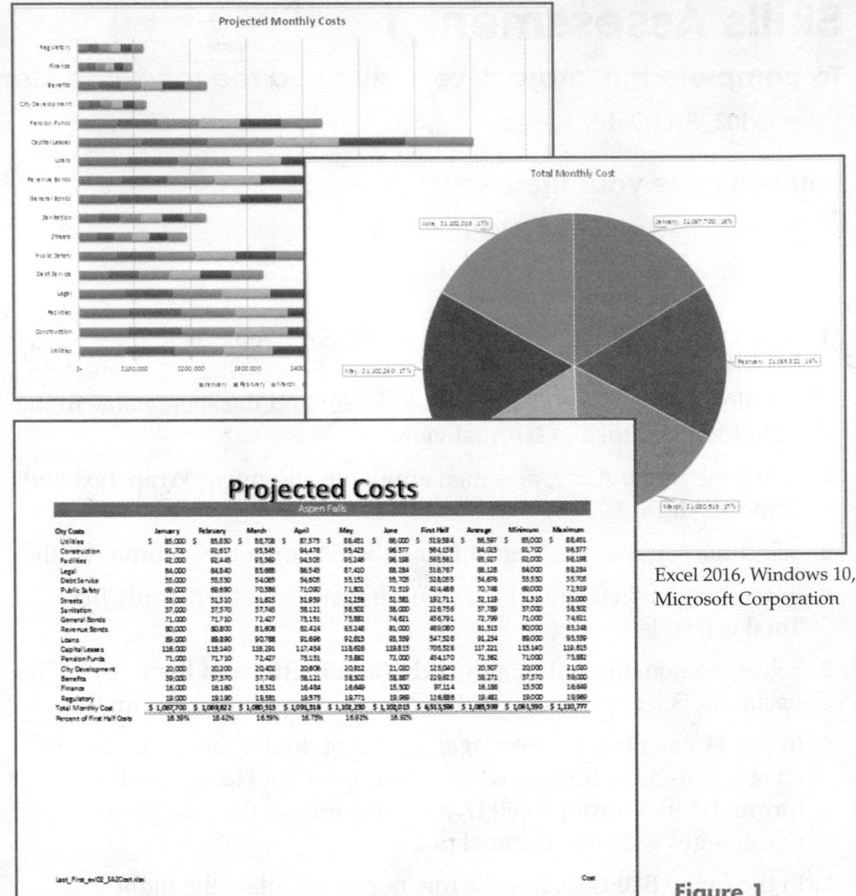

Excel 2016, Windows 10, Microsoft Corporation

Figure 1

9. On the **Cost** worksheet, insert four blank lines at the top of the worksheet. Insert a WordArt with the **Fill - Black, Text 1, Outline - Background 1, Hard Shadow - Background 1** style. In the WordArt, type the text Projected Costs and then change the **Font Size** to **44**. Move the WordArt to the top of the worksheet, centering it above the data.
10. Scale the **Cost** worksheet to print on **1 page**.
11. **Print Preview** the workbook, and then compare your screen with **Figure 1**.
12. **Save** the file, and then **Close** Excel. Submit the file as directed by your instructor.

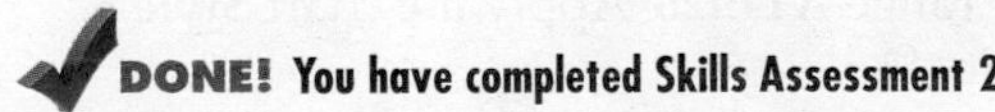

DONE! You have completed Skills Assessment 2

My Skills

To complete this project, you will need the following file:

- exl02_MYPersonalBudget

You will save your file as:

- Last_First_exl02_MYPersonalBudget

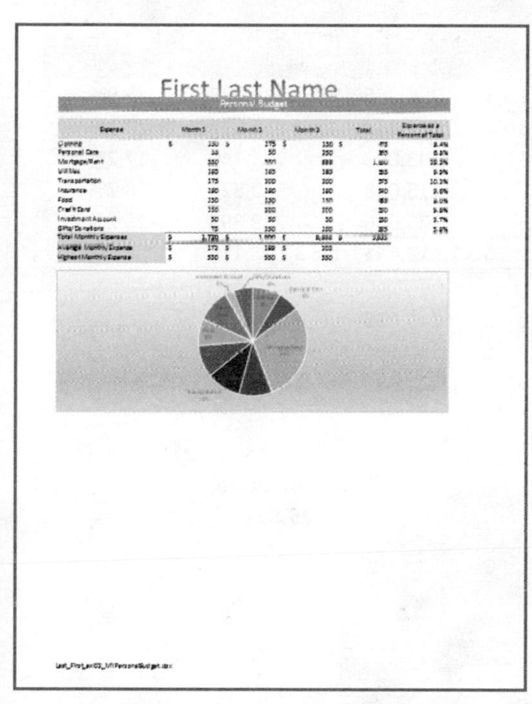

Excel 2016, Windows 10, Microsoft Corporation **Figure 1**

1. Start **Excel 2016**, and then open the file **exl02_MYPersonalBudget. Save** the file in your chapter folder as Last_First_exl02_MYPersonalBudget Add the file name in the worksheet's left footer, and then return to **Normal** view.
2. Change the alignments of the row **3** labels, and then indent the column **A** expense labels. In the range **B14:E14**, insert the column totals.
3. In the range **B15:D15**, insert a function to calculate the average monthly expense. In the range **B16:D16**, insert a function to calculate the maximum monthly expense.
4. In cell **F4**, calculate the *Expense as a Percent of Total*. In the formula, use an absolute cell reference when referring to the total. Format the results as percentages with one decimal, and then AutoFill the formula down through cell **F13**.
5. Apply the **Total** cell style where appropriate.
6. Insert a **Pie** chart based on the nonadjacent ranges **A3:A13** and **E3:E13**.
7. Move the pie chart to an appropriate location below your data, and then resize the chart.
8. Format the pie chart with any of the chart options of your choice including layout, style, or color.
9. At the top of the worksheet, insert three blank rows. Insert a WordArt using your first and last names as the WordArt text. Move the WordArt above the data, and then resize to fit in the blank rows.
10. Adjust the scaling to fit the data and the pie chart on one page when printed. **Print Preview** the workbook, and then compare your screen with **Figure 1**.
11. **Save** the file, and then **Close** Excel. Submit the file as directed by your instructor.

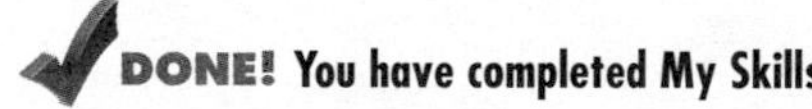
DONE! You have completed My Skills

Visual Skills Check

To complete this project, you will need the following file:

- exl02_VSNetAssets

You will save your file as:

- Last_First_exl02_VSNetAssets

Start **Excel 2016**, and then open the student data file **exl02_VSNetAssets**. **Save** the file in your chapter folder as Last_First_exl02_VSNetAssets Create the worksheet as shown in **Figure 1**. Calculate the *Percent of Total Net Assets* using an absolute cell reference. In rows **13:15**, insert the statistical functions that correspond with the row labels. Format the values and text as shown. Create the pie chart, and then move and resize the chart as shown in the figure. The chart uses the **Layout 4** chart layout, and **Color 8**, with data label font size **12** and **Bold**. Insert the file name in the worksheet's left footer. **Save** the file, and then **Close** Excel. Submit the file as directed by your instructor.

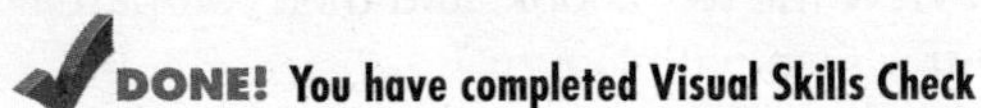

DONE! You have completed Visual Skills Check

Aspen Falls
Net Assets
Business-type Activities

Asset	July	August	September	Total	Percent of Total Net Assets
Transportation	$ 268,755	$ 275,082	$ 282,086	$ 825,923	25.9%
Port	242,886	245,688	247,253	735,827	23.1%
Water	175,885	180,256	193,008	549,149	17.2%
Power	117,006	108,832	115,038	340,876	10.7%
Hospital	213,468	250,865	275,066	739,399	23.2%
Total Net Assets	**$ 1,018,000**	**$ 1,060,723**	**$ 1,112,451**	**$ 3,191,174**	
Minimum Asset	$ 117,006	$ 108,832	$ 115,038		
Maximum Asset	$ 268,755	$ 275,082	$ 282,086		
Average Asset	$ 203,600	$ 212,145	$ 222,490		

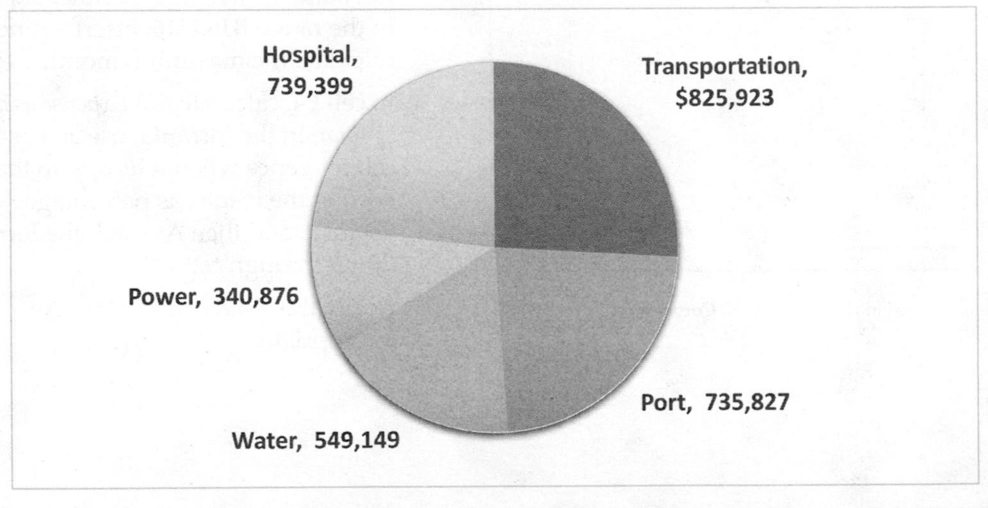

Figure 1

Excel 2016, Windows 10, Microsoft Corporation

Skills Challenge 1

To complete this project, you will need the following file:

- exl02_SC1Budget

You will save your file as:

- Last_First_exl02_SC1Budget

Start **Excel 2016**. Open the file **exl02_SC1Budget**, and then save the file in your chapter folder as Last_First_exl02_SC1Budget During the fourth quarter of this year, the Accounting Department developed a summary of the proposed Aspen Falls budget. Correct the errors in the statistical functions—you may want to display the formulas. Use an absolute cell reference when correcting the percentage. Correct the number formats, and format the labels appropriately. Modify the WordArt and the column chart. Verify that the WordArt, data, and column chart will print on one page. Add the file name in the worksheet's left footer. Save the file, and Close Excel. Submit the file as directed by your instructor.

DONE! You have completed Skills Challenge 1

Skills Challenge 2

To complete this project, you will need the following file:

- exl02_SC2Classes

You will save your file as:

- Last_First_exl02_SC2Classes

Start **Excel 2016**, and then open the workbook **exl02_SC2Classes**. Save the file in your chapter folder as Last_First_exl02_SC2Classes Carter Horikoshi, the Art Center Supervisor, created a workbook to track how many students attended the Community Center classes last summer. He wants to determine if he should offer more classes this summer based on the number of students from last summer. He wants to know the total enrollment and the average enrollment for each month and for each class. He would like to view a chart that summarizes the enrollment data. Using the skills you learned in this chapter, provide Mr. Horikoshi a workbook to assist him in his decision. Add the file name in the worksheet's left footer. Save the file and Close Excel. Submit the file as directed by your instructor.

DONE! You have completed Skills Challenge 2

More Skills Assessment

To complete this project, you will need the following files:

- exl02_MSARecycling (Excel)
- exl02_MSARecycling (Word)

You will save your files as:

- Last_First_exl02_MSARecycling (Excel)
- Last_First_exl02_MSARecycling (Word)
- Last_First_exl02_MSARecycling (JPG)

1. Start **Excel 2016**. Open the workbook **exl02_MSARecycling**, and then save the file in your chapter folder as Last_First_exl02_MSARecycling
2. Select the **Clustered Bar Chart**. Use the **Chart Tools** to change the **Chart Type** to a **Clustered Column** chart. Apply **Chart Style 7** to the chart.
3. Start **Word 2016**. Open the student data file **exl02_MSARecycling**, and then save the file in your chapter folder as Last_First_exl02_MSARecycling
4. At the bottom of the screen, on the taskbar, click the **Microsoft Excel** icon to display the Excel window. Copy the *Recycling Revenue* chart.
5. Display the **Microsoft Word** window. Move to the end of the document, and then paste the chart from Excel. Resize the chart so that the right edge is at the right margin.
6. Select the chart, and apply **Alt Text** using the title Recycling Chart Close the Format Chart pane. **Save** the file, and then **Close** the Word document.
7. At the bottom of the screen, on the taskbar, click the **Microsoft Excel** icon to open the Excel window, and then deselect the copied cells.

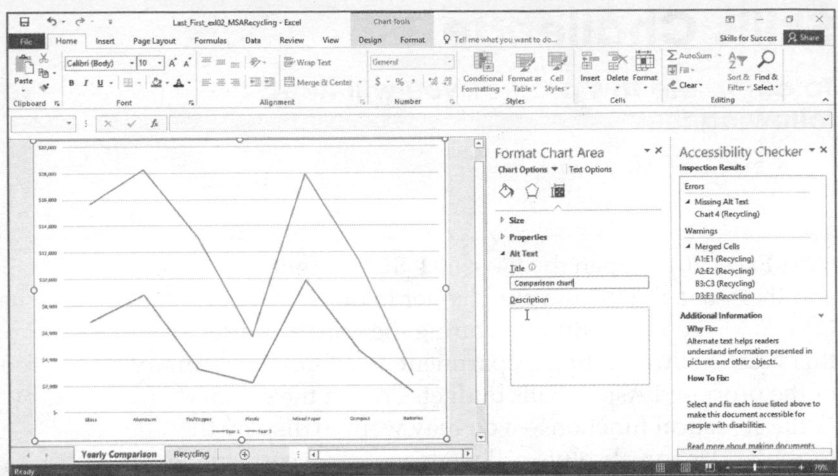

Figure 1 Excel 2016, Windows 10, Microsoft Corporation

8. Using data in the range **A5:C12**, create a **Stacked Line** chart. Move the Stacked Line chart to a chart sheet named Yearly Comparison and then clear the **Chart Title**. Click the **Recycling** sheet, and then **Save** the file.
9. Check Accessibility for the workbook. Format **Chart 1 (Yearly Comparison)** using Alt Text and apply Comparison Chart as the Title. Compare your screen with **Figure 1**.
10. Format **Chart 4 (Recycling)** using Alt Text and apply Recycling Revenue Chart as the Title.
11. Clear any warnings by unmerging cells as needed. Close all open panes.
12. **Save** the file, and then **Close** all open windows. Submit the files as directed by your instructor.

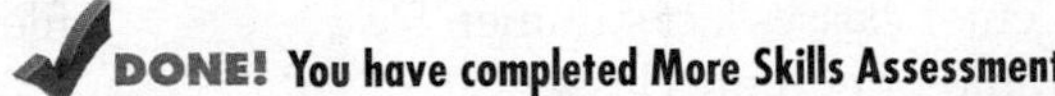

Collaborating with Google

To complete this project, you will need a Google account (refer to the Common Features chapter) and the following file:

- **exl02_GPRentalRevenue**

You will save your file as:

- **Last_First_exl02_GPRentalRevenue**

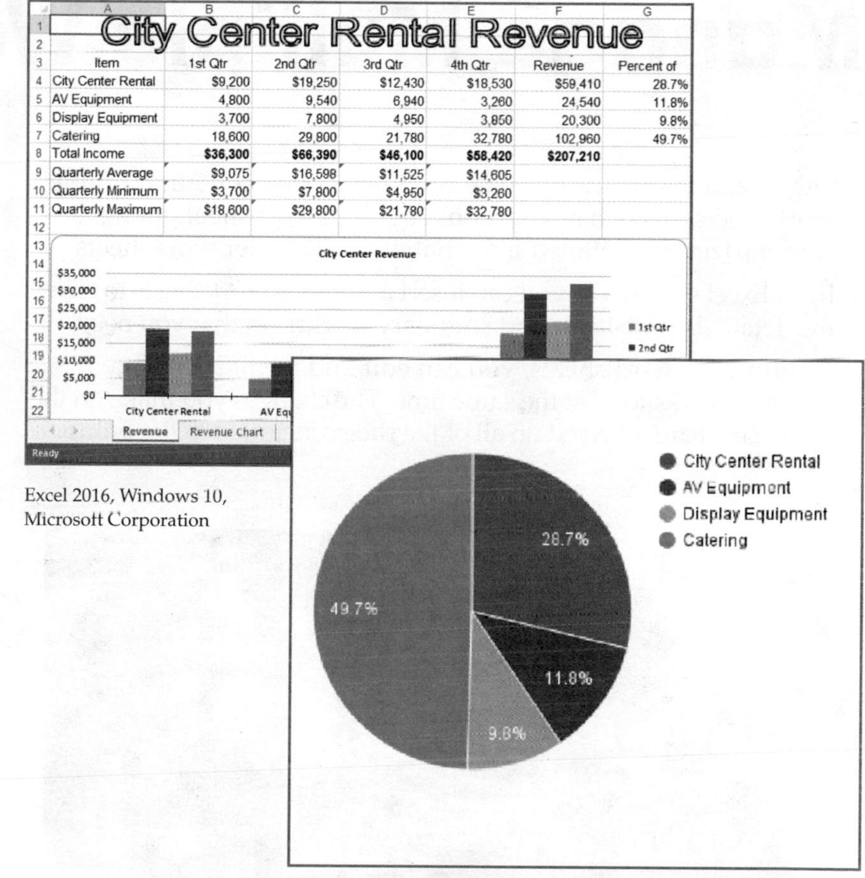

	A	B	C	D	E	F	G
1	City Center Rental Revenue						
2							
3	Item	1st Qtr	2nd Qtr	3rd Qtr	4th Qtr	Revenue	Percent of
4	City Center Rental	$9,200	$19,250	$12,430	$18,530	$59,410	28.7%
5	AV Equipment	4,800	9,540	6,940	3,260	24,540	11.8%
6	Display Equipment	3,700	7,800	4,950	3,850	20,300	9.8%
7	Catering	18,600	29,800	21,780	32,780	102,960	49.7%
8	Total Income	**$36,300**	**$66,390**	**$46,100**	**$58,420**	**$207,210**	
9	Quarterly Average	$9,075	$16,598	$11,525	$14,605		
10	Quarterly Minimum	$3,700	$7,800	$4,950	$3,260		
11	Quarterly Maximum	$18,600	$29,800	$21,780	$32,780		

Excel 2016, Windows 10, Microsoft Corporation

Figure 1

1. Log into your Google account, click **Google Apps**, and then click **Drive**. Create a new Google Sheet, and then replace the title with Rental Revenue
2. From the student data files, open **exl02_GPRentalRevenue**. Copy the range **A1:G9** from the *Revenue* worksheet, and then paste it in cell **A1** of the blank Google worksheet. Rename the sheet Revenue
3. Select the range **A1:G1**. Click **Center** align. Click **Format**, point to **Text wrapping**, and then click **Wrap**.
4. In cell **B7**, enter the **AVERAGE** function for the *1st Quarter*. Use AutoFill to copy the formula through **E7**.
5. In cell **B8**, enter the **MIN** function for the *1st Quarter*. Use AutoFill to copy the formula through **E8**.
6. In cell **B9**, enter the **MAX** function for the *1st Quarter*. Use AutoFill to copy the formula through **E9**.
7. In cell **G2**, calculate *Revenue as a Percent of Total Income* using absolute cell reference for **F6**. Format the result as a percentage with one decimal. AutoFill the formula down through **G5**.
8. Select rows **1** and **2**. Click **Insert**, and then click **2 Rows above**. Click **Insert**, click **Drawing**, click **Actions**, and then click **WordArt**. Type City Center Rental Revenue press Enter, and then click **Save & Close**. Move the WordArt to rows **1** and **2**. On the Insert tab, click Chart the data and resize.
9. Select the range **A3:E7**. Click **Insert**, and then click **Chart**. Verify the first thumbnail is selected, and then click **Insert**. Resize the chart to fit in cells **A13:G24**. Select the title, and then replace the current text with City Center Revenue
10. Select the nonadjacent ranges **A3:A7** and **F3:F7**. Click **Insert**, and then click **Chart**. Scroll down, select the **Pie Chart**, and then click **Insert**. In the upper right corner of the chart, click the arrow, and then select **Move to own sheet . . . .** Rename the sheet Revenue Chart Right click the chart title, and then click **Clear title**.
11. Click **File**, point to **Download as**, and then click **Microsoft Excel (.xlsx)**. Open the downloaded file, and then save the file in your chapter folder as Last_First_exl02_GPRentalRevenue Compare your screen with **Figure 1**.
12. Close all windows, and then submit your file as directed by your instructor.

DONE! You have completed Collaborating with Google

CHAPTER 3

Manage Multiple Worksheets

- Organizations typically create workbooks that contain multiple worksheets. In such a workbook, the first worksheet often summarizes the detailed information in the other worksheets.
- In an Excel workbook, you can insert and move worksheets to create the detailed worksheets and summary worksheet that you need.
- By grouping worksheets, you can edit and format the data in multiple worksheets at the same time. The changes you make on the active sheet are reflected on all of the sheets included in the group.
- You can create multiple worksheets quickly by copying and pasting information from one worksheet to other worksheets.
- You can color code each worksheet tab so that detailed information can be quickly located.
- When you use multiple math operators in a single formula, you must take care to ensure the operations are carried out in the intended order.
- When building a summary worksheet, you will typically use formulas that refer to cells in the other worksheets.

Franco Nadalin/Fotolia

Aspen Falls City Hall

In this chapter, you will work with a spreadsheet for Diane Payne, the Public Works Director in Aspen Falls. She wants to know the revenue generated from parking meters and parking tickets in different locations throughout the city. Understanding how much revenue is generated from the meters and tickets and the costs associated with park maintenance and upgrades will help Diane decide if more meters should be added and if more personnel should be hired to enforce parking regulations. She is also considering the removal of the parking meters in parts of the city and would like to know how much revenue would be lost.

A workbook, composed of multiple worksheets, allows Diane to collect data from different worksheets but analyze those worksheets grouped together as a whole. When you have a large amount of data to organize in a workbook, dividing the data into logical elements, such as locations or time periods, and then placing each element in a separate worksheet often makes sense. In other words, it is often better to design a system of worksheets instead of trying to fit all of the information on a single worksheet. You can then collect and input the data on an individual basis and see the summarized results with minimal effort.

In this project, you will work with grouped worksheets to enter formulas and apply formatting on all selected worksheets at the same time. You will create formulas that use multiple math operators, construct formulas that refer to cells in other worksheets, and create and format a clustered bar chart.

Time to complete all 10 skills—60 to 90 minutes

Outcome

Using the skills in this chapter, you will be able to move and clear cell contents using paste options, edit grouped worksheets, create summary sheets, create bar charts, and rename, delete, and organize worksheet tabs.

Objectives

3.1 Revise cell contents

3.2 Reorganize and edit worksheet tabs

3.3 Combine and edit data in grouped worksheets

3.4 Construct multiple operator and summary formulas

3.5 Design clustered bar charts

Student data file needed for this chapter:

exl03_Parking

You will save your file as:

Last_First_exl03_Parking

SKILLS

At the end of this chapter you will be able to:

Skill 1 Organize Worksheet Tabs
Skill 2 Enter and Format Dates
Skill 3 Clear Cell Contents and Formats
Skill 4 Move Cell Contents and Use Paste Options
Skill 5 Enter Data in Grouped Worksheets
Skill 6 Insert Multiple Math Operators in Formulas
Skill 7 Format Grouped Worksheets
Skill 8 Insert, Hide, Delete, and Move Worksheets
Skill 9 Create Summary Worksheets
Skill 10 Create Clustered Bar Charts

MORE SKILLS

Skill 11 Create SmartArt Organization Charts
Skill 12 Create and Insert Screen Shots
Skill 13 Modify the Quick Access Toolbar
Skill 14 Create and Edit Hyperlinks

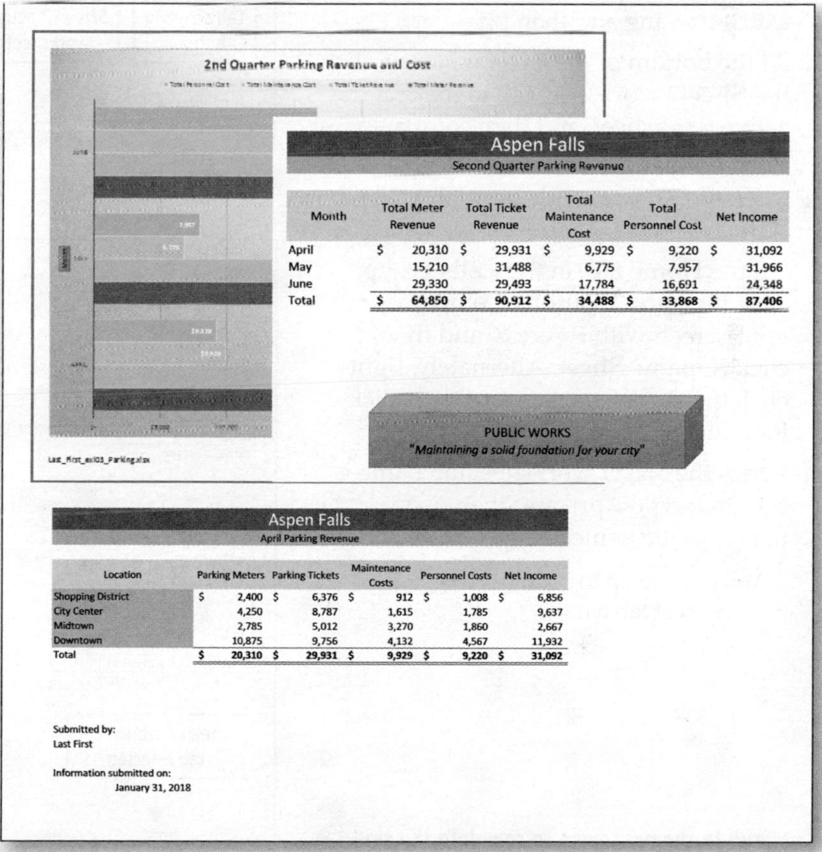
2nd Quarter Parking Revenue and Cost

Last_First_exl03_Parking.xlsx

Aspen Falls

Second Quarter Parking Revenue

Month	Total Meter Revenue	Total Ticket Revenue	Total Maintenance Cost	Total Personnel Cost	Net Income
April	$ 20,310	$ 29,931	$ 9,929	$ 9,220	$ 31,092
May	15,210	31,488	6,775	7,957	31,966
June	29,330	29,493	17,784	16,691	24,348
Total	$ 64,850	$ 90,912	$ 34,488	$ 33,868	$ 87,406

PUBLIC WORKS

"Maintaining a solid foundation for your city"

Aspen Falls

April Parking Revenue

Location	Parking Meters	Parking Tickets	Maintenance Costs	Personnel Costs	Net Income
Shopping District	$ 2,400	$ 6,376	$ 912	$ 1,008	$ 6,856
City Center	4,250	8,787	1,615	1,785	9,637
Midtown	2,785	5,012	3,270	1,860	2,667
Downtown	10,875	9,756	4,132	4,567	11,932
Total	$ 20,310	$ 29,931	$ 9,929	$ 9,220	$ 31,092

Submitted by:
Last First

Information submitted on:
January 31, 2018

SKILL 1: Organize Worksheet Tabs

- When a file contains more than one worksheet, you can move among worksheets by clicking the worksheet tabs.
- ***Tab scrolling buttons*** are buttons to the left of worksheet tabs used to display worksheet tabs that are not in view.

1. Start **Excel 2016**, and then open the student data file **exl03_Parking**. Click the **File tab**, and then click **Save As**. Click the **Browse** button, and then navigate to the location where you are saving your files. Click **New folder**, type Excel Chapter 3 and then press Enter two times. In the **File name** box, name the file Last_First_exl03_Parking and then press Enter.
2. At the bottom of the Excel window, click the **Sheet2** worksheet tab to make it the active worksheet, and then compare your screen with **Figure 1**.
3. Click the **Sheet1** worksheet tab to make it the active worksheet.
4. On the **Home tab**, in the **Cells group**, click the **Format** button. Compare your screen with **Figure 2**, and then click **Rename Sheet**. Alternately, right-click the worksheet tab, and then click Rename.
5. Verify the *Sheet1* worksheet tab name is selected, type April and then press Enter to accept the name change.

   MOS Obj 1.3.2 C

   You can use up to 31 characters in a worksheet tab name.

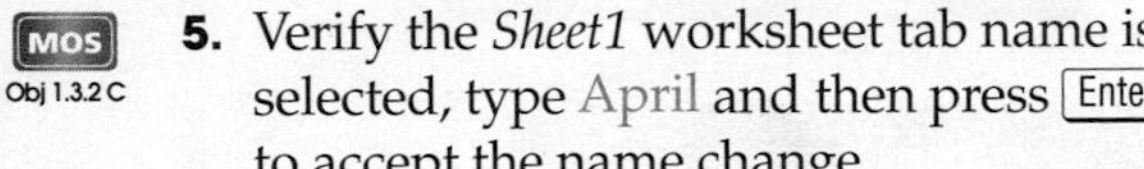

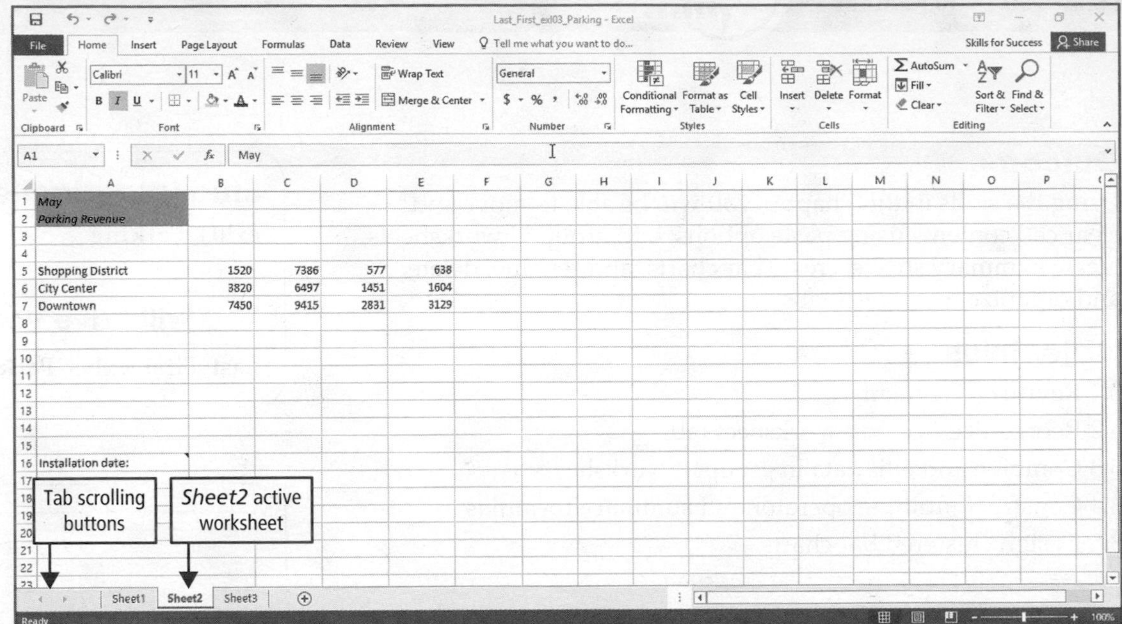

Figure 1

Excel 2016, Windows 10, Microsoft Corporation

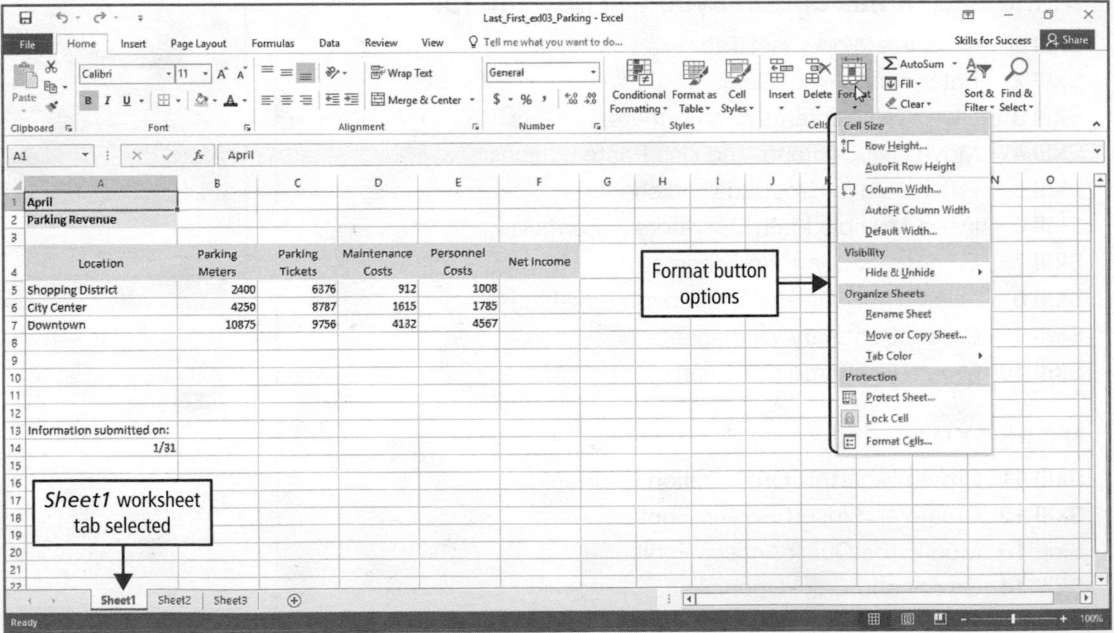

Figure 2

Excel 2016, Windows 10, Microsoft Corporation

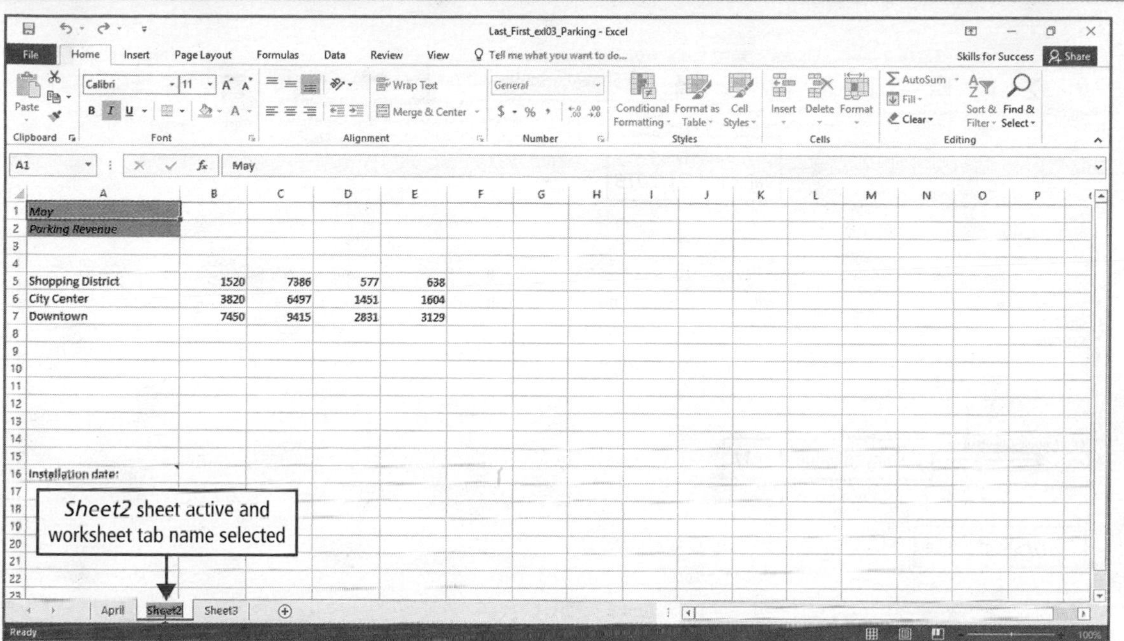

Excel 2016, Windows 10, Microsoft Corporation

Figure 3

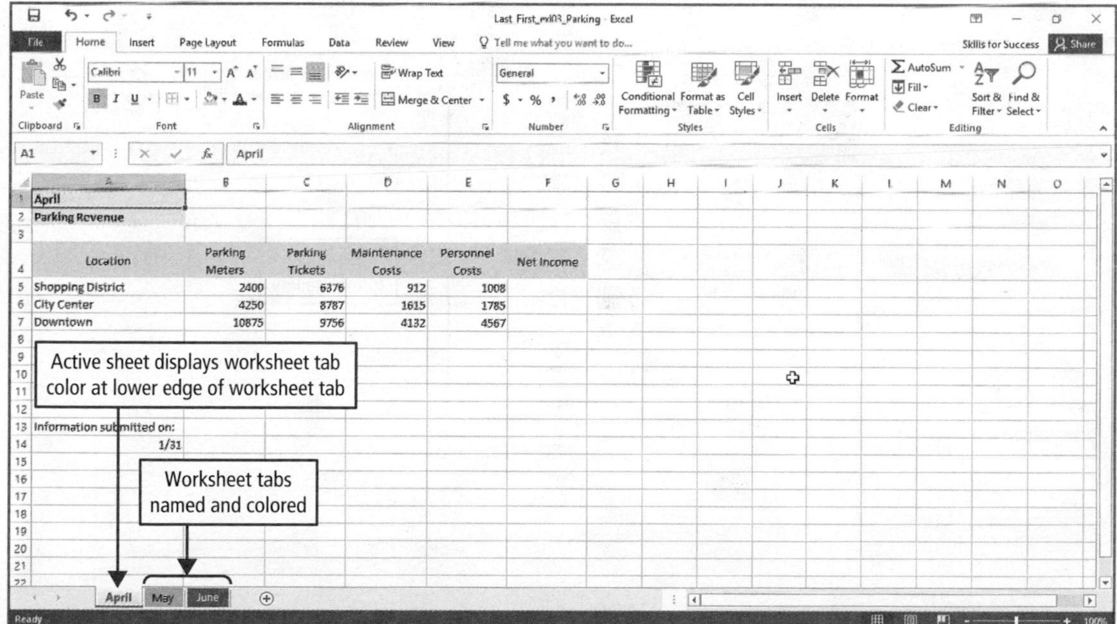

Excel 2016, Windows 10, Microsoft Corporation

Figure 4

6. Double-click the **Sheet2** worksheet tab to make it the active sheet and to select the sheet name. Compare your screen with **Figure 3**.
7. With the *Sheet2* worksheet tab name selected, type May and then press Enter.
8. Using either of the two methods just practiced, rename the **Sheet3** worksheet tab as June and then press Enter.
9. Verify that the *June* sheet is the active worksheet. Click the **Page Layout tab**, and then in the **Themes group**, click the **Colors** button. Scroll down, and then click **Slipstream** to change the theme colors for this workbook.

MOS Obj 1.3.6 C

10. Click the **Home tab**. In the **Cells group**, click the **Format** button, and then point to **Tab Color** to display the colors associated with the *Slipstream* theme colors. Click the fifth color in the first row—**Blue, Accent 1**. Alternately, right-click the worksheet tab, and then click Tab Color.

MOS Obj 1.3.1 C

    The gradient color on a worksheet tab indicates that the worksheet is active. When a worksheet is not active, the entire worksheet tab is filled with the selected color.

11. Use the technique just practiced to change the worksheet tab color of the **May** worksheet tab to the sixth color in the first row—**Turquoise, Accent 2**.
12. Change the worksheet tab color of the **April** worksheet tab to the seventh color in the first row—**Green, Accent 3**. Compare your screen with **Figure 4**.
13. **Save**  the file.

■ **You have completed Skill 1 of 10**

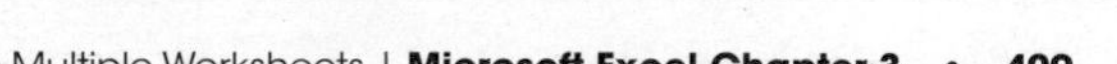

- When you enter a date, it is assigned a ***serial number***—a sequential number.
- Dates are stored as sequential serial numbers so they can be used in calculations. By default, January 1, 1900, is serial number 1. January 1, 2018, is serial number 43100 because it is 43,100 days after January 1, 1900. Serial numbers make it possible to perform calculations on dates, for example, to find the number of days between two dates by subtracting the older date from the more recent date.
- When you type any of the following values into cells, Excel interprets them as dates: 7/4/18, 4-Jul, 4-Jul-18, Jul-18. When typing in these dates formats, the [-] (hyphen) key and the [/] (forward slash) key function identically.
- You can enter months using the entire name or the first three characters. Years can be entered as two or four digits. When the year is left off, the current year will be inserted.

MOS Obj 1.4.8 C

1. On the **April** sheet, click cell **A14** to display the underlying value *1/31/2018* in the formula bar. Click the **Formulas tab**, and then in the **Formula Auditing group**, click the **Show Formulas** button. Compare your screen with **Figure 1**.

   The date, *January 31, 2018*, displays as 43131—the number of days since the reference date of January 1, 1900.

2. On the **Formulas tab**, in the **Formula Auditing group**, click the **Show Formulas** button to display the date.
3. Click the **Home tab**, and in the **Number group**, click the **Number Format arrow** (**Figure 2**).

   In the Number Format list, you can select common date, time, and number formats, or click *More Number Formats* to display additional built-in number formats.

■ Continue to the next page to complete the skill

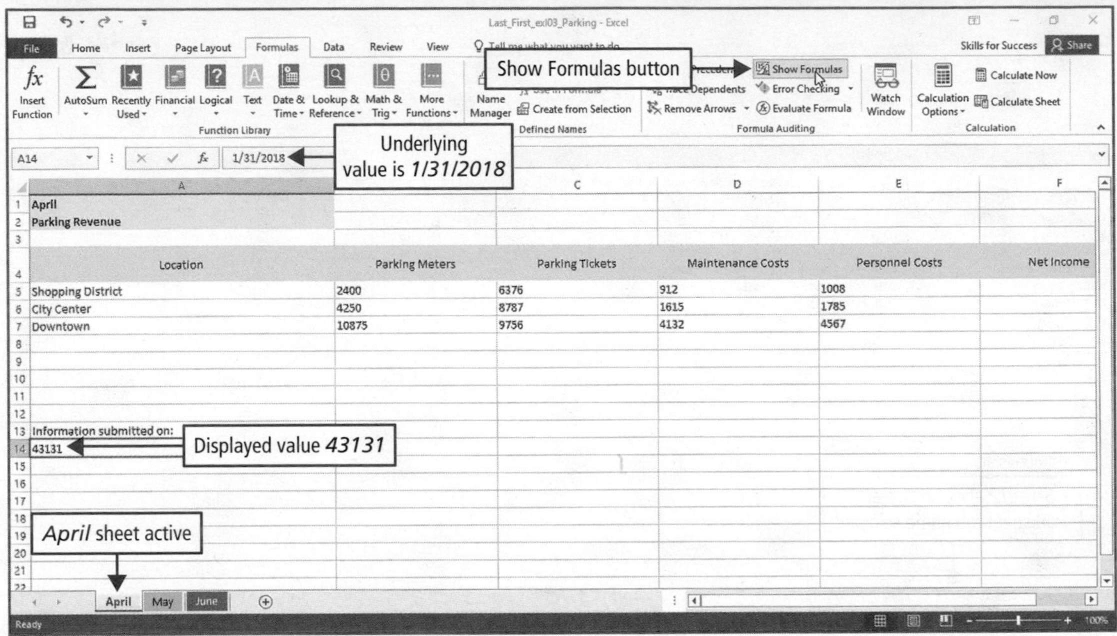

Figure 1

Excel 2016, Windows 10, Microsoft Corporation

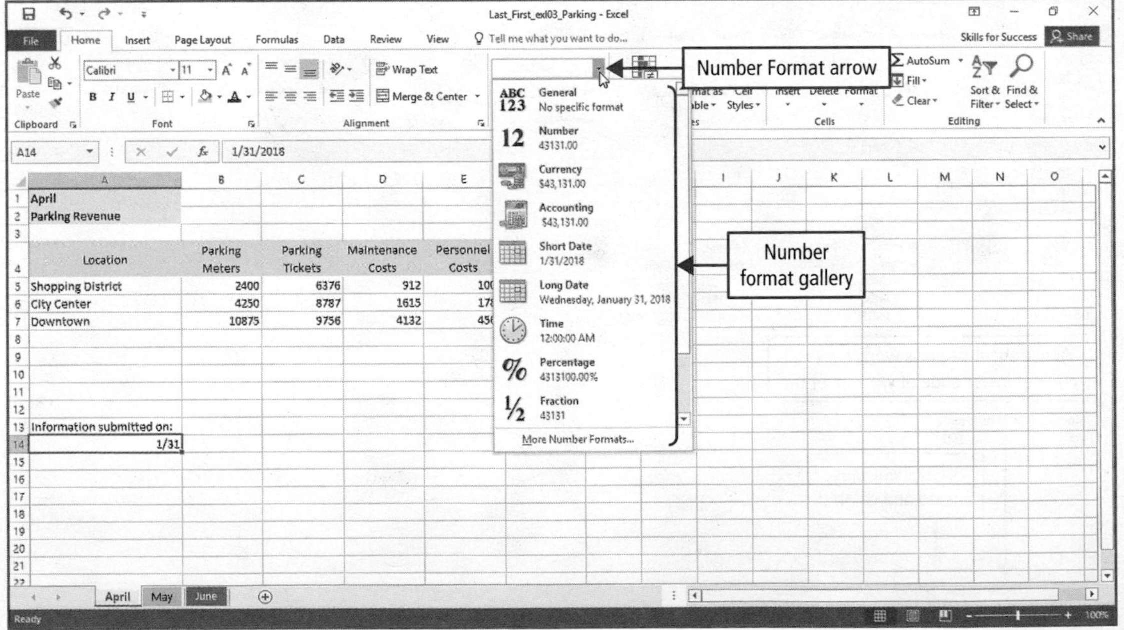

Figure 2

Excel 2016, Windows 10, Microsoft Corporation

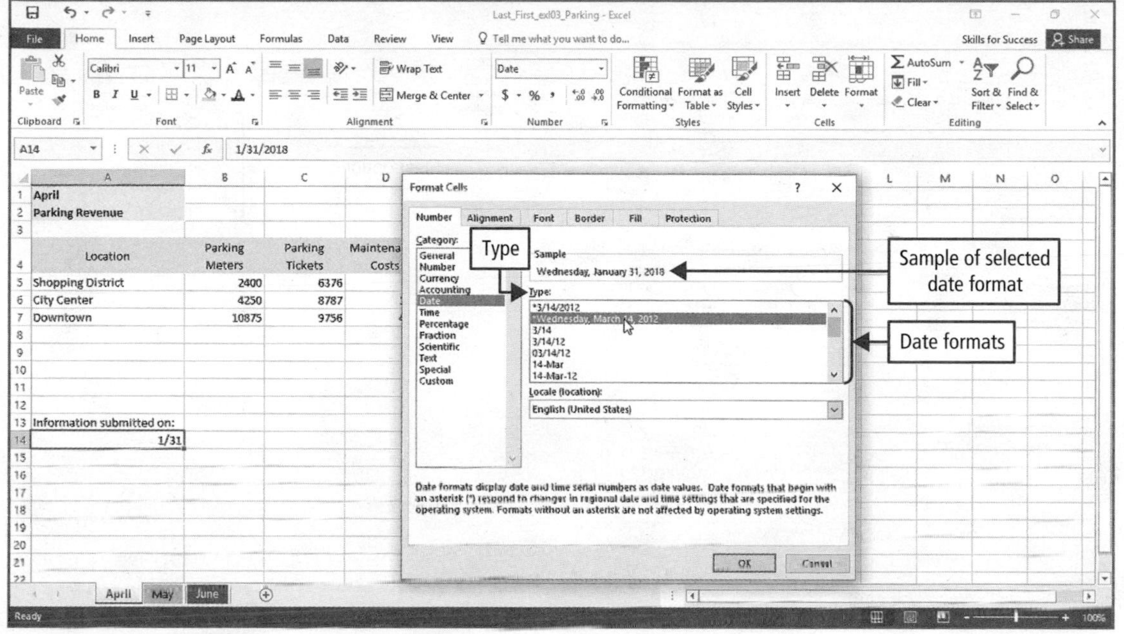

Excel 2016, Windows 10, Microsoft Corporation

Figure 3

Date Format AutoComplete	
Date Typed As	**Completed by Excel As**
7/4/18	7/4/2018
7-4-98	7/4/1998
7/4 or 7-4	4-Jul (current year assumed)
July 4 or Jul 4	4-Jul (current year assumed)
Jul/4 or Jul-4	4-Jul (current year assumed)
July 4, 1998	4-Jul-98
July 2018	Jul-18 (the first day of the month is assumed)
July 1998	Jul-98 (the first day of the month is assumed)

Figure 4

4. At the bottom of the **Number Format** list, click **More Number Formats**. On the **Number tab** of the **Format Cells** dialog box, notice Date is selected at the left. Under **Type**, click ***Wednesday, March 14, 2012** to show a sample of the selected date format. Compare your screen with **Figure 3**.

   The date *Wednesday, March 14, 2012* will not display in your worksheet. This is a sample of a format that can be applied to your current date.

5. Under **Type**, scroll down, click **March 14, 2012**, and then click **OK** to display the date in cell A14 as *January 31, 2018*.

6. Click the **May** worksheet tab to make it the active worksheet, and then click cell **A17**. Type 8/11/98 and then on the formula bar, click the **Enter** button [✓] to accept the entry and change the year from *98* to *1998*.

   When a two-digit year between 30 and 99 is entered, a twentieth-century date is applied to the date format—*8/11/1998*.

7. Click the **June** worksheet tab, and then click cell **A17**. Hold down [Ctrl] and press [;]—the semicolon key—to enter the current date. Press [Enter] to confirm the entry.

   The [Ctrl] + [;] shortcut enters the current date, obtained from your computer, into the selected cell using the default date format. The table in **Figure 4** summarizes how Excel interprets various date entries.

8. **Save** [save icon] the file.

■ **You have completed Skill 2 of 10**

- Cells can contain formatting, comments, hyperlinks, and ***content***—underlying formulas and data in a cell.
- You can clear the formatting, comments, hyperlinks, or contents of a cell.

1. Click the **April** worksheet tab, and then click cell **A1**. On the **Home tab**, in the **Editing group**, click the **Clear** button, and then compare your screen with **Figure 1**.
2. On the menu, click **Clear Contents**. Look at cell **A1**, and verify that the text has been cleared but that the fill color applied to the cell still displays.

   Alternately, to delete the contents of a cell, you can press Delete.
3. In cell **A1**, type Parking Revenue and then on the formula bar, click the **Enter** button ✓.
4. With cell **A1** still selected, in the **Editing group**, click the **Clear** button, and then click **Clear Formats** to clear the formatting from the cell. Compare your screen with **Figure 2**.
5. Click cell **A2**. On the **Home tab**, in the **Editing group**, click the **Clear** button, and then click **Clear All** to clear both the cell contents and the cell formatting.

   Alternately, tap a cell on a touchscreen, and then on the Mini toolbar, click Clear.

Continue to the next page to complete the skill

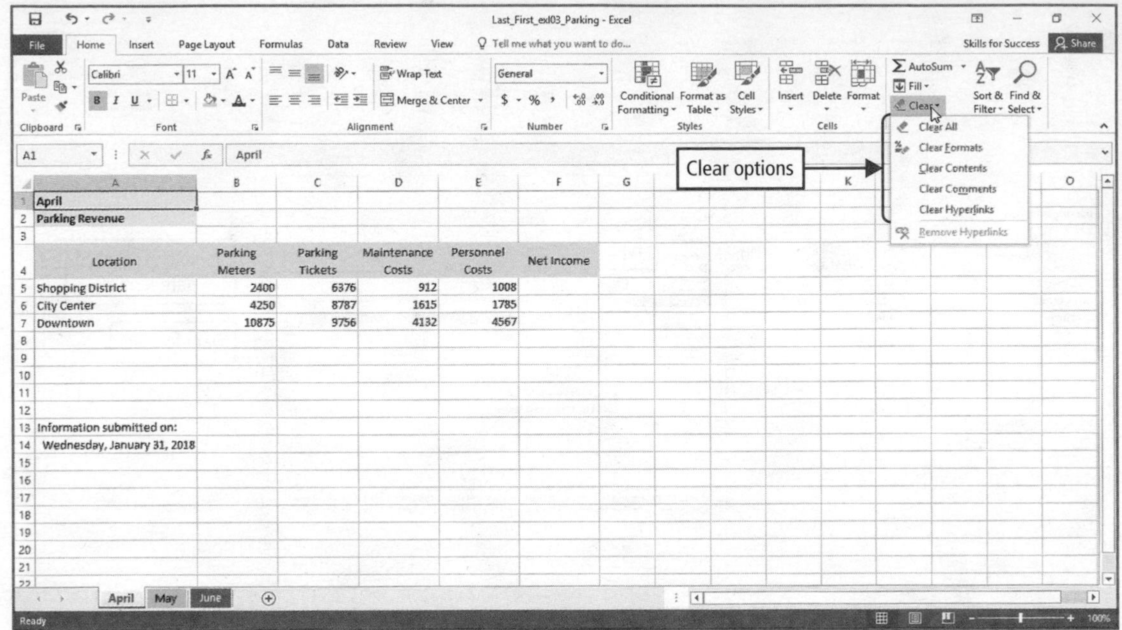

Figure 1 Excel 2016, Windows 10, Microsoft Corporation

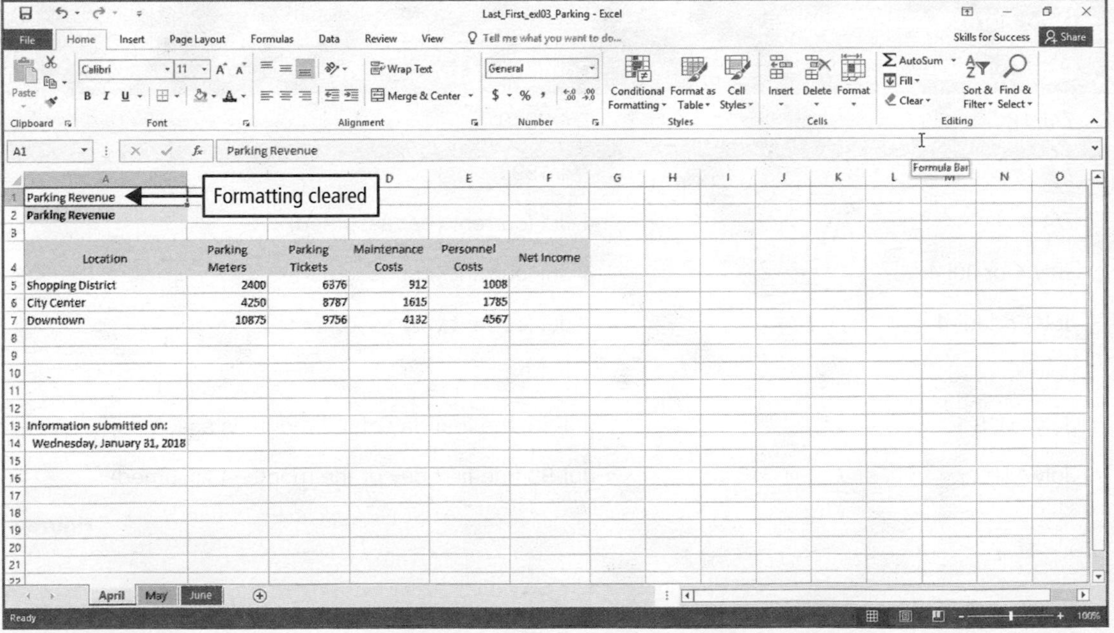

Figure 2 Excel 2016, Windows 10, Microsoft Corporation

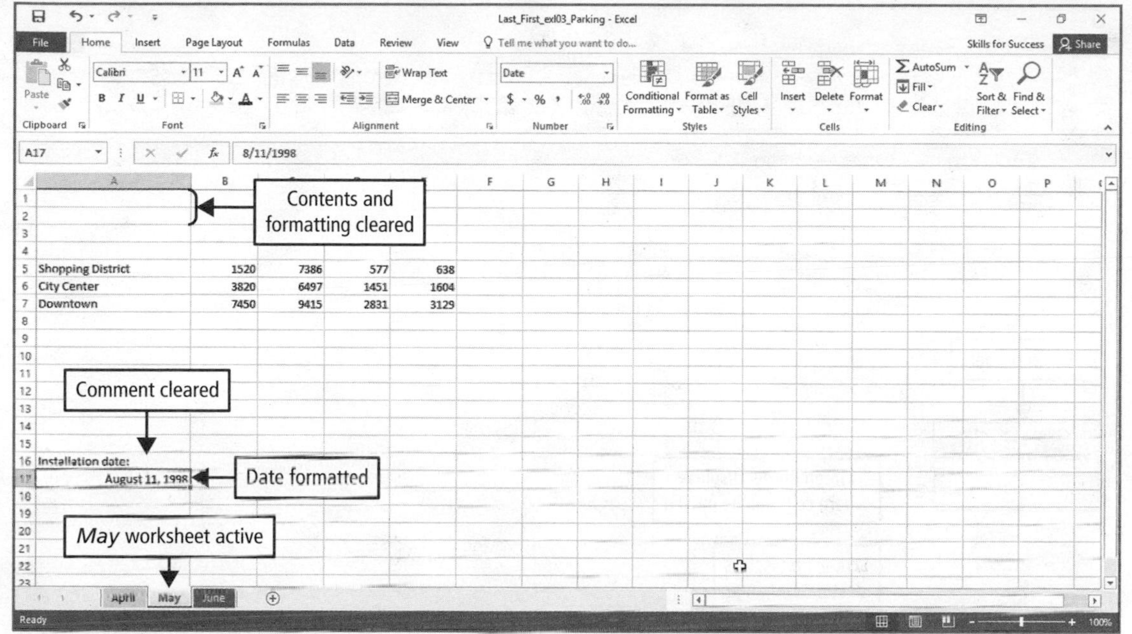

Excel 2016, Windows 10, Microsoft Corporation

Figure 3

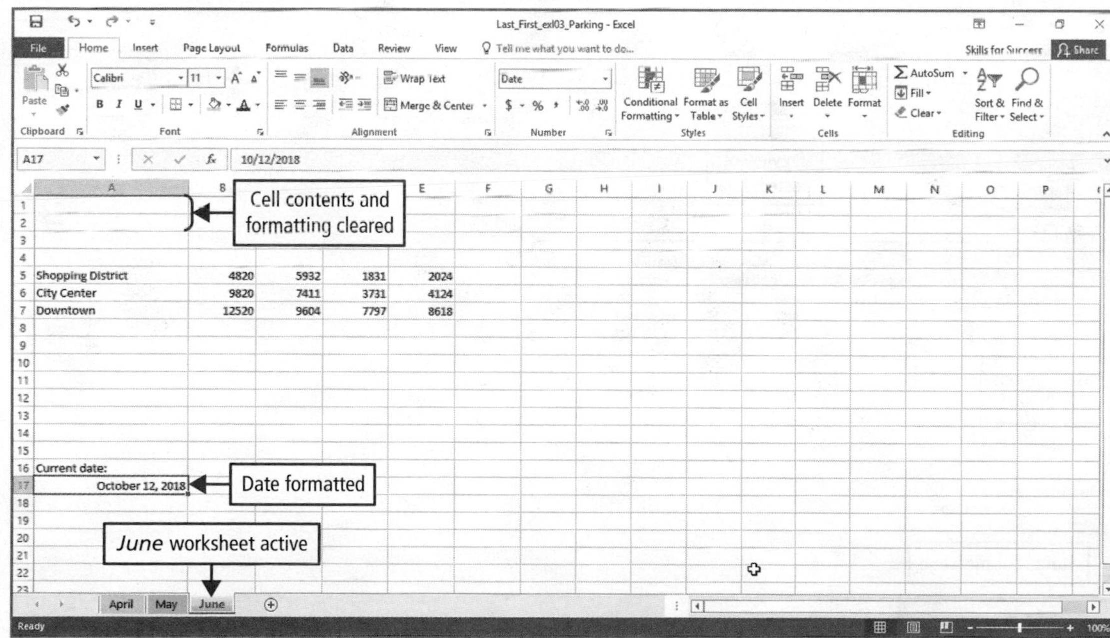

Excel 2016, Windows 10, Microsoft Corporation

Figure 4

6. Display the **May** worksheet, and then select the range **A1:A2**. In the **Editing group**, click the **Clear** button, and then click **Clear All**.
7. Click cell **A16** to display the comment. On the **Home tab**, in the **Editing group**, click the **Clear** button, and then click **Clear Comments** to clear the comment from the cell.
8. Click cell **A17**. On the **Home tab**, in the **Number group**, click the **Number Format arrow**. At the bottom of the **Number Format** list, click **More Number Formats**. In the **Format Cells** dialog box, under **Type**, scroll down, click **March 14, 2012**, and then click **OK** to display the date in cell A17 as *August 11, 1998*. Compare your screen with **Figure 3**.
9. Display the **June** worksheet. Select the range **A1:A2**, and then use the technique just practiced to clear the contents and formatting from the selected range.
10. Click cell **A17**, and then use the technique just practiced to apply the date format *March 14, 2012*, to the current date. Compare your screen with **Figure 4**.
11. Make **April** the active worksheet, and then **Save** the file.

■ **You have completed Skill 3 of 10**

- Data from cells and ranges can be copied and then pasted to other cells in the same worksheet, to other worksheets, or to worksheets in another workbook.
- The ***Clipboard*** is a temporary storage area for text and graphics. When you use either the Copy command or the Cut command, the selected data is placed in the Clipboard, from which the data is available to paste.

1. On the **April** sheet, select the range **A13:A14**. Point to the lower edge of the green border surrounding the selected range until the pointer displays. Drag downward until the ScreenTip displays *A16:A17*, as shown in **Figure 1**, and then release the left mouse button to complete the move.

   Drag and drop is a method of moving objects in which you point to the selection and then drag it to a new location.

2. Select the range **A4:F4**. In the **Clipboard group**, click the **Copy** button.

   A moving border surrounds the selected range, and a message on the status bar indicates *Select destination and press ENTER or choose Paste*, confirming that your selected range has been copied to the Clipboard.

3. Display the **May** sheet, and then click cell **A4**. In the **Clipboard group**, click the **Paste arrow** to display the **Paste Options** gallery. Point at the second option in the second row—**Keep Source Column Width** and then compare your screen with **Figure 2**.

■ Continue to the next page to complete the skill

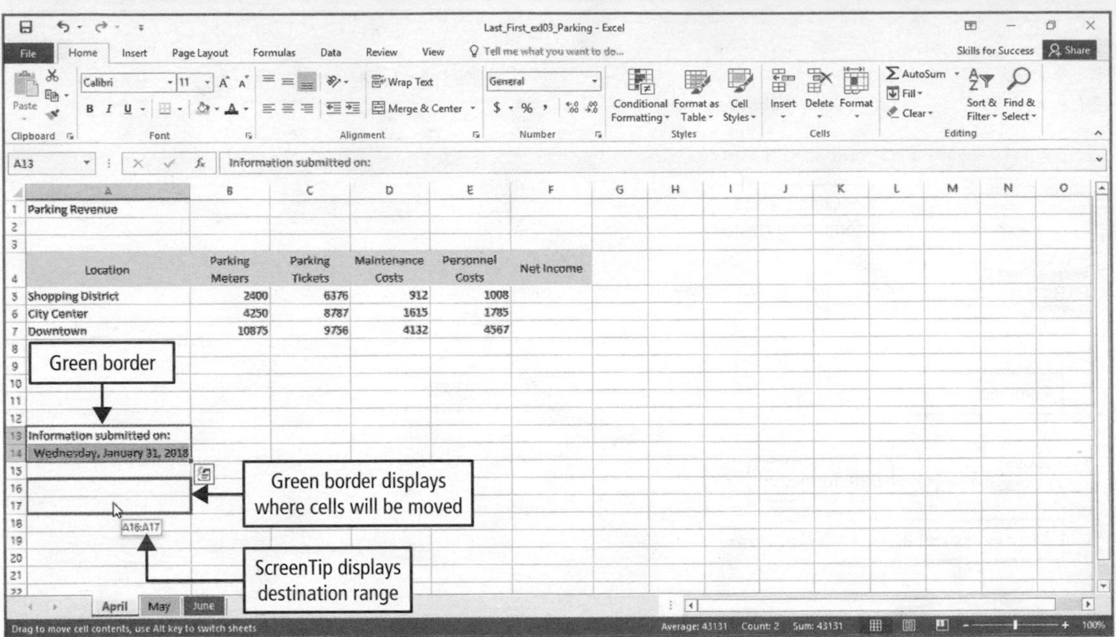

Figure 1

Excel 2016, Windows 10, Microsoft Corporation

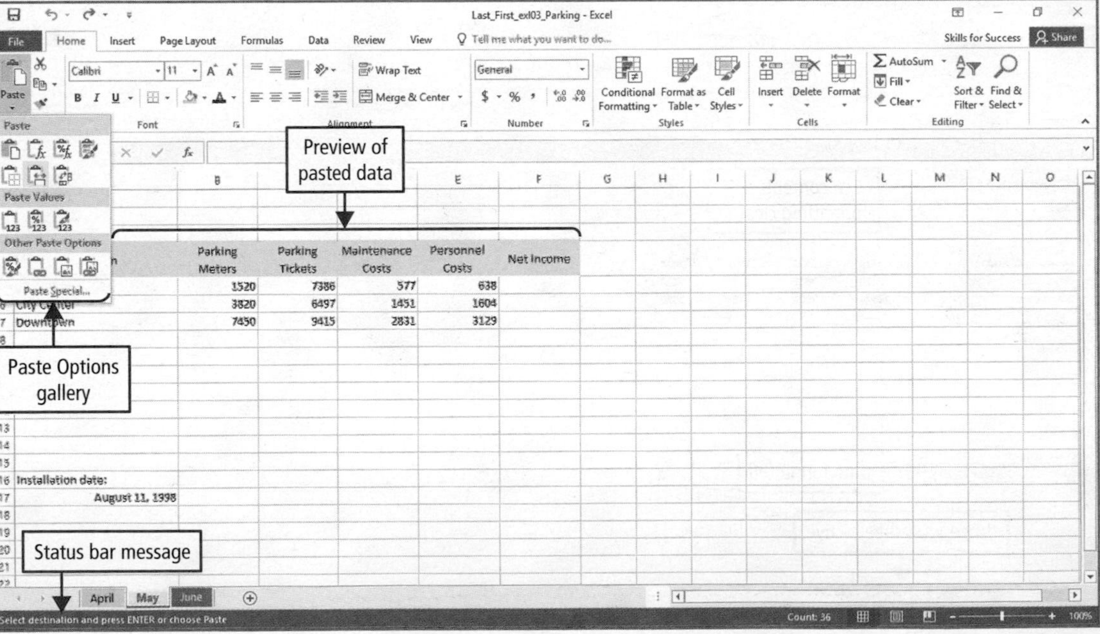

Figure 2

Excel 2016, Windows 10, Microsoft Corporation

Paste Options		
Option	**Icon**	**Content and format pasted**
Paste		Both the contents and cell formatting
Formulas		Only the formula
Formulas & Number Formatting		Both the formula and the number formatting
Keep Source Formatting		All content and cell formatting from original cells
No Borders		All content and cell formatting except borders
Keep Source Column Widths		All content and formatting including the column width format
Transpose		Orientation of pasted entries changes—data in rows are pasted as columns
Formatting		Only the formatting

Figure 3

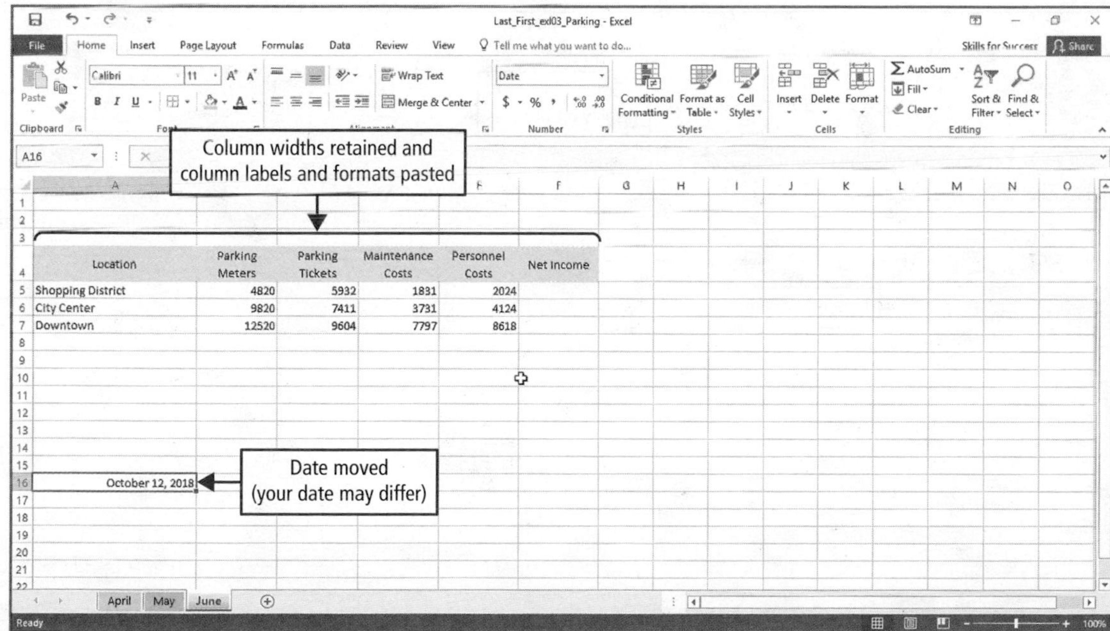

Excel 2016, Windows 10, Microsoft Corporation

Figure 4

4. In the **Paste Options** gallery, click the option **Keep Source Column Widths** to paste the column labels and to retain the column widths from the source worksheet. The table in **Figure 3** summarizes the Paste Options.

   When pasting a range of cells, you need to select only the cell in the upper left corner of the ***paste area***—the target destination for data that has been cut or copied. When an item is pasted, it is not removed from the Clipboard, as indicated by the status bar message.

5. Display the **June** sheet, and then click cell **A4**. Using the technique just practiced, paste the column labels using the Paste Option **Keep Source Column Widths**.
6. Click cell **A17**, and then point to the upper green border surrounding the cell to display the pointer. Drag up to move the cell contents to cell **A16**. In the message box *There's already data here. Do you want to replace it?* click **OK** to replace the contents. Compare your screen with **Figure 4**.
7. Click the **April** worksheet tab. **Save** the file.

- **You have completed Skill 4 of 10**

- You can group any number of worksheets in a workbook. After the worksheets are grouped, you can edit data in all of the grouped worksheets at the same time.
- Grouping worksheets is useful when you are creating or modifying a set of worksheets that are similar in purpose and structure.

1. Right-click the **April** worksheet tab, and then from the shortcut menu, click **Select All Sheets**.
2. At the top of the screen, on the title bar, verify that *[Group]* displays as shown in **Figure 1**.

   Here, all three worksheet tabs are shaded with a gradient color and *[Group]* displays on the title bar to indicate that the three worksheets are active as a group.
3. Select the range **A5:A7**, and then apply the **40% - Accent1** cell style.
4. Display the **May** worksheet to ungroup the sheets and to verify that the cell style you selected in the previous step displays as shown in **Figure 2**.

   In the worksheet tab area, both the *April* worksheet tab and the *June* worksheet tab display a solid color, indicating that they are no longer active in the group. At the top of your screen, *[Group]* no longer displays on the title bar.

   Selecting a single worksheet cancels a grouping. Because the worksheets were grouped, formatting was applied to all of the selected worksheets. In this manner, you can make the same changes to all selected worksheets at the same time.

■ **Continue to the next page to complete the skill**

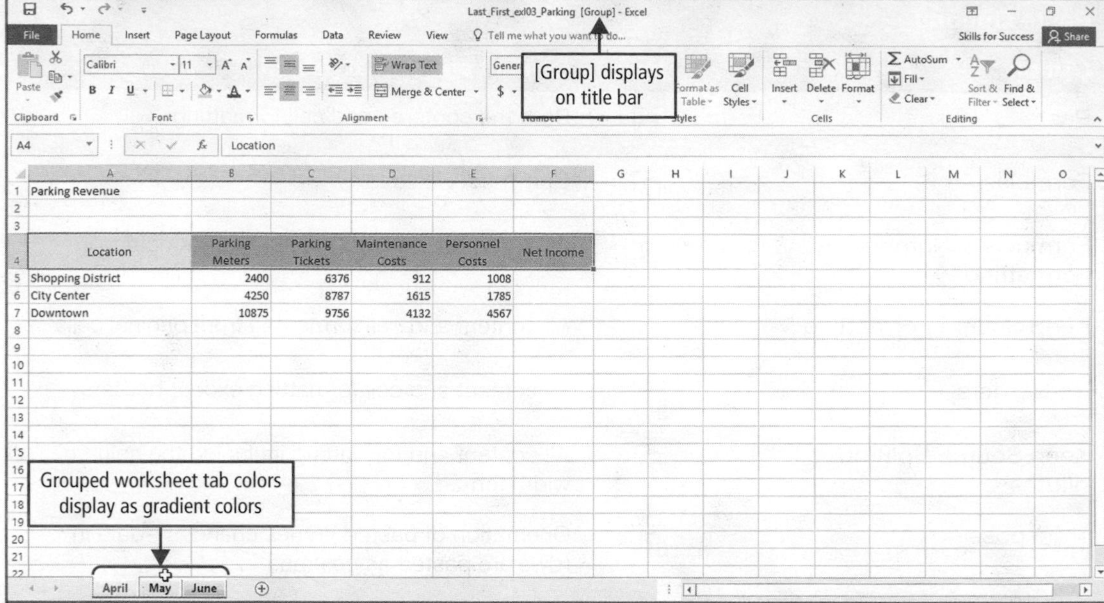

Figure 1 Excel 2016, Windows 10, Microsoft Corporation

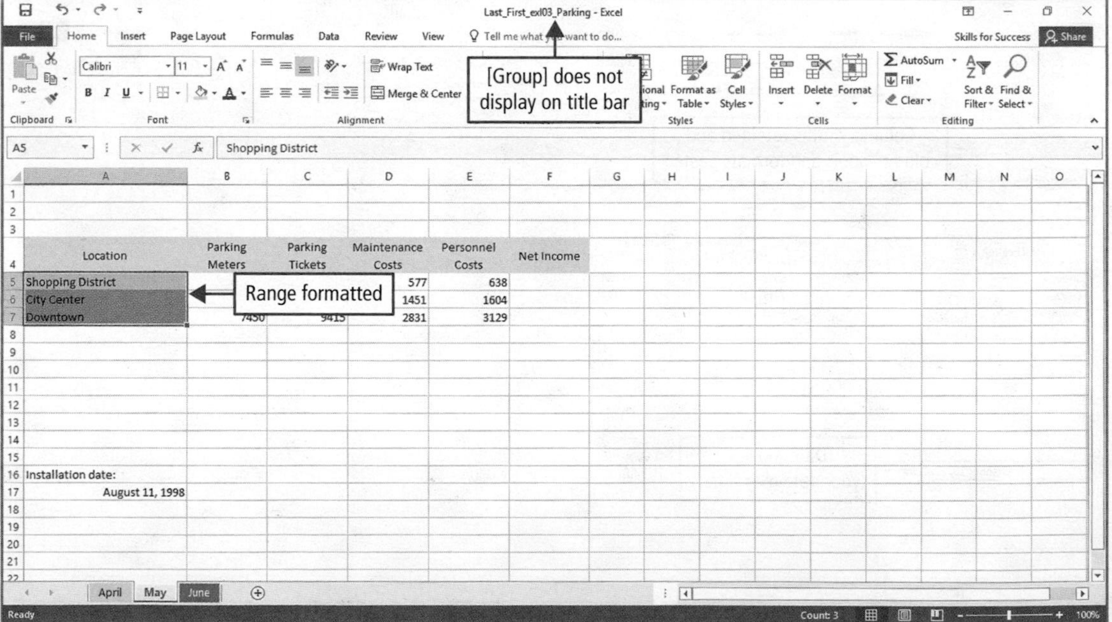

Figure 2 Excel 2016, Windows 10, Microsoft Corporation

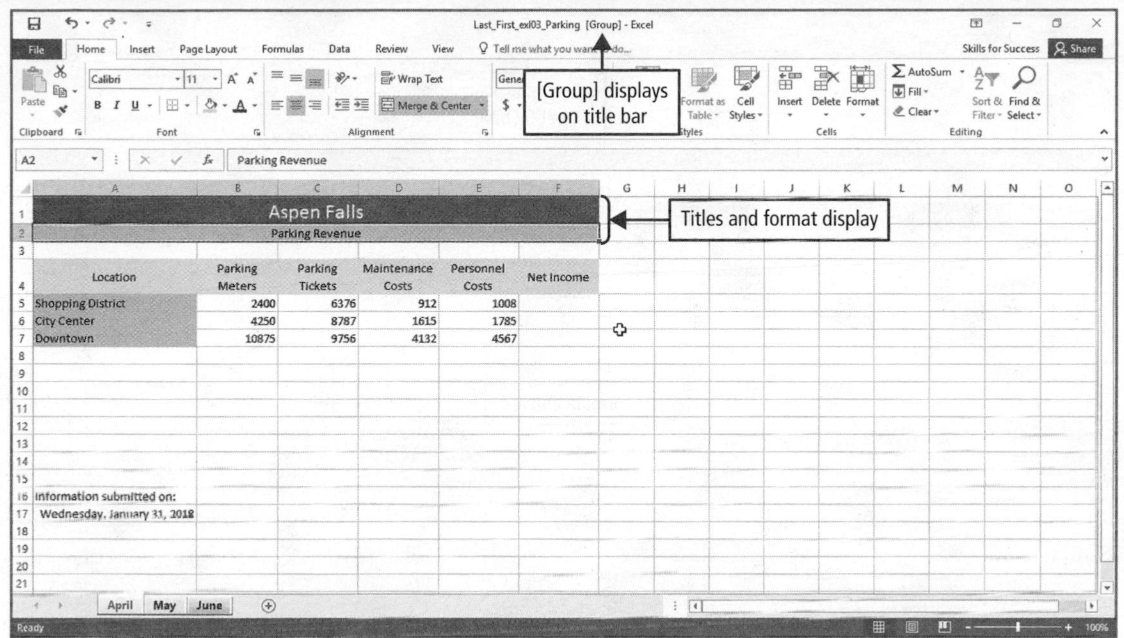

Excel 2016, Windows 10, Microsoft Corporation

Figure 3

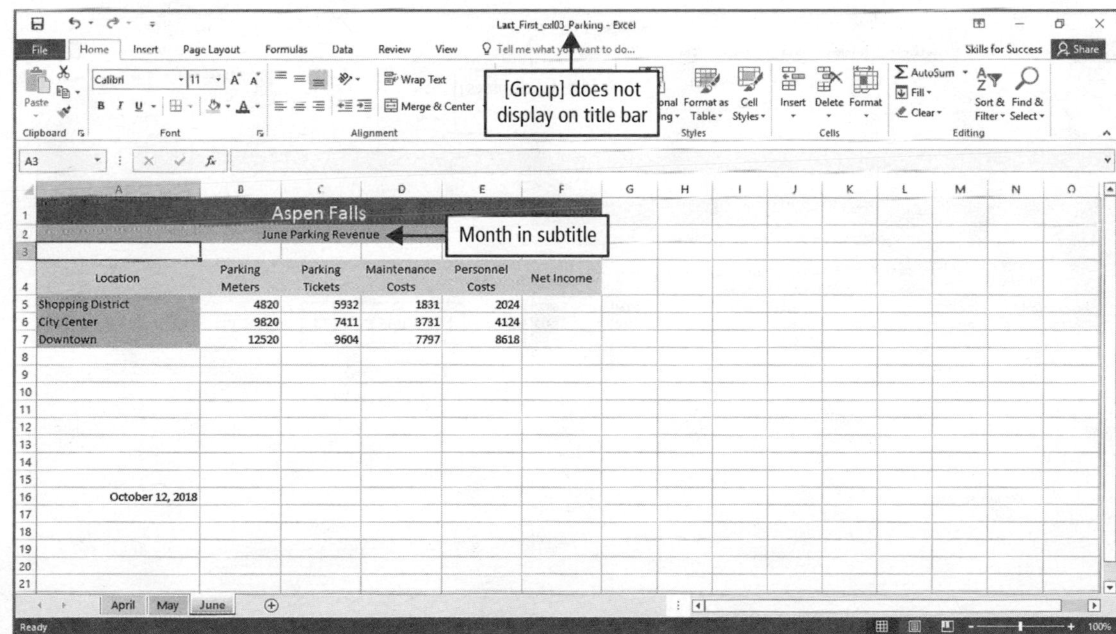

Excel 2016, Windows 10, Microsoft Corporation

Figure 4

5. Right-click the **April** worksheet tab, and then from the shortcut menu, click **Select All Sheets**.
6. Click cell **A1**, type Aspen Falls to replace the current text, and then press Enter. Select the range **A1:F1**, and then in the **Alignment group**, click the **Merge & Center** button. Apply the **Accent1** cell style. Click the **Font Size** button, and then click **18**.
7. In cell **A2**, type Parking Revenue and then press Enter. Select the range **A2:F2**, and then click the **Merge & Center** button. Apply the **40% - Accent1** cell style, and then compare your screen with **Figure 3**.
8. Right-click the **April** worksheet tab, and then from the shortcut menu, click **Ungroup Sheets**. Verify that [Group] no longer displays on the title bar.
9. Double-click cell **A2** to edit the cell contents. Use the arrow keys to move to the left of the word *Parking*. Type April and add a space, and then press Enter. Display the **May** worksheet. Using the same technique, edit cell **A2** to May Parking Revenue Display the **June** worksheet, and then edit cell **A2** to June Parking Revenue Compare your screen with **Figure 4**.
10. **Save** the file.

■ **You have completed Skill 5 of 10**

- When you combine several math operators in a single formula, ***operator precedence***—a set of mathematical rules for performing calculations within a formula—is followed. Expressions within parentheses are calculated first. Exponentials are calculated second. Then multiplication and division are performed before addition and subtraction.
- When a formula contains operators with the same precedence level, Excel evaluates the operators from left to right. Multiplication and division are considered to be on the same level of precedence. Addition and subtraction are considered to be on the same level of precedence.

1. Right-click the **June** worksheet tab, and then click **Select All Sheets**. Verify that *[Group]* displays on the title bar.
2. Click cell **F5**, enter the formula =(B5+C5)-(D5+E5) and then compare your screen with **Figure 1**.

   The formula *Net Income = Total Revenue – Total Cost* is represented by *(Parking Meters + Parking Tickets) – (Maintenance Cost + Personnel Cost)*. By placing parentheses in the formula, the revenue is first added together, the costs are added together, and then the total costs are subtracted from the total revenues. Without the parentheses, the formula would give an incorrect result.
3. On the formula bar, click the **Enter** button [✓]. AutoFill the formula down through cell **F7**. Compare your screen with **Figure 2**.

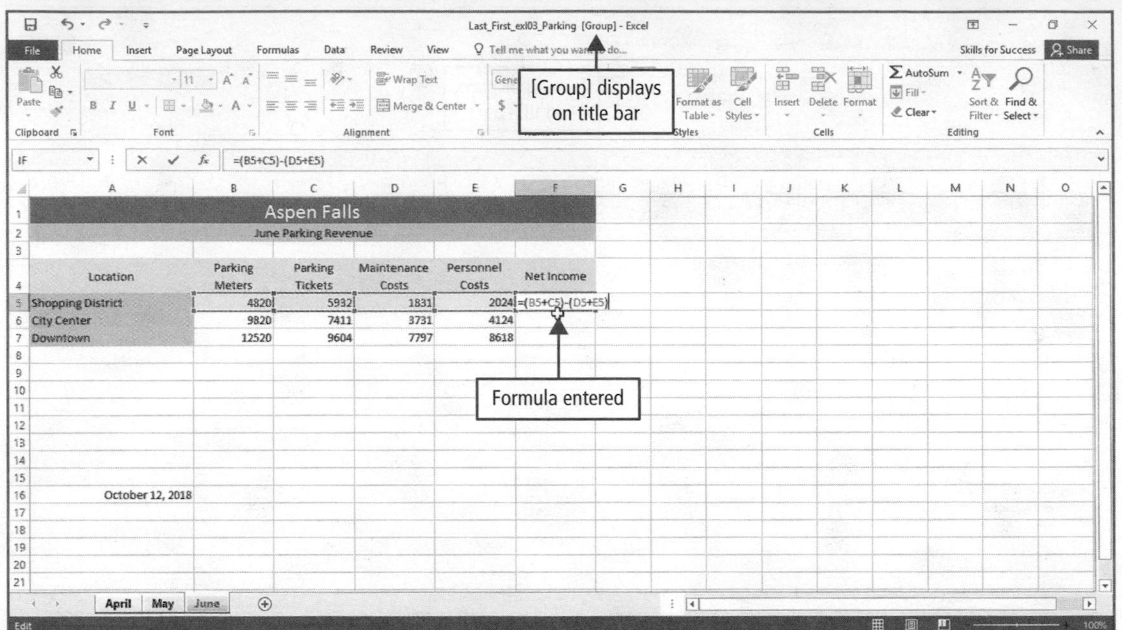

Figure 1 Excel 2016, Windows 10, Microsoft Corporation

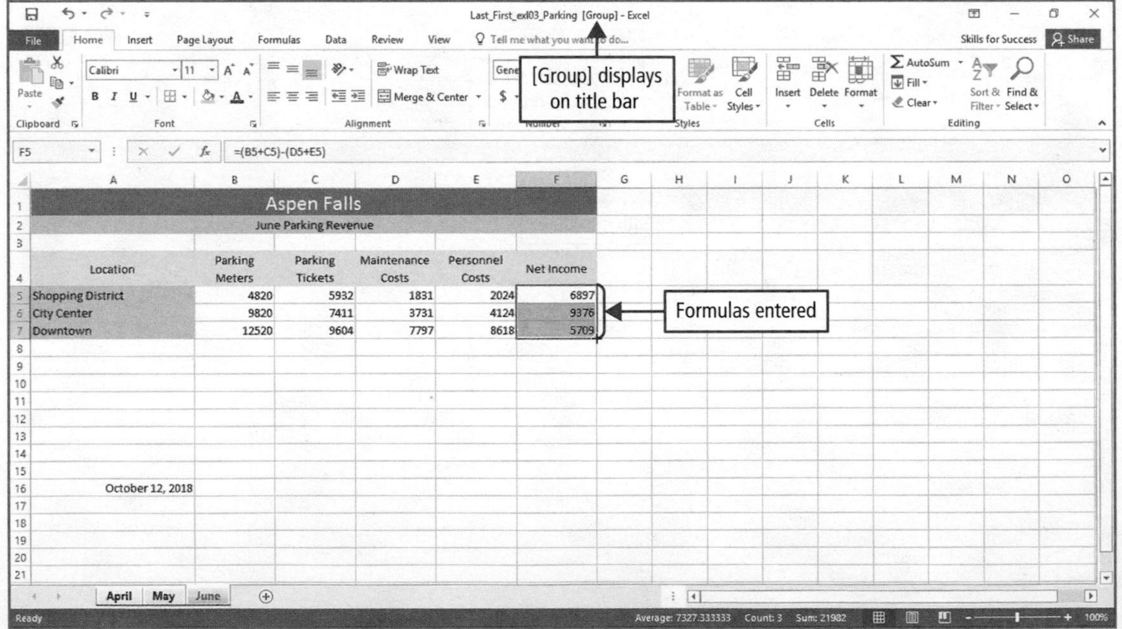

Figure 2 Excel 2016, Windows 10, Microsoft Corporation

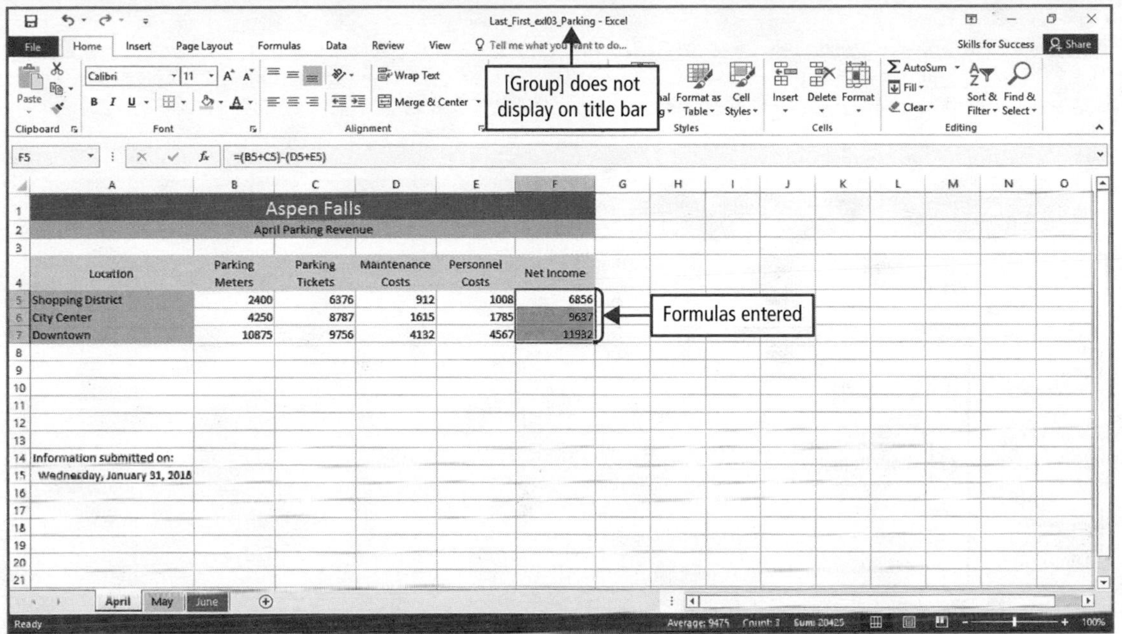

Excel 2016, Windows 10, Microsoft Corporation

Figure 3

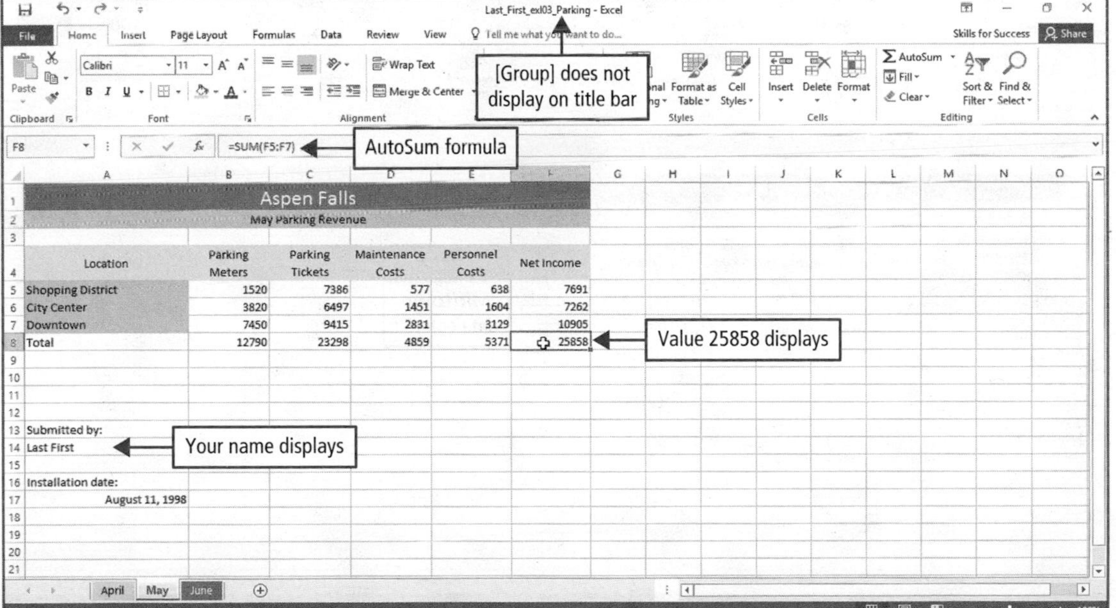

Excel 2016, Windows 10, Microsoft Corporation

Figure 4

4. Display the **April** worksheet to ungroup the sheets and to verify that the formula results display in the worksheet. Compare your screen with **Figure 3**.

   Because the worksheets were grouped, the formulas have been entered on all selected worksheets.

5. Right-click the **April** worksheet tab, and then click **Select All Sheets**. Verify that *[Group]* displays on the title bar.

6. In cell **A8**, type Total and then press Enter. Select the range **B8:F8**, and then on the **Home tab**, in the **Editing group**, click the **AutoSum** button to insert the column totals.

7. Click cell **A13**, type Submitted by: and then press Enter. In cell **A14**, using your name, type Last First and then press Enter.

8. Click the **May** worksheet tab. Click cell **F8**, and then compare your screen with **Figure 4**.

   On the *May* worksheet, the formula in cell F8 displays as the value *25858*.

9. **Save** the file.

■ **You have completed Skill 6 of 10**

- When worksheets are grouped, any formatting applied to a single worksheet is made to each worksheet in the group. For example, if you change the width of a column or add a row, all the worksheets in the group are changed in the same manner.

1. Right-click the **May** worksheet tab, and then click **Select All Sheets**.
2. In the row heading area, point to row 7 to display the [→] pointer. Right-click, and then compare your screen with **Figure 1**.
3. From the shortcut menu, click **Insert** to insert a new blank row above the *Downtown* row in all of the grouped worksheets. In cell **A7**, type Midtown and then press [Tab].
4. Click the **April** worksheet tab to make it the active worksheet and to ungroup the worksheets. Beginning in cell **B7**, enter the following *Midtown* data for April:

   2785 | 5012 | 3270 | 1860
5. Click the **May** worksheet tab, and then beginning in cell **B7**, enter the following *Midtown* data for May:

   2420 | 8190 | 1916 | 2586
6. Click the **June** worksheet tab, and then beginning in cell **B7**, enter the following *Midtown* data for June:

   2170 | 6546 | 4425 | 1925
7. Click each of the worksheet tabs, and then verify that you entered the values correctly. Click the **June** worksheet tab, and then compare your screen with **Figure 2**.

■ **Continue to the next page to complete the skill**

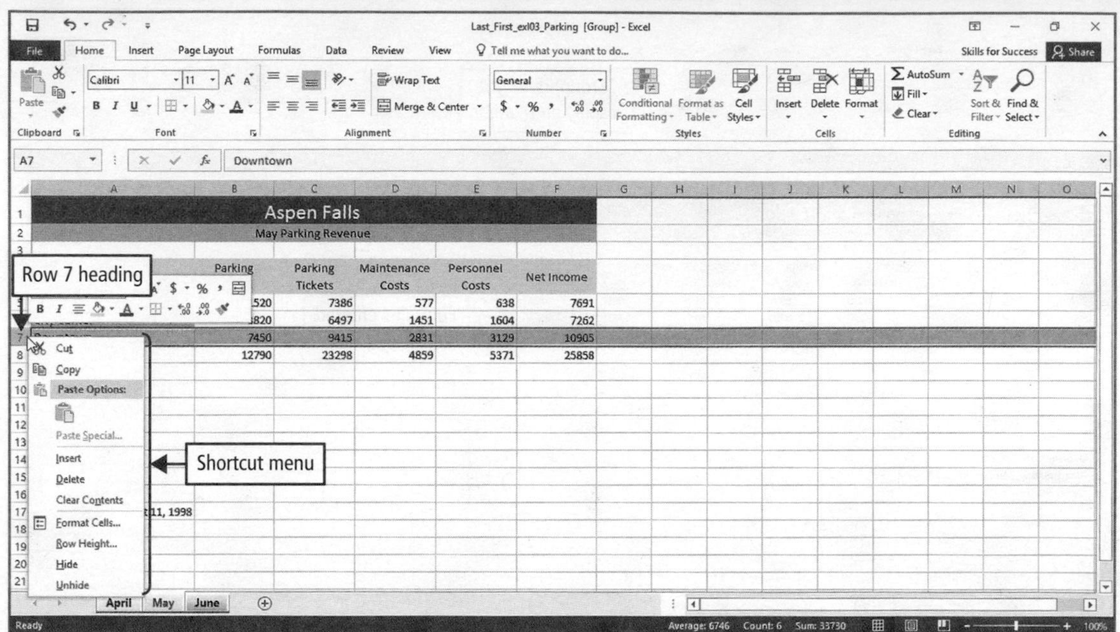

Figure 1

Excel 2016, Windows 10, Microsoft Corporation

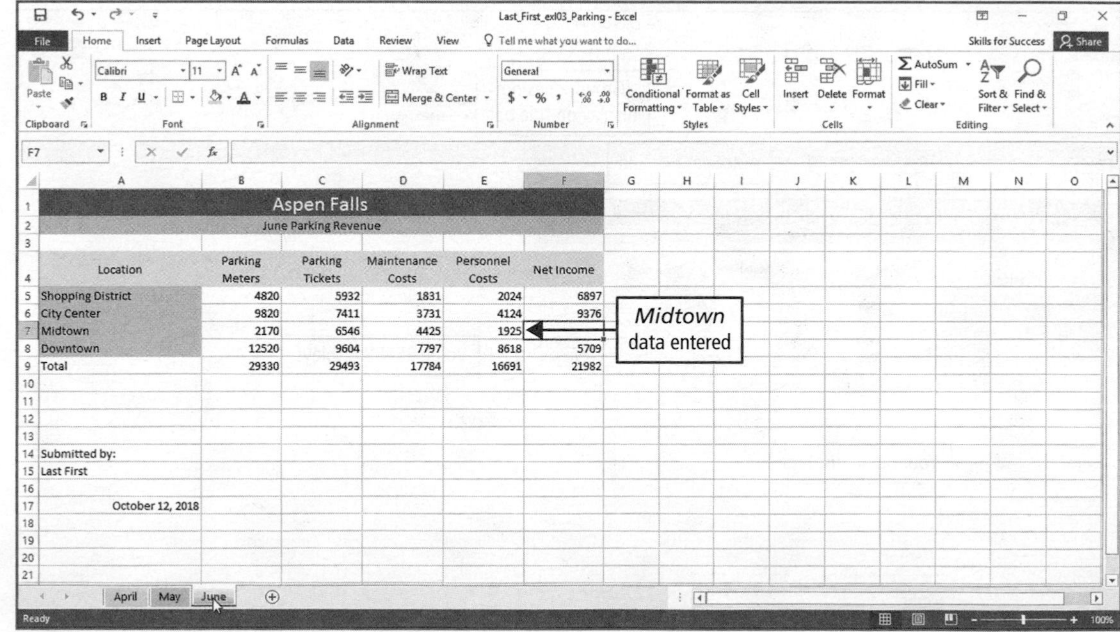

Figure 2

Excel 2016, Windows 10, Microsoft Corporation

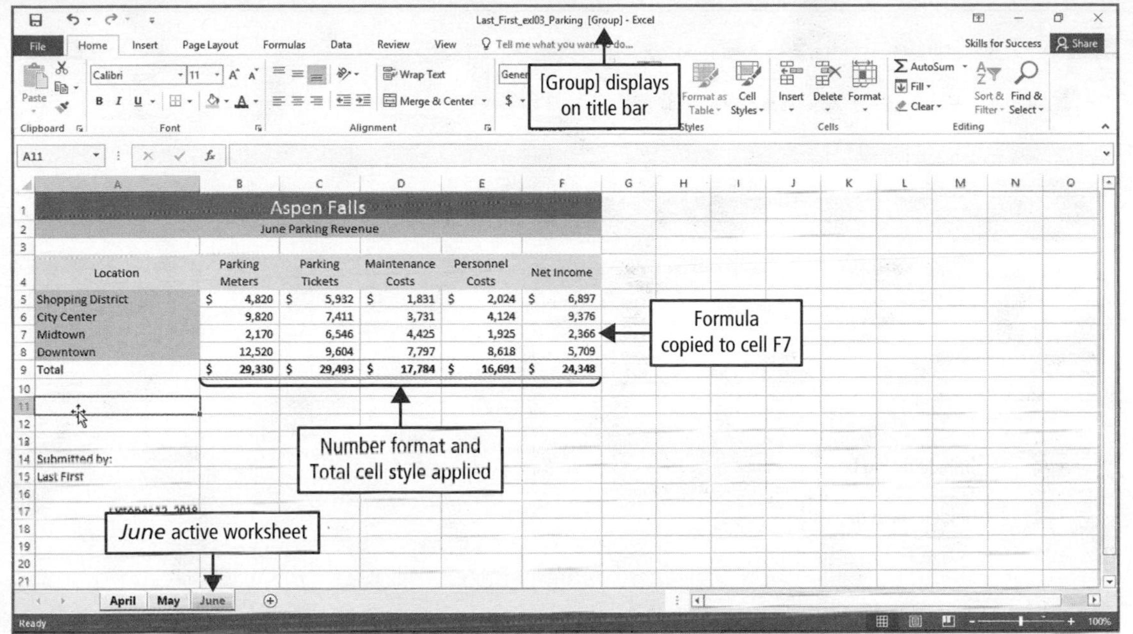

Excel 2016, Windows 10, Microsoft Corporation

Figure 3

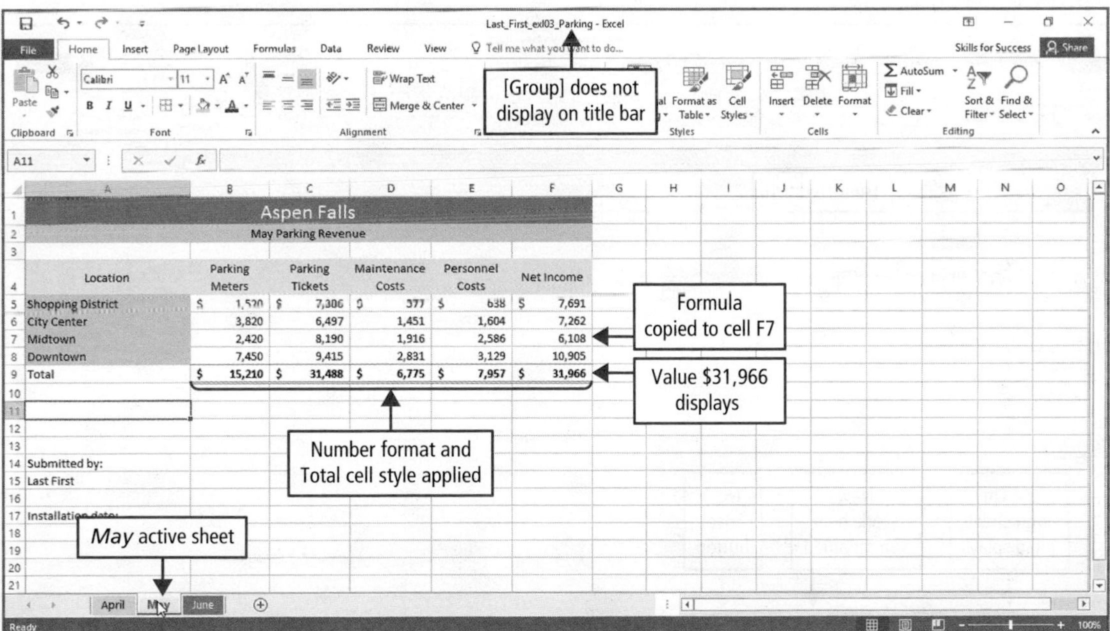

Excel 2016, Windows 10, Microsoft Corporation

Figure 4

8. Right-click the **June** worksheet tab, and then click **Select All Sheets**. Click cell **F6**, and then AutoFill the formula down to cell **F7**.

   On the *June* worksheet, the formula in cell *F9* displays as the value *24348*.

9. Select the range **B5:F5**, hold down Ctrl, and then select the range **B9:F9**. With the nonadjacent ranges selected, in the **Styles group**, click the **Cell Styles** button, and then click **Currency [0]**.

10. Select the range **B6:F8**, and then apply the **Comma [0]** cell style.

11. Select the range **B9:F9**, and then apply the **Total** cell style. Click cell **A11**, and then compare your screen with **Figure 3**.

12. Display the **April** sheet, and then verify that the same formatting was applied.

13. Click the **May** worksheet tab to make it the active worksheet, and then verify that the formulas and formatting changes were made. Compare your screen with **Figure 4**.

    On the *May* sheet, the formula in cell *F9* displays as the value *$31,966*.

14. **Save** the file.

- **You have completed Skill 7 of 10**

SKILL 8: Insert, Hide, Delete, and Move Worksheets

- To organize a workbook, you can position worksheet tabs in any order.
- You can add new worksheets to accommodate new information.

Obj 1.4.1 C

1. Right-click the **April** worksheet tab, and then from the shortcut menu, click **Unhide**. Compare your screen with **Figure 1**.
2. In the **Unhide** dialog box, verify *1st Qtr* is selected, and then click **OK**. Use the same technique to **Unhide** the **2015** and the **2016** worksheets.
3. Right-click the **2015** worksheet tab, and then click **Delete**. Read the message that displays, and then click **Delete**. Use the same technique to **Delete** the **2016** worksheet.

   Because you can't undo a worksheet deletion, it is a good idea to verify that you selected the correct worksheet before you click Delete.

Obj 1.1.3 C

4. To the right of the **June** worksheet tab, click the **New Sheet** button ⊕ to create a new worksheet. Rename the new worksheet tab as Summary
5. In cell **A2**, type Second Quarter Parking Revenue and then press Enter. In cell **A4**, type Month and then press Tab.
   Type the following labels in row **4**, pressing Tab after each label: Total Meter Revenue | Total Ticket Revenue | Total Maintenance Cost | Total Personnel Cost | Net Income
6. In cell **A5**, type April and then AutoFill the months down through cell **A7**.
7. Change the **Column Width** of **columns A:F** to 12 Click cell **A9**, and then compare your screen with **Figure 2**.

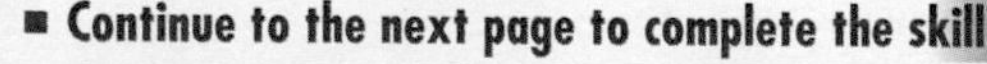

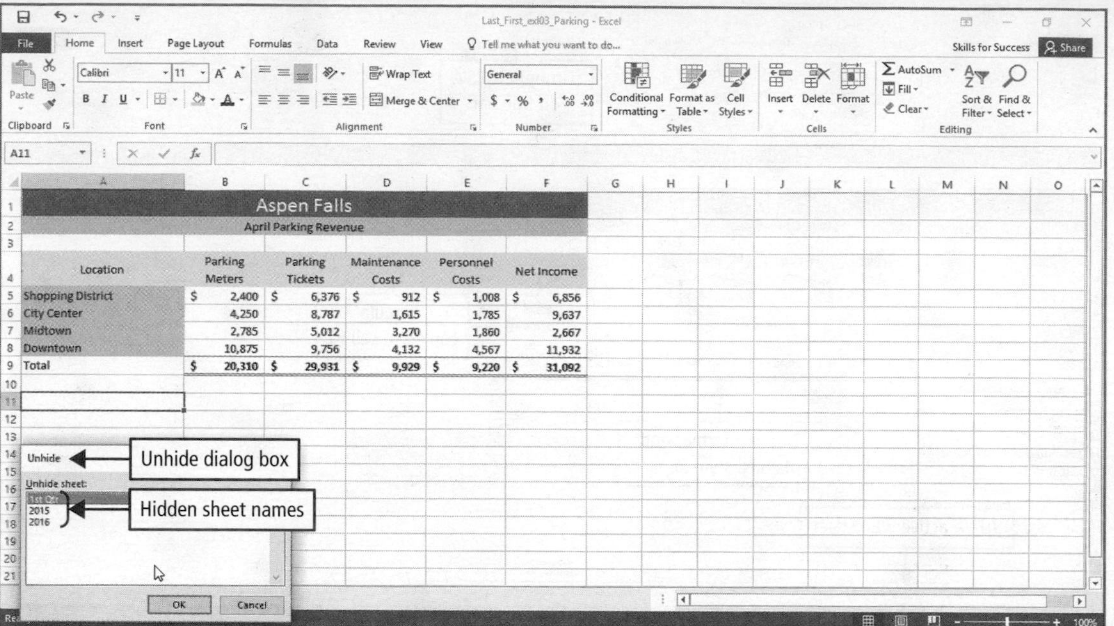

Figure 1

Excel 2016, Windows 10, Microsoft Corporation

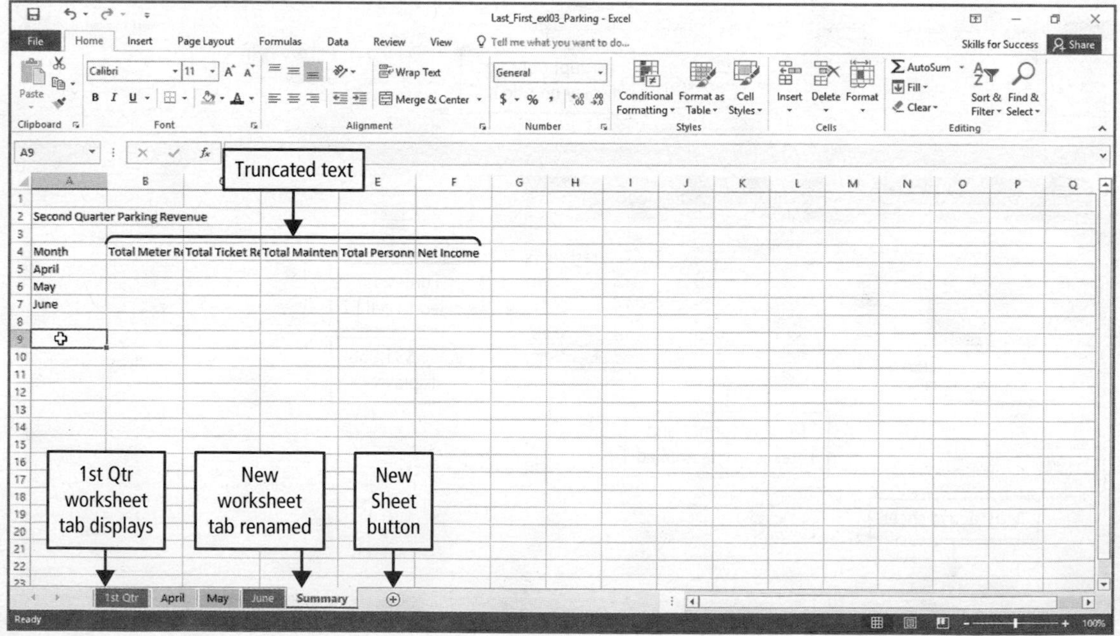

Figure 2

Excel 2016, Windows 10, Microsoft Corporation

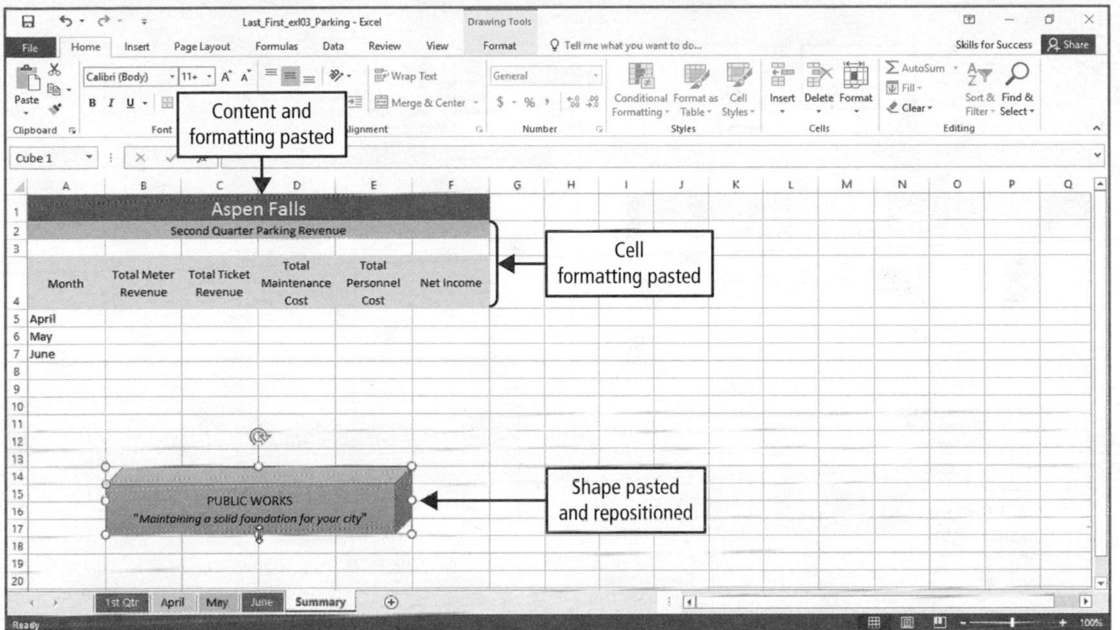

Excel 2016, Windows 10, Microsoft Corporation

Figure 3

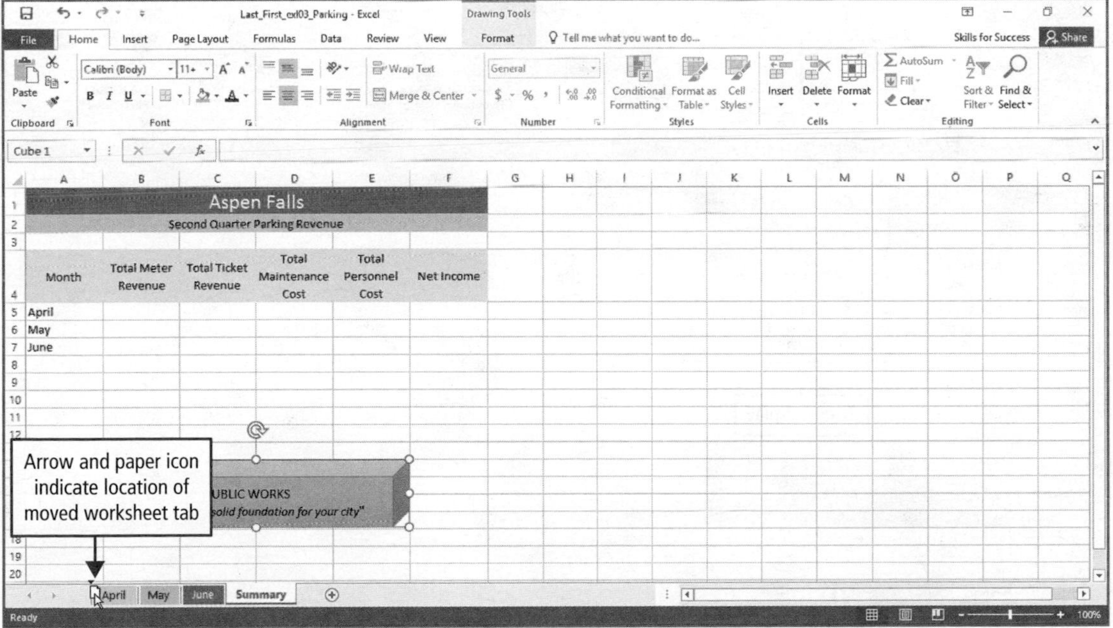

Excel 2016, Windows 10, Microsoft Corporation

Figure 4

8. Display the **June** sheet. Click cell **A1**, and then in the **Clipboard group**, click the **Copy** button. Display the **Summary** sheet. Click cell **A1**, and then click the **Paste** button to paste the cell content and format.

9. Display the **June** sheet, and then press Esc to remove the moving border. Select the range **A2:F4**, and then click the **Copy** button. Display the **Summary** sheet, and then click the cell **A2**. In the **Clipboard group**, click the **Paste arrow**. In the **Paste Options** gallery, under **Other Paste Options**, click the first option—**Formatting**—to paste only the format.
10. Display the **1st Qtr** sheet. Click the shape, and then click the **Copy** button. Display the **Summary** sheet. In the **Clipboard group**, click the **Paste** button. Move and resize the shape to approximately the range **B14:E17**. Compare your screen with **Figure 3**.
11. Right-click the **1st Qtr** worksheet tab, and then click **Hide**.

12. Click the **Summary** worksheet tab. Hold down the left mouse button and drag to the left to display an arrow and the pointer. Drag to the left until the arrow is to the left of the **April** worksheet tab, as shown in **Figure 4**.

13. Release the left mouse button to complete the worksheet move. **Save** the file.

■ **You have completed Skill 8 of 10**

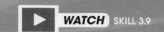

- A ***summary sheet*** is a worksheet that displays and summarizes totals from other worksheets. A ***detail sheet*** is a worksheet with cells referred to by summary sheet formulas.
- Changes made to the detail sheets that affect totals will automatically recalculate and display on the summary sheet.

Obj 4.1.1 C

1. On the **Summary** sheet, click cell **B5**. Type = and then click the **April** worksheet tab. On the **April** sheet, click cell **B9**, and then press Enter to display the April sheet B9 value in the Summary sheet B5 cell.
2. On the **Summary** sheet, click cell **B5**. In the formula bar, notice that the cell reference in the underlying formula includes both a worksheet reference and a cell reference, as shown in **Figure 1**.

   By using a formula that refers to another worksheet, changes made to the Total in cell *B9* of the *April* sheet will be automatically updated in this *Summary* sheet.
3. Click cell **B6**, type = and then click the **May** worksheet tab. On the **May** sheet, click cell **B9**, and then press Enter.
4. On the **Summary** sheet, repeat the technique just practiced to display the **June** sheet **B9** value in the **Summary** sheet **B7** cell.
5. On the **Summary** sheet, select the range **B5:B7**, and then AutoFill to the right through column **F**. Click cell **F7**, and then compare your screen with **Figure 2**.

■ Continue to the next page to complete the skill

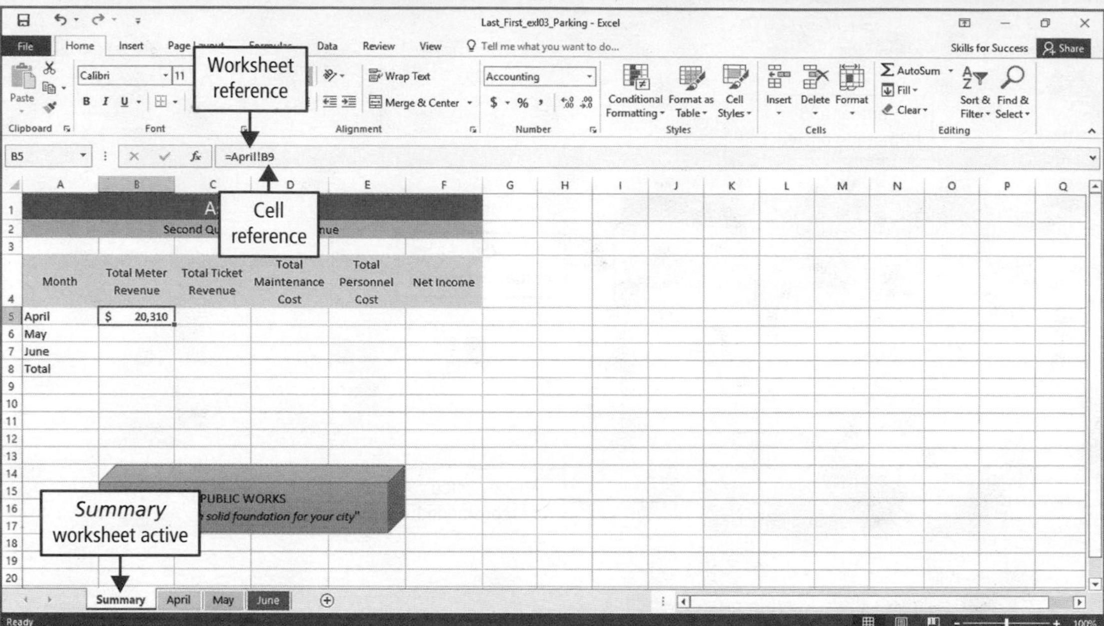

Figure 1

Excel 2016, Windows 10, Microsoft Corporation

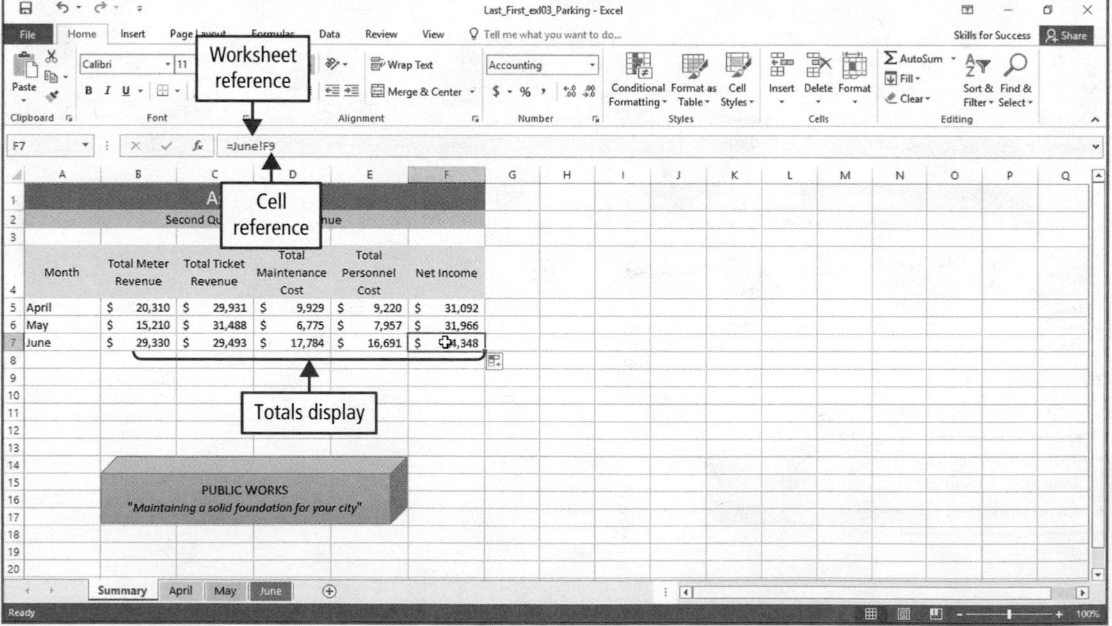

Figure 2

Excel 2016, Windows 10, Microsoft Corporation

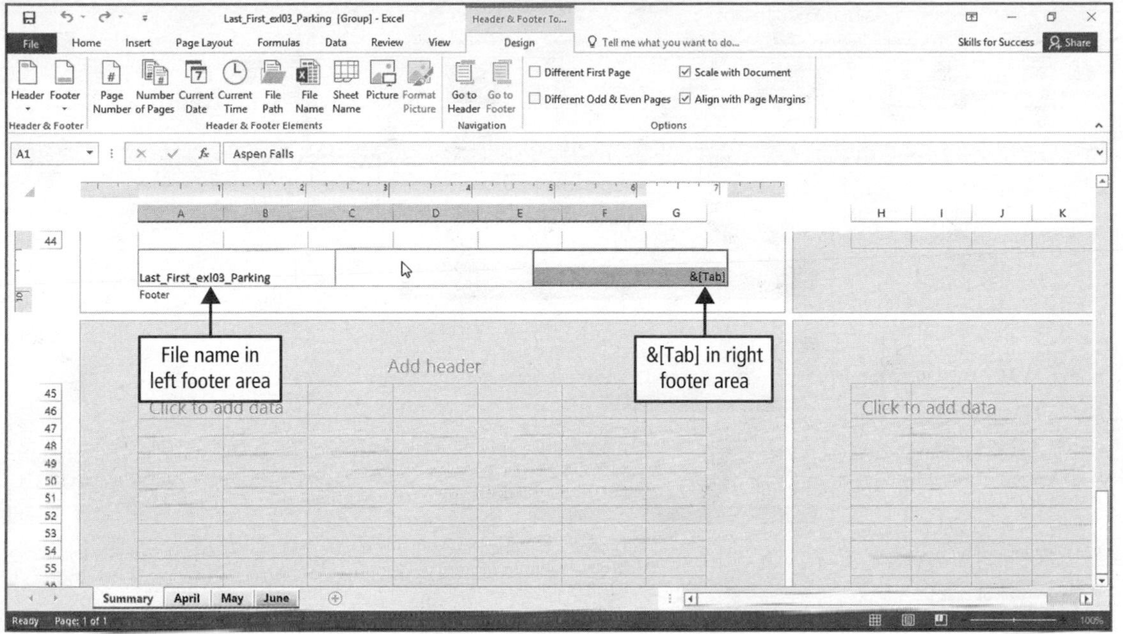

Excel 2016, Windows 10, Microsoft Corporation

Figure 3

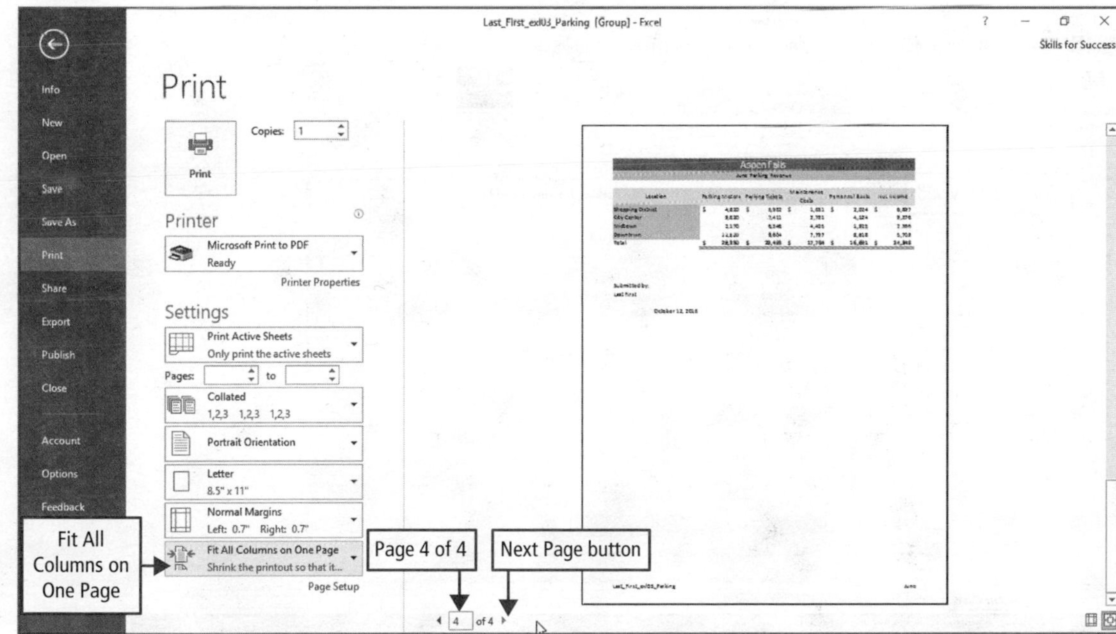

Excel 2016, Windows 10, Microsoft Corporation

Figure 4

6. On the **Summary** sheet, click cell **A8**, type Total and then select the range **B8:F8**. In the **Editing group**, click the **AutoSum** button 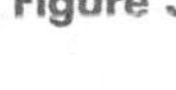, and then apply the **Total** cell style. Select the range **B6:F7** and then apply the **Comma [0]** cell style.
7. Right-click the **Summary** worksheet tab, and then click **Select All Sheets**.
8. Insert the File Name in the worksheet's left footer, and then insert the Sheet Name in the right footer. Compare your screen with **Figure 3**.

   By grouping worksheets, you can insert headers and footers into each worksheet quickly and consistently.

9. Click in a cell just above the footer to exit the **Footer** area. On the lower right side of the status bar, click the **Normal** button. Hold down Ctrl, and then press Home to make cell **A1** the active cell on all selected worksheets.
10. With the sheets still grouped, click the **File tab**, and then click **Print**. Under **Settings**, click the last option arrow, and then click **Fit All Columns on One Page**. At the bottom of the screen, click the **Next Page** button three times to view each of the four worksheets, and then compare your screen with **Figure 4**.

   Obj 1.5.4 C

   Because the worksheets are grouped, all four worksheets are included in the preview.

11. **Save** the file.

■ **You have completed Skill 9 of 10**

► A ***clustered bar chart*** is useful when you want to compare values across categories; bar charts organize categories along the vertical axis and values along the horizontal axis.

MOS Obj 5.1.1 C

1. Right-click the **Summary** worksheet tab, and then click **Ungroup Sheets**. On the **Summary** sheet, select the range **A4:E7**. Click the **Insert tab**, and then in the **Charts group**, click the **Recommended Charts** button. In the **Insert Chart** dialog box, verify the first choice is selected—**Clustered Bar**, and then click **OK**.

MOS Obj 5.2.4 C

2. On the **Design tab**, in the **Location group**, click the **Move Chart** button. In the **Move Chart** dialog box, select the **New sheet** option button, type 2nd Qtr Chart and then click **OK**.

MOS Obj 5.1.3 C

3. On the **Design tab**, in the **Data group**, click the **Switch Row/Column** button to display the months on the vertical axis. Compare your screen with **Figure 1**.

   Because you want to look at revenue and costs by month, displaying the months on the vertical axis is useful.

MOS Obj 5.2.3 C

4. In the **Chart Layouts group**, click the **Quick Layout** button, and then click **Layout 3**.
5. To the right of the chart, click the **Chart Styles** button, and then click **Style 3**.
6. Edit the **Chart Title** to 2nd Quarter Parking Revenue and Cost and then compare your screen with **Figure 2**.

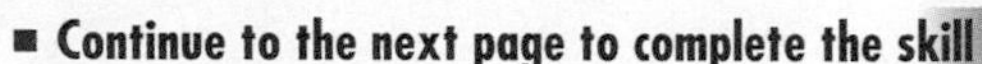
■ Continue to the next page to complete the skill

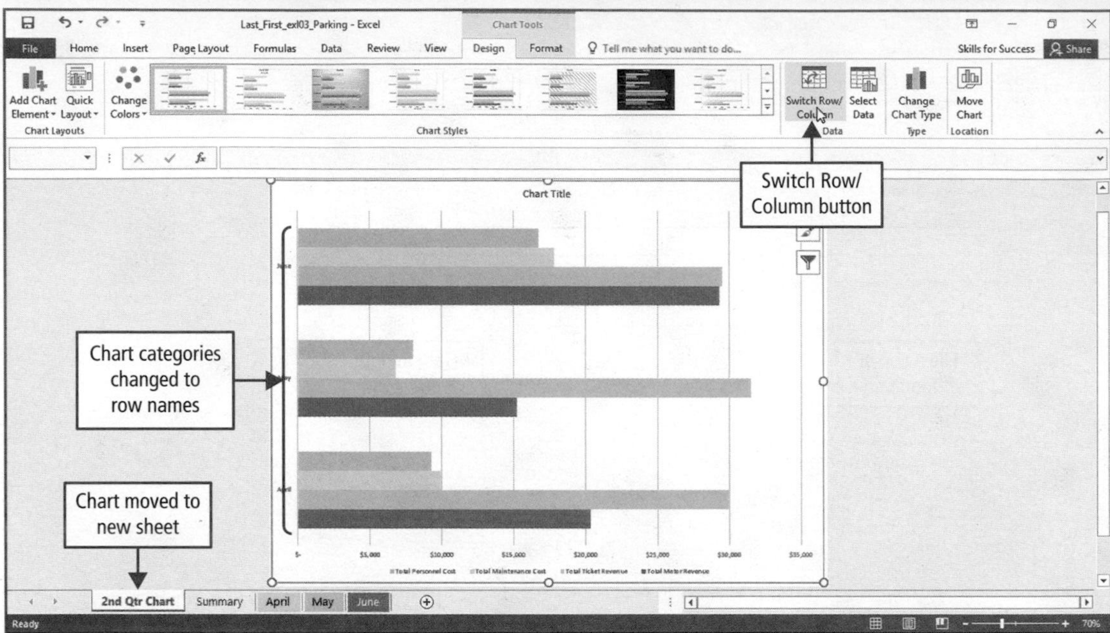

Figure 1

Excel 2016, Windows 10, Microsoft Corporation

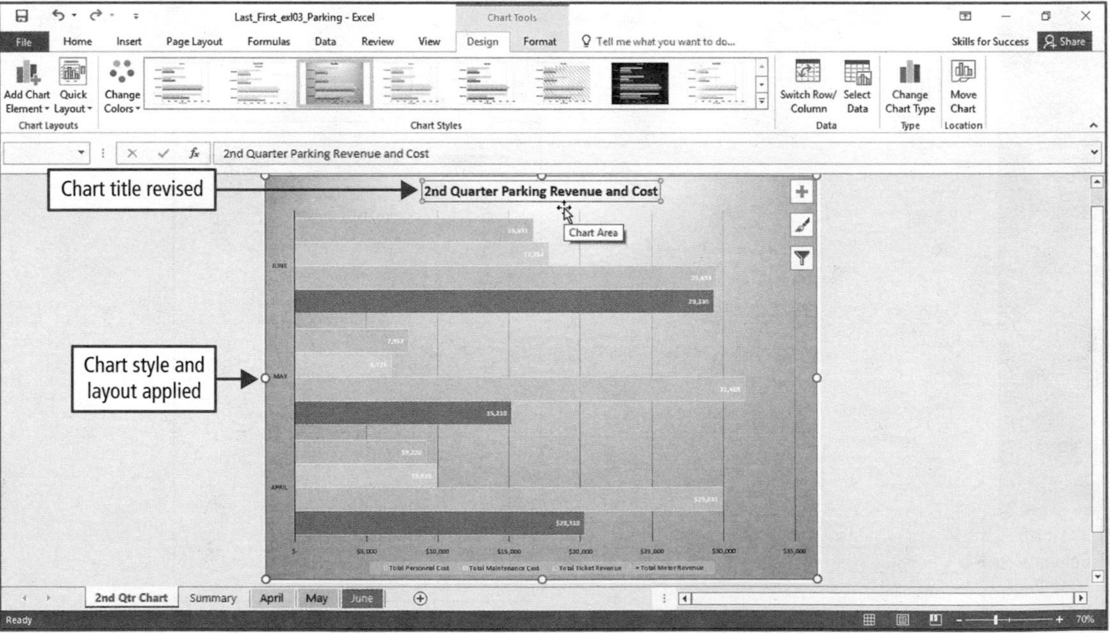

Figure 2

Excel 2016, Windows 10, Microsoft Corporation

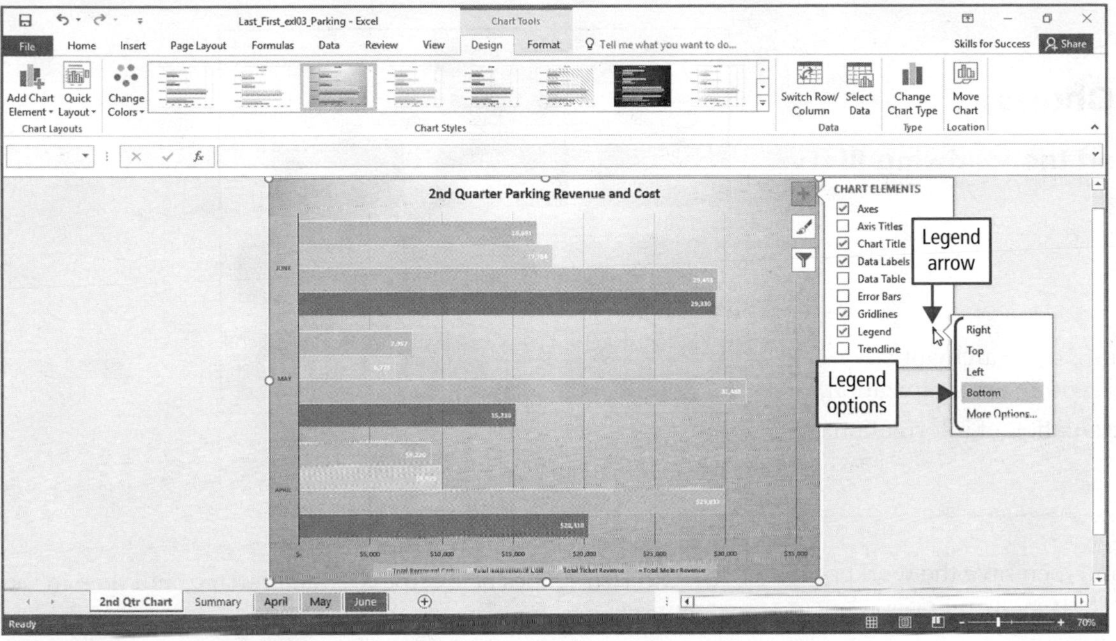

Excel 2016, Windows 10, Microsoft Corporation

Figure 3

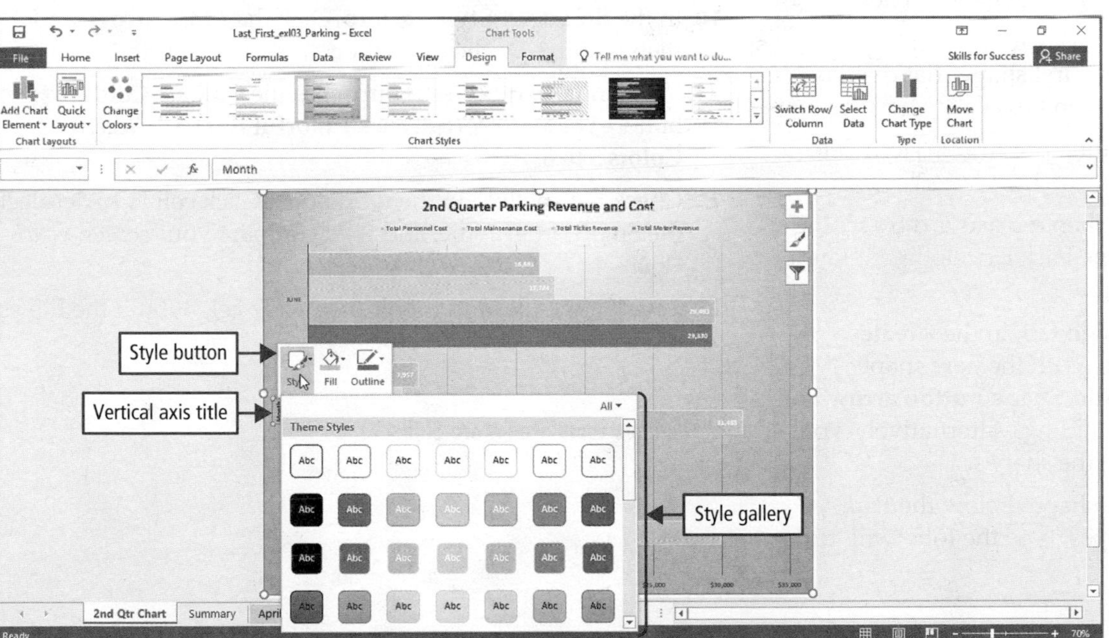

Excel 2016, Windows 10, Microsoft Corporation

Figure 4

7. At the top right corner of the chart, click the **Chart Elements** button. Point to **Legend**, and then click the **Legend arrow**. Compare your screen with **Figure 3**.
8. In the list, click **Top** to move the legend to the top of the chart sheet.

9. In the **Chart Elements** gallery, point to **Axis Titles**, and then click the **Axis Titles arrow**. Select the **Primary Vertical** check box to add the vertical axis title. Click the **Chart Elements** button to close the gallery.
10. On the left side of the chart, change the vertical **Axis Title** text to Month Right-click the *Month* title, and then on the Mini toolbar, click the **Style** button. Compare your screen with **Figure 4**.
11. In the **Style** gallery, click the second thumbnail in the fourth row—**Subtle Effect - Blue, Accent 1**.
12. Click the **Insert tab**, and then in the **Text group**, click the **Header & Footer** button. In the **Page Setup** dialog box, click the **Custom Footer** button. In the **Footer** dialog box, verify the insertion point is in the **Left section**, and then click the **Insert File Name** button. Click the **Right section** of the footer, and then click the **Insert Sheet Name** button. Click **OK** two times.

MOS Obj 1.3.8 C

13. **Save** the file, and then **Close** Excel. Submit the file as directed by your instructor.

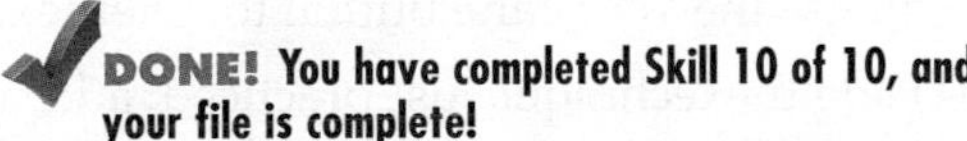

DONE! You have completed Skill 10 of 10, and your file is complete!

More Skills 11

Create SmartArt Organization Charts

To complete this project, you will need the following file:

- Blank Excel workbook

You will save your file as:

- Last_First_exl03_MS11Organization

- An ***organization chart*** graphically represents the hierarchy of relationships between individuals and groups within an organization.
- A ***SmartArt graphic*** provides a visual representation of information used to effectively communicate ideas.

Figure 1

1. Start **Excel 2016**. Open a blank workbook, and then save the workbook in your chapter folder as Last_First_exl03_MS11Organization
2. Click the **Insert tab**, and then in the **Illustrations group**, click the **Insert a SmartArt Graphic** button. In the **Choose a SmartArt Graphic** dialog box, click **Hierarchy**. In the **SmartArt Layout** gallery, click **Organization Chart**, and then click **OK**.
3. At the top of the SmartArt graphic, click the first shape that displays *Text*. Type Maria Martinez press Enter, and then type City Manager
4. Click the border of the second shape, and then press Delete to delete the text box.
5. Click the first shape in the second row, and then replace *Text* by typing Park Operations Repeat this process and type Park Development in the middle shape and Recreation in the last shape.
6. Click the *Park Operations* shape. On the **Design tab**, in the **Create Graphic group**, click the **Add Shape** button. With the new shape selected, type Grounds and then click the **Add Shape button arrow** and **Add Shape After**. In the new shape, type Buildings Alternatively, you can use the **Text Pane** button to enter text in the shapes.
7. Using the technique just practiced, add two shapes below the *Park Development* shape, and then in the two shapes, type the following text: Planning and Capital Development
8. Add two shapes below the *Recreation* shape, and then in the two shapes, type Sports and Aquatics
9. Move and size the SmartArt graphic to display in the range **A1:I22**.
10. In the **SmartArt Styles group**, click the **More arrow**, and then under **3-D**, click **Polished**.
11. In the **SmartArt Styles group**, click the **Change Colors** button. Under **Colorful**, click **Colorful Range – Accent Colors 5 to 6**. MOS Obj 5.3.3 C
12. Check the spelling in the workbook. Click cell **J1** to deselect the SmartArt graphic, and then compare your screen with **Figure 1**.
13. **Save** the file, and then **Close** Excel. Submit the file as directed by your instructor.

- **You have completed More Skills 11**

More Skills 12

Create and Insert Screen Shots

To complete this project, you will need the following file:

- **exl03_MS12Labor**

You will save your file as:

- **Last_First_exl03_MS12Labor**

► A ***screen shot*** is an image of the computer screen.

---

1. Close all open windows on your computer, and then open a web browser—for example, **Edge**. In the address bar, type aspenfalls.org and then press Enter to display the *City of Aspen Falls* web site. Click the link **Aspen Falls Labor Statistics.**

2. Start **Excel 2016**, and then open the file **exl03_MS12Labor**. Save the file in your chapter folder as Last_First_exl03_MS12Labor

3. Select cell **A1**. On the **Insert tab**, in the **Illustrations group**, click the **Take a Screenshot** button.

A ***screen clipping*** is a picture of a portion of the computer screen that can be inserted into a worksheet. It can be very small or as large as the entire screen.

4. In the **Available Windows** gallery, click the text **Screen Clipping**. The web page opens for *Aspen Falls Labor Statistics*, and then after a moment, the screen is dimmed.

5. Place the **Precision** select pointer at the top left of the BLS logo, and then drag to trace the logo outline. Release the mouse button.

The image that was captured is placed into cell A1, and is treated as a picture.

Obj 5.3.2 C

6. Select the image, and then on the **Picture Tools Format tab**, in the **Size group**, adjust the width to **1"**. The height will adjust to approximately 1.06" automatically.

7. In the **Picture Styles group**, apply the **Reflected Rounded Rectangle** style, which is the fifth option in row 1. Select an empty cell. Compare your screen with **Figure 1**.

8. **Save** the file, and then **Close** Excel. Submit the file as directed by your instructor.

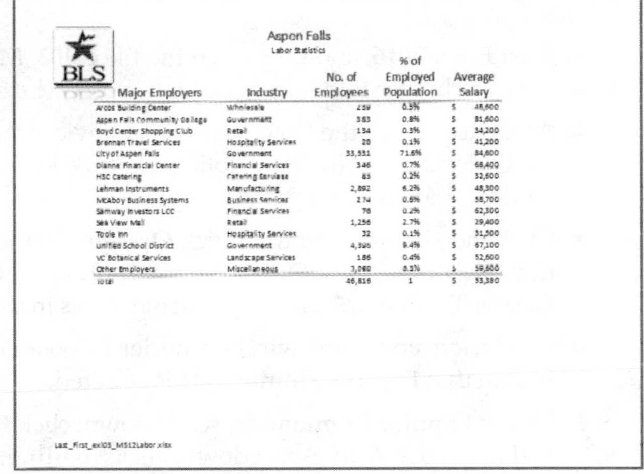

Aspen Falls
Labor Statistics

Major Employers	Industry	No. of Employees	% of Employed Population	Average Salary
Arcos Building Center	Wholesale	239	0.5%	$ 48,600
Aspen Falls Community College	Government	383	0.8%	$ 81,600
Boyd Center Shopping Club	Retail	134	0.3%	$ 34,200
Brennan Travel Services	Hospitality Services	28	0.1%	$ 41,200
City of Aspen Falls	Government	33,531	71.6%	$ 84,600
Dianne Financial Center	Financial Services	346	0.7%	$ 68,400
HSC Catering	Catering Services	85	0.2%	$ 32,600
Lehman Instruments	Manufacturing	2,892	6.2%	$ 48,300
McAboy Business Systems	Business Services	274	0.6%	$ 58,700
Samway Investors LCC	Financial Services	78	0.2%	$ 62,300
Sea View Mall	Retail	1,256	2.7%	$ 29,400
Toole Inn	Hospitality Services	32	0.1%	$ 31,500
Unified School District	Government	4,396	9.4%	$ 67,100
VC Botanical Services	Landscape Services	186	0.4%	$ 52,600
Other Employers	Miscellaneous	3,060	6.5%	$ 59,600
Total		46,816	1	$ 53,380

Last_First_exl03_MS12Labor.xlsx

Figure 1

■ **You have completed More Skills 12**

More Skills 13

Modify the Quick Access Toolbar

To complete this project, you will need the following file:

- exl03_MS13Members

You will save your files as:

- Last_First_exl03_MS13Members
- Last_First_exl03_MS13Snip

▸ The ***Quick Access Toolbar*** is a small toolbar that contains buttons for commonly used commands such as Save and Undo.

---

1. Start **Excel 2016**, and then open the file **exl03_MS13Members**. **Save** the file in your chapter folder as Last_First_exl03_MS13Members
2. At the top left of the Excel worksheet, review the current tools assigned to the Quick Access Toolbar. Notice the three icons on the toolbar, **Save**, **Undo**, and **Redo**.

Obj 1.4.3 C

3. Click the **File tab**, and then click **Options**. In the **Excel Options** dialog box, in the left pane, click **Quick Access Toolbar**. In the **Customize the Quick Access Toolbar** area, note the current tools in the pane.
4. On the left side of the window, under **Choose commands from arrow**, ensure that **Popular Commands** is selected.
5. Under **Popular Commands**, scroll down, click **Print Preview and Print**, and then click **Add**. Scroll down, click **Spelling**, and then click **Add**.
6. At the bottom of the **Excel Options** dialog box, click **OK**.
7. Review the Quick Access Toolbar located at the top left of the Excel window. Print Preview and Print and Spelling icons have been added to the ribbon. Compare your screen with **Figure 1**.
8. Using the **Snipping Tool**, take a **Full-screen Snip** of your screen. Save the file as Last_First_exl03_MS13Snip
9. **Save** the file, and then **Close** Excel. Submit the files as directed by your instructor.

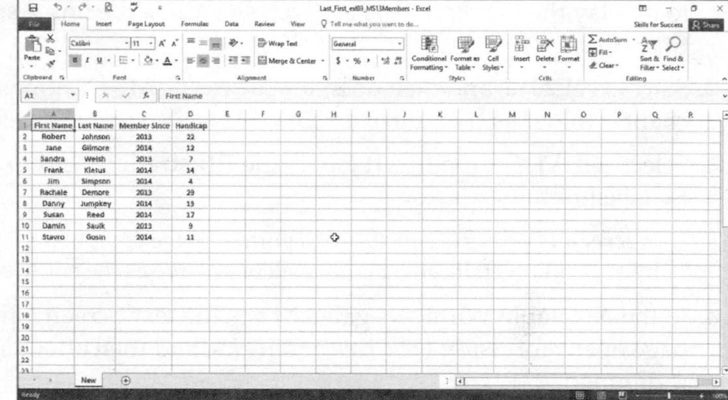

Figure 1

Excel 2016, Windows 10, Microsoft Corporation

- **You have completed More Skills 13**

More Skills 14

Create and Edit Hyperlinks

To complete this project, you will need the following file:

- exl03_MS14Weekends

You will save your file as:

- Last_First_exl03_MS14Weekends

▶ ***Hyperlinks*** are text or graphics that you click to go to a file, a location in a file, a web page on the World Wide Web, or a web page on an organization's intranet.

---

1. Start **Excel 2016**, open the student data file **exl03_MS14Weekends**, and then **Save** the file in your chapter folder as Last_First_exl03_MS14Weekends If a security warning appears, enable the content.
2. Verify that the **Summary** worksheet is the active worksheet. Click cell **A1**. Click the **Insert tab**, and then in the **Links group**, click the **Hyperlink** button.

Obj 1.2.3 C

3. At the left of the displayed **Insert Hyperlink** dialog box, under **Link to**, verify that **Existing File or Web Page** is selected.
4. At the bottom of the **Insert Hyperlink** dialog box, click in the **Address** box, and then if necessary, delete any text. Type www.aspenfalls.org

   As you type, Excel will try to assist you by inserting the name of websites you have previously visited.

5. In the dialog box, click **OK**, and then verify that *Aspen Falls* displays in a different color and is underlined.

   The different color and underline indicate that the word is a hyperlink.

6. Point to the hyperlink *Aspen Falls* to display the pointer and the ScreenTip with the URL. Click the hyperlink *Aspen Falls*.

   Your web browser opens to the home page of the City of Aspen Falls website.

7. **Close** the web browser. Notice that after you have clicked a hyperlink, the color of the hyperlink changes to indicate that you have visited the site.
8. Right-click cell **A1**, and then click **Edit Hyperlink**. In the **Edit Hyperlink** dialog box, click the **ScreenTip** button, and then enter the ScreenTip City of Aspen Falls Click **OK** two times.

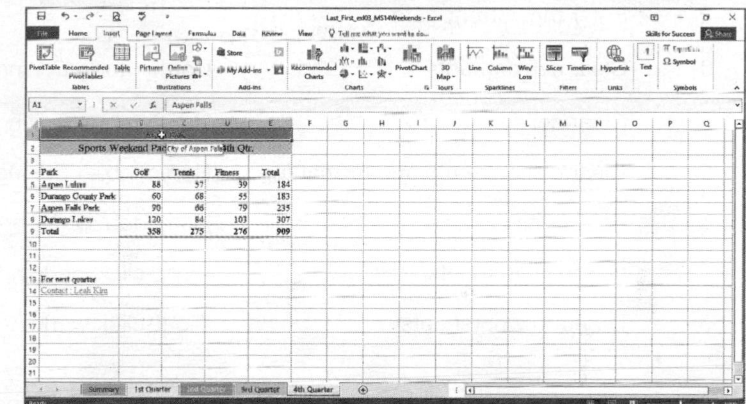

Excel 2016, Windows 10, Microsoft Corporation **Figure 1**

9. Point to the hyperlink *Aspen Falls* to display the ScreenTip, and notice there is no URL. Compare your screen with **Figure 1**.
10. **Save** the file, and then **Close** Excel. Submit the file as directed by your instructor.

- **You have completed More Skills 14**

The following table summarizes the **SKILLS AND PROCEDURES** covered in this chapter.

Skills Number	Task	Step	Icon	Keyboard Shortcut
1	Rename worksheet tab	Home tab → Cells group → Format → Rename Sheet → Type new name → Enter		
1	Rename worksheet tab	Double-click worksheet tab → Type new name → Enter		
1	Format worksheet tab	Home tab → Cells group → Format → Tab Color		
1	Format worksheet tab	Right-click worksheet tab → Tab Color		
2	Format dates	Home tab → Number group → Number Format arrow → More Number Formats		
2	Enter the current date			Ctrl + ;
3	Clear cell contents	Home tab → Editing group → Clear → Clear Contents		Delete
3	Clear cell formatting	Home tab → Editing group → Clear → Clear Formats		
3	Clear cell contents and formatting	Home tab → Editing group→ Clear → Clear All		
4	Paste with options	Home tab → Clipboard group → Paste arrow → Select desired option		
5	Group worksheets	Right-click worksheet tab → Select All Sheets		
5	Ungroup worksheets	Right-click worksheet tab → Ungroup Sheets or click a single worksheet tab		
8	Insert worksheet	Taskbar → New Sheet button	⊕	
8	Delete worksheet	Right-click worksheet tab → Delete		
8	Hide worksheet	Right-click worksheet tab → Hide		
8	Unhide worksheet	Right-click worksheet tab → Unhide → Worksheet name		
8	Move worksheet tab	Drag worksheet tab to new location		
MS11	Insert SmartArt	Insert tab → Illustrations group → Insert a SmartArt Graphic		
MS12	Create and insert screen shot	Insert tab → Illustrations group → Take a Screenshot		
MS13	Modify Quick Access Toolbar	File tab → Options → Quick Access Toolbar		
MS14	Insert hyperlink	Insert tab → Links group → Hyperlink		
MS14	Edit hyperlink	Right-click hyperlink → Edit Hyperlink		

Project Summary Chart

Project	Project Type	Project Location
Skills Review	Review	In Book & MIL MyITLab® Grader
Skills Assessment 1	Review	In Book & MIL MyITLab® Grader
Skills Assessment 2	Review	Book
My Skills	Problem Solving	Book
Visual Skills Check	Problem Solving	Book
Skills Challenge 1	Critical Thinking	Book
Skills Challenge 2	Critical Thinking	Book
More Skills Assessment	Review	In Book & MIL MyITLab® Grader
Collaborating with Google	Critical Thinking	Book

MOS Objectives Covered

1.1.3 C Add a worksheet to an existing workbook	2.1.2 C Cut, copy, or paste data
1.2.3 C Insert hyperlinks	2.1.3 C Paste data by using special paste options
1.3.1 C Change worksheet tab color	4.1.1 C Insert references
1.3.2 C Rename a worksheet	5.1.1 C Create a new chart
1.3.3 C Change worksheet order	5.1.3 C Switch between rows and columns in source data
1.3.6 C Change workbook themes	5.2.2 C Add and modify chart elements
1.3.8 C Insert headers and footers	5.2.3 C Apply chart layouts and styles
1.4.1 C Hide or unhide worksheets	5.2.4 C Move charts to a chart sheet
1.4.3 C Customize the Quick Access toolbar	5.3.2 C Insert images
1.4.8 C Display formulas	5.3.3 C Modify object properties
1.5.4 C Set print scaling	

Key Terms

1. Why should you arrive early for an interview?
2. What should you do at the end of an interview?

Online Help Skills

1. Start **Excel 2016**, and then in the upper right corner of the start page, click the **Help** button [?].
2. In the **Excel Help** window **Search help** box, type date function and then press [Enter].
3. In the search result list, click **DATE function**. **Maximize** the Help window, and then compare your screen with **Figure 1**.

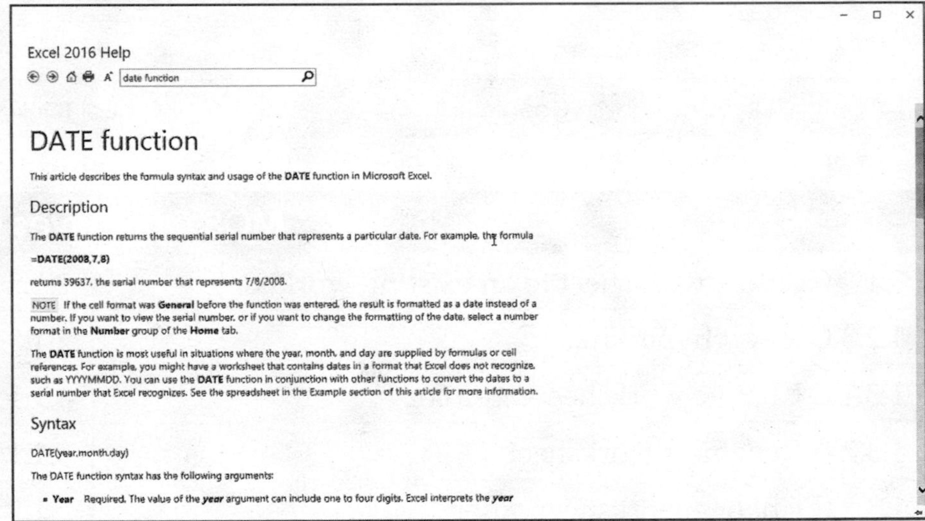

Figure 1 Excel 2016, Windows 10, Microsoft Corporation

4. Read the article to see if you can answer the following question: What cell format can be applied to stop changing numbers into dates?

Matching 

Match each term in the second column with its correct definition in the first column by writing the letter of the term on the blank line in front of the correct definition.

___ **1.** The labels along the lower edge of the workbook window that identify each worksheet.

___ **2.** Buttons to the left of the worksheet tabs used to display worksheet tabs that are not in view.

___ **3.** A sequential number assigned to a date.

___ **4.** A temporary storage area for text and graphics.

___ **5.** A method of moving or copying the content of selected cells in which you point to the selection and then drag it to a new location.

___ **6.** The target destination for data that has been cut or copied using the Clipboard.

___ **7.** The mathematical rules that specify the order that calculations are performed.

___ **8.** A worksheet that displays and summarizes totals from other worksheets.

___ **9.** A worksheet that contains the detailed information in a workbook.

___ **10.** A chart type that is useful when you want to compare values across categories.

A Clipboard
B Clustered bar chart
C Detail sheet
D Drag and drop
E Operator precedence
F Paste area
G Serial number
H Summary sheet
I Tab scrolling buttons
J Worksheet tabs

Multiple Choice

MyITLab®

Choose the correct answer.

1. An active tab color displays this way in the worksheet.
   A. With a solid tab color
   B. With a gradient tab color
   C. Always as the first worksheet

2. The method used to group worksheets in a workbook.
   A. Right-clicking a worksheet tab and then clicking Select All Sheets
   B. Double-clicking a worksheet tab
   C. Clicking the New Sheet button

3. This will be deleted when clearing the contents of a cell.
   A. Only the contents
   B. Only the formatting
   C. Both contents and formatting

4. When pasting a range of cells, this cell needs to be selected in the paste area.
   A. Bottom right cell
   B. Center cell
   C. Top left cell

5. The method used to hide worksheets.
   A. Move the worksheet as the last sheet
   B. Right-click a worksheet tab and then click Hide
   C. Double-click a worksheet tab

6. If a workbook contains grouped worksheets, this word will display on the title bar.
   A. [Collection]
   B. [Set]
   C. [Group]

7. When a formula contains operators with the same precedence level, the operators are evaluated in this order.
   A. Left to right
   B. Right to left
   C. From the center out

8. Addition and this mathematical operator are considered to be on the same precedence level.
   A. Multiplication
   B. Division
   C. Subtraction

9. Changes made in a detail worksheet will automatically recalculate and display on this sheet.
   A. Summary
   B. Final
   C. Outline

10. This will be pasted when the paste option Keep Source Column Widths is selected.
   A. The cell formatting
   B. Only the column width formatting
   C. All content and cell formatting including the column width format

Topics for Discussion

1. Some people in an organization will only view the summary worksheet without examining the detail worksheets. When might this practice be acceptable and when might it cause mistakes?

2. Illustrate some examples of how a formula's results will be incorrect if parentheses are not used to group calculations in the order they should be performed. Think of a class where you have three exam grades and a final exam grade. If the three tests together count as 50 percent of your course grade, and the final exam counts as 50 percent of your course grade, how would you write the formula to get the correct result?

Skills Review

To complete this project, you will need the following file:

- exl03_SRPayroll

You will save your file as:

- Last_First_exl03_SRPayroll

1. Start **Excel 2016**, and then open the file **exl03_SRPayroll**. Save the file in your chapter folder as Last_First_exl03_SRPayroll
2. Right-click the **Community Center** worksheet tab, and then click **Select All Sheets**. Click cell **A19**. On the **Home tab**, in the **Editing group**, click the **Clear** button, and then click **Clear All**. Select the range **A4:F4**, and then apply the **40% - Accent3** cell style. In the **Alignment group**, click the **Wrap Text** and the **Center** buttons.
3. In cell **F5**, type =B5-(C5+D5+E5) and then press Enter to compute Net Pay as *Total Gross Pay – (Income Tax + Social Security (FICA) Tax + Health Insurance)*. AutoFill the formula in cell **F5** down through cell **F12**, and then compare your screen with **Figure 1**.
4. Verify that the worksheets are still grouped. Select the range **B6:F12**, and then apply the **Comma [0]** cell style. Select the range **B13:F13**, and then apply the **Total** cell style.
5. To the right of the **Courthouse** worksheet tab, click the **New Sheet** button. Rename the new worksheet tab Summary and then change the **Tab Color** to **Orange** under **Standard Colors**. Click the **Summary** worksheet tab, and then drag it to the left of the **Community Center** worksheet tab.
6. Right click the **Summary** worksheet tab, and then click **Select All Sheets**. Add the file name to the worksheet's left footer. Click the **right footer section**, and then in the **Header & Footer Elements** group, click the **Sheet Name** button. Return to **Normal** view, and then press Ctrl + Home.
7. Display the **Community Center** sheet, select the range **A1:F4**, and then click **Copy**. Display the **Summary** sheet, and then click cell **A1**. Click the **Paste arrow**, and then click **Keep Source Column Widths**. In cell **A2**, replace the text with City Payroll In cell **A4**, replace the text with Location and then press Enter. Type the following labels in column A, pressing Enter after each label: Community Center | City Center | Courthouse | Total Compare your screen with **Figure 2**.

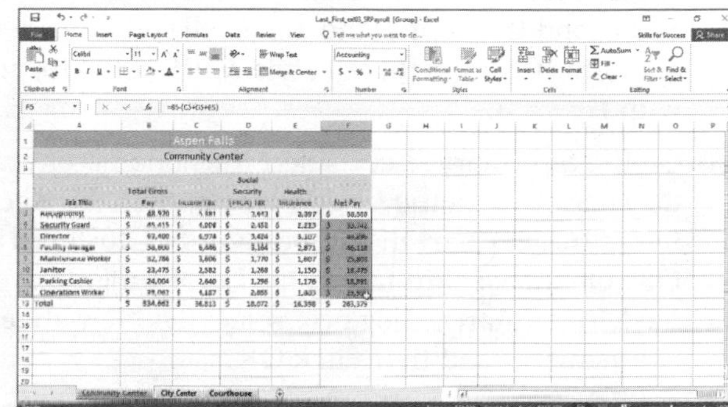

Excel 2016, Windows 10, Microsoft Corporation **Figure 1**

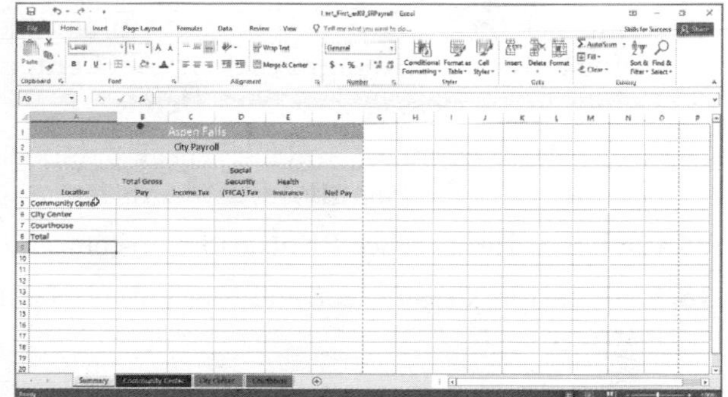

Excel 2016, Windows 10, Microsoft Corporation **Figure 2**

■ **Continue to the next page to complete this Skills Review**

8. On the **Summary** sheet, click cell **B5**, type = and then click the **Community Center** worksheet tab. On the **Community Center** sheet, click cell **B13**, and then press Enter. Use the same technique in cells **B6** and **B7** to place the *Total Gross Pay* amounts from the *City Center* and the *Courthouse* sheets on the *Summary* sheet.
9. On the **Summary** sheet, select the range **B5:B7**. Click the **Quick Analysis** button, click **Totals**, and then click the first option **Sum**. Select the range **B5:B8**, and then AutoFill the formulas to the right through column **F**. Select the range **B8:F8**, and then apply the **Total** cell style. Select the range **B6:F7**, and then apply the **Comma [0]** cell style. Click cell **A10**, and then compare your screen with **Figure 3**.
10. On the **Summary** sheet, select the nonadjacent ranges **A4:A7** and **C4:E7**. On the **Insert tab**, in the **Charts group**, click the **Recommended Charts** button. In the **Insert Chart** dialog box, verify **Clustered Bar** is selected, and then click **OK**. On the **Design tab**, in the **Location group**, click the **Move Chart** button. In the **Move Chart** dialog box, select the **New sheet** option button, type Payroll Adjustments and then click **OK**.
11. In the **Data group**, click the **Switch Row/Column** button. Click the **Chart Styles** button, and then click **Style 2**. Change the **Chart Title** to Payroll Adjustments by Location Click the **Chart Elements** button, click **Axis Title**, and then click the **Axis Title arrow**. Click the **Primary Horizontal** option box, and then type Deduction
12. On the **Summary** sheet, click cell **A12**, type Date Created and then click Enter. In cell **A13**, press Ctrl + ; (the semicolon), and then press Enter.
13. Right-click the **Summary** worksheet tab, and then click **Unhide**. In the **Unhide** dialog box, click **OK**. Right-click the **Art Center** worksheet tab, and then click **Delete**. In the message box, click **Delete**.
14. Group the worksheets, and then check the spelling. Ungroup the worksheets, and then click the **Payroll Adjustments tab**.
15. Click the **File tab**, click **Print**, and then compare your screen with **Figure 4**.
16. **Save** the file, **Close** Excel, and then submit the file as directed by your instructor.

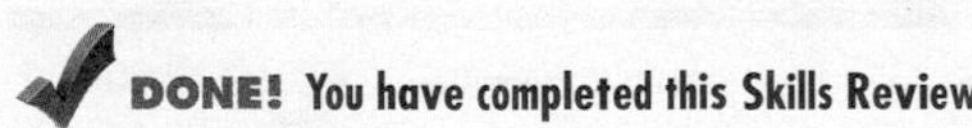

DONE! You have completed this Skills Review

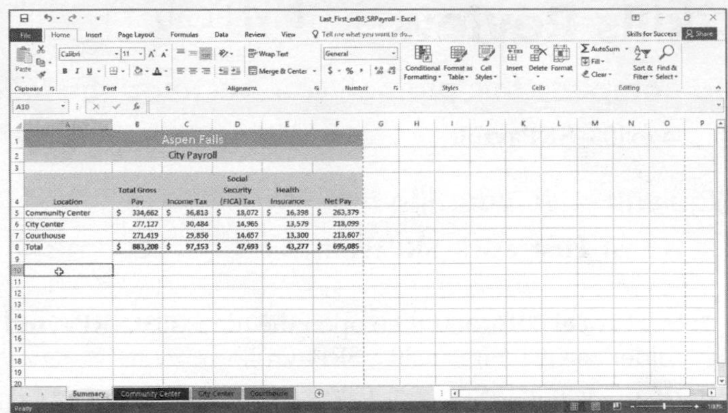

Figure 3 Excel 2016, Windows 10, Microsoft Corporation

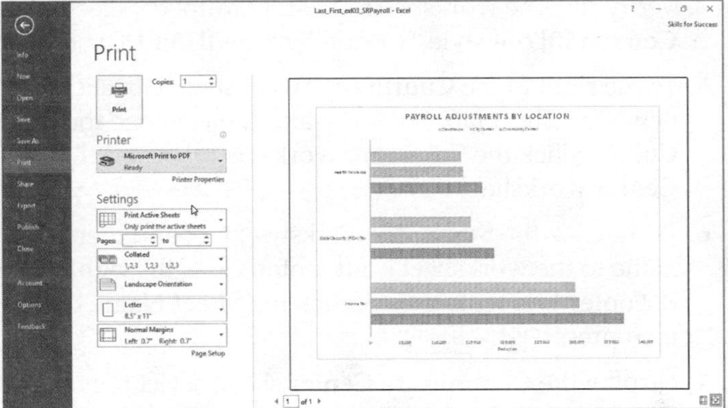

Figure 4 Excel 2016, Windows 10, Microsoft Corporation

Skills Assessment 1

To complete this project, you will need the following file:

- **exl03_SA1Center**

You will save your file as:

- **Last_First_exl03_SA1Center**

1. Start **Excel 2016**, and then open the file **exl03_SA1Center**. **Save** the file in your chapter folder as Last_First_exl03_SA1Center
2. Group the worksheets. In cell **E5**, construct a formula to compute *Net Income = Income – (Indirect Costs + Direct Costs)*. AutoFill the formula down through cell **E7**.
3. In the nonadjacent ranges **B5:E5** and **B8:E8**, apply the **Currency [0]** cell style.
4. Insert a new worksheet, and then rename the tab as Summary Apply the worksheet tab color **Gold, Accent 6**. Move the *Summary* sheet tab to make it the first worksheet in the workbook.
5. Copy the range **A1:E4** from any of the detail worksheets. On the **Summary** sheet, click cell **A1**, and then paste the range using the **Keep Source Column Widths** paste option. Change the subtitle of cell **A2** to City Center Annual Revenue and then change the label in cell **A4** to Quarter
6. In cell **A5**, type 1st Quarter and then AutoFill the labels through the range **A6:A8**. In cell **A9**, type Total
7. On the **Summary** worksheet, enter a formula in cell **B5** setting the cell to equal cell **B8** in the *1st Quarter* worksheet. On the **Summary** worksheet, enter the *Income* total from the *2nd Quarter*, the *3rd Quarter*, and the *4th Quarter* worksheets in the range **B6:B8**.
8. Select the range **B5:B8**, and then use the **Quick Analysis** button to insert the column total.
9. AutoFill the range **B5:B9** to the right through column **E**. In row **9**, apply the **Total** cell style to the range **B9:E9**. In the range **B6:E8**, apply the **Comma [0]** cell style.
10. Insert a **Clustered Bar** chart using the nonadjacent ranges **A4:A8** and **C4:D8** as the source data. Move the chart to a chart sheet with the sheet name City Center
11. Apply the **Style 10** chart style. Change the **Chart Title** to City Center Costs

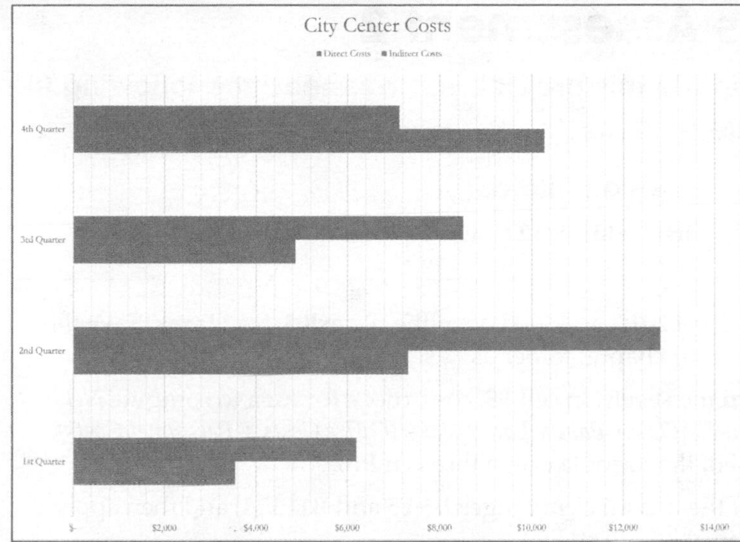

Aspen Falls				
City Center Annual Revenue				
Quarter	Income	Indirect Costs	Direct Costs	Net Income
1st Quarter	$ 17,700	$ 3,540	$ 6,195	$ 7,965
2nd Quarter	36,590	7,318	12,806	16,466
3rd Quarter	24,320	4,864	8,511	10,945
4th Quarter	25,604	10,270	7,126	8,208
Total	$ 104,214	$ 25,992	$ 34,638	$ 43,584

Aspen Falls				
City Center Rental Revenue: 1st Quarter				
Rental Item	Income	Indirect Costs	Direct Costs	Net Income
City Center Rental	$ 9,200	$ 1,840	$ 3,220	$ 4,140
AV Equipment	4,800	960	1,680	2,160
Display Equipment	3,700	740	1,295	1,665
Total	$ 17,700	$ 3,540	$ 6,195	$ 7,965

Figure 1

12. Group the worksheets using the *Summary* tab. Add the file name in the left footer and the sheet name in the right footer. Return to **Normal** view, and then press Ctrl + Home.
13. Check the spelling of the workbook, and then ungroup the sheets.
14. **Save** the file, and then compare your screen with **Figure 1**. **Close** Excel, and then submit the file as directed by your instructor.

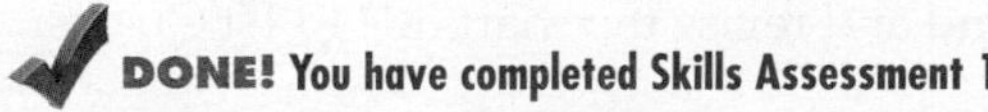

Skills Assessment 2

To complete this project, you will need the following file:

- exl03_SA2Taxes

You will save your file as:

- Last_First_exl03_SA2Taxes

1. Start **Excel 2016**, and then open the file **exl03_SA2Taxes**. **Save** the file in your chapter folder as Last_First_exl03_SA2Taxes
2. Group the sheets. In cell **F5**, construct a formula to compute *Net Revenue = (Taxes Paid + Late Fees) – (Office Costs + Personnel Costs).* AutoFill the formula down through **F10**.
3. Select the nonadjacent ranges **B5:F5** and **B11:F11**, and then apply the **Currency [0]** cell style.
4. Ungroup the worksheets, and then hide the April worksheet. Compare the *January* worksheet with **Figure 1**.
5. Insert a new sheet, rename the worksheet tab 1st Qtr Summary and then change the worksheet tab color to **Orange, Accent 1**. Move the worksheet to the first position in the workbook. Copy the range **A1:F4** from another worksheet, and then paste the range at the top of the *1st Qtr Summary* sheet using the **Keep Source Column Widths** paste option.
6. On the **1st Qtr Summary** sheet, change the subtitle in cell **A2** to 1st Quarter Tax Revenue and then change the label in cell **A4** to Month In the range **A5:A7**, enter the months January | February | March and in cell **A8**, type Total
7. In cell **B5**, enter a formula setting the cell to equal the total *Taxes Paid* in the *January* worksheet. In cells **B6** and **B7** of the *1st Qtr Summary* sheet, enter the total *Taxes Paid* from the *February* and the *March* worksheets.
8. Total column **B**, and then AutoFill the range **B5:B8** to the right through column **F**. In the range **B8:F8**, apply the **Total** cell style. In the range **B6:F7**, apply the **Comma [0]** cell style.
9. Select the range **A4:C7**, and then insert a **Clustered Bar** chart. Move and resize the chart to the range **A10:F24**. Switch the rows and columns in the chart.
10. Apply the **Layout 2** chart layout and the **Style 8** chart style. Change the data labels to **Inside End** and revise the chart title to 1st Quarter

Aspen Falls

January Tax Revenue

Tax	Taxes Paid	Late Fees	Office Costs	Personnel Costs	Net Revenue
Motor Vehicle	$ 82,831	$ 58,255	$ 2,879	$ 49,255	$ 88,952
Sales	154,520	47,280	3,796	51,529	146,475
Franchise	72,956	46,998	4,915	60,061	54,978
Utilities	98,750	35,107	5,688	38,378	89,791
Property	120,000	40,762	3,200	24,320	133,242
Other	101,033	46,125	2,879	61,086	83,193
Totals	$ **630,090**	$ **274,527**	$ **23,357**	$ **284,629**	$ **596,631**

Figure 1

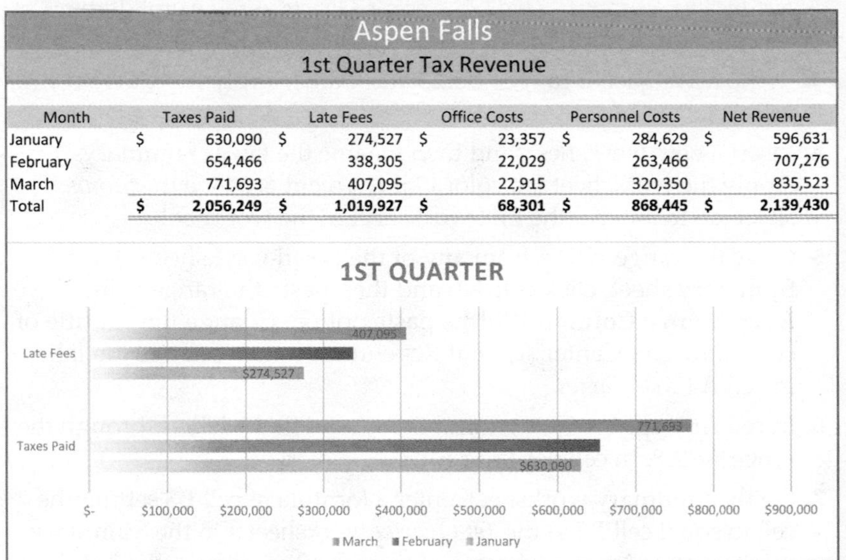

Aspen Falls

1st Quarter Tax Revenue

Month	Taxes Paid	Late Fees	Office Costs	Personnel Costs	Net Revenue
January	$ 630,090	$ 274,527	$ 23,357	$ 284,629	$ 596,631
February	654,466	338,305	22,029	263,466	707,276
March	771,693	407,095	22,915	320,350	835,523
Total	$ **2,056,249**	$ **1,019,927**	$ **68,301**	$ **868,445**	$ **2,139,430**

Figure 2

11. Group the worksheets, and then check the spelling of the workbook. Add the file name in the left footer and the sheet name in the right footer. Return to **Normal** view, and then press Ctrl + Home.
12. **Save** the file, and then compare your *1st Qtr Summary* sheet with **Figure 2**. **Close** Excel, and then submit the file as directed by your instructor.

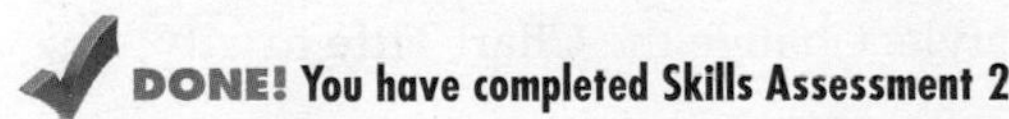

DONE! You have completed Skills Assessment 2

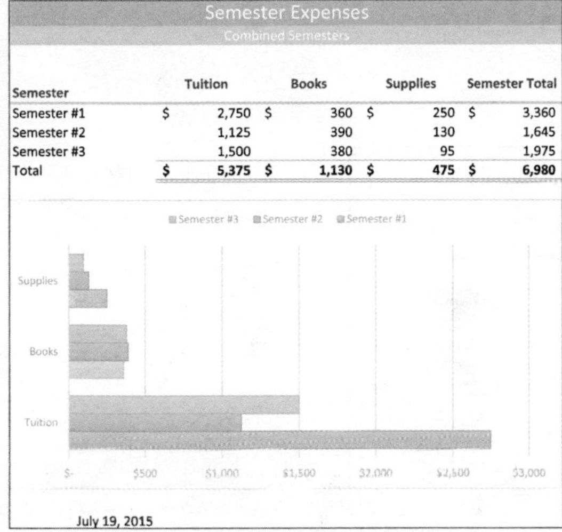

Semester Expenses
Combined Semesters

Semester		Tuition		Books		Supplies		Semester Total
Semester #1	$	2,750	$	360	$	250	$	3,360
Semester #2		1,125		390		130		1,645
Semester #3		1,500		380		95		1,975
Total	$	5,375	$	1,130	$	475	$	6,980

Semester Expenses
Semester #1

Class		Tuition		Books		Supplies		Class Total
Class 1	$	500	$	125	$	50	$	675
Class 2		250		50		55		355
Class 3		500		50		50		600
Class 4		750		75		45		870
Class 5		750		60		50		860
Total	$	2,750	$	360	$	250	$	3,360

Figure 1

My Skills

To complete this project, you will need the following file:

- **exl03_MYClasses**

You will save your file as:

- **Last_First_exl03_MYClasses**

1. Start **Excel 2016**, and then open the file **exl03_MYClasses**. **Save** the file in your chapter folder as Last_First_exl03_MYClasses
2. Group the worksheets. In cell **E5**, use the SUM function to total the row, and then AutoFill the formula down through cell **E9**. In row **10**, use the SUM function to total the columns. Apply the **Comma [0]** cell style to **E6:E9**.
3. Select cell **A2**, and then apply the **60% - Accent3** cell style.
4. Insert a new worksheet. Rename the new worksheet tab Semester Costs and then apply the worksheet tab color **Blue-Gray, Accent 6**. Move the new worksheet tab to make it the first worksheet in the workbook.
5. Copy the range **A1:E4** from any of the detail worksheets, and then on the **Semester Costs** worksheet, click cell **A1**. Paste the range using the **Keep Source Column Widths** paste option. Change the subtitle of cell **A2** to Combined Semesters and then change the label in cell **A4** to Semester and change the label in cell **E4** to Semester Total
6. In cell **A5**, type Semester #1 and then AutoFill the label down through **A7**. In cell **A8**, type Total
7. In cell **B5**, insert a formula to equal the value in cell **B10** in the *Semester #1* worksheet. In cells **B6** and **B7**, insert formulas that equal the *Tuition* total from the *Semester #2* and *Semester #3* worksheets.
8. Use **Quick Analysis** to insert the column **B** total, and then AutoFill the formulas in column **B** to the right through column **E**. Select the range **B8:E8**, and then apply the **Total** cell style. Apply the **Comma [0]** cell style to **B6:E7**.
9. Insert a **Clustered Bar** chart using the range **A4:D7** as the source data. Move and resize the chart to display below the data in approximately the range **A10:E24**.
10. Apply the **Style 4** chart style, and then delete the **Chart Title**. Move the legend to the top of the chart.
11. On the **Semester Costs** sheet, in cell **A26**, enter the current date, and then apply the **March 14, 2012** date format.
12. Group the worksheets. Add the file name in the left footer and the sheet name in the right footer. Return to **Normal** view, and then press Ctrl + Home.
13. Check the spelling of the workbook, and then ungroup the sheets. Compare your completed file with **Figure 1**.
14. **Save** the file, and then **Close** Excel. Submit the file as directed by your instructor.

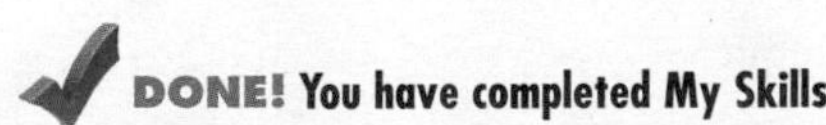

DONE! You have completed My Skills

Visual Skills Check

To complete this project, you will need the following file:

- exl03_VSWater

You will save your file as:

- Last_First_exl03_VSWater

Start **Excel 2016**, and then open the file **exl03_VSWater**. **Save** the file in your chapter folder as Last_First_exl03_VSWater Create a summary sheet as shown in **Figure 1** for the 4th Quarter with the totals from each month and the titles as shown in the figure. Name the worksheet tab 4th Qtr Summary and then apply the worksheet tab color **Teal, Accent 5**. Move the Summary sheet to be the first worksheet. Insert a **Clustered Bar** chart based on the range **A4:D7**, and then move the chart below the data. Apply **Layout 3** and **Chart Style 12**. Delete the chart title, and then move the legend to the **Top**. On all sheets, add a footer with the file name in the left section and the sheet name in the right section. **Save** the file, **Close** Excel, and then submit the file as directed by your instructor.

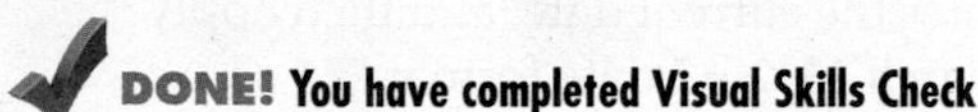

DONE! You have completed Visual Skills Check

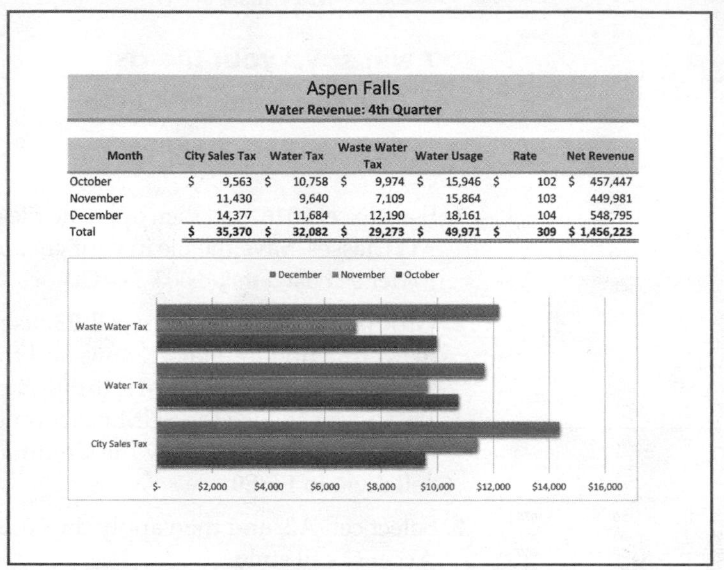

Aspen Falls
Water Revenue: 4th Quarter

Month	City Sales Tax	Water Tax	Waste Water Tax	Water Usage	Rate	Net Revenue
October	$ 9,563	$ 10,758	$ 9,974	$ 15,946	$ 102	$ 457,447
November	11,430	9,640	7,109	15,864	103	449,981
December	14,377	11,684	12,190	18,161	104	548,795
Total	$ 35,370	$ 32,082	$ 29,273	$ 49,971	$ 309	$ 1,456,223

Aspen Falls
Water Revenue: October

Building Type	City Sales Tax	Water Tax	Waste Water Tax	Water Usage	Rate	Net Revenue
Residential	$ 1,575	$ 1,890	$ 1,507	3,181	$ 19	$ 65,411
Commercial	4,233	5,762	5,671	5,440	27	162,546
Industrial	3,170	2,404	2,191	6,118	31	197,423
Apartments	585	702	605	1,207	25	32,067
Total	$ 9,563	$ 10,758	$ 9,974	15,946	$ 102	$ 457,447

Figure 1

Skills Challenge 1

To complete this project, you will need the following file:

- **exl03_SC1Visitors**

You will save your file as:

- **Last_First_exl03_SC1Visitors**

During each quarter, Carter Horikoshi, the Art Center Supervisor, tracked the revenue and costs at the Art Center. Open the file **exl03_SC1Visitors**, and then save the file in your chapter folder as Last_First_exl03_SC1Visitors Hide the Convention Center worksheet, and then move the remaining worksheets into the correct order. Assign a tab color to each worksheet tab. Group the worksheets, and then adjust the column widths to display all values. Format the labels in rows 1 through 4 consistently across all the worksheets. In cell F5, insert parentheses so that the sum of *Marketing Costs* and *Operating Costs* is subtracted from the sum of *Entrance Fees* and *Food Revenue*. Copy the corrected formula down. Format the numbers appropriately. Unhide the Annual Summary worksheet, and then move it as the first worksheet. Move and resize the bar chart to display below the data. On the Annual Summary sheet, format the values and the chart appropriately using the clustered bar chart and switching rows and columns. Move the Chart Legend to the top, and then delete the Chart Title. Verify that the formulas on the Summary sheet are correct. On all sheets, insert the file name in the left footer and the sheet name in the right footer. Check the spelling of the workbook, and then verify that all columns for each sheet will print on one page. Save the file, close Excel, and then submit the file as directed by your instructor.

DONE! You have completed Skills Challenge 1

Skills Challenge 2

To complete this project, you will need the following file:

- **exl03_SC2Durango**

You will save your file as:

- **Last_First_exl03_SC2Durango**

During each month of the summer season, Duncan Chueng, the Park Operations Manager, tracked the revenue and costs at the various locations in the Durango County Recreation Area. Open the file **exl03_SC2Durango**, and then save the file in your chapter folder as Last_First_exl03_SC2Durango Using the skills you learned in the chapter, create a new summary worksheet for the 3rd Quarter with an appropriate sheet name. Hide the worksheet tabs not included as part of the 3rd Quarter. Insert a clustered bar chart that displays the ticket revenue for each month, and then move it to a new sheet with an appropriate sheet name. Move the chart to the second position in the workbook. Format the chart appropriately. Move the summary sheet to the first position in the workbook. On all sheets, insert the file name in the left footer and the sheet name in the right footer. Adjust the page settings to print each worksheet on one page. Save the file, close Excel, and then submit the file as directed by your instructor.

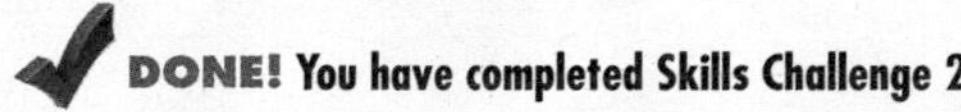
DONE! You have completed Skills Challenge 2

More Skills Assessment

To complete this project, you will need the following file:

- **exl03_MSAHierarchy**

You will save your files as:

- **Last_First_exl03_MSAHierarchy**
- **Last_First_exl03_MSASnip**

---

1. Start **Excel 2016**. Open the file **exl03_MSAHierarchy**, and then save the file in your chapter folder as Last_First_exl03_MSAHierarchy
2. On the **Org Chart** sheet, insert a SmartArt graphic, and then select the **Hierarchy** format. Move and resize the chart so the borders touch **B2:J20**. Compare your screen with **Figure 1**.
3. Using the employee names from the *Employees* sheet, insert the employees' first and last names in the chart. Enter Maria Martinez in the top shape, and then enter the remaining employees in the shapes using their level to guide you.
4. Format the SmartArt color as **Colorful - Accent Colors** and the style as **3-D Inset**.
5. On the **Employees** sheet, **hyperlink** the text in cell **A1** to www.aspenfalls.org and then set a **ScreenTip** to display as Aspen Falls City Hall
6. Select the link to open the website, and then click on the **Employee** link. In cell **B12**, insert a screen clipping of the organization chart graphic. Apply the **Simple Frame, White** style to the object. Adjust the height to 2″.
7. Open **Excel Options**, and then under *Popular Commands*, add **QuickPrint** and **Save As** to the Quick Access Toolbar.
8. View the new icons on the toolbar, and then compare your screen with **Figure 2**.
9. Using the **Snipping Tool**, take a **Full-Screen** snip of your screen. **Save** the file as Last_First_exl03_MSASnip
10. **Save** the file. **Close** all open windows, and then submit the files as directed by your instructor.

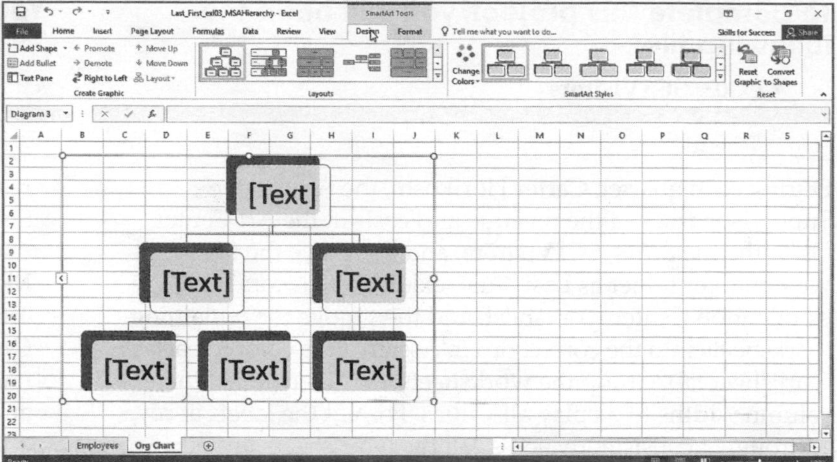

Figure 1 Excel 2016, Windows 10, Microsoft Corporation

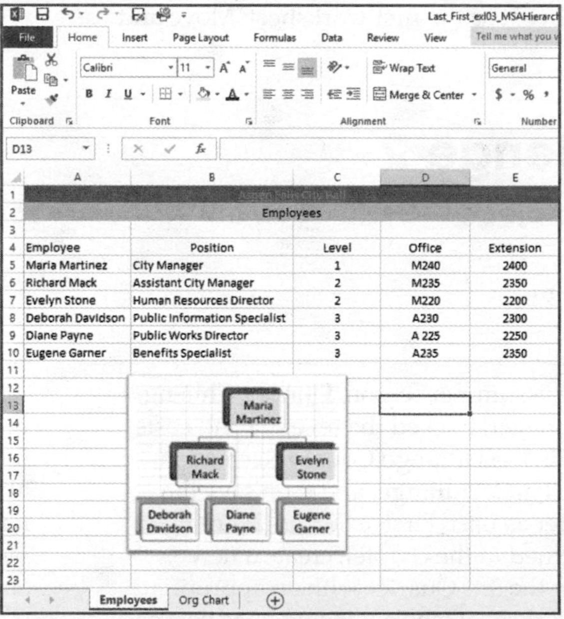

Figure 2 Excel 2016, Windows 10, Microsoft Corporation

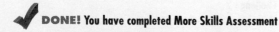

DONE! You have completed More Skills Assessment

Collaborating with Google

To complete this project, you will need a Google account (refer to the Common Features chapter) and the following file:

- **exl03_GPGarage**

You will save your file as:

- **Last_First_exl03_GPSnip**

---

1. Open the Google Chrome web browser. Log into your Google account, and then click **Google Apps** [icon].
2. Click **Drive** [icon] to open Google Drive.
3. Click the **New** button, and then click **Google Sheets** to open a blank spreadsheet.
4. Select the sheet title. In the dialog box, type Garage Revenue and then click **OK**. Rename the *Sheet1* worksheet tab as Summary Insert two tabs by clicking the **Add Sheet** button [icon], and then rename the tabs First Half | Second Half
5. Open the student data file **exl03_GPGarage**.
6. On the **Summary** sheet, copy the range **A4:F8**, and then paste it to cell **A1** in the **Summary** sheet in the **Garage Revenue** workbook. Use the technique just practiced to copy the **A4:F8** range from the **First Half** and **Second Half** sheets to the workbook. When finished, close the student data file **exl03_GPGarage** without saving changes if prompted.
7. Click the **Summary** sheet, and then select the range **A1:F1**. Click the **Format tab**, point to **Text wrapping**, and then click **Wrap**.
8. Click the **First Half** sheet, and then in cell **F2**, enter the formula =(B2+C2)-(D2+E2) Click cell **F2**, click the **Edit tab**, and then click **Copy**. Select the range **F3:F5**. Click the **Edit tab**, point to **Paste special**, and then click **Paste formula only**. Select the range **F2:F5**, and then using the technique just practiced, paste it to the range **F2:F5** in the **Second Half** worksheet.
9. Click the **Summary** worksheet, and then click cell **B2**. Type = click the **First Half** sheet, click cell **B5**, and then press Enter.

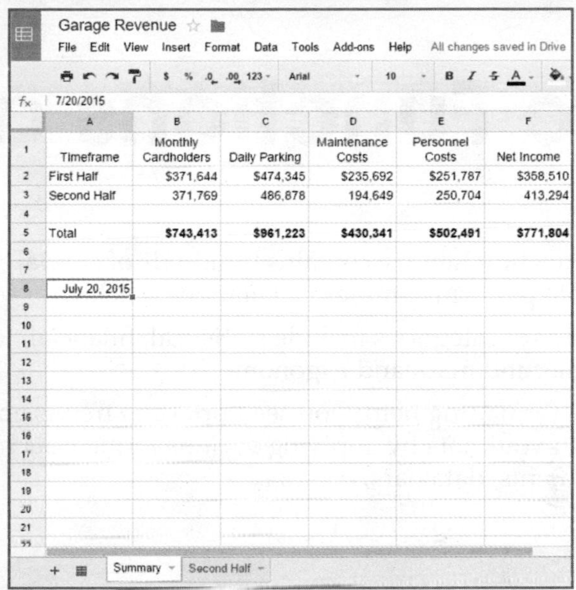

Garage Revenue
File Edit View Insert Format Data Tools Add-ons Help All changes saved in Drive
fx 7/20/2015

	A	B	C	D	E	F
1	Timeframe	Monthly Cardholders	Daily Parking	Maintenance Costs	Personnel Costs	Net Income
2	First Half	$371,644	$474,345	$235,692	$251,787	$358,510
3	Second Half	371,769	486,878	194,649	250,704	413,294
4						
5	Total	**$743,413**	**$961,223**	**$430,341**	**$502,491**	**$771,804**
6						
7						
8	July 20, 2015					

Summary | Second Half

Excel 2016, Windows 10, Microsoft Corporation **Figure 1**

10. On the **Summary** sheet, repeat the technique just practiced to display the **Second Half** sheet **B5** value in the **Summary** sheet **B3** cell. In cell **B5**, enter the SUM function for **B2:B3**.
11. On the **Summary** sheet, select the range **B2:B5**, and then AutoFill to the right through column **F**.
12. Click cell **A8**, and then enter today's date. With cell **A8** active, click the **Format tab**. Point to **Number**, **More Formats**, and then click **More date and time formats**. Scroll down the list, select the format **August 5, 1930**, and then click **Apply**.
13. On the **Summary** tab, click the **arrow**, and then select **Move Right**
14. Click the **First Half tab**, and then click **Hide sheet**. Compare your screen with **Figure 1**.
15. Using the **Snipping Tool**, take a **Full-Screen** snip of your screen. **Save** the file in your chapter folder as Last_First_exl03_GPSnip
16. **Close** all windows, and then submit your file as directed by your instructor.

DONE! You have completed Collaborating with Google

CHAPTER 4

More Functions and Excel Tables

- The Excel Function Library contains hundreds of special functions that perform complex calculations quickly.
- Function Library categories include statistical, financial, logical, date and time, and math and trigonometry.
- Conditional formatting helps you see important trends and exceptions in your data by applying various formats such as colored gradients, data bars, or icons.
- You can convert data that is organized in rows and columns into an Excel table that adds formatting, filtering, and AutoComplete features.
- An Excel table helps you manage information by providing ways to sort and filter the data and to analyze the data using summary rows and calculated columns.

Marcuspon/Fotolia

Aspen Falls City Hall

In this chapter, you will revise a spreadsheet for Jack Ruiz, the Aspen Falls Community Services Director. He has received permission from the City Council to create community gardens in open space areas in Aspen Falls. In order to promote the gardens, the city will provide materials to community members. He has a workbook with a list of materials and wants to know if any items need to be reordered and if new suppliers should be contacted for quotes when replacing the items. He is also tracking the donations received from local retail stores.

Using workbooks to track information is a primary function of a spreadsheet application. Because spreadsheets can be set up to globally update when underlying data is changed, managers often use Excel to help them make decisions in real time. An effective workbook uses functions, conditional formatting, summary statistics, and charts in ways that describe past trends and help decision makers accurately forecast future needs.

In this project, you will use the functions TODAY, NOW, COUNT, and IF to generate useful information for the director. You will apply conditional formatting to highlight outlying data and create sparklines to display trends. To update the underlying data, you will use the Find and Replace tool. Finally, you will create and format Excel tables, and then search the tables for data.

Time to complete all 10 skills — 60 to 90 minutes

Outcome

Using the skills in this chapter, you will be able to insert and move date and time functions, apply logical functions, format worksheets with borders, rotate text, lock panes, and apply conditional formatting. Also, you will insert sparkline charts, create, sort, and filter data in tables, and adjust print settings for large worksheets.

Objectives

4.1 Construct date and time functions
4.2 Apply logical conditions and formats to data
4.3 Modify worksheet formatting
4.4 Distinguish data using cell charts and filters
4.5 Understand large worksheet print options

Student data file needed for this chapter:
exl04_Garden

You will save your file as:
Last_First_exl04_Garden

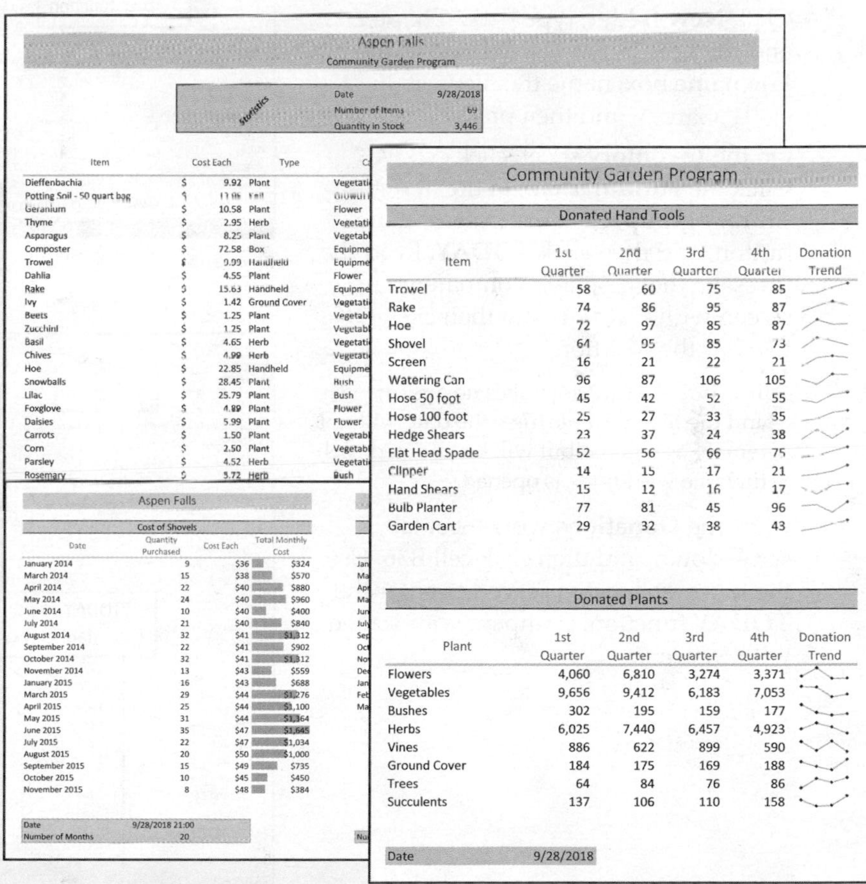

Excel 2016, Windows 10, Microsoft Corporation

SKILLS

Skill 1 Insert the TODAY, NOW, and COUNT Functions
Skill 2 Insert the IF Function
Skill 3 Move Functions, Add Borders, and Rotate Text
Skill 4 Apply Conditional Formatting
Skill 5 Insert Sparklines
Skill 6 Use Find and Replace
Skill 7 Freeze and Unfreeze Panes
Skill 8 Create and Sort Excel Tables
Skill 9 Filter Excel Tables
Skill 10 Convert Tables to Ranges and Adjust Worksheet Print Settings

MORE SKILLS

Skill 11 Add and Remove Table Columns and Rows
Skill 12 Insert the Payment (PMT) Function
Skill 13 Customize Workbook Views
Skill 14 Use Text and Lookup Functions

- The ***TODAY function*** returns the serial number of the current date.
- The ***NOW function*** returns the serial number of the current date and time.
- The ***COUNT function*** counts the number of cells that contain numbers.

1. Start **Excel 2016**, and then open the student data file **exl04_Garden**. Click the **File tab**, and then click **Save As**. Click the **Browse** button, and then navigate to the location where you are saving your files. Click **New folder**, type Excel Chapter 4 and then press Enter two times. In the **File name** box, name the file Last_First_exl04_Garden and then press Enter.
2. On the **Inventory** sheet, click cell **E4**. Click the **Formulas tab**, in the **Function Library group**, click the **Date & Time** button, and then click **TODAY**. Read the message that displays, compare your screen with **Figure 1**, and then click **OK** to enter the function.

   The TODAY function takes no arguments, and the result is ***volatile***—the date will not remain as entered but will be updated each time the workbook is opened.
3. Click the **Donations** worksheet tab, scroll down, and then click cell **B36**. Use the technique just practiced to enter the **TODAY** function. Compare your screen with **Figure 2**.

■ **Continue to the next page to complete the skill**

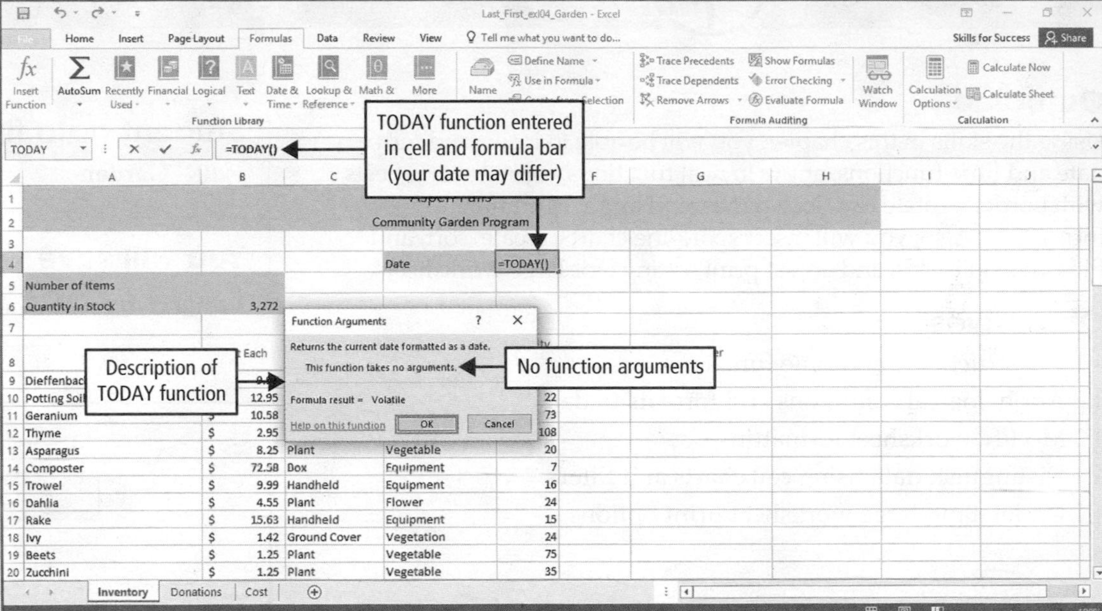

Figure 1

Excel 2016, Windows 10, Microsoft Corporation

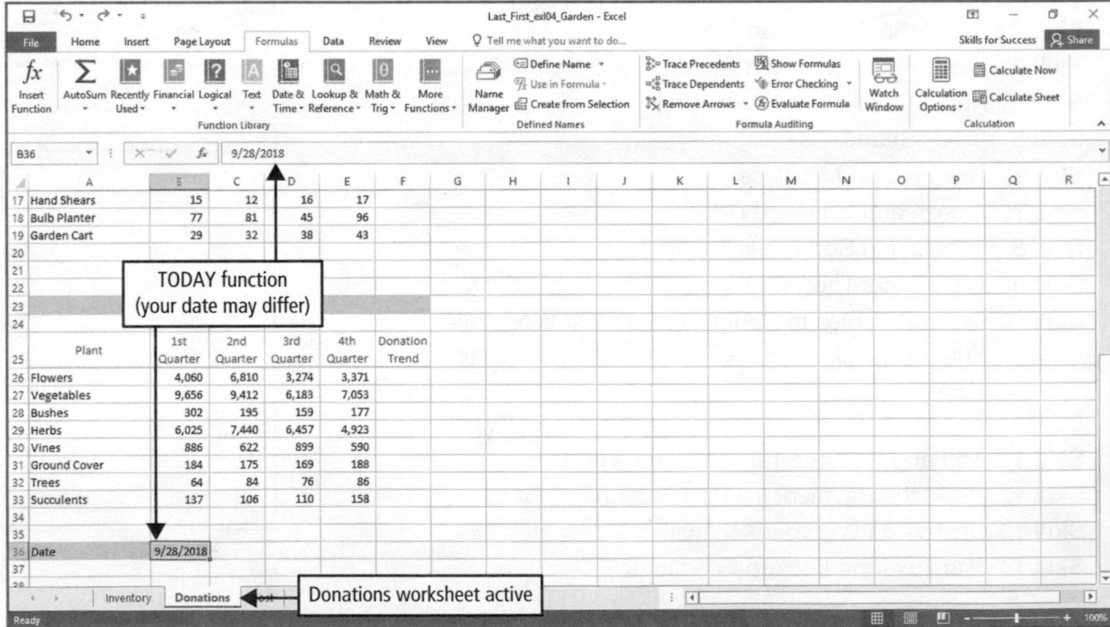

Figure 2

Excel 2016, Windows 10, Microsoft Corporation

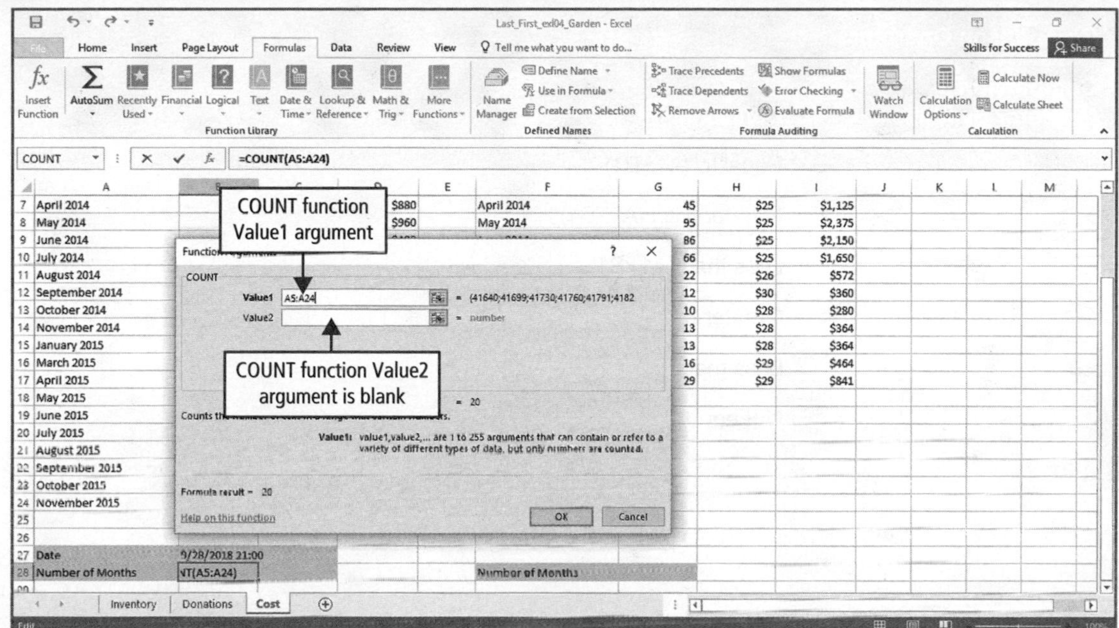

Excel 2016, Windows 10, Microsoft Corporation

Figure 3

=COUNT(B9:B77)

Count function entered in cell and formula bar

	A	B	C	D	E	F	G
5	Number of Items	69					
6	Quantity in Stock	3,272					
7							
8	Item	Cost Each	Type	Category	Quantity in Stock	Reorder	Supplier
9	Dieffenbachia	$ 9.92	Plant	Vegetation	58		
10	Potting Soil - 50 quart bag	$ 12.95	Soil	Growth medium	22		
11	Geranium	$ 10.58	Plant	Flower	73		
12	Thyme	$ 2.95	Earth Cover	Vegetation	108		
13	Asparagus	$ 8.25	Plant	Vegetable	20		
14	Composter	$ 72.58	Box	Equipment	7		
15	Trowel	$ 9.99	Handheld	Equipment	16		
16	Dahlia	$ 4.55	Plant	Flower	24		
17	Rake	$ 15.63	Handheld	Equipment	15		
18	Ivy	$ 1.42	Ground Cover	Vegetation	24		
19	Beets	$ 1.25	Plant	Vegetable	75		
20	Zucchini	$ 1.25	Plant	Vegetable	35		
21	Basil	$ 4.65	Earth Cover	Vegetation	87		
22	Chives	$ 4.99	Earth Cover	Vegetation	95		
23	Hoe	$ 22.85	Handheld	Equipment	12		
24	Snowballs	$ 28.45	Plant	Bush	28		
25	Lilac	$ 25.79	Plant	Bush	21		

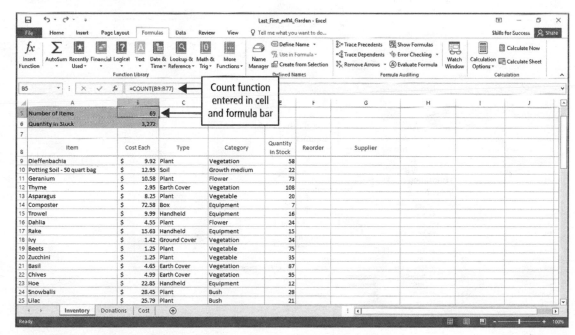

Excel 2016, Windows 10, Microsoft Corporation

Figure 4

4. Click the **Cost** worksheet tab, scroll down, and then click the merged cell **B27**. In the **Function Library group**, click the **Date & Time** button, and then click **NOW**. Read the message that displays, and then click **OK** to insert the function.
5. Click cell **B28**. In the **Function Library group**, click the **More Functions** button. Point to **Statistical**, and then click **COUNT**.
6. In the **Function Arguments** dialog box, in the **Value1** box, type A5:A24 and then compare your screen with **Figure 3**.

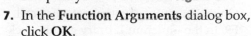

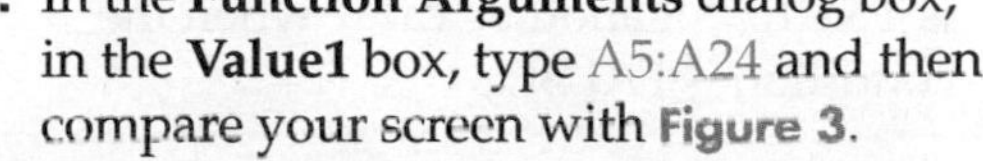

MOS Obj 4.1.4 C

7. In the **Function Arguments** dialog box, click **OK**.

   The number of cells in the range A5:A24 that contain values is *20*.

8. Click cell **G28**. Use the technique just practiced to enter a **COUNT** function with the range F5:F17 as the **Value1** argument.

   The result should be 13.

9. Click the **Inventory** worksheet tab, and then click cell **B5**. In the **Function Library group**, click the **More Functions** button, point to **Statistical**, and then click **COUNT**. If necessary, move the Function Arguments dialog box to the right to view column B. In the **Function Arguments** dialog box, with the insertion point in the **Value1** box, click cell **B9**. Press Ctrl + Shift + ↓ to select the range **B9:B77**. Click **OK** to display the result *69*. Compare your screen with **Figure 4**.
10. **Save** the file.

■ **You have completed Skill 1 of 10**

SKILL 2: Insert the IF Function

WATCH SKILL 4.2

- A ***logical function*** applies a logical test to determine whether a specific condition is met.
- A ***logical test*** is any value or expression that can be evaluated as TRUE or FALSE.
- ***Criteria*** are the conditions specified in the logical test.
- The ***IF function*** is a logical function that checks whether criteria are met, and then returns one value when the condition is TRUE and another value when the condition is FALSE.

1. On the **Inventory** worksheet, click cell **F9**. In the **Function Library group**, click the **Logical** button, and then on the list, click **IF**.

MOS Obj 4.2.1 C

2. In the **Function Arguments** dialog box, with the insertion point in the **Logical_test** box, type E9<10

   A ***comparison operator*** compares two values and returns either TRUE or FALSE. Here, the logical test *E9<10* uses the less than comparison operator, and will return TRUE only when the value in E9 is less than 10. The table in **Figure 1** lists commonly used comparison operators.

3. Press Tab to move the insertion point to the **Value_if_true** box, and then type Order
4. Press Tab to move the insertion point to the **Value_if_false** box, type Level OK and then compare your screen with **Figure 2**.

   In function arguments, text values are surrounded by quotation marks. Here, quotation marks display around *Order* and will automatically be inserted around *Level OK* after you click OK.

■ **Continue to the next page to complete the skill**

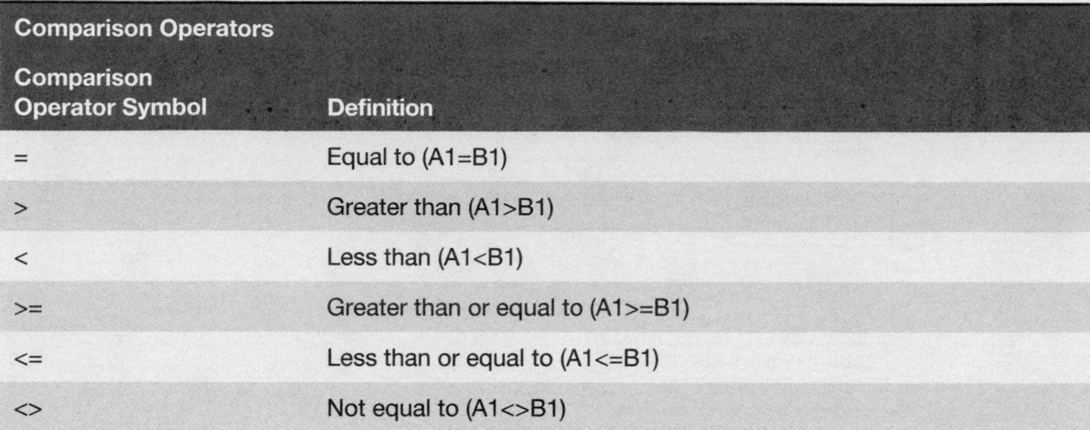

Comparison Operators

Comparison Operator Symbol	Definition
=	Equal to (A1=B1)
>	Greater than (A1>B1)
<	Less than (A1<B1)
>=	Greater than or equal to (A1>=B1)
<=	Less than or equal to (A1<=B1)
<>	Not equal to (A1<>B1)

Figure 1 Excel 2016, Windows 10, Microsoft Corporation

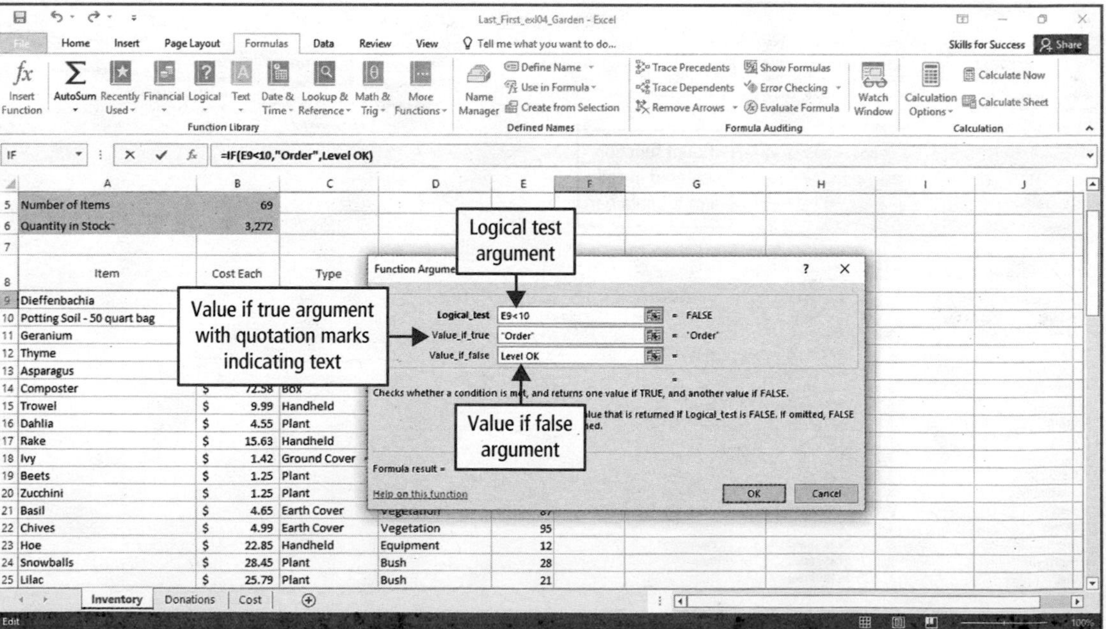

Figure 2 Excel 2016, Windows 10, Microsoft Corporation

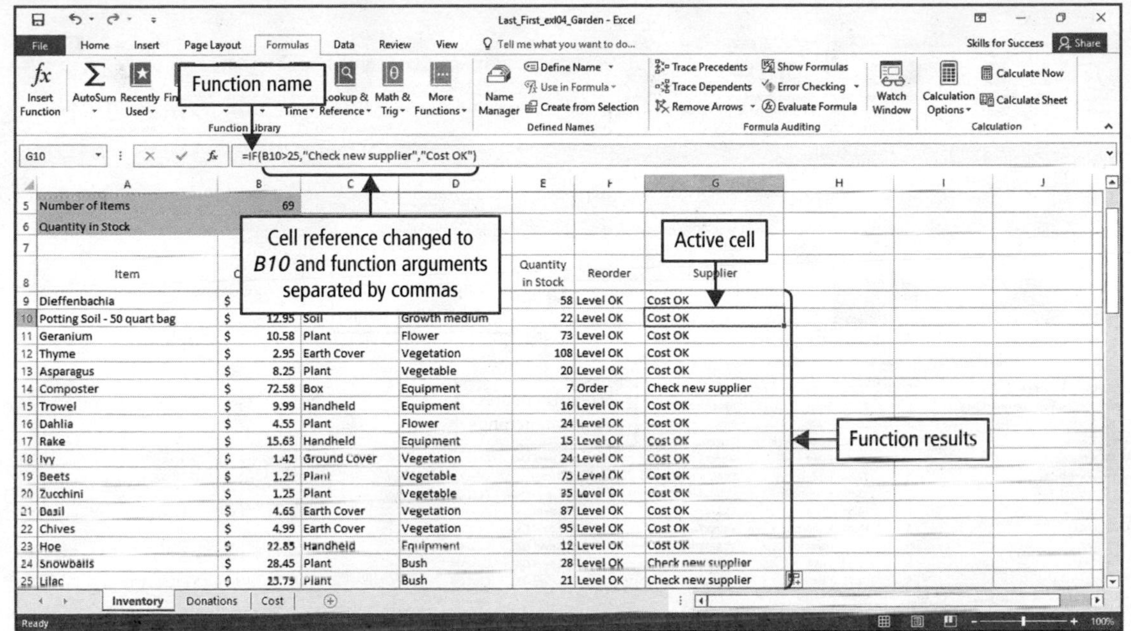

Excel 2016, Windows 10, Microsoft Corporation

Figure 3

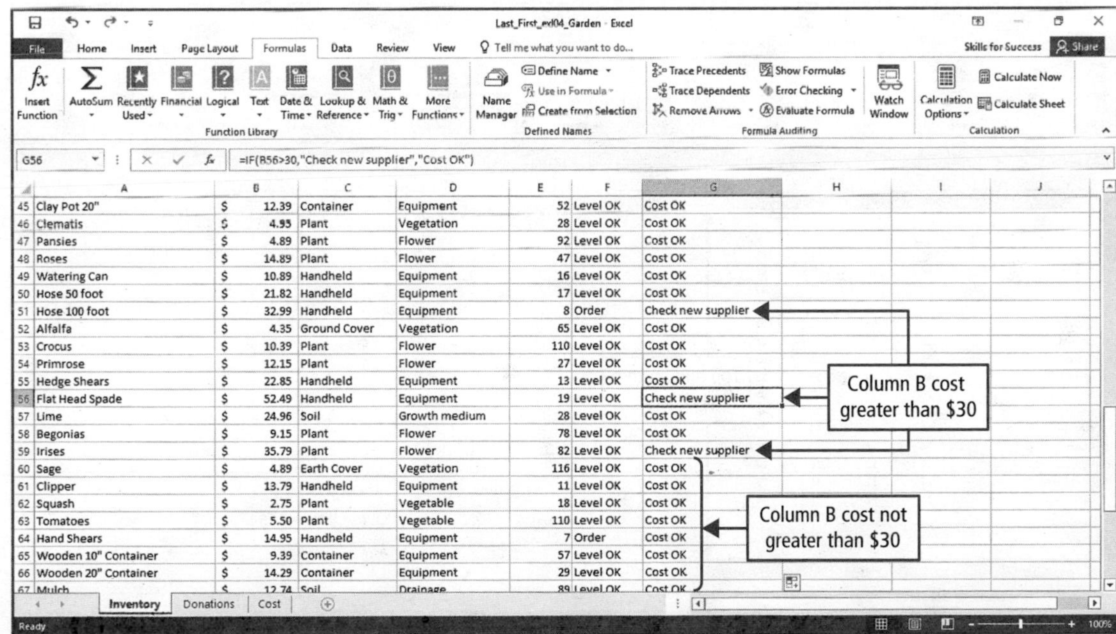

Excel 2016, Windows 10, Microsoft Corporation

Figure 4

5. Click **OK** to display the result *Level OK*.

   The IF function tests whether E9 is less than 10. When this condition is TRUE, *Order* will display. Because E9 contains the value *58*, the condition is FALSE, and *Level OK* displays.

6. Click cell **G9**. In the **Function Library group**, click the **Logical** button, and then click **IF**. In the **Logical_test** box, type B9>25 and then in the **Value_if_true** box, type Check new supplier In the **Value_if_false** box, type Cost OK and then click the **OK** button to display *Cost OK*.

7. Select the range **F9:G9**. Point to the fill handle to display the + pointer, and then double-click to AutoFill the functions down through row 77. Click **G10**, and then compare your screen with **Figure 3**.

   In each row of column G, the function evaluates the value in column B. When the value in column B is greater than $25, the text *Check new supplier* displays. Otherwise, the text *Cost OK* displays.

   When a function has multiple arguments, each argument is separated by a comma.

   When the function was copied down to G10, the cell reference changed from B9 to B10.

8. Scroll down and verify that nine items meet the condition and display the text *Check new supplier*. Click cell **G9**. In the formula bar, change the number *25* to 30 and then click the **Enter** button. AutoFill the function down through cell **G77**. Scroll down to verify that five items meet the changed condition. Click cell **G56**, and then compare your screen with **Figure 4**.

9. **Save** the file.

■ **You have completed Skill 2 of 10**

- When you move cells containing formulas or functions by dragging them, the cell references in the formulas or functions do not change.
- Borders and shading emphasize a cell or a range of cells, and rotated or angled text draws attention to text on a worksheet.

Obj 2.1.1 C

1. On the **Inventory** worksheet, press Ctrl + Home. Select the range **A5:B6**. Point to the top edge of the selected range to display the pointer. Drag the selected range to the right until the ScreenTip displays the range *D5:E6*, as shown in **Figure 1**, and then release the mouse button to complete the move.
2. Click cell **E5**. Notice that the cell references in the function did not change.
3. Click the **Donations** worksheet tab. Select the merged cell **A3**. Click the **Home tab**, and then in the **Font group**, click the **Border arrow**. In the center of the list, click **Top and Bottom Border**.
4. Click the merged cell **A23**. In the **Font group**, click the **Top and Bottom Border** button to apply a top and bottom border. Click cell **A5**, and then compare your screen with **Figure 2**.

   Once the border has been changed, the button on the ribbon will now show the new border format.
5. Click the **Cost** worksheet tab. Click the merged cell **A3**. Hold down Ctrl, and then click the merged cell **F3**. Release Ctrl, and then use the technique just practiced to apply a top and bottom border.

■ Continue to the next page to complete the skill

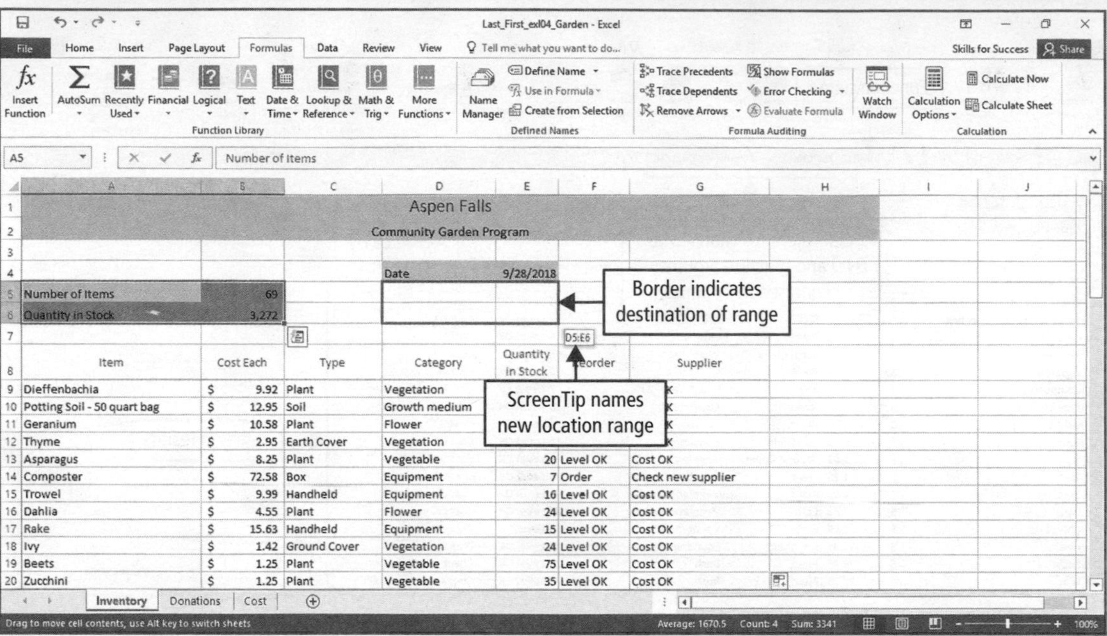

Figure 1

Excel 2016, Windows 10, Microsoft Corporation

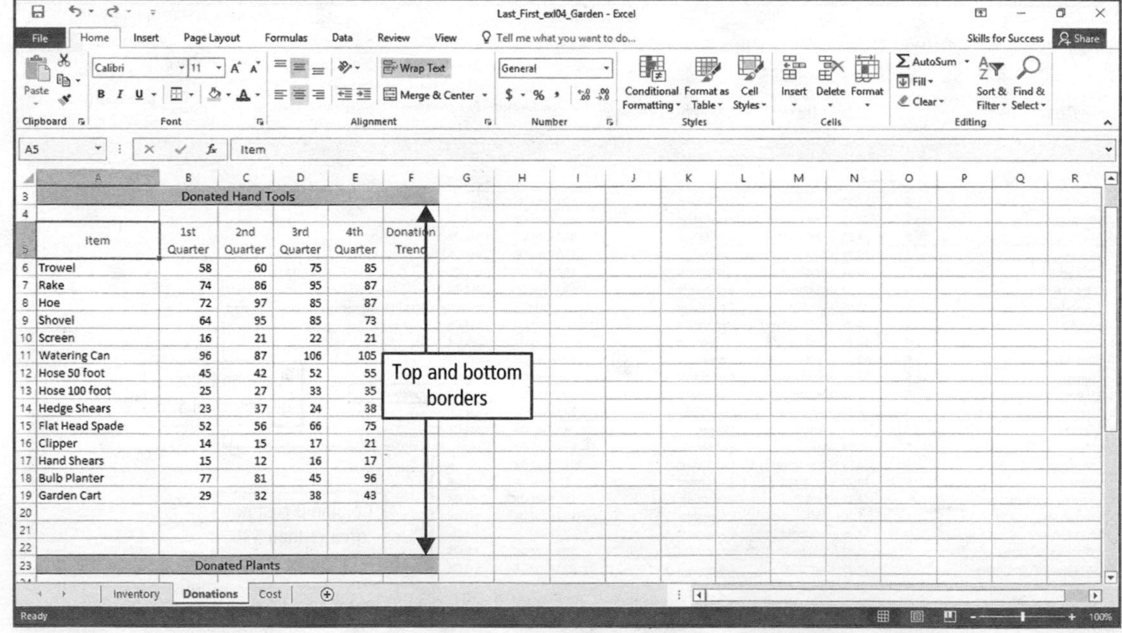

Figure 2

Excel 2016, Windows 10, Microsoft Corporation

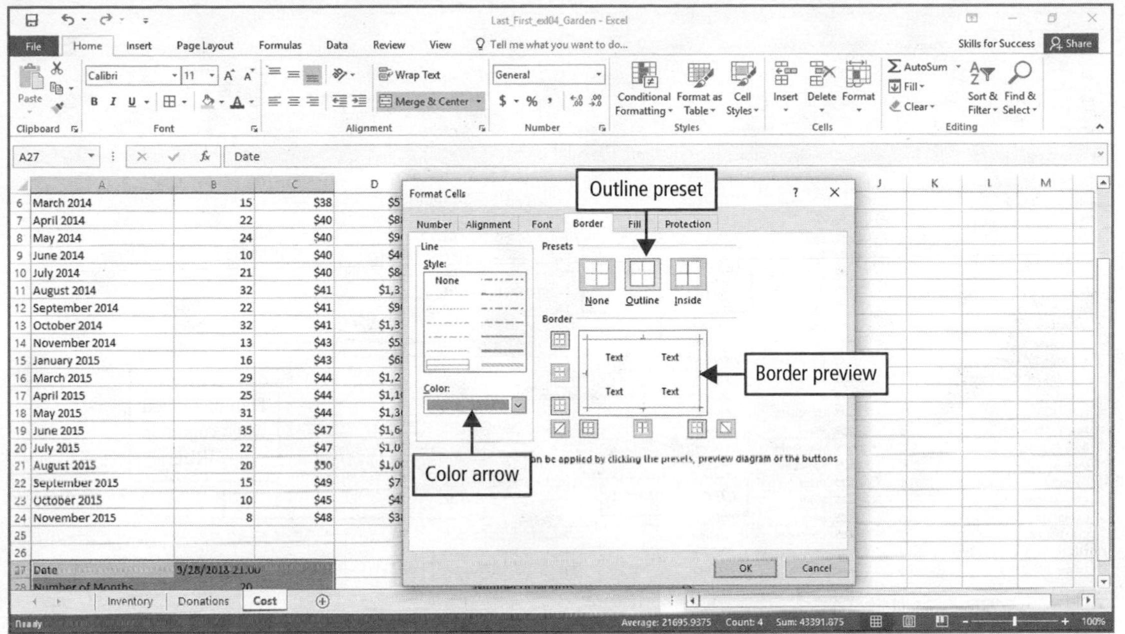

Excel 2016, Windows 10, Microsoft Corporation

Figure 3

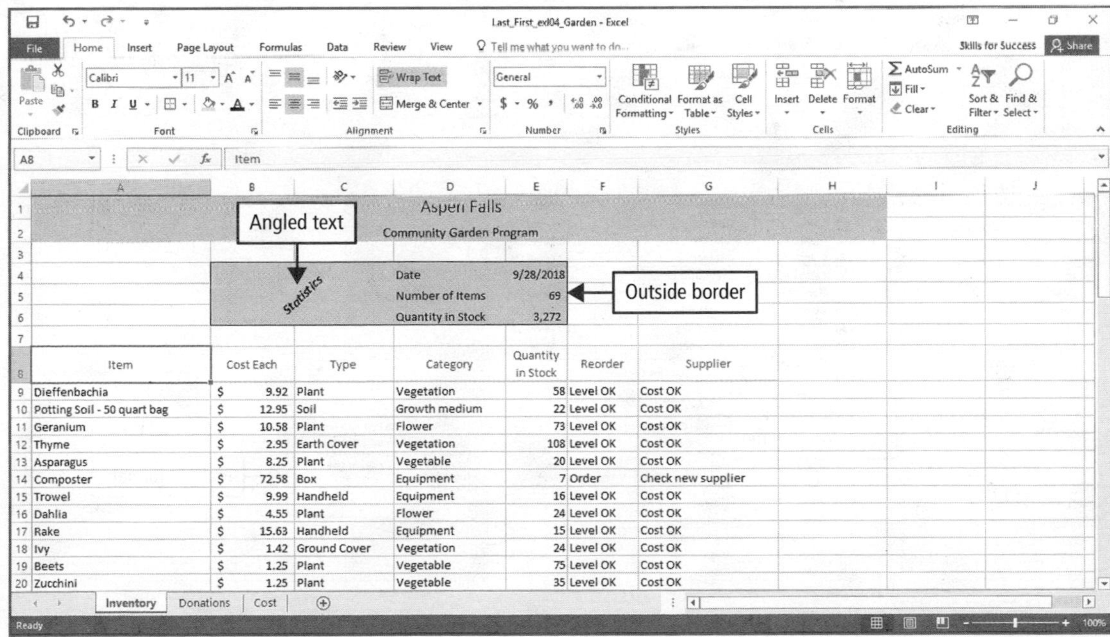

Excel 2016, Windows 10, Microsoft Corporation

Figure 4

6. Scroll down, and then select the range **A27:C28**. In the **Font group**, click the **Top and Bottom Border arrow** . At the bottom of the **Borders** gallery, click **More Borders**.
7. In the **Format Cells** dialog box, click the **Color arrow**, and then click the sixth color in the first row—**Orange, Accent 2**. Under **Presets**, click **Outline**. Compare your screen with **Figure 3**, and then click **OK**.
8. Select the range **F28:G28**. Press F4 to repeat the last command, and then click cell **F30**.

   Pressing F4 will repeat the last command. In this instance, it will apply an orange border to the selected range.

9. Click the **Inventory** worksheet tab. Click cell **B4**, type Statistics and then press Enter.
10. Select the range **B4:C6**. On the **Home tab**, in the **Alignment group**, click the **Merge & Center** button. Apply the **60% - Accent6** cell style, and then click **Middle Align** , **Bold** B, and **Italic** I. Click the **Font Color** arrow, and then click **Automatic**. MOS Obj 2.2.6 C

11. With the merged cell still selected, in the **Alignment group**, click the **Orientation** button , and then click **Angle Counterclockwise**. MOS Obj 2.2.2 C
12. Select the range **B4:E6**. In the **Font group**, click the **Border arrow** , and then click **Outside Borders**. Click cell **A8**, and then compare your screen with **Figure 4**.
13. **Save** the file.

■ **You have completed Skill 3 of 10**

SKILL 4: Apply Conditional Formatting

- ***Conditional formatting*** is a format, such as cell shading or font color that is applied to cells when a specified condition is true.
- Conditional formatting makes analyzing data easier by emphasizing differences in cell values.

1. On the **Inventory** worksheet, click cell **F9**. Press Ctrl + Shift + ↓ to select the range **F9:F77**.

Obj 2.3.4 C

2. Click the **Quick Analysis** button, and then click the first option under **Formatting**, **Text That Contains**. In the **Text That Contains** dialog box, replace the text in the first box, and type Order Compare your screen with **Figure 1**, and then click **OK**.

   Within the range F9:F77, cells that contain the text *Order* display with light red fill and dark red text formatting.

3. Using the technique just practiced, select the range **G9:G77**, and then open the **Text That Contains** dialog box. In the first box, type Check new supplier To the right of the format box, click the **arrow**, and then compare your screen with **Figure 2**.

   You can use the Text That Contains dialog box to specify the formatting that should be applied when a condition is true. If the formatting choice you need is not listed, you can open the Format Cells dialog box by clicking the Custom Format command.

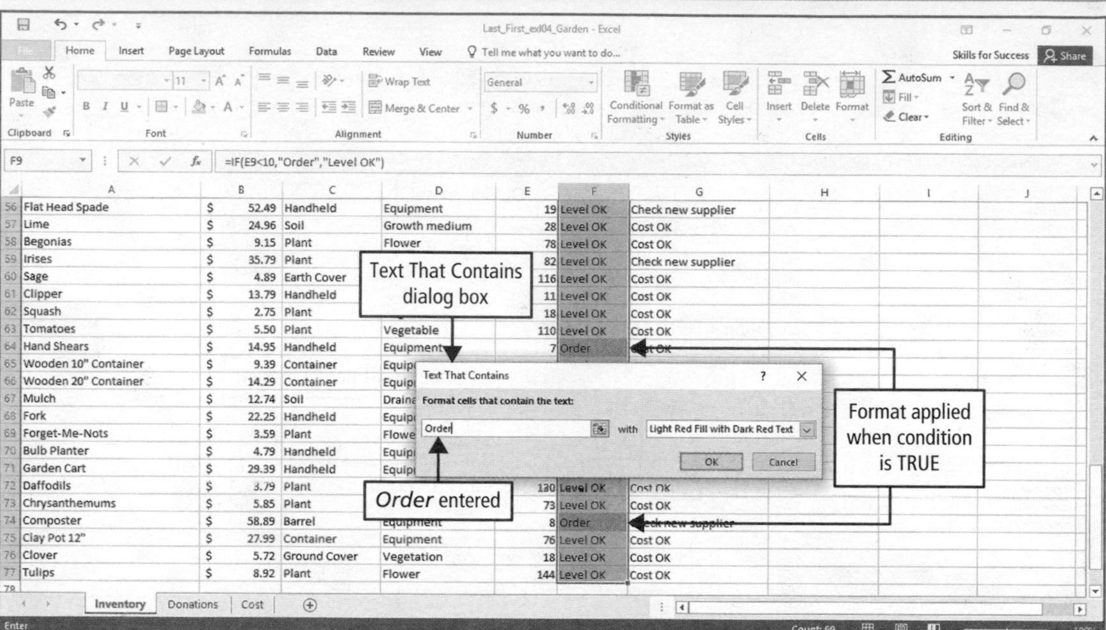

Figure 1 Excel 2016, Windows 10, Microsoft Corporation

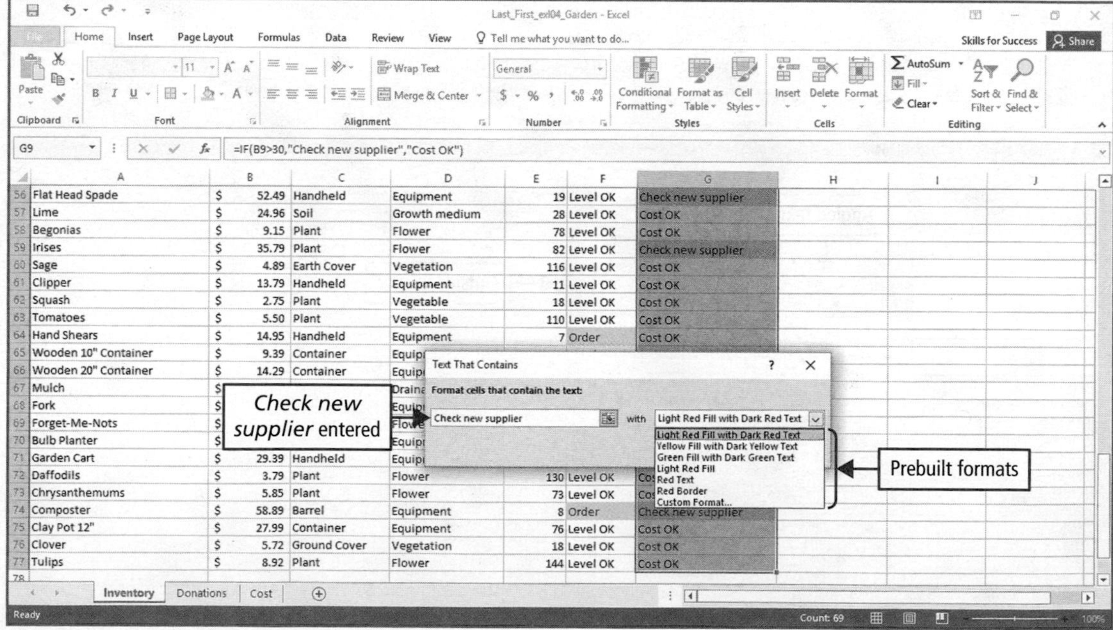

Figure 2 Excel 2016, Windows 10, Microsoft Corporation

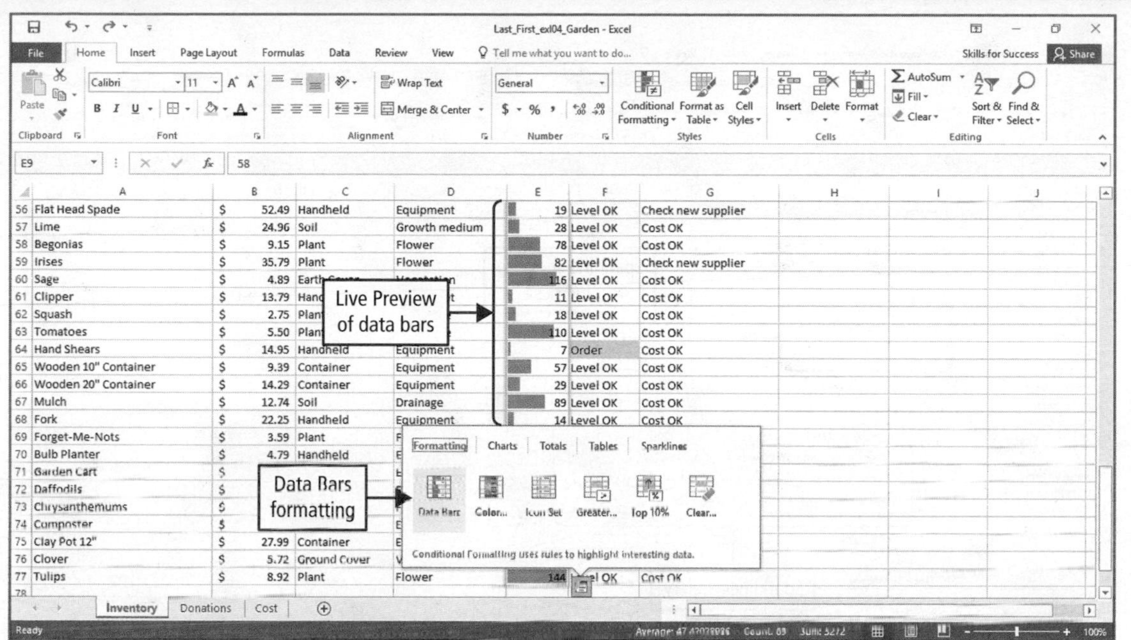

Excel 2016, Windows 10, Microsoft Corporation

Figure 3

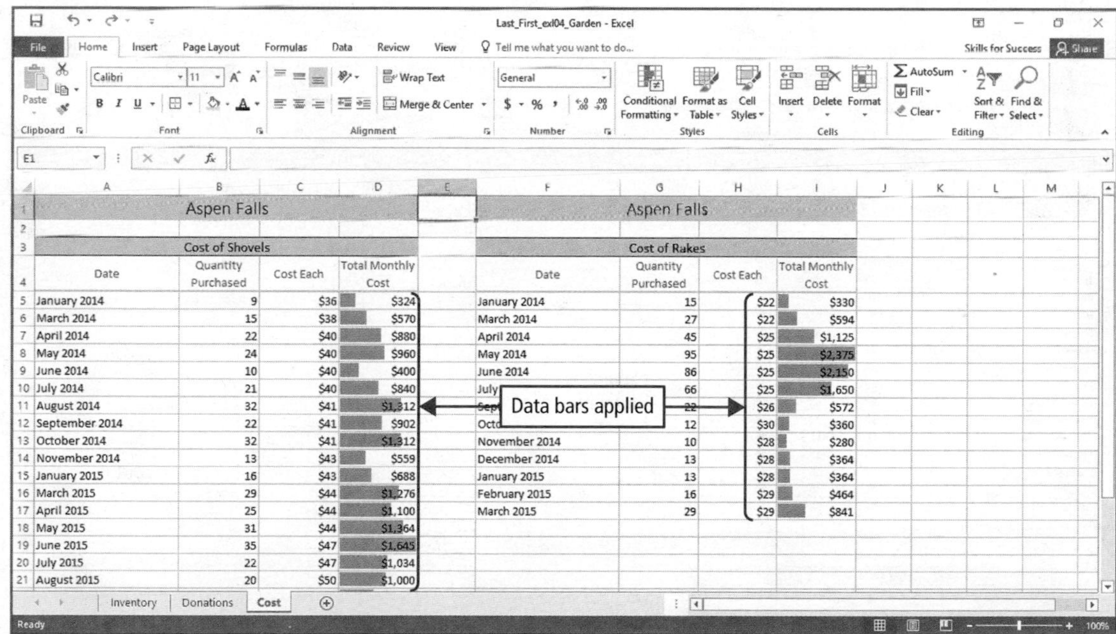

Excel 2016, Windows 10, Microsoft Corporation

Figure 4

4. In the list of conditional formats, click **Green Fill with Dark Green Text**, and then click **OK**.

5. Select the range **E9:E77**. Press Ctrl + Q, and then point to **Data Bars**. Compare your screen with **Figure 3**.

A ***data bar*** is a format that provides a visual cue about the value of a cell relative to other cells in a range. Data bars are useful to quickly identify higher and lower numbers within a large group of data, such as very high or very low levels of inventory.

6. In the **Quick Analysis** gallery, click **Data Bars** to apply the conditional formatting.

7. Scroll up, and then click cell **E15**. Type 190 and then press Enter to adjust all data bars to the new value.

Data bars are sized relative to the maximum value within a range. Here, when a new maximum value of 190 was entered, all the data bars adjusted.

8. Click the **Cost** worksheet tab. Select the range **D5:D24**, and then use the technique just practiced to apply the default data bar conditional format.

9. Select the range **I5:I17**, and then apply the default data bar conditional format. Click cell **E1**, and then compare your screen with **Figure 4**.

10. **Save** the file.

■ **You have completed Skill 4 of 10**

SKILL 5: Insert Sparklines

SKILL 4.5

- A ***sparkline*** is a chart contained in a single cell that is used to show data trends.

1. Click the **Donations** worksheet tab to make it the active sheet, and then select the range **B6:E19**.

Obj 2.3.1 C

2. Click the **Quick Analysis** button, and then click **Sparklines**. In the **Sparklines** gallery, point to **Line** to display sparklines in column F. Compare your screen with **Figure 1**, and then click **Line**.
3. With the range **F6:F19** selected, on the **Design tab**, in the **Show group**, click the **High Point** check box to mark the highest point of data on each sparkline.
4. In the **Style group**, click the **Sparkline Color** button, and then click the sixth color in the first row—**Orange-Accent 2**. Click cell **E20**, and then compare your screen with **Figure 2**.

   The sparklines in column F show that the donation levels of hand tools are generally increasing over time.

■ **Continue to the next page to complete the skill**

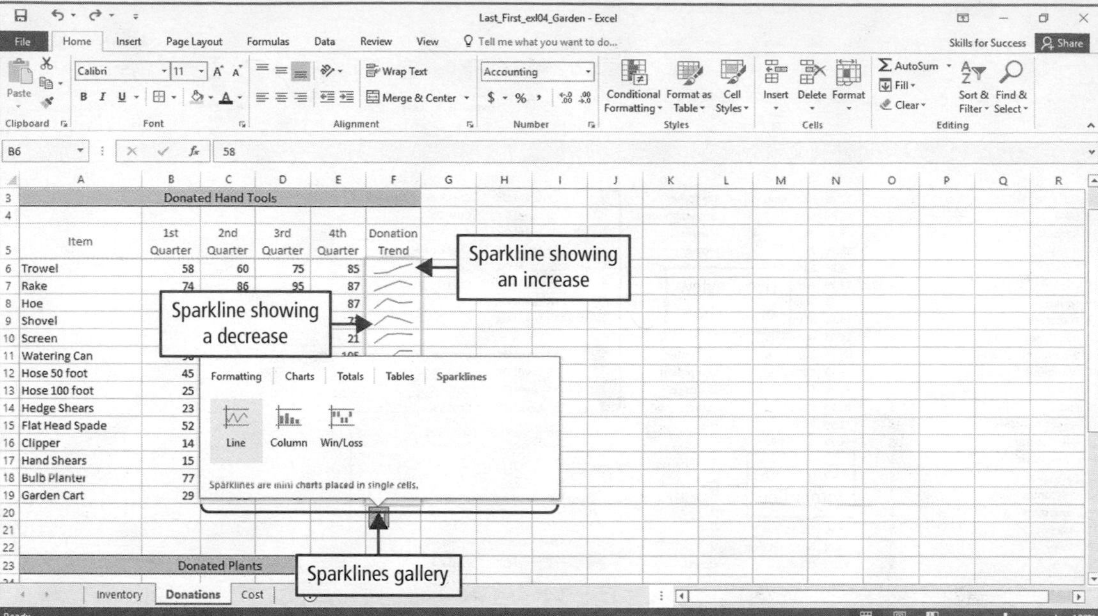

Figure 1

Excel 2016, Windows 10, Microsoft Corporation

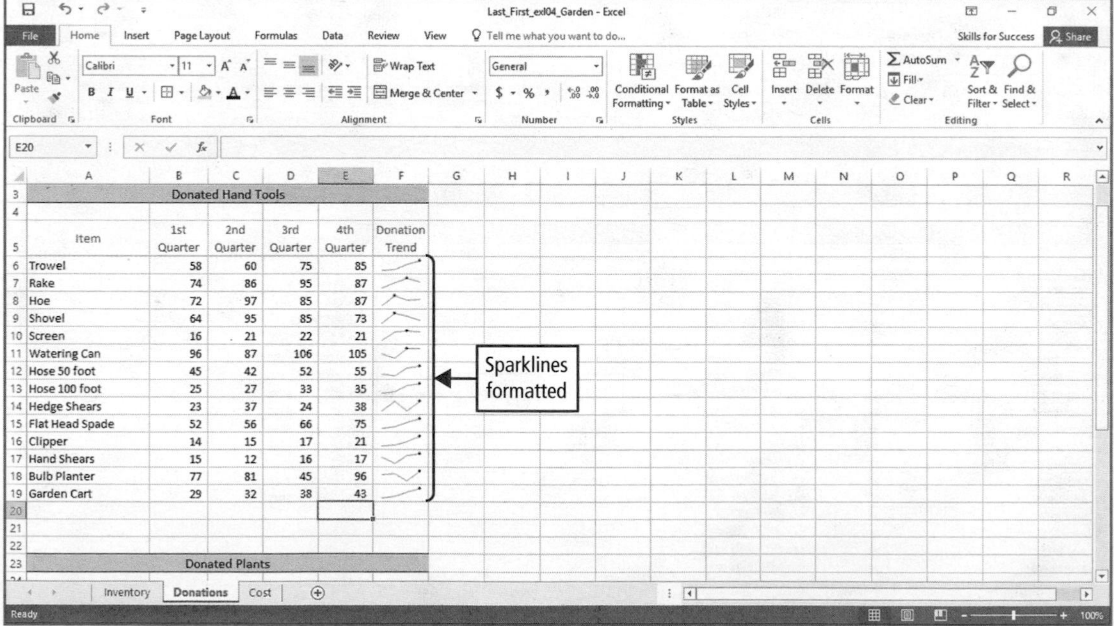

Figure 2

Excel 2016, Windows 10, Microsoft Corporation

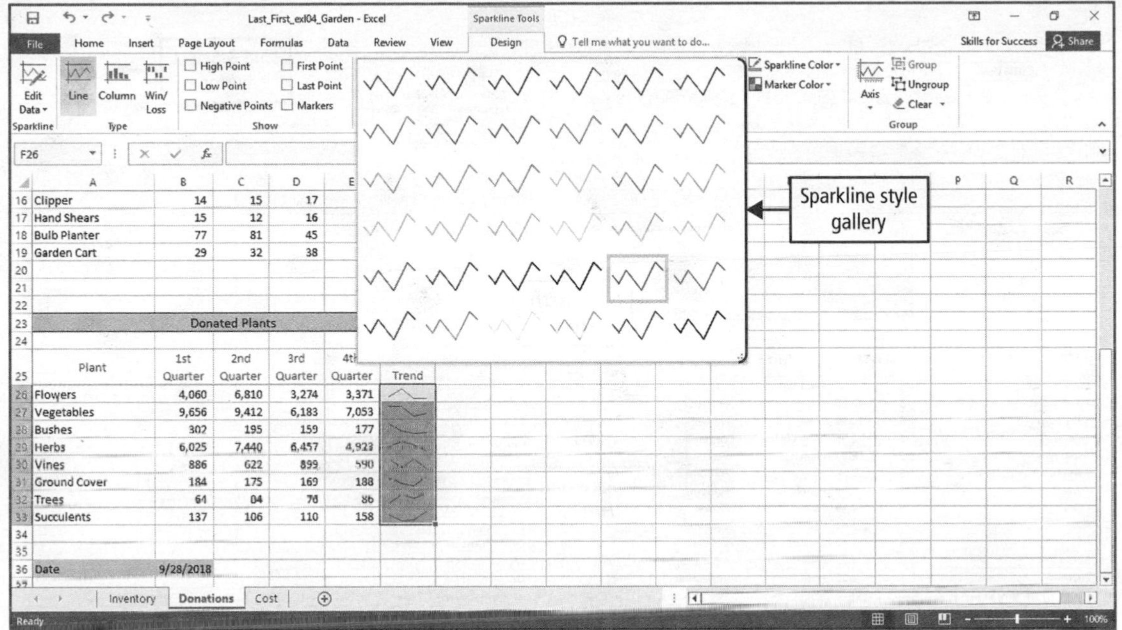

Excel 2016, Windows 10, Microsoft Corporation

Figure 3

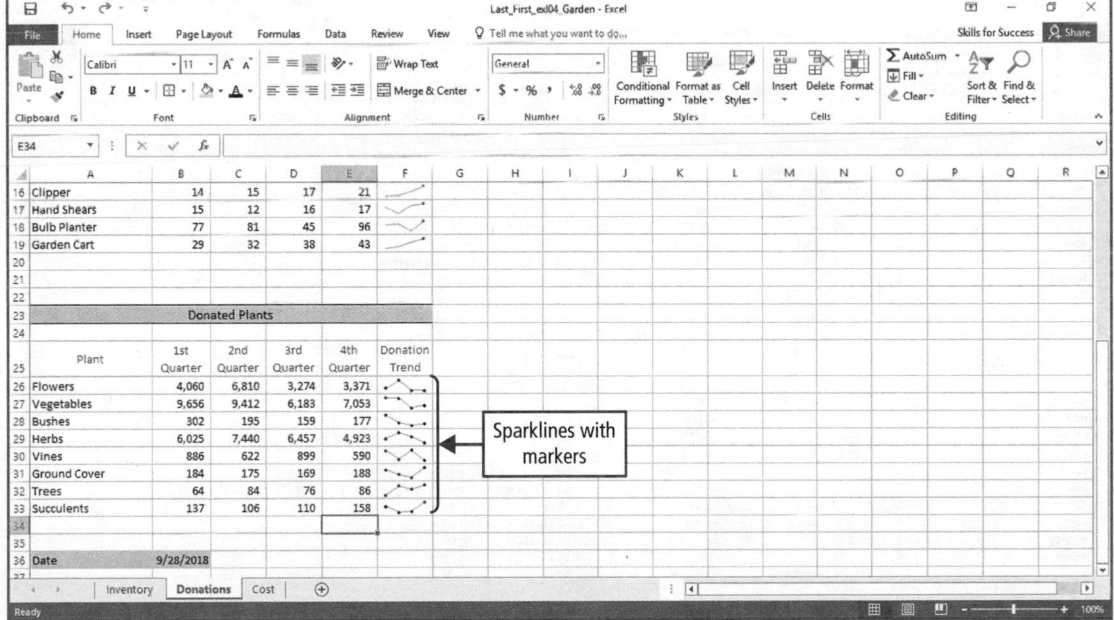

Excel 2016, Windows 10, Microsoft Corporation

Figure 4

5. Scroll down, and then select the range **B26:E33**. Use the technique just practiced to insert the default **Line** sparklines.
6. With the range **F26:F33** selected, on the **Design tab**, in the **Style group**, click the **More** button, and then compare your screen with **Figure 3**.
7. In the **Style** gallery, click the second color in the third row—**Sparkline Style Accent 2, (no dark or light)**.
8. In the **Style group**, click the **Marker Color** button. In the displayed list, point to **Markers**, and then click the second color in the first row—**Black, Text 1**—to mark each data point on the sparklines. Click cell **E34**, and then compare your screen with **Figure 4**.
9. Right-click the **Donations** worksheet tab, and then click **Select All Sheets**. Add the file name to the worksheet's left footer and the sheet name to the right footer. Return to **Normal** view, and then press Ctrl + Home to make cell **A1** the active cell on each of the grouped worksheets.
10. Right-click the **Donations** worksheet tab, and then click **Ungroup Sheets**.
11. **Save** the file.

■ **You have completed Skill 5 of 10**

► The ***Replace*** feature finds and then replaces a character or string of characters in a worksheet or in a selected range.

1. Click the **Inventory** worksheet tab, and then verify that cell **A1** is the active cell. On the **Home tab**, in the **Editing group**, click the **Find & Select** button, and then click **Replace**.

Obj 1.2.1 C

2. In the **Find and Replace** dialog box, in the **Find what** box, type Earth Cover and then press Tab. In the **Replace with** box, type Herb and then compare your screen with **Figure 1**.
3. Click the **Find Next** button, and then verify that cell **C12** is the active cell. In the **Find and Replace** dialog box, click the **Replace** button to replace the value in cell *C12* with *Herb* and to select the next occurrence of *Earth Cover* in cell *C21*.
4. In the **Find and Replace** dialog box, click the **Replace All** button. Read the message that displays. Compare your screen with **Figure 2**, and then click **OK**.

   The Replace All option replaces all matches of an occurrence of a character or string of characters with the replacement value. Here, six values were replaced. Only use the Replace All option when the search string is unique.

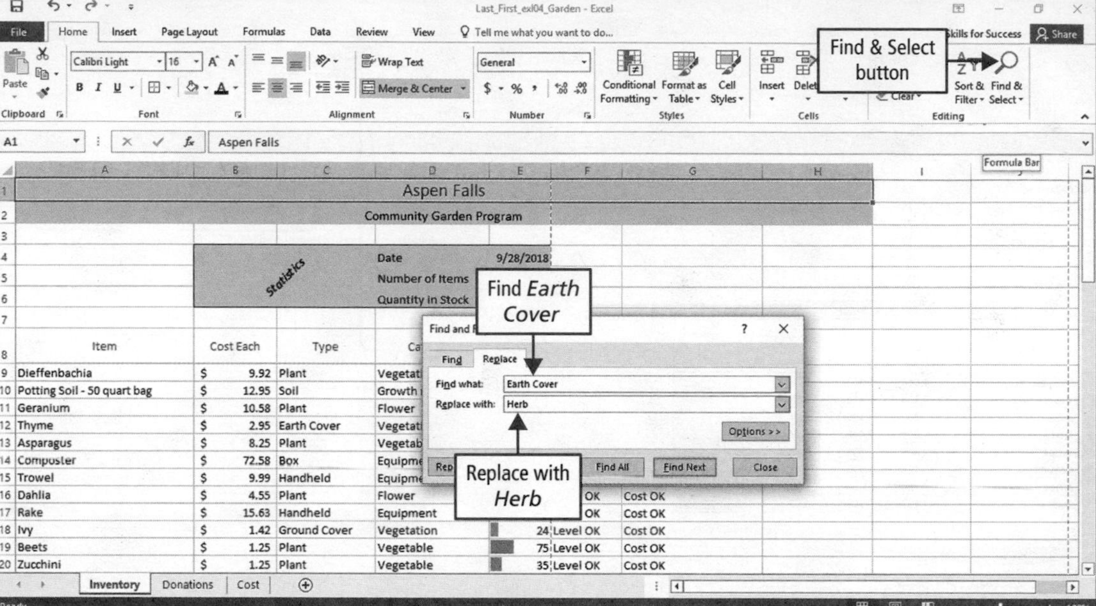

Figure 1

Excel 2016, Windows 10, Microsoft Corporation

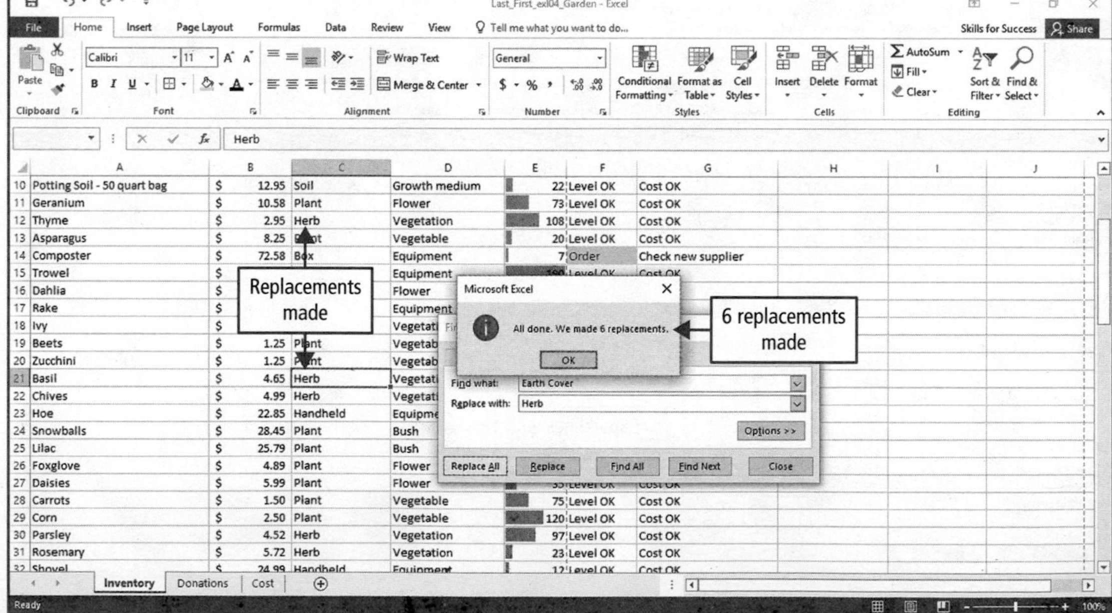

Figure 2

Excel 2016, Windows 10, Microsoft Corporation

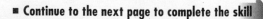

■ **Continue to the next page to complete the skill**

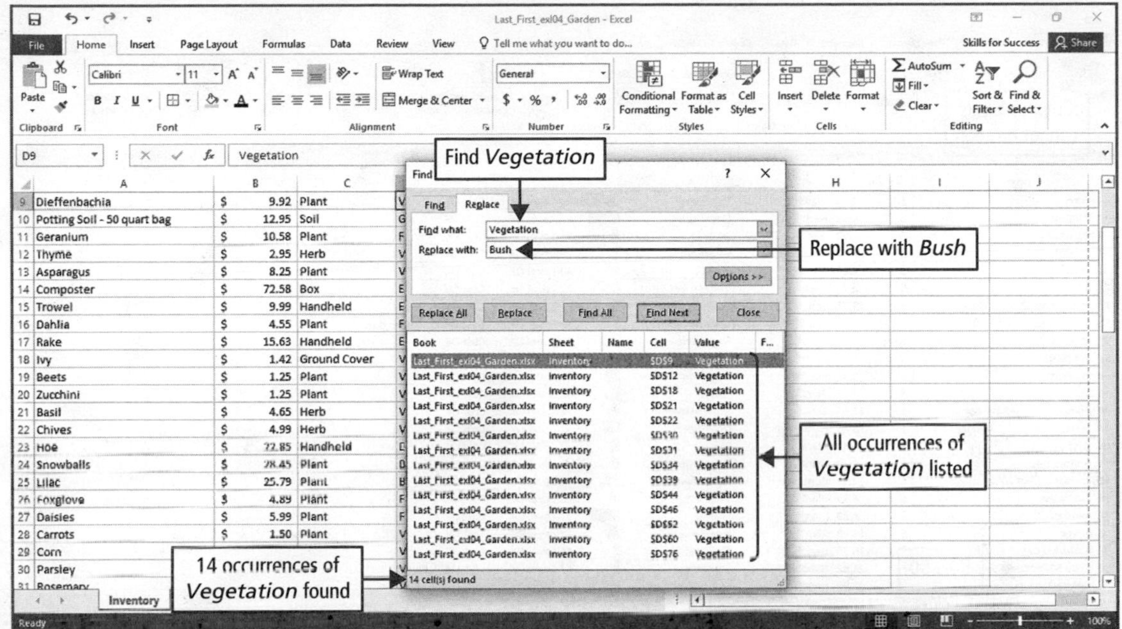

Excel 2016, Windows 10, Microsoft Corporation

Figure 3

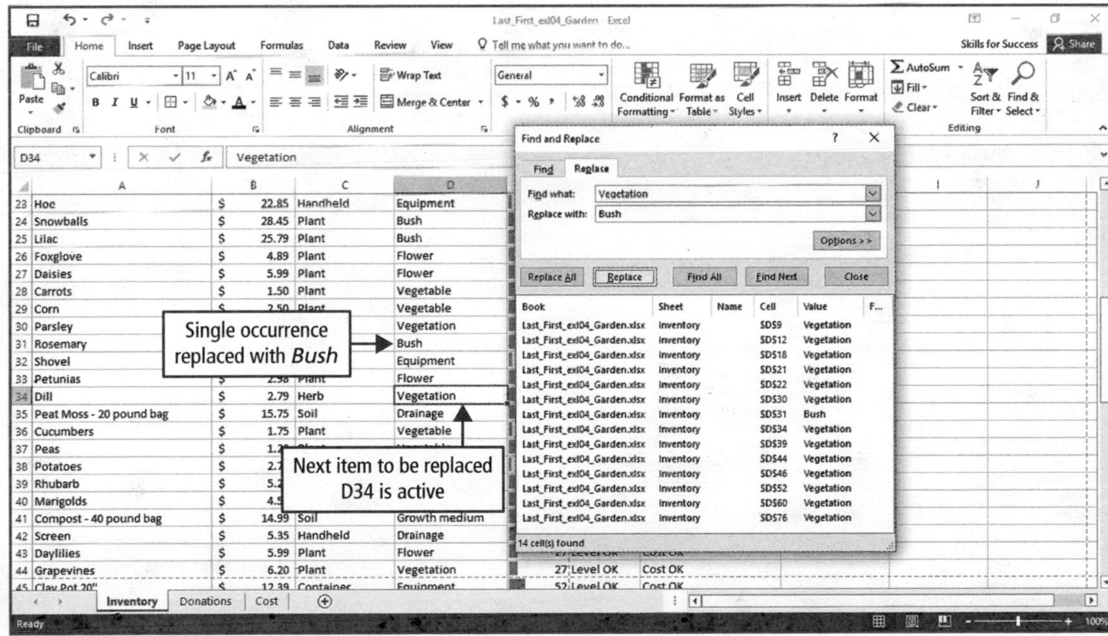

Excel 2016, Windows 10, Microsoft Corporation

Figure 4

5. In the **Find and Replace** dialog box, in the **Find what** box, replace the text *Earth Cover* with Vegetation and then press Tab. In the **Replace with** box, replace the text *Herb* with Bush and then click the **Find All** button.
6. In the **Find and Replace** dialog box, point to the bottom border, and then with the ⇕ pointer, drag down to resize the dialog box until each listed occurrence displays as shown in **Figure 3**. If necessary, move the dialog box to display all occurrences.

   The Find All option finds all occurrences of the search criteria.
7. In the lower portion of the **Find and Replace** dialog box, in the **Cell** column, click **$D$31** to make cell *D31* the active cell, and then click the **Replace** button. Compare your screen with **Figure 4**.

   In this manner, you can find all occurrences of cell text and use the list to replace only the occurrences you desire.
8. Use the technique just practiced to replace the two occurrences of the word Clay with the word Terracotta and then close all message and dialog boxes.
9. **Save** the file.

■ **You have completed Skill 6 of 10**

- The ***Freeze Panes*** command keeps rows or columns visible when scrolling in a worksheet. The frozen rows and columns become separate panes so that you can always identify rows and columns when working with large worksheets.

1. On the **Inventory** sheet, scroll until row **50** displays at the bottom of your window and the column labels are out of view. Compare your screen with **Figure 1**.

   When you scroll in large worksheets, the column and row labels may not be visible, which can make identifying the purpose of each row or column difficult.

Obj 1.4.5 C

2. Press Ctrl + Home, and then click cell **C15**. Click the **View tab**, and then in the **Window group**, click the **Freeze Panes** button. Click the first option **Freeze Panes** to freeze the rows above and the columns to the left of **C15**—the active cell.

   A line displays along the upper border of row 15 and on the left border of column C to show where the panes are frozen.

3. Click the **Scroll Down** ▾ and **Scroll Right** ▸ **arrows** to display cell **M80**, and then notice that the top and left panes remain frozen. Compare your screen with **Figure 2**.

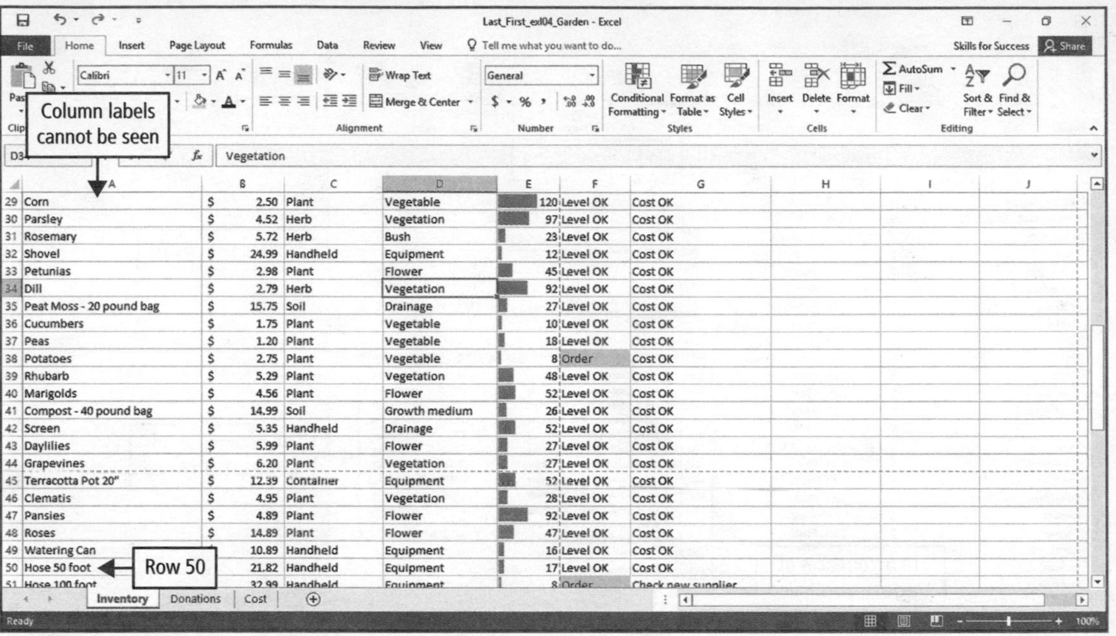

Figure 1

Excel 2016, Windows 10, Microsoft Corporation

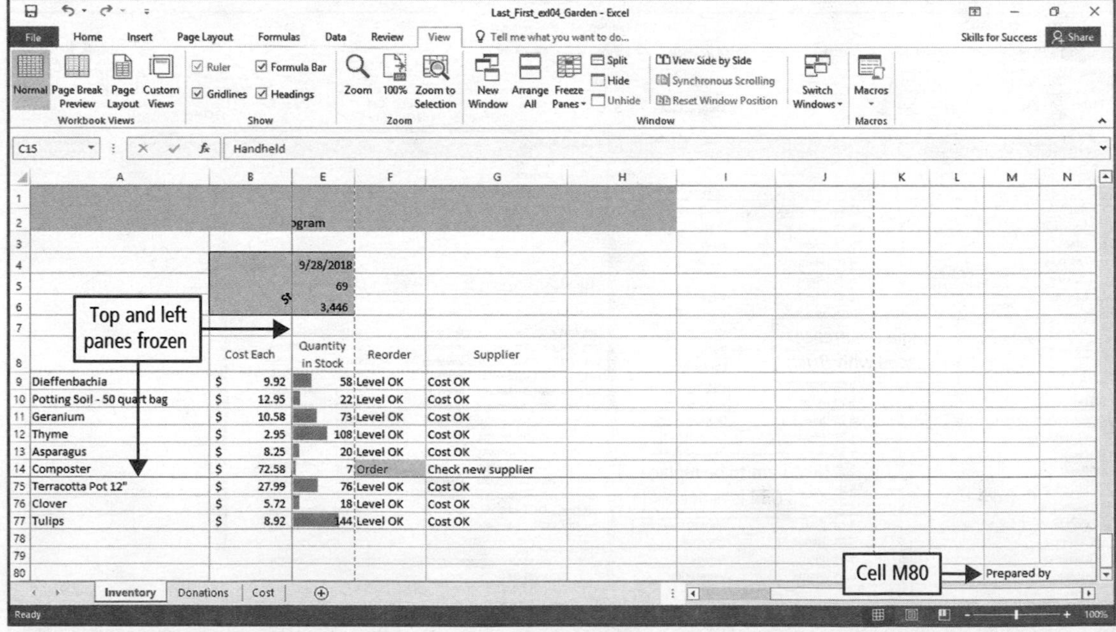

Figure 2

Excel 2016, Windows 10, Microsoft Corporation

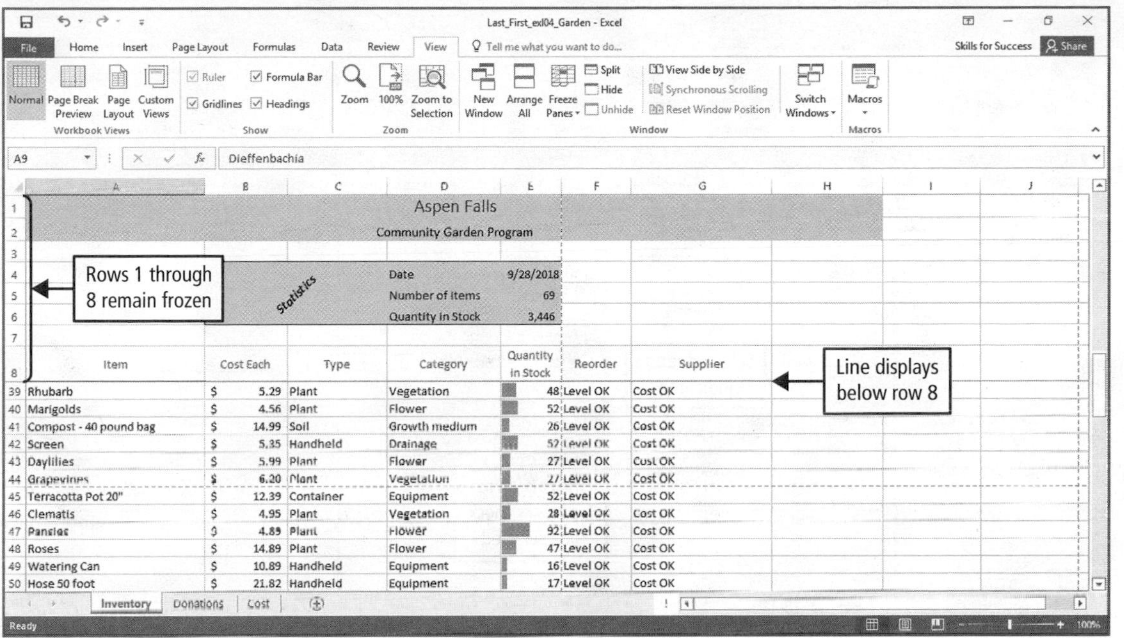

Excel 2016, Windows 10, Microsoft Corporation

Figure 3

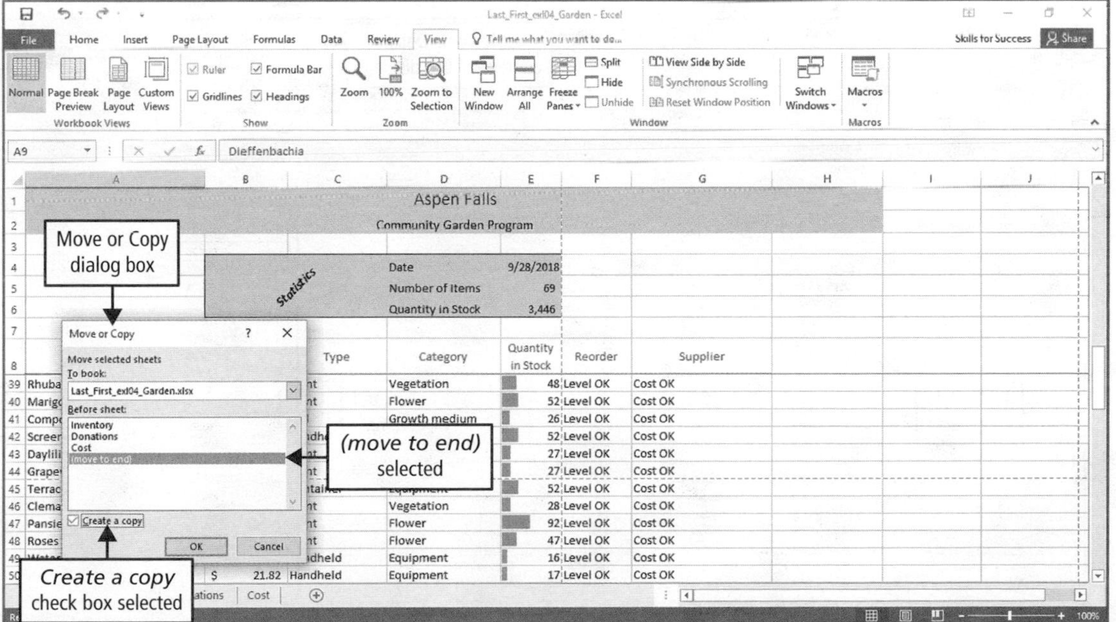

Excel 2016, Windows 10, Microsoft Corporation

Figure 4

4. Click cell **M80**, and then press Delete.
5. In the **Window group**, click the **Freeze Panes** button, and then click **Unfreeze Panes**.

   The rows and columns are no longer frozen, and the border no longer displays on row 15 and on column C.

6. Click cell **A9**. In the **Window group**, click the **Freeze Panes** button, and then click **Freeze Panes** to freeze the rows above **row 9**.
7. Watch the row numbers below **row 8** as you scroll down to **row 50**. Compare your screen with **Figure 3**.

   The labels in row 1 through row 8 stay frozen while the remaining rows of data continue to scroll.

8. Right-click the **Inventory** worksheet tab, and then from the list, click **Move or Copy**. In the **Move or Copy** dialog box, click **(move to end)**, and then click the **Create a copy** check box. Compare your screen with **Figure 4**.

MOS Obj 1.1.4 C

9. In the **Move or Copy** dialog box, click **OK** to create a copy of the worksheet named *Inventory (2)*.

   A (2) displays in the name because two sheets in a workbook cannot have the same name.

10. Right-click the **Inventory (2)** worksheet tab, click **Rename**, type Sort by Cost and then press Enter.
11. In the **Window group**, click the **Freeze Panes** button, and then click **Unfreeze Panes** to unfreeze the panes.
12. Click the **Inventory** worksheet tab, and then verify the panes are still frozen on this worksheet.
13. **Save** the file.

■ **You have completed Skill 7 of 10**

- To analyze a group of related data, you can convert a range into an ***Excel table***—a series of rows and columns that contain related data that have been formatted as a table. Data in an Excel table are managed independently from the data in other rows and columns in the worksheet.
- Data in Excel tables can be sorted in a variety of ways—for example, in ascending order or by color.

1. Click the **Sort by Cost** worksheet tab, and then click cell **A11**. On the **Home tab**, in the **Styles group**, click the **Format as Table** button. In the gallery, under **Light**, click the seventh choice in the first row—**Table Style Light 7**.

2. In the **Format as Table** dialog box, under **Where is the data for your table?**, verify that the range **=$A$8:$G$77** displays. Verify that the **My table has headers** check box is selected. Compare your screen with **Figure 1**, and then click **OK** to convert the range to an Excel table.

   When creating an Excel table, you only need to click in the data. The layout of column and row headings determines the default range provided in the Format As Table dialog box. If needed, the data range can also be edited in the dialog box, or alternatively, the user can click to drag and select the correct range.

3. Click cell **H8**, type Total Cost and then press Enter to automatically add the formatted column to the Excel table.
4. In cell **H9**, type =B9*E9 and then press Enter. Compare your screen with **Figure 2**.

   The new column is a ***calculated column***—a column in an Excel table that uses a single formula that adjusts for each row.

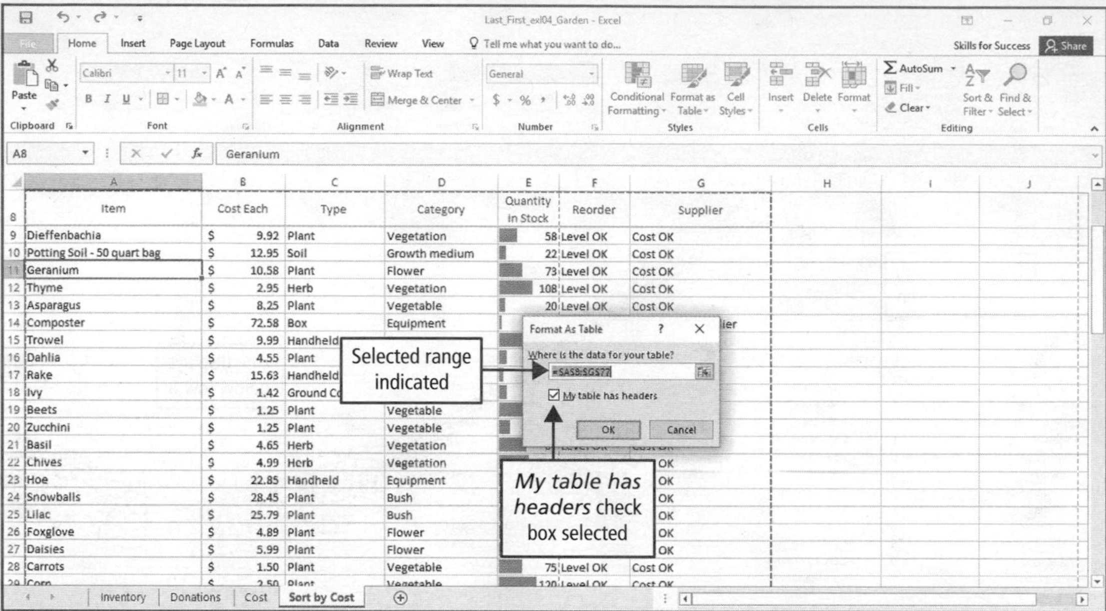

Figure 1

Excel 2016, Windows 10, Microsoft Corporation

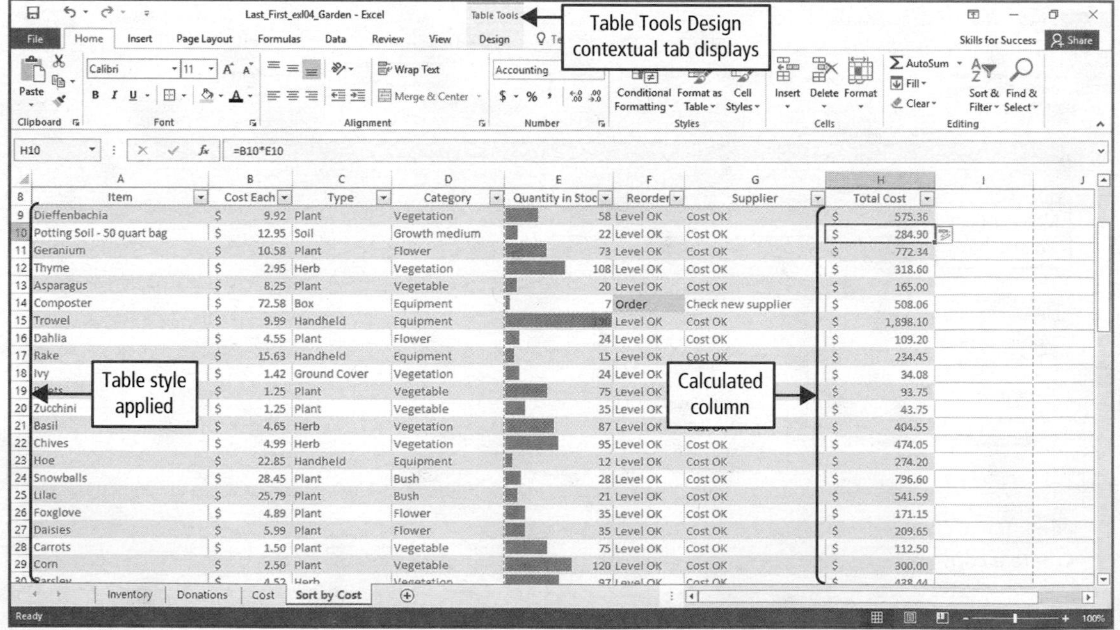

Figure 2

Excel 2016, Windows 10, Microsoft Corporation

■ Continue to the next page to complete the skill

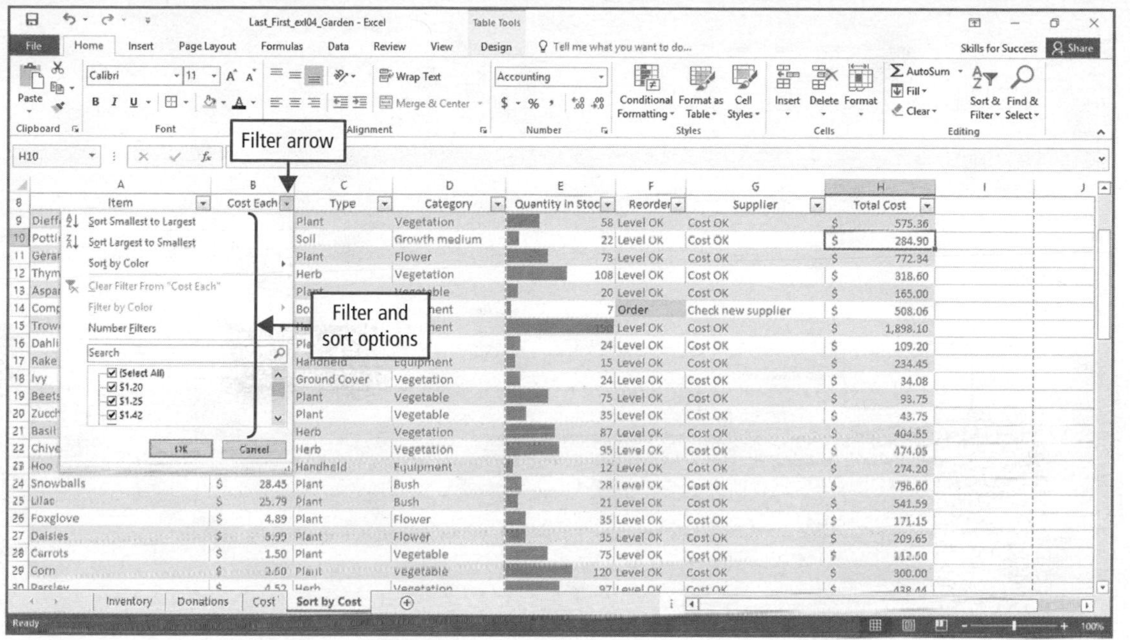

Excel 2016, Windows 10, Microsoft Corporation

Figure 3

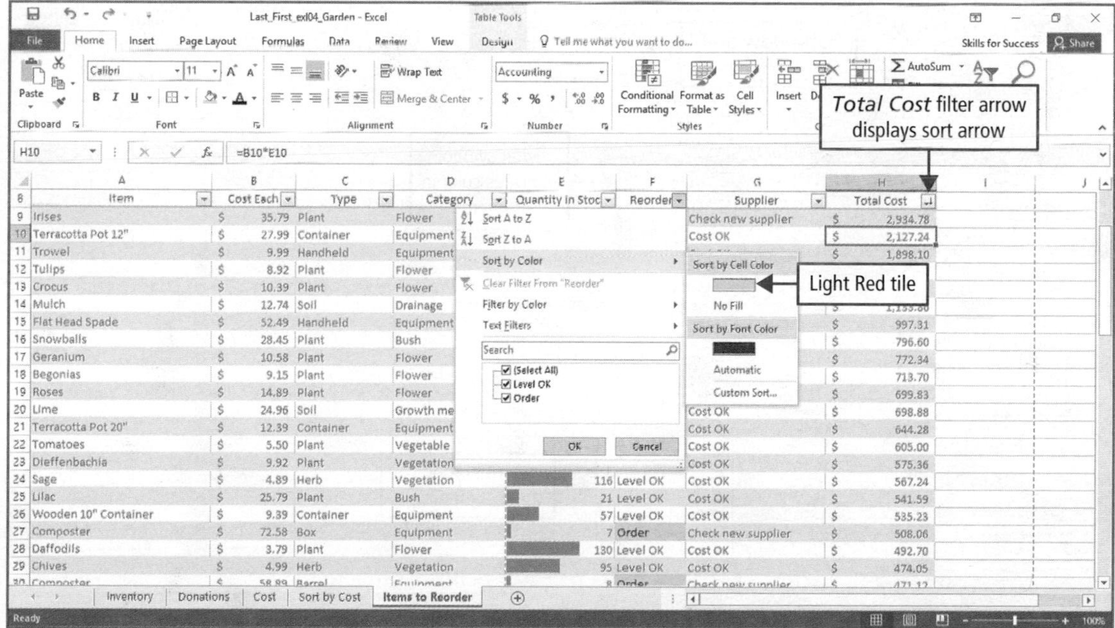

Excel 2016, Windows 10, Microsoft Corporation

Figure 4

5. In the header row of the Excel table, click the **Cost Each filter arrow**, and then compare your screen with **Figure 3**.

6. In the Filter gallery, click **Sort Smallest to Largest**.

Obj 3.3.3 C

   The rows in the table are sorted by the *Cost Each* values, from the lowest to the highest, as indicated by the up arrow on the column's filter button.

7. In the header row, click the **Total Cost filter arrow**, and then click **Sort Largest to Smallest**.

   The rows in the table are now sorted from the highest to lowest *Total Cost* value, and the small arrow in the Total Cost filter arrow points down, indicating a descending sort. The previous sort on the *Cost Each* column no longer displays.

8. Right-click the **Sort by Cost** worksheet tab, and then click **Move or Copy**. In the **Move or Copy** dialog box, click **(move to end)**, select the **Create a copy** check box, and then click **OK**.

Obj 1.1.4 C

9. Rename the **Sort by Cost (2)** worksheet tab as Items to Reorder

10. On the **Items to Reorder** worksheet, click the **Reorder filter arrow**, and then point to **Sort by Color**. Notice that the color formats in column F display in the list. Compare your screen with **Figure 4**.

    If you have applied manual or conditional formatting to a range of cells, you can sort by these colors.

11. In the list, under **Sort by Cell Color**, click the **Light Red** color to place the six items that need to be ordered at the top of the Excel table.

12. **Save** the file.

■ **You have completed Skill 8 of 10**

► You can ***filter*** data to display only the rows of a table that meet specified criteria. Filtering temporarily hides rows that do not meet the criteria.

MOS Obj 3.3.1 C

1. On the **Items to Reorder** worksheet, click the **Category filter arrow**. From the menu, clear the **(Select All)** check box to clear all the check boxes. Click the **Equipment** check box, as shown in **Figure 1**, and then click **OK** to display only the rows containing *Equipment*.

   The rows not meeting this criteria are hidden from view.

MOS Obj 3.2.3 C

2. Click the **Design tab**, and then in the **Table Style Options group**, click the **Total Row** check box to display the column total in cell **H78**. Select the range **H10:H72**. Click the **Home tab**, and then in the **Number group**, click the **Comma Style** button .

   The ***Total row*** displays as the last row in an Excel table and provides summary functions in drop-down lists for each column. Here, *Total* displays in cell A78. In cell H78, the number *$10,400.26* indicates the SUM of the Total Cost column for the filtered *Equipment* rows.

3. In the **Total** row, click cell **D78**, and then click the **arrow** that displays to the right of the selected cell. Compare your screen with **Figure 2**.

4. In the list of summary functions, click **Count** to count only the visible rows in column D—*20*.

MOS Obj 3.3.2 C

5. In the header row, click the **Type filter arrow**. From the menu, scroll down and clear the **Handheld** check box, and then click **OK**.

   Filters can be applied to more than one column. Here, both the Type and Category columns are filtered.

■ Continue to the next page to complete the skill

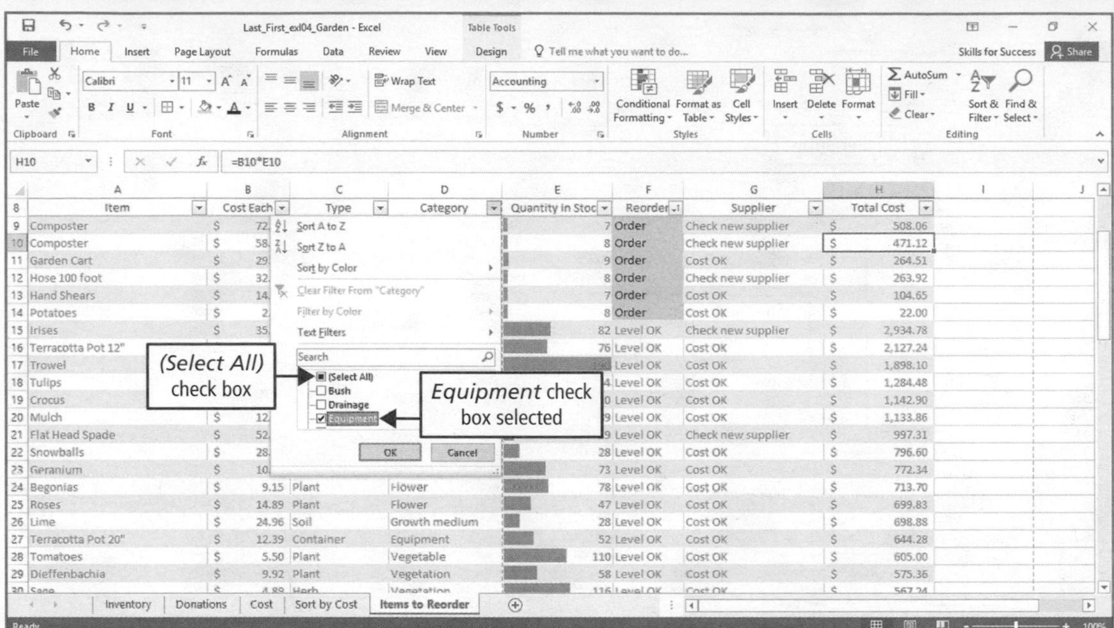

Figure 1 Excel 2016, Windows 10, Microsoft Corporation

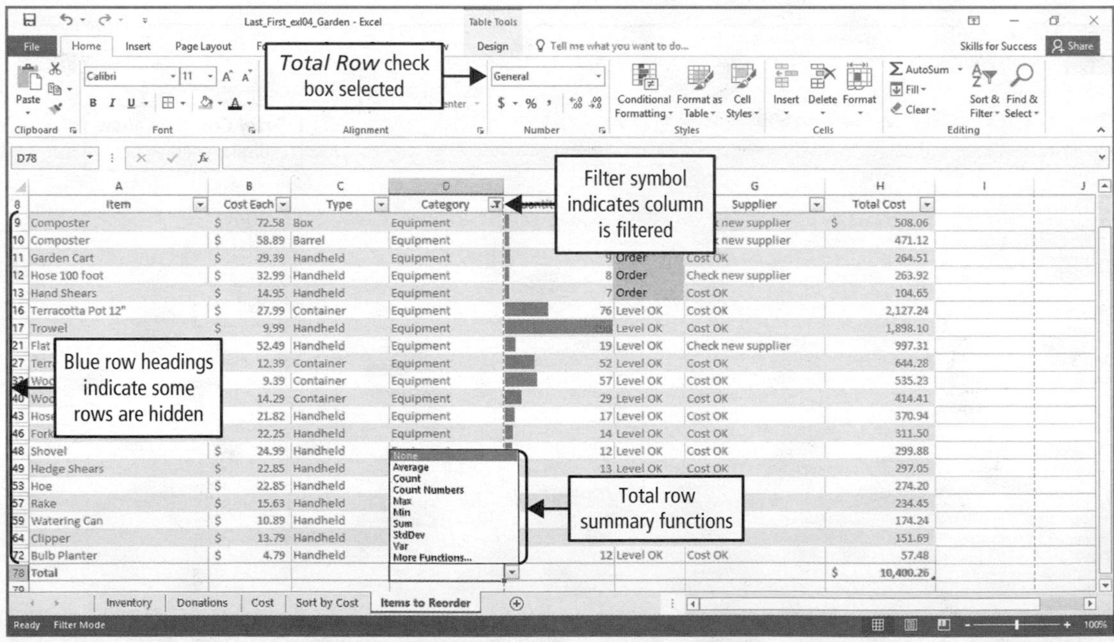

Figure 2 Excel 2016, Windows 10, Microsoft Corporation

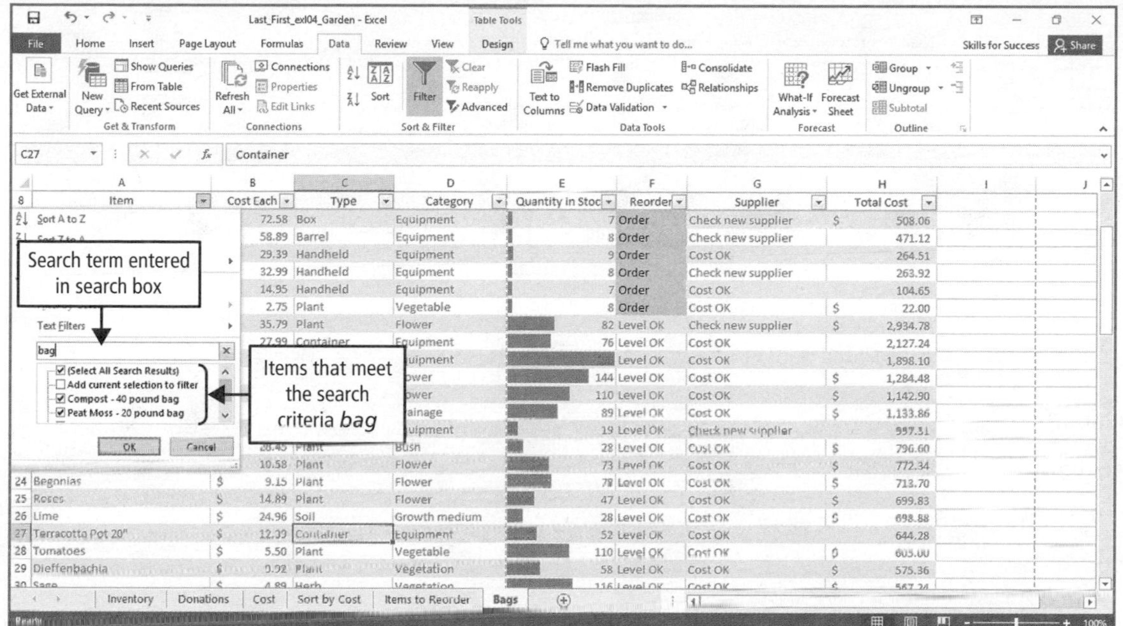

Excel 2016, Windows 10, Microsoft Corporation

Figure 3

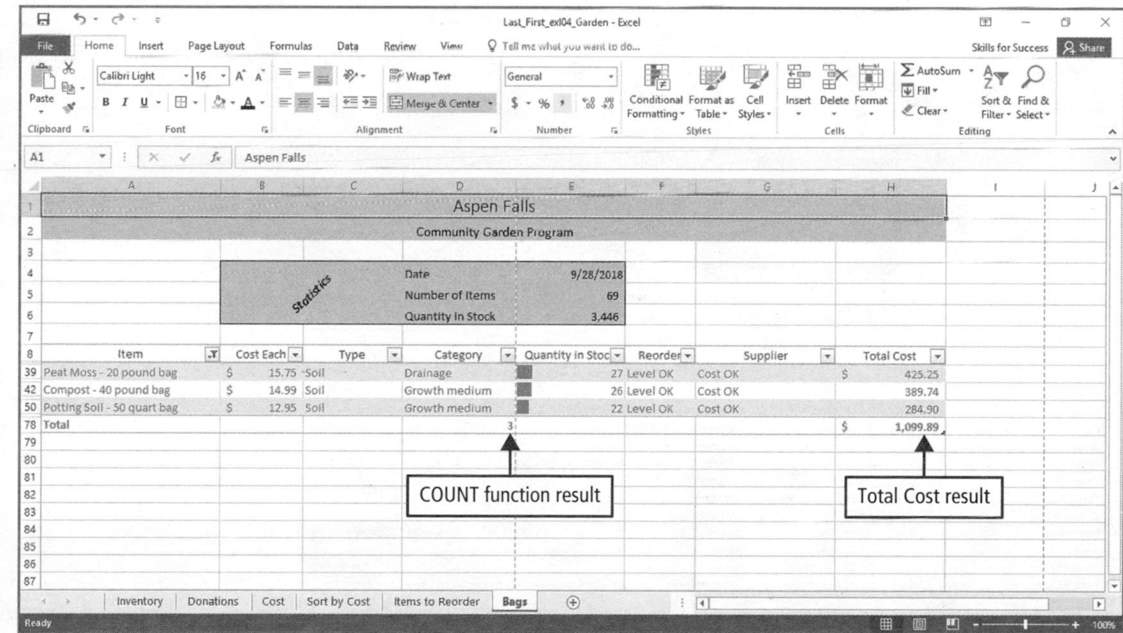

Excel 2016, Windows 10, Microsoft Corporation

Figure 4

6. Right-click the **Items to Reorder** worksheet tab, and then using the techniques previously practiced, create a copy of the worksheet, and move the sheet to the end. Rename the **Items to Reorder (2)** worksheet tab as Bags

7. With the **Bags** worksheet active, click any cell in the Excel table to make the Excel table active. Click the **Data tab**, and then in the **Sort & Filter group**, click the **Clear** button to clear all the filters and to display all the rows in the Excel table.

   The cells in column H show a mixture of Comma and Accounting Style format because cells were hidden when this column was formatted in step 2.

8. In the header row, click the **Item filter arrow**. In the **Filter** list, click in the **Search** box, type bag and then compare your screen with **Figure 3**.

MOS Obj 3.3.1 C

9. Click **OK** to display the three rows containing the text *bag* in the Item column. Click the range **H42:H50**. Click the **Home tab**, and then in the **Number group**, click the **Comma Style** button. Press Ctrl + Home, and then compare your screen with **Figure 4**.

   In the Total row, the Category count is in cell D78, and the Total Cost in cell H78 displays the results of the filtered rows.

10. **Save** the file.

■ **You have completed Skill 9 of 10**

SKILL 10: Convert Tables to Ranges and Adjust Worksheet Print Settings

- An Excel table can be converted into a range retaining the table format.
- When a worksheet is too wide or too long to print on a single page, row and column headings can be printed on each page.

1. Right-click the **Bags** worksheet tab, create a copy of the sheet, and then move it to the end of the workbook. Rename the **Bags (2)** worksheet tab as All Items

Obj 3.1.2 C

2. In the **All Items** sheet, click cell **A8**. On the **Design tab**, in the **Tools group**, click the **Convert to Range** button. Read the message box, as shown in **Figure 1**, and then click **Yes**.

   When converting a table into a range, all filters are removed and the heading row no longer displays filter buttons. Any existing sorts and formatting remain.

3. Click the **File tab**, and then click **Print**. Click the **Next Page** button ▶ three times to view the four pages.
4. Click the **Back** button ⊖. On the **Page Layout tab**, in the **Scale to Fit group**, click the **Width arrow**, and then click **1 page**. Click the **Height arrow**, and then click **1 page**.

Obj 1.5.4 C

5. Click the **Inventory** worksheet tab. In the **Scale to Fit group**, click the **Width arrow**, and then click **1 page**.

Obj 1.5.5 C

6. In the **Page Setup group**, click the **Print Titles** button, and then in the **Page Setup** dialog box, under **Print titles**, click in the **Rows to repeat at top** box. In the worksheet, click **row 8**, and then compare your screen with **Figure 2**.

■ **Continue to the next page to complete the skill**

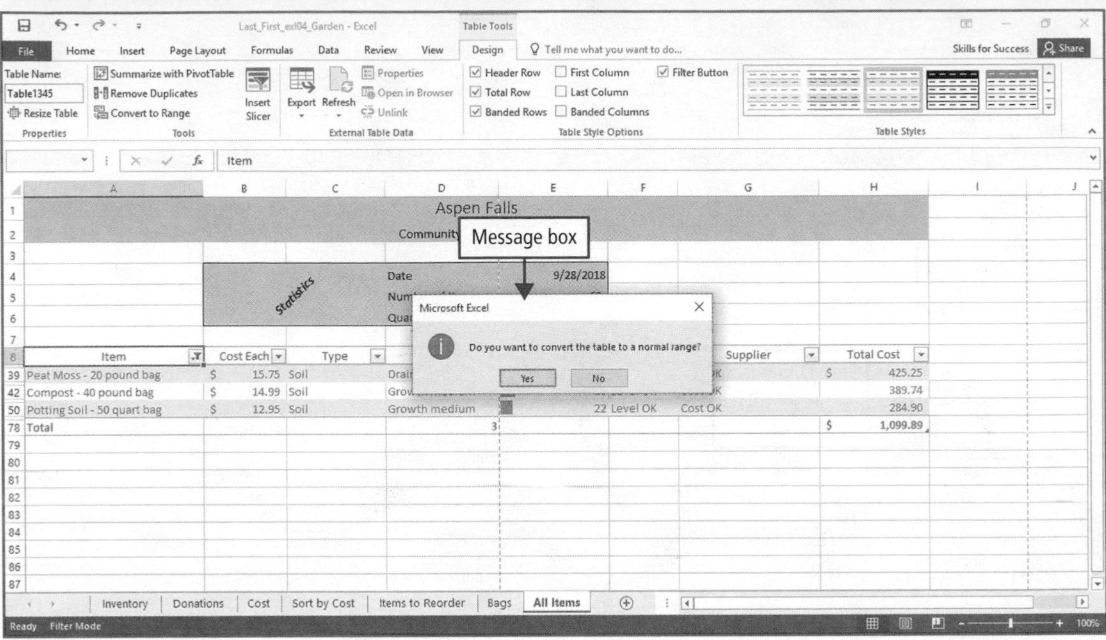

Figure 1

Excel 2016, Windows 10, Microsoft Corporation

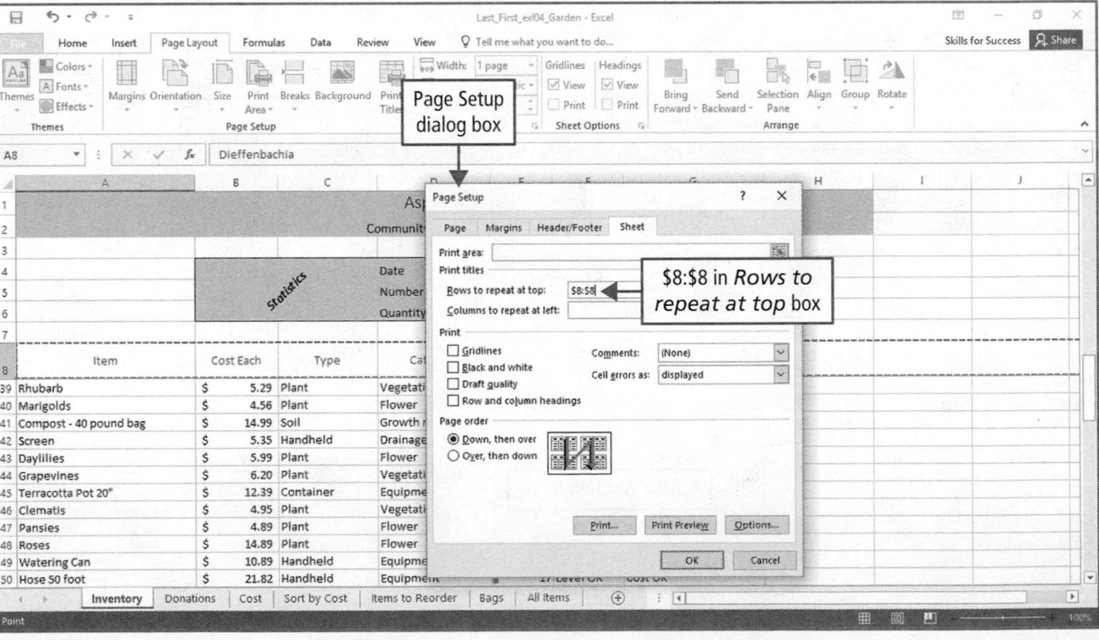

Figure 2

Excel 2016, Windows 10, Microsoft Corporation

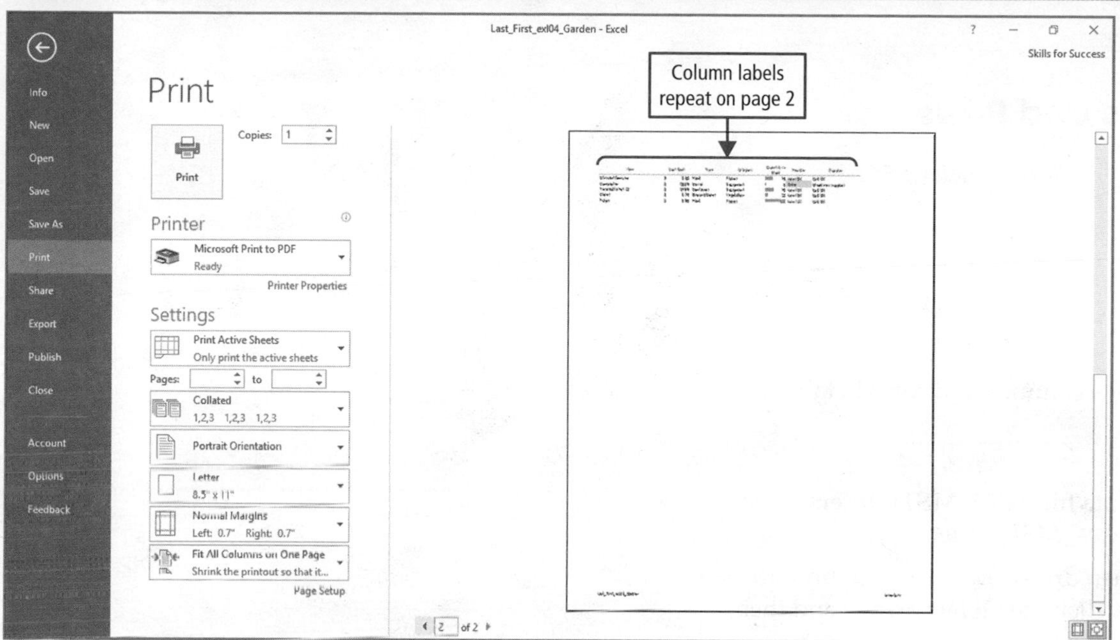

Excel 2016, Windows 10, Microsoft Corporation

Figure 3

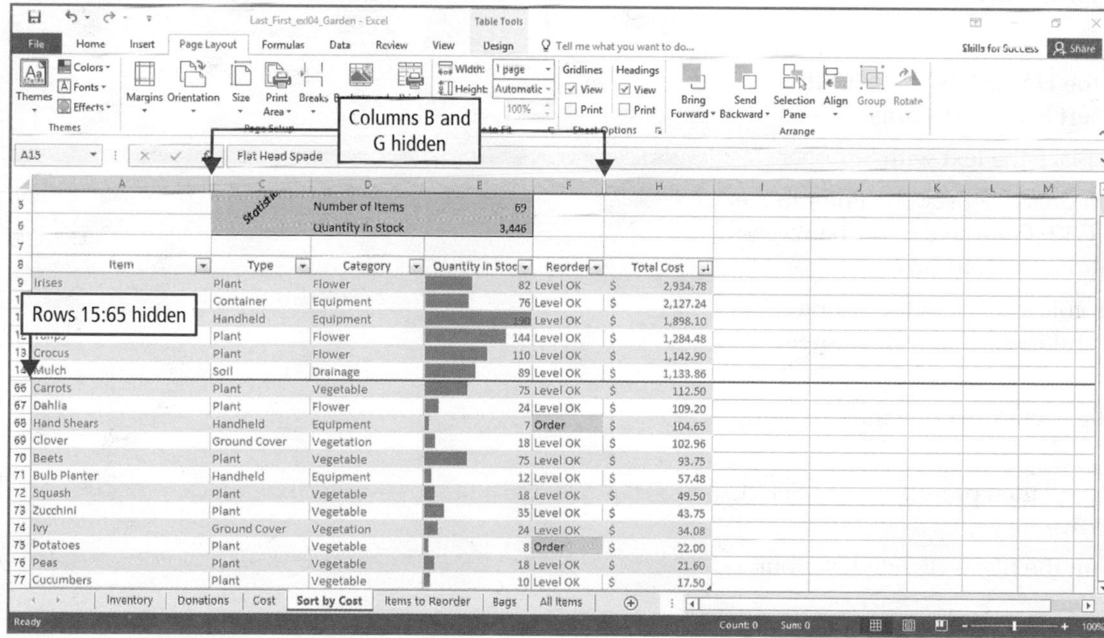

Excel 2016, Windows 10, Microsoft Corporation

Figure 4

7. In the **Page Setup** dialog box, click the **Print Preview** button. Click the **Next Page** button [▶] to verify that the column labels from **row 8** display at the top of Page 2. Compare your screen with **Figure 3**.
8. Click the **Back** button [←].
9. Click the **Cost** worksheet tab. Hold down [Ctrl], and then click the **Items to Reorder** and the **Bags** worksheet tabs to group the three worksheets. In the **Page Setup group**, click the **Orientation** button, and then click **Landscape**. In the **Scale to Fit group**, click the **Width arrow**, and then click **1 page**.

   With the worksheets grouped, the orientation and scaling are applied to all three worksheets.

10. Click the **Sort by Cost** worksheet tab to select the worksheet and ungroup the three worksheets. Click cell **B13**. On the **Home tab**, in the **Cells group**, click the **Format** button. In the list, point to **Hide & Unhide**, and then click **Hide Columns**. Use the technique just practiced to hide **column G**. MOS Obj 1.4.2 C
11. Select rows **15:65**. In the **Cells group**, click the **Format** button, point to **Hide & Unhide**, and then click **Hide Rows**.
12. On the **Page Layout tab**, in the **Page Setup group**, click the **Orientation** button, and then click **Landscape**. Compare your screen with **Figure 4**.
13. **Save** [💾] the file, and then **Close** [X] Excel. Submit the file as directed by your instructor.

DONE! You have completed Skill 10 of 10, and your file is complete!

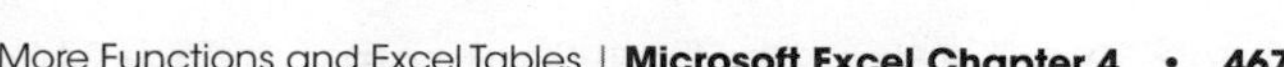

More Skills 11

Add and Remove Table Columns and Rows

To complete this project, you will need the following file:

- exl04_MS11Orders

You will save your file as:

- Last_First_exl04_MS11Orders

▶ Various methods can be used to add and remove columns and rows in tables.

---

1. Start **Excel 2016**, and then open the student data file **exl04_MS11Orders**. Save the file in your chapter folder as Last_First_exl04_MS11Orders

Obj 3.1.3 C

2. On the **Sort by Cost** sheet, click row **9**, and then drag down to select through row **71**. On the **Home tab**, in the **Cells group**, click the **Delete arrow**, and then click **Delete Sheet Rows**.
3. On the **Sort by Cost** sheet, select the range **A11:A12**. Right-click to open the shortcut menu, point to **Delete**, and then click **Table Rows**.

   Only the Order items remain in the table.

4. On the **Sort by Cost** sheet, click column **G**. On the **Home tab**, in the **Cells group**, click the **Insert arrow**, and then click **Insert Sheet Columns**.
5. Double-click the text *Column1* in cell **G8**, and replace the text with Supplier
6. Click cell **G9**, type Check new supplier and then press Ctrl + Enter. Point to the fill handle in **G9**, and then drag down through **G12**. Point to the line between columns **G** and **H,** and then double-click to AutoFit the column size.
7. Click the **Items to Reorder** sheet, and then click column **D**. On the **Home tab**, in the **Cells group**, click the **Delete arrow**, and then click **Delete Sheet Columns**.
8. Select the rows **16:40** as previously practiced. Right-click to open the shortcut menu, and then click **Delete Row**.
9. Click the **All Items** sheet. Select the rows **15:77**, and then press Ctrl + -. Select cell **A1**, and then compare your screen to **Figure 1**.
10. **Save** the file, and then **Close** Excel. Submit the file as directed by your instructor.

■ **You have completed More Skills 11**

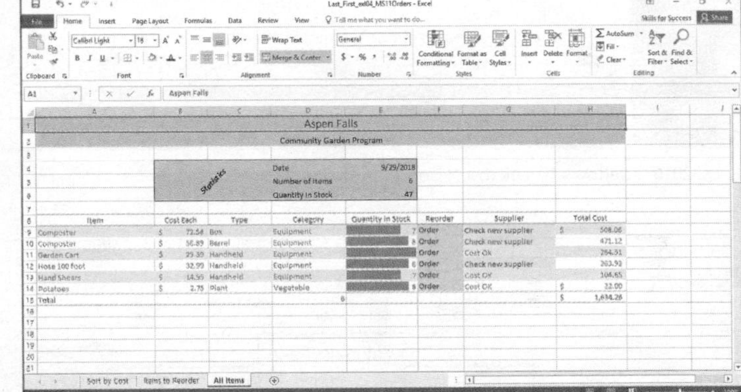

Figure 1 Excel 2016, Windows 10, Microsoft Corporation

More Skills 12

Insert the Payment (PMT) Function

To complete this project, you will need the following file:

- exl04_MS12Loans

You will save your file as:

- Last_First_exl04_MS12Loans

- The ***PMT function*** calculates the payment for a loan based on constant payments and a constant interest rate.
- The ***interest*** is the charge you pay for borrowing the money; it is generally a percentage of the amount borrowed. The ***rate*** is the percentage that is paid for the use of the borrowed money.
- The ***principal*** or ***Present value (Pv)*** of a loan is the initial amount of the loan—the total amount that a series of future payments is worth today.
- In the PMT function, the number of time periods, ***Nper***, is the total number of payments for the loan. The value at the end of the time periods is the ***Future value (Fv)***—the cash balance you want to attain after the last payment is made. The future value for a loan is usually zero.

1. Start **Excel 2016**, open the student data file **exl04_MS12Loans**, and then save the file in your chapter folder as Last_First_exl04_MS12Loans
2. Click cell **B8**. On the **Formulas tab**, in the **Function Library group**, click the **Financial** button. Scroll down, and then click **PMT**.

   The Function Arguments dialog box displays the arguments for the PMT function. When the insertion point is in an argument box, a description of that argument is provided in the Function Arguments dialog box.

3. If necessary, move the Function Arguments dialog box so you can view the data in columns A and B. Click in the **Rate** argument box, type B7/12 Press Tab.

   The payments on a loan are usually made monthly; however, when borrowing money, the interest rate and the number of periods are generally quoted in years. Here, the annual interest rate of 6 percent located in cell B7 is divided by 12—the number of months in a year—which results in a monthly interest rate.

4. In the **Nper** argument box, type B6*12 to calculate the number of monthly payments in the loan—*60*. Press Tab.
5. In the **Pv** argument box, type B5

Aspen Falls	
Construction Loans	
Garage Construction Loan	
Amount of Loan	$ 500,000.00
Period (years)	5
Interest rate (per year)	6%
Payment (per month)	$ 9,666.40
Hospital Construction Loan	
Amount of Loan	$ 8,500,000.00
Period (years)	20
Interest rate (per year)	5%
Payment (per month)	$ 56,096.24
Water Plant Construction Loan	
Amount of Loan	$ 2,500,000.00
Period (years)	15
Interest rate (per year)	10%
Payment (per month)	$ 26,865.13

Figure 1

6. In the **Function Arguments** dialog box, click **OK** to display the monthly payment amount, *($9,666.40)*.
7. On the formula bar, click in the function arguments to position the insertion point in front of *B5*. Type – (minus sign), and then press Enter. Compare your screen with **Figure 1**.

   By placing a minus sign in the function, the monthly payment amount displays as a positive number.

8. **Save** the file, and then **Close** Excel. Submit the file as directed by your instructor.

- **You have completed More Skills 12**

More Skills 13

Customize Workbook Views

To complete this project, you will need the following files:

- exl04_MS13Plants
- exl04_MS13Inventory

You will save your files as:

- Last_First_exl04_MS13Plants
- Last_First_exl04_MS13Snip

► The ***split window*** is a command that divides the window into separate panes so that each pane can be scrolled separately.

1. Start **Excel 2016**, and then open the file **exl04_MS13Plants**. Save the file in your chapter folder as Last_First_exl04_MS13Plants
2. Use the scroll bar on the right side of the windows to scroll down to view all of the rows in this worksheet, scroll up, and then click cell **E10**.
3. Click the **View tab**, and then in the **Window group**, click the **Split** button. MOS Obj 1.4.5 C Notice the spreadsheet is now split into four sections, and then compare your screen with **Figure 1**.

   Horizontal and vertical bars split the window. Vertical scrollbars display for the upper and lower panes, and horizontal scrollbars display for the left and right panes.

4. Drag the lower vertical scrollbar up to view **row 1**, and then drag the right horizontal scrollbar to the left to view the statistics in **B4:E9**.
5. Drag the upper vertical scrollbar down to view **row 80**.

   Statistics for the plant costs can be compared with the costs for plants to check for a new supplier.

6. **Save** the file, and then open **exl04_MS13Inventory**.
7. On the **View tab**, and then in the **Window group**, click the **View Side by Side** button. MOS Obj 1.4.5 C
8. In the top pane, in the **Window group**, click the **Synchronous Scrolling** button to turn it off.

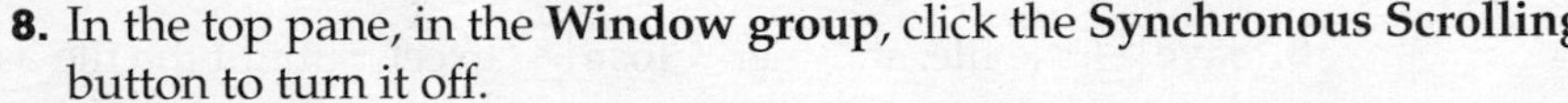

9. In the bottom pane, in the **Window group**, click the **Synchronous Scrolling** button to turn it off. Compare your screen with **Figure 2**.

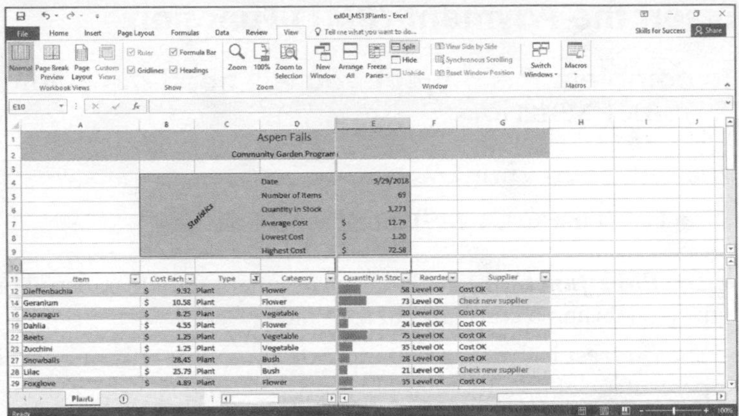

Figure 1 Excel 2016, Windows 10, Microsoft Corporation

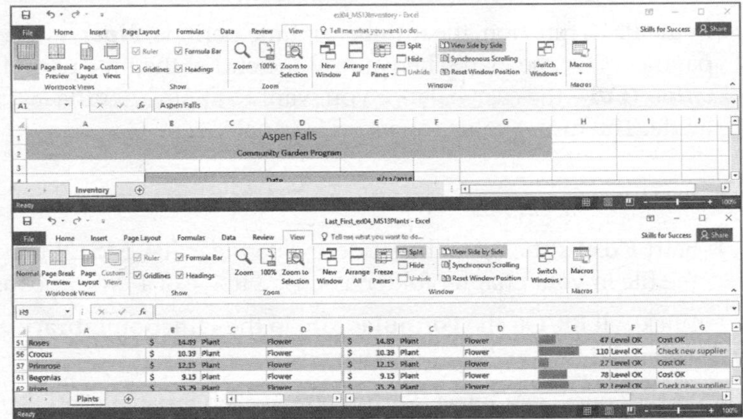

Figure 2 Excel 2016, Windows 10, Microsoft Corporation

   Both open workbooks display in the window. The workbooks can be compared side by side.

10. Using the Windows **Snipping Tool**, take a **Full-Screen** snip, and then **Save** the file to your chapter folder as Last_First_exl04_MS13Snip
11. **Close** all open windows, and then submit the files as directed by your instructor.

■ **You have completed More Skills 13**

More Skills 14

Use Text and Lookup Functions

To complete this project, you will need the following file:

- exl04_MS14Revenue

You will save your file as:

- Last_First_exl04_MS14Revenue

- The ***LOWER function*** is a text function used to convert a text string to all lowercase letters.
- The ***UPPER function*** is a text function used to convert a text string to all uppercase letters.
- The ***TRANSPOSE function*** is a lookup function used to convert a vertical range of cells to a horizontal range, or vice versa.

---

1. Start **Excel 2016**, and then open the student data file **exl04_MS14Revenue**. Save the file in your chapter folder as Last_First_exl04_MS14Revenue
2. On the **Home tab**, in the **Editing group**, click the **Find & Select** button. In the list, click **Go To**. In the **Go To** dialog box, click in the **Reference** box, and then type Location!A1 Click **OK**. MOS Obj 1.2.2 C
3. On the **Location** sheet, with cell **A1** active, click the **Formulas tab**. In the **Function Library group**, click the **Text** button, and then in the list, click **UPPER**. MOS Obj 4.3.2 C

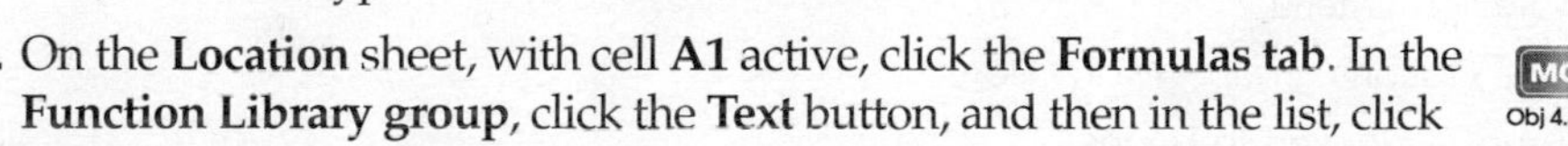

4. In the **Function Arguments** dialog box, with the insertion point in the **Text** box, type Quarter!A1 and then click **OK**.

   The text *Aspen Falls* from the Quarter worksheet is entered into cell A1 in all capital letters.

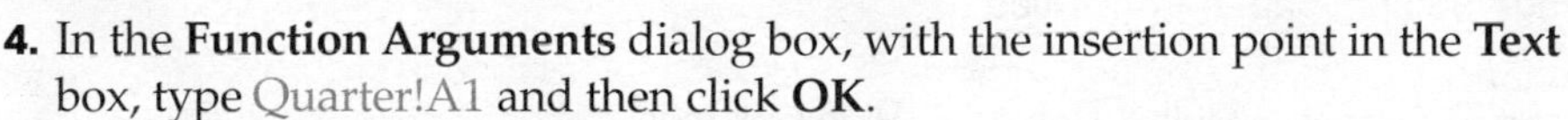

5. Click cell **A2**. In the **Function Library group**, click the **Text** button, and then in the list, click **LOWER**. MOS obj 4.3.2C
6. In the **Function Arguments** dialog box, with the insertion point in the **Text** box, type Quarter!A2 and then click **OK**.

   The text *Quarterly Revenue* from the Quarter worksheet is entered into cell A2 in all lowercase letters.

7. On the **Location** worksheet, select the range **A4:A8**. In the **Function Library group**, click the **Lookup & Reference** button, and then in the list, click **TRANSPOSE**.

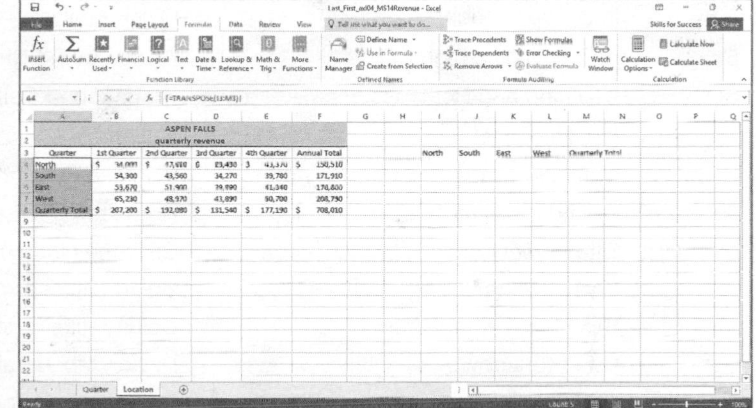

Excel 2016, Windows 10, Microsoft Corporation

Figure 1

8. With the insertion point in the **Array** box, drag to select the range **I3:M3**. Press and hold Ctrl and Shift, and then press Enter.
9. The data from I3:M3 appears in **A4:A8**, and the array function {=TRANSPOSE(I3:M3)} appears in the formula bar. Compare your screen to **Figure 1**.
10. **Save** the file, and then **Close** Excel. Submit the file as directed by your instructor.

- **You have completed More Skills 14**

The following table summarizes the **SKILLS AND PROCEDURES** covered in this chapter.

Skills Number	Task	Step	Icon	Keyboard Shortcut
1	Insert TODAY functions	Formula tab → Function Library group → Date & Time → TODAY		
1	Insert NOW functions	Formula tab → Function Library group → Date & Time → NOW		
1	Insert COUNT functions	Formula tab → Function Library group → More Functions → Statistical → COUNT		
2	Insert IF functions	Formula tab → Function Library group → Logical → IF		
3	Add borders	Home tab → Font group → Border arrow → Border		
3	Angle text	Home tab → Alignment group → Orientation		
4	Apply conditional formatting to text	Quick Analysis → Text Contains		Ctrl + Q
4	Apply conditional formatting data bars	Quick Analysis → Data Bars		Ctrl + Q
5	Insert sparklines	Quick Analysis → Sparklines		Ctrl + Q
5	Add sparkline high points	Design tab → Show group → High Point		
6	Use Find and Replace	Home tab → Editing group → Find & Select → Replace		Ctrl + H
7	Freeze panes	View tab → Window group → Freeze Panes		
7	Unfreeze panes	View tab → Window group → Unfreeze Panes		
8	Create Excel tables	Home tab → Styles group → Format as Table		
8	Filter Excel tables	Click the column filter arrow		
8	Sort Excel tables	Column filter arrow		
9	Search Excel tables	Column filter arrow → Search criteria		
9	Insert total rows	Design tab → Table Style Options group → Total Row		
10	Convert Excel tables to ranges	Design tab → Tools group → Convert to Range		
10	Repeat rows at the top of each printed page	Page Layout tab → Page Setup group → Print Titles		
10	Hide columns	Home tab → Cells group → Format → Hide & Unhide → Hide Columns		Ctrl + 0
10	Hide rows	Home tab → Cells group → Format → Hide & Unhide → Hide Rows		Ctrl + 9
MS11	Insert row/column	Home tab → Cells group → Insert		Ctrl + +
MS11	Delete row/column	Home tab → Cells group → Delete		Ctrl + −
MS12	Using financial functions	Formulas tab → Function Library group → Financial → PMT		
MS13	Split worksheet window	View tab → Window group → Split		
MS14	Use Go To	Home tab → Editing group → Find & Select → Go To		
MS14	Insert UPPER function	Formulas tab → Function Library group →Text → UPPER		
MS14	Insert LOWER function	Formulas tab → Function Library group →Text → LOWER		
MS14	Insert TRANSPOSE function	Formulas tab → Function Library group → Lookup & Reference → TRANSPOSE		

Project Summary Chart

Project	Project Type	Project Location
Skills Review	Review	In Book & MIL MyITLab® Grader
Skills Assessment 1	Review	In Book & MIL MyITLab® Grader
Skills Assessment 2	Review	Book
My Skills	Problem Solving	Book
Visual Skills Check	Problem Solving	Book
Skillls Challenge 1	Critical Thinking	Book
Skills Challenge 2	Critical Thinking	Book
More Skills Assessment	Review	In Book & MIL MyITLab® Grader
Collaborating with Google	Critical Thinking	Book

MOS Objectives Covered

1.1.4 C Copy and move a worksheet	3.1.1 C Create an Excel table from a cell range
1.2.1 C Search for data within a workbook	3.1.2 C Convert a table to a cell range
1.2.2 C Navigate to a named cell, range, or workbook element	3.1.3 C Add and remove table rows and columns
1.4.2 C Hide or unhide columns and rows	3.2.1 C Apply styles to tables
1.4.5 C Change window views	3.2.3 C Insert total rows
1.5.4 C Set print scaling	3.3.1 C Filter records
1.5.5 C Display repeating row and column titles on multipage worksheets	3.3.2 C Sort data by multiple columns
2.1.1 C Replace data	3.3.3 C Change sort order
2.2.2 C Modify cell alignment and indention	4.1.4 C Perform calculations by using the COUNT function
2.2.6 C Apply cell formats	4.2.1 C Perform logical operations by using the IF function
2.3.1 C Insert sparklines	4.3.2C Format text by using UPPER, LOWER, and PROPER functions
2.3.4 C Apply conditional formatting	

Key Terms

Term	Page
Calculated column	462
Comparison operator	450
Conditional formatting	454
COUNT function	448
Criteria	450
Data bar	455
Excel table	462
Filter	464
Freeze Panes	460
Future value (Fv)	469
IF function	450
Interest	469
Logical function	450
Logical test	450
LOWER function	471
NOW function	448
Nper	469
PMT function	469
Present value (Pv)	469
Principal	469
Rate	469
Replace	458
Sparkline	456
Split window	000
TODAY function	448
Total row	464
TRANSPOSE function	471
UPPER function	471
Volatile	448

1. What are some of the positive behaviors of the second applicant?
2. If you were the interviewer, which applicant would you hire, and why would you hire that person?

Online Help Skills

1. Start **Excel 2016**, and then in the upper right corner of the start page, click the **Help** button [?].
2. In the **Excel Help** window **Search** box, type formulas in Excel tables and then press [Enter].
3. In the search result list, click **Define and use names in formulas**, and then in **Learn more about using names**, scroll down and click the link under *Table name*—**Using structured references with Excel tables**. **Maximize** the **Excel Help** window, and then compare your screen with **Figure 1**.

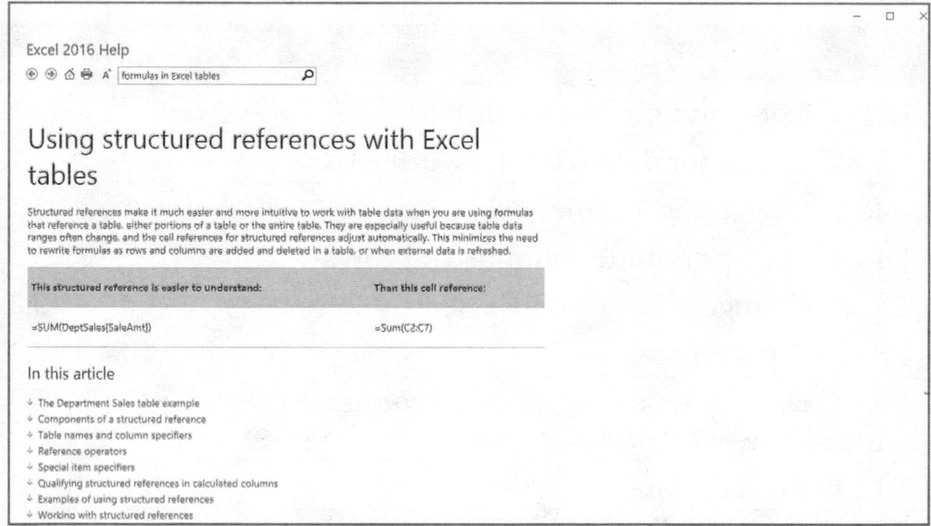

Figure 1 Excel 2016, Windows 10, Microsoft Corporation

4. Read the article to see if you can answer the following questions: What are structured references, and why would you use them?

Matching 

Match each term in the second column with its correct definition in the first column by writing the letter of the term on the blank line in front of the correct definition.

___ **1.** An Excel function that returns the serial number of the current date.

___ **2.** The result of a function that will be updated each time the workbook is opened.

___ **3.** The type of function that tests for specific conditions and typically uses conditional tests to determine whether specified conditions are TRUE or FALSE.

___ **4.** Conditions that determine how conditional formatting is applied or what values are returned in logical functions.

___ **5.** The cell shading or font color that is applied to cells when a specified circumstance is met.

___ **6.** A chart inside a single cell used to show data trends.

___ **7.** A series of rows and columns that are formatted together.

___ **8.** The column in an Excel table that uses a single formula that adjusts for each row.

___ **9.** A command to display only the rows of a table that meet specified criteria.

___ **10.** The row that provides summary functions in an Excel table.

A Calculated column

B Conditional formatting

C Criteria

D Excel table

E Filter

F Logical function

G Sparkline

H TODAY function

I Total row

J Volatile

Multiple Choice

Choose the correct answer.

1. The logical function that checks whether criteria are met and returns one value if TRUE and another value if FALSE.
   A. IF
   B. UNKNOWN
   C. NEW
2. These symbols are inserted into logical functions to determine whether a condition is true or false—(<) and (=), for example.
   A. Comparison operators
   B. Mathematical operators
   C. Logical symbols
3. Applying this format to text draws attention to the text on a worksheet.
   A. Angle
   B. Slope
   C. Slant
4. A format, such as cell shading, that is applied to cells when a specified condition is true.
   A. Filtered
   B. Conditional
   C. Calculated
5. The format that provides a visual cue about the value of a cell relative to other cells.
   A. Cell style
   B. Quick style
   C. Data bar
6. This command ensures that header rows and columns remain visible when a worksheet is scrolled.
   A. Total Panes
   B. Excel Panes
   C. Freeze Panes
7. Data in an Excel table can be sorted in this way.
   A. Large to largest
   B. Smallest to largest
   C. Small to smallest
8. A command to display only the rows of a table that meet specified criteria.
   A. Filter
   B. Standard
   C. Chart
9. The row that displays as the last row in an Excel table and provides summary statistics.
   A. Total
   B. Sorted
   C. Changeable
10. This word describes the result of a function that is updated each time the workbook is opened.
   A. Volatile
   B. Changeable
   C. Unstable

Topics for Discussion

1. Think about current news stories, including sports stories, and identify statistical data that is presented by the media. What are the advantages of using conditional formatting with this type of data?
2. Sorting and filtering are two of the most valuable ways to analyze data. If you were presented with an Excel table containing names and addresses, what are some of the ways you might sort or filter the data? If you were presented with an Excel table of a day's cash transactions at your college's cafeteria, what are some ways you could sort, filter, and total?

Skills Review

To complete this project, you will need the following file:

- exl04_SRAuction

You will save your file as:

- Last_First_exl04_SRAuction

1. Start **Excel 2016**, and then open the file **exl04_SRAuction**. Save the file in your chapter folder as Last_First_exl04_SRAuction
2. On the **Materials** sheet, click cell **B4**. On the **Formulas tab**, in the **Function Library group**, click the **Date & Time** button, and then click **TODAY**. In the message box, click **OK**. Click cell **B5**. In the **Function Library group**, click the **More Functions** button. Point to **Statistical**, and then click **COUNT**. In the **Value1** box, enter the range B9:B48 and then press Enter. Compare your screen with **Figure 1**.
3. Select the range **A4:B6**. Point to the right border of the selected range, and then move the data to the range **D4:E6**.
4. In cell **B4**, type Surplus and then merge and center the title in the range **B4:C6**. On the **Home tab**, in the **Alignment group**, click the **Middle Align** button. Click the **Orientation** button, and then click **Angle Counterclockwise**. Select the range **B4:E6**. In the **Font group**, click the **Border arrow**, and then click **Outside Borders**.
5. Click cell **A1**. In the **Editing group**, click the **Find & Select** button, and then click **Replace**. In the **Find what** box, type Sedan In the **Replace with** box, type Car and then click **Replace All**. Click **OK** for the message of 5 replacements, and then **Close** the dialog box.
6. Click cell **G9**. On the **Formulas tab**, in the **Function Library group**, click **Logical**. In the list, click **IF**, and then in the **Logical_test** box, type E9="Yes" In the **Value_if_true** box, type B9*F9 In the **Value_if_false** box, type 0 and then click **OK**. AutoFill the function down through **G48**, and then compare your screen with **Figure 2**.

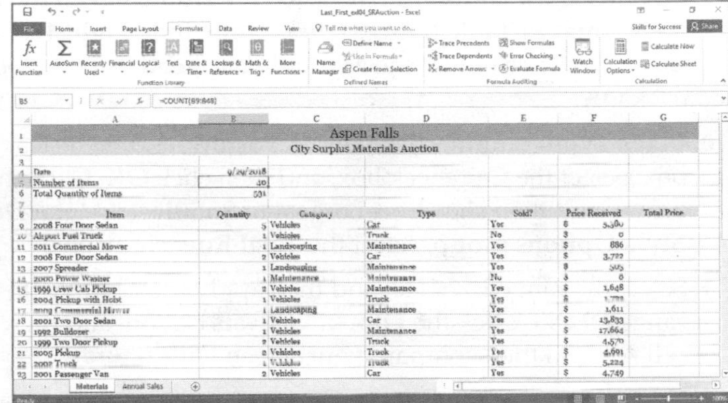

Excel 2016, Windows 10, Microsoft Corporation

Figure 1

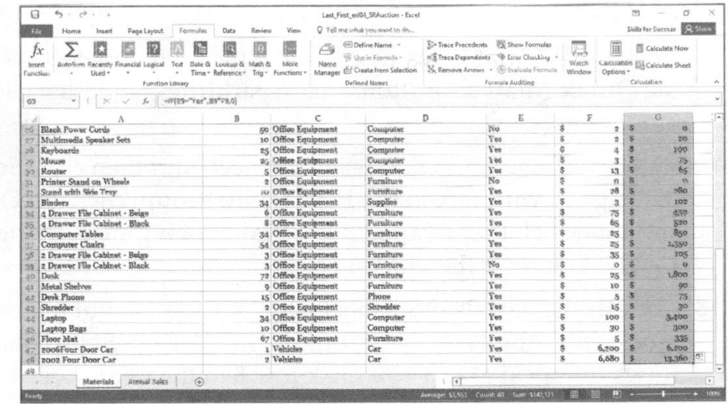

Excel 2016, Windows 10, Microsoft Corporation

Figure 2

■ **Continue to the next page to complete this Skills Review**

7. Click cell **A9**. On the **View tab**, in the **Window group**, click the **Freeze Panes** button. Click **Freeze Panes**.
8. Right-click the **Materials** worksheet tab, and then click **Move or Copy**. In the **Move or Copy** dialog box, click **(move to end)**, select the **Create a copy** check box, and then click **OK**. Rename the new worksheet tab as Price by Car
9. On the **Price by Car** sheet, in the **Window group**, click the **Freeze Panes** button, and then click **Unfreeze Panes**. On the **Home tab**, in the **Styles group**, click the **Format as Table** button. Click **Table Style Light 17**. In the **Format As Table** dialog box, verify that the **My table has headers** check box is selected, and then click **OK**.
10. In the **Type** column, click the **filter arrow**, and then clear the **(Select All)** check box. Select the **Car** check box, and then click **OK**. Click the **Total Price filter arrow**, and then click **Sort Largest to Smallest**. On the **Design tab**, in the **Table Style Options group**, select the **Total Row** check box.
11. Select the range **F12:G48**, and then apply the **Comma [0]** cell style. Select the range **F9:F48**. Click the **Quick Analysis** button, and then click **Data Bars**. Click cell **A9**, and then compare your screen with **Figure 3**.
12. Create a copy of the *Price by Car* sheet, move to the end, and then rename the worksheet tab to Pickups On the **Data tab**, in the **Sort & Filter group**, click the **Clear** button. Click the **Item filter arrow**. In the **Search** box, type Pickup and then click **OK**.
13. Click the **Annual Sales** worksheet tab, and then select the range **B4:F9**. Click the **Quick Analysis** button, click **Sparklines**, and then click the **Column** button.
14. Right-click the **Annual Sales** worksheet, and then click **Select All Sheets**. On the **Page Layout tab**, in the **Page Setup group**, click the **Orientation** button, and then click **Landscape**. In the **Scale to Fit group**, change the **Width** to **1 page**. Ungroup the worksheets.
15. Click the **Materials** worksheet. On the **Page Layout tab**, in the **Page Setup group**, click the **Print Titles** button. In the **Page Setup** dialog box, click in the **Rows to repeat at top** box, click row **8** in the worksheet, and then click **OK**.
16. **Save** the file. Click the **File tab**, and then click **Print**. Compare your screen with **Figure 4**. **Close** Excel, and then submit the file as directed by your instructor.

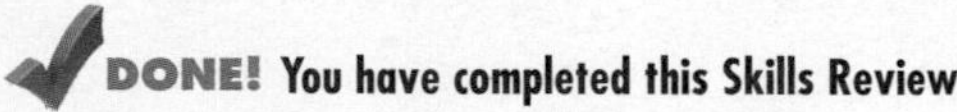
DONE! You have completed this Skills Review

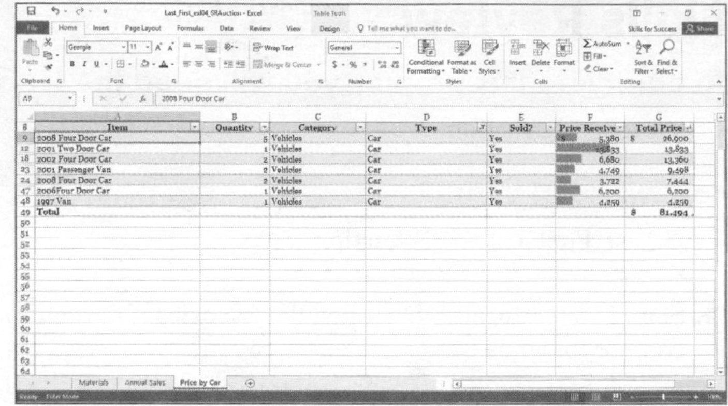

Figure 3 Excel 2016, Windows 10, Microsoft Corporation

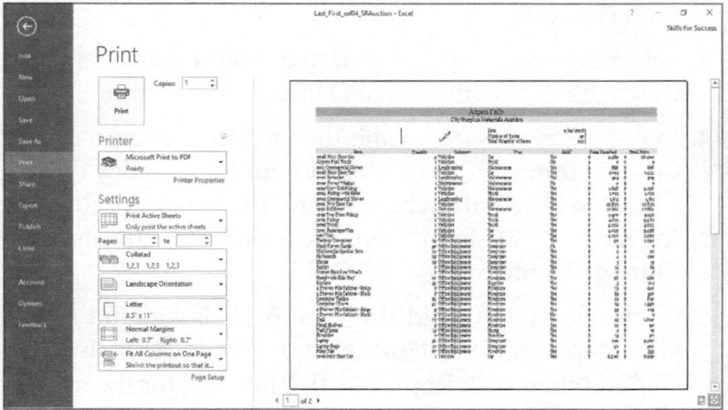

Figure 4 Excel 2016, Windows 10, Microsoft Corporation

Skills Assessment 1

To complete this project, you will need the following file:

- exl04_SA1Recycling

You will save your file as:

- Last_First_exl04_SA1Recycling

1. Start **Excel 2016**, and then open the file **exl04_SA1Recycling**. Save the file in your chapter folder as Last_First_exl04_SA1Recycling
2. In cell **E3**, insert the **NOW** function. Select **A5:G5**, and then apply a **Bottom Border**.
3. In range **F6:F27**, insert **Line Sparklines** using the data in columns **B:E**. Show the **Low Point**.
4. In cell **G6**, insert the **IF** function. For the logical test, check whether the **FY 2017** result is greater than the **FY 2016** value in the same row. If the logical test is TRUE, Yes should display, and if it is FALSE, Needs Work should display. **Center** the results, and then AutoFill **G6** down through **G27**.
5. In the **Improved from previous year** column, apply a **Text Contains** conditional format that will display any cells that contain *Needs Work* formatted with **Light Red Fill**.
6. Create a copy of the sheet, and then move the copy to the end of the workbook. Rename the new worksheet tab Improvements
7. On the **Improvements** sheet, format **A5:G27** as an Excel table using the **Table Style Light 16**. Filter column **G** to display only the rows that improved from the previous year.
8. Display the **Total** row, and then display the four **FY** sums. Apply **Currency [0]** to the totals. In **G28**, select **None**.
9. Sort the **FY 2017** column from the smallest to the largest value, and then hide column **B**.
10. On the **Improvements** sheet, click cell **A1**, and then change the **Height** scale to fit on 1 page. On the **Recycling** sheet, change the **Page Setup** to repeat the titles in row **5**.
11. Group the worksheets. Change the page orientation to **Landscape**. Add the file name in the left footer and the sheet name in the right footer. Return to **Normal** view.

Recycling Volumes
Aspen Falls (in tons)
8/15/2015 10:18

Type	FY 2014	FY 2015	FY 2016	FY 2017	Trend	Improved from previous year?
Glass	10,820	8,857	10,928	11,036		Yes
Tin Cans	825	650	833	842		Yes
White goods	11,010	12,250	11,120	11,230		Yes
Other ferrous	61,150	63,000	61,762	62,373		Yes
Aluminum cans	1,150	1,320	1,262	1,173		Needs Work
Non-ferrous	13,160	13,270	13,292	13,423		Yes
High Grade Paper	1,830	2,490	1,848	1,867		Yes
Newsprint	14,790	13,370	14,938	15,086		Yes
Cardboard	19,640	16,350	21,836	20,033		Needs Work
Other paper	4,340	5,900	4,383	4,427		Yes
PETE	703	960	710	717		Yes
HDPE	417	710	421	425		Yes
Other plastics	588	920	594	600		Yes
Yard waste	57,200	55,829	59,772	58,344		Needs Work
Wood waste	10,630	11,825	11,736	10,843		Needs Work
Batteries	2,900	3,030	2,929	2,958		Yes
Oil	8,840	6,360	8,928	9,017		Yes
Tires	1,010	806	1,020	1,030		Yes
Textiles	6,410	6,208	6,474	6,538		Yes
Gypsum	225	180	227	230		Yes
Electronics	1,850	1,050	1,869	1,887		Yes
Other	1,990	2,500	2,010	2,030		Yes

Figure 1

Recycling Volumes
Aspen Falls (in tons)
8/15/2015 10:18

Type	FY 2015	FY 2016	FY 2017	Trend	Improved from previous year?
Gypsum	180	227	230		Yes
HDPE	710	421	425		Yes
Other plastics	920	594	600		Yes
PETE	960	710	717		Yes
Tin Cans	650	833	842		Yes
Tires	806	1,020	1,030		Yes
High Grade Paper	2,490	1,848	1,867		Yes
Electronics	1,050	1,869	1,887		Yes
Other	2,500	2,010	2,030		Yes
Batteries	3,030	2,929	2,958		Yes
Other paper	5,900	4,383	4,427		Yes
Textiles	6,208	6,474	6,538		Yes
Oil	6,360	8,928	9,017		Yes
Glass	8,857	10,928	11,036		Yes
White goods	12,250	11,120	11,230		Yes
Non-ferrous	13,270	13,292	13,423		Yes
Newsprint	13,370	14,938	15,086		Yes
Other ferrous	63,000	61,762	62,373		Yes
Total	**$ 142,511**	**$ 144,287**	**$ 145,715**		

Figure 2

12. **Print Preview** the workbook, and then compare your screen with **Figure 1** and **Figure 2**. **Save** the file, and then **Close** Excel. Submit the file as directed by your instructor.

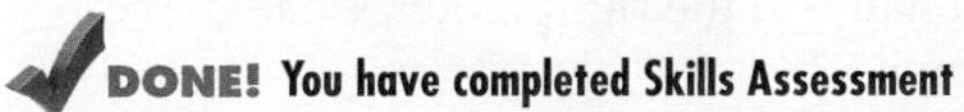

DONE! You have completed Skills Assessment 1

Skills Assessment 2

To complete this project, you will need the following file:

- exl04_SA2Equipment

You will save your file as:

- Last_First_exl04_SA2Equipment

1. Start **Excel 2016**, and then open the file **exl04_SA2Equipment**. Save the file in your chapter folder as Last_First_exl04_SA2Equipment
2. In cell **A2**, insert the **TODAY** function.
3. Apply **Thick Outside Borders** to the range **A4:G4**.
4. In the **Stock Level** column, insert the **IF** function. For the logical test, check whether the **Quantity in Stock** is less than **10**. If the logical test is TRUE, Order should display. If the logical test is FALSE, Level OK should display.
5. In the **Stock Level** column, apply a **Text Contains** conditional format that will display any cells that indicate *Order* formatted with **Red Text**.
6. In the worksheet, find all occurrences of Removal and replace with Extrication and then find all occurrences of Stick and replace with Baton
7. Format the range **A4:G63** as an Excel table using the **Table Style Medium 23** table style.
8. Create a copy of the worksheet, and then move the sheet to the end of the workbook. Rename the new sheet tab Safety On the **Safety** worksheet, **Sort** the table in alphabetical order by **Category**. **Filter** the Excel table to display the **Safety** type.
9. Display the **Total** row, and then in cell **B64**, display the count for column **B**, and apply **Currency [0]** cell style to **G64**. Hide column **D**.
10. On the **Equipment** sheet, convert the table to a normal range. Freeze the rows above **row 5**, and then set the titles in row **4** to repeat on each printed page.
11. Group the worksheets. Add a custom footer with the file name in the left footer and the sheet name in the right footer. Change the page orientation to **Landscape**.

Aspen Falls
11/24/2018

Quantity in Stock	Item	Cost Each	Type	Category	Stock Level	Total Cost
53	Coil Headphones	$30	Radio	Communication	Order	1,589
40	Radio Strap/Holder	$45	Radio	Communication	Order	1,800
3	Retractable Mic Keeper	$20	Radio	Communication	Level OK	60
41	Leather Radio Holder	$25	Radio	Communication	Order	1,025
20	10" Zipper Boots	$320	Boots	Footwear	Order	6,400
21	Leather Fire Boots	$340	Boots	Footwear	Order	7,140
26	Rubber Lug Boot	$109	Boots	Footwear	Order	2,834
27	Rubber Fire Boots	$169	Boots	Footwear	Order	4,563
28	Rubber Bunker Boots	$129	Boots	Footwear	Order	3,612
10	Hazmat Boot	$149	Boots	Footwear	Level OK	1,490
25	Fire Gloves	$89	Gloves	Outerwear	Order	2,225
27	Proximity Gear Gloves	$124	Gloves	Outerwear	Order	3,348
9	Extrication Gloves	$77	Gloves	Extrication Gear	Level OK	693
34	Rescue Glove Liners	$39	Gloves	Outerwear	Order	1,326
17	Extrication Coat	$223	Coat	Extrication Gear	Order	3,791
14	Extrication Pants	$189	Pants	Extrication Gear	Order	2,646
11	Extrication Coveralls	$359	Coveralls	Extrication Gear	Order	3,949
9	Gas Mask	$259	Safety	Safety Equipment	Level OK	2,331
9	Gas Mask Pouch	$35	Safety	Safety Equipment	Level OK	315
13	Respirator	$369	Safety	Safety Equipment	Order	4,797
19	Coverall with Hood	$159	Coveralls	Outerwear	Order	3,021
45	Disaster Safe Bag	$13	Safety	Safety Equipment	Order	585
10	Chemical Overboot	$52	Boots	Footwear	Level OK	520
10	Haz-Mat Boots	$89	Boots	Footwear	Level OK	890
57	Disaster Kit	$99	Safety	Safety Equipment	Order	5,643
10	Helmet	$229	Helmet	Outerwear	Level OK	2,290
51	Structural Fire Helmet	$179	Helmet	Outerwear	Order	9,129
25	Helmet with Eye Shield	$339	Shield	Safety Equipment	Order	8,475
8	Megaphone	$79	Megaphone	Communication	Level OK	632
53	Barrier Tape	$12	Tape	Traffic	Order	636
18	Fire Pants	$649	Pants	Outerwear	Order	11,682
19	Fire Coat	$989	Coat	Outerwear	Order	18,791
25	Proximity Coat	$1,299	Coat	Outerwear	Order	32,475
17	Proximity Pants	$1,059	Pants	Outerwear	Order	18,003
11	Radio Chest Harness	$35	Safety	Safety Equipment	Order	385
87	Rope Gloves	$32	Gloves	Outerwear	Order	2,784
28	Safety Harness	$199	Safety	Safety Equipment	Order	5,572
29	Chest Harness	$99	Safety	Safety Equipment	Order	2,871
35	EMS Jacket	$399	Coat	Outerwear	Order	13,965
47	EMS Pants	$289	Pants	Outerwear	Order	13,583
89	Breakaway Vest	$29	Vest	Outerwear	Order	2,581
15	Mesh Vest	$17	Vest	Outerwear	Order	255
25	Mesh Traffic Vest	$29	Vest	Outerwear	Order	725
89	Reflective Nylon Vest	$11	Vest	Outerwear	Order	979
16	Handheld Remote Siren	$289	Siren	Traffic	Order	4,624
19	Siren	$189	Siren	Traffic	Order	3,591
27	Traffic Baton	$19	Baton	Traffic	Order	513
37	Flare Beacon Kit	$305	Light	Traffic	Order	11,285
90	Flares with Stands	$99	Light	Traffic	Order	8,910
26	Traffic Flashlight	$18	Light	Traffic	Order	468
56	Night Barrier Tape	$15	Tape	Traffic	Order	840
17	Water Rescue Kit	$119	Safety	Water Rescue	Order	2,023
38	Water Rescue Vest	$99	Safety	Water Rescue	Order	3,762
4	Water Tether System	$59	Safety	Water Rescue	Level OK	236
18	Wildfire Helmet	$59	Helmet	Outerwear	Order	1,062
17	Full-Brim Helmet	$59	Helmet	Outerwear	Order	1,003
58	Firefighting Goggles	$49	Helmet	Safety Equipment	Order	2,842
31	Water Throw Bag	$59	Safety	Water Rescue	Order	1,829
32	Dry Bag	$18	Safety	Water Rescue	Order	576

Figure 1

Aspen Falls
11/24/2018

Quantity in Stock	Item	Cost Each	Category	Stock Level	Total Cost
9	Gas Mask	$259	Safety Equipment	Level OK	2,331
9	Gas Mask Pouch	$35	Safety Equipment	Level OK	315
13	Respirator	$369	Safety Equipment	Order	4,797
45	Disaster Safe Bag	$13	Safety Equipment	Order	585
57	Disaster Kit	$99	Safety Equipment	Order	5,643
11	Radio Chest Harness	$35	Safety Equipment	Order	385
28	Safety Harness	$199	Safety Equipment	Order	5,572
29	Chest Harness	$99	Safety Equipment	Order	2,871
17	Water Rescue Kit	$119	Water Rescue	Order	2,023
38	Water Rescue Vest	$99	Water Rescue	Order	3,762
4	Water Tether System	$59	Water Rescue	Level OK	236
31	Water Throw Bag	$59	Water Rescue	Order	1,829
32	Dry Bag	$18	Water Rescue	Order	576
Total	13				$ 30,925

Figure 2

12. **Print Preview** the workbook, and then compare your screen with **Figure 1** and **Figure 2**. **Save** the file, and then **Close** Excel. Submit the file as directed by your instructor.

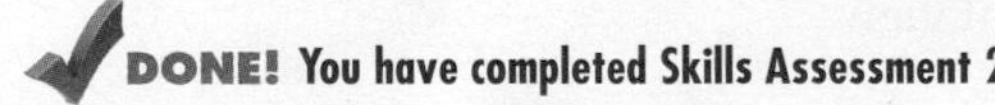

DONE! You have completed Skills Assessment 2

My Skills

To complete this project, you will need the following file:

- exl04_MYExpenses

You will save your file as:

- Last_First_exl04_MYExpenses

My Expenses

Current Date: 8/15/2018 12:33

Spending Category	Spending Type	February	March	April	Trend
Clothing	Work Uniform	85.00	90.00	92.00	
Clothing	Leisure Clothing	45.00	47.00	43.00	
Entertainment	Eating out	50.00	60.00	70.00	
Entertainment	Health Club	55.00	55.00	55.00	
Food	Groceries	155.00	145.00	147.00	
Housing	Rent	475.00	475.00	475.00	
Housing	Telephone	95.00	100.00	105.00	
Housing	Internet	85.00	90.00	90.00	
Housing	Electricity	75.00	80.00	90.00	
Housing	Renters Insurance	55.00	55.00	60.00	
Loans	Student Loan	65.00	65.00	65.00	
Loans	Credit Card	55.00	50.00	70.00	
Personal Care	Hair cut	50.00	-	55.00	
Pets	Pet Food	25.00	27.00	29.00	
Pets	Veterinarian	50.00	-	55.00	
Pets	Pet Toys	20.00	22.00	23.00	
Transportation	Car Payment	135.00	135.00	135.00	
Transportation	Fuel	50.00	60.00	70.00	
Transportation	Car Insurance	85.00	85.00	95.00	
Total		$ 1,710.00	$ 1,641.00	$ 1,826.00	

Figure 1

My Expenses

Current Date: 8/15/2018 12:33

Spending Category	Spending Type	February	March	April	Trend
Housing	Rent	475.00	475.00	475.00	
Food	Groceries	155.00	145.00	147.00	
Transportation	Car Payment	135.00	135.00	135.00	
Housing	Telephone	95.00	100.00	105.00	
Transportation	Car Insurance	85.00	85.00	95.00	
Clothing	Work Uniform	85.00	90.00	92.00	
Housing	Internet	85.00	90.00	90.00	
Housing	Electricity	75.00	80.00	90.00	
Entertainment	Eating out	50.00	60.00	70.00	
Loans	Credit Card	55.00	50.00	70.00	
Transportation	Fuel	50.00	60.00	70.00	
Loans	Student Loan	65.00	65.00	65.00	
Housing	Renters Insurance	55.00	55.00	60.00	
Entertainment	Health Club	55.00	55.00	55.00	
Total		$ 1,520.00	$ 1,545.00	$ 1,619.00	

Figure 2

1. Start **Excel 2016**, and then open the file **exl04_MYExpenses**. Save the file in your chapter folder as Last_First_exl04_MYExpenses
2. Click the merged cell **E2**, and then insert the **NOW** function.
3. Apply the **Outside Borders** to the range **D2:F2**.
4. Insert **Data Bars** to the data in the range **C5:E23**.
5. In the range **F5:F23**, insert **Line Sparklines** using the data in the columns **C:E**. On the sparklines, show the **High Point**.
6. Format the range **A4:F23** as an Excel table using **Table Style Light 19**. Sort the **Spending Category** column in alphabetical order.
7. Apply the **Total** row. Display the sums for **C24:E24**, and then apply the **Accounting** number format. In the **Trend** column total row, select **None**.
8. Select cell **A1**. Change the **Width** scale to fit on one page.
9. Create a copy of the worksheet, and then move the sheet to the end of the workbook. Rename the new tab High Expenses
10. On the **High Expenses** worksheet, sort the **April** column from largest to smallest. Hide **rows 19:23**.
11. Group the sheets, and then add the file name in the left footer and the sheet name in the right footer. Return to **Normal** view. Select cell **A1** in the **High Expenses** worksheet.
12. **Print Preview** the workbook, and then compare your screen with **Figure 1** and **Figure 2**. **Save** the file, and then **Close** Excel. Submit the file as directed by your instructor.

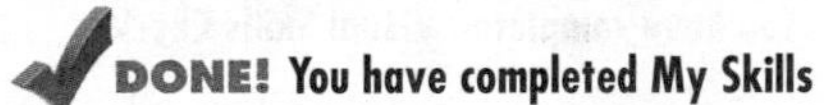
DONE! You have completed My Skills

Visual Skills Check

To complete this project, you will need the following file:

- exl04_VSArt

You will save your file as:

- Last_First_exl04_VSArt

Start **Excel 2016**, and then open the file **exl04_VSArt**. Save the file in your chapter folder as Last_First_exl04_VSArt Add the file name in the worksheet's left footer. Set the **Width** to scale to **1 page**. Insert the current date using a date function. Your date may be different than shown. Apply **Counterclockwise** orientation to the text **Artwork**. In the **Insurance** column, use a logical function indicating *Insure* for art with a value greater than $50,000; otherwise indicate *No*. The **conditional formatting** in the **Insurance column** for values to be Insured is **Light Red Fill with Dark Red Text**. Display **Data Bars** in the **Value** column. Format the data as an Excel table using the **Table Style Light 14** table style. Filter and sort the Excel table, and then display the functions on the **Total** row as shown in **Figure 1**. **Save** the file, and then **Close** Excel. Submit the file as directed by your instructor.

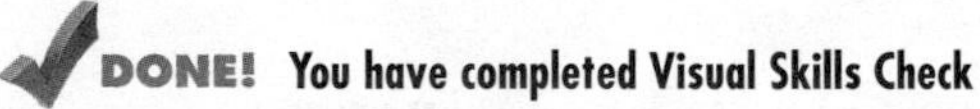
DONE! You have completed Visual Skills Check

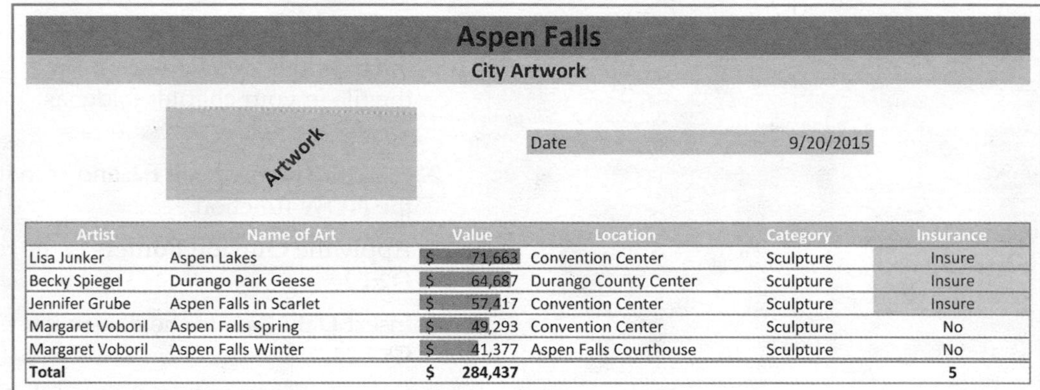

Aspen Falls

City Artwork

Artwork

Date	9/20/2015

Artist	Name of Art	Value	Location	Category	Insurance
Lisa Junker	Aspen Lakes	$ 71,663	Convention Center	Sculpture	Insure
Becky Spiegel	Durango Park Geese	$ 64,687	Durango County Center	Sculpture	Insure
Jennifer Grube	Aspen Falls in Scarlet	$ 57,417	Convention Center	Sculpture	Insure
Margaret Voboril	Aspen Falls Spring	$ 49,293	Convention Center	Sculpture	No
Margaret Voboril	Aspen Falls Winter	$ 41,377	Aspen Falls Courthouse	Sculpture	No
Total		$ 284,437			5

Figure 1

Skills Challenge 1

To complete this project, you will need the following file:

- exl04_SC1Classes

You will save your file as:

- Last_First_exl04_SC1Classes

Start **Excel 2016**, and then open the file **exl04_SC1Classes**. Save the file in your chapter folder as Last_First_exl04_SC1Classes Carter Horikoshi, the Art Center Supervisor, has started a workbook to track the art classes offered at different locations. He is concerned about large class sizes and wonders if he should hire an assistant for the instructors. Using the skills practiced in this chapter, on the Classes worksheet, correct the date function. The panes no longer need to be frozen. In the Excel table, display all rows. Data bars should be applied to all data in column D. In column E, the logical function should calculate whether a class needs a class assistant—a class needs a class assistant if the class size is greater than 30. Filter the worksheet to show the Computer Basics, Drawing, Painting, and Woodworking classes, and sorted from the largest to smallest class size. Repeat the titles in row 6 on each page, and the columns should fit on one page. For the Enrollment sheet, format the sparklines to emphasize the high and low values only in each row. The Enrollment sheet should print on one page. On both worksheets, add the file name in the left footer and the sheet name in the right footer. Save the file, and then Close Excel. Submit the file as directed by your instructor.

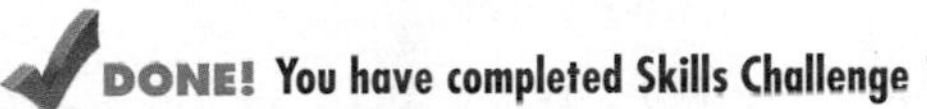
DONE! You have completed Skills Challenge 1

Skills Challenge 2

To complete this project, you will need the following file:

- exl04_SC2Water

You will save your file as:

- Last_First_exl04_SC2Water

Start **Excel 2016**, and then open the file **exl04_SC2Water**. Save the file in your chapter folder as Last_First_exl04_SC2Water Diane Payne, the Public Works Director, is responsible for testing the city water supply. She has started a workbook to track the water test results. Using the skills practiced in this chapter, insert functions in the Water worksheet that provide the current date and count the number of samples. Format the statistics shaded area with a border, and format the orientation and alignment of the text in the merged cells. Insert a logical function to determine if the High Test amount is greater than the Farm Water Limit for each quarter. Display Yes if TRUE and No if FALSE. Format the data as an Excel table using the table style of your choice, and then filter the table to display violations. On the Results worksheet, insert sparklines to display trends. On both worksheets, add the file name in the left footer and the sheet name in the right footer. Each worksheet should print on one page. Save the file, and then Close Excel. Submit the file as directed by your instructor.

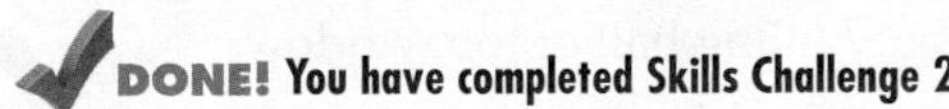
DONE! You have completed Skills Challenge 2

More Skills Assessment

MyITLab®
Grader

To complete this project, you will need the following files:

- exl04_MSAPayments
- exl04_MSAValues

You will save your files as:

- Last_First_exl04_MSAPayments
- Last_First_exl04_MSASnip

1. Start **Excel 2016**. Open the file **exl04_MSAPayments**, and then save the file in your chapter folder as Last_First_exl04_MSAPayments
2. On the **Loans** worksheet, enter a function in cell **B8** to calculate the monthly payment for the utility van. The **Rate** is the **Interest rate** divided by 12 The **Nper** is the **Period** multiplied by 12 The **Pv** is the current amount of the loan, entered as a negative value.
3. Enter a function in cell **B16** to calculate the monthly payment for the fire truck using the previous method and arguments provided.
4. On the **Utility Van** worksheet, in cell **A1**, use a function to enter the text from cell **A2** on the **Loans** sheet as all uppercase letters.
5. In cell **A2**, use a function to enter the text from cell **A4** on the **Loans** worksheet as all lowercase letters.
6. On the **Fire Truck** worksheet, use the previous method to enter uppercase text in cell **A1** from cell **A2** on the **Loans** sheet, and lowercase text in cell **A2** for the fire truck loan from the **Loans** sheet.
7. In the range **C7:F7**, use an array function to enter the labels from **A3:A6**, and then center and wrap the text.
8. On the **Utility Van** worksheet, repeat the previous method to enter the array function in the range **C7:F7**, and then format the text.
9. **Save** the file, and then open the file **exl04_MSAValues**.
10. Sort the **Values** worksheet, **Year Paid Off** column, smallest to largest, and then delete the loans for **2018**. Delete column **B**.
11. View the worksheets **Side by Side**, and then turn off **Synchronous Scrolling**. If necessary, resize both worksheets so that they are both viewable horizontally and evenly filling half of the window. Compare your screen with **Figure 1**.

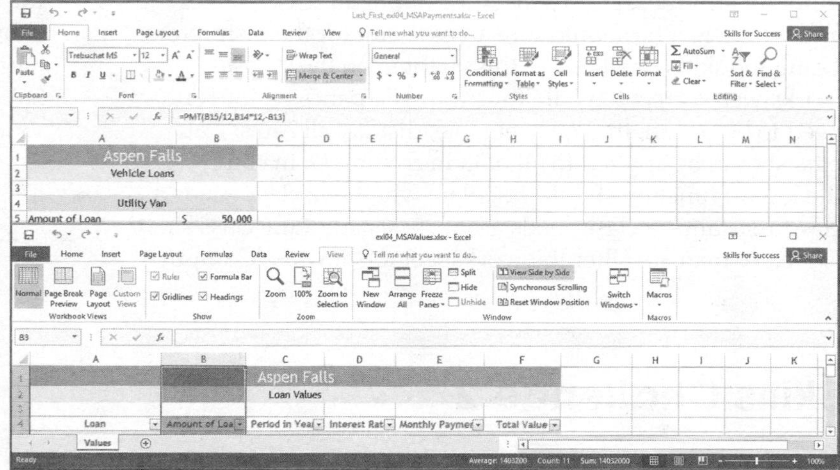

Figure 1 Excel 2016, Windows 10, Microsoft Corporation

12. Use the **Snipping Tool** to take a **Full-Screen** snip of your screen, and then save the file as Last_First_exl04_MSASnip
13. Close all of the windows without saving, except for **Last_First_exl04_MSAPayment**.
14. On the **Utility Van** worksheet, select cell **B7**, and then **Split** the window.
15. **Save** the file, and then **Close** Excel. Submit the files as directed by your instructor.

DONE! You have completed the More Skills Assessment

Collaborating with Google

To complete this project, you will need a Google account (refer to the Common Features chapter) and the following file:

- **exl04_GPRentals**

You will save your file as:

- **Last_First_exl04_GPRentals**

---

1. Open the Google Chrome web browser. Log into your Google account, and then click **Google Apps** ⊞.
2. Click **Drive** to open Google Drive.
3. Click **New**, and then click **File upload**. Navigate to the student data files and open **exl04_GPRentals**
4. Double-click the **exl04_GPRentals** file in **Google Drive**, and then click Open to view the workbook in **Google Sheets**.
5. On the **Rentals** worksheet, click cell **A203**. Type =TODAY to enter the current date.
6. Click cell **F2**, and then type =IF(E2>4, "Discount", "None") Autofill the formula down through **F201**.
7. Click **Format**, and then click **Conditional Formatting**. In the **Apply to range** box, verify **F2:F201** is entered. Click the **Format cells if arrow**, and then click **Text is exactly**. Replace the text *Value or formula* with Discount Click the **Formatting style arrow**, click **Red background**, and then click the **Bold** button. Click **Done**. Close the **Conditional Format rules** pane.
8. Click the **Rooms** worksheet. Click **Edit**, and then click **Find and replace**. In the **Find** box, type Gymnasium and in the **Replace with** box, type Athletic Center Click **Replace all**, and then click **Done**.
9. Click **Data**, and then click **Filter**.
10. Click the **Center** column **filter arrow**, clear the **Central, Northeast,** and **Northwest** checks, and then click **OK**.
11. Click the **Type** column **filter arrow**, and then click **Sort A → Z**. Compare your screen with **Figure 1**.

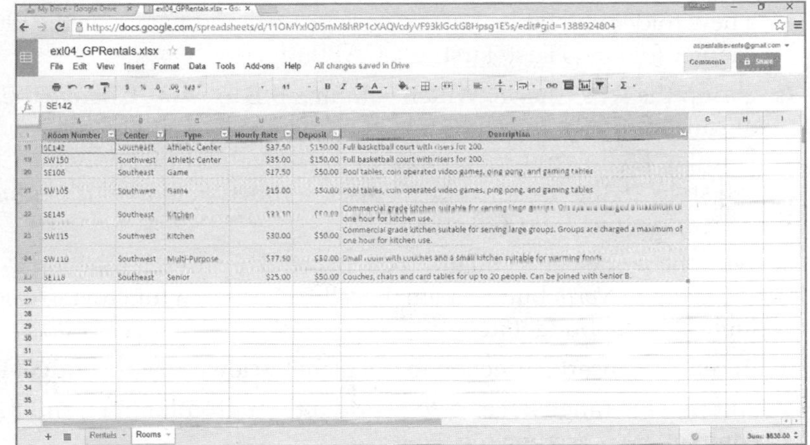

Figure 1

12. Click the **Rentals** worksheet, and then click cell **A2**. On the **View tab**, point to **Freeze,** and then click **1 row**.
13. Click **File**, point to **Download as**, and then click **Microsoft Excel (.xlsx)**.
14. Save the file in your chapter folder as Last_First_exl04_GPRentals
15. Close all windows, and then submit the file as directed by your instructor.

DONE! You have completed Collaborating with Google

CAPSTONE PROJECT

To complete this project, you will need the following file:

exl_CAPBudget

MyITLab® Grader

You will save your file as:

Last_First_exl_CAPBudget

1. Start **Excel 2016**, and then open the student data file **exl_CAPBudget**. Create a new folder named Excel Capstone Projects and then save the file in your chapter folder as Last_First_exl_CAPBudget
2. Group the worksheets. Widen columns **B:E** to *13.00*. Change the height of row **4** to *15.00*. In cell **E5**, insert a function to total the row, and then AutoFill **E5** down through **E14**. In the range **E6:E14**, apply the **Comma [0]** cell style. In the range **B15:E15**, insert a function to total the columns, and then apply the **Total** cell style.
3. With the worksheets still grouped, in cell **B16**, insert a function to calculate the average *North* budget item. In cell **B17**, insert a function to calculate the highest *North* budget item.
4. In cell **B18**, insert a function to calculate the lowest *North* budget item.
5. AutoFill the range **B16:B18** to the right through column **D**, and then compare your screen with **Figure 1**.
6. Ungroup the worksheets. Insert a new worksheet. Rename the new worksheet tab Summary and then apply the worksheet tab color **Orange, Accent 2**. Move the new worksheet tab to make it the first worksheet in the workbook.
7. Copy the range **A1:E4** from any of the quarter worksheets, and then on the **Summary** worksheet, paste the range into **A1:E4** using the **Keep Source Column Widths** paste option.
8. On the **Summary** worksheet, change the subtitle of cell **A2** to Annual Budget and then change the label in cell **A4** to Quarter
9. On the **Summary** worksheet, in cell **A5**, type 1st Quarter and then AutoFill **A5** down through cell **A8**. In cell **A9**, type Annual Total
10. On the **Summary** worksheet, enter a formula in cell **B5** setting the cell equal to cell **B15** in the *First Quarter* worksheet.
11. On the **Summary** worksheet, enter a formula for the *North* total from the *Second Quarter*, the *Third Quarter*, and the *Fourth Quarter* worksheets in the range **B6:B8**. AutoFill the range **B5:B8** to the right through column **E**. **Save** the file, and then compare your screen with **Figure 2**.

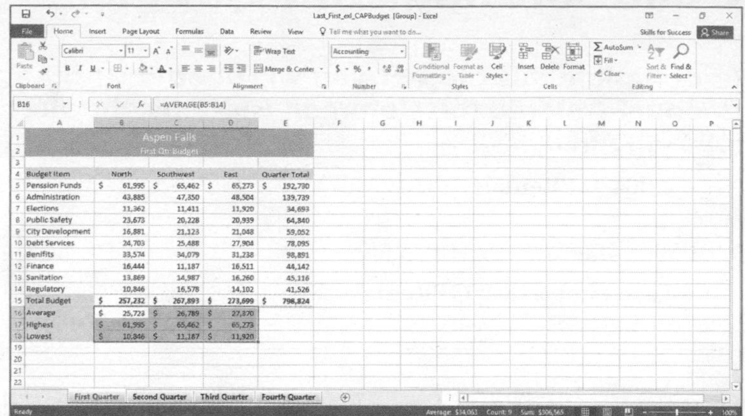

Figure 1 Excel 2016, Windows 10, Microsoft Corporation

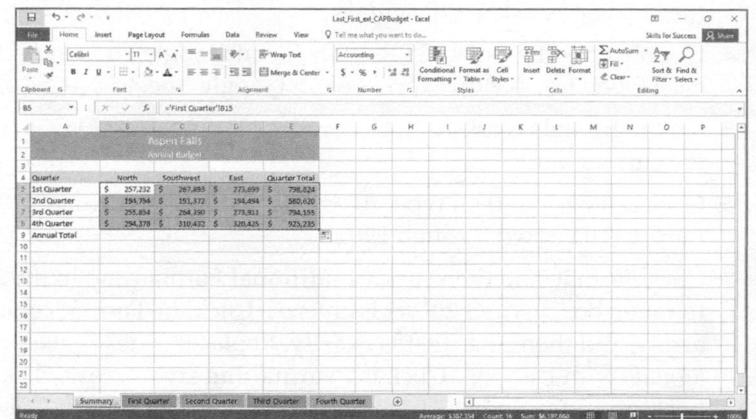

Figure 2 Excel 2016, Windows 10, Microsoft Corporation

12. On the **Summary** worksheet, in the range **B9:E9**, insert a function to calculate the column totals. Apply the **Comma [0]** cell style to **B6:E8**, and then apply the **Total** cell style to **B9:E9**.

■ **Continue to the next page to complete the skill**

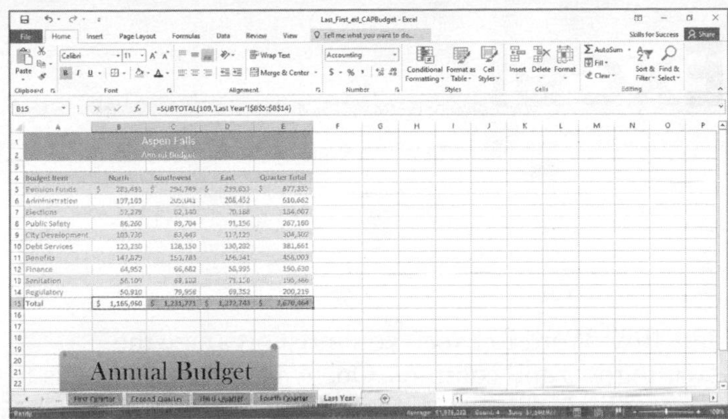

Excel 2016, Windows 10, Microsoft Corporation

Figure 3

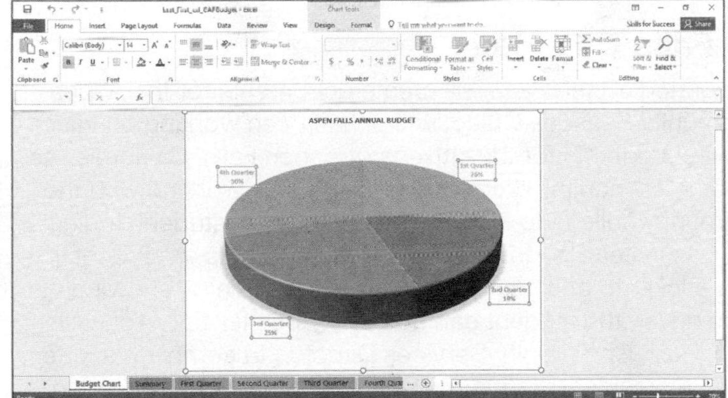

Excel 2016, Windows 10, Microsoft Corporation

Figure 4

13. In cell **A11**, type Bonus if less than and then in cell **A12**, type 1100000 and apply the **Accounting Number Format** with zero decimal places. Select the range **A11:A12**, and then apply **Outside Borders**.
14. In cell **B11**, insert the **IF** function. For the logical test, check whether the **North** total is less than the value in cell **A12**. If the logical test is true, 500 should display, and if the logical test is false, 50 should display. In the function, use an absolute cell reference when referring to cell **A12**.
15. In cell **B11**, apply the **Currency [0]** cell style, and then AutoFill cell **B11** to the right through cell **D11**.
16. Select the range **B5:D8**, and then insert the default **Data Bars** conditional format.
17. In cell **A17**, insert the **TODAY** function. Format the date with the **March 14, 2012** date format.
18. Unhide the **Last Year** worksheet. **Copy** the *Annual Budget* shape, and then paste the shape in the **Summary** worksheet. Move and resize the shape to approximately the range **A19:E23**.
19. On the **Last Year** worksheet, format the range **A4:E14** as a table, and then apply **Table Style Light 2**. Add a **Total row**, and then apply **Sum** to **B15:D15**. Convert the table to a normal range, and then apply the **Currency [0]** cell style to **B15:E15**. Compare your screen with **Figure 3**.
20. **Hide** the **Last Year** worksheet.
21. Group the worksheets, and then press Ctrl + Home. Find and replace the four occurrences of Qtr with Quarter
22. With the worksheets still grouped, check and correct any spelling errors. Add the file name to the left footer and the sheet name to the right footer. Return to **Normal** view, and then make cell **A1** the active cell. Ungroup the worksheets.
23. Make the **Summary** worksheet the active worksheet. Insert a **3-D Pie** chart based on the nonadjacent ranges **A4:A8** and **E4:E8**. Move the pie chart to a chart sheet with the sheet name Budget Chart
24. Format the chart. Apply **Layout 1**, and then apply **Chart Style 8**. Change the chart title to Aspen Falls Annual Budget and then change the data labels to a font size of **14**. Compare your screen with **Figure 4**.
25. **Save**, and then **Close** Excel. Submit the file as directed by your instructor.

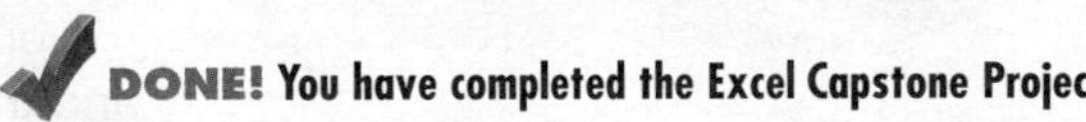

DONE! You have completed the Excel Capstone Project

INTEGRATED PROJECT 3

Copy Word Tables into Excel Worksheets

- Each Microsoft Office application has different strengths. For example, you can use Word to convert text into tables and Excel to insert functions and formulas into table cells.
- Exporting data from one application to another enables you to use the strengths of each application without having to retype the data.
- To move data from Word to Excel, you must organize the information into rows and columns. One way to format data is to create a table in Word.

Vitaly Krivosheev/Fotolia

Aspen Falls City Hall

In this Integrated Project, you will create documents for the Aspen Falls Community Services Office, which has been working on various sustainability programs for the citizens of Aspen Falls, California. As part of their sustainability program, Aspen Falls is working with the local community college to increase the number of students riding the city buses instead of driving their cars to campus. A student will be given a sticker to affix to his student ID, and then by showing his ID to a bus driver, the student can ride a city bus for free. You will assist Jack Ruiz, Community Services Director, to complete a letter to the college president stating more students will be permitted to participate in the free bus ride program.

In Word, you can use tabs to organize text into rows and columns. The tabbed text can be altered into a table, which can be formatted with table styles. A Word table can be copied and pasted into other applications such as Excel.

You will convert tabbed text into a table, add data to the table, and then format the table. You will then copy the table from the Word document and paste it into an Excel worksheet.

Time to complete this project — 30 to 60 minutes

Introduction

Outcome

Using the skills in this chapter, you will be able to adapt data to a Word table and then copy the table to an Excel workbook.

Objectives

3.1 Organize text

3.2 Summarize data in an Excel spreadsheet

Student data files needed for this project:

exl_IP03Riders (Word)
exl_IP03Pass (Excel)

You will save your files as:

Last_First_exl_IP03Riders (Word)
Last_First_exl_IP03Pass (Excel)

ASPEN FALLS COMMUNITY SERVICES
275 Elm Street, Room 122C
Aspen Falls, CA 93463

June 17, 2018

Dr. Dan Cheek
President
Aspen Falls Community College
817 Wisteria Lane
Aspen Falls, CA 93468

Dear Dr. Cheek:

We have been pleased with the involvement of the Aspen Falls Community College in our city wide sustainability programs. As you know, the city has been promoting "Ride the Bus for Free" which provides each student a sticker to affix to a student ID. By showing the student ID to a bus driver, the student can ride a city bus for free. Student participation in this program has exceeded our expectati

We still have funds available for this program and are pleased to inform you that the following stude who signed up after the deadline may now pick up a free city bus ride sticker from my office.

First Name	Last Name
Carmelina	Goforth
Florine	Dupont
Valentina	Blunt
Erik	Zook
Scotty	Whittle
Kareen	Whitehurst
First	Last

Thank you again for encouraging your students to take part in this sustainability program.

Sincerely,

Jake Ruiz
Community Services Director

Last_First_exl_IP03Riders.docx

Aspen Falls
Student Bus Passes

First Name	Last Name	Bus Pass Issued
Dane	Borders	Yes
Junko	Bachman	Yes
Donovan	Tisdale	Yes
Hugh	Tavares	Yes
Brandi	Schmid	Yes
Viviana	Pickard	Yes
Willy	Jasper	Yes
Denita	Gulley	Yes
Riley	Fonseca	Yes
Genevie	Condon	Yes
Sulema	Clancy	Yes
Errol	Batista	Yes
Dodie	Wicks	Yes
Delmer	New	Yes
Zoe	Martell	Yes
Misha	Lo	Yes
Yuki	Littleton	Yes
Cedrick	Ison	Yes
Lady	Haag	Yes
Joy	Folsom	Yes
China	Brumfield	Yes
Terence	Broyles	Yes
Gregg	Brito	Yes
Lane	Mireles	Yes
Glen	McDonnell	Yes
Valeria	LeClair	Yes
Lupe	Hamblin	Yes
Jonelle	Gough	Yes
Abel	Fanning	Yes
Freddie	Binder	Yes
Rueben	Winfield	Yes
Kathrine	Whitworth	Yes
Carmelina	Goforth	No
Florine	Dupont	No
Valentina	Blunt	No
Erik	Zook	No
Scotty	Whittle	No
Kareen	Whitehurst	No
First	Last	No

Last_First_exl_IP03Pass.xlsx

SKILLS

At the end of this project, you will be able to:

- Convert text to a table
- Copy a Word table into an Excel workbook
- Match destination formatting when pasting

1. Start **Excel 2016**, and then open the student data file **exl_IP03Pass**. **Save** the file in your chapter folder as Last_First_exl_IP03Pass
2. Add the file name in the worksheet's left footer, and then return to Normal view. Press Ctrl + Home. **Minimize** the Excel window.
3. Start **Word 2016**, and then open the student data file **exl_IP03Riders**. **Save** the file in your chapter folder as Last_First_exl_IP03Riders Add the file name to the footer, and then close the footer.
4. At the bottom of the Word document, beginning with the text *First Name*, select the seven lines of tabbed text. Do not select the blank line above or below the tabbed text.
5. Click the **Insert tab**. In the **Tables group**, click the **Table** button, and then click **Convert Text to Table**. Compare your screen with **Figure 1**.
6. In the **Convert Text to Table** dialog box, click **OK**.
7. On the Table Tools **Design tab**, in the **Table Styles group**, click the **More** button. In the **Table styles** gallery, scroll down, and then under **List Tables**, point to the fourth style—**List Table 1 Light - Accent 3**. Compare your screen with **Figure 2**, and then click the fourth style.
8. In the **Table Style Options group**, clear the **First Column** check box.
9. Click the **Table Tools Layout tab**. In the **Cell Size group**, click the **AutoFit** button, and then click **AutoFit Contents**.

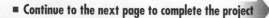

■ **Continue to the next page to complete the project**

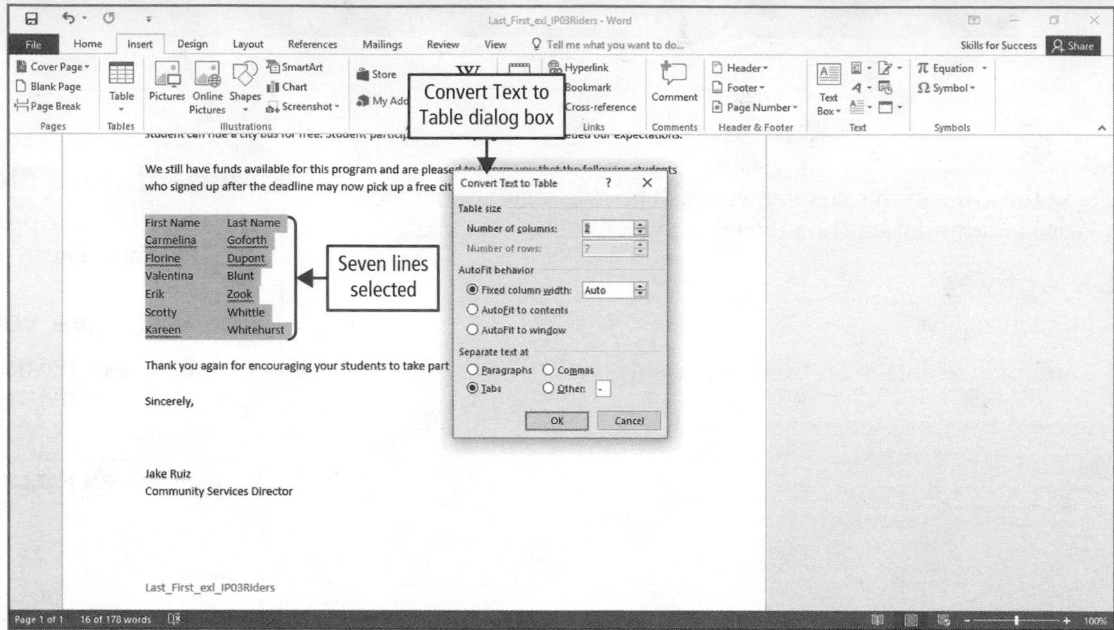

Figure 1

Excel 2016, Windows 10, Microsoft Corporation

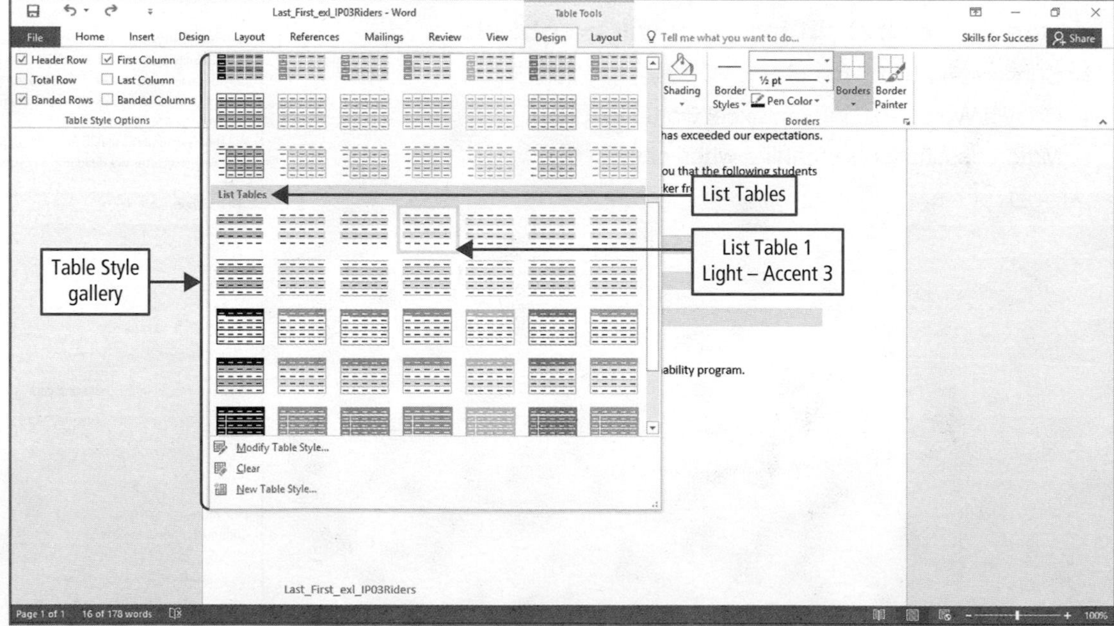

Figure 2

Excel 2016, Windows 10, Microsoft Corporation

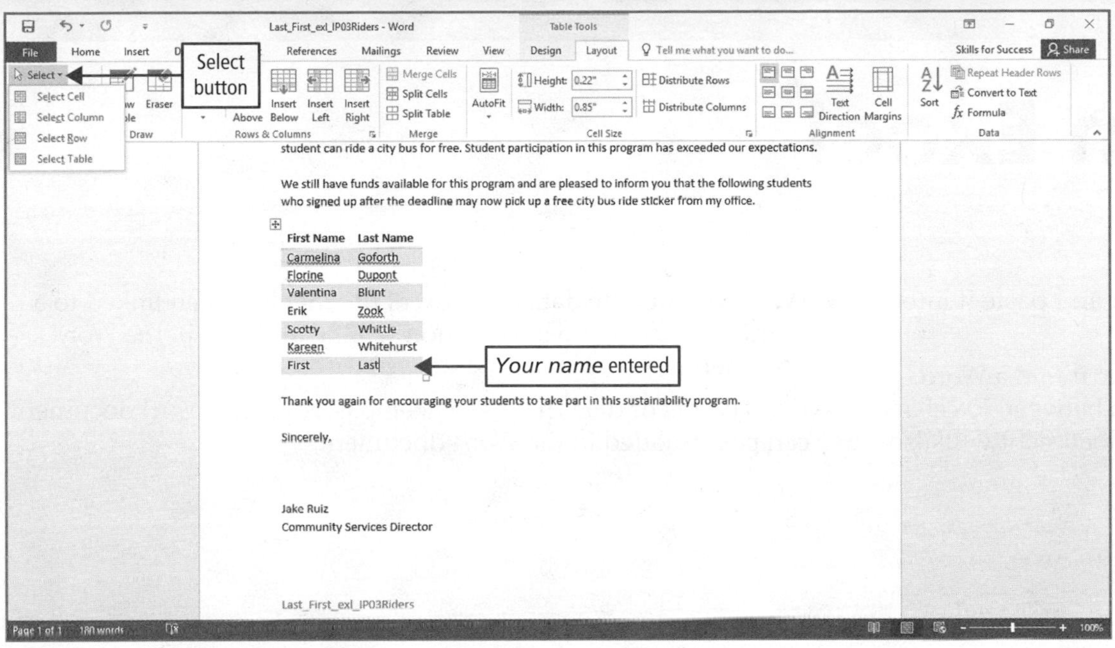

Excel 2016, Windows 10, Microsoft Corporation

Figure 3

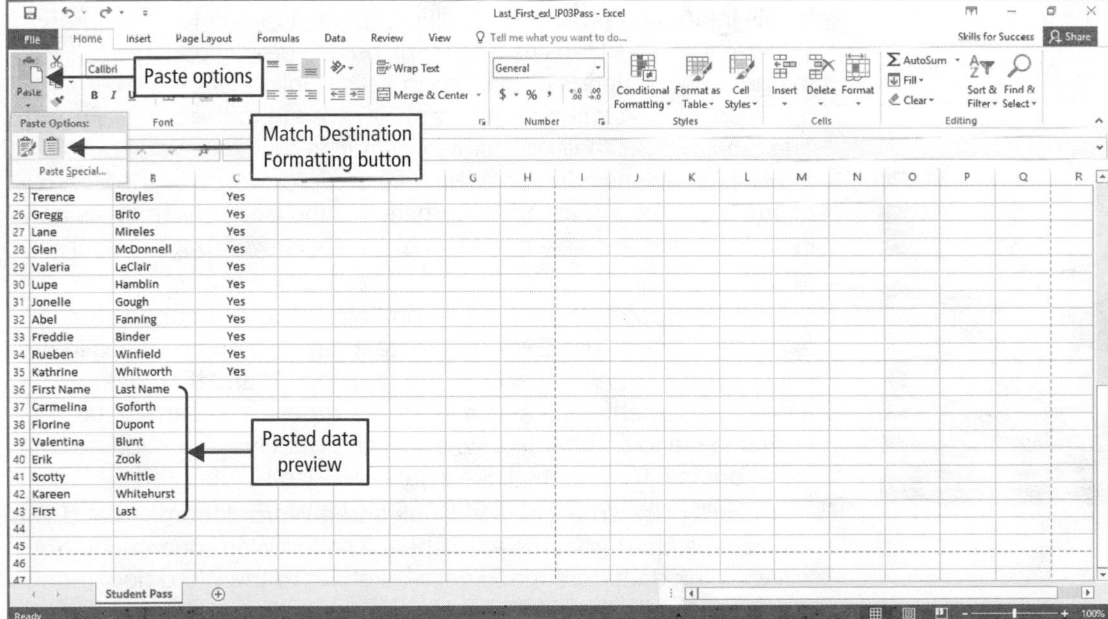

Excel 2016, Windows 10, Microsoft Corporation

Figure 4

10. In the last table row, click in the cell with the text *Whitehurst*, and then press Tab to insert a new row. Type your First name, press Tab, and then type your Last name. **Save** the Word document.
11. On the **Table Tools Layout tab**, in the **Table group**, click the **Select** button, and then compare your screen with **Figure 3**.
12. In the list, click **Select Table**. Click the **Home tab**, and then in the **Clipboard group**, click the **Copy** button.
13. Click the taskbar, and then click the **Excel** button to make the Excel window active.
14. Scroll as necessary, and then click cell **A36**. On the **Home tab**, in the **Clipboard group**, click the **Paste arrow**. Under **Paste Options**, point to the second button —**Match Destination Formatting**. Compare your screen with **Figure 4**.
15. Click the **Match Destination Formatting** button.
16. Click cell **A36**. In the **Cells group**, click the **Delete arrow**, and then click **Delete Sheet Rows** to delete the header row from the copied table.
17. Click cell **C36**, type No and then on the formula bar, click **Enter**. AutoFill cell **C36** down through **C42**.
18. **Save** the file, and then **Close** Excel. **Save** the Word document, and then **Close** Word. Submit the files as directed by your instructor.

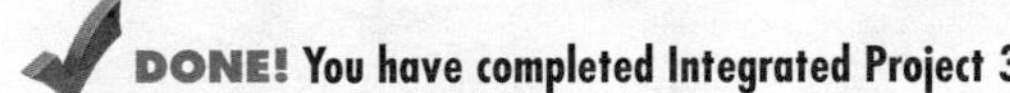

DONE! You have completed Integrated Project 3

Link Data from Excel

- You can copy a chart from an Excel workbook and paste it into a Word document.
- When you copy data from Excel, you can paste it into a Word document as a table, or you create a link open between Excel and Word so that any changes made in the Excel document will also be reflected in the Word table.
- When you update data in an Excel file that has been linked to a Word document, the information will be updated in the Word document.
- Excel charts or data that have been pasted into a Word document can be formatted in the Word document.

Africa Studio/Fotolia

Aspen Falls City Hall

In this Integrated Project, you will complete a memo for the Library Director, Douglas Hopkins. Mr. Hopkins has been working with the group, the Friends of the Aspen Falls Public Library. The group operates a bookstore and donates the revenue to the public library. The group tracks their bookstore revenue in an Excel workbook, and Mr. Hopkins plans to present the revenue information to the Board of Trustees. You will complete a memo to the Board of Trustees and include a chart and linked data from the Excel workbook in your memo.

Each Microsoft Office application has different strengths; for example, you can use Excel to create charts based on values in the Excel workbook. An Excel chart can be copied and then pasted into a Word document such as a memo or a report. You can link data from one file to another file. When linking data, you can update data in the original file and the linked data will also be updated.

You will open an Excel workbook and a Word document, and you will paste a chart from the worksheet into the Word document. You will also link data from the Excel worksheet to the Word document, and then update the link.

Time to complete this project — 30 to 45 minutes

Outcome

Using the skills in this chapter, you will be able to paste linked Excel data and charts to Word and update the linked data.

Objectives

4.1 Create linked data between Word and Excel

4.2 Apply revised data links

Student data files needed for this project:

exl_IP04Report (Word)
exl_IP04Book (Excel)

You will save your files as:

Last_First_exl_IP04Report (Word)
Last_First_exl_IP04Book (Excel)

SKILLS

At the end of this project, you will be able to:

- Copy Excel charts and paste them into Word documents
- Link Excel data to Word documents
- Link and keep the source formatting
- Update linked data

MEMORANDUM

TO: Library Board of Trustees
FROM: Douglas Hopkins, Library Director
DATE: September 4, 2018
RE: Friends of the Aspen Falls Library Book Sale

In the past four years, the book sales sponsored by the Friends of the Aspen Falls Public Library have grossed $73,818, nearly all of which have been donated to the Library for programming. The sales have increased steadily, as shown in the chart below:

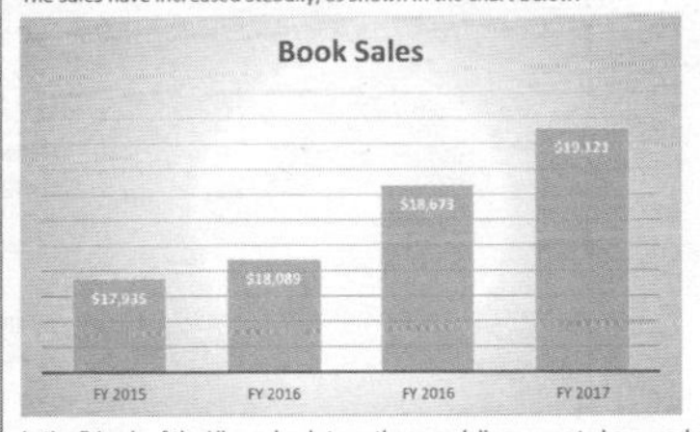

In the Friends of the Library bookstore, the remodeling seems to have worked wo
sales were low during the 3rd quarter of 2016 during the remodeling, the 2017 sa
above 2016 sales figures as shown in the table below:

Quarter	FY 2015	FY 2016	FY 2016	FY 2017
1st Quarter	$4,126	$4,989	$5,149	$5,615
2nd Quarter	4,735	4,852	4,819	5,646
3rd Quarter	4,886	3,483	4,638	1,621
4th Quarter	4,188	4,765	4,067	6,239
Total Sales	$17,935	$18,089	$18,673	$19,121

Last_First_exl_IP04Report

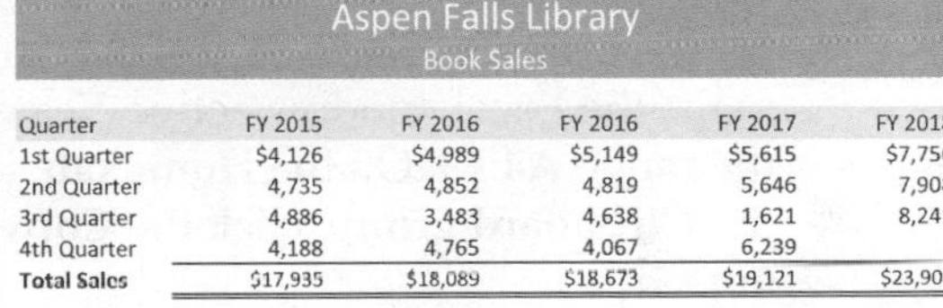

Aspen Falls Library
Book Sales

Quarter	FY 2015	FY 2016	FY 2016	FY 2017	FY 2018
1st Quarter	$4,126	$4,989	$5,149	$5,615	$7,756
2nd Quarter	4,735	4,852	4,819	5,646	7,908
3rd Quarter	4,886	3,483	4,638	1,621	8,241
4th Quarter	4,188	4,765	4,067	6,239	
Total Sales	$17,935	$18,089	$18,673	$19,121	$23,905

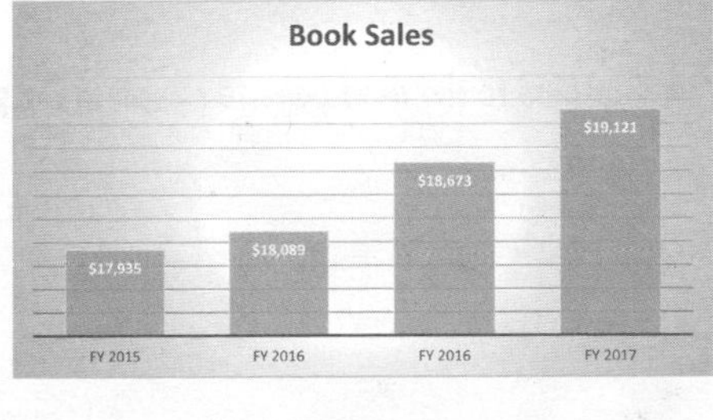

Last_First_exl_IP04Book

Excel 2016, Windows 10, Microsoft Corporation

1. Start **Word 2016**, and then open the student data file **exl_IP04Report**. **Save** the file in your chapter folder as Last_First_exl_IP04Report Add the file name to the footer, and then close the footer.
2. Start **Excel 2016**, and then open the student data file **exl_IP04Book**. **Save** the file in your chapter folder as Last_First_exl_IP04Book Add the file name in the worksheet's left footer, and then return to Normal view. Press Ctrl + Home.
3. In Excel, click the chart border to select the chart. If necessary, scroll down to see the chart. Compare your screen with **Figure 1**.
4. On the **Home tab**, in the **Clipboard group**, click the **Copy** button.
5. On the taskbar, click the **Word** button to make the Word window active. Position the insertion point in the first blank line below the paragraph that begins *In the past four years*.
6. In the **Clipboard group**, click the **Paste** button to paste the chart in the Word document. Compare your screen with **Figure 2**.
7. On the taskbar, click the **Excel** button to make the Excel window active. Select the range **A4:F9**. On the **Home tab**, in the **Clipboard group**, click the **Copy** button.

■ **Continue to the next page to complete the project**

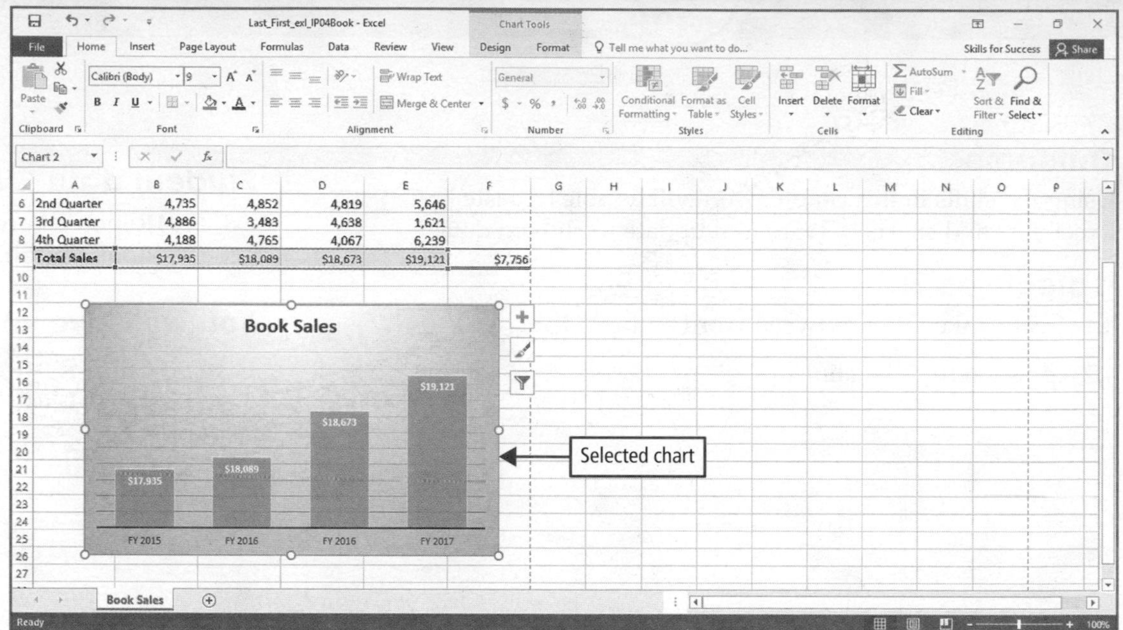

Figure 1

Excel 2016, Windows 10, Microsoft Corporation

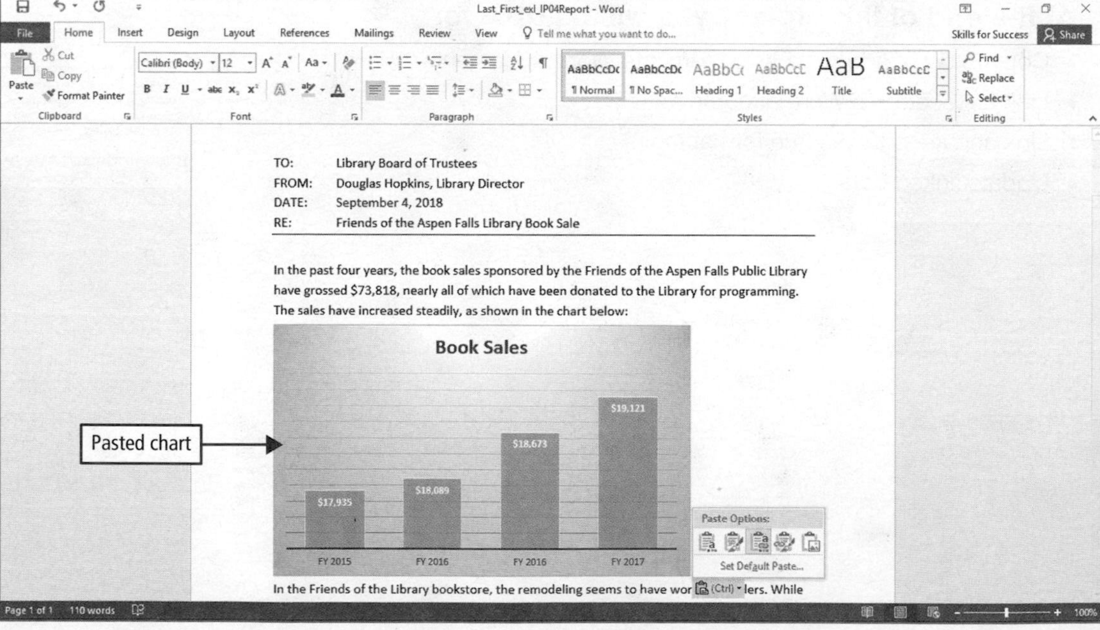

Figure 2

Excel 2016, Windows 10, Microsoft Corporation

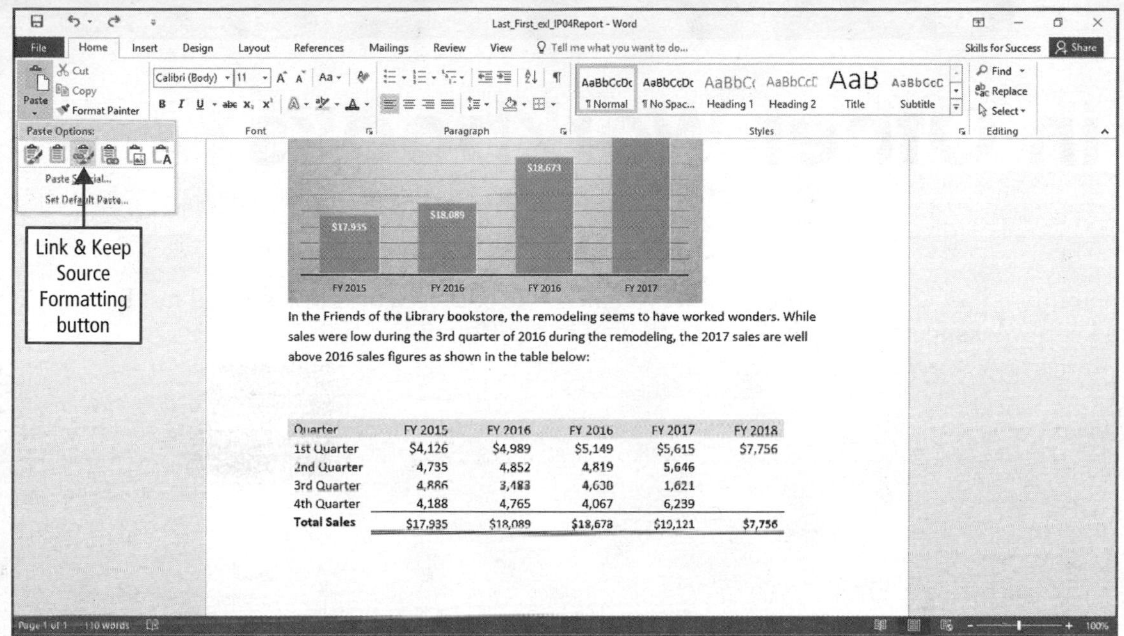

Excel 2016, Windows 10, Microsoft Corporation

Figure 3

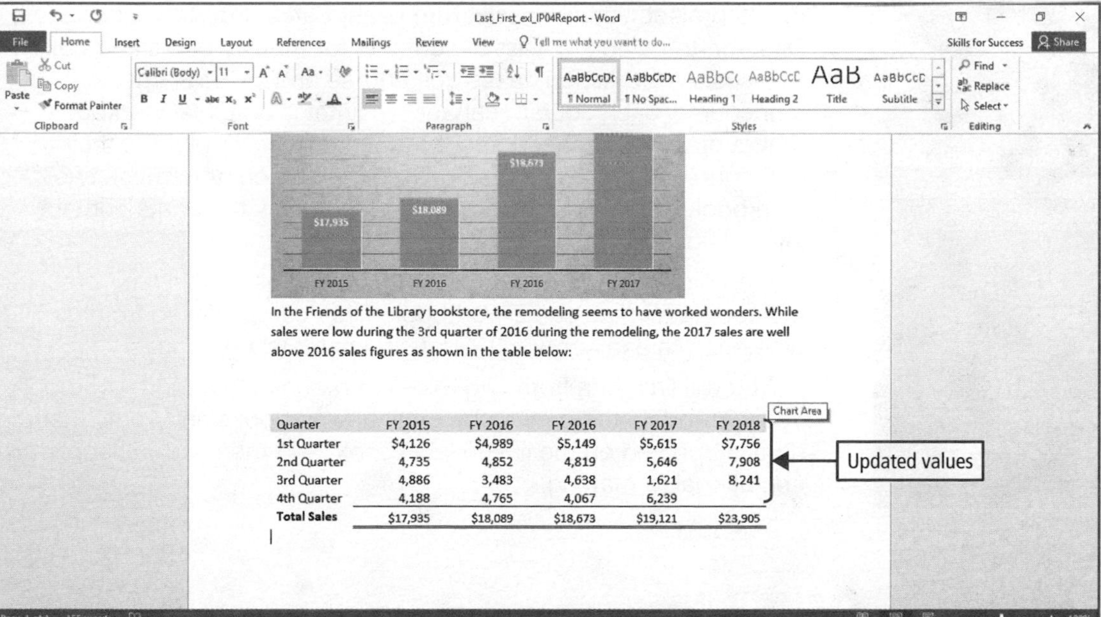

Excel 2016, Windows 10, Microsoft Corporation

Figure 4

8. On the taskbar, click the **Word** button.
9. Position the insertion point in the blank line at the end of the document. On the **Home tab**, in the **Clipboard group**, click the **Paste arrow**, and then under **Paste Options**, point to the third button —**Link & Keep Source Formatting**. Compare your screen with **Figure 3**.

   A preview of the data displays at the insertion point.
10. Click the **Link & Keep Source Formatting** button.
11. On the taskbar, click the **Excel** button. Press Esc to remove the moving border.
12. In cell **F6**, type 7908 and then press Enter. In cell **F7**, type 8241 and then press Enter.
13. **Save** the Excel file.
14. On the taskbar, click the **Word** button.
15. In the Word document, right-click the Excel table that you pasted previously, and then click **Update Link** to check for any changes in the linked Excel data. Compare your screen with **Figure 4**.

    In the Word document, the updated 2nd and 3rd Quarter values display, and the 2018 total is updated.
16. **Save** the Word document, and then **Close** Word. **Save** the Excel file, and then **Close** Excel. Submit the files as directed by your instructor.

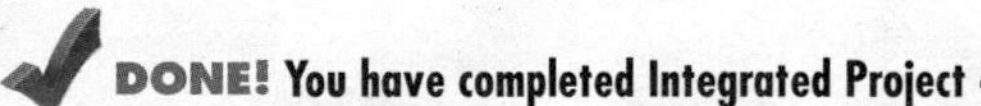

DONE! You have completed Integrated Project 4

INTEGRATED PROJECT 5

Refer to Cells in Other Workbooks

- An ***external reference***—a reference to a cell in another workbook—is useful when it is not practical to keep worksheets together in the same workbook.
- An external reference must include the name of the workbook and the name of the worksheet.
- After a link is created, the source workbook should not be renamed or moved to a different location.

Gunnar3000/Fotolia

Aspen Falls City Hall

In this project, you will assist Kim Leah, Parks and Recreation Director, to complete a list of contacts for the city parks and golf courses. At the Aspen Lakes golf course and at the Hamilton golf course, each course manager maintains an Excel workbook that contains information about the employees working at their golf course. You will link the contact information from these two workbooks into a third workbook that contains the parks contact information.

If employees are in different locations, sometimes it isn't practical to keep data in the same workbook. Data can be linked from one workbook to another workbook using external references.

You will link data from two Excel workbooks to a third workbook. You will update the data in the original workbooks and verify that the data is updated on the linked workbook, and then you will apply conditional formatting.

Time to complete this project — 30 to 60 minutes

Introduction

Outcome

Using the skills in this chapter, you will be able to paste linked Excel data and charts to other workbooks and update the linked data.

Objectives

5.1 Demonstrate linked data between Excel workbooks

5.2 Apply revised data links

Student data files needed for this project:

exl_IP05Golf
exl_IP05Hamilton
exl_IP05Contacts

You will save your files as:

Last_First_exl_IP05Golf
Last_First_exl_IP05Hamilton
Last_First_exl_IP05Contacts

SKILLS

At the end of this project, you will be able to:

- Link data from one Excel workbook to another
- Update linked data
- Insert conditional formatting

Aspen Falls Parks and Recreation

Employee Contact Information

First Name	Last Name	Position	Phone	Location
First	Last	Parks and Recreation Manager	(805) 555-1479	City Hall, Room 416
Amado	Pettinelli	Outdoor Recreation Supervisor	(805) 555-1417	City Hall, Room 440
Leah	Kim	Parks and Recreation Director	(805) 555-1410	City Hall, Room 412
Lorrine	Deely	Community Center Supervisor	(805) 555-1153	City Hall, Room 434
Booker	Berhe	Aquatics Supervisor	(805) 555-1350	City Hall, Room 432
Irving	Siravo	Capital Improvement Supervisor	(805) 555-1310	City Hall, Room 426
Keith	Hansen	Park Operations Manager	(805) 555-1112	City Hall, Room 414
Jacquetta	Ronald	Planning and Design Supervisor	(805) 555-1031	City Hall, Room 430
Neely	Ramsburg	Design and Development Manager	(805) 555-1403	City Hall, Room 420
Vic	Fowler	Aspen Lakes Course Manager	(805) 555-1010	Aspen Lakes Golf Course
Lee	Garrett	Golf Instructor	(805) 555-1787	Aspen Lakes Golf Course
Kyle	Burress	Golf Instructor	(805) 555-5851	Aspen Lakes Golf Course
Diego	Alvarez	Mechanic	(805) 555-7985	Aspen Lakes Golf Course
Ariana	Korpela	Landscaper	(805) 555-2775	Aspen Lakes Golf Course
Brooke	Whitlow	Bookkeeper	(805) 555-5595	Aspen Lakes Golf Course
Timothy	Dominik	Clubhouse Associate	(805) 555-2523	Aspen Lakes Golf Course
Jesse	Periera	Clubhouse Associate	(805) 555-6944	Aspen Lakes Golf Course
Chloe	Tauer	Maintenance Associate	(805) 555-3989	Aspen Lakes Golf Course
Rosaria	Cabiness	Food and Beverage	(805) 555-6814	Aspen Lakes Golf Course
Tracy	Lecroy	Hamilton Course Manager	(805) 555-1010	Hamilton Golf Course
Mandee	Covey	Golf Instructor	(805) 555-8675	Hamilton Golf Course
Ollie	Wizen	Golf Instructor	(805) 555-3593	Hamilton Golf Course
Dylan	Lee	Mechanic	(805) 555-9124	Hamilton Golf Course
Marissa	Madeiros	Landscaper	(805) 555-7781	Hamilton Golf Course
Sabrina	Mak	Bookkeeper	(805) 555-5221	Hamilton Golf Course
Chester	Schillinger	Clubhouse Associate	(805) 555-7279	Hamilton Golf Course
Byron	Hoese	Maintenance Manager	(805) 555-9737	Hamilton Golf Course

1. Start **Excel 2016**, and then open the student data file **exl_IP05Contacts**. **Save** the file in your chapter folder as Last_First_exl_IP05Contacts Add the file name in the worksheet's left footer, and then return to Normal view and press Ctrl + Home.
2. Click cell **A5**, type your First name, and then press Tab. In cell **B5**, type your Last name, and then press Enter. **Save** the file, and then compare your screen with **Figure 1**.
3. **Open** the student data file **exl_IP05Golf**. **Save** the workbook in your chapter folder as Last_First_exl_IP05Golf
4. Right-click the **Lessons** worksheet tab, and then click **Select All Sheets**. Add the file name in the worksheet's left footer, and then return to Normal view and press Ctrl + Home. Right-click the worksheet tab, and then click **Ungroup Sheets**.
5. Click the **Contacts** worksheet tab, and then select the range **A4:E13**. On the **Home tab**, in the **Clipboard group**, click the **Copy** button.
6. Make **Last_First_exl_IP05Contacts** the active workbook, and then click cell **A14**. On the **Home tab**, in the **Clipboard group**, click the **Paste arrow**. Under **Other Paste Options**, click the second button—**Paste Link**. Compare your screen with **Figure 2**.

   The reference to the source workbook, worksheet, and cell displays in the formula bar.
7. Make **Last_First_exl_IP05Golf** the active workbook. **Save** the file, and then **Close** the workbook.

■ **Continue to the next page to complete the project**

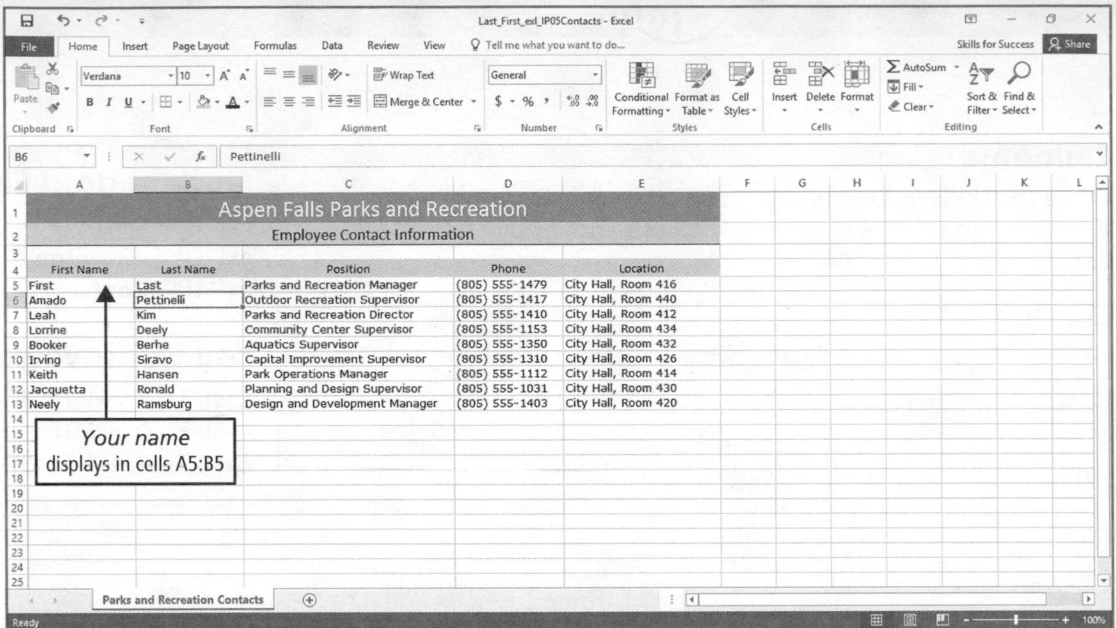

Figure 1 Excel 2016, Windows 10, Microsoft Corporation

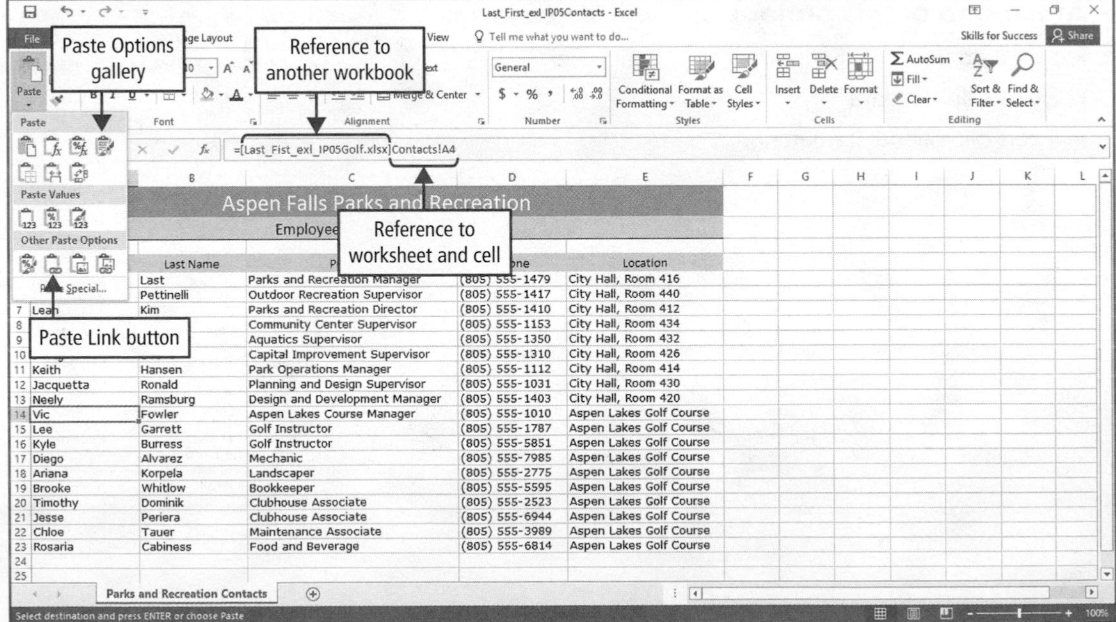

Figure 2 Excel 2016, Windows 10, Microsoft Corporation

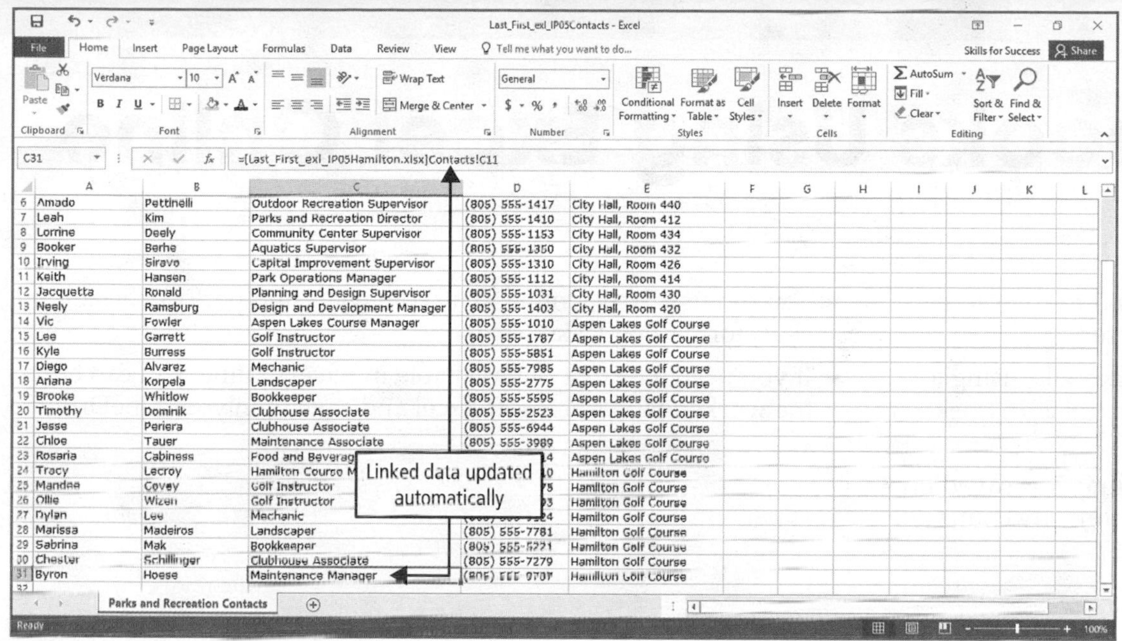

Excel 2016, Windows 10, Microsoft Corporation

Figure 3

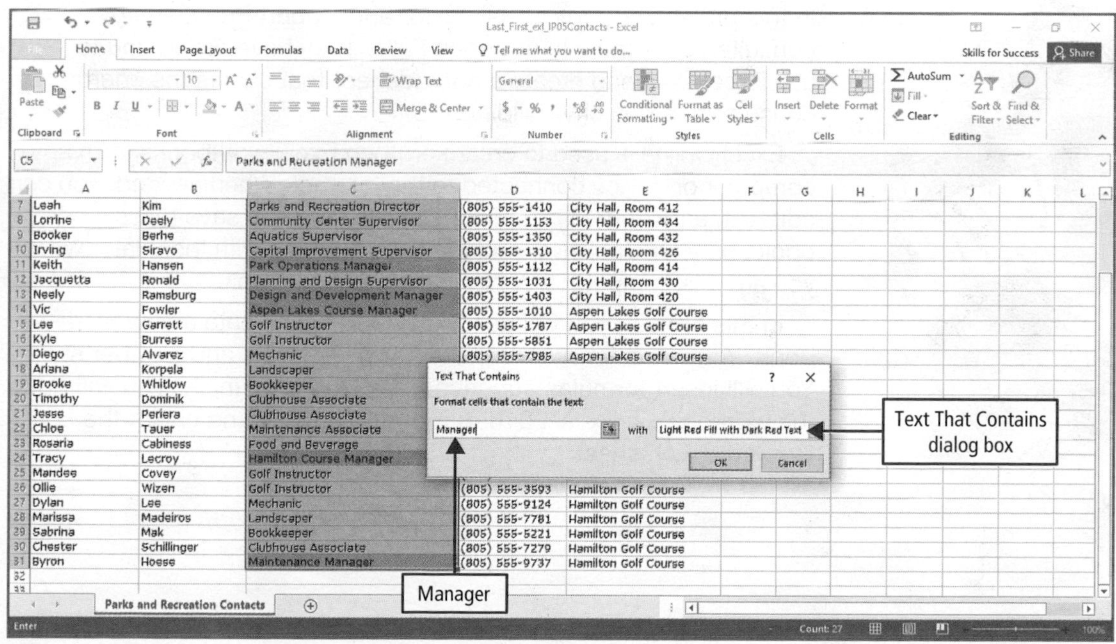

Excel 2016, Windows 10, Microsoft Corporation

Figure 4

8. **Open** the student data file **exl_IP05Hamilton**. **Save** the file in your chapter folder as Last_First_exl_IP05Hamilton
9. Using the techniques just practiced, enter the file name in the left footer of the grouped sheets, return to Normal view, press Ctrl + Home, and then **Ungroup Sheets**.
10. Click the **Contacts** worksheet tab, and then select the range **A4:E11**. On the **Home tab**, in the **Clipboard group**, click the **Copy** button.
11. Make **Last_First_exl_IP05Contacts** the active workbook, and then click cell **A24**. In the **Clipboard group**, click the **Paste arrow**. Under **Other Paste Options**, click the **Paste Link** button.
12. Make **Last_First_exl_IP05Hamilton** the active workbook, and then click cell **C11**. Type Maintenance Manager and then press Enter. **Save** the file.
13. Make **Last_First_exl_IP05Contacts** the active workbook. Click cell **C31**, and then compare your screen with **Figure 3**.
14. Select the range **C5:C31**. Click the **Quick Analysis** button, and then click the **Text Contains** button. In the **Text That Contains** dialog box, in the first box, replace the text with Manager Compare your screen with **Figure 4**, and then click **OK**.
15. **Save** the files, and then **Close** Excel. Submit the files as directed by your instructor.

DONE! You have completed Integrated Project 5

Create Workbooks Using Excel Online

- ***Excel Online*** is a cloud-based application used to complete basic spreadsheet formulas using a web browser.
- Excel Online can be used to create or edit workbooks using a web browser instead of the Excel program—Excel 2016 does not need to be installed on your computer.
- When you create a document using Excel Online, it is saved on your OneDrive so that you can work with it from any computer connected to the Internet.
- You can use Excel Online to insert a chart and perform basic chart formatting tasks.
- If you need a feature not available in Excel Online, you can edit the workbook in Microsoft Excel and save it on your OneDrive.

Maxim Kazmin/Fotolia

Aspen Falls City Hall

In this project, you will assist Taylor and Robert Price, energy consultants for the city of Aspen Falls. They have asked you to use Excel Online to create a spreadsheet that shows the energy consumption of a city building.

Excel Online is used to create or open Excel workbooks from any computer or device connected to the Internet. When needed, you can edit text, enter formulas, or insert charts. You can save these workbooks on your OneDrive, and continue working with them later when you are at a computer that has Excel 2016 available.

In this project, you will use Excel Online to create a new workbook. You will enter data and then apply formats and number styles. You will insert formulas, functions, and a chart. Finally, you will open the workbook in Excel 2016 to format the chart and check the spelling of the worksheet.

Time to complete this project—30 to 60 minutes

Outcome

Using the skills in this chapter, you will be able to build and edit Excel workbooks using Excel Online, and edit the workbooks using Excel 2016.

Objectives

1 Generate workbooks in Excel Online

2 Format workbooks in Excel Online

3 Analyze data using pie charts

4 Modify online workbooks

Student data file needed for this project:

New blank Excel Online workbook

You will save your file as:

Last_First_exl_OPEnergy

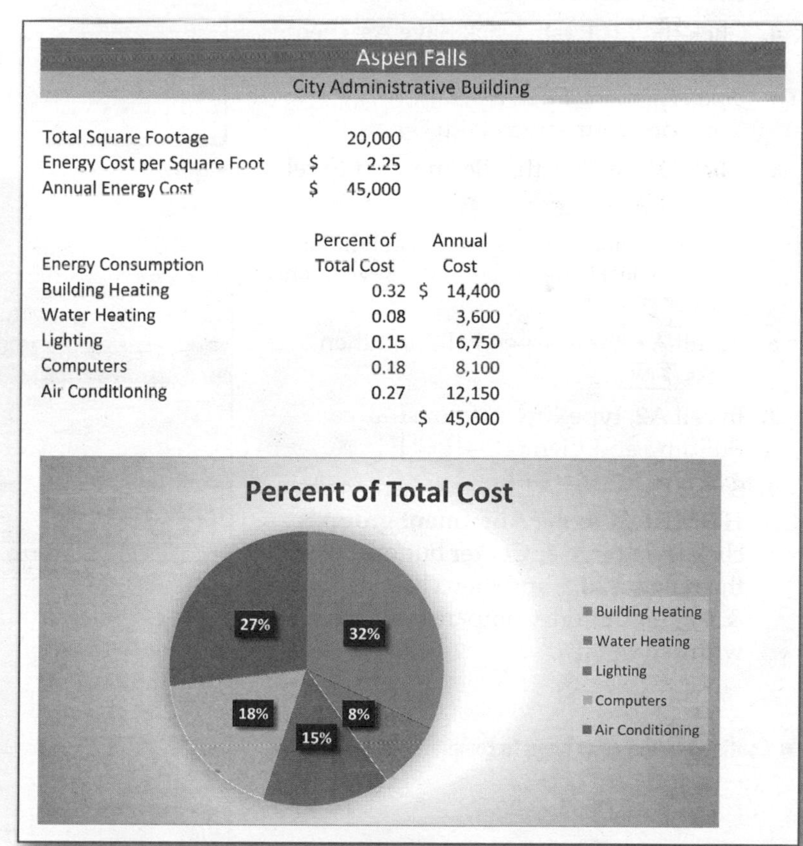

SKILLS

At the end of this project, you will be able to:

- Create new Excel workbooks using OneDrive
- Enter data in editing view
- Apply number styles
- Enter summary functions
- Enter formulas using absolute cell references
- Insert and format pie charts
- Edit workbooks created by Excel Online in Excel 2016

1. Start **Edge**, navigate to live.com and then log on to your Microsoft account. If you do not have an account, follow the links and directions on the page to create one.
2. After logging in, navigate as needed to display the OneDrive page.

   OneDrive and Office Online technologies are accessed through Web pages that can change often, and the formatting and layout of some pages may often be different than the figures in this book. When this happens, you may need to adapt the steps to complete the actions they describe.
3. On the toolbar, click **New**, and then click **Excel workbook**.
4. Click the **FILE tab**. Click **Save As**, then click the **Rename** button. In the **Rename** box, type Last_First_exl_OPEnergy Compare your screen with **Figure 1**.
5. Click **OK** to save the file and start Excel Online.

   Excel Online displays six tabs in Editing view: File, Home, Insert, Data, Review, and View.
6. In cell **A1**, type Aspen Falls and then press Enter.
7. In cell **A2**, type City Administrative Building and then press Enter.
8. Select the range **A1:F1**, and then on the **HOME tab**, in the **Alignment group**, click the **Merge & Center** button. Select the range **A2:F2**, and then click the **Merge & Center** button. Compare your screen with **Figure 2**.

■ **Continue to the next page to complete the project**

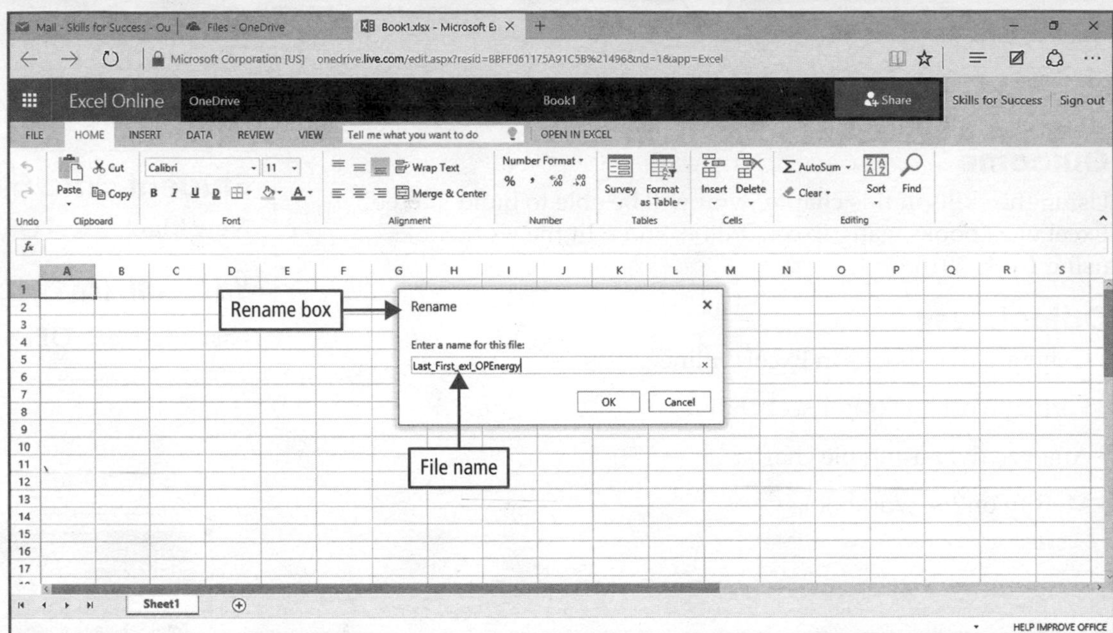

Figure 1

Excel 2016, Windows 10, Microsoft Corporation

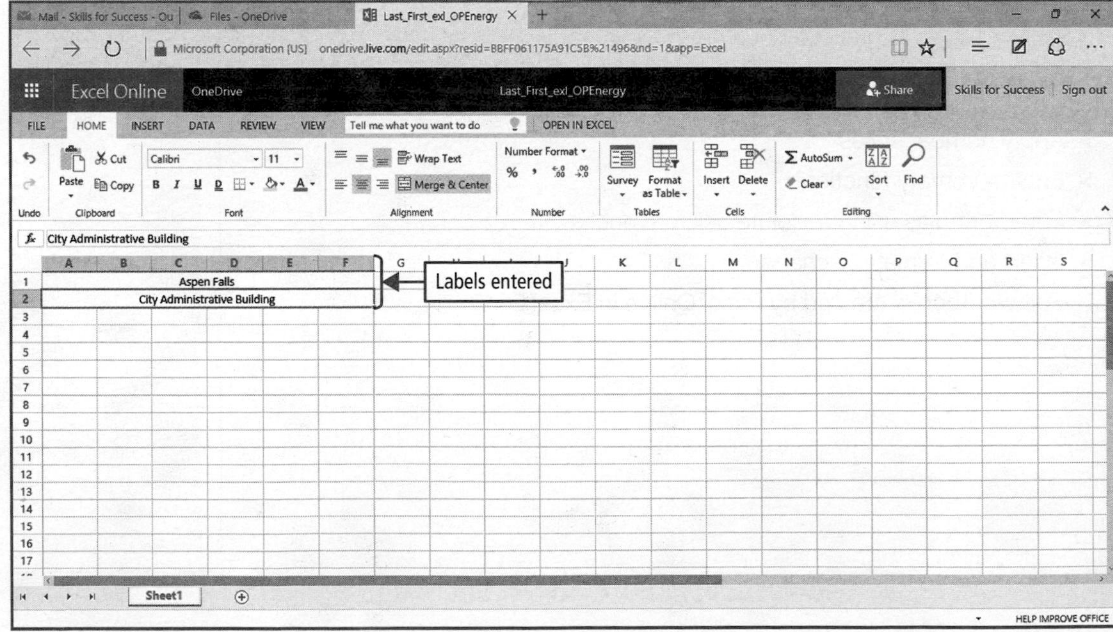

Figure 2

Excel 2016, Windows 10, Microsoft Corporation

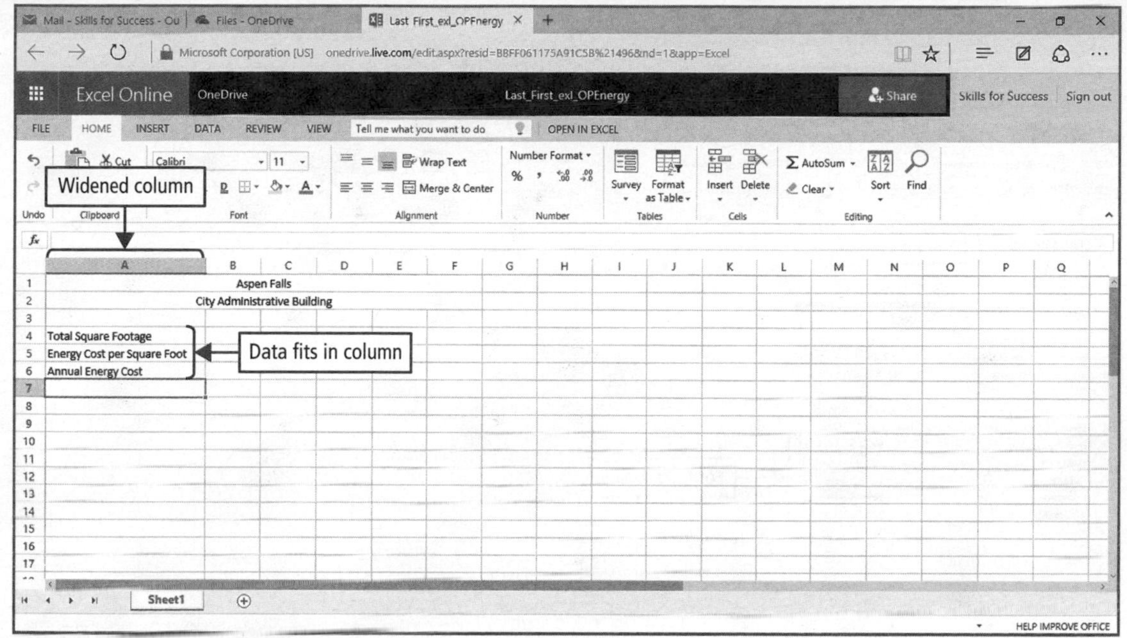

Excel 2016, Windows 10, Microsoft Corporation

Figure 3

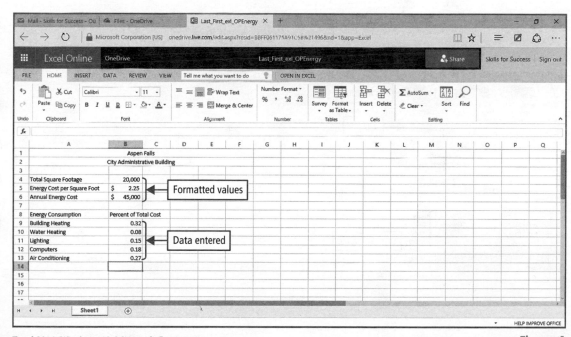

Excel 2016, Windows 10, Microsoft Corporation

Figure 4

9. In cell **A4**, type Total Square Footage and then press Enter.
10. In cell **A5**, type Energy Cost per Square Foot and then press Enter.
11. In cell **A6**, type Annual Energy Cost and then press Enter.
12. In the column heading area, point to the right boundary of column A to display the [+] pointer. Double-click the line between columns **A** and **B** to display all of the contents of cell **A5** in the column. Compare your screen with **Figure 3**.
13. Make cell **B4** the active cell. Type 20000 and then press Enter. Click cell **B4**, and then on the **HOME tab**, in the **Number group**, click the **Comma Style** button [,]. Click the **Decrease Decimal** button [.00→.0] two times.
14. In cell **B5**, type 2.25 and then press Enter.
15. In cell **B6**, type =B4*B5 and then press Enter.
16. Click cell **B5**. On the **HOME tab**, in the **Number group**, click the **Number Format** button, and then click **Accounting**.
17. Click cell **B6**, and then apply the **Accounting** number format. Click the **Decrease Decimal** button [.00→.0] two times.
18. Click cell **A8**, type Energy Consumption and then press Enter.
19. In the range **A9:A13**, pressing Enter after each entry, type Building Heating | Water Heating | Lighting | Computers | Air Conditioning
20. Click cell **B8**, type Percent of Total Cost and then press Enter.
21. In the range **B9:B13**, making sure you type the decimal in front of each number and pressing Enter after each entry, type the following values: .32 | .08 | .15 | .18 | .27 Compare your screen with **Figure 4**.

■ **Continue to the next page to complete the project**

22. Select the range **B9:B13**. In the **Number group**, click the **Number Format** arrow, and then click **Percentage**. Click the **Decrease Decimal** button two times.
23. Click cell **C8**, type Annual Cost and then press Enter.
24. Select the range **B8:C8**. In the **Alignment group**, click the **Wrap Text** button, click the **Middle Align** button, and then click the **Center** button.
25. Click cell **C9**, type =B9*$B$6 and then press Enter.
26. Click cell **C9**, point to the **fill handle**, and then drag the fill handle to copy the formula down through cell **C13**. Compare your screen with **Figure 5**.

    The absolute cell reference to $B$6 is copied to each of the other formulas.
27. Click cell **C14**. In the **Editing group**, click the **AutoSum** button, and then press Enter. Select the range **C10:C13**, and then in the **Number group**, click the **Comma Style** button. Click the **Decrease Decimal** button two times.
28. Select the range **A8:B13**. On the **INSERT tab**, in the **Charts group**, click the **Pie** button, and then point to the first chart—**2-D Pie**. Compare your screen with **Figure 6**, and then click the first chart.

    A contextual tab—the Chart Tools tab—displays on the ribbon.
29. Move the chart to approximately the range **A16:F30**.
30. To the right of the **Tell me what you want to do** box, click **OPEN IN EXCEL**. If prompted, click **OK** for the security warning, and then enter your ID and password.
31. If necessary, at the top of the screen, on the **Protected View** bar, click **Enable Editing**.

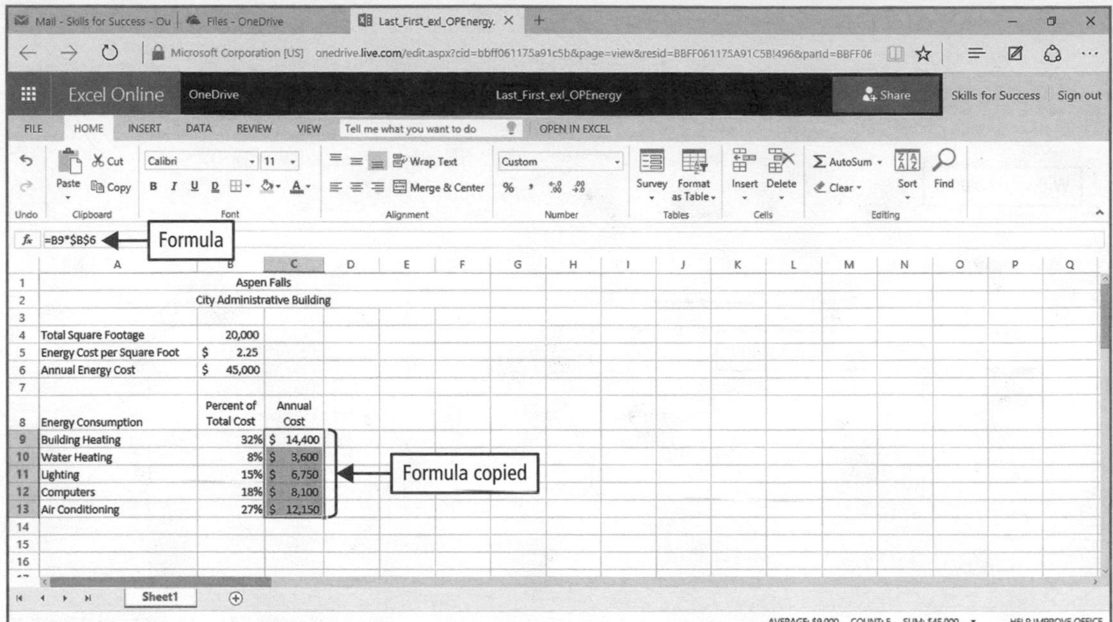

Figure 5

Excel 2016, Windows 10, Microsoft Corporation

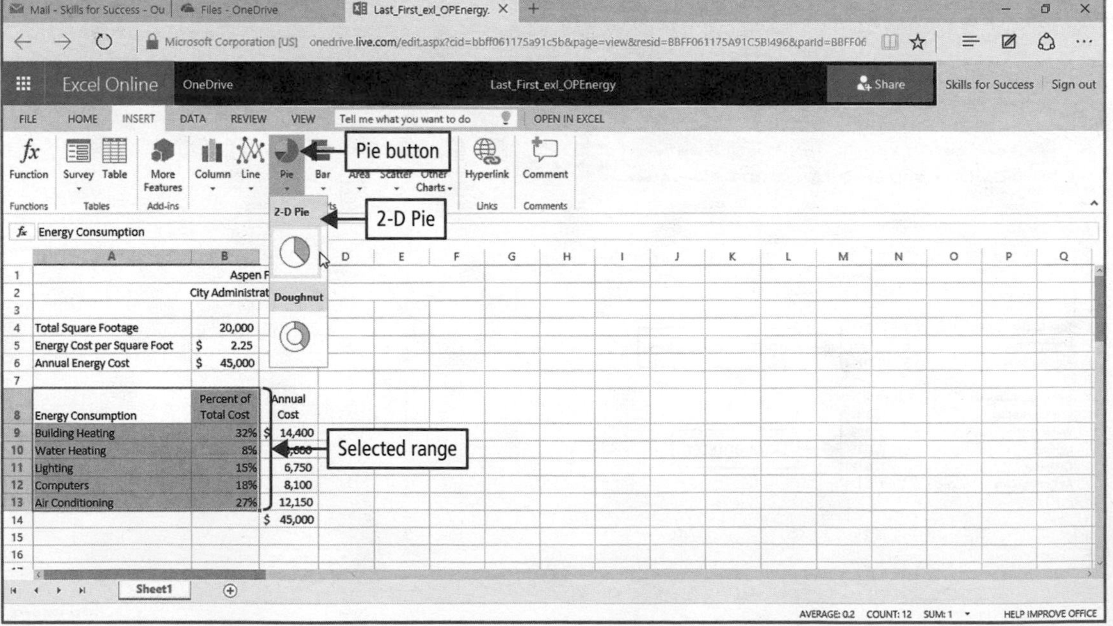

Figure 6

Excel 2016, Windows 10, Microsoft Corporation

■ **Continue to the next page to complete the project**

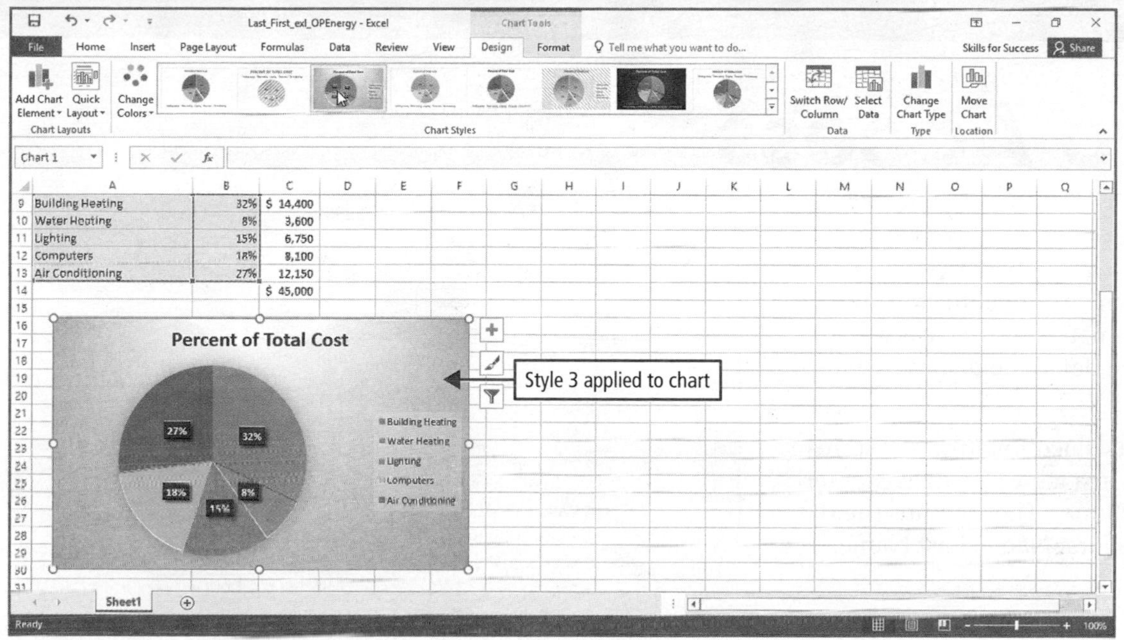

Excel 2016, Windows 10, Microsoft Corporation

Figure 7

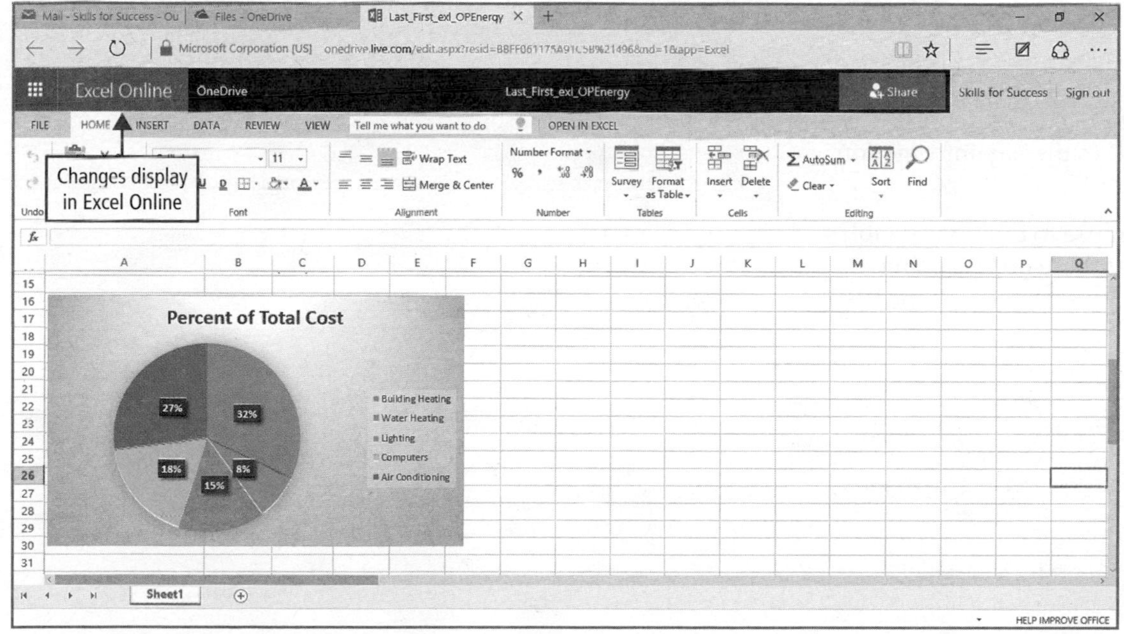

Excel 2016, Windows 10, Microsoft Corporation

Figure 8

32. Click cell **A1**. On the **HOME tab**, in the **Styles group**, click the **Cell Styles** button, and then click **Accent5**. In the **Font group**, click the **Font Size** button [11], and then click **14**. In the **Cells group**, click the **Format** button, and then click **Row Height**. In the **Row Height** dialog box, type 20 and then click **OK**.
33. Click cell **A2**. In the **Styles group**, click the **Cell Styles** button, and then click **40% - Accent5**. In the **Font group**, click the **Font Size** button [11], and then click **12**.
34. If necessary, scroll to view the chart. Click the chart, and then on the **Chart Tools Design tab**, in the **Chart Styles group**, click the third style—**Style 3**. Compare your screen with **Figure 7**.
35. Click the **REVIEW tab**. In the **Proofing group**, click the **Spelling** button to check and correct any spelling errors. **Save** the file, and then **Close** Excel.
36. On the **OneDrive** page, open the file in Excel Online. Scroll as necessary to compare your screen with **Figure 8**.

    The cell styles and the chart style 3 have been applied. Features not supported by Excel Online, such as styles, cannot be changed in the online application, but they can be viewed.
37. **Download** the file, and then **Save** the file to your chapter folder as Last_First_exl_OPEnergy or **Share** the file as directed by your instructor.
38. **Sign out** of your Microsoft account, and then **Close** the browser.

DONE! You have completed Excel Online Project

Introduction to Access

Microsoft Access is a ***database system***—a program used to both store and manage large amounts of data. In a database system, the ***database*** is a collection of structured tables designed to store the data. The data is managed using queries, forms, and reports.

Access tables organize data into rows and columns. Each row (record) stores data about each item in a collection. For example, in a table storing customer data, each row would represent an individual customer. The columns (fields) organize the types of data being collected, such as First Name, Last Name, Street, or City.

You can build a database from scratch or use one of the prebuilt templates provided by Microsoft. You can also add prebuilt tables, fields, and forms to an existing database.

After designing the tables, you are ready to enter data. Forms are built so that others can type the data quickly and accurately. You can also import data from other programs.

Queries are used to answer questions about the data. They filter and sort the data to display the information that answers these questions. Reports can be based on either tables or queries and are created to display information effectively.

Access has several wizards and views that you can use to build your tables, forms, queries, and reports quickly. You can format these objects using techniques similar to other Office programs.

Table field captions

Shelters

Shelter ID	Shelter Name	Park	Click to Add
1	Group Area A	Wiyot	
2	Central Picnic Area	Silver Lake	
3	Shelter East	Sunset Meadows	
4	Group Area A	Roosevelt	
5	Observation Point	Kellermann	
6	Willow Shelter	Aspen Falls Lake	
7	Franklin Shelter	Roosevelt	
8	Shelter in the Woods	Cedar Creek	
9	Aspen Shelter	Aspen Falls Lake	
10	Shelter North	Silver Lake	
11	Veteran's Picnic Area	Sunset Meadows	
12	Poplar Shelter	Aspen Falls Lake	
13	Manor Picnic Area	Squires Lake	
14	Eleanor Shelter	Roosevelt	
15	Group Area A	Cedar Creek	
16	Upriver Shelter	Yurok	
17	Group Area B	Wiyot	
18	Downriver Shelter	Yurok	
19	Shelter South	Silver Lake	
20	Group Area B	Cedar Creek	
21	Group Area C	Roosevelt	
22	Shelter West	Silver Lake	

Table record

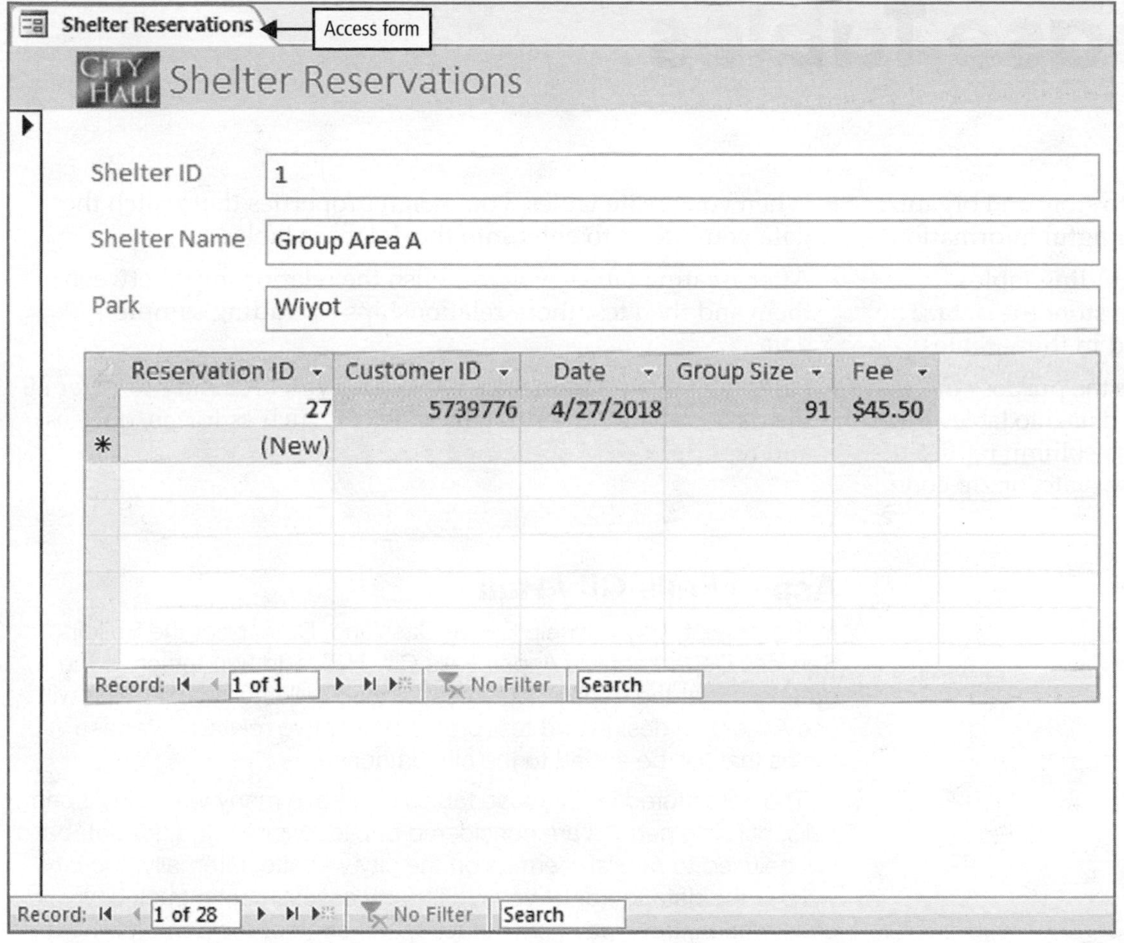

Shelter Reservations
Access form
City Hall
Shelter Reservations
Shelter ID
1
Shelter Name
Group Area A
Park
Wiyot
Reservation ID
Customer ID
Date
Group Size
Fee
27
5739776
4/27/2018
91
$45.50
(New)
Record: 1 of 1
No Filter
Search
Record: 1 of 28
No Filter
Search

CHAPTER 1

Create Database Tables

- Microsoft Office Access is an application used to store and organize data, and access and display that data as meaningful information.
- A single Access file contains many objects including tables, forms, queries, and reports. Tables are used to store the data. The other objects are used to access the data stored in those tables.
- When you create a database, you first determine the purpose of the database. You can then plan how to organize the data into tables. Each row in the table represents one record, and each column represents common characteristics of the data, such as city, state, or zip code.
- When you create tables, you assign properties that match the data you intend to enter into the database tables.
- After creating tables, you establish the relationships between them and then test those relationships by adding sample data.
- After the table relationships are tested, you are ready to enter all the data and add other database objects such as forms, queries, and reports.

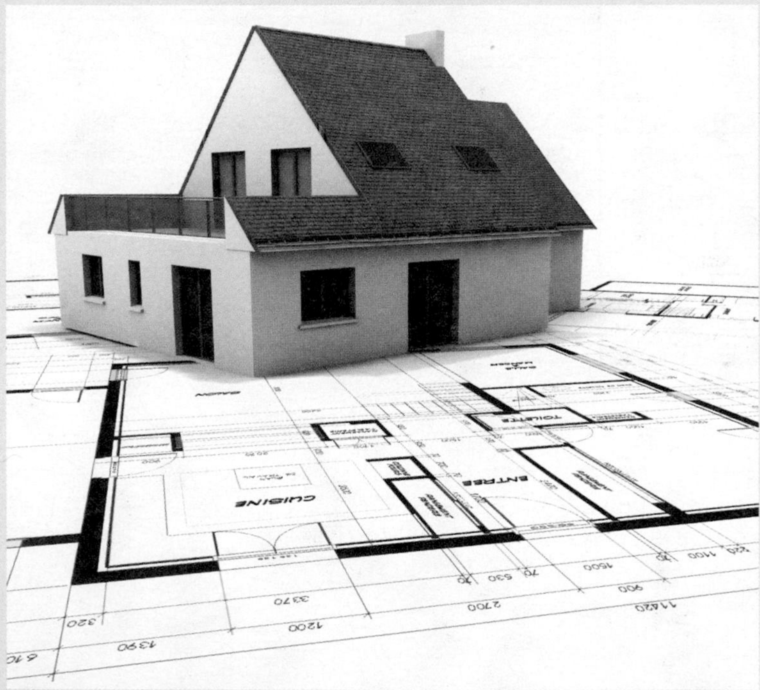

Aspen Falls City Hall

In this project, you will help Sadye Cassiano, Director of the Building Services Department of Aspen Falls City Hall, add two tables to the database that the department uses to track building permits. You will use Access to design and test prototypes of two related database tables that will be added to the city database.

The data stored in database tables is used in many ways. In Aspen Falls, building permits are considered public records, and the database will be used to publish permits on the city website. Internally, the city will use the data to adjust yearly property assessments, track city construction, track payments of fees, and contact the person filing a building permit. All of these tasks can be accomplished by accessing two tables in the database in different ways. Thus, the tables are the foundation of a database.

In this project, you will create a new database and then create one table in Datasheet view and a second table in Design view. In both tables you will add fields and assign properties to those fields, and create a relationship between the two tables. You will add data to one table by typing the data and add data to the second table by importing it from an Excel spreadsheet. Finally, you will use Datasheet view to filter, sort, format, and print the tables.

Outcome

Using the skills in this chapter, you will be able create a database, create tables and fields, edit field properties, import data into tables, filter and sort table records, and create table relationships.

Objectives

1.1 Create tables in different database views

1.2 Relate tables in a database

1.3 Manipulate data in tables

1.4 Format and import data in a database

Student data file needed for this chapter:

acc01_PermitsData (Excel)

You will save your files as:

Last_First_acc01_Permits (Access)
Last_First_acc01_PermitsData (Excel)

SKILLS

At the end of this chapter you will be able to:

Skill 1 Create Databases
Skill 2 Create Tables in Datasheet View
Skill 3 Enter Data into Datasheets
Skill 4 Create Tables in Design View
Skill 5 Relate Tables
Skill 6 Enter Data in Related Tables
Skill 7 Import Data into Tables
Skill 8 Filter and Sort Datasheets
Skill 9 Format Datasheets
Skill 10 Preview and Print Datasheets

MORE SKILLS

Skill 11 Compact and Repair Databases
Skill 12 Work with the Long Text Data Type
Skill 13 Work with the Attachment Data Type
Skill 14 Work with the Hyperlink and Yes/No Data Types

Permits

Permit Number	Start Date	Project Title	Location	Fee	Click to Add
B8756215ELEC	7/24/2017	REMODEL MALASKY RESIDENCE	4863 S Biltmore Av	$54.23	
B5666375ELEC	7/24/2017	ADDITION JAPP RESIDENCE	8493 N Bannock St	$44.20	
B3680115ELEC	7/24/2017	REMODEL AHRENDES RESIDENCE	3858 S Glenn Brook Pl	$51.79	
B1684124ELEC	7/24/2017	REMODEL HARTNETT RESIDENCE	8147 S 5Th St	$49.32	
B3849977ELEC	7/29/2017	ADDITION BRANDL RESIDENCE	6031 S Hinsdale Ct	$53.79	
B1090716ELEC	7/29/2017	REMODEL CUBIT RESIDENCE	3674 W Teabrook Av	$74.50	
B9568069ELEC	8/1/2017	ADDITION TRIEU RESIDENCE	8668 E Hopkirk Av	$55.06	
B4824848ELEC	8/1/2017	REMODEL MIYAGAWA RESIDENCE	515 E Birch	$64.67	
*				$0.00	

Access 2016, Windows 10, Microsoft Corporation

- When you start Access, the start screen displays so that you can either open an existing database or create a new blank database.
- Before you create a new database, you assign a name and location for the database file.

1. Start **Access 2016**, and then compare your screen with **Figure 1**.

   On the Access start screen, you can create a database from a template, open a recent database, or create a blank database.

Obj 1.1.1

2. On the Access start page, click **Blank desktop database**. In the **Blank desktop database** dialog box, using your own name, replace the suggested **File Name** with Last_First_acc01_Permits
3. To the right of the **File Name** box, click the **Browse** button to open the File New Database dialog box.
4. In the **File New Database** dialog box, navigate to the location where you will be saving your work for this chapter.
5. In the **File New Database** dialog box, click **New folder**, and then type Access Chapter 1 Press Enter two times to create and open the new folder. Compare your screen with **Figure 2**.

   The Microsoft Access 2007 - 2016 file format is the default file format for Access 2016.

■ Continue to the next page to complete the skill

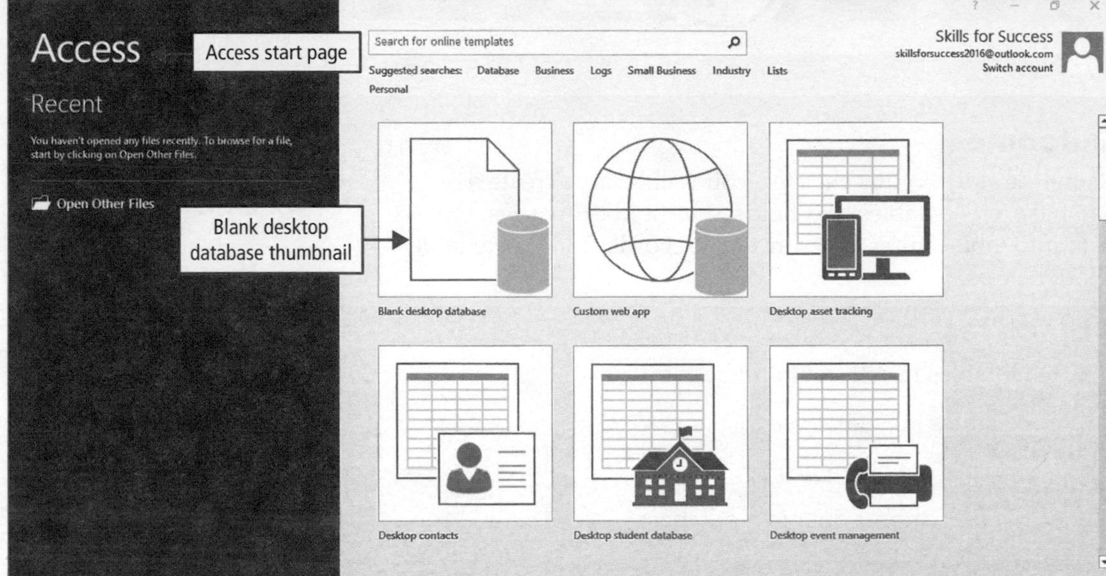

Figure 1 Access 2016, Windows 10, Microsoft Corporation

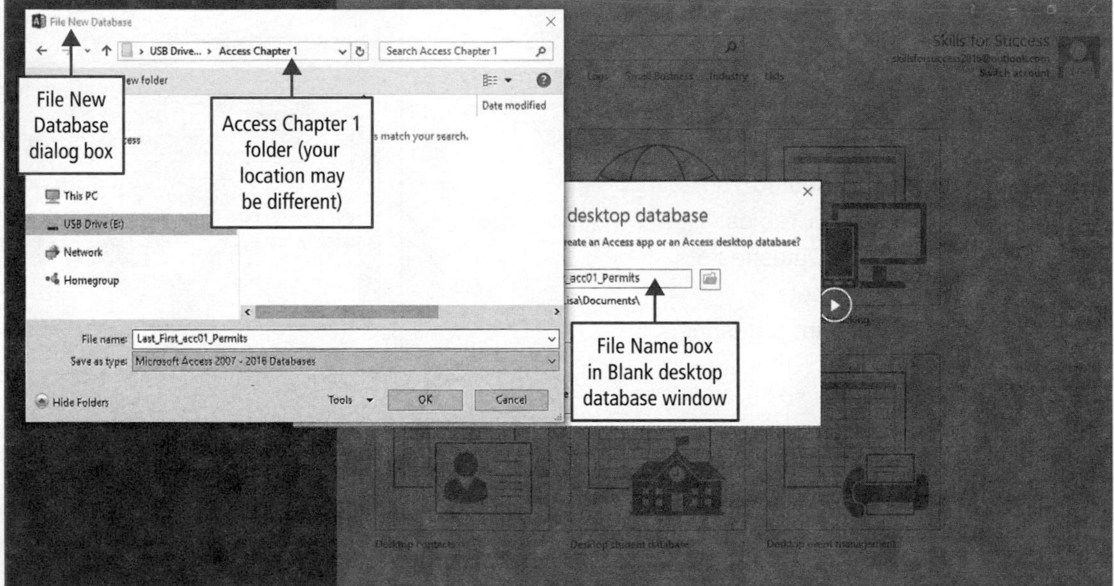

Figure 2 Access 2016, Windows 10, Microsoft Corporation

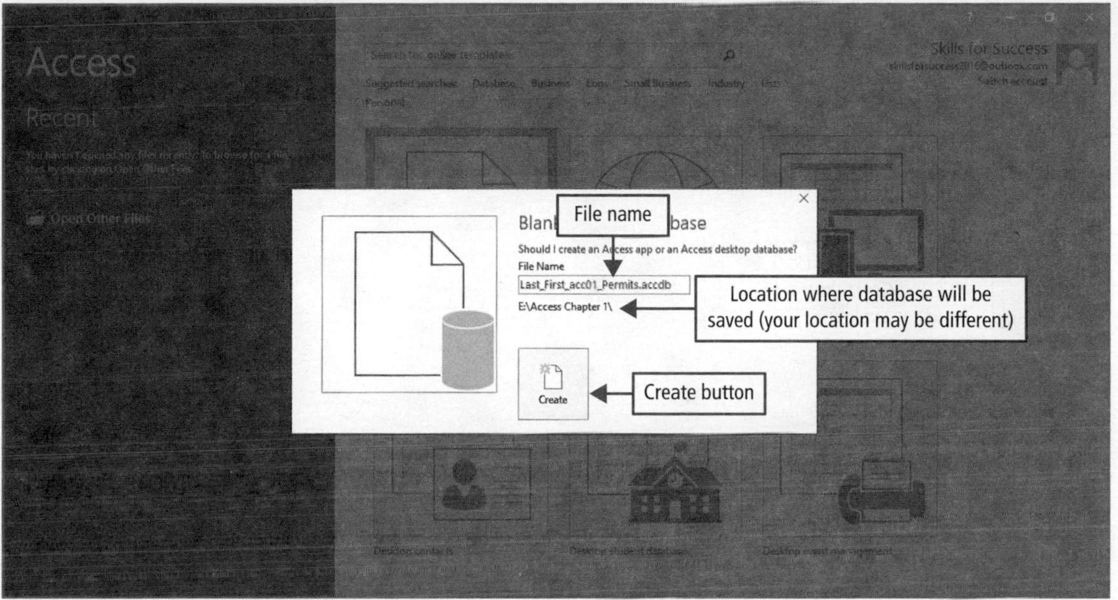

Access 2016, Windows 10, Microsoft Corporation

Figure 3

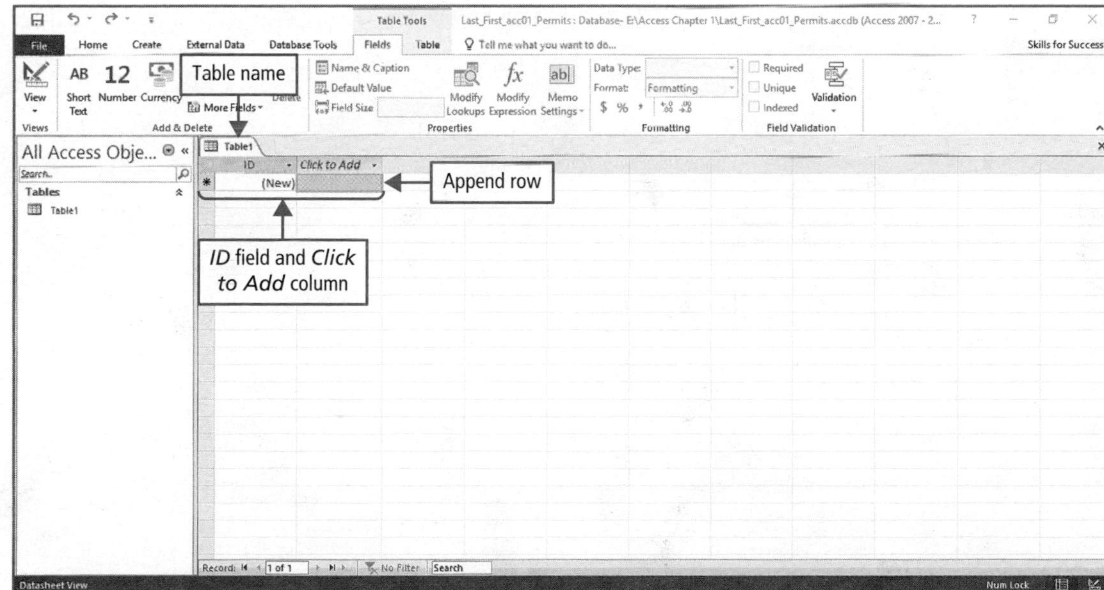

Access 2016, Windows 10, Microsoft Corporation

Figure 4

6. Click **OK** to accept the changes and close the **File New Database** dialog box.
7. Compare your screen with **Figure 3**, and then click the **Create** button.
8. Take a few moments to familiarize yourself with the Access window as described below and in **Figure 4**.

   When you create a blank database, a new table is automatically generated. The name *Table1* is temporarily assigned to the table, and the first column—*ID*—is the name of a ***field***—a common characteristic of the data that the table will describe, such as city, state, or postal code.

   Database ***tables*** are objects that store data by organizing it into rows and columns and are displayed in ***datasheets***. In a datasheet, each row is a ***record***—a collection of related data such as the contact information for a person. Each column is a field that each record will store such as city, state, or postal code.

   Table1 currently displays in ***Datasheet view***—a view that features the data but also has contextual tabs on the Ribbon so that you can change the table's design. In Datasheet view, the last row of the table is the ***append row***—the last row of a datasheet into which a new record is entered. *Table1* currently has no data.
9. Leave the table open for the next skill.

■ **You have completed Skill 1 of 10**

 WATCH SKILL 1.2

- When you design a table, you add field names and their properties.
- ***Data type*** is a field property that specifies the type of information that a field will contain; for example, text, number, date, or currency.

MOS Obj 2.1.1

1. In **Table1**, click the **ID** column header. On the **Fields tab**, in the **Properties group**, click **Name & Caption**. Replace the **Name** box value with ContractorID and then in the **Caption** box, type Contractor ID (include a space between the two words).
2. Compare your screen with **Figure 1**, and then click **OK**.

   Contractor ID—the field's caption—displays at the top of the column and is slightly truncated. You will widen the column in a later step. ***Captions*** determine what displays in all datasheet, form, and report labels. Actual field names should not contain spaces, but changing the caption to include spaces improves readability of forms, datasheets, and reports.

MOS Obj 2.4.1

3. In the second column, click the text ***Click to Add***, and then from the list of data types, click **Short Text**. Type CompanyName and then press Enter to move to the next column.

   The ***Short Text data type*** stores up to 255 characters of text.
4. On the **Fields tab**, in the **Add & Delete group**, click the **More Fields** button. Scroll to the last list of data types, click **Name**, and then compare your screen with **Figure 2**.

   Quick Start fields are a set of fields that can be added with a single click. For example, the Name Quick Start data type inserts the LastName and FirstName fields, assigns the Text data type, and adds a caption with a space between the two words.

■ Continue to the next page to complete the skill

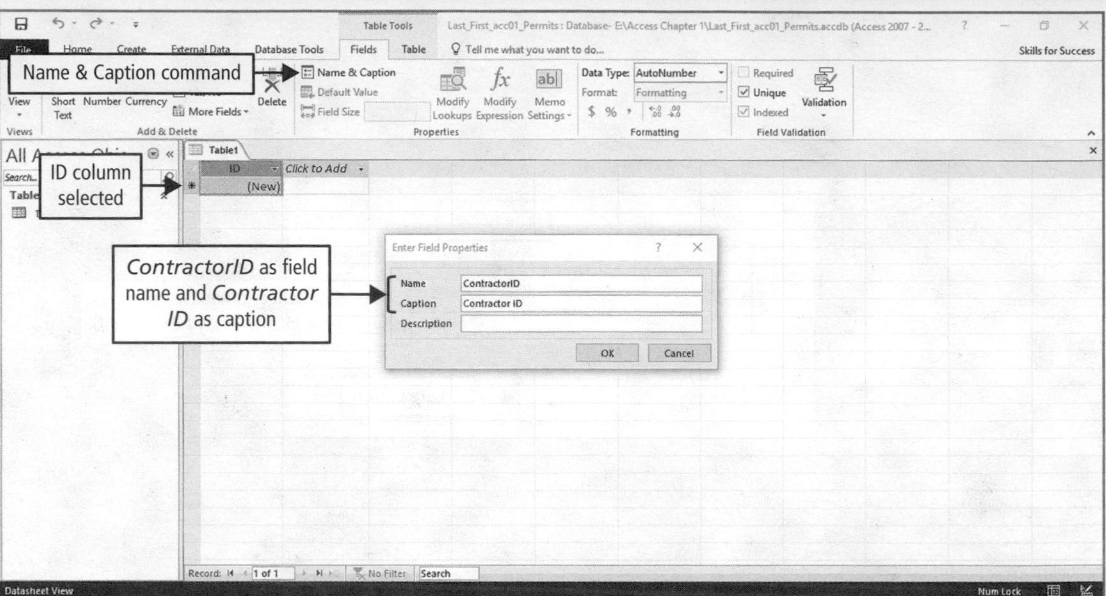

Figure 1

Access 2016, Windows 10, Microsoft Corporation

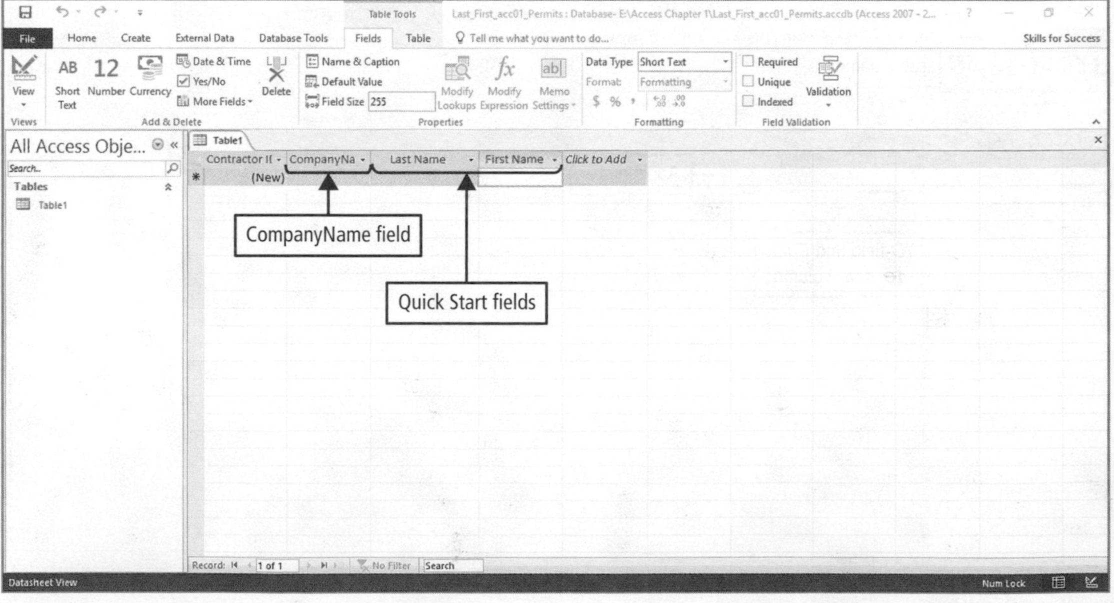

Figure 2

Access 2016, Windows 10, Microsoft Corporation

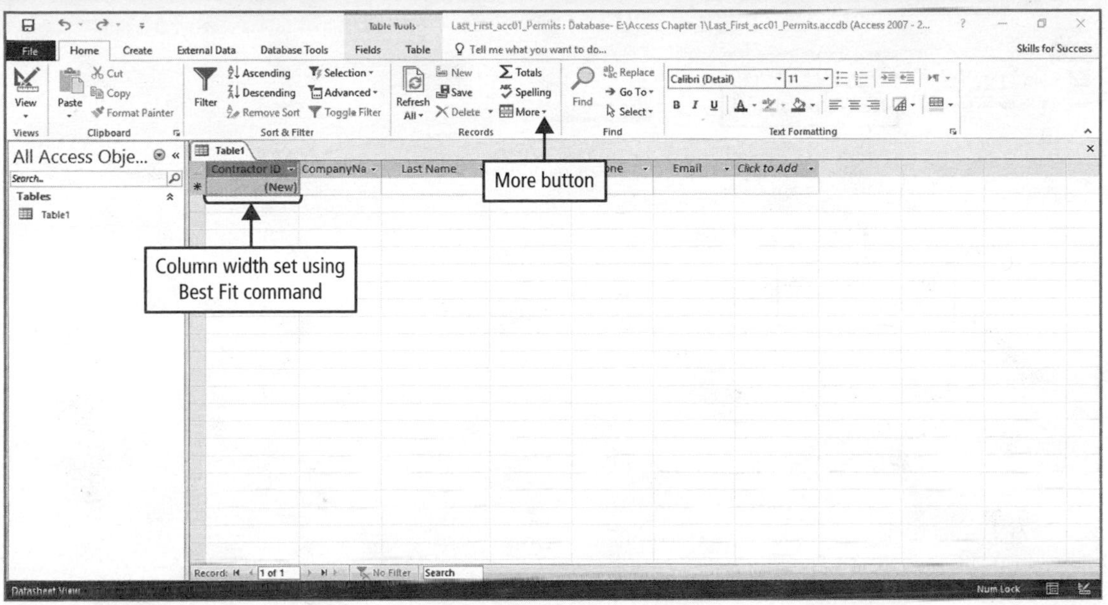

Access 2016, Windows 10, Microsoft Corporation

Figure 3

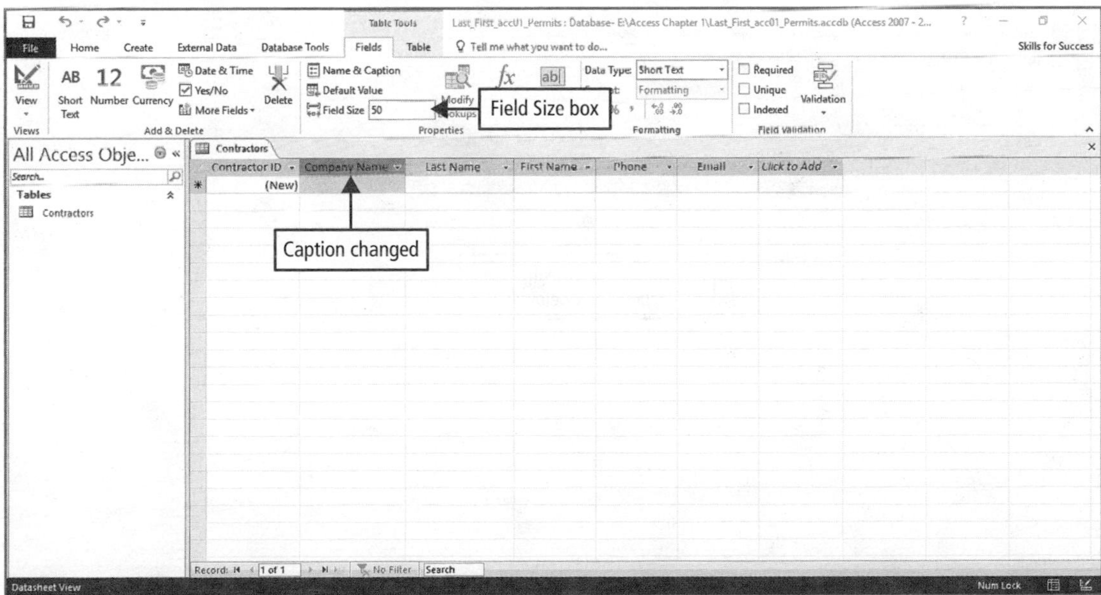

Access 2016, Windows 10, Microsoft Corporation

Figure 4

5. Click in the last column—*Click to Add*, and then click **Short Text**. Type Phone and then press Enter.
6. Repeat the technique just practiced to add a field name Email with the **Short Text** data type.
7. In the header row, click in the **Contractor ID** column. Click the **Home tab**. In the **Records group**, click **More**, and then click **Field Width**. In the **Column Width** dialog box, click **Best Fit**. Compare your screen with **Figure 3**.

   Column widths can be changed to match the width of their contents. As you add data, the widths may need to be adjusted.
8. Repeat the technique just practiced to adjust the **CompanyName** column width.
9. If necessary, click **CompanyName** to select the column, and then click the **Fields tab**. In the **Properties group**, change the **Field Size** value to 50

   MOS Obj 2.4.4

   Field size limits the number of characters that can be typed into a text or number field.
10. Click **Save**. In the **Save As** dialog box, type Contractors and then click **OK**.

    When you save a table that you have added or changed, its name displays in the Navigation Pane, and it becomes part of the database file.
11. With the CompanyName field selected, in the **Properties group**, click **Name & Caption**. Type the **Caption** Company Name and then click **OK**. Compare your screen with **Figure 4**.

    MOS Obj 2.4.3
12. Repeat the technique just practiced to change the **Field Size** property of the **Last Name**, **First Name**, **Phone**, and **Email** fields to 50 and then click **Save**.

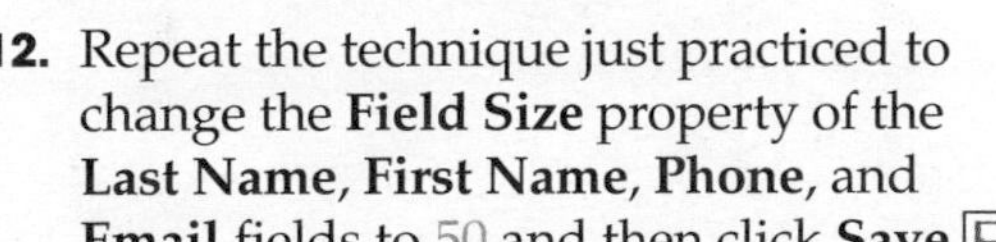

■ **You have completed Skill 2 of 10**

► When you are designing and building database tables, it is a good idea to enter some of the data that they will store. In this way, the design can be tested and adjusted if needed.

Obj 2.3.2

1. In the **Contractors** table datasheet, in the append row, click the first empty **Company Name** cell, and then type Front Poarch Construction Compare your screen with **Figure 1**.

   As soon as you enter data in the append row, it becomes a record, and the append row displays below the new record.

2. Press Enter to accept the data entry and move to the next column. Type Poarch Press Enter, and then in the **First Name** column, type Ken

3. Continue in this manner to enter the **Phone** number, (805) 555-7721 and the **Email** address, poarch.ken@poarchcontractors.com

4. Press Enter to finish the record and move the insertion point to the append row. Compare your screen with **Figure 2**.

   When you move to a different record or append row, the new or changed data is automatically saved to the database file on your storage device.

■ **Continue to the next page to complete the skill**

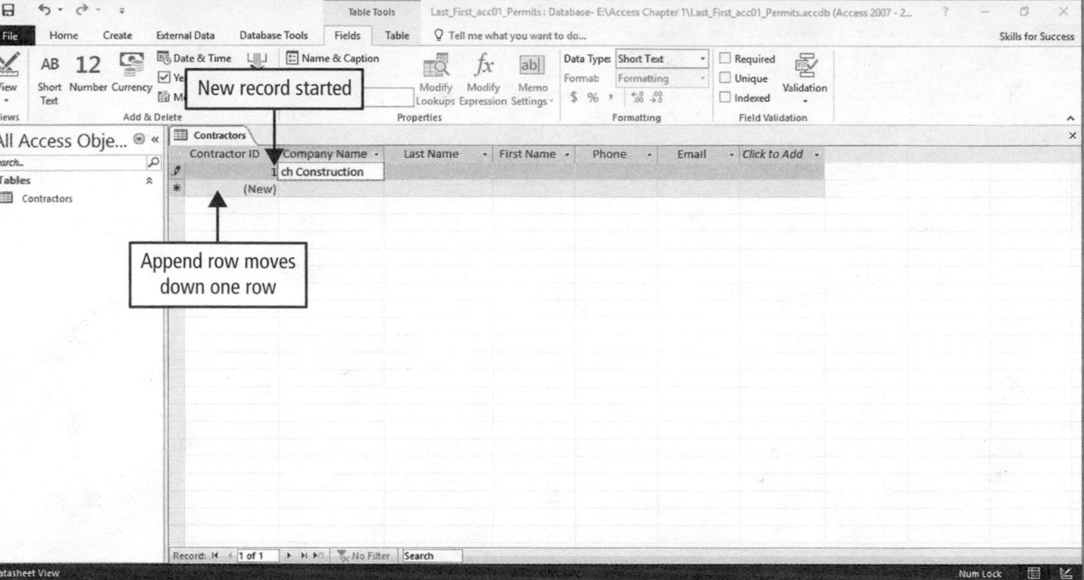

Figure 1

Access 2016, Windows 10, Microsoft Corporation

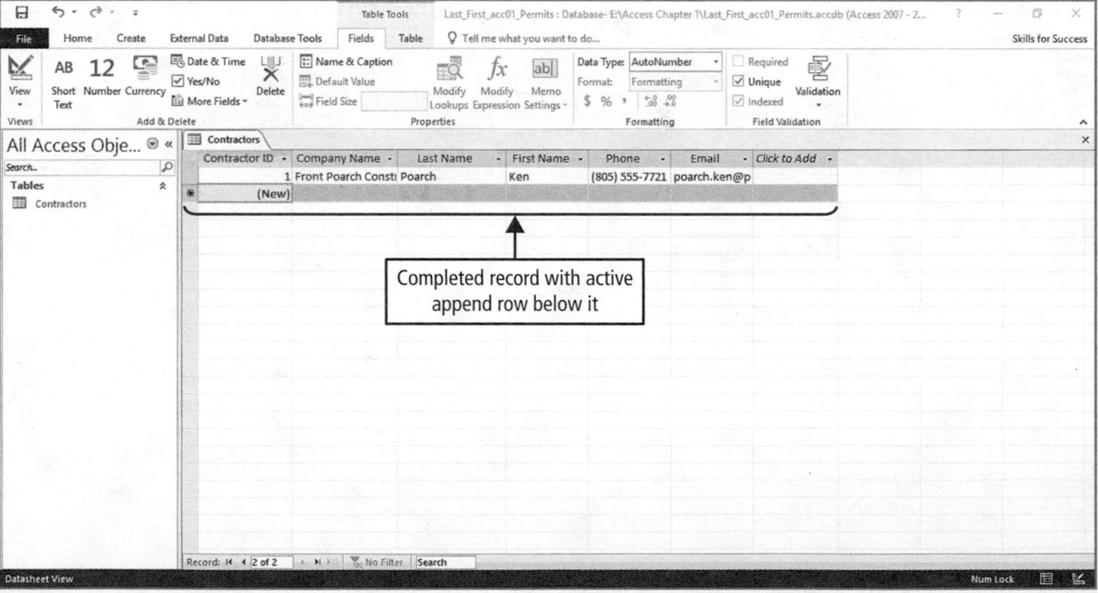

Figure 2

Access 2016, Windows 10, Microsoft Corporation

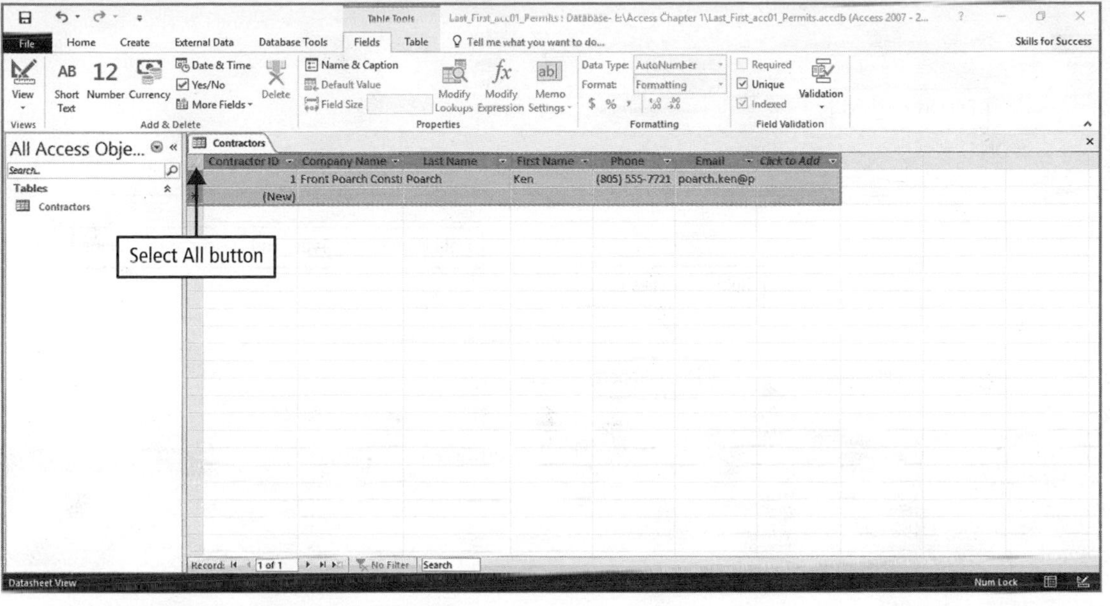

Access 2016, Windows 10, Microsoft Corporation

Figure 3

CompanyName	Last Name	First Name	Phone	Email
Front Poarch Construction	*Poarch*	*Ken*	*(805) 555-7721*	*poarch.ken@poarchconstruction.com*
Mikrot Construction	Mikrot	Kim	(805) 555-6795	kmikrot@mikrot.com
Sobata Contractors	Sobata	Jeri	(805) 555-4789	jeri@sobatacon.com
(leave blank)	Jestis	Mee	(805) 555-8506	mee.jestis@jestisandsons.com
Degasparre Remodelers	Degasparre	Artur	(805) 555-0770	artur@degasparre.com

Figure 4

5. To the left of the **Contractor ID** column heading, click the **Select All** button. Compare your screen with **Figure 3**.

   ContractorID is the table's ***primary key***—a field that uniquely identifies each record in a table. Primary key field names often include *ID* to help you identify them.

6. With all the cells still selected, repeat the technique practiced previously to apply **Best Fit** to the column widths.

   By selecting the entire datasheet, you can adjust column widths quickly. If your window is sized smaller than the datasheet, columns that are not in view will not be adjusted. You can adjust them by first maximizing the Access window or by scrolling to display them.

7. Starting with *Mikrot Construction*, add the records shown in the table in **Figure 4**. For the **Contractor ID**, accept the AutoNumber values.

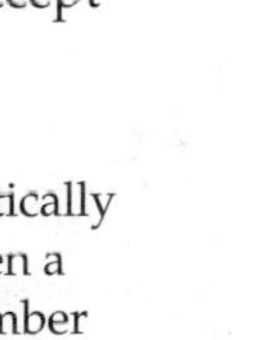

   The ContractorID data type is ***AutoNumber***—a field that automatically enters a unique, numeric value when a record is created. Once an AutoNumber value has been assigned, it cannot be changed. If your AutoNumber values differ from the ones shown in this chapter's figures, you do not need to change them.

8. Click **Save**, and then **Close** the table.

   When you close a database table, the database does not close. If you accidentally close the database, reopen it to continue.

■ **You have completed Skill 3 of 10**

- An alternate method for creating a table is to create it in ***Table Design view***—a view that features table fields and their properties.

1. Click the **Create tab**, and then in the **Tables group**, click the **Table Design** button.
2. With the insertion point in the **Field Name** column's first row, type PermitID and then press Enter to automatically assign the Short Text data type.

Obj 1.2.2

3. On the **Design tab**, in the **Tools group**, click **Primary Key**.
4. In the **Field Properties** pane, change the **Field Size** value to 50 and the **Caption** to Permit Number Compare your screen with **Figure 1**.

   When working with a table in Design view, the Field Name, Data Type, and Description data are entered in rows. Other field properties are entered in the Field Properties pane.

5. Click in the next blank **Field Name** box, and then type StartDate
6. Press Enter, click the **Data Type arrow**, and then click **Date/Time**. In the **Field Properties** pane, click the **Format** box, click the **Format arrow** that displays, and then click **Short Date**. Add the **Caption** property Start Date and then compare your screen with **Figure 2**.

   The ***Date/Time data type*** stores serial numbers that are converted and formatted as dates or times.

7. Add a third field named ProjectTitle with the **Short Text** data type and the **Caption** property Project Title
8. Add a fourth field named Location with the **Short Text** data type.

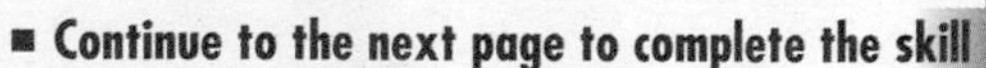
■ Continue to the next page to complete the skill

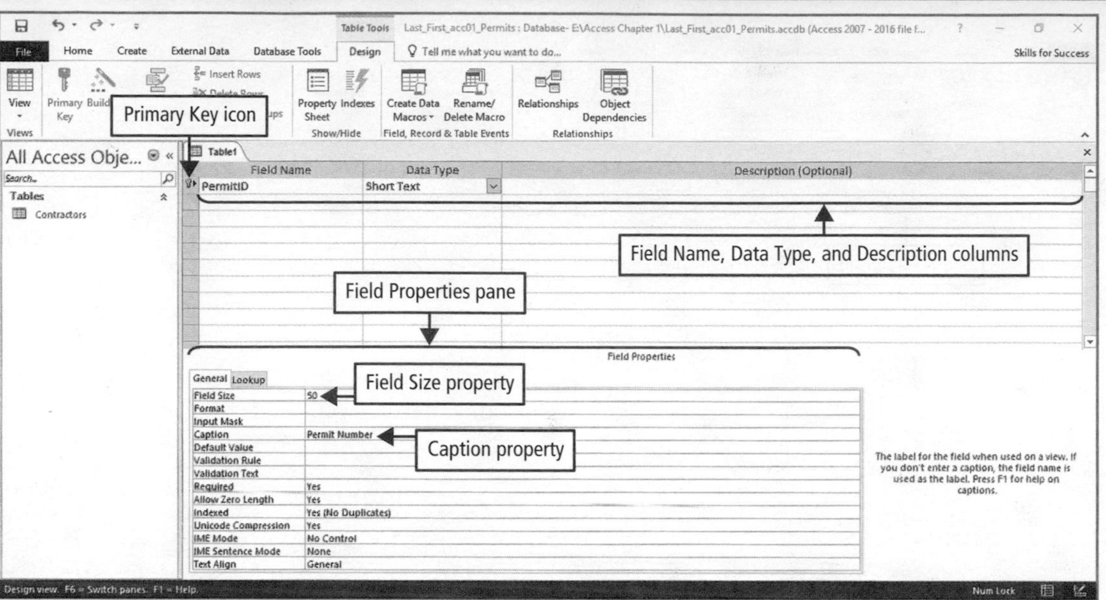

Figure 1 Access 2016, Windows 10, Microsoft Corporation

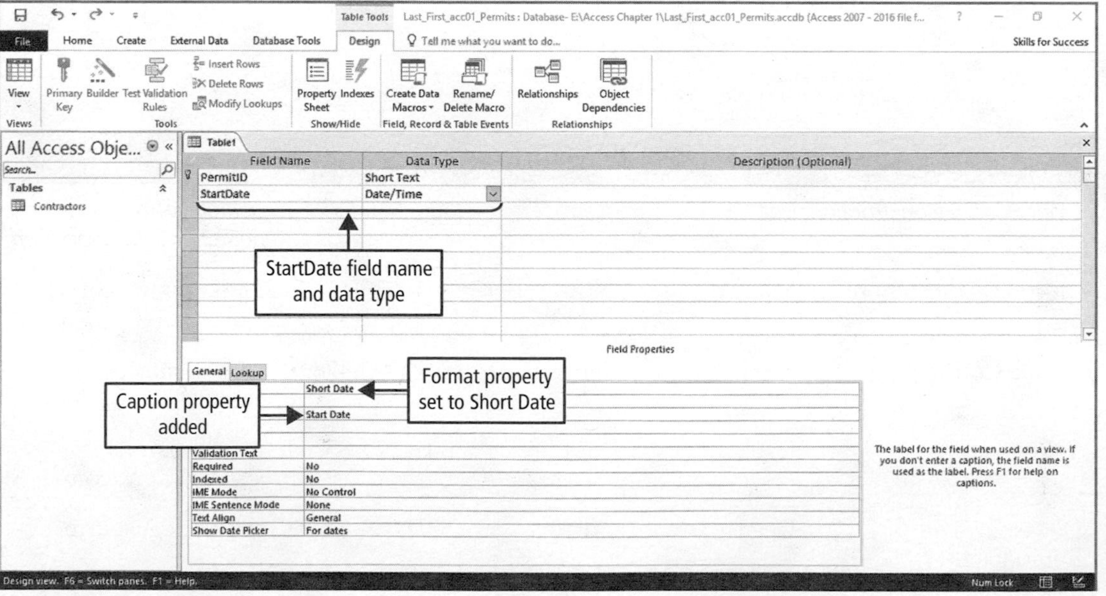

Figure 2 Access 2016, Windows 10, Microsoft Corporation

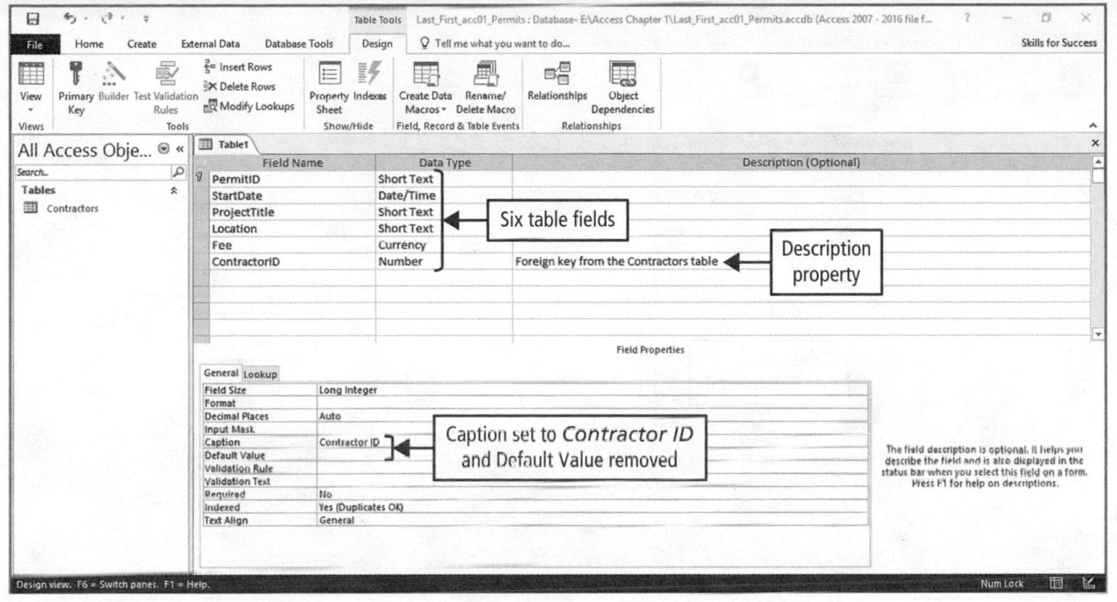

Access 2016, Windows 10, Microsoft Corporation

Figure 3

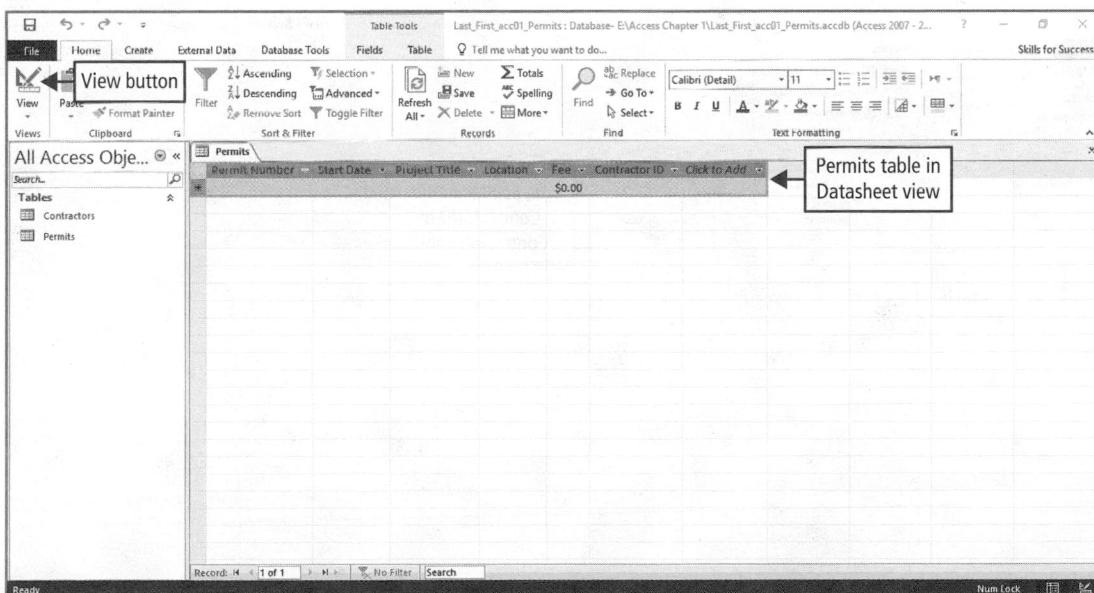

Access 2016, Windows 10, Microsoft Corporation

Figure 4

9. Add a fifth field named Fee with the **Currency** data type. Do not change any other field properties.

   The ***Currency data type*** stores numbers formatted as monetary values.

MOS Obj 1.2.4

10. Add a sixth field named ContractorID with the **Number** data type and the caption Contractor ID In the **Default Value** box, delete the *0*.

    The ***Number data type*** stores numeric values.

11. In the **ContractorID Description** box, type Foreign key from the Contractors table Compare your screen with **Figure 3**.

    A ***foreign key*** is a field that is used to relate records in a second related table. The foreign key field is often the second table's primary key. Here, ContractorID is the primary key of the Contractors table. The ContractorID field will be used to join this table to the Contractors table.

    When you join tables, the common fields must share the same data type. Because the Contractors table automatically assigns a number in the ContractorID field, the foreign key field should be assigned the Number data type.

12. Click **Save** [Save icon]. In the **Save As** dialog box, type Permits and then click **OK**.

13. On the **Design tab**, in the **Views group**, click the **View** button to switch to Datasheet view. Click the **Select All** button [Select All icon], and then adjust the column widths to **Best Fit**. Compare your screen with **Figure 4**.

14. **Save** [Save icon] and then **Close** [Close icon] the table.

■ **You have completed Skill 4 of 10**

- Records in two tables can be related by placing the same field in both tables and then creating a relationship between the common fields.

Obj 1.2.5

1. Click the **Database Tools tab**, and then in the **Relationships group**, click the **Relationships** button to display the Relationships tab and Show Table dialog box.

   If the Show Table dialog box does not display, you can open it by clicking the Show Table button in the Relationships group.

2. In the **Show Table** dialog box, double-click **Permits** to add it to the Relationships tab. In the **Show Table** dialog box, double-click **Contractors**. Alternately, you can add tables to the Relationships tab by dragging them from the Navigation Pane.
3. Compare your screen with **Figure 1**, and then close the Show Table dialog box.

Obj 1.2.1

4. From the **Permits** table, drag the **ContractorID** field to the **ContractorID** field in the **Contractors** table. When the Access Relationship pointer displays, as shown in **Figure 2**, release the mouse button.

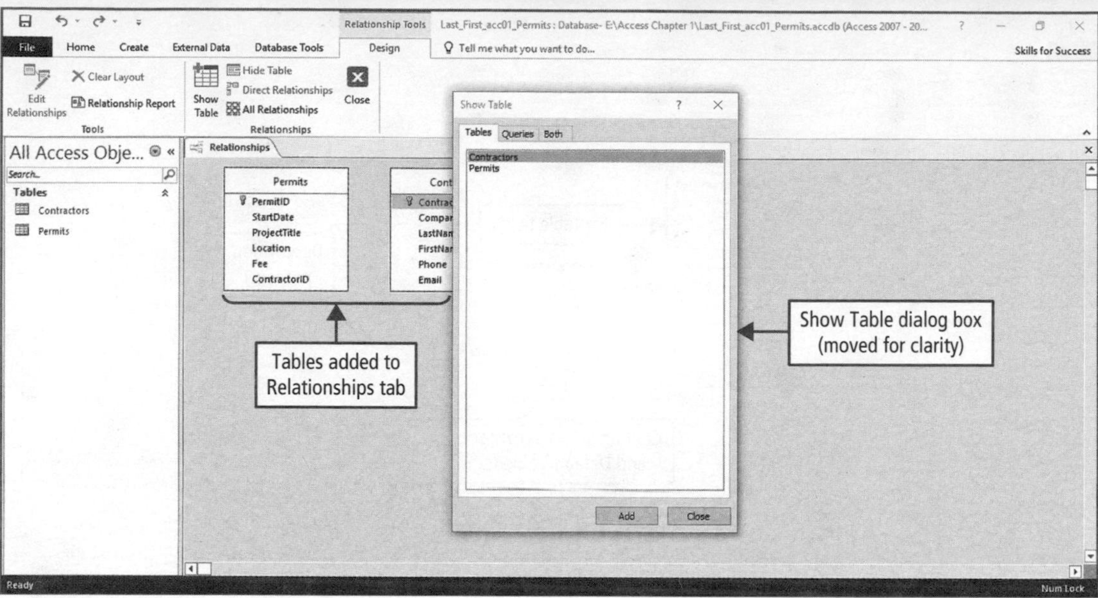

Figure 1

Access 2016, Windows 10, Microsoft Corporation

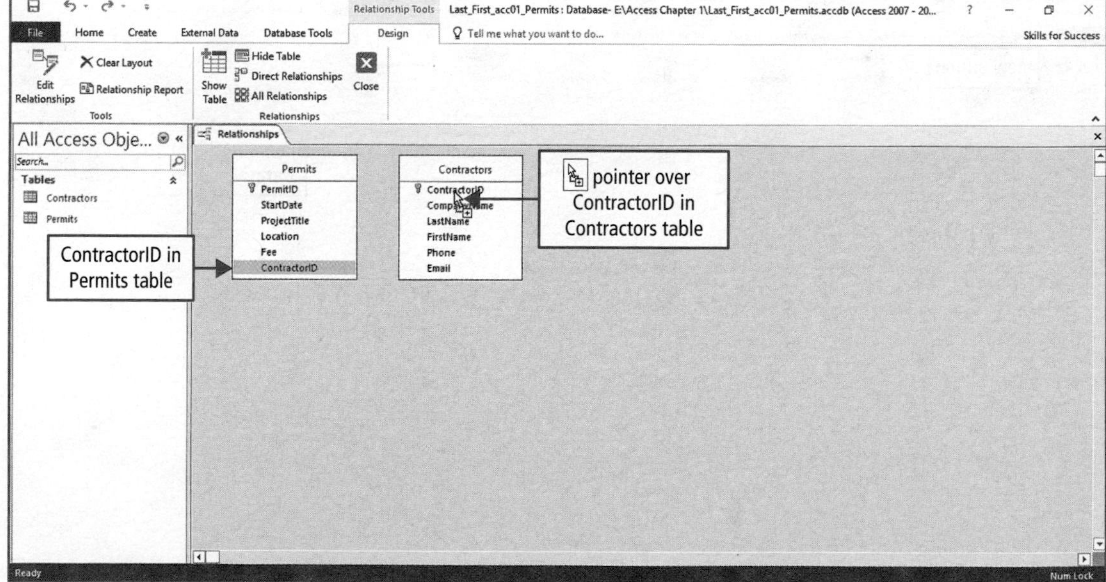

Figure 2

Access 2016, Windows 10, Microsoft Corporation

■ **Continue to the next page to complete the skill**

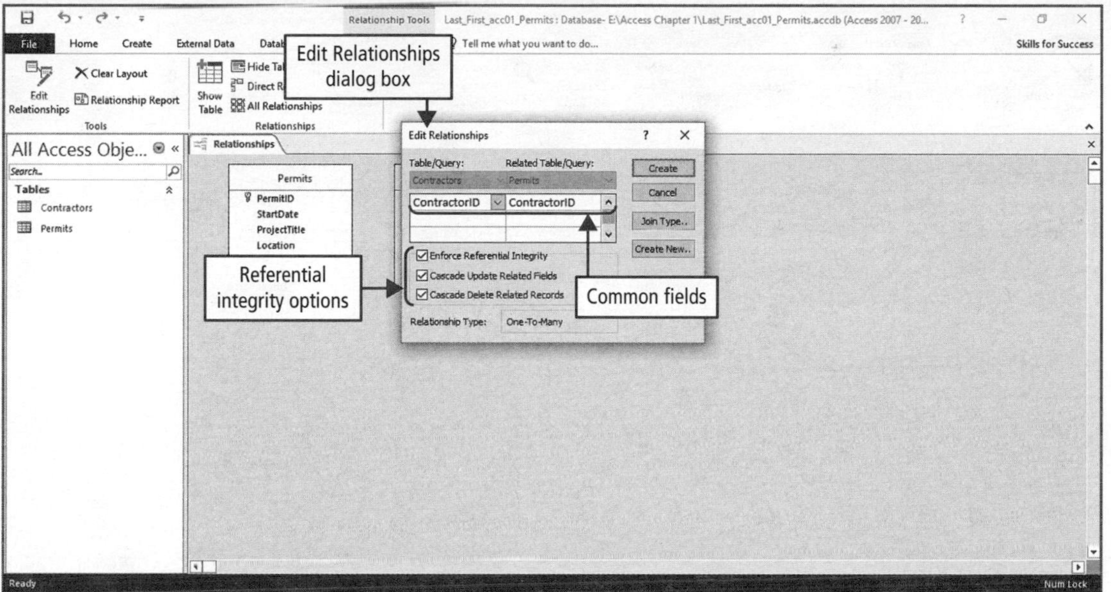

Access 2016, Windows 10, Microsoft Corporation

Figure 3

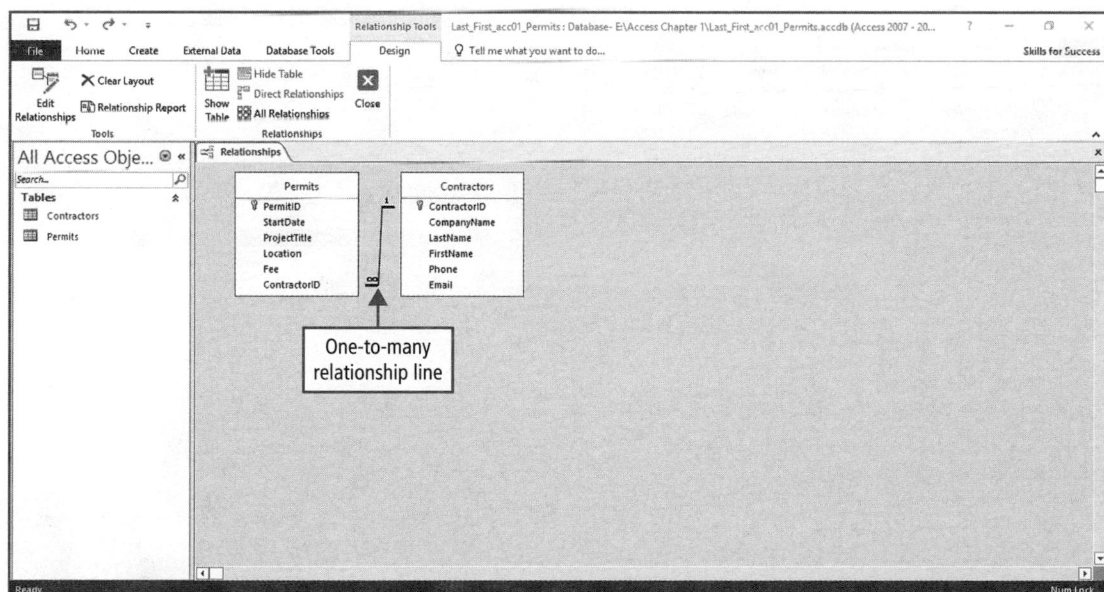

Access 2016, Windows 10, Microsoft Corporation

Figure 4

5. In the **Edit Relationships** dialog box, select the **Enforce Referential Integrity** check box. Select the **Cascade Update Related Fields** and **Cascade Delete Related Records** check boxes, and then compare your screen with **Figure 3**.

Obj 1.2.3

   Tables are typically joined in a ***one-to-many relationship***—a relationship in which a record in the first table can have many associated records in the second table.

   Referential integrity is a rule that keeps related values synchronized. For example, the foreign key value must be present in the related table. This option must be selected to create a one-to-many relationship.

   With a ***cascading update***, if you edit the primary key values in a table, all the related records in the other table will update accordingly.

   With a ***cascading delete***, you can delete a record on the *one* side of the relationship, and all the related records on the *many* side will also be deleted.

6. Click **Create**, and then compare your screen with **Figure 4**.
7. Click **Save** [Save]. On the **Design tab**, in the **Tools group**, click the **Relationship Report** button to create a report showing the database relationships.
8. If your instructor asks you to print your work for this chapter, print the report.
9. Click **Save** [Save], and then click **OK**. **Close** [X] the report, and then **Close** [X] the Relationships tab.

■ **You have completed Skill 5 of 10**

- When you enter data in related tables, referential integrity rules are applied. For example, a foreign key value must have a matching value in the related table.
- A ***subdatasheet*** displays related records from another table by matching the values in the field that relates the two tables. For example, all the permits issued to each contractor can be listed by matching the ContractorID value assigned to that permit.

1. In the **Navigation Pane**, double-click **Contractors** to open its datasheet.
2. Locate the record for Mee Jestis (Jestis, Mee), click the **Expand** button ⊞, and then compare your screen with **Figure 1**.

   When a table is on the *one* side of a relationship, a subdatasheet is available. Here, no permits have been issued to this contractor.

3. In the subdatasheet append row, under **Permit Number**, type B1018504RFSW
4. In the same record, under **Start Date**, click the cell, and then click the **Date Picker** button that displays. In the **Date Picker**, click the **Today** button.

   Fields that have been assigned the Date/Time data type display a Date Picker when they are selected.

5. In the same record, enter a **Project Title** of REMODEL CHITTESTER RESIDENCE a **Location** of 6088 W Devon Way and a **Fee** of $217.71 Compare your screen with **Figure 2**.

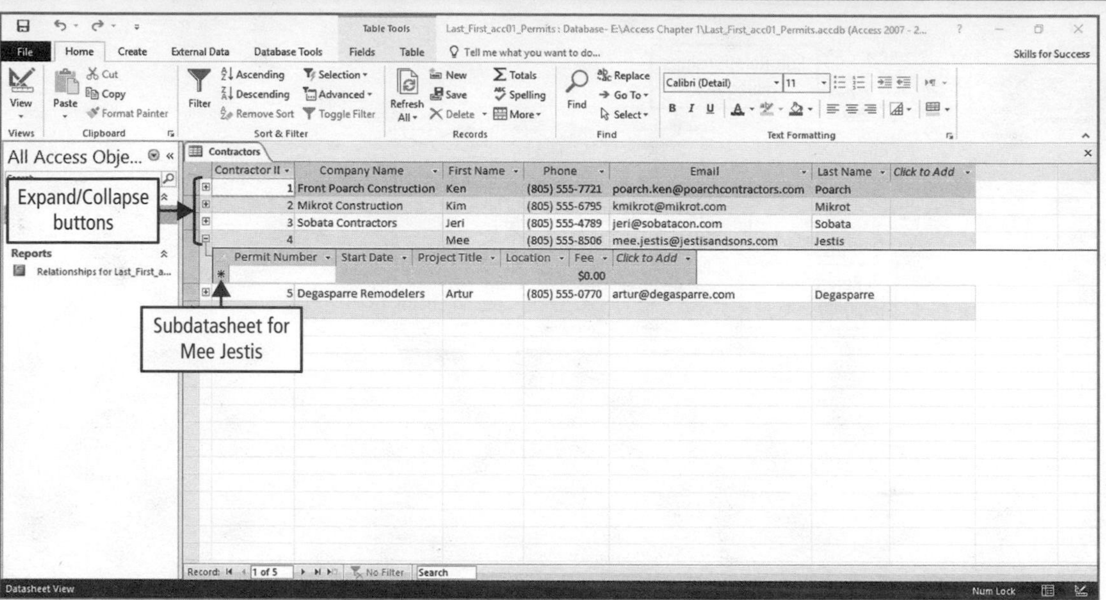

Figure 1

Access 2016, Windows 10, Microsoft Corporation

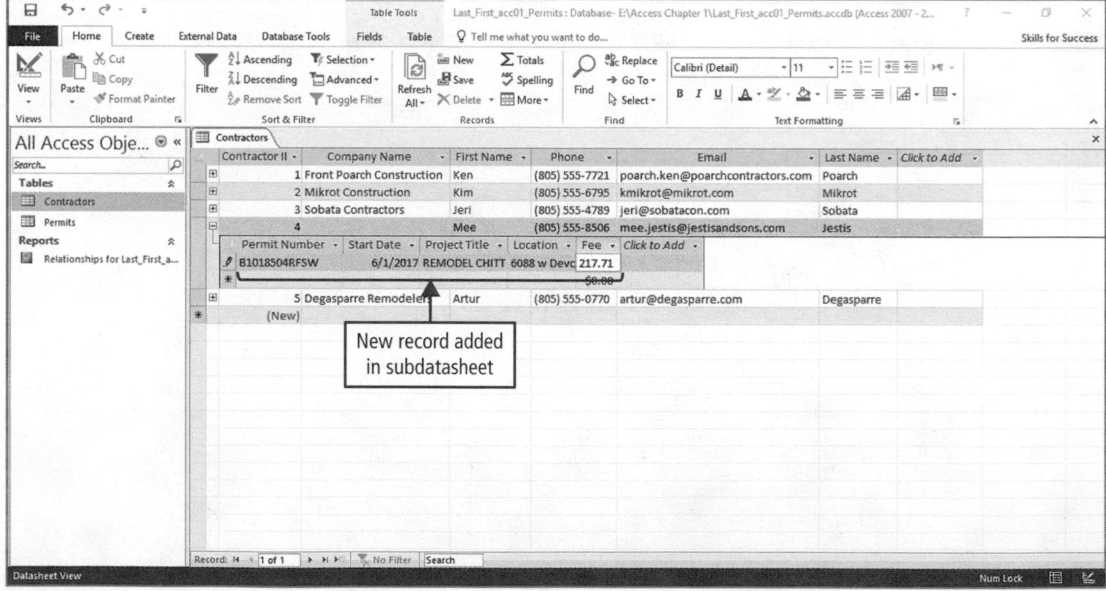

Figure 2

Access 2016, Windows 10, Microsoft Corporation

■ **Continue to the next page to complete the skill**

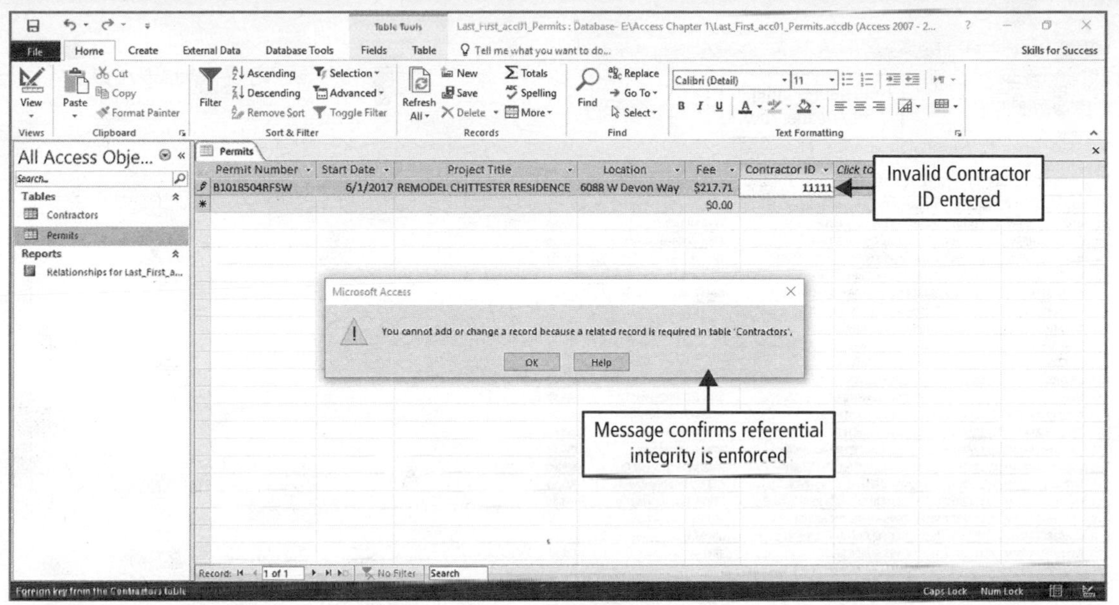

Access 2016, Windows 10, Microsoft Corporation

Figure 3

Permit Number	Start Date	Project Title	Location	Fee
B1018504RFSW	*Your date*	*REMODEL CHITTESTER RESIDENCE*	*6088 W Devon Way*	*217.71*
B1052521RFSW	7/21/2017	ROOF ABADIE RESIDENCE	5943 S Balivi Ln	208.65
B1090716ELEC	7/29/2017	REMODEL CUBIT RESIDENCE	3674 W Teabrook Av	74.50
B1071316PLMB	8/19/2017	REMODEL LAA RESIDENCE	5901 S Farnville Ln	58.00

Figure 4

6. **Close** [X] the table. In the **Navigation Pane**, under **Tables**, double-click **Permits** to open its datasheet.
7. Adjust the column widths to **Best Fit** to display all the data you previously entered in the subdatasheet.

   In this manner, records in a one-to-many relationship can be entered using a subdatasheet. Here, a new building permit record has been created, and the Contractor has been assigned.
8. In the first record, change the **Contractor ID** to 11111 Click in the append row, and then compare your screen with **Figure 3**.

   It is a good idea to test referential integrity. Here, referential integrity is working correctly. You are not allowed to enter a Contractor ID that does not exist in the related Contractors table.
9. Read the message, click **OK**, and then press [Esc] to cancel the change and return to the correct Contractor ID.
10. In the table, repeat the techniques just practiced to add the three records shown in **Figure 4**. For all records, use the same Contractor ID used in the first record.
11. If necessary, adjust the column widths to fit the contents. **Save** [Save] and then **Close** [X] the table.

■ **You have completed Skill 6 of 10**

SKILL 7: Import Data into Tables

SKILL 1.7

- When Excel tables are arranged as a datasheet, the data can be imported into Access tables.

1. Start **Excel 2016**, and then on the Excel start page, click **Open Other Workbooks**. On the **Open** page, click **Browse**. In the **Open** dialog box, navigate to the student data files for this chapter, and then open the Excel file **acc01_PermitsData**.
2. On the **File tab**, click **Save As**, and then click **Browse**. In the **Save As** dialog box, navigate to your chapter folder. Name the file Last_First_acc01_PermitsData and then click **Save**.
3. Click cell **A1**, type PermitID and then press Tab. Continue in this manner to enter the column labels in this order: StartDate | ProjectTitle | Location | Fee Compare your screen with **Figure 1**.

   When you import data from Excel, it is best practice to insert the table's field names in the spreadsheet's header row. In this project, you will not import any ContractorID data.

4. Click **Save**, and then **Close** Excel.

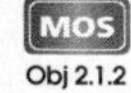
Obj 2.1.2

5. In **Access**, click the **External Data tab**, and then in the **Import & Link group**, click **Excel**.
6. In the **Get External Data - Excel Spreadsheet** dialog box, click the **Browse** button. In the **File Open** dialog box, navigate to your **Access Chapter 1** folder, select **Last_First_acc01_PermitsData**, and then click **Open**.

Obj 2.3.4

7. Click the **Append a copy of the records to the table** option button, click the **arrow**, and then select the **Permits** table as shown in **Figure 2**.

■ **Continue to the next page to complete the skill**

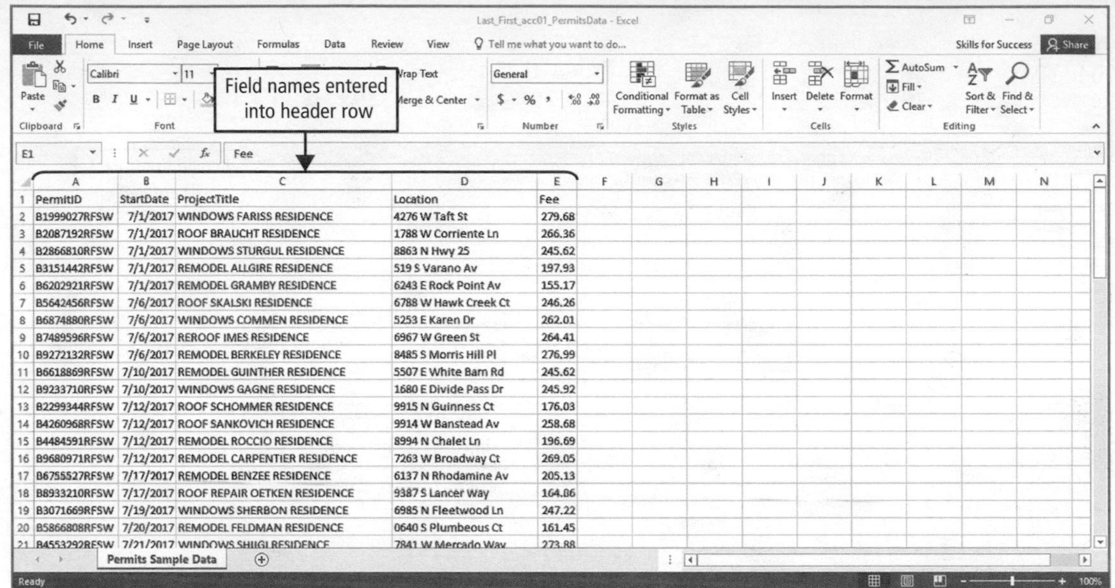

Figure 1

Access 2016, Windows 10, Microsoft Corporation

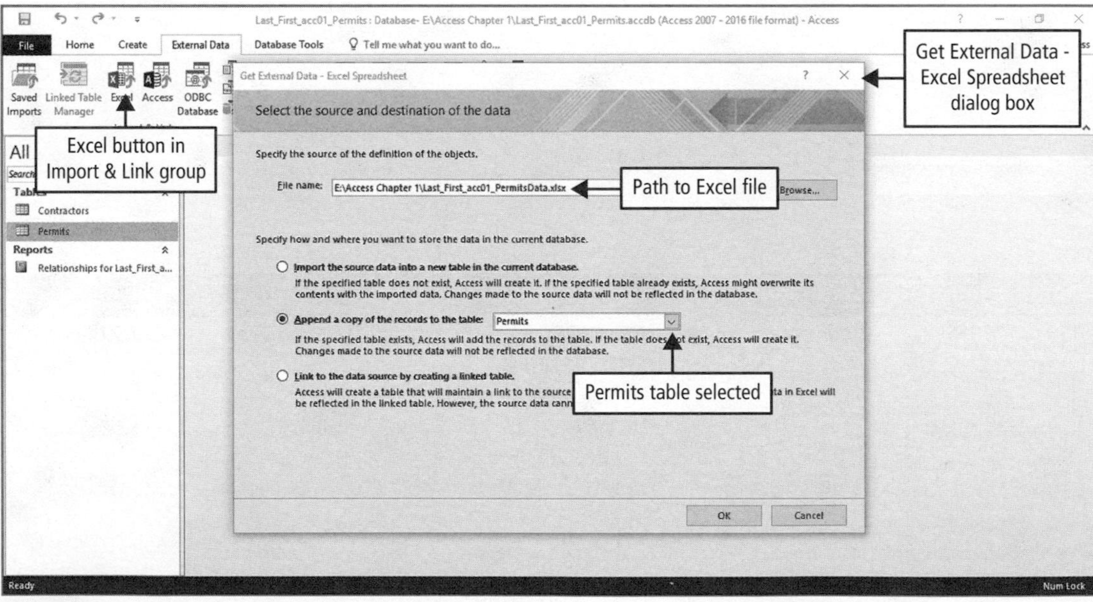

Figure 2

Access 2016, Windows 10, Microsoft Corporation

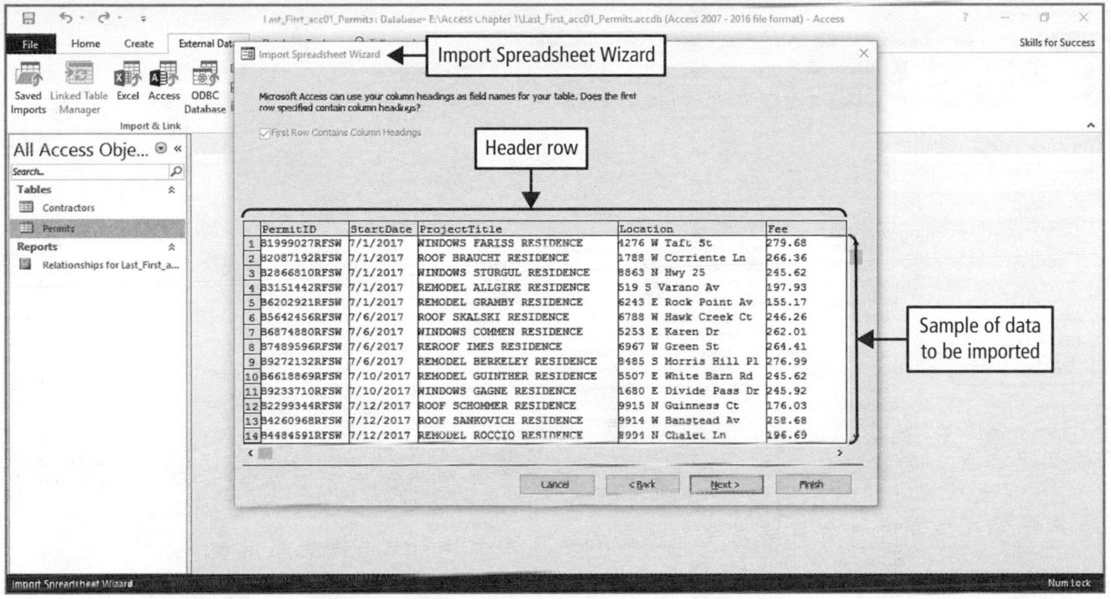

Access 2016, Windows 10, Microsoft Corporation

Figure 3

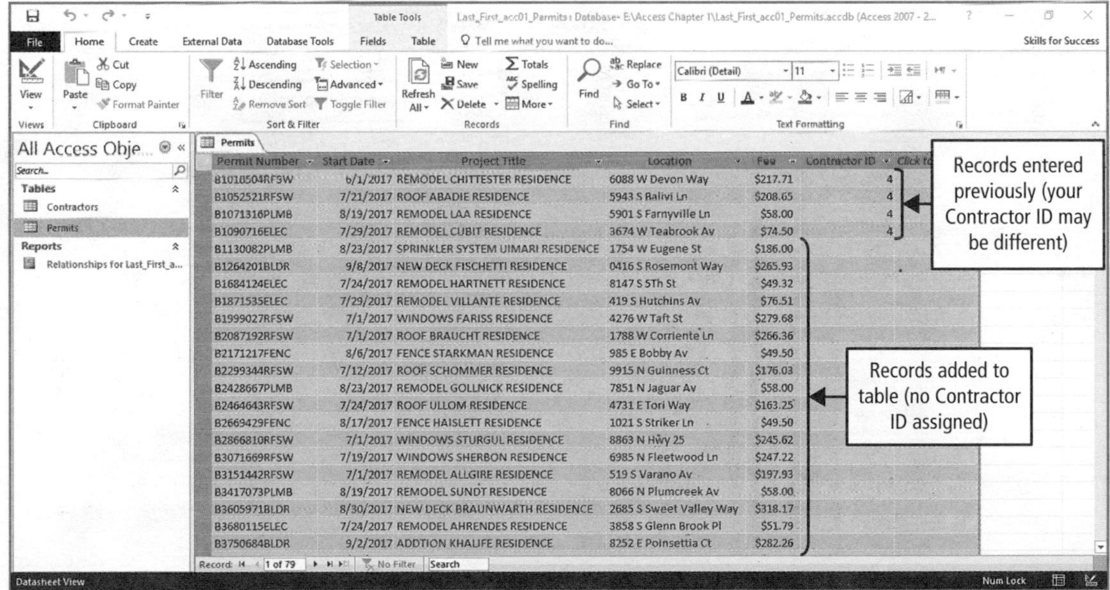

Access 2016, Windows 10, Microsoft Corporation

Figure 4

8. In the dialog box, click **OK** to open the **Import Spreadsheet Wizard** dialog box.

   Because a workbook can contain multiple worksheets, you are asked to select the worksheet that contains the data you wish to import.

9. In the first screen of the **Import Spreadsheet Wizard**, verify that the **Permits Sample Data** worksheet is selected, and then click **Next**. Compare your screen with **Figure 3**.

   In the wizard, it is recommended that you view the sample data and verify that it matches the field names in the header row. Here, the header that you previously inserted matches the field names in the Access table.

10. Click **Next** to display the last screen in the **Import Spreadsheet Wizard**. Verify that the **Import to Table** box displays the text *Permits*, and that the **I would like a wizard...** check box is cleared. Click **Finish** to complete the import.

11. In the **Save Import Steps** screen, verify that the **Save import steps** check box is cleared, and then click **Close**.

12. Open the **Permits** table in **Datasheet view**. Adjust the column widths to **Best Fit**, and then compare your screen with **Figure 4**.

    The records are added to the table and then sorted by the primary key—*Permit Number*. The Contractor ID is blank because these permits were issued to homeowners who are completing the work themselves.

13. Click **Save**, and then leave the table open for the next skill.

■ **You have completed Skill 7 of 10**

SKILL 8: Filter and Sort Datasheets

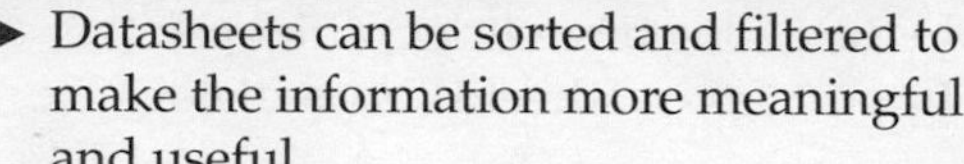

▸ Datasheets can be sorted and filtered to make the information more meaningful and useful.

Obj 2.3.6

1. With the **Permits** table open in **Datasheet view**, click anywhere in the **Start Date** column. On the **Home tab**, in the **Sort & Filter group**, click the **Ascending** button. Compare your screen with **Figure 1.**

   By default, tables are sorted by their primary key field. Here, the Start Date column arrow changes to a sort arrow to indicate that the records have been sorted in ascending order by date.

Obj 2.3.7

2. In the **Fee** column, click the **Fee arrow**. In the **Filter** menu that displays, clear the **(Select All)** check box, and then select the **$58.00** check box.
3. Compare your screen with **Figure 2**, and then click **OK** to view the eight records that result.

   In this manner, the Filter menu can be used to select records with the values you choose.

4. Click the **Fee arrow**, and then click **Clear filter from Fee**.
5. Click the **Fee arrow**, point to **Number Filters**, and then click **Less Than**. In the **Custom Filter** dialog box, type 75 and then click **OK** to display 31 records.

■ **Continue to the next page to complete the skill**

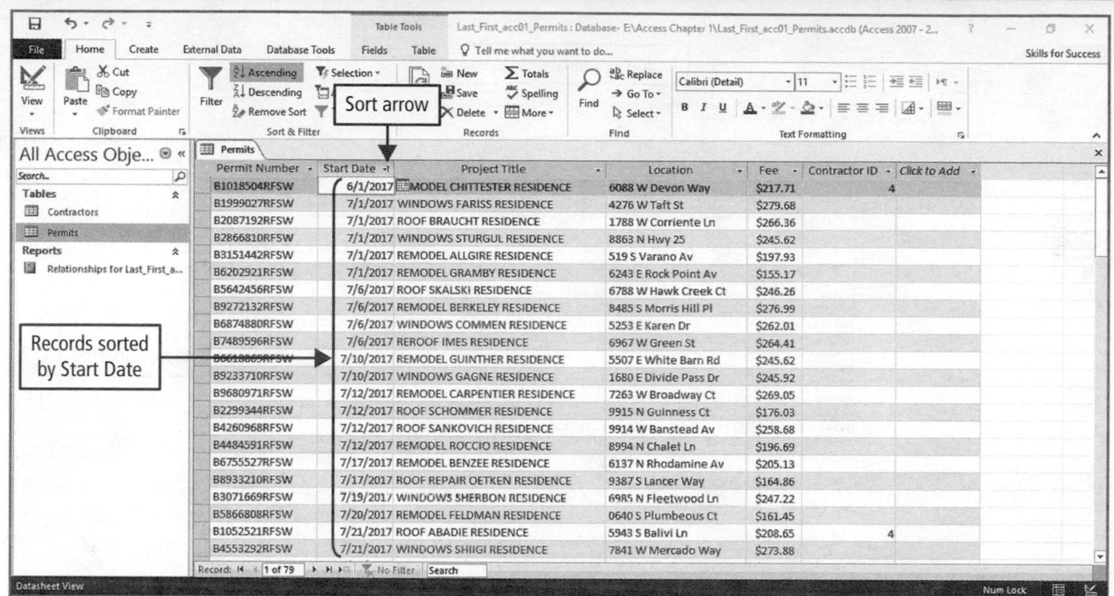

Figure 1

Access 2016, Windows 10, Microsoft Corporation

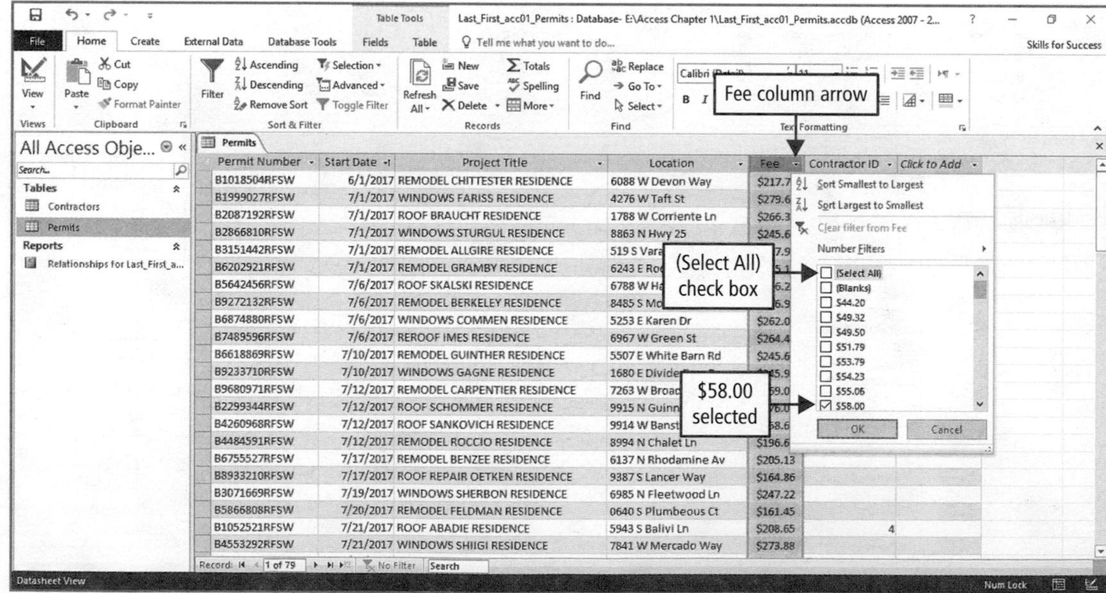

Figure 2

Access 2016, Windows 10, Microsoft Corporation

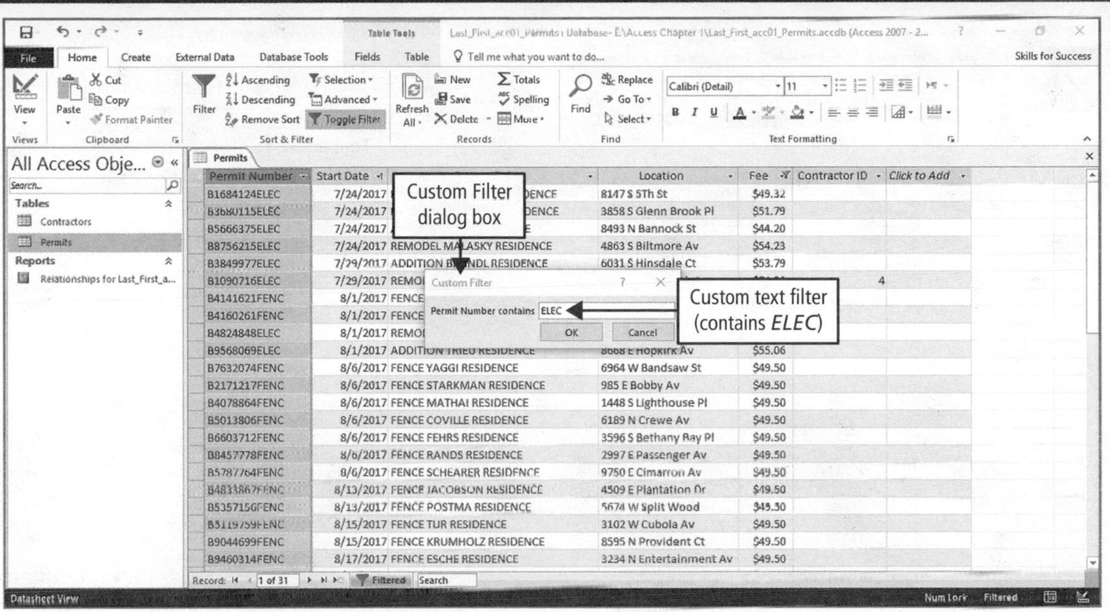

Access 2016, Windows 10, Microsoft Corporation

Figure 3

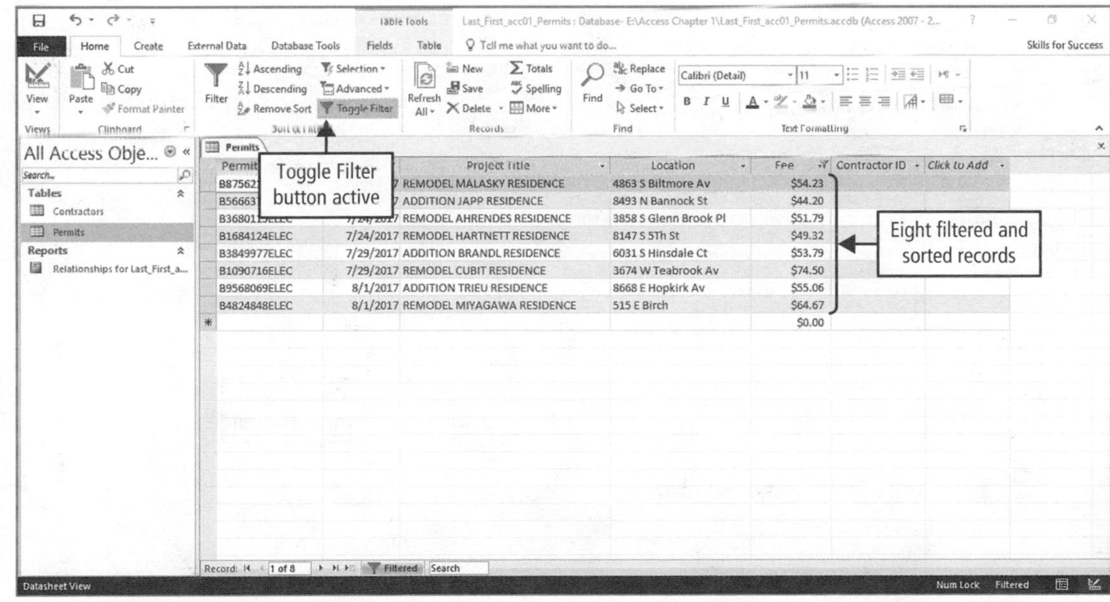

Access 2016, Windows 10, Microsoft Corporation

Figure 4

6. Click the **Permit Number arrow**. From the **Filter** menu, point to **Text Filters**, and then click **Contains**. In the **Custom Filter** dialog box, type ELEC

7. Compare your screen with **Figure 3**, and then click **OK** to display eight records.

   In this manner you can display records that contain the text or numbers you specify. Here, only the permits with permit numbers ending with ELEC and with fees less than $75 display.

8. Click **Save**, and then **Close** the table.

9. In the **Navigation Pane**, double-click **Permits** and notice that the 79 records are sorted by **Start Date** but the filters are not applied.

10. On the **Home tab**, in the **Sort & Filter group**, click **Toggle Filter** to reapply the filter. Compare your screen with **Figure 4**.

    The sort order and filter that you create in a datasheet are saved as part of the table's design. When you open a table, it sorts in the order you specified, but the filter is not applied.

11. Leave the table open for the next skill.

■ **You have completed Skill 8 of 10**

► Datasheets can be formatted to make the data easier to read.

1. If necessary, open the Permits table, and then toggle the filter on.
2. On the **Home tab**, in the **Text Formatting group**, click the **Font Size arrow** [11], and then click **10**.
3. In the **Text Formatting group**, click the **Font arrow** [Calibri (Detail)]. Scroll through the list of fonts as needed, and then click **Verdana**. Compare your screen with **Figure 1**.

   When you change the font size or font, the changes are applied to the entire datasheet.

4. Click the **Select All** button, and then apply the **Best Fit** column width.
5. With all the cells still selected, on the **Home tab**, in the **Records group**, click **More**, and then click **Row Height**.
6. In the **Row Height** dialog box, replace the existing **Row Height** value with 15 and then click **OK**.
7. Click anywhere in the **Contractor ID** column. On the **Home tab**, in the **Records group**, click **More**, and then click **Hide Fields**. Compare your screen with **Figure 2**.

MOS Obj 2.2.1

■ Continue to the next page to complete the skill

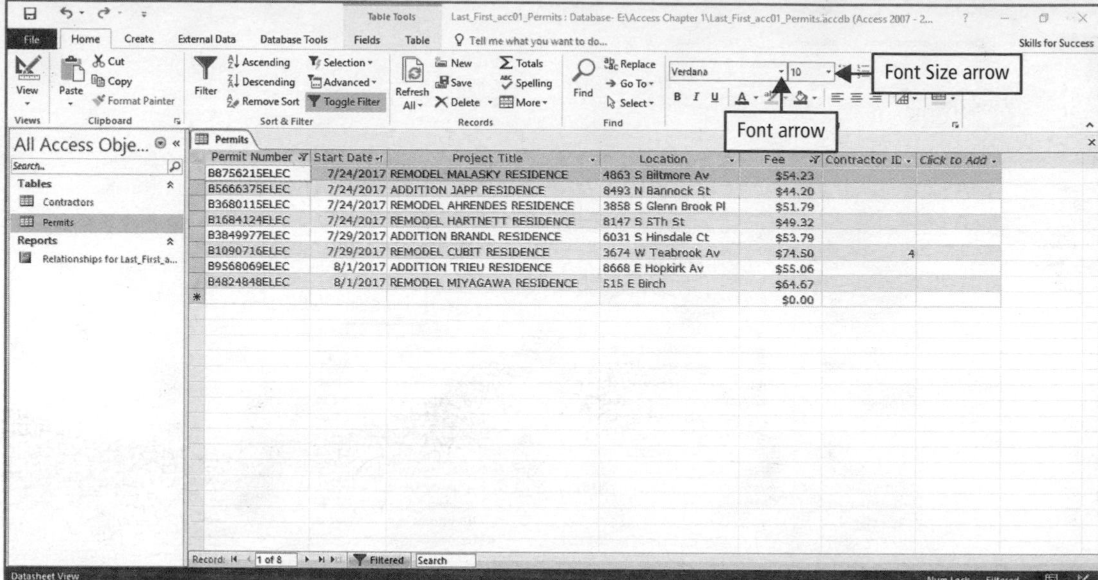

Figure 1

Access 2016, Windows 10, Microsoft Corporation

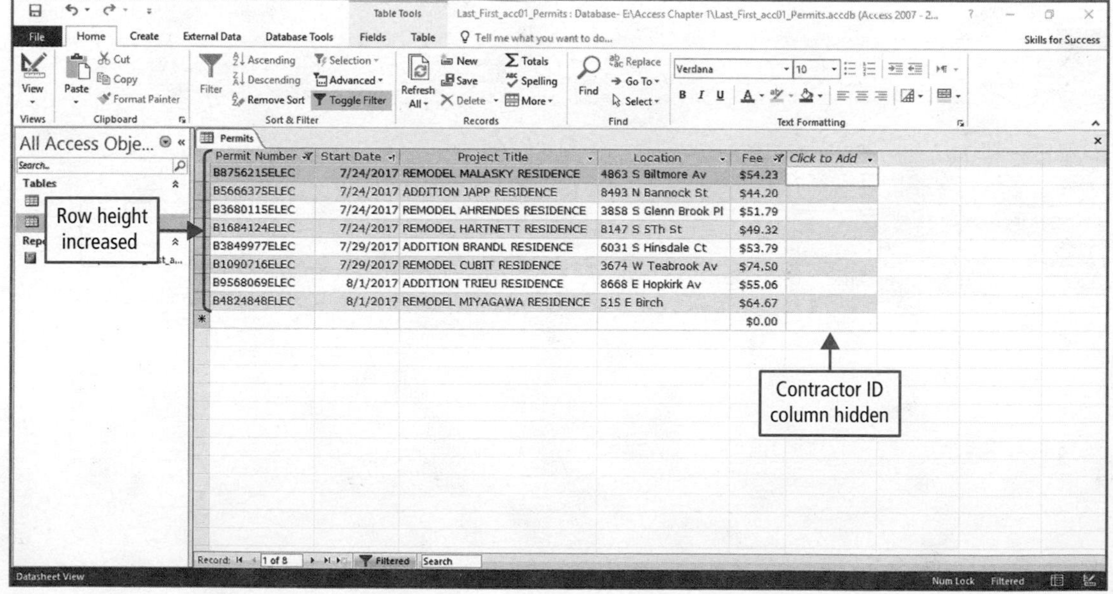

Figure 2

Access 2016, Windows 10, Microsoft Corporation

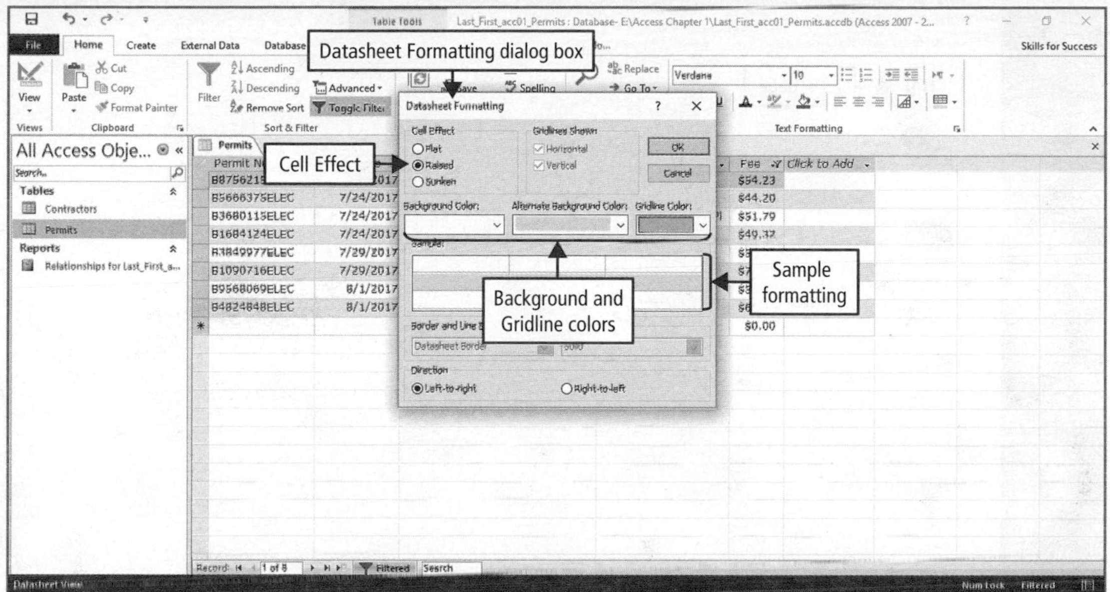

Access 2016, Windows 10, Microsoft Corporation

Figure 3

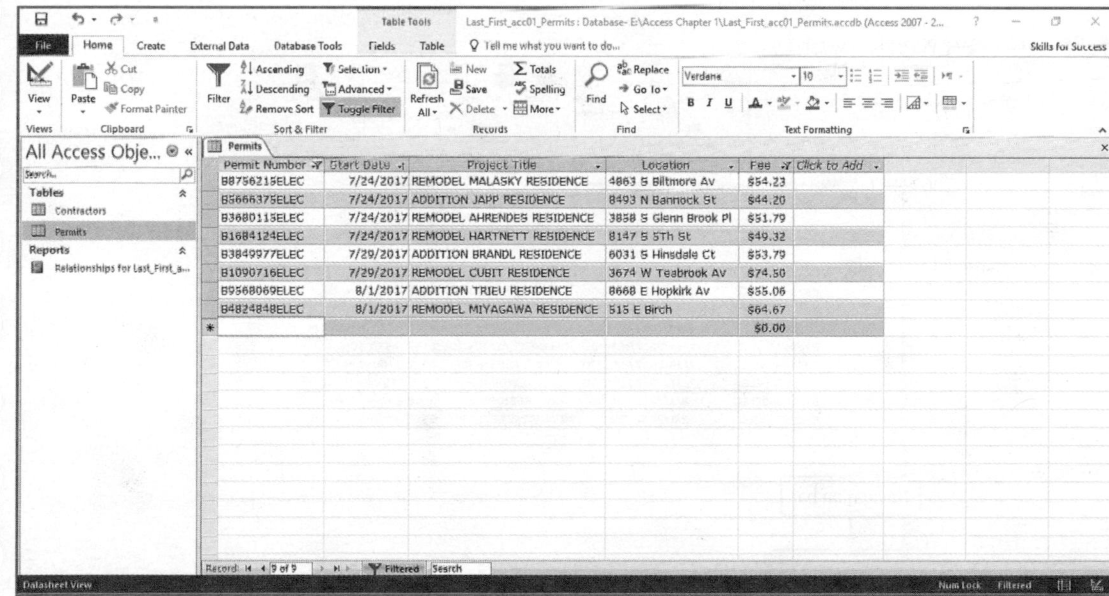

Access 2016, Windows 10, Microsoft Corporation

Figure 4

8. In the **Text Formatting group**, click the **Datasheet Formatting Dialog Box Launcher** ▫.
9. In the **Datasheet Formatting** dialog box, under **Cell Effect**, select the **Raised** option button.
10. Click the **Background Color arrow**. In the gallery, click **Automatic**.
11. Click the **Alternate Background Color arrow**. In the gallery, under **Theme Colors**, click the sixth color in the second row—**Orange, Accent 2, Lighter 80%**.
12. Click the **Gridline Color arrow**. In the gallery, under **Theme Colors**, click the eighth color in the first row—**Gold, Accent 4**. Compare your screen with **Figure 3**.

    In the Datasheet Formatting dialog box, a sample of the selected formatting displays.

13. Click **OK** to apply the changes and to close the dialog box. Click in the append row, and then compare your screen with **Figure 4**.
14. **Save** ▫ the table design changes, and leave the table open for the next skill.

■ **You have completed Skill 9 of 10**

SKILL 10: Preview and Print Datasheets

- Before printing, it is a good idea to preview the printed page(s) and make adjustments if necessary.

1. With the **Permits** table open in **Datasheet view**, click the **File tab**, and then click **Print**. Compare your screen with **Figure 1**.

   The ***Quick Print*** command prints the object directly. You cannot make any adjustments to the object, choose a different printer, or change the printer settings.

   The ***Print*** command opens the Print dialog box so you can select a different printer or different print options.

   The ***Print Preview*** command opens a preview of the table with Ribbon commands that you can use to make adjustments to the object you are printing.

2. On the **Print** page, click **Print Preview**. In the **Zoom group**, click the **Zoom arrow**, and then click **Zoom 100%**. Compare your screen with **Figure 2**. If necessary, scroll to the top of the page.

   The last column—Fee—will not print on page one. Tools in the navigation bar at the bottom of the preview are used to view the other printed pages.

■ Continue to the next page to complete the skill

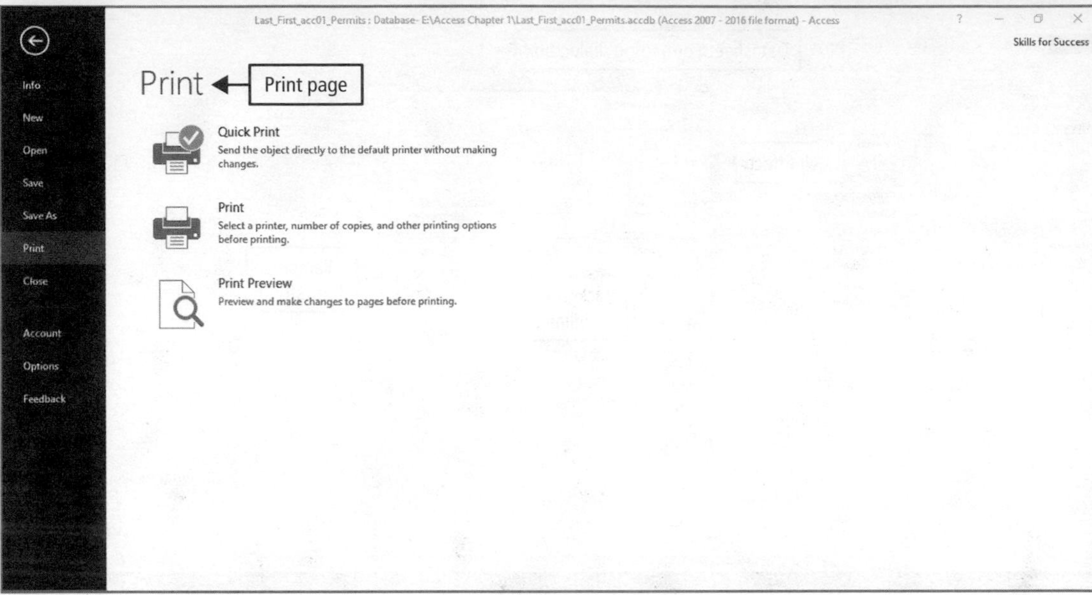

Figure 1 Access 2016, Windows 10, Microsoft Corporation

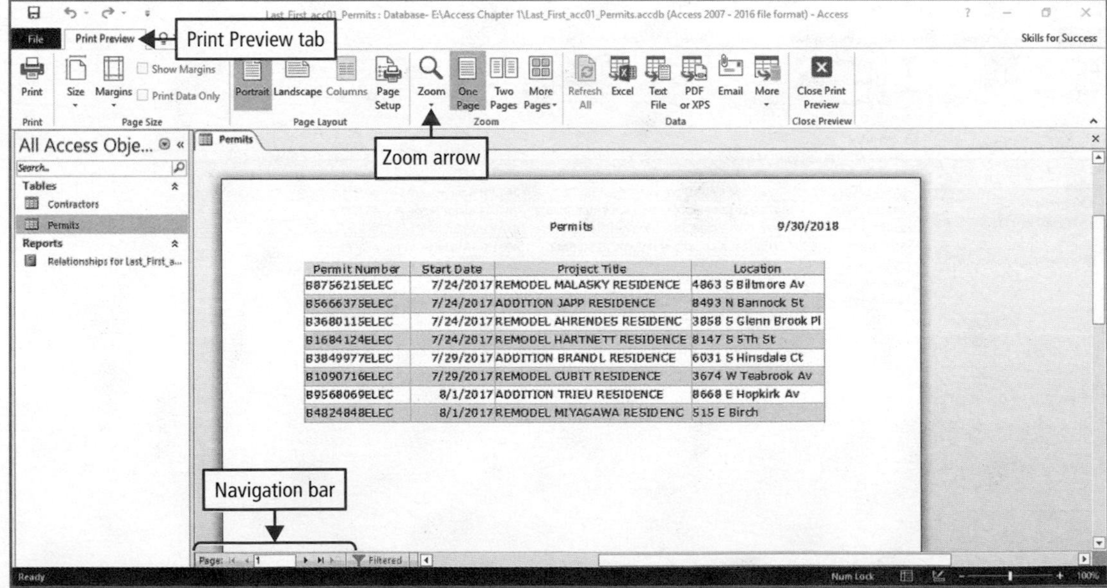

Figure 2 Access 2016, Windows 10, Microsoft Corporation

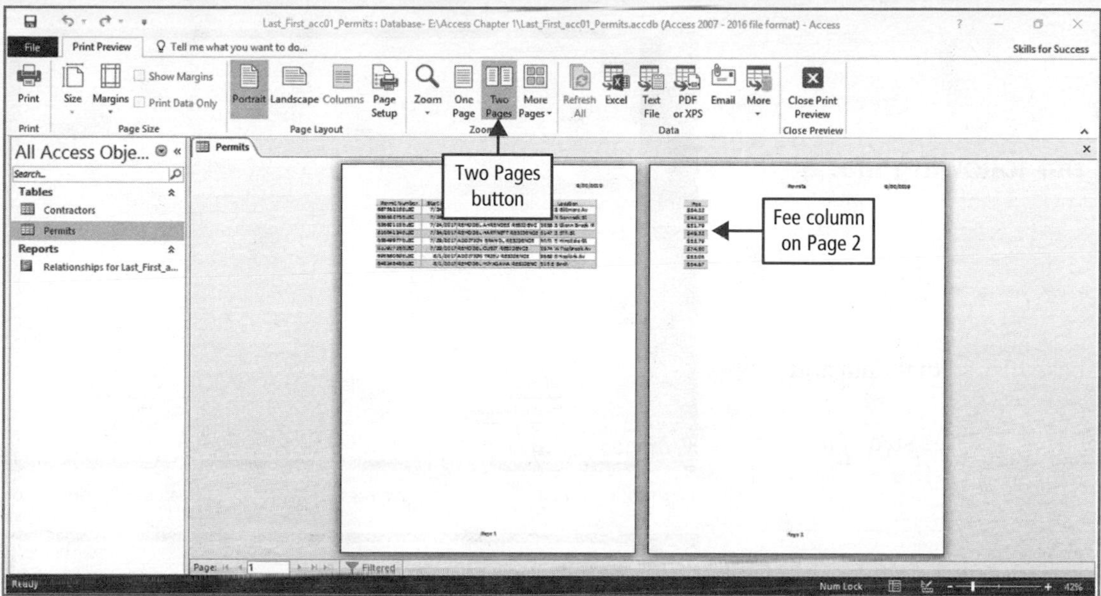

Access 2016, Windows 10, Microsoft Corporation

Figure 3

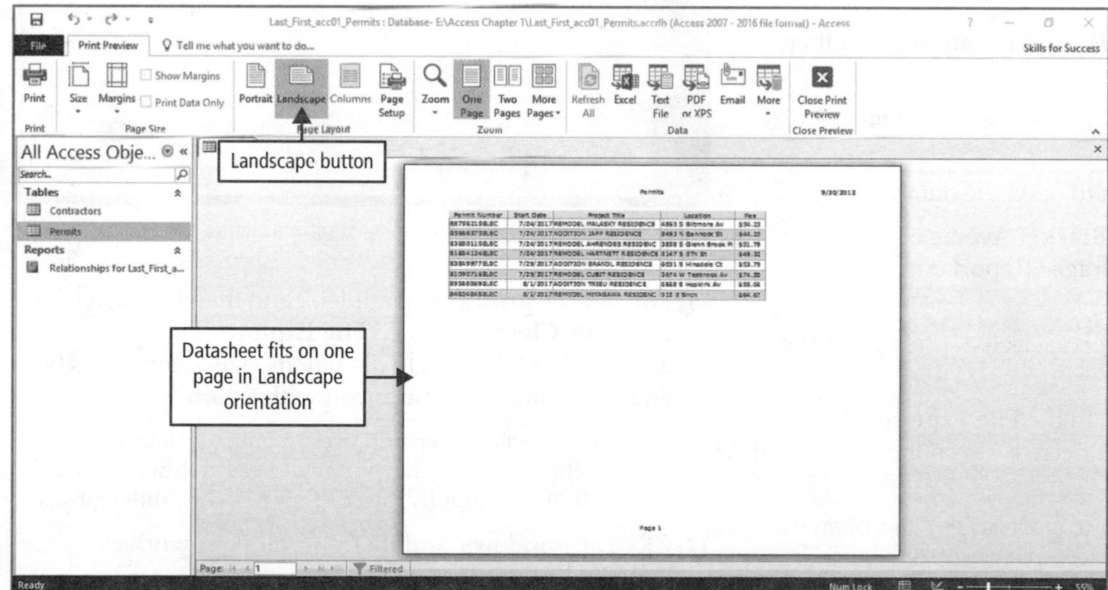

Access 2016, Windows 10, Microsoft Corporation

Figure 4

3. In the **Zoom group**, click **Two Pages**, and then compare your screen with **Figure 3**.

4. In the **Page Layout group**, click **Landscape**.

   By default, tables print in ***Portrait***—taller than wide. You can change the layout to ***Landscape***—wider than tall—to accommodate a wider table with few records.

5. In the **Zoom group**, click **One Page**, and then compare your screen with **Figure 4**.

   The buttons on the navigation bar are dimmed because the table now fits on one page.

6. If you are printing your work for this project, click the **Print** button, note the printer listed in the **Print** dialog box, and then click **OK**.

7. **Close** [X] the table.

   A table's page layout settings cannot be saved. The next time the table is opened, the default Portrait view will be applied. Typically, when you want to print data from a table, an Access report is created. Report layout settings can be saved.

8. If you are printing your work for this project, use the technique just practiced to print the **Contractors** table with the portrait orientation.

9. With all tables closed, **Close** [X] Access. Submit your work as directed by your instructor.

   All of the data and database objects are saved as you work with them, so you do not need to click Save before quitting Access.

DONE! You have completed Skill 10 of 10 and your databases are complete!

More Skills 11

Compact and Repair Databases

To complete this project, you will need the following file:

- acc01_MS11Triathlon

You will save your file as:

- Last_First_acc01_MS11Triathlon

- The ***Compact and Repair*** process rebuilds database files so that data and database objects are stored more efficiently.
- Applying the Compact and Repair Database tool decreases the size of a database file.

---

1. Start **Access 2016**, and then open the student data file **acc01_MS11Triathlon**.
2. On the **File tab**, click **Save As**, and then click the **Save As** button. In the **Save As** dialog box, navigate to your **Access Chapter 1** folder, and then **Save** the database as Last_First_acc01_MS11Triathlon If necessary, enable the content.
3. **Close** the Access window. Start **File Explorer**, and then navigate to your **Access Chapter 1** folder.
4. Click one time to select the file **Last_First_acc01_MS11Triathlon**, and then compare your screen with **Figure 1**.

   The size of the database file is approximately 952 KB. Your computer may display a different file size.
5. Double-click **Last_First_acc01_MS11Triathlon** to open the database.
6. In the **Navigation Pane**, under **Queries**, click **Bracket Averages** to select it. Press and hold Shift while clicking **Bracket Averages Report** one time, and then release Shift.
7. With the four queries, one form, and three reports selected, press Delete. Read the displayed message, and then click **Yes.**
8. **Close** the database, and then **Close** Access. In the **File Explorer** window, notice that the file size for the database did not decrease even though several database objects were deleted.
9. Double-click **Last_First_acc01_MS11Triathlon** to start Access and open the database.

10. Click the **File tab**, and then on the **Info** page, click the **Compact & Repair Database** button.

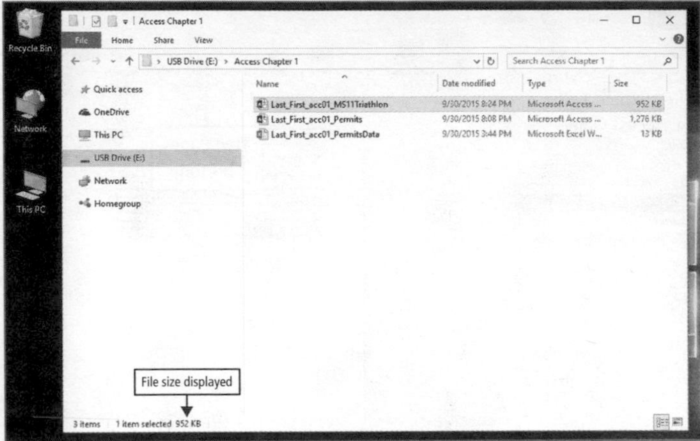

Figure 1 Access 2016, Windows 10, Microsoft Corporation

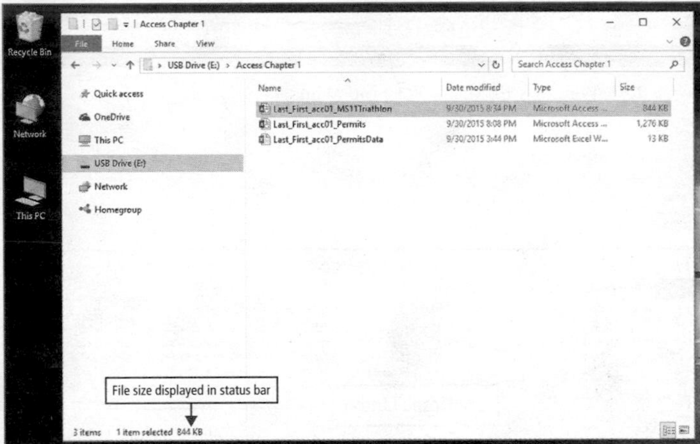

Figure 2 Access 2016, Windows 10, Microsoft Corporation

11. Wait for the process to complete, and then **Close** the database. **Close** Access. In **File Explorer**, click **Last_First_acc01_MS11Triathlon** to display its size in the status bar, and then compare your screen with **Figure 2**.

    The Compact and Repair process rebuilt the database file more efficiently, and the file size decreased to approximately 844 kB. Your computer may display a slightly different size.
12. Close all windows, and then submit your work as directed by your instructor.

- **You have completed More Skills 11**

More Skills 12

Work with the Long Text Data Type

To complete this project, you will need the following file:

- acc01_MS12Classes

You will save your file as:

- Last_First_acc01_MS12Classes

► Recall that the Short Text data type can store up to 255 characters per record. When you need to store more characters, you can use the ***Long Text data type***—a data type that can store up to 65,535 characters in each record.

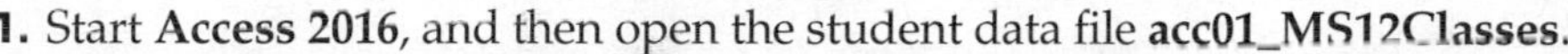

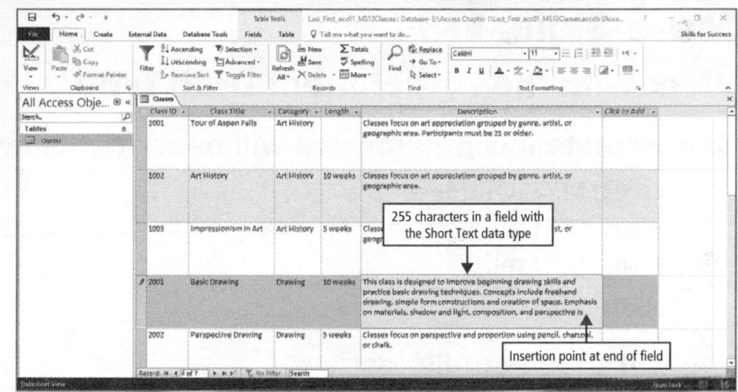

Access 2016, Windows 10, Microsoft Corporation **Figure 1**

1. Start **Access 2016**, and then open the student data file **acc01_MS12Classes.**
2. On the **File tab**, click **Save As**, and then click the **Save As** button. In the **Save As** dialog box, navigate to your **Access Chapter 1** folder, and then **Save** the database as Last_First_acc01_MS12Classes If necessary, enable the content.
3. Open the **Classes** table in Datasheet view. In the **Description** field of the fourth record—*Basic Drawing*—click to the right of the period in the sentence ending *creation of space.*
4. Add to the record by adding a space and then typing the following: Emphasis on materials, shadow and light, composition, and perspective is
5. Add a space, and then attempt to type the word also Compare your screen with **Figure 1**.

   A short text field contains 255 characters, so no more characters can be added to the field. Here, the Description field has reached its upper limit and the rest of the sentence cannot be entered.

6. In the **Description** column, click in a different row to complete the data entry in the *Basic Drawing* record. You will type the rest of the sentence in a later step.
7. With a **Description** field still active, click the **Fields tab**. In the **Formatting group**, click the **Data Type arrow**, and then click **Long Text**. MOS Obj 2.4.5
8. In the fourth record—*Basic Drawing*—click at the end of the **Description** text, and then complete the sentence by typing also included. Compare your screen with **Figure 2**.

   With the data type changed to Long Text, more than 255 characters can be entered, and the sentence can be completed. If you changed a Long Text field to a Short Text field, all extra characters would be permanently removed from the database.

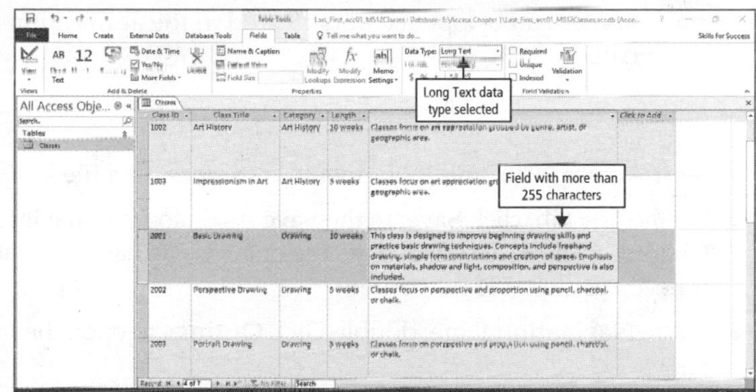

Access 2016, Windows 10, Microsoft Corporation **Figure 2**

9. **Save** the table design changes, **Close** the database, and then **Close** Access. Submit the database file as directed by your instructor.

- **You have completed More Skills 12**

More Skills 13

Work with the Attachment Data Type

To complete this project, you will need the following files:

- acc01_MS13Outings
- acc01_MS13Pic1
- acc01_MS13Pic2
- acc01_MS13Flyer

You will save your file as:

- Last_First_acc01_MS13Outings

- The ***Attachment data type*** is used to store files such as Word documents or digital photo files.
- Attached files can be opened and viewed in the application in which they were created.

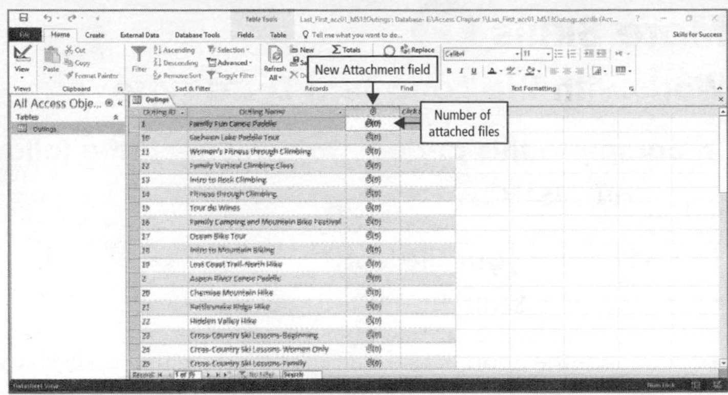

Figure 1 Access 2016, Windows 10, Microsoft Corporation

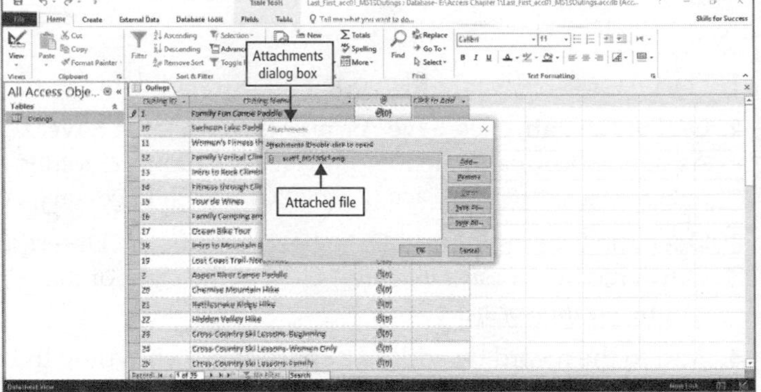

Figure 2 Access 2016, Windows 10, Microsoft Corporation

1. Start **Access 2016**, and then open the student data file **acc01_MS13Outings**.
2. On the **File tab**, click **Save**. In the **Save As** dialog box, navigate to your **Access Chapter 1** folder, and then **Save** the database as Last_First_acc01_MS13Outings If necessary, enable the content.
3. In the **Navigation Pane**, double-click **Outings** to open the table in Datasheet view.
4. In the datasheet's last column, click the **Click to Add arrow**, and then click **Attachment**. Compare your screen with **Figure 1**.

   The number in the parentheses indicates the number of files currently attached to each record.
5. In the record for **Family Fun Canoe Paddle**, double-click the **Paper Clip** icon. In the **Attachments** dialog box, click the **Add** button.
6. In the **Choose File** dialog box, navigate to the student files that came with this project. Click **acc01_MS13Pic1**, and then click **Open**. Compare your screen with **Figure 2**.

   The Attachments dialog box lists all files currently attached to the Family Fun Canoe Paddle record.
7. In the **Attachments** dialog box, click the **Add** button. In the **Choose File** dialog box, click **acc01_MS13Pic2**, and then click **Open**. Click **OK** to close the Attachments dialog box.
8. In the record for **Sacheen Lake Paddle Tour**, repeat the technique just practiced to attach the student data file **acc01_MS13Flyer**

   The numbers next to the Attachment icon indicate the number of files attached.
9. In the record for **Sacheen Lake Paddle Tour**, double-click the **Attachment** icon. In the **Attachments** dialog box, select **acc01_MS13Flyer.docx**, and then click **Open**.

   When you view an attached file, it is opened in the program associated with that file type.
10. **Close** [X] the Word document, **Close** [X] the Attachments dialog box, **Close** [X] the database, and then **Close** Access.
11. Submit the database file as directed by your instructor.

■ **You have completed More Skills 13**

More Skills 14

Work with the Hyperlink and Yes/No Data Types

To complete this project, you will need the following file:

- acc01_MS14Sponsors

You will save your file as:

- Last_First_acc01_MS14Sponsors

- The ***Hyperlink data type*** stores links to websites or files located on your computer.
- The ***Yes/No data type*** stores variables that can have one of two possible values—for example, yes or no, or true or false.

1. Start **Access 2016**, and then open the student data file **acc01_MS14Sponsors**.
2. On the **File tab**, click **Save As**, and then click the **Save As** button. In the **Save As** dialog box, navigate to your **Access Chapter 1** folder, and then **Save** the database as Last_First_acc01_MS14Sponsors If necessary, enable the content.
3. In the **Navigation Pane**, double-click **Sponsors : Table** to open the datasheet.
4. Click the **Click to Add arrow**, and then click **Hyperlink**. With the new field name selected, type Web Site and then press Enter.
5. Click **Web Site** two times to make it the active column. Click the **Fields tab**, and then compare your screen with **Figure 1**.
6. Click **Save** [save icon]. Click in the **Web Site** field for the first record, *National Park Service*, type www.nps.gov and then press Enter.
7. Place the pointer over the hyperlink just typed, but do not click it. Compare your screen with **Figure 2**.

   The Link Select pointer displays to indicate that clicking the hyperlink will open a website or file. For several seconds, a ScreenTip displays the web address for the hyperlink.

8. Click the hyperlink *www.nps.gov* to open your computer's default web browser and navigate to the home page for the National Park Service.
9. **Close** [X] the web browser window.
10. In **Access**, in the first blank column, click the **Click to Add arrow**, and then click **Yes/No**. Type Auto Renew and then press Enter.

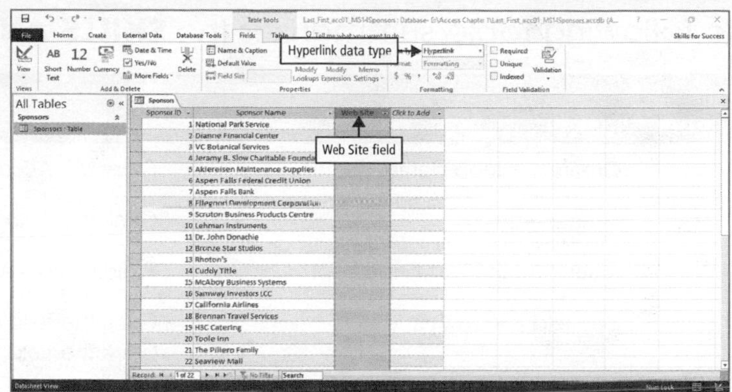

Access 2016, Windows 10, Microsoft Corporation **Figure 1**

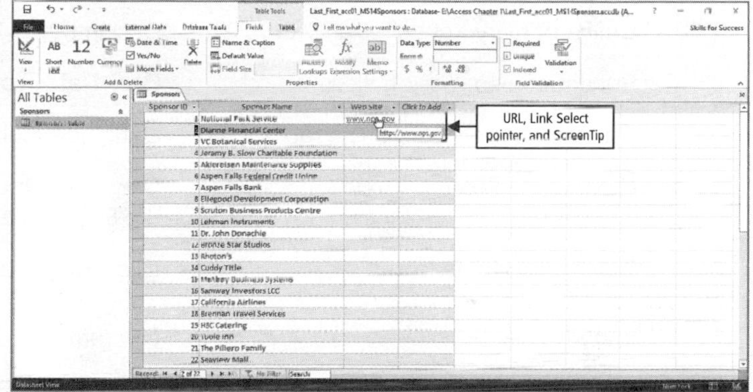

Access 2016, Windows 10, Microsoft Corporation **Figure 2**

11. In the first record, select the **Auto Renew** check box to set the value to *Yes*.

    Yes/No fields display a check box in each record so that each field's value can be set to Yes or No by checking or clearing its check box.

12. If your instructor asks you to print this project, print the datasheet.
13. **Save** [save icon] the table design changes, **Close** [X] the database, and then **Close** Access. Submit the database file as directed by your instructor.

- **You have completed More Skills 14**

The following table summarizes the **SKILLS AND PROCEDURES** covered in this chapter.

Skills Number	Task	Step	Icon
1	Create desktop databases	From the Access start screen, click Blank desktop database	
2	Create fields	Click the Click to Add column, and select the desired data type (Datasheet view)	
2	Insert Quick Start fields	Fields tab → Add & Delete group → More Fields	
2, 4	Set field properties	Click the field and use Fields tab commands Click the field and use Field Properties pane (Design view)	
2	Set Best Fit column widths	Home tab → Records group → More → Field Width	
3	Create new records in Datasheet view	Click append row, and type record data	
4	Define primary keys (Design view)	Design tab → Tools group → Primary Key	
4	Set data types (Design view)	Click Data Type arrow	
5	Add tables to Relationships tab	Database Tools → Relationships → Show Table	
5	Create a one-to-many relationship	Drag the primary key field from the table to the related field in the other table and select the Enforce Referential Integrity check box	
6	Display subdatasheets	Click the Expand button	⊞
7	Import Excel data	External Data → Import & Link → Excel	
8	Sort datasheets	Home tab → Sort & Filter group → Ascending (or Descending)	
8	Filter datasheets	Click column Filter arrow	
8	Disable or enable filters	Home tab → Sort & Filter group → Toggle Filter	
9	Change datasheet fonts and font sizes	Home tab → Text Formatting group	
9	Set datasheet row height	Home tab → Records group → More → Row Height	
9	Hide datasheet fields	Home tab → Records group → More → Hide Fields	
9	Apply alternate row shading	Home tab → Datasheet Formatting Dialog Box Launcher	⧉
10	Preview a printed table	File tab → Print → Print Preview	
10	Change orientation	Print Preview tab → Page Layout group	

Project Summary Chart

Project	Project Type	Project Location
Skills Review	Review	In Book & MIL MyITLab® Grader
Skills Assessment 1	Review	In Book & MIL MyITLab® Grader
Skills Assessment 2	Review	Book
My Skills	Problem Solving	Book
Visual Skills Check	Problem Solving	Book
Skills Challenge 1	Critical Thinking	Book
Skills Challenge 2	Critical Thinking	Book
More Skills Assessment	Review	In Book & MIL MyITLab® Grader
Collaborating with Google	Critical Thinking	Book

MOS Objectives Covered

1.1.1 Create a blank desktop database	2.2.1 Hide fields in tables
1.2.1 Create and modifying relationships	2.3.2 Add records
1.2.2 Set primary key field	2.3.4 Append records from external data
1.2.3 Enforce referential integrity	2.3.6 Sort records
1.2.4 Set foreign keys	2.3.7 Filter records
1.2.5 View Relationships	2.4.1 Add fields to tables
1.4.1 Compact databases	2.4.3 Change field captions
1.4.2 Repair databases	2.4.4 Changing field sizes
2.1.1 Create a table	2.4.5 Change field data types
2.1.2 Import data into tables	2.4.6 Configure fields to auto-increment

Key Terms

Append row 511
Attachment data type 532
AutoNumber 515
Caption 512
Cascade Delete 519
Cascade Update. 519
Compact and Repair 530
Currency data type 517
Data type. 512
Datasheet 511
Datasheet view 511
Date/Time data type 516
Field. 511
Field size. 513
Foreign key. 517
Hyperlink data type 533
Landscape. 529
Long Text data type 531
Number data type 517
One-to-many relationship . . 519
Portrait. 529
Primary key 515
Print. 528
Print Preview 528
Quick Print. 528
Quick Start field 512
Record 511
Referential integrity 519
Short Text data type 512
Subdatasheet 520
Table. 511
Table Design view. 516
Yes/No data type 533

BizSkills Video

1. Is there anything you would change about Theo's behavior at his performance evaluation? Why or why not?
2. How important do you think it is to set career development goals for yourself? Why?

Online Help Skills

1. Start **Access 2016**, and then in the upper-right corner of the Access start page, click the **Microsoft Access Help (F1)** button [?].
2. In the **Access Help** window **Search help** box, type table relationships and then press [Enter].
3. In the search result list, click **Introduction to tables**. Compare your screen with **Figure 1**.
4. Read the article to the answer to the following question: Why create table relationships?

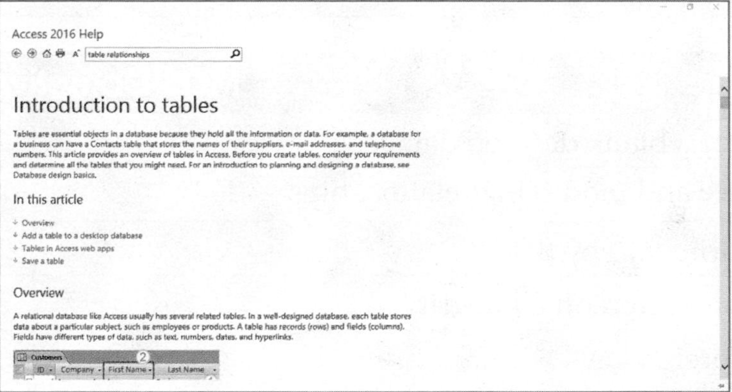

Figure 1 Access 2016, Windows 10, Microsoft Corporation

Matching 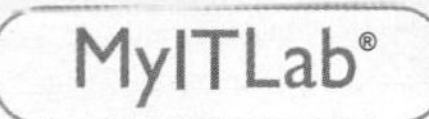

Match each term in the second column with its correct definition in the first column by writing the letter of the term on the blank line in front of the correct definition.

___ **1.** The object that stores the data by organizing it into rows and columns.

___ **2.** The collection of related information that displays in a single row of a database table.

___ **3.** This specifies the kind of information that a field will hold; for example, text or numbers.

___ **4.** A field property that determines what displays in datasheets, forms, and report labels.

___ **5.** A data type that automatically assigns a unique numeric value to a field.

___ **6.** A field that uniquely identifies each record in a table.

___ **7.** A data type that stores numbers formatted as monetary values.

___ **8.** A set of fields that can be added with a single click. For example, the Address data type inserts five fields for storing postal addresses.

___ **9.** An Access view that features table fields and their properties.

___ **10.** A field on the *many* side of a relationship used to relate to the table on the *one* side of the relationship.

A AutoNumber

B Caption

C Currency

D Data type

E Foreign key

F Primary key

G Quick Start

H Record

I Table

J Table Design

Multiple Choice

Choose the correct answer.

1. An Access view that displays records in rows and fields in columns.
   A. Database
   B. Data grid
   C. Datasheet

2. Each individual characteristic in a record that displays as a single column in a datasheet.
   A. Field
   B. Record
   C. Subset

3. A data type that stores up to 255 characters of text.
   A. Currency
   B. Number
   C. Short Text

4. The blank row at the end of a datasheet used to add records to a table.
   A. Append
   B. Data entry
   C. New record

5. An Access field property that limits the number of characters that can be typed into a text or number field.
   A. Character limit
   B. Character size
   C. Field size

6. A relationship in which a record in the first table can have many associated records in the second table.
   A. Cascading
   B. One-to-one
   C. One-to-many

7. A referential integrity option in which you can edit the primary key values in a table, and all the related records in the other table will update accordingly.
   A. Cascading delete
   B. Cascading update
   C. One-to-many relationship

8. A rule that keeps related values synchronized.
   A. Data duplication
   B. Data redundancy
   C. Referential integrity

9. A command that opens the Print dialog box so that you can select a different printer or different print options.
   A. Quick Print
   B. Print
   C. Print Preview

10. An orientation of the printed page that makes it wider than it is tall.
    A. Print Preview
    B. Landscape
    C. Portrait

Topics for Discussion

1. What kind of information do you think a small business or organization would organize into a database?

2. Each database object has a special purpose. For example, a query is used to filter and sort records. Why do you think the filter and sort tools are also available when you work with tables, forms, and reports?

Skills Review

To complete this project, you will need the following file:

- acc01_SREmployees

You will save your file as:

- Last_First_acc01_SRDepartments

1. Start **Access 2016**, and then click **Blank desktop database**. Replace the **File Name** with Last_First_acc01_SRDepartments Click **Browse**, navigate to your chapter folder, and then click **OK**. Finish the process by clicking the **Create** button.
2. In **Table1**, select the **ID** column. On the **Fields tab**, in the **Properties group**, click **Name & Caption**. Change the **Name** to EmployeeID and the **Caption** to Employee ID and then click **OK**.
3. Click the **Click to Add** column. In the **Add & Delete group**, click **More Fields**, scroll down, and then click **Name**.
4. Click the **Click to Add** column, click **Date & Time**, and then type DateHired Press **Enter**, and then repeat to add a **Short Text** field named DeptID
5. With the **DeptID** field selected, in the **Properties group**, click in the **Field Size** box, and then type 50
6. Click **Save**, type Employees and then click **OK**. Compare your screen with **Figure 1**, and then **Close** the table.
7. On the **External Data tab**, in the **Import & Link group**, click **Excel**. In the **Get External Data - Excel Spreadsheet** dialog box, click the **Browse** button. In the **File Open** dialog box, navigate to and select the student data file **acc01_SREmployees**, and then click **Open**. Click the **Append a copy of the records to the table** option button, and then click **OK**. In the first screen of the **Import Spreadsheet Wizard**, click **Finish**, and then click **Close** to complete the import process.
8. Double-click **Employees** to open the table in **Datasheet view**. Set the column widths to **Best Fit**.
9. Click the **DateHired** column, and then on the **Home tab**, in the **Sort & Filter group**, click **Ascending**.
10. Click the **DeptID arrow**, and then in the Filter list, clear the **(Select All)** check box. Select the **HR** check box, click **OK**, and then compare your screen with **Figure 2**.

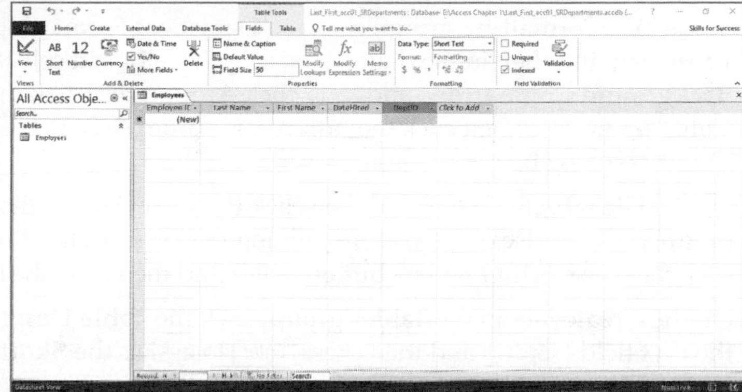

Figure 1 Access 2016, Windows 10, Microsoft Corporation

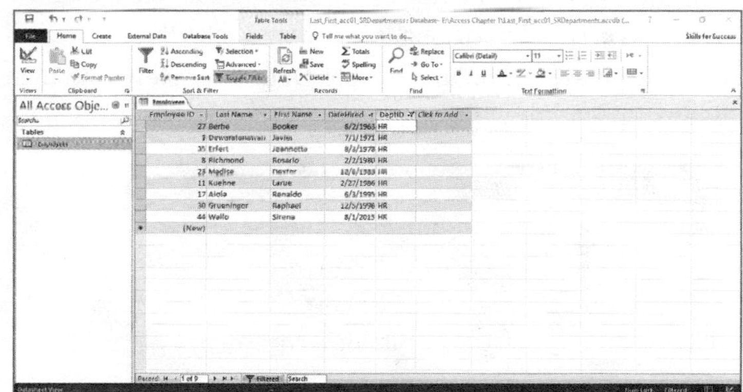

Figure 2 Access 2016, Windows 10, Microsoft Corporation

■ **Continue to the next page to complete this Skills Review**

11. On the **Home tab**, in the **Text Formatting group**, change the font size to **10** and the font to **Verdana**.
12. In the **Text Formatting group**, click the **Datasheet Formatting Dialog Box Launcher**, and then in the dialog box, select the **Raised** cell effect. Click the **Background Color arrow**, and then click **Automatic**. Click the **Gridline Color arrow**, and then click the fifth color—**Blue, Accent 1**. Click **OK** to close the dialog box.
13. On the **File tab**, click **Print**, and then click **Print Preview**. In the **Page Layout group**, click **Landscape**. If you are printing this project, click **Print**. Otherwise, click the **Close Print Preview button**. **Save**, and then close the table.
14. On the **Create tab**, in the **Tables group**, click the **Table Design** button. Name the first field DeptID and then press Enter to assign the **Short Text** data type. On the **Design tab**, in the **Tools group**, click **Primary Key**.
15. With the **DeptID** field still selected, in the **Field Properties** pane, change the **Field Size** value to 50 and the **Caption** to Department ID
16. Add a second field named Department with the **Short Text** data type.
17. Click **Save**, type Departments and then click **OK**.
18. Click the **View** button to switch to **Datasheet view**, and then add the following departments:

Department ID	Department
BG	Buildings and Grounds
CD	Community Development
CI	Capital Improvement
F2	Fire
HR	Human Resources
PR	Parks and Recreation

19. Set the column widths to **Best Fit**, and then compare your screen with **Figure 3**.
20. **Save**, and then **Close** the table. On the **Database Tools tab**, click the **Relationships** button. In the **Show Table** dialog box, add **Employees**, add **Departments**, and then click **Close**.
21. Drag the **DeptID** field from the **Employees** table, point to **DeptID** in the **Departments** table, and then release the left mouse button.
22. In the **Edit Relationships** dialog box, select the **Enforce Referential Integrity** check box, and then click **Create**. If you receive a message, open the Departments table and carefully check your typing.

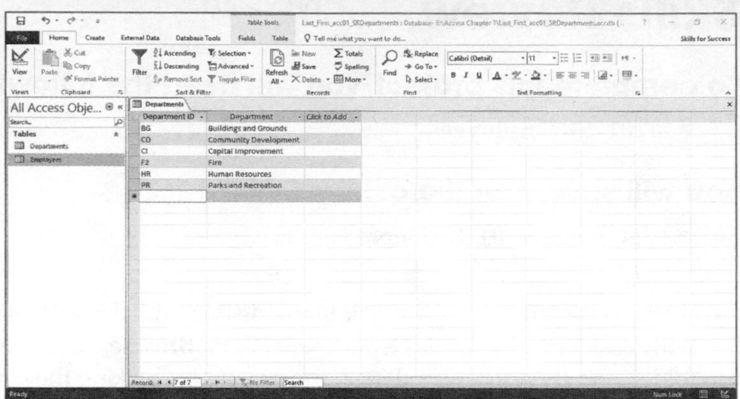

Figure 3 Access 2016, Windows 10, Microsoft Corporation

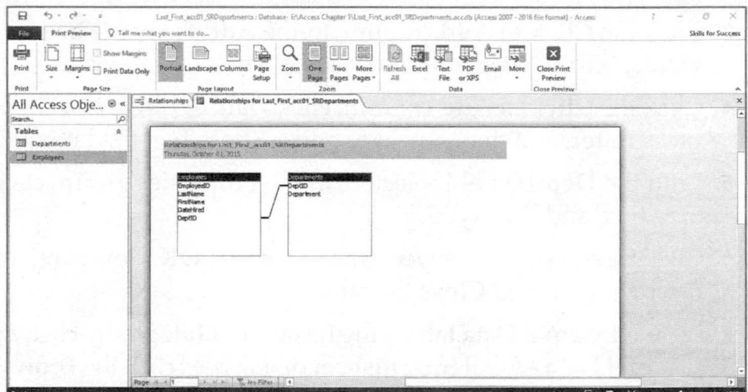

Figure 4 Access 2016, Windows 10, Microsoft Corporation

23. In the **Tools group**, click **Relationship Report**. Compare your screen with **Figure 4**. If you are printing this project, print the report.
24. Click **Save**, click **OK** to accept default name, and then **Close** the report.
25. **Save** and **Close** all open objects, and then **Close** Access. Submit your database files as directed by your instructor.

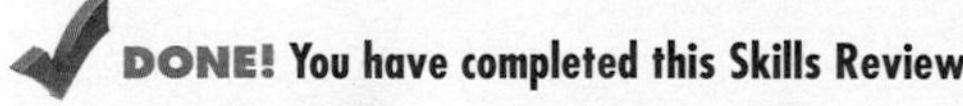

DONE! You have completed this Skills Review

Skills Assessment 1

MyITLab®
Grader

To complete this project, you will need the following file:

- **acc01_SA1UtilityData**

You will save your file as:

- **Last_First_acc01_SA1Utilities**

1. Create a blank desktop database. Name the file Last_First_acc01_SA1Utilities and then save it in your chapter folder.
2. In **Table1**, rename the **ID** field BillingID In the second column, add a **Short Text** field named AccountNumber
3. In the third column, add a **Date & Time** field with the name BillingDate In the fourth column, add a **Currency** field with the name Charge and then save the table as Billings **Close** the table.
4. Import the records in the **Electricity** worksheet from the student data file **acc01_SA1UtilityData**. Append the records to the **Billings** table.
5. Sort the **Billings** datasheet by the **Charge** column in descending order, and then filter the datasheet to display only the records from **Account Number** *2610-408376*.
6. Change the font to **Verdana**, the font size to **10**, and then set column widths to **Best Fit**.
7. Change the cell effect to **Raised**, the background color to **Automatic**, and the gridline color to **Blue-Gray, Text 2**. Compare your screen with **Figure 1**.
8. If you are printing this project, print the datasheet in Landscape orientation. **Save** and then close the table.
9. Create a new table in **Design view**. Name the first field AccountNumber Set the field as the table's primary key, assign the **Short Text** data type, and set its caption to Account Number
10. **Save** the table as Residents and then switch to **Datasheet view**. In the second and third columns, add the **Name Quick Start** fields. In the fourth column, add a **Short Text** field named Street
11. Add the following records to the table:

Account Number	Last Name	First Name	Street
1673-467266	Alloway	Dorris	56553 S Paddington Way
2610-408376	Klasen	Franklin	99721 E Powder River Dr
2790-748496	Cavagnaro	Crystle	72343 N Riverford Pl
3794-907351	Carie	Ryann	45340 N Gurdon Dr

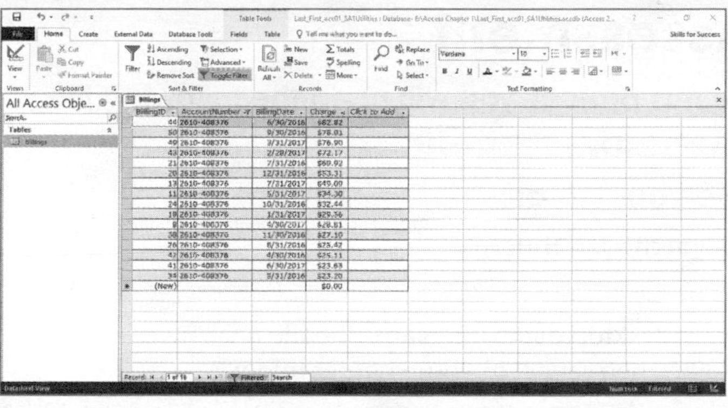

Access 2016, Windows 10, Microsoft Corporation

Figure 1

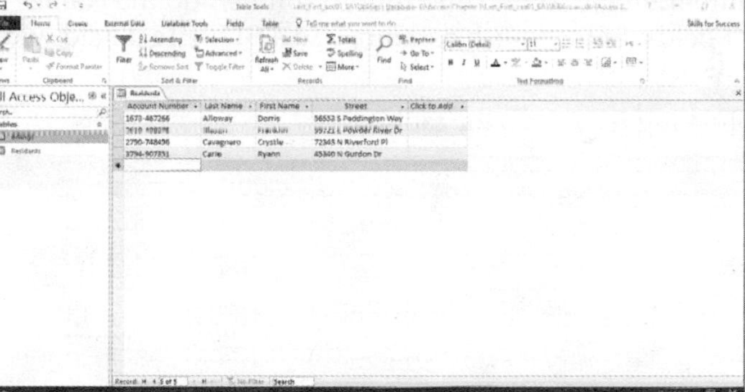

Access 2016, Windows 10, Microsoft Corporation

Figure 2

12. Set the column widths to **Best Fit**, and then compare your screen with **Figure 2**. **Save** and **Close** the table.
13. Add the **Billings** and then the **Residents** table to the **Relationships** tab. Create a one-to-many relationship using the **AccountNumber** field as the common field. Do not select the cascade update or delete options.
14. Create a relationship report. **Save** the report using the name suggested in the **Save As** dialog box. **Close** the report. **Save** and then **Close** the Relationships tab.
15. **Close** the Access window. Submit your work as directed by your instructor.

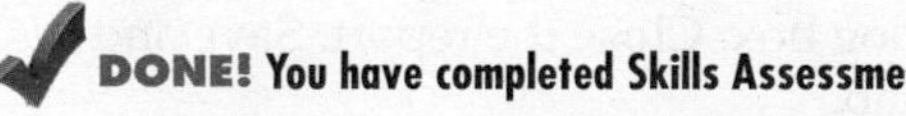
DONE! You have completed Skills Assessment 1

Skills Assessment 2

To complete this project, you will need the following file:

- acc01_SA2ClassData

You will save your file as:

- Last_First_acc01_SA2Interns

1. Create a blank desktop database. Name the file Last_First_acc01_SA2Interns and then save it in your chapter folder.
2. In **Table1**, rename the **ID** field as InternID and then change its data type to **Number**. In the second and third columns, add the **Name Quick Start** fields. In the fourth column, add a **Short Text** field with the name Phone
3. Add the following records to the table:

InternID	LastName	FirstName	Phone
1	Yerigan	Kenton	(805) 555-7928
2	Mostowy	Clarice	(805) 555-3107
3	Hemstreet	Caroline	(805) 555-5548
4	Marcantel	Almeda	(805) 555-7000
5	Shriver	Cheyenne	(805) 555-6991

4. Set the column widths to **Best Fit**, and then **Save** the table as Interns Compare your screen with **Figure 1**, and then **Save** and close the table.
5. Create a new table in **Design view**. Name the first field ClassID Set the field as the table's primary key, assign the **AutoNumber** data type, and then set its caption to Class ID
6. Add a **Short Text** field named Class as the second field. As the third field, add a **Date/Time** field named StartDate and then set its caption to Start Date
7. In the fourth row, add a **Number** data type named InternID and then set its caption to Intern ID **Save** the table as Sections and then close the table.
8. Add both tables to the **Relationships** tab. Create a one-to-many relationship using the **InternID** field as the common field. Do not select the cascade update or delete options.
9. Create a relationship report. **Save** the report using the name suggested in the **Save As** dialog box. **Close** the report. **Save** and then close the Relationships tab.

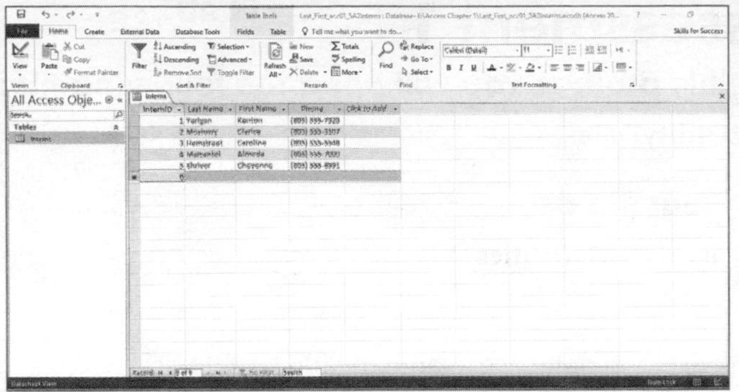

Access 2016, Windows 10, Microsoft Corporation

Figure 1

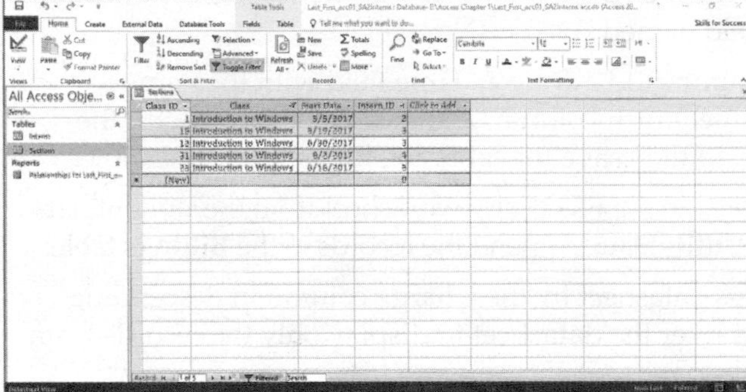

Access 2016, Windows 10, Microsoft Corporation

Figure 2

10. Import the records in the **Sections** worksheet from the Excel student data file **acc01_SA2ClassData**. Append the records to the **Sections** table.
11. Sort the **Sections** datasheet by the **InternID** column in ascending order, and then filter the datasheet to display only the records for the **Introduction to Windows** class.
12. Change the font to **Cambria**, the font size to **12**, and then set column widths to **Best Fit**.
13. Change the cell effect to **Raised**, the background color to **Automatic**, and the gridline color to **Blue-Gray, Text 2**. Compare your screen with **Figure 2**.
14. If you are printing this project, print the datasheet in Landscape orientation. **Save** and then close the table. **Close** Access.
15. Submit the database file as directed by your instructor.

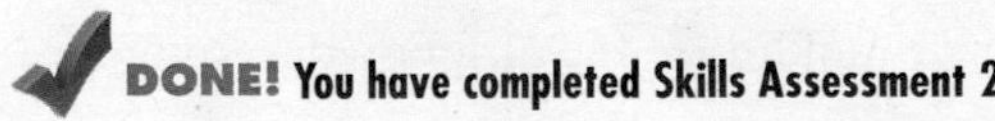

DONE! You have completed Skills Assessment 2

My Skills

To complete this project, you will need the following file:

- acc01_MYAddresses

You will save your file as:

- Last_First_acc01_MYContacts

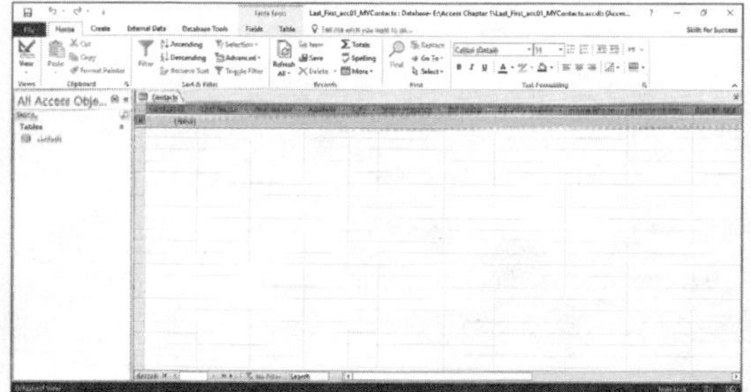

Access 2016, Windows 10, Microsoft Corporation **Figure 1**

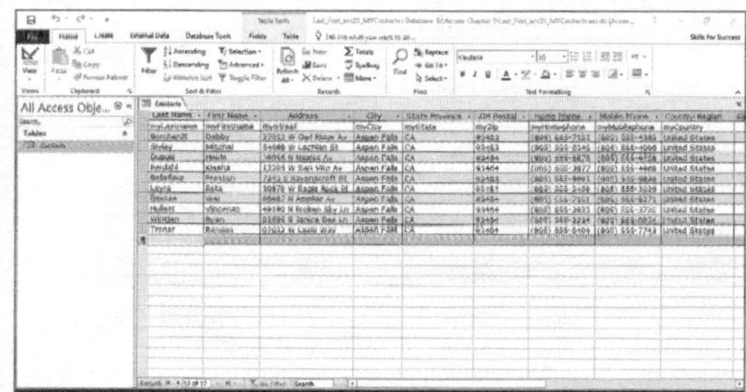

Access 2016, Windows 10, Microsoft Corporation **Figure 2**

1. Create a blank desktop database. Name the file Last_First_acc01_MYContacts and then save it in your chapter folder.
2. In **Table1**, rename the **ID** field as ContactID and then add a caption of Contact ID
3. In columns two and three, add the Quick Start **Name** fields.
4. In columns four through eight, add the Quick Start **Address** fields.
5. In columns nine through twelve, add the Quick Start **Phone** fields.
6. Delete the **Fax Number** and **Business Phone** fields.
7. Save the table as Contacts and then set the column widths to **Best Fit**. Compare your screen with **Figure 1**.
8. Complete the first record by inserting your own contact information, and then **Save** and close the table.
9. Import the contacts from the Excel student data file **acc01_MYAddresses**. Use the **Contacts** worksheet and append the data to the **Contacts** table.
10. Change the font to **Verdana** and the font size to **10**.
11. In the **Navigation Pane**, click the **Shutter Bar Open/Close Button** « to close the pane. Set the column widths to **Best Fit**.
12. Change the cell effect to **Raised**, the background color to **Automatic**, and the gridline color to **Blue-Gray, Text 2**.
13. Select the **Contact ID** column, and then on the **Home tab**, in the **Records group**, click **More**, and then click **Hide Fields**. **Save** the table changes.
14. Click the **Shutter Bar Open/Close Button** one time to display the Navigation Pane. Click in the append row, and then compare your screen with **Figure 2**.
15. If you are printing this project, print the datasheet in Landscape orientation. **Save** and then close the table.
16. **Close** Access. Submit your work as directed by your instructor.

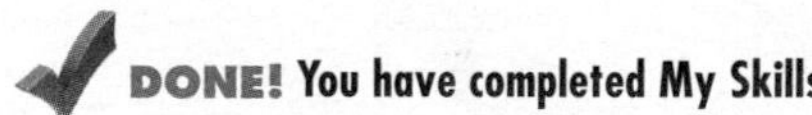
DONE! You have completed My Skills

Visual Skills Check

To complete this project, you will need the following file:

- acc01_VSAssessments

You will save your file as:

- Last_First_acc01_VSAssessments

Open the student data file **acc01_VSAssessments**. On the **File tab**, click **Save As**, and then under **Save Database As**, click **Save As**. Use the **Save As** dialog box to save the file in your chapter folder with the name Last_First_acc01_VSAssessments Sort, filter, and format the **Assessments** table datasheet as shown in **Figure 1**. The table is sorted by the **Parcel** column and filtered by the **AssessorID** column. The font is **Verdana** size **10**, the columns are set to **Best Fit**, and the row height is **15**. The cell effect is **Raised**, the background color is **Automatic**, and the gridline color is **Blue, Accent 1, Darker 50%**.

Set the table to print in the Landscape orientation, and then submit your database file as directed by your instructor.

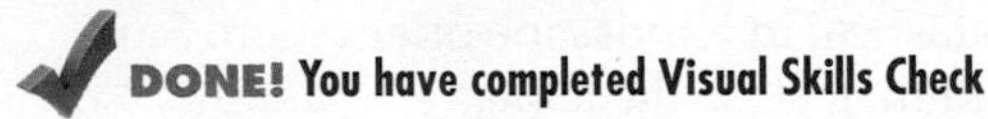

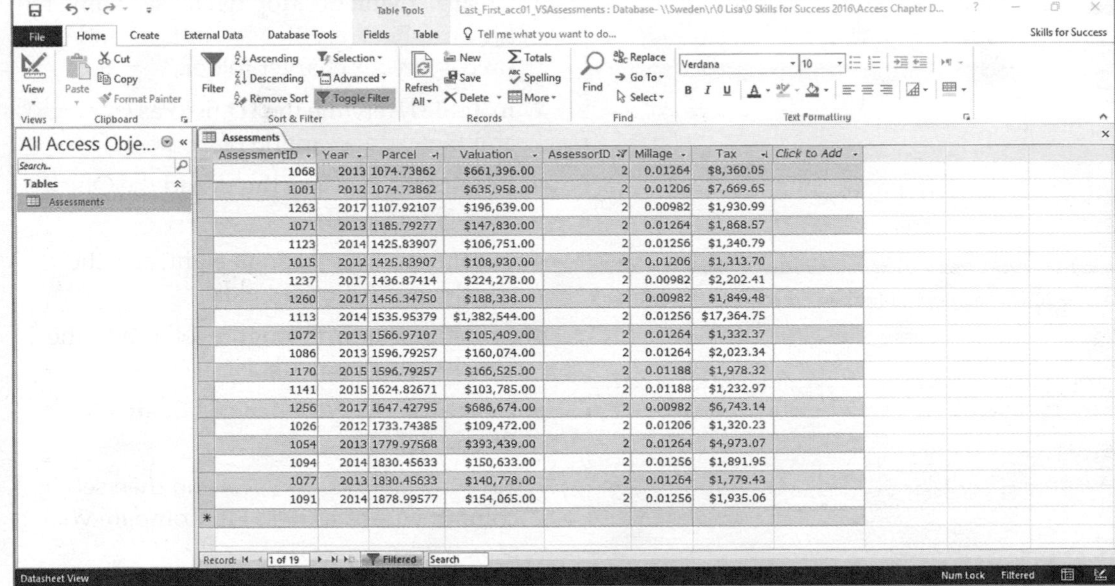

Figure 1

Access 2016, Windows 10, Microsoft Corporation

Skills Challenge 1

To complete this project, you will need the following file:

- acc01_SC1ZonesData

You will save your files as:

- Last_First_acc01_SC1ZonesData (Excel)
- Last_First_acc01_SC1Zones (Access)

Open the student data file **acc01_SC1ZonesData** in Excel, and then save it in your chapter folder as Last_First_acc01_SC1ZonesData View the data stored in the spreadsheet, which describes the zones used in Aspen Falls. Label each column with a label that describes the column and can be used as database field names, and then close the spreadsheet.

Create a new database named Last_First_acc01_SC1Zones and save it in your chapter folder. Create a table to store the data in the Excel spreadsheet. Assign field names, data types, and captions using the practices in this chapter's projects. Assign a primary key to the field that will uniquely identify each record. Name the table Zones and then import the Excel data into the table you just created. Set the field widths to Best Fit, and then close the table.

Set the table to print in the Landscape orientation, and then submit your database file as directed by your instructor.

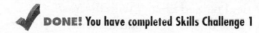

 **DONE! You have completed Skills Challenge 1**

Skills Challenge 2

To complete this project, you will need the following file:

- acc01_SC2Plants

You will save your file as:

- Last_First_acc01_SC2Plants

Open the student data file **acc01_SC2Plants**, and then save the file in your chapter folder with the name Last_First_acc01_SC2Plants View the **Relationships** tab, and notice that each plant is assigned a scientific name but the plant may have many common names—a one-to-many relationship. Open the Plants table, and then expand the subdatasheet for *Asarum caudatum* to display three of its common names. Use the subdatasheets for the other nine plants to enter the common names for each. To locate the common names, search the Internet using the plant's scientific name as the key term. For each plant, enter between one and three common names based on the information you find.

Submit your database file as directed by your instructor.

 **DONE! You have completed Skills Challenge 2**

More Skills Assessment

To complete this project, you will need the following files:

- acc01_MSAMuseum (Access)
- acc01_MSADonor (Word)

You will save your file as:

- Last_First_acc01_MSAMuseum

1. Start **Access 2016**, and **Open** the **acc01_MSAMuseum** file and then save it in your chapter folder as Last_First_acc01_MSAMuseum.
2. **Compact and Repair** the database.
3. In the **Museum Cars** table, add a field named Loaner with the **Yes/No** data type. Place a checkmark in the *Buick Electra* and *Chevrolet Master Eagle* **Loaner** fields.
4. Add a field named Donor with the **Attachment** data type. Change the **caption** of this field to Donor Compare your screen with **Figure 1**.
5. Attach the **acc01_MSADonor.docx** file to the **Chevrolet Master Eagle Donor** field.
6. Open the **Club Cars** table, and then change the **Notes** field to the **Long Text** data type.
7. At the end of the **Note** for the **Lincoln Sport Touring**, add the following text: This car will not be included in the 6/1/2018 car show. Compare your screen with **Figure 2**.
8. Change the field width of the **Club Cars** table to **Best Fit**.
9. In the **Museum Cars** table, add a field with the **Hyperlink** data type. Change the field name to MuseumWebsite and then adjust the field width to **Best Fit**.
10. In the Pontiac Chieftain record, change the MuseumWebsite to: www.aspenfalls.org
11. **Save** and **Close** any open objects, and then **Close** Access. Submit the file as directed by your instructor.

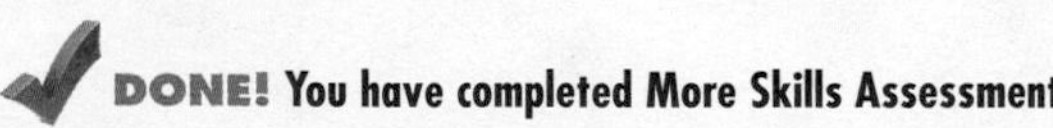

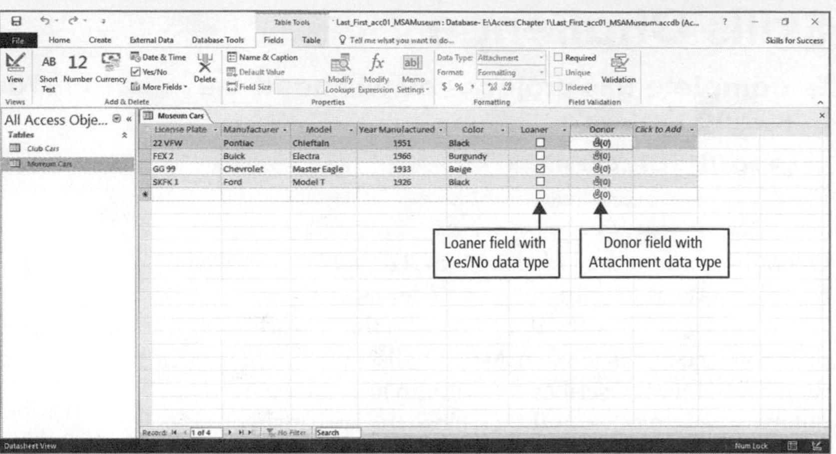

Figure 1 Access 2016, Windows 10, Microsoft Corporation

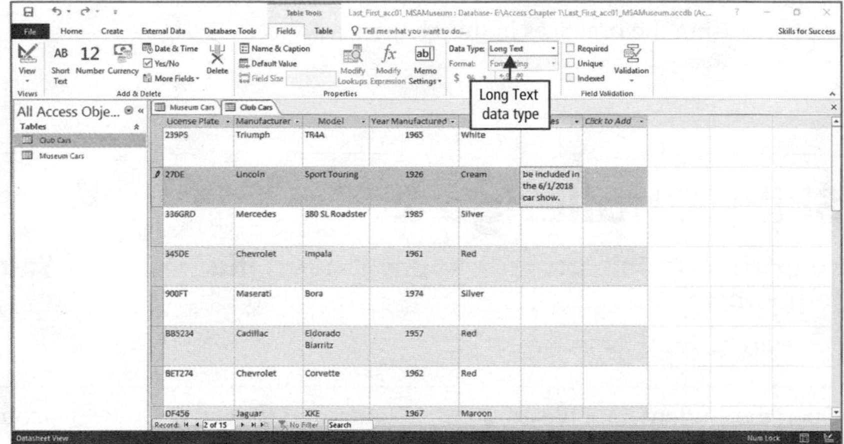

Figure 2 Access 2016, Windows 10, Microsoft Corporation

Collaborating with Google

To complete this project, you will need a Google account (refer to the Common Features chapter)

You will save your file as:

- **Last_First_acc01_GPSnip**

---

1. Open the Google Chrome web browser. Log into your Google account, and then click the **Apps** button.
2. Click the **Drive** button to open Google Drive. If you receive a pop-up message, read the message, and then click **Next**. Read each message, and then close the dialog box.
3. Click the **NEW** button, and then click **Google Sheets** to open a blank spreadsheet.
4. Click cell **A1**, type CustomerID and then press Tab. Continue in this manner to enter the column labels in this order: LastName | FirstName | Address | City | Zip | Phone | Email Compare your screen with **Figure 1**.
5. Click the spreadsheet title, *Untitled spreadsheet*. In the dialog box, type CustomerTable as the name of the spreadsheet, and then press **Enter**.

   If you are using a different web browser, you may need to click **File**, and then click **Rename**.
6. Click the **Share** button, and in the **Share with others** dialog box, type AspenFallsEvents@gmail.com to share the sheet with another user.
7. In the **Add a note** text box, type Please add the customer information to this spreadsheet. Once all the records are added I will import the information into the database. and then compare your screen with **Figure 2**.
8. Click **Send**. Click the **Share** button, and then click **Advanced**.
9. Press , type snip and then press Enter to start the **Snipping Tool**. Click the **New arrow**, and then click **Full-screen Snip**.
10. In the **Snipping Tool** mark-up window, click the **Save Snip** button. In the **Save As** dialog box, navigate to your Access Chapter 1 folder. Be sure the **Save as type** box displays **JPEG file**. Name the file Last_First_acc01_GPSnip and then press Enter. **Close** the Snipping Tool mark-up window.
11. Close all windows, and then submit your work as directed by your instructor.

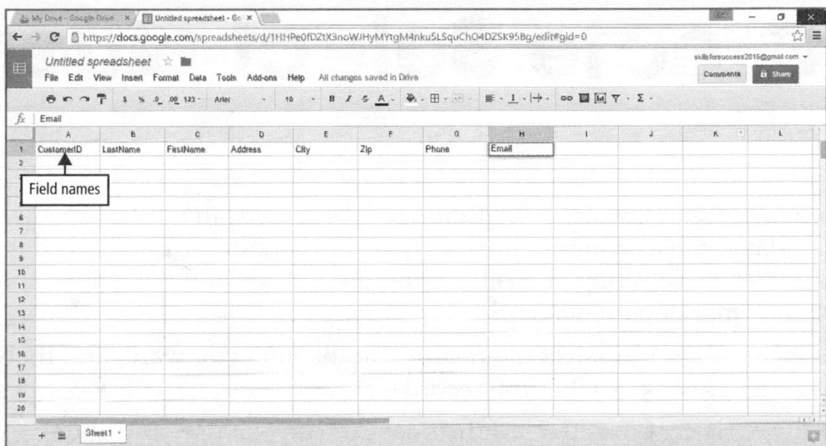

Figure 1

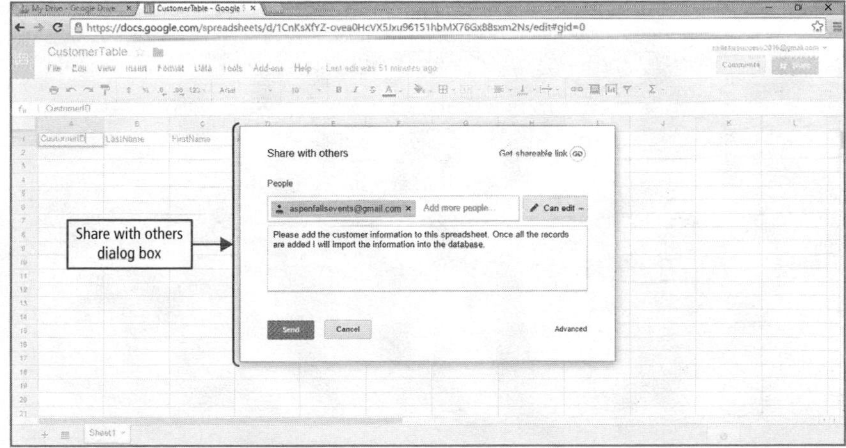

Figure 2

DONE! You have completed Collaborating with Google

CHAPTER 2

Create Select Queries

- Databases typically store thousands of records in multiple, related tables. Queries answer questions about the data stored in tables by selecting and presenting the records and fields with the information you need.
- In a query, you select the fields with the data you want, and then add criteria that filter the records.
- Criteria test to see if conditions are true or false, and then select only those records in which the results of those tests are true.
- When you run a select query, a datasheet is created with just the records and fields you selected. The data in the underlying tables is not changed or deleted.
- You can create new fields by calculating values derived from existing fields. These types of fields can be added to both tables and queries.
- Query results can also be grouped by one or more fields so that statistics such as totals and averages for each group can be calculated.

Arinahabich/Fotolia

Aspen Falls City Hall

In this chapter, you will create database queries for Aspen Falls City Hall, which provides essential services for the citizens and visitors of Aspen Falls, California. In this project, you will assist Diane Payne, Public Works Director, to answer several questions about the Water Utility monthly billing cycles.

For each monthly billing cycle, the Public Works Department needs to calculate charges—an amount that is derived from each resident's water usage and that month's rate for water. As payments are recorded in the database, the amount due should be automatically adjusted. You will complete both of these tasks by adding calculated fields to a table.

The Public Works Department needs to find records for specific residents by searching for their account number, name, or meter number. You will create select queries that can perform these searches. The department also needs to know which residents are late in their payments and add a late fee when appropriate. To do this, you will add a calculated field to a query.

Finally, the city needs to analyze water usage statistics. To do this, you will add grouping to a query, and then provide summary statistics such as count, average, and total. Throughout the project, you will test your queries using a small sample of the city database used to track resident utility bills.

Time to complete all 10 skills — 60 to 90 minutes

Outcome

Using the skills in this chapter, you will be able to create queries, add calculated fields to tables and queries, add comparison operators and date and time criteria to queries, group queries, and use logical operators and wildcards in queries.

Objectives

2.1 Create queries in a variety of views

2.2 Construct queries using logical operators and wildcards

2.3 Apply calculated fields to tables and queries

2.4 Adjust and add criteria to queries

Student data file needed for this chapter:

acc02_Water

You will save your file as:

Last_First_acc02_Water

Billing Date	Billing Count	Average Usage	Total Billing	Total Due
31-Jan-17	50	67.7	$778.09	($18.27)
28-Feb-17	55	68.4	$865.72	$0.00
31-Mar-17	60	78.8	$1,069.96	($1.00)
30-Apr-17	65	76.9	$1,149.54	$51.18
31-May-17	69	89.4	$1,541.50	$0.00
30-Jun-17	71	113.0	$2,006.00	$24.75
31-Jul-17	74	126.7	$2,312.25	$0.45
31-Aug-17	79	126.7	$2,702.43	$87.21
30-Sep-17	80	128.1	$2,743.20	$55.58
31-Oct-17	82	112.7	$2,279.00	$73.00
30-Nov-17	84	83.9	$1,761.00	$8.00
31-Dec-17	83	61.3	$1,170.24	$17.02
31-Jan-18	84	46.8	$903.67	$0.00
28-Feb-18	83	37.8	$753.60	$2.94
31-Mar-18	83	50.1	$1,039.75	$18.75
30-Apr-18	83	53.3	$1,312.22	($17.08)
31-May-18	82	73.7	$1,993.20	($32.01)
30-Jun-18	80	94.4	$2,643.90	$6.30
31-Jul-18	80	138.1	$4,199.38	$4,199.38

Statistics

Access 2016, Windows 10, Microsoft Corporation

SKILLS

At the end of this chapter you will be able to:

Skill 1 Create Queries with the Simple Query Wizard
Skill 2 Add Text Criteria
Skill 3 Add Calculated Fields to Tables
Skill 4 Create Queries in Design View
Skill 5 Add Comparison Operators
Skill 6 Add Date and Time Criteria
Skill 7 Group and Total Queries
Skill 8 Add Calculated Fields to Queries
Skill 9 Work with Logical Operators
Skill 10 Add Wildcards to Query Criteria

MORE SKILLS

Skill 11 Export Queries to Excel
Skill 12 Export Queries as Web Pages
Skill 13 Link to External Data Sources
Skill 14 Create Crosstab Queries

▸ ***Queries*** are used to ask questions about—query—the data stored in database tables. ***Select queries*** select and display the records that answer the question, without having to change the data in the underlying table or tables.

1. Start **Access 2016**. On the **Recent** page, click **Open Other Files**. On the **Open** page, click **This PC**, and then click **Browse**. In the **Open** dialog box, navigate to the student data files for this chapter, select **acc02_Water**, and then click the **Open** button.
2. On the **File tab**, click **Save As**. With **Save Database As** selected, click the **Save As** button. In the **Save As** dialog box, navigate to the location you are saving your files for this project. Click **New folder**, type Access Chapter 2 and then press Enter two times. Name the file Last_First_acc02_Water Compare your screen with **Figure 1**, and then click **Save**.
3. If the security warning message displays, click Enable Content.
4. In the **Navigation Pane**, under **Tables**, select **Residents**.
5. Click the **Create tab**, and then in the **Queries group**, click the **Query Wizard** button. In the **New Query** dialog box, with **Simple Query Wizard** selected, click **OK** to start the Simple Query Wizard. Compare your screen with **Figure 2.**

   The Simple Query Wizard's first screen is used to select the fields you want to display as columns in the query result. You can choose fields from any table or query, but they should be from tables that are related. Including unrelated tables will result in too many records in the query results.

■ **Continue to the next page to complete the skill**

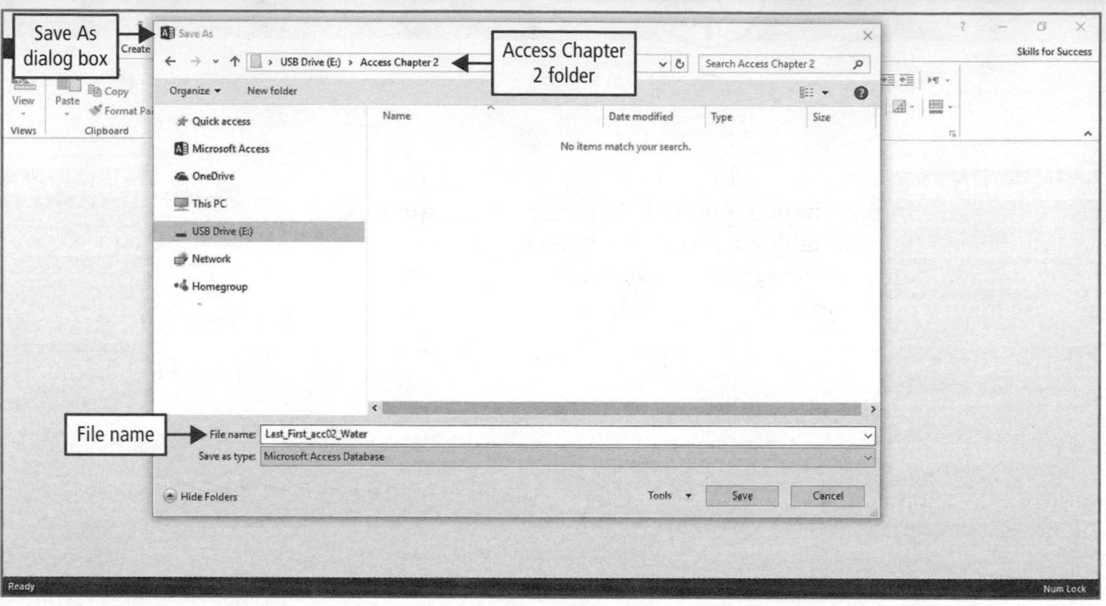

Figure 1

Access 2016, Windows 10, Microsoft Corporation

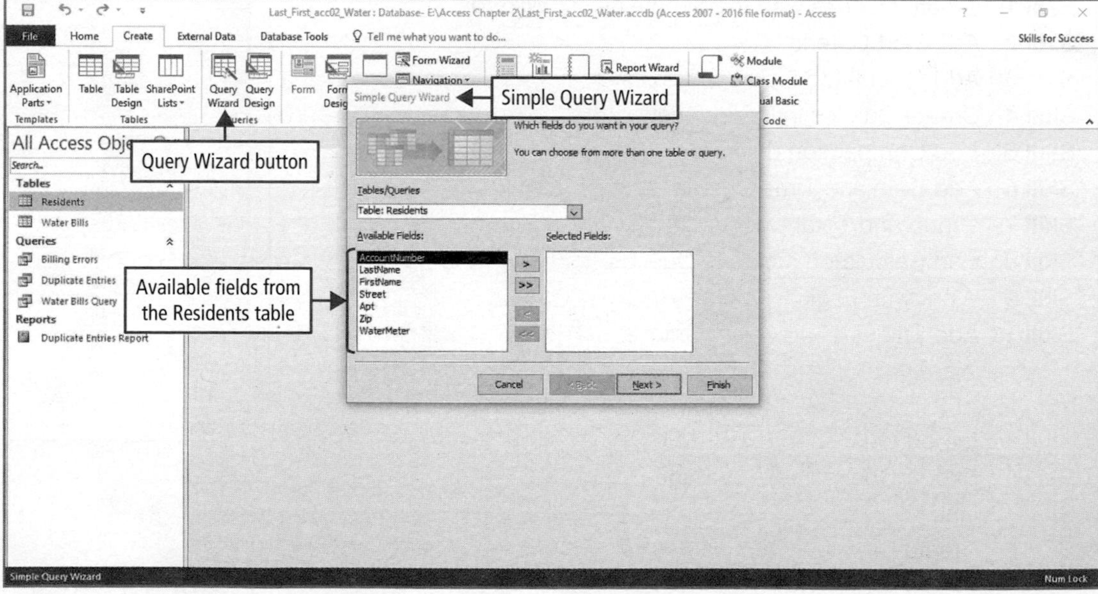

Figure 2

Access 2016, Windows 10, Microsoft Corporation

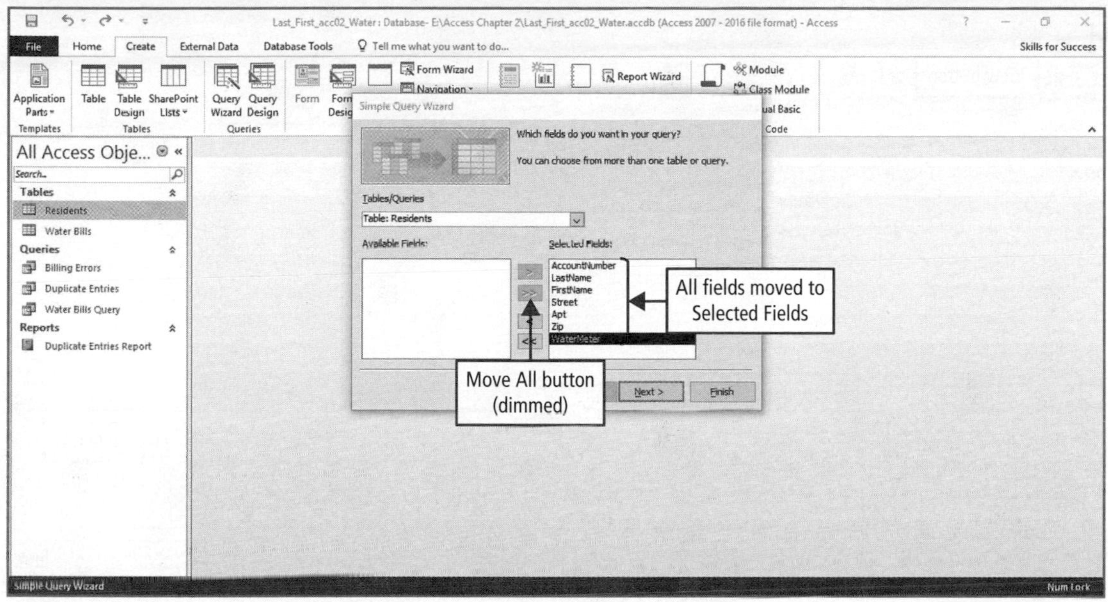

Access 2016, Windows 10, Microsoft Corporation

Figure 3

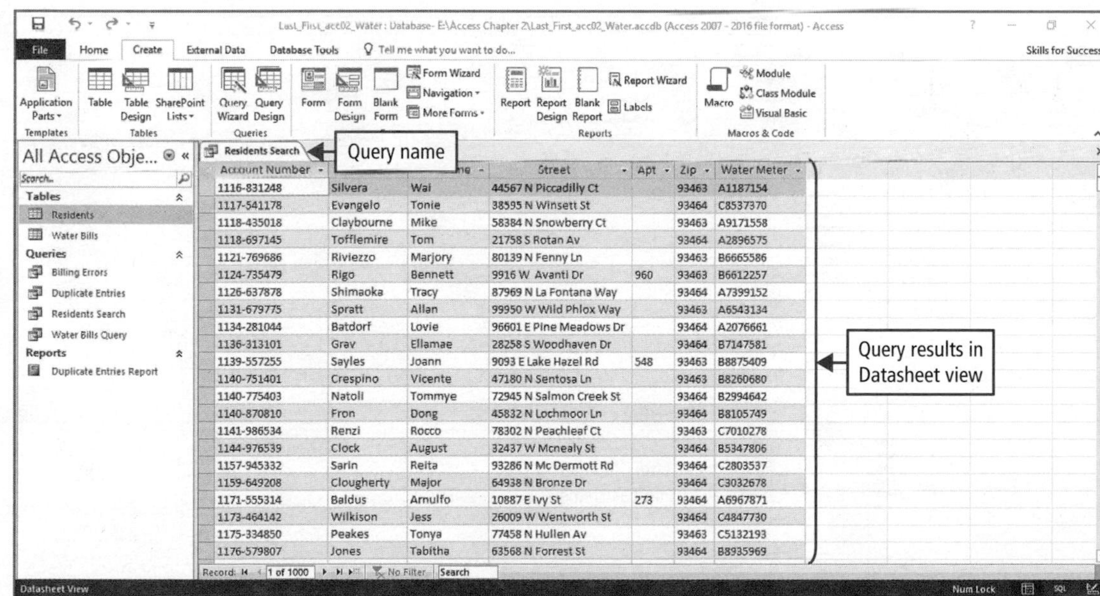

Access 2016, Windows 10, Microsoft Corporation

Figure 4

6. Click the **Move** button [>] one time, to move the **AccountNumber** field into Selected Fields.
7. Click the **Move All** button [>>] to move all the table's fields into Selected Fields. Compare your screen with **Figure 3**, and then click **Next**.
8. In the **What title do you want for your query** box, replace the existing text—*Residents Query*—with Residents Search

   In the last screen of the Simple Query Wizard, you type the name that will be given to the query and choose to either run the query or open it in Design view.

9. Click **Finish**, and then compare your screen with **Figure 4**.

   In this manner, the Simple Query Wizard quickly adds fields to a new query. When the query is run, the results display in Datasheet view. Here, all the records and fields from the Residents table have been selected and display. When the Run button is clicked, the query is automatically saved.

10. Leave the query open for the next skill.

- **You have completed Skill 1 of 10**

SKILL 2: Add Text Criteria

- ***Criteria*** are conditions in a query used to select the records that answer the query's question.

Obj 1.3.5

1. With the **Residents Search** query open in Datasheet view, click the **Home tab**. In the **Views group**, click the **View** button to switch to Design view. Alternatively, in the lower right corner of the window, click the Design View button. Compare your screen with **Figure 1**.

   Query Design view has two panes. The ***query design workspace*** displays the tables that the query will search. The ***query design grid*** displays the fields the query will display and the query settings that will be applied to each field.

2. If the table name—*Residents*—does not display under each field name in the design grid, on the Design tab, in the Show/Hide group, click Table Names so that it is selected.

3. In the intersection of the **LastName** column and **Criteria** row—the **LastName** column **Criteria** cell—type the letter h and then compare your screen with **Figure 2**.

   As you type in a criteria cell, ***IntelliSense***—Quick Info, ScreenTips, and AutoComplete boxes—displays guidelines for the feature you are typing. ***AutoComplete*** is a menu of commands that match the characters you type. The ***Quick Info*** message explains the purpose of the selected AutoComplete command.

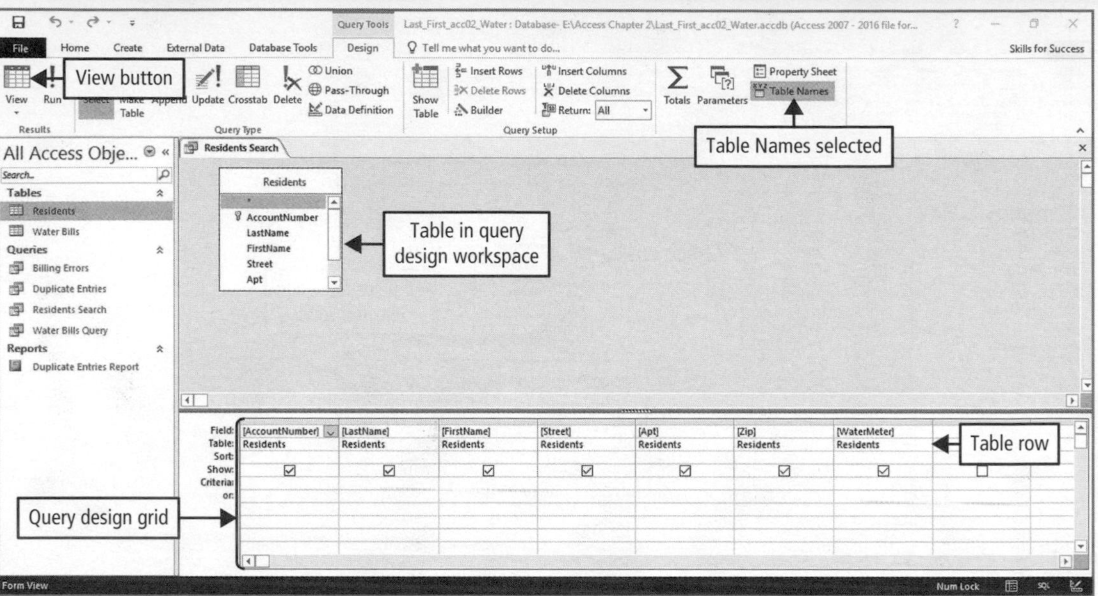

Figure 1

Access 2016, Windows 10, Microsoft Corporation

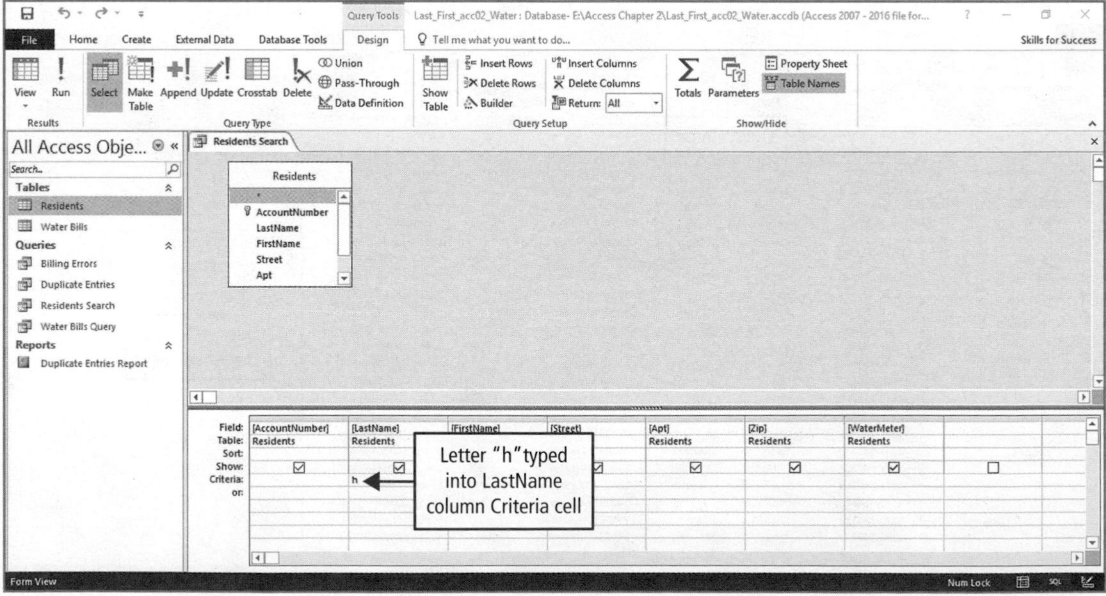

Figure 2

Access 2016, Windows 10, Microsoft Corporation

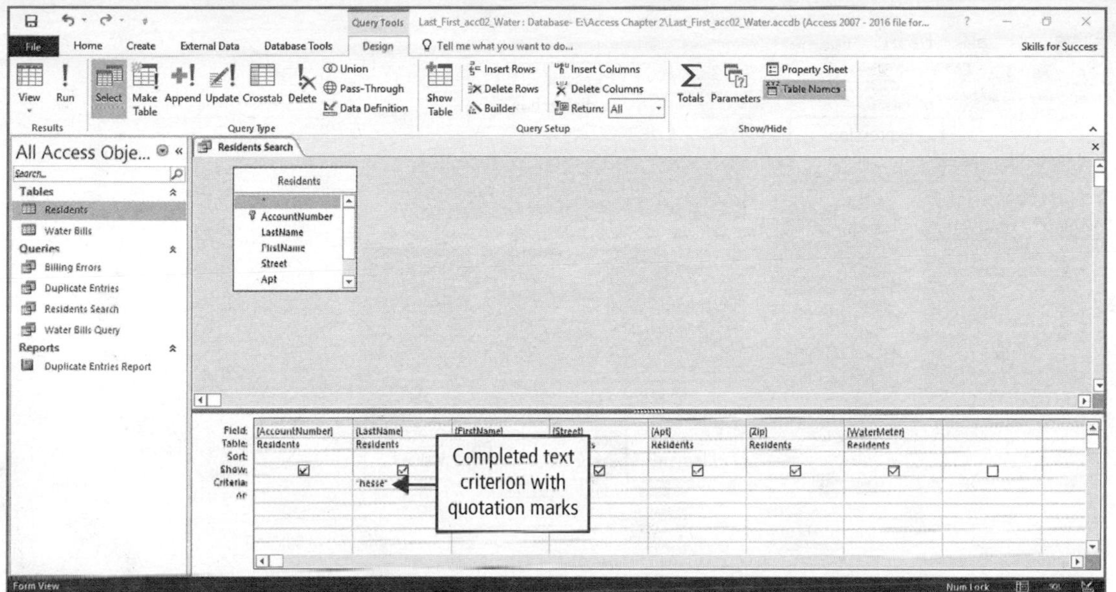

Access 2016, Windows 10, Microsoft Corporation

Figure 3

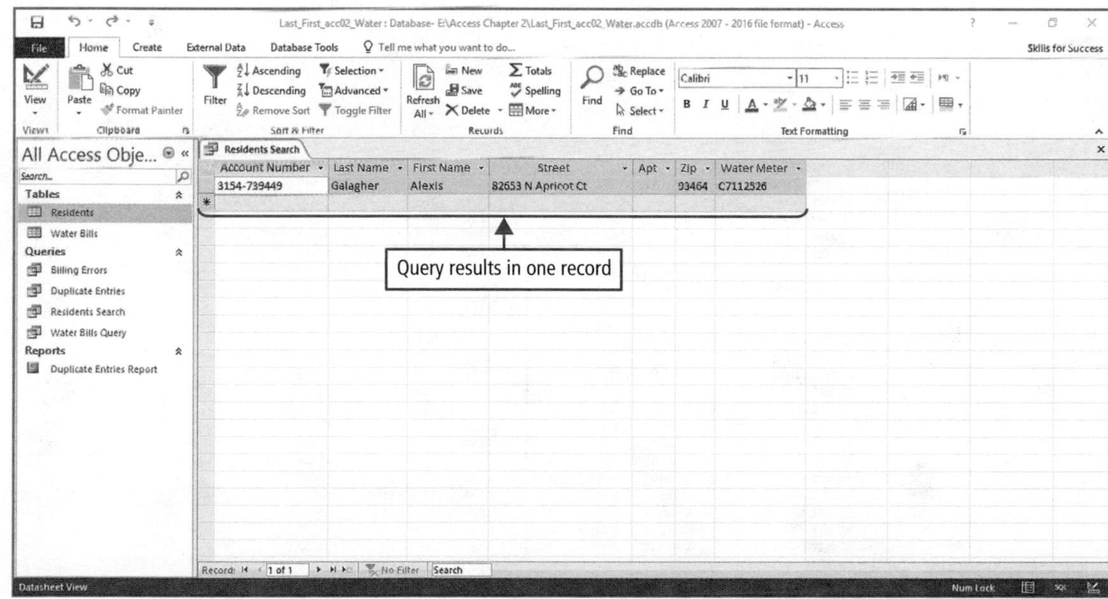

Access 2016, Windows 10, Microsoft Corporation

Figure 4

4. In the **LastName** column **Criteria** cell, complete the entry hesse Press Tab, and then compare your screen with **Figure 3**.

   Criteria that contain text must be surrounded by quotation marks. If you do not type the quotation marks, they will be automatically inserted before the query is run.

5. On the **Design tab**, in the **Results group**, click the **Run** button to display the three records that result.

   In this manner, criteria filter the data. Here, the query answers the question, *Which residents have a last name of Hesse?* By default, criteria are not case sensitive. Here, the criterion *hesse* matched the value *Hesse*.

6. On the **Home tab**, in the **Views group**, click the **View** button to return to Design view.
7. In the **LastName** column **Criteria** cell, delete the quotation marks and text *"hesse"*.
8. In the **WaterMeter** column **Criteria** cell, type the quotation marks and text "C7112526"

   When you include the quotation marks around criteria, the AutoComplete and Quick Info messages do not display.

9. On the **Design tab**, in the **Results group**, click the **Run** button, and then compare your screen with **Figure 4**.

   The query answers the following questions, *Who owns meter C7112526, and what is the address?*

10. If you are printing your work for this project, print the datasheet in Landscape orientation.
11. Click **Save**, and then **Close** the query.

■ **You have completed Skill 2 of 10**

- A ***calculated field*** is a field in a table or query that derives its values from other fields in the table or query.

1. In the **Navigation Pane**, under **Tables**, double-click **Water Bills** to open the datasheet.
2. Click anywhere in the **Usage** column to make it the active column.
3. Click the **Fields tab**, and then in the **Add & Delete group**, click **More Fields**. Near the bottom of the field list, point to **Calculated Field**, and then in the submenu that displays, click **Currency**.

MOS Obj 3.3.1

4. In the **Expression Builder** dialog box, under **Expression Categories**, double-click **Rate** to insert it into the expression.

   An ***expression*** is a combination of fields, mathematical operators, and prebuilt functions that calculates values in tables, forms, queries, and reports. In expressions, field names are enclosed between left and right square brackets.

5. Under **Expression Elements**, click **Operators**, and then under **Expression Categories**, click **Arithmetic**.
6. Under **Expression Values**, double-click the multiplication operator—the asterisk (*)—to insert it into the expression.
7. Under **Expression Elements**, click **Water Bills**, and then under **Expression Categories**, double-click **Usage**.
8. Compare your screen with **Figure 1**, and then click **OK**.
9. In the datasheet, with the text *Field1* still selected, type Billing Press Tab, and then compare your screen with **Figure 2**.

   The Billing column displays the result of multiplying each record's Rate by its Usage.

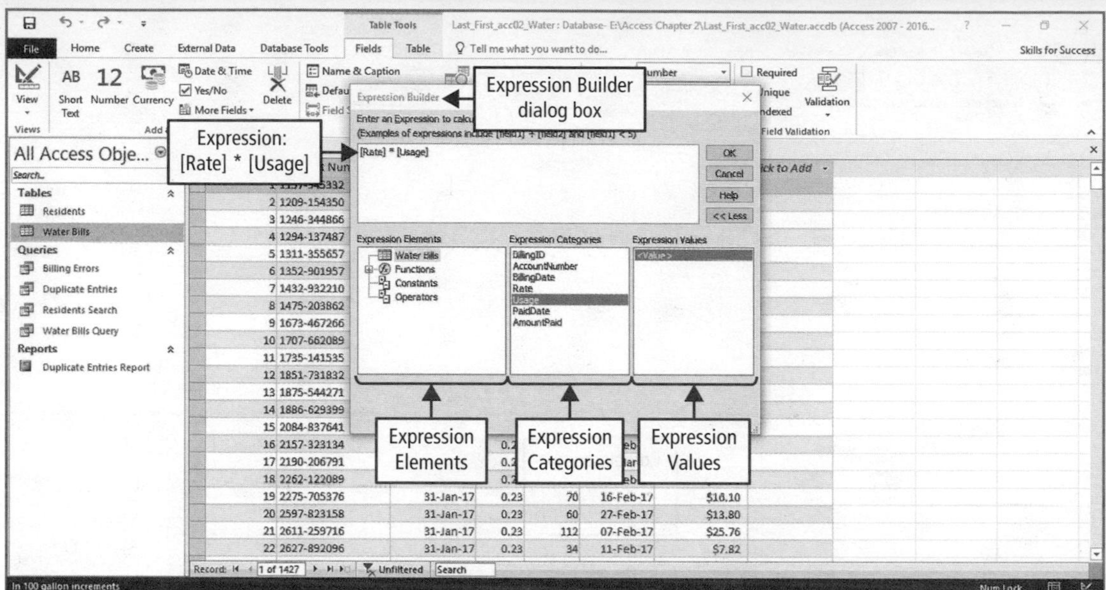

Figure 1

Access 2016, Windows 10, Microsoft Corporation

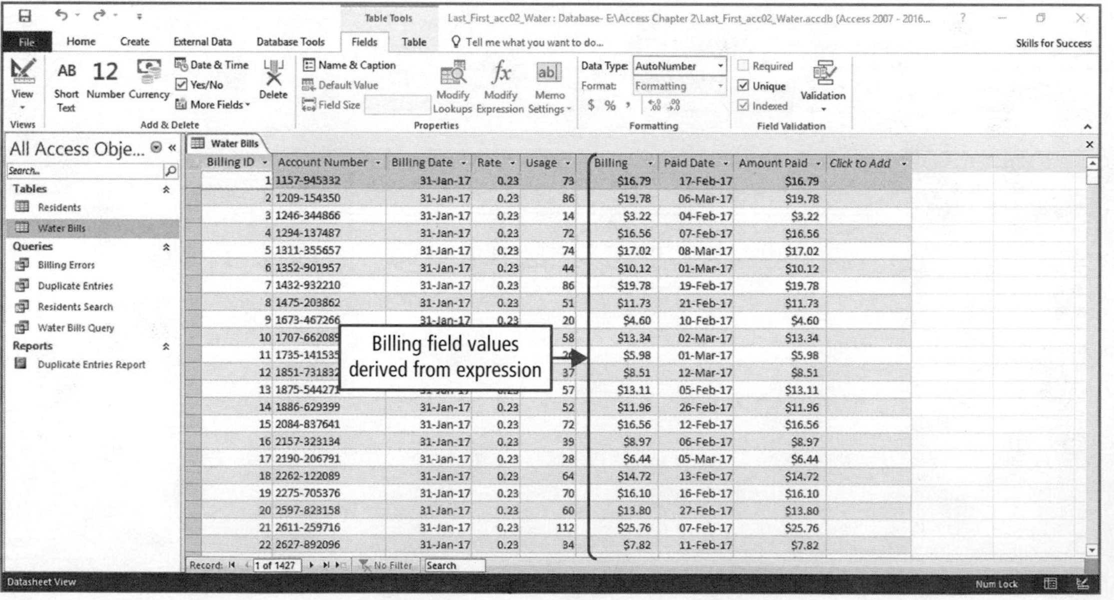

Figure 2

Access 2016, Windows 10, Microsoft Corporation

■ **Continue to the next page to complete the skill**

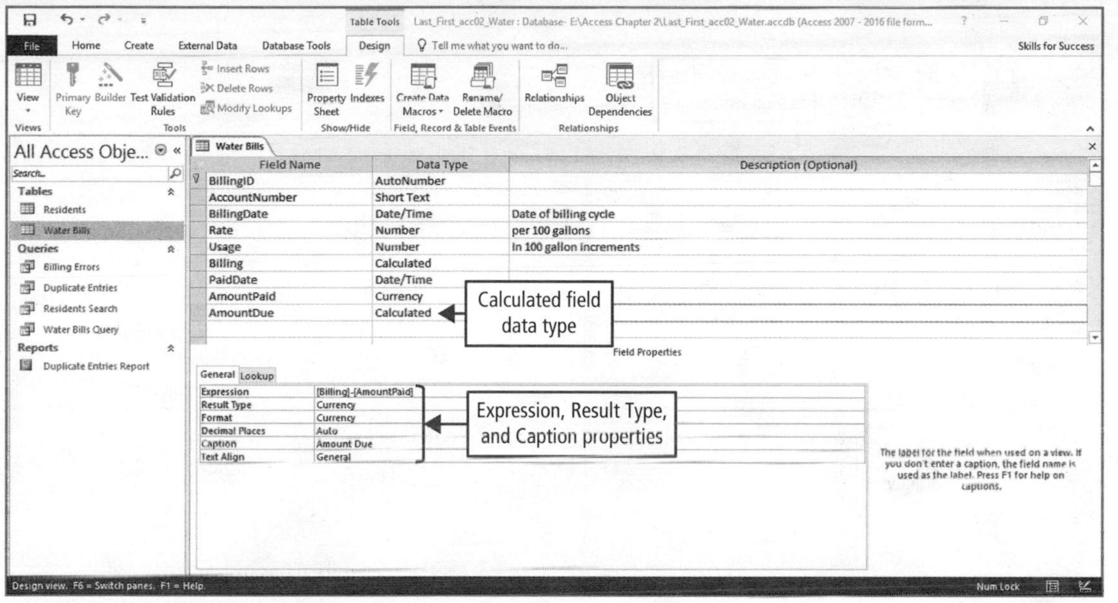

Access 2016, Windows 10, Microsoft Corporation

Figure 3

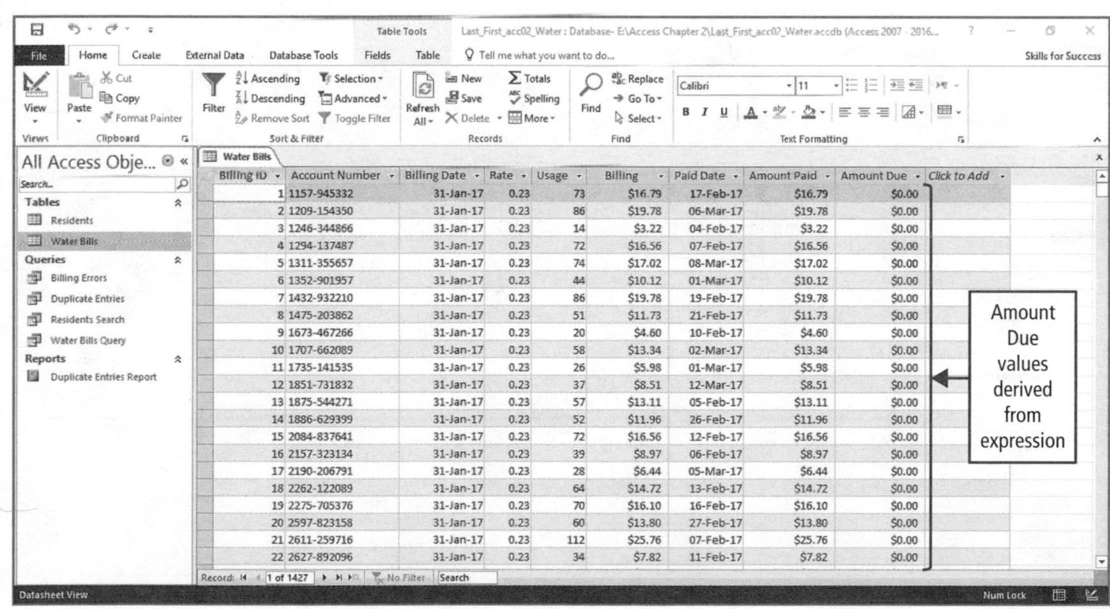

Access 2016, Windows 10, Microsoft Corporation

Figure 4

10. Click **Save** [Save]. On the **Home tab**, in the **Views group**, click **View** to switch to Design view.
11. In the **Field Name** column, click in the first empty cell, and then type AmountDue In the same row, display and click the **Data Type arrow**, and then click **Calculated** to open the Expression Builder.
12. In the **Expression Builder**, repeat the technique just practiced or type the following expression: [Billing] - [AmountPaid] and then click **OK**.
13. With the **AmountDue** field still active, in the **Field Properties** pane, click **Result Type**, click the **Result Type arrow**, and then click **Currency**.

    A calculated field can be assigned any of the data types other fields are assigned. Here, the Currency data type is the most appropriate data type.

14. In the **Field Properties** pane, click in the **Caption** cell, and then type Amount Due Compare your screen with **Figure 3**.
15. Click **Save** [Save], and then switch to Datasheet view. Set the **Amount Due** column width to **Best Fit**, and then compare your screen with **Figure 4**.

    It is best practice to exclude spaces from field names. Labels, however, can display spaces. Here, the *Amount Due* caption displays at the top of the last column instead of the field name—*AmountDue*.

16. Click **Save** [Save], and then **Close** [X] the table.

■ **You have completed Skill 3 of 10**

  SKILL 2.4

► To create a query in Design view, first add the necessary tables to the query design workspace. Then add the fields you want to use to the design grid.

1. Click the **Create tab**, and then in the **Queries group**, click the **Query Design** button.

MOS Obj 3.1.5

2. In the **Show Table** dialog box, double-click **Residents** to add the table to the query design workspace. Alternately, select the table in the dialog box, and then click the Add button.

3. Repeat the technique just practiced to add the **Water Bills** table. Compare your screen with **Figure 1**.

   Tables can be added to the query design workspace using the Show Table dialog box or by dragging them from the Navigation Pane.

4. **Close** the **Show Table** dialog box, and then compare your screen with **Figure 2**.

   This query needs to answer these questions: *What are the names of the customers who have an overdue balance, what are those balances, and from what time periods?* To answer these questions, fields from two tables are needed.

   When a query selects fields from multiple tables, the tables need to be related. By default, queries follow the relationship rules defined in the Relationships tab. Here, the two tables are joined in a one-to-many relationship using AccountNumber as the common field. A resident can have many water billing cycles.

■ Continue to the next page to complete the skill

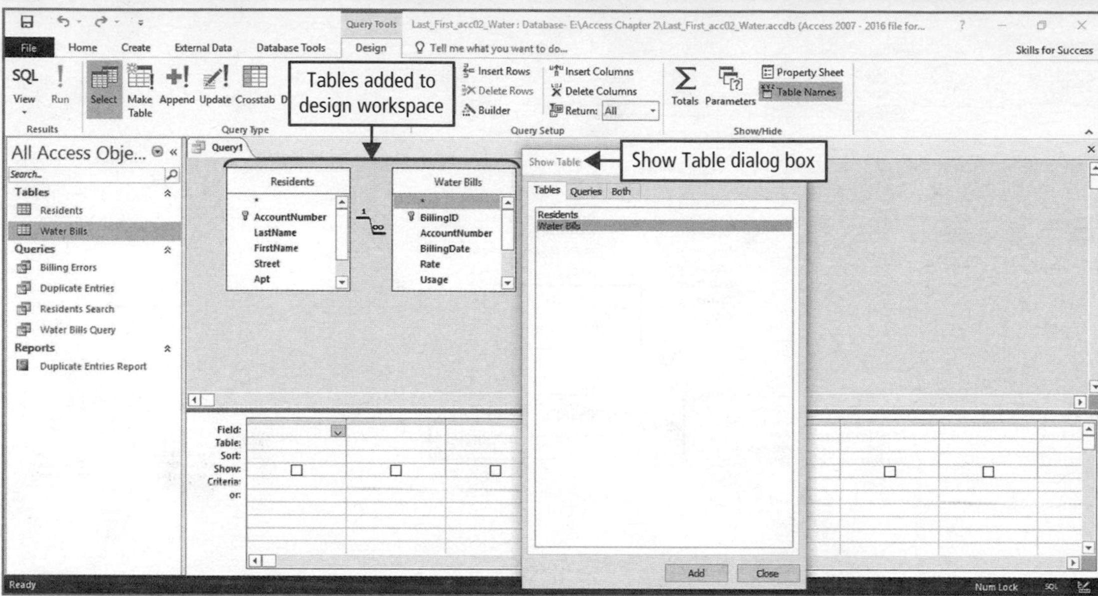

Figure 1 Access 2016, Windows 10, Microsoft Corporation

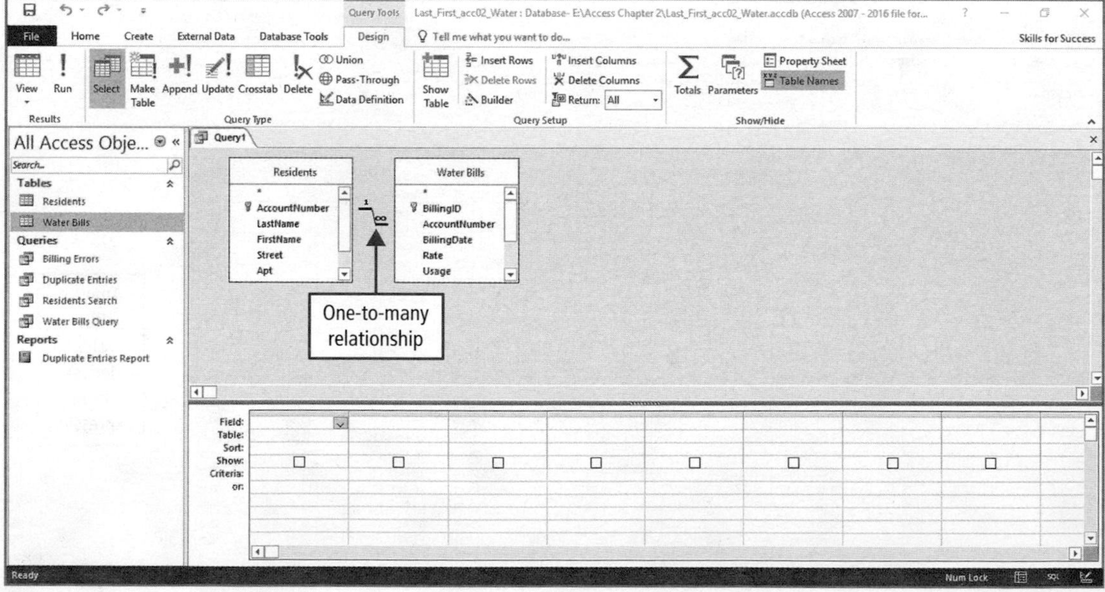

Figure 2 Access 2016, Windows 10, Microsoft Corporation

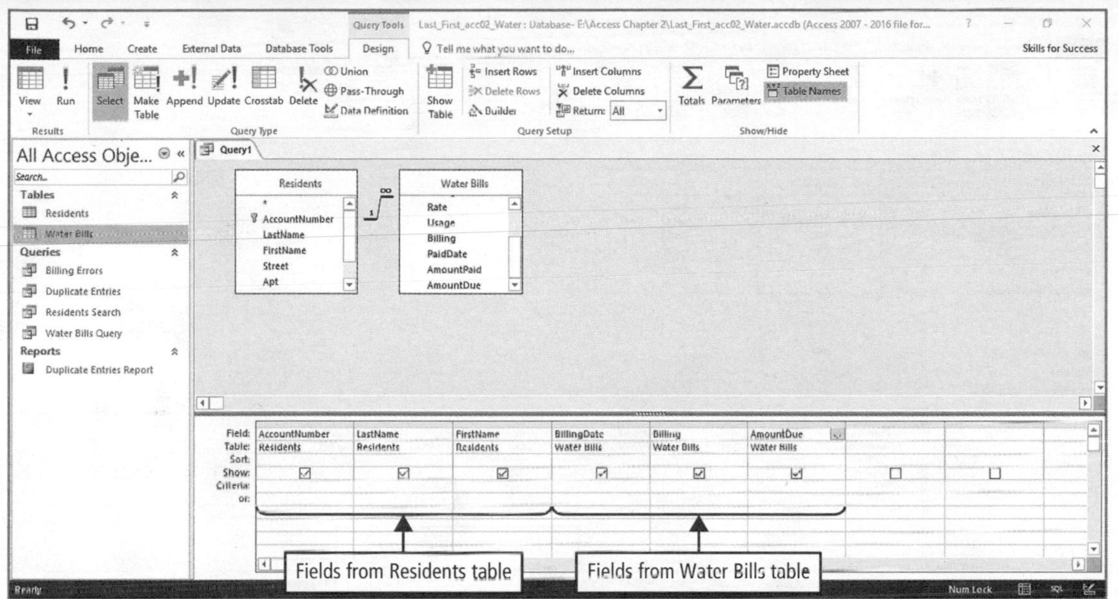

Access 2016, Windows 10, Microsoft Corporation

Figure 3

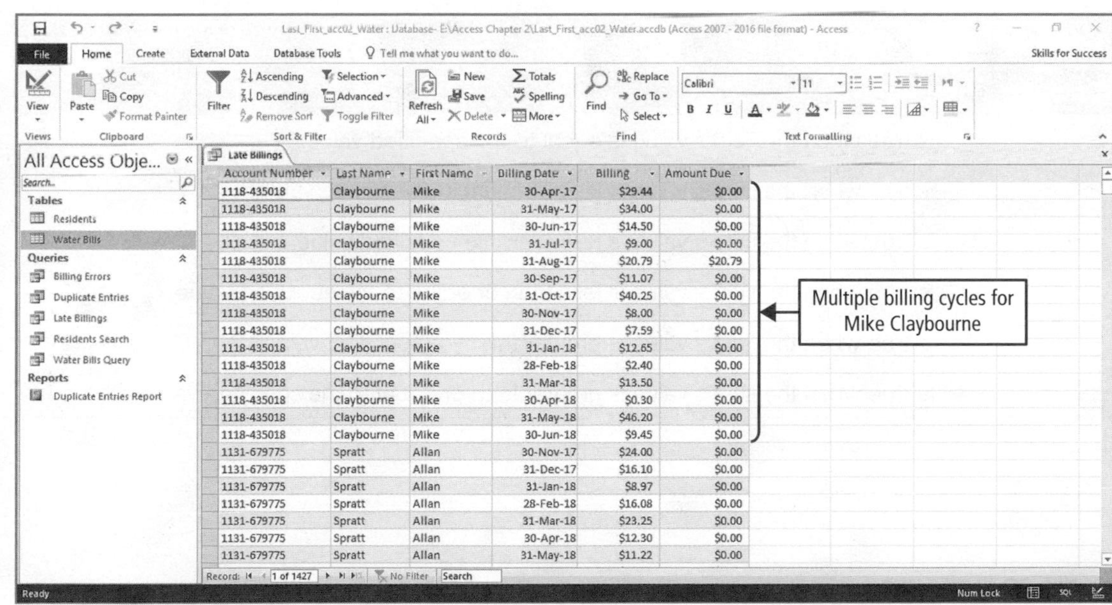

Access 2016, Windows 10, Microsoft Corporation

Figure 4

5. In the query design workspace, in the **Residents** table, double-click the **AccountNumber** field to add it to the first column of the design grid. Alternatively, drag the field into the first column Field cell.
6. Repeat the technique just practiced to add the **LastName** and **FirstName** fields to the second and third column of the design grid.

7. Scroll down the **Water Bills** table list as needed and add the following fields in this order: **BillingDate**, **Billing**, and **AmountDue**. Compare your screen with **Figure 3**.

MOS Obj 3.2.2

8. Click **Save**. In the **Save As** dialog box, type Late Billings and then press Enter.

MOS Obj 3.1.6

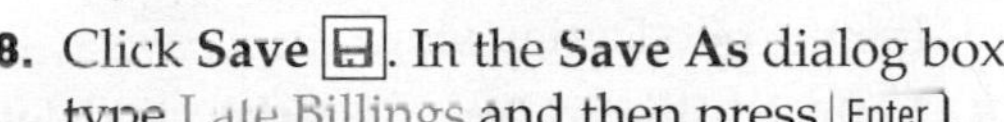

9. On the **Design tab**, in the **Results group**, click **Run**. Compare your screen with **Figure 4**.

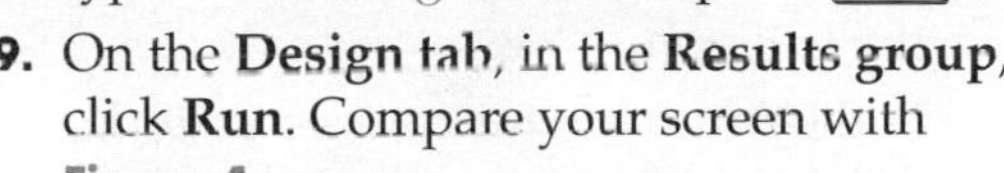

   Before adding criteria, it is a good idea to run the query to verify that it displays the fields you need. Here, you can see each billing cycle sorted by customer.

10. On the status bar, click the **Design View** button, and then leave the query open for the next skill.

■ **You have completed Skill 4 of 10**

- In query criteria, numbers are typically combined with ***comparison operators***—operators that compare two values including operators such as > (greater than) or < (less than).

1. If necessary, open the Late Billings query in Design view.

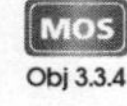

Obj 3.3.4

2. In the **Billing** column **Criteria** cell, type >80 Compare your screen with **Figure 1**.
3. On the **Design tab**, in the **Results group**, click the **Run** button to display the 15 records that answer the question, *Which billings are larger than 80?*
4. On the **Home tab**, click the **View** button to return to Design view.
5. In the **Billing** column **Criteria** cell, delete the criterion.
6. In the **Amount Due** column **Criteria** cell, type <0 and then **Run** the query to display the 12 records that answer the question, *Which customers have a negative balance?*
7. Switch to Design view. In the **Amount Due** column **Criteria** cell, replace the criteria with 0 **Run** the query to display the 1,314 records that answer the question, *Which billings have a balance of zero?*

   When a value is to match exactly, simply type the value. The equals (=) operator is not needed. The commonly used comparison operators are summarized in the table in **Figure 2**.

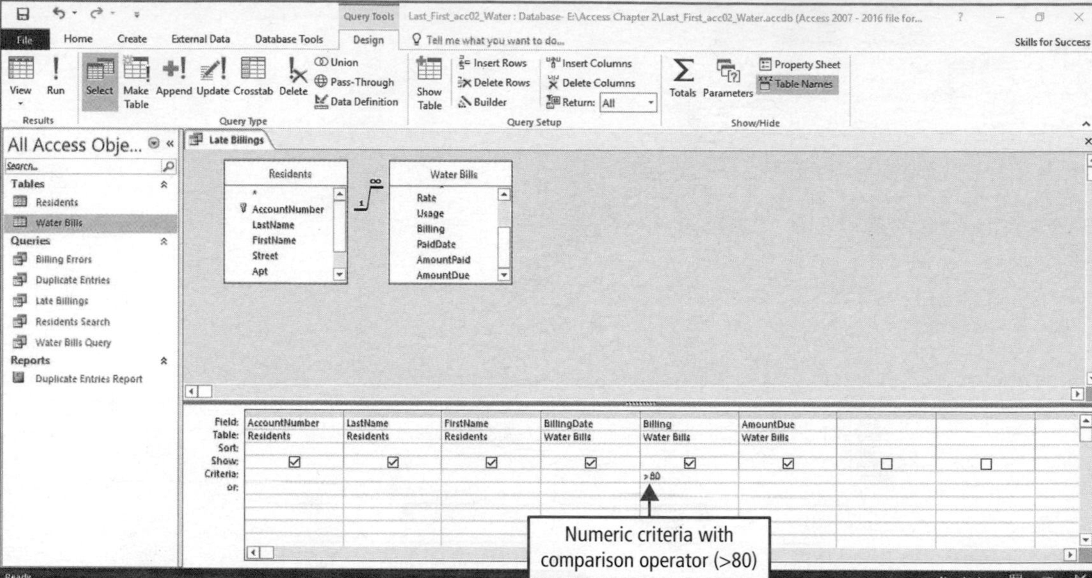

Figure 1

Access 2016, Windows 10, Microsoft Corporation

Common Comparison Operators	
Operator	**Purpose**
=	Is true when the field's value is equal to the specified value
<>	Is true when the field's value does not equal the specified value
<	Is true when the field's value is less than the specified value
<=	Is true when the field's value is less than or equal to the specified value
>	Is true when the field's value is greater than the specified value
>=	Is true when the field's value is greater than or equal to the specified value

Figure 2

■ **Continue to the next page to complete the skill**

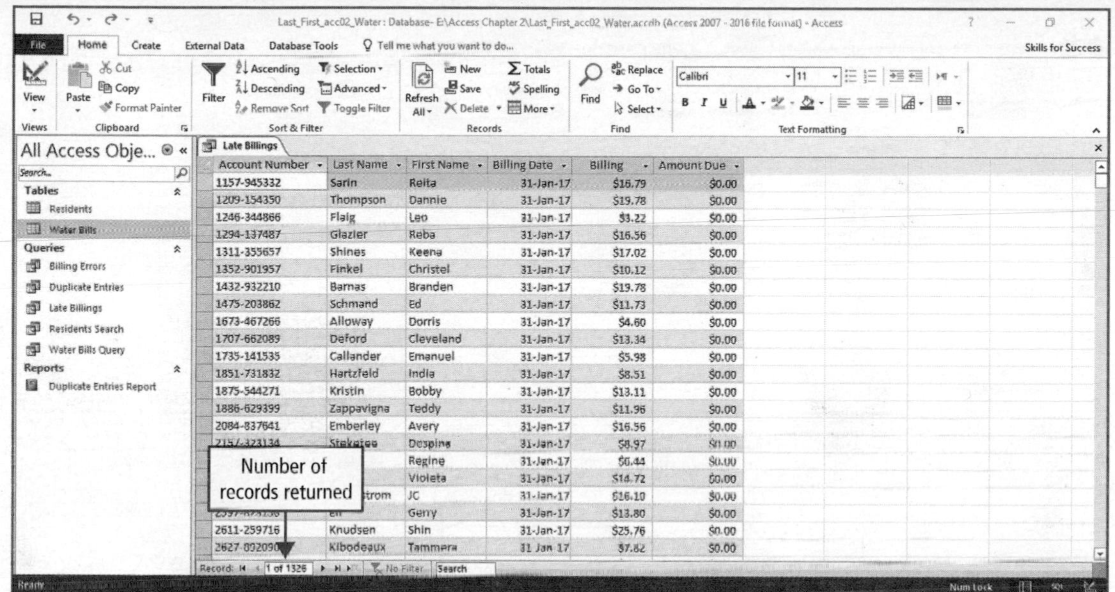

Access 2016, Windows 10, Microsoft Corporation

Figure 3

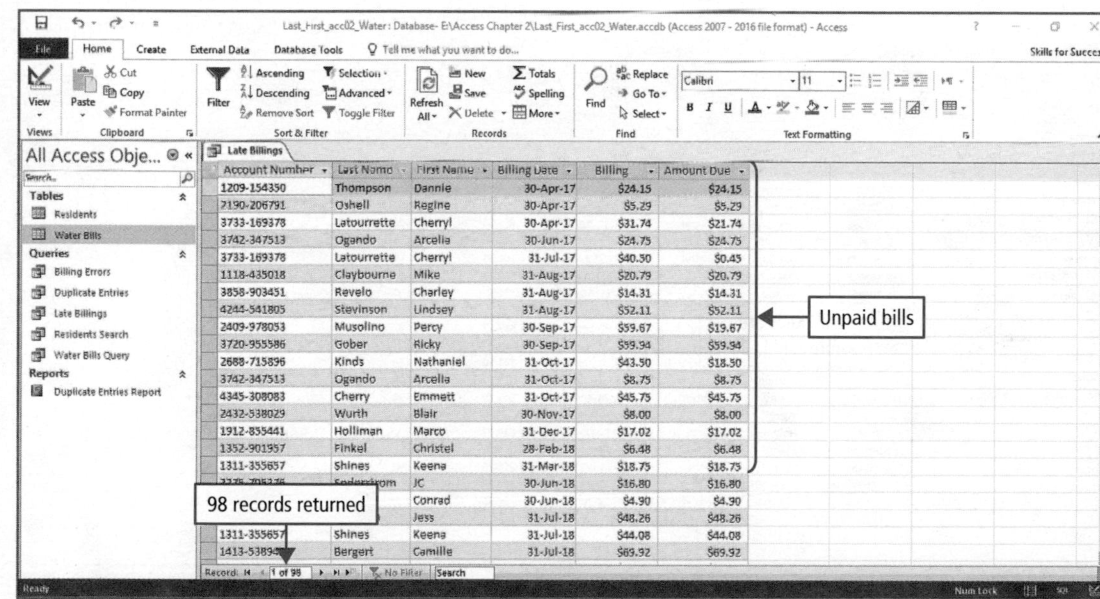

Access 2016, Windows 10, Microsoft Corporation

Figure 4

8. Switch to Design view. In the **Amount Due** column **Criteria** cell, replace the criteria with <=0 **Run** the query, and then compare your screen with **Figure 3**.

   The query returns records for which the amount due is zero and the records for which the amount due is negative. In this manner, the <= operator returns records that are equal to or less than the number following the criterion.

9. Switch to Design view. In the **Amount Due** column **Criteria** cell, replace the criteria with > 0 **Run** the query, and then compare your screen with **Figure 4**. Scroll down the datasheet to view the last records in the results.

   The query answers the question, *Which billings have a balance due?* An additional criterion is needed to return only those records for which the amount due is late.

10. Click **Save** [Save icon], return to Design View, and leave the query open for the next skill.

■ **You have completed Skill 5 of 10**

- In Access, dates and times are stored as numbers. The underlying numbers display as dates in database objects. For example, the number 37979 displays as *12/24/2003* if the Short Date format is assigned to the Date/Time field.
- When you add criteria to more than one query column, both criteria must be true if the record is to be included in the results.

1. With the **Late Billings** query open in Design view, click in the **BillingDate** column **Criteria** cell, and then type <7/1/2018 Press Tab, and then compare your screen with **Figure 1**.

   Years can be typed with four digits (2018) or two digits (18). When a year is entered as two digits, it will be converted to four digits when you press Tab. Dates are stored as serial numbers, so you can include arithmetic and comparison operators in your criteria.

   When dates are used as query criteria, they are enclosed in number signs (#). If you do not include them, they will be inserted when the query is run or when you press Tab.

2. On the **Design tab**, in the **Results group**, click the **Run** button, and then compare your screen with **Figure 2**.

   This query answers the question, *Which billings before July 1, 2018 still have a balance due?* In this manner, both the billing date and amount due comparisons must be true for the record to be included in the query results.

■ **Continue to the next page to complete the skill**

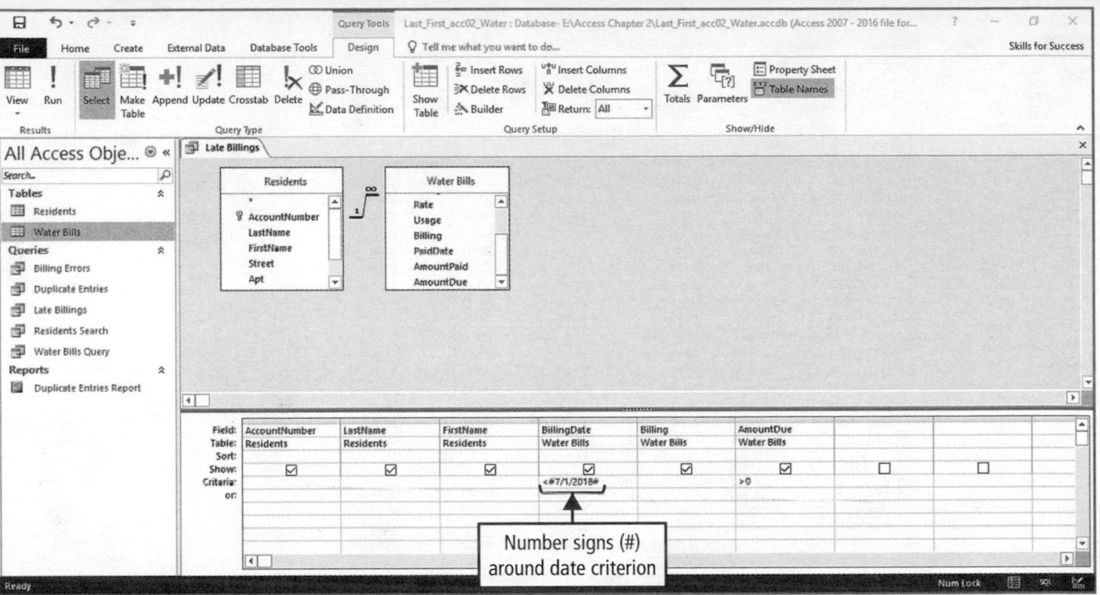

Figure 1 Access 2016, Windows 10, Microsoft Corporation

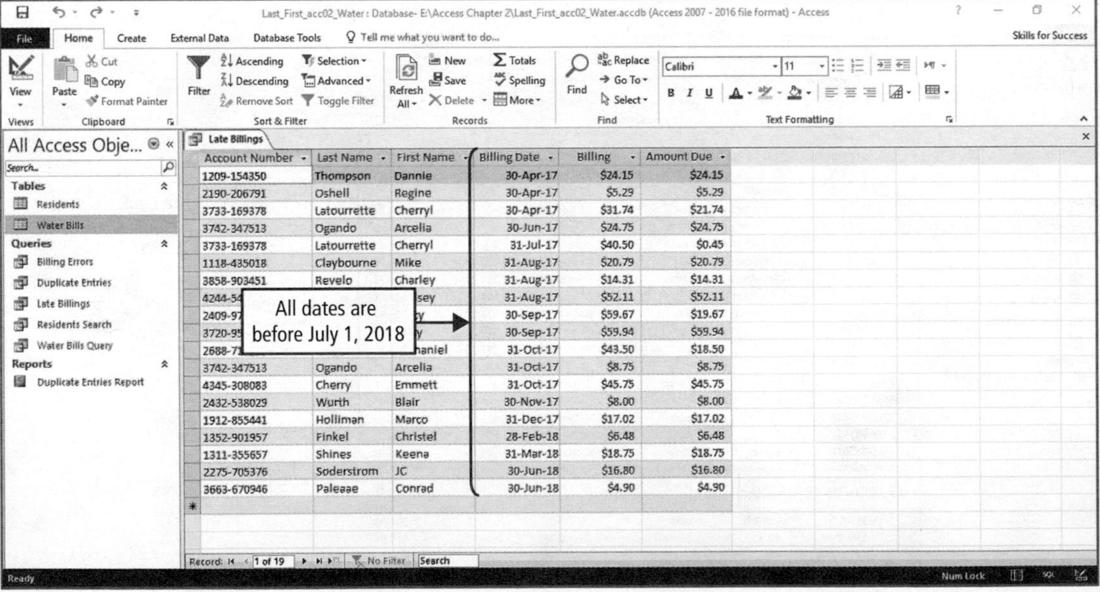

Figure 2 Access 2016, Windows 10, Microsoft Corporation

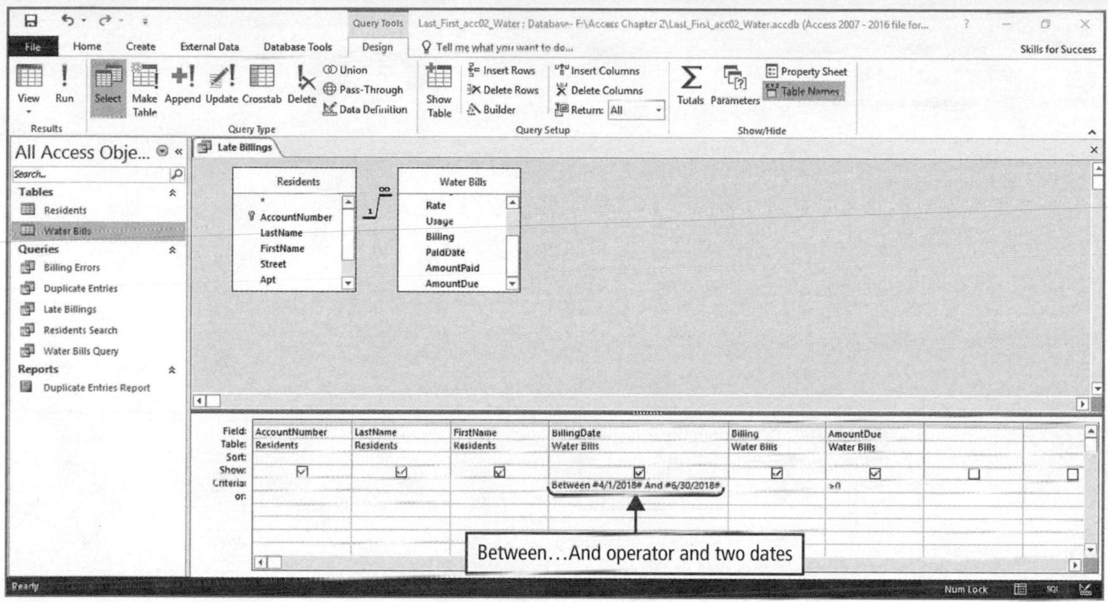

Access 2016, Windows 10, Microsoft Corporation

Figure 3

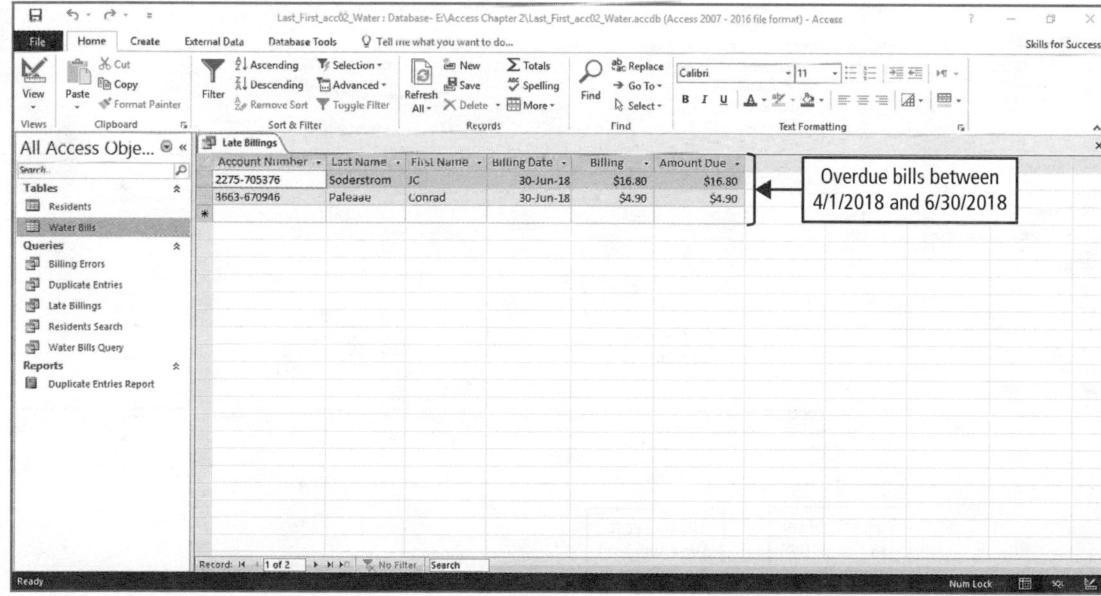

Access 2016, Windows 10, Microsoft Corporation

Figure 4

3. Switch to Design view. In the **BillingDate** column **Criteria** cell, replace the criteria with >=4/1/2018 **Run** the query to display the 81 billings with balances due that occurred on or after April 1, 2018.
4. Switch to Design view. In the **BillingDate** column **Criteria** cell, replace the existing criterion with Between 4/1/2018 And 6/30/2018
5. Click an empty cell, and then with the [+] pointer, increase the width of the **BillingDate** column to display all its criteria, and then compare your screen with **Figure 3**.

   The ***Between . . . And operator*** is a comparison operator that finds all numbers or dates between and including two values. Here, the billing cycle must be between April 1 and June 30, 2018, to display in the query.

   When you widen a query column in the design grid, the column will return to its original width when the query is closed.
6. **Run** the query, and then compare your screen with **Figure 4**.

   The query answers the question, *Which billings from the second quarter of 2018 have a balance due?*
7. Click **Save** [Save]. If you are printing this project, print the datasheet in Landscape view. **Close** [X] the query.

■ **You have completed Skill 6 of 10**

► The Total row is added to queries when you need ***summary statistics***—calculations for groups of data such as totals, averages, or counts.

1. On the **Create tab**, in the **Queries group**, click the **Query Design** button. In the **Show Table** dialog box, add the **Water Bills** table, and then **Close** the dialog box.
2. On the **Design tab**, in the **Show/Hide group**, click **Totals**. Add **BillingDate** to the first column, and then compare your screen with **Figure 1**.

   The Total row is used to determine how queries should be grouped and summarized. By default, each column is set to Group By. The ***Group By*** operator designates which query column contains the group of values to summarize as a single record, one for each set. Here, totals will be calculated for each month.

MOS Obj 3.3.3

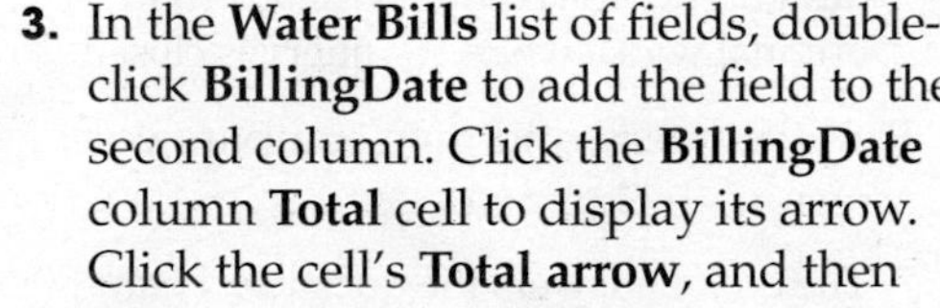

3. In the **Water Bills** list of fields, double-click **BillingDate** to add the field to the second column. Click the **BillingDate** column **Total** cell to display its arrow. Click the cell's **Total arrow**, and then from the menu, click **Count**.

   The ***Count*** operator calculates the number of records in each group. Here, the number of billings for each month will be calculated.
4. Repeat the technique just practiced to add the **Usage** field to the third column, and then change its **Total** cell value to **Avg**. Compare your screen with **Figure 2**.

   The ***Avg*** operator calculates the average of the values in each group.

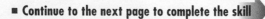

■ Continue to the next page to complete the skill

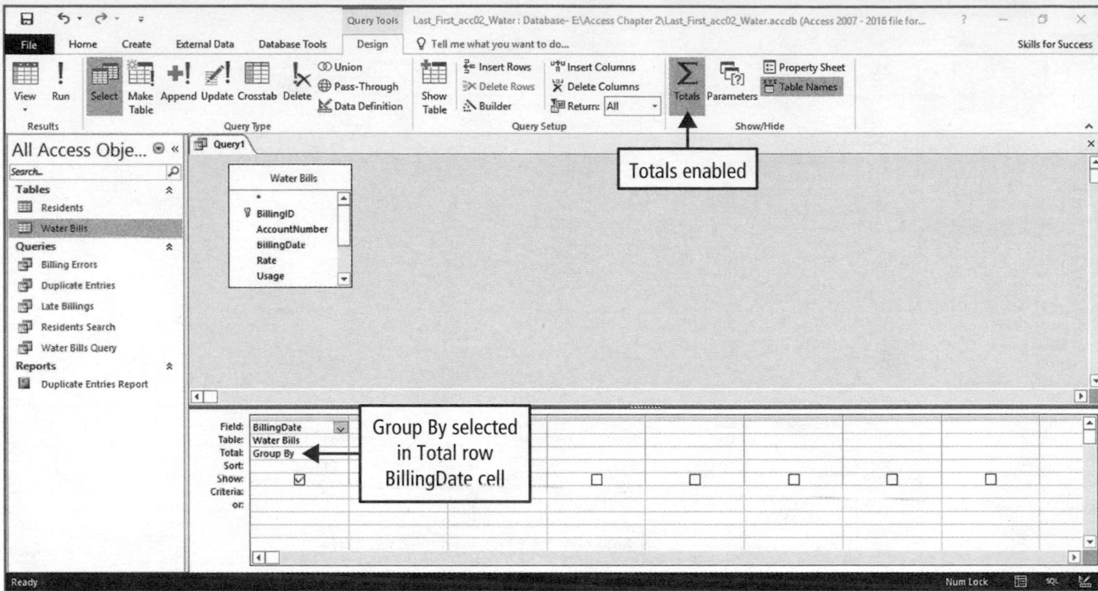

Figure 1 Access 2016, Windows 10, Microsoft Corporation

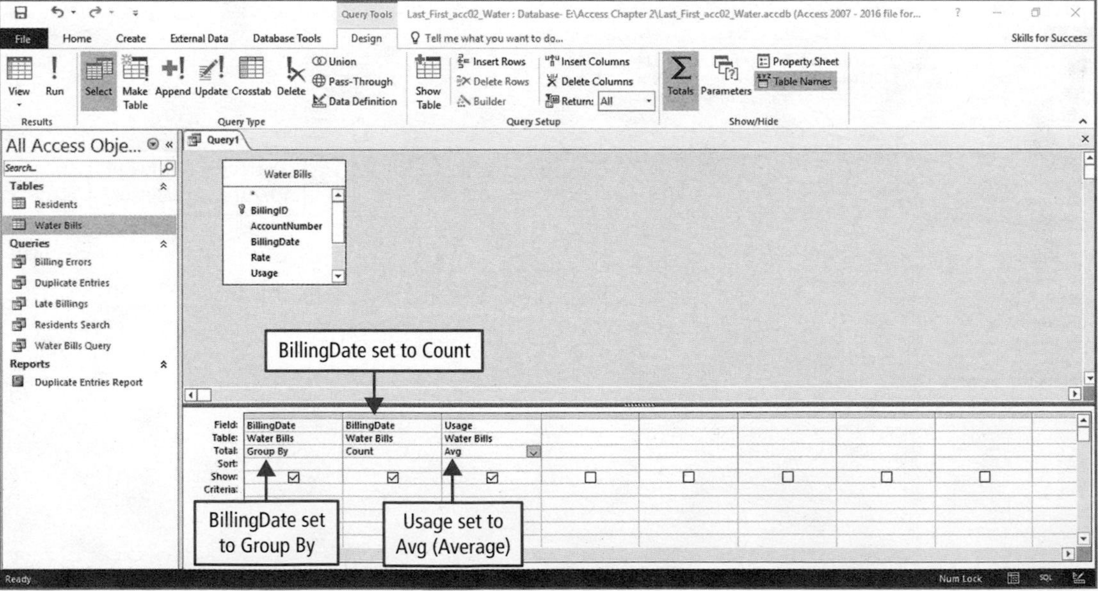

Figure 2 Access 2016, Windows 10, Microsoft Corporation

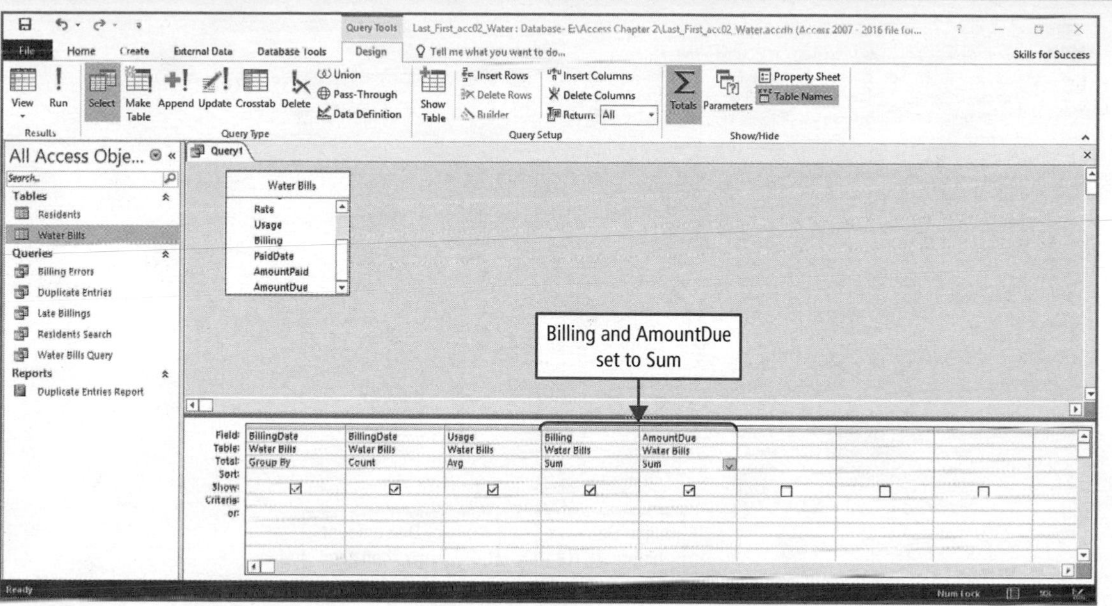

Access 2016, Windows 10, Microsoft Corporation

Figure 3

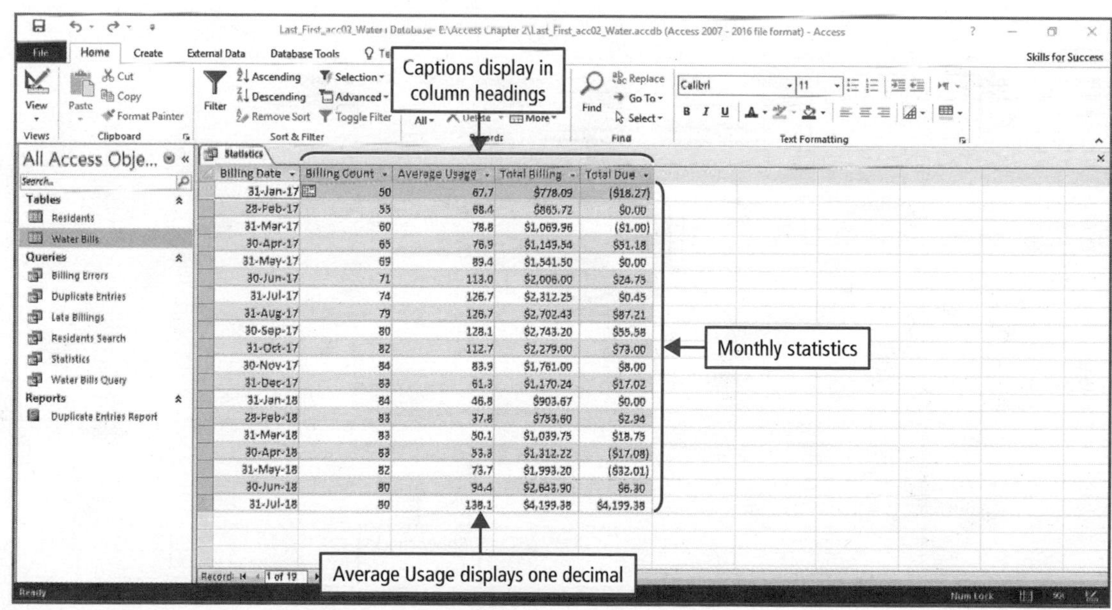

Access 2016, Windows 10, Microsoft Corporation

Figure 4

5. Add the **Billing** and **AmountDue** fields, and set their **Total** cells to **Sum**. Compare your screen with **Figure 3**.

   The ***Sum*** operator calculates the total of the values in each group.

6. Save the query with the name Statistics and then **Run** the query to display the statistics for each month.

   Pound signs in a numeric field indicate that the values are too wide for the column. Here, some of the averages have too many decimals for the number to display in the given column width.

7. Switch to Design view. Click in the **Usage** column to make it active, and then on the **Design tab**, in the **Show/Hide group**, click **Property Sheet**.

8. In the **Property Sheet**, click **Format**, click the **Format arrow** that displays, and then click **Fixed**. Display and click the **Decimal Places arrow**, and then click **1**. Click in the **Caption** cell, and then type Average Usage

9. Repeat the technique just practiced to change the caption of the second **BillingDate** to Billing Count Change the **Billing** caption to Total Billing and the **AmountDue** caption to Total Due

10. **Close** the Property Sheet. **Run** the query, set the column widths to **Best Fit**, and then compare your screen with **Figure 4**.

    The captions that were set previously in the property sheet display in the datasheet header row.

11. **Save** the query. If you are printing this project, print the datasheet in Landscape orientation.

12. **Close** the query.

■ **You have completed Skill 7 of 10**

SKILL 8: Add Calculated Fields to Queries

- You can insert calculated fields into queries. In queries, calculated fields need an ***alias***—a descriptive label used to identify a field in expressions, datasheets, forms, and reports.

1. Click the **Create tab**, and then in the **Queries group**, click the **Query Design** button. In the **Show Table** dialog box, add the **Residents** table, add the **Water Bills** table, and then **Close** the dialog box.
2. From the **Residents** table, add the **AccountNumber**, **LastName**, and **FirstName** fields to the design grid.
3. From the **Water Bills** table, add **BillingDate**, and then in the **BillingDate** column **Criteria** cell, type <4/1/18 and then press Tab.

MOS Obj 3.3.5

4. From the **Water Bills** table, add **AmountDue**, and then in the **AmountDue** column **Criteria** cell, type >0 **Run** the query, and then compare your screen with **Figure 1**.
5. Click **Save**, and then in the **Save As** dialog box, type Late Fees and then click **OK**.

MOS Obj 3.2.4

6. Switch to Design view. In the **AmountDue** column, clear the **Show** cell check box so that the column will not display in the datasheet.
7. Click in the first blank column **Field** row. On the **Design tab**, in the **Query Setup group**, click the **Builder** button.
8. In the **Expression Builder** dialog box, type the following expression Penalty:[AmountDue]*0.25 taking care to include the colon. Compare your screen with **Figure 2**.

   The alias in a calculated field ends with a colon. Here, *Penalty* will be the alias.

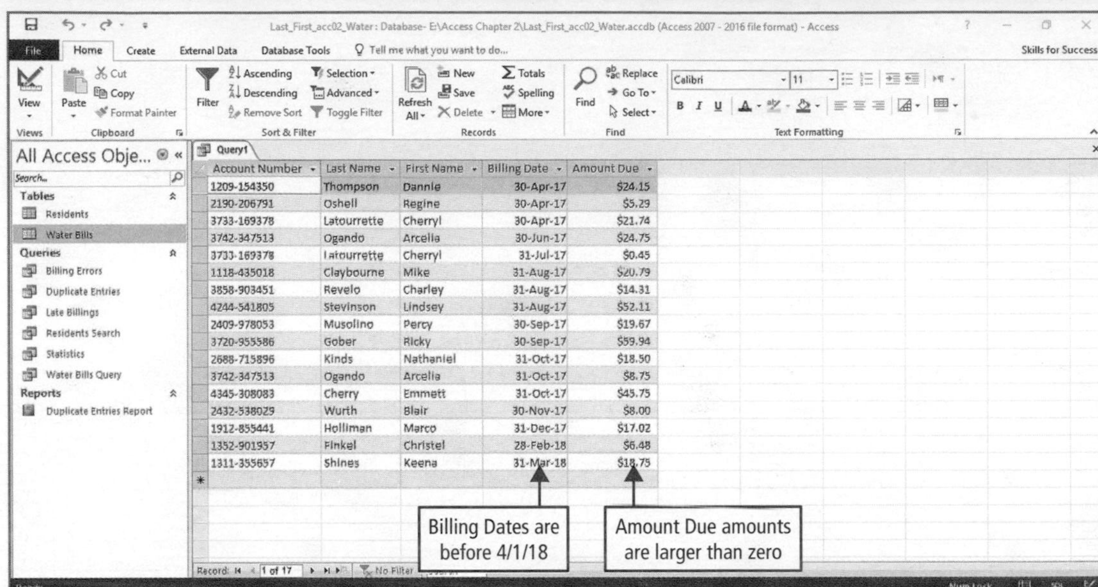

Figure 1 Access 2016, Windows 10, Microsoft Corporation

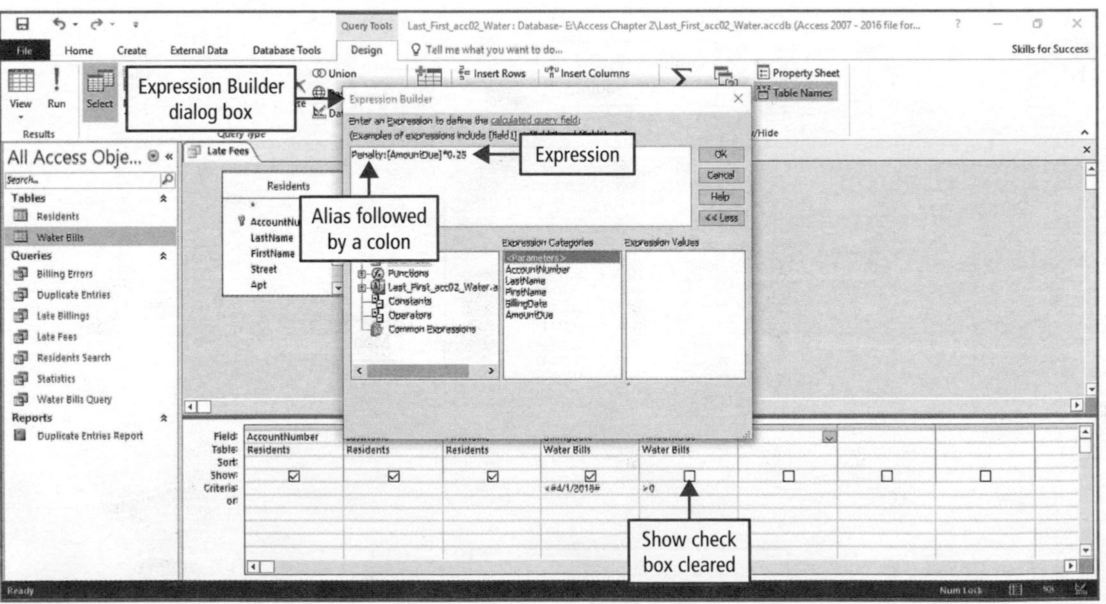

Figure 2 Access 2016, Windows 10, Microsoft Corporation

■ **Continue to the next page to complete the skill**

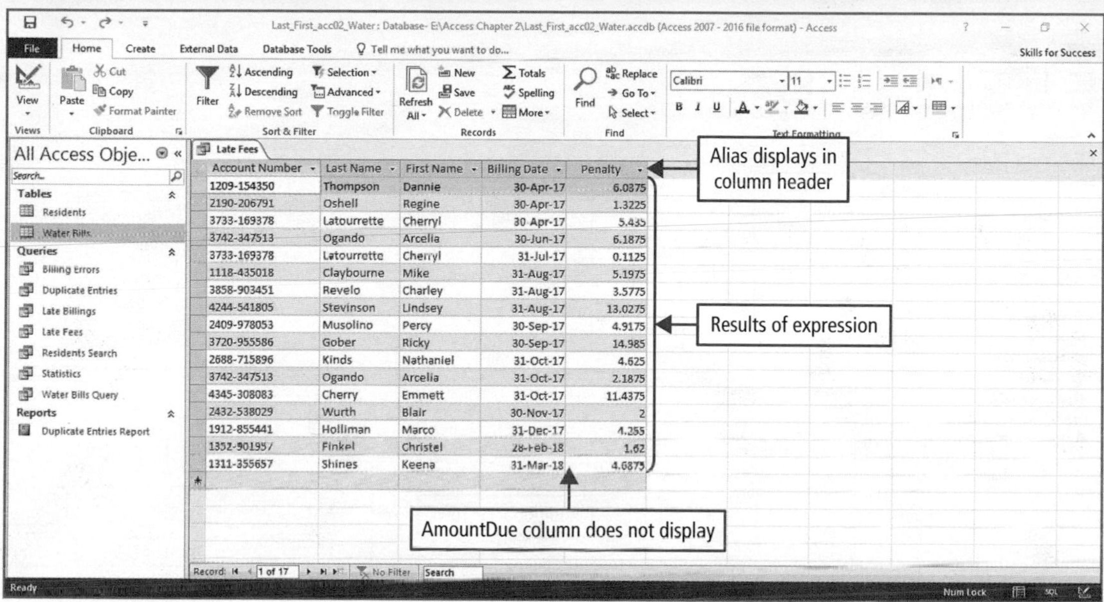

Access 2016, Windows 10, Microsoft Corporation

Figure 3

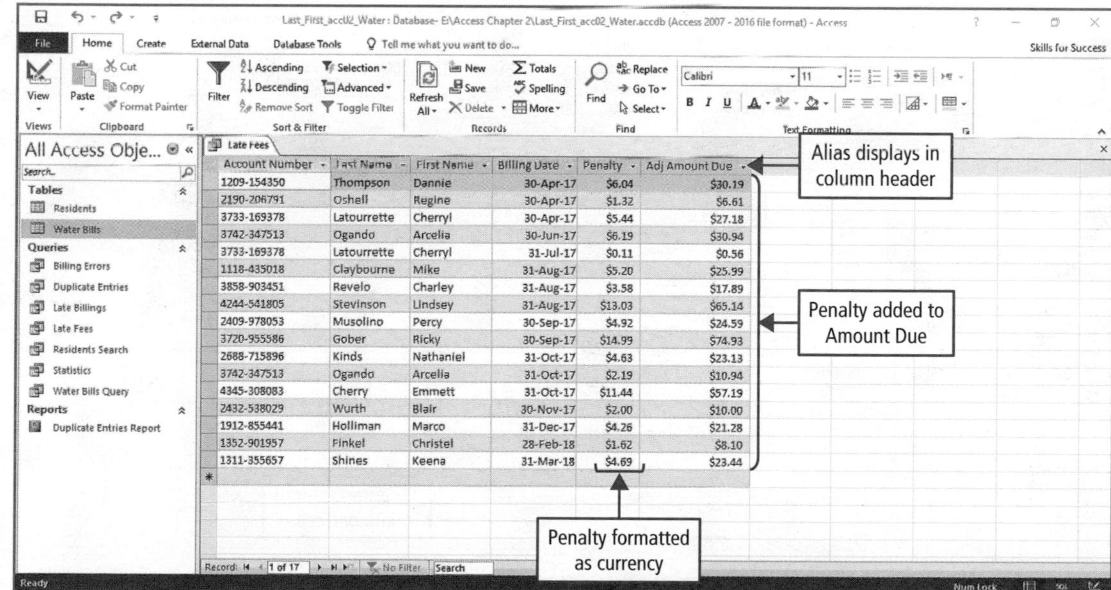

Access 2016, Windows 10, Microsoft Corporation

Figure 4

9. Click **OK** to close the Expression Builder and insert the expression.
10. **Run** the query, and then compare your screen with **Figure 3**. If the Enter Parameter dialog box displays, click Cancel, and then repeat steps 6 through 8, carefully checking your typing.

    In the last column, the alias *Penalty* displays in the header row. The result of the expression displays in each record. Here, a 25% penalty is derived by multiplying 0.25 by the amount due.
11. Click **Save**, and then switch to Design view. If necessary, click in the Penalty column to make it active.
12. Click the **Property Sheet** button to open it. In the **Property Sheet**, display and click the **Format arrow**, and then click **Currency**. **Close** the Property Sheet.

Obj 3.2.6

13. Click the first blank column **Field** cell, and then in the **Query Setup group**, click **Builder**.
14. In the **Expression Builder** dialog box, type the following alias and expression: Adj Amount Due:[AmountDue]+[Penalty]

    Because an alias represents a field name, when an alias is used in an expression, it is enclosed in square brackets. Here, the Penalty alias is used to add the penalty to the original amount due.
15. Click **OK**, and then **Run** the query. Set the column widths to **Best Fit**, and then compare your screen with **Figure 4**.
16. Click **Save**. If you are printing this project, print the datasheet in Landscape orientation.
17. **Close** the query.

- **You have completed Skill 8 of 10**

► When criteria are in more than one column, the placement of the criteria in the design grid rows determines whether one or both of the criteria must be true for the record to display.

1. In the **Navigation Pane**, under **Queries**, right-click **Billing Errors**, and then from the shortcut menu, click **Design View**.

MOS Obj 3.2.5

2. In the **Usage** column, click the **Sort** cell, click the **arrow** that displays, and then click **Ascending**.
3. **Run** the query, and notice that the **Usage** values that are empty or negative are listed first.
4. Switch to Design view. In the **Usage** column **Criteria** cell, type Is Null Below the value just typed, in the **Usage** column **or** cell, type <0 Compare your screen with **Figure 1**.

   The ***Is Null*** and ***Is Not Null*** operators test if a field is empty or not empty.

5. **Run** the query to display only the records for which the **Usage** value is empty or less than 0.
6. **Save**, and then **Close** the query. In the **Navigation Pane**, right-click **Billing Errors**, and then click **Design View**. Compare your screen with **Figure 2**.

   When two criteria are placed in *different* rows in the design grid, the ***Or logical operator***—a logical comparison of two criteria that is true if either of the criteria outcomes is true—applies. Because the two criteria in this query can be combined into a single row, they were automatically combined with the Or operator separating them.

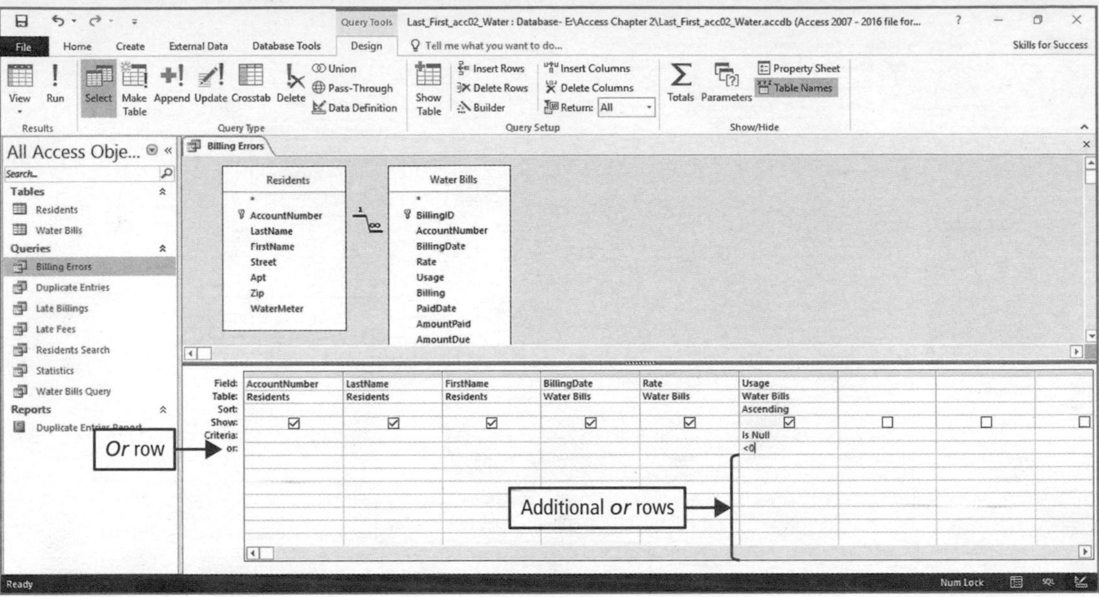

Figure 1 Access 2016, Windows 10, Microsoft Corporation

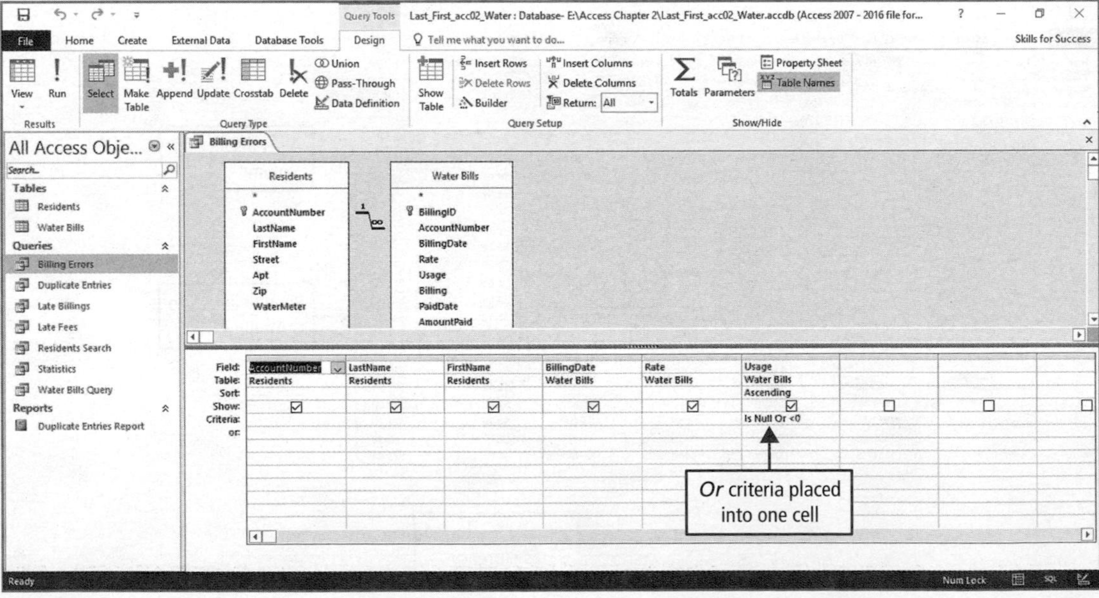

Figure 2 Access 2016, Windows 10, Microsoft Corporation

■ Continue to the next page to complete the skill

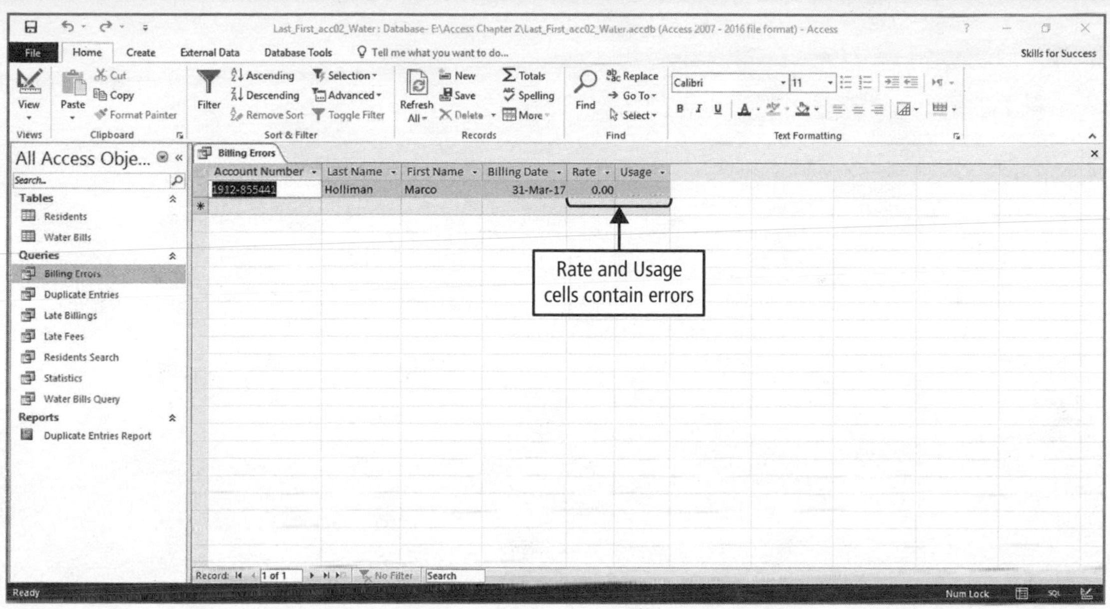

Access 2016, Windows 10, Microsoft Corporation

Figure 3

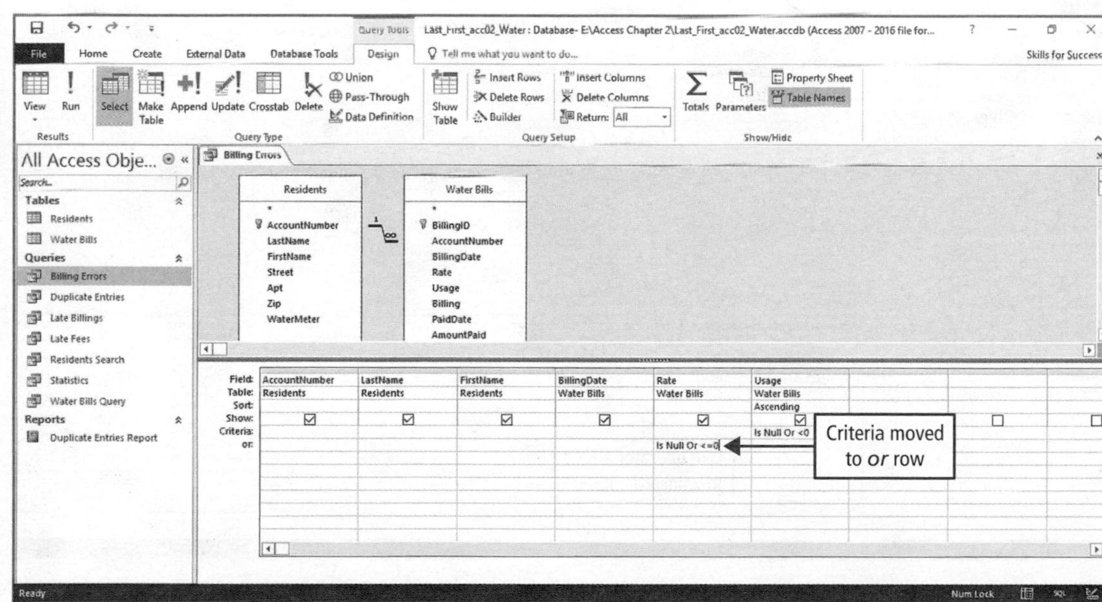

Access 2016, Windows 10, Microsoft Corporation

Figure 4

7. In the **Rate** column **Criteria** cell, type Is Null Or <=0

MOS Obj 3.3.4

8. **Run** the query, and notice that both the **Usage** and **Rate** columns contain errant values as shown in **Figure 3**.

   When two criteria are placed in the same row, the ***And logical operator***—a logical comparison of two criteria that is true only when both criteria outcomes are true—applies. Here, records are selected only where the Usage and Rate columns both have errors.

9. Switch to Design view. In the **Rate** column **Criteria** row, delete the criteria. In the **Rate** column **or** row (the row below the Criteria row), type Is Null Or <=0 and then compare your screen with **Figure 4**.

   Here, records are selected if either the Usage or Rate column has errors.

10. **Run** the query to display six records that match the criteria. If you are printing your work for this project, print the datasheet.

11. **Save** [Save icon], and then **Close** [Close icon] the query.

■ **You have completed Skill 9 of 10**

SKILL 10: Add Wildcards to Query Criteria

WATCH SKILL 2.10

- A ***wildcard*** is a special character, such as an asterisk, used in query criteria to allow matches for any combination of letters or characters.
- Using wildcards, you can expand your search criteria to find a more accurate subset of the data.

1. In the **Navigation Pane**, under **Queries**, right-click **Duplicate Entries**, and then, from the shortcut menu, click **Design View**.
2. In the **LastName** column **Criteria** cell, type Jones In the **FirstName** column **Criteria** cell, type William and then **Run** the query to display the record for William Jones.

   William Jones reports that he receives three bills each month. However, with the current criteria, his record is listed one time.

3. Switch to Design view. In the **FirstName** column **Criteria** cell, replace the existing criterion with Will* **Run** the query, and then compare your screen with **Figure 1**.

   The ***asterisk (*) wildcard*** character matches any combination of characters. Here, the two first names begin with *Will* but end differently.

4. Switch to Design view, and then compare your screen with **Figure 2**.

   When you include wildcards, the criterion needs to start with the Like operator. If you don't type the Like operator, it will be inserted automatically when the query is run.

■ Continue to the next page to complete the skill

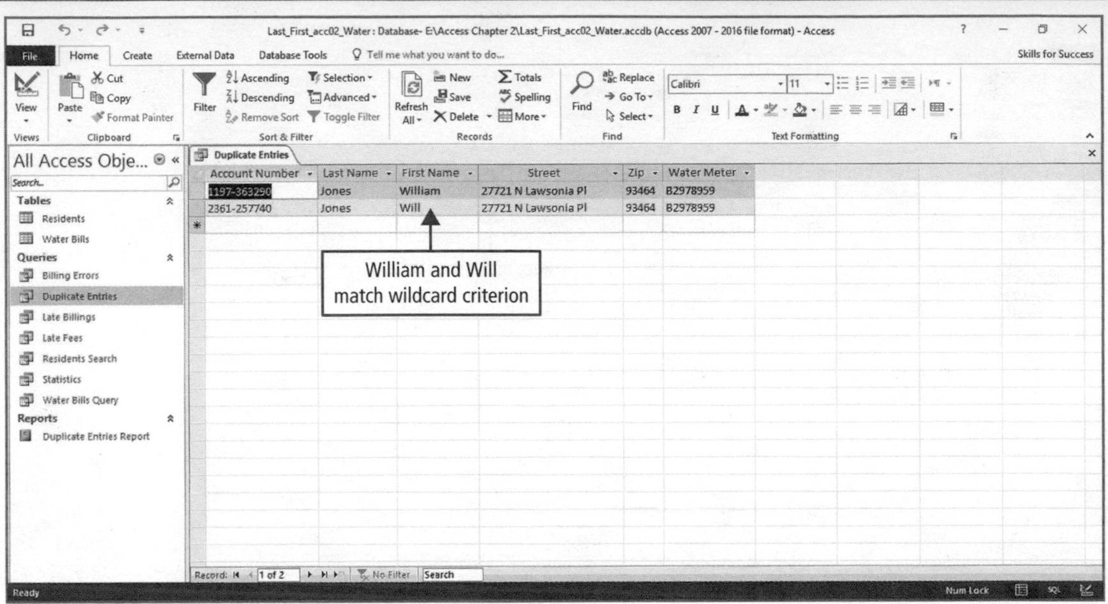

Figure 1 Access 2016, Windows 10, Microsoft Corporation

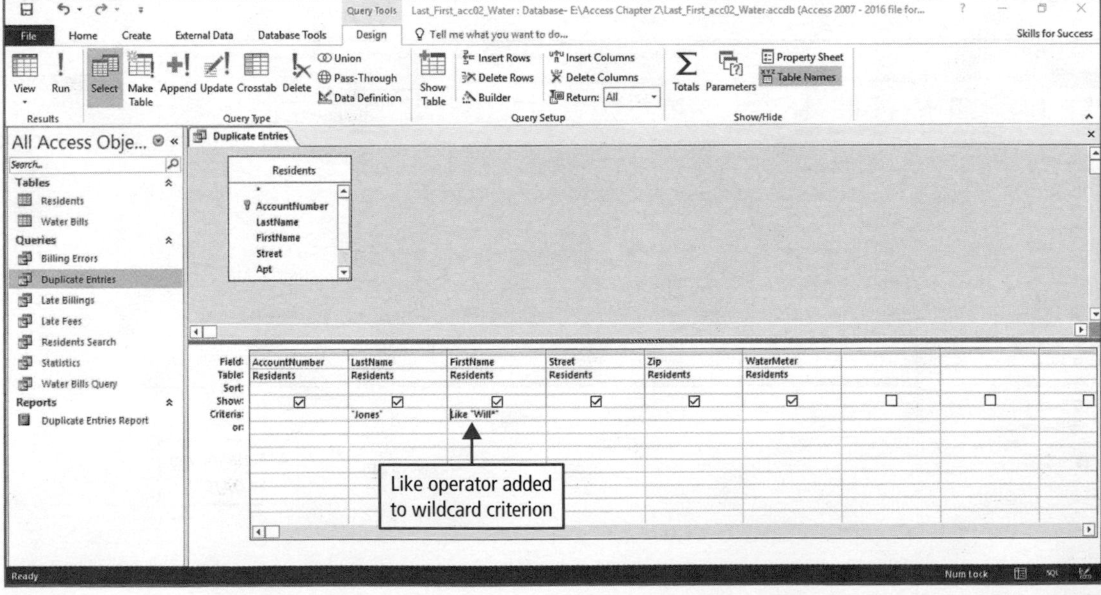

Figure 2 Access 2016, Windows 10, Microsoft Corporation

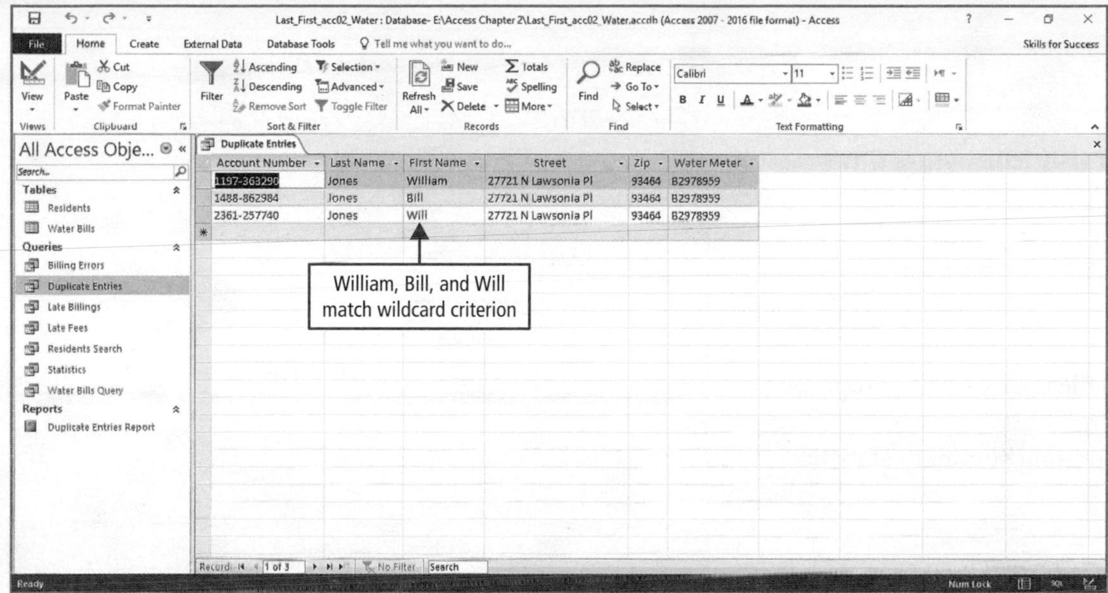

Access 2016, Windows 10, Microsoft Corporation

Figure 3

Common Access Wildcard Characters		
Character	**Description**	**Example**
*	Matches any number of characters.	Don* matches Don and Donna, but not Adonna.
?	Matches any single alphabetic character.	D?n matches Don and Dan, but not Dean.
[]	Matches any single character in the brackets.	D[ao]n matches Don and Dan, but not Den.
#	Matches any single numeric character.	C-#PO matches C-3PO, but not C-DPO.

Figure 4

5. In the **FirstName** column **Criteria** cell, replace the existing criterion with Like "?ill*" **Run** the query to display the three duplicate records for William Jones. Compare your screen with **Figure 3**.

   The ***question mark (?) wildcard*** character matches any single character. Common wildcard characters supported by Access are summarized in the table in **Figure 4**.

6. **Save**, and then **Close** the query.
7. In the **Navigation Pane**, under **Reports**, double-click **Duplicate Entries Report**. If you are printing this project, print the report.

   Recall that reports are often used to display the results of queries. Here, the report displays the results of the Duplicate Entries query.

8. **Close** the report.

   Because you did not make any design changes to the report, you do not need to save it.

9. **Close** Access. Submit your printouts or file as directed by your instructor.

DONE! You have completed Skill 10 of 10, and your database is complete!

More Skills 11

Export Queries to Excel

To complete this project, you will need the following file:

- acc02_MS11Results

You will save your files as:

- Last_First_acc02_MS11Results
- Last_First_acc02_MS11Excel

- ▶ Data from a table or query can be exported into file formats that are opened with other applications such as Excel and Word.
- ▶ In Excel, you can analyze the query results by adding summary statistics and charts.

---

1. Start **Access 2016**, and then open the student data file **acc02_MS11Results**. Save the database in your **Access Chapter 2** folder as Last_First_acc02_MS11Results If necessary, enable the content.
2. Open the **2018 DNF** query datasheet, and then replace the first and last names of the first racer *Lavette* and *Hoyle* with your own first and last names.
3. Switch to Design view. In the **Year** column **Criteria** cell, type 2018 In the **RunTime** column **Criteria** cell, type Is Null Compare your screen with **Figure 1**.
4. **Save** [Save icon], and then **Run** the query to display the 19 racers who did not finish—DNF. **Close** the query.
5. In the **Navigation Pane**, be sure that the **2018 DNF** query is still selected. Click the **External Data tab**, and then in the **Export group,** click the **Excel** button.
6. In the **Export - Excel Spreadsheet** dialog box, click the **File format arrow**.

   You can save a query in different Excel file formats.
7. Press Esc to close the menu, and then click the **Browse** button. In the **File Save** dialog box, navigate to your **Access Chapter 2** folder, name the file Last_First_acc02_MS11Excel and then click **Save**.
8. In the **Export - Excel Spreadsheet** dialog box, select the **Export data with formatting and layout** check box, and then select the **Open the destination file after the export operation is complete** check box, as shown in **Figure 2**.
9. Click **OK**. Wait a few moments for the data to display in Excel.

   When you export a table or query to Excel, the field names are included as column labels in the spreadsheet. In the taskbar, the Access button will flash to remind you to return to Access and close the dialog box that is open.

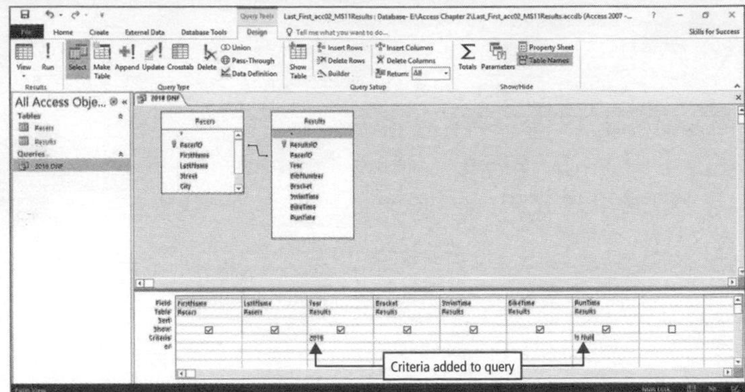

Figure 1 Access 2016, Windows 10, Microsoft Corporation

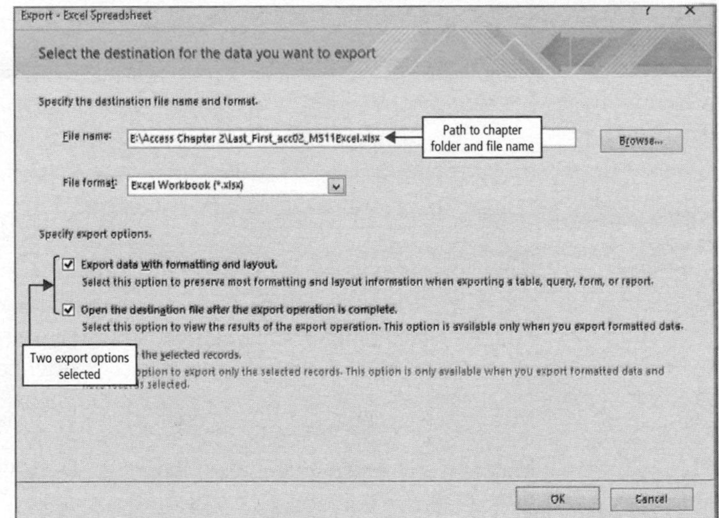

Figure 2 Access 2016, Windows 10, Microsoft Corporation

10. If your instructor asks you to print your work, print the worksheet.
11. **Close** [X] Excel. In the **Export - Excel Spreadsheet** dialog box, click the **Close** button.
12. **Close** [X] Access. Submit your files as directed by your instructor.

■ **You have completed More Skills 11**

More Skills 12

Export Queries as Web Pages

To complete this project, you will need the following file:

- acc02_MS12Females

You will save your files as:

- Last_First_acc02_MS12Females
- Last_First_acc02_MS12HTML

▸ By exporting a query as a web page, the file can be placed on a web server to make the results available on the web.

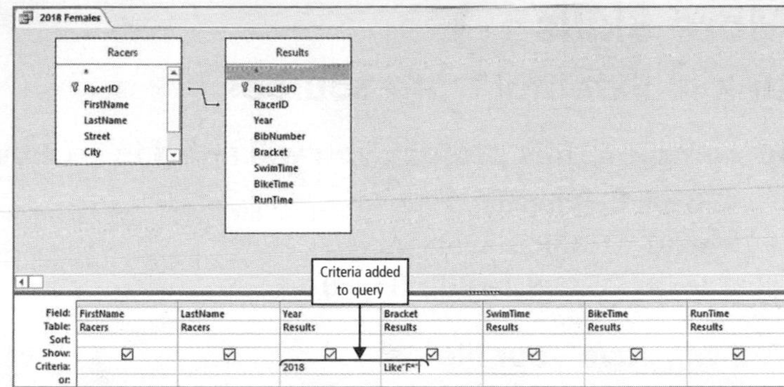

Access 2016, Windows 10, Microsoft Corporation

Figure 1

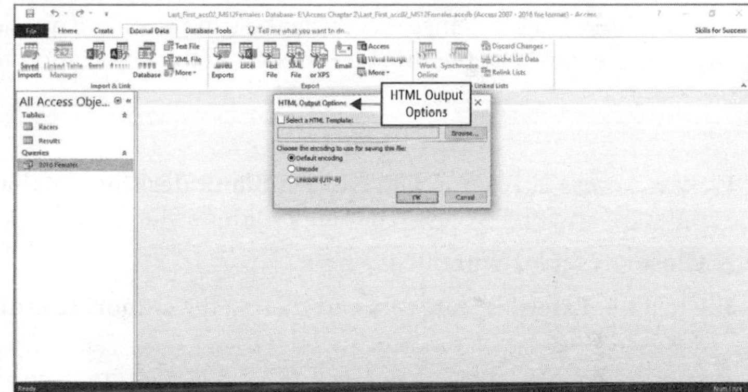

Access 2016, Windows 10, Microsoft Corporation

Figure 2

1. Start **Access 2016**, and then open the student data file **acc02_MS12Females**. Save the database in your **Access Chapter 2** folder as Last_First_acc02_MS12Females If necessary, enable the content.
2. Open the **2018 Females** query datasheet, and then replace the first and last names of the first racer *Luvette* and *Hoyle* with your own first and last names.
3. Switch to Design view. In the **Year** column **Criteria** box, type 2018 In the **Bracket** column **Criteria** cell, type Like "F*" Compare your screen with **Figure 1**.

   As you type *2018* IntelliSense will suggest *2018 Females* as an option. When you add a criterion, be careful to enter the correct data and not to accidentally select an IntelliSense suggestion that you do not want.

4. **Save** [Save], and then **Run** the query to display 158 records. **Close** [X] the query.
5. In the **Navigation Pane**, be sure that the **2018 Females** query is still selected. On the **External Data tab**, in the **Export group**, click the **More** button. In the list of file types, click **HTML Document**.

   An ***HTML document*** is a text file with instructions for displaying its content in a web browser. When the file is placed on a web server, the web page can be viewed on the Internet.

6. In the **Export - HTML Document** dialog box, click the **Browse** button. In the **File Save** dialog box, navigate to your **Access Chapter 2** folder. Name the file Last_First_acc02_MS12HTML and then click **Save**.
7. In the **Export - HTML Document** dialog box, select the **Export data with formatting and layout** check box. Select the **Open the destination file after the export operation is complete** check box, and then click **OK**. Compare your screen with **Figure 2**.
8. In the displayed **HTML Output Options** dialog box, click **OK** to accept the default settings and open the exported HTML file in a web browser. If necessary, select your browser on the toolbar to view the HTML file.
9. If your instructor asks you to print your work, print the web page.
10. **Close** [X] the web browser. Close the **Export - HTML Document** dialog box, and then **Close** [X] Access. Submit your files as directed by your instructor.

■ **You have completed More Skills 12**

More Skills 13

Link to External Data Sources

To complete this project, you will need the following files:

- Blank desktop database
- acc02_MS13Residents (Access)
- acc02_MS13WaterBills (Excel)

You will save your file as:

- Last_First_acc02_MS13Bills

▶ Access can use data stored in a ***linked table***—a table that exists in a different file created by an application such as Access or Excel.

▶ Once a linked table is inserted, it can be used to create queries and reports. To update the data, the file must be opened in the application that created it.

1. Start **Access 2016**, and then create a **Blank desktop database**. Save the database in your **Access Chapter 2** folder as Last_First_acc02_MS13Bills
2. **Close** ☒ Table1 without saving it.

Obj 2.1.3

3. Click the **External Data tab**, and then in the **Import & Link group**, click the **Excel** button.
4. In the **Get External Data - Excel Spreadsheet** dialog box, click the **Browse** button.
5. In the **File Open** dialog box, navigate to the student data files for this chapter. Click **acc02_MS13WaterBills**, and then click **Open**.
6. In the **Get External Data - Excel Spreadsheet** dialog box, select the **Link to the data source by creating a linked table** option button.
7. Click **OK** to start the Link Spreadsheet Wizard, compare your screen with **Figure 1**, and then click **Finish**. Read the message, and then click **OK**.
8. Double-click to open the **Water Bills** table. Set column widths to **Best Fit**.

   In the Navigation Pane, an arrow indicates that the data is linked, and the external application's icon displays.

9. **Save** 🖫, and then **Close** ☒ the table. On the **External Data tab**, in the **Import & Link group**, click the **Access** button.
10. In the **Get External Data - Access Database** dialog box, click the **Browse** button.
11. In the **File Open** dialog box, navigate to the student data files. Click **acc02_MS13Residents**, and then click **Open**.

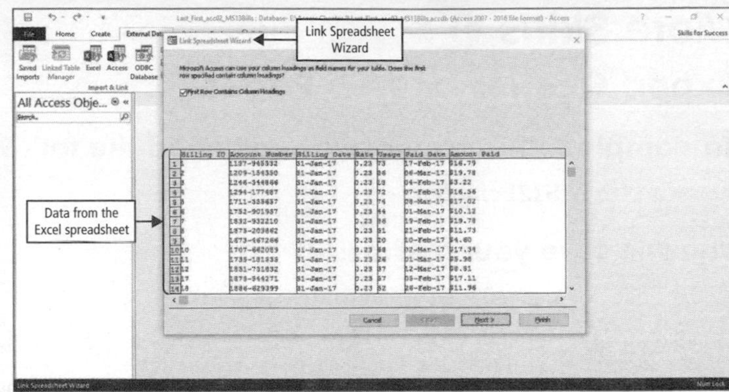

Figure 1 Access 2016, Windows 10, Microsoft Corporation

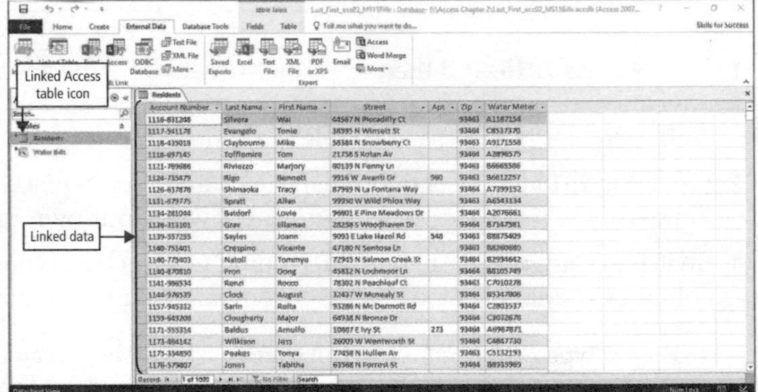

Figure 2 Access 2016, Windows 10, Microsoft Corporation

12. In the **Get External Data - Access Database** dialog box, select the **Link to the data source by creating a linked table** option button.
13. Click **OK**, and then in the **Link Tables** dialog box, click the **Residents** table. Click **OK** to link the table. **Close** the **Save Import Steps** dialog box.
14. Double-click to open the **Residents** table, and then compare your screen with **Figure 2**.
15. **Close** ☒ the table. **Close** ☒ Access, and then submit your file as directed by your instructor.

■ **You have completed More Skills 13**

More Skills 14

Create Crosstab Queries

To complete this project, you will need the following file:

- acc02_MS14Brackets

You will save your file as:

- Last_First_acc02_MS14Brackets

- A ***crosstab query*** is a select query that calculates a sum, an average, or a similar statistic and then groups the results by two sets of values.
- A crosstab query displays one group down the side of the datasheet and the other group across the top of the datasheet. For example, you could display racers' names on the left and race results at the top.

---

1. Start **Access 2016**, and then open the student data file **acc02_MS14Brackets.** Save the database in your **Access Chapter 2** folder as Last_First_acc02_MS14Brackets If necessary, enable the content.
2. In the **Navigation Pane**, under **Queries**, double-click **Male Results**. Be sure that the results for all males display as shown in **Figure 1**, and then **Close** [X] the query.
3. Click the **Create tab**, and then in the **Queries group**, click the **Query Wizard** button.
4. In the **New Query** dialog box, select **Crosstab Query Wizard**, and then click **OK**.
5. In the **Crosstab Query Wizard**, under **View**, select the **Queries** option button. Click **Query: Male Results**.

   A query can be built from another query. In this case, the crosstab query will use the data from the Male Results query.
6. Click **Next**, and then **Move** [>] **Year** into the **Selected Fields** list.
7. Click **Next**, and then, in the list of column headings, click **Bracket**.

   The column headings display at the top of each column in a crosstab query.
8. Click **Next**. Under **Functions**, click **Count**, and then compare your screen with **Figure 2**.

   The query will count the number of male racers for each year within each bracket. With the **Yes, include row sums** check box selected, the total count for each year will also be calculated.

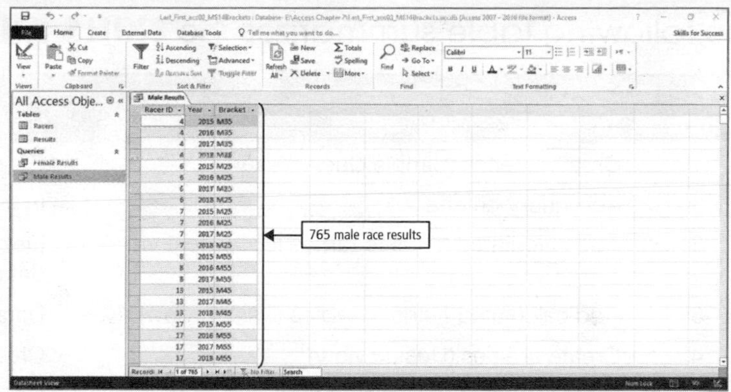

Access 2016, Windows 10, Microsoft Corporation **Figure 1**

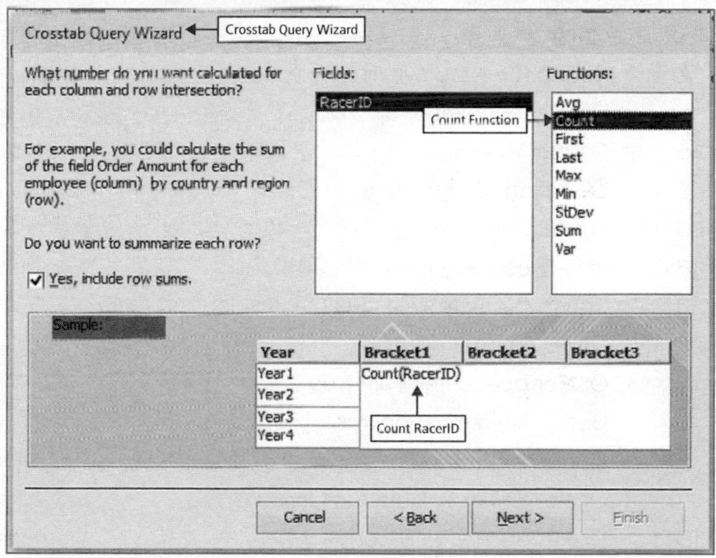

Access 2016, Windows 10, Microsoft Corporation **Figure 2**

9. Click **Next**, and then under **What do you want to name your query**, replace the text *Male Results_Crosstab* with Male Counts by Year
10. Click **Finish**.
11. Click **Save** [Save], **Close** [X] the query, and then **Close** [X] Access. Submit your file as directed by your instructor.

- **You have completed More Skills 14**

Review

The following table summarizes the **SKILLS AND PROCEDURES** covered in this chapter.

Skills Number	Task	Step
1	Create queries (Simple Query Wizard)	Create tab → Queries group → Query Wizard
2	Add query criteria	In the Criteria row, type the criteria in the column(s) with the values you wish to filter
3	Add calculated fields to tables (Datasheet view)	Fields tab → Add & Delete group → More Fields → Calculated Field → click the desired data type
3	Add calculated fields to tables (Design view)	Data Type arrow → Calculated
4	Create queries (Design view)	Create tab → Queries group → Query Design
4	Add tables to queries in Design view	Design tab → Query Setup group → Show Table
7	Group and total queries	Design tab → Show/Hide group → Totals Group first column(s), set Totals row to statistic for other column(s)
	Criteria:	
2	Equals the word *five*	"five"
5	Equals the number 5	5
5	Greater than 5	>5
5	Less than or equal to 5	<=5
6	Is after July 5, 2018	>#7/5/2018#
6	Is between July 5 and 10, 2018	Between #7/5/2018# And #7/10/2018#
8	Equals the *Rate* field plus 5 and is labeled *Extra*	Extra: [Rate]+5
9	Cell is empty	Is Null
9	One or both criteria are true	"Will" Or "Bill"
9	Both criteria must be true	"Will" And "Bill"
10	Contains the word *five*	Like "*five*"
10	Can be *Bill* or *Will* but not *Cerill*	Like "?ill"
MS11	Export queries to Excel	External Data tab → Export group → Excel button
MS12	Export queries as web pages	External Data tab → Export group → More button → HTML
MS13	Link to external sources	External Data tab → Import & Link group → Select external source
MS14	Create a crosstab query	Create tab → Queries group → Query Wizard → Crosstab Query Wizard

Project Summary Chart		
Project	**Project Type**	**Project Location**
Skills Review	Review	In Book & MIL MyITLab® Grader
Skills Assessment 1	Review	In Book & MIL MyITLab® Grader
Skills Assessment 2	Review	Book
My Skills	Problem Solving	Book
Visual Skills Check	Problem Solving	Book
Skillls Challenge 1	Critical Thinking	Book
Skills Challenge 2	Critical Thinking	Book
More Skills Assessment	Review	In Book & MIL MyITLab® Grader
Collaborating with Google	Critical Thinking	Book

MOS Objectives Covered	
1.3.5 Change views of objects	3.2.5 Sort data within queries
2.1.3 Create linked tables from external sources	3.2.6 Format fields within queries
3.1.1 Run a query	3.3.1 Add calculated fields
3.1.5 Create multi-table queries	3.3.3 Group and summarize data
3.1.6 Save a query	3.3.4 Group data by using comparison operators
3.2.2 Add fields	3.3.5 Group data by using arithmetic and logical operators
3.2.4 Hide fields	

Key Terms

BizSkills Video

1. If you could apply just one of the tips provided in this video to help manage your current priorities, which one would you choose? Why?
2. What techniques do you currently use to set a plan for your day? What other techniques could help you do this better?

Online Help Skills

1. Start **Access 2016**, and then in the upper right corner of the start page, click the **Help** button [?].
2. In the **Access Help** window **Search help** box, type query criteria and then press [Enter].
3. In the search result list, click **Create an expression**, and then compare your screen with **Figure 1**.

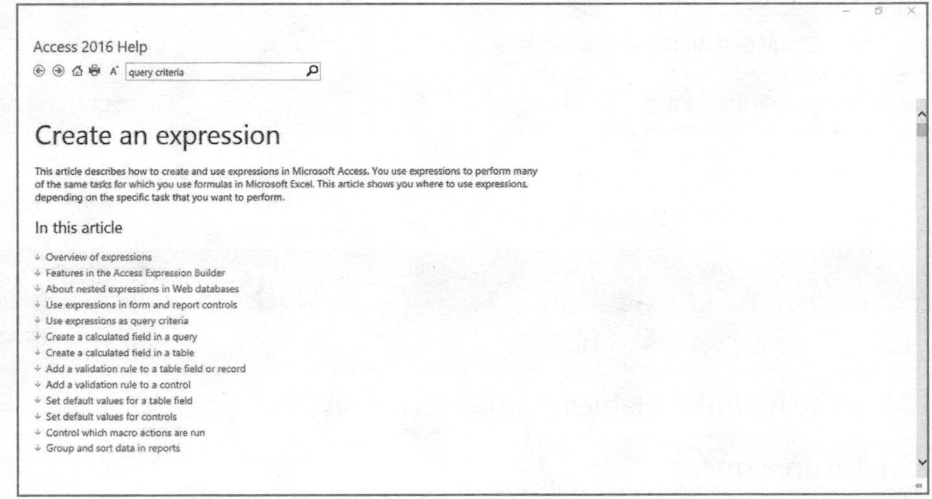

Figure 1 Access 2016, Windows 10, Microsoft Corporation

4. Read the article and answer the following question: Why would you set default values for controls?

Matching 

Match each term in the second column with its correct definition in the first column by writing the letter of the term on the blank line in front of the correct definition.

___ **1.** A database object used to ask questions about the data stored in database tables.

___ **2.** Conditions in a query used to select the records that answer the query's question.

___ **3.** A field in a table or query that derives its values from other fields in the table or query.

___ **4.** Less than (<) and greater than (>) are examples of this type of operator.

___ **5** In the query design grid, two criteria placed in the same row use this logical operator.

___ **6.** To add summary statistics to a query, this row must be added to the query.

___ **7.** When two criteria are placed in different rows in the query design grid, this logical operator will be applied.

___ **8.** An operator that tests if a field is empty.

___ **9.** This wildcard character can represent any combination of characters.

___ **10.** This wildcard character can represent any single character.

A And
B Asterisk (*)
C Calculated
D Comparison
E Criteria
F Or
G Query
H Question mark (?)
I Is Null
J Total

Multiple Choice

MyITLab®

Choose the correct answer.

1. A query that displays records without changing the data in a table.
   A. Select
   B. Simple
   C. View
2. In a query, criteria are added in this view.
   A. Datasheet
   B. Design
   C. Workspace
3. An IntelliSense box that explains the purpose of the selected AutoComplete.
   A. Balloon
   B. Quick Info
   C. ScreenTip
4. In a query, results are displayed in this view.
   A. Datasheet
   B. Design
   C. Design grid
5. A combination of fields, mathematical operators, and prebuilt functions that calculates values.
   A. Comparison operator
   B. Expression
   C. Quick Info
6. In query criteria, dates are surrounded by this character.
   A. >
   B. !
   C. #
7. A calculation for a group of data such as a total, an average, or a count.
   A. Calculated column
   B. Group formula
   C. Summary statistic
8. An operator that finds all numbers or dates between and including two values.
   A. And...Between
   B. Between...And
   C. In...Between
9. A descriptive label used to identify a field in expressions, datasheets, or forms and reports.
   A. Alias
   B. Label
   C. Name
10. The operator that is placed at the beginning of criteria that contain wildcards.
   A. Like
   B. Similar
   C. Wildcard

Topics for Discussion

1. You have created queries using the Simple Query Wizard and using Design view. Which method do you prefer, and why? What situations may be better suited to using the Simple Query Wizard? What situations may be better suited to using Design view?
2. Data that can be calculated from existing fields can be entered manually into its own field, or it can be included as a calculated field in a table or query. Which method would produce the most accurate results, and why?

Skills Review

To complete this project, you will need the following file:

- acc02_SRElectricity

You will save your file as:

- Last_First_acc02_SRElectricity

---

1. Start **Access 2016**, and then open the student data file **acc02_SRElectricity**. Save the file in your **Access Chapter 2** folder with the name Last_First_acc02_SRElectricity If necessary, enable the content.
2. Open the **Billing Cycles** table in Datasheet view. In the last column, click the **Click to Add arrow**, point to **Calculated Field**, and then from the submenu, click **Currency**.
3. In the **Expression Builder**, add the following expression: [UsageFee] - [AmountPaid]
4. Click **OK**, and then replace the selected text *Field1* with BalanceDue
5. Compare your screen with **Figure 1**, and then **Save** and **Close** the table.
6. On the **Create tab**, in the **Queries group**, click **Query Design**. **Add** both tables to the query workspace, and then **Close** the Show Table dialog box.
7. From the **Residents** table, add the **AccountNumber**, **LastName**, and **FirstName** fields to the design grid.
8. From the **Billing Cycles** table, add the **CycleDate**, **UsageFee**, and **BalanceDue** fields to the design grid.
9. In the **CycleDate** column **Criteria** cell, type Between 6/1/2018 And 6/30/2018
10. In the **BalanceDue** column **Criteria** cell, type > 1 Or Is Null
11. Click **Save**, type Penalties Query and then click **OK**.
12. Click the first blank **Field** cell, and then in the **Query Setup group**, click **Builder**. In the **Expression Builder**, add the following expression: Penalty: [BalanceDue] * 0.2 Click **OK**. In the **Show/Hide group**, click **Property Sheet**, and then change the calculated field's **Format** to **Currency**. **Close** the Property Sheet.
13. Run the query, compare your screen with **Figure 2**, and then **Save** and **Close** the query.

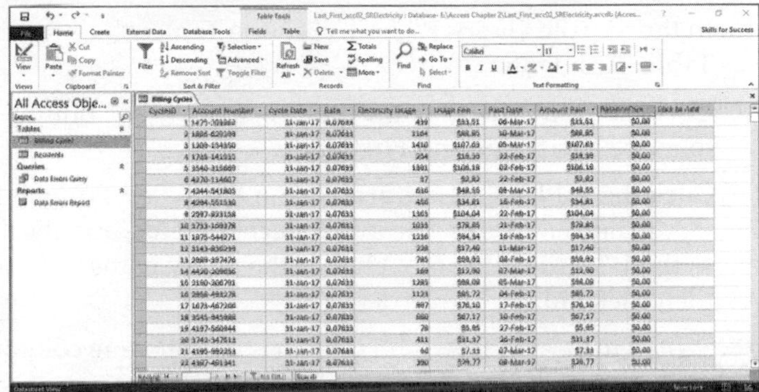

Access 2016, Windows 10, Microsoft Corporation **Figure 1**

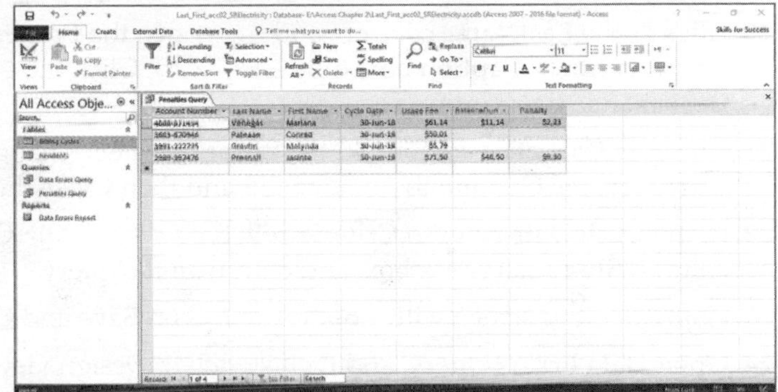

Access 2016, Windows 10, Microsoft Corporation **Figure 2**

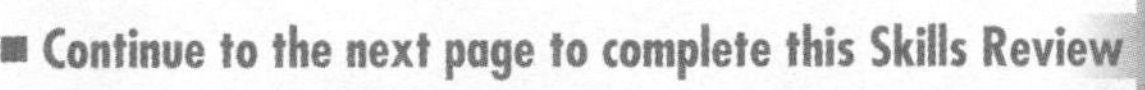
Continue to the next page to complete this Skills Review

14. On the **Create tab**, in the **Queries group**, click **Query Wizard**, and then in the **New Query** dialog box, click **OK**.
15. In the **Simple Query Wizard**, click the **Tables/Queries arrow**, and then click **Table: Residents**.
16. Click **AccountNumber**, and then click the **Move** button. Repeat the procedure to move **LastName** and **FirstName**.
17. Click the **Tables/Queries arrow**, and then click **Table: Billing Cycles**. Move **CycleDate** and **UsageFee** into **Selected Fields**, and then click **Next** two times. In the **Wizard** dialog box, change the query name to Resident Statistics and then click **Finish**.
18. Switch to Design view, and then in the **LastName** column **Sort** cell, set the value to **Ascending**.
19. On the **Design tab**, in the **Show/Hide group**, click **Totals**. Change the **LastName**, **FirstName**, and **CycleDate** columns **Total** cells to **First**. Change the **UsageFee** column **Total** cell to **Avg**.
20. Click in the **LastName** column, and then open the **Property Sheet**. In the **Property Sheet Caption** box, type Last Name Click the **FirstName** column, and then change the **Caption** property to First Name
21. Click the **UsageFee** column. In the **Property Sheet**, change the **Format** to **Currency**, the **Caption** to Average Bill and then **Close** the property sheet.
22. In the **CycleDate** column **Criteria** cell, type <1/1/2018 Clear the **CycleDate** column **Show** cell check box, and then **Run** the query.
23. Compare your screen with **Figure 3**, and then **Save** and **Close** the query.
24. Open **Data Errors Query**, and then switch to Design view. In the **LastName** column **Criteria** cell, type Like Thomps?n
25. In the **FirstName** column **Criteria** cell, type Ralph
26. In the **ElectricityUsage** column **or** cell, type Is Null
27. **Run** the query, and then compare your screen with **Figure 4**. **Save** and then **Close** the query.
28. Open **Data Errors Report**. If you are printing your work, print the report.
29. **Close** the report, and then **Close** Access. Submit your file as directed by your instructor.

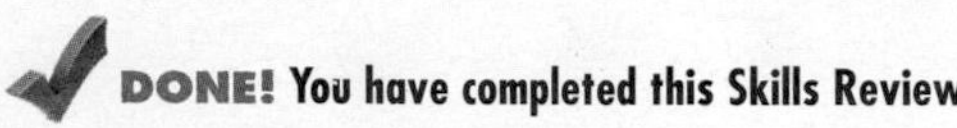
DONE! You have completed this Skills Review

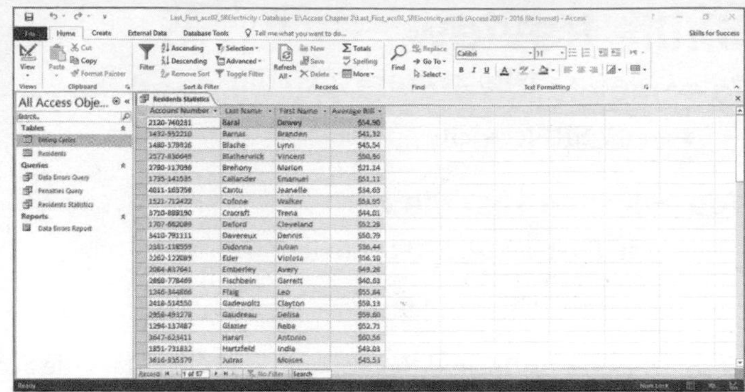

Figure 3 Access 2016, Windows 10, Microsoft Corporation

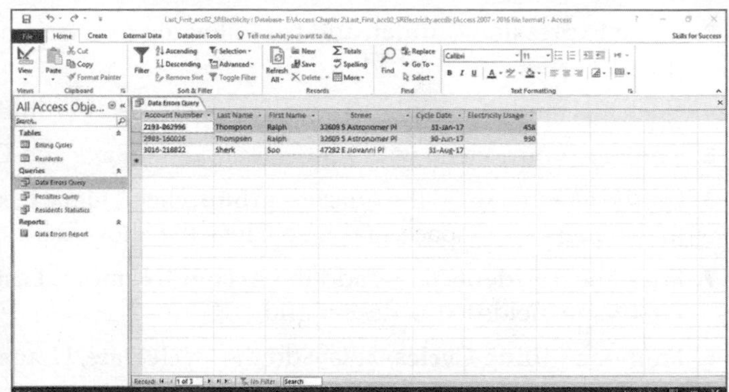

Figure 4 Access 2016, Windows 10, Microsoft Corporation

Skills Assessment 1

MyITLab®
Grader

To complete this project, you will need the following file:

- acc02_SA1Properties

You will save your file as:

- Last_First_acc02_SA1Properties

1. Start **Access 2016**, and then open the student data file **acc02_SA1Properties**. Save the file in your chapter folder as Last_First_acc02_SA1Properties
2. In the last column of the **Parcels** table datasheet, add a **Currency** calculated field that is derived by multiplying the **Value** field by 0.01206 Name the field Taxes and then **Save** and **Close** the table.
3. Use the **Simple Query Wizard** to start a query with the **Owner** field from the **Parcels** table and the **ZoneName** field from the **Zones** table. Name the query Tax Payments and then **Finish** the wizard.
4. In the **Tax Payments** query, add text criteria with a wildcard so that only records with *Residential* in their zone name result.
5. In the **Tax Payments** query, set the **ZoneName** column so that it does not show when the query is run.
6. Add a calculated field with the alias Payments that divides the **Taxes** field by two (Taxes/2). Set the field's **Format** property to **Currency**. **Run** the query, and then compare your results with **Figure 1**. **Save** and **Close** the query.
7. Create a new query in Design view, and then add the **Zones** and **Parcels** tables.
8. From the **Zones** table, add the **ZoneName** field, and then from the **Parcels** table, add the **Value** field three times.
9. Add the **Totals** row, and then group the query by **ZoneName**.
10. Set the first **Value** column summary statistic to **Count** each group, and then change its **Caption** property to Number of Parcels
11. Set the second **Value** column summary statistic to **Sum** each group, and then change its **Caption** property to Total Value
12. Set the third **Value** column summary statistic to average (**Avg**) each group, and then change its **Caption** property to Average Value
13. Set the third **Value** column **Sort** order to **Descending**.
14. **Save** the query with the name Zone Values and then **Run** the query. Set the datasheet column widths to **Best Fit**, and then compare your results with **Figure 2**. **Save**, and then **Close** the query.

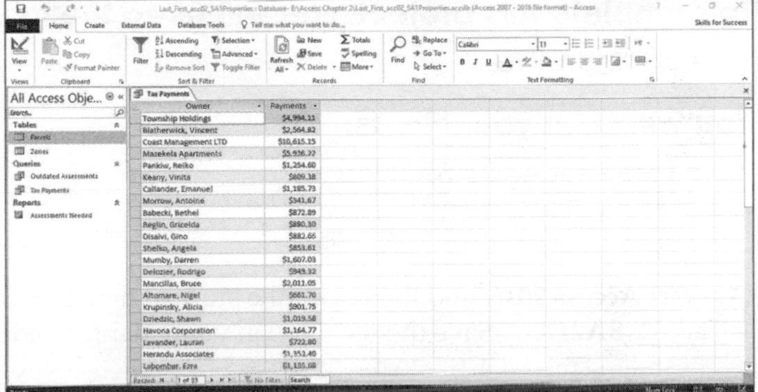

Access 2016, Windows 10, Microsoft Corporation **Figure 1**

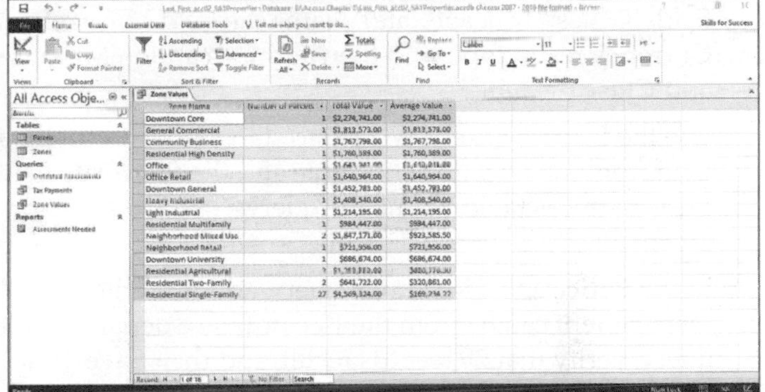

Access 2016, Windows 10, Microsoft Corporation **Figure 2**

15. Open the **Outdated Assessments** query in Design view. In the **LastAssessed** column, add criteria so that values that are either before 1/1/2017 *or* are empty (Null) will display in the query datasheet. Run the query, and verify that 24 records result. **Save** and **Close** the query.
16. Open the **Assessments Needed** report to view the 24 records from the Outdated Assessments query. If you are printing your work, print the report.
17. **Close** the report, and then **Close** Access. Submit your file as directed by your instructor.

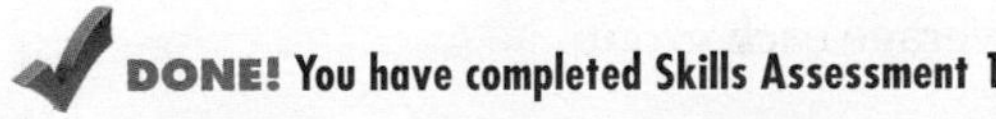
DONE! You have completed Skills Assessment 1

Skills Assessment 2

To complete this project, you will need the following file:

- acc02_SA2Fleet

You will save your file as:

- Last_First_acc02_SA2Fleet

1. Start **Access 2016**, and then open the student data file **acc02_SA2Fleet**. Save the database in your chapter folder as Last_First_acc02_SA2Fleet
2. In the last column of the **Fleet Services** table, add a calculated field that is derived from the product of the **Miles** and **MileageRate** fields (Miles * MileageRate). Name the field MileageFee assign it the **Currency** result type, and then add the caption Mileage Fee **Save** and **Close** the table.
3. Use the **Simple Query Wizard** to start a query with the **Department** field from the **Departments** table and the **StartDate** field from the **Fleet Services** table. Name the query Police and Fire Travel and then accept all other wizard defaults.
4. In the **Police and Fire Travel** query, add text criteria so that the **Department** can be from the Fire or Police department. Run the query, verify that 29 records result, and then **Save**.
5. In Design view, set the query to sort in ascending order by **StartDate**. Add criteria so that only records with a **StartDate** between 1/1/2018 *and* 7/31/2018 result.
6. Add a calculated field with the alias Charge that adds the BaseFee and MileageFee columns (BaseFee + MileageFee). **Run** the query, and then compare your results with **Figure 1**. **Save** and **Close** the query.
7. Create a new query in Design view, and then add the **Departments**, **Employees**, and **Fleet Services** tables.
8. From the **Departments** table, add the **Department** field, and then from the **Fleet Services** table, add the **ServiceID** field, and then add the **Miles** field two times.
9. Group the query by **Department**, and then **Count** the **ServiceID** in each group. Set the first **Miles** column to total each group and the second **Miles** column to average each group.

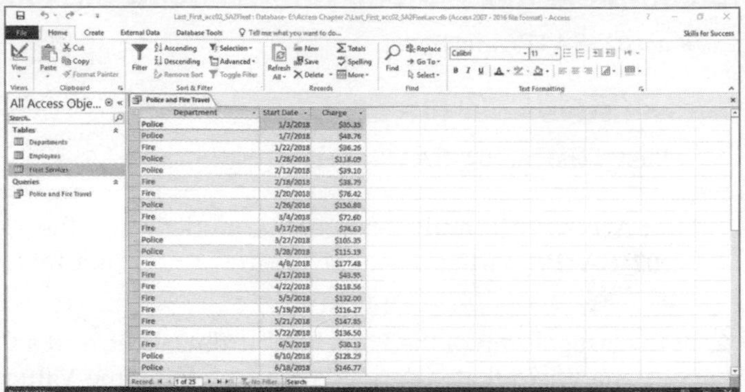

Figure 1 Access 2016, Windows 10, Microsoft Corporation

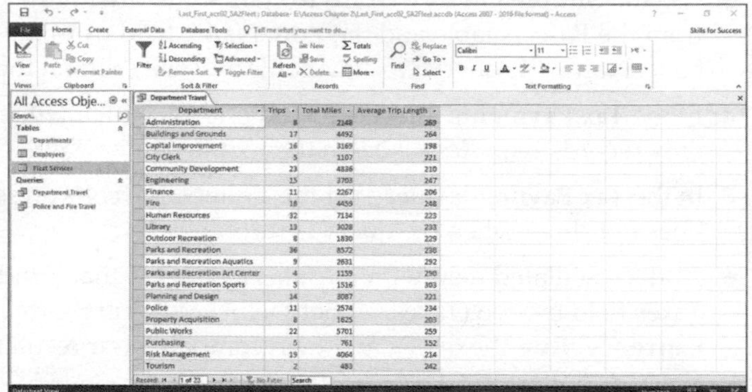

Figure 2 Access 2016, Windows 10, Microsoft Corporation

10. Set the **ServiceID** column **Caption** property to Trips and the first **Miles** column **Caption** property to Total Miles
11. Set the second **Miles** column properties so that the datasheet displays no decimals and the column's caption will be Average Trip Length
12. **Save** the query with the name Department Travel and then **Run** the query. Set the datasheet column widths to **Best Fit**, and then compare your results with **Figure 2**. **Save** and then **Close** the query.
13. **Close** Access, and then submit your file as directed by your instructor.

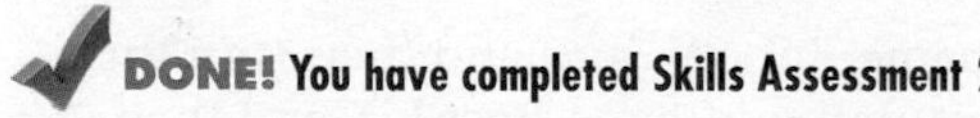

DONE! You have completed Skills Assessment 2

My Skills

To complete this project, you will need the following file:

- **acc02_MYBaseball**

You will save your file as:

- **Last_First_acc02_MYBaseball**

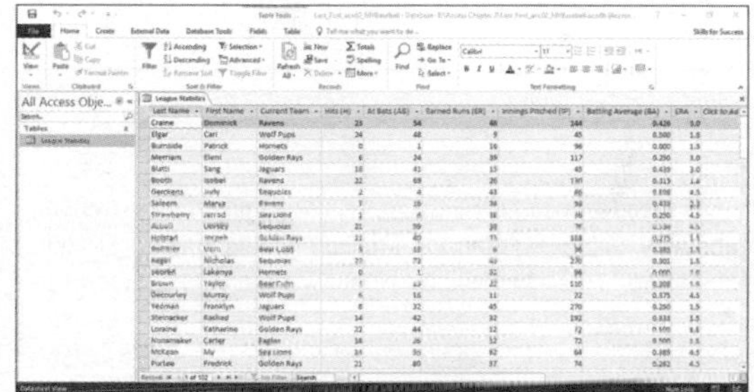

Access 2016, Windows 10, Microsoft Corporation **Figure 1**

Access 2016, Windows 10, Microsoft Corporation **Figure 2**

1. Start **Access 2016**, and then open the student data file **acc02_MYBaseball**. Save the database in your chapter folder as Last_First_acc02_MYBaseball
2. In the **League Statistics** table datasheet, click the **At Bats (AB)** column, and then add a **Number** calculated field. For the expression, divide the Hits field by the AtBats field. Name the field Batting Average You will format the numbers in a later step.
3. **Save** the table, and then switch to Design view. In the **BattingAverage Description (Optional)** cell, type Hits divided by AtBats
4. In the **BattingAverage** field properties, change the **Result Type** to **Single**, the **Format** to **Fixed**, and the **Decimal Places** to **3**. Add Batting Average (BA) as the field's caption.
5. In the first available row, add a new calculated field named ERA For the expression, multiply the EarnedRuns field by 9, and then divide by the InningsPitched field (EarnedRuns * 9 / InningsPitched).
6. In the **ERA Description (Optional)** cell, type Earned run average (EarnedRuns * 9 / InningsPitched)
7. In the **ERA** field properties, change the **Result Type** to **Single**, the **Format** to **Fixed**, and the **Decimal Places** to **1**.
8. **Save** the table, and then switch to Datasheet view. Set the column widths to **Best Fit**, and then compare your screen with **Figure 1**. **Save** and **Close** the table.
9. Create a new query in Design view that includes every field in the **League Statistics** table *except for* PlayerID, LastName, and FirstName. **Save** the query with the name Team Stats
10. Change the query to calculate the averages for each team.
11. Change the **Hits** column properties so that one decimal displays and the column heading displays as Avg Team Hits
12. Change the **AtBats** column properties so that one decimal displays and the column heading displays as Avg Team AB
13. Change the **BattingAverage** column properties so that three decimals display and the column heading displays as Team BA
14. Change the **EarnedRuns** column properties so that one decimal displays and the column heading displays as Avg Team ER
15. Change the **InningsPitched** column properties so that one decimal displays and the column heading displays as Avg Team IP
16. Change the **ERA** column properties so that one decimal displays and the column heading displays as Avg Team ERA
17. Run the query, set the column widths to **Best Fit**, and then compare your screen with **Figure 2**.
18. **Save** the query, and then **Close** Access. Submit your file as directed by your instructor.

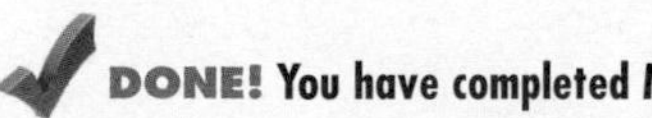

DONE! You have completed My Skills

Visual Skills Check

To complete this project, you will need the following file:

- acc02_VSPermits

You will save your file as:

- Last_First_acc02_VSPermits

Open the student data file **acc02_VSPermits**. Save the database in your chapter folder as Last_First_acc02_VSPermits

Create a query with the results shown in **Figure 1**. Name the query Fence Permits Due and add the columns as shown. Add a calculated field with the alias Balance and then add criteria that answer the question, *Which fencing projects have balances due*? Six records should result.

Submit your file as directed by your instructor.

Fence Permits Due

Record	Start Date	Project Title	Work Location	Fee	Paid to Date	Balance
B4078864FENC	8/6/2018	FENCE MATHAI RESIDENCE	1448 S Lighthouse Pl	$49.50	$0.00	$49.50
B4141621FENC	8/1/2018	JOBS RESIDENCE FENCE	4069 S Shaffer Meadow Ln	$49.50	$0.00	$49.50
B5119759FENC	8/15/2018	FENCE TUR RESIDENCE	3102 W Cubola Av	$49.50	$0.00	$49.50
B5357156FENC	8/13/2018	POSTMA RESIDENCE	5674 W Split Wood	$49.50	$25.00	$24.50
B6603712FENC	8/6/2018	FENCE FEHRS RESIDENCE	3596 S Bethany Bay Pl	$49.50	$15.00	$34.50
B9460314FENC	8/17/2018	FENCE ESCHE RESIDENCE	3234 N Entertainment Av	$49.50	$0.00	$49.50
*					$0.00	

Figure 1

Access 2016, Windows 10, Microsoft Corporation

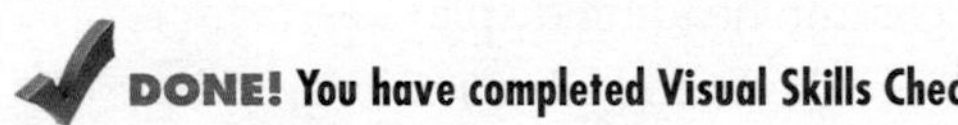
DONE! You have completed Visual Skills Check

Skills Challenge 1

To complete this project, you will need the following file:

- **acc02_SC1Classes**

You will save your file as:

- **Last_First_acc02_SC1Classes**

Open the student data file **acc02_SC1Classes**, and then save the file in your chapter folder as Last_First_acc02_SC1Classes Open the Instructor Class Counts query, and then add a column so that each instructor's first name is included after the last name field and the two interns with the last name of *Shriver* have an accurate count. Cheyenne Shriver should have a total of one, and Kenton Shriver should have a total of five.

Open the Intern Contacts List query, and then fix the query so that each intern is listed only once. To do this, you do not need to add any criteria, change any properties, use the Total row, or apply any filters to the datasheet. You will need to delete a table from the query to ensure each intern is only listed once.

Open the Word Classes query, and then fix the criteria and add columns so that it answers the question, *Where are all the Word classes offered, and what are their start dates and times?*

Submit your file as directed by your instructor.

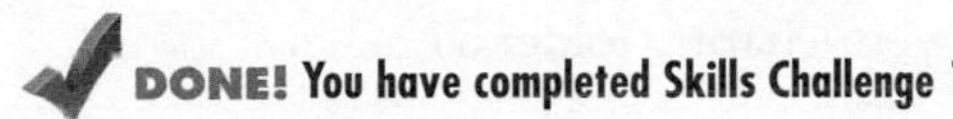
DONE! You have completed Skills Challenge 1

Skills Challenge 2

To complete this project, you will need the following file:

- **acc02_SC2Rentals**

You will save your file as:

- **Last_First_acc02_SC2Rentals**

Open student data file **acc02_SC2Rentals**, and then save the file in your chapter folder as Last_First_acc02_SC2Rentals Create a query named Refunds that answers the following question: *Which July renters of community center rooms get a refund?* Identify the renters by including the RenterID field. Display the date and hours each room was rented and the refund amount.

To calculate the balance due, subtract the deposit from the rental fee. The rental fee can be determined by multiplying the number of hours rented by the room's hourly rate. Define the calculated field's alias as Balance and format the column to display as currency. (The currency format encloses negative numbers—refunds—in parentheses instead of using a negative sign.) Be sure to limit the query results to July 2018 and only to those receiving a refund.

Submit your file as directed by your instructor.

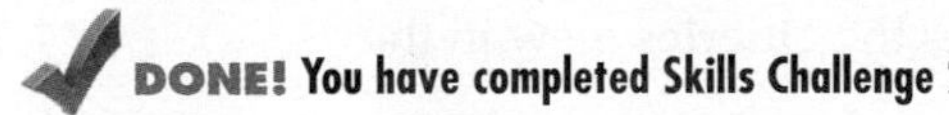
DONE! You have completed Skills Challenge 2

More Skills Assessment

To complete this project, you will need the following files:

- acc02_MSARacers
- acc02_MSAVolunteers (Excel)

You will save your files as:

- Last_First_acc02_MSARacers
- Last_First_acc02_MSAVolunteers (Excel)
- Last_First_acc02_MSARacers (Excel)
- Last_First_acc02_MSAResults (HTML)

1. Start **Access 2016**, and then open the student data file **acc02_MSARacers**. **Save** the database in your chapter folder as Last_First_acc02_MSARacers
2. Open the **Racers** table in Datasheet view. **Export the data with formatting and layout** to an **Excel Workbook**. **Save** the file as Last_First_acc02_MSARacers **Close** the **Export - Excel Spreadsheet** dialog box, and then **Close** the **Racers** table.
3. Open the **Results** table, and then **Export the data with formatting and layout** to an **HTML** file format. Save the file as Last_First_acc02_MSAResults Compare your screen with **Figure 1**, and then **Close** the **HTML Output Options** dialog box.
4. Navigate to your student data files and open the **acc02_MSAVolunteers** Excel file. **Save** the file as Last_First_acc02_MSAVolunteers Review the content, and then close the spreadsheet.
5. Return to Access, and in the **Import & Link group**, select **Link to the data source by creating a linked table** to link to the Volunteers Excel spreadsheet.
6. If necessary, select the **First Row Contains Column Headings** checkbox. Accept the remaining default settings.
7. Create a **Crosstabs Query** that uses the **Queries** view in the **Crosstab Query Wizard**.
8. In the **Crosstab Query Wizard**, select the **Query: 2018 Females** query.
9. Move the **Year** into the **Selected Fields**.

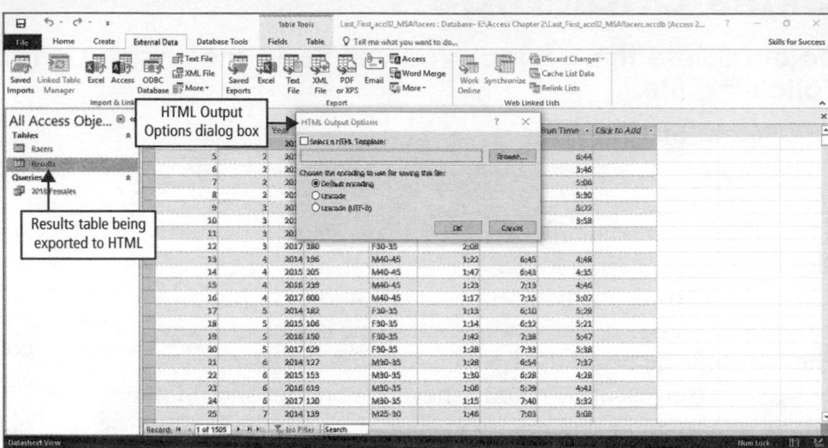

Figure 1 Access 2016, Windows 10, Microsoft Corporation

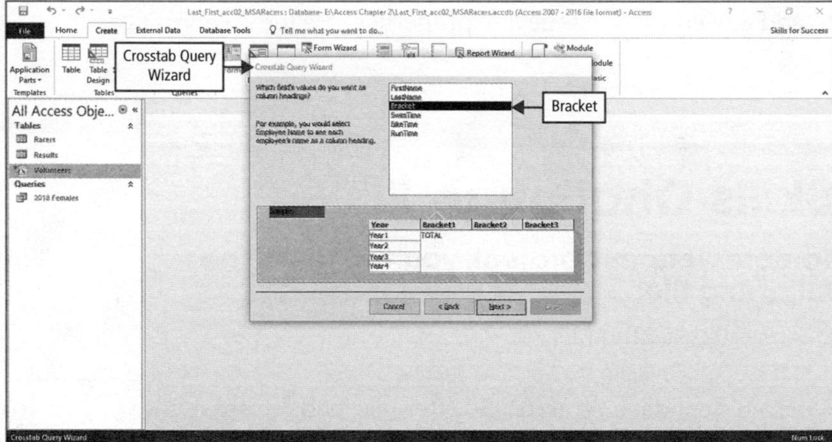

Figure 2 Access 2016, Windows 10, Microsoft Corporation

10. In **Which field's values do you want as column headings?** select **Bracket**, and then compare your screen to **Figure 2**.
11. Name the query 2018 Females_Crosstab
12. **Save** and **Close** the query.
13. **Close** Access, and submit the files as directed by your instructor.

Collaborating with Google

To complete this project, you will need a Google account (refer to the Common Features chapter) and the following file:

- acc02_GPMembers (Excel)

You will save your file as:

- Last_First_acc02_GPSnip

1. Open Google Chrome web browser. Log into your Google account, and then click the **Apps** button.
2. Click the **Drive** button to open Google Drive. If you receive a pop-up message, read the message, and then click **Next**. Read each message, and then close the dialog box.
3. Click the **New** button, and then click **Google Sheets** to open a blank spreadsheet.
4. Click the spreadsheet title, **Untitled spreadsheet**. In the dialog box, type Members as the name of the spreadsheet, and then click **OK**. Double-click the **Sheet1** worksheet tab. Rename the *Sheet1* worksheet tab as Members
5. Open the student data file **acc02_GPMembers**. Copy the range **A1:H80** from the *Members* worksheet and paste in cell **A1** of the blank Google worksheet.
6. Right-click the row 10 heading to display the shortcut menu, and then compare your screen with **Figure 1**.
7. Click **Delete Row** to delete the entire row and its contents.
8. In the second row, replace the existing **FirstName** and **LastName** with your first and last names.
9. In the fourth row, replace the existing **ZipCode** with the value 93463
10. Select the range **A1:H1**, and then click the **Bold** button to remove the Bold formatting.
11. Select cell **I1**, and then type Email
12. Press **Enter**.
13. Click the **Share** button, and in the **Share with others** dialog box, type AspenFallsEvents@gmail.com to share the sheet with another user.
14. In the **Add a note** text box, type Please review the contact information, and add email addresses as available. If any information is incorrect, please correct it. Compare your screen with **Figure 2**, and then click **Send**.
15. Press [Windows], type snip and then press [Enter] to start the **Snipping Tool**. Click the **New arrow**, and then click **Window Snip**. Point to the Google Chrome Browser, and when a red border displays around the window, click one time.
16. In the **Snipping Tool** mark-up window, click the **Save Snip** button. In the **Save As** dialog box, navigate to your Access Chapter 2 folder. Be sure the **Save as type** box displays **JPEG file**. Name the file Last_First_acc02_GPSnip and then press [Enter]. **Close** [X] the Snipping Tool mark-up window.
17. Close all windows, and then submit your file as directed by your instructor.

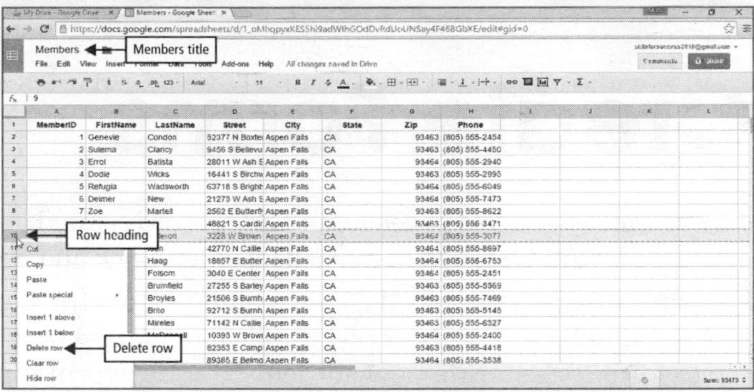

Figure 1

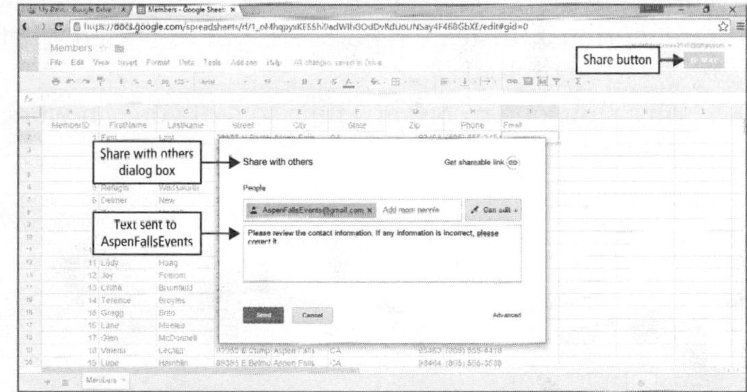

Figure 2

 **DONE! You have completed Collaborating with Google**

CHAPTER 3

Create Forms

- Forms are used to edit, delete, and add records stored in database tables and are designed to make data entry quick and accurate.
- Forms are often designed for entering data for the specific needs of the database. For example, a college database may provide one form for entering new students, another form for registering students for classes, and another form for assigning instructors to teach those classes.
- Forms are designed to be viewed on a computer screen and are rarely printed. Instead, reports are typically used when data needs to be printed.
- Forms show one record at a time so that you can work with just that data.
- Forms can take advantage of one-to-many relationships. The main form shows one record at a time from the first table, and below that, all the related records in the other table display in a subform.
- There are several methods for creating forms, including the Form Wizard and the Form Tool.
- Forms can be arranged in Word-like tables so that you can quickly position labels and text in cells to create a custom layout for your form.
- Forms can be based on queries so that you can work with a subset of the data.
- Some forms have buttons that open other database objects—tables, queries, other forms, and reports. These forms can be built quickly using the Navigation Form command.

Goodluz/Fotolia

Aspen Falls City Hall

In this chapter, you will create forms for Aspen Falls Utilities. You will work under the supervision of Diane Payne, Public Works Director, to design forms for entering records about city residents and their water bills. You will also build a form that data entry personnel will use to open and close the database forms.

There are several methods for creating forms in Access. The method you choose depends on the type of form you need and personal preference. No matter which method you choose, all forms need to provide a way to locate and update records quickly and accurately. Most forms also provide a way to add new records. The form's header displays information about the form's purpose, and the detail area displays labels and text boxes with values from the underlying table.

Some forms are used to open and close other forms and reports. These forms provide a way to navigate the database and can be set up in a way that hides the Navigation Pane. Using this method, you can provide a custom database interface based on the needs of the individuals who will use it.

To complete this project, you will create a form using a wizard and then format that form. You will use the form to edit records. You will create another form using the Form Tool that displays records from two related tables on the same screen and then enter new records using this form. You will also build a form based on a select query. Finally, you will create a Navigation Form that opens the other three forms, and then set up the form to hide the Navigation Pane when the form is in use.

Introduction

Time to complete all 10 skills — 60 to 90 minutes

Outcome

Using the skills in this chapter, you will be able to create various types of forms, add conditional formatting and controls to forms, work with tabular layouts, utilize input masks, validate fields, create databases in older formats, and backup databases.

Objectives

3.1 Create forms using various methods

3.2 Modify data within forms

3.3 Construct forms that use controls and conditional formatting

3.4 Generate forms that use input masks

Student data files needed for this chapter:

acc03_Water
acc03_WaterLogo

You will save your files as:

Last_First_acc03_Water
Last_First_acc03_WaterSnip (1 – 4)

SKILLS

At the end of this chapter you will be able to:

Skill 1 Use the Form Wizard
Skill 2 Use Forms to Modify Data
Skill 3 Format Forms in Layout View
Skill 4 Add Controls and Conditional Formatting
Skill 5 Use the Form Tool
Skill 6 Work with Tabular Layouts
Skill 7 Add Input Masks
Skill 8 Change Data in One-to-Many Forms
Skill 9 Create Forms from Queries
Skill 10 Create Navigation Forms

MORE SKILLS

Skill 11 Validate Fields
Skill 12 Create Databases from Templates
Skill 13 Import Objects from Other Databases
Skill 14 Back Up Databases

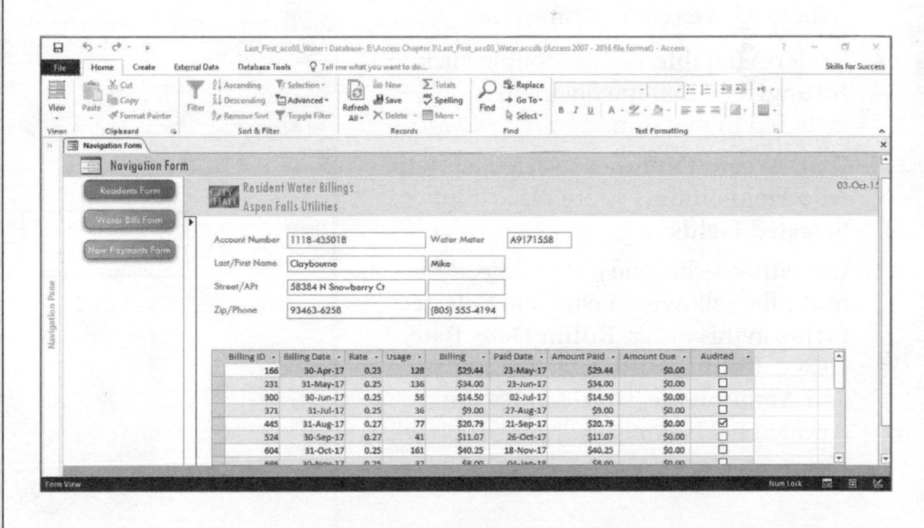

Access 2016, Windows 10, Microsoft Corporation

▸ Access has several tools for creating forms. The Form Wizard is an efficient method to create a form when you do not need to include all the fields from a table.

1. Start **Access 2016**, and then open the student data file **acc03_Water**. On the **File tab**, click **Save As**. With **Save Database As** selected, click the **Save As** button. In the **Save As** dialog box, navigate to the location where you are saving your files for this project. Click **New folder**, type Access Chapter 3 and then press Enter two times. Name the file Last_First_acc03_Water and then click **Save.**

2. If the Security Warning message displays, click the Enable Content button.

MOS Obj 4.1.1

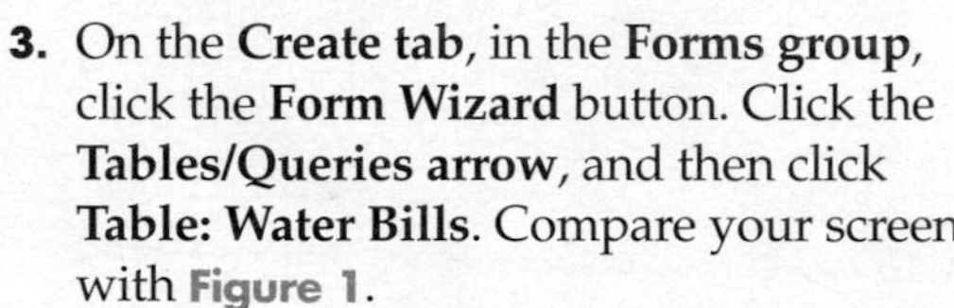

3. On the **Create tab**, in the **Forms group**, click the **Form Wizard** button. Click the **Tables/Queries arrow**, and then click **Table: Water Bills**. Compare your screen with **Figure 1**.

   By default, the table or query that is selected in the Navigation Pane will be selected in the first screen of the Form Wizard.

MOS Obj 4.2.2

4. Under **Available Fields**, double-click **BillingID** so that the field will be included in the form.

5. With **AccountNumber** selected, click the **Add Field** button > to place it into **Selected Fields**.

6. Use either technique just practiced to move the following fields into **Selected Fields** in this order: **BillingDate**, **Rate**, **Usage**, **Billing**, **PaidDate**, **AmountPaid**, and **AmountDue**. Do *not* move the Audited field. Compare your screen with **Figure 2.**

■ Continue to the next page to complete the skill

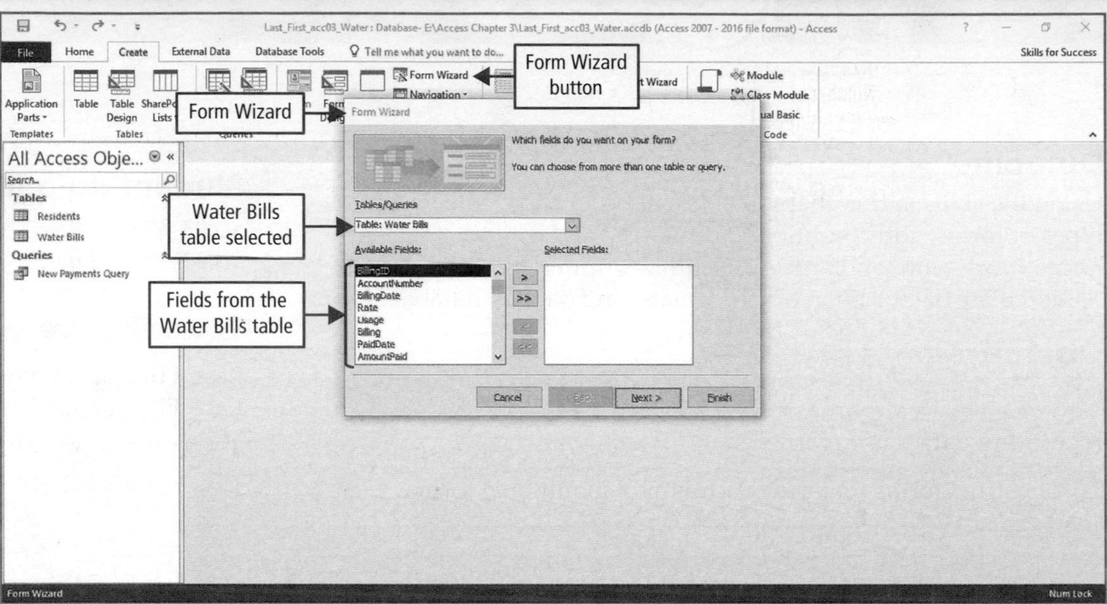

Figure 1 Access 2016, Windows 10, Microsoft Corporation

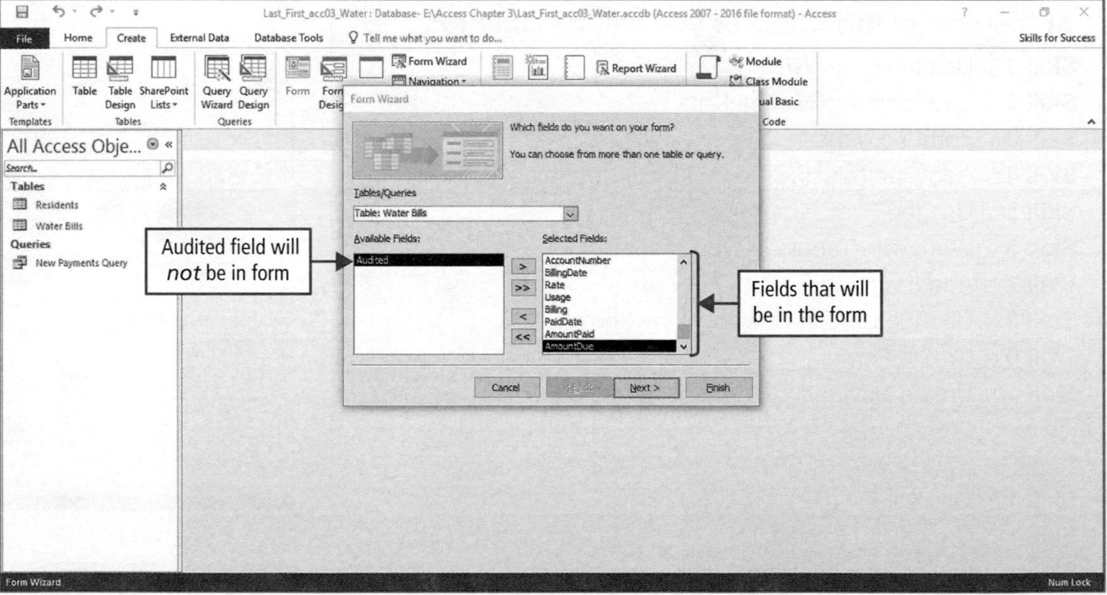

Figure 2 Access 2016, Windows 10, Microsoft Corporation

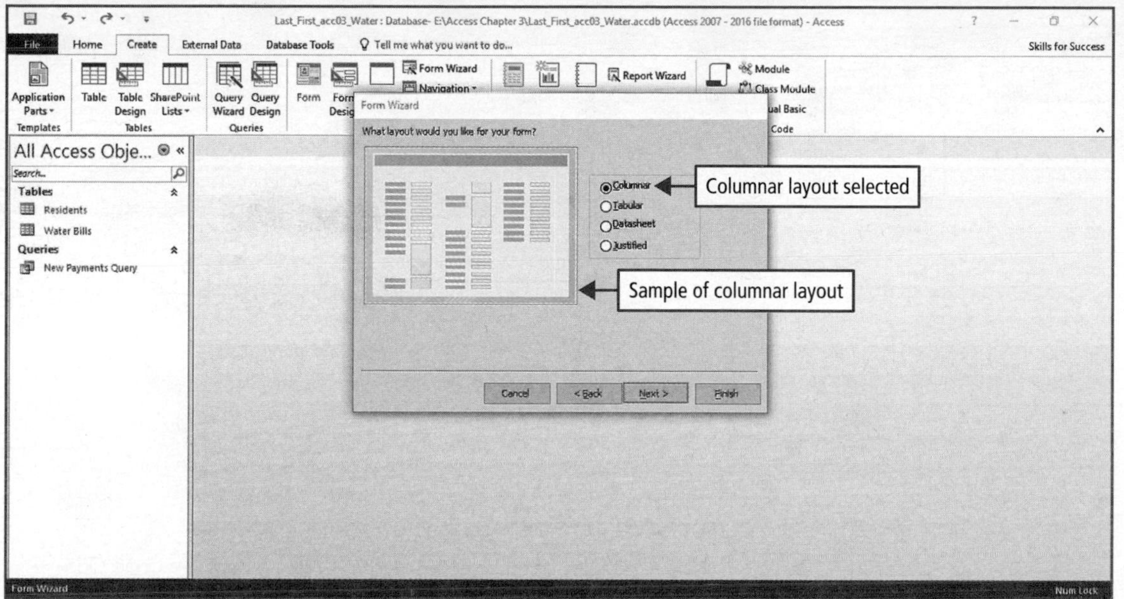

Access 2016, Windows 10, Microsoft Corporation

Figure 3

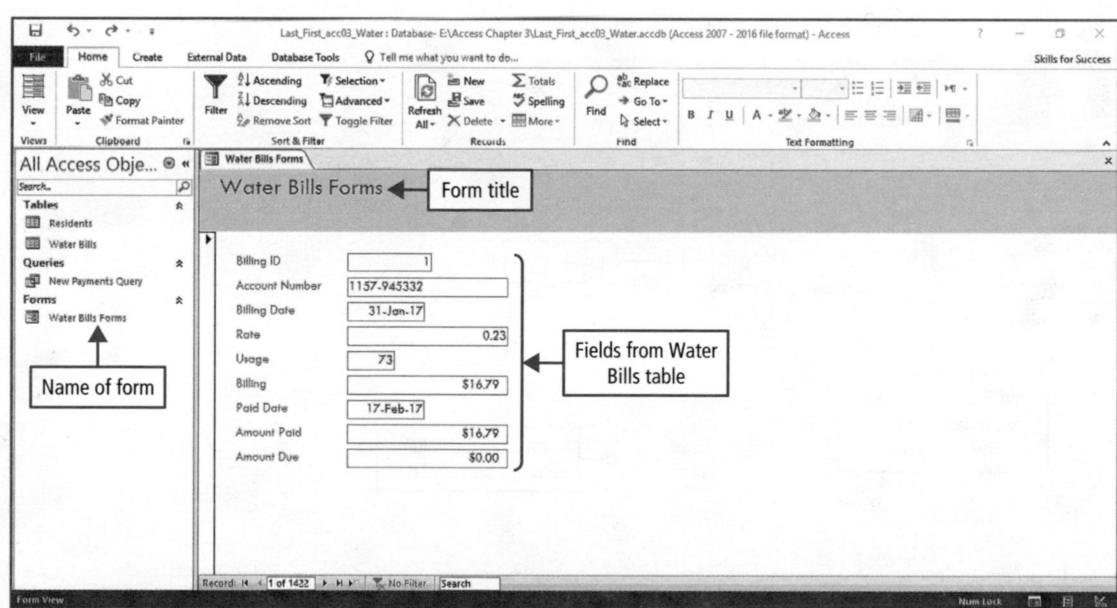

Access 2016, Windows 10, Microsoft Corporation

Figure 4

7. In the **Form Wizard**, click **Next**, and then compare your screen with **Figure 3**.

   You can use the Form Wizard to pick different layouts for your form. A ***layout*** determines how data and labels are arranged in a form or report. For example, the ***columnar layout*** places labels in the first column and data in the second column.

8. With **Columnar layout** selected, click **Next**. Under **What title do you want for your form**, change *Water Bills* to Water Bills Forms

9. In the **Forms Wizard**, click **Finish** to create the form and open it in **Form view**. Compare your screen with **Figure 4**.

   The title that you type in the last screen of the Form Wizard becomes the name of the form in the Navigation Pane, and the theme last used in the database is applied to the form.

10. Leave the form open for the next skill.

■ **You have completed Skill 1 of 10**

 WATCH SKILL 3.2

► Recall that forms are designed to input data into tables. When you edit data or add records, the changes are stored automatically in the underlying table.

1. Take a few moments to familiarize yourself with the **Water Bills Form**, as shown in **Figure 1**.

   Most forms display in ***Single Form view***—a view that displays one record at a time with field names in the first column and field values in the second column. If a field has a caption property assigned, that value will display in the label. For example, the *BillingID* field displays as *Billing ID*.

   At the bottom of the form, the Navigation bar shows how many records are in the underlying table and has buttons for moving from one record to another.

2. On the Navigation bar, click the **Next record** button [▸] to display record 2 of 1422—*Billing ID 2*.

3. Click the **Paid Date** box, and then type the date 06-Feb-17 Press Enter to move to the next field, **Amount Paid**, and then type 19.78 Watch the **Amount Due** value automatically update as you press Enter, and then compare your screen with **Figure 2**.

   The Amount Due field is a calculated field that automatically updates when the Rate, Usage, or AmountPaid fields are changed. The change you made to the AmountPaid field was changed in the table, and the AmountDue box updated to display the new value. In this manner, forms can be used to edit table data while viewing one record at a time.

■ **Continue to the next page to complete the skill**

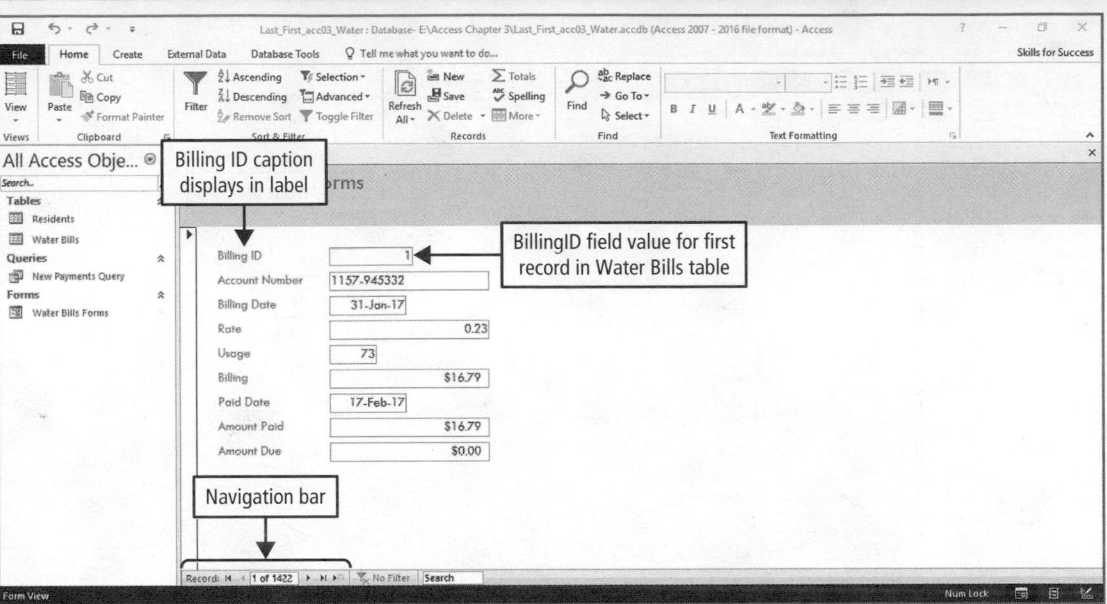

Figure 1 Access 2016, Windows 10, Microsoft Corporation

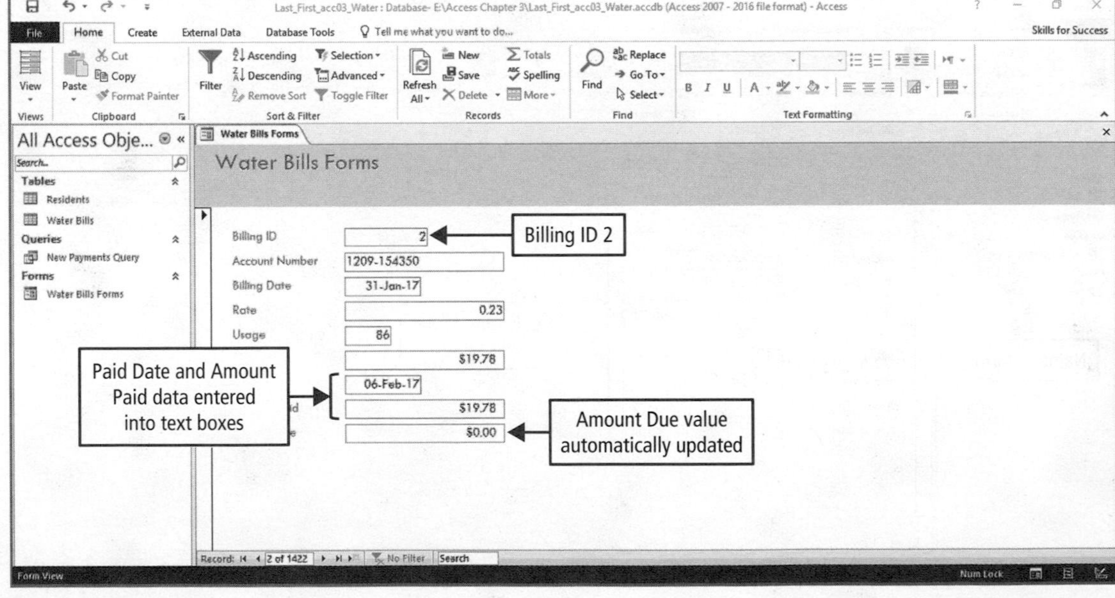

Figure 2 Access 2016, Windows 10, Microsoft Corporation

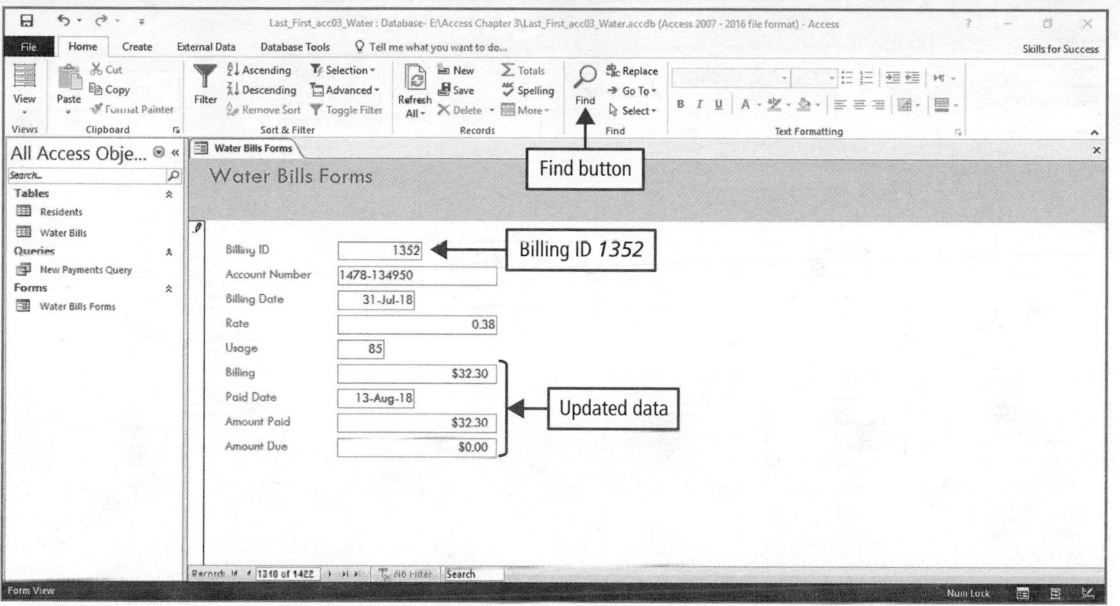

Access 2016, Windows 10, Microsoft Corporation

Figure 3

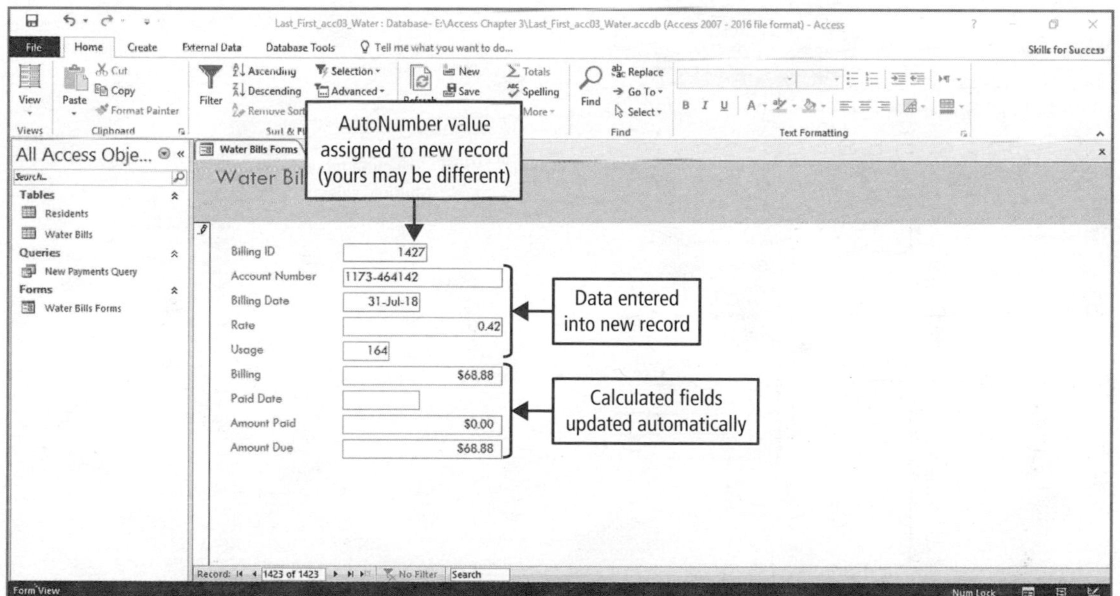

Access 2016, Windows 10, Microsoft Corporation

Figure 4

4. Press Enter to move to the next record—*Billing ID 3*. With **Billing ID** active, on the **Home tab**, in the **Find group**, click the **Find** button.

5. In the **Find and Replace** dialog box **Find What** box, type 1352 Press Enter, and then **Close** the dialog box.

Obj 1.3.1

6. In the record for *Billing ID 1352*, enter a **Paid Date** of 13-Aug-18 and an **Amount Paid** of 32.30 Press Enter to update the record. Compare your screen with **Figure 3**.

7. On the Navigation bar, click the **New (blank) record** button. Press Enter two times to move the insertion point to the **Account Number** box. Type 1173-464142 and then press Enter.

   You can move to the next field in a form by pressing Enter or Tab. In this way, you can continue typing values without having to use the mouse. Keeping your hands over the keyboard speeds data entry and increases accuracy.

8. In the **Billing Date** box, type 31-Jul-18 and then press Enter. In the **Rate** box, type 0.42 and then press Enter.

9. In the **Usage** box, type 164 Watch the **Billing** and **Amount Due** values update automatically as you press Enter, and then compare your screen with **Figure 4**.

   In the Water Bills table, the Billing field is a calculated field that multiplies the Rate value by the Usage value. Here, the July billing for this account is $68.88.

10. Leave the table open for the next skill.

    You do not need to save any changes because the data was automatically saved as you entered it.

■ **You have completed Skill 2 of 10**

- ***Layout view*** is used to format a form or report while you are viewing a sample of the data.

1. With the **Water Bills Form** open, on the **Home tab**, in the **Views group**, click the **View** button to switch to Layout view. If the Field List pane displays, **Close** [X] the pane.
2. On the **Design tab**, in the **Tools group**, click the **Property Sheet** button as needed to open the property sheet.
3. On the Navigation bar, click the **First record** button [⏮]. Click the **Account Number** text box, and then compare your screen with **Figure 1**.

   In Layout view, you can select individual ***controls***—objects in a form or report such as labels and text boxes—and format them. A ***label*** is a control in a form or report that describes other objects in the report or form. A ***text box*** is a control in a form or report that displays the data from a field in a table or query. Here, the label displays the caption *Account Number*, and the AccountNumber text box displays the value *1157-945332*.

4. With the **Account Number** text box control still selected, click the Ribbon **Format tab**. In the **Font group**, click the **Align Right** button.
5. Click the **Billing ID** text box to select it. Press and hold Shift while clicking the eight other text boxes with the [pointer] pointer. Release the Shift key, and then compare your screen with **Figure 2**.

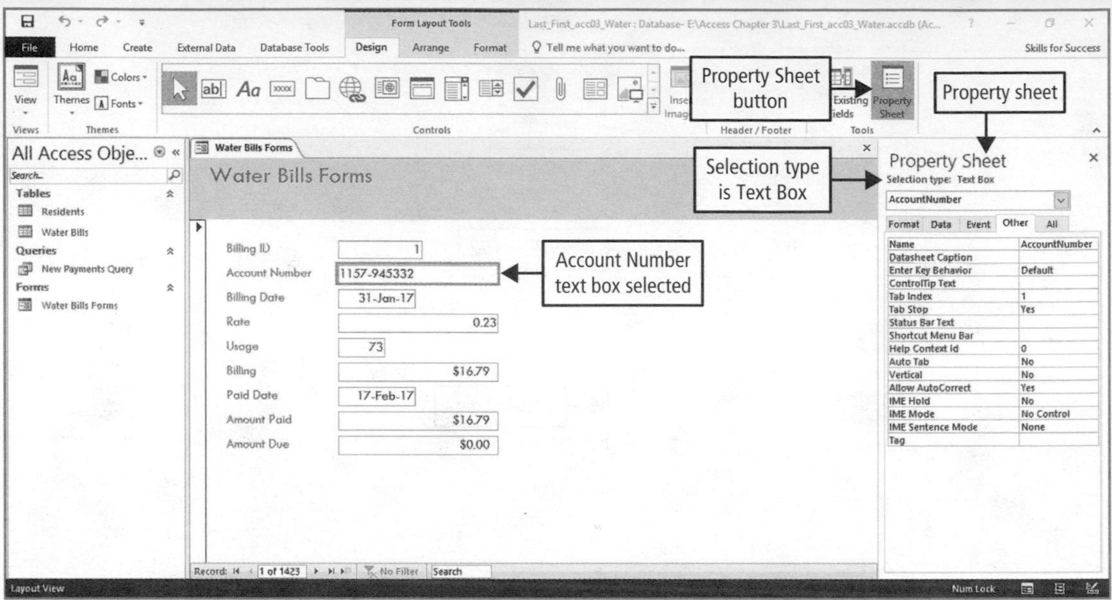

Figure 1

Access 2016, Windows 10, Microsoft Corporation

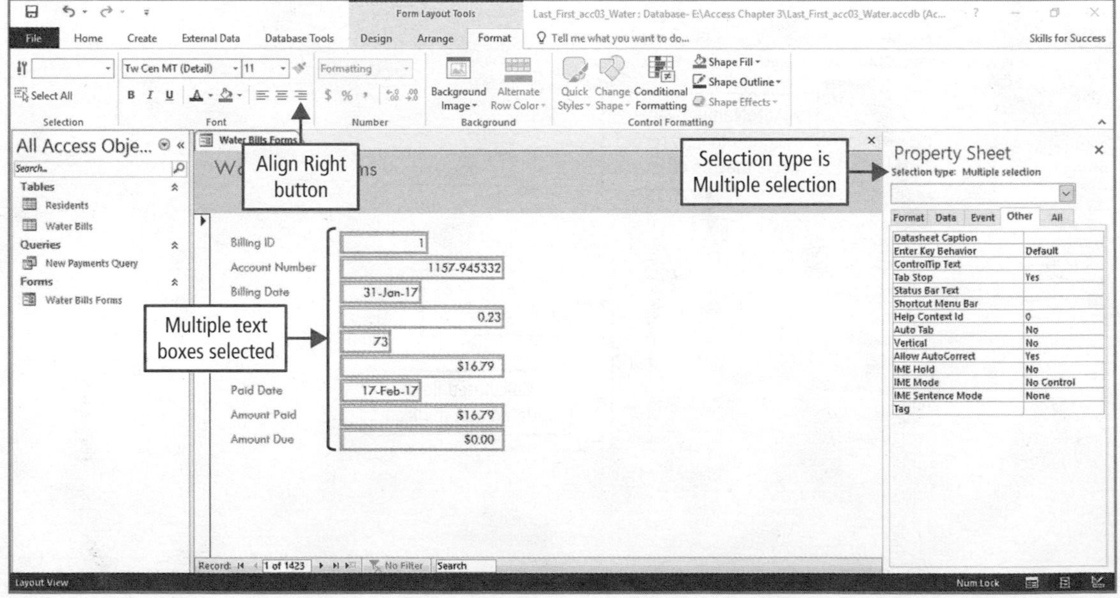

Figure 2

Access 2016, Windows 10, Microsoft Corporation

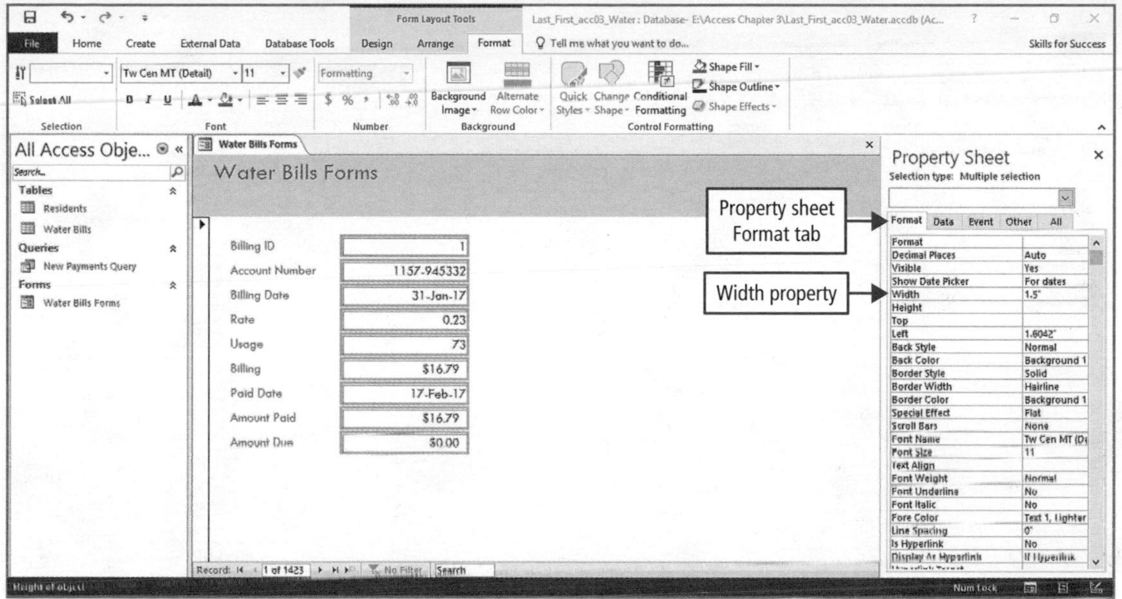

Access 2016, Windows 10, Microsoft Corporation

Figure 3

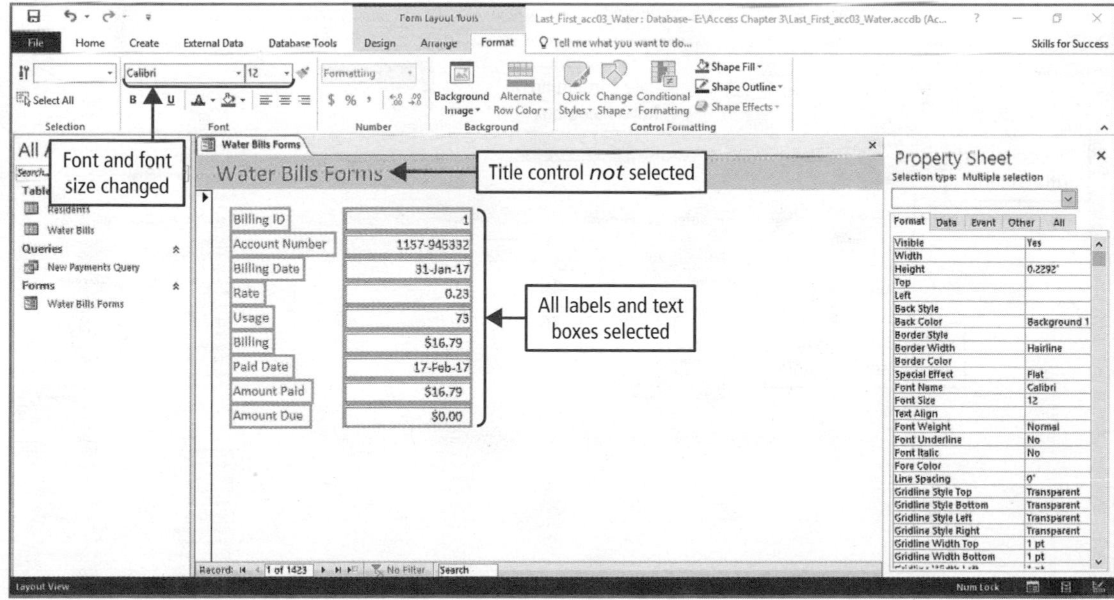

Access 2016, Windows 10, Microsoft Corporation

Figure 4

6. On the Property Sheet **Format tab**, click in the **Width** box, type 1.5" and then press Enter to simultaneously set the width of all nine text boxes. Compare your screen with **Figure 3.**

   In this manner, you can select multiple controls and then format them at the same time.

7. On the **Format tab**, in the **Selection group**, click **Select All** to select all the form controls. In the **Font group**, click the **Font arrow**. Scroll down the list of fonts, and then click **Calibri**.

8. With all the controls still selected, press and hold Ctrl while clicking the **Title** control with the text *Water Bills Form* to remove it from the current selection, and then release the Ctrl key.

9. On the **Format tab**, in the **Font group**, click the **Font size arrow** 11, and then click **12** to increase the font size by one point. Compare your screen with **Figure 4**.

10. Click **Save** to save the design changes, and then leave the form open for the next skill.

    When you make changes to the form's design, you need to save those changes. Here, the form's design was changed; however, none of the data was changed.

■ **You have completed Skill 3 of 10**

- Controls such as logos and titles can be added to forms to identify a company and the purpose of the form.
- You can format values so that when a condition is true, the value will be formatted differently than when the condition is false.

1. If it is not already open, open the Water Bills Form in Layout view.
2. In the form header, click the **Title** control with the text *Water Bills Form*. Be careful to select the control and not the text in the control—an orange border should surround the control as shown in **Figure 1**.
3. Press Delete to remove the Title control.

Obj 4.3.8

4. On the **Design tab**, in the **Header / Footer group**, click the **Logo** button. In the **Insert Picture** dialog box, navigate to the student data files for this project. Select **acc03_WaterLogo**, and then click **OK** to insert the control.
5. On the **Design tab**, in the **Header / Footer group**, click the **Title** button, and then type Monthly Billings
6. Click the **Amount Due** text box. Click the **Format tab**, and then in the **Control Formatting group**, click the **Conditional Formatting** button.
7. In the **Conditional Formatting Rules Manager** dialog box, click the **New Rule** button. In the **New Formatting Rule** dialog box, under **Format only cells where the**, click the second **arrow**. Compare your screen with **Figure 2**.

   The second box contains a drop-down list of ***comparison operators***—operators such as greater than and less than that compare two values.

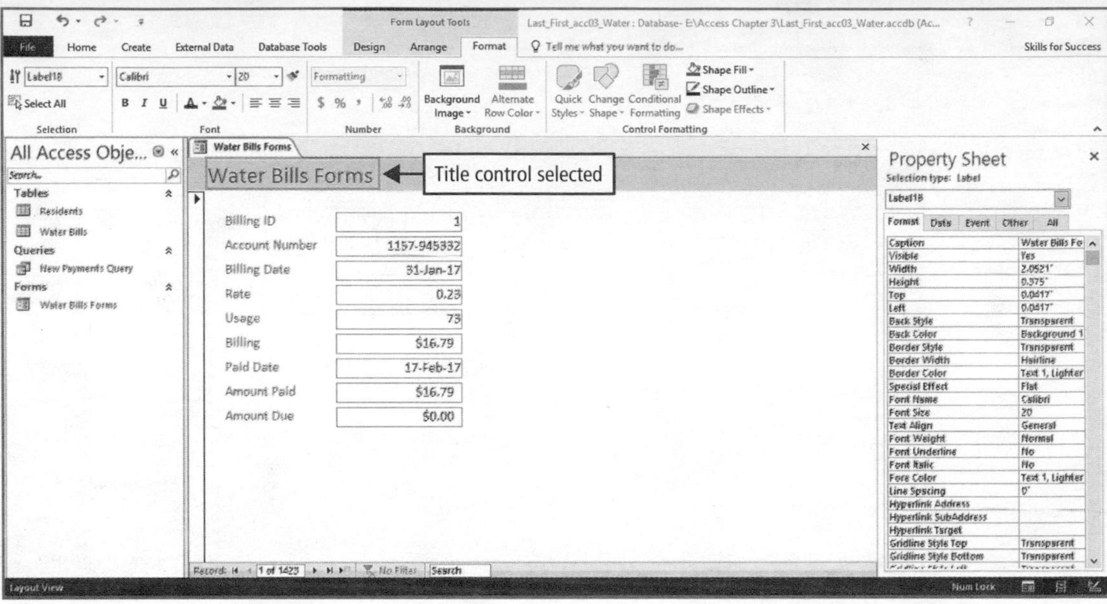

Figure 1

Access 2016, Windows 10, Microsoft Corporation

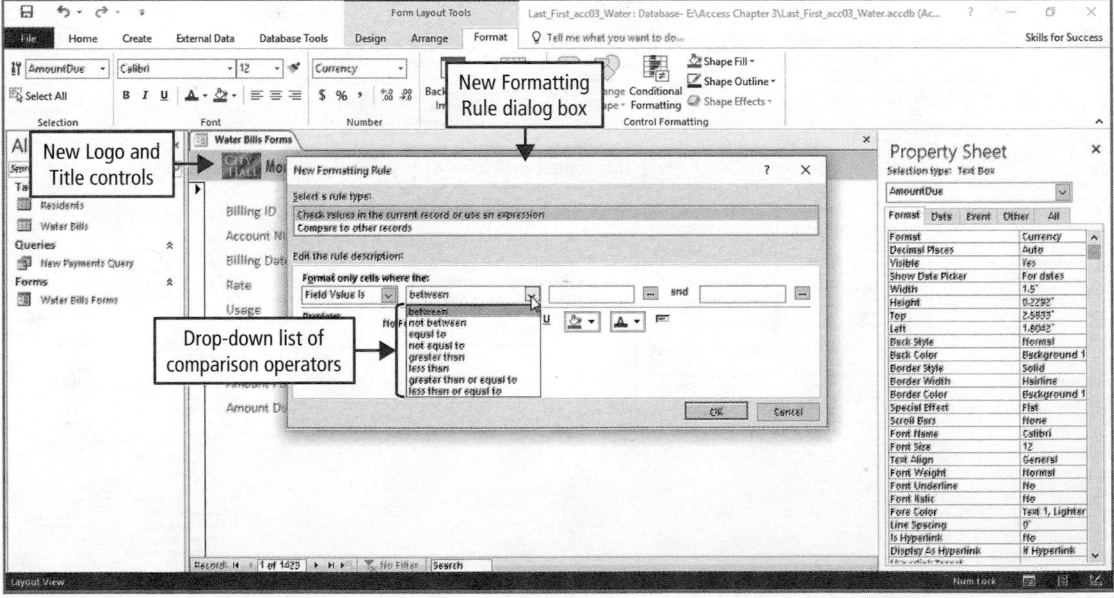

Figure 2

Access 2016, Windows 10, Microsoft Corporation

■ Continue to the next page to complete the skill

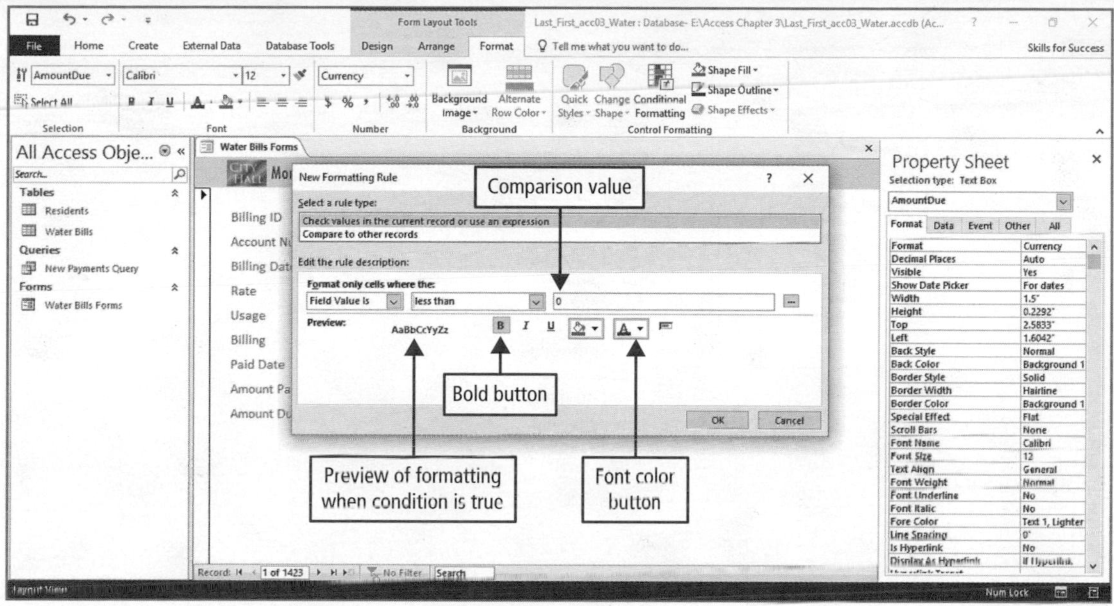

Access 2016, Windows 10, Microsoft Corporation

Figure 3

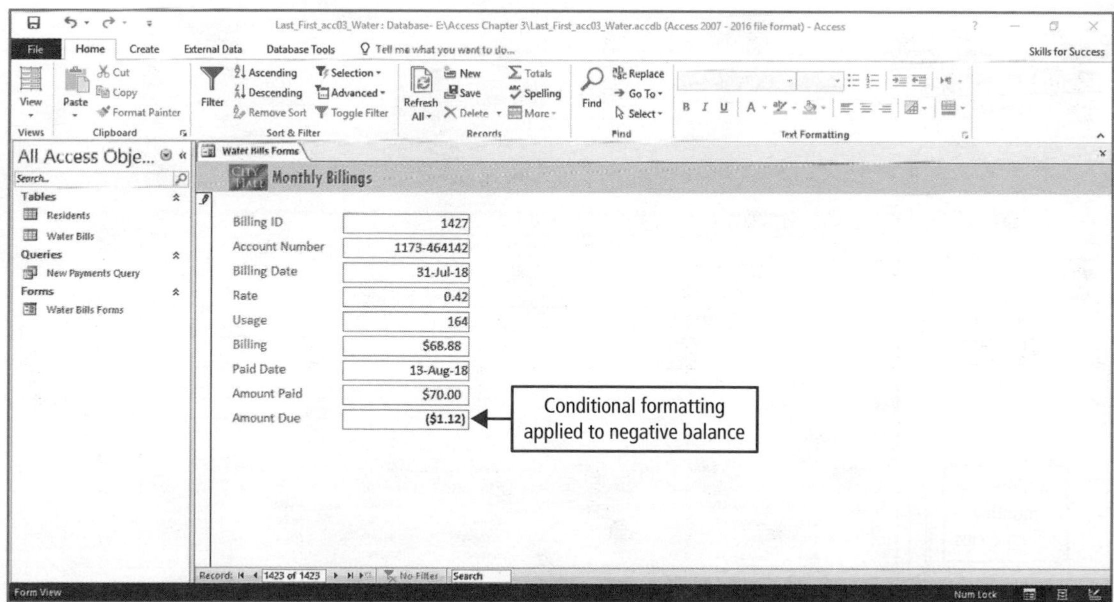

Access 2016, Windows 10, Microsoft Corporation

Figure 4

8. In the conditions list, click **less than**. Click in the third box, and then type 0
9. In the **New Formatting Rule** dialog box, click the **Font color arrow** [A ▾], and then click the second color in the last row—**Red**.
10. In the dialog box, click the **Bold** button [B], and then preview the conditional formatting, as shown in **Figure 3**.
11. Click **OK** two times to accept the changes, and **Close** the two dialog boxes. Click **Save** [Save icon], and then on the **Home tab**, click the **View** button to switch to Form view. Alternatively, on the status bar, click the Form View button [Form View icon].
12. On the Navigation bar, click the **Last record** button [▸|]. In the **Paid Date** field, type 13-Aug-18 Press Enter, and then in the **Amount Paid** box, type 70 Press Enter, click in the **Amount Due** box to deselect the text, and then compare your screen with **Figure 4**.
13. Press [Windows key], type snip and then press Enter to start the **Snipping Tool**. In the **Snipping Tool** window, click the **New arrow**, and then click **Full-screen Snip**.
14. Click the **Save Snip** button [Save Snip icon]. In the **Save As** dialog box, navigate to your **Access Chapter 3** folder, **Save** the snip as Last_First_acc03_WaterSnip1 and then **Close** [X] the Snipping Tool window.
15. **Save** [Save icon] the design changes, and then **Close** the form.

- **You have completed Skill 4 of 10**

SKILL 5: Use the Form Tool

► You can use the Form Tool to quickly create a form for any table or query that is selected in the Navigation Pane.

1. Click the **Database Tools tab**, and then click the **Relationships** button. Drag the **AccountNumber** field from the **Residents** table, point to the **AccountNumber** field in the **Water Bills** table, and then when the [icon] displays, release the left mouse button.

2. In the **Edit Relationships** dialog box, select the **Enforce Referential Integrity** check box. Compare your screen with **Figure 1**, and then click **Create**.

   The Residents and Water Bills tables need to have a one-to-many relationship so that each resident's account information can be linked to their monthly water bills.

Obj 4.2.7

3. **Close** [X] the Relationships tab.

4. In the **Navigation Pane**, select the **Residents** table. Click the **Create tab**, and then in the **Forms group**, click the **Form** button to create a one-to-many form. If necessary, **Close** [X] the property sheet. Compare your screen with **Figure 2**.

   When a one-to-many relationship exists, a main form and subform will be created when you use the Form Tool. In a ***one-to-many form***, the main form displays in Single Form view, and the related records display in a subform in Datasheet view. Here, a single resident displays in the main form, and that resident's monthly billings display in the subform.

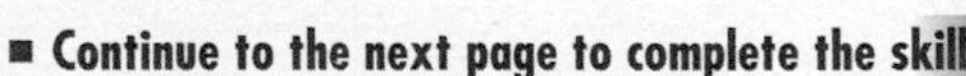

■ Continue to the next page to complete the skill

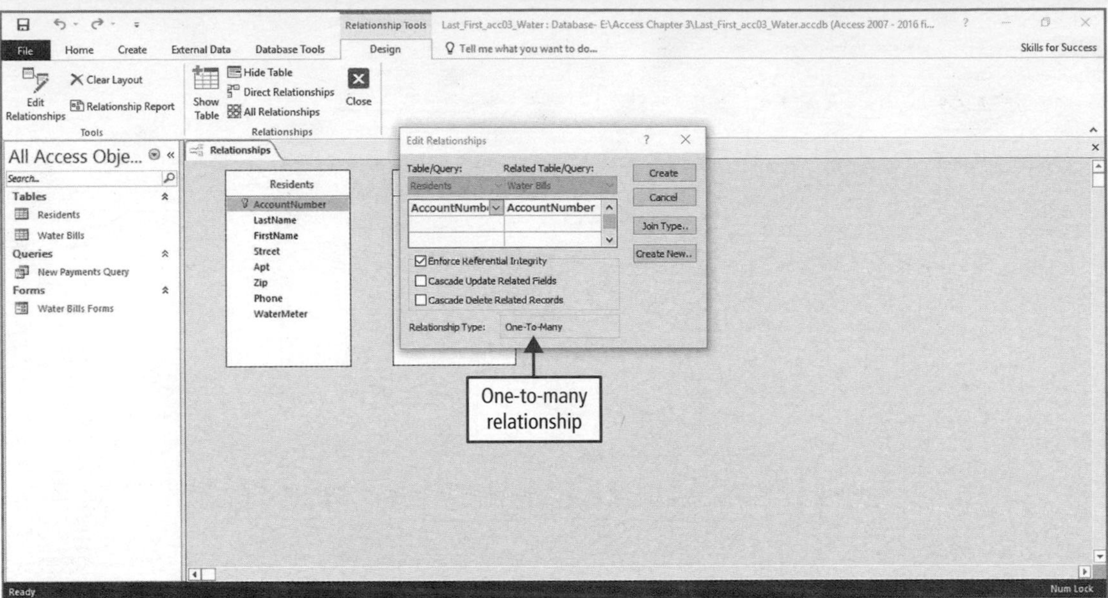

Figure 1 Access 2016, Windows 10, Microsoft Corporation

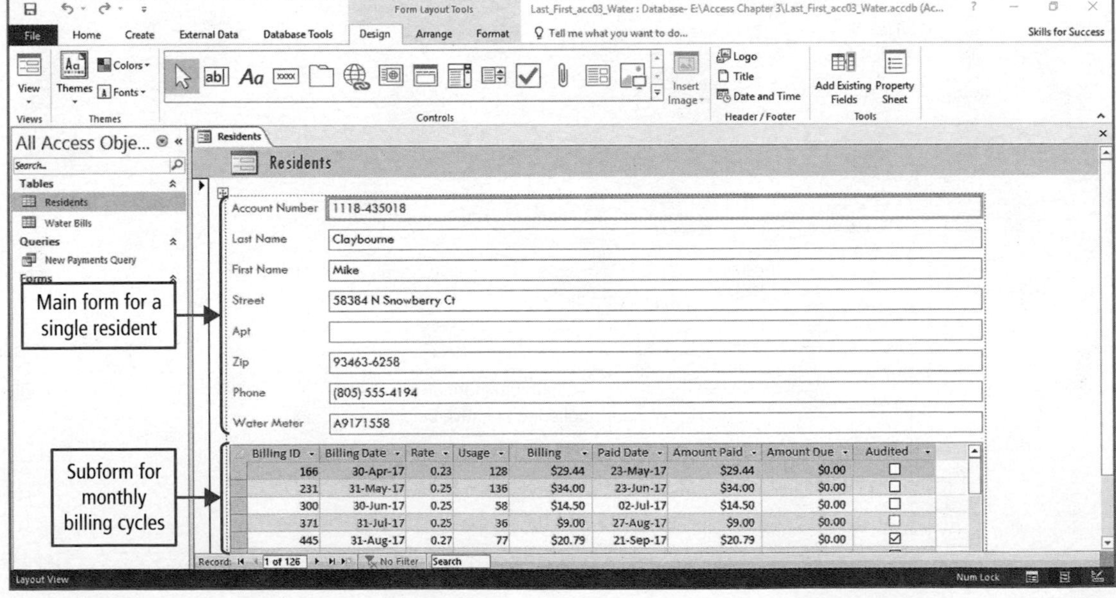

Figure 2 Access 2016, Windows 10, Microsoft Corporation

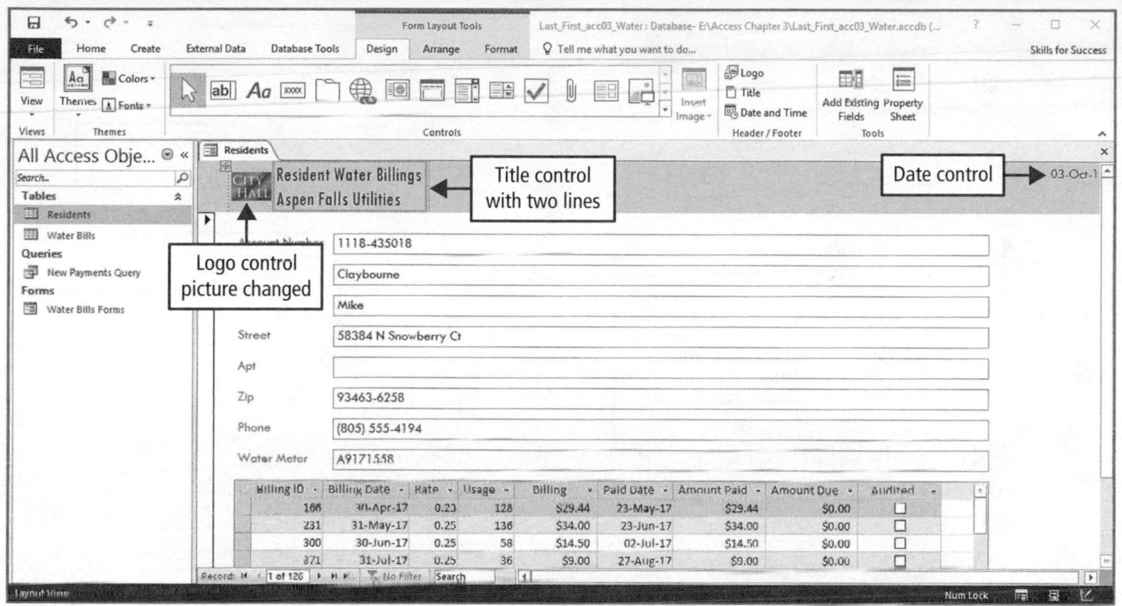

Access 2016, Windows 10, Microsoft Corporation

Figure 3

Access 2016, Windows 10, Microsoft Corporation

Figure 4

5. On the **Design tab**, in the **Header / Footer group**, click the **Logo** button, and then use the **Insert Picture** dialog box to insert **acc03_WaterLogo** as the form's logo.

6. In the **Header / Footer group**, click the **Date and Time** button. In the **Date and Time** dialog box, select the middle date—**dd-mmm-yy**—option button, clear the **Include Time** check box, and then click **OK**.

Obj 4.3.7

7. In the **Header / Footer group**, click the **Title** button to select the text in the form's **Title** control. Type Resident Water Billings and then press Ctrl + Enter to insert a new line in the control. Type Aspen Falls Utilities press Enter to finish editing the text, and then compare your screen with **Figure 3**.

   To change text in a control, you need to be in edit mode. ***Edit mode*** is a mode that selects the text inside a control, not the control itself. As you type in edit mode, the Title control adjusts its size to fit the new text.

8. With the **Title** control still selected, click the **Format tab**. In the **Font group**, click the **Font Color arrow**, and then click the last color in the first row—**Teal, Accent 6**.

9. In the header, click a blank area to the right of the form title to select the entire header. On the **Format tab**, in the **Font group**, click the **Background Color arrow**, and then click the last color in the second row—**Teal, Accent 6, Lighter 80%**. Compare your screen with **Figure 4**.

10. Click **Save**. In the **Save As** dialog box, type Residents Form and then press Enter. Leave the form open for the next skill.

■ **You have completed Skill 5 of 10**

► Forms created with the Form Tool use a ***tabular layout***—a layout in which the controls are positioned as table cells in rows and columns. You can insert, delete, and merge columns and then position controls within these tables as needed.

1. With **Residents Form** open in Layout view, click the **Account Number** text box to select the control.
2. Point to the selected control's right border to display the ⟺ pointer. Drag the right border to the left. When the column is aligned with the **Usage** column in the subform as shown in **Figure 1**, release the left mouse button to resize the entire column. (You will resize the subform later in this skill.)
3. With the **Account Number** text box still selected, click the **Arrange tab**. In the **Rows & Columns group**, click the **Insert Right** button two times to insert two new columns.

MOS Obj 4.2.6

4. Point to the label with the text *Water Meter*, and then with the ✥ pointer, drag and drop the label into the first cell in the first blank column.
5. Repeat the previous technique to move the **WaterMeter** text box—*A9171558*—into the blank cell to the right of the **Water Meter** label. Compare your screen with **Figure 2**.

MOS Obj 4.2.1

6. Move the **First Name** text box—*Mike*—into the blank cell to the right of the **Last Name** text box.
7. Double-click the **Last Name** label, change the label text to Last / First Name and then press Enter.

■ **Continue to the next page to complete the skill**

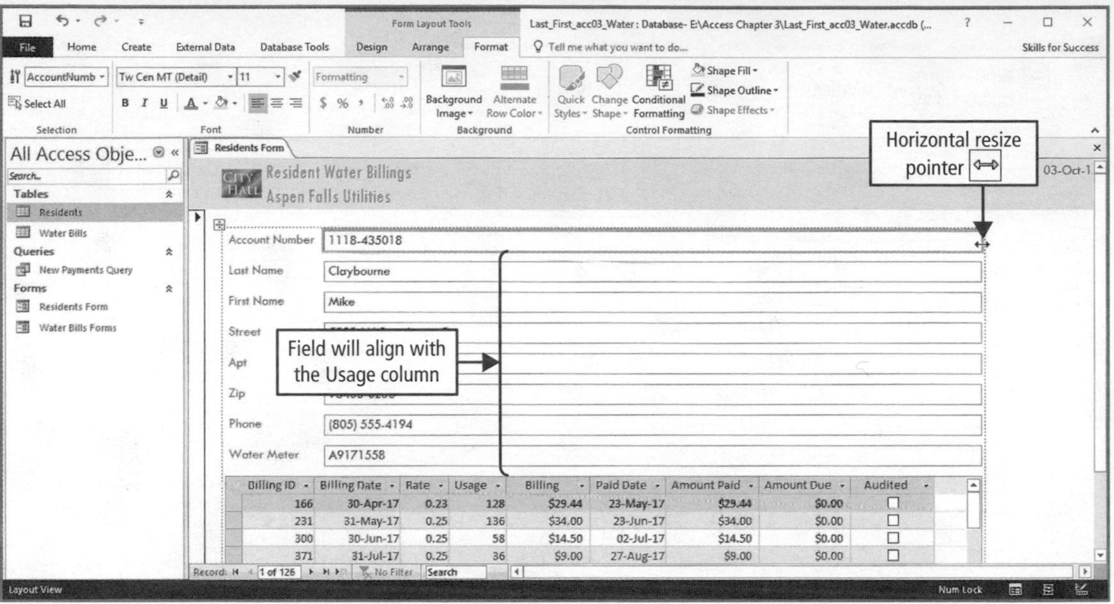

Figure 1

Access 2016, Windows 10, Microsoft Corporation

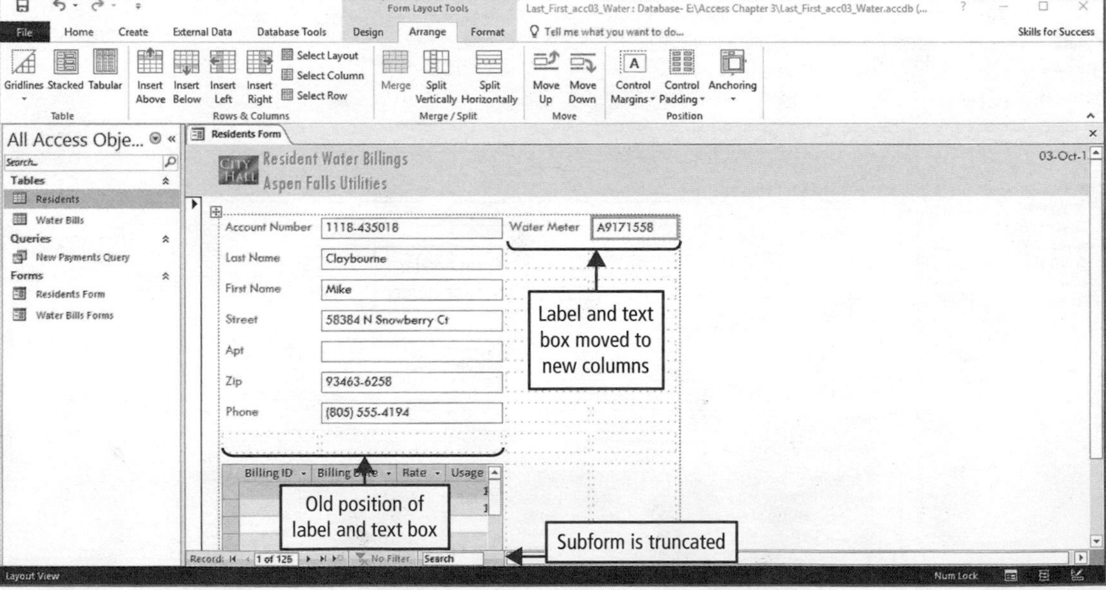

Figure 2

Access 2016, Windows 10, Microsoft Corporation

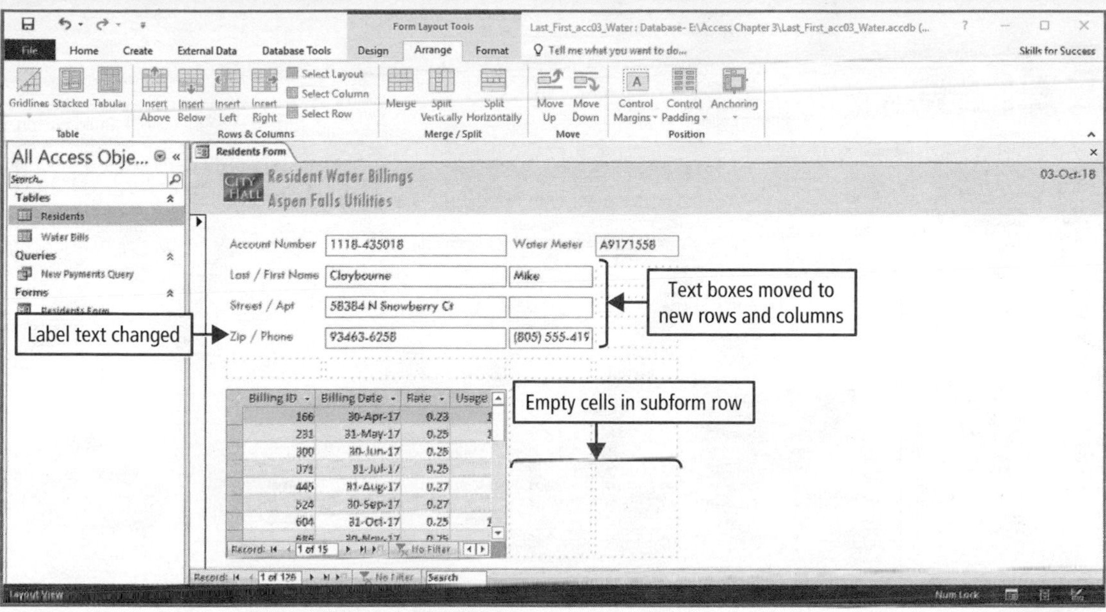

Access 2016, Windows 10, Microsoft Corporation

Figure 3

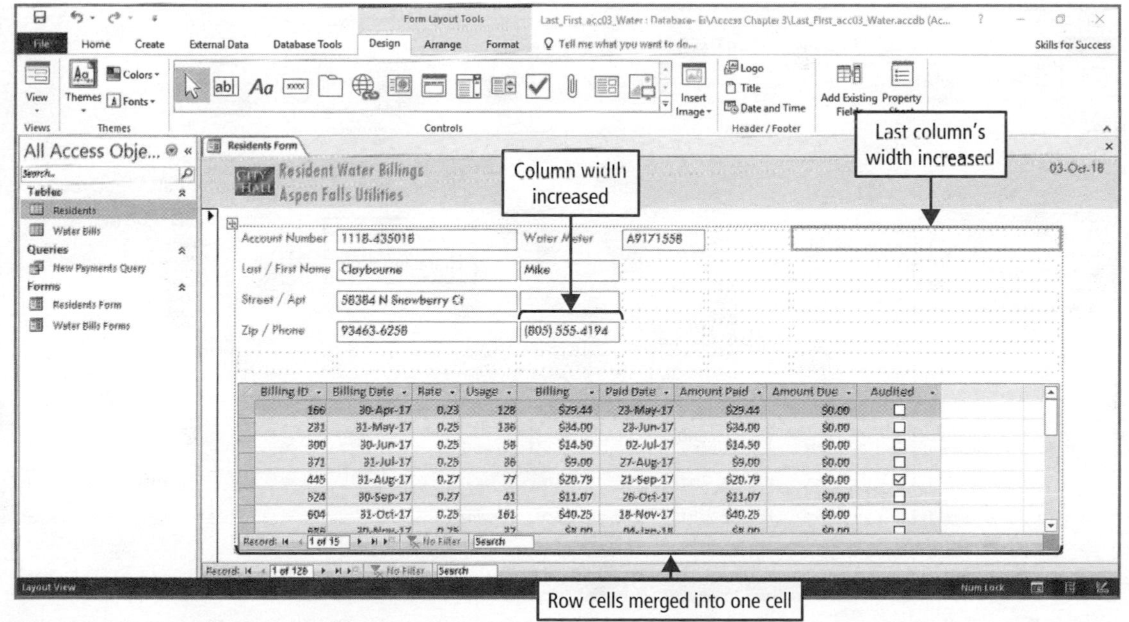

Access 2016, Windows 10, Microsoft Corporation

Figure 4

8. In the fifth row, click to select the **Apt** text box—it has a blank value. Drag to move the control into the empty cell to the right of the **Street** text box. In the first column of the same row, change the **Street** label text to Street / Apt
9. Move the **Phone** text box to the right of the **Zip** text box, and then change the **Zip** label text to Zip / Phone
10. In the third row, click the **First Name** label. On the **Arrange tab**, in the **Rows & Columns group**, click **Select Row**. With the row selected, press Delete to remove the unused row from the table. MOS Obj 4.2.4
11. Repeat the technique just practiced to delete the unused **Apt** and **Phone** rows. Compare your screen with **Figure 3**.
12. In the row with the subform, click in the last empty cell on the right, and then in the **Rows & Columns group**, click the **Insert Right** button two times to add two new columns. Click the **Select Row** button, and then with the five cells selected, in the **Merge / Split group**, click the **Merge** button.
13. In the main form, click the **PhoneNumber** text box to select it. On the **Design tab**, in the **Tools group**, click the **Property Sheet** button, and then change the **Width** value to 1.2"
14. Click in a blank cell in the last column, and then in the property sheet, change the **Width** value to 3.2" **Close** the property sheet, and then compare your screen with **Figure 4**.
15. Click **Save**, and leave the form open for the next skill.

■ **You have completed Skill 6 of 10**

► An ***input mask*** is a set of special characters that control what can and cannot be entered in a field.

1. With **Residents Form** open in Layout view, click the **Phone** text box. On the **Design tab**, in the **Tools group**, click the **Property Sheet** button.
2. On the property sheet **Data tab**, click **Input Mask**, and then click the **Build** button [...] that displays in the box. Compare your screen with **Figure 1**.

3. With **Phone Number** selected in the **Input Mask Wizard** dialog box, click **Next**. Click the **Placeholder character arrow**, and then click the number sign (#). Click in the **Try It** box, and then compare your screen with **Figure 2**.

   The Try It box displays a sample of the input mask in which you can try entering sample data. ***Placeholder characters*** are the symbols in an input mask that are replaced as you type data into the field. Here, the parentheses, space, and hyphen are in place, and number signs display where each number can be typed.

4. In the **Try It** box, click the first number sign, and then watch the box as you type ten digits—any digit can be typed in this preview.

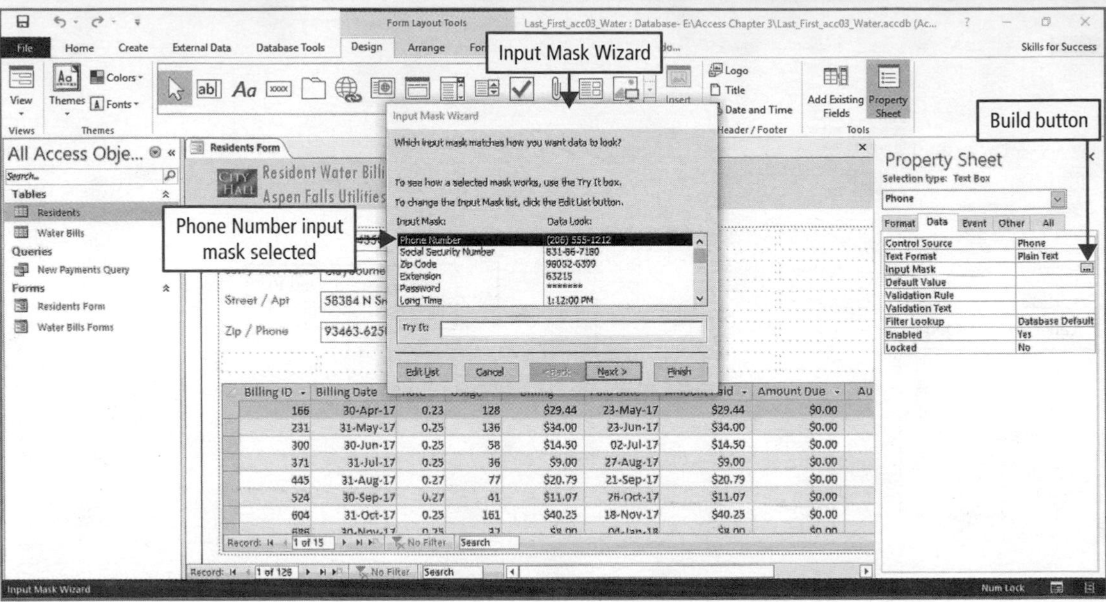

Figure 1

Access 2016, Windows 10, Microsoft Corporation

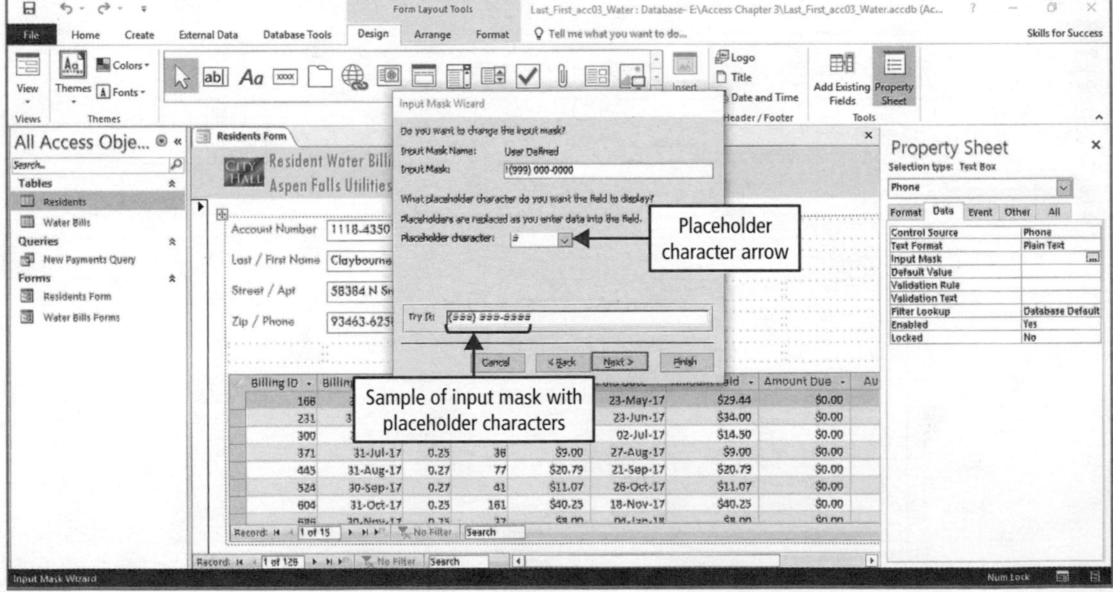

Figure 2

Access 2016, Windows 10, Microsoft Corporation

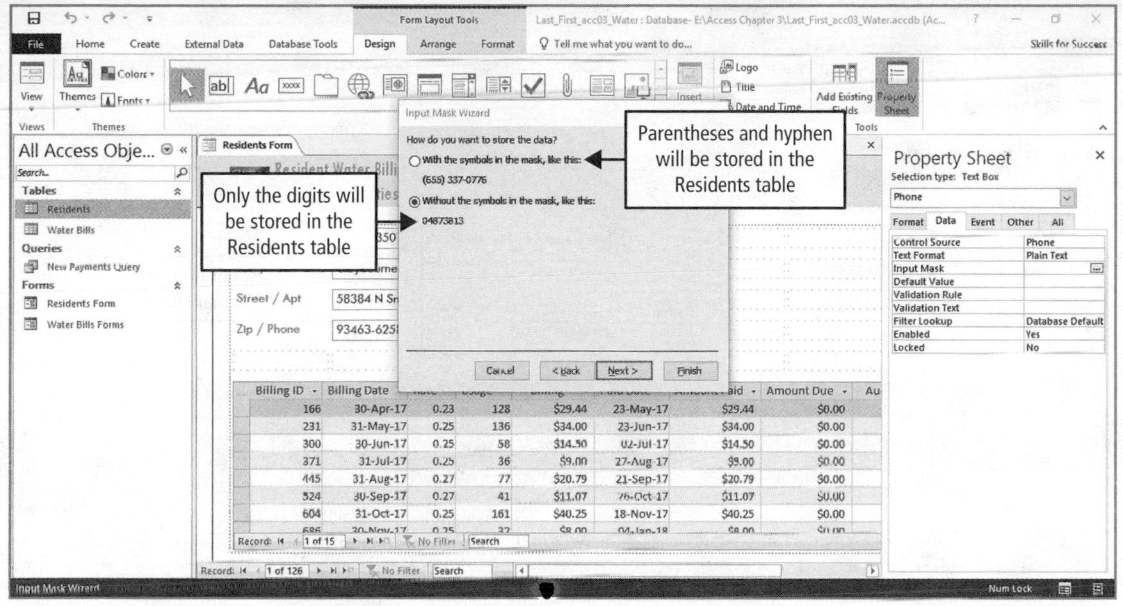

Access 2016, Windows 10, Microsoft Corporation

Figure 3

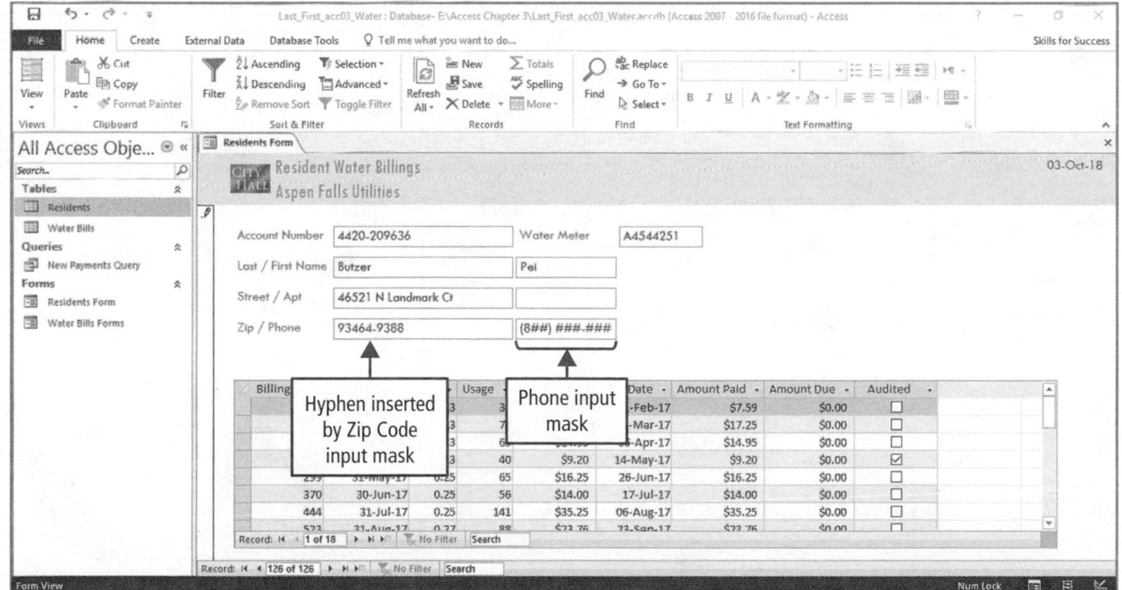

Access 2016, Windows 10, Microsoft Corporation

Figure 4

5. Click **Next**, and then compare your screen with **Figure 3**.

   The Phone Number input mask has one option that stores the number, parentheses, space, and hyphen in the table; the other option stores only the digits in the phone number.

6. Select the **With the symbols in the mask** option button, click **Next**, and then click **Finish**.

   In the property sheet Input Mask box, special characters have been inserted. These characters are needed for the input mask to perform correctly.

7. Select the **Zip** text box, and then use the property sheet to start the Input Mask Wizard. In the **Input Mask Wizard**, click **Zip Code**, and then accept the wizard defaults by clicking **Finish**.
8. **Close** [X] the property sheet, and then **Save** [Save] the form.
9. Click the **View** button to switch to Form view. In the main form's Navigation bar—the lower Navigation bar—click the **Last record** [▶|] button. Click in the left side of the **Zip** box, and then watch as you type 934649388
10. Press [Enter] to move to the **Phone** box, type 8 and then compare your screen with **Figure 4**.
11. Watch the **Phone** field as you type the rest of the phone number: 045556894

    The input mask converts the digits to *(804) 555-6894* and stores that value in the table.

12. Leave the form open for the next skill.

■ **You have completed Skill 7 of 10**

SKILL 8: Change Data in One-to-Many Forms

SKILL 3.8

► In a one-to-many form, you can work with the data from two tables on a single screen.

1. If necessary, open **Residents Form** in Form view.
2. Using the technique practiced in a previous skill, use the **Find and Replace** dialog box to navigate to the record for **Account Number** 4367-618513 and then **Close** the dialog box.
3. In the subform datasheet for Lizzette Middents, click in the third record's **Paid Date** cell, and then type 13-Aug-18
4. Press Enter, and then in the **Amount Paid** cell, type 7.98 Press Enter, and then compare your screen with **Figure 1**.

   A payment from Lizzette Middents has just been recorded in the Water Bills table.

5. In the main form's Navigation bar, click the **Next Record** button. In the subform Navigation bar for Pei Butzer, click the **New (blank) record** button to scroll to the bottom of the datasheet and create a new record.
6. Press Enter, and then in the **Billing Date** cell, type 31-Jul-18 Press Enter, and type 0.38 as the **Rate**. Press Enter, and then type 83 as the **Usage**. Press Enter to update the **Billing** and **Amount Due** columns, and leave the rest of the row blank. Compare your screen with **Figure 2**.

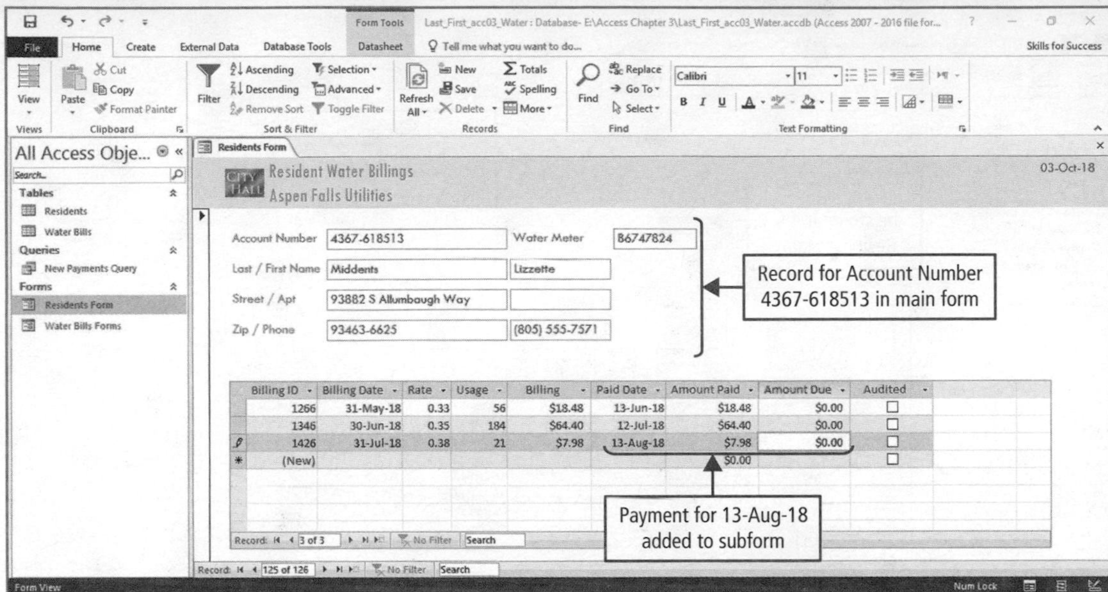

Figure 1

Access 2016, Windows 10, Microsoft Corporation

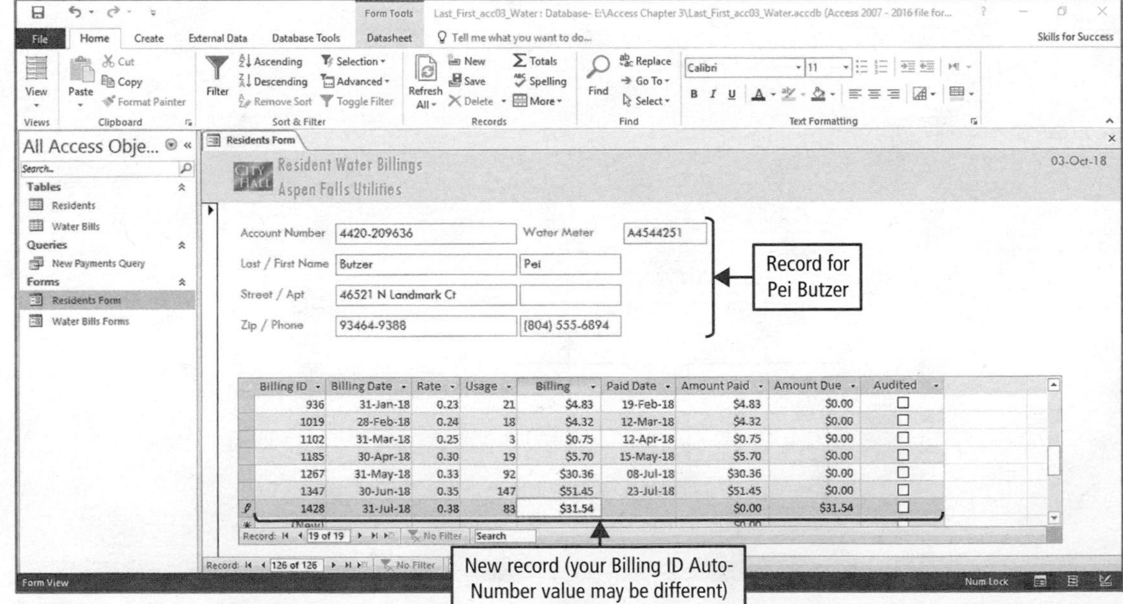

Figure 2

Access 2016, Windows 10, Microsoft Corporation

■ **Continue to the next page to complete the skill**

Account Number	4421-879567	Water Meter	C4847198
Last Name	Bransom	First Name	Alfred
Street	12133 S Azure Ln	Apt	A110
Zip	93464-5635	Phone	(805) 555-2685

Figure 3

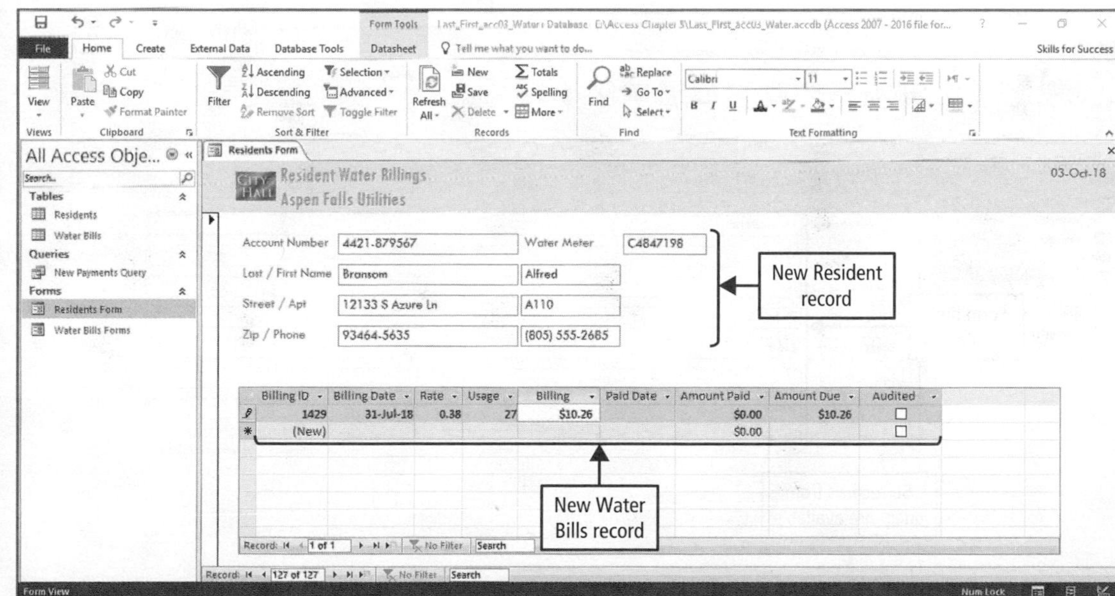

Access 2016, Windows 10, Microsoft Corporation

Figure 4

7. In the main form's Navigation bar, click the **New (blank) record** button to create a new Resident record.
8. In the main form, enter the data shown in **Figure 3**, pressing Enter to move to each text box.
9. In the subform for **Alfred Bransom**, click in the first row **Billing Date** cell. Type 31-Jul-18 and then press Enter. In the **Rate** cell, enter 0.38 and then in the **Usage** cell, enter 27 Press Enter, and then compare your screen with **Figure 4**.

   In this manner, a one-to-many form can add records to two tables. Here, a new resident was added to the Residents table, and then the first billing for that resident was added to the Water Bills table.

10. Repeat the skills practiced in a previous skill to start the **Snipping Tool** and create a **Full-screen Snip**. **Save** the snip in your chapter folder with the name Last_First_acc03_WaterSnip2 and then **Close** the Snipping Tool window.
11. **Close** the form.

■ **You have completed Skill 8 of 10**

- When you need to edit data for a specific subset of data, you can base the form on a query.
- A form based on a query displays only the records returned by the query's criteria.

1. In the **Navigation Pane**, under **Queries**, right-click **New Payments Query**, and then from the shortcut menu, click **Design View**. If the property sheet displays, **Close** [X] it.
2. In the **AmountDue** column **Criteria** cell, type >0 and then compare your screen with **Figure 1**.

   In the New Payments Query, fields from two related tables are selected. The criteria will filter only those records for which an amount is due.

3. Click **Save** [Save]. On the **Design tab**, in the **Results group**, click **Run** to display 50 records. **Close** [X] the query.
4. Under **Queries**, verify that **New Payments Query** is selected. Click the **Create tab**, and then in the **Forms group**, click the **Form** button. Compare your screen with **Figure 2**.

   The form displays all the fields from the select query. In this manner, you can build forms with fields from related tables in Single Form view or filter data by adding criteria to the query.

■ Continue to the next page to complete the skill

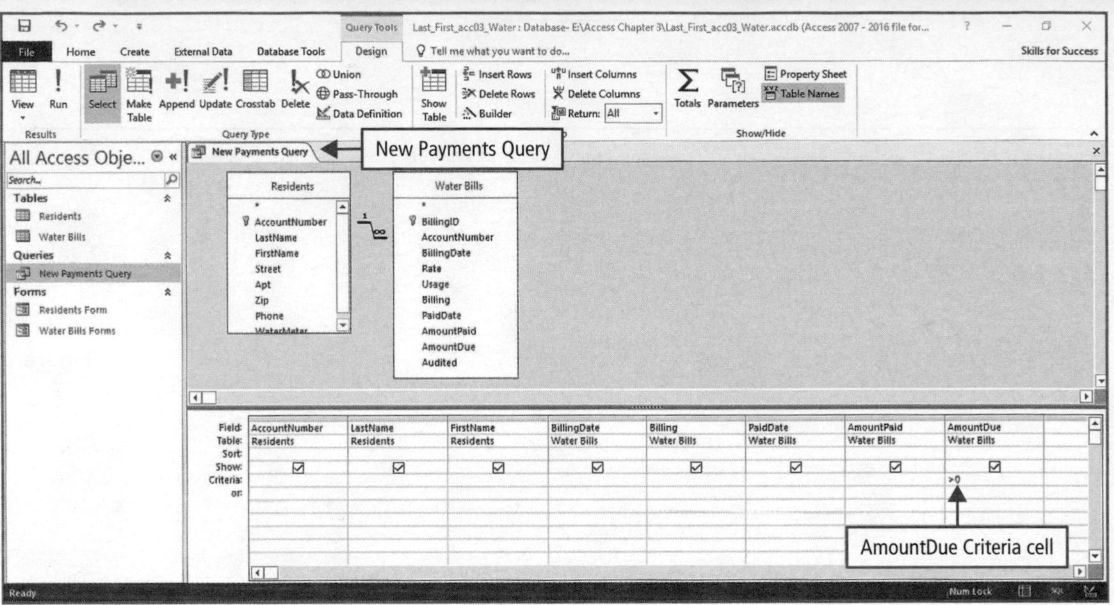

Figure 1 Access 2016, Windows 10, Microsoft Corporation

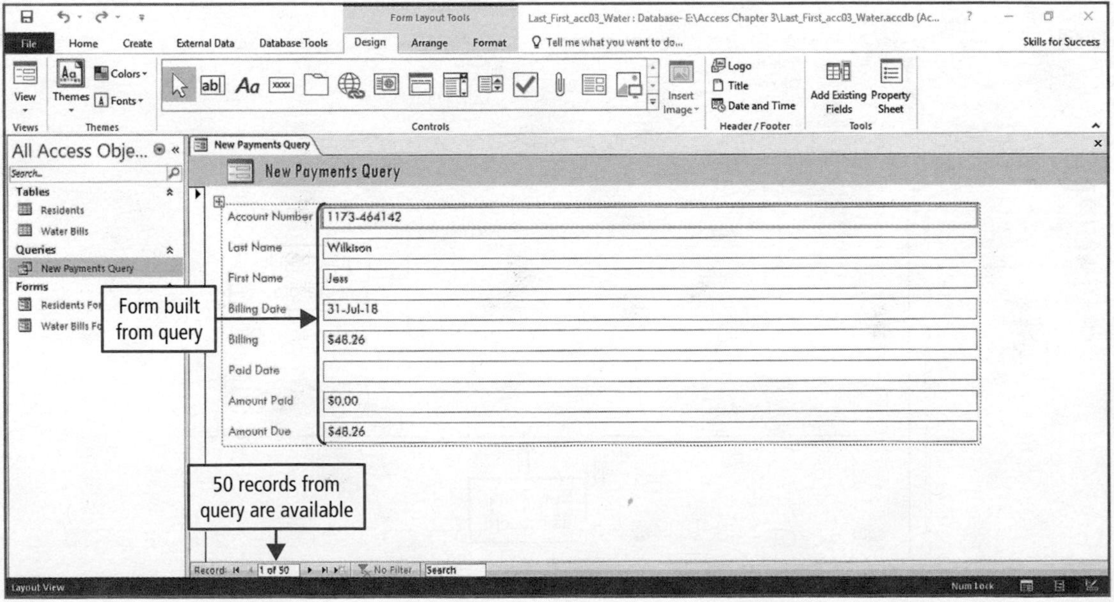

Figure 2 Access 2016, Windows 10, Microsoft Corporation

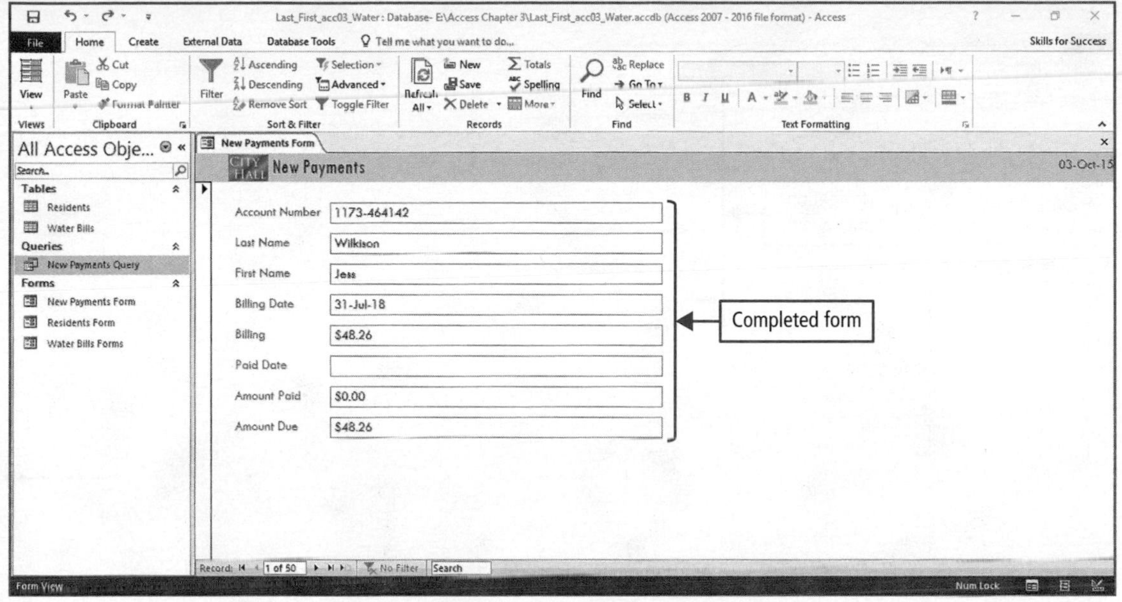

Access 2016, Windows 10, Microsoft Corporation

Figure 3

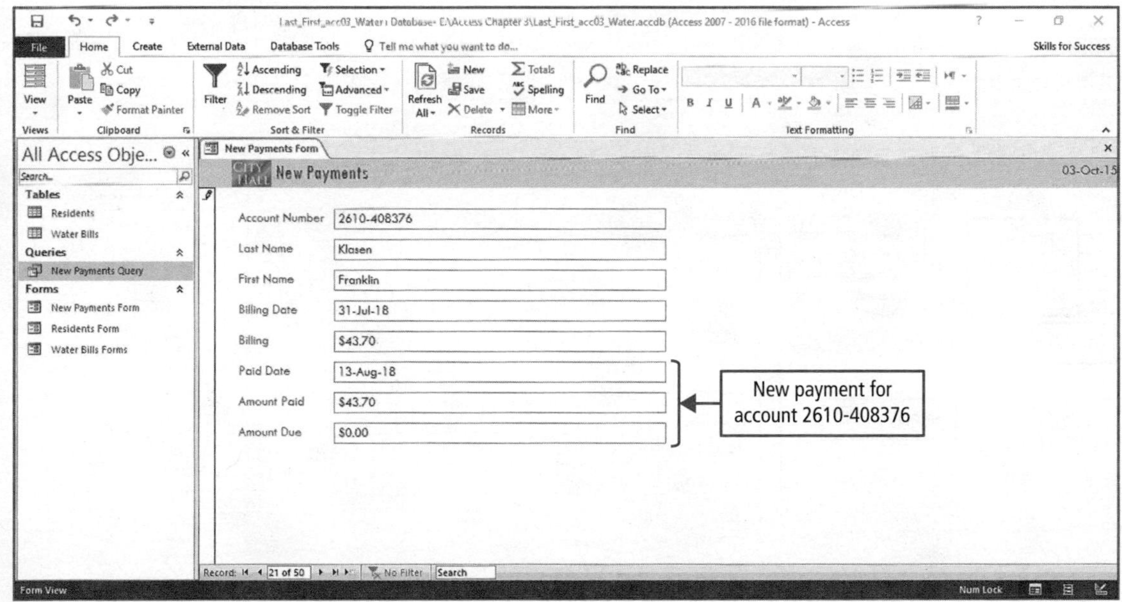

Access 2016, Windows 10, Microsoft Corporation

Figure 4

5. On the **Design tab**, in the **Tools group**, click the **Property Sheet** button to open the sheet. Verify that the first text box is selected, and then on the property sheet **Format tab**, change the **Width** value to 4" **Close** [X] the property sheet.
6. Repeat the technique practiced previously to insert the **acc03_WaterLogo** file as the form's logo, and then change the **Title** control's text to New Payments
7. Insert a **Date and Time** control with the middle date—**dd-mmm-yy**—option button selected and the **Include Time** check box cleared.
8. Click **Save** [Save]. In the **Save As** box, type New Payments Form and then press Enter.
9. Click the **View** button to switch to Form view, and then compare your screen with **Figure 3**.
10. **Find** the record for **Account Number** 2610-408376 In the **Paid Date** text box, enter 13-Aug-18 and then press Enter. In the **Amount Paid** field, enter 43.70 Press Enter, and then compare your screen with **Figure 4**.
11. Create a **Full-screen Snip**, **Save** the snip in your chapter folder as Last_First_acc03_WaterSnip3 and then **Close** [X] the Snipping Tool window.
12. **Close** [X] the form.

■ **You have completed Skill 9 of 10**

► ***Navigation forms*** are forms that contain a Navigation Control with tabs that you can use to quickly open forms and reports.

1. On the **Create tab**, in the **Forms group**, click the **Navigation** button, and then compare your screen with **Figure 1**.

   The gallery provides a visual summary of the several layouts available in a Navigation form.

2. In the **Navigation Form** gallery, click **Vertical Tabs, Left** to create the form.
3. Near the top left corner of the new form, click to select the **[AddNew]** button, and then click the **Format tab**. In the **Control Formatting group**, click the **Quick Styles** button, and then click the last style in the last row—**Intense Effect – Teal, Accent 6**.
4. With the button still selected, in the **Control Formatting group**, click the **Change Shape** button, and then click the third shape—**Rounded Rectangle**.
5. Drag **Residents Form** from the **Navigation Pane** to the **[Add New]** button in the Navigation form, and then release the left mouse button. Repeat this technique to add **Water Bills Form** and then **New Payments Form** to the Navigation form. Compare your screen with **Figure 2**. If the Field List list displays, **Close** [X] it.
6. Click the **Design tab**, and then click the **Property Sheet** button. In the property sheet, below **Selection type**, click the **arrow**, and then click **Form** to display the form's properties.

■ Continue to the next page to complete the skill

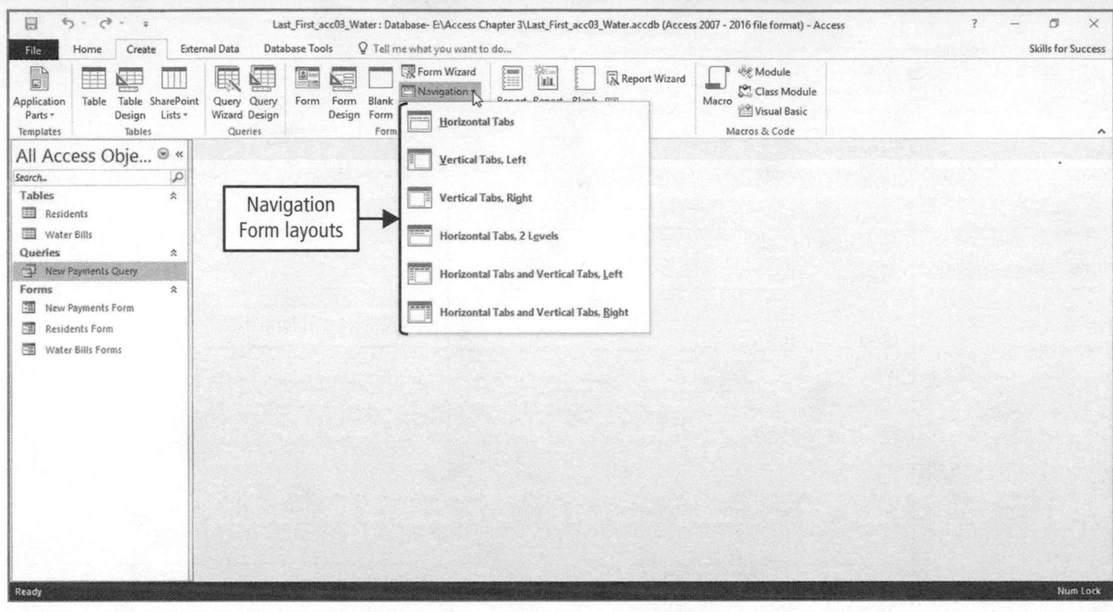

Figure 1 Access 2016, Windows 10, Microsoft Corporation

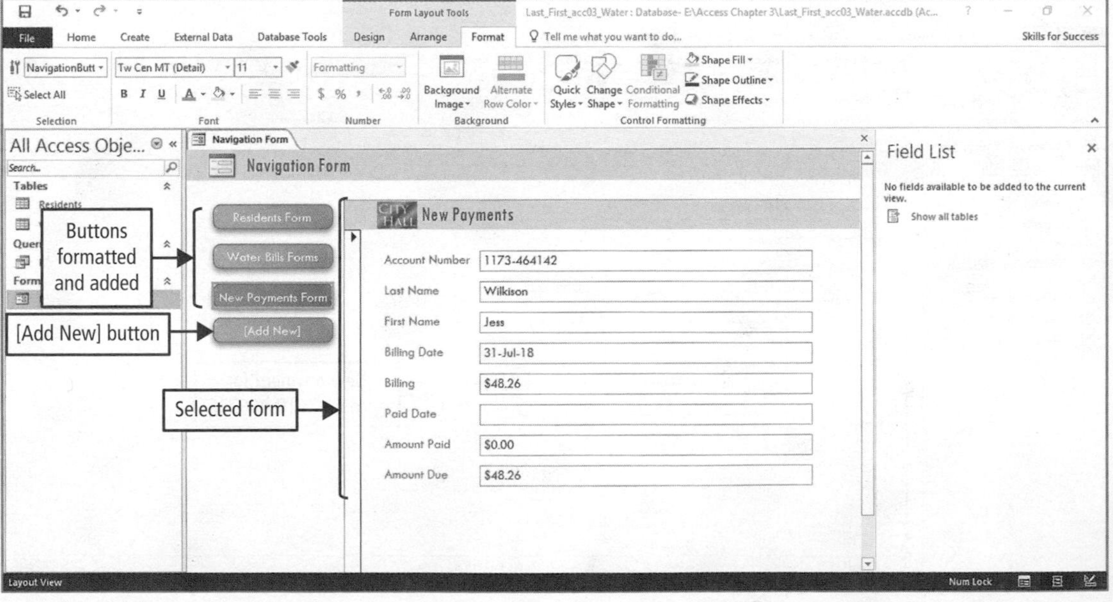

Figure 2 Access 2016, Windows 10, Microsoft Corporation

Selection type set to Form

Other tab

Modal property set to Yes

Access 2016, Windows 10, Microsoft Corporation

Figure 3

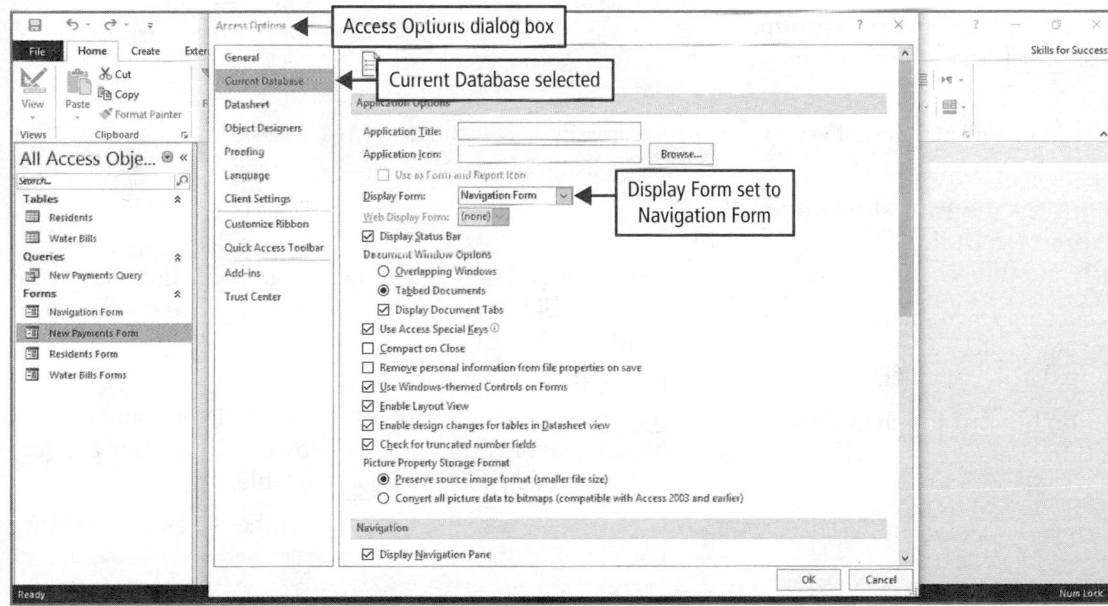

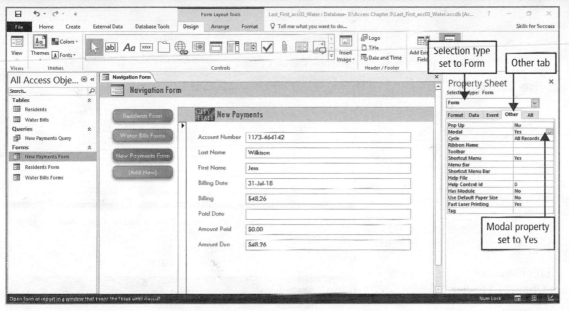

Access 2016, Windows 10, Microsoft Corporation

Figure 4

7. On the property sheet, click the **Other tab**, and then click **Modal**. Click the **Modal arrow**, and then click **Yes**. Compare your screen with **Figure 3**.

   When a form's ***Modal*** property is set to Yes, the Navigation Pane will collapse when the form is opened. When the form is closed, the Navigation Pane will display.

8. Click **Save** [Save icon], and then click **OK** to accept the default name for the form. **Close** [X] the property sheet, and then **Close** [X] the form.

9. Click the **File tab**, and then click **Options**. On the left side of the **Access Options** dialog box, click **Current Database**. Click the **Display Form arrow** to display a list of all the database forms, and then click **Navigation Form**. Compare your screen with **Figure 4**. MOS Obj 1.3.3

   In the Application Options dialog box, you can pick one form that opens automatically when the database is opened.

10. Click **OK**, read the message that displays, and then click **OK**.

11. **Close** [X] and then reopen the database to verify that Navigation Form opens as a modal form. MOS Obj 1.3.2

12. Create a **Full-screen Snip**, **Save** the snip in your chapter folder as Last_First_acc03_WaterSnip4 and then **Close** [X] the Snipping Tool window.

13. **Close** [X] the form to display the Navigation Pane, and then **Close** [X] Access.

14. If you are printing this project, open the snips and then print them. Otherwise, submit the files as directed by your instructor.

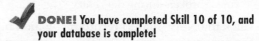

DONE! You have completed Skill 10 of 10, and your database is complete!

More Skills 11

Validate Fields

To complete this project, you will need the following file:

- acc03_MS11Employees

You will save your file as:

- Last_First_acc03_MS11Employees

▶ A ***validation rule*** is a field property that requires that specific values be entered into a field.

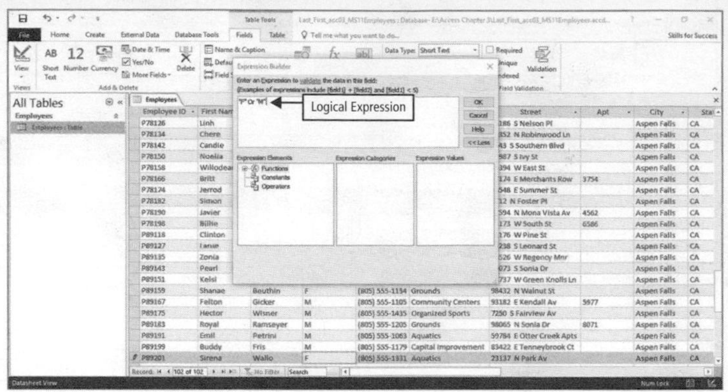

Figure 1 Access 2016, Windows 10, Microsoft Corporation

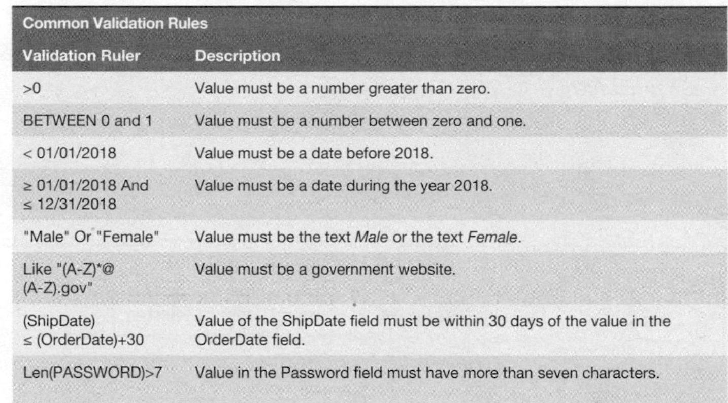

Common Validation Rules	
Validation Ruler	**Description**
>0	Value must be a number greater than zero.
BETWEEN 0 and 1	Value must be a number between zero and one.
< 01/01/2018	Value must be a date before 2018.
≥ 01/01/2018 And ≤ 12/31/2018	Value must be a date during the year 2018.
"Male" Or "Female"	Value must be the text *Male* or the text *Female*.
Like "(A-Z)*@(A-Z).gov"	Value must be a government website.
(ShipDate) ≤ (OrderDate)+30	Value of the ShipDate field must be within 30 days of the value in the OrderDate field.
Len(PASSWORD)>7	Value in the Password field must have more than seven characters.

Figure 2

1. Start **Access 2016**, and then open the student data file **acc03_MS11Employees**. **Save** the file in your **Access Chapter 3** folder as Last_First_acc03_MS11Employees
2. Open the **Employees** table in Datasheet view. In the Navigation bar, click the **Last record** navigation button [▸|].
3. In the record for Buddy Fris, change **Gender** to M and then, in the record for Sirena Wallo, change **Gender** to F
4. With a **Gender** field still active, click the **Fields tab**. In the **Properties group**, click in the **Field Size** box, type 1 and then press [Enter]. Read the message that displays, and then click **Yes**.

   This field size setting limits values to a single letter, but it will not prevent wrong letters from being entered into the field.

MOS Obj 2.4.2

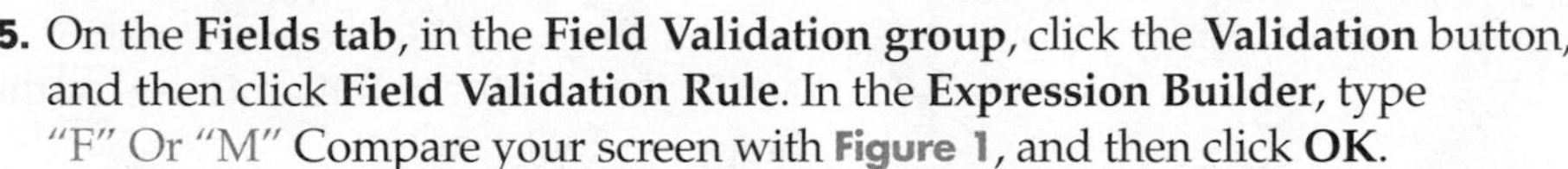

5. On the **Fields tab**, in the **Field Validation group**, click the **Validation** button, and then click **Field Validation Rule**. In the **Expression Builder**, type "F" Or "M" Compare your screen with **Figure 1**, and then click **OK**.

   Validation rules must be written precisely. Here, quotation marks indicate that the value can be the letter F or the letter M. No other values will be allowed during data entry. Common validation rules are summarized in the table in **Figure 2**.

6. In the **Field Validation group**, click the **Validation** button, and then click **Field Validation Message**. In the **Enter Validation Message** box, type Please enter an F or an M. Click **OK**, and then click **Save** [🖫].

   A validation message is the text that displays in a message box when a validation rule is broken during data entry.

7. Click the **New (blank) record** navigation button [▸*]. In the first column of the append row, type P90021 and then press [Enter]. In the next two fields, type your first and last name. Press [Enter], and then in the **Gender** field, type the letter q Press [Enter] to display the validation message.
8. In the displayed Access message, click **OK**. Press [Backspace], and then attempt to type male or female Notice that only one letter is allowed. Enter your gender as F or M and then **Close** [X] the table.
9. **Close** [X] Access, and then submit the file as directed by your instructor.

■ **You have completed More Skills 11**

More Skills 12

Create Databases from Templates

To complete this project, you will need the following file:

- **Blank desktop database**

You will save your file as:

- **Last_First_acc03_MS12Tasks**

- ▶ When you create a database, you can select a database from several prebuilt templates.
- ▶ Most database templates can provide all the tables, queries, forms, reports, and macros you need to begin entering data immediately after creating the database.

---

1. Start **Access 2016**. On the Access start screen, locate and then click the **Desktop task management** thumbnail. If necessary, type Desktop task management in the Search for online templates text box to locate the file. MOS Obj 1.1.2

2. In the **Desktop task management** preview, read the description, and then in the **File Name** box, replace the text with Last_First_acc03_MS12Tasks

3. Click the **Browse** button, and then in the **File New Database** dialog box, navigate to your **Access Chapter 3** folder. Click **OK**. Click the **Create** button to download and open the database file. If necessary, **Close** the **Getting Started with Tasks** dialog box.

4. Take a few moments to familiarize yourself with the database shown in **Figure 1**.

5. If necessary, in the security message, click **Enable Content** to display the Getting Started window.

6. **Close** [×] the Getting Started with Tasks dialog box.

7. **Close** [«] the Navigation Pane. In the **Task List** buttons row, click **New Task** to open the Task Details form.

8. In the **Task Details** form, in the **Task Title** box, type Interview college interns

9. In the **Assigned To** box, type Cathy Story Press [Enter], read the message that displays, and then click **Yes**.

   The Task Details form's List Items Edit Form property is set to Contact Details so that if you assign a task to a contact who is not in the Contacts table, the Contact Details form will automatically open. You can use this form to add that contact's information into the Contacts table.

10. In the **Contact Details** form, enter the following data:

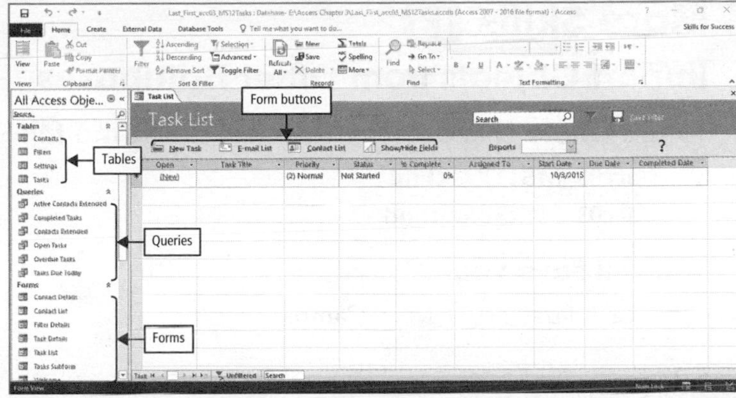

Access 2016, Windows 10, Microsoft Corporation **Figure 1**

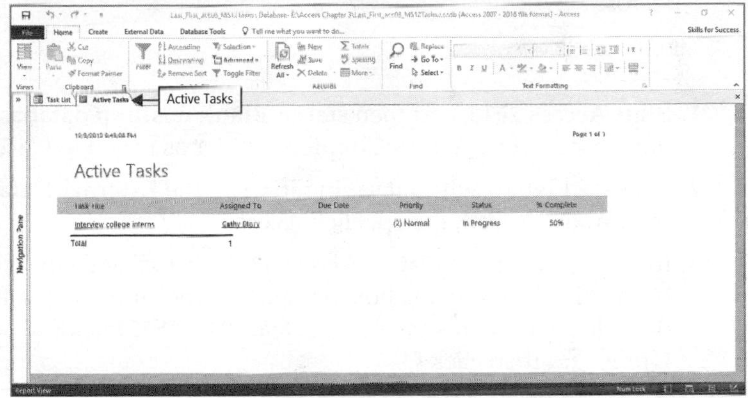

Access 2016, Windows 10, Microsoft Corporation **Figure 2**

   Company: IT Department
   Job Title: IT Services Supervisor
   Business Phone: (805) 555-1033
   E-mail: cstory@aspenfalls.org

11. Click **Close** to return to the Task Details form.

12. In the **Task Details** form, click the **Status arrow**, and then click **In Progress**. Click in the **% Complete** box, and then replace the existing text with 50% Click **Close** to update the Task List.

13. In the **Task List** form header, click the **Reports arrow**, and then click **Active Tasks** to open the Active Tasks report. Compare your screen with **Figure 2**.

14. **Close** [×] the Active Tasks report, and then **Close** [×] Access. Submit the file as directed by your instructor.

■ **You have completed More Skills 12**

More Skills 13

Import Objects from Other Databases

To complete this project, you will need the following files:

- acc03_MS13BackEnd
- acc03_MS13FrontEnd

You will save your file as:

- Last_First_acc03_MS13Camps

- You can build a database by importing objects from other Access databases.
- Commonly imported objects include tables, forms, queries, reports, and macros.

---

1. **Start Access 2016**, and then start a **Blank desktop database**. **Save** the database in your **Access Chapter 3** folder as Last_First_acc03_Camps
2. **Close** ☒ Table1 without saving it. Click the **External Data tab**, and then in the **Import & Link group**, click **Access**.

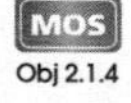
Obj 2.1.4

3. In the **Get External Data – Access Database** dialog box, click **Browse**. In the **File Open** dialog box, navigate to the student data files that you downloaded for this project. Click **acc03_MS13BackEnd**, and then click **Open,** and then click **OK**.

   The Get External Data - Access Database dialog box can be used to import Access objects into a database. It can also be used to create links to tables in another database file.

4. In the **Import Objects** dialog box, click the **Select All** button. Compare your screen to **Figure 1**, and then click **OK**.
5. **Close** the **Get External Data - Access Database** dialog box to import the tables into the database.

   When tables are imported from other databases, the fields, field properties, data, and relationships with other tables are imported. Here, four related tables were imported.

6. On the **External Data tab**, in the **Import & Link group**, click **Access**. In the **Get External Data – Access Database** dialog box, click **Browse,** and then open the student data file **acc03_MS13FrontEnd**. Click **OK** to open the Import Objects dialog box.
7. In the **Import Objects** dialog box, click the **Queries tab**, and then click **Select All** to add them to the import.

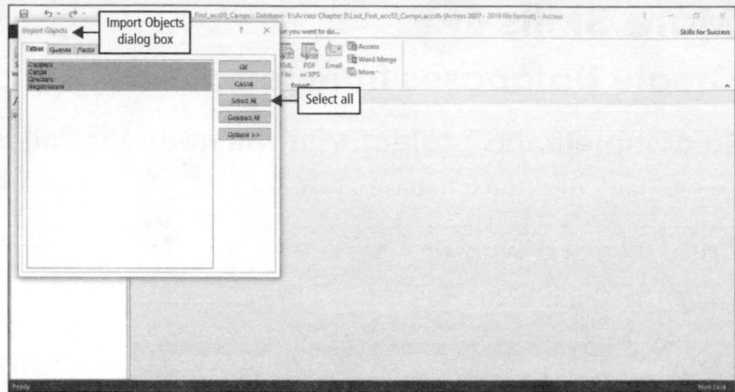

Figure 1 Access 2016, Windows 10, Microsoft Corporation

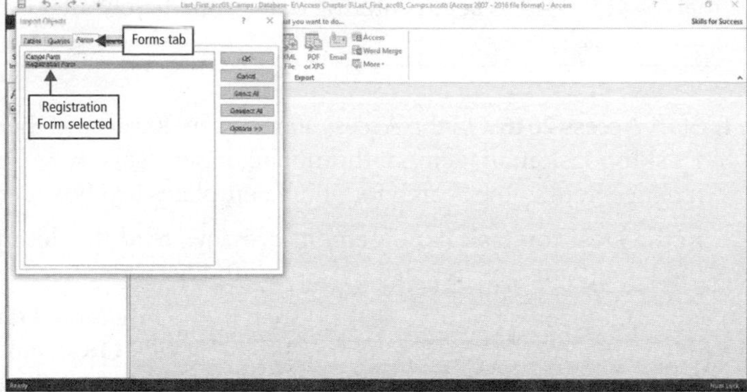

Figure 2 Access 2016, Windows 10, Microsoft Corporation

8. In the **Import Objects** dialog box, click the **Forms tab**, and then click **Registration Form** to add it to the import. Compare your screen with **Figure 2**.

   The queries selected in the previous step are still selected and will be included in the import. The Camps Form is not selected and will not be imported.

9. In the **Import Objects** dialog box, click the **Reports tab**, and then click **Select All** to add all the reports to the import.
10. In the **Import Objects** dialog box, click **OK**. **Close** the Get External Data - Access Data dialog box to complete the import.
11. **Close** ☒ Access. Submit the file as directed by your instructor.

- **You have completed More Skills 13**

More Skills 14

Back Up Databases

To complete this project, you will need the following file:

- acc03_MS14Art

You will save your files as:

- **Last_First_acc03_MS14Art**
- **Last_First_acc03_MS14Art_Backup**

▶ You can save a database as a template and back up databases. Missing tables, queries, or reports from a database can be restored from a backup.

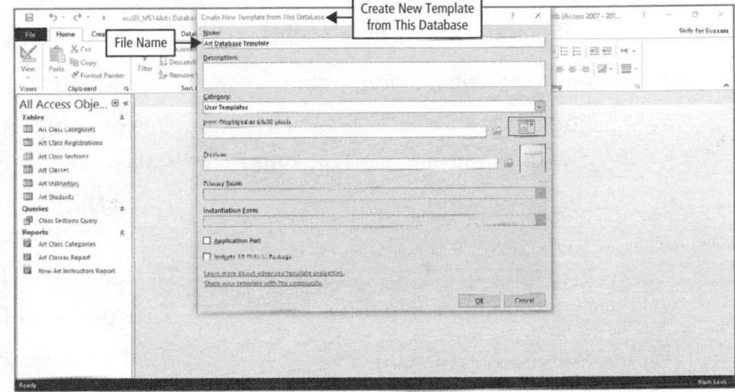

Access 2016, Windows 10, Microsoft Corporation **Figure 1**

1. Start **Access 2016**, and then open the student data file **acc03_MS14Art**. **Save** the file in your **Access Chapter 3** folder as Last_First_acc03_MS14Art If necessary, enable the content.
2. Click the **File tab**, and then click **Save As**. In the **Save Database As group**, click **Template**, and then click **Save As**. MOS Obj 1.5.3

   The Create New Template from This Database dialog box displays.

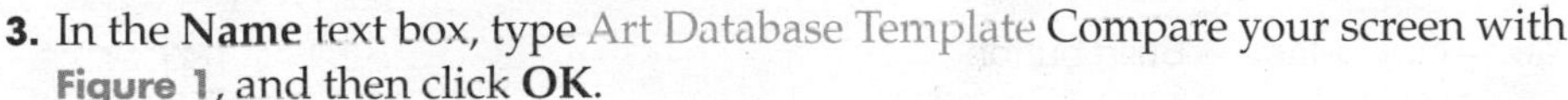

3. In the **Name** text box, type Art Database Template Compare your screen with **Figure 1**, and then click **OK**.
4. Read the message, and then click **OK**.
5. Click the **File tab**, and then click **Save As**. In the **Save Database As group**, click **Back Up Database**. Compare your screen with **Figure 2**, and then click **Save As**. MOS Obj 1.4.3
6. In the **Save As** dialog box, type Last_First_acc03_MS14Art_Backup and then click **Save**.
7. **Close** Access.
8. Submit your files as directed by your instructor.

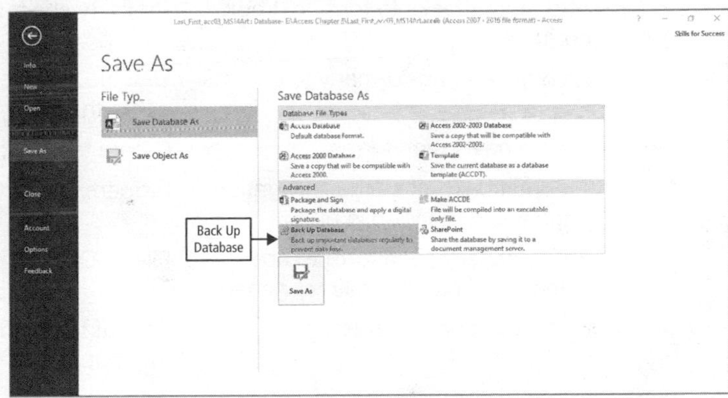

Access 2016, Windows 10, Microsoft Corporation **Figure 2**

■ **You have completed More Skills 14**

Review

Skills Number	Task	Step	Icon	Keyboard Shortcut
1	Create forms with the Form Wizard	Create tab → Forms group → Form Wizard		
2	Locate a record in a form	Click in the field to be searched. Then, Home → Find group → Find		Ctrl + F
2	Create new records	In the Navigation bar, click New (blank) record		
3	Format form controls	Select the control(s) in Layout view, and then use the groups on the Format tab		
3	Set control widths and heights	On the property sheet Format tab, change the Width or Height property		F4
4	Apply conditional formatting	Format tab → Control Formatting group → Conditional Formatting → New Rule		
4	Add logos	Design tab → Header / Footer group → Logo		
5	Create forms with the Form Tool	Select table or query in Navigation Pane. Then, Create tab → Forms group → Form		
5	Create one-to-many forms	In the Navigation Pane, select the table that will be the main form. Then, Create tab → Forms group → Form		
5	Add date and time controls	Design tab → Header / Footer group → Date and Time		
6	Insert columns and rows	Arrange tab → Rows & Columns group		
6	Delete columns and rows	Arrange tab → Rows & Columns group → Select Column or Select Row. Then, press Delete		
6	Merge columns and rows	Select cells or Select Row. Then, Arrange tab → Merge / Split group → Merge		
6	Edit label control text	Double-click the label control		
7	Add input masks to form text box controls	Property sheet Data tab → Input Mask → Build button		F4
8	Edit data in one-to-many forms	Use the main form Navigation bar to locate the desired record. Change data in either the main form or the subform datasheet		
10	Create navigation forms	Create tab → Forms group → Navigation Form		
10	Automatically close the Navigation Pane when the form is open	Property sheet Other tab → Modal → Yes		F4
10	Automatically set a form to open when the database is first opened	File → Options → Current Database → Display Form		
10	Format button controls	Format tab → Control Formatting group → Quick Styles (and other commands in the group)		
MS11	Create Validation rule	Fields tab → Field Validation group → Validation button → Expression Builder		
MS12	Create a database from a template	Access start screen → Select template		
MS14	Save database as a backup	File tab → Save As → Save Database As → Select Back Up Database		

Project Summary Chart

Project	Project Type	Project Location
Skills Review	Review	In Book & MIL MyITLab® Grader
Skills Assessment 1	Review	In Book & MIL MyITLab® Grader
Skills Assessment 2	Review	Book
My Skills	Problem Solving	Book
Visual Skills Check	Problem Solving	Book
Skillls Challenge 1	Critical Thinking	Book
Skills Challenge 2	Critical Thinking	Book
More Skills Assessment	Review	In Book & MIL MyITLab® Grader
Collaborating with Google	Critical Thinking	Book

MOS Objectives Covered

1.1.2 Create a database from a template	4.1.3 Save a form
1.3.1 Navigate to specific records	4.2.1 Move form controls
1.3.2 Create and modify a navigation form	4.2.2 Add form controls
1.3.3 Set a form as the startup option	4.2.4 Remove form controls
1.4.3 Back up a database	4.2.5 Set form control properties
1.5.3 Save a database as a template	4.2.6 Manage labels
2.1.4 Import tables from other databases	4.2.7 Add subforms
2.4.2 Add validation rules to fields	4.3.7 Insert headers and footers
2.4.8 Use input masks	4.3.8 Insert images
4.1.1 Create a form	

Key Terms

BizSkills Video

1. What do you think are the biggest sources of conflict in the meeting portrayed in the video?
2. What suggestions do you have to reduce the conflict in the group portrayed in the video?

Online Help Skills

1. Start **Access 2016**, and then in the upper right corner of the start page, click the **Help** button [?].
2. In the **Access Help** window **Search help** box, type form tool and then press [Enter].
3. In the search result list, click **Create a form by using the Form Tool**, and then compare your screen with **Figure 1**.

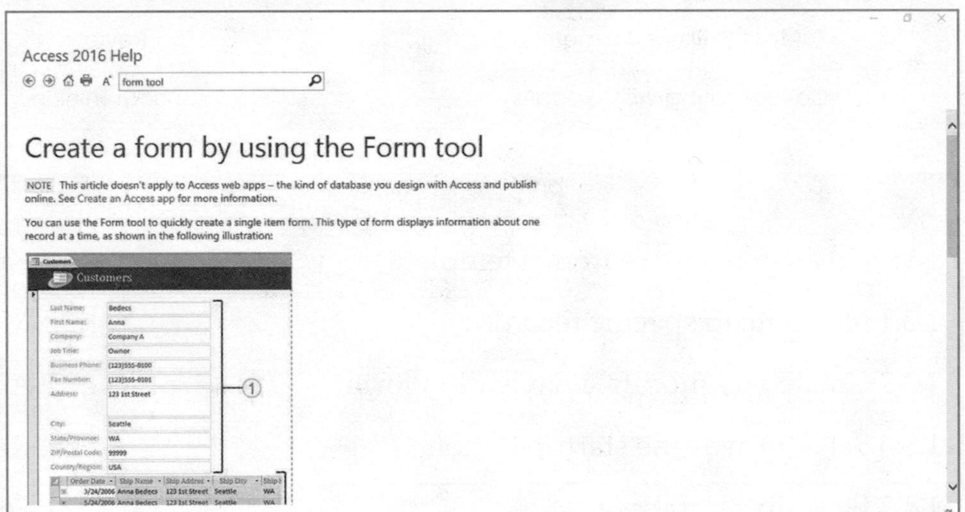

Figure 1 Access 2016, Windows 10, Microsoft Corporation

4. Read the article to see if you can answer the following questions: Under which circumstances would you use the Form Tool to create a form? Why would you use the Form Tool and not the Form Wizard?

Matching 

Match each term in the second column with its correct definition in the first column by writing the letter of the term on the blank line in front of the correct definition.

___ **1.** A tool used to create a form that provides a way to select tables and fields before the form is created.

___ **2.** The arrangement of data and labels in a form or report—columnar or tabular, for example.

___ **3.** A form control that displays the name of a form by default; the actual text can be edited later.

___ **4.** A set of special characters that control what can and cannot be entered in a field.

___ **5.** A layout with cells arranged in rows and columns into which controls are placed.

___ **6.** By default, subforms display in this view.

___ **7.** By default, main forms display in this layout.

___ **8.** A type of form that has a subform that displays related records from another table.

___ **9.** A form that can be used to quickly switch between forms and reports in the database.

___ **10.** To set a form to open automatically when the database is opened, open the Access Options dialog box, and then display the options for this category.

A Current Database
B Datasheet view
C Form Wizard
D Input mask
E Layout
F Navigation Form
G One-to-many form
H Single Form view
I Tabular layout
J Title

Multiple Choice 

Choose the correct answer.

1. An Access view used to format a form or report while you are viewing a sample of the data.
   A. Design view
   B. Form view
   C. Layout view
2. A layout that places labels in the first column and data in the second column.
   A. Columnar
   B. Datasheet
   C. Tabular
3. Controls on a form or report that describe each field—often the field name—in the underlying table.
   A. IntelliSense Quick Info boxes
   B. Labels
   C. Text boxes
4. Controls on a form or report that display the data from each field in the underlying table or query.
   A. Labels
   B. Text boxes
   C. Titles
5. The property sheet tab that contains the Input Mask property.
   A. Data
   B. Format
   C. Other
6. The symbol in an input mask that is replaced as you type data into the field.
   A. Data character
   B. Input character
   C. Placeholder character
7. Formatting that evaluates the values in a field and formats that data according to the rules you specify; for example, only values over 1,000 will have bold applied.
   A. Conditional formatting
   B. Logical formatting
   C. Rules-based formatting
8. A form contained within another form that contains records related to the record displayed in the main form.
   A. Parent form
   B. Relationship form
   C. Subform
9. When you want to build a form for a subset of table data, you can base the form on this.
   A. Blank Form tool
   B. Filtered table
   C. Query
10. To automatically close the Navigation Pane whenever the form is open, this form property needs to be set to *Yes*.
   A. Full Width
   B. Modal
   C. Open Exclusive

Topics for Discussion

1. You have created forms using two different methods: the Form Tool and the Form Wizard. Which method do you prefer, and why? What are the primary advantages of each method?
2. Recall that forms are used to enter data into a database. Consider the types of data businesses might store in a database. For example, a school needs a class registration form to enter students into classes. What type of forms might other businesses need to enter data?

Skills Review

To complete this project, you will need the following files:

- acc03_SRElectricity
- acc03_SRLogo

You will save your file as:

- Last_First_acc03_SRElectricity

1. Start **Access 2016**, and then open the student data file **acc03_SRElectricity**. **Save** the file in your **Access Chapter 3** folder with the name Last_First_acc03 SRElectricity If necessary, enable the content.
2. On the **Create tab**, in the **Forms group**, click the **Form Wizard** button. In the **Form Wizard** dialog box, select the **Billing Cycles** table, and then move **AccountNumber**, **CycleDate**, **Rate**, **ElectricityUsage**, and **UsageFee** into **Selected Fields**. Click **Next** two times, name the form Charges Form and then **Finish** the wizard.
3. On the **Home tab**, in the **Views group**, click **View** to switch to Layout view.
4. With the **Account Number** text box control selected, press and hold Ctrl, while clicking the other four text boxes. Click the **Format tab**, and then in the **Font group**, click the **Align Left** button.
5. Click the **Home tab**, and then click the **View** button to switch to Form view. In the Navigation bar, click **New (blank) record**, and then enter the following billing data: **Account Number** is 4420-209636, **Cycle Date** is 31-Jul-18, **Rate** is 0.07623, and **Electricity Usage** is 242. Click in the **Usage Fee** field, and then compare your screen with **Figure 1**.
6. **Save** and then **Close** the form. In the **Navigation Pane**, click **New Billings Query** one time to select it. Click the **Create tab**, and then in the **Forms group**, click the **Form** button.
7. Double-click the **Title** control, and then change the text to New Payments Form
8. Click the **Account Number** text box, and then click as needed to open the property sheet. On the property sheet **Format tab**, change the **Width** property to 4" and then compare your screen with **Figure 2**.
9. Click **Save**, type New Payments Form and then click **OK**. **Close** the form.

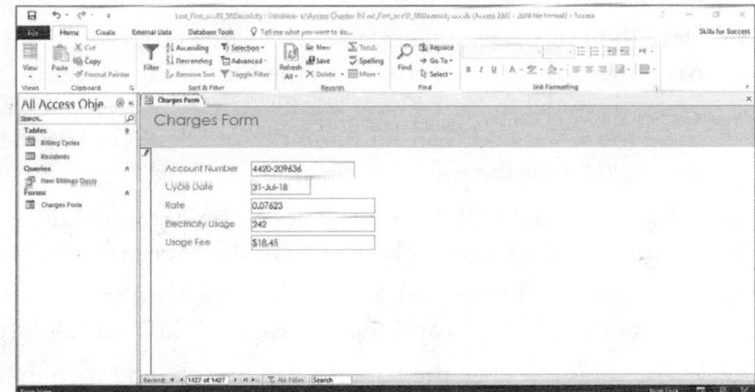

Access 2016, Windows 10, Microsoft Corporation **Figure 1**

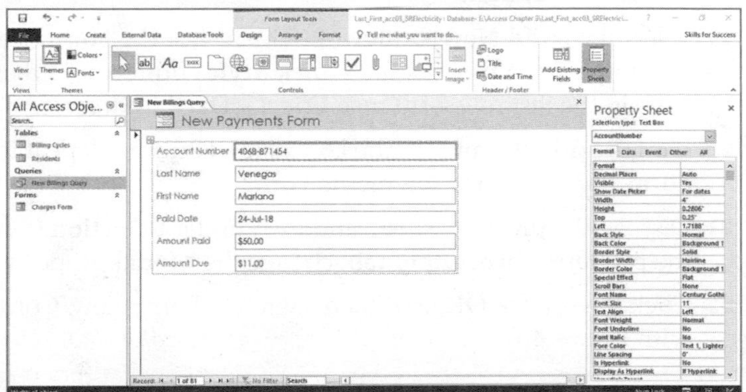

Access 2016, Windows 10, Microsoft Corporation **Figure 2**

■ **Continue to the next page to complete this Skills Review**

10. In the **Navigation Pane**, click the **Residents** table one time to select it. Click the **Create tab**, and then in the **Forms group**, click the **Form** button. Click **Save**, type Residents Form and then click **OK**.
11. On the **Design tab**, in the **Header / Footer group**, click **Logo**, and then use the **Insert Picture** dialog box to insert the file **acc03_SRLogo**.
12. Click the **Zip** text box, and then click the property sheet **Data tab**. Click the **Input Mask** box, and then click the displayed **Build** button. In the **Input Mask Wizard**, select **Zip Code**, and then click **Finish**.
13. Using the property sheet, set the width of the column of the **Account Number** text box to 4" With the column still active, click the **Arrange tab**, and then in the **Rows & Columns group**, click the **Insert Right** button three times.
14. Drag the **Electricity Meter** label to the first empty cell to the right of the **Account Number** text box. Drag the **Electricity Meter** text box control to the first empty cell to the right of the **Electricity Meter** label. Use the property sheet to set the width of the column with the **Electricity Meter** label to 1.5", and then **Close** the property sheet.
15. Click in the row with the subform. On the **Arrange tab**, in the **Rows & Columns group**, click **Select Row**. In the **Merge / Split group**, click **Merge**.
16. Click **Save**, and then switch to Form view. **Find** the record for **Account Number** 4420-209636 and then **Close** the Find and Replace dialog box.
17. In the subform, click the **Last Record** button, and then in the last record, record a **Paid Date** of 13-Aug-18 and an **Amount Paid** of 18.45 Compare your screen with **Figure 3**, and then **Close** the form.
18. On the **Create tab**, in the **Forms group**, click **Navigation**, and then click **Vertical Tabs, Left**.
19. Select the **[Add New]** button, and then click the **Format tab**. In the **Control Formatting group**, click the **Quick Styles** button, and then click the second style in the last row—**Intense Effect – Dark Red, Accent 1**.
20. Drag **Residents Form** to the **[Add New]** button. Repeat to add **Charges Form** and then **New Payments Form**.
21. Display the property sheet, and then under **Selection type**, select **Form**. On the property sheet **Other tab**, change the **Modal** property to **Yes**.
22. Click **Save**, click **OK**, and then switch to Form view. Compare your screen with **Figure 4**.

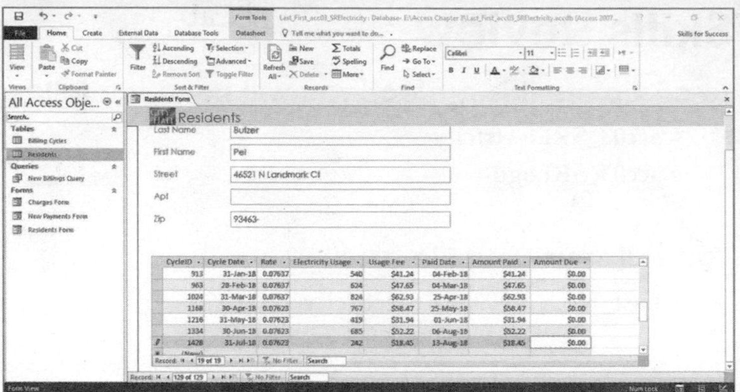

Figure 3 Access 2016, Windows 10, Microsoft Corporation

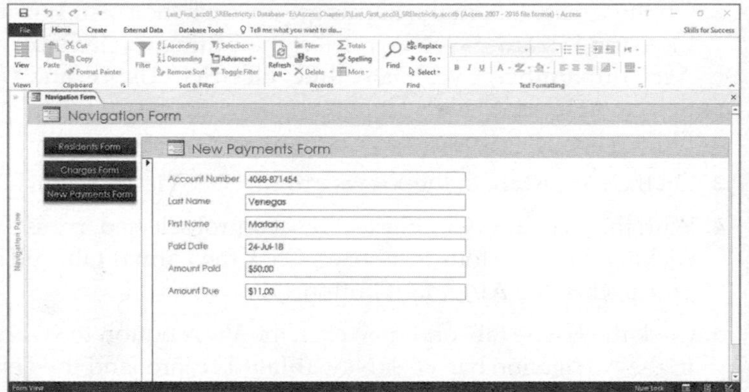

Figure 4 Access 2016, Windows 10, Microsoft Corporation

23. **Close** Access, and then submit the file as directed by your instructor.

DONE! You have completed this Skills Review

Skills Assessment 1

MyITLab®
Grader

To complete this project, you will need the following files:

- acc03_SA1Classes
- acc03_SA1Logo

You will save your file as:

- Last_First_acc03_SA1Classes

1. Start **Access 2016**, and then open the student data file **acc03_SA1Classes. Save** the file in your chapter folder with the name Last_First_acc03_SA1Classes If necessary, enable the content.
2. Use the **Form Wizard** to create a form with all the fields from the **Class Sessions** table *except* SessionID. Name the form Class Sessions Form and then accept all other wizard defaults.
3. Set the width of all the form's text boxes to 3" and their text alignment to left.
4. Use the form to add the following record: **Class Name** is Intermediate Microsoft Word **Community Center** is Central and **Intern ID** is 10 Leave the other fields blank. **Save** and then **Close** the form.
5. Use the **Form Tool** to create a form based on the **Word Classes** query. Change the **Title** control text to Word Classes Form **Save** the form as Word Classes Form and then **Close** the form.
6. Use the **Form Tool** to create a form with a main form based on the **Interns** table and with a subform based on the **Class Sessions** table. Change the form's logo using the file **acc03_SA1Logo**.
7. Add a **Phone Number** input mask to the **Phone** text box control that uses the number sign (#) as the placeholder character. Accept all other wizard defaults.
8. Add a column to the right of the table, and then move the **Last Name** text box control into the first cell to the right of the **First Name** text box.
9. Delete the unused row with the **Last Name** label, and then change the *First Name* label text to First / Last Name
10. Set the width of the table's first column to 1.5" and the width of the second and third columns to 2.6" In the subform row, merge all of the cells.

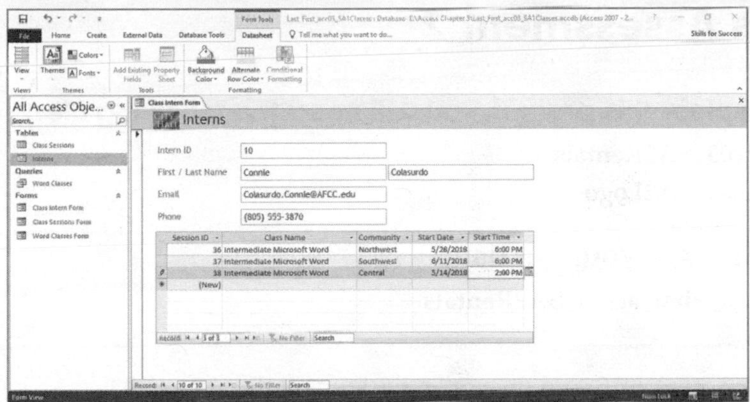

Access 2016, Windows 10, Microsoft Corporation **Figure 1**

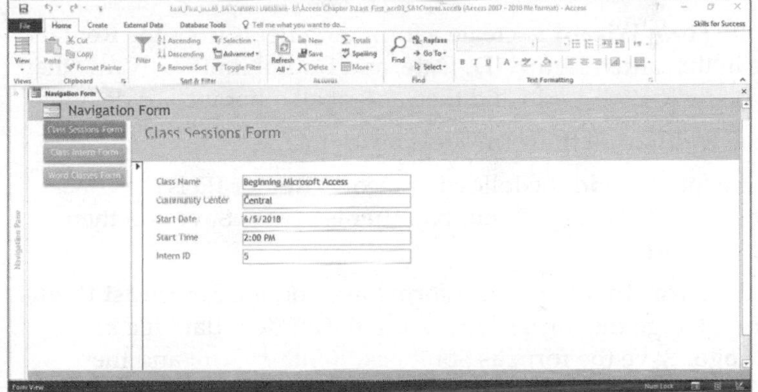

Access 2016, Windows 10, Microsoft Corporation **Figure 2**

11. **Save** the form with the name Class Intern Form and then switch to Form view. Navigate to the last **Intern** record, and then in the subform for Connie Colasurado, complete the last record by adding a **Start Date** of 5/14/2018 and **Start Time** of 2:00 PM Compare your screen with **Figure 1**, and then **Close** the form.
12. Create a **Navigation Form** with the **Vertical Tabs, Left** layout. Apply the **Intense Effect – Green, Accent 1** Quick Style to the [Add New] button, and then add buttons in the following order: **Class Sessions Form, Class Intern Form,** and **Word Classes Form.**
13. Set the form's **Modal** property to **Yes.** Click **Save,** and then click **OK.** Reopen the form, and then compare your screen with **Figure 2.**
14. **Close** the form, **Close** Access, and then submit the file as directed by your instructor.

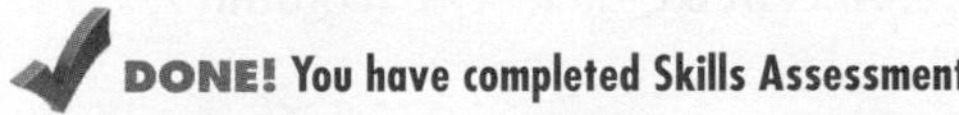
DONE! You have completed Skills Assessment 1

Skills Assessment 2

To complete this project, you will need the following files:

- acc03_SA2Rentals
- acc03_SA2Logo

You will save your file as:

- Last_First_acc03_SA2Rentals

---

1. Start **Access 2016**, and then open the student data file **acc03_SA2Rentals**. **Save** the file in your chapter folder with the name Last_First_acc03_SA2Rentals If necessary, enable the content.
2. Use the **Form Wizard** to create a form with fields from the **Rentals** table in this order: **RenterID**, **Date**, and **RoomNumber**. Name the form New Rentals Form and then accept all other wizard defaults.
3. Set the width of all the form's text boxes to 2"
4. Use the form to add the following record: **Renter ID** is CF38960 **Date** is 7/30/2018 and **Room Number** is SW115 **Save** and then **Close** the form.
5. Use the **Form Tool** to create a form based on the **Southeast Rentals** query. Change the form's logo using the student data file **acc03_SA2Logo**. **Save** the form as Southeast Rentals Form and then **Close** the form.
6. Use the **Form Tool** to create a form with a main form based on the **Rooms** table and with a subform based on the **Rentals** table.
7. For the **Deposit** text box control, create a new conditional formatting rule: If the field value is greater than 75 the font should be **Green** (column 6, last row) and **Bold**.
8. Use the property sheet to set the **Description** text box control's **Width** to 4.5" and the **Height** to 1"
9. **Save** the form with the name Rentals by Room Form and then switch to **Form view**. In the main form, navigate to **Room Number SW115**. In the subform for that room, complete the last record by entering 2 in the **Hours** field. Compare your screen with **Figure 1**, and then **Close** the form.
10. Create a **Navigation Form** with the **Horizontal Tabs** layout. Apply the **Colored Outline - Purple, Accent 6** Quick Style (column 7, row 1) to the [Add New] button, and then change its shape to **Round Same Side Corner Rectangle** (shape 5).
11. Add buttons in the following order: **New Rentals Form**, **Rentals by Room Form**, and **Southeast Rentals Form**.
12. Set the form's **Modal** property to **Yes**. Click **Save**, and then click **OK**. **Close** the form. Reopen the form, and then compare your screen with **Figure 2**.
13. **Close** the form, **Close** Access, and then submit the file as directed by your instructor.

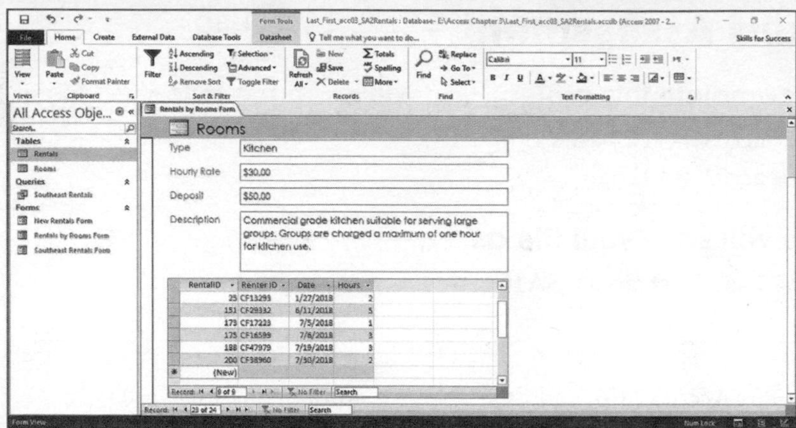

Figure 1 Access 2016, Windows 10, Microsoft Corporation

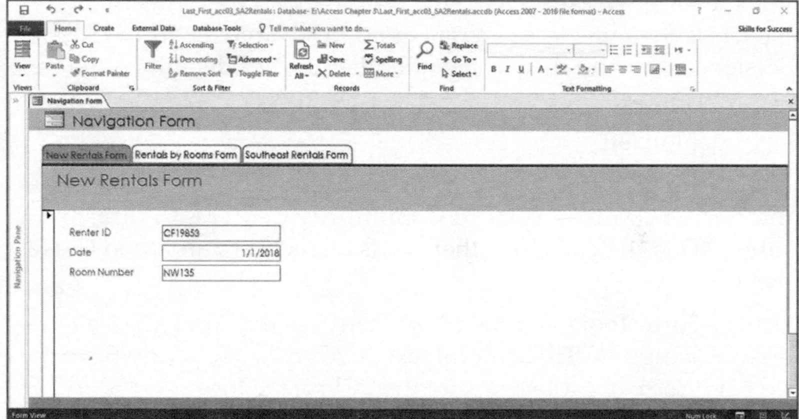

Figure 2 Access 2016, Windows 10, Microsoft Corporation

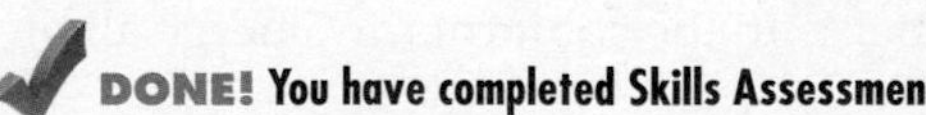
DONE! You have completed Skills Assessment 2

My Skills

To complete this project, you will need the following file:

- acc03_MYGrades

You will save your file as:

- Last_First_acc03_MYGrades

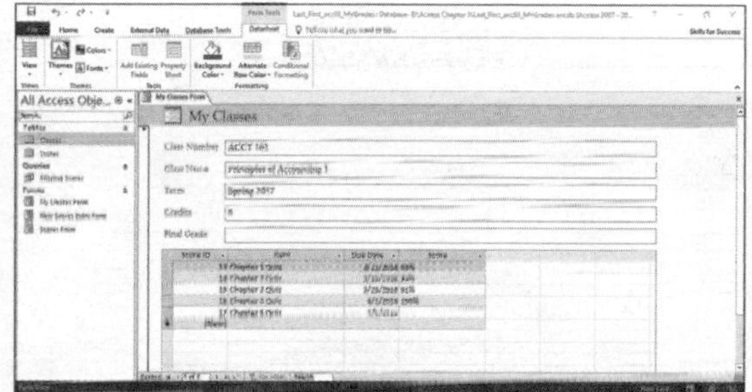

Access 2016, Windows 10, Microsoft Corporation **Figure 1**

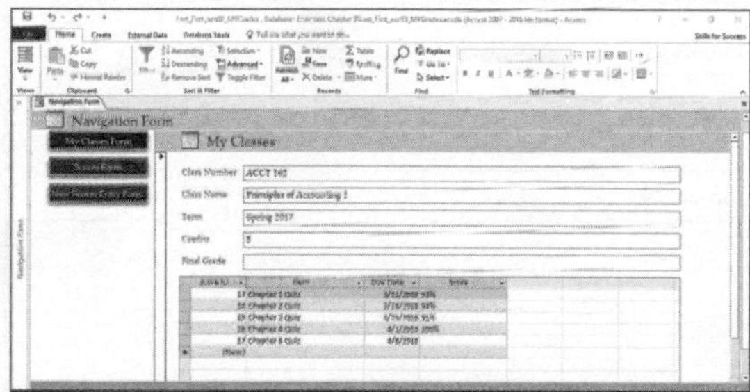

Access 2016, Windows 10, Microsoft Corporation **Figure 2**

1. Start **Access 2016**, and then open the student data file **acc03_MYGrades**. **Save** the file in your chapter folder with the name Last_First_acc03_MYGrades If necessary, enable the content.
2. Use the **Form Wizard** to create a form with all of the fields from the **Scores** table *except* ScoreID. Name the form Scores Form and then accept all other wizard defaults.
3. Set the width of all the form's text boxes to 2.5" and their text alignment to left. **Save** and then **Close** the form.
4. Use the **Form Tool** to create a form based on the **Missing Scores** query. Change the **Title** control text to New Scores
5. Set the width of the text box controls to 3.5" **Save** the form as New Scores Entry Form and then **Close** the form.
6. Use the **Form Tool** to create a form with a main form based on the **Classes** table and with a subform based on the **Scores** table.
7. In the main form, change the **Title** control to My Classes Click a blank cell on the right side of the subform, and then use the property sheet to set the **Height** of the row to 3.2"
8. **Save** the form with the name My Classes Form and then switch to Form view. Compare your screen with **Figure 1**.
9. In the main form, create a new record using the data from the class that is assigning this project to you. In the subform, fill in the data for all of the assignments, quizzes, tests, or other grading opportunities that have been posted for your class. If you received scores on any of these, enter those scores. When you are done, **Close** the form.
10. Create a **Navigation Form** with the **Vertical Tabs, Left** layout. Apply the **Moderate Effect - Brown, Accent 4** Quick Style (column 5, row 5) to the [Add New] button.
11. Add buttons in the following order: **My Classes Form**, **Scores Form**, and **New Scores Entry Form**.
12. Set the form's **Modal** property to **Yes**. Click **Save**, and then click **OK**. **Close** the form. Reopen the form, and then compare your screen with **Figure 2**.
13. **Close** the form, **Close** Access, and then submit the file as directed by your instructor.

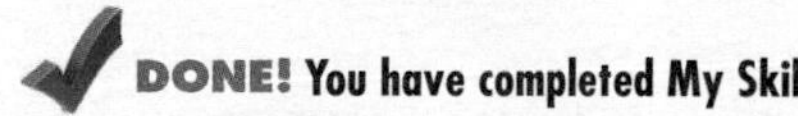

DONE! You have completed My Skills

Visual Skills Check

To complete this project, you will need the following files:

- acc03_VSArtCenter
- acc03_VSLogo

You will save your file as:

- Last_First_acc03_VSArtCenter

Open the student data file **acc03_VSArtCenter**, and then **Save** the file in your **Access Chapter 3** folder as Last_First_acc03_VSArtCenter

Open the **Students Form** in Layout view, and then arrange and format the label and text box controls as shown in Figure 1. The **First Name** and **Last Name** labels are bold, the **City** label text has been changed to City / State / Zip and unused rows have been deleted. Adjust the field widths to ensure all data displays.

Create the Navigation form shown in **Figure 1**. The form is named Navigation Form The title text has been changed to Art Classes Navigation Form and the logo was inserted from the student data file **acc03_VSLogo**. The buttons have been formatted with the **Subtle Effect - Dark Blue, Accent 1** Quick Style and the **Rounded Rectangle** shape, and the button text is bold. The form properties have been changed so that the Navigation Pane automatically closes whenever the form is open.

Submit the file as directed by your instructor.

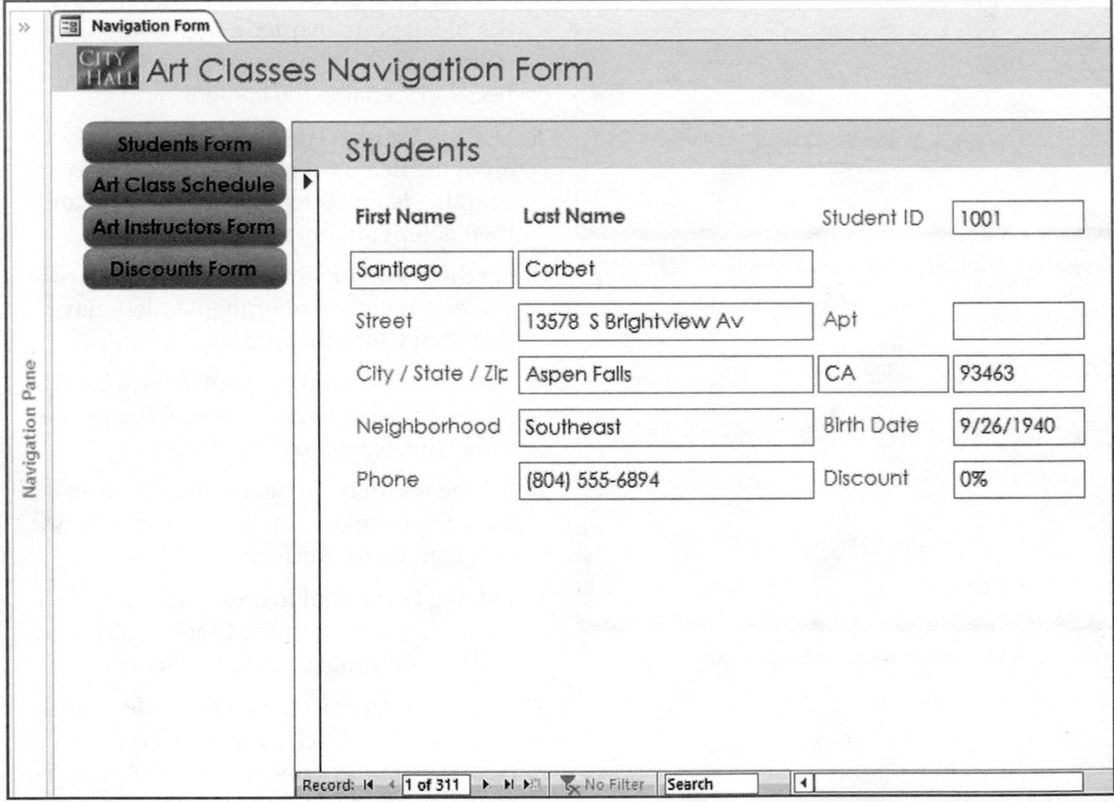

Figure 1

Access 2016, Windows 10, Microsoft Corporation

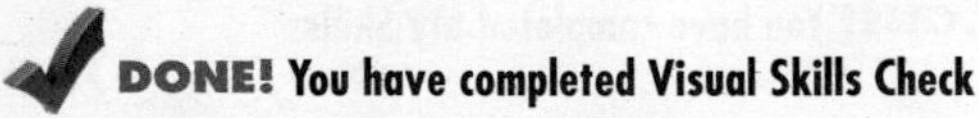

DONE! You have completed Visual Skills Check

Skills Challenge 1

To complete this project, you will need the following file:

- acc03_SC1Farms

You will save your file as:

- Last_First_acc03_SC1Farms

Open the student data file **acc03_SC1Farms**, and then save the file in your **Access Chapter 3** folder as Last_First_acc03_SC1Farms Use the Form Tool to create a form that displays all the records and fields from the Farms table. Using the techniques practiced in this chapter, arrange the labels and text boxes so that anyone who uses the form can fill in the data in a logical order. Add columns and rows and merge cells as needed, and resize them to better fit the data they contain. Delete any unused rows or columns. Update the label text so that the labels clearly describe the data. For example, add spaces between words and, where appropriate, describe all the controls in a single row. Format the controls with the farm's name to so they stand out from the rest of the controls.

Submit the file as directed by your instructor.

DONE! You have completed Skills Challenge 1

Skills Challenge 2

To complete this project, you will need the following file:

- acc03_SC2Wildlife

You will save your file as:

- Last_First_acc03_SC2Wildlife

Open the student data file **acc03_SC2Wildlife**, and then save the file as Last_First_acc03_SC2Wildlife Create a one-to-many form based on the Wildlife table in the main form and the Alternate Names table in the subform. Format the form to fit the data it will hold making sure to leave room for about five lines of text in the Description text box. Research each of the animals in the Wildlife table in order to complete the form. You can find the information you need at a website such as Wikipedia. Using the information you find, fill in the form. The first record—Tule Elk—has been completed as an example. Place alternate names in the subform. If an alternate name cannot be found, leave the subform blank for that animal. Submit the file as directed by your instructor.

DONE! You have completed Skills Challenge 2

More Skills Assessment

To complete this project, you will need the following files:

- Blank desktop database
- acc03_MSAResults

You will save your files as:

- Last_First_acc03_MSA
- Last_First_acc03_MSA_Backup

1. Start **Access 2016**, and then **Create** a **Desktop task management** database. **Save** the file in your **Access Chapter 3** folder as Last_First_acc03_MSA
2. Open the **Contacts** table in Datasheet view. Create a **Field Validation Rule** in the **Expression Builder** that verifies that either ND or SD is entered in the State/Province field. Compare your screen with **Figure 1**, and then click **OK** to close the **Expression Builder** dialog box.
3. Rename the **State/Province** field State and then test the field by typing MD in the **State** column. Enter the value ND in the **State** field in the first row.
4. **Save** the file as a **Back Up Database** with the file name Last_First_acc03_MSA_Backup
5. **Import** the **Racers** table from the **acc03_MSAResults** student data file, and then compare your screen to **Figure 2**.
6. **Close** the database, and then **Close** Access.
7. Submit your files as directed by your instructor.

DONE! You have completed More Skills Assessment

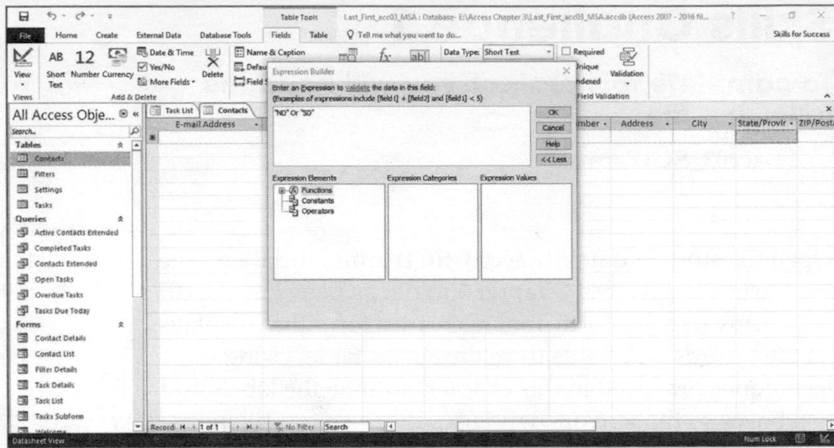

Figure 1 Access 2016, Windows 10, Microsoft Corporation

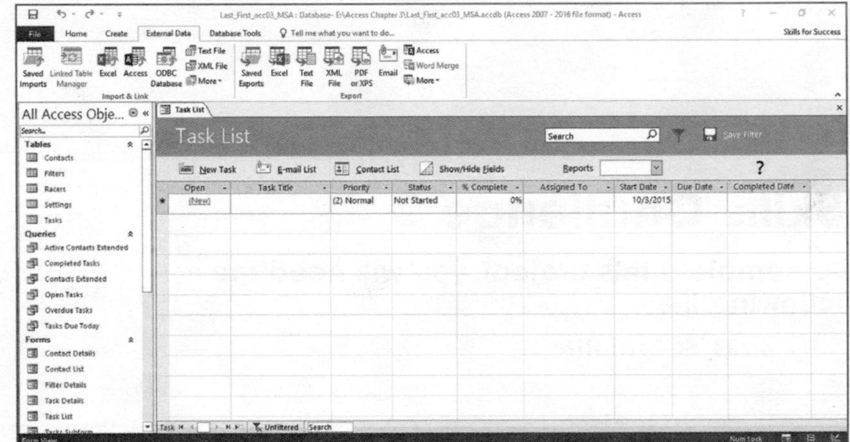

Figure 2 Access 2016, Windows 10, Microsoft Corporation

Collaborating with Google

To complete this project, you will need a Google account (refer to the Common Features chapter) and the following file:

- Blank Google form

You will save your file as:

- Last_First_acc03_GPSnip

1. Open Google Chrome web browser. Log into your Google account, and then click the **Apps** button.
2. Click the **Drive** button to open Google Drive, and then click the **NEW** button. Click **More**, and then click **Google Forms** to open a blank form.
3. Read the message, and then click **Get started**.
4. At the top of the web page, click the **Title** label, *Untitled form*, and then rename the form Customer Survey
5. Click the **Change theme** button. In the **Change theme** pane, scroll down and click the **Watercolors** theme. Compare your screen with **Figure 1**, and then click the **Edit questions** button.
6. In the **Form Description** text box, type Your feedback is appreciated!
7. In the first **Question** title, add the text Overall how satisfied are you with the service you received?
8. Below the **Question Type**, click **Add Option** as needed, and then type the following text as the three answer options: Very satisfied | Satisfied | Not satisfied
9. If necessary, below the first question, click the Add item button, and then click Multiple Choice.
10. In the second question textbox, type Would you recommend our services to a friend? and then type the follow answer options: Definitely | Maybe | No
11. Click **Done**, and then at the top of the screen, click the **View live form** button. Compare your screen with **Figure 2**, and then return to the Google Survey tab in your browser.
12. Click the **Send form** button, and then in **Send form** via email, type AspenFallsEvents@gmail.com to send the form to a customer.
13. In the **Custom message** text box, type Please take our two question survey.

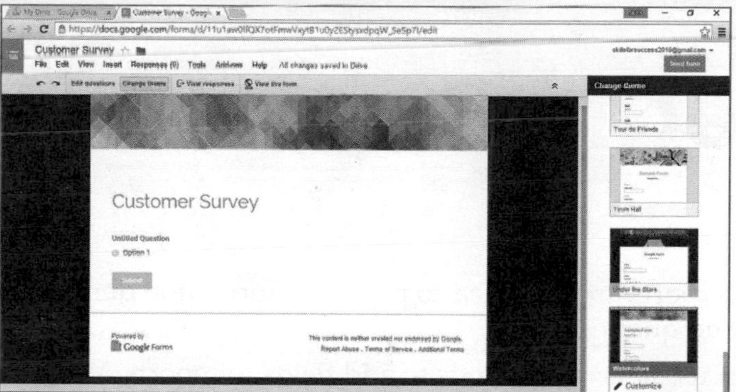

Figure 1

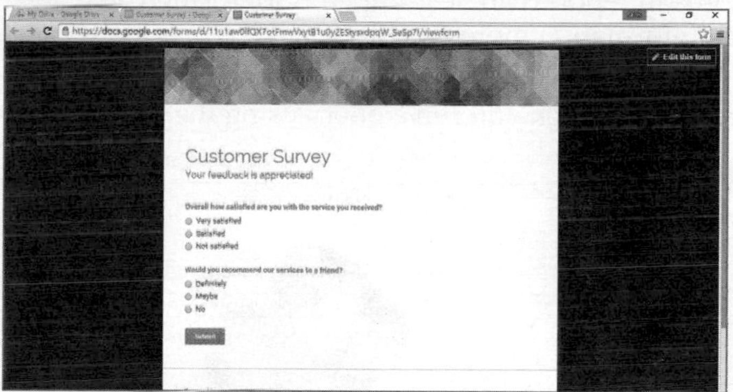

Figure 2

14. Click **Send**. If a confirmation page displays, click **OK**. Press [Windows], type snip and then press [Enter] to start the **Snipping Tool**. Click the **New arrow**, and then click **Window Snip**. Point to the Google Chrome window, and then when a red border displays around the window, click one time.
15. In the **Snipping Tool** mark-up window, click the **Save Snip** button. In the **Save As** dialog box, navigate to your Access Chapter 3 folder. Be sure the **Save as type** box displays **JPEG file**. Name the file Last_First_acc03_GPSnip and then press [Enter]. **Close** [x] the Snipping Tool mark-up window.
16. Click **Send**, read the message that displays, and then click **Create**. **Close** all windows, and then submit your file as directed by your instructor.

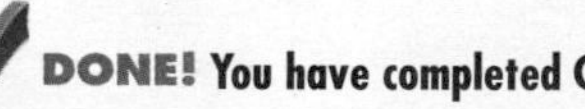

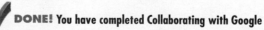

DONE! You have completed Collaborating with Google

CHAPTER 4

Create Reports

- Access reports are designed to present information derived from tables and queries.
- You can use several methods to add fields to reports. You can then format and arrange the fields to make the information more meaningful.
- The records in reports can be grouped, sorted, and filtered to make the information more useful.
- You can build a report with fields from an entire table or fields that are selected when you run a query using the Report tool.
- To select certain fields from one or more tables, you can create a report using the Blank Report tool.
- When you need to print addresses on self-adhesive labels, you can create a labels report.
- As you work with reports, each view has a special purpose. You can modify reports in Layout view. Report view shows the report's screen version and Print Preview shows the report's printed version.

Auremar/Fotolia

Aspen Falls City Hall

In this chapter, you will create reports for Aspen Falls Utilities. You will work under the supervision of Diane Payne, Public Works Director, to build a report about water bills for city residents and create mailing labels using resident addresses. You will also build a report that provides statistics about monthly water usage.

Good reports filter and sort the data found in the database tables in a way that provides useful information. Many reports are started by first creating a query so that the query can provide the fields and criteria needed by the report. After a report is created, you can add additional grouping, sorting, and filters so that just the records and fields you need will be displayed.

Reports can be designed in Layout view, and then viewed in Report view or printed. Reports that will be printed typically need to be narrower than reports that are designed to be viewed on a computer screen. For this reason, it is a good practice to view reports in Print Layout view and then make adjustments as needed to present the report effectively on the printed page.

You will create reports using the Report Wizard, Blank Report tool, Report tool, and Labels tool. You will also format, group, sort, and filter reports to display the information more effectively. Finally, you will summarize report data by adding totals.

Time to complete all 10 skills — 60 to 90 minutes

Outcome

Using the skills in this chapter, you will be able to create and format reports; add totals; group, sort, and filter reports; and create label reports.

Objectives

4.1 Create reports in different database views

4.2 Devise reports that include totals, groups, and filters

4.3 Modify and format reports

4.4 Construct reports based on queries

Student data files needed for this chapter:

acc04_Water (Access)
acc04_WaterLogo (JPG)

You will save your file as:

Last_First_acc04_Water

SKILLS

At the end of this chapter you will be able to:

Skill 1 Build Queries for Reports
Skill 2 Create Reports Using the Report Tool
Skill 3 Format Reports
Skill 4 Add Totals to Reports
Skill 5 Preview and Print Reports
Skill 6 Create Reports with the Blank Report Tool
Skill 7 Group and Sort Reports
Skill 8 Modify Report Layouts
Skill 9 Filter Reports
Skill 10 Create Label Reports

MORE SKILLS

Skill 11 Change Report Sort Order and Orientation
Skill 12 Export Reports to Word
Skill 13 Save Reports as PDF Documents
Skill 14 Save Reports as Web Pages

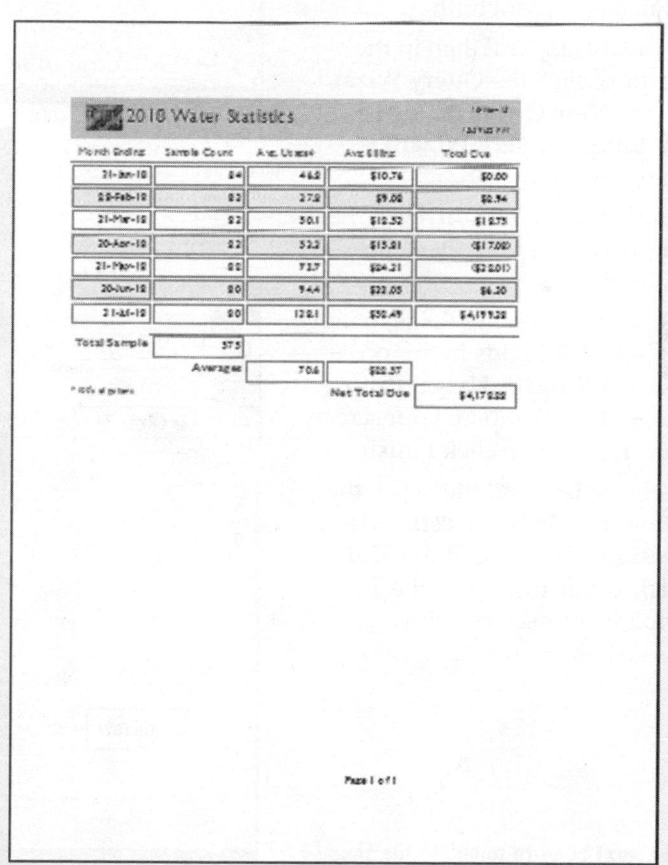

► Reports are often based on queries. You can create a query with fields, add criteria, and then build the report using the query as the data source.

1. Start **Access 2016**, and then open the student data file **acc04_Water**. On the **File tab**, click **Save As**. With **Save Database As** selected, click the **Save As** button. In the **Save As** dialog box, navigate to the location you are saving your files. Click **New folder**, type Access Chapter 4 and then press Enter two times. **Save** the file as Last_First_acc04_Water
2. If the Security Warning message displays, click the Enable Content button.
3. Click the **Create tab**, and then in the **Queries group**, click the **Query Wizard** button. In the **New Query** dialog box, verify that **Simple Query Wizard** is selected, and then click **OK**.
4. In the **Simple Query Wizard**, click the **Table/Queries arrow**, and then click **Table: Water Bills**.
5. Double-click the following fields to move them into **Selected Fields** in this order: **BillingDate**, **BillingID**, **Usage**, **Billing**, and **AmountDue**. Compare your screen with **Figure 1**, and then click **Finish**.
6. Click the **Home tab**, and then click the **View** button to switch to **Design view**. On the **Design tab**, in the **Show/Hide group**, click **Totals** to display the Total row. Compare your screen with **Figure 2**.

■ Continue to the next page to complete the skill

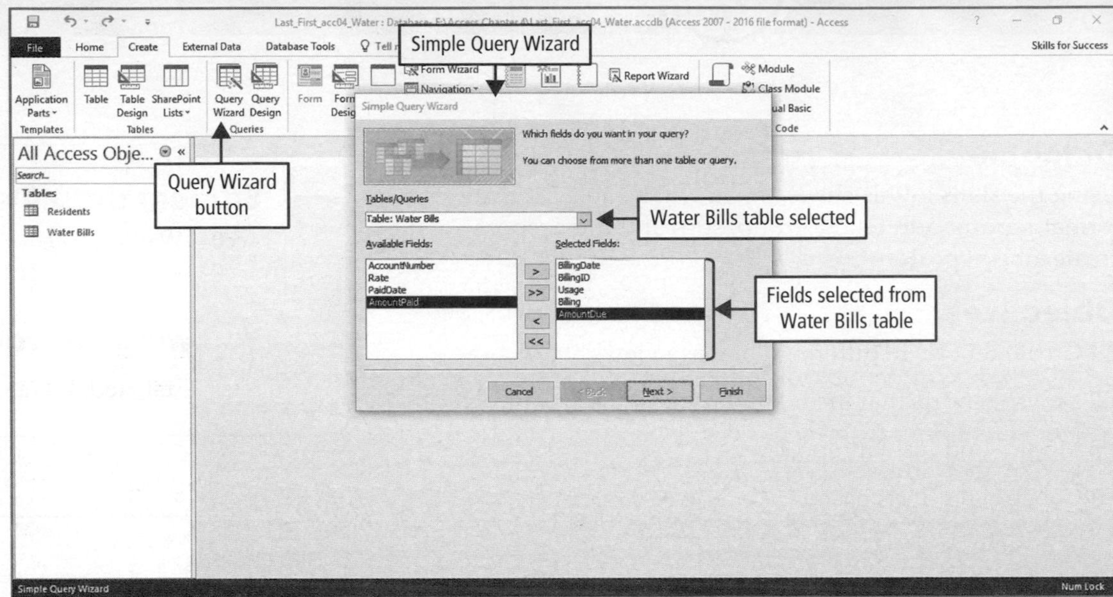

Figure 1

Access 2016, Windows 10, Microsoft Corporation

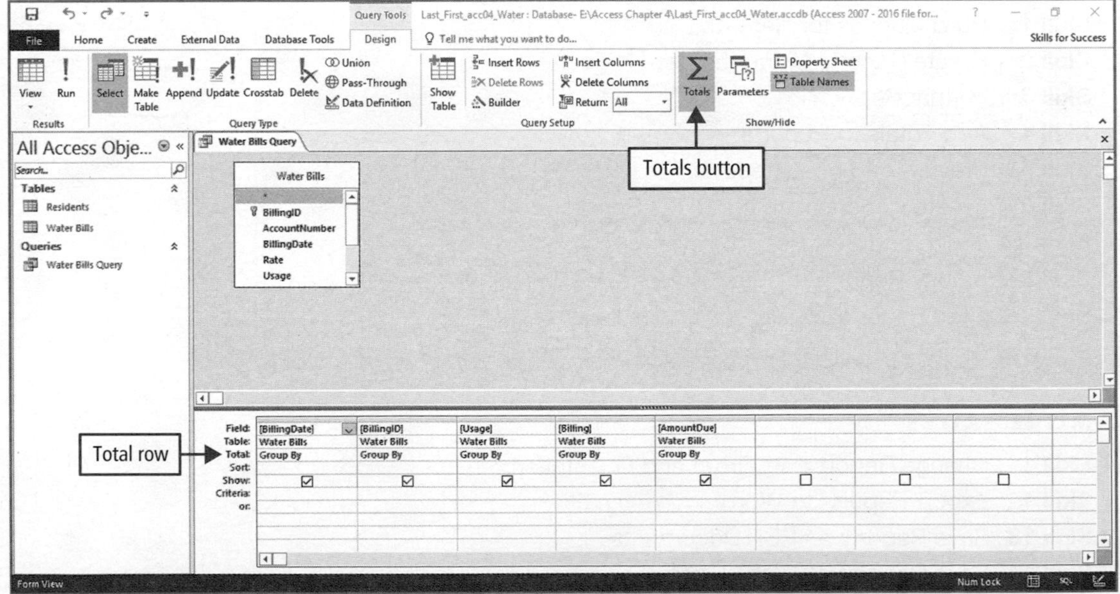

Figure 2

Access 2016, Windows 10, Microsoft Corporation

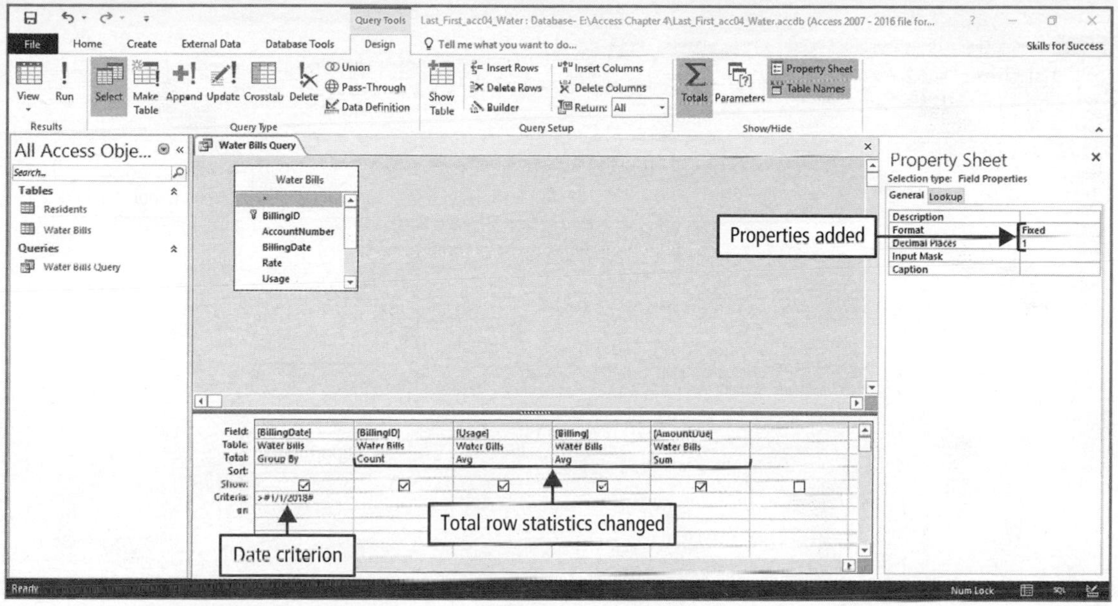

Access 2016, Windows 10, Microsoft Corporation

Figure 3

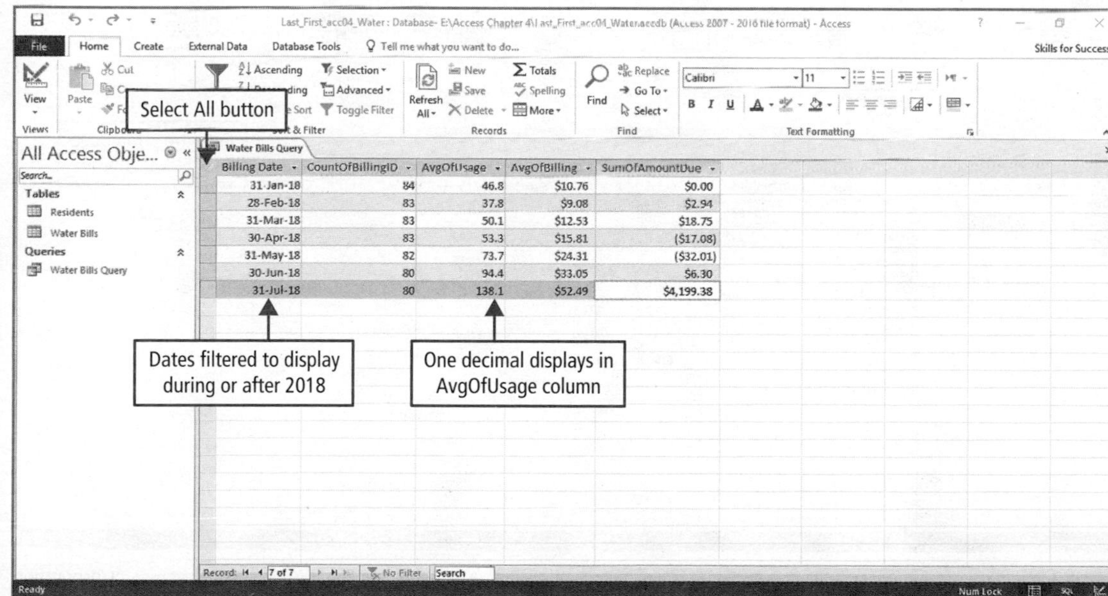

Access 2016, Windows 10, Microsoft Corporation

Figure 4

7. Click the **Total** cell for the **BillingID** column, click the arrow that displays, and then click **Count**.
8. Repeat the same technique to change the **Usage** column **Total** cell to **Avg**, the **Billing** column **Total** cell to **Avg**, and the **AmountDue** column **Total** cell to **Sum**.
9. In the **BillingDate** column **Criteria** cell, type >1/1/2018
10. Click in the **Usage** column **Criteria** cell, and then if necessary, in the Show/Hide group, click Property Sheet to open it. In the property sheet, change the **Format** to **Fixed** and the **Decimal Places** to **1**. Compare your screen with **Figure 3**.
11. **Close** the property sheet, and then **Run** the query.
12. In the upper left corner of the query datasheet, click the **Select All** button to select all the columns. On the **Home tab**, in the **Records group**, click the **More** button, and then click **Field Width**. In the **Column Width** dialog box, click **Best Fit**. Click a cell to deselect the columns, and then compare your screen with **Figure 4**.

    This query displays statistics about Aspen Falls water usage and bills for each month in 2018. This shows how a query can select the data that needs to be presented in a report.

13. Click **Save**, and then **Close** the query.

■ **You have completed Skill 1 of 10**

SKILL 2: Create Reports Using the Report Tool

► Reports can be created by selecting a table or query in the Navigation Pane and then clicking the Report button.

1. In the **Navigation Pane**, under **Queries**, click **Water Bills Query** one time to select it.

Obj 5.1.1

2. Click the **Create tab**, and then in the **Reports group**, click the **Report** button to create the report and open it in ***Report Layout view***—a view that can be used to format a report while viewing the report's data.
3. Click the **Save** button. In the **Save As** dialog box, replace the suggested report name with 2018 Statistics and then click **OK**. Compare your screen with **Figure 1**.

   Access reports have three main sections: the header(s), details, and footer(s). In each section, text boxes display the data, and label controls identify the text boxes. In this report, the labels are above each column in a tabular layout.

Obj 5.3.8

4. On the **Design tab**, in the **Themes group**, click the **Themes** button, and then click the last thumbnail—**Wisp**.
5. In the **Themes group**, click the **Colors** button, and then in the **Colors** gallery, click **Marquee**.
6. In the **Themes group**, click the **Fonts** button, and then near the bottom of the **Fonts** gallery, click **Gill Sans MT**. Compare your screen with **Figure 2**.

   You can refine a theme by changing its colors to a different color theme and its fonts to a different fonts theme.

■ **Continue to the next page to complete the skill**

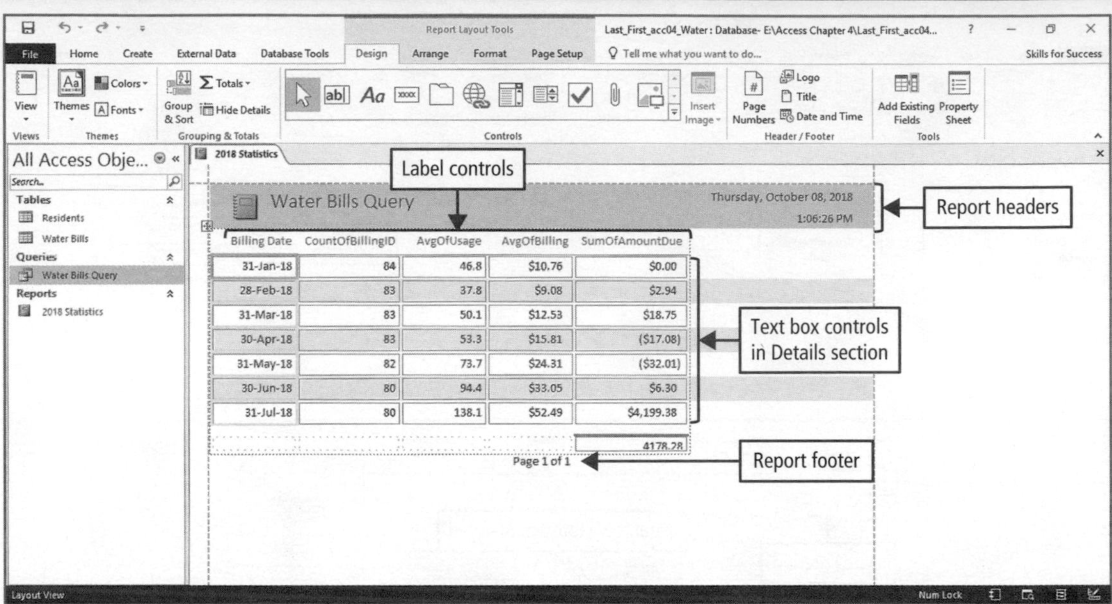

Figure 1 Access 2016, Windows 10, Microsoft Corporation

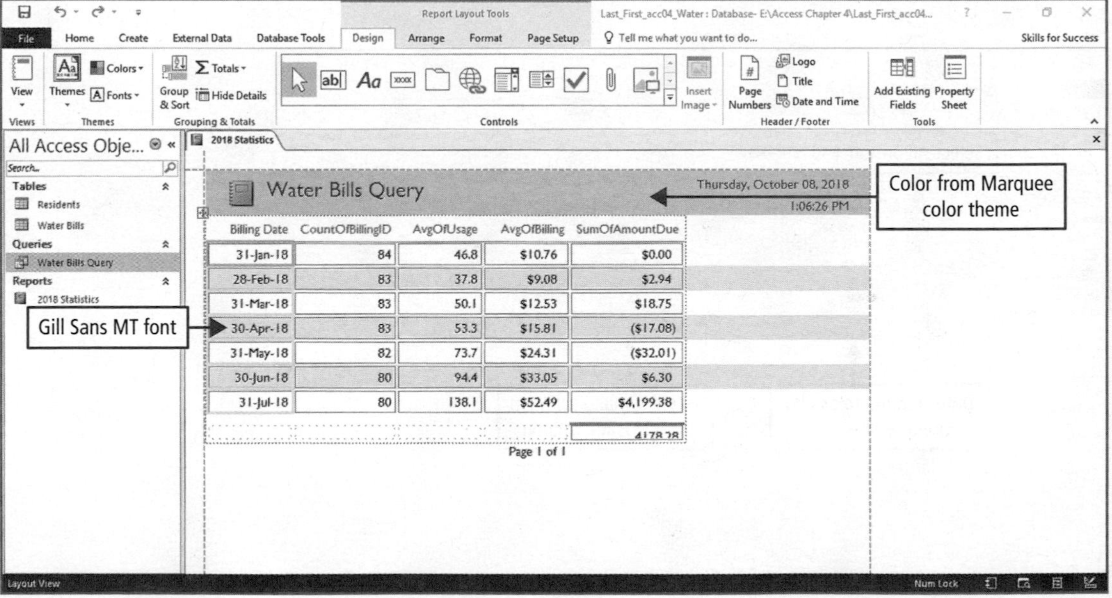

Figure 2 Access 2016, Windows 10, Microsoft Corporation

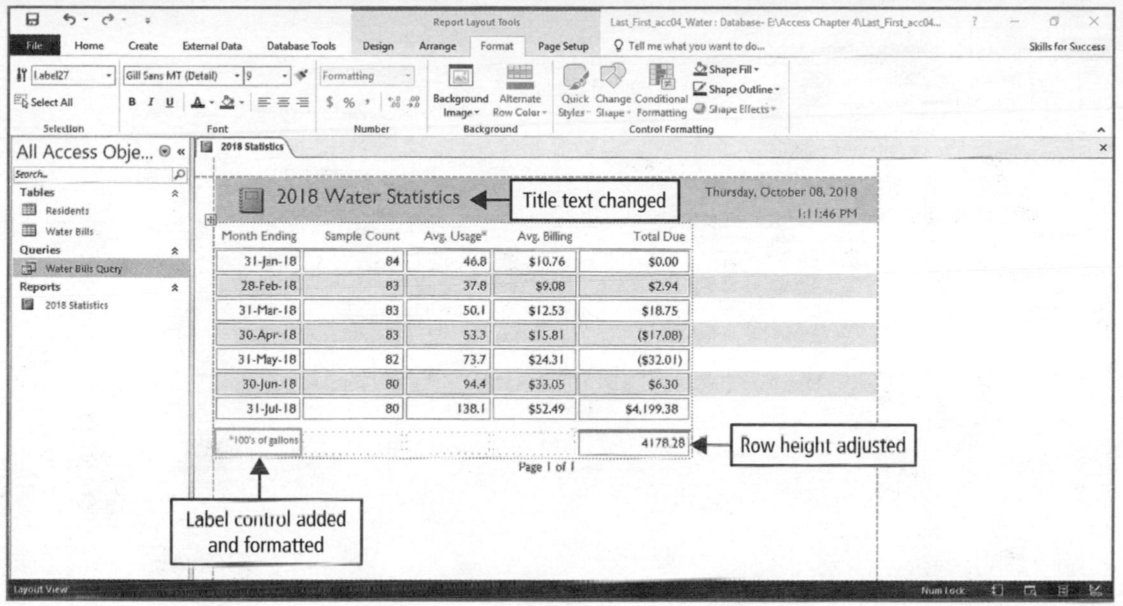

Access 2016, Windows 10, Microsoft Corporation

Figure 3

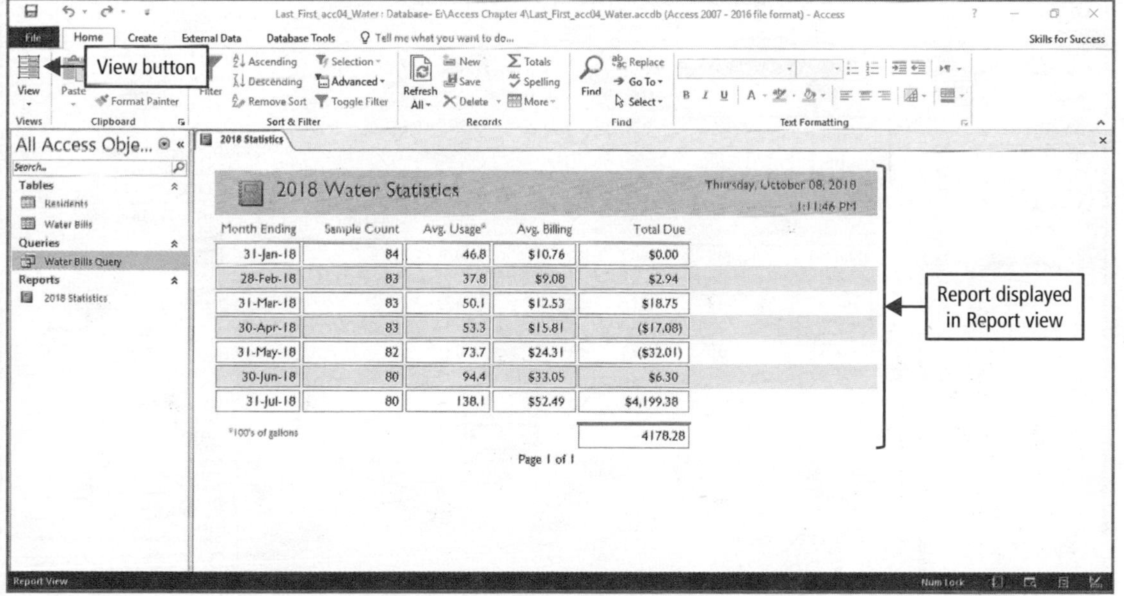

Access 2016, Windows 10, Microsoft Corporation

Figure 4

7. In the report header, double-click the title *Water Bills Query* to enter Edit mode, and then replace the text with 2018 Water Statistics

8. Double-click the **Billing Date** label control, change the label's text to Month Ending and then press Enter. Repeat this technique to change **CountOfBillingID** to Sample Count **AvgOfUsage** to Avg. Usage* **AvgOfBilling** to Avg. Billing and **SumOfAmountDue** to Total Due

Obj 5.2.4

9. Click the last cell—the cell with the value *4178.28*. Point to the cell's lower orange border to display the ↕ pointer, and then double-click to AutoSize the cell's height.

10. Click in the empty cell below the **Month Ending** column, and then type *100's of gallons Press Enter to complete the entry.

11. With the cell **100's of gallons* selected, click the **Format tab**. In the **Font group**, click the **Font Size arrow**, and then click 9. Compare your screen with **Figure 3**.

12. Click the **Home tab**, and then in the **Views group**, click the **View button** to switch to Report view. Alternately, in the status bar, click the Report View button. Compare your screen with **Figure 4**.

    Report view is a view optimized for onscreen viewing of reports.

13. Click **Save**, and then leave the report open for the next skill.

■ **You have completed Skill 2 of 10**

- Report controls can be formatted using the property sheet and the commands on the Format tab.

1. With the **2018 Water Statistics** report open, on the **Home tab**, click the **View** button to switch to Layout view. Alternately, on the status bar, click the Layout View button.

MOS Obj 5.3.7

2. On the **Design tab**, in the **Header / Footer group**, click the **Logo** button. In the **Insert Picture** dialog box, navigate to the student files, select **acc04_WaterLogo**, and then click **OK**.
3. Select the **Title** control, and then on the **Design tab**, in the **Tools group**, click **Property Sheet**.

MOS Obj 5.3.4

4. In the property sheet **Format tab**, change the **Title** control's **Width** to 2.6" In the report header, select the **Date** control, and then in the property sheet, change its **Width** to 2.4" Compare your screen with **Figure 1**.

   The Time control is in the same layout column as the Date control, so the width of both controls can be adjusted at the same time.

5. With the **Date** control still selected, click the Ribbon's **Format tab**. Change the **Font size** to **9**, and then apply **Italic**.
6. In the **Font group**, click the **Format Painter** button, and then with the pointer, click the **Time** control to apply the formatting from the previous step. Compare your screen with **Figure 2**.

■ Continue to the next page to complete the skill

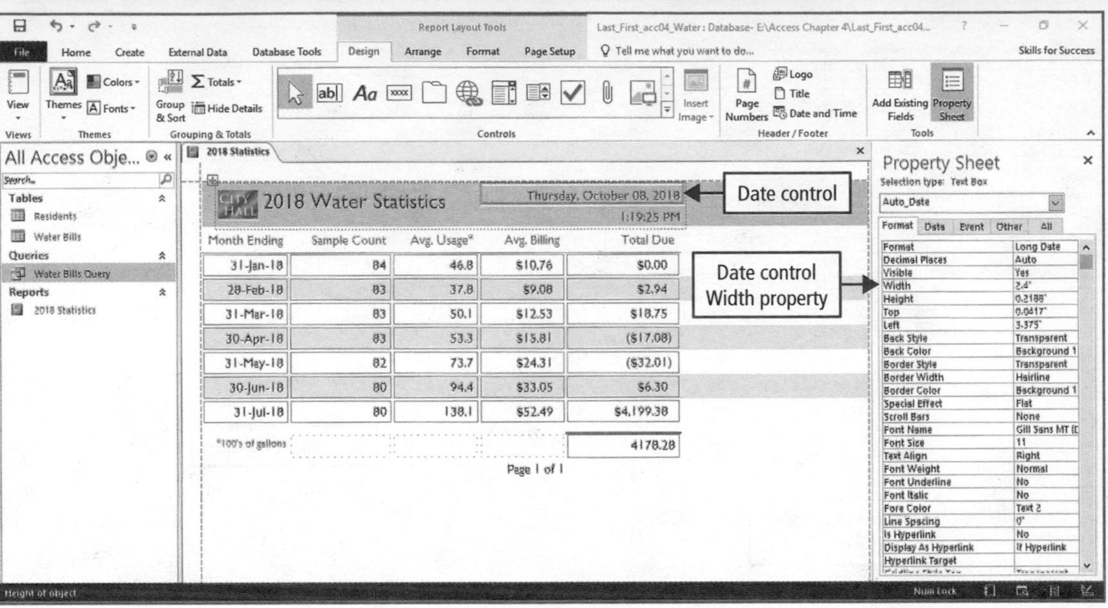

Figure 1

Access 2016, Windows 10, Microsoft Corporation

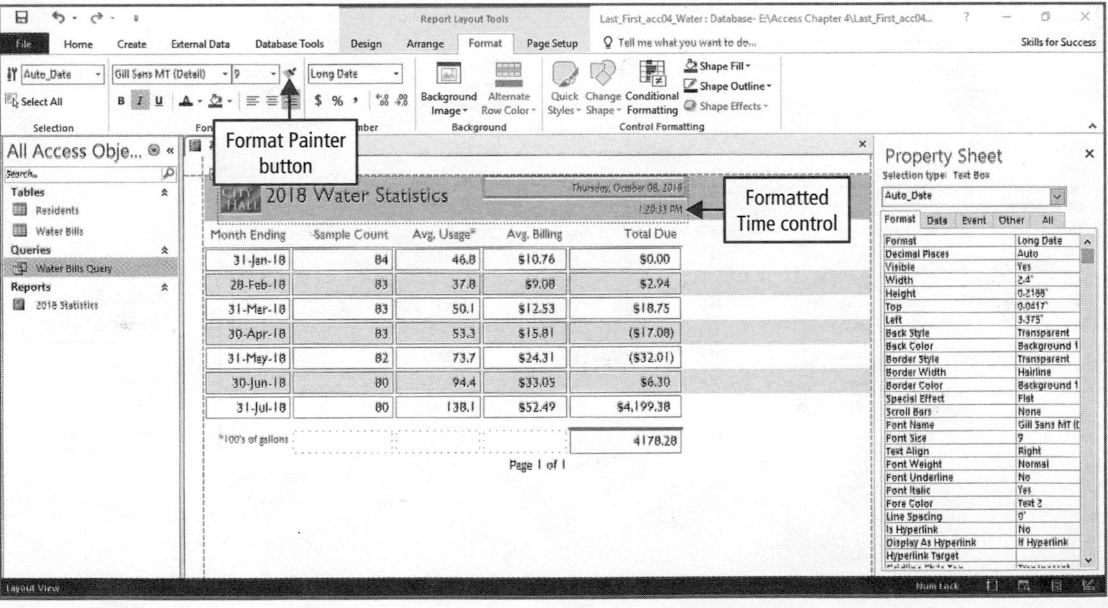

Figure 2

Access 2016, Windows 10, Microsoft Corporation

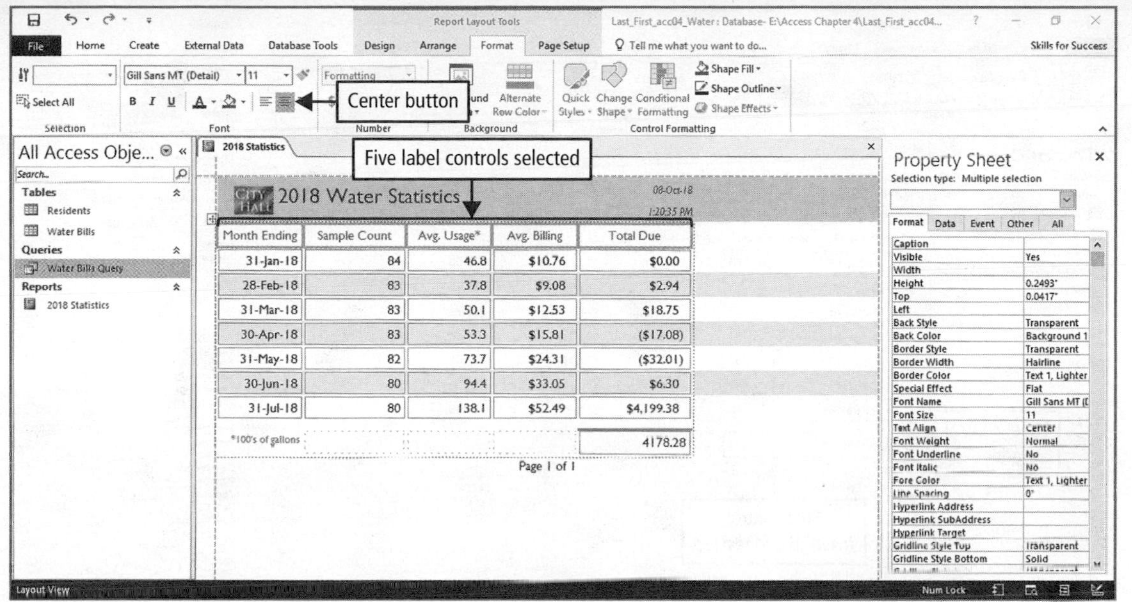

Access 2016, Windows 10, Microsoft Corporation

Figure 3

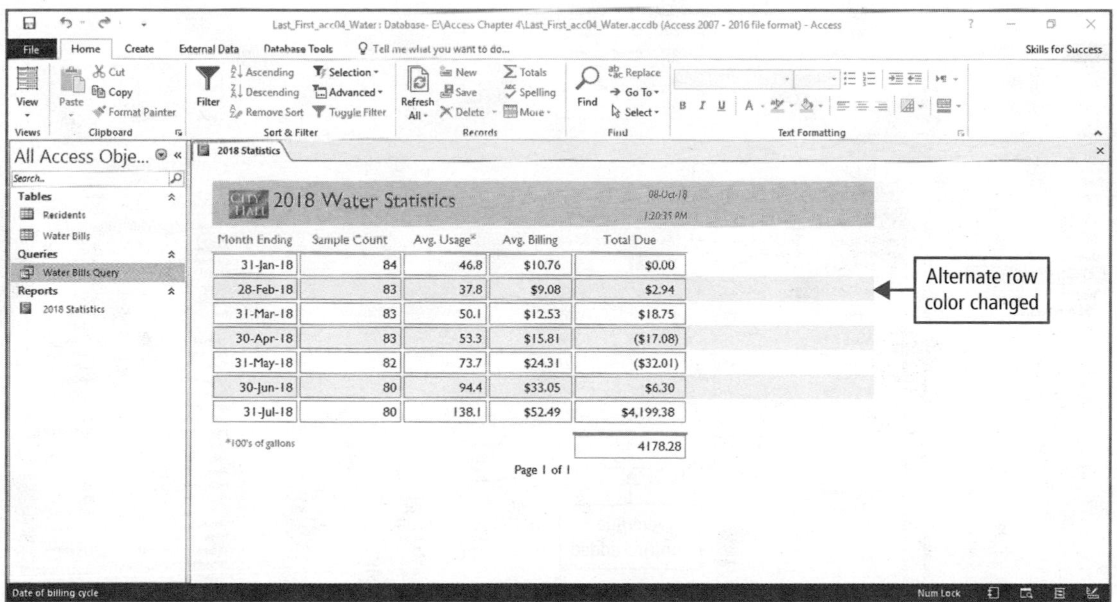

Access 2016, Windows 10, Microsoft Corporation

Figure 4

7. With the **Date** control still selected, on the Ribbon's **Format tab**, in the **Number group**, click the **Number Format arrow**, and then click **Medium Date**. Select the **Time** control, and then if necessary, change the **Number Format** to **Long Time**.
8. Above the first column, click the label control with the text *Month Ending*. Press and hold Shift while clicking the four other labels. Be careful not to move the mouse while clicking the left button.
9. With the five labels selected, on the **Format tab**, in the **Font group**, click the **Center** button. Compare your screen with **Figure 3**.
10. On the **Format tab**, in the **Selection group**, click the **Selection arrow**, and then click **Detail**. On the **Format tab**, in the **Background group**, click the **Alternate Row Color arrow**, and then in the color gallery's second row, click the sixth color—**Green, Accent 2, Lighter 80%**.

    To change the color of banded rows, you need to select the ***Detail control***—the area of a report that repeats for each record in the table or query.

11. On the status bar, click the **Report View** button, and then compare your screen with **Figure 4**.
12. Click **Save**, and then leave the report open for the next skill.

■ **You have completed Skill 3 of 10**

► You can add ***summary statistics***—calculations for groups of data such as totals, averages, and counts—to report columns.

1. With the **2018 Water Statistics** report still open, switch to Layout view.
2. In the report's last row, click in a blank cell, and then click the **Arrange tab**. In the **Rows & Columns group**, click the **Insert Above** button two times to insert two blank rows.
3. Click in the first cell of the upper blank row just inserted, and then type Total Sample
4. Click a number in the **Sample Count** column to make it active, and then click the **Design tab**. In the **Grouping & Totals group**, click the **Totals** button, and then click **Sum** to add a total for the active column.

MOS Obj 5.3.2

5. Click the **Sum** control just inserted, point to its lower border, and then double-click with the pointer to AutoFit the row's height. Compare your screen with **Figure 1**.
6. Click a number in the **Avg. Usage** column to make it active. On the **Design tab**, in the **Grouping & Totals group**, click the **Totals** button, and then click **Average**. Repeat this technique to add an average for the **Avg. Billing** column. Compare your screen with **Figure 2.**

■ Continue to the next page to complete the skill

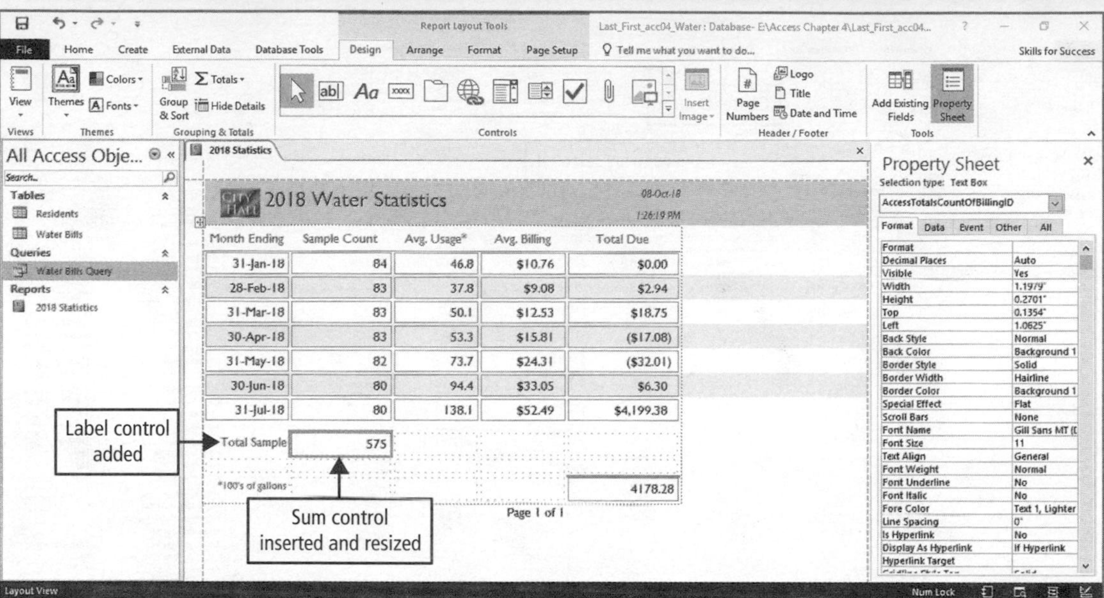

Figure 1 Access 2016, Windows 10, Microsoft Corporation

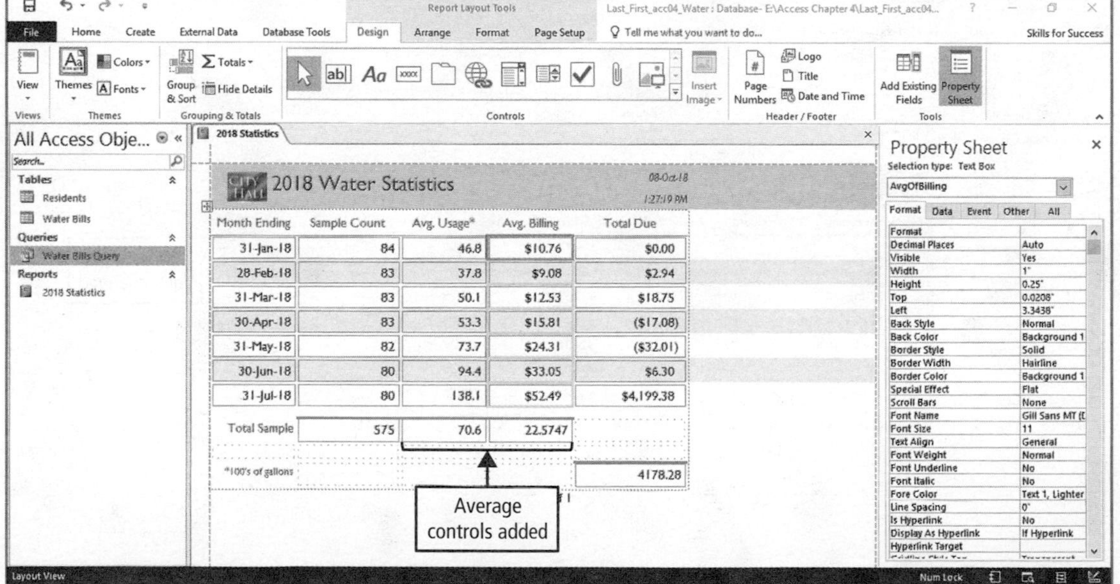

Figure 2 Access 2016, Windows 10, Microsoft Corporation

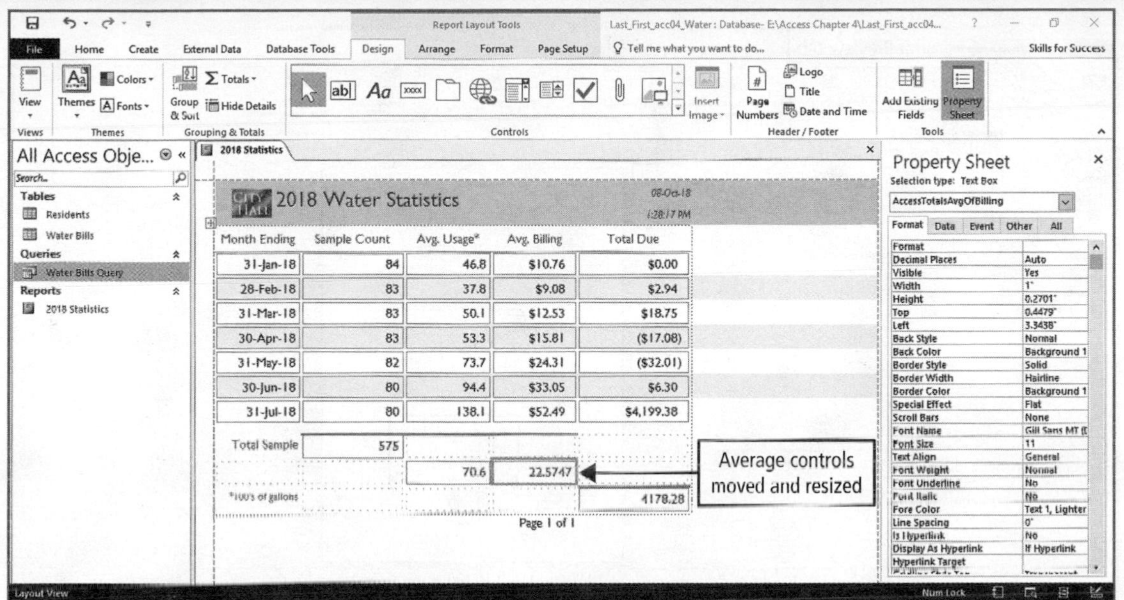

Access 2016, Windows 10, Microsoft Corporation

Figure 3

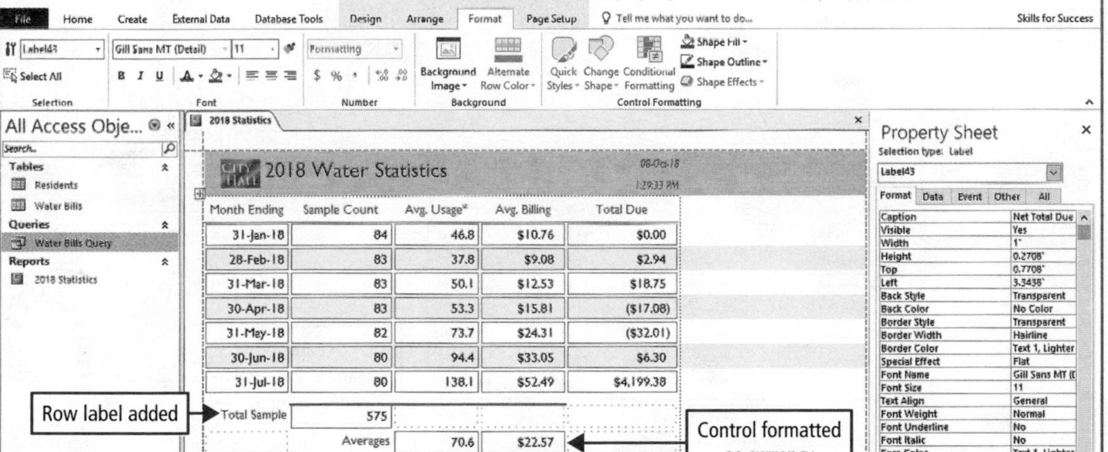

Access 2016, Windows 10, Microsoft Corporation

Figure 4

7. Point to the middle of the cell with the **Avg. Usage** column **Average** control—*70.6*. With the [+] pointer, drag the control down one cell. Repeat to move the **Average** control of the **Avg. Billing** column down one cell.
8. Point to the lower border of the selected Average control, and then double-click with the [↕] pointer to AutoFit the row's height. Compare your screen with **Figure 3**.
9. With the **Avg. Billing** column **Average** control still selected, click the Ribbon's **Format tab**, and then in in the **Number group**, click the **Apply Currency Format** button [$].
10. Click in the blank cell below the **Sample Count** column **Sum** control, and then type Averages
11. Click in the blank cell below the **Avg. Billing** column **Average** control, and then type Net Total Due Press [Enter]. Compare your screen with **Figure 4**.
12. Click **Save** [💾], and then leave the report open for the next skill.

- **You have completed Skill 4 of 10**

- It is good practice to preview reports before printing them to see if they need any formatting adjustments.

1. With the **2018 Water Statistics** report still open, click the **Home tab**. In the **Views group**, click the **View arrow**, and then click **Print Preview**. If the entire page does not display, in the Zoom group, click the One Page button. Compare your screen with **Figure 1**.

   In Print Preview view, the Print Preview tab is the only Ribbon tab, and the report displays as it will print on paper. Here, the page number footer—*Page 1 of 1*—displays at the bottom of the printed page.

2. In the **Close Preview group**, click the **Close Print Preview** button to return to Layout view. If your report displays in a different view, on the status bar, click the Layout View button.
3. Click the **Format tab**. In the **Selection group**, click the **Selection arrow**, and then click **Report** to select the report and display its properties in the property sheet. If necessary, open the property sheet.
4. Near the middle of the property sheet **Format tab**, double-click the **Fit to Page** box to change the value to **No**. Change the **Width** property to 5.8" Press Enter, and then compare your screen with **Figure 2**.

   By default, a report is set to the width of a printed sheet of paper. By removing this setting, you can decrease the width of the report to fit the contents.

■ **Continue to the next page to complete the skill**

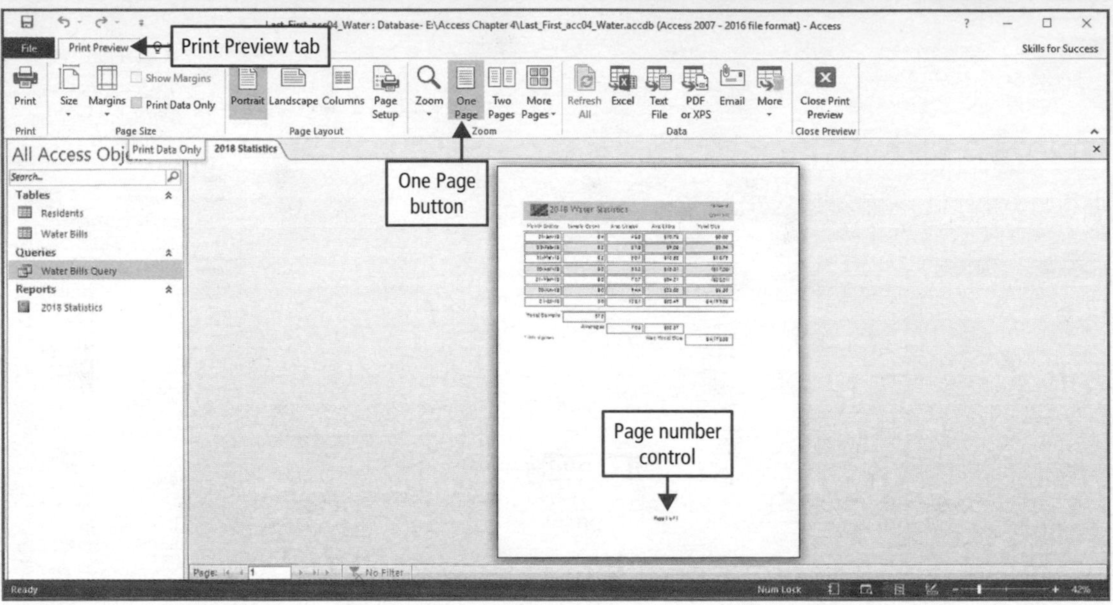

Figure 1 Access 2016, Windows 10, Microsoft Corporation

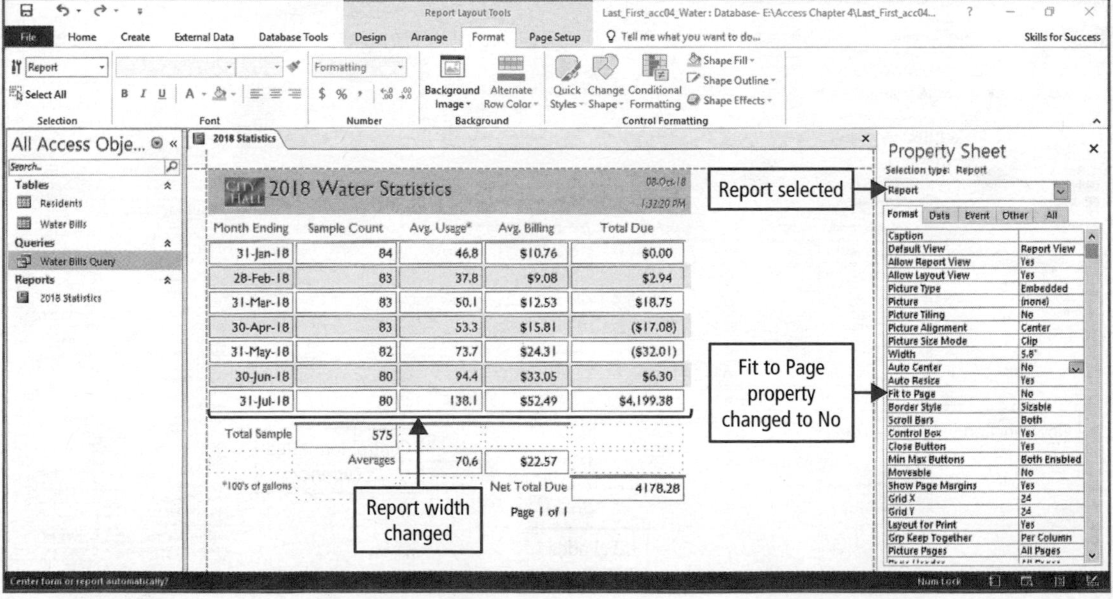

Figure 2 Access 2016, Windows 10, Microsoft Corporation

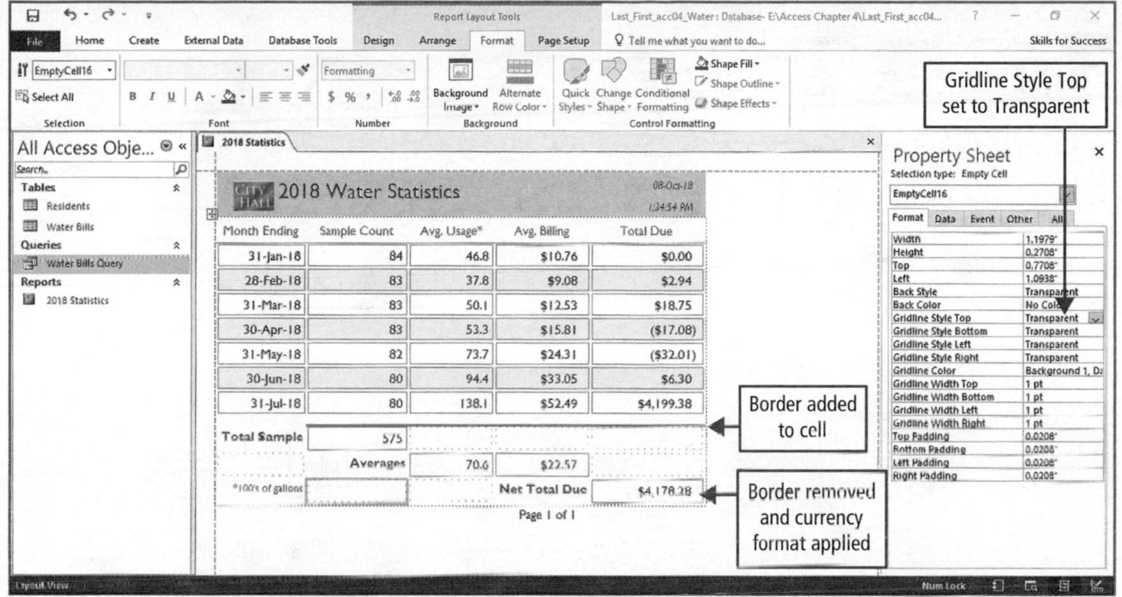

Access 2016, Windows 10, Microsoft Corporation

Figure 3

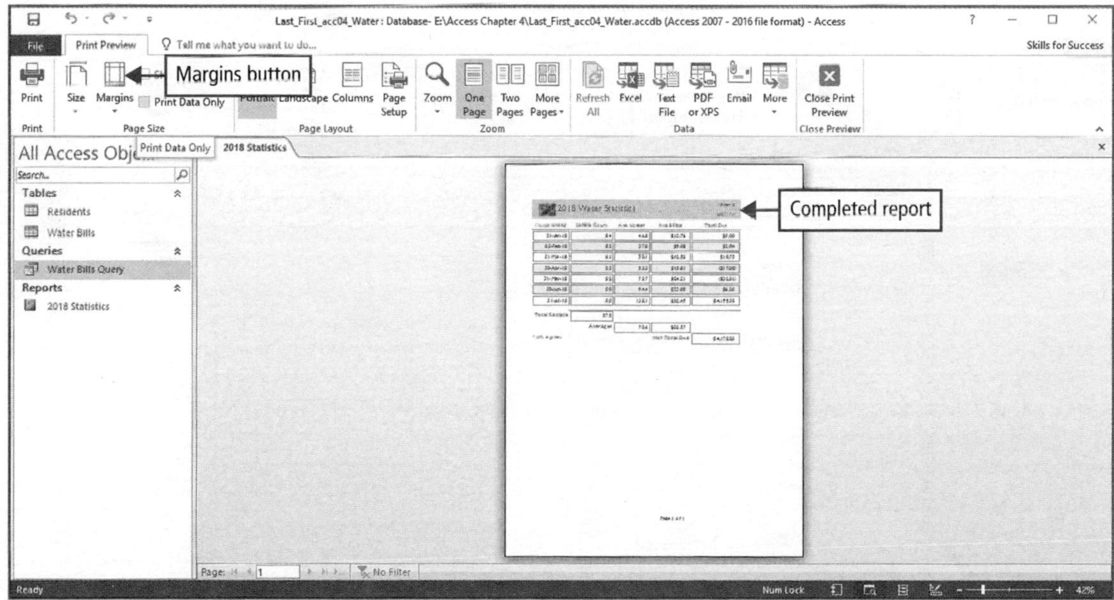

Access 2016, Windows 10, Microsoft Corporation

Figure 4

5. Below the **Month Ending** column, select the label with the text *Total Sample*. On the **Format tab**, in the **Font group**, click **Bold** [B], and then click **Align Right** [≡]. Double-click **Format Painter**, and then click the *Averages* and *Net Total Due* labels to apply the same formatting. Click the **Format Painter** button so that it is no longer active.
6. Click the *Net Total Due* label control, point to its right border, and then with the [↔] pointer, double-click to AutoFit the column width.
7. Click in the first empty cell below *$4,199.38*. On the property sheet **Format tab**, double-click **Gridline Style Top** to change its value to **Solid**. Double-click **Gridline Width Top** to change its value to **2 pt**.
8. Click in the last cell—*$4,178.28*. On the property sheet **Format tab**, click **Gridline Style Top** one time, click the displayed **arrow**, and then click **Transparent**. On the **Format tab**, in the **Number group**, click **Apply Currency Format** [$]. Click in a blank cell in the report, and then compare your screen with **Figure 3**.
9. **Close** [X] the property sheet. On the status bar, click the **Print Preview** button.
10. In the **Page Size group**, click the **Margins** button, and then click **Wide**. Click the **One Page** button. Compare your screen with **Figure 4**.

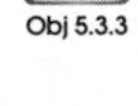

MOS Obj 5.3.3

11. If you are printing this project, click **Print**, and then use the **Print** dialog box to print the report.

MOS Obj 1.5.1

12. Click **Save**, and then **Close** [X] the report.

■ **You have completed Skill 5 of 10**

SKILL 6: Create Reports with the Blank Report Tool

► The Blank Report tool is used to build a report by adding fields one at a time.

1. On the **Create tab**, in the **Reports group**, click the **Blank Report** button.

2. In the **Field List** pane, click **Show all tables**. In the **Field List**, to the left of **Residents**, click the **Expand** button ⊞.

Obj 5.2.3

3. In the **Field List**, double-click **AccountNumber** to add the field to the report. Compare your screen with **Figure 1**.

   As you add fields with the Blank Report tool, the other tables move to the lower sections of the Field List pane. Here, the Water Bills table is a related table because it contains the AccountNumber as a foreign key.

Obj 5.2.4

4. In the **Field List**, double-click **LastName** and **FirstName** to add them to the report.

5. In the **Field List**, under **Fields available in related tables**, **Expand** ⊞ the **Water Bills** table.

6. Double-click **BillingDate**, and then compare your screen with **Figure 2**.

   When you add a field from another table, that table moves to the upper pane of the Field List.

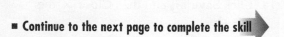

■ **Continue to the next page to complete the skill**

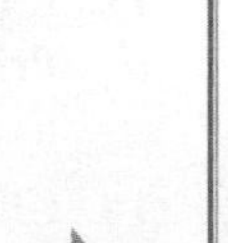

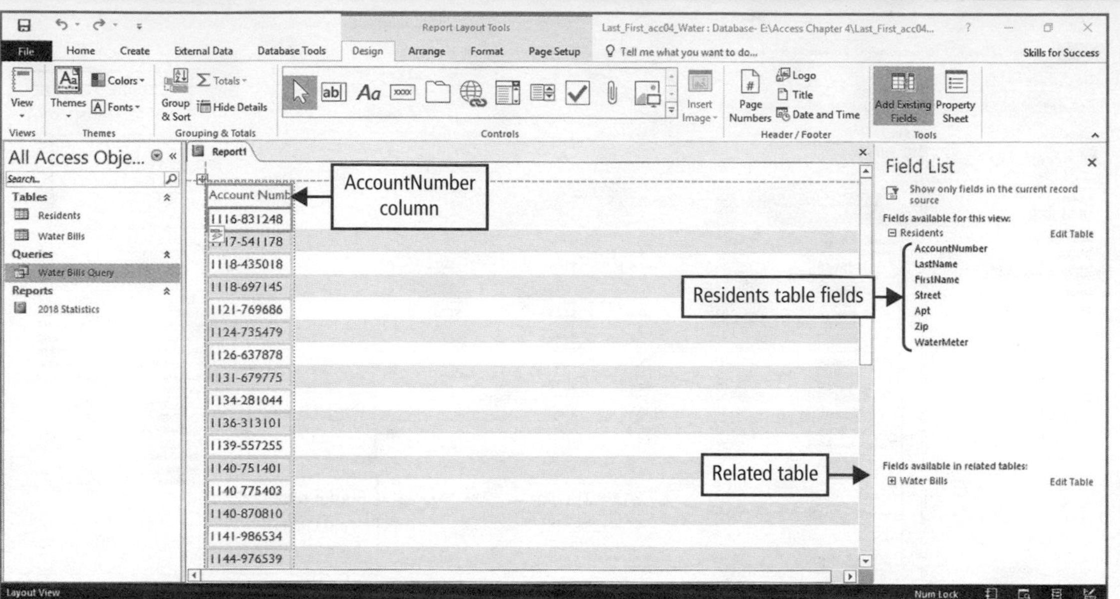

Figure 1

Access 2016, Windows 10, Microsoft Corporation

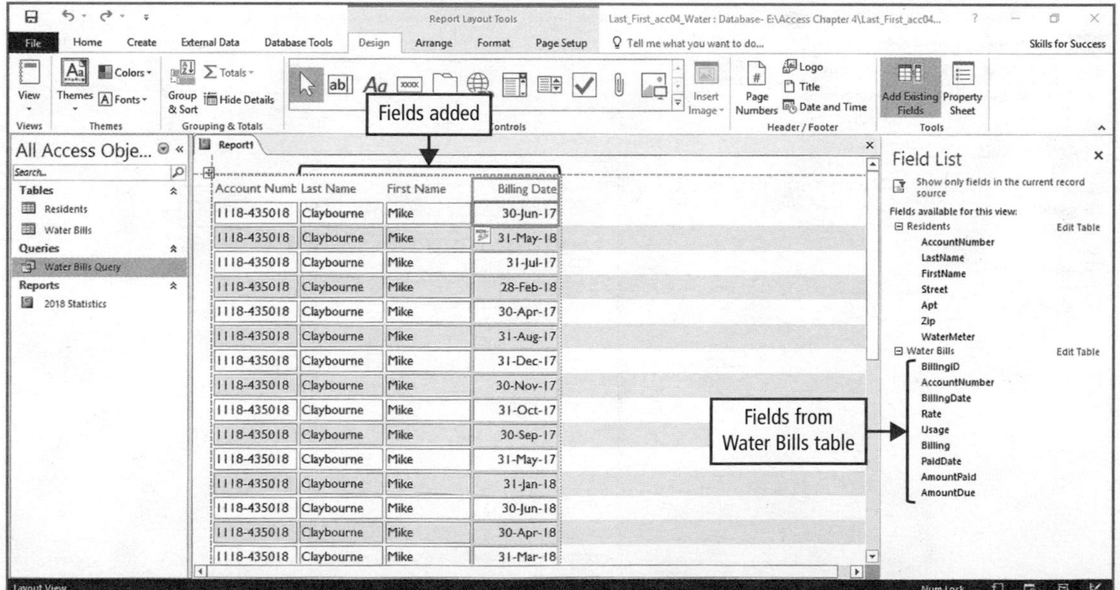

Figure 2

Access 2016, Windows 10, Microsoft Corporation

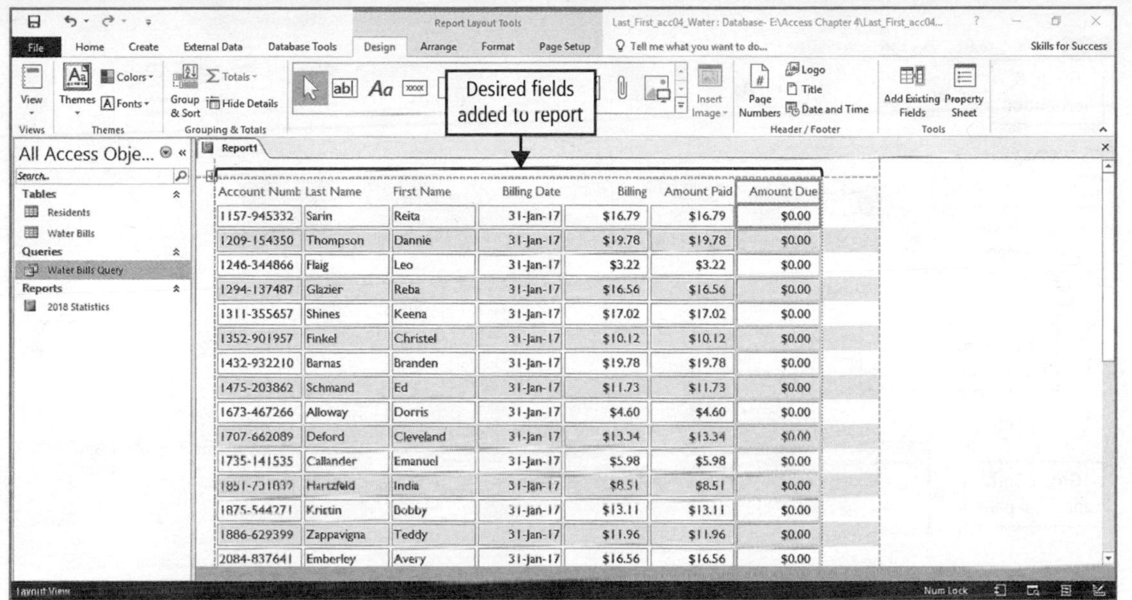

Access 2016, Windows 10, Microsoft Corporation

Figure 3

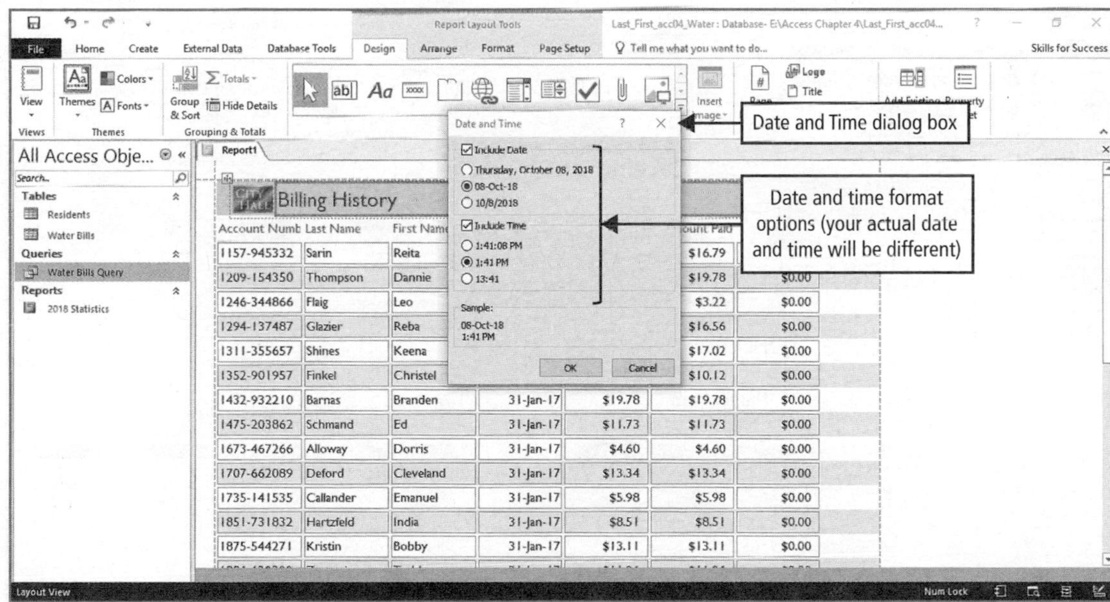

Access 2016, Windows 10, Microsoft Corporation

Figure 4

7. In the **Field List**, under **Water Bills**, double-click **Billing**, **AmountPaid**, and **AmountDue** to add the three fields to the report.
8. **Close** [X] the Field List pane, and then compare your screen with **Figure 3**.
9. On the **Design tab**, in the **Header / Footer group**, click the **Logo** button. In the **Insert Picture** dialog box, navigate to the student files, select **acc04_WaterLogo**, and then click **OK** to create a report header and insert the logo.
10. In the **Header / Footer group**, click the **Title** button, type Billing History and then press Enter.

Obj 5.3.6

11. In the **Header / Footer group**, click the **Date and Time** button. In the **Date and Time** dialog box, under **Include Date**, select the middle option button—**dd-mmm-yy**. Under **Include Time**, click the middle option button—**hh:mm PM**. Compare your screen with **Figure 4**, and then click **OK**.

Obj 5.3.6

12. Click **Save** [Save]. In the **Save As** dialog box, type Billing History Report and then press Enter. Leave the report open for the next skill.

■ **You have completed Skill 6 of 10**

 WATCH SKILL 4.7

- Report data can be grouped and sorted to make the report information more useful.
- Reports created with the Blank Report tool lay out controls in a table. You can position controls by dragging them into other cells, and you can format text controls by selecting the cell's location.

1. If necessary, open the *Billing History Report* in Layout view. On the **Design tab**, in the **Grouping & Totals group**, click the **Group & Sort** button as needed to display the **Group, Sort, and Total** pane.

Obj 5.2.1

2. In the **Group, Sort, and Total** pane, click the **Add a group** button. In the list of fields, click **AccountNumber** to group the billings within each account.
3. In the report, click **Account Number** to select the label. Point to the right border, and then with the [↕] pointer, double-click to AutoFit the label width. Compare your screen with **Figure 1**.
4. Click the first text box control with the text *Claybourne*, and then, with the [move] pointer, drag the control into the empty cell below the *Last Name* label.
5. Repeat this technique to move the control with the text *Mike* into the empty cell below the *First Name* label. Compare your screen with **Figure 2**.

   The resident names do not change within each group of account numbers, so they can be in the same row as the Account Number. As a result, the names are not repeated in each billing row.

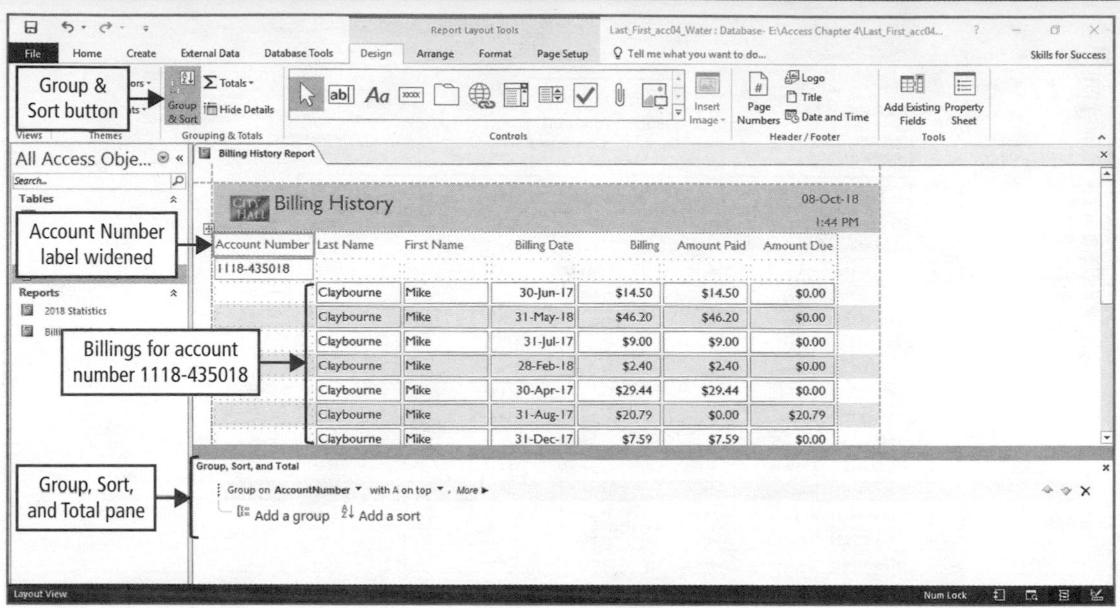

Figure 1 Access 2016, Windows 10, Microsoft Corporation

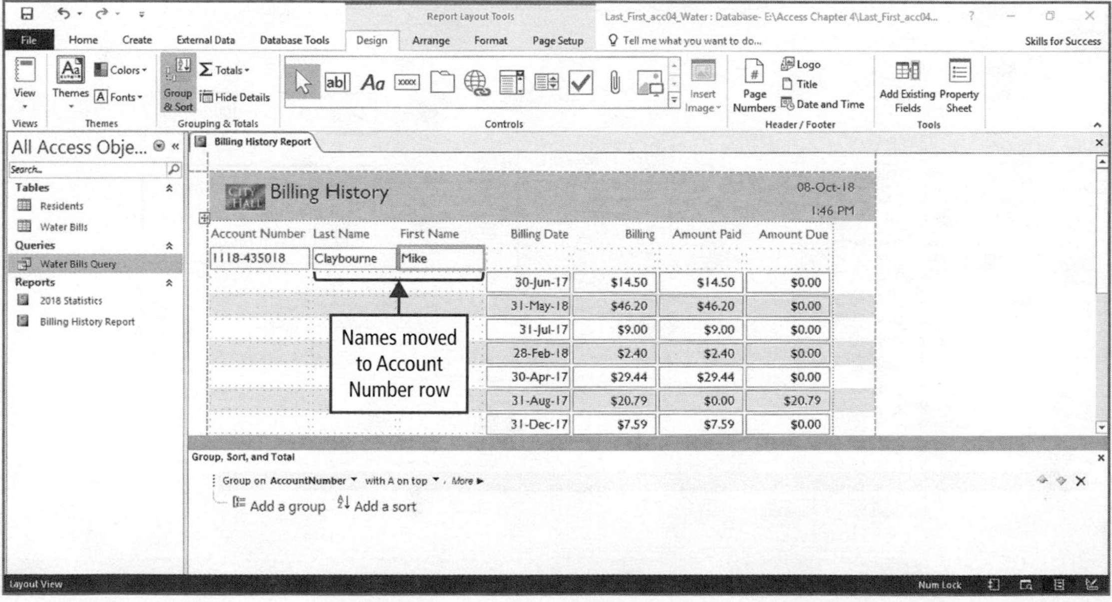

Figure 2 Access 2016, Windows 10, Microsoft Corporation

■ Continue to the next page to complete the skill

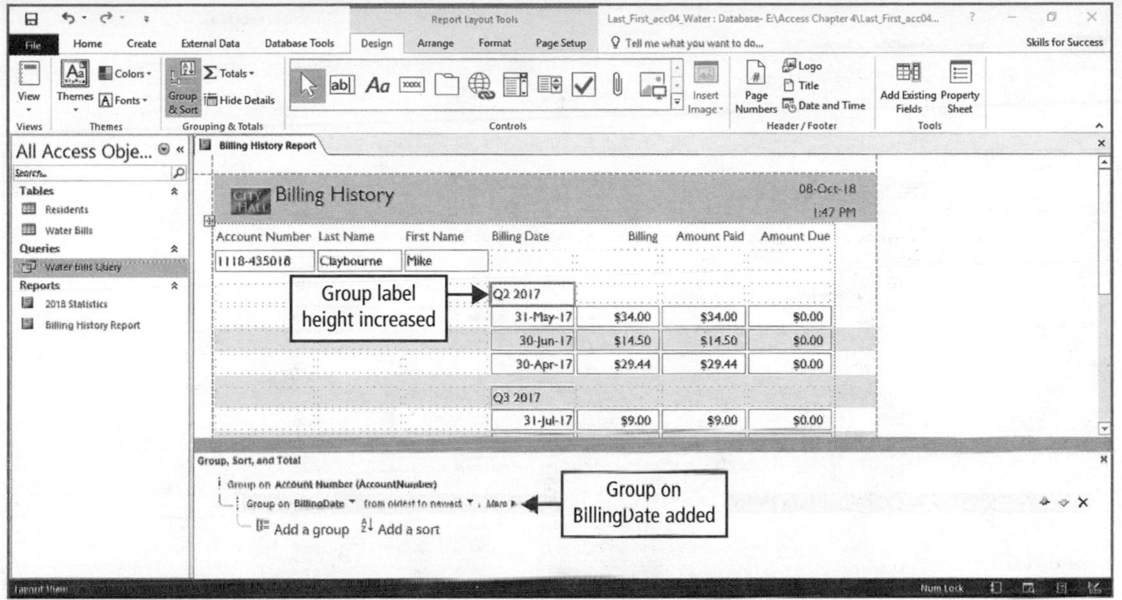

Access 2016, Windows 10, Microsoft Corporation

Figure 3

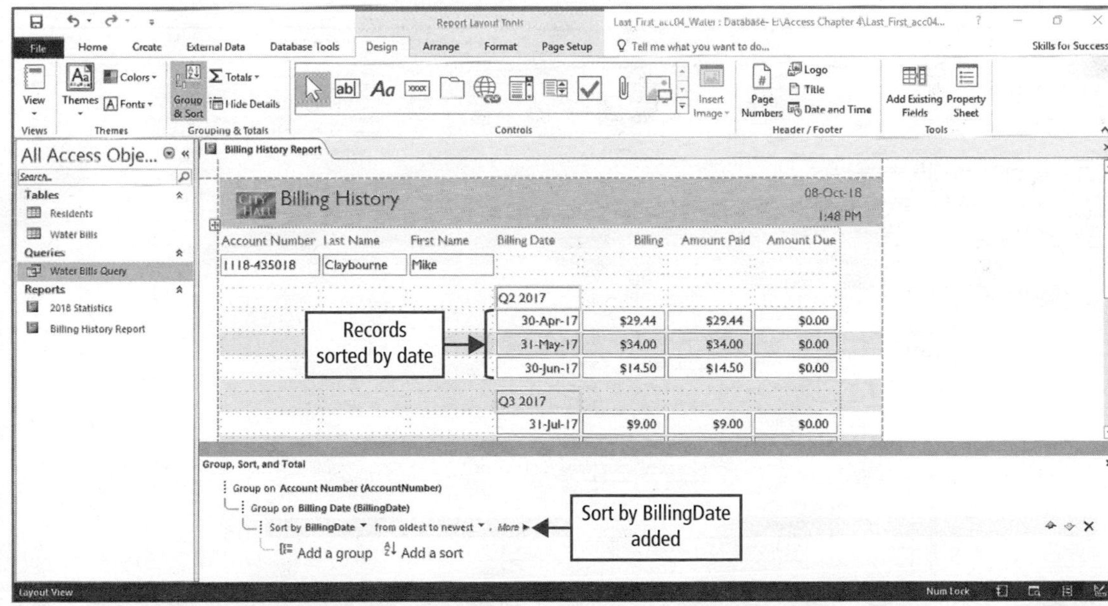

Access 2016, Windows 10, Microsoft Corporation

Figure 4

6. In the **Group, Sort, and Total** pane, click the **Add a group** button, and then in the list of fields, click **BillingDate** to group the Billing Cycles by quarter.

7. Click the first quarter label with the text *Q2 2017*. Point to the lower border, and then with the [pointer] pointer, double-click to AutoFit the row height. Compare your screen with **Figure 3**.

   Fields that contain dates can be grouped by several time intervals including days, months, quarters, and years. By default, they are grouped into yearly quarters with the oldest quarters displayed first.

8. In the **Group, Sort, and Total** pane, click the **Add a sort** button, and then in the list of fields, click **BillingDate** to sort by month within each yearly quarter. Compare your screen with **Figure 4**.

Obj 5.2.1

9. On the **Design tab**, in the **Grouping & Totals group**, click the **Group & Sort** button to close the pane.

10. **Save** [Save] the report, and then leave it open for the next skill.

■ **You have completed Skill 7 of 10**

SKILL 8: Modify Report Layouts

WATCH SKILL 4.8

- In a tabular layout, you can insert and delete rows and columns and then move controls so that they better communicate the report's information.

1. If necessary, open the *Billing History Report* in Layout view. Point to the cell with the text *Q2 2017*. With the [move] pointer, drag the control into the first empty cell below the cell with the text *Claybourne*.
2. Click in the first **Billing Date** cell with the text *30-Apr-17*. Press and hold Shift while clicking the **Amount Due** cell in the same row. Compare your screen with **Figure 1**.

Obj 5.3.1

3. With the four cells selected, point to the cell with the text *30-Apr-17*, and then drag the cell into the empty cell below the **Q2 2017** control. Compare your screen with **Figure 2**.
4. Below the report header, click the **Billing Date** label, and then press Delete to remove the label from the report.
5. Repeat the techniques practiced in this skill to move the **Billing** label to the empty cell to the right of the **Q2 2017** control.
6. Move the **Amount Paid** label to the empty cell to the right of the **Billing** label.

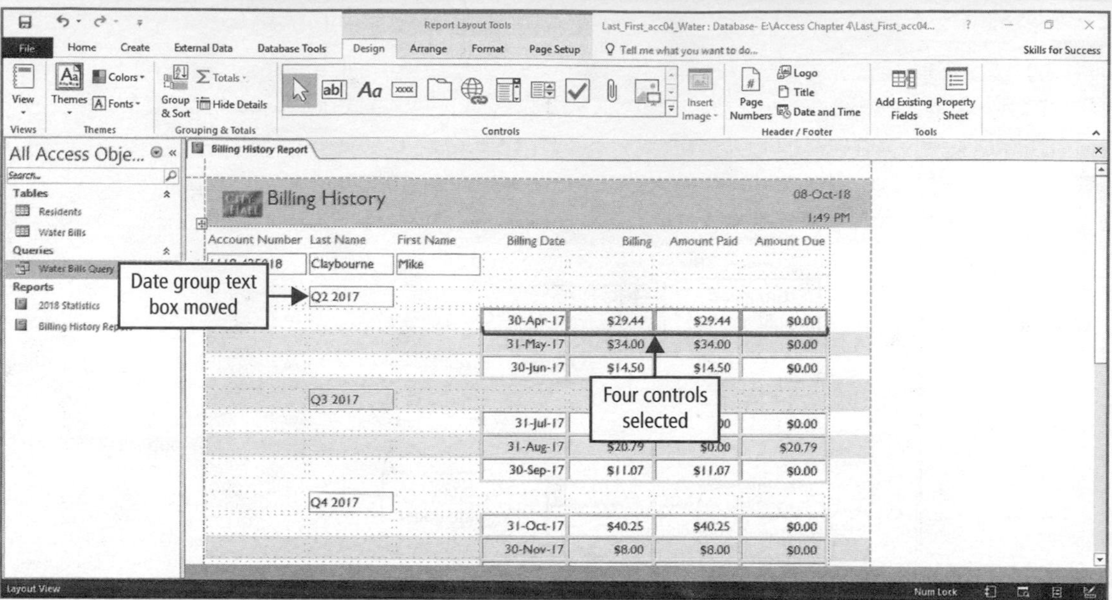

Figure 1

Access 2016, Windows 10, Microsoft Corporation

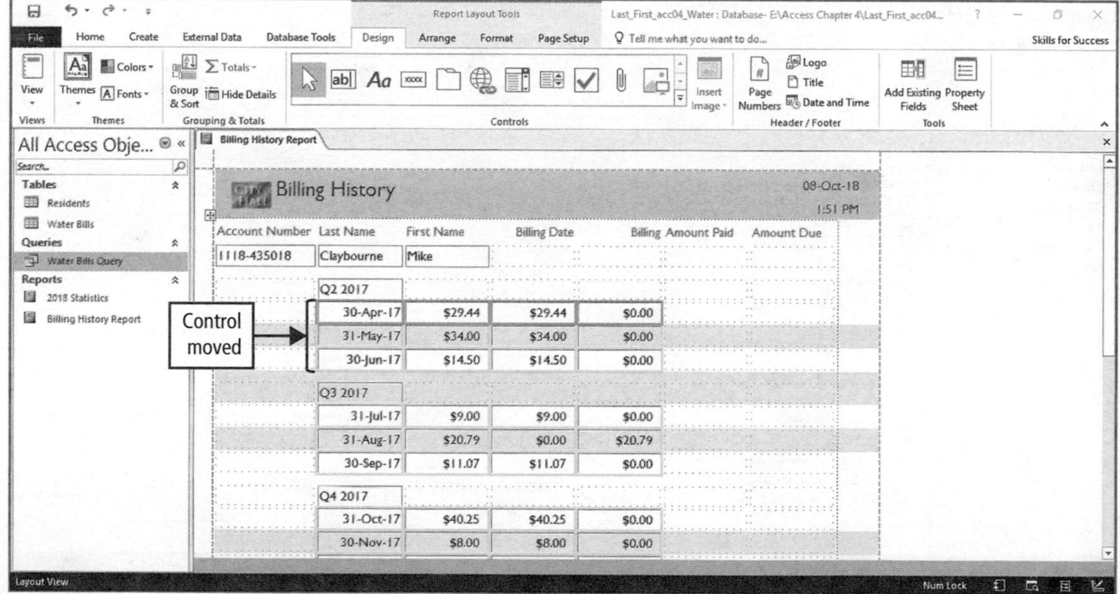

Figure 2

Access 2016, Windows 10, Microsoft Corporation

■ Continue to the next page to complete the skill

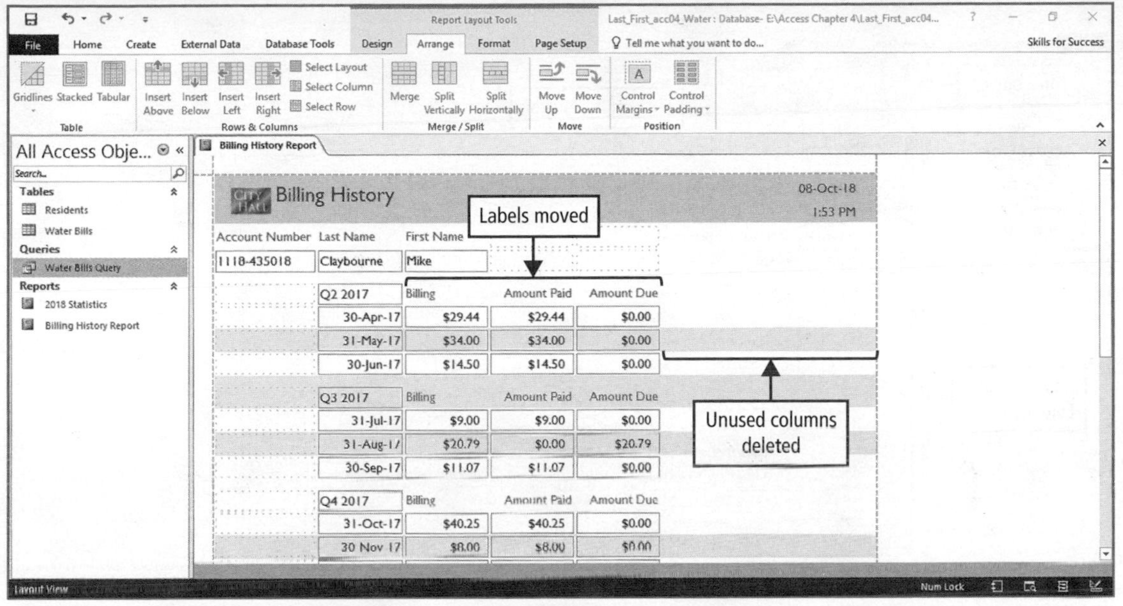

Access 2016, Windows 10, Microsoft Corporation

Figure 3

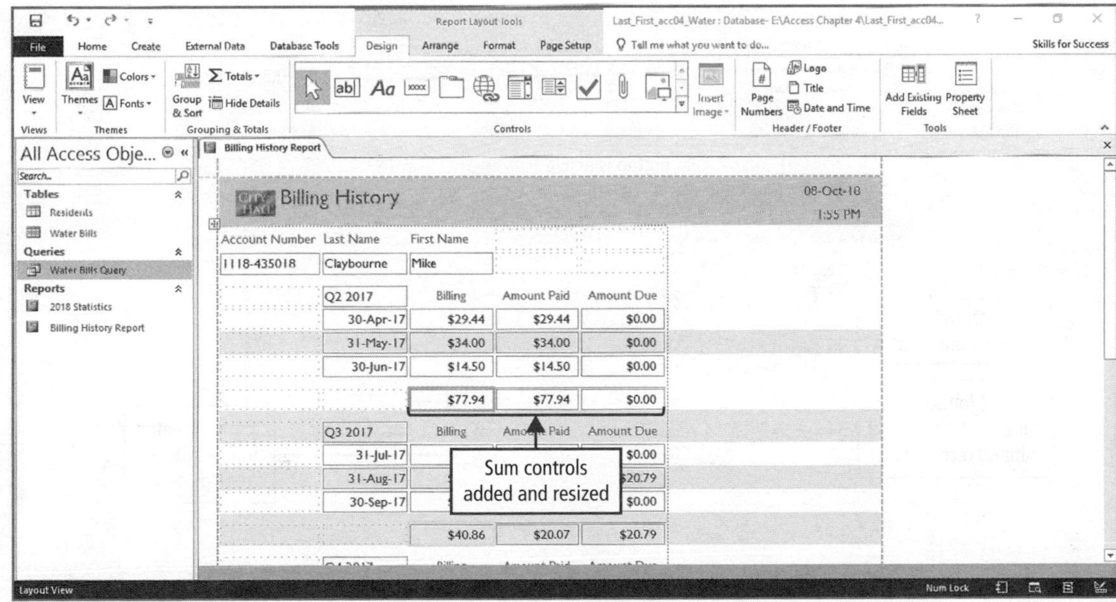

Access 2016, Windows 10, Microsoft Corporation

Figure 4

7. Move the **Amount Due** label to the empty cell to the right of the **Amount Paid** label.
8. Click in one of the blank columns on the right side of the report. Click the **Arrange tab**, and then in the **Rows & Columns group**, click **Select Column**. Press Delete to remove the column from the report. Repeat to this technique to delete the other blank column, and then compare your screen with **Figure 3**.
9. Use the Shift-click technique to select these labels: **Billing**, **Amount Paid**, and **Amount Due**. Click the **Format tab**, and then in the **Font group**, click the **Center** button.
10. Click in any cell below the **Billing** label to make the column active. Click the **Design tab**. In the **Grouping & Totals group**, click the **Totals** button, and then click **Sum** to add a summary statistic for each quarter.
11. Repeat the technique just practiced to insert the **Sum** total to the **Amount Paid** and **Amount Due** columns.
12. Click one of the cells with a Sum control that was inserted in the previous step. Point to the lower border, and then with the pointer, double-click to AutoFit the row's height. Compare your screen with **Figure 4**.
13. Click **Save**, and then leave the report open for the next skill.

■ **You have completed Skill 8 of 10**

► Reports can be filtered in a variety of ways so that you can view just the information you need.

1. With the **Billing Report** open in Layout view, switch to Report view.
2. Click in the text box with the last name *Claybourne*. Click the **Home tab**. In the **Sort & Filter group**, click the **Filter** button. In the **Filter** list, point to **Text Filters**, and then click **Equals**.
3. In the **Custom Filter** dialog box, type swickard and then click **OK**. Compare your screen with **Figure 1**.

   When you apply a filter, only the subset of records that match the filter criteria display and the Toggle Filter button is active. Here, only the billing history for Evie Swickard displays.

4. In the report, click in a control that displays a **Billing Date** value. On the **Home tab**, in the **Sort & Filter group**, click the **Filter** button. In the **Filter** list, point to **Date Filters**, and then click **Between**.
5. In the **Between Dates** dialog box, in the **Oldest** box, type 7/1/17 In the **Newest** box, type 9/30/17 Click **OK**, and then compare your screen with **Figure 2**.

   When you add filters, the previous filters remain in effect. Here, only the records for Evie Swickard in the third quarter of 2017 display. At the end of this report, three rows of totals display: one for the quarter, the account number, and the entire report.

■ **Continue to the next page to complete the skill**

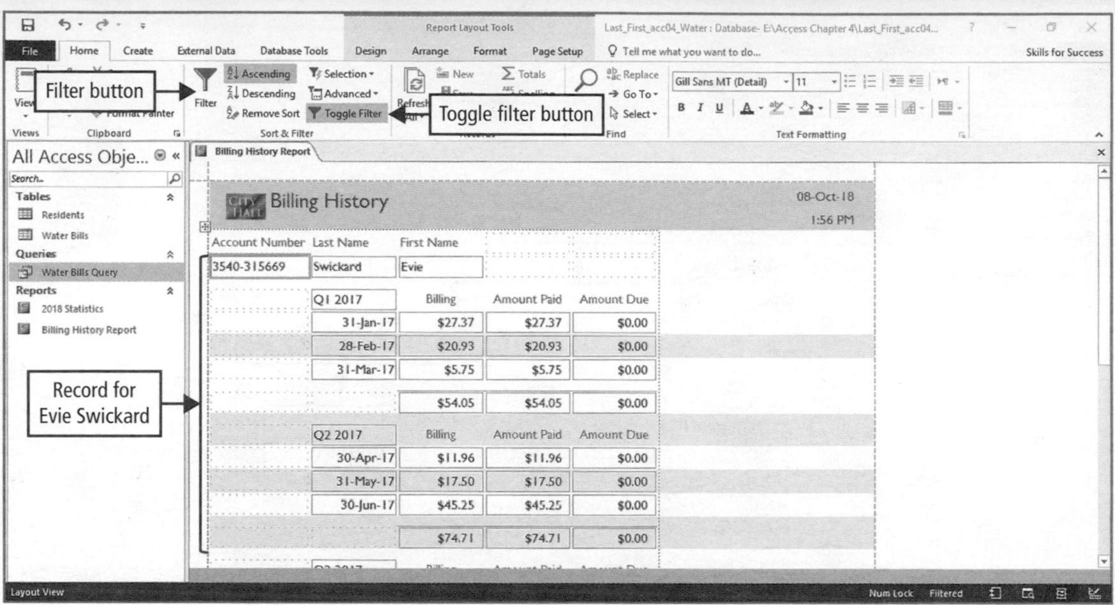

Figure 1

Access 2016, Windows 10, Microsoft Corporation

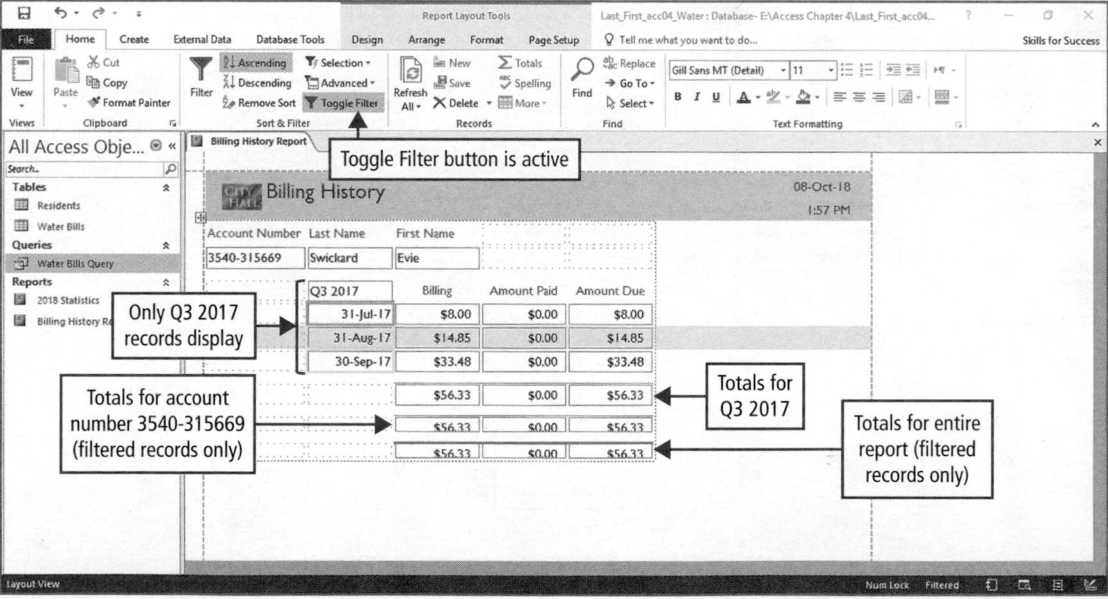

Figure 2

Access 2016, Windows 10, Microsoft Corporation

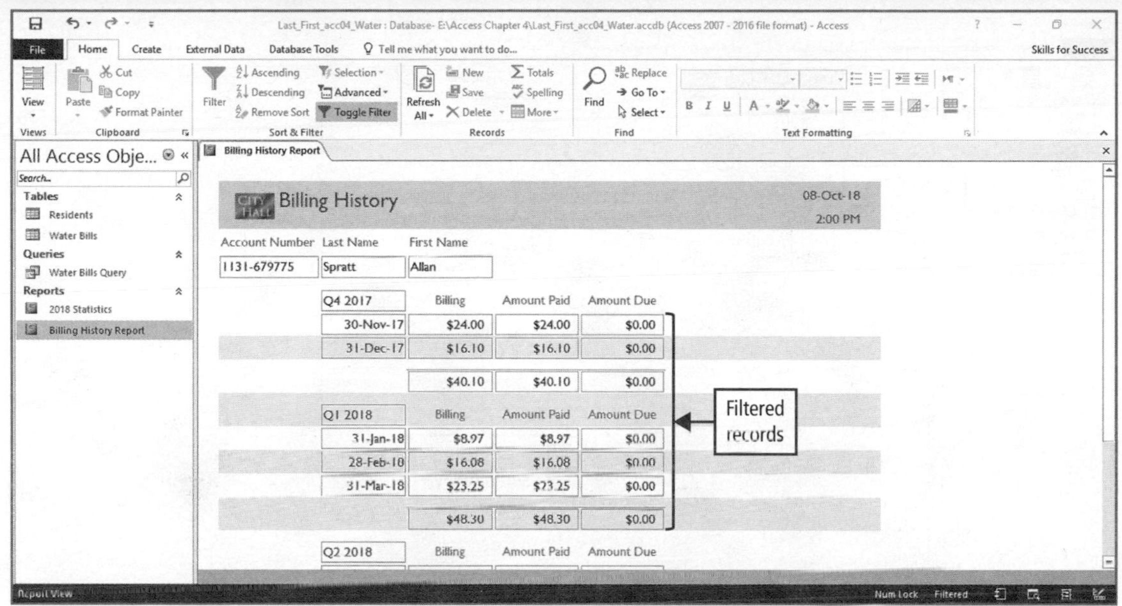

Access 2016, Windows 10, Microsoft Corporation

Figure 3

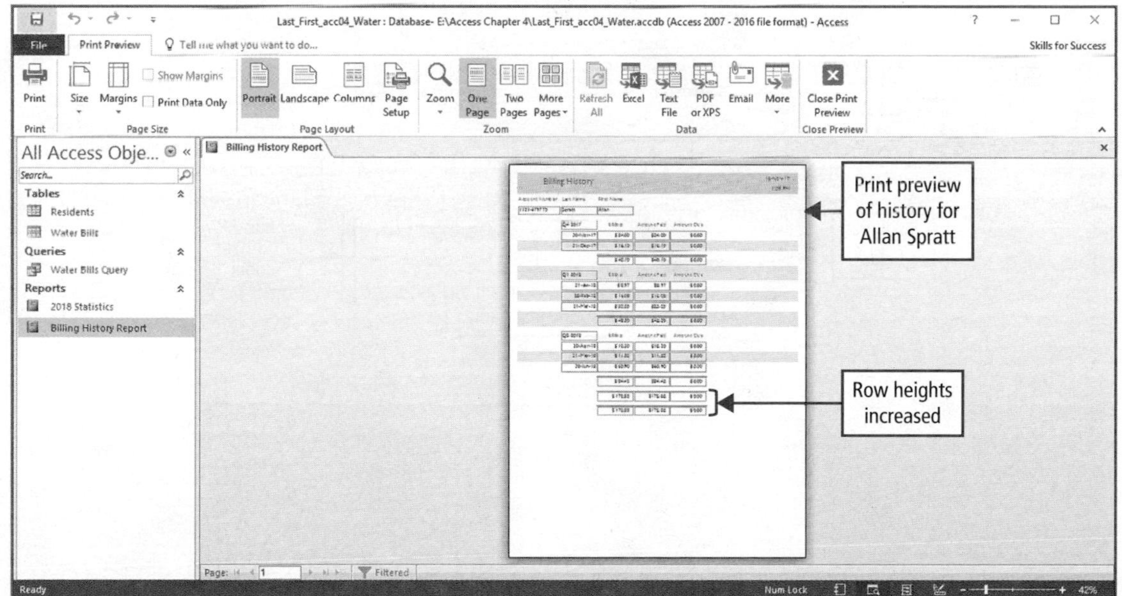

Access 2016, Windows 10, Microsoft Corporation

Figure 4

6. **Save** [icon], and then **Close** [icon] the report. In the **Navigation Pane**, double-click **Billing History Report** to open it in Report view. In the **Sort & Filter group**, click the **Toggle Filter** button to reapply the filter previously created.

   By default, any filters saved in a report are not active when you open the report.

7. In the **Sort & Filter group**, click **Advanced**, and then click **Clear All Filters**.

   The Clear All Filters command removes all filters from the report. Once the filter is cleared, it can no longer be enabled by clicking the Toggle Filter button.

8. Scroll down to the second account to display the history for *Allan Spratt*. Click in the text box with the text *Spratt*. On the **Home tab**, in the **Sort & Filter group**, click the **Selection** button, and then click **Equals "Spratt"**. Compare your screen with **Figure 3**.

9. On the status bar, click the **Layout View** button [icon]. Using the technique practiced previously, AutoFit the height of the last two rows—the rows with the Sum controls.

10. On the status bar, click the **Print Preview** button [icon]. If necessary, in the Zoom group, click One Page to display the entire page, and then compare your screen with **Figure 4**.

11. If you are printing your work, print the report.

12. Click **Save** [icon], and then **Close** [icon] the report.

■ **You have completed Skill 9 of 10**

SKILL 10: Create Label Reports

► A ***label report*** is a report formatted so that the data can be printed on a sheet of labels.

1. In the **Navigation Pane**, under **Tables**, click **Residents** one time to select the table.
2. On the **Create tab**, in the **Reports group**, click the **Labels** button.

Obj 5.1.3

3. In the **Label Wizard**, be sure that the **Filter by manufacturer** box displays the text **Avery**. Under **What label size would you like**, select the label size where **Product number** is **C2160**, as shown in **Figure 1**.

   Each manufacturer identifies its label sheets using a product number. Access formats the report to match the dimensions of the selected sheet size.

4. Click **Next**. If necessary, change the **Font name** to Arial, and the **Font weight** to Light. Change the **Font size** to **10**.
5. Click **Next**. Under **Available fields**, click **FirstName**, and then click the **Add Field** button [>] to add the field to the **Prototype label**.
6. With the insertion point in the **Prototype label** and to the right of *{FirstName}*, add a space, and then **Add Field** [>] the **LastName** field into the first line of the **Prototype label**.
7. Press [Enter], and then **Add Field** [>] the **Street** field into the second line of the **Prototype label**. Compare your screen with **Figure 2.**

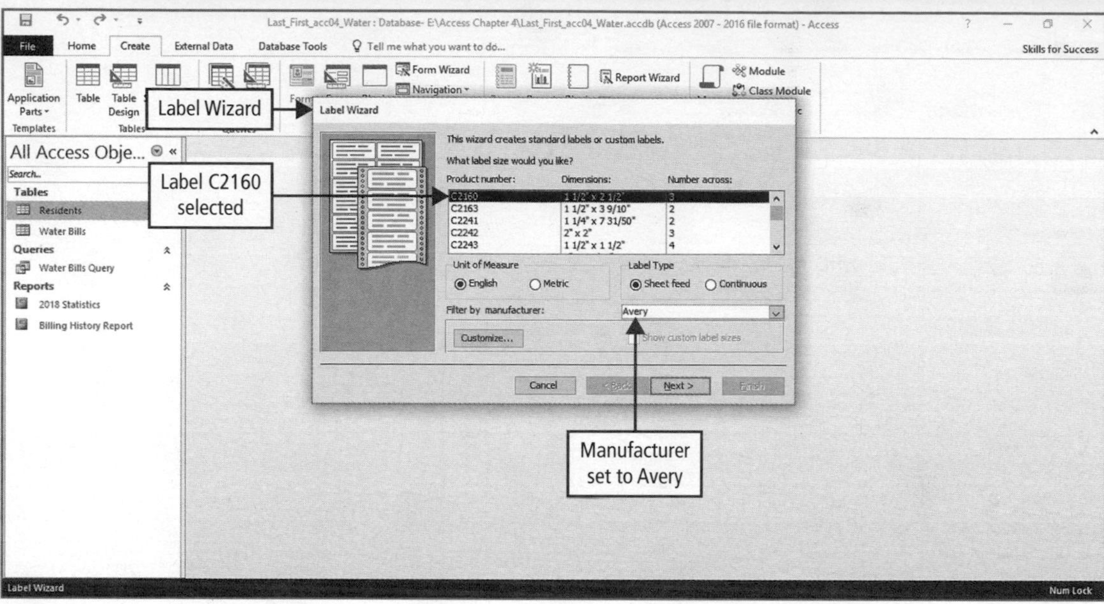

Figure 1 Access 2016, Windows 10, Microsoft Corporation

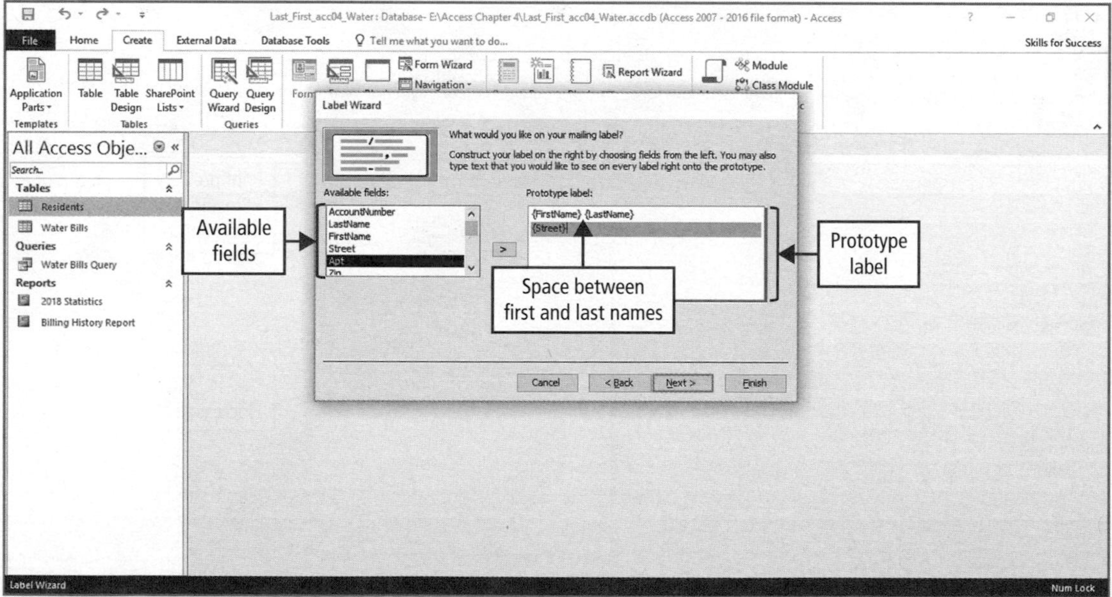

Figure 2 Access 2016, Windows 10, Microsoft Corporation

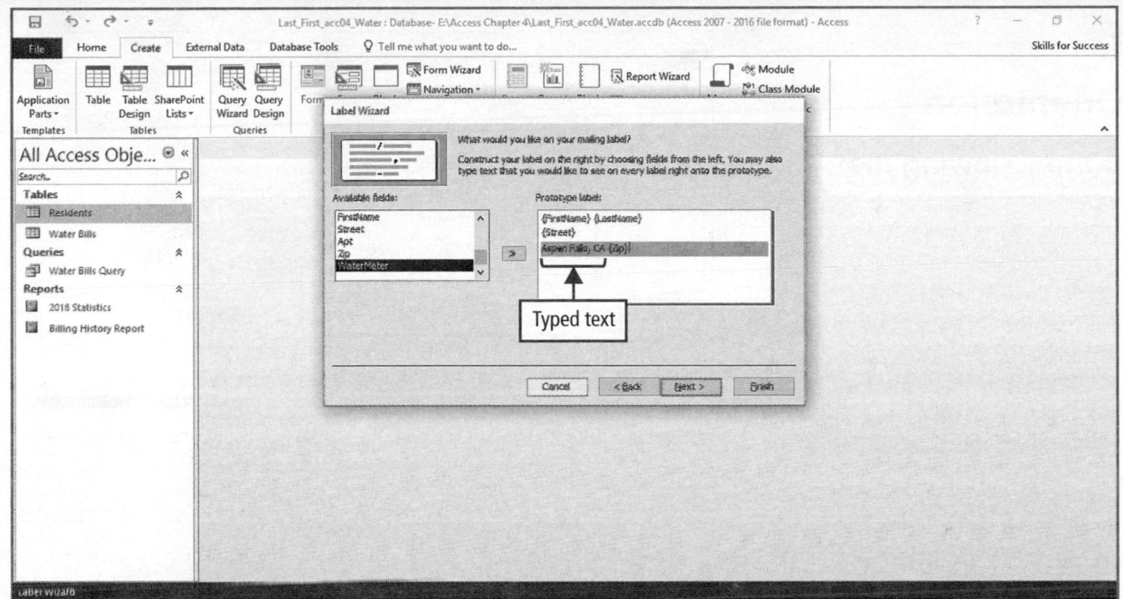

Access 2016, Windows 10, Microsoft Corporation

Figure 3

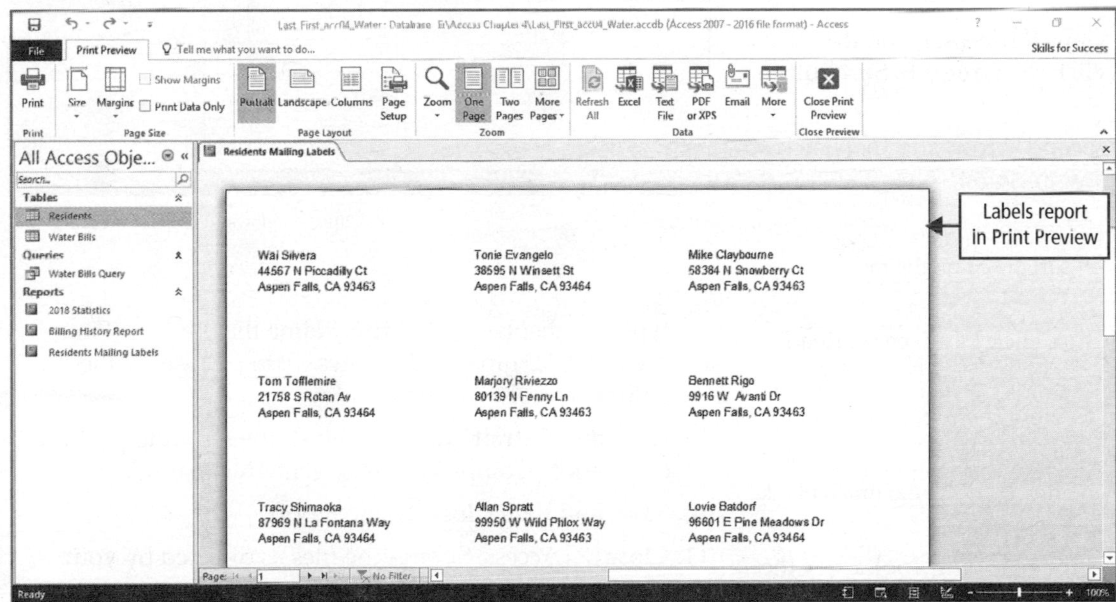

Access 2016, Windows 10, Microsoft Corporation

Figure 4

8. Press Enter, and then type Aspen Falls, CA Add a space, and then **Add Field** > the **Zip** field. Compare your screen with **Figure 3**.

   You can create labels using a combination of typed characters and fields from a table or query.

9. Click **Next** two times. Under **What name would you like for your report**, replace the existing name with Residents Mailing Labels

10. Click **Finish** to open the report in Print Preview. Compare your screen with **Figure 4**.

11. If you are printing your work for this project, print the first page of labels by setting the **From** and **To** values in the **Print** dialog box to *1*.

    When printing a label report, your printer may require additional steps. Most printers will not print until a sheet of labels or sheet of paper is placed in the manual feed tray. If you are working in a computer lab, check with your lab technician or instructor for what is required in your situation.

12. **Close** ✕ the report, and then **Close** ✕ Access. Submit your file as directed by your instructor.

DONE! You have completed Skill 10 of 10, and your file is complete!

More Skills 11

Change Report Sort Order and Orientation

To complete this project, you will need the following file:

- acc04_MS11Results

You will save your files as:

- Last_First_acc04_MS11Results
- Last_First_acc04_MS11Snip

- ▸ You can change the sort order of a report to present information in a more meaningful manner.
- ▸ Reports can be set to landscape or portrait orientation to allow the content to fit within the report page margins.

---

1. Start **Access 2016**, and then open the student data file **acc04_MS11Results**. **Save** the file in your **Access Chapter 4** folder as Last_First_acc04_MS11Results If necessary, enable the content.
2. Open the **2018 Race Results** report in Layout view. If necessary, on the **Design tab**, in the **Grouping & Totals group**, click the **Group & Sort** button to view the report's current sorting method.

MOS Obj 5.3.6

3. In the **Group, Sort, and Totals** pane, click the second arrow, and then click **from largest to smallest**. Compare your screen with **Figure 1**.
4. Click **Add a sort**, and then click **Bracket**.

   The report is now sorted by date, with a secondary sort based on the racer's bracket.

MOS Obj 5.3.5

5. Switch to Print Preview. In the **Page Layout group**, click **Landscape**. Read the message, and then click **OK**.
6. In the **Zoom group**, click the **One Page** button to view the report in landscape orientation.

   The report does not fit properly in landscape orientation. There is too much blank space on the right side of the report.

7. Press [Windows key], type snip and then press Enter to start the Snipping Tool. Click the **New arrow**, and then click **Window Snip**. Point to the Access window, and when a red border displays around the window, click one time.
8. In the **Snipping Tool** window, click the **Save Snip** button [Save Snip]. In the **Save As** dialog box, navigate to your Access Chapter 4 folder. Be sure the **Save as type** box displays **JPEG file**. Name the file Last_First_acc04_MS11Snip and then press Enter. **Close** [X] the Snipping Tool mark-up window.

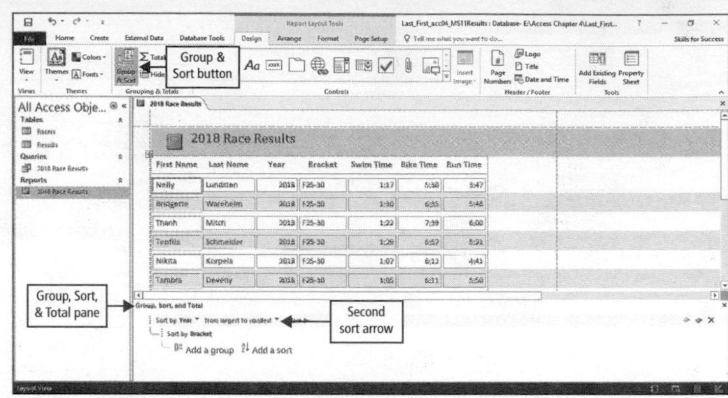

Figure 1 Access 2016, Windows 10, Microsoft Corporation

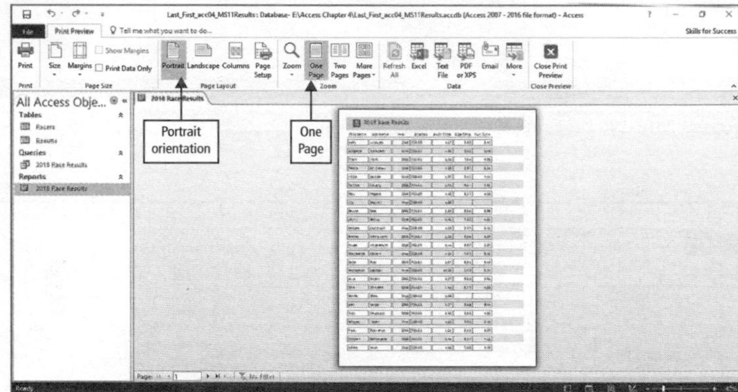

Figure 2 Access 2016, Windows 10, Microsoft Corporation

9. Click the **Portrait** button to return the report to portrait orientation. Compare your screen with **Figure 2**.
10. **Save**, and then **Close** [X] the report.
11. **Close** [X] Access. Submit the files as directed by your instructor.

■ **You have completed More Skills 11**

More Skills 12

Export Reports to Word

To complete this project, you will need the following file:

- acc04_MS12Reservations

You will save your file as:

- Last_First_acc04_MS12Reservations (Word)

- You can export reports to other file formats so that you can work with the data in other applications.
- When you export a report to Word, the report is saved as a ***Rich Text Format file***— a document file format designed to work with many different types of programs.

---

1. Start **Access 2016**, and then open the student data file **acc04_MS12Reservations**. If necessary, enable the content.
2. In the **Navigation Pane**, right-click **Shelter Reservations Report**, and then click **Print Preview**. If necessary, set the Zoom to **Zoom 100%**.
3. **Close** [X] the report. In the **Navigation Pane**, be sure that **Shelter Reservations Report** is selected.
4. On the **External Data tab**, in the **Export group**, click the **More** button, and then click **Word**. MOS Obj 1.5.4
5. In the **Export - RTF File** dialog box, click the **Browse** button. In the **File Save** dialog box, open your **Access Chapter 4** folder. In the **File name** box, type Last_First_acc04_MS12Reservations and then click **Save**.

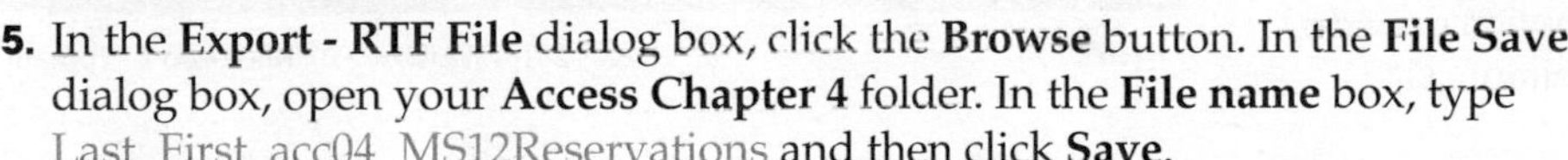

6. Select the **Open the destination file after the export operation is complete** check box. Compare your screen with **Figure 1**.

   Rich Text Format is often referred to as ***RTF***.

7. Click **OK**. Wait a few moments for the report to open in Word. In the **Word** window, click the **File tab**, and then click **Print**. Compare your screen with **Figure 2**.

   When you open an RTF file in Word 2013, it opens in ***Compatibility mode***—a mode that limits formatting and features to those supported in earlier versions of Office.

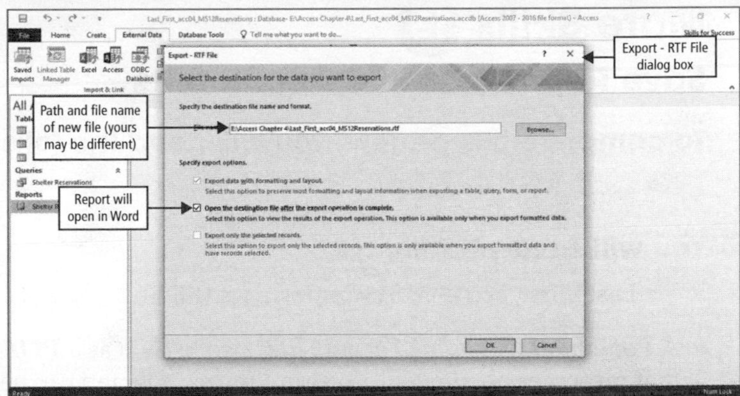

Access 2016, Windows 10, Microsoft Corporation **Figure 1**

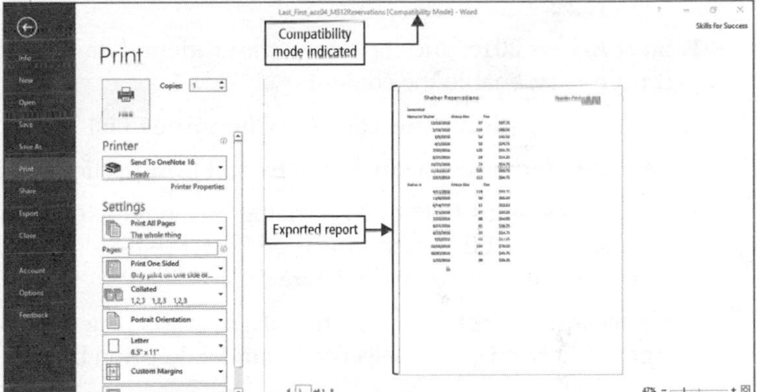

Access 2016, Windows 10, Microsoft Corporation **Figure 2**

8. If you are printing this project, print the Word document.
9. **Close** [X] Word. In Access, in the **Export - RTF File** dialog box, click the **Save export steps** checkbox, and then click **Save Export**.
10. **Close** [X] Access, and then submit the file as directed by your instructor.

- **You have completed More Skills 12**

More Skills 13

Save Reports as PDF Documents

To complete this project, you will need the following file:

- acc04_MS13Councils

You will save your file as:

- Last_First_acc04_MS13Committees (PDF)

► A ***Portable Document Format file***, also known as a ***PDF file***, is a file format that preserves document layout and formatting and can be viewed in Word, Windows Reader, or Adobe Acrobat Reader.

---

1. Start **Access 2016**, and then open the student data file **acc04_MS13Councils**. If necessary, enable the content.
2. In the **Navigation Pane**, click the **Committee List** report.
3. MOS Obj 1.5.4 On the **External Data tab**, in the **Export group**, click the **PDF or XPS** button.
4. In the **Publish as PDF or XPS** dialog box, navigate to your Access Chapter 4 folder. In the **File name** box, type Last_First_acc04_MS13Committees Compare your screen with **Figure 1**.

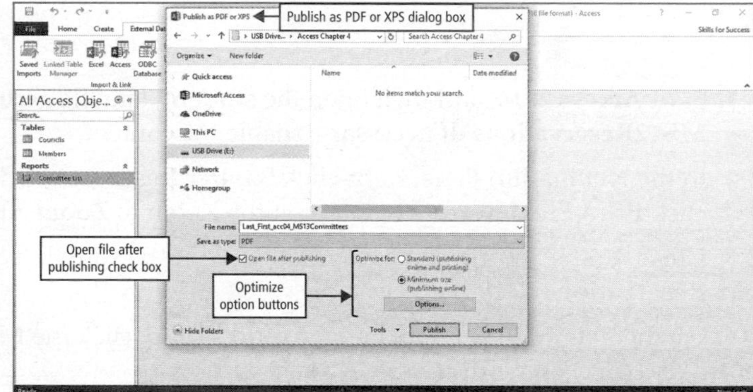

Figure 1 Access 2016, Windows 10, Microsoft Corporation

5. If necessary, select the **Open file after publishing** check box, and then to the right of **Optimize for**, select the **Standard** option button.

   When you export a report as a PDF file, it is a good idea to open it in a PDF reader application to verify the report looks as intended. The Standard option provides the best quality, but the file size may be larger than when the Minimum size option is used.

6. Click **Publish**, and then wait a few moments for the report to open in your computer's default reader application.
7. **Close** the PDF file. In Access, in the **Export - PDF** dialog box, click the **Save export steps** checkbox, and then click **Save Export**.
8. **Close** [X] Access, and then submit the file as directed by your instructor.

- **You have completed More Skills 13**

More Skills 14

Save Reports as Web Pages

To complete this project, you will need the following file:

- acc04_MS14Rosters

You will save your files as:

- Last_First_acc04_MS14Rosters (Access)
- Last_First_acc04_MS14Rosters (HTML file)

▶ You can export reports so that they can be opened in a web browser.

▶ A ***Hypertext Markup Language document*** (***HTML document***) is a text file with instructions for displaying its content in a web browser.

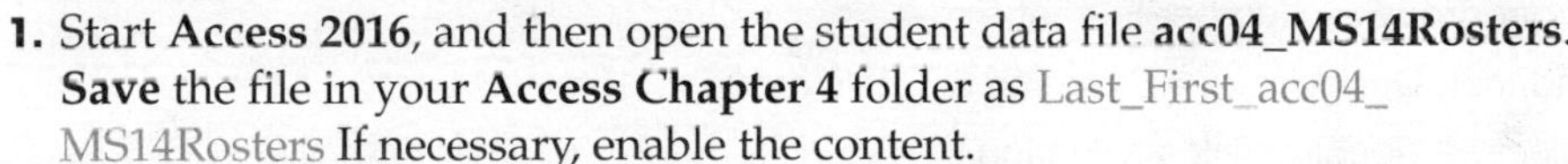

1. Start **Access 2016**, and then open the student data file **acc04_MS14Rosters**. **Save** the file in your **Access Chapter 4** folder as Last_First_acc04_MS14Rosters If necessary, enable the content.
2. In the **Navigation Pane**, select the **Camp Rosters** report.
3. On the **External Data tab**, in the **Export group**, click the **More** button, and then click **HTML Document**. MOS Obj 1.5.4
4. In the **Export - HTML Document** dialog box, click the **Browse** button. In the **File Save** dialog box, navigate to your Access Chapter 4 folder. In the **File name** box, type Last_First_acc04_MS14Rosters Compare your screen with **Figure 1**, and then click **Save**.

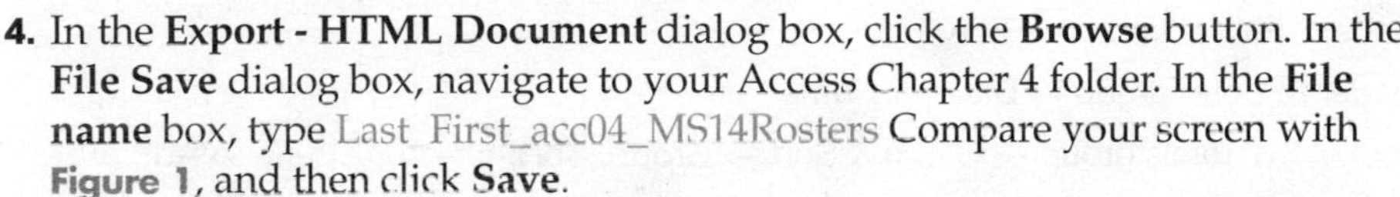

5. Select the **Open the destination file after the export operation is complete** check box.
6. Click **OK**. In the **HTML Output Options** dialog box, under **Choose the encoding to use for saving this file**, select the **Unicode (UTF-8)** option button, and then compare your screen with **Figure 2**. Click **OK**. Wait a few moments for the report to open in your web browser.

   Unicode (UTF-8) is a system for representing a large variety of text characters and symbols. It is used often in HTML documents.

7. If you are printing this project, print the web page. **Close** ☒ the web browser window.

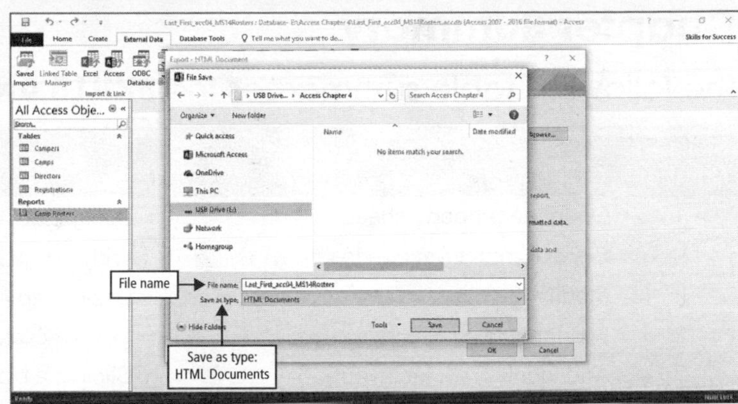

Access 2016, Windows 10, Microsoft Corporation **Figure 1**

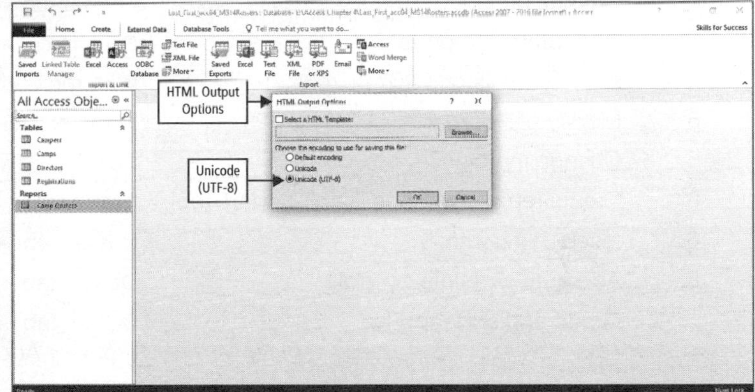

Access 2016, Windows 10, Microsoft Corporation **Figure 2**

8. In Access, in the **Export - HTML Document** dialog box, select the **Save export steps**, and then click **Save Export**.
9. **Close** ☒ Access, and then submit the files as directed by your instructor.

■ **You have completed More Skills 14**

Chapter Summary

The following table summarizes the **SKILLS AND PROCEDURES** covered in this chapter.

Skills Number	Task	Step
1	Open the property sheet	Design tab → Tools group → Property Sheet
2	Build reports from queries	With the query selected in the Navigation Pane, Create tab → Reports group → Report
2	Modify themes	Design tab → Themes group → Colors or Fonts
2	Edit label text	Double-click the label control to enter Edit mode
2	Add labels (Tabular layout)	Click in a blank table cell. Type the label text.
3	Format labels and text boxes	With the control selected, Format tab → Font group
3	Insert logos	Design tab → Header / Footer group → Logo
3	Select a specific control	Format tab → Selection group → Selection arrow
3	Change alternate row colors	Select Detail control, and then Format tab → Background group → Alternate Row Color
4	Change number formats	Format tab → Number group → Number Format arrow
4	Add totals to reports	Click in column, and then Design tab → Grouping & Totals group → Totals
4	AutoFit labels and text boxes	With the control selected, double-click a selection border
5	Modify cell borders	In the property sheet, on the Format tab, change Gridline Style properties
5	Change margins	Print Preview tab → Page Size group → Margins
6	Create reports with the Blank Report Tool	Create tab → Reports group → Blank Report. In the Field List, double-click or drag to add fields to the report.
6	Insert title controls	Design tab → Header / Footer group → Title
6	Add date and time controls	Design tab → Header / Footer group → Date and Time
7	Group and sort reports	Design tab → Grouping & Totals group → Group & Sort → Group, Sort, and Total pane → Add a group or Add a sort
8	Delete rows and columns	Arrange tab → Rows & Columns group → Select Column or Select Row → press Delete
9	Apply custom text and date filters	With field selected, Home tab → Sort & Filter group → Filter button → Text Filters or Date Filters
9	Remove filters	Home tab → Sort & Filter group → Advanced → Clear All Filters
9	Toggle filter on	Home tab → Sort & Filter group → Toggle Filter
9	Filter by selection	Click in field with desired value, Home tab → Sort & Filter group → Selection
10	Create label reports	Create tab → Reports group → Labels
MS11	Change sort order	Design tab → Grouping & Totals group → Group & Sort → Group, Sort, and Total Pane → Sort arrow
MS11	Change orientation	Print Preview → Page Layout group → select orientation
MS12	Export report to Word	External Data tab → Export group → More button → Word
MS13	Export report to PDF	External Data tab → Export group → PDF or XPS button
MS14	Export report to HTML	External Data tab → Export group → More button → HTML document

Project Summary Chart		
Project	**Project Type**	**Project Location**
Skills Review	Review	In Book & MIL MyITLab® Grader
Skills Assessment 1	Review	In Book & MIL MyITLab® Grader
Skills Assessment 2	Review	Book
My Skills	Problem Solving	Book
Visual Skills Check	Problem Solving	Book
Skillls Challenge 1	Critical Thinking	Book
Skills Challenge 2	Critical Thinking	Book
More Skills Assessment	Review	In Book & MIL MyITLab® Grader
Collaborating with Google	Critical Thinking	Book

MOS Objectives Covered	
1.5.1 Print reports	5.3.1 Format reports into multiple columns
1.5.3 Save a database as a template	5.3.2 Add calculated fields
1.5.4 Export objects to alternative formats	5.3.3 Control report positioning
5.1.1 Create a report	5.3.4 Format report elements
5.1.3 Create a report by using a wizard	5.3.5 Change report orientation
5.2.1 Group and sort fields	5.3.6 Insert header and footer information
5.2.3 Add report controls	5.3.7 Insert images
5.2.4 Add and modify labels	5.3.8 Apply a theme

Key Terms

Compatibility mode 651
Detail control 635
HTML document. 653
Hypertext Markup Language document 653
Label report 648
PDF file 652
Portable Document Format file 652
Report Layout view. 632
Report view 633
Rich Text Format file 651
RTF file 651
Summary statistics 636
Unicode (UTF-8) 653

BizSkills Video

1. What are some examples of good e-mail etiquette?
2. What are some things to avoid when e-mailing co-workers?

Online Help Skills

1. Start **Access 2016**, and then in the upper right corner of the start page, click the **Help** button .
2. In the **Access Help** window **Search help** box, type conditional formatting and then press Enter.
3. In the search result list, click **Introduction to reports in Access**. Scroll down the article and click **Highlight data with conditional formatting**, **Maximize** the Help window, and then compare your screen with **Figure 1**.

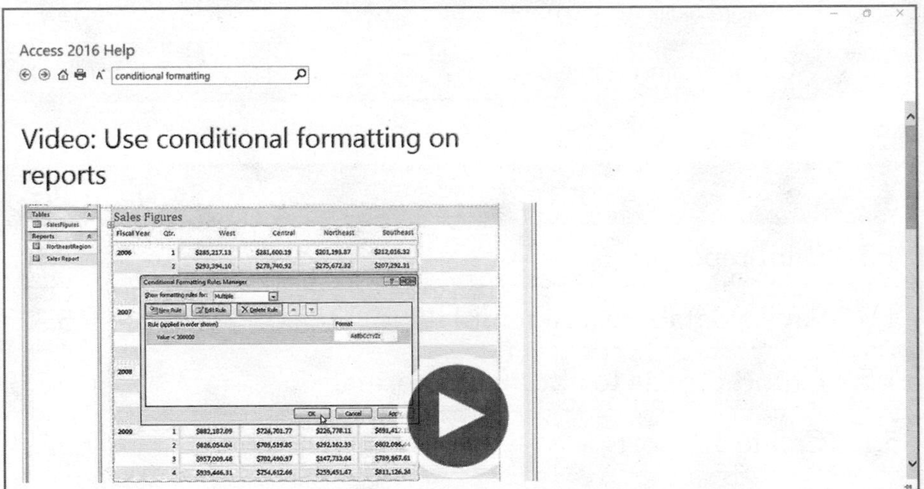

Figure 1 Access 2016, Windows 10, Microsoft Corporation

4. Read the article to answer the following question: How does adding conditional formatting add meaning to report data?

Matching MyITLab®

Match each term in the second column with its correct definition in the first column by writing the letter of the term on the blank line in front of the correct definition.

___ **1.** To change a theme, Colors theme, or Fonts theme, use this tab.

___ **2.** The Font group is located on this tab.

___ **3.** This is used when you want to build a report by adding fields one at a time or arrange them in a different layout.

___ **4.** A small picture that can be added to a report header, typically to the left of the title.

___ **5.** To set the width of a report control to a precise dimension in Layout view, this pane can be used.

___ **6.** An area at the beginning of a report that contains labels, text boxes, and other controls.

___ **7.** The Format Painter button can be found in this group.

___ **8.** To change the alternate row color, this report control should be selected.

___ **9.** To display a subset of records on a report that matches a given criterion.

___ **10.** This button creates and applies a filter automatically using the value in the active field.

A Blank Report tool
B Design
C Detail
D Filter
E Font
F Format
G Logo
H Property sheet
I Report header
J Selection

Multiple Choice

MyITLab®

Choose the correct answer.

1. A tool that can create a report with a single click.
   A. Blank Report tool
   B. Report tool
   C. Report Wizard
2. The method used to edit text in a label control in Layout view.
   A. Double-click the control
   B. Right-click the control, then click Edit
   C. Click the control, and then on the Design tab, click Edit
3. A method used to add a label control in Layout view.
   A. On the Design tab, in the Controls group, click Text Box
   B. Click in an empty cell and type the label text
   C. On the Insert tab, in the Labels group, click Add
4. This pane is used to add fields to a report in Layout view.
   A. Add Fields
   B. Blank Report
   C. Field List
5. Buttons to insert logo, title, and date and time controls are found in this group on the Design tab.
   A. Controls
   B. Header / Footer
   C. Tools
6. This pane is used to group and sort reports.
   A. Group pane
   B. Group and Sort pane
   C. Group, Sort, and Total pane
7. To delete a report column in Layout view, this method can be used.
   A. Click in the row, and then press Delete
   B. Click in the column, and then on the Arrange tab, click Delete Column
   C. Click in the column. On the Arrange tab, click Select Column, and then press Delete
8. To apply a custom filter, this method can be used.
   A. Click in the field, and then on the Home tab, click the Filter button
   B. Click in the field, and then on the Home tab, click the Custom button
   C. Click in the field, and then on the Home tab, click the Selection button
9. When a report is closed that has a filter applied, the following describes what happens when the report is opened the next time.
   A. The filter created previously was deleted
   B. The filter was saved, but it is not enabled
   C. The filter was saved, and it is enabled
10. A report formatted so that the data can be printed on a sheet of labels.
    A. Label report
    B. Mail report
    C. Merge report

Topics for Discussion

1. You have created reports using two different methods: the Report tool and the Blank Report tool. Which method do you prefer, and why? What are the primary advantages of each method?
2. You have filtered reports using two different methods: One method added criteria to a query and then built the report from the query. The other method added filters after the report was finished. Which method do you prefer, and why? What are the primary advantages of each method?

Skills Review

To complete this project, you will need the following files:

- acc04_SRElectricity (Access)
- acc04_SRLogo (JPG)

You will save your file as:

- Last_First_acc04_SRElectricity

---

1. Start **Access 2016**, and then open the student data file **acc04_SRElectricity**. **Save** the file in your **Access Chapter 4** folder as Last_First_acc04_SRElectricity If necessary, enable the content.
2. Click the **Create tab**, and then in the **Reports group**, click **Blank Report**. In the **Field List**, click **Show all tables**, and then expand the **Residents** table. Double-click to add these fields in the following order: **Account**, **LastName**, and **FirstName**.
3. In the **Field List**, expand the **Billing Cycles** table, and then double-click **CycleDate** and **Usage** to add them to the report.
4. Click **Save**, type Resident Usage Report and then click **OK**. **Close** the Field List, and then compare your screen with **Figure 1**.
5. On the **Design tab**, in the **Header / Footer group**, click **Title**, type Electricity Usage by Resident and then press Enter.
6. On the **Design tab**, in the **Grouping & Totals group**, click **Group & Sort**. In the **Group, Sort, and Total** pane, click **Add a group**, and then click **Account**. **Close** the Group, Sort, and Total pane.
7. Drag the field with the value *Claybourne* into the blank cell below the **Last Name** label. Drag the field with the value *Mike* into the blank cell below the **First Name** label.
8. Click the field displaying **Account** *1118-435018*, and then click the **Home tab**. In the **Sort & Filter group**, click **Selection**, and then click **Equals "1118-435018"**.
9. On the **Design tab**, in the **Views group**, click the **View arrow**, and then click **Print Preview**. Compare your screen with **Figure 2**. If you are printing this project, print the report. Click **Save**, **Close Print Preview**, and then **Close** the report.

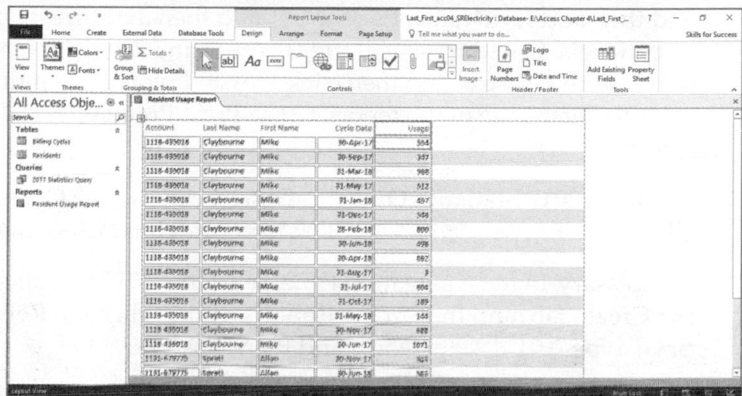

Access 2016, Windows 10, Microsoft Corporation **Figure 1**

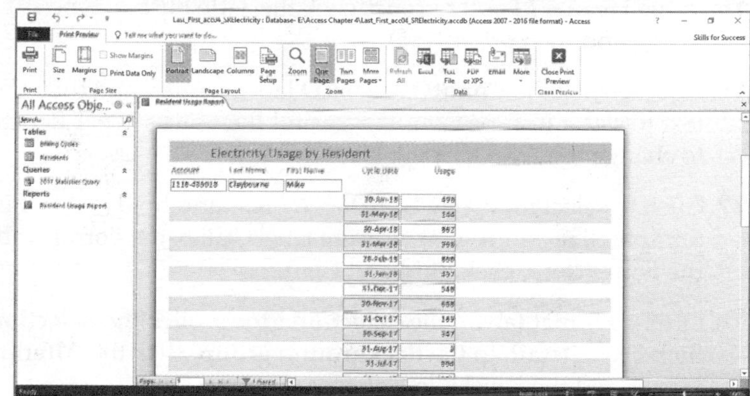

Access 2016, Windows 10, Microsoft Corporation **Figure 2**

10. In the **Navigation Pane**, select the **Residents** table. Click the **Create tab**, and then in the **Reports group**, click the **Labels** button.

■ Continue to the next page to complete this Skills Review

11. In the **Label Wizard**, verify **Avery C2160** is selected, and then click **Next** two times. Double-click **FirstName** to add it to the Prototype label. Add a space, and then add **LastName**. Press Enter, and then add **Street**. Press Enter, type Aspen Falls, CA add a space, and then add the **Zip** field. Compare your screen with **Figure 3**, and then click **Finish**. If you are printing your work, print the first page of the report. **Close Print Preview**, and then **Close** the report.

12. Open the **2017 Statistics Query** in Design view. In the **CycleDate** column **Criteria** cell, type <1/1/2018 Click **Save**, and then **Close** the query.

13. If necessary, in the Navigation Pane, select the 2017 Statistics Query. Click the **Create tab**, and then in the **Reports group**, click the **Report** button. Click **Save**, type 2017 Usage Report and then click **OK**.

14. In the **Header / Footer group**, click the **Logo** button. In the **Insert Picture** dialog box, navigate to the student files for this chapter, click **acc04_SRLogo**, and then click **OK**.

15. In the **Header / Footer group**, click the **Title** button, type 2017 Electricity Usage and then press Enter.

16. Double-click the **CountOfCycleID** label control, and then double-click the text to select it. Type Sample Size and then press Enter. Repeat this technique to change the **AvgOfUsage** label text to Average Usage

17. Click to select the **Cycle Date** label. Press and hold Shift while clicking the **Sample Size** and **Average Usage** labels. Click the **Format tab**, and then in the **Font group**, click **Bold** and **Center**.

18. On the **Format tab**, in the **Selection group**, click the **Selection arrow**, and then click **Detail**. In the **Background group**, click the **Alternate Row Color arrow**, and then click **No Color**.

19. Click a field in the **Sample Size** column, and then click the **Design tab**. In the **Grouping & Totals group**, click **Totals**, and then click **Sum**. Repeat this technique to add an **Average** total to the **Average Usage** column.

20. Below the **Sample Size** values, click the cell with the value *852*. Point to the top border, and then double-click to AutoFit the row. Click the total cell with the value *12*, and then press Delete to remove the control.

21. Compare your screen with **Figure 4**. If you are printing this project, print the report.

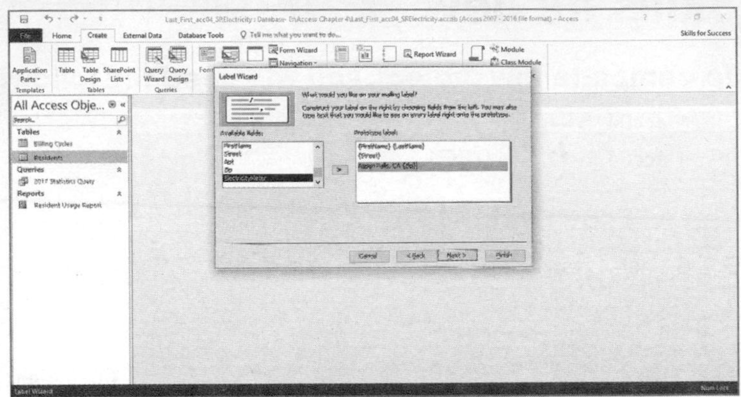

Figure 3 Access 2016, Windows 10, Microsoft Corporation

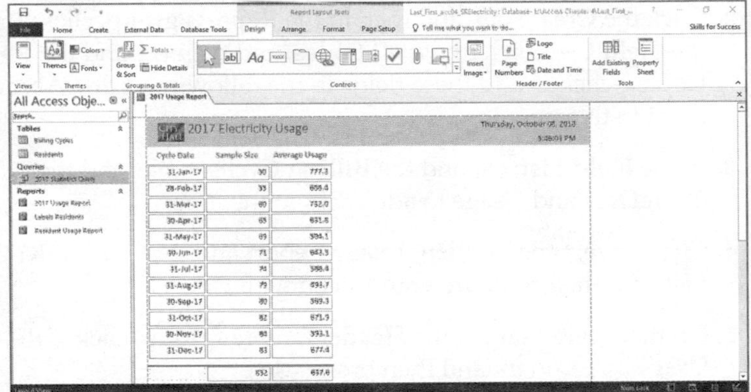

Figure 4 Access 2016, Windows 10, Microsoft Corporation

22. Click **Save**, **Close** the report, and then **Close** Access. Submit the file as directed by your instructor.

DONE! You have completed this Skills Review

Skills Assessment 1

To complete this project, you will need the following files:

- acc04_SA1Parcels (Access)
- acc04_SA1Logo (JPG)

You will save your file as:

- Last_First_acc04_SA1Parcels

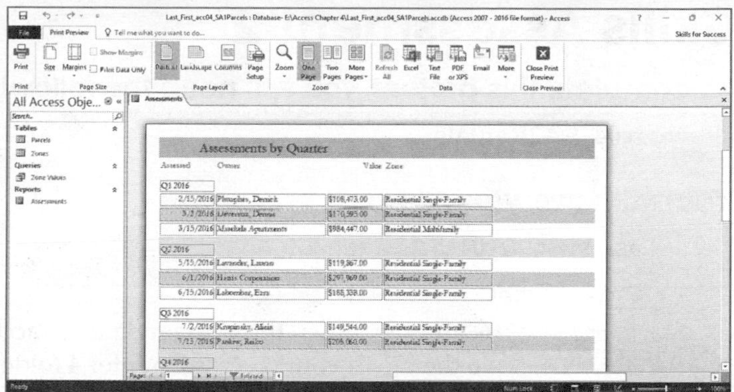

Access 2016, Windows 10, Microsoft Corporation **Figure 1**

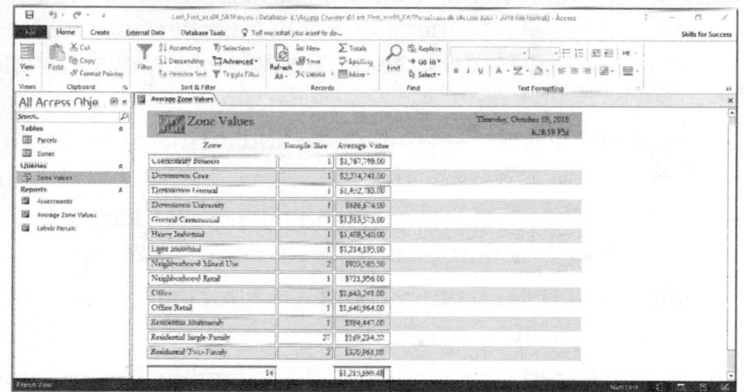

Access 2016, Windows 10, Microsoft Corporation **Figure 2**

1. Start **Access 2016**, and then open the student data file **acc04_SA1Parcels**. **Save** the file in your **Access Chapter 4** folder as Last_First_acc04_SA1Parcels If necessary, enable the content.
2. Use the **Blank Report** tool to create a report with these fields in the following order: **Owner**, **Value**, **Assessed**, and **Zone**. Save the report as Assessments
3. Apply the **Organic** theme, and then add a **Title** control with the text Assessments by Quarter
4. Group the report by the **Assessed** field, and then if necessary, sort the Assessed field within each group in oldest to newest order. AutoFit the control height of the quarter label controls.
5. Use the property sheet to set the width of the **Owner** column to **2"** and the width of the **Zone** column to **2"**. Change the alignment of the **Value** label to **Align Left**.
6. For the **Detail** control, change the **Alternate Row Color** to **Orange, Accent 5, Lighter 80%** (row 2, column 9).
7. Create a custom **Text Filter** to display only the records in which the **Zone** contains the word Residential
8. Switch to **Print Preview**, and then compare your screen with **Figure 1**. If you are printing this project, print the report. **Save**, and then **Close** the report.
9. Create a **Labels** report based on the **Parcels** table. In the **Label Wizard**, verify **Avery C2160** is selected, and then accept the default label format settings. In the first line of the **Prototype** label, add the **Owner** field. In the second line, add the **Street** field. In the third line, type Aspen Falls, CA add a space, and then add the **Zip** field. Accept all other wizard defaults, and then **Close** the report.
10. Modify the **Zone Values** query so that the second **Value** column computes an average for the group. **Save**, and then **Close** the query.
11. Use the **Report** tool to create a report based on the **Zone Values** query. **Save** the report as Average Zone Values
12. Add a logo using the file **acc04_SA1Logo**. Select the three column labels, and then apply **Bold** and **Center**.
13. Change the **AvgOfValue** label control text to Average Value and then add a control that calculates the column's average. Format the calculated control as **Currency**, and then AutoFit its height.
14. Switch to Report view, and then compare your screen with **Figure 2**. If you are printing this project, print the report.
15. Click **Save**, **Close** the report, and then **Close** Access. Submit the file as directed by your instructor.

DONE! You have completed Skills Assessment 1

Skills Assessment 2

To complete this project, you will need the following file:

- acc04_SA2Rentals

You will save your file as:

- Last_First_acc04_SA2Rentals

1. Start **Access 2016**, and then open the student data file **acc04_SA2Rentals**. **Save** the file in your **Access Chapter 4** folder as Last_First_acc04_SA2Rentals If necessary, enable the content.
2. Use the **Blank Report** tool to create a report with these fields in the following order: **Center** and **Room Number** from the **Rooms** table; and **Date** and **Hours** from the **Rentals** table. Save the report as Rentals Report
3. Apply the **Facet** theme, and then add a **Title** control with the text Community Center Rentals
4. Group the report by **Center**, and then group it again by **RoomNumber**. Sort by **Date** from oldest to newest.
5. Below the **Hours** column, add a control that calculates the column's total.
6. For the **Detail** control, change the **Alternate Row Color** to **Orange, Accent 4, Lighter 80%** (row 2, column 8).
7. Use filter by **Selection** to display only the rentals for Room CE110. AutoFit the height of the three summary controls in the **Hours** column.
8. Switch to Print Preview, and then compare your screen with **Figure 1**. If you are printing this project, print the report. **Save**, and then **Close** the report.
9. Create a **Labels** report based on the **Renters** table. In the **Label Wizard**, verify **Avery C2160** is selected, and then accept the default label format settings. In the **Prototype** label, add fields and spaces to create labels in the following format:

   FirstName LastName
   Street
   City, State Zip
   Accept all other wizard defaults. If you are printing this project, print the first page of the report. **Close** the report.

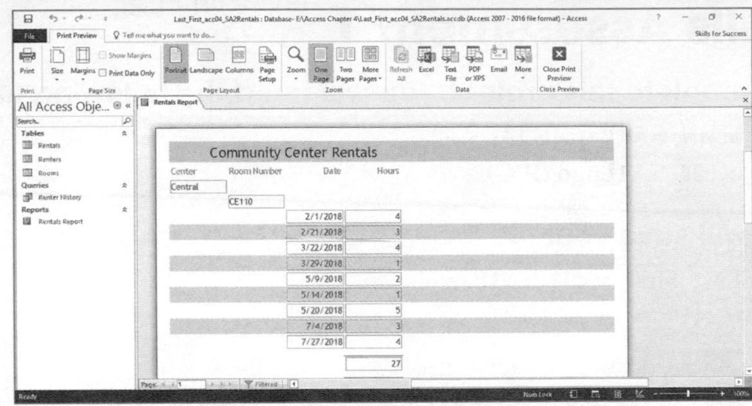

Figure 1 Access 2016, Windows 10, Microsoft Corporation

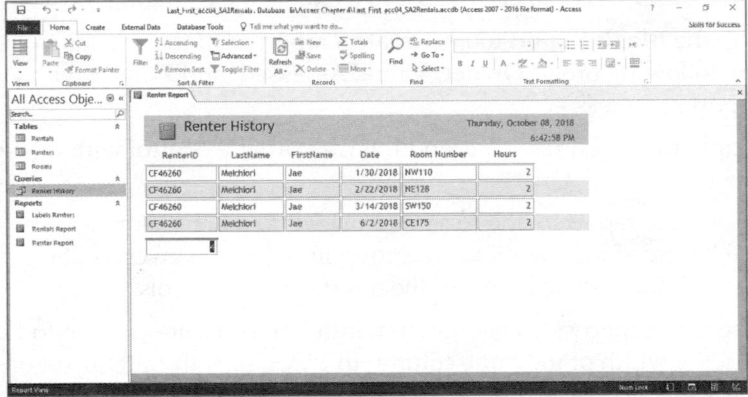

Figure 2 Access 2016, Windows 10, Microsoft Corporation

10. Modify the **Renter History** query to display only the records with **RenterID** CF46260 **Save**, and then **Close** the query.
11. Use the **Report** tool to create a report based on the **Renter History** query. **Save** the report as Renter Report
12. Resize the column widths so that the report is one page wide, and then delete the page number control.
13. Select the six column labels, and then apply **Bold** and **Center**. AutoFit the height of the **Count** control in the **RenterID** column.
14. Switch to Report view, and then compare your screen with **Figure 2**. If you are printing this project, print the report.
15. Click **Save**, **Close** the report, and then **Close** Access. Submit the file as directed by your instructor.

 **DONE! You have completed Skills Assessment 2**

My Skills

To complete this project, you will need the following file:

- acc04_MYBaseball

You will save your file as:

- Last_First_acc04_MYBaseball

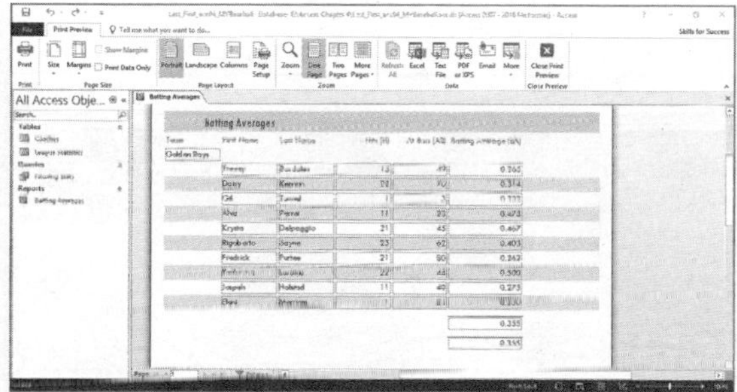

Access 2016, Windows 10, Microsoft Corporation **Figure 1**

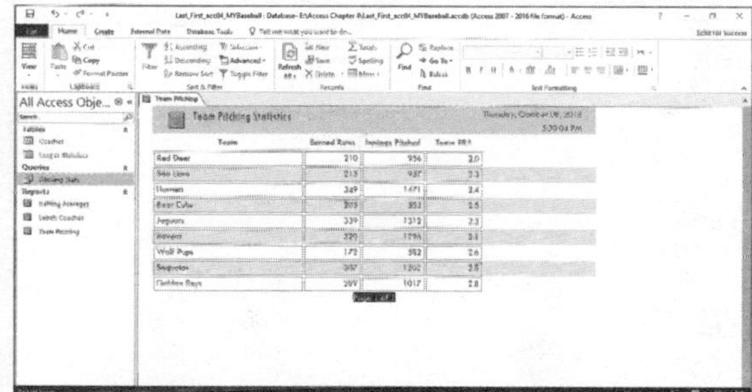

Access 2016, Windows 10, Microsoft Corporation **Figure 2**

1. Start **Access 2016**, and then open the student data file **acc04_MYBaseball**. **Save** the file in your **Access Chapter 4** folder as Last_First_acc04_MYBaseball If necessary, enable the content.
2. Use the **Blank Report** tool to create a report with these fields from the **League Statistics** table in the following order: **Team**, **FirstName**, **LastName**, **Hits (H)**, **AtBats (AB)**, and **BattingAverage (BA)**. Save the report as Batting Averages
3. Apply the **Integral** theme, and then add a **Title** control with the text Batting Averages
4. Group the report by **Team**, and then below the **Batting Average (BA)** column, add a control that calculates the column's averages.
5. For the **Detail** control, change the **Alternate Row Color** to **Teal, Accent 6, Lighter 80%** (row 2, last column).
6. Use filter by **Selection** to display only statistics for the *Golden Rays* team. Autofit the height of the two summary controls in the **Batting Average (BA)** column.
7. Switch to Print Preview, and then compare your screen with **Figure 1**. If you are printing this project, print the report. **Save**, and then **Close** the report.
8. Create a **Labels** report based on the **Coaches** table. In the **Label Wizard**, verify **Avery C2160** is selected, and then accept the default label format settings. In the **Prototype** label, add fields and spaces to create labels in the following format:
   FirstName LastName
   Street
   City, State Zip
   Accept all other wizard defaults. If you are printing this project, print the first page of the report. **Close** the report.
9. Modify the **Pitching Stats** query so that the **ERA** column calculates the average for each team. **Save**, and then **Close** the query.
10. Use the **Report** tool to create a report based on the **Pitching Stats** query. **Save** the report as Team Pitching
11. Change the **Title** control text to Team Pitching Statistics For the four column labels, apply **Bold** and **Center**.
12. Add a sort so that the **Team ERA** *(AvgOfERA)* column is ordered from smallest to largest. Delete the **Count** control in the **Team** column.
13. Switch to Report view, and then compare your screen with **Figure 2**. If you are printing this project, print the report.
14. Click **Save**, **Close** the report, and then **Close** Access. Submit the file as directed by your instructor.

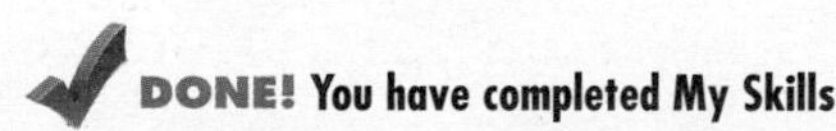

DONE! You have completed My Skills

Visual Skills Check

To complete this project, you will need the following files:

- acc04_VSPhones (Access)
- acc04_VSLogo (JPG)

You will save your file as:

- Last_First_acc04_VSPhones

Open the student data file **acc04_VSPhones**, and then save the file in your **Access Chapter 4** folder as Last_First_acc04_VSPhones

Use the Blank Report tool to create the report shown in **Figure 1**. In the report header, add the title, date, and time controls as shown. The logo is from the file **acc04_VSLogo**. Group the report by *Department* and sort it by *LastName*. Position, size, and delete controls as shown in **Figure 1**. Set the *Department* label control to size **14**, **Bold**, and merge cells so that the label spans the first two columns. Set the alternate row color of the group header row to **No Color**. Delete any unnecessary labels or rows, as needed.

Save the report as Phone List Print the report if needed. **Close** the report, **Close** Access, and then submit the file as directed by your instructor.

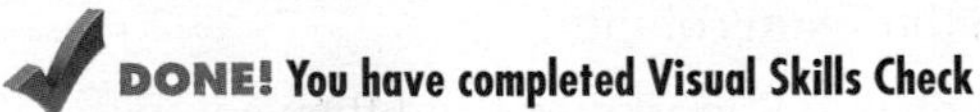

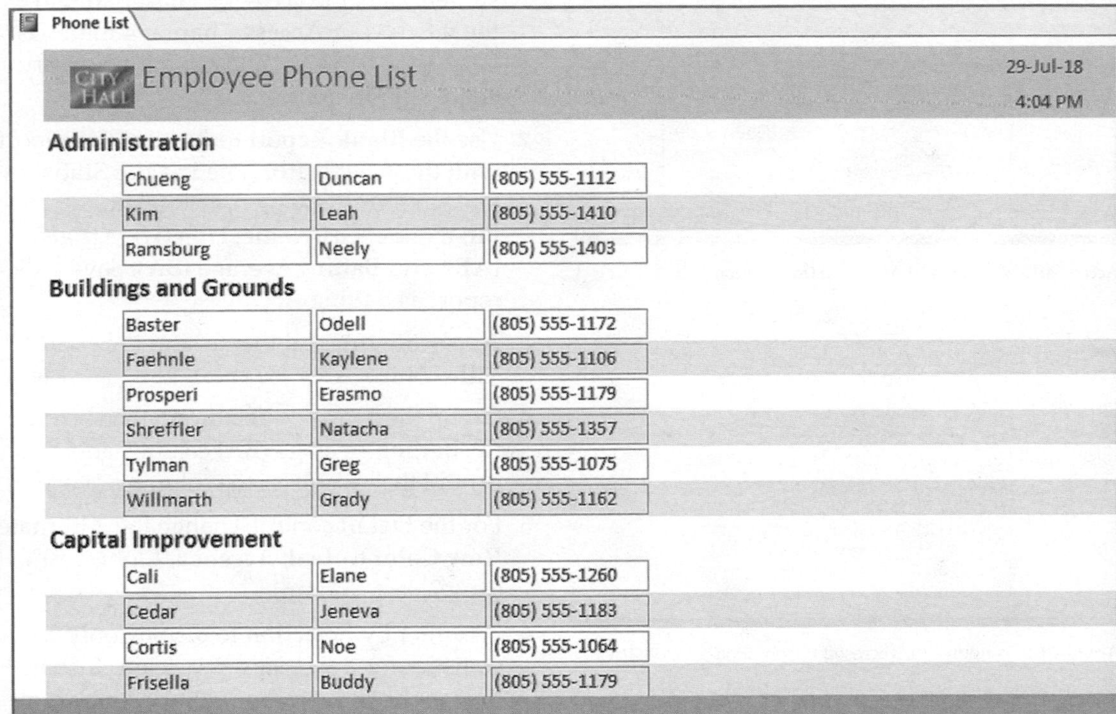

Figure 1

Skills Challenge 1

To complete this project, you will need the following file:

- acc04_SC1Reviews

You will save your file as:

- Last_First_acc04_SC1Reviews

Open the student data file **acc04_SC1Reviews**, and then save the file in your **Access Chapter 4** folder as Last_First_acc04_SC1Reviews Open Employee Evaluations in layout view, and then add grouping so that each employee's evaluations display under his or her name. Position and sort the fields and labels to make the report easier to understand. Add Totals to the Attendance and Customer Relations columns that calculate the average values for each column and format the numbers to display two decimals. Format the report to make it easier to read, and adjust the column widths and heights to fit the content each needs to display. Add a title control that describes the purpose of the report, and then filter the report to display the evaluations for Jack Hooley.

Print the report if needed. Close the report, Close Access, and then submit the file as directed by your instructor.

 **DONE! You have completed Skills Challenge 1**

Skills Challenge 2

To complete this project, you will need the following file:

- acc04_SC2Students

You will save your file as:

- Last_First_acc04_SC2Students

Open the student data file **acc04_SC2Students**, and then save the file in your **Access Chapter 4** folder as Last_First_acc04_SC2Students Create a query that can be used to create a mailing labels report. In the query, include the necessary name and address fields from the Students table, and then filter the query so that only participants from the Central neighborhood display. Save the query as Central Students Query. Use the Label Wizard to create a label report. Arrange the fields in the standard mailing address format. Include spacing and punctuation where appropriate. Do not include the Neighborhood field in the label. Accept all other default wizard settings.

Print the report if needed. Close the report, Close Access, and then submit the file as directed by your instructor.

 **DONE! You have completed Skills Challenge 2**

More Skills Assessment

To complete this project, you will need the following file:

- acc04_MSAClasses

You will save your files as:

- Last_First_acc04_MSAClasses (Access)
- Last_First_acc04_MSARTF (Rich Text Format)
- Last_First_acc04_MSAPDF (PDF)
- Last_First_acc04_MSAHTML (HTML)

---

1. Start **Access 2016**, and then open the student data file **acc04_MSAClasses**. **Save** the file in your **Access Chapter 4** folder as Last_First_acc04_MSAClasses
2. Open the **Sessions Report** in Layout view. Change the **Sort by Community Center** to **with Z on top**. Compare your screen with **Figure 1**, and then **Close** the **Group, Sort, and Total** dialog box. **Save**, and then **Close** the report.
3. Verify the Sessions Report is selected, and then export the report as a **Word** file. **Save** the Word file as Last_First_acc04_MSARTF in your **Access Chapter 4** folder. In the Access **Export - RTF File** dialog box, save the export steps as acc04_MSASessionsWord
4. With the Sessions Report still selected, export the report as a **PDF** file. During the export process, select **Optimize for Standard (publishing online and printing)**. **Save** the PDF file as Last_First_acc04_MSAPDF in your **Access Chapter 4** folder. In the Access **Export - PDF File** dialog box, save the export steps as acc04_MSASessionsPDF
5. With the Sessions Report still selected, export the report as an **HTML document** file. **Save** the HTML file as Last_First_acc04_MSAHTML in your **Access Chapter 4** folder. During the export process, **Choose the encoding to use for saving this file**: **Unicode (UTF-8)**. In the Access **Export - HTML File** dialog box, save the export steps as acc04_MSASessionsHTML

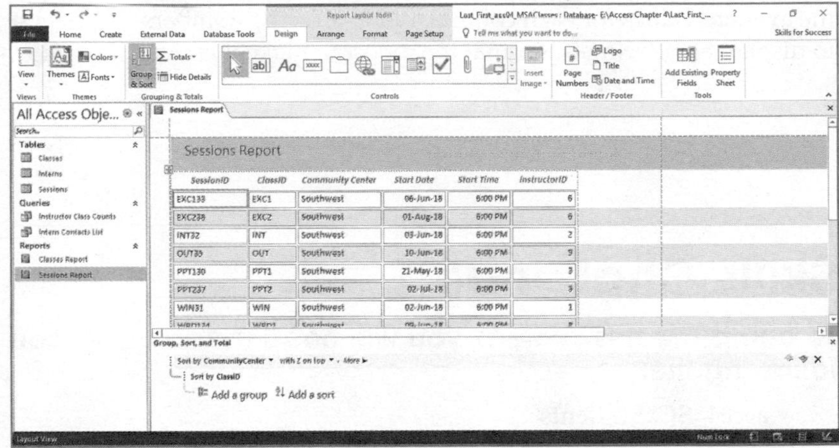

Figure 1 Access 2016, Windows 10, Microsoft Corporation

6. **Close** Access.
7. Submit the files as directed by your instructor.

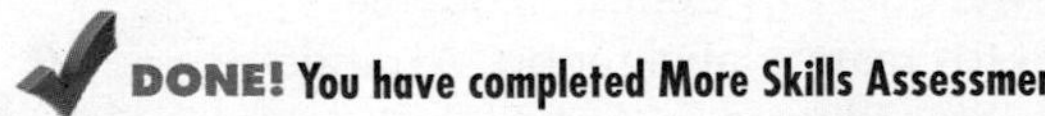

Collaborating with Google

To complete this project, you will need a Google account (refer to the Common Features chapter) and the following file:

- acc04_GPOutings

You will save your files as:

- **Last_First_acc04_GPReport (Word)**
- **Last_First_acc04_GPDownload (Word)**

1. Start **Access 2016**, and then open the student data file **acc04_GPOutings**.
2. In the **Navigation Pane**, select the **Outings Report**. On the **External Data tab**, in the **Export group**, click **More**, and then click **Word**. **Save** the Word file as Last_First_acc04_GPReport in your **Access Chapter 4** folder. During the export process, in the **Export - RTF File** dialog box, select **Open the designation file after the export operation is complete**.
3. When the Word file opens, switch to Access, **Close** the dialog box, and then **Close** Access. **Close** Word.
4. Open the Google Chrome web browser. Log into your Google account, and then click the **Apps** button. Click the **Drive** button to open Google Drive, and then click the **NEW** button. Click **File upload**.
5. Navigate to your Access Chapter 4 folder, and then double-click the **Last_First_GPReport** file.
6. In the bottom right portion of your browser, in the **Uploads completed** dialog box, click the **Last_First_acc04_GPReport** file. Compare your screen with **Figure 1**, and then click the **Open with Google Docs** button.
7. With your insertion point before the **Outings Report** title, if necessary, click the **More** button, and then click the **Center** button to center the title.
8. Select the title text **Outings Report**, and then change the font size to **24**.
9. Select the text **Outing ID** and **Outing Name**, click **Format**, and then click **Underline**.
10. Scroll down to view the second page of the document.

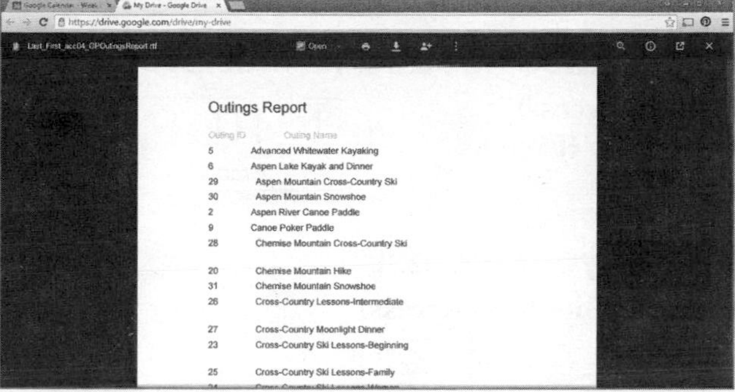

Figure 1

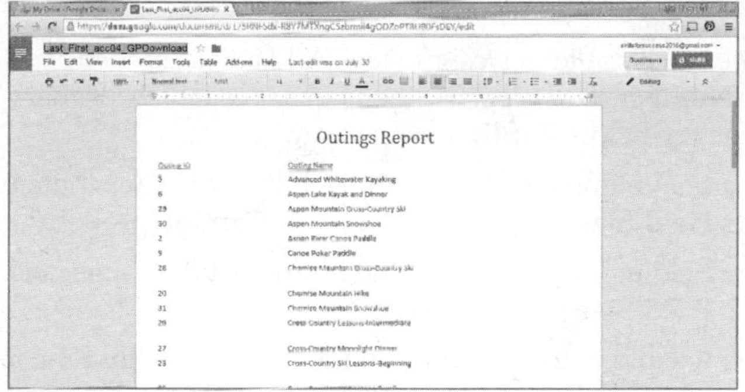

Figure 2

11. Select the text **Outing ID** and **Outing Name**, and then on the formatting toolbar, click **Underline**.
12. At the top of the browser, double-click the name of the document file.
13. Rename the document Last_First_acc04_GPDownload Compare your screen to **Figure 2**, and then click **OK**.
14. Click the **File tab**, and then point to **Download as**. In the submenu, click **Microsoft Word (.docx)**.
15. In the download bar, click the **arrow** next to the downloaded file, and then click **Open**. After the file opens in Microsoft Word, if necessary, Enable Editing, click the **File tab**, click **Save As**, and then save the file in your Access Chapter 4 folder.
16. **Close** both Word files, and then close Chrome. Submit the files as directed by your instructor.

DONE! You have completed Collaborating with Google

Student data files needed for this project:

acc_CSShelters (Access)
acc_CSShelterData (Excel)
acc_CSLogo (JPG)

You will save your file as:

Last_First_acc_CSShelters (Access)

---

1. Start **Access 2016**, and then open the student data file, **acc_CSShelters**. Use the **Save As** dialog box to save the file to your chapter folder as Last_First_acc_CSShelters If necessary, enable the content.
2. Create a new table in Design view. Add a field named ShelterID with the **AutoNumber** data type. Set the field as the table's primary key, and then change the field's **Caption** property to Shelter ID
3. Add a field named ShelterName with the **Short Text** data type. Change the field's **Field Size** property to 50 and its **Caption** property to Shelter Name
4. Add a field named Park with the **Short Text** data type, and then change the field's **Field Size** property to 50
5. **Save** the table with the name Shelters and then **Close** the table.
6. Import the data from the Excel file **acc_CSShelterData** by appending the data to the **Shelters** table.
7. Open the **Shelters** table, set the column widths to **Best Fit**, and then compare your screen with **Figure 1**. **Save**, and then **Close** the table.
8. Relate the database's two tables in a one-to-many relationship by enforcing referential integrity between the **ShelterID** fields. For the relationship, select both cascading options. **Save**, and then **Close** the Relationships tab.
9. Create a query in Design view, add both database tables, and then add the following fields: **ShelterName**, **ReservationDate**, **GroupSize**, and **Fee**. Add criteria so that only reservations for the month of July 2018 display. **Save** the query with the name July Reservations
10. **Run** the query. Compare your screen with **Figure 2**, and then **Close** the query.

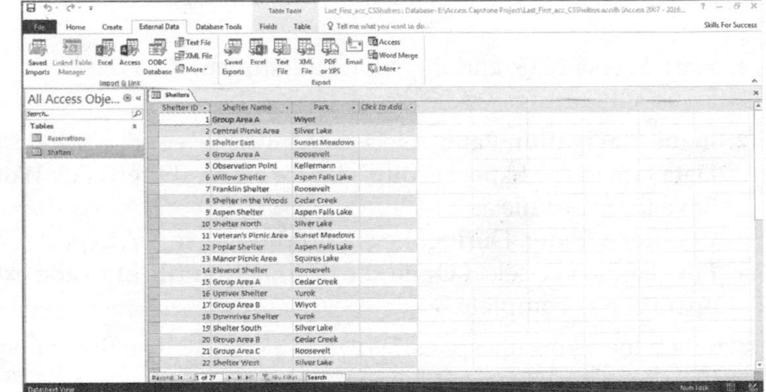

Figure 1 Access 2016, Windows 10, Microsoft Corporation

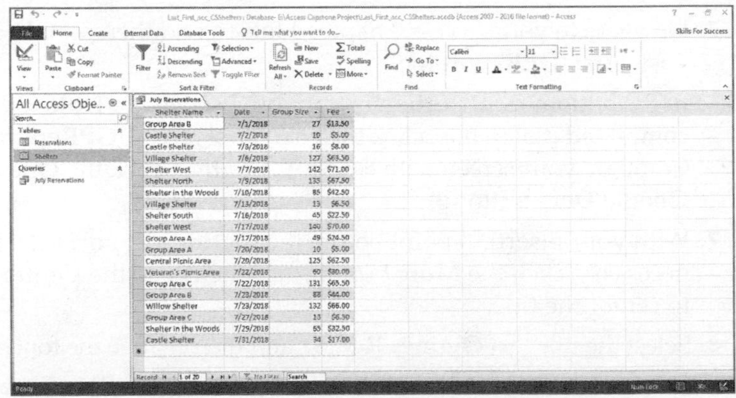

Figure 2 Access 2016, Windows 10, Microsoft Corporation

■ **Continue to the next page to complete the project**

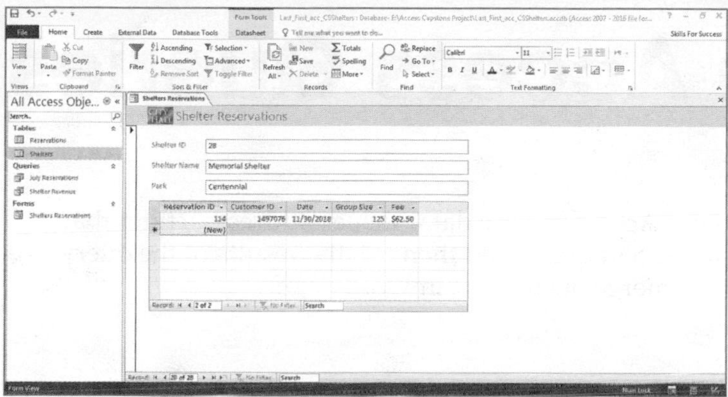

Access 2016, Windows 10, Microsoft Corporation

Figure 3

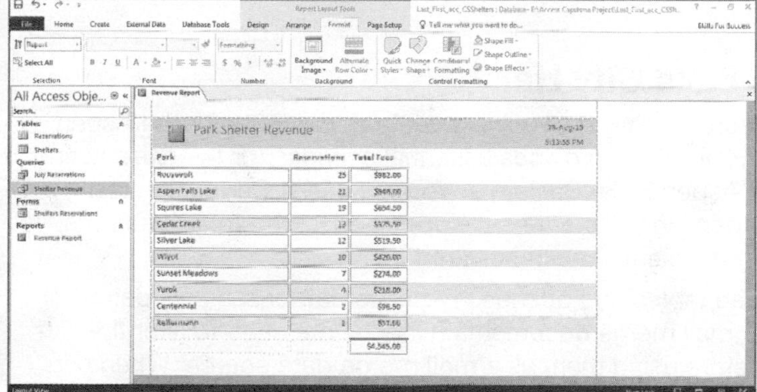

Access 2016, Windows 10, Microsoft Corporation

Figure 4

11. Create a query in Design view, add both database tables, and then add the following fields: **Park**, **ReservationDate**, and **Fee**. **Save** the query with the name Shelter Revenue
12. Group the **Shelter Revenue** query by **Park**. In the **ReservationDate** column, add a **Count** total, and then in the **Fee** column, add a **Sum** total.
13. **Save**, and then **Run** the query. Verify that 10 records display, and then **Close** the query.
14. Use the **Form** tool to create a form and subform with the main form based on the **Shelters** table. **Save** the form with the name Shelter Reservations
15. Apply the **Retrospect** theme, insert the logo from the file **acc_CSLogo**, and then change the form's title text to Shelter Reservations
16. Use the property sheet to change the width of the **Shelter ID** text box control to 4.8" and then **Close** the property sheet.
17. In the main form, add a new record with Memorial Shelter as the shelter name and Centennial as the park name. In the subform, add a reservation with a **Customer ID** of 1497076 The date is 11/30/2018 and the **Group Size** is 125
18. Compare your screen with **Figure 3**. **Save** all tables and forms, and then **Close** the form.
19. Use the **Report** tool to create a report based on the **Shelter Revenue** query. **Save** the report as Revenue Report
20. Change the report title to Park Shelter Revenue and then change the Date control's **Number Format** to **Medium Date**.
21. Add a sort that orders the **CountOfReservationDate** column from largest to smallest.
22. Change the second column label to Reservations and the third column label to Total Fees
23. For all three column labels, change the font size to **12**, apply **Bold**, and apply **Align Left**. **AutoFit** the second column's width.
24. Below the **Total Fees** column, **AutoFit** the height of the Total control, and then change the control's **Number Format** to **Currency**.
25. **Close** the Group, Sort, and Total pane, and then delete the control with the page number. Compare your screen with **Figure 4**.
26. **Save**, and then **Close** the report. **Close** Access, and then submit the file as directed by your instructor.

DONE! You have completed Access Capstone Project

Create Envelopes from Access Queries

- In Word, you can merge data into different types of documents such as letters, envelopes, mailing labels, or e-mail messages.
- You can use Access to store data such as addresses, filter that data in an Access query, and then use the results of the query to create mail merge documents in Word.

Tsiumpa | Fotolia

Aspen Falls City Hall

In this Integrated Project, you will create documents for the Aspen Falls City Hall, which provides essential services for the citizens and visitors of Aspen Falls, California. You will assist Carter Horikoshi, Art Center Supervisor, to create envelopes addressed to art students who live in the Central neighborhood.

You can use tables and queries in Access databases as a data source for mail merge documents. Queries are used to filter the records before using them as a mail merge data source. When you set a Word document as an envelope, the document changes to the size of a standard envelope with placeholders for the return and recipient address. Typically, the return address is typed, and the recipients' addresses are retrieved from the database table or query.

You will add criteria to an Access query, and then use that query as the data source for a mail merge. In Word, you will create a document that can print an envelope for each student who lives in the Central neighborhood.

Time to complete this project — 30 to 60 minutes

Introduction

Outcome

Using the skills in this project, you will be able to add criteria to a query, create an envelope as a mail merge document, use an Access query as the mail merge data source, and insert an address block merge field into a Word document.

Objectives

6.1 Construct envelopes from an Access query

6.2 Create a query to produce mail merge data

6.3 Generate an address block merge field in a Word document

Student data file needed for this project:

acc_IP06Addresses (Access)

You will save your files as:

Last_First_acc_IP06Addresses (Access)
Last_First_acc_IP06Merged (Word)

SKILLS

At the end of this project, you will be able to:

- Add criteria to an Access query
- Create an envelope as a mail merge document
- Use an Access query as a data source
- Type a return address and insert an address block merge field
- Preview and print an envelope for a selected record

First Last
500 S Aspen St
Aspen Falls, CA 93463

Eliseo Brennan
14824 W Dogwood Ln
Aspen Falls, CA 93463

1. Start **Access 2016**, and then open the student data file **acc_IP06Addresses**.
2. **Save** the file to your **Access App Level Projects** folder as Last_First_acc_IP06Addresses If necessary, enable the content.
3. In the **Navigation Pane**, right-click **Central Addresses**, and then click **Design View**. In the **Neighborhood** column **Criteria** cell, type Central and then compare your screen with **Figure 1**.
4. Click **Save** [Save], and then **Run** the query to display 10 records. **Close** [X] the query, and then **Close** [X] Access.
5. Start **Word 2016**, and then click **Blank document**. Click the **Mailings tab**. In the **Start Mail Merge group**, click the **Start Mail Merge** button, and then click **Envelopes**.

   When you start a mail merge, you need to choose a document type. Here, the document will be an envelope.
6. In the **Envelope Options** dialog box, verify that the **Envelope Size** is set to **Size 10**, and then click **OK**.
7. In the upper left corner of the envelope, type your First and Last names, and then press Enter. Type 500 S Aspen St and then press Enter. Type Aspen Falls, CA 93463 Compare your screen with **Figure 2**.

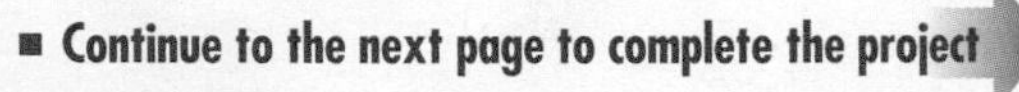

■ Continue to the next page to complete the project

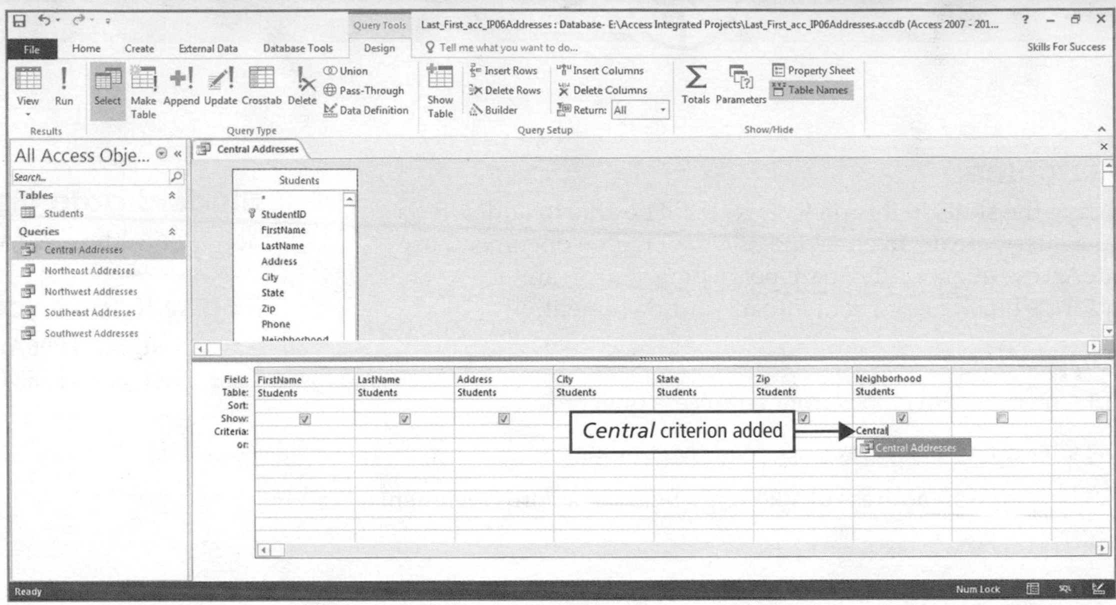

Figure 1

Access 2016, Windows 10, Microsoft Corporation

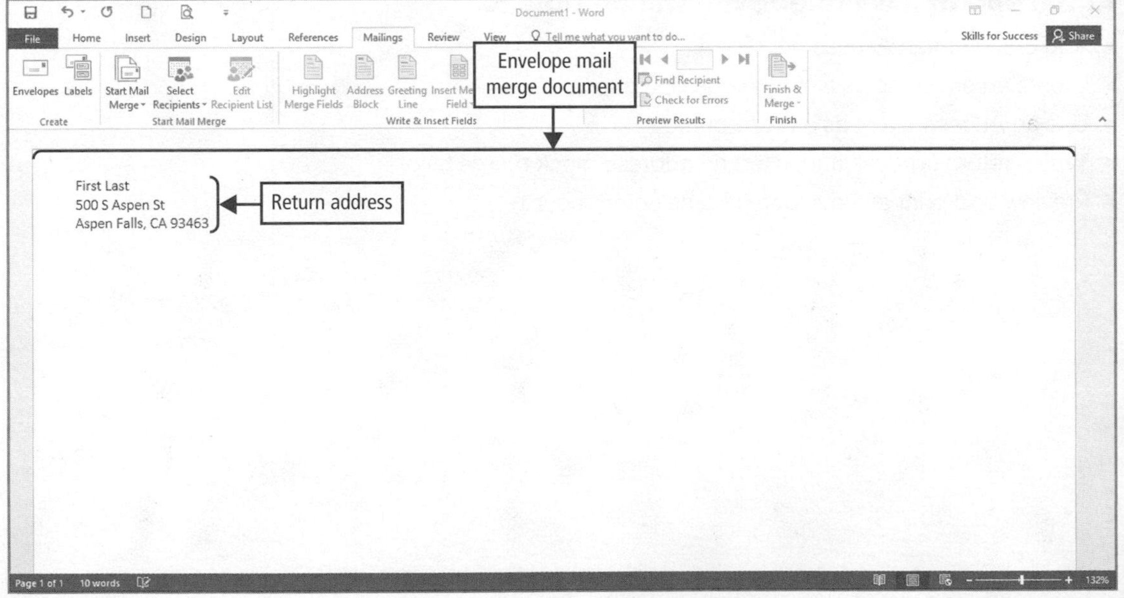

Figure 2

Word 2016, Windows 10, Microsoft Corporation

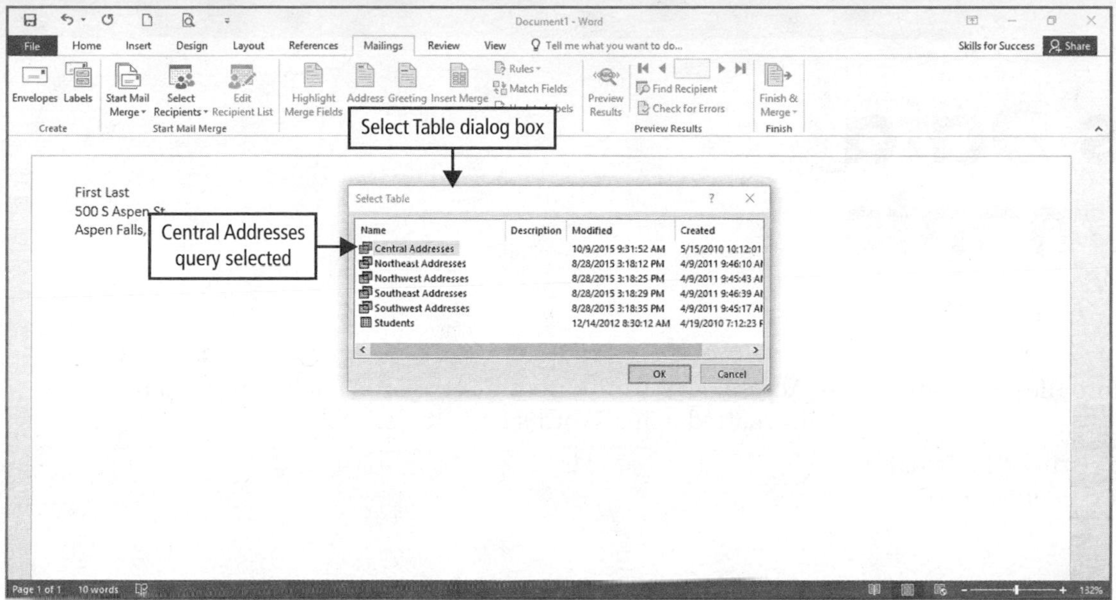

Word 2016, Windows 10, Microsoft Corporation

Figure 3

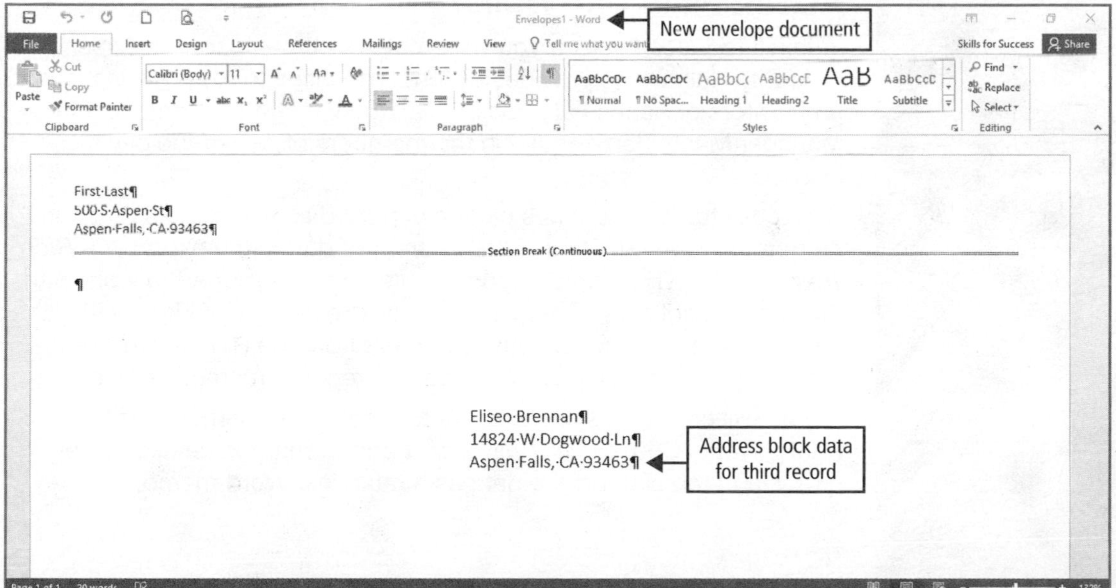

Word 2016, Windows 10, Microsoft Corporation

Figure 4

8. On the **Mailings tab**, in the **Start Mail Merge group**, click the **Select Recipients** button, and then click **Use an Existing List**.
9. In the **Select Data Source** dialog box, navigate to and click **Last_First_acc_IP06Addresses**, and then click **Open**. In the **Select Table** dialog box, verify that **Central Addresses** is selected. Compare your screen with **Figure 3**, and then click **OK**.
10. On the **Home tab**, in the **Paragraph group**, click the **Show/Hide** button to display the nonprinting characters. In the center of the envelope, click to left of the ¶ mark to display the address placeholder. Click the **Mailings tab**. In the **Write & Insert Fields group**, click the **Address Block** button, and then click **OK**.
11. In the **Preview Results group**, click **Preview Results**. In the **Preview Results group**, click the **Next Record** button ▶ two times.
12. In the **Finish group**, click the **Finish & Merge** button, and then click **Edit Individual Documents**. In the **Merge to New Document** dialog box, select the **Current record** option button, and then click **OK**. Compare your screen with **Figure 4**.
13. Click **Save**, and then in the **Save As** dialog box, navigate to the location you are saving your work. Name the file Last_First_acc_IP06Merged and then click **Save**. **Close** ✕ the document.
14. **Close** ✕ the original envelopes document without saving changes, and then submit the files as directed by your instructor.

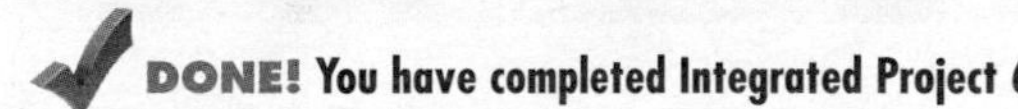
DONE! You have completed Integrated Project 6

Export Access Data to Word Documents

- Data stored in Access tables can be exported into files that can be opened by other programs.
- When Access tables or queries are exported as Rich Text Format (RTF) files, they can be imported into Word documents.
- Access data is imported into Word as a table that can be formatted using Word's table tools.

© Alsonh29 | Dreamstime.com

Aspen Falls City Hall

In this Integrated Project, you will create documents for the Aspen Falls City Hall, which provides essential services for the citizens and visitors of Aspen Falls, California. You will write a memo to City Manager Maria Martinez listing the members of one of the city's councils.

Access tables or queries can be exported as file formats that can be opened in Word. The file that is created during the export is a ***Rich Text Format*** (RTF) file—a document file format designed to work with many different types of programs. If you are already working with a Word document, you can import the text from the RTF file. In this manner, you can include Access data in reports, memos, and letters.

You will create an Access query to display the members of the Public Works Council. You will export and format the results of the query, and then import the data as a table in a Word memo.

Time to complete this project—30 to 60 minutes

Introduction

Outcome

Using the skills in this project, you will be able to export an Access query as an RTF file, modify a memo, and import data from an RTF file into Word.

Objectives

7.1 Modify a memo

7.2 Generate an RTF file from an Access query

7.3 Revise a document using imported data

Student data files needed for this project:

acc_IP07Councils (Access)
acc_IP07Memo (Word)

You will save your files as:

Last_First_acc_IP07Councils (Access)
Last_First_acc_IP07PublicWorks (RTF File)
Last_First_acc_IP07Memo (Word)

SKILLS

At the end of this project, you will be able to:

- Create an Access query in Design view, add criteria, and hide a column
- Export an Access query as an RTF file
- Modify a memo
- Import data from an RTF file into Word
- Adjust table column widths using Autofit

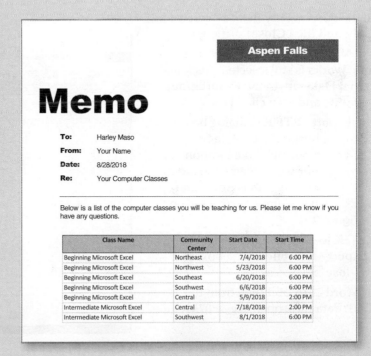

Aspen Falls

Memo

To: Harley Maso
From: Your Name
Date: 8/28/2018
Re: Your Computer Classes

Below is a list of the computer classes you will be teaching for us. Please let me know if you have any questions.

Class Name	Community Center	Start Date	Start Time
Beginning Microsoft Excel	Northeast	7/4/2018	6:00 PM
Beginning Microsoft Excel	Northwest	5/23/2018	6:00 PM
Beginning Microsoft Excel	Southeast	6/20/2018	6:00 PM
Beginning Microsoft Excel	Southwest	6/6/2018	6:00 PM
Beginning Microsoft Excel	Central	5/9/2018	2:00 PM
Intermediate Microsoft Excel	Central	7/18/2018	2:00 PM
Intermediate Microsoft Excel	Southwest	8/1/2018	6:00 PM

1. Start **Access 2016**, and then open the student data file **acc_IP07Councils**.
2. Use the **Save As** dialog box to save the file to your folder as Last_First_acc_IP07Councils If necessary, enable the content.
3. Click the **Create tab**, and then in the **Queries group**, click **Query Design**. **Add** the **Councils** and **Members** tables to the query, and then **Close** the dialog box.
4. Add the **FirstName**, **LastName**, and **CouncilName** fields to the query design grid.
5. In the **CouncilName** column **Criteria** cell, type Public Works In the **CouncilName** column **Show** cell, clear the check box.
6. Click **Save**, type Public Works and then click **OK**. Compare your screen with **Figure 1**.
7. **Run** the query, verify that seven records display, and then **Close** [X] the query.
8. In the **Navigation Pane**, verify that **Public Works** is still selected. Click the **External Data tab**. In the **Export group**, click **More**, and then click **Word**.
9. In the **Export - RTF File** dialog box, click the **Browse** button. In the **File Save** dialog box, navigate to the location you are saving your work. Name the file Last_First_acc_IP07PublicWorks and then click **Save**. Compare your screen with **Figure 2**.
10. Click **OK** to complete the export. **Close** the **Export - RTF File** dialog box, and then **Close** [X] Access.
11. Start **Word 2016**, and then from the student data files, open **acc_IP07Memo**.

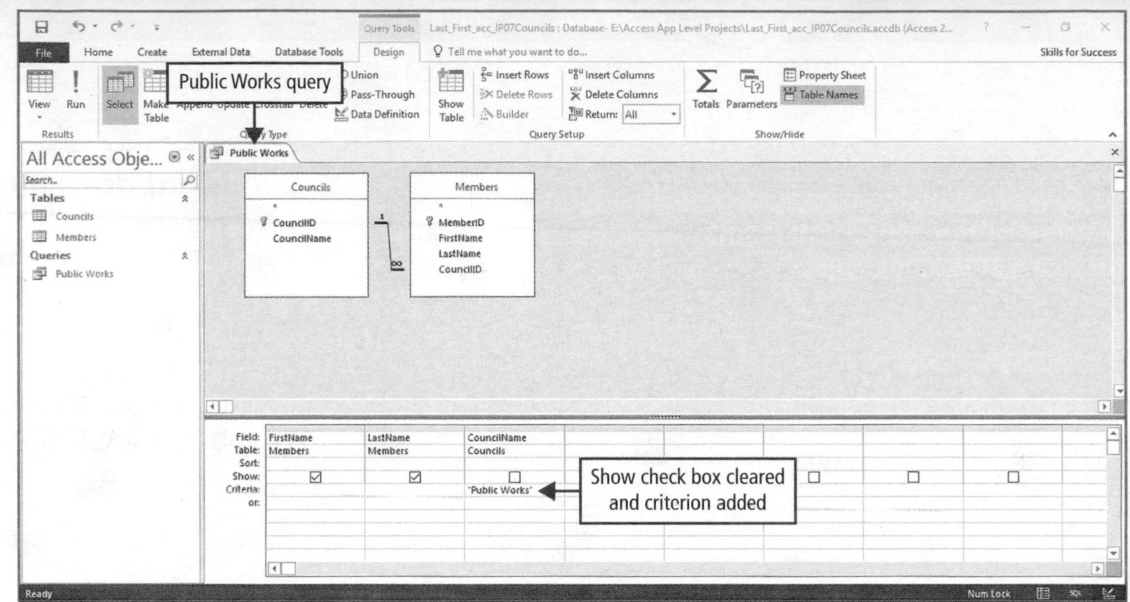

Figure 1

Access 2016, Windows 10, Microsoft Corporation

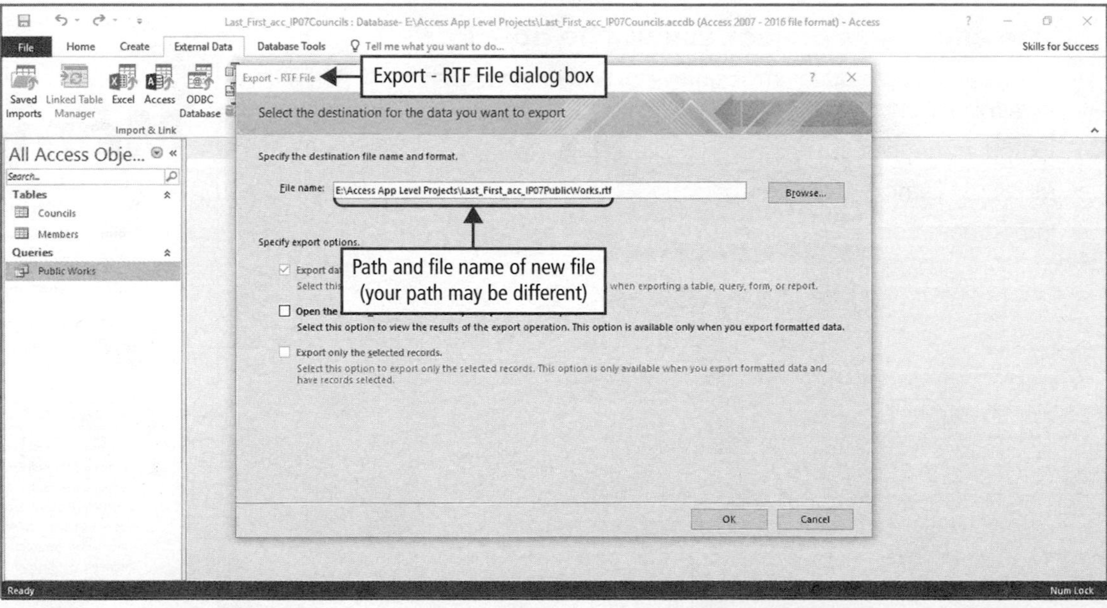

Figure 2

Access 2016, Windows 10, Microsoft Corporation

■ **Continue to the next page to complete the project**

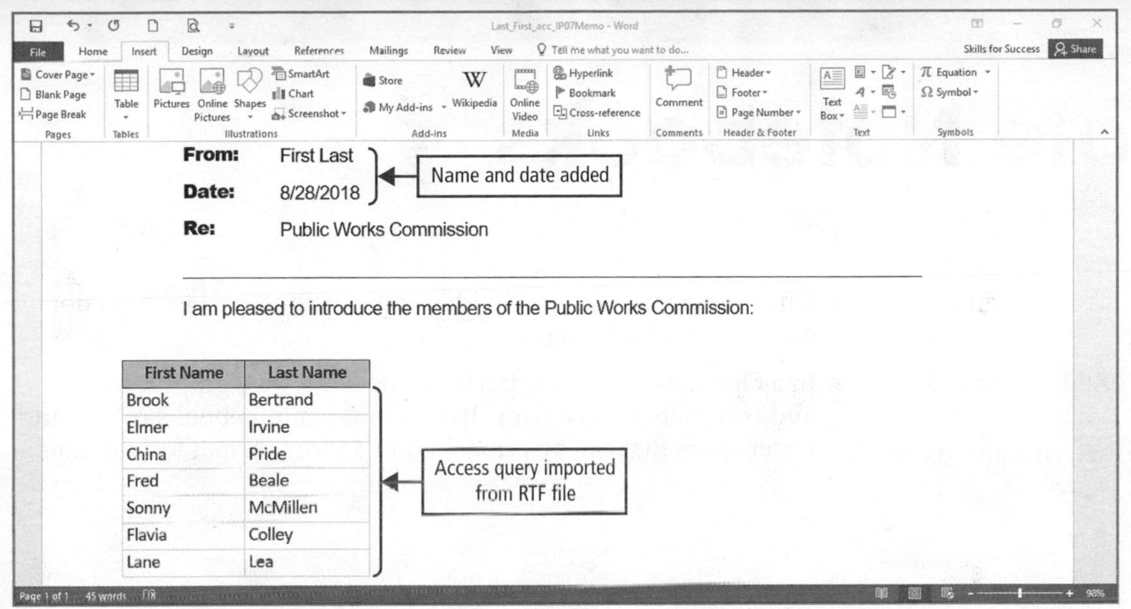

Access 2016, Windows 10, Microsoft Corporation

Figure 3

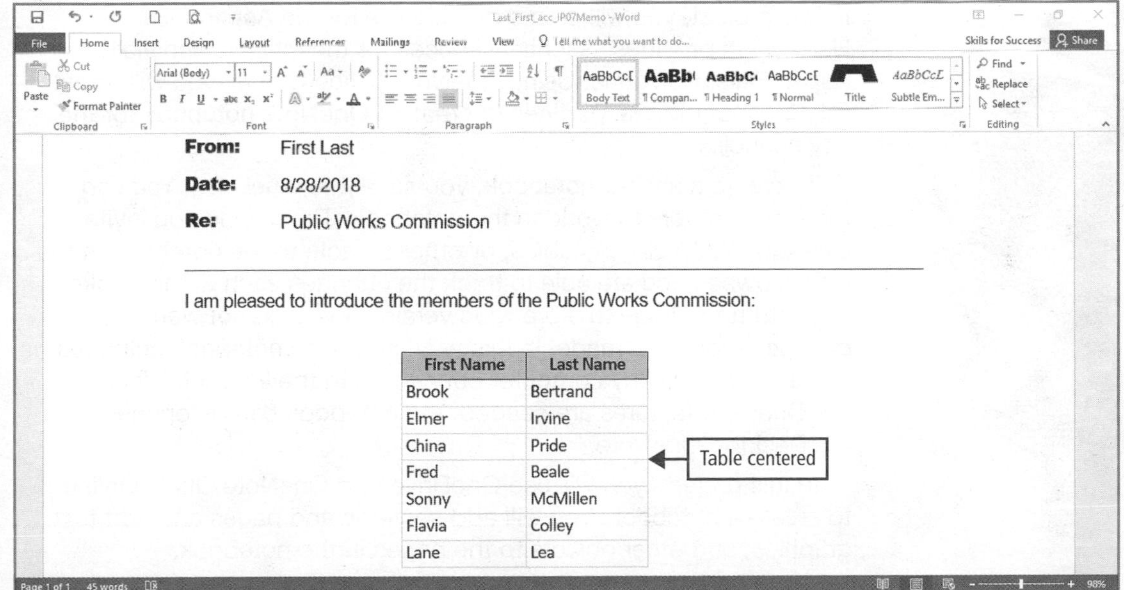

Access 2016, Windows 10, Microsoft Corporation

Figure 4

12. **Save** the file as Last_First_acc_IP07Memo
13. Click in the cell to the right of *From*, and then type your First and Last names. In the cell to the right of *Date*, type the current date in mm/dd/yyyy format.
14. Click in the blank paragraph below the table, and then type the following: I am pleased to introduce the members of the Public Works Commission:
15. Press Enter two times, and then click the **Insert tab**. In the **Text group**, click the **Object arrow**, and then click **Text from File**.
16. In the **Insert File** dialog box, select **Last_First_acc_IP07PublicWorks**, and then click **Insert**. Compare your screen with **Figure 3**.
17. Point to the imported table, and then click the table's **selector** button to select the table.
18. Click the **Table Tools Layout tab**, and then in the **Table group**, click the **Properties** button. In the **Table Properties** dialog box, under **Alignment**, click **Center**, and then click **OK**. Click to deselect the table, and then compare your screen with **Figure 4**.
19. **Save** the file, and then **Close** Word. Submit the files as directed by your instructor.

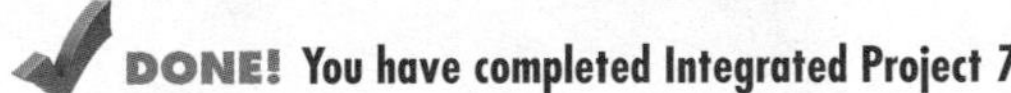

Create OneNote Notebooks

- ***OneNote*** is a program used to collect notes, drawings, and media from multiple participants.
- A OneNote document is a loose structure of digital pages called a ***notebook***.
- Notebooks can be shared by saving them to OneDrive and using OneNote Office Online to edit them.
- OneNote notebooks are divided into sections, and each section can have multiple pages.
- In a OneNote notebook, participants enter text, graphics, or audio anywhere on a page. In this manner, notebooks collect and foster ideas that can be published in a more formal format later.

© 3ddock / Fotolia

Aspen Falls City Hall

In this project, you will create documents for the Aspen Falls City Hall, which provides essential services for the citizens and visitors of Aspen Falls, California. Using OneNote Office Online, you will assist City Manager Maria Martinez to create a OneNote notebook for the city council.

To create a shared notebook, you save it to OneDrive. You can then invite others to work on the notebook. Those who you invite can add text, pictures, tables, or other objects to the notebook in the web browser. You are able to track the changes each author makes and return the page to a previous version if you do not want the changes they have made. In this way, an online notebook helps teams collaborate from any computer connected to the Internet. When all the OneNote features are needed, the notebook can be opened in the Desktop OneNote.

In this project, you will use OneDrive and OneNote Office Online to create a notebook. You will add sections and pages and add text, graphics, and other objects to the pages in the notebook.

Time to complete this project — 30 to 60 minutes

Outcome

Using the skills in this project, you will be able to create a OneNote notebook on OneDrive, add notebook sections and tables, add text and pictures to pages, and share notebooks.

Objectives

4.1 Construct a OneNote notebook

4.2 Produce notebook content

Student data file needed for this project:

acc_OPPhoto

You will save your files as:

City Council Notebook (OneDrive)
Last_First_acc_OPSnip1
Last_First_acc_OPSnip2

SKILLS

At the end of this project, you will be able to:

- Create a OneNote notebook on OneDrive
- Name notebook sections and pages
- Add notebook sections and pages
- Add text, tables, and pictures to pages
- Display pages in Reading view
- Show authors and share notebooks

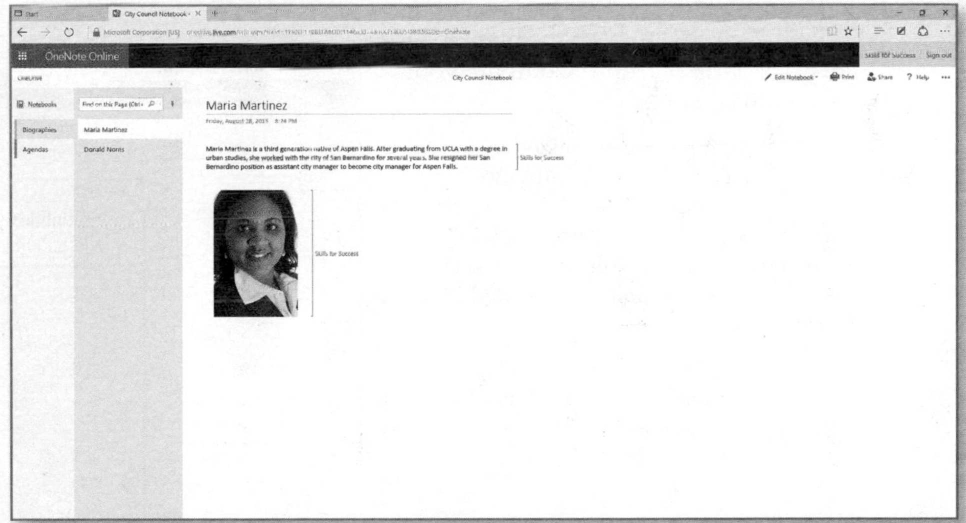

Access 2016, Windows 10, Microsoft Corporation

1. Start **Microsoft Edge**, navigate to onedrive.live.com and then log on to your Microsoft account. If you do not have an account, follow the links and directions on the page to create one.
2. After logging in, navigate as needed to display your **OneDrive** page. Compare your screen with **Figure 1**.

   OneDrive and Office Online technologies are accessed through web pages that can change often, and the formatting and layout of some pages may often be different than the figures in this book. You may need to adapt the steps to complete the actions they describe.
3. On the toolbar, click **New**, and then click **OneNote notebook**. In the **OneNote notebook** dialog box, name the file City Council Notebook and then click the **Create** button to save the document to your OneDrive and start OneNote Online.
4. With the insertion point in the blank page title, type Maria Martinez Compare your screen with **Figure 2**.

   In OneNote, notes are organized in notebooks. Each notebook is divided into sections, and each section can have multiple pages. Here, the notebook is named City Council Notebook, the section is untitled, and the first page is titled Maria Martinez.

   The changes you make in OneNote Online are automatically saved. For this reason, there is no save button.

■ **Continue to the next page to complete the skill**

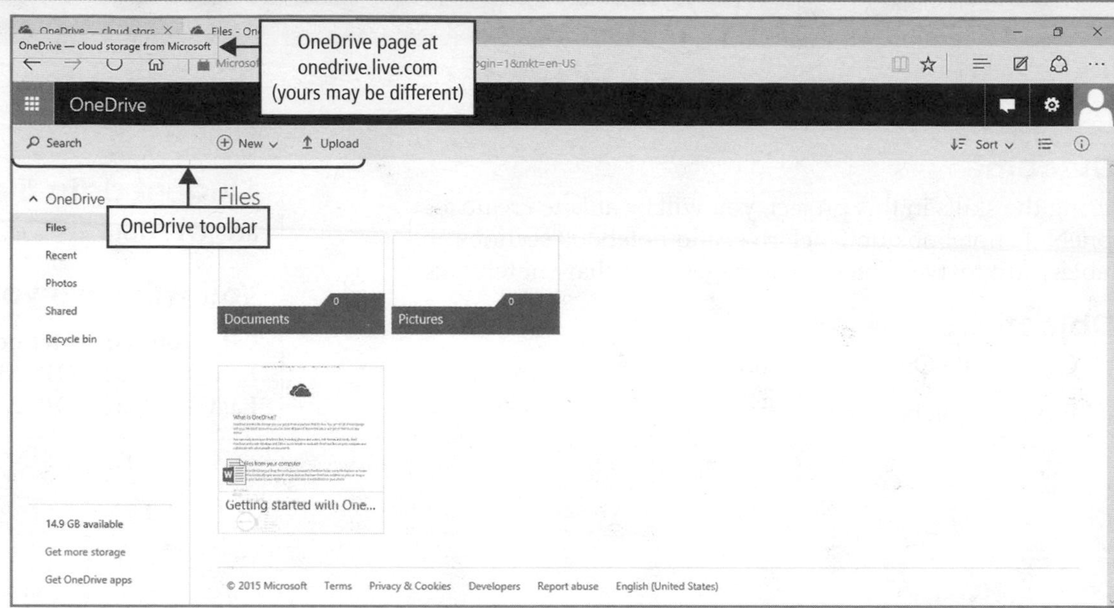

Figure 1 Access 2016, Windows 10, Microsoft Corporation

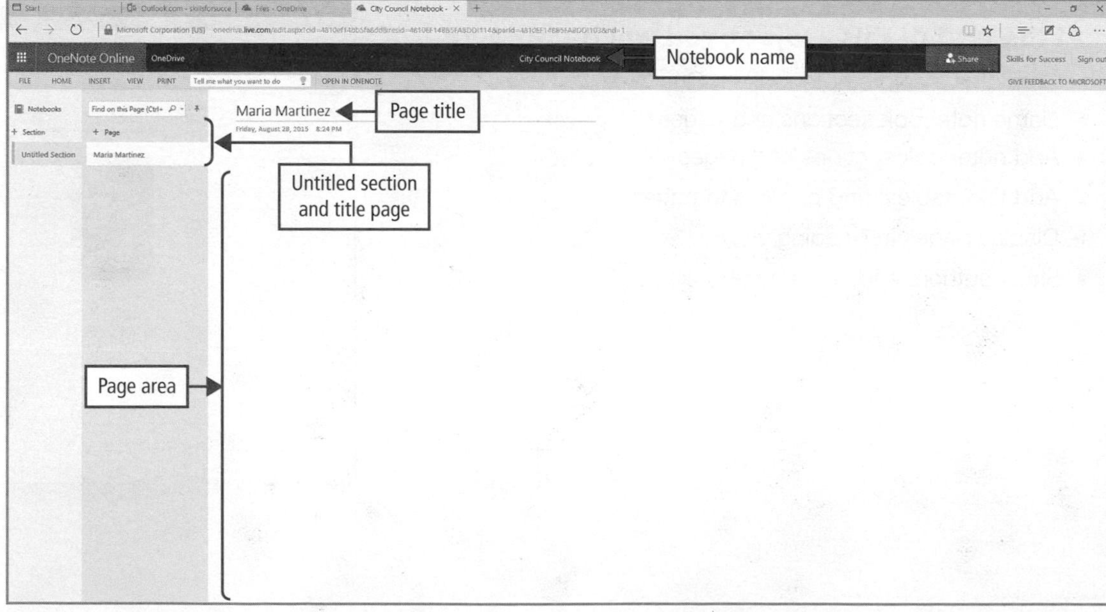

Figure 2 Access 2016, Windows 10, Microsoft Corporation

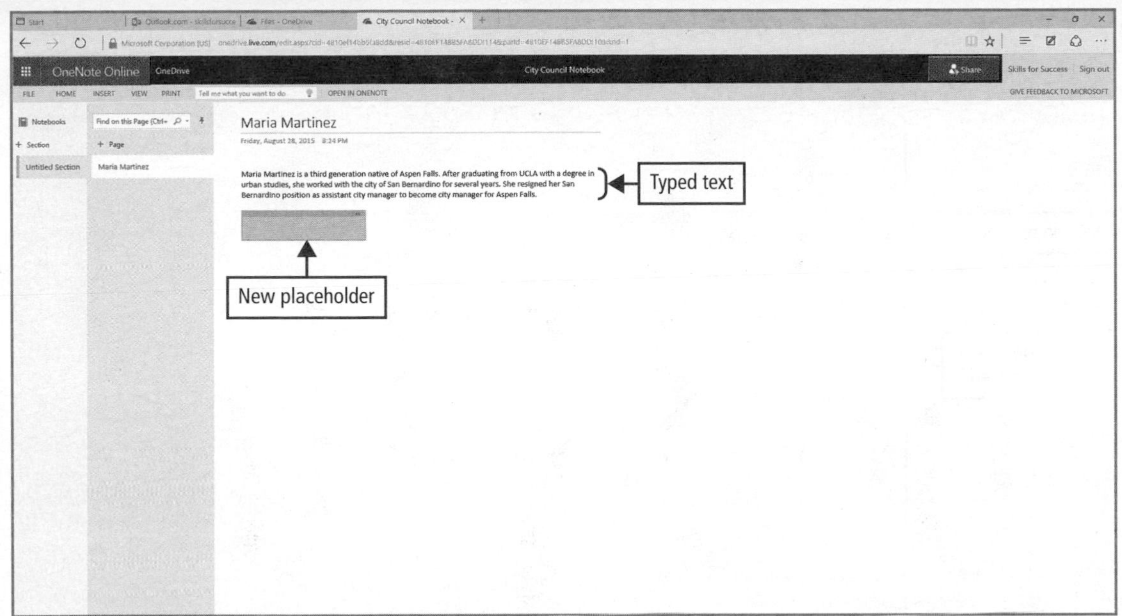

Access 2016, Windows 10, Microsoft Corporation

Figure 3

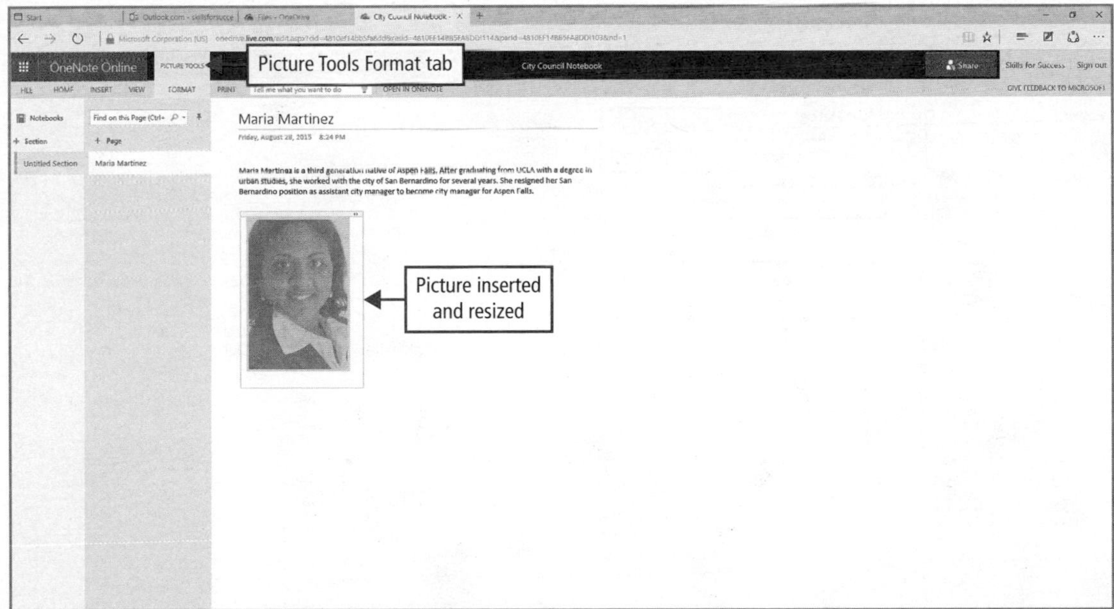

Access 2016, Windows 10, Microsoft Corporation

Figure 4

5. Press Tab to move the insertion point into the page, and then type the following: Maria Martinez is a third generation native of Aspen Falls. After graduating from UCLA with a degree in urban studies, she worked with the city of San Bernardino for several years. She resigned her San Bernardino position as assistant city manager to become city manager for Aspen Falls.
6. Click in a blank area in the middle of the page to create a new placeholder. Point to the title bar of the new placeholder, and then with the pointer, drag to position the placeholder below the text typed previously similar to the position shown in **Figure 3**.

   An object can be inserted anywhere on the page. It can then be moved by dragging its placeholder.
7. Click in the new placeholder positioned in the previous step. Click the **INSERT tab**, and then in the **Pictures group**, click **Picture**.
8. In the **Choose File to Upload** dialog box, navigate to the student data files that you downloaded for this project. Click **acc_OPPhoto**, and then click **Open**.
9. Wait a few moments for the picture to upload and display. Click the picture to select it and display the Picture Tools Format tab.
10. Click the **FORMAT tab**, and then in the **Image Size group**, select the value in the **Scale** box. Type 50% press Enter, and then compare your screen with **Figure 4**.

■ **Continue to the next page to complete the skill**

11. Click in the page to deselect the picture. In the left pane, right-click **Untitled Section**, and then from the shortcut menu, click **Rename**. In the **Section Name** dialog box, name the section Biographies and then click **OK**.
12. To the right of *Biographies*, click the **+ Page** button, and then type Donald Norris
13. Press Tab to move the insertion point into the page, and then type Donald, you need to post your bio. Thanks. Compare your screen with **Figure 5**.
14. Click the **INSERT tab**, and then in the **Notebook group**, click **New Section**. In the **Section Name** dialog box, type Agendas and then click **OK**.
15. With the insertion point in the title of the new Untitled Page, type April Meeting to title the page.
16. Press Tab to move the insertion point to the first line of the page. Click the **INSERT tab**, and then in the **Tables group**, click the **Table** button. In the **Table** gallery, click the second cell in the third row to insert a **2x3 Table**.
17. In the six table cells, type the following:

Item	Presenter
Aspen Falls Lake Flood Mitigation	Donald Norris
Community College Internships	Evelyn Stone and George Gato

18. Using the ⟺ pointer, drag the columns to the right until each cell's content fits on one line. Compare your screen with **Figure 6**.

■ **Continue to the next page to complete the skill**

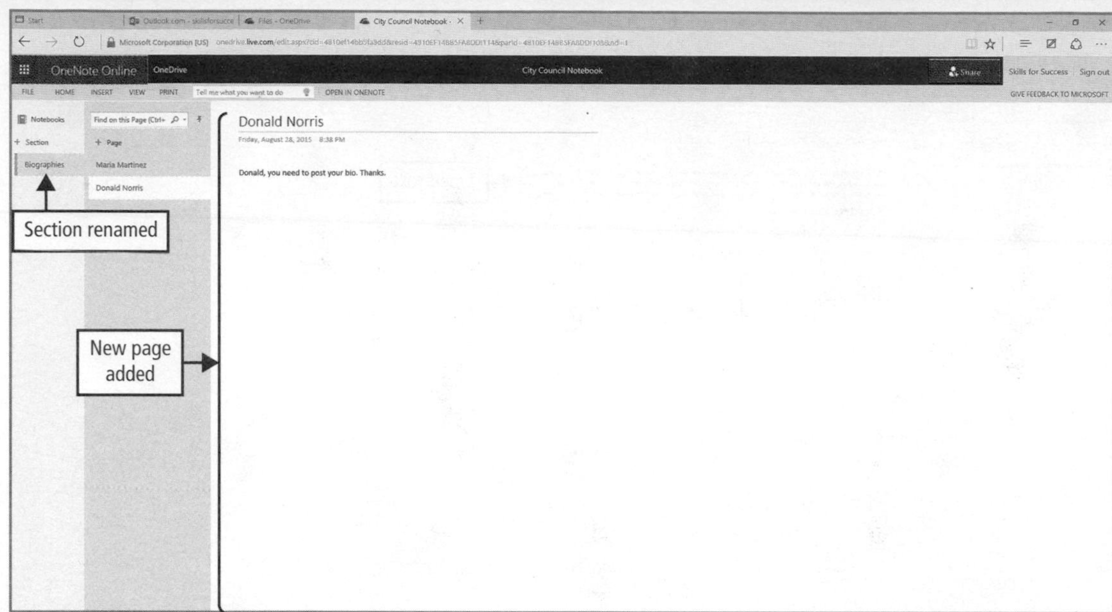

Figure 5 Access 2016, Windows 10, Microsoft Corporation

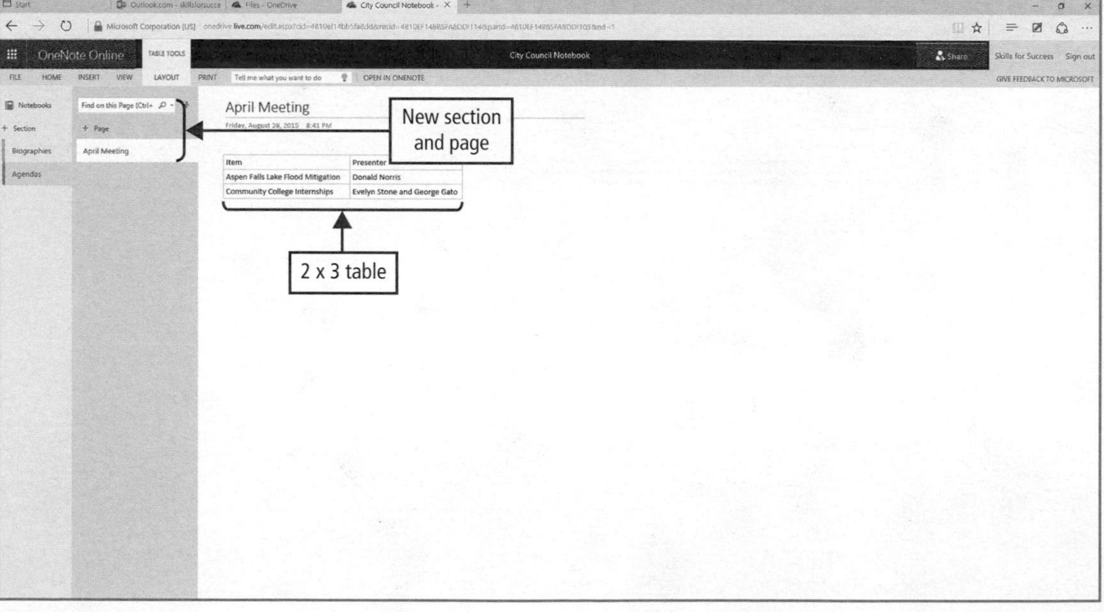

Figure 6 Access 2016, Windows 10, Microsoft Corporation

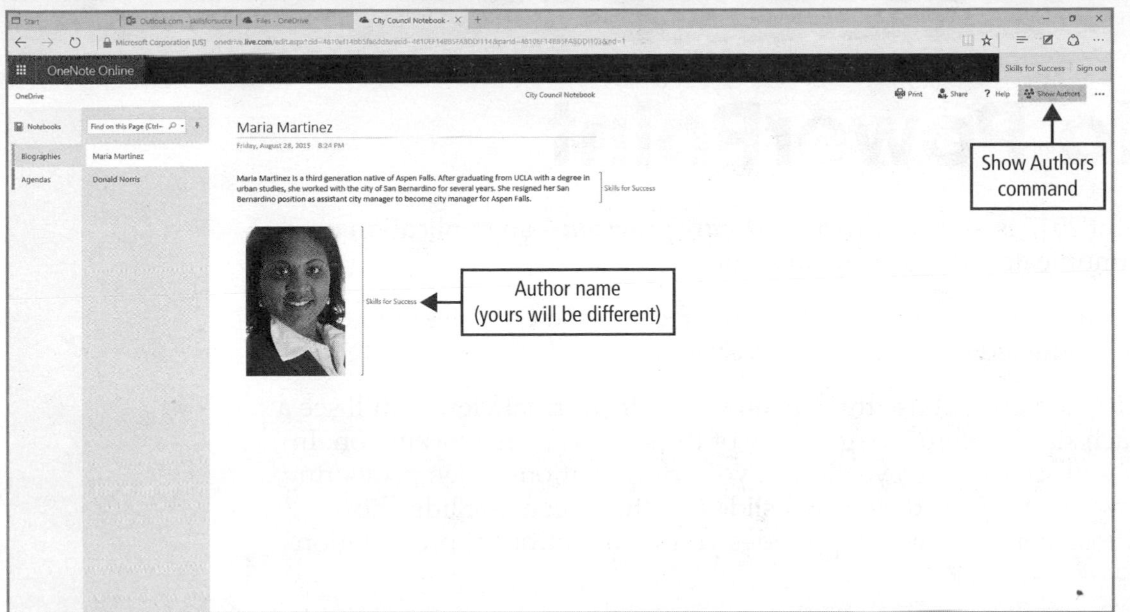

Access 2016, Windows 10, Microsoft Corporation

Figure 7

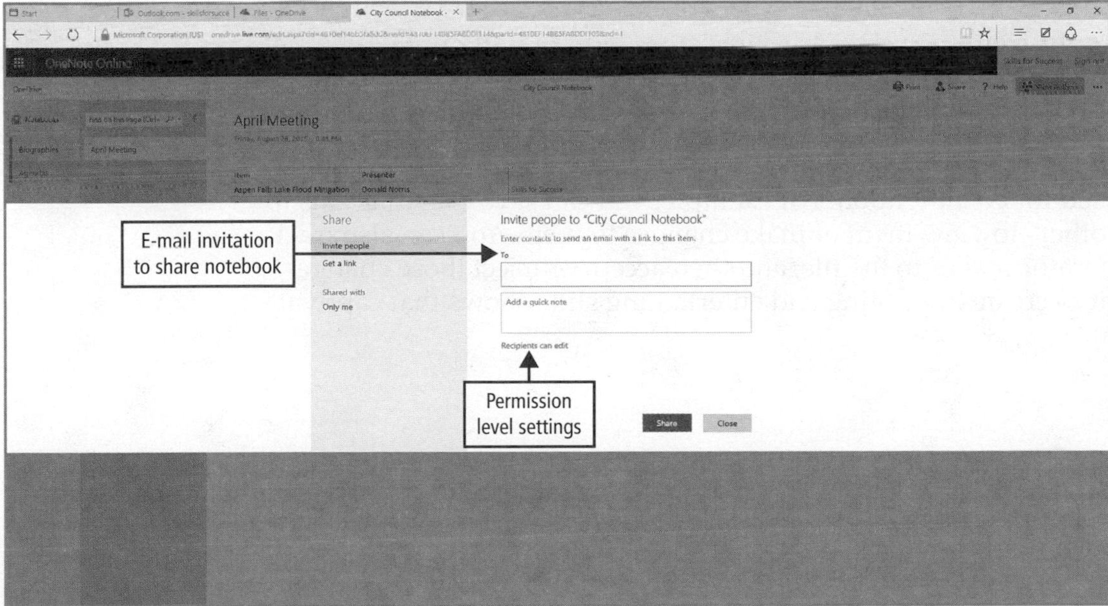

Access 2016, Windows 10, Microsoft Corporation

Figure 8

19. Click the **VIEW tab**, and then in the **Notebook Views group**, click **Reading View**. In the left pane, click **Biographies** to display the page. If necessary, click the **More** button, and then click **Show Authors**. Compare your screen with **Figure 7**.

    When you display the authors, each author's contributions are marked so that you can track each author's contributions to the notebook.

20. In the **Search** text box, type snip and then press Enter to start the Snipping Tool. Create a **Full-screen Snip**. **Save** the snip as Last_First_acc_OPSnip1 and then **Close** the Snipping Tool mark-up window.

21. In the left pane, click **Agendas** to display the page. Create a **Full-screen Snip** named Last_First_acc_OPSnip2 and then **Close** the Snipping Tool mark-up window.

22. Click the **Share** button, then compare your screen with **Figure 8**.

    In Reading view, you can click Share to invite others view the notebook. You can allow them to make changes as authors or limit them only to Reading view.

23. If your instructor has asked you to share the notebook, enter the e-mail address of the person you are to share with, and then click **Share**. Otherwise, click **Close**.

24. Click the **Sign out** link, and then **Close** your browser window. Submit the files as directed by your instructor.

DONE! You have completed Online Project 4

Introduction to PowerPoint

Microsoft PowerPoint 2016 is a ***presentation software program***—an application used to create slides to communicate a message to an audience.

You can use PowerPoint to insert, format, and add effects to text on slides. You can add text in the form of a bulleted or numbered list, captions, or titles.

When using PowerPoint, you will use three main views. In Normal view, you'll see a thumbnail image of each slide next to a larger view of the slide you are working on. In Slide Sorter view, you will see a bird's-eye view of your presentation. When presenting, you will use Slide Show view, where the current slide fills the screen. In Slide Show view, you can access Presenter view, which provides you with additional presentation information.

You can change layouts and add images to your slides. Images, either from your own files or from online sources, including office.com, can help to explain your message further, hold your audience's attention, and evoke an emotion or feeling. Slide layouts can be easily changed.

You can add other graphics into your slides using shapes with or without text, SmartArt graphics, or WordArt. Charts and tables can help you to present data in an organized and easy-to-understand format and make it easier for your audience to make comparisons.

PowerPoint can be used for collaboration. For example, you can save presentations to the Internet and invite others to view them or make changes to them. You can also track the changes each collaborator makes to the file, and then accept or reject those changes. You can use PowerPoint to create interesting and entertaining slide shows that captivate and inform your audience.

Image
Aspen Falls City Government
We are glad to have you on our team!
Text effects
Slide layout

© Yuri Arcurs

CHAPTER 1

Getting Started with PowerPoint 2016

- Microsoft PowerPoint is a presentation software program that can be used to effectively relay information, images, and video to an audience through a slide show.
- There are multiple views in PowerPoint: Normal, Slide Sorter, Reading, Slide Show, and Presenter. Each view is designed for particular tasks.
- Normal view is commonly used to create, edit, and format a presentation.
- Slide Show view is used to give a presentation; the slides are displayed as full screen.
- In Presenter view, a presenter can view upcoming slides and speaker notes while displaying the current slide to the audience on the screen.

Auremar/Fotolia

Aspen Falls City Hall

In this chapter, you will edit a presentation for Maria Martinez, the City Manager of Aspen Falls, California. Maria will use this presentation when representing the city to businesses, investors, and other agencies.

In your career, you may need to create professional presentations to help convey your message to an audience. Keep in mind that your audience will remember more information if you present it to them in a variety of ways—verbally, in writing, and visually. Using PowerPoint slides as a presentation aid will help you do this.

A slide, generally shown behind the presenter, can contain text to emphasize the most important information. Images can be used to emphasize a point, increase interest, or render an emotion. Animation or motion on the screen can attract—and help to hold—the audience's attention. You can create handouts from your slides and distribute them to your audience for reference.

A general rule of thumb for PowerPoint is to follow the 6 by 6 rule—a maximum of six lines per slide and no more than six words per line. Another PowerPoint standard is to use no font smaller than 18 to 24 points. Slides should always look uncluttered and use simple designs.

In this project, you will open and save an existing presentation and then edit the presentation, adding and adjusting text and images. You will change slide layouts, insert new slides, and rearrange slides. You will apply transitions, view the slide show, and create presentation handouts and notes.

Time to complete all 10 skills — 60 to 75 minutes

Introduction

Outcome

Using the skills in this chapter, you will be able to edit an existing PowerPoint presentation, insert new slides, add and adjust text and images, and work with slide shows.

Objectives

You will show mastery of the chapter material when you can:

1.1 Open, edit, and save an existing presentation
1.2 Apply various formats to slides with text and images
1.3 Check spelling and grammar throughout your presentation
1.4 Change layouts of slides
1.5 Define and use different PowerPoint views, including Normal, Slide Sorter, Presenter, and Slide Show
1.6 Add and utilize speaker notes
1.7 Use headers and footers on slides and handouts

Student data files needed for this chapter:

ppt01_Lifestyle
ppt01_Vision
ppt01_CityHall

You will save your files as:

Last_First_ppt01_Lifestyle
Last_First_ppt01_LifestyleSnip

SKILLS

At the end of this chapter, you will be able to:

Skill 1 Open, View, and Save Presentations
Skill 2 Edit and Replace Text
Skill 3 Format Slide Text
Skill 4 Check Spelling and Use the Thesaurus
Skill 5 Insert Slides and Modify Slide Layouts
Skill 6 Insert and Format Pictures
Skill 7 Organize Slides in Slide Sorter View
Skill 8 Apply Slide Transitions and View Slide Shows
Skill 9 Insert Headers and Footers and Print Handouts
Skill 10 Add Notes Pages and Use Presenter View

MORE SKILLS

Skill 11 Add Online Images
Skill 12 Print Presentations, Handouts, and Custom Ranges
Skill 13 Move and Delete Slides in Normal View
Skill 14 Change Slide Size and Orientation

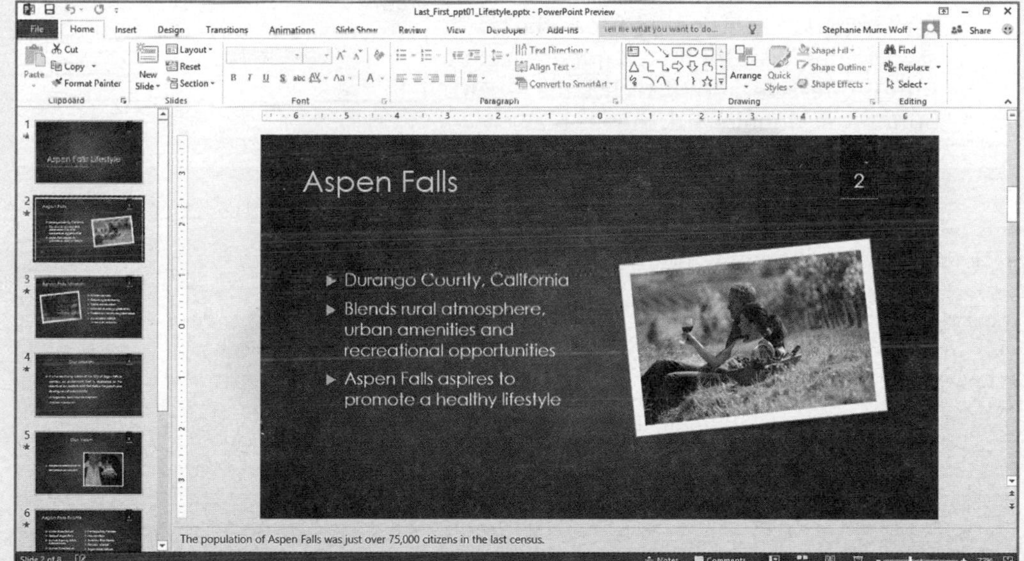

Auremar/Fotolia; PowerPoint 2016, Windows 10, Microsoft Corporation

- When you start PowerPoint 2016, the ***Start screen*** displays. From the Start screen, you can view a list of recently opened presentations, create a new presentation, or open an existing presentation.
- A ***slide*** is an individual page in a presentation and can contain text, pictures, tables, charts, and other multimedia objects.
- Save your changes frequently so that you do not lose any of your editing or formatting changes.

1. Start **PowerPoint 2016**, and then take a moment to familiarize yourself with the components of the PowerPoint Start screen as shown in **Figure 1**.
2. On the Start screen, click **Open Other Presentations**. On the **Open** page, click **This PC**, and then click **Browse**. In the **Open** dialog box, navigate to the student data files for this chapter. Select **ppt01_Lifestyle**, and then click the **Open** button—or double-click the file name—to open the presentation and display **Slide 1**.
3. Take a moment to identify the main parts of the PowerPoint window as shown in **Figure 2**.

   The PowerPoint window is divided into two main parts—the Slide pane and the left pane, which contains thumbnail images of the slides. In addition, the status bar indicates the displayed slide number and the number of slides in the presentation, and it contains buttons for the Notes and Comments panes, various views, zoom options, and Fit slide to current window.

■ **Continue to the next page to complete the skill**

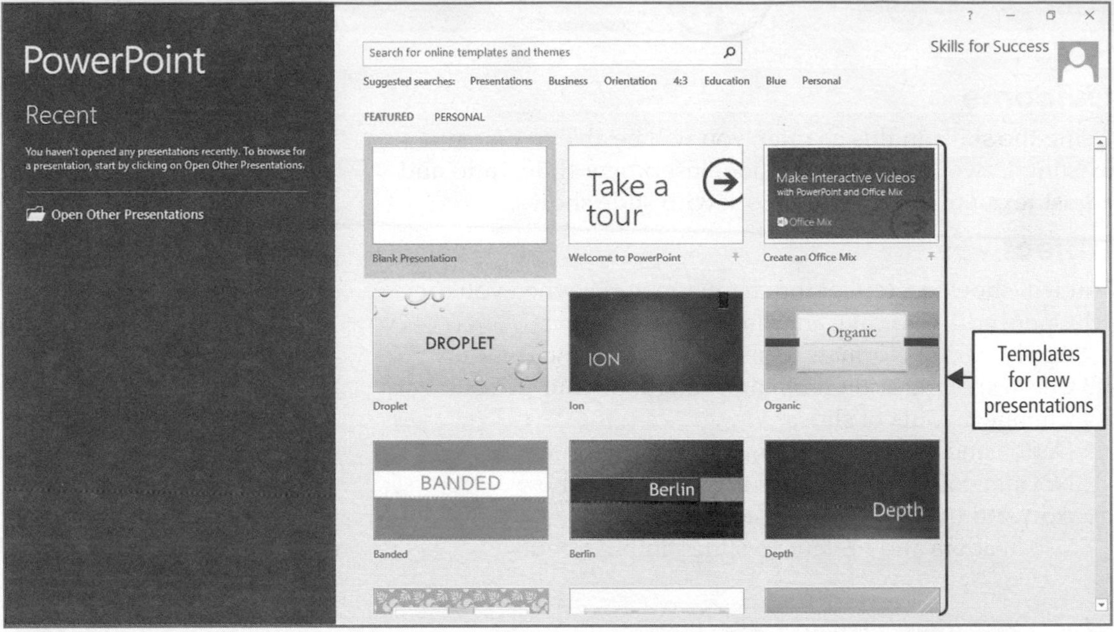

Figure 1 PowerPoint 2016, Windows 10, Microsoft Corporation

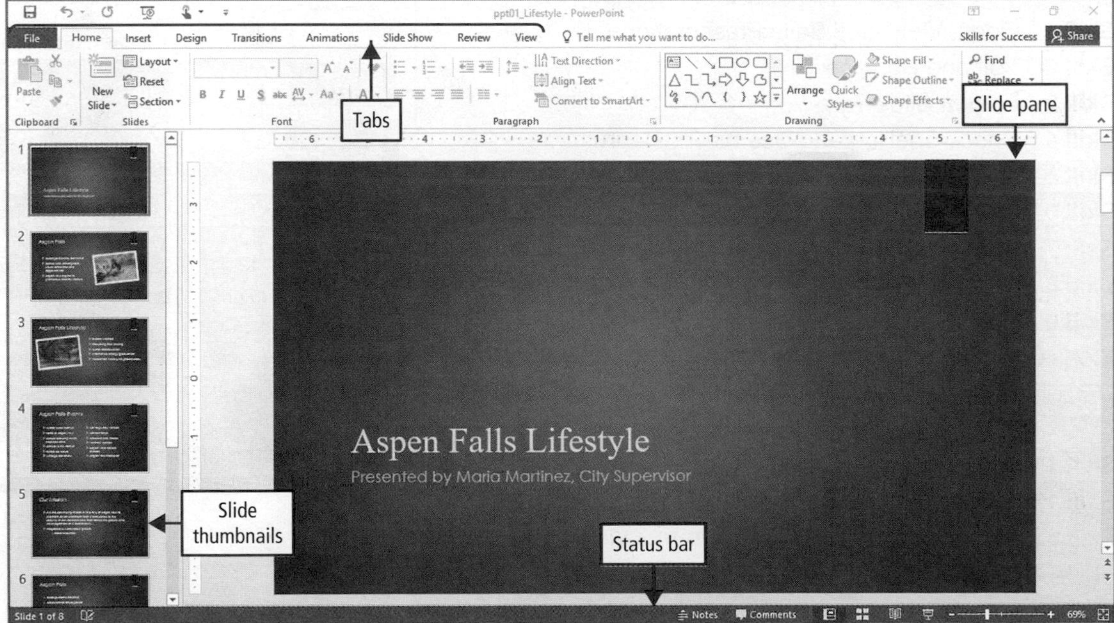

Figure 2 PowerPoint 2016, Windows 10, Microsoft Corporation

Microsoft PowerPoint Screen Elements	
Screen Element	**Description**
Tabs	In PowerPoint, the default tabs include File, Home, Insert, Design, Transitions, Animations, Slide Show, Review, and View
Slide thumbnails	Small preview images of each slide
Slide pane	An area of the Normal View window that displays the current slide
Status bar	A horizontal bar at the bottom of the window that displays the current slide number, number of slides in the presentation, and the Notes, Comments, View, Zoom, and Fit slide to current window buttons

Figure 3

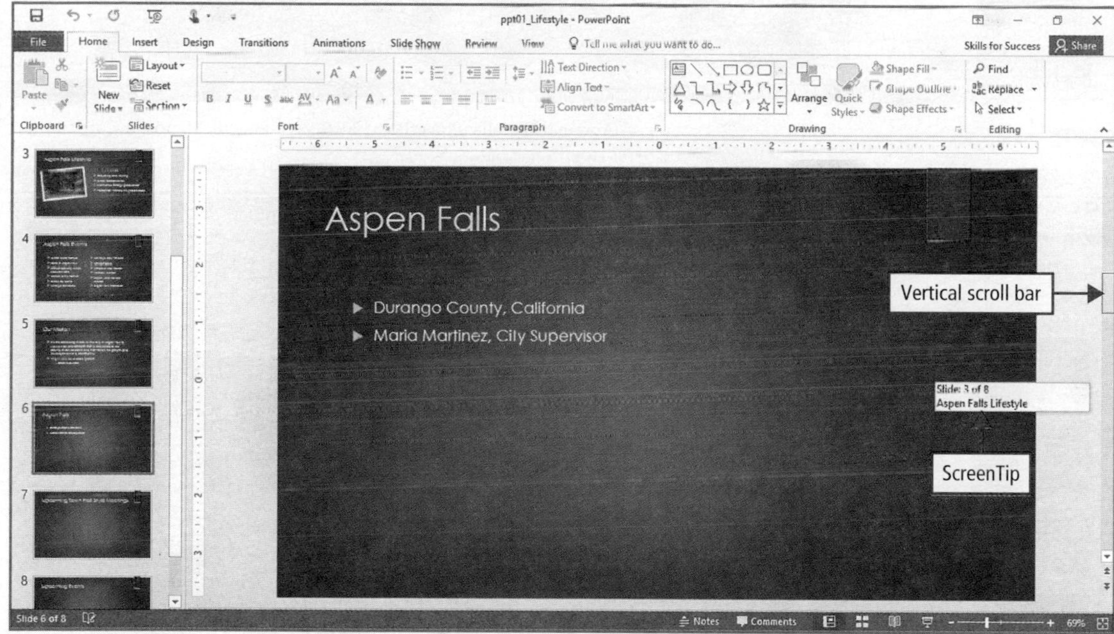

PowerPoint 2016, Windows 10, Microsoft Corporation

Figure 4

4. Locate the items described in **Figure 3**.

   At the left side of the PowerPoint window, the slide ***thumbnails***—miniature images of presentation slides—and slide numbers display. You can click a slide thumbnail to display it in the Slide pane. At the right side of the window, a scroll bar displays a scroll box.

5. At the left of the PowerPoint window, click the **Slide 2** thumbnail to display the slide in the Slide pane. Click the slide thumbnails for **Slides 3** through **6** to view each slide.

   As you view each slide, the vertical scroll box at the right side of the PowerPoint window moves, indicating the location of the slide that you are viewing. Several slides contain misspellings, which will be corrected later.

6. With **Slide 6** displayed, at the right side of the PowerPoint window, point to the vertical scroll box, and then hold down the mouse button. Drag up to display **Slide 3**, and then release the mouse button. A ScreenTip displays the slide number and slide title, as shown in **Figure 4**.

7. On the **File tab**, click **Save As**. Under Save As, click the **Browse** button and navigate to the location where you are saving your files, create a folder named PowerPoint Chapter 1 and then using your own name, save the file as Last_First_ppt01_Lifestyle

■ **You have completed Skill 1 of 10**

- In ***Normal view***, the PowerPoint window is divided into two areas—the Slide pane and the left pane, which contains thumbnails of each slide.
- Individual lines of bulleted text on a slide are referred to as ***bullet points***. To avoid overcrowding, slides should contain no more than six lines of bullet points.
- Bullet points are organized in list levels similar to an outline. A ***list level*** is a hierarchy of bullets and sub-bullets.
- You can use the Replace command to change multiple occurrences of the same text in a presentation.

---

1. Move to **Slide 2**, which contains two placeholders.

   Placeholders are indicated with dotted borders; they hold text or objects such as pictures, charts, and tables. The dotted border is not visible until you click, or place your insertion point in, the placeholder.

2. In the second bullet point, click to the left of the letter *o* in the word *opportunities* so that the insertion point displays before the word, as shown in **Figure 1**.

Obj 2.1.1

3. Type recreational and then press SpaceBar.
4. Move to **Slide 3**. In the right content placeholder, click at the end of the last bullet point—*Pedestrian friendly neighborhoods*—and then press Enter.

   Pressing Enter at the end of a bullet point adds a new bullet point at the same list level.

5. Type Sustainable lifestyle and then press Enter.
6. Press Tab to create a second-level, indented bullet point. Type Focus on tomorrow and then compare your slide with **Figure 2.**

■ **Continue to the next page to complete the skill**

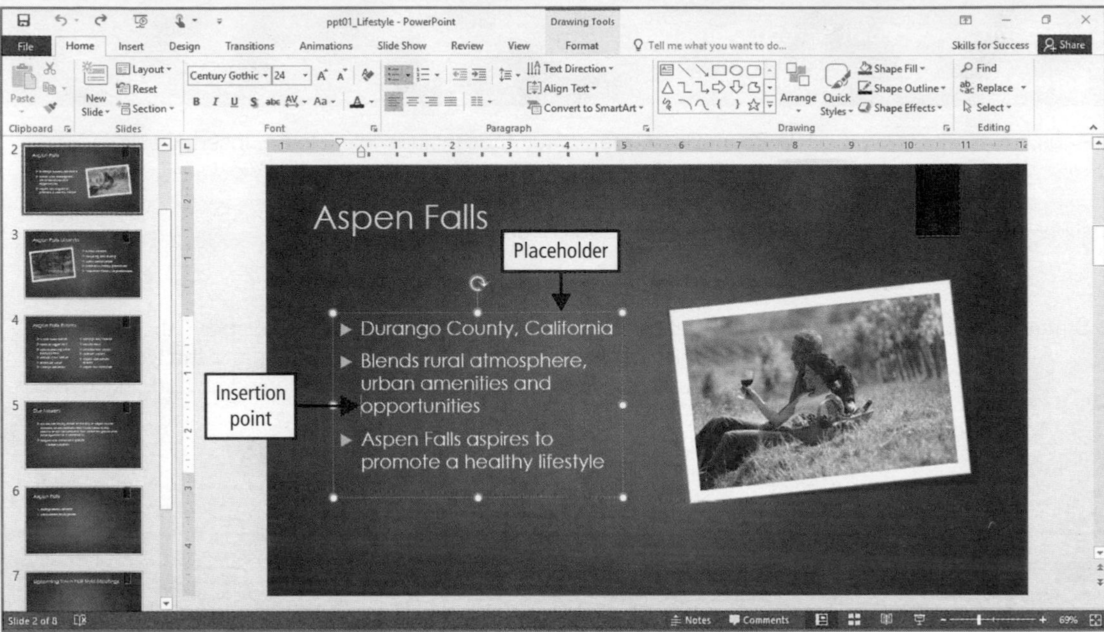

Figure 1

Auremar/Fotolia; PowerPoint 2016, Windows 10, Microsoft Corporation

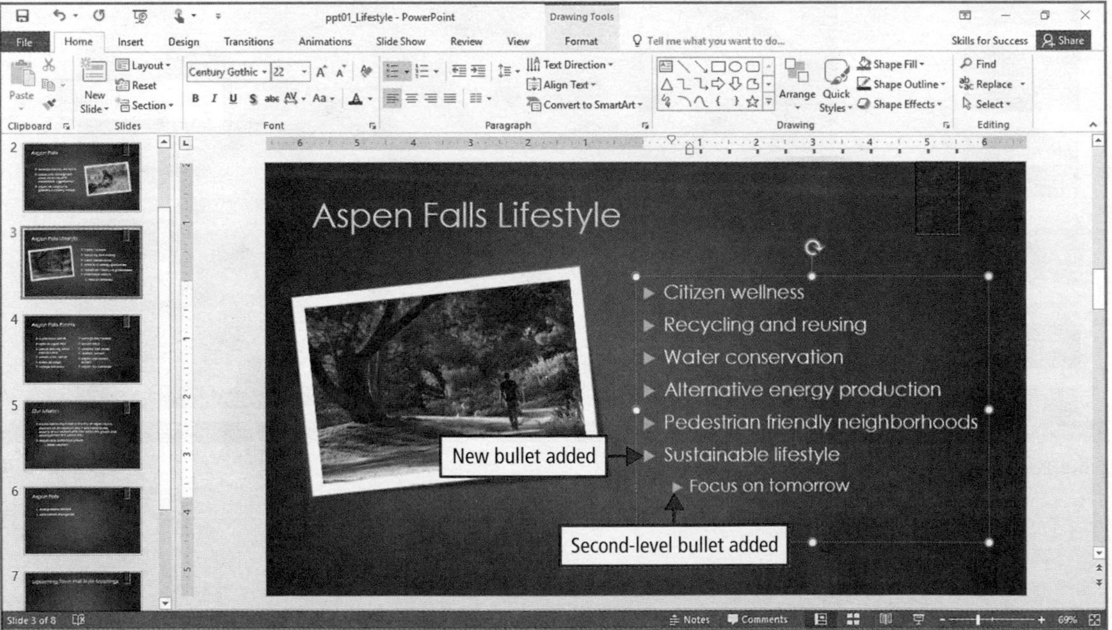

Figure 2

Charles Shapiro/Fotolia; PowerPoint 2016, Windows 10, Microsoft Corporation

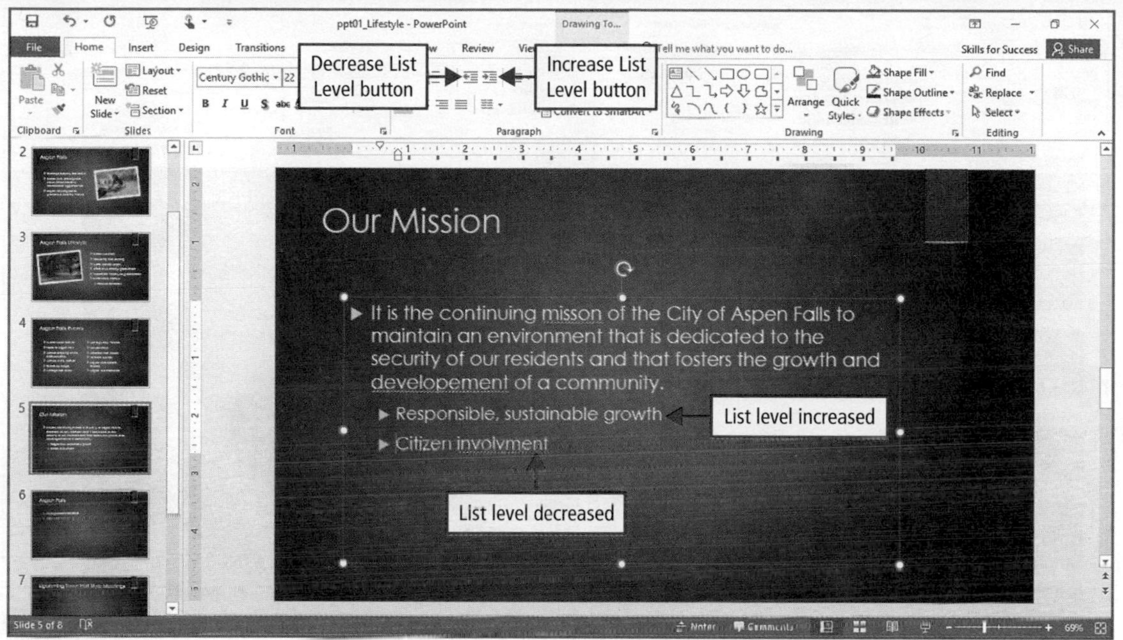

PowerPoint 2016, Windows 10, Microsoft Corporation

Figure 3

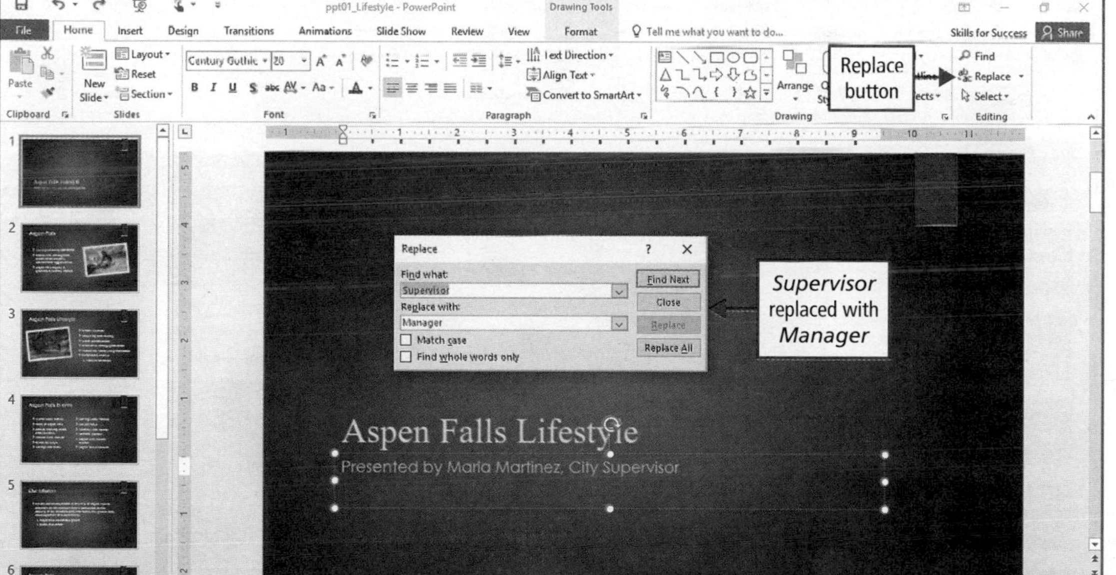

PowerPoint 2016, Windows 10, Microsoft Corporation

Figure 4

7. Move to **Slide 5**. Click anywhere in the second bullet point—*Responsible, sustainable growth*. On the **Home tab**, in the **Paragraph group**, click the **Increase List Level** button.

   The selection is formatted as a second-level bullet point, indicated by the indent and smaller font size.

8. Click anywhere in the third bullet point beginning with the word *Citizen*. On the **Home tab**, in the **Paragraph group**, click the **Decrease List Level** button. Compare your screen with **Figure 3**.

   A second-level bullet point is applied, as indicated by the decreased indent and the increased font size.

9. Move to **Slide 1** and notice the word *Supervisor* in the subtitle placeholder.

   This is the incorrect title for Maria. There is more than one instance in the presentation in which the word *Supervisor* is used instead of the word *Manager*.

10. On the **Home tab**, in the **Editing group**, click the **Replace** button. In the **Find what** box, type Supervisor and then click in the **Replace with** box. Type Manager and then compare your screen with **Figure 4**.

11. In the **Replace** dialog box, click the **Replace All** button, and then view a message box indicating that two replacements were made. Click **OK** to close the message box, and then in the **Replace** dialog box, click the **Close** button. **Save** the file.

- **You have completed Skill 2 of 10**

SKILL 3: Format Slide Text

- A ***font***, the size of which is measured in ***points***, is a set of characters—letters, numbers, and symbols—with the same design and shape.
- Font styles and effects emphasize text and include bold, italic, underline, shadow, small caps, and outline.
- The placement of text within a placeholder is referred to as ***text alignment***. Text can be aligned left, centered, aligned right, or justified.

1. On **Slide 1**, select the title text—*Aspen Falls Lifestyle*.
2. On the Mini toolbar, click the **Font Size arrow**, and then click 72.
3. With the title text still selected, on the **Home tab**, in the **Font group**, click the **Font arrow**. Scroll up through the **Font list**, and then point to **Century Gothic** to display the Live Preview of the font, as shown in **Figure 1**.
4. In the **Font list**, click **Century Gothic**.
5. Place your insertion point anywhere in the subtitle. Click a border of the subtitle placeholder, as shown in **Figure 2**.

   A solid border around a placeholder indicates that the entire placeholder and all of the contents within it are selected. With the placeholder selected, any formatting changes will be made to the contents of the placeholder.
6. In the **Font group**, click the **Launcher** to display the Font dialog box. Under **Effects**, select **Small Caps**, and then click **OK**.

   With small caps, lowercase characters are capitalized but are smaller than characters that are typed as capital letters.

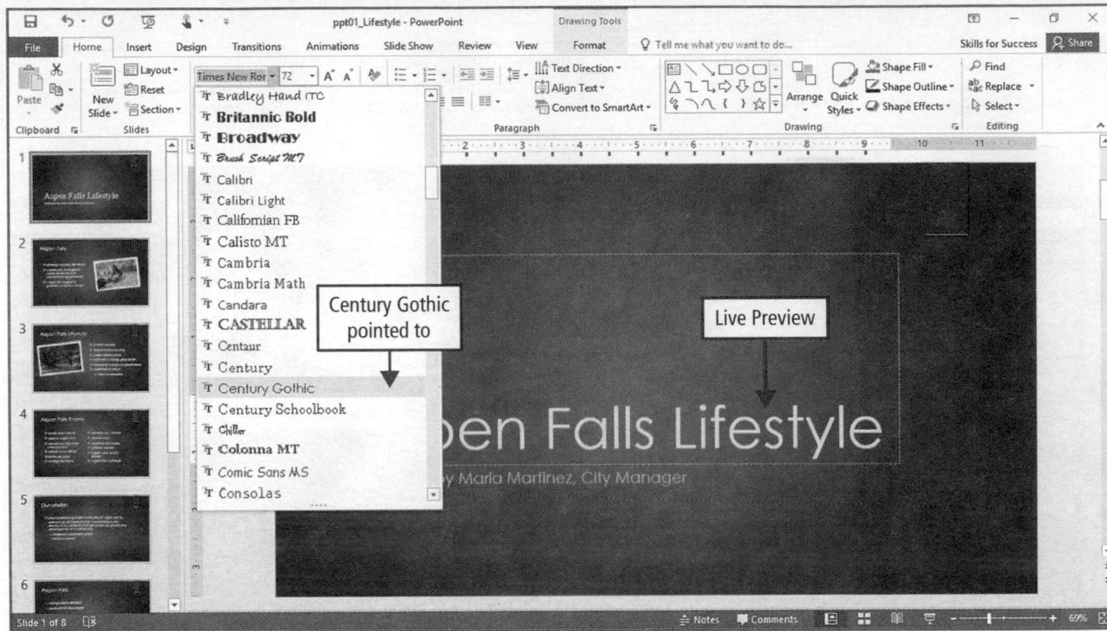

Figure 1

PowerPoint 2016, Windows 10, Microsoft Corporation

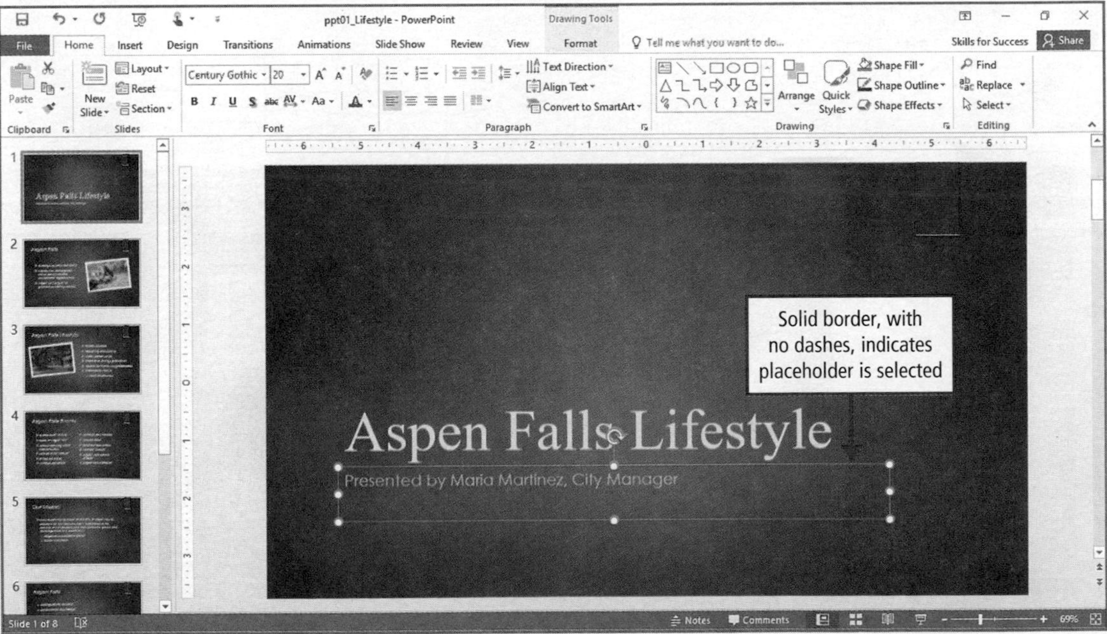

Figure 2

PowerPoint 2016, Windows 10, Microsoft Corporation

■ **Continue to the next page to complete the skill**

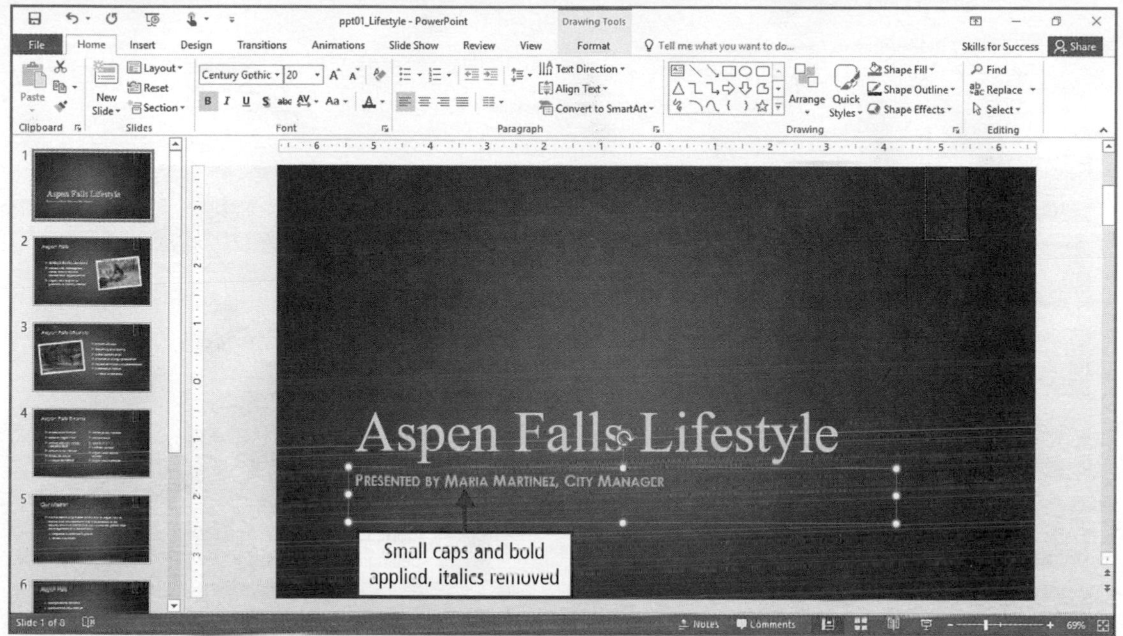

PowerPoint 2016, Windows 10, Microsoft Corporation

Figure 3

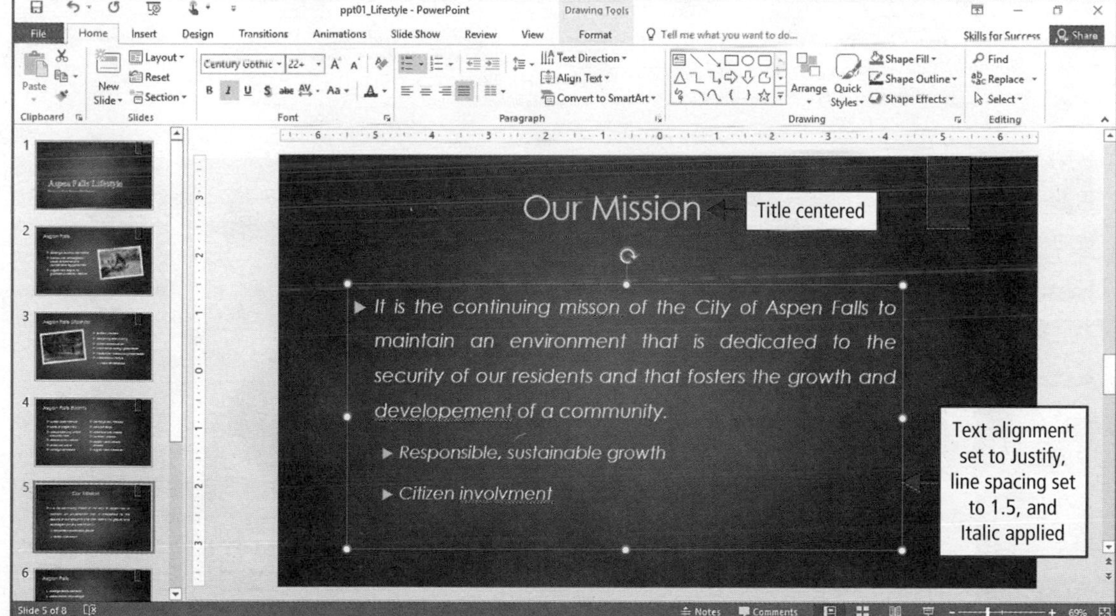

PowerPoint 2016, Windows 10, Microsoft Corporation

Figure 4

7. With the subtitle placeholder still selected, in the **Font group**, click the **Bold** button [B], and then click the **Italic** button [I].
8. Review the changes you have made, and then on the **Home tab**, in the **Font group**, click the **Italic** button [I] to turn off the italic formatting. Compare your slide with **Figure 3**.

   The italic formatting may have made the text more difficult to read, so it was removed. You can use the Mini toolbar, the Ribbon, or the Font dialog box to apply font styles and effects.

9. Move to **Slide 5** and click the title, and then click the border of the title placeholder to select it.
10. On the **Home tab**, in the **Paragraph group**, click the **Center** button to center align the title text.
11. Place your insertion point anywhere in the content placeholder. Click the border of the placeholder to select it. With the content placeholder selected, on the **Home tab**, in the **Paragraph group**, click the **Justify** button to distribute the bulleted text evenly between the placeholder margins.
12. With the content placeholder still selected, in the **Paragraph group**, click the **Line Spacing** button. In the displayed list, click **1.5** to increase the space between lines in the paragraph.
13. On the **Home tab**, in the **Font group**, click the **Italic** button [I]. Compare your slide with **Figure 4**.
14. **Save** the file.

■ **You have completed Skill 3 of 10**

- You can find spelling errors in a presentation by looking for words marked with a red wavy underline. These words are flagged because they are not in the Office 2016 main dictionary.
- You can also correct spelling errors using a shortcut menu or the spell check feature.
- The ***thesaurus*** is a research tool that provides a list of ***synonyms***—words with the same or similar meaning—for text that you select.

1. With **Slide 5** displayed in Normal view, notice that the word *involvment* is flagged with a red wavy underline, indicating that it is misspelled.
2. Point to *involvment*, and then right-click to display the shortcut menu with suggested solutions for correcting the misspelled word, as shown in **Figure 1**.
3. From the shortcut menu, click **involvement** to correct the spelling of the word.
4. Move to **Slide 4**. In the right content placeholder, notice the misspelled word or words.

   In the left content placeholder, if the word *Cinco* is flagged as misspelled, right-click and then click Ignore All. Proper names and non-English-language words are sometimes flagged as misspelled although they are spelled correctly. When you use the Ignore All command, the red wavy underline is removed for the current document only. If you are working on your personal computer, you can add words to the dictionary using the Add to Dictionary command. However, many colleges and workplaces do not allow this option.
5. Right-click the word *Triathalon*. From the shortcut menu, click **Triathlon**. Compare your slide with **Figure 2**.

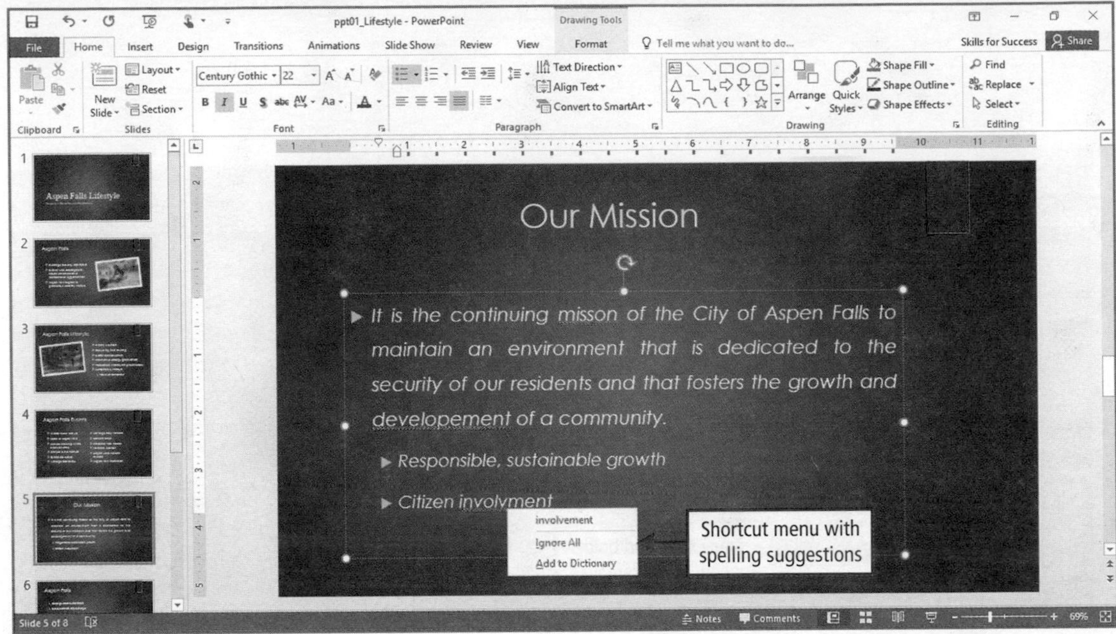

Figure 1

PowerPoint 2016, Windows 10, Microsoft Corporation

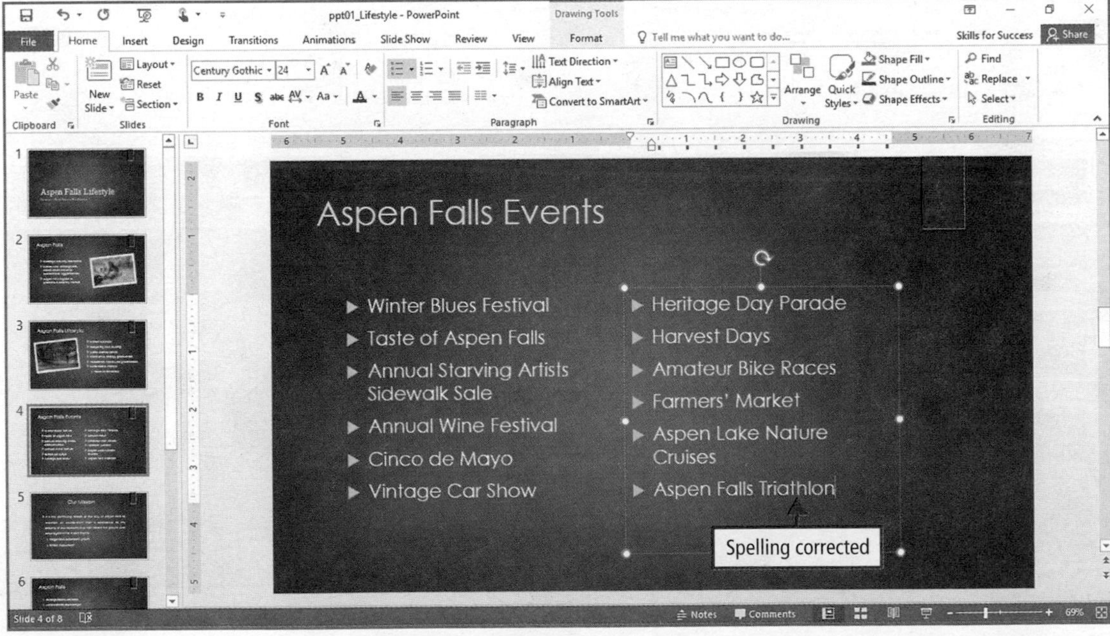

Figure 2

PowerPoint 2016, Windows 10, Microsoft Corporation

■ **Continue to the next page to complete the skill**

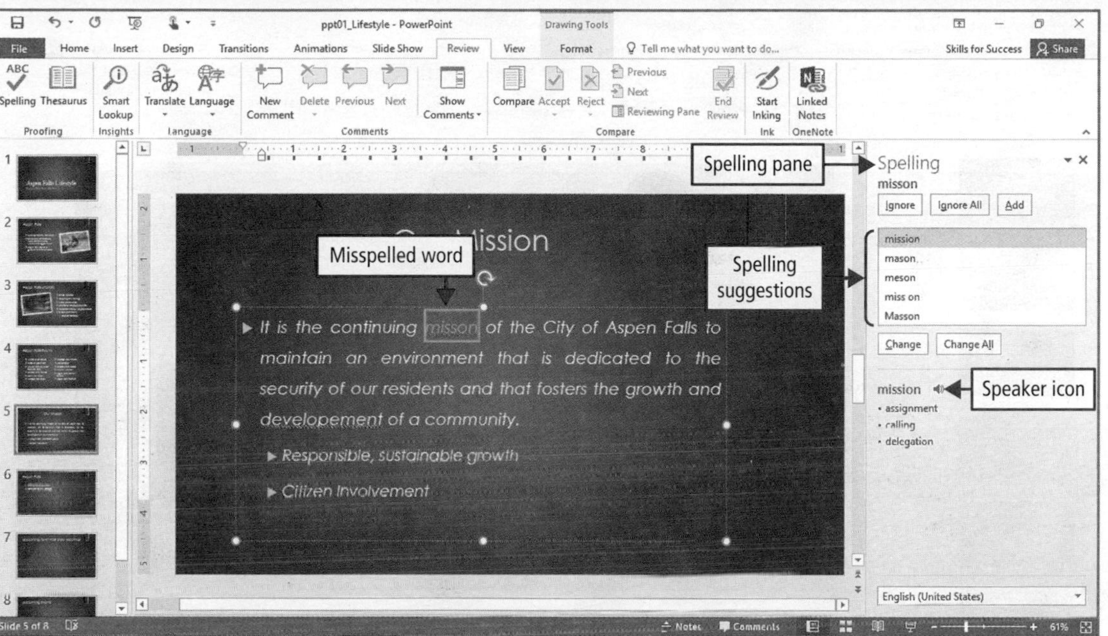

PowerPoint 2016, Windows 10, Microsoft Corporation

Figure 3

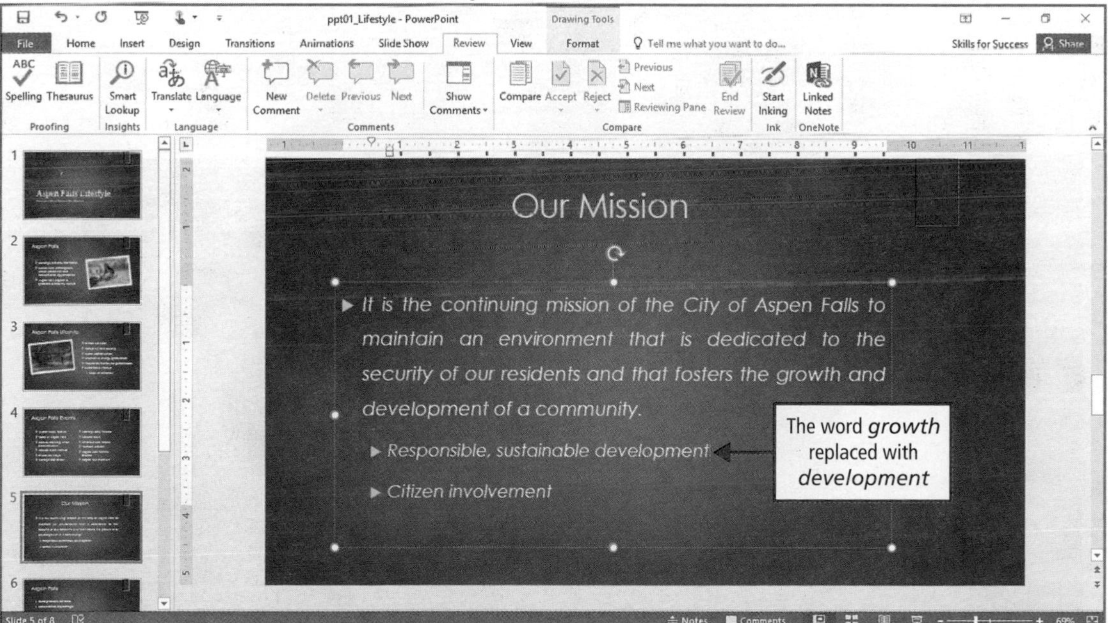

PowerPoint 2016, Windows 10, Microsoft Corporation

Figure 4

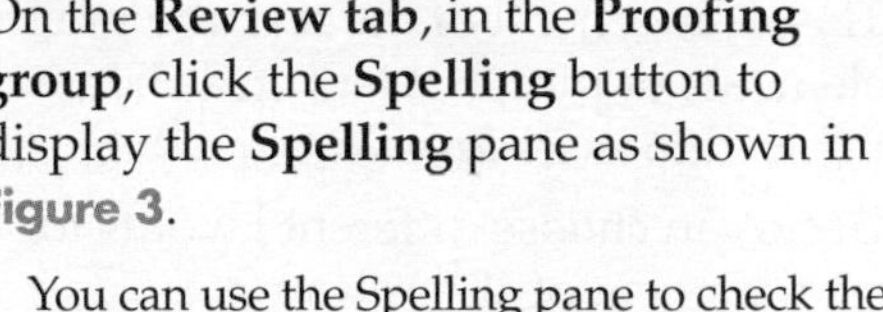

6. On the **Review tab**, in the **Proofing group**, click the **Spelling** button to display the **Spelling** pane as shown in **Figure 3**.

   You can use the Spelling pane to check the spelling of an entire presentation. Here, the incorrect spelling of the word *mission* on Slide 5 is highlighted on the slide and is also displayed in the Spelling pane. The Spelling pane provides options for correcting spelling, ignoring spelling, and adding words to the custom dictionary and contains the Speaker icon, which, when clicked, plays a recording of the spoken word. Pressing F7 is a shortcut for opening the Spelling pane.

7. Check that your computer's speakers are on and not muted, or plug in headphones. In the lower half of the **Spelling** pane, click the **Speaker** icon and listen to the correct pronunciation of the word. Then, in the box containing spelling suggestions, be sure that **mission** is selected, and then click the **Change** button.
8. Use the **Spelling** pane to correct the spelling of one more word. When a message box indicates that the spell check is complete, click **OK**.
9. On **Slide 5**, in the bullet point beginning with *Responsible*, point to the word *growth*, and right-click to display the shortcut menu.
10. Near the bottom of the shortcut menu, point to **Synonyms** to display the thesaurus list of suggested words to replace *growth*. Click **development** to replace *growth* with *development*. Compare your screen with **Figure 4**.
11. **Save** the file.

■ **You have completed Skill 4 of 10**

SKILL 5: Insert Slides and Modify Slide Layouts

- The arrangement of the text and graphic elements or placeholders on a slide is referred to as its ***layout***.
- Users can choose different layouts for the arrangement of slide elements.

1. With **Slide 5** displayed in Normal view, on the **Home tab**, in the **Slides group**, click the top half of the **New Slide** button to add a new slide with the same layout as the current slide. Alternately, you can press Ctrl + M to insert a new slide.
2. Click in the title placeholder, and then type Our Vision
3. On the **Home tab**, in the **Paragraph group**, click the **Center** button.
4. Place your insertion point in the content placeholder. Type Our goal is to become one of the best places to live in the world. In the text you just typed, place your insertion point before the *O* in *Our*, and then press Enter three times to move the text in the placeholder downward. Compare your slide with **Figure 1**.

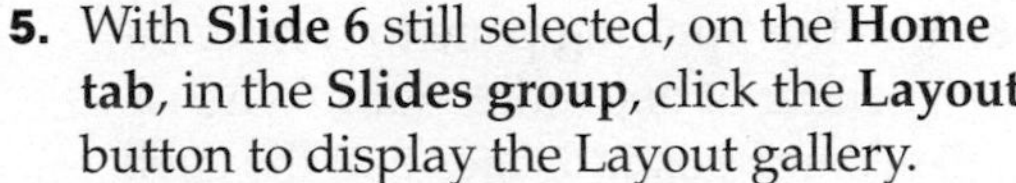

MOS Obj 1.2.5

5. With **Slide 6** still selected, on the **Home tab**, in the **Slides group**, click the **Layout** button to display the Layout gallery.

   The ***Layout gallery*** is a visual representation of the content layouts that you can apply to a slide. The Layout gallery varies with the slide design. Some slide designs have 17 layouts, whereas others have nine to choose from.

6. Click **Two Content**, and then compare your screen with **Figure 2**.

   The slide layout is changed to one that includes a title and two content placeholders. The existing text is arranged in the placeholder on the left side of the slide. For now, the placeholder on the right will remain empty.

■ **Continue to the next page to complete the skill**

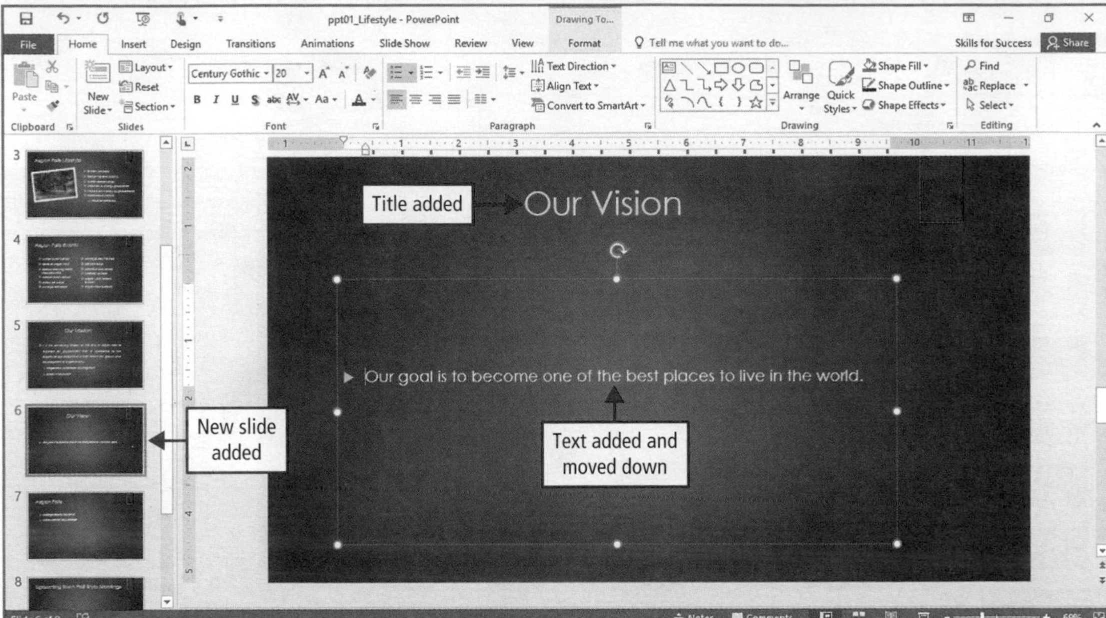

Figure 1

PowerPoint 2016, Windows 10, Microsoft Corporation

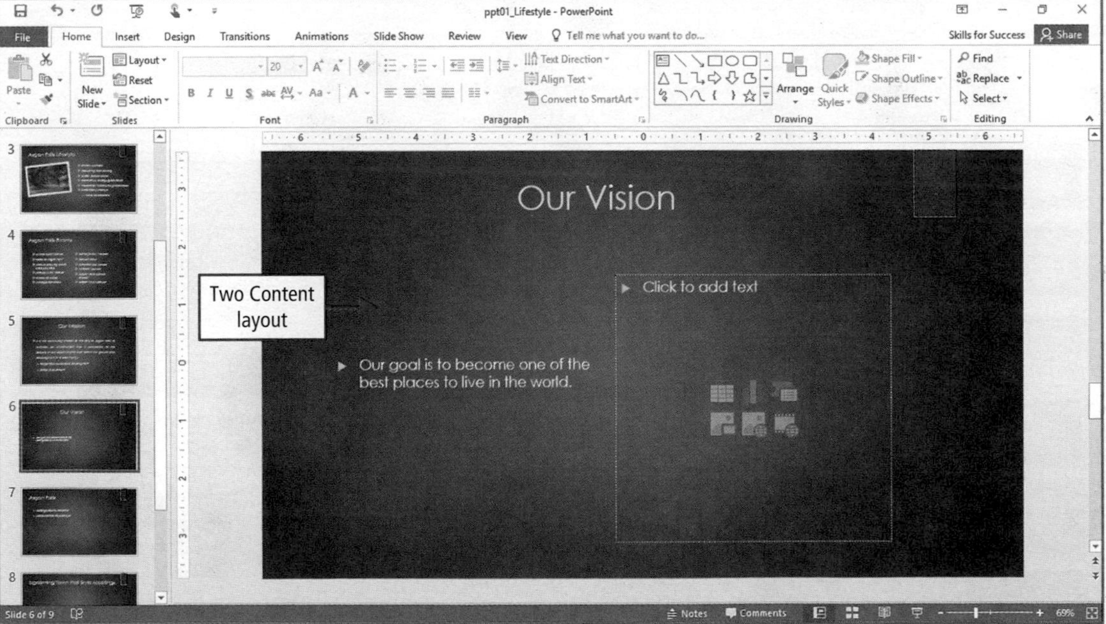

Figure 2

PowerPoint 2016, Windows 10, Microsoft Corporation

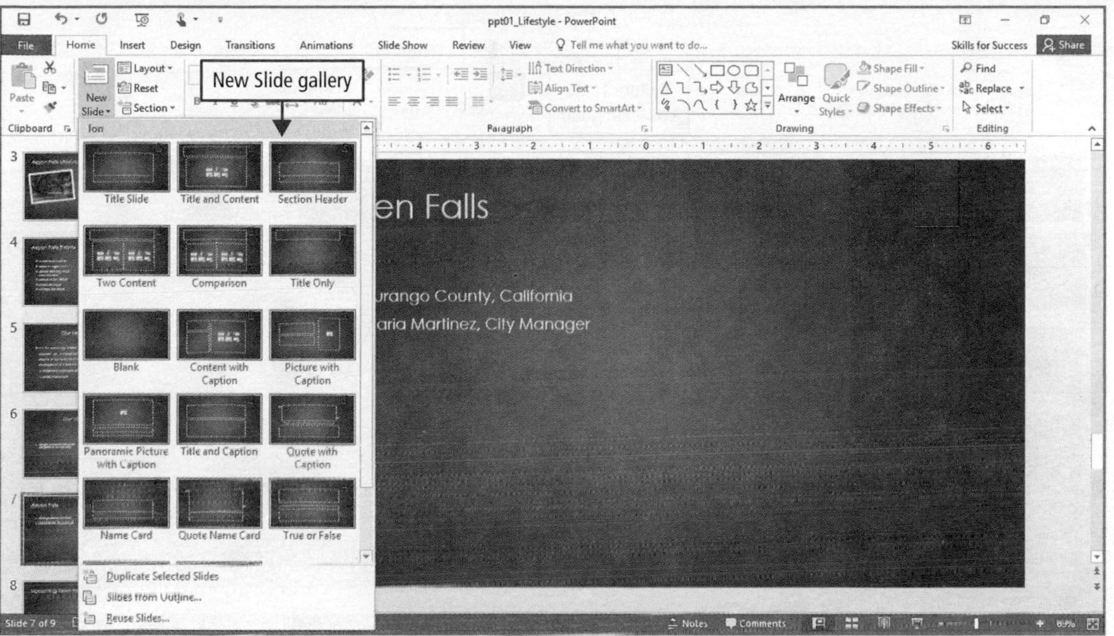

PowerPoint 2016, Windows 10, Microsoft Corporation

Figure 3

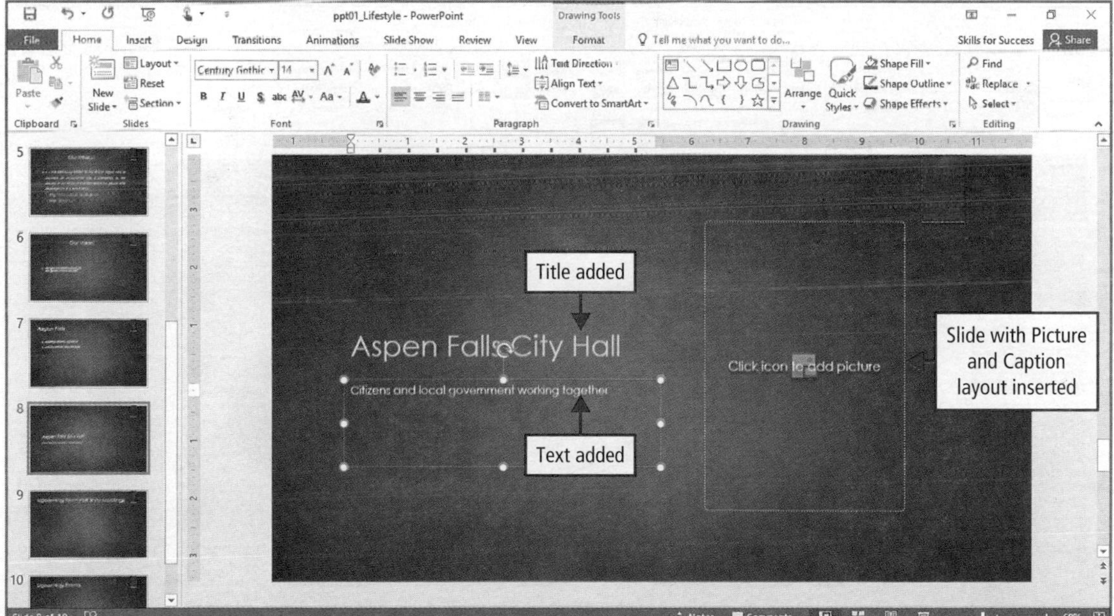

PowerPoint 2016, Windows 10, Microsoft Corporation

Figure 4

7. If necessary, scroll down, and then click **Slide 7**. On the **Home tab**, in the **Slides group**, click the lower half of the **New Slide** button—the **New Slide arrow**—and then compare your screen with **Figure 3**.

Obj 1.2.1

   When you click the upper half of the New Slide button, a new slide is inserted with the same layout as the previous slide. When you click the New Slide arrow, a gallery displays in which you can select a layout for the slide that you want to insert.

8. In the **Layout** gallery, click **Picture with Caption**.
9. Click in the title placeholder, and then type Aspen Falls City Hall
10. Select the title placeholder, and then on the **Home tab**, in the **Font group**, click the **Text Shadow** button.
11. In the text placeholder, type Citizens and local government working together and compare your screen with **Figure 4**.
12. Move to **Slide 7**. On the **Home tab**, in the **Slides group**, click the **Layout** button. In the **Layout** gallery, select **Name Card** to change the existing layout.

    You can set the layout when you insert a slide using the New Slide button, or you can adjust the layout of an existing slide using the Layout button.

13. **Save** the file.

■ **You have completed Skill 5 of 10**

SKILL 6: Insert and Format Pictures

- ***Pictures*** are images created with a scanner, digital camera, or graphics software and saved with a graphic file extension such as .jpg, .png, .tif, or .bmp.

Obj 2.3.1

1. On **Slide 6**, in the right content placeholder, click the **Pictures** button.
2. In the **Insert Picture** dialog box, navigate to your student files for this chapter, click **ppt01_Vision**, and then click **Insert**. Compare your screen with **Figure 1**.

   The picture is selected as indicated by the ***sizing handles***— circles surrounding a selected object that can be used to adjust its size. When you point to a sizing handle on a corner of the image, a resize pointer or displays, indicating that you can resize the image proportionally, both vertically and horizontally. When you point to a sizing handle in the middle of any side on the image, a vertical resize pointer or horizontal resize pointer displays, indicating the direction in which you can size the image.

3. With the image on Slide 6 still selected, point to the **Format tab**.

   The Picture Tools tab displays only when you have an image selected. This ***contextual tab*** contains commands related to the selected object.

Obj 2.3.3

4. On the **Format tab**, in the **Picture Styles group**, click the **More** button to display the **Picture Styles** gallery, and then compare your screen with **Figure 2**.

   A ***picture style*** is a prebuilt set of formatting borders, effects, and layouts applied to a picture.

■ **Continue to the next page to complete the skill**

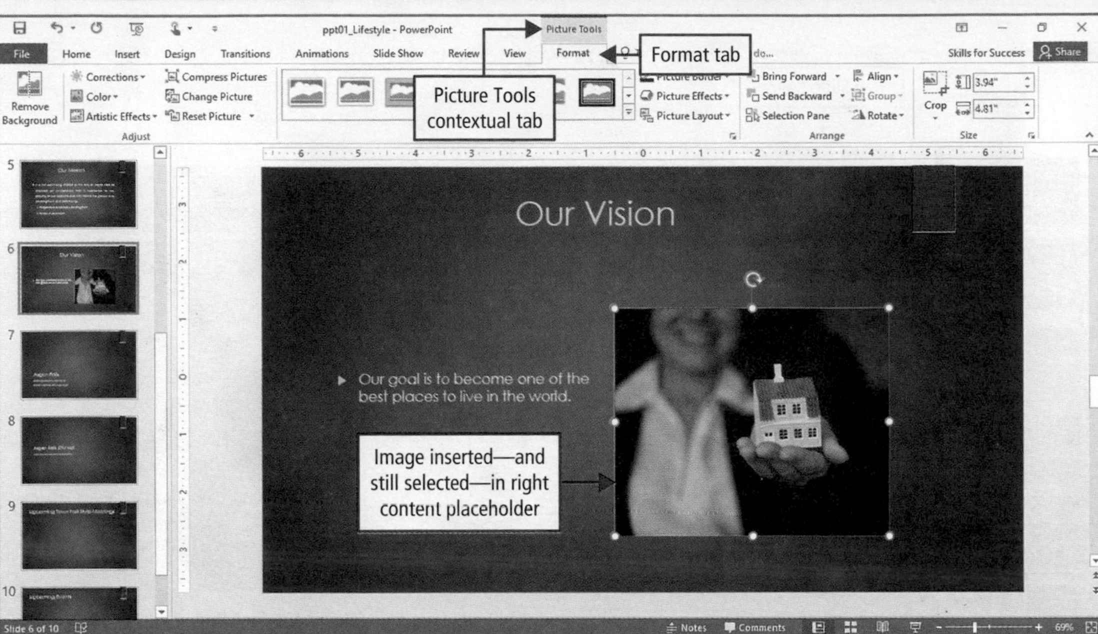

Figure 1

Fotoluminate LLC/Fotoliap; PowerPoint 2016, Windows 10, Microsoft Corporation

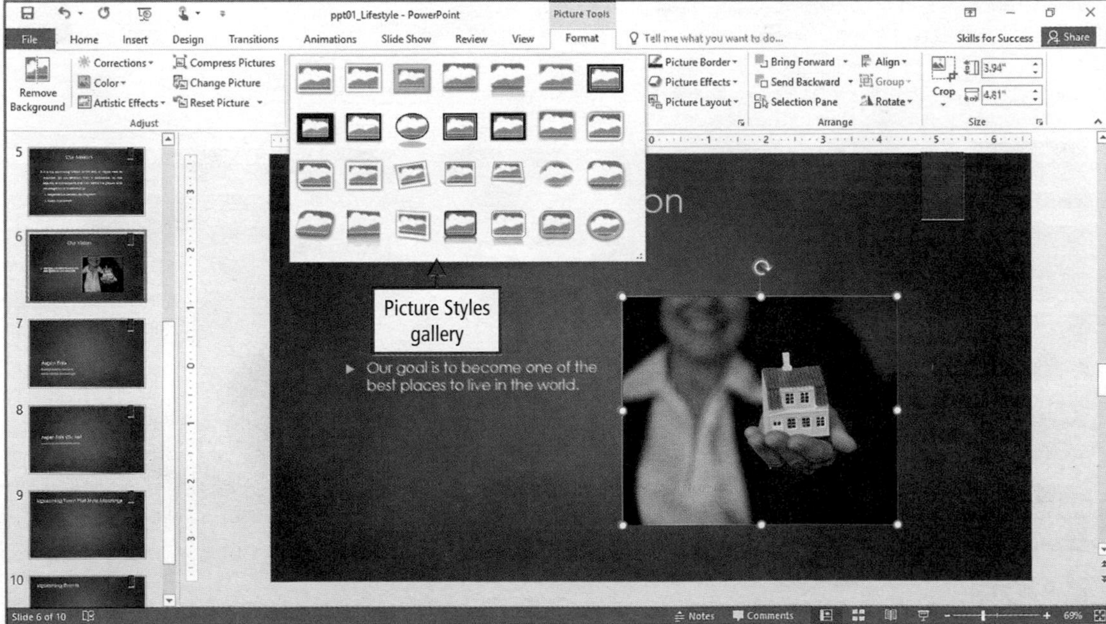

Figure 2

Fotoluminate LLC/Fotoliap; PowerPoint 2016, Windows 10, Microsoft Corporation

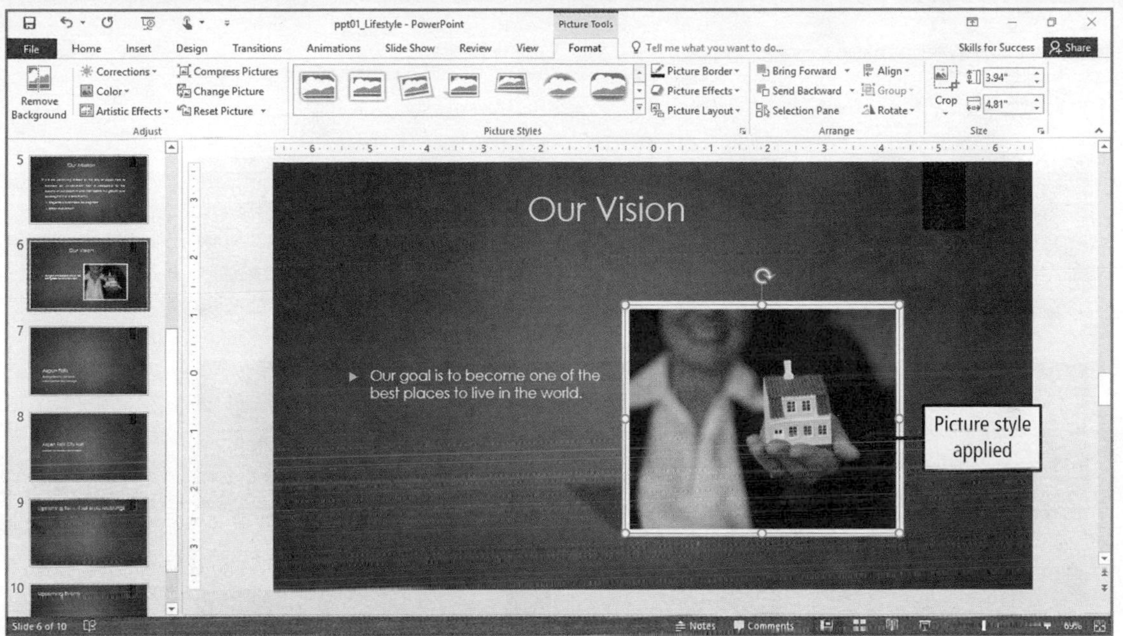

Fotoluminate LLC/Fotoliap; PowerPoint 2016, Windows 10, Microsoft Corporation

Figure 3

Fotoluminate LLC/Fotoliap; PowerPoint 2016, Windows 10, Microsoft Corporation

Figure 4

5. In the **Picture Styles** gallery, move your pointer over several of the thumbnails to preview the styles and display their names.
6. Using the ScreenTips to verify your selection, point to the fourth picture style in the third row—**Perspective Shadow, White**. Click to apply the picture style, and then compare your screen with **Figure 3.**
7. In the left placeholder, select both lines of bulleted text. On the **Home tab**, in the **Paragraph group**, click the **Line Spacing** button, and then click **2.0**. Compare your slide with **Figure 4**.

   2.0 line spacing means that the lines of text are double spaced. The additional line spacing balances the text with the picture.
8. Move to **Slide 8**. In the picture placeholder on the right, click the **Pictures** button. In the **Insert Picture** dialog box, navigate to your student files for this chapter, click **ppt01_CityHall**, and then click **Insert**.
9. On the **Format tab**, in the **Picture Styles group**, click the same style you applied to the previous picture—**Perspective Shadow, White**.
10. **Save** the file.

■ **You have completed Skill 6 of 10**

SKILL 1.7

- ***Slide Sorter view*** displays all of the slides in your presentation as thumbnails.
- Slide Sorter view can be used to rearrange and delete slides, apply formatting to multiple slides, or review and reorganize a presentation.
- In Slide Sorter view, you can select multiple slides by holding down Shift or Ctrl.

Obj 1.5.2

1. Display **Slide 1** in Normal view. On the status bar at the bottom of the PowerPoint window, locate the **View** buttons, and then click the **Slide Sorter** button to display the slide thumbnails. Compare your screen with **Figure 1**.
2. If necessary, scroll down in the presentation so that Slides 7 through 10 are visible. Click **Slide 7** and notice that a thick outline surrounds the slide, indicating that it is selected.

   On a touch screen device, you can tap—touch one time with your fingertip or stylus—to select a slide.
3. Press and hold Shift, and then click **Slide 10** so that Slides 7 through 10 are selected. Release Shift.

   Using Shift enables you to select a group of sequential slides.
4. With the four slides selected, press and hold Ctrl, and then click **Slides 7** and **8**. Notice that only Slides 9 and 10 are selected. Release Ctrl. Compare your screen with **Figure 2**.

   Using Ctrl enables you to select or deselect individual slides.

■ **Continue to the next page to complete the skill**

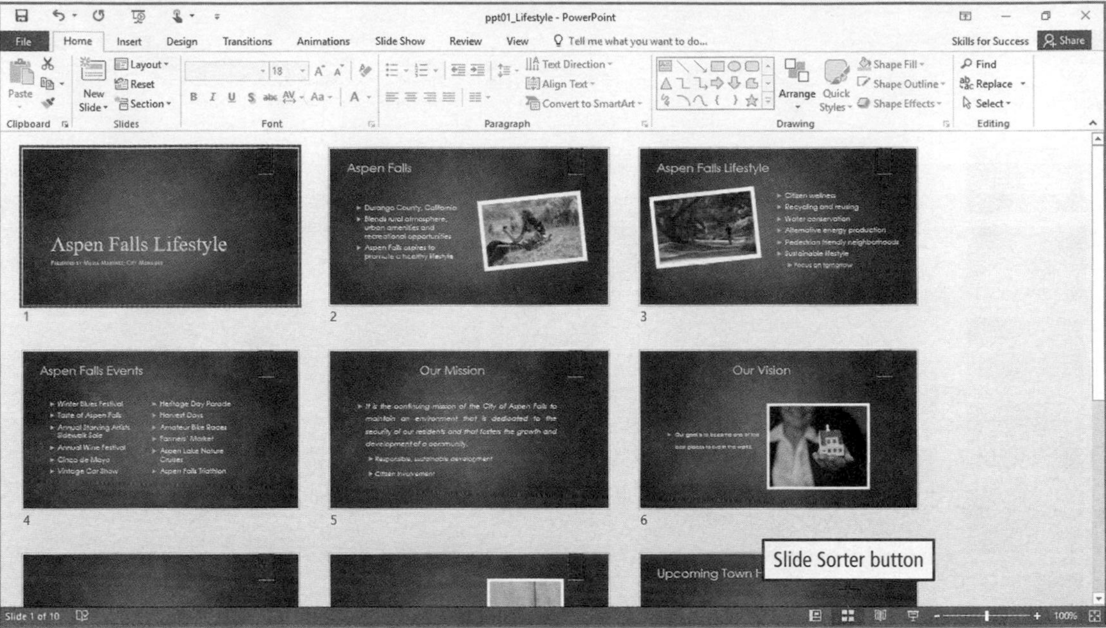

Figure 1

PowerPoint 2016, Windows 10, Microsoft Corporation

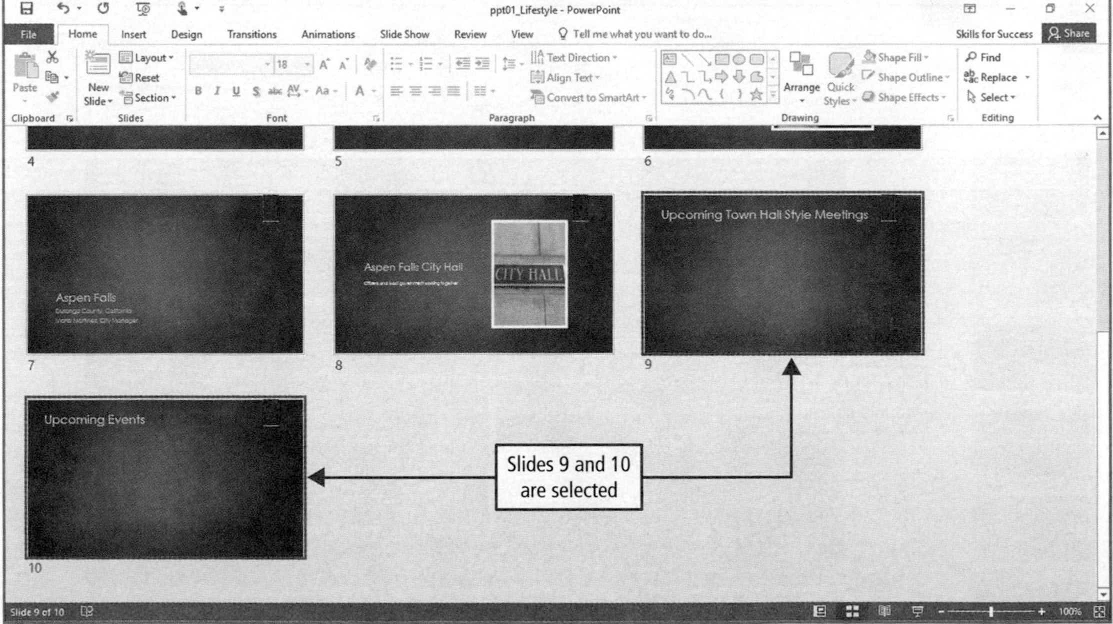

Figure 2

PowerPoint 2016, Windows 10, Microsoft Corporation

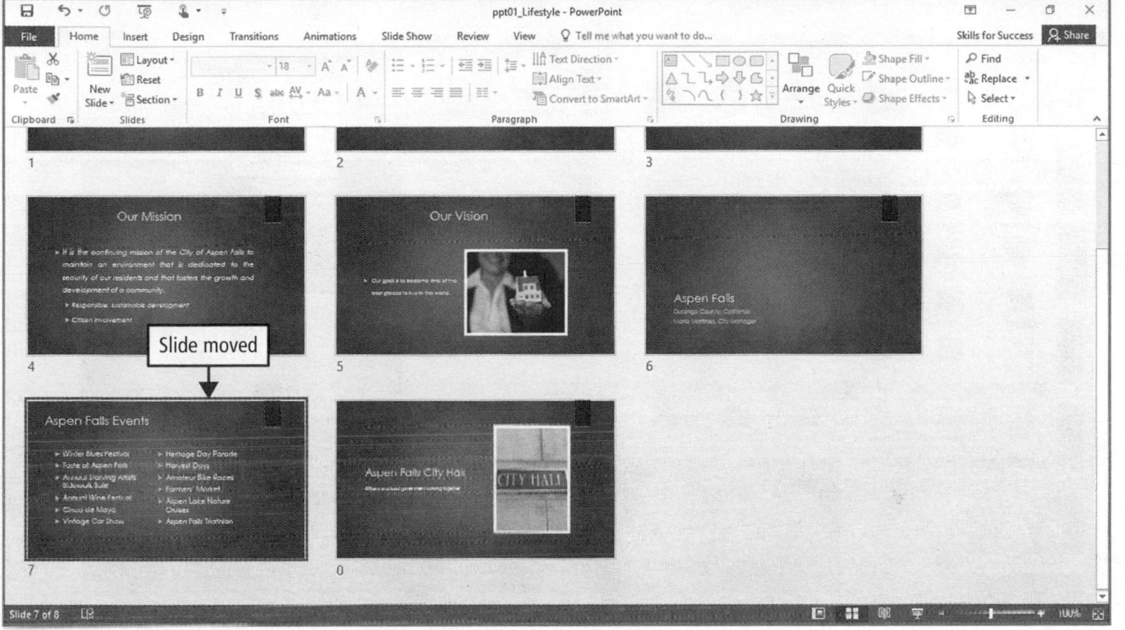

Thunder/Fotolia; Fotoluminate LLC/Fotolia; PowerPoint 2016, Windows 10, Microsoft Corporation

Figure 3

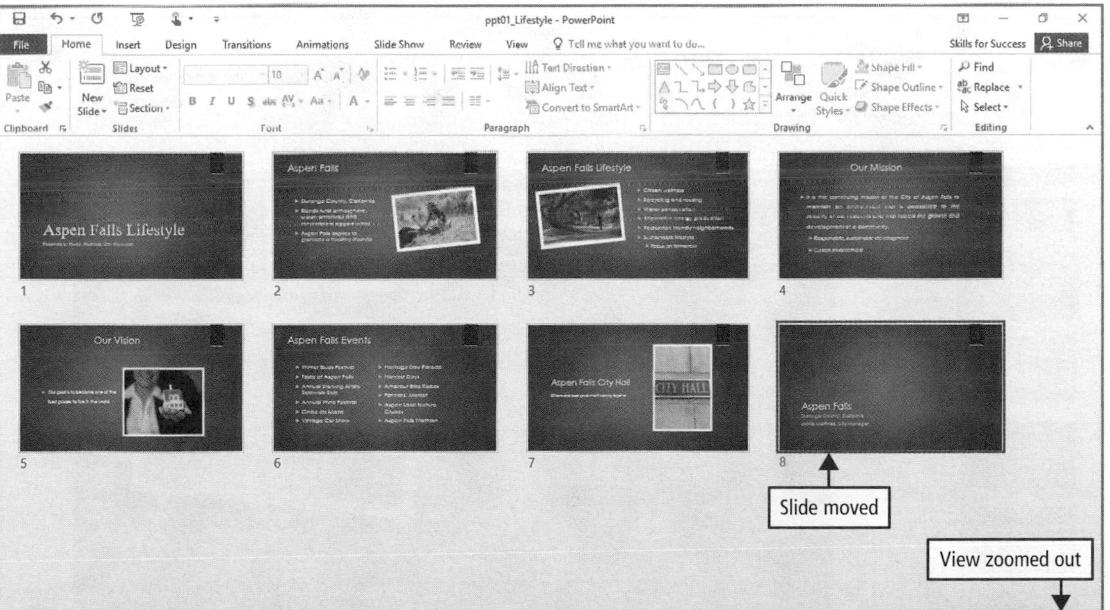

PowerPoint 2016, Windows 10, Microsoft Corporation

Figure 4

Obj 1.2.4

5. Press Delete to delete **Slides 9** and **10**. Notice that your presentation now contains eight slides because of the deletion.

6. If necessary, use the scroll bar so that **Slide 4** is visible, and then click **Slide 4** to select it.

MOS
Obj 1.4.2

7. Point to **Slide 4**, hold down the left mouse button, and then drag the slide straight down until it is positioned to the left of **Slide 8**. Release the mouse button, and then compare your screen with **Figure 3**.

   On a touch screen device, you can tap to select a slide and then tap and drag to move slide thumbnails.

8. Click the **Slide 6** thumbnail, and then drag it downward so that it displays as the last slide in the presentation.

9. On the status bar, locate the **Zoom Slider**. Notice that the current zoom level is 100%. On the left side of the zoom slider, click the **Zoom Out** button two times so that all slides are visible and the zoom level is **80%**. Compare your screen with **Figure 4**.

   On a touch screen device, you can zoom out by using a pinch gesture—placing two fingers apart on the screen and pinching them together. You can zoom in using a spread gesture—placing two fingers together on the screen and spreading them apart.

10. Double-click **Slide 1** to return the presentation to Normal view with Slide 1 displayed.

11. **Save** the file.

■ **You have completed Skill 7 of 10**

- When a presentation is viewed as a slide show, the entire slide fills the screen. When connected to a projection system, an audience can view your presentation on a large screen.
- ***Slide transitions*** are motion effects that occur in a slide show as you move from one slide to another.
- You can choose from a variety of transitions, and you can control the speed and method with which the slides advance during a presentation.

1. Display **Slide 2** in Normal view, and then click the **Transitions tab**. In the **Transition to This Slide group**, click the **More** button to display the **Transitions** gallery. Compare your screen with **Figure 1**.

   The slide transitions are organized in three groups—Subtle, Exciting, and Dynamic Content.

2. Click several of the transitions to view the transition effects, using the **More** button as necessary to redisplay the gallery.
3. In the **Transition to This Slide group**, click the **More** button, and then under **Exciting**, in the first row, click **Page Curl**.

4. In the **Transition to This Slide group**, click the **Effect Options** button, and then compare your screen with **Figure 2**. Click several of the effects to view them, clicking the Effect Options button to redisplay the gallery as needed.

   The Effect Options gallery lists the directions from which a slide transition displays and additional formats.

5. On the **Effect Options** list, click **Single Left** to change the effect.

■ **Continue to the next page to complete the skill**

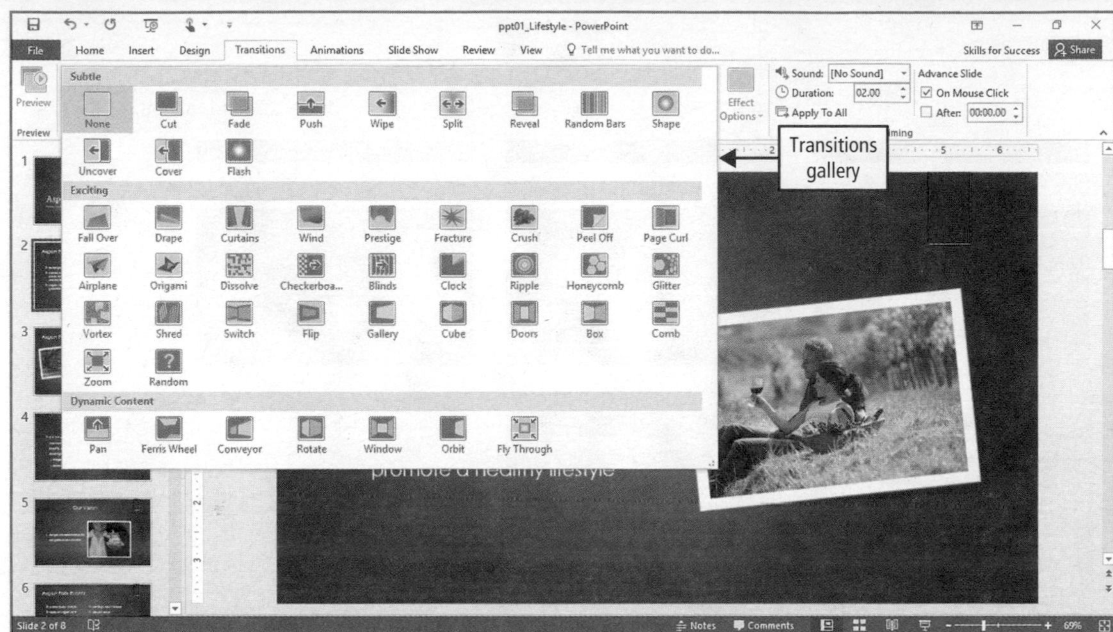

Figure 1

Auremar/Fotolia; PowerPoint 2016, Windows 10, Microsoft Corporation

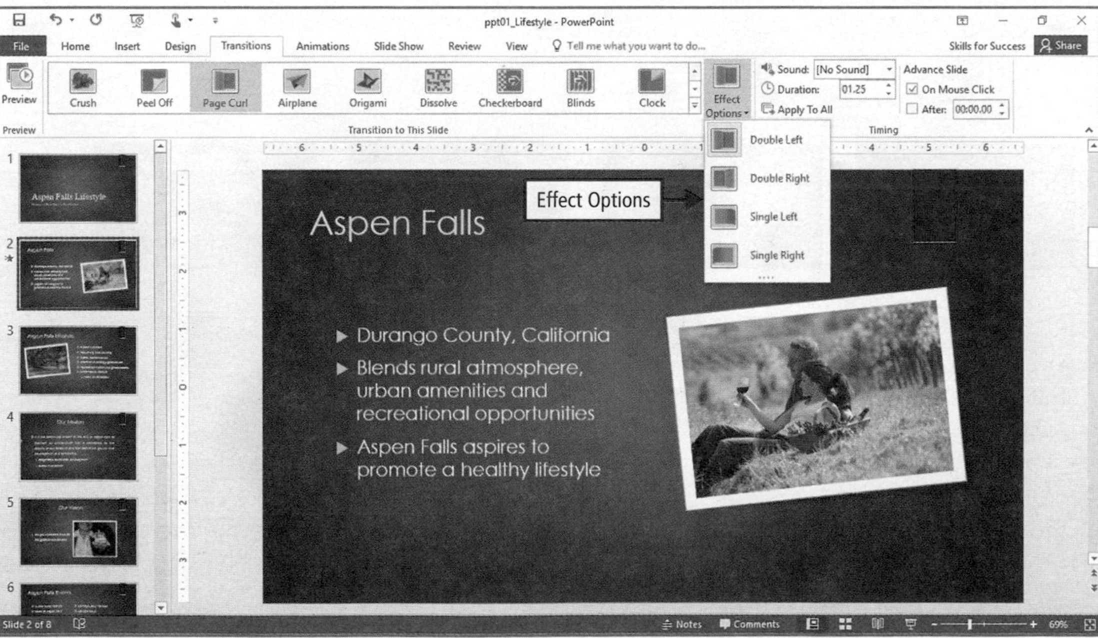

Figure 2

Auremar/Fotolia; PowerPoint 2016, Windows 10, Microsoft Corporation

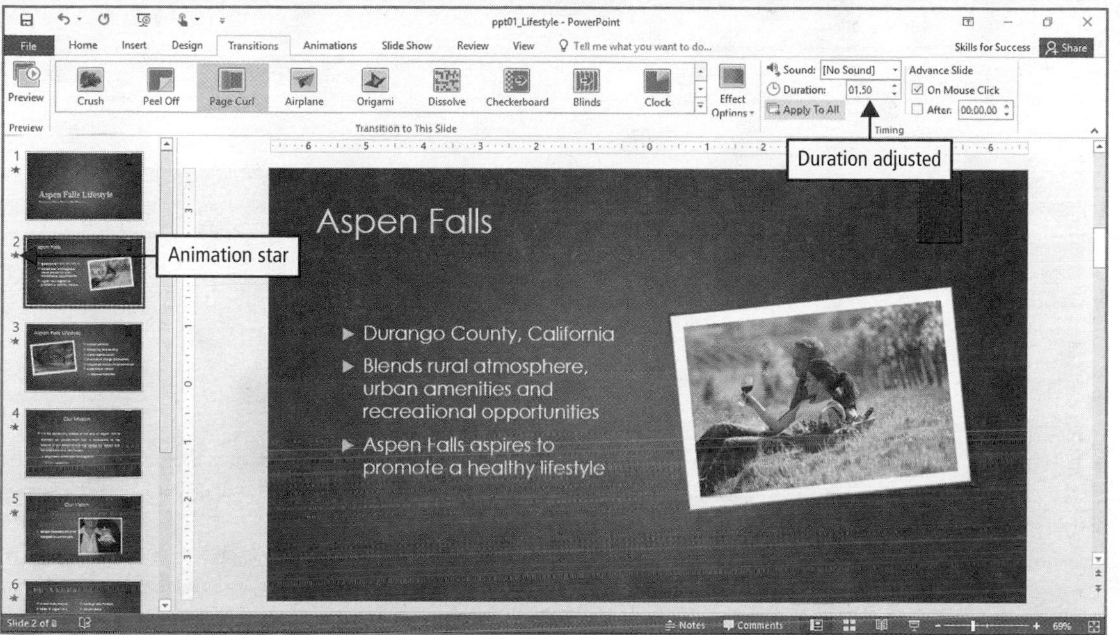

Auremar/Fotolia; PowerPoint 2016, Windows 10, Microsoft Corporation

Figure 3

PowerPoint 2016, Windows 10, Microsoft Corporation

Figure 4

6. In the **Timing group**, click the **Duration box up spin arrow** one time to display *01.50*.  MOS Obj 4.3.1
7. Verify that under **Advance Slide**, the **On Mouse Click** check box is selected so that the slides advance when the mouse button is clicked.
8. In the **Timing group**, click the **Apply To All** button to apply the transition setting to all of the slides. Compare your screen with **Figure 3**.

   The star that appears to the left of the slide thumbnails indicates that motion—in this case a transition—is present on the slide.

9. Click the **Slide Show tab**. In the **Start Slide Show group**, click **From Beginning**. Compare your screen with **Figure 4**. MOS Obj 4.3.2

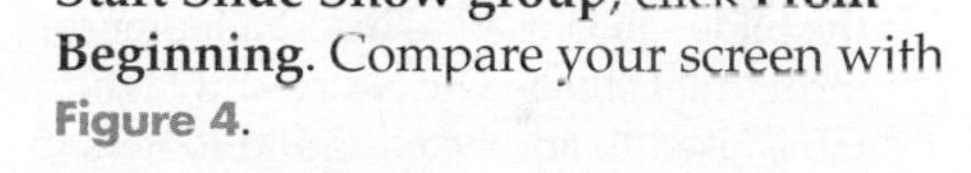

10. Click the left mouse button to advance to the second slide, noticing the transition.
11. On **Slide 2**, move the pointer to the lower left corner, and then locate the **Slide Controls**. Click the **Next Slide** button to advance to **Slide 3**.

    On a touch screen device, you can tap any of the Slide Controls to use them.

12. With **Slide 3** displayed, press SpaceBar or Enter to move to **Slide 4**. Continue to advance through the presentation using your preferred method.
13. After the last slide displays, click to display a black slide with the text *End of slide show, click to exit*.

    A ***black slide*** displays at the end of the slide show to indicate that the presentation is over.

14. Click the left mouse button to return to Normal view, and then **Save** the file.

- **You have completed Skill 8 of 10**

SKILL 9: Insert Headers and Footers and Print Handouts

- A ***header*** is text that prints at the top of each page of slide handouts. A ***footer*** is text that displays at the bottom of every slide or that prints at the bottom of a sheet of slide handouts or notes pages.
- The ***Snipping Tool*** is an application that is used to create screenshots called ***snips***.
- ***Slide handouts*** are printed images of slides on a sheet of paper.

Obj 1.2.7

1. Click the **Insert tab**, and then, in the **Text group**, click the **Header & Footer** button to display the Header and Footer dialog box.

   In the Header and Footer dialog box, the Slide tab is used to insert a footer on individual slides. The Notes and Handouts tab is used to add headers and footers to printouts.

2. In the **Header and Footer** dialog box, on the **Slides tab**, click the **Slide number** box to select it. Then, at the bottom of the dialog box, click **Don't show on title slide**. Compare your screen with **Figure 1**.

   A slide number will appear on each slide in the space indicated in the Preview section on the right. The placement of the slide number varies with the slide design.

3. Click the **Notes and Handouts tab**. Under **Include on page**, select—place a check mark in—the **Date and time** box, and then verify it is set to **Update automatically**.

4. Select the **Footer** check box, and then in the **Footer** box, using your own first and last name, type Last_First_ppt01_Lifestyle Compare your screen with **Figure 2**, and then click the **Apply to All** button.

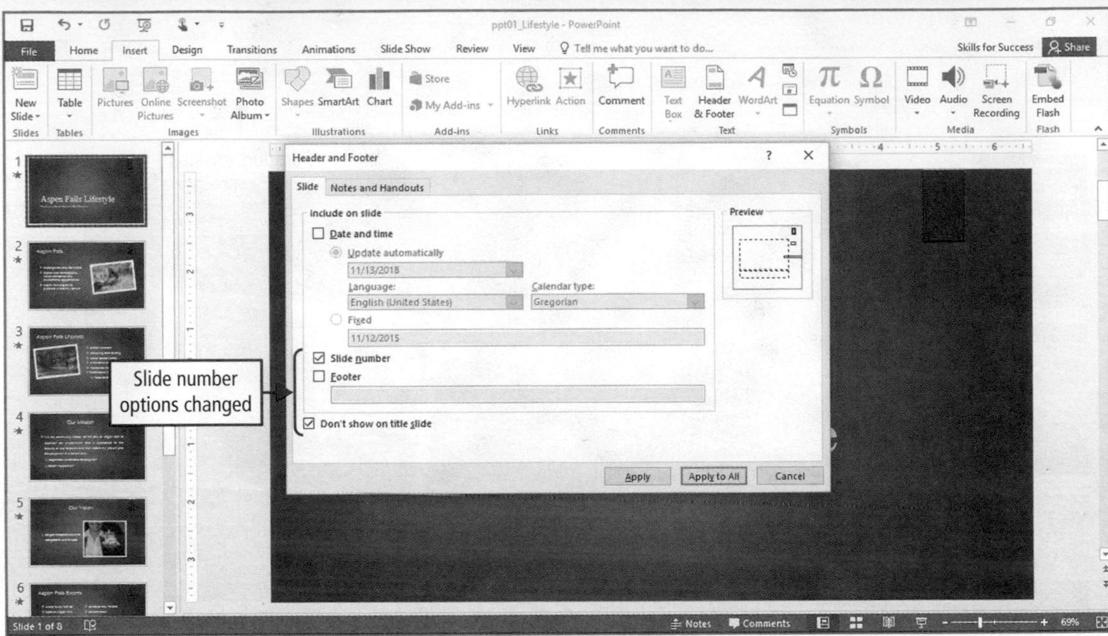

Figure 1

PowerPoint 2016, Windows 10, Microsoft Corporation

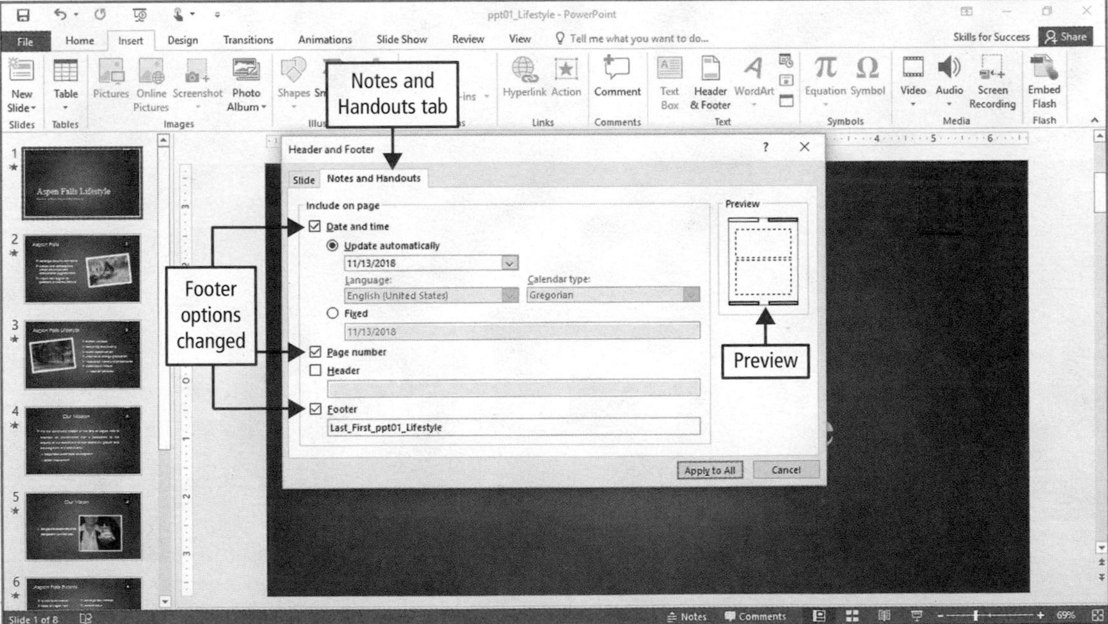

Figure 2

PowerPoint 2016, Windows 10, Microsoft Corporation

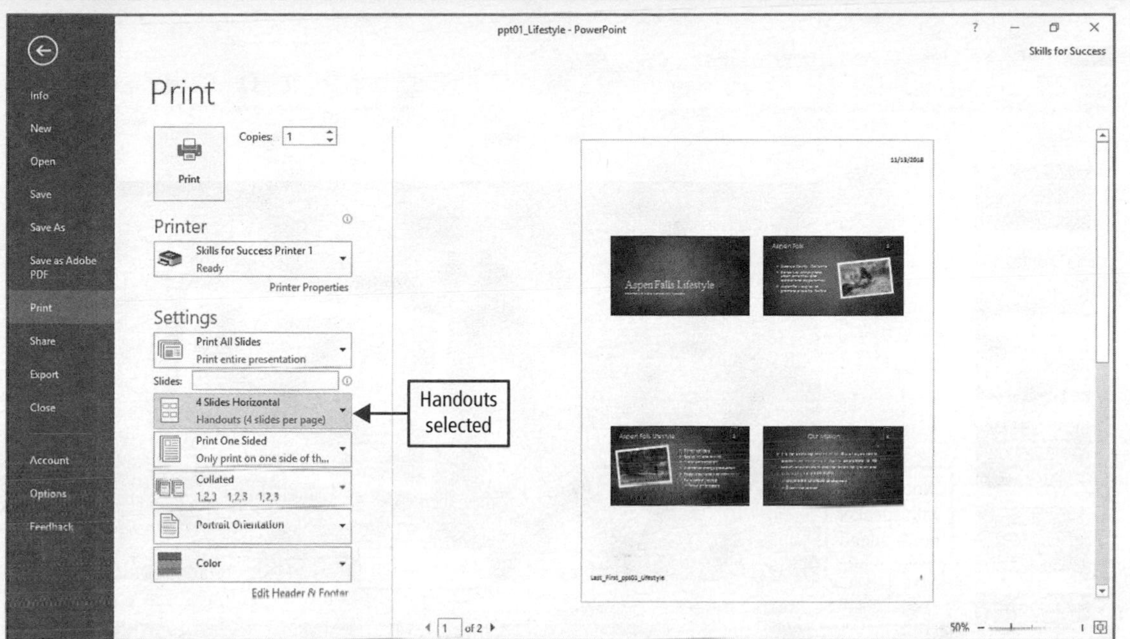

PowerPoint 2016, Windows 10, Microsoft Corporation

Figure 3

Print color changed

Next Page button

Second page of handouts displayed

PowerPoint 2016, Windows 10, Microsoft Corporation

Figure 4

5. On the **File tab**, click **Print**. MOS Obj 1.6.1

The Print page has tools you can use to select your desired print settings and displays a preview of your presentation exactly as it will print.

6. On the **Print page**, under **Settings**, click **Full Page Slides**. In the gallery, under **Handouts**, click **4 Slides Horizontal**. Compare your screen with **Figure 3**. MOS Obj 1.6.3

Depending on your printer, your slides may display in color, grayscale, or black and white. Your presentation includes eight slides, and the first handout displays the first four slides. The footer displays on the handouts, not on the slides.

7. On the left side of the window, under **Settings**, click the **Color** button, and then click **Pure Black and White**.  Obj 1.6.4

8. Toward the bottom of the screen, click the **Next Page** button [▶] to display the second page of slide handouts, containing Slides 5 through 8. Compare your screen with **Figure 4**.

9. Press [⊞] to display the **Start** menu. With the **Start** menu displayed, type Snip Open the **Snipping Tool** app. In the **Snipping Tool** dialog box, click the **New arrow**, and then click **Full-screen Snip**.

10. Click the **Save Snip** button [💾], and then in the **Save As** dialog box, navigate to your **PowerPoint Chapter 1** folder. **Save** the snip as Last_First_ppt01_LifestyleSnip and then **Close** the Snipping Tool mark-up window. Press [Esc] to return to the presentation, and then click **Save** [💾].

- **You have completed Skill 9 of 10**

- The ***Notes pane*** is an area of the Normal View window used to type notes for the presenter's reference. You can read your notes either on printed Notes pages or on screen using Presenter view.
- ***Notes pages*** are printouts that contain the slide image on the top half of the page and speaker notes on the lower half of the page.
- In ***Presenter view***, you can view your notes and the slide on the computer screen. Only the slide is projected to the audience. Presenter view requires only one monitor.
- During a presentation, you may find it helpful to refer to your notes for specific statistical information or important points.

1. Display **Slide 2**. On the status bar, click the **Notes** button as needed to display the **Notes** pane. Click in the **Notes** pane, and then type The population of Aspen Falls was just over 75,000 citizens in the last census. Compare your screen with **Figure 1**.
2. On **Slide 6**, click in the **Notes** pane, and then type Volunteers are needed, and welcomed, at all events. Please contact Deborah Davidson for more information at ddavidson@aspenfalls.org. Compare your screen with **Figure 2**.

3. Press F5 to start the presentation from the beginning, and then click to advance to the second slide.

   Notice that on Slide 2 the speaker notes you entered do not appear on screen. Your screen exactly matches the view being projected to the audience. If you are using dual monitors, your view may differ.

■ **Continue to the next page to complete the skill**

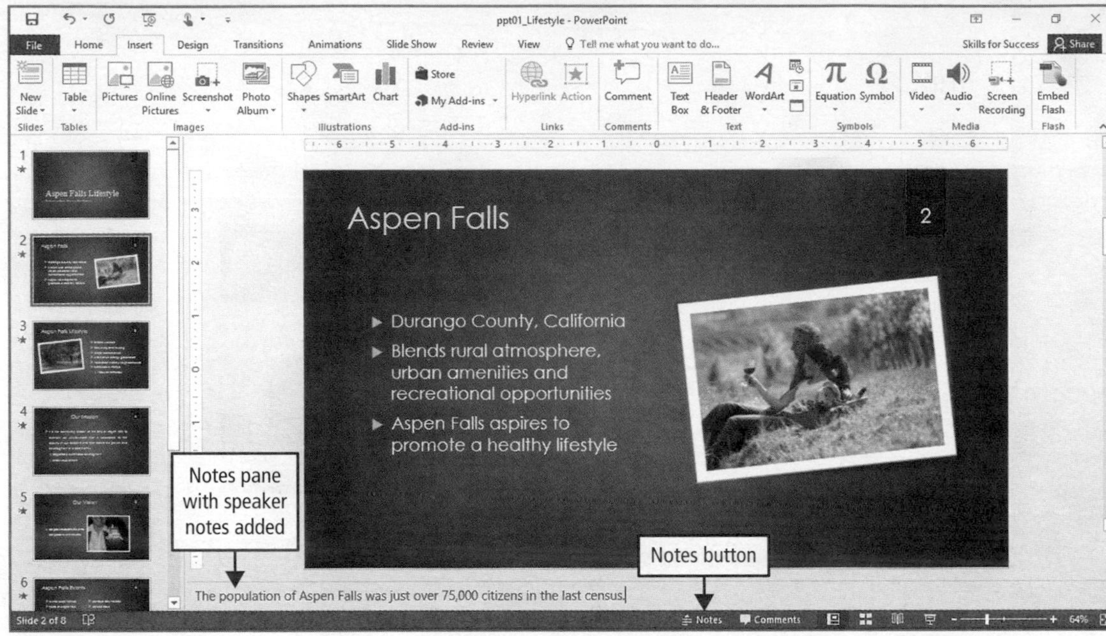

Figure 1

Auremar/Fotolia; PowerPoint 2016, Windows 10, Microsoft Corporation

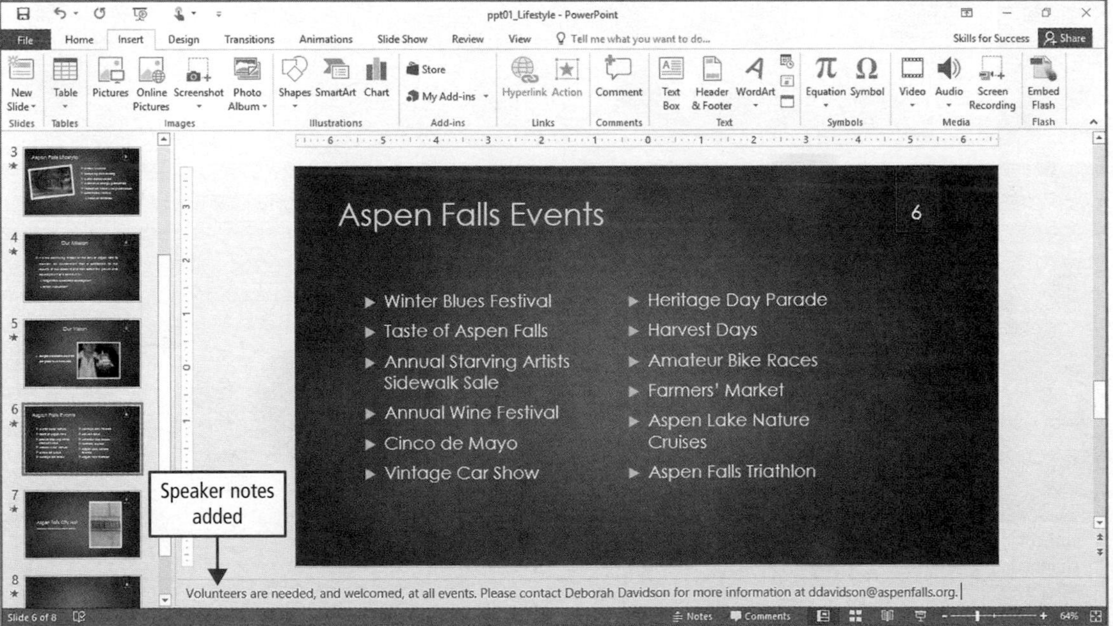

Figure 2

PowerPoint 2016, Windows 10, Microsoft Corporation

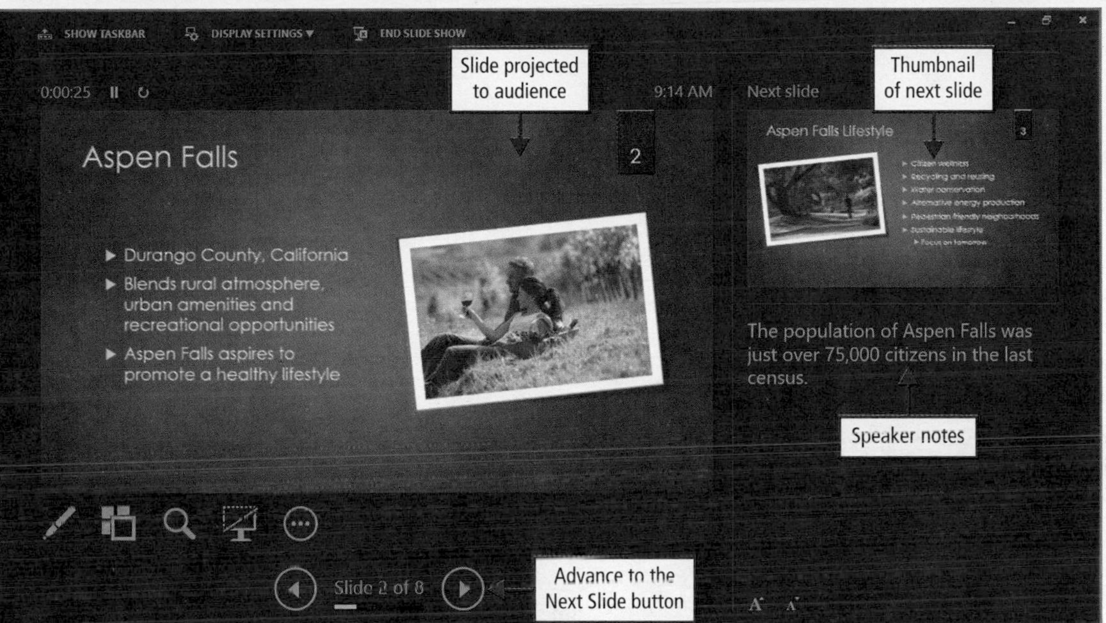

Auremar/Fotolia; PowerPoint 2016, Windows 10, Microsoft Corporation

Figure 3

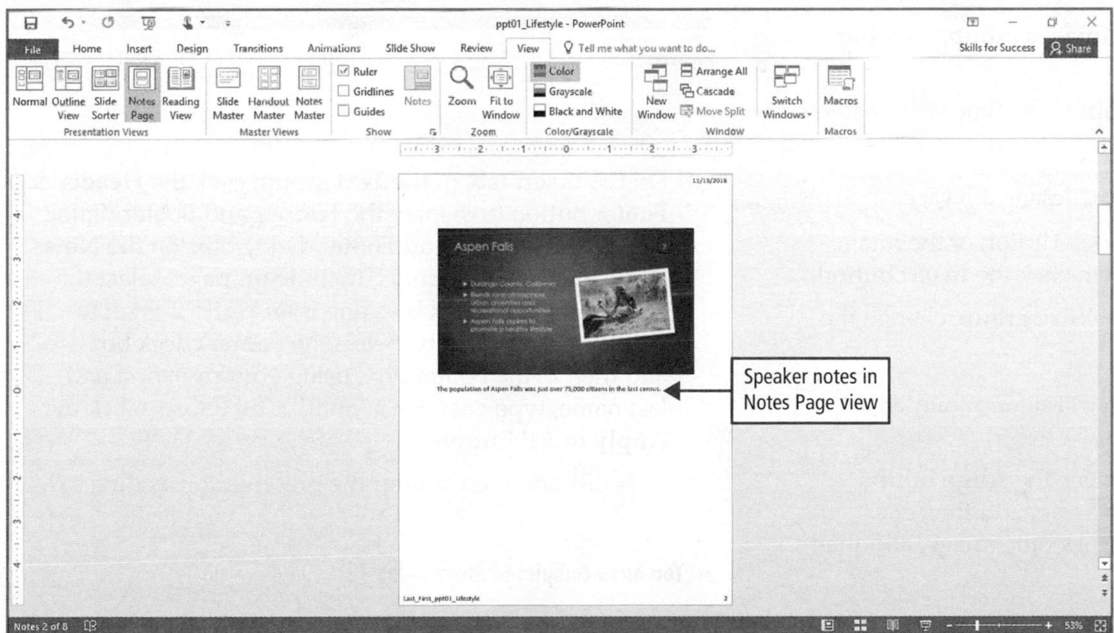

Auremar/Fotolia; PowerPoint 2016, Windows 10, Microsoft Corporation

Figure 4

4. Still in Slide Show view, with **Slide 2** displayed, right-click any area of the slide. From the shortcut menu, click **Show Presenter View**. Compare your screen with **Figure 3**.

   Presenter view displays three items—the current slide, speaker notes, and a thumbnail of the next slide. This view is shown only on the presenter's screen and is not projected on the screen the audience views. If you are using dual monitors, Presenter view may appear automatically, or the slide may appear on one monitor and the remaining information on the other. Keep these differences in mind as you use Presenter view.

5. Click the **Advance to the Next Slide** button to advance to Slide 3, and then continue to click to advance through the presentation, noticing the speaker notes on Slide 6. Click to end the slide show and return to Normal view.

6. On **Slide 1**, click the **View tab**. In the **Presentation Views group**, click **Notes Page**. Scroll down to display **Slide 2**, and then compare your screen with **Figure 4**.

   The lower half of Notes pages for any slides that do not contain notes will remain blank.

7. On the status bar, click the **Normal** button to return to Normal view.

8. On the **Quick Access Toolbar**, click **Save**, and then **Close** PowerPoint. Submit as directed by your instructor.

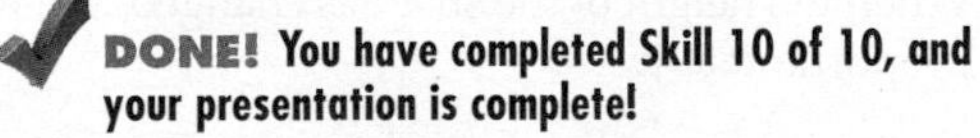

DONE! You have completed Skill 10 of 10, and your presentation is complete!

More Skills 11

Add Online Images

To complete this project, you will need the following file:

- ppt01_MS11Goals

You will save your file as:

- Last_First_ppt01_MS11Goals

- In PowerPoint, Online Pictures refers to ***online images***—a collection of images stored online and made available for use in presentations.
- Online images include graphics, drawings, or photographs accessed from Bing Image Search, OneDrive, or online search providers. These images can be included in your presentation to provide your audience with a visual representation of the slide topic.

---

1. Start **PowerPoint 2016**, and then open the student file **ppt01_MS11Goals**. Save the file in your **PowerPoint Chapter 1** folder as Last_First_ppt01_MS11Goals

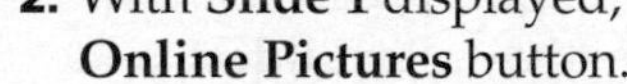

MOS Obj 2.3.1

2. With **Slide 1** displayed, on the **Insert tab**, in the **Images group**, click the **Online Pictures** button.
3. In the **Insert Pictures** dialog box, in the **Search Bing** box, type sustainable development and then press Enter.

   Related clips appear in the Insert Pictures dialog box. Results will vary.
4. Point to the images to view a ScreenTip or short description of the image. Click once to select an appropriate image, and then click the **Insert** button.
5. With the image selected, on the **Format tab**, in the **Size group**, change the **Shape Height** value to 2, and then press Enter.

   When the height of the shape is changed, the width will automatically adjust proportionately.
6. With the image still selected, on the **Format tab**, click the **Align** button, and then click **Align Top**. Click the **Align** button again, and then click **Align Right**. Click a blank area of the slide to deselect the image, and then compare your screen with **Figure 1**.

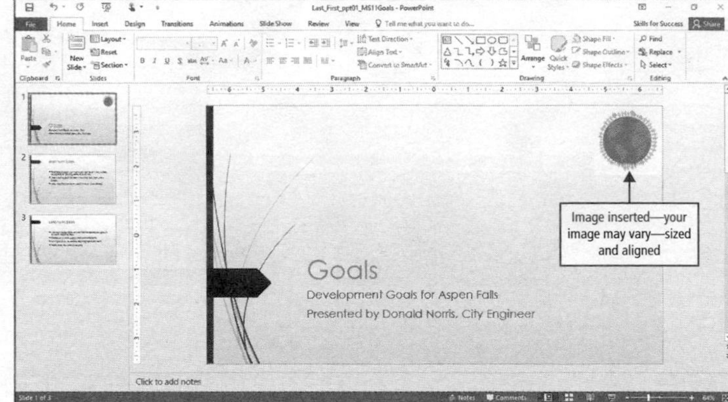

Figure 1 PowerPoint 2016, Windows 10, Microsoft Corporation

7. On the **Insert tab**, in the **Text group**, click the **Header & Footer** button to display the Header and Footer dialog box. In the **Header and Footer** dialog box, on the **Notes and Handouts tab**, under **Include on page**, select the **Date and time** check box, and then verify it is set to **Update automatically**. Select the **Footer** check box, and then in the **Footer** box, using your own first and last name, type Last_First_ppt01_MS11Goals Click the **Apply to All button**.
8. **Save**, and then submit the presentation as directed.

- **You have completed More Skills 11**

More Skills 12

Print Presentations, Handouts, and Custom Ranges

To complete this project, you will need the following file:

- ppt01_MS12Hiking

You will save your files as:

- Last_First_ppt01_MS12Snip1
- Last_First_ppt01_MS12Snip2

- Presentations can be printed in several formats—Full Page Slides, Notes pages, Outlines, or Handouts—in full color, grayscale, or pure black and white.
- You can print all of the slides in the presentation, or you can print a ***Custom Range*** that includes only a selection of slides.
- ***Full Page Slides*** are printouts in which the slide is fit to letter-size paper.
- ***Handouts*** are printouts that feature one or more slides on a single page. A handout can contain between two and nine slides per page.

---

1. Start **PowerPoint 2016**, and then open **ppt01_MS12Hiking**.
2. On the **File tab**, click **Print**. Under **Settings**, click **Print All Slides**, and then click **Custom Range**. In the **Slides** box, type 2-4 and then press Tab. At the bottom of the screen, click the **Next page** button ▸ two times to preview the slides as they will print. MOS Obj 1.6.1
3. Press ⊞, type snip and then press Enter to open the **Snipping Tool**. In the **Snipping Tool** dialog box, click the **New arrow**, and then click **Full-screen Snip**. In the **Snipping Tool** window, click **Save Snip**. In the **Save as** dialog box, navigate to your **PowerPoint Chapter 1** folder, name the snip Last_First_ppt01_MS12Snip1 and then click **Save**. **Close** the **Snipping Tool** mark-up window.
4. Under **Settings**, click the **Custom Range** button, and then click **Print All Slides**. Click the **Full Page Slides** button, and then under **Handouts**, preview several of the available options. Click **3 Slides**. Under **Settings**, click the **Color** button, and then click **Pure Black and White**. Compare your screen with **Figure 1**.

   The Pure Black and White color setting saves on ink and toner and creates a cleaner-looking handout.

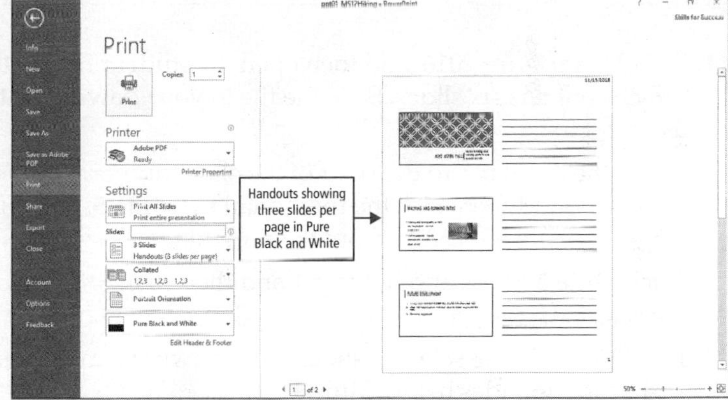

PowerPoint 2016, Windows 10, Microsoft Corporation **Figure 1**

5. Use the method previously practiced to capture a **Full-screen Snip** of the preview of the presentation as handouts with three slides per page in pure black and white. **Save** the snip as Last_First_ppt01_MS12Snip2 in your **PowerPoint Chapter 1** folder. **Close** the Snipping Tool.
6. **Close** the presentation without saving. Submit the snips as directed.

- **You have completed More Skills 12**

More Skills 13

Move and Delete Slides in Normal View

To complete this project, you will need the following file:

- ppt01_MS13Planning

You will save your file as:

- **Last_First_ppt01_MS13Planning**

▶ You can reorganize your presentation by moving and deleting slides in Normal view using the slide thumbnails.

---

1. Start **PowerPoint 2016**, and then open the student file **ppt01_MS13Planning**, which contains six slides. Save the file in your **PowerPoint Chapter 1** folder as Last_First_ppt01_MS13Planning

2. Using the scroll bar to the right of the slide thumbnails, scroll down if necessary, and then click the thumbnail for **Slide 5**. On your keyboard, press Delete to remove the slide from the presentation.
3. Click **Slide 3**. Press and hold Ctrl, and then click **Slide 4** so that both slides are selected.
4. Point to one of the selected slides, hold down the mouse button, drag up, and drop the slides below **Slide 1**.
5. Click the **Slide 5** thumbnail. Right-click, and then click **Delete Slide**. Click the **Slide 1** thumbnail. Compare your screen with **Figure 1**.
6. On the **Insert tab**, in the **Text group**, click the **Header & Footer** button, and then click the **Notes and Handouts tab**. Select the **Date and time**, and then set it to **Update automatically**. Select the **Page number** check box. Select the **Footer** check box, and then in the **Footer** box, type Last_First_ppt01_MS13Planning Click **Apply to All**.
7. **Save** your presentation, and then close it. Submit as directed.

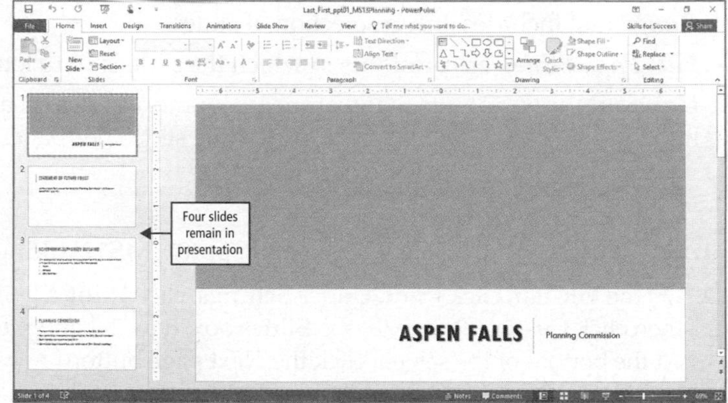

Figure 1 PowerPoint 2016, Windows 10, Microsoft Corporation

■ **You have completed More Skills 13**

More Skills 14

Change Slide Size and Orientation

To complete this project, you will need the following file:

- ppt01_MS14Downtown

You will save your files as:

- Last_First_ppt01_MS14Downtown
- Last_First_ppt01_MS14Snip

- ***Aspect ratio*** refers to the width-to-height ratio of a screen.
- PowerPoint 2016 is optimized to work with wide-screen monitors that have an aspect ratio of 16:9. Older monitors, or standard monitors, have a default aspect ratio of 4:3.
- The orientation of a slide can be switched from the default landscape format to a portrait format.

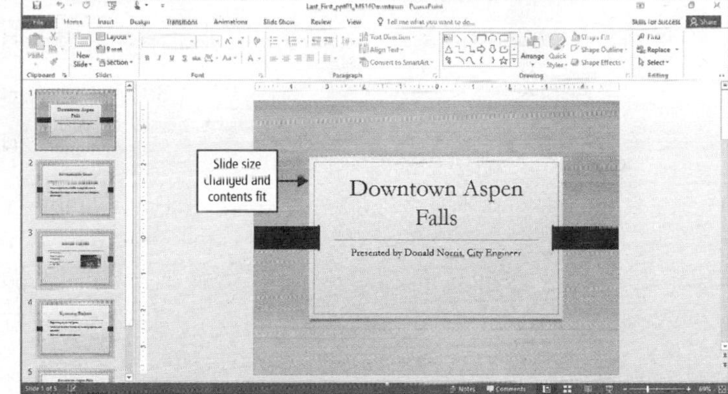

PowerPoint 2016, Windows 10, Microsoft Corporation **Figure 1**

1. Start **PowerPoint 2016**, and then open the student file **ppt01_MS14Downtown**. Save the file in your **PowerPoint Chapter 1** folder as Last_First_ppt01_MS14Downtown
2. On the **Insert tab**, in the **Text group**, click **Header & Footer**. On the **Notes and Handouts tab**, select the **Date and time** and **Page number** boxes. Select the **Footer** box, and then add the footer Last_First_ppt01_MS14Downtown Click **Apply to All**.
3. On the **Design tab**, in the **Customize group**, click the **Slide Size** button, and then click the **Standard (4:3)** button.  MOS Obj 1.5.1

   When changing the slide size, you can ***Maximize***—keep your content as large as possible while allowing some content to be cropped if needed. You can also ***Ensure Fit***—scale your information down so that it all appears on the slide.

4. In the dialog box, click **Ensure Fit**. Compare your screen with **Figure 1**.
5. On the **Design tab**, in the **Customize group**, click the **Slide Size** button. Click **Customize Slide Size**.
6. Under **Notes, Handouts & Outline**, select the **Landscape** option button, and then click **OK**.
7. On the **File tab**, click **Print**. Under **Settings**, click the button with the text **Full Page Slides**.
8. In the list, under **Handouts**, click **3 Slides**.
9. Press [Windows], type Snip and then press Enter. In the **Snipping Tool** dialog box, click the **New arrow**, and then click **Full-screen Snip**. Click **Save Snip**, navigate to your **PowerPoint Chapter 1** folder, and then save the snip as Last_First_ppt01_MS14Snip **Close** the Snipping Tool mark-up window.
10. **Save** [Save] the presentation, **Close** PowerPoint, and then submit as directed.

- **You have completed More Skills 14**

The following table summarizes the **SKILLS AND PROCEDURES** covered in this chapter.

Skills Number	Task	Step	Icon	Keyboard Shortcut
1	Save a presentation	File tab → Save As		Ctrl + S
2	Increase list level in a bulleted list	Select bullet point to be increased → Home tab → Paragraph group → Increase Indent button		Tab
2	Decrease list level in a bulleted list	Select bullet point to be decreased → Home tab → Paragraph group → Decrease Indent button		Shift + Tab
2	Replace text	Home tab → Editing group → Replace		Ctrl + H
3	Apply a font effect	Select text → Home tab → Font group → Launcher button → Select Font Effect		
3	Apply bold	Select text → Home tab → Font group → Bold button	B	Ctrl + B
3	Apply italic	Select text → Home tab → Font group → Italic button	I	Ctrl + I
3	Increase line spacing	Select text → Home tab → Paragraph group → Line Spacing button		
4	Check spelling	Review tab → Proofing group → Spelling button		F7 or Alt + R S
4	Find a synonym	Right-click word → Synonyms		
5	Insert a new slide	Home tab → Slides group → New Slide button		Ctrl + M
5	Change slide layout	Home tab → Slides group → Layout button		
6	Insert a picture	Insert tab → Images group → Pictures button		
6	Apply a Picture Style	Picture Tools Format tab → Picture Styles group		
7	Delete a slide	Select slide thumbnail → Right-click → Delete		Delete
7	Move a slide	Select slide → drag		
7	Select multiple slides	Select first slide → Press and hold Ctrl or Shift → Select next slide		Ctrl or Shift
7	Switch to Slide Sorter view	Status bar → Slide Sorter; or View tab → Presentation Views group → Slide Sorter		
8	Add a transition	Transitions tab → Transition to This Slide group → Transitions gallery		
8	Start slide show	Status bar → Slide Show; or Slide Show tab → Start Slide Show group		F5
9	Insert headers and footers	Insert tab → Text group → Header & Footer		
10	Use Presenter View	While in Slide Show, right-click → Show Presenter View		
10	Add speaker notes	Status bar → Notes button		
10	Print presentations and handouts	File tab → Print		Ctrl + P

Project Summary Chart		
Project Location	**Project**	**Project Type**
Skills Review	Review	In Book & MIL MyITLab® Grader
Skills Assessment 1	Review	In Book & MIL MyITLab® Grader
Skills Assessment 2	Review	Book
My Skills	Problem Solving	Book
Visual Skills Check	Problem Solving	Book
Skillls Challenge 1	Critical Thinking	Book
Skills Challenge 2	Critical Thinking	Book
More Skills Assessment	Review	In Book & MIL MyITLab® Grader
Collaborating with Google	Critical Thinking	Book

MOS Objectives Covered	
1.2.1 Insert specific slide layouts	1.7.4 Present a slide show by using presenter view
1.2.4 Delete slides	2.1.1 Insert text on a slide
1.2.5 Apply a different slide layout	2.3.1 Insert images
1.2.7 Insert slide headers, footers, and page numbers	2.3.3 Apply styles and effects
1.4.2 Modify slide order	4.1.1 Insert slide transitions
1.5.1 Change slide size	4.1.2 Set transition effect options
1.5.2 Change views of a presentation	4.3.1 Set transition effect duration
1.6.1 Print all or part of a presentation	4.3.2 Configure transition start and finish options
1.6.3 Print handouts	5.2.3 Proof a presentation
1.6.4 Print in color, grayscale, or black and white	

Key Terms

Aspect ratio 711
Black slide 703
Bullet point 690
Contextual tab 698
Custom Range 698
Ensure Fit 711
Font 692
Footer 704
Full Page Slide 709
Handout 709
Header 704
Layout 696
Layout gallery 696
List level 690
Maximize 711
Normal view 690
Notes page 706
Notes pane 706
Online images 708
Picture 698
Picture style 698
Placeholder 690
Point 692
Presenter view 706
Sizing handle 698
Slide 688
Slide handout 704
Slide Sorter view 700
Slide transition 702
Snip 704
Snipping Tool 704
Start screen 688
Synonym 694
Text alignment 692
Thesaurus 694
Thumbnail 689

BizSkills Video

1. After viewing the video, summarize some of the common elements of appropriate professional apparel for work.
2. How might a person's appearance impact his or her professional image? Is this fair?

Online Help Skills

1. Start **PowerPoint 2016**, and then open a blank presentation. On the **File tab**, in the upper right corner of the screen, click the **Microsoft PowerPoint Help** button [?], or press [F1].
2. In the **PowerPoint Help** window, use the Search box to locate and open the article *Turn your mouse into a laser pointer*. Maximize the window, and then compare your screen with **Figure 1**.

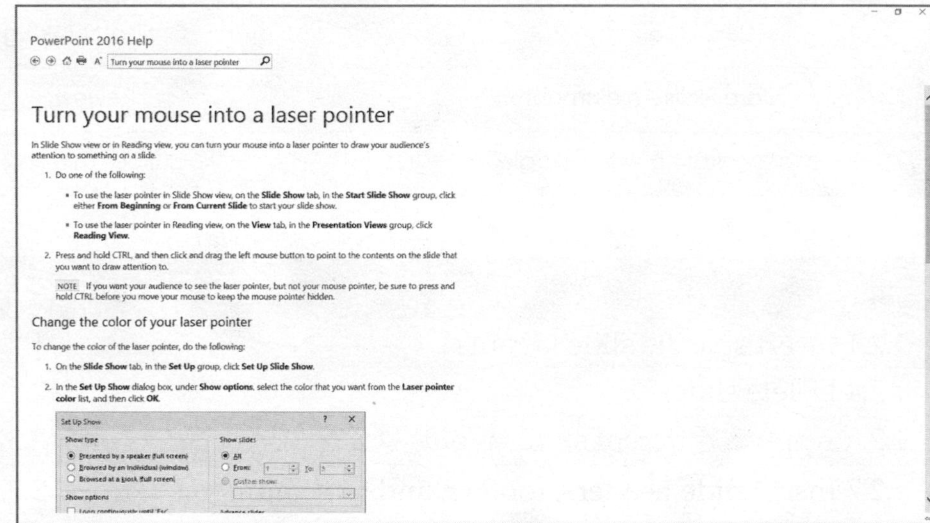

Figure 1 PowerPoint 2016, Windows 10, Microsoft Corporation

3. Read the article and answer the following questions: In what situation might you want to use your mouse as a laser pointer? How might this be beneficial?

Matching 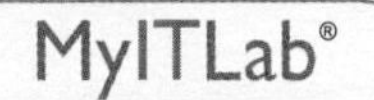

Match each term in the second column with its correct definition in the first column. Write the letter of the term on the blank line in front of the correct definition.

___ **1.** The initial screen that displays when you open PowerPoint 2016; from here you can open a recent file or create a new presentation from a template.

___ **2.** The setting that determines the indent, font size, and bullet type for slide bullets.

___ **3.** A line of text on a slide that starts with a special character and is assigned a specific indent.

___ **4.** The boxes on slides used to hold objects such as titles, subtitles, pictures, and other content.

___ **5.** A feature that changes the horizontal placement of text within a placeholder.

___ **6.** A set of characters with the same design and shape.

___ **7.** A circle surrounding a selected object that is used to adjust its size.

___ **8.** A slide that displays at the end of the slide show to indicate that the presentation is over.

___ **9.** An area of the Normal View window used to type notes that can be printed below a picture of each slide.

___ **10.** A printout that contains the slide image in the top half of the page and speaker notes typed in the Notes pane in the lower half of the page.

A Black slide
B Bullet point
C Font
D List level
E Notes page
F Notes pane
G Placeholder
H Sizing handle
I Start screen
J Text alignment

Multiple Choice

MyITLab®

Choose the correct answer.

1. The button that is used to move a bullet point, or line of text, to the right in preset increments.
 A. Increase List Level
 B. Decrease List Level
 C. Line Spacing

2. Words with the same meaning.
 A. Synonyms
 B. Antonyms
 C. Prepositions

3. The arrangement of the text and graphic elements or placeholders on a slide.
 A. Layout
 B. Gallery
 C. Design

4. The view in which all of the slides in your presentation are displayed as thumbnails.
 A. Outline view
 B. Slide Sorter view
 C. Reading view

5. Tabs that display only when certain objects such as pictures are selected.
 A. Contextual tabs
 B. ScreenTips
 C. Tool galleries

6. A prebuilt set of formatting borders, effects, and layouts applied to a picture.
 A. Artistic effects
 B. Picture styles
 C. Picture designs

7. A motion effect that occurs in Slide Show view when you move from one slide to the next during a presentation.
 A. Animation
 B. Slide transition
 C. Custom effect

8. Text that prints at the top of a sheet of slide handouts or notes pages.
 A. Page numbers
 B. Header
 C. Footer

9. Text that displays at the bottom of every slide or that prints at the bottom of a sheet of slide handouts.
 A. Page numbers
 B. Header
 C. Footer

10. View that displays the current slide, notes, and preview of upcoming slide to the presenter.
 A. Presenter view
 B. Slide Show view
 C. Notes Page view

Topics for Discussion

1. Review the design templates available from the Start screen in PowerPoint. How are presentations and templates designed for different audiences? For example, how might the design used in a presentation created for children differ from the design used in a presentation created for a group of financial investors?

2. How might adding speaker notes to a presentation be helpful? What are some best practices for using speaker notes?

Skills Review

To complete this project, you will need the following files:

- ppt01_SRSustainability
- ppt01_SRPlant

You will save your files as:

- Last_First_ppt01_SRSustainability
- Last_First_ppt01_SRSnip

1. Start **PowerPoint 2016**, and then open the student data file **ppt01_SRSustainability**. On the **File tab**, click **Save As**, and then click **Browse**. In the **Save As** dialog box, navigate to your **PowerPoint Chapter 1** folder, and then save the file as Last_First_ppt01_SRSustainability
2. Display **Slide 2**, and then click so that your insertion point appears to the left of the *p* in *printed*. Type Decrease and then press SpaceBar.
3. Display **Slide 1**. On the **Home tab**, in the **Editing group**, click the **Replace** button. In the **Find what** box, type Drive and then click in the **Replace with** box. Type Campaign and then click **Replace All**. Click **OK**, and then **Close** the Replace dialog box.
4. On **Slide 1**, select the title placeholder. On the **Home tab**, in the **Font group**, click the **Launcher**. Select **Small Caps**, and then click **OK**.
5. On the **Review tab**, in the **Proofing group**, click the **Spelling** button. Use the **Spelling** task pane to correct the spelling of two words, and then click **OK**.
6. On **Slide 2**, in the third bullet point, right-click the word *policy*, point to **Synonyms**, and then click the word **strategy**. Compare your screen with **Figure 1**.
7. Display **Slide 4**. On the **Home tab**, in the **Slides group**, click the **Layout** button, and then click **Two Content**.
8. In the right content placeholder, click the **Pictures** button. In the **Insert Picture** dialog box, navigate to your student files, and then click **ppt01_SRPlant**. Click **Insert**.
9. With the picture selected, on the **Format tab**, in the **Picture Styles group**, select **Rounded Diagonal Corner, White**.

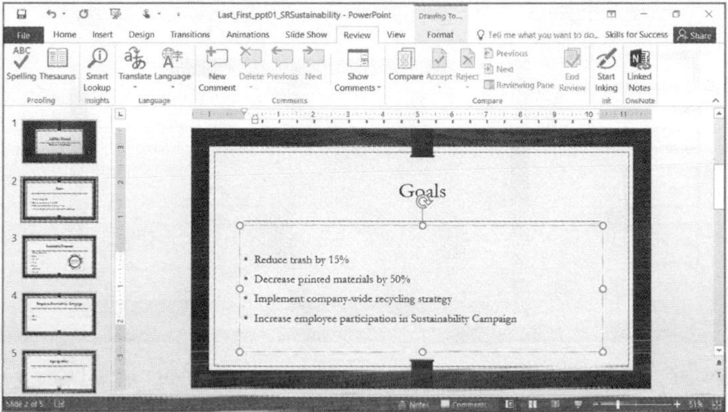

Figure 1 PowerPoint 2016, Windows 10, Microsoft Corporation

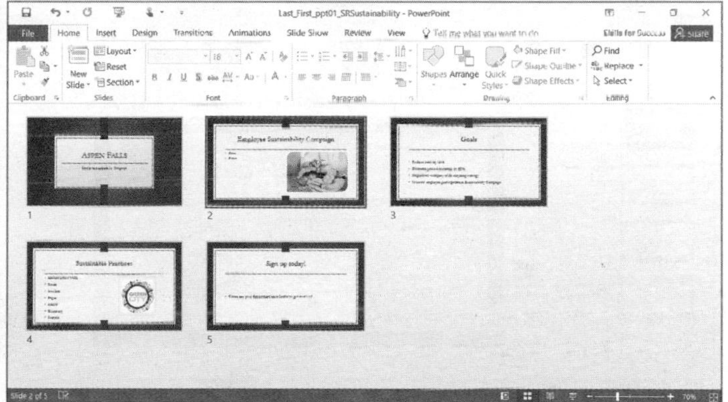

Figure 2 PowerPoint 2016, Windows 10, Microsoft Corporation

10. On the status bar, click the **Slide Sorter** button.
11. In **Slide Sorter** view, select **Slide 4**, and then drag it so that it appears directly after **Slide 1**. Compare your screen with **Figure 2**.

■ **Continue to the next page to complete this Skills Review**

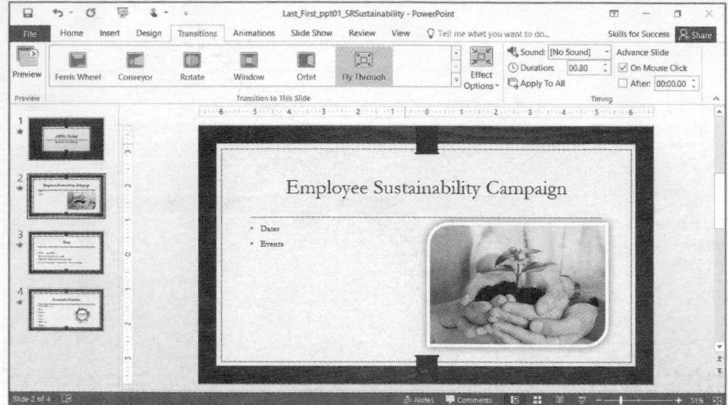

Astock/Fotolia; PowerPoint 2016, Windows 10, Microsoft Corporation **Figure 3**

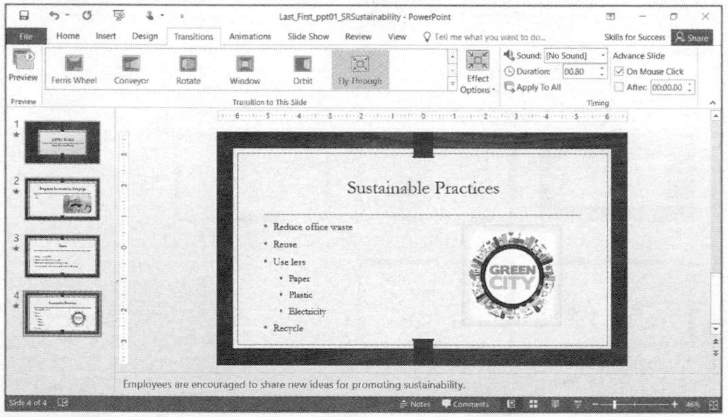

Marina Zlochin/Fotolia; PowerPoint 2016, Windows 10, Microsoft Corporation **Figure 4**

12. In **Slide Sorter** view, select **Slide 5**, and then press Delete.
13. Double-click **Slide 2** to return to Normal view. On the **Transitions tab**, in the **Transition to This Slide group**, click the **More arrow**. At the bottom of the gallery, click **Fly Through**.
14. On the **Transitions tab**, in the **Transition to This Slide group**, click the **Effect Options** button, and then select **In with Bounce**. In the **Timing group**, click **Apply To All**. Compare your screen with **Figure 3**.
15. Display **Slide 4**. Select the bullet points *Paper*, *Plastic*, and *Electricity*. With these three bullet points selected, press Tab.
16. On the status bar, click the **Notes** button. In the **Notes** pane, type Employees are encouraged to share new ideas for promoting sustainability. Compare your screen with **Figure 4**.
17. Display **Slide 3**. In the **Notes** pane, type Incentive programs to be announced.
18. On the **Insert tab**, in the **Text group**, click **Header & Footer**. On the **Slide tab**, select the **Slide number** check box. Select **Don't show on title slide**, and then click **Apply to All**.
19. On the **Insert tab**, in the **Text group**, click **Header & Footer**. On the **Notes and Handouts tab**, select **Date and time**, and then verify that **Update automatically** and **Page number** are selected. Check **Footer**, and then in the **Footer** box, type Last_First_ppt01_SRSustainability Click **Apply to All**.
20. On the **File tab**, click **Print**. Under **Settings**, click the **Full Page Slides** button, and then select **4 Slides Horizontal**. Under **Settings**, click the **Color** button, and then click **Pure Black and White**.
21. Press [Windows], type Snip and then press Enter. In the **Snipping Tool** dialog box, click the **New arrow**, and then click **Full-screen Snip**.
22. Click **Save Snip**, navigate to your **PowerPoint Chapter 1** folder, and then save the snip as Last_First_ppt01_SRSnip **Close** the Snipping Tool mark-up window.
23. Press Esc to return to the presentation, click **Save**, and then **Close** PowerPoint.
24. Submit as directed by your instructor.

DONE! You have completed this Skills Review

Skills Assessment 1

To complete this project, you will need the following files:

- ppt01_SA1Bike
- ppt01_SA1BikeLane
- ppt01_SA1BikePark

You will save your files as:

- Last_First_ppt01_SA1Bike
- Last_First_ppt01_SA1Snip

1. From your student data files, locate and open **ppt01_SA1Bike**. Save it in your **PowerPoint Chapter 1** folder as Last_First_ppt01_SA1Bike
2. On **Slide 2**, in the second bullet point, before the word *on*, add the word lane and then add a space.
3. Change the slide layout to **Two Content**. In the content placeholder on the right side of the slide, add the image **ppt01_SA1BikeLane**.
4. With the image still selected, apply the **Beveled Matte, White** picture style.
5. In the left content placeholder, select all of the text. Change the line spacing to **1.5** and the font size to **24**.
6. Select the last three bullet points, beginning with *Bike* and ending with *trails*, and then increase the list indent one level.
7. Add the sentence New development along parkway to be completed soon! as speaker notes on **Slide 2**. Compare your screen with **Figure 1**.
8. After **Slide 3**, insert a new **Slide 4** with the **Picture with Caption** layout. Add the title Bike Aspen Falls accepting the default title formatting.
9. In the picture placeholder, insert the image **ppt01_SA1BikePark**. Apply the **Beveled Matte, White** picture style. In the caption placeholder, type Off road trail at Aspen Lake Park and then increase the font size to **24**.
10. Move **Slide 3** so that it appears as the last slide in the presentation.
11. Use the **Spelling** pane to correct any spelling errors in the presentation.
12. On **Slide 4**, in the content placeholder, delete the word *fun* and replace it with the word family
13. On **Slide 4**, use the thesaurus to replace the word *Promotes* with the synonym Encourages

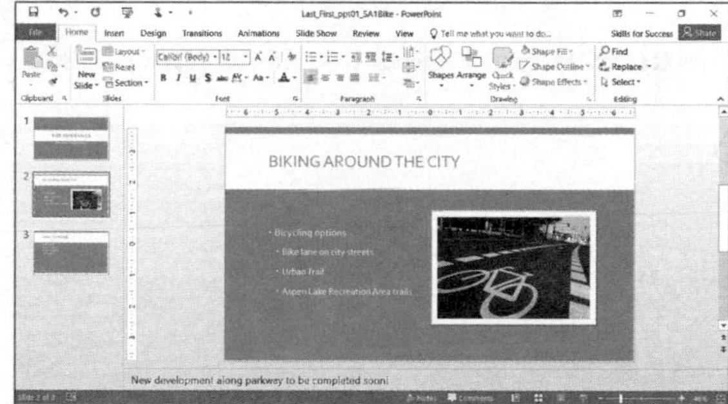

Figure 1 Marco Richter/Fotolia; PowerPoint 2016, Windows 10, Microsoft Corporation

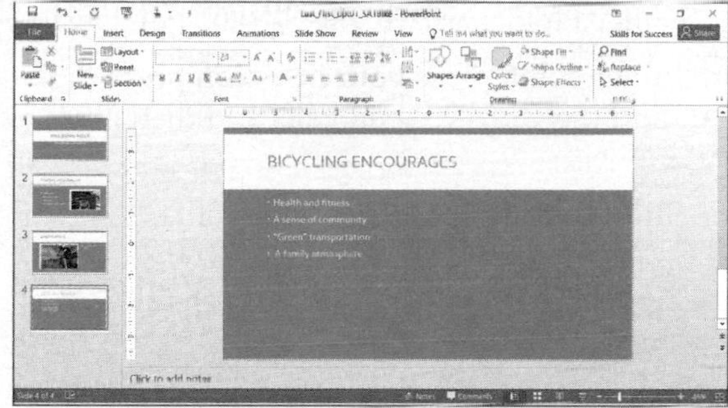

Figure 2 PowerPoint 2016, Windows 10, Microsoft Corporation

14. Use **Find and Replace** to replace all occurrences of the word *Biking* with the word Bicycling
15. On **Slide 4**, increase the font size for all bulleted text to **24**. Click a blank area of the slide to deselect the placeholder. Compare your screen with **Figure 2**.
16. Apply the **Push** transition to all slides.
17. Add the **Slide number** to all slides except for the title slide.
18. Add the **file name** to the **Footer** for the Notes and Handouts pages, and then add the **Date and time**, setting it to **Update automatically**.
19. Create a **Full Screen Snip** of **Handouts** with **Four Slides Vertical** per page, and then set to print in **Pure Black and White**. Save the Snip as Last_First_ppt01_SA1Snip
20. **Save** your presentation. **Close** PowerPoint, and then submit the files as directed by your instructor.

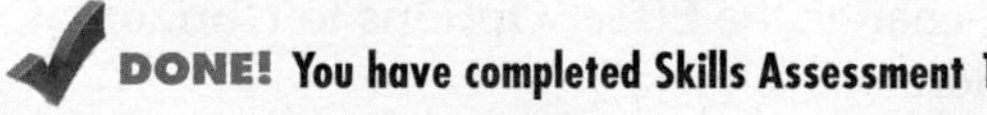

Skills Assessment 2

To complete this project, you will need the following files:

- **ppt01_SA2Health**
- **ppt01_SA2CheckUp**

You will save your file as:

- **Last_First_ppt01_SA2Health**

1. From your student data files, locate and open **ppt01_SA2Health**. Save it in your **PowerPoint Chapter 1** folder as Last_First_ppt01_SA2Health
2. On **Slide 2**, in the third bullet point, place your insertion point before the word *citizens*, add the words Aspen Falls and then press SpaceBar.
3. On **Slide 2**, change the **Slide Layout** to **Title and Content**.
4. On **Slide 3**, replace the word *Guidance* with the synonym Leadership
5. Use the **Spelling** pane to correct the spelling of one word. Ignore the spelling suggestions for any business names.
6. On **Slide 3**, in the left placeholder, insert the image **ppt01_SA2CheckUp**.
7. On **Slide 3**, select the image, and then apply the **Rounded Diagonal Corner, White** picture style. Repeat this process twice to add the same picture style to the images on Slides 4 and 5.
8. On **Slide 4**, increase the **Line Spacing** of all bulleted text to **2.0**. Click outside the placeholder, and then compare your screen with **Figure 1**.
9. On **Slide 5**, increase the **Font Size** for all bulleted text to **32**.
10. **Delete** the current **Slide 6**.
11. After **Slide 5**, insert a new **Slide 6** with the **Section Header** layout.
12. In the title placeholder, type Aspen Falls Healthy Living
13. In the text placeholder, type Contact Jack Ruiz, Community Services Director, for more information – jruiz@aspenfalls.org Compare your screen with **Figure 2**.
14. Add the **Blinds** transition, change the **Effect Options** to **Horizontal**, and then apply the transition to all slides.

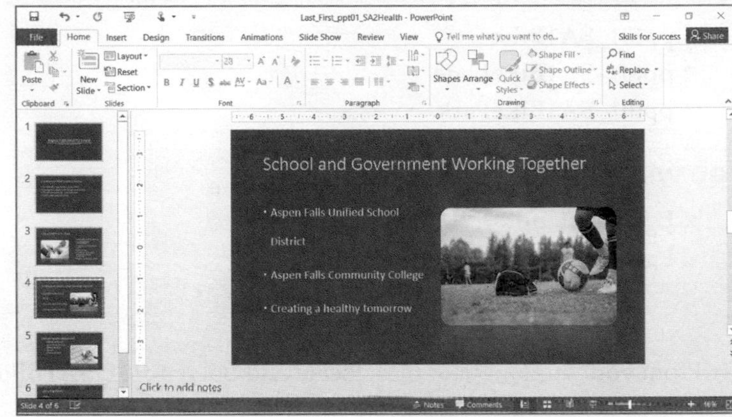

Figure 1 PowerPoint 2016, Windows 10, Microsoft Corporation

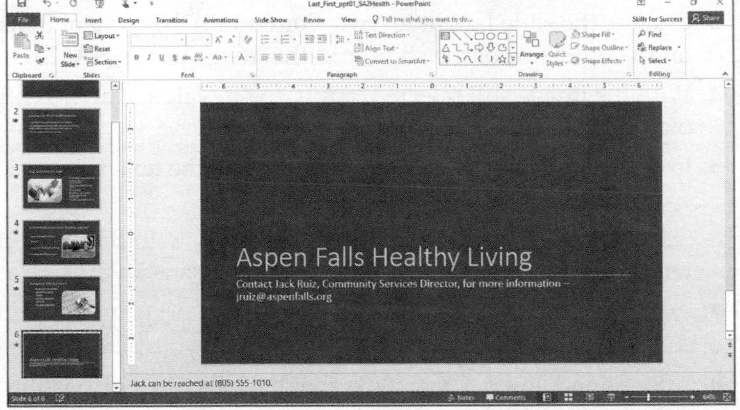

Figure 2 PowerPoint 2016, Windows 10, Microsoft Corporation

15. Add the date, page number, and file name as a footer to all the Notes and Handouts pages.
16. On **Slide 6**, using the **Notes** pane, add the speaker notes Jack can be reached at (805) 555–1010.
17. **Save**, and then submit the presentation as directed by your instructor. **Close** PowerPoint.

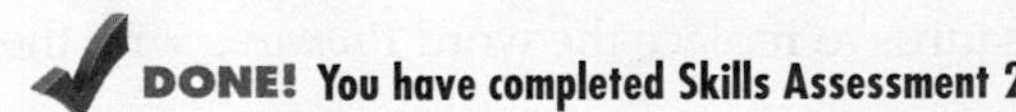

DONE! You have completed Skills Assessment 2

My Skills

To complete this project, you will need the following file:

- **ppt01_MSCareerDevelopment**

You will save your file as:

- **Last_First_ppt01_MSCareerDevelopment**

---

1. From your student data files, locate and open **ppt01_ MSCareerDevelopment**. Save it in your **PowerPoint Chapter 1** folder as Last_First_ppt01_MSCareerDevelopment
2. On **Slide 1**, in the subtitle placeholder, type your first and last names. Select the text in the subtitle placeholder, and then apply the **Font Effect** named **Small Caps**.
3. Insert a new **Slide 2** with the **Title and Content** layout.
4. In the title placeholder, type Career Development Strategies
5. In the content placeholder, type the following five bulleted points: Join professional organizations and Participate in ongoing education and Continue to develop new skills and Present a professional image and Utilize a mentor
6. Increase the **Font Size** to **28**. Increase the **Line Spacing** of all bulleted text to **1.5** lines.
7. Add the **Slide number** to all slides.
8. Add the **Transition** named **Random Bars** to both slides in the presentation. Compare your screen with **Figure 1**.
9. To all of the Notes and Handouts pages, add the date, page number, and file name as a footer. Save the presentation, and then submit as directed by your instructor.

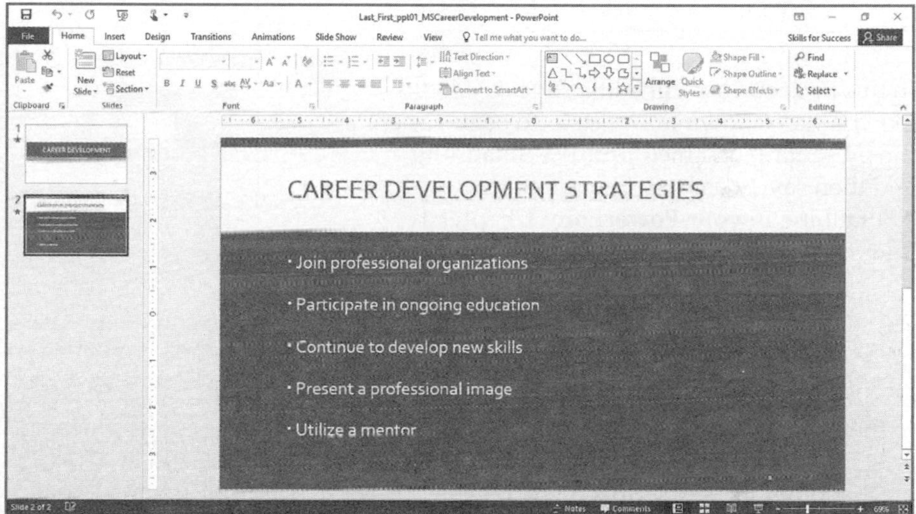

Figure 1 PowerPoint 2016, Windows 10, Microsoft Corporation

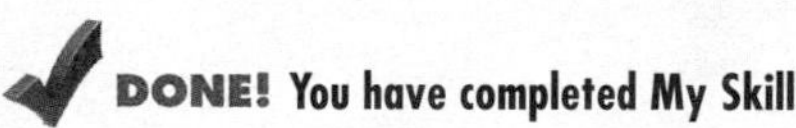

Visual Skills Check

To complete this project, you will need the following files:

- ppt01_VSPlanning
- ppt01_VSPlanningImage

You will save your file as:

- Last_First_ppt01_VSPlanning

In this project, you will edit a slide so it looks like the slide shown in **Figure 1**. To begin, open the presentation named **ppt01_VSPlanning**, and then save it as Last_First_ppt01_VSPlanning in your **PowerPoint Chapter 1** folder.

The slide layout is **Two Content**. Increase the title **Font Size** to **66**, and apply **Bold** and **Small Caps**. Apply the list levels as shown in the figure. The font size of the first bullet is **32** points; the remaining bullets' font sizes are **30** points. The **Line Spacing** is **1.5** lines. The image is **ppt01_VSPlanningImage**. The **Reflected Rounded Rectangle** style is applied to the picture. The **Transition** is named **Glitter**, and the **Effect Options** are set to **Hexagons from Bottom**. Correct spelling errors in the presentation. Add the date, page number, and file name in the footer of all of the Notes and Handouts pages. Submit the file as directed by your instructor.

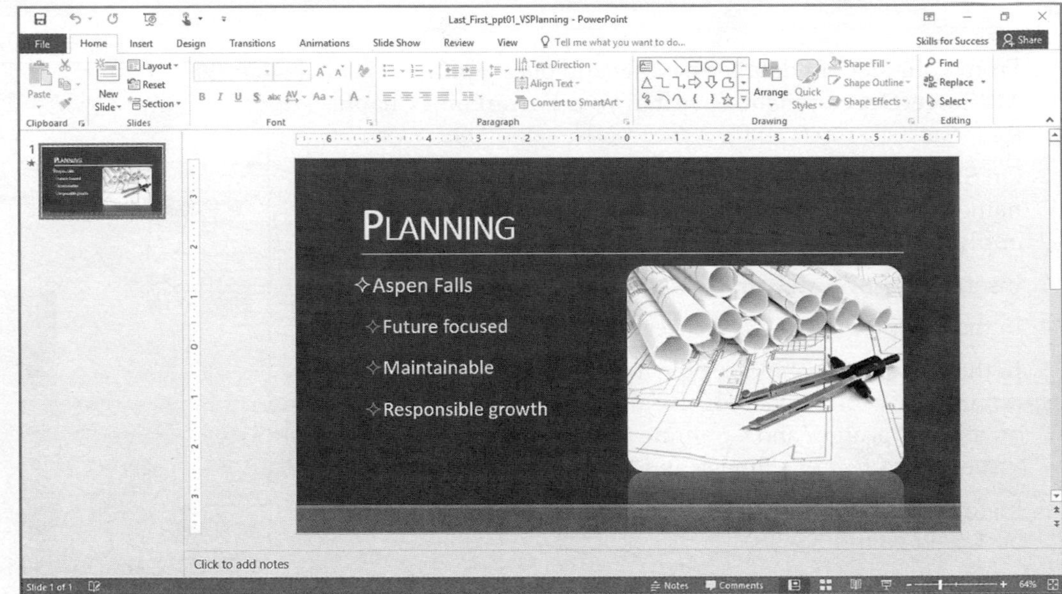

Figure 1

PowerPoint 2016, Windows 10, Microsoft Corporation

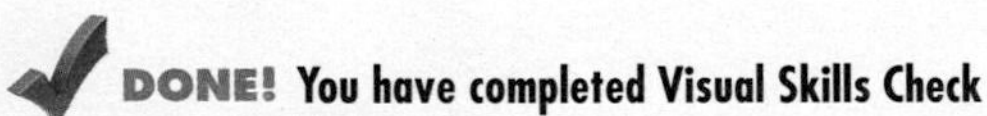

Skills Challenge 1

To complete this project, you will need the following files:

- **ppt01_SC1Invest**
- **ppt01_SC1InvestImage**

You will save your file as:

- **Last_First_ppt01_SC1Invest**

Locate and open the presentation **ppt01_SC1Invest**. Save the presentation in your chapter folder as Last_First_ppt01_SC1Invest Maria Martinez, City Manager, and Richard Mack, Assistant City Manager, will use this presentation when they meet with business investors who are considering investing in businesses in Aspen Falls. Using the skills you practiced in this chapter, adjust the font of the title on the title slide so that it appears on one line, and then adjust all other fonts in the presentation so they meet the standard rules of design listed in the chapter opening. Adjust the line spacing of all bulleted points so that the text fits well on the slides. Change the layout on Slide 3 so that on the right side of the slide you can add the image **ppt01_SC1InvestImage**. In the left content placeholder on Slide 3, increase the indent for all names, leaving the titles at their original level. Add a Picture Style to both images in the presentation. Correct all spelling errors in the presentation. To all of the Notes and Handouts pages, add the date, page number, and file name as a footer. Save the presentation, and then submit as directed by your instructor.

DONE! You have completed Skills Challenge 1

Skills Challenge 2

To complete this project, you will need the following file:

- **ppt01_SC2Events**

You will save your file as:

- **Last_First_ppt01_SC2Events**

Locate and open the presentation **ppt01_SC2Events**, and then save it in your chapter folder as Last_First_ppt01_SC2Events Add the current year in the appropriate place. Adjust the font sizes in the presentation, make at least one other enhancement to the fonts in the presentation—change fonts, apply bold, or apply a Font Effect—and correct the spelling errors. Increase the indent level of appropriate information on Slide 2, and then locate and add an appropriate image anywhere in the presentation. Apply a Picture Style to the image you inserted. Add a transition to both slides. To all of the Notes and Handouts pages, add the date, page number, and file name as a footer. Save the presentation, and then submit as directed by your instructor.

DONE! You have completed Skills Challenge 2

More Skills Assessment

To complete this project, you will need the following file:

- ppt01_MSASchool

You will save your files as:

- Last_First_ppt01_MSASchool
- Last_First_ppt01_MSASchoolSnip

---

1. From your student data files, locate and open **ppt01_MSASchool**. Save it in your chapter folder as Last_First_ppt01_MSASchool
2. On **Slide 2**, in the content placeholder, click the **Online Pictures** button.
3. In the **Search** box, type school supplies Choose an appropriate image to insert in the presentation.
4. In **Normal** view, select and then delete **Slide 3**.
5. Move **Slide 2** so that it becomes the last slide in the presentation.
6. On the **Design tab**, in the **Customize group**, click the **Slide Size** button, and then click **Custom Slide Size**.
7. Change the **Notes, Handouts & Outline** layout to landscape.
8. Click **Slide 1**. Click the **File tab**, and then click **Print**. Click the **Full Page Slides** button, and then under **Handouts**, click **1 Slide**.

   Compare your screen with **Figure 1**.

9. Press [Windows key], type snip and then press Enter to start the Snipping Tool. Click the **New arrow**, and then click **Full Screen Snip**.
10. In the **Snipping Tool** markup window, click the **Save Snip** button [Save Snip icon]. In the **Save As** dialog box, navigate to your **PowerPoint Chapter 1** folder. Name the file Last_First_ppt01_MSASchoolSnip and then press Enter. **Close** the Snipping Tool mark-up window.
11. **Save**, and then submit the presentation and snip file as directed. **Close** PowerPoint.

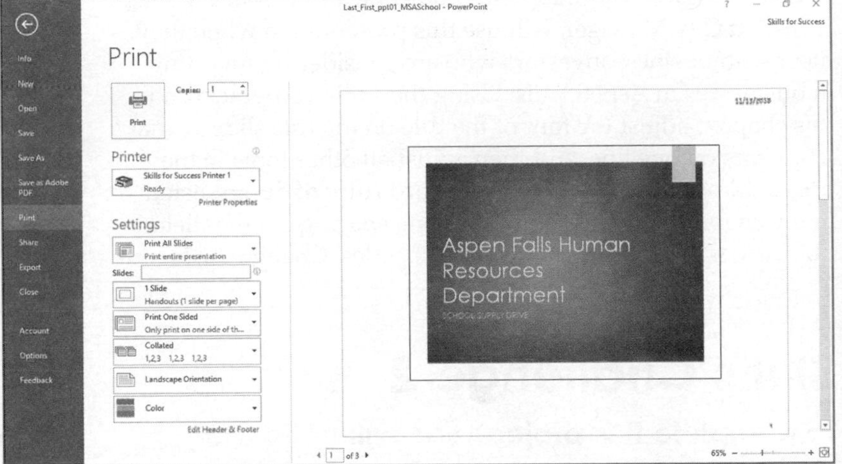

Figure 1 PowerPoint 2016, Windows 10, Microsoft Corporation

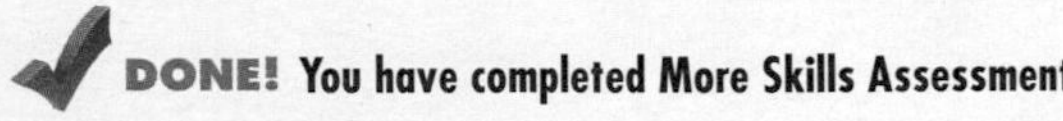
DONE! You have completed More Skills Assessment

Collaborating with Google

To complete this project, you will need a Google account (refer to the Common Features chapter) and the following file:

- ppt01_GPImage

You will save your files as:

- Last_First_ppt01_GPCareer
- Last_First_GPSnip

1. Open the Google Chrome web browser. Log in to your Google account, and then click the **Apps** button.
2. Click the **Drive** button to open Google Drive. If you receive a pop-up message, read the message, and then click **Next**. Read each message, and then close the dialog box.
3. Click the **New** button, and then click **Google Slides**.
4. In the **Themes** pane, click **Modern** or another theme. **Close** the Themes pane.
5. In the title placeholder, type Aspen Falls Career Fair
6. In the subtitle placeholder, type Aspen Falls Business and Technology Park Select the subtitle placeholder, and then change the **Font Size** to 24 Compare your screen with **Figure 1**.
7. Click the **Slide tab**, and then click **New slide**. In the title placeholder, type Featured Careers
8. In the content placeholder, type the following list

   Skilled Manufacturing
   Information Technology
   Healthcare Information Systems Management
   Accounting
9. Press Ctrl + M to insert a new slide. In the title placeholder, type Sign Up Online Today! In the content placeholder, type aspenfalls.org
10. Click the **Image** button. In the **Insert image** dialog box, click the **Choose an image to upload** button. Navigate to your student data files, and then click **ppt01_GPImage**.
11. With the image inserted on the slide, point to the center of the image, and then click, hold, and drag the image so that it is aligned with the lower right corner of the slide, as shown in **Figure 2**.

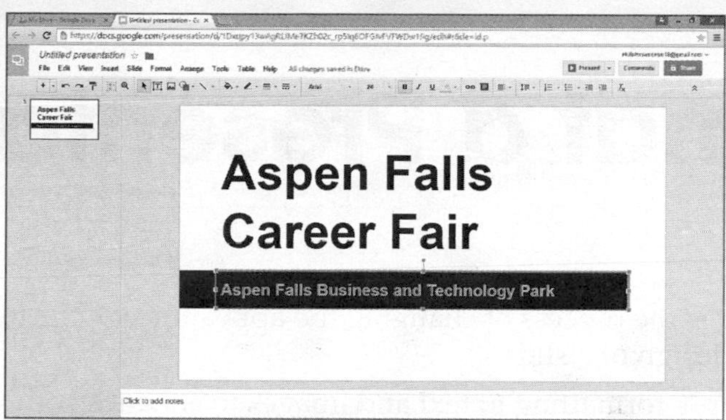

Figure 1

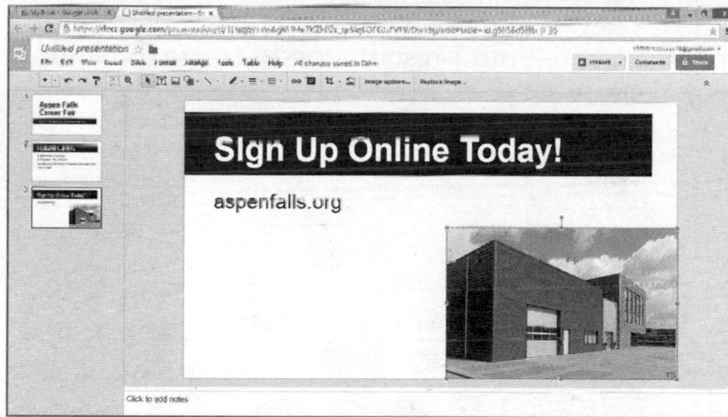

Figure 2

12. Click the **Share** button, and in the **Name before sharing** box, type Last_First_ppt01_GPCareer and then click **Save**. In the **Share with others** dialog box, type AspenFallsEvents@gmail.com to share the sheet with another user.
13. In the **Add a note** text box, type Please add slides regarding individual employers to this presentation. Click **Send**.
14. Press [Windows], type snip and then press Enter to start the Snipping Tool. Click the **New arrow**, and then create a **Full-screen Snip**.
15. In the **Snipping Tool** mark-up window, click the **Save Snip** button [Save]. In the **Save As** dialog box, navigate to your **PowerPoint Chapter 1** folder. Be sure the **Save as type** box displays **PNG file**. Name the file Last_First_ppt01_GPSnip and then press Enter. **Close** the Snipping Tool mark-up window.
16. Close all windows, and then submit your work as directed by your instructor.

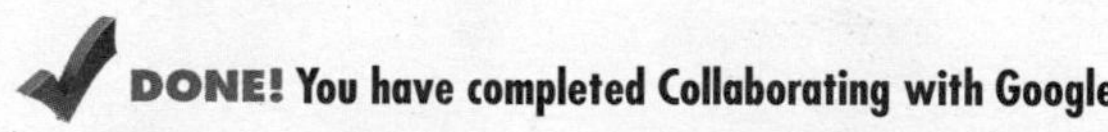

DONE! You have completed Collaborating with Google

CHAPTER 2

Format a Presentation

- Formatting is the process of changing the appearance of the text, layout, or design of a slide.
- You can apply formatting to text and images to enhance your slides in a manner that assists you in conveying your message to your audience.
- You can apply themes to your presentation to create dynamic and professional slides.
- The design of a presentation can be customized by changing font colors, bullet symbols, and slide backgrounds.
- Before applying formatting, you can use the Live Preview feature to view the effect of different formatting on your slides.

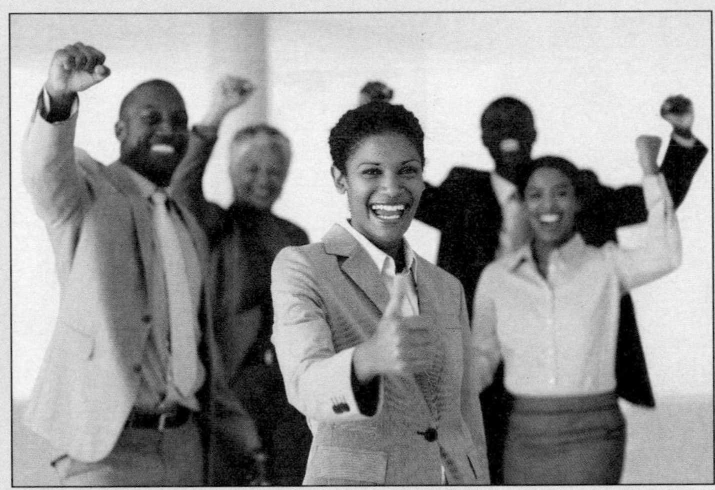

Yuri Arcurs/Fotolia

Aspen Falls City Hall

In this chapter, you will create a new presentation for Evelyn Stone, Director of Human Resources for Aspen Falls City Hall. This presentation will be shown during orientation for new employees. It contains important information to guide the new employees and will serve to inform and set a positive, welcoming atmosphere.

In your career, you may create presentations to guide an audience through a process or to provide an itinerary. When presenting this type of information, it is often best to break the information into numbered or bulleted lists. You can also add images and WordArt to attract and hold your audience's attention, emphasize information on the slide, and elicit a certain emotion.

Slide design is important to the success of your presentation. Uncluttered, clean-looking slides make it easier for your audience to understand your main points. To increase your own efficiency, you can insert slides from other presentations, copy formatting using the Format Painter, and copy and paste information. Design your presentation with your message in mind. Choose a theme, layout, and images that will appeal to and interest your audience.

In this project, you will create a new presentation and add slides with different layouts. You will apply a theme and then select a different variant for the entire presentation; later you will adjust the variant on a single slide.

Time to complete all 10 skills — 60 to 90 minutes

Outcome

Using the skills in this chapter, you will be able create a new presentation, select a new theme and variant, change the backgrounds of slides, use WordArt, and customize bullet points.

Objectives

2.1 Create presentations with different design themes and variants

2.2 Add images to presentations—to the slide layout and as slide backgrounds

2.3 Manipulate fonts with colors, effects, and WordArt

2.4 Format lists with bullets and numbers

Student data files needed for this chapter:

New PowerPoint presentation
ppt02_Photo1
ppt02_Photo2
ppt02_Photo3
ppt02_Photo4

You will save your file as:

Last_First_ppt02_Orientation

SKILLS

MyITLab® Skills 1-10 Training

At the end of this chapter, you will be able to:

Skill 1 Create New Presentations
Skill 2 Change Themes and Variants
Skill 3 Change Font Colors and Effects
Skill 4 Format Slide Backgrounds with Fill
Skill 5 Add Pictures and Textures to Slide Backgrounds
Skill 6 Format Text with WordArt
Skill 7 Change Character Spacing
Skill 8 Modify Bulleted and Numbered Lists
Skill 9 Move and Copy Text and Objects
Skill 10 Use Format Painter and Clear All Formatting

MORE SKILLS

Skill 11 Edit Slide Masters
Skill 12 Save and Apply Presentation Templates
Skill 13 Create Slides from Microsoft Word Outlines
Skill 14 Design Presentations with Contrast

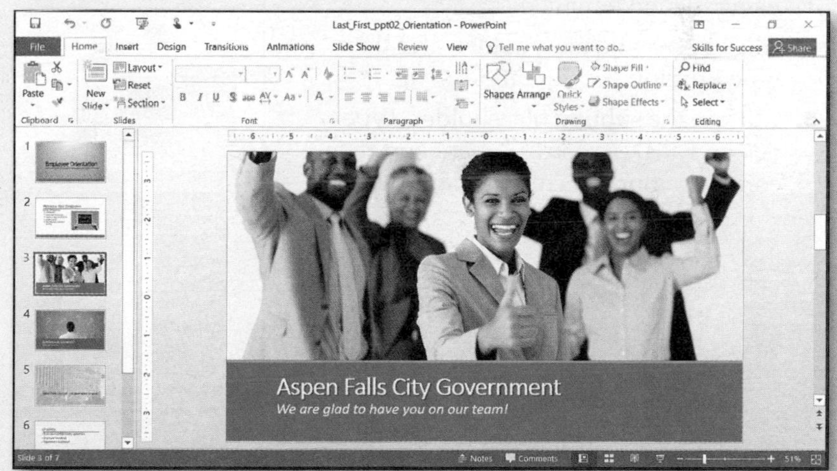

Yuri Arcurs/Fotolia; PowerPoint 2016, Windows 10, Microsoft Corporation

- When you start PowerPoint, you can search available templates and themes to find a look that fits your needs.
- When you select a template, a new, blank presentation in that design displays.

MOS Obj 1.1.1

1. Start **PowerPoint 2016**. Click **Open Other Presentations**, and then click **New**. On the **Start screen**, view the templates available, as shown in **Figure 1**.

   A ***template*** is a file upon which a presentation can be based.

MOS Obj 1.1.2

2. On the right side of the **Start screen**, click several template thumbnails to display a preview of each of the templates and the variants of the theme. After viewing the template, or templates, you selected, **Close** the preview window to return to the Start screen.
3. Click the **Ion** thumbnail. Along the bottom of the preview window, click the **More Images arrow** to view images of some of the slide layouts, and then click the **Create** button to create a presentation using the Ion template.
4. Click in the title placeholder, and then type Employee Orientation
5. Click in the subtitle placeholder. Type Aspen Falls City Government and then compare your screen with **Figure 2**.

■ Continue to the next page to complete the skill

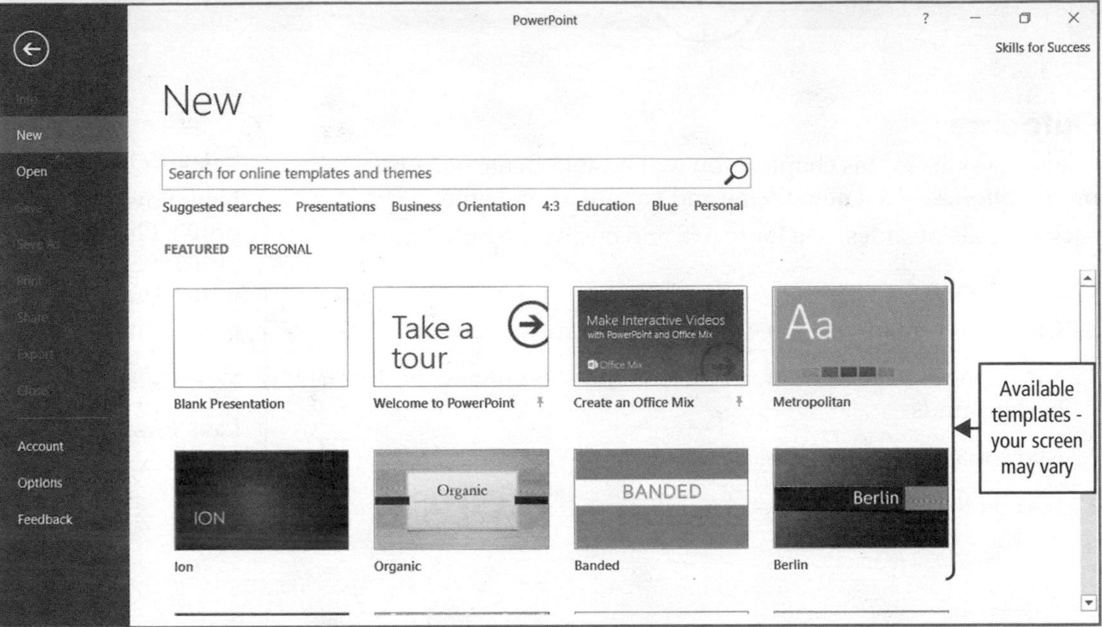

Figure 1 PowerPoint 2016, Windows 10, Microsoft Corporation

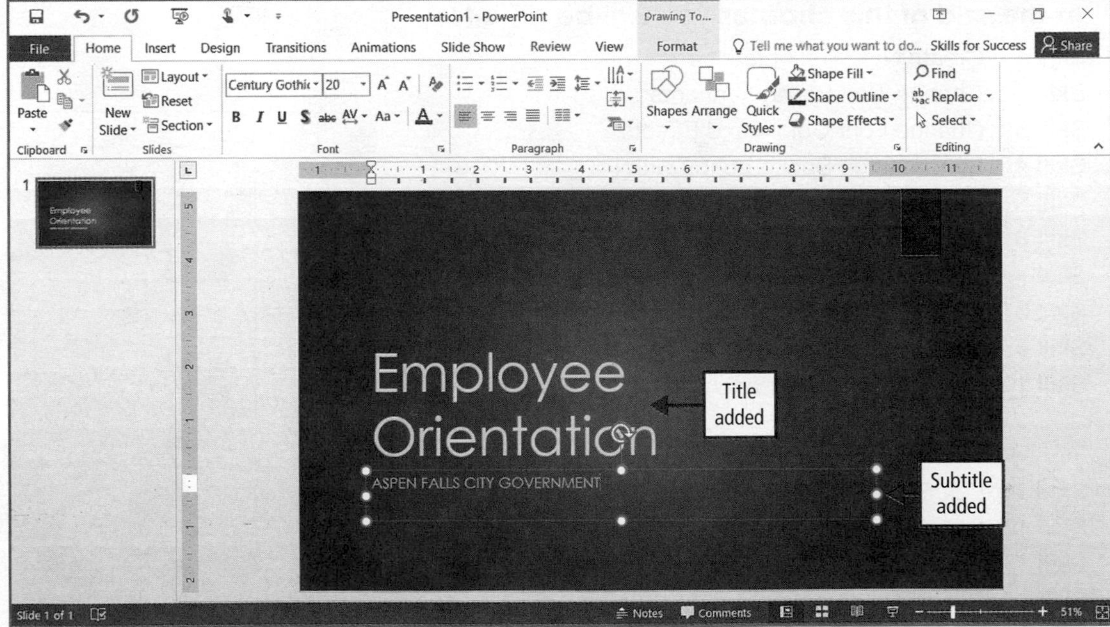

Figure 2 PowerPoint 2016, Windows 10, Microsoft Corporation

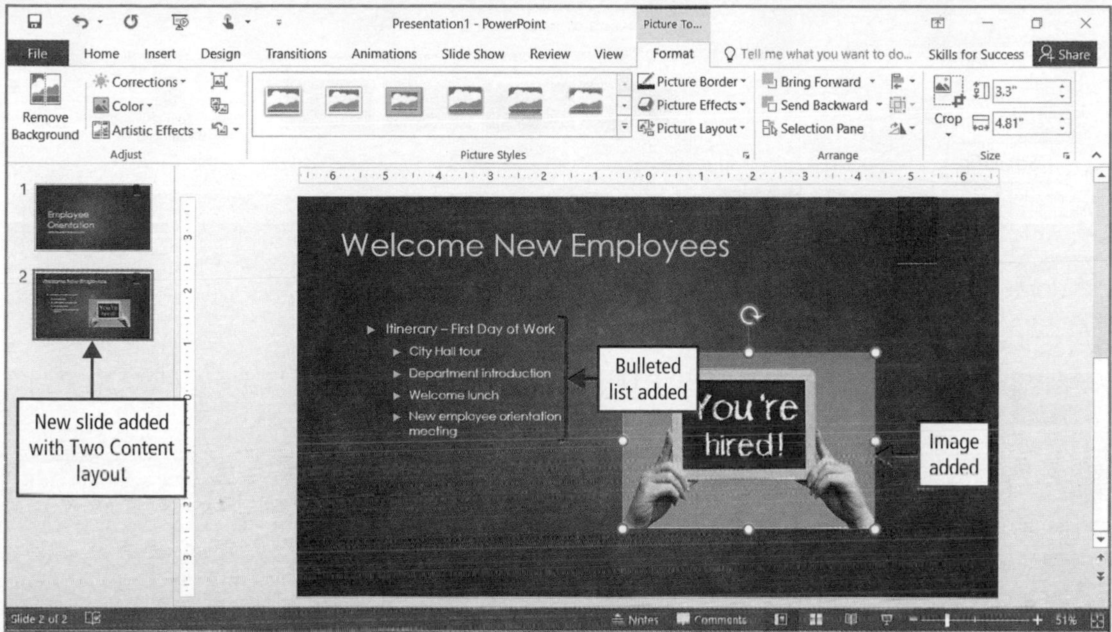

DOC RABE Media/Fotolia; PowerPoint 2016, Windows 10, Microsoft Corporation

Figure 3

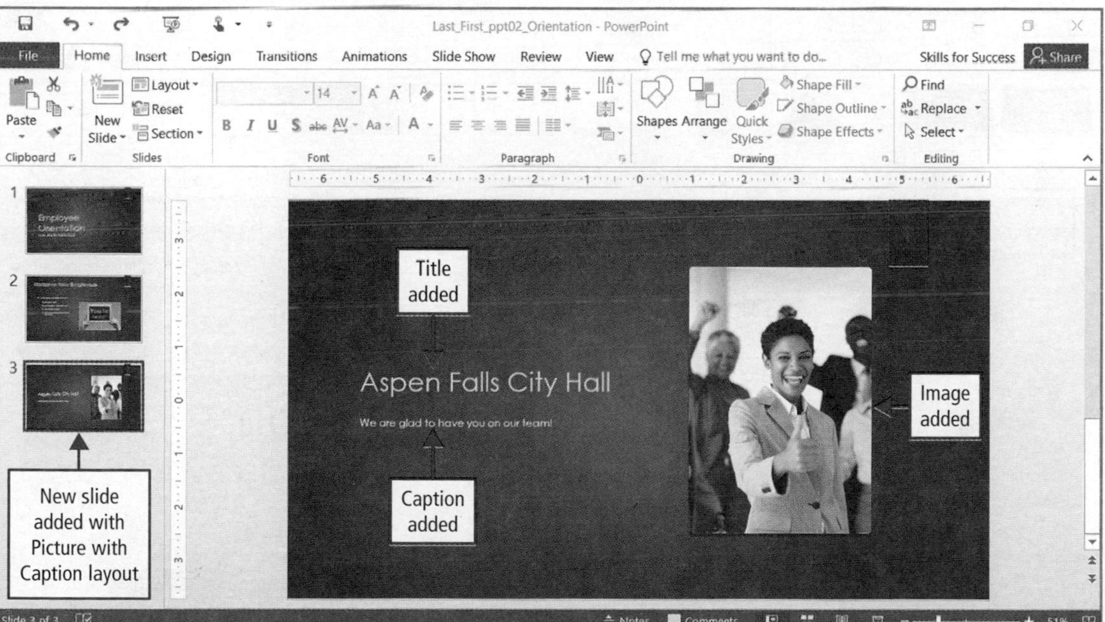

Yuri Arcurs/Fotolia; PowerPoint 2016, Windows 10, Microsoft Corporation

Figure 4

6. On the **Home tab**, in the **Slides group**, click the **New Slide arrow**. Click the **Two Content** thumbnail to insert a slide with the **Two Content** layout. In the title placeholder, type Welcome New Employees
7. In the left content placeholder, type Itinerary – First Day of Work and then press Enter.
8. Press Tab, and then type the following four bullet points, pressing Enter after each line:

   City Hall tour
   Department introduction
   Welcome lunch
   New employee orientation meeting
9. In the right content placeholder, click the **Pictures** button. In the **Insert Picture** dialog box, navigate to your student files for this chapter, click **ppt02_Photo1**, and then click **Insert**. Compare your screen with **Figure 3**.

10. On the **Home tab**, in the **Slides group**, click the **New Slide arrow**. In the gallery, click **Picture with Caption**. In the title placeholder, type Aspen Falls City Hall In the text placeholder, type We are glad to have you on our team!
11. In the picture placeholder, using the method described in Step 9, insert the student data file **ppt02_Photo2**. Compare your screen with **Figure 4**.
12. On the Quick Access Toolbar, click **Save**. On the **Save As** page, navigate to the location where you are saving your files, and then create a folder named PowerPoint Chapter 2 Using your own name, save the presentation as Last_First_ppt02_Orientation

■ **You have completed Skill 1 of 10**

- The presentation ***theme*** is a set of unified design elements—colors, fonts, and effects—that provides a unique look for your presentation. The theme can be selected as the presentation is created, or it can be applied later. Each template has a theme, and the types and numbers of slide layouts vary among templates.
- ***Theme variants*** are variations of the current theme, with different accent colors. You can change the variant for all slides in the presentation or for a single slide.

1. Display **Slide 1**. On the **Design tab**, in the **Themes group**, click the **More** button to display the Themes gallery.
2. Under **Office**, point to the first thumbnail—**Office Theme**, as shown in **Figure 1**.

   Theme names can be identified by their ScreenTips. The first theme in the Office group is the Office Theme, followed by other themes.

3. Point to several themes, and preview the changes to the first slide.

   Each theme includes background colors, font styles, colors, effects, and slide layouts specific to the theme.

4. In the **Themes** gallery, use ScreenTips to locate the **Retrospect** theme, and then click it to apply this theme to all of the slides in the presentation. Compare your screen with **Figure 2**.

■ Continue to the next page to complete the skill

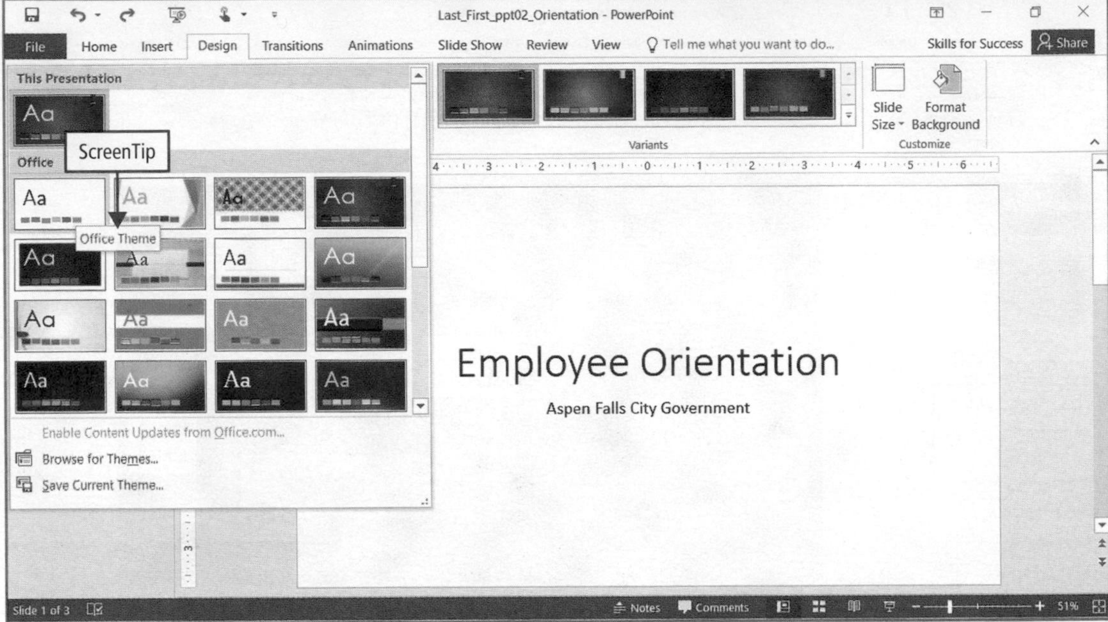

Figure 1 PowerPoint 2016, Windows 10, Microsoft Corporation

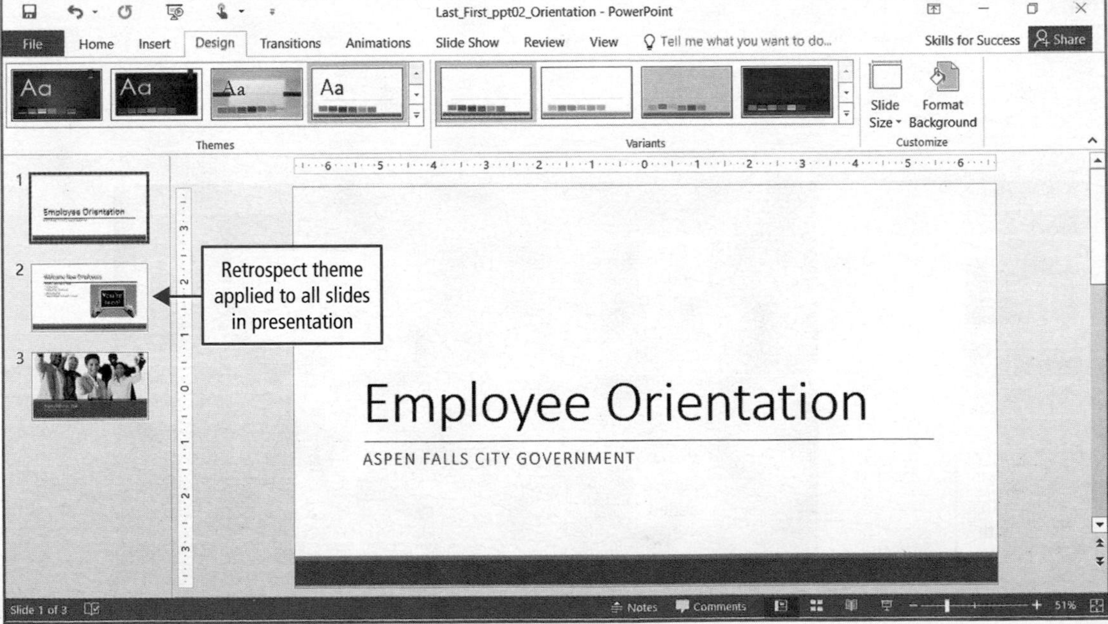

Figure 2 PowerPoint 2016, Windows 10, Microsoft Corporation

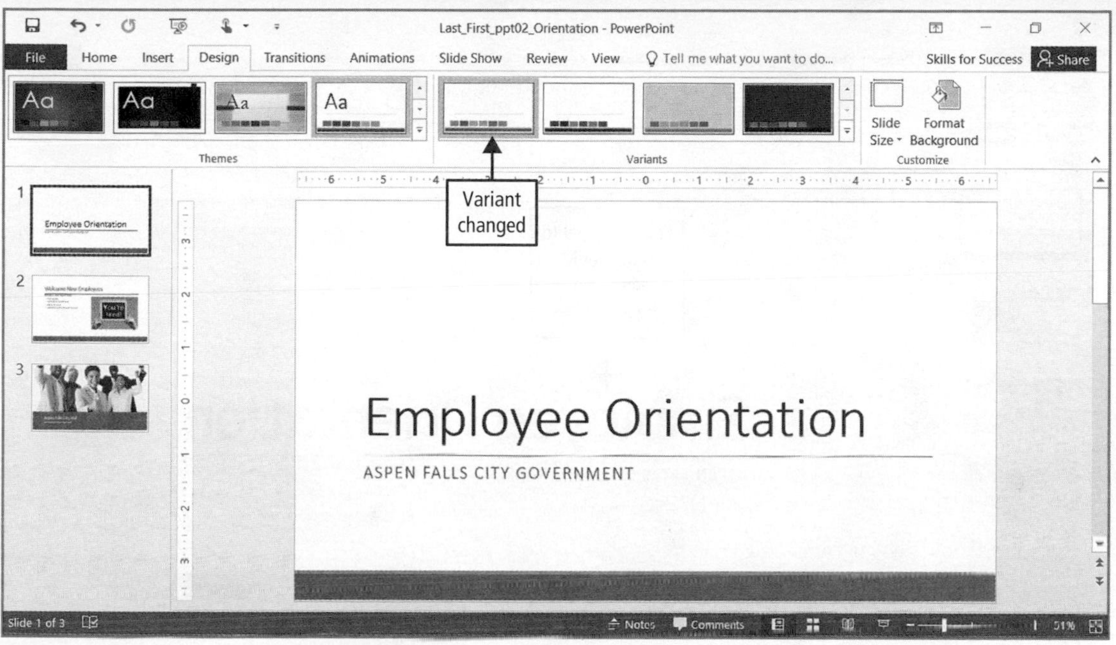

PowerPoint 2016, Windows 10, Microsoft Corporation

Figure 3

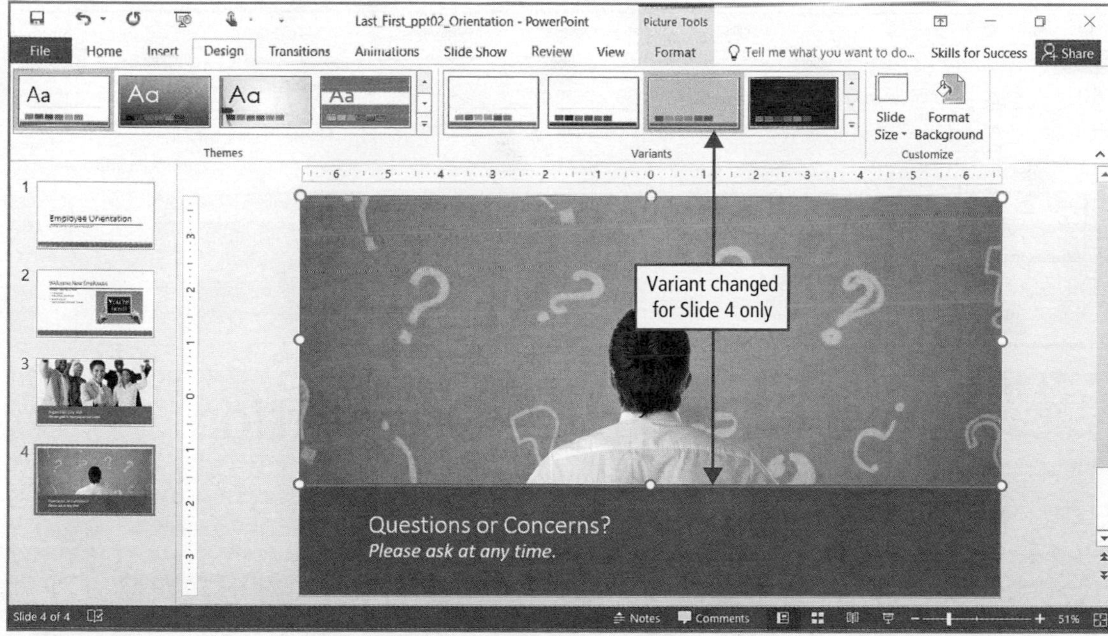

rangizzz/Fotolia; PowerPoint 2016, Windows 10, Microsoft Corporation

Figure 4

5. On the **Design tab**, in the **Variants group**, click the **More** button, click the first variant in the second row, and then compare your screen with **Figure 3**.

6. On **Slide 3**, select the caption *We are glad to have you on our team!* On the Mini toolbar, change the **Font Size** to **28**, and then click the **Italic** button.

   After applying a new theme to a presentation, you should review each slide and make formatting changes as necessary. The fonts, layouts, and spacing associated with one theme may require that existing text and objects be resized or moved to display in a manner that is consistent and attractive in the new theme.

7. On the **Home tab**, in the **Slides group**, insert a **New Slide** with the **Picture with Caption** layout. In the title placeholder, type Questions or Concerns? and then in the caption placeholder, type Please ask at any time. Select the text in the caption placeholder, and then increase the **Font Size** to **28** and add **Italic**.

8. In the picture placeholder, click the **Picture** button, and then insert the student data file **ppt02_Photo3**.

9. Still on **Slide 4**, on the **Design tab**, in the **Variants group**, click **More**, point to the third variant in the second row, and then right-click. On the shortcut menu, click **Apply to Selected Slides**, and then compare your slide with **Figure 4**. **Save** the file.

   The theme variant is changed for only the selected slide.

■ **You have completed Skill 2 of 10**

SKILL 3: Change Font Colors and Effects

- You can customize your presentation by changing the font colors and effects.
- When you are using several pictures in a presentation, choose font colors that complement the pictures you select.

Obj 2.1.2

1. Move to **Slide 1**. Click anywhere in the title placeholder, and then click the placeholder border to select it. On the **Home tab**, in the **Font group**, click the **Font arrow**. Scroll down and select **Trebuchet MS**.
2. With the text in the title placeholder still selected, on the **Home tab**, in the **Font group**, click the **Text Shadow** button [S].
3. Click a blank area of the slide to deselect the placeholder, and then compare your screen with **Figure 1**.

   Adding a text shadow helps the text to stand out from the slide background and adds additional depth to the presentation.

4. Select the subtitle placeholder, and then on the **Home tab**, in the **Font group**, click the **Text Shadow** button [S]. Compare your screen with **Figure 2**.

■ **Continue to the next page to complete the skill**

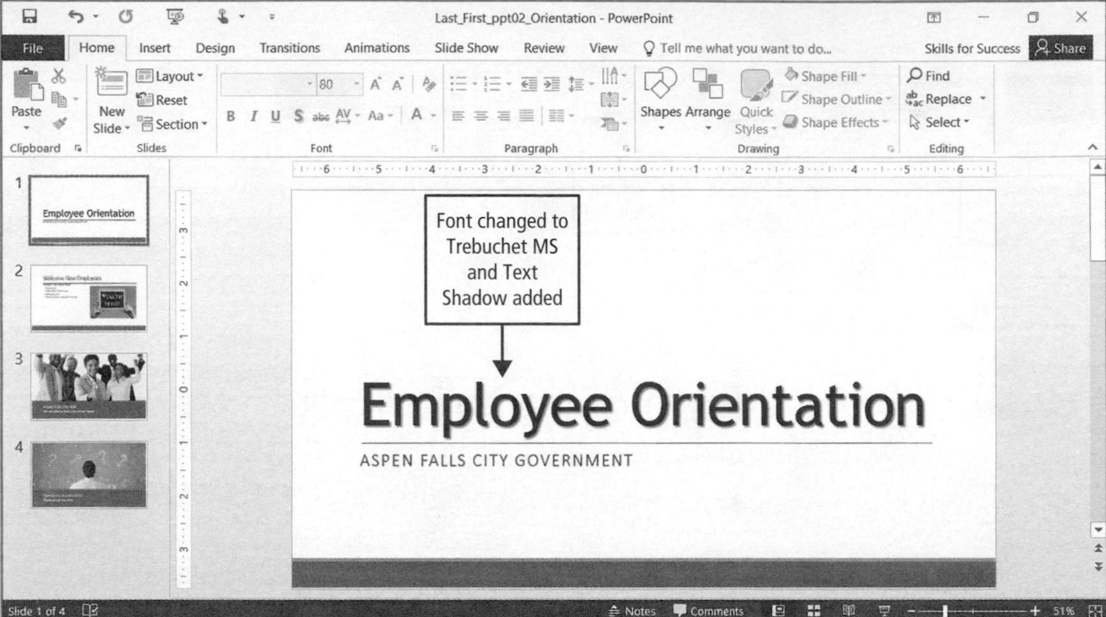

Figure 1 PowerPoint 2016, Windows 10, Microsoft Corporation

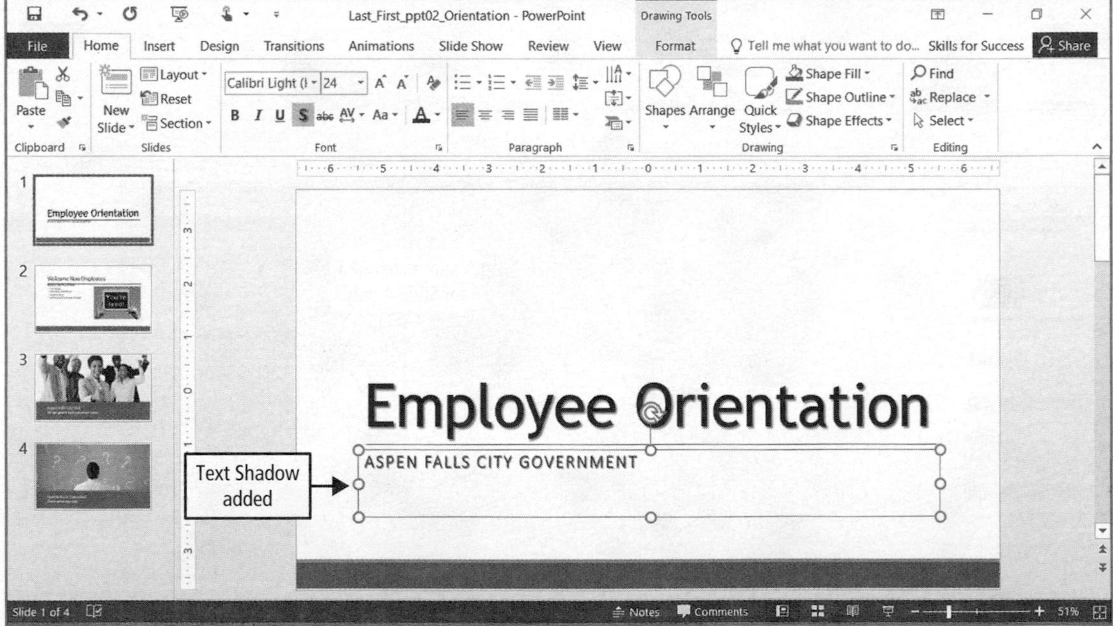

Figure 2 PowerPoint 2016, Windows 10, Microsoft Corporation

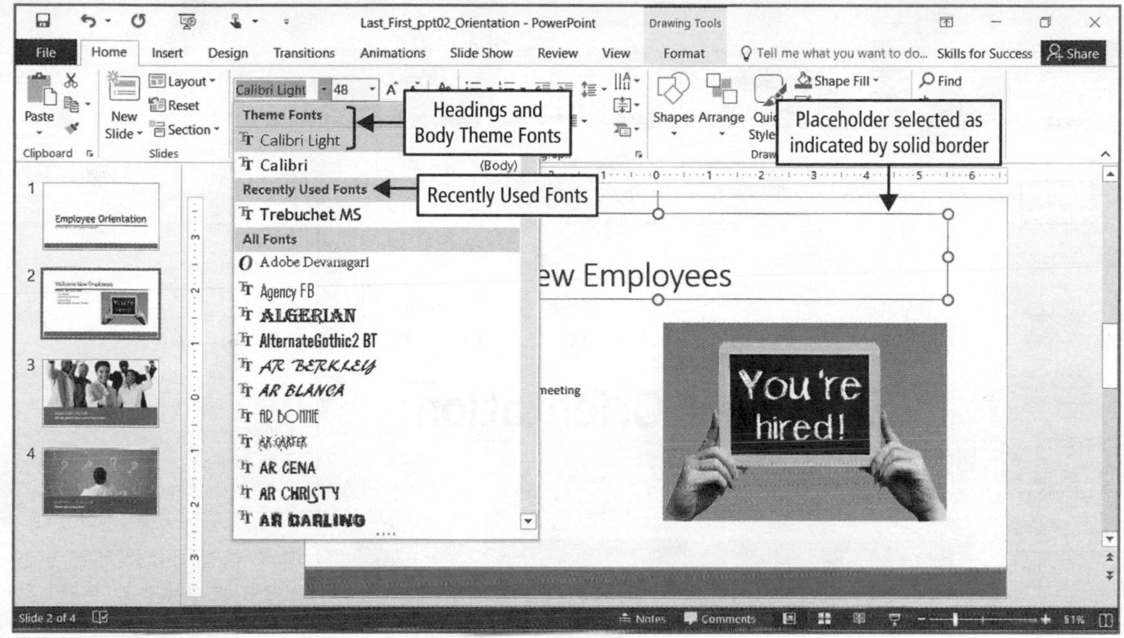

DOC RABE Media/Fotolia; PowerPoint 2016, Windows 10, Microsoft Corporation

Figure 3

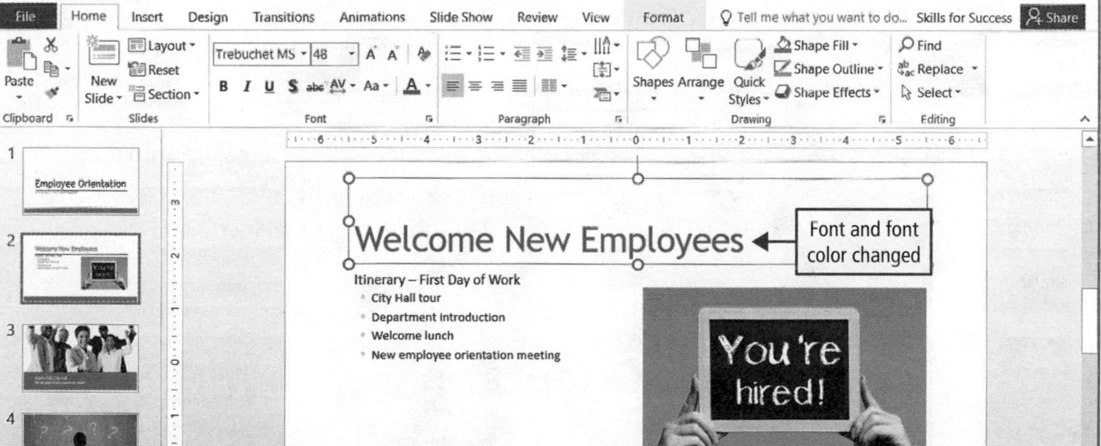

DOC RABE Media/Fotolia; PowerPoint 2016, Windows 10, Microsoft Corporation

Figure 4

5. On **Slide 2**, select the title placeholder. On the **Home tab**, and then in the **Font group**, click the **Font arrow**. Notice that at the top of the Font list, under Theme Fonts, *Calibri Light (Headings)* and *Calibri (Body)* display, as shown in **Figure 3**.

   The ***headings font*** is applied to slide titles, and the ***body font*** is applied to all other text. Sometimes the heading and body fonts are the same, but they are different sizes. In other font themes, the heading and body fonts are different. ***Recently Used Fonts*** is a listing of fonts you have selected and applied in the existing presentation. Using the Font list, you can apply theme fonts, recently used fonts, or a different font from the list of all fonts.

6. Under **Recently Used Fonts**, click **Trebuchet MS**.

7. With the title placeholder still selected, on the **Home tab**, in the **Font group**, click the **Font Color arrow**. Select the fifth color in the fifth row—**Turquoise, Accent 1, Darker 25%**. Compare your screen with **Figure 4**.

8. **Save** the file.

■ **You have completed Skill 3 of 10**

- You can customize the presentation design by changing the background of your slides.
- Modifications to slide backgrounds can be applied to a single slide or to all of the slides in the presentation.
- Previously modified backgrounds can be reset so that the original background associated with the presentation is applied to the slide.

Obj 1.2.6

1. Move to **Slide 1**. On the **Design tab**, in the **Customize group**, click **Format Background** to display the Format Background pane as shown in **Figure 1**.

   The Format Background pane is used to modify or reset the backgrounds for a single slide or for all slides in a presentation.

2. In the **Format Background** pane, under **Fill**, select **Gradient Fill** to display the gradient fill options.
3. Click the **Preset gradients** button, and then select the last color in the second row—**Top Spotlight - Accent 6**—and then compare your screen with **Figure 2**.

   The effects and color choices in the Format Background pane are based on the selected theme and variant. Here, the gradient choices all work well with the Retrospect theme and the selected color variant. Changes to the background may be made to a single slide, as you have done in this step, or to all slides in the presentation using the Apply to All button.

■ Continue to the next page to complete the skill

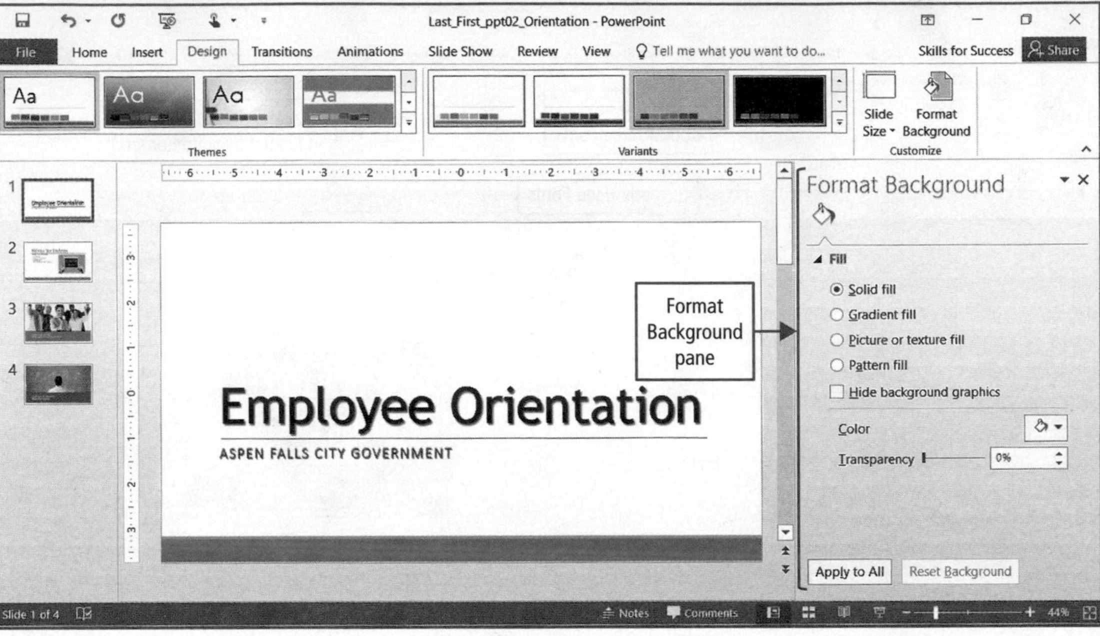

Figure 1 PowerPoint 2016, Windows 10, Microsoft Corporation

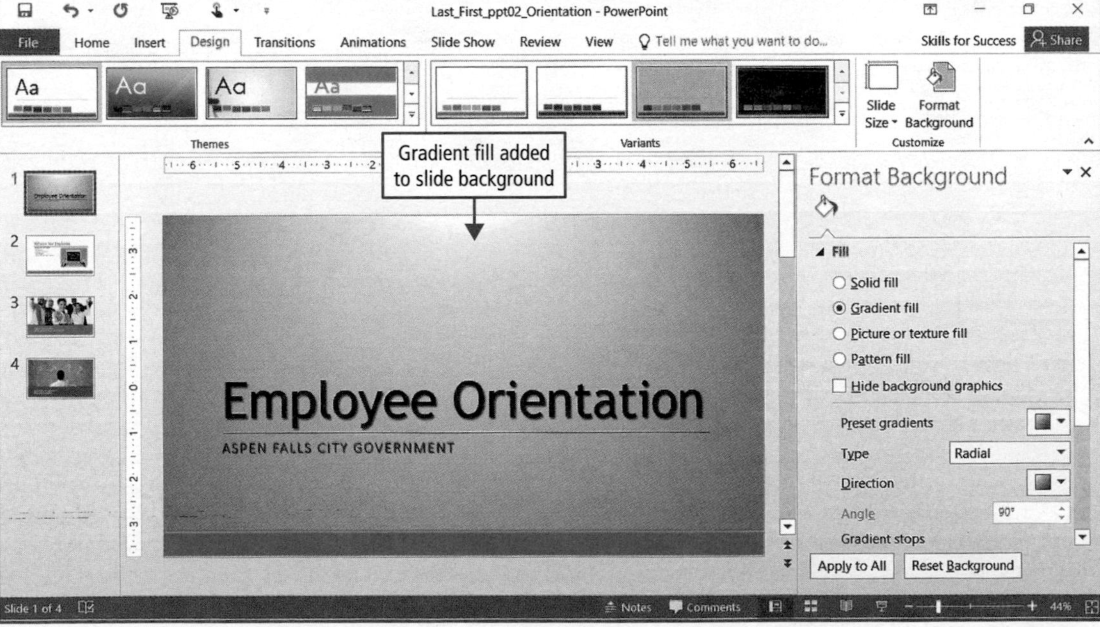

Figure 2 PowerPoint 2016, Windows 10, Microsoft Corporation

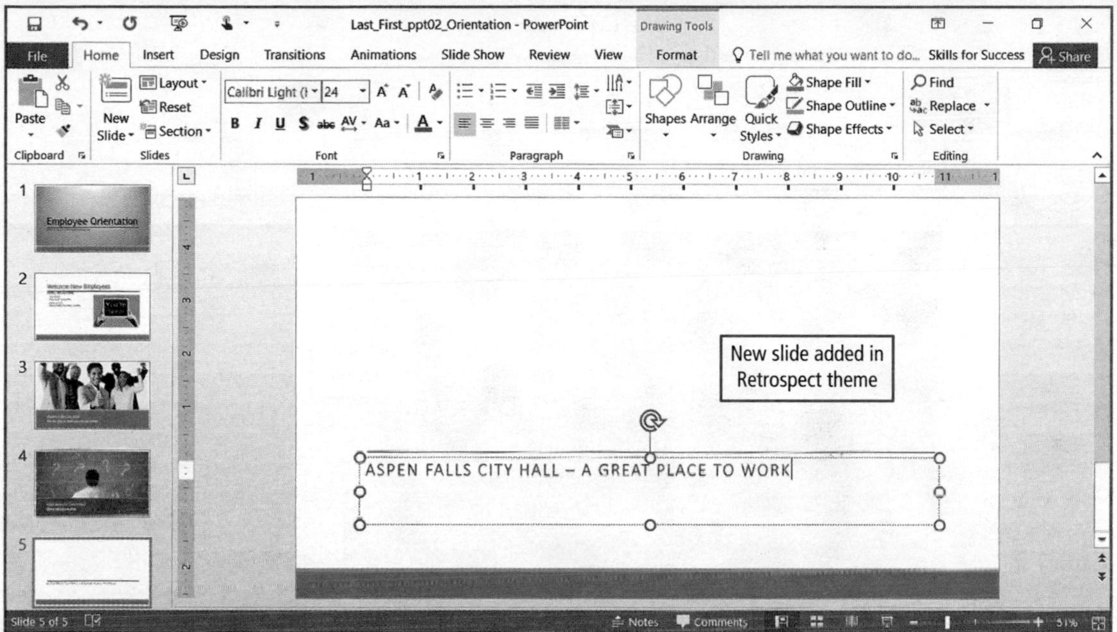

PowerPoint 2016, Windows 10, Microsoft Corporation

Figure 3

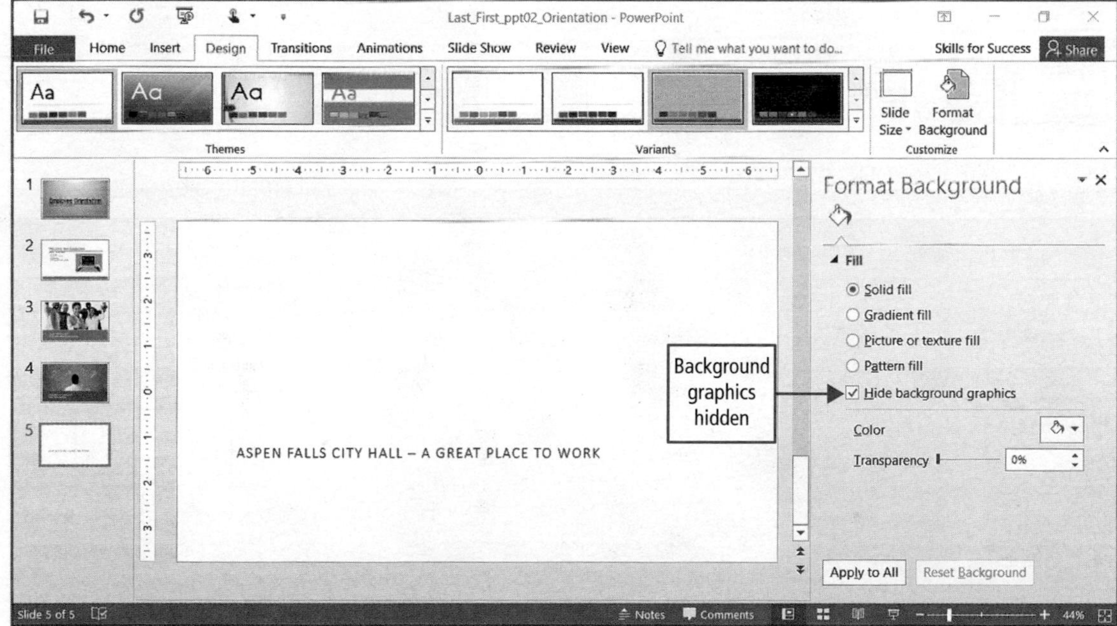

PowerPoint 2016, Windows 10, Microsoft Corporation

Figure 4

4. **Close** [×] the Format Background pane.

   The background style is applied only to Slide 1.

5. Display **Slide 4**, and then on the **Home tab**, in the **Slides group**, click the **New Slide arrow**.

   The slide layouts available are now broken into two groups. The first group shows the layouts with the customized background. The second group shows the original layouts.

6. In the **New Slide** gallery, under **Retrospect**, click **Section Header**. On the slide, click in the title placeholder, and then click a border of the placeholder. Press [Delete] to remove the placeholder. In the text placeholder, type Aspen Falls City Hall – A great place to work Compare your slide with **Figure 3**.

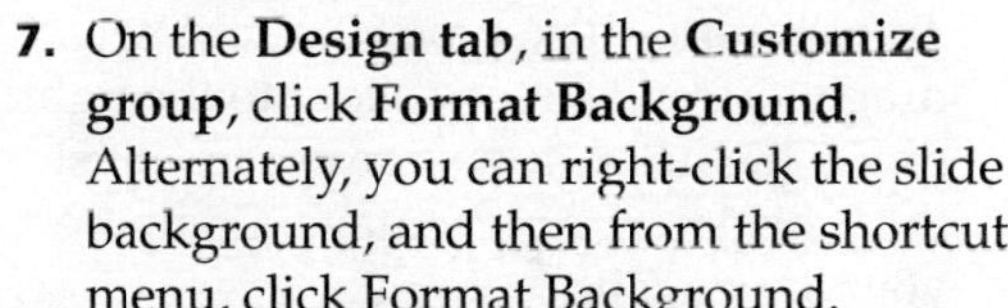

7. On the **Design tab**, in the **Customize group**, click **Format Background**. Alternately, you can right-click the slide background, and then from the shortcut menu, click Format Background.
8. In the **Format Background** pane, select the **Hide background graphics** check box, and then compare your screen with **Figure 4**.
9. **Close** [×] the Format Background pane, and then **Save** [💾] the file.

■ **You have completed Skill 4 of 10**

- You can add a picture or a texture to the slide background.
- When an image is inserted in the background, font colors, sizes, and effects may need to be adjusted so that the slide text is still easy to read.

Obj 1.2.6

1. With **Slide 5** displayed, on the **Design tab**, in the **Customize group**, click the **Format Background** button. In the **Format Background** pane, under **Fill**, select **Picture or texture fill**.
2. Under **Insert picture from**, click **File**. In the **Insert Picture** dialog box, navigate to the student files for this chapter, select **ppt02_Photo4**, and then click **Insert** to insert the picture as the slide background. Compare your screen with **Figure 1**.
3. In the **Format Background** pane, in the **Transparency** box, type 80 Alternately, drag the Transparency slider to the right or use the up or down arrows to adjust the transparency percentage. Compare your screen with **Figure 2**.

   You will format the slide text to stand out in a later skill. Here, the text is difficult to read due to lack of contrast between the font and the image in the background.

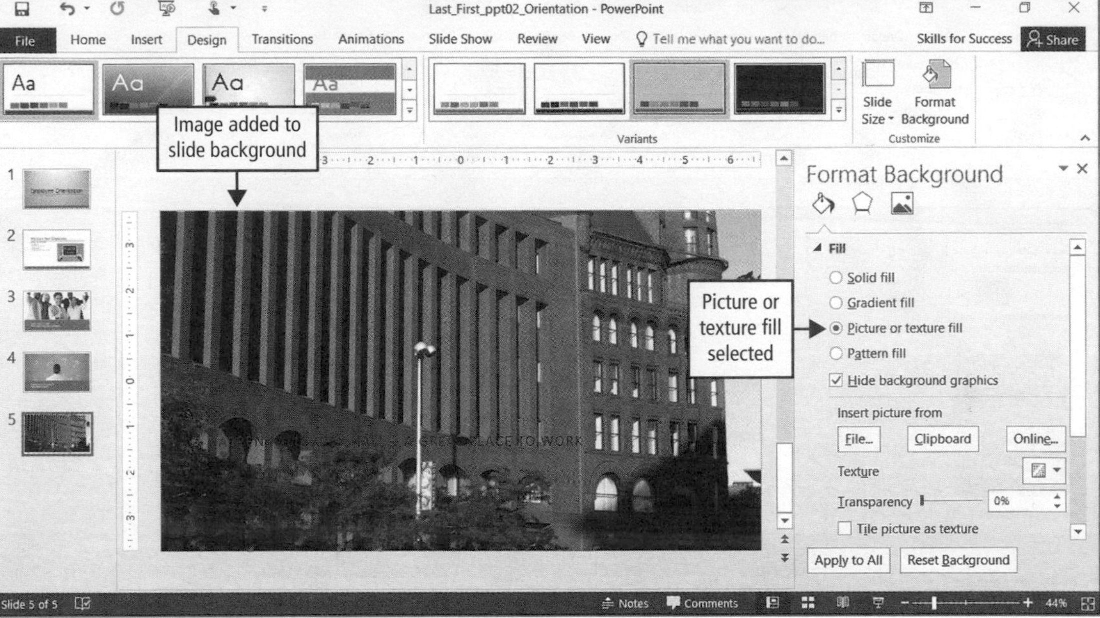

Figure 1 Courtesy of Kris Townsend; PowerPoint 2016, Windows 10, Microsoft Corporation

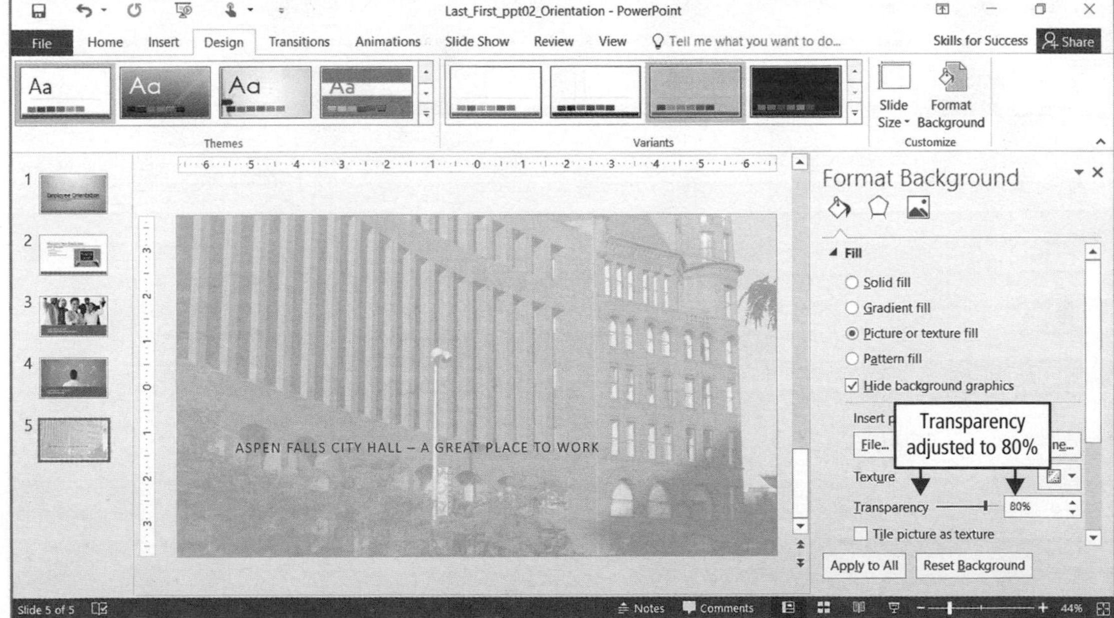

Figure 2 Courtesy of Kris Townsend; PowerPoint 2016, Windows 10, Microsoft Corporation

■ Continue to the next page to complete the skill

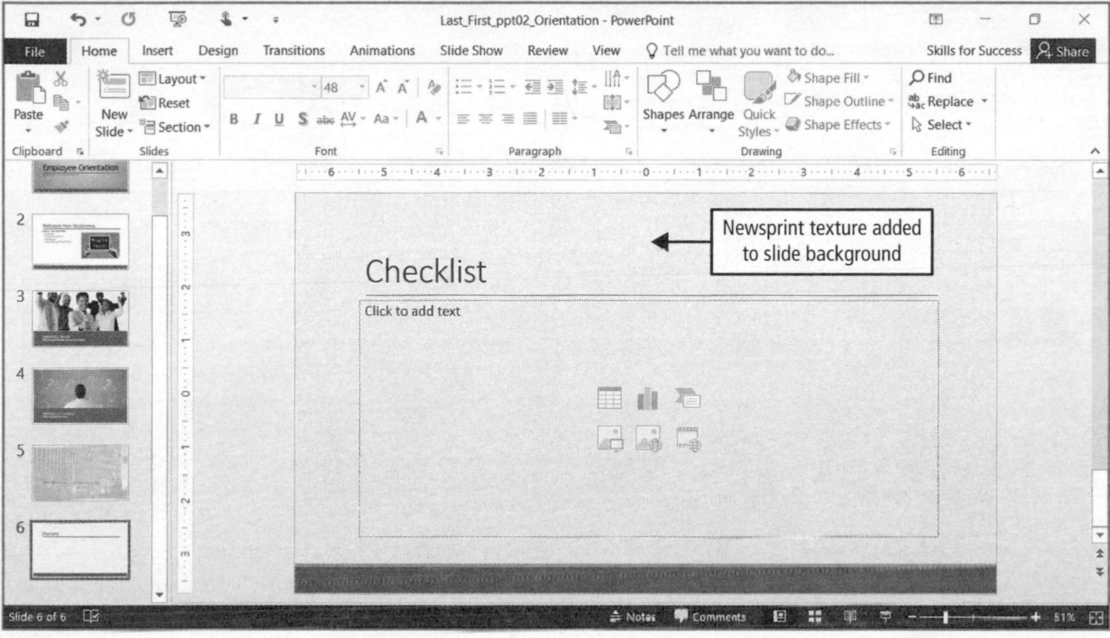

PowerPoint 2016, Windows 10, Microsoft Corporation

Figure 3

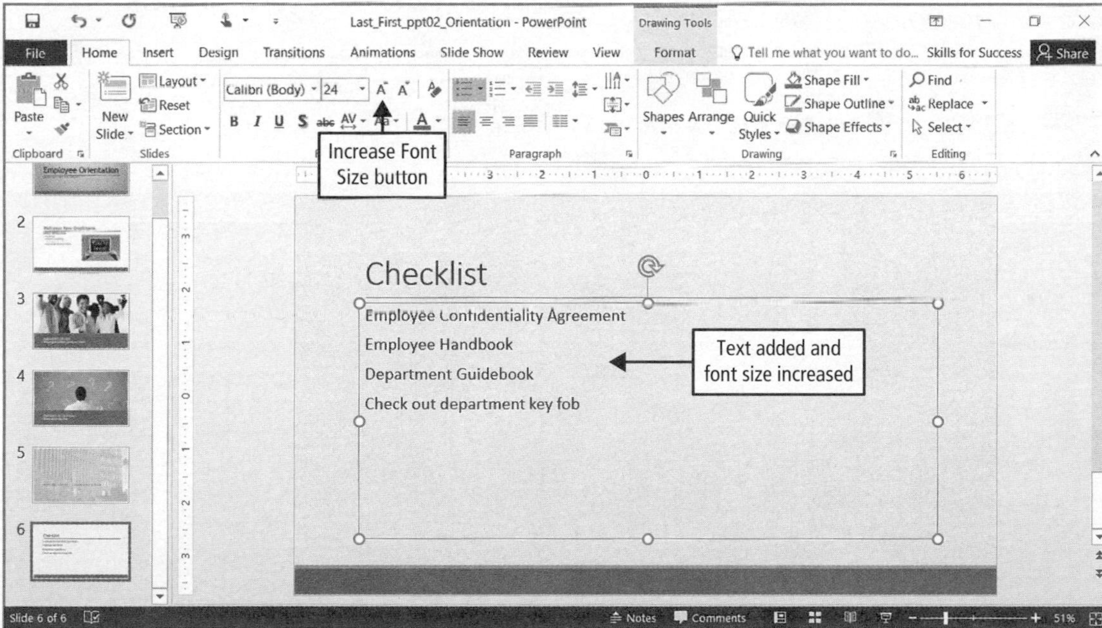

PowerPoint 2016, Windows 10, Microsoft Corporation

Figure 4

4. With **Slide 5** selected, on the **Home tab**, in the **Slides group**, click the **New Slide arrow**. Under **Retrospect**, click the **Title and Content** thumbnail. In the title placeholder, type Checklist and then press Esc two times so that no placeholders on the slide are selected.
5. In the **Format Background** pane, click **Picture or texture fill**. Click the **Texture** button, and then use ScreenTips to locate **Newsprint**. Click the **Newsprint** thumbnail to apply the texture. **Close** the Format Background pane, and then compare your screen with **Figure 3**.

   When applying a texture to the slide background, be sure to choose a texture that coordinates with the background colors and complements the content of your slide.
6. In the content placeholder, type Employee Confidentiality Agreement Press Enter. Type Employee Handbook Press Enter. Type Department Guidebook Press Enter. Type Check out department key fob
7. Select the content placeholder, and then on the **Home tab**, in the **Font group**, click the **Increase Font Size** button one time to change the **Font Size** to **24** points. Compare your screen with **Figure 4**.
8. **Save** the file.

■ **You have completed Skill 5 of 10**

- ***WordArt*** is a prebuilt set of fills, outlines, and effects used to create decorative text.
- You can convert existing text to WordArt or create new WordArt from scratch.

Obj 2.1.3

1. On **Slide 5**, select the text placeholder containing the text *Aspen Falls City Hall – A great place to work*. On the **Format tab**, in the **WordArt Styles group**, click the **More** button to display the WordArt gallery as shown in **Figure 1**.
2. Point to several WordArt styles to preview them with Live Preview.
3. In the **WordArt** gallery, click the second style in the second row—**Gradient Fill – Dark Green, Accent 1, Reflection**.
4. With the placeholder still selected, in the **WordArt Styles group**, click the **Text Fill** button, and then click the second color in the first row—**Black, Text 1**.

   In this manner, a WordArt style can be modified. Here the darker color provides more contrast between the text and slide background. Colors can be modified to match other font or theme colors in your presentation or to create a contrast with the slide background.
5. With the placeholder still selected, on the **Home tab**, in the **Font group**, click the **Font Size arrow**, click **44**, and then click **Bold** B. Compare your screen with **Figure 2**.

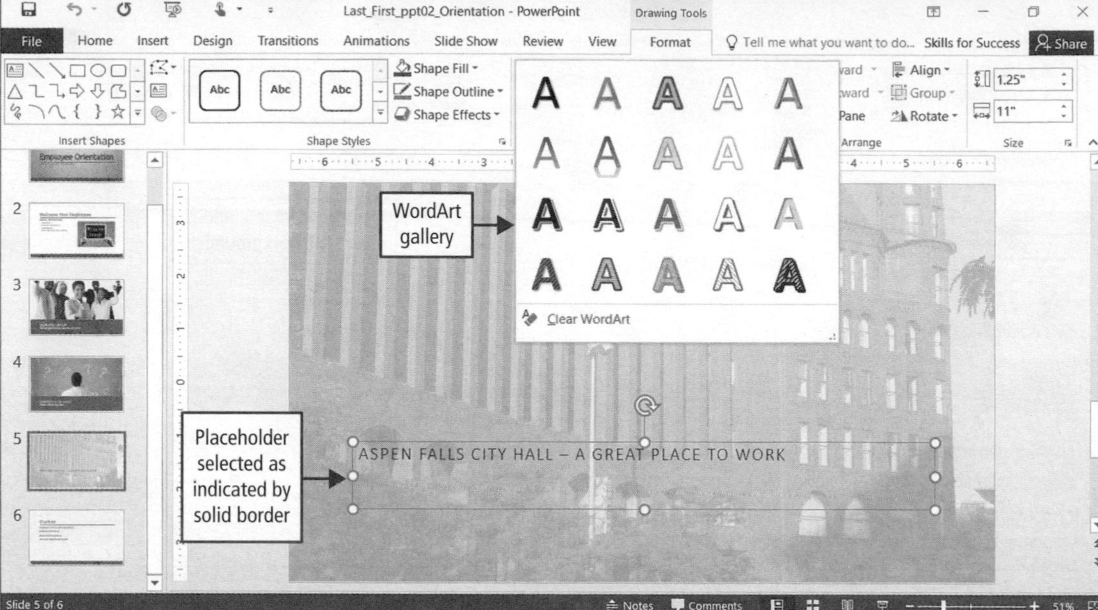

Figure 1

Courtesy of Kris Townsend; PowerPoint 2016, Windows 10, Microsoft Corporation

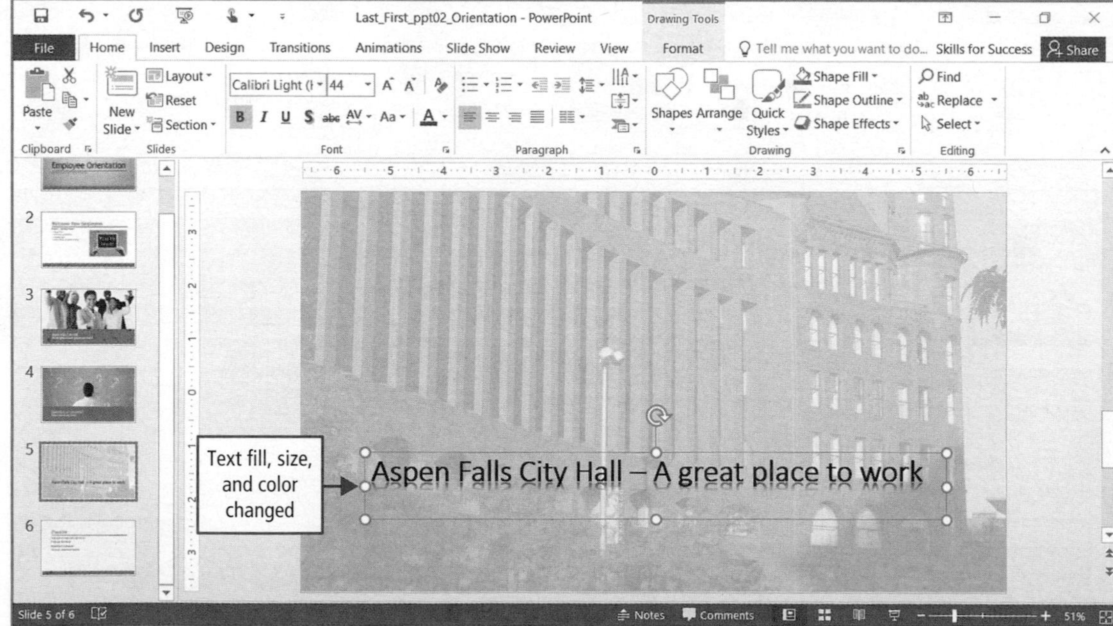

Figure 2

Courtesy of Kris Townsend; PowerPoint 2016, Windows 10, Microsoft Corporation

■ Continue to the next page to complete the skill

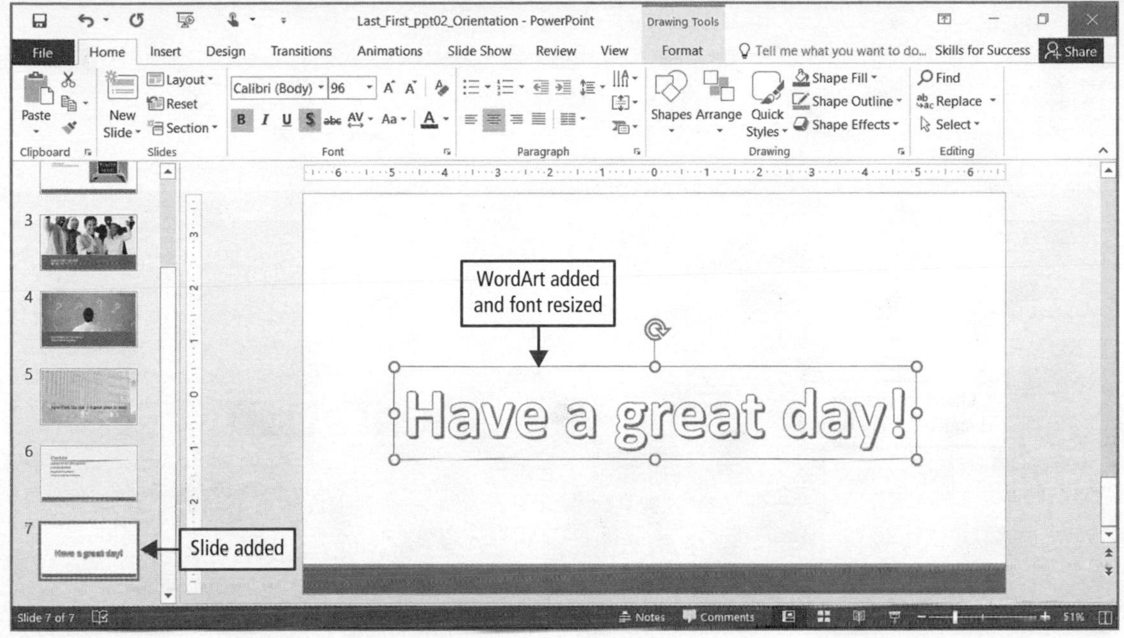

PowerPoint 2016, Windows 10, Microsoft Corporation

Figure 3

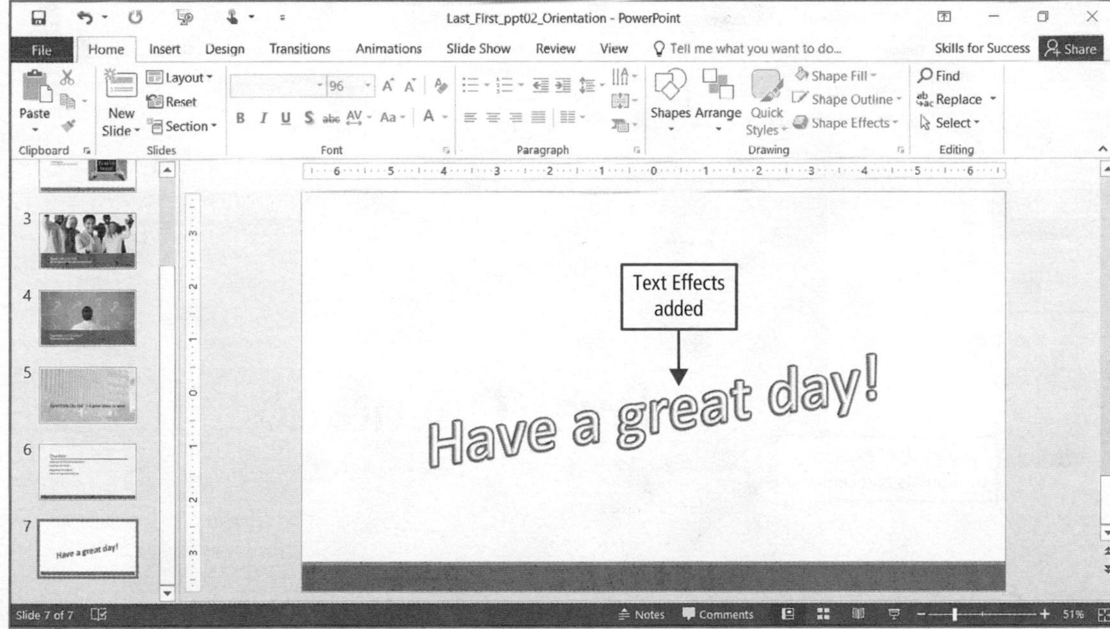

PowerPoint 2016, Windows 10, Microsoft Corporation

Figure 4

6. Move to **Slide 6**. On the **Home tab**, in the **Slides group**, click the **New Slide arrow**, and under **Retrospect**, click **Blank**.

   A blank slide layout contains no title or content placeholders.

7. On the **Insert tab**, in the **Text group**, click the **WordArt** button. In the **WordArt** gallery, click the fourth option in the third row—**Fill – White, Outline – Accent 2, Hard Shadow – Accent 2**. Type Have a great day! Select the text you just typed, on the Mini toolbar, click the **Font Size arrow**, and then click **96** to increase the **Font Size**. Compare your screen with **Figure 3**.
8. With the WordArt still selected, on the **Format tab**, in the **WordArt Styles group**, click the **Text Effects** button. Point to several of the options to view the available galleries. Point to **Bevel**, then point to several of the options to preview their effect on the text, and then click the first option in the second row—**Angle**.
9. On the **Format tab**, in the **WordArt Styles group**, click the **Text Effects** button. Point to **3-D Rotation**, and then point to several of the options to preview their effect on the text. Under **Parallel**, click the second option in the second row—**Off Axis 1 Right**. Click a blank area of the slide to deselect the WordArt placeholder. Compare your screen with **Figure 4**.
10. **Save** the file.

■ **You have completed Skill 6 of 10**

► Spacing between characters can be adjusted to change the look of the text or to adjust the text to better fit a placeholder.

1. Display **Slide 1**, and then select the title placeholder.
2. On the **Home tab**, in the **Font group**, click the **Character Spacing** button, and then in the list, select **Very Tight**. Compare your screen with **Figure 1**.

   The font size remains 80 points, but the spacing between characters has been decreased, allowing more text to fit into a smaller area.

3. Select the subtitle placeholder, and then on the **Home tab**, in the **Font group**, click the **Character Spacing** button. At the bottom of the list, click **More Spacing**.
4. In the **Font** dialog box, on the **Character Spacing tab**, click the **Spacing arrow**, and then next to **Expanded**, in the **By** box, type 6 Click **OK** to apply the Character Spacing. On the **Home tab**, in the **Paragraph group**, click the **Center** button. Compare your screen with **Figure 2**.

■ **Continue to the next page to complete the skill**

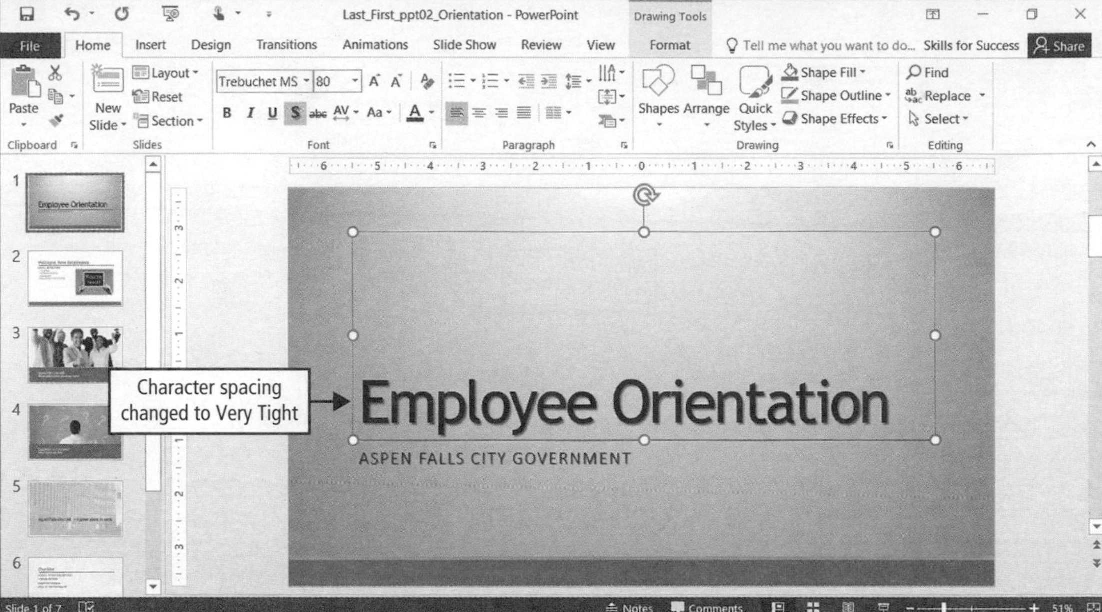

Figure 1 PowerPoint 2016, Windows 10, Microsoft Corporation

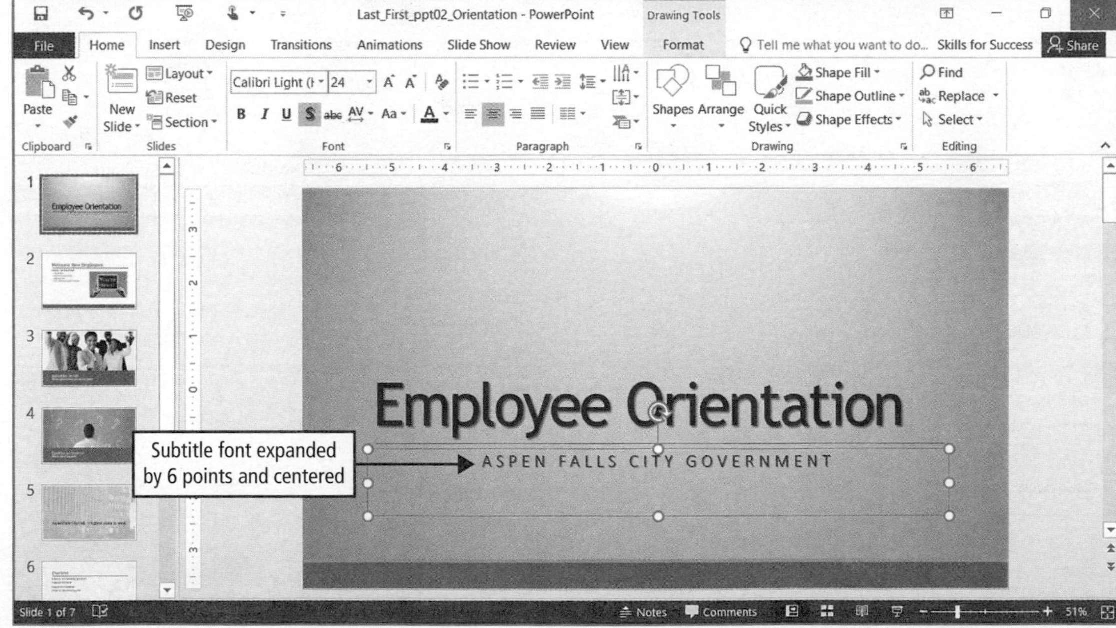

Figure 2 PowerPoint 2016, Windows 10, Microsoft Corporation

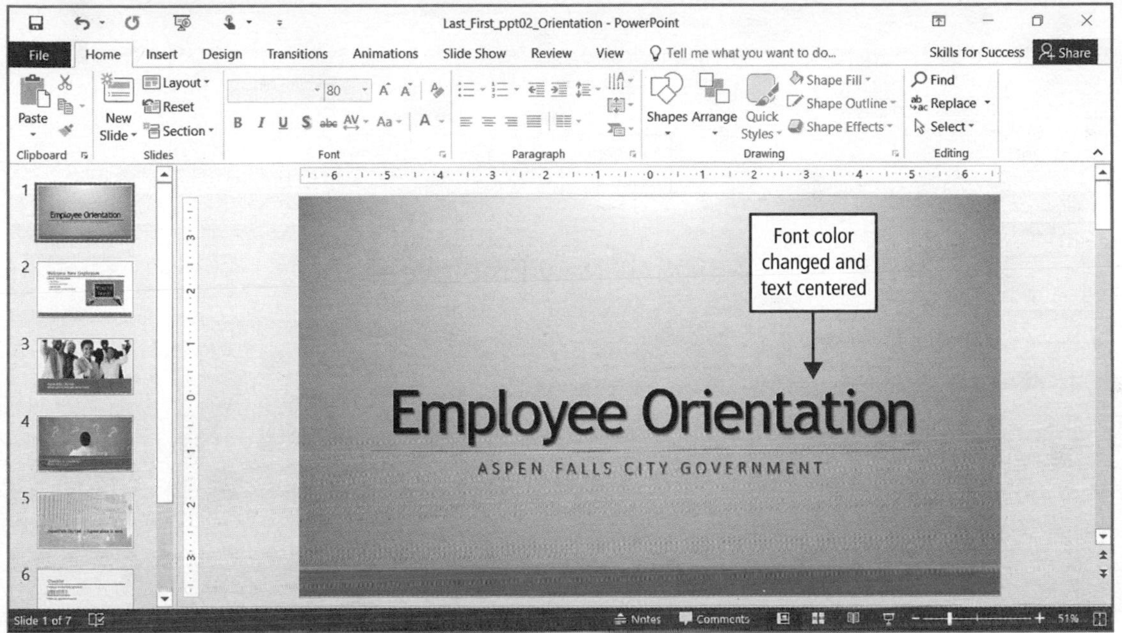

PowerPoint 2016, Windows 10, Microsoft Corporation

Figure 3

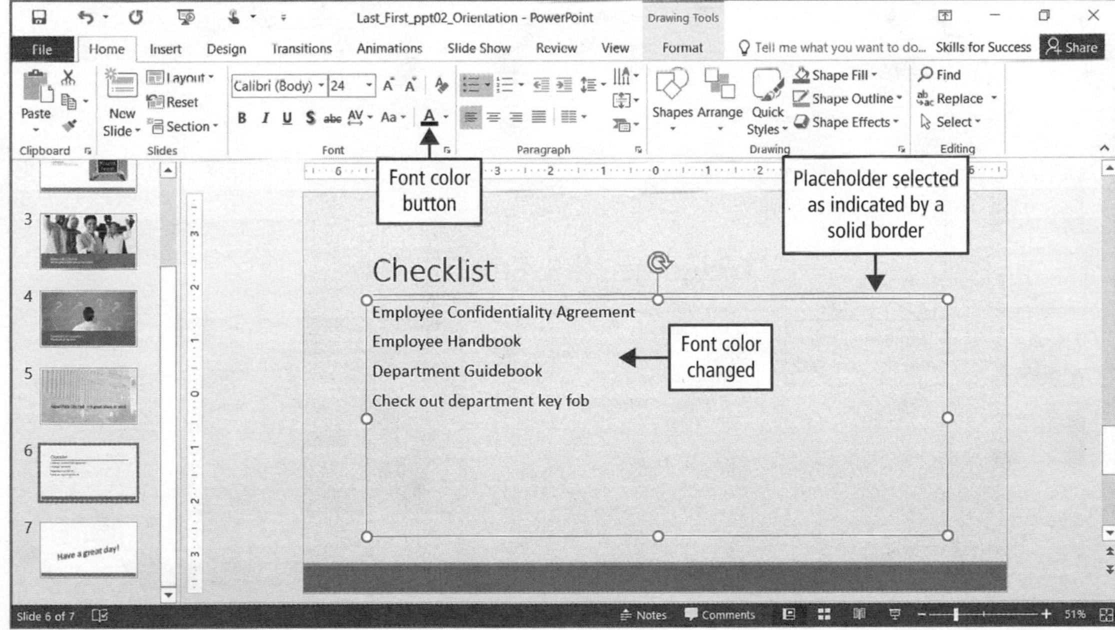

PowerPoint 2016, Windows 10, Microsoft Corporation

Figure 4

5. With **Slide 1** still displayed, select the text in the title placeholder, *Employee Orientation*.

   The modified background of this slide has decreased the contrast between the background color and the font color, which may make it difficult to read in poor lighting conditions or for viewers with visual impairments.

6. On the **Home tab**, in the **Paragraph group**, click the **Center** button. In the **Font group**, click the **Font Color arrow** to display the Font Color gallery.

7. In the first row of the gallery, click the second color—**Black, Text 1**—to change the color of the selected text, as shown in **Figure 3**.

   In the Font group, the Font Color button displays the color that you just applied to the selection. If you want to apply the same color to another selection, you can click the Font Color button without displaying the color gallery.

8. Display **Slide 6**, and then select the content placeholder. On the **Home tab**, in the **Font group**, click the **Font Color** button to change the font color to the same shade of black used in the previous step. Compare your slide with **Figure 4**.

9. **Save** the file.

■ **You have completed Skill 7 of 10**

  WATCH SKILL 2.8

▸ A presentation theme includes default bullet styles for the bullet points in content placeholders. You can customize a bullet symbol by changing its style, color, or size.

▸ A numbered list can be applied to bullet points in place of bullet symbols.

 MOS Obj 2.1.5

1. Display **Slide 2**, and then in the content placeholder, select the four lines of text, beginning with *City Hall tour*. On the **Home tab**, in the **Paragraph group**, click the **Numbering** button, and then compare your screen with **Figure 1**. If you clicked the Numbering arrow and a gallery displays, in the first row, click the second numbering option—1, 2, 3.

   The default color for the numbers just applied—Turquoise, Accent 1—is part of the current theme—Retrospect.

2. With the four numbered list items still selected, click the **Numbering arrow**, and then below the gallery, click **Bullets and Numbering**.

3. In the **Bullets and Numbering** dialog box, on the **Numbered tab**, click the **Color** button. Under **Theme Colors**, in the last row, click the fifth color—**Turquoise, Accent 1, Darker 50%**, and then click **OK**.

4. Select all of the text in the content placeholder—including the first line—click the **Font Size arrow**, and then click **24**. Click a blank area of the slide to deselect the text, and then compare your screen with **Figure 2**.

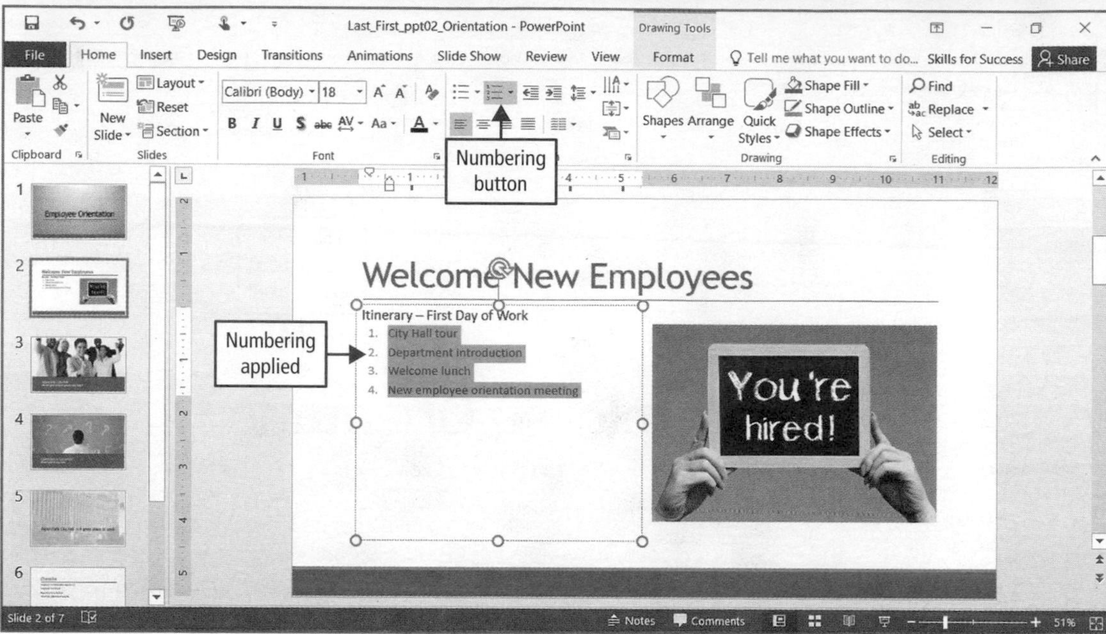

Figure 1 DOC RABE Media/Fotolia; PowerPoint 2016, Windows 10, Microsoft Corporation

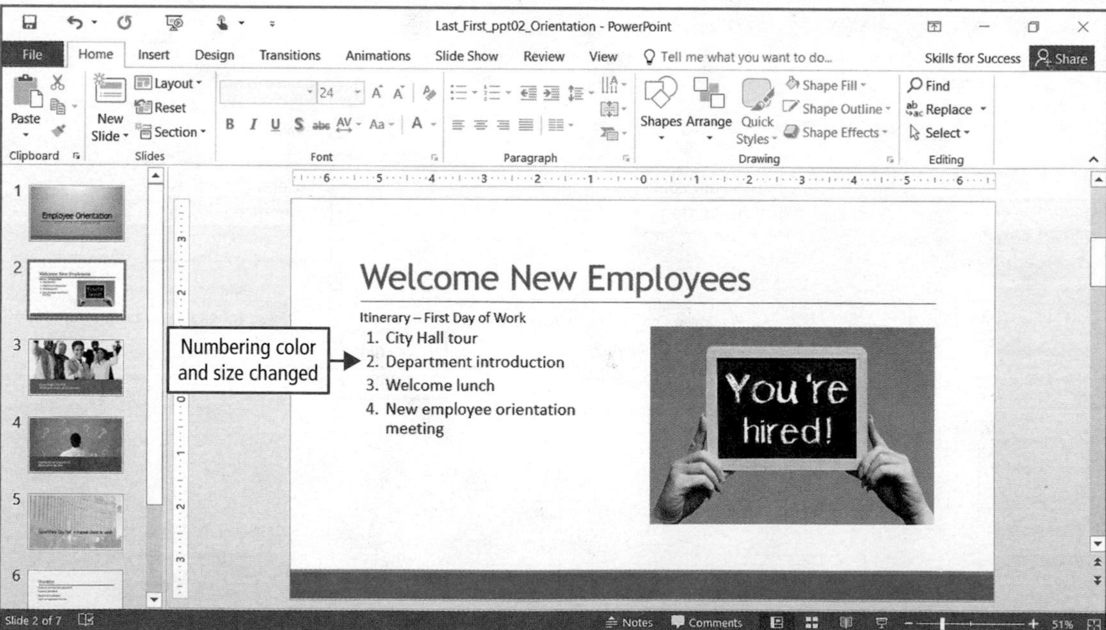

Figure 2 DOC RABE Media/Fotolia; PowerPoint 2016, Windows 10, Microsoft Corporation

■ Continue to the next page to complete the skill

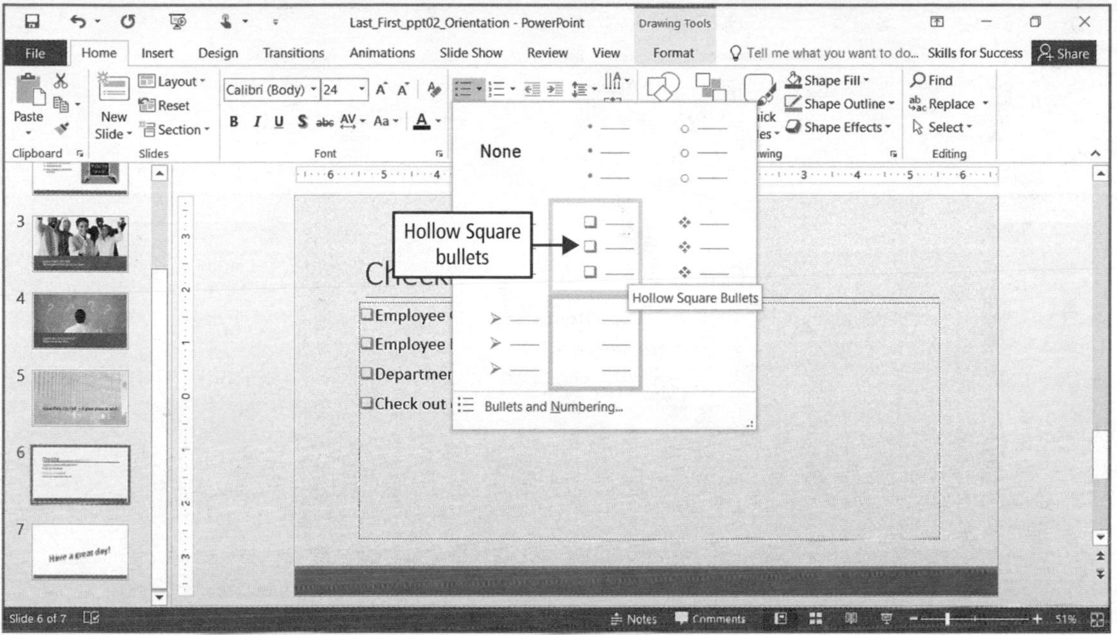

PowerPoint 2016, Windows 10, Microsoft Corporation

Figure 3

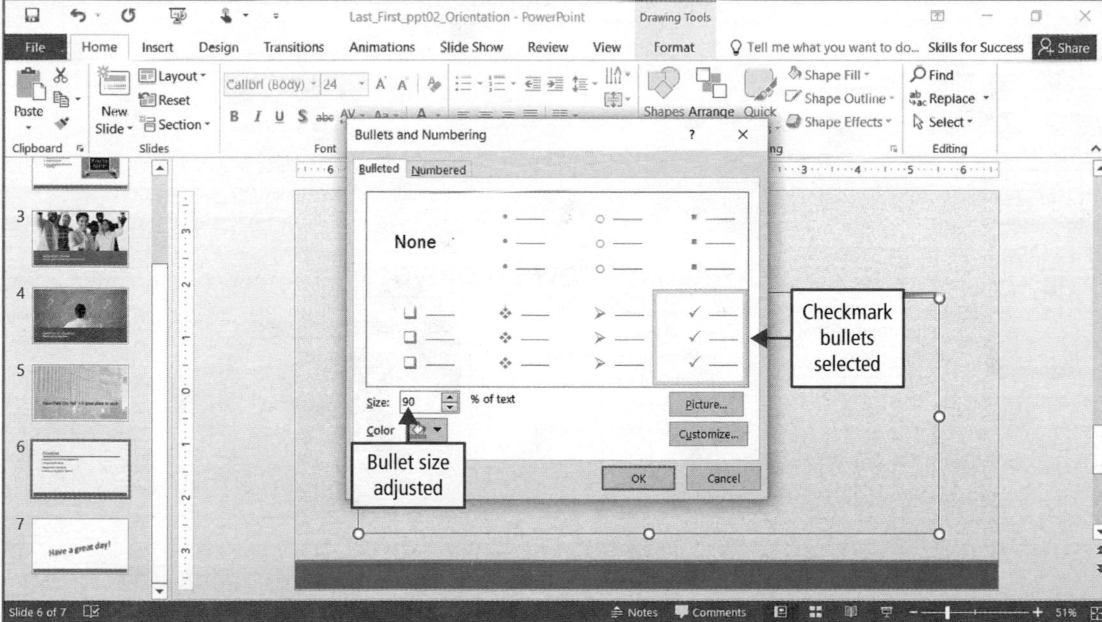

PowerPoint 2016, Windows 10, Microsoft Corporation

Figure 4

5. Move to **Slide 6**. Select the content placeholder.
6. On the **Home tab**, in the **Paragraph group**, click the **Bullets arrow** to display the Bullets gallery.

   The gallery displays several bullet characters that you can apply to the selection.

7. Point to the **Hollow Square Bullets** thumbnail as shown in **Figure 3**, and then click the thumbnail to apply the bullet style to the selection.
8. With the placeholder still selected, click the **Bullets arrow**, and then click **Bullets and Numbering**.
9. In the **Bullets and Numbering** dialog box, on the **Bulleted tab**, in the second row of the **Bullet** gallery, click **Checkmark Bullets**.
10. In the **Size** box, replace the number with 90 and then compare your screen with **Figure 4**. Click **OK** to apply the bullet style and size.

    The size of the checkmark bullets is adjusted to 90% of the size of the text after it. In this case, the size of the checkmarks will be 90% of the size of the 24-point font.

11. **Save** the file.

■ **You have completed Skill 8 of 10**

SKILL 9: Move and Copy Text and Objects

- The Cut command removes selected text or graphics from your presentation and places the selection in the Office Clipboard.
- The ***clipboard*** is a temporary storage area maintained by your operating system.
- The Copy command duplicates a selection and places it on the Office Clipboard.

1. On **Slide 6**, in the content placeholder, position the pointer over the fourth checkmark—the checkmark before *Check out department key fob*—to display the pointer [move pointer].
2. With the pointer [move pointer] positioned over the fourth checkmark, click to select the entire line of text. Compare your screen with **Figure 1**.

   Clicking a list number or bullet symbol is an efficient way to select the entire bullet point or list line.

3. On the **Home tab**, in the **Clipboard group**, click the **Cut** button [Cut] to remove the bullet from the slide and copy it to the clipboard.
4. Move to **Slide 2**. Place the insertion point before the third item in the numbered list, *Welcome lunch*. In the **Clipboard group**, click the **Paste** button to insert the selection and display the **Paste Options** [(Ctrl)] button as shown in **Figure 2**.

   The Paste Options button provides options for formatting pasted text. When you paste into a numbered list, the list automatically renumbers to accommodate the newly pasted information.

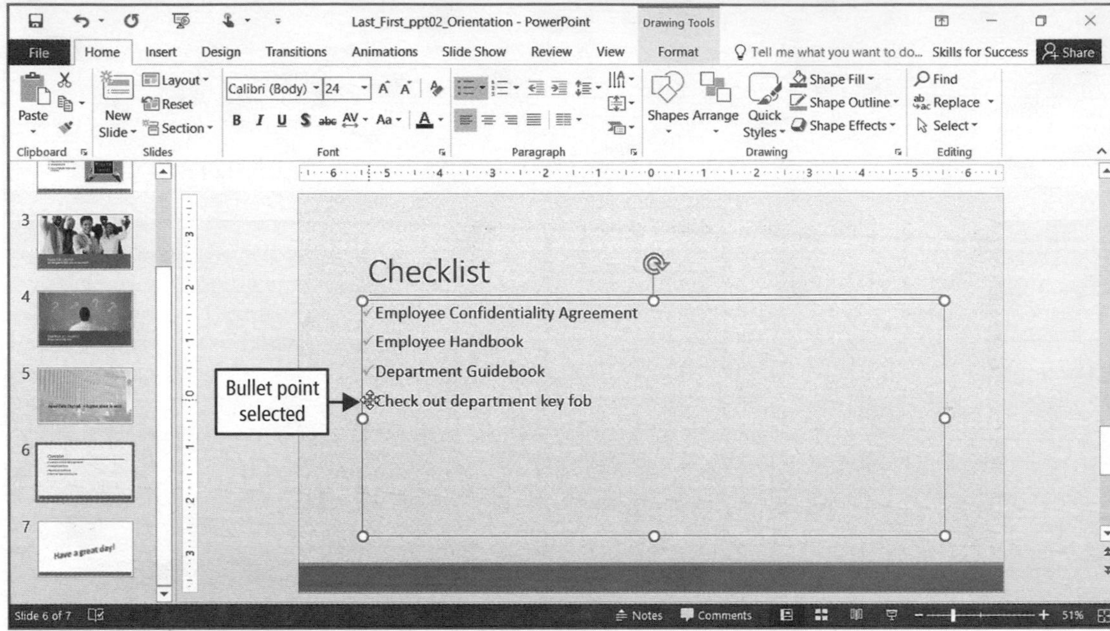

Figure 1

PowerPoint 2016, Windows 10, Microsoft Corporation

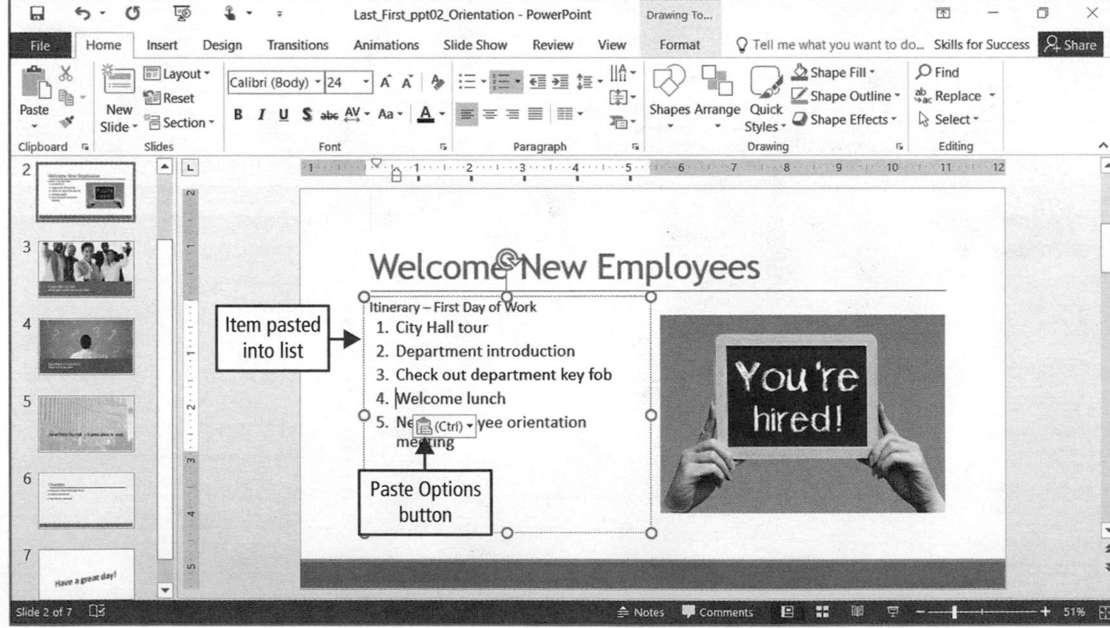

Figure 2

DOC RABE Media/Fotolia; PowerPoint 2016, Windows 10, Microsoft Corporation

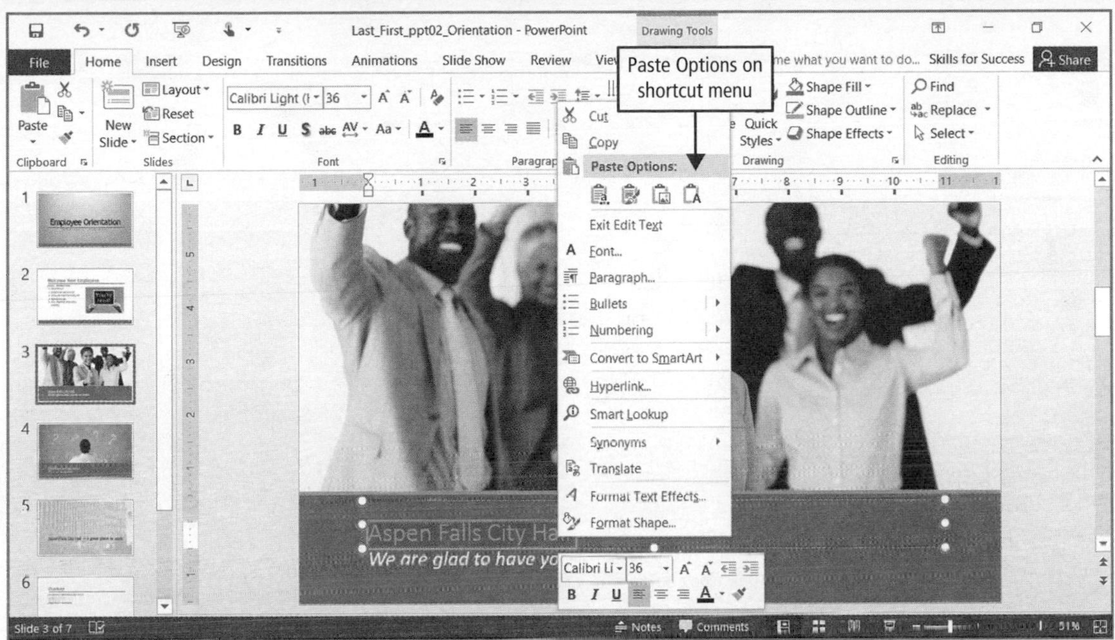

Yuri Arcurs/Fotolia; PowerPoint 2016, Windows 10, Microsoft Corporation

Figure 3

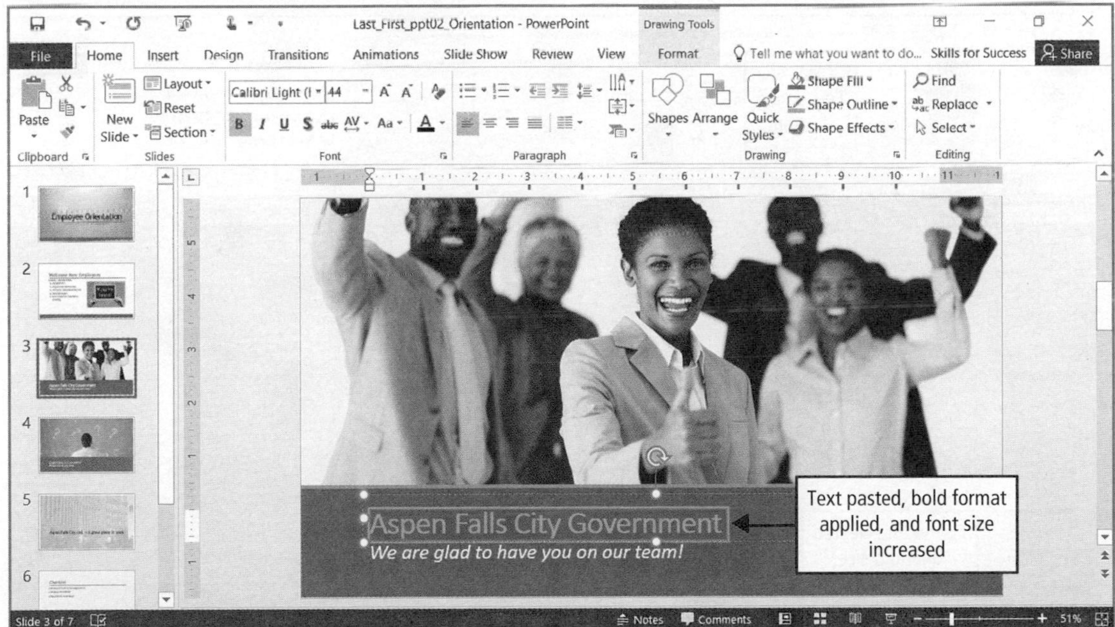

Yuri Arcurs/Fotolia; PowerPoint 2016, Windows 10, Microsoft Corporation

Figure 4

5. Click the **Paste Options** button [(Ctrl)] to view the four options. Click **Keep Text Only** [icon].

   Keep Source Formatting applies the original formatting of the pasted text. ***Use Destination Theme*** applies the formatting of the slide to which the text is pasted. ***Picture*** pastes the text as a picture. ***Keep Text Only*** removes all formatting from the selection. The Paste Options button remains on the screen until you perform another action.

6. Move to **Slide 1**, and then select the subtitle text *Aspen Falls City Government*. Point to the selection, and then right-click to display the shortcut menu. From the shortcut menu, click **Copy**.

   There are multiple methods you can use to cut, copy, and paste text, including the shortcut menu and the buttons in the Clipboard group. You can also use the keyboard shortcuts—Ctrl + X to cut, Ctrl + C to copy, and Ctrl + V to paste.

7. Move to **Slide 3**. Select the title text—*Aspen Falls City Hall*. Right-click the selected text to display the shortcut menu as shown in **Figure 3**, and then notice the four paste options.

8. On the shortcut menu, under **Paste Options**, point to each button to view how each paste option displays the text, and then click the last button—**Keep Text Only** [icon].

9. Select the title text. Apply **Bold** [B], and then change the **Font Size** to **44**. Compare your slide with **Figure 4**.

10. **Save** [icon] the file.

■ **You have completed Skill 9 of 10**

- ***Format Painter*** is used to copy formatting from one selection of text to another.
- When you need to copy formatting to multiple selections, double-click the Format Painter button. To copy formatting to a single selection, click the Format Painter one time.
- You can use the Clear All Formatting button to revert to the font formatting associated with the original slide layout.

1. Display **Slide 2**, and then click anywhere in the title placeholder. On the **Home tab**, in the **Clipboard group**, double-click the **Format Painter** button.
2. Click the **Slide 6** thumbnail to move to Slide 6. Point to the text in the title placeholder, and then compare your screen with **Figure 1**.

   When Format Painter is active, the pointer displays.

3. With the pointer, drag through the title text—*Checklist*.
4. In the content placeholder, select all three bulleted points to apply the same formatting to the bulleted text. Notice that the pointer is still active.
5. On **Slide 4**, use the same method to select and apply the same formatting to the text *Please ask at any time*. On the **Home tab**, in the **Clipboard group**, click the **Format Painter** button to turn off Format Painter. Alternately, press Esc.
6. With the text still selected, on the **Home tab**, in the **Font group**, click the **Clear All Formatting** button to revert to the default font formatting for this slide layout. Increase the **Font Size** to **24** and then compare your slide with **Figure 2**.

   Use the Clear All Formatting button to revert to the original formatting on a slide.

■ **Continue to the next page to complete the skill**

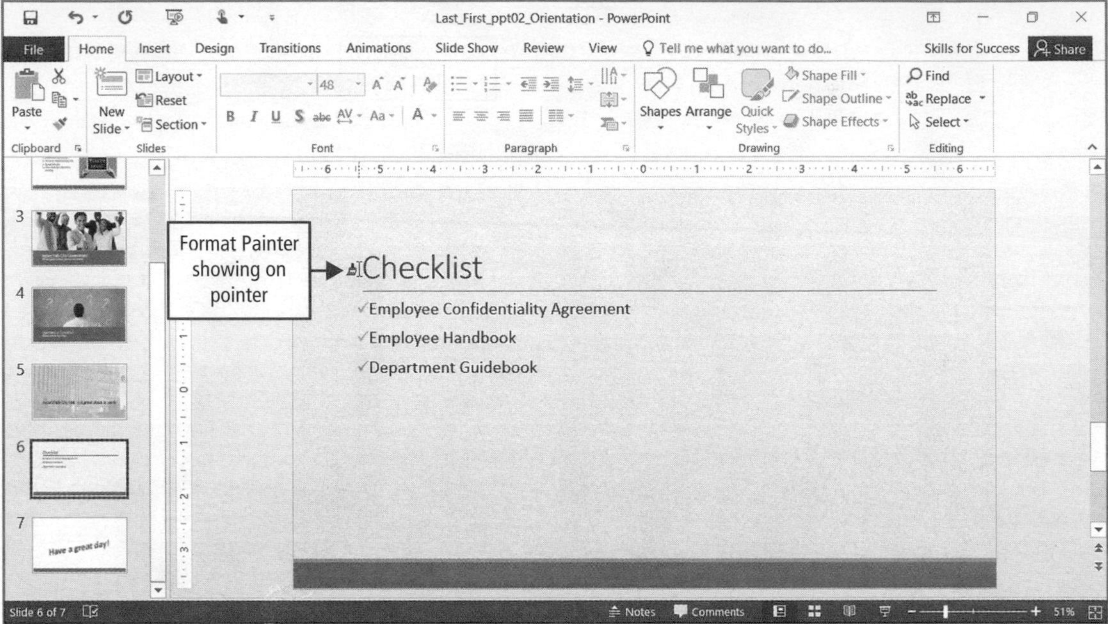

Figure 1

PowerPoint 2016, Windows 10, Microsoft Corporation

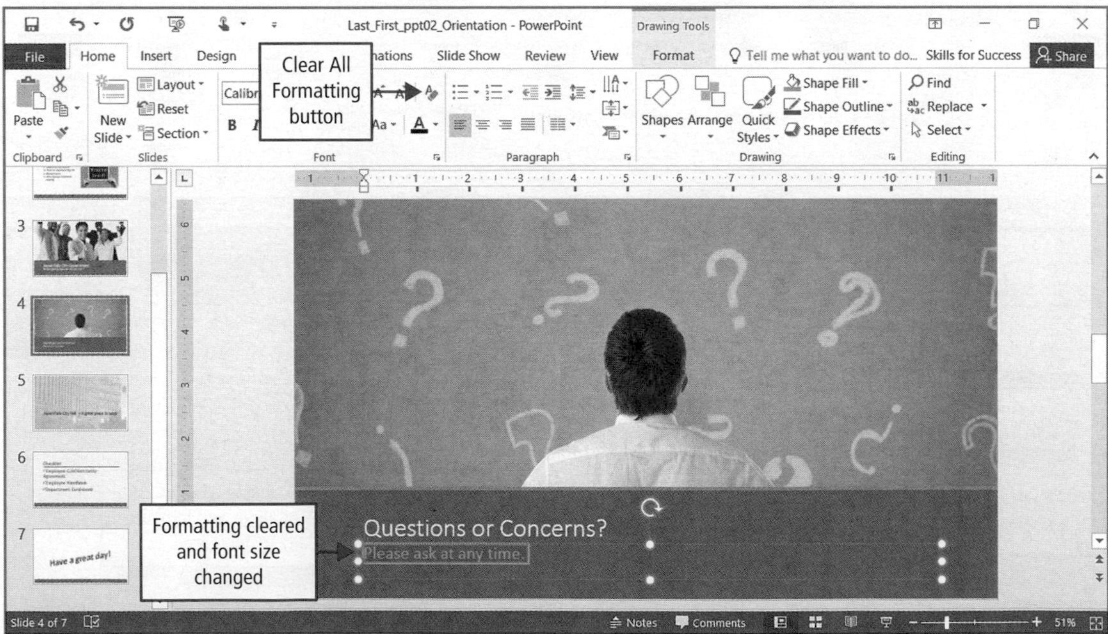

Figure 2

rangizzz/Fotolia; PowerPoint 2016, Windows 10, Microsoft Corporation

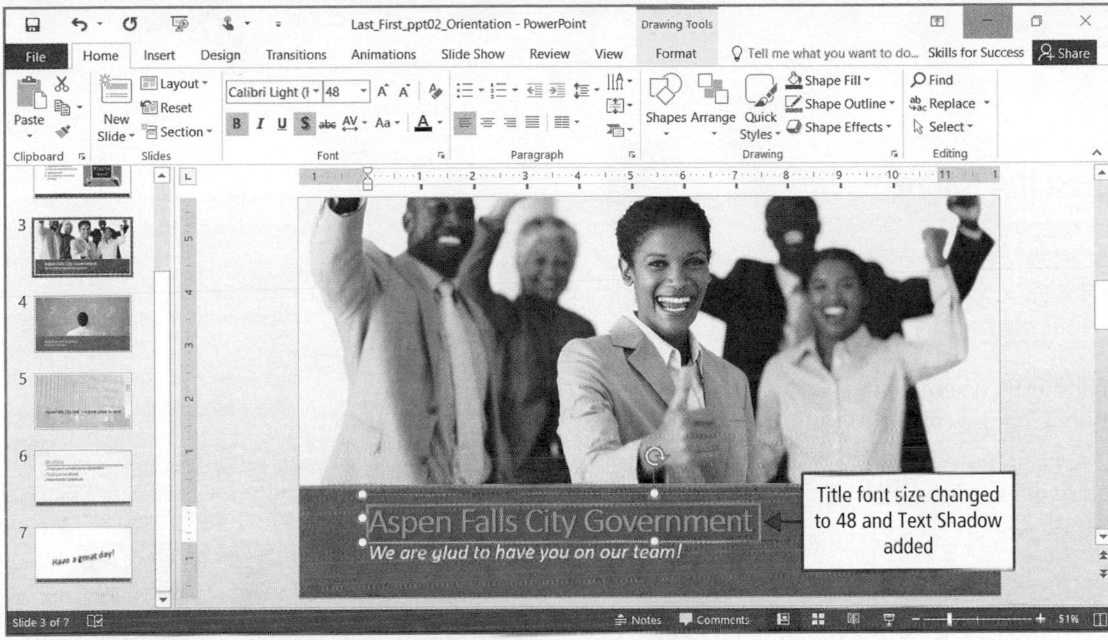

Yuri Arcurs/Fotolia; PowerPoint 2016, Windows 10, Microsoft Corporation

Figure 3

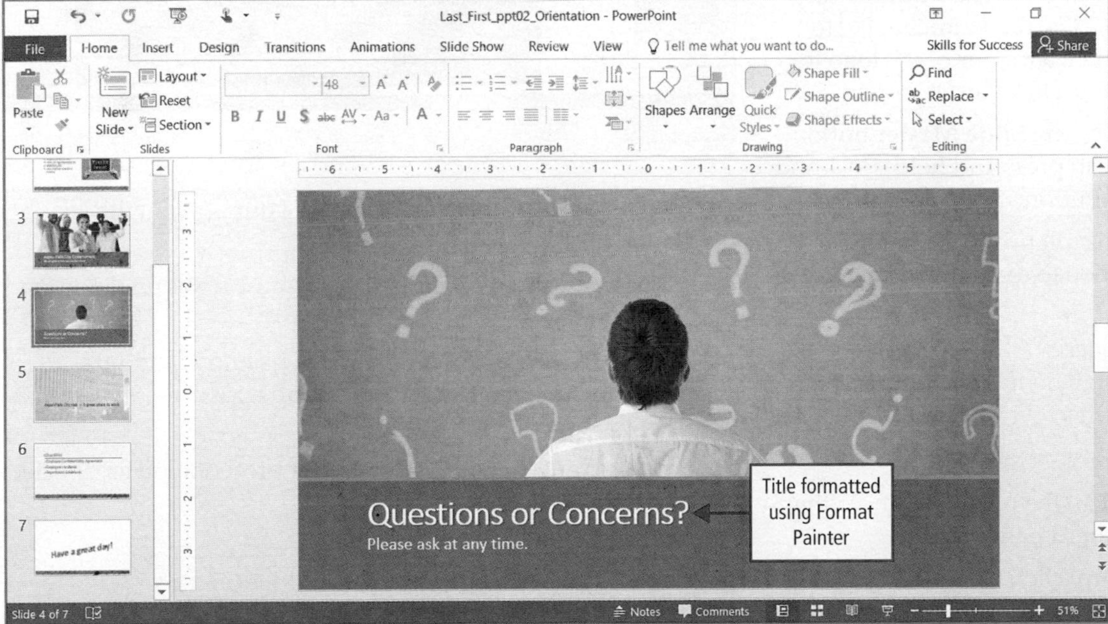

rangizzz/Fotolia; PowerPoint 2016, Windows 10, Microsoft Corporation

Figure 4

7. On **Slide 6**, select the bulleted list, and then change the **Font Size** to **36**.
8. Move to **Slide 3**. Select the title placeholder. On the **Home tab**, in the **Font group**, click the **Increase Font Size** button one time to change the font size to **48**, and then click the **Text Shadow** button. Compare your slide with **Figure 3**.
9. With the placeholder still selected, on the **Home tab**, in the **Clipboard group**, click the **Format Painter** button one time.
10. Display **Slide 4**, and then click the title placeholder *Questions or Concerns?* to apply the same formatting as the title text on Slide 3.

    Because the Format Painter button was clicked one time, Format Painter is no longer active after the formatting was copied one time.

11. Click a blank area of the slide to deselect the placeholder, and then compare your slide with **Figure 4**.
12. Insert a **Header & Footer** on all **Notes and Handouts** pages that includes the **Date and Time** updated automatically, a **Page Number**, and a **Footer** with the file name Last_First_ppt02_Orientation
13. **Save** the file. Submit your project as directed by your instructor. **Close** PowerPoint.

DONE! You have completed Skill 10 of 10, and your presentation is complete!

More Skills 11

Edit Slide Masters

To complete this presentation, you will need the following file:

- ppt02_MS11Software

You will save your file as:

- Last_First_ppt02_MS11Software

- ► The ***slide master*** is a slide that stores information about the theme and layouts applied to each type of slide in a presentation. Changes made to the slide master affect all layouts.
- ► When you want to add an image to the background of every slide, it is efficient to add that information to the slide master.

---

1. Start **PowerPoint 2016**, and then open **ppt02_MS11Software**. **Save** the file in your **PowerPoint Chapter 2** folder as Last_First_ppt02_MS11Software
2. Notice the IT Services Department logo in the lower right corner of the title slide. On the **Home tab**, in the **Clipboard group**, click the **Launcher** to display the Clipboard. Click the logo, and then click a border of the logo to select it. On the **Home tab**, in the **Clipboard group**, click **Cut**.
3. On the **View tab**, in the **Master Views group**, click the **Slide Master** button. Alternately, to switch to Slide Master view, you can press and hold Shift, and then on the status bar, click the Normal view button.
4. Toward the left side of the PowerPoint window, scroll up to display the top slide thumbnail, and then point to the first slide to display the *Ion Slide Master: used by slide(s) 1-4* ScreenTip.
5. Click the slide master—*Ion Slide Master: used by slide(s) 1-4*—so that it displays in the **Slide** pane. On the **Slide Master tab**, in the **Background group**, click the **Background Styles** button, and then click **Style 12**.

   The background is applied to each layout.
6. In the **Clipboard** pane, click the logo to paste it into the presentation. In the **Clipboard** Pane, click **Clear All**. **Close** the Clipboard pane.
7. On the **View tab**, in the **Presentation Views group**, click **Normal**. Alternately, on the status bar, click the Normal view button.

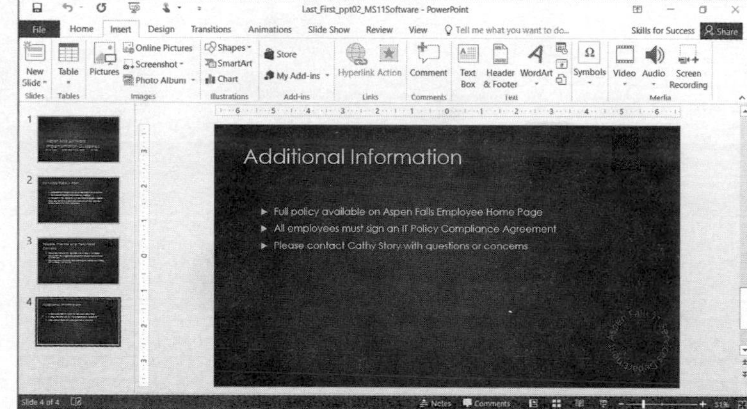

Figure 1 PowerPoint 2016, Windows 10, Microsoft Corporation

8. Display **Slide 4**, and then compare your screen with **Figure 1**.

   The logo will appear on all slides because it was pasted on the slide master.
9. Insert a **Header & Footer** on all **Notes and Handouts** pages. Include the **Date**, **Page Number**, and the **Footer text** Last_First_ppt02_MS11Software
10. **Save** the presentation. Submit your presentation as directed by your instructor.

- **You have completed More Skills 11**

More Skills 12

Save and Apply Presentation Templates

To complete this presentation, you will need the following file:

- ppt02_MS12Fire

You will save your files as:

- Last_First_ppt02_MS12Fire
- Last_First_ppt02_MS12FireTemplate
- Last_First_ppt02_MS12FireEvents

▸ You can create a presentation template—a file that contains standard formatting, layouts, color schemes, and logos.

▸ To create a new presentation from a template, open the file from File Explorer. The template will open as a new presentation, named Presentation 1.

---

1. Start **PowerPoint 2016**, and then open **ppt02_MS12Fire**. **Save** the file in your **PowerPoint Chapter 2** folder as Last_First_ppt02_MS12Fire
2. On **Slide 2**, select the text *Volunteer needs*, and then replace the text with Add topic or event here Select the text *Reception desk*, and then replace it with Topic/Event 1 Select all of the text in the line that begins with *5 – 10 hours*, and then replace it with Topic/Event description
3. On the **File tab**, click **Export**. Click **Change File Type**. Click the **Template** button. Click the **Save As** button, and then navigate to your **PowerPoint Chapter 2** folder and save the file as Last_First_ppt02_MS12FireTemplate

   The file is saved as a PowerPoint template with the file extension .potx. You can use this template to create new presentations with the same design, layouts, and images without changing the template file.
4. **Close** PowerPoint.
5. On the taskbar, click the **File Explorer** button, and then navigate to your **PowerPoint Chapter 2** folder.
6. Locate the template you created—**Last_First_ppt02_MS12FireTemplate.** Double-click the file name to open the presentation. MOS Obj 1.1.2

   A new presentation has been created from the template you saved earlier.
7. Display **Slide 2**. Replace the text *Add topic or event here* with Fall Open House Events

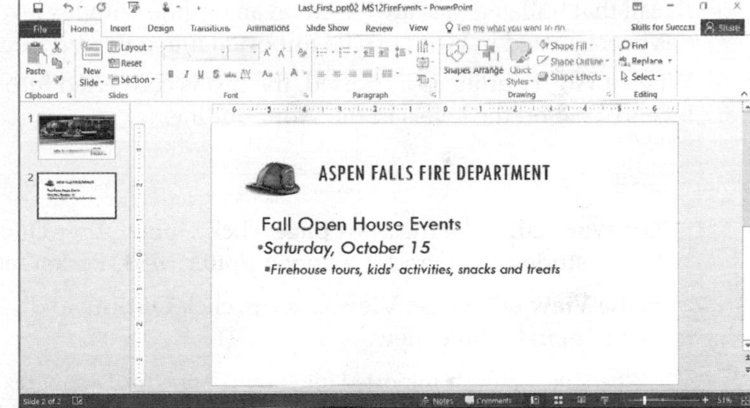

PowerPoint 2016, Windows 10, Microsoft Corporation **Figure 1**

8. Replace the text *Topic/Event 1* with Saturday, October 15 Replace the text *Topic/Event description* with Firehouse tours, kids' activities, snacks and treats
9. Insert a **Header & Footer** on the **Notes and Handouts** pages. Include the **Date**, **Page Number**, and the **Footer** Last_First_ppt02_MS12FireEvents
10. On the **File tab**, click **Save As**. **Save** the presentation in your **PowerPoint Chapter 2** folder as Last_First_ppt02_MS12FireEvents Compare your screen with **Figure 1**, and then submit your presentation as directed by your instructor.

■ **You have completed More Skills 12**

More Skills 13

Create Slides from Microsoft Word Outlines

To complete this presentation, you will need the following files:

- New PowerPoint presentation
- ppt02_MS13ParksOutline

You will save your file as:

- Last_First_ppt02_MS13ParksEvents

- Recall that bulleted lists are based on an outline with list levels. An outline that has been created in Word can be imported into a PowerPoint presentation.
- When a Word outline is imported, the text is converted into slide titles and list levels based on the levels in the Word outline.

---

1. Start **Word 2016**. On the **Start page**, click **Open Other Documents**. Navigate to your student files, and then open **ppt02_MS13ParksOutline**.
2. On the **View tab**, in the **Views group**, click **Outline** to display the Word document in Outline view.

   When the outline is imported into PowerPoint, the Level 1 text, indicated by a larger font size, will become the slide titles. The indented text will become the bullet points in the content placeholders.

3. **Close** Word without saving the file.
4. Start **PowerPoint 2016**. Click the **Wood Type** theme, and then click **Create** to create a new presentation. In the slide title placeholder, type Aspen Falls Parks and Recreation Department and then adjust the **Font Size** to **80**. In the subtitle placeholder, type Summer Events
5. **Save** the presentation in your **PowerPoint Chapter 2** folder as Last_First_ppt02_MS13ParksEvents

Obj 1.1.3

6. On the **Home tab**, in the **Slides group**, click the **New Slide arrow**, and then below the gallery, locate the **Slides from Outline** command.
7. Click **Slides from Outline**, and then in the **Insert Outline** dialog box, navigate to the student data files for this chapter. Click **ppt02_MS13ParksOutline**, click **Insert**, and then compare your screen with **Figure 1**.

   The Word outline is converted into three new slides, each with a slide title and several bullet points.

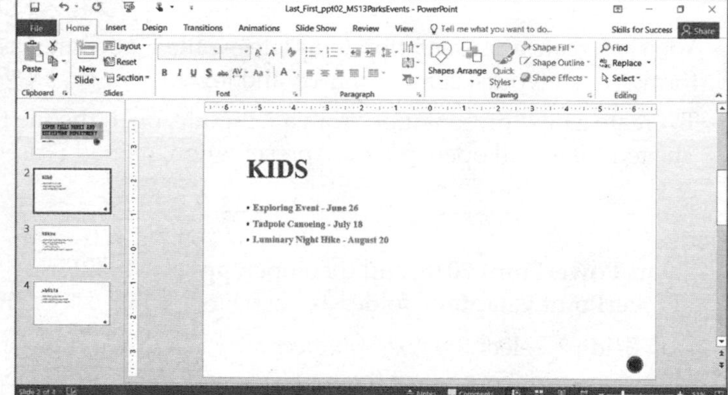

Figure 1 PowerPoint 2016, Windows 10, Microsoft Corporation

8. Insert a **Header & Footer** on the **Notes and Handouts** pages. Include the **Date**, **Page Number**, and the **Footer** Last_First_ppt02_MS13ParksEvents
9. **Save** the presentation, and then submit your presentation as directed by your instructor.

- **You have completed More Skills 13**

More Skills 14

Design Presentations with Contrast

To complete this presentation, you will need the following file:

- ppt02_MS14Clerk

You will save your file as:

- Last_First_ppt02_MS14Clerk

- ***Contrast*** is the difference in brightness between two elements on a slide, such as the background and the text or the background and a graphic. When a slide background and the slide objects or text do not have enough contrast, the message may be lost.
- High contrast increases the readability of the slide and focuses the viewer's attention on the message.
- The lighting in a room in which the presentation is viewed can affect the contrast in a presentation. In a dark room, a white background may be too bright. Conversely, in a bright room, a light background will display well.

---

1. Start **PowerPoint 2016**, and then open **ppt02_MS14Clerk**. **Save** the file in your **PowerPoint Chapter 2** folder as Last_First_ppt02_MS14Clerk
2. On **Slide 1**, note that the title and subtitle are readable, but the contrast is low. Move to **Slide 2**. Click in the title placeholder, and then click the title placeholder border to select it. On the **Home tab**, in the **Font group**, click the **Font Color arrow** [A], and then click the second option in the first row—**White, Text 1**. Click the **Bold** button [B].
3. Select the subtitle placeholder, and then on the **Home tab**, in the **Font group**, click the **Font Color** button [A] to apply the same color you applied to the title placeholder. With the placeholder still selected, click the **Bold** [B] and **Text Shadow** [S] buttons, and then click the **Increase Font Size** button [A] to increase the **Font Size** to **24**.

   In comparison to Slide 1, the contrast and readability are greatly increased.
4. Move to **Slide 3**. Right-click a blank area of the slide background, and then click **Format Background**. In the **Format Background** pane, select **Solid Fill** to increase contrast with the text. Compare your screen with **Figure 1**.
5. Press [F5] to view the presentation from the beginning, noticing the differences in design and contrast. Keep these presentation design ideas in mind as you develop your own PowerPoint presentations.

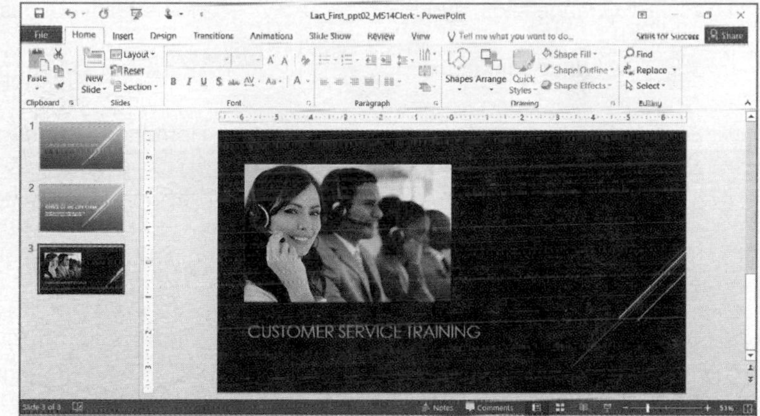

Wavebreak Media Ltd/123RF; PowerPoint 2016, Windows 10, Microsoft Corporation

Figure 1

6. Insert a **Header & Footer** on the **Notes and Handouts** pages. Include the **Date**, **Page Number**, and the **Footer** Last_First_ppt02_MS14Clerk
7. **Save** the presentation, and then submit your presentation as directed by your instructor.

- **You have completed More Skills 14**

The following table summarizes the **SKILLS AND PROCEDURES** covered in this chapter.

Skills Number	Task	Step	Icon	Keyboard Shortcut
1	Create new presentation	Start page → Template		
1	Add a new slide	Home tab → New Slide		Ctrl + M
2	Change theme	Design tab → Themes group		
2	Change theme variant	Design tab → Variants group		
2	Change slide layout	Home tab → Slides group → Layout button		
3	Change font color	Home tab → Font group → Font Color button		
3	Add text shadow	Home tab → Font group → Text Shadow button		
4	Change slide background	Design tab → Customize group → Format Background button		
6	Insert WordArt	Insert tab → Text group → WordArt button		
6	Convert text to WordArt	Select text → Format tab → WordArt Styles group → More button		
8	Add bullets	Home tab → Paragraph group → Bullets button		
8	Add numbering	Home tab → Paragraph group → Numbering button		
9	Cut text or object	Select text or object → Home tab → Clipboard group → Cut button		Ctrl + X
9	Copy text or object	Select text or object → Home tab → Clipboard group → Copy button		Ctrl + C
9	Paste text or object	Home tab → Clipboard group → Paste button		Ctrl + V
10	Copy formatting	Home tab → Clipboard group → Format Painter button		
10	Clear all formatting	Home tab → Font group → Clear All Formatting button		

Project Summary Chart		
Project	**Project Type**	**Project Location**
Skills Review	Review	In Book & MIL MyITLab® Grader
Skills Assessment 1	Review	In Book & MIL MyITLab® Grader
Skills Assessment 2	Review	Book
My Skills	Problem Solving	Book
Visual Skills Check	Problem Solving	Book
Skillls Challenge 1	Critical Thinking	Book
Skills Challenge 2	Critical Thinking	Book
More Skills Assessment	Review	In Book & MIL MyITLab® Grader
Collaborating with Google	Critical Thinking	Book

MOS Objectives Covered
1.1.1 Create a new presentation
1.1.2 Create a presentation based on a template
1.1.3 Import Word document outlines
1.2.1 Insert specific slide layouts
1.2.6 Modify individual slide backgrounds
2.1.2 Apply formatting and styles to text
2.1.3 Apply WordArt styles to text
2.1.5 Create bulleted and numbered lists
2.3.1 Insert images

Key Terms

BizSkills Video

1. Reflect on Joel and Sara's communication styles before, during, and after the meeting. List several ways in which each of them communicated in a nonprofessional or inappropriate manner.
2. Office communication includes not only speaking, but also written communication. What steps can you take to ensure that you come across professionally in written communication, including e-mail messages, reports, and presentations?

Online Help Skills

1. With PowerPoint open, click the **File** tab, and then in the upper right corner of the screen, click the **Microsoft PowerPoint Help** button [?], or press [F1].
2. In the **PowerPoint Help** window, use the **Search** box to locate and open the article *Use keyboard shortcuts to create your presentation*. Compare your screen with **Figure 1**.

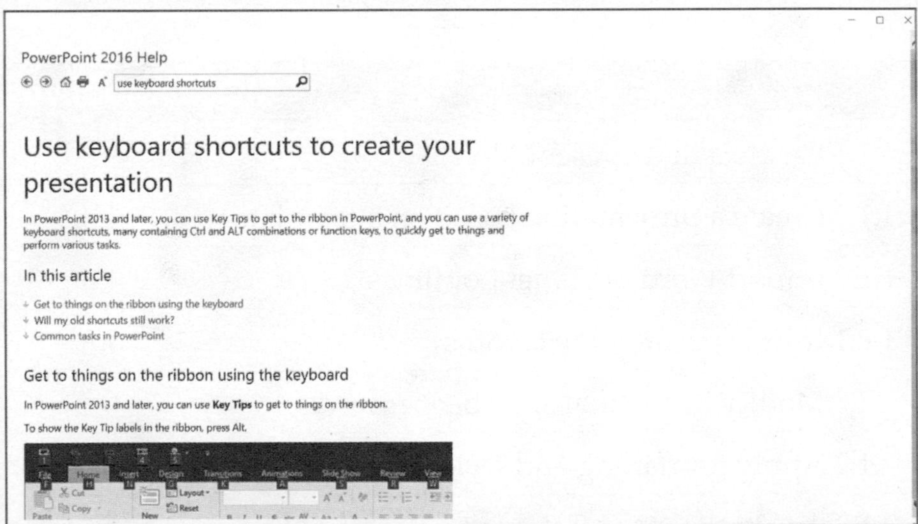

Figure 1 PowerPoint 2016, Windows 10, Microsoft Corporation

3. Read the article and answer the following question: What are two keyboard shortcuts that you might find most helpful, and why?

Matching 

Match each term in the second column with its correct definition in the first column by writing the letter of the term on the blank line in front of the correct definition.

___ **1.** When you point to an item in a gallery, this appears on screen and displays the name of the item.

___ **2.** A set of unified design elements that provides a look for your presentation using colors, fonts, and graphics.

___ **3.** Variations of the current theme, with different accent colors.

___ **4.** The Paste Option used to paste text as an image.

___ **5.** Listing of fonts you have selected and applied in the existing presentation.

___ **6.** Tool used to copy text formatting from one part of a presentation to another.

___ **7.** A text style used to create decorative effects in a presentation.

___ **8.** The font applied to all text in a presentation, except for the slide title.

___ **9.** A command that removes selected text or graphics from a presentation and then moves the selection to the clipboard.

___ **10.** A temporary storage area maintained by the operating system.

A Body font
B Clipboard
C Cut
D Format Painter
E Picture
F ScreenTip
G Theme
H Recently Used Fonts
I Theme variant
J WordArt

Multiple Choice

MyITLab®

Choose the correct answer.

1. The process of changing the appearance of the text, layout, or design of a slide.
   A. Editing
   B. Designing
   C. Formatting
2. On the Start screen, click these to display a preview of each of the templates and the variants of the theme.
   A. Template thumbnails
   B. Theme list
   C. Slide pane
3. Variations of the current theme, with different accent colors.
   A. Variant
   B. Color scheme
   C. Template
4. The effects and color choices in the Format Background pane are based on this.
   A. The image styles
   B. The slide layout
   C. The theme and variant
5. A slide layout that contains no title or content placeholders.
   A. Empty
   B. Normal
   C. Blank
6. The amount of room between letters of slide text.
   A. Alignment
   B. Character spacing
   C. Layout
7. The command used to duplicate a selection.
   A. Format Painter
   B. Cut
   C. Copy
8. In Paste Options, this selection removes all formatting from a selection of pasted text.
   A. Use Destination Theme
   B. Keep Source Formatting
   C. Keep Text Only
9. A command used to revert to font formatting associated with the original slide layout.
   A. Clear All Formatting
   B. Reset Format
   C. Reset Slide Layout
10. The mouse action necessary when Format Painter is to be used on multiple selections.
    A. Single-click
    B. Double-click
    C. Triple-click

Topics for Discussion

1. PowerPoint 2016 includes different design themes and variants. What should you consider when choosing a design theme for the presentations that you create?
2. Format Painter is an important tool used to maintain consistent formatting in a presentation. Why is consistency important when you format the slides in your presentations?

Skills Review

To complete this project, you will need the following files:

- New PowerPoint presentation
- ppt02_SRIntern1
- ppt02_SRIntern2

You will save your file as:

- Last_First_ppt02_SRInternship

---

1. Start **PowerPoint 2016**. On the **Start screen**, click the **Integral** theme thumbnail. Click the first variant in the second row. Click **Create**. Add the title Aspen Falls Internship Program and the subtitle 2018 On the **File tab**, click **Save As**, and then click **Browse**. In the **Save As** dialog box, navigate to your **PowerPoint Chapter 2** folder. Save the file as Last_First_ppt02_SRInternship
2. Insert a **New Slide** with the **Title and Content** layout. Add the title Program Goals and then apply **Bold** to the text in the title placeholder. In the content placeholder, type four points, pressing Enter after each except the last one: Professional growth | Beneficial service | Innovation | Skill development
3. Select the content placeholder. In the **Paragraph group**, click the **Numbering** button. Change the **Font Size** to **32**, and then apply **Bold** and **Text Shadow**. Click a blank area of the slide so that no placeholder is selected.
4. On the **Design tab**, in the **Customize group**, click the **Format Background** button. In the **Format Background** pane, select **Picture or texture fill**. Under **Insert picture from**, click the **File** button. From your student files, insert **ppt02_SRIntern1**. Compare your screen with **Figure 1**.
5. Insert a **New Slide** with the **Two Content** layout. Add the title Process and then apply **Bold**. In the left placeholder, type four points, pressing Enter after each entry except the last one: Complete application | Send letter of reference | Provide photo id | Participate in interview
6. On **Slide 2**, click the content placeholder. On the **Home tab**, in the **Clipboard group**, click the **Format Painter**.

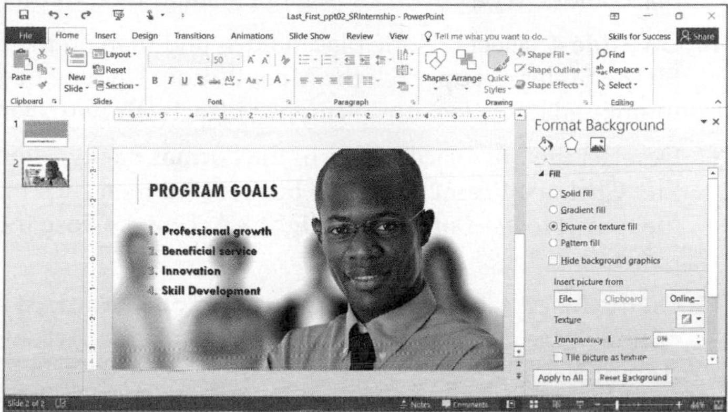

Minerva Studio/Fotolia; PowerPoint 2016, Windows 10, Microsoft Corporation **Figure 1**

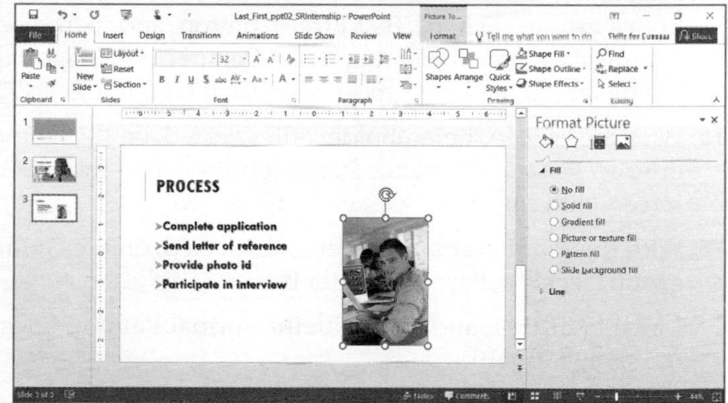

Goodluz/Fotolia; PowerPoint 2016, Windows 10, Microsoft Corporation **Figure 2**

7. On **Slide 3**, use the **Format Painter** to apply the formatting to all of the text in the left content placeholder. On the **Home tab**, in the **Paragraph group**, click the **Bullets arrow**, and then click **Bullets and Numbering**. Click **Arrow Bullets**, and then adjust the **Size** to 80% of text. Click **OK**.
8. In the right placeholder, click the **Pictures** button, and then insert the image **ppt02_SRIntern2**. Compare your screen with **Figure 2**.

■ **Continue to the next page to complete this Skills Review**

9. After Slide 3, insert a new **Slide 4** with the **Title Only** layout. In the title placeholder, type Aspen Falls City Hall and then **Center** and **Bold** the text.
10. On **Slide 4**, select the title placeholder, and then on the **Format tab**, in the **Shape Styles group**, click the **More** button. Under **Theme Styles**, click the first thumbnail in the last row—**Intense Effect – Brown, Dark 1**.
11. Deselect the title placeholder. In the **Format Background** pane, select **Gradient Fill**. Click the **Preset gradients** button, and then click the fourth thumbnail in the fourth row—**Bottom Spotlight – Accent 4**. **Close** the Format Background pane.
12. On the **Insert tab**, in the **Text group**, click the **WordArt** button. Select the fourth option in the third row—**Fill – White, Outline – Accent 2, Hard Shadow – Accent 2**.
13. Accept the default location, and then replace the WordArt text with Welcome college interns!
14. Select the WordArt placeholder. On the **Format tab**, in the **WordArt Styles group**, click the **Text Effects** button, and then click **Shadow**. Under **Perspective**, click the first option—**Perspective Diagonal Upper Left**. On the **Home tab**, in the **Font group**, increase the **Font Size** to **72**.
15. With the WordArt placeholder still selected, on the **Home tab**, in the **Font group**, click the **Character Spacing** button, and then click **Loose**. Compare your screen with **Figure 3**.
16. With the WordArt placeholder still selected, on the **Home tab**, in the **Clipboard group**, click the **Format Painter** button.
17. Move to **Slide 1**, and then with the **Format Painter**, select the text *2018* to apply the same formatting.
18. With the subtitle still selected, on the **Home tab**, in the **Font group**, click the **Font arrow**, and then click **Broadway**. Click a blank area of the slide so that no placeholders are selected.
19. Insert a **Header & Footer** on all **Notes and Handouts** pages with the **Date and Time**, the **Page Number**, and the **Footer** Last_First_ppt02_SRInternship
20. **Save** the presentation, and then compare your presentation with **Figure 4**. Submit the file as directed. **Close** PowerPoint.

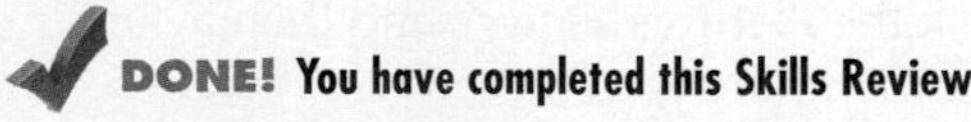

DONE! You have completed this Skills Review

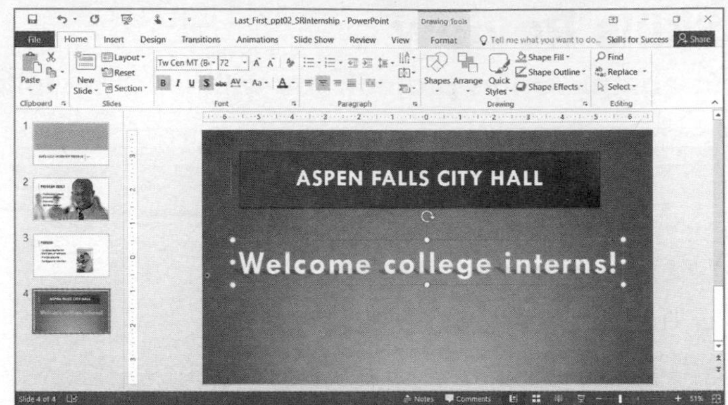

Figure 3 PowerPoint 2016, Windows 10, Microsoft Corporation

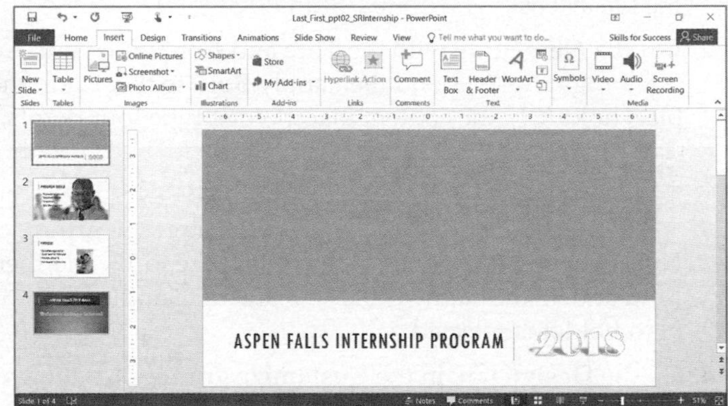

Figure 4 PowerPoint 2016, Windows 10, Microsoft Corporation

Skills Assessment 1

To complete this project, you will need the following files:

- New PowerPoint presentation
- ppt02_SA1Thumbs
- ppt02_SA1Phone

You will save your file as:

- Last_First_ppt02_SA1SocialMedia

---

1. Start **PowerPoint 2016**, and then create a new presentation with the **Mesh theme**. Do not change the variant. **Save** the file in your **PowerPoint Chapter 2** folder as Last_First_ppt02_SA1SocialMedia
2. In the title placeholder, type Social Media and then in the subtitle placeholder, type Aspen Falls City Hall Change the subtitle **Font Size** to 32, the **Character Spacing** to **Loose**, and the **Font Color** to **Light Blue**.
3. Insert a **New Slide** with the **Title and Content** layout. In the title placeholder, type Social Media and Local Government
4. In the content placeholder, type the following bullet points: Official Aspen Falls page | Open line of communication with citizens | Posts closely monitored and responded to
5. Use the **Format Painter** to apply the formatting from the subtitle on **Slide 1** to the bullet points on **Slide 2**.
6. Insert a **New Slide** with the **Picture with Caption** layout. **Copy** the title from **Slide 2**, and then **Paste** the selection to the title placeholder on **Slide 3**. In the picture placeholder, insert the image **ppt02_SA1Thumbs**. In the text placeholder, type Connecting citizens of Aspen Falls with local government Select the text placeholder, change the **Font Size** to **24**, and then apply **Italic**.
7. Insert a **New Slide** with the **Section Header** layout. In the title placeholder, type Information at our citizens' fingertips In the text placeholder, type Aspen Falls
8. Select the title placeholder. Use the **Format tab** to apply the WordArt style—**Fill – Blue-Gray, Background 2, Inner Shadow**. Change the **Font Size** to **54**. Select the text placeholder, and then apply the same WordArt style.

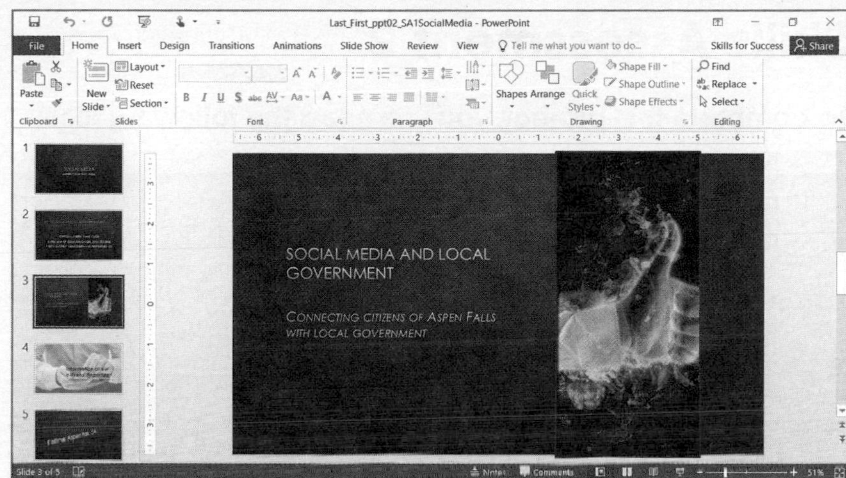

Detelina Petkova/Fotolia; PowerPoint 2016, Windows 10, Microsoft Corporation **Figure 1**

9. Insert the image **ppt02_SA1Phone** into the slide background, and then adjust the transparency to **50%**. **Close** the task pane.
10. Insert a new **Slide 5** with a **Blank** layout. Insert **WordArt** with the style **Fill – White, Text 1, Shadow**, with the text Follow Aspen Falls, CA! Include the exclamation point. Accept the default location for the WordArt. Increase the **Font Size** of the WordArt to **66**. To the WordArt, add the **Text Effect 3-D Rotation, Perspective Contrasting Right**.
11. Insert a **Header & Footer** on all **Notes and Handouts** pages. Include the date, page number, and the footer Last_First_ppt02_SA1SocialMedia
12. Compare your presentation with **Figure 1**. **Save** your presentation, and then submit the file as directed by your instructor. **Close** PowerPoint.

Skills Assessment 2

To complete this project, you will need the following files:

- New PowerPoint presentation
- ppt02_SA2Phone1
- ppt02_SA2Phone2

You will save your file as:

- Last_First_ppt02_SA2CallCenter

1. Start **PowerPoint 2016**, and then create a new presentation with the **Organic** theme. Do not change the variant. **Save** the file in your **PowerPoint Chapter 2** folder as Last_First_ppt02_SA2CallCenter
2. On **Slide 1**, in the title placeholder, type Call Center Training and then apply the second WordArt style in the second row—**Gradient Fill – Orange, Accent 1, Reflection**.
3. In the subtitle placeholder, type Aspen Falls City Hall Change the **Font** to **Verdana**, and then change the **Font Size** to **28**.
4. Insert a new **Slide 2** with the **Two Content** layout. Add the title Providing Phone Support In the left content placeholder, insert the image **ppt02_SA2Phone1**.
5. In the right content placeholder, type the following points: Answer within 4 rings | Offer a pleasant greeting | Transfer as appropriate | Follow up as needed
6. Select the four bullet points, and then change the **Font Color** to **Black, Text 1**, change the **Font Size** to **28**, and adjust the **Line Spacing** to **1.5**.
7. With the four bullet points still selected, change the bullets to **Checkmark Bullets**, and then adjust them to **75%** of text.
8. Insert a new **Slide 3** with the **Two Content** layout. Change the **Background** to **Gradient Fill**.
9. In the title placeholder, type Teamwork In the right content placeholder, insert the image **ppt02_SA2Phone2**. In the left content placeholder, type the following points and then format them as a numbered list: Attempt to assist | Ask a team member for input | Refer to a supervisor | Follow up Change the **Font Size** to **28** for all text in the left content placeholder.

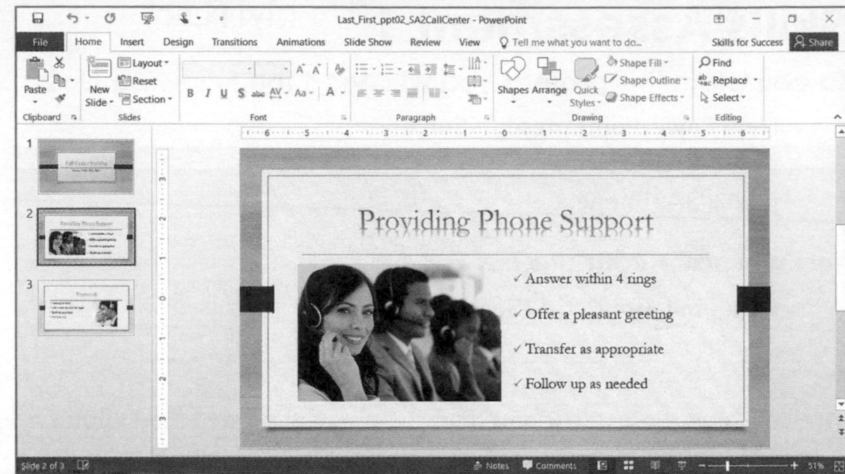

Figure 1 WavebreakmediaMicro/Fotolia; PowerPoint 2016, Windows 10, Microsoft Corporation

10. On **Slide 3**, select the text *Follow up* and change the **Font Color** to **Green, Accent 1**, apply **Bold**, and then change the **Character Spacing** to **Loose**.
11. Use the **Format Painter** to copy the formatting from the Slide 1 title—*Call Center Training*—to the titles on **Slides 2** and **3**.
12. Insert a **Header & Footer** on all **Notes and Handouts** pages. Include the date, page number, and the footer Last_First_ppt02_SA2CallCenter
13. Compare your completed presentation with **Figure 1**. **Save** your presentation, and then submit the file as directed by your instructor. **Close** PowerPoint.

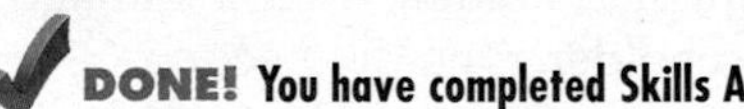

DONE! You have completed Skills Assessment 2

My Skills

To complete this presentation, you will need the following files:

- New PowerPoint presentation
- ppt02_MYMeeting1
- ppt02_MYMeeting2

You will save your file as:

- Last_First_ppt02_MYMeeting

1. Start **PowerPoint 2016**, and then create a new presentation with the **Facet** theme, with the second variant in the first row. **Save** the file in your **PowerPoint Chapter 2** folder as Last_First_ppt02_MYMeeting
2. On **Slide 1**, in the title placeholder, type Student Government Meetings
3. In the subtitle placeholder on **Slide 1**, type the name of your college, and then apply the first WordArt style—**Fill – Black, Text 1, Shadow**. Increase the **Font Size** to **24**.
4. Insert a new **Slide 2** with the **Two Content** layout. In the title placeholder, type Productive College Meeting Guidelines In the right content placeholder, insert the image **ppt02_MYMeeting1**.
5. On **Slide 2**, in the left content placeholder, type the following points: Send an invitation with agenda | Stay on track and on time | Involve all participants | Avoid creating a stressful meeting atmosphere
6. Select the left content placeholder, change the **Font Size** to **24**, and then adjust the **Line Spacing** to **1.5**.
7. With the four bullet points still selected, change the bullets to **Star Bullets**, and then change the size of the bullets to **70%** of text.
8. Insert a new **Slide 3** with the **Section Header** layout. Change the background for the newly inserted slide to **Picture Fill**, and then insert the image **ppt02_MYMeeting2**. Set the image's transparency to **50%**. Close the task pane.
9. In the title placeholder, type Productive Meetings Center the title text, and then apply bold and text shadow. Change the **Font Size** to 48.

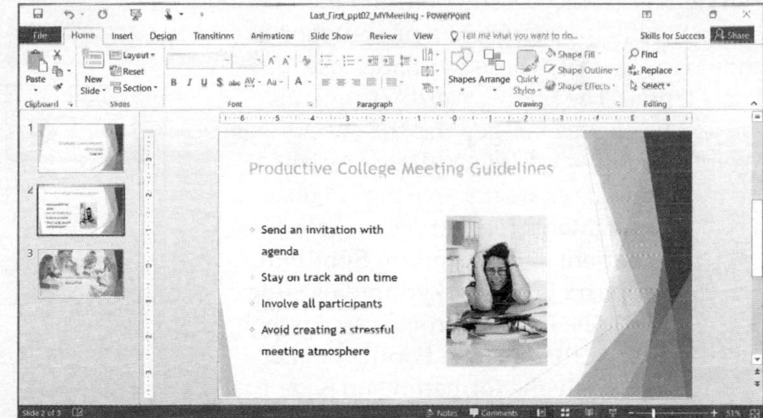

Picture-Factory/Fotolia; PowerPoint 2016, Windows 10, Microsoft Corporation

Figure 1

10. In the text placeholder, type Beneficial to all! Use the **Format Painter** to apply the **Slide 1** subtitle formatting to the text *Beneficial to all!*, and then **Center** the text.
11. Insert a **Header & Footer** on all **Notes and Handouts** pages. Include the date, page number, and the footer Last_First_ppt02_MYMeeting
12. Compare your completed presentation with **Figure 1**. **Save** your presentation, and then **Close** PowerPoint. Submit the file as directed by your instructor.

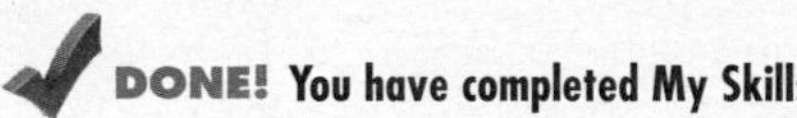

DONE! You have completed My Skills

Visual Skills Check

To complete this presentation, you will need the following files:

- New PowerPoint presentation
- ppt02_VSBadge

You will save your file as:

- Last_First_ppt02_VSNewHire

Start a new, blank presentation, and then create the first two slides of a presentation as shown in **Figure 1**. These two slides use the **Basis** theme. The Slide 1 WordArt contains the text Employee Badges and the style of this WordArt is **Fill – White, Outline – Accent 1, Shadow**, and its character spacing is **Loose**. The subtitle contains the text Aspen Falls City Hall The gradient named **Bottom Spotlight – Accent 1** appears in the background of **Slide 1**. On **Slide 2**, the image is from your student files—**ppt02_VSBadge**. The Format Painter was used to apply the formatting on Slide 1 to the title on Slide 2. For the numbered list, the font color is **Green, Accent 1, Darker 50%**, and the numbers are sized at **90%** and are the same font color as the text. **Save** the presentation as Last_First_ppt02_VSNewHire and then insert the date, file name, and page number in the **Notes and Handouts** footer. Submit the file as directed by your instructor.

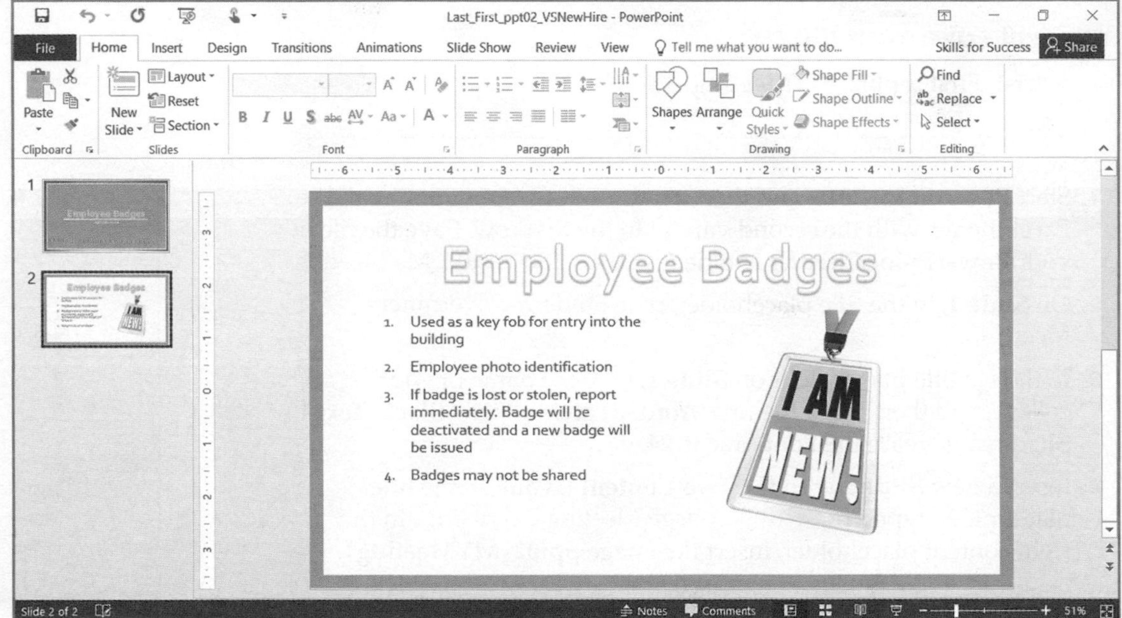

Figure 1 iQoncept/Fotolia; PowerPoint 2016, Windows 10, Microsoft Corporation

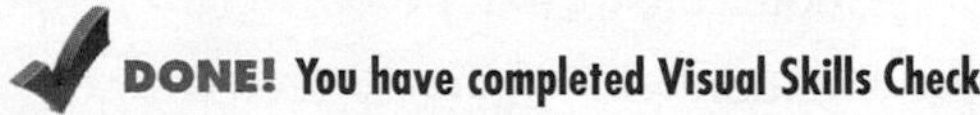
DONE! You have completed Visual Skills Check

Skills Challenge 1

To complete this presentation, you will need the following files:

- ppt02_SC1CellPhone
- ppt02_SC1CellPicture

You will save your file as:

- Last_First_ppt02_SC1CellPhone

Using the skills you have practiced in this chapter, correct the errors and issues with the presentation named **ppt02_SC1CellPhone**. Add the image named **ppt02_SC1CellPicture** to the Slide 1 slide background. Pick a theme and variant that have a background that complements the image used on Slide 1. Adjust the fonts or background so that the text is easy to read. On Slide 2, add numbering to the bullet points that begin with the text *No surfing*, *No texting*, *Limit personal*, and *Phones must be.* Adjust the numbers so that they are smaller than the text.

Resize the fonts on Slide 2 so they are easy to read, and adjust the line spacing so that the text fills the placeholder. Use WordArt to enhance the appearance of one of the titles in the presentation. Change the font color, and add one other enhancement to the text *Please use your break times for these activities*. Insert a new Slide 3 with the Section Header layout. Copy the title and subtitle from Slide 1. Paste them into the appropriate placeholders on Slide 3, and adjust font colors and sizes as needed. **Save** the presentation as Last_First_ppt02_SC1CellPhone Add a footer to the Notes and Handouts pages with the date, file name, and page number, and then check spelling in the presentation. Submit the file as directed by your instructor.

DONE! You have completed Skills Challenge 1

Skills Challenge 2

To complete this presentation, you will need the following file:

- New blank presentation

You will save your file as:

- Last_First_ppt02_SC2College

Using the skills you have practiced in this chapter, create a presentation with six slides describing a college at which you would like to continue your education after graduating from your current program. Apply an appropriate theme, and change the fonts and colors themes. On at least one slide, format the slide background with a picture that depicts the college that you choose. On the first slide, format the slide title by using a WordArt style. Include in your presentation a numbered list that indicates at least four reasons why you would like to attend this college. The remaining slides may include information about the programs, culture, and benefits of attending this college.

Format the last slide with the Section Header layout, and enter text that briefly summarizes your presentation. Check the spelling in the presentation. Add a footer to the Notes and Handouts pages with the date, page numbers, and footer text Last_First_ppt02_SC2College **Save** the presentation as Last_First_ppt02_SC2College and then submit as directed by your instructor.

DONE! You have completed Skills Challenge 2

More Skills Assessment

To complete this project, you will need the following files:

- ppt02_MSABudget
- ppt02_MSABudgetOutline

You will save your file as:

- Last_First_ppt02_MSABudget (template)

1. From your student data files, locate and open **ppt02_MSABudget**.
2. On **Slide 1**, to increase contrast, select the title, and then change the **Font Color** to **White, Text 1**. Add **Text Shadow** to the title.
3. Click the **New Slide arrow**, and then use **Slides from Outline** to insert new slides from the Word document named **ppt02_MSABudgetOutline**.
4. Switch to **Slide Master** view. Scroll to the top of the thumbnail pane, and then click the top slide—**Slide Master**.
5. Select the title placeholder, change the **Font** to **Century Gothic**, and then switch back to Normal view.
6. Display **Slide 2**. Place your insertion point after the word *employees* in the last bullet point and then press Enter. Add a new bullet point with the text Enter meeting dates and times here
7. Display **Slide 3**. Place your insertion point after the word *plan* in the last bullet point, and then press Enter. Add a new bullet point with the text Enter action plan deadline here Compare your screen with **Figure 1**.
8. Insert a **Header & Footer** on the **Notes and Handouts** pages. Include the date, page number, and the footer Last_First_ppt02_MSABudget
9. Click the **File tab**, and then **Export** the presentation as a template. **Save** the template in your **PowerPoint Chapter 2** folder as Last_First_ppt02_MSABudget **Close** PowerPoint.
10. Submit the file as directed.

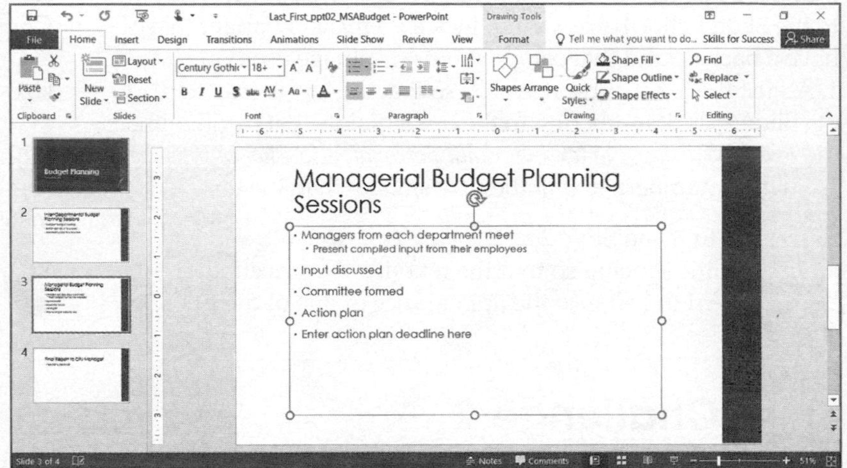

Figure 1 PowerPoint 2016, Windows 10, Microsoft Corporation

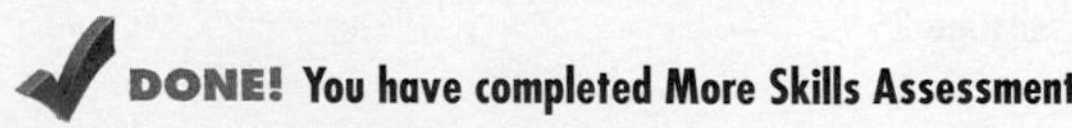

DONE! You have completed More Skills Assessment

Collaborating with Google

To complete this project, you will need a Google account (refer to the Common Features chapter) and the following files:

- **ppt02_GoogleImage**
- **ppt02_GoogleSlides**

You will save your file as:

- **Last_First_ppt02_GPSnip**

---

1. Open the Google Chrome web browser. Log into your Google account, and then click the **Google Apps** button.
2. Click the **Drive** button to open Google Drive. If you receive a pop-up message, read the message, and then click **Next**. Read each message, and then close the dialog box.
3. Click the **New** button, and then click **Google Slides**.
4. In the **Choose a Theme** pane, scroll down and click **Spotlight** or another theme, and then click **OK**. **Close** the Themes pane.
5. Click the **Background** button.
6. Click the **Image Choose** button. Click the **Choose an image to upload** button. Navigate to your student data files and click **ppt02_GoogleImage**, and then click **Open**. In the **Background** dialog box, click **Done**.
7. Select the title placeholder, click the **Text color** button, and then change the text color to **white**. Repeat the same process to change the color of the subtitle placeholder to **white**.
8. In the title placeholder, type Email Safety Select the placeholder, click the **Align button**, and then click **Right**.
9. In the subtitle placeholder, type Aspen Falls IT Select the placeholder, click the **Align** button, and then click **Right**. Compare your screen with **Figure 1**.
10. Click the **File tab**, and then click **Import slides**. Click the **Upload tab**, and then click the **Select a file from your computer** button. Navigate to your student data files, click **ppt02_GoogleSlides**, and then click **Open**.
11. Toward the right side of the **Import slides** dialog box, click the **Select slides: All** link to select both slides.
12. Click the **Import Slides** button, and then compare your screen with **Figure 2**.

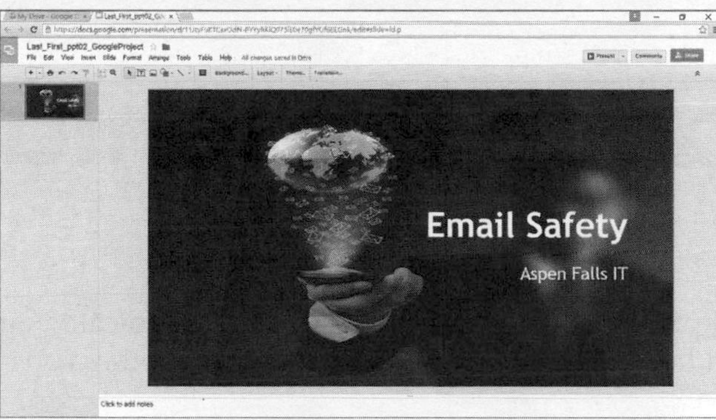
Email Safety
Aspen Falls IT

Figure 1

Email Safety

Aspen Falls IT

Figure 2

13. Click the **Share** button. In the **Name before sharing** box, type Last_First_ppt02_GoogleProject and then click **Save**. In the **Share with others** dialog box, type AspenFallsEvents@gmail.com to share the sheet with another user.
14. In the **Add a note** text box, type Slides from IT were imported; please import slides from HR.
15. Click **Send**.
16. Press [Windows], type snip and then press [Enter] to start the Snipping Tool. Click the **New arrow**, and then click **Full-screen Snip**.
17. In the **Snipping Tool** mark-up window, click the **Save Snip** button [Save]. In the **Save As** dialog box, navigate to your **PowerPoint Chapter 2** folder. Be sure the **Save as type** box displays **JPEG file**. Name the file Last_First_ppt02_GPSnip and then press [Enter]. **Close** [X] the Snipping Tool mark-up window.
18. Close all windows, and then submit your work as directed by your instructor.

DONE! You have completed Collaborating with Google

CHAPTER 3

Enhance Presentations with Graphics

- Appropriate presentation graphics visually communicate your message and help your audience understand the points you want to convey.
- It is a good practice to evaluate the graphics that you use, the text on your slides, and your spoken words to ensure that your presentation is coherent, precise, and accurate.
- It is helpful to review the procedures in your organization so that you are familiar with how presentations are shared using slide libraries and other file-sharing procedures.
- When effective and illustrative diagrams are needed, you can use SmartArt graphics to list information and show processes and relationships.
- Replacing bullet points with SmartArt graphics can add interest and variety to a presentation.

auremar/fotolia

Aspen Falls City Hall

In this chapter, you will create a presentation promoting Aspen Falls' new employee enrichment program. This program aims to improve career satisfaction and productivity for employees. It is being modeled after a similar program created at a local company—Samway Investments. It was so successful in increasing productivity that Maria Martinez, the City Manager, asked managers at Samway for permission to use their information. The managers agreed and have provided some of their materials, including a presentation.

In your career, you may reuse materials, including slides, created for a previous project. This will save you time and allow you to work efficiently and cooperatively. To keep your presentations engaging and appealing, you can search Microsoft's Online Pictures gallery and insert pictures. You may insert shapes to communicate your message and modify those shapes to add interest. With SmartArt, you can take a plain bulleted list and change it to an easy-to-read diagram with clear separation between different elements. Videos add interest to your presentation, and you can use PowerPoint to add borders and styles and to correct the colors.

In this project, you will start with a new blank presentation and reuse slides from another presentation. You will insert, size, move, and align images and shapes, add text, and apply styles to shapes. You will also insert and format a SmartArt graphic and a video.

Time to complete all 10 skills—60 to 90 minutes

Outcome

Using the skills in this chapter, you will be able to import slides from other presentations, insert and enhance images to add interest, work with text in shapes to organize information, use SmartArt to convey your message, and add videos to your slide show.

Objectives

3.1 Collaborate and combine presentations by reusing slides from other presentations

3.2 Compose presentations using graphics and videos to enhance your message

3.3 Use SmartArt graphics to create diagrams that show lists and processes

3.4 Modify images, SmartArt, and videos to enhance their appearance

Student data files needed for this chapter:

New PowerPoint presentation
ppt03_EnrichmentSamway
ppt03_EnrichmentProductivity
ppt03_EnrichmentVideo

You will save your file as:

Last_First_ppt03_Enrichment

SKILLS

MyITLab® Skills 1-10 Training

At the end of this chapter, you will be able to:

Skill 1 Insert Slides from Other Presentations
Skill 2 Insert, Size, and Move Online Pictures
Skill 3 Modify Picture Shapes, Borders, and Effects
Skill 4 Insert, Size, and Move Shapes
Skill 5 Add Text to Shapes and Insert Text Boxes
Skill 6 Apply Gradient Fills and Group and Align Graphics
Skill 7 Convert Text to SmartArt Graphics and Add Shapes
Skill 8 Modify SmartArt Layouts, Colors, and Styles
Skill 9 Insert Video Files
Skill 10 Apply Video Styles and Adjust Videos

MORE SKILLS

Skill 11 Compress Pictures
Skill 12 Save Groups as Picture Files
Skill 13 Change Object Order
Skill 14 Insert a Screen Shot in a Presentation

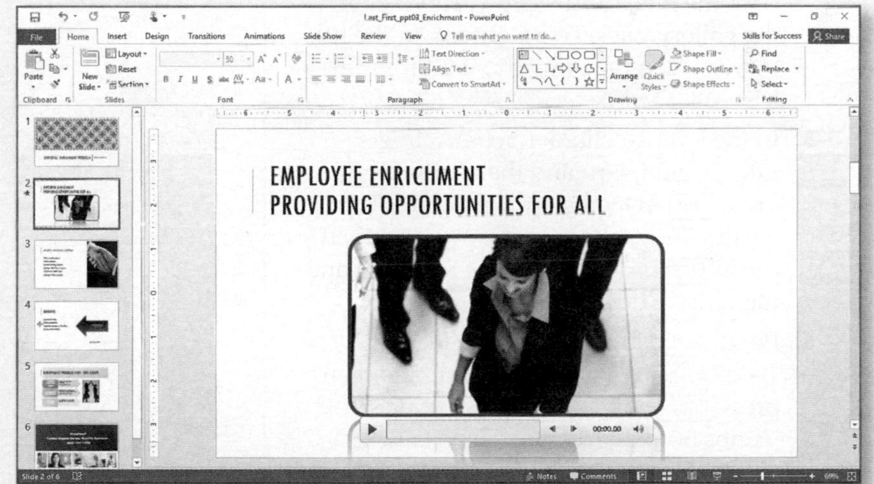

Minerva Studio/Fotolia

► Presentation slides can be shared so that frequently used content does not need to be recreated.

1. Start **PowerPoint 2016**, and then create a new presentation with the **Integral** template and default variant.
2. In the title placeholder, type Employee Enrichment Program and then in the subtitle placeholder, type Aspen Falls City Hall Compare your screen with **Figure 1**.

   When a placeholder has text formatted in all caps, it is a good idea to type the text with normal capitalization in case you change the formatting or theme later.

3. On the Quick Access Toolbar, click **Save** [Save icon]. Navigate to the location where you are saving your files, create a folder named PowerPoint Chapter 3 and then using your own name, **Save** the document as Last_First_ppt03_Enrichment
4. On the **Home tab**, in the **Slides group**, click the **New Slide arrow**, and then in the gallery, click **Two Content**. In the title placeholder, type Enrichment Program Kick-Off Events
5. In the left placeholder, type Wellness Lunch and Learn and then press Enter. Press Tab to increase the list level. Type Health and wellness presenter and then press Enter. Type Lunch by Toole Inn and then press Enter.
6. Press Shift + Tab to decrease the list level. Type De-Stress for Less Seminar and then press Enter. Press Tab. Type Products and demos from merchants at Sea View Mall and then press Enter. Type Aromatherapy classes Compare your screen with **Figure 2**.

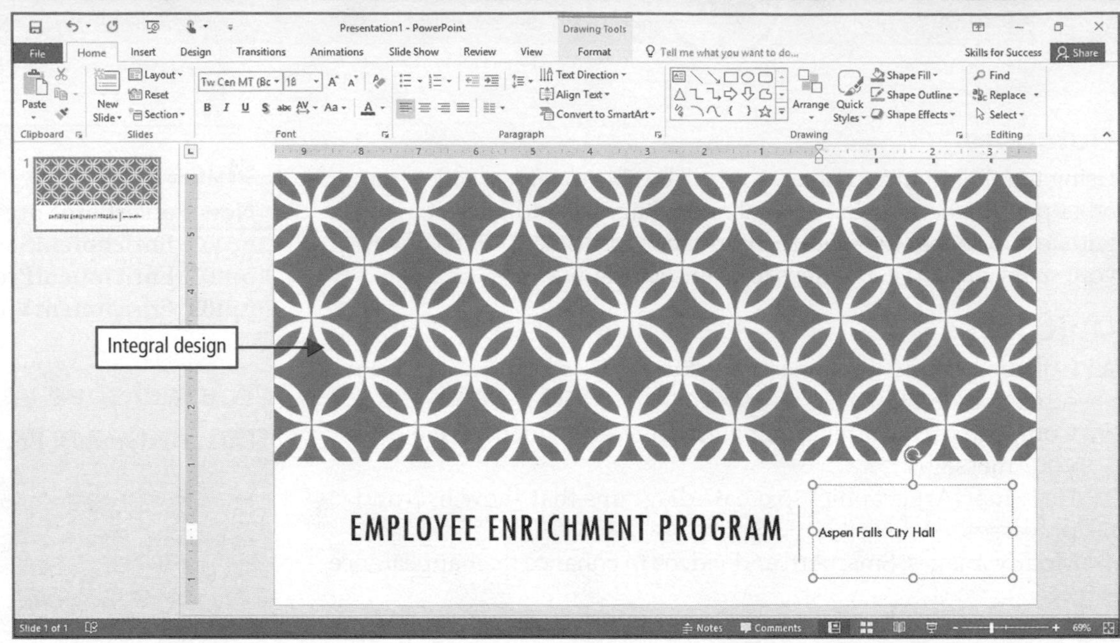

Figure 1

PowerPoint 2016, Windows 10, Microsoft Corporation

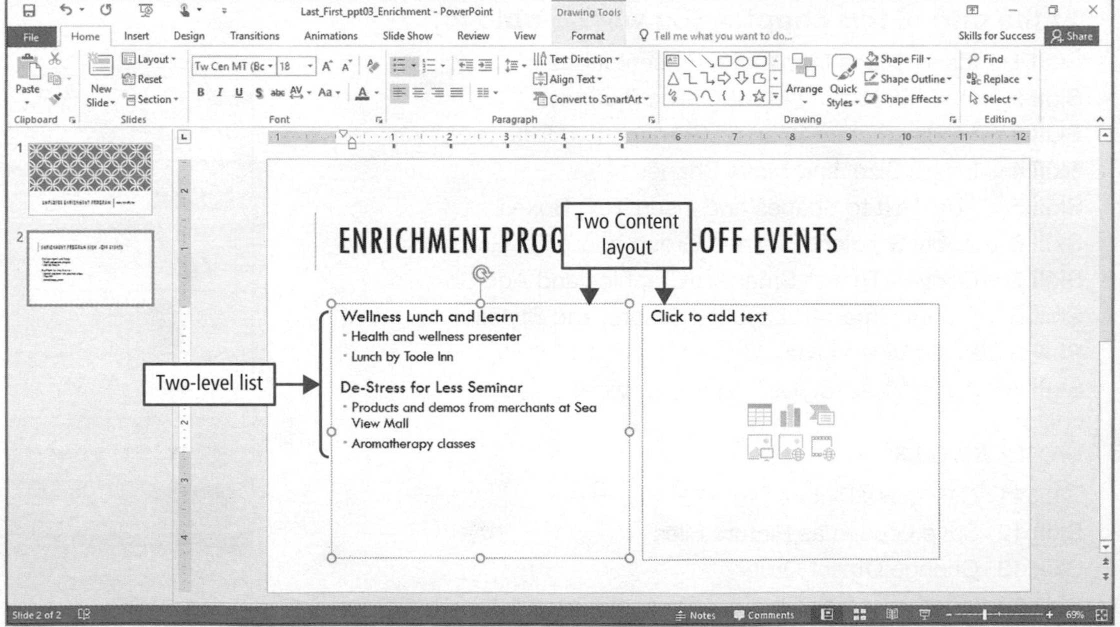

Figure 2

PowerPoint 2016, Windows 10, Microsoft Corporation

■ Continue to the next page to complete the skill

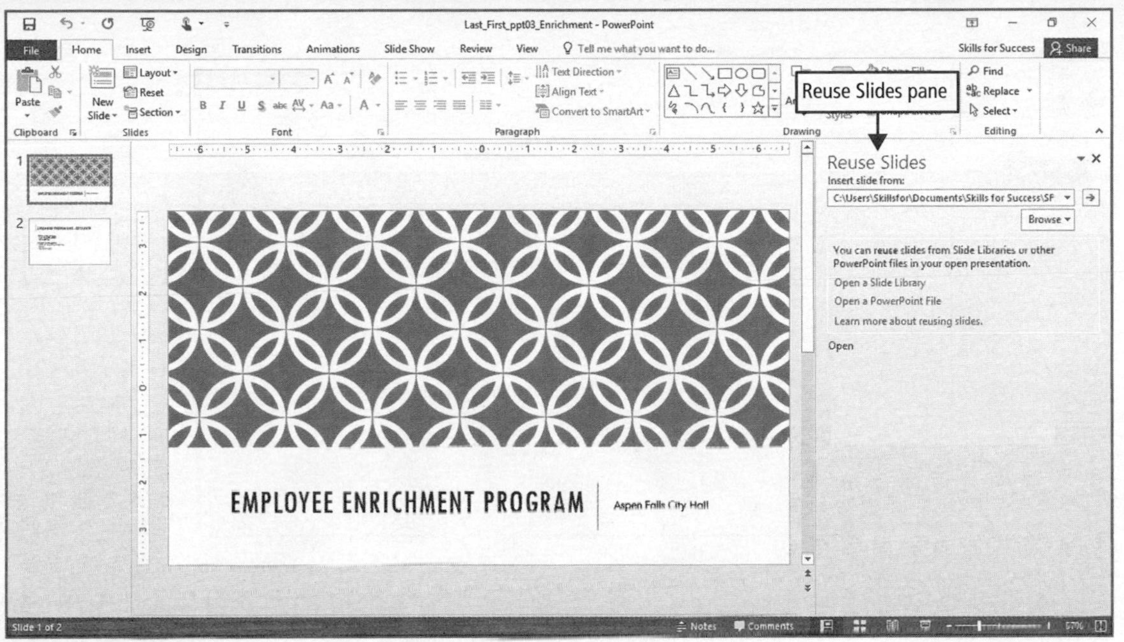

PowerPoint 2016, Windows 10, Microsoft Corporation

Figure 3

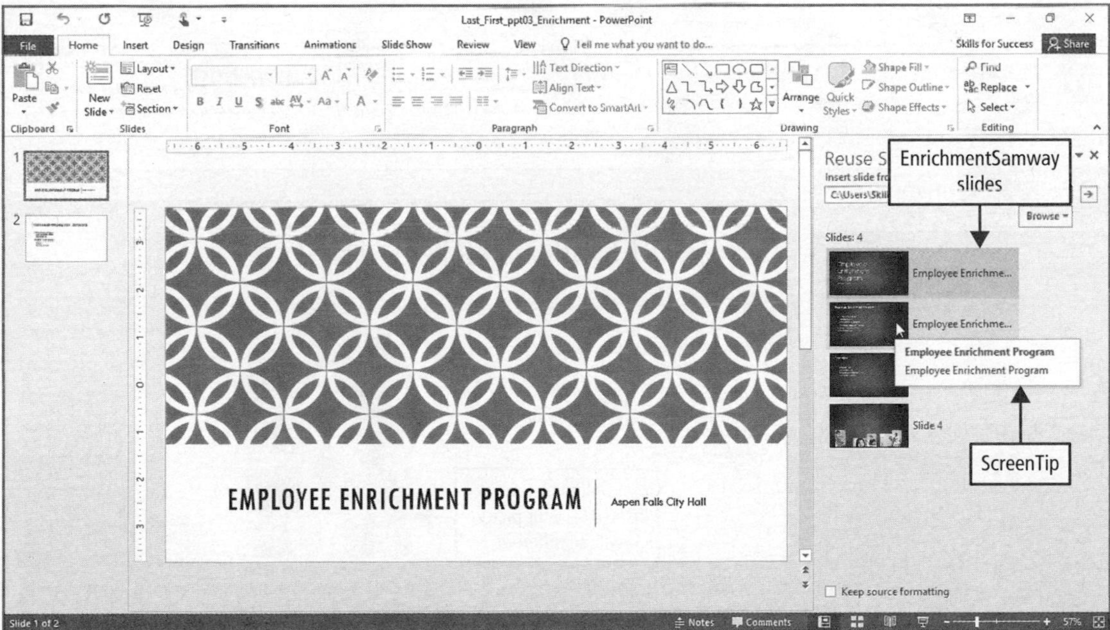

PowerPoint 2016, Windows 10, Microsoft Corporation

Figure 4

7. Move to **Slide 1**. On the **Home tab**, in the **Slides group**, click the **New Slide arrow**. Below the gallery, click **Reuse Slides** to display the **Reuse Slides** pane as shown in **Figure 3**.

8. In the **Reuse Slides** pane, click **Browse**, and then click **Browse File**. In the **Browse** dialog box, navigate to the student files for this chapter, click **ppt03_EnrichmentSamway**, and then click **Open**.

MOS Obj 5.1.1

You can use the Reuse Slides pane to insert all of the slides from another presentation or insert only the slides you need.

9. At the bottom of the **Reuse Slides** pane, verify that the **Keep source formatting** check box is cleared. Point to the second slide thumbnail—*Employee Enrichment Program*—to view a ScreenTip with the slide title as shown in **Figure 4**.

10. Still pointing to the second slide in the **Reuse Slides** pane, click the **Employee Enrichment Program** slide—the second slide—to insert it in the current presentation.

With the *Keep source formatting* option cleared, the formatting of the current presentation is applied to the inserted slide.

11. In the **Reuse Slides** pane, right-click the third slide—*Benefits*.

On the shortcut menu, you have the option to insert only the selected slide or to insert all of the slides in the current presentation.

12. Click **Insert Slide**, and then in the upper right corner of the **Reuse Slides** pane, click the **Close** button [X] to close the pane.

13. **Save** [save icon] the file.

■ **You have completed Skill 1 of 10**

► Online images are available from a variety of sources in many different formats, including .jpg, .tif, and .bmp files.

MOS Obj 2.3.1

1. Display **Slide 4**. In the right content placeholder, click the **Online Pictures** button to display the **Insert Pictures** dialog box. Compare your screen with **Figure 1**.

   Online pictures include images, such as graphics, drawings, or photographs, accessed from Bing Image Search, OneDrive, or online providers.

2. In the **Insert Pictures** dialog box, in the **Bing** search box, type teamwork success and then press Enter.

3. In the **Search Results**, locate an image related to teamwork and success. Click any image to select it. Click the **Insert** button to insert the image into the right content placeholder in your presentation. Your image will vary from the picture shown in the figure. Compare your screen with **Figure 2**.

   The image is inserted into the right content placeholder and sized to fit.

4. With the image selected, on the **Format tab**, in the **Size group**, in the **Height** box, type 3.5 and then press Enter. If needed, resize your image to fit it onto the slide.

   When a shape's height is changed, the width is automatically adjusted, unless the aspect ratio is unlocked.

■ **Continue to the next page to complete the skill**

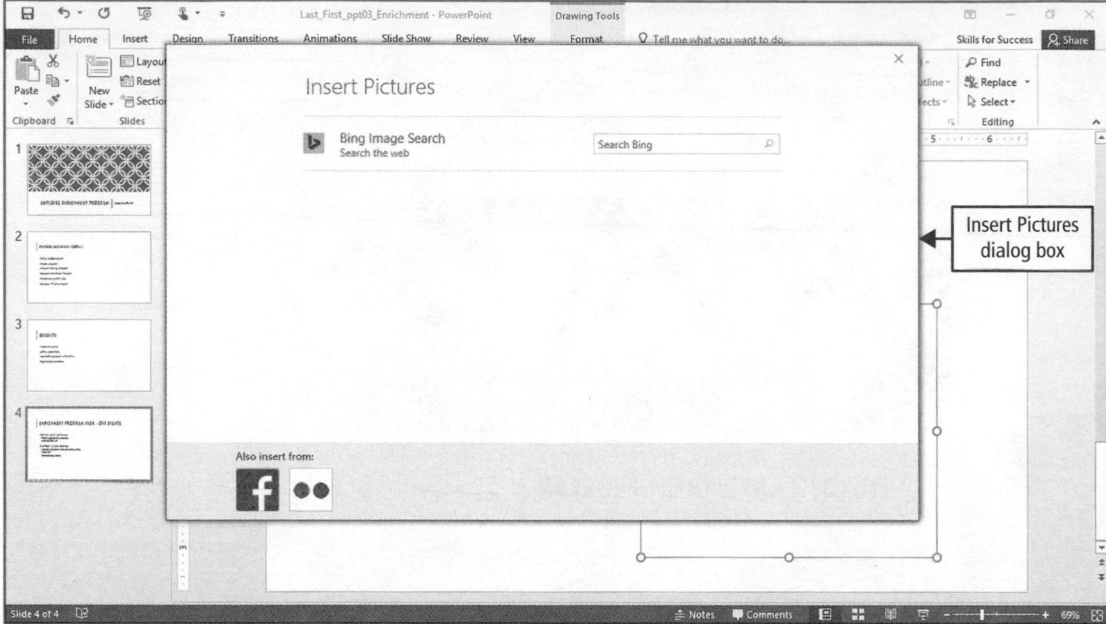

Figure 1

PowerPoint 2016, Windows 10, Microsoft Corporation

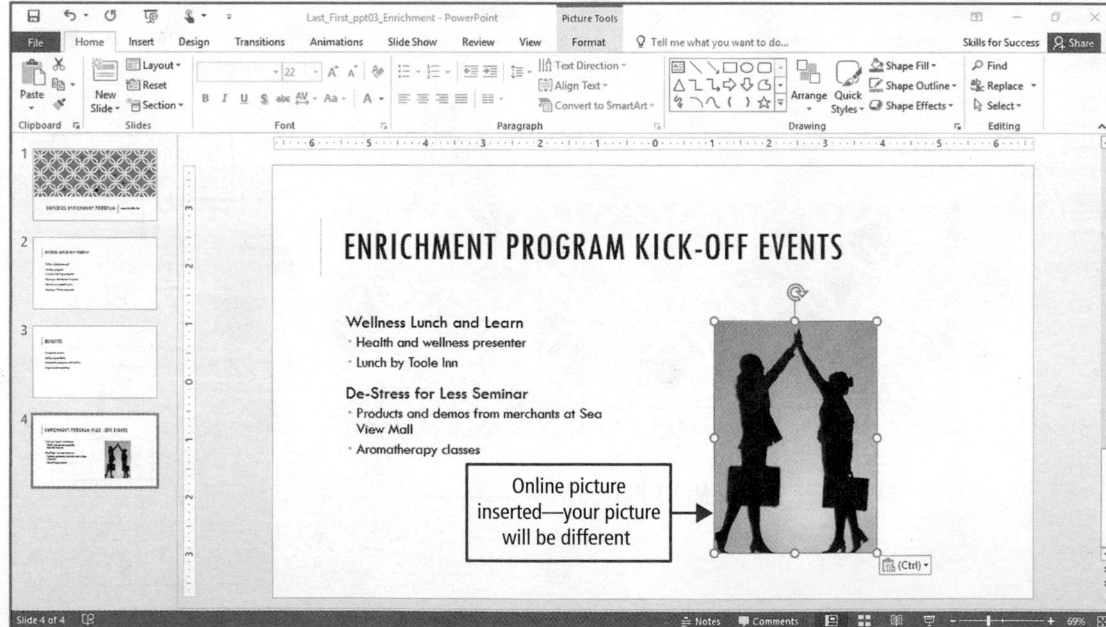

Figure 2

PowerPoint 2016, Windows 10, Microsoft Corporation

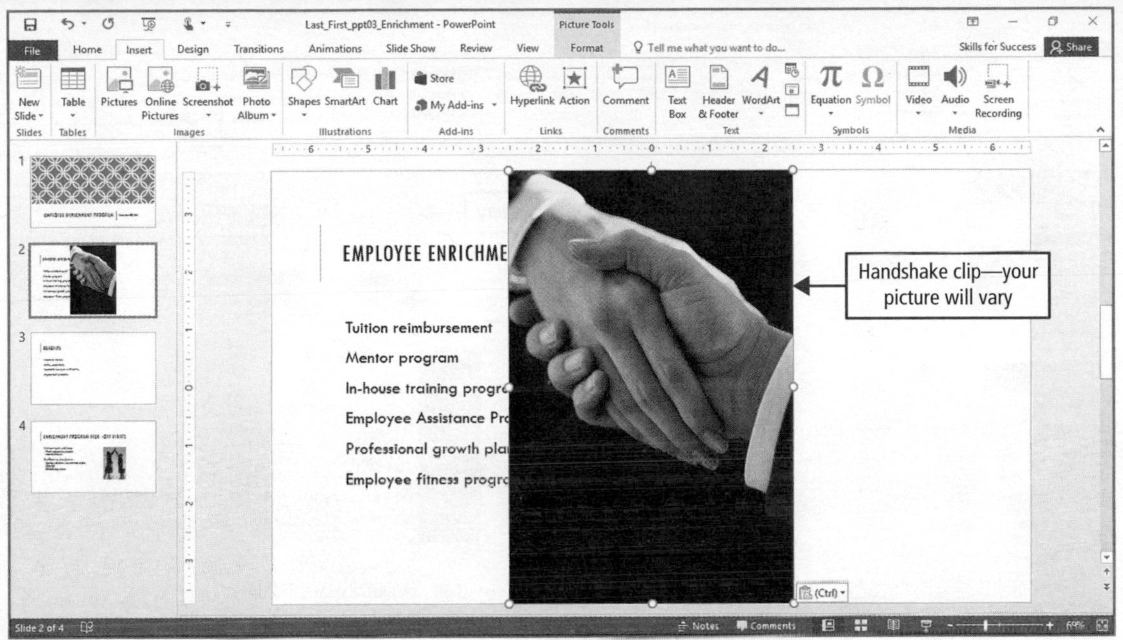

PowerPoint 2016, Windows 10, Microsoft Corporation

Figure 3

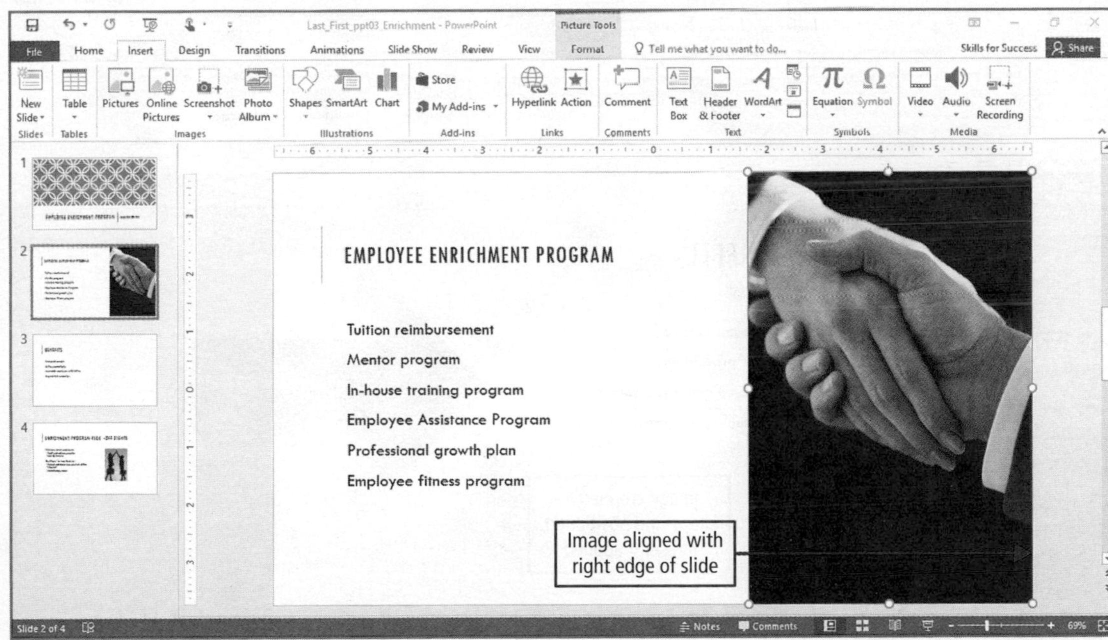

PowerPoint 2016, Windows 10, Microsoft Corporation

Figure 4

5. Display **Slide 2**. On the **Insert tab**, in the **Images group**, click the **Online Pictures** button. In the **Bing** search box, type handshake and then press Enter.
6. In the search results, point to any of the images to display information about the image—the name of the clip containing the search words you entered, the size of the clip, and, if applicable, the author or company—in the lower left corner of the search box.
7. Locate an image similar to the one shown in the figure and choose a picture with a vertical layout—an image that is tall in length, and narrow in width. Select an image of a handshake, and then click **Insert**. Compare your screen with **Figure 3**. Locate an image similar to the one.
8. Point to the picture to display the pointer. With the pointer, drag the image to the right so that it is aligned with the top, right, and bottom edges of the slide, resizing if needed. Compare your screen with **Figure 4**.
9. **Save** the file.

- **You have completed Skill 2 of 10**

SKILL 3: Modify Picture Shapes, Borders, and Effects

- Pictures are usually rectangular, but they can be changed to a number of different shapes available in PowerPoint.
- ***Picture effects*** are picture styles that include shadows, reflections, glows, soft edges, bevels, and 3-D rotations.

---

1. Display **Slide 3**. In the right content placeholder, click the **Pictures** button. From your student data files, insert the image named **ppt03_EnrichmentProductivity**.

Obj 2.3.2

2. On the **Format tab**, in the **Size group**, click the **Crop arrow**. Point to **Crop to Shape** to display the **Shape** gallery, and then compare your screen with **Figure 1**.
3. Under **Block Arrows**, click the second shape—**Left Arrow**—to change the shape of the picture.
4. In the **Picture Styles group**, click the **Picture Effects** button. Point to **Preset**, and then point to each thumbnail to preview the effects on the cropped image using Live Preview.
5. Click the last option in the first row—**Preset 4**. Point to the picture to display the pointer, and then drag to position the picture as shown in **Figure 2**.

Obj 2.3.3

6. Display **Slide 4**, and then select the picture. On the **Format tab**, in the **Picture Styles group**, click the **Picture Effects** button. Point to **Shadow**, and then point to, but do not click, several of the options to preview the shadow effects.

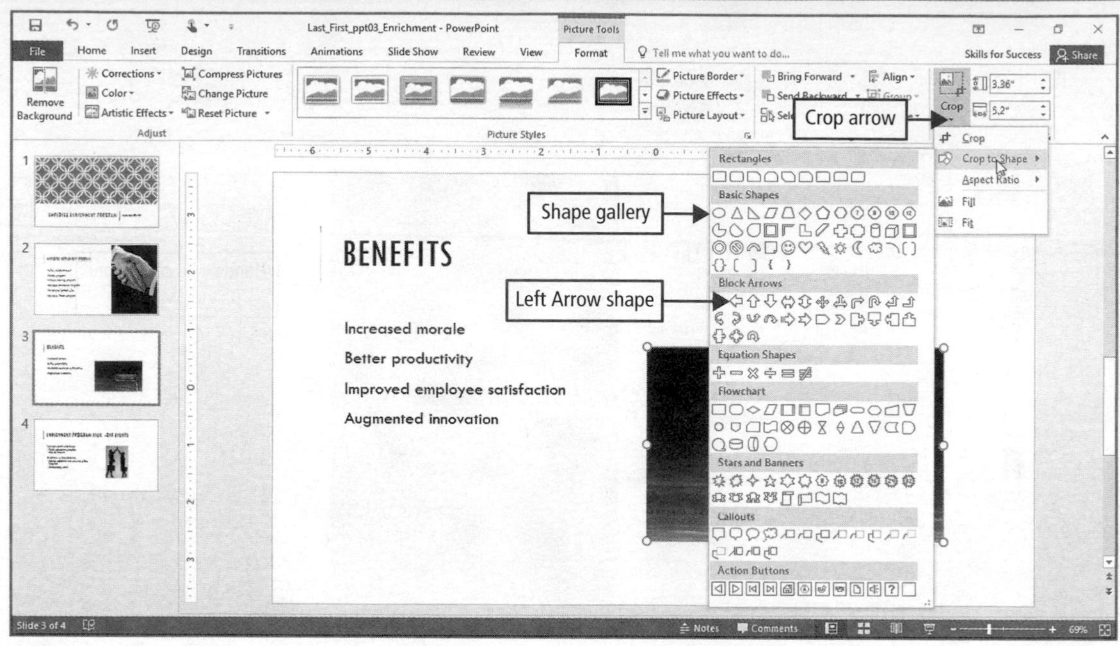

Figure 1

PowerPoint 2016, Windows 10, Microsoft Corporation

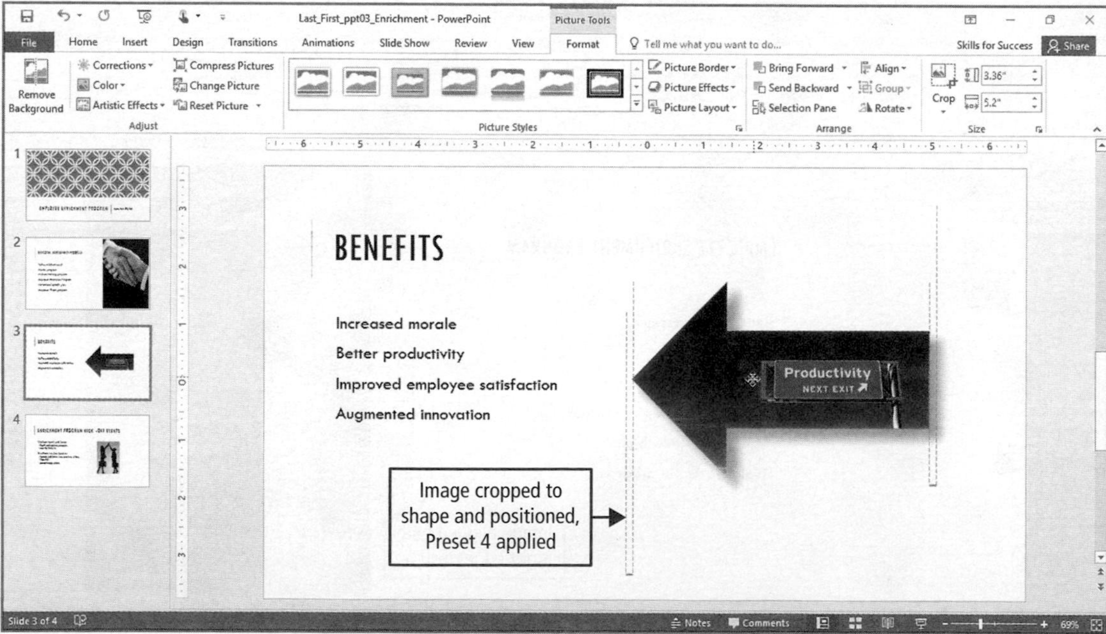

Figure 2

Eyeidea/Fotolia; PowerPoint 2016, Windows 10, Microsoft Corporation

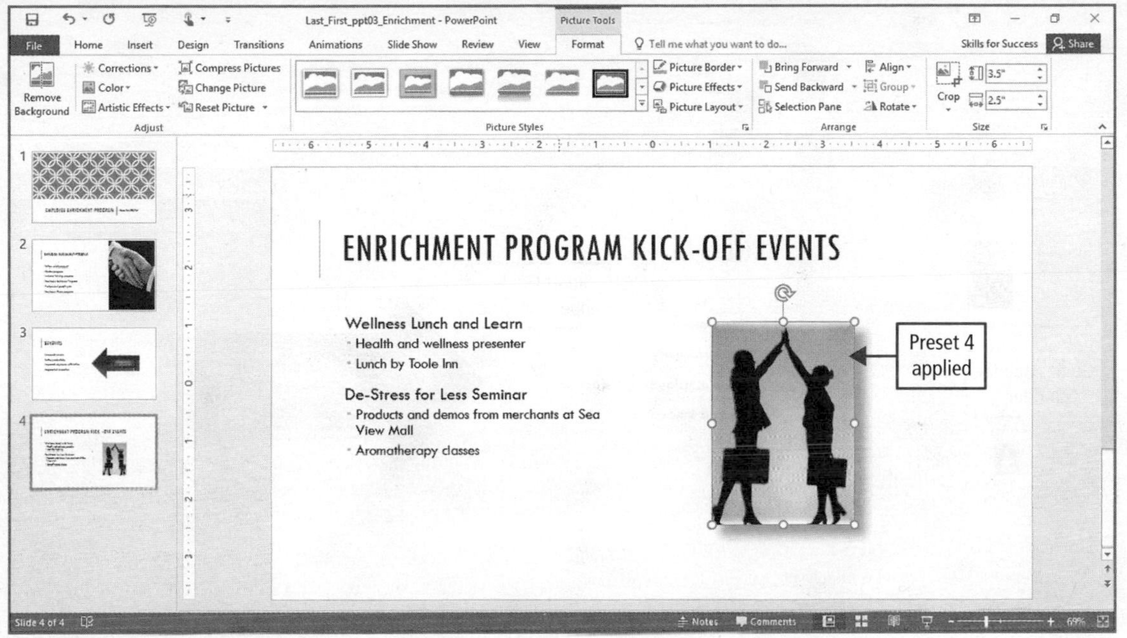

PowerPoint 2016, Windows 10, Microsoft Corporation

Figure 3

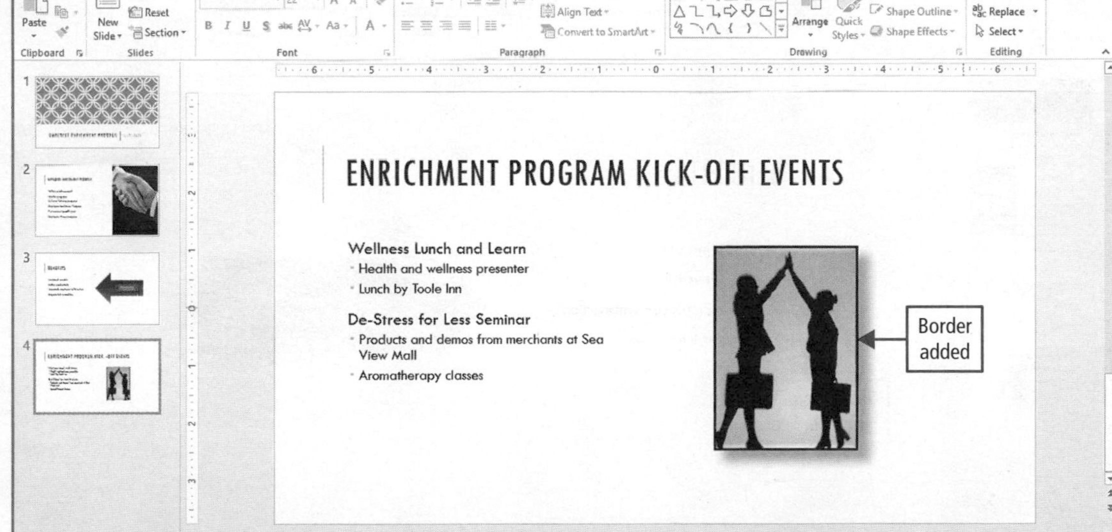

PowerPoint 2016, Windows 10, Microsoft Corporation

Figure 4

7. Point to **Reflection**, and then preview the various reflection effects. View the effects in several other galleries.
8. Point to **Preset** to display the gallery. Click the last option in the first row—**Preset 4**—to apply the same effect as applied on **Slide 3**. Compare your screen with **Figure 3**.

   Preset effects are a combination of other effects, like a bevel and a shadow.
9. With the picture still selected, on the **Format tab**, in the **Picture Styles group**, click the **Picture Border** button. Under **Theme Colors**, click the second color in the first row—**Black, Text 1**—to add a narrow border to the image.

   When you apply multiple effects to an image in this manner, choose effects that complement the picture, other effects, and the presentation theme.
10. Click the **Picture Border** button again, and then point to **Weight**. Click **3 pt** to apply a thicker border.
11. Click a blank area on the slide so that nothing is selected, and then compare your screen with **Figure 4**.
12. **Save** the file.

■ **You have completed Skill 3 of 10**

► You can use shapes as design elements, particularly on slides with a simple background design.

1. Move to **Slide 3**. If the rulers are not displayed in the **Normal view** slide pane, on the **View tab**, in the **Show group**, select the **Ruler** check box.

Obj 2.2.1

2. On the **Insert tab**, in the **Illustrations group**, click the **Shapes** button, and then under **Equation Shapes**, click the first shape—**Plus**.

3. Click anywhere near the bottom center of the slide to insert the shape. Point to the center of the shape to display the pointer, and then drag up and to the left, as shown in **Figure 1**.

Obj 2.4.4

Smart Guides are dashed lines that appear automatically on the slide when pictures, shapes, text, or placeholders are nearly even or evenly spaced. They are used to help align and space images evenly. The ruler displays ***guides***—lines that give you a visual indication of where the pointer is positioned.

Obj 2.2.4

4. With the shape selected, on the **Format tab**, in the **Shape Styles group**, click the **More** button to display the gallery. In the **Theme Styles group**, click the third option in the last row—**Intense Effect - Blue, Accent 2**.

Obj 2.2.3

5. On the **Format tab**, in the **Size group**, change the shape **Height** to 1.1" Adjust the **Width** to 1.1" Compare your screen with **Figure 2**.

When a shape's height or width is changed, only that dimension, and not the other, is changed.

■ **Continue to the next page to complete the skill**

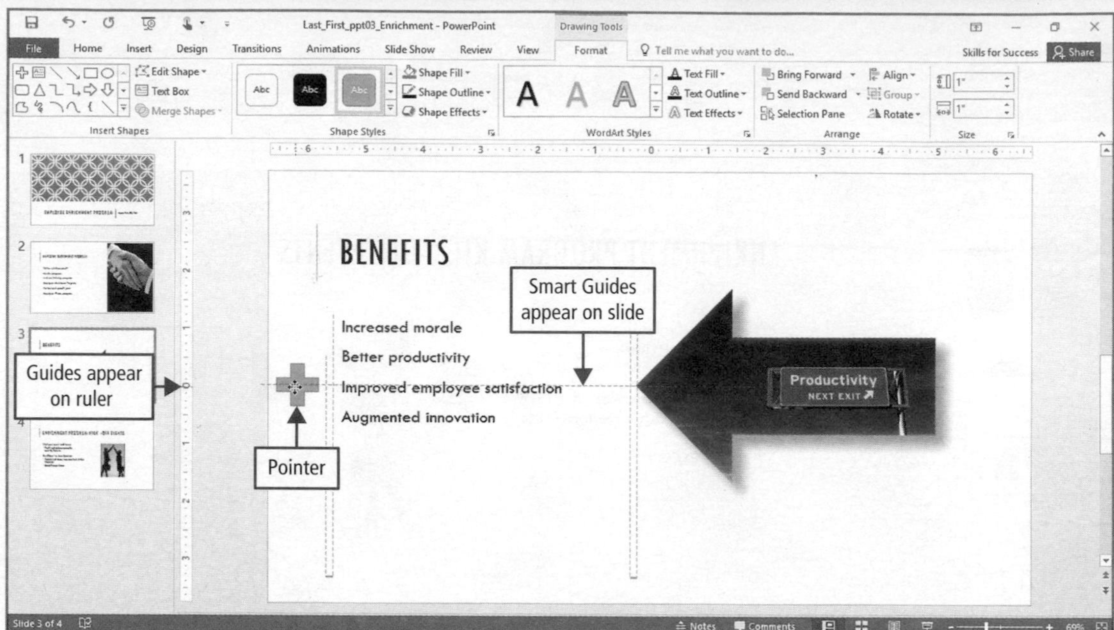

Figure 1

Eyeidea/Fotolia; PowerPoint 2016, Windows 10, Microsoft Corporation

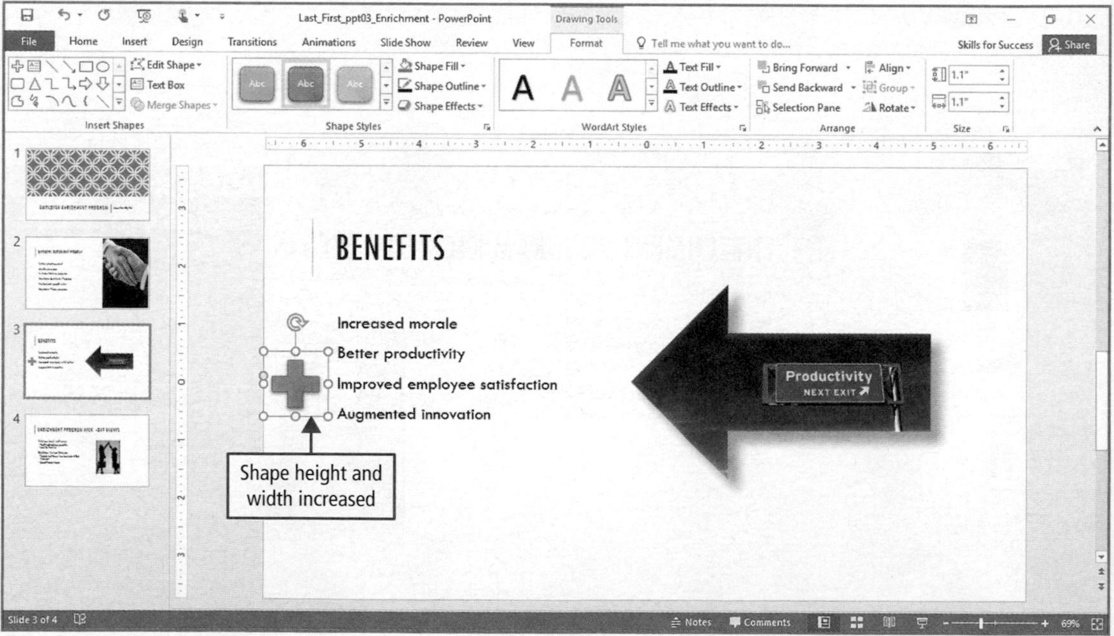

Figure 2

Eyeidea/Fotolia; PowerPoint 2016, Windows 10, Microsoft Corporation

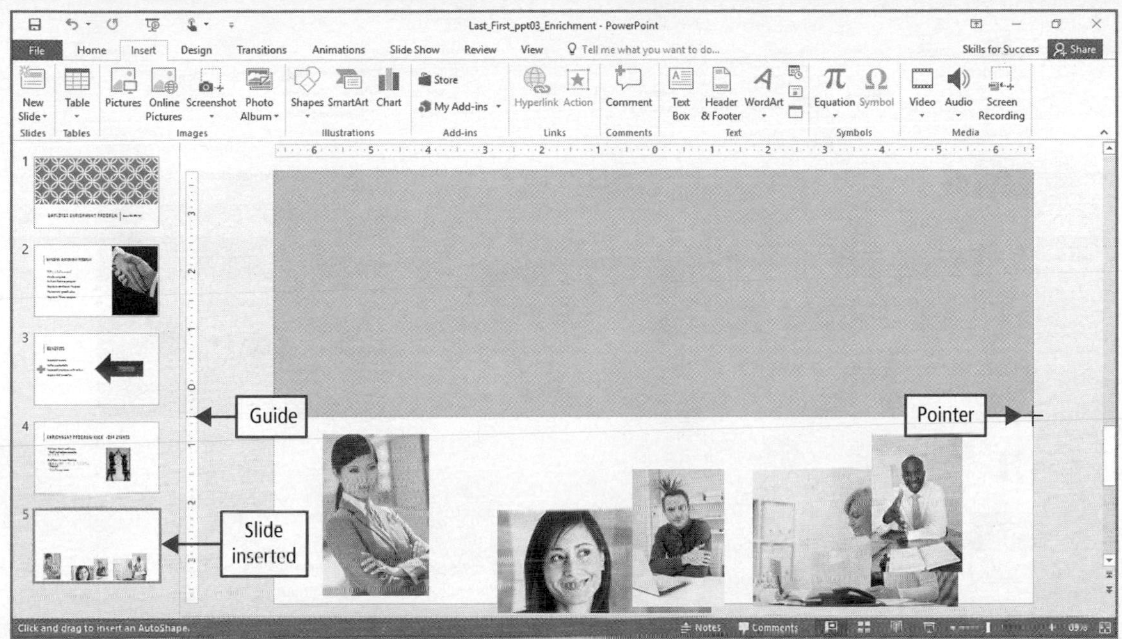

Alliance/Fotolia; Minerva Studio/Fotolia; Jeanette Dietl/Fotolia; Momentimages/Fotolia; Minerva Studio/Fotolia
PowerPoint 2016, Windows 10, Microsoft Corporation

Figure 3

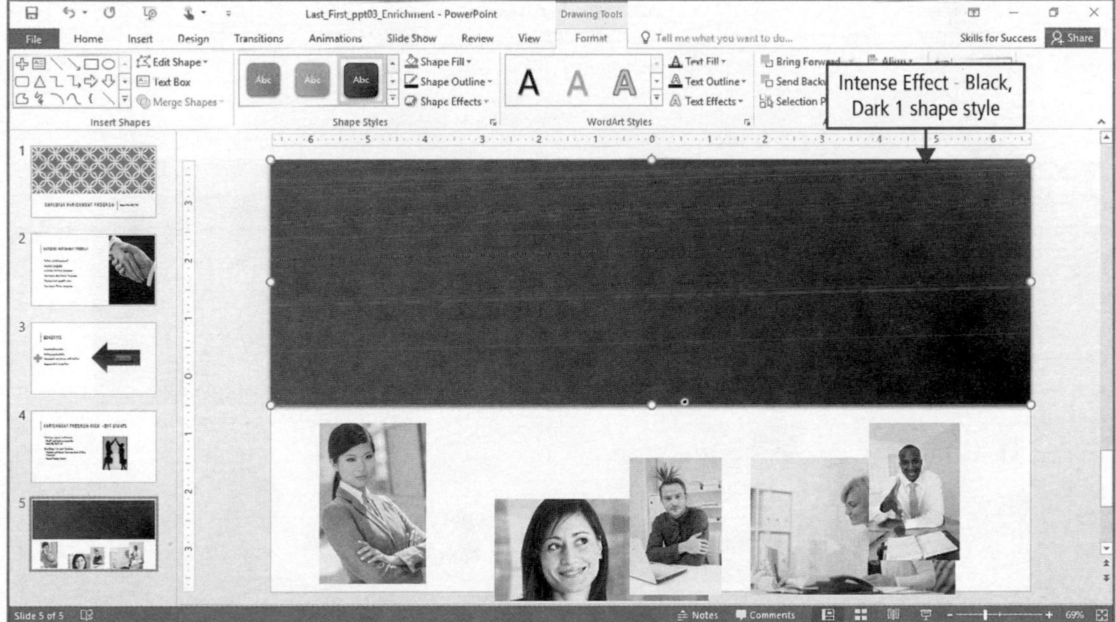

Alliance/Fotolia; Minerva Studio/Fotolia; Jeanette Dietl/Fotolia; Momentimages/Fotolia; Minerva Studio/Fotolia
PowerPoint 2016, Windows 10, Microsoft Corporation

Figure 4

6. Move to **Slide 4**. On the **Home tab**, in the **Slides group**, click the **New Slide arrow**, and then click **Reuse Slides** to display the **ppt03_EnrichmentSamway** slides in the **Reuse Slides** pane. If the slides from **ppt03_EnrichmentSamway** do not display in the **Reuse Slides** pane, click the **Browse** button, click **Browse File**, navigate to your student files, and then open **ppt03_EnrichmentSamway**.
7. In the **Reuse Slides** pane, click **Slide 4** to insert it in the presentation, and then **Close** [×] the pane.
8. On the **Insert tab**, in the **Illustrations group**, click the **Shapes** button. Under **Rectangles**, click the first shape—**Rectangle**. With the [+] pointer, drag from the upper left corner of the slide to the right edge of the slide and down to the half-inch mark—**0.5** inches below **0** on the vertical ruler. Compare your screen with **Figure 3**.
9. With the rectangle selected, on the **Format tab**, in the **Shape Styles group**, click the **More** button [▾], and then click the first style in the last row of the **Theme Styles group**—**Intense Effect - Black, Dark 1.**
10. Compare your screen with **Figure 4**, and if necessary, drag the rectangle so that it is positioned as shown in the figure.
11. **Save** [💾] the file.

■ **You have completed Skill 4 of 10**

SKILL 5: Add Text to Shapes and Insert Text Boxes

SKILL 3.5

- A ***text box*** is an object used to position text anywhere on a slide.
- In addition to being used as design elements, shapes can also be used as containers for text.

1. On **Slide 5**, if necessary, select the rectangle.

   To insert text in a shape, select the shape, and then begin to type.

2. Type Questions? Press Enter, and then type Contact Eugene Garner, Benefits Specialist Press Enter, type (805) 555–1020 and then compare your screen with **Figure 1**.

   When you type text in a shape, it is centered both horizontally and vertically within the shape.

3. Select the three lines of text, and then change the **Font Size** to **40**.
4. With the three lines of text still selected, on the **Format tab**, in the **WordArt Styles group**, click the **More** button. Click the last style in the third row—**Fill - Ice Blue, Background 2, Inner Shadow**.
5. In the **WordArt Styles group**, click the **Text Fill arrow** to display the gallery. Click the first color in the first row—**White, Background 1**. Click a blank area of the slide so that nothing is selected, and then compare your screen with **Figure 2**.

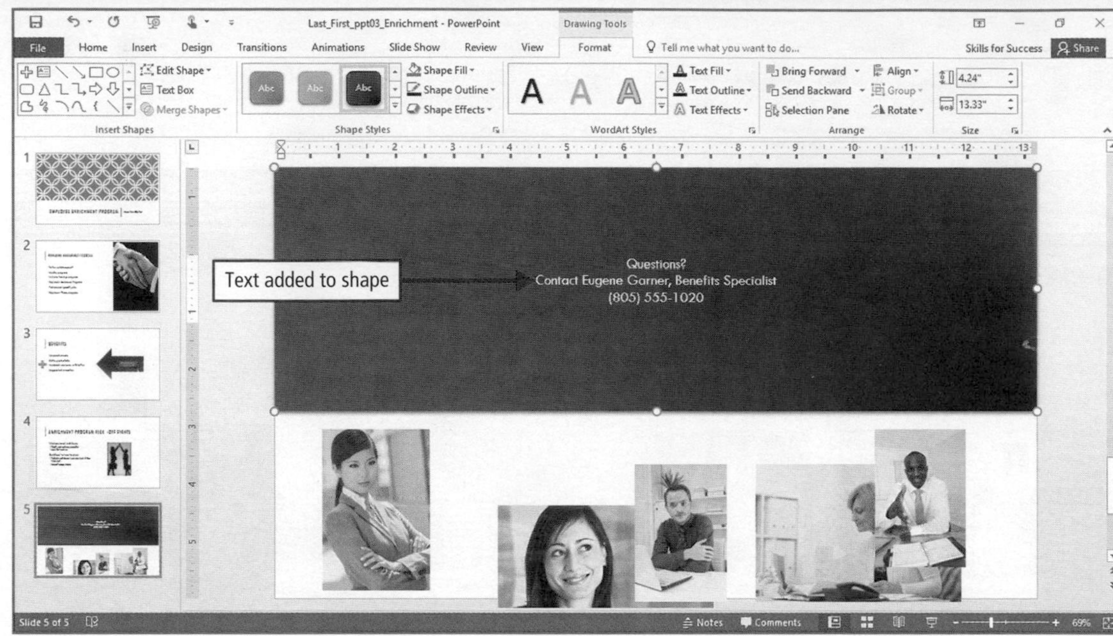

Figure 1 Alliance/Fotolia; Minerva Studio/Fotolia; Jeanette Dietl/Fotolia; Momentimages/Fotolia; Minerva Studio/Fotolia
PowerPoint 2016, Windows 10, Microsoft Corporation

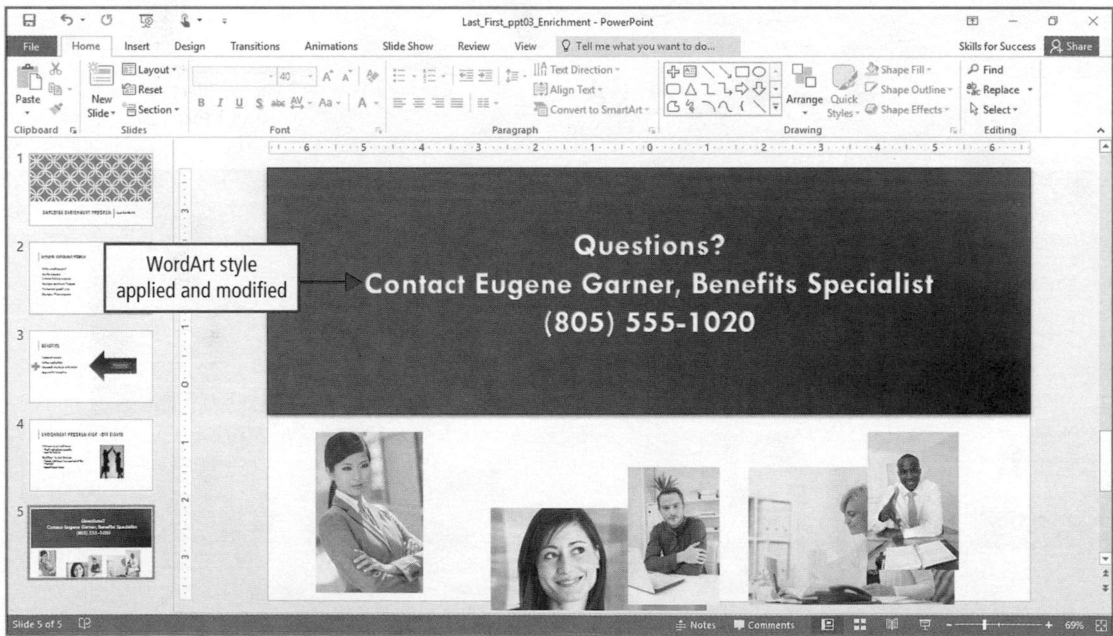

Figure 2 Alliance/Fotolia; Minerva Studio/Fotolia; Jeanette Dietl/Fotolia; Momentimages/Fotolia; Minerva Studio/Fotolia
PowerPoint 2016, Windows 10, Microsoft Corporation

■ **Continue to the next page to complete the skill**

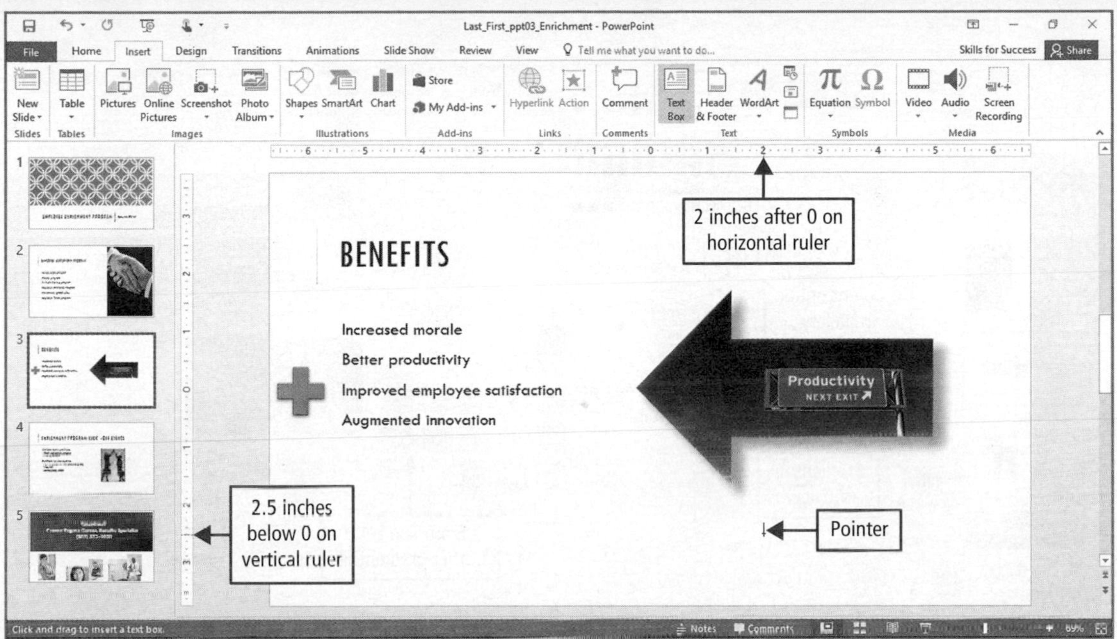

Eyeidea/Fotolia; PowerPoint 2016, Windows 10, Microsoft Corporation

Figure 3

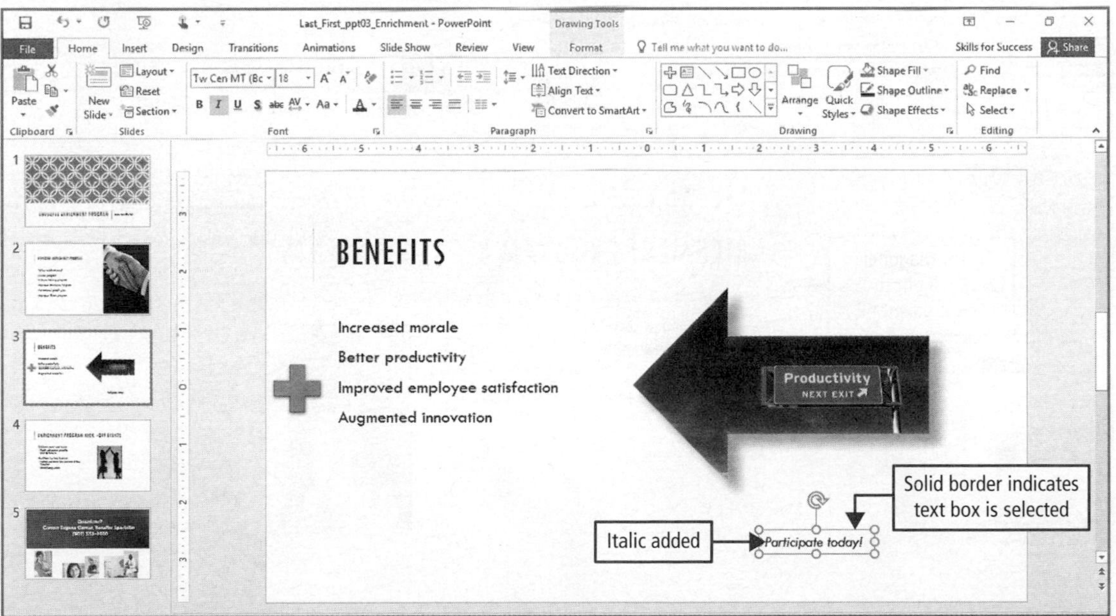

Eyeidea/Fotolia; PowerPoint 2016, Windows 10, Microsoft Corporation

Figure 4

MOS Obj 2.2.2

6. Display **Slide 3**. On the **Insert tab**, in the **Text group**, click the **Text Box** button [Text Box]. Position the [↓] pointer on the slide aligned at **2** inches after **0** on the horizontal ruler and at **2.5** inches below **0** on the vertical ruler, as shown in **Figure 3**.

7. Without moving the pointer, click one time to insert a text box. Type Participate today!

   Text boxes automatically resize to fit the text you type. If needed, text boxes can be resized using the sizing handles or moved by clicking and dragging.

8. Click anywhere on the slide so that the text box is not selected.

   Unlike shapes, when a text box is inserted, it does not include borders or fill colors. Text inserted in a text box appears to be floating on the slide and is formatted in the same font as the body font used in content placeholders.

9. Click the text in the text box, and then click a border of the text box to select it. Recall that a solid border indicates that the object is selected. On the **Home tab**, in the **Font group**, click the **Italic** button [I]. Compare your screen with **Figure 4**. If your text box is not positioned as shown in the figure, select the text box and then use the [↑], [↓], [←], or [→] keys on your keyboard to ***nudge***—move an object in small increments using the directional arrow keys—the text box so that it is positioned as shown.

10. **Save** [Save] the file.

- **You have completed Skill 5 of 10**

- A ***group*** is a collection of multiple objects treated as one unit that can be copied, moved, or formatted.

1. On **Slide 3**, select the plus sign shape. On the **Format tab**, in the **Shape Styles group**, click the **Shape Fill** button. Preview the styles, and then, under **Theme Colors**, click the fourth option in the second row—**Dark Teal**, **Text 2**, **Lighter 80%**.
2. In the **Shape Styles group**, click the **Shape Fill** button. Point to **Gradient**, and then under **Variations**, in the second row, point to the last thumbnail—**From Top Left Corner**—as shown in **Figure 1**, and click to apply a gradient fill to the shape.

   A ***gradient fill*** is a gradual progression of colors and shades, usually from one color to another or from one shade to another shade of the same color. A gradient fill is used to add a fill to a shape or placeholder. Gradients come in light and dark variations.
3. Display **Slide 4**. Click the title placeholder, and then click the placeholder border to select it. On the **Format tab**, in the **Shape Styles group**, click the **Shape Fill** button, and then point to **Gradient**. Under **Light Variations**, click the last option in the last row—**Linear Diagonal - Bottom Right to Top Left**. Compare your screen with **Figure 2**.

■ Continue to the next page to complete the skill

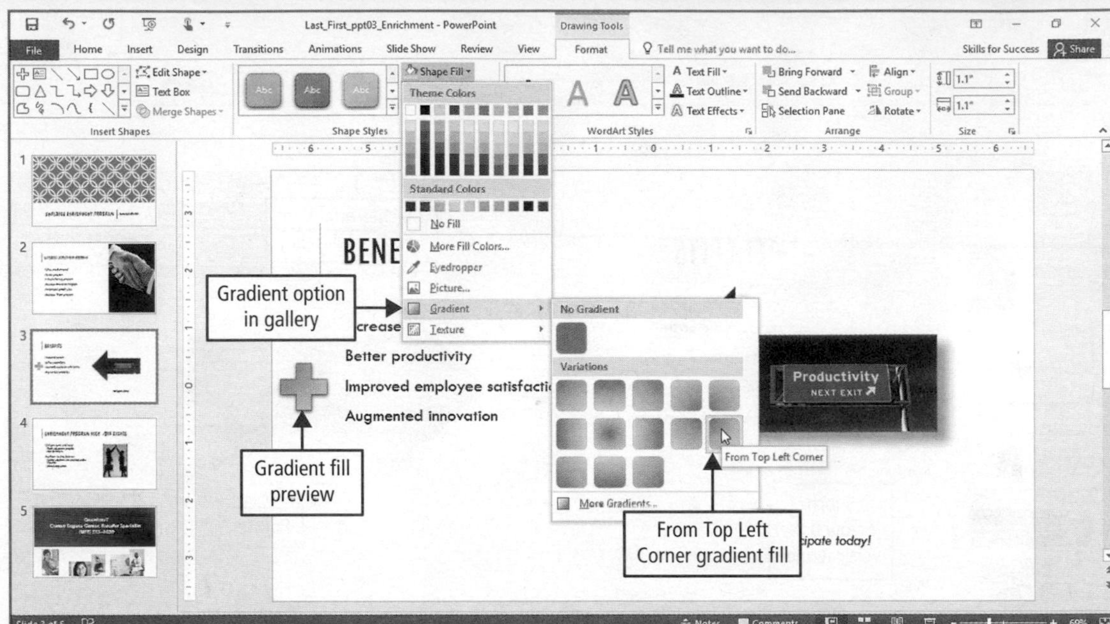

Figure 1 PowerPoint 2016, Windows 10, Microsoft Corporation

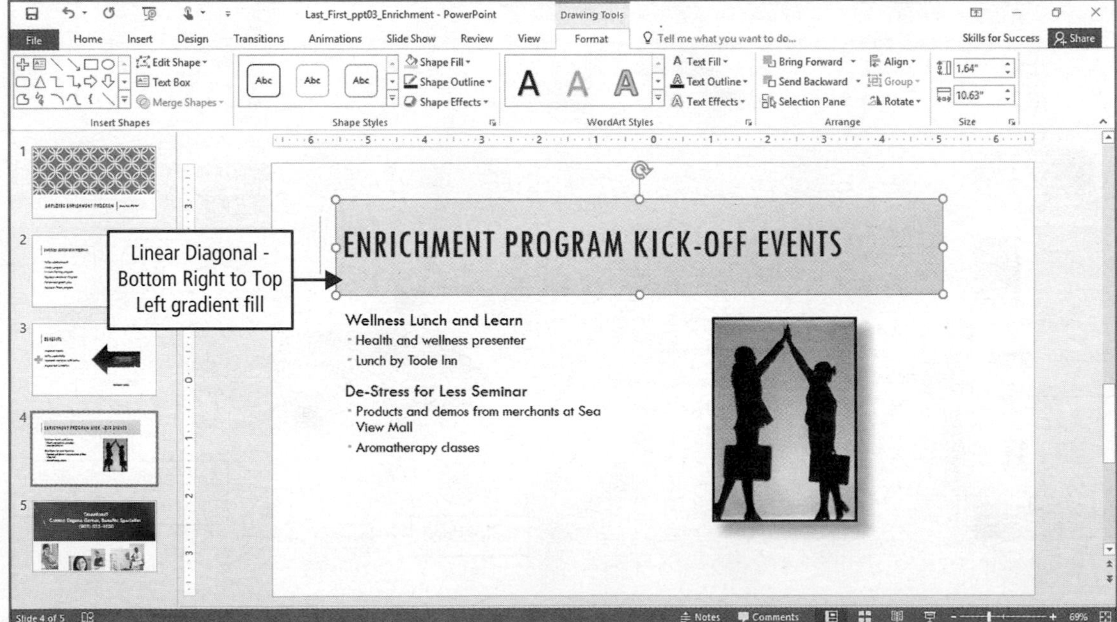

Figure 2 PowerPoint 2016, Windows 10, Microsoft Corporation

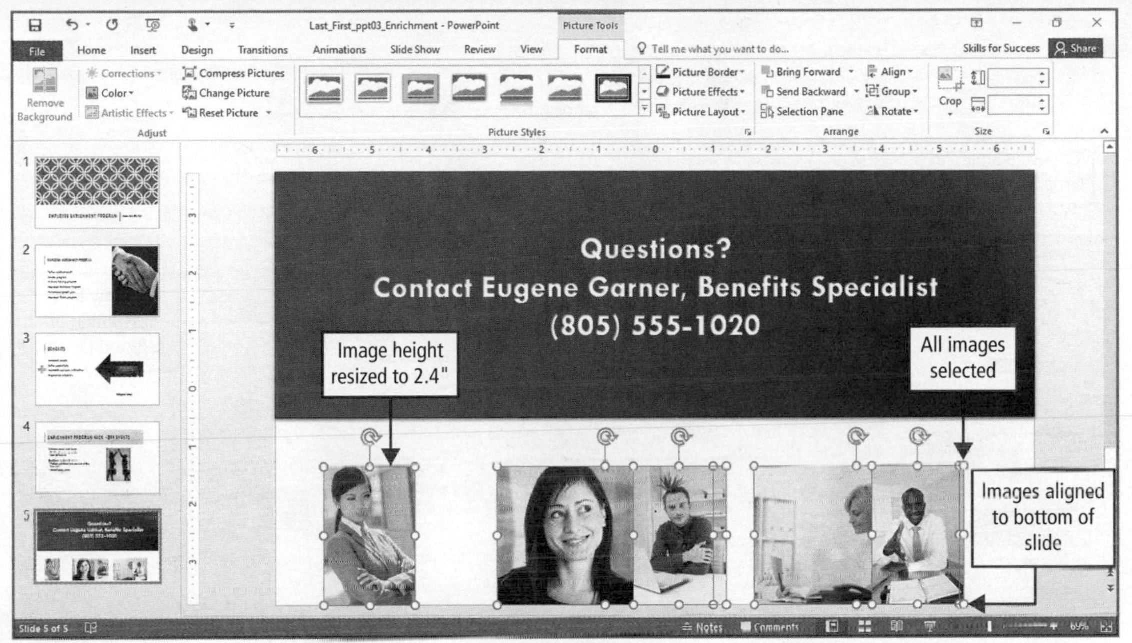

Alliance/Fotolia; Minerva Studio/Fotolia; Jeanette Dietl/Fotolia; Momentimages/Fotolia; Minerva Studio/Fotolia
PowerPoint 2016, Windows 10, Microsoft Corporation

Figure 3

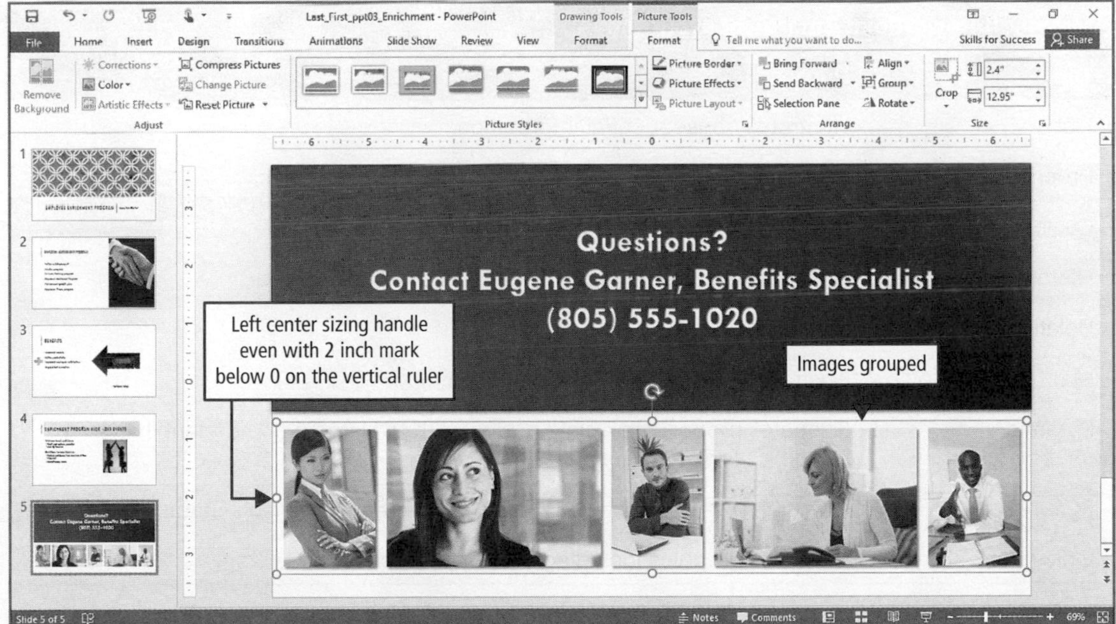

Alliance/Fotolia; Minerva Studio/Fotolia; Jeanette Dietl/Fotolia; Momentimages/Fotolia; Minerva Studio/Fotolia
PowerPoint 2016, Windows 10, Microsoft Corporation

Figure 4

4. Display **Slide 5**. Select the furthest left image, and then on the **Format tab**, in the **Size group**, change the **Height** to 2.4"
5. Hold down Ctrl, and then click each picture at the bottom of the slide so that all five of the images are selected.
6. On the **Format tab**, in the **Arrange group**, click the **Align** button, and verify that **Align to Slide** is selected. If it is not, select it, and then click the Align button again. Click **Align Bottom**. Compare your screen with **Figure 3**. MOS Obj 2.4.2

   The Align Bottom option aligns the selected objects to the bottom of the slide.
7. With the pictures selected, on the **Format tab**, in the **Picture Styles group**, click the **Picture Effects** button. Point to **Shadow**, and then under **Outer**, click the first option in the first row—**Offset Diagonal Bottom Right**.
8. With the pictures selected, on the **Format tab**, in the **Arrange group**, click the **Align** button, and then click **Distribute Horizontally**. MOS Obj 2.4.1

   When aligned to the slide, the pictures are evenly distributed horizontally.
9. With the pictures selected, in the **Arrange group**, click the **Group** button, and then click **Group**. With the grouped pictures selected, press and hold the Shift key and use the pointer to drag the images straight up, so that the left center sizing handle is aligned with the **2** inch mark below **0** on the vertical ruler. Compare your screen with **Figure 4**.

   When Shift is held while moving an object, the object moves precisely in the direction you are dragging.
10. **Save** the file.

■ **You have completed Skill 6 of 10**

SKILL 7: Convert Text to SmartArt Graphics and Add Shapes

- A ***SmartArt graphic*** is a visual representation of information that can be used to communicate your message or ideas effectively.
- SmartArt graphics can be created from scratch by inserting the graphic and then adding text.
- You can convert text that you have already typed—such as a list—into a SmartArt graphic, add additional text and pictures, and then apply colors, effects, and styles that coordinate with the presentation theme.

Obj 3.3.2

1. Display **Slide 4**, and then click anywhere in the bulleted list in the left content placeholder. On the **Home tab**, in the **Paragraph group**, click the **Convert to SmartArt Graphic** button. At the bottom of the gallery, click **More SmartArt Graphics** to open the **Choose a SmartArt Graphic** dialog box. Compare your screen with **Figure 1**.

   The Choose a SmartArt Graphic dialog box is divided into three sections. The left pane lists the SmartArt graphic types. The center section displays the layouts for the selected type. The right section displays a preview of the selected layout along with a description of the layout.

2. In the left pane of the **Choose a SmartArt Graphic** dialog box, click each of the SmartArt graphic types to view the layouts in each category, and then in the center pane, click several layouts to view their descriptions.

   The nine types of SmartArt layouts are summarized in **Figure 2**.

■ **Continue to the next page to complete the skill**

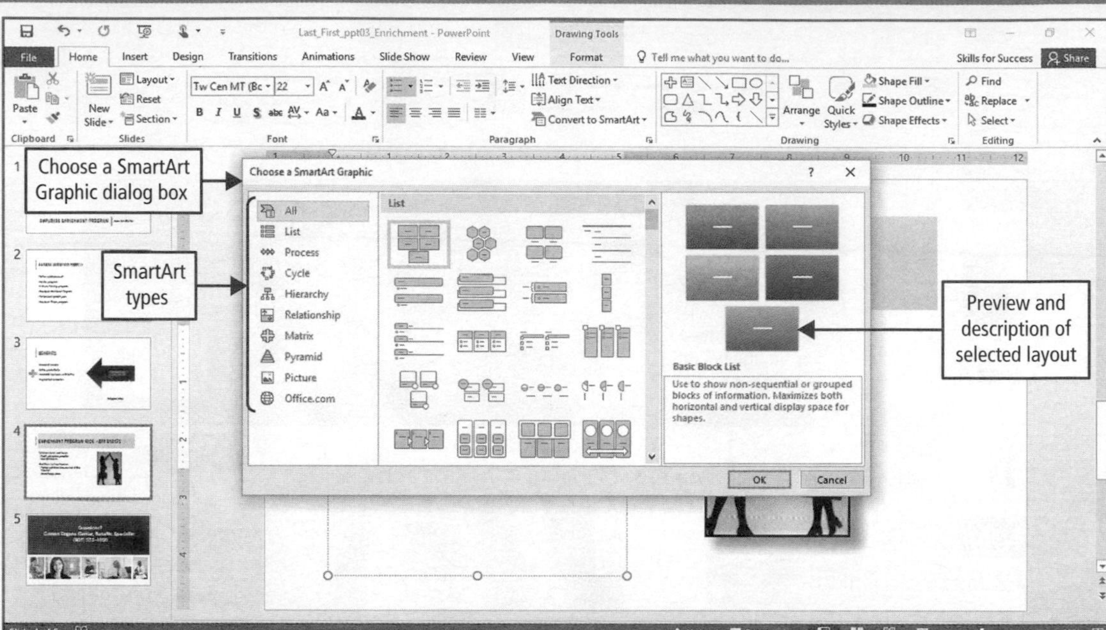

Figure 1

PowerPoint 2016, Windows 10, Microsoft Corporation

Microsoft PowerPoint SmartArt Layout Types	
Type	**Purpose**
List	Illustrates nonsequential information.
Process	Illustrates steps in a process or timeline.
Cycle	Illustrates a continual process.
Hierarchy	Illustrates a decision tree or creates an organization chart.
Relationship	Illustrates a connection.
Matrix	Illustrates how parts relate to a whole.
Pyramid	Illustrates proportional relationships, with the largest component in the bottom or top.
Picture	Communicates message and ideas using pictures in each shape.
Office.com	Variety of graphics including charts, processes, and lists.

Figure 2

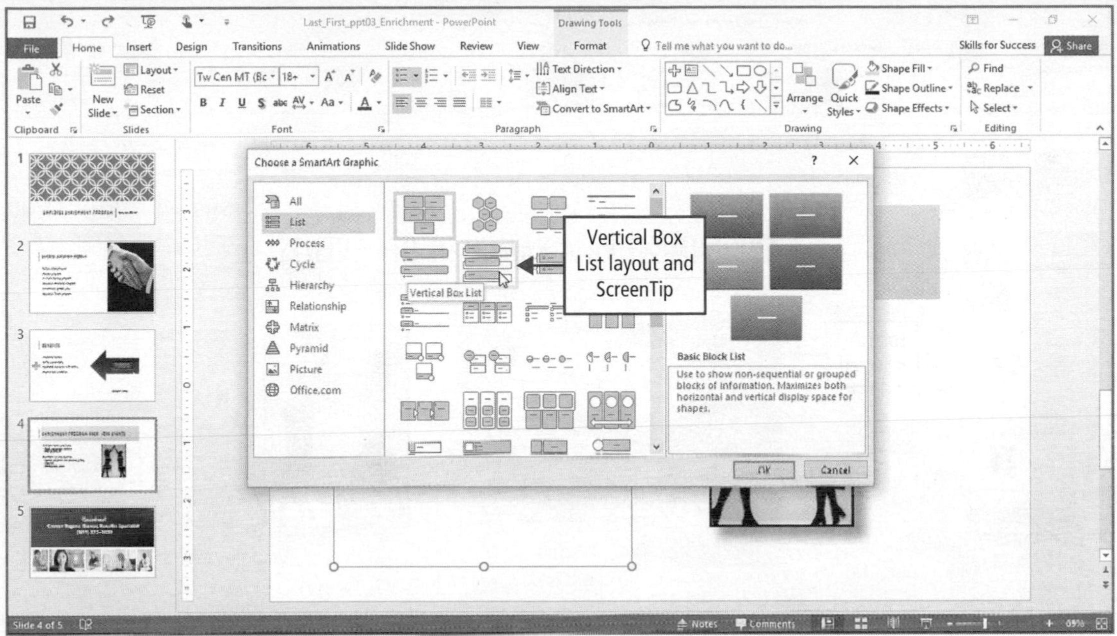

PowerPoint 2016, Windows 10, Microsoft Corporation

Figure 3

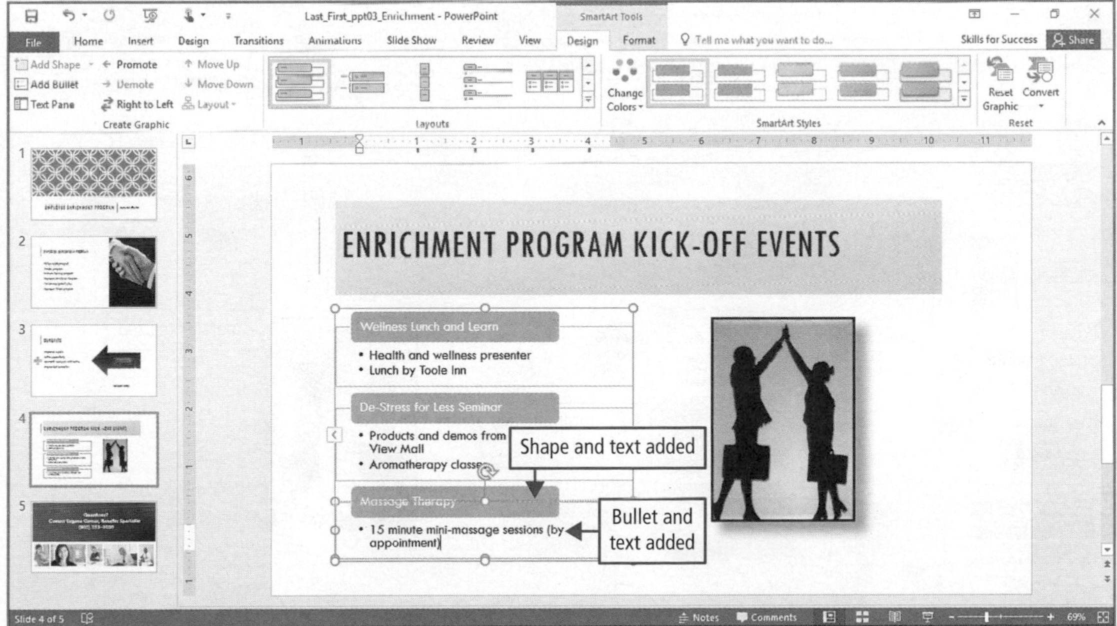

PowerPoint 2016, Windows 10, Microsoft Corporation

Figure 4

3. In the left pane of the **Choose a SmartArt Graphic** dialog box, click **List**, and then in the center pane, use the ScreenTips to locate **Vertical Box List**. Compare your screen with **Figure 3**.

4. Click **Vertical Box List**, and then click **OK** to convert the bulleted list to a SmartArt graphic.

   The Text Pane button may be selected on the Ribbon, and the Text pane may display to the left of the SmartArt graphic.

5. If the **Type your text here** pane displays, **Close** [×] it.

6. Click anywhere in the text *De-stress for Less Seminar*. On the **SmartArt Tools Design tab**, in the **Create Graphic group**, click the **Add Shape** button. Type Massage Therapy

   MOS Obj 3.3.3

7. On the **SmartArt Tools Design tab**, in the **Create Graphic group**, click the **Add Bullet** button. Type 15 minute mini-massage sessions (by appointment) Compare your screen with **Figure 4**.

   The contents are automatically resized to fit the new bullet point.

8. **Save** [💾] the file.

■ **You have completed Skill 7 of 10**

SKILL 8: Modify SmartArt Layouts, Colors, and Styles

- After you create a SmartArt graphic, you can change the layout to one that provides the best visual representation of your information.
- The colors that you apply to a SmartArt graphic are coordinated with the presentation color theme.
- SmartArt styles include gradient fills and 3-D effects.

1. On **Slide 4**, if necessary, select the SmartArt graphic. On the **SmartArt Tools Design tab**, in the **Layouts group**, click the **More** button, and then use ScreenTips to locate and click **Vertical Arrow List**.
2. Click anywhere in the text *Health and wellness presenter* in the first arrow shape. On the **Home tab**, in the **Font group**, notice that the font size is 17 points. Recall that in a professional presentation, all fonts should be at least 18 to 24 points.
3. Click a blank area of the SmartArt graphic to select the entire graphic—individual shapes should not be selected. Compare your screen with **Figure 1**.
4. With the pointer, drag the SmartArt's right center sizing handle to the right to align the side with the **0.5** inch mark after **0** on the horizontal ruler.
5. Click anywhere in the text *Health and wellness presenter* in the first arrow shape. On the **Home tab**, in the **Font group**, notice that the font size is **18** points. Compare your screen with **Figure 2**.

   The font was automatically resized to fit the larger size of the SmartArt and now meets design standards.

■ **Continue to the next page to complete the skill**

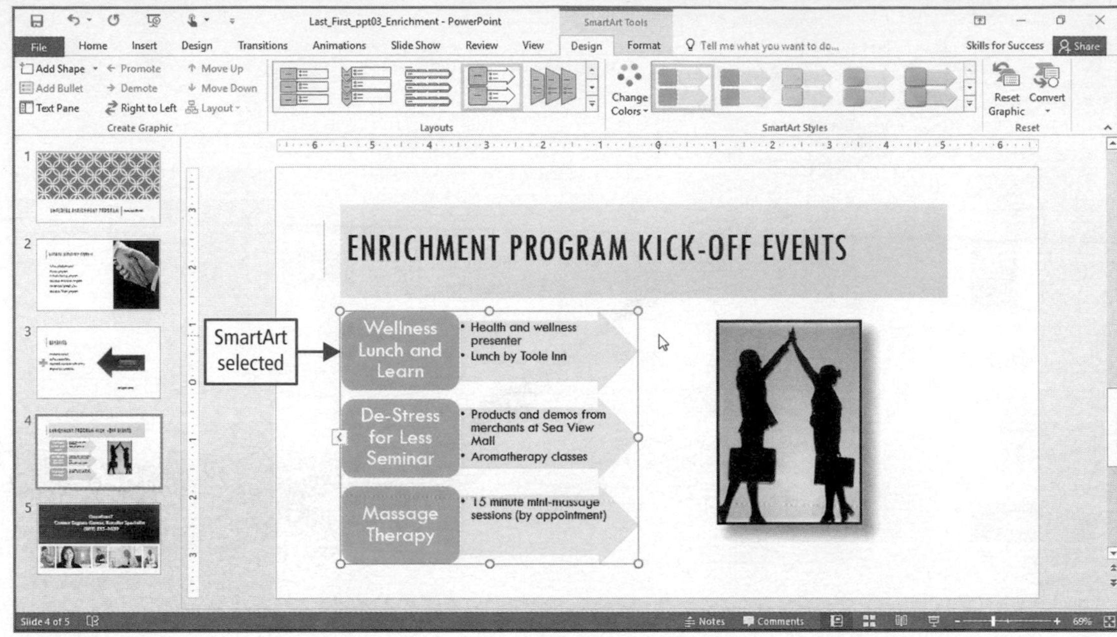

Figure 1 PowerPoint 2016, Windows 10, Microsoft Corporation

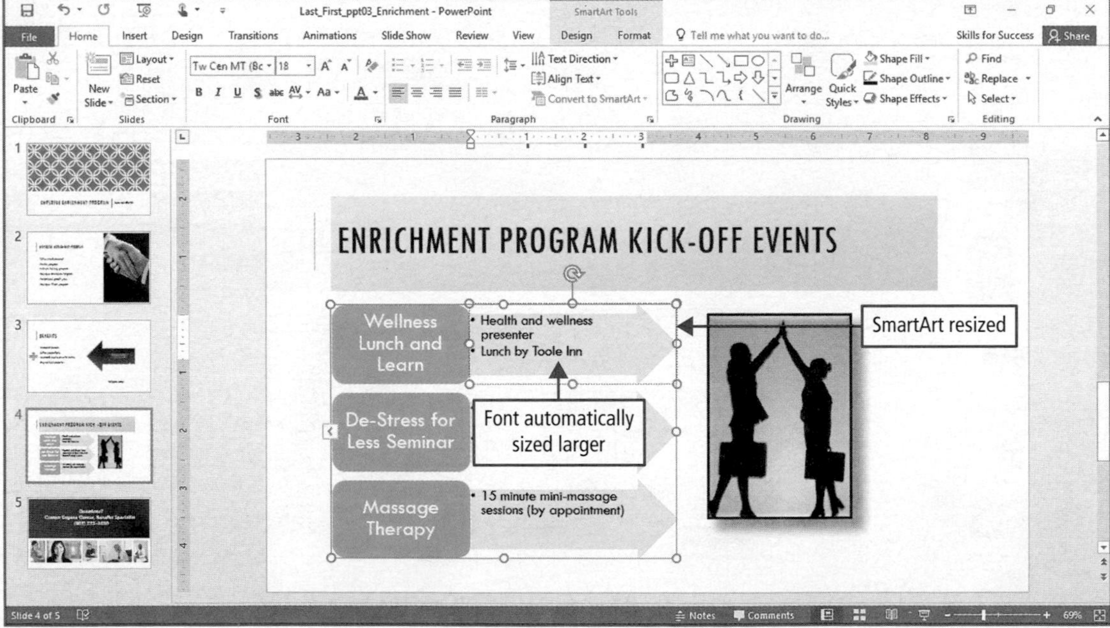

Figure 2 PowerPoint 2016, Windows 10, Microsoft Corporation

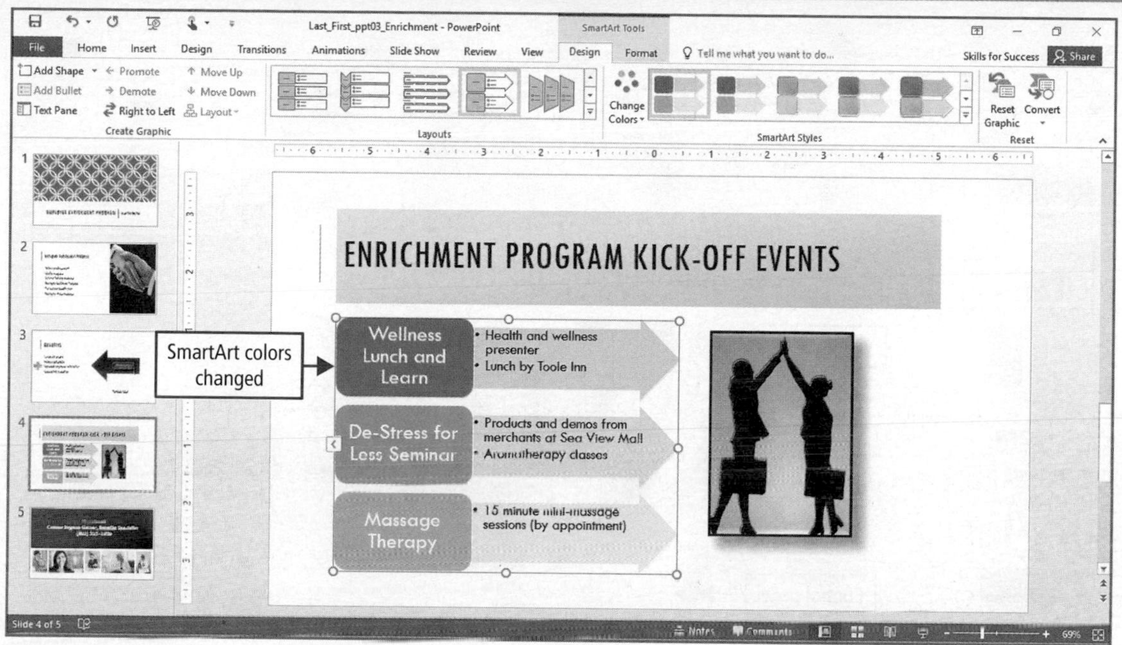

PowerPoint 2016, Windows 10, Microsoft Corporation

Figure 3

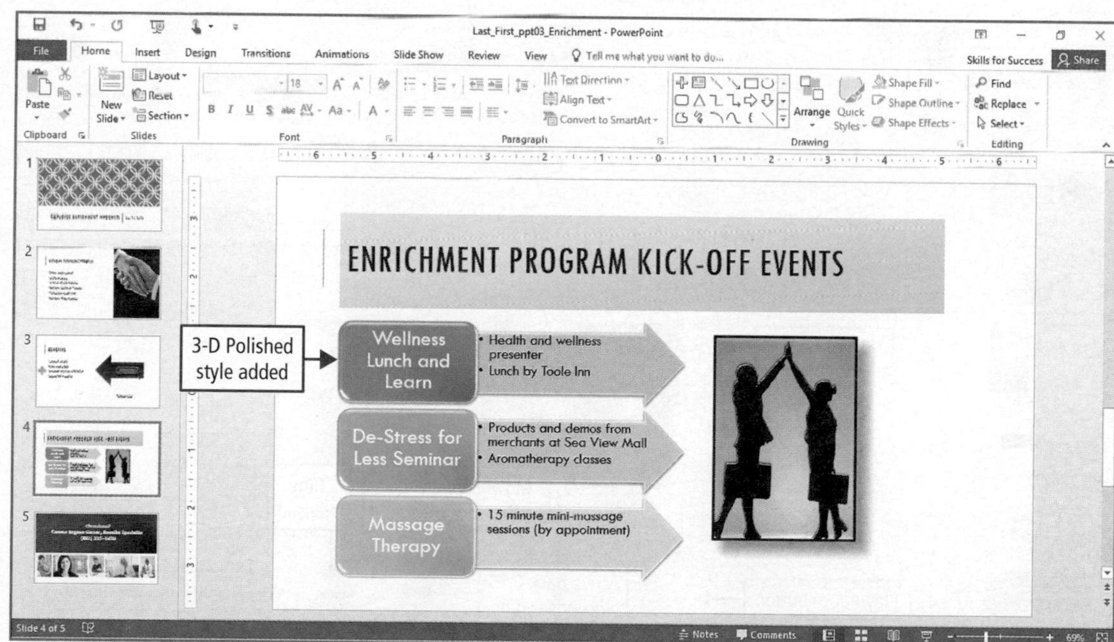

PowerPoint 2016, Windows 10, Microsoft Corporation

Figure 4

6. On the **SmartArt Tools Design tab**, in the **SmartArt Styles group**, click the **Change Colors** button to display the **Color** gallery. Point to several options to preview the colors.

   The colors that display in the gallery coordinate with the slide design.

7. Under **Colorful**, click the second style—**Colorful Range - Accent Colors 2 to 3**. Compare your screen with **Figure 3**.
8. On the **SmartArt Tools Design tab**, in the **SmartArt Styles group**, click the **More** button [▾] to display the **SmartArt Styles** gallery. Point to several of the styles to view their effects on the SmartArt. Then, under **3-D**, click the first style—**Polished**. Click in a blank area of the slide, and then compare your screen with **Figure 4**.
9. **Save** [💾] the file.

- **You have completed Skill 8 of 10**

► You can insert, size, and move video files in a presentation, and you can control when the video will begin to play during a slide show.

1. Display **Slide 1**, and then insert a **New Slide** with the **Title and Content** layout. In the title placeholder, type Employee Enrichment Press Enter, and then type Providing Opportunities for All

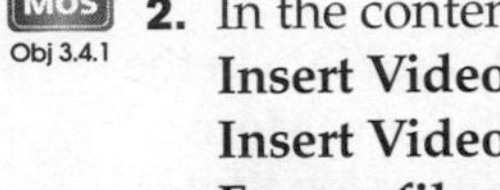

2. In the content placeholder, click the **Insert Video** button, and then in the **Insert Video** dialog box, to the right of **From a file**, click the **Browse** button. Navigate to your student files, and then click **ppt03_EnrichmentVideo**. Click **Insert**. Compare your screen with **Figure 1**.

   The video displays in the center of the slide, and playback and volume controls display in the control panel below the video. Video formatting and editing tools display on the Ribbon. On the Insert tab, in the Media group, clicking the Video button is an alternate method to insert videos.

3. On the control panel below the video, point to the **Play/Pause** button so that it is highlighted as shown in **Figure 2**.

4. Click the **Play/Pause** button to view the video. Alternately, press Alt + P.

   As the video plays, the control panel displays the time that has elapsed since the start of the video. This video contains no audio.

■ **Continue to the next page to complete the skill**

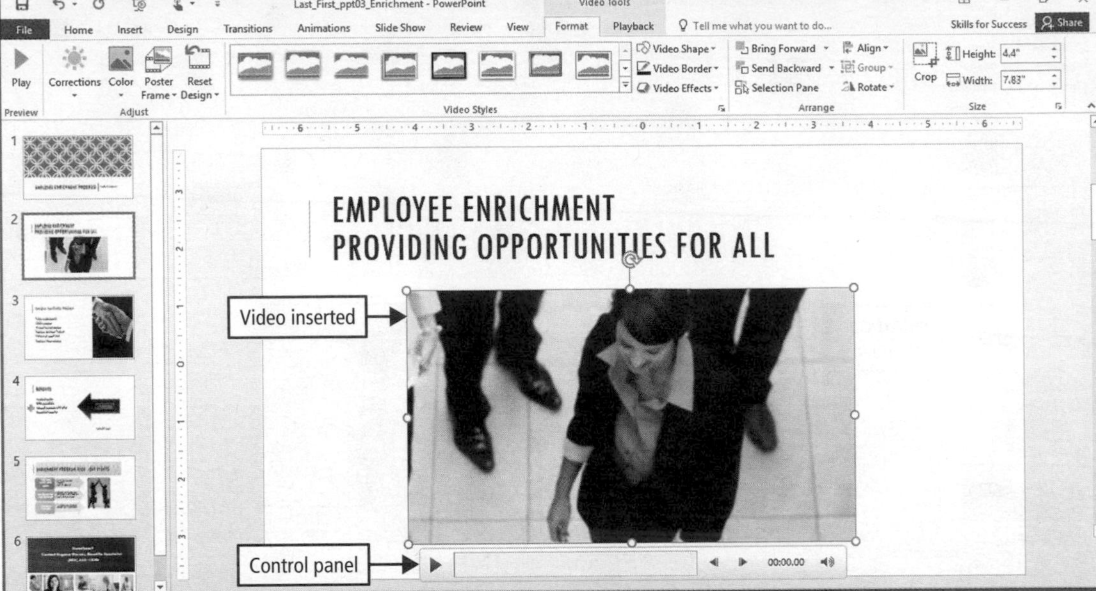

Figure 1

Minerva Studio/Fotolia; PowerPoint 2016, Windows 10, Microsoft Corporation

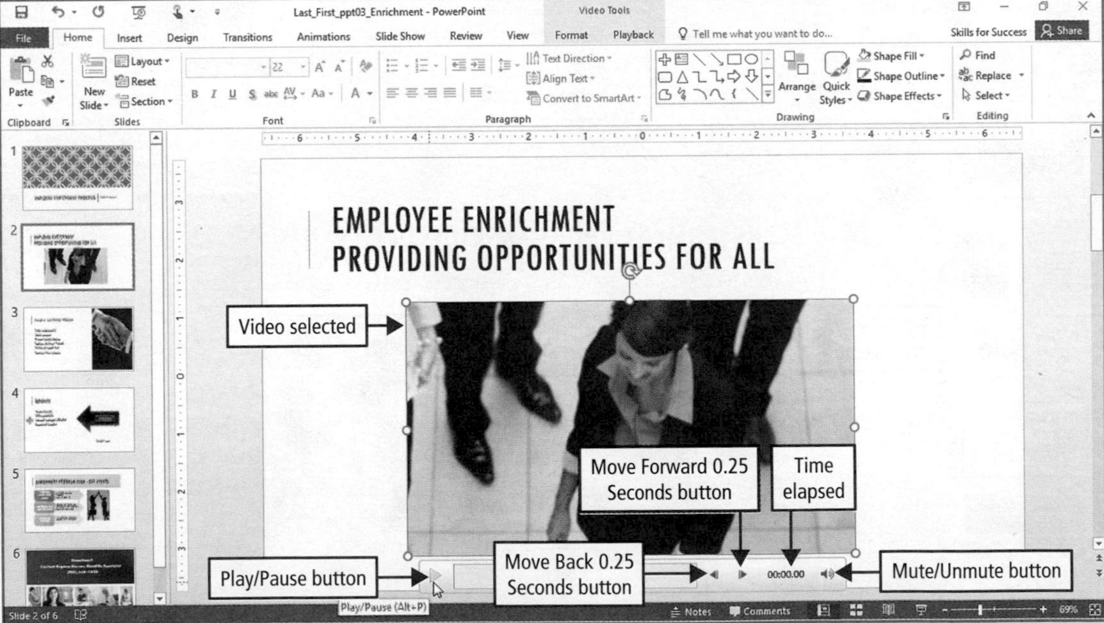

Figure 2

Minerva Studio/Fotolia; PowerPoint 2016, Windows 10, Microsoft Corporation

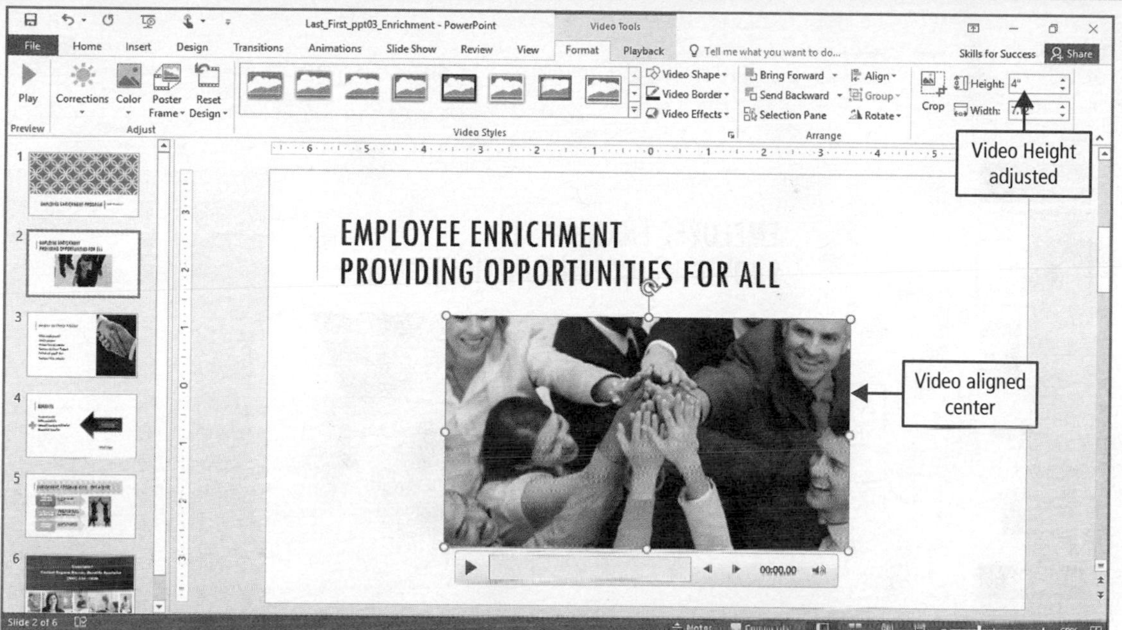

Yuri Arcurs/Fotolia; PowerPoint 2016, Windows 10, Microsoft Corporation

Figure 3

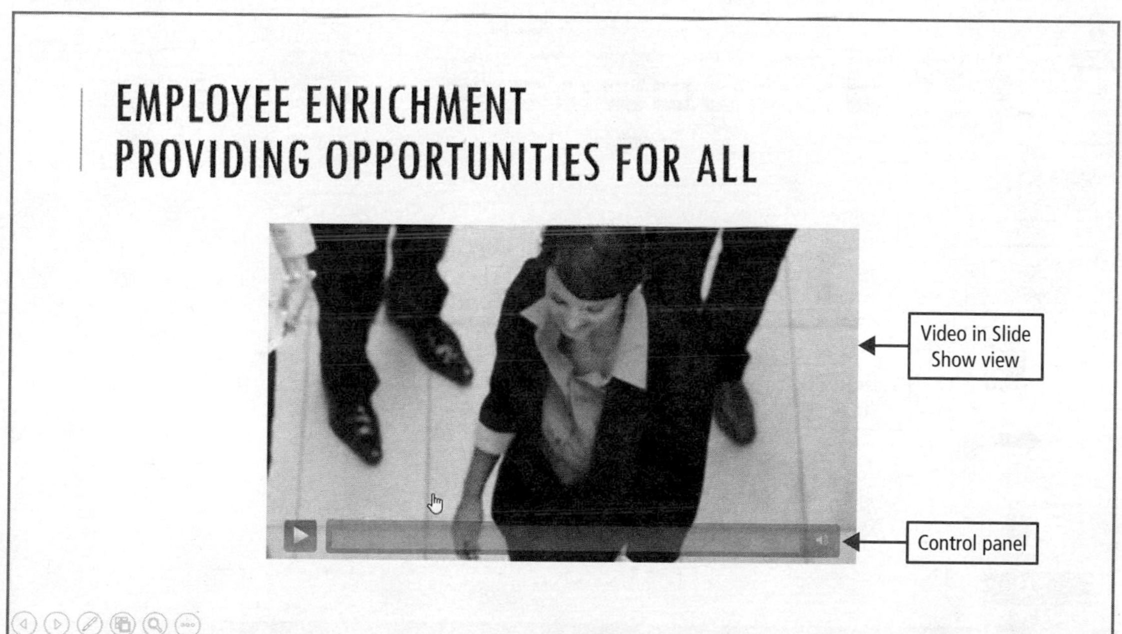

Minerva Studio/Fotolia; PowerPoint 2016, Windows 10, Microsoft Corporation

Figure 4

5. On the **Format tab**, in the **Size group**, click in the **Height** box . Type 4" and then press Enter. Notice that the video width adjusts proportionately.  MOS Obj 3.4.3

6. On the **Format tab**, in the **Arrange group**, click the **Align** button, and then click **Align Center** to center the video horizontally on the slide. Compare your screen with **Figure 3**.

7. Toward the right side of the status bar, click the **Slide Show** button to display **Slide 2** in the slide show. Point to the video to display the pointer, and then compare your screen with **Figure 4**.

   When you point to the video during the slide show, the player controls display.

8. With the pointer displayed, click the mouse button to view the video. When the video is finished, press Esc to exit the slide show.

9. If necessary, select the video. On the **Playback tab**, in the **Video Options group**, click the **Start arrow**, and then click **Automatically**. On the **Slide Show tab**, in the **Start Slide Show group**, click the **From Current Slide** button to display **Slide 2** in the slide show. When the video is finished, press Esc to exit the slide show. MOS Obj 3.4.2

   When you set a video to start automatically, the video will play when the slide displays in the slide show. You can use this option if you want the video to begin playing without clicking the mouse button.

10. **Save** the file.

■ **You have completed Skill 9 of 10**

- You can apply styles and effects to a video and change the video shape and border.
- You can recolor a video so that it coordinates with the presentation theme.

1. On **Slide 2**, if necessary, select the video. On the **Format tab**, in the **Video Styles group**, click the **More** button [▾]. In the **Video Styles** gallery, under **Intense**, click the third style—**Reflected Rounded Rectangle**. Click a blank area of the slide to view the style you just applied, and then compare your screen with **Figure 1**.
2. Select the video. On the **Format tab**, in the **Video Styles group**, click the **Video Border** button. Under **Theme Colors**, click the fourth option in the first row—**Dark Teal, Text 2**.
3. Click the **Video Border** button again, and then point to **Weight** and click **6 pt**.
4. With the video selected, on the **Format tab**, in the **Adjust group**, click the **Color** button.

   The Recolor gallery displays colors from the presentation theme that you can apply to the video.
5. Point to several of the thumbnails to view the color change, and then click the second thumbnail—**Grayscale**—to change the color of the video. Compare your slide with **Figure 2**.
6. On the **Format tab**, in the **Adjust group**, click the **Color** button, and then click the first thumbnail—**No Recolor**—to change the video color back to the original.

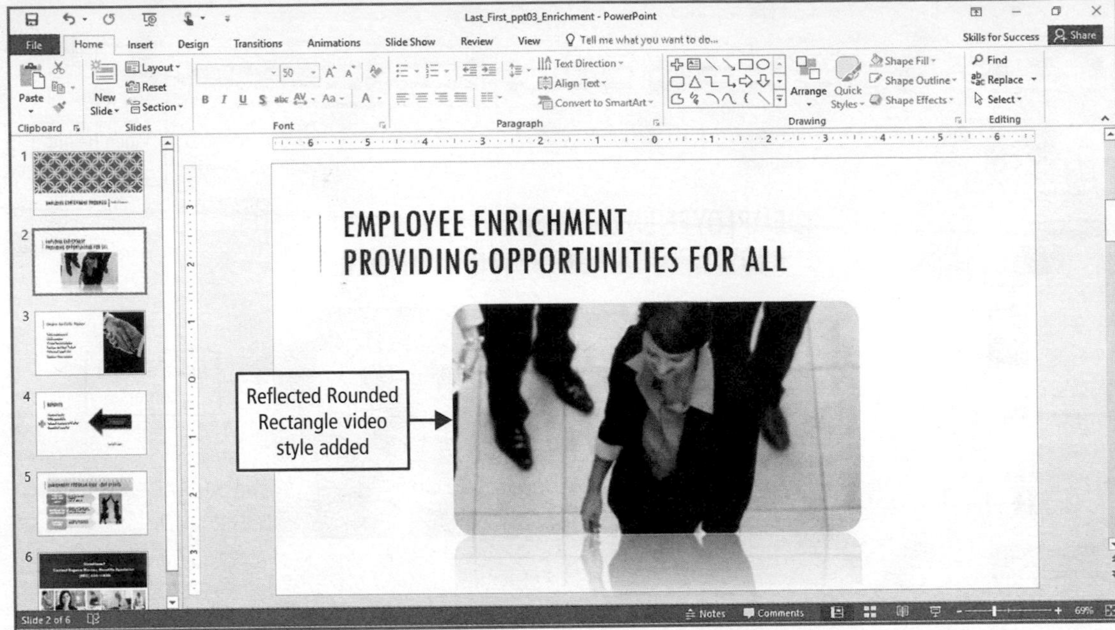

Figure 1 Minerva Studio/Fotolia; PowerPoint 2016, Windows 10, Microsoft Corporation

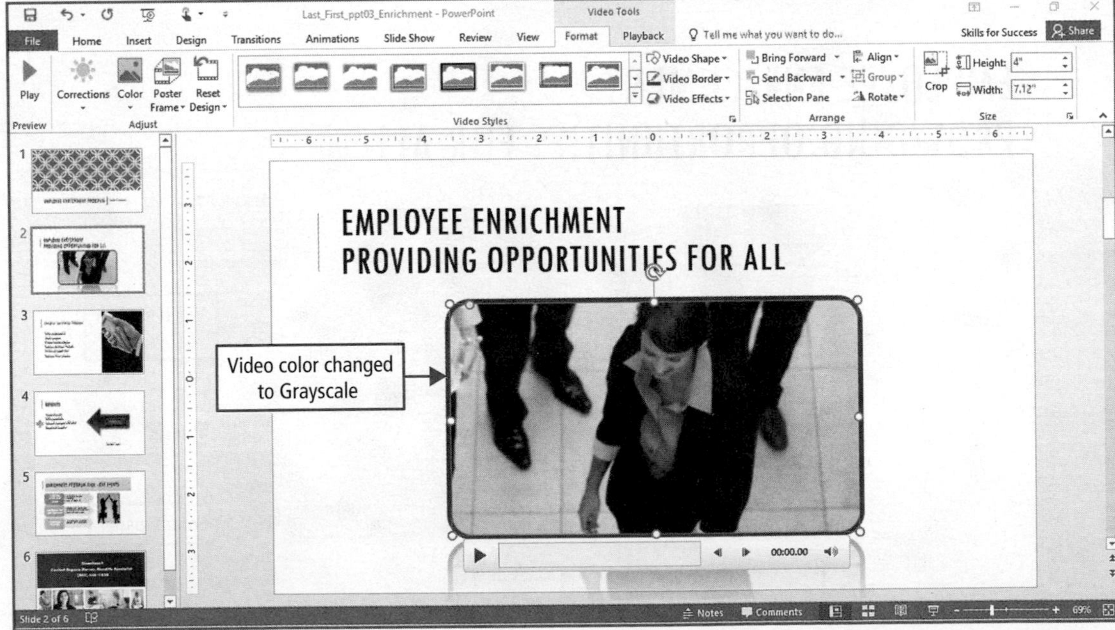

Figure 2 Minerva Studio/Fotolia; PowerPoint 2016, Windows 10, Microsoft Corporation

■ **Continue to the next page to complete the skill**

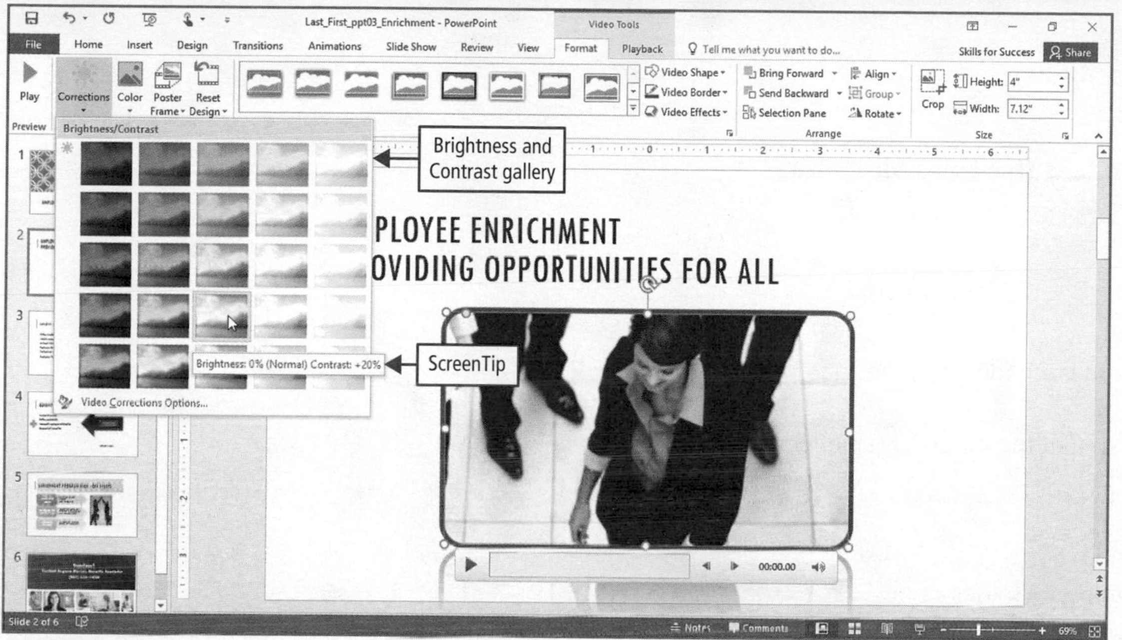

Minerva Studio/Fotolia; PowerPoint 2016, Windows 10, Microsoft Corporation

Figure 3

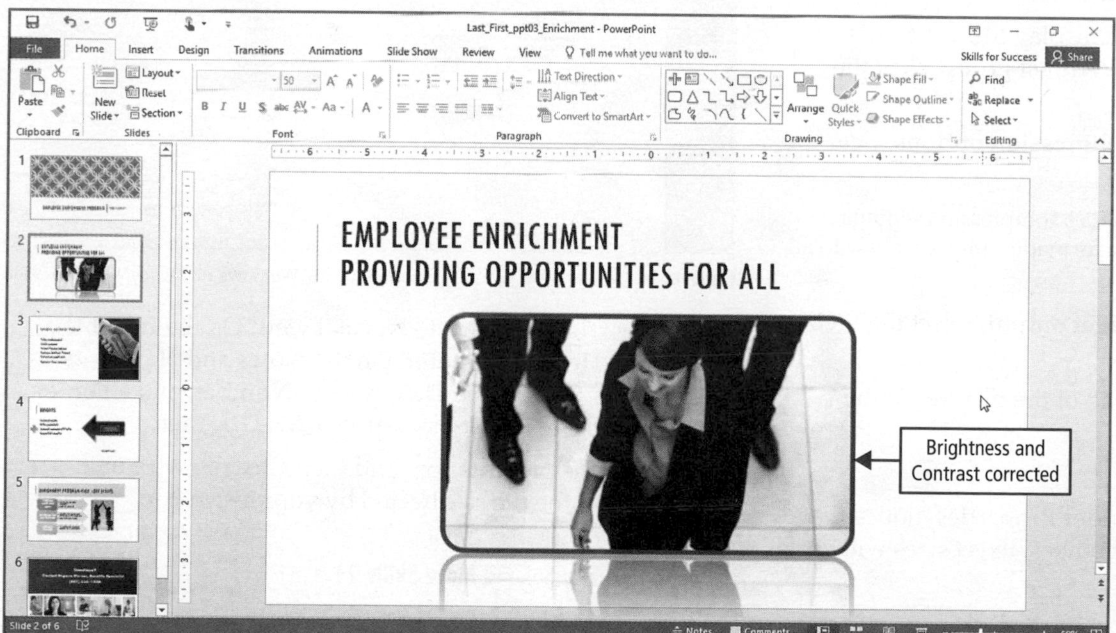

Minerva Studio/Fotolia; PowerPoint 2016, Windows 10, Microsoft Corporation

Figure 4

7. With the video selected, on the **Format tab**, in the **Adjust group**, click the **Corrections** button to display the **Brightness and Contrast** gallery.

   The Brightness and Contrast gallery displays combinations of brightness and contrast adjustments that you can apply to a video to improve color and visibility.

8. In the third column, point to the fourth thumbnail to display the ScreenTip **Brightness: 0% (Normal) Contrast: +20%**, as shown in **Figure 3**.
9. Click **Brightness: 0% (Normal) Contrast: +20%** to apply the correction to the video, and then click anywhere on the slide so that the video is not selected. Compare your screen with **Figure 4**.
10. On the **Slide Show tab**, in the **Start Slide Show group**, click **From Beginning**, and then advance through the presentation. When the black slide displays, click one more time to return to Normal view.
11. Insert a **Header & Footer** on the **Notes and Handouts** pages. Include the **Date and time**, the **Page Number**, and a **Footer** with the text Last_First_ppt03_Enrichment **Apply to All** pages.
12. **Save** the file. **Close** PowerPoint. Submit as directed by your instructor.

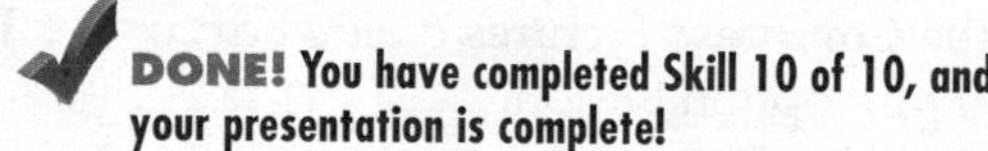

DONE! You have completed Skill 10 of 10, and your presentation is complete!

More Skills 11

Compress Pictures

To complete this presentation, you will need the following file:

- ppt03_MS11Garden

You will save your file as:

- Last_First_ppt03_MS11Garden

- ▸ When a presentation contains several pictures with large file sizes, the delivery of a presentation may be slow.
- ▸ You can compress the pictures in a presentation so that the file size is smaller.

---

1. Start **PowerPoint 2016**. Locate and open **ppt03_MS11Garden**. **Save** your presentation in your **PowerPoint Chapter 3** folder as Last_First_ppt03_MS11Garden
2. Click the **File tab**, and then on **Info page**, under **Properties**, notice that the **Size** of the file is approximately 16.3 MB—megabytes.

Obj 5.2.4

3. Click Esc to return to the presentation, and then display **Slide 2**. Select the picture, and then click the **Format tab**. In the **Adjust group**, click the **Compress Pictures** button.
4. In the **Compress Pictures** dialog box, under **Compression options**, clear the **Apply only to this picture** check box.

   Clearing the *Apply only to this picture* check box applies compression settings to all pictures in the presentation so that the changes are made simultaneously to all images in the presentation.

5. In the **Compress Pictures** dialog box, under **Target output**, select the **Web (150 ppi)** option button.
6. Click **OK** to close the dialog box and compress all of the pictures in the presentation.
7. On the Quick Access Toolbar, click **Save** .
8. Click the **File tab**, and then on the **Info** page, under **Properties**, notice that the **Size** of the file is approximately 780 KB—kilobytes. Exact sizes will vary. Compare your screen with **Figure 1**.

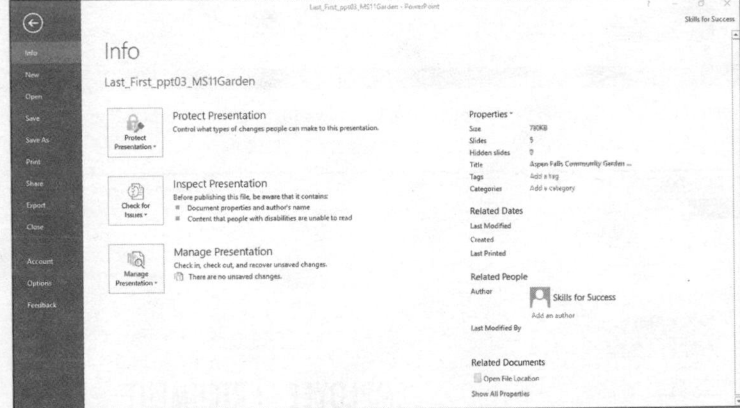

Figure 1 PowerPoint 2016, Windows 10, Microsoft Corporation

9. Press Esc to return to Normal view. On the **Insert tab**, click **Header & Footer**. On the **Notes and Handouts** pages, include the **Date**, a **Page Number**, and a **Footer** with the text Last_First_ppt03_MS11Garden
10. **Save** the presentation, and then **Close** PowerPoint. Submit the file as directed by your instructor.

- **You have completed More Skills 11**

More Skills 12

Save Groups as Picture Files

To complete this presentation, you will need the following file:

- ppt03_MS12Parks

You will save your files as:

- Last_First_ppt03_MS12Parks
- Last_First_ppt03_MS12ParksLogo

- A group can be saved as a picture file.
- Saving a group as a picture facilitates easy sharing among presentations and applications.

---

1. Start **PowerPoint 2016**, and then open **ppt03_MS12Parks**. **Save** the presentation in your **PowerPoint Chapter 3** folder as Last_First_ppt03_MS12Parks

2. On **Slide 1**, toward the top right corner of the slide, click the rectangle shape containing the words *Aspen Falls Parks Department* to select it. Hold down Ctrl, and then click the picture so that both the picture and the text box are selected.

   Without grouping, each of these items would move separately.

3. On the **Picture Tools Format tab**, in the **Arrange group**, click the **Group** button, and then click **Group**. Point to the grouped image, and then right-click. On the shortcut menu, click **Save as Picture**.

   Grouping the rectangle and picture combines them into a single image that can be saved or moved.

4. In the **Save As Picture** dialog box, navigate to your **PowerPoint Chapter 3** folder. Click the **Save as type arrow**, and then click **JPEG File Interchange Format**. In the **File name** box, type Last_First_ppt03_MS12ParksLogo and then click **Save** to save the group as a picture file.

   Saving the file as a JPEG image results in a good-quality picture with a smaller file size than other picture file types.

5. Display **Slide 2**. On the **Insert tab**, in the **Images group**, click the **Pictures** button. Navigate to your **PowerPoint Chapter 3** folder, and then click **Last_First_ppt03_MS12ParksLogo**. Click **Insert** to insert the picture.

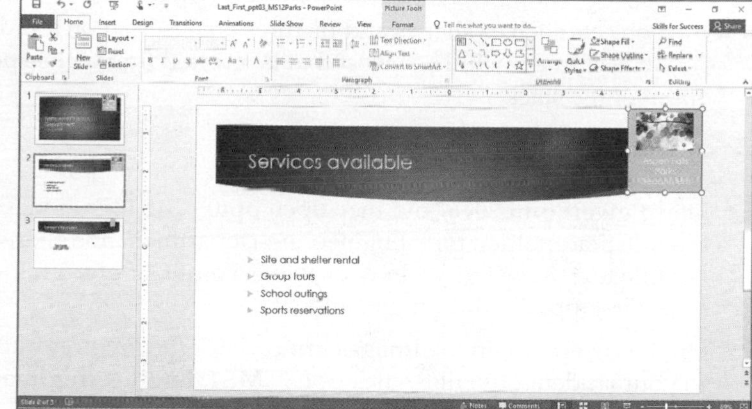

PowerPoint 2016, Windows 10, Microsoft Corporation **Figure 1**

6. On the **Format tab**, in the **Size group**, replace the number in the **Height** box with 2.2" and then press Enter to resize the picture. Drag the picture to the upper right corner of the slide as shown in **Figure 1**.

7. On **Slide 3**, repeat the techniques just practiced to insert, size, and position the **Last_First_ppt03_ParksLogo** picture.

8. On the **Notes and Handouts** pages, include the **Date**, a **Page Number**, and a **Footer** with the text Last_First_ppt03_MS12Parks

9. **Save** and then submit your files as directed. **Close** PowerPoint.

- **You have completed More Skills 12**

More Skills 13

Change Object Order

To complete this presentation, you will need the following files:

- ppt03_MS13EngineeringImage
- ppt03_MS13Engineering

You will save your file as:

- Last_First_ppt03_MS13Engineering

▶ When objects such as shapes and pictures are inserted on a slide, they often overlap as if in a stack. The object that is inserted first will be positioned at the bottom of the stack.

---

1. Start **PowerPoint 2016**, and then open **ppt03_MS13Engineering.** In the title placeholder, type Engineering Department and then center the title text. **Save** the file in your **PowerPoint Chapter 3** folder as Last_First_ppt03_MS13Engineering
2. On the **Insert tab**, in the **Images group**, click the **Pictures** button. Navigate to your student data files, click **ppt03_MS13EngineeringImage**, and then click **Insert**.
3. On the **Format tab**, in the **Size group**, replace the number in the **Height** box with 2.5" and then press Enter.
4. On the **Format tab**, in the **Arrange group**, click the **Align** button, and then click **Align Center**. In the **Arrange group**, click the **Align** button again, and then click **Align Middle**.
5. Click the **Picture Effects** button, and then point to **Preset**. Under **Presets**, click the second style in the first row—**Preset 2.**
6. On the **Insert tab**, in the **Illustrations group**, click the **Shapes** button. Under **Rectangles**, click the first shape—**Rectangle**. Click anywhere on the slide. On the **Format tab**, in the **Size group**, change the number in the **Height** box to 3" Change the number in the **Width** box to 3.5" and then press Enter.
7. On the **Format tab**, in the **Arrange group**, click the **Align** button. Click **Align Center**. In the **Arrange group**, click the **Align** button again, and then click **Align Middle**.

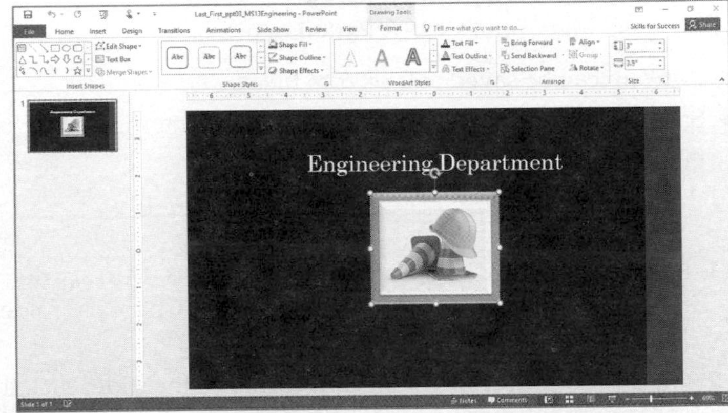

Figure 1 PowerPoint 2016, Windows 10, Microsoft Corporation

8. On the **Format tab**, in the **Shape Styles group**, click the **More** button, and then under **Theme Styles**, click the sixth option in the last row—**Intense Effect – Gold, Accent 5.**
9. With the rectangle still selected, click the **Shape Effects** button, and then point to **Preset**. Under **Presets**, click the second style in the first row—**Preset 2.**
10. On the **Format tab**, in the **Arrange group**, click the **Send Backward** button, and then compare your slide with **Figure 1**. MOS Obj 2.4.1
11. Insert a **Header & Footer** on the **Notes and Handouts** pages. Include the **Date and time**, the **Page Number**, and the **Footer** Last_First_ppt03_MS13Engineering
12. **Save** the presentation. Submit the file as directed.

■ **You have completed More Skills 13**

More Skills 14

Insert a Screen Shot in a Presentation

To complete this presentation, you will need the following files:

- ppt03_MS14Finance
- ppt03_MS14FinanceMemo

You will save your file as:

- **Last_First_ppt03_MS14Finance**

► You can insert a ***screen shot***—a snapshot of any window that is open on your desktop—into your presentation. A screen shot can be used to clarify exactly what a user should be seeing on their screen.

---

1. Start **PowerPoint 2016**. Locate and open the file **ppt03_MS14Finance**. **Save** the presentation in your **PowerPoint Chapter 3 folder** as Last_First_ppt03_MS14Finance
2. Move to **Slide 2**.
3. Start **Word 2016**. Navigate to your student data files, and then open **ppt03_MS14FinanceMemo**. Review the contents of the memo template, and then at the bottom of your screen, on the taskbar, click the **PowerPoint** button to display the **Last_First_ppt03_MS14Finance** presentation.
4. On **Slide 2**, click the right content placeholder.
5. On the **Insert tab**, in the **Images group**, click the **Screenshot** button. Under **Available Windows**, click the image of the Word memo. Compare your screen with **Figure 1**.

   The image of the Finance Memo, opened in Word 2016, is inserted into the content placeholder.

6. Insert a **Header & Footer** on the **Notes and Handouts** pages with the **Date**, **Page Number**, and the **Footer** text Last_First_ppt03_MS14Finance
7. **Save** the presentation. **Close** PowerPoint, and then **Close** Word. Submit the file as directed.

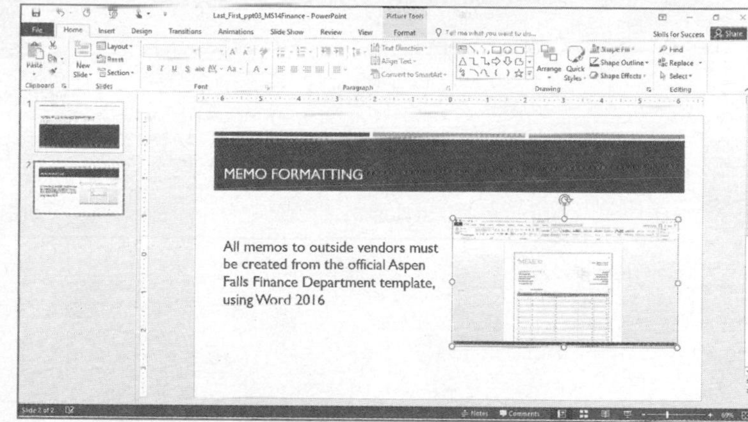

PowerPoint 2016, Windows 10, Microsoft Corporation **Figure 1**

■ **You have completed More Skills 14**

Review

The following table summarizes the **SKILLS AND PROCEDURES** covered in this chapter.

Skills Number	Task	Step	Icon
1	Insert slides from other presentations	Home tab → New Slide arrow → Reuse Slides	
2	Insert online pictures	Insert tab → Online Pictures	
3	Crop a picture to a shape	Format tab → Crop arrow → Crop to Shape	
3	Add picture effects	Format tab → Picture Effects	
3	Add a border to pictures	Format tab → Picture Border	
4	Insert shapes	Insert tab → Shapes	
5	Add text to shapes	Select shape → type text	
5	Insert text boxes	Insert tab → Text Box	
6	Group objects	Press Ctrl, select items → Format tab → Group → Group	
7	Convert text to SmartArt	Place insertion point in text → Home tab → Convert to SmartArt	
9	Insert videos	Insert tab → Video	
10	Apply video styles	Format tab → Video Styles	

Project Summary Chart		
Project	**Project Type**	**Project Location**
Skills Review	Review	In Book & MIL MyITLab® Grader
Skills Assessment 1	Review	In Book & MIL MyITLab® Grader
Skills Assessment 2	Review	Book
My Skills	Problem Solving	Book
Visual Skills Check	Problem Solving	Book
Skillls Challenge 1	Critical Thinking	Book
Skills Challenge 2	Critical Thinking	Book
More Skills Assessment	Review	In Book & MIL MyITLab® Grader
Collaborating with Google	Critical Thinking	Book

MOS Objectives Covered	
2.2.1 Insert or replace shapes	2.4.4 Display alignment tools
2.2.2 Insert text boxes	3.3.2 Convert lists to SmartArt graphics
2.2.3 Resize shapes and text boxes	3.3.3 Add shapes to SmartArt graphics
2.2.4 Format shapes and text boxes	3.4.1 Insert audio and video clips
2.3.1 Insert images	3.4.2 Configure media playback options
2.3.2 Resize and crop images	3.4.3 Adjust media window size
2.3.3 Apply styles and effects	5.1.1 Insert slides from another presentation
2.4.1 Order objects	5.2.4 Preserve presentation content
2.4.2 Align objects	

Key Terms

BizSkills Video

1. How is customer service important to customer retention? How does this impact the overall success, or failure, of a company?
2. If a company provides customer service training to all of its customer service staff, how might photos and videos help to communicate its message?

Online Help Skills

1. With PowerPoint open, on the **File tab**, near the upper right corner of the screen, click the **Microsoft PowerPoint Help** button [?], or press [F1].
2. In the **PowerPoint Help** window, use the **Search** box to locate and open the article *Video and audio file formats supported in PowerPoint*. Maximize the window, and then compare your screen with **Figure 1**.

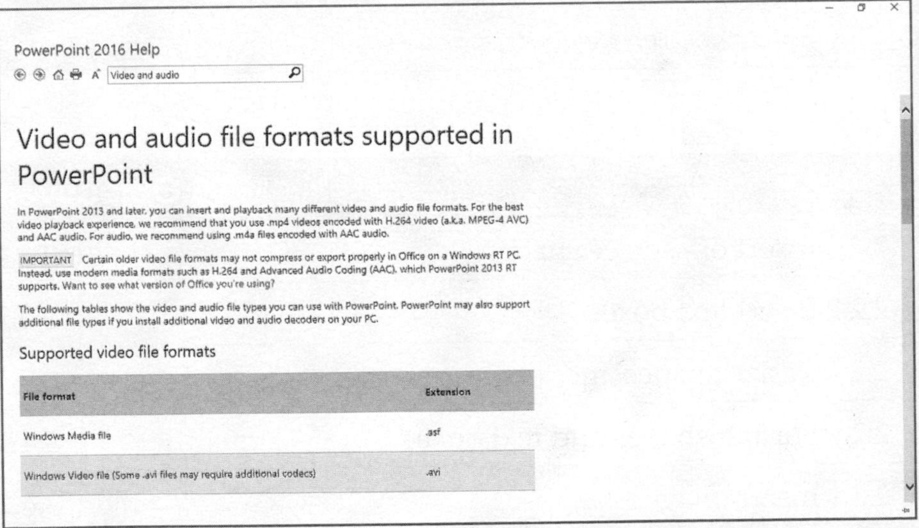

Figure 1 PowerPoint 2016, Windows 10, Microsoft Corporation

3. Read the article and answer the following questions: What video format does Microsoft recommend for use in PowerPoint presentations? List at least two other types of video files that could be inserted into a presentation. **Close** the Help window, and then **Close** PowerPoint.

Matching 

Match each term in the second column with its correct definition in the first column by writing the letter of the term on the blank line in front of the correct definition.

___ **1.** The command used to insert slides from another presentation.

___ **2.** Formatting options applied to pictures that include shadows, reflections, glows, soft edges, bevels, and 3-D rotations.

___ **3.** Lines that display in the rulers to give you a visual indication of where the pointer is positioned.

___ **4.** Objects such as lines, rectangles, and circles that can be used as design elements on a slide.

___ **5.** An object used to position text anywhere on a slide.

___ **6.** The action of moving an object in small increments by using the directional arrow keys.

___ **7.** Multiple objects treated as one unit that can be copied, moved, or formatted.

___ **8.** A fill effect in which one color fades into another.

___ **9.** A visual representation of information that you can use to communicate your message or ideas effectively by choosing from many different layouts.

___ **10.** A command used to change a list into a SmartArt graphic.

A Convert to SmartArt Graphic
B Gradient fill
C Group
D Guides
E Nudge
F Picture effects
G Reuse Slides
H Shapes
I SmartArt graphic
J Text box

Multiple Choice

MyITLab®

Choose the correct answer.

1. The task pane that is used to insert slides from another presentation.
   - A. Insert Slides
   - B. Browse Slides
   - C. Reuse Slides
2. This does not automatically include borders or shading when inserted on a slide.
   - A. Rectangle shape
   - B. Text box
   - C. SmartArt
3. The default alignment applied to text typed in a shape.
   - A. Left
   - B. Center
   - C. Right
4. A SmartArt layout type that illustrates nonsequential information.
   - A. Process
   - B. Cycle
   - C. List
5. A SmartArt layout type that illustrates a continual process.
   - A. Hierarchy
   - B. Cycle
   - C. Process
6. A SmartArt layout type that illustrates a decision tree or creates an organization chart.
   - A. Relationship
   - B. Hierarchy
   - C. Pyramid
7. A SmartArt layout type that illustrates connections.
   - A. Relationship
   - B. Hierarchy
   - C. Pyramid
8. The tab in which video Start options are found.
   - A. Format
   - B. Playback
   - C. Design
9. The button that displays video Brightness and Contrast options.
   - A. Color
   - B. Design
   - C. Corrections
10. The button that displays the video Recolor gallery.
    - A. Color
    - B. Design
    - C. Corrections

Topics for Discussion

1. Some PowerPoint presenters advocate using only slides that consist of a single statement and a graphic so that the presentation reads like a story. Other presenters advocate using slides that combine the "single statement and graphics" approach with slides that include detail in the form of bullet points, diagrams, and pictures. What is the advantage of each of these approaches? Which approach would you prefer to use?
2. Sharing presentation slides among employees in an organization is a common practice. What types of information and objects do you think should be included on slides that are shared within an organization?

Skills Review

To complete this presentation, you will need the following files:

- ppt03_SRPastTuition
- ppt03_SRVideo

You will save your file as:

- Last_First_ppt03_SRTuition

1. Start **PowerPoint 2016**, and then create a new presentation using the **Facet** theme and the default variant. On **Slide 1**, in the title placeholder, type Tuition Reimbursement Plan Change the **Font Size** for the text in the title placeholder to **44**. In the subtitle placeholder, type An Aspen Falls Employee Benefit
2. On the **Home tab**, in the **Slides group**, click the **New Slide arrow**, and then click **Reuse Slides**.
3. In the **Reuse Slides** pane, click the **Browse** button, and then click **Browse File**. From your student files, click **ppt03_SRPastTuition**, and then click **Open**. In the **Reuse Slides** pane, click **Slides 2**, **3**, and **4** to insert them, and then **Close** the pane. **Save** your presentation in your **PowerPoint Chapter 3** folder as Last_First_ppt03_SRTuition
4. On **Slide 2**, in the right content placeholder, click the **Online Pictures** button. In the **Insert Pictures** dialog box, in the **Search Bing** box, type textbook and then press Enter. Click a square or rectangular image featuring textbooks. Click the **Insert** button. Compare your screen with **Figure 1**. Your image will vary.
5. With the picture selected, on the **Format tab**, in the **Size group**, change the **Height** to 4"
6. On the **Format tab**, in the **Size group**, click the **Crop arrow**, and then click **Crop to Shape**. Under **Rectangles**, click **Round Diagonal Corner Rectangle**. In the **Picture Styles group**, click the **Picture Effects** button, point to **Bevel**, and then under **Bevel**, click **Soft Round**.
7. On the **Insert tab**, in the **Text group**, click **Text Box**. Align the pointer at **0.5** inches before **0** on the horizontal ruler and at **3** inches below **0** on the vertical ruler, and then click one time to insert the text box. Type Earn your college degree Adjust the placement of your textbox if needed. Click a blank area of the slide, and then compare your slide with **Figure 2**.

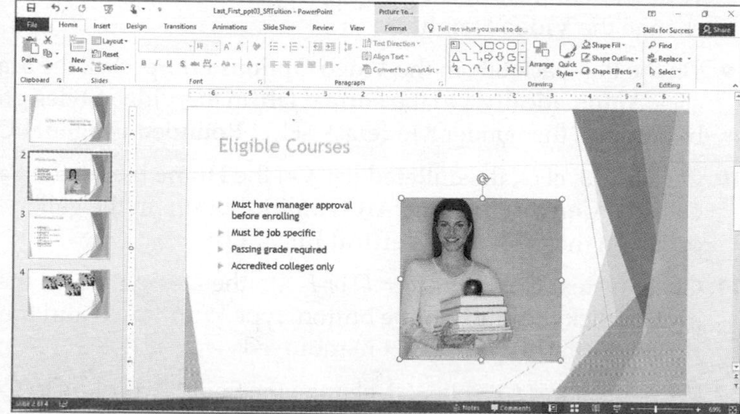

Xy/Fotolia; PowerPoint 2016, Windows 10, Microsoft Corporation **Figure 1**

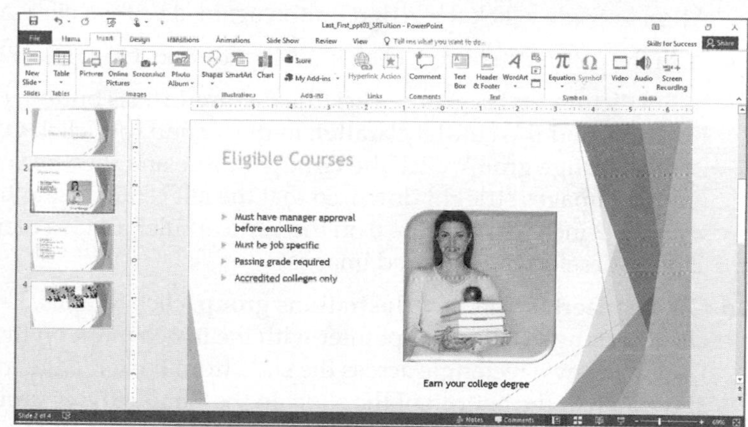

Xy/Fotolia; PowerPoint 2016, Windows 10, Microsoft Corporation **Figure 2**

■ **Continue to the next page to complete this Skills Review**

8. On **Slide 3**, in the right content placeholder, click the **Insert Video** button. From your student files, insert **ppt03_SRVideo**. On the **Format tab**, in the **Size group**, change the **Video Height** to 3.6"

9. On the **Playback tab**, in the **Video Options group**, click the **Start arrow**, and then click **Automatically**. On the **Format tab**, in the **Video Styles group**, click the **More** button, and then under **Moderate**, select **Rounded Diagonal Corner, White**.

10. On **Slide 3**, click the bulleted list. On the **Home tab**, in the **Paragraph group**, click the **Convert to SmartArt Graphic** button. In the gallery, click the second option in the first row—**Vertical Block List**.

11. Click the text *Grade earned = D or F*. On the **Design tab**, in the **Create Graphic group**, click the **Add Shape** button, type Withdrawn and then click the **Add Bullet** button. Type 0%; not reimbursed

12. With the SmartArt selected, change the SmartArt colors to **Colorful - Accent Colors**, and then apply the first **3-D** SmartArt style—**Polished**. Click a blank area of the slide, and then compare your slide with **Figure 3**.

13. Display **Slide 4**. Hold down Ctrl, and then click each picture. On the **Format tab**, in the **Arrange group**, click the **Align** button, and then, if necessary, select **Align to Slide**. Click the **Align** button again, and then click **Align Top**.

14. With the pictures selected, click the **Align** button. Click **Distribute Horizontally**.

15. In the **Picture Styles group**, click the **Picture Effects** button. Point to **3-D Rotation**, and then under **Parallel**, in the second row, click **Off Axis 1 Right**. In the **Arrange group**, click the **Group** button, and then click **Group**. Drag the grouped images straight down, so that the left center sizing handle is aligned with the **2** inch mark before **0** on the vertical ruler. Click a blank area of the slide to deselect the grouped images.

16. On the **Insert tab**, in the **Illustrations group**, click **Shapes**. Under **Rectangles**, click **Rectangle**. Align the pointer with the **0** inch mark on the vertical ruler. Drag to draw a rectangle across the slide from the left edge to the right edge and down to the bottom of the slide. In the **Shape Styles group**, click the **Shape Fill** button, and then under **Standard Colors**, click **Light Green**. Click **Shape Fill**, and then click **Gradient**. Under **Dark Variations**, click **From Center**.

17. In the shape, type Congratulations graduates! and then change the **Font Size** to **40** for all of the text in the shape.

18. View the slide show. Insert a **Header & Footer** on all **Notes and Handouts** pages with the date, page number, and the footer text Last_First_ppt03_SRTuition Compare your presentation with **Figure 4**, and then **Save** the presentation. **Close** and then submit the file as directed by your instructor.

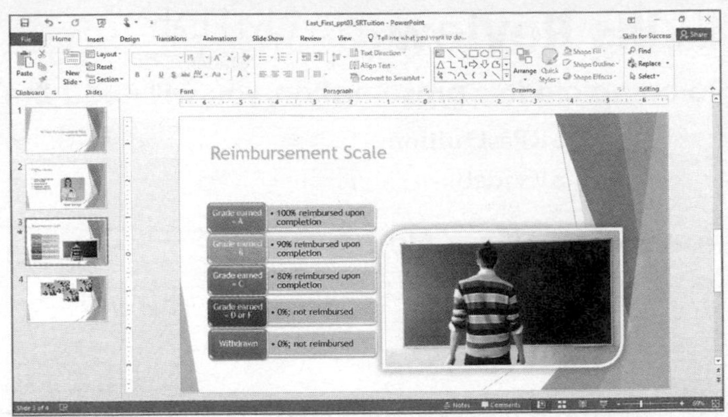

Figure 3 PowerPoint 2016, Windows 10, Microsoft Corporation

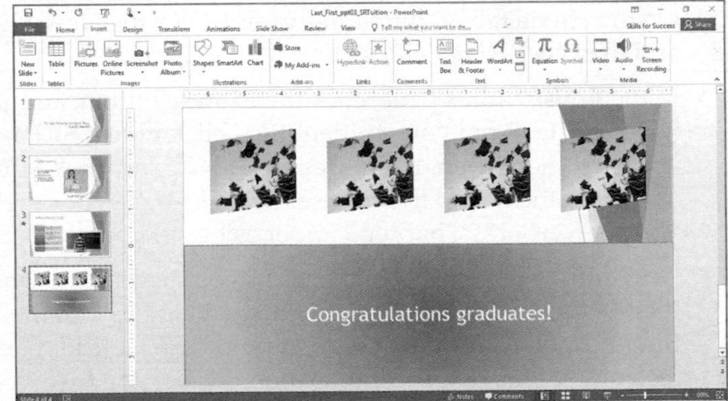

Figure 4 xy/Fotolia; PowerPoint 2016, Windows 10, Microsoft Corporation

DONE! You have completed this Skills Review

Skills Assessment 1

To complete this presentation, you will need the following files:

- ppt03_SA1Online
- ppt03_SA1OnlineCourses
- ppt03_SA1Video

You will save your file as:

- Last_First_ppt03_SA1Online

1. Start **PowerPoint 2016**, and then from your student files, open **ppt03_SA1Online**. With **Slide 1** showing in Normal view, display the **Reuse Slides** pane, and then insert **Slide 2—Course Offerings**—from the student data file **ppt03_SA1OnlineCourses**. **Save** your file in your **PowerPoint Chapter 3** folder as Last_First_ppt03_SA1Online
2. On **Slide 2**, convert the text in the right content placeholder to SmartArt in the **Target List** layout. Change the SmartArt **Color** to **Colorful Range - Accent Colors 5 to 6**, and then apply the **3-D, Inset** SmartArt style.
3. On **Slide 2**, in the left content placeholder, use **Online Pictures** to search for online education images. Insert an image related to online education. Compare your screen with **Figure 1**—your image may vary.
4. On **Slide 3**, insert a **Left Arrow** shape. Draw the shape, adjusting the size to a **Height** of 2" and a **Width** of 3" Move the shape so that the tip of the arrow is at the **1** inch mark to the right of **0** on the horizontal ruler and the bottom of the shape is even with the **2** inch mark below **0** on the vertical ruler.
5. In the shape, type Enroll today! Increase the **Font Size** to **24**. Apply the **Brown, 18 pt glow, Accent color 1** glow shape effect.
6. On **Slide 3**, in the left content placeholder, insert the video named **ppt03_SA1Video** from your student files. Adjust the **Video Height** to 3.2" and then add the **Simple Frame, White** video style.
7. With the video still selected, change the video **Color** to **Grayscale**. Compare your screen with **Figure 2**.

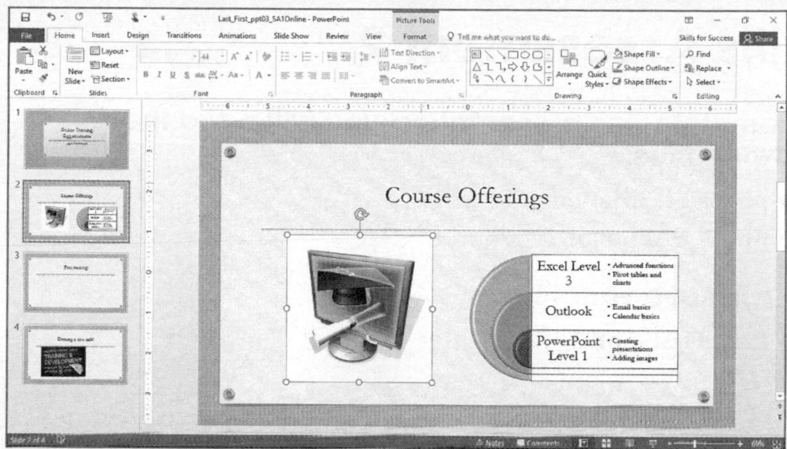

PowerPoint 2016, Windows 10, Microsoft Corporation **Figure 1**

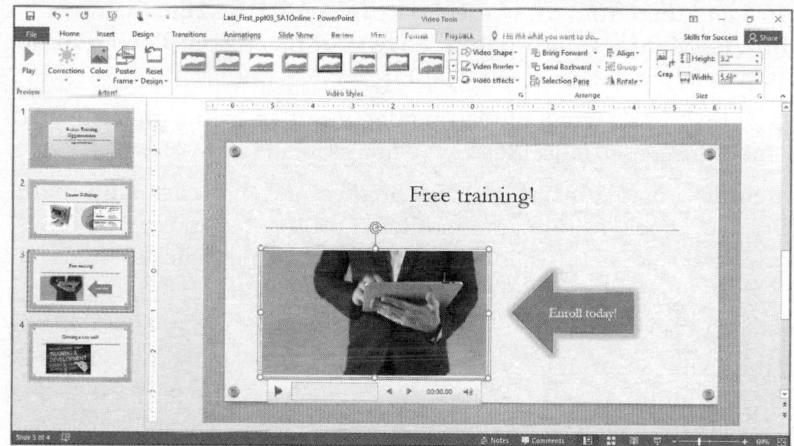

Doc Rabe Media/Fotolia; PowerPoint 2016, Windows 10, Microsoft Corporation **Figure 2**

8. On **Slide 4**, select the image, click **Align**, and then click **Align Center**. With the image still selected, crop it to the **Flowchart: Document** shape.
9. On the **Notes and Handouts** pages, include the date, a page number, and a footer with the text Last_First_ppt03_SA1Online **Save** and **Close** the presentation, and then submit it as directed by your instructor.

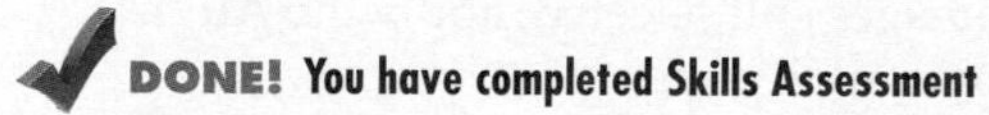

Skills Assessment 2

To complete this presentation, you will need the following files:

- ppt03_SA2Mentor
- ppt03_SA2Email

You will save your file as:

- Last_First_ppt03_SA2Mentor

---

1. Start **PowerPoint 2016**, and then from your student files, open **ppt03_SA2Mentor**. Move to **Slide 2**. Display the **Reuse Slides** pane, and then from the student data file **ppt03_SA2Email**, insert **Slide 1—Mentor Coordinators**. **Save** your file in your **PowerPoint Chapter 3** folder as Last_First_ppt03_SA2Mentor
2. On **Slide 2**, in the content placeholder, insert an online image related to mentoring assistance Resize the image to a **Height** of 3.1"
3. On **Slide 2**, on the **Insert tab**, click **Shapes**, and then click **Flowchart: Punched Tape**. Position your pointer at the intersection of **0** on the horizontal ruler and **0** on the vertical ruler, and then click to insert the shape. Change the **Height** to 2" and the **Width** to 3.5" If needed, adjust or move the image you inserted earlier to avoid an overlap.
4. In the shape, insert the text Climb to the top! Apply the **Intense Effect - Plumb**, **Accent 1** shape style, and then increase the **Font Size** to 28. Apply the **Circle Bevel** shape effect. Select the image and the shape, use the **Align** button to **Align to Slide**, and then select **Distribute Horizontally**. Click a blank area of the slide, and then compare your screen with **Figure 1**. The image on your slide may vary.
5. On **Slide 3**, convert the content placeholder text to the **Segmented Process** SmartArt—found in the **List** or **Process** layouts. Change the SmartArt **Color** to **Primary Theme Colors Dark 2 Fill**, and then apply the **Powder** 3-D SmartArt style.
6. On **Slide 4**, select all of the images, and then crop all of them at once to the **Basic Shape** named **Folded Corner**.
7. On **Slide 4**, with all of the images still selected, apply the **Align Middle** and **Distribute Horizontally** alignment options.
8. On **Slide 4**, apply the **Full Reflection, 8 pt offset** picture effect to all of the pictures, and then compare your screen with **Figure 2**.

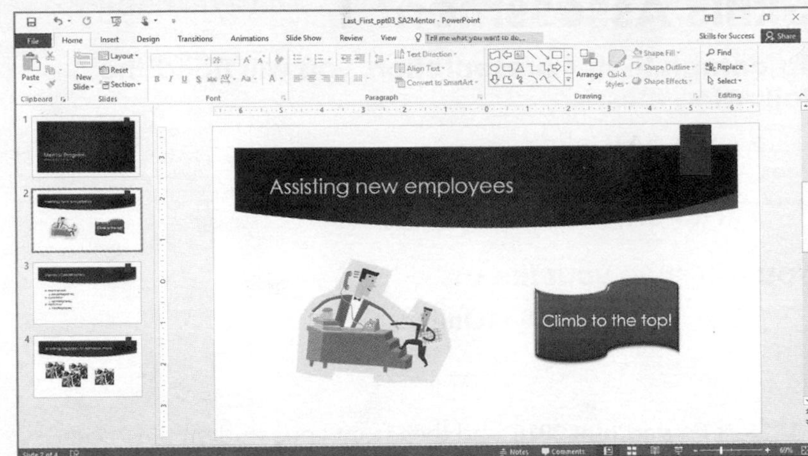

Figure 1 PowerPoint 2016, Windows 10, Microsoft Corporation

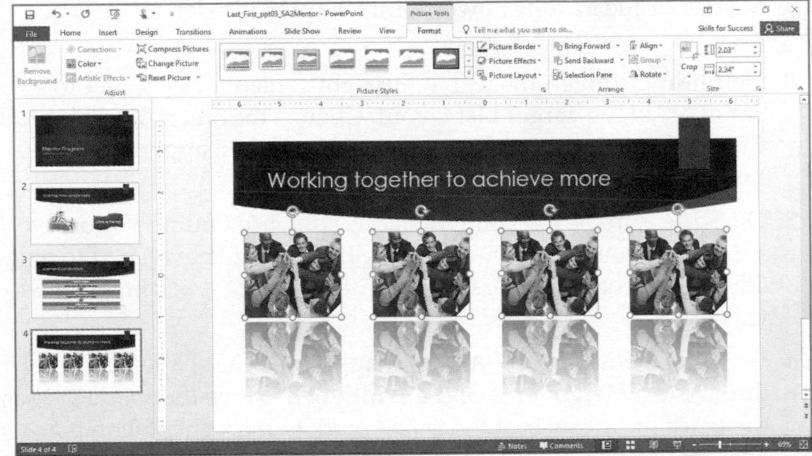

Figure 2 Yuri Arcurs/Fotolia; PowerPoint 2016, Windows 10, Microsoft Corporation

9. On the **Notes and Handouts** pages, include the date, a page number, and a footer with the text Last_First_ppt03_SA2Mentor **Save** and **Close** the presentation, and then submit it as directed by your instructor.

DONE! You have completed Skills Assessment 2

My Skills

To complete this presentation, you will need the following files:

- **ppt03_MYCareerSearch**
- **ppt03_MYCareerAdvice**

You will save your file as:

- **Last_First_ppt03_MYCareerSearch**

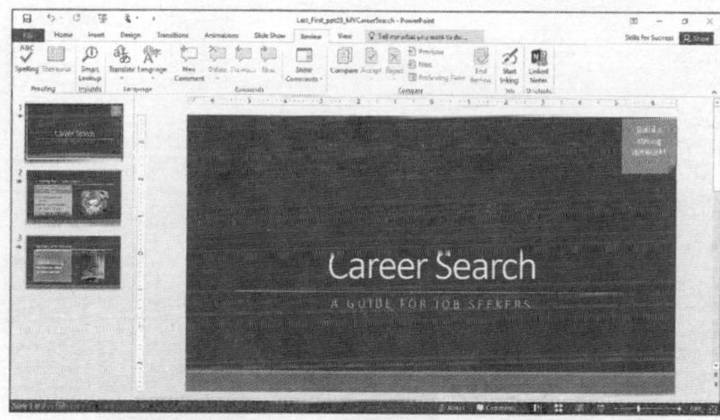

Career Search

PowerPoint 2016, Windows 10, Microsoft Corporation **Figure 1**

1. Start **PowerPoint 2016**, and then from your student files, open **ppt03_MYCareerSearch**. Select **Slide 2**. Display the **Reuse Slides** pane, and then from the student data file **ppt03_MYCareerAdvice**, insert **Slide 1—Making it to the top**. **Save** the presentation in your **PowerPoint Chapter 3** folder as Last_First_ppt03_MYCareerSearch
2. On **Slide 1**, insert the **Folded Corner** basic shape. Change the shape's height to 1.5" and its width to 1.5" Move the shape to the upper right corner of the slide, and then insert the text Build a strong network!
3. On **Slide 2**, in the right content placeholder, insert an online picture related to a job interview—use the search term interview Resize the image to a height of **3.5"**.
4. On **Slide 2**, in the left content placeholder, convert the text to a **Horizontal Bullet List** SmartArt graphic, and then apply the **Polished** 3-D SmartArt style.
5. On **Slide 3**, select the left content placeholder, apply a **Gradient** with a **Dark Variation From Center** shape fill, and then apply the **Preset 4** shape effect. For the placeholder text, increase the font size to **24** and apply **Bold**.
6. On **Slide 3**, crop the image to the **Round Diagonal Corner Rectangle** shape, and then apply the **Preset 4** picture effect.
7. On the **Notes and Handouts** pages, include the date, a page number, and a footer with the text Last_First_ppt03_MYCareerSearch
8. **Save** the presentation, and then compare your screen with **Figure 1**. Your images may vary. **Close** PowerPoint, and then submit the file as directed by your instructor.

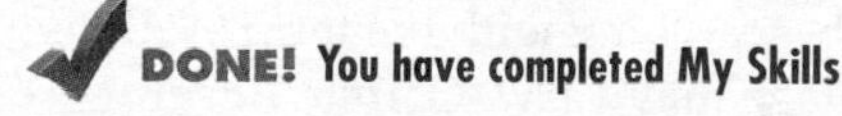

DONE! You have completed My Skills

Visual Skills Check

To complete this presentation, you will need the following file:

- ppt03_VSPark

You will save your file as:

- Last_First_ppt03_VSPark

Start **PowerPoint 2016**, and then from your student files, open **ppt03_VSPark**. Format and edit the slide as shown in **Figure 1**. **Save** the file as Last_First_ppt03_VSPark in your **PowerPoint Chapter 3** folder.

The list in the left content placeholder has been converted to SmartArt. An additional shape and bullet have been added, with the text shown. The SmartArt's color has been changed to **Colorful Range – Accent Colors 4 to 5**, and the **Polished 3-D** SmartArt style has been applied. An image was inserted from Bing Image Search, searching with the term Walking Path Your image may vary. A **Circle Bevel Picture Effect** has been applied to the image. The **Dark Variation From Center** gradient fill was added to the title placeholder, the font size was changed to **60** points, and the text was centered. On the **Notes and Handouts** pages, include the date, a page number, and a footer with the text Last_First_ppt03_VSPark **Save** and **Close** the presentation, and then submit it as directed by your instructor.

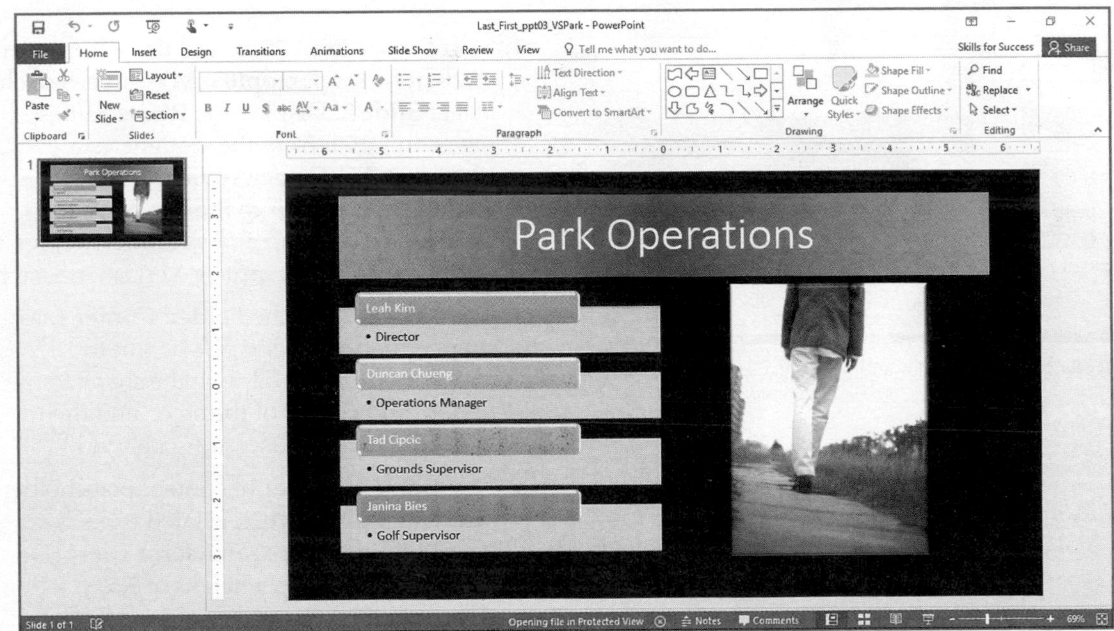

Figure 1 Anetlanda/Fotolia; PowerPoint 2016, Windows 10, Microsoft Corporation

DONE! You have completed Visual Skills Check

Skills Challenge 1

To complete this presentation, you will need the following file:

- **ppt03_SC1Fire**

You will save your file as:

- **Last_First_ppt03_SC1Fire**

Locate and open the presentation **ppt03_SC1Fire**. Save the presentation in your chapter folder as Last_First_ppt03_SC1Fire Rachel Brewer, the city's Fire Marshall, will use these slides as she presents at a volunteer recognition event. Using the skills you practiced in this chapter, add a gradient fill to the subtitle placeholder on Slide 1, and then adjust the font style, size, and color so that the subtitle will be easy for the audience to read. On Slide 2, convert the text in the left content placeholder into SmartArt. Choose a layout that effectively conveys the slide's message, applying styles and colors as needed. Select the video, and then correct the color by increasing the brightness and contrast. Apply a video style.

On the Notes and Handouts pages, include the date, a page number, and a footer with the text Last_First_ppt03_SC1Fire Save, close, and then submit the presentation as directed by your instructor.

DONE! You have completed Skills Challenge 1

Skills Challenge 2

To complete this presentation, you will need the following files:

- **ppt03_SC2EAP**
- **ppt03_SC2EAPVideo**

You will save your file as:

- **Last_First_ppt03_SC2EAP**

Locate and open the presentation **ppt03_SC2EAP**, and then save it in your chapter folder as Last_First_ppt03_SC2EAP Add a shape to Slide 1 with the text EAP Size the shape appropriately, so that it draws attention and is easily readable. Add an effect and a gradient to the shape and position it in an appropriate place on the slide. Search online for an image that complements the slide design and the content of the presentation and insert it on Slide 2 in the right content placeholder. Add a border that matches the color of the image you added, adjust the weight of the border, and add an effect to the picture. Convert the text in the left content placeholder to SmartArt, using a style that emphasizes the information in the placeholder. Adjust the size of the SmartArt as needed.

Insert a new Slide 3 with the Title and Content layout. In the title placeholder, type Your EAP – Here to help In the content placeholder, insert the video from your student file named **ppt03_SC2_EAPVideo**. Add a complementary style to the video and size it to better fill the space on the slide.

Save the presentation. On the Notes and Handouts pages, include the date, a page number, and a footer with the text Last_First_ppt03_SC2EAP and then check the spelling in the presentation. Save, close, and then submit the presentation as directed by your instructor.

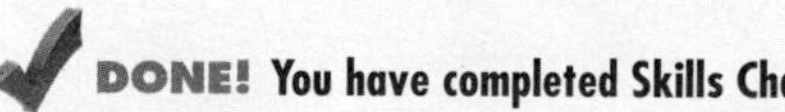
DONE! You have completed Skills Challenge 2

More Skills Assessment

To complete this presentation, you will need the following files:

- **ppt03_MSAParkProposal**
- **ppt03_MSAParkFees**

You will save your files as:

- **Last_First_ppt03_MSAParkProposal**
- **Last_First_ppt03_MSAParkProposalLogo**

---

1. From your student data files, locate and open **ppt03_MSAParkProposal**. **Save** it in your chapter folder as Last_First_ppt03_MSAParkProposal
2. On **Slide 1**, select the rectangle shape that contains the text *Aspen Falls Parks and Recreation Department*. Align the shape with the right side of the slide.
3. Select the image on the slide. Align the image with the right side of the slide.
4. Select the rectangle shape that contains the text *Aspen Falls Parks and Recreation Department*. Send the shape backward, so that it appears behind the image.
5. With the shape still selected, press Ctrl, and then select the image. With both selected, **Group** the objects.
6. Right-click the grouped object, and then click **Save as Picture**. **Save** as a JPEG image in your **PowerPoint Chapter 3** folder, naming it Last_First_ppt03_MSAParkProposalLogo
7. Click a blank area of the slide, and then compare your screen with **Figure 1**.
8. Display **Slide 4**, and then select the content placeholder.
9. Open **Word 2016**, and then from your student data files, open the file named **ppt03_MSAParkFees**.
10. Switch back to PowerPoint. On **Slide 4**, insert a screenshot of the Word document **ppt03_MSAParkFees**, and then **Close** Word.
11. Move to **Slide 2**. Select the picture, and then **Compress** all pictures in the presentation, using the **Target output**, **Web (150 ppi)**. If this resolution is not available, select another option.

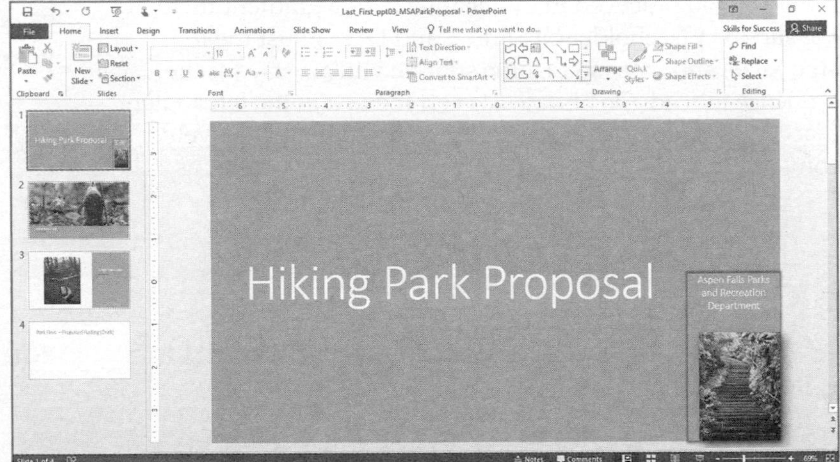

Figure 1 lkunl/Fotolia; PowerPoint 2016, Windows 10, Microsoft Corporation

12. On the **Notes and Handouts** pages, include the date, a page number, and a footer with the text Last_First_ppt03_MSAParkProposal
13. **Save** and then submit the file as directed. **Close** PowerPoint.

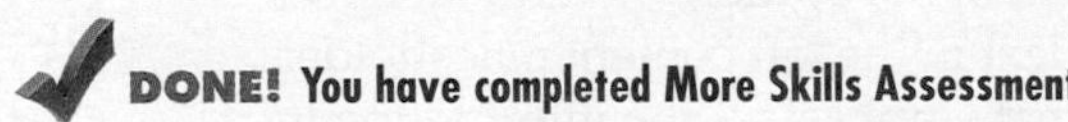

Collaborating with Google

To complete this project, you will need a Google account (refer to the Common Features chapter).

To complete this presentation, you will need the following file:

- **New Google Slides presentation**

You will save your files as:

- **Last_First_ppt03_GoogleProject**
- **Last_First_ppt03_GPSnip**

1. Open the Google Chrome web browser. Log into your Google account, and then click the **Google Apps** button.
2. Click the **Google Drive** button to open Google Drive. If you receive a pop-up message, read the message, and then click **Next**. Read each message, and then close the dialog box.
3. Click the **New** button, and then click **Google Slides**.
4. In the **Themes** pane, scroll down and click **Simple Dark** or another theme, and then **Close** the Themes pane.
5. In the title placeholder, type Mapping Tools
6. In the subtitle placeholder, type Aspen Falls Parks Department
7. Click the **New Slide arrow**, and then click **Title only**. In the title placeholder, type Mapping App and then click a blank area of the slide.
8. Click the **Insert tab**, and then click **Video**. In the **YouTube** search box, type MapMaster from Pearson Press Enter, and then, in the search results, click the **MapMaster from Pearson** video. If this video is not available, search for another video containing content related to mapping software. Click the **Select** button.
9. Drag the video straight down on the slide so that it appears centered vertically between the title placeholder and the bottom of the slide.
10. Double-click the video to preview it. With the video still selected, on the **Insert tab**, click **Comment**. In the **Comment** box, type Let me know if you think this app would be helpful for Parks employees. Press Enter. Click the comment, and then compare your screen with **Figure 1**.

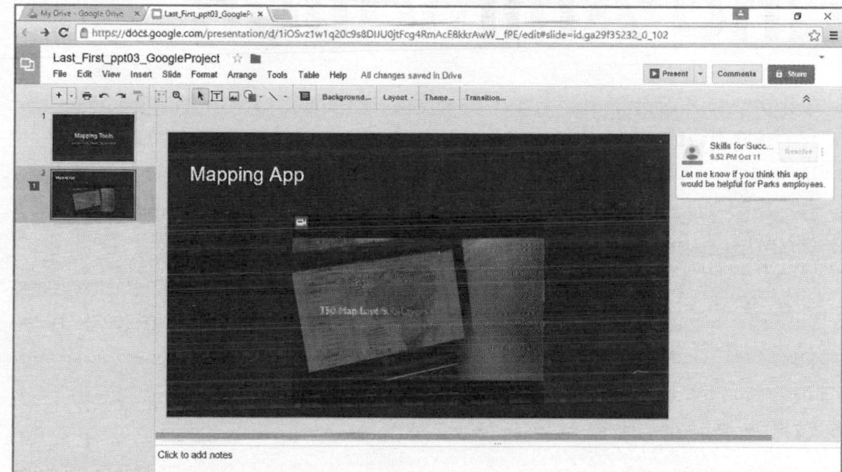

Figure 1

11. Click the **Share** button. In the **Name before sharing** box, type Last_First_ppt03_GoogleProject and then click **Save**. In the **Share with others** dialog box, type AspenFallsEvents@gmail.com to share the sheet with another user.
12. In the **Add a note** text box, type Draft of mapping app presentation.
13. Click **Send**.
14. Press [Windows], type snip and then press Enter to start the Snipping Tool. Click the **New arrow**, and then click **Full-screen Snip**.
15. In the **Snipping Tool** mark-up window, click the **Save Snip** button. In the **Save As** dialog box, navigate to your **PowerPoint Chapter 3** folder. Be sure the **Save as type** box displays **JPEG file**. Name the file Last_First_ppt03_GPSnip and then press Enter. **Close** the Snipping Tool mark-up window.
16. **Close** all windows, and then submit your work as directed by your instructor.

DONE! You have completed Collaborating with Google

CHAPTER 4

Present Data Using Tables, Charts, and Animation

- Tables and charts are used to present information in a graphic format that helps the audience to better understand the data being presented.
- Presenters can use charts to display numeric data, particularly when making comparisons between data.
- Styles can be used to format the chart or table and corresponding data in a manner that matches and complements the rest of the presentation.
- Animation effects are used to draw attention to important slide elements.
- Timing can be used to precisely control the pace of a slide show and the order in which each element of the presentation appears.

Shutterstock/Alex Brylov

Aspen Falls City Hall

In this chapter, you will enrich a presentation regarding business growth in Aspen Falls, California. This presentation will be used to inform the audience about industries with high-growth potential and to encourage continued expansion of businesses. Statistical data about these issues will be easier to understand when presented in tables and charts.

In your career, you may need to present numerical or comparative information to an audience. You can use a table or chart to present this information. Tables and charts will help your audience to understand growth trends, make comparisons, or understand the composition of a whole.

Animations can help to draw your audience's attention to the screen. During a slide show, you can use annotations to draw on a slide.

When adding tables, charts, animations, and annotations to your presentation, keep in mind the axiom that "less is more." Summarize data as much as possible, and present only the most important information. If needed, detailed studies can be presented to your audience in the form of handouts.

In this project, you will add a table and charts to a presentation. You will then add and modify animations. Finally, you will work with the presentation in Slide Show view, moving through the presentation and creating an annotation on a slide.

Time to complete all 10 skills — 60 to 75 minutes

Outcome

Using the skills in this chapter, you will be able to create, format, and edit tables and charts, use and modify animations, and work with animations and annotations during a slide show.

Objectives

You will show mastery of the chapter material when you can:

4.1 Compile data into tables and format the information

4.2 Compose charts, adding and editing data

4.3 Design animations to retain the audience's interest and increase understanding

4.4 Generate a slide show with ink annotations

Student data file needed for this chapter:

ppt04_Growth

You will save your file as:

Last_First_ppt04_Growth

SKILLS

At the end of this chapter, you will be able to:

- **Skill 1** Insert Tables
- **Skill 2** Modify Table Layouts
- **Skill 3** Apply Table Styles
- **Skill 4** Insert Column Charts
- **Skill 5** Edit and Format Charts
- **Skill 6** Insert Pie Charts
- **Skill 7** Apply Animation Effects and Change Duration
- **Skill 8** Modify Animation Timing and Use Animation Painter
- **Skill 9** Delay or Remove Animation
- **Skill 10** Navigate Slide Shows

MORE SKILLS

- **Skill 11** Download Microsoft Office Mix
- **Skill 12** Create an Office Mix
- **Skill 13** Getting Started with Microsoft Sway
- **Skill 14** Importing Slides into Sway

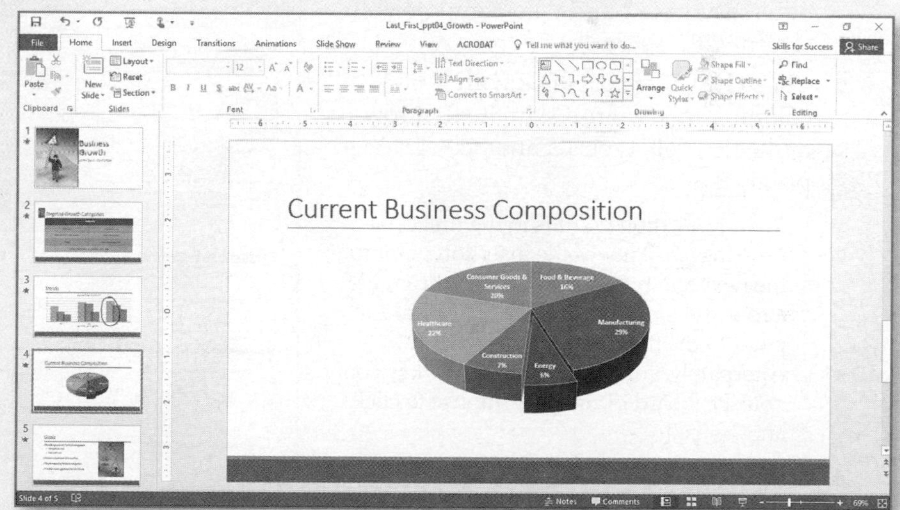

- In a presentation, a ***table*** is used to organize and present information in columns and rows.
- In tables, text is typed into a ***cell***—the intersection of a column and row.

1. Start **Microsoft PowerPoint 2016**, and then from the student data files for this chapter, open **ppt04_Growth**. On the **File tab**, click **Save As**. Navigate to the location where you are saving your files, create a folder named PowerPoint Chapter 4 and then using your own name, **Save** the file as Last_First_ppt04_Growth
2. Move to **Slide 2**, and then in the title placeholder, type Targeted Growth Categories
3. MOS Obj 3.1.1 In the content placeholder, click the **Insert Table** button.
4. In the **Insert Table** dialog box, in the **Number of columns** box, type 2 and then press Tab. In the **Number of rows** box, if necessary, type 2 and then compare your screen with **Figure 1**.
5. Click **OK** to create a table with two columns and two rows. In the first row, in the first cell, type Technology and then press Tab.

   If your insertion point is in the first cell, pressing Tab moves the insertion point to the next cell in the same row. At the end of a row, pressing Tab moves your insertion point to the first cell in the next row. Alternately, you can use the arrow keys on your keyboard or use your mouse to click another cell.
6. Type Home Health Care and then compare your screen with **Figure 2**.

■ **Continue to the next page to complete the skill**

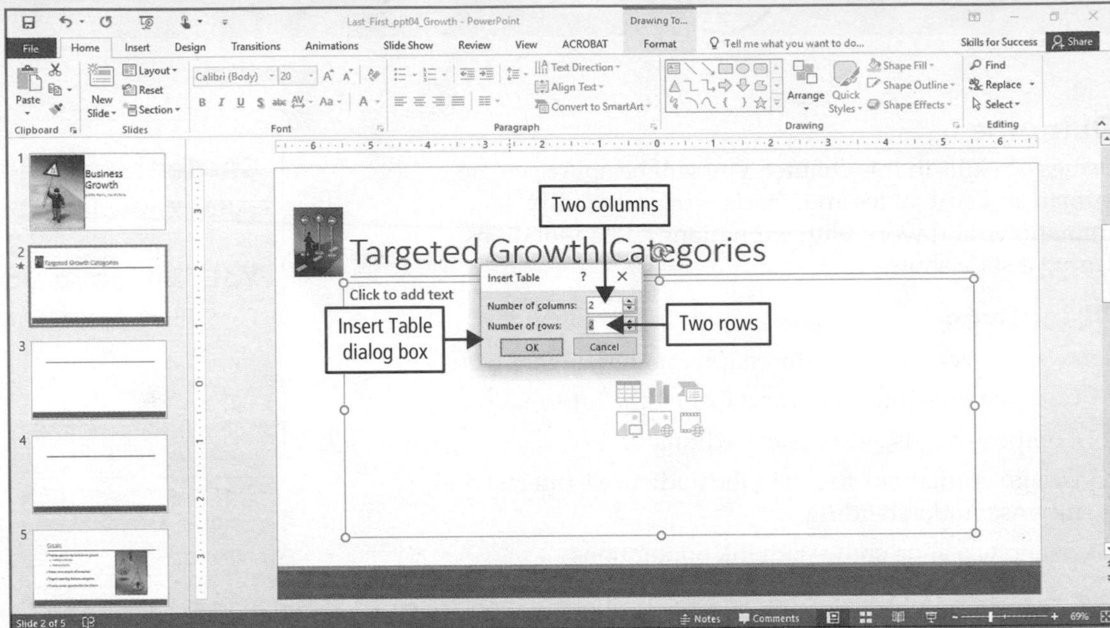

Figure 1

PowerPoint 2016, Windows 10, Microsoft Corporation

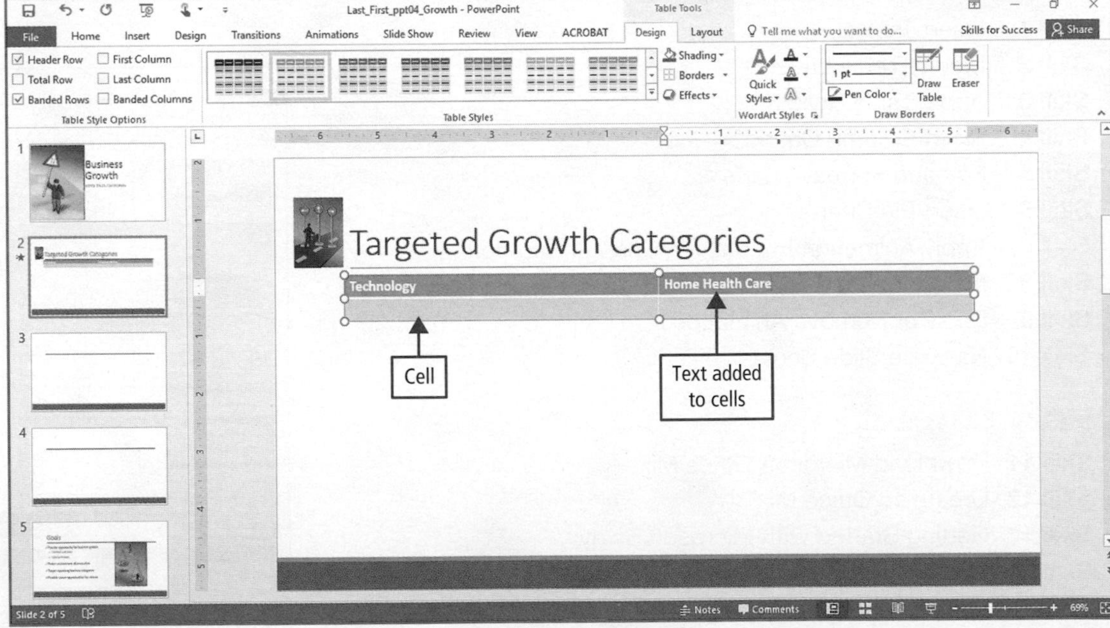

Figure 2

PowerPoint 2016, Windows 10, Microsoft Corporation

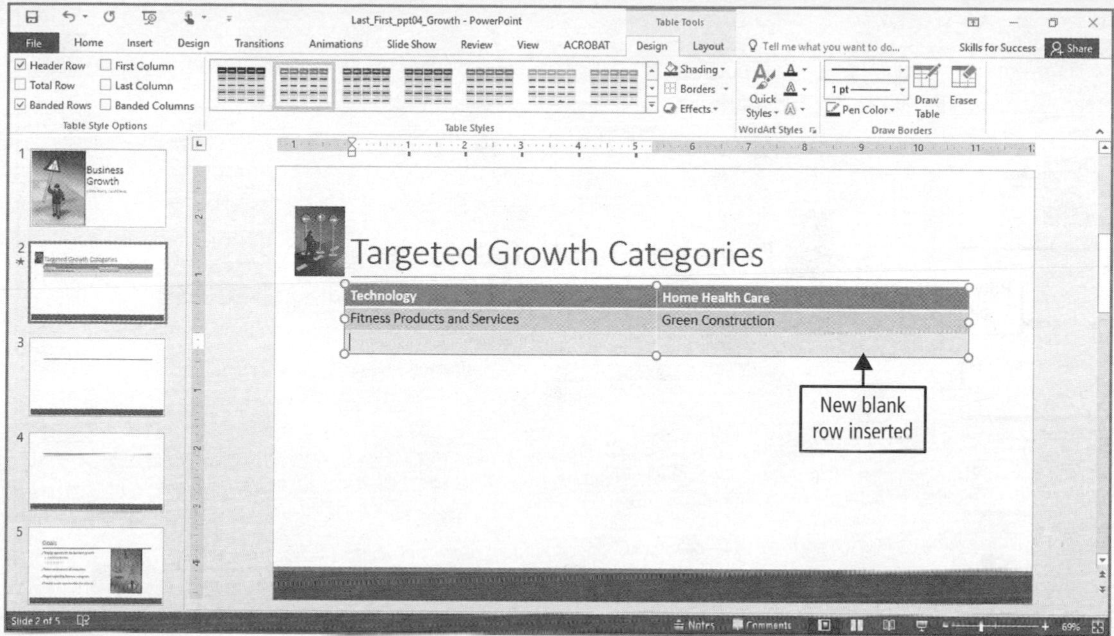

PowerPoint 2016, Windows 10, Microsoft Corporation

Figure 3

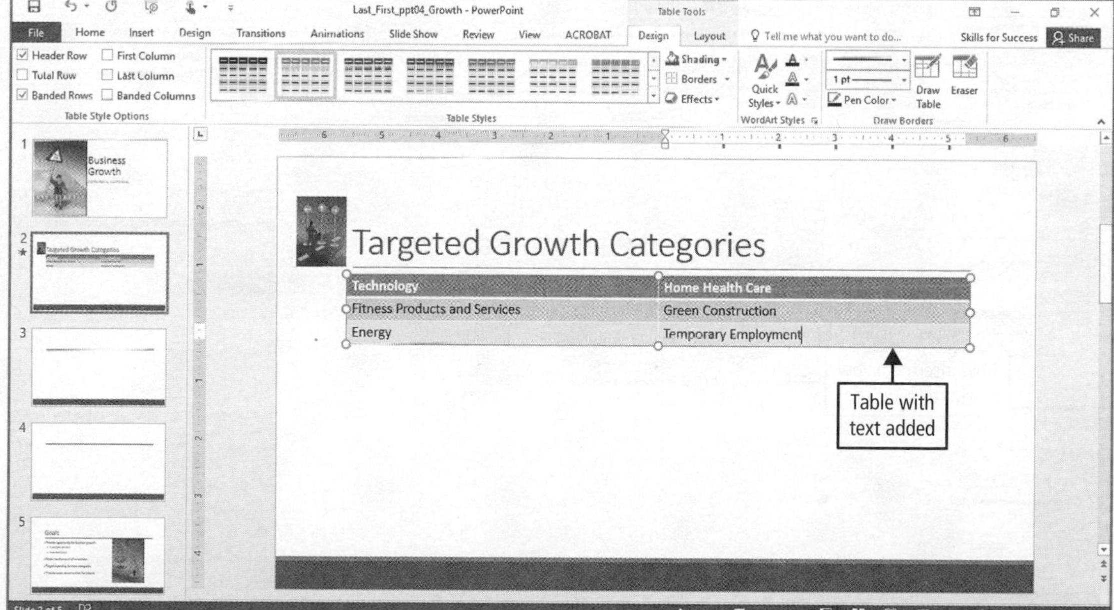

PowerPoint 2016, Windows 10, Microsoft Corporation

Figure 4

7. Press Tab to move the insertion point to the first cell in the second row. With the insertion point positioned in the first cell of the second row, type Fitness Products and Services

8. Press Tab. Type Green Construction and then press Tab to insert a new blank row. Compare your table with **Figure 3**.

   When the insertion point is positioned in the last cell of a table, pressing Tab inserts a new blank row at the bottom of the table. Alternately, on the Table Tools Layout tab, in the Rows & Columns group, you can click the Insert Below button to add a new row below the current row.

9. In the first cell of the third row, type Energy and then press Tab. Type Temporary Employment and then compare your screen with **Figure 4**.

10. Save the file.

- **You have completed Skill 1 of 10**

- You can modify the layout of a table by inserting or deleting rows and columns and by changing the height and width of rows and columns.
- The height and width of the entire table can also be modified.

MOS Obj 3.1.2

1. In the first row of the table, click in any cell. On the **Layout tab**, in the **Rows & Columns group**, click the **Insert Above** button.

   A new first row is inserted.

2. Type Industry and then compare your screen with **Figure 1**.
3. Click so that your insertion point appears anywhere in the last row of the table, and then on the **Layout tab**, in the **Rows & Columns group**, click **Insert Below**.
4. In the last row of the table, in the first cell, type Aspen Falls Chamber of Commerce Study, 2018 Compare your screen with **Figure 2**.
5. At the center of the lower border surrounding the table, point to the center sizing handle to display the pointer.
6. With the pointer, drag down until the lower edge of the table extends to the **2.5 inch** mark below zero on the vertical ruler, and then release the mouse button to resize the table. If your ruler is not displayed, on the View tab, in the Show group, select Ruler.

■ **Continue to the next page to complete the skill**

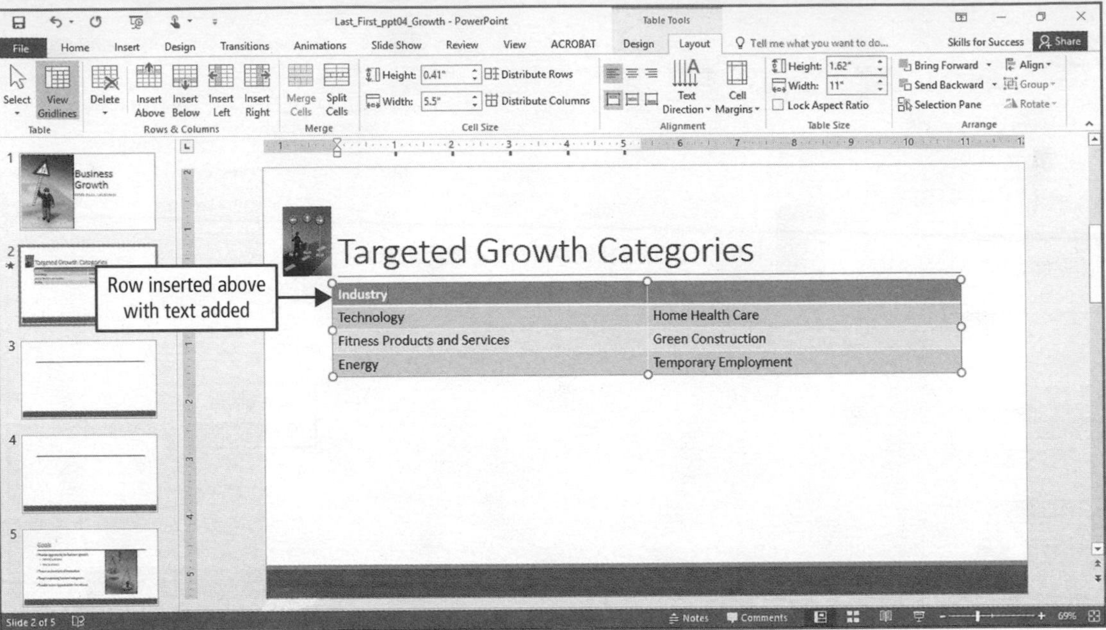

Figure 1

PowerPoint 2016, Windows 10, Microsoft Corporation

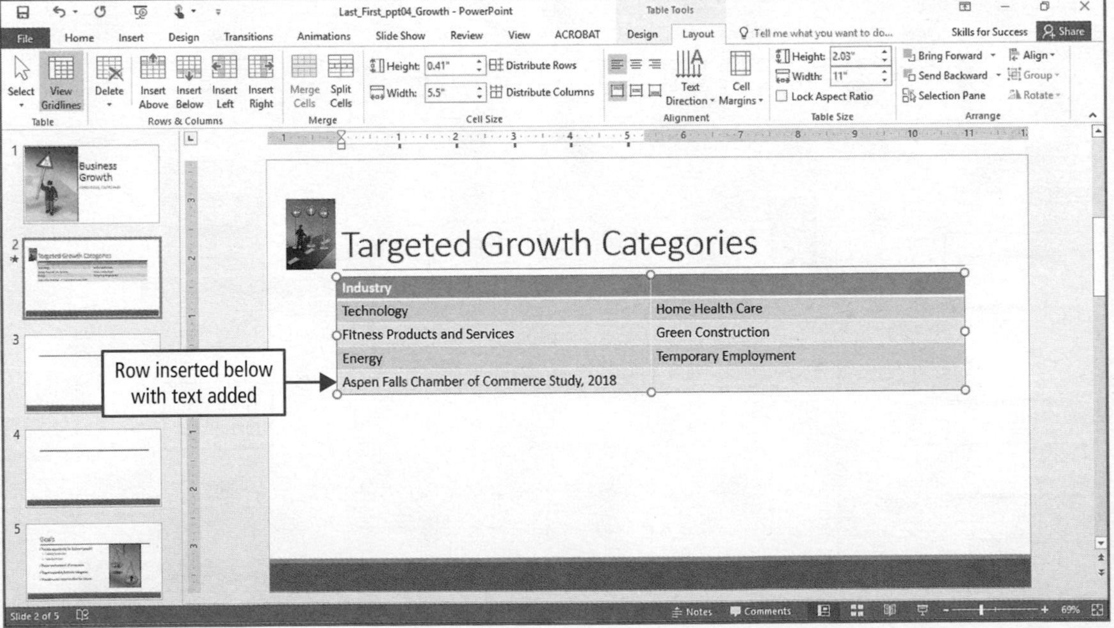

Figure 2

PowerPoint 2016, Windows 10, Microsoft Corporation

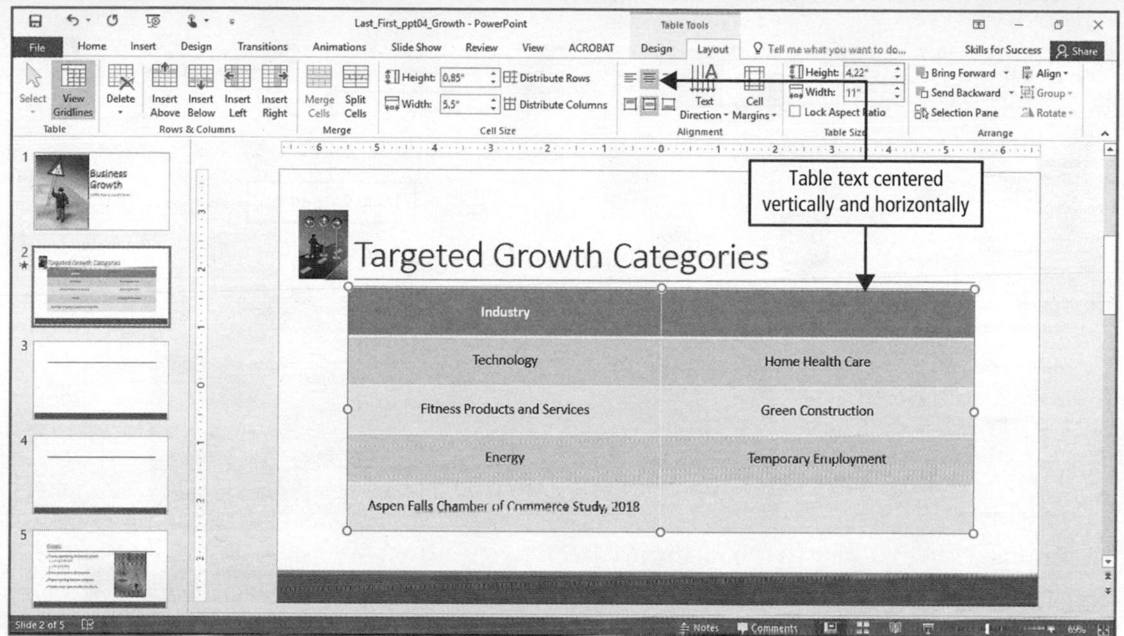

PowerPoint 2016, Windows 10, Microsoft Corporation

Figure 3

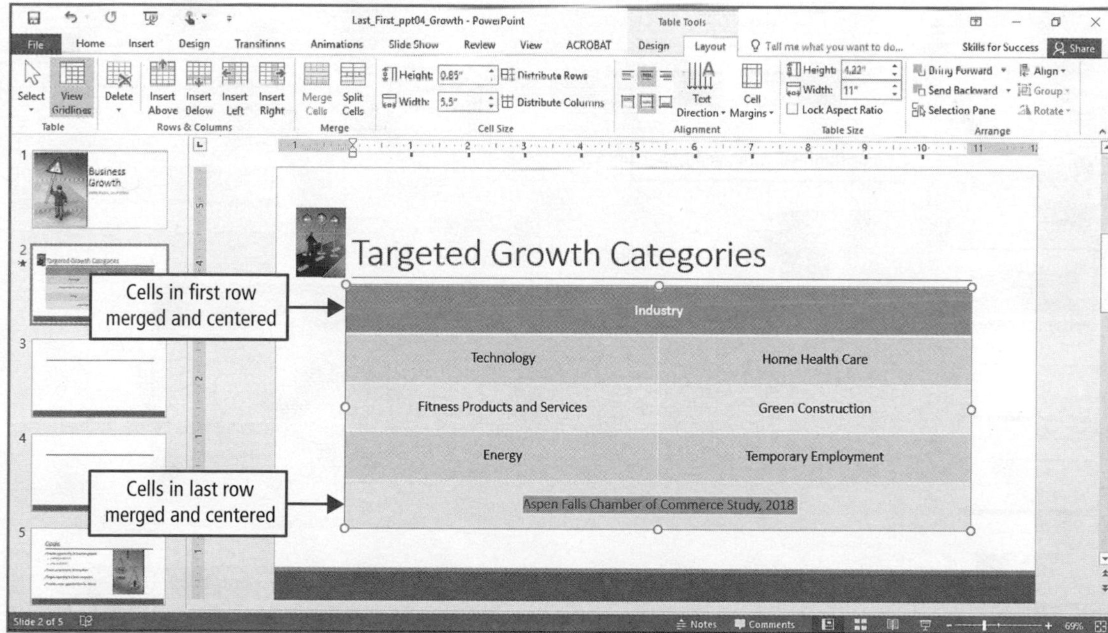

PowerPoint 2016, Windows 10, Microsoft Corporation

Figure 4

7. With the table selected, on the **Layout tab**, in the **Alignment group**, click the **Center** button.

8. In the **Alignment group**, click the **Center Vertically** button. Compare your screen with **Figure 3**.

   All of the text in the table is centered horizontally and vertically within the cells.

9. Position the pointer to the left of the first row in the table to display the **Select Row** pointer. Click to select the entire first row. On the **Layout tab**, in the **Merge group**, click **Merge Cells**. Repeat this process to merge the cells in the last row of the table, and then compare your screen with **Figure 4**.

   When ***merged***, selected cells are combined into a single cell. Alternately, you can select a row of cells by clicking and dragging to select with your mouse. When merging selected cells, only the top, leftmost cell should contain data; otherwise, the data in the remaining cells will be lost.

10. **Save** the file.

- **You have completed Skill 2 of 10**

- A ***table style*** includes borders and fill colors that are applied to the entire table in a manner consistent with the presentation theme.
- The styles and color categories available vary depending on the presentation's theme.

Obj 3.1.3

1. On **Slide 2**, click in any cell in the table. On the **Table Tools Design tab**, in the **Table Styles group**, click the **More** button. In the **Table Styles** gallery, point to several styles and watch as Live Preview displays the table with the selected style. Scroll all the way to the bottom of the gallery to view all of the styles.
2. Scroll up to the top of the gallery. Under **Best Match for Document**, click the fifth style in the first row—**Themed Style 1 - Accent 4**—and compare your screen with **Figure 1**.
3. Click anywhere in the first row of the table. On the **Table Tools Design tab**, in the **Table Styles group**, click the **Shading arrow**. Click **Eyedropper**. In the upper portion of the slide, in the image, with the **Eyedropper**, click in the dark area beneath one of the signs and the figure of a man, in the area shown in **Figure 2**.

   With the color-matching ***eyedropper***, you can select color from any object or image on your slide and apply the color to another area of your slide, creating a cohesive color scheme.

■ Continue to the next page to complete the skill

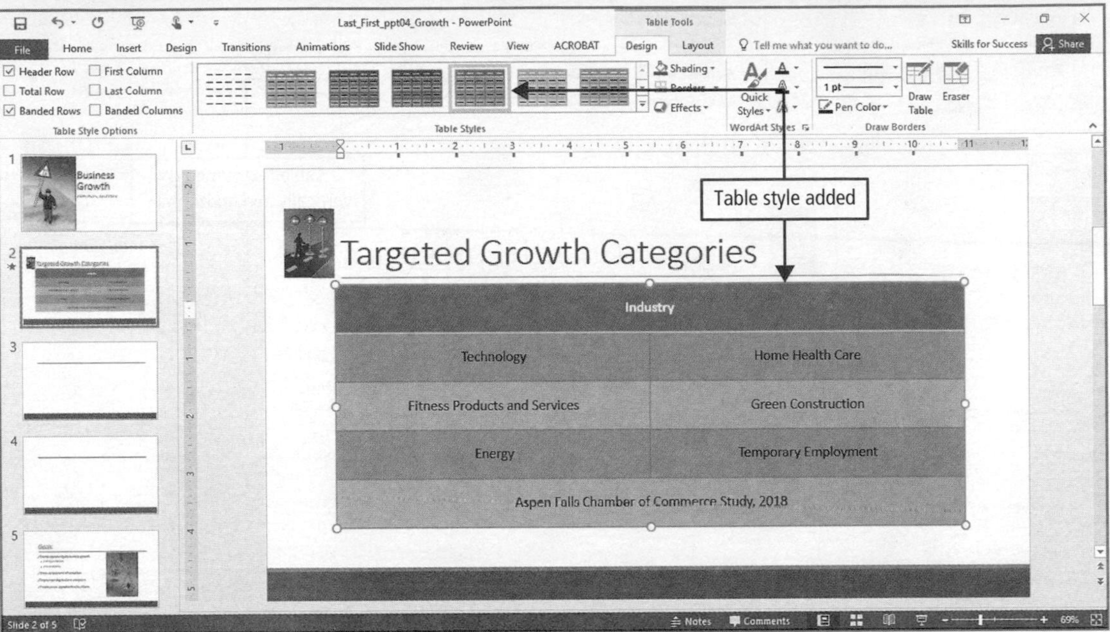

Figure 1

PowerPoint 2016, Windows 10, Microsoft Corporation

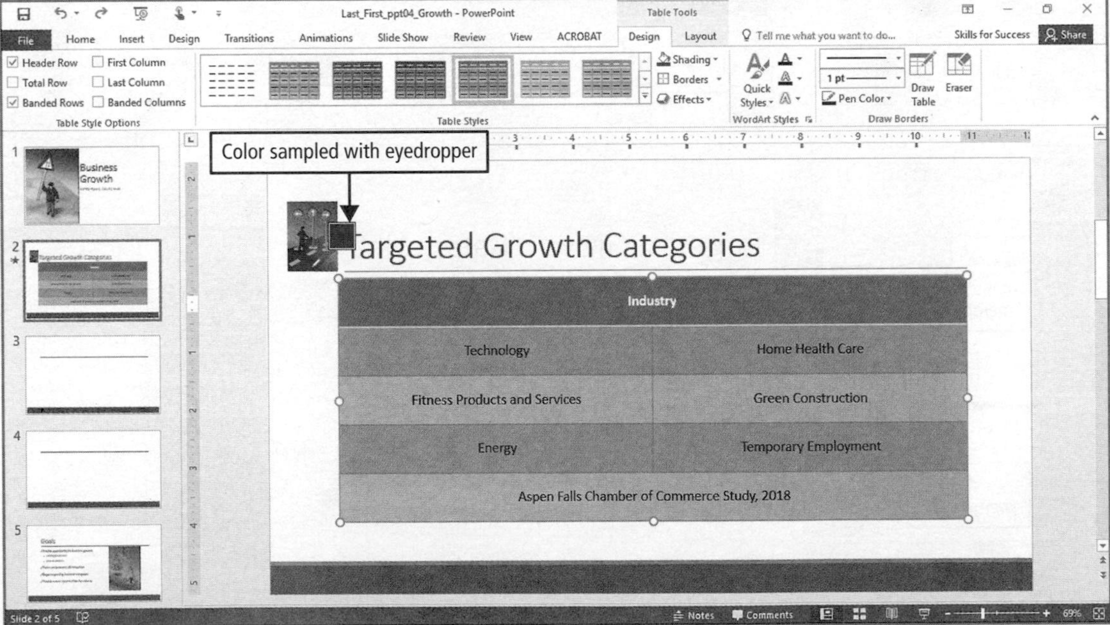

Figure 2

PowerPoint 2016, Windows 10, Microsoft Corporation

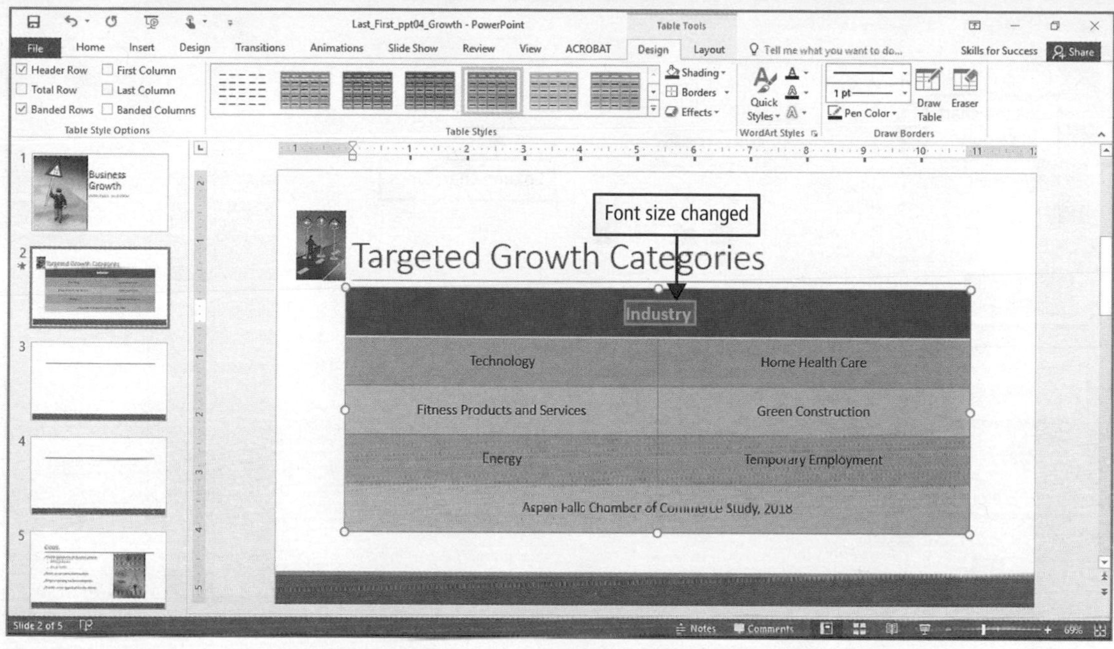

PowerPoint 2016, Windows 10, Microsoft Corporation

Figure 3

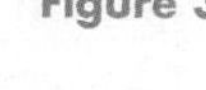

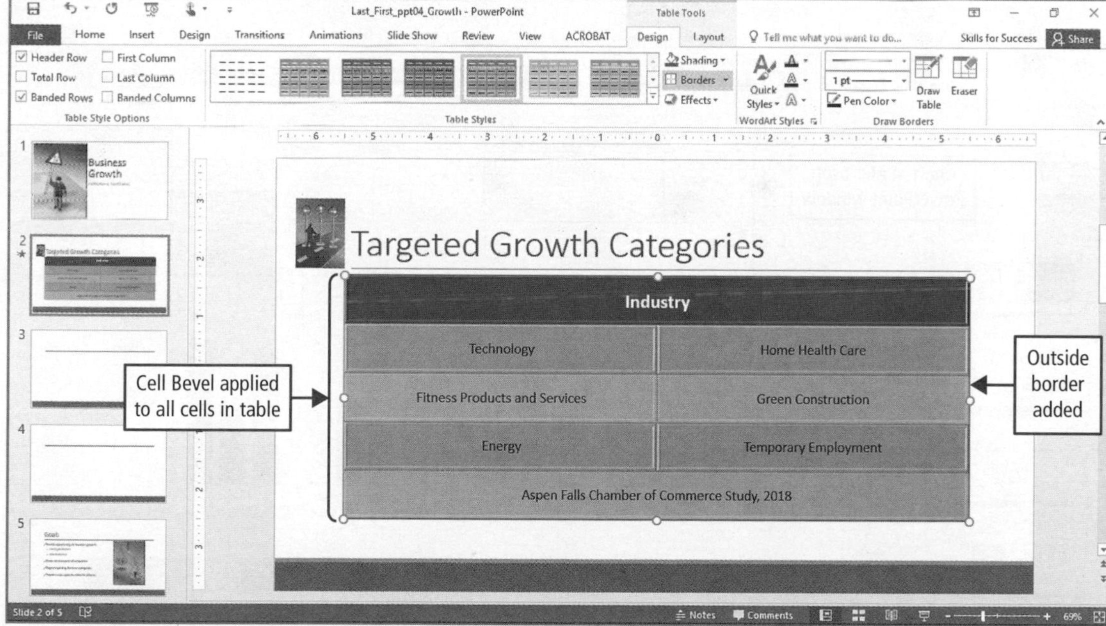

PowerPoint 2016, Windows 10, Microsoft Corporation

Figure 4

4. Move the pointer to the left of the first row in the table to display the **Select Row** pointer.
5. With the **Select Row** pointer pointing to the first row in the table, click to select the entire row and to display the **Mini toolbar**. On the **Mini toolbar**, change the **Font Size** to **24**. Compare your screen with **Figure 3**.
6. Click a border of the table to select the entire table. On the **Table Tools Design tab**, in the **Table Styles group**, click the **Effects** button. Point to **Cell Bevel**, and then point to several bevels to view the effect on the table.
7. Under **Bevel**, click the second thumbnail in the first row—**Relaxed Inset**—to apply the effect to the entire table.
8. With the table still selected, on the **Table Tools Design tab**, in the **Table Styles group**, click the **Borders arrow**, and then click **Outside Borders**. Compare your screen with **Figure 4**.
9. **Save** the file.

■ **You have completed Skill 3 of 10**

- A ***chart*** is a graphic representation of numeric data.
- A ***column chart*** is useful for illustrating comparisons among related categories.
- When creating a chart, you may need to delete unwanted data from the worksheet so that it does not display in the chart.

1. Display **Slide 3** in Normal view. In the title placeholder, type Trends

MOS Obj 3.2.1

2. In the content placeholder, click the **Insert Chart** button. In the left pane of the **Insert Chart** dialog box, click several of the chart types to view the chart gallery and a preview of the selected chart type. Then click **Column**, as shown in **Figure 1**.
3. With the first chart—**Clustered Column**—selected, click **OK**. Compare your screen with **Figure 2**.

   The Chart in Microsoft PowerPoint window contains sample data. The column headings—*Series 1*, *Series 2*, and *Series 3*—display in the chart ***legend***, which identifies the patterns or colors that are assigned to the data in the chart. The row headings—*Category 1*, *Category 2*, *Category 3*, and *Category 4*—display along the bottom of the chart as ***category labels***—labels that identify the categories of data in a chart.

MOS Obj 3.2.4

4. In the **Chart in Microsoft PowerPoint** window, click cell **B1**, which contains the text *Series 1*. Type Technology and then press Tab to move to the next cell. In cell **C1**, type Healthcare Press Tab and then in cell **D1**, type Staffing Press Enter.

   On the slide, notice that the chart legend is updated to reflect the change.

■ **Continue to the next page to complete the skill**

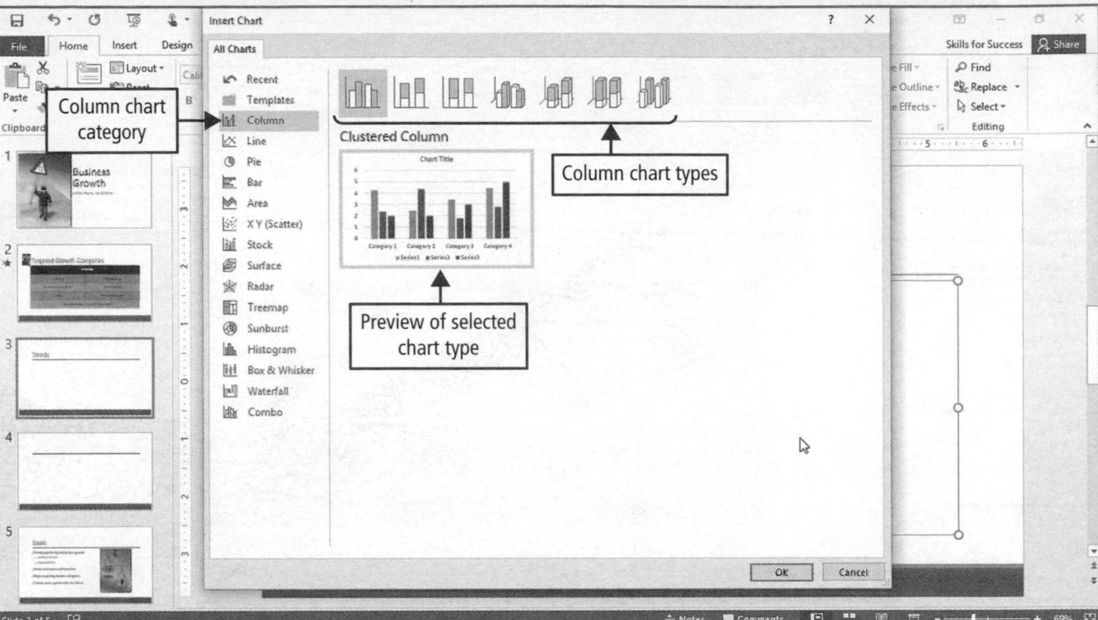

Figure 1

PowerPoint 2016, Windows 10, Microsoft Corporation

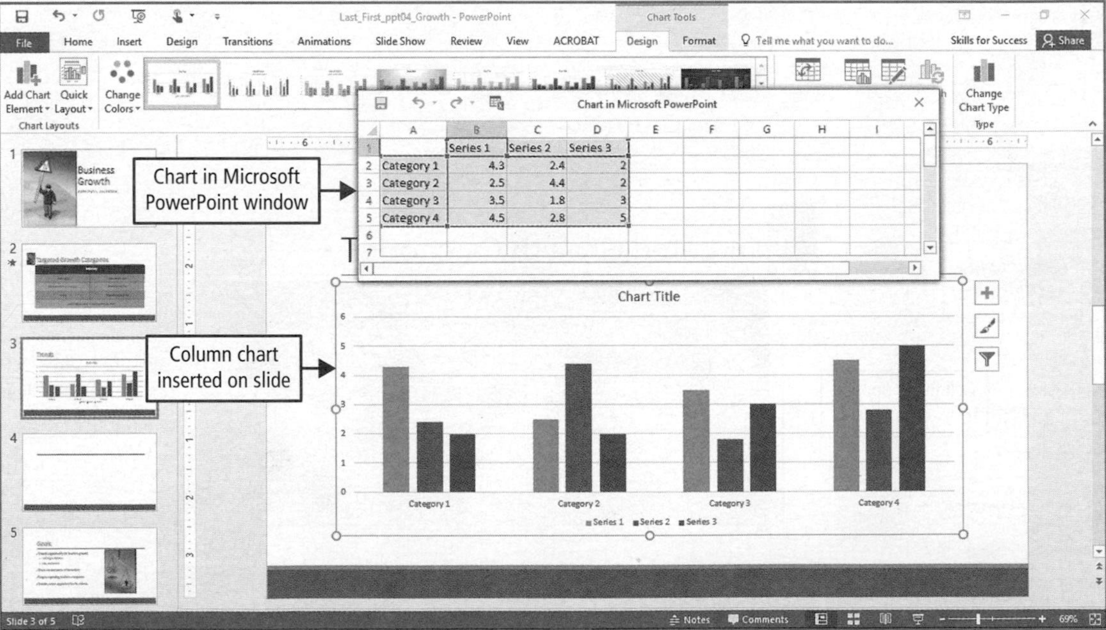

	A	B	C	D
1		Series 1	Series 2	Series 3
2	Category 1	4.3	2.4	2
3	Category 2	2.5	4.4	2
4	Category 3	3.5	1.8	3
5	Category 4	4.5	2.8	5

Figure 2

PowerPoint 2016, Windows 10, Microsoft Corporation

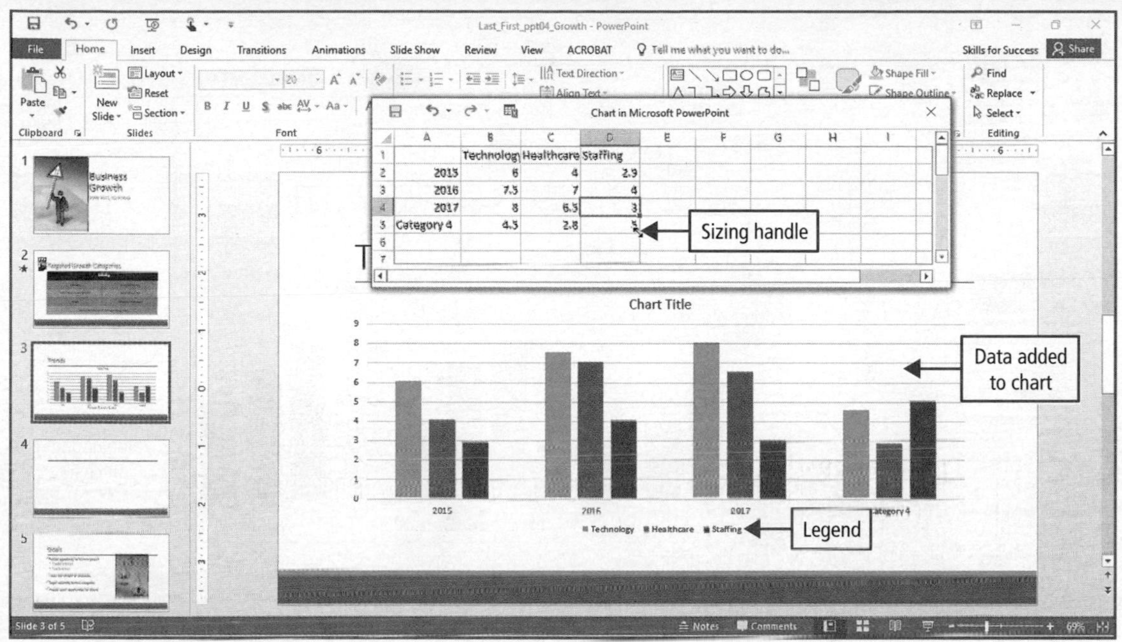

PowerPoint 2016, Windows 10, Microsoft Corporation

Figure 3

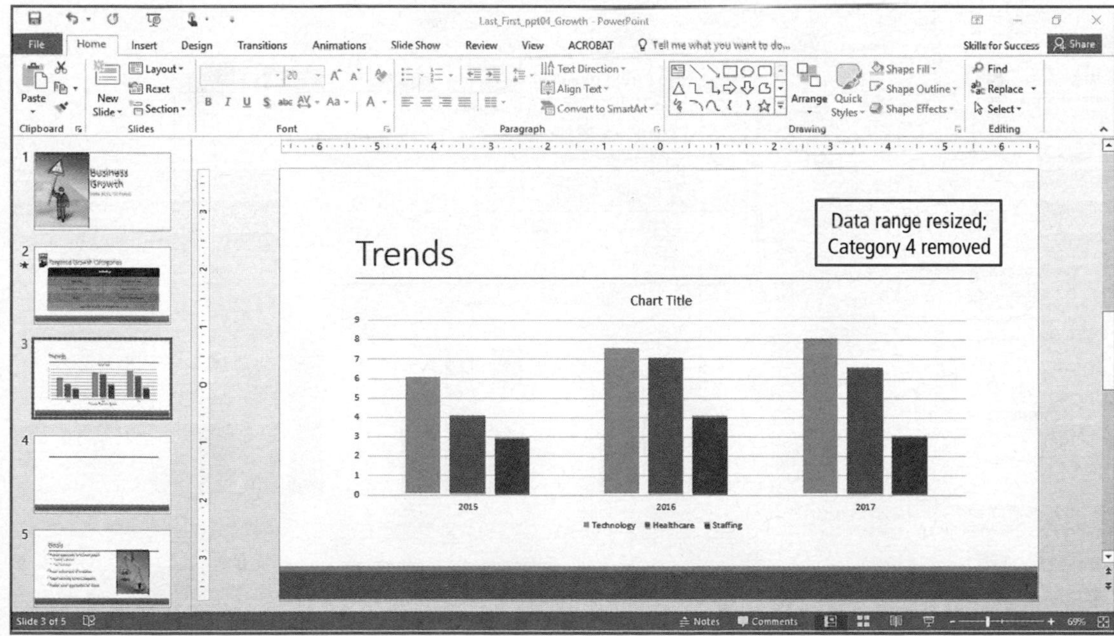

PowerPoint 2016, Windows 10, Microsoft Corporation

Figure 4

5. In cell **A2**, type 2015 Press Enter and type 2016 Press Enter and type 2017

6. Click cell **B2**, type 6 Press Enter to move to cell **B3**, and then type 7.5 Press Enter and type 8 Click cell **C2**, and then type 4 Press Enter and type 7 Press Enter and type 6.5 Click cell **D2**, and then type 2.9 Press Enter and type 4 Press Enter and type 3.

7. Still in the **Chart in Microsoft PowerPoint** window, point to the lower right corner of cell **D5** to display the pointer, as shown in **Figure 3**.

8. With the pointer, drag straight up so that only the range **A1:D4** is selected. Release the mouse button. Select the data in cells **A5:D5**, and then press Delete. **Close** the Chart in Microsoft PowerPoint window, and then compare your screen with **Figure 4**.

   Alternately, in the Chart in Microsoft PowerPoint window, you can right-click the row 5 heading—the number 5 that appears on the left side of the worksheet—and then, on the shortcut menu, click Delete to remove the entire row and resize the data range.

9. **Save** the file.

- **You have completed Skill 4 of 10**

SKILL 5: Edit and Format Charts

- After a chart is created, you can edit the data values using the Chart in Microsoft PowerPoint window. Changes made immediately display in the PowerPoint chart.
- Charts are formatted by applying predefined styles and by modifying chart elements.

1. On **Slide 3**, if necessary, click the chart so that it is selected. On the **Chart Tools Design tab**, in the **Data group**, click the **Edit Data** button to display the **Chart in Microsoft PowerPoint** window.

   Each of the cells containing the data that you entered are ***data points***—individual data plotted in a chart. Each data point is represented in the chart by a ***data marker***—a column, bar, or other symbol that represents a single data point. Related data points form a ***data series*** and are assigned a unique color or pattern represented in the chart legend.

2. In the **Chart in Microsoft PowerPoint** window, click cell **D4**, which contains the value *3*. Type 5 and then press Enter. Compare your screen with **Figure 1**.

   In the chart, the last column is increased to reflect the change to the data.

3. In the **Chart in Microsoft PowerPoint** window, click cell **C1**, which contains the text *Healthcare*. Type Health and then watch the chart legend as you press Enter. Compare your screen with **Figure 2**.

4. In the **Chart in Microsoft PowerPoint** window, click the **Close** button ☒.

■ **Continue to the next page to complete the skill**

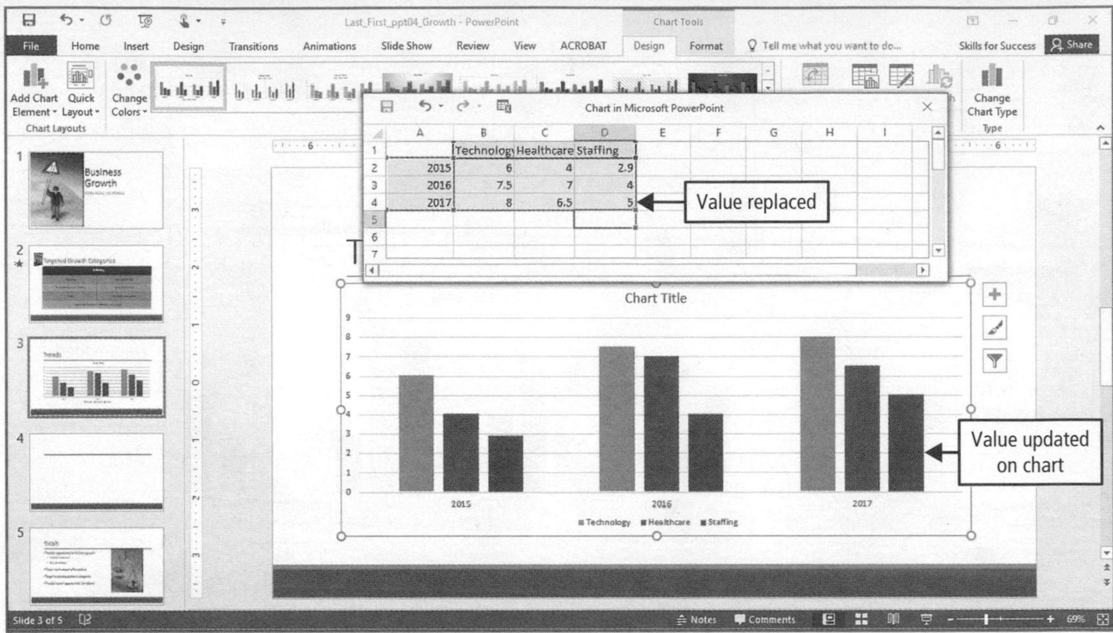

Figure 1

PowerPoint 2016, Windows 10, Microsoft Corporation

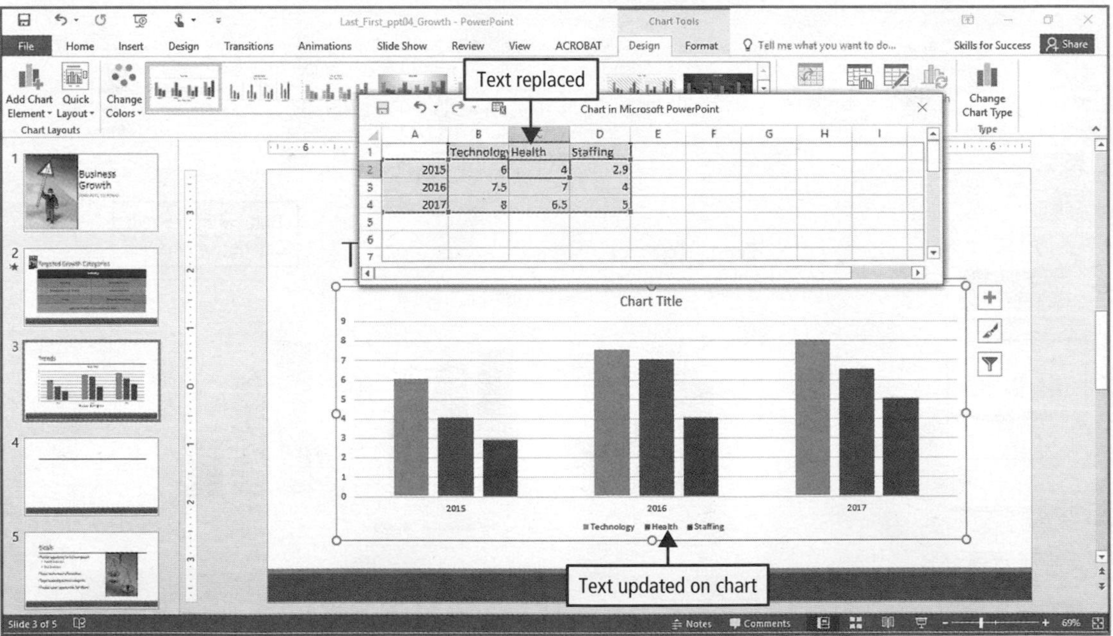

Figure 2

PowerPoint 2016, Windows 10, Microsoft Corporation

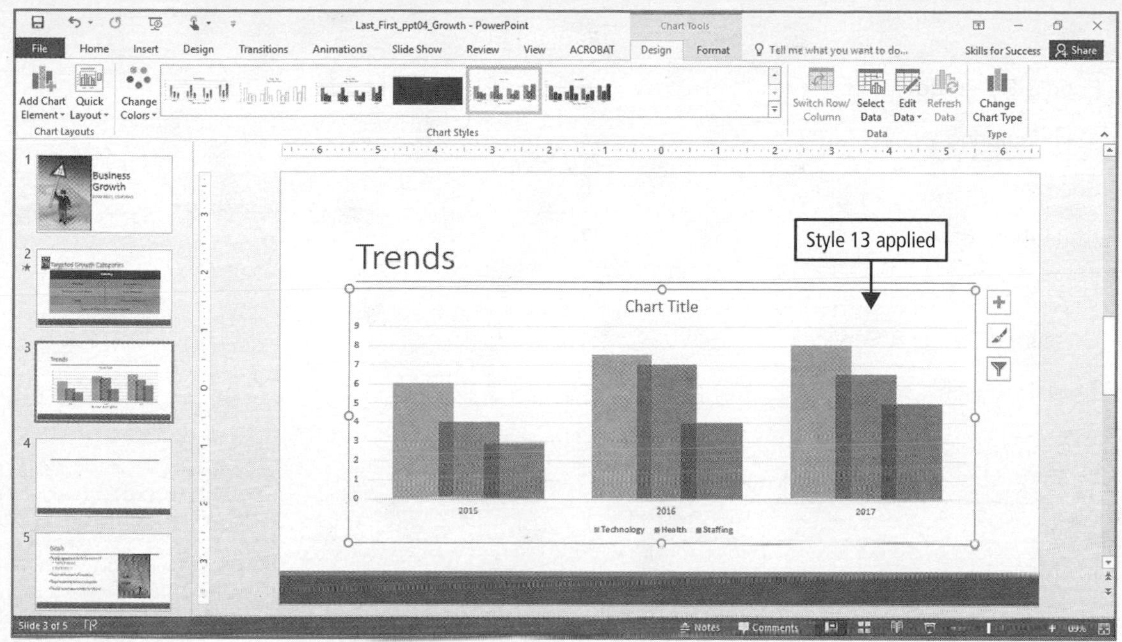

PowerPoint 2016, Windows 10, Microsoft Corporation

Figure 3

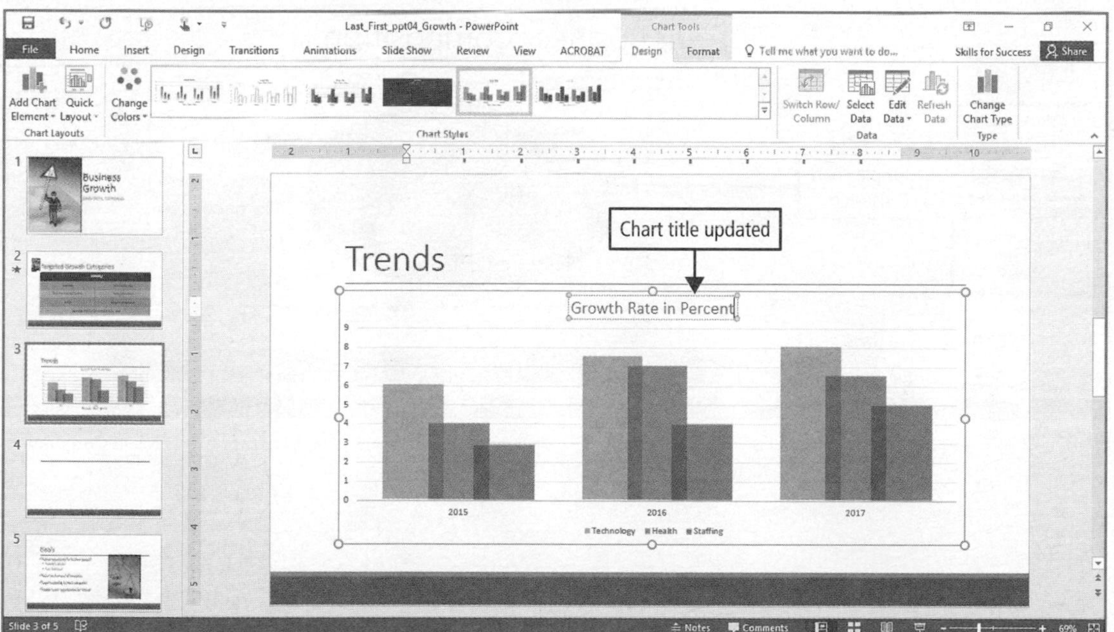

PowerPoint 2016, Windows 10, Microsoft Corporation

Figure 4

5. With the chart still selected, on the **Chart Tools Design tab**, in the **Chart Styles group**, click the **More** button [▾] to display the **Chart Styles** gallery.

   A ***chart style*** is a prebuilt set of effects, colors, and backgrounds designed to work with the presentation theme. For example, you can have flat or beveled columns, colors that are solid or transparent, and backgrounds that are dark or light.

6. The thumbnails in the **Chart Styles** gallery are numbered sequentially. Locate and click **Style 13**. Compare your slide with **Figure 3**.
7. Click the **Chart Title** placeholder, and then type Growth Rate in Percent Compare your screen with **Figure 4**.
8. **Save** [💾] the file.

■ **You have completed Skill 5 of 10**

▸ A ***pie chart*** is used to illustrate percentages or proportions and includes only one data series.

1. Display **Slide 4**. In the title placeholder, type Current Business Composition
2. In the content placeholder, click the **Insert Chart** button. In the left pane of the **Insert Chart** dialog box, click **Pie**. Toward the top of the dialog box, click the second chart—**3-D Pie**—and then click **OK**.
3. In the **Chart in Microsoft PowerPoint** window, in cell **B1**, type Percentage and then in cells **A2:B7**, enter the remaining data as shown in **Figure 1**, pressing Enter after each entry.

   As you press Enter, the data range expands to include the new data.

4. **Close** the Chart in Microsoft PowerPoint window, and then compare your screen with **Figure 2**.

	Percentage
Food & Beverage	16
Manufacturing	29
Energy	6
Construction	7
Healthcare	22
Consumer Goods & Services	20

Figure 1

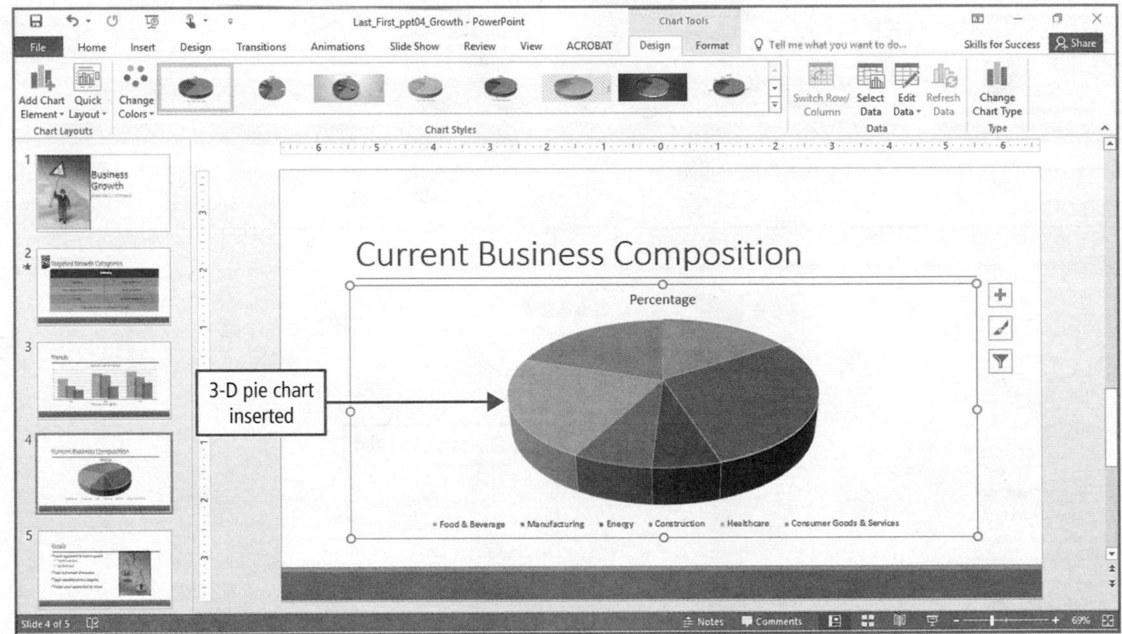

Figure 2

PowerPoint 2016, Windows 10, Microsoft Corporation

■ Continue to the next page to complete the skill

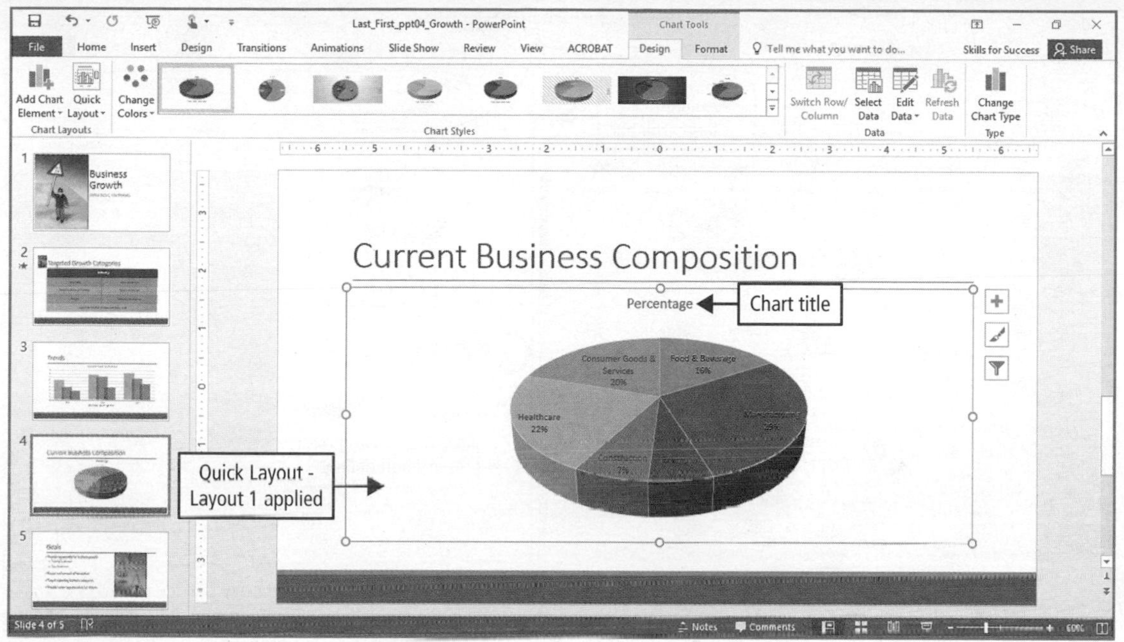

PowerPoint 2016, Windows 10, Microsoft Corporation

Figure 3

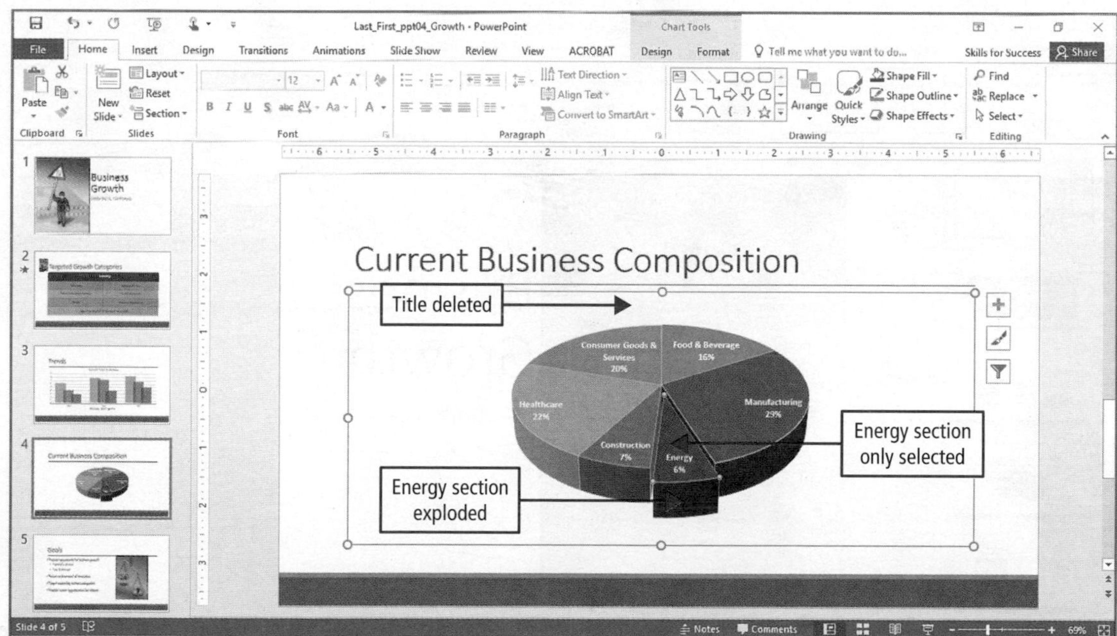

PowerPoint 2016, Windows 10, Microsoft Corporation

Figure 4

5. With the chart still selected, on the **Chart Tools Design tab**, in the **Chart Layouts group**, click the **Quick Layout** button, and then click the first layout—**Layout 1**. Compare your screen with **Figure 3**.

   Recall that a pie chart includes one data series. Thus, the legend is often omitted, and ***data labels***—text that identifies data markers—are positioned on or outside of the pie slices. Layout 1 displays a title and the category names and the percentage that each slice represents of the total.

6. Click a border of the chart title, and then press Delete so that the title is removed.

   When the title is deleted, the chart is resized to fill the space.

7. With the chart still selected, on the **Home tab**, in the **Font group**, click the **Font Color arrow**. In the first row, click the first color—**White, Background 1**—and then click **Bold**.

   When the chart is selected, formatting changes can be made to the text using the Home tab and Font group.

8. To emphasize the growth in the *Energy* category, click any section of the pie, and then click the *Energy* section so that just the *Energy* section is selected. Be sure that you are not selecting the label placeholder. Click, hold, and drag the Energy section straight down slightly to explode the section. Compare your screen with **Figure 4**.

   To ***explode*** a section of the pie, select and then drag it out to add emphasis.

9. **Save** the file.

- **You have completed Skill 6 of 10**

SKILL 7: Apply Animation Effects and Change Duration

- ***Animation*** adds a special visual effect to an image, chart, or text on a slide.
- An ***entrance effect*** is an animation that appears as an object or text is moved onto the screen. An ***emphasis effect*** is an animation that emphasizes an object or text that is already displayed. An ***exit effect*** is an animation that appears as an object or text is moved off the screen.
- You can change the duration of an animation effect by making it longer or shorter.

1. Display **Slide 1**. On the **Transitions tab**, in the **Transition to This Slide group**, click the **More** button [▾], and then click **Peel Off**. Click the **Effect Options** button, and then click **Right**.
2. In the **Timing group**, in the **Duration** box, type .75 and then press Enter to speed up the animation effect. In the **Timing group**, click the **Apply To All** button.

   You can set the duration of a transition or animation by typing a value in the Duration box, or you can use the up and down spin arrows to increase and decrease the duration in increments.

MOS Obj 4.2.1

3. On **Slide 1**, click to select the image on the left side of the slide. On the **Animations tab**, in the **Animation group**, click the **More** button [▾] to display the **Animation** gallery. Scroll through the Animation gallery to view the types of animation effects. Compare your screen with **Figure 1**.
4. Under **Entrance**, click **Fly In** to apply the effect. Compare your screen with **Figure 2**.

   The number 1 displays to the left of the image, indicating that the image is the first object in the slide animation sequence and it will appear on the first mouse click during the slide show. The number will not display during the slide show.

■ **Continue to the next page to complete the skill**

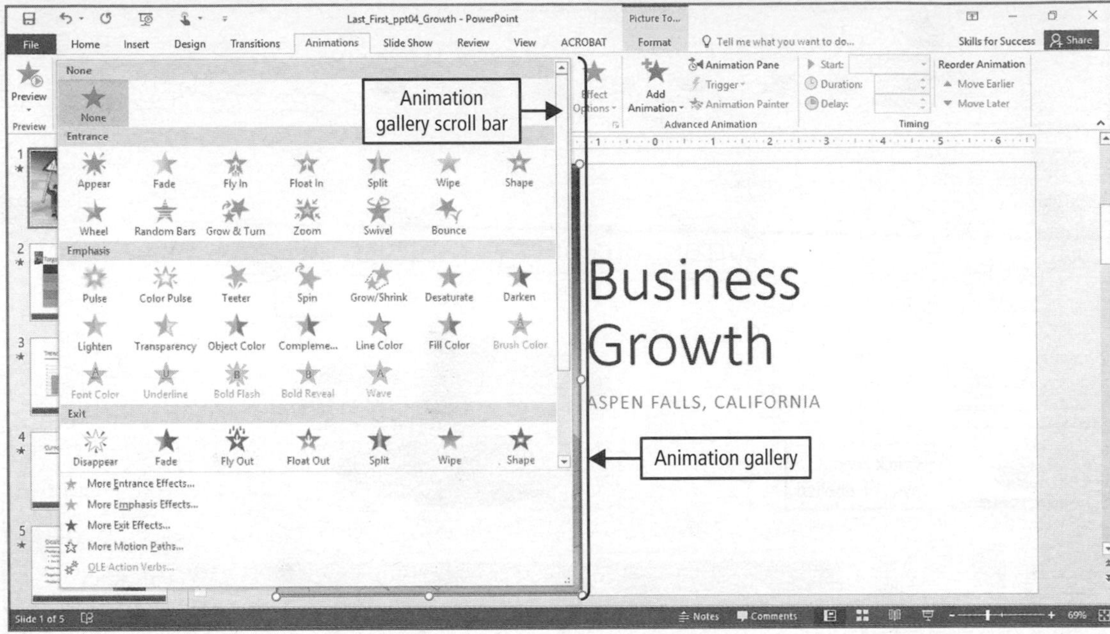

Figure 1

PowerPoint 2016, Windows 10, Microsoft Corporation

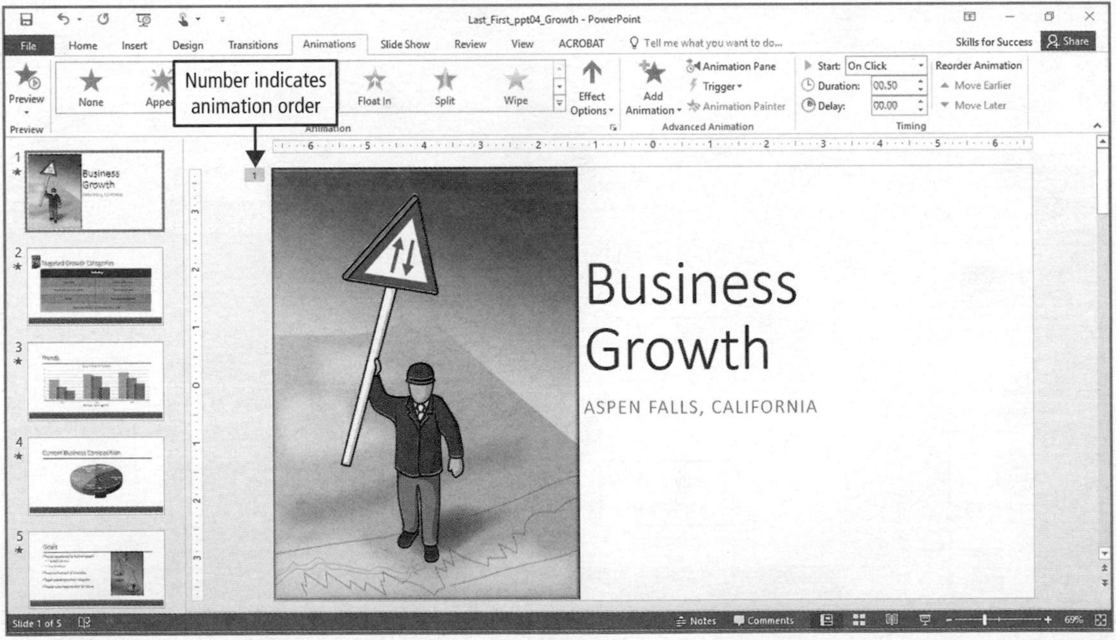

Figure 2

PowerPoint 2016, Windows 10, Microsoft Corporation

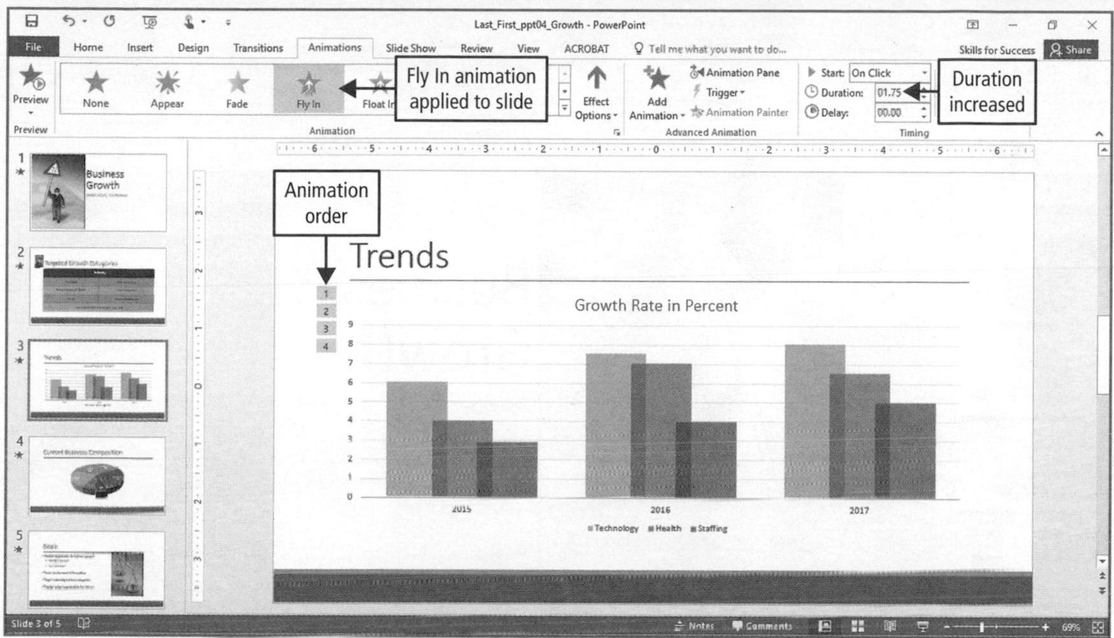

PowerPoint 2016, Windows 10, Microsoft Corporation

Figure 3

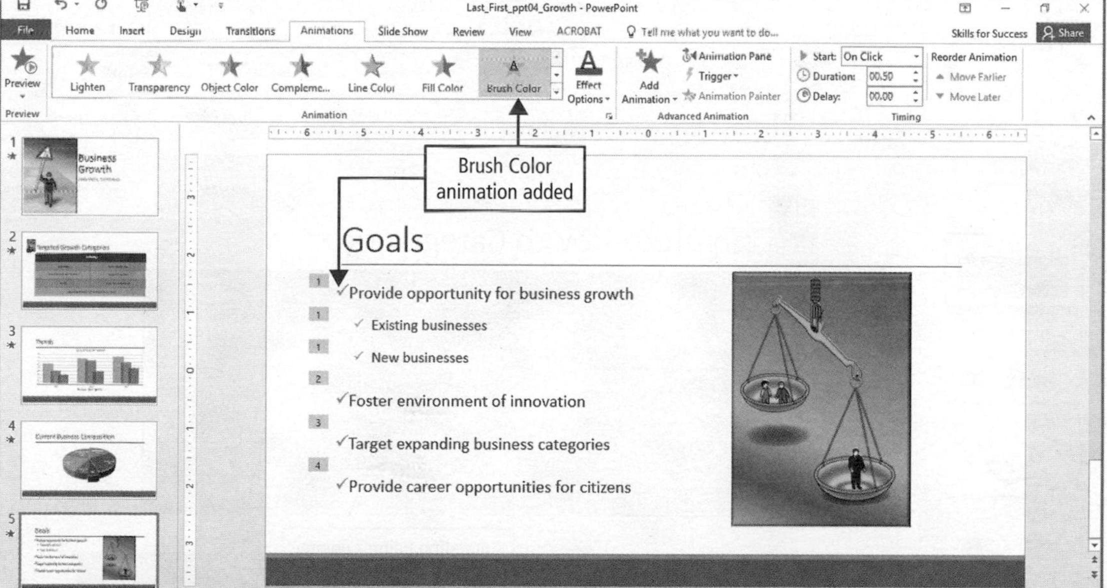

PowerPoint 2016, Windows 10, Microsoft Corporation

Figure 4

5. Move to **Slide 3**. Click the upper right corner of the chart placeholder so that the entire chart, and no individual element of the chart, is selected. On the **Animations tab**, in the **Animation group**, click **Fly In**.
6. On the **Animations tab**, in the **Animation group**, click the **Effect Options** button. Under **Sequence**, click **By Series**. Preview the effect as it appears automatically on the slide. In the **Duration** box, type 1.75 press Enter, and then compare your screen with **Figure 3**. (MOS Obj 4.2.3)

   The numbers 1, 2, 3, and 4 display to the left of the content placeholder, indicating the order in which the animation will display. The number 1 indicates the animation of the chart area or background. Numbers 2, 3, and 4 indicate the animation of the data series. Providing this animation in a slower duration helps the viewer to see the overall increase in growth.

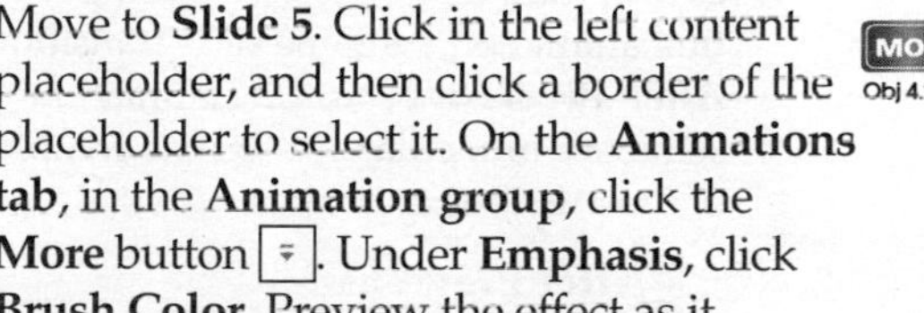

7. Move to **Slide 5**. Click in the left content placeholder, and then click a border of the placeholder to select it. On the **Animations tab**, in the **Animation group**, click the **More** button. Under **Emphasis**, click **Brush Color**. Preview the effect as it appears automatically on the screen, and then compare your screen with **Figure 4**. (MOS Obj 4.2.2)
8. Still on **Slide 5**, select the image in the right content placeholder. In the **Animation group**, click the **More** button. Under **Exit**, click **Wheel**.
9. Press F5 to view the show from the beginning, using your mouse button to click through the animations, noticing all of the animations—the ones you added and the one that was already in the presentation on Slide 2. When you reach the black slide, click one more time to return to Normal view.
10. **Save** the file.

■ **You have completed Skill 7 of 10**

- Timing options control when animated items appear in the animation sequence.
- ***Animation Painter*** is a tool used to copy animation settings from one object to another.

1. Display **Slide 1**, and then select the image. Recall that the number 1 displayed to the left of the image indicates that the image is first in the slide animation sequence.

Obj 4.2.3

2. On the **Animations tab**, in the **Timing group**, click the **Start arrow** to display three options—*On Click*, *With Previous*, and *After Previous*. Compare your screen with **Figure 1**.

   On Click begins the animation sequence when the mouse button is clicked or the SpaceBar is pressed. ***With Previous*** begins the animation sequence at the same time as any animation preceding it or, if it is the first animation, with the slide transition. ***After Previous*** begins the animation sequence immediately after the completion of the previous animation.

3. Click **After Previous**.

   The number 1 is changed to 0, indicating that the animation will begin immediately after the slide transition; the presenter need not click the mouse button or press SpaceBar to display the image.

4. With the image selected, on the **Animations tab**, in the **Advanced Animation group**, click the **Animation Painter** button. Move to **Slide 2**, and then point to the table to display the **Animation Painter** pointer, as shown in **Figure 2**.

■ **Continue to the next page to complete the skill**

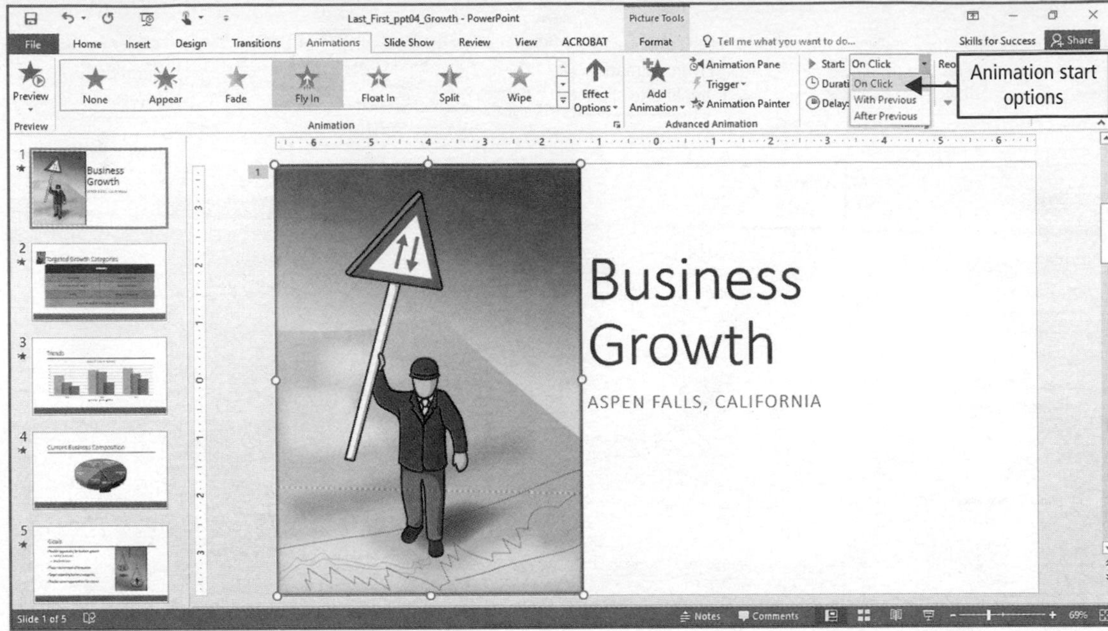

Figure 1

PowerPoint 2016, Windows 10, Microsoft Corporation

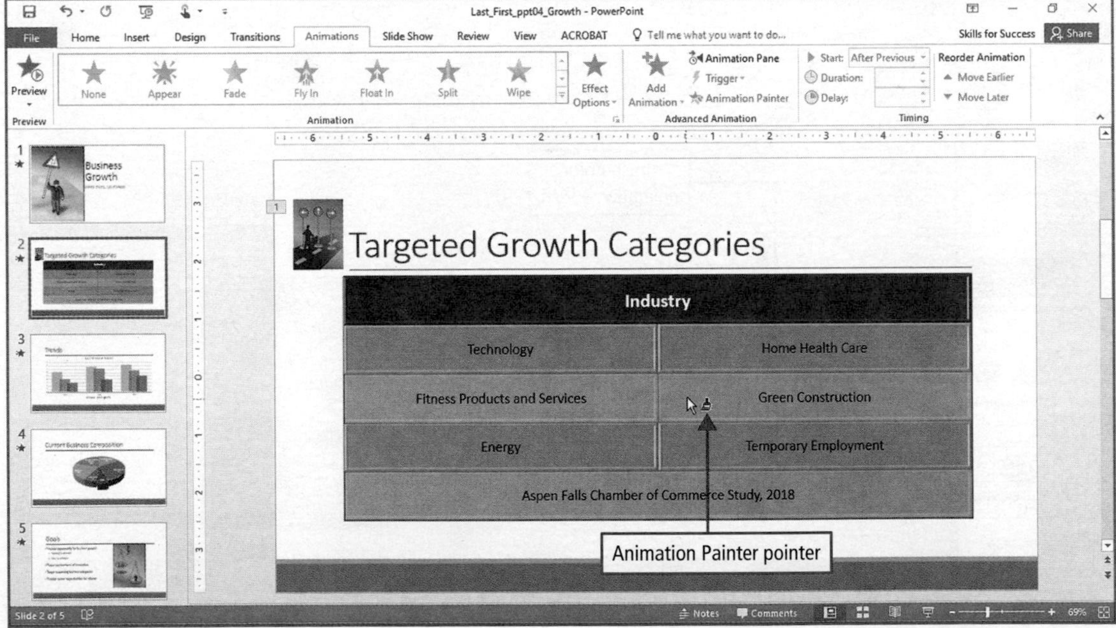

Figure 2

PowerPoint 2016, Windows 10, Microsoft Corporation

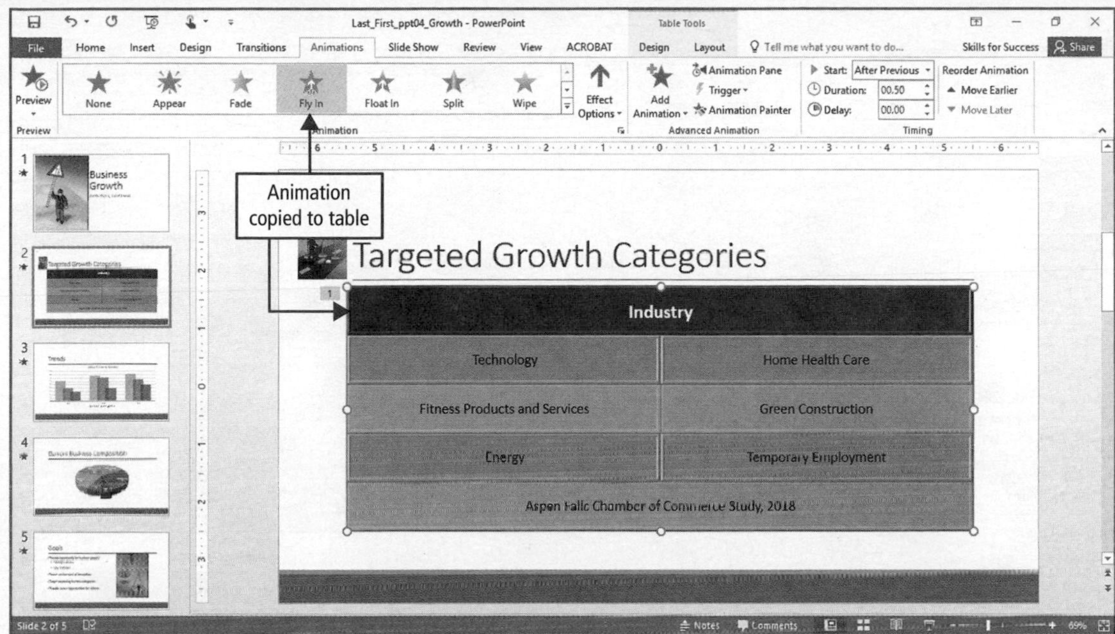

PowerPoint 2016, Windows 10, Microsoft Corporation

Figure 3

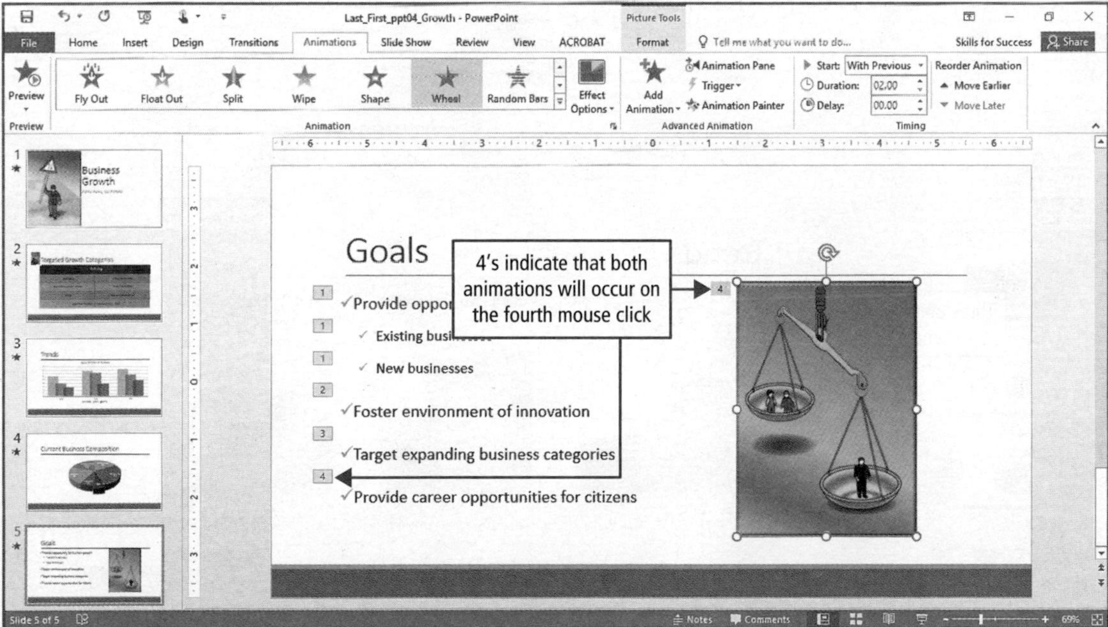

PowerPoint 2016, Windows 10, Microsoft Corporation

Figure 4

5. With the **Animation Painter** pointer, click the table to apply the same animation to it. Compare your screen with **Figure 3.**

   The table displays a number 1, indicating that the animation will begin with the animation applied to the image in the upper left corner of the slide. This animation was included in the original file.

6. Move to **Slide** 5. Click the image in the right content placeholder to select it. Notice that this image is currently the fifth animation—the Exit effect will be applied on the presenter's fifth mouse click.

MOS Obj 4.3.3

7. With the image selected, on the **Animations tab**, in the **Timing group**, click the **Start arrow**. Click **With Previous**, and then compare your screen with **Figure 4.**

   The image animation number changes to 4, indicating that this animation will appear with the animation of the fourth bullet point. Alternately, in the Timing group, you can use the Move Earlier and Move Later buttons to change the animation order of selected objects.

8. On your keyboard, press F5 to view the slide show. Click through the presentation in Slide Show view to view the entire presentation.

9. **Save** the file.

■ **You have completed Skill 8 of 10**

SKILL 9: Delay or Remove Animation

- When an animation effect interferes with the flow of the presentation, you can remove the effect.
- Animation can be ***delayed*** so that it starts after a predetermined amount of time.

1. Display **Slide 2** in Normal view. Select the image in the upper left corner of the slide. Notice that this image contains animation.
2. With the image selected, on the **Animations tab**, in the **Animation group**, click the **More** button. To remove the animation, at the top of the gallery, under **None**, click the first thumbnail—**None**. Compare your screen with **Figure 1**.

   It is not necessary to animate every object on every slide. In this slide, the slide transition and table animation draw sufficient attention to the table. The animation of the image detracted from the emphasis on the table.

3. Move to **Slide 3**, and then click to select the chart. On the **Animations tab**, in the **Preview group**, click **Preview**.

   The preview shows the sequence automatically, without the need to click. When in Slide Show view, each of the animations would appear on a mouse click, including the chart area.

4. To the left of the chart, click the **1**, which indicates the first mouse click. With the **1** selected, on the **Animations tab**, in the **Animation group**, click **None**. On the **Animations tab**, in the **Preview group**, click **Preview** to view the modified animation. Compare your screen with **Figure 2.**

   The animation was removed from the background of the chart so that it appears automatically, rather than requiring a click.

■ **Continue to the next page to complete the skill**

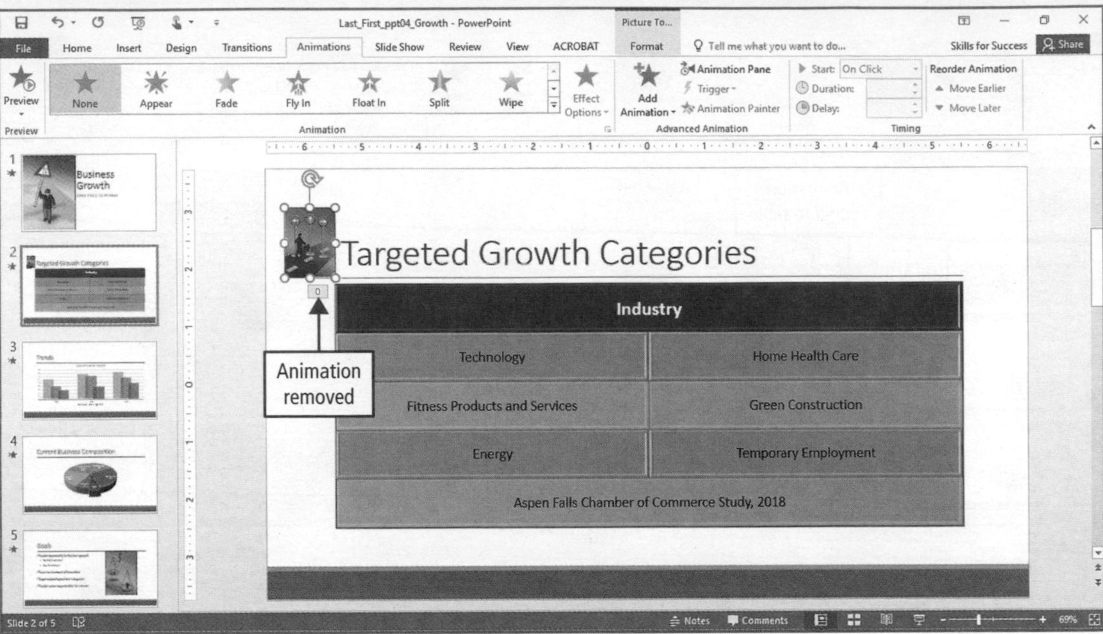

Figure 1

PowerPoint 2016, Windows 10, Microsoft Corporation

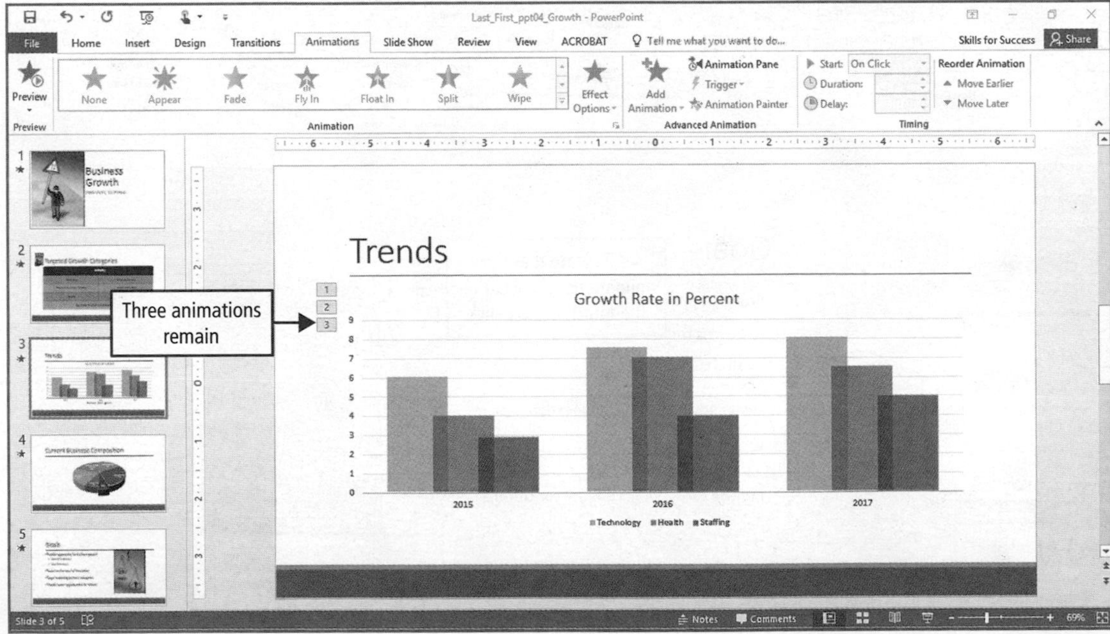

Figure 2

PowerPoint 2016, Windows 10, Microsoft Corporation

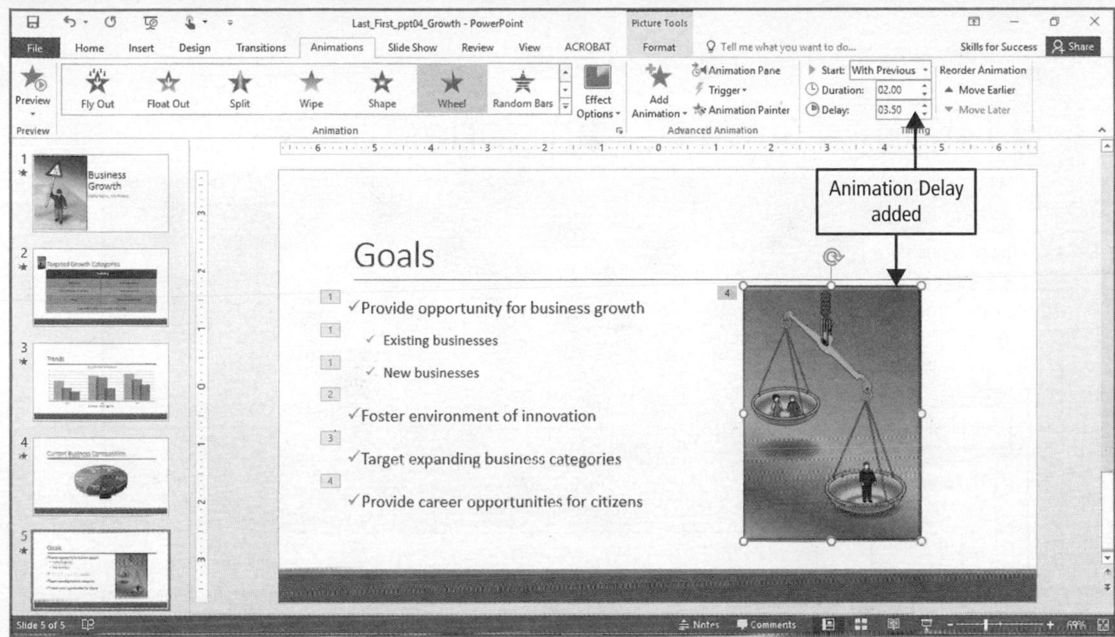

PowerPoint 2016, Windows 10, Microsoft Corporation

Figure 3

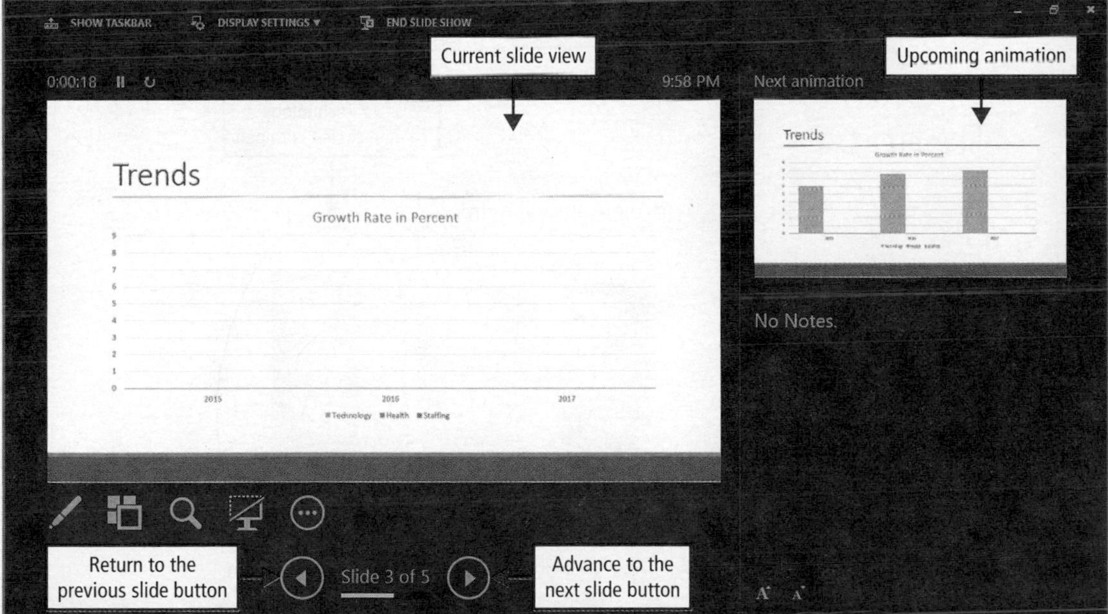

PowerPoint 2016, Windows 10, Microsoft Corporation

Figure 4

5. Move to **Slide 5**. Select the image in the right content placeholder. On the **Animations tab**, in the **Timing group**, in the **Delay** box, type 3.5 Press Enter, and then compare your screen with **Figure 3**.

   The image will be animated on Exit effect 3.5 seconds after the last mouse click.

6. Click a blank area of the slide so that nothing is selected. Press F5 to start the slide show from the beginning. While **Slide 1** is displayed, right-click, and then click **Show Presenter View**. Click the **Advance to the next slide arrow** to move through the presentation, until you reach **Slide 3**. Compare your screen with **Figure 4**.

   The upcoming animations not just the next slide—are shown on the preview on the right side of the presenter view window.

7. Finish viewing the slide show, and then return to Normal view.

8. **Save** the file.

- **You have completed Skill 9 of 10**

► During a slide show, when you move your mouse pointer, a ***navigation toolbar*** displays in the lower left corner of the slide. You can use the navigation toolbar to go to any slide while the slide show is running. You can use this toolbar, Presenter View, or simply click your mouse, spacebar, or Enter key to move through a presentation in Slide Show view.

1. On the **Slide Show tab**, in the **Start Slide Show group**, click the **From Beginning** button. Click the mouse button to display **Slide 2**.
2. Point to the lower left corner of the slide, and notice that left- and right-pointing arrows display, as shown in **Figure 1**.

   The left-pointing arrow—the Return to the previous slide button —is a navigation tool that, when clicked, displays the previous slide or animation. The right-pointing arrow—the Advance to the next slide button —displays the next slide or animation.

3. In the lower left corner of the slide, in the navigation toolbar, notice that a pen displays.

   The pen can be used to ***annotate***—write on the slide—while the slide show is running.

4. Move the pointer to the right, and notice that a **See all slides** button displays. Click this button, and then click the **Slide 3** preview to move to that slide. Click one time to display the animation of the *Technology* category.
5. Click the **Pen** button , and then click **Pen**. With the pen pointer, circle the *2017 Technology* column as shown in **Figure 2**.

   Ink annotations can be kept or discarded at the end of a presentation.

■ **Continue to the next page to complete the skill**

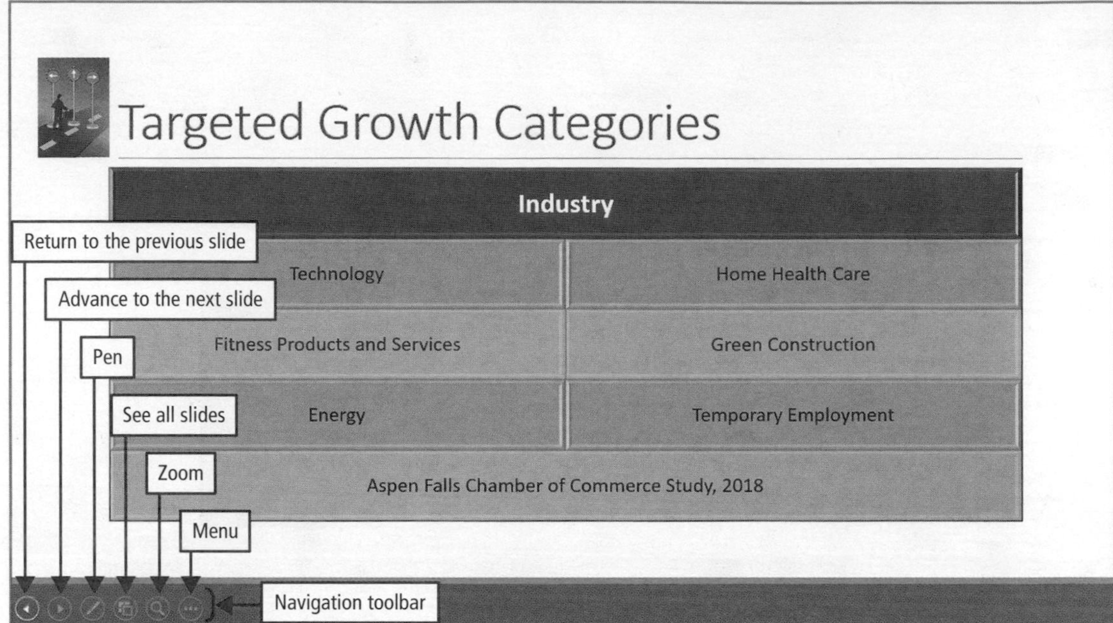

Figure 1

PowerPoint 2016, Windows 10, Microsoft Corporation

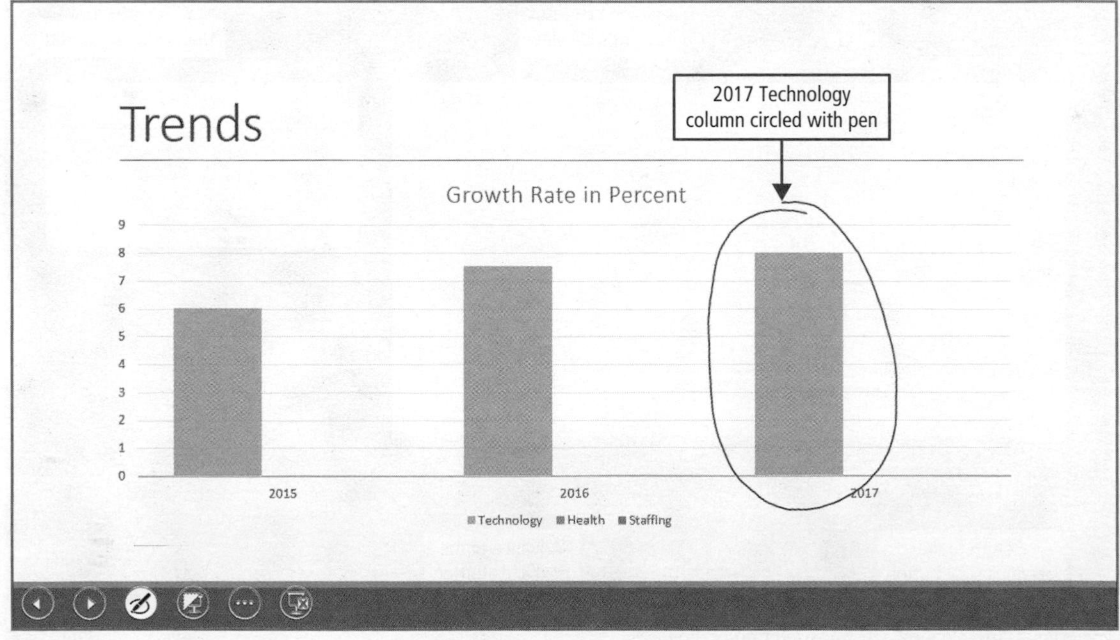

Figure 2

PowerPoint 2016, Windows 10, Microsoft Corporation

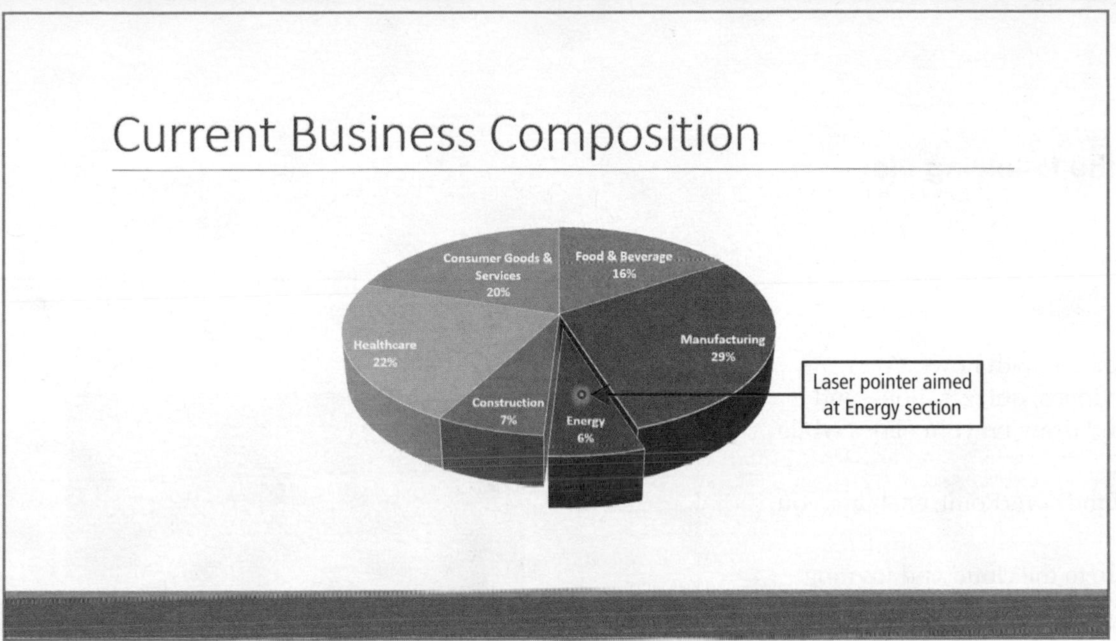

PowerPoint 2016, Windows 10, Microsoft Corporation

Figure 3

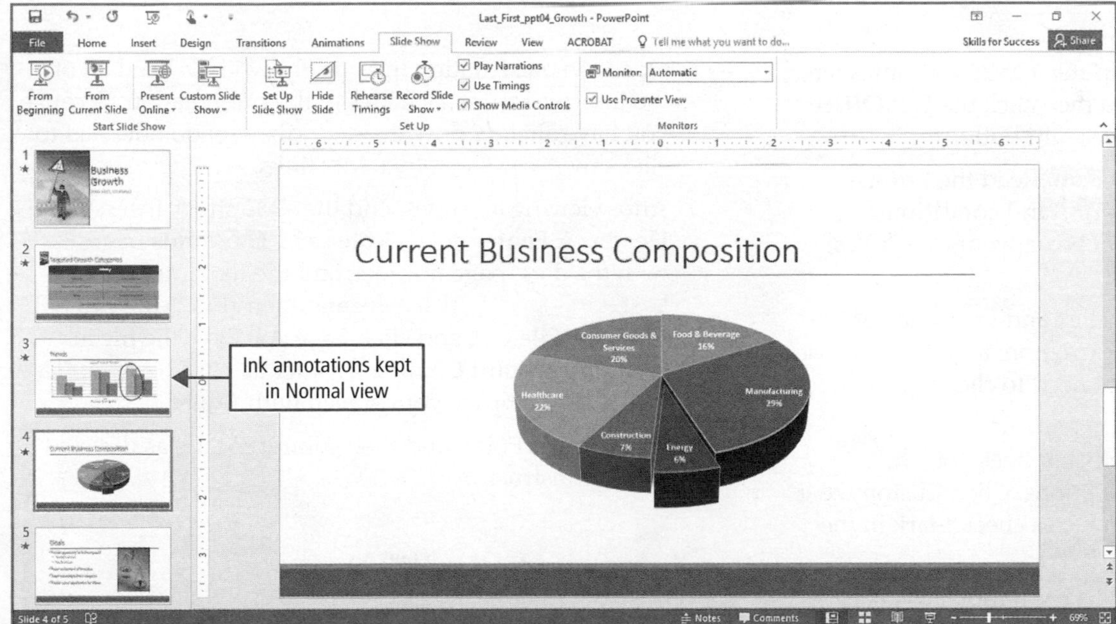

PowerPoint 2016, Windows 10, Microsoft Corporation

Figure 4

6. In the navigation toolbar, click the **Advance to the next slide** button three times to go through the animations on Slide 3 and display Slide 4 in Slide Show view.
7. With **Slide 4** displayed, click the **Pen** button, and then click **Laser Pointer**. Point to the *Energy* section of the pie chart, and then compare your screen to **Figure 3**.
8. Press Esc to turn the laser pointer off.
9. On your keyboard, press B.

   The B key is a toggle key that displays a black screen. During a slide show, you can pause a presentation so that a discussion can be held without the distraction of the slide elements. Rather than turning off the projection system or ending the slide show, you can display the slide as a black screen and then redisplay the same slide when you are ready to resume the presentation. Alternately, the W key will display a white screen.

10. On your keyboard, press B to redisplay **Slide 4**. Press Esc to end the slide show.
11. When prompted, click to **Keep** your ink annotations. Compare your screen with **Figure 4**.
12. Insert a **Header & Footer** on the **Notes and Handouts** pages. Include the **Page Number** and a **Footer** with the text Last_First_ppt04_Growth and **Apply to All** pages.
13. **Save** the file. **Close** PowerPoint. Submit the file as directed by your instructor.

DONE! You have completed Skill 10 of 10 and your presentation is complete!

More Skills 11

Download Microsoft Office Mix

To complete this project, you will need the following file:

- Create an Office Mix template

You will save your file as:

- Last_First_ppt04_MS11Mix

- Microsoft Office ***Mix*** is a downloadable add-in for use with PowerPoint. With it, you can add interactive content—audio, videos, quizzes, polls, and inking—to your presentation, as well as record and draw on your slides while presenting.
- After downloading Mix, a new tab will be added to PowerPoint, enabling you to use the features of the Mix app.
- Mixes can be shared by saving a newly created file to the cloud and inviting others to collaborate.
- For an overview, open your Internet browser and navigate to https://mix.office.com/ and then click the How to make your first mix video.

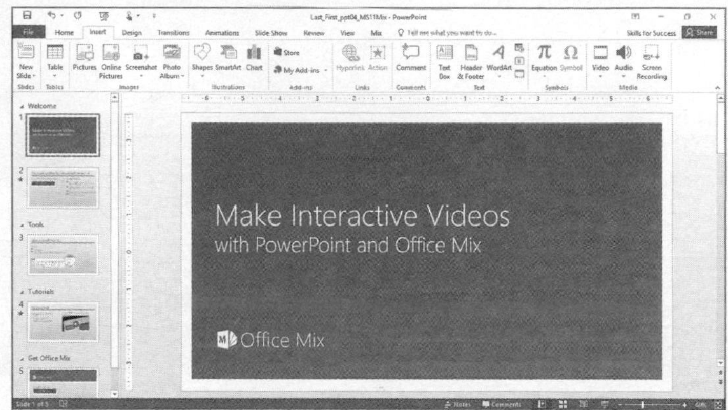

Figure 1 PowerPoint 2016, Windows 10, Microsoft Corporation

---

1. Be sure that PowerPoint is no open on your computer. Open your Internet browser, navigate to https://mix.office.com/ and then click the **Get Office Mix** button. Click the **Sign in with a Microsoft account** button.
2. On the taskbar, click **OfficeMix.Setup.exe**. Click **Run**. Read the License Terms, and then click the **I agree to the license terms and conditions checkbox**. Click **Install**. If a User Account Control box appears, click **Yes**, and then wait as the app is installed.
3. In the Mix pane on the right side of your screen, click and view each of the Quick Start Video Tutorials. View the videos to learn more about Mix. Close your browser to return to PowerPoint. You do not need to click the Create Your First Mix link.
4. If the Mix tab appears, proceed to step 5. If the Mix tab does not automatically open, click the File tab, then click Options. Click Customize Ribbon, and then on the right side of the screen, place a check mark in the Mix box. Click OK.
5. Click the **File tab**, and then click **New**. Click the design template **Make Interactive Videos - Create an Office Mix**. Click **Create**.
6. Open the presentation in Slide Show view. Read all of the information on all slides in the presentation. Because you have already downloaded Mix, you do not need to click any of the Get Office Mix links.
7. After viewing all slides, end the slide show. Insert a **Header & Footer** on all **Notes and Handouts** pages with the date, page number, and the footer text Last_First_ppt04_MS11Mix and then click **Apply to All**. Click the **File tab**, and click **Save As**. **Save** the file in your **PowerPoint Chapter 4** folder as Last_First_ppt04_MS11Mix Compare your screen with **Figure 1**.
8. **Close** PowerPoint, and then submit the file as directed by your instructor.

- **You have completed More Skills 11**

More Skills 12

Create an Office Mix

To complete this project, you will need the following file:

- ppt04_MS12Streets

You will save your file as:

- Last_First_ppt04_MS12Streets

- ▶ Using Mix, you can capture your voice and ink annotations as you present a slide show.
- ▶ Mixes can be saved and shared in the traditional manner, or they can be saved to the cloud.

---

1. Start **Microsoft PowerPoint 2016**, and then from the student data files for this chapter, open **ppt04_MS12Streets**. **Save** the file in your **PowerPoint Chapter 4** folder as Last_First_ppt04_MS12Streets
2. With your speakers on and a microphone available—either built in or plugged in—on the **Mix tab**, in the **Record group**, click **Slide Recording**.
3. With the first slide displayed, in the upper left corner, click the **Record** button. Speak the following sentence in a clear voice: "Thank you for joining us for an overview of our upcoming street projects."
4. While recording, on your keyboard, press the → key to move to **Slide 2**. On the right side of the screen, click the last color button—**Red**. Speak the following sentences: "These are the projects for this fiscal quarter. Most are on budget, however, the 4th Street project is running about 10% over budget." As you say 4th Street, use your mouse pointer—or your finger on a touch screen device—to circle the 4th *St* cell. Speak the following sentence: "This is attributed to an increase in the cost of construction material delivery."
5. On your keyboard, press the → key to move to the next slide. Draw an arrow pointing to the 4th *St* section of the pie. Speak the following sentence: "Because this project consumes the largest portion of our budget, we will be closely monitoring this situation."
6. On your keyboard, press the → key to move to the next slide. Speak the following sentence: "Please join us at our next meeting for a detailed update."

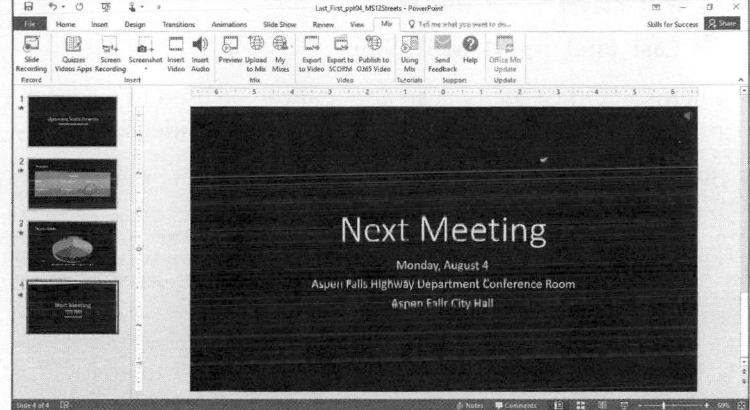

PowerPoint 2016, Windows 10, Microsoft Corporation **Figure 1**

7. In the upper left corner of the screen, click the **Stop Recording** button.
8. In the upper right corner, click the **Close** button to return to PowerPoint.
9. Click the **Slide 1** thumbnail to display Slide 1 in Normal view. On the **Mix tab**, in the **Mix** group, click the **Preview** button. After viewing your Mix, click the **Close** button in the lower left corner of the screen. Compare your screen with **Figure 1**.
10. Insert a **Header & Footer** on all **Notes and Handouts** pages with the date, page number, and the footer text Last_First_ppt04_MS12Streets and then **Save**. **Close** PowerPoint, and then submit the file as directed by your instructor.

■ **You have completed More Skills 12**

More Skills 13

Getting Started with Microsoft Sway

To complete this project, you will need the following file:

- New, blank Sway

You will save your file as:

- Last_First_ppt04_MS13Snip

- ▶ Microsoft Office ***Sway*** is an app that can be used to create storylines and presentations. You can add text, images, and videos.
- ▶ Sways are stored online and can be shared with others by sending a link. Sways work across devices.
- ▶ For an overview, go to https://sway.com and view any of the tutorial videos.

---

1. To work with Sway, use your Internet browser to go to https://sway.com/ and then click **Get started**.
2. On the **Sign in** screen, enter your e-mail address, press Enter, and then click the **Get Started** button. Click **Create New**.
3. In the **Title your Sway** box, type Hiking Trails in Aspen Falls
4. Click the **Background** button, and then click **Suggested**. Review the information about copyright and then click any of the suggested categories. Click any of the suggested images in the **Suggested** pane, and then drag the image to the **Drag a picture here** box. Images will vary. **Close** the Suggested pane.
5. Click the **Design tab**, and then in the **Design** pane, use screentips to locate and then click **Style: 4, Variation: 4**. **Close** the Design pane.
6. Click the **Insert tab**, and then in the center of the screen, under the *Hiking Trails in Aspen Falls* title, click the **+**.
7. Click **Heading**, and then type The Aspen Falls area contains over 300 miles of groomed hiking trails.
8. In the **Suggested pane**, select an image of a hiking trail, and then drag this image to the left of the text you just entered.
9. **Close** the **Suggested** pane, and then click **Preview** to preview your Sway. Toward the bottom of the screen, click the Move Forward arrow. Compare your screen with **Figure 1**, noting that your images will vary.

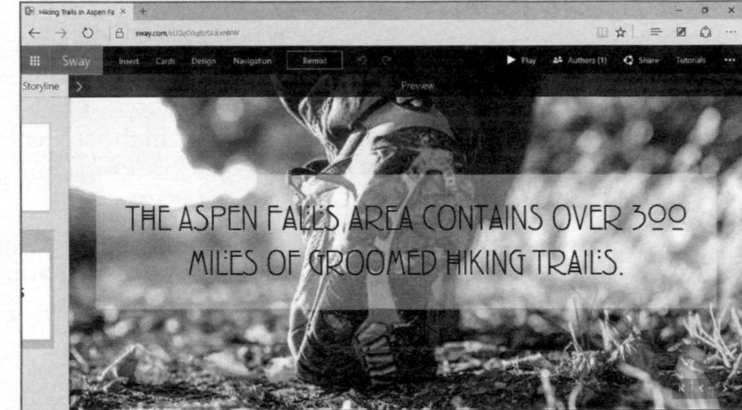

Figure 1 Anetlanda/Fotolia; PowerPoint 2016, Windows 10, Microsoft Corporation

Additional images and text could be added to this Sway.

10. Press [Windows], type snip and then press Enter to start the **Snipping Tool**. Click the **New arrow**, and then click **Full-screen Snip**.
11. In the **Snipping Tool** mark-up window, click the **Save Snip** button. In the **Save As** dialog box, navigate to your **PowerPoint Chapter 4** folder. Be sure the **Save as type** box displays JPEG file. Name the file Last_First_ppt04_MS13Snip and then press Enter. **Close** the Snipping Tool mark-up window. **Close** Sway. Submit the file as directed by your instructor.

- **You have completed More Skills 13**

More Skills 14

Importing Slides into Sway

To complete this project, you will need the following files:

- ppt04_MS14Directory
- ppt04_MS14DirectoryImage

You will save your file as:

- **Last_First_ppt04_MS14Snip**

▶ Files created in other programs—including slides created in Microsoft PowerPoint—can be imported into a Sway.

1. Open your Internet browser, and then go to https://sway.com/. Sign in with your e-mail address as needed, and then, in the upper right corner of the screen, if needed, click My Sways.
2. Click **Import**. Navigate to your student data files, and then open **ppt04_MS14Directory**. Wait as the presentation loads.
3. Click the **Background** button, and then click **Upload**. In the **Open** dialog box, click **ppt04_MS14DirectoryImage**, and then click **Open**. **Close** the Suggested pane.
4. Below the title, in the newly imported text, select *City Manager*, and then click **Emphasize**. Repeat the same process to emphasize these titles in the directory—*Assistant City Manager*, *Public Information Specialist*, *Human Resources Director*, *Parks and Recreation Director*, and *Park Operations Manager*.
5. Select the text *Grounds Supervisor*, and then click **Accent**. Repeat this process to accent *Building Supervisor*. The layout of your Sway screen may vary slightly.
6. Click **Preview** to preview your Sway. Scroll to right to view the Directory heading. Compare your screen with **Figure 1**.

   The link to this Sway—a phone and contact directory for Aspen Falls employees—could be linked to a web page, sent to a citizen, or shared in many other ways. The information in the Sway can easily be updated.

7. Press [Windows], type snip and then press [Enter] to start the **Snipping Tool**. Click the **New arrow**, and then click **Full-screen Snip**.

Anetlanda/Fotolia; PowerPoint 2016, Windows 10, Microsoft Corporation **Figure 1**

8. In the **Snipping Tool** mark-up window, click the **Save Snip** button [Save]. In the **Save As** dialog box, navigate to your **PowerPoint Chapter 4** folder. Be sure the **Save as type** box displays JPEG file. Name the file Last_First_ppt04_MS14Snip and then press [Enter]. **Close** [×] the Snipping Tool mark-up window. **Close** [×] Sway. Submit the file as directed by your instructor.

■ **You have completed More Skills 14**

The following table summarizes the **SKILLS AND PROCEDURES** covered in this chapter.

Skills Number	Task	Step	Icon	Keyboard Shortcut
1	Insert table	Placeholder → Insert table button		
2	Add a Table Style	Table Tools Design tab → Table Styles group → More button → Table Styles gallery		
2	Center text in a table horizontally	Select table → Layout tab → Alignment tab → Center button		Ctrl + E
2	Center text in a table vertically	Select table → Layout tab → Alignment tab → Center Vertically button		
4	Insert chart	Placeholder → Insert Chart button		
4	Add a Chart Style	Chart Tools Design tab→ Chart Styles group→ More button → Chart Styles gallery		
5	Edit an existing chart	Chart Tools Design tab → Data group → Edit Data → Chart in Microsoft PowerPoint window → Edit data		
7	Add slide transition	Transitions tab → Transition to This Slide group → Transition → Effect Options button → Select Effect option → Timing group → Apply To All		
7	Add animation	Select object → Animations tab → Animation group → More button → Animation gallery		
8	Use Animation Painter	Select object with animation → Animations tab → Advanced Animation group → Animation Painter button → Select object to be animated		
9	Remove animation	Select object → Animations tab → Animation group → More button → Animation gallery → None		
10	Next Slide - Slide Show	Left mouse click, spacebar, Enter, or Next Slide arrow		
10	Previous Slide - Slide Show	Previous Slide arrow		
10	Pen - Slide Show	Navigation toolbar → Pen → Pen		
10	Laser Pointer - Slide Show	Navigation toolbar → Pen → Laser Pointer		Ctrl + Mouse Click and hold
10	Black Slide - Slide Show	End of slide show, or press B		B
10	White Slide – Slide Show	Press W while in Slide Show view		W

Project Summary Chart		
Project	**Project Type**	**Project Location**
Skills Review	Review	In Book & MIL MyITLab® Grader
Skills Assessment 1	Review	In Book & MIL MyITLab® Grader
Skills Assessment 2	Review	Book
My Skills	Problem Solving	Book
Visual Skills Check	Problem Solving	Book
Skills Challenge 1	Critical Thinking	Book
Skills Challenge 2	Critical Thinking	Book
More Skills Assessment	Review	In Book & MIL MyITLab® Grader
Collaborating with Google	Critical Thinking	Book

MOS Objectives Covered	
3.1.1 Create a table	4.2.1 Apply animations to objects
3.1.2 Insert and delete table rows and columns	4.2.2 Apply animations to text
3.1.3 Apply table styles	4.2.3 Set animation effect options
3.2.1 Create a chart	4.3.3 Reorder animations on a slide
3.2.4 Add a legend to a chart	

Key Terms

BizSkills Video

1. In the video, professionals reflected on the lessons they learned from mistakes made in their career. Think of a mistake you made in your college career or a job you have had. What have you learned from that mistake, and how will this knowledge help you in your future career?
2. What setbacks have you experienced in your college career? How did you, or will you, overcome them?

Online Help Skills

1. With PowerPoint open, on the **File tab**, in the upper right corner of the screen, click the **Microsoft PowerPoint Help** button [?], or press [F1].
2. In the **PowerPoint Help** window, use the **Search** box to locate and open the article *Add a trend or moving average line to a chart*. Compare your screen with **Figure 1**.

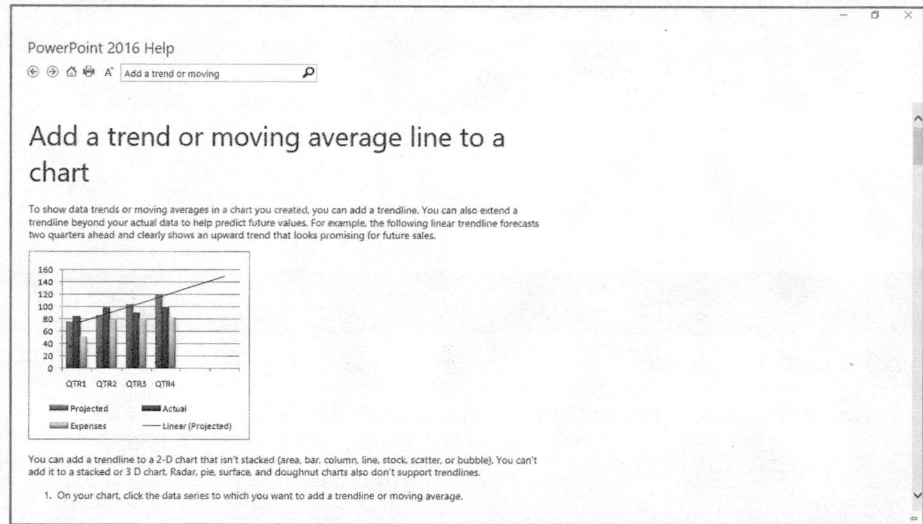

Figure 1 PowerPoint 2016, Windows 10, Microsoft Corporation

3. Read the article and answer the following questions: Why might it be beneficial to add a trend or average line to a chart? How might this help your audience to understand the data you are presenting?

Matching 

Match each term in the second column with its correct definition in the first column by writing the letter of the term on the blank line in front of the correct definition.

___ **1.** In a table or worksheet, the intersection of a column and row.

___ **2.** A format used to organize and present information in columns and rows.

___ **3.** Predefined formatting that applies borders and fill colors to a table so that it is consistent with the presentation theme.

___ **4.** A graphic representation of numeric data.

___ **5.** Text that identifies the categories of data in a chart.

___ **6.** A chart type useful for illustrating comparisons among related categories.

___ **7.** Individual data plotted in a chart.

___ **8.** Text that identifies a data marker in a chart.

___ **9.** A column, bar, area, dot, pie slice, or other symbol that represents a single data point.

___ **10.** Visual or motion effects added to an object on a slide.

A Animation
B Cell
C Chart
D Column chart
E Category label
F Data label
G Data marker
H Data point
I Table
J Table style

Multiple Choice MyITLab®

Choose the correct answer.

1. A prebuilt set of effects, colors, and backgrounds applied to a chart that is designed to work with the presentation theme.
   A. Chart layout
   B. Chart style
   C. Chart effect
2. Tool used to copy color from one slide object to another.
   A. Eyedropper
   B. Animation Painter
   C. Copy button
3. A chart element that identifies the patterns or colors that are assigned to the data in the chart.
   A. Data series
   B. Data label
   C. Legend
4. A type of chart used to illustrate percentages or proportions using only one series of data.
   A. Column chart
   B. Line chart
   C. Pie chart
5. A type of animation that appears as a slide element comes onto the screen.
   A. Entrance effect
   B. Emphasis effect
   C. Exit effect
6. Animation that emphasizes an object or text that is already displayed.
   A. Entrance effect
   B. Emphasis effect
   C. Exit effect
7. Postpone animation, so that it appears at a predetermined amount of time after the last animation.
   A. Delay
   B. Duration
   C. Exit effect
8. A feature that copies animation settings from one object to another.
   A. Format Painter
   B. Animation Painter
   C. Copy and Paste
9. The action of writing on a slide while the slide show is running.
   A. Annotate
   B. Edit
   C. Navigation
10. A pointer used while a slide show is in progress.
    A. Animation
    B. Highlighter
    C. Laser pointer

Topics for Discussion

1. You can apply multiple animations to each slide. Is it a good idea to limit the amount of animation you use? Why or why not?
2. Recall that a column chart is used to compare data and a pie chart is used to illustrate percentages or proportions. Give examples of the types of data that an organization might use in a column or a pie chart.

Skills Review

To complete this presentation, you will need the following file:

- **ppt04_SRGiving**

You will save your file as:

- **Last_First_ppt04_SRGiving**

1. Start **Microsoft PowerPoint 2016**, and then from the student data files for this chapter, open **ppt04_SRGiving**. On the **File tab**, click **Save As**. Navigate to your **PowerPoint Chapter 4** folder, and then using your own name, **Save** the file as Last_First_ppt04_SRGiving
2. Move to **Slide 2**. In the content placeholder, click the **Insert Table** button. In the **Insert Table** dialog box, in the **Number of columns** box, type 3 and then click **OK**.
3. In the first cell, type Literacy Council and then press Tab. Type Food Pantry Press Tab and then type Aspen Falls Youth Club Press Tab. With the insertion point positioned in the first cell of the second row, type Green Aspen Falls and then press Tab. Type Aspen Falls Cultural Committee and then press Tab. Type Advocates Group
4. Click any cell in the first row. On the **Layout tab**, in the **Rows & Columns group**, click the **Insert Above** button. In the first cell of the new row, type Employee-Selected Charities Compare your screen with **Figure 1**.
5. With your insertion point still in the first cell of the table, on the **Layout tab**, in the **Cell Size group**, click the **Distribute Rows** button. On the **Layout tab**, in the **Table group**, click the **Select** button, and then click **Select Table**. In the **Alignment group**, click the **Center** button, and then click the **Center Vertically** button.
6. Select all of the cells in the first row of the table. On the **Layout tab**, in the **Merge group**, click **Merge Cells**.
7. On the **Table Tools Design tab**, in the **Table Styles group**, click the **More** button. Under **Best Match for Document**, click the second style in the second row—**Themed Style 2 - Accent 1**. Compare your screen with **Figure 2**.

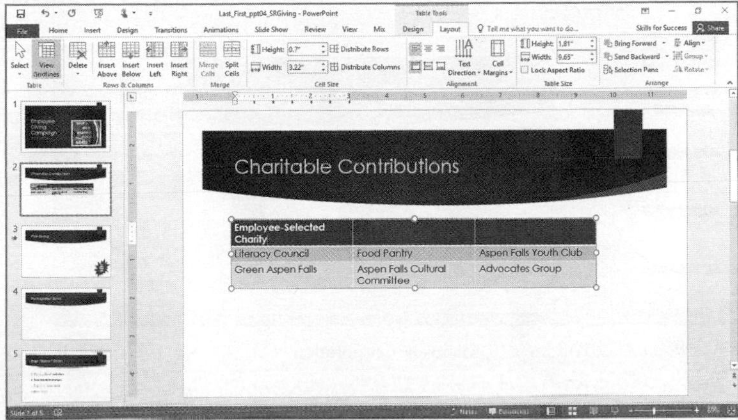

Figure 1 PowerPoint 2016, Windows 10, Microsoft Corporation

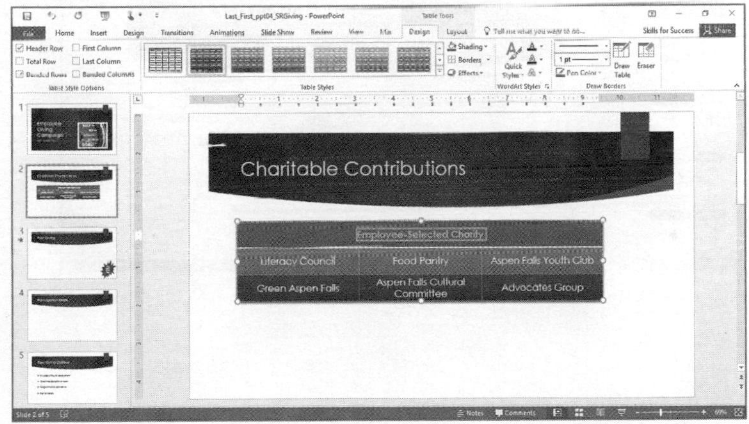

Figure 2 PowerPoint 2016, Windows 10, Microsoft Corporation

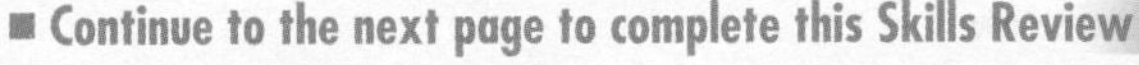
■ **Continue to the next page to complete this Skills Review**

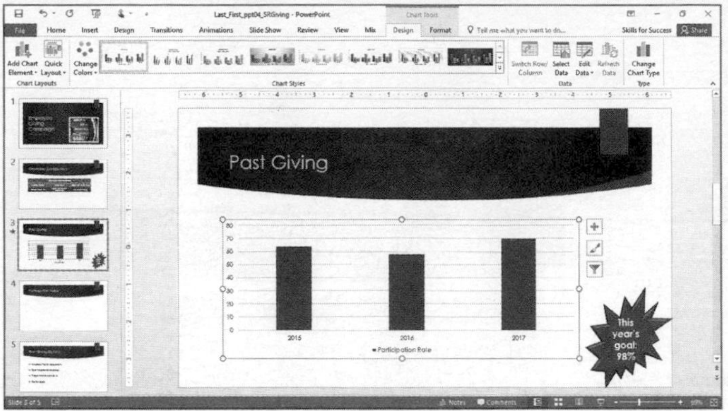

PowerPoint 2016, Windows 10, Microsoft Corporation **Figure 3**

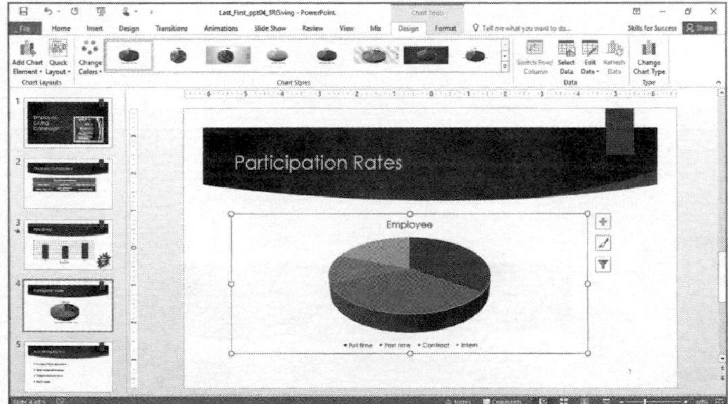

PowerPoint 2016, Windows 10, Microsoft Corporation **Figure 4**

8. Move to **Slide 3**. In the content placeholder, click the **Insert Chart** button. On the left side of the **Insert Chart** dialog box, if necessary, click Column. With the first chart—**Clustered Column**—selected, click **OK**.
9. In the **Chart in Microsoft PowerPoint** window, click cell **B1**. Type Participation Rate In cell **A2**, type 2015 Press [Enter] and type 2016 Press [Enter] and type 2017 In cell **B2**, type 64 Press [Enter] and type 58 Press [Enter] and type 70 Press [Enter] Point to the sizing handle in the lower right corner of cell **D5**, and then drag up and to the left so that only the range **A1:B4** is selected. **Close** the Chart in Microsoft PowerPoint window.
10. Select the chart title placeholder, press [Delete], and then compare your screen with **Figure 3**.
11. Move to **Slide 4**. In the content placeholder, click the **Insert Chart** button. On the left side of the **Insert Chart** dialog box, click **Pie**, click **3-D Pie**, and then click **OK**. In the worksheet, in cell **B1**, type Employee In cell **A2**, type Full time In cell **A3**, type Part time In cell **A4**, type Contract In cell **A5**, type Intern In cell **B2**, type 35 In cell **B3**, type 34 In cell **B4**, type 12 In cell **B5**, type 19 **Close** the Chart in Microsoft PowerPoint window, and then compare your screen with **Figure 4**.
12. Move to **Slide 5**. Select the content placeholder, and then on the **Animations tab**, in the **Animation group**, click the **More** button. Under **Entrance**, click **Zoom**.
13. Select the content placeholder. On the **Animations tab**, in the **Advanced Animation group**, click the **Animation Painter** button. Move to **Slide 1**. Click the picture on the right side of the slide to apply the animation from the bulleted list on Slide 5 to the picture on Slide 1.
14. With the image on Slide 1 selected, on the **Animations tab**, in the **Timing group**, in the **Duration** box, type 2 and then press [Enter].
15. With the image still selected, in the **Timing group**, click the **Start arrow**, and then click **With Previous**. In the **Delay** box, type 2 and then press [Enter].
16. Move to **Slide 3**. Select the starburst shape in the lower right corner of the slide. On the **Animations tab**, in the **Animation group**, click the **More** button, and then click **None** to remove the animation from this shape.
17. View the slide show. Insert a **Header & Footer** on all **Notes and Handouts** pages with the date, page number, and the footer text Last_First_ppt04_SRGiving and then **Save**. **Close** PowerPoint, and then submit the file as directed by your instructor.

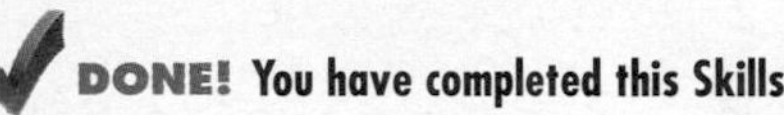

Skills Assessment 1

To complete this presentation, you will need the following file:

- ppt04_SA1Community

You will save your file as:

- Last_First_ppt04_SA1Community

1. Start **Microsoft PowerPoint 2016**. From your student files, open **ppt04_SA1Community**. **Save** the file in your **PowerPoint Chapter 4** folder as Last_First_ppt04_SA1Community
2. Display **Slide 3**. In the content placeholder, insert a table with 3 columns and 3 rows. In the three cells in the first row, type 2015 and 2016 and 2017 In the second row, type the following from left to right: 2% and 1% and 3% In the first cell in the third row, type County Real Estate Records 2017
3. Size the table so that its lower edge aligns at the **3 inch** mark below zero on the vertical ruler. **Distribute** the rows, and then apply the **Themed Style 2 - Accent 4** table style. Center the text horizontally and vertically within the cells. Increase the font size to **28** for the entire table. Add a **Soft Round** Cell Bevel to all cells in the table. **Merge** the cells in the bottom row.
4. Display **Slide 4**. Insert a **Pie** chart. In the **Chart in Microsoft PowerPoint** window, in cell **B1**, verify the word *Sales* appears. Beginning in cell **A2**, enter the following data:

New	37
Existing	63

5. In the **Chart in Microsoft PowerPoint** window, delete any extra data, and then resize the data range so that only **A1:B3** appear. **Close** the Chart in Microsoft PowerPoint window. Change the chart style to **Style 10**, and then delete the chart title. Increase the size of all fonts in the chart to 18
6. Animate the pie chart by applying the **Swivel** entrance effect, and then change the **Effect Options** to **By Category**.

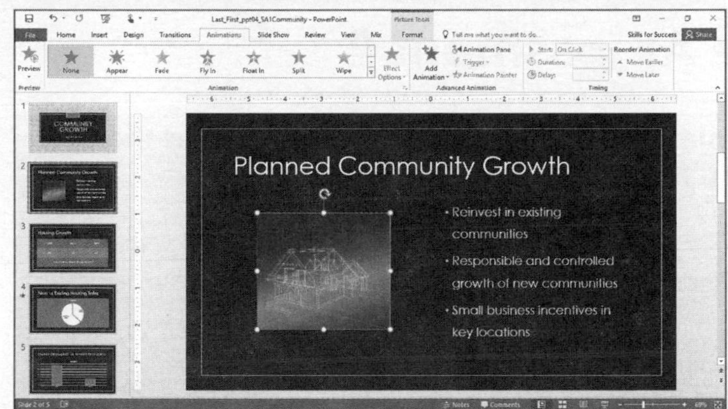

Figure 1 AlexZel/Fotolia; PowerPoint 2016, Windows 10, Microsoft Corporation

7. Display **Slide 5**. Add a **Clustered Column** chart with the following data; delete any extra data and change the data range so only this data displays:

	Resident
Owner	74
Tenant	26

8. **Delete** the legend below the clustered column chart.
9. Display **Slide 2**, and then remove the animation effect from the image in the left content placeholder.
10. Insert a **Header & Footer** on all **Notes and Handouts** pages with the date, page number, and the footer text Last_First_ppt04_SA1Community
11. **Save**, and then compare your presentation with **Figure 1**. **Close** PowerPoint. Submit the file as directed by your instructor.

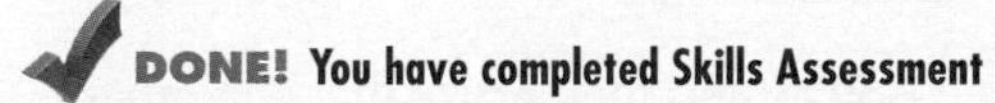
DONE! You have completed Skills Assessment 1

Skills Assessment 2

To complete this presentation, you will need the following file:

- ppt04_SA2Invest

You will save your file as:

- Last_First_ppt04_SA2Invest

---

1. Start **Microsoft PowerPoint 2016**. From your student files, open **ppt04_SA2Invest**. **Save** the file in your **PowerPoint Chapter 4** folder as Last_First_ppt04_SA2Invest
2. On **Slide 2**, apply the **Wipe** entrance effect to the text in the left content placeholder. Use the **Animation Painter** to copy the same formatting to the image in the right content placeholder.
3. Move to **Slide 3**. In the content placeholder, insert a table with 3 columns and 2 rows. In the first row, type the following heading: Available Plans and then **Merge** the cells in the first row. In the second row, type Pretax and Traditional and Tiered
4. Size the table so that its lower edge aligns at the **1 inch** mark below zero on the vertical ruler. Apply the **Themed Style 2 - Accent 5** table style. **Center** the table text horizontally and vertically. Change the **Font Size** to **28** for the entire table. Apply the **Circle** Cell Bevel effect to the entire table. **Animate** the table by applying the **Entrance Wipe** animation.
5. Move to **Slide 4**, and then remove the animation from the title placeholder. In the content placeholder, insert a **Clustered Column** chart. In the **Chart in Microsoft PowerPoint** window, in cell **B1**, type Pretax In cell **C1**, type Traditional and then in cell **D1**, type Tiered Beginning in cell **A2**, enter the following data:

2015	6%	6%	5%
2016	6%	5%	9%
2017	5%	4%	8%

6. Delete the values in the range **A5:D5**, and then resize the data range so that only **A1:D4** appear on the chart. Apply the **Style 14** chart style.

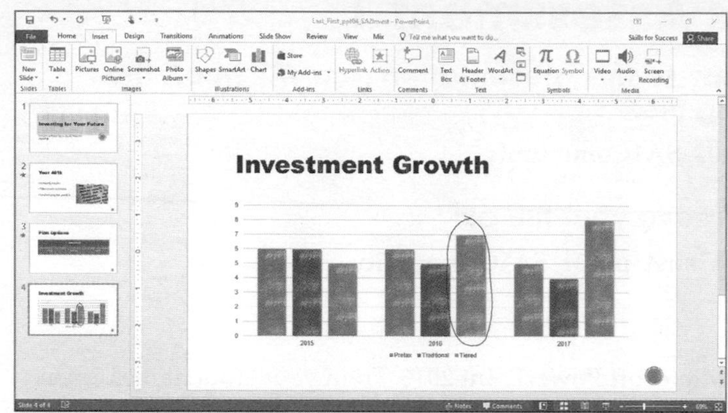

PowerPoint 2016, Windows 10, Microsoft Corporation **Figure 1**

7. Edit the chart data by changing the *2016 Tiered* data in cell **D3** to 7%
8. Delete the chart title.
9. Open the presentation in Slide Show view, and then on **Slide 4**, use the **Pen** to circle the *2016 Tiered* column. **End** the slide show. **Keep** your ink annotations.
10. Insert a **Header & Footer** on all **Notes and Handouts** pages with the date, page number, and the footer text Last_First_ppt04_SA2Invest
11. **Save**, and then compare your screen with **Figure 1**. **Close** PowerPoint. Submit the file as directed by your instructor.

 **DONE! You have completed Skills Assessment 2**

My Skills

To complete this presentation, you will need the following file:

- ppt04_MYCollege

You will save your file as:

- Last_First_ppt04_MYCollege

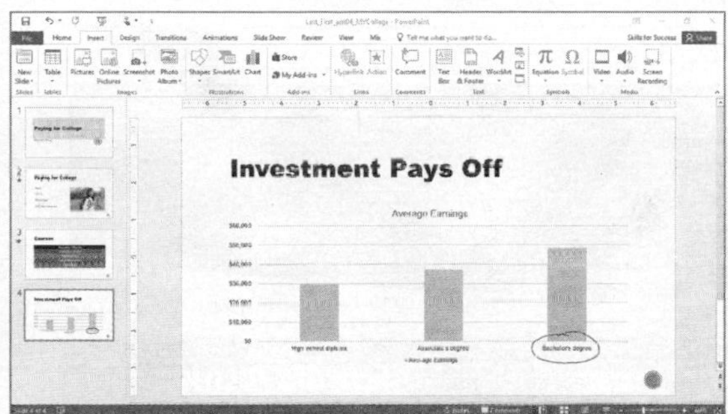

PowerPoint 2016, Windows 10, Microsoft Corporation

Figure 1

1. Start **Microsoft PowerPoint 2016**. From your student data files, open **ppt04_MYCollege**. **Save** the file in your **PowerPoint Chapter 4** folder as Last_First_ppt04_MYCollege Add your first and last names to the subtitle placeholder.
2. On **Slide 2**, apply the **Fly In** animation to the text in the left content placeholder. Adjust the **Duration** of the animation to 01.25 seconds.
3. Move to **Slide 3**. In the content placeholder, insert a table with enough rows and columns to list all of the courses in which you are enrolled this semester. Enter the name of each course in the table.
4. Size the table so that its lower edge aligns at the **2 inch** mark below zero on the vertical ruler. Apply the **Dark Style 1 - Accent 2** table style. **Center** the table text horizontally and vertically. Change the **Font Size** to **28** for the entire table. Apply the **Cool Slant** Cell Bevel effect to the entire table. Use the **Animation Painter** to copy the animation from the bulleted list on Slide 2 to the table.
5. Move to **Slide 4**, and then remove the animation from the title placeholder. In the content placeholder, insert a **Clustered Column** chart. In the **Chart in Microsoft PowerPoint** window, add the following data (source: nces.ed.gov/fastfacts), resizing the data range as needed:

	Average Earnings
High school diploma	$30,000
Associate's degree	$37,540
Bachelor's degree	$48,530

6. Open the presentation in Slide Show view, and then on **Slide 4**, use the **Pen** to circle the text *Bachelor's degree*. **End** the Slide Show. **Keep** your ink annotations.
7. Insert a **Header & Footer** on all **Notes and Handouts** pages with the date, page number, and the footer text Last_First_ppt04_MYCollege
8. **Save**, and then compare your screen with **Figure 1**. Submit your presentation as directed. **Close** PowerPoint.

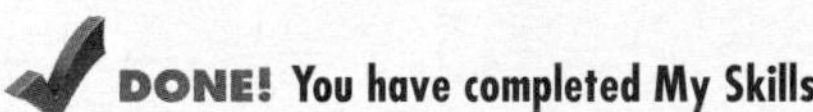

Visual Skills Check

To complete this presentation, you will need the following file:

- New blank PowerPoint presentation

You will save your file as:

- **Last_First_ppt04_VSHealthcare**

Start **PowerPoint 2016**. Create a new presentation in the **Ion Boardroom** theme. Add the slide title and create the table as shown in **Figure 1**. **Save** the file as Last_First_ppt04_VSHealthcare in your **PowerPoint Chapter 4** folder. To complete this presentation, use the **Title and Content** layout. Type and align the text as shown in the figure, and then apply the **Dark Style 1 - Accent 1** table style. In the first table row, change the **Font Size** to **24** and, if needed, **Bold**. If needed, change the font size of the remaining data in the table to **18**. Apply the **Divot** Cell Bevel effect to the entire table, and then add an outside border to the table. Insert a **Header & Footer** on all **Notes and Handouts** pages with the date, page number, and the footer text Last_First_ppt04_VSHealthcare Submit your presentation as directed.

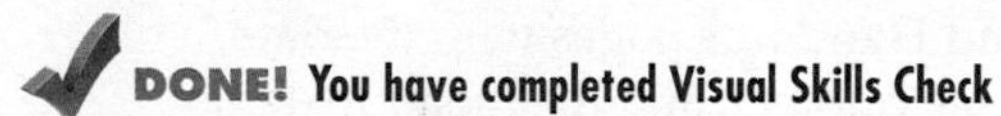

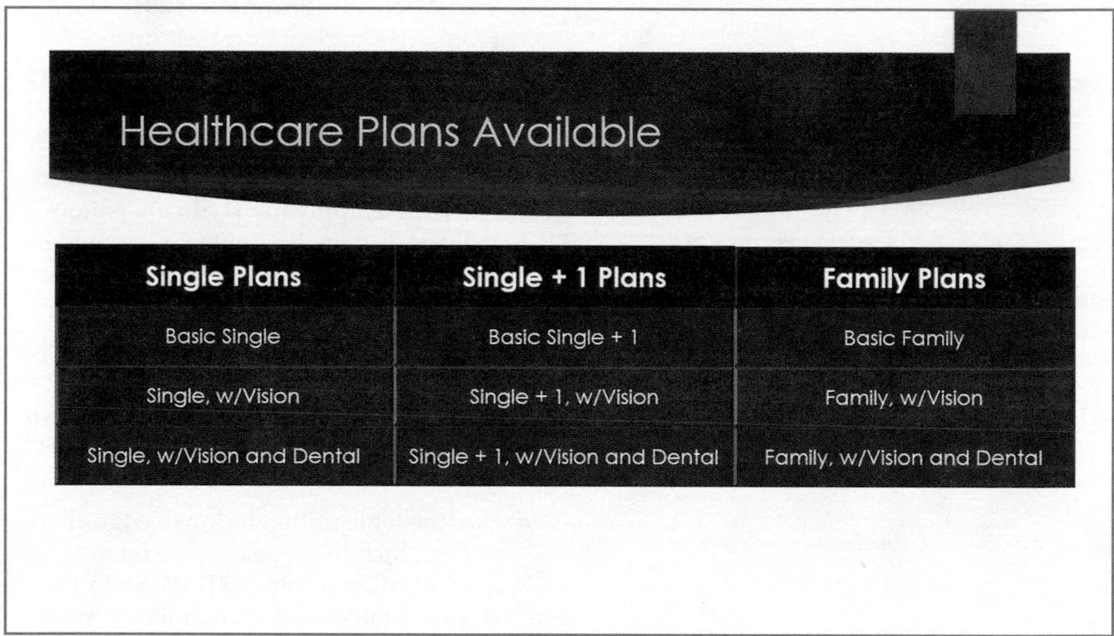

Figure 1

Skills Challenge 1

To complete this presentation, you will need the following file:

- ppt04_SC1Winery

You will save your file as:

- Last_First_ppt04_SC1Winery

Start **PowerPoint 2016**. From your student files, open **ppt04_SC1Winery**. Save the file in your PowerPoint Chapter 4 folder as Last_First_ppt04_SC1Winery Using the skills you have practiced in this chapter, add a transition to both slides in the presentation. To the first image on the first slide, add animation. Using the Animation Painter, copy the animation from the first image to the other two images on the slide. Adjust the animation of all three images so that they appear With Previous. Use the Animation Painter again to copy the same animation to the chart on Slide 2. On Slide 2, change the Animation Effects so that the data appears By Category. Insert a Header & Footer on all Notes and Handouts pages with the date, page number, and the footer text Last_First_ppt04_SC1Winery If necessary, change the chart animation so that the background of the chart appears With Previous and each of the other animations appears On Click. With the chart selected, change the Chart Style. In Slide Show view, use the Highlighter to highlight the category label that represents the category with the highest percentage of visitors. Keep your ink annotations. Save your file, and then submit as directed by your instructor.

DONE! You have completed Skills Challenge 1

Skills Challenge 2

To complete this presentation, you will need the following file:

- ppt04_SC2Forum

You will save your file as:

- Last_First_ppt04_SC2Forum

Start **PowerPoint 2016**. From your student files, open **ppt04_SC2Forum**. Save the file in your PowerPoint Chapter 4 folder as Last_First_ppt04_SC2Forum View the presentation in Slide Show view, and notice the animation on Slide 2. In Normal view, edit the chart data to remove the Consultants category, and resize the data range so that only the Small, Medium, and Large categories appear. Change the Chart Style. Remove the animation from the chart on Slide 2, and replace it with something less obtrusive. Change the animation so that all of the data appears at the same time. Use the Animation Painter to copy the new formatting you applied to the chart to the title on the first slide. Insert a Header & Footer on all Notes and Handouts pages with the date, page number, and the footer text Last_First_ppt04_SC2Forum Save and then submit your file as directed by your instructor. Close PowerPoint.

DONE! You have completed Skills Challenge 2

More Skills Assessment

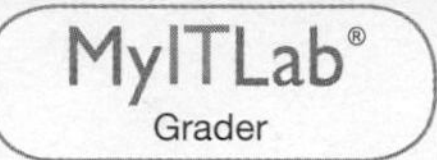

To complete this presentation, you will need the following file:

- **ppt04_MSAWater**

You will save your file as:

- **Last_First_ppt04_MSAWaterMix**

1. Start **Microsoft PowerPoint 2016**, and then from the student data files for this chapter, open **ppt04_MSAWater**. **Save** the file in your **PowerPoint Chapter 4** folder as Last_First_ppt04_MSAWaterMix
2. Be sure that your speakers are on and that you have a microphone available—either built in or plugged in. On the **Mix tab**, in the **Record group**, click **Slide Recording**.
3. With the first slide displayed, in the upper left corner, click the **Record** button. Speak the following sentences in a clear voice: "Thank you for joining us. We are here to discuss our new Water Quality Initiative."
4. While recording, on your keyboard, press the → key to move to **Slide 2**. On the right side of the screen, click the last color button—**Red**. With **Slide 2** displayed, speak the following sentence: "As you can see, we have experienced an increase in water usage each quarter for the past year." As you say *increase*, use your mouse pointer—or your finger on a touch screen device—to trace the increase line on the chart. Speak the following sentence: "We need to begin a water conservation initiative to reduce our overall water consumption."
5. On your keyboard, press the → key to move to the next slide. Speak the following sentence: "We all know that conservation of our fresh water supply is key."
6. On your keyboard, press the → key to move to the next slide. Speak the following sentence: "This process will address our current needs. We are adding new equipment to our current facility." As you speak this sentence, use your mouse pointer—or your finger on a touch screen device—to draw a circle around the first shape in the SmartArt graphic.
7. Speak the following sentence: "We will also start a new public awareness campaign, using commercials and social media to inform our citizens about the importance of conservation and how they can help." As you speak this sentence, use your mouse pointer—or your finger on a touch screen device—to draw a circle around the second shape in the SmartArt graphic.
8. Speak the following sentence: "Lastly, we are working with Aspen Falls Community College to form a research task force to explore new options." As you speak this sentence, use your mouse pointer—or your finger on a touch screen device—to draw a circle around the third shape in the SmartArt graphic.
9. In the upper left corner of the screen, click the **Stop Recording** button.
10. In the upper right corner, click the **Close** button to return to PowerPoint. Compare your screen with **Figure 1**.
11. Insert a **Header & Footer** on all **Notes and Handouts** pages with the date, page number, and the footer text Last_First_ppt04_MSAWaterMix and then **Save**. **Close** PowerPoint. Submit the file as directed by your instructor.

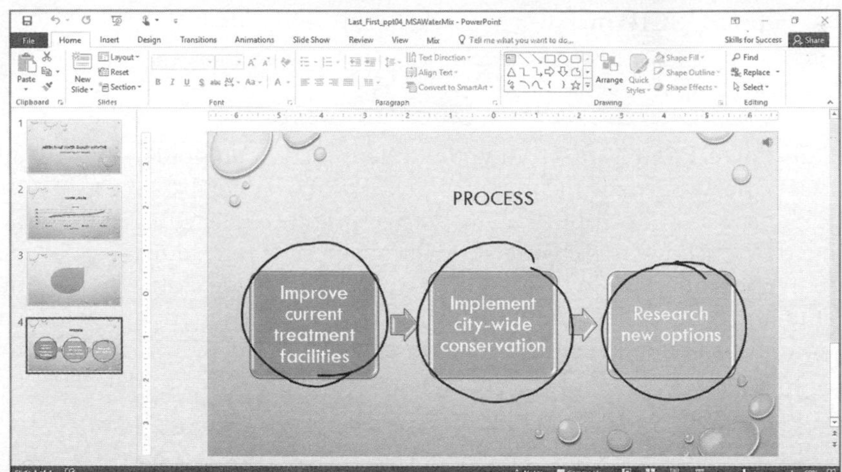

Figure 1 PowerPoint 2016, Windows 10, Microsoft Corporation

DONE! You have completed More Skills Assessment

Collaborating with Google

To complete this project, you will need a Google account (refer to the Common Features chapter) and the following file:

- New Slide presentation

You will save your files as:

- Last_First_ppt04_GPSnip
- Last_First_ppt04_GPInterns

1. Open the Google Chrome web browser. Log into your Google account, and then click the **Google Apps** button.
2. Click the **Drive** button to open Google Drive. If you receive a pop-up message, read the message, and then click **Next**. As needed, read each message, and then close the dialog box.
3. Click the **New** button, and then click **Google Slides**.
4. In the **Themes** pane, click **Biz** or another theme, and then **Close** the Themes pane.
5. In the title placeholder, type Internship Placement
6. In the subtitle placeholder, type Aspen Falls Community College and City Hall Collaboration
7. Click the **New Slide arrow**, and then click **Title Only**. In the title placeholder, type Career Success
8. Click outside of the title placeholder, and then click the **Insert tab**. Click **Table**, and then use your pointer to drag over a **2 x 3** area of the grid to create a table with 2 columns and 3 rows.
9. In the first cell of the first row of the table, type Internship Program Press Tab, and then type Percent of Interns with Full Time Employment After Graduation
10. In the first cell of the second row, type Summer Residency Press Tab, and then type 93%
11. In the first cell of the third row, type Semester Work Study Press Tab, and then type 95%
12. Select the first row, and then click **Bold** and increase the **Font Size** to 18. Click the **Text color arrow**, and then click the seventh color in the second row—**cornflower blue**.

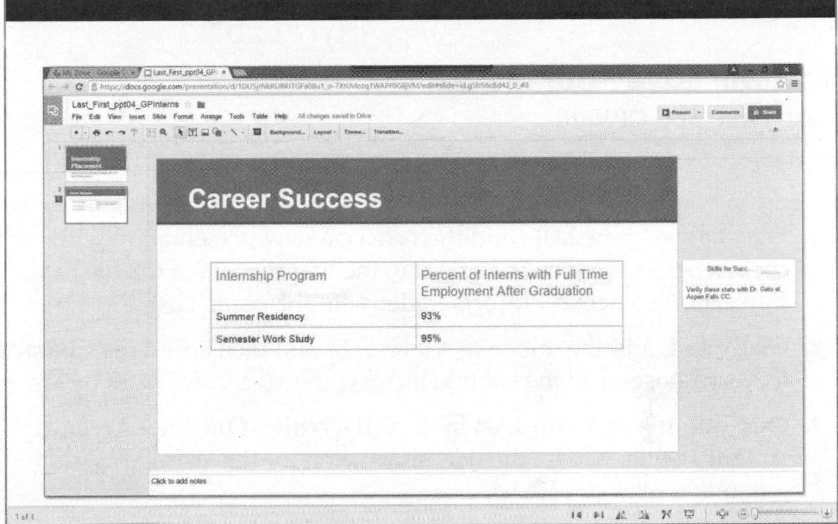

Figure 1

13. Click the outer border of the table to select it. Click the **Arrange tab**, and then point to **Center on page**. Click **Vertically**.
14. With the table still selected, click the **Comments** button. Type Verify these stats with Dr. Gato at Aspen Falls CC. and then click **Comment**.
15. In the upper left corner, click the **Untitled presentation** box, and then change the name of the presentation to Last_First_ppt04_GPInterns Press Enter.
16. Press [Windows], type snip and then press Enter to start the **Snipping Tool**. Click the **New arrow**, and then click **Full-screen Snip**. Compare your screen with **Figure 1**.
17. In the **Snipping Tool** mark-up window, click the **Save Snip** button [Save]. In the **Save As** dialog box, navigate to your **PowerPoint Chapter 4** folder. Be sure the **Save as type** box displays **JPEG file**. Name the file Last_First_ppt04_GPSnip and then press Enter. **Close** [×] the Snipping Tool mark-up window.
18. **Close** all windows, and then submit your files as directed by your instructor.

 **DONE! You have completed Collaborating with Google**

Student data file needed for this project:
ppt_CPVote

MyITLab® Grader

You will save your file as:
Last_First_ppt_CPVote

1. Start **PowerPoint 2016**, and then create a new presentation with the **Dividend theme**. Select the second variant in the first row. **Save** the file to your **PowerPoint Special Projects** folder with the name Last_First_ppt_CPVote
2. On **Slide 1**, add the title Vote Aspen Falls and then adjust the **Character Spacing** to **Very Loose**. Add the subtitle Increase the Vote Campaign, By Maria Martinez
3. On **Slide 1**, insert **WordArt** in the **Fill - White, Outline - Accent 1, Glow - Accent 1** style. Accept the default location for the WordArt. Add the text Get out and vote! to the WordArt.
4. Insert a new **Slide 2** with the **Two Content** layout. Add the title Voter Information
5. In the left content placeholder, add the photo **ppt_CPVote** from your student data files.
6. In the right content placeholder, add the following two-level bulleted list:
   Who is qualified to vote
      Resident for minimum of 28 days
      US citizen
      At least 18 years of age
      Registered or registering
7. Increase the **Line Spacing** for the bulleted list to **1.5**, and then compare your screen with **Figure 1**.
8. Insert a new **Slide 3** with the **Two Content** layout. Add the title Poll Location
9. In the left content placeholder, add **SmartArt** with the **Vertical Box List** layout. In the top shape, type Aspen Falls City Hall Add a **Bullet** with the text 500 S Aspen St, Aspen Falls, CA Delete all other shapes in the SmartArt placeholder.
10. In the right content placeholder, insert an online image from **Bing Image Search** located using the term Voter.
11. Change the **Height** of the image to **2.5 inches**. Compare your screen with **Figure 2**, noting that your image will vary.

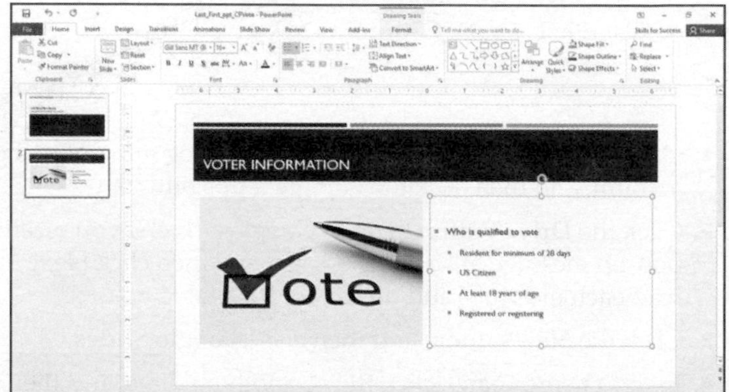

Figure 1 Nfsphoto/Fotolia; PowerPoint 2016, Windows 10, Microsoft Corporation

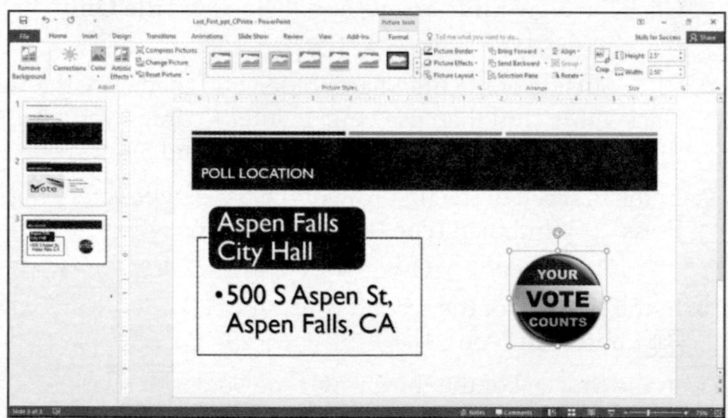

Figure 2 PowerPoint 2016, Windows 10, Microsoft Corporation

■ **Continue to the next page to complete the skill**

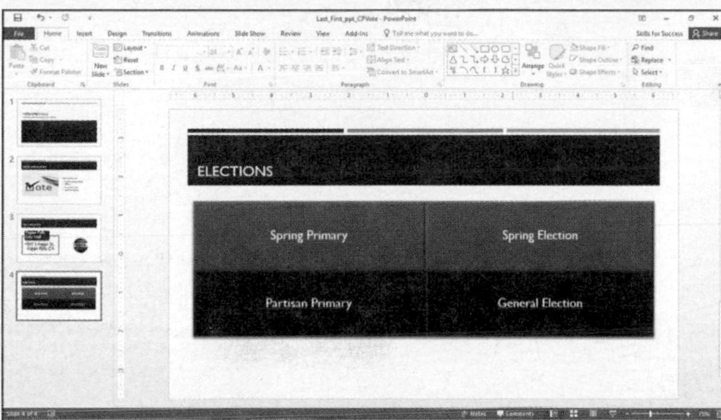

PowerPoint 2016, Windows 10, Microsoft Corporation

Figure 3

12. Insert a new **Slide 4** with the **Title and Content** layout. Add the title Elections

13. In the content placeholder, insert a **Table** with two columns and two rows, and then add the following text:

Spring Primary	Spring Election
Partisan Primary	General Election

14. Change the **Table Style Options** so that **Header Row** is not selected, and then change the **Table Style** to **Themed Style 2 - Accent 1**. Add a **Circle Cell Bevel** effect to the table.

15. With the table selected, increase the table **Height** to **3.5 inches**, and then **Center** the text **Vertically** and **Horizontally**. Increase the **Font Size** to **24**. Click a blank area of the slide so that the table is no longer selected, and then compare your screen with **Figure 3**.

16. Insert a new **Slide 5** with the **Title and Content** layout. Add the title Voter Demographics

17. On **Slide 5**, in the content placeholder, insert a **Pie Chart** with the following data:

	Race
White	46
Asian	25
African American	12
Native American	0.6
Pacific Islander	0.2
Other	10
Two or More	5

18. Apply **Chart Style 12** to the pie chart.

19. Use the **Format Painter** to copy the formatting from the WordArt on **Slide 1** to the titles on **Slides 2, 3, 4,** and **5**, and then compare your screen with **Figure 4**.

20. Add the **Fly-In Animation** to the pie chart on **Slide 5**.

21. Add the **Wind Transition**, and then adjust the **Effect Options** to **Left**. Apply the transition to all slides.

22. Add a footer to the **Notes and Handouts** pages with the date, page number, and file name.

23. **Save**  and then **Close** [×] PowerPoint. Submit the project as directed by your instructor.

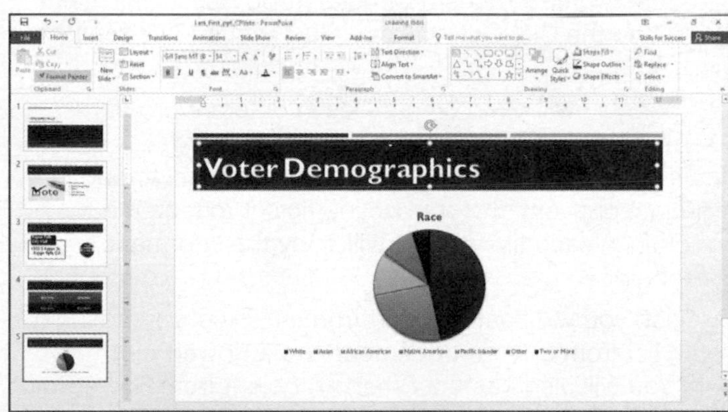

PowerPoint 2016, Windows 10, Microsoft Corporation

Figure 4

DONE! You have completed the PowerPoint Capstone Project

Copy and Paste Between Office Programs

- You can copy a chart from Excel and paste it into a PowerPoint presentation.
- When you copy a chart from Excel, the chart data can be saved with the PowerPoint presentation.
- You can also paste text from a Word document into a PowerPoint presentation.
- Objects created in PowerPoint can be pasted into Word. For example, you can copy a SmartArt graphic from a PowerPoint presentation and paste it into a Word document.

Alisonhancock/Fotolia

Aspen Falls City Hall

In this Integrated Project, you will prepare a PowerPoint presentation and a Word handout for the Aspen Falls City Council about trends in attendance at events in Aspen Falls. City planners are working with the Tourism Department and the City Council to update the venues, dates, and security needed based on attendance at each event. Tourism Director Todd Austin will make the presentation to the City Council, city planners, and citizens of Aspen Falls.

In your career, you will often create files in different programs about the same topic. You may create a report in Word, a presentation in PowerPoint, and a spreadsheet in Excel about an upcoming project or event. It would be inefficient to recreate the same information in each file, so you will copy the information from one file to another.

In this project, you will paste a chart from an Excel spreadsheet and a bulleted list from a Word document into a PowerPoint presentation. You will also paste a SmartArt object from PowerPoint into Word.

Time to complete this project — 30 to 45 minutes

Introduction

Outcome

Using the skills in this chapter, you will be able to paste a chart from Excel and text from Word into a presentation. You will also paste a SmartArt graphic from PowerPoint into a document.

Objectives

8.1 Design a presentation with bulleted lists, charts, and SmartArt

8.2 Combine information from PowerPoint, Excel, and Word

8.3 Adjust themes and designs to create a cohesive presentation

Student data files needed for this project:

ppt_IP08AttendanceReport (Word)
ppt_IP08Attendance (PowerPoint)
ppt_IP08AttendanceTrends (Excel)

You will save your files as:

Last_First_ppt_IP08Attendance (PowerPoint)
Last_First_ppt_IP08AttendanceReport (Word)

SKILLS

At the end of this project, you will be able to:

- Copy an Excel chart and paste it into a PowerPoint presentation
- Copy a bulleted list from a Word document and paste it into a PowerPoint presentation
- Copy a SmartArt graphic from a PowerPoint presentation and paste it into a Word document

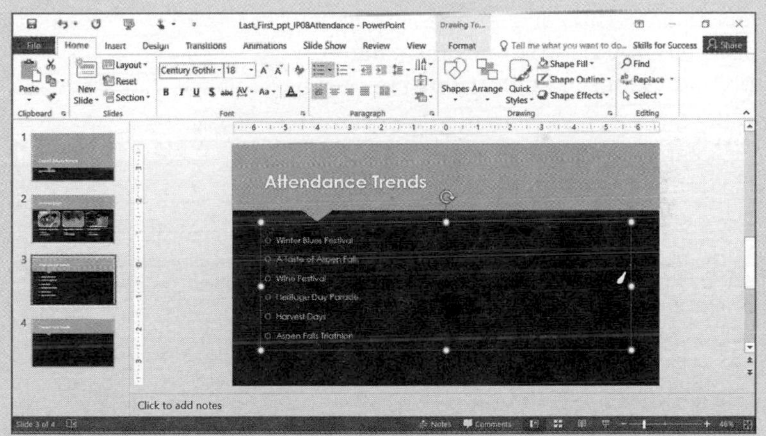

PowerPoint 2016, Windows 10, Microsoft Corporation

1. Start **Microsoft PowerPoint 2016**. Navigate to your student data files for this chapter. Open **ppt_IP08Attendance**. On the **File tab**, click **Save As**. Navigate to the location where you are saving your files, create a folder named PowerPoint Special Projects and then using your own name, save the presentation as Last_First_ppt_IP08Attendance in the new folder.
2. Start **Word 2016**, open **ppt_IP08AttendanceReport**, and then save it in your **PowerPoint Special Projects** folder as Last_First_ppt_IP08AttendanceReport If necessary, on the **Home tab**, in the **Paragraph group**, click the **Show/Hide** button to display nonprinting characters.
3. With the **Last_First_ppt_IP08_AttendanceReport** Word document displayed, locate and then select the six lines of bulleted text, beginning with *Winter Blues Festival* and ending with *Aspen Falls Triathlon*. On the **Home tab**, in the **Clipboard group**, click the **Copy** button.
4. On the taskbar, switch to the **PowerPoint** presentation, and then display **Slide 3**. Click in the content placeholder, and then on the **Home tab**, in the **Clipboard group**, click the **Paste** button.
5. Click a border of the placeholder to select it, and then on the **Home tab**, in the **Paragraph group**, click the **Line Spacing arrow**. Click **1.5** to increase the spacing between lines, and then compare your screen with **Figure 1**.
6. Display **Slide 2**, and then select the SmartArt object. Verify that none of the shapes in the SmartArt object are selected. If any of the shapes are selected, click a blank area of the SmartArt boundary box to deselect the shape and select the SmartArt object. Display the text pane if necessary. Compare your screen with **Figure 2**.

■ **Continue to the next page to complete the project**

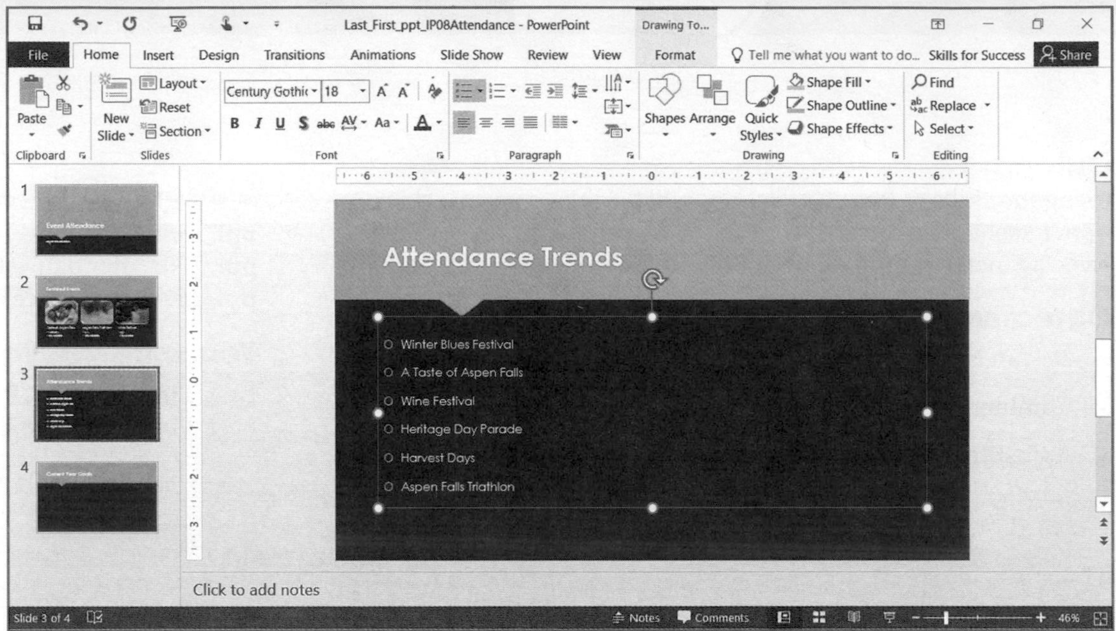

Figure 1

PowerPoint 2016, Windows 10, Microsoft Corporation

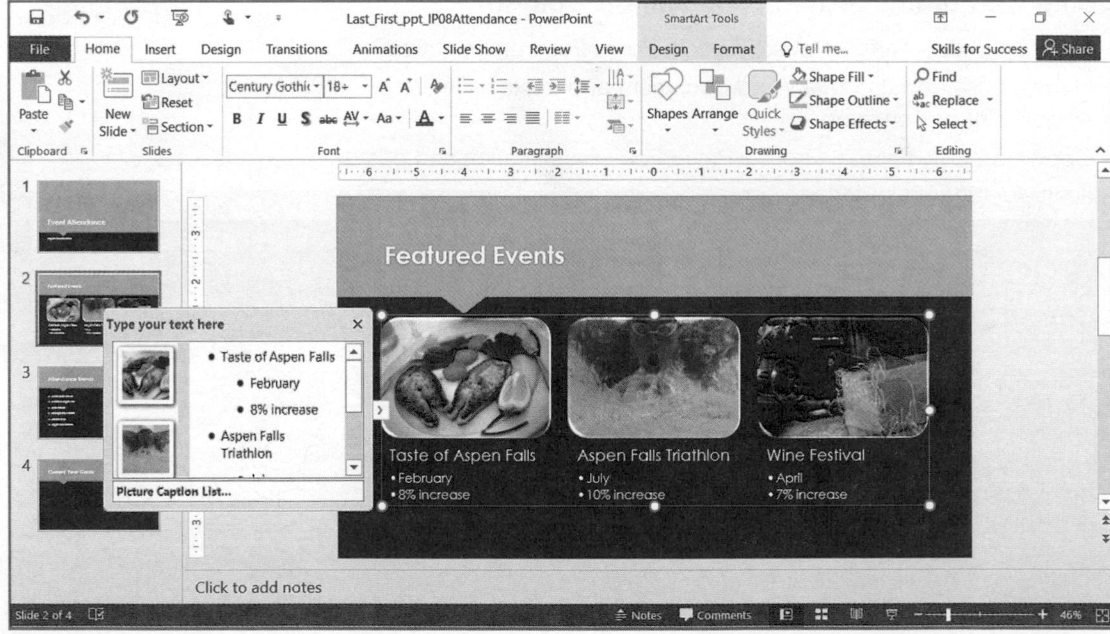

Figure 2

PowerPoint 2016, Windows 10, Microsoft Corporation

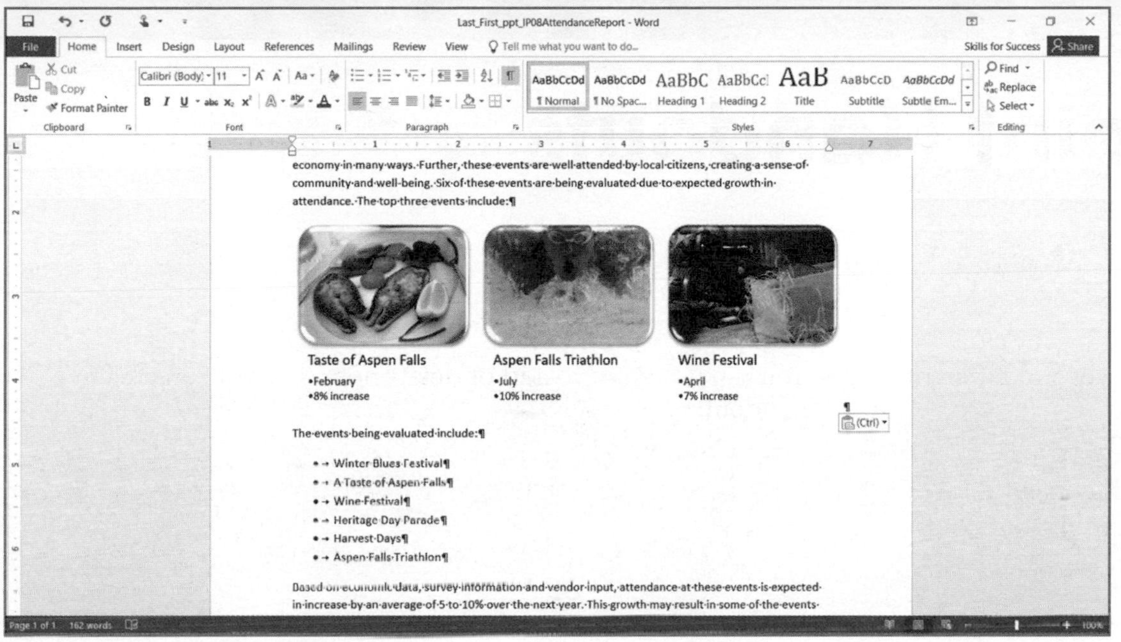

PowerPoint 2016, Windows 10, Microsoft Corporation

Figure 3

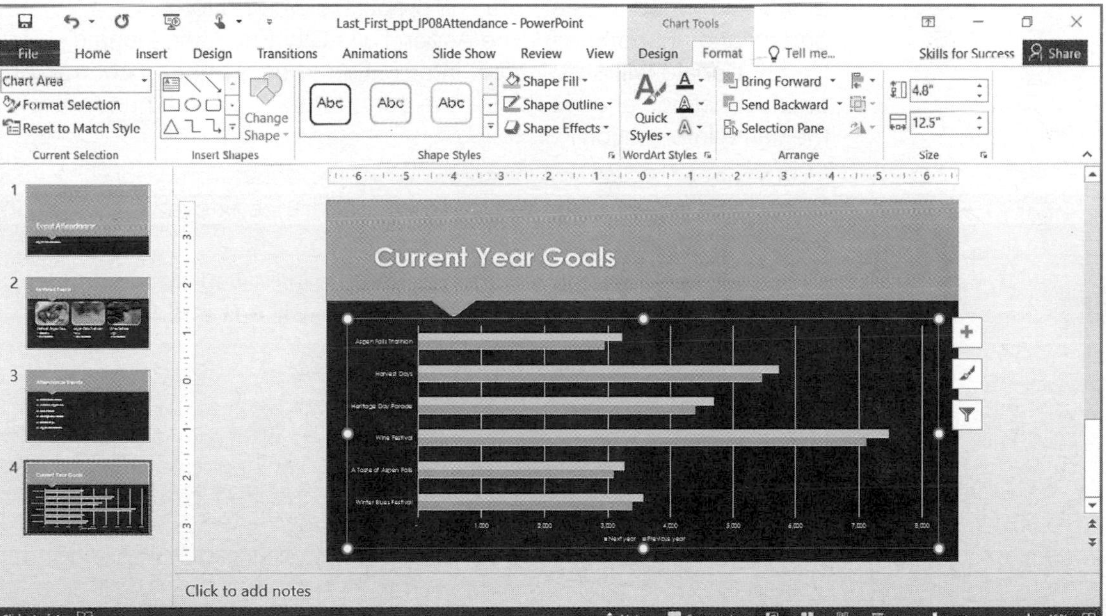

PowerPoint 2016, Windows 10, Microsoft Corporation

Figure 4

7. With the SmartArt object selected, press Ctrl + C to copy the SmartArt object.
8. On the taskbar, switch to **Word**. Click the blank line below the first paragraph, and then press Ctrl + V to paste the SmartArt object. Compare your screen with **Figure 3**.
9. Insert a footer in the Word document that displays the file name. **Save** and then **Close** the Word document.
10. Start **Excel 2016**, and then from your student files, open **ppt_IP08_AttendanceTrends**.
11. Right-click in a blank area of the chart to display the shortcut menu, and then click **Copy**.
12. On the taskbar, click the **PowerPoint** button, and then display **Slide 4**. Right-click a border of the content placeholder on **Slide 4**, and then from the shortcut menu, under **Paste Options**, point to the first button—**Use Destination Theme & Embed Workbook**.
13. Click **Use Destination Theme & Embed Workbook** to paste the chart. With the chart selected, on the **Format tab**, in the **Shape Height** box, type 4.8 and then press Enter. In the **Shape Width** box, type 12.2 and then press Enter. In the **Arrange group**, click the **Align** button, and then click **Align Center**. On the chart, delete the title. Compare your screen with **Figure 4**.
14. Insert a footer on all **Notes and Handouts** that displays the date and time, page number, and file name. **Save** and **Close** the presentation, and then **Close** the Excel file without saving. Submit the Word and PowerPoint files as directed by your instructor.

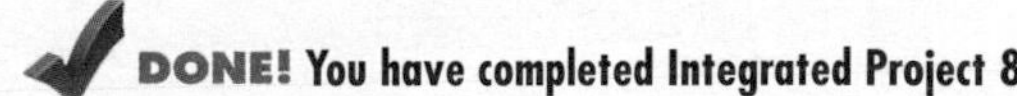
DONE! You have completed Integrated Project 8

INTEGRATED PROJECT 9

Send PowerPoint Handouts to Word

- Presentation handouts can be sent to Word in several different formats.
- When you send handouts to Word, you can use Word's document formatting features to format the document appropriately.
- You can use Word to add or delete notes to create an effective handout.

Courtesy of Kris Townsend

Aspen Falls City Hall

In this Integrated Project, you will prepare, edit, and format presentation handouts for the Aspen Falls City Engineer, Donald Norris. Donald will present this information to construction contractors at city meetings and would like the contractors to have a handout with the same information.

In your career, you might create Word handouts from your PowerPoint presentation to give to your audience or even attach to an e-mail message.

You will use the Create Handouts feature in PowerPoint to send the handouts to Microsoft Word, where you will edit and format the handouts.

Time to complete this project — 30 to 45 minutes

Outcome

Using the skills in this project, you will be able to create a Word document containing images of PowerPoint slides as well as notes. The files will be linked, so that changes to one file will be reflected in the other.

Objectives

9.1 Create Word handouts for a PowerPoint presentation

9.2 Apply changes to handouts

Student data file needed for this project:

ppt_IP09Construction (PowerPoint)

You will save your files as:

Last_First_ppt_IP09Construction (PowerPoint)
Last_First_ppt_IP09ContractorHandout (Word)

SKILLS

At the end of this project, you will be able to:

- Create handouts in Word from a PowerPoint presentation
- Edit presentation handouts in Word
- Format presentation handouts in Word

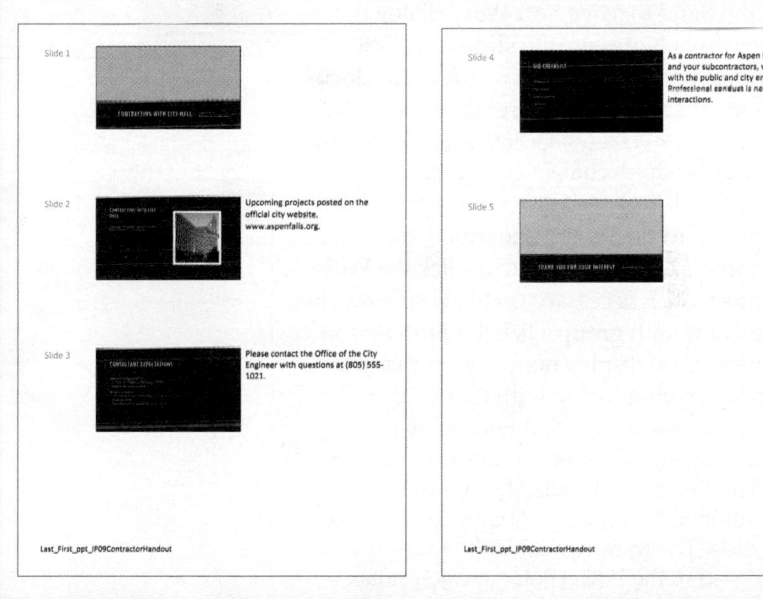

Courtesy of Kris Townsend

1. Start **PowerPoint 2016**, and then open the student data file **ppt_IP09Construction**. Save the file in your **PowerPoint Special Projects** folder with the file name Last_First_ppt_IP09Construction
2. On the **File tab**, click **Export**, and then click **Create Handouts**. Compare your screen with **Figure 1**.

   On the Export page, you can choose several different save and delivery options. The Create Handouts option is used to create a Word document with slides and presentation notes.
3. On the right side of the **Export page**, click the **Create Handouts** button.

   In the Send to Microsoft Word dialog box, you can choose how the presentation will be displayed in Microsoft Word.
4. In the **Send to Microsoft Word** dialog box, verify that **Notes next to slides** is selected. Under **Add slides to Microsoft Word document**, select **Paste link**, and then click **OK**.

   When you create a link between the presentation and the document, if the original file is updated, the linked file will also be updated.
5. If the Word document does not display automatically, on the taskbar, click the **Word** button. If necessary, on the **Home tab**, in the **Paragraph group**, click the **Show/Hide** button ¶ to display nonprinting characters. Compare your screen with **Figure 2**.

   The slides are inserted into the Word document in a three-column table format. The first column indicates the slide number. The second column displays the slide. The third column contains notes typed in the PowerPoint speaker notes pane. If notes are not created for a slide, then the cell in the third column is blank.
6. Scroll down to view each slide. Notice that the document contains two pages with a three slides per page layout, and that for Slides 3 and 4, notes display in the third column.

■ **Continue to the next page to complete the project**

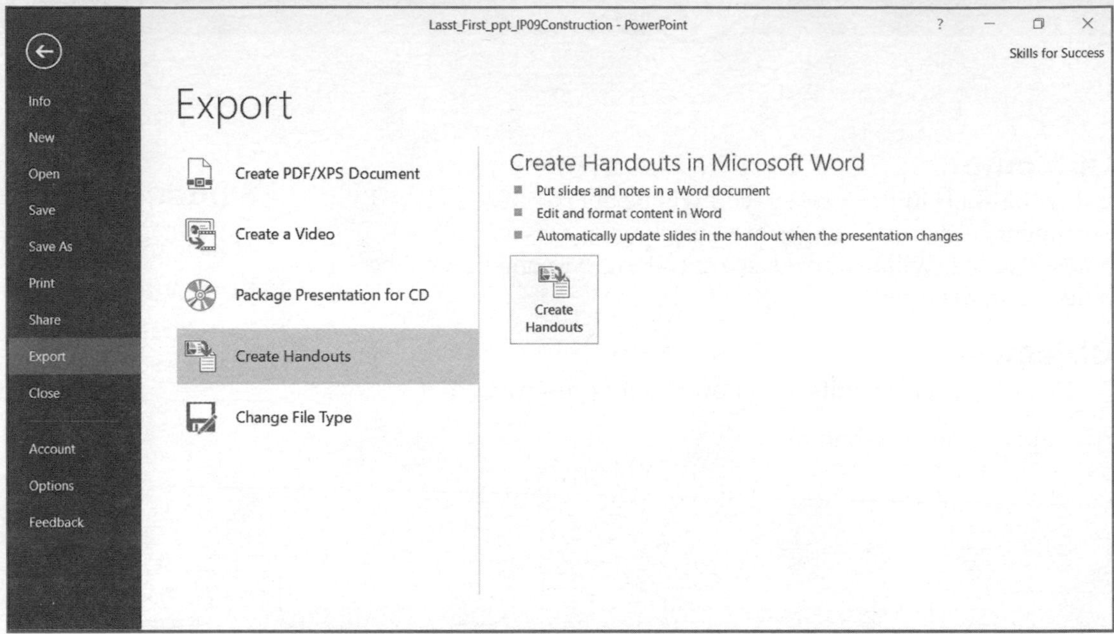

Figure 1 PowerPoint 2016, Windows 10, Microsoft Corporation

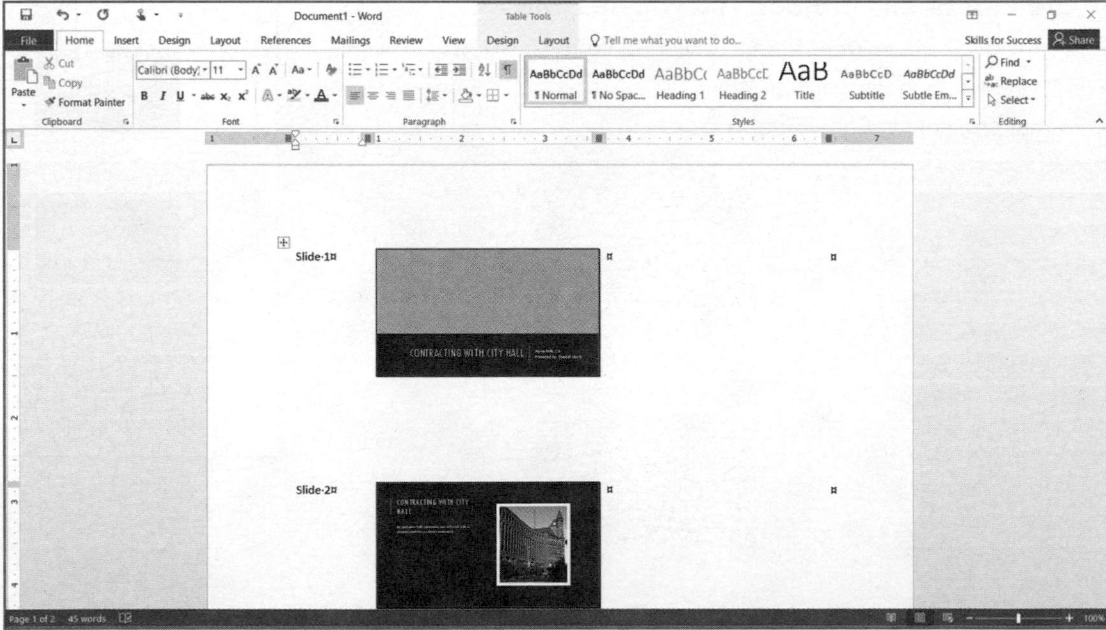

Figure 2 PowerPoint 2016, Windows 10, Microsoft Corporation

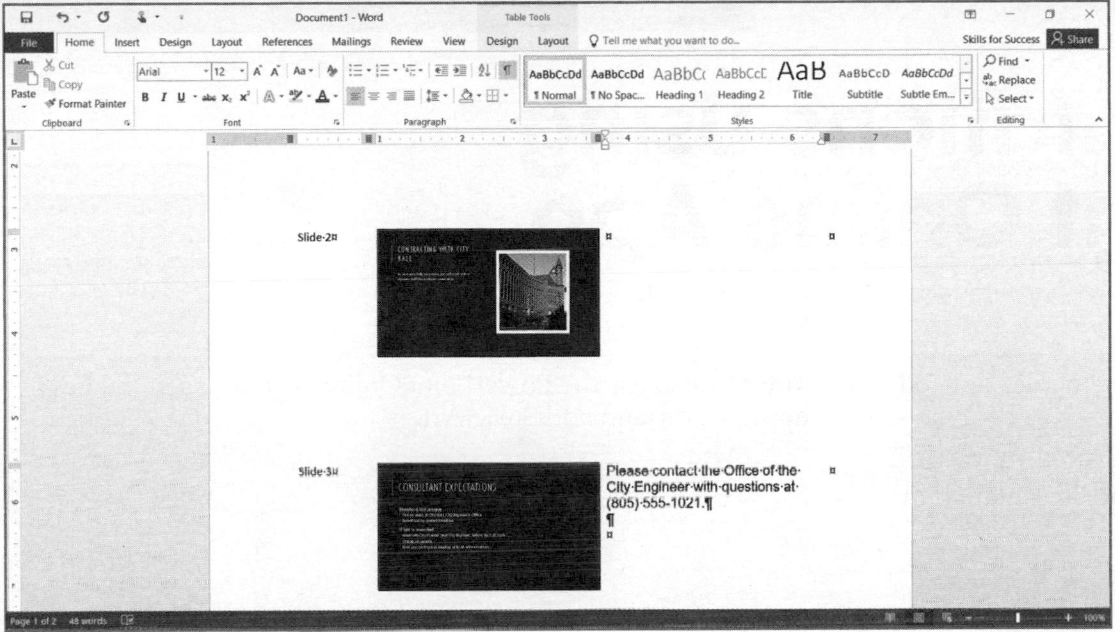

PowerPoint 2016, Windows 10, Microsoft Corporation

Figure 3

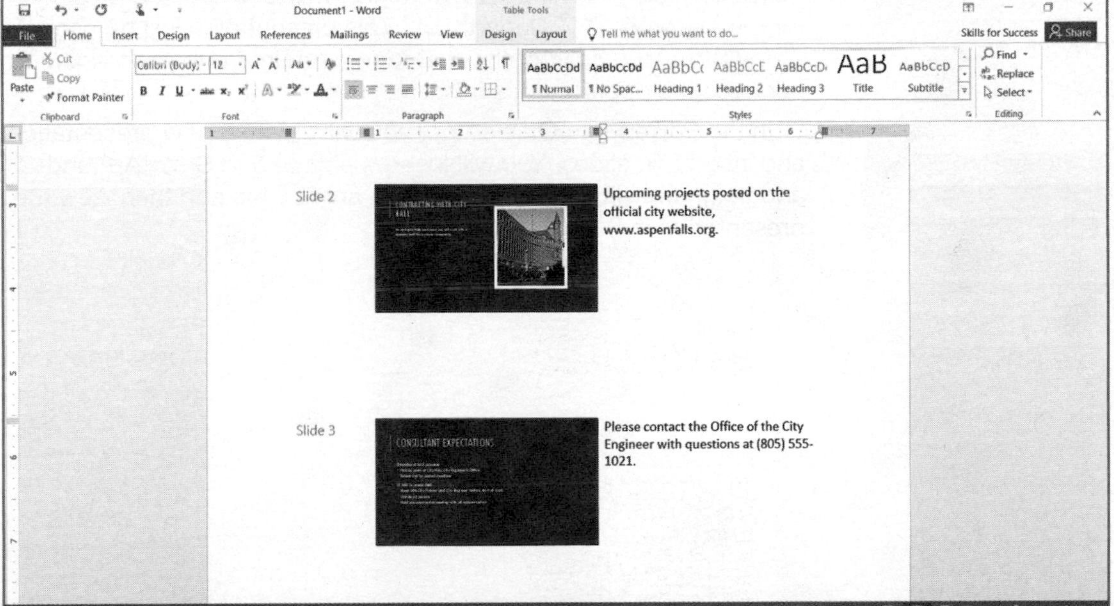

PowerPoint 2016, Windows 10, Microsoft Corporation

Figure 4

7. In the Word document, scroll to display **Slide 3**. Click at the end of the text in the third column following the word *questions* but before the period, press SpaceBar, and then type at (805) 555-1021 Compare your screen with **Figure 3**.
8. Click anywhere in the first column. On the **Table Tools Layout tab**, in the **Table group**, click the **Select** button, and then click **Select Column** to select all of the cells in the first column. On the **Home tab**, in the **Styles group**, click **Heading 2** to apply the style to all of the slide numbers.
9. If needed, scroll to display **Slide 2**. Click in the third column, and then type Upcoming projects posted on the official city website, www.aspenfalls.org.

   Notice that the font, font size, and spacing of the text that you typed are different than the notes that were part of the PowerPoint presentation.
10. With the insertion point positioned in the third column, on the **Table Tools Layout tab**, in the **Table group**, click the **Select** button, and then click **Select Column** to select all of the third column. Change the **Font** to **Calibri** and the **Font Size** to **12**. Click the **Show/Hide** button to turn off the nonprinting characters. Click a blank area of the document so that no text is selected. Compare your screen with **Figure 4**.
11. **Save** the Word document in your **PowerPoint Special Projects** folder with the file name Last_First_ppt_IP09ContractorHandout
12. Insert a footer in the Word document that displays the file name, and then **Save** the document.
13. **Close** the Word document, and then **Close** PowerPoint. Submit the Word document and the linked PowerPoint presentation as directed by your instructor.

DONE! You have completed Integrated Project 9

Create Presentations Using the PowerPoint Online App

- The Office Online Apps can be used to create new files or to edit files that were created in Office programs.
- In the PowerPoint Online App, you can create or edit a presentation in Editing view, and you view the presentation in Slide Show view.
- You can also use the PowerPoint Online App to insert images, apply styles, and add SmartArt.

Goldenkb | Dreamstime.com

Aspen Falls City Hall

In this project, you will use PowerPoint Online to create a presentation for the Aspen Falls IT Department. This presentation will be used by Cathy Story, the head of the IT Department, in employee training to reinforce the department's mission.

In the PowerPoint Online App, you will create a new presentation, and insert two slides. You will insert a picture and SmartArt, and add text. You will add transitions and animations and then view the presentation in Slide Show view.

Time to complete this project — 30 to 60 minutes

Introduction

Outcome

Using the skills in this project, you will be able to create and edit a presentation with text and images, using PowerPoint Online.

Objectives

1 Create presentations using the PowerPoint Online App

2 View presentations in Slide Show view

3 Add slides, themes, images, transitions, and animations

To complete this project, you will need the following file:

New, blank PowerPoint Online presentation

You will save your file as:

Last_First_ppt_OATechnology

SKILLS

At the end of this project, you will be able to:

- Create a presentation using the PowerPoint Online App
- Add a presentation theme
- Add new slides
- Insert Pictures
- Add transitions
- Add animations
- View a presentation in Slide Show view

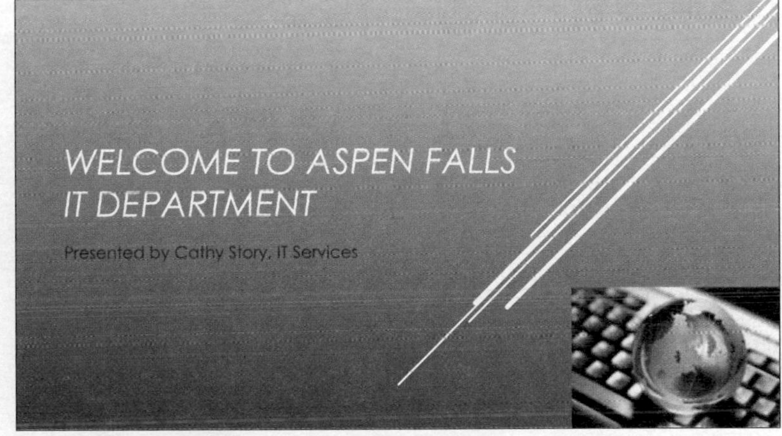

1. Start your internet browser, navigate to onedrive.live.com and then log on to your Windows Live account. If you do not have a Windows Live account, follow the links and instructions on the onedrive.live.com Home page to create one.
2. At the top, left side of the screen, click the **Apps** button, and then click **PowerPoint Online**. Scroll down, as needed, and then click the **Slice** thumbnail.
3. To name the presentation, toward the top of the window, replace the text *Presentation* with Last_First_ppt_OATechnology and then compare your screen with **Figure 1**.
4. On **Slide 1**, in the title placeholder, type Welcome to Aspen Falls Press Enter, and then type IT Department Select all of the text in the placeholder, and then on the **Home tab**, in the **Font group**, change the **Font Size** to 44. Select the text *IT Department*, and then in the **Font group**, click **Italic** *I*.
5. In the subtitle placeholder, type Presented by Cathy Story, IT Services Click a blank area of the slide so that no placeholder is selected. Compare your screen with **Figure 2**.

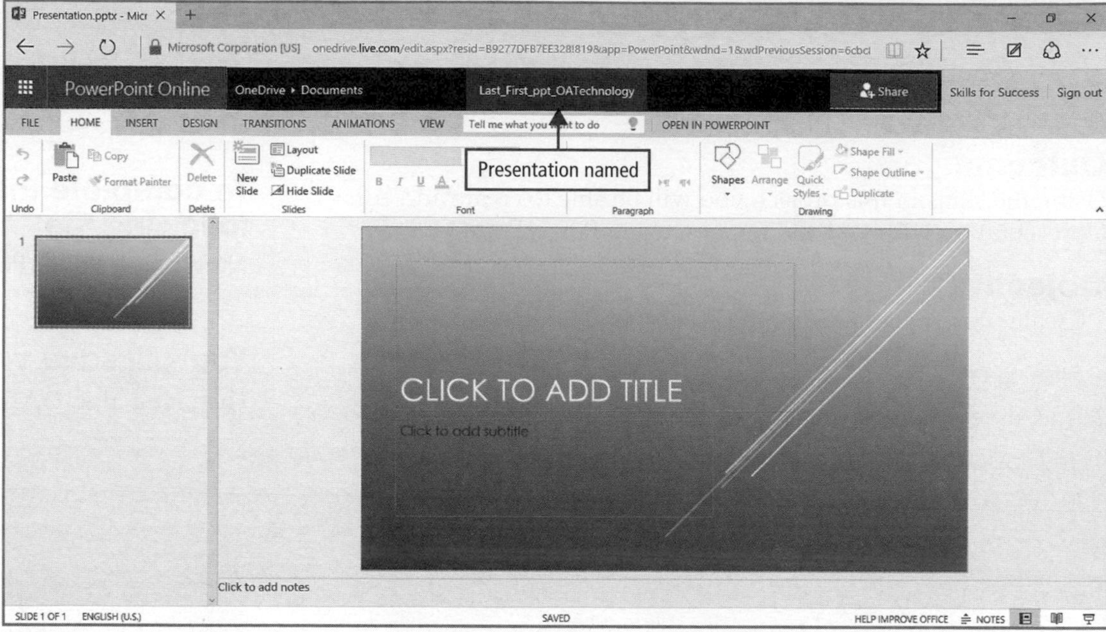

Figure 1

PowerPoint 2016, Windows 10, Microsoft Corporation

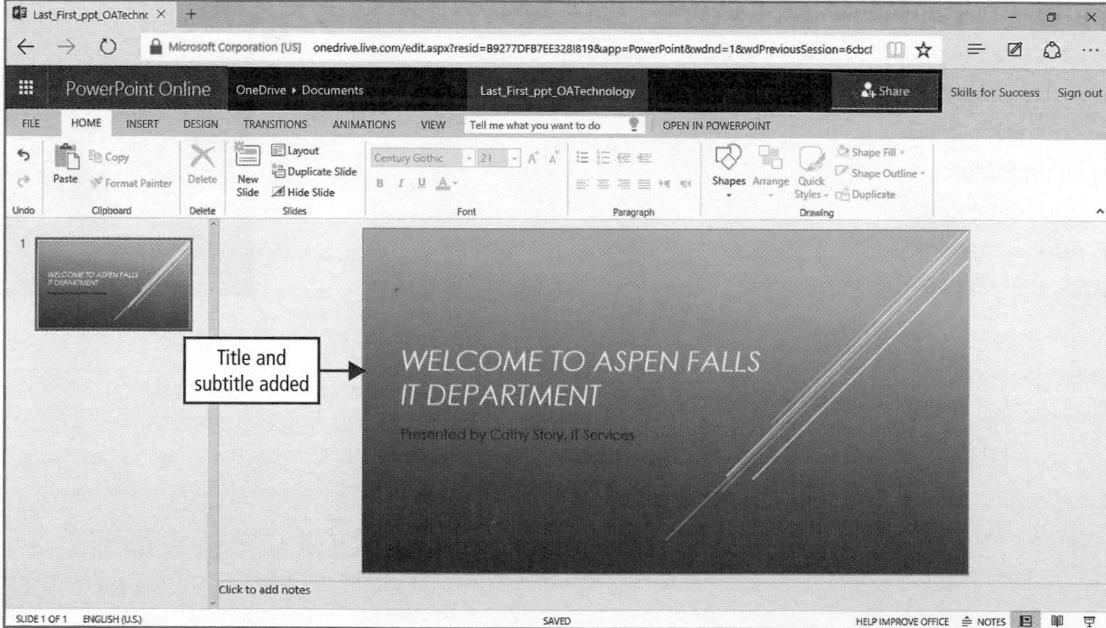

Figure 2

PowerPoint 2016, Windows 10, Microsoft Corporation

■ **Continue to the next page to complete the project**

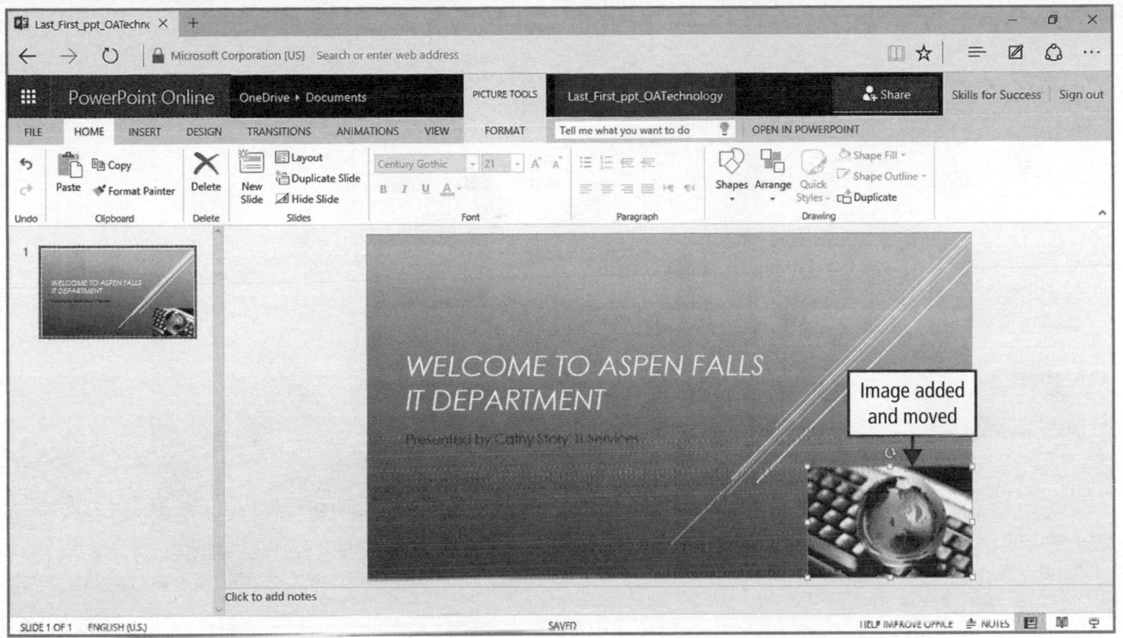

PowerPoint 2016, Windows 10, Microsoft Corporation

Figure 3

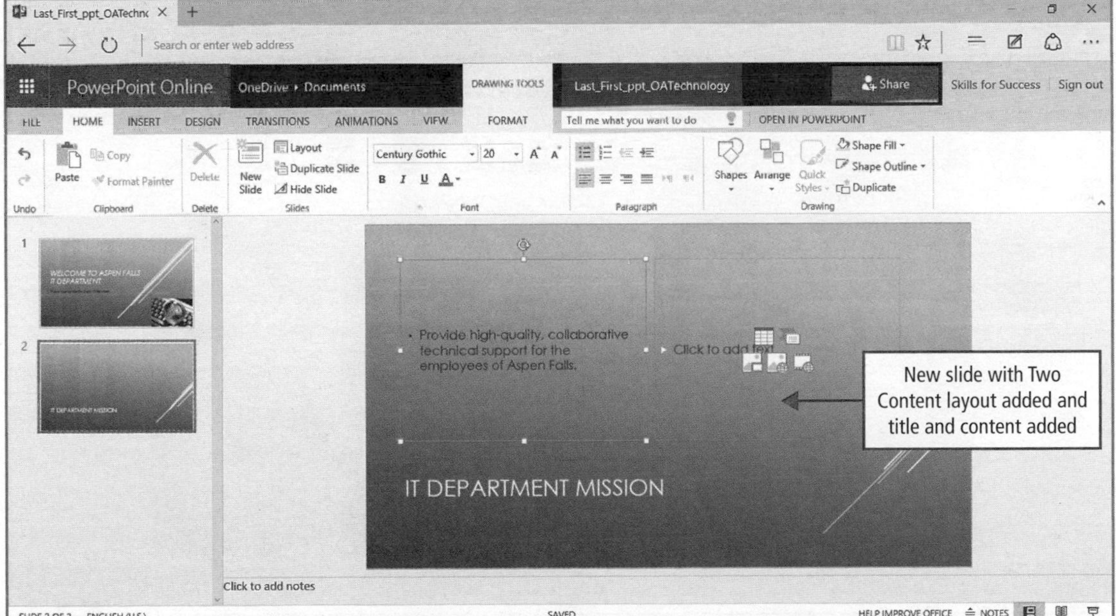

PowerPoint 2016, Windows 10, Microsoft Corporation

Figure 4

6. On the **Insert tab**, in the **Images group**, click **Picture**. Navigate to your student data files, and then click **ppt_OATechnologyImage**. Click **Open**. With the [pointer icon] pointer, drag the image to the lower right corner of the slide, and then compare your screen with **Figure 3**.
7. On the **Home tab**, in the **Slides group**, click **New Slide**. In the **New Slide** dialog box, click **Two Content**, and then click **Add Slide**.
8. On **Slide 2**, in the title placeholder, type IT Department Mission
9. In the left content placeholder, type Provide high-quality, collaborative technical support for the employees of Aspen Falls. Compare your screen with **Figure 4**.
10. In the right content placeholder, click the **Insert SmartArt** button. On the **SmartArt Tools Design tab**, click the **More Layouts arrow**, and then in the second row, click the second layout, **Basic Cycle**.
11. On the **SmartArt Tools Design tab**, in the **Create Graphic group**, click the **Edit Text** button.

■ **Continue to the next page to complete the project**

12. In the content placeholder, at each of the bullet points, type the following list, and then compare your screen with **Figure 5**, deleting any extra bullets as needed.

    Employee
    Help Desk
    IT Technician
    IT Supervisor

13. Click a blank area of the slide to update the SmartArt graphic, and then click the SmartArt graphic in the right content placeholder to select it.

14. With the SmartArt selected, on the **SmartArt Tools Design tab**, in the **SmartArt Styles group**, click the **Change Colors** button. Under **Colorful**, click the first option **Colorful - Accent Colors**.

15. In the **SmartArt Styles group**, click the **More arrow**, and then in the second row, click the fourth style—**Powder**. Compare your screen with **Figure 6**.

16. On the **Transitions tab**, in the **Transition to This Slide group**, click **Push**. In the **Transitions group**, click **Apply to All**.

■ **Continue to the next page to complete the project**

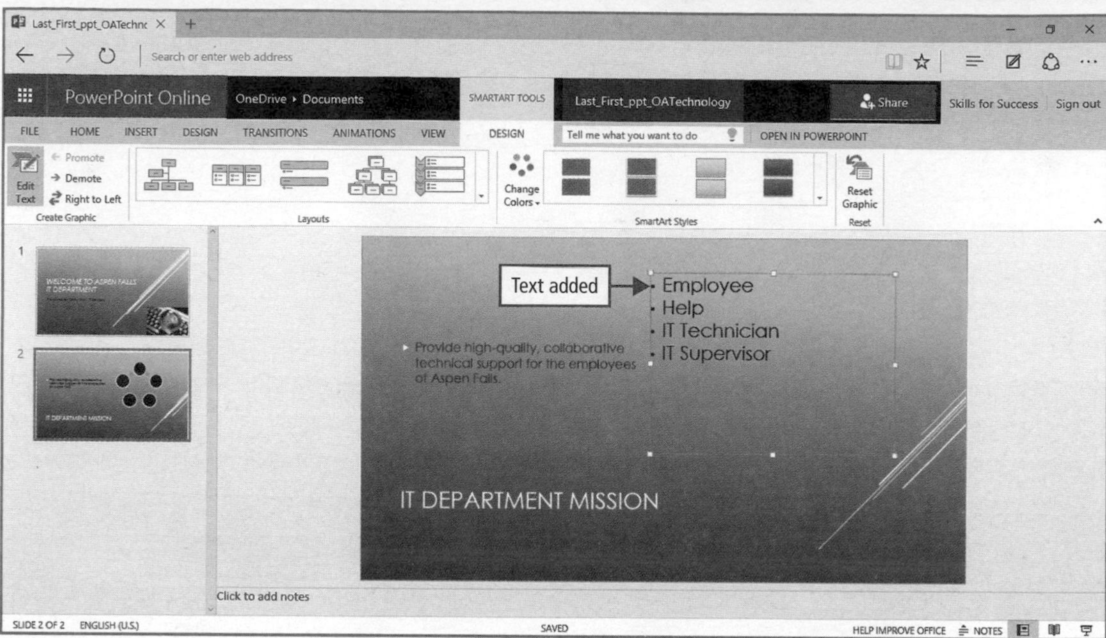

Figure 5

PowerPoint 2016, Windows 10, Microsoft Corporation

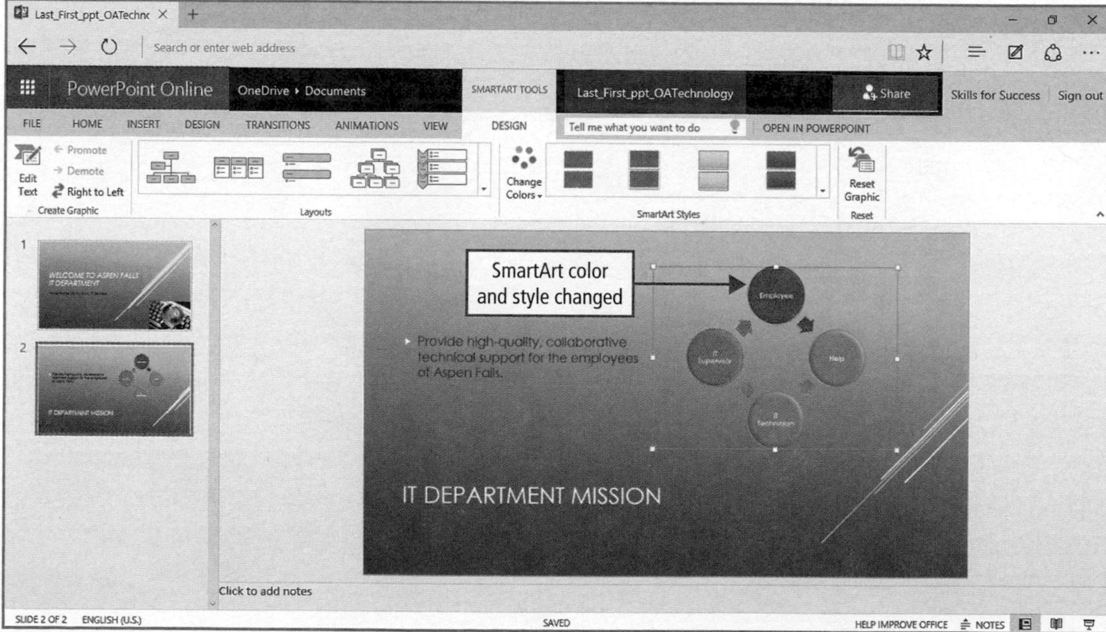

Figure 6

PowerPoint 2016, Windows 10, Microsoft Corporation

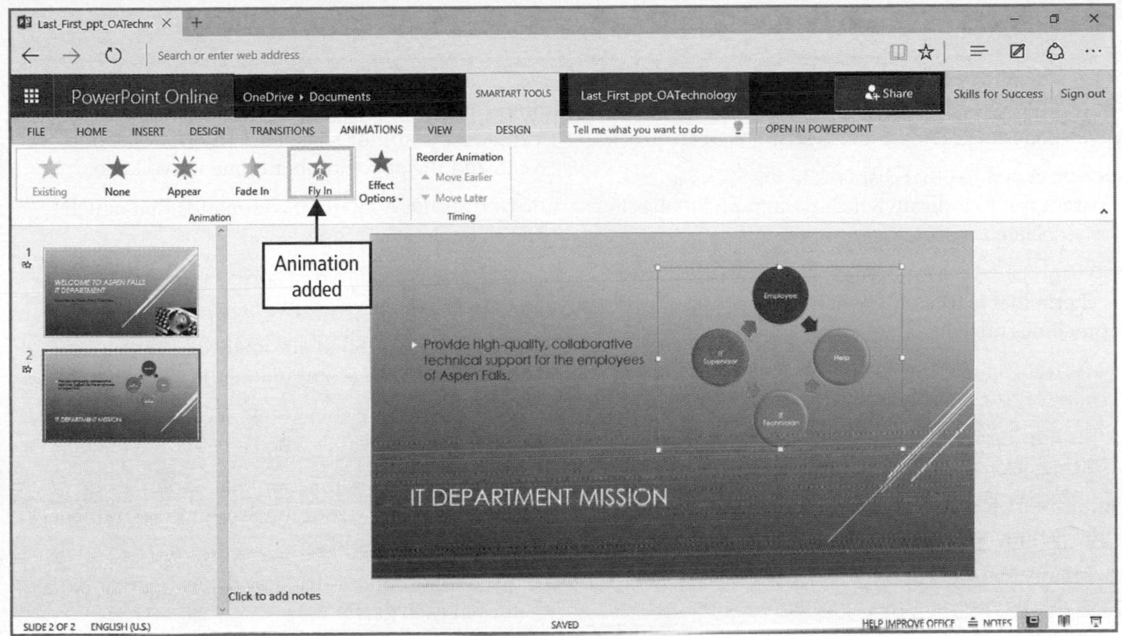

PowerPoint 2016, Windows 10, Microsoft Corporation

Figure 7

17. With the SmartArt still selected, on the **Animations tab**, in the **Animation group**, click **Fly-In**. Compare your screen with **Figure 7**.

18. On the **View tab**, in the **Presentation Views group**, click the **Slide Show** button. If necessary, allow the pop-up to appear. Click to move to the second slide, and then click to make each SmartArt animation appear.

19. End the slide show, and then return to the online app.

20. **Submit** the document as directed by your instructor.

In PowerPoint Online, there is no Save button because your presentation is saved automatically.

21. In the top right corner of the **browser** window, click the **Sign out** link, and then **Close** [X] the browser window.

DONE! You have completed the PowerPoint Online Project

Glossary

.docx extension The file extension typically assigned to Word documents.

.pdf extension The file extension assigned to PDF documents.

3-D Short for three-dimensional.

Absolute cell reference A cell reference address that remains the same when it is copied or filled to other cells. To make a cell reference absolute, insert a dollar sign ($) before the row and column references.

Accelerator A feature that searches the web for information related to text that you type/enter.

Accessibility Technologies that adapt the display for nonvisual users.

Accessibilty Checker Finds potential accessibility issues and creates a report.

Action Center A feature that is used to let you know the status of various settings and apps, as well as when you have updates for your device available to download.

Active cell The cell outlined in green in which data is entered when you begin typing.

Active content A program downloaded with a web page that provides additional functionality.

ActiveX script A small program that allows Internet Explorer to load other software applications in the browser.

Activity reporting A family account feature that provides a report to the account owner with the length of time your child spent using the device and your child's online searches, including what apps and games have been installed and played.

After Previous Begins the animation sequence immediately after the completion of the previous animation.

Alias A descriptive label used to identify a field in expressions, datasheets, forms and reports.

Alignment Guide A line that displays when an object is aligned with a document object such as a margin or heading.

Alternative (Alt) text Text used in documents and web pages to provide a text description of an object.

Anchor A symbol that displays to the left of a paragraph to indicate which paragraph an object is associated with.

And logical operator A logical comparison of two criteria that is true only when both criteria outcomes are true.

Animation Special visual effect added to an image, chart, or text on a slide.

Animation Painter Tool used to copy animation settings from one object to another.

Annotate Pen used to write on the slide while the slide show is running.

App Short for application, often a program purchased through the computer or device application store.

Append row The last row of a datasheet into which a new record is entered.

Apple Safari A free web browser created by Apple for use on both Macintosh and Windows operating systems as well as the iPad, iPhone, and iPod.

Application software Software used to accomplish specific tasks such as word processing and surfing the Internet.

Apps, games & media A family account feature used to determine what apps and games can be downloaded for a specific age.

Area chart A chart type that emphasizes the magnitude of change over time.

Argument The values that a function uses to perform operations or calculations.

Arithmetic operator A symbol that specifies a mathematical operation such as addition or subtraction.

Aspect ratio The width-to-height ratio of a screen.

Asterisk (*) wildcard A wildcard character that matches any combination of characters.

Attachment data type A data type used to store files such as Word documents or digital photo files.

Author-date citation A short citation format that contains the author's last name, the publication year, and the page number if one is available.

AutoComplete A menu of commands that match the characters you type.

AutoCorrect A feature that corrects common spelling errors as you type.

AutoFit A command that automatically changes the column width to accommodate the longest entry.

AutoNumber A field that automatically enters a unique, numeric value when a record is created.

AVERAGE function A function that adds a group of values and then divides the result by the number of values in the group.

Avg An operator that calculates the average of the values in each group.

Axis A line bordering the chart plot area used as a frame of reference for measurement.

Backstage view A collection of pages on the File tab used to open, save, print, and perform other file management tasks.

Bar chart A chart type that illustrates comparisons among individual items. The categories are displayed on the vertical axis, and the values are displayed on the horizontal axis.

Between . . . And operator A comparison operator that finds all numbers or dates between and including two values.

Bibliography A compilation of sources referenced in a report and listed on a separate page.

Black Slide Slide that displays at the end of a slide show to indicate that the presentation is over.

Block style A business letter format that begins all lines at the left margin except for letterheads, tables, and block quotes. Also known as full-block style.

Bluetooth A wireless technology that connects devices using radio waves over short distances.

Body font Font applied to all text on the slide, except for the title.

Bookmark Identifies the exact location of an object, a table, or text that you name for future reference.

Browser software Software used to view web pages on the World Wide Web.

Browsing history The information that a browser stores as you browse the web.

Bullet point An individual line of bulleted text on a slide.

Bulleted list A list of items with each item introduced by a symbol—such as a small circle or check mark—in which the list items can be presented in any order.

Button Another word for icon.

C drive The internal drive that stores the operating system. It is commonly assigned the letter "C."

Cached data and files Webpage data stored on your computer and used to decrease the time it takes for frequently-visited pages to display.

Calculated column A column in an Excel table that uses a single formula that adjusts for each row.

Calculated field A field in a table or query that derives its values from other fields in the table or query.

Caption A field property that determines what displays in datasheet, form, and report labels.

Card reader A collection of ports designed to accept flash-based memory cards.

Cascading delete A referential integrity option in which you can delete a record on the one side of the relationship and all the related records on the many side will also be deleted.

Cascading update A referential integrity option in which you can edit the primary key values in a table and all the related records in the other table will update accordingly.

Category axis The axis that displays the category labels.

Category label (Excel) Nonnumeric text that identifies the categories of data.

Category label (PowerPoint) Label that identifies the category of data in a chart.

Cell A box formed by the intersection of a row and column into which text, objects, and data can be inserted.

Cell address The column letter and row number that identify a cell; also called the cell reference.

Cell reference The column letter and row number that identify a cell; also called a cell address.

Cell style A prebuilt set of formatting characteristics, such as font, font size, font color, cell borders, and cell shading.

Central processing unit The hardware responsible for processing data according to the computer instructions.

Chart A graphic representation of data used to show comparisons, patterns, and trends.

Chart layout A prebuilt set of chart elements that can include a title, legend, or labels.

Chart sheet A workbook sheet that contains only a chart and is useful when you want to view a chart separately from the worksheet data.

Chart style (Excel) A prebuilt chart format that applies an overall visual look to a chart by modifying its graphic effects, colors, and backgrounds.

Chart style (PowerPoint) Prebuilt set of effects, colors, and backgrounds designed to work with the presentation theme.

Chart type A specific design of how data is displayed or compared in a chart.

Citation A note in the document that refers the reader to a source in the bibliography.

Click To press the left mouse button.

Clipboard A temporary storage area that holds text, graphics, or an object that has been cut or copied; maintained by your operating system

Cloud backup A service that copies your files to a server so that you can recover them, if needed.

Cloud computing A service such as file storage or an application provided via the Internet.

Cloud-based protection A Windows Defender feature that sends Microsoft information about potential security problems found in Windows Defender.

Clustered bar chart A chart type that is useful when you want to compare values across categories; bar charts organize categories along the vertical axis and values along the horizontal axis.

Column break A nonprinting character that forces the text following the break to flow into the next column.

Column chart (Excel) A chart type useful for illustrating comparisons among related numbers.

Column chart (PowerPoint) Used to show comparison among related categories.

Column heading The letter that displays at the top of a column.

Columnar layout A layout that places labels in the first column and data in the second column.

Compact and Repair A process that rebuilds database files so that data and database objects are stored more efficiently.

Comparison operator (Access) An operator that compares two values, such as > (greater than) or < (less than).

Comparison operator (Excel) Compares two values and returns either TRUE or FALSE.

Compressed folder A file or group of files reduced into a single file.

Computer A programmable electronic device that can receive input, process, output, and store data.

Conditional formatting A format, such as cell shading or font color, that is applied to cells when a specified condition is true.

Content Underlying formulas and data in a cell.

Contextual tab A tab that displays on the Ribbon only when a related object such as a graphic or chart is selected. Contains commands related to the selected object.

Contrast The difference in brightness between two elements on a slide, such as the background and the text or the background and a graphic.

Control An object on a form or in a report such as a label or a text box.

Cookie A small text file written by a website that you visit. It is used to add functionality to the page or to analyze the way that you use the website and to track what websites you visit next.

Copy A command that places a copy of the selected text or object in the Office Clipboard.

Cortana A built-in feature of Windows 10 that opens apps, files, and settings, provides appointment reminders, and shares results of keyed or spoken questions or commands for items located on your computer devices and in Bing.

Cortana Notebook A location on your device used to store the results of previous searches.

Count An operator that calculates the number of records in each group.

COUNT function A function that counts the number of cells that contain numbers.

CPU Central processing unit.

CPU cache A storage area dedicated to the processor.

CPU speed A computer specification measured in calculations per second.

Criteria (Access) Conditions in a query used to select the records that answer the query's question.

Criteria (Excel) The conditions specified in the logical test.

Crosstab query A select query that calculates a sum, an average, or a similar statistic, and then groups the results by two sets of values.

Currency data type A data type that stores numbers formatted as monetary values.

Custom Range A user-determined selection of slides that will print; does not include all of the slides in the presentation.

Custom scan A Windows Defender feature that checks only the files, folders, and programs that you identify.

Cut A command that deletes the selected text or object and places a copy in the Office clipboard.

Data bar A format that provides a visual cue about the value of a cell relative to other cells in a range.

Data label Text that identifies data markers in a chart.

Data marker A column, a bar, an area, a dot, a pie slice, or another symbol that represents a single data point.

Data point A chart value that originates in an Excel worksheet cell. Also, individual data plotted in a chart.

Data series Related data points on a chart; assigned a unique color or pattern represented in the chart legend.

Data source The file that contains the information—such as names and addresses—that changes with each letter or label in the main mail merge document.

Data type A field property that specifies the type of information that the field will hold; for example, text, number, date, or currency.

Database A collection of structured tables designed to store data.

Database software Software used to store large amounts of data and retrieve that data in useful and meaningful ways.

Database system A program used to both store and manage large amounts data.

Datasheet The presentation of a database table.

Datasheet view An Access view that features the data but also has contextual tabs on the Ribbon so that you can change the table's design.

Date/Time data type A data type that stores serial numbers that are converted into and formatted as dates or times.

Default home page The page that first displays when you open a web browser.

Default printer The printer that is automatically selected when you do not choose a different printer.

Delay (animation) Animation starts after a predetermined amount of time.

Desktop A graphical user interface element that simulates a real desktop in which files are placed.

Desktop application A program that can display information on the desktop but that is not actually "running" on the desktop.

Desktop computer A computer designed to be placed permanently on a desk or at a work station.

Desktop publishing software Software designed to produce professional publications such as newsletters, letterheads, business cards, and brochures.

Detail control The area of a report that repeats for each record in the table or query.

Detail sheet A worksheet with cells referred to by summary sheet formulas.

Device A common term for a portable computer like a smartphone or tablet.

Disk cleanup A Windows feature that removes unnecessary files from the hard drive of the PC to allow for better storage and file retrieval.

Displayed value Data displayed in a cell.

Document properties Information about a document that can help identify or organize files, such as the name of the document author, the file name, and key words.

Domain name A unique name assigned to a website on the World Wide Web.

Dot leader A series of evenly spaced dots that precede a tab stop.

Double-click To click the left mouse button two times quickly without moving the mouse.

Double-spacing The equivalent of a blank line of text displays between each line of text.

Double-tap To tap the screen in the same place two times quickly.

Download history A list of all the files you have downloaded to your computer from the webpages you have visited.

Drag To press and hold the left mouse button while moving the mouse.

Drag and drop A method of moving objects in which you point to the selection and drag it to a new location.

Drop cap The first letter (or letters) of a paragraph, enlarged and either embedded in the text or placed in the left margin.

DVD A type of optical data storage.

DVD drive A storage device that uses optical laser technology to read and write data.

Edit To insert, delete, or replace text in an Office document, workbook, or presentation.

Edit mode A mode that selects the text inside a control, not the control itself.

Em dash A long dash based on the width of the capital letter M in the current font and font size. It marks a break in thought, similar to a comma but stronger.

E-mail software Software used to receive and send e-mail. Many e-mail programs also include tools for managing appointments, contacts, and tasks.

Embedded chart A chart that is placed on the worksheet containing the data.

Embedded computer A small, specialized computer built into a larger component such as an automobile or appliance.

Embedded system Computer hardware and software used to control many devices.

Emphasis effect Animation that emphasizes an object or text that is already displayed.

Endnote A note or comment placed at the end of a section or a document.

Ensure Fit (Slide Size) A setting that scales information down so that it all appears on the slide.

Entrance effect Animation that appears as an object or text is moved onto the screen.

Error indicator A green triangle that indicates a possible error in a formula.

Error value A message that displays whenever a formula or function cannot perform its calculations.

Excel table A series of rows and columns that contain related data that have been formatted as a table.

Exit effect Animation that appears as an object or text is moved off the screen.

Explode To drag a section of a pie chart out to add emphasis.

Expression A combination of fields, mathematical operators, and prebuilt functions that calculates values in tables, forms, queries, and reports.

External drive Any storage drive connected to an eSATA port.

Eyedropper Tool used to select color from any object or image on a slide and apply the color to another area of the slide; often used to create a cohesive color scheme.

Favorite A stored web address that can be clicked to quickly navigate to that page.

Field (Access) A common characteristic of the data that the table will describe, such as city, state, or postal code.

Field (Word) A category of data—such as a file name, a page number, or the current date—that can be inserted into a document.

Field size A field property that limits the number of characters that can be typed into a text or number field.

File Explorer A Windows application that is used to view, find, and organize files and folders.

File system An organized method to save and retrieve files.

Fill handle The small green square in the lower right corner of the selection.

Filter A command to display only the rows of a table that meet specified criteria. Filtering temporarily hides rows that do not meet the criteria.

Fingerprint scanner An input device that reads fingerprints to authorize computer users.

First line indent The location of the beginning of the first line of a paragraph in relation to the left edge of the remainder of the paragraph.

Flagged error A wavy line indicating a possible spelling, grammar, or style error.

Flash Fill Recognizes a pattern in data and automatically enters the rest of the data.

Flash-based memory card Solid state drive designed for devices such as digital cameras and video recorders.

Floating object An object that you can move independently of the surrounding text.

Folder window A File Explorer window that displays files and folders.

Font A set of characters with the same design and shape.

Footer (PowerPoint) The text that displays at the bottom of every slide or that prints at the bottom of a sheet of slide handouts or notes pages.

Footer (Word) A reserved area for text, graphics, and fields that displays at the bottom of each page in a document.

Footnote A note or comment placed at the bottom of the page.

Foreign key A field that is used to relate records in a second related table. The foreign key field is often the second table's primary key.

Form data Information that you have typed into forms, such as your username, e-mail address, and street address.

Format To change the appearance of the text—for example, changing the text color to red.

Format Painter A tool that copies formatting from selected text to apply that formatting to other text.

Formatting The process of specifying the appearance of cells or the overall layout of a worksheet.

Formatting mark A character that displays in your document to represent a nonprinting character such as a paragraph, space, or tab.

Formula An equation that performs mathematical calculations on number values in the worksheet.

Formula AutoComplete A feature that suggests values as you type a function.

Formula bar A bar below the Ribbon that displays the value contained in the active cell and is used to enter or edit values or formulas.

Freeze Panes A command used to keep rows or columns visible when scrolling in a worksheet. The frozen rows and columns become separate panes.

Full Page Slide A printout in which the slide is fit to an 8.5" by 11", or letter-size, sheet of paper.

Full scan A Windows Defender feature that checks all files and running programs for viruses, spyware, and infected software.

Full-block style A business letter format that begins all lines at the left margin except for letterheads, tables, and block quotes. Also known as block style.

Function A prewritten Excel formula that takes a value or values, performs an operation, and returns a value or values.

Future value (Fv) In a loan, the value at the end of the time periods, or the cash balance you want to attain after the last loan payment is made.

Gallery A visual display of selections from which you can choose.

Gateway A network device through which different networks communicate.

GB The abbreviation for gigabyte.

General format The default number format. It does not display commas or trailing zeros to the right of a decimal point.

Gesture Dragging with your finger over the touch screen to form circles, straight lines, and taps in a specific order. Also a bodily motion that is interpreted as a command.

Gigabyte A unit of measure for storage devices. One gigabyte can store about one billion bytes, or one thousand digital photos.

Google Chrome A free web browser created by Google for use on Android, Windows, and Macintosh systems.

GPU A graphics processing unit.

Gradient fill Gradual progression of colors and shades, usually from one color to another or from one shade to another shade of the same color, used to add a fill to a shape or placeholder. Gradients come in light and dark variations.

Graphical user interface A visual system used to interact with the computer.

Graphics processing unit A card attached to the computer's main board to improve computer performance, usually for gamers and video developers.

Group A collection of multiple objects treated as one unit that can be copied, moved, or formatted.

Group By An operator that designates which query column contains the group of values to summarize as a single record, one for each set.

GUI Graphical user interface.

Guide A line that displays in the ruler to give you a visual indication of where the pointer is positioned.

Handout A printout that features one or more slides on a single page; can contain between two and nine slides per page.

Hanging indent An indent where the first line extends to the left of the rest of the paragraph.

Hard disk drive A common storage device in desktop computers that stores data using magnetic charges.

HDD Hard disk drive.

Header (PowerPoint) The text that prints at the top of each page of slide handouts.

Header (Word) A reserved area for text, graphics, and fields that displays at the top of each page in a document.

Headings font Font used in a slide title.

Home page The starting point for the remainder of the pages at a website.

HomeGroup A Windows networking tool that makes it easy to share pictures, videos, music, documents, and devices such as printers.

Hosted e-mail A service used to provide e-mail addresses and related resources.

Hover over To point to a link to display additional information.

HTML document A Hypertext Markup Language document; a text file with instructions for displaying its content in a web browser.

Hyperlink Text or a graphic that you click to go to a file, a location in a file, a web page on the World Wide Web, or a web page on an organization's intranet.

Hyperlink data type A data type that stores links to websites or files located on your computer.

Hypertext Markup Language document A text file with instructions for displaying its content in a web browser.

Icon A picture representation for an application, file, folder, or command on your device.

IF function A logical function that checks whether criteria are met, and then returns one value when the condition is TRUE and another value when the condition is FALSE.

Indent The position of paragraph lines in relation to the page margins.

Information processing cycle The four basic computer functions that work together in a cycle: input, process, output, and storage.

InPrivate Browsing A Microsoft Edge search window that limits the browsing history that is stored to a device.

Input device Computer hardware that provides information to the computer, such as keyboards, mice, touch displays, and microphones.

Input The process of gathering information from the user or other sources through an input device.

Input mask A set of special characters that control what can and cannot be entered in a field.

Insertion point A flashing vertical line that indicates where text will be inserted when you start typing.

Install To add new programs to your computer.

Integrated graphics card A graphics card built into the computer's motherboard.

IntelliSense A feature that displays Quick Info, ToolTips, and AutoComplete boxes as you type.

Interest The charge for borrowing money; generally a percentage of the amount borrowed.

Internet A collection of networks distributed throughout the world.

Internet service provider An organization that provides Internet connections, typically for a fee.

Internet zone The default security zone in Internet Explorer applied to all websites.

Intranet A private network that is accessed by only individuals within the organization.

IP address A unique set of numbers assigned to each device on the Internet.

Is Not Null An operator that tests if a field contains a value—is not empty.

Is Null An operator that tests if a field is empty.

ISP Internet service provider.

Justified text A paragraph alignment that aligns the text with both the left and right margins.

Keep Source Formatting Paste option that applies the original formatting of the pasted text.

Keep Text Only Paste option that removes all formatting from the pasted selection.

Keyboard An input device used to type characters and perform common commands.

Keyboard shortcut A combination of CTRL, ALT, WINDOWS, and character keys that performs a command when pressed.

Keyword A word or phrase to help identify the file when you do not know the file name during a File Explorer search.

Label (Access) A control on a form or in a report that describes other objects in the form or report.

Label (Excel) Text data in a cell that identifies a number value.

Label report A report formatted so that the data can be printed on a sheet of labels.

Landscape An orientation that is wider than it is tall.

Laptop A portable computer with a built-in screen, keyboard, and touchpad.

Layout (Access) A format that determines how data and labels are arranged in a form or report.

Layout (PowerPoint) The arrangement of the text and graphic elements or placeholders on a slide.

Layout gallery The visual representation of several content layouts that you can apply to a slide.

Layout view An Access view used to format a form or report while you are viewing a sample of the data.

Leader A series of characters that form a solid, dashed, or dotted line to fill the space preceding a tab stop.

Leader character The symbol used to fill the space in a leader.

Legend (Excel) A box that identifies the patterns or colors that are assigned to the data series or categories in the chart.

Legend (PowerPoint) Identifies the patterns or colors that are assigned to the data in the chart.

Line chart A chart type that illustrates trends over time, with time displayed along the x-axis and the data point values connected by a line.

Line spacing The vertical distance between lines of text in a paragraph; can be adjusted for each paragraph.

Linked table A table that exists in a different file from the one you are working on created by an application such as Access or Excel but that can be opened as a table in Access.

List level A hierarchy of bullets and sub-bullets; each level has its own formatting.

Live Preview A feature that displays what the results of a formatting change will be if you select it.

Local intranet zone A security zone for web content stored on internal networks that is accessed only by those within the organization.

Lock screen A screen that displays shortly after a computer or device is turned on that is running Windows 10. It may display after a period of inactivity or when not signed in to prevent unauthorized individuals from using your account.

Logical function Applies a logical test to determine whether a specific condition is met.

Logical test Any value or expression that can be evaluated as TRUE or FALSE.

Long Text data type A data type that can store up to 65,535 characters in each record.

LOWER function A text function used to convert a text string to all lowercase letters.

Mail merge A Word feature used to customize letters or labels by combining a main document with a data source.

Main document The mail merge document that contains the text that remains constant.

Malware A type of program designed to harm your computer, control your computer, or discover private information.

Manual page break A document feature that forces a page to end at a location you specify.

Margins The spaces between the text and the top, bottom, left, and right edges of the paper.

Masked character Text that is hidden by displaying characters such as bullets.

MAX function A function that returns the largest value in a range of cells.

Maximize (Slide Size) A setting that keeps slide content as large as possible, while allowing some content to be cropped if needed.

Merge Selected cells are combined into a single cell.

Merge field A field that merges and displays data from a specific column in the data source.

Metadata Information and personal data that is stored with your document.

MHTML file Another name for a web archive.

Microsoft account Personal account that you use to access your files, settings, and online services from devices connected to the Internet.

Microsoft Edge The default web browser in Windows 10 that replaces Internet Explorer by Microsoft.

Microsoft Office A suite of productivity programs.

MIN function A function that returns the smallest value in a range of cells.

Mini toolbar A toolbar with common formatting commands that displays near selected text.

Mix Downloadable add-in for use with PowerPoint, with which you can add interactive content—audio, videos, quizzes, polls, and inking—to your presentation, as well as record and draw on your slides while presenting.

Modal When a form's Modal property is set to Yes, the Navigation Pane will collapse when the form is opened. When the form is closed, the Navigation Pane will display.

Modem A device that translates signals from analog to digital or digital to analog.

Mouse An input device used to point to and click screen elements.

Mozilla Firefox A free and open-source web browser created by Mozilla Foundation and Mozilla Corporation.

Name Box An area that displays the active cell reference.

Navigation bar A vertical or horizontal bar with hyperlinks to the main pages of a website.

Navigation form A form that contains a Navigation Control with tabs that you can use to quickly open forms and reports.

Navigation toolbar Displays in the lower left corner of the slide while in Slide Show or Presenter view; may be used to go to any slide while the slide show is running.

Network drive A hard drive that is accessed through a network.

Network interface card A card that connects a computer to a network.

NIC Network interface card.

Normal view (Excel) A view that maximizes the number of cells visible on the screen.

Normal view (PowerPoint) A view in which the PowerPoint window is divided into two areas—the Slide pane and the left pane containing thumbnails of each slide.

Notebook The name given to a OneNote document. It is a loose structure of digital pages.

Notes page Printout that contains the slide image in the top half of the page and speaker notes in the lower half of the page.

Notes pane The area of the Normal View window used to type notes that can be printed below an image of each slide.

NOW function A function that returns the serial number of the current date and time.

Nper The total number of payments for the loan.

Nudge To move an object in small increments by pressing one of the arrow keys.

Number data type A data type that stores numeric values.

Number format A specific way that Excel displays numbers.

Number value Numeric data in a cell.

Numbered list A list of items with each item introduced by a consecutive number or letter to indicate definite steps, a sequence of actions, or chronological order.

Office 365 A Cloud-based service built around the Office suite of programs.

Office Add-in A plugin that adds extra features or custom commands to Office programs.

Office Clipboard A temporary storage area that holds text or an object that has been cut or copied.

Office on Demand A streaming version of Office that you can work with using a computer that does not have Office installed.

Office RT An app version of Office designed to work on tablets with an ARM processor.

On Click Begins the animation sequence when the mouse button is clicked or the spacebar is pressed.

OneDrive A free storage space on the cloud that is automatically created when you create your Microsoft account.

OneNote A program used to collect notes, drawings, and media from multiple participants.

One-to-many form A two-part form in which the main form displays in Single Form view and the related records display in a subform in Datasheet view.

One-to-many relationship A relationship in which a record in the first table can have many associated records in the second table.

Online app A program that runs in a web browser.

Online image A graphic, drawing, or photograph accessed from Bing Image Search or other online providers. Also a collection of images stored online and made available for use in presentations.

Online picture An image, such as a graphic, drawing, or photograph, provided from a variety of online sources, such as Bing Image Search.

Onscreen keyboard A virtual keyboard that displays on a touch screen.

Open source software Software that can be sold or given away as long as the source code is provided for free.

Operating system software Software that controls the way the computer works while it is running.

Operator precedence A set of mathematical rules for performing calculations within a formula.

Or logical operator A logical comparison of two criteria that is true if either of the criteria outcomes is true.

Organization chart A chart that graphically represents the hierarchy of relationships between individuals and groups within an organization.

Orphan The first line of a paragraph that displays as the last line of a page.

Outline A Word feature that is used to plan and organize longer documents such as formal reports.

Output The computer process of displaying information through an output device.

Output device Hardware that provides information to the user such as monitors, speakers, and printers.

Page Layout view A view used to adjust how a worksheet will look when it is printed.

Paint A drawing program that is installed with most versions of Windows.

Paragraph spacing The vertical distance above and below each paragraph; can be adjusted for each paragraph.

Parent folder The folder that contains student data files.

Password A series of letters, numbers, symbols, and spaces that you type to gain access to a computer, file, or program to help ensure you are authorized.

Password protect To require a password to open a shared file.

Paste A command that inserts a copy of the text or object from the Office Clipboard.

Paste area The target destination for data that has been cut or copied.

PDF document An image of a document that can be viewed using a PDF reader such as Adobe Acrobat Reader instead of the application that created the original document.

PDF file A Portable Document Format file.

Peer-to-peer network A small network that connects computers and devices without the need for a server.

Permission level The privilege to read, rename, delete, or change a file.

Personal identification number A four-digit code used when signing in to Windows 10.

Phishing website A dishonest website posing as a legitimate site to gain personal information, such as your logon and bank account number.

Picture An image created with a scanner, digital camera, or graphics software and saved with a graphic file extension such as .jpg, .png, .tif, or .bmp.

Picture Also paste option that pastes copied text as a picture.

Picture effect A picture style that includes prebuilt shadows, reflections, glows, soft edges, bevels, and 3-D rotations.

Picture style Prebuilt set of formatting borders, effects, and layouts applied to a picture.

Pie chart (Excel) A chart type that displays the relationship of parts to a whole.

Pie chart (PowerPoint) Used to illustrate percentages or proportions and includes only one data series.

PIN Another word for personal identification number.

Placeholder (Common Features) A reserved, formatted space into which you enter your own text or object. If no text is entered, the placeholder text will not print.

Placeholder (PowerPoint) A box with dotted borders; holds text or objects such as pictures, charts, and tables.

Placeholder character A symbol in an input mask that is replaced as you type data into the field.

PMT function A function that calculates the payment for a loan based on constant payments and a constant interest rate.

Point A unit of measure with 72 points per inch typically used for font sizes and character spacing.

Pop-up A small window that displays in addition to the web page you are viewing.

Port A connector on the outside of the computer to which you connect external devices.

Portable Document Format file A file format that preserves document layout and formatting and can be viewed in Word, Windows Reader, or Adobe Acrobat Reader.

Portrait An orientation that is taller than it is wide.

Present value (Pv) The initial amount of the loan, and the total amount that a series of future payments is worth today.

Presentation software Software used to arrange information in slides that can be shared with and viewed by others.

Presenter view A view available when slides are projected in Slide Show view; shows notes and slide on computer screen while only the slide is being projected to the audience; requires only one monitor.

Preset effects A combination of other effects, like a bevel and a shadow.

Primary key A field that uniquely identifies each record in a table.

Principal The initial amount of the loan, and the total amount that a series of future payments is worth today. Also called the present value (Pv) of a loan.

Print A command that opens the Print dialog box so that you can select a different printer or different print options.

Print Preview A command that opens a preview of the table with Ribbon commands that you can use to make adjustments to the object you are printing.

Process The computer process of transforming, managing, and making decisions about data and information.

Productivity software Software used to accomplish tasks such as reading and composing e-mail, creating documents, and managing tasks.

Program Another word for an application.

Protected Mode A feature that makes it more difficult for malware to be installed on your computer.

Protected View A view applied to files downloaded from the Internet that allows you to decide if the content is safe before working with the file.

Public A shared file that does not require a password.

Public computer A computer that is available to others when you are not using it.

Public website A website designed for public access.

Quarantined item A file or program found to have a potential security issue that is isolated in a special location on your PC and prevented from running on your PC during a Windows Defender scan.

Query A database object used to ask questions about—query—the data stored in database tables.

Query design grid The lower half of the Query Design view window that contains the fields the query will display and the query settings that should be applied to each field.

Query design workspace The upper half of the Query Design view window that displays the tables that the query will search.

Question mark (?) wildcard A wildcard character that matches any single character.

Quick Access A list of favorite and/or frequently-visited locations and files on your computer.

Quick Access Toolbar A small toolbar that contains buttons for commonly used commands such as Save and Undo.

Quick Info An IntelliSense box with a message that explains the purpose of the selected AutoComplete command.

Quick Print A command that prints the object directly. You cannot make any adjustments to the object, choose a different printer, or change the printer settings.

Quick scan A Windows Defender feature that checks only the areas on your PC that are most likely to be affected by viruses, spyware, and infected software.

Quick Start field A set of fields that can be added with a single click. For example, the Name Quick Start data type inserts the LastName and FirstName fields and assigns the Text data type to each.

Quick Style A style that can be accessed from a Ribbon gallery of thumbnails.

RAM Random access memory—the computer's short-term memory.

Random access memory An electronic chip that provides temporary storage.

Range Two or more cells in a worksheet that are adjacent.

Range finder An Excel feature that outlines all of the cells referenced in a formula. It is useful for verifying which cells are used in a formula and for editing formulas.

Rate The percentage that is paid for the use of the borrowed money.

Read Mode A view that is used when you need to read, but not edit, electronic documents.

Read privilege A permission level that allows you to open the document, but you cannot save any changes that are made.

Reader A tablet-like computer designed to bring entertainment features such as books and movies.

Reading view A webpage view that provides the webpage text without the navigation bars and hyperlinks displayed.

Real-time protection A Windows Defender feature that checks for malware all the time.

Recently Used Fonts Listing of fonts you have selected and applied in the existing presentation.

Record A collection of related data, such as the contact information for a person.

Recycle Bin An area on your drive that stores files you no longer need.

Referential integrity A rule that keeps related values synchronized. For example, the foreign key value must be present in the related table.

Refresh Reload, or update, the current webpage with any changes that have been made since the browser session started.

Relative cell reference Refers to cells based on their position in relation to (relative to) the cell that contains the formula.

Replace A feature that finds and then replaces a character or string of characters in a worksheet or in a selected range.

Report A database object that presents tables or query results in a way that is optimized for onscreen viewing or printing.

Report Layout view A view that can be used to format a report while viewing the report's data.

Report view A view optimized for onscreen viewing of reports.

Restore Used to reduce the window size to what it was previously.

Restricted sites zone A security zone in which you place sites that you explicitly do not trust.

Ribbon Contains commands placed in groups that are organized by tabs so that you can quickly find the tools you need.

Rich Text Format A document file format designed to work with many different types of programs.

Rich Text Format file A document file format designed to work with many different types of programs.

Right-click To press the right mouse button.

Router A device for connecting networks.

Row heading The number that displays at the left of a row.

RTF file Rich Text Format file.

Sample submission A Windows Defender feature that sends Microsoft malware samples found on your PC so Microsoft can learn about potential security issues.

Sans serif font A font where the letters do not have serifs.

Scanner An input device that can convert paper images into a digital image.

Screen clipping A picture of a portion of the computer screen that can be inserted into a worksheet.

Screen shot (Word) A picture of the computer screen, a window, or a selected region saved as a file that can be printed or shared electronically. Also a snapshot of any window that is open on your desktop.

Screen time A family account feature used to set the start, end time, and total time the device can be used each day.

Script Code downloaded with a web page that provides additional functionality.

Scroll To place the mouse in the scroll bar and move the mouse up or down or side-to-side to view parts of the window that do not display at the same time.

Scroll bar An area at the far right or bottom of a window indicating there is more to be displayed.

Search box An area located on the taskbar used to find applications, files, computer settings, or results on the Internet.

Search provider A website that provides a way for you to search for information on the web.

Search suggestion The words and phrases that display as you type in a search box.

Section A portion of a document that can be formatted differently from the rest of the document.

Section break A nonprinting character that marks the end of one section and the beginning of another section.

Select query A type of query that selects and displays the records that answer a question without changing the data in the table.

Separator character A character such as a tab or comma designated as the character to separate columns of unformatted text.

Serial number A sequential number. Dates are stored as sequential serial numbers so they can be used in calculations.

Series A group of numbers, text, dates, or time periods that come one after another in succession. For example, the months January, February, March.

Serif An extra detail or hook at the end of a character stroke.

Serif font A font where the letters have extra details or hooks at the end of each stroke.

Server A computer dedicated to providing services to other computers on a network.

SharePoint A web application server designed for organizations to develop an intranet.

Short Text data type A data type that stores up to 255 characters of text.

Shortcut A link to a specific application, file, or folder.

Sign in The process of connecting to a device by keying a Microsoft account username and then entering a password or PIN or using a picture password.

Sign-in screen The screen displayed for logging in to a computer.

Single Form view A view that displays one record at a time with field names in the first column and field values in the second column.

Site index *See* Site map.

Site map A page of hyperlinks that outline a website.

Sizing handle A small circle surrounding a selected on an object's border that is used to resize the object by dragging.

Slide An individual page in a presentation that contains text, pictures, tables, charts, and other multimedia or graphic objects.

Slide (PowerPoint) An individual page in a presentation that can contain text, pictures, or other objects.

Slide handout A printed image of slides on a sheet of paper.

Slide master The highest level slide in a hierarchy of slides that stores theme and slide layout information.

Slide Sorter view The view that displays all of the slides in your presentation as thumbnails.

Slide transition A motion effect that occurs in a slide show as you move from one slide to another.

Small caps A font effect that displays all characters in uppercase while making any character originally typed as an uppercase letter taller than the ones typed as lowercase characters.

Smart Guide A guideline that appears automatically when you move objects on your slide and helps to align and space images equally.

SmartArt graphic A pre-built visual representation of information that you can use to communicate your message or ideas effectively.

Smartphone A cellular phone with an operating system.

SmartScreen Filter A feature that helps protect you from online threats.

Snap To quickly position a window to either half of the screen by dragging its title bar and the pointer to the screen's edge.

Snip A screen shot created with the Snipping Tool application.

Snipping Tool An application that creates screen shots called snips.

Social media A Cloud service where content is shared through the interactions of people connected through social networks.

Software A set of instructions stored on your computer.

Solid-state drive A drive that stores data using electricity and retains the data when the power is turned off.

Source The reference used to find information or data.

Sparkline A chart contained in a single cell that is used to show data trends.

Speech recognition An input technology that performs commands or types text based on words spoken into a microphone.

Split bar A bar that splits a document into two windows.

Split window A command that divides the window into separate panes so that each pane can be scrolled separately.

Spreadsheet The primary document that you use in Excel to store and work with data, also called a worksheet.

Spreadsheet software Software used to organize information in a tabular structure with numeric data, labels, formulas for calculations, and charts.

SQL select query A command that selects data from a data source based on the criteria you specify.

SSD Solid-state drive.

Start screen The initial screen that displays when starting PowerPoint 2016.

Statistical function A predefined formula that describes a collection of data; for example, averages, maximums, and minimums.

Storage The location where data resides on a computer.

Storage device Computer hardware that stores information while the computer is in use or after it is powered off. Storage devices include magnetic hard drives, solid-state drives, optical drives, USB flash drives, and other types of permanent storage.

Streaming media A Cloud-based service that provides video and music as you watch or listen to it.

Student data file A file that you need to complete a project in a textbook.

Style A prebuilt collection of formatting settings that can be assigned to text.

Stylus A pen-like pointing device used with touch screens.

Subdatasheet A datasheet that displays related records from another table by matching the values in the field that relates the two tables. In a datasheet, the subdatasheet displays below each record.

Sum (Access) An operator that calculates the total of the values in each group.

SUM (Excel) An Excel function that adds all the numbers in a range of cells.

Summary sheet A worksheet that displays and summarizes totals from other worksheets.

Summary statistic A calculation for each group of data, such as a total, an average, or a count.

Superscript Text that is positioned higher and smaller than the other text.

Sway An app that can be used to create storylines and presentations.

Switch Connects the devices on a network.

Synonym Word with the same or similar meaning.

Tab scrolling buttons The buttons to the left of the worksheet tabs used to display worksheet tabs that are not in view.

Tab stop A specific location on a line of text marked on the Word ruler to which you can move the insertion point by pressing the Tab key.

Tabbed browsing A feature that you use to open multiple web pages in the same browser window.

Table Design view An Access view that features table fields and their properties.

Table style Borders and fill colors applied to the entire table in a manner consistent with the presentation theme.

Table The object that stores the data by organizing it into rows and columns. Each column is a field, and each row is a record.

Tablet A portable computer built around a single touch screen.

Tabular layout A layout in which the controls are positioned as table cells in rows and columns.

Tag Another name for a keyword.

Tap Touch the device display once with your finger.

Taskbar A toolbar located at the bottom of the desktop used to view an application, file, or folder, search the Internet, and view updates.

TB The abbreviation for terabyte.

Template (Excel) Prebuilt workbook used as a pattern for creating new workbooks.

Template (PowerPoint) A file upon which a presentation can be based.

Terabyte A unit of measure for storage devices. One terabyte is one trillion bytes, or approximately one thousand gigabytes.

Text alignment The horizontal placement of text within a placeholder.

Text box (Access) A control on a form or in a report that displays the data from a field in a table or query.

Text box A movable, resizable container for text or graphics. Also an object used to position text anywhere on a slide.

Text effect A pre-built set of decorative formats, such as outlines, shadows, text glow, and colors, that make text stand out in a document.

Text value Character data in a cell that usually labels number values.

Text wrap A format that displays text on multiple lines within a cell.

The Cloud An Internet technology used to store files and to work with programs that are stored in a central location.

Theme (Common Features) A prebuilt set of unified formatting choices including colors and fonts.

Theme (PowerPoint) Set of unified design elements—colors, fonts, and effects—that provides a unique look for your presentation.

Theme variants Variations of the current theme, with different accent colors.

Thesaurus A reference that lists words that have the same or similar meaning to the word you are looking up. Also a research tool that provides a list of synonyms.

This PC Part of File Explorer that is used to access devices, drives, and folders on your computer.

Three-dimensional Refers to an image that appears to have all three spatial dimensions—length, width, and depth.

Thumb drive Another name for a USB flash drive.

Thumbnail (PowerPoint) A miniature image of a presentation slide.

Thumbnail (Windows) A miniature window of the open app, file, or folder that when hovered over contains the Close button in the top-right corner.

TODAY function A function that returns the serial number of the current date.

Toggle button A button used to turn a feature both on and off.

Top-level domain Letters after a domain name that specify the organization type sponsoring a website and follow the period after a website's domain name—*.gov,* for example.

Total row A row that displays as the last row in an Excel table and provides summary functions in drop-down lists for each column.

Touch display A screen that interprets commands when you touch it with your finger.

Touchpad A flat area on which you can move the finger to position the pointer.

Tracking cookie A cookie that gathers information about your web browsing behaviors across multiple websites. They are used to provide ads and services based on your interests.

TRANSPOSE function A lookup function used to convert a vertical range of cells to a horizontal range, or vice versa.

Truncated Cut off.

Trusted sites zone A security zone in which you place sites you trust to not harm your computer.

Underlying formula The formula as displayed in the formula bar.

Underlying value Data displayed in the formula bar.

Unicode (UTF-8) A system for representing a large variety of text characters and symbols. It is used often in HTML documents.

Uniform Resource Locator The unique address of a page on the Internet.

Uninstall To remove a program from your computer.

Unsecured network A network that does not require a password to connect to it.

Unzip The process of opening and extracting the files from the zipped folder.

UPPER function A text function used to convert a text string to all uppercase letters.

URL An acronym for Uniform Resource Locator.

USB flash drive A small, portable solid-state drive about the size of the human thumb.

Use Destination Theme Paste option that applies the formatting of the slide to which the text is pasted.

Utility program A small program designed to perform a routine task or computer housekeeping task.

Validation rule A field property that requires that specific values be entered into a field.

Value Data in a cell.

Value axis The axis that displays the worksheet's numeric data.

Vertical alignment The space above and below a text or object in relation to the top and bottom of a table cell or top and bottom margins.

Volatile The result of a function will not remain as entered, but will be updated each time the workbook is opened.

Web Another name for World Wide Web.

Web album A Cloud-based service that you use to store, organize, and share photos and video.

Web archive A file that saves web page text and pictures in a single file, typically assigned the *.mht* file extension.

Web browser A program used to navigate the World Wide Web.

Web browsing A family account feature used to restrict websites from your child's viewing.

Web note An item on a website you can highlight, clip, or annotate to read about later.

Web page archive A file that saves web page text and its pictures in a single file. These files are typically assigned the *.mht* file extension.

Website A collection of connected pages located at a single domain name.

Widow The last line of a paragraph that displays as the first line of a page.

Wildcard A special character, such as an asterisk, used in query criteria to allow matches for any combination of letters or characters.

Windows 10 Store app Software that is downloaded and installed from the Windows 10 Store and that runs and displays information in the Start screen. Also a program used to perform a similar set of tasks that run on the Start screen.

Windows background The image that displays on the desktop.

Windows Defender Software automatically included in Microsoft Windows that is used to check for and help prevent viruses, spyware, and other unwanted software from being installed on your device without your knowledge.

Windows Update A feature that lets you know when your computer was last modified with newer settings. You can also check for any new updates and view what was recently downloaded or installed.

Wired network A network that transmits signals through wires.

Wireless network A network that transmits signals via radio waves.

With Previous Begins the animation sequence at the same time as any animation preceding it or, if it is the first animation, with the slide transition.

Word processing software Software used to create, edit, format, and print documents.

WordArt A set of graphic text styles that can be used to make text look like a graphic. Also a prebuilt set of fills, outlines, and effects used to create decorative text.

Workbook A file that you can use to organize various kinds of related information.

Worksheet The primary document that you use in Excel to store and work with data, also called a spreadsheet.

Worksheet tab The labels along the lower border of the workbook window that identify each worksheet.

World Wide Web A collection of linked pages designed to be viewed from devices, such as your laptop, tablet, or SmartPhone, connected to the Internet.

Word wrap Words at the right margin automatically move to the beginning of the next line if they do not fit.

WWW An acronym for World Wide Web.

X-axis The horizontal axis of a chart.

Y-axis The vertical axis of a chart.

Yes/No data type A data type that stores variables that can have one of two possible values—for example, yes or no or true or false.

Zipped folder Another name for a compressed folder.

Online materials can be found in the Student Resources located at www.pearsonhighered.com/skills

Microsoft Office Specialist Word 2016				C = CORE
Chapter	MOS Obj #	Objective	Skills Heading	Page
1	**Create and Manage Documents**			
	1.1 C	**Create a Document**		
Ch1	1.1.1 C	Create a Blank Document	Create a New Document	148
Online	1.1.2 C	Create a Blank Document Using a Template	Work with Templates	
Online	1.1.3 C	Open a PDF in Word for Editing	Save and Close a Document	
Ch3	1.1.4 C	Insert Text from a File or External Source	Insert Text from Another Document	229
	1.2 C	**Navigate Through a Document**		
Ch2	1.2.1 C	Search for Text	Proofread a Document	189
Online	1.2.2 C	Insert Hyperlinks	Use a Style Guide to Format a Newsletter	
Ch4	1.2.3 C	Create Bookmarks	Document Inspector	290
Ch4	1.2.4 C	Move to a Specific Location or Object in a Document	Use GoTo	290
	1.3 C	**Format a Document**		
Ch4	1.3.1 C	Modify Page Setup	Change Page Setup	270
Ch3/Ch4	1.3.2 C	Apply Document Themes	Use Themes	228 /268
Online	1.3.3 C	Apply Document Style Sets		
Ch1/Ch2	1.3.4 C	Insert Headers and Footers	Insert a Header and Footer	164/169/ 207
Ch2	1.3.5 C	Insert Page Numbers		206
Online	1.3.6 C	Format Page Background Elements	Change Page Background	
	1.4 C	**Customize Options and Views for Documents**		
Ch2/Ch4	1.4.1 C	Change Document Views	Explore the Word Interface	204/288/ 289/290
Ch1/Ch4	1.4.2 C	Customize Views by Using Zoom Settings	Insert and Delete Text	166/271
Online	1.4.3 C	Customize the Quick Access Toolbar		
Ch1	1.4.4 C	Split the Window	Split the Window	170
Ch1	1.4.5 C	Add Document Properties	Insert and Delete Text	168
Ch1/Ch4	1.4.6 C	Show or Hide Formatting Marks	Explore the Word Interface	148/273

Chapter	MOS Obj #	Objective	Skills Heading	Page
	1.5 C	**Print and Save Documents**		
Online	1.5.1 C	Modify Print Settings	Print a Document	
Ch1	1.5.2 C	Save Documents in Alternative File Formats	Save and Close a Document	166/240
Ch1	1.5.3 C	Print All or Part of a Document	Print a Document	166
Ch1	1.5.4 C	Inspect a Document for Hidden Properties or Personal Information		168
Online	1.5.5 C	Inspect a Document for Accessibility Issues		
Online	1.5.6 C	Inspect a Document for Compatibility Issues		
2	**Format Text, Paragraphs, and Sections**			
	2.1 C	**Insert Text and Paragraphs**		
Ch2	2.1.1 C	Find and Replace Text	Proofread a Document	189
Ch1	2.1.2 C	Cut, Copy and Paste Text	Create a New Document	154
Ch2	2.1.3 C	Replace Text by Using Autocorrect	Proofread a Document	208
Ch1	2.1.4 C	Insert Special Characters	Add Bullets, Numbers, and Symbols	171
	2.2 C	**Format Text and Paragraphs**		
Ch1/Ch4	2.2.1 C	Apply Font Formatting	Format Characters	160/162/ 272/274
Ch1	2.2.2 C	Apply Formatting by Using Format Painter	Copy and Clear Formats	160
Ch2	2.2.3 C	Set Line and Paragraph Spacing and Indentation	Working with Paragraph Spacing	198/200
Online	2.2.4 C	Clear Formatting	Copy and Clear Formats	
Online	2.2.5 C	Apply a Text Highlight Color to Text Selections		
Ch1	2.2.6 C	Apply Built-in Styles to Text	Understand Word Styles	150
Ch3	2.2.7 C	Change Text to WordArt	Use WordArt	249
Online	2.2.9 C	Insert WordArt		
	2.3 C	**Order and Group Text and Paragraphs**		
Ch4	2.3.1 C	Format Text in Multiple Columns	Work with Columns	269
Ch4	2.3.2 C	Insert Page, Section, or Column Breaks	Work with Page Breaks Work with Columns	271
Online	2.3.3 C	Change Page Setup Options for a Section	Work with Page Breaks	

Chapter	MOS Obj #	Objective	Skills Heading	Page
3	**Create Tables and Lists**			
	3.1 C	**Create a Table**		
Ch3	3.1.1 C	Convert Text to Tables	Create a Table	250
Online	3.1.2 C	Convert Tables to Text		
Ch3	3.1.3 C	Create a Table by Specifying Rows and Columns	Create a Table	240
Ch3	3.1.4 C	Apply Table Styles	Create a Table	238
	3.2 C	**Modify a Table**		
Online	3.2.1 C	Sort Table Data	Create a Table	
Online	3.2.2 C	Configure Cell Margins and Spacing		
Ch3	3.2.3 C	Merge and Split Cells	Create a Table	246
Ch3	3.2.4 C	Resize Tables, Rows, and Columns	Create a Table	239
Online	3.2.5 C	Split Tables		
Online	3.2.6 C	Configure a Repeating Row Header		
	3.3 C	**Create and Modify a List**		
Ch2	3.3.1 C	Create a Numbered or Bulleted List	Add Bullets, Numbers, and Symbols	196
Online	3.3.2 C	Change Bullet Characters or Number Formats for a List Level	Add Bullets, Numbers, and Symbols	
Online	3.3.3 C	Define a Custom Bullet Character or Number Format	Add Bullets, Numbers, and Symbols	
Ch2	3.3.4 C	Increase or Decrease List Levels		196
Ch2	3.3.5 C	Restart or Continue List Numbering		210
Online	3.3.6 C	Set Starting Number Value		
4	**Create and Manage References**			
	4.1 C	**Create and Manage Reference Markers**		
Ch2	4.1.1 C	Insert Footnotes and Endnotes	Format a Research Report	190
Online	4.1.2 C	Modify Footnote and Endnote Properties	Format a Research Report	
Ch2	4.1.3 C	Create Bibliography Citation Sources	Develop a Bibliography or Works Cited Page	192
Online	4.1.4 C	Modify Bibliography Citation Sources	Develop a Bibliography or Works Cited Page	
Ch2	4.1.5 C	Insert Citations for Bibliographies		194

Chapter	MOS Obj #	Objective	Skills Heading	Page
Online	4.1.6 C	Insert Figure and Table Captions	Add Captions	
Online	4.1.7 C	Modify Caption Properties	Set Caption Positions Change Caption Formats Change Caption Labels Exclude Labels from Captions	
	4.2 C	**Create and Manage Simple References**		
Online	4.2.1 C	Insert a Standard Table of Contents		
Online	4.2.2 C	Update a Table of Contents		
Online	4.2.3 C	Insert a Cover Page		
Online	4.3.5 C	Proofing		
5	**Insert and Format Graphic Elements**			
	5.1 C	**Insert Graphic Elements**		
Online	5.1.1 C	Insert Shapes	Insert Simple Shapes	
Ch3/Ch4	5.1.2 C	Insert Pictures	Insert Graphics	228/278
Ch1	5.1.3 C	Insert a Screen Shot or Screen Clipping		169
Ch3	5.1.4 C	Insert Text Boxes	Insert a Text Box	248
	5.2 C	**Format Graphic Elements**		
Ch3	5.2.1 C	Apply Artistic Effects	Insert Graphics	233
Ch3	5.2.2 C	Apply Picture Effects	Insert Graphics Apply Picture Effects	232/233
Online	5.2.3 C	Remove Picture Backgrounds		
Ch3/Ch4	5.2.4 C	Format Objects		231/279
Ch3	5.2.5 C	Apply a Picture Style	Add Quick Styles to Images	232
Ch3/Ch4	5.2.6 C	Wrap Text Around Objects	Insert Graphics	231/279
Ch3	5.2.7 C	Position Objects	Work with Columns	231
Online	5.2.8 C	Add Alternative Text to Objects for Accessibility		
	5.3 C	**Insert and Format SmartArt Graphics**		
Ch4	5.3.1 C	Create a SmartArt Graphic	Create SmartArt	280
Ch4	5.3.2 C	Format a SmartArt Graphic	Create SmartArt	282/283
Ch4	5.3.3 C	Modify SmartArt Graphic Content	Create SmartArt	281

Chapter	MOS Obj #	Objective	Skills Heading	Page
		Microsoft Office Specialist Excel 2016		C = CORE
1	**Create and Manage Worksheets and Workbooks**			
	1.1 C	**Create Worksheets and Workbooks**		
Ch1	1.1.1 C	Create a Workbook	Creating a New Workbook	328
Online	1.1.2 C	Import Data From a Delimited Text File	Import Files	
Ch3	1.1.3 C	Add a Worksheet to an Existing Workbook	Deleting, Inserting, Renaming, and Coloring Worksheet Tabs	422
Ch4	1.1.4 C	Copy and Move a Worksheet	Moving or Copying a Worksheet	461/463
	1.2 C	**Navigate in Worksheets and Workbooks**		
Ch4	1.2.1 C	Search for Data within a Workbook	Find and replace data	458
Ch1/Ch4	1.2.2 C	Navigate to a Named Cell, Range, or Workbook Element	Navigating within Worksheets	331/ 348/471
Ch3	1.2.3 C	Insert and Remove Hyperlinks	Insert Hyperlinks	431
	1.3 C	**Format Worksheets and Workbooks**		
Ch3	1.3.1 C	Change Worksheet Tab Color	Deleting, Inserting, Renaming, and Coloring Worksheet Tabs	409
Ch1/Ch3	1.3.2 C	Rename a Worksheet	Deleting, Inserting, Renaming, and Coloring Worksheet Tabs	344/408
Ch3	1.3.3 C	Change Worksheet Order	Moving or Copying a Worksheet	423
Ch1/Ch2	1.3.4 C	Modify Page Setup	Insert a Header and Footer	345/ 346/385
Online	1.3.5 C	Insert and Delete Columns or Rows	Inserting and Deleting Columns or Rows	
Ch3	1.3.6 C	Change Workbook Themes	Changing Themes	409
Ch1	1.3.7 C	Adjust Row Height and Column Width	Adjusting Column Width and Row Height	336
Ch1/Ch3	1.3.8 C	Insert Headers and Footers	Adding Headers and Footers	344/427
	1.4 C	**Customize Options and Views for Worksheets and Workbooks**		
Ch3	1.4.1 C	Hide or Unhide Worksheets		422/423
Ch4	1.4.2 C	Hide or Unhide Columns and Rows	Hiding Worksheet Rows	467
Ch3	1.4.3 C	Customize the Quick Access Toolbar		430
Ch1	1.4.4 C	Change Workbook Views	Using Worksheet Views	345/347
Ch4	1.4.5 C	Change Window Views		460/470

Chapter	MOS Obj #	Objective	Skills Heading	Page
Ch1	1.4.6 C	Modify Document Properties		344/351
Online	1.4.7 C	Change Magnification by Using Zoom Tools		
Ch1/Ch3	1.4.8 C	Display Formulas	Showing Functions and Formulas	346/410
	1.5 C	**Configure Worksheets and Workbooks for Distribution**		
Ch1	1.5.1 C	Set a Print Area	Changing Page Orientation and Print Range	348
Ch1	1.5.2 C	Save Workbooks in Alternative File Formats	Exporting a Workbook to PDF	350
Ch1/Ch2	1.5.3 C	Print All or Part of a Workbook	Using Print Preview and Printer Selection	387
Ch1/Ch2/Ch3/Ch4	1.5.4 C	Set Print Scaling	Changing Page Margins and Scaling	347/386/425/466
Ch4	1.5.5 C	Display Repeating Row and Column Titles on Multipage Worksheets	Using Print Titles	466
Online	1.5.6 C	Inspect a Workbook for Hidden Properties or Personal Information		
Ch2	1.5.7 C	Inspect a Workbook for Accessibility Issues		388
Ch2	1.5.8 C	Inspect a Workbook for Compatibility Issues		388
2	**Manage Data Cells and Ranges**			
	2.1 C	**Insert Data in Cells and Ranges**		
Ch4	2.1.1 C	Replace Data	Dragging and Dropping Modifying Cell Information	452
Ch1/Ch3	2.1.2 C	Cut, Copy, or Paste Data	Paste Options/Paste Special	335/423
Ch3	2.1.3 C	Paste Data by Using Special Paste Options	Paste Options/Paste Special	414
Ch1	2.1.4 C	Fill Cells by Using Autofill	Using Series (AutoFill)	340/341/349/350
Online	2.1.5 C	Insert and Delete Cells	Inserting and Deleting Cells, Clearing Cells, and Cell Ranges	
	2.2 C	**Format Cells and Ranges**		
Ch1	2.2.1 C	Merge Cells	Merging and Centering Versus Centering Across	331
Ch2/Ch4	2.2.2 C	Modify Cell Alignment and Indentation	Aligning Cell Content	369/453
Online	2.2.3 C	Format Cells by Using Format Painter	Copying Formats	
Ch2	2.2.4 C	Wrap Text within Cells	Wrapping Text and Line Breaks	369
Ch1/Ch2	2.2.5 C	Apply Number Formats	Number Formatting	342/372

Chapter	MOS Obj #	Objective	Skills Heading	Page
Ch1/ Ch2/Ch4	2.2.6 C	Apply Cell Formats	Cell Formats	337/369/ 453
Ch1/Ch2	2.2.7 C	Apply Cell Styles	Using Built-In Cell Styles	337/342/ 343/373
	2.3 C	**Summarize And Organize Data**		
Ch4	2.3.1 C	Insert Sparklines	Exploring Sparklines	456
Online	2.3.2 C	Outline Data	Create Outlines Collapse Groups of Data in Outlines	
Online	2.3.3 C	Insert Subtotals	Using Tables and the Total Row	
Ch4	2.3.4 C	Apply Conditional Formatting	Highlighting Values in a Range with Conditional Formatting	454/455
3	**Create Tables**			
	3.1 C	**Create and Manage Tables**		
Ch4	3.1.1 C	Create an Excel Table from a Cell Range	Applying Table Styles	462
Ch4	3.1.2 C	Convert a Table to a Cell Range	Applying Table Styles	466
Ch4	3.1.3 C	Add or Remove Table Rows and Columns		468
	3.2 C	**Manage Table Styles and Options**		
Ch4	3.2.1 C	Apply Styles to Tables	Applying Table Styles	462
Ch4	3.2.2 C	Configure Table Style Options	Applying Table Styles	
Ch4	3.2.3 C	Insert Total Rows	Using Tables and the Total Row	464
	3.3 C	**Filter and Sort a Table**		
Ch4	3.3.1 C	Filter Records	Using Tables and the Total Row	464/465
Ch4	3.3.2 C	Sort Data by Multiple Columns	Sort data on Multiple Columns	464
Ch4	3.3.3 C	Change Sort Order	Applying Table Styles	463
Online	3.3.4 C	Remove Duplicate Records	Remove Duplicates	
4	**Perform Operations with Formulas and Functions**			
	4.1 C	**Summarize Data by Using Functions**		
Ch1/ Ch2/Ch3	4.1.1 C	Insert References	Using Relative Cell Referencing Using Absolute Cell Referencing Using Mixed Cell Referencing	340/371 424
Ch1	4.1.2 C	Perform Calculations by Using the SUM Function	Using the SUM Function by Selecting Destination Cells	338

Chapter	MOS Obj #	Objective	Skills Heading	Page
Ch2	4.1.3 C	Perform Calculations by Using MIN and MAX Functions	Using MIN and MAX	376
Ch4	4.1.4 C	Perform Calculations by Using the COUNT Function	Using COUNT and AVERAGE	449
Ch2	4.1.5 C	Perform Calculations by Using the AVERAGE Function	Using COUNT and AVERAGE	374
	4.2 C	**Perform Conditional Operations by Using Functions**		
Ch4	4.2.1 C	Perform Logical Operations by Using the IF Function	Using Logical Functions	450
Online	4.2.2 C	Perform Logical Operations by Using the SUMIF Function	The SUMIF Function	
Online	4.2.3 C	Perform Logical Operations by Using the AVERAGEIF Function	The AVERAGEIF Function	
Online	4.2.4 C	Perform Statistical Operations by Using the COUNTIF Function	The COUNTIF Function	
	4.3 C	**Format and Modify Text by Using Functions**		
Online	4.3.1 C	Format Text by Using RIGHT, LEFT, and MID Functions	Using Text Functions	
Ch4	4.3.2 C	Format Text by Using UPPER, LOWER, and PROPER Functions	Using Text Functions	471
Online	4.3.3 C	Format Text by Using the CONCATENATE Function	Using Text Functions	
5	**Create Charts and Objects**			
	5.1 C	**Create Charts**		
Ch2/Ch3	5.1.1 C	Create a New Chart	Creating Charts in an Existing Worksheet	378/382/389/391/426
Online	5.1.2 C	Add Additional Data Series	Add a Data Series to a Chart	
Ch3	5.1.3 C	Switch Between Rows and Columns in Source Data	Correcting a Confusing Chart	426
Ch2	5.1.4 C	Analyze Data by Using Quick Analysis	Creating Pie Charts	370/378
	5.2 C	**Format Charts**		
Ch2	5.2.1 C	Resize Charts	Modifying a Chart's Position Properties	379/389

Chapter	MOS Obj #	Objective	Skills Heading	Page
Ch2/Ch3	5.2.2 C	Add and Modify Chart Elements	Modifying an Existing Chart	380/383/391/427
Ch2/Ch3	5.2.3 C	Apply Chart Layouts and Styles	Creating Charts in an Existing Worksheet Changing the Data and Appearance of a Chart	380/383/389/426
Ch2/Ch3	5.2.4 C	Move Charts to a Chart Sheet	Placing Charts on a Chart Sheet	382/391/426
	5.3 C	**Insert and Format Objects**		
Online	5.3.1 C	Insert Text Boxes and Shapes	Inserting Objects	
Ch3	5.3.2 C	Insert Images	Inserting a Picture	429
Ch3	5.3.3 C	Modify Object Properties	Add Styles and Effects to Objects Change Object Colors	428
Ch2	5.3.4 C	Add Alternative Text to Objects for Accessibility		388

Microsoft Office Specialist PowerPoint 2016

Chapter	MOS Obj #	Objective	Skills Heading	Page
1	**Create and Manage Presentations**			
	1.1	**Create a Presentation**		
Ch2	1.1.1	Create a New Presentation	Develop a Presentation from a Custom Template and Outline	728
Ch2	1.1.2	Create a Presentation Based on a Template	Develop a Presentation from a Custom Template and Outline	728/749
Ch2	1.1.3	Import Word Document Outlines	Develop a Presentation from a Custom Template and Outline	750
	1.2	**Insert and Format Slides**		
Ch1/Ch2	1.2.1	Insert Specific Slide Layouts	Add, Reuse, and Rearrange Slides and Change Slide Layouts	697/735
Online	1.2.2	Duplicate Existing Slides		
Online	1.2.3	Hide And Unhide Slides	Create Hyperlinks within a Presentation	
Ch1	1.2.4	Delete Slides	Navigate in Slide Show View and Outline View	701/710

Chapter	MOS Obj #	Objective	Skills Heading	Page
Ch1	1.2.5	Apply a Different Slide Layout	Add, Reuse, and Rearrange Slides and Change Slide Layouts	696
Ch2	1.2.6	Modify Individual Slide Backgrounds	Create a Custom Template Using the Slide Master	734/736
Ch1	1.2.7	Insert Slide Headers, Footers, and Page Numbers	Understand the Purpose and Benefits of Using Themes	704
	1.3	**Modify Slides, Handouts, And Notes**		
Online	1.3.1	Change the Slide Master Theme or Background	Understand the Purpose and Benefits of Using Themes	
Online	1.3.2	Modify Slide Master Content	Create a Custom Template Using the Slide Master	
Online	1.3.3	Create a Slide Layout	Create a Custom Template Using the Slide Master	
Online	1.3.4	Modify a Slide Layout	Add, Reuse, and Rearrange Slides and Change Slide Layouts	
Online	1.3.5	Modify the Handout Master	Customize the Handout Master	
Online	1.3.6	Modify the Notes Master	Customize the Notes Master	
	1.4	**Order and Group Slides**		
Online	1.4.1	Create Sections	Use Slide Sections to Organize and Prepare a Presentation	
Ch1	1.4.2	Modify Slide Order		701
Online	1.4.3	Rename Sections	Use Slide Sections to Organize and Prepare a Presentation	
	1.5	**Change Presentation Options and Views**		
Ch1	1.5.1	Change Slide Size	Work with PowerPoint Windows and Views	711
Ch1	1.5.2	Change Views of a Presentation	Navigate in Slide Show View and Outline View	700/706
Online	1.5.3	Set File Properties		
	1.6	**Configure a Presentation for Print**		
Ch1	1.6.1	Print All or Part of a Presentation	Preview and Print a Presentation	705/709
Online	1.6.2	Print Notes Pages		
Ch1	1.6.3	Print Handouts	Preview and Print a Presentation	705

Chapter	MOS Obj #	Objective	Skills Heading	Page
Ch1	1.6.4	Print in Color, Grayscale, or Black and White	Preview and Print a Presentation	705
	1.7	**Configure and Present a Slide Show**		
Online	1.7.1	Create Custom Slide Shows	Create a Custom Slide Show	
Online	1.7.2	Configure Slide Show Options	Create a Custom Slide Show	
Online	1.7.3	Rehearse Slide Show Timing		
Ch1	1.7.4	Present a Slide Show by Using Presenter View	Create and Use Speaker Notes	707
2	**Insert and Format Text, Shapes, and Images**			
	2.1	**Insert and Format Text**		
Ch1	2.1.1	Insert Text on a Slide	Create a Custom Template Using the Slide Master	690
Ch2	2.1.2	Apply Formatting and Styles to Text	Modify Text	732
Ch2	2.1.3	Apply WordArt Styles to Text	Work with Shape and Line Graphics	738
Online	2.1.4	Format Text in Multiple Columns	Create Multiple Columns in a Single Shape	
Ch2	2.1.5	Create Bulleted and Numbered Lists	Use Text Hierarchy to Convey Organization	742
Online	2.1.6	Insert Hyperlinks	Create Hyperlinks within a Presentation	
	2.2	**Insert and Format Shapes and Text Boxes**		
Ch3	2.2.1	Insert or Replace Shapes	Create Hyperlinks within a Presentation	774
Ch3	2.2.2	Insert Text Boxes	Work with Shape and Line Graphics	777
Ch3	2.2.3	Resize Shapes and Text Boxes	Work with Shape and Line Graphics	774
Ch3	2.2.4	Format Shapes and Text Boxes	Work with Shape and Line Graphics	774
Online	2.2.5	Apply Styles to Shapes and Text Boxes	Work with Shape and Line Graphics	
	2.3	**Insert and Format Images**		
Ch1/ Ch2/Ch3	2.3.1	Insert Images	Work with Images and Art	698/770
Ch3	2.3.2	Resize and Crop Images	Work with Images and Art	772
Ch1/Ch3	2.3.3	Apply Styles and Effects	Work with Images and Art	698/708/ 729/770
	2.4	**Order and Group Objects**		
Ch3	2.4.1	Order Objects	Work with Shape and Line Graphics	779
Ch3	2.4.2	Align Objects	Work with Shape and Line Graphics	779/790

Chapter	MOS Obj #	Objective	Skills Heading	Page
Online	2.4.3	Group Objects		
Ch3	2.4.4	Display Alignment Tools	Work with Shape and Line Graphics	774
3	**Insert Tables, Charts, SmartArt, and Media**			
	3.1	**Insert and Format Tables**		
Ch4	3.1.1	Create a Table	Create a Table	808
Ch4	3.1.2	Insert and Delete Table Rows and Columns		810
Ch4	3.1.3	Apply Table Styles	Create a Table	812
Online	3.1.4	Import a Table	Import Tables from External Sources	
	3.2	**Insert and Format Charts**		
Ch4	3.2.1	Create a Chart	Create and Insert Charts	814
Online	3.2.2	Import a Chart	Import Charts from External Sources	
Online	3.2.3	Change the Chart Type	Create and Insert Charts	
Ch4	3.2.4	Add a Legend to a Chart	Create and Insert Charts	814
Online	3.2.5	Change the Chart Style of a Chart	Create and Insert Charts	
	3.3	**Insert and Format SmartArt Graphics**		
Online	3.3.1	Create SmartArt Graphics	Create a SmartArt Graphic	
Ch3	3.3.2	Convert Lists to SmartArt Graphics	Convert Lists to SmartArt	780
Ch3	3.3.3	Add Shapes to SmartArt Graphics		781
Online	3.3.4	Reorder Shapes in SmartArt Graphics		
Online	3.3.5	Change the Color of SmartArt Graphics	Navigate Comments	
	3.4	**Insert and Manage Media**		
Ch3	3.4.1	Insert Audio and Video Clips	Apply and Modify Multimedia in Presentations	784
Ch3	3.4.2	Configure Media Playback Options	Apply and Modify Multimedia in Presentations	785
Ch3	3.4.3	Adjust Media Window Size	Apply and Modify Multimedia in Presentations	785
Online	3.4.4	Set the Video Start and Stop Time	Apply and Modify Multimedia in Presentations	
Online	3.4.5	Set Media Timing Options	Apply and Modify Multimedia in Presentations	

Chapter	MOS Obj #	Objective	Skills Heading	Page
4	**Apply Transitions and Animations**			
	4.1	**Apply Slide Transitions**		
Ch1	4.1.1	Insert Slide Transitions	Use Transitions and Animations	702
Ch1	4.1.2	Set Transition Effect Options	Use Transitions and Animations	702
	4.2	**Animate Slide Content**		
Ch4	4.2.1	Apply Animations to Objects	Use Transitions and Animations	820
Ch4	4.2.2	Apply Animations to Text	Use Transitions and Animations	821
Ch4	4.2.3	Set Animation Effect Options	Use Transitions and Animations	821/822
Online	4.2.4	Set Animation Paths	Use Transitions and Animations	
	4.3	**Set Timing for Transitions and Animations**		
Ch1	4.3.1	Set Transition Effect Duration	Create Hyperlinks within a Presentation	703
Ch1	4.3.2	Configure Transition Start and Finish Options	Create Hyperlinks within a Presentation	703
Ch4	4.3.3	Reorder Animations on a Slide		823
5	**Manage Multiple Presentations**			
	5.1	**Merge Content from Multiple Presentations**		
Ch3	5.1.1	Insert Slides from Another Presentation	Merge Multiple Presentations and Compare and Review Changes	769
Online	5.1.2	Compare Two Presentations	Merge Multiple Presentations and Compare and Review Changes	
Online	5.1.3	Insert Comments	Create Comments	
Online	5.1.4	Review Comments	Create Comments	
	5.2	**Finalize Presentations**		
Online	5.2.1	Protect a Presentation	Mark Presentations as Final and Apply Password Protection	
Online	5.2.2	Inspect a Presentation		
Ch1	5.2.3	Proof a Presentation		695
Ch3	5.2.4	Preserve Presentation Content	Restrict Permissions	788
Online	5.2.5	Export Presentations to Other Formats	Save a Presentation	

Microsoft Office Specialist Access 2016				
Chapter	**MOS Obj #**	**Objective**	**Skills Heading**	**Page**
1	**Create and Manage a Database**			
	1.1	**Create and Modify Databases**		
Ch1	1.1.1	Create a Blank Desktop Database		510
Ch3	1.1.2	Create a Database from a Template	Using Quick Start Templates	611
Online	1.1.3	Create a Database by Using Import Objects or Data from Other Sources	Merge Databases Created Linked Tables from External Data Sources	518
Online	1.1.4	Delete Database Objects	Delete Tables, Queries, Forms, and Reports	
	1.2	**Manage Relationships and Keys**		
Ch1	1.2.1	Create and Modify Relationships	Create a One-to-Many Relationship Create a Many-to-Many Relationship	518
Ch1	1.2.2	Set the Primary Key	Understand and Designate Keys	516
Online	1.2.3	Enforce Referential Integrity	Understand Referential Integrity	519
Ch1	1.2.4	Set Foreign Keys	Understand and Designate Keys	517
Ch1	1.2.5	View Relationships	Understand Relationships Between Tables	518
	1.3	**Navigate Through a Database**		
Ch3	1.3.1	Navigate Specific Records	Understand the Purpose of a Table	593
Ch3	1.3.2	Create and Modify a Navigation Form	Use Navigation Forms	609
Ch3	1.3.3	Set a Form as the Startup Option	Set a Form as the Startup Option	609
Online	1.3.4	Display Objects in the Navigation Pane	Maneuver in the Navigation Pane	
Ch2	1.3.5	Change Views of Objects	Maneuver in the Navigation Pane	552
	1.4	**Protect and Maintain Databases**		
Ch1	1.4.1	Compact a Database	Compact and Repair Database	530
Ch1	1.4.2	Repair a Database	Compact and Repair Database	530
Ch3	1.4.3	Back Up a Database	Back Up a Database	613
Online	1.4.4	Split a Database	Split a Database	
Online	1.4.5	Encrypt a Database with a Password	Encrypt a Database with a Password	
Online	1.4.6	Recover Data from Backup		
	1.5	**Print and Export Data**		
Ch4	1.5.1	Print Reports	Create a Report Using the Report Wizard	639

Chapter	MOS Obj #	Objective	Skills Heading	Page
Online	1.5.2	Print Records		
Ch3	1.5.3	Save a Database as a Template	Save Databases as Templates	613
Ch4	1.5.4	Export Objects to Alternative Formats		651/ 652/653
2	**Build Tables**			
	2.1	**Create Tables**		
Ch1	2.1.1	Create a Table	Create a Table in Design View	512
Ch1	2.1.2	Import Data into Tables	Import Data from Other Sources	522
Ch2	2.1.3	Create Linked Tables from External Sources		572
Ch3	2.1.4	Import Tables from Other Databases	Understand the Purpose of a Table	612
Online	2.1.5	Create a Table from a Template with Application Parts		
	2.2	**Manage Tables**		
Ch1	2.2.1	Hide Fields in Tables	Hide Fields in Tables	526
Online	2.2.2	Add Total Rows		
Online	2.2.3	Add Table Descriptions		
Online	2.2.4	Rename Tables		
	2.3	**Manage Records in Tables**		
Online	2.3.1	Update Records	Navigate and Edit Records in Datasheets	
Ch1	2.3.2	Add Records	Understand the Purpose of a Table	514
Online	2.3.3	Delete Records	Enter Data Manually	
Ch1	2.3.4	Append Records from External Data	Import Data from Other Sources	522
Online	2.3.5	Find and Replace Data	Find and Replace Records in the Datasheet	
Ch1	2.3.6	Sort Records	Sort Tables and Query Results	524
Ch1	2.3.7	Filter Records	Find and Replace Records in the Datasheet	524
	2.4	**Create and Modify Fields**		
Ch1	2.4.1	Add Fields to Tables	Understand Masks and Formatting	512
Ch3	2.4.2	Add Validation Rules to Fields	Add a Validation Rule to Fields	610
Ch1	2.4.3	Change Field Captions	Change Field Captions	513
Ch1	2.4.4	Change Field Sizes	Create a Table in Design View	513
Ch1	2.4.5	Change Field Data Types	Create a Table in Design View	531
Ch1	2.4.6	Configure Fields to Auto-Increment	Configure Fields to Auto-Increment	515

Chapter	MOS Obj #	Objective	Skills Heading	Page
Online	2.4.7	Set Default Values	Set Default Values	
Ch3	2.4.8	Using Input Masks	Understand Masks and Formatting	602
Online	2.4.9	Delete Fields	Enter Data Manually	
3	**Create Queries**			
	3.1	**Create a Query**		
Ch2	3.1.1	Run a Query	Understand the Purpose of Queries	553
Online	3.1.2	Create a Crosstab Query	Create Crosstab Queries	
Online	3.1.3	Create a Parameter Query	Create Parameter Queries	
Online	3.1.4	Create an Action Query	Create Action Queries	
Ch2	3.1.5	Create a Multi-Table Query	Create Queries in Design View	556
Ch2	3.1.6	Save a Query	Create Queries in Design View	557
	3.2	**Modify a Query**		
Online	3.2.1	Rename a Query		
Ch2	3.2.2	Add Fields	Create Queries in Design View	557
Online	3.2.3	Remove Fields		
Ch2	3.2.4	Hide Fields	Define Selection Criteria for Queries	564
Ch2	3.2.5	Sort Data within Queries	Understand the Purpose of Queries	566
Ch2	3.2.6	Format Fields within Queries	Create Aggregate Functions	565
	3.3	**Create Calculated Fields and Grouping within Queries**		
Ch2	3.3.1	Add Calculated Fields	Create Calculated Fields	554
Online	3.3.2	Set Filtering Criteria	Understand the Purpose of Queries	
Ch2	3.3.3	Group and Summarize Data	Create Aggregate Functions	562
Ch2	3.3.4	Group Data by Using Comparison Operators	Define Selection Criteria for Queries	558/567
Ch2	3.3.5	Group Data by Using Arithmetic and Logical Operators	Define Selection Criteria for Queries	564
4	**Create Forms**			
	4.1	**Create a Form**		
Ch3	4.1.1	Create a Form	Understand the Purpose of Forms	590
Online	4.1.2	Create a Form from a Template with Application Parts	Understanding Application Parts	

Chapter	MOS Obj #	Objective	Skills Heading	Page
Ch3	4.1.3	Save A Form	Understand the Purpose of Forms	591
	4.2	**Configure Form Controls**		
Ch3	4.2.1	Move Form Controls		600
Ch3	4.2.2	Add Form Controls		590
Online	4.2.3	Modify Data Sources		
Ch3	4.2.4	Remove Form Controls		601
Ch3	4.2.5	Set Form Control Properties		607
Ch3	4.2.6	Manage Labels		600
Ch3	4.2.7	Add Subforms	Create a Form Using the Form Wizard	598
	4.3	**Format a Form**		
Online	4.3.1	Modify Tab Order	Modify Tab Order in Forms Auto Order Forms	
Online	4.3.2	Configure Print Settings	Modify a Form's Design	
Online	4.3.3	Sort Records by Form Field	Sort Records	
Online	4.3.4	Apply a Theme	Modify a Form's Design	
Online	4.3.5	Control Form Positioning		
Online	4.3.6	Insert Backgrounds	Insert Backgrounds	
Ch3	4.3.7	Insert Headers and Footers	Modify a Form's Design	599
Ch3	4.3.8	Insert Images	Modify a Form's Design	596
5	**Create Reports**			
	5.1	**Create a Report**		
Ch4	5.1.1	Create a Report Based on the Query or Table	Understand Referential Integrity	632
Online	5.1.2	Create a Report in Design View		
Ch4	5.1.3	Create a Report by Using a Wizard	Understand the Purpose of Reports	648
	5.2	**Configure Report Controls**		
Ch4	5.2.1	Group and Sort Fields	Customize a Report	642/643
Online	5.2.2	Modify Data Sources	Modify Data Sources	
Ch4	5.2.3	Add Report Controls	Create a Report Using the Report Wizard Add Report Controls	640
Ch4	5.2.4	Add and Modify Labels	Create a Report Using the Report Wizard	633/640

Chapter	MOS Obj #	Objective	Skills Heading	Page
	5.3	**Format a Report**		
Ch4	5.3.1	Format a Report into Multiple Columns	Format Reports into Multiple Columns	644
Ch4	5.3.2	Add Calculated Fields	Create a Report Using the Report Wizard	636
Ch4	5.3.3	Control Report Positioning		639
Ch4	5.3.4	Format Report Elements	Customize a Report	634
Ch4	5.3.5	Change Report Orientation	Change Report Orientation	650
Ch4	5.3.6	Insert Header and Footer Information	Insert Headers and Footers	641/650
Ch4	5.3.7	Insert Images	Insert Images	634
Ch4	5.3.8	Apply a Theme		632

Index